MW00649364

SIXTH EDITION

Theoretical **Models** and **Processes** of Reading

Donna E. Alvermann
Norman J. Unrau
Robert B. Ruddell
EDITORS

INTERNATIONAL
Reading Association
800 Barksdale Road, PO Box 8139
Newark, DE 19714-8139, USA
www.reading.org

Executive Editor, Publications Shannon Fortner
Acquisitions Manager Tori Mello Bachman
Managing Editors Susanne Viscarra and Christina M. Lambert
Editorial Associate Wendy Logan
Creative Services/Production Manager Anette Schuetz
Design and Composition Associate Lisa Kochel

Cover Frank Pessia and © Hemera/Thinkstock

Library of Congress Cataloging-in-Publication Data
Theoretical models and processes of reading / Donna E. Alvermann, University of Georgia, Norman J. Unrau, California State University, Los Angeles, Robert B. Ruddell, University of California, Berkeley, editors. — Sixth edition.
pages cm
Includes bibliographical references and index.
ISBN 0-87207-710-1 (978-0-87207-710-2 : alk. paper) 1. Reading. 2. Reading—Research. I. Alvermann, Donna E. II. Unrau, Norman. III. Ruddell, Robert B.
LB1050.T48 2013
428.4—dc23

2012048890

Suggested APA Reference
Alvermann, D.E., Unrau, N.J., & Ruddell, R.B. (Eds.). (2013). *Theoretical models and processes of reading* (6th ed.). Newark, DE: International Reading Association.

We dedicate this sixth edition of *Theoretical Models and Processes of Reading* to

Harold L. "Hal" Herber,

an individual whose scholarship spanned many years of reading research and who touched many lives as a teacher, teacher educator, mentor, and friend.

CONTENTS

Part 2. Foundations for Literacy Development

Part 3. Comprehension Development From Words to Worlds

ABOUT THE EDITORS

Donna E. Alvermann is an appointed Distinguished Research Professor in the Department of Language and Literacy Education at The University of Georgia, Athens. She was formerly a classroom teacher in Texas and New York. Her research focuses on young people's literacy practices in classrooms, out-of-school settings (e.g., libraries), and digital environments.

The author of over 150 articles in journals such as *American Educational Research Journal*, *Reading Research Quarterly*, and *Journal of Literacy Research*, Donna codirected the National Reading Research Center, funded by the U.S. Department of Education, from 1992 to 1997. Her coauthored/edited books include *Content Area Reading and Literacy: Succeeding in Today's Diverse Classrooms* (7th ed., Pearson, 2013); *Reconceptualizing the Literacies in Adolescents' Lives* (3rd ed., Routledge, 2012); *Adolescents' Online Literacies: Connecting Classrooms, Digital Media, and Popular Culture* (Peter Lang, 2010); *Adolescents and Literacies in a Digital World* (Peter Lang, 2004); and *Bring It to Class: Unpacking Pop Culture in Literacy Learning* (Teachers College Press, 2010). She also coedited the International Reading Association's premier research journal, *Reading Research Quarterly* (2003–2007), and served as president of the National Reading Conference (now the Literacy Research Association).

Currently a member of the Intermediate and Adolescent Literacy Advisory Group of the Alliance for Excellent Education in Washington, DC, Donna has been the recipient of the Literacy Research Association's Oscar S. Causey Award for Outstanding Contributions to Reading Research, the Literacy Research Association's Albert J. Kingston Award for Distinguished Service, and the ALER Laureate Award. Elected to the Reading Hall of Fame in 1999, she was also awarded the International Reading Association's highest honor, the William S. Gray Citation of Merit, in 2006. From 2008 to 2010, Donna was the U.S. advisor to the international ADORE Project, funded by the European Commission/EU, that researched teacher education involving adolescent readers in Germany, Belgium, Estonia, Finland, Hungary, Italy, Norway, Poland, Romania, and Switzerland.

In her spare time, Donna listens to bluegrass and folk, takes long road trips with Jack, and plays with Jazz, her 3-year-old golden retriever.

Norman J. Unrau is a professor emeritus of California State University, Los Angeles, where he served in the Division of Curriculum and Instruction and taught courses on literacy, cognition, and learning in the credential and M.A. programs. He also served as the coordinator of the M.A. in Education program with a focus on middle and high school curriculum and instruction. He continues to teach graduate students, engage in research, and serve on California State University committees to promote academic literacy in schools.

Norm completed his master's degree at Columbia University's Teachers College. After teaching high school English and social studies for nearly 25 years, he completed his doctorate in education at the University of California, Berkeley. His work at Berkeley focused on cognition in reading and writing. Norm has served as editor of the International Reading Association's *Journal of Adolescent & Adult Literacy* and is the author of *Content Area Reading and Writing: Fostering Literacies in Middle and High School Cultures* (2nd ed., Pearson, 2008) and *Thoughtful Teachers, Thoughtful Learners: Helping Students Think Critically* (2nd ed., Pippin, 2008). He served as coeditor of the fifth edition (2004) of *Theoretical Models and Process of Reading* with Bob Ruddell. Norm has also published articles on reading, writing, critical thinking, assessment, motivation, and graduate programs in education that have appeared in the *Journal of Adolescent & Adult Literacy*, *The Journal of Educational Research*, *Reading Psychology*, *Teacher Education Quarterly*, *Issues in Teacher Education*, and other professional journals.

When not teaching, reading, or writing, Norm enjoys playing tennis and the saxophone, traveling with his wife, Cherene, who teaches piano, and biking by the ocean with his daughter, Amy.

Robert B. Ruddell is a professor emeritus in the Language, Literacy, and Culture faculty group at the University of California, Berkeley. He began his teaching career at age 18 in a one-room schoolhouse in a coal mining community in the Appalachian Mountains of his home state of West Virginia. His work with the primary-grade students in that school was the genesis of his interest in understanding the nature of the reading process. (While in that school, he dismissed school early one day each month to visit the homes and families of each of his 32 students; he is still in contact with six of them.)

Bob received a combined M.A. degree from West Virginia University and George Peabody College for Teachers. After completing his doctorate at Indiana University, he taught credential and graduate courses in reading and language development and directed the Advanced Reading and Language Leadership Program at the University of California, Berkeley. Over the years, he has worked closely with his doctoral students, advising and directing the research and dissertations of 86 of these Ed.D. and Ph.D. students. Bob has successfully mixed consultation in public schools with his university teaching and research, working with teachers in both inner city and rural schools. He has lectured and conducted workshops for teachers in each of the 50 states, as well as in England, Sweden, Germany, Australia, Canada, and the Ivory Coast.

Bob is the recipient of the International Reading Association's William S. Gray Citation of Merit, which recognizes lifetime achievement and leadership contributions to the field of reading and literacy development. He also received the

Oscar S. Causey Research Award from the National Reading Conference, recognizing his research on effective and influential literacy teachers. He received the Marcus Foster Memorial Reading Award from the California Reading Association for his teaching and research and was the recipient of the Indiana University Citation Award presented to former graduate students who have made outstanding contributions to literacy. He has served as the president of the Reading Hall of Fame and on the IRA Board of Directors.

Bob is the author of the fifth edition of the widely used literacy methods text *How to Teach Reading to Elementary and Middle School Students: Practical Ideas From Highly Effective Teachers* (Pearson, 2009). Along with his coeditorship of the present edition of *Theoretical Models and Processes of Reading* (*TMPR6*), he also was coeditor with M.R. Ruddell and Harry Singer of *TMPR4* (1994) and with Norman Unrau of *TMPR5* (2004). Bob coedited the earlier volumes, *TMPR* (1970), *TMPR2* (1976), and *TMPR3* (1985), with Harry Singer.

Bob's articles have appeared in *The Reading Teacher* and *Language Arts*, as well as in a variety of research journals and yearbooks. He was senior editor of the Pathfinder reading program series (Allyn & Bacon, 1978). His research and teaching interests focus on the study of comprehension and critical thinking, word identification strategies, reading motivation, and ways in which highly effective and influential teachers develop these skills in their students.

Bob and his wife, Sandra, enjoy traveling throughout the United States and internationally. They especially enjoy visits from their three grandchildren: Rebecca, Grace, and Madeline. Bob delights in conversations with his former students, and he relaxes with suspense and mystery novels and a good round of golf.

CONTRIBUTORS

Marilyn Jager Adams
Department of Cognitive, Linguistic, and Psychological Sciences
Brown University
Providence, Rhode Island, USA

Patricia A. Alexander
College of Education
University of Maryland, College Park
College Park, Maryland, USA

Donna E. Alvermann
Department of Language and Literacy Education
The University of Georgia
Athens, Georgia, USA

Meaola Amituanai-Toloa
Woolf Fisher Research Centre
University of Auckland
Auckland, New Zealand

Daniel K. Anderson
Sharecare
Burlington, Vermont, USA

Richard C. Anderson (Emeritus)
College of Education
University of Illinois at Urbana-Champaign
Champaign, Illinois, USA

Bonnie B. Armbruster (Emerita)
Center for the Study of Reading
University of Illinois at Urbana-Champaign
Champaign, Illinois, USA

Patricia Azuara
College of Education and Human Development
University of Arizona
Tucson, Arizona, USA

Ann L. Brown (Deceased)
Graduate School of Education
University of California, Berkeley
Berkeley, California, USA

Nancy Brynelson
Center for the Advancement of Reading
Office of the Chancellor
California State University
Sacramento, California, USA

Patricia A. Carpenter
Psychology Department
Carnegie Mellon University
Pittsburgh, Pennsylvania, USA

Jill Castek
College of Liberal Arts and Sciences
Portland State University
Portland, Oregon, USA

Dina C. Castro
Frank Porter Graham Child Development Institute
University of North Carolina at Chapel Hill
Chapel Hill, North Carolina, USA

Courtney B. Cazden (Emerita)
Graduate School of Education
Harvard University
Cambridge, Massachusetts, USA

Julie L. Coiro
School of Education
University of Rhode Island
Kingston, Rhode Island, USA

Richard L. Coulson (Emeritus)
Southern Illinois University School of Medicine
Carbondale, Illinois, USA

Deborah R. Dillon
Department of Curriculum and Instruction
University of Minnesota
Minneapolis, Minnesota, USA

Mary Anne Doyle
Neag School of Education
University of Connecticut
Storrs, Connecticut, USA

Nell K. Duke
School of Education
University of Michigan
Ann Arbor, Michigan, USA

KaiLonnie Dunsmore
National Center for Literacy Education
Urbana, Illinois, USA

Anne Haas Dyson
College of Education
University of Illinois at Urbana-Champaign
Champaign, Illinois, USA

John R. Edlund
Department of English and Foreign Languages
California State Polytechnic University, Pomona
Pomona, California, USA

Linnea C. Ehri
Graduate Center
City University of New York
New York, New York, USA

Paul J. Feltovich
Florida Institute for Human and Machine Cognition
Pensacola, Florida, USA

Ellice A. Forman
School of Education
University of Pittsburgh
Pittsburgh, Pennsylvania, USA

Emily Fox
College of Education
University of Maryland, College Park
College Park, Maryland, USA

James R. Gavelek
College of Education
University of Illinois at Chicago
Chicago, Illinois, USA

James Paul Gee
Mary Lou Fulton Teachers College
Arizona State University
Phoenix, Arizona, USA

Celia Genishi
Teachers College
Columbia University
New York, New York, USA

Kenneth S. Goodman (Emeritus)
College of Education
University of Arizona
Tucson, Arizona, USA

Yetta M. Goodman (Emerita)
College of Education
University of Arizona
Tucson, Arizona, USA

Usha Goswami
Centre for Neuroscience in Education
University of Cambridge
Cambridge, UK

John T. Guthrie (Emeritus)
College of Education
University of Maryland, College Park
College Park, Maryland, USA

Kris D. Gutiérrez
School of Education
University of Colorado at Boulder
Boulder, Colorado, USA

M.A.K. Halliday (Emeritus)
Department of Linguistics
University of Sydney
New South Wales, Sydney, Australia

Brenda Hannon
College of Liberal and Fine Arts
Texas A&M University–Kingsville
Kingsville, Texas, USA

Shirley Brice Heath
Department of English
Stanford University
Stanford, California, USA

Elizabeth E. Heilman
College of Education
Michigan State University
East Lansing, Michigan, USA

Laurie A. Henry
College of Education
University of Kentucky
Lexington, Kentucky, USA

Elfrieda H. Hiebert
TextProject
Santa Cruz, California, USA
Division of Social Sciences
University of California, Santa Cruz
Santa Cruz, California, USA

George G. Hruby
College of Education
University of Kentucky
Lexington, Kentucky, USA

Selena Hsiao
Woolf Fisher Research Centre
University of Auckland
Auckland, New Zealand

Glynda Hull
Graduate School of Education
University of California, Berkeley
Berkeley, California, USA

Marcel Adam Just
Center for Cognitive Brain Imaging
Carnegie Mellon University
Pittsburgh, Pennsylvania, USA

Mira-Lisa Katz
Department of English
Sonoma State University
Rohnert Park, California, USA

Walter Kintsch (Emeritus)
Institute of Cognitive Science
University of Colorado at Boulder
Boulder, Colorado, USA

Charles K. Kinzer
Teachers College
Columbia University
New York, New York, USA

Gunther Kress
Institute of Education
University of London
London, UK

Melanie R. Kuhn
School of Education
Boston University
Boston, Massachusetts, USA

Mei Kuin Lai
Woolf Fisher Research Centre
University of Auckland
Auckland, New Zealand

Carol D. Lee
School of Education and Social Policy
Northwestern University
Evanston, Illinois, USA

Donald J. Leu
Neag School of Education
University of Connecticut
Storrs, Connecticut, USA

Christopher J. Lonigan
Florida Center for Reading Research
Florida State University
Tallahassee, Florida, USA

Marla H. Mallette
Graduate School of Education
Binghamton University, State University of New York
Binghamton, New York, USA

Sandra McCormick (Emerita)
College of Education
The Ohio State University
Columbus, Ohio, USA

Stuart McNaughton
Woolf Fisher Research Centre
University of Auckland
Auckland, New Zealand

Mary B. McVee
Graduate School of Education & Center for Literacy and Reading Instruction
University at Buffalo, State University of New York
Buffalo, New York, USA

Elizabeth Birr Moje
School of Education
University of Michigan
Ann Arbor, Michigan, USA

William E. Nagy
School of Education
Seattle Pacific University
Seattle, Washington, USA

Katherine Nelson (Emerita)
Graduate Center
City University of New York
New York, New York, USA

David G. O'Brien
Department of Curriculum and Instruction
University of Minnesota
Minneapolis, Minnesota, USA

Kate Pahl
School of Education
University of Sheffield
Sheffield, UK

Allan Paivio (Emeritus)
Department of Psychology
University of Western Ontario
London, Ontario, Canada

Annemarie Sullivan Palincsar
School of Education
University of Michigan
Ann Arbor, Michigan, USA

Giovanni Parodi
Department of Linguistics
Pontificia Universidad Católica de Valparaíso
Valparaíso, Chile

P. David Pearson
Graduate School of Education
University of California, Berkeley
Berkeley, California, USA

Iliana Reyes
College of Education and Human Development
University of Arizona
Tucson, Arizona, USA

Louise M. Rosenblatt (Deceased)
School of Education
New York University
New York, New York, USA

Jennifer Rowsell
Department of Teacher Education
Brock University
St. Catharines, Ontario, Canada

Robert B. Ruddell (Emeritus)
Graduate School of Education
University of California, Berkeley
Berkeley, California, USA

Robert Rueda
Rossier School of Education
University of Southern California
Los Angeles, California, USA

David E. Rumelhart (Deceased)
School of Humanities and Sciences
Stanford University
Stanford, California, USA

Mark Sadoski
Texas A&M Health Science Center
Texas A&M University
College Station, Texas, USA

S. Jay Samuels
College of Education and Human Development
University of Minnesota
Minneapolis, Minnesota, USA

Judith A. Scott
Education Department
University of California, Santa Cruz
Santa Cruz, California, USA

Timothy Shanahan
College of Education
University of Illinois at Chicago
Chicago, Illinois, USA

Louise Spear-Swerling
Special Education and Reading Department
Southern Connecticut State University
New Haven, Connecticut, USA

Rand J. Spiro
College of Education
Michigan State University
East Lansing, Michigan, USA

Steven A. Stahl (Deceased)
College of Education
University of Illinois at Urbana-Champaign
Champaign, Illinois, USA

Laura Sterponi
Graduate School of Education
University of California, Berkeley
Berkeley, California, USA

Amy Stornaiuolo
Graduate School of Education
University of Pennsylvania
Philadelphia, Pennsylvania, USA

Stephanie L. Strachan
College of Education
Michigan State University
East Lansing, Michigan, USA

Brian Street (Emeritus)
Department of Education and Professional Studies
King's College London
London, UK

Ana Taboada Barber
College of Education and Human Development
George Mason University
Fairfax, Virginia, USA

Alfred W. Tatum
College of Education
University of Illinois at Chicago
Chicago, Illinois, USA

Stephen M. Tonks
College of Education
Northern Illinois University
DeKalb, Illinois, USA

Rolf Turner
Department of Statistics
University of Auckland
Auckland, New Zealand

Norman J. Unrau (Emeritus)
Charter School of Education
California State University, Los Angeles
Los Angeles, California, USA

Chad H. Waldron
College of Education
Michigan State University
East Lansing, Michigan, USA

Lynne M. Watanabe
College of Education
Michigan State University
East Lansing, Michigan, USA

Allan Wigfield
College of Education
University of Maryland, College Park
College Park, Maryland, USA

Marlene Zepeda (Emerita)
College of Health and Human Services
California State University, Los Angeles
Los Angeles, California, USA

Welcome, once again, to the world of reading and literacy research. We invite you to join us in the exciting investigation and discovery of reading theory, models, and processes. The reading process constitutes what Edmund Burke Huey, a pioneer in reading theory, called "the most intricate workings of the human mind, as well as...the most remarkable specific performance that civilization has learned in all its history" (1908/1968, p. 6). In this sixth edition of *Theoretical Models and Processes of Reading* (*TMPR6*), over half of the chapters have never appeared in any earlier edition. Eight of these new chapters were specially commissioned for this volume. Twenty percent of the chapters that have appeared earlier have been revised and/or updated by their authors to reflect current research and instructional developments in the field.

The following are our goals for this preface:

- To explain the overall purposes that guided the development of *TMPR6*
- To share a brief background of the past editions of *TMPR* (1970, 1976, 1985, 1994, and 2004) that led to the current sixth edition
- To describe the criteria used in the selection of chapters for the current volume and to offer a brief summary of the sixth edition's content
- To acknowledge those who assisted us in *TMPR6*'s development

Purposes for This Volume

In searching the research literature for current trends in theoretical models and processes of reading, we were careful to negotiate a balance between this newer material and chapters from earlier editions that have retained their relevancy well into the 21st century. We did so with the following purposes in mind:

- To provide an updated volume of carefully selected pieces that offer insight into reading and literacy research
- To offer an expanded range of research designs and their applications to both basic and applied research
- To be inclusive of reading processes and literacy practices studied through cognitive, sociocultural, critical, transactional, and poststructural theorizing
- To develop the ability to understand and critique a comprehensive body of research literature spanning more than five decades
- To make connections among a wide range of literacy theories and their associated models
- To apply the knowledge base assembled here in generating new research studies and models that inform instructional decision making

A Brief Background on *TMPR*

The first edition of *TMPR* emerged from a 1969 symposium presented at the 14th annual convention of the International Reading Association in Kansas City, Missouri. Robert Ruddell of the University of California, Berkeley, and Harry Singer of the University of California, Riverside, discussed the idea that a book might evolve from invited speakers' informative research presentations at the convention. The idea of honoring Professor Jack Holmes of the University of California, Berkeley, was at the center of the volume's creation. Holmes, who passed away in 1969, had been Singer's doctoral advisor and mentor and Ruddell's former senior colleague at Berkeley.

In 1970, the collection of papers, which were edited by Singer and Ruddell, became the first edition of *TMPR*. The first part contained six papers and reactions that came directly from the symposium and dealt with linguistic, perceptual, and cognitive components of the reading process. Contributors to that part included S. Jay Samuels, Joanna Williams, George Spache, Russell Stauffer, Roy Kress, and Albert Kingston. The second part of the first edition included nine selected articles that developed theoretical models of the reading process, including Jack Holmes's substrata-factor theory, Kenneth Goodman's psycholinguistic guessing game, Richard Venezky and Robert Calfee's reading competency model, and Eleanor Gibson's classic article on learning to read. Graduate students in reading programs throughout the United States were quick to use that first 348-page volume.

The second edition (1976) was approximately 75% new and doubled in length to 768 pages. Several new ideas grew from conversations between Singer and Ruddell as they planned the new edition. For example, the editors decided to include focusing questions at the beginning of each section as well as research articles that would illustrate various research traditions. The second edition was dedicated to researchers who had contributed to an understanding of the reading process. That 1976 edition had four sections:

- "Introduction," which highlighted pioneers in reading research and the nature of the reading process
- "Processes of Reading," which contained subsections on language, visual processing, perception, word recognition, cognition, affect, and cultural interaction
- "Models," which included pieces based on psycholinguistics (Ruddell and Goodman), information processing (including Gough and Anderson), developmental differences (Holmes and Singer), and affect (Mathewson)
- "Teaching and Research Issues," with pieces by Harry Singer, Richard Venezky and colleagues, George Miller, and Irene Athey, which focused

on teaching, modeling, text comprehension, and developmental processes, respectively

The third edition of TMPR was published in 1985, again edited by Singer and Ruddell, and dedicated to professors, researchers, and graduate students who formulate theories of reading and literacy, test hypotheses, and generate new knowledge in the field. With 70% new selections, the four main sections of this 976-page volume are "Historical Changes in Reading," "Processes of Reading," "Models of Reading," and "Teaching and Research Issues." Examination of the third edition's content reveals the impact of theory and research from literacy's allied disciplines, ranging from cognitive psychology with emphasis on schema theory and metacognition to sociolinguistics emphasizing greater concern for cultural and ethnic diversity in literacy learning. New to that volume, each part in the "Processes of Reading" section included at least one research exemplar article to complement each major theory piece.

Following a growing trend, the fourth edition, edited by Ruddell, Ruddell, and Singer, expanded to 1,296 pages, but like the previous editions, most of the content provided new frameworks and insights, with more than 80% of the selected articles having not appeared in any earlier volumes. Like earlier editions, this edition retained four themed sections: "Historical Changes in Reading: Researchers and Their Research," "Processes of Reading and Literacy," "Models of Reading and Literacy Processes," and "New Paradigms: Theory, Research, and Curriculum." The selections in these four sections made evident the explosion of knowledge in our field during the prior decade with new and revised theoretical perspectives, new paradigms, the use of multiple research stances, and new research findings.

The fifth edition, edited by Ruddell and Unrau, was by far the largest in the history of *TMPR*'s publication and reflected the aspirations of its editors to extend the coverage and depth of *TMPR*. It consisted of 56 chapters within 1,728 pages. Retaining the four main themes of the fourth edition, the fifth included a supplementary CD that contained several *TMPR* classics and more recent pieces that we could not include in that already expansive edition. During the book's editing, we strove to assemble an expanded collection of classical and up-to-date chapters to inform readers about not only the history of research in reading but also the spectrum of challenges that educators were encountering and engaging in their research.

When beginning work on the fifth edition, we developed a set of questions that we used to generate feedback and suggestions from professors and instructors around the world who taught with *TMPR4* and earlier editions. Many of those suggestions were incorporated into *TMPR5*, such as coverage of second-

language learning, critical literacy, and delayed or struggling readers. Results from that survey also informed the design of the Questions for Reflection to encourage the integration of research, theory, and practice.

New to that fifth edition's first section were a conversation between Richard Allington and Anne McGill-Franzen, who identified key trends and influences in literacy instruction; an exploration by Patricia Alexander and Emily Fox of five eras of literacy research and practice over the past 50 years; and a chapter by Sheila Valencia and Karen Wixson that developed a base of understanding about policy, standards, assessment, and instruction that reflected educators' interests in the nationwide standards and accountability movement. New to the second section, which focused on reading and literacy processes, were chapters that brought greater emphasis to the roles of sociocognition and literacy development by an array of authors, including James Gee, Anne Haas Dyson, Robert Jiménez, Patton Tabors, and Catherine Snow. An entirely new Part 6 was added to the Section Two, "Instructional Effects on Literacy Development," and included work by Robert Ruddell, Rachel Brown and her colleagues, Judith Langer, and Jill Fitzgerald.

Section Three contained a dozen models representing a wide range of reading and writing theories. Many models were brought forward from earlier editions of *TMPR*, such as those by Jay Samuels, David Rumelhart, Marilyn Adams, and Louise Rosenblatt. Others were new additions, including the chapters by Marcel Just and Patricia Carpenter and by Walter Kintsch. Mark Sadoski and Allan Paivio's dual coding model was updated, as was the sociocognitive-processing model by Robert Ruddell and Norman Unrau, and a radically revised model for understanding cognition and affect in writing by John Hayes replaced an earlier cognitive process model of writing.

Section Four contained five new chapters with each focusing on a different segment of literacy's future horizon. A chapter by Deborah Dillon and her colleagues called for a move toward a more pragmatic stance with more concentration on pressing problems in literacy that were calling for solutions and that would promote growth in the field rather than preoccupation with narrow paradigm conflicts and political agendas. A chapter from the then newly published RAND Reading Study Group's report on strategies to develop a research program on reading comprehension was included, along with a chapter envisioning a theory of new literacies written by Donald Leu and his colleagues. With assessment on the minds of educators worldwide, Lorrie Shepard's chapter on the role that assessment plays in learning cultures was added because it provided a historical framework for assessment practices and urged educators to examine the purposes of assessment and its relation to learning outcomes. Concluding this section, Claude Goldenberg reviewed research on literacy learning for children from low-income families and presented implications for research and instruction designed to enhance their literacy development.

The scope of *TMPR5* was perhaps broader and more comprehensive than any of its earlier companion volumes. It identified a range of essential factors critical to our continued progress in helping individuals read more proficiently and in helping educators understand reading processes more deeply. The new edition of *TMPR* continues in the pursuit of that progress. As we move into the sixth edition of *TMPR*, it is interesting to note that the International Reading Association has recorded sales of over 54,000 volumes of the first five editions.

Selection Criteria and Content of the Sixth Edition

As has been the case with earlier editions of *TMPR*, the editors gathered an abundance of information from a wide range of sources and discussed at great length how this new edition should be structured and what content should fill that structure. We looked for new publications that reflect developments during the past decade and are likely to have significant and enduring effects on the literacy field. While shortening this new edition, we also strived to extend its reach into domains of research and instruction that affect practitioners, graduate students, literacy teacher educators, and researchers. We discovered new pieces that presented new findings and perspectives, and we commissioned several new chapters to address those areas in which we could not find appropriate scholarship.

Guidelines we used to help in the selection of chapter content included the following:

- The chapters for each of the four sections must demonstrate the finest scholarship in the field.
- Selection of pieces for Sections One ("Perspectives on Literacy Research and Its Application") and Four ("Literacy's New Horizons: An Emerging Agenda for Tomorrow's Research and Practice") must reflect a historical perspective that reveals key changes in the literacy field, be well conceptualized, and identify important emerging trends in research and practice.
- Selections for Sections Two ("Processes of Reading and Literacy") and Three ("Models of Reading and Writing Processes") must offer a balance between theoretical and research pieces, exemplify a well-reasoned rationale grounded in theory, demonstrate varied methodologies, and provide implications for future research and practice.
- Research pieces need to provide a clear theory-based rationale that is connected to a well-constructed research design, present well-formulated conclusions and implications that advance the literacy field, and be accessible to graduate students and professionals alike.

TMPR6, like its predecessors, seeks to represent earlier and current scholarship that is among the best in the field. It builds on the classics of earlier editions in two important ways. First, the sixth edition's content is largely reflective of a user survey that showed what the literacy field deemed necessary to retain from earlier editions of *TMPR* as well as several perceived gaps that needed closing.

Looking to the field to inform their selection of content for this edition, the editors took into account the results of 640 completed surveys distributed and analyzed by the International Reading Association. Survey respondents included faculty and graduate students in literacy education departments across the United States. The editors also initiated small focus groups at several annual meetings of key literacy organizations to determine new topics that professionals in the field wished to see represented in the new edition. Finally, the editors used data compiled from the surveys and focus groups to assist them in making decisions about the content that would be included in the sixth edition. This decision-making process was aimed at negotiating a balance between their sense of new trends in the field and earlier classics that have retained relevancy well into the 21st century.

The titles of the four sections remain intact from earlier editions. Within each section, there is a rich blend of newly commissioned chapters, reprints of recently published articles, and updates to chapters that have been brought forward to preserve the historical value of *TMPR* over the past five decades.

In Section One, "Perspectives on Literacy Research and Its Application," Patricia Alexander and Emily Fox have updated their earlier chapter on historical perspective in reading research and practice while simultaneously offering a rationale for where they see the field headed. A new chapter by Norman Unrau and Donna Alvermann traces the evolving contexts for models of reading and writing, especially in relation to what counts as a model in an ever widening field of theoretical stances. Just as theories have entered the field from disciplines such as psychology, sociology, and anthropology, so also have new methodologies for studying a broader array of reading and writing practices. Capturing this latter trend is a new chapter by Marla Mallette, Nell Duke, Stephanie Strachan, Chad Waldron, and Lynne Watanabe in which they explore the synergy that exists among several well-known research methodologies.

Section Two, "Processes of Reading and Literacy," contains 13 new chapters (including commissioned pieces and reprints), plus updates for another three chapters (Melanie Kuhn and Steven Stahl; Louise Spear-Swerling; and Ann Brown, Annemarie Sullivan Palincsar, and Bonnie Armbruster) that were brought forward from earlier editions of *TMPR*. In a newly commissioned chapter, Anne Haas Dyson and Celia Genishi report on their research on social talk and imaginative play in the development of young children's language and literacy. Another newly commissioned piece for the sixth edition is Shirley Brice Heath's chapter that builds on her earlier work *Ways With Words*. Iliana Reyes and Patricia Azuara's chapter on emergent biliteracy in young Mexican immigrant children is a reprint of their article by the same name. Another reprint, this one by Carol Lee, uses a Vygotskian lens to explore a group of underachieving urban adolescents' growth in literacy and language. On a somewhat similar topic, Mei Kuin Lai, Stuart McNaughton, Meaola Amituanai-Toloa, Rolf Turner, and Selena Hsiao examine the sustained acceleration of students' achievement in reading comprehension, but this time within a New Zealand context. Two reprints from a special issue of *Educational Researcher* on early literacy learners address the field's concern that more research is needed on young learners' literacy skill development (Christopher Lonigan and Timothy Shanahan) and dual-language learning (Kris Gutiérrez, Marlene Zepeda, and Dina Castro). In two updated chapters on fluency (Melanie Kuhn and Steven Stahl) and reading disabilities (Louise Spear-Swerling), the authors add insights and practices that have appeared in the literature since their earlier reviews of the literature.

Part 3 of Section Two contains a reprint from Katherine Nelson's work on communities of mind as well as a reprint of Mary McVee, KaiLonnie Dunsmore, and James Gavelek's effort to align key concepts of schema theory with sociocultural theory. This part concludes with a newly commissioned chapter by George Hruby and Usha Goswami on the implications of educational neuroscience for reading researchers. Although one might argue that the processes associated with motivation and engagement in Part 4 could be integrated into earlier parts of Section Two, we chose to highlight the importance of these processes by adding two new chapters that extend the work of the National Reading Research Center. Both are reprints, with the first of the two (Ana Taboada, Stephen Tonks, Allan Wigfield, and John Guthrie) providing evidence that a reader's desire to comprehend a printed text stimulates metacognitive processing, background knowledge activation, and the use of relevant cognitive-based strategies. The second reprint, a chapter by Alfred Tatum, focuses on the role of enabling texts—that is, texts which engage youths in certain sociocultural, political, spiritual, and economic issues that they find relevant to their lives. Part 5, which concludes Section Two, addresses the requests of several focus group members who asked for theoretically grounded research on students' literacy development in instructional contexts. In a newly commissioned chapter (Mary Anne Doyle), the author explores the theoretical basis for Marie Clay's Reading Recovery approach to early literacy intervention. Finally, a postscript by Annemarie Sullivan Palincsar to her coauthored chapter with Ann Brown and Bonnie Armbruster addresses the adaptations that have been made to reciprocal teaching since its inception.

Section Three, "Models of Reading and Writing Processes," contains a wide range of models that represent markedly different reading and writing theories. A number of these are retained from earlier editions of *TMPR* and are derived from cognitive-processing theories; others draw from transactional, sociocultural, and sociocognitive theories. Of the six chapters in Part 1 of Section Three on cognitive-processing models, one is an update by Walter Kintsch on his construction–integration model of text comprehension. His influence on Brenda Hannon's model of reading comprehension performance in proficient adult readers is evident in a new reprint that concludes the part. In Part 2 of this section, Mark Sadoski and Allan Paivio update their dual coding theory of reading, and in Part 3, we have retained Louise Rosenblatt's chapter on the transactional theory of reading and writing. Part 4 on integrating reading and writing models contains two new chapters: one is a reprint of Giovanni Parodi's article on reading–writing connections in discourse-oriented research, and the other is a commissioned piece by Mira-Lisa Katz, Nancy Brynelson, and John Edlund that focuses on the reading and writing of expository text—a curriculum that guides students' ability to enact rhetorical literacies and also promotes college access and success. In Part 5, Robert Ruddell and Norman Unrau integrate two of their chapters from earlier editions of *TMPR* to show how the classroom teacher figures prominently into their sociocognitive model of reading as a meaning-construction process involving reader, text, and teacher.

Section Four, "Literacy's New Horizons: An Emerging Agenda for Tomorrow's Research and Practice," contains four new chapters, two chapter updates, and one reprint. A new chapter by Donna Alvermann and Elizabeth Birr Moje deconstructs the discourse of "every teacher a teacher of reading" to point out the need for a model of adolescent literacy instruction that takes into account the complexities of 21st-century teaching and learning in subject matter classrooms. An updated chapter from an earlier edition of *TMPR* by Deborah Dillon, David O'Brien, and Elizabeth Heilman reexamines how literacy scholars' preoccupation with paradigmatic debates resulted in fewer practical advances in the field of literacy education than might have been the case had pragmatism been adopted as a viable alternative. In a reprint of an article focused on the National Early Literacy Panel's recommendations for teaching young children how to read, David Pearson and Elfrieda Hiebert critique what they describe as a "basic-skills conspiracy of good intentions" (p. 1145). In an updated chapter on information technologies and the changing nature of literacy, Donald Leu, Charles Kinzer, Julie Coiro, Jill Castek, and Laurie Henry reinforce their earlier work in *TMPR5* that literacy today is deictic, multiple, multimodal, and multifaceted. In a newly commissioned chapter, Jennifer Rowsell, Gunther Kress, Kate Pahl, and Brian Street offer for the first time an integrated perspective on new literacies and a social semiotic approach to multimodality. In the remaining two commissioned chapters, the authors suggest an agenda for future research. For example, Glynda Hull, Amy Stornaiuolo, and Laura Sterponi provide a new taxonomy of textual strategies—one that specifically invites participation in online communication through designfulness, overture, reciprocity, and resonance. Finally, Robert Rueda takes into account the new and multiple literacies needed in an interconnected global economy in which information-driven work environments depend on an individual's ability to adapt quickly and creatively while simultaneously attending to factors that influence a reader's motivation to read and write.

Acknowledgments

As we conclude our work on the sixth edition, we would like to recognize and express our appreciation to a number of people who have helped us complete this multiyear project. We first want to thank a very long list of literacy researchers and theory builders who have contributed to this edition. Second, we want to express our appreciation to the many professors, graduate students, and literacy specialists who responded to our survey, participated in focus groups, and provided us with feedback that helped us shape this volume's content. They enabled us to see the past and the future more clearly. Third, we must acknowledge the extensive and impressive help we received from our graduate research assistants who enabled us to include graduate student perspectives throughout the process of creating this edition. Our gratitude goes to Gurupreet Kahlsa, a doctoral student at the University of Southern Alabama, who worked closely with Norman Unrau, and to Andrew Huddleston and Jairus Joaquin, both of whom were graduate students at The University of Georgia and worked closely with Donna Alvermann. Their thoughtful input will be long remembered.

We also wish to thank our families for their care and encouragement during this four-year endeavor: To Jack and Jazz, who excel in the world of humans and golden retrievers when it comes to patience and loyalty in dealing with Donna's projects. To Norm's wife, Cherene, to her listening ear, and to her understanding as we moved step by step through the creation of this work go boundless appreciation. To Bob's wife, Sandra, who has provided her support, understanding, and love throughout the completion of this important research volume, go special thoughts, gratitude, and respect.

Our appreciation also goes out to many individuals at IRA headquarters, past and present. When we began this endeavor, Anne Fullerton helped us take many of the critical first steps involved in creating this book, including facilitation with surveys and focus groups, setting up early meetings at conventions, and creating a road map to this project's completion. We were then fortunate to work with Shannon Fortner, who directed IRA's collaboration on the project seamlessly, answered our stream of questions in a timely and fully comprehensible manner, and exercised her editorial skills as the book moved toward production. We also valued the contributions of the Publications Division and many of its individual members, including Susanne Viscarra, Tori Bachman, Christina Lambert, and Cindy Held.

Finally, we want to thank the International Reading Association's Board of Directors and other IRA personnel for their support, which enabled the production of this sixth edition of *Theoretical Models and Processes of Reading.*

Donna E. Alvermann
Norman J. Unrau
Robert B. Ruddell

REFERENCE

Huey, E.B. (1968). *The psychology and pedagogy of reading.* Cambridge, MA: MIT Press. (Original work published 1908)

SECTION ONE

Perspectives on Literacy Research and Its Application

In the introductory section for this edition of *Theoretical Models and Processes of Reading*, we have focused more intently on the construct of theory, its manifestations and transformations throughout the history of literacy research, and methods considered useful in its development. The three chapters in this section serve as lenses to look on three separate but interacting spheres: perspectives of research and theory over the past 60 years, the roles that theory and models have had in the evolution of literacy research and instruction, and research methodologies best used to address research topics or the problems of practice in literacy and to build theory that illuminates.

Where were we? Where are we? Where are we going? Answers to these questions come from Patricia Alexander and Emily Fox, who provide us with "A Historical Perspective on Reading Research and Practice, Redux" (Chapter 1). In their chapter, the authors survey the past 60 years of reading history and identify six perspectives on learning beginning with the "Era of Conditioned Learning" that started in the 1950s and progressing to our current "Emergent Era of Goal-Directed Learning" that commenced in 2006. The authors then distill lessons learned from those 60 years. Their review of six decades of reading research and instruction magnifies and clarifies factors, such as trends in research, that have guided and shaped the identity and evolution of the field of reading.

Because absolute truth often eludes our pursuit, we rely on theoretical lenses to focus our beliefs and practices. It is from theories that researchers build models in attempts to explain complex cognitive, cultural, and social processes. As in Plato's cave, where what is seen is but a reflection of reality, models are representations through which we make sense of abstractions. In "Literacies and Their Investigation Through Theories and Models" (Chapter 2), Norman Unrau and Donna Alvermann assay the paradigms, theories, and models through which researchers have studied reading and literacies over the last half century, including constructivism, social constructionism, information/cognitive processing theories, sociocultural perspectives, sociocognitive theory, structuralism, poststructuralism, pragmatism, and motivational theories. In a discussion of how literacy theories have given rise to theoretical models and perspectives, research directions and methodologies, instructional practices, and interventions, the authors clarify how views of literacy continue to evolve as the 21st century witnesses massive changes in the way communication takes place in a global society.

An interesting proposal from Marla Mallette, Nell Duke, Stephanie Strachan, Chad Waldron, and Lynne Watanabe in "Synergy in Literacy Research Methodology" (Chapter 3) outlines a new way of thinking about research design classifications used in literacy research. Rather than the traditional quantitative, qualitative, or mixed-methods typologies, the authors suggest a classification based on the type of insights that various methodologies provide. Categories of what is, what was, what happens when, and what can be are described, with recent studies examined for how they illuminate these insights. A classification system such as the authors' outline can provide continuity for specific foci of research over time, no matter what methodological approach is selected for a study.

These three chapters also serve as an introduction to the next three sections of this edition. Section Two provides a spectrum of studies that focus on literacy processes and that often contribute to knowledge that has been synthesized into the reading and other literacy theories and models presented in Section Three. Section Four then provides us with a view of the multiple challenges that lie on the horizon as we build our knowledge base, develop perspectives, and deepen understandings that enrich literacy and learning.

A Historical Perspective on Reading Research and Practice, Redux

Patricia A. Alexander and Emily Fox, University of Maryland, College Park

In this chapter, we have been asked to revisit the past eras and future directions that we have identified for the domain of reading, beginning with the creation of the International Reading Association in 1956, an event regarded as transformational in the history of this field (Monaghan & Saul, 1987). Without question, the efforts of researchers during that formative period gave rise to extensive literature on learners and the learning process that remains an enduring legacy. Yet, this was not the only period of significant change the reading community has experienced in the past 60 years. In fact, reading has periodically responded to internal and external forces, resulting in both gradual and dramatic transformations to the domain—transformations that have altered reading study and practice. Our purpose here is to position those transformations within a historical framework. As with others (VanSledright, 2002), we hold that such a historical perspective allows for reasoned reflection and a certain wisdom that can be easily lost when one is immersed in ongoing study and practice. That is because a historical perspective broadens the vista on reading and adds a critical dimension to the analysis of present-day events and issues.

To capture this historical perspective, we surveyed eras in reading research and practice that have unfolded in the past 60 years and that symbolize alternative perspectives on learners and learning. For each, we described certain internal and external conditions that helped frame that period, as well as the views of and principles of learning that are characteristic of that era. Moreover, we explored both the prevailing views of learning within those periods and rival stances that existed as educational undercurrents. To bring this historical vista into focus, we highlighted exemplary and prototypic works that encapsulated the issues and concerns of the time. Of course, we recognize that the boundaries and distinctions we have drawn between these eras are approximations of permeable and overlapping periods of reading research and practice. Nonetheless, these eras remain a useful platform from which the subsequent contributions in this volume can be explored.

In revisiting the historical perspective offered in our initial venture (Alexander & Fox, 2004), we considered the degree to which our interpretation of past and emergent perspectives adopted by the field might be expected to remain stable

This chapter is adapted from "A Historical Perspective on Reading Research and Practice," in *Theoretical Models and Processes of Reading* (5th ed., pp. 33–68), edited by R.B. Ruddell and N.J. Unrau, 2004, Newark, DE: International Reading Association.

over time (i.e., from one edition of *Theoretical Models and Processes of Reading* to the next). It was our sense that our view of the distant eras could be expected to remain relatively stable. What we saw as characterizing the view of the learner by the field during a given time period and what we considered to be the forces for change pushing toward a new perspective on learning and a new view of the learner were not likely to change significantly in the absence of any major influx of new information or transformative new worldview that would cast these eras and their progressive unfolding in a radically different light. However, where we did expect that change could occur would be in our provisional characterization of the emergent era, and our view of where the field was heading.

When we first undertook this historical analysis (Alexander & Fox, 2004), we held that the reading research community was poised at a new juncture in its history—a juncture that was formed in part by the juxtaposition of increasingly varied forms of reading engaged in by globally networked students with a seemingly unwavering investment in the high-stakes testing of reading skills and competencies. Herein, we not only return to our description of past eras and evaluate our skills at prognostication when it came to the then-emergent period, but we also consider the onset of a new era only now taking form.

The Era of Conditioned Learning (1950–1965)

The Conditions for Change

As early as the first decades of the 20th century, during the nascence of psychology, the processes of reading were already of passing interest to educational researchers (e.g., Buswell, 1922; Huey, 1908; Thorndike, 1917). However, it was not until somewhat later in that century that reading became a recognized field of study with systematic programs of research aimed at ascertaining its fundamental nature and the processes of its acquisition. Although reading had long been a basic component of formal schooling in the United States, attention to and efforts toward marrying research knowledge and instructional practice regarding the processes entailed in reading acquisition underwent a significant increase during the 1950s. Instigation for that marked change came as a result of a confluence of social, educational, political, and economic factors occurring in that decade.

Postwar America was fertile ground for transformations in reading research and practice for several reasons. For one, the high birthrate during and immediately following World War II resulted in record numbers of children entering the public school system (Ganley, Lyons, & Sewall, 1993). This baby boom contributed to both quantitative and qualitative changes to the school population. One of those qualitative changes was a seeming rise in the number of children experiencing difficulties in learning to read. Such reading problems, while nothing new to teachers, took on particular significance in the age of Sputnik, as America's ability to compete globally became a defining issue (Allington & McGill-Franzen, 2000). The outcome was a growing public pressure on the educational community to find an answer to the "problem" of reading acquisition.

One of the groundbreaking but controversial publications of this period was *Why Johnny Can't Read—and What You Can Do About It* by Rudolf Flesch (1955). This publication exemplified a growing interest in reading research and its relevance to educational practice (Ruddell, 2002). In arguments reminiscent of contemporary debates, Flesch attacked the prevailing look–say method of reading instruction as a contributor to the reading problems experienced by many American students. As the basis for his attack, he referred to research that established the effectiveness of phonics-based techniques over those that relied on a whole-word approach. Before long, volumes like the *See Dick...* and *See Jane...* books with their look–say approach gave way to controlled vocabulary readers and synthetic phonics drill and practice in such approaches as the Lippincott Basic Reading Program, Reading With Phonics, and Phonetic Keys to Reading (Chall, 1967).

The burgeoning interest in finding an answer to children's reading problems interfaced with psychological research in the guise of Skinnerian behaviorism, the prevailing research orientation at the time (Goetz, Alexander, & Ash, 1992). With its promise of bringing a scientific perspective to the reading problem, behaviorism seemed suited to the task at hand (Glaser, 1978). In effect, it was time to turn the attention of the research community to the fundamental task of learning to read, and to apply the same principles of analysis that explained and controlled the behavior of animals in the laboratory to children's language learning. Such an analysis would presumably result in pedagogical techniques based on an understanding of the physiological and environmental underpinnings of human behavior (Glaser, 1978).

Based on this perspective, the processes and skills involved in learning to read could be clearly defined and broken down into their constituent parts. Those constituent parts could then be practiced and reinforced in a systematic and orderly fashion during classroom instruction (Pearson & Stephens, 1994). With this analytic view, there was a growing tendency for problems in the reading act to be looked upon as deficiencies in need of remediation, just as physical ailments require medical remedies. Indeed, it was a medical metaphor of reading, with its diagnosis, prescription, and remediation, that came to the foreground in the 1950s. Moreover, despite the claims of some within the reading research community that little of significance occurred in reading until the 1960s (Weaver & Kintsch, 1991), the continued influence of behaviorism on educational practice remains evident today.

Guiding View

Because of the prevailing influences of behavioristic theory in educational research and practice, reading during this period was conceptualized as conditioned behavior and just another process susceptible to programming. The Skinnerian or strict behaviorist perspective was that learning should not be conceived as growth or development, but rather as acquiring behaviors as a result of certain environmental contingencies. As Skinner (1976) states,

> Everyone has suffered, and unfortunately is continuing to suffer, from mentalistic theories of learning in education....The point of education can be stated in behavioral terms: a teacher arranges contingencies under which the student acquires behavior

> which will be useful to him under other contingencies later on....Education covers the behavior of a child or person over many years, and the principles of developmentalism are therefore particularly troublesome. (pp. 202–203)

In this theoretical orientation, learning results from the repeated and controlled stimulation from the environment that comes to elicit a predictable response from the individual. This repeated pairing of stimulus/response, often linked with the application of carefully chosen rewards and punishments, leads to the habituation of the reading act. For example, the child presented with the symbols C-A-T immediately produces the desired word, *cat*, seemingly without cognitive involvement.

The philosophical grounds for this stance lay in the works of the empiricist David Hume (1777/1963) and his narrow conception of knowledge as perception and learning as habituated association (Strike, 1974). The investigation of academic learning, thus, involved identification of the requisite desired behaviors and determination of the environmental conditions (i.e., training) that produced them. Depending on how strictly the behaviorist paradigm was followed, hypotheses and conclusions were more or less restricted to discussion of observable behaviors and the environmental stimuli that preceded them (Strike, 1974).

The task for this generation of reading researchers, therefore, was to untangle the chained links of behavior involved in reading so learners could be trained in each component skill. The act of reading consisted of the competent and properly sequenced performance of that chain of discrete skills. Research was additionally concerned with the structuring and control of materials effective in the delivery of environmental stimulation and practice opportunities (Glaser, 1978; Monaghan & Saul, 1987). There was also a concomitant interest in the identification and remediation of problems in skill acquisition, which would require even finer grained analysis of the appropriate behaviors so skill training could proceed in the smallest of increments (Glaser, 1978).

Resulting Principles

Out of the labors of the reading researchers of this era came a body of literature on the multitude of subskills required for reading. The interest in the study of the components of reading processes was exemplified by such efforts as the interdisciplinary studies at Cornell University that became the Project Literacy program (Levin, 1965; Venezky, 1984). As a result of the behaviorist emphasis on studying observable behavior, there was a particular focus on reading as a perceptual activity. Such perceptual activities included the identification of visual signals, the translation of these signals into sounds, and assembly of these sounds into words, phrases, and sentences (Pearson & Stephens, 1994). Phonics instruction came to be seen as part of the logical groundwork for beginning to read (Chall, 1967, 1995) and had the desirable attribute of being eminently trainable. The counterpart of this emphasis on skills was an interest in developing and validating diagnostic instruments and remedial techniques (C.E. Smith & Keogh, 1962).

Where there were problems in skill acquisition, the solution was likely to be an individually paced training program (Glaser, 1978).

Rival Views of Learner and Learning Process

Although the behaviorist perspective dominated the psychological research of the time, alternative theories of human learning operated beneath the surface. The legacy of William James (1890) endures in the notion that human thought mattered in human action and that introspection and self-questioning were effective tools for uncovering those thoughts. According to James, reading would best be described as a mindful habit. As such, reading would best be examined through a psychological lens via introspection rather than through the behaviorists' physiological lens of observation of measurable behaviors. From such mental inspection, hypotheses as to the nature of reading could be forged (Jenkinson, 1969). This approach stood directly against the behaviorist antagonism to mentalism and insistence on observation of overt behavior only. When researchers addressed questions about the reasoning involved in reading, they leaned toward a Jamesian stance and away from strict behaviorism (Alexander, 2003).

From another angle, the reductionist aspect of behaviorism, with its intended training program of bottom-up assembly of linked sets of behaviors to create a coherent activity such as learning to read, stood in opposition to Gestalt theory (Wertheimer, 1945/1959). For Gestalt theory, understanding phenomena as wholes was essential and could never be achieved by concatenation of individual facts, skills, or observations (Wulf, 1922/1938). Although explanation of perceptual processes occupied much of the attention of Gestalt theorists, their focus was on the phenomenon as a whole rather than on its elements. Human beings brought to the tasks of perception the propensity and ability to synthesize and make coherent sense out of their perceptual data. Such coherence and sense could not be achieved by assembly alone.

The top-down perspective emphasized by Gestalt theorists was evident in the developmental approach to learning to read, a competing stance taken by reading researchers leading into and during this era (e.g., Gray, 1951; Gray & Rogers, 1956; Russell, 1961; Strang, McCullough, & Traxler, 1955). These developmentalists were identified by Chall (1967) as linguistic proponents who emphasized whole-word recognition, the importance of context in comprehension and word identification, and the consideration of reading as a unique human activity with its own definitive characteristics. They viewed learning to read as a lifespan developmental process, and they saw reading development as an important contributor to and reflection of the individual's development as a person. The developmental approach decried by Skinner assumed that reading was an intrinsically intentional activity aimed at the fulfillment of meaningful purposes, with adult purposes for reading having high educational interest and potential social value. This mindfulness or purposefulness of reading involved multiple aspects of reading, including its function as communication between individuals as well as the essential roles of interest and motivation in what and how people read. From this perspective, even at its earliest stages, reading development was never merely a matter of acquisition of skills but entailed an understanding of reading as meaning making and as ultimately aimed toward achievement of the reader's own purposes.

The Era of Natural Learning (1966–1975)

The Conditions for Change

By the mid-1960s, there was already a general unrest with the precepts of Skinnerian behaviorism (Ryle, 1949) and with the conceptualization of reading as discrete skills passively drilled and practiced until reflexively demonstrated. Several factors served to hasten the transition in research on the learner and the learning process. One of those factors was an increased interest in internal mental structures and processes sparked by advances in neurology and artificial intelligence (Ericsson & Smith, 1991). Both of these movements turned attention back inside the human mind and away from the environment.

Another factor in this theoretical transformation was the fact that the dissatisfaction with behaviorism as an explanatory system was shared by diverse segments of the educational research community whose views on many other issues were frequently at odds (Pearson & Stephens, 1994). In the mid-1960s, a federally funded nationwide cooperative research venture, the First Grade Studies (Bond & Dykstra, 1967), brought together researchers on 27 different reading projects in a systematic comparison of various approaches to instruction in beginning reading. The attention of researchers in a wide range of disciplines had been drawn to the investigation of the reading process, the effect of which was an interdisciplinary perspective on the nature of reading and the teaching of reading that remains a hallmark of the field.

Two communities of theorists and researchers were especially influential in setting the stage for this period of reading research: linguists and psycholinguists. On the one hand, linguists following in the tradition of Chomsky (1957, 2002) held to a less environmentally driven and more hardwired view of language acquisition, and hence of reading. Psycholinguistic researchers, on the other hand, felt that the attention to discrete aspects of reading advocated in behaviorism destroyed the natural communicative power and inherent aesthetic of reading (Goodman & Goodman, 1979; F. Smith, 1973, 1978). Given these circumstances, the stage was set for a new era of reading research.

Guiding View

In this new era of reading research, the conceptualization that served as the formative stance was of learning as a natural process. Language, as with other innate human capacities, was to be developed through meaningful use, not practiced to the point of mindless reaction, as behaviorists proposed. This notion of hardwired capacities blended the explanatory language of physiology and psychology (Chomsky, 1965). It was assumed that human beings are biologically programmed to acquire language under favorable conditions. This programming involved the existence of mental structures designed to perform the complex task of assimilating and integrating the particular linguistic cues provided by a given language community (Chomsky, 1975).

Such a view of the language learner was strongly influenced by the writings of linguist Noam Chomsky (e.g., 1998, 2002) and marked a dramatic shift from the behaviorist view of learning as conditioning. In his classic volume *Syntactic Structures*, Chomsky (1957) helped establish the field of generative grammar, which focused on the assumed innate mental structures that allowed for language use. He argued that it was critical to separate human mental competencies from subsequent performance, an argument that distinguished him from the majority of linguists of the time concerned with the performance end of language (i.e., transformational grammar). In framing his theory, Chomsky was influenced by the emerging research in neuroscience and cognitive science (Baars, 1986). He saw unquestionable relations between the universality of neurological structures and the universality of grammatical structures. His assertion was that humans emerge from the womb with a preexisting template that guides language use. "Languaging" was thus perceived to unfold naturally, to follow a developmental trajectory, and to involve not just the action of the environment on the individual but also the individual's contribution in the form of a predisposition or innate capacity (Chomsky, 1957, 1998). This shift in the view of language acquisition from conditioned behavior to natural process inevitably reverberated in the reading research community in the form of psycholinguistics (Goodman, 1965; F. Smith, 1973). As with the generative grammarians, psycholinguists argued that because all human languages follow similar production rules, the capacity for language must be built in. Psycholinguists carried this assumption beyond oral language into print or reading. They also focused on semantics or meaning and how meaning is acquired, represented, and used during the process of reading. Consequently, learning to read, the written counterpart of acquiring an oral language, came to be viewed as an inherent ability rather than a reflective act involving the laborious acquisition of a set of skills (Harste, Burke, & Woodward, 1984). Just as children came to understand the spoken language of their surrounding community (Halliday, 1969), they would come to understand its written language given enough exposure in meaningful situations (Goodman & Goodman, 1979).

While generative grammarians and psycholinguists sought the universals underlying human language acquisition and use, others during this time period became interested in the interaction of language as a system and language in its particular social uses. Sociolinguistic investigations such as those of Labov (1966) and Shuy (1968) began to explore variations in everyday language use and the relation of those variations to social roles (Labov, 1972). The contrast between the everyday language of children growing up in different social settings and the language demanded in an educational setting began to surface as an issue for educational research and practice (Labov, 1976; Shuy, 1969).

Resulting Principles

With the view that language development was a native capacity of human beings came significant changes not only in perceptions of the nature of reading but also in the position of reading relative to other language processes and in preferred modes of diagnosis and instruction. Specifically, because the premise underlying this "natural movement" was that language had a natural and rule-governed structure, it became essential to unite all manner of language acquisition and use. To assume that the process of acquiring and using written language was somehow unique from that of speaking or listening would be disruptive to the theoretical premises upon which this perspective was founded. Thus, in this period and for subsequent eras of reading research, we see a tendency toward the aggregation of the language arts into the unified field of literacy (Halliday & Hasan, 1974).

Concurrent with this new view of reading as a natural process, investigations into the inferred mental structures and processes of reading in relation to performance took shape. For one, the learner was cast in the role of an active participant, a constructor of meaning who used many forms of information to arrive at comprehension (Halliday, 1969). Learning to read was not so much a matter of being taught but a matter of arriving at facility as a result of a predisposition to seek understanding within a language-rich environment.

For another, reading diagnosis within this period was less about isolating and correcting problems in the underlying skills of reading than it was about understanding how readers arrived at their alternative interpretations of written text (Clay, 1967, 1976). Unlike the diagnostic studies of the preceding period (Christenson & Barney, 1969; C.E. Smith & Keogh, 1962; Snyder & Freud, 1967), this new model of diagnosis did not focus on identifying and eradicating the source of readers' errors. Rather, the goal was to ascertain how the unexpected responses readers produced were reflective of their attempts at meaning making (Goodman & Goodman, 1979). The groundbreaking work by Kenneth Goodman and colleagues on miscue analysis was prototypic of this reconceptualization occurring in reading diagnosis (e.g., Goodman, 1965).

Rival Views of Learner and Learning Process

Interestingly, some of the very conditions that sparked the "reading as a natural process" movement helped establish a rival view of reading that came to dominate in the subsequent decade (Fodor, 1964; Fodor, Miller, & Langendoen, 1980). Specifically, a number of individuals invested in cognitive science and artificial intelligence were equally as fascinated with the internal structures and processes of the human mind as were generative grammarians and psycholinguists. However, for these researchers, the focus was more on how those processes and procedures could be best represented symbolically and transferred into computer programs that could approximate human performance (Fodor, 2001). In effect, these individuals were interested in creating "intelligent machines" that mimicked the problem solving of intelligent humans (Alexander, 2003).

What was significant about this alternative view of learners and learning was the lack of any presumption that the mental structures and processes being uncovered via neuroscience meant that resulting performance was somehow innate or hardwired. To the contrary, the variability in human performance that these researchers observed and documented suggested that seeming similarities in human language processes were likely the result of acquired or learned knowledge and processes combined with innate mental capabilities. This seemed especially true for written language, which required the manipulation of a symbolic system not required in oral communication or in other problem-solving domains, such as history or biology (Chi, Glaser, & Farr, 1988).

Although human neurology had a role to play, it was not as a regulator of language use. Within this rival group, there was a growing interest in text-based performance because of the opportunity it provided to investigate the subtle and not-so-subtle differences between experts and novices in terms of their memory, recall, and problem-solving approaches. The level of detail required to approximate even the simplest of human actions resulted in a growing appreciation for the power of individual differences and for the degree to which the specific domain of study and the task altered mental processes (Chase & Simon, 1973). For example, researchers of this period found chess to be an excellent venue for study because it is a game with a rigid and limited rule structure. Yet, there were clearly those who excelled at this mental game. Researchers studied the knowledge and processes of expert chess players to understand how experts visualize tasks, anticipate the moves of their opponents, and act to counter those moves. From this vantage point, any attempt to unify all forms of language acquisition and performance would be discounted within the rival group. Rather, reading as the processing of written text needed to be examined in its own right and not subsumed under the process of acquiring and using oral language.

The Era of Information Processing (1976–1985)

The Conditions for Change

By the mid-1970s, the reading research community was again poised for theoretical transformation. Conditions for that change included the growing attention to the structure and processes of the human mind and increased federal funding for basic reading research (Alexander, 1998a). The effects of these converging conditions were the creation of research centers dedicated to reading research and, concomitantly, a significant influx of theorists and researchers into the reading community whose interests were more basic than applied research and whose roots were primarily in cognitive psychology (Pearson & Stephens, 1994). The interdisciplinary character of these centers, most notably the Center for the Study of Reading under Richard Anderson, involved individuals from psychology and reading-related fields such as English, literature, communications, and writing.

Given their more basic research agenda and their strong cognitive roots, these alliances forwarded a perspective on reading that deviated markedly from the orientation that had dominated. Specifically, this new perspective held little regard for the innateness or naturalness of reading and little interest in the amalgamation of literacy fields. As would be expected, some within the reading research community felt uneasy about this basic research emphasis, arguing that it had the "deleterious" effects of "squeezing out" reading educators and undervaluing instructional practice (Vacca & Vacca, 1983, p. 383).

Guiding View

On the basis of research published between 1976 and 1985, it was cognitive psychology, and more specifically information-processing theory, that dominated the domain of reading (R.C. Anderson, 1977). However, a psycholinguistic undercurrent remained evident during this period and gained momentum as new constituents joined the reading community. Even given the continuing presence of psycholinguistics, this remained the era of cognitive psychology characterized by unprecedented research on knowledge, especially the construct of prior knowledge (Alexander, 1998a). Much of this knowledge research was influenced by the philosophy of Immanuel Kant (1787/1963). Kantian philosophy was significant for its distinction between the sensible world and the intelligible world as varied sources of human knowledge:

> By "sensible world" [Kant] meant the world as perceived by the senses; he would later call this also the phenomenal world, or world of appearances. By "intelligible world" he meant the world as conceived by the intellect or reason....Here Kant already laid down his basic theses: that space and time are not objective or sensible objects, but are forms of perception inherent in the nature and structure of the mind; and that the mind is no passive recipient and product of sensations, but is an active agent—with inherent modes and laws of operation—for transforming sensations into ideas. (Durant & Durant, 1967, p. 534)

This new generation of reading researchers searched for general processes or "laws" that explained human language as an interaction between symbol system and mind. With the burgeoning studies in expert/novice differences and artificial intelligence (Chi, Feltovich, & Glaser, 1981; Ericsson & Smith, 1991; Schank & Abelson, 1977), the medical metaphor of diagnosis, prescription, and remediation that reigned in the 1950s and the "reading as a natural process" metaphor of the 1960s were replaced with a mechanistic information-processing metaphor (Reynolds, Sinatra, & Jetton, 1996). Text-based learning was about knowledge, which was organized and stored within the individual mind and resulted from the input, interpretation, organization, retention, and output of information from the individual's environment (Samuels & Kamil, 1984).

Resulting Principles

As noted, the construct of prior knowledge and its potent influence on students' text-based learning were enduring legacies of this era (Alexander, 1998a; Alexander & Murphy, 1998). Specifically, the readers' knowledge base was shown to be *powerful*, *pervasive*, *individualistic*, and *modifiable*. Prior knowledge was linked to individuals' perspectives on what they read or heard (Pichert & Anderson, 1977), their allocation of attention (R.C. Anderson, Pichert, & Shirey, 1983), and their interpretations and recall of written text (Bransford & Franks, 1971; Lipson, 1983). In addition, significant associations were established between readers' existing knowledge and their subsequent reading performance (Stanovich, 1986), comprehension (Alvermann, Smith, & Readence, 1985), memory (R.C. Anderson, Reynolds, Schallert, & Goetz, 1977), and strategic processing (Alexander & Judy, 1988; Garner, 1987).

Because of the primacy of reading-specific studies during this period, an extensive literature on text-based factors arose, particularly in relation to comprehension. Writings on story grammar, text cohesion, text structure, and text genres proliferated (Armbruster, 1984; Kintsch & van Dijk, 1978; Mandl, Stein, & Trabasso, 1984; Meyer, 1975; Taylor & Beach, 1984). Further, in parallel with the foci within the broader cognitive field, reading theorists and researchers investigated the organization of knowledge in the mind (R.C. Anderson, 1977; Rumelhart, 1980) and how that organization distinguished novice readers from more expert readers (Allington, 1980; August, Flavell, & Clift, 1984; Lundeberg, 1987; Paris & Myers, 1981).

The information-processing research of this period resulted in a multitude of cognition-related constructs. Of the many constructs articulated in this decade, schema theory remains one of the most potent legacies of the time. In fact, Baldwin et al. (1992) described schema theory as "one of the hottest topics in the history of NRC" (p. 507). The theoretical construct of schemata, what Rumelhart (1980) calls the building blocks of cognition, drew explicitly on the philosophy of Kant (R.C. Anderson et al., 1977) and embodied the power, pervasiveness, individuality, and modifiability of knowledge previously mentioned. Even those forwarding alternative explanations for the structure of human knowledge and the processing of information have had to counter the tenets of schema theory and the body of supporting evidence (Sadoski, Paivio, & Goetz, 1991).

One of the distinguishing characteristics of this research period was its focus on the individual mind. Such an individualistic perspective was understandable for several reasons. First, the computer-based viewpoint that shaped this era was fundamentally a model of individual knowledge acquisition and use. There was little, if any, consideration of sociocultural or contextual influences on the processing of linguistic information. Second, the research studies generated during this period strongly supported individualistic interpretations of written text. In effect, any presumption that one and only one interpretation would result from reading text was empirically disputed (Brewer, 1980).

Finally, the research activities of this period demonstrated that students' knowledge could be significantly modified through direct intervention, training, or explicit instruction (Paris & Winograd, 1990; Pressley, Goodchild, Fleet, Zajchowski, & Evans, 1989; Weinstein, Goetz, & Alexander, 1988). This body of strategy research highlighted the modifiability of individuals' knowledge bases and their approaches to information processing. These studies targeted a spectrum of general text-processing strategies, including summarization, mapping, self-questioning, and predicting (Brown, Campione, & Day, 1981; Hansen, 1981; Raphael & Wonnacott, 1985; Tierney, Readence, & Dishner, 1990). There was also consideration of instructional environments and pedagogical techniques that contributed to improved comprehension of text (Duffy, Roehler, Meloth, & Vavrus, 1986; Lysynchuk, Pressley, D'Ailly, Smith, & Cake, 1989; Pearson, 1984).

Rival Views of Learner and Learning Process

Among the most vocal critics of the information-processing approach to reading research were those who held to a more naturalistic and holistic view of reading (e.g., F. Smith, 1985). Many of the psycholinguists who had fueled the "reading as natural process" movement were significant forces in this rival perspective. However, there were several important distinctions between this iteration of the natural movement and its predecessor. For one, there was a shift away from the neurological or physiological arguments central to that earlier period and more concern for naturalism in the materials and procedures used to teach reading. One reason for this shift in emphasis was the new alliances that invigorated this alternative view. Specifically, there was an influx of literature and writing researchers into the reading community who were more interested in the unity within the language arts than in any potential dissimilarities. The expanding literature on the common bases of reading and writing was indicative of this integrated view (Spivey & King, 1989; Tierney, Soter, O'Flahavan, & McGinley, 1989), as were the studies on discussion (Alvermann & Hayes, 1989; Bloome & Green, 1984; Heath, 1982).

Characteristic of this rival view was an increased concern for the aesthetic of reading over the rational (Rosenblatt, 1978/1994). One outcome of this philosophical reorientation was a rather negative attitude toward knowledge as the "residue" of information getting or fact finding (p. 23). This unfavorable view of knowledge as information getting is well represented in the writings of Louise Rosenblatt, especially her classic treatise *The Reader, the Text, the Poem: The Transactional Theory of the Literary Work*. With her writings, Rosenblatt frames several decades of literacy research around the notion of reader stances or responses to text (e.g., Britton, 1982; Cox & Many, 1992; Fish, 1980).

Rosenblatt (1978/1994) contends that depending on the goal of the learner and the instructor, an individual's response to a text falls along a continuum from an efferent to an aesthetic stance. Those assuming a more efferent stance seek to uncover the truths voiced by some invisible or anonymous author:

> In nonaesthetic reading, the reader's attention is focused primarily on what will remain as the residue *after* the reading—the information to be acquired, the logical solution to a problem, the actions to be carried out. As the reader responds to the printed words or symbols, his attention is directed outward so to speak, toward concepts to be retained, ideas to be tested, actions to be performed after the reading. (p. 23)

By contrast, readers holding to an aesthetic stance focus on the literary experience and allow themselves to discover the pleasure and beauty of the story:

> In aesthetic reading, in contrast, the reader's primary concern is with what happens *during* the actual reading event....*In aesthetic reading, the reader's attention is centered directly on what he is living through during his relationship with that particular text.* (pp. 24–25)

This contrast between the aesthetic and efferent stances that Rosenblatt describes had the effect of casting learning from text, central to the information-processing orientation, in an unfavorable light and countered the seemingly analytic, less personal perspective of reading forwarded by cognitive researchers (Benton, 1983; Britton, 1982; Rosenblatt, 1938/1995). In effect, the goal was to lose oneself *in* the text and not specifically to learn *from* it. For those who espoused this goal, a "learning from text" perspective transformed a natural literary, aesthetic experience into an unnatural, overly analytic act.

The Era of Sociocultural Learning (1986–1995)

The Conditions for Change

As the mid-1980s came along, there were indications that the reading community was positioned for further change. The explanatory adequacy of the computer metaphor that had guided the information-processing–based research of the previous decade was perceived as diminishing, even by those in the field of artificial intelligence who had fostered this metaphor (J.R. Anderson, Reder, & Simon, 1996). For instance, within cognitive psychology, the earlier information-processing approach was replaced by a constructivist theory that acknowledged learning as individualistic while rejecting the mechanistic and computerlike aspects of learning implicit in this stance (Reynolds et al., 1996).

This shift in emphasis may have come to pass as the applications of the information-processing approach in such areas as expert systems development and classroom training programs were seen to have less-than-ideal outcomes. The expert systems that were designed to imitate human decision-making processes (e.g., Clancey, 1983) did not always live up to their claims (Chipman, 1993). In the realm of reading education, the application of information-processing theory in cognitive training programs also proved less promising than anticipated, which engendered doubt as to the feasibility of these training approaches (Harris, 1996). Many students failed to benefit from the explicit instruction in strategies or components of reading that was intended to improve their text-based learning. For some students, no improvements were produced by this instruction, while for others, the benefits did not endure or transfer (Paris, Wasik, & Turner, 1991). Although the prior era of information-processing researchers had embraced general "laws" of text processing, these laws did not appear to account for the behaviors and results seen in specific applications, such as with particular populations, types of textual materials, and in variable classroom conditions (Paris et al., 1991).

A further force for change was the increased influence of alternative perspectives and research traditions speaking from outside the realm of cognitive psychology. Writings in social and cultural anthropology, such as the works of Vygotsky (1934/1986), Lave (1988), and others (Heath, 1983; Rogoff, 1990) provided a new viewpoint for literacy researchers, as well as those in the larger educational research community. These writings sparked a growing acceptance in the literacy community of the ethnographic and qualitative modes of inquiry advocated in social and cultural anthropology. Along with these modes of inquiry came the practice of studying literacy with naturally occurring texts in natural settings, such as classrooms, homes, and workplaces (R.C. Anderson, Wilson, & Fielding, 1988). These new approaches brought the methodology of literacy research more in line with the holistic and aesthetic school of thought. Reflecting this shift in emphasis, the *Journal of Reading Behavior* became first the *Journal of Reading Behavior: Journal of Literacy* in 1991 and then the *Journal of Literacy Research* in 1996. That is, the behavioral orientation toward reading of the 1950s and 1960s, reflected in the title for the journal of the National Reading Conference for many years thereafter, was fully abandoned in favor of a more integrated designation at the beginning of the 1990s.

An additional impetus to change was the development of a systematic attitude of distrust or devaluing of formal knowledge, and of the traditional mode of scientific inquiry. It might be said that the outcome of learning came to be less important than the learning process (Sfard, 1998). The goal of learning was no longer seen as the development of an individually held body of knowledge, but rather the creation of a mutual understanding arising in the social interaction of particular individuals in a particular context at a particular time. At the extremes of the research community, there were those who portrayed the knowledge gained in school settings as an oppressive tool of political and cultural authorities seeking to maintain their dominance over the disempowered (McLaren, 1998). At another extreme were those who characterized schooled knowledge as the currently agreed-upon interpretation of a reality that was essentially unknowable and unverifiable (von Glasersfeld, 1991). A common thread in these theoretical movements active during this time, such as critical theory, postmodernism, and radical constructivism, was the denial of privileged status to formal or schooled knowledge (Gee, 1989; Woods & Murphy, 2002). This multitude of divergent voices and interacting factors pushed research on learning toward a new stage in its development.

Guiding View

As a result of the aforementioned forces, group orientations came to replace the earlier focus on individualistic learning and instruction seen in the prior era (Alexander, Murphy, & Woods, 1996). Literacy research now sought to capture the shared understanding of the many rather than the private knowledge of the one. From detection of the universal laws of learning, the goal became the description of the "ways of knowing" unique to particular social, cultural, and educational groups. The shared literacy experiences advocated in the aesthetic stance of the prior era were enthusiastically taken up, extended, and more broadly accepted with this adoption of social and cultural perspectives on literacy learning. The dominant perspective during this time became the view of learning as a sociocultural, collaborative experience (Alexander, 1996; Reynolds et al., 1996), and of the learner as a member of a learning community (Brown & Campione, 1990). The widespread popularity of such concepts as cognitive apprenticeship, shared cognition, and social constructivism during this time period are evidence of the power of this view.

Resulting Principles

In this era of literacy research, the ongoing movement was toward increased sophistication of the conception of knowledge. Reviews of the knowledge terms used by literacy researchers and in broader educational contexts (Alexander, Schallert, & Hare, 1991; de Jong & Ferguson-Hessler, 1996; Greene & Ackerman, 1995) revealed that literacy involved a multitude of "knowledges." Knowledge was not a singular construct but existed in diverse forms and interactive dimensions (Paris, Lipson, & Wixson, 1983; Prawat, 1989). These various knowledges had to be coordinated or reconciled in the performance of any nontrivial literacy act.

A primary locus for this adaptive activity was in the reconciliation of schooled and unschooled knowledge (Gardner, 1991). Students arrive at school with an extensive prior body of conceptual knowledge guiding their understanding and use of language. This unschooled knowledge (also known as informal knowledge or spontaneous concepts) could differ markedly in character from more formally acquired understandings (i.e., scientific concepts or schooled knowledge; Alexander, 1992; Vygotsky, 1978). Research in the field of conceptual change and misconceptions showed that this unschooled knowledge could be a more salient factor in students' learning from texts than their formally acquired knowledge (Alexander, 1998b; Guzzetti & Hynd, 1998; Vosniadou, 1994). The relative dominance of informal knowledge over formal understandings could be because what is learned in a school setting appears of limited relevance and therefore limited value to students (Alexander & Dochy, 1995; Cognition and Technology Group at Vanderbilt, 1990; Whitehead, 1929/1957). Unschooled knowledge might also possess a concrete and personal referent lacking in much of school learning (Alexander et al., 1996).

Beyond the recognition of knowledge's multiple forms, there was a growing awareness that one's knowledge was not always a positive force in subsequent learning and development. One's existing knowledge could impede or interfere with future learning in the form of misconceptions or barriers to conceptual change (Chinn & Brewer, 1993; Perkins & Simmons, 1988; Roth, 1985). Research on persuasion also provided insight into the possible negative role of preexisting knowledge (Alexander, Murphy, Buehl, & Sperl, 1997; Chambliss, 1995; Garner & Hansis, 1994). Specifically, those who approached arguments and evidence presented in text with little relevant knowledge or with a strong opinion proved more resistant to the author's persuasive message.

Besides these investigations of the complexity of knowledge, research on knowledge and learning in this era also turned to investigation of the conditionality of knowledge. This conditionality could arise from domain specificity or task specificity, as well as from social or contextual factors. The new awareness of the salience of social and contextual contributions to learning was evident in the proliferation of such terms as *learning communities* (Brown & Campione, 1990), *socially shared cognition* (Resnick, Levine, & Teasley, 1991), *distributed cognition* (Salomon, 1993), *shared expertise* (Brown & Palincsar, 1989), *guided participation* (Rogoff, 1990), *situated action* (Greeno & Moore, 1993), or *anchored instruction* (Cognition and Technology Group at Vanderbilt, 1990). Most members of the literacy research community agreed that schooling, at least, was a social and cultural phenomenon along with its resultant knowledge (e.g., Cognition and Technology Group at Vanderbilt, 1996; Lave, 1988; Rogoff, 1990). Schools clearly functioned as social institutions centered on the interactions of students and teachers. Designed to serve socially contrived goals, schools operated as unique socially sanctioned contexts in which students were to build the requisite knowledge base for our postindustrialized societies (e.g., Perret-Claremont, Perret, & Bell, 1980).

Certain researchers made the sociocultural nature of schools and classrooms the focus of their efforts, developing instructional procedures that engendered optimal social interchanges in the classroom (e.g., Bereiter & Scardamalia, 1989; Collins, Brown, & Newman, 1989; Palincsar & Brown, 1984). Teachers, in these approaches, played the essential role of facilitator or guide (Rogoff & Gauvain, 1986; Vygotsky, 1934/1986), with the scaffolding provided by the teacher diminishing in proportion to the students' increasing knowledge, interest, and strategic abilities in a particular area (e.g., Alexander, 1997b; Brown & Palincsar, 1989) so students could develop self-direction and autonomy (Deci & Ryan, 1991).

Conditionality came into play as well in investigations of possible domain specificity of knowledge and learning. Domains made up the realm of academic learning and provided the settings against which choices of vocation and avocation were framed (Alexander, 1998c). The question of the possible relationship of these domains to some objective reality remained (Bereiter, 1994; Matthews, 1994). Nonetheless, these domains differed significantly from one another (Spiro, Feltovich, Jacobson, & Coulson, 1992; Spiro & Jehng, 1990), with these differences strongly affecting the inscription, perception, communication, and learning of the associated knowledge in such domains (Alexander, 1998c; Nolen, Johnson-Crowley, & Wineburg, 1994; Stahl, Hynd, Glynn, & Carr, 1996). One attempt to characterize this diversity was the use of the term *structuredness*, involving the grouping of problems typical of the domain in terms of their form and content or in having an optimal algorithmic or heuristic solution strategy (Frederiksen, 1984).

Some of these domain differences would no doubt seem obvious from even a superficial comparison of such representative texts as a mathematics textbook or a historical account (Ball, 1993; Putnam, Heaton, Prawat, & Remillard, 1992; VanSledright, 1996). Other differences were more deeply imprinted in the beliefs of students and teachers about the domain itself, and also about their own competencies in that domain (Alexander & Dochy, 1995; Pajares, 1992). The answers to questions about what it meant to *know* mathematics versus history or what doing well required in literature versus science diverged (Matthews, 1994; Wineburg, 1996) along pathways determined by beliefs about the epistemological characteristics of different domains, including the certainty of their central concepts or fundamental principles (Schommer, 1990, 1993).

Because domains vary in significant ways, it was logical for researchers to assume that students' knowledge, strategic thinking, and motivations would likewise vary along domain lines (Alexander, 1997b; Murphy & Woods, 1996). This meant that a global label such as "good" or "poor student" would be perceived as too general and in need of qualification. The critical question was, Good at what, or poor at what? Such domain-specific or task-specific qualification of student ability added to the conditionality of learning.

Rival Views of the Learner and the Learning Process

In this era, what characterized rival theories of learning were not dichotomous viewpoints on the nature of literacy, such as the earlier split along the dimension of rational versus aesthetic. During this period, predominant and rival views were in agreement on the value of considering social and contextual forces in literacy. The distinction between the predominant and rival stances came in the relative importance attached to the context or to social interactions. Specifically, for certain segments of this community, the situated character or social nature of knowledge and knowing became the central focus (Sfard, 1998).

Research on situativity or situated action (e.g., Greeno & the Middle School Mathematics Through Applications Project Group, 1998; Greeno & Moore, 1993) was grounded in the perceptual investigations of Gibson (1966) and in the symbolic processing theory developed by researchers in artificial intelligence and technology (Greeno & Moore, 1993). From this foundation, researchers evolved an emphasis on the learning affordances offered in the conditions of the immediate learning environment and saw knowledge as nontransferable between situations or contexts (Sfard, 1998). Within this perspective, learning could not be separated from the situation in which it occurred, so knowledge came to reside in the context itself rather than in the individual learners. From the standpoint of human interactions, as well, certain sociocultural researchers came to the position that knowledge was not merely shaped or colored by social experiences and interactions but actually existed in those interchanges rather than in individual minds (Sfard, 1998). For those holding to this view, knowledge would be present when students are socially engaged in discussion or collaborative learning activities. With these varied sociocultural perspectives on literacy came a radical shift from the prior era's location of knowledge in the mind and emphasis on individuality of knowledge and the process of knowing.

The Era of Engaged Learning (1996–2005)

The Conditions for Change

As the 1990s moved along, there were forces at work that boded a change in the way learners and learning were perceived and studied within the literacy community. Those forces led to changing perceptions of text, readers, and the reading process. Prior to this period, texts were generally defined as printed materials (e.g., books, magazines) read in linear fashion (Wade & Moje, 2000). Further, readers targeted in the research were most often young children acquiring the ability to decode and comprehend written language or older students struggling with the demands of traditional text-based learning (Hiebert & Taylor, 2000; Pigott & Barr, 2000). Moreover, outside the concern for readers' efferent or aesthetic response to literature or the creation of a stimulating print-rich learning environment, there was little regard for motivation in the form of readers' goals, interests, and involvement in the learning experience (Oldfather & Wigfield, 1996). However, several conditions conspired to change these typical perceptions of text, reader, and reading, ushering in a new era of reading research.

First, with the growing presence of hypermedia and hypertext, the reading community began to consider the effects of the nature and form of these nonlinear and less traditional forms of text on students' learning (Alexander, Kulikowich, & Jetton, 1994; Bolter, 1991). The term *nonlinear text* refers to discourse accompanied by a database management system that guides or prompts readers to other informational sites and sources (Gillingham, Young, & Kulikowich, 1994). This influx of hypermedia and hypertext became coupled with an increased attention to classroom discourse and its role in students' academic development (Alvermann, Commeyras, Young, Randall, & Hinson, 1997). Researchers considered the form and content of that discourse and its relation to reading performance, as well as to subject-matter learning (Jetton & Alexander, 1998). Collectively, the interest in hypermedia and classroom discourse extended notions of text to both traditional and alternative forms (Alexander & Jetton, 2003).

Second, during this time, the rich and impressive body of literature on motivation that had formed over the past several decades found its way into the reading community (Guthrie & Wigfield, 2000). This infusion of motivation research led to the consideration of such critical factors as learners' interest, goals, and self-efficacy beliefs, as well as their self-regulation and active participation in reading and text-based learning (Almasi, McKeown, & Beck, 1996; Ames, 1992; Hidi, 1990; Schallert, Meyer, & Fowler, 1995; Schraw, Bruning, & Svoboda, 1995; Turner, 1995). One of the characteristics of this motivational research was its social cognitive perspective on student learning (Pintrich & Schunk, 2001). In other words, these motivational factors were not considered in isolation but were studied in relation to other factors such as students' knowledge, strategic abilities, and sociocultural background and features of the learning context. The result of this infusion of motivation theory and research into the reading literature was a reconceptualization of the student as an engaged or motivated reader (Guthrie & Wigfield, 2000). This motivational focus was especially apparent in the activities of the National Reading Research Center funded by the U.S. Department of Education.

Finally, for many reasons, including a deepening understanding of human development, the increased longevity of the population, and the mounting demands of functioning within a postindustrial, information-technological age, the literacy community's view of reading shifted (Alexander et al., 1996; Reinking, McKenna, Labbo, & Kieffer, 1998). Throughout the previous eras of reading research, activities, debates, and stances revolved primarily around the acquisition of reading processes and whether reading could best be understood as a discrete set of skills or as a more natural unfolding of competence fostered by meaningful, aesthetic engagement. What became apparent, however, was that neither orientation toward reading effectively captured the complexity of reading or recognized the changing nature of reading as individuals continue their academic development (Alexander, 2003). In other words, it became increasingly more difficult to ignore that reading is a domain that relates not only to the young or struggling reader but also to readers of all abilities and ages. Further, reading extends beyond the initial phase of acquisition and across the lifespan as readers engage in a range of reading-related, goal-directed activities. Initiatives directed toward adolescent and adult readers were evidence of the expanded view of reading (Moje, Young, Readence, & Moore, 2000; RAND Reading Study Group, 2002). Thus, the earlier dichotomization of reading into "learning to read" and "reading to learn" stages (Chall, 1995) was shifting back to a more integrated and developmental perspective.

Guiding View

The guiding view of the learner during this era highlighted the importance of the blending of affect, knowledge, and strategic processing that characterized the nature of the learner's interaction with the learning situation, with this blending being termed *engagement* (Guthrie & Wigfield, 2000). The label "engaged" captured several of the aforementioned forces that shaped perceptions of reading and informed research toward the end of the 20th century. For one, it acknowledged that reading is not confined to traditional print materials but extends to the texts students encounter daily, including the nonlinear, interactive, dynamic, and visually complex materials conveyed via audiovisual media (Alexander & Jetton, 2003). It also entails the discussions that occur around both traditional and alternative texts (Alvermann et al., 1997; Wade, Thompson, & Watkins, 1994).

Of course, understanding how students learn by means of alternative forms of text was still emergent, and the nature of reading online has remained a topic of controversy (Alexander, Graham, & Harris, 1998; Lankshear & Knobel, 2003; Wade & Moje, 2000). As our history in dealing with other forms of nonprint modes of communication (e.g., television; Neuman, 1988) indicated, there was indeed a great deal to learn about the potentials of alternative, nonlinear media. For example, as these alternative forms of text became more prevalent, literacy researchers and practitioners began to consider possible implications for such fundamental concepts as learning, memory, and strategic processing (Bolter, 1991; Garner & Gillingham, 1996; Goldman, 1996; Salomon, Perkins, & Globerson, 1991). Those who wanted to forward claims about "new literacies" (Leu, Kinzer, Coiro, & Cammack, 2004) not only acknowledged this need for closer examination of online reading but also perceived the distinctions between the processing of traditional and hypermedia text to be so extensive as to require fundamentally new forms of reading knowledge, skills, and strategies. They strove to open the door on alternative texts and text processing to a degree not seen previously. An additional research area that began to be recognized was the need to examine how pedagogical techniques and learning environments could be adapted to assist not only readers who struggle with traditional text but also those who get lost in hyperspace (Alexander et al., 1994; Lawless & Kulikowich, 1996; Reinking et al., 1998).

Engagement also pertained directly to students' meaningful participation in text-based learning. While the philosophical writings of Skinner, Chomsky, Kant, and Vygotsky were central to prior eras of reading research, the writings of John Dewey (e.g., 1910/1991, 1913) were key to this era. Dewey's notions of experiential learning and interest were evident in the conceptions of engagement framed within the burgeoning motivation research and resulted in a unification of once oppositional stances. In this era of literacy research, the learner was conceptualized as a motivated knowledge seeker (Alexander, 1997a). Such a perception differed from the Kantian (1787/1963) distinction between the sensible and the intelligible worlds inherent in information-processing theory and the efferent/aesthetic distinction underlying the psycholinguistic perspective of reading (Goodman & Goodman, 1979). Specifically, it was assumed that a search for understanding or the act of learning via text involved the integration of cognitive and motivational forces.

The research on reader engagement further established that learners are more than passive receptacles of information (Guthrie & Wigfield, 2000). They are active and willful participants in the construction of knowledge (Alexander, 1997a; Reed & Schallert, 1993; Reed, Schallert, & Goetz, 1993). However, the picture of engagement emerging during this decade deviated from prior sociocultural interpretations in terms of the focus on the individual learner within the educational environment (Alexander & Murphy, 1999). In particular, while the learner still resided and operated within a sociocultural context, attention was once more turned to the individual working to create a personally meaningful and socially valuable body of knowledge. Thus, the portrait of the engaged reader framed by the research had both individualistic and collective dimensions, a reconciliation of information-processing and sociocultural perspectives of past decades (Guthrie, McGough, Bennett, & Rice, 1996; Guthrie, Van Meter, et al., 1996).

A further consequence of this view of the learner as actively engaged in the process of learning was a rekindled interest in strategic processing. In contrast to the habituated skills of earlier eras, the effective use of strategies was understood to require reflection, choice, and deliberate execution on the part of the learner (Alexander et al., 1998). Strategy use by its nature calls for engaged learners who are willing to put forth effort and who can knowledgeably respond to the demands of a particular situation. The body of literature on learning strategies, particularly reading comprehension strategies, grew in these years in response to this new view of the engaged learner (Pressley, 2002).

Finally, the view of learners as actively engaged allowed for a return to the developmental perspective on reading. Developmentally, individuals were viewed as continually in the process of learning to read and had a direct role to play in their literacy. From this vantage point, students are not yet complete as readers when they can demonstrate basic linguistic skills or fluency in reading. Rather, they continue to grow as readers as their linguistic knowledge, subject-matter knowledge, strategic capabilities, and motivations expand and mature (Alexander, 1997b). This developmental perspective on reading extended concern beyond the early elementary years into adolescence and adulthood.

This developmental orientation toward reading was evident in major reports and the activities of the Center for the Improvement of Early Reading Achievement. For example, in its summary report entitled "Adolescent Literacy—Research Informing Practice: A Series of Workshops," the Partnership for Reading (2002) identifies development as a superordinate principle for organizing the research agenda on adolescent literacy. Similarly, the RAND Reading Study Group (2002), in its publication *Reading for Understanding: Toward an R&D Program in Reading Comprehension*, described learning to read well as "a long-term developmental process" (p. xiii) and recognized the need for research that "will contribute to better theories of reading development" (p. 29).

Resulting Principles

Several principles appeared to guide this decade of reading research. One of those principles pertained to the complexity and multidimensional nature of reading. Specifically, notions that reading is cognitive, aesthetic, *or* sociocultural in nature were set aside. Instead, all these forces were seen to be actively and interactively involved in reading development (Alexander & Jetton, 2000). For example, there is a significant relation between learners' knowledge and their interests (Alexander, Jetton, & Kulikowich, 1995; Csikszentmihalyi, 1990). Similarly, encountering personally relevant texts promotes deeper student engagement in learning (Guthrie & Wigfield, 2000).

Another guiding principle of this era was that students encounter a range of textual materials, both traditional and alternative, that should be reflected in the learning environment (Wade & Moje, 2000). Although their views on the merits of technology differed, educational researchers acknowledged that technology had transformed learning and teaching (Cuban, 1993; Postman, 1993; Scardamalia, Bereiter, McLean, Swallow, & Woodruff, 1989). Computer-based technologies were now commonplace in the lives of K–12 students in postindustrial societies. They regularly surfed the Web, e-mailed, and communicated via text messages—acts that changed the face of information processing and human communication (Alexander & Knight, 1993; Garner & Gillingham, 1996). This technological revolution produced an unimaginable proliferation of information sources and text types. This proliferation further complicated perceptions of reading and placed new demands on readers (Gillingham et al., 1994). For instance, effective readers now had to become capable of assessing credibility, identifying possible biases, analyzing persuasive or literary techniques, and locating and selecting optimal sources (Rouet, Vidal-Abarca, Erboul, & Millogo, 2001). However, these new technologies also held promise for reading in what Reinking et al. (1998) call a posttypographic world.

Because reading was viewed as multidimensional in character, with significant relations among readers' knowledge, strategic processing, and motivation, simple models or theories based on a "learning to read" and "reading to learn" distinction needed to be supplanted with more complex, reciprocal models of reading development (Alexander, 2003). Specifically, investigation of the initial stages of reading acquisition could not be isolated from the issues emerging when comprehension of texts became the focus. This required a genuinely developmental theory of reading, spanning preliteracy reading readiness to proficient adult reading. This developmental vision of reading was reflected in the report of the RAND Reading Study Group (2002): "a vision of proficient readers who are capable of acquiring new knowledge and understanding new concepts, are capable of applying textual information appropriately, and are capable of being engaged in the reading process and reflecting on what is read" (p. xiii).

Rival Views of Learner and Learning Process

In this era, the view in the literacy research community of the learner as a motivated, engaged knowledge seeker and of the learning process as developmental and anchored in a sociocultural context stood in sharp contrast to a trend that had been gaining momentum over the previous several decades. We chose to label this rival perspective as learning as reconditioning. The choice of the term *reconditioning* signaled several significant features of this rival undercurrent. First, as in the early conditioning period, this rival stance was invested in the identification, teaching, and remediation of the subskills or components underlying reading acquisition (e.g., Foorman, Francis, Fletcher, Schatschneider, & Mehta, 1998). In addition, the emphasis in this rival orientation was on beginning or struggling readers who had yet to master these reading fundamentals. In many ways, "why Johnny *still* can't read" was a suitable anthem for adherents to this strong minority perspective.

Unlike the earlier "learning as conditioning" era, the concentration on reading subskills and components at this point was less driven by theory than by other forces. One of those forces was the drive toward accountability, primarily in the form of high-stakes testing and the push for national standards (Paris & Urdan, 2000). From the stance of learning as engagement, assessments that fostered knowledge seeking around challenging, valuable, and meaningful problems and issues would be warranted (American Psychological Association Presidential Task Force on Psychology in Education, 1993). However, such problems were not readily measurable or as predictive of reading difficulties in the early years. Moreover, the effort to institute national standards that seemingly prescribed the content and skills learners should have acquired at given points in their school careers thus constrained the views of learners and learning (Paris & Urdan, 2000).

Another difference between the conditioning and reconditioning perspectives was the alliances each represented. Specifically, the investment in basic skills and components of reading gained support from researchers in special education and others who worked with struggling readers (Foorman et al., 1998; Torgesen, 1998, 1999). These researchers were joined by those engaged in neuroscience. In particular, advancements in neuroimaging techniques allowed researchers to examine the neurological structures and processes of struggling readers and readers with special needs (Shaywitz et al., 2000). On the basis of such neuroimaging studies, still in a formative stage, researchers attempted to pinpoint the specific neurobiological or physiological patterns related to specific reading outcomes or documented conditions (Pugh et al., 1997; Shaywitz, Fletcher, Holahan, & Shaywitz, 1992).

The Emergent Era of Goal-Directed Learning (2006–Present)

The Conditions for Change

It is always a bit risky to project the era that is currently taking shape, because hindsight is always more accurate than foresight. However, given the coalescence of conditions both internal and external to the reading community, we feel that there is now sufficient materialization to give the present period a name and a character. The first set of conditions that turned the attention of the field beyond the era of engagement and led to the current emergent era can be characterized as concerns and doubts directed specifically toward engagement: What is it really, and what did it actually promise for literacy development (Mayer, 2004; Nystrand & Gamoran, 1991)? Such rumblings were conjoined with three interrelated conditions. The first pertained to the expanding presence of technologies and the complications that arose from living in a hypermedia age (Leu et al., 2004; Leu, O'Byrne, Zawilinski, McVerry, & Everett-Cocapardo, 2009). The second was the unrelenting obsession with testing within American schools, as exemplified by the growing popularity of standards-based assessment and the effects of this obsession on the perceptions and intentions of students (Valli, Croninger,

Chambliss, Graeber, & Buese, 2008). At the intersection of these two was the third: the rising concerns about the ability of our school-age population to think deeply or critically about information, whether that information is contained in their textbooks, encountered on the Internet, or shared through expanding social media (e.g., Facebook, Twitter; Bereiter & Scardamalia, 2005).

Thus, despite the presumed benefits that were to be realized from focusing on readers' active participation with a range of traditional and nontraditional forms of text, and even in the face of a growing presence for hypermedia in the lives of students both in school and out of school, there were voices of concern that arose at the turn of the 21st century (Bereiter, 2002; VanSledright, 2002). In subsequent years, those voices became clearer and stronger to the point that we can now see the emergence of a new era that we speculate will carry forward into the second decade of this century.

What precisely were the concerns and doubts directed toward reader engagement? The first pertained to the very nature of engagement that was sought. As we find throughout the history of educational research and practice, there is often an inverse relation between the growing popularity of certain terms or labels within a community and the specificity of their meanings (Afflerbach, Pearson, & Paris, 2008; Dinsmore, Alexander, & Loughlin, 2008). For instance, it is not surprising to find volumes devoted to clarifying the meaning of *constructivism*, *comprehension*, or even *text*, just three examples of often used but variably defined terms (Bloome & Enciso, 2006; Fox & Alexander, 2009; Phillips, 1995). This same problem occurred with the notion of engagement. With the rising popularity of the idea, there were increasing questions as to what precisely one meant by *engagement*. Is it some underlying shift in learners' motivation toward reading, or is it the frequencies with which learners physically or verbally participate in classroom activities (Guthrie & Wigfield, 2000; Nystrand & Gamoran, 1991)?

Along with the serious inspection of the meaning of the construct came a concomitant issue that cast even longer shadows on the engagement era. That is, even if we could have come to some agreed-upon definition of *engagement* and could reliably identify its features, what benefits should be realized from reader engagement? In effect, there were questions as to whether engagement was itself an end goal or should be viewed as a means to some other end (Dochy, Segers, Van den Bossche, & Gijbels, 2003; Loyens & Gijbels, 2008; Mayer, 2004). Should it be expected that more engaged readers attain a deeper comprehension of the texts they encounter, for example, or should readers who report or exhibit more positive motivations toward reading manifest a level of performance or comprehension that seemingly less motivated readers do not, especially when other explanatory factors such as reading proficiency or socioeconomic status are removed from the equation?

Researchers who began to examine such engagement questions or to consider the evidence or justification offered by "engaged" students illuminated the problems of assuming that engagement alone would be the avenue to more competent readers. The data were not especially encouraging and suggested that engagement alone (i.e., higher manifest participation, self-reported motivations) was not adequate to foster reading development (Chinn & Anderson, 1998; Kim, Anderson, Nguyen-Jahiel, & Archodidou, 2007; Murphy, Wilkinson, & Soter, 2011). For instance, in one extensive meta-analysis of classroom discussion and its effects on literacy learning, Murphy, Wilkinson, Soter, Hennessey, and Alexander (2009) found that the only significant effect for most classroom discussion approaches in reading classrooms was a rise in student talk for an initial period. There was no concomitant rise in student learning or comprehension performance over time. For those hoping to enhance students' learning through engagement, such findings proved troubling.

The doubts that arose about the nature and benefits of engagement were exacerbated by two other conditions endemic to the educational system and to the broader sociocultural milieu. First, the culture of testing within contemporary educational systems was driving students and teachers toward beliefs about knowledge and knowing (i.e., epistemic beliefs), such as the certainty of knowledge, that are not particularly conducive to optimal development in reading and other academic domains (Alexander, 2010; Hofer & Pintrich, 2002). When so much of what counts in schools are basic processes and reading abilities that can easily be captured in right–wrong, multiple-choice questions, deeper and more reflective dimensions of reading may be sacrificed; the knowledge and processes associated with competent or proficient reading may be shuffled aside (Noddings, 2004; Valli et al., 2008). With the increased interest in reading in the content areas and in adolescent and adult reading development, the rather constrained view of text processing and comprehension promoted by high-stakes assessments led to worries that more complex linguistic processing and deeper forms of thinking and reasoning were being irreparably damaged (Alexander & Riconscente, 2005).

Such ruminations over the potential effects of the assessment culture of schools were additionally amplified when the benefits of technological engagement were put under the empirical microscope during the early years of the 21st century (Alexander & the Disciplined Reading and Learning Research Laboratory [DRLRL], 2010). Clearly, the amount of time school-age learners spend with hypermedia continues to rise, and the time they are engaged with traditional print wanes; of such trends, there is little doubt (Rideout, Foehr, & Roberts, 2010). What is also apparent is that the manner of that engagement is more apt to be in a passive than active mode; that is, these students are more apt to be listening to music or watching videos than reading online (Rideout et al., 2010)

Collectively, these conditions—concerns about the notion of engagement, the side effects of the assessment culture, and expanding but often passive engagement with technology—contributed to a realization that the view of engagement as key to learning must be reconsidered in light of the demands of the new century. It appeared that not only engagement but also the nature of the learner's goals and purposes in entering into such engagement must be considered, with higher order goals of critical and analytical evaluation receiving increasing attention (Kulikowich & Alexander, 2010).

Guiding View

Our purpose in labeling this emergent period as the era of goal-directed learning is to highlight the strong push to bring yet another dimension to the idea of learner engagement. It is not so much that the principles of the prior era have been set aside or abandoned, quite to the contrary. Instead, what was pragmatically sound about the goal of engendering a more participatory model of learning and more motivated learners has been subsequently refined and augmented to value the outcome of that participation and to regard carefully the nature of the intentions that promote competent learning. In effect, beliefs about the importance of students' enhanced social and emotional engagement in classroom literacy activities were amplified by an increased call for ensuring that the cognitive and academic outcomes of such engagement were equally valued and nurtured. Thus, the theme of this present era is engagement as a means not only to students willing and empowered to engage socially and emotionally in the literacy activities within their classrooms but also to students who manifest the ability to think deeply and critically about the ideas conveyed in the written and oral texts that are part of those literacy activities.

What marks this emergent era of reading research more than anything else is the appreciation that the aim in reading development is not solely a person capable of breaking the linguistic code or even someone motivated to do so—a concern that also carries forward from the prior era. Rather, the competent reader recognizes that there are authors who construct texts (traditional or alternative) for some explicit or implied purpose and that within the linguistic code is a meaning or message that must be recognized and also queried (Fox, 2009; Fox, Dinsmore, & Alexander, 2010). Thus, the competent reader appreciates that comprehension entails more than the processing of texts as if they were authorless or decontextualized amalgamations of words or phrases (Fox, Dinsmore, Maggioni, & Alexander, 2009). Rather, competent readers' intentions are to ponder and interrogate text, to regard the content of that text relative to questions they are presented with or formulate themselves. In other words, their goal is to read critically and analytically for the purpose of learning *about*, *with*, and *from* text (Alexander et al., 2011).

The growing number of research programs that focus on critical, analytical talk and text processing across subject-matter areas are ample evidence that this era of goal-directed reading has taken root. For instance, there is the work of Anderson, Chinn, Murphy, Wilkinson, and others that seeks to raise the quality of talk and discussion taking place within classrooms, so as to ensure that deeper comprehension and significant learning result (Chinn & Anderson, 1998; Kim et al., 2007; Murphy et al., 2009). Similarly, there are extensive intervention programs in history and science for teachers and for students that seek to improve students' ability to deal with disciplinary text structures (Moje, Tucker-Raymond, Varelas, & Pappas, 2007; Wijekumar & Meyer, 2006) and to examine and challenge the ideas that are forwarded in those texts (Felton & Kuhn, 2007; Maggioni, VanSledright, & Alexander, 2009).

Critical and analytic reading is evidentiary in nature (Wilkinson, Soter, & Murphy, 2010). There is an old Yiddish proverb that loosely translates: "For example, is not proof." The ability to talk about text, to offer an illustration or example from one's own experience or to forward an opinion, is not in and of itself proof that text of any sort has been adequately understood or comprehended. Bloom's taxonomy aside, evaluation in the form of unsubstantiated opinion does not require higher forms of cognitive thought than inferring an unstated relation or even finding a specific fact within a complex piece of text (Bereiter & Scardamalia, 2005). The ability to offer reasoned and reasonable justification does not occur spontaneously or without provocation for many developing readers (Alexander et al., 2011). Critical and analytic reading and evidentiary reasoning, as with other complex and demanding ways of thinking, are more apt to take shape under the tutelage of more competent others and when the value of such analytic processing is mirrored in the time dedicated and the assessments administered within school settings (Murphy et al., 2009).

As suggested, this emerging concern over critical and analytic reading and the importance of considering the reader's goals in the learning situation has the advantage of tying together threads that are evident not just in the work on engagement but also in the research pertaining to content area reading and online or hypermedia text processing. For example, the long-term interest in content area reading and expository text processing within the reading community has made it evident that there are features to the nature of domain exposition that prove challenging to students. It is not solely the structural or linguistic demands (e.g., specialized terminology, complex paragraph structures; Ozuru, Dempsey, & McNamara, 2009) of disciplinary or informational text that are at issue. It is also that the role texts play in varied disciplines or domains can be markedly different, as can the disciplinary standards for what constitutes pertinent evidence (Alexander et al., 2011).

Take, for example, the distinctions between reading within history and reading within science. Within the discipline of history, textual documents are core. Reading often entails the identification of relevant primary and secondary sources and the building of a defensible interpretation of a historical event or personage on the basis of those located sources. The information extracted or inferred from those textual sources must be thoughtfully synthesized and reconciled, often by means of established processing strategies such as corroboration and sourcing. Further, there is no one historical interpretation that can be crafted from available sources, and thus, readers must be competent at judging the quality of evidence vis-à-vis the source and weighing competing explanations.

While the role of text within science may be less in the foreground, the processing of written evidence to understand the patterns and relations that exist within the physical world is no less essential. Whereas the complexity of processing historical texts may come, in part, from readers' struggles to search out sources or to make sense of the language or references from another time and place, the complexity of processing scientific texts may come from the specialized terminology populating these texts or from the common infusion of nonlinguistic materials such as numeric data or graphic representations. Further, while a strongly defensible interpretation of the past based on evidence may be an end within historical thinking, it is more about finding the best causal explanation for scientific phenomena given the physical evidence that is associated with scientific reasoning.

In neither aforementioned case are these laudable ends apt to be achieved unless the reader is competent enough to handle the textual content and to contemplate that content in a manner that is in concert with the discipline. Reading and thinking historically, in sum, is not the same as reading and thinking scientifically, and each entails a level of critical, analytic reading that is not developmentally assured even if one has the necessary phonological abilities or even the motivation to engage.

Moreover, the ever-expanding technological presence in the lives of students, both in and out of school, and their ability to navigate through the deluge of information remains a growing concern in this era (Strømsø, Bråten, & Samuelstuen, 2008). Perhaps there is less concern that students will become lost in hypermedia space because of the unfamiliarity or complexity of technology. It would appear that hypermedia and Internet technologies are truly commonplace in students' lives (Rideout et al., 2010). Yet, there is the real possibility that students can still get lost in hypermedia space for other reasons. For one, there is little evidence that today's students are well equipped for or deeply invested in separating the wheat from the chaff when it comes to online content. They seem relatively unaware of how to judge the credibility of online sources or to seek corroboration (Flanagin & Metzger, 2007). Therefore, the focus on learners' goals and the consequent attention to critical, analytical reading cannot restrict itself to traditional texts but must out of necessity consider the application of these competences online and offline, as well as for personal and academic purposes.

Resulting Principles

The convergence of factors that frame the current era have helped forge several basic principles that undergird this focus on learning as goal directed. First and foremost, there is the reconceptionalization of competence (Fox, 2009; Fox et al., 2009). This new conceptualization encompasses the competent learner's predictable and appropriate manifestation of critical and analytic thought and evidentiary-based reasoning relevant to the tasks and texts at hand. This expanded view of competence builds on the contention of Alexander and the DRLRL (2010) that competence in a domain "should be marked by adaptive and consistent...thinking" and "by performance that is principled in its focus and disciplined in its processing" (p. 26).

For the domain of reading, competence would thus entail a particular configuration of the reader's knowledge of text structures and conventions, knowledge of the topic or domain that the text addresses, strategies for interrogating the content or claims made within the text, and the motivation to put forth the effort that this level of processing demands (Alexander, 1997b). Further, competent reading, so described, would require readers' sensitivity to the form and quality of evidence that given questions framed within certain domains (e.g., history, science, mathematics) would warrant (Moje, 2007; Shanahan & Shanahan, 2008). Learners' awareness of, selection of, and movement toward appropriate goals are thus key elements in their competent reading.

The perspective on learning as goal directed foregrounds the learner's understanding of the task situation and all that that entails. It is not enough to assume that learners or readers are doing what the intended aim of the task is; we must also consider what they see the goal as being (Kulikowich & Alexander, 2010; McCrudden, Magliano, & Schraw, 2010). Thus, it is also learners' intentionality that matters in this new era. In this way, the foregrounding of the learner's view in this perspective differs from previous iterations, such as schema theory, where it was the learner's perception of the situation that structured his or her engagement in the learning situation. The focus here is on the entire chain—epistemic beliefs, perceptions, intentions, and corresponding goals—on the learner's side, as well as what is afforded by the specific object of knowledge and suggested by the specific learning context on the other.

Rival Views of the Learner and Learning Process

The dominant rival view that was present during the engagement era and grew in strength with the ascendance of testing-driven education has certainly carried forward into the current historical era. Those who are inclined toward a view of learning as a set of basic processes and skills are still evident in the research community (Foorman et al., 2006). The simple model of reading (Gough & Tunmer, 1986), with its diagnostically oriented separation of reading into decoding and oral language comprehension, remains a widely used and studied explanatory paradigm (e.g., Cartwright, 2007; Vellutino, Tunmer, Jaccard, & Chen, 2007; Verhoeven & van Leeuwe, 2008). The neurological aspects of learning and text processing are also still objects of research attention and recipients of research funding (Schlaggar & McCandliss, 2007). Yet, one group that was a catalyst to the formation of the engagement era now stands somewhat in opposition to the general view of competence and intentionality that marks the era of goal-directed learning we project.

For these individuals, who strongly promote the notion of new literacies, there is not a unified view of reading that can embrace both traditional and online or hypermedia texts—and, consequentially, not a unified view of reading competence that can be forwarded to capture all manner of text processing in this hypermedia age (Coiro, Knobel, Lankshear, & Leu, 2008). Instead, it is their argument that the demands of reading and learning online are so unique that there must, by default, be knowledge, skills, and strategies that apply uniquely to hypermedia texts. Such a viewpoint is presented in Kellner's (2001) essay on new literacies and new technologies:

> Genuine computer literacy involves not just technical knowledge and skills, but refined reading, writing, research, and communicating ability. It involves heightened capacities for critically accessing, analyzing, interpreting, processing, and storing both print-based and multimedia material. In a new information/entertainment society, immersed in transformative multimedia technology, knowledge and information come not merely in the form of print and words, but through images, sounds, and multimedia material as well. Computer literacy thus also involves the ability to discover and access information and intensified abilities to read, to scan texts and computer data bases and websites, and to access information and images in a variety of forms, ranging from graphics, to visual images, to audio and video materials, to good old print media. The creation of new multimedia websites, data bases, and texts requires accessing, downloading, and organizing digitized verbal, imagistic, and audio and video material that are the new building blocks of multimedia culture. (pp. 73–74)

It remains to be seen whether those who champion the notion of new literacies will be able to identify truly unique forms of textual knowledge and processes that are not manifest in any form in the competent reading of traditional text. For now, we remain with those who do not dismiss the growing presence and power of the Internet or hypermedia technologies but perceive the variability of processing across text types as iterations of already existing knowledge and processes rather than as unique forms—as variations on a theme rather than as an entirely new melody (Afflerbach & Cho, 2009).

Emergent Premises: Lessons From the Past

In this overview of the past 60 years of reading research, our discussion has been anchored by the conception of the learner and learning process underlying the approach to reading research in a given time period. Investigations of learning are, of necessity, situated in the context of a particular slant on the nature of the learner and on how learning occurs. Identifying that context allows the essential character of the research endeavors in different time periods and from different theoretical orientations to emerge from the myriad of studies and reported findings.

As we look across the eras of reading research on learners and learning and consider the characteristics and guiding principles unique to each, we cannot help but recognize that there are patterns evident in the fabric of that literature on learners and learning that bind those eras together. Those patterns, what we refer to as the emergent premises, are among the most important lessons to be derived from this historical analysis.

• Membership within the reading community is flexible and alters the basic identity of that community and its orientation toward research and practice. Characterizing the prototypic reading researcher would be a difficult task because the membership of the reading community has remained in flux. Over the past 60 years, those considered to be among the leading reading researchers have ranged from reading specialists to psycholinguists, from literature researchers to cognitive scientists, and from special educators to generative grammarians. Because of the interdisciplinary and fluid nature of the reading community, the issues and perspectives on research and practice forwarded by its members have similarly been interdisciplinary and fluid in nature. If one were interested in predicting the future of reading research, it would be wise to look carefully at community demographics. Who is being drawn to the reading field, and what special orientations, interests, and methodologies do they bring into this community of practice?

• Prevailing trends within the research literature reflect the influence of sociopolitical forces outside the reading community. While forces within the reading community, such as its membership, have been influential in shaping the eras of reading research, forces outside the community have also served as change agents. Consider the transformational effect of baby boomers and Sputnik on reading research and practice in the 1950s and 1960s, for example, or the impact that significant governmental funding for cognitive research had on the reading research agenda in the 1970s and 1980s. Further, as with the broader educational community, reading has not been immune to the effects of technology or the accountability movement, nor have its members been oblivious to the needs of the linguistically and culturally diverse students populating America's classrooms in increasing numbers. Such sociopolitical influences combine with forces within the reading community to transform the reading landscape and give each era of research its distinctive character (Valencia & Wixson, 2001). What is not clear in this historical analysis is the degree to which the reading community is proactive or reactive in relation to such powerful external forces.

• There is a recurrence of issues and approaches to reading research and practice across the decades. The ebb and flow of reform movements have been well documented in the educational literature (Alexander et al., 1996). This iterative reform pattern is also evident in the reading research literature in terms of perspectives on learners and learning. Perhaps the most obvious recurrence is the shifting emphasis on whole-word or phonetic instructional approaches. Despite periodic calls for balanced or integrated programs of research and practice in the literature (Stahl & Miller, 1989), the debate over the "right" or "most effective" approach continues unabated (Goodman, 1996). Other such recurring themes in the extant literature include more individualistic or more social emphases, variable interest in the use of controlled vocabulary readers or "authentic" literature (Rosenblatt, 1978/1994), and the valuing or devaluing of knowledge (Alexander, 1998a). The renewal of interest in readers other than children and in reading processes and practices other than those related to reading acquisition similarly represents a return to themes forwarded in the lifespan developmental perspective (Gray, 1951).

It would seem that knowledge of reading's history might serve to temper some of the unabashed support for particular "new" reform efforts that are, in actuality, iterations or reincarnations of past reading approaches with qualified or questionable records of success. At the very least, such a historical perspective would remind us that many current initiatives have legacies that deserve consideration.

• The history of reading research reveals a shifting emphasis on the physiological, the psychological, and the sociological. While reading always involves physiological, psychological, and sociological dimensions, each era weighs these dimensions differently. When we look across the eras of reading research described in this chapter, it becomes apparent that each is distinguished by the relative weight placed on body, mind, or society when understanding the nature of learners and learning. In effect, while reading invariably entails human physiology, psychological processing, and social engagement, it is their relative importance that becomes a defining feature for each era. For example, physiology, which focuses on the biological, chemical, and neurological dimensions of human performance, was clearly present in the behavioral orientations of Skinner and others, where reading was conditioned response. The physiological perspective was evident again in the Chomskian views of language as a hardwired capacity and more recently in the growing interest in neurological structures and reading performance.

Psychological orientations, which deal with the mental processes of the mind, were most apparent in the era of information processing. This orientation continues in the studies of expertise, motivation, and learner development. Here the focus is squarely on process and functioning (the mental software) rather than on the physical or neurochemical structures (the mental hardware) from which these processes and functions may arise. The burgeoning interest in metacognition in the form of epistemic beliefs and the learner's own perspective on learning is similarly grounded in a psychological orientation.

Finally, throughout reading history, there have been periods when the concern has not been centered on the individual student or his or her mental structures or processes. Rather, the focus has been on the student in relation to others (human-to-human interactions) or the learning of groups who share history (e.g., gender or ethnic groups) or geography (e.g., classroom communities). We see this sociological framework clearly in the rising interest in sociocultural perspectives and in research on cooperative or collaborative learning, and it is beginning to be explored as well in relation to the social world that is constructed and encountered online.

To understand the history of reading research, we need to appreciate the impact of these varied perspectives on learner and learning that become mirrored in the research questions posed, the methodologies applied, and the interpretations made. Indeed, the tensions felt within and across each of the eras described in this chapter arise, in part, because of the contrasting perspectives held by segments of the reading community.

Yet, as we stated, reading is invariably physiological, psychological, *and* sociological, suggesting the need for an integrated orientation. Reading invariably involves the physical, from the appropriation of visual stimuli through the neurological processing of those stimuli. Moreover, reading embraces the psychological in terms of the interpretation, storage, and retrieval of text; the formulation of goals and expression of interests; and much more. Finally, reading is sociological in that it involves intra- and interindividual communication through linguistic media which are themselves socioculturally influenced. Therefore, a meaningful integration of these orientations will require a broad yet fine-grained view of reading that can incorporate information about brain structures and mental activities into an account of individual and social behavior.

• The cycle of changes observed in the history of reading research involves developmental maturation of the field. The movement from era to era in the past 60 years has represented an overall positive trend. Comparing the respective views of the learner and learning process of each era, we see that they have become progressively more sophisticated and also more inclusive. Each succeeding generation of researchers has investigated a wider range of phenomena, and often at a greater level of complexity. Similarly, the recurrence of themes has functioned iteratively, not merely reiteratively, in that the terms of the debate have been redefined and expanded as dictated by the prevailing perspective on learners and learning. The view of learning and of reading has become increasingly differentiated and integrated, indicative of a developmental progression toward greater understanding (Marton & Booth, 1997). The broader categories of membership in the reading research community over time and the acceptance of multidisciplinary techniques and forms of evidence also argue that the field is not merely changing but also maturing.

• Without an overarching, developmental theory of reading, differential perspectives on research and practice may be judged as conflicting rather than complementary. Despite the promising activities of recent eras, reading researchers have still not produced a well-accepted developmental theory that looks broadly at the nature of reading across the lifespan. The barriers to such a grand theory have been many, including the continuing focus on early reading, especially phonics and phonological awareness; difficulties in assessing deep and complex processes; and the requirement of interdisciplinary cooperation (Alexander, 2003; Ruddell, 2002).

In the absence of such a grand theory, it is highly likely that overly simplistic models or rival camps will continue to characterize the decades of reading. For example, across these eras, it has been commonplace to conceptualize the stages of reading under the banners of "learning to read" and "reading to learn" (Chall, 1995). However, more recent research makes it evident that these two hypothesized stages are, in fact, inextricably intertwined throughout reading development (Alexander, 2003). Even as readers begin to unravel the mysteries of language, they are constructing their knowledge base. Simultaneously, as readers pursue knowledge in academic domains, they are building a richer understanding of language.

A unifying theory of reading development would supersede such overly simplistic stage theories, just as it would potentially illustrate how the seemingly conflicting or rival views of reading we have described herein are complementary parts of a complex whole. Increasing inclusiveness, complexity, and specificity can be considered as markers of more advanced levels of understanding (Marton & Booth, 1997). Perhaps, if current trends continue, the reading research community will achieve the articulated developmental orientation that has eluded it for so long. Having moved away from the earlier and relatively holistic and undifferentiated instantiation of the developmental perspective forwarded by earlier theorists (e.g., Gray, 1951), and having explored and detailed various aspects of reading—cognitive, linguistic, social, and motivational, each of which competed to be central in reading—perhaps we can now take up the demanding task of seeing how these aspects belong together in such a developmental view of reading.

Concluding Thoughts

Our purpose in this historical analysis of the past 60 years of reading research is to provide readers a lens through which to view current theory and practice. Such a retrospective comes with no assurances. Historical analysis, after all, is an interpretative science. However, a glance backward at where reading research has been may serve to remind us that today's research and practice is a legacy with roots that reach into the past. Moreover, by paying our respects to that past, we may better understand the activities of the present and envision the paths for reading research that lie ahead.

QUESTIONS FOR REFLECTION

1. How does understanding the history of reading research and practice provide insight into the issues and trends in the field today?
2. In what ways did theoretical beliefs guide researchers in understanding reading throughout the various eras of research and practice?
3. How has the interdisciplinary nature of reading research impacted research findings throughout its history?

REFERENCES

Afflerbach, P., & Cho, B.-Y. (2009). Identifying and describing constructively responsive comprehension strategies in new and traditional forms of reading. In S.E. Israel & G.G. Duffy (Eds.), *Handbook of research on reading comprehension* (pp. 69–90). New York: Routledge.

Afflerbach, P., Pearson, P.D., & Paris, S.G. (2008). Clarifying differences between reading skills and reading strategies. *The Reading Teacher, 61*(5), 364–373. doi:10.1598/RT.61.5.1

Alexander, P.A. (1992). Domain knowledge: Evolving themes and emerging concerns. *Educational Psychologist*, 27(1), 33–51. doi:10.1207/s15326985ep2701_4

Alexander, P.A. (1996). The past, present, and future of knowledge research: A reexamination of the role of knowledge in learning and instruction. *Educational Psychologist, 31*(2), 89–92.

Alexander, P.A. (1997a). Knowledge-seeking and self-schema: A case for the motivational dimensions of exposition. *Educational Psychologist*, 32(2), 83–94. doi:10.1207/s15326985ep3202_3

Alexander, P.A. (1997b). Mapping the multidimensional nature of domain learning: The interplay of cognitive, motivational, and strategic forces. In M.L. Maehr & P.R. Pintrich (Eds.), *Advances in motivation and achievement* (Vol. 10, pp. 213–250). Greenwich, CT: JAI.

Alexander, P.A. (1998a). Knowledge and literacy: A transgenerational perspective. In T. Shanahan & F.V. Rodríguez-Brown (Eds.), *The forty-seventh yearbook of the National Reading Conference* (pp. 22–43). Chicago: National Reading Conference.

Alexander, P.A. (1998b). Positioning conceptual change within a model of domain literacy. In B. Guzzetti & C. Hynd (Eds.), *Perspectives on conceptual change* (pp. 55–76). Mahwah, NJ: Erlbaum.

Alexander, P.A. (1998c). The nature of disciplinary and domain learning: The knowledge, interest, and strategic dimensions of learning from subject-matter text. In C. Hynd (Ed.), *Learning from text across conceptual domains* (pp. 263–287). Mahwah, NJ: Erlbaum.

Alexander, P.A. (2003). Profiling the developing reader: The interplay of knowledge, interest, and strategic processing. In C.M. Fairbanks, J. Worthy, B. Maloch, J.V. Hoffman, & D.L. Schallert (Eds.), *The fifty-first yearbook of the National Reading Conference*. Oak Creek, WI: National Reading Conference.

Alexander, P.A. (2010). Through myth to reality: Reframing education as academic development. *Early Education and Development, 21*(5), 633–651. doi:10.1080/10409289.2010.497433

Alexander, P.A., Dinsmore, D.L., Fox, E., Grossnickle, E.M., Loughlin, S.M., Maggioni, L., et al. (2011). Higher order thinking and knowledge: Domain-general and domain-specific trends and future directions. In G. Schraw (Ed.), *Assessment of higher order thinking skills* (pp. 47–88). Charlotte, NC: Information Age.

Alexander, P.A., & the Disciplined Reading and Learning Research Laboratory. (2010). *The challenges of developing competent literacy in the 21st century*. Washington, DC: The National Academy of Sciences.

Alexander, P.A., & Dochy, F.J.R.C. (1995). Conceptions of knowledge and beliefs: A comparison across varying cultural and educational communities. *American Educational Research Journal, 32*(2), 413–442.

Alexander, P.A., & Fox, E. (2004). A historical perspective on reading research and practice. In R.B. Ruddell & N.J. Unrau (Eds.), *Theoretical models and processes of reading* (5th ed., pp. 33–68). Newark, DE: International Reading Association. doi:10.1598/0872075028.2

Alexander, P.A., Graham, S., & Harris, K.R. (1998). A perspective on strategy research: Progress and prospects. *Educational Psychology Review, 10*(2), 129–154. doi:10.1023/A:1022185502996

Alexander, P.A., & Jetton, T.L. (2000). Learning from text: A multidimensional and developmental perspective. In M.L. Kamil, P.B. Mosenthal, P.D. Pearson, & R. Barr (Eds.), *Handbook of reading research* (Vol. 3, pp. 285–310). Mahwah, NJ: Erlbaum.

Alexander, P.A., & Jetton, T.L. (2003). Learning from traditional and alternative texts: New conceptualization for an information age. In A. Graesser, M. Gernsbacher, & S. Goldman (Eds.), *Handbook of discourse processes* (pp. 199–241). Mahwah, NJ: Erlbaum.

Alexander, P.A., Jetton, T.L., & Kulikowich, J.M. (1995). Interrelationship of knowledge, interest, and recall: Assessing a model of domain learning. *Journal of Educational Psychology, 87*(4), 559–575. doi:10.1037/0022-0663.87.4.559

Alexander, P.A., & Judy, J.E. (1988). The interaction of domain-specific and strategic knowledge in academic performance. *Review of Educational Research, 58*(4), 375–404.

Alexander, P.A., & Knight, S.L. (1993). Dimensions of the interplay between learning and teaching. *The Educational Forum, 57*(3), 232–245. doi:10.1080/00131729309335422

Alexander, P.A., Kulikowich, J.M., & Jetton, T.L. (1994). The role of subject-matter knowledge and interest in the processing of linear and nonlinear texts. *Review of Educational Research, 64*(2), 201–252.

Alexander, P.A., & Murphy, P.K. (1998). The research base for APA's learner-centered principles. In N.M. Lambert & B.L. McCombs (Eds.), *Issues in school reform: A sampler of psychological perspectives on learner-centered schools* (pp. 25–60). Washington, DC: American Psychological Association.

Alexander, P.A., & Murphy, P.K. (1999). Learner profiles: Valuing individual differences within classroom communities. In P.L. Ackerman, P.C. Kyllonen, & R.D. Roberts (Eds.), *The future of learning and individual differences research: Processes, traits, and content* (pp. 413–431). Washington, DC: American Psychological Association. doi:10.1037/10315-018

Alexander, P.A., Murphy, P.K., Buehl, M.M., & Sperl, C.T. (1997, December). *The influence of prior knowledge, beliefs, and interest in learning from persuasive text*. Paper presented at the annual meeting of the National Reading Conference, Scottsdale, AZ.

Alexander, P.A., Murphy, P.K., & Woods, B.S. (1996). Of squalls and fathoms: Navigating the seas of educational innovation. *Educational Researcher, 25*(3), 31–36, 39.

Alexander, P.A., & Riconscente, M.M. (2005). A matter of proof: Why achievement ≠ learning. In J.S. Carlson & J.R. Levin (Eds.), *The No Child Left Behind legislation: Educational research and federal funding* (pp. 27–36). Greenwich, CT: Information Age.

Alexander, P.A., Schallert, D.L., & Hare, V.C. (1991). Coming to terms: How researchers in learning and literacy talk about knowledge. *Review of Educational Research, 61*(3), 315–343.

Allington, R.L. (1980). Teacher interruption behaviors during primary-grade oral reading. *Journal of Educational Psychology, 72*(3), 371–377. doi:10.1037/0022-0663.72.3.371

Allington, R.L., & McGill-Franzen, A. (2000). Looking back, looking forward: A conversation about teaching reading in the 21st century.

Reading Research Quarterly, 35(1), 136–153. doi:10.1598/RRQ.35.1.10

Almasi, J.F., McKeown, M.G., & Beck, I.L. (1996). The nature of engaged reading in classroom discussions of literature. *Journal of Literacy Research*, 28(1), 107–146. doi:10.1080/10862969609547913

Alvermann, D.E., Commeyras, M., Young, J.P., Randall, S., & Hinson, D. (1997). Interrupting gendered discursive practices in classroom talk about texts: Easy to think about, difficult to do. *Journal of Literacy Research*, 29(1), 73–104. doi:10.1080/10862969709547950

Alvermann, D.E., & Hayes, D.A. (1989). Classroom discussion of content area reading assignments: An intervention study. *Reading Research Quarterly*, 24(3), 305–335. doi:10.2307/747772

Alvermann, D.E., Smith, L.C., & Readence, J.E. (1985). Prior knowledge activation and the comprehension of compatible and incompatible text. *Reading Research Quarterly*, 20(4), 420–436. doi:10.2307/747852

American Psychological Association Presidential Task Force on Psychology in Education. (1993). *Learner-centered psychological principles: Guidelines for school redesign and reform.* Washington, DC: American Psychological Association.

Ames, C. (1992). Classrooms: Goals, structures, and student motivation. *Journal of Educational Psychology*, 84(3), 261–271. doi:10.1037/0022-0663.84.3.261

Anderson, J.R., Reder, L.M., & Simon, H.A. (1996). Situated learning and education. *Educational Researcher*, 25(4), 5–11.

Anderson, R.C. (1977). The notion of schemata and the educational enterprise. In R.C. Anderson, R.J. Spiro, & W.E. Montague (Eds.), *Schooling and the acquisition of knowledge* (pp. 415–431). Hillsdale, NJ: Erlbaum.

Anderson, R.C., Pichert, J.W., & Shirey, L.L. (1983). Effects of reader's schema at different points in time. *Journal of Educational Psychology*, 75(2), 271–279. doi:10.1037/0022-0663.75.2.271

Anderson, R.C., Reynolds, R.E., Schallert, D.L., & Goetz, E.T. (1977). Frameworks for comprehending discourse. *American Educational Research Journal*, 14(4), 367–381.

Anderson, R.C., Wilson, P.T., & Fielding, L.G. (1988). Growth in reading and how children spend their time outside of school. *Reading Research Quarterly*, 23(3), 285–303. doi:10.1598/RRQ.23.3.2

Armbruster, B.B. (1984). The problem of "inconsiderate texts." In G.G. Duffy, L.R. Roehler, & J. Mason (Eds.), *Theoretical issues in reading comprehension* (pp. 202–217). New York: Longman.

August, D.L., Flavell, J.H., & Clift, R. (1984). Comparison of comprehension monitoring of skilled and less skilled readers. *Reading Research Quarterly*, 20(1), 39–53. doi:10.2307/747650

Baars, B.J. (1986). *The cognitive revolution in psychology.* New York: Guilford.

Baldwin, R.S., Readence, J.E., Schumm, J.S., Konopak, J.P., Konopak, B.C., & Klingner, J.K. (1992). Forty years of NRC publications: 1952–1991. *Journal of Reading Behavior*, 24(4), 505–532.

Ball, D.L. (1993). With an eye on the mathematical horizon: Dilemmas of teaching elementary school mathematics. *The Elementary School Journal*, 93(4), 373–397. doi:10.1086/461730

Benton, M.G. (1983). Secondary worlds. *Journal of Research and Development in Education*, 16(3), 68–75.

Bereiter, C. (1994). Constructivism, socioculturalism, and Popper's World 3. *Educational Researcher*, 23(7), 21–23.

Bereiter, C. (2002). *Education and mind in the knowledge age.* Mahwah, NJ: Erlbaum.

Bereiter, C., & Scardamalia, M. (1989). Intentional learning as a goal of instruction. In L.B. Perret (Ed.), *Knowing, learning, and instruction: Essays in honor of Robert Glaser* (pp. 361–392). Hillsdale, NJ: Erlbaum.

Bereiter, C., & Scardamalia, M. (2005). Beyond Bloom's taxonomy: Rethinking knowledge for the knowledge age. In M. Fullan (Ed.), *Fundamental change: International handbook of educational change* (pp. 5–22). Dordrecht, The Netherlands: Springer.

Bloome, D., & Enciso, P. (2006). Looking across Columbus: What we mean by "multiple literacies." *Theory Into Practice*, 45(4), 296–303. doi:10.1207/s15430421tip4504_2

Bloome, D., & Green, J. (1984). Directions in the sociolinguistic study of reading. In P.D. Pearson, R. Barr, M.L. Kamil, & P. Mosenthal (Eds.), *Handbook of reading research* (pp. 395–422). New York: Longman.

Bolter, J.D. (1991). *Writing space: The computer, hypertext, and the history of writing.* Hillsdale, NJ: Erlbaum.

Bond, G.L., & Dykstra, R. (1967). The Cooperative Research Program in First-Grade Reading Instruction. *Reading Research Quarterly*, 2(4), 5–142. doi:10.2307/746948

Bransford, J.D., & Franks, J.J. (1971). The abstraction of linguistic ideas. *Cognitive Psychology*, 2(4), 331–350. doi:10.1016/0010-0285(71)90019-3

Brewer, W.F. (1980). Literary theory, rhetoric, and stylistics: Implications for psychology. In R.J. Spiro, B.C. Bruce, & W.F. Brewer (Eds.), *Theoretical issues in reading comprehension* (pp. 221–243). Hillsdale, NJ: Erlbaum.

Britton, J.N. (1982). *Prospect and retrospect.* Montclair, NJ: Boynton/Cook.

Brown, A.L., & Campione, J.C. (1990). Communities of learning and thinking: Or, a context by any other name. *Human Development*, 21, 108–125.

Brown, A.L., Campione, J.C., & Day, J.D. (1981). Learning to learn: On training students to learn from text. *Educational Researcher*, 10(2), 14–21.

Brown, A.L., & Palincsar, A.S. (1989). Guided, cooperative learning and individual knowledge

acquisition. In L.B. Resnick (Ed.), *Knowing, learning, and instruction: Essays in honor of Robert Glaser* (pp. 393–451). Hillsdale, NJ: Erlbaum.
Buswell, G.T. (1922). *Fundamental reading habits: A study of their development*. Chicago: University of Chicago Press.
Cartwright, K.B. (2007). The contribution of graphophonological-semantic flexibility to reading comprehension in college students: Implications for a less simple view of reading. *Journal of Literacy Research, 39*(2), 173–193.
Chall, J.S. (1967). *Learning to read: The great debate*. New York: McGraw-Hill.
Chall, J.S. (1995). *Stages of reading development* (2nd ed.). New York: Wadsworth.
Chambliss, M. (1995). Text cues and strategies successful readers use to construct the gist of lengthy written arguments. *Reading Research Quarterly, 30*(4), 778–807. doi:10.2307/748198
Chase, W.G., & Simon, H.A. (1973). Perception in chess. *Cognitive Psychology, 4*(1), 55–81. doi:10.1016/0010-0285(73)90004-2
Chi, M.T.H., Feltovich, P., & Glaser, R. (1981). Categorization and representation of physics problems by experts and novices. *Cognitive Science, 5*(2), 121–152. doi:10.1207/s15516709cog0502_2
Chi, M.T.H., Glaser, R., & Farr, M. (1988). *The nature of expertise*. Hillsdale, NJ: Erlbaum.
Chinn, C.A., & Anderson, R.C. (1998). The structure of discussions intended to promote reasoning. *Teachers College Record, 100*(2), 315–360.
Chinn, C.A., & Brewer, W.F. (1993). The role of anomalous data in knowledge acquisition: A theoretical framework and implications for science instruction. *Review of Educational Research, 63*(1), 1–49.
Chipman, S.F. (1993). Gazing once more into the silicon chip: Who's revolutionary now? In S.P. Lajoie & S.J. Derry (Eds.), *Computers as cognitive tools* (pp. 341–367). Mahwah, NJ: Erlbaum.
Chomsky, N. (1957). *Syntactic structures*. New York: Mouton de Gruyter.
Chomsky, N. (1965). *Aspects of the theory of syntax*. Cambridge, MA: MIT Press.
Chomsky, N. (1975). *Reflections on language*. New York: Pantheon.
Chomsky, N. (1998). *On language: Chomsky's classic works* Language and Responsibility *and* Reflections on Language. New York: New.
Chomsky, N. (2002). *On nature and language*. New York: Cambridge University Press. doi:10.1017/CBO9780511613876
Christenson, A., & Barney, L. (1969). Oral reading errors among intermediate children. *Education, 89*(4), 307–311.
Clancey, W.J. (1983). The epistemology of a rule-based expert system: A framework for explanation. *Artificial Intelligence, 20*(3), 215–251. doi:10.1016/0004-3702(83)90008-5
Clay, M.M. (1967). The reading behavior of five-year-old children: A research report. *New Zealand Journal of Educational Studies, 2*(1), 11–31.
Clay, M.M. (1976). *Young fluent readers*. London: Heinemann.
Cognition and Technology Group at Vanderbilt. (1990). Anchored instruction and its relationship to situated cognition. *Educational Researcher, 19*(6), 2–10.
Cognition and Technology Group at Vanderbilt. (1996). Looking at technology in context: A framework for understanding technology and education research. In D.C. Berliner & R.C. Calfee (Eds.), *Handbook of educational psychology* (pp. 807–840). New York: Macmillan.
Coiro, J., Knobel, M., Lankshear, C., & Leu, D.J. (2008). Central issues in new literacies and new literacies research. In J. Coiro, M. Knobel, C. Lankshear, & D.J. Leu (Eds.), *Handbook of new literacies* (pp. 1–21). New York: Taylor & Francis.
Collins, A., Brown, J.S., & Newman, S.E. (1989). Cognitive apprenticeships: Teaching the crafts of reading, writing, and mathematics. In L.B. Resnick (Ed.), *Knowing, learning, and instruction: Essays in honor of Robert Glaser* (pp. 453–494). Hillsdale, NJ: Erlbaum.
Cox, C., & Many, J.E. (1992). Towards an understanding of the aesthetic response to literature. *Language Arts, 69*(1), 28–33.
Csikszentmihalyi, M. (1990). *Flow: The psychology of optimal experience*. New York: Cambridge University Press.
Cuban, L. (1993). *How teachers taught: Constancy and change in American classrooms, 1890–1980*. New York: Teachers College Press.
Deci, E.L., & Ryan, R.M. (1991). A motivational approach to self: Integration in personality. In R.A. Dienstbier (Ed.), *Nebraska Symposium on Motivation, 1990: Perspectives on motivation* (Vol. 38, pp. 237–288). Lincoln: University of Nebraska Press.
de Jong, T., & Ferguson-Hessler, M.G.M. (1996). Types and qualities of knowledge. *Educational Psychologist, 31*(2), 105–113. doi:10.1207/s15326985ep3102_2
Dewey, J. (1913). *Interest and effort in education*. Boston: Riverside.
Dewey, J. (1991). *How we think*. Buffalo, NY: Prometheus. (Original work published 1910)
Dinsmore, D.L., Alexander, P.A., & Loughlin, S.M. (2008). Focusing the conceptual lens on metacognition, self-regulation, and self-regulated learning. *Educational Psychology Review, 20*(4), 391–409. doi:10.1007/s10648-008-9083-6
Dochy, F., Segers, M., Van den Bossche, P., & Gijbels, D. (2003). Effects of problem-based learning: A meta-analysis. *Learning and Instruction, 13*(5), 533–568. doi:10.1016/S0959-4752(02)00025-7
Duffy, G., Roehler, L.R., Meloth, M.S., & Vavrus, L.G. (1986). Conceptualizing instructional explanation. *Teaching and Teacher Education, 2*(3), 197–214. doi:10.1016/S0742-051X(86)80002-6

Durant, W., & Durant, A. (1967). *The story of civilization: Part X: Rousseau and revolution.* New York: Simon & Schuster.

Ericsson, K.A., & Smith, J. (1991). *Toward a general theory of expertise: Prospects and limits.* New York: Cambridge University Press.

Felton, M.K., & Kuhn, D. (2007). How do I know? The epistemological roots of critical thinking. *Journal of Museum Education, 32*(2), 101–123.

Fish, S.F. (1980). *Is there a text in this class?* Cambridge, MA: Harvard University Press.

Flanagin, A.J., & Metzger, M.J. (2007). The role of site features, user attributes, and information verification behaviors on the perceived credibility of web-based information. *New Media & Society, 9*(2), 319–342. doi:10.1177/1461444807075015.

Flesch, R. (1955). *Why Johnny can't read—and what you can do about it.* New York: Harper & Brothers.

Fodor, J.A. (1964). *The structure of language: Readings in the philosophy of language.* New York: Prentice-Hall.

Fodor, J.A. (2001). *The mind doesn't work that way: The scope and limits of computational psychology.* Cambridge, MA: MIT Press.

Fodor, J.A., Miller, G.A., & Langendoen, D.T. (1980). *Language of thought.* Cambridge, MA: Harvard University Press.

Foorman, B.R., Francis, D.J., Fletcher, J.M., Schatschneider, C., & Mehta, P. (1998). The role of instruction in learning to read: Preventing reading failure in at-risk children. *Journal of Educational Psychology, 90*(1), 37–55. doi:10.1037/0022-0663.90.1.37

Foorman, B.R., Schatschneider, C., Eakin, M.N., Fletcher, J.M., Moats, L.C., & Francis, D.J. (2006). The impact of instructional practices in grades 1 and 2 on reading and spelling achievement in high poverty schools. *Contemporary Educational Psychology, 31*(1), 1–29. doi:10.1016/j.cedpsych.2004.11.003

Fox, E. (2009). The role of reader characteristics in processing and learning from informational text. *Review of Educational Research, 79*(1), 197–261. doi:10.3102/0034654308324654

Fox, E., & Alexander, P.A. (2009). Text comprehension: A retrospective, perspective, and prospective. In S.E. Israel & G.G. Duffy (Eds.), *Handbook or research on reading comprehension* (pp. 227–239). New York: Routledge.

Fox, E., Dinsmore, D.L., & Alexander, P.A. (2010). Reading competence, interest, and reading goals in three gifted young adolescent readers. *High Ability Studies, 21*(2), 165–178. doi:10.1080/13598139.2010.525340

Fox, E., Dinsmore, D.L., Maggioni, L., & Alexander, P.A. (2009, April). *Factors associated with undergraduates' success in reading and learning from course texts.* Paper presented at the annual meeting of the American Educational Research Association, San Diego.

Frederiksen, N. (1984). Implications of cognitive theory for instruction in problem solving. *Review of Educational Research, 54*(3), 363–407.

Ganley, A.C., Lyons, T.T., & Sewall, G.T. (1993). *The U.S.A. since 1945: After Hiroshima* (3rd ed.). White Plains, NY: Longman.

Gardner, H. (1991). *The unschooled mind.* New York: Basic.

Garner, R. (1987). *Metacognition and reading comprehension.* Norwood, NJ: Ablex.

Garner, R., & Gillingham, M.G. (1996). *Conversations across time, space, and culture.* Mahwah, NJ: Erlbaum.

Garner, R., & Hansis, R. (1994). Literacy practices outside of school: Adults' beliefs and their responses to "street texts." In R. Garner & P.A. Alexander (Eds.), *Beliefs about text and instruction with text* (pp. 57–73). Hillsdale, NJ: Erlbaum.

Gee, J.P. (1989). Literacy, discourse, and linguistics: Essays by James Paul Gee [Special issue]. *Journal of Education, 171*(1).

Gibson, J.J. (1966). *The senses considered as perceptual systems.* Boston: Houghton Mifflin.

Gillingham, M.G., Young, M.F., & Kulikowich, J.M. (1994). Do teachers consider nonlinear text to be text? In R. Garner & P.A. Alexander (Eds.), *Beliefs about text and instruction with text* (pp. 201–219). Hillsdale, NJ: Erlbaum.

Glaser, R. (1978). The contributions of B. F. Skinner to education and some counterinfluences. In P. Suppes (Ed.), *Impact of research on education: Some case studies* (pp. 199–265). Washington, DC: National Academy of Education.

Goetz, E.T., Alexander, P.A., & Ash, M. (1992). *Educational psychology: A classroom perspective.* Columbus, OH: Charles E. Merrill.

Goldman, S.R. (1996). Reading, writing, and learning in hypermedia environments. In H. Van Oostendorp & S. de Mui (Eds.), *Cognitive aspects of electronic text processing* (pp. 7–42). Norwood, NJ: Ablex.

Goodman, K.S. (1965). A linguistic study of cues and miscues in reading. *Elementary English, 42,* 639–643.

Goodman, K.S. (1996). *On reading.* Portsmouth, NH: Heinemann.

Goodman, K.S., & Goodman, Y.M. (1979). Learning to read is natural. In L.B. Resnick & P.A. Weaver (Eds.), *Theory and practice of early reading* (Vol. 1, pp. 137–154). Hillsdale, NJ: Erlbaum.

Gough, P.B., & Tunmer, W.E. (1986). Decoding, reading, and reading disability. *Remedial and Special Education, 7*(1), 6–10. doi:10.1177/074193258600700104

Gray, W.S. (1951). Foundation stones in the road to better reading. *The Elementary School Journal, 51*(8), 427–435. doi:10.1086/459271

Gray, W.S., & Rogers, B. (1956). *Maturity in reading, its nature and appraisal.* Chicago: University of Chicago Press.

Greene, S., & Ackerman, J.M. (1995). Expanding the constructivist metaphor: A rhetorical perspective on literacy research and practice. *Review of Educational Research, 65*(4), 383–420.

Greeno, J.G., & the Middle School Mathematics Through Applications Project Group. (1998). The situativity of knowing, learning, and research. *American Psychologist, 53*(1), 5–26. doi:10.1037/0003-066X.53.1.5

Greeno, J.G., & Moore, J.L. (1993). Situativity and symbols: Response to Vera and Simon. *Cognitive Science, 17*(1), 49–59. doi:10.1207/s15516709cog1701_3

Guthrie, J.T., McGough, K., Bennett, L., & Rice, M.E. (1996). Concept-Oriented Reading Instruction: An integrated curriculum to develop motivations and strategies for reading. In L. Baker, P. Afflerbach, & D. Reinking (Eds.), *Developing engaged readers in school and home communities* (pp. 165–190). Mahwah, NJ: Erlbaum.

Guthrie, J.T., Van Meter, P., McCann, A., Wigfield, A., Bennett, L., Poundstone, C., et al. (1996). Growth of literacy engagement: Changes in motivations and strategies during Concept-Oriented Reading Instruction. *Reading Research Quarterly, 31*(3), 306–332. doi:10.1598/RRQ.31.3.5

Guthrie, J.T., & Wigfield, A. (2000). Engagement and motivation in reading. In M.L. Kamil, P.B. Mosenthal, P.D. Pearson, & R. Barr (Eds.), *Handbook of reading research* (Vol. 3, pp. 403–422). Mahwah, NJ: Erlbaum.

Guzzetti, B., & Hynd, C. (1998). *Theoretical perspectives on conceptual change*. Mahwah, NJ: Erlbaum.

Halliday, M.A.K. (1969). Revelant models of language. *Educational Review, 22*(1), 26–37. doi:10.1080/0013191690220104

Halliday, M.A.K., & Hasan, R. (1974). *Cohesion in English*. London: Longman.

Hansen, J. (1981). The effects of inference training and practice on young children's reading comprehension. *Reading Research Quarterly, 16*(3), 391–417. doi:10.2307/747409

Harris, K.R. (1996, April). *The state of strategy research: Is this old territory or are there new frontiers?* Panel discussion presented at the annual meeting of the American Educational Research Association, New York.

Harste, J.C., Burke, C., & Woodward, V. (1984). *Language stories and literacy lessons*. Portsmouth, NH: Heinemann.

Heath, S.B. (1982). What no bedtime story means: Narrative skills at home and school. *Language in Society, 11*(1), 49–76. doi:10.1017/S0047404500009039

Heath, S.B. (1983). *Ways with words: Language, life, and work in communities and classrooms*. New York: Cambridge University Press.

Hidi, S. (1990). Interest and its contribution as a mental resource for learning. *Review of Educational Research, 60*(4), 549–571.

Hiebert, E.H., & Taylor, B.M. (2000). Beginning reading instruction: Research on early interventions. In M.L. Kamil, P.B. Mosenthal, P.D. Pearson, & R. Barr (Eds.), *Handbook of reading research* (Vol. 3, pp. 455–482). Mahwah, NJ: Erlbaum.

Hofer, B.K., & Pintrich, P.R. (2002). *Personal epistemologies: The psychology of beliefs about knowledge and knowing*. Mahwah, NJ: Erlbaum.

Huey, E.B. (1908). *The psychology and pedagogy of reading*. New York: Macmillan.

Hume, D. (1963). *An enquiry concerning human understanding and selections from a treatise of human nature*. La Salle, IL: Open Court. (Original work published 1777)

James, W. (1890). *Principles of psychology* (Vols. 1–2). New York: Holt.

Jenkinson, M.D. (1969). Sources of knowledge for theories of reading. *Journal of Reading Behavior, 1*(Winter), 11–29.

Jetton, T.L., & Alexander, P.A. (1998, April). *Teachers' views of discussion: Issues of control, time, and ability*. Paper presented at the annual meeting of the American Educational Research Association, San Diego.

Kant, I. (1963). *Critique of pure reason* (N. Kemp Smith, Trans.). London: Macmillan. (Original work published 1787)

Kellner, D. (2001). New technologies/new literacies: Reconstructing education for the new millennium. *International Journal of Technology and Design Education, 11*(1), 67–81. doi:10.1023/A:1011270402858

Kim, I.-H., Anderson, R.C., Nguyen-Jahiel, K., & Archodidou, A. (2007). Discourse patterns during children's collaborative online discussions. *Journal of the Learning Sciences, 16*(3), 333–370. doi:10.1080/10508400701413419

Kintsch, W., & van Dijk, T.A. (1978). Toward a model of text comprehension and production. *Psychological Review, 85*(5), 363–394. doi:10.1037/0033-295X.85.5.363

Kulikowich, J.M., & Alexander, P.A. (2010). Intentionality to learn in an academic domain. *Early Education and Development, 21*(5), 724–743. doi:10.1080/10409289.2010.508210

Labov, W. (1966). *The social stratification of English in New York City*. Washington, DC: Center for Applied Linguistics.

Labov, W. (1972). *Sociolinguistic patterns*. Philadelphia: University of Pennsylvania Press.

Labov, W. (1976). Systematically misleading data from test questions. *The Urban Review, 9*(3), 146–170. doi:10.1007/BF02172509

Lankshear, C., & Knobel, M. (2003). *New literacies: Changing knowledge and classroom learning*. Buckingham, UK: Open University Press.

Lave, J. (1988). *Cognition in practice: Mind, mathematics and culture in everyday life*. New York: Cambridge University Press. doi:10.1017/CBO9780511609268

Lawless, K.A., & Kulikowich, J.M. (1996). Understanding hypertext navigation through cluster analysis. *Journal of Educational Computing Research, 14*(4), 385–399. doi:10.2190/DVAP-DE23-3XMV-9MXH

Leu, D.J., Kinzer, C.K., Coiro, J.L., & Cammack, D.W. (2004). Toward a theory of new literacies emerging from the Internet and other information and communication technologies. In R.B. Ruddell & N.J. Unrau (Eds.), *Theoretical models and processes of reading* (5th ed., pp. 1570–1613). Newark, DE: International Reading Association. doi:10.1598/0872075028.54

Leu, D.J., O'Byrne, W.I., Zawilinski, L., McVerry, J.G., & Everett-Cocapardo, H. (2009). Expanding the new literacies conversation. *Educational Researcher, 38*(4), 264–269. doi:10.3102/0013189X09336676

Levin, H. (Ed.). (1965). *Planning for a reading research program.* Ithaca, NY: Cornell University.

Lipson, M.Y. (1983). The influence of religious affiliation on children's memory for text information. *Reading Research Quarterly, 18*(4), 448–457. doi:10.2307/747379

Loyens, S.M.M., & Gijbels, D. (2008). Understanding the effects of constructivist learning environments: Introducing a multi-directional approach. *Instructional Science, 36*(5/6), 351–357. doi:10.1007/s11251-008-9059-4

Lundeberg, M. (1987). Metacognitive aspects of reading comprehension: Studying the understanding in legal case analysis. *Reading Research Quarterly, 22*(4), 407–432. doi:10.2307/747700

Lysynchuk, L.M., Pressley, M., D'Ailly, H., Smith, M., & Cake, H. (1989). A methodological analysis of experimental studies of comprehension strategy instruction. *Reading Research Quarterly, 24*(4), 458–470. doi:10.2307/747607

Maggioni, L., VanSledright, B., & Alexander, P.A. (2009). Walking on the borders: A measure of epistemic cognition in history. *Journal of Experimental Education, 77*(3), 187–214. doi:10.3200/JEXE.77.3.187-214

Mandl, H., Stein, N.L., & Trabasso, T. (Eds.). (1984). *Learning and comprehension of text.* Hillsdale, NJ: Erlbaum.

Marton, F., & Booth, S. (1997). *Learning and awareness.* Mahwah, NJ: Erlbaum.

Matthews, M.R. (1994). *Science teaching: The role of history and philosophy of science.* New York: Routledge.

Mayer, R.E. (2004). Should there be a three-strikes rule against pure discovery learning? The case for guided methods of instruction. *American Psychologist, 59*(1), 14–19. doi:10.1037/0003-066X.59.1.14

McCrudden, M.T., Magliano, J.P., & Schraw, G. (2010). Exploring how relevance instructions affect personal reading intentions, reading goals and text processing: A mixed methods study. *Contemporary Educational Psychology, 35*(4), 229–241. doi:10.1016/j.cedpsych.2009.12.001

McLaren, P. (1998). *Life in schools* (3rd ed.). New York: Longman.

Meyer, B.J.F. (1975). *The organization of prose and its effects on memory.* Amsterdam: North-Holland.

Moje, E.B. (2007). Developing socially just subject matter instruction: A review of the literature on disciplinary literacy teaching. *Review of Research in Education, 31*(1), 1–44. doi:10.3102/0091732X07300046

Moje, E.B., Tucker-Raymond, E., Varelas, M., & Pappas, C. (2007). Giving oneself over to science: Exploring the roles of subjectivities and identities in learning science. *Cultural Studies of Science Education, 1*(3), 593–601. doi:10.1007/s11422-006-9016-y

Moje, E.B., Young, J.P., Readence, J.E., & Moore, D.W. (2000). Reinventing adolescent literacy for new times: perennial and millennial issues. *Journal of Adolescent & Adult Literacy, 43*(5), 400–410.

Monaghan, E.J., & Saul, E.W. (1987). The reader, the scribe, the thinker: A critical look at the history of American reading and writing instruction. In T.S. Popkewitz (Ed.), *The formation of school subjects: The struggle for creating an American institution* (pp. 85–122). Philadelphia: Falmer.

Murphy, P.K., Wilkinson, I.A.G., & Soter, A.O. (2011). Instruction based on discussion. In R.E. Mayer & P.A. Alexander (Eds.), *Handbook of research on learning and instruction* (pp. 382–407). Oxford, UK: Taylor & Francis.

Murphy, P.K., Wilkinson, I.A.G., Soter, A.O., Hennessey, M.N., & Alexander, J.F. (2009). Examining the effects of classroom discussion on students' high-level comprehension of text: A meta-analysis. *Journal of Educational Psychology, 101*(3), 740–764. doi:10.1037/a0015576

Murphy, P.K., & Woods, B.S. (1996). Situating knowledge in learning and instruction. *Educational Psychologist, 31*(2), 141–145. doi:10.1207/s15326985ep3102_6

Neuman, S.B. (1988). The displacement effect: Assessing the relation between television viewing and reading performance. *Reading Research Quarterly, 23*(4), 414–440. doi:10.2307/747641

Noddings, N. (2004). High stakes testing: Why? *Theory and Research in Education, 2*(3), 263–269. doi:10.1177/1477878504046520

Nolen, S.B., Johnson-Crowley, N., & Wineburg, S.S. (1994). Who is this "I" person, anyway? The presence of a visible author in statistical text. In R. Garner & P.A. Alexander (Eds.), *Beliefs about text and instruction with text* (pp. 41–55). Hillsdale, NJ: Erlbaum.

Nystrand, M., & Gamoran, A. (1991). Instructional discourse, student engagement, and literature achievement. *Research in the Teaching of English, 25*(3), 261–290.

Oldfather, P., & Wigfield, A. (1996). Children's motivations to read. In L. Baker, P. Afflerbach, & D. Reinking (Eds.), *Developing engaged readers in school and home communities* (pp. 89–113). Mahwah, NJ: Erlbaum.

Ozuru, Y., Dempsey, K., & McNamara, D.S. (2009). Prior knowledge, reading skill, and text cohesion in the comprehension of science texts. *Learning and Instruction, 19*(3), 228–242. doi:10.1016/j.learninstruc.2008.04.003

Pajares, M.F. (1992). Teacher's beliefs and educational research: Cleaning up a messy construct. *Review of Educational Research, 62*(3), 307–332.
Palincsar, A.S., & Brown, A.L. (1984). Reciprocal teaching of comprehension-fostering and comprehension-monitoring activities. *Cognition and Instruction, 1*(2), 117–175. doi:10.1207/s1532690xci0102_1
Paris, S.G., Lipson, M.Y., & Wixson, K.K. (1983). Becoming a strategic reader. *Contemporary Educational Psychology, 8*(3), 293–316. doi:10.1016/0361-476X(83)90018-8
Paris, S.G., & Myers, M. (1981). Comprehension monitoring, memory, and study strategies of good and poor readers. *Journal of Reading Behavior, 13*(1), 5–22.
Paris, S.G., & Urdan, T. (2000). Policies and practices of high-stakes testing that influence teachers and schools. *Issues in Education, 6*(1/2), 83–107.
Paris, S.G., Wasik, B.A., & Turner, J.C. (1991). The development of strategic readers. In R. Barr, M.L. Kamil, P. Mosenthal, & P.D. Pearson (Eds.), *Handbook of reading research* (pp. 609–640). New York: Longman.
Paris, S.G., & Winograd, P. (1990). Dimensions of thinking and cognitive instruction. In B.F. Jones & L. Idol (Eds.), *How metacognition can promote academic learning and instruction* (pp. 15–51). Hillsdale, NJ: Erlbaum.
Partnership for Reading. (2002). *Adolescent literacy—Research informing practice: A series of workshops.* Washington, DC: National Institute for Literacy. Retrieved May 9, 2012, from novel.nifl.gov/partnershipforreading/adolescent/research_needs.html
Pearson, P.D. (1984). Direct explicit teaching of reading comprehension. In G.G. Duffy, L.R. Roehler, & J. Mason (Eds.), *Comprehension instruction: Perspectives and suggestions* (pp. 222–233). New York: Longman.
Pearson, P.D., & Stephens, D. (1994). Learning from literacy: A 30-year journey. In R.B. Ruddell, M.R. Ruddell, & H. Singer (Eds.), *Theoretical models and processes of reading* (4th ed., pp. 22–42). Newark, DE: International Reading Association.
Perkins, D.N., & Simmons, R. (1988). Patterns of misunderstanding: An integrative model for science, math, and programming. *Review of Educational Research, 58*(3), 303–326.
Perret-Claremont, A., Perret, J., & Bell, N. (1980). The social construction of meaning and cognitive activity in elementary school children. In L.B. Resnick, J.M. Levine, & S.D. Teasley (Eds.), *Perspectives on socially shared cognition* (pp. 41–62). Washington, DC: American Psychological Association. doi:10.1037/10096-002
Phillips, D.C. (1995). The good, the bad, and the ugly: The many faces of constructivism. *Educational Researcher, 24*(7), 5–12.
Pichert, J.W., & Anderson, R.C. (1977). Taking different perspectives on a story. *Journal of Educational Psychology, 69*(4), 309–315. doi:10.1037/0022-0663.69.4.309
Pigott, T.D., & Barr, R. (2000). Designing programmatic interventions. In M.L. Kamil, P.B. Mosenthal, P.D. Pearson, & R. Barr (Eds.), *Handbook of reading research* (Vol. 3, pp. 99–108). Mahwah, NJ: Erlbaum.
Pintrich, P.R., & Schunk, D.H. (2001). *Motivation in education: Theory, research, and applications* (2nd ed.). Englewood Cliffs, NJ: Prentice Hall.
Postman, N. (1993). *Technopoly.* New York: Vintage.
Prawat, R.S. (1989). Promoting access to knowledge, strategy, and disposition in students: A research synthesis. *Review of Educational Research, 59*(1), 1–41.
Pressley, M. (2002). Comprehension strategies instruction: A turn-of-the-century report. In C.C. Block & M. Pressley (Eds.), *Comprehension instruction: Research-based best practices* (pp. 11–27). New York: Guilford.
Pressley, M., Goodchild, F., Fleet, J., Zajchowski, R., & Evans, E.D. (1989). The challenges of classroom strategy instruction. *The Elementary School Journal, 89*(3), 301–342. doi:10.1086/461578
Pugh, K.R., Shaywitz, B.A., Shaywitz, S.E., Shankweiler, D.P., Katz, L., Fletcher, J.M., et al. (1997). Predicting reading performance from neuroimaging profiles: The cerebral basis of phonological effects in printed word identification. *Journal of Experimental Psychology: Human Perception and Performance, 23*(2), 299–318. doi:10.1037/0096-1523.23.2.299
Putnam, R.T., Heaton, R.M., Prawat, R.S., & Remillard, J. (1992). Teaching mathematics for understanding: Discussing case studies of four fifth-grade teachers. *The Elementary School Journal, 93*(2), 213–228. doi:10.1086/461723
RAND Reading Study Group. (2002). *Reading for understanding: Toward an R&D program in reading comprehension.* Santa Monica, CA: RAND.
Raphael, T.F., & Wonnacott, C.A. (1985). Heightening fourth-graders' sensitivity to sources of information for answering comprehension questions. *Reading Research Quarterly, 20*(3), 282–296. doi:10.2307/748019
Reed, J.H., & Schallert, D.L. (1993). The nature of involvement in academic discourse. *Journal of Educational Psychology, 85*(2), 253–266. doi:10.1037/0022-0663.85.2.253
Reed, J.H., Schallert, D.L., & Goetz, E.T. (1993, April). *Interest happens but involvement takes effort: Distinguishing between two constructs in academic discourse tasks.* Paper presented at the annual meeting of the American Educational Research Association, Atlanta, GA.
Reinking, D., McKenna, M.C., Labbo, L.D., & Kieffer, R.D. (Eds.). (1998). *Handbook of literacy and technology: Transformations in a post-typographic world.* Mahwah, NJ: Erlbaum.
Resnick, L.B., Levine, J.M., & Teasley, S.D. (Eds.). (1991). *Perspectives on socially shared cognition.* Washington, DC: American Psychological Association. doi:10.1037/10096-000

Reynolds, R.E., Sinatra, G.M., & Jetton, T.L. (1996). Views of knowledge acquisition and representation: A continuum from experience centered to mind centered. *Educational Psychologist, 31*(2), 93–104. doi:10.1207/s15326985ep3102_1

Rideout, V.J., Foehr, U.G., & Roberts, D.F. (2010). *Generation M2: Media in the lives of 8- to 18-year-olds.* Menlo Park, CA: H.J. Kaiser Family Foundation.

Rogoff, B. (1990). *Apprenticeship in thinking: Cognitive development in social context.* New York: Oxford University Press.

Rogoff, B., & Gauvain, M. (1986). A method for the analysis of patterns illustrated with data on mother–child instructional interaction. In J. Valsiner (Ed.), *The individual subject and scientific psychology* (pp. 261–290). New York: Plenum.

Rosenblatt, L.M. (1994). *The reader, the text, the poem: The transactional theory of the literary work.* Carbondale: Southern Illinois Press. (Original work published 1978)

Rosenblatt, L.M. (1995). *Literature as exploration.* New York: Modern Language Association. (Original work published 1938)

Roth, K.J. (1985). Developing meaningful conceptual understanding in science. In B.F. Jones & L. Idol (Eds.), *Dimensions of thinking and cognitive instruction* (pp. 139–175). Hillsdale, NJ: Erlbaum.

Rouet, J.-F., Vidal-Abarca, E., Erboul, A.B., & Millogo, V. (2001). Effects of information search tasks on the comprehension of instructional texts. *Discourse Processes, 31*(2), 163–186. doi:10.1207/S15326950DP3102_03

Ruddell, R.B. (2002). *Teaching children to read and write: Becoming an effective literacy teacher* (3rd ed.). Boston: Allyn & Bacon.

Rumelhart, D.E. (1980). Schemata: The building blocks of cognition. In R.J. Spiro, B.C. Bruce, & W.F. Brewer (Eds.), *Theoretical issues in reading comprehension* (pp. 33–58). Hillsdale, NJ: Erlbaum.

Russell, D.H. (1961). *Children learn to read* (2nd ed.). New York: Ginn.

Ryle, G. (1949). *The concept of mind.* London: Hutchinson.

Sadoski, M., Paivio, A., & Goetz, E.T. (1991). A critique of schema theory in reading and a dual coding alternative. *Reading Research Quarterly, 26*(4), 463–484. doi:10.2307/747898

Salomon, G. (1993). *Distributed cognition: Psychological and educational considerations.* Cambridge, UK: Cambridge University Press.

Salomon, G., Perkins, D.N., & Globerson, T. (1991). Partners in cognition: Extending human intelligence with intelligent technologies. *Educational Researcher, 20*(3), 2–9.

Samuels, S.J., & Kamil, M.L. (1984). Models of the reading process. In P.D. Pearson, R. Barr, M.L. Kamil, & P. Mosenthal (Eds.), *Handbook of reading research* (pp. 185–224). New York: Longman.

Scardamalia, M., Bereiter, C., McLean, R.S., Swallow, J., & Woodruff, E. (1989). Computer-supported intentional learning environments. *Journal of Educational Computing Research, 5*(1), 51–68.

Schallert, D.L., Meyer, D.K., & Fowler, L.A. (1995). The nature of engagement when reading in and out of one's discipline. In K.A. Hinchman, D.J. Leu, & C.K. Kinzer (Eds.), *Perspectives on literacy research and practice: Forty-fourth yearbook of the National Reading Conference* (pp. 119–125). Chicago: National Reading Conference.

Schank, R.C., & Abelson, R.P. (1977). *Scripts, plans, goals, and understanding: An inquiry into human knowledge structures.* Hillsdale, NJ: Erlbaum.

Schlaggar, B.L., & McCandliss, B.D. (2007). Development of neural systems for reading. *Annual Review of Neuroscience, 30,* 475–503. doi:10.1146/annurev.neuro.28.061604.135645

Schommer, M. (1990). Effects of beliefs about the nature of knowledge on comprehension. *Journal of Educational Psychology, 82*(3), 498–504. doi:10.1037/0022-0663.82.3.498

Schommer, M. (1993). Epistemological development and academic performance among secondary students. *Journal of Educational Psychology, 85*(3), 406–411. doi:10.1037/0022-0663.85.3.406

Schraw, G., Bruning, R., & Svoboda, C. (1995). Sources of situational interest. *Journal of Reading Behavior, 27*(1), 1–17.

Sfard, A. (1998). On two metaphors for learning and the dangers of choosing just one. *Educational Researcher, 27*(2), 4–13.

Shanahan, T., & Shanahan, C. (2008). Teaching disciplinary literacy to adolescents: Rethinking content-area literacy. *Harvard Educational Review, 78*(1), 40–59.

Shaywitz, B.A., Fletcher, J.M., Holahan, J.M., & Shaywitz, S.E. (1992). Discrepancy compared to low achievement definitions of reading disability: Results from the Connecticut Longitudinal Study. *Journal of Learning Disabilities, 25*(10), 639–648. doi:10.1177/002221949202501003

Shaywitz, B.A., Pugh, K.R., Jenner, A.R., Fulbright, R.K., Fletcher, J.M., Gore, J.C., et al. (2000). The neurobiology of reading and reading disability (dyslexia). In M.L. Kamil, P.B. Mosenthal, P.D. Pearson, & R. Barr (Eds.), *Handbook of reading research* (Vol. 3, pp. 229–249). Mahwah, NJ: Erlbaum.

Shuy, R.W. (1968). Detroit speech: Careless, awkward, and inconsistent, or systematic, graceful, and regular? *Elementary English, 45*(5), 565–569.

Shuy, R.W. (1969). Some considerations for developing beginning reading materials for ghetto children. *Journal of Reading Behavior, 1*(2), 33–43.

Skinner, B.F. (1976). *About behaviorism.* New York: Vintage.

Smith, C.E., & Keogh, B.K. (1962). The group Bender-Gestalt as a reading readiness screening instrument. *Perceptual and Motor Skills, 15*(3), 639–645.

Smith, F. (1973). *Psycholinguistics and reading*. New York: Holt, Rinehart & Winston.
Smith, F. (1978). *Understanding reading* (2nd ed.). New York: Holt, Rinehart & Winston.
Smith, F. (1985). A metaphor for literacy: Creating worlds or shunting information? In D.R. Olson, N. Torrance, & A. Hildyard (Eds.), *Perceiving, acting, and knowing: Toward an ecological psychology* (pp. 1–39). Hillsdale, NJ: Erlbaum.
Snyder, R.T., & Freud, S.L. (1967). Reading readiness and its relation to maturational unreadiness as measured by the spiral aftereffect and other visual-perceptual techniques. *Perceptual and Motor Skills, 25*(3), 841–854.
Spiro, R.J., Feltovich, P.J., Jacobson, M.J., & Coulson, R.L. (1992). Cognitive flexibility, constructivism, and hypertext: Random access instruction for advanced knowledge acquisition in ill-structured domains. In T.M. Duffy & D.H. Jonassen (Eds.), *Constructivism and the technology of instruction* (pp. 57–75). Cambridge, UK: Cambridge University Press.
Spiro, R.J., & Jehng, J.C. (1990). Cognitive flexibility and hypertext: Theory and technology for the nonlinear and multidimensional traversal of complex subject matter. In D. Nix & R.J. Spiro (Eds.), *Cognition, education, and multimedia* (pp. 163–205). Hillsdale, NJ: Erlbaum.
Spivey, N.N., & King, J.R. (1989). Readers as writers composing from sources. *Reading Research Quarterly, 24*(1), 7–26. doi:10.1598/RRQ.24.1.1
Stahl, S.A., Hynd, C.R., Glynn, S.M., & Carr, M. (1996). Beyond reading to learn: Developing content and disciplinary knowledge through texts. In L. Baker, P. Afflerbach, & D. Reinking (Eds.), *Developing engaged readers in school and home communities* (pp. 139–163). Mahwah, NJ: Erlbaum.
Stahl, S.A., & Miller, P.D. (1989). Whole language and language experience approaches for beginning reading: A quantitative research synthesis. *Review of Educational Research, 59*(1), 87–116.
Stanovich, K.E. (1986). Matthew effects in reading: Some consequences of individual differences in the acquisition of literacy. *Reading Research Quarterly, 21*(4), 360–407. doi:10.1598/RRQ.21.4.1
Strang, R., McCullough, C.M., & Traxler, A.E. (1955). *Problems in the improvement of reading* (2nd ed.). New York: McGraw-Hill.
Strike, K.A. (1974). On the expressive potential of behaviorist language. *American Educational Research Journal, 11*(2), 103–120.
Strømsø, H.I., Bråten, I., & Samuelstuen, M.S. (2008). Dimensions of topic-specific epistemological beliefs as predictors of multiple text understanding. *Learning and Instruction, 18*(6), 513–527. doi:10.1016/j.learninstruc.2007.11.001
Taylor, B.M., & Beach, R.W. (1984). The effects of text structure instruction on middle-grade students' comprehension and production of expository text. *Reading Research Quarterly, 19*(2), 134–146. doi:10.2307/747358
Thorndike, E.L. (1917). Reading as reasoning: A study of mistakes in paragraph reading. *Journal of Educational Psychology, 8*(6), 323–332. doi:10.1037/h0075325
Tierney, R.J., Readence, J.E., & Dishner, E.K. (1990). *Reading strategies and practices: A compendium* (3rd ed.). Boston: Allyn & Bacon.
Tierney, R.J., Soter, A., O'Flahavan, J.F., & McGinley, W. (1989). The effects of reading and writing upon thinking critically. *Reading Research Quarterly, 24*(2), 134–173. doi:10.2307/747862
Torgesen, J.K. (1998). Instructional interventions for children with reading disabilities. In B.K. Shapiro, P.J. Accardo, & A.J. Capute (Eds.), *Specific reading disability: A view of the spectrum* (pp. 197–200). Parkton, MD: York.
Torgesen, J.K. (1999). Reading disabilities. In R. Gallimore, A. Bernheimer, G. MacMillan, D. Speece, & S. Vaughn (Eds.), *Developmental perspectives on children with high incidence disabilities: Papers in honor of Barbara K. Keogh* (pp. 157–182). Mahwah, NJ: Erlbaum.
Turner, J.C. (1995). The influence of classroom contexts on young children's motivation for literacy. *Reading Research Quarterly, 30*(3), 410–441. doi:10.2307/747624
Vacca, R.T., & Vacca, J.L. (1983). Two less than fortunate consequences of reading research in the 1970's. *Reading Research Quarterly, 18*(4), 382–383. doi:10.2307/747374
Valencia, S.W., & Wixson, K.K. (2001). Literacy policy and policy research that makes a difference. In J.V. Hoffman, D.L. Schallert, C.M. Fairbanks, J. Worthy, & B. Maloch (Eds.), *Fiftieth yearbook of the National Reading Conference* (pp. 21–43). Chicago: National Reading Conference.
Valli, L., Croninger, R.G., Chambliss, M.H., Graeber, A.O., & Buese, D. (2008). *Test-driven: High-stakes accountability in elementary schools*. New York: Teachers College Press.
VanSledright, B.A. (1996). Closing the gap between school and disciplinary history? Historian as high school history teacher. In J. Brophy (Ed.), *Advances in research on teaching* (Vol. 6, pp. 257–289). Greenwich, CT: JAI.
VanSledright, B.A. (2002). *In search of America's past: Learning to read history in elementary school*. New York: Teachers College Press.
Vellutino, F.R., Tunmer, W.E., Jaccard, J.J., & Chen, R. (2007). Components of reading ability: Multivariate evidence for a convergent skills model of reading development. *Scientific Studies of Reading, 11*(1), 3–32.
Venezky, R.L. (1984). The history of reading research. In P.D. Pearson, R. Barr, M.L. Kamil, & P. Mosenthal (Eds.), *Handbook of reading research* (pp. 3–38). New York: Longman.
Verhoeven, L., & van Leeuwe, J. (2008). Prediction of the development of reading comprehension: A longitudinal study. *Applied Cognitive Psychology, 22*(3), 407–423. doi:10.1002/acp.1414

von Glasersfeld, E. (1991). *Radical constructivism in mathematics education*. Dordrecht, The Netherlands: Kluwer Academic.

Vosniadou, S. (1994). Capturing and modeling the process of conceptual change. *Learning and Instruction*, 4(1), 45–69. doi:10.1016/0959-4752(94)90018-3

Vygotsky, L. (1978). *Mind in society: The development of higher psychological processes* (M. Cole, V. John-Steiner, S. Scribner, & E. Souberman, Eds. & Trans.). Cambridge, MA: Harvard University Press.

Vygotsky, L. (1986). *Thought and language* (A. Kozulin, Trans.). Cambridge, MA: MIT Press. (Original work published 1934)

Wade, S.E., & Moje, E.B. (2000). The role of text in classroom learning. In M.L. Kamil, P.B. Mosenthal, P.D. Pearson, & R. Barr (Eds.), *Handbook of reading research* (Vol. 3, pp. 609–627). Mahwah, NJ: Erlbaum.

Wade, S.E., Thompson, A., & Watkins, W. (1994). The role of belief systems in authors' and readers' constructions of texts. In R. Garner & P.A. Alexander (Eds.), *Beliefs about text and instruction with text* (pp. 265–293). Hillsdale, NJ: Erlbaum.

Weaver, C.A., & Kintsch, W. (1991). Expository text. In R. Barr, M.L. Kamil, P.B. Mosenthal, & P.D. Pearson (Eds.), *Handbook of reading research* (Vol. 2, pp. 230–245). Mahwah, NJ: Erlbaum.

Weinstein, C.E., Goetz, E.T., & Alexander P.A. (Eds.). (1988). *Learning and study strategies: Issues in assessment, instruction, and evaluation*. San Diego, CA: Academic.

Wertheimer, M. (1959). *Productive thinking*. New York: Harper & Row. (Original work published 1945)

Whitehead, A.N. (1957). *The aims of education and other essays*. New York: Macmillan. (Original work published 1929)

Wijekumar, K., & Meyer, B.J.F. (2006). Design and pilot of a web-based intelligent tutoring system to improve reading comprehension in middle school students. *International Journal of Technology in Teaching and Learning*, 2(1), 36–49.

Wilkinson, I.A.G., Soter, A.O., & Murphy, P.K. (2010). Developing a model of quality talk about literary text. In M.G. McKeown & L. Kucan (Eds.), *Bringing reading research to life* (pp. 142–169). New York: Guilford.

Wineburg, S.S. (1996). The psychology of learning and teaching history. In D.C. Berliner & R.C. Calfee (Eds.), *Handbook of educational psychology* (pp. 423–437). New York: Simon & Schuster Macmillan.

Woods, B.S., & Murphy, P.K. (2002). Thickening the discussion: Inspecting constructivist theories of knowledge through a Jamesian lens. *Educational Theory*, 52(1), 43–59. doi:10.1111/j.1741-5446.2002.00043.x

Wulf, F. (1938). Tendencies in figural variation. In W.D. Ellis (Ed. & Trans.), *A source book of Gestalt psychology* (pp. 136–148). New York: Routledge & Kegan Paul. doi:10.1037/11496-010 (Original work published 1922)

CHAPTER 2

Literacies and Their Investigation Through Theories and Models

Norman J. Unrau, California State University, Los Angeles

Donna E. Alvermann, The University of Georgia

Theory and theoretical models have the power to cast both light and shadow on our understanding of literacies. They seem to exercise their powers not absolutely but on a continuum of degrees of illumination, so we sometimes get from a theory only a narrow shaft of light that provides an insight into a literacy process, such as reading. Furthermore, the intensity of light that a narrow shaft provides changes in its intensity, so a theory's powers to illuminate can rise or fall, depending on our capacity to grasp a particular theory or model, its individual components, their interactions, and the potential outcomes of those interactions. In this sense, all theories are relative. Their explanatory powers fluctuate, depending on our ability to appreciate their assumptions, subtleties, and implications.

While theories of reading, both conscious and unconscious, affect readers generally, specialized readers, such as researchers, graduate students, and reading specialists, activate and use their own theories of reading. Their use of theory may affect a wide range of activities and decisions. Regarding the identification of issues in reading to investigate, seasoned and newly emerging researchers often turn to theory and theoretical models to provide a theoretical framework for their investigations and to identify key issues that they plan to examine in detail. Theories and models may also provide researchers with knowledge organized into structures that can frame the discussion of a study's results, their bearing on current instructional practices, and their implications for subsequent research. In addition, researchers often use their findings to provide documentation for a theory's validity, to reject a theory in part or in its entirety, to modify aspects of it, and to posit new theories that more powerfully and comprehensively explain reading processes or outcomes. In fact, the importance of findings often comes to life when seen within a particular theoretical perspective.

For those interested in literacy research or engaged in it, grappling with literacy theory or theoretical models of reading is unavoidable. Addressing theoretical considerations for a research project arises in most educational research textbooks included in undergraduate and graduate courses (Creswell, 2008). Research studies on reading and articles published in professional journals commonly begin with a review of literature relevant to the research questions posed and to the theory used to frame the study. Answering a call for proposals from a governmental agency or private organization also necessitates the articulation of a theoretical framework for the proposed research. For example, research grants or contracts funded through the U.S. Institute of Educational Sciences (IES) to study reading require that applicants clearly describe their intervention and the theory (or theories) framing the intervention. The key components of the intervention must be identified along with a description of how those components relate to one another theoretically, as well as pedagogically and operationally. Applicants are also urged to provide a strong theoretical and empirical justification for their intervention. Developing a deep understanding of theory and its uses in literacy studies can serve a broad audience comprised of researchers, teachers, teacher educators, graduate students, and reading specialists.

In this chapter, we first clarify the meanings of *theory* and *model*, particularly in relation to literacy studies. We then explore meanings of *paradigm* and their shifts relevant to the field of literacy research over the past half century or so. Subsequently, we review central theories and associated models that influence literacy research, especially reading, including constructivism, social constructionism, information/cognitive processing theory, sociocultural perspectives, sociocognitive theory, structuralism, poststructuralism, and motivational theory relevant to reading. Finally, we speculate on the evolution of literacy theories and models for future research.

Theory and Model: Their Meanings and Relationship

A word's roots often reveal its essence, and to some degree, that is what the ancient Greek word root of *theory* affords. Our modern theory is rooted in the Greek word *theōria* (θεωρία), which, when translated, means "a looking at, viewing, contemplation, speculation, also a sight, a spectacle" (McPherson, 2012). Aspects of our current use of the word *theory*, certainly as viewing and speculation, are reflected in these ancient meanings. However, when we take a Wittgensteinian view of language and look at the meanings of words in the context of their use in the current game of language (Wittgenstein, 1953), we soon discover a fascinating range of meanings when people, including educators, speak of theory. In living rooms, offices, and classrooms, we hear people providing us with a description or explanation for how and why events have occurred the way they did, including why the Yankees lost the World Series. Not infrequently, we hear listeners respond to these descriptions and explanations with comments such as, "That's an interesting theory," "I've heard that theory before," or "I don't think that theory works here, Albert." In classrooms, especially those in which science is taught, we are more likely to hear explanations for events that are grounded in a hypothesis, but because that hypothesis has been vigorously tested, speakers refer to it as a theory, perhaps with accompanying laws. The theory has been so carefully developed and tested that it not only describes and explains events but can also be used to predict them, sometimes to an impressive degree of mathematical precision. With this usage of the word *theory* in mind, we would be comfortable assuming that in some contexts, when people are talking about theory, they are describing, explaining, and attempting to predict events. When used by natural or physical scientists, a theory usually refers to an explanation of some aspect of reality, such as the behavior of gases under pressure, that has been subjected to extensive testing, survived falsification, and become widely accepted by the scientific community in which the theory is germane.

In science broadly and in literacy research in particular, theories are propositional networks commonly used to help members of a community of researchers and practitioners understand, explain, and make predictions about key concepts and processes in a particular field of study. Theories themselves can be expressed in natural language, in mathematical terms, or in some other symbolic language, such as that used in chemistry. Darwin (1859/1988), for example, presented his theory of evolution to the general public in his book *On the Origin of Species*. He introduced the theory that populations evolve over time through the process of natural selection, and he presented evidence, much of which he collected during his voyage on the *Beagle*, that life's diversity came about through a branching pattern of common descent. However, a theory need not be completely developed and verified at birth. Although we have come to understand many of the branches that Darwin sketched for us, we will undoubtedly be filling in the missing sprouts and myriad details in our understanding of that evolutionary process for generations.

We can get some ideas about what theory means to educators when we look at how they invoke theory in relationship to research. Creswell (2008), in his educational research textbook, defines theory in quantitative research as that which "explains and predicts the probable relationship between independent and dependent variables" (p. 131) and encourages his readers to think about theory as a bridge between the independent and dependent variables in research. In general, he writes, theories are simply broad explanations of what researchers anticipate finding when they relate variables to one another. Although not all research using quantitative methods tests a theory, he believes that testing a theory represents quantitative research at its most rigorous because it tests a broadly investigated explanation rather than a researcher's hunch. As for the location of theories in a quantitative study, they typically appear in either the literature review or research question/hypothesis sections.

The role of theory in qualitative research is more complex and evolving than is its role in quantitative research (Dressman, 2007). Whereas some scholars hold that qualitative research can expand theoretical knowledge and understanding through interaction between theory and inquiry, others believe that qualitative research is solely inductive, with its validity depending on the degree to which preconceived theory is set aside (Mitchell & Cody, 1993). For example, when using grounded theory (Glaser & Strauss, 1967; Strauss & Corbin, 1990) to discover and explain what reading specialists working with second-grade teachers do in a professional development program, theory would be induced from field notes based on observations of participants in a study, transcriptions of interviews with them, or other data points contributing to theory building. When using ethnography, researchers may build a thick description of lived experience in a culture to explain what lies behind human behavior (Geertz, 1973), with little or no attention to theory building. However, scholars have argued that theory is itself already embedded in whatever qualitative method a researcher adopts, whether it be grounded theory, ethnography, or phenomenology (Mitchell & Cody, 1993). Researchers using the ethnographic method, for example, commonly theorize that language and other modes of communication, such as images, sounds, and gestures, will reflect their users' values, beliefs, and customs (Pelto & Pelto, 1978; Rowsell, Kress, Pahl, & Street, Chapter 43 this volume).

Overt and Tacit Theories

All of us are theoreticians, according to Gee (2012), but some of us are more mindful of our immersion in theory than others. When introducing the importance of theory in ethical discourse, Gee defined *theory* as "a set of generalizations about an area...in terms of which descriptions of phenomena in that area can be couched and explanations can be offered" (p. 13). With that meaning, he asserted that theories provide the foundation for beliefs, even though individuals may not be cognizant of the theory or theories that they are using to ground their beliefs and claims. Theories, once articulated, give us critical information about what counts as evidence to support them and where we might discover that evidence. Undoubtedly, some theories that serve as a base for our beliefs and claims are sound. However, many, if not all of us, are likely to use generalizations that, if put to a thorough analysis and testing, would prove to be unsupportable and so undermine the credibility of our theories.

Our ability to clarify and explain the theories and generalizations on which our beliefs and claims rest is to Gee (2012) of moral and ethical importance because theories can cause damage to other people, especially in the form of social injustice. Noting that individuals, when presenting their arguments, vary in the degree to which they articulate or are capable of articulating the theories underlying beliefs and claims included in those arguments, Gee observes that theories in discourse can be viewed as lying on a continuum from overt to tacit. Individuals using tacit theories to ground beliefs and claims are, to varying degrees, unaware or unconscious of the generalizations contributing to their positions' theoretical foundations. Individuals using overt theories are more conscious of their theories' supporting generalizations. These two qualities of theory, tacit and overt, cannot be viewed as absolutes because individuals may understand the grounding for their theory to a large degree but still not be entirely conscious of all the theory's underlying generalizations or may be troublingly unaware of their theory's foundation but still have a limited understanding of several generalizations supporting it.

People, according to Gee (2012), also operate with primary or nonprimary theories. Those who have analyzed, researched, and reflected on the generalizations that support their theories and have discussed and debated over them with others hold what he calls primary theories and primary generalizations that support those theories. Those who have nonprimary theories have not put their supporting generalizations under rigorous examination to discover their truth value. Furthermore, generalizations not exposed to examination, debate, and discussion are said to be nonprimary. Nonprimary theories and generalizations are usually adopted by individuals from beliefs and claims that they have heard or read others espousing. Although Gee does not argue that these primary and nonprimary theories can also lie on a continuum, they most likely can because a primary theory could be grounded by some durable generalizations that were well examined but undermined by others more tacit in nature and less carefully explored for their quality of truth.

Meaning of Theory in Pre-1990s Literacy Research

Prior to the advent of change in literacy studies during the 1990s, the meaning of *theory* in literacy mirrored the meaning as used in the hard sciences and the meaning reflected in writings on the history of science (Dressman, 2007; Kuhn, 1996; Popper, 1959/2002). Considered one of the most important documents of the 20th century, Popper's *The Logic of Scientific Discovery* presents two fundamental issues in the theory of knowledge: the distinction of science from non-science and the clarification of induction's role in the development of scientific knowledge.

Popper (1959/2002) presumed that theories arise from creative processes and that there is no "logical method of having new ideas" (p. 8). He pointed out that discoveries of all kinds have irrational elements and referred to Einstein, who thought that universal laws, such as those in physics, arose from intuition and love of experience. That belief contributed to Popper's rejection of a logic of induction that would enable us to empirically test universal laws and theories. Even though we find that a multitude of empirical experiments provide evidence for a theory, the full verification of the theory will always await the next experiment that may falsify the theory. Every theory, therefore, is characterized by and subject to falsifiability.

Popper (1959/2002) also provided us with a model of the quasi-inductive evolution of science in the form of an image: particles suspended in a fluid.

> Testable science is the precipitation of these particles at the bottom of the vessel: they settle down in layers (of universality). The thickness of the deposit grows with the number of these layers, every new layer corresponding to a theory more universal than those beneath it. As the result of this process ideas previously floating in higher metaphysical regions may sometimes be reached by the growth of science, and thus make contact with it, and settle. (pp. 277–278)

He then gave us the example of the layering of theories in physics, from atomism to the fluid theory of electricity. While contributing a sense of order to our world picture, these ideas could only acquire scientific status when offered in falsifiable form that would allow opening the door to rival theories. Asserting that science can never claim truth, Popper wrote that we can only guess. And what we formulate as a guess, we try to falsify or overthrow with all the tools of research available to us. "The wrong view of science," he wrote, "betrays itself in the craving to be right; for it is not his *possession* of knowledge, of irrefutable truth, that makes the man of science, but his persistent and recklessly critical *quest* for truth" (p. 281).

The importance of educational theory and theories about literacy, more specifically, is reflected in studies of theory's impact on research in literacy. Dressman (2007) spent several years investigating changes in the use of the word *theory* in literacy research and in the conceptualization of literacy itself. That inquiry enabled him to explore how theory and its use affected the generation of knowledge about literacy, especially as a social practice, in major research journals. Although earlier literacy research from the 1960s through the late 1980s was dominated by empirical studies using experimental methods that focused on reading and writing as cognitive activities (Shannon, 1989), the language of literacy research has changed. According to Dressman, researchers reconceived literacy, changing what being literate means and how researchers theorized the relationship between literacy and other human activities. Researchers also expanded their use of the term *theory* itself and the ways they used theories to construct knowledge about literacy.

Before getting too deeply into Dressman's discoveries, we need to look deeper into the relationship between theory and model and into the historical contributions to literacy research that these concepts have added to our understanding of reading and reading processes.

What Is a Model?

As *theory* has taken on different meanings from user to user and from context to context, so has *model*. In the context of the artist's studio, a model can inspire the representation of the human form on canvas. In other contexts, a model is a prototype in design of what is to be produced or emulated. Car designers create models of automobiles that enable them to envision the lines and curves of the next year's fleet. In scientific contexts, scientists create models to depict scientific processes or structures that are often invisible, such as the model of an atom. In yet another context, economists design models to render in mathematical terms a network of complex variables, such as an economic model of international trade. These examples of the use of the word *model* hardly exhaust the variations we find in its application.

With the term *model* having such a rich array of meanings, we might expect it to have different meanings even in a single rich field of research, such as that of literacy. For example, a journal article can provide an explanation and discussion of professional development models that have demonstrated their effectiveness in helping teachers address language and literacy challenges that students present; however, individual components of the models may never have been subject to any form of independent or interdependent assessment. In the fourth edition of *Theoretical Models and Processes of Reading* (Ruddell, Ruddell, & Singer, 1994), the editors wrote in the introduction to the section on models of reading and literacy processes that while a theory is an explanation of a phenomenon,

> a model serves as a metaphor to explain and represent the theory. This representation often takes the form of a depiction of the interrelationships among a theory's variables and may even make provision for connecting the theory to observations. The theory is thus more dynamic in nature than the model but describes the way the model operates; the model is frequently static and represents a snapshot of a dynamic process. (p. 812)

Theory may also be seen as a model of reality. Reality serves as the ultimate model of how things work. All human-created models are then replicas that mimic or represent reality's perfect form and function. The degree to which a human-designed model, such as a model of the reading process, represents or at least reflects the reality of a complex and invisible process varies widely. All models are theoretical because they are an imitation of reality, an effort to describe or explain it—not reality itself. So, calling a model of the reading process a theoretical model may be a redundancy because a model, in this instance of its use, is already theoretical. Nevertheless, a model of reading, writing, or both represents in ordinary language or graphic form the components of a process and explains how those components function and interact with one another.

In the broader literacy field, we now encounter models as metaphors that represent abstract constructs that might be quite difficult to operationalize and calibrate as well as those that represent theoretical variables that have been operationalized and quantified. Models embodying abstract constructs have emerged from qualitative research, as we see in the case of Lee (Chapter 10 this volume), and render less quantifiable constructs into conceptual or graphic formats. In comparison, a model depicting theoretical variables that have been quantified can be found in a structural equation model, such as that depicting the contributions of word processing, working memory, text-based processing, and knowledge access to reading comprehension (see Hannon, 2012/Chapter 33 this volume).

So, Where Are the Paradigms?

In *The Structure of Scientific Revolutions*, Kuhn (1996) writes that science does not fit the vision of knowledge generated by the steady accumulation of discoveries. Rather, the history of science has proceeded through peaceful, relatively long episodes of tradition-framed normal science ruptured by powerful intellectual revolutions in which one widely accepted conceptual view was overthrown by another. For example, the discovery of oxygen by Lavoisier resulted in the displacement of theoretical ideas about an imaginary element called phlogiston that was believed to be the cause of combustion, and Newton's widely accepted concepts and laws of physics were eventually revised radically by Einstein's theory of relativity. In his book, Kuhn presents the image of the scientist as a rather conservative person who accepts the knowledge and theoretical views that he was taught and applies them to solving new problems that arise before him. In doing so,

Kuhn argues, the scientist adopts a paradigm and will extend the knowledge base of his students by solving problems within that paradigm and so extend its reach. However, situations, scientific puzzles, and problems will arise that could simply not be accounted for within a given paradigm. In fact, a new situation, problem, or discovery might contradict an accepted paradigm, ushering in a revolution, such as those brought about by Lavoisier and Einstein. These new paradigms could not be based on the old ones. Because the two paradigms were what Kuhn calls incommensurable, the new paradigm could only displace or replace the old. The description and explanation of paradigm led critics to accuse Kuhn of depicting science as a form of mob rule in which truth was thrown under the wheels of a powerful paradigm's progress.

While most of us are likely to believe that scientists, including literacy researchers, are dedicated to the pursuit of truth through the methods of science, some, especially those who have read and resonate with Kuhn's (1996) work, hold the belief that scientists are far more interested in maintaining the principles and theories embraced by fellow scientists in their research community than in discovering truth. This view of the scientist, which may diverge greatly from the more widely embraced one of scientist as truth seeker, should be understood within Kuhn's conception of paradigms in science and of their shifts as new discoveries, theories, and the solution to scientific puzzles become inexplicable within principles and theories of old paradigms.

So, what is the difference between a paradigm and a theory? It is not merely a theory that sustains a paradigm but a network of theoretical, conceptual, instrumental, methodological, and sociocultural sources that serve scientists broaching scientific puzzles in their research community. This network of resources enables the scientist practicing normal science to frame experiments, carry them out, record them, and distribute empirical findings to others in the research community who share a common paradigm. Many theoretical models of reading and other literacy processes have been proposed over the past 50 years. However, in many instances, earlier models of reading served as explanations on which later models elaborated, sometimes extensively.

Over the past five or six decades, one primary paradigm shift—although some may identify more—has occurred that had a profound effect on research in reading and literacy in general. That shift, often referred to as a revolution in the psychological sciences from behaviorism to cognitive psychology, began in the 1950s and extended into the 1960s and beyond (Gardner, 1985; Miller, 2003). The shift enabled psychologists to adopt new theoretical frameworks to explain mental events, such as learning, memory, and language processes, and to use new, empirical methods to investigate them.

Over roughly the same five or six decades, a second development often related to paradigms occurred in the realm of research methodologies used in literacy studies. That development was the tension between quantitative and qualitative methods of research that we discussed earlier in relation to the meaning of *theory*. Literacy and social science researchers have been engaged in debates about the capacity of these two methods to represent reality faithfully and accurately. The competition between them has even been termed a paradigm war (Symonds & Gorard, 2010). Their differences entail more than merely methods. To some, the two paradigms compete as epistemological frameworks. During the 1970s and into the 1980s, the epistemological assumptions and differences between quantitative and qualitative methods led many researchers to view them as incommensurable. When viewed as epistemological frameworks or ways to think about and explain events, these two methods present competing worldviews (Maxwell & Loomis, 2003).

In these debates, quantitative methods are commonly viewed as objective, empirical, scientific, positivistic, and decontextualized. Conversely, qualitative methods are seen as subjective, interpretive, social, and contextualized. Furthermore, differences between these paradigms extend beyond methods and into beliefs about theory. For example, quantitative methods commonly rely on the use of statistical procedures and tests that are mathematically based in probability theory. If a researcher does not believe in probability theory or the application of certain statistical tests to data, then that researcher might have serious qualms about working in the quantitative paradigm. With respect to the qualitative paradigm, should a researcher not resonate with grounded theory or interpretive methods, that researcher would probably struggle with significant dissonance in adopting and applying qualitative methods to answer research questions.

While viewing quantitative and qualitative methods as paradigms has been doubted because they may not embody all the characteristics typically assigned to paradigms (Gorard, 2004; Kuhn, 1996), the resolution of their being incommensurable may arise from their simultaneous use in mixed methods research (Symonds & Gorard, 2010). That combination of the two paradigms, often in tension with each other, has been seen as a third paradigm that combines elements of both quantitative and qualitative perspectives and methods to answer research questions and corroborate those answers (Johnson & Onwuegbuzie, 2004; Johnson, Onwuegbuzie, & Turner, 2007).

Before the late 1980s, positivistic perspectives and quantitative methods tended to dominate literacy research; however, the mushrooming of socially constructed or nonpositivist perspectives and qualitative methods in many fields, especially sociology and psychology, during the 1960s, 1970s, and 1980s contributed to an expanding influence and importance in literacy research of qualitative methods by the 1990s (Dressman, 2007). This change in perspective and method, evidence for which appears to be more than sufficient, seems still to be progressing with significant tensions arising in the field of literacy research over the credibility and validity of quantitative or qualitative methods. About the same time in the mid-1990s that the literacy field witnessed the publication of increasing numbers of qualitative studies, a new journal, *The Scientific Study of Reading*, emerged with an editorial staff dedicated to the publication of empirically sound research on reading and related literacy processes. While the scientific study of reading and related literacy processes and federal funding of literacy research based on a scientific standard that fosters scientifically valid research with randomized controlled trials and closely matched comparison groups (Coalition for Evidence-Based Policy, 2003) appear to be far from dropping over the western horizon, new light arising in the east has clearly illuminated aspects of reading and literacy processes formerly cloaked in various degrees of darkness. Many in the literacy field would assert that new theories and new ways to generate theory have brought new light to the world of literacy.

In the field of reading and literacy research over the past half century, the exact location of reality and the most trustworthy methods of discovering truth have become significantly more problematic. Does reality reside in a constant world outside ourselves waiting to be discovered? Is reality constructed through language as we interact with others in an array of social contexts, enabling us to define ourselves and discover truth by examining language and how we use it? To varying degrees, do we both inhabit a reality and construct it? Do we find truth through various methods in both an assumed outer reality and a reality that we socially construct? An array of literacy researchers and theorists over the past 50 years have created influential theories and models that give us opportunities to explore the realities they investigated or constructed and the discoveries they made that generated knowledge that we can use to search deeper into literacy's problems, perplexities, and puzzles.

Theories Influencing Reading and Literacy Research

A remarkably wide range of theories has influenced research on reading, including theoretical models and their related reading processes. Whereas some of these theories, particularly in more recent years, arose from the field of literacy research, many others originated in fields outside the domain of literacy research but frequently allied with it, such as psychology and literary theory. This should come as no surprise because psychology has long been a breeding ground for inquiry into learning and learning-related processes, such as memory and cognition. Among the broad and influential theories that have had a significant impact on reading research are constructivism, social constructionism, transactional theory, information/cognitive processing theories, sociocultural perspectives, sociocognitive theory, structuralism, poststructuralism, pragmatism, and reading motivation theory. An introduction, brief though it may be, to these theoretical frameworks and perspectives provides readers with knowledge to help them understand concepts that appear frequently in this volume and in literacy research. Although significant analysis, reconnaissance, and reflection preceded the placement of individuals and their work within particular categories, these placements may not be consistent with each reader's understanding or remain accurate over time as ideologies evolve.

Constructivism

Among educators, constructivism is a widely applied theory of learning that explains how knowledge and meanings are constructed, rather than transmitted or absorbed, through our interaction with others and the environment. In the light of constructivist theory, learners control the process of resolving tensions between personally constructed models of the world held in memory and socially constructed representations of new experiences. Typically, learners construct new knowledge when they interact with others or objects in their surroundings, activate existing background knowledge in response to interactions, build new knowledge from prior knowledge, or transform older knowledge into newer information. Constructivists view that negotiated knowledge as "temporary, developmental, nonobjective, internally constructed, and socially and culturally mediated" (Fosnot, 1996, p. ix). To the constructivist, contexts for learning are inseparable from what is learned, the learner has significant capacity to regulate the knowledge construction process, and meanings are negotiated in social settings (Cambourne, 2002).

In her exploration of the constructivist metaphor, Spivey (1997) argues that what distinguishes constructivism from other perspectives is an underlying metaphor of building that guides thought and inquiry. Constructivists, she believes, look at individuals as agents "whose *ways* of knowing, seeing, understanding, and valuing influence what is known, seen, understood, and valued" (p. 3). Arising from a review of constructivism's historical antecedents, Spivey found differences in focal points for constructivist agents that varied across individuals, small groups or dyads, and communities. Forms of constructivism that focus on individuals as agents include cognitive constructivism with its emphasis on schema theory and cognitive-developmental constructivism with its emphasis on Piaget's theory of cognitive development (Piaget & Inhelder, 1969). Forms of constructivism that focus on small groups or pairs as agents are usually based on Vygotsky's theories, wherein two people, such as a child and her mother, collaborate to build knowledge, especially through language. Additionally, forms of constructivism that focus on larger communities are exemplified in the work of the sociologist Durkheim (1982), who developed the notion of a collective consciousness, and literary theorist Fish (1980), who studied interpretive communities and the meaning-making discourses that transpired in them.

Two theories or frameworks under the umbrella of constructivism and applicable to the investigation of reading demonstrate the broad and deep importance of this perspective to literacy research. These frameworks include schema theory and psycholinguistics.

Schema Theory. During the mid-1970s, schema theory made its appearance as part of the cognitive revolution that resurrected the study in psychology of internal mental events and became an important theoretical resource for reading research and pedagogy. Although sometimes considered a theory of reading comprehension, schema theory is about how we structure knowledge and represent it in memory. A schema is a hypothetical knowledge structure—hypothetical because it is difficult to examine empirically. However, we can infer the existence of schema from the study of memory and its influence on the interpretation of new experience. Schemata have been compared with scripts, file cabinets, storage slots, and containers (Anderson, 1984/Chapter 19 this volume). Anderson has identified and explained several functions of schemata and their effects on learning and remembering when interacting with texts. Among these functions are a schema's capacity to provide scaffolding as we process text, to allow effective memory searches while reading, and to facilitate inference making. A chapter in this volume (McVee, Dunsmore, & Gavelek, 2005/Chapter 20 this volume) has been dedicated to revisiting schema theory, its impact on literacy research, and an evaluation of its continuing usefulness as a theoretical framework to understand and investigate reading processes and to inform practice.

Researchers have identified risks inherent in adhering to a constricted or rigid conceptualization of schemata as fixed and inflexible structures. While fixed or mechanical views of knowledge structures or mental representations may be more likely to appear when learners first acquire knowledge in a field, more advanced understanding and application of knowledge structures in complex knowledge domains, such as medicine, need to be developed. Cognitive flexibility theory (Spiro, Coulson, Feltovich, & Anderson, 1988/Chapter 22 this volume), as a successor of schema theory, provides themes, especially in realms of advanced knowledge acquisition and applications, that encourage liberation from the risks of schema rigidity. Among those themes are the avoidance of oversimplification of complex problem domains, the importance of constructing multiple representations of complex concepts, and the capacity to assemble schemata in novel configurations rather than merely retrieving them from memory and applying them. For researchers advancing knowledge generation in the field of literacy, as in all other complex domains, this move from generic schema activation to situation-specific assembly of knowledge is of critical importance.

Psycholinguistic Theory. In the late 1950s, behaviorist theories of language acquisition proposed by Skinner (1957) were radically critiqued by the linguist Chomsky (1959) in an essay that signaled the beginning of the cognitive revolution in the psychological sciences. Chomsky proposed that human beings have a universal grammar or an innate language acquisition device that enables them to generate an infinite variety of sentences typical of their language's syntactical structures. Children could not acquire the rich diversity of language by simply imitating the sentences that they heard their parents utter. Instead, they construct sentences using their steadily growing knowledge of words and their inborn universal grammar. Although all children have an inborn language acquisition device, that is not enough for the development of normal language function. Children also need a language acquisition support system that enables their inborn language potential to be activated and realized through social interaction (Bruner, 1986).

Psycholinguistic theory enabled reading educators to look at reading as a "psycholinguistic guessing game" (Goodman, 1967, p. 126) in which readers predict what will be coming next in sentences as they read text and try to construct meaning. Miscues can then be viewed not as errors but as keys to the kinds of problems that children may be having in learning to read. Goodman and Goodman (1994/Chapter 21 this volume) have found that the concept of schema is helpful in exploring the role of miscues in learning language. They explore two kinds of miscues in the light of schema theory and two schema processes: schema-forming and schema-driven miscues. The constructivist conceptions of assimilation and accommodation (Piaget, 1977) clarify the function of the two kinds of miscues. When a schema-forming miscue occurs, a reader is working toward accommodation or the modification of an existing schema to adjust to new language experiences, but when a schema-driven miscue takes place, the reader reveals assimilation or the understanding of new language experiences with existing schema.

Schema-forming miscues reveal a reader's development of rules for language use, the application of those rules, and their limits. For example, before a child has developed the alphabetic principle, he may read the title of a frequently read story by guiding his finger across the words and saying, "Gooooodniiiiightmoooooon." Schema-driven miscues result from the activation of existing schemata to either construct or comprehend language. For example, when a child is learning the plural form of *mouse*, she may read "mices" rather than "mice," revealing that she believes, because of preexisting schema, that the -*s* must be added to generate a plural noun. As the Goodman and Goodman (1994/Chapter 21 this volume) point out, these miscues may not always be easily distinguished, but the miscues that children make reveal not only the construction and reconstruction of schema but also the contributions of miscues to the development of self-regulated reading.

In sum, constructivism as a theory covers several interrelated theoretical frameworks for the investigation and understanding of reading and reading processes. Schema theory and psycholinguistics share the central concepts of constructivism and demonstrate the active role that learners have in the acquisition and application of knowledge that contributes to the development of reading and readers.

Social Constructionism

Although Berger and Luckmann (1966) are widely acknowledged as the voices of authority on social constructionism, Bruffee (1986), a notable figure in the field of rhetoric and composition pedagogy, explicitly aligns a social constructionist view of knowledge building with our purpose in writing this section of the chapter. In his 1986 essay in *College English* titled "Social Construction, Language, and the Authority of Knowledge," Bruffee argues the following: "A social constructionist position in any discipline assumes that any entities we normally call reality, knowledge, thought, facts, texts, selves and so on are constructs generated by communities of like-minded peers" (p. 774). Implications of this argument for English teachers' goals and practices, which were of interest to Bruffee over 25 years ago, are of no less interest to literacy researchers and teachers today.

Basically, Bruffee (1986) shows in his essay how cognitivist beliefs in a foundational structure for knowledge building is antithetical to a nonfoundational, social constructionist view in which "concepts, ideas, theories, the world, reality, and facts are all language constructs generated by knowledge communities and used by them to maintain community coherence" (p. 777). These opposing views of knowledge building and their implications for practice are important to understand, especially in a chapter that purports to investigate theoretical models of multiple literacies. As Bruffee cogently argues, educators' tendency to classify knowledge into two distinct categories, theory and practice, has its beginnings in a cognitivist approach to understanding. That is to say, if one believes in a foundational mode of knowledge building (as the cognitivists do), then it follows that one views theory as the grounding or sanctioning of literacy practices. Conversely, if one views knowledge building through a social constructionist lens, then it stands to reason that theory and practice are no longer treated as opposites, with theory holding sway over practice.

Social constructionism arose initially from inquiry focusing on social processes and their effects on the construction of knowledge. Everyday life, as Berger and Luckmann (1966) posited, presents us with a reality that we interpret, find subjectively meaningful as a coherent world, and share intersubjectively with others. The reality of everyday life is filled with objectivations of subjective processes, most often through language, that make the intersubjective world possible. Everyday life is lived in and through language that we share with others, making our understanding of language essential for our understanding of reality.

With language as its sine qua non, social constructionism may be understood as a theoretical orientation with several assumptions. In describing four key assumptions, Gergen (1985) informed readers of the growing influence that the turn toward social processes was having in his field of psychology. Membership in the social constructionism movement, according to Burr (2003), need not require the acceptance of all of these assumptions. Just accepting one could be sufficient. Among the assumptions constituting social constructionism, according to Gergen, are the following:

1. In an atmosphere of increasing criticism of positivist and empiricist beliefs about knowledge generation, social constructionism "begins with radical doubt in the taken-for-granted world" and works as a social critic. Constructionism asks us to suspend our belief that "commonly accepted categories or understandings receive their warrant through observation. Thus, it invites one to challenge the objective basis of conventional knowledge" (p. 267). Social constructionists question the power of the words we use to capture reality and render it as we do. This assumption about the limits of language casts doubt on much of our knowledge base, including that formed through positivistic or scientific methods.
2. Understandings about the world arise from interaction among people in relationships. That epistemological perspective invites inquiry into how cultural and historical beliefs and processes construct the world.

3. Our ways of understanding the world as we believe it to be are sustained through daily interactions in social settings, especially those that involve language. Communication in communities, negotiation, and rhetoric have greater influence on prevailing and continuing understandings than the empirical validity of a perspective.
4. Social constructionists believe that conceptions and understandings of the world are deeply and directly associated with social actions in that world. A form of social action might be simply a description and explanation of the world as an individual perceives it. To change that description and explanation might well change decisions we make about actions that we take in the world.

Serving to summarize our discussion and provide a view of social constructionists, Gergen (2002) notes that

> constructionists do not draw a strong distinction between the observing scientist and the world observed. Rather, they see scientists engaged in a collaborative construction of what they will take to be the world. Armed with a set of shared assumptions, a language of description and explanation, and a set of related practices, a world of particulars is established. Thus, we may anticipate the development of multiple realities, depending on one's discipline....Because disciplinary practices are inevitably linked to preferred ways of life, claims to knowledge are never neutral in their societal ramifications. Reality claims are inherently saturated with visions of the good. (pp. 188–189)

Transactional Theory

Although some educators believe an objective meaning exists in a text, others (Bleich, 1980; Culler, 1980) have argued that the meanings for a text are to be found in the reader's personal responses. This perspective aligns somewhat with Rosenblatt's (1978; 1994/Chapter 35 this volume) articulation of transactional theory. According to Rosenblatt, every act of reading is a transaction between a particular reader and a particular text at a particular time in a particular context. The reader and the text compose a transactional moment. The meaning does not preexist in the text or in the reader but results from the transaction between reader and text. Meaning is the result of the reader's meaning construction that engages his or her unique background knowledge and cognitive processing. When readers transact with a text, they create an evocation or mental representation of the text that can be observed, analyzed, reflected on, pondered, explained, and savored. While exploring and clarifying the evocation, readers assemble meanings for or interpretations of the text.

When Rosenblatt (1978) created the transactional theory, she developed a theoretical perspective that, she believed, explained all modes of reading. The theory covered all modes of reading because she took into account the range of stances that a reader could adopt toward a text. The two stances that she identified were the efferent and aesthetic stances. When adopting the efferent stance, the reader transacts with texts to construct information, to create an evocation believed to represent the text. When transacting with a text from an aesthetic stance, the reader's attention is focused on the lived experiences depicted in a reading event, such as a poem. According to her theory, these two stances exist on a continuum to acknowledge that readers might take stances that include both efferent and aesthetic qualities.

Information/Cognitive Processing Theories and Models of Reading

The first edition[1] of *Theoretical Models and Processes of Reading* (Singer & Ruddell, 1970) contains the first published theory of reading. That first theory, which reflects a cognitive processing perspective of reading, was created by Holmes (1953), to whom the first edition was dedicated by its editors, Singer and Ruddell. According to Singer (1994), prior research in reading had been atheoretical, largely because of the dominance of behaviorism. In his chapter, Holmes (1960/1970) proposed to answer the question, "Just how complex is this ability we call reading, what are its dimensions, and how do they operate?" (p. 187). Using a statistical procedure called substrata-factor analysis, Holmes created a substrata-factor theory of reading in which he identified variables correlated with levels of reading proficiency. Furthermore, he identified subvariables in four variable categories to predict speed and power of reading. Holmes designed the investigation to discover relationships between speed and power of reading and the 37 subabilities categorized under intelligence, linguistic ability, oculomotor ability, and personality traits. He found that his theoretical model explained reading through the interaction of 13 of the initial 37 variables tested. Of the 13 key variables, knowledge of vocabulary in context played a significant role in both speed and power of reading. Holmes concluded his chapter on a theory of reading with the assertion that he was justified in formalizing the hypothesis into a generalized theory and that although the theory he presented was complex, his methodology highlighted important dimensions of reading that deepened our knowledge of the dynamics of reading.

The information processing or cognitive perspective of reading influenced research most intensely from the mid-1970s to the mid-1980s but continues to pervade theories and models today. Reading researchers using this theoretical framework hoped to discover and explain how the individual reader interacted with print to construct meaning. Often using a computer metaphor, interested in artificial intelligence, and sometimes striving toward a mathematical representation of reading processes, researchers investigated several related cognitive processes, such as sensory input, attention allocation, symbol interpretation, strategy use, the organization of knowledge, its storage in short- and long-term memory, and outputs, especially in the form of text representation or comprehension. Although schema theory along with its effects on knowledge construction plays an important part in the information-processing perspective, usually missing from the menu of investigated processes were the effects of the reader's sociocultural environment, both historical and current, on cognition, a reflection of the emphasis on individual and internal mental events within this theoretical framework.

Two information processing models of reading appeared in the second edition of *Theoretical Models and Processes of Reading* (Singer & Ruddell, 1976): Gough's (1972/1976) "One Second of Reading" and LaBerge and Samuels's (1974/1976) "Toward a Theory of Automatic Information Processing in Reading." Included in that volume's section on information processing models are two other papers by Anderson and his colleagues (Anderson, 1974/1976; Anderson, Goldberg, & Hidde, 1971/1976), who explored sentence processing. Here, our focus is on the two information processing models themselves, both of which are bottom-up models, meaning that they focus on graphic input and its processing without recognizable attention to prior knowledge activation and its effects on text processing and comprehension.

Gough's Information Processing Model. Gough's (1972/1976) "One Second of Reading" includes a reading model whose key features are in italics in the following (hypercondensed) description of the model (see Rumelhart, 1985/Chapter 29 this volume). Following an eye fixation and focus on *graphemic input*, the *visual system* forms an *icon* and retains it while a *scanner* with a *pattern recognizer* reviews the icon. The pattern recognition component identifies the letters that compose the icon that was formed from graphemic input. The letters, which are transferred into a *character register*, are decoded by a *decoder* with the help of a *code book* and transformed into a *phonemic tape* or representation. The phonemic representation becomes input to the *librarian* that compares the phonemic string with a *lexicon* and that puts the lexical activation into *primary memory*. The activated lexical symbols in primary memory become input for *Merlin*, a system that applies *rules of semantics and syntax* to construct the input's meaning or deep structure. That meaning is then transferred to what Gough called *The Place Where Sentences Go When They Are Understood* (also known as TPWSGWTAU). The text has been read once the initial graphemic input has found its way to TPWSGWTAU, a process that takes about one second.

In a postscript to his "one second of reading" model that is in the third edition of *Theoretical Models and Processes of Reading*, Gough (1985) announced that the model was wrong. He renounced the explicit claim that readers always read letter by letter or serially (at the rate of 10–20 milliseconds per letter) but asserted that letters do mediate word recognition. He also renounced the claim that phonological recoding mediates all word recognition because he had realized that proficient readers have direct access to high-frequency or sight words, at the least, but he held that phonological recoding mediates recognition of most words. While agreeing that his bottom-up model failed, he believed it pointed educators and researchers in the right direction.

LaBerge–Samuels Information Processing Model. The LaBerge–Samuels (1974/1976) automatic information processing model is composed of three memory systems that hold three different representations of graphemic input as it is processed (see Rumelhart, 1985/Chapter 29 this volume; Samuels, 1994/Chapter 28 this volume). The first, the visual memory system, holds visual representations of letters or their features, spelling groups, words, and groups of words. The second, the phonological memory system, holds phonological representations of spelling groups, words, and word groups. The third, the semantic memory system, holds the meaning representations of the words, word groups, and sentences. The registration of a visual signal on the sensory surface initiates the reading process. A set of feature detectors analyzes the information and identifies lines, angles, curves, and intersections. The feature detectors feed into letter codes that feed into spelling-pattern codes that, in turn, feed into visual word codes. While some features map as spelling-pattern codes, others map onto visual word codes. Words can be transferred into meanings by means of several different routes: Visual word codes usually pass through a phonological word code and then into word-meaning codes, visual word codes may feed into word-meaning codes to discriminate between homophonic similarities (e.g., *chute/shoot*), and word groups (e.g., "...on the...") can be translated immediately into phonological spelling patterns and eventually into word-meaning codes. When the complete set of initial inputs has been processed, the reader constructs a word-group meaning and comprehends the input. Of historical significance, Samuels (1977) soon realized that the bottom-up, linear design of this model needed to be revisited and modified it to include feedback loops to account for prior knowledge in semantic memory and its interaction with the processing of input as it moved toward comprehension.

Rumelhart's Interactive Model. Important to note when reviewing the Gough (1972/1976) and LaBerge–Samuels (1974/1976) models in their original form is that both were bottom-up models and that with some variation, a similar pattern occurs: from the processing of letters to the construction of meaning for a word. Rumelhart (1985/Chapter 29 this volume) believed that the concept of information flow and the use of flowcharts to represent that information's processing became vehicles for the design of early models of reading that attempted to approximate the reading process. However, recognizing various problems with bottom-up processing models, Rumelhart designed an interactive model of reading that was published in the third edition of *Theoretical Models and Processes of Reading* (Singer & Ruddell, 1985). That model took into account the perception of words in their semantic environment, the selection of syntax depending on the semantic context, and the interpretation of dependent clauses and complete sentences depending on context. Rumelhart's bottom-up/top-down interactive model and the chapter in which he initially described it can be found in Chapter 29 of this volume.

Rumelhart (1985/Chapter 29 this volume) was troubled by the early bottom-up representations of the reading process because they did not fully account for evidence from research on the perception of letters that depended on surrounding letters and the context effects of those letters (Nash-Webber, 1975). Top-down processing would be needed to account for the context effects of letter and word processing. Furthermore, the syntactic environment in which words appear affects our perception of them (Kolers, 1970; Weber, 1970). Top-down information about the syntactical development of sentences in which words appear should have been accounted for but was not in the early information-processing models. To compound Rumelhart's concerns, he found that semantic context was not taken into account in the early models even though research had shown convincingly that the semantic environment had affected word recognition.

The aforementioned discrepancies between research findings and their lack of representation in existing models of reading led Rumelhart (1985/Chapter 29 this volume) to construct his interactive, bottom-up and top-down model of reading. That model takes into account not only bottom-up graphemic input but also orthographic, syntactical, semantic, and lexical knowledge, all of which fed into a hypothesized pattern synthesizer that can generate probable interpretations of a text. The pattern synthesizer, however, is the key component of the model because all that is interesting occurs there. To represent all the interesting parallel and interacting reading processes, Rumelhart established a message center that has five hypotheses levels: letter feature, letter, letter-cluster, lexical, and syntactical. As information moves through the message center, the message center constructs and evaluates hypotheses generated at each level with the purpose of accepting the most likely meanings and nullifying the least likely. Essentially, reading as represented in Rumelhart's model is a complex hypothesis-testing process that operates interactively, bottom up and top down.

In spite of the model's advances, Rumelhart (1985/Chapter 29 this volume) was not satisfied with his functional depiction of the reading process. He also wanted to design a mathematical model for the evaluation of each hypothesis at each of the five levels. Although not satisfied with his equations, he concluded that the model could be quantified and could generate predictions in spite of the model's complexity.

Several other cognitive processing models that still exercise a significant influence on researchers' perspectives and reading pedagogy appeared during the 1970s and 1980s. These include models developed by Kintsch and by Just and Carpenter.

Construction–Integration Model. During the era dominated by the emergence of cognition in psychological studies, other information or cognitive processing models of reading also appeared. An early rendition of Kintsch's (Chapter 32 this volume) construction–integration model of reading was presented in the late 1970s. In that model, the authors (Kintsch & van Dijk, 1978) assumed that texts can be described at microlevels (local) and macrolevels (global). That model accounts for the construction of a semantic textbase that is generated by a cyclical process limited by working memory and a situation model that represents information given by the text and integrated with the reader's background knowledge. The model they proposed includes macro-operators that reduce text information to its gist, or what they termed its theoretical macrostructure. *Schemata* in this model refers to text structures, such as an argument, or to reader's goals, such as discovering how women were treated in the 14th century by reading stories in Giovanni Boccaccio's *The Decameron.* Such schemata control the macro-operators that transform the textbase into a hierarchical structure of macropropositions that represent the text's gist and determine which micropropositions are relevant to that gist. Although the model does not explain how inferences occur while reading, it assumes that they occur as schemata are activated and developed to represent a text. The full representation of the text constructed by the reader constitutes his or her comprehension. This model's description of the reading process as constructive provides a foreshadowing of Kintsch's later construction–integration model of reading.

Just and Carpenter Reading Model. Just and Carpenter (1980/Chapter 30 this volume) drew on research that they and others had conducted, especially in the field of eye-movement studies, and a theoretical framework based on production systems while reading to design their bottom-up and top-down model. Unlike earlier information processing models that researchers had proposed, the architectural features of Just and Carpenter's model account for reading time on words, clauses, and sentences; for events at several levels of processing, such as those at the word encoding and lexical access levels; and for the complexities of processing during top-down and bottom-up interactions.

Dual Coding Theory Model. Before it was extended to explain reading comprehension, Dual Coding Theory (DCT) was an established theory of cognition that takes into account both verbal and nonverbal memory processes. Sadoski and Paivio (2004/Chapter 34 this volume) present the DCT and how it explains decoding, comprehension, and responses to texts. The DCT model provides an alternative to information processing models based primarily on schema theory and verbal processes. One of the basic assumptions of the DCT model is that every mental representation retains qualities, linguistic or nonlinguistic, of the original experience from which it arose. According to the DCT, the different characteristics of verbal and nonverbal codes lead to their development into two different processing systems, one for language processing and another for processing the imagery of events and objects. Combined, the two systems or codes can take into account all knowledge of language and the world. For Sadoski and Paivio, models of reading that omit basic units of nonverbal information, or *imagens*, are unable to capture the rich sensory contribution that reality makes to comprehension and memory. Acknowledging, explaining, and integrating mental imagery into their model provides, they believe, a more accurate depiction of how the mind, especially that of the reader, processes and remembers sensory experience. Absent a thorough consideration of mental imagery, other models of reading are limited to a single code, verbal processing, and to a solely abstract representation of knowledge gained through interaction with texts.

Sociocultural Perspectives

Sociocultural perspectives in the literature on literacy commonly refers to both a specific theoretical perspective, that of Vygotsky, and a set of related theoretical perspectives that share assumptions about the mind, the world, and their relationship (Gavelek & Bresnahan, 2009). The term *sociocultural*, in its more inclusive application, refers to a group of perspectives that includes sociolinguistics, pragmatism, and second-generation cognitive science and that commonly manifest themes distilled from Vygotsky's cultural-historical theory. Those themes include the beliefs that the mind emerges from social interaction with other minds, that activities of the mind are mediated by tools and symbol systems (languages), and that to understand a mental function, one must understand the roots and processes contributing to that function's development. Among the sociocultural theorists explored here are Vygotsky, Scribner and Cole, Halliday, Heath, Gee, and Street. These individuals and their colleagues have provided researchers with theoretical frameworks for inquiring into a substantive body of knowledge about language and literacies.

Vygotsky, Society, and Language. Among Vygotsky's (1978, 1986) many ideas, three are of particular importance for understanding the connections among society, culture, and the development of minds. First, he embraced the idea that we must understand the historical, social, and cultural contexts of a child's experiences to truly understand that person's intellectual or cognitive development. Second, Vygotsky believed that our individual development depends on language that allows us to interact with others in our culture and to strive for self-mastery. Language and our writing system enable us to develop skills and higher mental functions progressively. Third, Vygotsky believed that every step in a child's cultural development appears twice: first as a process between people and second as an individual process within the child. Interpersonal processes, like our use of language to communicate with one another, are transformed into intrapersonal ones, like our use of inner speech when we talk our way through to the solution of a complex problem. If in reading about this two-stage concept of development a reader only experienced the first stage and did not internalize it for individual use, then it has not and cannot contribute to mental development.

For Vygotsky, Bruner notes (1986), "language was an agent for altering the powers of thought—giving thought new means for explicating the world. In turn, language became the repository for new thoughts once achieved" (p. 143). In contrast to Piaget, Vygotsky believed that language could provide a path to a " 'higher ground' " (p. 143), by which he seems to have meant a more elevated level of abstraction or a wider perspective of one's culture. As Bruner notes, Vygotsky bestows on language "both a cultural past and a generative present, and assigns it a role as the nurse and tutor of thought" (p. 145).

In sum, Vygotsky (1978, 1986) expressed the belief that we internalize our culture's sign systems. As we internalize these sign systems, especially our culture's language, they function as a bridge that enables us to transform our behavior and our consciousness. Because we become competent members of our society largely through language and its acquisition, the investigation of how that bridge is built and how it functions has been a dominant interest to literacy researchers and teachers. On our way toward competence, we interact with and learn from others. One of Vygotsky's key ideas, the zone of proximal development (ZPD), emphasizes the importance of the interactive, socially based nature of learning. The ZPD is the difference between what one can achieve alone and what one can achieve with the help of a more knowledgeable or capable person. As a result of interactions in the ZPD, children internalize culturally appropriate knowledge and behaviors that they can eventually demonstrate independently. In Vygotsky's words, "An essential feature of learning is that it creates the zone of proximal development" (1978, p. 90). Where and how his cultural historical theory is being challenged in terms of understanding the minds of both dominant and nondominant groups of children are the issues in an edited volume titled *Vygotsky in 21st Century Society: Advances in Cultural Historical Theory and Praxis With Nondominant Communities* (Portes & Salas, 2011).

Scribner and Cole: The Vai People of Liberia. The benefits attributed to literacy were both explicit and implicit in Vygotsky's work. More explicit claims of literacy's effects on cognition and higher order reasoning came through his work with Luria in South Central Asia at a time when the Soviet Union was striving to bring literacy to peoples of that region. Vygotsky and Luria (Luria, 1976) compared the performance of newly literate and nonliterate people on reasoning tasks, including working through syllogisms, and found significant differences between the groups favoring the reasoning and higher order thinking skills of the newly literate population. Benefits of literacy like those alleged by Luria and Vygotsky have been aligned with similar and even far broader claims about the cognitive benefits of literacy in books like *The Domestication of the Savage Mind* (Goody, 1977), *The Literate Revolution in Greece and Its Cultural Consequences* (Havelock, 1982), and *Orality and Literacy: The Technologizing of the Word* (Ong, 1982). Some scholars, such as Scribner and Cole (1981), have questioned the validity of the cognitive effects supposedly arising from literacy and wondered about the contributions of culture, especially the culture of schooling, that sometimes came with literacy's benefits.

In their research with the Vai people in Liberia, Scribner and Cole (1981) attempted to answer two crucial questions: (1) Is the difference in mental functioning of literate versus nonliterate groups the result of literacy or attending school? and (2) Is it possible to detect differences in the effects of different forms of literacy that are used for different purposes in an individual's life or a society's functioning? Conditions of language learning and use among the Vai provided the researchers with an exceptional opportunity to address these questions. Three conditions for acquisition of literacy existed in Vai society: (1) English could be acquired in a formal school environment, (2) the Vai have a language and script that is learned outside of school settings, and (3) the Vai have a form of Arabic literacy. Of additional importance, for each of these literacies, the Vai have a distinct set of uses: English for government and education, Vai literacy for keeping records and writing letters (usually commercial), and Arabic for reading, writing, and memorizing the Koran.

Fortunately, some Vai are literate in one, two, or all three of these languages, whereas others are nonliterate. That meant Scribner and Cole (1981) could disaggregate their data and address their questions to discover if literacy was having an effect on mental functioning. If schooling was the critical variable, then only literates who attended school would show the cognitive benefits of literacy. To generate data, the researchers administered tests to their participants, many with items similar to those that Vygotsky and Luria had used, to detect improvements in abstract thinking, taxonomic categorization, memory, logical reasoning, and reflective knowledge about language.

Scribner and Cole (1981) found that only English literacy was associated with the kinds of abstract thinking and cognitive skills tested. Neither the Vai script nor Arabic had a significant effect on higher order thinking and reasoning. Because English literacy among the Vai was acquired in the school setting, schooling appeared to be the key variable affecting higher order thinking abilities. That finding suggests that literacy alone is not the path to better cognitive or intellectual functioning. The culture of schooling while acquiring literacy has its own effects on cognitive abilities.

With regard to detecting the effects of different forms of literacy that were used for different purposes in the Vai culture, Scribner and Cole (1981) found that each form of literacy was related to some specific skills. For example, Arabic literacy had a positive effect on memory tasks, and literacy in the Vai script conferred more skill in integrating syllables and using grammar rules. While a specific literacy enhanced these practice-related skills, no literacy alone generated evidence to support claims that literacy improved higher order cognitive abilities.

The acquisition of literacy alone appears to have no predictable effects on the quality of an individual's cognitive or reasoning skills—or on the acquisition of capacities that lead to a good life. According to Scribner and Cole's (1981) findings, literacy could not substitute for formal schooling when it came to performance on the cognitive tasks measured. However, school effects were not enduring; being out of school for a few years or away from school-like occupations led to significantly weaker performance on the intellectual operations measured.

Scribner and Cole vaporized the myth of literacy. The belief that learning to read and write, outside of any school context, will bring significant improvements in higher order thinking and reasoning could not be supported with the findings that their study generated. Currently, a new myth of literacy and schooling prognosticates that given the opportunity in school, children will gain the literacy that they require to achieve success. However, that new myth also has its significant doubters who believe that deeper social changes must occur for deeper effects of schooling to become manifest (Gee, 2012).

Halliday: Every Child a Meaning Maker. Sociolinguists, who study language as a social phenomenon, frequently explore language use in communities, how language functions to initiate and carry out social action, and how that language contributes to the development of literacy, power structures, and identity. From very early in life, children participate in meaning making through interaction with mothers, fathers, siblings, and significant others. The children may be oblivious to their meaning making when playing dialogue games of all kinds, but they are nonetheless obviously creating meaning collaboratively. While engaged in these dialogues, children are also constructing an identity (Halliday, 1991/Chapter 5 this volume). In the first weeks of life, infants form bonds that become the basis both for a sense of self and for language. In nonverbal dialogues, such as smile-to-smile or glee-to-glee, child and mother establish moments of attention exchanges that contribute to the verbal exchanges that initiate language acquisition.

The four- or five-month-old, while interacting with one of the significant others, engages in what Halliday (1991/Chapter 5 this volume) calls systematic symbolic constructions. These symbolic encounters with the persons and objects in the child's world constitute moments when meaning is mutually constructed. These acts of meaning making occur, for example, when a child, excited by a pigeon rising from a park walkway and flying over his head, points and shouts in glee as the mother says, "Did you see a pigeon?" That moment of interaction between mother, child, and flying object constructs meaning in the child's mind for that rush of feathers and wings. Halliday further observed that the child, in seeing his own body separate from the bird and from the mother who labeled the bird, is constructing a sense of self, differentiated from his mother and from the pigeon. In a multitude of these symbolic moments, the child develops a protolanguage that employs a system of signs, signals, and symbols and that will enable him to take future linguistic steps into the realm of real language and a far more complex symbolic system. All the preliterate symbolic events that are developed in dialogue with others contribute to the development of language systems and systems of meaning. Eventually, those systems of meaning will enable the child to use language to define his world and eventually himself.

Having evolved a protolanguage that enables the child to communicate with his mother, father, and others in the world and that feeds a growing sense of self, the child is ready to transition not only from crawling to walking but also from protolanguage to human language. The big difference between protolanguage and language itself is that language has a grammar and a lexical system. For English, that includes morphology, vocabulary, and syntax. The emerging language enables the child to interface with people and objects in the world, receive information about that world, and communicate information to all the individuals who populate his world.

Early in the development of real language, according to Halliday (1991/ Chapter 5 this volume), the child gains the capacity to convey information in two dialogic modes or moods. They are dialogic because they occur between two people who are communicating. They are modes (and moods) because they convey information in two different forms: the pragmatic mode and the mathetic mode. The pragmatic (also known as the imperative) mode conveys information about how conditions in the world should be. The mathetic (also known as the declarative) mode conveys information about how conditions in the world actually are. With the evolution of pragmatic and mathetic modes, conversation emerges as collaboration in constructing shared experiences. As a child grows in language capacity from protolanguage to shared construction of meaning out of experiences not materially shared, we can see that language and conversation lay the groundwork for meaning making and for literacy developments yet to come.

Heath: Language Acquisition in Three Communities. Heath (1983) has carefully depicted the influence of family and culture on literacy development, especially the place of early reading and language use during childhood. In her book *Ways With Words: Language, Life, and Work in Communities and Classrooms*, she describes three Appalachian communities: Trackton (a black mill community), Roadville (a white mill community), and Gateway (a mainstream urban community).

In Trackton, children experienced a social environment in which the black community shared in teaching and uniting the youngsters with the community. Few children's books or book-reading activities with children were found in the homes, so oral storytelling styles influenced story creation. Although storytellers in Trackton based their stories on real events, they fictionalized details around those real events so the outcome might not resemble what really happened. The good storytellers were good at "talking junk" (p. 200) that included wildly exaggerated compliments and comparisons. Almost never heard in Trackton was a straightforward, unembellished rendering of an event. Children learned to value a good story, and storytelling was quite competitive. As children, especially the boys, got older, they prized stories, playsongs, and dialogue that included double entendres that sounded harmless on the surface but snapped with irony, insult, or innuendo beneath.

Although the timing, purpose, and content of stories in Roadville differed significantly from stories in Trackton, people in Roadville also spent time telling them. Roadville stories had to be based in fact with a minimum of embellishment. Stories were characterized by truthfulness and carried a moral message. They were intended to confirm membership in the community and the community's behavioral norms. Stories acknowledged their tellers' weaknesses and their attempts to overcome those weaknesses. Furthermore, Roadville children were reared in an environment where parents talked with their babies, modified their language to involve their children, and used interactional patterns that included answering questions, labeling, and naming objects. The children of Roadville were expected to accept the power of print through association with alphabet letters and workbooklike activities.

In Gateway, the townspeople placed a high value on schools and schooling for both black and white children. Families nurtured their children's interest in children's literature from an early age. Parents frequently asked their children information-type questions and developed book-sharing routines. The children often saw parents and siblings reading for a variety of purposes. Heath (1983) concluded that Gateway children acquired values about reading and writing that the Trackton and Roadville children found strange. The Gateway children were familiar not only with book-reading routines, such as those reflected in Sulzby's (1985/1994) study of storybook reading, but with comprehension strategies as well. The discourse and literacy practices of Trackton and Roadville children needed to be bridged by the teachers in the school context, whereas the Gateway children were more school-ready because of the alignment between their experiences with reading and the expectations of teachers.

Heath (Chapter 8 this volume) has followed the history and development of citizens living in and moving from these Appalachian communities over decades. She has documented the lives of the children of Trackton's children as they moved to urban centers and the effects of those moves on the meanings of cultural membership to members of the community and how the socialization of children can alter radically in transitions to urban communities where cultural resources for adaptation may deteriorate (Heath, 1983, 1990/2004). Her more recent work has followed the changes in families and family life following transitions to larger urban areas and the deterioration of interactions between children and family members that supported and sustained socialization and language development within the family and community. With friends often replacing family as the heart of daily life, intimate strangers providing after-school supervision in activities, and an onrush of electronic media alluring to adolescents, relationships between parents and their children interlaced with extended conversations became, in general, less intimate and interactive, more tenuous and distant. Heath has many concerns about the impact of these deep social changes in our cultural and communal life, especially during a time of global upheavals and economic shifts.

Gee and Discourse Development. The perspective of reading that permeates the work of Gee (2012, 2001/Chapter 4 this volume) is founded in the belief that reading is always situated in a social environment where knowledge construction, language, motives, values, societies, and cultures interact. While linguistic processes, such as phonemic awareness and letter-sound relationships, decoding, and word recognition, are essential for reading to occur, reading is, nevertheless, embedded or situated in complex sociocultural systems that shape and support reading and its emergence in children. Each literacy event that we experience is composed not only of a text that needs to be read but also of a social language, a Discourse, and a cultural world in which the text exists. Literacy and languages have no meaning outside their particular cultural world.

As children acquire social languages, they become socialized into what Gee (1996, 2012, 2001/Chapter 4 this volume) calls Discourses (with a capital *D* to distinguish it from discourse as just language use). Although Discourses always involve language, they also involve ways of using words—ways of talking, writing, interacting, believing, valuing, and feeling to enact "meaningful socially situated identities and activities" (Gee, 2001/2004, p. 124). Discourses, as identity kits, reflect who we are and how we behave as a teacher, special-education student, gang member, third grader, or feminist. These Discourses can also blend or conflict, as happens, for example, with some African American students who adopt the Discourse of a gifted middle school science student during class time but access a street-savvy, hip-hop adolescent Discourse during time in the home community. During a lifetime, each of us is quite likely to master and mix a number of Discourses.

While we become socialized into a Discourse, we also develop an accompanying theory about the world that is shared by people who are socialized into that Discourse. That cultural model (Gee, 1999, 2012) informs people of what the world looks like from the viewpoint of a particular Discourse. Furthermore, a cultural model embodies a Discourse of parenting that includes various aspects of parent–child relations for the group socialized into that model, including model-appropriate patterns of childhood behaviors and development. Gee (2012) points out that middle class and working-class models of childhood vary and that child-rearing guidebooks and other materials help parents realize the cultural model that they have internalized. Theories, beliefs, and images of childhood development and early literacy within a cultural model guide practices that contribute to each child's early reading, writing, speaking, and listening. In Heath's investigation of language use in Trackton, Roadville, and middle class Gateway, we have seen the profound influence of these cultural models and the development of Discourse that they inform.

Social Semiotic Theory. Semiosis is a process for meaning making through the use of signs, which include both the observable signifier (e.g., the color red) and the signified meaning (e.g., danger). Because in the field of social semiotics what a sign stands for is not a pre-given (Hodge & Kress, 1988; van Leeuwen, 2005), the term *resource* is preferred. According to van Leeuwen,

> Semiotic resources are not restricted to speech and writing and picture making. Almost everything we do or make can be done or made in different ways and therefore allows, at least in principle, the articulation of different social and cultural meanings. Walking could be an example. We may think of it as...basic locomotion, something we have in common with other species. But there are many different ways of walking....Different ways of walking can seduce, threaten, impress and much more....
>
> As soon as we have established that a given type of physical activity or a given type of material artefact constitutes a semiotic resource, it becomes possible to describe...its potential for making meaning. (p. 4)

Although it is fairly common among literacy researchers to refer to multimodal frameworks as theoretical constructs, the actual theory behind such constructs is semiotic theory, or more specifically, *social* semiotic theory for researchers who view people as having agency in using and shaping semiotic resources (Halliday, 1978; Hodge & Kress, 1988). Multimodality is but the field to which a theory of social semiotics is applied (Jewitt & Kress, 2003).

Social semiotic theory is useful for explaining the ways in which people play a central role in meaning making—how they use various resources (signs) to represent through different modes (e.g., oral and written language, still and moving images, sound, gesture, performance) what it is they wish to communicate to others (Kress & van Leeuwen, 1996). Said another way, it is through the representations that people make of the resources available to them that researchers and teachers are able to infer what matters to their participants and students (Jewitt & Kress, 2003). Inferences of this kind have particular relevance when they contradict a prevailing community's expectations about reading and reading instruction.

For example, in *Before Writing: Rethinking the Paths to Literacy*, Kress (1997) challenges the field to rethink commonly held assumptions about language and literacy that privilege a linguistic mode of communication over other modes. Of particular interest is his thinking on semiotic mediation and its implications for modal reach (Kress, 2009):

> What is done by speech in one culture may be done by gesture in another; what may be well done through image in one culture may be better done in three-dimensional forms in another; and so on. We cannot assume that translations from one mode to the "same" mode in another culture can draw on the same resources. In other words, the implicit assumption that "languages" (and now modes) can deal broadly with the same domains in different cultures—even if differently—is likely to be unfounded. It may be that a meaning expressed by gesture in this culture has to be *spoken* in that other culture; what may be handled by image here, may need to be *written* there. (pp. 57–58)

Social semiotic theory is particularly germane to research conducted as part of the New Literacy Studies. To read *Social Linguistics and Literacies: Ideology in Discourses*, in which Gee (2012) overviews the sociocultural approaches to language and literacy that came together in the last decade or two of the 20th century, is to better understand the relationship of the New Literacy Studies to social semiotic theory. It is also to understand how two competing models of literacy—the autonomous and ideological models—have been instrumental in shaping literacy instruction as we know it today.

The autonomous model, which is prevalent in U.S. schools, is the existing paradigm that views reading and writing as neutral processes that are largely explained by individual variations in cognitive and physiological functioning. It is a view that assumes a universal set of reading and writing skills for decoding and encoding printed text. Its persistence is notable, especially given Heath's (1983) influential research, which showed that it is *how* children are socialized into different literacies that matters (e.g., their different ways with words and whether those ways match the school's approach to reading instruction).

In critiques of the autonomous model, Street (1984, 1995) draws from his work as an anthropologist in Iran during the 1970s. Based on that research and the earlier research of Scribner and Cole (1981) among the Vai in West Africa, Street specifically questions the assumption that reading and writing are neutral processes, thereby laying the groundwork for his ideological model. Street (1995), whose research continues to link the cultural dimension of language and literacy to contemporary practices in education, explains the autonomous model this way:

> A great deal of the thinking about literacy...has assumed that literacy with a big "L" and single "y" [is] a single autonomous thing [with] consequences for personal and social development....One of the reasons for referring to this position as an autonomous model of literacy is that it represents itself as though it is not a position located ideologically at all, as though it is just natural. One of the reasons why I want to call the counter-position ideological is precisely in order to signal that we are not simply talking here about technical features of the written process or the oral process. What we are talking about are competing models and assumptions about reading and writing processes, which are always embedded in power relations. (pp. 132–133)

As used here, *power* refers not to something that is seized and held on to by a person seeking to suppress the rights of others, but rather as something that circulates and speaks through silences as well as utterances (Foucault, 1997).

Just prior to Street's (1995) critique of the autonomous model of literacy, Gee's (1990) seminal publication *Social Linguistics and Literacies: Ideology in Discourses* was helping to reshape the field's thinking about reading and why it was no longer adequate to think of it as a process residing solely in one's head. Then, in 1996, the New London Group published its treatise on multiliteracies. This work drew attention to the need for a multiplicity and integration of communication modes (e.g., language, still and moving images, speech, sound, gesture, movement) in the context of a culturally and linguistically diverse world grown significantly more attached to new communication technologies, although multiliteracies need not involve digital technologies (Lankshear & Knobel, 2006). Typically, the term *multiliteracies* denotes more than "mere literacy" (Cope & Kalantzis, 2000, p. 5), which remains language- and print-centered in conventional classroom instruction. Over time, however, the notion of literacy with a "big 'L' and single 'y'" has loosened to make room for the plural form, literacies or multiliteracies. In addition, terms such as *situated literacies* (Barton, Hamilton, & Ivanič, 2000), *digital literacies*, and the *New Literacy Studies* (Gee, 1996; New London Group, 1996) have become part of a burgeoning research literature, as have multimodal texts that are part and parcel of New Literacy Studies.

Sociocognitive Theory and Models of Reading

Beginning in the mid-1980s, as increased attention and interest were given to sociocultural influences on literacy, models of reading and writing began to appear in which cognitive processes were increasingly embedded and integrated with social and cultural influences. Kucer's (1985) mid-1980s model of reading and writing processes had cognitive processes and strategies to describe the parallel processes of reading and writing at its core. However, he recognized that knowledge was culturally coded, reflecting Vygotsky's belief that minds are embedded in the history and culture of their time. Because objects, events, and processes are culturally based, cultural knowledge is integrated with the knowledge that we construct when reading and writing (Kucer, 2001). Along with other designers of models who viewed society and culture as inseparable from reading and writing, Kucer created an integrated model that reflected not only top-down and bottom-up cognitive processes but also the inherent, ever-present impact of social and cultural life on literacy.

An interactive reading process model designed by Ruddell and Speaker (1985) and published in the third edition of *Theoretical Models and Processes of Reading* includes components for declarative and procedural knowledge, knowledge utilization and control, and reader output that reflected information processing factors. However, it also takes into account the influence of the reader's social and cultural environment in which reading processes are embedded. Later models of reading (Ruddell & Unrau, 1994, Chapter 38 this volume) that evolved from this model expand on the importance of the social and cultural environment by integrating an elaborated description and analysis of the teacher's role in developing an instructional environment for reading and learning. Those later models also depict a complex meaning negotiation process with texts affected by an array of social and cultural factors, such as a community of students' interpretations of texts of many kinds in the classroom social context.

Sociocognitive models of writing also emerged from earlier cognitive processing models of writing (Flower & Hayes, 1981) that explain writing as a set of thinking processes guided by a writer's growing network of self-constructed goals. Hayes (1996/2004) designed an individual-environment writing model that contains two major components: the task environment, which is both social and physical, and the individual. The individual component of the model includes cognitive processes, working memory, long-term memory, and motivation. While the first three of these features represent the cognitive processing dimensions of writing, the last feature, motivation, was newly added to take into account the writer's affective states.

While these sociocognitive models of reading and writing reflect the concerns and interests of researchers and other educators in the literacy field, the expansion of researchers' attention to the socially grounded investigation of reading and reading processes is evident in work published from the mid-1990s onward. In attempts to provide support for students, teachers, and English departments in urban schools, Lee (Chapter 10 this volume) developed a system of cultural modeling that draws on students' mental models of language use. In the case of African American students who speak an African American English vernacular, she believes that readers approach texts with mental models of language play that they acquire through interaction outside the classroom, often on the playgrounds and playing fields of their communities. The particular genre of talk that she explored as a mental model was signifying, a form of language that always involves double entendre and indirection, frequently in the service of ritualized insults. Her intention was to use these language modes as an instructional resource that would enable students to respond to literature. She developed an instructional strategy that guides students in the analysis of signifying dialogues so they can discover the implications and meanings of each turn in a dialogue. This process can then be transferred to the analysis of other literary texts. In short, students' vernacular serves as a bridge for the scaffolding of response to literature and other texts. Through cultural modeling, teachers can transform what might have been viewed as a deficit into an asset for the development of academic literacy. Although the model that emerged from Lee's work is quite different from other sociocognitive models that we have explored, it suggests once again the range of meanings that the term *model* has acquired in literacy studies.

Structuralism

As a theory, structuralism operates on an underlying assumption that structures exist in the events, texts, or processes under study; that those structures can be identified; and that their functions, often within other larger structures, can be described or explained. Two structuralists who have influenced literacy studies over the years illustrate the theory in action: Saussure and Lévi-Strauss. Saussure, often considered the "father of structuralism" (Spivey, 1997, p. 99), was a late 19th- and early 20th-century linguist who approached the study of language with the purpose of discovering its structures. He derived several principles about language from his inquiry. Among them was the precept that there is a language system belonging to a social group (*langue*), that there is also a language used by an individual when communicating (*parole*), and that *parole* should be studied to understand the abstract structure of the *langue*.

Lévi-Strauss was an anthropologist who was familiar with Saussurian principles but focused his interests on mythology. Interested in myth's universal structures, Lévi-Strauss examined specific myths (*parole*) to discover their more abstract structure (*langue*). In part, he studied myth to discover rules governing them within and across cultures. Through the examination of myths, he was able to understand both their internal structure and how they coalesced as constellations of related myths for the cultures to which they belonged. While both of these illustrative structuralists have, to some degree, influenced studies in literacy, we present next a group of critical theorists along with Bourdieu whose perspectives have been used as theoretical frameworks for many studies in literacy and reading, including those that have investigated the accumulation of cultural capital and the effects of its expression on marginalized social groups.

Critical Theory. When knowledge is conveyed to others, especially when that knowledge is presented to less powerful individuals or social groups by those with more power, critical theorists are likely to challenge personal or group preferences that may appear in the conveyance of information. Founding critical theorists believed that repressive (and oppressive) institutions manipulate masses of citizens for the benefit of the few at the cost of the many and that growing awareness of the structure and function of those repressive institutions can impel social change and foster individual freedom. The impetus for this movement in social theory coalesced in Frankfurt a decade or two before the rise of fascism in Germany and other European nations. Scholars associated with the Frankfurt School, including Adorno (2001), Habermas (1989), Horkheimer (2002), and Marcuse (1964), often applied Marxist categories (e.g., social class differences) in their analysis and critique of hegemonic social and cultural institutions. Applied to education, Marx's theory of capitalism focuses on "the process whereby the members of the working class will come to see themselves as members of this class and, as such, in direct opposition not only to members of the bourgeoisie but to capitalism itself" (Fay, 1987, p. 35).

Ideas rooted in critical theory have served as the foundation for critical pedagogy and critical literacy. Educators who have focused on these theoretical fields have analyzed the ways in which cultural institutions, including schools, express dominance, and have evolved theories about teaching and learning literacy that contribute to emancipation and social justice.

Critical Pedagogy and Critical Literacy. Freire (1970/1993), a founding father of critical pedagogy and critical literacy, presented in *Pedagogy of the Oppressed* his method for developing critical consciousness, or the capacity to perceive social, political, and economic contradictions and act against oppressive forces. He focused on the roots of oppression and methods of unearthing them for close examination. Through reflection on the forces of oppression, the oppressed can be liberated. Liberation can arise through critical dialogue with the oppressed that aims at reflection on an individual's specific situation.

A considerable body of theory beyond that of Freire (e.g., Morrell's 2008 work on Othered critical traditions) has arisen around critical literacy and its pursuit of social justice. Recognizing how language shapes social interaction (Bourdieu, 1991; Gee, 2012, 2001/Chapter 4 this volume; Janks, 2000; Lankshear & McLaren, 1993; Luke, 2000) is a common denominator in critical literacy research. For example, researchers (Lewison & Leland, 2002) have identified five dimensions of critical literacy: "interrogating the everyday world, questioning power relationships, appreciating multiple realities and viewpoints, analyzing popular culture and media, and taking action to promote social justice" (p. 109).

Critical literacy as theory translates into ways in which reading and writing enable individuals to understand daily social and political processes for the purpose of living more freely in a democratic society. Engaging in critical literacy practices enables readers to see their world more clearly, understand how it works, rewrite that world with their interests written in, and take more liberating action within it. Critical literacy's intent is to emancipate and empower those who have become subordinated and marginalized. Morrell (2009), for example, has drawn on critical theory to design curricula that students and teachers along with university researchers can implement and investigate in classrooms, especially in those classrooms where students' academic literacies are underdeveloped.

Bourdieu. Reading researchers (e.g., Alvermann, Friese, Beckmann, & Rezak, 2011; Jiménez, Smith, & Martínez-León, 2003; Marsh, 2006) who draw on Bourdieu's (Bourdieu, 1991; Bourdieu & Passeron, 1990) work are typically interested in exposing structural hierarchies that perpetuate inequalities in educational opportunities. Like Bourdieu, they are less interested in theory for theory's sake, especially theory that distances itself from the social world and institutional practices associated with schooling. From Bourdieu's perspective, fields are social sites characterized by specific rules and logics that determine the resources to which individuals in those fields have access (e.g., a high school classroom). *Resources*, in Bourdieu's terms, refers to several forms of capital (e.g., cultural, symbolic) that are used as thinking tools in analyzing data. Another thinking tool common to Bourdieu's work is "misrecognition, an alienated cognition that looks at the world through categories the world imposes, and apprehends the social world as a natural world" (Bourdieu, 1990, pp. 140–141). Misrecognition is perpetuated by beliefs and understandings held by individuals in social fields that are assumed to be natural but are in fact arbitrary and often in need of reexamination (Bourdieu, 1991).

Poststructuralism

Texts are usually thought to signify meaning—meaning that is contingent on the interaction of reader and context. Less typical is Deleuze and Guattari's (1987) concept of a text. In their poststructural decentering project, Deleuze and Guattari avoid any orientation toward a culmination or ending point. In their sense of the term, a text is neither signifier nor the signified; therefore, it is inappropriate to think of interpreting or understanding texts in the conventional way. As Grosz (1993/1994) explains,

> It is...no longer appropriate to ask what a text means, what it says, what is the structure of its interiority, how to interpret or decipher it. Instead, one must ask what it does, how it connects with other things (including its reader, its author, its literary and nonliterary context). (p. 199)

The conventional modes of interpretation and analysis espoused by linguists, literacy theorists, and semioticians do not hold when analyzing texts from Deleuze and Guattari's perspective. Instead, it is how texts function outside themselves that is of interest. This interest stems from the view that texts, like rhizomes, connect with other things. For instance, "a rhizome ceaselessly establishes connections between semiotic chains, organizations of power, and circumstances relative to the arts, sciences, and social struggles" (p. 7).

Moreover, from Deleuze and Guattari's (1987) perspective, researchers interested in theory building would do well to make maps, not tracings. In their metaphoric use of the terms, a map is "a part of the rhizome...open and connectable in all of its dimensions...[with] multiple entryways, as opposed to the tracing, which always comes back 'to the same'" (p. 12). Maps, unlike tracings, are always becoming; they have no beginnings and endings, just middles. It is by looking at the middles that we begin to see how, in perspective, everything else changes. Dimitriadis and Kamberelis (1997) explain the process this way:

> In drawing maps, the theorist works at the surface, "creating" possible realities by producing new articulations of disparate phenomena and connecting the exteriority of objects to whatever forces or directions seem potentially related to them. As such, maps exceed both individual and collective experiences of what seems "naturally" real. (p. 150)

Looking for middles, rather than beginnings and endings, makes it possible to decenter key linkages and find new ones, not by combining old ones in new ways but by remaining open to the proliferation of ruptures and discontinuities that in turn create other linkages (Alvermann, 2000; Leander, Phillips, & Taylor, 2010). Rhizomatic cartography is a spatial methodology for studying a range of literacy practices, such as adolescents' uses of popular cultural texts to renegotiate their identities (Hagood, 2004), a Christian faith-based school's literacy practices (Eakle, 2007), and students' multimodal/embodied classroom performances that have implications for literacy pedagogy (Leander & Rowe, 2006).

Pragmatism

In the face of an array of approaches and theoretical frameworks to literacy research and to what they view as the sometimes deleterious effects of overzealous adherence to particular paradigms, some educators have advocated for a far more pragmatic approach to inquiry. Although often avoided by educational researchers because of its conceptual vagueness and misapplications, pragmatism has had a long history in American philosophy and education with its reflection in the works of Dewey, James, and Rorty. In its application to literacy research, pragmatism translates into an engagement with inquiry that results in useful outcomes rather than in the discovery of knowledge that promotes one's ideology or epistemology. For a fuller description of pragmatism and its applications to literacy research, see Dillon, O'Brien, and Heilman (Chapter 40 this volume).

Reading Motivation Theory

Several motivational theories or perspectives have been applied in the past few decades by researchers as a framework for research on motivation for reading. Frequently, these motivational theories have influenced the development of instruments to measure students' motivation for or engagement in reading. Probably the most influential of these has been Guthrie and Wigfield's (2000) engagement theory. Guthrie and Wigfield argue that engaged reading occurs when readers coordinate cognition, in the form of knowledge and strategies, within a social context to satisfy or achieve motivational ends, such as readers' goals, wishes, and intentions. According to this perspective, "motivation is the foundational process for reading engagement and is a major contributor...to disengagement from reading" (p. 405). Thus, reading engagement theory is focused on explaining how instructional, motivational, and engagement variables interact to explain reading outcomes.

In their engagement model of reading development, Guthrie and Wigfield (1997, 2000) illustrate how instructional processes, such as strategy instruction, interesting texts, and autonomy support, impact engagement processes, which ultimately influence reading and learning outcomes. These processes may overlap and interact in any instructional context, creating greater instructional cohesion that theoretically could augment engagement, conceptual mastery, and reading achievement. Engagement processes include social interactions, conceptual knowledge, strategy use, and motivation. According to the model, reading engagement processes mediate the effects of instructional context on student outcomes. Thus, the instructional context does not directly influence reading outcomes; rather, the effects of the instructional context depend on levels of student engagement. Finally, achievement, knowledge, and practices are the focal outcomes in the model. Achievement might take the form of standardized test results, knowledge the form of student portfolios of work, and practices the form of independent reading. In testing their engagement theory, Wigfield, Guthrie, and their associates (2008) confirmed empirically that engaged reading mediated the effects of instruction on comprehension.

Among other motivational theories that have served as frameworks for research are self-determination theory, behaviorial theory, social cognitive theory, expectancy–value theory, and control–value theory. Although a nuanced explanation of the use of these theories in reading research is not possible here, we can describe some of the theories' basic features and explain their capacity to energize reading. Table 1 identifies several of these theories, provides brief descriptions, and includes references for the theorists who created or advocated each theory. Although other motivational theories, such as attribution and goal theory, have also been applied to research and to classroom practice related to reading, the motivational theories covered in Table 1 offer a glimpse of the work that has been and remains to be done on motivation, its effects on reading and reading processes, and its relationships with engagement in reading.

Literacy Theory and Models in Evolution

The importance of educational theory and, more specifically, theories about literacy is reflected in studies of theory's impact on literacy research. Dressman (2007), whose discoveries we alluded to earlier in this chapter, investigated changes in the conceptualization of literacy and in the use of the word *theory* in research. That inquiry enabled him to explore how theory and its use affected the generation of knowledge about literacy, especially as a social practice, in major research

Table 1. Description of Motivational Theories and Their Capacity to Energize Reading

Motivational Theory	Brief Conceptual Description and Capacity to Energize Reading	Theorists
Self-determination theory	Self-determination theory explains motivation in terms of three basic human needs: the need to feel autonomous, competent, and related to others. Contexts that support these needs have been found to positively impact intrinsic motivation and reading.	• Deci, E.L., & Ryan, R.M. (1985). *Intrinsic motivation and self-determination in human behavior.* New York: Plenum. • Deci, E.L., & Ryan, R.M. (2000). The "what" and "why" of goal pursuits: Human needs and the self-determination of behavior. *Psychological Inquiry, 11*(4), 227–268. • Ryan, R.M., & Deci, E.L. (2000). Self-determination theory and the facilitation of intrinsic motivation, social development, and well-being. *American Psychologist, 55*(1), 68–78.
Behavioral theory	Reading motivation, as seen in the light of behavioral theory, depends on changes in rate, frequency, or form of reading behaviors that occur in response to stimuli or events in an environmental context, such as a classroom.	• Thorndike, E.L. (1913). *Educational psychology: Vol. 2. The psychology of learning.* New York: Teachers College Press.
Social cognitive theory	Social cognitive theory explains motivation in terms of the social influences on self-processes, such as self-efficacy. Motivation, including that related to reading, is influenced by expectations about the consequences of one's actions, specifically one's self-efficacy regarding the performance of those actions.	• Bandura, A. (1986). *Social foundations of thought and action: A social cognitive theory.* Englewood Cliffs, NJ: Prentice-Hall.
Expectancy–value theory	Contemporary expectancy–value theory explains student motivation for reading in terms of two distinct and interrelated components: expectancy of success and task value. The subcomponents of the theory are comprised of many different motivational constructs that have been found to predict students' expectations for success and the amount of value placed on engaging and/or succeeding at a task, such as reading.	• Wigfield, A., & Eccles, J.S. (2000). Expectancy–value theory of achievement motivation. *Contemporary Educational Psychology,* 25(1), 68–81. *(continued)*

Table 1. Description of Motivational Theories and Their Capacity to Energize Reading (*Continued*)

Motivational Theory	Brief Conceptual Description and Capacity to Energize Reading	Theorists
Control–value theory	Control–value theory is grounded in the assumption that individuals' appraisals of their control and values are key to the activation of achievement emotions and outcome emotions. In an effort to succinctly summarize how students' appraisals of current achievement activities and of past and future outcomes arouse achievement emotions, Pekrun (2009) states that "students experience emotions when they feel being in control of, or out of control of, achievement-related activities and outcomes that are subjectively important to them" (pp. 591–592).	• Pekrun, R. (2006). The control–value theory of achievement emotions: Assumptions, corollaries, and implications for educational research and practice. *Educational Psychology Review, 18*(4), 315–341. • Pekrun, R. (2009). Emotions at school. In K.R. Wentzel & A. Wigfield (Eds.), *Handbook of motivation at school* (pp. 575–604). New York: Routledge.

journals. Although earlier literacy research from the 1960s through the late 1980s was dominated by empirical studies using experimental methods that focused on reading and writing as cognitive activities (Shannon, 1989), the language of literacy research has changed. According to Dressman, researchers reconceived literacy, changing what being literate means and how researchers theorized the relationship between literacy and other human activities. Researchers also expanded their use of the term *theory* itself and the ways they used theories to construct knowledge about literacy.

Dressman (2007) compared the uses of the term *theory* in articles published in three major journals (*Reading Research Quarterly, Research in the Teaching of English*, and the *Journal of Literacy Research*) before and after the early 1990s. He analyzed a pre-1990s article (Fitzgerald & Spiegel, 1986) that included in its literature review section a comment that "overall structure, plan, or schema is a necessary condition for coherence" (p. 264). The authors followed with 10 citations by theorists or researchers on text cohesion. Fitzgerald and Spiegel then set up the purpose of their study: to document in their research the theoretically established relationship between cohesion and coherence. As Dressman commented, in papers like those, "the dance between theory and empirical evidence was close and well coordinated, more like a tango than the twist" (p. 335). In similar papers, theories that offered explanations for a process or phenomenon became open to criticism, reevaluation, and sometimes loss of dominance, as Dressman suggests was the fate of schema theory in the early 1990s when researchers complained that it was "too vague, too ill-defined, and too idealistic" (p. 336) to serve as the base for a model of reading comprehension.

Dressman (2007) then looked at the use of the word *theory* in papers published from the mid-1990s to about 2007. Instead of theory operating as bookends for research papers by appearing prominently in the front-end literature review and the rear-end discussion of a theory's fate in the face of empirical findings, theory frequently moved to the center of all sections of studies, particularly those that focused on literacy as social action and that were mainly qualitative.

As an example of theory's new centrality in published literacy research, Dressman (2007) analyzed the structure of a paper on critical inquiry in an urban high school English class. In that paper, Fecho (2001) cited several theorists and multiple theories throughout all sections of his article. The research done was not to serve the purpose of validating and extending a theory or challenging the validity of a theory or set of theories. Instead, Fecho used theory to align with his findings. Theorists and theories (Bakhtin, 1981; Freire & Macedo, 1995; hooks, 1990) substantiated observations made in the classrooms and confirmed that discourse occurring there resonated with current concepts in critical literacy and with critical literacy theorists.

The more recent studies that focus on literacy as social action, according to Dressman (2007), use theory in at least three significantly different ways from earlier empirical or analytical research. First, theories in the more recent studies were brought up and applied with greater distance between a study's empirical foundation and the phenomenon being examined. Theory acquired a metaphorical dimension rather than being used as a generalization under siege or defended with new data. Second, theory was evoked in more ways. Instead of merely being supported or denounced with a researcher's new evidence, theory had multiple functions, far beyond its mere verification or rejection. Those multiple functions included service (1) as a foundational platform where theory appeared in the introduction and framed the study, (2) as a focus point where theory framed the introduction and was referred to in the discussion section, (3) as a discursive scaffold where theory was integrated throughout the study to frame it and make sense of its findings, or (4) as a dialectical scaffold where theory was used to both interrogate and be interrogated by the study's data. Third, theories took on personal importance to researchers in the later studies, so discussion of theory acquired sociocultural, sociopolitical, and self-defining significance, allowing educators to view themselves and their work through a fresh perspective. While acknowledging the many benefits of theoretically framed research, including the expansion of a study's significance and implications as well as the building of grand theories of literacy-centered social interaction, Dressman (Dressman & McCarthey, 2011) has also emphasized the importance of interrogating theories used to justify arguments so researchers are more aware of the assumptions, interpretations, and consequences of theories they use to generate knowledge.

Whether or not these changes in the appearance and function of theory that Dressman has identified will evolve further so theory and its use in research continues to change along the lines that he has observed remains to be seen. Not long ago, researchers using qualitative or ethnographic methods often worried about where they could get their work published—or even if they could get it published. However, we are far beyond that condition in literacy research today.

Tensions over theories, including the information that they convey and the impact that they have on literacy research and instruction, have torn groups apart and pulled them together. New theories in science, such as Darwin's theory of evolution, have altered the way scientists in a community have understood the foundation of their field; explained how and why things work as they do; solved common, perplexing problems; and made predictions about the future of a discipline. Although tensions between competing or conflicting theories can spur contention and disputes, they can also stimulate creative resolution, stir new insights, and spawn new understandings to explain how things work. Although theory and theoretical models have brought light to the invisible processes of reading both within our minds and in our social environment, they have also distorted our vision, even bringing episodes of blindness that made the accurate perception of processes both internal and external impossible. Yet, it is abundantly clear that encouraging the generation of theory and providing justification for theory in the form of evidence, discussion, and debate—practices that Gee (2012) considers ethically responsible—can immeasurably enrich our work, move us further toward understanding the issues that arise, and perplex us in our investigation of literacy and reading processes.

Theories structure and guide literacy practice—whether we are aware of those theories or not. While degrees of awareness about theory and the depth of their influence on teaching or research vary enormously, we have little variance in our belief that it is vitally important to discover which theories are structuring and driving practice in our classrooms and our research. As a vehicle with its lights on, theory can help us see better where we are going, why we are going there, and how we might get safely to our destination. However, theory can be misleading. It has the power to influence our decisions and shape our interpretation of events. So, with a degree of vigilance, we need to monitor theory's impact on our work and heighten our awareness of its influence while always being ready to reframe its structure, even on the move.

QUESTIONS FOR REFLECTION

1. How are the concepts of theory and model related in research on literacy?
2. How did the conception of theory and its use change in late 20th-century literacy research?
3. How do the theories of constructivism and social constructionism differ?
4. Which of the theories presented in this chapter have helped you understand literacy and reading processes the most? Why?

NOTE

[1] The first edition of *Theoretical Models and Processes of Reading* (Singer & Ruddell, 1970) includes several other papers that emerged from a symposium given at the 14th International Reading Association convention in 1969 and several selected articles that developed theoretical models of the reading process. A paper by Goodman on the psycholinguistic guessing game appears in the book, along with a reading competency model by Venezky and Calfee. Following that first endeavor, which brought newly emerging theoretical models of reading and an analysis of specific aspects of the reading processes to graduate students, researchers, teachers, and scholars, *Theoretical Models and Processes of Reading* went through five subsequent editions, including this sixth edition. Over more than 40 years, theoretical models of reading and of writing have proliferated.

REFERENCES

Adorno, T. (2001). *The culture industry: Selected essays on mass culture.* New York: Routledge.

Alvermann, D.E. (2000). Researching libraries, literacies, and lives: A rhizoanalysis. In E.A. St. Pierre & W.S. Pillow (Eds.), *Working the ruins: Feminist poststructural theory and methods in education* (pp. 114–129). New York: Routledge.

Alvermann, D., Friese, E., Beckmann, S., & Rezak, A. (2011). Content area reading pedagogy and domain knowledge: A Bourdieusian analysis. *Australian Educational Researcher, 38*(2), 203–220. doi:10.1007/s13384-011-0024-x

Anderson, R.C. (1976). Concretization and sentence learning. In H. Singer & R.B. Ruddell (Eds.), *Theoretical models and processes of reading* (2nd ed., pp. 588–596). Newark, DE: International Reading Association. (Reprinted from *Journal of Educational Psychology*, 1974, 66(2), 179–183)

Anderson, R.C., Goldberg, S.R., & Hidde, J.L. (1976). Meaningful processing of sentences. In H. Singer & R.B. Ruddell (Eds.), *Theoretical models and processes of reading* (2nd ed., pp. 580–587). Newark, DE: International Reading Association. (Reprinted from *Journal of Educational Psychology*, 1971, 62(5), 395–399)

Bakhtin, M. (1981). *The dialogic imagination: Four essays* (M. Holquist, Ed.; C. Emerson & M. Holquist, Trans.). Austin: University of Texas Press.

Bandura, A. (1986). *Social foundations of thought and action: A social cognitive theory.* Englewood Cliffs, NJ: Prentice-Hall.

Barton, D., Hamilton, M., & Ivanič, R. (Eds.). (2000). *Situated literacies: Reading and writing in context.* New York: Routledge.

Berger, P.L., & Luckmann, T. (1966). *The social construction of reality: A treatise in the sociology of knowledge.* Garden City, NY: Doubleday.

Bleich, D. (1980). Epistemological assumptions in the study of response. In J.P. Tompkins (Ed.), *Reader-response criticism: From formalism to post-structuralism* (pp. 134–163). Baltimore: Johns Hopkins University Press.

Bourdieu, P. (1990). *The logic of practice* (R. Nice, Trans.). Stanford, CA: Stanford University Press.

Bourdieu, P. (1991). *Language and symbolic power* (J.B. Thompson, Ed.; G. Raymond & M. Adamson, Trans.). Cambridge, MA: Harvard University Press.

Bourdieu, P., & Passeron, J. (1990). *Reproduction in education, society and culture* (2nd ed.; R. Nice, Trans.). Thousand Oaks, CA: Sage.

Bruffee, K.A. (1986). Social construction, language, and the authority of knowledge: A bibliographical essay. *College English, 48*(8), 773–790. doi:10.2307/376723

Bruner, J. (1986). *Actual minds, possible worlds.* Cambridge, MA: Harvard University Press.

Burr, V. (2003). *Social constructionism* (2nd ed.). New York: Routledge.

Cambourne, B. (2002). Holistic, integrated approaches to reading and language arts instruction: The constructivist framework of an instructional theory. In A.E. Farstrup & S.J. Samuels (Eds.), *What research has to say about reading instruction* (pp. 25–47). Newark, DE: International Reading Association. doi:10.1598/0872071774.2

Chomsky, N. (1959). A review of B.F. Skinner's *Verbal Behavior. Language,* 35(1), 26–58. doi:10.2307/411334

Coalition for Evidence-Based Policy. (2003). *Identifying and implementing educational practices supported by rigorous evidence: A user friendly guide.* Washington, DC: National Center for Education Evaluation and Regional Assistance, Institute of Education Sciences, U.S. Department of Education. Retrieved July 13, 2012, from www2.ed.gov/rschstat/research/pubs/rigorousevid/rigorousevid.pdf

Cope, B., & Kalantzis, M. (2000). Introduction: Multiliteracies: The beginning of an idea. In B. Cope & M Kalantzis (Eds.), *Multiliteracies: Literacy learning and the design of social futures* (pp. 3–8). New York: Routledge.

Creswell, J.W. (2008). *Educational research: Planning, conducting, and evaluating quantitative and qualitative research* (3rd ed.). Upper Saddle River, NJ: Pearson.

Culler, J. (1980). Literary competence. In J.P. Tompkins (Ed.), *Reader-response criticism: From formalism to post-structuralism* (pp. 101–117). Baltimore: Johns Hopkins University Press.

Darwin, C. (1988). *On the origin of species.* Washington Square: New York University Press. (Original work published 1859)

Deci, E.L., & Ryan, R.M. (1985). *Intrinsic motivation and self-determination in human behavior.* New York: Plenum.

Deci, E.L., & Ryan, R.M. (2000). The "what" and "why" of goal pursuits: Human needs and the self-determination of behavior. *Psychological Inquiry, 11*(4), 227–268. doi:10.1207/S15327965PLI1104_01

Deleuze, G., & Guattari, F. (1987). *A thousand plateaus: Capitalism and schizophrenia* (B. Massumi, Trans.). Minneapolis: University of Minnesota Press.

Dimitriadis, G., & Kamberelis, G. (1997). Shifting terrains: Mapping education within a global landscape. *The Annals of the American Academy of Political and Social Science, 551*(1), 137–150. doi:10.1177/0002716297551001010

Dressman, M. (2007). Theoretically framed: Argument and desire in the production of general knowledge about literacy. *Reading Research Quarterly, 42*(3), 332–363. doi:10.1598/RRQ.42.3.1

Dressman, M., & McCarthey, S.J. (2011). Toward a pragmatics of epistemology, methodology, and social theory. In N.K. Duke & M.H. Mallette (Eds.), *Literacy research methodologies* (2nd ed., pp. 441–463). New York: Guilford.

Durkheim, E. (1982). *The rules of sociological method and selected texts on sociology and its method* (S. Lukes, Ed.; W.D. Halls, Trans.). New York: Free.

Eakle, A.J. (2007). Literacy spaces of a Christian faith-based school. *Reading Research Quarterly, 42*(4), 472–510. doi:10.1598/RRQ.42.4.3

Fay, B. (1987). The basic scheme of critical social science. In *Critical social science: Liberation and its limits* (pp. 27–41). Ithaca, NY: Cornell University Press.

Fecho, B. (2001). "Why are you doing this?": Acknowledging and transcending threat in a critical inquiry classroom. *Research in the Teaching of English, 36*(1), 9–37.

Fish, S. (1980). *Is there a text in this class? The authority of interpretive communities.* Cambridge, MA: Harvard University Press.

Fitzgerald, J., & Spiegel, D.L. (1986). Textual cohesion and coherence in children's writing. *Research in the Teaching of English, 20*(3), 263–280.

Flower, L., & Hayes, J.R. (1981). A cognitive process theory of writing. *College Composition and Communication, 32*(4), 365–387. doi:10.2307/356600

Fosnot, C.T. (Ed.). (1996). *Constructivism: Theory, perspectives, and practice.* New York: Teachers College Press.

Foucault, M. (1997). *Essential works of Foucault: 1954–1984: Vol. 1. Ethics: Subjectivity and truth* (P. Rabinow, Ed.; R. Hurley et al., Trans.). New York: New.

Freire, P. (1993). *Pedagogy of the oppressed* (Rev. ed.; M.B. Ramos, Trans.). New York: Continuum. (Original work published 1970)

Freire, P., & Macedo, D.P. (1995). A dialogue: Culture, language, and race. *Harvard Educational Review, 65*(3), 377–402.

Gardner, H. (1985). *The mind's new science: A history of the cognitive revolution.* New York: Basic.

Gavelek, J., & Bresnahan, P. (2009). Ways of meaning making: Sociocultural perspectives on reading comprehension. In S.E. Israel & G.G. Duffy (Eds.), *Handbook of research on reading comprehension* (pp. 140–176). New York: Routledge.

Gee, J.P. (1990). *Social linguistics and literacies: Ideology in Discourses.* New York: Falmer.

Gee, J.P. (1996). *Social linguistics and literacies: Ideology in Discourses* (2nd ed.). Bristol, PA: Taylor & Francis.

Gee, J.P. (1999). *An introduction to Discourse analysis: Theory and method.* New York: Routledge.

Gee, J.P. (2004). Reading as situated language: A sociocognitive perspective. In R.B. Ruddell & N.J. Unrau (Eds.), *Theoretical models and processes of reading* (5th ed., pp. 116–132). Newark, DE: International Reading Association. (Reprinted from *Journal of Adolescent & Adult Literacy*, 2001, *44*(8), 714–725)

Gee, J.P. (2012). *Social linguistics and literacies: Ideology in Discourses* (4th ed.). New York: Routledge.

Geertz, C. (1973). *The interpretation of cultures.* New York: Basic.

Gergen, K.J. (1985). The social constructionist movement in modern psychology. *American Psychologist, 40*(3), 266–275. doi:10.1037/0003-066X.40.3.266

Gergen, K.J. (2002). Beyond the empiricist/constructionist divide in social psychology. *Personality and Social Psychology Review, 6*(3), 188–191. doi:10.1207/S15327957PSPR0603_2

Glaser, B.G., & Strauss, A.L. (1967). *The discovery of grounded theory: Strategies for qualitative research.* Chicago: Aldine.

Goodman, K.S. (1967). Reading: A psycholinguistic guessing game. *Journal of the Reading Specialist, 6*(4), 126–135. doi:10.1080/19388076709556976

Goody, J. (1977). *The domestication of the savage mind.* New York: Cambridge University Press.

Gorard, S. (2004). Sceptical or clerical? Theory as a barrier to the combination of research methods. *Journal of Educational Enquiry, 5*(1), 1–21.

Gough, P.B. (1976). One second of reading. In H. Singer & R.B. Ruddell (Eds.), *Theoretical models and processes of reading* (2nd ed., pp. 509–535). Newark, DE: International Reading Association. (Reprinted from *Visible Language*, 1972, *6*(4), 291–320)

Gough, P.B. (1985). One second of reading: Postscript. In H. Singer & R.B. Ruddell (Eds.),

Theoretical models and processes of reading (3rd ed., pp. 687–688). Newark, DE: International Reading Association.
Grosz, E. (1994). A thousand tiny sexes: Feminism and rhizomatics. In C.V. Boundas & D. Olkowski (Eds.), *Gilles Deleuze and the theater of philosophy* (pp. 187–210). New York: Routledge. (Reprinted from *Topoi*, 1993, *12*(2), 167–179)
Guthrie, J.T., & Wigfield, A. (Eds.). (1997). *Reading engagement: Motivating readers through integrated instruction*. Newark, DE: International Reading Association.
Guthrie, J.T., & Wigfield, A. (2000). Engagement and motivation in reading. In M.L. Kamil, P.B. Mosenthal, P.D. Pearson, & R. Barr (Eds.), *Handbook of reading research* (Vol. 3, pp. 403–422). Mahwah, NJ: Erlbaum.
Habermas, J. (1989). *The structural transformation of the public sphere: An inquiry into a category of bourgeois society* (T. Burger, Trans.). Cambridge, MA: MIT Press.
Hagood, M.C. (2004). A rhizomatic cartography of adolescents, popular culture, and constructions of self. In K.M. Leander & M. Sheehy (Eds.), *Spatializing literacy research and practice* (pp. 143–160). New York: Peter Lang.
Halliday, M.A.K. (1978). *Language as social semiotic: The social interpretation of language and meaning*. London: Edvard Arnold.
Havelock, E.A. (1982). *The literate revolution in Greece and its cultural consequences*. Princeton, NJ: Princeton University Press.
Hayes, J.R. (2004). A new framework for understanding cognition and affect in writing. In R.B. Ruddell & N.J. Unrau (Eds.), *Theoretical models and processes of reading* (5th ed., pp. 1399–1430). Newark, DE: International Reading Association. (Reprinted from *The science of writing: Theories, methods, individual differences, and applications*, pp. 1–27, by C.M. Levy & S. Ransdell, Eds.,1996, Mahwah, NJ: Erlbaum)
Heath, S.B. (1983). *Ways with words: Language, life, and work in communities and classrooms*. New York: Cambridge University Press.
Heath, S.B. (2004). The children of Trackton's children: Spoken and written language in social change. In R.B. Ruddell & N.J. Unrau (Eds.), *Theoretical models and processes of reading* (5th ed., pp. 187–209). Newark, DE: International Reading Association. (Reprinted from *Cultural psychology: Essays on comparative human development*, pp. 496–519, by J.W. Stigler, R.A., Shweder, & G. Herdt, Eds., 1990, New York: Cambridge University Press)
Hodge, R., & Kress, G. (1988). *Social semiotics*. New York: Cornell University Press.
Holmes, J.A. (1953). *The substrata-factor theory of reading*. Berkeley, CA: California Book.
Holmes, J.A. (1970). The substrata-factor theory of reading: Some experimental evidence. In H. Singer & R.B. Ruddell (Eds.), *Theoretical models and processes of reading* (pp. 187–197). Newark, DE: International Reading Association. (Reprinted from *New frontiers in reading*, by J.A. Figurel, Ed., 1960, New York: Scholastic Magazines)
hooks, b. (1990). *Yearning: Race, gender, and cultural politics*. Boston: South End.
Horkheimer, M. (2002). Traditional and critical theory. In C. Calhoun, J. Gerteis, J. Moody, S. Pfaff, K. Schmidt, & I. Virk (Eds.), *Classical sociological theory* (pp. 304–318). Malden, MA: Blackwell.
Janks, H. (2000). Domination, access, diversity and design: A synthesis for critical literacy education. *Educational Review, 52*(2), 175–186. doi:10.1080/713664035
Jewitt, C., & Kress, G. (Eds.). (2003). *Multimodal literacy*. New York: Peter Lang.
Jiménez, R.T., Smith, P.H., & Martínez-León, N. (2003). Freedom and form: The language and literacy practices of two Mexican schools. *Reading Research Quarterly, 38*(4), 488–508. doi:10.1598/RRQ.38.4.4
Johnson, R.B., & Onwuegbuzie, A.J. (2004). Mixed methods research: A research paradigm whose time has come. *Educational Researcher, 33*(7), 14–26. doi:10.3102/0013189X033007014
Johnson, R.B., Onwuegbuzie, A.J., & Turner, L.A. (2007). Toward a definition of mixed methods research. *Journal of Mixed Methods Research, 1*(2), 112–133. doi:10.1177/1558689806298224
Kintsch, W., & van Dijk, T.A. (1978). Toward a model of text comprehension and production. *Psychological Review, 85*(5), 363–394. doi:10.1037/0033-295X.85.5.363
Kolers, P.A. (1970). Three stages of reading. In H. Levin & J.P. Williams (Eds.), *Basic studies on reading* (pp. 90–118). New York: Basic.
Kress, G. (1997). *Before writing: Rethinking the paths to literacy*. New York: Routledge.
Kress, G. (2009). What is mode? In C. Jewitt (Ed.), *The Routledge handbook of multimodal analysis* (pp. 54–67). New York: Routledge.
Kress, G., & van Leeuwen, T. (1996). *Reading images: The grammar of visual design*. New York: Routledge.
Kucer, S.B. (1985). The making of meaning: Reading and writing as parallel processes. *Written Communication, 2*(3), 317–336. doi:10.1177/0741088385002003006
Kucer, S.B. (2001). *Dimensions of literacy: A conceptual base for teaching reading and writing in school settings*. Mahwah, NJ: Erlbaum.
Kuhn, T.S. (1996). *The structure of scientific revolutions* (3rd ed.). Chicago: University of Chicago Press.
LaBerge, D., & Samuels, S.J. (1976). Toward a theory of automatic information processing in reading. In H. Singer & R.B. Ruddell (Eds.), *Theoretical models and processes of reading* (2nd ed., pp. 548–579). Newark, DE: International Reading Association. (Reprinted from *Cognitive Psychology*, 1974, 6(2), 293–323)

Lankshear, C., & Knobel, M. (2006). *New literacies: Everyday practices and classroom learning* (2nd ed.). New York: Open University Press.

Lankshear, C., & McLaren, P.L. (Eds.). (1993). *Critical literacy: Politics, praxis, and the postmodern*. Albany: State University of New York Press.

Leander, K.M., Phillips, N.C., & Taylor, K.H. (2010). The changing social spaces of learning: Mapping new mobilities. *Review of Research in Education, 34*(1), 329–394. doi:10.3102/0091732X09358129

Leander, K.M., & Rowe, D.W. (2006). Mapping literacy spaces in motion: A rhizomatic analysis of a classroom literacy performance. *Reading Research Quarterly, 41*(4), 428–460. doi:10.1598/RRQ.41.4.2

Lewison, M., & Leland, C. (2002). Critical literacy. In B.J. Guzzetti (Ed.), *Literacy in America: An encyclopedia of history, theory and practice* (Vol. 1, pp. 108–111). Santa Barbara, CA: ABC-CLIO.

Luke, A. (2000). Critical literacy in Australia: A matter of context and standpoint. *Journal of Adolescent & Adult Literacy, 43*(5), 448–461.

Luria, A.R. (1976). *Cognitive development: Its cultural and social foundations*. Cambridge, MA: Harvard University Press.

Marcuse, H. (1964). *One-dimensional man: Studies in the ideology of advanced industrial society*. London: Routledge & Kegan Paul.

Marsh, J. (2006). Popular culture in the literacy curriculum: A Bourdieuan analysis. *Reading Research Quarterly, 41*(2), 160–174. doi:10.1598/RRQ.41.2.1

Maxwell, J.A., & Loomis, D.M. (2003). Mixed methods design: An alternative approach. In A. Tashakkori & C. Teddlie (Eds.), *Handbook of mixed methods in social and behavioral research* (pp. 241–271). Thousand Oaks, CA: Sage.

McPherson, F. (Ed.). (2012). Theory. In *Oxford English Dictionary*. New York: Oxford University Press. Retrieved July 19, 2012, from www.oed.com/view/Entry/200431?rskey=MTujDX&result=1

Miller, G.A. (2003). The cognitive revolution: A historical perspective. *Trends in Cognitive Sciences, 7*(3), 141–144. doi:10.1016/S1364-6613(03)00029-9

Mitchell, G.J., & Cody, W.K. (1993). The role of theory in qualitative research. *Nursing Science Quarterly, 6*(4), 170–178. doi:10.1177/089431849300600405

Morrell, E. (2008). *Critical literacy and urban youth: Pedagogies of access, dissent, and liberation*. New York: Routledge.

Morrell, E. (2009). Critical research and the future of literacy education. *Journal of Adolescent & Adult Literacy, 53*(2), 96–104. doi:10.1598/JAAL.53.2.1

Nash-Webber, B. (1975). The role of semantics in automatic speech understanding. In D.G. Bobrow & A. Collins (Eds.), *Representation and understanding: Studies in cognitive science* (pp. 351–382). New York: Academic.

New London Group. (1996). A pedagogy of multiliteracies: Designing social futures. *Harvard Educational Review, 66*(1), 60–92.

Ong, W.J. (1982). *Orality and literacy: The technologizing of the word*. New York: Methuen.

Pekrun, R. (2006). The control–value theory of achievement emotions: Assumptions, corollaries, and implications for educational research and practice. *Educational Psychology Review, 18*(4), 315–341. doi:10.1007/s10648-006-9029-9

Pekrun, R. (2009). Emotions at school. In K.R. Wentzel & A. Wigfield (Eds.), *Handbook of motivation at school* (pp. 575–604). New York: Routledge.

Pelto, P.J., & Pelto, G.H. (1978). *Anthropological research: The structure of inquiry*. New York: Cambridge University Press. doi:10.1017/CBO9780511607776

Piaget, J. (1977). *The development of thought: Equilibration of cognitive structures* (A. Rosin, Trans.). New York: Viking.

Piaget, J., & Inhelder, B. (1969). *The psychology of the child* (H. Weaver, Trans.). New York: Basic Books.

Popper, K. (2002). *The logic of scientific discovery*. New York: Routledge. (Original work published 1959)

Portes, P.R., & Salas, S. (Eds.). (2011). *Vygotsky in 21st century society: Advances in cultural historical theory and praxis with non-dominant communities*. New York: Peter Lang.

Rosenblatt, L.M. (1978). *The reader, the text, the poem: The transactional theory of the literary work*. Carbondale: Southern Illinois University Press.

Ruddell, R.B., Ruddell, M.R., & Singer, H. (Eds.). (1994). *Theoretical models and processes of reading* (4th ed.). Newark, DE: International Reading Association.

Ruddell, R.B., & Speaker, R.B. (1985). The interactive reading process: A model. In H. Singer & R.B. Ruddell (Eds.), *Theoretical models and processes of reading* (3rd ed., pp. 751–793). Newark, DE: International Reading Association.

Ruddell, R.B., & Unrau, N.J. (1994). Reading as a meaning-construction process: The reader, the text, and the teacher. In R.B. Ruddell, M.R. Ruddell, & H. Singer (Eds.), *Theoretical models and processes of reading* (4th ed., pp. 996–1056). Newark, DE: International Reading Association.

Ryan, R.M., & Deci, E.L. (2000). Self-determination theory and the facilitation of intrinsic motivation, social development, and well-being. *American Psychologist, 55*(1), 68–78. doi:10.1037/0003-066X.55.1.68

Samuels, S.J. (1977). Introduction to theoretical models of reading. In W. Otto, C. Peters, & N. Peters (Eds.), *Reading problems: A multidisciplinary perspective* (pp. 7–41). Reading, MA: Addison-Wesley.

Scribner, S., & Cole, M. (1981). *The psychology of literacy*. Cambridge, MA: Harvard University Press.

Shannon, P. (1989). Paradigmatic diversity within the reading research community. *Journal of Reading Behavior, 21*(2), 97–107.

Singer, H. (1994). The substrata-factor theory of reading. In R.B. Ruddell, M.R. Ruddell, & H. Singer (Eds.), *Theoretical models and processes of reading* (4th ed., pp. 895–927). Newark, DE: International Reading Association.

Singer, H., & Ruddell, R.B. (Eds.). (1970). *Theoretical models and processes of reading*. Newark, DE: International Reading Association.

Singer, H., & Ruddell, R.B. (Eds.). (1976). *Theoretical models and processes of reading* (2nd ed.). Newark, DE: International Reading Association.

Singer, H., & Ruddell, R.B. (Eds.). (1985). *Theoretical models and processes of reading* (3rd ed.). Newark, DE: International Reading Association.

Skinner, B.F. (1957). *Verbal behavior*. New York: Appleton-Century-Crofts.

Spivey, N.N. (1997). *The constructivist metaphor: Reading, writing, and the making of meaning*. San Diego, CA: Academic.

Strauss, A., & Corbin, J. (1990). *Basics of qualitative research: Grounded theory procedures and techniques*. Newbury Park, CA: Sage.

Street, B.V. (1984). *Literacy in theory and practice*. New York: Cambridge University Press.

Street, B.V. (1995). *Social literacies: Critical approaches to literacy in development, ethnography and education*. New York: Longman.

Sulzby, E. (1994). Children's emergent reading of favorite storybooks: A developmental study. In R.B. Ruddell, M.R. Ruddell, & H. Singer (Eds.), *Theoretical models and processes of reading* (4th ed., pp. 244–280). Newark, DE: International Reading Association. (Reprinted from *Reading Research Quarterly*, 1985, *20*(4), 458–481)

Symonds, J.E., & Gorard, S. (2010). Death of mixed methods? Or the rebirth of research as a craft. *Evaluation & Research in Education*, 23(2), 121–136. doi:10.1080/09500790.2010.483514

Thorndike, E.L. (1913). *Educational psychology: Vol. 2. The psychology of learning*. New York: Teachers College Press.

van Leeuwen, T. (2005). *Introducing social semiotics*. New York: Routledge.

Vygotsky, L.S. (1978). *Mind in society: The development of higher psychological processes* (M. Cole, V. John-Steiner, S. Scribner, & E. Souberman, Eds. & Trans.). Cambridge, MA: Harvard University Press.

Vygotsky, L.S. (1986). *Thought and language* (Rev. ed.; A. Kozulin, Trans.). Cambridge, MA: MIT Press.

Weber, R. (1970). First-graders' use of grammatical context in reading. In H. Levin & J.P. Williams (Eds.), *Basic studies on reading* (pp. 147–163). New York: Basic.

Wigfield, A., & Eccles, J.S. (2000). Expectancy–value theory of achievement motivation. *Contemporary Educational Psychology*, 25(1), 68–81. doi:10.1006/ceps.1999.1015

Wigfield, A., Guthrie, J.T., Perencevich, K.C., Taboada, A., Klauda, S.L., McRae, A., et al. (2008). Role of reading engagement in mediating effects of reading comprehension instruction on reading outcomes. *Psychology in the Schools*, 45(5), 432–445. doi:10.1002/pits.20307

Wittgenstein, L. (1953). *Philosophical investigations* (G.E.M. Anscombe, Trans.). Oxford, UK: Basil Blackwell.

CHAPTER 3

Synergy in Literacy Research Methodology

Marla H. Mallette, Binghamton University*

Nell K. Duke, University of Michigan*

Stephanie L. Strachan, Chad H. Waldron, and Lynne M. Watanabe, Michigan State University

Although a single research study can make a difference (Russell, 1961; Shanahan & Neuman, 1997), it typically takes a long line or lines of research to significantly deepen understanding of a phenomenon or to meaningfully inform practice (Duke & Martin, 2011; Shanahan, 2002). Thus, rather than perpetuating divisions in the field, we argue that lines of research work best when we marshal different methodologies to address the research topic or the problem of practice. The complexity of literacy teaching, learning, and development is such that no single research methodology is sufficient for understanding. Rather, insights garnered through one methodological approach must inform the pursuit of questions by another, and so on, creating a synergy of methodology over time (Duke & Mallette, 2004, 2011).

We begin this chapter with an overview of the rich array of methodologies that have been brought to bear in literacy research. We then present three insights about literacy teaching and learning that have resulted from research of several methodologies, each study building on the next. In the third section of the chapter, we discuss how theoretical constructs can develop through the application of research of multiple methodologies, taking emergent literacy theory as a case. We conclude with recommendations for enabling and encouraging synergy across research methodologies.

An Overview of Literacy Research Methodologies

In perusing research methods textbooks (e.g., Creswell, 2012; Johnson & Christensen, 2012), we found that the most common categorizations of research tend to be quantitative, qualitative, and mixed. However, like Shavelson and Towne (2002), we view this categorization approach as problematic:

> It is common to see quantitative and qualitative methods described as being fundamentally different modes of inquiry—even as being different paradigms embodying quite different epistemologies (Howe, 1988; Phillips, 1987). We regard this view as mistaken. Because we see quantitative and qualitative scientific inquiry as being epistemologically quite similar (King, Keohane, and Verba, 1994; Howe and Eisenhart, 1990), and as we recognize that both can be pursued rigorously, we do

> not distinguish between them as being different forms of inquiry. We believe the distinction is outmoded, and it does not map neatly in a one-to-one fashion onto any group or groupings of disciplines. (p. 19)

Instead, we suggest more nuanced categorization systems that emphasize the type of insights that methodologies can provide. One example of such a categorization system is to group methodologies by those that primarily tell us what is, what was, what happens when, and what can be. In Table 1, we group 15 research methodologies into these four categories (recognizing that in some cases, some could fall within another category instead or as well depending on the focus of the study). Each of the 15 specific methodologies is regularly employed in literacy research. Table 1 includes recent examples gleaned from the methodology described. An important point to make is that many studies in literacy research employ combinations of these methodologies within a single study. This is true, by definition, of mixed research, but it is also true of research that would not fit that designation. For example, an experimental study might employ verbal protocols as an outcome measure, or a case study may also be historical. In our view, this is not problematic but, in fact, to be encouraged, as it provides us with a greater range of tools to address the complex questions and problems facing our field.

Insights About Literacy Gained From Multiple Methodologies

Keeping the vast array of literacy research methodologies and the kinds of questions that they can address in mind, we now turn to three specific examples of important insights in the field of literacy research that have resulted from synergy across studies employing different methodologies. When multiple methodological approaches inform the formulation of new questions, and therefore the methodological design of future studies, our understanding of the complexities of literacy has the potential to expand in ways that relying on only one methodology does not allow.

Insight 1: Developing Children's Phonological Awareness Improves Word Reading

Current understanding in the field of literacy is that developing children's phonological awareness skills improves their ability to read words (e.g., Ehri et al., 2001; National Institute of Child Health and Human Development, 2000). To what researcher or study can we attribute this important insight? No one study or methodology can account for this knowledge; rather, multiple studies and methodologies, including research using technologies, linguistic analysis, correlational research, experimental studies, and quantitative meta-analysis, enabled this insight.

The development of this insight began with research seeking to describe children's phonological knowledge. Hoping to ascertain the conditions underlying individuals' perceptions of the speech stream, Liberman, Cooper, Shankweiler,

Table 1. Some Key Research Methodologies Used in Literacy Research

Research Methodology	Description[a]	A Recent Example of Findings Gleaned From This Methodology
What Is?		
Case study	"Case studies seek to describe naturally occurring phenomena. These studies often focus on a single or small number of cases, such as one classroom or three reading groups at one grade level. Researchers typically identify themes or patterns, rather than making claims about cause–effect relationships."[a]	A study of two Sunni madrassahs in Mauritius has revealed that contrary to stereotype, local vernacular literacies and secular identities were both enacted in and influenced by practices within the madrassahs.[b]
Content analysis	"Content analysis is a methodology for examining the content of something, such as instruction (e.g., how much instructional time is devoted to vocabulary instruction) or texts (e.g., what kinds of text, and in what proportions, are included in basal readers). Content analysis is more about the *what* in language, whereas discourse analysis is more about the *how* with language."[a]	A study of available print materials and activities involving written language in second-, third-, and fourth-grade classrooms showed an average of 1 minute per day of instructional time with informational text in grade 2 and 16 minutes per day in grades 3 and 4.[c]
Correlational	"This kind of research examines relationships among variables. Researchers often conduct these studies when they are interested in causes and effects but are unable to control or alter the variables. For example, correlational research might examine the relationship between exposure to lead paint and reading difficulties."[a]	A study finds that adults' morphological awareness, syntactic awareness, and vocabulary knowledge are all predictive of their reading comprehension, with syntactic awareness predicting both directly and indirectly through vocabulary knowledge.[d]
Discourse analysis	"This methodology tries to gain insight into the structures and meanings that underlie conversations and written texts. Researchers examine previously or newly recorded texts and develop systems for uncovering patterns in the texts."[a]	A study examined college students' instant messages and found 15 instant-messaging features used at specific reported frequencies; many paralinguistic cues were employed.[e]
Ethnography	"Ethnography is a specific type of case study. Like case study research, ethnographic research explores phenomena by looking closely at specific examples. This kind of research typically involves extended, intense observations and emphasizes cultural contexts. Researchers often attempt to represent the perspectives of insiders."[f]	A study of three Sudanese refugee families over 18 months revealed a variety of insights regarding the role of television in their lives, including the role that it played in helping the families learn about the U.S. context, as well as staying connected with their heritage culture.[g] *(continued)*

Table 1. Some Key Research Methodologies Used in Literacy Research (*Continued*)

Research Methodology	Description[a]	A Recent Example of Findings Gleaned From This Methodology
Neuroimaging	"This kind of research tries to answer questions about neurological structure and/or function. Researchers examine images of the brain and brain activity. These studies are characterized by the use of specialized medical equipment and processes, such as electroencephalography or functional magnetic resonance imaging."[f]	A study found that children with word-reading difficulties showed less neurophysiological activity in some parts of the brain and more neurophysiological activity in other parts of the brain as compared with typically performing readers.[h]
Survey	"Survey research usually elicits reports from participants about themselves. The purpose of this kind of research is usually to understand something about the larger group to which the participants belong. For example, researchers might survey 100 kindergarten teachers across a state to learn about the beliefs of the kindergarten teachers in that state. This kind of research may involve different kinds of interactions, such as face-to-face or telephone interviews and computerized or mailed surveys."[i]	A study surveyed high school teachers about their preparation for teaching writing and their writing instruction and assessment. Included in the findings was that most teachers did not believe they were adequately prepared to teach writing and that almost half did not assign at least one multiparagraph piece of writing per month.[j]
Verbal protocol analysis	"Verbal protocols, also referred to as think-aloud studies, typically gather information about people's thought processes. Researchers often ask participants to complete a specific task, such as reading a book, and report what they are thinking. Participants from second grade to adulthood have participated in verbal protocol research."[i]	A study of the processes prompted by the graphics in informational text read by second graders revealed 17 distinct processes, many similar to those used with written text but others unique to graphics.[k]
What Was?		
Historical	"In historical research, researchers attempt to address a question about the past. They examine artifacts from or about the time period, such as diaries, photographs, court records, or legal documents. Researchers may also interview people associated with the event or topic. This kind of research often searches for patterns or themes that might inform current issues. For example, a researcher might examine past educational policies for the purpose of revising or creating present-day policy initiatives."[f]	A study examined the growth and impact of reading groups (e.g., book clubs), libraries, and other book-based institutions in Georgian England and found that they greatly increased the number and breadth of the reading public and made long-lasting contributions to literary life.[l]

Research Methodology	Description[a]	A Recent Example of Findings Gleaned From This Methodology
What Happens When?		
Experimental and quasi-experimental	"These designs investigate cause–effect relationships. Researchers typically identify a focus, such as the use of a particular instructional approach, and measure its outcomes. Researchers attempt to eliminate alternative explanations for outcomes by creating groups of participants who differ in only one way—for example, in receiving or not receiving a particular instructional approach. In experiments, researchers typically create groups by randomly assigning participants. In contrast, researchers use groups that already exist for quasi-experiments."[f]	A study found that collaborative strategic reading, a specific approach to reading comprehension instruction, improves the reading comprehension of seventh- and eighth-grade students as compared with business-as-usual instruction in English/language arts classrooms.[m]
Meta-analysis	"Researchers use this methodology to synthesize the results of previous research. Researchers systematically collect studies that have addressed the same or similar questions, then conduct statistical analyses to identify trends across the collected studies. Quantitative meta-analyses often focus on the relative magnitudes of outcomes, such as the average effect of a particular instructional intervention."[i]	A study examined the impact of morphological instruction on literacy skills across 22 studies and found that morphological instruction improves reading, spelling, vocabulary, and morphological skill regardless of age group studied, particularly for less skilled readers and when part of a broader intervention.[n]
Single-subject experimental	"In this design, individuals are (or an individual is) studied in such a way that they each comprise their own comparison group. For example, in an ABA withdrawal design, repeated baseline assessments are administered (A), then an intervention is introduced and the subject assessed repeatedly again (B), and finally, the intervention is withdrawn and the subject assessed additional times (A). Differences in A and B suggest a possible impact of the intervention."[i]	A study used a multiple-baseline design to examine the impact of a computer-based sight-word reading intervention on the sight-word reading of a sixth-grade student with an autism spectrum disorder and found that the impact was both positive and maintained.[o] *(continued)*

Table 1. Some Key Research Methodologies Used in Literacy Research (*Continued*)

Research Methodology	Description[a]	A Recent Example of Findings Gleaned From This Methodology
What Can Be?		
Formative or design	"In this methodology, data are collected systematically for the purpose of informing design or practice to reach specified goals. Often, researchers and teachers work together to implement an instructional approach, investigate factors that might influence its outcomes, modify the approach to account for what they have discovered, and implement the revised instructional approach. This implement-investigate-and-revise process might continue for several rounds or until the original goal is achieved."[f]	A study aimed to improve understanding of how word selection and word organization might facilitate vocabulary acquisition among preschool children through the iterative implementation and analysis of a specific vocabulary intervention in preschool classrooms.[p]
Instrument development	This methodology explores what can be measured and how. "These studies examine the reliability and validity of assessments, attitude surveys, and other research tools. Along with other activities, researchers typically give the assessment to a number of participants and then perform statistical analyses to examine its validity and reliability."[a]	A series of studies examined the validity, reliability, and effectiveness of a formative and summative assessment tool that provides computer-generated evaluations of the substantive content and expository quality of writing.[q]
Other		
Mixed	"Mixed methods research is the type of research in which a researcher or team of researchers combines elements of qualitative and quantitative research approaches (e.g., use of qualitative and quantitative viewpoints, data collection, analysis, inference techniques) for the broad purposes of breadth and depth of understanding and corroboration."[r]	A study examined both the quality and quantity of comprehension instruction in special education classrooms and found that these special education teachers rarely taught students complex strategies and seemed unaware of teaching techniques to develop students' comprehension.[s]

[a]From "10 Things Every Literacy Educator Should Know About Research," by N.K. Duke and N.M. Martin, 2011, *The Reading Teacher, 65*(1), p. 14.
[b]"Multilingual Language and Literacy Practices and Social Identities in Sunni Madrassahs in Mauritius: A Case Study," by A.M.A. Owodally, 2011, *Reading Research Quarterly, 46*(2), 134–155.

[c]"Availability and Use of Informational Texts in Second-, Third-, and Fourth-Grade Classrooms," by J. Jeong, J.S. Gaffney, and J. Choi, 2010, *Research in the Teaching of English*, *44*(4), 435–456.

[d]"The Relation of Morphological Awareness and Syntactic Awareness to Adults' Reading Comprehension: Is Vocabulary Knowledge a Mediating Variable?" by Y. Guo, A.D. Roehrig, and R.S. Williams, 2011, *Journal of Literacy Research*, *43*(2), 159–183.

[e]"Young People's Everyday Literacies: The Language Features of Instant Messaging," by C. Haas and P. Takayoshi (with B. Carr, K. Hudson, and R. Pollock), 2011, *Research in the Teaching of English*, *45*(4), 378–404.

[f]From Duke and Martin, p. 15.

[g]"Television, Language, and Literacy Practices in Sudanese Refugee Families: 'I Learned How to Spell English on Channel 18,'" by K.H. Perry and A.M. Moses, 2011, *Research in the Teaching of English*, *45*(3), 278–307.

[h]"The Timing and Strength of Regional Brain Activation Associated With Word Recognition in Children With Reading Difficulties," by R. Rezaie, P.G. Simos, J.M. Fletcher, J. Juranek, P.T. Cirino, Z. Li, et al., 2011, *Frontiers in Human Neuroscience*, *5*, article 00045.

[i]From Duke and Martin, p. 16.

[j]"Teaching Writing to High School Students: A National Survey," by S.A. Kiuhara, L.S. Hawken, and S. Graham, 2009, *Journal of Educational Psychology*, *101*(1), 136–160.

[k]"Picture This: Processes Prompted by Graphics in Informational Text," by R.R. Norman, 2010, *Literacy Teaching and Learning*, *14*(1/2), 1–39.

[l]*A Nation of Readers: The Lending Library in Georgian England*, by D. Allan, 2009, Chicago: University of Chicago Press.

[m]"Efficacy of Collaborative Strategic Reading With Middle School Students," by S. Vaughn, J.K. Klingner, E.A. Swanson, A.G. Boardman, G. Roberts, S.S. Mohammed, et al., 2011, *American Educational Research Journal*, *48*(4), 938–964.

[n]"The Effects of Morphological Instruction on Literacy Skills: A Systematic Review of the Literature," by P.N. Bowers, J.R. Kirby, and S.H. Deacon, 2010, *Review of Educational Research*, *80*(2), 144–179.

[o]"Extending Research on a Computer-Based Sight-Word Reading Intervention to a Student With Autism," by J.S. Yaw, C.H. Skinner, J. Parkhurst, C.M. Taylor, J. Booher, and K. Chambers, 2011, *Journal of Behavioral Education*, *20*(1), 44–54.

[p]"Developing Vocabulary and Conceptual Knowledge for Low-Income Preschoolers: A Design Experiment," by S.B. Neuman and J. Dwyer, 2011, *Journal of Literacy Research*, *43*(2), 103–129.

[q]"A New Formative Assessment Technology for Reading and Writing," by T.K. Landauer, K.E. Lochbaum, and S. Dooley, 2009, *Theory Into Practice*, *48*(1), 44–52.

[r]From "Toward a Definition of Mixed Method Research," by R.B. Johnson, A.J. Onwuegbuzie, and L.A. Turner, 2007, *Journal of Mixed Methods Research*, *1*(2), p. 123.

[s]"Teaching Reading in the 21st Century: A Glimpse at How Special Education Teachers Promote Reading Comprehension," by J.K. Klingner, J. Urbach, D. Golos, M. Brownell, and S. Menon, 2010, *Learning Disability Quarterly*, *33*(2), 59–74.

and Studdert-Kennedy (1967) engaged in research using the technologies of synthetic speech and spectrograms. At the Haskins Laboratories in New York, the researchers found that

> the acoustic cues for successive phonemes are intermixed in the sound stream to such an extent that definable segments of sound do not correspond to segments at the phoneme level. Moreover, the same phoneme is most commonly represented in different phonemic environments by sounds that are vastly different. (p. 432)

Therefore, as a perception task, it is difficult for children to identify individual phonemes within spoken words.

Building on this work, and using an alternative way to investigate children's phonological awareness, researchers analyzed children's early writing attempts to ascertain how children categorized sounds in the speech stream (e.g., Chomsky, 1970; Read, 1971). First, using a naturalistic design, Read conducted linguistic analyses of preschool children's written productions, with particular attention to their spelling, to better understand how children heard sounds within words. The children in this study had not received spelling instruction in their homes or preschools; they primarily attempted to represent the sounds they heard in relation to the names of the letters they knew. By analyzing the estimated spellings of children who had relatively limited letter-sound knowledge, Read hoped to determine which phonological differences the children were able to parse out, thereby revealing certain features of their phonological awareness. Read found common patterns throughout these spellings, concluding that the children were developing a systematic and logical understanding of the relationship between the speech stream and orthography.

In recognizing a limitation of his naturalistic study (i.e., the data were collected from children who spontaneously wrote on their own), Read (1975) built on his own work with a series of studies in which "the experiments typically employed an XAB paradigm, in which the subjects were given sound X and were then asked, 'Is X more like A or B?'" (p. 21). Read elicited knowledge from children with more diverse backgrounds and a greater age range to examine the consistency of the patterns found in his original study. Taken together and using different methodologies, his research supported the notion that children are able to categorize phonemes and identify phonological relationships.

Armed with a better grasp of young children's developing and systematic understanding of phonemic awareness, researchers designed correlational studies to investigate the potential relationship between students' phonological awareness and their ability to read words, while accounting for possible confounding factors (e.g., Cunningham, 1990; Ehri & Wilce, 1979; Share, Jorm, Maclean, & Matthews, 1984; Stahl & Murray, 1994; Uhry & Shepherd, 1993). For example, in a correlational study examining the relationship among 39 individual attributes and reading ability, Share and colleagues found that phonemic segmentation was the most consistent and significant attribute in predicting students' reading ability at the end of kindergarten and first grade. Similarly, in their research with first-grade students, Stanovich, Cunningham, and Feeman (1984) examined the relationship between reading comprehension and phonological awareness (among other constructs) and concluded at the end of the school year that phonological awareness was moderately and independently related to reading comprehension.

The understanding of the need for and development of phonological awareness through naturalistic and descriptive studies, along with the establishment of a strong and predictive relationship between phonological awareness and reading, provided a solid framework for research designed to investigate causation. Researchers have used experimental, quasi-experimental, and some mixed research designs to examine the effects of phonological awareness instruction on reading (e.g., Ball & Blachman, 1991; Bradley & Bryant, 1983; Ehri & Wilce, 1985; Lundberg, Frost, & Petersen, 1988; Treiman & Baron, 1983; Williams, 1980).

As one example of a quasi-experimental study, Lundberg and colleagues (1988) provided 235 preschool children with a training program designed to improve children's phonological awareness. The children had not received reading instruction prior to taking part in this eight-month program, nor did they receive any reading instruction while involved in the program. Consisting of metalinguistic games and exercises, the program statistically significantly improved children's phonological and phonemic awareness skills, such as rhyming and phonemic segmentation, as compared with the control group. Further, by following both the control and the experimental groups for several years, the researchers found that children who had received the phonological awareness training outperformed the control group on reading measures in the second grade.

Similarly, Ball and Blachman (1991) conducted an experimental study in which they randomly assigned 90 kindergartners from three urban public schools to receive (a) training in both letter-sound relationships and segmenting words into phonemes, (b) training in only letter-sound relationships, or (c) no intervention. After seven weeks, the researchers found that the group receiving both letter-sound training and instruction in phonemic segmentation statistically significantly outperformed students who only received letter-sound instruction, as well as the control group, on measures of spelling and early word reading. Overall, these studies have contributed to the field by demonstrating that phonological awareness can be taught to young students and that this instruction benefits their word reading.

With such a large mass of individual studies examining the impact of phonological awareness instruction on word reading, some researchers in the field began to ask questions regarding what the body of evidence as a whole says about the effects of phonological awareness instruction on children's word reading (e.g., Bus & van IJzendoorn, 1999; Ehri et al., 2001). To address these questions, a different methodology became appropriate: quantitative meta-analysis. In their quantitative meta-analysis, Ehri and colleagues (2001) examined 52 peer-reviewed studies and concluded that phonological awareness instruction significantly affects both the reading and spelling of early readers. The researchers found instruction in phonological awareness to be most effective when (a) instruction also included letters, (b) students learned in small groups, and (c) it did not make up the main or only focus of literacy teaching (e.g., instruction for 5 to 18 hours of the year was most beneficial). These results have helped us better understand that phonological awareness plays an important role in early reading instruction as well as the circumstances under which phonological awareness instruction is most effective.

Our current understanding of how developing children's phonological awareness improves their word reading arose over time as researchers built on the findings of one another, created new questions, and explored these inquiries through multiple methodologies.

Insight 2: Text Structure Instruction Improves Reading Comprehension

A variety of instructional factors influence students' reading comprehension development, such as discussions of text in class (e.g., McKeown, Beck, & Blake, 2009) and rich vocabulary instruction that includes a wide variety of words taught in meaningful contexts (e.g., Stahl & Nagy, 2006). Similar to our insights about phonological awareness, the insight that text structure instruction can improve reading comprehension originated through studies of various research methodologies.

Research on text structure is commonly recognized as beginning with a discourse analysis and experimental study published by Meyer in 1975 in a book entitled *The Organization of Prose and Its Effects on Memory*. This study examined the structure of texts, at the time referred to as their "content structure," and the ideas that readers recall from the text. As Meyer noted,

> structure variables have been demonstrated to have an influence on the learning and retention of information in lists of words, but little research has been done investigating the effects of structure variables on the learning and retention of information in normal text. (p. 1)

Meyer's (1975) study included 105 undergraduates enrolled in a psychology course at Cornell University, randomly divided into five 21-subject groupings. Each subject grouping read three different sets of long passages. In two sessions, a free-written recall and a recall with signaling words from the passage were implemented to test each subject grouping's capacity to recall the text based on the content structure. The content structure proved to have a definite impact on the recall of information within a text.

As literacy and language research entered the 1980s, Meyer, Brandt, and Bluth (1980) conducted a correlational study investigating the relationship between reading ability and use of text structure in reading comprehension. The participants were 102 ninth-grade students divided into reading proficiency groups, as determined by the SAT and a district-developed reading comprehension test. The researchers found a strong relationship between comprehension skills and use of text structure; stronger readers made greater use of text structure.

In a subsequent quasi-experimental study, McGee (1982) examined the comprehension of third- and fifth-grade good and poor readers. Students read 125-word passages with expository themes and provided oral recalls, which were audiorecorded for measurement of superordinate, subordinate, and total idea units recalled within each passage. Fifth-grade good readers demonstrated greater awareness of text structure and recalled more total and superordinate ideas than other groups, suggesting that use of text structure is facilitative of comprehension even for elementary-age readers.

Research demonstrating the importance of text structures in proficient reading led to research investigating whether teaching readers to use text structure improves comprehension. A series of quasi-experimental and experimental studies addressing this question were conducted throughout the 1980s. For example, a quasi-experimental study by Taylor (1982) investigated the impact of teaching fifth graders to attend to text structure and verbalize a macrostructure for expository text. Specifically, the experimental group used a series of summarization tasks focused on text structure. The control group received more conventional reading instruction, with traditional comprehension questions to be completed after reading an expository text. Taylor concluded that instruction in text structure improved understanding of text organization and recall of text ideas.

Shortly afterward, Taylor and Beach (1984) published an experimental study examining the effect of seven weeks of text structure instruction on seventh-grade students in the context of social studies textbooks. The experimental treatment group received seven weeks of instruction in text structure, which improved "students' recall for relatively unfamiliar social studies material" (p. 143).

Around this same time, building on the findings of Meyer (1975), Taylor (1982), and others, Englert and Hiebert (1984) shed further light on the relation of structure knowledge to reading comprehension. Their study involved readers of two age groups (third and sixth grade), three reading ability levels, and four text structures (comparison/contrast, description, enumeration, sequence), with a measure focusing on how well students could distinguish statements related to the text from those that were unrelated. Again, older readers and more skilled readers were more attuned to text structure, and they were better able to distinguish statements that were related to the text from those that were unrelated. The researchers also found some differences in performance patterns for different text structures, which was an important point for the field. This study further motivated research on instructional interventions around text structure.

Building on Englert and Hiebert's (1984) and Taylor and Beach's (1984) research, Armbruster, Anderson, and Ostertag (1987) designed an experimental study to investigate the impact of providing seventh graders with instruction in a specific text structure—problem/solution—and use of a hierarchical summary procedure with social studies text. As compared with a group receiving instruction in answering questions after reading social studies material as well as a business-as-usual control, the intervention was effective at improving students' text comprehension. The major findings of these quasi-experimental and experimental studies in the 1980s involved various contexts for using text structure to improve reading comprehension. Studies using text structure instruction with various instructional audiences continue today (e.g., Gaddy, Bakken, & Fulk, 2008).

Now into the 21st century, a variety of methodologies are being used to deepen understanding of the role of text structure in reading comprehension. For example, Kendeou and van den Broek (2007) designed a study "to investigate the effects of readers' prior knowledge, as well as text structure, and the possible interaction of the two, online—that is, during comprehension of text" (p. 1568). This study employed verbal protocols, as used by Meyer (1975), as well as a quasi-experimental design. The findings revealed an interaction between college students' prior knowledge and use of text structure when reading.

Teaching students to recognize and understand text structure improves reading comprehension. This insight has been developed through studies of several different research methodologies, including discourse analysis, verbal protocols, correlational studies, quasi-experimental research, and experimental research. Collectively, these studies have provided us with another set of instructional practices to support the development of reading comprehension.

Insight 3: Teaching a Process Approach to Writing Fosters Writing Development

The complex definition and multifaceted understanding of a process approach to writing has evolved over time. Pritchard and Honeycutt (2006) explained, "Today, most researchers of the process model recognize that it involves both procedural knowledge and many other kinds of strategies that can be nurtured and directly taught" (p. 276). Additionally, the writing process is an act of problem solving that is recursive in nature. As writers develop, they come to understand and employ procedural, strategic knowledge in more efficient and automatized ways (Pritchard & Honeycutt, 2006). More specifically, Graham and Sandmel (2011) have delineated the following fundamental principles of the process writing approach:

> Students engage in cycles of planning (setting goals, generating ideas, organizing ideas), translating (putting a writing plan into action), and reviewing (evaluating, editing, revising). They write for real purposes and audiences, with some of their writing projects occurring over an extended period of time. Students' ownership of their writing is stressed, as is self-reflection and evaluation. Students work together collaboratively, and teachers create a supportive and nonthreatening writing environment. (p. 396)

The current understanding of process writing and the nature of implementing a process model of writing to foster writing development derive from the synergy of writing research over time and across methodologies.

Emig's (1971) case study of 12th graders' composing processes is often referred to as the first empirical study of students' writing processes. The eight

16- and 17-year-old students participated in four individual sessions in which they talked about their own composing processes (i.e., verbal protocols). This enabled Emig to identify various components of composition and their role in the writing process. She also found the writing instruction within classrooms to be abstract, simplified, and teacher centered, thereby illustrating the need for writing instruction that recognizes process and accounts for individual development and progress. Emig explained that one of the major contributions of this study was its "unique effort to utilize case studies for eliciting data about how students behave as they write" (p. 5). Making the composing process more visible contributed to the knowledge base regarding the writing process.

Building on Emig's (1971) work, Graves (1975) used a mixed design to examine and explain the writing process. Data collection and analysis occurred in four phases and included several methodological techniques. In phase 1, Graves analyzed the writing of 94 students, whereas phase 2 included observations of 14 students. In phase 3, he conducted interviews of 17 children, and phase 4 focused solely on a 7-year-old boy. Graves explained that

> this approach made it possible to follow findings from the several larger settings to an individual case and, conversely, from the case and/or small group findings to all-class profiles and to the entire group of seven year old children studied. (p. 229)

Concurrently, Shaughnessy (1977) implemented an informal content-analysis approach to examine the errors of 4,000 New York City College basic writing students. Through an examination of their writing, she found distinct patterns in their errors. Shaughnessy suggested that these errors reflected their "linguistic situation" (p. 121); the students were quite proficient in their language use, yet as writers, they were beginners. Shaughnessy's work broadened the construct of the writing process to include a sociocultural lens; however, early on, reference to her work focused on how categories of errors informed an understanding of writing as a process.

Flower and Hayes (1980) expanded on this pioneering work of studying the process of writing, with the aim to examine writing as a "problem-solving, cognitive process" (p. 22). They used verbal protocol methodology to examine the composing process of expert and novice adult writers. The novice writers were college students, and the experts were teachers of writing and rhetoric. The verbal protocol included the writers recording their composing process for the same problem. The problem consisted of a situation that participants needed to solve through their writing process (e.g., writing for a particular audience or assignment). Flower and Hayes found that composing is a problem-solving process that is influenced by purpose and goals. The purpose includes the audience and the assignment itself, whereas the goals include the reader, the persona, creating meaning, and the text. By identifying the importance of purpose and goals, reseachers found this problem-solving process to be describable and teachable. Students could be taught to think about the writing problem in a different way by attending to purpose and goals, which Flower and Hayes (1981) referred to as the "cognitive process theory of writing" (p. 365).

Perl and colleagues (1983) framed their research in this process theory of writing (Flower & Hayes, 1981) to explore the writing process from the perspective of the teacher. They conducted an ethnographic study of 10 teachers as they developed their own writing process. The researchers found that the teachers' level of implementation and understanding of a process approach influenced the process approach that they used within their own classrooms. Ethnography enabled Perl et al. to fully describe and account for the teachers' experiences as writers and as teachers of writing. This methodology enhanced the knowledge base about how writers enacted the writing process by also accounting for the teacher's perspective and suggesting important possible characteristics of writing pedagogy, including establishing a community of writers and providing models of a writing process.

Bereiter and Scardamalia (1984, 1987; Scardamalia, Bereiter, & Goelman, 1982) also built on the findings of Flower and Hayes (1980, 1981) to focus on factors that influence the writing process. They conducted several studies with writers of varying ages (from third graders to graduate students) to identify the cognitive and production factors that enhance or inhibit the writing process, particularly in relation to mentor texts. Bereiter and Scardamalia (1987; Scardamalia et al., 1982) employed verbal protocols and what they termed clinical-experimental actions within their work. Interviews were used in conjunction with written products and questionnaires. Students were assigned to groups writing different mentor texts (e.g., explicit lists, examples) to see their influence on the writing process. An individual's schema was found to influence the way that he or she implemented the writing process and the written products created. Additionally, the importance of the cognitive factors influencing a process approach to writing was emphasized.

In 1994, Needels and Knapp sought to learn whether adherence to a writing process pedagogy was associated with writing quality. They conducted a correlational study of 26 fourth-grade and 16 sixth-grade students to examine the relationship between writing quality and a process approach to teaching writing. Researchers used writing samples, daily teacher logs, observation coding forms, and classroom reports. Using regression analysis, they found that more than 40% of variance on writing quality was accounted for by adherence to a process approach model. Additionally, the implementation of the model did not have negative effects on writing mechanics. Further, the process approach implemented in this study incorporated skills and strategies, while emphasizing a sociocognitive perspective. The researchers built on the understandings illustrated through the case studies, verbal protocols, and ethnography by quantifying a relationship between writing quality and a process approach to writing.

Goldstein and Carr (1996) employed a survey to examine the relationship between writing quality and a process approach to writing. They looked at the National Assessment in Educational Progress writing data of fourth, eighth, and twelfth graders from 1992 in conjunction with a survey that each student filled out about the instructional writing practices of their teachers. The researchers found that the students of teachers who encouraged the elements of process writing were generally better writers and averaged higher scores on writing than the students of teachers who did not. Their findings support the relationship between instruction encouraging a process approach to writing and writing quality.

Experimental and quasi-experimental studies were conducted to study the effectiveness of process writing instruction on writing quality. Graham and Sandmel (2011) examined these findings in a meta-analysis, which included 29 studies published through 2009, that met their criteria for inclusion (i.e., experimental or quasi-experimental design; quasi-experimental included a pretest; control condition was defined; treatment was the process writing approach as defined; outcome measures were writing quality, motivation, or both; students were in grades 1–12; effect size could be calculated). The results of their meta-analysis revealed a statistically significant effect, demonstrating that with general education students, instruction using a process writing approach improved writing quality. However, no other significant effects were found in their meta-analysis (e.g., process writing instruction did not produce significant improvement in writing quality with struggling writers; process writing instruction also did not significantly improve motivation). With the limited number of studies that examined struggling writers ($n = 5$) and that measured motivation ($n = 7$), Graham and Sandmel's findings accentuate shortcomings in the quantity of experimental and quasi-experimental research that has investigated the effectiveness of process writing instruction. Yet, equally important, their meta-analysis highlighted weaknesses with the quality of these studies.

The findings from Graham and Sandmel's (2011) meta-analysis clearly underscore the need for more experimental and quasi-experimental research on the effectiveness of process writing instruction as well as the importance of returning to mixed research studies, such as those conducted by Emig (1971), Graves (1975), and Bereiter and Scardamalia (1987), to better understand student responses to writing process instruction.

Our knowledge of the process approach to writing as a complex combination of cognitive and social problem solving, procedural knowledge, and strategies, which can be influenced by instruction, developed over time and arose from studies of several different methodologies. The insights gained from each study have contributed to a greater understanding of process writing as a whole. However, work still needs to be done to better understand the factors, processes, and practices influencing process writing, and a variety of methodologies will undoubtedly be helpful to continued work in this area.

It is important to note that although a single study could influence practice or spark interest in a new area of research, insights about literacy phenomena develop over time and are strengthened and enriched when examined from lines of research through the use of multiple methodologies. For the insights detailed in this chapter, we purposely represented each line of research chronologically, by selecting representative studies, to demonstrate how individual studies build on one another. However, within each insight, the studies highlighted often represent a sample of an individual's or group's research, as scholars' lines of research often comprise numerous contributions across the span of their careers. Thus, it is important to consider that the richness of theories within these insights resulted from a synergy of research methodologies that is both linear and recursive.

As an illustrative example, the cognitive process theory of writing (Flower & Hayes, 1981), as described in insight 3, provided a theoretical framework for research on process writing. However, the development of this framework was grounded in the earlier research of scholars who subsequently expanded and investigated this construct. That is, Flower and Hayes credited Scardamalia and Bereiter in conducting "some of the most exciting and extensive research in this area," as they "have looked at the ways children cope with the cognitive demands of writing" (p. 374), through verbal protocol and experimental methodologies. Further, Flower and Hayes cited Perl's case study research in contributing to their understanding of writing as goal directed. In addition to these and numerous other studies, Flower's and Hayes's own prior studies, using verbal protocol methodologies, influenced the development of their cognitive theory of writing. Thus, synergy in the development of literacy constructs is dynamic; it is created linearly as newer research builds on the methodologies of previous research and recursively as scholars use studies and methodologies informed by their research in developing new research.

Understanding Theoretical Constructs of Literacy Through Multiple Methodologies

To examine how synergy of research methodologies informs broad literacy theories, we explore emergent literacy. Emergent literacy research has been, and continues to be, fraught with dissention among researchers (see, e.g., McGill-Franzen, 2010; Stanovich, 1990). Scholars have debated issues of methodology (e.g., what counts, or counts more, as research) and philosophy (e.g., development, or what is most important to develop). In addition, current scholarship on emergent literacy is often embedded in early literacy or literacy learning in early childhood, both of which take a broader focus on literacy from birth to age 8. Yaden, Rowe, and MacGillivray (2000) described emergent literacy as "an identifiable, though changing theoretical stance" (p. 445). The evolving and contested nature of emergent literacy theory makes it a rich example for our purposes. That is, the wide array of methodologies used in emergent literacy research provide compelling support for how multiple research methodologies advance theory.

Emergent Literacy

The construct of emergent literacy (Clay, 1966; Teale & Sulzby, 1986) marked an ideological shift away from the idea that reading development does not occur until a particular age when children are *ready* to read. Rather, emergent literacy theory posits that literacy develops from birth, with many important steps toward reading occurring in the years leading up to conventional reading and writing.

Methodologies in Emergent Literacy Research

To demonstrate the breadth of research methodologies that have contributed to understanding emergent literacy, this subsection focuses on the methodologies used in the research reviews conducted by Mason and Allen (1986) and Whitehurst and Lonigan (1998). These reviews are, of course, products of their time. Examining long-standing reviews allows us to see the range of research methodologies that were influential relatively early in the development of emergent literacy theory. Current research on emergent literacy is both diverse and voluminous. Consider, for example, that the *Handbook of Early Literacy Research* (Dickinson & Neuman, 2006; Neuman & Dickinson, 2003, 2011) has generated three comprehensive editions of research reviews published in the course of just seven years. Thus, with the proliferation of research in emergent literacy, more current reviews tend to focus on subtopics within emergent literacy.

Mason and Allen (1986) conducted a review of emergent literacy research to provide a conceptual understanding of emergent literacy, along with implications for instruction. They categorized the research into the following four areas: (1) social and linguistic contexts, (2) oral and written language, (3) emergent reading and writing skills and knowledge, and (4) instructional practices. Interestingly, they reflected on the importance of methodology:

> More descriptive than experimental research is reviewed. One reason is that emergent literacy represents a new perspective. Establishing this perspective involves the development of new constructs and linkages among causative factors, a step that is usually initiated with descriptive research techniques. In addition, a larger number of Emergent Literacy variables that affect later reading and writing success are being studied. These include oral language, story listening comprehension, and error patterns in early attempts to write and read. (p. 4)

Twelve years later, Whitehurst and Lonigan (1998) theorized that emergent literacy encompasses two distinct, yet related, domains (i.e., outside-in skills and inside-out skills), which they explained through a modified version of Whitehurst's (1996) theoretical model. It is important to note that Whitehurst and Lonigan recognized the limitations of their model, and that their model was not completely embraced in the field. Further, their notion of two distinct domains, and what constitutes each domain, remains unsettled. Whitehurst and Lonigan's review focused on: (a) addressing the multitude of skills, behaviors, and experiences of emergent literacy theory; and (b) the inclusivity of a range of methodologies used in emergent literacy research.

In juxtaposing these two reviews, it is evident that both include similar aspects of emergent literacy (i.e., context, oral and written language, book reading, emergent reading, emergent writing, skills, interventions), which still represent the areas reflected in recent work. For example, the first five sections of the latest edition of the *Handbook of Early Literacy Research* (Neuman & Dickinson, 2011) focus on these same topics: (1) developmental processes, (2) family and sociocultural contexts, (3) pedagogy, (4) interventions and professional development, and (5) policy.

Another similarity between the two reviews is in how they conceptualized and defined emergent literacy. Mason and Allen (1986) suggested that

> this area of study, which is becoming known as "emergent literacy," replaces the terms "reading readiness" and "early reading and writing." According to Teale and Sulzby (1986), the phrase "emergent literacy" was coined by Clay (1966). "Emergent" denotes the process of becoming, and "literacy" denotes the interrelatedness of writing and reading in young children's development. The study of emergent literacy represents "a new perspective which stresses that legitimate, conceptual, developmental literacy learning is occurring during the first years of a child's life" (Teale & Sulzby, 1986, p. 28). (p. 3)

Whitehurst and Lonigan (1998) stated,

> The term "emergent literacy" is used to denote the idea that the acquisition of literacy is best conceptualized as a developmental continuum, with its origins early in the life of a child, rather than an all-or-none phenomenon that begins when children start school....For instance, the "reading readiness" approach, which preceded an emergent literacy perspective and is still dominant in many educational arenas, has as its focus the question of what skills children need to have mastered before they can profit from formal reading instruction. Such perspectives create a boundary between the "prereading" behaviors of children, and the "real" reading that children are taught in educational settings....A second distinction between an emergent literacy perspective and other perspectives on literacy is the assumption that reading, writing, and oral language develop concurrently and interdependently from an early age from children's exposure to interactions in the social contexts in which literacy is a component, and in the absence of formal instruction....the term "emergent literacy" is typically attributed to Clay (1966). A more formal introduction of the term and field of inquiry was heralded by Teale and Sulzby's (1986) book, *Emergent Literacy: Writing and Reading*. (pp. 848–849).

Table 2 provides an overview of the research methodologies used in the studies reviewed by Mason and Allen (1986) and Whitehurst and Lonigan (1998), organized chronologically by the areas of emergent literacy in the two reviews.

In examining the bodies of research in these two reviews, we found a difference in the time between them. Mason and Allen (1986) focused on research from 1970 to 1986, whereas Whitehurst and Lonigan (1998) predominantly focused on research from 1980 to 1997. As such, the overlap of time was only about six to seven years, with approximately 35% of the studies during this time frame reviewed by both groups. In addition, in several areas, they reviewed different studies by the same researchers. The underlying similarities are striking and provide a strong research-based foundation of knowledge in (a) the

Table 2. Emergent Literacy Research Reviewed by Mason and Allen[a] (M&A) and Whitehurst and Lonigan[b] (W&L)

Reviewer	Research Reviewed	Method[c]	Focus
Context/Experiences			
M&A	Clay, M.M. (1970). Research on language and reading in Pekeha and Polynesian children. In D.K. Bracken & E. Malmquist (Eds.), *Improving reading ability around the world* (pp. 132–141). Newark, DE: International Reading Association.	Descriptive, observation	Cultural, social
M&A	Goodacre, E. (1973). Great Britain. In J.A. Downing (Ed.), *Comparative reading: Cross-national studies of behavior and processes in reading and writing* (pp. 360–382). New York: Macmillan.	Correlation	Cultural, social
M&A	Sakamoto, T., & Makita, K. (1973). Japan. In J.A. Downing (Ed.), *Comparative reading: Cross-national studies of behavior and processes in reading and writing* (pp. 440–465). New York: Macmillan.	Correlation	Cultural, social
M&A	Thorndike, R. (1976). Reading comprehension in 15 countries. In J.E. Merritt (Ed.), *New horizons in reading* (pp. 500–507). Newark, DE: International Reading Association.	Correlation	Cultural, social
M&A	Chesterfield, R. (1978). Effects of environmentally specific materials on reading in Brazilian rural primary schools. *The Reading Teacher*, *32*(3), 312–315.	Quasi-experimental	Classroom (instructional materials)
W&L	Ninio, A. (1980). Picture-book reading in mother–infant dyads belonging to two subgroups in Israel. *Child Development*, *51*(2), 587–590.	Mixed methods	Home and classroom experiences
M&A	Wells, C.G. (1981). *Learning through interaction: The study of language development*. New York: Cambridge University Press.	Discourse analysis	Cultural, social
Both	Heath, S.B. (1982). What no bedtime story means: Narrative skills at home and school. *Language in Society*, *11*(1), 49–76.	Ethnography	Home experiences, socioeconomic status, story reading
Both	White, K.R. (1982). The relation between socioeconomic status and academic achievement. *Psychological Bulletin*, *91*(3), 461–481.	Meta-analysis	Home and classroom experiences, socioeconomic status

(continued)

Table 2. Emergent Literacy Research Reviewed by Mason and Allen[a] (M&A) and Whitehurst and Lonigan[b] (W&L) (*Continued*)

Reviewer	Research Reviewed	Method[c]	Focus
Both	Anderson, A.B., & Stokes, S.J. (1984). Social and institutional influences on the development and practice of literacy. In H. Goelman, A. Oberg, & F. Smith (Eds.), *Awakening to literacy* (pp. 24–37). Exeter, NH: Heinemann.	Descriptive, observation	Home experiences, socioeconomic status
M&A	Dyson, A.H. (1984). Emerging alphabetic literacy in school contexts: Toward defining the gap between school curriculum and child mind. *Written Communication*, *1*(1), 5–55.	Case study	Home and classroom experiences, writing
M&A	Allen, J. (1985). Inferential comprehension: The effects of text source, decoding ability, and mode. *Reading Research Quarterly*, *20*(5), 603–615.	Correlation, comparative	Classroom (instructional materials)
M&A	Evans, M.A., & Carr, T.H. (1985). Cognitive abilities, conditions of learning, and the early development of reading skill. *Reading Research Quarterly*, *20*(3), 327–350.	Correlation, comparative	Classroom (instructional approach)
M&A	Juel, C., & Roper/Schneider, D. (1985). The influence of basal readers on first grade reading. *Reading Research Quarterly*, *20*(2), 134–152.	Correlation, comparative	Classroom (instructional materials)
Both	Wells, G. (1985). Preschool literacy-related activities and success in school. In D.R. Olson, N. Torrance, & A. Hildyard (Eds.), *Literacy, language, and learning: The nature and consequences of reading and writing* (pp. 229–255). New York: Cambridge University Press.	Correlation	Home experiences, socioeconomic status, story reading
Both	Feitelson, D., & Goldstein, Z. (1986). Patterns of book ownership and reading to young children in Israeli school-oriented and nonschool-oriented families. *The Reading Teacher*, *39*(9), 924–930.	Descriptive, observation	Home experiences, socioeconomic status
M&A	Heath, S.B. (1986). Separating "things of the imagination" from life: Learning to read and write. In W.H. Teale & E. Sulzby (Eds.), *Emergent literacy: Writing and reading* (pp. 156–172). Westport, CT: Ablex.	Ethnography	Home experiences, socioeconomic status, story reading

Reviewer	Research Reviewed	Method[c]	Focus
W&L	Stevenson, H.W., & Newman, R.S. (1986). Long-term prediction of achievement and attitudes in mathematics and reading. *Child Development*, *57*(3), 646–659.	Correlation	Experiences
Both	Teale, W.H. (1986). Home background and young children's literacy development. In W.H. Teale & E. Sulzby (Eds.), *Emergent literacy: Writing and reading* (pp. 173–206). Westport, CT: Ablex.	Descriptive, observation	Home experiences, socioeconomic status, story reading
W&L	Raz, I.S., & Bryant, P. (1990). Social background, phonological awareness and children's reading. *British Journal of Developmental Psychology*, *8*(3), 209–225.	Correlation	Home experiences, socioeconomic status
W&L	Snow, C., Barnes, W.S., Chandler, J., Goodman, I.F., & Hemphill, L. (1991). *Unfulfilled expectations: Home and school influences on literacy*. Cambridge, MA: Harvard University Press.	Mixed methods	Home experiences, language
W&L	Bryant, D.M., Lau, L.B., Burchinal, M., & Sparling, J.J. (1994). Family and classroom correlates of Head Start children's developmental outcomes. *Early Childhood Research Quarterly*, *9*(3/4), 289–309.	Correlation	Home and classroom experiences
W&L	Dickinson, D.K., & Smith, M.W. (1994). Long-term effects of preschool teachers' book readings on low-income children's vocabulary and story comprehension. *Reading Research Quarterly*, *29*(2), 104–122.	Correlation	Classroom (book reading, teacher talk)
W&L	Bus, A.G., van IJzendoorn, M.H., & Pellegrini, A.D. (1995). Joint book reading makes for success in learning to read: A meta-analysis on intergenerational transmission of literacy. *Review of Educational Research*,*65*(1), 1–21.	Meta-analysis	Home story reading
W&L	Purcell-Gates, V. (1996). Stories, coupons, and the "TV Guide": Relationships between home literacy experiences and emergent literacy knowledge. *Reading Research Quarterly*, *31*(4), 406–428.	Mixed methods	Home practices, knowledge, socioeconomic status
Emergent Reading			
M&A	Clay, M.M. (1967). The reading behavior of five-year-old children: A research report. *New Zealand Journal of Educational Studies*, 2, 11–31.	Descriptive, observation	
Both	Ferreiro, E., & Teberosky, A. (1982). *Literacy before schooling* (K.G. Castro, Trans.). Exeter, NH: Heinemann.	Content analysis	

(continued)

Table 2. Emergent Literacy Research Reviewed by Mason and Allen[a] (M&A) and Whitehurst and Lonigan[b] (W&L) (*Continued*)

Reviewer	Research Reviewed	Method[c]	Focus
M&A	Ehri, L.C., & Wilce, L.S. (1985). Movement into reading: Is the first stage of printed word learning visual or phonetic? *Reading Research Quarterly*, *20*(2), 163–179.	Correlation	
W&L	Ehri, L.C. (1988). *Movement in word reading and spelling: How spelling contributes to reading* (Technical Report No. 408). Champaign: Center for the Study of Reading, University of Illinois at Urbana-Champaign.	Experimental	
W&L	Tunmer, W.E., Herriman, M.L., & Nesdale, A.R. (1988). Metalinguistic abilities and beginning reading. *Reading Research Quarterly*, *23*(2), 134–158.	Correlation (path analysis)	
W&L	Whitehurst, G.J. (1996, April). *A structural equation model of the role of home literacy environment in the development of emergent literacy skills in children from low-income backgrounds*. Paper presented at the annual meeting of the American Educational Research Association, New York.	Correlation (structural equation modeling)	
Emergent Writing			
M&A	Clay, M.M. (1975). *What did I write?* Exeter, NH: Heinemann.	Content analysis	
M&A	Bissex, G.L. (1980). *Gnys (genius) at wrk (work): A child learns to write and read*. Cambridge, MA: Harvard University Press.	Case study	
Both	Ferreiro, E., & Teberosky, A. (1982). *Literacy before schooling* (K.G. Castro, Trans.). Exeter, NH: Heinemann.	Content analysis	
M&A	Temple, C.A., Nathan, R.G., & Burris, N.A. (1982). *The beginnings of writing*. Boston: Allyn & Bacon.	Content analysis	
M&A	Graves, D.H. (1983). *Writing: Teachers and children at work*. Exeter, NH: Heinemann.	Mixed methods	
Both	Harste, J.C., Woodward, V.A., & Burke, C.L. (1984). *Language stories and literacy lessons*. Portsmouth, NH: Heinemann.	Descriptive, observation	
M&A	Goodman, Y.M. (1986). Children coming to know literacy. In W.H. Teale & E. Sulzby (Eds.), *Emergent literacy: Writing and reading* (pp. 1–14). Westport, CT: Ablex.	Content analysis	

Reviewer	Research Reviewed	Method[c]	Focus
Both	Sulzby, E. (1986). Writing and reading: Signs of oral and written language organization in the young child. In W.H. Teale & E. Sulzby (Eds.), *Emergent literacy: Writing and reading* (pp. 50–89). Westport, CT: Ablex.	Content analysis	
W&L	Sulzby, E., Barnhart, J., & Hieshima, J. (1988). *Forms of writing and rereading from writing: A preliminary report* (Technical Report No. 437). Champaign: Center for the Study of Reading, University of Illinois at Urbana-Champaign.	Content analysis	
Intervention			
Both	Clay, M.M. (1979). *Reading: The patterning of complex behavior.* Portsmouth, NH: Heinemann.	Quasi-experimental, instrument development	Reading Recovery
Both	McCormick, C.E., & Mason, J.M. (1984). *Intervention procedures for increasing preschool children's interest in and knowledge about reading* (Technical Report No. 312). Champaign: University of Illinois at Urbana-Champaign; Cambridge, MA: Bolt Beranek & Newman.	Quasi-experimental	Book reading
M&A	Tharp, R.G., Jordan, C., Speidel, G.E., Au, K.K., Klein, T.W., Calkins, R.P., et al. (1984). Product and process in applied developmental research: Education and the children of a minority. In M.E. Lamb, A.L. Brown, & B. Rogoff (Eds.), *Advances in developmental psychology* (Vol. 3, pp. 91–142). Hillsdale, NJ: Erlbaum.	Mixed methods, formative design	Kamehameha Early Education Program
M&A	Huck, C., & Pinnell, G.S. (1985). *Reading Recovery in Ohio: An early intervention effort to reduce reading failure.* Unpublished manuscript.	Quasi-experimental	Reading Recovery
M&A	Feitelson, D., Kita, B., & Goldstein, Z. (1986). Effects of listening to series stories on first graders' comprehension and use of language. *Research in the Teaching of English, 20*(4), 339–356.	Quasi-experimental	Teacher read-aloud
W&L	Whitehurst, G.J., Falco, F.L., Lonigan, C.J., & Fischel, J.E. (1988). Accelerating language development through picture book reading. *Developmental Psychology, 24*(4), 552–559.	Experimental	Dialogic reading (shared book reading)

(continued)

Table 2. Emergent Literacy Research Reviewed by Mason and Allen[a] (M&A) and Whitehurst and Lonigan[b] (W&L) (*Continued*)

Reviewer	Research Reviewed	Method[c]	Focus
W&L	Valdez-Menchaca, M.C., & Whitehurst, G.J. (1992). Accelerating language development through picture book reading: A systematic extension to Mexican day care. *Developmental Psychology, 28*(6), 1106–1114.	Experimental	Dialogic reading (shared book reading)
W&L	Neuman, S.B., & Roskos, K. (1993). Access to print for children of poverty: Differential effects of adult mediation and literacy-enriched play settings on environmental and functional print tasks. *American Educational Research Journal, 30*(1), 95–122.	Experimental	Literacy-enriched play
W&L	Sénéchal, M., & Cornell, E.H. (1993). Vocabulary acquisition through shared reading experiences. *Reading Research Quarterly, 28*(4), 360–374.	Correlation, comparative	Shared book reading
W&L	Arnold, D.H., Lonigan, C.J., Whitehurst, G.J., & Epstein, J.N. (1994). Accelerating language development through picture book reading: Replication and extension to a videotape training format. *Journal of Educational Psychology, 86*(2), 235–243.	Experimental	Dialogic reading (shared book reading)
Language			
M&A	Chomsky, C. (1972). Stages in language development and reading exposure. *Harvard Educational Review, 42*(1), 1–33.	Correlation	Story reading
Both	Ninio, A., & Bruner, J. (1978). The achievement and antecedents of labelling. *Journal of Child Language, 5*(1), 1–15.	Content analysis	Story reading
Both	Snow, C.E. (1983). Literacy and language: Relationships during the preschool years. *Harvard Educational Review, 53*(2), 165–189.	Correlation	Story reading
W&L	Butler, S.R., Marsh, H.W., Sheppard, M.J., & Sheppard, J.L. (1985). Seven-year longitudinal study of the early prediction of reading achievement. *Journal of Educational Psychology, 77*(3), 349–361.	Correlation (path analysis)	Literacy
Both	Sulzby, E. (1985). Children's emergent reading of favorite storybooks: A developmental study. *Reading Research Quarterly, 20*(4), 458–481.	Content analysis	Written, narrative

Reviewer	Research Reviewed	Method[c]	Focus
W&L	Purcell-Gates, V. (1986). Lexical and syntactic knowledge of written narrative held by well-read-to kindergartners and second graders. *Research in the Teaching of English*, 22(2), 128–160.	Descriptive	Written, narrative
M&A	Snow, C.E., & Ninio, A. (1986). The contracts of literacy: What children learn from learning to read books. In W.H. Teale & E. Sulzby (Eds.), *Emergent literacy: Writing and reading* (pp. 116–138). Westport, CT: Ablex.	Content analysis	Story reading
W&L	Dickinson, D.K., & Snow, C.E. (1987). Interrelationships among prereading and oral language skills in kindergartners from two social classes. *Early Childhood Research Quarterly*, 2(1), 1–25.	Correlation	Story reading
W&L	Pappas, C.C., & Brown, E. (1988). The development of children's sense of the written story register: An analysis of the texture of kindergarteners' "pretend reading" texts. *Linguistics and Education*, *1*(1), 45–79.	Content analysis	Written, narrative
M&A	Lartz, M.N., & Mason, J.M. (1989). *Jamie: One child's journey from oral to written language* (Technical Report No. 453). Champaign: University of Illinois at Urbana-Champaign.	Case study	Written, narrative
W&L	Pikulski, J.J., & Tobin, A.W. (1989). Factors associated with long-term reading achievement of early readers. In S.McCormick & J. Zutell (Eds.), *Cognitive and social perspectives for literacy research and instruction: Thirty-eighth yearbook of the National Reading Conference* (pp. 135–143). Chicago: National Reading Conference.	Correlation	Literacy
W&L	Scarborough, H.S. (1989). Prediction of reading dysfunction from familial and individual differences. *Journal of Educational Psychology*, *81*(1), 101–108.	Correlation	Story reading
W&L	Bishop, D.V., & Adams, C. (1990). A prospective study of the relationship between specific language impairment, phonological disorders and reading retardation. *Journal of Child Psychology and Psychiatry*, *31*(7), 1027–1050.	Correlation	Literacy
W&L	Dickinson, D.K., & Tabors, P.O. (1991). Early literacy: Linkages between home, school and literacy achievement at age five. *Journal of Research in Childhood Education*, 6(1), 30–46.	Correlation	Literacy

(continued)

Table 2. Emergent Literacy Research Reviewed by Mason and Allen[a] (M&A) and Whitehurst and Lonigan[b] (W&L) (*Continued*)

Reviewer	Research Reviewed	Method[c]	Focus
W&L	Crain-Thoreson, C., & Dale, P.S. (1992). Do early talkers become early readers? Linguistic precocity, preschool language, and emergent literacy. *Developmental Psychology, 28*(3), 421–429.	Correlation	Story reading
W&L	Payne, A.C., Whitehurst, G.J., & Angell, A.L. (1994). The role of home literacy environment in the development of language ability in preschool children from low-income families. *Early Childhood Research Quarterly, 9*(3/4), 427–440.	Correlation	Story reading
W&L	Sénéchal, M., Cornell, E.H., & Broda, L.S. (1995). Age-related differences in the organization of parent–infant interactions during picture-book reading. *Early Childhood Research Quarterly, 10*(3), 317–337.	Discourse analysis, comparative	Story reading
W&L	Sénéchal, M., LeFevre, J., Hudson, E., & Lawson, E.P. (1996). Knowledge of storybooks as a predictor of young children's vocabulary. *Journal of Educational Psychology, 88*(3), 520–536.	Correlation	Story reading
W&L	Sénéchal, M., LeFevre, J., Thomas, E.M., & Daley, K.E. (1998). Differential effects of home literacy experiences on the development of oral and written language. *Reading Research Quarterly, 33*(1), 91–116.	Correlation	Story reading
Skills			
M&A	Mason, J.M. (1977). *Reading readiness: A definition and skills hierarchy from preschoolers' developing conceptions of print* (Technical Report No. 59). Champaign: University of Illinois at Urbana-Champaign; Cambridge, MA: Bolt Beranek & Newman.	Descriptive, observation	Alphabetic principle (training, intervention)
Both	Mason, J.M. (1980). When do children begin to read? An exploration of four year old children's letter and word reading competencies. *Reading Research Quarterly, 15*(2), 203–227.	Descriptive, observation	Alphabetic principle
Both	Bradley, L., & Bryant, P.E. (1983). Categorizing sounds and learning to read—a causal connection. *Nature, 301*(5899), 419–421.	Quasi-experimental	Phonological awareness

Reviewer	Research Reviewed	Method[c]	Focus
W&L	Jorm, A.F., Share, D.L., Maclean, R., & Matthews, R.G. (1984). Phonological recoding skills and learning to read: A longitudinal study. *Applied Psycholinguistics*, *5*(3), 201–207.	Correlation	Alphabetic principle
M&A	Lundberg, I. (1984). Learning to read. *School Research Newsletter* (National Board of Education, Sweden), *August*.	Correlation	Phonological awareness
W&L	Mann, V.A., & Liberman, I.Y. (1984). Phonological awareness and verbal short-term memory. *Journal of Learning Disabilities*, *17*(10), 592–599.	Correlation	Phonological awareness
M&A	Perfetti, C.A. (1984). Reading acquisition and beyond: Decoding includes cognition. *American Journal of Education*, *93*(1), 40–60.	Correlation	Phonological awareness
M&A	Peterman, C., & Mason, J.M. (1984, November). *Kindergarten children's perceptions of the form of print in labeled pictures and stories*. Paper presented at the annual meeting of the National Reading Conference, St. Petersburg, FL.	Correlation	Alphabetic principle
W&L	Share, D.L., Jorm, A.F., MacLean, R., & Matthews, R. (1984). Sources of individual differences in reading acquisition. *Journal of Educational Psychology*, *76*(6), 1309–1324.	Correlation	Phonological awareness
W&L	Stanovich, K.E., Cunningham, A.E., & Feeman, D.J. (1984). Intelligence, cognitive skills, and early reading progress. *Reading Research Quarterly*, *19*(3), 278–303.	Correlation	Phonological awareness
M&A	Juel, C., Griffith, P.L., & Gough, P.B. (1985). Acquisition of literacy: A longitudinal study of children in first and second grade. *Journal of Educational Psychology*, *78*(4), 243–255.	Correlation	Phonological awareness
W&L	Perfetti, C.A., Beck, I., Bell, L.C., & Hughes, C. (1987). Phonemic knowledge and learning to read are reciprocal: A longitudinal study of first grade children. *Merrill Palmer Quarterly*, *33*(3), 283–319.	Correlation	Phonological awareness
W&L	Wagner, R.K., & Torgesen, J.K. (1987). The nature of phonological processing and its causal role in the acquisition of reading skills. *Psychological Bulletin*, *101*(2), 192–212.	Correlation	Other cognitive (rapid naming)
W&L	Ball, E.W., & Blachman, B.A. (1988). Phoneme segmentation training: Effect on reading readiness. *Annals of Dyslexia*, *38*(1), 208–225.	Experimental	Phonological awareness (training, intervention)

(continued)

Table 2. Emergent Literacy Research Reviewed by Mason and Allen[a] (M&A) and Whitehurst and Lonigan[b] (W&L) (*Continued*)

Reviewer	Research Reviewed	Method[c]	Focus
W&L	Juel, C. (1988). Learning to read and write: A longitudinal study of 54 children from first through fourth grades. *Journal of Educational Psychology, 80*(4), 437–447.	Correlation	Phonological awareness
W&L	Lundberg, I., Frost, J., & Petersen, O. (1988). Effects of an extensive program for stimulating phonological awareness in preschool children. *Reading Research Quarterly*, 23(3), 263–284.	Quasi-experimental	Phonological awareness (training, intervention)
W&L	Byrne, B., & Fielding-Barnsley, R. (1991). Evaluation of a program to teach phonemic awareness to young children. *Journal of Educational Psychology, 83*(4), 451–455.	Experimental	Phonological awareness (training, intervention)
W&L	Gathercole, S.E., Willis, C., & Baddeley, A.D. (1991). Differentiating phonological memory and awareness of rhyme: Reading and vocabulary development in children. *British Journal of Psychology, 82*(3), 387–406.	Correlation	Other cognitive (phonological memory)
W&L	Gough, P.B., & Walsh, M.A. (1991). Chinese, Phoenicians, and the orthographic cipher of English. In S.A. Brady & D.P. Shankweiler (Eds.), *Phonological processes in literacy: A tribute to Isabelle Y. Liberman* (pp. 199–210). Hillsdale, NJ: Erlbaum.	Correlation	Alphabetic principle
W&L	Gathercole, S.E., Willis, C.S., Emslie, H., & Baddeley, A.D. (1992). Phonological memory and vocabulary development during the early school years: A longitudinal study. *Developmental Psychology, 28*(5), 887–898.	Correlation	Other cognitive (phonological memory)
W&L	Torgesen, J.K., Morgan, S.T., & Davis, C. (1992). Effects of two types of phonological awareness training on word learning in kindergarten children. *Journal of Educational Psychology, 84*(3), 364–370.	Experimental	Phonological awareness (training, intervention)
W&L	Byrne, B., & Fielding-Barnsley, R. (1993). Evaluation of a program to teach phonemic awareness to young children: A 1-year follow-up. *Journal of Educational Psychology, 85*(1), 104–111.	Experimental	Phonological awareness (training, intervention)
W&L	Bowey, J.A. (1994). Phonological sensitivity in novice readers and nonreaders. *Journal of Experimental Child Psychology, 58*(1), 134–159.	Correlation	Phonological awareness

Reviewer	Research Reviewed	Method[c]	Focus
W&L	Stahl, S.A., & Murray, B.A. (1994). Defining phonological awareness and its relationship to early reading. *Journal of Educational Psychology, 86*(2), 221–234.	Correlation (factor analysis)	Phonological awareness
W&L	Wagner, R.K., Torgesen, J.K., & Rashotte, C.A. (1994). Development of reading-related phonological processing abilities: New evidence of bidirectional causality from a latent variable longitudinal study. *Developmental Psychology, 30*(1), 73–87.	Correlation (latent variable modeling)	Other cognitive (phonological memory, rapid naming)
W&L	Byrne, B., & Fielding-Barnsley, R. (1995). Evaluation of a program to teach phonemic awareness to young children: A 2- and 3-year follow-up and a new preschool trial. *Journal of Educational Psychology, 85*(1), 104–111.	Experimental	Phonological awareness (training, intervention)
W&L	Rohl, M., & Pratt, C. (1995). Phonological awareness, verbal working memory and the acquisition of literacy. *Reading and Writing, 7*(4), 327–360.	Correlation	Other cognitive (phonological memory)
W&L	Johnston, R.S., Anderson, M., & Holligan, C. (1996). Knowledge of the alphabet and explicit awareness of phonemes in prereaders: The nature of the relationship. *Reading and Writing, 8*(3), 217–234.	Correlation	Phonological awareness, alphabetic principle
W&L	McBride-Chang, C., & Manis, F.R. (1996). Structural invariance in the associations of naming speed, phonological awareness, and verbal reasoning in good and poor readers: A test of the double deficit hypothesis. *Reading and Writing, 8*(4), 323–339.	Correlation (structural equation modeling)	Other cognitive (rapid naming)
W&L	Wagner, R.K. (1996, April). *Meta-analysis of the effects of phonological awareness training with children.* Paper presented at the annual meeting of the American Educational Research Association, New York.	Meta-analysis	Phonological awareness (training, intervention)

Note. The reviews are organized chronologically by the areas of emergent literacy in the two reviews.
[a]"A Review of Emergent Literacy With Implications for Research and Practice in Reading," by J.M. Mason and J. Allen, 1986, *Review of Research in Education, 13*(1), 3–47.
[b]"Child Development and Emergent Literacy," by G.J. Whitehurst and C.J. Lonigan, 1998, *Child Development, 69*(3), 848–872.
[c]Descriptive research is a broad "what is?" methodology in which researchers "describe or enumerate a phenomenon" (according to Shanahan) without attempting to change the context. (Quotation from *What Research Has to Say About Reading Instruction* [3rd ed., p. 10], edited by A.E. Farstrup and S.J. Samuels, 2002, Newark, DE: International Reading Association.)

development of emerging reading and writing; (b) the importance of context, experiences, and language; and (c) the relationships between skills and reading outcomes.

Yet, most important given the focus of this chapter is the breadth of methodologies used by researchers whose work has contributed to the influential conceptualization and theorization of emergent literacy presented by Mason and Allen (1986) and Whitehurst and Lonigan (1998). In examining Table 2, readers can clearly see that a broad perspective, which embraces the methodological affordances of numerous research studies, is necessary to understand the complexity of emergent literacy. For example, understanding the importance of children's context and experiences in their emergent literacy development and growth has been advanced through research using descriptive, correlational, meta-analysis, ethnographic, content analysis, and discourse analysis methodologies. It is through the plethora of methodological lenses, offering more sophistication than would be possible with a singular methodological focus, that our understanding of emergent literacy has developed.

As noted earlier, the reviews that were the focus of our analysis are from 1986 and 1998, demonstrating that multiple methodologies informed the early development of emergent literacy theory. Since the publication of those reviews, emergent literacy theory continues to develop and expand.

In 1997, McGee and Purcell-Gates suggested, "the field of emergent literacy is alive and well" (p. 317). A decade and a half later, this sentiment still applies and is reflected in the sheer volume of research published in the past 20 years. Further, as Sulzby and Teale (1991) noted, "one strength of emergent literacy research currently is the openness of researchers to use many different methodologies," (p. 749) another view that is still relevant and clearly reflected in research today. The following studies, which feature a small sampling of methodologies currently used in research, exemplify the continuous development of emergent literacy theory:

- *Case study:* Exploring story dictation and vocabulary development (Christ, Wang, & Chiu, 2011)
- *Correlation:* Used in cluster analysis to create profiles of at-risk preschool children (Cabell, Justice, Konold, & McGinty, 2011)
- *Experimental study:* Using randomized design to determine the effectiveness of curricular approaches (Lonigan, Farver, Phillips, & Clancy-Menchetti, 2011)
- *Formative experiment:* Designed to explore, develop, and modify an intervention for children ages 3–5 and their low-literate parents (J. Anderson, Purcell-Gates, Jang, & Gagné, 2010)
- *Instrument development:* Examining a measure of emergent literacy learners with special needs (Baker, Spooner, Ahlgrim-Delzell, Flowers, & Browder, 2010)

- *Meta-analysis:* Examining the effects of instruction on alphabetic knowledge (Piasta & Wagner, 2010)
- *Mixed methods:* Using a longitudinal design to explore the relationship between young children's home culture and their literacy development (Sonnenschein, Baker, & Serpell, 2010)

In reflecting on the current state of emergent literacy, Teale et al. (2009) noted, "We *have* come a long way" (p. 93), an insight clearly supported through multifaceted research. At the same time, however, there still remains much to learn. We look forward to the continued evolution of understanding, following in what is now a long tradition of contributions from rich and diverse methodological resources.

Moving Forward

The examples of synergy of research methodologies presented in this chapter were made possible because scholars read and drew on work of multiple methodologies. In each of the three insights, as well as theory development, scholars have contextualized their research in extant research reflective of numerous methodologies. Interesting, and noteworthy to future scholars, is that the groundbreaking work in each example was indeed dissertation research (e.g., Clay, 1966; Emig, 1971; Graves, 1975; Meyer, 1975; Read, 1971).

To continue, and expand, the degree to which a broad range of methodologies inform development of insights and theory in the field, we must continue to ensure that scholars read and work from and across a broad range of research methodologies. This task is in some respects more daunting now than it has been in the past. However, one way to encourage synergy of research methodology is for journal editors to actively seek representation of a broad range of methodologies within their journals or edited volumes. Editors can also encourage reviewers, and act themselves, to draw authors' attention to cases in which relevant work of different methodologies is not included within their literature reviews. Grantors can fund work of multiple methodologies and bring together scholars working within the same topic using different methodological approaches. Professional organizations and conference organizers can do the same, encouraging symposia, for example, in which multiple methodologies are represented.

Still, the greatest responsibility for culling from research using a range of methodologies lies with the individual scholar. Reading widely, seeking to understand the methodologies, findings, and perspectives of scholars working in related areas, even if in seemingly unrelated ways, is an important responsibility. As argued at the outset of this chapter, the complexity of literacy teaching, learning, and development is such that no single research methodology will be sufficient for understanding.

QUESTIONS FOR REFLECTION

1. How does synergy in literacy research contribute to the development and confirmation of theory?
2. How did the accumulation of evidence from methodologically different studies form the foundation of theory and practice in emergent literacy?
3. How can you conceptualize a study using synergistic methods that would add to the body of research literature on emergent literacy or process writing?
4. What benefits accrue from synergistic approaches to literacy research?

NOTE

*When this chapter was written, Mallette was at Southern Illinois University, and Duke was at Michigan State University.

REFERENCES

Allan, D. (2009). *A nation of readers: The lending library in Georgian England*. Chicago: University of Chicago Press.

Allen, J. (1985). Inferential comprehension: The effects of text source, decoding ability, and mode. *Reading Research Quarterly, 20*(5), 603–615.

Anderson, A.B., & Stokes, S.J. (1984). Social and institutional influences on the development and practice of literacy. In H. Goelman, A. Oberg, & F. Smith (Eds.), *Awakening to literacy* (pp. 24–37). Exeter, NH: Heinemann.

Anderson, J., Purcell-Gates, V., Jang, K., & Gagné, M. (2010). *Implementing an intergenerational literacy program with authentic literacy instruction: Challenges, responses, and results*. Ottawa, ON: Canadian Council on Learning.

Armbruster, B.B., Anderson, T.H., & Ostertag, J. (1987). Does text structure/summarization instruction facilitate learning from expository text? *Reading Research Quarterly*, 22(3), 331–346. doi:10.2307/747972

Arnold, D.H., Lonigan, C.J., Whitehurst, G.J., & Epstein, J.N. (1994). Accelerating language development through picture book reading: Replication and extension to a videotape training format. *Journal of Educational Psychology, 86*(2), 235–243.

Baker, J.N., Spooner, F., Ahlgrim-Delzell, L., Flowers, C., & Browder, D.M. (2010). A measure of emergent literacy for students with severe developmental disabilities. *Psychology in the Schools*, 47(5), 501–513. doi:10.1002/pits.20486

Ball, E.W., & Blachman, B.A. (1988). Phoneme segmentation training: Effect on reading readiness. *Annals of Dyslexia, 38*(1), 208–225.

Ball, E.W., & Blachman, B.A. (1991). Does phoneme awareness training in kindergarten make a difference in early word recognition and developmental spelling? *Reading Research Quarterly, 26*(1), 49–66. doi:10.1598/RRQ.26.1.3

Bereiter, C., & Scardamalia, M. (1984). Learning about writing from reading. *Written Communication, 1*(2), 163–188. doi:10.1177/0741088384001002001

Bereiter, C., & Scardamalia, M. (1987). *The psychology of written composition*. Hillsdale, NJ: Erlbaum.

Bishop, D.V., & Adams, C. (1990). A prospective study of the relationship between specific language impairment, phonological disorders and reading retardation. *Journal of Child Psychology and Psychiatry, 31*(7), 1027–1050.

Bissex, G.L. (1980). *Gnys (genius) at wrk (work): A child learns to write and read*. Cambridge, MA: Harvard University Press.

Bowers, P.N., Kirby, J.R., & Deacon, S.H. (2010). The effects of morphological instruction on literacy skills: A systematic review of the literature. *Review of Educational Research, 80*(2), 144–179. doi:10.3102/0034654309359353

Bowey, J.A. (1994). Phonological sensitivity in novice readers and nonreaders. *Journal of Experimental Child Psychology, 58*(1), 134–159.

Bradley, L., & Bryant, P.E. (1983). Categorizing sounds and learning to read—a causal connection. *Nature, 301*(5899), 419–421. doi:10.1038/301419a0

Bryant, D.M., Lau, L.B., Burchinal, M., & Sparling, J.J. (1994). Family and classroom correlates of Head Start children's developmental outcomes. *Early Childhood Research Quarterly*, 9(3/4), 289–309.

Bus, A.G., & van IJzendoorn, M.H. (1999). Phonological awareness and early reading: A meta-analysis of experimental training studies. *Journal of Educational Psychology, 91*(3), 403–414. doi:10.1037/0022-0663.91.3.403

Bus, A.G., van IJzendoorn, M.H., & Pellegrini, A.D. (1995). Joint book reading makes for success in learning to read: A meta-analysis on intergenerational transmission of literacy. *Review of Educational Research, 65*(1), 1–21.

Butler, S.R., Marsh, H.W., Sheppard, M.J., & Sheppard, J.L. (1985). Seven-year longitudinal study of the early prediction of reading achievement. *Journal of Educational Psychology, 77*(3), 349–361.

Byrne, B., & Fielding-Barnsley, R. (1991). Evaluation of a program to teach phonemic awareness to young children. *Journal of Educational Psychology, 83*(4), 451–455.

Byrne, B., & Fielding-Barnsley, R. (1993). Evaluation of a program to teach phonemic awareness to young children: A 1-year follow-up. *Journal of Educational Psychology, 85*(1), 104–111.

Byrne, B., & Fielding-Barnsley, R. (1995). Evaluation of a program to teach phonemic awareness to young children: A 2- and 3-year follow-up and a new preschool trial. *Journal of Educational Psychology, 85*(1), 104–111.

Cabell, S.Q., Justice, L.M., Konold, T.R., & McGinty, A.S. (2011). Profiles of emergent literacy skills among preschool children who are at risk for academic difficulties. *Early Childhood Research Quarterly, 26*(1), 1–14. doi:10.1016/j.ecresq.2010.05.003

Chesterfield, R. (1978). Effects of environmentally specific materials on reading in Brazilian rural primary schools. *The Reading Teacher, 32*(3), 312–315.

Chomsky, C. (1970). Reading, writing, and phonology. *Harvard Educational Review, 40*(2), 287–309.

Chomsky, C. (1972). Stages in language development and reading exposure. *Harvard Educational Review, 42*(1), 1–33.

Christ, T., Wang, X.C., & Chiu, M.M. (2011). Using story dictation to support young children's vocabulary development: Outcomes and process. *Early Childhood Research Quarterly, 26*(1), 30–41. doi:10.1016/j.ecresq.2010.06.002

Clay, M.M. (1966). *Emergent reading behavior.* Unpublished doctoral dissertation, University of Auckland, New Zealand.

Clay, M.M. (1967). The reading behavior of five-year-old children: A research report. *New Zealand Journal of Educational Studies, 2*, 11–31.

Clay, M.M. (1970). Research on language and reading in Pekeha and Polynesian children. In D.K. Bracken & E. Malmquist (Eds.), *Improving reading ability around the world* (pp. 132–141). Newark, DE: International Reading Association.

Clay, M.M. (1975). *What did I write?* Exeter, NH: Heinemann.

Clay, M.M. (1979). *Reading: The patterning of complex behavior.* Portsmouth, NH: Heinemann.

Crain-Thoreson, C., & Dale, P.S. (1992). Do early talkers become early readers? Linguistic precocity, preschool language, and emergent literacy. *Developmental Psychology, 28*(3), 421–429.

Creswell, J.W. (2012). *Educational research: Planning, conducting, and evaluating quantitative and qualitative research* (4th ed.). Boston: Pearson.

Cunningham, A.E. (1990). Explicit versus implicit instruction in phonemic awareness. *Journal of Experimental Child Psychology, 50*(3), 429–444. doi:10.1016/0022-0965(90)90079-N

Dickinson, D.K., & Neuman, S.B. (Eds.). (2006). *Handbook of early literacy research* (Vol. 2). New York: Guilford.

Dickinson, D.K., & Smith, M.W. (1994). Long-term effects of preschool teachers' book readings on low-income children's vocabulary and story comprehension. *Reading Research Quarterly, 29*(2), 104–122.

Dickinson, D.K., & Snow, C.E. (1987). Interrelationships among prereading and oral language skills in kindergartners from two social classes. *Early Childhood Research Quarterly, 2*(1), 1–25.

Dickinson, D.K., & Tabors, P.O. (1991). Early literacy: Linkages between home, school and literacy achievement at age five. *Journal of Research in Childhood Education, 6*(1), 30–46.

Duke, N.K., & Mallette, M.H. (Eds.). (2004). *Literacy research methodologies.* New York: Guilford.

Duke, N.K., & Mallette, M.H. (Eds.). (2011). *Literacy research methodologies* (2nd ed.). New York: Guilford.

Duke, N.K., & Martin, N.M. (2011). 10 things every literacy educator should know about research. *The Reading Teacher, 65*(1), 9–22.

Dyson, A.H. (1984). Emerging alphabetic literacy in school contexts: Toward defining the gap between school curriculum and child mind. *Written Communication, 1*(1), 5–55.

Ehri, L.C. (1988). *Movement in word reading and spelling: How spelling contributes to reading* (Technical Report No. 408). Champaign: Center for the Study of Reading, University of Illinois at Urbana-Champaign.

Ehri, L.C., Nunes, S.R., Willows, D.M., Schuster, B.V., Yaghoub-Zadeh, Z., & Shanahan, T. (2001). Phonemic awareness instruction helps children learn to read: Evidence from the National Reading Panel's meta-analysis. *Reading Research Quarterly, 36*(3), 250–287. doi:10.1598/RRQ.36.3.2

Ehri, L.C., & Wilce, L.S. (1979). The mnemonic value of orthography among beginning readers. *Journal of Educational Psychology, 71*(1), 26–40. doi:10.1037/0022-0663.71.1.26

Ehri, L.C., & Wilce, L.S. (1985). Movement into reading: Is the first stage of printed word learning visual or phonetic? *Reading Research Quarterly, 20*(2), 163–179. doi:10.2307/747753

Emig, J. (1971). *The composing processes of twelfth graders* (Research Report No. 13). Urbana, IL: National Council of Teachers of English.

Englert, C.S., & Hiebert, E.H. (1984). Children's developing awareness of text structures in expository materials. *Journal of Educational Psychology, 76*(1), 65–74. doi:10.1037/0022-0663.76.1.65

Evans, M.A., & Carr, T.H. (1985). Cognitive abilities, conditions of learning, and the early development of reading skill. *Reading Research Quarterly, 20*(3), 327–350.

Feitelson, D., & Goldstein, Z. (1986). Patterns of book ownership and reading to young children in Israeli school-oriented and nonschool-oriented families. *The Reading Teacher, 39*(9), 924–930.

Feitelson, D., Kita, B., & Goldstein, Z. (1986). Effects of listening to series stories on first graders' comprehension and use of language. *Research in the Teaching of English, 20*(4), 339–356.

Ferreiro, E., & Teberosky, A. (1982). *Literacy before schooling* (K.G. Castro, Trans.). Exeter, NH: Heinemann.

Flower, L., & Hayes, J.R. (1980). The cognition of discovery: Defining a rhetorical problem. *College Composition and Communication, 31*(1), 21–32. doi:10.2307/356630

Flower, L., & Hayes, J.R. (1981). A cognitive process theory of writing. *College Composition and Communication, 32*(4), 365–387. doi:10.2307/356600

Gaddy, S.A., Bakken, J.P., & Fulk, B.M. (2008). The effects of teaching text-structure strategies to postsecondary students with learning disabilities to improve their reading comprehension on expository science text passages. *Journal of Postsecondary Education and Disability, 20*(2), 100–119.

Gathercole, S.E., Willis, C., & Baddeley, A.D. (1991). Differentiating phonological memory and awareness of rhyme: Reading and vocabulary development in children. *British Journal of Psychology, 82*(3), 387–406.

Gathercole, S.E., Willis, C.S., Emslie, H., & Baddeley, A.D. (1992). Phonological memory and vocabulary development during the early school years: A longitudinal study. *Developmental Psychology, 28*(5), 887–898.

Goldstein, A.A., & Carr, P.G. (1996). Can students benefit from process writing? *NAEPfacts, 1*(3), 1–6.

Goodacre, E. (1973). Great Britain. In J.A. Downing (Ed.), *Comparative reading: Cross-national studies of behavior and processes in reading and writing* (pp. 360–382). New York: Macmillan.

Goodman, Y.M. (1986). Children coming to know literacy. In W.H. Teale & E. Sulzby (Eds.), *Emergent literacy: Writing and reading* (pp. 1–14). Westport, CT: Ablex.

Gough, P.B., & Walsh, M.A. (1991). Chinese, Phoenicians, and the orthographic cipher of English. In S.A. Brady & D.P. Shankweiler (Eds.), *Phonological processes in literacy: A tribute to Isabelle Y. Liberman* (pp. 199–210). Hillsdale, NJ: Erlbaum.

Graham, S., & Sandmel, K. (2011). The process writing approach: A meta-analysis. *Journal of Educational Research, 104*(6), 396–407. doi:10.1080/00220671.2010.488703

Graves, D.H. (1975). An examination of the writing processes of seven year old children. *Research in the Teaching of English, 9*(3), 227–241.

Graves, D.H. (1983). *Writing: Teachers and children at work.* Exeter, NH: Heinemann.

Guo, Y., Roehrig, A.D., & Williams, R.S. (2011). The relation of morphological awareness and syntactic awareness to adults' reading comprehension: Is vocabulary knowledge a mediating variable? *Journal of Literacy Research, 43*(2), 159–183. doi:10.1177/1086296X11403086

Haas, C., & Takayoshi, P. (with Carr, B., Hudson, K., & Pollock, R.). (2011). Young people's everyday literacies: The language features of instant messaging. *Research in the Teaching of English, 45*(4), 378–404.

Harste, J.C., Woodward, V.A., & Burke, C.L. (1984). *Language stories and literacy lessons.* Portsmouth, NH: Heinemann.

Heath, S.B. (1982). What no bedtime story means: Narrative skills at home and school. *Language in Society, 11*(1), 49–76.

Heath, S.B. (1986). Separating "things of the imagination" from life: Learning to read and write. In W.H. Teale & E. Sulzby (Eds.), *Emergent literacy: Writing and reading* (pp. 156–172). Westport, CT: Ablex.

Huck, C., & Pinnell, G.S. (1985). *Reading Recovery in Ohio: An early intervention effort to reduce reading failure.* Unpublished manuscript.

Jeong, J., Gaffney, J.S., & Choi, J. (2010). Availability and use of informational texts in second-, third-, and fourth-grade classrooms. *Research in the Teaching of English, 44*(4), 435–456.

Johnson, R.B., & Christensen, L. (2012). *Educational research: Quantitative, qualitative, and mixed approaches* (4th ed.). Thousand Oaks, CA: Sage.

Johnson, R.B., Onwuegbuzie, A.J., & Turner, L.A. (2007). Toward a definition of mixed method research. *Journal of Mixed Methods Research, 1*(2), 112–133. doi:10.1177/1558689806298224

Johnston, R.S., Anderson, M., & Holligan, C. (1996). Knowledge of the alphabet and explicit awareness of phonemes in prereaders: The nature of the relationship. *Reading and Writing, 8*(3), 217–234.

Jorm, A.F., Share, D.L., Maclean, R., & Matthews, R.G. (1984). Phonological recoding skills and learning to read: A longitudinal study. *Applied Psycholinguistics, 5*(3), 201–207.

Juel, C. (1988). Learning to read and write: A longitudinal study of 54 children from first through fourth grades. *Journal of Educational Psychology, 80*(4), 437–447.

Juel, C., Griffith, P.L., & Gough, P.B. (1985). Acquisition of literacy: A longitudinal study of children in first and second grade. *Journal of Educational Psychology, 78*(4), 243–255.

Juel, C., & Roper/Schneider,D. (1985). The influence of basal readers on first grade reading. *Reading Research Quarterly, 20*(2), 134–152.

Kendeou, P., & van den Broek, P. (2007). The effects of prior knowledge and text structure on comprehension processes during reading of scientific texts. *Memory & Cognition, 35*(7), 1567–1577. doi:10.3758/BF03193491

Kiuhara, S.A., Hawken, L.S., & Graham, S. (2009). Teaching writing to high school students: A national survey. *Journal of Educational Psychology, 101*(1), 136–160. doi:10.1037/a0013097

Klingner, J.K., Urbach, J., Golos, D., Brownell, M., & Menon, S. (2010). Teaching reading in the 21st century: A glimpse at how special education teachers promote reading comprehension. *Learning Disability Quarterly, 33*(2), 59–74.

Landauer, T.K., Lochbaum, K.E., & Dooley, S. (2009). A new formative assessment technology for reading and writing. *Theory Into Practice, 48*(1), 44–52. doi:10.1080/00405840802577593

Lartz, M.N., & Mason, J.M. (1989). *Jamie: One child's journey from oral to written language* (Technical Report No. 453). Champaign: University of Illinois at Urbana-Champaign.

Liberman, A.M., Cooper, F.S., Shankweiler, D.P., & Studdert-Kennedy, M. (1967). Perception of the speech code. *Psychological Review, 74*(6), 431–461. doi:10.1037/h0020279

Lonigan, C.J., Farver, J.M., Phillips, B.M., & Clancy-Menchetti, J. (2011). Promoting the development of preschool children's emergent literacy skills: A randomized evaluation of a literacy-focused curriculum and two professional development models. *Reading and Writing, 24*(3), 305–337. doi:10.1007/s11145-009-9214-6.

Lundberg, I. (1984). Learning to read. *School Research Newsletter* (National Board of Education, Sweden), *August*.

Lundberg, I., Frost, J., & Petersen, O. (1988). Effects of an extensive program for stimulating phonological awareness in preschool children. *Reading Research Quarterly, 23*(3), 263–284. doi:10.1598/RRQ.23.3.1

Mann, V.A., & Liberman, I.Y. (1984). Phonological awareness and verbal short-term memory. *Journal of Learning Disabilities, 17*(10), 592–599.

Mason, J.M. (1977). *Reading readiness: A definition and skills hierarchy from preschoolers' developing conceptions of print* (Technical Report No. 59). Champaign: University of Illinois at Urbana-Champaign; Cambridge, MA: Bolt Beranek & Newman.

Mason, J.M. (1980). When do children begin to read? An exploration of four year old children's letter and word reading competencies. *Reading Research Quarterly, 15*(2), 203–227.

Mason, J.M., & Allen, J. (1986). A review of emergent literacy with implications for research and practice in reading. *Review of Research in Education, 13*(1), 3–47.

McBride-Chang, C., & Manis, F.R. (1996). Structural invariance in the associations of naming speed, phonological awareness, and verbal reasoning in good and poor readers: A test of the double deficit hypothesis. *Reading and Writing, 8*(4), 323–339.

McCormick, C.E., & Mason, J.M. (1984). *Intervention procedures for increasing preschool children's interest in and knowledge about reading* (Technical Report No. 312). Champaign: University of Illinois at Urbana-Champaign; Cambridge, MA: Bolt Beranek & Newman.

McGee, L.M. (1982). Awareness of text structure: Effects on children's recall of expository text. *Reading Research Quarterly, 17*(4), 581–590. doi:10.2307/747572

McGee, L.M., & Purcell-Gates, V. (1997). "So what's going on in research on emergent literacy?" *Reading Research Quarterly, 32*(3), 310–318. doi:10.1598/RRQ.32.3.5

McGill-Franzen, A. (Ed.). (2010). The National Early Literacy Panel report: Summary, commentary, and reflections on policies and practices to improve children's early literacy [Special issue]. *Educational Researcher, 39*(4).

McKeown, M.G., Beck, I.L., & Blake, R.G.K. (2009). Rethinking reading comprehension instruction: A comparison of instruction for strategies and content approaches. *Reading Research Quarterly, 44*(3), 218–253. doi:10.1598/RRQ.44.3.1

Meyer, B.J.F. (1975). *The organization of prose and its effects on memory*. Amsterdam: North-Holland.

Meyer, B.J.F., Brandt, D.M., & Bluth, G.J. (1980). Use of top-level structure in text: Key for reading comprehension of ninth-grade students. *Reading Research Quarterly, 16*(1), 72–103. doi:10.2307/747349

National Institute of Child Health and Human Development. (2000). *Report of the National Reading Panel. Teaching children to read: An evidence-based assessment of the scientific research literature on reading and its implications for reading instruction: Reports of the subgroups*. Washington, DC: U.S. Government Printing Office.

Needels, M.C., & Knapp, M.S. (1994). Teaching writing to children who are underserved. *Journal of Educational Psychology, 86*(3), 339–349. doi:10.1037/0022-0663.86.3.339.

Neuman, S.B., & Dickinson, D.K. (Eds.). (2003). *Handbook of early literacy research*. New York: Guilford.

Neuman, S.B., & Dickinson, D.K. (Eds.). (2011). *Handbook of early literacy research* (Vol. 3). New York: Guilford.

Neuman, S.B., & Dwyer, J. (2011). Developing vocabulary and conceptual knowledge for low-income preschoolers: A design experiment. *Journal of Literacy Research, 43*(2), 103–129. doi:10.1177/1086296X11403089

Neuman, S.B., & Roskos, K. (1993). Access to print for children of poverty: Differential effects of adult mediation and literacy-enriched play

settings on environmental and functional print tasks. *American Educational Research Journal*, *30*(1), 95–122.
Ninio, A. (1980). Picture-book reading in mother–infant dyads belonging to two subgroups in Israel. *Child Development*, *51*(2), 587–590.
Ninio, A., & Bruner, J. (1978). The achievement and antecedents of labelling. *Journal of Child Language*, *5*(1), 1–15.
Norman, R.R. (2010). Picture this: Processes prompted by graphics in informational text. *Literacy Teaching and Learning*, *14*(1/2), 1–39.
Owodally, A.M.A. (2011). Multilingual language and literacy practices and social identities in Sunni madrassahs in Mauritius: A case study. *Reading Research Quarterly*, *46*(2), 134–155. doi:10.1598/RRQ.46.2.3
Pappas, C.C., & Brown, E. (1988). The development of children's sense of the written story register: An analysis of the texture of kindergarteners' "pretend reading" texts. *Linguistics and Education*, *1*(1), 45–79.
Payne, A.C., Whitehurst, G.J., & Angell, A.L. (1994). The role of home literacy environment in the development of language ability in preschool children from low-income families. *Early Childhood Research Quarterly*, *9*(3/4), 427–440.
Perfetti, C.A. (1984). Reading acquisition and beyond: Decoding includes cognition. *American Journal of Education*, *93*(1), 40–60.
Perfetti, C.A., Beck, I., Bell, L.C., & Hughes, C. (1987). Phonemic knowledge and learning to read are reciprocal: A longitudinal study of first grade children. *Merrill Palmer Quarterly*, *33*(3), 283–319.
Perl, S., Pekala, R., Schwartz, J., Graves, A., Silver, B., & Carter, J. (1983). How teachers teach the writing process. *The Elementary School Journal*, *84*(1), 18–44. doi:10.1086/461340
Perry, K.H., & Moses, A.M. (2011). Television, language, and literacy practices in Sudanese refugee families: "I learned how to spell English on Channel 18." *Research in the Teaching of English*, *45*(3), 278–307.
Peterman, C., & Mason, J.M. (1984, November). *Kindergarten children's perceptions of the form of print in labeled pictures and stories*. Paper presented at the annual meeting of the National Reading Conference, St. Petersburg, FL.
Piasta, S.B., & Wagner, R.K. (2010). Developing early literacy skills: A meta-analysis of alphabet learning and instruction. *Reading Research Quarterly*, *45*(1), 8–38. doi:10.1598/RRQ.45.1.2.
Pikulski, J.J., & Tobin, A.W. (1989). Factors associated with long-term reading achievement of early readers. In S. McCormick & J. Zutell (Eds.), *Cognitive and social perspectives for literacy research and instruction: Thirty-eighth yearbook of the National Reading Conference* (pp. 135–143). Chicago: National Reading Conference.
Pritchard, R.J., & Honeycutt, R.L. (2006). The process approach to writing instruction: Examining its effectiveness. In C.A. MacArthur, S. Graham, & J. Fitzgerald (Eds.), *Handbook of writing research* (pp. 275–290). New York: Guilford.
Purcell-Gates, V. (1986). Lexical and syntactic knowledge of written narrative held by well-read-to kindergartners and second graders. *Research in the Teaching of English*, *22*(2), 128–160.
Purcell-Gates, V. (1996). Stories, coupons, and the "TV Guide": Relationships between home literacy experiences and emergent literacy knowledge. *Reading Research Quarterly*, *31*(4), 406–428.
Raz, I.S., & Bryant, P. (1990). Social background, phonological awareness and children's reading. *British Journal of Developmental Psychology*, *8*(3), 209–225.
Read, C. (1971). Pre-school children's knowledge of English phonology. *Harvard Educational Review*, *41*(1), 1–34.
Read, C. (1975). *Children's categorization of speech sounds in English* (Vol. 1). Urbana, IL: National Council of Teachers of English.
Rezaie, R., Simos, P.G., Fletcher, J.M., Juranek, J., Cirino, P.T., Li, Z., et al. (2011). The timing and strength of regional brain activation associated with word recognition in children with reading difficulties. *Frontiers in Human Neuroscience*, *5*, Article 00045. doi:10.3389/fnhum.2011.00045.
Rohl, M., & Pratt, C. (1995). Phonological awareness, verbal working memory and the acquisition of literacy. *Reading and Writing*, *7*(4), 327–360.
Russell, D.H. (1961). Reading research that makes a difference. *Elementary English*, *38*, 64–68.
Sakamoto, T., & Makita, K. (1973). Japan. In J.A. Downing (Ed.), *Comparative reading: Cross-national studies of behavior and processes in reading and writing* (pp. 440–465). New York: Macmillan.
Scarborough, H.S. (1989). Prediction of reading dysfunction from familial and individual differences. *Journal of Educational Psychology*, *81*(1), 101–108.
Scardamalia, M., Bereiter, C., & Goelman, H. (1982). The role of production factors in writing ability. In M. Nystrand (Ed.), *What writers know: The language, process, and structure of written discourse* (pp. 173–210). Orlando, FL: Academic.
Sénéchal, M., & Cornell, E.H. (1993). Vocabulary acquisition through shared reading experiences. *Reading Research Quarterly*, *28*(4), 360–374.
Sénéchal, M., Cornell, E.H., & Broda, L.S. (1995). Age-related differences in the organization of parent–infant interactions during picture-book reading. *Early Childhood Research Quarterly*, *10*(3), 317–337.
Sénéchal, M., LeFevre, J., Hudson, E., & Lawson, E.P. (1996). Knowledge of storybooks as a predictor of young children's vocabulary. *Journal of Educational Psychology*, *88*(3), 520–536.
Sénéchal, M., LeFevre, J., Thomas, E.M., & Daley, K.E. (1998). Differential effects of home literacy experiences on the development of oral and

written language. *Reading Research Quarterly, 33*(1), 91–116.
Shanahan, T. (2002). What reading research says: The promises and limitations of applying research to reading education. In A.E. Farstrup & S.J. Samuels (Eds.), *What research has to say about reading instruction* (3rd ed., pp. 8–24). Newark, DE: International Reading Association. doi:10.1598/0872071774.1
Shanahan, T., & Neuman, S.B. (1997). Literacy research that makes a difference. *Reading Research Quarterly, 32*(2), 202–210. doi:10.1598/RRQ.32.2.5.
Share, D.L., Jorm, A.F., Maclean, R., & Matthews, R. (1984). Sources of individual differences in reading acquisition. *Journal of Educational Psychology, 76*(6), 1309–1324. doi:10.1037/0022-0663.76.6.1309
Shaughnessy, M.P. (1977). *Errors and expectations: A guide for the teacher of basic writing.* New York: Oxford University Press.
Shavelson, R.J., & Towne, L. (Eds.). (2002). *Scientific research in education.* Washington, DC: National Academy Press.
Snow, C.E. (1983). Literacy and language: Relationships during the preschool years. *Harvard Educational Review, 53*(2), 165–189.
Snow, C., Barnes, W.S., Chandler, J., Goodman, I.F., & Hemphill, L. (1991). *Unfulfilled expectations: Home and school influences on literacy.* Cambridge, MA: Harvard University Press.
Snow, C.E., & Ninio, A. (1986). The contracts of literacy: What children learn from learning to read books. In W.H. Teale & E. Sulzby (Eds.), *Emergent literacy: Writing and reading* (pp. 116–138). Westport, CT: Ablex.
Sonnenschein, S., Baker, L., & Serpell, R. (2010). The Early Childhood Project: A 5-year longitudinal investigation of children's literacy development in sociocultural context. In D. Aram & O. Korat (Eds.), *Literacy development and enhancement across orthographies and cultures* (pp. 85–96). New York: Springer. doi:10.1007/978-1-4419-0834-6_6
Stahl, S.A., & Murray, B.A. (1994). Defining phonological awareness and its relationship to early reading. *Journal of Educational Psychology, 86*(2), 221–234. doi:10.1037/0022-0663.86.2.221
Stahl, S.A., & Nagy, W.E. (2006). *Teaching word meanings.* Mahwah, NJ: Erlbaum.
Stanovich, K.E. (1990). A call for an end to the paradigm wars in reading research. *Journal of Reading Behavior, 22*(3), 221–231. doi:10.1080/10862969009547708
Stanovich, K.E., Cunningham, A.E., & Feeman, D.J. (1984). Intelligence, cognitive skills, and early reading progress. *Reading Research Quarterly, 19*(3), 278–303. doi:10.2307/747822
Stevenson, H.W., & Newman, R.S. (1986). Long-term prediction of achievement and attitudes in mathematics and reading. *Child Development, 57*(3), 646–659.
Sulzby, E. (1985). Children's emergent reading of favorite storybooks: A developmental study. *Reading Research Quarterly, 20*(4), 458–481.
Sulzby, E. (1986). Writing and reading: Signs of oral and written language organization in the young child. In W.H. Teale & E. Sulzby (Eds.), *Emergent literacy: Writing and reading* (pp. 50–89). Westport, CT: Ablex.
Sulzby, E., Barnhart, J., & Hieshima, J. (1988). *Forms of writing and rereading from writing: A preliminary report* (Technical Report No. 437). Champaign: Center for the Study of Reading, University of Illinois at Urbana-Champaign.
Sulzby, E., & Teale, W. (1991). Emergent literacy. In R. Barr, M.L. Kamil, P. Mosenthal, & P.D. Pearson (Eds.), *Handbook of reading research* (Vol. 2, pp. 727–758). New York: Longman.
Taylor, B.M. (1982). Text structure and children's comprehension and memory for expository material. *Journal of Educational Psychology, 74*(3), 323–340. doi:10.1037/0022-0663.74.3.323
Taylor, B.M., & Beach, R.W. (1984). The effects of text structure instruction on middle-grade students' comprehension and production of expository text. *Reading Research Quarterly, 19*(2), 134–146. doi:10.2307/747358
Teale, W.H. (1986). Home background and young children's literacy development. In W.H. Teale & E. Sulzby (Eds.), *Emergent literacy: Writing and reading* (pp. 173–206). Westport, CT: Ablex.
Teale, W.H., Hoffman, J., Paciga, K., Lisy, J.G., Richardson, S., & Berkel, C. (2009). Early literacy: Then and now. In J.V. Hoffman & Y.M. Goodman (Eds.), *Changing literacies for changing times: An historical perspective on the future of reading research, public policy, and classroom practices* (pp. 76–97). New York: Routledge.
Teale, W.H., & Sulzby, E. (Eds.). (1986). *Emergent literacy: Writing and reading.* Norwood, NJ: Ablex.
Temple, C.A., Nathan, R.G., & Burris, N.A. (1982). *The beginnings of writing.* Boston: Allyn & Bacon.
Tharp, R.G., Jordan, C., Speidel, G.E., Au, K.K., Klein, T.W., Calkins, R.P., et al. (1984). Product and process in applied developmental research: Education and the children of a minority. In M.E. Lamb, A.L. Brown, & B. Rogoff (Eds.), *Advances in developmental psychology* (Vol. 3, pp. 91–142). Hillsdale, NJ: Erlbaum.
Thorndike, R. (1976). Reading comprehension in 15 countries. In J.E. Merritt (Ed.), *New horizons in reading* (pp. 500–507). Newark, DE: International Reading Association.
Torgesen, J.K., Morgan, S.T., & Davis, C. (1992). Effects of two types of phonological awareness training on word learning in kindergarten children. *Journal of Educational Psychology, 84*(3), 364–370.
Treiman, R., & Baron, J. (1983). Phonemic-analysis training helps children benefit from spelling-sound rules. *Memory & Cognition, 11*(4), 382–389. doi:10.3758/BF03202453

Tunmer, W.E., Herriman, M.L., & Nesdale, A.R. (1988). Metalinguistic abilities and beginning reading. *Reading Research Quarterly*, *23*(2), 134–158.

Uhry, J.K., & Shepherd, M.J. (1993). Segmentation/spelling instruction as part of a first-grade reading program: Effects on several measures of reading. *Reading Research Quarterly*, *28*(3), 218–233. doi:10.2307/747995

Valdez-Menchaca, M.C., & Whitehurst, G.J. (1992). Accelerating language development through picture book reading: A systematic extension to Mexican day care. *Developmental Psychology*, *28*(6), 1106–1114.

Vaughn, S., Klingner, J.K., Swanson, E.A., Boardman, A.G., Roberts, G., Mohammed, S.S., et al. (2011). Efficacy of collaborative strategic reading with middle school students. *American Educational Research Journal*, *48*(4), 938–964. doi:10.3102/0002831211410305

Wagner, R.K. (1996, April). *Meta-analysis of the effects of phonological awareness training with children*. Paper presented at the annual meeting of the American Educational Research Association, New York.

Wagner, R.K., & Torgesen, J.K. (1987). The nature of phonological processing and its causal role in the acquisition of reading skills. *Psychological Bulletin*, *101*(2), 192–212.

Wagner, R.K., Torgesen, J.K., & Rashotte, C.A. (1994). Development of reading-related phonological processing abilities: New evidence of bidirectional causality from a latent variable longitudinal study. *Developmental Psychology*, *30*(1), 73–87.

Wells, C.G. (1981). *Learning through interaction: The study of language development*. New York: Cambridge University Press.

Wells, G. (1985). Preschool literacy-related activities and success in school. In D.R. Olson, N. Torrance, & A. Hildyard (Eds.), *Literacy, language, and learning: The nature and consequences of reading and writing* (pp. 229–255). New York: Cambridge University Press.

White, K.R. (1982). The relation between socioeconomic status and academic achievement. *Psychological Bulletin*, *91*(3), 461–481.

Whitehurst, G.J. (1996, April). *A structural equation model of the role of home literacy environment in the development of emergent literacy skills in children from low-income backgrounds*. Paper presented at the annual meeting of the American Educational Research Association, New York.

Whitehurst, G.J., Falco, F.L., Lonigan, C.J., & Fischel, J.E. (1988). Accelerating language development through picture book reading. *Developmental Psychology*, *24*(4), 552–559.

Whitehurst, G.J., & Lonigan, C.J. (1998). Child development and emergent literacy. *Child Development*, *69*(3), 848–872.

Williams, J.P. (1980). Teaching decoding with an emphasis on phoneme analysis and phoneme blending. *Journal of Educational Psychology*, 72(1), 1–15. doi:10.1037/0022-0663.72.1.1

Yaden, D.B., Rowe, D.W., & MacGillivray, L. (2000). Emergent literacy: A matter (polyphony) of perspectives. In M.L. Kamil, P.B. Mosenthal, P.D. Pearson, & R. Barr (Eds.), *Handbook of reading research* (Vol. 3, pp. 425–454). Mahwah, NJ: Erlbaum.

Yaw, J.S., Skinner, C.H., Parkhurst, J., Taylor, C.M., Booher, J., & Chambers, K. (2011). Extending research on a computer-based sight-word reading intervention to a student with autism. *Journal of Behavioral Education*, *20*(1), 44–54. doi:10.1007/s10864-010-9118-1

SECTION TWO

Processes of Reading and Literacy

This section includes a spectrum of chapters that provide a foundation in socially embedded language and cognitive processes upon which readers build knowledge, skills, and strategies. Most emergent readers evolve through identifiable phases of reading growth, acquire word knowledge, develop comprehension, and become self-regulating as they gain metacognitive skills. All of these aspects of a reader's growth are explored in these chapters. But that is not the end of the story. Because the ways readers respond to and engage with texts vary widely, we include chapters exploring motivation and engagement. Furthermore, engaged, responsive teachers using effective instructional strategies can have profound, enduring effects on children's development as readers, including those who struggle to master the process. Here we provide an overview of each part's content and contribution to our understanding of reading processes. Questions suitable for reflection and discussion follow each chapter.

Part 1: Language and Cognition in Sociocultural Contexts

For this introductory section on literacy processes, we selected chapters that represent a sociolinguistic base from which reading emerges and the subsequent effects of that base on reading. We sought perspectives that go beyond reading solely as a network of cognitive processes to a view of reading as a sequence of meaning-construction events capable of defining us, others, and our world.

James Paul Gee's "Reading as Situated Language: A Sociocognitive Perspective" (Chapter 4) reflects the view that reading is far more than processing skills; it is a process embedded in a context of social interaction and culture. As children learn social languages—such as the language of rap, street gangs, classrooms, or law—they also are socialized into Discourses, which Gee also calls "communities of practice" (p. 142) or "identity kits" (p. 143). While socialized into Discourses, children build cultural models that inform Discourse members of what is linguistically, socially, and culturally acceptable practices for that community. A Discourse establishes a reader's/writer's world and suggests that the reader's/writer's work in that world is to gain a critical consciousness of how he or she is defined by texts.

Acknowledging that meanings are socially constructed, M.A.K. Halliday looks closely at a child's developing discourse skills in language. Through "The Place of Dialogue in Children's Construction of Meaning" (Chapter 5), he shows us how a Discourse, in Gee's sense, contributes to a child's grasp of language and formation of personal identity.

In "Social Talk and Imaginative Play: Curricular Basics for Young Children's Language and Literacy" (Chapter 6), Anne Haas Dyson and Celia Genishi explore the tension between the official school curriculum and the more natural learning that takes place through children's imaginative play and social activities. The authors describe how dominant official language arts curricula have focused on individualized basic skills and raising test scores for minority children from low-income families, including those learning English as an additional language. The demands of the official curriculum have frequently discouraged imaginative play and talk. The authors present data from two case studies to demonstrate how basic childhood processes allow children to engage cross-culturally in their social worlds.

In "Exploring Vygotskian Perspectives in Education: The Cognitive Value of Peer Interaction" (Chapter 7), Ellice Forman and Courtney Cazden reveal how adult–child interactions differ from child–child interactions in school settings and so emphasize the importance of providing children with classroom interactions, such as peer tutoring and collaborative work. Those forms of peer exchange provide opportunities to practice questioning and direction giving, language activities that young children rarely perform in school-situated child–teacher transactions.

The next two chapters in this part of Section Two demonstrate the intersubjective defining powers of language. Shirley Brice Heath's "It's a Book! It's a Bookstore! Theories of Reading in the Worlds of Childhood and Adolescence" (Chapter 8) examines the ways in which researchers study the value of reading books to children, and particularly the degree of influence such reading practices have had on educators. Heath's brief summation of her latest longitudinal ethnographic study provides the background necessary for understanding the relation of extended talk to academic language. She concludes with a cautionary note about expecting too much of media and multitasking, especially in light of the "toxic stress" (p. 222) such activity can induce.

In "Emergent Biliteracy in Young Mexican Immigrant Children" (Chapter 9), Iliana Reyes and Patricia Azuara report on three case studies that reveal the metalinguistic awareness and strategies their biliterate student participants demonstrated. The studies offer a glimpse into how daily bilingual family interactions positioned the young students into multiple roles as teacher and student, and as novice and expert. Reyes and Azuara expressed hope that their study would challenge the stereotype that Mexican immigrant families fail to provide home environments that prepare their children for formal literacy learning at school. Their findings also challenge a deficit view of bilingualism and biliteracy.

Carol Lee's "Revisiting Is October Brown Chinese? A Cultural Modeling Activity System for Underachieving Students" (Chapter 10) recounts how a group of African American students move from being disengaged underachievers to active participants in their school's ninth-grade English curriculum. Using cultural modeling activity theory, the author (who doubles as their teacher) analyzes a day of English language arts instruction in their urban high school. Lee focuses her analysis on a class discussion that involved signifying—a form of discourse that requires participants to engage in innuendo, satire, and other forms of figurative language. How this discourse ignited students' engagement with canonical texts is one of several highlights in the chapter.

As a group, the chapters in Part 1 demonstrate how literacy development is embedded in social and cultural contexts whose influence persists from a child's earliest moments of language acquisition, throughout the self-shaping school years, and well into adult life in college and the workplace. As we move toward a closer inspection of cognitive processes, including phonological processing, word recognition, fluency, comprehension, and metacognition, we suggest keeping in mind that each phase of reading growth and each instant of reading occur within a social and cultural theater that contributes to every child's role and sense of reality.

Part 2: Foundations for Literacy Development

The chapters in this part of Section Two are concerned with individual differences in reading acquisition and achievement across age levels. We were particularly interested in research that addresses the long-term consequences to readers going off track in their progress toward proficiency.

Focusing on sustained acceleration of achievement in reading comprehension, chapter authors Mei Kuin Lai, Stuart McNaughton, Meaola Amituanai-Toloa, Rolf Turner, and Selena Hsiao discovered that despite New Zealand students' relatively high scores on international assessments of reading comprehension, large disparities remain in the distribution of achievement scores. These disparities lie between indigenous (Māori) and immigrant (Pasifika) children and other children who live in urban communities. In "Sustained Acceleration of Achievement in Reading Comprehension: The New Zealand Experience" (Chapter 11), the authors argue that sustaining accelerated rates of achievement for students in poor communities is dependent on the development of professional learning communities capable of analyzing the effectiveness of instruction and then making the necessary adjustments. Collaboration between the researchers and teachers yielded increased rates of student achievement that was sustained over a period of three years.

In "Phases of Word Learning: Implications for Instruction With Delayed and Disabled Readers" (Chapter 12), Linnea Ehri and Sandra McCormick describe five phases and their accompanying reading behaviors. These phases progress from pre-alphabetic, so called because these children do not use alphabetic knowledge to read words, to automatic, in which readers manifest proficient word reading. The authors also provide instructional practices that contribute to delayed and disabled readers' growth in each phase as they learn new strategies to decipher words.

Attempting to address yet another ripple in the long-standing debate about code-emphasis versus meaning-emphasis instructional approaches in early literacy development, Christopher Lonigan and Timothy Shanahan's "Developing

Early Literacy Skills: Things We Know We Know and Things We Know We Don't Know" (Chapter 13) defends the National Early Literacy Panel's (NELP) findings on oral language. Although the critiques of the NELP's report have been plentiful (see also Chapters 14 and 41), the authors maintain that both code-related and meaning-related skills are necessary in developing a young child's ability to comprehend written texts.

In "Advancing Early Literacy Learning for All Children: Implications of the NELP Report for Dual-Language Learners" (Chapter 14), Kris Gutiérrez, Marlene Zepeda, and Dina Castro advocate the use of the term *dual-language learners* (DLLs) rather than *limited English proficient students* or *English learners*. The term *DLLs*, they argue, does a better job of capturing these students' linguistic repertoires and defines them by more than simply their proficiency in English. Citing the dearth of studies on DLLs from birth to age 4 as a limitation of the NELP's report, the authors caution that care should be taken when drawing policy implications from general studies that do not address the unique variations among DLLs.

Melanie Kuhn and Steven Stahl's "Fluency: Developmental and Remedial Practices—Revisited" (Chapter 15) is situated within Chall's (1996) stage theory of children's growth in reading. Noting the importance of a "rapid, accurate, and expressive rendering of text" (p. 385) as opposed to word-by-word reading, the authors review the literature on fluency as a factor in the reading process. The contributions of automaticity, prosody, and fluency instruction are examined. Kuhn and Stahl conclude that fluency instruction improves reading achievement among children in first and second grades, but they also note that the role of fluency in helping readers move from simply decoding to comprehending is an area that needs more classroom-based research.

In "A Road Map for Understanding Reading Disabilities and Other Reading Problems, Redux" (Chapter 16), Louise Spear-Swerling traces how the Individuals with Disabilities Education Act of 2004 has permitted schools to use Response to Intervention criteria to identify reading disabilities rather than the IQ–achievement discrepancy model. An important feature of this chapter is a table of common cognitive profiles and patterns of reading difficulties that distinguish between three major types: specific word-recognition difficulties, specific comprehension difficulties, and mixed reading difficulties.

Part 3: Comprehension Development From Words to Worlds

The seven articles that compose this part of the section on processes of reading and literacy extend from the role of language in the development of young children's theory of mind to an investigation of the neurological correlates of reading processes and reading development. Many of the entries between these fresh and insightful end pieces are classics that enrich our understanding of schema theory and efforts to revisit and refresh our understanding of that theory's contributions to literacy research and theory. Even though some of these pieces were originally published 30 or more years ago, they afford a rich grounding in research and theory applicable to literacy studies today.

In "Language Pathways Into the Community of Minds" (Chapter 17), Katherine Nelson argues that the "'theory of mind'" (p. 437), as it relates to cognitive development, has been too narrowly constructed and instead suggests a construct she terms the "community of minds" (p. 439) to describe the cognitive developmental process made possible through the use, comprehension, and production of language. Within this community of minds, language enables the child to develop higher order cognitive processes, including those that enable the development of a theory of mind during a child's preschool years. This is a gradual process as the child learns that knowledge is not a private matter but is shared among members of a community.

William Nagy and Judith Scott provide a comprehensive review of vocabulary acquisition processes in "Vocabulary Processes" (Chapter 18). Their interest lies in answering two related questions: How do children add words to their reading and writing vocabularies, and how do they learn the meanings of new words? The authors reveal the complexities of word knowledge and the value of metalinguistic awareness in learning words.

The next three chapters explore the forms and functions of background knowledge, including the effects of contexts and word knowledge on miscues. Richard Anderson's classic piece "Role of the Reader's Schema in Comprehension, Learning, and Memory" (Chapter 19) explains schema theory, provides examples of evidence supporting the theory, and makes recommendations for its application to classroom instruction.

In "Schema Theory Revisited" (Chapter 20), Mary McVee, Kailonnie Dunsmore, and James Gavelek revisit schema theory by reinterpreting it through sociocultural perspectives. Schema theory, they argue, is worth revisiting because it is a concept that is frequently used in textbooks for preservice and inservice teachers. However, it is often discussed as an in-the-head phenomenon separate from sociocultural theories of learning. In reviewing the critiques of schema theory, the authors argue that cultural and social factors should be integral components of schema and not just seen as background variables. A sociocultural view of schema suggests that meanings for words and images do not exist solely in the head but also within actions, talk, experiences, and culturally situated knowledge. Schemata originate from social interactions between individuals and their environments. Although connections to prior knowledge are important, schema theory must include attention to the cultural material students bring to interactions with texts, and teachers must learn to attend to this in their instruction.

In "To Err Is Human: Learning About Language Processes by Analyzing Miscues" (Chapter 21), Yetta and Kenneth Goodman develop the role of schema in meaning construction through their exploration of miscue analysis. Arguing that there is nothing random about miscues, the Goodmans explain the role of schema-forming miscues as a kind of struggle toward accommodation of new information and explain schema-driven miscues as those reflecting assimilation of either old or new information into a preexisting schema. A reader's linguistic and conceptual schematic background manifests itself in both miscues and the reader's conceptual understanding of texts.

In "Cognitive Flexibility Theory: Advanced Knowledge Acquisition in Ill-Structured Domains" (Chapter 22), Rand Spiro, Richard Coulson, Paul Feltovich, and Daniel Anderson explore the learning of complex concepts and identify cognitive elements that interfere with advanced learning. The outgrowth of that exploration is cognitive flexibility theory, a view of cognition that emphasizes multiple representations of concepts, multiple linkages between knowledge structures, and the promotion of schema assembly rather than the activation of schema as prepacked, monolithic units of knowledge in memory. For learning in ill-structured domains where we encounter sometimes-overwhelming complexity, such as learning to read or teaching reading, Spiro's theory, along with its situation-specific orientation, is a remarkably insightful and organic accommodation to earlier, more mechanistic views of schema form and function.

In "Educational Neuroscience for Reading Researchers" (Chapter 23), George Hruby and Usha Goswami review recent promising advances in neuroscientific research on cognitive processes involved in reading, noting that over the last 30 years of brain research, only the surface has been scratched to date regarding areas of neural activation that function when a reader is making sense of text. Neuroscience is an exciting field, as understanding how brains operate when learning occurs offers enormous potential for educators, and could very well upend established literacy theories. However, much more research will be needed to merge brain, social, cognitive, and cultural perspectives in ways beneficial for reading education.

Part 4: Motivation and Engagement

In this part, we include studies addressing literacy engagement for different purposes and with varying effects. All reflect concerns about reader motivation, an often neglected but integral dimension of the reading process. In the mid-1990s, a flood of research on motivation found its way into the literacy community, partly through the work of the National Reading Research Center at the University of Maryland and the University of Georgia. This recognition of the importance of motivation in the reading process led to further studies of engaged readers who bring to class not only their cognitive capacities and skills but also individual identities and entire cultural worlds that affect how and what they learn.

For example, Ana Taboada, Stephen Tonks, Allan Wigfield, and John Guthrie offer "Effects of Motivational and Cognitive Variables on Reading Comprehension" (Chapter 24). They examined how both motivational and cognitive variables predict upper elementary school students' reading comprehension while controlling for another set of variables. Based on multiple regression analyses of their data, the authors concluded that the desire to comprehend text stimulates a reader to be metacognitive, activate background knowledge, and implement relevant cognitive strategies.

In "Toward a More Anatomically Complete Model of Literacy Instruction: A Focus on African American Male Adolescents and Texts" (Chapter 25), Alfred Tatum presents a qualitative case study of an African American adolescent male student with whom he worked for more than a 10-month period. The study was designed to gather data on the student's motivation for reading written texts and how they affected the ways in which the student viewed himself, both in his home and in community contexts. Tatum used what he referred to as enabling texts, or texts that move beyond a solely cognitive focus and include social, cultural, political, spiritual, and economic issues that are relevant to adolescents' lives.

Part 5: Instructional Effects on Literacy Development

The chapters in this part are in response to several readers' requests for examples of theoretically grounded research on children and young people's literacy development that have application for classroom instruction. In "Marie M. Clay's Theoretical Perspective: A Literacy Processing Theory" (Chapter 26), Mary Anne Doyle traces the development of a well-known literacy intervention: Reading Recovery. Although much has been written about Clay's research and theoretical undertakings, Doyle pulls together all the complex pieces of Clay's work and applies them to instructional decision making. For readers who have asked why Reading Recovery is effective, this chapter provides answers.

The second chapter in this part on instructional effects on children's literacy development answers another reader-posed question: What processes did the authors of reciprocal teaching go through to create reciprocal teaching? Ann Brown, Annemarie Sullivan Palincsar, and Bonnie Armbruster address this question in "Instructing Comprehension-Fostering Activities in Interactive Learning Situations" (Chapter 27), which also appeared in the fifth edition of *Theoretical Models and Processes of Reading*. For this new edition, however, we invited Palincsar to provide a postscript. Her response, which is included at the end of the original article, discusses two noteworthy transformations that reciprocal teaching has undergone since its inception. She also addresses her disagreement with some recent attacks that have been directed toward strategy-based instruction.

REFERENCE

Chall, J.S. (1996). *Stages of reading development* (2nd ed.). Fort Worth, TX: Harcourt Brace.

CHAPTER 4

Reading as Situated Language: A Sociocognitive Perspective

James Paul Gee, Arizona State University*

My main goal here is to situate reading within a broad perspective that integrates work on cognition, language, social interaction, society, and culture. In light of recent reports on reading (National Reading Panel, 2000; Snow, Burns, & Griffin, 1998) that have tended to treat reading quite narrowly in terms of psycholinguistic processing skills, I argue that such a broad perspective on reading is essential if we are to speak to issues of access and equity in schools and workplaces. I also argue that reading and writing cannot be separated from speaking, listening, and interacting, on the one hand, or using language to think about and act on the world, on the other. Thus, it is necessary to start with a viewpoint on language (oral and written) itself, a viewpoint that ties language to embodied action in the material and social world.

I have organized this article into four parts. First, I develop a viewpoint on language that stresses the connections among language, embodied experience, and situated action and interaction in the world. In the second part, I argue that what is relevant to learning literacy is not English in general, but specific varieties of English that I call "social languages." I then go on to discuss notions related to the idea of social languages, specifically Discourses (with a capital *D*) and their connections to socially situated identities and cultural models. In the third part, I show the relevance of the earlier sections to the development of literacy in early childhood through a specific example. Finally, I close the article with a discussion of the importance of language abilities (construed in a specific way) to learning to read.

A Viewpoint on Language

It is often claimed that the primary function of human language is to convey information, but I believe this is not true. Human languages are used for a wide array of functions, including but by no means limited to conveying information (Halliday, 1994). I will argue here that human language has two primary functions through which it is best studied and analyzed. I would state these functions as follows: to scaffold the performance of action in the world, including social activities and interactions; to scaffold human affiliation in cultures and social groups and institutions through creating and enticing others to take certain

This chapter is reprinted from *Journal of Adolescent & Adult Literacy*, 44(8), 714–725.

perspectives on experience. *Action* is the most important word in the first statement; *perspectives* is the most important word in the second. I will discuss each of these two functions in turn.

Situated Action

Traditional approaches to language have tended to look at it as a closed system (for discussion, see Clancey, 1997). Any piece of language is treated as representation (re-presenting) of some information. On the traditional view, what it means to comprehend a piece of language is to be able to translate it into some equivalent representational system, either other language (one's own words) or some mental language or language of thought that mimics the structure of natural languages (e.g., is couched in terms of logical propositions).

However, there are a variety of perspectives today on language that tie its comprehension much more closely to experience of and action in the world. For example, consider these two remarks from work in cognitive psychology: "comprehension is grounded in perceptual simulations that prepare agents for situated action" (Barsalou, 1999a, p. 77); "to a particular person, the meaning of an object, event, or sentence is what that person can do with the object, event, or sentence" (Glenberg, 1997, p. 3).

These two quotes are from work that is part of a family of related viewpoints. For want of a better name, we might call the family "situated cognition studies" (e.g., Barsalou, 1999a, 1999b; Brown, Collins, & Dugid, 1989; Clancey, 1997; Clark, 1997; Engestrom, Miettinen, raij Punamaki, 1999; Gee, 1992; Glenberg, 1997; Glenberg & Robertson, 1999; Hutchins, 1995; Latour, 1999; Lave, 1996; Lave & Wenger, 1991; Wenger, 1998). While there are differences among the members of the family (alternative theories about situated cognition), they share the viewpoint that meaning in language is not some abstract propositional representation that resembles a verbal language. Rather, meaning in language is tied to people's experiences of situated action in the material and social world. Furthermore, these experiences (perceptions, feelings, actions, and interactions) are stored in the mind or brain, not in terms of propositions or language but in something like dynamic images tied to perception both of the world and of our own bodies, internal states, and feelings: "Increasing evidence suggests that perceptual simulation is indeed central to comprehension" (Barsalou, 1999a, p. 74).

It is almost as if we videotape our experiences as we are having them, create a library of such videotapes, edit them to make some prototypical tapes (or set of typical instances), but stand ever ready to add new tapes to our library. We re-edit the tapes based on new experiences or draw out of the library less typical tapes when the need arises. As we face new situations or new texts we run our tapes—perhaps a prototypical one, or a set of typical ones, or a set of contrasting ones, or a less typical one, whatever the case may be. We do this to apply our old experiences to our new experience and to aid us in making, editing, and storing the videotape that will capture this new experience, integrate it into our library, and allow us to make sense of it (both while we are having it and afterwards).

These videotapes are what we think with and through. They are what we use to give meaning to our experiences in the world. They are what we use to give meaning to words and sentences. But they are not language or *in* language (not even in propositions). Furthermore, since they are representations of experience (including feelings, attitudes, embodied positions, and various sorts of foregrounds and backgrounds of attention), they are not just information or facts. Rather, they are value-laden, perspective-taking movies in the mind. Of course, talking about videotapes in the mind is a metaphor that, like all metaphors, is incorrect if pushed too far (see Barsalou, 1999b for how the metaphor can be cashed out and corrected by a consideration of a more neurally realistic framework for "perception in the mind").

On this account, the meanings of words, phrases, and sentences are always situated, that is, customized to our actual contexts (Gee, 1999a). Here context means not just the words, deeds, and things that surround our words or deeds, but also our purposes, values, and intended courses of action and interaction. We bring out of our store of videotapes those that are most relevant to understanding our current context or those that allow us to create and construe that context in a certain way. We can see this in even so trivial an example as the following: If you hear "The coffee spilled, go get the mop" you run a quite different set of images (that is, assemble a quite different situated meaning) than when you hear "The coffee spilled, go get a broom."

On this account, too, the meaning of a word (the way in which we give it meaning in a particular context) is not different than the meaning of an experience, object, or tool in the world (i.e., in terms of the way in which we give the experience, object, or tool meaning):

> The meaning of the glass to you, at that particular moment, is in terms of the actions available. The meaning of the glass changes when different constraints on action are combined. For example, in a noisy room, the glass may become a mechanism for capturing attention (by tapping it with a spoon), rather than a mechanism for quenching thirst. (Glenberg, 1997, p. 41)

While Glenberg here is talking about the meaning of the glass as an object in one's specific experience of the world at a given time and place, he could just as well be talking about the meaning of the word *glass* in one's specific experience of a piece of talk or written text at a given time and place. The meaning of the word *glass* in a given piece of talk or text would be given by running a simulation (a videotape) of how the glass fits into courses of action being built up in the theater of our minds. These courses of action are based on how we understand all the other words and goings on in the world that surrounds the word *glass* as we read it: "[T]he embodied models constructed to understand language are the same as those that underlie comprehension of the natural environment" (Glenberg, 1997, p. 17).

If embodied action and social activity are crucially connected to the situated meanings oral or written language convey, then reading instruction must move well beyond relations internal to texts. Reading instruction must be rooted in the connections of texts to engagement in and simulations of actions, activities, and interactions—to real and imagined material and social worlds.

Perspective-Taking

Let me now turn to the second function of language already mentioned. Consider, in this regard, the following quote from Tomasello (1999):

> [T]he perspectivial nature of linguistic symbols, and the use of linguistic symbols in discourse interaction in which different perspectives are explicitly contrasted and shared, provide the raw material out of which the children of all cultures construct the flexible and multi-perspectival—perhaps even dialogical—cognitive representations that give human cognition much of its awesome and unique power. (p. 163)

Let's briefly unpack what this means. From the point of view of the model Tomasello was developing, the words and grammar of a human language exist to allow people to take and communicate alternative perspectives on experience (see also Hanks, 1996). That is, words and grammar exist to give people alternative ways to view one and the same state of affairs. Language is not about conveying neutral or objective information; rather, it is about communicating perspectives on experience and action in the world, often in contrast to alternative and competing perspectives: "We may then say that linguistic symbols are social conventions for inducing others to construe, or take a perspective on, some experiential situation" (Tomasello, 1999, p. 118).

Let me give some examples of what it means to say that words and grammar are not primarily about giving and getting information but are, rather, about giving and getting different perspectives on experience. I open Microsoft's Web site: Is it selling its products, marketing them, or underpricing them against the competition? Are products I can download from the site without paying for them free, or are they being exchanged for having bought other Microsoft products (e.g., Windows), or are there strings attached? Note also how metaphors (like "strings attached") add greatly to, and are a central part of, the perspective-taking we can do. If I use the grammatical construction "Microsoft's new operating system is loaded with bugs" I take a perspective in which Microsoft is less agentive and responsible than if I use the grammatical construction "Microsoft has loaded its new operating system with bugs."

Here is another example: Do I say that a child who is using multiple cues to give meaning to a written text (i.e., using some decoding along with picture and context cues) is reading, or do I say (as some of the pro-phonics people do) that she is not really reading, but engaged in emergent literacy? (For those latter people, the child is only really reading when she is decoding all the words in the text and not using nondecoding cues for word recognition). In this case, contending camps actually fight over what perspective on experience the term *reading* or *really reading* ought to name. In the end, the point is that no wording is ever neutral or just "the facts." All wordings—given the very nature of language—are perspectives on experience that comport with competing perspectives in the grammar of the language and in actual social interactions.

How do children learn how words and grammar line up to express particular perspectives on experience? Here, interactive, intersubjective dialogue with more advanced peers and adults appears to be crucial. In such dialogue, children come to see, from time to time, that others have taken a different perspective on what is being talked about than they themselves have. At a certain developmental level, children have the capacity to distance themselves from their own perspectives and (internally) simulate the perspectives the other person is taking, thereby coming to see how words and grammar come to express those perspectives (in contrast to the way in which different words and grammatical constructions express competing perspectives).

Later, in other interactions, or when thinking, the child can re-run such simulations and imitate the perspective-taking the more advanced peer or adult has done by using certain sorts of words and grammar. Through such simulations and imitative learning, children learn to use the symbolic means that other persons have used to share attention with them: "In imitatively learning a linguistic symbol from other persons in this way, I internalize not only their communicative intention (their intention to get me to share their attention) but also the specific perspective they have taken" (Tomasello, 1999, p. 128).

Tomasello (1999) also pointed out—in line with my previous discussion that the world and texts are assigned meanings in the same way—that children come to use objects in the world as symbols at the same time (or with just a bit of a time lag) as they come to use linguistic symbols as perspective-taking devices on the world. Furthermore, they learn to use objects as symbols (to assign them different meanings encoding specific perspectives in different contexts) in the same way they learn to use linguistic symbols. In both cases, the child simulates in his head and later imitates in his words and deeds the perspectives his interlocutor must be taking on a given situation by using certain words and certain forms of grammar or by treating certain objects in certain ways. Thus, meaning for words, grammar, and objects comes out of intersubjective dialogue and interaction: "[H]uman symbols [are] inherently social, intersubjective, and perspectival" (Tomasello, 1999, p. 131).

If value-laden perspectives on experience are connected to the situated meanings oral or written language convey, then, once again, we have an argument that reading instruction must move well beyond relations internal to texts. Reading instruction must be rooted in the taking and imagining of diverse perspectives on real and imagined material and social worlds. The moral of both the functions of language that we have discussed is this: Our ways with words (oral or written) are of the same nature as our ways with ways of understanding and acting on the material and social world. In a quite empirical sense, the moral is one Freire (1995) taught us long ago: Reading the word and reading the world are, at a deep level, integrally connected—indeed, at a deep level, they are one and the same process.

Social Languages

The perspective taken thus far on language is misleading in one respect. It misses the core fact that any human language is not one general thing (like English), but composed of a great variety of different styles, registers, or social languages. Different patterns of vocabulary, syntax (sentence structure), and discourse connectors (devices that connect sentences together to make a whole integrated text) constitute different social languages, each of which is connected to specific sorts of social activities and to a specific socially situated identity (Gee, 1999a). We recognize different social languages by recognizing these patterns (in much the way we recognize a face through recognizing a certain characteristic patterning of facial features).

As an example, consider the following, taken from a school science textbook: "1. The destruction of a land surface by the combined effects of abrasion and removal of weathered material by transporting agents is called erosion.... The production of rock waste by mechanical processes and chemical changes is called weathering" (Martin, 1990, p. 93).

A whole bevy of grammatical design features mark these sentences as part of a distinctive social language. Some of these features are heavy subjects (e.g., "The production of rock waste by mechanical processes and chemical changes"); processes and actions named by nouns or nominalizations, rather than verbs (e.g., "production"); passive main verbs ("is called") and passives inside nominalizations (e.g., "production...by mechanical processes"); modifiers that are more "contentful" than the nouns they modify (e.g., "transporting agents"); and complex embedding (e.g., "weathered material by transporting agents" is a nominalization embedded inside "the combined effects of...," and this more complex nominalization is embedded inside a yet larger nominalization, "the destruction of...").

This style of language also incorporates a great many distinctive discourse markers, that is, linguistic features that characterize larger stretches of text and give them unity and coherence as a certain type of text or genre. For example, the genre here is explanatory definition, and it is characterized by classificatory language of a certain sort. Such language leads adept readers to form a classificatory scheme in their heads something like this: There are two kinds of change (erosion and weathering) and two kinds of weathering (mechanical and chemical).

This mapping from elements of vocabulary, syntax, and discourse to a specific style of language used in characteristic social activities is just as much a part of reading and writing as is the phonics (sound-to-letter) mapping. In fact, more people fail to become successful school-based, academic, or work-related readers or writers because of failing to master this sort of mapping than the phonics one.

There are a great many different social languages—for example, the language of medicine, literature, street gangs, sociology, law, rap, or informal dinner-time talk among friends (who belong to distinctive cultures or social groups). To know any specific social language is to know how its characteristic design features are combined to carry out one or more specific social activities. It is to know, as well, how its characteristic lexical and grammatical design features are used to enact a particular socially situated identity, that is, being, at a given time and place, a lawyer, a gang member, a politician, a literary humanist, a "bench chemist," a radical feminist, an everyday person, or whatever. To know a particular social language is either to be able to "do" a particular identity, using that social language, or to be able to recognize such an identity, when we do not want to or cannot actively participate.

Let me give two further examples of social languages at work. First, I'll use an example I've used in this journal before. It's about a young woman telling the same story to her parents and to her boyfriend (*JAAL*, February 2000; Gee, 1996). To her parents at dinner she says, "Well, when I thought about it, I don't know, it seemed to me that Gregory should be considered the most offensive character." But to her boyfriend later she says, "What an ass that guy was, you know, her boyfriend." In the first case, the young woman is taking on the identity of an educated and dutiful daughter engaged in the social activity of reporting to her parents her viewpoints on what she has learned in school. In the second case, she is taking on the identity of a girlfriend engaged in the social activity of bonding with her boyfriend.

Here is a second example from Myers (1990, p. 150): A biologist wrote in a professional science journal, "Experiments show that *Heliconius* butterflies are less likely to oviposit on host plants that possess eggs or egg-like structures." Writing about the same thing in a popular science magazine, the same biologist wrote, "*Heliconius* butterflies lay their eggs on *Passiflora* vines. In defense the vines seem to have evolved fake eggs that make it look to the butterflies as if eggs have already been laid on them." In the first case, the biologist is taking on the identity of professional scientist engaged in the social activity of making experimental and theoretical claims (note, for instance, the subject "Experiments") to professional peers. In the second case, the biologist is taking on the identity of a popularizer or scientific journalist engaged in the social activity of telling the educated public a factual story about plants and animals (note, for instance, the subjects "butterflies" and "vines").

Now here is the bite of social languages and genres: When we talk about social languages and genres, oral and written language are inextricably mixed. Some social languages are written; some are spoken. Some have both spoken and written versions; written and spoken versions are often mixed and integrated within specific social practices. Furthermore, social languages are always integrally connected to the characteristic social activities (embodied action and interaction in the world), value-laden perspectives, and socially situated identities of particular groups of people or communities of practice. If discussions about reading are not about social languages (and thus, too, about embodied action and interaction in the world, value-laden perspectives, and socially situated identities), then they are not, in reality, about reading as a semiotic meaning-making process (and it is hard to know what reading is if it is not this).

Here is another part of the bite of talk about social languages and genres. Both inside and outside school, most social languages and genres are clearly not acquired by direct instruction. While some forms of (appropriately timed) scaffolding, modeling, and instructional guidance by mentors appear to be important, immersion in meaningful practice is essential. Social languages and genres are acquired by processes of socialization, an issue to which I will turn below.

It is inevitable, I would think, that someone at this point is going to object that social languages are really about the later stages of the acquisition of literacy. It will be pointed out that the current reading debates are almost always about small children and the earlier stages of reading. What, it will be asked, has all this talk of social languages got to do with early literacy? My answer is, everything. Social languages (and their connections to action, perspectives, and identities) are no less relevant to the first stages of learning to read than they are to the later ones (and there are not so much stages here as the same things going on over time at ever deeper and more complex levels). However, before I turn to the relevance of social languages to early childhood at the end of this article, I need to develop briefly a few more theoretical notions related to social languages.

Discourses

I said earlier that social languages are acquired by socialization. But now we must ask, socialization into what? When people learn new social languages and genres—at the level of being able to produce them and not just consume them—they are being socialized into what I will call Discourses with a big "D" (I use discourse with a little "d" to mean just language in use, Gee, 1996, 1999a; see also Clark, 1996). Even when people learn a new social language or genre only to consume (interpret), but not produce it, they are learning to recognize a new Discourse. Related but somewhat different terms others have used to capture some of what I am trying to capture with the term *Discourses* are communities of practice (Wenger, 1998), actor-actant networks (Latour, 1987, 1991), and activity systems (Engestrom, Miettinen, raij Punamaki, 1999; Leont'ev, 1978).

Discourses always involve language (i.e., they recruit specific social languages), but they always involve more than language as well. Social languages are embedded within Discourses and only have relevance and meaning within them. A Discourse integrates ways of talking, listening, writing, reading, acting, interacting, believing, valuing, and feeling (and using various objects, symbols, images, tools, and technologies) in the service of enacting meaningful socially situated identities and activities. Being-doing a certain sort of physicist, gang member, feminist, first-grade child in Ms. Smith's room, special ed (SPED) student, regular at the local bar, or gifted upper-middle-class child engaged in emergent literacy are all Discourses.

We can think of Discourses as identity kits. It's almost as if you get a toolkit full of specific devices (i.e., ways with words, deeds, thoughts, values, actions, interactions, objects, tools, and technologies) in terms of which you can enact a specific identity and engage in specific activities associated with that identity. For example, think of what devices (e.g., in words, deeds, clothes, objects, attitudes) you would get in a Sherlock Holmes identity kit (e.g., you do not get a "Say No to

Drugs" bumper sticker in this kit; you do get both a pipe and lots of logic). The Doctor Watson identity kit is different. And we can think of the Sherlock Holmes identity kit (Discourse) and the Doctor Watson identity kit (Discourse) as themselves parts of a yet larger Discourse, the Holmes-Watson Discourse, because Watson is part of Holmes's identity kit and Holmes is part of Watson's. Discourse can be embedded one inside another.

One Discourse can mix or blend two others. For example, Gallas (1994) created a sharing-time Discourse (a way of being a recognizable sharer in her classroom) that mixed Anglo and African American styles. Discourses can be related to each other in relationships of alignment or tension. For example, Scollon and Scollon (1981) have pointed out that school-based Discourses that incorporate essayist practices and values conflict with the values, attitudes, and ways with words embedded in some Native American home and community-based Discourses (i.e., ways of being a Native American of a certain sort). These latter Discourses value communicating only when the sender knows the receiver of the communication and his or her context and do not value the sorts of fictionalizing (generalizing) of sender and receiver that essayist practices involve.

Cultural Models

Within their socialization into Discourses (and we are all socialized into a great many across our lifetimes), people acquire cultural models (D'Andrade & Strauss, 1992; Gee, 1999a; Holland & Quinn, 1987; Shore, 1996; Strauss & Quinn, 1997). Cultural models are everyday theories (i.e., storylines, images, schemas, metaphors, and models) about the world that people socialized into a given Discourse share. Cultural models tell people what is typical or normal from the perspective of a particular Discourse (or a related or aligned set of them).

For example, certain types of middle-class people in the United States hold a cultural model of child development that goes something like this (Harkness, Super, & Keefer, 1992): A child is born dependent on her parents and grows up by going through (often disruptive) stages toward greater and greater independence (and independence is a high value for this group of people). This cultural model plays a central role in this group's Discourse of parent-child relations (i.e., enacting and recognizing identities as parents and children).

On the other hand, certain sorts of working-class families (Philipsen, 1975) hold a cultural model of child development that goes something like this: A child is born unsocialized and with tendencies to be selfish. The child needs discipline from the home to learn to be a cooperative social member of the family (a high value of this group of people). This cultural model plays a central role in this group's Discourse of parent-child relations.

These different cultural models, connected to different (partially) class-based Discourses of parenting, are not true or false. Rather, they focus on different aspects of childhood and development. Cultural models define for people in a Discourse what counts as normal and natural and what counts as inappropriate and deviant. They are, of course, thereby thoroughly value laden.

Figure 1. Summary of Tools for Understanding Language and Literacy in Sociocultural Terms

Discourses: Ways of combining and coordinating words, deeds, thoughts, values, bodies, objects, tools, and technologies, and other people (at the appropriate times and places) so as to enact and recognize specific socially situated identities and activities.

Social languages: Ways with words (oral and written) within Discourses that relate form and meaning so as to express specific socially situated identities and activities.

Genres: Combinations of ways with words (oral and written) and actions that have become more or less routine within a Discourse in order to enact and recognize specific socially situated identities and activities in relatively stable and uniform ways (and, in doing so, we humans reproduce our Discourses and institutions through history).

Cultural models: Often tacit and taken-for-granted schemata, storylines, theories, images, or representations (partially represented inside people's heads and partially represented within their materials and practices) that tell a group of people within a Discourse what is typical or normal from the point of view of that Discourse.

Cultural models come out of and, in turn, inform the social practices in which people in a Discourse engage. Cultural models are stored in people's minds (by no means always consciously), though they are supplemented and instantiated in the objects, texts, and practices that are part and parcel of the Discourse. For example, many guidebooks supplement and instantiate the above middle-class cultural model of childhood and stages. On the other hand, many religious materials supplement and instantiate the above working-class model of childhood.

Figure 1 summarizes the discussion so far, defining all the theoretical tools and showing how they are all related to one another.

Early Literacy as Socioculturally Situated Practice

I turn now to a specific example involving early literacy from my own research. I do this both to give a more extended example of the perspective I have developed so far and to show the relevance of this perspective to early childhood and the earliest stages of the acquisition of literacy. The event is this: An upper-middle-class, highly educated father approaches his 3-year-old (3:10) son who is sitting at the kitchen table. The child is using an activity book in which each page contains a picture with a missing piece. A question is printed under the picture. The child uses a "magic pen" to rub the missing piece and "magically" uncovers the rest of the picture. The part of the picture that is uncovered is an image that constitutes the answer to the question at the bottom of the page, though, of course, the child must put this answer into words.

In the specific case I want to discuss here, the overt part of the picture was the top half of the bodies of Donald and Daisy Duck. The question printed at the bottom of the page was "In what are Donald and Daisy riding?" (Note the social language in which this question is written. It is not the more vernacular form: "What are Donald and Daisy riding in?") The child used his pen to uncover an old fashioned Model T sort of car with an open top. Donald and Daisy turn out to be sitting in the car.

The father, seeing the child engaged in this activity, asks him, after he has uncovered the car, to read the question printed below the picture. Notice that the father has not asked the child to give the answer to the question, which is a different activity. The father is confident the child can answer the question and has a different purpose here. It is to engage in an indirect reading lesson, though one of a special and specific sort.

The father is aware that the child, while he knows the names of the letters of the alphabet and can recognize many of them in words, cannot decode print. He is also aware that the child has on several previous occasions, in the midst of various literacy-related activities, said that he is "learning to read." However, in yet other activities, at other times, the child has said that he "cannot read" and thereafter seemed more reluctant to engage in his otherwise proactive stance toward texts. This has concerned the father, who values the child's active engagement with texts and the child's belief, expressed in some contexts and not others, that he is not just learning to read, but is in fact "a reader."

We might say that the father is operating with a however tacit theory (cultural model) that a child's assuming a certain identity ("I am a reader") facilitates the acquisition of that identity and its concomitant skills. I believe this sort of model is fairly common in certain sorts of families. Parents co-construct an identity with a child (attribute, and get the child to believe in, a certain competence) before the child can actually fully carry out all the skills associated with this identity (competence before performance).

So, the father has asked the child to read the printed question below the picture of Donald and Daisy Duck sitting in the newly uncovered car. Below, I give the printed version of the question and what the child offered as his "reading" of the question:

Printed version: In what are Donald and Daisy riding?

Child's reading: What is Donald and Daisy riding on?

After the child uttered the above sentence, he said, "See, I told you I was learning to read." He seems to be well aware of the father's purposes. The child, the father, the words, and the book are all here in sync to pull off a specific practice, and this is a form of instruction, but it's a form that is typical of what goes on inside socialization processes.

The father and son have taken an activity that is for the child now a virtual genre—namely, uncovering a piece of a picture and on the basis of it answering a question—and incorporated it into a different *metalevel activity*. That is, the father and son use the original activity not in and for itself but as a platform with which to discuss reading or, perhaps better put, to co-construct a cultural model of what reading is. The father's question and the son's final response ("See, I told you I was learning to read") clearly indicate that they are seeking to demonstrate to and for each other that the child can read.

Figure 2, which will inform my discussion that follows, (partially) analyzes this event in terms of the theoretical notions we have developed above.

From a developmental point of view, then, what is going on here? Nothing so general as acquiring literacy. Rather, something much more specific is going on. First, the child is acquiring, amidst immersion and adult guidance, a piece of a particular type of *social language*. The question he has to form—and he very well knows this—has to be a *classificatory question*. It cannot be, for instance, a narrative-based question (e.g., something like "What are Donald and Daisy doing?" or "Where are Donald and Daisy going?"). Classificatory questions (and related syntactic and discourse resources) are a common part of many school-based (and academic) social languages, especially those associated with nonliterary content areas (e.g., the sciences).

The acquisition of this piece of a social language is, in this case, scaffolded by a genre the child has acquired, namely to uncover the piece of the picture, form a classificatory question to which the picture is an answer (when the parent isn't there to read the question for the child), and give the answer. This genre bears a good deal of similarity to a number of different non-narrative language and action genres (routines) used in the early years of school.

Finally, in regard to social languages, note that the child's question is uttered in a more vernacular style than the printed question. So syntactically it is, in one sense, in the wrong style. However, from a discourse perspective (in terms of the function its syntax carries out), it is in just the right style (i.e., it is a classificatory question). It is a mainstay of child language development that the acquisition of a function often precedes acquisition of a fully correct form (in the sense of contextually appropriate, not necessarily in the sense of grammatically correct).

Figure 2. Partial Analysis of a Literacy Event

Text	=	Written:	In what are Donald and Daisy riding?
		Read:	What is Donald and Daisy riding on?
		Remark:	See, I told you I was learning to read.
Social language	=	Classificatory question	
Genre	=	Uncover the piece of the picture, form a classificatory question to which the picture is an answer, and give the answer	
Cultural model	=	Reading is the proactive production of appropriate styles of language (e.g., here a classificatory question) and their concomitant meanings in conjunction with print	
Discourse (identity)	=	Emergent reader of a certain type (filtering school-aligned practice into primary Discourse)	

In addition to acquiring a specific piece of certain sorts of social languages, the child is also, as part and parcel of the activity, acquiring different cultural models. One of these is a cultural model about what reading is. The model is something like this: Reading is not primarily letter-by-letter decoding but the proactive production of appropriate styles of language (e.g., here a classificatory question) and their concomitant meanings in conjunction with print. This is a model that the father (at some level quite consciously) wants the child to adopt, both to sustain the child's interest in becoming a reader and to counteract the child's claims, in other contexts, that he can't read. Of course, the child's claim that he can't read in those other contexts reflects that, in other activities, he is acquiring a different cultural model of reading, namely one something like this: Reading is primarily the ability to decode letters and words, and one is not a reader if meaning is not primarily driven from decoding print. As his socialization proceeds, the child will acquire yet other cultural models of reading (or extend and deepen ones already acquired).

The genres, social languages, and cultural models present in this interaction between father and son existed, of course, in conjunction with ways of thinking, valuing, feeling, acting, interacting and in conjunction with various mediating objects (e.g., the book and the "magic pen"), images (the pictures of Donald, Daisy, and the car), sites (kitchen table), and times (morning as father was about to go to work). In and through the social practices that recruit these genres, social language, and cultural models, the 3-year-old is acquiring a Discourse. The father and the child are co-constructing the child as a reader (and, indeed, a person) of a particular type, that is, one who takes reading to be the proactive production of appropriate styles of language and meanings in conjunction with print. This socially situated identity involves a self-orientation as active producer (not just consumer) of appropriate meanings in conjunction with print; meanings that, in this case, turn out to be school and academically related.

However, this Discourse is not unrelated to other Discourses the child is or will be acquiring. I have repeatedly pointed out how the social language, genre, and cultural models involved in this social practice are in full alignment with some of the social languages, genres, cultural models, and social practices the child will confront in the early years of school (here construing schooling in fairly traditional terms).

At the same time, this engagement between father and child, beyond being a moment in the production of the Discourse of a certain type of reader, is also a moment in the child's acquisition of what I call his primary Discourse. The child's primary Discourse is the ways with words, objects, and deeds that are associated with his primary sense of self formed in and through his (most certainly class-based) primary socialization within the family (or other culturally relevant primary socializing group) as a "person like us." In this case, the child is learning that "people like us" are "readers like this."

Now consider what it means that the child's acquisition of the reader Discourse (being-doing a certain type of reader) is simultaneously aligned with (traditional) school-based Discourses and part of his acquisition of his primary Discourse. This ties school-related values, attitudes, and ways with words, at a specific and not some general level, to his primary sense of self and belonging. This will almost certainly affect how the child reacts to, and resonates with, school-based ways with words and things.

Reading and Early Language Abilities

Many of the recent reading reports (e.g., see Gee, 1999b; National Reading Panel, 2000; Snow, Burns, & Griffin, 1998) have stressed that there is significant correlation between early phonological awareness and later success in learning to read and, thus, called for early phonemic awareness training in schools and early sustained and overt instruction on phonics. However, some of these reports are aware that a good many other things, besides early phonological awareness, correlate with successfully learning to read in the early years of school. It turns out, for instance, that the correlation between early language abilities and later success in reading is just as large as, if not larger than, the correlation between early phonological awareness and success in reading. Indeed, as one might suspect, early language abilities and early phonological awareness are themselves correlated (Snow, Burns, & Griffin, 1998):

> [P]erformance on phonological awareness tasks by preschoolers was highly correlated with general language ability. Moreover it was measures of semantic and syntactic skills, rather than speech discrimination and articulation, that predicted phonological awareness differences. (p. 53)
>
> . . .
>
> What is most striking about the results of the preceding studies is the power of early preschool language to predict reading three to five years later. (pp. 107–108)
>
> . . .
>
> On average, phonological awareness (r. = .46) has been about as strong a predictor of future reading as memory for sentences and stories, confrontation naming, and general language measures. (p. 112)

So what are these early language abilities that seem so important for later success in school? According to the National Research Council's report (Snow, Burns, & Griffin, 1998), they are things like vocabulary—receptive vocabulary, but more especially expressive vocabulary—the ability to recall and comprehend sentences and stories, and the ability to engage in verbal interactions. Furthermore, I think that research has made it fairly clear what causes such verbal abilities. What appears to cause enhanced school-based verbal abilities are family, community, and school language environments in which children interact intensively with adults and more advanced peers and experience cognitively challenging talk and texts on sustained topics and in different genres of oral and written language.

However, the correlation between language abilities and success in learning to read (and in school generally) hides an important reality. Almost all children—including poor children—have impressive language abilities. The vast majority of children enter school with large vocabularies, complex grammar, and deep understandings of experiences and stories. It has been decades since anyone believed that poor and minority children entered school with "no language" (Gee, 1996; Labov, 1972).

The verbal abilities that children who fail in school lack are not just some general set of such abilities, but rather specific verbal abilities tied to specific school-based practices and school-based genres of oral and written language of just the sort I looked at in the earlier example of the 3-year-old making up a classificatory question. This 3-year-old will have been exposed to a great number of such specific, but quite diverse, practices, each offering protoforms of later school-based and academic social languages and genres. These protoforms, always embedded in specific social practices connected to specific socially situated identities (and useless when not so embedded), are the stuff from which success in school-based and academic reading flows. These are the sorts of protoforms that must be delivered to all children—amidst ample practice within socialization in specific Discourses—if we are to have true access and equity for all children.

QUESTIONS FOR REFLECTION

1. Why is it important to think about reading from a broader perspective than a set of psycholinguistic processing skills?
2. How is language used for perspective-taking and not just giving and getting information?
3. How does a Discourse (note the capital *D*) contribute to a student's grasp of language and the formation of personal identity?

NOTE

*When this chapter was written, Gee was at the University of Wisconsin–Madison.

REFERENCES

Barsalou, L.W. (1999a). Language comprehension: Archival memory or preparation for situated action. *Discourse Processes, 28*, 61–80.

Barsalou, L.W. (1999b). Perceptual symbol systems. *Behavioral and Brain Sciences*, 22, 577–660.

Brown, A.L., Collins, A., & Dugid, P. (1989). Situated cognition and the culture of learning. *Educational Researcher, 18*, 32–42.

Clancey, W.J. (1997). *Situated cognition: On human knowledge and computer representations.* Cambridge, England: Cambridge University Press.

Clark, A. (1997). *Being there: Putting brain, body, and world together again.* Cambridge, MA: MIT Press.

Clark, H.H. (1996). *Using language.* Cambridge, England: Cambridge University Press.

D'Andrade, R., & Strauss, C. (Eds.). (1992). *Human motives and cultural models.* Cambridge, England: Cambridge University Press.

Engestrom, Y., Miettinen, R., & raij Punamaki (Eds.). (1999). *Perspectives on activity theory.* Cambridge, England: Cambridge University Press.

Freire, P. (1995). *The pedagogy of the oppressed.* New York: Continuum.

Gallas, K. (1994). *The languages of learning: How children talk, write, dance, draw, and sing their understanding of the world.* New York: Teachers College Press.

Gee, J.P. (1992). *The social mind: Language, ideology, and social practice.* New York: Bergin & Garvey.

Gee, J.P. (1996). *Social linguistics and literacies: Ideology in Discourses* (2nd ed.). London: Taylor & Francis.

Gee, J.P. (1999a). *An introduction to discourse analysis: Theory and method.* London: Routledge.

Gee, J.P. (1999b). Reading and the New Literacy Studies: Reframing the National Academy of Sciences report on reading. *Journal of Literacy Research, 31,* 355–374.

Glenberg, A.M. (1997). What is memory for? *Behavioral and Brain Sciences, 20,* 1–55.

Glenberg, A.M., & Robertson, D.A. (1999). Indexical understanding of instructions. *Discourse Processes, 28,* 1–26.

Halliday, M.A.K. (1994). *Functional grammar* (2nd ed.). London: Edward Arnold.

Hanks, W.F. (1996). *Language and communicative practices.* Boulder, CO: Westview Press.

Harkness, S., Super, C., & Keefer, C.H. (1992). *Learning to be an American parent: How cultural models gain directive force.* In R. D'Andrade & C. Strauss (Eds.), *Human motives and cultural models* (pp. 163–178). Cambridge, England: Cambridge University Press.

Holland, D., & Quinn, N. (Eds.). (1987). *Cultural models in language and thought.* Cambridge, England: Cambridge University Press.

Hutchins, E. (1995). *Cognition in the wild.* Cambridge, MA: MIT Press.

Labov, W. (1972). *Language in the inner city.* Philadelphia, PA: University of Pennsylvania Press.

Latour, B. (1987). *Science in action.* Cambridge, MA: Harvard University Press.

Latour, B. (1991). *We have never been modern.* Cambridge, MA: Harvard University Press.

Latour, B. (1999). *Pandora's hope: Essays on the reality of science studies.* Cambridge, MA: Harvard University Press.

Lave, J. (1996). Teaching, as learning, in practice. *Mind, Culture, and Activity, 3,* 149–164.

Lave, J., & Wenger, E. (1991). *Situated learning: Legitimate peripheral participation.* New York: Cambridge University Press.

Leont'ev, A.N. (1978). *Activity, consciousness, and personality.* Englewood Cliffs, NJ: Prentice-Hall.

Martin, J.R. (1990). Literacy in science: Learning to handle text as technology. In F. Christe (Ed.), *Literacy for a changing world* (pp. 79–117). Melbourne, NSW, Australia: Australian Council for Educational Research.

Myers, G. (1990). *Writing biology: Texts in the social construction of scientific knowledge.* Madison, WI: University of Wisconsin Press.

National Reading Panel. (2000). *Report of the National Reading Panel: Teaching children to read.* Washington, DC: Author. Available online: www.nationalreadingpanel.org.

Philipsen, G. (1975). Speaking "like a man" in Teamsterville: Culture patterns of role enactment in an urban neighborhood. *Quarterly Journal of Speech, 61,* 26–39.

Scollon, R., & Scollon, S.W. (1981). *Narrative, literacy, and face in interethnic communication.* Norwood, NJ: Ablex.

Shore, B. (1996). *Culture in mind: Cognition, culture, and the problem of meaning.* New York: Oxford University Press.

Snow, C.E., Burns, M.S., & Griffin, P. (Eds.). (1998). *Preventing reading difficulties in young children.* Washington, DC: National Academy Press.

Strauss, C., & Quinn, N. (1997). *A cognitive theory of cultural meaning.* Cambridge, England: Cambridge University Press.

Tomasello, M. (1999). *The cultural origins of human cognition.* Cambridge, MA: Harvard University Press.

Wenger, E. (1998). *Communities of practice: Learning, meaning, and identity.* Cambridge, England: Cambridge University Press.

CHAPTER 5

The Place of Dialogue in Children's Construction of Meaning

M.A.K. Halliday, University of Sydney

Meaning as a Social Phenomenon

Much of the discussion of children's language development in the last quarter of a century, especially in educational contexts, has been permeated by a particular ideological construction of childhood. This view combines individualism, romanticism, and what Martin calls "childism": the Disneyfied vision of a child that is constructed in the media and in certain kinds of "kiddie lit."[1] Each child is presented as a freestanding autonomous being; and learning consists in releasing and bringing into flower the latent awareness that is already there in the bud. This is the view that was embodied in the "creativity" and "personal growth" models of education by James Britton, John Dixon, and David Holbrook in Great Britain; and more recently, from another standpoint, in the United States in Donald Graves's conception of children's writing as process and of their text as property to be individually owned.[2] It has been supported theoretically first by Chomskyan innatism and latterly by cognitive science models which interpret learning as the acquisition of ready-made information by some kind of independent processing device (cf. Kintsch, 1988).

What these various discourses have in common is that they are all essentially antisocial—or perhaps "asocial," to be more accurate. In this they contrast with interpretations of development and learning that would make reference to Vygotsky, to Bernstein, and, in linguistics, to the functional, social-semantic tradition that derives from European scholarship, especially the Prague and London schools, from glossematics, and from the American anthropological linguists.[3] In this view, meaning is a social and cultural phenomenon and all construction of meaning is a social process. We can use the term "intersubjective" for it provided we do not take this to imply that the "subject" comes into existence first and then proceeds to interact with other subjects. There is no subject until construed by social meaning-making practices (see Thibault, in press).

This chapter is reprinted from *Theoretical Models and Processes of Reading* (4th ed., pp. 70–82), edited by R.B. Ruddell, M.R. Ruddell, and H. Singer, 1994, Newark, DE: International Reading Association. (Adapted from *Dialoganalyse III: Referate der 3: Arbeitstagung, Bologna 1990* [3rd International Conference on Dialogue Analysis] (Vol. 2, pp. 417–430), edited by S. Stati, E. Weigand, and E. Hundsnurscher, Tübingen, Germany: Niemeyer.)

Developmental Stages

In studying child language development some 20 years ago I was struck by how clearly this social-semantic perspective stands out once you observe how children begin to communicate—especially if you observe it from birth and in a natural form, without eliciting or experimenting and without using too many technical aids. These practices tend to obscure the social nature of semiotic development, whereas the traditional diary method of child language studies brings it out. In this context, some fairly clearly defined developmental stages seemed to me to emerge:[4]

1. presymbolic ("primary intersubjectivity"), typically birth to 0;5

1 to 2. transition stage, typically 0;5 to 0;8

2. symbolic—protolinguistic ("secondary intersubjectivity"), typically 0;8 to 1;4

2 to 3. transition stage, typically 1;4 to 2;0

3. symbolic—linguistic, typically 2;0 and on

Since I was focusing specifically on the development of language I concentrated on the last three, referring to them as "phases":

2. symbolic—protolinguistic = Phase 1, "protolanguage"

2 to 3. transition = Phase II, "transition"

3. symbolic—linguistic = Phase III, "language"

Since then detailed studies of early language development have been carried out in comparable terms, based on intensive observation of children in their homes, by Clare Painter and by Jane Oldenburg; and Qiu Shijin has observed a population of Chinese children living in Shanghai, over a short period but covering different ages within the range. All have used the same theoretical framework for their interpretations (see Oldenburg, 1990; Painter, 1984; Qiu, 1985).

From the beginning of life a child's acts of meaning are joint constructions, dialogically enacted between himself and some "significant other" by reference to whom he is achieving a personal identity. Colwyn Trevarthen documented this process for the presymbolic stage many years ago when he showed that a newborn infant within 2 or 3 weeks of birth takes part in exchanging attention.[5] This exchange of attention is the beginning of language. It has no "content" in the adult sense; but it has meaning. For the child, the meaning is "we are together and in communication; there is a 'you'—and a 'me.'" "You" and "me" are, of course, mutually defining; neither can exist without the other. I shall not dwell on this stage here; but I have found it fascinating to take part in, and have been amazed by the semogenic potential of these early microencounters. They are not entirely without content, as a matter of fact; but there is as yet no *systematic* construing of experience.

When the child begins to control his material environment, typically at 'round about 4 to 5 months, he begins the transition to *systematic* symbolic construction. He can reach out and grasp an object that is in view; and this coincides with his first *symbolic* encounter with the environment, which takes the form of an act of meaning that is something like "that's interesting!—what is it?" This introduces a "third person" into the protoconversation alongside the "you" and the "me." The act itself may take any accessible form (my own subject Nigel produced a high-pitched squeak)—anything that can engage the child and the other in shared attention to some third party. This third party, which is construed as "neither you nor me," is typically not, in fact, an object but a happening—a commotion of some kind like a sudden noise or a bright light coming into the child's attention. But the act of meaning is clearly *addressed*; the meaning is jointly constructed, and the material phenomenon is construed as experience only through the shared act of exchanging a symbol. The mother, of course, or whoever is sharing in the act, responds in her own tongue; she says, "Yes, those were pigeons," or "That's a bus," or "See, they've put the lights on." But the semogenic process is dialogic, in two distinct respects: on the one hand *interpersonally*, in that the two acts define each other as question and answer, and on the other hand *experientially*, in that some kind of perturbation in the environment is construed dialogically as a phenomenon of experience. In other words, it is through language that this "third party" acquires the status of reality.

The child is also at the same time construing his own body; the first *symbolic* construction of self versus environment coincides more or less with the first construction of this same opposition in *material* terms. What is "out there" is what can be grasped, "grasping" being both a material process and a process of consciousness. But it has to be actively explored, on both these planes; and the transition to the systematic symbolic stage, that of the protolanguage, takes place only after the child has learnt that he can detach himself from the material environment (by rolling over). This protolanguage phase, that of "secondary intersubjectivity," is then reached, typically at somewhere between 7 and 10 months of age, through a change in both forms of his dialogue with the environment. On the one hand, in his *bodily* engagement the child learns to propel himself from one place to another, by some form of crawling. He now has the freedom of space-time; and at the same time he achieves the semiotic freedom of construing meanings into systems—that is, on both planes he achieves paradigmatic choice. This choice of meaning is the essential characteristic of protolanguage.

Protolanguage is the form of language that we humans share with what we think of as the "higher" mammals: mainly primates and cetaceans, but it also appears in our two most favored pets, cats and dogs, at least when they interact with us. All these are, of course, different languages; but all have the same formal structure, as systems of simple signs. In the process of his symbolic activity, the child construes meaning into *systems*; and the systems are functional in different contexts—I referred to these as "microfunctions" in my analysis. The process is, of course, dialogic; the others share in construing the meaning potential. In this protolinguistic phase we can see clearly how meaning is created at the point of impact of the material and the conscious, in the dialectic engagement between these two domains of experience. Consider a typical protolinguistic dialogue such as the following:

[Mother is holding child in her lap, throwing his toy rabbit in the air and catching it. The child is watching attentively.]

Child: [∂̆̃∂̆̃]

Mother: There he goes!

Child: [∂̆̃∂̆̃∂̆̃]

Mother: Oh, you want me to throw him up again, do you? All right. There he goes!

Child: [loudly] [ḿn͡g̀]

Mother: No, that's enough. Let's find something else to do.

Here the material processes taking place in space-time (the mother throwing up the rabbit and catching it) impact on the conscious processes whereby both parties are attending, with shared positive affect, both to the other and to the third party, the rabbit-commotion. It is the interpenetration of these two that generates a *meaning*, such as "that's fun; I want you to do it again"; and also a contrasting meaning of "I *insist* that you do it again!" These evolve dialogically as part of a shared *system* of meanings in different microcontexts, which includes others such as "I want/don't want that object," "let's be (you and me) together/let's attend to this (third party) together," "I like/am curious about that," and so on.

It is in protolanguage, then, that the activity of *meaning* comes to be construed in the form of a system, such that there is an ongoing dialectic relationship between the *system* and the *instance*. The system is the potential for generating instances; and by the same token each new instance perturbs the system.[6] The system is a dynamic open system, metastable in character, that persists only through constantly changing in interaction with its environment; and each new instance constitutes an incursion from the environment, since the material conditions that engender it are never totally identical. (We may note that this impacting of the conscious with the material takes place at both "ends" of the symbolic process, the semantic and the phonetic; so that the system is evolving at both these interfaces, both in the construction of content and in the construction of expression. In the latter, the material conditions are those of the child's own body, his physiological potential—which also, of course, is constantly changing.)

The second major transition is that from protolanguage into language—into the distinctively human semiotic that is not, as far as we know, shared by other species. In the course of this transition the resource for making meaning is further transformed, this time into a system of another, significantly different kind. In the context of overall development, while protolanguage goes with crawling, language goes with walking; and both these activities are carried out by specialized organs—mouth and legs—leaving arms and hands free for other purposes. But the criterial, and critical, difference between protolanguage and language is that language is *stratified*: that is, it has a *grammar*. A grammar (strictly, "lexicogrammar"—syntax, vocabulary, morphology if any) is a purely symbolic system that is introduced "in between" the content and the expression; that is, it is a distinct level of semiotic organization located between the two material interfaces. Unlike a protolanguage, a language cannot be described as a system of signs; it is a system based on the more complex principle of *realization*, which cannot be reduced to pairs of *signifiant/signifié*. The grammar thus does not interface directly with either material environment. But at the same time it is not neutral between the two; it is biased toward the content plane. The grammar is a "natural" grammar which has evolved as the primary means for construing experience and enacting social processes—still, of course, in dialogic contexts.

Only a system that is stratified in this way can construe meaning in the form of "information"—as a specifically linguistic commodity that can be *exchanged*, on the model of the exchange of goods-&-services that evolves with protolanguage. Without a grammar there can be no information. Once a grammar has evolved, I can tell you things and we can argue about them. The critical final step leading to the joint construction of information is the complex one of *arguing about*: the combination of mood with transitivity, in grammatical terms. But the child cannot reach this point in one giant leap. Let us try to enumerate the main steps in his progress.

Dialogic Construction of Meaning

It seems that children have a favorite strategy for achieving the transition from child tongue to mother tongue. It may be universal, or some aspects of it may be; and it may well have been the course taken by language in its evolution. The grammar makes it possible to construe experience, through the system of transitivity and its lexical counterpart in naming.[7] But at the same time, because the grammar is a purely abstract system at one remove from the material interfaces it also makes it possible simultaneously to construe two contrasting dialogic modes (when they become grammaticalized we know them as "moods"): the imperative, or "pragmatic" mode, meaning "this is how things *should* be; you bring them about!" and the declarative, or "mathetic" mode, meaning "this is how things *are*; you can check whether you agree." Early examples of pragmatic utterances from my records were:

1. water ón (turn the water on!), squeeze órange (squeeze an orange!)
   get dówn (I want to get down!), play tráin (let's play with the train!)

All had rising tone, and demanded a response. Contrast these with mathetic utterances such as the following, all on falling tone:

2. big bàll (that's a big ball), new rècord (here's a new record)
   red sweàter (I've got my red sweater), two hàmmer (I'm holding two hammers)

These were from 1;7. A later example (1;9) shows the two modes in syntagmatic sequence:

3. no room walk on wàll...walk on óther wall (there's no room to walk on [this] wall; I want to walk on the other wall!).

The three English-speaking children who were recorded intensively by natural language diaries all made this distinction systematically as the primary semantic option in the protolanguage-language transition. All three expressed it prosodically, by intonation and/or voice quality; and in all three the pragmatic was the marked option. The Chinese-speaking children also made it and also expressed it prosodically; however there were not enough data to establish the markedness pattern.[8]

The pragmatic is a demand for goods-&-services; it seeks a response, in the form of action, and the "others" involved in the dialogue recognize and construe it as such (unconsciously, of course). That does not mean that they always accede to the request; but they show that they have got the message, and in that respect "no" is as effective as "yes." Gradually, during the course of the transition, the pragmatic evolves into a demand for information; thus ontogenetically (and perhaps also phylogenetically) the interrogative, although in the adult grammar it pairs with the declarative, is derived by splitting off from the imperative—a demand for action becomes a demand for verbal action. The mathetic, on the other hand, does not demand any action. What it does do is invite confirmation: "Yes, that's a big ball," "It's not a big ball; it's a little ball," "It's not a ball; it's a melon," and so on. And here an important question arises: what is the essential condition for entering into a dialogue of this kind, in which one interactant corroborates, or disputes, what the other one has just said? It is that the experience must have been *shared*. You cannot corroborate or dispute what happened unless you also were there to see it.

Thus the basic form of information is *turning shared experience into meaning*: that is, telling someone something that they already know. I can construe an experience semiotically, and offer the construction to you, provided I know that you have shared the experience; and you then share in construing it. Thus the construction is again dialogic: meaning is created by the impact between a material phenomenon and the shared processes of consciousness of those who participated in it.

Every parent is familiar with the situation where their child is asked to give information to someone about an experience that person has not shared, and the child is unable to do it. Mother has taken the child to the zoo; when she comes home she says, "Tell Daddy what you saw at the zoo today." Daddy is attending, but the child cannot oblige—either he remains silent, or he turns back to Mummy and tells her. Why? Because she was the one with whom he shared the experience. How can he tell Daddy about it, when Daddy wasn't there?

Conversation, then, evolves as the joint construal of shared experience, whereby phenomena that are accessible to the consciousness of both parties—things both can see, events both have experienced—are turned dialogically into meanings. This is how conversation begins; and how it continues, for a child, until he is well on the way from protolanguage to mother tongue. No doubt conversation continued in that way for many generations in the history of the human species, before its further potential was taken up. But the potential is there once the *system* of meaning-making is in place; this is what enables the listener to construe phenomena that only the speaker has actually witnessed. And in the course of time each child makes this same discovery: that language can *create* information—it can take the place of shared experience. It is not necessary for the listener to have been there and seen the thing too; the experience can be *reconstrued* out of the language. This is such a major discovery that Nigel, at least, consistently used a different grammar for the two situations: he had one form for "I'm telling you something we shared," which was his original context for giving information, and another form for "I'm telling you something that happened, even though you weren't there to see it." This grammatical distinction is not made in the adult language, so after a few months Nigel gave it up. We do not distinguish between telling people what (we think) they know and telling them what (we think) they don't know; the declarative covers both. But at the same time, we do not stop using language in the earlier way. In communication models the concept of information is usually taken to imply that knowledge is being transmitted from a knower to a nonknower: "I know something that you don't know; I 'mean' it, and as a result you now know it." Where this happens, language is operating as a surrogate for shared experience—a way of sharing semiotically what has not been shared materially. Prototypically this is monologic, since only the knower takes part in transforming it into meaning. But it is mainly in rather specialized uses of language, like an academic lecture, that information is constructed and imparted in this monologic way. Most of the time when we are in the indicative mood we are construing meanings interactively on the basis of shared experience. The prototypical form of this process is the dialogic one, in which the construction proceeds by argument. Arguing is the shared construction of experiential meaning; it occupies the space from consensus to conflict, and interactants will typically move between the two as they extend their dialogue into conversation.[9]

In *Learning How to Mean* I gave an example of the joint construction of *narrative* in a dialogue between Nigel and his parents, when Nigel was 1;8. Nigel had been taken to the zoo, and had picked up a lid from a plastic cup which he was clutching in one hand while stroking a goat with the other hand. The goat started to eat the lid; the keeper intervened, saying that the goat shouldn't eat the lid—it wasn't good for it. Some hours later, back home, Nigel recalled the incident:

Nigel:	try eat lìd
Father:	What tried to eat the lid?
Nigel:	[repeating] try eat lìd
Father:	What tried to eat the lid?
Nigel:	goàt...man said nò...goat try eat lìd...man said nò

A few hours later again he returned to the story, this time with his mother:

Nigel:	goat try eat lìd...man said nò
Mother:	Why did the man say no?
Nigel:	goat shòuldn't eat lid...[shaking his head] goòdfor it

Mother: The goat shouldn't eat the lid; it's not good for it.

Nigel: goat try eat lìd...man said nò...goat shòuldn't eat lid...[shaking head] goòdfor it

We tend to think of narrative and dialogue as opposed forms of discourse; but this type of text suggests that in its early development narrative itself is dialogic. The material experience had been shared between child and parents; the child then takes the initiative in verbalizing it so that it becomes part of a shared construction of reality. The parents join in, their turns taking the form of questions; but these are not simply interpersonal prompts—because they are *wh*-type questions, they contain experiential information: "What tried to eat the lid?" says, "There was a doer [grammatically, an actor]; you identify it"; "Why did the man say no?" says, "There was a reason [grammatically, some expression of cause]; you identify it." Thus there is joint participation in the construing of this experience.

We may compare this with the sequence of texts shown in the figure, taken from the record of conversations over a period of about 8 months, when Nigel was between 2;10 and 3;6. These are not narratives of events, but rather the ongoing construction of a general concept, in this case that of "cats." The child is older now, and in these instances he is asking the questions; many of these are yes/no questions, but there are also *wh*-type questions of "how?" and "why?" In both types, of course, the child is also *contributing* information:

"Do cats like meat/bones/marrow?"—constructing and testing out a taxonomy of potential foods.

"How do the cat's claws come out?"—they come out and go in again.

"Does it go with [i.e., walk on] its claws?"—they come out and go in in different contexts and functions.

The Construction of "Cats" (Nigel From 2;10 to 3;6)

Text A1: Nigel at 2;10;22

Nigel: And you [that is, "I"] saw a cat in Chania Falls.
Mother: Yes, you saw a cat in Chania Falls.
Nigel: And you picked the cat up. Mummy, do cats like meat?
Mother: Yes, they do.
Nigel: Do cats like bones? Do cats like marrow?

Text A2: Nigel at 2;10;26

Nigel: Can I stroke the cat? You ["I"] want to stroke the cat...you want to scratch it...it's drinking its milk...it's moving its tail out...it's moving its tail outside...it's scratching...it's putting its tail up...what's this?
Mother: I don't know; I suppose it's its elbow.
Nigel: It's waggling its tail...it's lapping it with its tongue...you can go near its elbow...you *can* go near its elbow...but you can't go too near its face...because it thinks you might take away its milk...it was just a bit frightened...it thinked that you might take away its milk...has it finished its milk?

(continued)

The Construction of "Cats" (Nigel From 2;10 to 3;6) (*Continued*)

Text A3: Nigel at 2;11;5

Nigel:	[thinking about "The House That Jack Built"] What is a rat?
Father:	It's a sort of big mouse.
Nigel:	Does the rat go when the cat has killed it?
Father:	No, it doesn't go any more then.
Nigel:	Why did the cat kill the rat?
Father:	Cats do kill rats.
Nigel:	Why do they?
Father:	[formula] You'll have to wait to understand that till you're a bit bigger.
Nigel:	No, I can understand it now.
Father:	Well, cats just like to eat rats and mice.
Nigel:	Why do they like to eat them?
Father:	They just do.

Text A4: Nigel at 2;11;15

Nigel:	Why did the cat go out? Mummy, why did the cat go out?
Mother:	It gets fed up, having its tail squashed.

Text A5: Nigel at 3;0;26

Nigel:	How do the cat's claws come out?
Father:	They come out from inside its paws. Look, I'll show you.
Nigel:	Does it go with its claws?
Father:	Not if it's going along the ground.
Nigel:	And not if it's climbing up a tree.
Father:	Yes, if it's climbing up a tree it does go with its claws.

Text A6: Nigel at 3;2;7

Nigel:	Will the cat eat the grape?
Father:	I don't think so. Cats like things that go, not things that grow.

Text A7: Nigel at 3;5;12

Nigel:	Cats have no else to stop you from trossing them...cats have no other way to stop children from hitting them...so they bite. Cat, don't go away! When I come back I'll tell you a story. [He does so.]

Text A8: Nigel at 3;6;12

Nigel:	Can I give the cat some artichoke?
Mother:	Well, she won't like it.
Nigel:	Cats like things that go; they don't like things that grow.

Text A9: Nigel at 3;6;14

Nigel:	I wish I was a puppet so that I could go out into the snow in the night. Do puppets like going out into the snow?
Father:	I don't know. I don't think they mind.
Nigel:	Do cats like going out in the snow?
Father:	Cats don't like snow.

(continued)

The Construction of "Cats" (Nigel From 2;10 to 3;6) (*Continued*)

Nigel:	Do they die? [He knows that some plants do.]
Father:	No, they don't die; they just don't like it.
Nigel:	Why don't puppets mind snow?
Father:	Well [hesitating]...puppets aren't people.
Nigel:	Yes, but...cats also aren't people.
Father:	No, but cats are alive; they go. Puppets don't go.
Nigel:	Puppets do go.
Father:	Yes, but you have to make them go; like trains.
Nigel:	Trains have wheels. Puppets have legs.
Father:	Yes, they have legs; but the legs don't go all by themselves. You have to make them go.

From M.A.K. Halliday (1984a).

But the conversations achieve much more than that. Experientially, for example, the dialogue constructs the general taxonomy of plants and animals ("things that grow" versus "things that go"); compare the complex argument around a four-way distinction of cats, puppets, people, and trains at 3;6. Interpersonally, it evolves into a dynamic modeling of question, answer, challenge, contradiction, and the like that is the essential component of the resources out of which all conversation is constructed.

I have given various examples elsewhere from my own records (cf. Halliday, 1978); many more will be found in the writings of Oldenburg and Painter, as well as throughout the now extensive literature on child language (but note that very little of this takes any account of protolanguage). It is instructive both to examine single instances and to track conversational motifs through time, as in the cat extracts just cited. For example, in wondering how Nigel had construed his experience of time and space I was able to put together conversational fragments extending over several years, while Joy Phillips, from intensive study of the earlier data, showed how he had developed the fundamental semantic strategies of comparison and contrast. And the extraordinarily rich body of natural conversation between mothers and their children of 3;6 to 4;0 that Ruqaiya Hasan has assembled, which is reported on briefly in her paper given at this conference [i.e., "Analisi del Dialogo," Bologna, May 2 to 5, 1990], adds a significant new dimension to our understanding of the development of dialogue. In all these early discourses we see clearly how the text interacts with its environment, such that meaning is created at the intersection of two contradictions: the experiential one, between the material and the conscious modes of experience, and the interpersonal one, between the different personal histories of the interactants taking part. Thus from the ontogenesis of conversation we can gain insight into human learning and human understanding.

QUESTIONS FOR REFLECTION

1. If meaning is socially and culturally constructed, how does that idea challenge earlier notions of learning as the acquisition of ready-made information?
2. How do joint constructions between parent and child facilitate the development of meaning within children's early language development?
3. How do humans transition from protolanguage to systematic language?
4. In what ways are narrative discourses dialogic in children's constructions of meaning?

NOTES

[1] This ideology is particularly characteristic of what has been called the "manipulative capitalist" society. See Martin (1989, especially Chapter 4, *passim*).

[2] See, for example, Dixon (1967), Graves (1983). For an excellent critique, see Rothery (1990, chapter entitled "The Pedagogies of Traditional School Grammar: Creativity, Personal Growth, and Process"); see also Rothery (in press).

[3] Among contemporary linguists an outstanding contributor to the development of this tradition is Claude Hagège. See, for example, Hagège (1985).

[4] The initial interpretation of my observations is contained in Halliday (1975). The data to age 2;7 is available in Halliday (1984a). See also Bullowa (1979).

[5] Colwyn Trevarthen's important work in this field is presented in a number of his papers; see especially (1979) and (1980). For his work on the protolanguage phase, see (1978). Bruner's work provides a valuable general theoretical underpinning from a psychological standpoint; compare Bruner (1977).

[6] Contrast genetically transmitted communication systems (like the dances of bees), where instances do not perturb the system. This fundamental feature of semiotic systems is obscured in adult language by the massive quantitative effects to which it contributes (cf. Halliday, 1987); but it is seen very clearly at the protolanguage phase of development.

For language as a dynamic open system, see Lemke's articles "Towards a model of the instructional process," "The formal analysis of instruction," and "Action, context, and meaning," in Lemke (1984).

[7] Naming (lexicalized denotation) and transitivity are the cornerstones of the potential of language for construing experience (the experiential metafunction, in the terms of systemic theory). They were first explicitly linked in this way by Mathesius; see, for example, (1936). For naming in the development of conversation, see Halliday (1984b).

[8] It may seem surprising that, with children learning a tone language, a major distinction such as this could be realized by intonation. In fact, of course, Chinese uses intonation (grammatical tone) as well as lexical tone; but this is irrelevant. The protolanguage is "child tongue," not mother tongue; you cannot tell, when a child is speaking protolanguage, what language his mother tongue is going to be, and although by the time children introduce this distinction they are already launched into the mother tongue, this particular contrast is still their own invention.

In some instances, in fact, their system runs counter to the pattern of the mother tongue. Thus in Nigel's grammar proto-imperatives, being pragmatic, were rising in tone, whereas in English the informal imperative is typically falling; while when he first used dependent clauses, which have no macrofunction, he gave them the unmarked (falling) tone. Thus when, at just under 1;9, he said, "When New-World finish, song about bús!" ("When the *New World* [symphony] is finished, sing me the song about a bus"), the first clause was falling and the second rising; whereas in adult English the tones would have been the other way 'round.

[9] From her study of long conversations among groups of adults, Suzanne Eggins postulates that it is in fact the periodicity of consensus and conflict that is the major factor in keeping conversations going. See Eggins (1990).

REFERENCES

Bruner, J.S. (1977). Early social interaction and language acquisition. In H.R. Shaffer (Ed.), *Studies in mother-infant interaction*. London: Academic.

Bullowa, M. (1979). Infants as conversational partners. In T. Myers (Ed.), *The development of conversation and discourse*. Edinburgh: Edinburgh University Press.

Dixon, J. (1967). *Growth through English*. Oxford, UK: Oxford University Press.

Eggins, S. (1990). *Keeping the conversation going: A systemic-functional analysis of conversational structure in casual sustained talk*. Doctoral dissertation, University of Sydney, Australia.

Graves, D.H. (1983). *Writing: Teachers and children at work*. Portsmouth, NH: Heinemann.

Hagège, C. (1985). *L'homme de paroles: contribution linguistique aux sciences humaines*. Paris: Fayard.

Halliday, M.A.K. (1975). *Learning how to mean: Explorations in the development of language*. London: Edward Arnold. (New York: Elsevier, 1977)

Halliday, M.A.K. (1978). Meaning and the construction of reality in early childhood. In H.L. Pick, Jr. & E. Saltzman (Eds.), *Modes of perceiving and processing of information*. Hillsdale, NJ: Erlbaum.

Halliday, M.A.K. (1984a). *Listening to Nigel: Conversations of a very small child*. Sydney: University of Sydney, Linguistics Department.

Halliday, M.A.K. (1984b). Language as code and language as behaviour: A systemic-functional interpretation of the nature and ontogenesis of dialogue. In R.P. Fawcett et al. (Eds.), *The semiotics of culture and language* (Vol. 1). London: Frances Pinter.

Halliday, M.A.K. (1987). Language and the order of nature. In N. Fabb et al. (Eds.), *The linguistics of writing*. Manchester, UK: Manchester University Press.

Kintsch, W. (1988). The role of knowledge in discourse comprehension: A construction-integration model. *Psychological Review, 95*(2).

Lemke, J.L. (1984). *Semiotics and education*. Toronto: Victoria College, University of Toronto.

Martin, J.R. (1989). *Factual writing: Exploring and challenging social reality*. Oxford, UK: Oxford University Press.

Mathesius, V. (1936). On some problems of the systematic analysis of grammar. *Travaux du Cercle Linguistique de Prague, 6*.

Oldenburg, J. (1990). Learning the language and learning through language in early childhood. In M.A.K. Halliday, J. Gibbons, & H. Nicholas (Eds.), *Learning, keeping and using language: Selected papers from the Eighth World Congress of Applied Linguistics*. Amsterdam: Benjamins.

Painter, C. (1984). *Into the mother tongue: A case study of early language development*. London: Frances Pinter.

Qiu S. (1985). Transition period in Chinese language development. *Australian Review of Applied Linguistics, 8*(1).

Rothery, J. (1990). *"Story" writing in primary school: Assessing narrative type genres*. Doctoral dissertation, University of Sydney, Australia.

Rothery, J. (in press). Making changes: Developing an educational linguistics. In R. Hasan & G. Williams (Eds.), *Literacy in society*. London: Longman.

Thibault, P.J. (1990). *Social semiotics as praxis: Test, social meaning making and Nabokov's "Ada."* Minneapolis, MN: University of Minnesota Press.

Trevarthen, C. (1978). Secondary intersubjectivity: Confidence, confiding and acts of meaning in the first year. In A. Lock (Ed.), *Action, gesture and symbol: The emergence of language*. London: Academic.

Trevarthen, C. (1979). Communication and cooperation in early infancy: A description of primary intersubjectivity. In M. Bullowa (Ed.), *Before speech: The beginning of interpersonal communication*. Cambridge, UK: Cambridge University Press.

Trevarthen, C. (1980). The foundations of intersubjectivity: Development of interpersonal and cooperative understanding in infants. In D. Olson (Ed.), *The social foundations of language and thought: Essays in Honor of Jerome S. Bruner*. New York: Norton.

CHAPTER 6

Social Talk and Imaginative Play: Curricular Basics for Young Children's Language and Literacy

Anne Haas Dyson, University of Illinois at Urbana-Champaign

Celia Genishi, Teachers College, Columbia University

It is writing time in the kindergarten class. As she does every day, Mrs. Bee (all names are pseudonyms), the teacher, urges her young charges to "think" before they write, to make a "quick sketch" of their idea, and then to write that idea, "stretching their words" and listening to their sounds, bravely spelling the best they can. Each child should do their "own" text based on their "own" true life, Mrs. Bee cautions. No one should copy anyone else, and most certainly, they should not spend the period drawing and talking.

After Mrs. Bee's directions, the children begin to draw and talk; among the children are LaTrell and his tablemates, Cici and Della:

LaTrell: I seen a balloon when I went on my—

Cici: I seen a air balloon! It was up in the sky.

LaTrell: It was the color blue. Yeah, it went all the way in the sky.

Cici: It was over by my day care. MRS. BEE, WE SEEN THE AIR BALLOON!

Della: ME, TOO! I saw the air balloon.

["Me, too" echoes from other students in the room.]

Mrs. Bee: Everybody didn't see an air balloon, now. ["I did!" can be heard all around.] Only the things you really did see.

LaTrell: I'm gonna make a air balloon.

Cici: I seen an air balloon. Red, yellow, different colors!

Soon a virtual flock of balloons are taking off on children's papers. As for LaTrell's balloons, they sprout appendages and become *him* flying, propelled by his mother, who tosses him up in the air. "This how I went up in the sky when I was a baby... I didn't know I couldn't come down," he says. (See Figure 1; see Dyson, 2010a, for the complete vignette.)

In the opening months of the school year, Mrs. Bee's children were collectively finding a new kind of playground, one that existed on paper. From an

Figure 1. A Kindergartner's Transformed Balloons

official point of view, though, they drew too much, copied from each other, did not focus on a true event, and indeed did not listen. They were unruly children who did not fall in line with the mandated curriculum, a commercial writing program that had been paced by Mrs. Bee's school district and choreographed with expected benchmarks.

This view of Mrs. Bee's children, and Mrs. Bee's own view of her teaching challenges, were filtered through the demands of that district curriculum, which discouraged imaginative play and talk and emphasized individuals doing their work "by yourself" and thereby achieving basic skills (e.g., knowing letters and sounds and applying that knowledge to encode a brief narrative).

Language arts curricula focused on the basics are not uncommon in young children's classrooms. Although a move toward more academic curricula for young children has been clearly evident since the 1970s, it has become increasingly dominant over the last 20 years (Russell, 2011). This is especially so in schools like Mrs. Bee's that serve children labeled as at risk (e.g., children from low-income and minority families, including those learning English as an additional language). In such schools, academic curricula are designed to raise young children's test scores and close achievement gaps with the more economically privileged (Pappano, 2010). Indeed, federal funds for, and the very survival of, many central city public schools are dependent on achievement test scores tied to the basics.

Given these trends, time-honored curricular basics for young children have not fared well. Among these lost basics are time and space for play, for nonlinguistic forms of communication, such as drawing, and for extended talk among children themselves.

In this chapter, we are interested in curricularly unruly children, especially children who are not considered mainstream and who bring to the classroom a diversity of experiences with language and literacy. That diversity challenges the organized curricular path to academic success. Our purpose is not to call for a return to some mythic early childhood past. Indeed, narrow curricula focused on the perceived literacy basics have long been a part of what Haberman (1991) has called "the pedagogy of poverty" (p. 290; e.g., Bereiter & Engelmann, 1966). Rather, our aims are threefold.

First, we aim to reposition children and childhoods at the center of the curriculum. Drawing on the interdisciplinary field of childhood studies, we approach children not simply as putty for society's structures but as people of substance who respond to the institutional and societal structures in which they live. In this way, they have agency in the construction of their own childhoods.

Second, conceiving of children in this way entails taking seriously basic childhood processes through which children cross-culturally engage with their worlds. As we argue herein, this in turn brings new support for social talk and multimodal play, which may not be basic in many classrooms but are, nonetheless, basic to childhoods themselves (Montgomery, 2009).

Third, drawing on sociocultural and dialogic theories, we aim to illustrate the complex interplay between childhoods' basics (e.g., social participation, play) and official school basics (e.g., working independently, using standard English, demonstrating orthographic knowledge and textual sense). This interplay has consequences for learning paths and teaching possibilities. Most striking, an awareness of this interplay allows teachers to read the signs of childhood actions and decipher unexpected childhood resources.

To illustrate this interplay, we draw on data from recent projects. Dyson's (in press) was a study of the ideologies about language and childhood that undergirded the basics in two urban schools serving at-risk students. She focused on official writing curricula, highlighting how first graders and kindergartners interpreted those curricula. She met LaTrell during the kindergarten phase of that study. Falchi, Axelrod, and Genishi's (2012) project was a longitudinal one in which four collaborators followed six children of Mexican and indigenous Mixteco heritage between the ages of 3 and 7 years old from Head Start through second grade in a public school with a Spanish/English dual-language program. The children's collective story took them from emergent bilingualism in a prekindergarten program that emphasized children's own pace of development in a play-based context to early literacy in English and Spanish in a structured program.

Ultimately, we aim herein to contribute quite literally to a level playing field on which children can enact diverse learning paths to academic success and, moreover, assume some social agency in their lives in formation.

Unruly Children in a Basics World

> Children are born not into a "society" *per se* but into a childhood, that is, a particular configuration of ongoing relations that give social shape and cultural meaning to their initial membership in the human world. (Cook, 2002, p. 2)

Childhood is not simply a developmental period or a time of transition to adulthood. As Cook (2002) explains, it is a cultural institution influenced by societal forces, among them history, economics, technology, and the power-ridden dynamics of race, gender, class, and geography. How does the proper child show respect to elders, spend time, and relate to siblings? How does a well-mannered child interact with strangers, relatives, and neighbors? How does a normal child behave in gender-appropriate ways? There is not one answer to such questions; childhoods are part of the sociocultural worlds into which children are interactively guided (Ochs & Schieffelin, 2001). Think of such directives as "be a big boy/good girl," "don't be a baby," "give Grandma a hug," and "don't talk to strangers"; all are admonitions undergirded by ideologies of proper childhoods in relation to others.

In school, there are similar conceptions of what proper children should know and do, and these have changed dramatically in language and literacy education (Hirsh-Pasek, Golinkoff, Berk, & Singer, 2009). In Mrs. Bee's district, a recent newspaper article (reference not provided to maintain the anonymity of those named herein) voiced worries about unprepared kindergartners, estimated by local teachers to comprise about a third of the new entrants. Such children, the article declared, do not know their ABCs, cannot provide at least some letter–sound connections, nor follow two or three steps in directions. Children are thus positioned as individuals in hierarchical relationships with one another based not on social negotiations in particular contexts but on relative placement on a graded list of skills beginning at their very entry into school.

Our focus herein, though, is not only on the nature of the official curriculum but also on the nature of the unofficial one, the one governed by children. To borrow once again from Cook (2002), one aim of the relatively recent interdisciplinary field of childhood studies is to "dismantle the epistemological hegemony that has regarded children as being *merely* in transition, as nothings and nobodies in the here and now" (p. 5). These studies illustrate that within and against societal and institutional structures, children exercise agency in selectively attending to, resisting, and transforming their local worlds as they interpret them (e.g., Beresin, 2010; Corsaro, 2010; Dyson, 1999, 2007; Genishi, Dyson, & Russo, 2011; James & James, 2008; Thorne, 2005). In other words, whatever the curricular demands, young children do not just do as they are told.

Childhood Agency: Playing in School

Children's agency, and their relationships with other children, is central to the concept of childhood cultures. These cultures entail the communicative and often playful social practices that children produce as they respond to the adult-introduced social practices that comprise, and constrain, their everyday experiences in time and space (Corsaro, 2010; James, Jenks, & Prout, 1998). Playgrounds are spaces where children are relatively free to organize their own activities; thus, they are prime sites for the study of childhood cultures (e.g., Beresin, 2010; Corsaro, 1985; Opie, 1993; Opie & Opie, 1959).

Classrooms are spaces where children are not so free. Nonetheless, in these spaces, large numbers of children spend a great deal of time side by side. Whether they should or should not, young children tend to be drawn to other children and to play. Even in highly structured literacy activities, children may engage in playful banter and spontaneous competitions, as humble as "My H is better than your H" (refer to Glupczynski, 2007). In this way, official school tasks are driven not only by official demands but also by peer relationships, childhood practices, and their valued cultural resources, including the characters, themes, plots, and images from varied forms of popular media (Dyson, 2007, 2010b; Genishi & Dyson, 2009).

These practices within the unofficial community of children may contrast those in the official world in striking ways. Children, after all, may differ from their teachers (and from curriculum regulators) not only in age but also in aesthetic taste, sense of humor, communicative repertoire, and dominant intentions (including to play)—factors that are themselves shaped by the sociocultural particularities of everyday life (Chudacoff, 2007). To place children center stage in the classroom curriculum requires a view of them as complex social actors in childhood worlds.

Learning in Childhoods

From a sociocultural perspective, the adults in children's lives shape their learning through the recurrent social activities of everyday life, with their embodied human relationships, their material resources, their symbolic mediators (especially talk), and their enacted values (Cole, 1996; Rogoff, 2003; Vygotsky, 1978). Through their participation, children learn to focus on a common topic and to infer the relevance of their own actions; they learn to coordinate with others, anticipating others' moves and acting accordingly themselves. In these ways, they become communicators and active participants, meaning makers in a shared life.

Children, though, learn not only through enacting activities with guiding adults but also through observing, listening to stories (real and invented) about how the world works, *and* through their own play (Rogoff, 2003). In that play, children assume control over what can be a confusing world; they examine the workings of the world around them, then assume roles, appropriate the language of those roles, negotiate actions, and face the consequences of their actions as pretend parents and children, superheroes and victims, party givers and invitees, and so forth. Cross-culturally, these are children's ways of learning, even though their opportunities to observe, the nature of their interaction with others, the cultural material they play with, and even how that play is viewed by others may all vary (Konner, 1991).

In school, then, teachers organize practices through which children will learn. Even if the intention is to teach this skill or that one, from children's points of view, the teacher is offering a kind of event, a social happening. Children are to figure out its purpose, what is relevant in that activity given their drive to make sense and to make relationships (Nelson, 2007), and what resources they have—that is, what basis they have for participation.

Because oral and written language use is infused with social and cultural meanings (e.g., Collins & Blot, 2003; Ochs & Schieffelin, 2001; Schieffelin, 2000), children come to school—the official space for the public's children—with different kinds of resources, among them languages, communicative experiences, and knowledge about symbol systems, including kinds of texts (González, Moll, & Amanti, 2005; Kenner, 2000; Levinson, 2007). Whatever their nature, these provide the basis for young children's entry into school practices.

Moreover, children are not making sense alone but in the company of other children. Within these relationships themselves may be unexpected symbolic and thematic resources, from the stuff of popular media to that of age-old playground games, like chase-escape, attack-defend, escape-capture (Sutton-Smith, 1995), not to mention rhymes and chase games involving play with gender, violence, and love (Beresin, 2010; Dyson, 2007; Thorne, 1993).

Children's social actions in school activities are thus oriented to official *and* unofficial worlds. Their actions in language and literacy activities cannot be understood only by studying them as lone actors or as apprentices to adult experts. If we do that, we destroy the composing act itself; its symbolic vehicles—its images and words—are addressed to (indeed, in dialogue with) a voice-filled world (Bakhtin, 1981). Even a child acting alone is situated in a practice and, so situated, has intentions and resources linked to other experiences, other people, and other social places.

In the following case studies, we bring our focus close in on two small boys who were kindergartners, peers, friends, and initiates into school literacy. They were both students who tried, in the main, to "do good," as LaTrell put it (if only to avoid "trouble," finish their work, get lunch recess in LaTrell's case, or get "choice" time in Miguel's). Both boys sometimes found themselves outside the boundaries of a mandated curriculum, with its notion of proper children keeping pace with the benchmarks of basics to be mastered. As we looked from the sidelines, we sometimes found them playing alone and with others, lost in imagined worlds. The cases of these two unruly children are drawn from studies that reflect particular and potentially overlapping concerns of ours: children who are emergent bilinguals and engaged in learning English and children, glossed as nonmainstream, who are engaged in learning to use written language.

LaTrell: A Social Player in an Individualistic Writing Curriculum

LaTrell, the small boy who was surprised that he could stay in the air, was an earnest student and a playful peer in Mrs. Bee's kindergarten class. His urban school is located in a small Midwestern metropolitan area (population of approximately 226,000, according to the 2010 U.S. census). All 21 of his classmates were, like him, African American, as was his teacher, Mrs. Bee.

Dyson observed, audiotaped, and collected child products in LaTrell's class twice weekly over the course of an academic year (for methods, see Dyson, 2010b). He was one of three focal children, each of whom allowed entry into different classroom friendship groups; in the end, she came to know all the children in the class.

Mrs. Bee, like LaTrell himself, was relatively new to the public elementary school. She had spent years teaching preschool in a rural area, where the curriculum was play based; she had not expected, she told me, the pressure that she faced to get her kindergartners reading and writing. She followed official guidelines, which allowed no play period other than a short recess after lunch (if the weather and the school lunch behavior monitors allowed).

The mandated and district-paced writing curriculum was undergirded by particular ideologies or values and beliefs about childhood and language. The proper child should learn the basics of written language as early as possible, and this belief was evident in the benchmarked skills involving orthographic spelling and organized texts. Moreover, the proper child was diligent and reflective and concentrated on writing. That child did not play around with seatmates. The text was not a playground; it was a private drive on a benchmarked road.

The approach to both childhood and written language could be described by what Appiah (2005) refers to as an unattractive view of individualism. In this ideology, individuality and sociality are competing goals. Although there were times when peers were directed to share their writing plans, the overriding notion was that the proper child went inside the self, thought about an experience, and then, quite deliberately, crafted that true experience on paper. The child was supposed to write a text (and by extension, a life) in which the self mattered most.

When the children met on the classroom rug at the beginning of writing time, Mrs. Bee often talked to them about "working independently," writing only about what was "really real," and not copying a story that she might model, that another child might tell, or that the popular media may have presented. Those were not their own "true" stories; indeed, such copying was "illegal," Mrs. Bee told them; in adult terms, it was plagiarism. Moreover, they were told to try to spell independently, although she and adult volunteers would help when necessary.

As LaTrell and his peers have already shown, the children were not so proper. They listened dutifully to Mrs. Bee as they sat on the rug. Then, they made their way to their work tables, where they negotiated, and even argued over, supplies and jointly invented worlds and sought help for "making words." They learned fairly quickly that Spider-Man, Superman, and SpongeBob were banned topics. Such topics could elicit a peer's "ooo" if anyone so ventured on his or her page (although writing about having, say, a Tinker Bell doll or Hannah Montana video seemed OK; commercial possession was fine, even if imaginative play was not).

On True Stories of the True Self

The air balloon vignette illustrates Mrs. Bee's worries about the "realness" of the children's stories and their veracity for individuals. "Everybody didn't see an air balloon, now," she said. Yet, the children's proliferating balloons suggested that even if "everybody" did not see an air balloon, most of the children would like to see such appealing flying objects (and LaTrell, of course, became a flying object).

The air balloon event, which happened in the fifth week of school, also illustrates how LaTrell and his peers could participate in composing as if it were a form of play. LaTrell's topics came not so much from inner reflection, nor from straightforward copying, but from social interaction with paper and peers. Indeed, his writing seemed at times situated, at least in part, in playful practices appropriated from his childhood world, as in the opening of the snowmen event described below.

Shortly after the balloon event, LaTrell initiated another event with what seemed a variant of "playing the dozens," a verbal game of the African American oral tradition. Although playing the dozens typically involves competitive insults about the other's mother (Smitherman, 2000), the opening of LaTrell's event seemed a truncated version, reminiscent of childhood versions of the game that did not seem particularly insulting (see Jemie, 2003):

LaTrell is sitting by Alicia, who is in her second year of kindergarten and previously solicited his involvement in an evolving scene of her own. While Alicia once again draws her extended family at birthday parties, LaTrell first draws a snowman and then moves to add a person hanging on to what turns out to be a broom:

LaTrell: Your mama's gonna hit the snowman.

Alicia: [laughing] No, that's your mama.

LaTrell: [adds a small snowman] Your mama's gonna hit the other snowman. Your mama hit the other snowman, hit the baby snowman. That's your mama.

Alicia looks and smiles but does not respond. She is drawing the relatives who are at her sister's and her birthday parties at the park.

LaTrell: [to the table] Her mama hit the head with a broom.

LaTrell adds more snowmen and then, like Alicia, begins to draw his relatives amid the invading snowmen. When Alicia adds a baby brother, LaTrell does, too. When he draws his brother being bitten by a dog, she creates her own dog. When LaTrell adds a sun, so does Alicia (although his spells doom for the snowmen). In this dialogic way, LaTrell's yard full of wild snowmen and Alicia's park full of celebrating relatives take shape together.

When Earnest, sitting nearby, decides that he will make a snowman, the more experienced Alicia sees trouble ahead:

Alicia: Ooo. He copied offa you.

LaTrell: So?

With this last comment, LaTrell suggested that he (like Earnest, among others) did not seem initially to understand that he was to do more than learn to write. He was to transform his relationship to his peers, as well as to his own imagination. In fact, Alicia was copying LaTrell, and he was copying her. They were both contributing to and appropriating from the conversational gathering of ideas—referred to years ago by Britton (1970) as a "sea of talk" (p. 29; see Salvio & Boldt, 2009). This was a common dynamic among the children, who were supposedly doing their work independently.

On Making Words Independently

During the air balloon event, LaTrell, like most of his peers, did not "make the words" on the bottom of his paper to go with the picture, which itself was linked to different told stories. The basic skill of "stretching and sounding the words out," a major emphasis of rugtime lessons, did not quite capture the children's difficulty. The children were beginning to associate letters with sounds, but the link between those associations and the production of meaning was not clear (Bialystok, 1991; Ferreiro & Teberosky, 1982; Tolchinsky, 2003). The whole business of putting speech, not an image, on paper was tenuous. This is hardly atypical (e.g., Clay, 1975, 1998), but given the new basics demands, it was locally a sign of parents not doing their job and children not meeting benchmarks (as per the newspaper article noted earlier).

As the curricular guide urged, Mrs. Bee aimed for the children to spell as best they could, to be independent. Still, as learners do when they are faced with a new task (Rogoff, 2003), the children sought help despite the curricular guidelines. They pooled their collective knowledge. In fact, sometimes a child got caught up and joined in the repetitive monitoring of a peer trying to put talk on paper syllable by syllable; their written messages could thus merge, just as Alicia's relatives and LaTrell's snowmen did.

In the snowmen event, LaTrell sought help from Alicia, who was going through kindergarten for the second time and initially had relatively more encoding knowledge than LaTrell. In the episode, she shifts roles from responsive peer to good teacher, using her speech as a meditational tool to model, guide, and generally be supportive (Vygotsky, 1978):

LaTrell is trying to write *snowman*, the name of the objects most salient to him in his drawing (cf. Ferreiro & Teberosky, 1982; Tolchinsky, 2003). He knows that he needs an s, but he also knows that a single letter is not enough for *snowman*. He relies on Alicia's experience:

LaTrell: What else?

Alicia: /Sno/ /m/ /m/ /m/ *m*.

LaTrell: How you write *m*?

Alicia: Like this. Line down. Like that. [makes an *m* on her paper]

As Alicia models how to write an *m*, LaTrell watches and then tries it himself.

Alicia: Yep. Like that.

LaTrell: Now what else?

Alicia: /Snowma/ /n/ /n/ /n/.

LaTrell: What?

Alicia: *N*. Want me to show you?

LaTrell: I can write it like this.

Alicia: Ooo. That good.

Although the above interaction was quite serious, sometimes LaTrell manipulated the sounds of words in quite playful ways, as in the following exchange with Earnest. The two boys have been arguing about whose turn it is to use the eraser, when seemingly out of the blue, LaTrell changes the subject:

LaTrell: Yippeeo jibeeo jibeeoo.

Earnest: Cheerio cheerio cheerio.

LaTrell: Jibeeo.

On Being a Good Writer

The children's imaginative play and social responsiveness could be viewed as the beginnings of what we as authors are doing right now, writing to respond to others' voices on a topic. The children were engaged in a kind of exploratory play that could conceivably be channeled into such relations as text performers and audience members (through sharing times), authors and actors (through dramatizing of texts), and official collaborators who share a page.

Or, their sociability, the linking of their individual papers into a social networking of ideas and relations, could be viewed as simply unruly. Their imaginative exploits could be deemed a distraction from the real stuff of life. To be a proper child, LaTrell would have to learn, as he did, that official writing was a kind of individual competition; one had to get a topic first, before anybody else did, like getting the ball first on the playground. Moreover, one had to produce true (or apparently true) sentences. Any playful imaginings had to stay in the free space of drawing or the social space of talk. Thus, in his dialogic storytelling with peers, LaTrell was bitten by a shark in the local pool, his friend Charles had a baby lion as a pet, and in her drawing, his peer Odette rode an elephant to the local mall.

By spring of the school year, LaTrell's collective play, and mutual helping, during writing time did not stop, but the composing of imagined worlds did. He could use his growing orthographic knowledge to write straightforward sentences (e.g., "I GO T [to] The Prc…and I GO T The Hos [house] and I a [had] Jos [juice]"). His texts about playing in the park, swimming in the pool, and going to his grandma's house were like those of other children in his room.

The very individuality that the curriculum seemed to desire was more apparent when a child could fly and snowmen could invade. The curricular guide's insistence that children stretch out true narrative moments with details seemed to make little sense to the children, who were still exploring lines and curves and figuring out connections between sounds and graphics. Ironically, such details were the stuff of the intricate details of drawing, the lively rounds of child storytelling, and the moment-to-moment enactments of worlds in formation.

As we leave LaTrell's classroom for Miguel's, we leave these thoughts for now and return to our reflections on curriculum and assessment in the last section of our chapter.

Miguel: A Player for Whom the Social Is Complex

We now turn our attention to Miguel, a multilingual child with a rich imagination that he sometimes kept to himself and sometimes opened up to others. His family had immigrated to the United States from southwestern Mexico before he was born, and his language story reflected the family's history. He understood but did not speak Mixteco, the indigenous language that he heard at home, and began to speak both Spanish and English in a Head Start program with a largely Latino population. He helps us illustrate the complex relationships among talk, play, and the basics of written language.

As a preschool child, Miguel was characterized as "not a talker." We surmised that as a preschooler, he was in the process of learning Spanish and English and that he also preferred activities he could do on his own. Because Genishi and her collaborators followed him since his prekindergarten days as a 3- then 4-year-old, we documented his path from the textual playground of pre-K to what we earlier called "a private drive on a benchmarked road," the road of the prescribed kindergarten literacy curriculum.

But first, we examine scenes from the playground. The administrators and teachers at the Head Start center that Miguel attended were committed to maintaining a play-based curriculum, in which adults honored children's choices. The teachers followed the HighScope curricular structure of plan-do-review (Hohmann, Banet, & Weikart, 1979), as mandated by Head Start. Within that structure, children in this center chose activities ranging from the family area to tabletop toys to the block area. During the 4s year, the computer was an area of choice. Children could transform any of the multiple areas into stages for sociodramatic play, but the family and block areas were especially open to it.

Miguel most often chose the block area, where he preferred action or nonlinguistic activities over talk. Thus, he became notable for his constructive play with blocks and trucks and for his gestures and the creation of his own soundtrack, on which sound effects like "beep beep" and growls predominated. His friends, or associates, were the boys who also liked the block area, but his usually independent actions seemed to be impelled by his imagination and not motivated by friendships. Still, his pre-K days unfolded on the indoor and outdoor playgrounds of the Head Start center, which featured ample space and time for child choice. Like his classmates, Miguel was able to choose activities, playmates, and languages that came together via a fluid curriculum supported by flexible teachers. This confluence of complex curricular pieces formed a social web prior to the onset of school: the kindergarten of today, with its academic curriculum and the attendant pressures that we were introduced to in Mrs. Bee's room (see also Graue, 2011; Hu, 2008, 2011).

Signs of a Social Miguel

As in real estate, location matters in schooling. Miguel's kindergarten teacher, Mrs. Em, was required to use the same balanced literacy curriculum that Mrs. Bee used. However, because the teachers and their kindergartners lived in different states within the United States, the ways in which they implemented the curriculum varied by school district, neighborhood, school, and classroom. Despite curricular prescriptions, teachers, of course, had their own ways of implementing them. Miguel was in a classroom and school where kindergarten teachers were able to fit time for play into the daily schedule. In short, he had sanctioned opportunities to keep alive or extend the playful social web that was constructed in pre-K.

In this space, where there was room for social talk and play, Miguel was still a bit of a loner, often choosing to work or play alone and following his own timeline. Peer relationships only occasionally seemed important to him, as this poem about his friendship with Josué, a friend from Head Start, reflects (conventional Spanish spellings and English translations are in parentheses):

> *Yo soi (soy) su* (I am his)
> *amgo (amigo) Di (de)* (friend of)
> *Josue (Josué)*
> *Yo si soi* (Yes I am)
> *su amgo* (his friend)
> *con Jose (Josué)* (with Josué)
> *Yo me une* [uní?] (joined with?)
> *soi amgo Di Jose* (Josué)
> *sha sha sha.*
>
> (Genishi & Dyson, 2009, p. 51)

This songlike poem, an index of a newly social Miguel, was one of a number of pieces of creative writing that contrast with what he produced during writing time. The creative writing assignment was in fact not part of the balanced literacy curriculum, but rather a teacher insertion. Moreover, it was an insertion that Miguel responded to with long stories, as compared with his peers' pieces. His tendency to be independent revealed itself again.

Picture a Sad Frog Versus Talk With a Purpose: "You Need More Dinosaurs"

Miguel's teacher, Mrs. Em—and the school's dual-language program—modified the balanced literacy units of study so children could begin to read and write in both English and Spanish. She also included choice time in the daily schedule, when children could choose to play as long as they completed their work. That is, choice time could be withheld if, for example, a child had not completed an assigned writing task.

As in playful and creative settings, in the prescribed curricular context, Miguel also worked on his own, following Mrs. Em's suggestions as best as he could. When he talked, he was often reading aloud what he had written, apparently for himself. "*Yo tengo que jugar con mi hermano*" ("I have to play with my brother") was a sentence that the teacher dictated and Miguel dutifully wrote with quite a few hints from his teacher, a child co-author, and the word wall (field notes, 2/08). The orientation of the curriculum toward individual learners and learning was clearly reflected here. Thus, as a student who mostly liked to work alone, Miguel should have been a good match for this curricular feature.

Still, we could rely on him to show how hard it is to categorize a child as a loner, not a talker, or a good match for a curricular approach when we looked at his writing. The following are two examples from his writing journal:

> ~~Frogs~~ *rana le* ~~*tongo*~~ *quiero cet* [*comer?*] *a* ~~flies~~ *para no le* ~~*tengo*~~ *a* worms

The text is accompanied by a drawing of a frog with its tongue out and flies and a drawing of a sad frog with a worm. Falchi, the observing researcher, thinks the message is that the frog doesn't like worms.

> *A rana le gusta comer.* (The frog likes to eat.)

Miguel wrote with difficulty, even when the topic was appealing to him, as animals were.

Indeed, when Mrs. Em assessed him early and then later in the kindergarten year, he did not meet the expected benchmarks for the balanced literacy curriculum. (Whether these were reasonable benchmarks for children who were learning to read and write in two languages is an open question, of course.) In sum, Miguel may not have shone as he engaged in scripted literacy lessons, but because of opportunities for creative writing and the inclusion of choice time, he had notable moments of spoken and written expression about topics that interested him. As we saw above, a favorite topic was animals of all kinds.

While playing with plastic animals, this time of the extinct kind, Miguel and another kindergartner spoke to each other in English, occasionally making their dinosaurs fight with each other (field notes, 3/24/08). At one point, Miguel asserted, "You need more dinosaurs," surely a promising line to launch a prehistoric minidrama. However, because the substitute teacher then told the two boys in Spanish that they should be building something with their LEGOs—being literally constructive in their play—their conversation stopped, and they proceeded to build things individually. Hence, the social was unintentionally curtailed, and both boys then appeared to be loners.

At other times, when children were able to develop their play, dinosaurs reappeared (field notes, 4/28/08). In response to his peer Marco, who asks where the bad guys are, Miguel tells him that his dinosaur is "the good guy." The two dramatists have the dinosaurs attack each other while the boys provide a soundtrack with occasional explosions. Miguel later says, "My dinosaur has spikes," which is true because his plastic dinosaur is a stegosaurus. In a few minutes, Tommy joins them, and suddenly the dinosaurs are dead or dying, so Marco says to one of the animals, "Run for your life!" This play seems unremarkable as the boys animate the plastic dinosaurs and invest the energy of invented dramas in their scene, an energy quite invisible in a dictated sentence like "*Yo tengo que jugar con mi hermano*" ("I have to play with my brother"), which sounds like the weary complaint of an older brother about a younger one. Actually, Miguel has two sisters and no brothers, making his diligence in writing the sentence all the more impressive. Additionally, perhaps the contrasting scene in which dinosaurs are in demand is remarkable because it could only have happened in a context that allowed for playful, social talk, a context that is increasingly rare in kindergarten classrooms.

Curricula for Young Children: We Need More Dinosaurs

> "You are to be in all things regulated and governed," said the gentleman, "by fact. We hope to have, before long, a board of fact, composed of commissioners of fact, who will force the people to be a people of fact, and of nothing but fact. You must discard the word Fancy altogether." (Dickens, as quoted in McDermott & Hall, 2007, p. 11)

We could not help but sense a kinship between the mandated language arts curricula of today and Mr. Gradgrind's proposal for "commissioners of fact" in Charles Dickens's (1854/2007) 19th-century novel *Hard Times*. The administrators monitoring children's progress according to the No Child Left Behind Act and the updated Race to the Top must feel as if they have been given fact sheets, containing, for instance, the number of letters a child should know to be ready for kindergarten or the number of words that must be correctly spelled in order to reach a writing benchmark.

The facts appear to be suffocating "Fancy altogether" as reading and writing become the center of early childhood curricula. Resistance to the transformation of the kindergarten into the first grade, traditionally where most children learned to read, seems to be disappearing. Experienced teachers are leaving the classroom, states are eviscerating public employees' unions (Karp, 2011), and teacher educators seek to align themselves with steadfast teachers like Mrs. Bee and Mrs. Em who do the best they can.

What is also disappearing is the vision of teachers as professionals, or more accurately put, teachers' abilities and voices are disappearing as administrators are pushed to measure the quality of teaching via the facts of students' test scores. Teachers are no longer able to make judgments within the context of children's own social and cultural realities, to decide that LaTrell and his peers were not plagiarizing but collegially, even collaboratively, constructing graphic worlds or that Miguel could create his own sentences to later write correctly. Neither curriculum developers nor diligent teachers can easily destroy childhood imagination and play, so central are they to the essence of childhoods. But curriculum developers and teachers can drive them underground, denying teachers the opportunities to know and build on children's interests, predilections, and ways of working. Indeed, in the wider educational world now, youths are forging ahead outside of school in social networks oriented to participation in newly evolving (and sometimes virtual) communities (e.g., Kirkland, 2011); school is marginal to their literacy practices.

Teachers Measure Their Teaching: Partnering Curriculum With Assessment

The balanced literacy curriculum that shaped much of LaTrell's and Miguel's school days had means of assessment embedded in benchmarks and book levels. These constraints lined the private drives that children were to take as they became readers and writers. In some schools, teachers are assessed by the degree of fidelity to the details of a prescribed curriculum. In some schools, at a given hour, say 10:00 a.m., the topic must be nonfiction because at other times in the 90-minute literacy block, teachers must address other topics. That is one meaning of *fidelity of implementation*, which enables administrators to state that benchmarked measures are valid because the curriculum was faithfully taught. (See Snyder, Bolin, & Zumwalt, 1992, for a comprehensive definition of *fidelity of implementation*, and see National Research Center on Learning Disabilities, 2007, for an evidence-based definition linked to Response to Intervention.) Of course, teachers and children vary in their ability (and willingness) to be faithful to curricular prescriptions. Children often veer away from prescriptions; they take detours off the drive as they use multiple modes, such as drawing, moving, and gesturing, to express or help themselves arrive at their own literacy benchmarks of fanciful air balloons or sad frogs.

The stuff of teacher-based assessment, then, incorporates drawings, the children's talk about them, and the printed text, which are all inseparable from literacy learning. Particularly for emergent bilinguals (García, Kleifgen, & Falchi, 2008) and multilingual children, assessment should feature their talk. How much and in what context do children speak their home language, English, or both? What do they talk about? What kind of talk does the prescribed curriculum engender? Despite Miguel's tendency to be independent and not especially talkative, choice time allowed him a verbal range beyond assigned texts. His growing knowledge of the social world and its print counterparts often depended on the fanciful dramas of choice time, when children traded dinosaurs or warned the plastic creatures to run for their lives. LaTrell's verbally elaborate stories needed the imaginative space of textual playgrounds, complete with companions. Without them, his texts bespoke just another little boy who didn't do anything "special," as he explained it; he just rode his bike to the park.

Teachers, whose children need the time and space to create the social and imaginative contexts in which literacy begins to make sense to them, in turn need the time and space to be professional observers—to listen, watch, sense, and make sense of children's spoken and written texts. Such observations tell teachers what pieces of the curriculum their children need. Just as young children need private drives to reading and writing much less than they need the public spaces of imaginative play, teachers need the time to observe those spaces, to see how the happenings in play might productively connect to new understandings in literacy lessons. Further, when what teachers observe is puzzling, or when they are faced with their own set of facts, they feel stuck because a child seems stuck, and they need the time and space to collaborate, to build on their own sociability to ask peers or staff developers where they might consider going next (Genishi & Dyson, 2009, ch. 6).

Talk of "might consider going" puts us on the expansive stage of the imagination. Unfortunately, that fanciful stage is shrinking, as the lament becomes more and more familiar: In early childhood classrooms, time and space for talk and play are hard to find; they're going the way of the dinosaurs. Yet, just as children continually revive these extinct creatures, adults can take their cue from Miguel and Marco to affirm the need for literal and figurative playgrounds where children can control dinosaurs and their eventual textual representations of them.

As we close this chapter, we leave readers with these questions about facts and fancy in early childhood schooling: Given the curricula we have described, their uniform pacing toward set benchmarks, are kindergartners learning what we as a society want them to learn? Are play and childhood imagination curricular problems or basic forces for individual growth as societal participants? It is past time for us as a society to dialogically construct these exam questions as we aim to intervene in these educational "hard times" for the very young.

QUESTIONS FOR REFLECTION

1. What are the values and beliefs embedded within mandated language curricula?
2. What do the stories of LaTrell and Miguel tell the researchers?
3. To what degree does your interpretation of these students' stories correspond to the researchers' interpretation?

REFERENCES

Appiah, K.A. (2005). *The ethics of identity*. Princeton, NJ: Princeton University Press.

Bakhtin, M.M. (1981). Discourse in the novel. In M. Holquist (Ed.), *The dialogic imagination: Four essays* (E. Emerson & M. Holquist, Trans.; pp. 259–422). Austin: University of Texas Press.

Bereiter, C., & Engelmann, S. (1966). *Teaching disadvantaged children in the preschool*. Englewood Cliffs, NJ: Prentice-Hall.

Beresin, A.R. (2010). *Recess battles: Playing, fighting, and storytelling*. Jackson: University Press of Mississippi.

Bialystok, E. (1991). Letters, sounds, and symbols: Changes in children's understanding of written language. *Applied Psycholinguistics, 12*(1), 75–89. doi:10.1017/S0142716400009383

Britton, J. (1970). *Language and learning*. Harmondsworth, Middlesex, England: Penguin.

Chudacoff, H.P. (2007). *Children at play: An American history*. New York: New York University Press.

Clay, M.M. (1975). *What did I write?* Auckland, New Zealand: Heinemann.

Clay, M.M. (1998). *By different paths to common outcomes*. York, ME: Stenhouse.

Cole, M. (1996). *Cultural psychology: A once and future discipline*. Cambridge, MA: Belknap.
Collins, J., & Blot, R.K. (2003). *Literacy and literacies: Texts, power, and identity*. New York: Cambridge University Press. doi:10.1017/CBO9780511486661
Cook, D.T. (Ed.). (2002). *Symbolic childhood*. New York: Peter Lang.
Corsaro, W.A. (1985). *Friendship and peer culture in the early years*. Norwood, NJ: Ablex.
Corsaro, W.A. (2010). *The sociology of childhood* (3rd ed.). Thousand Oaks, CA: Pine Forge.
Dyson, A.H. (1999). Transforming transfer: Unruly children, contrary texts, and the persistence of the pedagogical order. In A. Iran-Nejad & P.D. Pearson (Eds.), *Review of research in education* (Vol. 24, pp. 141–171). Washington, DC: American Educational Research Association.
Dyson, A.H. (2007). School literacy and the development of a child culture: Written remnants of the "gusto of life." In D. Thiessen & A. Cook-Sather (Eds.), *International handbook of student experience in elementary and secondary school* (pp. 115–142). Dordrecht, The Netherlands: Springer.
Dyson, A.H. (2010a). Childhoods left behind? Official and unofficial basics of child writing. In N. Yelland (Ed.), *Contemporary perspectives on early childhood education* (pp. 159–176). Berkshire, England: Open University Press.
Dyson, A.H. (2010b). Writing childhoods under construction: Re-visioning 'copying' in early childhood. *Journal of Early Childhood Literacy, 10*(1), 7–31. doi:10.1177/1468798409356990
Dyson, A.H. (in press). *Writing "basics"? Views from children's worlds*. New York: Teachers College Press.
Falchi, L., Axelrod, Y., & Genishi, C. (2012). *Seeking time and space for children's multimodal practices*. Manuscript submitted for publication.
Ferreiro, E., & Teberosky, A. (1982). *Literacy before schooling* (K.G. Castro, Trans.). Exeter, NH: Heinemann.
García, O., Kleifgen, J.A., & Falchi, L. (2008). *From English language learners to emergent bilinguals* (Research Review No. 1). New York: The Campaign for the Educational Equity, Teachers College, Columbia University. Retrieved May 14, 2012, from www.tc.columbia.edu/i/a/document/6468_Ofelia_ELL__Final.pdf
Genishi, C., & Dyson, A.H. (2009). *Children, language, and literacy: Diverse learners in diverse times*. New York: Teachers College Press.
Genishi, C., Dyson, A.H., & Russo, L. (2011). Playful learning: Early education that makes sense to children. In B.S. Fennimore & A.L. Goodwin (Eds.), *Promoting social justice for young children* (pp. 59–70). New York: Springer. doi:10.1007/978-94-007-0570-8_6
Glupczynski, T. (2007). *Understanding young children's experiences with a scripted literacy curriculum*. Unpublished dissertation, Teachers College, Columbia University, New York.
González, N., Moll, L.C., & Amanti, C. (2005). Introduction: Theorizing practices. In N. González, L.C. Moll, & C. Amanti (Eds.), *Funds of knowledge: Theorizing practices in households, communities, and classrooms* (pp. 1–24). Mahwah, NJ: Erlbaum.
Graue, E. (2011). Are we paving paradise? *Educational Leadership, 68*(7), 12–17.
Haberman, M. (1991). The pedagogy of poverty versus good teaching. *Phi Delta Kappan, 73*(4), 290–294.
Hirsh-Pasek, K., Golinkoff, R.M., Berk, L.E., & Singer, D.G. (2009). *A mandate for playful learning in preschool: Presenting the evidence*. New York: Oxford University Press.
Hohmann, M., Banet, B., & Weikart, D.P. (1979). *Young children in action: A manual for preschool educators*. Ypsilanti, MI: High/Scope.
Hu, W. (2008, August 6). Where the race now begins at kindergarten. *The New York Times*, p. B1.
Hu, W. (2011, May 28). Too young for kindergarten? Tide turning against 4-year-olds. *The New York Times*, p. A1.
James, A., & James, A.L. (2008). *Key concepts in childhood studies*. Los Angeles: Sage.
James, A., Jenks, C., & Prout, A. (1998). *Theorizing childhood*. New York: Teachers College Press.
Jemie, O. (2003). *Yo' mama! New rap, toasts, dozens, jokes, and children's rhymes from urban black America*. Philadelphia: Temple University Press.
Karp, S. (2011). Who's bashing teachers and public schools and what can we do about it? *Rethinking Schools, 25*(3), 28–33.
Kenner, C. (2000). *Home pages: Literacy links for bilingual children*. Stoke on Trent, Staffordshire, England: Trentham.
Kirkland, D.E. (Ed.). (2011). Teaching English in a sea of change: Linguistic pluralism and the new English [Special issue]. *English Education, 42*(3).
Konner, M. (1991). *Childhood*. Boston: Little, Brown.
Levinson, M.P. (2007). Literacy in English Gypsy communities: Cultural capital manifested as negative assets. *American Educational Research Journal, 44*(1), 5–39. doi:10.3102/0002831206298174
McDermott, R., & Hall, K.D. (2007). Scientifically debased research on learning, 1854–2006. *Anthropology & Education Quarterly, 38*(1), 9–15. doi:10.1525/aeq.2007.38.1.9
Montgomery, H. (2009). *An introduction to childhood: Anthropological perspectives on children's lives*. Malden, MA: Wiley-Blackwell.
National Research Center on Learning Disabilities. (2007). *Fidelity of implementation*. Retrieved June 18, 2011, from www.nrcld.org/rti_practices/fidelity.html
Nelson, K. (2007). *Young minds in social worlds: Experience, meaning, and memory*. Cambridge, MA: Harvard University Press.
Ochs, E., & Schieffelin, B.B. (2001). Language acquisition and socialization: Three developmental stories and their implications. In A. Duranti (Ed.), *Linguistic anthropology: A reader* (pp. 263–301). Malden, MA: Blackwell.

Opie, I. (1993). *The people in the playground*. New York: Oxford University Press.
Opie, I., & Opie, P. (1959). *The lore and language of schoolchildren*. Oxford, UK: Oxford University Press.
Pappano, L. (2010). Kids haven't changed; kindergarten has. *Harvard Education Letter, 26*(5), Article 479.
Rogoff, B. (2003). *The cultural nature of human development*. New York: Oxford University Press.
Russell, J.L. (2011). From child's garden to academic press: The role of shifting institutional logics in redefining kindergarten education. *American Educational Research Journal, 48*(2), 236–267. doi:10.3102/0002831210372135
Salvio, P.M., & Boldt, G.M. (2009). "A democracy tempered by the rate of exchange": Audit culture and the sell-out of progressive writing curriculum. *English in Education, 43*(2), 113–128. doi:10.1111/j.1754-8845.2009.01043.x
Schieffelin, B.B. (2000). Introducing Kaluli literacy: A chronology of influences. In P.V. Kroskrity (Ed.), *Regimes of language: Ideologies, politics, and identities* (pp. 293–328). Sante Fe, NM: School of American Research Press.
Smitherman, G. (2000). *Talkin that talk: Language, culture, and education in African America*. New York: Routledge. doi:10.4324/9780203254394
Snyder, J., Bolin, F., & Zumwalt, K. (1992). Curriculum implementation. In P.W. Jackson (Ed.), *Handbook of research on curriculum* (pp. 402–435). New York: Macmillan.
Sutton-Smith, B. (1995). Introduction: What is children's folklore? In B. Sutton-Smith, J. Mechling, T.W. Johnson, & F.R. McMahon (Eds.), *Children's folklore: A source book* (pp. 3–9). New York: Garland.
Thorne, B. (1993). *Gender play: Girls and boys in school*. New Brunswick, NJ: Rutgers University Press.
Thorne, B. (2005). Unpacking school lunchtime: Structure, practice, and the negotiation of differences. In C.R. Cooper, C.G. Coll, W.T. Bartko, H.M. Davis, & C. Chatman (Eds.), *Developmental pathways through middle childhood: Rethinking contexts and diversity as resources* (pp. 63–88). Mahwah, NJ: Erlbaum.
Tolchinsky, L. (2003). *The cradle of culture and what children know about writing and numbers before being taught*. Mahwah, NJ: Erlbaum.
Vygotsky, L.S. (1978). *Mind in society: The development of higher psychological processes* (M. Cole, V. John-Steiner, S. Scribner, & E. Souberman, Eds. & Trans.). Cambridge, MA: Harvard University Press.

LITERATURE CITED

Dickens, C. (2007). *Hard times*. New York: Simon & Schuster. (Original work published 1854)

CHAPTER 7

Exploring Vygotskian Perspectives in Education: The Cognitive Value of Peer Interaction

Ellice A. Forman, University of Pittsburgh

Courtney B. Cazden, Harvard University

Two important and related themes in Vygotsky's writings are the social foundations of cognition and the importance of instruction in development:

> An important point to note about Vygotsky's ideas on the social origins of cognition is that it is at this point that he uses the notion of internalization. He is not simply claiming that social interaction leads to the development of the child's abilities in problem-solving, memory, etc.; rather, he is saying that the very means (especially speech) used in social interactions are taken over by the individual child and internalized. Thus, Vygotsky is making a very strong statement here about internalization and the social foundations of cognition (Wertsch, 1981, p. 146).

> If all the development of a child's mental life takes place in the process of social intercourse, this implies that this intercourse and its most systematized form, the teaching process, forms the development of the child, creates new mental formations, and develops higher processes of mental life. Teaching, which sometimes seems to wait upon development, is in actual fact its decisive motive force.... The assimilation of general human experience in the teaching process is the most important specifically human form of mental development in ontogenesis. This deeply significant proposition defines an essentially new approach to the most important theoretical problem of psychology, the challenge of actively developing the mind. It is in this that the main significance of this aspect of Vygotsky's enquiries lies (Leontiev & Luria, 1968, p. 365).

In all of Vygotsky's writings with which we are familiar, the social relationship referred to as "teaching" is the one-to-one relationship between one adult and one child. When we try to explore Vygotskian perspectives for education, we immediately confront questions about the role of the student peer group. Even if formal education takes place in a group context only for economic reasons, because no society can afford a teacher for each individual child, the presence of

This chapter is reprinted from *Culture, Communication and Cognition: Vygotskian Perspectives* (pp. 323–347), edited by J.V. Wertsch, New York: Cambridge University Press.

peers should not be ignored or relegated only to discussions of issues in classroom management and control.

We see two separate but related issues concerning the group presence. First, there are the problems posed for the teacher in carrying out direct teaching to a group of students; second, there are the questions raised for the teacher's more indirect planning for the social organization of all work-related talk in the classroom setting, specifically the contribution that peers can make to each other. We focus on the second set of questions in this chapter. This is not to underestimate the importance of the first. If teaching is conceived as assistance to the child in the child's zone of proximal development, then teaching to a group of children whose "zones" overlap only in part, or not at all, poses obvious problems. But to state the problem thus seems mainly to give new labels to the familiar problem of within-group variation in any group being taught. We focus instead on the less-discussed problem of the potential contribution of social interactions among the children themselves.

Understanding this contribution has both practical and theoretical significance. Practically, despite the fact that school classrooms are unusually crowded social environments, group work is rarely encouraged (Galton, Simon, & Croll, 1980), perhaps in part because there has been no clear rationale for its value. (See Sharan, 1980, for one review of arguments and evidence.) Theoretically, most developmental research studies in the United States have traditionally focused on the value of peer interactions in the socialization of behavior and personality and have said less about their possible value for cognition and intellectual learning. According to Lawler (1980), until recently the same has been true of most writing on education in the Soviet Union—for example, the work of Makarenko.

Interactions among peers focused on intellectual content can be placed on a continuum, depending on the distribution of knowledge or skill among the children, and therefore on the roles they take toward each other. At one extreme, one child knows more than the others and is expected to act as a peer tutor (or "consultant" in the recent Soviet work of M.D. Vinogradova and I.B. Pervin, summarized in Lawler [1980]). In the contrasting case, knowledge is equal, or at least not intentionally unequal, and the give and take of equal status collaboration is expected. We present research first on two different forms of peer tutoring and then on collaboration. Because empirical as well as theoretical analysis of peer interactions is at such a beginning stage, we include excerpts from interaction protocols, not only as evidence for our interpretations, but to provide material for alternative interpretations as well.

Peer Tutoring

The report of Vygotsky's pupil, Levina, points to possible cognitive benefits to a tutor from the activity of giving verbal instructions to peers:

> Vygotsky said that speech does not include within itself the magical power to create intellectual functioning. It acquires this capacity only through being used in its instrumental capacity (Levina, 1981, p. 296).

To the extent that this is true, then what Levina calls the "intellectualization" as well as the internalization of speech should be promoted by the use of instrumental speech to others. Levina suggests exactly that

> what is silently perceived as something unitary and whole is immediately broken up into its component elements in any attempt to make a verbal formulation of it. It is easy to be convinced of this as soon as one tries to introduce the clarity of a verbal characterization into an unconscious impression. What are the motivating forces behind this type of verbal formulation? What is it that compels the child to represent his/her perceptions verbally and to formulate and label his/her actions? In answering this question, Vygotsky laid great stress on factors having to do with the social order. He thought that in labeling an ongoing action, the child initially pays tribute to people in the environment by means of verbal representation. He/she makes this representation accessible to them, as if to clarify it. Vygotsky believed that the very act of labeling arose out of the necessity for giving one's own actions a specialized form comprehensible to others (Levina, 1981, p. 288-289).

Levina's examples of labeling stimulated by the need to communicate to another, taken from notes and protocols collected under Vygotsky's supervision, contain only child speech that is directed back to the experimenter. Though the need to communicate to peers is not mentioned, it seems consistent with the Levina–Vygotsky perspective that the need to communicate to a less knowledgeable other—such as a peer—would motivate the identical process at least as strongly. Instruction of peers could, in this respect, be an intermediate step between receptively being directed by the speech of another and productively and covertly directing one's own mental processes via inner speech.

The first analysis of peer tutoring comes from research in an inner-city multigrade primary classroom in San Diego. Twelve peer tutoring sequences called instructional changes (ICs) were videotaped for analysis (Carrasco, Vera, & Cazden, 1981; Cazden et al., 1978; Mehan & Riel, 1982). Briefly, in each IC the teacher (T) taught a lesson to one child who then taught the same lesson to one or more peers. Leola, a black third grader, was asked to learn and then teach a language arts task. Here are the first three items on her worksheet in completed form.

1. new	1. Y ø ł o đ u	2. t ɏ ɇ o l ꞩ d	3. m ø n̸ e
2. no			
3. off	You	told	me

Following is a transcription, minus repetitions, corrections, and so on, of the teacher's (T) direction as she talked to Leola (L) through the first two items on the task:

Item 1

T: Okay, now number one here says *new*. What's the opposite of *new*?

L: Old.

T: *Old*. How would you spell *old*?

L: O-L-D.

T: Okay, in the letters that are on this paper, cross out the letters you just used for spelling *old*.

L: (*L does it.*)

T: Good. What word is left?

L: Y-O-U.

T: What does it spell?

L: You.

T: Okay, and down here you'll write *you*.

Item 2

T: Okay, now number two there says...

L: No.

T: *No*. What's the opposite of *no*?

L: Yes.

T: Okay, how do you spell *yes*?

L: Y-E-S

T: All right. Now what are you going...

L: (*L crosses out the letters Y-E-S*) Told.

Note first that the T's questions serve to talk Leola through the task until she can do it herself, as Wertsch (1978) has shown for mothers' help to their preschool children in a puzzle-copying task. That such aid does help Leola work independently is shown by a comparison of T's instructions for the first and second items. The first three questions are repeated, but then a much vaguer and incomplete question, "Now what are you going...," is sufficient, and Leola takes off on her own.

The second noteworthy aspect of this IC from the Levina–Vygotsky perspective is the development of increased articulateness and precision in Leola's verbalizations of the task. If one considers the entire instructional chain as a "discourse imitation test," the T's instructions must be reconstructed by the tutor's cognitive, linguistic, and sociolinguistic system. Whereas T taught with questions, Leola teaches with statements, often "You gotta X." (Mehan & Riel, 1982, show that his contrast in teaching styles was characteristic of all 12 ICs.)

It was not immediately easy for Leola to put the directions for this task into words. When Leola first tried to explain to T, pretask, what she was going to tell the group, she included explicit reference to only one of the four essential components, the idea of having some letters "left":

T: Tell me what you are going to tell them to do.

L Spell these letters, and then put out that letter, and then have another letter left.

T goes over the instructions again, this time asking Leola specifically to say the word "opposite." Leola then includes that word, but with the vague verb "do":

T: You want to cross out the opposite of "new." You better say that, because it's going to be really important. They are going to read "new," and then what are they going to do?

L: Do the opposite of it.

Leola achieves the clearest explanation in round 3 (without hesitations and self-repairs):

L: The opposite of *off* is *on*, so on number three, you gotta cross *on* off. O-N. And it is *me* left, M-E.

Overall, one is tempted to argue that the changes in Leola's instructions constitute an example of what Wertsch and Stone (1978), following the Soviet psychologists, call microgenesis—that is, development within an observable time period, and it is a kind of development that Leola seemed to need. In the nine lessons analyzed by Mehan (1979), some 3 hours of talk in all, she spoke four times, and only twice more than one word. This is not to say she was in any way nonverbal, but is to suggest that she could benefit from challenges to formulate academic content in words, and that the demands of tutoring, including the need for repeated formulation and for corrections of others, provide that challenge well. If there is any validity to the internalization hypothesis, practice in explicit overt formulation should ultimately aid inner speech as well. Vague, inexplicit speech—or a unitary and unformulated perception, in Levina's words—is not the same as predication and "sense" in inner speech.

Finally, there is an interesting reduction of information in Leola's instructions after round 3. With two exceptions, in all the rounds after 3 Leola is talking out loud, head down, while she does her own work. In the reduced rounds 4–5 and 7–10, the reduction in information is more by alternative formulations of the components than by deletion of them altogether. For example, the critical word "opposite" is spoken only in rounds 1–3, and then when the first item has to be repeated (IR) and round 6. In the other rounds, Leola says only "out is in" (presupposing that *is* means *is the opposite of*) or, even more briefly, simply places the two words in juxtaposition: "west east." In the two exceptions, IR and 6, explicitness returns as Leola corrects her tutees and she notices that they have made a mistake.

Two alternative explanations are possible for the decreased explicitness in the reduced rounds. It may be due either to Leola's understanding that the concept of "opposites" can now be assumed or to the decreased explicitness that characterizes speech to oneself. As Wertsch (1979) points out, the decay of old or "given" information is functionally equivalent in dialogue and private speech.

The second analysis of peer tutoring comes from observations by Kamler (1980) in a second-grade classroom in New Hampshire in which Donald Graves's research team was observing the teaching of writing. The teacher, Egan, held regular conferences with individual children. In addition, she encouraged the children to hold "peer conferences" about their writing with each other. Here is one observer's account of the conferences between two children, Jill and Debbie:

> On March 11, Jill was one of six children scheduled for a writing conference....At Egan's direction, Jill and the other conferees went to the language table. Egan had requested that Jill first spend time with 7-year-old Debbie going over the book to be sure it was ready for a conference....
>
> Jill began by reading each page aloud to Debbie....As Jill listened to her own words, she made changes on pages 1, 2, and 3 without any prompting or comment from Debbie, and on pages 4, 5, and 8 in direct response to questions Debbie asked....
>
> At the conclusion of this half-hour conference, Jill had made six content changes which affected the overall meaning of the piece. She had deleted information which made no sense or which she could not support; she added information to clarify or explain. Debbie's presence was crucial to the content revisions of the draft. Her physical presence forced Jill to reread the book for the first time since composing; Debbie seemed to make the concept of audience visible for Jill. Jill also needed an active reader to ask questions....
>
> [Later] Debbie claimed her time: "O.K., Jill, you help me now!" They reversed roles, returned to the language table to work on Debbie's book *Ice Follies*, until Egan was ready to see Jill 20 minutes later. (Kamler, 1980, pp. 683–685)

Note first that this is a more reciprocal model of peer assistance. The roles of writer and helpful questioner are interchangeable among the children. All the children can learn what to do and say in the questioner role from the teacher's model in the conferences with her, a consistent model of how to ask helpful questions that are focused on the content of writing, not form. The teacher believes that questions focused on content are more helpful than questions about form; they are also the kind of questions that children can understandingly ask of each other. The teacher's model thus makes it possible for the children to take turns performing the teacher's role for each other—to the benefit of each child as author, who can have so many more experiences with a responsive audience; and to the benefit of each child as critic, who can internalize such questions through the process of not only answering them to the teacher, but of asking them of peers as well.

For these benefits to occur, the teacher's model must be learnable by the children. Graves reports (personal communication) that the conference structure of another teacher in the same school was not as learnable by the children, and so there was less of a multiplier effect via peer conferences in his classroom. This comparison suggests that the intellectual value of peer interactions in a classroom will be enhanced when the teacher consistently models a kind of interaction in which the children can learn to speak to each other.

As Kamler points out, the child writer benefits in two different ways from the peer's presence. Most obviously, the peer asks questions, following the adult model but with content appropriate to the writing at hand; some of Jill's changes (pages 4, 5, and 8) were in direct response to Debbie's questions. Less obviously, the peer silently but no less effectively represents the needs of an audience and makes "the concept of audience visible."

We can locate the effect of such a silent audience in the otherwise empty cell created by Wertsch and Stone's (personal communication) separation of the interpsychological/intrapsychological and external/internal dimensions in Vygotsky's analysis. Wertsch and Stone separated the two dimensions in order to make a place for egocentric speech. In Vygotsky's words, "Egocentric speech is internal speech in its psychological function and external speech physiologically" (1956, p. 87)—that is, intrapsychological in function but external in form. We suggest that the changes Jill made in response to Debbie's silent presence are exactly the opposite: internal in form (though recorded in writing) and interpsychological in function, to make the writing more informative to another.

Peer Collaboration

In comparison with peer tutoring, even less is understood about the intellectual value of peer collaboration. This may be partly due to the fact that collaboration requires a work environment that is even further from traditional classroom organization. Peer tutoring tasks tend to resemble common classroom activities: filling in workbooks, reading aloud, editing written assignments, and so forth. In these activities the tutor helps inform, guide, and/or correct the tutee's work. Collaboration requires a mutual task in which the partners work together to produce something that neither could have produced alone. Given the focus on individual achievement in most Western industrial societies, curricula that promote collaboration are rarely found in schools or studied by educators or psychologists.

Research on peer collaboration has thus been sparse. The major exception to this generalization is a body of research conducted by a group of Genevan psychologists (Doise, Mugny, & Perret-Clermont, 1975, 1976; Mugny & Doise, 1978; Perret-Clermont, 1980). They have conducted a series of experiments to examine the effect of peer collaboration on logical reasoning skills associated with the Piagetian stage of concrete operations: perspective taking, conversation, and so on.

Most of the Genevan research employs a training study design in which subjects are randomly assigned to treatment or control groups in which they are exposed to different social contexts. For example, the subjects in the treatment group may be asked to solve a conservation task in a small peer group composed of conservers and nonconservers, while subjects in the control group are asked to solve the same problem alone. All subjects are individually pretested and posttested on some standard measure of concrete-operational reasoning, and the effect of exposure to peer collaboration is assessed by comparing the pretest-to-posttest gains in concrete-operational reasoning found in each group. The Genevans have employed this same training study design across a number of studies in which the particular reasoning task chosen, the social groups assembled, and the criteria used to evaluate cognitive growth are systematically varied. After reviewing this entire body of research, Perret-Clermont (1980) concludes that peer interaction enhances the development of logical reasoning through a process of active cognitive reorganization induced by cognitive conflict. She claims also that cognitive conflict is most likely to occur in situations where children with moderately discrepant perspectives (e.g., conservers and transitional subjects) are asked to reach a consensus.

Two Russian researchers, Lomov (1978) and Kol'tsova (1978), and two Japanese investigators, Inagaki and Hatano (Inagaki, 1981; Inagaki & Hatano, 1968, 1977), have reached similar conclusions—that peer interaction helps individuals acknowledge and integrate a variety of perspectives on a problem, and that this process of coordination, in turn, produces superior intellectual results. For Kol'tsova, the results are precise, rich, and logically rigorous definitions of a social science concept. For Inagaki and Hatano, the results are generalizable and stable conservation concepts. For Perret-Clermont, the results are increased ability to use concrete operational logic.

In none of these studies were subjects' interactions during collaborative problem solving systematically observed. The studies provide only anecdotal evidence to support the hypothesis that peer interaction is capable of enhancing intellectual performance because it forces individuals to recognize and coordinate conflicting perspectives on a problem. To test this hypothesis, one would need to examine the process of social coordination that occurs during problem solving in order to isolate the social conditions that are the most responsible for cognitive growth. For example, one could observe the interactions that occur while the group is working in order to differentiate those groups in which members work closely together and frequently attempt to coordinate their differing perspectives from those in which members work largely on their own. Then one could examine how these different group interactional patterns affect the problem-solving strategies used. Just this approach is advocated by Perret-Clermont:

> We have also shown that, for the task to have educational value, it is not sufficient for it merely to engage children in joint activity; there must also be confrontation between different points of view. Are all the activities described as "cooperation" by research workers such as to induce real interindividual coordinations which are the source of cognitive conflict? This question can only be answered by the systematic observation which remains to be done. (1980, p. 196)
>
> In further studies of the psychology of intelligence, we should envisage not solely the effect of interindividual coordination on *judgment* behavior, or on *performance* as an index of development...but also the impact of different types of social interaction, and in particular of partner's strategies, on the *strategy* which the subject adopts in order to carry out the task. (1980, p. 192)

We will describe a recent study (Forman, 1981) in which videotapes of collaborative problem-solving sessions were analyzed for the social interactional patterns used and the problem-solving strategies employed. In addition, individual measures of logical reasoning were collected on this sample of collaborative problem solvers that were compared with similar measures collected on a previous sample of solitary problem solvers.

The research design used by Forman is a modification of the training study design utilized by Perret-Clermont and her colleagues. Instead of providing only one opportunity for children to solve a problem in a collaborative fashion, Forman exposed her subjects to a total of 11 problem-solving sessions. There are several reasons for using a longitudinal design to assess children's problem-solving skills. One can observe the process of cognitive growth directly, rather than having to infer it from pretest-posttest performance; and children can develop stable working relationships. In addition, a longitudinal design was chosen for this study so that the data collected on collaborative problem solving could be compared with similar longitudinal data collected by Kuhn and Ho (1980) on solitary problem solving. [See Kuhn and Phelps (1979) and Forman (1981) for a more detailed explanation of the strengths of this kind of longitudinal design.]

Forman's study thus provides two kinds of information about collaboration: how the reasoning strategies of collaborative problem solvers differ from those of solitary problem solvers and how some collaborative partnerships differ from others in both social interactional patterns and cognitive strategy usage. In the following discussion, we will focus on these two kinds of data: comparisons of collaborators with solitary problem solvers and comparisons among different collaborative partnerships. We will then discuss the findings of Forman's study in light of Perret-Clermont's hypothesis and what seems to us the essential and complementary theory of Vygotsky.

Forman's Study

Like Perret-Clermont, Forman asked children to cooperate in the solution of a logical reasoning task. Unlike Perret-Clermont, Forman selected a chemical reaction task that has been used to assess the ability to isolate variables in a multivariate context (Kuhn & Phelps, 1982). In addition, her subjects were older (approximately 9 years of age) than those selected by Perret-Clermont (4–7 years).

In both the study conducted by Forman (1981) and that conducted by Kuhn and Ho (1980) the subjects were fourth- to fifth-grade, middle-class children—15 singletons (Kuhn and Ho) and 4 pairs (Forman)—who showed no ability to isolate variables in a multivariate task known as the "simple plant problem." In addition to the pretest used for subject selection, all subjects were given an additional pretest: a combinations problem in which subjects were asked to arrange five kinds of snacks in all possible combinations. The singletons and pairs participated in 11 problem-solving sessions, approximately once a week over a 3-month period. The two pretest measures were readministered as posttests within a week after the final problem-solving session. All pretests and posttests were administered individually.

The chemical reaction problem consisted of a series of seven chemical problems that were ordered in terms of logical complexity. Problem 1, the simplest, requires that subjects identify the one chemical from a set of five odorless, colorless chemicals that is necessary and sufficient for producing a specified color change when mixed with a reagent. In problems 2 and 3, two or three of the five chemicals are capable of producing the color change, either separately or together. In problem 4, two chemicals are capable of producing the change, but only when *both* of them are present; and so forth.

Problem 1, with a different operative chemical each time, was presented for the first four sessions. This procedure ensured that the children were repeatedly exposed to the simplest problem in the series before more difficult problems were introduced. After the fourth session, a new problem in the series was presented whenever the previous problem had been solved once. Thus, progress through the problem series is one measure of the effectiveness of the subjects' problem-solving strategies.

Each of the 11 problem-solving sessions in both studies followed the same format. First, two demonstration experiments were performed by the experimenter. Then, the children were asked a standard set of questions about the demonstration, for example, "What do you think makes a difference in whether it turns purple or not?" Next, the children were invited to set up the experiments they wanted to try in order to determine what chemicals were responsible for the change. No mixing of chemicals was permitted during this setting-up phase of the task. After the experiments were set up and some additional questions about them were posed, the children were permitted to mix together the combinations they had selected. In Forman's study, the dyads were encouraged to work together on setting up and mixing the chemical experiments. Finally, after the results from the experiments had been observed, the experimenter repeated the original set of questions in order to assess whether the correct chemicals had been identified.

Forman analyzed only the part of the sessions devoted to planning and setting up the experiments. Four sessions for each of three subject pairs (George and Bruce: sessions 3, 5, 8, 11; Lisa and Linda: sessions 3, 5, 9, 11; Matt and Mitch: sessions 3, 5, 8, 10)—12 tapes in all—were coded. (The fourth pair had been included only as insurance against illness, etc.) The two coding systems used in the analysis consisted of one set of social interactional categories and one set of experimentation categories. In this chapter, we will discuss only one type of social behavior code (procedural interactions) and three types of experimentation strategies (random, variable isolation, and combinatorial).

Procedural interactions occurred during most of the problem-solving sessions coded (a range of 71 percent to 100 percent of the available time). They were defined as all activities carried out by one or both children that focus on getting the task accomplished.[1] Examples of procedural interactions were distributing and arranging task materials, choosing chemical experiments, and recording experiments. Three levels of procedural interactions were identified: parallel, associative, and cooperative (adapted from Parten's 1932 study of social interaction). These three levels represent three qualitatively different approaches to the sharing of ideas and the division of labor. During parallel procedural interactions, children share materials and exchange comments about the task. However, they make few if any attempts to monitor the work of the other or to inform the other of their own thoughts and actions. Associative procedural interactions occur when children try to exchange information about some of the combinations each one has selected. However, at the associative level, no attempt is made to coordinate the roles of the two partners. Cooperative interactions require that both children constantly monitor each other's work and play coordinated roles in performing task procedures.

The experimentation strategy codes were adapted from Kuhn and Phelps (1982). Three basic types of experimentation strategies were observed: a random or trial-and-error strategy; an isolation-of-variables strategy; and a combinatorial strategy. The random experiments strategy represents a relatively ineffective, unsystematic approach to experimentation. The variable-isolation strategy is effective for solving the first three problems only. The more advanced problems, 4 through 7, require both experimental isolation and combinatorial strategies. Thus, this experimentation coding system was devised to identify when or if this strategy shift (from only variable isolation to both variable isolation and combinatorial) occurred.

Experimental strategy codes were assigned to a dyad based solely on the type of chemical experiments set up. Neither the type of social organization used to select these experiments nor the kinds of conversations that occurred during the setting-up process affected the assignment of an experimentation code. Thus, the coding of experimentation strategies constituted an assessment of each dyad's behavior that was independent of that obtained by coding their social interactions.

For the comparisons of the problem-solving achievements of collaborators versus singletons, two kinds of data are available: the number of chemical problems solved during the 11 sessions and pretest-to-posttest change scores. The first comparison produced striking differences between collaboration and solitary problem solving. While Kuhn and Ho found that only 4 of the 15 singletons solved problems 1 through 3 in the 11 sessions, all 4 of Forman's dyads solved problems 1 through 4 in the same amount of time. In addition, one dyad (George and Bruce) solved problems 1 through 6 during this three-month period, an achievement approached by none of Kuhn and Ho's subjects.

The pretest-posttest comparison between singletons and dyads produced more mixed results. These results are displayed in Tables 1 and 2 (ignoring for now the initials in parentheses). On the simple plant problem (Table 1), the singletons showed greater progress than the pairs between the pretest and posttest. In contrast, subjects who had worked in pairs seemed to show greater progress on the combinations problem (Table 2) than did the subjects who had worked alone.[2] Thus, while the pairs seemed able to master the series of chemical problems at a much faster rate than did the singletons, they did not show consistently greater pretest–posttest gains.

One clear difference between these two comparisons (progress through the problems versus posttest performance) is that both partners were able to contribute to the solution of each chemical problem presented, but on the pretest–posttest measures the partners were on their own. The relatively sophisticated problem-solving strategies that collaborators were able to display when they could assist

Table 1. **Pretest and Posttest Category Frequencies on the Simple Plant Problem**

Group	Predominantly Concrete	Transitional	Predominantly Formal	Total *N*
Pretest				
Singletons	15	0	0	15
Pairs	8	0	0	8
Posttest				
Singletons	4	5	6	15
Pairs	6 m1, l2, m2, g, k1, k2	1 (b)	1 (l1)	8

Table 2. **Pretest and Posttest Category Frequencies on the Combination Problem**

Group	Predominantly Concrete	Transitional	Predominantly Formal	Total *N*
Pretest				
Singletons	15	0	0	15
Pairs	8	0	0	8
Posttest				
Singletons	12	3	0	15
Pairs	5 k2, l1, m1, k1, g	3 l2, m2, b	0	8

each other were not as apparent when each partner was asked to work alone on similar problems.

Another reason why collaborators did not always outperform the singletons may lie in difference among the partnerships. Due to the very small number of dyads examined, large differences between dyads may obscure all but massive differences between dyads and singletons. Therefore, we turn to the second set of comparisons: those among dyads. First, we will discuss the types of social interactions that occurred over time in the three collaborative partnerships examined. Second, we will look at the experimentation strategies used by those same dyads. Third, we will reexamine their pretest-posttest data.

The most obvious difference among the social behaviors of the three dyads concerned the development of procedural interactions patterns. All procedural interactions were classified as either parallel, associative, or cooperative. Table 3 shows that all three dyads engaged in predominantly parallel and associative interactions during the first session coded (session 3 for all three dyads). Only Lisa and Linda showed any degree of cooperative behavior during this session. However, by sessions 5, 8, and 11, George and Bruce were entirely cooperative. Lisa and Linda retained some associative interaction patterns in session 5, but by sessions 9 and 11 they too were engaging in cooperative interactions. In contrast, Matt and Mitch never cooperated throughout the 3-month period. The interaction pattern that Matt and Mitch seemed to prefer was either predominantly or entirely parallel in nature.

Table 3. Percentage of Procedural Time Spent in Parallel, Associative, and Cooperative Activities

	Type of Procedural Activity (%)		
Subject Pair	Parallel	Associate	Cooperative
George and Bruce			
Session 3	61	39	0
Session 5	0	0	100
Session 8	0	0	100
Session 11	0	0	100
Lisa and Linda			
Session 3	42	26	32
Session 5	0	44	55
Session 9	0	0	100
Session 11	0	0	100
Matt and Mitch			
Session 3	90	10	0
Session 5	85	15	0
Session 8	100	0	0
Session 10	100	0	0

Table 4 summarizes the differences in experimentation strategies used in each pair's last two sessions. All three pairs used similar kinds of experimentation strategies during the earlier sessions. George and Bruce, the dyad who solved the greatest number of problems, used both an isolation of variables and a combinatorial strategy in the two later sessions. Lisa and Linda used only the variable-isolation strategy in session 9 but both strategies by session 11. In contrast, Matt and Mitch produced either random experiments or experiments capable of isolating single variables throughout the study, despite the fact that neither of these strategies was sufficient for solving the advanced problems that were presented to them during sessions 8 and 10.

Returning to the pretest-posttest measures, we find that George and Bruce, who worked so well together, did not maintain this high degree of performance when they were tested individually. The initials on Tables 1 and 2 show the posttest status of the six children whose tapes were analyzed: George (G), Bruce (B), Lisa (L1), Linda (L2), Matt (M1), Mitch (M2), plus the remaining unanalyzed fourth pair (K1 and K2). On the simple plant problem (Table 1), the children receiving the highest scores were Bruce and Lisa; on the combinations problem (Table 2), Bruce, Linda, and Mitch exhibited the most advanced/reasoning skills. Thus, the clear differences among dyads that were apparent on the videotapes of collaborative problem-solving sessions were not reflected in the posttest results.

In summary, when pairs were compared with singletons, the pairs solved the chemical combination problems at a much faster rate. However, the pairs did not do better than the singletons on all of the posttest measures. Singletons appeared to outperform the pairs on the simple plant problem, a test of a subject's ability

Table 4. Experimentation Strategies Used in Chemical Problems 4–7

Subject Pair	Random Combinations	Isolation-of-Variables Strategy	Systematic Combinational Strategy
George and Bruce			
Session 8		X	X
Session 11		X	X
Lisa and Linda			
Session 9		X	
Session 11		X	X
Matt and Mitch			
Session 8	X	X	
Session 10		X	

to isolate variables, whereas the pairs seemed to do better on the combinations problem.

When comparisons were made between the pairs, it was found that George and Bruce solved more chemical combination problems than did the other pairs. In addition, George and Bruce were the first pair to switch to an entirely cooperative interaction pattern and to use a combinatorial experimentation strategy. On some of these variables, that is, the degree of cooperation shown and the use of a combinatorial strategy, Lisa and Linda appeared to hold an intermediate position between the two pairs of boys. However, these fairly consistent differences in interactional style and problem-solving strategy use were not reflected in the posttest performance of these children. In general, George and Bruce did not exhibit consistently higher levels of reasoning on their individual posttests than did the other subjects.

Discussion

What can these results tell us about the hypothesis proposed by Perret-Clermont that peer interaction can induce cognitive conflict that, in turn, results in cognitive restructuring and growth? Forman did find an association between high levels of social coordination (cooperative procedural interactions) and the use of certain experimentation strategies (combinatorial strategies). However, she did not devise a measure of cognitive conflict for her study, and her findings thus cannot establish that social coordination results in cognitive conflict, which then affects problem-solving skills.

One reason why cognitive conflict was not assessed was that overt indices of conflict, that is, arguments, were relatively rare during the portion of the problem-solving session examined—the setting-up phase of the task during which experimentation strategies were most apparent. In this portion of the session, hypotheses concerning the experiments could be proposed but not tested. During most of the setting-up time, children were busy working, separately or together, on laying out and sharing task materials and on planning and choosing experiments. Among the children who interacted at a cooperative level, a great deal of mutual support, encouragement, correction, and guidance was exchanged. For example, one child would select chemical combinations while the other checked for duplicates. Instead of conflicting points of view, one saw two people attempting to construct and implement a joint experimentation plan to be tested later on in the task.

Conflicting points of view were apparent later in the problem-solving session, when most or all of the results of the experiments were visible. At that time, one could observe children forming distinct and sometimes opposing conclusions about the problem solution. Just such a conflict occurred in problem-solving session 3 between George and Bruce: Here is a summary of their interaction taken from a videotape record.

> In this session, chemical C alone was the solution to the chemical problem. The two boys set up and mixed the following set of experiments: B, C, BE, CD, CE, DE, BDE, CDF, DEF. In addition, they could examine the results of the two demonstration experiments: BCE, DEF. All the experiments containing chemical C turned purple, the rest remained clear.
>
> After all the experiments were mixed, the experimenter asked both children, "What makes a difference in whether it turns purple?" Bruce initially concluded that the answer was C and E. George expressed his surprise that a single element, for example C, produced the desired color change. In response to the standard prompt from the experimenter, "Can you be sure it's C and E?" Bruce reexamined some experiments and found one that contained E (and not C) that did not change color. Bruce, however, did not conclude at this point that C was the only operative chemical. George then asked Bruce whether all the experiments containing C produced the desired color change. Bruce scanned each experiment containing C and announced that each did change color.
>
> Based on the experimental evidence and some information remembered from previous sessions, George concluded that C was the solution to the problem. Bruce, however, contradicted George by asserting it was F. At this point, they both reexamined the experiments. Afterward, George still concluded it was C and Bruce concluded it was C and F.
>
> The experimenter asked whether they could be sure of their answers. George replied that he was sure of C but not of F. Once again, the evidence was examined. This time, Bruce identified the experiment CDF as indicating that F was an operative chemical. George countered this argument by comparing it with experiment DEF that did not produce the desired reaction. Bruce responded that D and E were more powerful liquids than F and therefore prevented F from working. George then tried another approach by asking Bruce how he could tell it was F and not C that made the mixture CDF turn purple. Bruce replied by asking George how he could tell it wasn't both C and F that made CDF turn purple. George's concluding remark was an assertion that he just knew it was C alone.

This interchange shows the kinds of activities that conflicting solutions to the problem seemed to induce. The children returned repeatedly to the experimental evidence for supporting data. Because their conclusions differed, they were forced to acknowledge information that refuted their own inferences as well as data that supported them. These data then had to be integrated into a convincing argument in support of their own point of view. Counterarguments to their partner's position also had to be constructed. Bruce, in particular, was forced to revise his conclusions based on the evidence George brought to his attention. Despite his efforts, George was unable to convince Bruce to accept his conclusion. Unfortunately, they had not provided themselves with enough of the appropriate experimental evidence in session 3 to enable them to reach a consensus about the solution.

Collaboration on the chemical reaction task thus seems to involve two different types of social interactive processes. The first process, which occurs during the setting-up or planning stage of the task, involves either separate (parallel) working patterns or closely coordinated cooperative patterns. Cooperation during the setting-up stage consists of mutual guidance, encouragement, and support. Often during this phase of the task, complementary problem-solving roles are assumed.

Later on in the task, when experimental evidence is being examined, the second kind of interactive process occurs. At this time, each child seems to be reaching independent conclusions about the solution of the task that are based on all or only some of the available experimental evidence. After each child comes to a conclusion, he or she may find that his or her partner does not agree. In this circumstance, overt conflicting perspectives on the experimental evidence are expressed in the form of an argument. Arguments capable of producing a consensus seemed to be those that made use of appropriate supporting evidence.

It appears that Perret-Clermont's notion that cognitive conflict is the mediator between peer interaction and cognitive reorganization can be tested best in contexts where overt manifestations of conflict are likely. These contexts seem to occur when children have access to a wealth of empirical evidence, when this evidence is capable of suggesting at least two distinct solutions to the problem, and when a consensual solution is solicited.

Perret-Clermont's hypothesis about the importance of cognitive conflict comes from Piaget's theory concerning the role of social factors in development. Most of the past research on the topic of peer collaboration has been based upon Piaget's ideas. Piaget placed more importance on peer interaction than upon adult-child interaction, so it is not surprising that the bulk of research on collaboration has shared a Piagetian perspective.

In order to understand the limitations as well as the strengths of this perspective on collaboration, one needs to appreciate the role that peer interaction plays in Piaget's theory. Piaget (1970) identified four factors that he believed are necessary for a theory of cognitive development: maturation, experience with the physical environment, social experiences, and equilibration or self-regulation. In addition, Piaget claimed that equilibration is the most fundamental of the four factors. Peer interaction, and social experiences in general, derive their importance from the influence they can exert on equilibration through the introduction of cognitive conflict. Perret-Clermont shares this view of development when she writes:

> Of course, cognitive conflict of this kind does not create the *forms* of operations, but it brings about the disequilibriums which make cognitive elaboration necessary, and in this way cognitive conflict confers a special role on the social factor as one among other factors leading to mental growth. Social-cognitive conflict may be figuratively likened to the catalyst in a chemical reaction: it is not present at all in the final product, but it is nevertheless indispensible if the reaction is to take place. (Perret-Clermont, 1980, p. 178)

When Piaget looks at peer interaction, therefore, he looks for evidence of disequilibrium, that is, cognitive conflict. He is not interested in describing or explaining social interactional processes as a whole. Piaget's theory is most helpful in explaining those situations where cognitive conflict is clearly and overtly expressed in external social behaviours, for example, arguments. However, in situations where overt conflict is not apparent and where mutual guidance and support are evident, his theory provides few clues concerning the role of social factors in development. Fortunately, Vygotsky's writings on adult-child interaction offer insights into the intellectual value of these kinds of peer interactions.

To illustrate how Vygotsky's ideas shed light on some of the processes involved in peer collaboration, we will discuss another set of observations of George and Bruce. One of the most puzzling findings from Forman's study was the discrepancy between how a dyad functions as a unit and how the partners function separately. George and Bruce were clearly the most successful collaborators, yet they did not show the same consistently high level of functioning when they were posttested separately. This discrepancy between dyadic and individual performance levels was also apparent when subjects who collaborated were compared with those who worked alone. On the posttest measures, which were individually administered, collaborative problem solvers did not do better than solitary problem solvers. Nevertheless, collaborative partners were able to solve many more chemical problems than could solitary problem solvers during the same period of time.

Vygotsky acknowledged that a discrepancy might exist between solitary and social problem solving when he developed his notion of the zone of proximal development. He defined this zone as "*the distance between the actual developmental level as determined by independent problem solving and the level of potential development as determined through problem solving under adult guidance or in collaboration with more capable peers*" (1978, p. 86). Thus, Vygotsky hypothesized that children would be able to solve problems with assistance from an adult or more capable peer before they could solve them alone. This seemingly obvious observation was then used to reach several original conclusions. One conclusion was that the zone of proximal development could be used to identify those skills most amenable to instruction. Another was that learning consists of the internalization of social interactional processes. According to Vygotsky, development proceeds when interpsychological regulation is transformed into intrapsychological regulation.

Returning to Forman's data, it appears that a similar process of interpsychological to intrapsychological regulation may also occur in collaborative contexts where neither partner can be seen as objectively "more capable," but where the partners may assume separate but complementary social roles. One child may perform an observing, guiding, and correcting role while the other performs the task procedures. This observing partner seems to provide some of the same kinds of assistance that has been called scaffolding by Wood, Bruner, and Ross (1976). Such support from an observing partner seems to enable the two collaborators to solve problems together before they are capable of solving the same problems alone. When collaborators assume complementary roles, they begin to resemble the peer tutors described earlier. For example, the observer/performer roles are functionally similar to the critic/author roles observed in Egan's New Hampshire classroom.

In addition, one can see in Forman's data instances where problem-solving strategies first appear as social interactional procedures and are later internalized. Remember that a combinatorial problem was administered to each child individually at three different times (as a pretest, as an immediate posttest, and as a delayed posttest). In addition, these same children were presented with a similar combinatorial problem in each problem-solving session when they were asked to decide jointly which chemical mixtures to set up. Therefore, a comparison can be made between the combinations generated by each child when he or she worked alone or in pairs.

> Both George and Bruce used an empirical strategy to generate combinations during their pretest—for example, selecting a combination at random and then basing the next combination on the first by adding, subtracting, or substituting one of its elements. The third combination would then be produced by copying, with another minor revision, the second combination. Pairwise checking of each new combination with each previous combination was the empirical procedure used for guarding against duplications.
>
> In their early collaborative problem-solving sessions, George and Bruce worked in parallel and each used an empirical strategy similar to the one used on the pretest to generate combinations. After about a month of working together, they devised a social procedure for generating combinations empirically by assuming complementary problem-solving roles: one selected chemicals and the other checked their uniqueness.
>
> After two months, they had begun to organize their combinations into groups based on their number of elements. In addition, they had devised a deductive system for generating two-element combinations. This deductive procedure enabled the child who had previously done the checking to prompt, correct, and reinforce the selections of his partner. Higher-order combinations were produced empirically using the familiar social procedure.
>
> At the last session, the boys continued to assume complementary roles but now used the blackboard as a recording device. They produced combinations in a highly organized fashion—singles, two-element combinations, three-element combinations, and so on—and were able to generate almost all of the 31 possible combinations. They used a deductive procedure for generating the two-element combinations but still relied on their empirical procedure for the higher order combinations.
>
> At the first posttest one week after the last collaborative session, the degree to which each boy had internalized a deductive combinatorial system was assessed by asking

> them to generate combinations independently. Bruce was able to generate all 10 two-element combinations deductively on his own, but George was not. George used an empirical system to generate combinations. On the second posttest 4 months later, however, both boys had internalized a deductive procedure for producing two-element combinations.

It appears that these two boys were able to apply a preexisting intrapsychological rule, an empirical combinatorial procedure, to a collaborative context by dividing the procedure into complementary problem-solving roles. With repeated exposure to the problem, these boys were able to progress to a deductive procedure for generating simple, two-element combinations. At first, deductive reasoning was clearly a social activity for George and Bruce. Each time one partner selected a series of combinations, the other guided, prompted, and corrected his selections. Later, one partner was able to demonstrate that he had internalized this deductive procedure by using it to generate all possible two-element combinations on his own. Four months later, both partners were able to generate all possible pairs of five objects deductively by themselves. Thus, for these two boys, deductive combinatorial reasoning first appeared in a collaborative context. Only one of the two boys was initially able to show that he had internalized this procedure when he generated combinations alone. Months later, however, both boys had internalized this deductive process.

In summary, a Piagetian perspective on the role of social factors in development can be useful in understanding situations where overt indices of cognitive conflict are present. However, if one wants to understand the cognitive consequences of other social interactional contexts, Vygotsky's ideas may be more helpful. In tasks where experimental evidence was being generated and where managerial skills were required, by assuming complementary problem-solving roles, peers could perform tasks together before they could perform them alone. The peer observer seemed to provide some of the same kinds of "scaffolding" assistance that others have attributed to the adult in teaching contexts.

Thus, the Vygotskian perspective enables us to see that collaborative tasks requiring data generation, planning, and management can provide another set of valuable experiences for children. In these tasks, a common set of assumptions, procedures, and information needs to be constructed. These tasks require children to integrate their conflicting task conceptions into a mutual plan. One way to achieve a shared task perspective is to assume complementary problem-solving roles. Then each child learns to use speech to guide the actions of her or his partner and, in turn, to be guided by the partner's speech. Exposure to this form of social regulation can enable children to master difficult problems together before they are capable of solving them alone. More importantly, experience with social forms of regulation can provide children with just the tools they need to master problems on their own. It enables them to observe and reflect on the problem-solving process as a whole and to select those procedures that are the most effective. When they can apply this social understanding to themselves, they can then solve, independently, those tasks that they had previously been able to solve only with assistance.

Thus, collaborative problem solving seems to offer some of the same experiences for children that peer tutoring provides: the need to give verbal instructions to peers, the impetus for self-reflection encouraged by a visible audience, and the need to respond to peer questions and challenges. The reciprocal model of peer assistance that characterized the children in Egan's classroom is even more apparent in collaborative problem-solving contexts, similar to those observed by Forman.

Conclusion

In conclusion, in these analyses we are not talking about a children's culture separate from adults. What Leont'ev and Luria discuss as the "most important specifically human form of mental development"—namely, "the assimilation of general human experience in the teaching process"—must ultimately be grounded in adult–child interactions. But peer (and cross-age) relationships can function as intermediate transforming contexts between social and external adult–child interactions and the individual child's inner speech.

Although such peer interactions take place in home and community as well as at school, they may be especially important in school because of limitations and rigidities characteristic of adult–child interactions in that institutional setting. Cazden (1983) argues for the value to child development of a category of parent–child interactions of which the peek-a-boo game and picture book reading are familiar examples. In interactions such as these, there is a predictable structure in which the mother initially enacts the entire script herself and then the child takes an increasingly active role, eventually speaking all the parts initially spoken by the mother. The contrast between such learning environments and the classroom is striking. In school lessons, teachers give directions and children nonverbally carry them out; teachers ask questions and children answer them, frequently with only a word or a phrase. Most importantly, these roles are not reversible, at least not within the context of teacher–child interactions. Children never give directions to teachers, and questions addressed to teachers are rare except for asking permission. The only context in which children can reverse interactional roles with the same intellectual content, giving directions as well as following them, and asking questions as well as answering them, is with their peers.

QUESTIONS FOR REFLECTION

1. Why does it make sense that Vygotsky's perspectives for education would apply to a student peer group and not solely to one-on-one adult–child interactions?
2. What factors influence a student's learning in the zone of proximal development?
3. How is a Vygotskian perspective useful in understanding the value of peer collaboration?

NOTES

Forman's research was supported, in part, by a grant from Radcliffe College; by a grant to Deanna Kuhn from the Milton Fund, Harvard University; and by NIMH Grant No. 5 T32 MH15786 to the Department of Psychology, Northwestern University. We would like to thank the students, faculty, and principal of the Straton Elementary School, Arlington, Massachusetts for their generous participation in this research; and Leonard Scinto, Addison Stone, and Jim Wertsch for their helpful comments on earlier drafts of this chapter.

[1] Other social interactional codes were used to identify conversations that served to plan, reflect upon, or organize these procedural activities (metaprocedural interactions), task-focused jokes (playful interactions), task-focused observations (shared observations), and off-task behavior.

[2] A second set of posttests was administered to both samples 4 months after the first posttest. The pairs constantly outperformed the singletons on both second posttest measures. However, the interpretation of these findings is problematic due to the fact that this 4-month period occurred during the school year for the pairs but during the summer for the singletons.

REFERENCES

Carrasco, R. L., Vera, A., and Cazden, C.B. 1981. Aspects of bilingual students' communicative competence in the classroom: A case study. In R. Duran (Ed.), *Latino language and communicative behavior. Discourse processes: Advances in research and theory* (Vol. 6). Norwood, N.J.: Ablex.

Cazden, C. B. 1983. Peekaboo as an instructional model: Discourse development at school and at home. In B. Bain (Ed.), *The sociogenesis of language and human conduct: A multi-disciplinary book of readings*. N.Y.: Plenum, pp. 33–58.

Cazden, C. B., Cox, M., Dickinson, D., Steinberg, Z., and Stone, C. 1978. "You all gonna hafta listen": Peer teaching in a primary classroom. In W. A. Collins (Ed.), *Children's language and communication*. 12th Annual Minnesota Symposium on Child Development. Hillsdale, N.J.: Erlbaum, pp. 183–231.

Doise, W., Mugny, G., and Perret-Clermont, A. N. 1975. Social interaction and the development of cognitive operations. *European Journal of Social Psychology*, 5(3), 367–383.

Doise, W., Mugny, G., and Perret-Clermont, A. N. 1976. Social interaction and cognitive development: Further evidence. *European Journal of Social Psychology*, 6, 245–247.

Forman, E. A. 1981. *The role of collaboration in problem-solving in children*. Doctoral dissertation, Harvard University, Cambridge, MA.

Galton, M., Simon, B., and Croll, P. 1980. *Inside the primary classroom*. Boston, MA: Routledge & Kegan Paul.

Inagaki, K. 1981. Facilitation of knowledge integration through classroom discussion. *Quarterly Newsletter of the Laboratory of Comparative Human Cognition*, 3(3), 26–28.

Inagaki, K., and Hatano, G. 1968. Motivational influences on epistemic observation. *Japanese Journal of Educational Psychology*, 6, 191–202.

Inagaki, K., and Hatano, G. 1977. Amplification of cognitive motivation and its effects on epistemic observation. *American Educational Research Journal*, *14*, 485–491.

Inhelder, B., and Piaget, J. 1958. *The growth of logical thinking from childhood to adolescence*. New York: Basic Books.

Kamler, B. 1980. One child, one teacher, one classroom: The story of one piece of writing. *Language Arts*, *57*, 680–693.

Kol'tsova, V. A. 1978. Experimental study of cognitive activity in communication (with specific reference to concept formation). *Soviet Psychology*, *17*, 23–38.

Kuhn, D., and Ho, V. 1980. Self-directed activity and cognitive development. *Journal of Applied Developmental Psychology*, *1*(2), 119–133.

Kuhn, D., and Phelps, E. 1979. A methodology for observing development of a formal reasoning strategy. *New Directions for Child Development*, 5, 45–58.

Kuhn, D., and Phelps, E. 1982. The development of problem-solving strategies. In H. Reese (Ed.), *Advances in child development* (Vol. 17). New York: Academic.

Lawler, J. 1980. Collectivity and individuality in Soviet educational theory. *Contemporary Educational Psychology*, 5, 163–174.

Leont'ev, A. N. 1981. The problem of activity in psychology. In J. V. Wertsch (Ed.), *The concept of activity in Soviet psychology*. Armonk, N.Y.: Sharpe, pp. 37–71.

Leontiev, A. N., and Luria, A. R. 1968. The psychological ideas of L. S. Vygotsky. In B. Wolman (Ed.), *Historical roots of contemporary psychology*. New York: HarperCollins.

Levina, R. E. 1981. L. S. Vygotsky's ideas about the planning function of speech in children. In J. V. Wertsch (Ed.), *The concept of activity in Soviet psychology*. Armonk, N.Y.: Sharpe, pp. 279–299.

Lomov, B. F. 1978. Psychological processes and communication. *Soviet Psychology, 17*, 3–22.
Mehan, H. 1979. *Learning lessons*. Cambridge, MA: Harvard University Press.
Mehan, H., and Riel, M. M. 1982. Teachers' and students' instructional strategies. In L. Adler (Ed.), *Cross-cultural research at issue*. New York: Academic.
Mugny, G., and Doise, W. 1978. Socio-cognitive conflict and structure of individual and collective performances. *European Journal of Social Psychology, 8*, 181–192.
Parten, M. 1932. Social participation among preschool children. *Journal of Abnormal and Social Psychology, 27*, 243–269.
Perret-Clermont, A. N. 1980. *Social interaction and cognitive development in children*. New York: Academic.
Piaget, J. 1970. Piaget's theory. In P. H. Mussen (Ed.), *Carmichael's manual of child psychology* (3rd ed., Vol. 1. New York: Wiley, pp. 703–732.
Sharan, S. 1980. Cooperative learning in small groups: Recent methods and effects on achievement, attitudes, and ethnic relations. *Review of Educational Research, 50*, 241–271.
Simon, B. (Ed.). 1957. *Psychology in the Soviet Union*. Stanford, CA: Stanford University Press.
Simon, B., and Simon, J. (Eds.). 1963. *Educational psychology in the USSR*. Stanford, CA: Stanford University Press.
Slavina, L. S. 1957. Specific features of the intellectual work of unsuccessful pupils. In. B. Simon (Ed.), *Psychology in the Soviet Union*. Stanford, CA: Stanford University Press, pp. 205–212.
Vygotsky, L. S. 1956. *Izbrannye psikhologicheskie issledovaniya* [Selected psychological research]. Moscow: Izdatel'stzo Akademii Pedagogicheskikh Nauk RFSFR.
Vygotsky, L. S. 1978. *Mind in society*. Edited by M. Cole, V. John-Steiner, S. Scribner, and E. Souberman. Cambridge, MA: Harvard University Press.
Vygotsky, L. S. 1981. The genesis of higher mental functions. In J. V. Wertsch (Ed.), *The concept of activity in Soviet psychology*. Armonk, N.Y.: Sharpe.
Wertsch, J. V. 1978. Adult–child interaction and the roots of metacognition. *Quarterly Newsletter of the Institute for Comparative Human Development*, 2(1), 15–18.
Wertsch, J. V. 1979. The regulation of human action and the given-new organization of private speech. In G. Zivin (Ed.), *The development of self-regulation through private speech*. New York: Wiley, pp. 79–98.
Wertsch, J. V. (Ed.). 1981. *The concept of activity in Soviet Psychology*. Armonk, N.Y.: Sharpe.
Wertsch, J. V., and Stone, C. A. 1978. Microgenesis as a tool for developmental analysis. *Quarterly Newsletter of the Laboratory of Comparative Human Development, 1*(1), 8–10.
Wood, D., Bruner, J. S., and Ross, G. 1976. The role of tutoring in problem-solving. *Journal of Child Psychology and Psychiatry, 17*, 89–100.

CHAPTER 8

It's a Book! It's a Bookstore! Theories of Reading in the Worlds of Childhood and Adolescence

Shirley Brice Heath, Stanford University

Our Bookshop Manifesto

WE BELIEVE IN THE BOOK. We believe in quieting the noise and listening to the stories. We believe in traveling far and wide between paper pages. We believe in touching the words, scribbling in the margins, and dogging the ears. We believe in surrounding ourselves with books long finished and books not yet read; in revisiting our young selves each time we pull old favorites off the shelf.

We believe in five-year-olds inking their names in big letters on the flyleaf. We believe in becoming someone else for four hundred pages. We believe in turning off the screens and unplugging the networks once in a while. We believe in meeting the author, reading the footnotes, looking up the words and checking the references. We believe in holding our children on our laps and turning the pages together.

We believe in standing shoulder to shoulder in comfortable silence with our fellow citizens before a good shelf of books; we believe in talking face to face with friends and strangers in the aisles of a good bookstore. We believe that together, readers, writers, books and bookstores can work magic. (Day, 2010)

As the first decade of the 21st century drew to a close, everyone (or so it seemed) jumped in to declare the death of the book and, by implication, of reading, writing, and bookstores as well. From cognitive theorists to devotees of books, this theme stirred either outright rebellion fed by nostalgia or acquiescence moderated by positive projections for the future role of technology in the learning lives of former booklovers. This chapter sets out several perspectives that permit insight into the threads of thinking that run between those in rebellion and those who have agreed to let books live alongside other technological inventions. In five sections, the chapter draws from the epigraph with the hope of leading education researchers, teachers, and parents to bring into balance new and old ways of learning to read and of reading to learn along the life span.

All sections of the chapter bear the influence of social scientists who focus their research on what happens to those who read with different kinds of technologies. Representing primarily the disciplines of anthropology and linguistics, the social scientists whose work is discussed here have been heavily influenced by ideas from cognitive neuroscience and the information sciences. In general, these scholars have given an unprecedented amount of attention to advances in understanding both the brain and the ways in which socialization processes and environmental contexts influence neurological development.

The first section takes a look at the ways in which researchers have considered the value of reading books with young children. The following section considers how overly simplistic ideas about what happens in these reading interactions have had an undeserved influence on educators' ideas about early reading and its relationship to family life, socioeconomic class, and language development. The next section offers a brief summation of a longitudinal ethnographic study of how 300 working-class families in the United States used reading in their lives as they navigated the tumultuous economic twists and turns of the final two decades of the 20th century and the opening decade of the next. The fourth section carries on from the prior discussion of extended talk, especially deliberative discourse and its relationship to academic language. The final section speaks of the magic of words in all media and modes with cautions. No magic ever fully reveals itself to those beyond the wizard's curtain. Hence, we must never believe that magic brings us full goodness and light or that it will lead us into pure evil.

"Traveling Far and Wide Between Paper Pages"

I begin this section with a personal story from my experiences as a writer and scholar. In 2009, the editors of the *Handbook of Research on Children's and Young Adult Literature* (S.A. Wolf, Coats, Enciso, & Jenkins, 2011) asked me to write a chapter for the volume under the title "The Book as Home." The editors quickly rejected the chapter I wrote by saying that they wanted something personal. As a model for me to follow, they sent several other chapters that they had already approved for the volume. After I read those, I knew exactly what the editors had expected from me: a quiet, soothing piece about how much I had, as a child, found solace, peace, and a home in books. If I were diligent in following the model of other chapters, I would even point out how I had found, in my early experiences with children's literature, the power of literacy that had guided me to become a well-known scholar.

The only problem was that the biographical portrayals of the other chapters did not fit me. Moreover, I was uneasy with the implications that I saw in those chapters, suggesting that rich early literacy experiences were somehow critical to fostering oral language development and habituating key mental traits. As an anthropologist who has worked in communities around the world in which children have no early access to books, I knew that (a) these children learned to talk, often in several languages; (b) many of them learned to read later in life after only the barest early foundation of literacy learning in their primitive impoverished schools; and (c) these children did not lack imagination, analytical skills, or playful wit. Thus, not only did the biographical portrayals of other chapters of the handbook not match my own, but they also bore little relationship to the lives of most of the world's children living either in developing nations or in under-resourced neighborhoods and communities of modern economies.

I decided to write a chapter, goaded not only by my discomfort with the aforementioned points but also by findings from my own longitudinal study of working-class families in the United States (summarized in the third section herein). The chapter's eventual title carried only a portion of the original title assigned to me by the editors. My chosen title, which the editors let stand, was "The Book as Home? It All Depends" (Heath, 2011).

I did not grow up with books or, indeed, surrounded by many people who could or did read at all. I never saw a room with bookshelves until I was in secondary school, and that was the school library. My response to these books? I was not impressed, only puzzled. The point of the chapter that finally evolved for the handbook reminded readers that if we look around the world, the majority of children never have the opportunity to think of books as instruments or ladders of power for them. Most have little incentive to think that learning to read will bring them power. They have little evidence in their everyday worlds to convince them that reading will give them something in exchange for the time and effort it takes to learn to read well enough to travel "far and wide between paper pages." Indeed, most of these children would fear the idea of such travel, and they have never met anyone who learned a significant amount of what they know through reading "paper pages."

My intention in the chapter that I wrote for the handbook was not to berate or diminish the experiences of those fortunate enough to grow up with books and adults who spend time reading and talking about books with children. Instead, I thought it important then, just as I do now in this chapter, to remind readers of two basic sets of facts.

The first is that for decades, research has shown that although individuals do not grow up with books or reading, they can and often do learn to read later in life. If and when the need arises and discretionary money and time become available, individuals have for centuries shown that they can readily (and often quite suddenly) learn to love and cherish books in adulthood (as I did). They can even become authors (as I did).[1] Only when I became a mother did I become aware of the role of children's books in the lives of my peers who were also parents. They bought and read books to their children on a regular basis and expected their children to know stories found in books.

I, however, followed the pattern that I had known in my own childhood of hearing and telling oral stories; we quieted the house and listened to stories. My children and I shared stories not only at bedtime but also on other occasions, when we did chores together, rode in the car, or waited in the offices of dentists and doctors. Once I began buying and reading books to my children, they and I, in fact, came to enjoy, even relish, not only reading books but also talking about them and using them as springboards for generating our own stories as sequels or counternarratives. However, the powers of literacy that my children gained from having books introduced to them carried no particular benefits over those I was able to achieve as an adult in spite of my not having books as "home" when I was a child.

As researchers around the world look at how and when literacy is acquired and what people do with it, they recognize that individuals do not *learn to read* with sufficient competence to be able to *read to learn* until both the practice of reading and the artifact of the scroll, manuscript, or book carry meaning for the role that they are playing in life. Moreover, readers across the ages have had to have not only a place for reading in their lives but also dedicated time and space. The initial cost is not the only investment that artifacts of reading require. They must be kept in safe, dry spaces. Reading requires sufficient light, as well as relative quiet. For individuals or families who change their location often, reading materials are heavy burdens (literally). Moreover, reading is one of the few activities that almost entirely rules out any simultaneous activity. One cannot ride a horse, peel potatoes, drive a car, help a child with homework, or hoe a garden while reading a book. The intense demand for full attention that reading requires may account for the fact that throughout the history of literacy, those who take up books have often been portrayed as lazy, secretive, and even dangerous. Many children's books feature the reading child as the naughty one in a family. In the history of fine arts, women reading books or letters have often been interpreted as up to no good, subject to the temptations of nature, and likely to be led into transgressions (cf. Bollmann, 2008; Updike, 2005; B.J. Wolf, 2001).

The second set of facts behind my wanting the handbook chapter to depart from the usual biographical script expected by advocates and authors of children's literature relates to what we know about oral language competencies (Duranti, Ochs, & Schieffelin, 2012; Schieffelin & Ochs, 1986). As children mature, what is usually called for in school-based teaching of reading has little or no influence on the development of facility and fluency with oral language(s). Instructional modes that surround the teaching of reading in schools around the world give much less attention to how readers talk and think about what they are reading than they do to the oral performance of reading. Teacher requests that pupils read aloud dominate over their queries about visual details of illustrations, interpretive and comparative analyses surrounding the content of what has been read, or speculations about the intentions of the author. When the key focus is on teaching the young to show that they can read by doing so aloud, the free-flowing language interactions, mental images, and hand-drawn sketches that make books live in the memory of readers receive little time or focus. Yet, neuroscience research on how the brain processes and stores words of printed texts has pointed to the vital importance of surrounding the physical act of reading with oral language and other creative forms of representation, such as dramatic action, drawing, and extending textual ideas.[2]

"Holding Our Children on Our Laps and Turning the Pages Together"

During the second half of the 20th century, cycles of attention from researchers featured arguments that pointed to social class differences in reading achievement. Many of these arguments remain in place in textbooks, in reports on the declining health and welfare of families living in poverty, and in the minds of teachers and education policymakers. These arguments highlight ways that lower class families lack features of middle class families that are often equated with successful trajectories of learning to read (Blanchard & Moore, 2010). These features include aspects of home life that range from leisure time preferences to extent of lexical input and quantity and type of reading materials. This contrastive view often seeks justification for arguments that point to deficits in the language input and adult–child reading materials, time, and values of families either oriented to working-class values or caught in the spiral of cross-generational poverty. These deficits are often made to stand in sharp contrast to pictures of middle class families, many of whom include one or both parents who have higher education credentials and identities as professionals. Within these families, both the quantity and quality of language input, especially during reading time with children, can often be viewed as providing children with strong preparation for success in school. The quantitative bases of much of this research come from morpheme counts per stretches of time as well as frequency counts of certain types of vocabulary. Counts of literacy artifacts in the home that are available to children and also used by parents are also often seen as contributing to the sense of a literacy environment in which children grow up.[3]

The socioeconomic status of families quickly becomes linked to readiness for learning to read and to work hard for school success. Many studies have focused on children's opportunities in their family life to build their spoken vocabulary and be familiar with book reading. These opportunities have often been seen as essential to children's ability to respond positively to the school's instruction in learning to read and to succeeding in primary schooling. Decontextualized quantitative factors of families' available time, artifacts, and habits of conversation around books have sometimes been characterized as cultural values. Populist versions of the culture of poverty have led many educators to think of impoverished families as having little to offer their children and as uncaring and irresponsible with regard to their children's schooling.

Few studies have considered the interdependence of home language habits with the extent and type of parental employment, access to transportation and community resources, and established age- and gender-related roles within families from different ethnic, religious, and cultural contexts. Moreover, research since the explosion of new technologies in the 1990s that points to extended work hours, higher work demands, and reduced labor forces has generally been ignored by educators who insist that families must do more to support their children's work at school (Hochschild, 1997; Robinson & Godbey, 1999; Schor, 1991). The squeezing of family time and the increase of overlapping demands make more time a mounting impossibility. Yet, many educators persist in making judgmental assessments about families living in or near the poverty line and claim that certain cultural traits are ineffective conduits for young children who enter formal schooling.[4]

In the 1980s, some studies began to point to specific differences between home values and habits of literacy of lower class families and those of the school (Heath, 1983/1996; Philips, 1983; Schieffelin & Gilmore, 1986). By the next decade, however, several researchers of child language development began to caution against viewing this contrast as accounting for all the critical factors that contribute to literacy and academic achievement. Indeed, these studies argued that the matter is much more complex than studies of either socioeconomic class or cultural norms of home and school have attested. Multiple bundles of factors must be taken into account, and how these factors are bundled shifts not only as children age but also continuously across the life span for both children and parents.[5] Moreover, intensity and reach of literacy habits link to developmental maturation, physical and mental health, felt need, and other motivational incentives, as well as the extent to which facility with different types of reading and writing supports the maintenance of economic status and positioning within key social niches of family members (Heath, 2012).

By the opening of the 21st century, researchers from across a variety of disciplines agreed in general on the following key supports for children's successful experiences with oral language development as well as reading and writing. For neurologically normal children to reach young adulthood with oral language fluency, competency, and confidence in reading and writing, they must have the following:

- Within and beyond formal education, supportive intimate models of readers, widely varying types and modes of reading materials, and meaningful incentives to draw, write, act, and talk before, during, and after reading
- Mentors and teachers who are well trained and motivated to keep their own learning attuned to ongoing research on language development of monolingual and bilingual or multilingual children
- Teachers and parents who are oriented to different modes and media of presentation for young children and adolescents and open to talking with and learning from young people about reading and writing with recent technologies
- Safe and reliable access by children and their families to libraries staffed by personnel who are familiar with and fond of a host of technologies that make books and magazines available
- After-school and summer opportunities that are rich in time for adults and young learners to plan, create, and evaluate projects together using a range of art forms and various types of scientific experimentation
- Regular access of parents, teachers, and young learners from preschool into young adulthood to museums, zoos, environmental centers, parks, and playgrounds and the multiple forms of literature in pamphlets, children's literature, science and art books, and on the Internet that complement visits to such places[6]

Cutting across these conclusions is the common thread of meaningful interactions of adults, children, and adolescents working and learning together within a variety of contexts and times and through different combinations of modes and media for different purposes and audiences.

These conclusions regarding key supports render moot past assertions that literacy learning relies on a small bundle of factors, such as the nature and extent of language input from parents to children, the quantity and nature of literacy artifacts in the home, and characteristics of conversational routines between children and adults. Research in the first decade of the 21st century has made clear the vital importance of sustaining as long as possible joint parent–child interests, activities, informational and entertainment sources, and projects of work and play. Middle childhood and adolescence are periods of development in which critical jumps in powers of judgment, understanding of responsibility, and deliberative conversational skills take place. During these years, young learners critically need conversational time and project development with caring adults and opportunities for exploring sports, arts, and science activities together. With startling regularity, since the turn of the 21st century, neuroscience research has pointed to the impact of quality time spent by young and old in joint pursuits during the years of middle childhood and adolescence. Regardless of cultural or religious background or economic standing, adults who surround children as they grow up need to acknowledge their responsibilities to talking, playing, and working with the young and to being alert to how the young so often guide and instruct those elders who are willing listeners and observers open to new understandings (Bell, Lewenstein, Shouse, & Feder, 2009).[7]

"Turning Off the Screens and Unplugging the Networks Once in a While"

This section follows on the key supports noted in the preceding section by providing a summation of an ethnographic study of three decades of family and community life.[8] The cross-generational analysis lays out the extent to which habits and values of oral and written language changed in relation to times, spaces, and interactants of the play and work of daily life. Critical to questions of values and behaviors surrounding literacy are changes in housing and consumerism patterns that do not show up as significant in short-term studies of life in families and communities. However, longitudinal examination of everyday habits surrounding child socialization has revealed the significant influence of economic pressures, employment, family structure, and household location shifts. Looking across the years at the pathways of change for habits and values means appreciating the extent to which factors previously unacknowledged as influential have risen in significance. Such is especially the case with family practices around meal preparation and clean-up, homework and other after-dinner pursuits, and technologies of communication, especially hand-held devices.

Ways With Words: Language, Life, and Work in Communities and Classrooms (Heath, 1983/1996) documented the lifeways of two communities of working-class families living near each other in the Piedmont Carolinas in the first decade after the Civil Rights era. One of these communities, Trackton, was black; the other, Roadville, was white. In both communities, parents worked, often on alternating shifts, in the local textile mills. In addition, young and old family members planted backyard gardens, helped during harvest times on nearby tobacco farms, and bought their meat in the fall when farmers butchered calves and pigs. Hard work, church attendance, and entertainment at home with friends and family filled their days.

Following the legislative changes brought by the Civil Rights movement, schools in their region were desegregated, and teachers in elementary schools immediately perceived differences in how children from different communities used language. Middle-class children, black and white, came to school familiar with the questioning habits of formal schooling and the key role of learning to read for success in school. However, children from working-class communities, black and white, came to school using language in different ways.

White working-class communities, such as Roadville, were closely tied to agrarian life, local churches, and wage labor in manufacturing. Their homes were set apart from one another, and mothers and their young children walked to the homes of neighbors for visits and play time after school or on summer days when chores at home were completed. In good weather, children played outside while their mothers visited on the porch or in the house. On rainy days, children played quietly in the kitchen or a bedroom while adults talked together in an adjacent room. When adults and children read together at home or in church, they closely attended to the texts and their meanings. In the presence of their elders, children spoke when they were addressed by an adult; otherwise, they listened and played quietly. Adults asked straightforward questions; children answered as directly and fully as possible. Book reading between adults and young children at home was a time of naming pictures, talking about events portrayed in illustrations, and memorizing titles of books and stories, many of which carried a moral or lesson. In church services, the pastor and Sunday School superintendent did most of the talking, while the congregation listened and responded in recitation of prayers and scriptural readings. Using hymnals, the congregation sang under the direction of the choir leader.

Children from black working-class communities, such as Trackton, lived in houses in close proximity to one another. In the open plaza that ran in front of their homes, children played in cross-age groups, subject to the watchful eye of any adults who were around. Children incorporated numerous language games in their play. Adults and children teased one another openly. Children entered into adult conversations frequently, often overlapping and interrupting the talk of adults. Multiparty talk surrounded babies from birth, and oral storytelling and repetition of jump-rope rhymes and taunts matched the pace of play activities on the open plaza. Questions directed to children sought new information, not affirmation, and written texts entered family life primarily in the form of documents from bureaucracies, landlords, and utility companies. Church services emphasized performance over literal reading of texts, and members participated freely in the raising of hymns, a practice in which words sung often bore relatively little relation to the words printed in hymnals. Members, young and old, also took part in scriptural readings, choral recitations, and oral affirmations of the words of the preacher.

Ways With Words (Heath, 1983/1996) documents how these community ways of using language played out for Roadville and Trackton children in classrooms. Roadville children tended to do very well in their early elementary years, finding familiarity in teachers' questions designed to test children's comprehension of their reading texts. The children learned the alphabet quickly and had relatively little difficulty understanding the concept of grapheme–phoneme correspondence. As they reached the upper grades, however, questions in their texts and from their teachers sought interpretations and actions from their reading of texts. These tasks stumped many of the Roadville children, especially those with little experience in hearing conversations that debated ways in which the same text could carry different meanings.

Trackton children, however, faced immediate difficulties in desegregated schools in which most of their teachers were from white or black middle class neighborhoods. Trackton children did not know how to respond to teachers' questions that asked children to repeat information the teachers already knew. Having grown up as conversationalists and information creators, Trackton children often responded to teachers' questions in ways that could be interpreted as insolent and disrespectful. Well before they reached the upper grades of their primary schools, where questions asked for interpretations, many Trackton children opted out of trying to learn school ways. Instead, they settled in to just getting by until they were old enough to drop out of school.

However, in the early 1980s, just over a decade after the Civil Rights era, drastic economic changes for their parents jolted Trackton and Roadville children into new lifeways. Foreign takeover led to the closure of textile mills, and tobacco subsidies that had been in place since the Great Depression were severely reduced. Along with these local economic setbacks, the nation suffered a double-dip recession in the early 1980s. Factory workers and farmworkers from the Southeastern states had to scatter to find new kinds of employment. Leaving their rural homes and small communities, they settled their families in new types of neighborhoods and schools. Residents of Roadville and Trackton relocated initially to towns in the Southeast with populations of 50,000 to 250,000. There, male family members had some chance of finding work that capitalized on their handyman mechanical skills. Some men took advantage of their do-it-yourself competencies and started their own small businesses, often in automotive, television, or small-engine repair work.

However, the costs of rent, food, and other goods needed in their new lives soon led mothers to seek work outside the home. Some took advantage of their caregiving skills and entered programs leading to certificates as nursing or teacher aides. Some chose to stay at home and take in washing, ironing, mending, and dressmaking for more well-to-do families. With these changes in times, places, and means of earning a living came an increasing number of shifts in patterns of time and space surrounding cooking and eating, spending family time at home, playing and reading with young children, and worshiping. During the 1980s, these and other changes in daily life marked the start of a roller coaster of changes that accelerated during the 1990s and through the first decade of the 21st century.

The generation that moved away from Roadville and Trackton when they were parents of young children increasingly adopted the attitude that only education could ensure their children's achievement of a better future or the American Dream. These parents insisted that their children work hard in school, be involved in as many extracurricular activities as possible, and look ahead to further education. Most parents did all they could to keep their children from having to do work in the house or yard or to seek employment that might curtail participation in after-school and weekend activities that they now saw as critical to building social capital. As the 1990s opened, young people old enough to enter the military service, nursing school, colleges, or apprenticeship programs did so, while encouraging their younger siblings to stay in school and plan to move on to a college or university.

With the dot-com era came further impetus to understanding the power of learning by doing while also undertaking specialized advanced study. Four years of higher education needed to be supplemented by internships and apprenticeships, work experience, or self-start projects that held promise as start-up companies. Reading of all types and through multiple media came to be accepted as the norm for young adults who wanted to get away from home and explore possibilities in new parts of the country, especially urban centers known for their technology companies. The generation that was too young when their parents left to remember Roadville and Trackton grew up never looking back. They accepted their futures as full of opportunities, good jobs, big homes, and faraway vacations. They had time for reading and writing, primarily as means to an end and as supplements to learning by doing, talking with and watching others, and keeping up on the Internet with key personalities, companies, and trends in the fast-moving global economy. Their literacies had exchange value, giving them something they wanted in return for their time, effort, and dedication.

Along with the rapid economic changes of the 1990s came changes in definitions of *family* and *family life*. The extensive and rapid inclusion of women in the labor force and professional life meant that children and adolescents were growing up primarily in the care of intimate strangers. Paid by parents, these individuals watched over, guided, entertained, and fed the children of parents whose hours of work outside the home meant that they themselves could not fulfill these responsibilities. Day care centers for infants and preschool children extended their hours, sometimes operating around the clock, to accommodate parents who worked two shifts or long, unpredictable hours. Regardless of the level of material goods and other resources of these venues, children engaged face to face in extended sessions of play and talk with caregivers far less than the prior generation's children had in their own homes and communities.

Families who started the decade of the 1980s with working-class identities moved through the 1990s with growing confidence that they could live in middle class neighborhoods and join the mainstream of modern economic life. As those who had been children when their parents left Roadville and Trackton entered adulthood, went off to seek further education, married, and started their own families during the 1990s, they acquired more material goods, larger homes, and greater familiarity with commercial entertainers than their parents ever thought possible. Often created through loans and sustained with mounting credit card debt, their fairy tale worlds meant that their children filled their out-of-school hours as avid soccer, baseball, and football players; videogame experts; and budding pianists and dancers. Complementing achievement in school, these pursuits, along with volunteer hours in community service, meant to the young that the promise of college entry would be fulfilled for them.

Meanwhile, parents and children spent fewer hours playing and working together, undertaking joint responsibilities for maintaining household and meal chores, and exploring the outdoors or taking vacations as families. Once they reached their final years of primary school, children saw more interest in their friends than in their parents. Through the tween and teen years, they moved primarily in the company of their peers, often within activities, including travel, that were organized and supervised by intimate strangers. By 2000, the majority of the children of the children of Trackton and Roadville had never planned and cooked a meal, mowed a lawn, repaired anything around the house, seen a family member change a tire, or helped the family plant a tulip bed, fruit tree, or garden.

In place of not only these activities with their elders but also many other types of undertakings dependent on joint decision making, verbal negotiation, and trial and error, the young spent the majority of their time with their friends. They created among themselves conversational forms of entertainment that reflected their updated information about entertainment figures, forms of music, developments in technology, gossip surrounding boy–girl relationships, and short-term plans for getting together at one another's homes. As they moved through middle school and into secondary school, a few found after-school work on some days of the week, primarily to earn money to pay for their own clothes or special equipment that they wanted for particular sports activities, such as tennis, soccer, baseball, hockey, and golf.

In these adolescents' talk, they reflected features listed in Table 1 in contrast with features called for in academic written discourse, such as research papers, laboratory reports, and honors papers.[9] The interactional talk of young people was cut through with multiple forms of enactment, ranging from voice modulation to gestural exaggeration. These enactments often carried introductions, such as, "And we're, like, really, yeah, like...." In conversations, *like* plus the use of the present tense to report past actions brought listeners into a sense of reality surrounding the events being narrated. When they talked in groups of more than

Table 1. Features of Adolescent Peer Talk and Requirements of Written Academic Language

Feature	Requirement
Layering of symbol systems including gestural, musical, and body decorative	*Required:* Extended written texts; images (e.g., charts, tables, figures, and photographs), if included, must be labeled and their contents referenced within the written text
Repetition of layered collaborative narratives based on shared experiences	*Proscribed:* Repetition of content, other than in limited uses (such as transitions or summations)
Repetitive commentary on the same range of topics	*Required:* Attribution to original retrievable reference of any content repeated (cited) from a source other than current author
Strong preference for narrative genre over explanation or description	*Required:* Expository, reportative, and persuasive texts including an argument of key points with limited use of narratives to illustrate points
Sequencing of events within narratives marked by coordinating conjunctions	*Required:* Clauses linked primarily through causal and temporal conjunctions; introduction of additive points permitted with the use of *furthermore, in addition* (etc.) and summative points with the use of *thus, therefore, as a consequence* (etc.)
Frequent use of judgment in absolute terms	*Proscribed:* Author's value judgments and adverbs leading the reader to assess judgments of content (e.g., *unfortunately, even, obviously*)
Redundant use of "shallow" syntactic constructions and familiar vocabulary	*Required:* Technical or specialized lexical items and dependent and independent clauses
Dominance of present tense with narrow range of past or future tense	*Required:* Fluency with range of tenses needed to indicate relationships among ideas and events
Frequent use of *if-then* propositions as threats or challenges	*Proscribed:* Use of second person pronoun (implied or stated), thereby precluding use of hypotheticals as threats or challenges
Preference for use of hypotheticals for recast events rather than future projections	*Required:* If-then propositions ranging across past, present, and future
Preference for unbalanced *if-then* propositions with one variable on one side of the proposition and several on the other side	*Preferred:* Balanced hypotheticals with variables on either side of the *if-then* proposition relatively equal in number and semantic weight

Note. From *Words at Work and Play: Three Decades in Family and Community Life* (p. 139), by S.B. Heath, 2012, New York: Cambridge University Press. Copyright 2012 by Shirley Brice Heath. Reprinted with permission.

two or three, young speakers entertained one another with collaborative narratives that replayed their shared experiences. They punctuated their talk with repetition, narratives, and chains of actions linked by coordinating conjunctions, such as *and*. Statements using *if-then* often came as warnings or threats issued with only one or two variables on either side of the *if-then* proposition (e.g., "'n he's goin' right up to the door, and, like, he don't look right or left or nutn'. If'n the cops come by, he better be a fast runner right then").

By the time they enter middle school, young people in conversational groups learn the importance of understanding rap lyrics, crossover musical styles, and advertisements that adults often find puzzling. The young communicate through multiple media at the same time: text messaging while talking on the phone, watching videos, doing their homework, or talking with friends on the way to the bus. They layer their speech genres in multiple ways, embedding song lyrics and jokes in what appear to be serious treatises on local shopping centers or new car models.

Close study of the language, work, and play of descendant families from Roadville and Trackton living in the commodified world that came with the 1990s reveals several key patterns:

- Times of dedicated play, planning, and project time between adult family members and their children across ages dropped dramatically, whereas participation of the young within community organizational and peer activities increased significantly.
- With each year, young people increased the number of hours they spent in one another's homes or engaged in rule-governed sports and community service activities directed by intimate strangers. Before entering secondary school, the norm was between 12 and 15 hours each week. For most students in secondary school, this number surpassed 20 hours each week.
- Models of dress, talk, and choices of entertainment forms favored by the young grew more distant and commercialized throughout the 1990s. Peers were monitors and judges of fashion for children as young as 8 years of age.
- Voluntary pursuits of expertise among the young depended increasingly on intent participation or learning a role through observing (Rogoff, Paradise, Arauz, Correa-Chavez, and Angelillo, 2003). Such learning brought vertical and horizontal gains. Learners zeroed in on what they wanted to learn and why, and they sought advice from peers in both face-to-face and online consultations.
- During the first decade of the 21st century, interactional talk time between adults and children in households dropped to less than an hour each week for children under the age of 12. Young people between the ages of 12 and 18 spent about seven minutes each week engaged in extended talk on the same topic with adults at home.

During the 1980s, family members planned and scripted activities, such as cleaning out the attic or garage, planning the summer vacation, or making a cake and card for a favorite relative's birthday. By the 1990s, adults purchased or paid others to undertake these tasks. As separate bedrooms with isolated entertainment stations came to characterize households, "turning off the screens and unplugging the networks" became more and more difficult. Young people learning on their own time increasingly mixed and layered texts, music, images, and interactive technologies to build strong performative frameworks for communications that they transmitted to their peers via the Internet. Only in relatively rare instances did parents join in these productions and share space, time, entertainment, or informational sources with the young.

Throughout secondary school and beyond, young people engaged in collaborative peer work using electronic media and creating opportunities to learn how to use new software for mixing, editing, and producing materials, often for niche or highly selected audiences among their friends at school or within their special interest niches online. As they entered universities, they continued this pattern of connecting through writing whenever possible. Between 2007 and 2010, secondary school students of descendant Roadville and Trackton families could claim some level of expertise with an average of 60 different genres. When their older siblings in college reviewed the list, they claimed that they created twice as many genres in the course of their academic year. They reported to their younger siblings that writing figured in everything they did and certainly exceeded in frequency, variation, and quantity the amount of writing they did for their course assignments.[10] For both groups, functions and audience generated and influenced experimentation with style, length, layering of media, and follow-up genres.

The developmental trajectory of talk among teenagers engaged in video games, communicating, and creating multimedia performances for their online exchanges showed some surprising results. Only young people who spent hours and hours developing their technical expertise, especially their programming expertise and understanding of writing code in various programs, moved much beyond a level that most of their friends regarded as OK or mediocre. Standards were high for those who became recognized experts among their peers. These were readers who consulted an array of online sources (and occasionally print materials) about computers, programming, and animation techniques and creators. Some hung out in bookstores in the computer and graphic novel sections (Heath & Wolf, forthcoming). On some occasions, they talked with their friends about specific books or other sources. Those who read graphic novels or had been early fans of comic book artists during elementary school had select friends with whom they shared resources and opinions. Certain authors and artists and their styles were frequent topics of conversation. Often, these young people were known as geeks beyond their immediate circle of friends. It was not uncommon for the most resourceful geeks to set up informal consulting businesses for their parents' friends who needed computer help or for their own classmates who wanted term papers embellished with computer art.

Many of the geeks, female and male, increased their hours of searching digital space each year. As they did so, they spent more and more time balancing occasions of involvement in brief bits of interaction with extended hours of checking out the Internet, perfecting projects that they had created on the Internet to their satisfaction, and exploring new video games and types of animation, along with breaking news about specific technology industries. These learners mastered a substantial corpus of specialized vocabulary, meta-awareness about their own learning strategies, and for some, a readiness to explain the pros and cons of specific programs, games, and new technology products. Those who worked long hours to reach the expert level tended, however, not to talk extensively with friends who were outside their relatively closed worlds of adult clients and peer geekdom.

The written language that teenagers produced in their interactions with electronic media featured a preponderance of short (often incomplete) sentences, with highly redundant chunks of material. Only rarely did they write and arrange multiparagraph extended texts on one topic. Their writing reflected a mix of given or previously scripted texts, and their inclusion of written language with other media showed substantial borrowing of special effects from their more creative counterparts whose work they found online. Many resisted attempts by teachers to involve them in sustained engagement with extended printed or oral language. Outside of their participation in activities of their own interest, they were often characterized as having short attention spans and inadequate comprehension as measured by standard classroom means. Yet, many geeks did well on standardized tests and engaged with enthusiasm in projects of mathematics or science at school. Only occasionally would they argue with teachers and academic texts, even when their group project work proved the text to be incorrect. In effect, they did not involve themselves sufficiently in the substance of issues raised in their academic schoolwork to bring their own knowledge and skills to bear in oral or written argument (cf. Kuipers & Viechnicki, 2008).

"We Believe in Talking Face to Face With Friends"

The matter of extended talk, particularly on topics for which numerous sources and forms of information, including books, are available, merits thoughtful consideration in any discussion of reading. Extended talk can take place only when interlocutors want to learn from one another. This situation usually occurs only when speakers feel the need to talk about something that is, to some extent, within the same frame of reference for all participants. Within extended talk, speakers engage in not only explication and evaluation but also movement across time frames of past, present, and future. Such talk takes time and involves narratives, clarifying questions, requests for justification of claims, and deliberation of ideas, values, and behaviors.

The deliberation behind scientific, religious, political, and social decisions becomes implanted in the minds of the young primarily through times of listening to and taking part in extended talk from someone whom young speakers feel they trust. Even more vital to such talk by younger speakers is their conviction that they have the respect of their interlocutors.

An examination of the right-hand column of Table 1 indicates features of written academic discourse, many of which also characterize extended talk. Here, speakers must be able to indicate the source of information that they reference; otherwise, listeners tend to regard this information as merely opinion. Causal and temporal conjunctions are needed to support additive points, as are a range of tenses to indicate relationships among ideas and events. Finally, in both oral and written extended discourse, individuals engage in hypothetical reasoning, juxtaposing the here and now as well as the future against past or universal happenings and postulates.

Since the time of Aristotle and Socrates, Western traditions of oratory and written exposition have prized deliberative language as the major carrier of moral and ethical codes. Those who engage in deliberation reason "if X, then Y," or "better yet, if A, B, and C, then D, and E; what might happen if...?" The power of deliberative discourse is its valuation of the strength of the argument over the status of the individual putting forth the argument. The capacity for reasoned judgment must prevail so different positions and views can be asserted, and self-interest will give way to the common good.[11] To gain the fluency of language that is necessary to take part in written and oral deliberative discourse, individuals need extensive experience in situations where they observe and work in thinking collectives with others of different ages and levels and types of knowledge, skills, and experience. Literature, film, dramatic productions, and other art forms have long been accepted as providing vicarious means of safe observation and participation with the lives of others. Authors and scholars of young adult literature have pointed to this value as especially important for adolescents.[12]

To learn to make ethical decisions, the young need to see the values and skills involved when individuals interpret and create analogies, contrast one situation to another, and consider responses or outcomes that result from similar and different circumstances. Young people need the intimacy of extended times of talk and reading (which involves talking with the text) if they are to learn to empathize and perceive the intentions and needs of others. To recognize, as well as to deliberate, possible actions and consequences of playing out moral obligations, children need years of moral discourse—everyday interactions along with written and performed texts that extend beyond the immediate desires of those observing or taking part. The development of autonomy of the child derives from practices embedded in learning how to talk and think about topics beyond the child's own self-interests and the here and now. All of these dimensions of human development come within children's theater, Readers Theatre, and participation in the literary and visual life of art and science museums and the musical life of ensemble performance.[13]

Anthropologists who have studied language development in cultures around the world in the past three decades have looked closely at situations within socialization that foster the concept of responsibility among children. Social awareness, empathy, and self-monitoring are key properties, and social scientists argue that only through participation in joint tasks are these human features developed.[14] The young must gain a sense of interdependence with others, simultaneously feeling the importance of empathy, consequential thinking, and "a generative cross-situational awareness of and responsiveness to others' needs and desires" (Ochs & Izquierdo, 2009, p. 391). If we consider literature and its many instances of deliberation and examination of personhood, we recognize deeply why the reading of literature has been a mainstay of formal schooling. Here, the academy attempts to reinforce what teachers have long expected children to learn from both exposure to children's literature and direct participation in work and play with adults.

Yet, educators increasingly point out that readers in middle and secondary school have difficulty with and little patience for interpreting passages from literary writers of the past. The right-hand column of Table 1 makes clear some of the grounds for young readers' impatience and frustration. If readers have neither taken part in nor witnessed deliberative discourse around them, they will lack the oral language fluency necessary to interpret not only literary texts but also other texts that are central to academic life. Without experience in the decision making of partnered work, play, and talk with adults, the level of receptive and productive competency that is necessary to grasp how extended texts work eludes them. The young need some degree of immersion in language that goes beyond the here and now of everyday talk and action to reflection and retrospection about human feelings. Consider, for example, the distance of everyday language centered on current self-interests from the following sentence in Robert Frost's statement on poetry from the preface to his *Collected Poems* (1939):

> It begins in delight, it inclines to the impulse, it assumes direction with the first line laid down, it runs a course of lucky events, and ends in a clarification of life—not necessarily a great clarification, such as sects and cults are founded on, but in a momentary stay against confusion. (n.p.)

Here, Frost (1939) draws parallels between the shape of love and "the figure a poem makes" (n.p.). As in so many passages of English literature, the interior mind moves back and forth across time and experience, with backdrop and foreshadowing, and consternation over life's contradictions. Such texts rest on a deep grasp of temporality and causality, metaphor and analogy. The hypothetical underlies literature, enabling readers to practice the mental and linguistic performances necessary to support what could be their own actions to come.

"Together, Readers, Writers, Books and Bookstores Can Work Magic"

The irony is that the falling away during the 1990s of deliberative interactions between adults and the young and between the young and extended written texts, including literary works, preceded a decade of unprecedented life-altering and world-changing events for families living in modern economies. Descendants of

Roadville and Trackton experienced these changes and were forced to assess the nature and extent of their emotional and intellectual resources for handling the shifts in daily life that hit them hard as the first decade of the 21st century moved to its end.

Following the attack on New York City in September of 2001 through the end of the decade, the economic stability for families who had held on to their fragile middle class lives in the prior decade turned shaky. By 2007–2008, many had seen their pensions, benefits, salaries, and bonuses either decline or disappear entirely. Some saw the loss of their homes through foreclosure followed in short succession by alterations in family relationships that came with lifestyle shifts and dwindling hopes of college education for their children. Separation, divorce, remarriage, or partnering in new arrangements altered habits surrounding homework, dinnertime, after-school activities, and allegiances to one or the other parent and adaptation to new siblings.

These changes intensified the appeal of the flood of new technologies that fed the desires of the young for isolation from their immediate world and for unceasing connections with peers near and far. For many children, familial disruptions shut down any opportunities to objectively weigh positions or sides. Children now increasingly found themselves sent to counselors and child psychologists—intimate strangers hired to listen to children and ask questions that might help them gain the emotional maturity to empathize with others, take on moral responsibility, and manage their own feelings of abandonment, disillusion, and exclusion. Lacking, in many cases, extensive positive experiences in playing, planning, and working alongside caring adults before family breakups, many young people had no guidelines or habits to lead them to plan and act responsibly toward their own futures as young adults. Moreover, in 2012, barely half of U.S. citizens were married, and children were increasingly being raised in households that did not include either or both of their biological parents. More and more children grew up living under separation and divorce agreements of joint custody. Their own parents had, in many cases, disconnected themselves to a great extent from their own mothers and fathers. Often relocated far from extended family members, children and parents preferred family vacations that did not include visits to grandparents or other relatives.

By the end of the first decade of the 21st century, questions asked in the prior century about literacy seemed quaint, simplistic, and decidedly removed from realities in the contemporary world. By this time, most young people who managed to get their hands on several different types of technologies had no difficulty identifying what was needed not only to make these devices work but also to figure out how they worked.

Increasingly, the greater the facility young people had with technology, the more they read and wrote. However, this *more* refers to genres of text, almost all multimodal and directed to and received from a widening array of other writers and readers across an expanding span of topics. Self-directed and peer-influenced young people felt the need to learn and be "on top of what's happenin' *now*," leading them to multitudes of sources on the Internet. Those with access to transport and discretionary income also congregated in commercial and other venues where they talked with experts who shared their special interests. Many young people in troubled families turned their attention more and more away from family issues toward engagement with activities and interests that had no evident role to play in helping them ground plans for the future.

The young in families trying to adjust to both new economic and interpersonal arrangements found themselves mired in option stress and multitasking. All around them came directives to "go to college," "start your own company," and "explore the world." Start-up and established corporations dedicated to social networking recognized the special learning qualities of these young people, many of them just out of secondary school. By 2012, many of these companies made a point of recruiting young, fresh employees who had little or no higher education, only inventive skills and techniques learned through their own voluntary pursuits. The young accepted the achievements of robots and avatars and were willing to set aside ethical considerations.[15]

Meanwhile, as manufacturing continued to take place in newly developing nations, the United States and other advanced economies struggled to recruit secondary-level students to the study of sciences to support advanced manufacturing that would go beyond production of short-lived products built for consumer consumption. Examples of advanced manufacturing included development of alternative energy sources, medical equipment and pharmaceutical drugs to extend independence of the aging population, and synthetic materials to take the place of rare metals critical to technologies, such as that of smartphones. These technological needs came along with an increasing rate of growth of the proportion of families living in poverty and a jump in the national sense of sharp class divisions between the rich and the poor.

These major societal changes and their effects on family life and child development in the first decades of the 21st century explain to a great extent why it is that in the next generation, when people speak of education, they will not be referring primarily to sites of formal instruction. The dramatic transformations of the social and economic circumstances of family life mean that levels of toxic stress, particularly for young children, are likely to keep increasing year by year.[16] Scientists, educators, and the general public will be unable to escape the enlarging institutional gap between families and schools. Together they are not strong enough to overcome the pressures on normal child development brought about by the radical and rapidly changing situations of child and adolescent development. New strategies and agents need to emerge.

In many ways, young people began to take the lead in this charge during the years following 1990. Youth-based community organizations, often spurred by small groups of young people, came into being, particularly in urban areas where public transport made it possible for young people to move about their city and know what was happening in neighborhoods other than their own. In these sites, since the 1990s, young leaders and supportive adults have created learning organizations for after-school and summer hours that help young people negotiate their changing demands and possibilities. Creativity, play, collaborative work, and shoulder-to-shoulder interactions of professionals, mentors, and novice learners take place in these organizations. Flexibility and adaptability characterize these organizations so they keep pace with shifting demographics, interests of the young, job and further education possibilities, and small business developments. Here, reading, writing, financial literacy, reflective talk, and public critique take place within high-pressure contexts that demand on-time high performance from the young. These organizations range from social entrepreneurship dedicated to both local and international causes to arts and science organizations that create products and services for the public and for private sector businesses.[17]

Quietly and largely outside the notice of educational institutions, community organizations such as those described here work in collaboration with parental groups, businesses, and social service agencies dedicated to health, environmental sustainability, and civic learning. The wide range of resources, agents, and environments available in different communities means that standardization of ways of teaching and learning and ideas about the monolinearity of learning pathways have given way to creativity and creative industries. Learning for individuals and small groups in these sites takes place voluntarily and is linked with motivations and visions of the future for the organization and those within. Horizontal connections that include learners of different ages, persuasions, and levels of knowledge and skill characterize these learning environments, as does recognition of different kinds of talents.[18]

Variously termed pro-ams (professional amateurs), citizen scientists and artists, and participants in the knowledge society, individuals within these organizations are likely to see themselves as linked to the collective interests of local communities.[19] Voluntarily formed and maintained, these playful learning environments emphasize integrity and the exercise of judgment in ways that integrate intellectual and technical knowledge, on the one hand, and moral and civic responsibility, on the other. Playful learning in the relentless work that it takes to keep these organizations going calls on a myriad of interconnections rather than just a few power relationships. In their playful work, learning and teaching, trying and failing, and imagining and dreaming become community properties.

A robust understanding of how humans learn requires simultaneous emphases on widely varying types of learning environments. Such understanding grows increasingly vital for the design and sustenance of learning environments that enable learners to develop adaptive habits that are imperative for lifelong learning. As new sources, types, and formats of information emerge with the accelerating pace of innovative technologies, previously unimagined problems and possibilities inevitably follow. The health of the planet will increasingly be interrelated with how humans identify and respond with flexible thinking grounded in commitment not to individual interests but to communal well-being. Young and old together have to recognize the imperative of action over apathy, agency over nostalgia, and caring creativity over care-less passivity.[20]

QUESTIONS FOR REFLECTION

1. In your classroom, how can you foster talking about reading as opposed to the "performance of reading"?
2. How does the author explain the current generation of schoolchildren's increasing difficulty with the experience of "deliberative discourse"?
3. What, if any, preconceptions about developing literacy has this chapter challenged for you?

NOTES

[1] Watson (2003) tells the story of the makers of illuminated manuscripts who came to their tasks with little or no familiarity with what it meant to have meanings conveyed through letters and vignettes (sidebar drawings). Drawing on long-term fieldwork among indigenous learners, Walker (1981) portrays the development of scripts, written texts, and reading habits of adults who had known little or nothing about written languages as children.

[2] By the end of the first decade of the 21st century, research from neuroscientists increased in frequency and complexity as well as interdisciplinarity. Two summary sources for reading researchers are Hruby and Goswami (2011) and Strauss, Goodman, and Paulson (2009). An equally active and fast-moving topic for research by cognitive neuroscientists relates to spatial understanding that results from drawing and sketching, as well as reading and interpreting illustrations. Embedded within this work has been the growing focus on the direct use of the digits and full hand in creating meaning through visual art forms, such as sketching, sculpting, and modeling (see Ramadas, 2009; Wilson, 1998).

[3] In spite of extensive scholarly writing on this topic, the most comprehensive and balanced perspective comes from Snow, Barnes, Chandler, Goodman, and Hemphill (1991) and Snow, Burns, & Griffin (1998). Works often cited to prove the deleterious effects of growing up in homes of families living in poverty include Hart and Risley (1995, 1999) and Lareau (2003). These studies emphasize lexical deficiencies, in particular, that result in families whose parents have neither discretionary time nor financial resources to put toward experiences such as those offered by libraries, museums, zoos, city park programs, and youth organizations.

[4] Messages related to these topics package easily and draw interest from school administrators. Tracing the career of enterprising individuals eager to meet this market demand during the 1990s and the first decade of the 21st century is readily done (see, e.g., aha! Process [www.ahaprocess.com], the website of Ruby Payne).

[5] Those issuing such cautions speak on the basis of studies that are highly interdisciplinary and often involve research seeking to understand reading problems of children diagnosed as being dyslexic, hyperactive, language delayed, or on the autism disorder spectrum (see, e.g., M. Wolf, 2007, especially ch. 4 and 6).

[6] Chapter 8 of Snow et al. (1991) lays out many of the underpinnings of these premises. Since the early 1990s, nonprofits dedicated to learning during the after-school hours have intensified attention to these premises (see, e.g., the website of the After-School Corporation [www.tascorp.org] in New York).

[7] Ironically, anthropologist Margaret Mead (1970) predicted this need more than half a century before the introduction of the Internet and technologies through which the young so often teach their elders. She referred to the phenomenon as prefigurative socialization,

interactional relationships that differed from those of postfigurative learning in which elders passed on their knowledge to the young. Within prefigurative learning, elders learn from the young.

[8] No claim is made here or in the full study (Heath, 2012) that the families followed for three decades represent average or typical families. Those whose lives are reported in the full study would be the first to assert the uniqueness of their characteristics, situations, and ways of coping. In fact, they would argue that every family has its own stories to tell in its own way.

[9] Methods used to collect data on interactive talk among young people are laid out in Heath (2012, App. B) and Heath and Street (2008).

[10] For a survey of university students' writing during their college years, in and out of their classrooms, visit the Stanford Study of Writing website (ssw.stanford.edu). Numerous other modes worked alongside and often led their writing, and their lives beyond the classroom demanded more writing of them than their classrooms did (see also Fishman, Lunsford, McGregor, & Otuteye, 2005).

[11] Since the 1990s, the concept of deliberative democracy has been broadly considered on university campuses and in think tanks of different political persuasions (Gutmann & Thompson, 2004).

[12] In a time of mounting attention to technology and science, philosophers and other humanists increasingly feel compelled to argue for the benefits of the humanities (see, e.g., Nussbaum, 1997, 2010).

[13] Materials advocating the value of the arts for children flooded the world of after-school providers from the 1990s forward. It is surprising, therefore, that relatively little long-term research has looked at the human development dimensions of participation in the arts. Winner and Hetland (2000) have made this point to the consternation of arts advocates.

[14] In contemporary advanced economies, families of the middle class experience difficulty in providing the young with opportunities to make mistakes and learn from them and to take responsibility in the family context (see Ochs & Izquierdo, 2009).

[15] Blascovich and Bailenson (2011) examine the edginess of virtual worlds, especially the reading powers of avatars that discern and reflect facial expressions, for example, well beyond the abilities of humans to do so. Avatars read symbol systems and situations, and they can take action based on their interpretations of what they read. The capacities of their virtual worlds, however, are not neutral.

[16] In a National Research Council report, Shonkoff and Phillips (2000) point to many of the same factors indicated in Heath's (2012) study of three decades in family and community life. The council and numerous policy reports strongly argue the impact on children of sensing threats all around them to both their present and their future. Advances in technologies and long-term record keeping show that children who grow up with toxic stress suffer long-lasting biological effects, as well as a greater likelihood of social struggles throughout adolescence.

[17] To a great extent, the changing nature of community youth-led organizations means that written accounts and extensive websites are scarce. Workers within these sites have no time to write their own social histories or do much by way of "getting our story out there." Grants, donations, and occasional funds from local civic organizations and governments constitute their primary means of financial support, along with sales from their products and services (see Bornstein, 2004; Elizabeth & Young, 2006; Heath & Smyth, 1999; and the Artists for Humanity website [www.afhboston.com]).

[18] These sites of youth play and work illustrate horizontal learning that reflects expanding interests and niche seeking and complements vertical learning (see Engeström, 1987, for more on the critical context of work for such learning).

[19] The idea of professional amateurs holds considerable prominence in the worlds of both the humanities and political policy (see Finnegan, 2005; Garber, 2001; Leadbetter & Miller, 2004).

[20] In 1995, McKnight wrote *The Careless Society: Community and Its Counterfeits*, expressing many of the views of the final section of this chapter. His advice in that volume is likely to remain as needed in the future as it was in the mid-1990s.

REFERENCES

Bell, P., Lewenstein, B., Shouse, A.W., & Feder, M.A. (Eds.). (2009). *Learning science in informal environments: People, places, and pursuits.* Washington, DC: National Academies Press.

Blanchard, J., & Moore, T. (2010). *The digital world of young children: Impact on emergent literacy* [White paper]. New York: Pearson Foundation.

Blascovich, J., & Bailenson, J. (2011). *Infinite reality: Avatars, eternal life, new worlds, and the dawn of the virtual revolution.* New York: HarperCollins.

Bollmann, S. (2008). *Women who read are dangerous.* London: Merrell.

Bornstein, D. (2004). *How to change the world: Social entrepreneurs and the power of new ideas.* New York: Oxford University Press.

Day, C.O. (2010). *Our bookshop manifesto.* Retrieved June 24, 2012, from www.mendocino.com/?id=4104&url=www.gallerybooks.com

Duranti, A., Ochs, E., & Schieffelin, B.B. (Eds.). (2012). *The handbook of language socialization.* Malden, MA: Wiley-Blackwell.

Elizabeth, L., & Young, S. (Eds.). (2006). *Works of heart: Building village through the arts.* Oakland, CA: New Village.

Engeström, Y. (1987). *Learning by expanding: An activity-theoretical approach to developmental research.* Helsinki: Orienta-Konsultit.

Finnegan, R. (Ed.). (2005). *Participating in the knowledge society: Researchers beyond the university walls.* New York: Palgrave Macmillan. doi:10.1057/9780230523043

Fishman, J., Lunsford, A., McGregor, B., & Otuteye, M. (2005). Performing writing, performing literacy. *College Composition and Communication, 57*(2), 224–252.

Garber, M. (2001). *Academic instincts.* Princeton, NJ: Princeton University Press.

Gutmann, A., & Thompson, D. (2004). *Why deliberative democracy?* Princeton, NJ: Princeton University Press.

Hart, B., & Risley, T.R. (1995). *Meaningful differences in the everyday experience of young American children.* Baltimore: Paul H. Brookes.

Hart, B., & Risley, T.R. (1999). *The social world of children learning to talk.* Baltimore: Paul H. Brookes.

Heath, S.B. (1996). *Ways with words: Language, life, and work in communities and classrooms.* New York: Cambridge University Press. (Original work published 1983)

Heath, S.B. (2011). The book as home? It all depends. In S.A. Wolf, K. Coats, P. Enciso, & C.A. Jenkins (Eds.), *Handbook of research on children's and young adult literature* (pp. 32–47). New York: Routledge.

Heath, S.B. (2012). *Words at work and play: Three decades in family and community life.* New York: Cambridge University Press.

Heath, S.B., & Smyth, L. (1999). *ArtShow: Youth and community development.* Washington, DC: Partners for Livable Communities.

Heath, S.B., & Street, B.V. (2008). *On ethnography: Approaches to language and literacy research.* New York: Teachers College Press.

Heath, S.B., & Wolf, J.L. (forthcoming). Brain and behavior: The coherence of teenage responses to young adult literature. In M. Hilton & M. Nikolajeva (Eds.), *Contemporary adolescent literature and culture: The emergent adult.* Burlington, VT: Ashgate.

Hochschild, A.R. (1997). *The time bind: When work becomes home and home becomes work.* New York: Metropolitan.

Hruby, G.G., & Goswami, U. (2011). Neuroscience and reading: A review for reading education researchers. *Reading Research Quarterly, 46*(2), 156–172. doi:10.1598/RRQ.46.2.4

Kuipers, J., & Viechnicki, G. (2008). Special issue on objectification and the inscription of knowledge in science classrooms. *Linguistics and Education, 19*(3), 203–205. doi:10.1016/j.linged.2008.06.005

Lareau, A. (2003). *Unequal childhoods: Class, race, and family life.* Berkeley: University of California Press.

Leadbetter, C., & Miller, P. (2004). *The pro-am revolution: How enthusiasts are changing our society and economy.* London: Demos.

McKnight, J. (1995). *The careless society: Community and its counterfeits.* New York: Basic.

Mead, M. (1970). *Culture and commitment: A study of the generation gap.* London: Bodley Head.

Nussbaum, M.C. (1997). *Cultivating humanity: A classical defense of reform in liberal education.* Cambridge, MA: Harvard University Press.

Nussbaum, M.C. (2010). *Not for profit: Why democracy needs the humanities.* Princeton, NJ: Princeton University Press.

Ochs, E., & Izquierdo, C. (2009). Responsibility in childhood: Three developmental trajectories. *Ethos, 37*(4), 391–413. doi:10.1111/j.1548-1352.2009.01066.x

Philips, S.U. (1983). *The invisible culture: Communication in classroom and community on the Warm Springs Indian Reservation*. New York: Longman.
Ramadas, J. (2009). Visual and spatial modes in science learning. *International Journal of Science Education, 31*(3), 301–318. doi:10.1080/09500690802595763
Robinson, J.P., & Godbey, G. (1999). *Time for life: The surprising ways Americans use their time* (2nd ed.). University Park: Pennsylvania State University Press.
Rogoff, B., Paradise, R., Arauz, R.M., Correa-Chavez, M., & Angelillo, C. (2003). Firsthand learning through intent participation. *Annual Review of Psychology, 54*, 175–203. doi:10.1146/annurev.psych.54.101601.145118
Schieffelin, B.B., & Gilmore, P. (Eds.). (1986). *The acquisition of literacy: Ethnographic perspectives*. Norwood, NJ: Ablex.
Schieffelin, B.B., & Ochs, E. (Eds.). (1986). *Language socialization across cultures*. New York: Cambridge University Press.
Schor, J. (1991). *The overworked American: The unexpected decline of leisure*. New York: Basic.
Shonkoff, J.P., & Phillips, D.A. (Eds.). (2000). *From neurons to neighborhoods: The science of early childhood development*. Washington, DC: National Academy Press.
Snow, C.E., Barnes, W.S., Chandler, J., Goodman, I.F., & Hemphill, L. (1991). *Unfulfilled expectations: Home and school influences on literacy*. Cambridge, MA: Harvard University Press.
Snow, C.E., Burns, M.S., & Griffin, P. (Eds.). (1998). *Preventing reading difficulties in young children*. Washington, DC: National Academies Press.
Strauss, S.L., Goodman, K.S., & Paulson, E.J. (2009). Brain research and reading: How emerging concepts in neuroscience support a meaning construction view of the reading process. *Educational Research and Reviews, 4*(2), 21–33.
Updike, J. (2005). *Still looking: Essays on American art*. New York: Knopf.
Walker, W. (1981). Native American writing systems. In C.A. Ferguson & S.B. Heath (Eds.), *Language in the USA* (pp. 145–174). New York: Cambridge University Press.
Watson, R. (2003). *Illuminated manuscripts and their makers*. London: V&A.
Wilson, F.R. (1998). *The hand: How its use shapes the brain, language, and human culture*. New York: Pantheon.
Winner, E., & Hetland, L. (Eds.). (2000). The arts and academic achievement: What the evidence shows [Special issue]. *Journal of Aesthetic Education, 34*(3/4).
Wolf, B.J. (2001). *Vermeer and the invention of seeing*. Chicago: University of Chicago Press.
Wolf, M. (2007). *Proust and the squid: The story and science of the reading brain*. New York: HarperCollins.
Wolf, S.A., Coats, K., Enciso, P., & Jenkins, C.A. (Eds.). (2011). *Handbook of research on children's and young adult literature*. New York: Routledge.

LITERATURE CITED

Frost, R. (1939). *Collected poems*. New York: Henry Holt.

CHAPTER 9

Emergent Biliteracy in Young Mexican Immigrant Children

Iliana Reyes and Patricia Azuara, University of Arizona

In this article, we explore the relationship between emergent biliteracy and growing up in a biliterate environment. Our research particularly considers and describes some of the paths that young Spanish-speaking emergent bilingual children follow depending on their specific learning experiences and how these experiences shape their biliteracy development. We adopt the term *emergent bilinguals* instead of *English-language learners* to more accurately describe young children (ages 3 to 5 years) who speak a native language other than English and are in the dynamic process of developing bilingual and biliterate competencies with the support of their communities (e.g., parents, school, community; García, Kleifgen, & Falchi, 2008; Reyes, 2006). We began with the following two research questions:

1. What knowledge of biliteracy (including but not limited to story reading) do young emergent bilingual children (4- and 5-year-olds) develop in the early years?
2. How do context and specific language environments (e.g., home, community) influence the development of biliteracy in young Mexican Spanish–English bilingual children?

Theoretical Frameworks

We situate our study within two major theoretical frameworks: (1) a sociocultural framework and (2) an ecology of language framework. We describe each of these in relation to the purpose of our study.

A sociocultural framework foregrounds how children learn language through interactions with people in their immediate contexts (Harste, Woodward, & Burke, 1984; Pérez, 2004; Vygotsky, 1978). Learning is viewed as a process in which the child's existing knowledge interacts with mediating tools available in the environment to promote the development of new understandings (Rogoff, 1990; Vygotsky, 1978). Children learn through direct interactions with people and what they observe in their sociocultural context (Rogoff, 1990; Vygotsky, 1978). Specific to literacy development, children's understanding and inventions of written language are not individual; rather, they reflect the cultural conventions

This chapter is reprinted from *Reading Research Quarterly*, 43(4), 374–398.

and ideologies within the social contexts of which they are a part (Moll, Saez, & Dworin, 2001). In this regard, the construct of the zone of proximal development by Vygotsky is helpful in identifying the social guidance and scaffolding that "experts"—defined as those adults or peers who are more competent on specific abilities or knowledge; on the other hand, "novices" are those members of a community whose capabilities can be extended via the zone of proximal development by interacting with a more competent member (Williams, 2004)—provide to children who are participating in literacy activities beyond their current abilities (Gregory, Long, & Volk, 2004). It is this scaffolding in social contexts that helps the young bilingual child to advance his or her language and literacy development and independent thinking in two languages (Dworin & Moll, 2006; Moll, 1990; Rogoff, 1990; Tharp & Gallimore, 1988). Writing and literacy development emerges as a result not only of children's interactions with objects and people but also of their own internal representations and transformation of thoughts and ideas and the biological basis that allows this learning (Ferreiro & Teberosky, 1982; Tolchinsky, 2003; Vygotsky, 1978). The emergence of literacy, like a child's development, is characterized by "spurts, plateaus, and regressions...development typically is not smoothly uniform and cumulative, but asynchronous and nonlinear" (Yaden, 2008, p. 10).

The second major theoretical perspective that guides our understanding of biliteracy is the ecology of language framework adapted from the work by Haugen (1953/1969) and later used by a number of scholars (e.g., Barton, 1994; Bronfenbrenner, 1986; Hornberger, 1989; Hornberger & Skilton-Sylvester, 2000). Barton argued that an ecological approach to literacy is useful because "it takes as its starting point this interaction between individuals and their environments" (p. 29). This ecological framework also integrates insights from anthropology, biology, educational linguistics, and psychology that "enable an appreciation of the interdisciplinary nature of literacy and language studies" (Pahl, 2008, p. 306). We adopt this perspective to the study of biliteracy to shed light on the ecological environments and the complex interrelationships among the different factors within these environments (e.g., languages used, their speakers, their interpretations of text) that influence young emergent bilinguals' biliteracy development in Spanish and English.

From Literacy to Biliteracy Development Studies

In this section, we review studies that inform current knowledge of early literacy, including but not limited to development of concepts of print, print awareness, and metalinguistic awareness in monolingual populations. Next, we review biliteracy studies with young children, highlighting those from the sociocultural or ecology of language traditions. Because the research on young bilingual children has tended to focus on oral language development, there is still a great need to understand the relatively underexplored phenomenon of emergent biliteracy (but see Dworin & Moll, 2006; Gregory et al., 2004; Jiménez, 2003; Kenner, 2000; Kenner, Kress, Hayat, Kam, & Tsai, 2004).

Although our focus in this study is early biliteracy development, we recognize that bilingualism and biliteracy cannot be separated, and bilingualism influences biliteracy development. We also believe that the key to understanding young children's development of biliteracy is to consider both languages as interacting together. Therefore, we purposely avoid comparing these children's biliteracy development with the literacy development of monolingual children (see Grosjean, 1998, for further discussion on this point).

Early Literacy

Literacy acquisition is a multifaceted process that is different for every child (Whitmore, Martens, Goodman, & Owocki, 2004). Although children exposed to a writing system develop print knowledge, the age at which they become aware of this knowledge and the processes of development vary. Young children are active participants in the learning process, making hypotheses and constructing knowledge about the writing systems they are exposed to and attempting to derive meaning from print in their environments (Ferreiro, 2007; Goodman, 1986). Children interact with print by constructing, organizing, and analyzing its meaning and connecting it with their own personal experiences (Goodman, 1984, 1986; Kirkland, Aldridge, & Kuby, 1991).

From an early age, children begin noticing print through being exposed to it at home and in their communities (e.g., on signs, posters, and flyers). In addition to making discoveries on their own, children are influenced by feedback from others around them as they attempt to understand print in their environment and eventually in different writing systems (Ferreiro & Teberosky, 1982; Tolchinsky, 2003). Although research findings have not pinpointed a direct correlation between the ability to read environmental print and later conventional reading abilities (e.g., word identification, letter–sound correspondence), it has been shown that children acquire knowledge about the written environment through multiple experiences before they enter school (Kassow, 2006). Later, as part of school reading instruction, children learning alphabetic writing systems are guided to pay attention to the one-to-one correspondence between letters and sounds. However, research on phonological awareness has been unclear regarding when, where, and how exactly it develops regardless of the context (Chaney, 1994; Morris, Bloodgood, Lomax, & Perney, 2003; Snow, Burns, & Griffin, 1998). In addition, young children begin developing metalinguistic awareness, that is, the ability to use language to think about, play with, talk about, and analyze language in its different domains (e.g., phonology, pragmatics, semantics; Snow et al., 1998).

Recently, Justice and Ezell's (2001) work has illuminated the impact that low income in a family has on children's emergent literacy. They found that preschool English monolingual children (3- to 5-year-olds) from low-income families "demonstrated difficulty with many of the written language awareness tasks" (p. 130). They concluded that disparities in the experiences and opportunities available to them as compared with children from more financially privileged backgrounds were significant contributors to their lower academic literacy knowledge (see also

Chaney, 1994; Dickinson & Snow, 1987). However, reviewing multiple literacy studies in which not only schooled literacy was valued, we found that even those children who seem "disadvantaged," such as those from economically marginalized communities, early in their lives do develop knowledge about oral and written language through daily interactions in their home and community contexts (Heath, 1983; Taylor & Dorsey-Gaines, 1988).

Studies have confirmed that preschool children develop environmental print awareness, integrating their existing knowledge with contextual cues in the environment to understand and make sense of, or read, print in signs, logos, or product labels (Goodman & Altwerger, 1981; Manning, Manning, Long, & Wolfson, 1987; Teale, 1986). Whereas children develop environmental print awareness through natural interactions, they develop concepts of print related to books through multiple experiences with print. These concepts of print include a variety of conventions about books, including how a book is held, directionality of print, and one-to-one correspondence between letter and sound (Clay, 1989).

Biliteracy Studies

Edelsky and Jilbert's (1985) early work on naturalistic observations in bilingual classrooms provided descriptions of the writing development of bilingual children and how these children use their bilingual skills when reading and writing in school contexts. However, due to the complexity of such research, only a few researchers have explored young children's biliteracy development in multiple contexts (Dworin, 2003; Kenner et al., 2004; Schwarzer, 2001; Tabors, Paez, & Lopez, 2002; Yaden & Tardibuono, 2004; Zentella, 2005).

In a recent study, Kenner et al. (2004) explored the "keys" to biliteracy and found that "when children have access to more than one writing system, children's ability to distinguish between different scripts is found to develop at an early age" (p. 126). Not only could children in their study distinguish between different writing systems (e.g., alphabetic, logographic), but they also made use of cues in their native languages (Chinese, Arabic, and Spanish) to constantly reinterpret their concepts of writing in what the authors described as engagement in "the process of appropriating the principles [of writing] for themselves" (p. 137). These children used the information presented to them in their school, home, and community contexts to work out some of the underlying principles of different writing systems. From an ecological perspective, Kenner (2004) described how immigrant families in Britain act as supportive "literacy ecosystems" in promoting their children's development of biliteracy, which allows young children and their families to adapt and integrate new forms of literacy related to new life in Britain.

It is important to note that the scripts of some languages share many characteristics in common, whereas others differ greatly. In the case of English and Spanish, they both share an alphabetic script, which makes it easier for Spanish-speaking children to identify the letters, although the frequency and sound of certain letters vary between the two languages. Even when children can identify certain universal features across the alphabetic systems of their two languages (e.g., syllabic structure, number of letters in the alphabet), they also make a cognitive effort to understand the particular written symbols (e.g., the graphic variations in size and shape, the differing lengths of strings) that distinguish each language (Ferreiro & Teberosky, 1982; Tolchinsky, 2003; Verona, 1993).

In terms of the development of print awareness in emergent bilinguals, Romero (1983) addressed preschool (4- to 5-year-olds) Spanish–English bilinguals, a very similar population to our study. The preschoolers in her study showed that they were print aware, and they began reading print in signs and labels using contextual cues. In line with results of previous studies with monolingual children, she observed that as she systematically removed contextual cues from labels, children's ability to recognize and identify the words diminished. In terms of language use, more than 75% of children's responses were in Spanish, 23% were in English, and only 2% were bilingual (i.e., in a mixture of Spanish and English). Romero concluded that the children had associated each item's specific function with a particular language and used that language to respond. As described later, we used a modification of Romero's environmental print task (EPT) with the children in our study.

In Latin America, Ferreiro and Teberosky (1982) studied the emergent literacy of monolingual Spanish-speaking children living in Argentina. They evaluated children at different ages (4- to 6-year-olds) and from different socioeconomic groups on emergent writing and reading tasks (e.g., letter and number identification task, name writing, word reading task). They found that when entering school, and long before knowing how to read and write, young children are capable of creating their own hypotheses about how to write and distinguish between letters, numbers, and words. Later, Yaden and Tardibuono (2004) replicated Ferreiro and Teberosky's study on Piagetian writing tasks with bilingual Latino children living in Los Angeles, California. They found that 4-year-old bilingual children follow the same patterns and construct the same hypotheses about early concepts of writing as do monolingual Spanish-speaking children. Although their findings were not qualitatively different from Ferreiro and Teberosky's, they did find that their children's understanding of different features of written language was similar to that of 5-year-old middle class Argentinian children but more advanced than that of Argentinian children from low-income families. One could speculate that this difference might be due to the children's level of bilingualism; however, Yaden and Tardibuono did not investigate what children understood about the principles of the two written languages to which they were exposed in their different contexts. Nonetheless, their findings argue that being exposed to two languages does not hinder the natural development of literacy (see also Hakuta, 1986).

Li (2006) and Reyes (2006) described the biliterate and trilingual practices of Chinese–Canadian and Spanish–Mexican children and their families, respectively. Of relevance for the present study is that the home context was found to be a crucial environment for children's successful development of biliteracy. Both studies showed that children's bilingualism and development of biliteracy allowed them to participate in different literacy practices regardless of their level of fluency in either language. These children used their bilingual abilities to participate in various family and academic activities both at home and at school. In general, these studies point to a multitude of factors, including language ideologies of parents and teachers, that shape the development of biliteracy.

If we want to move toward a more integrated view of biliteracy, it is important to adopt an ecological perspective to account for the different individual and social factors and their effect on children's biliteracy development (Dworin, 2003; Grosjean, 1998).

Multiple-Approach Method to the Study of Biliteracy

In our study, children participated in reading assessment tasks and an interview at school to elicit their concepts of print and environmental print awareness. They were also observed in their home environments during literacy interactions with family and community members. By using a multiple-approach analysis within an ecological framework, we can identify how family, community, educational practices, and macro-level forces (such as English-only laws) may influence biliteracy development in young emergent bilinguals.

Participants

The participants were twelve 4- and 5-year-old (*M* age = 5 years, 4 months) emergent bilingual children (7 girls, 5 boys) whose first language (L1) was Spanish and second language (L2) was English and who had been exposed to both languages from an early age. The children and their families live in an urban setting in the U.S. Southwest and are part of a larger cohort of children who are participating in a 3-year longitudinal study (the Emergent Biliteracy and Language Development project with Mexican immigrant families in Tucson, AZ) focusing on the study of literacy practices at home (Reyes, 2006; Reyes, Alexandra, & Azuara, 2007). In this article, we focus on data collected during the 1st year, when children were in preschool. These 12 children were selected randomly from among the children whose parents gave permission for participation in the larger study at the beginning of the school year. The 12 children participated in all literacy assessments conducted in the classroom.

The Community, Home, and School Contexts of Children's Bilingualism

The Community. The families in this project are part of the Tucson, Arizona, community, which is more than 30% Latino. The children live in a predominantly bilingual and bicultural neighborhood with a strong presence of Mexican culture. Signs and announcements are typically printed in both Spanish and English (e.g., at the supermarket, local library, tax offices, clothing store). Thus, the children and their families are exposed to bilingual print in their environment. In addition, the families participated in several organized social and community events, such as *carne asada* barbeques, rodeo weekend, bilingual library time, and religious practices (e.g., attending Spanish-language catechism classes).

The Preschool Program. The 12 children attended a public, state-funded preschool that is part of an early childhood education program in the local school district. All children qualified for a free- or reduced-cost school lunch. Although English was the language of instruction in this preschool program, the classroom teacher and teacher's aide did use Spanish during social interactions and to provide clarification during instruction (about 40% during classroom interactions). Moreover, the native language was honored when parents volunteered in the classroom; as many of them were Spanish dominant, the teacher invited them to use Spanish in their classroom interactions.

During an interview with the teacher, we learned that Ms. Vásquez (all names are pseudonyms) is a fluent bilingual though nonnative Spanish speaker who had lived in Mexico for more than 20 years. She was committed to promoting the children's bilingual and bicultural abilities. Although her program was not officially bilingual at the time of our data collection, she incorporated Spanish in her instruction. Because of her training as a bilingual teacher and her experiences living in Mexico, she empathized with students' and families' specific needs and tried to support the children's native language development within the parameters of a state-level English-only law and concordant district policies. In keeping with these restrictions, she shifted from liberal use of both Spanish and English in the fall semester to almost exclusive use of English for instruction during the spring semester, with Spanish used only when needed for clarification. In explaining her decision to shift to English during the spring semester, Ms. Vásquez stated that she was preparing the students to make the transition to an English-only kindergarten classroom the following fall (Teacher interview, January 14, 2005).

To assess the children's language development in Spanish and English at the beginning of the school year, we administered the English and Spanish versions of the Peabody Picture Vocabulary Test—Revised (Dunn & Dunn, 1981; Dunn, Padilla, Lugo, & Dunn, 1986), to obtain a basic index of their comprehension ability (receptive vocabulary) in each language. All reading and writing assessment tasks were administered at school during regular school hours. We learned about the children's family and community language environments by interviewing their parents and teachers. According to the teacher, who assessed the children using the State of Arizona Language Assessment test, most children were either Spanish monolinguals or Spanish dominant. We corroborated this information with parents' own assessment of their children's language fluency. Table 1 shows that, with two exceptions, the children were Spanish dominant in that their vocabulary scores were higher in Spanish than they were in English (10 out of 12). One exception was Dariana, whose scores were similar in each language; we learned that she was a simultaneous bilingual who had been exposed to both languages at home since birth. The other was Adam, also a simultaneous

Table 1. Children's English and Spanish Assessment Scores and Profiles

Participant	Age (yrs; mos)	PPVT standard score Spanish	PPVT standard score English	CAP score	Parent's and teacher's language assessment
1	5; 1	104	72	9	Spanish dominant
2	4; 11	86	40	13	Spanish dominant
*3	5; 0	91	87	18	Balanced bilingual
4	4; 7	95	68	13	Spanish dominant
5	4; 7	68	49	11	Spanish dominant
6	5; 1	62	87	15	English dominant
*7	4; 11	77	40	11	Spanish dominant
*8	4; 4	87	53	9	Spanish dominant
9	4; 5	82	66	10	Spanish dominant
10	4; 4	80	58	8	Spanish dominant
11	5; 1	73	43	7	Spanish dominant
12	4; 5	73	40	13	Spanish dominant

Note. PPVT = Peabody Picture Vocabulary Test; CAP = concepts about print.
*Case-study children

bilingual, who scored higher in English vocabulary than he did in Spanish. Both his mom and teacher considered him English dominant at the beginning of the school year.

Our Roles as Bilingual Mexican "Maestras" and Researchers

We engaged in the study through multiple positions. First, we are also immigrants to the United States. Through this common experience (although under very different circumstances), we could identify with the parents and their families in different ways; I, Iliana Reyes, shared with the families that I self-identify as a *Norteña*, from the state of Sinaloa, from which many of the families in our study come; Patricia Azuara is from Mexico City but has lived in Arizona for more than 10 years and has worked in the local schools in various roles, including as an elementary literacy teacher. Families were aware of our advanced education and at times had asked us to serve as resources (e.g., by making referrals to services). In addition, they have trusted us not only because they see us as a special kind of *maestra* (teacher) but also because, having been in contact with them for more than 3 years now, they see us as friends of the family who are genuinely interested in learning about their day-to-day family successes and challenges.

Data Collection and Analyses of Reading and Writing Assessment Tasks

We presented the 12 children with various reading and writing assessment tasks during the beginning of the preschool academic year, assessing environmental print, book handling, and concepts of print. During the spring semester, we also interviewed them about their knowledge of print and writing. To maintain ecological validity, we administered these assessments at school while children were involved in center activities; the children viewed the reading and writing assessment tasks as part of the established daily classroom routine.

EPT. To find out what these 12 children knew about the print in their environment, we adapted the environmental print awareness task developed by Goodman and Altwerger (1981) and later used by Romero (1983) with bilingual children. Based on our home observations and information parents provided, we selected labels in Spanish and English that the children frequently saw in their everyday bilingual/bicultural context, such as a can of Rosarita refried beans and a bag of *Dos Ranchitos* tortillas (see Appendix A for a complete list of items).

The task was divided into two parts that were presented in two different sessions conducted a few days apart. In the first session, we presented the actual objects and asked children to identify each item. In the second session, children were presented with pictures showing only the labels from these items without the product; thus, they had to rely on the print, format, and color of the label for cues.

We developed a coding scheme for the children's responses, based on both the actual responses we received in this study and the coding schemes of Goodman and Altwerger (1981) and Romero (1983). That is, we identified patterns and grouped children's responses into six different categories: (1) not recognized, (2) named only the function of the object, (3) used the generic name of the item, (4) used another brand name to name the product, (5) partially recognized the brand, and (6) named the exact print on the label (see Appendix B for the complete coding scheme).

We were also interested in the hypotheses children made regarding the languages used in their environment. Therefore, we asked them during the first and second administration of the task to identify the language of each label and rationalize their answer. (*¿En que idioma está escrito? ¿Porqué crees que está escrito en español [o inglés]*? "In what language is this written? Why do you think this is written in Spanish [or English]?"). Children's responses were audiotaped and later transcribed and analyzed to identify the language they selected and their reasons for identifying it as Spanish or English.

Concepts About Print (CAP) and Book-Handling Knowledge. To get a general sense of the children's understanding of books and their use, we administered a book-handling task adapted from the work of Clay (1972) and translated to Spanish by Escamilla, Andrade, Basurto, and Ruiz (1996). We also adopted items from the book-handling task developed by Goodman and Altwerger (1981) and translated into Spanish as "*Conocimiento pre-escolar del manejo de libros*" by Romero (1983) in her dissertation. We used Spanish and English editions of the same book—*Stones* by Clay (1979) and *Las Piedras* translated by Andrade, Ruiz, and Basurto (1995). Based on each child's relative proficiency in the two languages, 11 of the 12 children were presented with the Spanish edition of this book, *Las Piedras*.

The task was administered to each of the 12 children individually in one session during center time at the preschool. Each child was presented with the book and asked to read it for the researcher. If the child refused to read or said she or he could not read, then the researcher read the book, asking the child to help by following along and pointing to the text with one finger. Following Clay's (1972) procedures, the researcher then asked questions to elicit the child's understanding of general concepts of print.

For coding, we followed Clay's (1972) and Goodman's (1986) criteria: "1" for a correct answer or "0" when the child either gave the incorrect answer or did not respond at all. We computed the total points for each child and then averaged the number of correct responses that were identified under several categories, such as book format, directionality of print, identification of word sequence, and book terminology (e.g., page, author) among other concepts (e.g., letter–sound correspondence, letter and word concepts, and punctuation), to derive the total percentage correct.

Interview About Children's Metalinguistic Awareness of Concepts of Print and Writing. Eleven of the 12 children (1 participant was absent on the day this interview was conducted) participated in a one-on-one interview conducted in the child's dominant language by a bilingual researcher. The interview protocol, based on Owocki and Goodman's (2002) interview, was designed to explore children's perceptions and attitudes about concepts of print, writing, and the process and functions of writing. Some of the questions included the following: *¿Sabes escribir? ¿Cómo aprendiste a escribir?* (Do you know how to write? How did you learn to write?); *¿Escribes en inglés o en español, o en los dos?* (In what language do you write, in Spanish, English, or both?); *¿Por qué escribe la gente?* (Why do people write?; see Owocki & Goodman [2002] for additional questions). The children were also asked to produce samples of writing and of drawing. As previously mentioned, we conducted these interviews during the spring semester at the same time that we were conducting observations at home.

Data Collection and Analyses From Home Observations

During the first year of the study, we collected data through participant observations in all 12 children's homes and during their preschool classroom interactions. One of the researchers visited each family an average of twice a month, for at least two hours per visit, and videotaped children's interactions in different contexts (e.g., mealtime, playtime, school-related activities). We also interviewed the parents individually at the beginning of the project, which allowed us to understand each family's ideologies about language and their literacy practices and how these impacted children's language environment at home. Through ongoing conversations and continuous contact with the families, we additionally obtained anecdotal information that gave us a representative picture of the literacy practices and activities children engaged in with their families. We scheduled our visits at different times and days of the week, including weekends, to capture a wide range of the child's and family's routines. We videotaped continuously for about an hour, following the target child as he or she moved through various activities (this included going from an activity inside the house to one in an outside area, such as the backyard, a nearby park, or the store). Our observations were written down as part of our field notes.

Case Studies. From the 12 children, we selected 3 to describe in detail as case studies. We selected these 3 children, Dariana, Frida, and Sercan, because according to the teacher's and parents' assessments, they could be considered representative of the diverse range of language and literacy experiences and competencies of the children. We used a case study approach (Dyson & Genishi, 2005) to facilitate the examination and interpretation of the literacy events in which children and their families participated during daily activities at home. Through a triangulation process, we analyzed our field notes and coded video data from observations of these children participating in different literacy events at home with adults, with peers, and on their own (Howe, 2003). The conversations during family interactions were transcribed for analysis using Gumperz and Berenz's (1993) transcription conventions and the TRANSANA video software (Wood & Fassnacht, 2005). With regard to participation in family literacy events at home, we wrote detailed field notes of instances where these case study children were observed engaging with and around print at home with adults (parents, grandparents, relatives) and other children (siblings and peers). Decisions regarding what to record in our field notes and later to analyze from these notes and the videotapes were made according to a coding scheme we developed based on Heath's (1983) and Teale's (1986) categories of literacy events (e.g., daily living routines, entertainment, school-related activity), as well as from categories that we identified when the target child was participating in a literacy event (see Appendix C for details about literacy categories).

Results and Discussion

Reading and Writing Assessment Tasks

All findings presented and discussed in this section relate to the 12 children who participated in the reading and writing assessment tasks. We describe and discuss particular patterns of responses as well as general solutions children provided when faced with particular challenges in some of the stimuli (no further statistical analyses were conducted due to the small *N* of 12).

EPT. In the EPT, we observed that the children's responses did not differ significantly depending on whether they were presented with the actual objects or labels alone (see Figure 1 for frequency of responses; we only analyzed the responses of 10 of the 12 participants as we were not able to complete two of the

Figure 1. Frequency of Children's Responses to Food Objects and Product Labels

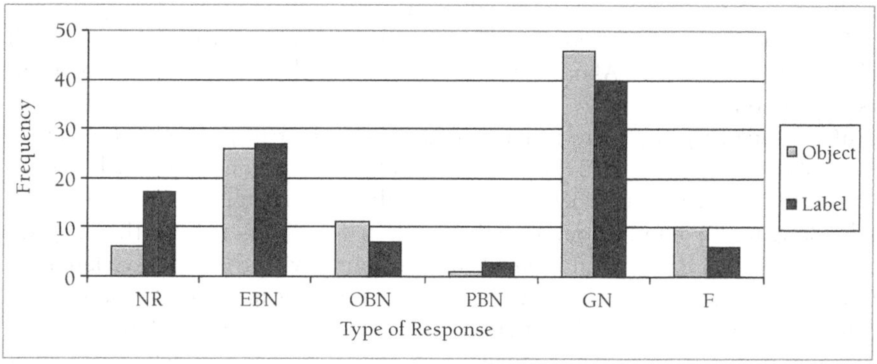

children's assessments). Out of children's 100 responses, 46 of the responses to objects (RO), and 40 of the responses to labels (RL) provided the generic name (e.g., "*pasta* [toothpaste]" for Colgate, "*frijoles* [beans]" for Rosarita, and "soda" for Coca-Cola).

Children gave responses that exactly matched the print on the label (26 times for RO and 27 for RL) for only three of the objects: McDonald's fries, Food City grocery bag, and stop sign. A few children identified an item and then labeled it using a different brand name (11 times for RO and 7 times for RL) with which they were more familiar (e.g., "Pepsi " for Coca-Cola and "Peter Piper's" for Domino's Pizza). On some occasions, a child used a different brand name from the one shown as the generic name for an object (e.g., "ChocoMilk" for Nesquik). Less frequently, some children described the function of the item (10 times for RO and 6 times for RL) instead of the printed label, as in the following examples:

- "*Para lavarse los dientes*" (to brush your teeth) for Colgate toothpaste
- "*Para parar los carros*" (to stop the cars) for the stop sign
- "*Para que pasen los niños*" (for kids to pass) also for the stop sign

In these responses to the EPT, children focused on the functions of the items rather than their specific brand names. As adults do, these 5-year-olds typically used generic names to identify the objects presented. It is not uncommon for people to use generic referents, such as "toothpaste" or "milk," except in very specific situations, such as when choosing among specific brands in a store (Romero, 1983). It was interesting to observe that two of the children already associated the examples of print with product advertisements. For example, in his responses, Sercan changed his tone of voice to mimic that used in media advertisements while pointing to the print on the Colgate toothpaste box and saying, "*lava los dientes* [brush your teeth]."

In terms of language use, from our observations, children's identifications of the language of print were not based on the size or style of the font or on the product itself. Based on previous findings with young Spanish-speaking children (Romero, 1983), we had expected that children would say that the products most familiar to them in their environment were written in Spanish, such as the can of Rosarita beans and the Food City grocery bag (a local grocery store where all of these families shop). About equal percentages of children identified the print as English (46 for RO and 39 for RL) or as Spanish (44 for RO and 42 for RL). We could not identify any pattern that would predict their responses. For example, 8 out of the 10 children said the print on the object was in one language but when later presented with the label for that item alone, identified it as written in the other language. For only 3 out of all the children did we observe that the language they identified for the print seemed to correspond with their relative language fluency. We speculate that these three children might be becoming metalinguistically aware by associating the language they can speak the best with the one they can read from the articles and labels presented to them in this activity. In addition, when asked to rationalize their responses, none of the children used specific features of print or context-related cues as an explanation for the language chosen. This is not surprising as Spanish and English are closely related languages with similar scripts, differing only in diacriticals and letter frequency. Instead, children created hypotheses, such as

- "*porque aquí dice*" (because it says so here) while pointing to small print
- "*porque mi papi me dijo*" (because my father told me)
- "*[porque] en inglés no sé como se llama*" ([because] I don't know what it's called in English)

Less frequently (8 for RO and 10 for RL out of 100 responses), children identified the print in the label as bilingual and provided explanations using their two languages. For example, one child pointed to the print on the can of beans and read "*frijoles*" (beans) with a Spanish pronunciation, reporting that the word was in Spanish; then he pointed to the same word and changed his pronunciation and elongated the second syllable to indicate he was speaking in English: "frijool" (bean). This example led us to speculate that this child knew that there are cognates for English and Spanish words, and given the cognitive demand of the question, he was attempting to find an explanation by making generalizations and marking one of his languages with a different pronunciation.

In addition, three children indicated that one part of the print was written in English and another part in Spanish. For example, when asked about the Coca-Cola label, Sercan read "soda" while pointing to the word "Coca," and he said "Pepsi" while pointing to the word "Cola," explaining "*Aquí dice soda Pepsi, pero soda es en español y Pepsi es en inglés*" (Here it says soda Pepsi, but soda is in Spanish, and Pepsi is in English). Responses like this one suggest that children are metalinguistically aware that languages are represented in different ways, although they do not use features of the print to identify the language of writing. Children who identified the print on the label as bilingual seemed to have internalized that, in their particular sociocultural context, it is not unusual to find print in both languages in books, labels, or advertisements (Ernst-Slavit & Mulhern, 2003). Another possible explanation for the language identification is that it seemed the fewer the cues that were available on the label, the more likely the child was to identify it as bilingual. It might be that the child was less willing to take a chance on identifying the label as Spanish or English when no contextual cues were available.

CAP and Book-Handling Knowledge. The preschool book-handling task allowed us to identify what concepts children have developed relative to books and their use in Spanish and English. When they were shown the book and the researcher asked, "*¿Qué es esto?*" (What is this?) all the children responded in Spanish with "*libro*" (book). Eleven out of 12 also demonstrated an understanding of the function of books with responses such as "*para leerlo*" (for reading) when asked, "*¿Qué haces con el?*" (What do you do with it?) Because we were interested in the children's ability to differentiate whether a book was written in Spanish or English, we placed the two books (*Stones* and *Las Piedras*) in front of each child and asked him or her to select the book that was in Spanish ("*Por favor, escoge el que está en español*" [Please select the one that is in Spanish]). The presentation of books was counterbalanced, so that the Spanish version appeared on the child's left for half of the participants and on the right for the other half. In addition, we manipulated the book covers to include orthographic markers in the Spanish version of the book (e.g., ¡!). We matched the size, color, and font of the print in both languages. Overall, 9 out of the 12 children (75%) selected the correct book. However, they gave a variety of rationales for how they knew that the book was in Spanish and not English:

- "*porque lo ando leyendo*" (because I'm reading it)
- "*porque aquí dice que está en español*" (because it says here that it's in Spanish) while pointing to the title of the book
- "*porque mi mamá me lo lee en español*" (because my mom reads it to me in Spanish)

From these responses, we could not draw any conclusions in terms of whether children could distinguish Spanish from English print based on particular grammatical or orthographic aspects. They were not necessarily able to explain to the researcher how they were able to identify the language of the books. Instead, they could provide general information about the language they used when reading at school or at home with their mom or dad (see Example 9 above). Of interest here is the children's ability to talk about their two languages in relation to print, interlocutors, and context. That is, they demonstrate metalinguistic awareness about which language they speak with particular individuals and in specific contexts (Baker, 2001).

Most of the children (10 of 12) demonstrated knowledge that the print carried the message when asked to show the researcher where to start reading the book. Specifically, they pointed directly to the title of the book and then opened the book and indicated where the beginning and end of the text was. In addition, they also paid attention to the pictures throughout the book, showing recognition that pictures also help construct the meaning of the story (see Whitehurst et al., 1994 for similar results). On encountering a page that was purposefully placed upside down, 8 out of 12 children either turned the book to read the text or pointed out the mistake. This indicates that the children were using many cues—such as color, size, shape of print, and pictures—to decode the print in the book (Goodman, 1986).

In terms of directionality, 83% of children had developed this concept in both languages. They knew that in both Spanish and English, people read from left to right and top to bottom. To determine whether the children had developed the concepts of letters and words, we asked them to show us first one letter and then two letters. All the children were able to do so correctly. However, in this task, only one child was able to identify a word when asked to "*Ahora enséñame nada más una palabra*" (Now show me one word) on the last sentence of the CAP *Stones* book. This result shows that these 5-year-olds have developed some knowledge about letters but are still developing their letter and word knowledge (Justice, Pence, Bowles, & Wiggins, 2006). We will come back to this point in the General Discussion section.

In sum, these young emergent bilinguals showed general knowledge of book handling (e.g., they identified correctly the beginning and end of the text, the title, and how to turn the pages). They had also developed the concept of directionality of print; none, however, was able to point word by word as the adult read or to attend to letter or word order in the text (see Reyes & Hernández, 2006, on word-order development). In terms of punctuation conventions, these emergent bilingual children had started to formulate hypotheses about some marks. Specifically, three of the children noticed that some phrases throughout the book had question marks or exclamation points at the beginning and end (e.g., ¡Las Piedras!, *¿Va a parar en el cerco?* [*Stones*! Will the stone stop by the fence?]). Children identified these as print errors, explaining that the punctuation mark was *al revés* (upside down) or *se equivocaron las señoras* (the ladies made a mistake—presumably referring to the authors). We interpret these responses as indicating that the children had developed more familiarity with punctuation conventions of written English than of Spanish. This conclusion is corroborated by both our observations in the classroom, in which we documented teachers' direct explanations about English punctuation to the children, as well as the dominant presence of English written materials in the preschool classroom. Some of the children were also developing hypotheses about the function of the period; four of them said that the period was "*para parar*" (for stopping) but were unable to explain the functions of any other punctuation conventions (e.g., comma, accent mark, capital and lowercase letters).

The results from this task are in line with Clay's (1989) findings that, in general, young children develop some knowledge and hypotheses about the function of the period and a few about initial letters and sounds in words to finger-point while they read a story. Young children may not be able to complete all the different aspects of this task until they have developed conventional literacy through direct instruction at school.

Interview About Children's Metalinguistic Awareness of CAP and Writing. During the interview, all children responded that they could write and provided examples of writing and drawing (*M* age at time of interview = 5 years, 3 months). All children produced different kinds of representations when asked to write versus draw. As observed in earlier studies (Ferreiro & Teberosky, 1982; Goodman, 1986), in addition to scribbles, they could make actual letters or symbols that represented letters. Children distinguished between drawing and writing when asked to identify each sample for us. Figure 2 shows Jazlynn's examples, which show clear differentiation between writing and drawing.

The children also demonstrated different levels of metalinguistic awareness of their biliteracy abilities during the interview. For example, 10 of the 11 children said that they were able to write in both languages. The other child said she could write only in Spanish because that was the language her family used at home. Each of these children provided examples where they indicated which language they used for writing during specific interactions. In terms of their awareness of language use according to context, children's responses clearly differentiated between the language they use when writing at home and the language they use at school. At home, most children (7 out of 11) reported writing in Spanish, 2 in English, and 2 in both languages. The children's responses about their language

Figure 2. Jazlynn's Drawing and Writing Samples

use at school are less straightforward because they are fairly evenly split among English only, Spanish only, and both English and Spanish. Interestingly, from our observations at home, we corroborated that children's responses regarding the language used for writing at home were consistent with their language use during family interactions. However, their responses regarding school language use did not necessarily correspond with their language competencies but instead seemed to relate to their language preference. This is an important observation because the children were older at the time of this interview (compared to when they participated in the other two assessments); therefore, they seemed to be able to better express some of their theories and preferences about language and literacy use.

In addition, all of the children had developed hypotheses about the functions of writing when asked for what purpose people write. Their responses fit one of the following categories:

- *para aprender* (to learn; 3 children)
- *para escribirle a mi mamá* (to write to my mom; 2 children)
- *porque les gusta escribir* (because [people] like to write; 4 children)
- did not respond (2 children)

These responses suggest awareness of three different functions of writing: to learn, to communicate with others, and for entertainment. Of interest here is that children seemed to connect the functions of writing with the immediate contexts where they use writing: to learn at school and to write to Mom at home. Two of them, Dariana and Jimena, responded that they used only English when writing at school or when writing to the teacher. On the other hand, Frida and Sercan said that they used both languages, Spanish and English, for writing in the classroom. Interestingly, they said they used English with their main teacher but "*las dos*" (the two [languages]) when writing to us, the researchers. In fact, we did interact with the participant children in the classroom using both languages because we wanted to let them know that it was acceptable to speak both languages with us and that we valued their two languages; therefore, the children seem to have identified us as being bilingual and recognized that they could use either or both languages with us. In contrast, they seem to have associated the lead teacher, the main authority figure in the classroom, with English. From our classroom and home observations, we learned that for these children English is the language of communication in formal interactions with teachers. During our classroom visits, we observed that children were not encouraged to write in Spanish; however, Spanish was often used for clarification and disciplinary purposes (field notes, February 5, 2005). These children had developed the awareness that English was the dominant language of instruction within the school context, implicitly recognizing that English had more power and prestige than did their native language (Li, 2006).

Home Observations of Children's Biliteracy Development

In addition to assessing the children's performance on specific tasks, we were also interested in observing their development of early biliteracy in their natural contexts. As indicated earlier, we selected 3 out of the 12 children, Dariana, Frida, and Sercan, to describe in detail as case studies. (We limited the analysis to three case studies due to space limitations.) These children's performances on the reading and writing assessment tasks yielded a score that indicates they, like the remaining children in the cohort of 12, have not yet developed all concepts of print (see scores in Table 1). These 3 young emergent bilinguals showed general knowledge of book handling by correctly identifying the beginning and end of the story, the title, how to turn the pages, and the concept of directionality of print. However, only Dariana was able to point to a word in a sentence when asked. From both the CAP task and the EPT, we learned that these emergent bilingual children had started to formulate hypotheses about the functions of some punctuation conventions. Based on their responses in the EPT, we can determine that they are not yet able to indicate whether a particular text is in Spanish or English. The reading assessments yielded a low score for each child (based on a total score of 34), but that does not tell us about *how* these young emergent bilingual children are constructing meaning from their two linguistic resources and whether they might demonstrate greater literacy knowledge within their natural contexts; it is for this reason that we turn to the home observations.

Table 2 presents the types of literacy events we observed during our first year of home visits across the three case-study families. In our case-study description and discussion, we also include information about parents' beliefs about bilingualism. We interviewed parents individually at the beginning of the project to understand the families' ideologies about language and their literacy practices and how these influenced the children's language environments at home. As we will share in the following case studies, each child's language environment influenced his or her own individual solutions and family strategies in relation to bilingualism and biliteracy. Some solutions were considered "localized" to a particular language environment, whereas others seemed more general because they recurred across case studies.

The three case-study children made remarkable progress in terms of their oral language development throughout the year and were able to develop their bilingual competencies to near native fluency. The children's bilingual environment varied (see Table 3 for details on the bilingual environment of each case-study family), and because of the nature of this study, it is important to highlight children's bilingual support (or lack thereof) at school and in their community.

Sercan: "Que rico de los que me gustan a mi" (How delicious, like the ones I like). Sercan was born in a rural area of Oaxaca, Mexico, and migrated to the United States with his family when he was 1 year old. Sercan's family lives in a trailer park where there is a large concentration of Mexican-origin residents. He lives with his mom, dad, and 1-year-old sister. The primary language of the

Table 2. Domains of Family Literacy Practices (Observed Events Across Case-Study Participants)

Daily living routines	Entertainment/ recreation	Educational/ school-related	Religion	Interpersonal communication	Literacy for the purpose of teaching or learning
1. Commercial: receipts, flyers, product labels 2. Work: job applications 3. Medical: labels on prescription medication, thermometer instructions, appointment reminders, letters from hospital after baby delivery	1. Family cards (e.g., Christmas and Mother's Day) 2. Storybook readings 3. Instructional manuals 4. Internet reading 5. Song lyrics	1. Report cards 2. Fieldtrip letters (bilingual) 3. Monthly calendar and notices 4. Homework for target child and siblings, homework for parent (ESL or early childhood classes) 5. Internet reading	1. Church newsletters 2. Catechism course materials	1. Reading the newspaper 2. Writing letters to relatives or friends 3. Writing e-mails	1. Child wanting to practice the ABC's while writing 2. Playing *la escuelita*

Table 3. Bilingual Backgrounds of the Three Case-Study Children

Child	Place of birth	Family and community language environment	Language used by parents and caretaker	Early childhood education setting
Frida	Sonora, Northern Mexico	Spanish at home; bilingual in community	Spanish	English-dominant with some L1 use
Dariana	Arizona, Southwestern United States	Bilingual at home and in community	Spanish and English	English-dominant with some L1 use
Sercan	Oaxaca, Southern Mexico	Spanish at home; bilingual in community	Spanish	English-dominant with some L1 use

Note. L1 = first language.

household is Spanish, although there are some English influences. The family's bilingual community context and Sercan's formal schooling in English permeate their home interactions. Sercan uses some phrases (e.g., "whatever" and "never mind") and borrows some English words (especially for academic concepts related to colors and numbers) in his conversations with his parents. Sercan's mom and dad try to learn English words from their son, and we frequently observed them asking him to translate words or phrases. From a sociocultural perspective, this type of everyday interaction points to the switching between expert and novice roles by Sercan and his parents depending on whether the interaction is in Spanish or English (Reyes, 2006; Rogoff, 1990).

The family's physical living space is very constrained, and they do not have easy access to public recreational spaces (transportation is also an issue as they do not own a car). During our conversations, Sercan's mom stated that she does not allow her children to play out in the streets because she is "scared they will be run over by a car" (field notes, September 1, 2006). We believe that this constraint has in fact been of benefit to the children's literacy development because their mother provides them with reading and writing materials to explore almost every evening, such as books in English and Spanish, pencils, coloring books, and notebooks. The family enjoys engaging in reading and writing activities, and it was not uncommon during our home visits to find all members of the family writing in their personal notepads. For this family, daily experiences literally become stories, and the living room walls become canvases on which drawings and letters are printed. Children scribbled in their pads and on couches and the walls, but even though Mom complained about having to wash the walls, she also laughed about and expressed pride in the children's attempt to write (field notes, February 9, 2005). During an interview, the mother and father reported that they promoted Spanish maintenance at home. Specifically, they emphasized speaking Spanish at home with the children, but because of their limited proficiency in English, they relied on the school system to teach their children reading and writing in English (interview, November 27, 2004).

In one home observation, the family had just returned from the grocery store. Mom gave the children a yogurt to eat while she finished unpacking the groceries. Sercan showed his container of yogurt to the researcher and asked what color it was, initiating the following conversation:

> Child begins eating his yogurt (S = Sercan, R = Researcher, M = Mom. Translations from Spanish in parentheses; # = commentary).
>
> S: *Ven mira. ¿Mira, qué color tiene (el yogurt)...¿Qué, qué color tiene?* (Look, look. What color is [my yogurt]?...What color is it?)
>
> R: *¿Qué color es?* (What color is it?)
>
> S: *Yo no se...es* blue? (I don't know...is blue?)
>
> #"Blue," he said, answering his own question.#
>
> R: Uh huh.
>
> S: *Mira esto. Se está saliendo.* (Look at this. It's coming off.)

R: *¿De qué sabor es?* (What flavor is it?)
#S starts to open his yogurt.#
< Three-second pause >
M: *¿No sabes qué sabor es?* (You do not know what flavor it is?)
S: Ay!
#He spits out the plastic he bit off in order to open the container and then notices that the print is upside down and turns the package around.#
S: *Es sabor de... de, mira.* (The flavor is of...of, look.)
#He shows the researcher the writing on the yogurt container.#
R: *¿Qué dice? ¿De qué sabor es?* (What does it say? What flavor is it?)
#S studies the package and label for a few seconds and then, with a marked change in his discourse intonation, "reads"#
S: *Es sabor de...de...es de...de...de que rico de los que me gustan a mi.* (The flavor is...is... is how delicious, like the ones I like.)
R: *¿Eso dice?* (That's what it says?)
S: Uh huh.
#He nods his head yes.#
(March 6, 2005, video clip 03)

During this interaction, we learn about Sercan's knowledge of print awareness and some concepts about print he is able to use spontaneously. When the researcher asks him what the label says about the flavor of the yogurt, Sercan looks at the package and immediately turns it around. We assume he noticed that the print was upside down because, by turning the package around, he could read it from left to right. He studies the label for a few seconds and then changes his intonation to "read" the label in the style of a television commercial. From this example, we can infer that Sercan has developed various concepts of print. First, he knows that the print on the package carries meaning and that it provides the information requested from him, the flavor of the yogurt. In addition, he knows that the letters need to be oriented in a certain direction to read them from left to right (evidence of the concept of directionality and of word identification). Although he was not able to decode the message on the package, he predicted what the label might say. He also used style shifting as a discourse strategy to mimic an advertisement, thereby demonstrating his knowledge of how this genre is used in food packaging and television advertisements. Sercan demonstrated the same strategy when identifying toothpaste during the EPT, showing the importance of the media in mediating his use of the two languages (Dyson, 1993). Of significance here is that within this linguistic environment, Sercan takes risks to explore the print and make hypotheses about it without any constraints. We learned that he can indeed identify a word, something we were not able to observe from his responses in the controlled tasks. The advantage of analyzing these data across multiple methods is that in naturalistic activities relevant to the children's daily lives, they are able to demonstrate knowledge that they cannot show in the more artificial setting of the reading assessment tasks.

In another event, Sercan was playing with markers and paper early in the morning (field notes, November 10, 2005). He made several pictures and an ABC chart. When the researcher came to look at his pictures, he showed her a picture of a tree with monkeys in the branches. He explained that the monkeys were making noise in the tree. The researcher then prompted him to write a story. He eagerly took a marker and attempted to write the word "*chango*" (monkey) in Spanish. Sercan sounded out the word and wrote "EHGg" (reversed first "G"). Then he looked at his writing and got frustrated with the product. To encourage him, the researcher then turned the page over and asked him to try again. On the flip side of the paper he had drawn a face. "*Este es un chango*" (This is a monkey), he explained to the researcher (see top of Figure 3). She responded to the drawing by saying playfully "*un chango marango*" and prompted him to label his picture. The word *marango* is not found in most Spanish dictionaries; however, it is used as an adjective in Mexican popular songs and jokes to refer to a funny monkey. Sercan then wrote near the top of the paper something that he identified as "*Chango Marrano,*" using one letter to represent each syllable of the words. He continued by adding two more faces to his drawing. The researcher then asked him what language he had used to write the phrase. The child explained, "*Lo escribí en español*" (I wrote it in Spanish). Taking him a step further, she then asked whether he could write it in English. Sercan paused for a second and then answered, "*Oh...con los chiquitos lo hago en inglés*" (Oh...with the small ones [letters] I write it in English). He then copied the same combination of letters, this time in lower case. Finally, he read rapidly with no change in intonation "CHANGO MARRANO [first line], chango marrano [second line]."

This example can be analyzed at two linguistic levels. On the first level, Sercan evidently was not familiar with the word *marango*, so he changed the researcher's *marango* to *marrano* (pig), a word familiar to him that is similar in terms of the

Figure 3. Sercan's *Chango Marango* (Funny Monkey) Writing Sample

patterns of sounds and number of syllables. By exploring the sounds in the word *chango* and finding a word that rhymes with it, Sercan demonstrates that he is developing an awareness of the phonological structure of Spanish. In addition, this example suggests that Sercan has developed a hypothesis in terms of his two languages. He knows that to write the same word in two different languages, he needs to write an additional string of letters and that somehow he needs to differentiate between the two languages. To mark this distinction, he uses uppercase letters to write in Spanish and lowercase letters to write in English. This emergent bilingual boy has internalized that languages are represented differently, and he has found a *local,* that is, context-specific, solution to mark these differences. Sercan was not able to use this solution when participating in the concepts of print task because there he was presented with specific stimuli that did not differ in case. As will be evident in the next two case studies, each child came up with individual solutions to the problem of representing Spanish versus English text.

Frida: "La 'i' no es; es la 'e'!" [It's not the "i"; it's the "e"!]. Frida was born in a small town in Sonora, Mexico, and migrated with her parents and grandparents when she was 2 years old. Frida speaks mostly Spanish at home with her parents and grandparents but speaks some English with relatives (her aunt and younger cousin) who visit their home every evening. Frida lives with her parents, baby sister, and grandparents in a trailer park located on a busy street just a couple of blocks south of her preschool. The family's physical living space is very limited, with four adults and two children living in a two-bedroom trailer. However, the yard space in front of the trailer has enough space for the children to play, and they have a jumping platform where Frida and her cousins spend their afternoons playing.

At school, Frida is a curious and attentive student. According to her teacher, she is "ahead of her class" and has been able to develop fluent bilingual competencies. We visited Frida and her family in the evenings. During these visits, we observed how Frida and her cousin, Raúl (a year younger than Frida), played together at home, participating in different literacy events, including coloring, writing, and reading together (see Table 2 for a summary of these events across families). Her mom, Ceci, explained that the cousins like to play together often and that they spontaneously gather around the dining table to color and write with different materials. Frida, according to her mom, always plays the role of the more expert writer when interacting with Raúl. She also reported that Frida is able to spell some words and recognize sound–letter correspondences in both Spanish and English, particularly when dictating to Raúl how to spell words. We were able to confirm these abilities during our home visits. We consider in detail a transcript of a conversation between Frida and her cousin while they wrote and colored from an activity book. Frida's mom, Ceci, and aunt, Isela, interact with the children by providing scaffolding and supporting their biliterate abilities.

Participants: F = Frida, RL = cousin Raúl, M = Frida's mom, T = Tía, Frida's aunt

	Conversation (Translation in parentheses)	Clarification and nonverbal behavior
F:	*Yo no sé escribir* Iliana. #researcher's name# (I do not know how to write *Iliana.*)	
M:	Iliana, Iliana.	Mom corrects Frida's Spanish pronunciation.
T:	*Mira, yo les voy a decir. Pues, escribe* Miss *y después yo te voy a decir como se escribe* Iliana. (Okay, I'll tell you how to do it. [First] write *Miss* and then I'll tell you how to write *Iliana.*)	Aunt points to Frida's paper, so she starts writing.
RL:	*¿Y después que sigue?* (And after that, what is next?)	
F:	*Tienes que saber tu nombre.* (You have to know how to write your name.)	Frida talks to cousin.
M:	*Ahora si pon* Miss Iliana *pues.* (Now you can write *Miss Iliana.*)	Mom tells Frida what to write next.
F:	Miss	Frida reads aloud what she is writing.
T:	*Luego, la I...la I* (Then the I...the I)	Spanish pronunciation Frida thinks for a second and then writes the letter "E" instead of "I"
T:	*No, la "I"* (No, the I)	Spanish pronunciation
	la I (the I)	English pronunciation
	No, esa es la "e." (No, that one is the "e.")	English pronunciation
	La "I" de mi nombre así como se escribe Isela (Like the "I" in my name, Isela)	Spanish pronunciation
	Pon la "I," luego la "s." (Write the "I" and then the "s.")	Spanish pronunciation and then English pronunciation for "s"
	La "I"...*vez ahí dice* Miss Iliana. (The "I"...see it says there *Miss Iliana.*)	Aunt continues to pronounce and spell all the letters in English for the child.
F:	*Y aquí le voy a poner...* (and later I'll write here...)	Child covers the whole page and starts writing something. Then she shows us her finished letter.
#Interaction continues.#		

(From field notes and video clip, April 7, 2005)

The aunt helps both Frida and Raúl to spell and write letters and names on the activity sheet. In a later exchange, Frida's mom also helps by reading aloud what Frida is writing. Of significance here is the fact that Frida and Raúl are becoming aware of print and pronunciation in two languages because of the direct teaching and scaffolding by adults that mediate their learning of writing during the activity. In this example, Frida is able first to write her own name independently and then to write the researcher's name with the help of her aunt and mom. During this interaction, we observe how the aunt's distinction between the Spanish and English pronunciations of a couple of letters (the vowels "i" and "e") helps the child realize that even when the sounds are similar in the two languages, the sound–letter correspondence is different for each language. Specifically, the letter "i" in Spanish sounds like the letter "e" in English. In this instance, Frida reacts by stopping what she is writing; after she listens to her aunt, she thinks for a few seconds and then rewrites the first letter of the name she's spelling. She is making use of her phonological awareness to connect the sound representation to the printed letters on her paper. Frida's metalinguistic awareness and phonological awareness are enhanced by her active use of two languages to write names and by her aunt relating the spelling of Spanish letters to proper names already familiar to Frida in both English and Spanish. From this home interaction, we learned that this literacy practice and the strategy of identifying the sounds that correspond with particular letters in the two languages were very common activities in this family; often while the mom and aunt made flour tortillas with the grandma, the children engaged in this type of literacy event to entertain themselves. The data show how learning is embedded and mediated within this particular situation in which the children sometimes engage in literacy activities for entertainment and at other times to complete school homework (school-related activity). When we compare the demands of various home literacy events with those of the various reading assessment tasks in which children participated, it becomes clear that these contexts are different, and the options available to children are constrained by the context.

In terms of language use, both adults help Frida and her cousin to spell in Spanish, but they also draw from English to help them—even though the mom and aunt do not consider themselves bilingual. This shift reflects the adults' acknowledgment of the children's biliterate competencies. This interpretation is based on our comparisons with previous home observations where Mom helped Frida with homework and school assignments using Spanish exclusively (field notes, January 2005). The adults provide the language environment and context to support and encourage the children's biliteracy knowledge. Mom explained during an interview that Spanish was the main language of interactions at home and that she liked to help Frida read and write in the language she knows best, Spanish; however, she considered English "vital" as it would open better job opportunities for Frida in the future. The mother's scaffolding and support increase Frida's level of understanding in both languages. Later on, during the concepts of writing interviews at school, we observed Frida using the same strategy of drawing from her L1 to write and spell in the L2. For example, when we asked Frida to

Figure 4. Frida's "July" Writing Sample

write something, she wrote the word "July" (see Figure 4), and when asked immediately after she finished writing in what language she had written this word, she responded that it was in Spanish. Of interest here is that when Frida was asked to read the word, she actually read the word "July" in English and spelled it as "LLULi," using double "L" to indicate the same sound in both English and Spanish (in Spanish, double "L" makes a similar sound as the "Y" in English). This example illustrates that she is becoming phonologically aware in her two languages and that she uses her knowledge of Spanish when spelling in English (using the resources in her L1 helps her to produce and interpret written language in the L2), the same strategy we had observed at home with the interactions among Frida, her mom, aunt, and cousin.

Dariana's Bilingual Prayer Book

Dariana was born and grew up in the southwestern United States. She is exposed to both languages at home and switches from one language to the other comfortably, depending on the interlocutor and context. Dariana has grown up close to her grandma and grandpa, who are Spanish-dominant speakers. Grandma takes care of Dariana and her younger sister (2 years old) every afternoon until Mom and Dad return from work. This language environment, as we will see in the following examples, has a significant impact on supporting Dariana's biliteracy.

During our home visits, we observed that Dariana loves to write, make signs containing her name to decorate her room, and read books to her sister. Dariana's mother is a paraprofessional; thus, even though she does not always read to her daughters at night, they engage together in different literacy activities, such as writing notes to each other and writing letters. Books (mainly in English) are part of her home environment, and the girls have numerous educational toys (e.g., minicomputers, alphabet puzzles).

During our observations, we learned that English was the primary language used between mother and daughter; however, when the grandparents were present (practically every afternoon during the week) the family conversed in Spanish. The mother explained to us, "*me gusta que ella [Dariana] pueda comunicarse con sus abuelos*" (I like for her to be able to communicate with her grandparents). At the time of one visit in the fall, Dariana had recently observed her mother and grandmother grieving over her great-grandmother's death (field notes, November 27, 2005). In accordance with the *novena* tradition in the Catholic religion, Dariana's grandmother had been praying for the great-grandmother's soul for several days (for nine consecutive days, family and relatives get together to pray for the soul of the deceased). Later on, while visiting her grandmother, Dariana reported feeling sad and went to write by herself. Without the adults noticing, she took her grandmother's prayer book and made a bilingual prayer book for herself (see Figures 5a & 5b).

This literacy event illustrates what Dariana knows about written language, her knowledge of the function of writing, and her transformation of this practice in a syncretic way that integrates her resources in the two languages (Gregory et al., 2004; Orellana, Reynolds, Dorner, & Meza, 2003). First, she uses both drawings and print to convey meaning. Second, Dariana knows the conventions of writing, such as directionality, use of spaces between words, and use of commas and periods. In addition, Dariana has learned the use and function of written language for a specific cultural practice: praying in remembrance of and grief over the loss of a loved one. Literacy in this family has a religious function. Finally, when analyzing at the micro level the written language Dariana used in her prayer book, we see that both languages are present. The grandmother's original prayer book was written only in Spanish, but in Dariana's version, she copied a fragment in Spanish for the inside of the book and used English to design and write on the front cover. Later, when she showed her prayer book to her grandmother, a monolingual Spanish speaker, the grandmother modeled for her how to write "Jesus" in Spanish with an accent mark: *Jesús* (see Figure 5a). This example clearly shows how family members mediate children's learning by differentiating particular words in the two scripts, and how intergenerational learning is part of this family's literacy practices as literacy "experts" help and scaffold the young child's learning.

General Discussion

In this section, we begin with a summary of the three main findings from this study. We then interpret these findings using both sociocultural and ecology of language frameworks. Finally, we offer an ecological model of emergent biliteracy.

First, we found that children were developing knowledge and metalinguistic awareness about print in both their languages. From the different reading and writing assessments these children participated in, we learned that young bilingual children are beginning to understand that Spanish and English are written in distinct ways; however, these 5-year-olds do not necessarily come up with the same solutions to particular problems, such as identifying the language in which a specific sample of print is written. For example, in the print awareness task,

Figure 5. Dariana's Bilingual Prayer Book

a. Dariana's Cover for Bilingual Prayer Book

b. Dariana's Religious Text and Drawing

many children focused on the function of the items presented rather than on their specific forms (i.e., brand names). In describing the function of specific objects, they used mostly Spanish with the researcher; moreover, some of the children used style shifting as a discourse strategy, indicating their knowledge of the genre of media advertisements (Ervin-Tripp, 2001). Here we see how children's access and exposure to communication media (newspapers, television, etc.) in their environment influence the kinds of strategies they develop to interpret print in and out of their school surroundings.

In terms of identifying the language of print, none of the children seemed to use specific orthographic or diacritic features. It could have been that some children were in fact using information from the text or the print when they identified it as English or Spanish, but they gave no evidence of this from their explanations at this point in their development. Instead, some children used other strategies, such as pointing to the same word and stating that it was written in different languages, depending on the intonation and phonology used to pronounce the word. This strategy demonstrates metalinguistic awareness that two languages, Spanish and English, are present in the child's environment and that they are distinct from each other. In other assessments, children demonstrated metalinguistic awareness by inventing solutions, using strategies, and creating hypotheses, expending considerable cognitive efforts to understand print by drawing on their resources in both linguistic systems (e.g., children hypothesized that upper versus lowercase letters signaled whether a word was in English or Spanish). That a high degree of variability is present in "normal" emergent biliteracy is itself an important finding in terms of guiding teachers' expectations in the school environment. As Yaden pointed out, "variation in the data is the data" (D.B. Yaden, Jr., personal communication, April 25, 2008) and should be considered as such when describing linguistic profiles of emergent bilinguals.

Second, we found that families demonstrated a wide variety of communicative practices and ways in which they used written materials in the two languages. Based on our ethnographic observations, we learned that these emergent bilingual children participate in different literacy events at home. This participation in a variety of literacy events (e.g., daily living routines, entertainment, literacy for literacy's sake, storybook time, interpersonal communication) helps young children develop biliteracy. Of interest here is that in each individual family, certain kinds of literacy practices tend to take place consistently in a particular language (or combination of languages) and that this pattern varies across families depending on their specific activities and contexts. Moreover, these parents support their children's emergent biliteracy with various practices and resources at home. They recognize the importance of their children learning to read and write in English, but many also seek to maintain the home language for personal or cultural reasons, such as to maintain relationships with monolingual Spanish-speaking relatives. Children are involved in different everyday literacy routines with their parents, such as writing and reading general notes, cards, letters, and religious texts.

Most of the literacy events in these children's homes involved the use of the native language (i.e., Spanish) to interpret English printed material. The language used by parents and siblings during these literacy events and the function of these events contribute to language learning and socialization in the community where these young children are growing up bilingual. Interestingly, we observed instances where children modeled English for their parents, an activity that helped them develop higher-order thinking. In addition, differentiating between what is English and what is Spanish in explanations and translations to their parents promotes metalinguistic knowledge (Orellana & Reynolds, 2008). Therefore, both adults and children draw upon a range of linguistic and cultural resources to meet various challenges in their day-to-day activities (Reyes & Moll, 2008).

Third, we found that intergenerational learning occurred in both directions among family members. Adults and more advanced peers, often siblings, serve as experts who scaffold print knowledge as the young child progresses toward biliteracy (Kenner, 2004). Yet parents, peers, and children may switch between expert and novice roles in specific contexts, for example, when a child translates an English word into Spanish for his parents. We conclude that children do not construct meaning on their own but rather transform and build on it while actively participating in literacy events during interactive play and learning with peers and family members, something we could not have observed from the classroom literacy tasks alone (see Rowe, 2006, for a discussion of children's participatory role in literacy learning). Some researchers have referred to this transformation of knowledge during interaction as hybrid, or syncretic, literacy practices (Gregory et al., 2004; Gutiérrez, 2008); however, we focus here on the *process* of transformation as part of the natural development of children's emergent biliteracy. The strategies these children used provide evidence that parent–child and peer interactions, parents' and teachers' literacy practices, and children's own interpretation and transformation of language interact to facilitate literacy development. The fluidity and dynamic nature of biliteracy were evident in the scaffolding and intergenerational learning among family members.

As indicated earlier, in this study we have drawn on sociocultural and ecology of language perspectives to explore and explain children's knowledge and development of emergent biliteracy. In addition, the application of a multiple-methods approach to both the analysis and interpretation of the data allows us to examine how children solve particular literacy problems in reading and writing assessments and natural settings, to compare children's performance in formal tasks versus naturalistic activities, and to identify particular hypotheses that bilingual children develop as they construct meaning from environmental print and learn about conventions and concepts of print in two languages with alphabetic scripts.

The case studies provided evidence that these emergent bilingual children's development of biliteracy is dynamic and mediated by their immediate sociocultural contexts. Through our observations of children participating in different literacy events at home, we documented that the development of bilingual print concepts and awareness is mediated through social interaction and does not necessarily come about through exposure alone (Kassow, 2006; Neuman & Roskos, 1993). In other words, children's biliteracy development is highly situated and is influenced, mediated, and transformed in particular ways during peer and family interactions. Even though these students were living in a bicultural community in the Southwest where they used Spanish during their everyday lives, they had limited opportunities to develop their oral and written Spanish proficiency in the classroom.

The naturalistic observations in combination with the reading and writing assessment tasks contributed to a better understanding of the process of biliteracy than would have been evident through either observation or reading and writing assessments alone. If we had evaluated these emergent bilingual children's literacy knowledge from the literacy assessments alone, as is the case in many schools, we would have assumed that they lacked several basic early literacy concepts; however, observation in their natural home environments allowed us to identify concepts that were emerging. We also were able to explore and learn from an ecological perspective about the process and mediation of learning involved in developing biliteracy during experiences embedded in meaningful contexts (Hornberger & Skilton-Sylvester, 2000) in their home environment (such as writing a prayer to come to terms with the death of a family member).

Although this study provides evidence that children's biliteracy development is a complex and dynamic process that is mediated by their everyday participation in various literacy events and learning environments at home and at school, a few words of caution are in order. First, this study involved a limited number of participants. Second, all the participants were Spanish–English bilinguals. Future studies with a larger group of participants and including children with different home languages would allow a more detailed examination of the different linguistic environments and activities that support the development of biliteracy and how these might vary by culture or home language.

Furthermore, we do not claim that the characteristics and profiles of these children can be generalized to all emergent Spanish–English bilingual children. In fact, based on these case studies we would predict great variability, even across Spanish–English bilinguals from similar backgrounds. Nevertheless, these children can be considered representative of the diverse range of language and literacy experiences and competencies developed throughout their particular contexts.

Finally, we argue that the findings contribute toward the development of a theoretical model focusing on the ecology of emergent biliteracy in early childhood. Such a model should consider not only *what* children learn but also *how* they learn their native language at home and their second language at school and in the community (Moll, 1990; Tabors & Snow, 2001). Although the preschool children described in this study had not yet developed conventional writing and reading competencies in either language, the bilingual, and in some cases biliterate, interactions in which they participate support them in beginning to construct meaning from print they encounter in their bilingual surroundings (Gregory et al., 2004).

Our work contributes to the field of biliteracy by adopting an ecological perspective to interpret young children's pathways to biliteracy. This perspective has yielded richer information in the interpretation of the data than we could have gleaned from children's responses to the reading and writing literacy assessment tasks alone. These findings have theoretical implications for rethinking how we view children's interactions within the contexts that mediate their learning. This approach to the study of biliteracy development of young children has allowed us to look at how various environments and interactions among participants, contexts, and sociocultural forces shape young immigrant children's biliteracy development. These Mexican-origin parents overwhelmingly support biliteracy and deliberately use Spanish at home to talk, read, and write, while also encouraging their children to become proficient in written and spoken English. Regardless of government-mandated English-only policies and programs that may constrain children's classroom experiences, their daily learning experiences are permeated with bilingualism and biliteracy. The findings in this study point to the potential to develop biliteracy that apparently exists within each child's immediate environment and is enhanced when community members (e.g., parents, peers, schoolteachers, neighbors) provide direct scaffolding during linguistic interactions.

Although previous studies in the field have laid some groundwork toward developing an ecological model of biliteracy, models such as Hornberger's (1989) have focused on the continuum of biliteracy among adult bilinguals and its application to language-planning purposes. No previous studies have embraced an ecological approach to early childhood biliteracy development.

We argue for a model that describes the biliteracy process as part of the natural development of young Spanish–English emergent bilinguals. This model should include theory and research that document the interplay of factors at multiple levels and how they impact the development of biliteracy. Moreover, an ecological model of emergent biliteracy needs to account for time- and place-specific influences from home, community, and school and predict how these would influence children's literacy development (Barton, 1994). Finally, this ecological model should acknowledge that children's development is dynamic, malleable, and influenced by naturalistic opportunities in the environment that tap into any child's potential to acquire multiple languages and literacies.

An ecological model of emergent biliteracy in early childhood can bring benefits to the field by challenging deficit perspectives that tend to devalue bilingualism and biliteracy as impediments rather than potential assets in academic achievement and that stereotype Mexican immigrant families as failing to provide stimulating home environments that prepare children for formal literacy learning at school (Reyes, 2001; Zentella, 2005). An ecological model of emergent biliteracy has implications for pedagogical practice, in terms of helping educators to provide more effective instruction, to understand children's individual ways of responding to school activities and assignments, and to recognize alternate and more nuanced strategies for evaluating children's biliteracy knowledge.

QUESTIONS FOR REFLECTION

1. In what ways do young emerging biliterate children demonstrate metalinguistic awareness about print in both their languages?
2. How does linguistic intergenerational teaching and learning occur in emerging bilingual families?
3. What are the limitations of traditional or standardized reading and writing assessments in determining biliterate students' literacy competencies?

NOTES

This work was supported by a grant from the Foundation for Child Development Young Scholars Program to the first author. We wish to thank David Bloome, Ian Wilkinson, David Yaden, and especially the anonymous reviewers for their thoughtful and useful feedback. All opinions and conclusions expressed in this article are those of the authors.

REFERENCES

Andrade, A.M., Ruiz, O.A., & Basurto, A.G. (1995). *Las piedras*. Auckland, New Zealand: Heinemann.

Baker, C. (2001). *Foundations of bilingual education and bilingualism* (3rd ed.). Buffalo, NY: Multilingual Matters.

Barton, D. (1994). *Literacy: An introduction to the ecology of written language*. Oxford, England: Blackwell.

Bronfenbrenner, U. (1986). Ecology of the family as a context for hum a n development: Research perspective s. *Developmental Psychology*, 22(6), 723–742. doi:10.1037/0012-1649.22.6.723

Chaney, C. (1994). Language development, metalinguistic awareness, and emergent literacy skills of 3-year-old children in relation to social class. *Applied Psycholinguistics*, 15(3), 371–394.

Clay, M. (1972). *Reading: The patterning of complex behaviour*. Auckland, New Zealand: Heinemann.

Clay, M. (1979). *Stones: The concepts about print test*. Auckland, New Zealand: Heinemann.

Clay, M. (1989). Concepts about print in English and other languages. *The Reading Teacher*, 42(4), 268–276.

Dickinson, D.K., & Snow, C.E. (1987). Interrelationships among prereading and oral language skills in kindergartners from two social classes. *Early Childhood Research Quarterly*, 2(1), 1–25. doi:10.1016/0885-2006(87)90010-X

Dunn, L.M., & Dunn, L.M. (1981). *Peabody Picture Vocabulary Test—Revised*. Circle Pines, MN: American Guidance Service.

Dunn, L.M., Padilla, E.R., Lugo, D.E., & Dunn, L.M. (1986). *Test de vocabulario en imágenes Peabody (TVIP) [Peabody picture vocabulary test]*. Circle Pines, MN: American Guidance Service.

Dworin, J.E. (2003). Insights into biliteracy development: Toward a bidirectional theory of bilingual pedagogy. *Journal of Hispanic Higher Education*, 2(2), 171–186. doi:10.1177/1538192702250621

Dworin, J.E ., & Moll, L .C . (2006). Guest editors' introduction . *Journal of Early Childhood Literacy*, 6 (3), 234–240. doi:10.1177/1468798406069795

Dyson, A.H. (1993). *Social worlds of children learning to write in an urban primary school*. New York: Teachers College Press.

Dyson, A.H., & Genishi, C. (2005). *On the case: Approaches to language and literacy research*. New York: Teachers College Press.

Edelsky, C., & Jilbert, K. (1985). Bilingual children and writing: Lessons for all of us. *The Volta Review*, 87(5), 57–72.

Ernst-Slavit, G., & Mulhern, M. (2003). Bilingual books: Promoting literacy and biliteracy in the second-language and mainstream classroom. *Reading Online*, 7(2). Retrieved June 10, 2008, from www.readingonline.org/articles/art_index.asp?HREF=ernst-slavit/index.html

Ervin-Tripp, S. (2001). Variety, style-shifting, and ideology. In P. Eckert & J.R. Rickford (Eds.), *Style and sociolinguistic variation* (pp. 44–56). New York: Cambridge University Press.

Escamilla, K., Andrade, A.M., Basurto, A., & Ruiz, O.A. (1996). *Instrumento de observación: De los logros de la lecto-escritura inicial*. Portsmouth, NH: Heinemann.

Ferreiro, E. (2007). Letters and numbers in early literacy. In Y. Goodman & P. Martens (Eds.), *Critical issues in early literacy: Research and pedagogy* (pp. 59–77). Mahwah, NJ: Erlbaum.

Ferreiro, E., & Teberosky, A. (1982). *Literacy before schooling*. Portsmouth, NH: Heinemann.

García, O., Kleifgen, J.A., & Falchi, L. (2008). From English language learners to emergent bilinguals. In *Equity matters: Research review No. 1*. New York: Teachers College, Columbia University.

Goodman, Y. (1984). The development of initial literacy. In H. Goelman, A. Oberg, & F. Smith (Eds.), *Awakening to literacy* (pp. 102–109). Exeter, NH: Heinemann.

Goodman, Y. (1986). Children coming to know literacy. In W. Teale & E. Sulzby (Eds.), *Emergent literacy: Writing and reading* (pp. 1–14). Norwood, NJ: Ablex.

Goodman, Y., & Altwerger, B. (1981). *Print awareness in preschool children: A study of the development of literacy in preschool children* (Occasional Paper No. 4). Tucson: University of Arizona, College of Education, Program in Language and Literacy, Arizona Center for Research and Development.

Gregory, E., Long, S., & Volk, D. (2004). *Many pathways to literacy: Learning with siblings, peers, grandparents, and in community settings*. London: Routledge.

Grosjean, F. (1998). Studying bilinguals: Methodological and conceptual issues. *Bilingualism: Language and Cognition, 1*(2), 131–149. doi:10.1017/S136672899800025X

Gumperz, J.J., & Berenz, N. (1993). Transcribing conversational exchanges. In J.A. Edwards & M.D. Lampert (Eds.), *Talking data: Transcription and coding in discourse research* (pp. 91–122). Hillsdale, NJ: Erlbaum.

Gutiérrez, K.D. (20 0 8). Developing a sociocritical literacy in the Third Space. *Reading Research Quarterly, 43*(2), 148–164. doi:10.1598/RRQ.43.2.3

Hakuta, K. (1986). *Mirror of language: The debate on bilingualism*. New York: Basic.

Harste, J.C., Woodward, V.A., & Burke, C.L. (1984). *Language stories and literacy lessons*. Portsmouth, NH: Heinemann.

Haugen, E. (1969). *The Norwegian language in America: A study in bilingual behavior* (Vols. 1–2). Bloomington, IN: Indiana University Press. (Original work published 1953)

Heath, S.B. (1983). *Ways with words: Language, life, and work in communities and classrooms*. New York: Cambridge University Press.

Hornberger, N.H. (1989). Continua of biliteracy. *Review of Educational Research, 59*(3), 271–296.

Hornberger, N.H., & Skilton-Sylvester, E. (2000). Revisiting the continua of biliteracy: International and critical perspectives. *Language and Education: An International Journal, 14*(2), 96–122.

Howe, K.R. (2003). *Closing methodological divides: Toward democratic educational research*. Dordrecht, The Netherlands: Kluwer Academic.

Jiménez, R.T. (2003). Literacy and Latino students in the United States: Some considerations, questions, and new directions. *Reading Research Quarterly, 38*(1), 122–128.

Justice, L.M., & Ezell, H.K. (2001). Written language awareness in preschool children from low-income households: A descriptive analysis. *Communication Disorders Quarterly, 22*(3), 123–134. doi:10.1177/152574010102200302

Justice, L.M., Pence, K., Bowles, R.B., & Wiggins, A. (2006). An investigation of four hypotheses concerning the order by which 4-year-old children learn the alphabet letters. *Early Childhood Research Quarterly, 21*(3), 374–389. doi:10.1016/j.ecresq.2006.07.010

Kassow, D. (2006). *Environmental print awareness in young children*. Seattle, WA: Talaris Research Institute.

Kenner, C. (2000). *Home pages: Literacy links for bilingual children*. Stoke-on-Trent, England: Trentham.

Kenner, C. (2004). *Becoming biliterate: Young children learning different writing systems*. Stoke-on-Trent, England: Trentham.

Kenner, C., Kress, G., Hayat, A.-K., Kam, R., & Tsai, K.-C. (2004). Finding the keys to biliteracy: How young children interpret different writing systems. *Language and Education, 18*(2), 124–144.

Kirkland, L., Aldridge, J., & Kuby, P. (1991). Environmental print and the kindergarten classroom. *Reading Improvement, 28*(4), 219–222.

Li, G. (2006). Biliteracy and trilingual practices in the home context: Case studies of Chinese–Canadian children. *Journal of Early Childhood Literacy, 6*(3), 355–381. doi:10.1177/1468798406069797

Manning, M.M., Manning, G.L., Long, R., & Wolfson, B.J. (1987). *Reading and writing in the primary grades*. Washington, DC: National Education Association.

Moll, L.C. (Ed.). (1990). *Vygotsky and education: Instructional implications and applications of sociohistorical psychology*. New York: Cambridge University Press.

Moll, L.C., Saez, R., & Dworin, J. (2001). Exploring biliteracy: Two student case examples of writing as a social practice. *The Elementary School Journal, 101*(4), 435–449. doi:10.1086/499680

Morris, D., Bloodgood, J.W., Lomax, R.G., & Perney, J. (2003). Developmental steps in learning to read: A longitudinal study in kindergarten and first grade. *Reading Research Quarterly, 38*(3), 302–328. doi:10.1598/RRQ.38.3.1

Neuman, S.B., & Roskos, K. (1993). Access to print for children of poverty: Differential effects of adult mediation and literacy-enriched play settings on environmental and functional print tasks. *American Educational Research Journal, 30*(1), 95–122.

Orellana, M.F., & Reynolds, J.F. (2008). Cultural modeling: Leveraging bilingual skills for school paraphrasing tasks. *Reading Research Quarterly, 43*(1), 48–65. doi:10.1598/RRQ.43.1.4

Orellana, M.F., Reynolds, J., Dorner, L., & Meza, M. (2003). In other words: Translating or "paraphrasing" as a family literacy practice in immigrant households. *Reading Research Quarterly, 38*(1), 12–34. doi:10.1598/RRQ.38.1.2

Owocki, G., & Goodman, Y. (2002). *Kidwatching: Documenting children's literacy development.* Portsmouth, NH: Heinemann.

Pahl, S. (2008). The ecology of literacy and language: Discourses, identities and practices in homes, schools and communities. In A. Creese, P. Martin, & N.H. Hornberger (Eds.), *Encyclopedia of language and education: Vol. 9. Ecology of language* (pp. 305–315). Berlin, Germany: Springer.

Pérez, B. (Ed.). (2004). *Sociocultural contexts of language and literacy.* Mahwah, NJ: Erlbaum.

Reyes, I. (2006). Exploring connections between emergent biliteracy and bilingualism. *Journal of Early Childhood Literacy,* 6(3), 267–292. doi:10.1177/1468798406069801

Reyes, I., Alexandra, D., & Azuara, P. (2007). Las prácticas de lectoes-critura en los hogares de inmigrantes mexicanos [Home literacy practices in Mexican immigrant households]. *Cultura y Educación, 19*(4), 395–407. doi:10.1174/113564007783237760

Reyes, I., & Hernández, A.E. (2006). Sentence interpretation strategies in emergent bilingual children and adults. *Bilingualism: Language and Cognition,* 9(1), 51–69. doi:10.1017/S1366728905002373

Reyes, I., & Moll, L. (2008). Bilingual and biliterate practices at home and school. In B. Spolsky & F. Hult (Eds.), *The handbook of educational linguistics* (pp. 147–160). Malden, MA: Blackwell.

Reyes, M.L. (2001). Unleashing possibilities: Biliteracy in the primary grades. In M. Reyes de la Luz & J.J. Halcón (Eds.), *Best for our children: Critical perspectives on literacy for Latino students* (pp. 96–121). New York: Teachers College Press.

Rogoff, B. (1990). *Apprenticeship in thinking: Cognitive development in social context.* New York: Oxford University Press.

Romero, G. (1983). *Print aware ness of the preschool bilingual Spanish–English speaking child.* Unpublished doctoral dissertation, University of Arizona, Tucson.

Rowe, D. (2006, April). *Expanding the agenda for early literacy research: The potentials of reframing early literacy learning as social practice.* Paper presented at the annual meeting of the American Educational Research Association, San Francisco, CA.

Schwarzer, D. (2001). *Noah's ark: One child's voyage into multiliteracy.* Portsmouth, NJ: Heinemann.

Snow, C.E., Burns, M.S., & Griffin, P. (Eds.). (1998). *Preventing reading difficulties in young children.* Washington, DC: National Academy Press. Retrieved April 10, 2008, from www.nap.edu/catalog.php?record_id=6023#toc

Tabors, P., Paez, M., & Lopez, L. (2002, February). *Early childhood study of language and literacy development of Spanish-speaking children: Theoretical background and preliminary results.* Paper presented at the annual meeting of the National Association of Bilingual Education, Philadelphia, PA.

Tabors, P., & Snow, C.E. (2001). Young bilingual children and early literacy development. In S.B. Neuman & D.K. Dickinson (Eds.), *Handbook of early literacy research* (pp. 159–178). New York: Guilford.

Taylor, D., & Dorsey-Gaines, C. (1988). *Growing up literate: Learning from inner-city families.* Portsmouth, NH: Heinemann.

Teale, W.H. (1986). Home background and young children's literacy development. In W.H. Teale & E. Sulzby (Eds.), *Emergent literacy: Writing and reading* (pp. 173–206). Norwood, NJ: Ablex.

Tharp, R.G., & Gallimore, R. (1988). *Rousing minds to life: Teaching, learning, and schooling in social context.* Cambridge, England: Cambridge University Press.

Tolchinsky, L. (2003). *The cradle of culture and what children know about writing and numbers before being taught.* Mahwah, NJ: Erlbaum.

Verona, S. (1993). Initial sound/letter correspondence in children's early written productions. *Journal of Research in Childhood Education,* 8(1), 12–22.

Vygotsky, L.S. (1978). *Mind in society: The development of higher psychological processes* (M. Cole, V. John-Steiner, S. Scribner, & E. Souberman, Eds. & Trans.). Cambridge, MA: Harvard University Press.

Whitehurst, G.J., Epstein, J.N., Angell, A.L., Payne, A.C., Crone, D.A., & Fischel, J.E. (1994). Outcomes of an emergent literacy intervention in Head Start. *Journal of Educational Psychology, 86*(4), 542–555. doi:10.1037/0022-0663.86.4.542

Whitmore, K.F., Martens, P., Goodman, Y.M., & Owocki, G. (2004). Critical lessons from the transactional perspective on early literacy research. *Journal of Early Childhood Literacy,* 4(3), 291–325. doi:10.1177/1468798404047291

Williams, A. (2004). "Right, get your book bags!": Siblings playing school in multiethnic London. In E. Gregory, S. Long, & D. Volk (Eds.), *Many pathways to literacy: Young children learning with siblings, grandparents, peers and communities* (pp. 52–65). New York: Routledge.

Wood, D., & Fassnacht, C. (2005). *Transana software.* Wisconsin Center for Education Research, University of Wisconsin-Madison. Retrieved March 14, 2005, from transana.org

Yaden, D.B., Jr. (2008, February). *Some considerations on the nature and determinants of developmental change in the acquisition and growth of early literacy from developmental science.* Paper presented at the Martha King Colloquium Series, Ohio State University, Columbus.

Yaden, D.B., Jr., & Tardibuono, J.M. (2004). The emergent writing development of urban Latino preschoolers: Developmental perspectives and instructional environments for second-language learners. *Reading & Writing Quarterly,* 20(1), 29–61. doi:10.1080/10573560490242723

Zentella, A.C. (Ed.). (2005). *Building on strength: Language and literacy in Latino families and communities.* New York: Teachers College Press.

APPENDIX A

List of Items Used for the Environmental Print Task

Generic Name	Brand Name	Language
Tortillas	Dos Ranchitos	Bilingual
Refried beans	Rosarita	Bilingual
Chocolate drink mix	Nestle/Nesquik	English
Grocery bag	Food City	English
Cereal	Kellogg's Corn Flakes	English
Toothpaste	Colgate	Bilingual
Soda	Coca-Cola	Bilingual
Fries	McDonald's	English
Pizza	Domino's Pizza	English
Street sign	Stop sign	English

APPENDIX B

Coding Scheme for Environmental Print Task

1. Not recognized (NR): The response was not related to the item shown.
2. Function (F): The child named the function of the item (e.g., "*para lavarte los dientes*" [to brush your teeth] instead of Colgate).
3. Generic (GN): The child's response included the generic name of the item but not the exact brand name (e.g., toothpaste instead of Colgate).
4. Other brand name (OBN): The child responded with the name of a different brand (e.g., Pepsi instead of Coca-Cola).
5. Partial brand name (PBN): The child's response included part of the brand name (e.g., Coca instead of Coca-Cola).
6. Exact brand name (EBN): The child responded with the exact brand of the item as printed on the label (e.g., Domino's Pizza).

APPENDIX C

Domains of Activity Related to Literacy

The following is adapted from Heath (1983) and Teale (1986).

1. Daily Living Routines. This domain of activity is concerned with the ongoing recurrent practices of everyday life: obtaining food, maintaining shelter, participating in what is required by social institutions, maintaining the social organization of the family, and so forth (e.g., shopping, cooking, paying bills, traveling from one place to another, maintaining welfare assistance, washing clothes, getting appliances or automobiles repaired).

2. Entertainment. Literacy can mediate entertainment activities in three different ways. First, literacy itself can be the *source* of the entertainment (reading a novel, doing a crossword puzzle). Second, literacy can be instrumental to entertainment when it is used to select, find out about, or in some other way facilitate or maintain participation in an entertaining activity (e.g., reading a television guide). Third, literacy can be incidental to entertainment (e.g., if a child is watching cartoons on television and there are several written signs that appear at various times during the cartoon).
3. School-Related Activity. This domain of activity is directly related to the social institution of school (e.g., letters from the principal, consent forms, announcements, as well as homework that involve reading and/or writing).
4. Work. This domain of literacy relates directly to employment (e.g., filling out forms for catalog orders or receipts for rent collected, reading a technical manual). Also, literacy related to securing or maintaining employment (e.g., reading classified advertisements, reading a flyer from the employer explaining work-force cutback procedures).
5. Religion. This domain of literacy relates to family members' religious activities linked directly to the social institution of church (e.g., Bible reading, Bible study sessions, the use of the Bible study/interpretation guides, and reading of children's pamphlets from Sunday school).
6. Interpersonal Communication. Literacy is used to communicate with friends, relatives, or other persons physically or temporally distant (e.g., sending Christmas and birthday cards with handwritten messages on them, reading a letter from a friend in another state, and writing a letter to grandparents).
7. Participating in "Information Networks." Literacy in this case is used to gain information for which there is no immediately discernible use and no direct link to any of the previously mentioned social institutions, school, church, or work (e.g., reading regularly or irregularly the sports section of the newspaper).
8. Storybook Time. This activity consists of book-reading episodes in which an adult (e.g., parent, grandparent) or an older sibling reads to the child at bedtime or at another time during the day.
9. Literacy for the Sake of Teaching/Learning Literacy. In this category, the focus of the activity is to help another person to learn to read and/or write or when the target child reads/writes or attempts to read/write for the sake of learning about reading/writing.
10. Cultural Heritage. In this category, the literacy event directly relates to an aspect of the family's cultural background (e.g., learning about a family tradition, such as *posadas*, an Hispanic Christian feast that commemorates the journey of Mary and Joseph to Bethlehem in preparation for the birth of Jesus and can include a piñata, Mexican hot chocolate, *pan dulce* [sweet bread], and music in its celebration).

CHAPTER 10

Revisiting Is October Brown Chinese? A Cultural Modeling Activity System for Underachieving Students

Carol D. Lee, Northwestern University

As individuals, we problem solve in the world by drawing on what Wertsch (1991) calls a psychological tool kit or what Bruner (1990) calls a communal tool kit, which includes symbol systems that are inherited and reinterpreted across generations, rooted deeply in culture and history. Language is perhaps the most ubiquitous tool kit we have for sense making, an extraordinarily complex resource that inherently entails what Bakhtin (1981) calls dialogicality, that is, the ways in which our utterances are influenced by the voices behind and ahead of that which we hear and say. I explore these ideas about the semiotic potential and dialogic nature of learning through language in relation to instructional discourse in a freshman English language arts classroom in an underachieving African American high school.

There are commonalities in the arguments articulated by Wertsch, Bruner, and Bakhtin. First, the quality of thought demonstrated by individuals is constructed out of interactions with others. Second, these others include those with whom individuals have direct contact as well as historical others from whom cultural forms of talk, reasoning, and artifacts have been embedded in traditions.

This article is about a group of African American high school freshmen. By all traditional criteria, they would be considered underachievers. They are disengaged from schooling and speak variations of English that many see as indices of underdevelopment. However, if the claims of Vygotsky, Bakhtin, Wertsch, Bruner, and others are reasonable, then African American students who speak African American English Vernacular both participate in and inherit semiotic potential grounded in their use of language, ways of reasoning, thinking about the world, and thinking about story. If these claims are reasonable, then the quality of academic work produced by underachieving students must be understood not only in terms of what occurs in their homes, with their families, and with their peers in neighborhood life but also in terms of what goes on in the daily life of classrooms in which they participate year in and year out. In the effort to teach students who speak varieties of English not valued by the academy or languages other than English, or students whose families live in poverty, it is very important to understand the intersections

This chapter is adapted from "Is October Brown Chinese? A Cultural Modeling Activity System for Underachieving Students," *American Educational Research Journal, 38*(1), 97–141.

between the ways that students use language and reason in their home and community experiences and the routine practices of classrooms.

This article offers an analysis of a day of instruction in an English language arts classroom in an underachieving high school, Fairgate, serving African American students. I provide an analysis of the activity of the day in question and document the history of the classroom activity that led to the development of an intellectual community within the class. I also describe the ways in which the students' cultural funds of knowledge (Moll & Greenberg, 1990) were incorporated to support learning. I use as a unit of analysis Bourdieu's (1990) construct of *habitus*, which is defined by Duranti (1997) as "a system of dispositions with historical dimensions through which novices acquire competence by entering activities through which they develop a series of expectations about the world and about ways of being in it" (p. 44). I document the historical antecedents that shaped the students' expectations about participation in the culture of this classroom, as well as the ways in which the culture of this classroom was explicitly linked to particular routine practices from the students' experiences in their home communities. Although this article concentrates on the teaching of literature, the principles of curriculum design, instructional routines, and pedagogical knowledge apply across subject matters.

Background

Fairgate High School is in an urban district that has been known historically for its poor schools. Over the past two decades, middle class White and Black families have left the city to avoid sending their children to the public schools in that area. In the last 12 years, the district has undergone radical reorganization. One major focus of this reorganization has been to shift increasing power to the local school community, including parents, community residents, and teachers. Although this reform has been useful in engaging parents and community members in a number of schools, it has had marginal large-scale impact on the quality of education for most students in the district, especially at the high school level. Even though there has been substantive improvement across years of accountability-based reform efforts, students still achieve well below national norms, the discrepancies being greatest for African American and Latino youngsters.

Fairgate High School is an all-Black high school. Sixty-nine percent of its students are from low-income families. At the time of the intervention described in this article, the 1994–1995 graduation rate was 65%, in contrast to the state graduation rate of 80%. In 1995, 73% of Fairgate's sophomores did not meet the basic goals of the state-mandated achievement test in reading, 25% met state goals, and only 2% exceeded those goals. The average ACT score in reading for all students who took the exam was 15.4. For students who completed a core high school program, their average was 13.7. These numbers are in contrast to the state reading average of 23.1. This is a school in transition, with a faculty and administration who are working hard to transform the school. One of the school's reform programs is the Cultural Modeling Project.

The class described in this article is part of the Cultural Modeling Project, which supports the empowerment of the English departments in urban high schools through curriculum development, technology infusion, professional development, and assessment. It is based on the premise that students bring to the language arts classroom a rich array of knowledge that is useful for learning generative concepts and strategies in reading and writing. Although the project focuses on African American students who speak African American English Vernacular, it has implications for students from other speech communities whose language variety is devalued in the broader U.S. culture (Lee & Slaughter-Defoe, 1995). The framework on which the project is based posits that strategic knowledge of the ways that literary authors embed meaning in tropes and certain literary forms is necessary to negotiate rich literary texts. The quality of response to literature that the project seeks to develop goes beyond summaries of plot. An idealized response includes personal, empathetic responses, as well as responses to form and structure. Readers must come to the literary text with a mental model (Perkins, 1992) of language play as a worthwhile end in itself for communication. Adolescents who speak African American English Vernacular demonstrate in their daily language use outside of classrooms a rich understanding of and appreciation for language play. This language play is demonstrated most directly in a genre of talk known as signifying, although it is evident in many other forms of talk that are part of the African American rhetorical tradition (Smitherman, 1977).

Signifying has been passed down from one generation to another within the African American speech community since the Holocaust of Enslavement, referred ubiquitously by many simply as slavery (with the implicit assumption that *slave* and *African American* are synonymous). Signifying may involve, but is not limited to, ritual insult. One specialized category of signifying is called playing the dozens, as exemplified in phrases like "Your mother is so fat, she got hit by a car and the car sued for body damages" (Percelay, Ivey, & Dweck, 1994, p. 49). Other categories of signifying include rapping, loud talking, and marking (Mitchell-Kernan, 1981; Smitherman, 1977). Signifying always involves indirection and double entendre and invites participants to look beyond the surface meaning to subtle interpretations to be inferred. It is vivid in its use of metaphor and often involves satire, irony, and shifts in point of view. African American adolescents who routinely participate in such talk make tacit use of strategies for interpreting metaphors, symbols, irony, and satire. These same strategies are required to negotiate literary texts in which such tropes and literary constructs operate to communicate meaning that must be inferred. Lee (1992, 1993, 1995a, 1995b, 1996, 1997) developed an instructional strategy that involves having students analyze samples of signifying dialogues to determine the intended meanings for each turn of talk, and then extrapolate the strategies they used to construct these inferred meanings. Through this process, the students make public and explicit their knowledge of strategies they routinely use that have been intuitive and implicit. They then apply the same strategies to literary texts in which characters communicate using African American English Vernacular and in which signifying and other oral genres are appropriated and manipulated by writers for literary purposes. Such texts have included works by Zora Neale Hurston, Alice Walker, Toni Cade Bambara, and Toni Morrison. Jones (1991) offers an excellent analysis of the appropriation of oral forms in African American fiction, and Gates (1988) provides an excellent analysis of the appropriation of signifying as a literary trope in African American fiction. The idea behind the Cultural Modeling Project is that African American English Vernacular offers a fertile bridge for scaffolding literary response, rather than a deficit to be overcome.

Another view of the project is that prior knowledge is powerful in the reader's negotiation with rich literary texts. Literature constructs a social world that the reader is invited to enter. Readers are expected to enter a subjunctive world, which may be very different from their experiences. The readers' skill, use of reading strategies, and history of reading other texts allow them to enter a text world that is distant from their own experiences. The negotiation process with unfamiliar story worlds is difficult for novice readers, those who lack strong reading strategies, and those who have little history of reading many different kinds of literary texts. This difficulty often results in disengagement on the part of novice readers and an inability to generate an efferent aesthetic response to the text (Rosenblatt, 1978). For this reason, a strategy of the Cultural Modeling Project is to sequence texts so the initial set of texts for any unit are ones for which they have relevant knowledge of the social codes operating in the text while they are developing powerful strategies for reading literature. Texts in later units are ones for which students have less prior social knowledge, but for which over time they have developed a set of strategies that help them compensate for limitations of prior social knowledge relevant to a given text.[1] In the class discussion that is the focus of this article, the students have consequential prior knowledge that enhances the quality of interpretations they offer and their level of engagement with the text.

The class in question is taught by this researcher. During the first year of the project at Fairgate, four other teachers from the English department implemented the framework with the entire freshman class at the school. Teachers met over the summer prior to the school year and read a variety of materials on African American English Vernacular, response to literature, composition, and constructivist learning theories. They were asked to confront their assumptions about the language spoken by their students and to understand what intellectual and cultural capital their students contributed to the English language arts classroom that could be productively tapped. This researcher taught one class in the school for two reasons: (1) to understand the process of implementing such a framework and (2) to develop a peerlike relationship with the faculty in order to promote mutual understanding and communication over the three years of the project. The second year of the project focused on the sophomore and junior classes, and the third year focused on the seniors. By the end of the third year of the project, the entire school had used the framework of the Cultural Modeling Project. By the second year of the project, the entire English department faculty participated.

The classes taught by this researcher were videotaped daily. The videotapes and student work provided the data on which the analysis in this article is based.

Is October Brown Chinese?

Rattlebone by Maxine Claire (1994) was the first novel selected for the freshman class. *Rattlebone* is an imaginatively structured novel that consists of a series of related short stories that cohere around the experiences of a girl named Irene Wilson and her family and friends during the 1950s in Kansas City. The novel employs extraordinarily vivid language, with an imaginative use of African American English Vernacular, and illustrates a subtle unearthing of sociocultural values grounded in African American historical experiences. On this particular day of instruction, the class had completed several days of activities involving answering questions about the opening chapter, "October Brown," that required close reading. "October Brown" is told from the point of view of a child narrator, Irene. October Brown is the teacher in a segregated African American elementary school. Not only is she educated, but also she has tastes that distinguish her from the working-class families of the children she teaches. Below is a summary of key elements in the story, which is necessary to understand the class discussion.

October Brown teaches in a segregated school in Kansas City in the 1950s. Her students are from poor families. However, October Brown is well educated and dresses and eats her lunch in ways that clearly distinguish her from the working-class families whose children she teaches. There is a running reference to rumors that suggest the children and their families are jealous of October Brown. In the beginning of the story, we are told that "We heard it from our friends, who got it from their near-eye-witness grandmothers and their must-be-psychic neighbor ladies" that when she was a child, October Brown's father killed her mother in a fit of rage. Thereafter, the rumor goes, the Devil visited October Brown and marked her face with a white spot the neighbors called "a Devil's kiss" (Claire, 1994, p. 3).

The child protagonist, Irene Wilson, is sent to school after her mother and father had a fight. Her mother is pregnant, and during the fight, the father inadvertently pushed her down the steps. He reports the accident over the party line telephone. Thus, Irene is embarrassed when she is called to the blackboard because she believes her rumor-mongering classmates are aware that her father pushed her mother down the stairs, and Irene sucks the chalk while standing at the blackboard.

Later in the school year, there is a huge snow blizzard. For the first time, Irene's father visits school to bring food for the children in the class from the mothers in the neighborhood. October Brown, who wears dresses "draped at her waist or flounced, crepe with sequined dragons and peacocks, glittery butterflies, dresses that shone like the sun in the drab circle of dark clothes dark girls wore at the rear of the classroom" (Claire, 1994, p. 6), offers Irene's father, James, part of her lunch:

> She peeled her orange, dangled her legs in the aisle. She held it out to him, a flower offering on a china plate. He shook his head no. She ate one section, cherry-slick fingertips into cherry-red lips, so proper....
>
> Smiling, she touched the many-colored, parrot-appliquéd shoulder of her dress. (p. 12)

There is a subtle allusion suggesting that October Brown may be trying to seduce Irene's father.

This article offers an analysis of one day of class discussion of the opening chapter, "October Brown," and a history of the culture of class activity out of which this day was constructed over time. For analytical purposes, the discussion is divided into three episodes, each of which revolves around one or more discussion questions.

In the first episode, the teacher[2] asks the question, "What does the narrator mean when she says they were on opposite ends of the same track?" This question refers to the scene where Irene's mother and father were fighting:

> They were on opposite ends of the same track, and I knew from time and again that they would both speed up, bear down until they had only inches left between them, then they would both fall back and rumble until silence prevailed. (Claire, 1994, pp. 7–8)

The students were required to attend to the metaphor and symbolism of these lines.

In the second episode, one question is posed by the teacher, and two are posed independently by students. The teacher's question, "Why does Irene suck chalk?," refers to the section in the story where Irene is called to the front of the class while embarrassed, imagining that particular students whose families share the party line telephone with her family are aware that Irene's father pushed her pregnant mother down the stairs, and at the same time worried about her mother and the baby. Again, this question demands attention to an image that is both metaphorical and symbolic: "Certain that my mother's fall was preface to disaster, I stood there at the blackboard with the chalk in my mouth, sucking on the fact that one or the other, mother or baby, would die" (Claire, 1994, p. 8). The teacher's question is followed by two questions initiated by students. The first student question on the surface is unrelated to the focus the teacher is attempting to establish. The student asks, "How come *a*, *l*, and *b* are capitalized on the cover of the book?" This is a reference to the graphics of the title on the cover of the book, *rAttLeBOnE*. A second student asks a question that implicitly directs the class's attention to the similarities between the fact that Irene's father pushed her pregnant mother down the stairs and the rumor that October Brown's father killed her mother:

> We heard it from our friends, who got it from their near-eye-witness grandmothers and their must-be-psychic neighbor ladies, that when she was our same age, our teacher, Miss October Brown, watched her father fire through his rage right on into her mother's heart....The story went on that immediately thereafter, Satan himself had made a visitation to October Brown, and from that time until the year she became our grown-woman schoolteacher, the burnt brown of her left cheek was marked by a wavery spot of white: a brand, a Devil's kiss. (Claire, 1994, p. 3)

The third episode is driven entirely by an assertion posed by a student: "I think October Brown is Chinese." Although it is never explicitly stated, the clear inference is that October Brown and her students are Black. Thus, a highly provocative volley of discussion follows this young man's assertion.

Analysis of Discourse

I have analyzed the transcript from that day's discussion to determine the underlying structure of what occurred that day. The focus of the discussion was driven by the questions on the floor. The transcript was divided into three instructional episodes, each focusing on a question or series of related questions. The analysis then examines student and teacher talk in order to make assertions about the reasoning processes in which these students engaged as well as the sources of support for that reasoning.

Episode 1: On Opposite Ends of the Same Track

The first episode revolves around a teacher-generated question: "What does the narrator mean when she says, 'They were on opposite ends of the same track'?" (p. 7). The question refers to a scene in which Irene's parents had been arguing. To arrive at a warrantable response, readers must engage in analogical reasoning. Readers must reject a literal interpretation of the line "they were on opposite ends of the same track" and infer an unstated relationship between the image of trains on a railroad track and the relationship between Irene's parents. Table 1 summarizes associations that can be made between references to the track image in the text and patterns of activity carried out by the parents.

I provide an idealized model of text analysis to attack the question as well as the pattern of reasoning in which the students engaged. Students had to recognize pronoun referents, use prior knowledge, and hypothesize a warrantable generalization.

- Students had to recognize that "they" in paragraph 2 refers to Irene's parents.
- Students had to recognize that the reference to people being on the opposite ends of the same track does not fit what had been described in the scene so far.
- Students had to reason that the reference to the tracks must not be literal.
- Students had to note patterns in the text that relate to the image of the people on the track.

Table 1. Question 1: *Rattlebone* by Maxine Claire[a]

Track References in the Text	Parallel Patterns in the Text Related to Irene's Parents' Relationship	Prior Knowledge Associations
1. "opposite ends" (p. 7)	1. Parents arguing	1. Two train cars
2. "speed up" (p. 7)	2. Mother follows father up stairs, "not letting up."	2. Engine moving
3. "fall back" (p. 8)	3. Later father would bring home sherbet, and mother would rub his back.	3. Social relationships
4. "same track" (p. 7)	4. Same text as 3	4. Railroad track

[a]Claire, M. (1994). *Rattlebone*. New York: Penguin.

- Students had to use prior knowledge of tracks and make warrantable potential associations between what they know about tracks and the pattern they notice in the text.
- Students had to hypothesize a generalization based on the analysis of the patterns and their world knowledge.
- Students had to test that hypothesis against the scenario in the text.

I note the pattern of reasoning in which the students successfully engaged for several reasons. With few exceptions, these students score in the bottom two quartiles of the distribution in standardized scores of reading comprehension. However, the practices in which they engage in order to respond to the teacher's question are consistent with research on the strategies that more expert readers invoke (Pearson & Fielding, 1991), the self-monitoring that characterizes better readers (Garner, 1987), and the literary inferences that more experienced readers of fiction routinely construct (van den Broek, 1996). The script is clearly teacher directed in this episode (Gutierrez, Rymes, & Larson, 1995), but the reasoning is still at a high level. Although the level of reasoning is advanced, the distribution of talk is limited to a few students. What should be the balance between teacher-directed scripts and student-initiated norms for discourse remains an open question, which is of particular import when orchestrating intellectually rigorous discussions among low-achieving students (Delpit, 1986; Gutierrez et al., 1995; Nystrand & Gamoran, 1997; Wells, 1995).

Episode 2: A Shift to Student-Generated Questions

The second instructional episode differs from the first in that the questions on which the discussion focuses are generated by both the teacher and students. The emergence of student-generated questions marks an important shift in the activity of the class and in the level and distribution of student engagement in the discussion. The student-generated questions are complex in at least two ways. One question is explicitly stated. Shanee[3] asked, "How come *a*, *l*, and *b* are capitalized on the cover of the book?" Gutierrez et al. (1995) writes about the need to examine the "counterscripts" of classroom discourse. Counterscripts focus on issues that are different from the immediate goals of the teacher. Often, they are pockets of activity viewed by the teacher as being disruptive. Although the student-generated questions are not direct outgrowths of the focus initially established by the teacher, in a sense constituting a counterscript, they are still consistent with the larger, long-range goals of the teacher in terms of apprenticing the students into sophisticated literary analyses.

In addition, during the second instructional episode, Shanee and Marilyn coconstructed two additional questions. The coconstruction evolves from an interchange they initiate with each other. The questions are actually implied rather than directly stated. Shanee said, "In the beginning, October Brown's father killed her mother, right? Her mama and father arguing. Her dad made her fall down the steps." As will happen again in the next instructional episode, a creative attention to "errors" opens up space for provocative literary debate. Marilyn corrected Shanee: "That's Irene." Shanee has linked two parallel incidents in the story, namely, the fight between October Brown's parents and the resulting violence reported as rumor in the very beginning of the story, and the fight between Irene's parents that resulted in Irene's mother falling down the steps of the house while she is pregnant. Implicit in the interchange that ensues are the following questions:

- What are we to make of the similarities between what happened between October Brown's parents and what is happening between Irene's parents?
- Who is talking when it is reported that Irene's daddy made her mama fall down the steps, and how was this incident known by a student in Irene's class?

In the process of exploring these two questions as well as the question explicitly asked by the teacher ("Why does Irene suck chalk?"), the students end up focusing on and interpreting oxymorons, text that represent subtle interpretations of point of view, as well as attending to warnings in the narrator's voice. The paragraph that described Irene's chagrin when fellow student Jewel Hicks, "the pink-ribboned, talks-too-much, needs-her-butt-beat Jewel daughter of the on-our-party-line Mrs. Hicks" (p. 8), shouts out, "Her daddy made her mama fall down the steps and her mama's going to have a baby" (p. 9), is replete with oxymorons:

> Wailing is the sound you make to straighten out a **tangled throat** so that you can breathe, and to spill tears from **boiling eyes** so that you can see your "**Come on, Irene**" **way out into the hall**. Our janitor pushing his T-broom nodded, "How do, Miss Brown" in the dimness of the hallway, and the **cedar-sawdust-muted click of her high-heeled shoes** comforted me as much as her arm around my shoulders all the way to the girl's restroom while I cried myself into hiccups. (Claire, 1994, p. 9, emphases added)

I have marked in boldface the oxymorons and metaphors that posed interpretive challenges to the students. The students had to link problems of prior knowledge, in this case the use of the old-fashioned party telephone line, as warrants in arguments about problems of point of view. For example, how did Jewel Hicks's mother think she knew what had happened between Irene's parents? Additional problems of point of view are encountered through warnings in the author's or narrator's voice, as when Irene says (reflecting not merely her point of view but also that of the author), "Certain that my mother's fall was preface to disaster" (p. 8). This is a problem of point of view because the narrator shifts throughout the story from the voice of Irene to that of an omniscient narrator who shares values with the author. The disaster being foreshadowed is more than the physical health of Irene's mother and the baby in the womb. Jewel Hicks's revelation that Irene's father made Mrs. Wilson fall down the steps leads students to question whether the assertions made about October Brown's parents are believable, which in turn is a question about point of view and the reliability of the point of view of characters. Problems of point of view are among the most sophisticated and challenging of enduring literary questions (Booth, 1983). The focus on interpretive problems of point of view in this episode was not initiated by the teacher but by students—students with standardized reading scores that would not predict their initiation of such complex interpretive problems, let alone their ability to handle such problems with rigor.

The second instructional episode is revealing as a transitional phase in the interactions of this day's activity. First, the questions posed by the teacher in this and the first episode as well as the questions posed explicitly and implicitly by students share crucial attributes. They are questions for which there are no simple right or wrong answers. Each requires complex inferencing, and two focus on actions in the plot that serve symbolic functions in the text (in addition to the book cover question posed by Shanee). These shared norms represent an evolving epistemological stance being constructed in the culture of this classroom. Although the questions are posed by two students, there is widespread conversation initiated by the students in response to these questions. If the student-initiated questions were only relevant or valued by the two students who posed them, the level of student interaction in responding to the questions likely would not have occurred. This happens often in classrooms where teachers pose interpretive questions that mean little to the students who do not respond. In addition, the norms for arguing or debating these questions are shared by other students in the class. For example, using the interchange around the teacher's question, "Why did Irene suck chalk?," Trevor, Shanee, Marilyn, and Anthony all offer competing interpretations, cite textual evidence to support their claims, and recall real-world warrants to argue for the reasonableness of their interpretations. Figure 1 offers a graphic representation of the epistemological norms for interpretation in this episode.

Episode 3: Error as Opportunity

The third instructional episode is initiated and dominated by a question posed by a young man, Yetu. Yetu believes that October Brown is Chinese. For the purposes of analysis, I have divided the course of discussion into these three distinct episodes, categorized according to the questions on the floor. However, the divisions are arbitrary. Once the students have begun to pursue the questions raised by Shanee and Marilyn, which occurs about midway through the second episode, the interactional space has completely changed since the first episode. The discussion abounds with multiparty talk. Students are talking at the same time, responding to one another, and responding to several questions on the floor at once. The role of the teacher has dramatically shifted from one who directs conversation in the classroom to that of a coach who tries to make space for each voice to be heard by the entire group. Although not the specific focus of this article, it is important to note that the talk among the students is entirely in African American English Vernacular, not simply in terms of vernacular syntax forms, but more importantly in terms of the performance of the discourse.

Figure 1. Episode 2: Establishing Epistemological Norms for Interpretation and Classroom Discourse: *Rattlebone* by Maxine Claire[a]

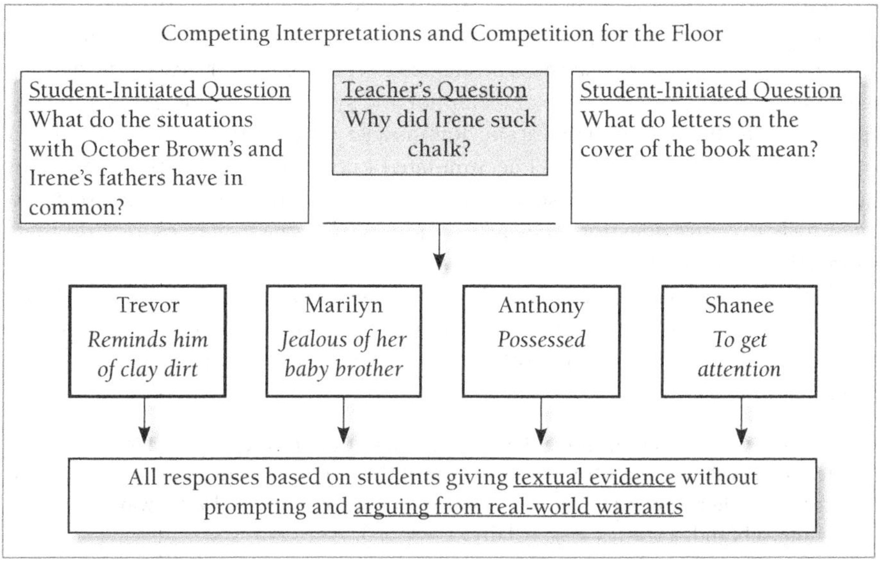

[a]Claire, M. (1994). *Rattlebone*. New York: Penguin.

Students signify on one another,[4] display body language for emphasis, and reflect a rhythm and prosody in their speech that is dramatic and culturally Black. When Yetu hypothesized that October Brown was Chinese, he was bombarded with responses from students.

Yetu's question is exciting for several reasons. As with Shanee's earlier question about possible parallels between October Brown's parents and Irene's parents, Yetu's question easily can be construed as an error (although I have no doubt that a deconstructionist critic could well launch a warrantable argument that October Brown could be Chinese). As is the case with pedagogical techniques in some reform mathematics classrooms (Lampert, 1990; Stevenson & Stigler, 1992), attention to errors may reveal complex forms of reasoning pursued by students, even though they do not get the "right" answer. Yetu had paid attention to particular details used to describe October Brown:

> She peeled her orange, dangled her legs in the aisle. She held it out to him, a flower offering on a china plate....She looked eyes-through-hair at him. She snapped straight and threw the mass of hair back....
>
> Smiling, she touched the many-colored, parrot-appliquéd shoulder of her dress. (Claire, 1994, p. 12)

Underlying Yetu's claim is an implicit process of literary reasoning in which he (a) infers that an abundance of detail signifies importance, (b) looks for patterns in the detail, (c) makes real-world associations with the patterns in the textual details, (d) hypothesizes a generalization that supports the patterns he sees, (e) evaluates the reasonableness of his hypothesis based on the details in the text and what he knows about the world, and (f) infers that external or physical images may represent an internal trait of the character. Strategies b–e are both literary and generic. Readers use these strategies to construct inferences, and literary readers use them to make sense of metaphor and symbolism. Strategies a and f are specialized to literary interpretation. Rabinowitz (1987) argues that specialized strategies are part of the pool of accumulated knowledge from which readers of fiction draw as they make sense of diverse texts. As all but four students respond vigorously to Yetu's question, they also summon the same strategies to build their supporting and counterclaims.

Yetu is asked by the teacher why he believes October Brown is Chinese. Yetu directs the class to the details cited above. Several students (not Shanee or Marilyn) contradict Yetu, citing other textual evidence from the beginning of the story:

> The story went on that immediately thereafter, Satan himself had made a visitation to October Brown, and from that time until the year she became our grown-woman schoolteacher, the burnt brown of her left cheek was marked by a wavery spot of white: a brand, a Devil's kiss. (Claire, 1994, p. 3)

Students reference this section of the text as proof that October Brown has "burnt brown" colored skin.

At that point, an intense debate ensues about how to determine whether a person is Chinese. A young man, Marcus, who has been so disruptive that he has been escorted out of the class to sit for a while in the hall, reenters the discussion. On the videotape of the class on that day, Marcus can be seen consciously making markedly grimaced faces at the camera, making faces at a female student sitting next to him, and generally acting out the essence of what Gutierrez et al. (1995) characterizes as student counterscripts. As Marcus is being escorted out of the class by the teacher and other students are talking "out of turn," Marilyn shouts out, "HEY, excu::se me. y'a::ll so RUDE!...> ^You [referring to the teacher] need to kick his BUTT <ou::t this class."[5] Persons without insider knowledge of the nature and history of the raucously loud, overlapping, multiparty talk would most likely view the interchanges as out of turn and disruptive. Marcus returns to class in the midst of the debate over whether October Brown is Chinese. Monica says, after quoting from the text about the burnt brown color of October Brown's skin, "Chinese people ain't brown." Marcus responds for the first time in the class discussion, "Yeah they is....They brown; they brown skinnded." Marcus's comment is interesting because what he is doing, albeit unconsciously, is refuting the textual evidence referring to the color of October Brown's skin as sufficient proof of her being Black rather than Chinese. He essentially questions the warrants on which definitions of being Chinese are based. Marcus suggests that if Chinese people have "colored" skin, then that reference in the text is not sufficient evidence to prove Monica's

position. Patricia then introduces a different body of textual evidence based on a different set of warrants: "Chinese women have the dresses where they have the like, uhh, sequined dragons and glittery butterflies and, you know, all that. Like the sun." Another student responds to Patricia, "Maybe she just like Chinese customs." A hotly debated conversation continues around the central question of what it means to be Chinese. This debate is significant because it is an intellectual argument over warrants in pursuit of literary inquiry. Both Kuhn (1991) and Toulmin, Rieke, and Janik (1984) contend that appeals to warrants represent the most sophisticated forms of argumentative reasoning. A debate over literary warrants—that is, what counts as credible evidence for a hypothesis when the text itself is insufficient—was initiated and sustained by low-achieving high school freshmen. The class debate provides additional evidence that an epistemology of literary inquiry was evolving as routine practice in this classroom.

The interactional space typical of the second and especially the third episode is represented by one stretch of talk captured in Figure 2. The interactional space is entirely dominated and directed by students. Students initiate comments to one another, contradict one another, and always cite textual evidence and real-world warrants to support their claims.

Figure 2. Episode 3: Typical Interactional Space Dominated by Students

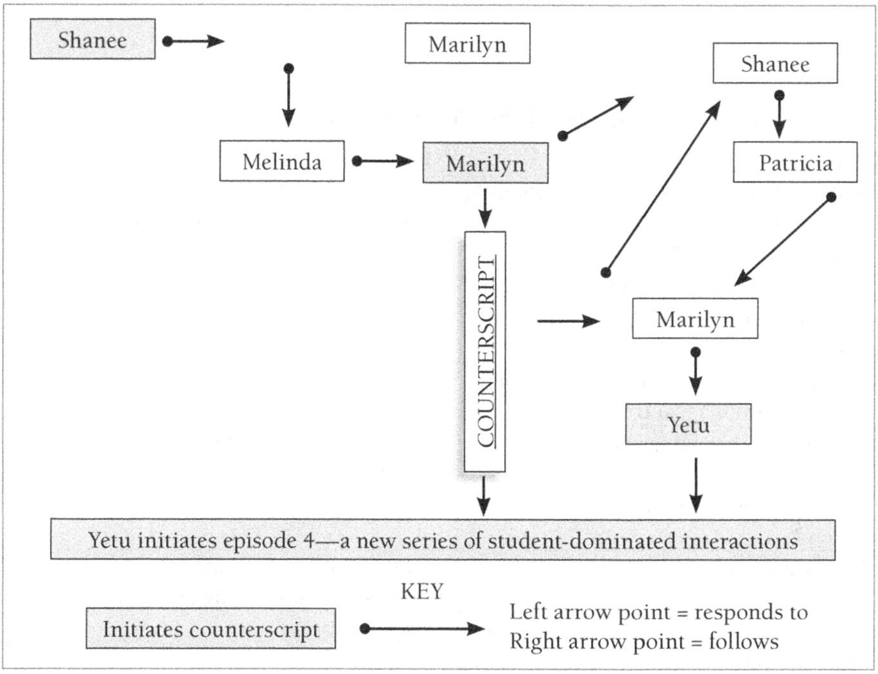

Shifts in Who Scaffolds Learning Across Episodes

The beginning and ending of the episodes are marked by changes in the questions around which instructional discussion occurs. One pattern that marks the shifts is the movement from interpretive discussion initiated by questions posed by the teacher to questions posed by both the teacher and students, and finally to questions posed by students. After ascertaining this pattern, the shifts in who was scaffolding within each episode emerged in the analysis. Scaffolding may be viewed as activities by a more knowledgeable person to provide temporary support for those who are learning. The temporary support may focus on strategies, norms for reasoning, and generally more expertlike ways of solving a kind of problem (Collins, Brown, & Newman, 1989).[6]

After the first question posed by the teacher ("Why does Irene suck chalk?"), there is not the multiparty overlapping enthusiastic talk that is typical of Episodes 2 and 3. The teacher poses a series of questions that break down the steps in order to figure out a way of thinking about a question about a symbol in the text. The questions posed by the teacher (Table 2) model for the students how to reason. The questions invoke the need to examine the text for evidence and to weigh the reasonableness of one's propositions. Posed by the teacher, the questions scaffold the reasoning processes from which students draw. Each student responds to the reasoning questions, but there is little interaction among students.

By the second episode, scaffolding is shared by two other students, Marilyn and Shanee. When Shanee raises the question about October Brown's parents and Irene's parents, implying that there were parallels in the two subplots, Marilyn challenges her.

Table 2. Scaffolding Sequence 1: *Rattlebone* by Maxine Claire[a]

Episode 1	Function
1. What does the narrator mean when she says, "They were on opposite sides of the same track"? (p. 7)	(Nos. 1–4) Model and coach—how to reason through a question based on interpreting a symbol.
2. Who are they talking about?	
3. What are the mother's and father's names?	
4. When they talk about tracks, are they talking about a real track?	
5. Let's read that paragraph.	(No. 5) Examine text for supporting evidence.
6. What is the comparison being made here?	
7. How do you know?	(No. 7) Weigh reasonableness of your proposition by drawing on text and world knowledge.

[a]Claire, M. (1994). *Rattlebone*. New York: Penguin.

Shanee: At the beginning of this book it said that October Brown's father had killed her mother. Right?

T: Uh huh.

Shanee: And then it's a part in this book where uhh I forget, let me see [flips through pages in her book], it says when her mama was going to, no her mother and her father was arguing, and then she said her daddy made her mama fall down the steps and she going to have her baby.

Marilyn: That's Irene, uhh, mother and father.

Shanee: I know but then at the beginning on the first page it say

Marilyn: That's October's father did that to her mother,

Shanee: I know but then at the beginning on the first page it say

Marilyn: That's October's father did that to her mother.

Shanee: I know but it but I believe that it's something in common because it say [inaudible comment from a student out of the camera's view. The camera pans around the room. Most students are looking at their books and quietly listening.]

Shanee: Yeah, her father.

Marilyn: But now that wasn't done on purpose. Read through it. That was not done on purpose. That was a rumor, that was a rumor. She accidentally fell down the steps. That was a rumor that uhh, that he made her uhh fall down the steps. (transcript, lines 361–381, November 1, 1995)

In this interchange between Marilyn and Shanee, Shanee models a powerful strategy for literary interpretation based on structuralist principles (Culler, 1975). She notes parallels in elements of the plot, attends to the details through which those elements are communicated, and is ready to hypothesize a generalization that the two elements may represent a common proposition or at least have something in common as Shanee notes. In her role as coach in this evolving apprenticeship,[7] the teacher makes public and explicit what Shanee has done so she and others in the class may have access to this as strategic knowledge that is applicable to other cases in this reading and future texts they may study or read.

Marilyn adds another dimension of modeling in the full interchange. She models that the norms for interpretation and discussion, at least in this class, impart that it is okay to challenge others and that the warrants on which counterclaims are made should be based on textual evidence. Marilyn says to Shanee, "Read it through. It was not done on purpose. That was a rumor." Marilyn also weighs alternative interpretations, again against textual evidence:

T: What about October Brown and her father?

Marilyn: That's a fact; probably is not because kids said that. (transcript, lines 384–385, November 1, 1995)

Marilyn is willing to change her interpretation when confronted with disconfirming textual evidence; she also seeks the evidence on her own. In the scaffolding

Table 3. Scaffolding Sequence 2: *Rattlebone* by Maxine Claire[a]

Episode 2	Function
Marilyn: Read it through. It was not done on purpose. That was a rumor.	Marilyn invokes norms for evidence—read it.
Teacher: What about October Brown and her father?	
Marilyn: That's a fact; probably is not because kids said that.	Marilyn weighs evidence and alters her hypothesis.
Teacher: You've (referring to Marilyn and Shanee) done something powerful; looking for things happening to different characters, but seem to be the same; they're there for a purpose; good readers think about that.	Teacher makes explicit the powerful heuristic students have invoked without being conscious of the heuristic.
Marilyn: People spread rumors about Irene, but that was just rumors; and they spread rumors about October Brown.	
Teacher: If the author consciously put details there, why; who is the author trying to say something about? These are wonderful details.	Teacher makes explicit through the question another set of important assumptions about literary texts necessary for close textual analysis.

[a]Claire, M. (1994). *Rattlebone.* New York: Penguin.

sequence in Episode 2, the major modeling is carried out by two students in the class rather than by the teacher. Table 3 summarizes the key scaffolding moves by the two students and the teacher and the function each serves in moving the instructional conversation forward.

The shift in who is modeling and scaffolding from the first to the second episodes lays the preparation for the intense interactional space of the third episode. The third episode is totally run by the students in terms of the focus of discussion, the complex interactions of multiparty overlapping talk, and the norms for argumentation. It would be possible to highlight only the talk of the third episode as evidence of the quality of reasoning shown by the students. However, my interest in this article is to construct an argument to account for the interactional spaces in the third episode, namely, that one must understand the history behind the evolution of the activity. The explication in the "Analysis of Discourse" section of this article offers an analysis of the microhistory behind Episode 3. This day is representative of a history of classroom routines and activities that constitute what has now become classroom culture.

The History Out of Which the Culture of This Classroom Is Constituted

The Santa Barbara Discourse Group (Green & Dixon, 1994) has made a convincing contribution to understanding the activity of classroom life. I chose this exemplary day of classroom discussion to illustrate literary reasoning and interpretation carried out by a group of African American high school freshmen who by most traditional standards would be seen as underachieving. I also chose this layered discussion because it is carried out entirely in African American English Vernacular, not only in terms of syntax and phonology but also in terms of prosody and discourse style. The discussion focuses on a noncanonical African American work of fiction. Using the three criteria (students, language use, and text), the illustration embodies subjugated knowledge and persons. The literature on classroom instruction needs more exemplars of this type. However, at least as important as the exemplars are the insights into the development of this quality of intellectual activity. Did students come in on the first day of instruction eager and ready to engage literary texts in this way? They did not. Thus, while privileging the cultural capital or funds of knowledge (Moll & Greenberg, 1990) that the students brought to the classroom from their home and community lives, I must also address how a particular culture of inquiry was constructed over time in this classroom. To address this issue, it is necessary to trace and analyze the history of activity, the nature of interactions, and the artifacts and routines through which certain habits—habits of mind (Perkins, 1992)—evolved.

From the beginning to the end of the school year, this was a very difficult class to manage. Students complained that the teacher gave too much work and that the work was too difficult. They rarely completed homework, and getting them to complete written assignments was always a major chore. They came into the class with clear epistemologies about school and school knowledge. School was a place where teachers told you what they wanted you to know, and your job was to fill in blanks on worksheets or write single-sentence answers that you could copy from the book. The answers were always either right or wrong, and the arbiter of correctness was always the teacher. In classrooms, if you sit long enough, the teacher will tell you what she wants you to know. If you are good, you will sit quietly, passively, and listen. If you are more aggressive, you will try to institute countermeasures in the form of disruptive behavior to change the agenda of the class to one more palatable to you. These students had experienced school in this way for at least eight long years and had well-established ideas about what you do in school. There was a clear culture that they expected to find when they entered the classroom on the first day. The challenge for the teacher was to alter these cultural expectations, to craft a classroom culture over time and with the support of students that operated from a different set of norms.

The Santa Barbara Discourse Group (Green & Dixon, 1994) believes that classroom culture is constituted through talk, activities, and artifacts. Norms for talk tell which members can talk, when, and about what. Routine activities show members the interactions that are valued, the problems that are worth addressing, and useful ways of attacking these worthwhile problems. Artifacts provide members with tools, in the Vygotskian sense (Vygotsky, 1978), with which to conduct inquiry. In the context of this instructional model, artifacts included books, computer-based supports, and cognitively guided graphic organizers and journal prompts. Talk, routine activities, and artifacts are the stuff out of which classroom culture is constructed over time. Classrooms are highly resonant and potentially dialogic interactional spaces. Students, in particular adolescents, contribute as much to classroom culture as teachers because students either engage or resist the classroom norms. Because of these last two premises, I argue that what students bring from their home and community lives is as important as the hybrid space that is constructed in the classroom.

Through analysis of videotapes of classroom instruction over time, of artifacts of student work, and of the teacher's journals and lesson plans, six categories are offered for analyzing over time how this class came to where it was on November 1, 1995. I argue that classroom culture was shaped by creating community, building new norms for reading, valuing complex problems, modeling strategies for solving complex literary problems, building intertextual links, and using routine artifacts to support critical thinking.

Creating Community

When discussions began on any given day, students were fairly active and unsettled as they came in from the rowdy, noisy halls between classes. Because it was not unusual for some students to talk about off-task subjects while instructional discussion was going on and because some students were quiet and shy, the teacher routinely asked something like, "Patricia, did you hear what Brian said? Brian, speak up so Patricia can hear what you have to say." Time was taken on all days to make sure every student had a book and was looking at the appropriate passage under discussion. Although this may seem commonplace, it was not uncommon to walk through the halls of this high school and look through the windows of classrooms to see teachers lecturing to students who were sleeping with their heads on their desks, looking out the window, or talking to other students. This daily routine established a set of expectations for participation in this class; that is, students at least must look at the book and give the appearance of being alert. Second, the teacher made efforts daily to engage the most disengaged. A student like Marcus who acted out daily in class was asked to sit outside in the hall for a while until he was prepared to participate productively. Although the school provided teachers with the option of sending disruptive students to the discipline office for in-school suspension, parent conferences, or regular suspension for several days out of school, the teacher never opted to use these forms of discipline. She wanted Marcus and the several other students who routinely acted out to believe that they were members of this class community, that they had the choice of engaging or not engaging, but they did not have the right to prevent others from learning. During the November 1 discussion, Marcus's comments, which added another dimension to the argument over whether October Brown is Chinese, came after he returned to class from one of his regular respites in the hall. Had Marcus seen himself only as part of the castigated other, I do not believe that he would have come back and directly entered the evolving debate. Several students in the class were labeled as learning disabled, went to a special resource class, and as remedial readers demonstrated problems with vocabulary, fluency, and comprehension well beyond the reading problems of the rest of the class. Again, special efforts were made to bring them into the discussion. Special assignments were designed for them that were consistent with the work that the rest of the class was doing, but in smaller chunks so they would better cope.

Two other crucial routines through which a sense of community evolved included linking the texts to students' prior experience and providing routines that made students take responsibility for their own reading. Again, daily the teacher asked each student to write down ideas about a passage in question on one of the routine artifacts used in the class. Daily routines might involve asking questions about a target passage, making observations of salient details from a passage, or making inferences from a character's actions or descriptions. This was always done *before* the class discussion. The teacher understood that the students, despite their low achievement, valued grades. They saw the work they produced and the efforts they extended in class as having a utilitarian function for getting good grades. They had high expectations for themselves in terms of grades. Knowing that their initial reflections in response to the close reading of a text would be collected and graded gave them a reason that they valued to extend effort. From the teacher's point of view, this routine activity socialized the students into taking responsibility for their own thinking and did not privilege the habit of sitting and waiting for others to think for them.

In the midst of counterscripts, the most intense and interactional discussions occurred when students had opportunities to link their home and community experiences in meaningful ways to extend their thinking about a passage. For example, on November 1, the class was asked to hypothesize about what particular books October Brown might be reading to her class. During the days of legal school segregation and explicit second-class resources to schools serving Black youngsters, October Brown brings books from her own library to read to her students, but no titles are given in the text. Some students suggest that she reads the Bible, and others suggest history books. In all cases, they offer textual evidence to support their claims. Shanee says she thinks October Brown brings the poem "Invictus." The teacher invites Shanee to bring in a copy of "Invictus" by William Ernest Henley to share with the class the next day and indicates that she [the teacher] will bring in another poem that she thinks October Brown reads to her students. The next day, Shanee dutifully brings in "Invictus" and renders a moving reading of the poem, and the teacher brings in a copy of "The Creation" by James Weldon Johnson and reads that poem in the rhetorical manner of a Black preacher from the pulpit. On another day before the November 1 discussion, the students are working to interpret a phrase from the chapter "October Brown": "intuition is the guardian of childhood" (Claire, 1994, p. 4). Marilyn tells a story about being invited to a party given by a close friend and having an intuitive feeling that she ought not go. She follows that intuition and does not go. There is a shooting at the party, and her friend is hurt. A history of links to the students' prior knowledge and experiences contributes strongly to the collective understanding of the text and assists in the evolution of an intellectual community in the classroom. This may be why on the November 1 videotape, Marilyn literally shouts to the teacher and to the class, "That's not important. You need to kick his BUTT <out::t this class." Marilyn is trying to make an important point and is responding to Marcus, who is acting out and diverting the teacher's attention away from the class as she escorts him from the classroom for his daily hall visit.

Building New Norms for Reading

Listening to comments that students make, especially at the beginning of the school year, clearly suggests that students in many cases did not see reading as requiring an effort to make meaning. Reading in school involved looking at or saying the words, often to find a set of words that matched the words in the question from the back of the story in the anthology on the worksheet and writing down the sentences that contained the matching phrase. One certainly did not read the same text or passage more than once. The routine activities and artifacts used from the very beginning of the school year encouraged students to complete multiple readings of the same text or passage, consider multiple points of view, provide textual evidence to support claims, attend to unusual details in the text, and link the text to life experiences.

Statements like the following were routinely made by the teacher:

T: I know that you did [read it]. I've read it more times than you have. (transcript, line 50, October 23, 1995)

T: There are lots. There's not one unusual thing; there are lots of unusual statements about those marigolds. (transcript, lines 122–123, October 23, 1995)

T: You have to read the book. You can't answer the questions without reading the story carefully. (transcript, lines 223–224, October 31, 1995)

Every day the teacher responded to students' replies with the question, "How do you know?" These statements were made by the teacher and communicated daily from the beginning of the school year. They were reinforced by activities in which all students were expected to engage. This approach helped develop habits, which Perkins (1992) calls habits of mind.[8]

At Fairgate High School, the teacher must commit a great deal of energy to ensure that even the most resistant students participate in the intellectual activity of the class. Teachers who believe that these students cannot learn, that they contribute nothing of value from their home and community lives, and that their language is inferior are not likely to invest the energy, the tenacity, and the sheer will demanded to reengage students who have disengaged from school over the course of nearly a decade. During my 34-year career in education and my three-year experience of teaching and conducting research at Fairgate High School, I have seen teachers who fit both categories. This observation speaks to the uneven nature of the school experience for such students. The inconsistency of expectations and in the quality of intellectual and emotional experience with schooling may explain students' conceptions of school and how they learn to adapt.

This brief interchange from October 23 shows that the ways of reading and interpreting seen on November 1 were emergent and not part of how students perceived school-based reading before this class:

T: And third I want you to look again for unusual statements, used to describe the act of what they did. You know what they did. They took some stones and threw them to destroy the flowers, but Eugenia Collier describes what they did using some unusual words. Words you wouldn't normally think of to describe kids throwing rocks at flowers...

S: Describe some words?

T: ...but she uses some words to describe what they are doing that seem bigger than what they did. They are unusual ways to describe throwing rocks at flowers.

S: I don't understand this.

T: I'll come over there. (transcript, lines 179–199, October 23, 1995)

Using the strengths of highly verbal students like Shanee and Marilyn in whole-group and small-group work and interacting individually with students over time were part of the activity through which the culture of this classroom was constructed. Lave and Wenger (1991) describes the quality of participation by those who are learning the activity of a community of practice as "peripheral participation" (p. 14). These students were learning to read literary texts in ways valued by literary critics (Rabinowitz, 1987) and sophisticated readers of canonical literature. This statement is not meant to suggest that all literary critics or readers of canonical literature agree on norms for interpretation. Reader response (Langer, 1990; Rosenblatt, 1978), structuralist (Culler, 1975), deconstructionist (Bloom, deMan, Derrida, & Hartman, 1987), feminist (Donovan, 1975), and Black aesthetic (Gayle, 1972) traditions of literary interpretation are distinct communities of practice. Fish (1980) argues that the norms for interpretation constitute interpretive communities. Although I accept these differences, I believe strongly that two fundamental stances are required for participation in any of these traditions, especially for novice readers: close reading of the text, attributing generalizations beyond the text to what the tradition signifies as salient details, and a willingness to critique the text (Rabinowitz, 1987). Other empirical studies have suggested common stances among expert readers of fiction (Graves & Frederiksen, 1996; van den Broek, 1996).

Valuing Complex Problems and Building Intertextual Links

Table 4 lists examples of the intellectual problems posed by texts and tackled by the students. The texts were chosen thematically because the students contributed much from their life experiences to the texts and because each story revolved around central images, metaphors, and vivid figurative language through which essential symbols and points of view are communicated. The sequence of the texts provided a history of common practice by posing similar rhetorical and interpretive problems over time. Bloome and Egan-Robertson (1993) argue for

Table 4. Valuing Complex Problems and Intertextual Links

Marshall, P. (1992). To Da-Duh, in memoriam. In *African American literature: Voices in a tradition* (pp. 499–512). Austin, TX: Harcourt Brace Jovanovich.	• What do the images used to describe the shed in the beginning of the story and the images used to describe Da-Duh's orchard have in common? • What might images of light and dark stand for in this story? • What do you think the tree in the orchard might symbolize? • What do you think Da-Duh's garden symbolizes in the story?
Collier, E. (1992). Marigolds. In *African American literature: Voices in a tradition* (pp. 485–498). Austin, TX: Harcourt Brace Jovanovich.	• Looking closely at the descriptions of the marigolds, what do you think the marigolds represent to Miss Lottie? To the children? • Why do you think the author uses the term "beheaded" to describe Joey's destruction of the garden? • What does the narrator mean when she says in retrospect, "And I too have planted marigolds"? • Why do you think the scene between the mother and father is in the story?
Claire, M. (1994). *Rattlebone*. New York: Penguin.	• Whose point of view is represented in the statement "Intuition is the guardian of childhood; it was keen in us, and we were right"? • In the context of the story, what does the phrase "They were on opposite ends of the same track" mean? • Why does Irene suck chalk?

the importance of intertextual links in classroom instruction and discourse. It is important to note again that the questions highlighted probably reflect a structuralist (Culler, 1975) or New Critics' (Ransom, 1941) close textual analysis. Some may argue that a more personalized reader response (Tompkins, 1980) approach would be more appropriate where students primarily make personal and affective responses to the text. I absolutely agree with Rosenblatt (1978) that an aesthetic response to the texts allows students to subjunctively enter the text world. I am also convinced that they negotiate that subjunctivity through close textual analysis and an ability to link the world of the text to some anchors in their own personal experiences. This is particularly so for underachieving, disengaged novice readers who are asked to read canonical texts that are obtuse in syntax and vocabulary and removed in terms of the social codes that operate in the world of the texts. In some sense, the most widespread effect of the traditional English language arts curriculum at the high school level for most students is tremendous disengagement. The net result for most students is to dedicate themselves after high school never to read Shakespeare, Keats, or Faulkner ever again in life. The focus over time on problems of symbolism, points of view, and interpretation of complex inferences in this class was cultural modeling's curriculum design to apprentice these students into a community of intellectual inquiry that valued problems that demanded close textual analysis.

Modeling Strategies for Solving Complex Literary Problems

A young man at Fairgate High School talked to me about his math class. He complained that the teacher would give the class problems, but when students experienced difficulties, the teacher would tell them to try to discover how to tackle the problem on their own. He said, "She won't tell us." Included in the questions at the end of selections in the anthologies once used by the English Language Arts Department (which I am sure are representative of literature anthologies generally) were product questions. The questions are posed after the student has read the story or poem, and they presume that a process of close reading has preceded. Langer (1990) talks about the horizons of possibility that emerge while one is reading. The modeling strategies and the artifacts used over time from the beginning of the school year were aimed at helping students learn how to construct horizons of possibilities while they read. When the broader questions were encountered that spanned episodes and details across the text, the students were already engaged in paying close attention to details and thinking about them while reading. Using the artifacts and the modeling strategies is one attempt to address Delpit's (1986) challenge about the need to be explicit in instruction.

From the beginning of the school year, the class analyzed samples of signifying dialogues. As previously stated, signifying is a form of discourse in the African American speech community that involves innuendo, double entendre, satire, and irony and is dense in figurative language. It often involves forms of ritual insult but is not limited to insult. An example of signifying might be "Yo mama so skinny, she can do the hula hoop in a Cheerio." African American adolescents and adults who speak African American English Vernacular participate in this form of language play (Abrahams, 1970; Kochman, 1972; Labov, 1972; Mitchell-Kernan, 1981; Smitherman, 1977). This discourse form privileges indirection, multiple layers of meaning, and language play as valuable in their own right. The routine practice of this kind of talk necessarily engages participants in reasoning about issues of irony and satire and socializes participants into valuing certain aesthetic stances toward language that are central to the practice of literary interpretation (Lee, 1991, 1992, 1993, 1995a, 1995b, 1996, 1997). In other studies using signifying as a model for strategies to detect the need to reject literal interpretations and to reconstruct an inferred interpretation, students have achieved statistically significant gains in achievement (Lee, 1993, 1995a, 1995b).

The modeling activities were central to the construction of an intellectual community in the class. The modeling activities are a form of guided participation (Rogoff, 1995). Through the use of modeling activities, students practice the strategies that will be used to solve problems in canonical texts while receiving guidance and support from the teacher and more knowledgeable others (e.g., other students in small-group work). African American adolescents who speak African American English Vernacular and participate in signifying dialogues in their everyday lives have a form of tacit knowledge that is applicable to the analysis of canonical literary texts. This tacit knowledge, however, is limited to the circumstances of their everyday talk. When students face problems of interpreting figurative language, symbols, irony, and satire in canonical literary texts, they do not consciously refer to the strategies they use to understand and participate in signifying dialogues outside the school. This is because that everyday knowledge is not linked to other instantiations and is, therefore, inert and not generalizable. Through the instructional conversations in which students analyze stretches of signifying dialogues, the teacher asks the students to make public how they know the meaning of each turn of talk in a signifying dialogue. The teacher then provides the students with a more abstract language in which to couch the strategies they use. The teacher also helps the students make connections between the strategies they make public regarding their interpretation of the signifying dialogues and the application of the strategies to the canonical texts that follow in the instructional unit. These modeling activities were characterized by metacognitive talk in which students focus on their processes of reasoning.

Students were asked to hypothesize, weigh evidence, and alter their hypotheses as evidence warranted. In addition to analyzing samples of signifying dialogues in order to construct a mental model of the norms for interpretation that were valued in this class, the modeling continued in the form of coaching students as they engaged daily in the practice of interpretation. This coaching involved offering students feedback as they attended to details that stood out because they were unusual or because they were densely repeated in the context. The artifacts routinely used across time coupled with the verbal coaching from the teacher and eventually from other students in small groups were the tools that students used to act on the complex problems posed.

Using Routine Artifacts to Support Critical Thinking

The artifacts used routinely from the first few weeks of instruction are likened to tools to support thinking. Vygotsky (1934/1987) argued that tools augmented and extended the possibilities of thought. For example, hypertext technology restructures how we think about linearity in texts. The traditional sense of story grammar may be historically altered by the evolution of this technological tool. Although the tradition of stream-of-consciousness fiction was a conceptual tool that restructured how readers think about the structure of storytelling, the universe of readers of such texts is relatively small. The computer tools that support hypertext environments are more accessible, used more widely, and likely to have a more distributed impact on thinking. In cultural-historical activity theory (Cole, 1996), tools or mediating artifacts are not only material (e.g., a hammer or a computer) but ideational (e.g., software programs; theorems in geometry; or literary constructs, e.g., symbolism and unreliable narrators). Although some of the artifacts routinely employed in this class were physical (e.g., the use of computers), most were ideational, such as routine categories of questions, graphic organizers, and software programs that scaffolded literary response.[9]

In an attempt to distribute expertise (Salomon, 1993), students were asked to answer detailed questions about each page of an assigned text in order to influence active attention to salient details while reading, rather than after they had completed reading. Students had to answer the questions in writing before class discussions occurred. The teacher walked around the room while students responded to the questions in order to provide support for problems individual students were having. Although some of the activity occurred as homework, much of it took place in class to ensure that each student engaged in the activity. Especially at the beginning of the school year, the teacher could not depend on the majority of students to complete homework assignments. If the teacher had depended on homework to move along the pace of instruction, she would also have lost many students who were disengaged from school.

In addition to the categories of close reading questions answered while students were in the process of reading, students almost daily used another tool or artifact aimed at apprenticing them into taking responsibility for monitoring their own emerging understandings. Reading research documents that poor readers do not engage in metacognitive or executive control over whether they are understanding in order to take active steps to resolve their lack of comprehension (Garner, 1987). The reflective journal was used each time students began a new reading assignment. In this journal, students recorded questions they had while reading, posited possible responses to those questions, described evidence that might support what they thought was a reasonable response to their questions, and wrote what others might say to counter that position. Because the journal was so detailed, students did not complete all sections all the time. The process yielded thoughtful and complex question posing. After five weeks of instruction, students read the short story "Marigolds" by Eugenia Collier (1992). The quality of questions raised by the students in their journals reflected their understanding of the quality of questions this community had come to value. They are not questions about plot but rather about the internal motivations of characters that must be inferred and about the meaning of specific figurative language in the story. Table 5 includes a sample of questions generated by students weeks before November 1, during the analysis of "Marigolds." These questions became the source of whole- and small-group discussions.

As preparation for the complex literary questions listed in Table 5, students used various graphic organizers developed by the Cultural Modeling Project to record observations from their close reading and to structure ways of reasoning about particular categories of questions. For example, students recorded details from descriptions of the marigolds in "Marigolds" or details from descriptions of Da-Duh's garden in "To Da-Duh, in Memoriam" by Paule Marshall (1992). The visual record became an object about which hypothesizing about generalizations and significance occurred. The activity occurred in small- and whole-group work.

Table 5. Student-Generated Questions: "Marigolds" by Eugenia Collier[a]

Questions Generated by Students During the Fifth Week of Instruction	Quality of Questions
1. If Lizabeth hates the marigolds, why does she talk about them as rising "suddenly and shockingly a dazzling strip of bright blossoms, clumped together in enormous mounds, warm and passionate and sun-golden?"	These questions do not have simple right or wrong answers. They focus on the internal states of characters that must be inferred from the story. They also focus explicitly on interpreting the specific language of the text, with a clear attention to figurative language, as in questions 1, 7, and 9. Raising questions of this sort indicates that students are engaging in metacognitive strategies, monitoring their understanding of the story as it evolves. The discussion that followed focused on their questions rather than the teacher's.
2. Why did Lizabeth feel ashamed after acting so mean?	
3. Why do they want to bother Miss Lottie's flowers?	
4. Why don't they want something in their neighborhood to look nice?	
5. Why was Miss Lottie so overprotective with her flowers?	
6. Why would Miss Lottie put flowers in front of her yard instead of remodeling her house?	
7. What did Lizabeth mean by "my favorite gesture of phony bravado"?	
8. What did the narrator mean when she said the marigolds interfered with the perfect ugliness of the place?	
9. What does Lizabeth mean when she says "we children were not consciously aware of how thick were the bars of our cage"?	
10. Why did the children think Miss Lottie was a witch?	

[a]Collier, E. (1992). Marigolds. In *African American literature: Voices in a tradition* (pp. 485–498). Austin, TX: Harcourt Brace Jovanovich.

It recurred from the first weeks of instruction, almost daily, not only through the November 1 class, which is the subject of this article, but through the end of the school year.

One particular graphic organizer tool was a table structure. When students were given questions about symbolic images, they were asked to list in a two- or three-column table all the references that were associated with that image in one column. In a second column, they were asked to hypothesize about the patterns they saw in the details listed in the first column. Through discussion in whole- and small-group work, students weighed the evidence that supported their hypotheses. Whole-group discussions invited multiple and often rival hypotheses for debate, not debate aimed at one right conclusion but rather at the reasonableness of multiple possible points of view.

Finally, it was understood that vocabulary was an important variable in negotiating texts. Although it was equally important that students memorize vocabulary, it was also important that they be empowered to decipher the meaning of unfamiliar words from the contexts in which they are used. Thus, another routine artifact used was sheets of paper on which were listed sentences and paragraphs from the assigned texts with vocabulary highlighted. Students were asked to make predictions from the context about the meanings of words and to match that prediction with the definitions from the dictionary. Again, the attempt was to teach the students to fish, rather than simply to feed them directly.

The culture of this classroom of African American underachieving freshmen that is evident in the discussion that occurred on November 1, 1995, evolved slowly over an eight-week period. The evolution continued during the school year as patterns of interactions, strategies for attacking interpretive problems in canonical literature, categories and qualities of problems, and patterns of rhetorical possibilities across texts were negotiated between the teacher and students and among students. The talk, problems, modes of reasoning, texts, and artifacts constituted the activity system (Engeström, Miettinen, & Punamaki, 1999; Leontiev, 1981) through which classroom culture was constructed. Table 6 summarizes each of these categories.

Table 6. Activity Through Which Classroom Culture Is Constituted

Creating Community	Building New Norms for Reading	Valuing Complex Problems	Modeling Strategies	Building Intertextual Links	Artifacts
• Expect all to read text. • Speak so others can hear you. • Praise the disengaged. • Link prior experience. • Take responsibility.	• Value multiple readings. • Multiple points of view • Invoke textual evidence. • Attend to unusual details. • Link to life experiences. • Close reading of text	• Symbolism • Point of view • Complex inferences	• Signifying strategies • Close reading • Attention to details • Hypothesizing • Weighing evidence	• Common problems across "To Da-Duh, in Memoriam" by Paule Marshall,[a] "Marigolds" by Eugenia Collier,[b] and *Rattlebone* by Maxine Claire[c]	• Reflective journals • Tables to analyze symbols • Close reading questions • Graphic organizers • Using context vocabulary sheets

[a]Marshall, P. (1992). To Da-Duh, in memoriam. In *African American literature: Voices in a tradition* (pp. 499–512). Austin, TX: Harcourt Brace Jovanovich.
[b]Collier, E. (1992). Marigolds. In *African American literature: Voices in a tradition* (pp. 485–498). Austin, TX: Harcourt Brace Jovanovich.
[c]Claire, M. (1994). *Rattlebone*. New York: Penguin.

Conclusion

The activity system out of which the quality of literary meaning making evolved included using routines that support the creation of a sense of community or shared norms, building new norms for reading as a process, valuing complex problems, modeling strategies by drawing on knowledge the students had constructed from their language experiences outside of school, building links across texts, and using artifacts that help structure how students reason. A second important dimension concerns the knowledge base of the teacher that informed how she designed the instruction and, less obviously, how she responded in the moment of the minute-by-minute performance on the classroom floor. Because I am the teacher, hopefully there is some validity to my deconstruction of my own thinking processes as I engaged in this complex practice of teaching.

The teacher's knowledge base must be dynamic and adaptive as she cannot fully anticipate what students will say or how they will respond. Among the problems teachers must address are (a) uptake of students' ideas and misconceptions (the teacher's response to Yetu's claim that October Brown was Chinese); (b) managing instructional discourse, in this case, managing multiparty overlapping talk (understanding its functions regarding engagement and opportunities for simultaneous participation); (c) managing counterscripts (e.g., responding to Marcus's resistance in ways that sustain him as a member of the intellectual community and encouraging hybridity through multiple points of view); (d) planning to address the human dimensions of teaching and learning (e.g., addressing the holistic needs—cognitive, social, emotional—of students and resisting negative stereotypes that lead to low expectations); and (e) understanding student resistance from a developmental point of view. This holistic vision of teaching is consistent with the socialization focus of Black schools in the South under segregation (Billingsley, 1968; Irvine & Irvine, 1983; Siddle Walker, 1993) and the kinds of culturally responsive teachers documented by Ladson-Billings (1994) and Foster (1997).

In this article, I have chosen Bourdieu's (1988) construct of habitus as a conceptual unit of analysis, the historical dimensions of the dispositions that participants bring to an activity. There are multiple historical dimensions impacting the novices reported in this article. These dimensions include their ethnic cultural history, their personal histories, and the history of practices over time within this classroom. Much of this history is instantiated through language and modes of interaction. The challenge in designing instructional interventions is to consider in strategically informed ways the generativity of what students bring to the space of classrooms, the psychological (Wertsch, 1991) and communal (Bruner, 1990) tool kits of their experiences. Design challenges are further complicated by the demands of the disciplines taught and the difficulties of orchestrating a system of practices in classrooms that invite and support meaningful forms of guided participation in intellectually demanding problems.

QUESTIONS FOR REFLECTION

1. What strategies employed by the Cultural Modeling Project could support effective classroom discussions of text and help your own teaching of underachieving students?
2. The author mentions the concept of "instructional space." How can you take advantage of student errors or changes in the instructional space to advance student comprehension?
3. What insights do you gain from this chapter about building a shared culture of inquiry in a classroom?

NOTES

The research was funded by the McDonnell Foundation's Cognitive Studies in Educational Practice and the Spencer Foundation. Any opinions expressed in this article represent those of the author and do not necessarily reflect positions of the funding agencies.

[1] For example, a reader who does not understand the assumptions about the role of fate in Greek life is not likely to view the experiences of characters like Oedipus in *Oedipus Rex* as making much sense. Similarly, a reader who is not aware of the social norms under which Hester Prynne would have operated is likely to have a less sympathetic response to Hawthorne's *A Scarlet Letter*. Knowledge of the social codes assumed to be operating in the social world of the text is an important element of the knowledge a skilled reader brings to a literary text (Rabinowitz, 1987). Such knowledge allows the reader to enter the subjunctive world of the text but does not preclude the reader from assuming a critical stance and rejecting the social codes, as many generations of readers have done with *A Scarlet Letter*. However, novice readers cannot assume the role of informed critic when they do not recognize the social codes operating in the text, and assume the work to be nonsensical instead.

[2] Throughout this article, I shift point of view. I refer to myself in the third-person voice as "the teacher" when reporting on observable actions as part of classroom activity. When interpreting those actions of myself as "the teacher," I use the first-person point of view. The reason for this shift is that I play two separate roles. When I was in the classroom teaching daily, I was not thinking analytically as a researcher. Rather, I was thinking analytically as a classroom teacher. My critique as the author of the analysis reported in this article is separate from my role as the teacher. I use the pronoun referent *we* when referring to the work of the Cultural Modeling Project as a whole, reflecting the collective thinking of the many persons who have worked as researchers and teachers on that project.

[3] All names of students and teachers are pseudonyms.

[4] Signifying is an oral genre of talk within the African American English Vernacular speech community that involves indirection, double entendre, and a high degree of figurative language.

[5] The following transcription codes are used: < > faster pace than surrounding talk; ^ rising intonation (data from Jefferson, 1979); CAPS emphatic stress; :: elongation of vowel sound (data from Tannen, 1989).

[6] In this case, scaffolding supports were provided by people, but they may also be provided through the design of smart computer-based tools that dynamically respond to changes in competence evidenced by users.

[7] It will be useful here to distinguish among modeling, coaching, and the acts of scaffolding that constitute cognitive apprenticeship (Collins et al., 1989). In modeling, one with more or at least equal knowledge demonstrates the strategy, heuristic, or mode of reasoning. The act of coaching involves providing advice and commentary on the problem-solving activity of the learner or more novice other. Such commentary often involves an expertlike explanation of the usefulness of the moves made by the learner, advice on how the move could be improved, or a comment on how what the novice or peer has done may be linked to other powerful strategies or kinds of knowledge. The process of providing more modeling and coaching at the beginning and removing those sources of support dynamically across time as needed is scaffolding.

[8] Perkins (1992) defines habits of mind as dispositions "to be broad and adventurous," "toward sustained intellectual curiosity," "to clarify and seek understanding," "to be planful and strategic," "to be intellectually careful," "to seek and evaluate reasons," and "to be metacognitive" (p. 116).

[9] A version of the Collaboratory Notebook (Edelson & O'Neill, 1994) was especially designed for the Cultural Modeling Project and used by students. The software program provides an environment in which links to relevant prior knowledge useful to a section of a text being read in class and opportunities to respond to one another's responses are accessible (Lee, 2003).

REFERENCES

Abrahams, R. (1970). *Deep down in the jungle: Negro narrative folklore from the streets of Philadelphia.* Chicago: Aldine.

Bakhtin, M.M. (1981). *The dialogic imagination: Four essays* (M. Holquist, Ed.; C. Emerson & M. Holquist, Trans.). Austin: University of Texas Press.

Billingsley, A. (1968). *Black families in white America.* Englewood Cliffs, NJ: Prentice Hall.

Bloom, H., deMan, P., Derrida, J., & Hartman, G.M.J.H. (1987). *Deconstructionism and criticism.* New York: Continuum.

Bloome, D., & Egan-Robertson, A. (1993). The social construction of intertextuality in classroom reading and writing lessons. *Reading Research Quarterly, 28*(4), 305–333. doi:10.2307/747928

Booth, W. (1983). *A rhetoric of fiction.* Chicago: University of Chicago Press.

Bourdieu, P. (1988). *The political ontology of Martin Heidegger.* Stanford, CA: Stanford University Press.

Bourdieu, P. (1990). *The logic of practice* (R. Nice, Trans.). Stanford, CA: Stanford University Press.

Bruner, J. (1990). *Acts of meaning.* Cambridge, MA: Harvard University Press.

Cole, M. (1996). *Cultural psychology: A once and future discipline.* Cambridge, MA: Belknap.

Collins, A., Brown, J., & Newman, S. (1989). Cognitive apprenticeship; Teaching the craft of reading, writing, and mathematics. In L.B. Resnick (Ed.), *Knowing, learning, and instruction: Essays in honor of Robert Glaser* (pp. 453–493). Hillsdale, NJ: Erlbaum.

Culler, J. (1975). *Structuralist poetics: Structuralism, linguistics, and the study of literature.* New York: Cornell University Press. doi:10.4324/9780203449769

Delpit, L. (1986). Skills and other dilemmas of a progressive Black educator. *Harvard Educational Review, 56*(4), 379–385.

Donovan, J. (1975). *Feminist literary criticism.* Lexington: University Press of Kentucky.

Duranti, A. (1997). *Linguistic anthropology.* New York: Cambridge University Press. doi:10.1017/CBO9780511810190

Edelson, D.C., & O'Neill, D.K. (1994, June). The Co-Vis Collaboratory Notebook: Supporting collaborative scientific inquiry. In A. Best (Ed.), *Proceedings of the 1994 National Educational Computing Conference* (pp. 146–152). Eugene, OR: International Society for Technology in Education.

Engeström, Y., Miettinen, R., & Punamaki, R.L. (Eds.). (1999). *Perspectives on activity theory.* New York: Cambridge University Press. doi:10.1017/CBO9780511812774

Fish, S. (1980). *Is there a text in this class? The authority of interpretive communities.* Cambridge, MA: Harvard University Press. doi:10.2307/1772220

Foster, M. (1997). *Black teachers on teaching.* New York: New.

Garner, R. (1987). *Metacognition and reading comprehension.* Norwood, NJ: Ablex.

Gates, H.L. (1988). *The signifying monkey: A theory of Afro-American literary criticism.* New York: Oxford University Press.

Gayle, A., Jr. (1972). *The Black aesthetic.* Garden City, NY: Doubleday.

Graves, B., & Frederiksen, C.H. (1996). A cognitive study of literary expertise. In R.J. Kruez & M.S. MacNealy (Eds.), *Empirical approaches to literature and aesthetics* (pp. 397–418). Norwood, NJ: Ablex.

Green, J.L., & Dixon, C.N. (1994). Talking knowledge into being: Discursive and social practices in classrooms. *Linguistics and Education*, *5*(3/4), 231–239.

Gutierrez, K., Rymes, B., & Larson, J. (1995). Script, counterscript, and underlife in the classroom: James Brown versus *Brown v. Board of Education*. *Harvard Educational Review*, *65*(3), 445–471.

Irvine, R.W., & Irvine, J.J. (1983). The impact of the desegregation process on the education of Black students: Key variables. *The Journal of Negro Education*, *52*(4), 410–422. doi:10.2307/2294948

Jefferson, G. (1979). A technique for inviting laughter and its subsequent acceptance/declination. In G. Psathas (Ed.), *Everyday language: Studies in ethnomethodology* (pp. 79–96). New York: Irvington.

Jones, G. (1991). *Liberating voices: Oral tradition in African American literature*. New York: Penguin.

Kochman, T. (Ed.). (1972). *Rappin' and stylin' out: Communication in urban Black America*. Urbana: University of Illinois Press.

Kuhn, D. (1991). *The skills of argument*. New York: Cambridge University Press. doi:10.1017/CBO9780511571350

Labov, W. (1972). *Language in the inner city: Studies in the Black English vernacular*. Philadelphia: University of Pennsylvania Press.

Ladson-Billings, G. (1994). *The dreamkeepers: Successful teachers of African American children*. San Francisco: Jossey-Bass.

Lampert, M. (1990). When the problem is not the question and the solution is not the answer: Mathematical knowing and teaching. *American Educational Research Journal*, *27*(1), 29–64.

Langer, J. (1990). The process of understanding: Reading for literary and informative purposes. *Research in the Teaching of English*, *24*(3), 229–260.

Lave, J., & Wenger, E. (1991). *Situated learning: Legitimate peripheral participation*. New York: Cambridge University Press.

Lee, C.D. (1991). Big picture talkers/words walking without masters: The instructional implications of ethnic voices for an expanded literacy. *The Journal of Negro Education*, *60*(3), 291–305. doi:10.2307/2295483

Lee, C.D. (1992). Literacy, cultural diversity, and instruction. *Education and Urban Society*, *24*(2), 279–291. doi:10.1177/0013124592024002008

Lee, C.D. (1993). *Signifying as a scaffold for literary interpretation: The pedagogical implications of an African American discourse genre*. Urbana, IL: National Council of Teachers of English.

Lee, C.D. (1995a). A culturally based cognitive apprenticeship: Teaching African American high school students skills in literary interpretation. *Reading Research Quarterly*, *30*(4), 608–631. doi:10.2307/748192

Lee, C.D. (1995b). Signifying as a scaffold for literary interpretation. *The Journal of Black Psychology*, *21*(4), 357–381. doi:10.1177/00957984950214005

Lee, C.D. (1996). *Cultural modeling in reading comprehension: An analysis of African American students' responses to culturally familiar and culturally less familiar fiction*. Unpublished manuscript, Northwestern University.

Lee, C.D. (1997). Bridging home and school literacies: A model of culturally responsive teaching. In J. Flood, S.B. Heath, & D. Lapp (Eds.), *A handbook for literacy educators: Research on teaching the communicative and visual arts* (pp. 330–341). New York: Macmillan.

Lee, C.D. (2003). Toward a framework for culturally responsive design in multimedia computer environments: Cultural modeling as a case. *Mind, Culture, and Activity, 10*(1), 42–61.

Lee, C.D., & Slaughter-Defoe, D. (1995). Historical and sociocultural influences on African American education. In J. Banks & C. Banks (Eds.), *Handbook of research on multicultural education*. New York: Macmillan.

Leontiev, A.N. (1981). The problem of activity in psychology. In J.V. Wertsch (Ed.), *The concept of activity in Soviet psychology* (pp. 37–71). Armonk, NY: Sharpe.

Mitchell-Kernan, C. (1981). Signifying, loud-talking and marking. In A. Dundes (Ed.), *Mother wit from the laughing barrel: Readings in the interpretation of Afro-American folklore* (pp. 310–328). Englewood Cliffs, NJ: Prentice-Hall.

Moll, L., & Greenberg, J.B. (1990). Creating zones of possibilities: Combining social contexts for instruction. In L. Moll (Ed.), *Vygotsky and education: Instructional implications and applications of sociohistorical psychology* (pp. 319–348). New York: Cambridge University Press. doi:10.1017/CBO9781139173674.016

Nystrand, M., & Gamoran, A. (1997). The big picture: The language of learning in dozens of English lessons. In M. Nystrand (Ed.), *Opening dialogue: Understanding the dynamics of language and learning in the English classroom*. New York: Teachers College Press.

Pearson, P.D., & Fielding, L. (1991). Comprehension instruction. In R. Barr, M.L. Kamil, P. Mosenthal, & P.D. Pearson (Eds.), *Handbook of reading research* (Vol. 2, pp. 815–860). New York: Longman.

Percelay, J., Ivey, M., & Dweck, S. (1994). *Snaps*. New York: William Morrow.

Perkins, D. (1992). *Smart schools: Better thinking and learning for every child*. New York: Free.

Rabinowitz, P. (1987). *Before reading: Narrative conventions and the politics of interpretation*. Ithaca, NY: Cornell University Press.

Ransom, J.C. (1941). *The new criticism*. Norfolk, CT: New Directions.

Rogoff, B. (1995). Observing sociocultural activity and three planes: Participatory appropriation, guided participation, and apprenticeship. In J. Wertsch, P. del Rio, & A. Alvarez (Eds.),

Sociocultural studies of mind (pp. 139–164). New York: Cambridge University Press. doi:10.1017/CBO9781139174299.008
Rosenblatt, L. (1978). *The reader, the text, the poem: The transactional theory of the literary work.* Carbondale: Southern Illinois University Press.
Salomon, G. (1993). *Distributed cognitions: Psychological and educational considerations.* New York: Cambridge University Press.
Siddle Walker, E.V. (1993). Caswell County Training School, 1933–1969: Relationships between community and school. *Harvard Educational Review,* 63(2), 161–182.
Smitherman, G. (1977). *Talkin and testifyin: The language of Black America.* Boston: Houghton Mifflin.
Stevenson, H.W., & Stigler, J.W. (1992). *The learning gap: Why our schools are failing and what we can learn from Japanese and Chinese education.* New York: Simon & Schuster.
Tannen, D. (1989). *Talking voices: Repetition, dialogue, and imagery in conversational discourse.* Cambridge, UK: Cambridge University Press.
Tompkins, J. (1980). *Reader-response criticism: From formalism to post structuralism.* Baltimore: Johns Hopkins University Press.
Toulmin, S., Rieke, R., & Janik, A. (1984). *An introduction to reasoning.* New York: Macmillan.
van den Broek, P. (1996). Causal inferences in the comprehension of literary texts. In R.J. Kreuz & M.S. MacNealy (Eds.), *Empirical approaches to literature and aesthetics* (pp. 179–200). Norwood, NJ: Ablex.
Vygotsky, L. (1978). *Mind in society: The development of higher psychological processes* (M. Cole, V. John-Steiner, S. Scribner, & E. Souberman, Eds. & Trans.). Cambridge, MA: Harvard University Press.
Vygotsky, L. (1987). Thinking and speech (N. Minick, Trans.). In R.W. Rieber & A.S. Carton (Eds.), *The collected works of L.S. Vygotsky. Vol. 1: Problems of general psychology* (pp. 37–285). New York: Plenum. (Original work published 1934)
Wells, G. (1995). Language and the inquiry-oriented curriculum. *Curriculum Inquiry, 25,* 233–269.
Wertsch, J. (1991). *Voices of the mind: A sociocultural approach to mediated action.* Cambridge, MA: Harvard University Press.

LITERATURE CITED

Claire, M. (1994). *Rattlebone.* New York: Penguin.
Collier, E. (1992). Marigolds. In *African American literature: Voices in a tradition* (pp. 485–498). Austin, TX: Harcourt Brace Jovanovich.
Marshall, P. (1992). To Da-Duh, in memoriam. In *African American literature: Voices in a tradition* (pp. 499–512). Austin, TX: Harcourt Brace Jovanovich.

CHAPTER 11

Sustained Acceleration of Achievement in Reading Comprehension: The New Zealand Experience

Mei Kuin Lai, Stuart McNaughton, Meaola Amituanai-Toloa, Rolf Turner, and Selena Hsiao, University of Auckland*

Schooling improvement interventions for culturally and linguistically diverse students from poorer communities need to solve a set of theoretical challenges relating to more effective literacy instruction. Although recent commentaries have suggested that some of the pressing issues in beginning reading instruction have been resolved, overall effectiveness in teaching reading comprehension is limited, and that research has not had much impact on effective comprehension instruction (Pressley, 2002; Sweet & Snow, 2003).

The need to address effectiveness in teaching reading comprehension is particularly significant for schools serving culturally and linguistically diverse populations (Garcia, 2003). The challenge to meet these needs is pressing in New Zealand where—despite the fact that, on average, students in the middle years of school have high levels of reading comprehension judged by international comparisons—there are large disparities in the distribution of achievement (Alton-Lee, 2004). These disparities are between children from both Māori (indigenous) and Pasifika (immigrants from the Pacific Islands) communities in urban schools with the lowest employment and income levels, and other children. Māori and Pasifika children score lower in reading comprehension measures than children from other ethnic groups. Since at least the 1950s, numerous reports have identified these disparities (e.g., Openshaw, Lee, & Lee, 1993), with one in 1981 calling them a crisis in urgent need of a solution (Ramsay, Sneddon, Grenfell, & Ford, 1981).

Like other countries, New Zealand is concerned with disparities in literacy achievement and has responded to this enduring "education debt" (Ladson-Billings, 2006, p. 3) with programs of schooling improvement and reform at local, district, and even national levels. Since 1998, New Zealand has focused on resolving these disparities. The national policy shifts have led to deployment of resources and to fine-tuning of early literacy programs. These changes have been associated with reductions in the disparities in accuracy and fluency of early reading at a national level (Crooks & Flockton, 2005). Experimental evidence supports the conclusion that specific changes in beginning instruction that have been implemented in groups of schools have been effective (e.g., Phillips, McNaughton, & MacDonald, 2004).

This chapter is reprinted from *Reading Research Quarterly*, *44*(1), 30–56.

However, the evidence—some of it presented in this report—also indicates that there has been little, if any, impact on reading comprehension from Year 4 of schooling. Indeed, it appears that the gaps may have increased nationally (Crooks & Flockton, 2005). Although depressing, this is not surprising theoretically. Much of the knowledge and many of the skills required for early fluency and accuracy in reading come from acquiring discrete bodies of knowledge. Paris (2005) called these *constrained* skills, which he claimed are learned relatively easily. The more language-based and content-dependent nature of comprehension requires *unconstrained* skills, which are more difficult to both teach and learn. In developmental terms, becoming a good decoder is a necessary but not sufficient condition for good comprehension, and effective instruction for decoding does not necessarily presage later development (McNaughton, 2002).

There has been little evidence that the issue of disparities in literacy achievements between groups can be solved easily in schools. In the United States, Borman (2005) showed that national reforms of schools to boost the achievement of children in low-performing schools serving the poorest communities have produced small gains in the short term, with effect sizes of the order of less than 0.20. For those few schools that sustained reforms over a longer period of around seven years, the effects increased (estimated effect sizes of about 0.50). Borman concluded that although nationally some achievement gains have occurred, they have typically been low and need to be accumulated over long periods of time. At a more specific level, individual studies from the United States have shown that clusters of schools serving minority children have been able to increase the achievement of children in reading comprehension. In one set of studies, Taylor, Pearson, Peterson, and Rodriguez (2005) intervened in high-poverty schools with carefully designed professional development research and development. They reported small cumulative gains across two years.

Implementing effective interventions poses a major challenge in New Zealand schools serving poorer communities with high numbers of Māori and Pasifika students. The goal is not just to produce achievement gains with acceptable effect sizes. The issue is accelerated achievement. Students need to make more than just an expected rate of gain.

This need for acceleration was recognized by the designer of Reading Recovery. Clay's (1979, 2005) developmental argument was that in order for an early intervention program to be functional for an individual, it needed to change the rate of acquisition to a rate of progress faster than the cohort to whom the individual belonged. This acceleration was needed so that over the brief but intensive period of the individualized intervention, a learner would come to function within the average bands required for his or her classroom. Groups of students from particular cultural groups who have not been well served by school instruction also need to make accelerated gains, to come to function like other students at equivalent levels. Their rate of progress needs to be higher than comparison cohorts. The issue for these students is not the same as in Reading Recovery in that the target is not for a group of students to come to function as a group within average bands. Rather, in the ideal case, the distribution of students needs to approximate an expected distribution—in the case of New Zealand students, the New Zealand national distribution. The probability of being in the lower (or indeed the upper) "tail" of the distribution should be no more than what would be expected for the population as a whole.

The idea of acceleration in terms of faster-than-normal rates of progress so that the changed distribution comes to match an expected distribution implies several criteria for judging the effectiveness of an intervention. Acceleration needs to be robust in the sense that the rate of gain is increased relative to expected gain across a defined period of time, say over a school or a chronological year. The gain needs to approximate an expected distribution, which likely means the gains need to be sustainable, at least in the medium term, say two to three years. Finally, because of the issue of approximating an expected distribution, there is a need to know that different subgroups within the total group have gained similarly. There is evidence that some interventions and school reforms can have differential effects for different level groups (Correnti, Rowan, & Camburn, 2003; Hubbard, Mehan, & Stein, 2006). Similarly, the ubiquitousness of "Matthew effects" (Stanovich, 1986, p. 381) is well known in educational interventions. Such effects should be avoided in the microcosm of an intervention, where differences among subgroups may become further exacerbated and all groups should make accelerated gains.

The presence of subgroup differences in reading comprehension achievement in mainstream schooling is well documented (Snow, Burns, & Griffin, 1998). In New Zealand, these differences include gender and ethnicity differences as well as differences associated with language background. For example, national monitoring data for 9-year-olds (Crooks & Flockton, 2005) shows that females outperform males on average by an effect size of 0.22 across a range of reading tasks, but most of the differences between males and females are on comprehension tasks. Similarly, the average effect size for the difference between Māori and Anglo-European students across tasks was 0.38, again most of the differences attributable to reading comprehension measures. The effect size favoring students for whom English was the predominant language at home was 0.23. From the general experimental literature, we also know that interventions can produce Matthew effects where those children who know or can do more learn more from a new procedure, an example being instruction designed to boost vocabulary learning (Penno, Wilkinson, & Moore, 2002).

The impact of schooling improvement interventions on such subgroups is not well known (Borman, 2005). There is some evidence that different types of programs are differentially effective with the age or year level of student (Correnti et al., 2003), which might suggest that in a highly prescribed intervention, some students would benefit more than others or that some students would learn less than others. For example, more advanced students might benefit from a program with more advanced instructional elements that allow them to develop unconstrained skills, but they may be limited by a program focused mainly on constrained skills (Paris, 2005). The intervention we will describe in this research was not initially prescribed but nevertheless was, through a process of development with the schools, highly specific. The process, which led to a controlled fine-tuning of existing instruction, was predicted to be both generic and adaptable enough to serve the needs of the subgroups.

An added problem for schooling improvement interventions designed to produce accelerated gains in achievement over several years is the presence of summer effects, the differential growth in learning over the months when schools are closed (Cooper, Charlton, Valentine, Muhlenbruck, & Borman, 2000; Entwisle, Alexander, & Olson, 1997). Students from poorer communities and minority students make less progress than other students do over this period, contributing to a widening gap in achievement. In Heyns's (1978) classic study, sixth-grade low-income black students lost almost a quarter of a grade on the word knowledge subtest of the Metropolitan Achievement Test, and lowest income white students made almost no gains. Heyns showed that between half and two thirds of the annual learning gap between white children from high-income homes and black children from the poorest homes accrued during the summer months. The gains over the school year were much closer for all groups.

Although there is no New Zealand study that has taken repeated measures over successive years on which to draw, the extent of the effect captured in reviews suggests that similar summer effects would likely be present. This poses two potential issues for the present study: First, a methodological issue is modeling the growth, taking these assumed effects into account. When achievement is measured at the beginning and end of each academic year, the likely shape of growth over three years is therefore likely to be a staircase of some sort (Borman, 2000). The more substantive issue is the sheer challenge of designing powerful school effects that over time are greater than these assumed summer effects. This is an added challenge to meeting the criteria of effective acceleration.

Can an intervention be designed within the framework of schooling improvement that solves the problem of acceleration meeting criteria for effectiveness? We approached this challenge in the following way. We started with known attributes of effective schooling improvement in reading comprehension that are assumed to apply equally for culturally and linguistically diverse students from poorer communities. Several dimensions have been identified in the school reform literature. They include the form and function of professional learning communities; the specificity of the program; the level and quality of implementation; the relationships between the developer and the local school and school district; the coordination and fit of the model to local circumstances; and the degree to which the program is articulated and elaborated (Borman, 2005; Cohen & Ball, 2007; Datnow & Stringfield, 2000; Raphael, Goldman, Au, & Hirata, 2006). Given the finding that more collaborative programs in literacy focused on teachers' knowledge and problem solving of their practices in professional learning communities may be more effective in the later years, we argue that the complexity associated with effective instruction for reading comprehension requires much more localized and informed adaptive expertise (Bransford, Derry, Berliner, & Hammerness, 2005).

Our reading of this literature suggests two major hypotheses for how instruction for culturally and linguistically diverse students in poor urban schools might accelerate achievement gains over a sustained period of time. The first is that instructional practices drawing on evidence about teaching and learning requirements in specific contexts need to be developed, and the second is that professional learning communities need to be able to fine-tune their practices through analyses of achievement data and problem solving. In what follows, we provide a detailed rationale for these two hypotheses.

According to Block and Pressley (2002), to comprehend written text a reader needs to be able to decode accurately and fluently and to have a wide and appropriate vocabulary, appropriate and expanding topic and world knowledge, active comprehension strategies, and active monitoring and fix-up strategies. So it follows that children who make relatively little progress may have difficulties in one or more of these areas. According to Slavin, Cheung, Groff, and Lake (2008), effective instruction also provides direct and explicit instruction for skills and strategies for comprehension. Effective teaching actively engages students in a great deal of actual reading and writing and instructs in ways that make expertise generalizable and enable students to self-regulate independently.

In addition, researchers have also identified the teacher's role in incorporating cultural resources, including event knowledge (Ladson-Billings, 1994; Lee, 2007; McNaughton, 2002), and in building students' sense of self-efficacy and more general engagement and motivation (Guthrie & Wigfield, 2000; Wang & Guthrie, 2004). Quantitative and qualitative aspects of teaching convey expectations about students' ability that affect their levels of engagement and sense of being in control. Culturally and linguistically diverse students seem to be especially likely to encounter teaching that conveys low expectations (Dyson, 1999). A number of studies that focused not directly on reading comprehension but on schooling improvement have shown how these expectations can be changed and how they influence instruction and learning. In general, both changes to beliefs about students and more evidence-based decisions about instruction are implicated, often in the context of schoolwide or even clusterwide initiatives (Bishop, Berryman, Tiakiwai, & Richardson, 2003; Phillips et al., 2004; Taylor et al., 2005).

It follows that low progress could be associated with a variety of teaching and learning needs in one or more of these areas. Out of this array of teaching and learning needs, those for students and teachers in any particular instructional context may therefore have a context-specific profile. Although our research-based knowledge means there are well-established relationships, the patterns of these relationships in specific contexts may vary. A simple example might be whether the groups of students who make relatively low progress in a particular context, say in a cluster of similar schools serving similar communities, have difficulties associated with decoding or using comprehension strategies or both, and how the teaching that occurs in those schools is related to those difficulties. Buly and Valencia (2002) provided a case study from a policy perspective on the importance of basing any intervention on specific profiles, rather than on assumptions about what children need (and what instruction should look like). In that study, a policy mandating phonics instruction for all students in the state of Washington who fell below literacy proficiency levels was shown to have missed the needs of the majority of students, whose decoding was strong but who struggled with comprehension or language requirements for the tests.

In the context examined in the current research, several explanations were possible for the low levels of reading comprehension. One was that children's comprehension levels were low because of low levels of accurate and fluent decoding (Tan & Nicholson, 1997). A second explanation was that the children may have learned a limited set of strategies; for example, they may have been able to recall well but were weaker in more complex strategies for drawing inferences, synthesizing, and evaluating, or the children may not have been taught well enough to control and regulate the use of strategies (Pressley, 2002). Other possible contributing reasons might have been more language-based—that children's vocabulary may have been insufficient for the texts used in classroom tasks (Biemiller, 1999) or that the children were less familiar with text genres. The patterns of Matthew effects may also have been present in classrooms, where culturally and linguistically diverse children receive more fragmented instruction that is overly focused on decoding or relatively simple forms of comprehending or receive relatively less dense instruction, all of which compounds low progress (McNaughton, 2002; Stanovich, West, Cunningham, Cipielewski, & Siddiqui, 1996). There was also a set of possible hypotheses around whether the texts, instructional activities, and the pedagogy of the classroom enabled cultural and linguistic expertise to be incorporated into and built on in classrooms (Lee, 2000; McNaughton, 2002). But each of these needed to be checked against the localized patterns of instruction in the classrooms in order for the relationships to be tested.

Our argument is that using detailed evidence to affect instructional changes in a sustained way requires more than an intervention that prespecifies these changes. As Pressley (2006) recently noted, we need to know about being effective at the school level too. Collaborative analysis around evidence from teachers' own classrooms has been implicated as an important component of professional development aimed at improving teaching and student achievement. In their review of effective professional development, Hawley and Valli (1999) identified such collaborative analysis as a more effective form of professional development than traditional workshop models.

Further research evidence suggests that approaches in which professional development focuses on joint problem solving around agreed evidence result in improvements in student achievement, particularly reading comprehension (e.g., Cawelti & Protheroe, 2001; Taylor et al., 2005). Cawelti and Protheroe identified teacher analysis and use of achievement data as critical factors responsible for student reading achievement gains in six formerly underperforming districts with successful school improvement efforts.

There are several critical features of professional learning communities that can effectively analyze evidence to improve teaching practices and raise student achievement (Coburn, 2003; Robinson & Lai, 2006; Toole & Seashore-Louis, 2002). One is the need for the community's shared ideas, beliefs, and goals to be theoretically rich. This shared knowledge is about the target domain (in the present case, that of comprehension), but it also entails detailed understanding of the nature of teaching and learning related to that domain (Timperley, Wilson, Barrar, & Fung, 2007), such as the research-based evidence on effective teaching of comprehension described earlier (e.g., Block & Pressley, 2002). However, being theoretically rich requires not just consideration of researchers' theories but the engagement of teachers' tacit ones (Robinson & Lai, 2006; Timperley et al., 2007). Engaging the teachers' theories uncovers the reasons and conditions that have resulted in their current practices. This allows the reasons to be challenged if, for example, they are based on inaccurate assumptions and permits the necessary conditions to be taken into account to improve practice (see Robinson & Lai, 2006, for more details). A recent review of the literature indicates that this process is strongly linked to interventions that have improved achievement (Timperley et al., 2007).

Not only do teachers' theories need be engaged alongside researchers' theories, but any theory competition needs be resolved without a particular theory being privileged (Robinson & Lai, 2006). This process increases the validity of the emerging theories by allowing for disconfirming evidence from all parties to be treated and tested equally, rather than privileging researchers or teachers' theories. Robinson and Lai provided the framework by which different theories can be examined using four standards of theory evaluation: accuracy (empirical claims about practice are well founded in evidence), effectiveness (theories meet the goals and values of those who hold them), coherence (competing theories from outside perspectives are considered), and improvability (theories and solutions can be adapted to meet changing needs or incorporate new goals, values, and contextual constraints).

This framework also means that a second feature of an effective learning community is that the goals and practices of a community are based on evidence. That evidence should draw on descriptions of children's learning as well as descriptions of instruction and teaching practices. However, what is also crucial is the validity of the inferences drawn or claims made about that evidence, as meanings and implications of evidence are not self-evident (Coburn, Touré, & Yamashita, in press). Robinson and Lai (2006) suggested that all inferences be treated as competing theories and evaluated using the evaluation framework detailed previously.

So this requires a further feature, which is an analytic stance to the collection and use of evidence. A research framework needs to show whether and how planned interventions do influence teaching and learning, enabling the community to know how effective interventions are in meeting goals. Therefore, the research framework adopted by the community needs to be staged so that the effect of interventions can be determined.

A final feature of an effective professional learning community is that the researchers' and teachers' ideas and practices need to be culturally located. By this, we mean that the ideas and practices that are developed and tested should entail an understanding of children's language and literacy practices, as these reflect children's local and global cultural identities. It is important to know how these practices relate (or do not relate) to classroom practices (McNaughton, 2002; New London Group, 1996).

In summary, we claim that sustaining accelerating rates of achievement in reading comprehension for culturally and linguistically diverse students in the schools of poorer communities is dependent on two developments: the first is the development of professional learning communities focused on critically analyzing the effectiveness of instruction, and the second is the fine-tuning of instruction to better meet the learning needs of students in the communities. We report here on a three-phase schooling improvement study with these elements that was aimed at accelerating achievement. Elsewhere we have described in detail the processes occurring in each of the phases (Lai & McNaughton, 2008; Lai, McNaughton, MacDonald, & Farry, 2004; McNaughton, Lai, MacDonald, & Farry, 2004). Here our focus is on the outcomes of the intervention in terms of trajectories of change over time and distributions of achievement across groups using the concept of acceleration.

Method

The project was designed as a collaboration involving schools in a New Zealand Ministry of Education schooling improvement initiative, the initiative leaders in the schools, the Woolf Fisher Research Centre (The University of Auckland) and representatives of the New Zealand Ministry of Education. The Ministry of Education representatives were long-standing members of the professional learning community and were invited by the schools to participate. They had no control over the funding for the research, and their role was to learn from the emerging results to facilitate greater research–policy–practice links (Annan, 2007). Seven Decile 1 schools (i.e., schools with the highest proportion of students from the lowest socioeconomic communities) from urban centers in the South Auckland area took part. Two of these schools were contributing schools (Year 1–Year 6); three were full primary schools (Year 1–Year 8); one was an intermediate school (Year 7–Year 8); and one was a middle school (Year 7–Year 9). The schools' sizes ranged from 292 students to 593 students.

The schooling improvement initiative had been running for five years prior to this project. In those five years, the Ministry of Education and researchers have been working with schools on addressing student behavior and staffing, developing a shared focus on student outcomes, forming partnerships with each other and the community, and establishing more effective teaching and management practices (Annan, 2007; Lai, 2003).

Participants (Students and Teachers)

We report two overlapping groups of students. One group comprised all the students present at the beginning of the three-year study (baseline sample, *N* = 1,975 students). A second group comprised three cohorts of students, initially from School Year 4 (comparable to grade 3 in the United States; students were 9-year-olds), Year 5 (10-year-olds), and Year 6 (11-year-olds) who were followed longitudinally for three years (total *N* = 238).

The baseline data (February 2003) were collected from the 1,975 students in six of the schools (one school that joined the project was unable to participate in the first round of data collection). The total group consisted of equal proportions of males and females (50% and 50%, respectively) from 14 ethnic groups. Four main groups from indigenous and ethnic minority Pasifika communities made up 87% of the sample. These groups were Samoan (33%), Māori (20%), Tongan (19%), and Cook Island (15%) ethnic groups. Approximately half the children had a home language other than English. A number of students dropped out and reentered the project during the period of the intervention (*n* = 536), with the majority of those students having missed at least half of the intervention.

The second group comprised three cohorts of students who were followed longitudinally from Time 1 to Time 6 and who were present at all six data collection time points. The total of 238 students is indicative of the high turnover of students in these schools, between 25% and 30% on average per year. The three cohorts were Cohort 1 (*n* = 114) students who were Year 4 at Time 1; Cohort 2 (*n* = 56) students who were Year 5 at Time 1, and Cohort 3 (*n* = 68) students who were Year 6 at Time 1. These students were a subset of the students included in the baseline sample.

Approximately 70 teachers were involved in each year of the project, including school-appointed literacy leaders who were normally the deputy or associate principal. Characteristics of the teachers varied somewhat year to year, but in general around two thirds had five or more years of experience, and 10% were beginning teachers. Eleven percent taught in bilingual classes (including Samoan, Tongan, and Māori bilingual classes). A third of the teachers were Pasifika (from different Pacific Island communities) or Māori (indigenous).

Design

At the core of the following analyses is a quasi-experimental design from which qualified judgments about possible causal relationships are made. Schools are open and dynamic systems. Day-to-day events change the properties of teaching and learning and the conditions for teaching and learning effectively. This variability is inherent to human behavior generally (see Sidman, 1960) and specifically is present in applied settings (Risley & Wolf, 1973). These circumstances require a design that deliberately incorporates variability and the sources of the variability and that has longitudinal properties. The quasi-experimental design described is appropriate to the circumstances of testing effectiveness over a period of time, given that variability is an important property (Raudenbush, 2005).

It was appropriate also given that the question is the effectiveness of the intervention in terms of an expected rate of gain for a particular cluster of schools if the intervention had not occurred and given that the obtained rate of gain should match a national distribution.

Repeated measures of children's achievement were collected in February 2003 (Time 1), November 2003 (Time 2), February 2004 (Time 3), November 2004 (Time 4), February 2005 (Time 5), and November 2005 (Time 6) as part of the quasi-experimental design. The design uses single-case logic within a developmental framework of cross-sectional and longitudinal data. The measures at Time 1 generated a cross-section of achievement across year levels (Years 4–5–6–7–8), which provides a baseline forecast of what the expected trajectory of development would be if the planned interventions had not occurred (Risley & Wolf, 1973). Successive stages of the intervention can then be compared with the baseline forecast and judgments about acceleration that are contextually valid can be made. In the present case, the first of these planned interventions was the analysis and discussion of data. The second was the development of instructional practices through workshops. The third was a phase in which sustainability was promoted. This design, which includes replication across cohorts, provides a high degree of both internal and external validity. The internal validity comes from the in-built testing of treatment effects described further below and the external validity comes from the systematic analysis of replication across cohorts within the cluster.

Two sorts of general analyses are possible with the repeated measures. Analyses can be conducted within each year. These are essentially pre- to post-test measures. However, because the measures we use can be corrected for age through transformation into stanine scores (Elley, 2001), they provide an indicator of the impact of the three phases against national distributions at similar times of the school year and hence a measure of acceleration. A more robust analysis of relationships between the intervention and achievement is provided by repeated measures within the quasi-experimental design format. They show change over repeated intervals and acceleration relative to expected change across school months and summer breaks.

Good science requires replications (Sidman, 1960). In quasi-experimental research, the need to systematically replicate effects and processes is heightened because of the reduced experimental control gained with the design. This need is specifically identified in discussions about alternatives to experimental randomized designs (Borko, 2004; Chatterji, 2005; Raudenbush, 2005). For example, McCall and Green (2004) argued that in applied developmental contexts, evaluation of program effects requires a variety of designs including quasi-experimental, but our knowledge is dependent on systematic analyses across sites. Replication across sites can add to our evaluation of program effects, particularly when it is inappropriate or premature to conduct experimental randomized designs. Such systematic replication is also needed to determine issues of sustainability (Coburn, 2003) and scaling up (McDonald, Keesler, Kauffman, & Schneider, 2006).

The design used with this cluster of schools has in-built replications across age levels within the quasi-experimental design format. These provide a series of demonstrations of possible causal relationships. However, there are possible competing explanations for the conclusions of the clusterwide results that are difficult to counter with the quasi-experimental design. These are the well-known threats to internal validity, two of which are particularly threatening in the design adopted here. (Some of the threats to internal validity, such as regression, testing, and instrumentation, are handled by other aspects of the methods. For example, all students in all achievement bands were in the cohorts, and we present analyses of these subgroups; similarly repeated testing occurred but with instruments that were designed for the interval of repetition and with alternative forms.)

The first of these major threats is that an unknown combination of factors unique to these schools and this cluster—that is, the immediate historical, cultural, and social context for these schools and this particular cluster—determined the outcomes; technically, this is partly an issue of ambiguous temporal precedence and partly an issue of history and maturation effects (Shadish, Cook, & Campbell, 2002). For example, the nature of students might have changed in ways that were not captured by the general descriptions of families and students, or perhaps, given that the immediate history included a number of New Zealand Ministry of Education initiatives (Annan, 2007), the schools were developing more effective ways of teaching anyway.

A second major threat is that the students who were followed longitudinally and were continuously present over several data points were different in achievement terms from those students who were only present in the baseline and subsequently left. It might be, for example, that the comparison groups contained students who were more transient and had lower achievement scores. Hence over time, as the cohort followed longitudinally is made up of just those students who are continuously and consistently at school, scores rise. Researchers such as Bruno and Isken (1996) reported lower levels of achievement for some types of transient students. This is partly an issue of potential selection bias and partly an issue of attrition (Shadish et al., 2002). As the projections on the projected baseline are based on the assumption that the students at baseline are similar to the cohort students, having a lower projected baseline may result in finding large improvements due to the design of the study, rather than any real effects.

There are three ways of adding to the robustness of the design in addition to the in-built replications that meet the two major threats. The first is to use, as a comparison, a similar cluster of schools that has not received the intervention. It was possible to identify such a cluster post hoc and examine the baseline levels in schools after a year of intervention against the levels in the second cluster that had not experienced the intervention. The second cluster of schools was in a neighboring suburb that was part of a different Ministry of Education schooling improvement initiative. The second cluster was similar in geographical location, in type (all Decile 1 schools), in number of schools (n = 7), in number of students (n = 1,161), in ethnic and gender mix (equal proportions of males and females from more than 12 ethnic groups; the major groups being Samoan [37%], Māori [22%], Cook Island [18%], and Tongan [15%]), in starting levels of achievement, and in prior history of interventions. This cluster was to participate in the same three-year intervention as part of a staggered replication series and was scheduled to begin the intervention a year later than the one reported here. Therefore, all target year levels (School Year 4–School Year 8) in the second cluster were measured exactly one year after the baseline was established in the first cluster reported here (Lai, McNaughton, MacDonald, Amituanai-Toloa, & Farry, 2006).

The two achievement baselines are shown in Figure 1 and Figure 2. The baselines are cross-sectional data collected at the beginning of the first year of the intervention in each cluster but a year apart. They are in the form of normalized scores (stanines) from the Supplementary Tests of Achievement in Reading (STAR; Elley, 2001). The raw scores have been converted into 9-point stanine scores based on school level norms. The comparison shows that a year after the intervention had started in the first cluster of schools, the second cluster of schools continued to have levels of achievement similar to those that the first cluster of schools originally had.

This comparison adds to the design conclusions by establishing that there was not some general impact on similar neighboring area Decile 1 schools operating over the time period of the intervention and that if no intervention had taken place in the first cluster of schools, the levels of achievement would have remained around stanine 3.0.

A second way of adding to the believability of the design is by checking the characteristics of students who are included in the cross-sectional (baseline) analysis but not included in the longitudinal analysis because they were not present

Figure 1. Baseline for Cluster 1 (2003): Student Achievement Across Year Levels (n = 1,975)

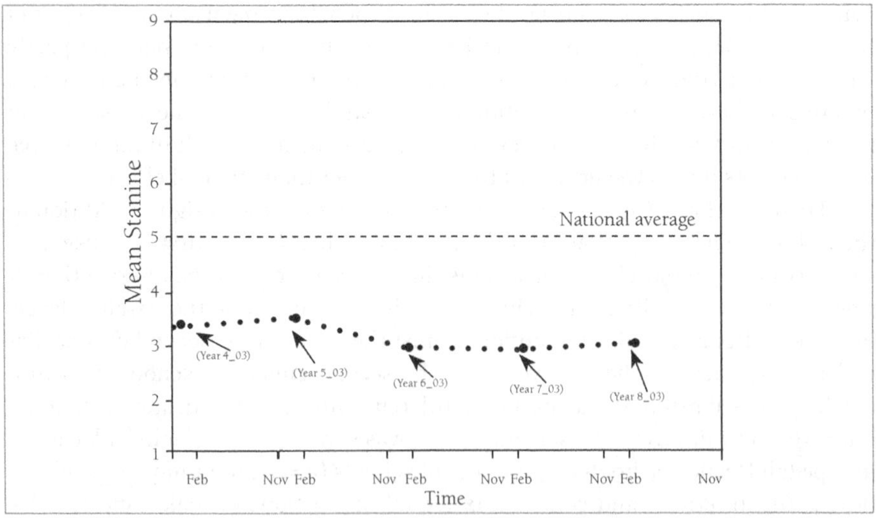

Figure 2. Baseline for Cluster 2 (2004): Student Achievement Across Year Levels (n = 1,161)

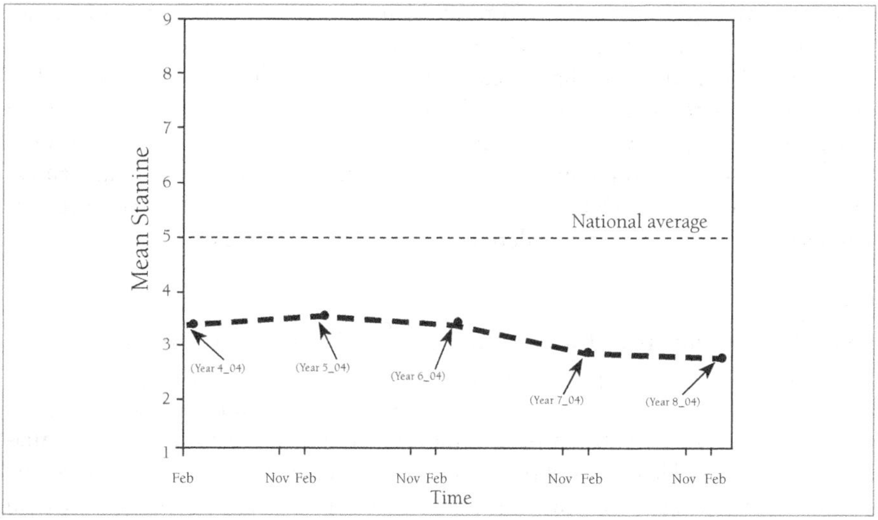

in subsequent repeated measures. We accomplished this for the first year data by checking the achievement data for those students who were present at two time points (Time 1 and Time 2) versus those students who were only present in the cross-sectional baseline established at Time 1 (Time 1 only).

The results of this checking are given in Table 1 for raw scores. The comparisons indicate that in each of all but one comparison, the two groups of students were not significantly different.

These two additional checks add to the robustness of the design by showing that the intervention cannot easily be explained as arising from external and general effects on Decile 1 schools in these suburbs or the immediate histories

Table 1. Reading Achievement (Raw Scores on STAR): Students Present Only at Time 1 (February 2003) and Present at Both Time 1 and Time 2 (November 2003) by Year Level

	Time 1 Only			Time 1 and Time 2				
Raw Score	*N*	*M*	*SD*	*N*	*M*	*SD*	*t*	*d*
Year 4	34	16.26	7.57	205	16.9	6.82	0.50	0.09
Year 5	34	18.94	9.42	208	21.96	8.13	1.96	0.34
Year 6	30	23.6	9.58	265	24.09	8.87	0.28	0.05
Year 7	33	30.61	10.70	267	30.16	12.26	0.20	0.04
Year 8	34	32.68	13.18	271	37.41	13.11	1.99*	0.36

* $p < 0.05$.

of interventions and resourcing. In addition, they do not support the competing explanation that the students analyzed in the longitudinal design were higher achievers anyway and hence any "progress" simply reflected their usual levels of reading achievement compared with all other students.

The design had three phases, each occurring over the course of a year. The first phase was the collaborative analysis of evidence phase, the second phase added to this targeted workshops, and in the third phase, a program of building the professional learning community replaced the workshops while the critical analysis introduced in the prior two phases continued. In repeated-measures design terms, these could be considered an A - A + B - A + C design.

Procedures

Phase One: Analysis of Data, Feedback, and Critical Discussion. The first phase introduced both hypothesized components (analysis and change in instructional practices) within the professional learning community without targeted workshops. Areawide data on both achievement and instruction were first analyzed by the school leaders and researchers in two meetings and then analyzed by senior managers and senior teachers with each school using their specific school data. Additional meetings at school level were conducted with support from Lai.

The format of the meetings was identical: The researchers presented achievement and teacher observation data collected as part of the intervention and then facilitated a discussion about the data and their implications for classroom practice. The analysis, feedback, and discussion process involved two key steps. The first step was a close examination of students' strengths and weaknesses and of current instruction to understand learning and teaching needs, and the second was a discussion of competing theories about the problem and evaluation of the evidence for these competing theories. This meant using evaluation standards of accuracy, effectiveness, coherence, and improvability (Robinson & Lai, 2006). This process ensured that the collaboration was a critical examination of practice and that valid inferences were drawn from the information.

An example of a data discussion using this process is as follows: In New Zealand, there has been considerable debate about the causes of low reading achievement. One school of thought is that it is primarily constrained skills, such as students' decoding, that are the cause of the low reading achievement whereas another view is that it is primarily unconstrained skills that are the cause. In a meeting, the professional learning community tested these two theoretical positions (the latter being held predominantly by the school leaders in the community) by carefully examining profiles of students' needs from the achievement data. In other words, the community engaged and tested teachers' and researchers' theories using the standard of accuracy (empirical claims about practice are well founded in evidence). The profiles indicated that students were high decoders but were weak in other aspects of reading comprehension, thereby ruling out one of the opposing theories (decoding was the reason for low comprehension) and ruling in the other (students could decode but not comprehend texts). In addition, analysis of achievement and classroom observation data revealed other more pressing issues. Students were not checking the text for evidence when comprehending, and teachers were not prompting students to do so (Lai & McNaughton, 2008). So the community realized that they did not need an intensive focus on decoding but rather a focus on the other areas of reading comprehension, such as checking for textual evidence. The feedback procedures with examples are described fully in Lai and McNaughton (2008) and Robinson and Lai (2006).

Prior to the project, a review of each of the school leaders' capacity to critically analyze student achievement data was undertaken as part of the New Zealand Ministry of Education's assessment of the initiative (Lai, 2003). In that review, school leaders were evaluated twice. They were first required to bring student achievement data from their school and demonstrate to the reviewer in an interview that they could analyze it accurately and make appropriate links to aspects of their teaching practice. They were then required to write a case study documenting how their school had used student achievement data to change an aspect of school practice to raise achievement. The results of those two evaluations indicated that the school leaders were accurate in their analysis of achievement data but needed further support in making links based on evidence between their achievement information and their practices. The first phase of this project therefore built on these existing skills and extended them further by helping teachers to make connections between specific teaching practices and student achievement.

Phase Two: Targeted Professional Development. The collection, feedback, and discussion of profiles continued in the second phase in the second year, but in addition targeted professional development consisting of 10 sessions over half a year occurred. The professional development was designed from the profiles and known dimensions of effective teaching and was led by McNaughton. The curriculum for the sessions was a mixture of theoretical and research-based ideas as well as teachers' investigations and examples from their own classrooms.

Session 1 introduced theoretical concepts of comprehension and related these to the profiles of teaching and learning. A theoretical model was presented that drew on Sweet and Snow (2003) and developmental analyses such as Whitehurst and Lonigan (2001). A task was set to examine individual classroom profiles of achievement and how these mirrored or differed from school and cluster patterns. Each session from this point started with group discussion of the task that had been set and sharing of resources relating to the topic. Session 2 focused on strategies, in particular, the issues of checking for meaning, fixing up threats to meaning, and strategy use in texts. A task to increase the instructional focus on checking and fixing was set. Session 3 introduced theories and research relating the role of vocabulary in comprehension. Readings used were Biemiller (1999), Pressley (2000), and others that identified features of effective teaching of vocabulary. The task for this session was to design a simple study carried out in the classroom that built vocabulary through teaching. Sessions 4 and 5 identified the significance of the density of instruction and repeated practice with a particular focus on increasing access to rich texts including electronic texts (Block & Pressley, 2002). The task mirrored this emphasis with an analysis by the teacher on the range and types of books available in classrooms and engagement by different students. Sessions 6 and 7 introduced concepts of incorporating cultural and linguistic resources and building students' awareness of the requirements of classroom tasks and features of reading comprehension (from McNaughton, 2002). Tasks relating to observing and analyzing these features of instructions were set. In Sessions 8 and 9, transcripts of the video classroom lessons were used to exemplify patterns of effective teaching in different settings, such as guided reading and shared reading, and the practice of examining and critiquing each others' practices was developed. The ninth session also covered some specific topics that the groups had requested, such as the role of homework and teaching and learning in bilingual settings. Session 9 also involved planning to create learning circles within schools, where colleagues observed in each others' classrooms aspects of teaching, such as building vocabulary, and discussed what these observations indicated about effectiveness. The final session reviewed these collaborative teaching and learning observations.

Phase Three: Sustaining the Intervention. The third phase was planned by the literacy leaders and researchers jointly. It added to the two core components in several ways. The cluster collection and feedback and critical discussion of achievement data continued. In addition, the school leaders continued to guide the learning circles developed in the professional development phase, focusing on the dimensions of instruction developed through the sessions. A major new feature was the development and use of planned inductions into the focus and patterns of teaching and professional learning in the schools. The schools experienced staff turnover of differing degrees from year to year, but on average around a third of the staff changed from year to year. This component was designed to maintain and build on the focus with new staff.

Another new feature was a teacher-led conference, designed to build the effectiveness of the professional communities across schools even further. School teams developed action research projects often with pre- and posttesting components to check various aspects of their programs. The questions for these projects were generated by teams within schools. The researchers helped shape the questions and the processes for answering the questions. Two research meetings took place at each of six schools (the seventh had a change of principal and literacy leader and declined to develop projects, although staff attended the conference). Several of the research topics were concerned with increasing vocabulary both in language programs and in instructional reading and writing programs. Others included increasing factual information in narrative writing (to build awareness of use of factual information), teaching of skimming and scanning in the reading program, use of instructional strategies to increase the use of complex vocabulary in writing, the effects of using a new assessment tool for writing to inform teaching, redesigning homework to raise literacy levels, and the use of critical thinking programs. In each case, the projects involved use of formal or informal assessments of student outcomes. A total of 11 projects were presented (conference format) at a teacher-led conference in the fourth term of the school year that 90% of the teachers attended. Other professional colleagues such as literacy advisors attended the conference also.

Measures

Baseline data on reading comprehension were collected using both the revised Progressive Achievement Tests (PAT) in Reading (reading comprehension section only; Reid & Elley, 1991) and the STAR (Elley, 2001). These tests were designed for repeated measurement, are used by schools, and provide a recognized, standardized measure of reading comprehension that can be reliably compared across schools. Both tests have high reliability and validity (Elley, 2001; Reid & Elley, 1991). In addition to these assessments, the schools used other reading measures for both diagnostic and summative purposes, and the baseline results for these are reported elsewhere (McNaughton et al., 2004).

The revised PAT in Reading measures both factual and inferential comprehension of prose material in Years 4–9. Each prose passage consists of 100–300 words and is followed by four or five response options that are multichoice. The prose passages are narrative, expository, and descriptive, and different year levels complete different combinations of prose passages. Different year levels complete different parts of the PAT. The proportion of factual to inferential items per passage is approximately 50%–50% in each year level. Depending on test parts, the test–retest reliability ranged from 0.85 to 0.88, and the split-half reliability ranged from 0.88 to 0.92.

The STAR was designed to supplement the assessments that teachers make about students' close reading ability in Years 4–9 in New Zealand (Elley, 2001). It has parallel forms and can be given at three points during the school year. The raw scores can be converted to 9-point stanine scores based on New Zealand national norms. In Years 4–6, the test consists of four subtests measuring word recognition (decoding of familiar words through identifying a word from a set of words that describe a familiar picture), sentence comprehension (completing sentences by selecting appropriate words), paragraph comprehension (replacing words that have been deleted from the text in a Cloze format), and vocabulary range (finding a synonym for an underlined word). Only the paragraph-comprehension subtest is not multichoice and consists of 20 items, 10 more than in the rest of the subtests. In Years 7 and 8, students complete two more subtests, which involve understanding the language of advertising (identifying emotive words from a series of sentences) and reading different genres or styles of writing (selecting phrases in paragraphs of different genres that best fit the purpose and style of the writer). In Years 7 and 8, there are 12 items per subtest except for in the paragraph-comprehension subtest, which consists of 20 items. The test–retest reliability was 0.91, and the split-half reliability was 0.91 for the total scores.

The correlation between the two tests was 0.62 ($p < 0.01$). Elley (2001) reported correlations between 0.70 and 0.78 for Years 4–8 students on these tests, indicating that the tests measure similar but not identical facets of reading comprehension. After the initial testing, schools focused on using the STAR data, and the outcome data on reading comprehension reported here for the overall project are from across the six time points in which the STAR data were used.

Reliability

At the beginning of the project, the schools and researchers developed an intra-school standardized process of administering the test and moderating the accuracy of teacher scoring. This involved standardizing the week and time (morning) of testing and creating a system of randomly checking a sample of teachers' marking for accuracy of scoring. Accuracy of scoring was further checked by the data-entry team from the Woolf Fisher Research Centre during data entry and during analysis. The STAR and PAT were administered as part of schools' normal assessment cycle at the beginning of the school year, and thereafter STAR was administered at the end of each year also (using the parallel form). Additional assessments conducted at Time 1 (February 2003) involved analyzing student scores on factual and inferential questions from the PAT and from the STAR and qualitatively coding the types of errors that students made on the Cloze passage according to the types of errors reported in the STAR manual (Elley, 2001). Four raters were trained to code errors. These raters subsequently discussed how to code the errors and collectively rated a sample of tests so that the reliability of coding could be determined. The coding was subsequently checked, and interobserver agreement on 10% of students' subtests (across ages) was 90.5% (for more details, see Lai et al., 2004).

Description of the Instructional Program

Observations of reading sessions in a sample of classrooms were conducted early in the first year to provide a general description of classrooms and a sample of how features of teaching and learning might map onto the achievement data. The initial observations involved in situ running records of each component of the reading lessons by trained observations and tape recordings of selected group work in 15 classrooms. Subsequent observations in the second year involved systematic observations from video transcripts of classroom lessons using a coding protocol based on the focus of the instructional program (see Lai et al., 2004; McNaughton, Amituanai-Toloa, & Lai, 2008).

Generally, the program was similar across classes and schools and similar to the general descriptions of the New Zealand teaching in the middle grades (Ministry of Education, 2006; Smith & Elley, 1994). Class sizes generally ranged from 21 to 26 students. A 10- to 15-minute whole-class activity, which involved mostly introducing and sharing a text, often a narrative text, or reviewing the previous day's work, was then usually followed by a 30- to 40-minute guided reading session in small groups led by the teacher using an instructional text.

These included text study and analysis (such as studying plot or character in narrative texts and extracting and using information in informational texts), specific group or paired forms of instructional/guided reading (such as reciprocal teaching, Palincsar & Brown, 1984), and individual or group project work (such as developing taxonomies of categories introduced in science topics). Typically, the teacher worked with two groups over this time period and held conferences on the run with other groups.

Levels of engagement were generally high, with routines well established and many instances of teacher–student and student–student interactions. The general organization meant whole-class activities occurred three to five days per week and small-group work with one or two groups occurred often daily, so that each group had at least one session but up to three sessions with direct teacher guidance each week. However, there was some variation in frequency of contact with each group among schools. When not with the teacher, groups did a range of activities. Some had developed to the point of being able to operate just with peer guidance in reciprocal teaching arrangements (Palincsar & Brown, 1984). In most classrooms, worksheets sometimes related to texts were used, which contained questions about a text and often contained sentence, word, or subword studies.

The detailed observations were used together with the assessments and achievement data to generate hypotheses about instructional changes. The hypotheses followed partly from a general view that a new program of instruction was not needed, rather existing practices needed to be fine-tuned. The reasons for this view included evidence from the baseline that instruction was sufficiently effective to enable students to make about a year's gain for one year at school across the age levels, but on average students consistently remained two years below at each level. Also, the national and international data relating to literacy instruction and achievement in New Zealand suggest generally effective instruction that is not as effective with Māori and Pasifika students (Alton-Lee, 2004).

One hypothesis was that more explicit and incidental instruction of vocabulary was needed. This was not surprising, given that about half of the students had a home language other than English. The evidence from the profiling tests was that the students had a limited vocabulary range, and vocabulary instruction was seen as essential to boosting reading comprehension (Pearson, Hiebert, & Kamil, 2007). However, classroom observations revealed high rates of explicit instruction. Analyses suggested that these rates reflected a focus on technical and topic-related words and that a focus was needed on more literary or academic words of idiomatic usage, figurative language, and familiar words used in unfamiliar ways (Pearson et al., 2007).

A second hypothesis was about strategy instruction. Analyses of achievement tests revealed difficulties with comprehending connected text. A solid research base provides considerable evidence for the significance of developing strategies (Pressley, 2002). However, the analyses of classroom instruction revealed the presence of high rates of explicit teaching of strategies. More analyses indicated a specific problem with strategy instruction: the limited use of text evidence to detect confusions or threats to meaning or to check and corroborate meanings. The hypothesis was that strategies such as prediction and clarification needed to be linked to checking and discussing meanings from texts.

A third hypothesis had two components. One was that students' learning would be improved if instruction capitalized more on students' cultural and linguistic resources (Ladson-Billings, 1994; Lee, 2007). That is, more effective instruction would incorporate children's event knowledge and interests through judicious selection and matching of texts and use of familiar language and culturally based forms of teaching. The evidence was that this did occur in classrooms but that a more deliberate focus was needed. However, complementing this form of teaching would be instruction that increased students' awareness of the goals and formats of classroom activities and the relevance of their skills and knowledge to these activities. Classroom observations had shown instances in which students were confused about what they were required to do.

The fourth hypothesis concerned the general issue of practice (Sweet & Snow, 2003). Each of the previous hypotheses is dependent on the extent of practice within texts and planned variation in exposure across types of texts. Observations also revealed a tendency for a large proportion of time to be spent in explicit instruction outside of actual reading and for the teacher to be dominant in extended interactions of questioning, often involving Initiation Response and Evaluation sequences (Cazden, 2001), which took time away from reading. Adolescent readers identify independent reading and access to high-quality and diverse reading materials as especially motivating (Ivey & Broaddus, 2001).

These hypotheses and the observations on which they were based were systematically discussed along with the achievement data with the teacher leaders and the staff in the schools in the first year and formed the basis for specific professional development in the second year. Further observations conducted at the beginning and end of the second year provided a check on the integrity of the intervention at the level of classroom instruction. A full description is contained in McNaughton et al. (2008). The observations showed that changes had occurred in most areas consistent with the hypotheses: an increased focus on vocabulary, increased use of strategies to maintain and check meanings, increased instruction to cue students' awareness of tasks and strategies, and increased presence of the four elements of the instructional focus in each teacher's instructional exchange. The planned focus on incorporating students' background had not increased beyond levels present at the beginning of Year 1.

Data Analysis

Repeated measures using both raw scores and normalized scores in stanines provide descriptions of achievement patterns over time. Standard statistical tests for mean differences were used as appropriate, such as Hotelling's T^2 tests (corrected through Bonferroni procedures as needed), chi-square tests, effect sizes (Cohen's d), and multivariate analyses of variance. The calculation of the effect size indexes (Cohen's d) was based on Cohen's 1988 and 1992 equations:

$$d = \frac{m_A - m_B}{\sigma_{pooled}} \quad \text{and} \quad \sigma_{pooled} = \sqrt{\frac{\sigma_A^2 + \sigma_B^2}{2}}$$

National expectations were determined from the national norms provided in the assessment tool and the test developer's guidelines for expected national progress. The stanine scale is age adjusted, so it would be expected that students making expected progress over time would remain at the same stanine level. Data from all testing periods were recorded and stored in SPSS, which was used as the primary analysis tool for these statistics.

Testing the effectiveness of the interventions in terms of acceleration proceeded in several steps. The first step was to establish the effectiveness within the limits of the quasi-experimental design. We use the logic of the quasi-experimental design described earlier and compare actual levels of cohorts and the total group against what was projected by the baseline. As described earlier, we have increased the robustness of this basic design in several ways, including replications across cohorts and checks on subject bias and on history and maturation effects via a lagged comparison with a cluster of similar schools. In addition, we examine the distribution of achievement for the cohorts of students at Time 1 and their distributions after three years at Time 6. This is essentially a pre- to posttest analysis, but because we have used stanines that are normalized and therefore age adjusted, any consistent shifts mean that change has occurred relative to normal expected growth.

Testing the generalized effectiveness across subgroups in the cohorts followed longitudinally involved comparisons between subgroups. We first examined differences across ethnic groups. The comparison based on ethnic groups was binary. Students were categorized into two ethnic groups: Māori for indigenous New Zealand Māori (20% of the sample) and non-Māori, who were primarily students from Pacific Island nations (74% of the sample). There were insufficient numbers of students from the other ethnicities to allow comparisons with other ethnic groups (New Zealand European, 2%; Asian, 3%; and other, 1%). The analyses of achievement group differences were also binary. Low-start students were those in the "low" and "below average" bands of achievement in the baseline test as indicated by the STAR manual (Elley, 2001). High-start students were those in the "average," "above average," and "excellent" bands of achievement as indicated by the STAR manual. We were unable to analyze the data according to low, medium, and high start due to the few number of students (< 10) in the high-start bands at the beginning of the study.

Modeling the Data. We attempted to fit growth curves to the longitudinal data (over six data points) to model the changes and to analyze subgroups. There were six repeated measures for each student with many missing values, resulting in a total of 6,117 records in the data set across seven schools. The obvious hierarchical structure of such data would be students (Level 1) nested in classrooms (Level 2) nested in schools (Level 3). Two difficulties with this structure stem from the characteristics of classes. Class 1 in Calendar Year 1 was not the same class as Class 1 in Calendar Year 2 because it often would have a completely different set of students and possibly a different teacher. We could impose a hierarchical structure by replacing the *class* label by the *class–calendar year* label. But even then, there are difficulties brought on by the fact that some students changed classes between the first and the second tests in a given calendar year. The indications are that 25 students changed classes in Calendar Year 1, 129 changed classes in Calendar Year 2, and 283 changed classes in Calendar Year 3. We could remove these students, but these changes are not anomalous; rather they are a typical feature of the schools, and moreover, this would result in the loss of at most 437 students (out of 6,117 records of data)—"at most" because there may be overlap among the groups changing classes in the three calendar years. Dropping these students may cause a biasing effect on the data.

As a consequence, we attempted to develop an appropriate model, taking account of as much of the hierarchical structure as is actually present, leaving both school and class in the first model. We found no variance attributable to school and almost no proportion of variance attributable to classes (< 10%). Given the issues with defining the class label, and the fact that so little of the variance was attributable to school and class, we dropped those from subsequent models of growth over the six data points.

The data set we used for the subsequent models were a subset of the total data set, composed of only the students with all six data points. The students in this subset were not statistically significantly different from other students at the baseline (see previous section on Design). However, from Year 2 onwards, there were statistically significant differences between these students and a number of students with missing values who were either absent or transient (Lai, McNaughton, & Timperley, 2007). This is most likely attributable to the effects of the intervention, given the lack of statistically significant differences at baseline. Hence, our model only included students with all six time points to avoid any confounding effects from students with differential exposure to the intervention. We also did not include in our modeling two schools (intermediate and middle school) that would have, at most, cohorts participating in two years of our intervention.

It would have been possible to use imputation methods, such as multiple imputation, to handle the missing data, but the assumption of missing-at-random missingness and monotone missingness (Horton & Kleinman, 2007) was not applicable to the data collected. The purpose of the modeling was to describe the growth in reading skills over the three-year period for the intervention, so including students' data that were not missing at random could bias the model. So we decided that the analysis would lean on the conservative side and base the growth model on those students who had completed all six tests to avoid the potential bias if we misspecified the imputation model.

From this data set, we first attempted to model growth over the six data points (three years) using the statistical package Minitab. We began by testing a model that assumed no theoretical reason for a difference in the interval of testing between school years, in this case between Test 2 (end of year) and Test 3 (beginning of year), between Test 4 (end of year) and Test 5 (beginning of year), and within school years. We tested for goodness of fit for a linear model, treating time as a continuous covariate against the six-parameter model. Given the test statistic $F(4, 1149) = 6.89$, $p < 0.001$, we rejected this model. Similarly, we tested a quadratic (in time) model against the six-parameter model and obtained $F(3, 1149) = 8.38$, $p < 0.001$. Hence, the quadratic model was also rejected.

In the research literature, one model of growth over time suggests a staircase-shaped model, with achievement increasing in the calendar year and decreasing or increasing (depending on the population being examined) over the summer holidays (Borman, 2000). With students similar to ours, Borman found a decrease in achievement over summer. However, a preliminary analysis of our data for the cluster of schools suggested that achievement reached a plateau instead, with no further gains or losses over the first summer (Lai & McNaughton, 2008). So we tested a subsequent model that took into account the possible differences between and across the school year. With the subsequent, generalized model, we could predict that given our intervention, we would improve achievement across the school year, but that average achievement would plateau (students would not make any progress) between school years.

To gain a more detailed understanding of our data and to test whether the intervention process successfully avoided having differential effects, we applied hierarchical linear modeling (HLM) with repeated measures, as implemented by the MIXED procedure in SAS, as an extension to the generalized model. The variances and correlation structure of the repeated measures were modeled first and then the generalized least-square estimates of the factors, such as students' initial achievements and cohort groups; time differences were obtained by optimizing residual likelihood functions with the Newton–Raphson algorithm (Littell, Henry, & Ammerman, 1998; Wolfinger, Tobias, & Sall, 1994) and Satterthwaite approximation for the modifications of the degrees of freedom. Throughout the process of model extensions, the Akaike's information criterion (AIC) and Bayesian information criterion (BIC) were used to determine which combination of factors provided better models.

Results

Establishing the Baseline and Initial Profiles

At the beginning of the project, the stanine distributions of both tests, STAR and PAT, indicated that the average student experienced considerable difficulty on these measures of reading comprehension (see Figure 3). The average student in both tests scored in the below-average (Stanines 2 and 3) band of achievement. For both the PAT and STAR tests, the mean stanine was 3.10, indicating that achievement was about two years below-average levels. Over 60% of students scored in the low (Stanine 1) or below-average (Stanines 2 and 3) bands,

Figure 3. Progressive Achievement Test (PAT) and Supplementary Tests of Achievement (STAR) in Reading Stanine Distribution Across All Year Levels at Time 1 (February 2003)

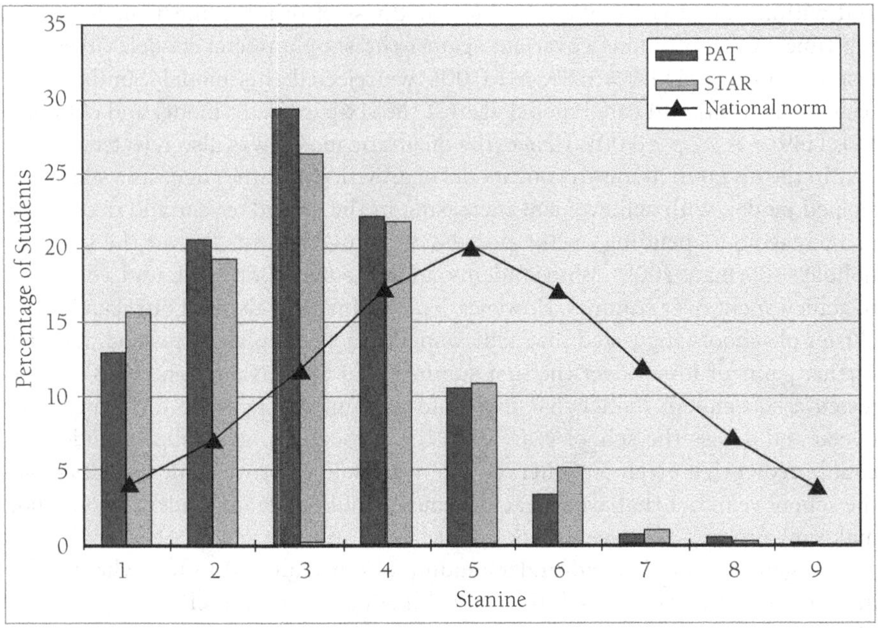

and less than 5% were in the above-average (Stanines 7 and 8) or superior bands (Stanine 9). Twenty-three percent of students would be expected at these lower (Stanines 1–3) or higher (Stanines 7–9) extremes.

At Time 1 across the year levels, the pattern was the same in both tests, with the median in every year level at Stanine 3. Figure 1 (see page 37) shows these cross-sectional data, and the means and standard deviations for these cross-sectional data are given in Table 1. The near stable pattern across year levels indicates that the students made on average one year of progress for one chronological year at school (including both school months and summer months). Two implications can be drawn from this: The teaching was sufficient to maintain expected progress, albeit consistently at two years below average levels, and the teaching was not effective enough to accelerate progress.

Design-Based Analysis of Acceleration

Gains were analyzed, first as parallel comparisons with the projected means for each year established by the cross-sectional baseline, and then against a comparison group of similar schools. The three-year longitudinal data for cohorts plotted against the initial baseline are shown in Figure 4. Visual inspection suggests that the cohorts accelerated gains against the projections provided by the

Figure 4. Stanine Means of Time 1–6 Cohorts Against 2003 Baseline Mean

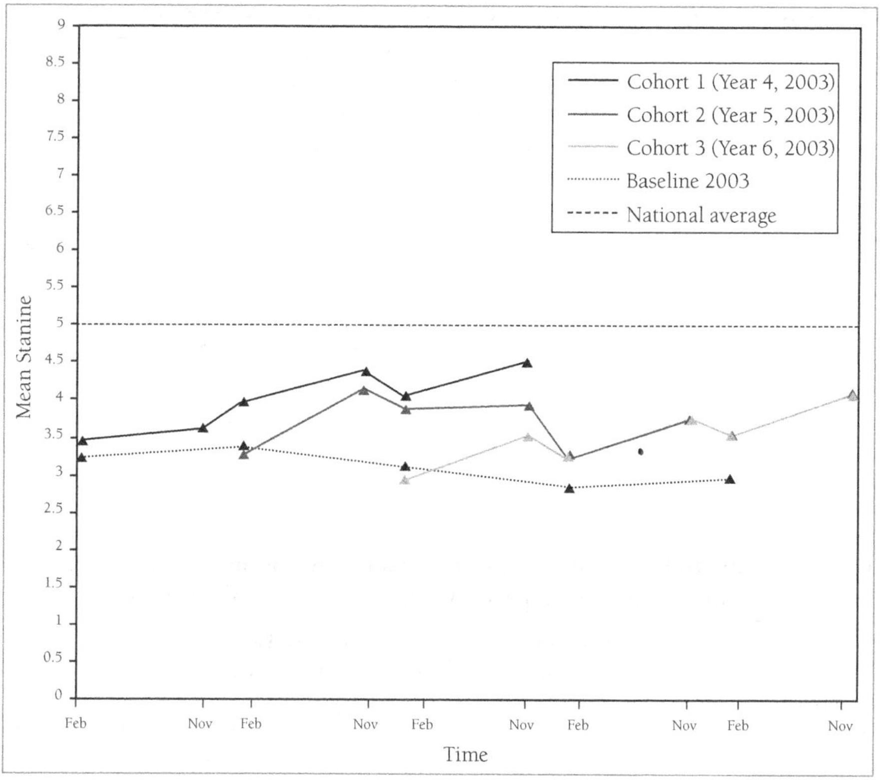

cross-sectional data after one year, two years, and three years. Planned comparisons after one year and after two years confirm the visual inspection.

After one year of the intervention, all cohorts were statistically significantly higher than the baseline projected from the cross-sectional data at Time 1 (see Table 2). This provides the initial design-based evidence that the intervention can be systematically attributed to the intervention.

Further analysis shows that after two years of the intervention, all cohorts were not just statistically significantly higher than the projected baseline (see Table 3) but that the difference between their scores and those of students in the same year level two years previously had increased. The effect sizes were now up to 0.59 as compared with 0.44 after one year of the intervention. This suggests that the intervention had a cumulative and positive effect on achievement.

As noted in the description of the design, we added two features to increase the robustness of the design. The first was to test the issue of subject selection bias, and we showed that the students in the longitudinal cohorts did not generally differ from all students in terms of initial achievement levels (see Table 1).

Table 2. Mean Student Achievement in Comprehension (in Stanines) After One Year of Intervention Compared With Cross-Sectional Baseline

Comparison Year		Cross-Sectional Baseline (Time 1, February 2003)	Cohorts After One Year of Intervention (Time 3, February 2004)		*t*	*d*
Baseline Year 5	*M*	3.42	Year 4→5	3.96	3.12*	0.37
	SD	1.57		1.35		
	N	241		114		
Baseline Year 6	*M*	3.15	Year 5→6	3.84	3.04**	0.44
	SD	1.55		1.62		
	N	296		56		
Baseline Year 7	*M*	2.83	Year 6→7	3.26	2.51*	0.34
	SD	1.29		1.22		
	N	307		68		

*$p < 0.05$. **$p < 0.01$.

Table 3. Mean Student Achievement in Comprehension (in Stanines) After Two Years of Intervention Compared With Cross-Sectional Baseline

Comparison Year		Cross-Sectional Baseline (Time 1, February 2003)	Cohorts After Two Years of Intervention (Time 5, February 2005)		*t*	*d*
Baseline Year 6	*M*	3.15	Year 4→6	4.04	5.28***	0.59
	SD	1.55		1.45		
	N	296		114		
Baseline Year 7	*M*	2.83	Year 5→7	3.23	2.12*	0.31
	SD	1.29		1.29		
	N	307		56		
Baseline Year 8	*M*	2.95	Year 6→8	3.53	3.04**	0.42
	SD	1.45		1.29		
	N	299		68		

* $p < 0.05$. ** $p < 0.01$. *** $p < 0.001$.

A second design feature was to compare the baseline projections with a cross-sectional baseline from a similar cluster of schools after a year had elapsed, thereby controlling for general history and maturation and other associated confounding variables. We have compared the outcomes of the intervention in the first cluster with the baseline of the second cluster established at the same time. After one year of the intervention, all year-level cohorts scored statistically significantly higher than the comparison cluster that had not experienced this intervention (see Table 4). The effect sizes were between 0.33 and 0.45. After two years,

Table 4. Mean Student Achievement in Comprehension (in Stanines) After One Year of Intervention Compared With Cross-Sectional Comparison Cluster

Comparison Year		Cross-Sectional Baseline Cluster 2 (February 2004)	Intervention Cohorts After One Year of Intervention (Time 3, February 2004)		*t*	*d*
Year 5	*M*	3.39	Year 4→5	3.96	3.42**	0.40
	SD	1.53		1.35		
	N	248		114		
Year 6	*M*	3.32	Year 5→6	3.84	2.28*	0.33
	SD	1.51		1.62		
	N	237		56		
Year 7	*M*	2.71	Year 6→7	3.26	3.43**	0.45
	SD	1.22		1.22		
	N	360		68		

* $p < 0.05$. ** $p < 0.01$.

Table 5. Mean Student Achievement in Comprehension (in Stanines) After Two Years of Intervention Compared With Cross-Sectional Comparison Cluster

Comparison Year		Cross-Sectional Baseline Cluster 2 (February 2004)	Intervention Cohorts After Two Years of Intervention (Time 5, February 2005)	*t*	*d*
Year 6	*M*	3.32	4.04	4.21***	0.49
	SD	1.51	1.45		
	N	237	114		
Year 7	*M*	2.71	3.23	2.95**	0.41
	SD	1.22	1.29		
	N	360	56		
Year 8	*M*	2.75	3.53	4.6***	0.61
	SD	1.26	1.29		
	N	305	68		

** $p < 0.01$. *** $p < 0.001$.

all year-level cohorts continued to score statistically significantly higher than the comparison cluster that had not experienced this intervention, with effect sizes between 0.41 and 0.61 (see Table 5).

Distributional Analysis of Acceleration

The criterion for acceleration included shifting the distribution to match national norms. The following analyses examine the shift in distribution from Time 1 to Time 6 against the expected distribution.

Gains Time 1–Time 6, Total Group and Year Cohorts. There was a statistically significant acceleration in achievement for the total cohort ($n = 238$) from Time 1 to Time 6 of 0.97 stanine. The total gain represents about one year's progress in addition to expected national progress over the three-year period (Table 6 presents the mean stanine and raw scores for the cohorts of students tracked across the three phases of the project, and this is shown graphically in the form of an overall shift in the stanine distribution in Figure 5). Each cohort also made significant gains compared with expected gains. By the end of the project, the average student scored in the average band of achievement, and now 10% of the students were in the above-average and superior stanine bands (Stanines 7–9). All cohorts made statistically significant accelerations in achievement across the three years, with the effect sizes for the age-adjusted scores between 0.36 and 0.76.

The obtained stanine distributions at Time 1 and Time 6 can be compared with the expected (normal) distribution. Because of small cell sizes at Time 1 in the banded stanines, the band cells were combined into two cells: number of students in Stanines 1–3 and number in Stanines 4–9. The distributions at Time 1 were significantly different from the expected norms, $\chi^2(1, N = 238) = 176.5$, $p < 0.001$. At Time 6, the obtained distribution yielded $\chi^2(1, N = 238) = 9.72$, $p < 0.01$. When a much more stringent test is used rather than the conventional $p < 0.05$ criteria, the observed distribution at Time 6 was not significantly different from the expected. However, the difference detected with the conventional, less stringent test ($p < 0.05$) supports the conclusion that more gains are needed to better approximate the expected distribution.

Table 6. Stanine and Raw Score Means by Cohort at Time 1 (February 2003) and Time 6 (November 2005)

		Stanine				Raw Scores			
Cohort		Time 1	Time 6	*t*	*d*	Time 1	Time 6	*t*	*d*
Cohort 1 (N = 114)	*M*	3.41	4.5	6.68***	0.66	17.71	34.33	23.49***	2.16
(Year 4, 2003)	*SD*	1.32	1.94			6.69	8.59		
Cohort 2 (N = 56)	*M*	3.25	3.75	3.1**	0.36	20.77	42.23	17.95***	2.16
(Year 5, 2003)	*SD*	1.31	1.43			7.21	12.04		
Cohort 3 (N = 68)	*M*	2.94	4.09	7.57***	0.76	22.49	50.66	22.49***	2.59
(Year 6, 2003)	*SD*	1.52	1.50			9.8	11.83		
Total (N = 238)	*M*	3.24	4.21	9.86***	0.62	19.79	40.86	32.49***	2.00
	SD	1.39	1.73			8.06	12.53		

** $p < 0.01$. *** $p < 0.001$.

Figure 5. Stanine Distribution at Time 1 (February 2003) and Time 6 (November 2005) Against National Norms

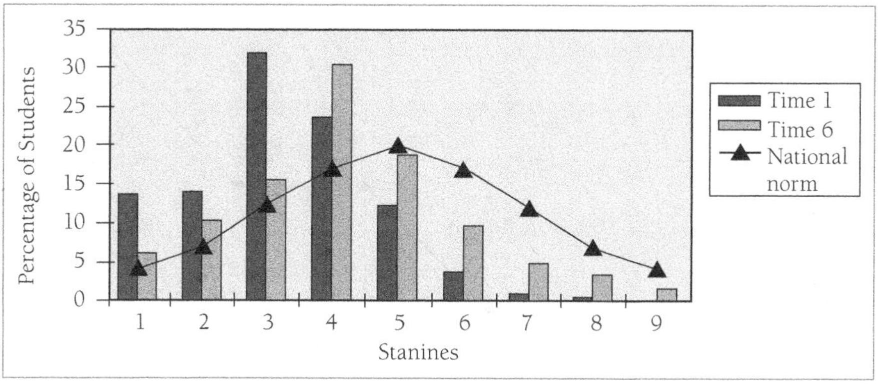

Growth Modeling

In modeling the growth over time, we first theorized that on the basis of initial exploratory analyses of our data (Lai & McNaughton, 2008), we would improve achievement across the school year but that achievement would plateau (further progress would not occur) between school years. Hence a reasonable null model would be a four-stage model specified by the parameter vector (μ_1, μ_2, μ_2, μ_3, μ_3, μ_4) indicated by Figure 6. (This is similar to other models tracking achievement over time, such as Borman, 2000.) When the full six-parameter model was tested against this null model, the null hypothesis was not rejected, $F(2, 1149) = 2.68$, $p = 0.07$.

We refined the model to give the most generalized representation, one in which the increase within a year was constant for all year levels. The fixed-effect part of this model was $\mu + \theta \times i$, where i is the number of successive interventions that a student had experienced prior to taking the observation. The point estimate of intervention effect on achievement changes over time indicated that for every additional intervention a student received, the mean stanine level was raised by 0.42 ($SD = 0.04$), yielding a 95% confidence interval (CI) of 0.34, 0.49. This reduced generalized model estimates that each intervention raised the mean stanine level by between 0.34 and 0.49. The reduced generalized model was not statistically different from the first model, $F(4, 1149) = 2.07$, $p = 0.08$.

Hierarchical Linear Modeling (HLM) and Generalized Effects of the Intervention. The intervention was designed from the profiles of the local students and their instruction and contained elements that were designed to be both generic and personalized using cultural and linguistic resources. A telling indicator of the effectiveness of the intervention would be its generalized effectiveness. To further incorporate the notion of the reasonable null model with other factors and provide better modeling for the correlation structure of the repeated measures, HLM

Figure 6. Estimated Generalized Intervention Effect Model

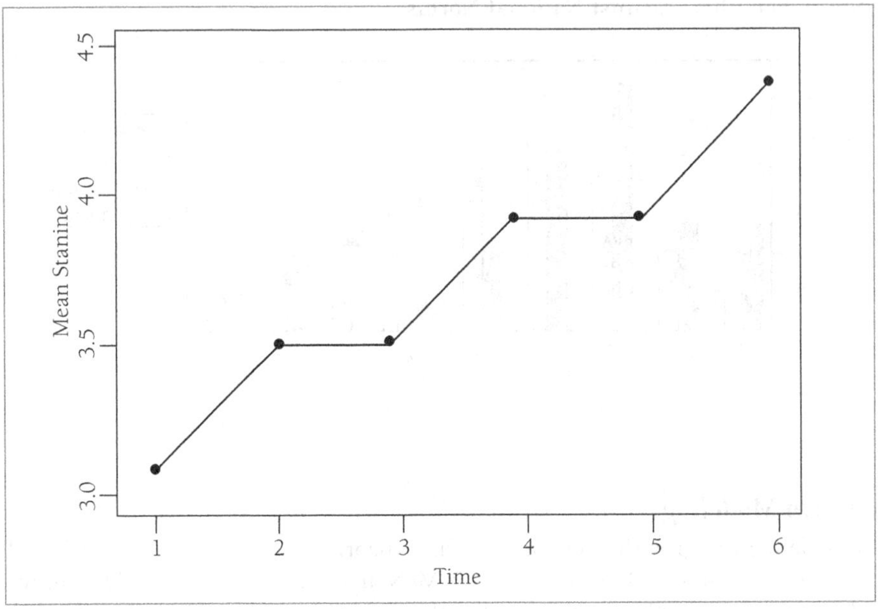

was used to develop the growth curves. The Level 1 within-students' correlations between repeated measures was fitted with an unstructured variance–covariance structure. This means that we made no assumptions regarding equal variances or correlations about the distribution of the measured data. The reasonable null model was refitted with the HLM structure, where this HLM version of the reasonable null model can be written mathematically as follows:

$$y_{it} = \beta_0 \times \beta_1 x_{1t} + e_{it} \quad (1),$$

where y_{it} is the stanine results for Student i at Time t; β_0 is the Level 1 intercept, defined here as the expected achievement level; β_1 is the expected rate of increase in reading skills measured by stanine per each intervention received by Student i; x_{1i} indicates the number of successive interventions Student i had experienced prior to Time t; and is the within-student error of prediction for Student i at Time t with the variance of $e_{it} = \Sigma$. The point estimate of intervention effect on reading achievement changes over time indicated that for every successive intervention a student received, the mean stanine level was raised by 0.30 (SE = 0.03; 95% CI = 0.24, 0.35), $t(237) = 9.86$, $p < 0.001$. This model yielded an AIC of 4,273.4 and a BIC of 4,363.3. Thus, the model depiction in Figure 6 also applied to this HLM basic model. This level of gain is within the CIs of the original generalized model in Figure 6, establishing that it can be applied to the data. The slight differences in level of gain are due to the specificity of the HLM model to subgroups of students.

To improve the model fits further and provide generalized inferences to more specific student characteristics, we added two factors to the model specified by Equation 1 after a series of model selections. The two added factors combined examined the effectiveness of the intervention for different year levels and students with different initial reading achievement as well as the changes in their reading achievements over the summer holidays in greater detail. The final complex growth model can therefore be written as follows:

$$y_{ijt} = \beta_{0ij} + \beta_1 x_{1ij} + \beta_2 x_{2ij} + e_{it} \quad (2),$$

where β_{0ij} is now the Level 1 intercept, definable by the expected achievement level for Cohort j to which Student i belongs, with the student's initial achievement level; β_1 is the expected rate of increase in reading skills (in stanine) per each intervention received by Student i of Cohort j; x_{1i} indicates the number of successive interventions Student i had experienced prior to Time t; x_{2ij} indicates the number of successive summers that Student i of Cohort j has had since the first intervention, with β_2 being the expected rate of change in reading skills (in stanine) per each summer break for the respective cohort. The complex model yielded an AIC of 4,006.4 and a BIC of 4,079.3 and is a better model fit.

The estimates for the complex model with respective CIs are summarized in Table 7. Initially low-achieving students made more gain than did initially high-achieving students. For example, the point estimate for initially low-achieving students in Cohort 1 (Year 4 at Time 1) indicated that for every additional intervention experienced, their average stanine improved by 0.45; high-achieving students at the same cohort gained 0.22 of a stanine in their reading achievement. Similar patterns were found for the other two cohorts.

There was a differential effect on the students' reading achievements over the summer holidays. For Cohort 1 (the largest cohort), regardless of initial reading achievement, the average stanine dropped by only 0.05 over the summer, consistent with the earlier plateau hypothesis. However, for Cohorts 2 and 3, the estimated stanine drops over the summer holidays were 0.54 and 0.24, respectively. There were no differences between students with different initial achievements over summer.

Throughout the model-selection process, gender and ethnicity (in terms of whether a student was New Zealand Māori or non-Māori) were not found to be significant effects in determining reading achievement levels, as including these factors did not improve the model fit. A series of statistical tests of significance indicated these factors were not statistically significant.

Discussion

The question asked in this article was whether a long-standing challenge for more effective teaching in a particular context of schools serving culturally and linguistically diverse poorer communities could be addressed. The challenge has been to accelerate levels of achievement in reading comprehension for Māori and Pasifika

Table 7. Estimation of Fixed Effects for the Complex Growth Model

Fixed Effects	Estimates	*SE*	*t*	95% Confidence Interval	
Intercept (Cohort 3 Initial Achievement): β_{0ij}					
Cohort 1					
Low	2.64	0.09	30.41***	2.47	2.81
High	4.59	0.11	41.98***	4.37	4.81
Cohort 2					
Low	2.45	0.13	19.06***	2.19	2.70
High	4.68	0.15	31.58***	4.39	4.97
Cohort 3					
Low	2.01	0.12	17.27***	1.78	2.24
High	4.23	0.13	31.38***	3.96	4.49
Intervention effect: β_1					
Cohort 1					
Low	0.45	0.07	6.34***	0.31	0.59
High	0.22	0.08	2.73**	0.06	0.38
Cohort 2					
Low	0.50	0.10	4.87***	0.30	0.71
High	0.34	0.11	3.01**	0.12	0.56
Cohort 3					
Low	0.65	0.09	6.90***	0.46	0.83
High	0.39	0.10	3.76***	0.18	0.59
Summer effect: β_2					
Cohort 1	-0.05	0.07	-0.70	-0.20	0.09
Cohort 2	-0.54	0.10	-5.17***	-0.75	-0.34
Cohort 3	-0.24	0.10	-2.57*	-0.43	-0.06

* $p < 0.05$. ** $p < 0.01$. *** $p < 0.001$.

students in Decile 1 urban schools in New Zealand. Low achievement in literacy has a long history, and there is some evidence that gains have occurred recently in beginning literacy instruction. But national and international evidence about New Zealand children suggest that large disparities in reading comprehension achievement remain (Crooks & Flockton, 2005; Flockton & Crooks, 2001). This pressing local problem has a more global significance, which is addressing gaps in reading comprehension for cultural and language minority students in schools serving the poorest communities (August & Shanahan, 2006; Sweet & Snow, 2003).

A proposed solution with two general components was tested within our research practice collaboration. We predicted that together the two components would effect changes in instruction that would result in changed achievement. We argue that although the two components draw on different theoretical traditions, each are necessary to an effective solution, echoing in part an argument about thinking about both instruction and schools recently mounted by Pressley (2006) when identifying what the future of reading research could be. The components were the need to design effective instruction from contextualized evidence of teaching and learning and to systematically and collaboratively collect, analyze, and discuss evidence, which then is acted on to change practices. Other researchers have noted the assumed significance of the first component in comprehensive school reform (Borman, 2005), and research in the professional development literature also signals the significance of the second component (Timperley et al., 2007). These two general components were present in the three-phase collaboration implemented with the cluster of seven schools. The quasi-experimental design with its in-built replication and comparison with a matched cluster and controls for differential participant loss provides qualified support for the claim that the significant changes that did take place in reading comprehension achievement resulted from the intervention.

Here our concern was to test whether the intervention addressed the acceleration problem. Essentially, this is a benchmark for effectiveness. Did the intervention produce accelerated gains relative to expected gains, such that the distribution of students over a medium term of three years came to match a normal distribution? Moreover, was the intervention designed well enough so that there were generalized positive effects on particular groups of students who, under some circumstances, were likely to be differentially affected?

Gains did occur, and the evidence based on the quasi-experimental design format strongly suggests that the three-phase process was instrumental. The effect sizes associated with these gains were higher than those reported internationally for short-term gains in schooling improvement (effect sizes < 0.2) and were comparable and in some instances higher than those reported for sustained reforms over several years of about 0.5 (Borman, 2005). More important here was finding that significant acceleration in achievement had occurred. The students made approximately one year's gain in addition to expected progress over the three years. The generalized growth model fitted to the data suggested a rate of school year gain of between 0.30 and 0.50 stanine occurring year by year, with a plateau between school years. The students who had been on average in the below-average bands were after three years on average within the average bands, with the chi-square analysis indicating that the achievement distribution now closely resembled the national distribution, unlike at the beginning of the intervention. Seventy-one percent were now in middle to upper bands of reading comprehension for age level compared with only 40% at the start and 77% nationally, an educationally significant achievement given the long-standing nature of the challenge to effective instruction.

The improvements are even more significant considering the national picture of improvements in these age bands. There is no national testing in New Zealand in primary and middle school. However, a recent study examining trends in national databases for students of the same age range as those reported here revealed that nationally, scores in reading comprehension have remained relatively stable for many years despite substantial changes in oral reading accuracy (Elley, 2005). A recent national review of all government-funded schooling improvement initiatives further indicates that only one initiative has been able to improve achievement for culturally and linguistically diverse communities (Annan, 2007). That initiative is the one we are reporting in this article. In other words, there is little evidence, either nationally in the age range on which we have focused or locally in interventions in the communities with which we are working, of a general improvement that could have contributed to the achievement gains seen here.

The intervention was designed from the profiles of the local students and their instruction and contained elements that were designed to be both generic and personalized using cultural and linguistic resources. A telling indicator of the effectiveness of the intervention would be its generalized effectiveness. The intervention showed generalized effects across gender and ethnicity. There were, however, some year-level variations, particularly over the summer holidays. Previous studies (e.g., Lai & McNaughton, 2008) have reported consistent year-level differences, particularly a drop in scores between Year 6 and Year 7 over the summer holidays unlike in other year levels, and have investigated several possibilities for the drop, including a change in the test format. However, the differences in year level in our study do not follow the same consistent pattern, and further investigation is required to understand these differences.

The analysis of growth over time suggests that change was not smoothly linear or quadratic. Rather, it had a more staircase shape, like a double sigmoid, brought about by the tendency for achievement to plateau over summer and for accelerated gains to be made during the school year. This model is similar to the one produced by Borman (2000), who noted a similar staircase shape for disadvantaged students, albeit with sharper drops over summer for students not attending summer school and a plateau with minor gains for students who had attended summer school. The summer effect, in which gains in school literacy, especially those of children in lower socioeconomic and minority communities, decrease from the end of one school year to the beginning of the next, has been related to family, social, and cultural practices that provide differential exposure to school-related literacy activities (Cooper et al., 2000). The generalized model developed from the data reported here showed a plateau rather than a drop over the summer, which may suggest that the family practices in New Zealand communities over the summer may have different features than those of the communities represented in data used by Borman and others. Anecdotal reports from the present schools implicate the importance of local community libraries and of encouragement of students' love of recreational reading as influential over summer.

The nonlinearity of growth across successive years is consistent with a model of reading in which development in the middle school years was constructed through practices both in school and out of school. To better understand how relationships between school and home over summer determine patterns of progress, we clearly need to add an ecological dimension to the model of reading development (Bronfenbrenner, 1979). Previous studies have identified the importance of continued access to and engagement in school-like literacy practices in family and neighborhood contexts, such as recreational reading (Anderson, Wilson, & Fielding, 1988) and practices described in the classic longitudinal study by Heyns (1978). The notion of increasing independent engagement by the middle year needs to be tempered with how that increasing independence is constructed or supported by practices and resources both at school and at home. The development processes suggest the likelihood that both schools and families (Anderson et al., 1988) may be sites at which to directly measure the probability of access to and use of specific practices. The presence of variations in growth patterns across cohorts and at different times clearly indicates the potential for development changes.

The intervention produced gains during the school year that were substantial enough to overcome the plateau associated with the summer holidays. Increasingly higher levels were achieved by the end of each successive year, meeting the tough challenge for judging effectiveness. We have not analyzed the phase-by-phase data separately here, but we are currently analyzing the relationships between gains during the year and over the summer and relating these to reports from the schools about community literacy activities over the summer. What is apparent is that the drop is not inevitable.

These data also signal the importance of including the summer break when modeling growth across school years to gauge implementation effectiveness. It is possible to test at a single point in the year over multiple years, thereby reducing the unequal time intervals, accounting for the effects of the summer, and enabling a different model to be fitted to the data. However, this ignores an important source of information about the changes between school years that affect literacy growth over time. It may also conflate the efficacy of the intervention with possible community, social, and family effects over summer. The need to understand this variation further and specifically to consider the role of the school in promoting community and family literacy activities is signaled in these data (Cooper et al., 2000). This is all the more pressing given that the data suggest that, by and large, the summer drop affects students of different genders and ethnicities and students from low- and high-starting achievement levels in similar ways.

Both the general outcomes and the growth curve also show the need for continued gains because the match with the normal distribution was not perfect, and the predicted time to reach normal levels was longer than three years. Extrapolating from the fitted model, we would need another two to three years of sustained acceleration, given a continuing plateau over each summer. Borman's (2005) summary of general effects for schooling improvement suggests modest gains in a first year may be followed by an implementation dip and that greater gains accrue over the medium to longer term, around five to seven years. One implication of these findings is a view of research and development collaborations in which sustainability is built into the collaboration rather than assuming that it will occur independently.

The intervention was based on two components that have been described and analyzed fully in other publications. But it is worth noting that our results support the predicted significance of both components. Other studies have linked the analysis of data to improving achievement (e.g., Cawelti & Protheroe, 2001), and Hawley and Valli's (1999) review of professional development identifies problem solving around evidence gathered from one's own school as a more effective form of professional development than traditional workshop models. Further details on how such a process can be developed and what it should look like are contained in Robinson and Lai (2006), who presented the methodology underpinning the analysis processes used in this study and provided detailed descriptions of the analysis process. This process includes a close examination of students' strengths and weaknesses and of current instruction to understand learning and teaching needs as well as drawing valid inferences from the information through raising competing theories of the "problem" and evaluating the evidence for these competing theories using standards of accuracy, effectiveness, coherence, and improvability.

What this suggests is that, in general, the teachers through the professional communities within schools had the capacity to change practices but needed support to identify the locus of change and test their theories about raising achievement. Given the close collaboration with researchers, this also confirms the importance of external support in particular research–practice collaborations (e.g., Annan, 2007; Robinson & Lai, 2006). However, identifying collaborative problem solving as important is not an argument against the need for specificity in interventions. In many respects, the analysis process was quite detailed and specific around the hypotheses for more effective instruction. Moreover, the level of detail required to fine-tune strategy instruction, for example, meant that the teachers were required to act more like the "adaptive experts" described by Bransford et al. (2005, p. 48), with detailed pedagogical content knowledge.

Moreover, the complexities in our data around change over time in subgroups highlight the need for more research to better understand the locus of change in student outcomes and the impact of schools and teachers on those changes. A number of research programs (e.g., Taylor et al., 2005) use some combination of teacher analysis of data and fine-tuning of instructional practices within a variety of research–policy–practice partnerships. Far less is known about how various components of these combinations work together to explain the results with different cohorts and in different school contexts. The complexity of our findings on the locus of change suggests that we can enhance our impact if we better understand these complexities and their impact on achievement.

The second component of the intervention involved the targeting of specific strengths and needs, using evidence from the local achievement data and teaching practices. The need to contextualize the evidence is both to better inform problem solving and to add to theoretical understandings of instruction in cultural and linguistically diverse contexts (Garcia, 2003; Sweet & Snow, 2003). The analysis of profiles of teaching and learning provided specific instructional hypotheses. It showed that low decoding levels were generally not a problem. Instead, patterns of checking and detecting threats to meaning in paragraph comprehension, the size and knowledge of vocabulary, incorporation of students' familiar knowledge complemented by building students' awareness, and finally the density of instruction were areas of concern. The four areas to enhance were identified through the problem analysis process and then were targeted more specifically in the professional development workshops in the second phase. The evidence from the measures of integrity was that the focus and fine-tuning in practices occurred around these four areas of concern, although there were still low levels of use of cultural and linguistic resources (McNaughton, MacDonald, Amituanai-Toloa, Lai, & Farry, 2006).

An example of how research grounded in the contextualized problem solving can contribute to our understanding of teaching and learning can be found in the analyses of strategy instruction. A solid research base provides considerable evidence for the significance of developing comprehension strategies (Pressley, 2002). But what was not initially anticipated from that research base was the specific problem with strategy instruction that we found in this context. Having reexamined the literature, we note that previous commentators had signaled the same problem with strategy instruction. The problem was repeated explicit instruction out of the context of reading connected text for meaning (Baker, 2002; Moats, 2004).

The problem is likely derived from the tendency for instructional packages to be presented and then deployed in a formulaic way as routines to be run off rather than as strategic acts whose use and properties are determined by the overarching goal of enabling readers to construct and use appropriate meanings from texts (Pressley, 2002). The increased focus on checking and building awareness of use over the intervention was associated with the gains in component tests, including paragraph comprehension (McNaughton et al., 2008). Our hypothesis is that maintaining the focus on using texts to clarify, confirm, or resolve meanings and avoiding the risk of making strategies ends in themselves may be particularly important to the continued effectiveness of strategy instruction in our context.

The solution to this risk lay in the collective evidence-based problem solving and the increased knowledge that teachers developed to understand the nature of comprehending, learning, and teaching and the characteristics of effective teaching. These are features of effective programs that have been identified by other researchers too (Taylor et al., 2005). More generally, this carries implications for the features of effective teacher education and professional development. The issue here is the balance between teachers learning and carrying out predetermined patterns of instruction known to be effective or developing as adaptive experts with a body of knowledge and practices who can use and modify known instructional practices to solve issues of effective practice (Bransford et al., 2005; Robinson & Lai, 2006).

The three-phase model for the intervention was implemented readily in the schools, as indicated by the take-up of the problem solving in and across schools in the first year. Successful implementation of the model was also indicated by no noticeable increase in teacher turnover and no school dropout as in the early stages of some of the school reform programs (Slavin & Madden, 2001). We attribute this to two features of the context. One is the general New Zealand context, where historically there has been problem solving and innovation at the local level. One example is the development of the "natural language" text, primarily by teachers dissatisfied with texts with little relevance to or familiarity with local children (McNaughton, 2002). A second feature is that our research team had been working with these schools on related projects for five years prior to this study (Phillips et al., 2004), and considerable mutual trust and protocols for collaboration had developed, a feature of effective longer term school reform efforts (Taylor et al., 2005).

The data we have examined here were longitudinal, which meant that the analyses were restricted to just those students who were present over three years. A significant issue facing the sustainability of schooling improvement projects is to test the impact on new cohorts of students and those students who are present intermittently over a period of time against the acceleration criterion. Analyses will need to be conducted to check the applicability of the model of growth for new and transient students to make further judgments about the effectiveness.

Another significant issue is scaling up the intervention to different schools and different contexts. Our intervention model is an alternative to prescribed instructional programs, based on a specified process of contextualizing instruction to unique profiles of needs and analyzing and discussing these profiles in professional learning communities. Although successful in accelerating achievement, the difficulty with scaling up comes from guaranteeing fidelity. If fidelity is to the content of the instructional program, then scaling up is not possible, as the program of instruction may differ across contexts due to the unique profile of needs. However, if fidelity is to the process, then scaling up requires replicating the specified process, which may result in different instructional programs appropriate to local needs. We have been engaged in replicating the process, scaling up this intervention to like schools (similar socioeconomic and ethnic groups with low-starting achievement) and unlike schools (different socioeconomic groups and ethnic groups with average-starting achievement). In the replication series, we have found that achievement has accelerated across the 40 schools examined (Lai, McNaughton, & Hsiao, 2008).

In conclusion, we revisit the primary question asked in this article: whether a long-standing challenge for more effective teaching in a particular context of cultural and linguistic diversity could be addressed. The results from our study provide further evidence that the low achievement results for such students are neither inevitable nor immutable. Rather, with effective instruction from contextualized evidence of teaching and learning and with systemic collection, analysis, and discussion of evidence that is acted on to change practices, culturally and linguistically diverse students can succeed. Most important, the acceleration criterion enables us to better judge what it will take and how long it will take to achieve equitable outcomes for all our students.

QUESTIONS FOR REFLECTION

1. Why is the disparity of reading comprehension achievement a problem of global significance?
2. How can educators design interventions that address the "summer slumps" in reading achievement?
3. Why is the collaborative model that the researchers implemented in this study an example of theory generation and revision?
4. How can researchers assist and support teachers who work with language-minority high-poverty urban students?

NOTES

*When this chapter was written, Turner was in the Starpath Project at the University of Auckland.

The Woolf Fisher Research Centre receives support from the Woolf Fisher Trust, the University of Auckland, and Manukau Institute of Technology. The research reported here was funded by the Teaching and Learning Research Initiative (New Zealand Council for Educational Research), the Ministy of Education and the Woolf Fisher Trust. We thank all the schools, teachers, and children who took part in this research.

REFERENCES

Alton-Lee, A. (2004, November). *A collaborative knowledge building strategy to improve educational policy and practice: Work in progress in the Ministry of Education's Best Evidence Synthesis Programme.* Paper presented at the meeting of the New Zealand Association for Research in Education National Conference, Wellington, New Zealand.

Anderson, R.C., Wilson, P.T., & Fielding, L.G. (1988). Growth in reading and how children spend their time outside of school. *Reading Research Quarterly*, 23(3), 285–303. doi:10.1598/RRQ.23.3.2

Annan, B. (2007). *A theory for schooling improvement: Consistency and connectivity to improve instructional practice.* Unpublished doctoral thesis, University of Auckland, New Zealand.

August, D., & Shanahan, T. (Eds.). (2006). *Executive summary: Developing literacy in second-language learners: Report of the National Literacy Panel on Language-Minority children and youth.* Retrieved August 31, 2007, from www.cal.org/projects/archive/nlpreports/Executive_Summary.pdf

Baker, L. (2002). Metacognition in comprehension instruction. In C.C. Block & M. Pressley (Eds.), *Comprehension instruction: Research-based best practices* (pp. 77–95). New York: Guilford.

Biemiller, A. (1999). *Language and reading success.* Cambridge, MA: Brookline.

Bishop, R., Berryman, M., Tiakiwai, S., & Richardson, C. (2003). *Te kōtahitanga phase 1: The experiences of year 9 & 10 Maori students in mainstream classrooms.* Retrieved September 29, 2008, from www.educationcounts.govt.nz/publications/series/9977/5375

Block, C.C., & Pressley, M. (Eds.). (2002). *Comprehension instruction: Research-based best practices.* New York: Guildford.

Borko, H. (2004). Professional development and teacher learning: Mapping the terrain. *Educational Researcher*, 33(8), 3–15. doi:10.3102/0013189X033008003

Borman, G.D. (2000). The effects of summer school: Questions answered, questions raised. *Monographs of the Society for Research in Child Development*, 65(1, Serial No. 260).

Borman, G.D. (2005). Chapter 1: National efforts to bring reform to scale in high-poverty schools: Outcomes and implications. *Review of Research in Education*, 29(1), 1–27. doi:10.3102/0091732X029001001

Bransford, J., Derry, S., Berliner, D., & Hammerness, K. (2005). Theories of learning and their role in teaching. In L. Darling-Hammond & J. Bransford (Eds.), *Preparing teachers for a changing world* (pp. 40–87). San Francisco: Jossey-Bass.

Bronfenbrenner, U. (1979). *The ecology of human development*. Cambridge, MA: Harvard University Press.

Bruno, J.E., & Isken, J.A. (1996). Inter–intra school site student transiency: Practical and theoretical implications for instructional continuity at inner city schools. *Journal of Research and Development in Education, 29*(4), 239–252.

Buly, M.R., & Valencia, S.W. (2002). Below the bar: Profiles of students who fail state reading assessments. *Educational Evaluation and Policy Analysis, 24*(3), 219–239. doi:10.3102/01623737024003219

Cawelti, G., & Protheroe, N. (2001). *High student achievement: How six school districts changed into high-performance systems*. Arlington, VA: Educational Research Service.

Cazden, C. (2001). *Classroom discourse: The language of teaching and learning* (2nd ed.). Portsmouth, NH: Heinemann.

Chatterji, M. (2005). Achievement gaps and correlates of early mathematics achievement: Evidence from the ECLS K–first grade sample. *Education Policy Analysis Archives, 13*(46), 1–38.

Clay, M.M. (1979). *The early detection of reading difficulties*. Auckland, New Zealand: Heinemann.

Clay, M.M. (2005). *Literacy lessons designed for individuals: Part one. Why? when? and how?* Portsmouth, NH: Heinemann.

Coburn, C.E. (2003). Rethinking scale: Moving beyond numbers to deep and lasting change. *Educational Researcher, 32*(6), 3–12. doi:10.3102/0013189X032006003

Coburn, C.E., Touré, J., & Yamashita, M. (in press). Evidence, interpretation and persuasion: Instructional decision making at the district central office. *Teachers College Record.*

Cohen, D.K., & Ball, D.L. (2007). Educational innovation and the problem of scale. In B. Schneider & S. McDonald (Eds.), *Scale up in education: Ideas in principle* (Vol. 1, pp. 19–36). Lanham, MD: Rowman & Littlefield.

Cohen, J. (1988). *Statistical power analysis for the behavioral sciences* (2nd ed.). Hillsdale, NJ: Erlbaum.

Cohen, J. (1992). A power primer. *Psychological Bulletin, 112*(1), 155–159. doi:10.1037/0033-2909.112.1.155

Cooper, H., Charlton, K., Valentine, J.C., Muhlenbruck, L., & Borman, G.D. (2000). Making the most of summer school: A meta-analytic and narrative review. *Monographs of the Society for Research in Child Development, 65*(1, Serial No. 260).

Correnti, R., Rowan, B., & Camburn, E. (2003, April). *Variation in 3rd grade literacy instruction and its relationship to student achievement among schools participating in comprehensive school reforms*. Paper presented at 5th annual meeting of the American Educational Research Association, Chicago, IL.

Crooks, T., & Flockton, L. (2005). *Reading and speaking assessment results 2004: National Education Monitoring Project Report 34*. Dunedin, New Zealand: Educational Assessment Research Unit, University of Otago.

Datnow, A., & Stringfield, S. (2000). Working together for reliable school reform. *Journal of Education for Students Placed at Risk, 5*(1–2), 183–204. doi:10.1207/s15327671espr0501&2_11

Dyson, A.H. (1999). Transforming transfer: Unruly students, contrary texts and the persistence of the pedagogical order. *Review of Research in Education, 24*(1), 141–171.

Elley, W. (2001). *STAR Supplementary Test of Achievement in Reading: Years 4–6*. Wellington: New Zealand Council for Educational Research.

Elley, W. (2005). On the remarkable stability of student achievement standards over time. *New Zealand Journal of Educational Studies, 40*(1 & 2), 3–23.

Entwisle, D.R., Alexander, K.L., & Olson, L.S. (1997). *Children, schools, and inequality*. Boulder, CO: Westview.

Flockton, L., & Crooks, T. (2001). *Reading and speaking assessment results 2000: National Education Monitoring Project Report No 19*. Dunedin: Otago University for the Ministry of Education, New Zealand.

Garcia, G.E. (2003). *The reading comprehension development and instruction of English-language learners*. In A.P Sweet & C. Snow (Eds.), Rethinking reading comprehension (pp. 30–50). New York: Guilford.

Guthrie, J.T., & Wigfield, A. (2000). Engagement and motivation in reading. In M.L. Kamil, P.B. Mosenthal, P.D. Pearson, & R. Barr (Eds.), *Handbook of reading research* (Vol. 3, pp. 403–422). Mahwah, NJ: Erlbaum.

Hawley, W.D., & Valli, L. (1999). The essentials of effective professional development: A new consensus. In L. Darling-Hammond & G. Sykes (Eds.), *Teaching as a learning profession* (pp. 127–150). San Francisco: Jossey-Bass.

Heyns, B. (1978). *Summer learning and the effects of schooling*. New York: Academic.

Horton, N.J., & Kleinman, K.P. (2007). Much ado about nothing: A comparison of missing data methods and software to fit incomplete data regression models. *The American Statistician, 61*(1), 79–90. doi:10.1198/000313007X172556

Hubbard, L., Mehan, H., & Stein, M.K. (2006). *Reform as learning: School reform organizational culture, and community politics in San Diego*. New York: Routledge.

Ivey, G., & Broaddus, K. (2001). "Just plain reading": A survey of what makes students want to read in middle school classrooms. *Reading Research Quarterly, 36*(4), 350–377. doi:10.1598/RRQ.36.4.2

Ladson-Billings, G. (1994). *The dreamkeepers: Successful teachers of African American children*. San Francisco: Jossey-Bass.

Ladson-Billings, G. (2006). From the achievement gap to the education debt: Understanding achievement in U.S. schools. *Educational Researcher, 35*(7), 3–12. doi:10.3102/0013189X035007003

Lai, M.K. (2003). *Review of Mangere AUSAD School Improvement initiative: Analysis of student achievement data and school capacity data.* Wellington, New Zealand: Ministry of Education.

Lai, M.K., & McNaughton, S. (2008). Raising student achievement in poor, urban communities through evidence-based conversations. In L. Earl & H. Timperley (Eds.), *Professional learning conversations: Challenges in using evidence* (pp. 13–27). Dordrecht, the Netherlands: Kluwer Academic.

Lai, M.K., McNaughton, S., & Hsiao, S. (2008). *Sustaining acceleration of achievement in reading comprehension: Scaling up across diverse contexts.* Manuscript in preparation, University of Auckland, New Zealand.

Lai, M.K., McNaughton, S., MacDonald, S., Amituanai-Toloa, M., & Farry, S. (2006, April). *Replication of a process.* Paper presented at the annual meeting of the American Educational Research Association, San Francisco, CA.

Lai, M.K., McNaughton, S., MacDonald, S., & Farry, S. (2004). Profiling reading comprehension in Mangere schools: A research and development collaboration. *New Zealand Journal of Educational Studies, 27*(3), 184–197.

Lai, M.K., McNaughton, S., & Timperley, H. (2007). *Sustainability of professional learning: Final milestone.* Wellington, New Zealand: Ministry of Education.

Lee, C.D. (2000). Signifying in the zone of proximal development. In C.D. Lee & P. Smagorinsky (Eds.), *Vygotskian perspectives on literacy research: Constructing meaning through collaborative inquiry* (pp. 191–225). Cambridge, England: Cambridge University Press.

Lee, C.D. (2007). *Culture, literacy, and learning: Taking bloom in the midst of the whirlwind.* New York: Teachers College Press.

Littell, R.C., Henry, P.R., & Ammerman, C.B. (1998). Statistical analysis of repeated measures data using SAS procedures. *Journal of Animal Science, 76*(4), 1216–1231.

McCall, R.G., & Green, B.L. (2004). Beyond the methodological gold standards of behavioural research: Considerations for practice and policy. *Social Policy Report: Giving Child and Youth Development Knowledge Away, 18*(2), 3–17.

McDonald, S.-K., Keesler, V.A., Kauffman, N.J., & Schneider, B. (2006). Scaling-up exemplary interventions. *Educational Researcher, 35*(3), 15–24. doi:10.3102/0013189X035003015

McNaughton, S. (2002). *Meeting of minds.* Wellington, New Zealand: Learning Media.

McNaughton, S., Amituanai-Toloa, M., & Lai, M.K. (2008). *Plotting effective instruction: Context specific relationships in a cluster wide intervention.* Manuscript submitted for publication.

McNaughton, S., Lai, M.K., MacDonald, S., & Farry, S. (2004). Designing more effective teaching of comprehension in culturally and linguistically diverse classrooms in New Zealand. *Australian Journal of Language and Literacy, 27*(3), 184–197.

McNaughton, S., MacDonald, S., Amituanai-Toloa, M., Lai, M.K., & Farry, S. (2006). *Enhanced teaching and learning of comprehension in Years 4–9: Mangere Schools.* Auckland, New Zealand: Uniservices Ltd, University of Auckland, Woolf Fisher Research Centre.

Ministry of Education. (2006). *Effective literacy practices in years 5 to 8.* Wellington, New Zealand: Learning Media Ltd.

Moats, L.C. (2004). Science, language, and imagination in the professional development of reading teachers. In P. McCardle & V. Chhabra (Eds.), *The voice of evidence in reading research* (pp. 269–287). Baltimore: Paul H. Brookes.

New London Group. (1996). A pedagogy of multiliteracies: Designing social futures. *Harvard Educational Review, 66*(1), 60–92.

Openshaw, R., Lee, G., & Lee, H. (1993). *Challenging the myths: Rethinking New Zealand's educational history.* Palmerston North, New Zealand: The Dunmore Press.

Palincsar, A.S., & Brown, A.L. (1984). Reciprocal teaching of comprehension-fostering and comprehension-monitoring activities. *Cognition and Instruction, 1*(2), 117–175. doi:10.1207/s1532690xci0102_1

Paris, S.G. (2005). Reinterpreting the development of reading skills. *Reading Research Quarterly, 40*(2), 184–202. doi:10.1598/RRQ.40.2.3

Pearson, P.D., Hiebert, E.H., & Kamil, M.L. (2007). Vocabulary assessment: What we know and what we need to learn. *Reading Research Quarterly, 42*(2), 282–296. doi:10.1598/RRQ.42.2.4

Penno, J.F., Wilkinson, I.A.G., & Moore, D.W. (2002). Vocabulary acquisition from teacher explanation and repeated listening to stories: Do they overcome the Matthew effect? *Journal of Educational Psychology, 94*(1), 23–33. doi:10.1037/0022-0663.94.1.23

Phillips, G., McNaughton, S., & MacDonald, S. (2004). Managing the mismatch: Enhancing early literacy progress for children with diverse language and cultural identities in mainstream urban schools in New Zealand. *Journal of Educational Psychology, 96*(2), 309–323. doi:10.1037/0022-0663.96.2.309

Pressley, M. (2000). What should comprehension instruction be the instruction of? In M.L. Kamil, P.B. Mosenthal, P.D. Pearson, & R. Barr (Eds.), *Handbook of reading research* (Vol. 3, pp. 545–561). Mahwah, NJ: Erlbaum.

Pressley, M. (2002). Comprehension strategies instruction: A turn-of-the-century status report. In C.C. Block & M. Pressley (Eds.), *Comprehension instruction: Research-based best practices* (pp. 11–27). New York: Guilford.

Pressley, M. (2006, April 29). *What the future of reading research could be.* Paper presented at the of the International Reading Association Reading Research 2006 conference, Chicago, IL.

Ramsay, P.D.K., Sneddon, D.G., Grenfell, J., & Ford, I. (1981). *Tomorrow may be too late. Final report of the Schools with Special Needs Project.* Hamilton,

New Zealand: University of Waikato, Education Department.

Raphael, T.E., Goldman, S.R., Au, I.K.H., & Hirata, S. (2006, April). *A developmental model of the standards-based change process: A case study of school literacy reform.* Paper presented at the annual meeting of American Educational Research Association, San Francisco, CA.

Raudenbush, S.W. (2005). Learning from attempts to improve schooling: The contribution of methodological diversity. *Educational Researcher, 34*(5), 25–31. doi:10.3102/0013189X034005025

Reid, N.A., & Elley, W.B. (1991). *Progressive Achievement Tests: Reading comprehension* (Rev. ed.). Wellington, New Zealand: New Zealand Council for Educational Research.

Risley, T.R., & Wolf, M.M. (1973). Strategies for analyzing behavioral change over time. In J.R. Nesselroade & H.W. Reese (Eds.), *Life-span developmental psychology: Methodological issues* (pp. 175–183). New York: Academic.

Robinson, V., & Lai, M.K. (2006). *Practitioner research for educators: A guide to improving classrooms and schools.* Thousand Oaks, CA: Corwin.

Shadish, W.R., Cook, T.D., & Campbell, D.T. (2002). *Experimental and quasi-experimental designs for generalized causal inference.* Boston: Houghton Mifflin.

Sidman, M. (1960). *Tactics of scientific research: Evaluating experimental data in psychology.* New York: Basic.

Slavin, R.E., Cheung, A., Groff, C., & Lake, C. (2008). Effective reading programs for middle and high schools: A best-evidence synthesis. *Reading Research Quarterly, 43*(3), 290–322. doi:10.1598/RRQ.43.3.4

Slavin, R.E., & Madden, N. (2001). *One million children: Success for all.* Thousand Oaks, CA: Corwin.

Smith, J.W.A., & Elley, W.B. (1994). *Learning to read in New Zealand.* Auckland, New Zealand: Longman Paul.

Snow, C.E., Burns, M.S., & Griffin P. (Eds.). (1998). *Preventing reading difficulties in young children.* Washington, DC: National Academy Press.

Stanovich, K.E. (1986). Matthew effects in reading: Some consequences of individual differences in the acquisition of literacy. *Reading Research Quarterly, 21*(4), 360–407. doi:10.1598/RRQ.21.4.1

Stanovich, K.E., West, R.F., Cunningham, A.E., Cipielewski, J., & Siddiqui, S. (1996). The role of inadequate print exposure as a determinant of reading comprehension problems. In C. Cornoldi & J. Oakhill (Eds.), *Reading comprehension difficulties: Processes and intervention* (pp. 15–32). Mahwah, NJ: Erlbaum.

Sweet, A.P., & Snow, C.E. (Eds.). (2003). *Rethinking reading comprehension.* New York: Guilford.

Tan, A., & Nicholson, T. (1997). Flashcards revisited: Training poor readers to read words faster improves their comprehension of text. *Journal of Educational Psychology, 89*(2), 276–288. doi:10.1037/0022-0663.89.2.276

Taylor, B.M., Pearson, P.D., Peterson, D.S., & Rodriguez, M.C. (2005). The CIERA School Change Framework: An evidence-based approach to professional development and school reading improvement. *Reading Research Quarterly, 40*(1), 40–69. doi:10.1598/RRQ.40.1.3

Timperley, H., Wilson, A., Barrar, H., & Fung, I. (2007). *Teacher professional learning and development: Best Evidence Synthesis (BES).* Wellington, New Zealand: Ministry of Education.

Toole, J.C., & Seashore-Louis, K. (2002). The role of professional learning communities in international education. In K. Leithwood & P. Hallinger (Eds.), *Second international handbook of educational leadership and administration* (pp. 245–279). Dordrecht, the Netherlands: Kluwer Academic.

Wang, J., & Guthrie, J.T. (2004). Modeling the effects of intrinsic motivation, extrinsic motivation, amount of reading, and past reading achievement on text comprehension between U.S. and Chinese students. *Reading Research Quarterly, 39*(2), 162–186. doi:10.1598/RRQ.39.2.2

Whitehurst, G.J., & Lonigan, C.J. (2001). Emergent literacy: Development from pre-readers to readers. In S.B. Neuman & D.K. Dickinson (Eds.), *Handbook of early literacy research* (pp. 11–29). New York: Guilford.

Wolfinger, R.D., Tobias, R.D., & Sall, J. (1994). Computing Gaussian likelihoods and their derivatives for general linear mixed models. *SIAM Journal on Scientific Computing, 15*(6), 1294–1310. doi:10.1137/0915079

Phases of Word Learning: Implications for Instruction With Delayed and Disabled Readers

Linnea C. Ehri, City University of New York

Sandra McCormick, The Ohio State University

During the last 20 years, many researchers have conducted studies to understand how children learn to read. The focus of their research has been on the cognitive and linguistic processes that are central to the development of reading ability rather than on methods of instruction (Adams, 1990; Gough, Ehri, & Treiman, 1992). It is important to distinguish between learner processes and teacher methods, because very often these are confused. For example, some educators interpret *phonics* to mean worksheets or skill and drill; in other words, a method of instruction. To other educators, however, this term refers to the graphophonic knowledge and decoding procedures that beginners must acquire to become competent readers. Many methods of instruction besides worksheets and skill and drill can promote the acquisition of these reading processes. The present article explains the processes that students acquire in learning to read and then considers their implications for instruction.

In portraying the course of acquisition of reading processes suggested by research findings, various schemes have been proposed for distinguishing stages or phases of development through which all readers pass on their way from prereading to skilled reading (e.g., Chall, 1983; Ehri, 1987, 1991, 1994; Ehri & Wilce, 1985, 1987a; Frith, 1985; Goswami, 1986, 1988; Gough & Hillinger, 1980; Juel, 1983, 1991; Juel, Griffith, & Gough, 1985; Mason, 1980; Soderbergh, 1977; Stuart & Coltheart, 1988). Of interest in the present article are schemes that portray the development of word-reading processes and their instructional implications for students who have word-identification difficulties.

Information about word-learning processes can assist teachers of problem readers in several ways. First, it can help them understand and interpret the word-reading behaviors they see in delayed and disabled readers. Behaviors that might be regarded as bizarre, atypical reactions to print are in most cases just behaviors that typify less-mature readers who are at an earlier phase of development. Information about development can help to clarify the reading processes used by students in a particular phase and also the constraints that limit their word learning.

This chapter is reprinted from *Reading & Writing Quarterly: Overcoming Learning Difficulties, 14*(2), 135–163.

Second, information about word-learning processes can clarify the locus of difficulties that students have in learning to read words. Various studies have indicated that some students, called *delayed readers*, take longer to learn to read because of absence from school or lack of adequate instruction. Other students, referred to as *disabled readers*, are thought to possess a processing deficiency that makes it harder to learn to read. These deficits may involve greater difficulty in processing words phonologically or slower processing speeds (Bowers & Wolf, 1993; Wimmer, 1993). Both types impede the word-learning processes described below, making explicit instruction and practice much more important for acquiring reading competence.

Third, information about phases of development can help teachers determine how to support, scaffold, and guide their students to the next phase. Too often, instruction in word identification is unsuccessful with problem readers because it requires capabilities that students have not yet acquired. Taking account of the properties of word-learning processes at each phase helps to ensure that instruction does have utility for learners. Recognizing signs of progress, or lack of it, in learners can help teachers decide whether their teaching techniques are working or whether a different approach might better address a learner's difficulties. Space does not allow us to consider the variety of techniques that teachers might use with problem readers and how these techniques relate to phases of development. However, if teachers understand the processes to be cultivated at each phase, they have a basis for judging whether a teaching technique might work in a particular instance. As teachers gain experience relating their methods of instruction to students' phases of development, they will become more skilled at this trouble shooting, problem-solving approach to reading instruction (Ehri & Williams, 1996).

Ways to Read Words

Before describing the phases of development, it is important to characterize the various ways that words might be read by mature readers (Ehri, 1991, 1994, 1995). A goal of instruction is to enable readers to read words in all of the following ways:

1. Decoding. Words can be read by applying decoding or word-attack strategies. A decoding strategy enables readers to read words that are unfamiliar in print. Decoding involves identifying the sounds of individual letters, holding them in mind, and blending them into pronunciations that are recognized as real words. A more mature form of decoding that requires more alphabetic knowledge is to pronounce and blend familiar clusters of letters, such as phonograms, common affixes, syllables, and spelling patterns. In English, this strategy works sometimes, but not always. It is more effective when combined with other strategies.
2. Analogy. Another way to attack unfamiliar words is to read them by analogy, that is, by recognizing how the spelling of an unfamiliar word is similar to a word already known. To analogize, readers access the known word

in memory and then adjust the pronunciation to accommodate the new word, for example, reading *fountain* by analogy to *mountain* (Gaskins et al., 1988; Goswami, 1986).

3. Prediction. A third way to attack unknown words is to guess what the words might be by using initial letters in the words, preceding and succeeding words in the text, or context cues such as pictures (Goodman, 1976). Prediction, however, does not explain how most words in text are read because most words, particularly content words, cannot be guessed very accurately (Gough & Walsh, 1991).
4. Sight. A very different way to read words is by sight, which involves using memory to read words that have been read before. Sight of the word immediately activates its spelling, pronunciation, and meaning in memory. When sight words are known well enough, readers can recognize their pronunciations and meanings automatically, without expending any attention or effort figuring out the word (LaBerge & Samuels, 1974). This property makes sight-word reading especially valuable for text reading because it allows word-reading processes to operate unobtrusively, with the reader's attention focused on the meaning of print.

It is important to understand what sight-word learning involves because recent findings have challenged traditional views (Ehri, 1992). To account for sight-word learning, we must explain how readers are able to look at printed words they have read before and recognize those specific words while bypassing thousands of other words also stored in memory, including words with very similar spellings or meanings. Moreover, we must explain how readers are able to store and remember new words easily after reading them only a few times. The kind of process we have found to be at the heart of sight-word learning is a *connection-forming process*. Connections are formed that link the written forms of words to their pronunciations and meanings. This information is stored in the reader's mental dictionary or lexicon.

What kinds of connections are formed to store sight words in memory? The traditional view holds that readers memorize connections between the visual shapes of words and their meanings. However, Ehri's (1992) work suggests that this view is incorrect. Her findings indicate that readers learn sight words by forming connections between graphemes in the spellings and phonemes underlying the pronunciations of individual words. The connections are formed out of readers' general knowledge of grapheme–phoneme correspondences that recur in many words. Graphemes are the functional letter units symbolizing phonemes. Phonemes are the smallest units of "sound" in words. Readers look at the spelling of a particular word, pronounce the word, and apply their graphophonic knowledge to analyze how letters symbolize individual phonemes detectable in the word's pronunciation. This secures the sight word in memory.

Figure 1 reveals how beginners might analyze several different words to secure them as sight words in memory. In this figure, uppercase letters designate

Figure 1. Connections Formed in Memory Between Graphemes and Phonemes in Specific Words Learned by Sight

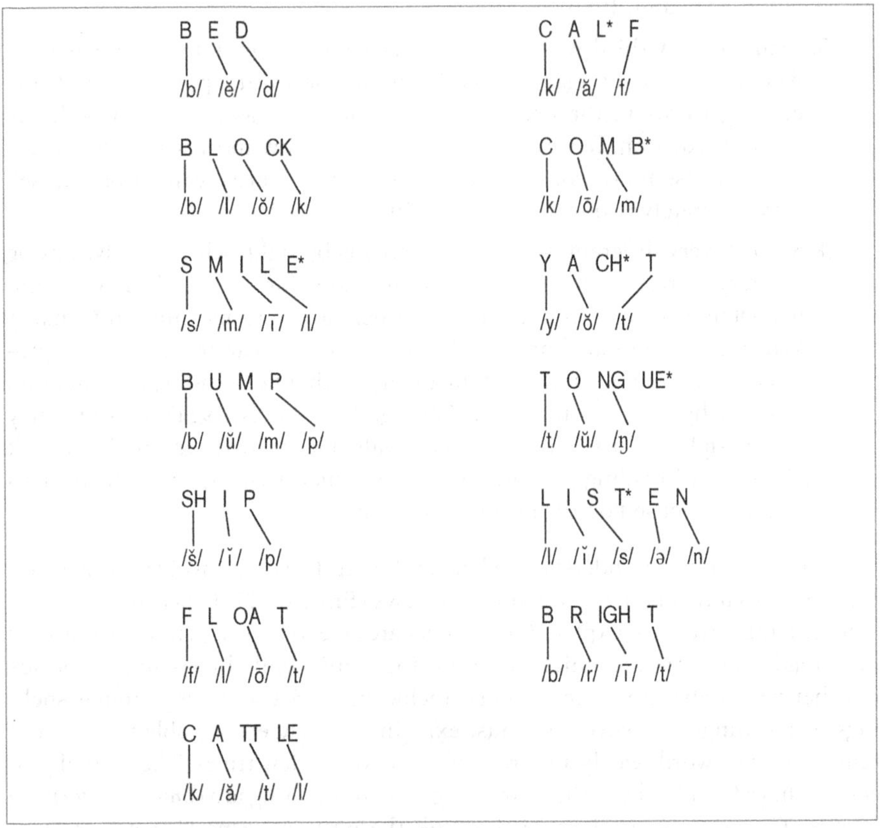

Uppercase letters indicate graphemes, lowercase letters between slashes indicate phonemes, lines indicate graphophonic connections, asterisks indicate unpronounced letters.

spellings, lowercase letters between slashes indicate phonemes, and lines linking letters to phonemes indicate connections. To secure sight words in memory in this way, readers must possess alphabetic knowledge, including letter shapes, how to segment pronunciations into phonemes, and which graphemes typically symbolize which phonemes (Ehri, 1997).

The process of forming connections allows readers to remember how to read not only words containing conventional letter–sound correspondences but also words that have less regular spellings. Connections that might be formed to remember irregular words are included in Figure 1. Note that the same types of connections are evident. In fact, most of the letters in irregular words conform to grapheme–phoneme conventions. In remembering letters that do not correspond to phonemes, readers may remember them as extra visual forms, or they may flag them as silent in memory, or they may remember a special spelling pronunciation that includes the silent letter—for example, remembering *listen* as "lis-ten" or *chocolate* as "choc-o-late." Or they may see them as part of a larger spelling pattern, for example, the *gh* in -ight.

Spellings of words are like maps that visually lay out their phonological forms. Skilled readers are able to compute these mapping relations very quickly when they read words. Knowledge of letter–sound relations provides a powerful mnemonic system that bonds the written forms of specific words to their pronunciations in memory. When readers acquire working knowledge of the alphabetic spelling system, they can build a lexicon of sight words easily as they encounter new words in their reading (Ehri, 1992).

To explain the development of word-reading ability, we need to take account of these various ways to read practiced and unpracticed words—by decoding, by analogizing, by predicting, and by sight—and to specify how these processes are acquired.

Phases of Word Learning

Researchers have applied different terminology to describe stages or phases of development. In this piece we borrow from Ehri's (1991, 1994, 1995) scheme to distinguish five phases of word learning. Each phase is characterized by learners' understanding and use of the alphabetic system in their word reading. The five phases are (1) the pre-alphabetic phase, (2) the partial-alphabetic phase, (3) the full-alphabetic phase, (4) the consolidated-alphabetic phase, and (5) the automatic-alphabetic phase. We prefer the concept of phase, which is a less-stringent way to characterize periods of development than the concept of stage. One phase may overlap with the next phase, and mastery of one phase may or may not be a prerequisite for movement to the next. Each phase highlights a characteristic of word learning that becomes prominent.

To give an overview, the pre-alphabetic phase characterizes preschoolers and older severely disabled readers who have little working knowledge of the alphabetic system. The partial-alphabetic phase characterizes kindergartners, first graders, and older disabled readers who have rudimentary working knowledge of the alphabetic system but lack full knowledge, particularly vowel knowledge. The full-alphabetic phase characterizes students in first grade and beyond who have working knowledge of the major grapheme–phoneme units in English. The consolidated-alphabetic phase characterizes students, usually in second grade and beyond, who possess working knowledge of the major graphophonic relations, who have used this knowledge to build a sizable sight vocabulary, and who as a result have learned how to decode commonly recurring letter patterns as units. Their reading is faster and more fluent. The automatic-alphabetic phase characterizes mature readers who recognize most words in text automatically by sight and who are facile if not automatic in applying the various strategies to attack unfamiliar words.

Pre-Alphabetic Phase

The first phase is called *pre-alphabetic* because alphabetic knowledge is not used to read words. Children at this phase have very limited knowledge of letters, and they do not understand that letters in written words map onto sounds in oral language. Pre-alphabetic readers are limited to sight-word reading, that is, reading words from memory, and to guessing words from context. They have no ability to decode words or to analogize because they lack any working knowledge of the alphabetic system.

This phase has been called the *selective-cue* stage (Juel, 1991) because children attend to selected cues in remembering how to read words. It has been labeled the *paired-associate* stage (Gough & Hillinger, 1980) to denote that arbitrarily chosen associations are formed to link some feature of a written word to its spoken form or meaning. It has also been termed the *logographic* phase (Ehri, 1991; Frith, 1985) because readers focus on nonalphabetic graphic features of words that have nothing to do with sounds in the words—for example, the length of the word or its shape.

The following word-reading behaviors are in evidence during the pre-alphabetic phase of development (Ehri, 1987, 1991, 1994; Ehri & Wilce, 1985; Gough & Hillinger, 1980; Juel et al., 1985; Soderbergh, 1977):

1. Children may read words that they encounter frequently in their environment, for example, *stop*, *Burger King*, *Pepsi*, *milk*. However, when environmental cues such as logos and distinctive print are removed and the word is presented by itself, children can no longer read it (Mason, 1980). If a trick is played by showing children familiar words in their environment with one letter altered—for example, changing the *p* to an *x* on a can of *Xepsi*—children fail to detect the change and read the print as *Pepsi* (Masonheimer, Drum, & Ehri, 1984). This indicates that children "read the environment" rather than the print. They remember nonalphabetic visual cues rather than letters. This has been called *visual cue reading* (Ehri & Wilce, 1985).
2. Children have trouble learning to read words that are written without any context clues such as pictures or logos. With practice they may learn some words, but the words are quickly forgotten (Mason, 1980). This is because the associations formed are arbitrary and hard to hold in memory. When students remember how to read words, they use visual cues and rote learning. Bits of the word, such as its length or shape, or other gross cues, are selected rather than the sequence of letters.
3. Students may select meaning-bearing cues in remembering how to read words, for example, remembering the word *look* because it has two "eyes" in the middle. This makes it easier to remember the word. However, because letters are not linked to sounds in memory, the letters do not constrain how the meaning is labeled. As a result, the student may read it as *see* rather than *look*. Another problem is that similarly spelled words, such as *book*, *moon*, and *tool*, may also be mistaken as the same word. Because

meaning-bearing cues are absent in most words, this is not effective for building a sight vocabulary. Teachers who have observed delayed and disabled readers produce misreadings such as these, which are way off base, have attributed them to cognitive processing difficulties. However, there is a simpler explanation. The students are pre-alphabetic–phase readers. The only cues they have available for remembering how to read words are nonphonetic, visual cues.

4. Connected text cannot be read independently; however, readers may "pretend read" text that they have heard several times and memorized.
5. The strategy of guessing from context cues is used to read words. For example, students who see a picture of a Ford convertible may read the written word *wheels* printed beneath it as *car.* Letters exert little influence on the word that is guessed because students lack knowledge of letter–sound relations.

The pre-alphabetic phase of word learning is typical in preschool and kindergarten. The most telling sign that students are in this phase is their lack of letter knowledge. Children who know few letter names or sounds are shut off from reading words alphabetically, so by default they process words as strictly visual forms. Another telling sign is lack of awareness of constituent sounds in words.

When behaviors indicative of this phase are present in older students, these learners may be labeled *nonreaders*, *severely delayed readers*, or *severely disabled readers* (McCormick, 1994). Instruction is needed to help them become alphabetic readers of print. Basically, they need to acquire letter knowledge and phonemic awareness, and they need to engage in activities that strengthen this knowledge and incorporate it into their literacy activities.

To ensure that letter use is possible, students need to learn both lowercase and uppercase letters. Practice should include opportunities to print as well as name the letters because this improves letter-recognition learning (Adams, 1990). Accurate, immediate letter-name recognition is one of the best predictors of success in learning to read (Biemiller, 1977/1978; Blachman, 1984; Chall, 1967; Share, Jorm, Maclean, & Matthews, 1984).

Studying letters in words is important. When teachers detect students focusing on unprofitable cues, their focus should be redirected. For example, when Jim says, "I know that word is *look* because it has eyes," the teacher can say, "Yes, it has two letter *o*s in the middle. Now, can you name the letters of this word?" Scott and Ehri (1989) found that having novice beginners count or name letters in words helped them remember how to read the words. Many of the letter names contain relevant sounds (e.g., /s/ in *ess*, /t/ in *tee*, /m/ in *em*, but not /y/ in *wie*), so students who know names can use this knowledge to discover relations between letters they see in spellings of words and sounds they detect in the word pronunciations (Ehri, 1986, 1987).

Teaching phonemic awareness to students, that is, awareness that spoken words are made up of separate sounds, also is important in moving them to the next phase. Phonemic awareness is a crucial precursor to the development of skill in processing grapheme–phoneme relations in words (Juel, Griffith, & Gough, 1986; Share et al., 1984). Many studies have indicated that a deficiency in phonemic awareness is a principal cause of word-identification difficulties (e.g., see Pratt & Brady, 1988). Several tasks to assess the extent of beginners' phonemic awareness have been identified: saying the first and final sounds in words, counting the number of sounds in short words, listening to a sequence of two to three sounds and blending them to form a word, identifying different words with the same initial or final sounds, and removing the first or final sound from a word and saying what remains (e.g., see Stahl & Murray, 1994).

If phonemic awareness is weak in a pre-alphabetic–phase reader, there are many research-based activities that can be used to train students in these important understandings (e.g., Ball & Blachman, 1991; Griffith & Olson, 1992). Gamelike listening and sound manipulation activities can be used to help students segment words into their component syllables or phonemes (analysis activities) or to give students practice in blending sounds to form words (synthesis activities). Students' attention should be directed at articulatory gestures as well as acoustic properties of sounds. Mouth positions and movements involving the lips, tongue, and teeth to produce sounds provide a reliable basis for discovering the sound segments in words, particularly for disabled readers who have phonological segmentation difficulties (Lindamood & Lindamood, 1975). Segmentation as well as blending exercises are important antecedents that prepare learners to process print alphabetically.

Because prevention is the best antidote to disabled reading, it is crucial for kindergarten teachers to offer effective letter instruction and to make sure that all their students master letters by the end of the year before formal reading instruction begins. For students who enter school knowing few letters, a program such as Letterland (Wendon, 1993) can make the task of remembering the shapes and sounds of letters much easier. Mnemonics that help children form memorable links between letters and sounds are used in this program. Letters are drawn to resemble animate characters shaped like the letter with a name whose initial sound is symbolized by that letter—for example, *s* drawn as Sammy Snake, *c* as Clever Cat, *m* as Mike the Munching Monster. Alliteration in the name draws attention to the relevant sound. These names provide a way of referring to the letters that avoids problems arising from conventional letter names that do not always contain relevant sounds.

Exercises that give pre-alphabetic readers practice using their letter knowledge to invent spellings of words directs their attention to letter–sound relations. It also helps them acquire not only letter knowledge but also phonemic awareness (Ehri & Wilce, 1987b). Teachers can help students stretch out the pronunciations of words, listen for initial and final sounds in the words, and select letters for those sounds. With this knowledge, students are equipped to move from the pre-alphabetic to the partial-alphabetic phase of development.

Partial-Alphabetic Phase

Word-reading behaviors in this phase may typify kindergartners, novice first-grade readers, and older problem readers. Students can remember how to read words by sight using partial-alphabetic cues. They can use guessing strategies to read words. However, they are weak at decoding words and reading words by analogy because both of these strategies require more working knowledge of the alphabetic system than they possess.

Mason (1980) called this the *visual recognition* stage because children begin to detect letters in words. This phase has also been labeled the *rudimentary-alphabetic* phase because beginners can match some of the letters in words to sounds in their pronunciations (Ehri, 1991). The following capabilities characterize readers in the partial-alphabetic phase (Ehri, 1991, 1994; Ehri & Wilce, 1985, 1987a; Mason, 1980):

1. Students use partial letters combined with context cues to guess the identities of unfamiliar words (Stahl & Murray, 1998). For example, on seeing a picture of a farm with a word beginning with *b* printed beneath the picture, students might read it as *barn*. This contrasts with the previous phase, in which alphabet letters were ignored in guessing words. Words are often misread as other words having similar letters, for example, *man* for *men*, *this* for *that*, *horse* for *house*.
2. Students who read words backwards—for example, *was* for *saw*—are not seeing them backwards but simply have not acquired a strong left-to-right orientation in their word reading (Vellutino, 1979). One important achievement at this phase involves practicing the reading direction until it becomes automatic.
3. Students can remember how to read words by sight more effectively in this phase than in the previous phase. This is because they have available some alphabetic knowledge to use in forming connections between letters and sounds in words. However, because their knowledge of the system is limited, and because they lack full phonemic segmentation ability, they process only partial letter–sound relations to form connections in learning sight words. For example, in remembering how to read *block*, they might link the initial and final letters *b* and *k* to sounds /b/ and /k/ in the pronunciation of the word. However, other letters and sounds in the word are overlooked. Although it is easier to retain words in memory in this phase than in the previous phase, the problem is that other similarly spelled words, such as *book* and *black*, may be mistaken for *block*. Ehri and Wilce (1985, 1987a, 1987b) have called the use of partial graphophonic cues to read words *phonetic cue reading.*
4. At this phase, readers typically know the sounds of consonants whose letter names contain these sounds: *b*, *d*, *f*, *j*, *k*, *l*, *m*, *n*, *p*, *r*, *s*, *t*, *v*, *z*, including the "soft" sounds of *c* (/s/) and *g* (/j/). However, they may not know the hard sounds of *c* (/k/) and *g* (/g/), or the sounds of *h*, *w*, and *y*, whose names

are not informative about sounds and may even mislead (e.g., initial /w/ sound in the name of Y *wie*). Also, they may not know graphemes involving more than one letter to symbolize a phoneme: *sh*, *wh*, *th*, *ch*, *ck*.

5. Decoding strategies are not available for reading unfamiliar words. Also, analogizing is not operable because sight words are not represented in memory in sufficient detail to recognize that new words have similar spelling patterns to known words. Rather than read new words by analogy, the new words are often misread as the known words because of a partial resemblance between letters (Ehri & Robbins, 1992).

Instructional Implications. The following instructional activities are useful in helping older delayed or disabled readers become full alphabetic readers.

To ensure that readers acquire working knowledge of the major grapheme–phoneme relationships in their word processing, direct instruction is necessary because the graphophonic system is too complicated for most readers, particularly disabled readers, to figure out on their own. Explicit instruction in letter–sound correspondences should be provided in a way that links the correspondences to their occurrence in specific words. Although phonic analysis instruction has historically been the subject of much controversy, careful consideration of research studies addressing this controversy points definitively to the benefits of instruction in phonics when it is carried out appropriately. In a comprehensive review of this research, Adams (1990) summarizes these conclusions:

> The best differentiator between good and poor readers is repeatedly found to be their knowledge of spelling patterns and their proficiency with spelling–sound translations. Phonic mastery is not only highly correlated with phonic coverage, but for low-readiness children—for those who lack it most—it is strongly and directly dependent on it. (p. 290)

Learners in this phase already use letter–sound associations to some extent; however, because their focus is on initial and final letters in words rather than on all the letters, they need to learn to process letters in words more completely. When words contain grapheme–phoneme relations known but overlooked by a student, the teacher should direct attention to these sounds. For example, when a student reads *black* as *back*, the teacher might say, "Yes, this word does begin with the *b* sound and ends with the *k* sound, but here is the letter *l*. What is that sound?" Then, the teacher should model the blending of all the sounds while sliding a finger under each to produce the correct word and have the student copy the procedure immediately.

Knowledge of the vowel spelling system, particularly short vowels, can be promoted by teaching students mnemonics that link the shapes of letters to their sounds in the fashion of alliterative Letterland characters (Wendon, 1991). For example, *a* can be drawn in the shape of an apple and labeled *Annie Apple*, *e* in the shape of an elephant head and trunk labeled *Eddy Elephant*, *i* in the shape of an ink pen labeled *Impy Ink*, *o* in the shape of an octopus labeled *Oscar Octopus*, and *u* in the shape of an umbrella called *Uppy Umbrella*. Ehri, Deffner, and Wilce (1984) found that such mnemonics were effective ways to teach letter–sound associations to beginners; adaptations that are age appropriate can be made for older delayed readers.

It also is helpful for partial-alphabetic readers to engage in writing activities. Dual approaches to writing should be adopted; for example, when students are writing their own stories or other creative pieces, *invented spellings* (also called *temporary spellings*) may be encouraged if correct spellings of words are unknown (Henderson, 1981; Read, 1970). Studies have indicated that teaching students to stretch out the sounds in spoken words and to select letters representing those sounds helps them acquire skills that are useful for reading words (Ehri & Wilce, 1987b). As students analyze words to spell them, teachers can intervene and use the opportunity to scaffold students' learning. The beauty of interacting with students about their invented spellings is that the spellings make visible the difficulties that students are having with the graphophonic system. Teachers can help students find hard-to-detect sound segments such as consonant clusters (e.g., the /l/ in *black*). They can help them identify more conventional letters for the sounds detected, for example, *w* rather than *y* to spell the sound /w/ as in *witch*. Teachers can list other known words spelled with that sound in the initial position to show how common the grapheme–phoneme relation is in words.

If teachers notice students reversing *b*s and *d*s, they can teach them a mnemonic for distinguishing the two letter shapes—for example, by using one's fists and thumbs to form the shape of a bed, with *b* on the left and *d* on the right. (To create this mnemonic, make two fists with your thumbs extended upward; bring the two fists together with knuckles touching to form the shape of a bed that also looks like the word *bed*, with the left *b* hand at the beginning and the right *d* hand at the end of the word.) Students can quickly form this *bed* mnemonic on their own to remind themselves which letter is which.

The aim of guiding students as they invent spellings is to help them use conventional grapheme–phoneme relations to produce phonetically complete spellings. Teaching students to invent spellings is particularly helpful for novice beginning readers (Ehri & Wilce, 1987b) and for older delayed readers (Baron & Treiman, 1980).

The other aspect of the dual approach to writing instruction involves making students aware that each word has a unique, prescribed sequence of letters that constitutes that word's identity and that distinguishes it from similarly spelled words. To this end, the second part of this dual approach is to teach students to write, conventionally, words that have been targeted for their reading instruction. Students can be prompted to write these words conventionally by posting the words on charts in the classroom and by placing an alphabetized word bank on each student's desk. However, it is unrealistic to expect partial-alphabetic readers to remember the correct spellings of words if they cannot make graphophonic sense of letters in the spelling. To be easily remembered, spellings must fall within students' knowledge of the alphabetic system. For this reason, the production of correct spellings of words from memory will not be very common until the next phase of development, when students' knowledge of the alphabetic system is more extensive (Ehri, 1997).

Other ways to heighten students' understanding of the spellings of specific words are to have them engage in gamelike and manipulative activities. For example, students might spell targeted words with magnetic letters; or write words on small handheld chalkboards or Magic Slates; or play word games, such as Hangman, that focus attention on the internal letters in words.

When students analyze the spellings of specific words, they need to recognize how letters match up to sounds in the pronunciation of the words. This helps to establish the words in memory as fully analyzed forms. Teachers at Benchmark School (Gaskins, Ehri, Cress, O'Hara, & Donnelly, 1996/1997) have devised activities to help students do this. Each day, time is set aside for students to practice analyzing words targeted for that week, for example, *tent*, *skate*, and *round*. Several steps are performed to help students learn the words. First, the teacher pronounces the word. Then he or she has children stretch out their pronunciations and segment the word into its sounds. They do this by saying each sound as they raise a finger; for example: "*Skate*: /s/-/k/-/a/-/t/: I hear four sounds." Benchmark teachers found that segmenting had to be done before the spelling of the word was presented to get children to attend to sounds and not to letters. After segmentation, a card showing the spelling is placed on the board, and children state the number of letters they see. The teacher asks why there are five letters but only four sounds, and the students reconcile the discrepancy by replying that very often when final *e* occurs in words, it does not make a separate sound, but rather it makes the preceding vowel say its own name. Students are then prompted to search the list of key words they have already learned to find another word with the same vowel sound. For *skate*, they might find *place*. Students practice writing the words from memory as well. They might stretch out the word with the teacher and write the letters needed for each sound, or they might stretch out the word and insert letters into Elkonin (1973) boxes to show how each letter goes with a sound.

To speed word learning in this phase, it is advisable to teach similarly spelled words in separate sets—for example, *on* and *no*; *what*, *want*, and *that*; *for* and *from*. Otherwise, the words become confused, and learning time is increased (Gough & Hillinger, 1980).

Readers are able to read connected text by applying their sight-word knowledge and guessing strategies. Their reading is bolstered substantially if they have heard or read the text before because they can incorporate their memory for the text into their reading (Sulzby, 1985). In assessing students' independent reading skill, it is important to observe them reading unfamiliar rather than familiar text. In selecting unfamiliar books that are not frustrating for students to read, it is important to assess the match between their sight-word repertoires and words in the books because students have very limited word-attack skills. In this phase it is important for students to be weaned from excessive reliance on text memory in their reading. To develop into independent readers, they must acquire and use their alphabetic knowledge to process graphophonic cues when they read words in text.

In sum, the instruction given to partial-alphabetic readers should be aimed at helping them expand their working knowledge of grapheme–phoneme relations for writing as well as for reading, to make use of this knowledge in building a sight vocabulary, and to use their growing sight vocabulary and prediction strategies to read connected text independently.

Full-Alphabetic Phase

Readers at the full-alphabetic phase of development differ from partial-alphabetic readers in a number of respects (Ehri, 1991, 1994; Frith, 1985). The full-alphabetic phase has also been called the *spelling-sound* stage (Juel, 1991) and the *cipher reading* stage (Gough & Hillinger, 1980) to convey the point that learners acquire and use orderly relationships for associating sounds to the letters they see in words. In terms of development, there is a marked contrast between the previous two phases and this phase. The pre- and partial-alphabetic phases occur inevitably among beginners who lack full knowledge of the alphabetic system and who, as a result, grapple with word reading in ways that are not completely effective. In contrast, the full-alphabetic phase is an essential beginning point that enables beginners to acquire the foundation for attaining mature reading skill in an alphabetic writing system. Mastery of this phase is essential for moving into the next two phases. Beginners who are taught to read words in writing systems whose spelling–sound correspondences are more regular than English—for example, German—and who receive systematic phonics instruction spend little if any time in the pre- and partial-alphabetic phases once they learn how letters symbolize sounds (Wimmer, 1993; Wimmer & Goswami, 1994).

The following word-reading responses characterize students at the full-alphabetic phase (Ehri, 1991, 1994; Gough & Hillinger, 1980; Juel, 1991; Juel et al., 1985; Soderbergh, 1977):

1. Learners possess working knowledge of the major grapheme–phoneme correspondences, including vowels, and they possess phonemic awareness, which enables them to match up phonemes in pronunciations of words to graphemes seen in the conventional spellings of words. This knowledge enables them to decode unfamiliar words, to perform complete graphophonic analyses on words to store them as sight words in memory, and to read unfamiliar words by analogy to familiar words.
2. Early in this phase, decoding operations are executed slowly. The slow, nonfluent reading seen initially has been called *gluing to print* because learners consciously and deliberately sound out and blend letter–sound associations in their word reading (Chall, 1983). Painstaking decoding is a typical, temporary aspect of reading development often traceable to direct instruction in sequential decoding as a means of attacking unfamiliar words (e.g., Barr, 1974/1975; Chall, 1983; Clay, 1967; Monaghan,

1983; Soderbergh, 1977). Beginners become more rapid in applying this strategy as they practice decoding words and as their knowledge of fully analyzed sight words grows. They become familiar with the most frequent sounds symbolized by letters and how these sounds are typically blended in words. Their decoding fluency increases with practice.

3. One very important development at this phase is the sizable growth that occurs in students' sight vocabularies as a result of reading practice. Much of this practice involves reading words in the context of stories. As indicated above, students must possess working knowledge of the alphabetic system to be able to look at words in text and perform the matching operations linking graphemes to phonemes. Students who have practiced reading new words in this way, perhaps as few as four times (Reitsma, 1983), retain the new words in memory and can read them by sight. As a result, the learner's sight vocabulary grows steadily and rather substantially during the full-alphabetic phase.
4. At this phase, students become able to read unfamiliar words by analogy to familiar words they know by sight, for example, reading *beak* by analogy to *peak*. Goswami (1986, 1988) has shown that beginners can analogize early in their reading development when the analogs are present to prompt word reading. However, for beginners to read new words by analogy to sight words retrieved from memory, they must have some decoding skill (Ehri & Robbins, 1992). This enables them to store the sight words in memory in sufficient letter detail to recognize that the new words resemble but are not identical to the known words and to adapt their knowledge of known words in blending sounds to form new words. Although analogizing becomes possible at this phase, it is more common at the next phase as readers' knowledge of sight words grows and as their decoding skills become easier to execute.
5. Text reading is initially slow and laborious even though students know most grapheme–phoneme relations. How laborious it is depends on how many unfamiliar words the text contains and how accessible its meaning is. According to conventional wisdom based on work by Betts (1954) and others, for text reading to be sufficiently comfortable and productive, students must be able to read most of the words accurately, with comprehension at or above 75%. Texts that students can read independently are those whose words are read at accuracy levels above 95%. Texts at an instructional level are read with about 95% accuracy, allowing teachers to observe students' miscues and fluency, identify difficulties, and provide help. Texts become frustrating when word reading accuracy drops below 95%.

Text reading practice is essential for acquiring reading skill, particularly in English, which involves retaining the specific forms of words in memory to read them effectively (Share & Stanovich, 1995). Students must be exposed to these words to learn how to read them. They must have the decoding and prediction skills to read the unfamiliar words accurately and to activate connection-forming processes that will retain the words in memory as sight words. Because each book they read contains only a few unfamiliar words, they need to read many books for their sight vocabularies to grow.

Instructional Implications. To promote learning in the full-alphabetic phase, and to help students move into the next phase, a number of instructional suggestions can be offered.

To help learners move from slow, deliberate decoding to faster decoding that involves less overt attention to each grapheme–phoneme relation, the key is practice. Beginners must read—a lot. Much practice in analyzing letter–sound associations within words is necessary so that these associations become rapidly executed and automatic.

Accuracy levels in reading words in text can be enhanced by having students read books that they have heard or read before. However, the problem is that if students rely mainly on their memory for the text and do not pay sufficient attention to the print, this form of reading will contribute little to strengthening their text reading fluency or their sight-word acquisition. The alternative is to have students practice reading texts that they have not read before. However, the problem here is that texts must be found in which the words can be read by sight, by decoding, or by prediction with at least 95% accuracy. It is especially hard to find such books for beginners with small sight vocabularies and slow decoding skill.

In this phase the strategy of reading new words by analogy to known words can be strengthened by teaching students to divide words into syllabic and subsyllabic units. Monosyllabic words can be divided into onsets and rimes (Treiman, 1985). An *onset* is the part of a syllable that comes before a vowel (e.g., the *h* in *hall*), while the *rime* is the rest of the syllable (i.e., the *all* in *hall*). Teachers have often called the rime a *phonogram*. The term *word family* applies to word sets that contain a commonly spelled and pronounced rime, for example, *hall*, *ball*, *tall*, *call*.

Recent findings suggest the importance of helping students recognize and practice reading words using onsets and rimes (e.g., see Treiman, 1985). Students might experiment with the spellings of rimes by substituting alternative onsets in front of the rimes (sometimes called *consonant substitution*) and then reading the product to determine whether it is a recognizable word, or students might be given an assortment of new words that are analogous to words they already know, with the task of identifying the familiar analog and showing how it can be applied to read the new word—for example, using the known word *book* to read the unknown word *cook*. Use of rimes to promote analogizing is considered particularly serviceable because research findings indicate that it is easier for beginners to make an analogy between the ending portions of words than between the beginning portions, for example, b*ook* → c*ook* versus *hea*t → *hea*p (Goswami, 1986).

Gaskins and her staff at Benchmark School (Gaskins et al., 1988) have developed a word-identification program that teaches students to read words by analogy. The program was developed to address the word reading problems of children having difficulty learning to read. Students are taught over the course of the first year of instruction to read and spell a set of 93 key words in the way described above, by fully analyzing the graphophonic relations in the words so that they are retained in memory as sight words. The words are selected to exhibit major grapheme–phoneme relations and common rime spellings. As each key word is learned, students are asked to identify its spelling pattern—for example, in *skate*, the letters *ate*—and to think of other words with the same pattern. Students are given much practice using key words to read unfamiliar words, multisyllabic as well as monosyllabic. Students are especially proud when they are successful at decoding "college level" words in this way—for example, reading *temperature* by recognizing the following analogies and stating aloud, "If I know *ten* then I know *tem*, if I know *her* then I know *per*, if I know *fur* then I know *tur*." Lovett et al. (1994) found that this approach helps disabled readers make progress in learning to read.

At this phase, it is important for students to practice reading words in connected text in a way that combines graphophonic processing with comprehension. One characteristic of disabled readers is that they slight graphophonic cues and rely excessively on context for reading words in text. As a result, their sight vocabularies may fail to develop adequately. The antidote to this is to strengthen disabled readers' working knowledge of the alphabetic system sufficiently so that graphophonic connections in words are processed spontaneously during text reading.

In observing students read text orally, teachers should look for signs of the following behaviors. Students should use sight-word memory to read familiar words. They should apply decoding or analogizing strategies mainly to read unfamiliar words. They should use a prediction strategy to confirm the accuracy of the words that are identified by the other strategies. (Failure to do this is evidenced by miscues that do not make sense and that are not self-corrected.) Prediction can also be used to aid in identifying words that are resistant to the other strategies. However, if students rely on prediction as the primary means of identifying words and skip over words so predicted without processing their graphophonic connections, then text reading practice will fall short as a means of building students' word-reading skills.

Consolidated-Alphabetic Phase

The consolidated-alphabetic phase actually begins during the full-alphabetic phase. Its onset is characterized by the consolidation of larger units out of grapheme–phoneme relations that recur in different words. This phase has also been referred to as the *orthographic* phase to indicate that the focus is on spelling patterns (Ehri, 1991; Frith, 1985). Word learning becomes more mature in several respects (Ehri, 1991, 1994; Juel, 1983).

1. The important acquisition at this phase involves learning chunks of letters that recur in different words and how they are pronounced. These letter chunks might include affixes, root words, onsets, rimes, and syllables. The patterns might be linked to their linguistic origins—Anglo-Saxon, Greek, and Latin—to clarify the distinctions and regularities (Henry, 1989). The

value of these chunks is that they facilitate word-decoding accuracy and speed (Juel, 1983) as well as sight-word learning (Ehri, 1995). Whereas full-alphabetic readers operate primarily with grapheme–phoneme relations, consolidated-alphabetic readers can operate with larger units as well, hence reducing the total number of units to be processed in words. For example, the word *interesting* contains 10 graphophonic units (including *ng*, symbolizing one phoneme) but only 4 graphosyllabic units.

2. Among the first spellings that are likely to become consolidated are those that occur most frequently in children's texts. These include the morphemic suffixes *-ed*, *-ing*, *-er*, and *-est* (Bryant, 1997) as well as spelling patterns that recur in many words and are high-frequency words themselves: *-it*, *-at*, *-in*, *-an*, *-and*, *-all*.
3. Students' sight vocabularies continue to grow. It is easier to store longer words in memory because learners can form connections between familiar letter chunks; they are not limited to grapheme–phoneme connections. Readers in the consolidated-alphabetic phase recognize sight words by remembering connections involving multiletter combinations as well as single graphemes. When words are learned in this way, they are seldom confused with other words having similar spellings.
4. Students who learn the strategy of reading words by analogy are assisted in recognizing spelling patterns that recur in different words and in building neighborhoods of words organized by spelling pattern in memory (Laxon, Coltheart, & Keating, 1988). This facilitates the consolidation of letter sequences into units.
5. To read unfamiliar words, decoding strategies are expanded to include hierarchical decoding as well as sequential decoding. In hierarchical decoding, more complex understandings are acquired about the influence of graphemes occurring in one part of the word on the sounds of graphemes in other parts of the word—for example, the influence of final *-e* on the preceding vowel (e.g., *fine* vs. *fin*, *pane* vs. *pan*, *cone* vs. *con*), the influence of *e* and *i* on the preceding consonant *g* or *c* (e.g., *wage* vs. *wag*, *cent* vs. *cant*, *face* vs. *fact*, *city* vs. *cat*), and the influence of double consonants on a preceding vowel (e.g., *cutter* vs. *cuter*, *latte* vs. *late*) (Venezky, 1970; Venezky & Johnson, 1973). Students acquire working knowledge, that is, implicit knowledge, of these relations. Teaching students explicitly stated rules may promote acquisition of working knowledge, but it is no guarantee (Beck, 1981). Evidence that students have acquired working knowledge is revealed in tasks requiring them to read real words they have never read before (such as *gather*) or nonwords (such as *cibe*) containing the patterns.

Instructional Implications. Signs that average readers are using consolidated units in their reading become apparent typically in second grade (Bowey & Hansen, 1994; Ehri, 1991; Juel, 1983, 1991). Acquisition of more complex relationships may continue to mature through at least the eighth grade (Juel, 1991; Venezky, 1976).

Although the analogy strategy may be taught in the full-alphabetic phase, continued attention is warranted during the consolidated-alphabetic phase. To direct students' attention to common spelling patterns, they can practice dividing written words into onsets and rimes and practice the strategy of reading words by analogy. As this phase progresses, students should be helped to make the transition from (a) analogizing with prompts to (b) analogizing consciously on their own to (c) analogizing unconsciously on their own.

Students should learn to break apart multisyllabic words into separate syllables by locating vowel nuclei and pronouncing each vowel with its adjacent consonants as a separate syllable. Some syllables can be read by analogy to familiar words. As students practice decoding multisyllabic words, they acquire implicit awareness that syllable breaks tend to come between certain letters and not between others. Practice is much more effective for learning this than having students memorize syllabication rules. Segmenting spelling patterns into syllables and pronouncing them can be done not only to decode unfamiliar words but also to analyze the spellings of lengthy words whose identities have already been determined, perhaps from context. This type of analysis should help students form the connections needed to retain the words in memory as sight words.

Additional regularities of the English spelling system will become apparent to students who engage in word-study activities that involve distinguishing the linguistic roots of spellings and then analyzing words with these roots to discover relationships between the meanings of words and the meanings of their parts (Henry, 1989). For example, students can learn to identify and analyze words containing Anglo-Saxon parts, such as *hood*, *ful*, *ness*, *ship*, and *ish*; or Greek parts, such as *tele*, *graph*, *ology*, *phon*, and *auto*; or Latin parts, such as *tion*, *ture*, *scrib*, *struct*, and *rupt*. They can explore whether different words having the same parts bear any similarities in their meanings as a result. Word-study activities such as these can be quite fascinating to students.

Delayed readers may gain control of graphophonic word-identification strategies with carefully planned programs, but their progress is often halted around the fourth grade, when they encounter increasing numbers of multisyllable words—not just two-syllable words, but words having three, four, and five syllables or more. Orthographic recoding through application of word-pattern analysis, use of typical word units, and recognition of prefixes and suffixes must receive direct practice for disabled readers to become skillful in identifying these words. Providing recoding models ("look for affixes, then look for a base word"), teaching students to detect analogies, giving practice dividing words into syllables, using word sorts designed to point up common syllables, building longer words from shorter ones, and other activities can develop skill in processing multisyllabic words. (See Cunningham, 1998, for additional specific suggestions.)

Students should engage in much practice using the various knowledge sources and strategies to read words during text reading so that word reading becomes automatic and fluent. This is important so that word reading operates unobtrusively as an integral part of text reading with the reader's attention focused on comprehension.

Automatic Phase

This is the phase of proficient word reading. Chall (1983) termed this the *automatic phase* because of readers' highly developed automaticity and speed in identifying unfamiliar as well as familiar words. The majority of words that readers at this phase encounter are words in their sight vocabularies, enabling them to read most words effortlessly in or out of context. On the occasions when an uncommon, technical, or foreign word is met, these readers have several strategies at their disposal for identifying the word. There is some evidence that when automatic-phase readers recognize words by sight, the other word-reading strategies are at work as well, though at an unconscious level, and contribute to efficient reading by confirming the identities of words and thus creating redundancy in the processing of text (Perfetti, 1985). The presence of multiple sources to verify word recognition maintains a high level of reading accuracy. Automatic, fluent word recognition frees the reader's attention to focus on text meaning.

Conclusion

In this review we have indicated that as readers progress from the earliest phase of reading to the most proficient phase, they learn to read words by several different means: by using context, by decoding through use of letter–sound associations or spelling patterns, by analogy, and by sight. At each phase, reading improves as new mechanisms for recognizing words are added to the learner's repertoire. When readers reach the automatic phase, all of these systems are under their control. It is important for teachers to recognize which systems are operational at each phase and which are beyond reach at that phase.

Knowledge of the characteristics of each phase can provide teachers with a basis for assessing the strategies available to readers when they respond to print. As a first step, teachers can examine the list of characteristics typical of each phase and compare them to the predominant responses of a learner. Once the probable phase is identified, a program of word learning can be tailored to capitalize on the student's learning strengths, to avoid instruction that requires processes the learner has not yet acquired, and to provide lessons that will move the student through that phase into the next. In this way, knowledge about the phases of word learning allows teachers of delayed and disabled readers to move beyond generalized prescriptions for word learning. It provides them with a basis for designing lessons that more precisely make contact with each student's word-reading knowledge and strategies.

In the past, a common approach to instruction has been to determine which specific skill needs to be taught to students—for example, developing a larger sight vocabulary, or increasing knowledge of letter–sound relationships, or increasing fluency. Once determined, a rather standard group of activities has typically been used with all students. In contrast, according to phase theory, what is taught depends on a student's phase of development. Although all facets of word learning may need to be addressed in some fashion, the specific type of instruction that facilitates reading for students in one word-learning phase may not advance learning for students in a different phase. Vellutino and Scanlon (1987) provide one example of this disparity. Teachers may expedite breakthroughs into reading during the pre-alphabetic phase of development by giving students immediate access to word names through whole-word instruction. However, this will not contribute to students' development in the next phase. For progress to continue, teachers must provide opportunities for students to develop skill in analyzing words into their sound-symbol constituents. Another example is the teacher who attempts to teach letter–sound decoding to students who lack phonemic awareness or knowledge of all the letter shapes and sounds. This is destined to result in slow and incomplete learning as well as frustration for both teacher and student.

It is important to recognize that, compared to normally developing readers, delayed and disabled readers have more difficulty learning to read words in most of the ways we have described. They are slower to acquire a sight vocabulary (Ehri & Saltmarsh, 1995). They have limited knowledge and use of decoding and analogizing strategies (Rack, Snowling, & Olson, 1992). One reason why multiple word-reading deficiencies are apparent in these students is that the various ways of reading words develop together and are mutually interdependent throughout development, as we have indicated. If one way does not develop adequately, then the other ways will not develop adequately either. Decoding skill is needed to retain fully analyzed sight words in memory. A sight vocabulary is needed to read words by analogy. Familiarity with analogous relations among sight words helps in learning spelling patterns that are useful for more efficient decoding. This means that students having difficulty learning to read need instruction that is thorough in covering all aspects of word reading. Very little can be left to self-discovery or chance. Clues about how growth can be promoted at each phase of development are found in the cognitive and instructional descriptions we offer in this piece. With practice applying this phase theory in their teaching, we hope that teachers can acquire a more refined sense of their students, of how far they have progressed in their ability to read words, and of what types of instruction are most helpful for advancing their development as readers.

QUESTIONS FOR REFLECTION

1. How do students form connections among written text, pronunciation, and meanings?
2. Why might it be preferable to conceptualize word learning as phases as opposed to stages?
3. What is the role of direct instruction in the different phases of word learning?

REFERENCES

Adams, M. (1990). *Beginning to read: Thinking and learning about print.* Cambridge, MA: MIT Press.

Ball, E., & Blachman, B. (1991). Does phoneme awareness training in kindergarten make a difference in early word recognition and developmental spelling? *Reading Research Quarterly, 26,* 49–66.

Baron, J., & Treiman, R. (1980). Use of orthography in reading and learning to read. In J. Kavanaugh & R. Venezky (Eds.), *Orthography, reading, and dyslexia* (pp. 155–170). Baltimore: University Park Press.

Barr, R. (1974/1975). The effect of instruction on pupil reading strategies. *Reading Research Quarterly, 10,* 555–582.

Beck, I. (1981). Reading problems and instructional practices. In G. Mackinnon & T. Waller (Eds.), *Reading research: Advances in theory and practice* (Vol. 2, pp. 55–95). New York: Academic Press.

Betts, E. (1954). *Foundations of reading instruction* (3rd ed.). New York: American Book Co.

Biemiller, A. (1977/1978). Relationship between oral reading rates for letters, words, and simple text in the development of reading achievement. *Reading Research Quarterly, 13,* 223–253.

Blachman, B. (1984). Relationship of rapid naming ability and language analysis skills to kindergarten and first-grade reading achievement. *Journal of Educational Psychology, 76,* 610–622.

Bowers, P., & Wolf, M. (1993). Theoretical links among naming speed, precise timing mechanisms and orthographic skill in dyslexia. *Reading and Writing: An Interdisciplinary Journal, 5,* 69–85.

Bowey, J., & Hansen, J. (1994). The development of orthographic rimes as units of word recognition. *Journal of Experimental Child Psychology, 58,* 465–488.

Bryant, P., Nunes, T., & Bindman, M. (1997). Children's understanding of the connection between grammar and spelling. In B. Blachman (Ed.), *Foundations of reading acquisition and dyslexia: Implications for early intervention* (pp. 219–240). Mahwah, NJ: Erlbaum.

Chall, J. (1967). *Learning to read: The great debate.* New York: McGraw-Hill.

Chall, J. (1983). *Stages of reading development.* New York: McGraw-Hill.

Clay, M. (1967). The reading behaviour of five-year-old children: A research report. *New Zealand Journal of Educational Studies, 2*(1), 11–31.

Cunningham, P.M. (1998). The multisyllabic word dilemma: Helping students build meaning, spell, and read "big" words. *Reading & Writing Quarterly, 14,* 191–218.

Ehri, L. (1986). Sources of difficulty in learning to spell and read words. In M. Wolraich & D. Routh (Eds.), *Advances in developmental and behavioral pediatrics* (Vol. 7, pp. 121–195). Greenwich, CT: JAI Press.

Ehri, L. (1987). Learning to read and spell words. *Journal of Reading Behavior, 19,* 5–31.

Ehri, L. (1991). Development of the ability to read words. In R. Barr, M.L. Kamil, P. Mosenthal, & P.D. Pearson (Eds.), *Handbook of reading research* (Vol. 2, pp. 383–417). White Plains, NY: Longman.

Ehri, L. (1992). Reconceptualizing the development of sight word reading and its relationship to recoding. In P. Gough, L. Ehri, & R. Treiman (Eds.), *Reading acquisition* (pp. 107–143). Hillsdale, NJ: Erlbaum.

Ehri, L. (1994). Development of the ability to read words: Update. In R.B. Ruddell, M.R. Ruddell, & H. Singer (Eds.), *Theoretical models and processes of reading* (4th ed., pp. 323–358). Newark, DE: International Reading Association.

Ehri, L. (1995). Phases of development in learning to read words by sight. *Journal of Research in Reading, 18,* 116–125.

Ehri, L. (1997). Learning to read and learning to spell are one and the same, almost. In C. Perfetti, L. Rieben, & M. Fayol (Eds.), *Learning to spell: Research, theory and practice across languages* (pp. 237–269). Mahwah, NJ: Erlbaum.

Ehri, L. (1997). Sight word learning in normal readers and dyslexics. In B. Blachman (Ed.), *Foundations of reading acquisition and dyslexia: Implications for early intervention* (pp. 163–189). Mahwah, NJ: Erlbaum.

Ehri, L., Deffner, N., & Wilce, L. (1984). Pictorial mnemonics for phonics. *Journal of Educational Psychology, 76,* 880–893.

Ehri, L., & Robbins, C. (1992). Beginners need some decoding skill to read words by analogy. *Reading Research Quarterly, 27,* 12–26.

Ehri, L., & Saltmarsh, J. (1995). Beginning readers outperform older disabled readers in learning to read words by sight. *Reading and Writing: An Interdisciplinary Journal, 7,* 295–326.

Ehri, L., & Wilce, L. (1985). Movement into reading: Is the first stage of printed word learning visual or phonetic? *Reading Research Quarterly, 20,* 163–179.

Ehri, L., & Wilce, L. (1987a). Cipher versus cue reading: An experiment in decoding acquisition. *Journal of Educational Psychology, 79,* 3–13.

Ehri, L., & Wilce, L. (1987b). Does learning to spell help beginners learn to read words? *Reading Research Quarterly, 22,* 47–65.

Ehri, L., & Williams, J. (1996). Learning to read and learning to teach reading. In F. Murray (Ed.), *The teacher educator's handbook: Building a knowledge base for the preparation of teachers* (pp. 231–244). San Francisco: Jossey-Bass.

Elkonin, D. (1973). U.S.S.R. In J. Downing (Ed.), *Comparative reading* (pp. 551–579). New York: Macmillan.

Frith, V. (1985). Beneath the surface of developmental dyslexia. In K.E. Patterson, J.C. Marshall, & M. Coltheart (Eds.), *Surface dyslexia: Neuropsychological and cognitive studies of phonological reading* (pp. 301–330). London: Erlbaum.

Gaskins, I., Downer, M., Anderson, R., Cunningham, P., Gaskins, R., Schommer, M., et al. (1988). A metacognitive approach to phonics: Using what you know to decode what you don't know. *Remedial and Special Education, 9,* 36–41.

Gaskins, I., Ehri, L., Cress, C., O'Hara, C., & Donnelly, K. (1996/1997). Procedures for word learning: Making discoveries about words. *The Reading Teacher, 50,* 312–327.

Goodman, K. (1976). Reading: A psycholinguistic guessing game. In H. Singer & R.B. Ruddell (Eds.), *Theoretical models and processes of reading* (2nd ed., pp. 497–508). Newark, DE: International Reading Association.

Goswami, U. (1986). Children's use of analogy in learning to read: A developmental study. *Journal of Experimental Child Psychology, 42,* 73–83.

Goswami, U. (1988). Orthographic analogies and reading development. *Quarterly Journal of Experimental Psychology, 40,* 239–268.

Gough, P., Ehri, L., & Treiman, R. (Eds.). (1992). *Reading acquisition.* Hillsdale, NJ: Erlbaum.

Gough, P., & Hillinger, M. (1980). Learning to read: An unnatural act. *Bulletin of the Orton Society, 30,* 179–196.

Gough, P., & Walsh, S. (1991). Chinese, Phoenicians, and the orthographic cipher of English. In S. Brady & D. Shankweiler (Eds.), *Phonological processes in literacy: A tribute to Isabelle Y. Liberman* (pp. 199–209). Hillsdale, NJ: Erlbaum.

Griffith, P., & Olson, M. (1992). Phonemic awareness helps beginning readers break the code. *The Reading Teacher, 45,* 516–523.

Henderson, E. (1981). *Learning to read and spell: The child's knowledge of words.* DeKalb: Northern Illinois University Press.

Henry, M. (1989). Children's word structure knowledge: Implications for decoding and spelling instruction. *Reading and Writing: An Interdisciplinary Journal, 2,* 135–152.

Juel, C. (1983). The development and use of mediated word identification. *Reading Research Quarterly, 18,* 306–327.

Juel, C. (1991). Beginning reading. In R. Barr, M.L. Kamil, P. Mosenthal, & P.D. Pearson (Eds.), *Handbook of reading research* (Vol. 2, pp. 759–788). White Plains, NY: Longman.

Juel, C., Griffith, P., & Gough, P. (1985). Reading and spelling strategies of first-grade children. In J. Niles & R. Lalik (Eds.), *Issues in literacy: A research perspective* (pp. 306–309). Rochester, NY: National Reading Conference.

Juel, C., Griffith, P., & Gough, P. (1986). Acquisition of literacy: A longitudinal study of children in first and second grade. *Journal of Educational Psychology, 78,* 243–255.

LaBerge, D., & Samuels, J. (1974). Toward a theory of automatic information processing in reading. *Cognitive Psychology, 6,* 293–323.

Laxon, V., Coltheart, V., & Keating, C. (1988). Children find friendly words friendly too: Words with many orthographic neighbours are easier to read and spell. *British Journal of Educational Psychology, 58,* 103–119.

Lindamood, C., & Lindamood, P. (1975). *Auditory discrimination in depth: The ADD program.* Austin, TX: Pro-Ed.

Lovett, M., Borden, S., DeLuca, T., Lacerenza, L., Bensen, N., & Brackstone, D. (1994). Treating the core deficits of developmental dyslexia: Evidence of transfer of learning after phonologically- and strategy-based reading training programs. *Developmental Psychology, 30,* 805–822.

Mason, J. (1980). When do children learn to read? An exploration of four-year-old children's letter and word reading competencies. *Reading Research Quarterly, 15,* 202–227.

Masonheimer, P., Drum, P., & Ehri, L. (1984). Does environmental print identification lead children into word reading? *Journal of Reading Behavior, 16,* 257–272.

McCormick, S. (1994). A nonreader becomes a reader: A case study of literacy acquisition by a severely disabled reader. *Reading Research Quarterly, 29,* 156–177.

Monaghan, J. (1983, April). *A four-year study of the acquisition of letter–sound correspondences.* Paper presented at the annual meeting of the American Educational Research Association, Montreal, Quebec, Canada.

Perfetti, C. (1985). *Reading ability.* New York: Oxford University Press.

Pratt, A., & Brady, S. (1988). Relation of phonological awareness to reading disability in children and adults. *Journal of Educational Psychology, 80,* 319–323.

Rack, J., Snowling, M., & Olson, R. (1992). The nonword reading deficit in developmental dyslexia: A review. *Reading Research Quarterly, 27,* 28–53.

Read, C. (1970). Pre-school children's knowledge of English phonology. *Harvard Educational Review, 41,* 1–34.

Reitsma, P. (1983). Printed word learning in beginning readers. *Journal of Experimental Child Psychology, 75,* 321–339.

Scott, J., & Ehri, L. (1989). Sight word reading in prereaders: Use of logographic vs. alphabetic access routes. *Journal of Reading Behavior, 22,* 149–166.

Share, D., Jorm, A., Maclean, R., & Matthews, R. (1984). Sources of individual differences in reading acquisition. *Journal of Educational Psychology, 76,* 1309–1324.

Share, D., & Stanovich, K. (1995). Cognitive processes in early reading development: Accommodating individual differences into a model of acquisition. *Issues in Education: Contributions From Educational Psychology, 1,* 1–57.

Soderbergh, R. (1977). *Reading in early childhood: A linguistic study of a preschool child's gradual acquisition of reading ability.* Washington, DC: Georgetown University Press.

Stahl, S., & Murray, B. (1994). Defining phonological awareness and its relationship to early reading. *Journal of Educational Psychology, 86,* 221–234.

Stahl, S., & Murray, B. (1998). Issues involved in defining phonological awareness and its relation to early reading. In J.L. Metsala & L.C. Ehri (Eds.), *Word recognition in beginning literacy* (pp. 65–88). Hillsdale, NJ: Erlbaum.

Stuart, M., & Coltheart, M. (1988). Does reading develop in a sequence of stages? *Cognition, 30,* 139–181.

Sulzby, E. (1986). Children's emergent reading of favorite storybooks: A developmental study. *Reading Research Quarterly, 20,* 458–481.

Treiman, R. (1985). Onsets and rimes as units of spoken syllables: Evidence from children. *Journal of Experimental Child Psychology, 39,* 161–181.

Vellutino, F. (1979). *Dyslexia: Theory and research.* Cambridge, MA: MIT Press.

Vellutino, F., & Scanlon, D. (1987). Phonological coding, phonological awareness, and reading ability: Evidence from a longitudinal and experimental study. *Merrill-Palmer Quarterly, 27,* 321–363.

Venezky, R. (1970). *The structure of English orthography.* The Hague, the Netherlands: Mouton.

Venezky, R. (1976). *Theoretical and experimental base for teaching reading.* The Hague, the Netherlands: Mouton.

Venezky, R., & Johnson, D. (1973). Development of two letter–sound patterns in grades one through three. *Journal of Educational Psychology, 64,* 109–115.

Wendon, L. (1991). *First steps in Letterland.* Cambridge, UK: Letterland Ltd.

Wendon, L. (1993). Literacy for early childhood: Learning from the learners. *Early Child Development and Care, 86,* 11–22.

Wimmer, H. (1993). Characteristics of developmental dyslexia in a regular writing system. *Applied Psycholinguistics, 14,* 1–33.

Wimmer, H., & Goswami, U. (1994). The influence of orthographic consistency on reading development: Word recognition in English and German children. *Cognition, 51,* 91–103.

CHAPTER 13

Developing Early Literacy Skills: Things We Know We Know and Things We Know We Don't Know

Christopher J. Lonigan, Florida State University

Timothy Shanahan, University of Illinois at Chicago

It is important to remember that what members of the National Early Literacy Panel (NELP) and the commentators in this issue of *Educational Researcher* (*ER*) have in common is the goal of improving our understanding of children's early development related to literacy and advancing the field of early childhood education so that children gain the maximum benefit of their education. We were struck by the either–or approach of many of these commentaries. The panel's report does not present a choice between code-focused and meaning-focused instruction, and we do not view early childhood education in this either–or fashion. Nevertheless, we applaud the time and effort these authors have expended stating their views and raising questions for the field, and we are heartened that many of the issues raised by them are the same as those explicitly stated in the report *Developing Early Literacy* (NELP, 2008; available at http://www.nifl.gov/earlychildhood/NELP/NELPreport.html). We have divided our comments into two articles: This one addresses the critics' conceptual concerns, and the other is on methodological and statistical issues (see Schatschneider & Lonigan, this issue of *ER*, pp. 347–351).

We Said Too Much; We Haven't Said Enough

Several critiques took exception either to things the commentators believe that we suggested (and shouldn't have) or to what they think we should have suggested (but didn't). Perhaps these contradictory concerns indicate that we struck an appropriate balance. Teale, Hoffman, and Paciga (this issue of *ER*, pp. 311–315) and Dickinson, Golinkoff, and Hirsh-Pasek (pp. 305–310) are concerned that the report will narrow the instruction of early childhood educators. The report is a synthesis of research and not a practitioner's guide on how to teach early literacy, although we believe that it does have value for informing practice.

We were disappointed that Pearson and Hiebert's comments (this issue of *ER*, pp. 286–294) failed to reflect the distinctions among early childhood education environments (e.g., kindergarten, family child care, center-based child care).

Their failure to acknowledge these variations prevents them, perhaps, from recognizing how the report advances the field. Unlike the National Reading Panel (NRP) report (National Institute of Child Health and Human Development, 2000), our focus was on children of kindergarten age or younger. These reports relied on some of the same studies of code-based teaching (about 75% of the studies were unique to either NELP or NRP), but our focus was on understanding the impacts of interventions specifically with younger children.

Pearson and Hiebert were concerned that we did not examine the results of large-scale federal studies, such as the Reading First or Early Reading First evaluations. We did not do so because these reports were not peer reviewed and thus fell outside the scope of our review parameters, were not yet available when we wrote the report, or did not include preschool or kindergarten outcomes (Reading First), or because the reports evaluated the impact of a funding stream. Hiebert and Pearson are correct that there are ways that such studies could have been included in a meta-analysis. However, the Early Childhood Longitudinal Program–Kindergarten study (Denton & West, 2002) neither evaluated the effectiveness of any intervention nor included correlations of early skills with later achievement (its multivariate results were consistent with the NELP findings).

One consideration in determining the scope of the NELP report was to avoid the controversies surrounding the NRP conclusions. Our aim was solely to present a rigorous synthesis of research findings. The report was intended as a first step in a process to develop practice recommendations; it was never intended to be a practice document. Some critics decried the interpretations of NELP findings in publications such as *Early Beginnings*, but the panelists neither wrote nor approved that publication. So we have no response to that. However, such publications highlight legitimate differences in interpretation of research results, and rather than complaining that we failed to impose our interpretations, we are amazed that the commentaries in this issue failed to articulate their own interpretations (an exception is Schickedanz and McGee's article, pp. 323–329, which focuses on how the NELP findings can be used to better help children). Although we agree that the NELP report could be misinterpreted, that is not a flaw of the report. We hope that attempts to use the report to advance practice would attend to the entirety of the report and that these uses would neither base recommendations on selected findings nor overextend the evidence.

Language Development and the Development of Skilled Reading

Several critics in this issue of *ER* (Dickinson et al.; Neuman, pp. 301–304; Teale et al.) express concern that the NELP report did not sufficiently highlight the role of oral language in later literacy. We believe that we reviewed the language evidence thoroughly, but we were constrained by the available evidence from making the claims that these critics would have preferred. The panel did not neglect language: We included more than 90 correlational studies on its relationship with literacy (including data from nearly 10,000 children). In each instructional chapter, language outcomes were reported and discussed, and an entire chapter was devoted to studies of interventions aimed at teaching language. We further analyzed these studies, finding that some oral language measures are more closely related to reading than others and that language measures differed in relationship with comprehension and decoding. These findings are consistent with longitudinal studies (e.g., Sénéchal & LeFevre, 2002; Storch & Whitehurst, 2002) and theoretical frameworks (e.g., Whitehurst & Lonigan, 1998). The differences were not small: Some measures of oral language consistently explained less than 10% of the variance in later reading, whereas other measures explained about 50% of this variance.

Our conclusions concerning the importance of language were as follows:

> Such results are potentially instructive about the focus of early childhood education. They suggest that a focus on building vocabulary alone is unlikely to be sufficient for improving outcomes not only in literacy but also in oral language itself. Although, these results should not be taken to imply that well-developed vocabularies are *unimportant* for literacy. The results suggest that well-developed vocabularies are *insufficient* for literacy. More complex oral-language skills are dependent on vocabulary. For instance, a child with strong grammatical knowledge but limited vocabulary would have a difficult time understanding a text or writing a meaningful narrative. Vocabulary provides the foundation for grammatical knowledge, definitional vocabulary, and listening comprehension. (Lonigan, Schatschneider, & Westberg, 2008, p. 75)

Furthermore,

> The results suggest a need for more careful study of the role of oral language in literacy development....These results suggest that an instructional focus on vocabulary during the preschool and kindergarten years is likely a necessary but insufficient approach to promoting later literacy success. (Lonigan et al., 2008, p. 78)

Far from saying that oral language skills were unimportant to the development of literacy, our call was to move beyond the narrow focus on vocabulary or creating "language-rich environments" often found in discussions of early childhood education to a broader and more detailed account of what aspects of oral language require attention and how these skills can be promoted. Indeed, the modest correlations between the global oral language category and later decoding, reading comprehension, and spelling suggest that a general focus on something labeled *oral language* is unlikely to provide much literacy benefit to young children.

In many ways, these critiques appear to be echoing what we highlighted in the NELP report: that oral language skills are substantially more important for reading comprehension than for decoding, that a broader array of oral language skills beyond vocabulary appears to be required for reading comprehension, that more research on these dimensions of oral language is needed, and that there is substantially more evidence of positive impacts of instruction for increasing young children's simple vocabulary than there is for promoting oral language skills beyond simple vocabulary (e.g., grammar, deep vocabulary knowledge, listening comprehension). Many of the critiques in this issue of *ER* were written as if we had argued that oral language skills were unimportant for literacy or that we failed to review such research. We clearly did neither. We welcome the concurrence on these significant points, and we hope that this level of concern and agreement translates into efforts designed to fill these gaps in research evidence.

Nevertheless, the authors of the critiques of the NELP report have gone well beyond what current evidence supports. Dickinson et al. seem to suggest that we excluded evidence that would have demonstrated that oral language skills are substantially more important than code-related skills because the importance of oral language skills increases over time, whereas the importance of code-related skills diminishes. We are unaware of such evidence, and they do not provide any support for their claims. In considering these claims, we examined studies from the report's meta-analysis of predictive relations for early literacy skills. We identified studies that included long-term reading outcomes and both language- and code-related predictors, or that assessed reading outcomes at multiple grades and included language predictors, code-related predictors, or both.

A summary of the results of these studies (i.e., zero-order or partial correlations with reading comprehension or reading composite variables) is shown in Table 1. MacDonald and Cornwell (1995) administered reading and spelling measures to

Table 1. Summary of Predictive Relations Between Code- and Meaning-Related Predictors Measured in Preschool or Kindergarten and Reading Outcomes Measured Across Grades

		Grade for Reading Outcome						
Study	Predictor Variable	K	1	2	3	6	7	10
MacDonald & Cornwall (1995)	PA							.49/.20[a]
	PPVT-R							.21/.12[a]
Badian (2001)	Verbal IQ		.50		.50		.60	
	PA (syllable)		.47		.25		.46	
	PA (rhyme)		.47		.49		.51	
	Orthography		.40		.47		.44	
Butler et al. (1985)	Psycholinguistic		.44	.40	.49	.47		
	Language		.40	.47	.49	.48		
Walker et al. (1994)	MLU	.55	.36	.58	.43			
	Number of words	.62	.32	.63	.43			
Sénéchal & LeFevre (2002)	PPVT-R		.14		.53			
	Listening comprehension		.16		.38			
	PA		.50		.73			
	Alphabet knowledge		.44		.39			

Note. PA = phonological awareness; PPVT-R = Peabody Picture Vocabulary Test–Revised; MLU = mean length of utterance.

[a]Partial correlations for decoding/reading comprehension controlling for socioeconomic status and alternative predictor variable (i.e., for PA, PPVT-R scores were controlled).

24 students at age 17 who had completed reading, vocabulary (Peabody Picture Vocabulary Test–Revised), and phonological awareness measures when they were in kindergarten. Partial correlations (controlling for socioeconomic status and the alternative predictive variable) with decoding and reading comprehension show a stronger role for phonological awareness than for vocabulary measured in kindergarten for reading outcomes in high school. Badian (2001) administered a verbal IQ (Wechsler Preschool and Primary Scale of Intelligence) and an orthographic matching measure to 96 children 6 months before kindergarten entry and two phonological awareness measures when the children were in kindergarten. In first, third, and seventh grades, the same children were administered reading measures. Zero-order correlations of the preschool and kindergarten measures with the reading comprehension measures at Grades 1, 3, and 7 demonstrate significant predictive relations for orthographic knowledge in preschool and phonological awareness in kindergarten with reading at each grade. Moreover, for all code-related predictors, correlations with reading comprehension were statistically significant when verbal IQ was controlled.

Butler, Marsh, Sheppard, and Sheppard (1985) examined the predictive relations of a psycholinguistic factor that included scores from an auditory closure test and a sound-blending test, and a language factor with a composite reading measure that included both decoding and reading comprehension tasks. Measures that comprised the psycholinguistic and language factors were administered to 392 kindergarteners. Reading measures were administered to the same children in Grades 3 and 6. Zero-order correlations for the two factors with the composite reading measure show roughly equal and stable predictive relations for both language and code-related skills across time. Moreover, in multiple regressions, both the psycholinguistic factors and the language factors were significant predictors of reading at each grade level. Sénéchal and LeFevre (2002) reported correlations between vocabulary, listening comprehension, phonological awareness, and alphabet knowledge measured in kindergarten and reading outcomes in first and third grades. Although the results of Sénéchal and LeFevre's study suggested a larger role for language skills at the later reading assessment, code-related skills continued to be as strongly or more strongly related to reading from the first- to third-grade assessments. Data from the Walker, Greenwood, Hart, and Carta (1994) study, which was cited by Dickinson et al. in support of their position, do not suggest an increasing importance of oral language or stronger relations with reading than do the code-related skills included in other studies.

Although this is not an exhaustive summary of such results, the studies summarized in Table 1 are consistent with the findings of all the studies on this topic summarized by NELP, and they provide no evidence of an increasing role for oral language across time, more durable predictive relations between oral language and reading than between code-related skills and reading, or a diminishing role of code-related skills; nor do they provide evidence that oral language skills are more important for reading comprehension than are code-related skills. As demonstrated by Storch and Whitehurst (2002), children's oral language skills have increasing importance as measures of reading move from those that primarily measure decoding to those that measure reading comprehension; however, code-related skills remain important throughout. Consequently, there is no support for the claims of Teale et al. that (a) we did not address how what is taught in preschool and kindergarten relates to literacy in third grade and beyond, (b) the predictor skills we identified are unlikely to be related to more mature reading comprehension (they are), or (c) the most significant factor in upper grade reading comprehension is background knowledge (this may be true; however, no studies support the claim).

Although one could work backward and create a hypothetical chain of causal links from highly proficient reading comprehension skills in mature readers through well-developed background knowledge to strong language skills to something taught in preschool (e.g., see Neuman's commentary in this issue), such a chain of causal links would merely represent a hypothesis. This hypothesis would need to be tested and supported by data. At present, there are few (if any) studies that would allow tests of these hypotheses. We do wonder, however, what the relation between solving science problems and reading comprehension is—which is the meta-analytic evidence cited by Neuman as supporting her hypothesis. Curiously, the results of that meta-analysis indicate that interventions that emphasized declarative knowledge had little to no impact on students' abilities to solve problems, which "varied from algorithmic trigonometry problems to complex but closed physics and chemistry problems" (Taconis, Ferguson-Hessler, & Broekkamp, 2001, p. 461). Although the study by Taconis et al. found that interventions that emphasized "strategic knowledge" negatively affected problem solving, this seems a bit different from providing the skills necessary to decode words. The importance of code-related skills to reading does not imply that language skills should be ignored; similarly, the importance of language skills to reading does not imply that code-related skills should be ignored.

Impacts of Shared Reading Activities

Schickedanz and McGee provide an alternative summary of the shared reading interventions included in the NELP report. Their conclusions are largely consistent with those of the panel; however, they suggest a greater impact of shared reading interventions for younger children and for expressive language measures than for older children and receptive measures. These are reasonable interpretations of the studies. During its review, the panel also considered alternative groupings of studies and effects. As the report noted, it is impossible to unambiguously attribute anything to these differences given that this variable was confounded with others, such as risk status.

Regarding a stronger impact of shared reading on expressive measures than on receptive measures, we have noted this pattern in our own shared reading studies (e.g., Arnold, Lonigan, Whitehurst, & Epstein, 1994; Lonigan, Anthony, Bloomfield, Dyer, & Samwel, 1999; Lonigan & Whitehurst, 1998)—although it is not a consistent finding. However, we are at a loss to provide a theoretical rationale for why such a finding should be expected. Similarly, we did not include some outcomes in our analyses because the measure was often confounded with the experimental condition. Schickedanz and McGee also question the noninclusion of some studies. We could not include studies in our analyses if they had serious design or analytic problems that precluded calculating appropriate effect sizes or interpreting the study results, and we could not include studies that fell outside our inclusion criteria (such as dissertations or foreign-language publications)—the studies the various critics question were not included for these reasons. We agree completely with Schickedanz and McGee that if shared reading is to be used as an instructional vehicle for improving children's language, there needs to be more high-quality research using a broad range of outcome measures beyond vocabulary.

Effects of Parent and Home Programs

Dail and Payne (this issue of *ER*, pp. 330–333) lament that our summary of parent and home intervention programs included studies of such a wide array of approaches. Given the limited research evidence concerning such programs, we thought it prudent to be inclusive, rather than adopting a narrow ideological stance that would have precluded consideration of relevant data. We were disappointed in the number of well-conducted studies that allowed estimation of causal impacts that had been published in peer-reviewed outlets; it was also disappointing that the retrieved studies had little in common that would allow much meaningful analysis to examine the effects of various factors. Had we included non-peer-reviewed studies, we would not have substantially increased the yield but would have included the several randomized evaluations of Even Start that show few beneficial effects of these programs.

Dail and Payne assert causal claims without appropriate evidence and even seem a bit chagrined at the panel's unwillingness to endorse this approach. They claim their family literacy program "works" and explain why it must work but fail to show evidence of success—not a surprising failure, given that their research methods cannot prove a learning impact (without control groups it is impossible to determine an advantage for a program, particularly at these age levels when children are learning so fast). They say we erred in examining studies of programs that did not match their ideological stance. Without taking any position on their beliefs, how does one explain the positive benefits obtained from studies of the instructional approaches that Dail and Payne eschew for ideological reasons?

Early Literacy and English-Language Learners

We agree completely with Gutiérrez, Zepeda, and Castro (this issue of *ER*, pp. 334–339) that there is a need for more research on the early literacy of children who are English-language learners (ELLs). One of our frustrations was the inability to address questions that were specifically about children who are ELLs because there were insufficient data. Gutiérrez et al.'s critique reflects a common misunderstanding of meta-analysis. Although the researchers who published the studies summarized in the NELP report often included diverse samples of children (including ELLs) in their studies, they rarely reported their data separately; therefore, we were blocked from evaluating the relative impact of these instructional approaches on these groups. Thus ELLs contributed data to these analyses, and when there were sufficient subgroup data to allow comparison we found scant evidence that child or family characteristics moderated the overall conclusions. The lack of data on ELLs is evident with studies of older students as well (Shanahan & Beck, 2006), although not to the extent that NELP uncovered with preschool and kindergarten children.

Because there was little evidence that child or family characteristics moderated the conclusions concerning the skills that predicted later literacy or concerning the identified instruction that promoted these skills, we argued that there was no reason to withhold these educational opportunities from any children. Gutiérrez et al. take exception to this recommendation. The majority of their critique concerns the ways that children whose home language is not English may differ from children whose home language is English. They correctly note that there is insufficient empirical evidence to determine whether a host of potential linguistic, sociocultural, and family factors changes the nature of the relations between early skills and later reading or, even to determine whether a set of skills different from those identified for children whose home language is English would be identified. What troubles us is that although they question how these results apply to young ELLs, they do not offer any concrete alternatives. We wonder, then, what an early childhood professional is to do when faced with one or more children whose home language is not English.

Research published subsequent to the NELP synthesis provides insight into the development of early literacy skills of children who are ELLs. Similar to the findings of studies with school-age ELLs (August & Shanahan, 2006), some of this recent research indicates that there is significant consistency in the structure and function of code-related skills between monolingual and bilingual children (Anthony et al., 2009; Anthony et al., 2006; Branum-Martin et al., 2006). A recent study reported by Branum-Martin et al. (2009) indicates that measuring language-related skills across languages is complicated by child factors, instructional factors, and type of measure, with more within-language consistency than between-language consistency. Data from prediction studies indicate that within-language predictions are stronger than between-language predictions (e.g., Anthony et al., 2009; Farver, Nakamoto, & Lonigan, 2007; Gottardo & Mueller, 2009), and these studies suggest that the skills identified as strong predictors of later literacy work similarly for children who are ELLs.

There are still few studies that evaluate the effectiveness of instructional practices in promoting early literacy skills with these children. An exception is the study by Farver, Lonigan, and Eppe (2009) with Spanish-speaking ELLs. This study found that interventions like those identified in the NELP report as effective for promoting oral language skills and code-related skills yielded moderate to large and statistically significant effects (i.e., effect sizes ranged from .40 to .94) relative to a group of children who participated only in their Head Start activities. These results support the panel's conclusion that there is no reason that the code-focused and shared reading instructional activities identified as effective should not be used with children whose home language is not English.

As far as we can tell, Orellana and D'warte's primary critiques (in this issue of *ER*, pp. 295–300) of the NELP report are that our analyses were directed at answering questions concerning the predictors of reading and writing and that we did not focus on the types of skills on which they conduct research. We agree completely. Orellana and D'warte wonder who determines which skills matter in literacy. They want to impose a definition of literacy politically, which is markedly different from the empirical approach adopted by NELP. The panel rejected the idea of using expertise or standing to impose a vision of what panel members thought might be important but instead provided a thorough examination of the relevant empirical data measuring the relation of skills to later conventional literacy. Orellana and D'warte suggest that we erred in not including measures of aesthetic sensibilities, critical awareness, or the ability to tailor messages to particular audiences as prerequisite literacy skills for 3- and 4-year-old children—a list drawn apparently, given the citations, from studies of high school students and opinion pieces.

When everything is literacy, the term *literacy* no longer has any useful meaning. At what point should skills that are useful for something not be included in the category *things that are literacy*? Things beyond the usage of the term that has its roots in the word's etymology (i.e., from Middle English, *literat;* from Latin *litteratus*—marked with letters; literate, from *litterae*—letters; literature, from plural of *littera*) typically are contextualized by a modifier, as in *computer literacy, mathematical literacy, artistic literacy,* or *transcultural literacy.* Each of these things is useful to someone and a worthy topic of investigation; however, they are not reading and writing per se, which is how we defined *conventional literacy.* Without doubt, the pragmatics of being able to read or write different genres, for different purposes or audiences, or to be able to negotiate differences in written versus spoken grammar belong in the domain of conventional literacy; however, there are no longitudinal studies that would help identify the precursors to these things.

The State of Early Childhood Education Today

We agree with Teale et al. that the evidence summarized in the NELP report does not constitute a mandate to teach code-related skills to the exclusion of meaning-related skills like vocabulary, grammar, and background knowledge. Indeed, we believe that the evidence in the report indicates a need to go beyond simple vocabulary and nebulous recommendations to create "language-rich environments." At present, there is strong evidence for instructional activities that promote code-related skills. Unfortunately, evidence for instructional activities that promote oral language skills is less compelling. Whereas there is clear support for shared reading interventions resulting in improved vocabulary skills, there is less evidence concerning effective instructional strategies for other meaning-related skills such as listening comprehension or background knowledge, and no evidence that even the most powerful of the shared reading interventions results in improved reading skills. This gap in the research base needs to be filled.

There is a degree of resistance to literacy instruction in the early childhood community. Much early childhood education eschews the idea of teachers determining instructional content and activities. Between 59% and 70% of Head Start and other early childhood education programs serving children who are at risk of later academic difficulties use either the High/Scope Curriculum or the Creative Curriculum (Jackson et al., 2007; U.S. Department of Health and Human Services, 2005). Neither curriculum has causally interpretable research evidence to indicate that its use results in increased development of early literacy or other preacademic or socioemotional skills relative to alternative curricula. Much of this "instructional tension" in early childhood education probably owes its genesis to the expert consensus recommendations embodied in the practice guides concerning "developmentally appropriate practice" produced by the National Association for the Education of Young Children. Whereas these guides have increased in their focus on specific skills and intentional instruction, the fact that the early guides, which were not based on meaningful evidence, declared such educational practices "developmentally inappropriate" has created a legacy that will continue for some time.

Although NELP highlighted strong evidence for promoting both code- and meaning-focused skills through the use of focused, teacher-directed, and intentional instruction, the report also explicitly noted that none of the studies on effective instructional practices involved a model of instruction that relied on whole-group choral recitation. The implication of the evidence summarized by NELP is that what one would observe in "a really good preschool" (Neuman, p. 301) should depend on the strengths and needs of children in the classroom. Many children are likely to do well in a traditional early childhood classroom with relatively little teacher-directed instruction. Some will not, however, and the evidence summarized by the NELP report provides a guide to identify those children who are not on a developmental trajectory to succeed. Evidence for effective instructional strategies summarized in the report provides a starting point for actions that can help put all children on a trajectory of success. Some of those things will look like "fiddling around with sounds associated with printed letters," playing with sounds in words, and engaging in meaningful and extended language interactions with the teacher. Such a preschool will be "really good" because it is responsive to the needs of individual real children—not just to the idealized children who come to preschool well equipped to seek out the knowledge they will need and who have the tools to do much of the work on their own.

Conclusion

As noted by Whitehurst and Lonigan (1998), there are many "pleasing ideas" in the realm of early literacy. When these ideas are subjected to the light of empirical scrutiny, however, not all emerge unscathed. It is almost a certainty that when a set of studies is subjected to the rigors of a meta-analysis, someone's sacred cow will be threatened. These critics are correct that the NELP report does not provide simple answers or espouse a mandate for early childhood education. It summarizes the available evidence, with all of its nuances and blemishes. We welcome the fact that the report has researchers, practitioners, and policy makers discussing the implications of current evidence for improving early childhood education, and we look forward to continuing the conversation.

QUESTIONS FOR REFLECTION

1. What are the dangers of presenting literacy instruction as a choice between code-focused and meaning-focused instruction?
2. Why do the authors feel it was important that the NELP report limit itself to peer-reviewed studies that allowed estimation of causal impacts?
3. How were the limited data on early literacy skills for English learners incorporated into the NELP report findings?

REFERENCES

August, D., & Shanahan, T. (Eds.). (2006). *Developing literacy in second-language learners: Report of the National Literacy Panel on Language-Minority Children and Youth*. Mahwah, NJ: Lawrence Erlbaum.

Anthony, J. L., Solari, E. J., Williams, J. M., Schoger, K. D., Zhang, A., Branum-Martin, L., et al. (2009). Development of bilingual phonological awareness in Spanish-speaking English language learners: The roles of vocabulary, letter knowledge, and prior phonological awareness. *Scientific Studies of Reading, 13*, 535–564.

Anthony, J. L., Williams, J. M., McDonald, R., Corbitt-Shindler, D., Carlson, C. D., & Francis, D. J. (2006). Phonological processing and emergent literacy in Spanish-speaking preschool children. *Annals of Dyslexia, 56*, 239–270.

Arnold, D. S., Lonigan, C. J., Whitehurst, G. J., & Epstein, J. N. (1994). Accelerating language development through picture-book reading: Replication and extension to a videotape training format. *Journal of Educational Psychology, 86*, 235–243.

Badian, N. A. (2001). Phonological and orthographic processing: Their roles in reading prediction. *Annals of Dyslexia, 51*, 179–202.

Branum-Martin, L., Mehta, P. D., Fletcher, J. M., Carlson, C. D., Ortiz, A., Carlo, M., et al. (2006). Bilingual phonological awareness: Multilevel construct validation among Spanish-speaking kindergarteners in transitional bilingual education classrooms. *Journal of Educational Psychology, 98*, 170–181.

Branum-Martin, L., Mehta, P. D., Francis, D. J., Foorman, B. R., Cirino, P. T., Miller, J. F., et al. (2009). Pictures and words: Spanish and English vocabulary in classrooms. *Journal of Educational Psychology, 101*, 897–911.

Dail, A. R., & Payne, R. L. (2010). Recasting the role of family involvement in early literacy development: A response to the NELP report. *Educational Researcher, 39*, 330–333.

Denton, K., & West, J. (2002). *Children's reading and mathematics achievement in kindergarten and first grade*. Washington, DC: U.S. Department of Education, National Center for Education Statistics. Retrieved from http://nces.ed.gov/pubs2002/2002125.pdf

Dickinson, D. K., Golinkoff, R. M., & Hirsh-Pasek, K. K. (2010). Speaking out for language: Why language is central to reading development. *Educational Researcher, 39*, 305–310.

Farver, J. M., Lonigan, C. J., & Eppe, S. (2009). Effective early literacy skill development for young English language learners: An experimental study of two methods. *Child Development, 80*, 703–719.

Farver, J. M., Nakamoto, J., & Lonigan, C. J. (2007). Assessing preschoolers' emergent literacy skills in English and Spanish with the Get Ready to Read! screening tool. *Annals of Dyslexia, 57*, 161–178.

Gottardo, A., & Mueller, J. (2009). Are first- and second-language factors related in predicting second-language reading comprehension? A study of Spanish-speaking children acquiring English as a second language from first to second grade. *Journal of Educational Psychology, 101*, 330–344.

Gutiérrez, K. D., Zepeda, M., & Castro, D. C. (2010). Advancing early literacy learning for all children: Implications of the NELP report for dual-language learners. *Educational Researcher, 39*, 334–339.

Jackson, R., McCoy, A., Pistorino, C., Wilkinson, A., Burghardtm, J., Clark, M., et al. (2007). *National evaluation of Early Reading First: Final report to Congress*. Washington, DC: Institute of Education Sciences.

Lonigan, C. J., Anthony, J. L., Bloomfield, B., Dyer, S. M., & Samwel, C. (1999). Effects of two preschool shared reading interventions on the emergent literacy skills of children from low-income families. *Journal of Early Intervention, 22*, 306–322.

Lonigan, C. J., Schatschneider, C., & Westberg, L. (2008). Identification of children's skills and abilities linked to later outcomes in reading, writing, and spelling. In National Early Literacy Panel, *Developing early literacy: Report of the National Early Literacy Panel* (pp. 55–106). Washington, DC: National Institute for Literacy. Available at http:// www.nifl.gov/earlychildhood/NELP/NELPreport.html

Lonigan, C. J., & Whitehurst, G. J. (1998). Relative efficacy of parent and teacher involvement in a shared-reading intervention for preschool children from low-income backgrounds. *Early Childhood Research Quarterly, 17*, 265–292.

MacDonald, G. W., & Cornwall, A. (1995). The relationship between phonological awareness and reading and spelling achievement eleven years later. *Journal of Learning Disabilities, 28*, 523–527.

National Early Literacy Panel. (2008). *Developing early literacy: Report of the National Early Literacy Panel*. Washington, DC: National Institute for Literacy. Available at http://www.nifl.gov/earlychildhood/NELP/ NELPreport.html

National Institute of Child Health and Human Development. (2000). *Report of the National Reading Panel. Teaching children to read: An evidence-based assessment of the scientific research literature on reading and its implications for reading instruction* (NIH Pub. No. 00-4769). Washington, DC: U.S. Government Printing Office.

Neuman, S. B. (2010). Lessons from my mother: Reflections on the National Early Literacy Panel report. *Educational Researcher, 39*, 301–304.

Orellana, M. F., & D'warte, J. (2010). Recognizing different kinds of "Head Starts." *Educational Researcher, 39*, 295–300.

Pearson, P. D., & Hiebert, E. H. (2010). National reports in literacy: Building a scientific base for practice and policy. *Educational Researcher, 39*, 286–294.

Schatschneider, C., & Lonigan, C. J. (2010). Misunderstood statistical assumptions undermine criticism of the National Early Literacy Panel's report. *Educational Researcher, 39*, 347–351.

Schickedanz, J. A., & McGee, L. M. (2010). The NELP report on shared story reading interventions (chapter 4): Extending the story. *Educational Researcher, 39*, 323–329.

Sénéchal, M., & LeFevre, J. (2002). Parental involvement in the development of children's reading skill: A five-year longitudinal study. *Child Development, 73*, 445–460.

Shanahan, T. (in press). Review of *Interdisciplinary Approaches to Literacy and Development. Comparative Education Review*.

Shanahan, T., & Beck, I. (2006). Effective literacy teaching for English-language learners. In D. August & T. Shanahan (Eds.), *Developing literacy in second-language learners: Report of the National Literacy Panel on Language-Minority Children and Youth* (pp. 415–488). Mahwah, NJ: Lawrence Erlbaum.

Storch, S. A., & Whitehurst, G. J. (2002). Oral language and code-related precursors to reading: Evidence from a longitudinal structural model. *Developmental Psychology, 38*, 934–947.

Street, B. V. (1984). *Literacy in theory and practice*. Cambridge, UK: Cambridge University Press.

Taconis, R., Ferguson-Hessler, M. G. M., & Broekkamp, H. (2001). Teaching science problem solving: An overview of experimental work. *Journal of Research in Science Teaching, 38*, 442–468.

Teale, W. H., Hoffman, J., & Paciga, K. A. (2010). Where is NELP leading preschool literacy instruction? Potential positives and pitfalls. *Educational Researcher, 39*, 311–315.

U.S. Department of Health and Human Services, Administration for Children and Families.

(2005, May). *Head Start impact study: First year findings*. Washington, DC: Author.
Walker, D., Greenwood, C., Hart, B., & Carta, J. (1994). Prediction of school outcomes based on early language production and socioeconomic factors. *Child Development*, *65*, 606–621.
Whitehurst, G. J., & Lonigan, C. J. (1998). Child development and emergent literacy. *Child Development*, *69*, 848–872.

CHAPTER 14

Advancing Early Literacy Learning for All Children: Implications of the NELP Report for Dual-Language Learners

Kris D. Gutiérrez, University of Colorado at Boulder

Marlene Zepeda, California State University, Los Angeles

Dina C. Castro, University of North Carolina at Chapel Hill

Children who are learning English often are characterized in ways that do not capture their linguistic repertoires. They are referred to as limited English proficient students or English learners, defining this group of children by a single feature, their proficiency in English. Young learners who are acquiring two languages simultaneously or who are developing their primary language as they learn a second language are better understood as dual-language learners (DLLs). Four-year-old children who have developed language skills in their home language and who enroll in early childhood educational settings with no English skills are also known as early sequential bilinguals (Peña & Kester, 2004). A significant number of children of immigrant families grow up in bilingual environments where an estimated 84% of individuals age 5 and older speak a language other than English (Pew Hispanic Center, 2009). Capturing the bicultural nature of DLLs' lives not only provides a more accurate representation of children's everyday practices but also is important to the development of sound and appropriate educational policies that support their full development as language and literacy learners. The purpose of this article is to discuss the implications of findings reported by the National Early Literacy Panel (NELP) for the early care and education of children who are DLLs. We begin with a discussion of the participation of young DLLs in early care and education research, including gaps in knowledge. Then we examine the relevance of the NELP report for young DLLs and conclude with a discussion of the implications of the report for future research.

Dual-Language Learners in Early Care and Education Research

There is a dearth of studies that focus on children from birth to age 4 from which policy implications can be drawn. This is particularly the case for DLLs, one of

This chapter is reprinted from *Educational Researcher*, 39(4), 334–339.

the fastest growing student populations in the United States, with approximately 2 million DLLs enrolled in the prekindergarten to Grade 3 cohort (Kindler, 2002); however, young DLLs remain largely understudied, often excluded from studies of early learning and among the least understood from a policy perspective. When included, these children often are subsumed under a broader "at-risk" category, making it difficult to understand underlying learning processes or to tease out relevant differences and factors.

DLLs are a diverse group, yet one of the most common misconceptions is that all DLLs are immigrants. Nearly four fifths of children in immigrant families (79%) are U.S. citizens by birth (Hernandez, Denton, & McCartney, 2008). DLLs also are highly variable in terms of their socioeconomic status, first-language practices, and experiences with literacy. Thus meaningful statements about intergroup comparability between DLLs and monolinguals must do more than rely on simple comparisons and generalizations; they must account for their variability. Often, conceptions of these young learners—whose home practices and histories of involvement with literacy differ widely, in ways that matter—are so flattened out that they become meaningless as guides for developing policy and practice.

Despite limited empirical evidence, there is a tendency to extrapolate implications for the education of DLLs based on a broader population of children. Moreover, studies of older DLLs or monolingual English-speaking children serve as the basis for drawing implications for policy and practices for young DLLs. As we discuss in the next section, in some cases the authors of studies of young language and literacy learners employ the universalist principle: If it works for mainstream children, it must work for English learners and DLLs.

Yet the achievement gap between DLLs and monolingual English-speaking children persists even after 5 to 6 years of schooling in the United States and is exacerbated by a constellation of factors that constrain DLLs' opportunities to learn (Ballantyne, Sanderman, D'Emilio, & McLaughlin, 2008; Reardon & Galindo, 2006). DLLs are more likely to live in high-poverty communities and thus are more likely to lack access to health care services and to libraries and enrichment opportunities; they also are less likely to attend preschool (Ballantyne et al., 2008; Dolan, 2009), where forms of support known to have a positive influence on children's early learning are available (Bowman, Donovan, & Burns, 2000).

Given the vulnerability of these young learners, we must insist on an evidence-based approach to policy and practice for DLLs, as we would for all children. Research that focuses on preschool-age and younger DLLs is needed to understand how early language and literacy learning unfolds. In particular, we call attention to the need for more studies that examine how the home language supports second-language learning in English, including how early biliteracy supports learning in formal schooling environments. Presently, much of what is known either is based on short-term studies that stress English acquisition over the continued use of the home language or is derived from school-age populations (August & Shanahan, 2006; Genesee, Lindholm-Leary, Saunders, & Christian, 2006).

A related topic in need of a more expansive understanding is the "dynamics of transfer across different language systems" (Castro, Espinosa, & Páez, in press); that is, which language and early literacy skills do and do not transfer and under what conditions (Snow, 2006). Research building on studies that focus on specific aspects of language development would provide a deeper understanding of cross-linguistic transfer. As some studies have shown, transfer varies by linguistic similarities and differences and between writing systems, as well as the relations between languages. Further research on the role of early bilingualism in children's cognitive processing, including the cognitive benefits of bilingualism/biliteracy independent of the transfer issue, would be an important contribution (e.g., Bialystok, 2009; Carlson & Choi, 2009; de Villiers, de Villiers, & Hobbs, 2009).

Another often-ignored topic is the relationship between socioemotional development and dual-language and literacy development. Young DLLs experience additional developmental demands in comparison with their monolingual English-speaking peers. Depending on the language-learning context, negative emotions such as anxiety and self-consciousness may interfere with learning and limit the child's ability to benefit from instructional strategies developed for his or her support (Espinosa, 2009). Understanding language development in young DLLs involves understanding both the mechanics of language transfer and the social context of children's learning.

Many children in the United States participate in early childhood programs; however, DLLs remain underrepresented, especially in assessments of program and instructional effectiveness. Given the increased federal interest in early learning, DLLs can no longer be ignored in early childhood federal policies and programs or omitted from relevant assessments, as their exclusion significantly affects the validity of local, state, and federal policies and practices designed to meet their needs.

The National Early Literacy Panel Report and Young Dual-Language Learners

Given the imperatives described above, we turn to an examination of *Developing Early Literacy: Report of the National Early Literacy Panel* (NELP, 2008; available at http://www.nifl.gov/earlychildhood/NELP/NELPreport.html) and its implications for DLLs. We argue for more relevant and rigorous study and discuss the relationship between extant early learning literature and relevant studies needed to develop appropriate and robust policies and programs for DLLs. We argue that the NELP report is yet another example of a national research synthesis that does not address the issues of prekindergarten DLLs, and we recommend that the report not be used as a guide for making policy for this population of children. Colleagues in this issue of *Educational Researcher* address the merits and limitations of the report for English-speaking populations. Our focus is on its limitations for young children who are DLLs.

We argue that there is insufficient empirical evidence to support generalizing NELP's findings to DLL populations, as they were not the focus of the meta-analysis. Generalizing the predictive significance of NELP's conclusions to DLLS or drawing implications about effective instructional strategies for this population without qualification is a practice inconsistent with the American Educational Research Association (AERA) standards for reporting on empirical social science research (AERA Task Force, 2006; Laosa, 1990), because what is effective pedagogy and practice for DLLs remains an unanswered empirical question. Few studies with sizeable samples or studies of DLLs were included in NELP's analyses, so there is little attention to the particular developmental demands associated with acquiring two languages and becoming literate in the early years. One related concern is that the report's findings may be seen as suggesting interventions for DLLs and other educationally vulnerable student populations, for example, poor urban or rural students who also were not represented in the report's studies. Specifically, the report does not contribute evidence about the effectiveness of particular instructional practices, social arrangements, and interventions for DLLs.

Let us examine how the report addresses the issue of underrepresentation of DLLs. Regarding code-focused studies, the authors state that extant studies did not allow for sufficient examination of the "relative effectiveness of code-focused instruction for specific subpopulations of children" (NELP, 2008, p. 119). The authors then argue that it makes good sense to suggest this particular intervention for all populations of young children:

> Although the early childhood education field is interested in specific questions about which interventions will work best for children living in poverty, children from traditionally underrepresented ethnic groups, children who are English-language learners, or children growing up in rural or urban environments, there are not yet studies focusing on these specific subpopulations or that allow examination of these subpopulations to answer these questions. Given the clear success of code-focused instruction with these mixed populations, it seems prudent to make such instruction available to all populations of young children, at least until research more directly addresses this question. (p. 120)

Here the NELP study first argues that its studies include mixed samples of children from various ethnic and racial groups, socioeconomic backgrounds, and population centers but that the studies lack sufficient specificity to examine differences across groups. Nevertheless the report recommends the intervention for all children until there are sufficient studies to support or proffer other claims. The report makes a similar argument regarding the positive effect of shared-reading interventions:

> At present, the number of studies in the literature that have examined specific groups of children (such as children from different SES backgrounds, different ethnicities, home languages, or living circumstances—i.e., rural versus urban) is not

sufficient to allow an adequate analysis of how shared-reading interventions may result in larger or smaller effects on these groups. (p. 164)

As before, the study's authors find it reasonable to recommend that shared reading would help all or most subgroups of children:

> Studies focusing on shared reading with these groups have not yet been reported in sufficient frequency to allow definitive answers to these questions. Nevertheless, the existing studies provide no reason to expect substantially different patterns of results for these variables in future research. (p. 164)

The issue here is not whether shared reading is inappropriate for DLLs; that is an empirical question. Rather, the point is that we currently do not have a sufficient evidence base to support the claim. Researchers need to provide appropriate caveats and proceed with care when extrapolating findings on monolingual English-speaking children, or samples that have insufficient numbers of subpopulations, to subgroup populations with distinct characteristics, such as DLLs, that would benefit from appropriate and robust forms of instruction and support. For instance, questions about shared reading for DLLs should ask how this strategy should be implemented to be effective with DLLs at different stages in their English acquisition (e.g., language or languages used, in which sequence, how many times, for how long).

Further, the report makes a number of claims about what works that could be interpreted in ways that have unintended consequences for children who are most in need of robust literacy practices. As Dickinson, Hirsh-Pasek, Neuman, Burchinal, and Golinkoff (2009) observed, the report may suggest a prescription for early literacy that privileges narrow skills at the expense of "oral language skills, vocabulary, and background knowledge that form the foundation for early and long-term literacy" (p. 1). This is consequential, as large studies of the effects of early language on reading development illustrate the relation between language and code-related skills (Dickinson et al., 2009) and the role that language plays in subsequent reading comprehension (Vellutino, Tunmer, Jaccard, & Chen, 2007).

Although NELP's synthesis notes that oral language skills are a moderate to strong predictor of emergent literacy, the report also suggests that indices of oral language development were moderate to weak predictors of later reading skills and less predictive than conventional reading skills (e.g., phonological processing skills). Despite the attention to language studies, NELP's core findings do not emphasize the development of oral language as being critical to later reading, as are decoding skills.

More specifically, the main table reporting predictors of reading comprehension measured at or before kindergarten lists oral language with an average *r* of only .33. However, this is misleading. A secondary analysis reported later in the chapter shows that some oral language measures have a much higher average *r*, including overall language comprehension (.70), receptive language (.52), expressive language (.48), and grammar (.47), and some others have an average *r* at least somewhat higher than the .33 reported in the initial table (definitional vocabulary: .38; verbal knowledge: .36; verbal IQ: .35; receptive vocabulary: .34). The average correlation for *overall language comprehension is in fact the strongest predictor of reading comprehension reported in the chapter*, well above such constructs as alphabet knowledge (.48) and phonological awareness (.44; N. Duke, personal communication, December 2, 2009).

Although we applaud the panel for conducting the secondary analysis that revealed these higher average correlations for measures of oral language, we are concerned that they will be overlooked. There have been no headlines or claims based on the report that highlight overall language comprehension as the strongest predictor of later reading comprehension; the executive summary of the report itself does not list any oral language variable among the constructs with "medium to large predictive relationships with later measures of literacy development" (NELP, 2008, p. vii).

Overemphasizing decoding skills and minimizing the role of oral language in literacy development is problematic for all young children and consequential for DLLs, as their need for deep knowledge of words (Francis, Rivera, Lesaux, Kieffer, & Rivera, 2006; Verhallen & Schoonen, 1998) is addressed by providing them with ongoing opportunities to learn word meanings explicitly in a range of linguistic contexts and with repeated practice in using them (Collins, 2005; Silverman, 2007). Most DLLs simultaneously acquire oral proficiency and second-language literacy (Castro, Páez, Dickinson, & Frede, in press), highlighting the mutually reinforcing nature of second-language learners' reading, writing, and oral skills (Brisk & Harrington, 2007). Thus language and literacy development involves the lamination of component skills and sociocultural variables that help form the social situation of development.

Research with older populations of DLLs identifies the importance of English oral language development, especially in relation to mastery of question forms and word meaning (Saunders & O'Brien, 2006). Further, transference theory, well established in the language development field, posits that children learning two languages will use information from their first language (L1) to build their understanding of how language functions in their second language (L2); transfer is also bidirectional from L1 to L2 and L2 to L1 (e.g., Dickinson, McCabe, Clark-Chiarelli, & Wolf, 2004). Thus oral language development in the home language has important implications for understanding the general cognitive functioning of young DLLs (García, Kleifgen, & Falchi, 2008). The National Literacy Panel of Language-Minority Children and Youth (August & Shanahan, 2006) identified oral language proficiency as a key component of more advanced reading skills and found that students may apply decoding skills with only a basic minimal knowledge of the phonological structures of English. However, oral English proficiency correlates with the ability to comprehend more difficult texts and to apply word- and test-level skills (August & Shanahan, 2006). As Ballantyne et al. (2008) suggest, "These findings help explain why many language-minority students can keep pace with their native English-speaking peers when the instructional focus is on word-level skills, but lag behind when the instructional focus turns to reading comprehension and writing" (pp. 24–25).

Currently, there is no empirical base to support the assumption that factors that predict later conventional reading skills will function similarly across ethnic and socioeconomic status levels. However, a recurrent and related theme in the NELP report was that no differences were identified in conventional reading skills by ethnicity or socioeconomic status. Although NELP does acknowledge that many studies lacked adequate demographic sample descriptions and that more focused research for English-language-learner populations is needed, the concern is that consumers of the report will view the "no difference" findings as justification for a narrow drill-and-skills approach to literacy development over other approaches that are essential to more robust language and literacy. Further, little is learned about the relation between the development of the home language and a second language, as most studies that include DLLs measure outcomes only in English.

The NELP report also places significant weight on phonemic awareness (PA). We agree that the development of PA is important for young DLLs and acknowledge that PA shows some overlap in certain instructional contexts; however, the limitations of existing evidence make it difficult to generalize. We have some indication of how PA develops for Spanish speakers learning English but have relatively little knowledge of its functioning in other languages, particularly for 3- and 4-year-olds. Because PA is influenced by the quality and quantity of language input at home and school, research that documents these factors merits attention.

A long-term view of literacy development places an emphasis on the foundational skills, avoiding the either–or dichotomies that are neither productive nor supported by the extant literature. As summarized in a recent review,

> For dual language learners, the development of language and literacy involves the integration of *component skills* (e.g., sound–symbol awareness, grammatical knowledge, vocabulary knowledge), as well as more elusive sociocultural variables critical to the development of reading and writing. (Castro, Espinosa, et al., in press)

To understand these relationships, valid, reliable, and culturally sound assessment instruments normed for young DLLs should be developed to effectively monitor children's English language acquisition and development across different developmental domains.

Moreover, research that examines language and literacy development in DLLs younger than 5 is needed, as recent research on DLLs focuses primarily on school-age populations (e.g., August & Shanahan, 2006). One shortcoming of the NELP review is that it also did not include children younger than the age of 4, limiting its findings to children 4 and older. Similarly, as the analyses found no differences between these 4-year-olds and kindergarteners, the findings are aggregated for these populations and important distinctions blurred. For example, the analyses do not acknowledge distinctions between many programs for

4-year-olds and kindergarten classrooms and thus neglect important differences attributable to the early education philosophy.

In the discussion above, we address the efficacy of the NELP report for young DLLs. We note that there is insufficient evidence to adequately apply its findings to pedagogical practice. We take issue with the universalist principle at work in the report in which findings are generalized to DLLs, despite the acknowledgement that more research is in order. Of course, we are not suggesting that it would be better to withhold educational opportunities for DLLs; rather, we argue that educational practices for DLLs should be based on relevant empirical evidence. This research lacuna suggests further consideration of how first-language development relates to second-language development. We also emphasize that oral language development is critical for all young children but has particular salience for DLLs, who need more time and practice with receptive and productive skills.

Conclusion and Implications for Research

The NELP (2008) report calls attention to the need for research to "determine whether certain interventions would be effective with particular groups of children" (p. 18). The growing population of young DLLs merits immediate attention. We are hopeful that the present article serves as a call for a more expansive research agenda for young DLLs. The field would benefit significantly from longitudinal studies that examine how children exposed to two languages from an early age develop in relation to their specific individual differences and sociocultural contexts, including different types of educational interventions. There is also need for studies that examine how early literacy skills in the first language influence literacy development in English and how the development of academic literacy unfolds. Similarly, we need empirical work that examines the effects of specific instructional practices and approaches with a different language of instruction on DLLs' first- and second-language development. Such studies are essential to building a knowledge base that can guide the development of evidence-based policies and practices. Currently, there is a dearth of research about which program configurations, instructional models, and curricular approaches are most successful with prekindergarten DLLs.

Space limitations constrain us from addressing the important policy implications of the NELP review. In sum, we advise policy makers and practitioners to proceed cautiously as they consider implementing NELP's findings vis-à-vis DLLs, as more definitive research is needed to provide evidence-based interventions for this educationally vulnerable population. In the interim, there is an emerging body of research on DLLs' language and literacy development that should be taken into account when discussing instruction for young DLLs. Several research syntheses of studies targeting DLLs have identified specific instructional practices to promote language and literacy (August & Shanahan, 2006; Gersten et al., 2007), and recommendations have been given for using research on older DLLs prudently and strategically (Castro, Páez, et al., in press).

In conclusion, we highlight the need for a robust research agenda that focuses on young simultaneous bilinguals. We also encourage the development of language and literacy interventions that serve as cultural amplifiers (Cole & Griffin, 1980) that extend rather than constrain children's repertoires of practice—repertoires that can be leveraged to ensure full participation in meaningful literacy practices across learning contexts (Gutiérrez & Rogoff, 2003). To accomplish this research agenda, there is significant need for researchers who have the relevant expertise to examine the language and literacy practices of young DLLs. We advocate studies that push for more nuanced understandings of DLLs, studies that capture the cognitive and sociocultural complexities of becoming literate and biliterate, and policies that promote robust language and literacy learning, rather than seeking silver-bullet solutions for this important child population.

QUESTIONS FOR REFLECTION

1. What are the dangers of assuming that literacy practices that work for general education students will work for DLLs as well?
2. What evidence did the NELP report find of the importance of oral language skills as a predictor of emergent literacy?
3. How might the assumptions made in the NELP report be used to support narrow drill-and-skills approaches to literacy development with DLLs?

REFERENCES

AERA Task Force on Reporting of Research Methods in AERA Publications. (2006). Standards for reporting on empirical social science research in AERA publications. *Educational Researcher, 35*(6), 33–40.

August, D., & Shanahan, T. (Eds.). (2006). *Developing literacy in second-language learners: Report of the National Literacy Panel on Language-Minority Children and Youth.* Mahwah, NJ: Lawrence Erlbaum.

Ballantyne, K. G., Sanderman, A. R., D'Emilio, T., & McLaughlin, N. (2008). *Dual language learners in the early years: Getting ready to succeed in school.* Washington, DC: National Clearinghouse for English Language Acquisition and Language Instruction Educational Programs.

Bialystok, E. (2009). Claiming evidence from non-evidence: A reply to Morton and Harper. *Developmental Science, 12*(4), 499–450.

Bowman, B. T., Donovan, M. S., & Burns, M. S. (2000). *Eager to learn: Educating our preschoolers.* Washington, DC: National Academy Press.

Brisk, M. E., & Harrington, M. M. (2007). *Literacy and bilingualism: A handbook for all teachers* (2nd ed.). Mahwah, NJ: Lawrence Erlbaum.

Carlson, S. M., & Choi, H. P. (2009, April). *Bilingual and bicultural: Executive function in Korean and American children.* Paper presented at the 2009 Biennial Meeting of the Society for Research in Child Development, Denver, Colorado.

Castro, D.C., Espinosa, L., & Paéz, M. (in press). Defining and measuring quality in early childhood practices that promote dual language learners' development and learning. In M. Zaslow, I. Martinez-Beck, K. Tout, & T. Halle (Eds.), *Measuring quality in early childhood settings.* Baltimore: Paul H. Brookes.

Castro, D. C., Páez, M., Dickinson, D., & Frede, E. (in press). Promoting language and literacy in young dual language learners: Research, practice and policy. *Child Development Perspectives.*

Cole, M., & Griffin, P. (1980). Cultural amplifiers reconsidered. In D. R. Olson (Ed.), *The social foundations of language and thought: Essays in honor of Jerome S. Bruner* (pp. 343–364). New York: Norton.

Collins, M. F. (2005). ESL preschoolers' English vocabulary acquisition from storybook reading. *Reading Research Quarterly, 40*(4), 406–408.

de Villiers, P., de Villiers, J. G., & Hobbs, K. (2009, April). *False belief reasoning in low-income bilingual preschoolers: Is there an effect of bilingualism?* Paper presented at the 2009 Biennial Meeting of the Society for Research in Child Development, Denver, Colorado.

Dickinson, D., Hirsh-Pasek, K., Neuman, S., Burchinal, M., & Golinkoff, R. (2009, January 12). *The language of emergent literacy: A response to the National Institute for Literacy report on early literacy.* New Brunswick, NJ: National Institute for Early Education Research.

Dickinson, D. K., McCabe, A., Clark-Chiarelli, N., & Wolf, N. (2004). Cross-language transfer of phonological awareness in low-income Spanish and English bilingual preschool children. *Applied Psycholinguistics, 25,* 323–347.

Dolan, S. L. (2009). *Missing out: Latino students in America's schools.* Washington, DC: National Council de la Raza.

Espinosa, L. M. (2009). *Getting it right for young children from diverse backgrounds: Applying research to improve practice.* Boston: Pearson.

Francis, D. J., Rivera, M., Lesaux, N. K., Kieffer, M., & Rivera, H. (2006). *Practical guidelines for the education of English language learners: Research-based recommendations for instruction and academic interventions* (Vol. 24, p. 64). Portsmouth, NH: RMC Research Corporation, Center on Instruction.

García, O., Kleifgen, J., & Falchi, L. (2008). *From English language learners to emergent bilinguals: A research initiative of the Campaign for Educational Equity.* New York: Teachers College Press.

Genesee, F., Lindholm-Leary, K., Saunders, W. M., & Christian, D. (2006). *Educating English language learners: A synthesis of research evidence.* New York: Cambridge University Press.

Gersten, R., Baker, S. K., Shanahan, T., Linan-Thompson, S., Collings, P., & Scarcella, R. (2007). *Effective literacy and English language instruction for English learners in the elementary grades: A practice guide* (NCEE 2007–2011). Washington, DC: National Center for Education Evaluation and Regional Assistance, Institute of Education Sciences, U.S. Department of Education. Retrieved from http://ies .ed.gov/ncee

Gutiérrez, K., & Rogoff, B.(2003).Cultural ways of learning: Individual traits or repertoires of practice. *Educational Researcher, 32*(5), 19–25.

Hernandez, D. J., Denton, N. A., & McCartney, S. E. (2008). The lives of America's youngest children in immigrant families. *Zero to Three, 29,* 5–12.

Kindler, A. (2002). *Survey of the states' limited English proficient students and available educational programs and services, 2000–2001.* Summary report. Washington, DC: National Clearinghouse for English Language Acquisition and Language Instruction Educational Programs.

Laosa, L. M. (1990). Population generalizability, cultural sensitivity and ethical dilemmas. In C. B. Fisher & W. W. Tryon (Eds.), *Ethics in applied developmental psychology: Emerging issues in an emerging field* (pp. 227–251). Westport, CT: Ablex.

National Early Literacy Panel. (2008). *Developing early literacy: Report of the National Early Literacy Panel.* Washington, DC: National Institute for Literacy. Available at http://www.nifl.gov/earlychildhood/NELP/NELPreport.html

Peña, E. D., & Kester, E. S. (2004). Semantic development in Spanish-English bilinguals: Theory, assessment, and intervention. In B. A. Goldstein (Ed.), *Bilingual language development and disorders in Spanish-English speakers* (pp. 105–128). Baltimore: Paul H. Brookes.

Pew Hispanic Center. (2009). *Statistical portrait of Hispanics in the United States, 2007.* Washington, DC: Author.

Reardon, S., & Galindo, C. (2006, April 11). *K–3 academic achievement patterns and trajectories of Hispanics and other racial/ethnic groups.* Paper presented at the annual meeting of the American Educational Research Association, San Francisco, CA.

Saunders, W. M., & O'Brien, G. (2006). Oral language. In F. Genesee, K. Lindholm-Leary, W. M. Saunders, & D. Christian (Eds.), *Educating English language learners: A synthesis of research evidence* (pp. 14–63). New York: Cambridge University Press.

Silverman, R. D. (2007). Vocabulary development of English-language and English-only learners in kindergarten. *Elementary School Journal, 107*(4), 365–384.

Snow, C. E. (2006). Cross-cutting themes and future research directions. In D. August & T. Shanahan (Eds.), *Developing literacy in second-language learners: Report of the National Literacy Panel on Language-Minority Children and Youth* (pp. 631–652). Mahwah, NJ: Lawrence Erlbaum.

Vellutino, F. R., Tunmer, W. E., Jaccard, J. J., & Chen, R. (2007). Components of reading ability: Multivariate evidence for a convergent skills model of reading development. *Scientific Study of Reading, 11*(1), 3–32.

Verhallen, M., & Schoonen, R. (1998). Lexical knowledge in L1 and L2 of third and fifth graders. *Applied Linguistics, 19*(4), 452–470.

CHAPTER 15

Fluency: Developmental and Remedial Practices—Revisited

Melanie R. Kuhn, Boston University

Steven A. Stahl, University of Illinois at Urbana-Champaign

The process of becoming literate can be conceptualized as a series of qualitatively different stages through which learners progress as they become increasingly proficient with print (Chall, 1996b; Harris & Sipay, 1990). One of the primary advances in this process involves the shift from dealing with words on a word-by-word basis to a rapid, accurate, and expressive rendering of text. In other words, learners develop such familiarity with print that they achieve fluency in their reading. Fluent reading may underlie or assist in effective engagement with text (LaBerge & Samuels, 1974). The purpose of this chapter is a review of the literature examining how children move toward fluent reading. It will incorporate both theoretical discussions and practical studies relating to fluency research. Specifically, to accomplish this purpose, we have reviewed the theoretical accounts of reading that include an important role for fluency in the reading process and studies that have attempted to facilitate its development.

Fluency as a Factor in the Reading Process

Given that the ultimate goal of reading is the construction of meaning (Anderson, Hiebert, Wilkinson, & Scott, 1985), it is important to assess the role fluency plays in comprehension. There are two primary theories regarding fluency contribution to a reader's understanding of text, each of which emphasizes one of fluency's component parts. The first and better known of the two theories stresses the contribution of automaticity to fluent reading, whereas the second focuses on the role of prosody.

There seems to be a consensus regarding the primary components of fluency: (a) accuracy in decoding, (b) automaticity in word recognition, and (c) the appropriate use of prosodic features such as stress, pitch, and appropriate text phrasing. When reviewing the theories relating to fluency's role in the overall reading process, it is important to tease out the various ways these components may contribute to a learner's ability to interpret text. There is a rich literature about the contribution of accurate word recognition to reading comprehension (Johns, 1993) and enjoyment

This chapter has been adapted by Melanie R. Kuhn from "Fluency: A Review of Developmental and Remedial Practices," by Melanie R. Kuhn and Steven A. Stahl, *Journal of Educational Psychology*, 95(1), 3–21.

of reading (Nell, 1988). This will not be reviewed here. Instead, we will concentrate on the relative importance of automaticity and prosody to comprehension.

Contribution of Automaticity

Proficient readers have certain features in common; they not only read accurately, but also their recognition of words is automatic. The question is, How does this automaticity contribute to the primary goal of reading, which is comprehension of text? An individual has a limited amount of attention available for any given cognitive task (LaBerge & Samuels, 1974; Perfetti, 1985; Stanovich, 1980). This being the case, attention expended on one activity is, necessarily, attention unavailable for another.

In the case of reading, an individual is required to perform at least two interdependent tasks: The reader must determine what words compose the text while simultaneously constructing meaning. As such, the greater the amount of attention expended on decoding, the less that is available for comprehension. To ensure that readers have enough attention to understand texts adequately, the argument continues, it is necessary for them to develop decoding to the point where each word is recognized instantaneously. Once this occurs, they will have the necessary attention to focus on the sense or meaning of the text.

According to Stanovich's (1980) interactive-compensatory model, information from multiple sources is available for aiding readers in their construction of meaning. This is true at each stage of development and presumes that learners will make use of information from orthographic, phonological, semantic, and syntactic sources. However, if a reader is less adept at gleaning information from one source, he or she may become overreliant on other sources. It follows that until readers achieve automaticity in word recognition, they will necessarily depend more on alternative knowledge sources to make sense of what is being read. In other words, they are more likely to rely on context as an aid to word recognition and comprehension than are fluent readers. (This refers only to the use of context as an aid to identifying words already in a child's lexicon, not to the use of context in learning new word meanings. Stanovich would argue that automatic word recognition allows readers to concentrate on the meaning of text, rather than on identifying words. Thus, automatic word recognition allows one to focus contextual analysis on constructing meaning rather than decoding [see also Adams, 1990].)

The question then becomes, How do learners make the shift from decoding accurately but deliberately to decoding automatically? According to the automaticity theorists, the best way to ensure this transition is through extensive practice. As with any skill that requires an individual to coordinate a series of smaller actions to create a unified process, it is practice that allows the learner to develop expertise. In terms of reading, this practice consists primarily in providing successive exposures to print. As letters, and later words, become increasingly familiar to the learner, less and less attention needs to be directed toward processing text at the orthographic level. This ability to complete a process without conscious attention fulfills LaBerge and Samuels's (1974) criterion for automaticity. In this way, the automaticity theory accounts for two of the components of fluent reading: accurate decoding at a sufficient rate. It further posits an explanation for automaticity's role in text comprehension. However, there is an important aspect of fluency that this theory does not attend to, that of prosody.

Contribution of Prosody

Although the automaticity theory accounts for the accurate and effortless decoding that fluent readers exhibit, it fails to provide a sufficient explanation for the role that prosody plays in the reading process. When an individual provides a fluent rendering of a text, there is a tacit understanding that he or she is doing more than simply reading the words quickly and accurately; he or she is also reading with expression. Implicit in the phrase *reading with expression* is the use of those prosodic features that account for the tonal and rhythmic aspects of language (Dowhower, 1991).

Prosody comprises a series of features including pitch or intonation, stress or loudness, and duration or timing, all of which contribute to an expressive rendering of a text (Allington, 1983; Dowhower, 1991; Schreiber, 1980, 1987, 1991). Additionally, prosodic reading includes appropriately chunking groups of words into phrases or meaningful units in accordance with the syntactic structure of the text. Taken together, these features are classified as *suprasegmental* because they extend over more than one speech sound and contribute to meaning. Given this understanding of what constitutes prosody, it is necessary to determine the role that prosody plays in the development of fluency and the ways in which these features contribute to the construction of meaning from a text.

Prosody may provide a link between fluency and comprehension. Chafe (1988) speculates that to read a sentence with intonation, one must assign syntactic roles to the words in the sentence. The assignment of syntactic roles is a key component of microprocessing, or the mental parsing of a text into hierarchically ordered propositions (Kintsch, 1998). Schreiber (1987) also suggests that the explicit presence of prosodic cues may be one crucial difference between speech and reading and one of the reasons that speech is easier to understand. However, he reports that the evidence supporting a link between prosody and microprocessing is weak, with some studies finding links between the use of prosodic features and syntactic comprehension, and others failing to find such an effect.

Dowhower (1991) identifies six distinct markers that compose prosodic reading: pausal intrusions, length of phrases, appropriateness of phrases, final phrase lengthening, terminal intonation contours, and stress. From a linguistic perspective, readers who use these markers appropriately are capable of making the connection between written and oral language. In other words, they are able to transfer their knowledge of syntax from speech to text by effectively applying these features to their reading. Such readers can produce a rendering of text that maintains the important features of expressive oral language in addition to reading it accurately and at an appropriate rate.

Children who have not achieved fluency read either in a word-by-word manner or by grouping words in ways that deviate from the type of phrasing that occurs naturally in oral language (Allington, 1983; Chall, 1996b; Clay & Imlach, 1971; Dowhower, 1991; Samuels, 1988). Young children are highly attuned to the use of prosodic features in speech (Dowhower, 1991; Schreiber, 1987; Schreiber &

Read, 1980). In fact, research indicates that infants under a year old use prosodic features as a primary cue to the syntactic structure of their language and that their babbling follows the characteristics inherent in the prosody of their primary language. Further, Read and Schreiber (1982) and Schreiber (1987) have determined that children are not only highly attuned to prosodic elements in oral language but also actually more reliant on them for determining meaning than are adults.

Given children's sensitivity to prosody in oral language, it seems reasonable to assume that they are equally dependent on these features in determining the meaning of text (Allington, 1983; Dowhower, 1991; Schreiber, 1991). In fact, appropriate phrasing, intonation, and stress are all considered to be indicators that a child has become a fluent reader (Chomsky, 1978; Rasinski, 1990b; Samuels, Schermer, & Reinking, 1992). The reasoning behind this emphasis is that such readings provide clues to an otherwise invisible process; they act as indicators of the reader's comprehension. Given that a fluent reader is one who groups text into syntactically appropriate phrases, this parsing of text signifies that the reader has an understanding of what is being read.

Research on Fluency Instruction

Rather than incorporate precursors to fluency in this version of our chapter (e.g., developing phonemic awareness or automaticity in letter recognition), we restrict our discussion to a few different approaches used to improve children's fluency. Among these are approaches primarily used with clinical populations or children with reading problems, such as repeated reading (Samuels, 1979) and assisted reading (Chomsky, 1978; Heckelman, 1969, 1986), and approaches used with entire classes, such as the oral recitation lesson (Hoffman, 1987) and fluency-oriented reading instruction (Stahl, Heubach, & Cramond, 1997). There have been other studies that attempted to improve children's speed of word recognition in isolation (e.g., Fleisher, Jenkins, & Pany, 1979) and approaches that segmented text to enable children to identify pausal units in the text (e.g., O'Shea & Sindelar, 1983). We use these studies to inform our knowledge of the issues related to fluency development.

To obtain a large corpus of studies relating to instructional approaches to fluency development, we first undertook a search of both the ERIC and PsycLIT databases for any articles that referred to reading fluency. As we began to locate these articles, we either read through the abstract or briefly scanned the article to confirm that the contents were appropriate for further review and analysis. In addition, if the article was to be included, the reference list was used as a means of cross-checking sources. In this way, we were able to locate a number of articles that were not identified in the initial search. The articles that emerged from this search process fell into four broad categories: theoretical bases of fluency development, research pertaining to the validity of these theories, recommendations for classroom practice, and intervention studies. Given our purpose, we chose to concentrate on intervention studies to determine the overall effectiveness of fluency instruction.

When deciding whether a given article should be included as part of this review, we had both inclusionary and exclusionary criteria. We selected studies that focused on evaluating strategies designed to promote readers' fluency development, such as the development of either the automaticity or prosodic components of fluent reading or some combination of the two. Methods and representative studies are presented for each type of intervention, along with a summarization of the results.

We chose not to consider articles that dealt with either external or self-correction strategies because such studies focus on components of the reading process that lead to more effectively attending to the text rather than on a fluent rendition of the reading (e.g., Mudre & McCormick, 1989). Nor did we include studies that focused exclusively on training accurate word recognition. It is reasonably well established that teaching children to be more accurate at recognizing words leads to improved comprehension (e.g., Chall, 1996a; see Table 1).

We intended to conduct a meta-analysis but did not, for three reasons. First, we found relatively few studies with control groups. Baseline studies can be submitted to meta-analytic techniques (e.g., Scruggs, 1987), but these studies cannot be combined with control group studies. Two separate analyses are more likely to be confusing than enlightening. Second, the effect sizes we calculated fluctuated widely, from 0.13 to 2.79. High effect sizes likely are due to a lack of variance in the control condition, leading to exaggerated estimates of effect. These few effect sizes over 1.00 would have to be eliminated from the analysis to avoid their having an excessive influence on the calculated effect. Finally, there were a number of different conditions used as controls, from no treatment to having the students spend an equivalent amount of time in nonrepetitive reading. These different control conditions made it difficult to come up with a common metric, as should be done in a meta-analysis. Instead, we used vote-counting procedures to analyze the data, combined with qualitative synthesis of the studies themselves.

Studies

We found 58 studies dealing with assisted reading, repeated reading, or classroom interventions designed to improve fluency. In addition, we found nine studies dealing with segmented text and four studies dealing with speeded isolated word recognition. This is a total of 71 studies.

Segmented text and isolated word-recognition studies were analyzed separately. Our logic in doing so was as follows: If fluency-based instruction affects microprocessing, then we might also expect to find effects in studies using segmented text, that is, text broken up by phrases. If fluency instruction improves comprehension by helping students develop automatic word recognition, then we might see similar effects from studies in which readers' word recognition was speeded up through practice of reading words in isolation.

There are several reasons for the preponderance of studies without control groups. Repeated reading and assisted readings were developed as clinical approaches for working with children with reading problems (e.g., Dahl, 1979). Thus, testing their effectiveness with targeted children using baseline or multiple

Table 1. Repeated-Reading Studies

Study	Criteria (Multiple Readings vs. Criteria)	Grade of Participants	Reading Level of Participants[a]	Initial Fluency of Participants	Level of Material Read	Fluency Results	Microprocessing Comprehension (Results)	General Comprehension	Notes
Bell, Markley, Yonker (1990)	Set number of readings (3)	2–3	Average	Not given	Instructional	Improvement over time			No effect on attitudes
Bohlen (1988)	Criterion (until he or she could read the text fluently)	3	Below grade level (2.5–3.4)	Not given	Instructional	No significant improvement over time			Small *n*, good effect size
Carver & Hoffman (1981)		High school	4th–6th grade		2nd–9th grade	Improvement over time	Improvement over time	No improvement over time	
Dahl (1979)	Criterion (100 wpm)	2	Below grade level	Disfluent (35–60 wpm)	Difficult	T > C	T > C	T = C	No effect on tahistoscopic recognition of words (automaticity)
Dowhower (1987)	Criterion (100 wpm)	2	Average	Disfluent (less than 50 wpm)	2nd grade	Improvement over time	Improvement over time (4/5 groups)		
Hannah (1994)	Criterion	2	Low achieving	Disfluent	Not given	T = C	T = C		
Herman (1985)	Criterion (85 wpm)	4–6	2nd–17th percentile	Disfluent (35–50 wpm)	Instructional	Improvement over time	Improvement over time	T = C; improvement over time	

Study	Criteria (Multiple Readings vs. Criteria)	Grade of Participants	Reading Level of Participants[a]	Initial Fluency of Participants	Level of Material Read	Fluency Results	Microprocessing Comprehension (Results)	General Comprehension	Notes
Homan, Klesius, & Hite (1993)	Set number of readings (4)	6	Below grade level high 4th-grade, beginner 5th-grade levels	Not given	Instructional (5th grade)	T = C; improvement over time			
Knupp (1988)	Criterion (85 wpm)	4–6	2nd–4th grade (2–4 levels below placement)	Disfluent	45–65 wpm; 4–8 incorrect words per 100; 50–75% comprehension	Improvement over time	Improvement over time		
Koch (1984)	Set number of readings (variable)	2	Low achieving	Not given	Above grade	T > C			2x group read faster than 6x or control[b]
Koskinen & Blum (1984)	Set amount of time	3	Below average (1.7–4.5)	Disfluent	On grade	T > C	T > C		
Levy, Barnes, & Martin (1993)	Set number of readings	College	Above average	Probably high	Appropriate	Improvement over time			
Levy, Newell, Snyder, & Timmins (1986)	Set number of readings	College	Above average	Probably high	Appropriate	Improvement over time	Improvement over time		
Mathes & Fuchs (1993)	Set number of readings	4–6	Learning disabled	Not given	Easy	T = C	T = C	T = C	
Mathes & Fuchs (1993)	Set number of readings	4–6	Learning disabled	Not given	Instructional	T = C	T = C	T = C	

(continued)

Table 1. Repeated-Reading Studies (*Continued*)

Study	Criteria (Multiple Readings vs. Criteria)	Grade of Participants	Reading Level of Participants[a]	Initial Fluency of Participants	Level of Material Read	Fluency Results	Microprocessing Comprehension (Results)	General Comprehension	Notes
O'Shea, Sindelar, & O'Shea (1985)	Set number of readings	3	At or above grade level	Average (70–119 wpm)	Above grade	Improvement over time	Improvement over time	Improvement over time	
O'Shea, Sindelar, & O'Shea (1987)	Set number of readings	5–8	Learning disabled (3rd-grade level average)	Below average to above average (34–156 wpm)	Above grade	Improvement over time			
Person & Burke (1984)	Set number of readings (3)	2–4	Not given	Not given	Easy	T = C			
Rashotte & Torgesen (1985)	Set number of readings	2–5	Below average	Disfluent (less than 6.5 wpm)	2nd grade (low overlap)	T = C	T = C		Text with high overlap produced better fluency
Rashotte & Torgesen (1985)	Set number of readings	2–5	Below average	Disfluent (less than 6.5 wpm)	2nd grade (high overlap)	T = C	T = C		
Rasinski (1990a)	Set amount of time	3	Above average	4th grade (above level)	Improvement over time				
Simmons, Fuchs, Fuchs, Mathes, & Hodge (1995)	3 readings	2–5	Learning disabled and low performing (2nd–3rd grade)	Disfluent (67 wcpm)	Appropriate		T > C	T = C	

Study	Criteria (Multiple Readings vs. Criteria)	Grade of Participants	Reading Level of Participants[a]	Initial Fluency of Participants	Level of Material Read	Fluency Results	Microprocessing Comprehension (Results)	General Comprehension	Notes
Stoddard, Valcante, Sindelar, O'Shea, & Algozzine (1993)	Set number of readings (7); measurement at 1st, 3rd, & 7th reading	4–5	Low achieving	Fluent (70 wpm)	Instructional	Improvement over time			
Tingstrom, Edwards, & Olmi (1995)	Criterion (100 wpm with no errors)	3–4	Low achieving	Disfluent (40–69 wpm)	Instructional	Improvement over time	Improvement over time		Found that previewing improved repeated reading for 2 out of 3 students
Turpie & Paratore (1995)	Set number of readings (7)	1	Low achieving	Not given	On grade	Improvement over time	Improvement over time (2 out of 4 students)		
Van Bon, Boksebeld, Font Freide, & Van den Hurk (1991)	Set number of readings (4)	3	Learning disabled		1 year above	T > C for familiar text, but T = C for transfer text			Compared repeated readings with readings while listening with nonrepeated text
van der Leij (1981), Experiment 1	Set number of readings (5)	5–7	1st grade	Not given		T = C			

(continued)

Table 1. Repeated-Reading Studies (*Continued*)

Study	Criteria (Multiple Readings vs. Criteria)	Grade of Participants	Reading Level of Participants[a]	Initial Fluency of Participants	Level of Material Read	Fluency Results	Microprocessing Comprehension (Results)	General Comprehension	Notes
van der Leij (1981), Experiment 3	Set number of readings (4)	5–7	1st grade	Not given		C > T; T = C			
Weinstein & Cooke (1992)	Criterion (90 wpm)	2–5 (ages 7–10)	Below average (1.0–1.3)	Disfluent	1st grade (on level)	Improvement over time	Improvement over time		No difference between criteria
Weinstein & Cooke (1992)	3 successive improvements	2–5 (ages 7–10)	Below average (1.0–1.3)	Disfluent	1st grade (on level)				
Young, Bowers, & MacKinnon (1996)	Set number of readings (3)	5	Low achieving	Not given	Instructional	T > C			

Note. The technique used for all studies was repeated reading. C > T = the control produced a significantly higher score than the treatment on this measure. T > C = the treatment produced a significantly higher score than a control on the measure. T = C = the difference between the treatment and a control was not statistically significant. wcpm = words correct per minute. wpm = words per minute.

[a] Numbers in parentheses refer to the tested level of participants.

[b] The group that read the passage(s) two times read faster than the group that read the passage(s) six times or the control.

baseline designs is appropriate. In other cases, researchers compared different variations of repeated reading (Rashotte & Torgesen, 1985). In another case, students involved in a pilot study made so much gain as to make a control group seem to be unethical (Stahl et al., 1997).

Authors who used baseline designs did test for statistical significance, but the lack of studies with a control in this literature as a whole is problematic. Baseline designs are useful in evaluating the effectiveness of approaches for children who are in small, heterogeneous populations, such as learning-disabled children or children with reading problems. There is an assumption in such designs of a null hypothesis in which the child would make no growth over the period of instruction. This may be tenable in the case of children with severe reading problems but not tenable with a more average population. Chomsky (1978) illustrates this point. She used a set of taped readings to bring children with reading problems to fluent reading, finding significant improvement over time. But this improvement was equivalent to six months over a 10-month school year. Thus, her students, although ahead of where they started, were further behind their classmates. Similarly, in Blum et al.'s (1995) study, although all children made significant progress, only one of the five children in the study progressed beyond the preprimer level during the 19 weeks of the intervention. Neither result would be the accelerated progress needed by children who are behind their classmates in reading (Clay, 1993).

Fluency Instruction as Remediation

The studies of fluency instruction fell into two overarching categories: those that build on independent learning, or what Dowhower (1989) labels *unassisted strategies*, and assisted-reading strategies that provide learners with a model of fluent reading behaviors. Further, these studies consist of two types of interventions: those that dealt with fluency training as a means of remediation for individuals and those designed for classrooms. Additionally, researchers looked at a range of indicators to determine reading improvement, including measures of accuracy, rate, prosody, and comprehension. The studies are categorized here, first according to the type of intervention provided and then in terms of whether their reading methods were designed for individual learners, dyads, or groups. We discuss both near transfer, that is, improvement on fluency measures such as increased reading rate on previously unread texts, and far transfer, for example, improvement in comprehension on new material.

Unassisted Repeated Reading

Perhaps the best known of the reading interventions designed to support fluency development is that of repeated reading. This is a strategy that relies on independent practice of text. The basic method of repeated reading was developed by Samuels (1979) and Dahl (1979) in an attempt to apply LaBerge and Samuels's (1974) automaticity theory to practice. Samuels and Dahl note that classroom practice often consists of students reading new text on a daily basis in the hope that they will improve their word-recognition skills. However, it struck the researchers that by increasing the amount of practice on a given passage, students might be able to improve not only their accuracy but also their fluency. We found a total of 33 comparisons dealing with repeated reading, over half of the total population of studies dealing with fluency reading instruction. These studies are summarized in Table 1. The vast majority dealt with either students at the second- or third-grade level or older children with reading problems who could be presumed to be reading at a primary level.

Effects of Repeated Reading on Fluency and Comprehension

We found 15 studies that assessed the effects of repeated reading on fluency using a control group. We did a vote count (Light & Pillemer, 1984) of these studies, vote counting in two ways. First, we counted each study once, using the majority of comparisons to assign it depending on whether there was evidence of repeated-reading effectiveness. In six studies, repeated reading produced significantly greater achievement than the control did; eight studies had no such effect, and in one, repeated reading improved fluency for familiar passages but not for a transfer passage. In the second vote-counting procedure, we counted each individual comparison. This procedure gave added weight to studies with multiple comparisons. In eight comparisons, the repeated-readings group performed significantly higher than the control did, whereas 21 comparisons did not. Overall, repeated reading did not produce significantly greater achievement than a control did. However, this may be the result of the type of control group involved. In some cases, students were assigned to a no-treatment control group, whereas in others, students were expected to read an amount of connected text equivalent to the amount read by the intervention group but not in a repeated manner (e.g., Mathes & Fuchs, 1993; Rashotte & Torgesen, 1985). As discussed later in the chapter, the two types of controls are likely to produce very different outcome measures.

Criteria. The majority of studies had students read each passage a set number of times, usually three readings, rather than using the criterion suggested by Samuels (1979; i.e., 100 wpm). Of the 15 studies with a control group, two used criteria. Of these two, one had a significant treatment difference, and one did not. Of the remaining 13 studies in which students read a set number of times, three found significant differences, nine did not, and two had mixed findings. Overall, there were too few studies that used a criterion to evaluate its effectiveness.

Difficulty. We also examined the relative difficulty of the passages. It could be argued that having students read and reread relatively easy passages would improve their fluency (e.g., Clay, 1993). It could also be argued that the rereadings scaffold children's word-recognition abilities so they can read more difficult material.

Mathes and Fuchs (1993) compared the use of easy and difficult materials and found no effect for the difficulty of materials. However, they also failed to find a difference between a repeated-reading treatment and a control group. Rashotte and Torgesen (1985) used relatively easy reading materials and also failed to find significant differences between their repeated-readings treatment and a control group. The remainder of the studies used materials at or above the child's instructional level. Six of the 11 remaining studies found differences favoring the treatment group. Our best guess is that more difficult materials would lead to greater gains in achievement, but more research is needed on this question.

Comprehension. As noted in Table 1, the basic results for comprehension mirror those for fluency. Generally, where an increase in fluency was found, there was also an increase in comprehension. The exceptions were in Carver and Hoffman's (1981) study and Dahl's (1979) study, in which there were effects for microcomprehension (generally cloze) measures but not for more general comprehension measures (e.g., standardized tests). This is consonant with the notion that fluent reading would affect the reader's microcomprehension processes, through the assignment of syntactic relations in sentences, but might not affect macrocomprehension processes, which are affected more by prior knowledge and more global comprehension strategies (see Stahl, Jacobson, Davis, & Davis, 1989). It also may be that the more general measures of comprehension, such as standardized achievement tests, are more resistant to change.

Other Findings. Dowhower (1987) not only used rate and accuracy as measures of fluency but also found that repeated reading had measurable effects on speech pauses and intonation. Herman (1985) found not only effects on speech pauses and rate for read material but also that repeated-readings treatment transferred to previously unread material.

Rashotte and Torgesen (1985) found that students reading texts with a high overlap of words improved in rate and accuracy more than did students reading texts with a low overlap. Although these two groups differed significantly, neither was significantly more fluent than a group engaged in nonrepetitive reading. However, Rashotte and Torgesen limited students to four readings of each text; they might have found stronger effects had they had students read to a fluency criterion for each text.

Assisted-Reading Strategies

As with the unassisted repeated reading, assisted readings emphasize practice as a means of improving accuracy, automaticity, and prosody as well as the learner's understanding of a text. Further, they provide extensive exposure to print. However, unlike traditional repeated reading, assisted-reading methods provide learners with a model of fluent reading (Dowhower, 1989). There is also a greater amount of variation among the intervention strategies. To maintain a sense of cohesion, we outline the various methods along with several studies that evaluate the effectiveness of these methods. We found 15 studies involving assisted reading. Of these, seven had a control group to evaluate effectiveness of the treatment, and eight did not. These studies are summarized in Table 2.

Neurological Impress Method or Assisted Reading. Heckelman (1969) suggests the neurological impress method as a remedial strategy for disfluent readers, although the term may go back further. Currently, it is called *assisted reading* or even *choral reading* because a tutor and tutee read the same material chorally. Although assisted reading is quite successful in improving the reading fluency of struggling readers, the procedure is time-consuming in nature. Given the requirement of one-on-one teacher support for the method, it was feasible for assisted reading to be used primarily in tutoring situations but did not provide a viable approach for integration into most traditional classrooms. As such, Hollingsworth (1970) redesigned the procedure so it could be used with a tape recording of a text while allowing the teacher to monitor students' reading.

Reading-While-Listening. Chomsky (1978) and Carbo (1981) also used tapes for an assisted-reading approach called *reading-while-listening*. This intervention differs from Hollingsworth's (1970, 1978) modified assisted-reading approach insofar as there is less direct monitoring from the teacher, and students are responsible for determining the length and frequency of their sessions. One of the primary concerns regarding such read-along techniques is that there is no way to ensure active engagement on the part of the learners. Indeed, in a number of classroom observation studies (e.g., Evans & Carr, 1985; Leinhardt, Zigmond, & Cooley, 1981), time spent listening to tapes in class did not significantly affect achievement. In these reading-while-listening studies, however, students were held responsible for being able to read the text fluently, so they did actively participate in the process.

Closed-Caption Television. Rather than designing material that needed to be used in conjunction with a television monitor, Koskinen, Wilson, and Jensema (1985) made use of the closed-caption option available on a number of television programs with remedial readers in an exploratory study.

Results. Using the same vote-counting procedure as for repeated reading, five of the seven studies using assisted reading with a control group had significant treatment differences. When analyzed by number of comparisons, six of the nine comparisons proved significant treatment effects.

Finally, comparisons of assisted and unassisted forms of repeated reading (Dowhower, 1987; Rasinski, 1990a) found both to be effective. For Dowhower's study, both approaches showed gains in rate, accuracy, and comprehension on practiced and similar nonpracticed passages and gains in prosody for the reading-while-listening group. Similarly, Rasinski found that both approaches led to significant gains in speed and accuracy, but he favored reading-while-listening because it was easier to implement and, as a result, may be a more efficient aid to fluency development.

Table 2. Assisted-Reading Studies

Study	Criteria (Multiple Readings vs. Criteria)	Number of Participants	Grade Level	Reading Level of Participants	Initial Fluency of Participants	Level of Material Read	Fluency Results	Microprocessing Comprehension (Results)	General Comprehension	Notes
Carbo (1978)		8	2–6	Learning disabled	Not given	Difficult	Improvement over time			
Chomsky (1978)	Criterion ("achieve fluency")	5	3	Below grade level	Disfluent	Difficult	Mean gain lower than expected (.60 in 1 year)		Mean gain lower than expected (.75 in 1 year)	
Dowhower (1987)	Criterion (100 wpm)		2	Average	Disfluent (<50 wpm)	2nd grade	Improvement over time	Improvement over time (2/5 groups)		
Eldredge (1990)	Criterion (until students could read it expressively without teacher assistance)	18	3	Low achieving	Not given	3rd–6th-grade readability			T > C	Significant effect on Gates–MacGinitie vocabuary
Gardner (1965)			5–8	Below grade level					T > C	
Gilbert, Williams, & McLaughlin (1996)	Set number of readings (4)	3	1–2	Learning disabled	Low (28–58 wpm)	Unclear				
Heckelman (1969)		24	7–10	3 years below grade level		Unclear			Improvement over time	Growth in oral reading accuracy also

(continued)

Table 2. Assisted-Reading Studies (*Continued*)

Study	Criteria (Multiple Readings vs. Criteria)	Number of Participants	Grade Level	Reading Level of Participants	Initial Fluency of Participants	Level of Material Read	Fluency Results	Microprocessing Comprehension (Results)	General Comprehension	Notes
Hollingsworth (1970)	Set amount of time	8	4	Average		Varied from 1 year below grade to 1 year above	T = C	T = C		
Hollingsworth (1978)	Set amount of time	20	4–6	Below average		Varied from 1 year below grade to 1 year above			T > C	
Langford, Slade, & Burnett (1974)		2	4–6	Below average	Disfluent		Improvement over time			
Mefferd & Pettegrew (1997)	Set number of readings	3	4–5	Developmentally handicapped	Low (14, 48, & 89 wpm)	Above grade	Improvement over time	Improvement over time		
Rasinski (1990a)	Set amount of time	20	3	Above average		4th grade (above grade)	Improvement over time			
Richek & McTeague (1988)	Set number of readings	37	2–3	Chapter 1	Not given	Difficult	T > C		T > C	
Strong & Traynelis-Yurek (1983)	Not given	26	2–6	Not given			T = C			
Young, Bowers, & MacKinnon (1996)	Set number of readings (3)	10	5	Low achieving	Not given	Instructional	T > C			

Note. T > C = the treatment produced a significantly higher score than a control on the measure. T = C = the difference between the treatment and a control was not statistically significant. wpm = words per minute.

Classroom Approaches

Two general approaches have been taken when attempting to adapt the principles of fluency instruction to the classroom. First, authors have tried to adapt clinical approaches directly. Assisted-reading approaches, rather than unassisted repeated reading, have been adapted because of the ability to incorporate social interaction within a classroom setting. Alternatively, authors have used a variety of techniques, such as echo reading, repeated reading, and partner reading, in an integrated lesson plan. Both approaches show promise.

Classroom Extensions of Assisted Reading

Although the assisted-reading approaches outlined previously incorporate models of fluent reading as an aid to reading development, an alternative to individual repeated reading involves the use of a partner as a means of facilitating fluency development. When the repeated-reading approach is modified so two readers can work together, students are able to receive the type of immediate feedback that is not available when working on unassisted readings or prerecorded models. It is also a technique that can be effectively adopted in traditional classrooms.

Eldredge and Quinn (1988; Eldredge, 1990) examined a modified version of assisted reading (Heckelman, 1969) in which a classmate was chosen to be the lead reader. The struggling reader, known as the "assisted reader," received support and feedback from a partner. Pairs were changed weekly. The lead readers were selected on the basis of their ability to render the chosen texts fluently. They set the pace for the pair, read in phrases, and indicated each word as it was read. As a result of the intervention strategy, students read with assistance material that would have been beyond their instructional level had they been working independently. Eventually, this led to independent reading of grade-level text.

Koskinen and Blum (1984) implemented a procedure that allowed for paired repeated reading of texts with below-average third graders. Students in the repeated-reading condition worked in pairs where they learned to select their own texts, to follow the strategy, and to provide both self-evaluations and evaluations of their partners (the procedure is fully described in Koskinen & Blum, 1986).

Hoskisson and Krohm (1974) provided a transition from assisted readings to partner reading. Second-grade students were presented a series of tape-recorded stories at a read-along center. Tapes were prepared for a number of books; reading levels and pace of narration were adjusted to the individual reading abilities of students to assure that struggling readers did not get lost and that better readers would remain engaged in the activity. Additionally, students were provided with weekly opportunities to read one of these stories to a peer. Their lessons were extended to a home reading program.

Another effective way of encouraging students to read a text repeatedly is by giving them a real purpose for doing so. Such a purpose is provided by the cross-age reading strategy suggested by Labbo and Teale (1990). In this study, the authors invited fifth graders to read aloud to kindergartners from books that were appropriate for the younger participants. Students in the cross-age reading group were prepared for their reading performances in three ways: They were taught to select appropriate texts for their audience, they were given opportunities to develop fluency with the books, and they determined ways in which they could involve kindergartners in discussions of the texts.

We found two other studies that examined cross-age tutoring but with less salutary results. Sutton (1991) examined the effects of cross-age tutoring with first and second graders. She reported improvement over time in fluency and the amount of time spent engaged in reading, but she did not have a control group. Ramunda (1994) used above-average second graders as tutors, but she did not find a significant effect on comprehension compared with a control group.

It seems that cross-age tutoring appears to be successful with below-grade-level tutors but does not seem to affect above-grade-level tutors. This may be because the below-grade-level tutors in Labbo and Teale's (1990) study were reading relatively difficult materials, but the above-grade-level tutors in Ramunda's (1994) study were reading relatively easy texts. It could also indicate that the procedure aids fluency development in struggling readers but does not assist readers who are already considered to be fluent.

Integrated Fluency Lessons

Hoffman (1987) developed an oral recitation lesson format as an alternative means of presenting a traditional basal reader story. The goal of the lesson was to use oral reading as a means of developing students' prosody rather than treating it as a form of assessment. In this procedure, the teacher began by reading the basal story aloud. This reading was followed by a group discussion to deal with comprehension prior to the students' oral reading of the text. The teacher then reread the story, paragraph by paragraph, with the children following along and echoing back each paragraph. Next, the students chose or were assigned a portion of the text to master, with the understanding that their reading was to be expressive. They were provided with opportunity to practice this text until they could read it at an adequate rate with few errors (2 errors per 100 words). The final step involved the students reading their passage to the group before going on to the next story.

Morris and Nelson (1992) created a program based on the oral recitation lesson for a group of struggling second-grade readers. The goal was to incorporate the modeling of fluent reading along with the opportunity for practice into the students' reading lessons. The lessons took place for a 20-minute period, three times a week. On the first day, the teacher read a text aloud to the students and discussed the story with them. This was followed with an echo reading of the text. On the second day, the students completed a paired reading of the text. They then practiced a 100-word passage from the story until they could read it fluently with few errors. On the last day, the students read the passage they selected aloud while the teacher took a running record of the text.

Rasinski, Padak, Linek, and Sturtevant (1994) used a similar format in their fluency development lesson, but instead of using basal reader stories, they used

50–150-word texts. The researchers specifically suggested short texts so the teachers were able to complete the entire lesson in a 15-minute session. In this way, the lessons could be incorporated into the current reading curriculum. Teachers read each passage aloud, students and teachers discussed the material and then read the texts chorally, and students practiced reading in pairs. During the final component, partners gave each other positive feedback.

Another program based on Hoffman's (1987) work is the fluency-oriented reading instruction program (Stahl et al., 1997). This approach is an attempt to use repeated reading in a classroom program to develop fluent and automatic word recognition in second graders. The resulting program had three aspects: a redesigned basal reading lesson, a free-reading period at school, and a home reading program.

The redesigned basal reading lesson used the story from the children's second-grade reading text. This text would be difficult for children reading below grade level. With the support provided by the program, however, children who entered second grade with some basic reading ability could profit from a conventional second-grade text. The teacher began by reading the story aloud to the class and discussing it to put comprehension right in front so the children were aware that they were reading for meaning. The rest of the week involved choral, echo, and partner reading of the text with extension activities upon completion of the story.

Results. In terms of the vote-counting procedure, out of six studies that examined the effects of lessons designed to increase fluency, only three had a control group. Of the controlled studies, only one found clear evidence that the fluency-oriented lessons produced significantly better achievement than did traditional instruction or a shared-book experience (which was commonly used in basal reading programs at the time). The effects of this instruction were suggestive, especially given the large gains reported by Stahl et al. (1997), but these approaches need to be examined in more controlled research.

Discussion

When fluency instruction was compared with the traditional instruction used with a basal reader, fluency instruction improved children's reading fluency and comprehension. When different approaches to fluency instruction were compared, the results were less clear-cut. Overall, these strategies seem, to a greater or lesser degree, effective in assisting readers making the transition to fluent reading. These include normally achieving students at the point where they are making this transition and those who are experiencing difficulties in becoming fluent.

This finding is subject to a caveat. Relatively few studies had conventional experimental or quasi-experimental designs. Many of the studies, from a special education tradition, used single or multiple baseline designs, in which progress is examined over a period of time. These studies can be robust (Neuman & McCormick, 1995), but we find the reliance on this design in an entire body of research to be problematic. Also, in a number of studies in which progress could be compared with a norm, students' progress fell below what would be expected (e.g., Blum et al., 1995; Chomsky, 1978).

Conclusions

Fluency Instruction and the Stage Model. According to Chall's (1996b) stage model, one would expect that fluency instruction would be most effective for children in the confirmation and fluency stage, from the end of first grade to third grade. This proposition is difficult to test because practically all studies used either normally achieving second graders or older children with reading problems who were reading at the second-grade level. That is, nearly all of the researchers working with fluency instruction implicitly accepted a stage view and acted accordingly. Of the few studies that used populations outside of this range, the results supported the stage model. Hollingsworth (1970) used average fourth graders, who should have been in the learning-the-new stage and not in need of fluency instruction, and found that the treatment did not produce significant improvement over a control. Hollingsworth (1978) replicated this study with below-average fourth graders, who would have been predicted to benefit from this training, and found that they did. Stahl et al. (1997) found that their fluency-oriented reading instruction program was highly effective with children reading at a primer level or higher at the beginning of second grade. Nearly all of those students were reading at the second-grade level by the end of the year. With children reading below the primer level, the approach brought only half to that level. Teachers dropped children who were reading at an emergent stage from the program because it did not seem to benefit them. Blum et al. (1995) found that only children who entered their assisted-reading treatment with some reading ability (a preprimer level) benefited from the treatment. Both Marseglia (1997) and Turpie and Paratore (1995) found that their repeated-readings treatment seemed to work better for the higher level first graders that they worked with than with the lower achieving first graders.

Therefore, the research results are consistent with the stage model. Fluency instruction seems to work best with children between a late preprimer level and late second-grade level. Beyond or below that level, the results are not as strong. Children need to have some entering knowledge about words to benefit from rereading but not be so fluent that they cannot demonstrate improvements.

Effects of Rereading. We stressed approaches that involved rereading of text through assisted reading, repeated reading, or approaches that integrated a number of activities into a classroom lesson design. Although these approaches all seem to be effective, it is not clear why they are effective. Specifically, it is not clear whether these studies have their effects because of any particular instructional activities or through the general mechanism of increasing the volume of children's reading. Fluency instruction may work only by increasing the amount of reading children do relative to traditional instruction. If so, then there may be other approaches that work as well or better. We know that increasing the amount of reading children do will improve their achievement (Anderson, Wilson, & Fielding, 1988; Berliner, 1981; Taylor, Frye, & Maruyama, 1990). Repeated reading and assisted readings may enable children to read more difficult material than they might otherwise be able to read or may provide a manageable structure to enable increased amounts of reading.

Several studies compared repeated and nonrepeated reading. Homan et al. (1993), Mathes and Fuchs (1993), Rashotte and Torgesen (1985), and Van Bon et al. (1991) found no difference in effects between repeated reading of a small number of texts and nonrepetitive reading of a larger set of texts. This indicates that it is not the repetition that leads to the effect but the amount of time spent reading connected text.

Relative Difficulty of the Text. What level should the text be? Some have argued that having children read easy text improves fluency (e.g., Clay, 1993), but it seems that the most successful approaches involved children reading instructional-level text or even text at the frustration level with strong support (see Stahl et al., 1997). Mathes and Fuchs (1993), however, used both relatively easy and relatively difficult texts and found no effect for text difficulty. More directed work needs to be done to assess the effects of the relative difficulty of text on learning.

Next, both practice and support are essential to the development of fluent reading and can be provided either through repetition or modeling. Whether this provision comes through the use of taped narrations, another individual, or repetition seems to be less crucial a matter than the fact that it exists, for such support seems to allow learners to work within their zone of proximal development (Vygotsky, 1978), offering the scaffolding that allows learners to successfully move beyond the point at which they are able to work independently.

An Irony

The method of repeated reading, as discussed by Samuels (1979, 1988; Samuels et al., 1992), was developed as an approach to translate LaBerge and Samuels's (1974) automatic information processing model into an instructional approach. LaBerge and Samuels's model is based on the notion that automatic processing of words will free up attentional resources that can then be devoted to comprehension. Samuels contends that through repeated reading, children will develop automatic word recognition, thus allowing them to be able to improve their comprehension. As shown in this review, repeated reading and other fluency-oriented approaches do improve comprehension. However, the irony is that they do not appear to improve automatic word recognition, as measured by conventional experimental psychology measures. Dahl (1979) failed to find that repeated reading improved tachistoscopic recognition of words, and neither Dowhower (1989) nor McFalls, Schwanenflugel, and Stahl (1996) found that fluency-oriented instruction improved children's response latency to words. Thus, fluency-oriented instruction seems to have salutary effects in a number of areas but not in the area that it was intended for, rapid recognition of isolated words.

Prosody, Automaticity, and Comprehension

Both the assisted and unassisted methods of fluency interventions have been generally effective in facilitating reading rate and accuracy. Given the amount of repetition or practice with print that they require on the part of learners, these results are not surprising. However, they also lead to improvements on measures of learners' comprehension. The following question then arises: Does this understanding develop simply from the amount of practice students undergo with regard to word recognition, or is there something more specific to their reading of connected text and their emerging sense of its relation to oral language that allows for this understanding to develop?

If comprehension were improved only by improved automatic word recognition, then teaching children to identify words faster would have an effect on comprehension. A number of studies have examined teaching children to say words faster (Fleisher et al., 1979; Levy, Abello, & Lysynchuk, 1997; Spring, Blunden, & Gatheral, 1981). Although in all of these studies children's passage reading fluency improved, in none of these studies did their comprehension significantly differ from that of a control group. In these studies, children were taught to say the words in a list that they knew faster. In contrast, preteaching words that children did not know seems to improve comprehension (e.g., Blanchard, 1981; Tan & Nicholson, 1997). Thus, it seems that more than speed of recognition is involved in the effects of repeated and assisted readings on comprehension.

Another source of information is the research on parsing or segmenting texts. Beginning with Cromer (1970), a number of researchers have found that presenting students with text segmented by phrase units seems to produce better comprehension than conventional text does. This effect is especially pronounced for children who are slow but accurate readers (Cromer, 1970; O'Shea & Sindelar, 1983). Segmenting the text may provide the same cues to phrasal structure as prosody does in oral language (Schreiber, 1980, 1987). However, nearly all researchers studied the effects of segmenting text with older children, fourth grade and higher, a different population than we are concerned with. O'Shea and Sindelar were the only researchers we found who worked with primary-grade children. They found that segmented text produced better comprehension than conventional text did, as measured by a maze-type cloze test. Being able to segment text by phrasal boundaries may improve comprehension in primary-grade children, but we are reluctant to infer from the results of one study that fluency instructional effects on comprehension are due to their effects on prosody.

Given that assisted and repeated reading and parsing of texts both seem to aid learners' comprehension, and speeded recognition of isolated words does not, we would argue that it is more than simply automaticity and accuracy that allow this understanding to develop. Further, the discussion surrounding prosody as a necessary component in children's ability to understand oral language and its role in language acquisition all add to the argument that prosody is equally necessary to developing an understanding of written text. Finally, given that fluent oral reading is considered to be expressive as well as quick and accurate and that prosodic features are, to a large extent, responsible for such expression, it is important to consider a definition of *fluency* that encompasses more than rate and accuracy.

Directions for Future Research

Fluency instruction seems to be a promising approach to teaching children in the confirmation and fluency stage of reading, especially those in late first and second grades but also children with reading problems who are disfluent. Although the basic approaches have been around for over 30 years, there are many unanswered questions. We are still not sure of the role of repetitive reading, whether increasing the amount of reading done would have similar effects, what the effects are of reading texts at a range of difficulties, whether fluency instruction works by improving automatic word recognition or whether it affects perception of phrasal boundaries, and how improved fluency affects comprehension. These are questions worth exploring.

These issues all relate to the larger notion of practice. It has been argued that practice in reading is vital to develop as a reader (e.g., Berliner, 1981). But what kind of practice is needed? We know that time spent reading is an important variable in learning to read, but time spent reading what? Is reading difficult material more useful than reading easy material? Is reading the same material repeatedly as useful as reading new material? Does repeated reading lead to improved self-monitoring and correction? Are there different effects for oral and silent reading?

From this review, we have come to view fluency instruction as successful in improving the reading achievement of children at a certain point in their reading development. However, we have seen relatively little of this instruction in the schools. To help more readers move from labored decoding to the construction of meaning, we consider it important that educators integrate these techniques in the classroom more frequently.

QUESTIONS FOR REFLECTION

1. Why is an understanding of speech syntax important in the development of reading comprehension?
2. Why might assisted reading show more statistically significant results than unassisted repeated-reading intervention methods do?
3. Of the several reading fluency interventions discussed in this chapter, which method resonates with your concept of ideal literacy instruction?

REFERENCES

Adams, M.J. (1990). *Beginning to read: Thinking and learning about print*. Cambridge, MA: MIT Press.

Allington, R.L. (1983). Fluency: The neglected reading goal. *The Reading Teacher, 36*(6), 556–561.

Anderson, R.C., Hiebert, E.H., Wilkinson, I.A.G., & Scott, J. (1985). *Becoming a nation of readers: The report of the Commission on Reading*. Washington, DC: National Institute of Education.

Anderson, R.C., Wilson, P.T., & Fielding, L.G. (1988). Growth in reading and how children spend their time outside of school. *Reading Research Quarterly, 23*(3), 285–303. doi:10.1598/RRQ.23.3.2

Bell, D.M., Markley, B.K., & Yonker, R.J. (1990). *The effect of repeated reading on elementary students' attitude toward reading*. East Lansing, MI: National Center for Research on Teacher Learning. (ERIC Document Reproduction Service No. ED326844)

Berliner, D.C. (1981). Academic learning time and reading achievement. In J.T. Guthrie (Ed.), *Comprehension and teaching: Research reviews* (pp. 203–226). Newark, DE: International Reading Association.

Blanchard, J.S. (1981). A comprehension strategy for disabled readers in the middle school. *Journal of Reading, 24*, 331–336.

Blum, I.H., Koskinen, P.S., Tennant, N., Parker, E.M., Straub, M., & Curry, C. (1995). *Using audiotaped books to extend classroom literacy instruction into the homes of second-language learners* (Reading Research Report No. 39). Athens, GA: National Reading Research Center.

Bohlen, L. (1988). *Building fluency through repeated reading in the third grade*. East Lansing, MI: National Center for Research on Teaching Learning. (ERIC Document Reproduction Service No. ED294158)

Carbo, M. (1978). Teaching reading with talking books. *The Reading Teacher, 32*(3), 267–273.

Carbo, M. (1981). Making books talk to children. *The Reading Teacher, 35*(2), 186–189.

Carver, R.P., & Hoffman, J.V. (1981). The effect of practice through repeated reading on gain in reading ability using a computer-based instructional system. *Reading Research Quarterly, 16*(3), 374–390. doi:10.2307/747408

Chafe, W. (1988). Punctuation and the prosody of written language. *Written Communication, 5*(9), 395–426. doi:10.1177/0741088388005004001

Chall, J.S. (1996a). *Learning to read: The great debate* (3rd ed.). New York: McGraw-Hill.

Chall, J.S. (1996b). *Stages of reading development* (2nd ed.). Fort Worth, TX: Harcourt Brace.

Chomsky, C. (1978). When you still can't read in third grade. After decoding, what? In S.J. Samuels (Ed.), *What research has to say about reading instruction* (pp. 13–30). Newark, DE: International Reading Association.

Clay, M.M. (1993). *Reading recovery: A guidebook for teachers in training*. Portsmouth, NH: Heinemann.

Clay, M.M., & Imlach, R.H. (1971). Juncture, pitch, and stress as reading behavior variables. *Journal of Verbal Learning and Verbal Behavior, 10*(2), 133–139. doi:10.1016/S0022-5371(71)80004-X

Cromer, W. (1970). The difference model: A new explanation for some reading difficulties. *Journal of Educational Psychology, 61*(6), 471–483. doi:10.1037/h0030288

Dahl, P.R. (1979). An experimental program for teaching high speed word recognition and comprehension skills. In J.E. Button, T. Lovitt, & T. Rowland (Eds.), *Communications research in learning disabilities and mental retardation* (pp. 33–65). Baltimore: University Park.

Dowhower, S.L. (1987). Effects of repeated reading on second-grade transitional readers' fluency and comprehension. *Reading Research Quarterly, 22*(4), 389–406. doi:10.2307/747699

Dowhower, S.L. (1989). Repeated reading: Theory into practice. *The Reading Teacher, 42*(7), 502–507.

Dowhower, S.L. (1991). Speaking of prosody: Fluency's unattended bedfellow. *Theory Into Practice, 30*(3), 165–175. doi:10.1080/00405849109543497

Eldredge, J.L. (1990). Increasing the performance of poor readers in the third grade with a group-assisted strategy. *The Journal of Educational Research, 84*(2), 69–77.

Eldredge, J.L., & Quinn, D.W. (1988). Increasing reading performance of low-achieving second graders with dyad reading groups. *The Journal of Educational Research, 82*(1), 40–46.

Evans, M.A., & Carr, T.H. (1985). Cognitive abilities, conditions of learning and the early development of reading skill. *Reading Research Quarterly, 20*(3), 327–350. doi:10.2307/748022

Fleisher, L.S., Jenkins, J.R., & Pany, D. (1979). Effects on poor readers' comprehension of training in rapid decoding. *Reading Research Quarterly, 15*(1), 30–48. doi:10.2307/747430

Gardner, C. (1965). *Experimental use of the impress method of reading rehabilitation*. East Lansing, MI: National Center for Research on Teacher Learning. (ERIC Document Reproduction Service No. ED003838)

Gilbert, L.M., Williams, R.L., & McLaughlin, T.F. (1996). Use of assisted reading to increase correct reading rates and decrease error rates of students with learning disabilities. *Journal of Applied Behavior Analysis, 29*(2), 255–257. doi:10.1901/jaba.1996.29-255

Hannah, A.M. (1994). *The effects of repeated readings on the reading fluency and comprehension of second-grade, Chapter 1 students*. Unpublished doctoral dissertation, University of Delaware, Newark.

Harris, A.J., & Sipay, E. (1990). *How to increase reading ability* (10th ed.). White Plains, NY: Longman.

Heckelman, R.G. (1969). A neurological-impress method of remedial-reading instruction. *Academic Therapy Quarterly, 4*, 277–282.

Heckelman, R.G. (1986). N.I.M. revisited. *Academic Therapy, 21*(4), 411–420.

Herman, P.A. (1985). The effect of repeated readings on reading rate, speech pauses, and word recognition accuracy. *Reading Research Quarterly, 20*(5), 553–565. doi:10.2307/747942

Hoffman, J. (1987). Rethinking the role of oral reading. *The Elementary School Journal, 87*(3), 367–373. doi:10.1086/461501

Hollingsworth, P.M. (1970). An experiment with the impress method of teaching reading. *The Reading Teacher, 24*(2), 112–114.

Hollingsworth, P.M. (1978). An experimental approach to the impress method of teaching reading. *The Reading Teacher, 31*(6), 624–626.

Homan, S., Klesius, P., & Hite, S. (1993). Effects of repeated readings and nonrepetitive strategies on students' fluency and comprehension. *The Journal of Educational Research, 87*(2), 94–99. doi:10.1080/00220671.1993.9941172

Hoskisson, K., & Krohm, B. (1974). Reading by immersion: Assisted reading. *Elementary English, 51*(6), 832–836.

Johns, J.L. (1993). *Informal reading inventories.* DeKalb, IL: Communitech International.

Kintsch, W. (1998). *Comprehension: A paradigm for cognition.* Cambridge, UK: Cambridge University Press.

Knupp, R. (1988). *Improving oral reading skills of educationally handicapped elementary school-aged students through repeated readings.* East Lansing, MI: National Center for Research on Teacher Learning. (ERIC Document Reproduction Service No. ED297275)

Koch, K.A. (1984). *The effects of oral repeated reading on second grade students' oral reading accuracy, rate, and comprehension.* Unpublished doctoral dissertation, Purdue University, West Lafayette, IN.

Koskinen, P.S., & Blum, I.H. (1984). Repeated oral reading and the acquisition of fluency. In J.A. Niles & L.A. Harris (Eds.), *Changing perspectives on research in reading/language processing and instruction* (33rd yearbook of the National Reading Conference, pp. 183–187). Rochester, NY: National Reading Conference.

Koskinen, P.S., & Blum, I.H. (1986). Paired repeated reading: A classroom strategy for developing fluent reading. *The Reading Teacher, 40*(1), 70–75.

Koskinen, P.S., Wilson, R.M., & Jensema, C. (1985). Closed-captioned television: A new tool for reading instruction. *Reading World, 24*(4), 1–7. doi:10.1080/19388078509557842

Labbo, L.D., & Teale, W.H. (1990). Cross age reading: A strategy for helping poor readers. *The Reading Teacher, 43*(6), 363–369.

LaBerge, D., & Samuels, S.J. (1974). Toward a theory of automatic information processing in reading. *Cognitive Psychology, 6*(2), 293–323. doi:10.1016/0010-0285(74)90015-2

Langford, K., Slade, B., & Burnett, E. (1974). An examination of impress techniques in remedial reading. *Academic Therapy, 9*(5), 309–319.

Leinhardt, G., Zigmond, N., & Cooley, W. (1981). Reading instruction and its effects. *American Educational Research Journal, 18*(3), 343–361.

Levy, B.A., Abello, B., & Lysynchuk, L. (1997). Transfer from word training to reading in context: Gains in fluency and comprehension. *Learning Disability Quarterly, 20*(3), 173–188. doi:10.2307/1511307

Levy, B.A., Barnes, L., & Martin, L. (1993). Transfer of fluency across repetitions and across texts. *Canadian Journal of Experimental Psychology, 47*(2), 401–427. doi:10.1037/h0078821

Levy, B.A., Newell, S., Snyder, J., & Timmins, K. (1986). Processing changes across reading encounters. *Journal of Experimental Psychology, 12*(4), 467–478.

Light, R.J., & Pillemer, D.B. (1984). *Summing up: The science of reviewing research.* Cambridge, MA: Harvard University Press.

Marseglia, P. (1997). *The effect of repeated readings on the fluency of high and low ability readers in a first grade class.* East Lansing, MI: National Center for Research on Teacher Learning. (ERIC Document Reproduction Service No. ED405562)

Mathes, P.G., & Fuchs, L.S. (1993). Peer-mediated reading instruction in special education resource rooms. *Learning Disabilities Research & Practice, 8*(4), 233–243.

McFalls, E.L., Schwanenflugel, P.J., & Stahl, S.A. (1996). The influence of word meaning on the acquisition of a reading vocabulary in second grade children. *Reading and Writing, 8*(3), 235–250. doi:10.1007/BF00420277

Mefferd, P.E., & Pettegrew, B.S. (1997). Fostering literacy acquisition of students with developmental disabilities: Assisted reading with predictable trade books. *Reading Research and Instruction, 36*(3), 177–190. doi:10.1080/19388079709558237

Morris, D., & Nelson, L. (1992). Supported oral reading with low achieving second graders. *Reading Research and Instruction, 32*(1), 49–63. doi:10.1080/19388079209558105

Mudre, L.H., & McCormick, S. (1989). Effects of meaning-focused cues on underachieving readers' context use, self-corrections, and literal comprehension. *Reading Research Quarterly, 24*(1), 89–113. doi:10.2307/748012

Nell, V. (1988). *Lost in a book: The psychology of reading for pleasure.* New Haven, CT: Yale University Press.

Neuman, S.B., & McCormick, S. (1995). *Single-subject experimental research: Applications for literacy.* Newark, DE: International Reading Association.

O'Shea, L.J., & Sindelar, P.T. (1983). The effects of segmenting written discourse on the reading comprehension of low- and high-performance readers. *Reading Research Quarterly, 18*(4), 458–465. doi:10.2307/747380

O'Shea, L.J., Sindelar, P.T., & O'Shea, D. (1985). The effects of repeated readings and attentional cues on reading fluency and comprehension. *Journal of Reading Behavior, 17*(2), 129–142.

O'Shea, L.J., Sindelar, P.T., & O'Shea, D. (1987). The effects of repeated readings and attentional cues on the reading fluency and comprehension of learning disabled readers. *Learning Disabilities Research, 2*(2), 103–109.

Perfetti, C.A. (1985). *Reading ability*. New York: Oxford University Press.

Person, M.E., & Burke, D.M. (1984, October). *Oral reading in the classroom*. Paper presented at the annual meeting of the Northern Rocky Mountain Educational Research Association, Jackson Hole, WY. (ERIC Document Reproduction Service No. ED251796)

Ramunda, J.M. (1994). *A cross-age reading program: Building fluency and comprehension*. Unpublished master's thesis, Kean College, Union, NJ. (ERIC Document Reproduction Service No. ED366940)

Rashotte, C.A., & Torgesen, J.K. (1985). Repeated reading and reading fluency in learning-disabled children. *Reading Research Quarterly, 20*(2), 180–188. doi:10.1598/RRQ.20.2.4

Rasinski, T.V. (1990a). Effects of repeated reading and listening-while-reading on reading fluency. *The Journal of Educational Research, 83*(3), 147–150.

Rasinski, T.V. (1990b). Investigating measures of reading fluency. *Educational Research Quarterly, 14*(3), 37–44.

Rasinski, T.V., Padak, N., Linek, W., & Sturtevant, B. (1994). Effects of fluency development on urban second-grade readers. *The Journal of Educational Research, 87*(3), 158–165. doi:10.1080/00220671.1994.9941237

Read, C., & Schreiber, P.A. (1982). Why short subjects are harder to find than long ones. In E. Wanner & L. Gleitman (Eds.), *Language acquisition: The state of the art* (pp. 78–101). Cambridge, UK: Cambridge University Press.

Richek, M.A., & McTeague, B.K. (1988). The "Curious George" strategy for students with reading problems. *The Reading Teacher, 42*(3), 220–226.

Samuels, S.J. (1979). The method of repeated readings. *The Reading Teacher, 32*(4), 403–408.

Samuels, S.J. (1988). Decoding and automaticity: Helping poor readers become automatic at word recognition. *The Reading Teacher, 41*(8), 756–760.

Samuels, S.J., Schermer, N., & Reinking, D. (1992). Reading fluency: Techniques for making decoding automatic. In S.J. Samuels & A.E. Farstrup (Eds.), *What research has to say about reading instruction* (2nd ed., pp. 124–144). Newark, DE: International Reading Association.

Schreiber, P.A. (1980). On the acquisition of reading fluency. *Journal of Reading Behavior, 12*(3), 177–186.

Schreiber, P.A. (1987). Prosody and structure in children's syntactic processing. In R. Horowitz & S.J. Samuels (Eds.), *Comprehending oral and written language* (pp. 243–270). New York: Academic.

Schreiber, P.A. (1991). Understanding prosody's role in reading acquisition. *Theory Into Practice, 30*(3), 158–164. doi:10.1080/00405849109543496

Schreiber, P.A., & Read, C. (1980). Children's use of phonetic cues in spelling, parsing, and—maybe—reading. *Bulletin of the Orton Society, 30*, 209–224. doi:10.1007/BF02653719

Scruggs, T.E. (1987). The quantitative synthesis of single subject research: Methodology and validation. *Remedial and Special Education, 8*(2), 24–33. doi:10.1177/074193258700800206

Simmons, D.C., Fuchs, L.S., Fuchs, D., Mathes, P., & Hodge, J.P. (1995). Effects of explicit teaching and peer tutoring on the reading achievement of learning-disabled and low-performing students in regular classrooms. *The Elementary School Journal, 95*(5), 387–408. doi:10.1086/461851

Spring, C., Blunden, D., & Gatheral, M. (1981). Effect on reading comprehension of training to automaticity in word-reading. *Perceptual and Motor Skills, 53*(3), 779–786. doi:10.2466/pms.1981.53.3.779

Stahl, S.A., Heubach, K., & Cramond, B. (1997). *Fluency-oriented reading instruction*. Athens, GA: National Reading Research Center; Washington, DC: Educational Resources Information Center, Office of Educational Research and Improvement, U.S. Department of Education.

Stahl, S.A., Jacobson, M.G., Davis, C.E., & Davis, R.L. (1989). Prior knowledge and difficult vocabulary in the comprehension of unfamiliar text. *Reading Research Quarterly, 24*(1), 27–43. doi:10.2307/748009

Stanovich, K.E. (1980). Toward an interactive-compensatory model of individual differences in the development of reading fluency. *Reading Research Quarterly, 16*(1), 32–71. doi:10.2307/747348

Stoddard, K., Valcante, G., Sindelar, P., O'Shea, L., & Algozzine, P. (1993). Increasing reading rate and comprehension: The effects of repeated readings, sentence segmentation, and intonation training. *Reading Research and Instruction, 32*(4), 53–65. doi:10.1080/19388079309558133

Strong, M.W., & Traynelis-Yurek, E. (1983). *Behavioral reinforcement within a perceptual-conditioning program of oral reading*. East Lansing, MI: National Center for Research on Teacher Learning. (ERIC Document Reproduction Service No. ED233328)

Sutton, P.A. (1991). *Strategies to increase oral reading fluency of primary resource students*. East Lansing, MI: National Center for Research on Teacher Learning. (ERIC Document Reproduction Service No. ED335660)

Tan, A., & Nicholson, T. (1997). Flashcards revisited: Training poor readers to read words faster improves their comprehension of text. *Journal of Educational Psychology, 89*(2), 276–288. doi:10.1037/0022-0663.89.2.276

Taylor, B.M., Frye, B.J., & Maruyama, G.M. (1990). Time spent reading and reading growth. *American Educational Research Journal, 27*(2), 351–362.

Tingstrom, D.H., Edwards, R.P., & Olmi, D.J. (1995). Listening previewing in reading to read: Relative effects on oral reading fluency. *Psychology in the Schools, 32*(2), 318–327. doi:10.1002/1520-6807(199510)32:4<318::AID-PITS2310320410>3.0.CO;2-2

Turpie, J.J., & Paratore, J.R. (1995). Using repeated readings to promote reading success in a heterogeneously grouped first grade. In K.A. Hinchman & D.J. Leu (Eds.), *Perspectives on literacy research and practice* (44th yearbook of the National Reading Conference, pp. 255–264). Chicago: National Reading Conference.

Van Bon, W.H., Boksebeld, L.M., Font Freide, T.A., & Van den Hurk, A.J. (1991). A comparison of three methods of reading-while-listening. *Journal of Learning Disabilities, 24*(8), 471–476. doi:10.1177/002221949102400805

van der Leij, A. (1981). Remediation of reading-disabled children by presenting text simultaneously to eye and ear. *Bulletin of the Orton Society, 31*, 229–243. doi:10.1007/BF02658613

Vygotsky, L.S. (1978). *Mind in society: The development of higher psychological processes* (M. Cole, V. John-Steiner, S. Scribner, & E. Souberman, Eds. & Trans.). Cambridge, MA: Harvard University Press.

Weinstein, G., & Cooke, N.L. (1992). The effects of two repeated reading interventions on generalization of fluency. *Learning Disability Quarterly, 15*(1), 21–28. doi:10.2307/1510562

Young, A.R., Bowers, P.G., & MacKinnon, G.E. (1996). Effects of prosodic modeling and repeated reading on poor readers' fluency and comprehension. *Applied Psycholinguistics, 17*(1), 59–84. doi:10.1017/S0142716400009462

CHAPTER 16

A Road Map for Understanding Reading Disabilities and Other Reading Problems, Redux

Louise Spear-Swerling, Southern Connecticut State University

When asked to revise this chapter for the latest edition of *Theoretical Models and Processes of Reading,* I thought about changes in the field of reading disabilities (RD) that have occurred since my initial writing of the chapter a number of years ago. Perhaps the most important changes have involved those spurred by the Individuals with Disabilities Education Improvement Act, popularly termed IDEA 2004, which permitted schools to adopt Response to Intervention (RTI) criteria in identification of RD and to eliminate the use of the IQ–achievement discrepancy model. The latter model, long the centerpiece of identification criteria for RD and other learning disabilities (LD), requires students to have IQ scores substantially higher than their achievement scores to be eligible for special education services in the category of LD. In contrast, RTI criteria do not require the routine use of IQ tests; rather, they involve providing research-based interventions to students who need them as part of the general education system. RTI models conceptualize students with LD as those failing to make adequate progress even in interventions effective for most other struggling students.

A fourth-grade student who I'll call Jamie captures the type of experience I often had in schools a decade ago. Jamie's teachers were considering him for special education services in the category of LD. He had had trouble in reading since early first grade but had not previously been eligible for services because he did not meet IQ–achievement discrepancy criteria. Reports in Jamie's file indicated that he had a full-scale IQ score of 90, the lower end of the average range but well above the range for intellectual disabilities (below 70). After several years of struggling in reading and falling further and further behind—because special education was the main avenue for intervention in the district and required a disability classification—Jamie finally had a sufficiently large IQ–achievement discrepancy to qualify for LD services. As I spoke to the district administrator involved in his case to provide recommendations for helping him in reading, she seemed impatient. Finally, she made a comment that stunned me. "Well, you know," she remarked dismissively, "it's not like his IQ is 120."

This chapter is adapted from "A Road Map for Understanding Reading Disability and Other Reading Problems: Origins, Prevention, and Intervention," in *Theoretical Models and Processes of Reading* (5th ed., pp. 517–573), edited by R.B. Ruddell and N.J. Unrau, 2004, Newark, DE: International Reading Association.

In recent years, educational policy in my state, as in some other states, has emphasized the use of RTI models in general education, required the use of RTI criteria in identification of LD, and eliminated IQ–achievement discrepancy criteria. Although implementation of RTI involves many challenges, now I rarely encounter students going without intervention because they lack a special education label, and educators no longer spend valuable assessment time documenting IQ–achievement discrepancies. Instead, educators tend to focus heavily on questions such as the following: What is the most effective intervention for this student? What is the best way to monitor his or her progress? How can we accelerate progress? These questions do not always have straightforward answers. However, at least the questions are educationally meaningful, based on the expectation that struggling students can learn, and focused on how to teach those students successfully.

There are indeed children who have unusual difficulty learning to read, whose reading problems cannot be accounted for by other disabilities, broad intellectual limitations, an impoverished home environment, or inadequate instruction. Many of these children require ongoing, intensive educational support to learn to read, and special education often is the appropriate avenue for providing this support. These students, as well as other struggling readers who do not meet formal criteria for RD but often benefit from similar interventions, are the focus of this chapter.

The chapter begins by considering core features of all definitions of RD, as well as the influence of RTI criteria on identification of RD in recent years. This first section reviews research on reading development and common patterns of reading difficulties and describes a theoretical model for understanding both typical reading and reading problems. The second section of the chapter considers the educational implications of the model, including the role of RTI in differentiating RD from other reading difficulties. The third section explores important challenges of RTI implementation for educators in relation to identification of RD. The chapter closes with conclusions and future directions for research.

What Are RD?

Core Features of RD

Most current legislation and identification guidelines subsume RD under the umbrella category of LD. In the United States, LD constitutes by far the largest single category of special education, with approximately 44% of students receiving special education classified as having LD in 2007 (Cortiella, 2009), often because of reading difficulties. IDEA 2004 specifies three areas of reading in which a student with LD can be eligible for services: basic reading (i.e., word-level reading skills), reading fluency, and reading comprehension. A student must have low achievement in at least one of these three areas to be identified with a learning disability in reading.

Historically, three core concepts have been central to RD. First, RD involves intrinsic, presumably biologically based, reading difficulties, as opposed to reading failure associated mainly with extrinsic causes such as poverty or poor instruction. Behavior-genetic studies of children's reading development suggest substantial genetic influences on both word recognition and language comprehension (Byrne et al., 2007; Olson et al., 2011). Converging evidence from functional brain imaging studies also suggests a neurobiological basis for some cases of RD (Lyon, Shaywitz, & Shaywitz, 2003). These findings do not mean that children with RD are incapable of learning to read; however, they support the view that some children find learning to read intrinsically difficult, even with good instruction and extensive literacy experiences.

A second core concept is that RD involve unexpected reading failure: reading difficulties not accounted for by other disabilities or lack of opportunity to learn. Finally, a third concept, related to the idea of unexpectedness, is that a specific cognitive deficit or set of deficits, not generalized learning problems, characterize RD. Recent research with middle elementary children (Compton, Fuchs, Fuchs, Lambert, & Hamlett, 2012) confirms the existence of struggling students with difficulties specific to either reading or mathematics and with distinctive patterns of cognitive and academic strengths and weaknesses, not attributable to broad cognitive limitations such as intellectual disabilities.

RTI Approaches to Identification of RD

Specific features of RTI models vary, but all involve a combination of population-based systems approaches to education (e.g., routine screening of entire school populations for early detection of reading difficulties) coupled with the use of research-based interventions for students who need them. Interventions entail tiers of increasing intensity, with greater intensity—for example, more intervention time and a smaller teacher–student ratio—for students at greater levels of risk. Educators consider students failing to respond to the most intensive interventions for special education services in a variety of categories, including LD. Rather than conceptualizing the unexpectedness of LD in relation to IQ, RTI models conceptualize it in relation to expected progress under intervention (Fletcher, Lyon, Fuchs, & Barnes, 2007). RTI-based definitions of LD typically retain the use of exclusionary criteria. Exclusionary criteria require that in order to be eligible for services in the category of LD, a student's learning difficulties cannot primarily be due to another disability, such as sensory impairment or intellectual disabilities, or to environmental factors such as economic disadvantage, lack of instruction, or limited experience with English.

The changes in IDEA 2004 involving the discrepancy requirement stemmed at least in part from long-standing criticisms of this requirement in the scientific community (e.g., Siegel, 1988; Spear-Swerling & Sternberg, 1996; Stanovich, 1991). Criticisms include concerns about the use of IQ tests as measures of overall potential for learning, the exclusion of children who lack discrepancies from educational services, psychometric problems such as regression effects, and the fact that discrepancy criteria make early identification of reading problems difficult, because it often takes time for children to accumulate a significant discrepancy. As in Jamie's case, some educators may erroneously view poor readers who have difficulty meeting discrepancy criteria as lacking the capacity for improvement. Perhaps most important, the discrepancy approach provides little insight into the best way to help children with reading difficulties. Approaches that target individual poor readers' specific component weaknesses—such as word reading versus comprehension—appear to lead to improved outcomes relative to the discrepancy model (Aaron, Joshi, Gooden, & Bentum, 2008).

Although not without their own challenges, RTI approaches to identification of RD address many of the aforementioned concerns. These approaches conceptualize children with RD as those who experience persistent reading difficulties over time, despite receiving intervention that is generally effective for most struggling readers. RTI approaches do not require the routine use of IQ tests, they emphasize prevention and early intervention, and they do not necessitate a label for extra help.

Most research on RTI has focused on primary-grade reading. In general, this research (e.g., Blachman et al., 2004; Denton, Fletcher, Anthony, & Francis, 2006; Denton et al., 2010; Simmons et al., 2011; Speece, Case, & Molloy, 2003; Vellutino & Scanlon, 2002) shows that early intervention in reading is very effective in ameliorating or preventing many children's reading difficulties. Not surprisingly, longer interventions produce a higher percentage of intervention responders. Nevertheless, even high-quality, sustained RTI efforts do not eliminate all reading difficulties. A subgroup of at-risk readers requires long-term intervention, a finding supporting the view that genuine RD exist and a continued role for special education in serving these students, as well as those with other disabilities (D. Fuchs, Fuchs, & Stecker, 2010).

RTI approaches to identification of LD and RD have proliferated across states since the passage of IDEA 2004. However, because IDEA 2004 permitted multiple options for LD eligibility criteria, identification practices are highly variable. As of this writing, 15 states require the use of RTI criteria in identification of LD, either alone or in combination with other criteria such as an IQ–achievement discrepancy. Most states permit both RTI and discrepancy models, essentially leaving the choice to individual school districts (Zirkel & Thomas, 2010). Furthermore, most states implementing RTI do not prescribe a particular duration of interventions, decision rules for movement across tiers, or other implementation details (Zirkel, 2011).

Because of their focus on prevention, early intervention, and instructionally relevant information, RTI-based approaches to identification of LD are much more educationally useful than the discrepancy approach. In addition, an analysis of the specific cognitive profiles and patterns typical of struggling readers is extremely helpful for early identification and planning instruction, both for students with RD and poor readers in general. An important foundation for interpreting cognitive patterns and profiles involves understanding the development of typical readers, reviewed in the following section. Readers interested in further detail about typical reading development may wish to consult Ehri (2005) and the previous version of this chapter (Spear-Swerling, 2004a).

Abilities Involved in Reading Development

A number of reading development models emphasize the importance of two broad types of abilities in reading: oral language comprehension and word recognition (e.g., Adams, 1990; Chall, 1983; Hoover & Gough, 1990). Each of these two broad areas includes numerous component abilities. For instance, oral language comprehension includes vocabulary knowledge and grammatical understanding, whereas word recognition includes knowledge of letter–sound relationships, the ability to decode unfamiliar words, and automatic as well as accurate recognition of words. Reading fluently in text taps both types of broad abilities, not only automatic word recognition but also integrating a range of important subword-, word-, and comprehension-level processes (L.S. Fuchs, Fuchs, Hosp, & Jenkins, 2001). Fluency development is associated with improvements in prosody of oral reading, such as appropriate pauses and intonation while reading text. In young children, reading prosody predicts reading comprehension independent of reading rate (e.g., words read correctly per minute), and children may sometimes use good reading prosody to assist comprehension, especially when reading difficult material (Benjamin & Schwanenflugel, 2010; Kuhn, Schwanenflugel, & Meisinger, 2010).

One central set of linguistic processes in reading involves phonological processes. Phonological processes involve the use of phonological codes (abstract mental representations of speech sounds), or of actual speech, in a variety of cognitive and linguistic tasks, including memory and oral language as well as written language (Scarborough & Brady, 2002). Phonological processes play a key role in word recognition, especially in an alphabetic language such as English, in which the printed letters correspond primarily to sounds in spoken words. For example, *phonemic awareness*, which involves awareness and manipulation of individual sounds in spoken words (e.g., being able to segment a spoken word such as *fish* into three separate sounds: /f/, /i/, /sh/), greatly facilitates learning to decode printed words. *Phonological awareness* encompasses a more rudimentary level of awareness that includes the ability to perform tasks such as rhyming and alliteration. Other phonological processes directly influence working memory and comprehension, such as *phonological memory*, which facilitates holding words in memory to integrate meaning while reading or listening to text, although working memory also may play a role in decoding, especially of long, complex words (Compton et al., 2012). Phonological processes are a core difficulty in many cases of RD and other reading problems.

Although many abilities are ultimately important in learning to read, abilities involved in word recognition are especially important in the early elementary grades, when word-recognition skill is developing most rapidly, and the comprehension demands of most texts are relatively low. By fourth grade, typical readers already have acquired reasonably automatic, accurate word recognition for most common words, and the comprehension demands of texts escalate substantially, so oral language comprehension begins to account for more of the variance in reading comprehension (Chall, 1983; Rupley, Willson, & Nichols, 1998; Vellutino, Tunmer, Jaccard, & Chen, 2007).

A Model of Typical Reading Development

An extensive research base exists on the cognitive processes involved in reading development, and the following model owes much to the work of other researchers (e.g., Adams, 1990; Chall, 1983; Ehri, 1991, 2005; Hoover & Gough, 1990; Perfetti, 1985; Rupley et al., 1998; Stanovich, 2000). An earlier version of this model was developed collaboratively by myself and Robert Sternberg (Spear-Swerling & Sternberg, 1994, 1996) and involves a series of six phases that constitute a road to proficient reading. The phases of typical reading development in the model appear on the left-hand side of Figure 1. These phases are intended to be specific to English, with the age and grade ranges approximations based on research involving mainly middle class samples of English-speaking youngsters, although children learning a variety of alphabetic languages seem to progress through a series of phases roughly similar to those outlined here.

Oral language comprehension develops prior to and simultaneously with word-level reading abilities, beginning during the early preschool years and continuing into adulthood. For most children, oral language comprehension substantially exceeds reading comprehension until about seventh or eighth grade (Biemiller, 1999). Even among typical readers, there are individual differences in oral language comprehension that influence and set limits on reading comprehension, especially after word-recognition skills have developed. Moreover, children's own reading experiences and volume of reading exert important influences on their oral language development. Thus, oral language and reading development interact and are mutually facilitative.

Visual-Cue Word Recognition. This phase of reading, termed *visual-cue* or *prealphabetic word recognition* (Ehri, 1991, 2005), is characteristic of very young children, primarily preschoolers. Children do not yet grasp the alphabetic principle—the fundamental insight that written English involves a code in which printed letters map on to speech sounds in spoken words—and also often lack phonological awareness and knowledge of most letter–sound relationships. Instead, they rely on a salient visual cue, such as a distinctive logo or word shape, to recognize words and are heavily dependent on context in word recognition. For instance, a typical preschooler might recognize the word *stop* on a red, octagonal sign, or the word *McDonald's* from the golden arches, but would not recognize those words if they were printed on a page.

Phonetic-Cue Word Recognition. Ehri (1991, 2005) terms this second phase of reading *phonetic-cue word recognition* or *partial alphabetic reading.* This phase is typical of kindergartners and first graders but also may occur in some preschoolers, especially those with extensive exposure to literacy. Phonetic-cue readers can use partial phonetic cues in word recognition because they grasp the alphabetic

Figure 1. A Road Map for Understanding Patterns of Reading Difficulties and Disabilities

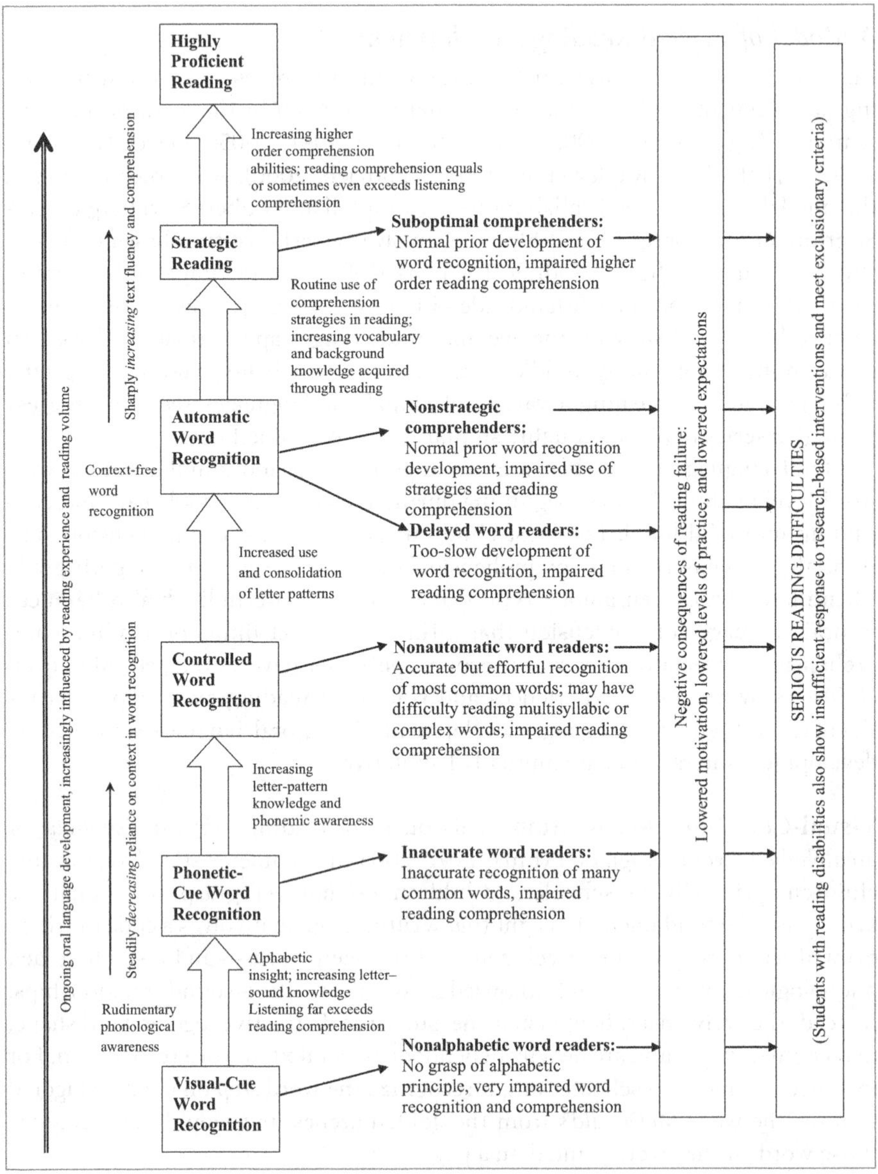

principle, have at least a rudimentary level of phonological awareness (e.g., recognizing spoken words with similar beginning or ending sounds), and know at least some letter–sound relationships, especially for single consonants such as *m* and *s*. Often they attend to the first few letters of a word, or to the first and last letters, but not to the middle part of a word. Hence, they may confuse similarly spelled words such as *boat* and *boot*. Because they do not make full use of all the letters in a word, phonetic-cue readers remain dependent on pictures or sentence context to aid word recognition.

Controlled Word Recognition. Children in this phase of reading development, often those in late first to second grade, can read a variety of common words accurately. They make full use of phonetic cues in word recognition, and therefore this phase has been termed *full alphabetic* (Ehri, 2005). Children with controlled word recognition have more advanced levels of phonemic awareness than do children in previous phases of reading; they also know a wide range of letter–sound relationships, including those for many common letter patterns (e.g., *sh*, *th*, *ck*, *oa*, *ay*) as well as single letters. However, they may have difficulty reading complex multisyllabic words, especially those tapping relatively sophisticated morphemic and linguistic knowledge, and they must expend mental effort to recognize many words, so their word recognition is not automatic. Thus, they may continue to rely on context cues, especially to speed word recognition.

Automatic Word Recognition. In this phase, children recognize a wide range of common words automatically as well as accurately. Consolidation and use of larger letter patterns, such as prefixes, suffixes, and common rimes (e.g., *ight*), appear to facilitate automatic word recognition. Hence, this phase is roughly analogous to one that has been termed *consolidated alphabetic* (Ehri, 2005). Children in this phase, usually late second to third graders, have greater ability to decode multisyllabic words than do children in previous phases of reading, and they integrate automatic word recognition with a variety of comprehension processes to achieve fluent reading of text. They depend on context only infrequently to aid recognition of unfamiliar words. Limits on reading comprehension begin to revolve less around word recognition and increasingly around language comprehension abilities and background knowledge.

Strategic Reading. Strategic readers have the ability to use routinely at least some reading comprehension strategies, such as summarization and making use of context to determine what a word means (as opposed to using context to read words). For instance, a strategic reader reading the sentence "Her scarlet cape flashed red in the crowd" would be able to recognize all the words in the sentence accurately and easily, including *scarlet*, but would concurrently use sentence context to figure out that the word *scarlet* means *red*. Children's improved morphological awareness also facilitates their vocabulary development. Morphological awareness involves sensitivity to the morphological structure of words (e.g., the ability to recognize constituent morphemes in words like *motherhood*, *unspeakable*, and *plentiful* and to use morphemic knowledge to infer word meanings; see Carlisle, 2010). Children may develop and use some comprehension strategies in listening well before the phase of strategic reading, and they certainly have some morphological awareness prior to this phase; for instance, a typical first grader would recognize the use of final *-s*, not *-z*, to denote plurality in a word like *dogs*. However, in the phase of strategic reading, children make routine use of strategies in their reading as well as their listening, and they have greatly increased morphemic awareness. Automatic word recognition facilitates these achievements because it allows children to focus more of their mental resources on comprehension of the text and provides a foundation of knowledge about common word parts, such as common base words and affixes. Children can now use reading extensively as a tool for gathering information, and their own reading contributes increasingly to development of vocabulary and background knowledge (Cunningham & Stanovich, 1991). Strategic reading typically begins around the middle elementary grades (third to fourth grade) and continues to develop in subsequent grades.

Proficient Reading. The primary distinction between strategic reading and proficient reading involves the development of higher order comprehension abilities. Examples of the latter include the ability to read critically, understand more profound literary themes, and evaluate and integrate different kinds of information. Although reading volume certainly affects background knowledge in previous phases of reading, its cumulative effects are greatest in this final phase. Thus, over time, reading volume may contribute to growth in broad verbal abilities and to overall cognitive development (Stanovich, 2000). By this phase, oral and reading comprehension are comparable, and reading comprehension may even exceed oral comprehension for certain texts, such as dense informational texts (Biemiller, 1999). Proficient reading typically begins in adolescence and continues throughout adulthood.

I should highlight several general points about the preceding model. First, although the focus here is on reading, many of the cognitive processes typical of a given phase of reading also reveal themselves in children's spelling. (See Ehri, 2005, for a detailed discussion.) Second, although skilled readers clearly use context to aid *comprehension* and have more mental resources free for doing so because their word recognition is automatic, using context to aid *word recognition* is a hallmark of unskilled reading (Stanovich, 2000). Third, the phases describe an individual's general approach to most, but not necessarily all, words and reading tasks within a given phase. A child in the phase of controlled word recognition might recognize automatically a few very common words; a proficient adult reader who recognizes the vast majority of words automatically might use controlled processing for a very unusual or technical word, such as unfamiliar science terminology. Finally, the last four phases in the model overlap. For example, by the phase of strategic reading, children have acquired the ability to use routinely at least some comprehension strategies in reading, but further development in strategy knowledge and strategy use continues into the phase of proficient reading.

Research on Common Profiles of Reading Difficulties

Table 1 displays three broad profiles common among poor readers: specific word-recognition difficulties (SWRD), specific comprehension difficulties (SCD), and mixed reading difficulties (MRD). Reading comprehension difficulties of students with SWRD relate entirely to their word-reading problems; with appropriate intervention for these problems, these students' reading comprehension should be commensurate with their oral language comprehension. Students with SCD have the opposite profile; they have reading comprehension difficulties despite grade-appropriate word-recognition and phonological skills, with no history of word-recognition difficulties. Often these reading comprehension difficulties are associated with problems involving verbal working memory, defined as the ability to maintain a set of items in memory while processing an additional task (Daneman & Carpenter, 1980), and oral language comprehension (Cain, Oakhill, & Bryant, 2004; Catts, Adlof, & Weismer, 2006). However, oral language weaknesses of students with SCD can be mild, and frequently these students are not identified for speech/language services (Catts et al., 2006; Nation, 2005). Furthermore, some students with SCD function well within the average range on measures of broad oral language comprehension (e.g., Leach, Scarborough, & Rescorla, 2003). These latter students may have circumscribed language weaknesses not detected by broad language measures, or they may have limitations in other areas influencing comprehension, such as use of specific reading comprehension strategies (e.g., Garner, 1990).

Finally, students with MRD have trouble with word recognition, but they also have reading comprehension problems that cannot be fully accounted for by their word-recognition weaknesses; for example, they may have poor comprehension even when reading relatively easy text that they can decode well because of limitations in vocabulary, working memory, or strategic knowledge. To put it another way, SWRD involves a reading problem specific to word recognition, and SCD involves a reading problem specific to reading comprehension, but MRD involves problems in both word-recognition and core comprehension abilities.

Research suggests a nontrivial prevalence of each profile (Catts, Compton, Tomblin, & Bridges, 2012; Catts et al., 2006; Catts, Hogan, & Adlof, 2005; Compton et al., 2012; Leach et al., 2003; Nation & Snowling, 1997; Spear-Swerling, 2004b). However, the relative frequency of each profile varies across studies depending on methodology (e.g., whether SCD are defined in relation to reading comprehension or listening comprehension), as well as on the age and characteristics of the population studied. For example, Leach et al. studied a group of fourth and fifth graders from schools that included both affluent and socioeconomically diverse populations, but few ethnic-minority children and no English learners. These investigators found that a specific comprehension deficit, defined in terms of reading comprehension, constituted only about 6% of reading problems that had been identified in third grade or earlier, whereas SWRD and MRD involved approximately 49% and 46% of reading difficulties in third grade or earlier, respectively. However, proportions of SWRD, MRD, and SCD were roughly similar

Table 1. Common Cognitive Profiles and Patterns of Reading Difficulties

	Pattern	Word-Recognition Skills	Oral Language Comprehension	Reading Comprehension	Overall Intervention Needs[a]
Specific word-recognition difficulties	Nonalphabetic word reader	Well below average	Average or better	Below average	Systematic phonemic awareness and phonics instruction, with fluency building
	Inaccurate word reader	Below average	Average or better	Usually below average; may perform adequately on undemanding texts	Systematic phonics instruction (with phonemic awareness instruction if phonemic awareness is weak), with fluency building
	Nonautomatic word reader	Below average, especially in automaticity and sometimes also in decoding of multisyllabic words	Average or better	Usually below average; may perform adequately on undemanding texts	Instruction focused on structural analysis and decoding of multisyllabic words if needed, as well as on automaticity of word recognition and fluency building
	Delayed word reader	Average or better, but with a history of word-recognition problems	Average or better	Below average	Explicit instruction in comprehension strategies and other specific areas of comprehension in which student is weak (e.g., vocabulary or inferencing)
Specific comprehension difficulties	Nonstrategic comprehender	Average or better, with no history of word-recognition difficulties	Varies, but often mildly below average	Below average; lacks strategic comprehension skills	Explicit instruction in comprehension strategies and other specific areas of comprehension in which student is weak (e.g., vocabulary)
	Suboptimal comprehender	Average or better, with no history of word-recognition difficulties	Varies, but often mildly below average	Lacks higher order comprehension abilities	Explicit instruction in higher order comprehension abilities (e.g., evaluating and synthesizing information)
Mixed reading difficulties	Varies depending upon the pattern of word-recognition difficulties and specific types of comprehension difficulties	Difficulties with word recognition: nonalphabetic, inaccurate, nonautomatic, or delayed	Varies, but often mildly below average	Below average because of a combination of weaknesses in word-recognition and core comprehension abilities	Explicit instruction in word-recognition skills depending on pattern (see above), coupled with explicit instruction in comprehension strategies and other specific areas of comprehension in which student is weak

[a]Interventions should occur in the context of a comprehensive curriculum of reading and English language arts instruction. For example, although nonalphabetic, inaccurate, and nonautomatic word readers do not need *interventions* in the area of vocabulary and comprehension, like all students, they require *instruction* in these areas; usually this instruction would occur as part of their core reading program.

for cases identified after grade 3—each profile constituted about one-third of the poor reading group. In contrast, Lesaux and Kieffer (2010), studying a population of low-SES (socioeconomic status), sixth-grade struggling readers that included a large number of English learners, classified about 79% with SCD, about 21% with MRD, and essentially none with SWRD. Vocabulary weaknesses were ubiquitous in this sample and likely accounted for the absence of students identified with SWRD; some students did have word-reading difficulties, but they also had consistent vocabulary weaknesses, yielding a MRD rather than SWRD profile.

SWRD often emerge in the early grades, when children must acquire a foundation of basic word-recognition skills, and SCD in the later grades, when comprehension demands increase. However, all three profiles can be found across a wide range of grade levels. For instance, several studies have found evidence for late-emerging cases of SWRD (e.g., Catts et al., 2012; Leach et al., 2003; Lipka, Lesaux, & Siegel, 2006), usually defined as manifesting after third grade. Catts and colleagues documented almost all cases of these late-emerging word-reading difficulties by fourth grade, with word-reading difficulties involving problems in accuracy, automaticity, or both. These investigators suggest that late-emerging cases of SWRD may relate to changing expectations for word reading as children enter the middle elementary grades and must read greater proportions of complex multisyllabic words that place higher demands on children's phonological skills, morphological awareness, and working memory. Vocabulary knowledge also influences accurate reading of many multisyllabic words; for example, a pure decoding process can yield an approximation of words like *sedimentary* and *canopy*, but oral familiarity with these words facilitates accurate reading of them.

Children with late-emerging cases of SWRD may have relatively mild phonological, language, or working memory difficulties that enable them to perform adequately in the earliest phases of reading development, especially if they have certain compensatory strengths available to them. However, they may begin to have more difficulties with word reading in the middle elementary grades, when word-reading demands become more complex. Late-emerging cases of SWRD in Catts et al. (2012) typically involved children who in kindergarten had had relatively mild weaknesses in phonological awareness and expressive vocabulary coupled with strengths in receptive vocabulary and letter knowledge. Likewise, late-emerging cases of SWRD in Lipka et al. (2006) involved children with phonological weaknesses, who appeared better able to compensate for these weaknesses in the earliest grades than later on.

Specific Patterns of Reading Difficulties Within Each Profile: A Model of RD

As the previous discussion shows, difficulties of poor readers at various ages have been studied extensively (e.g., Catts et al., 2005; Shankweiler, Crain, Brady, & Macaruso, 1992; Siegel, 1988; Stanovich, 1986; Stanovich & Siegel, 1994; Torgesen et al., 2001; Vellutino & Scanlon, 2002; Vellutino et al., 2007; Wolf & Bowers, 1999). The patterns of reading difficulties discussed below are founded in this research and involve a revision of a model originally described by Spear-Swerling and Sternberg (1994, 1996). The model conceptualizes reading difficulties as involving deviations from the path to proficient reading at various phases in development (Spear-Swerling & Sternberg, 1994, 1996). Figure 1 depicts this model, with the patterns of reading difficulties also described in Table 1. The further children go off track and fall increasingly behind their age cohort because of lack of intervention, the harder it is for them to get back on the road to proficient reading. For all struggling readers, the negative consequences of reading failure, such as decreased motivation, practice, and expectations—shown on the right-hand side of Figure 1—tend to complicate reading difficulties. These complications may begin as early as first grade (Stanovich, 1986). Specific patterns of reading difficulties associated with various profiles depend on the point at which a struggling reader has gone off track. Four patterns relate to SWRD and two patterns to SCD, shown in the center of Figure 1 and discussed next.

Patterns Related to SWRD

Nonalphabetic Word Readers. Nonalphabetic word readers have trouble very early in the process of reading development, in the phase of visual-cue word recognition. Like typically developing readers in this phase, they do not grasp the alphabetic principle, have limited letter–sound knowledge, and lack phonological awareness, so they must rely on visual cues alone, such as word shape, to recognize words. Because it is impossible to progress very far in an alphabetic language such as English without understanding the alphabetic code and acquiring some ability to use phonetic cues, nonalphabetic readers have extremely impaired word recognition and reading comprehension. They are often young children and are likely to be noticed because of the severity of their difficulties.

Inaccurate Word Readers. These children go off track in the phase of phonetic-cue word recognition. They have grasped the alphabetic principle, have some knowledge of letter sounds, and perhaps have a rudimentary level of phonological awareness, which enables them to use some phonetic cues in attempting to read words. However, they do not make full use of phonetic cues, and therefore their word recognition is inaccurate. Their difficulties may relate to poor phonemic awareness, insufficient knowledge of letter–sound relationships, or both areas. Inaccurate word readers may continue to rely on context cues, such as pictures or sentence context, to aid word recognition. In relatively easy texts, they may sometimes achieve adequate reading comprehension. However, as text demands escalate, it will become increasingly difficult for inaccurate readers to compensate effectively for their poor word recognition, and their reading comprehension will likely be impaired.

Nonautomatic Word Readers. Nonautomatic word readers go astray in the phase of controlled word recognition. As with typically developing readers in the controlled word-recognition phase, nonautomatic word readers have the ability to read most common words accurately, but their word reading is effortful, and they may also have difficulty reading complex multisyllabic words. Their speed of reading text may remain very slow, and their use of mental resources to speed word recognition (e.g., via use of context cues) tends to impair reading comprehension, especially in more demanding texts. Nonautomatic word readers may have underlying deficits in rapid naming (e.g., Wolf & Bowers, 1999), although the interpretation of naming speed deficits, especially whether such deficits reflect a core phonological weakness, remains a matter of dispute (Kirby, Georgiou, Martinussen, & Parrila, 2010; Scarborough & Brady, 2002). Some nonautomatic word readers may have late-emerging SWRD (Catts et al., 2012; Lipka et al., 2006), whereas others may have had early word-reading difficulties that only partially resolved or responded to intervention.

Delayed Word Readers. This pattern of SWRD involves delayed development of word-recognition skills and not poor oral language comprehension (i.e., the "delay" pertains specifically to word recognition, not overall language development). Delayed word readers have a history of word-recognition difficulties that they eventually overcame, but at a cost: While these readers struggled to develop word recognition, they missed other kinds of reading experiences and instruction important to the development of reading comprehension, such as the use of comprehension strategies. Comprehension strategies require a proactive rather than passive stance on the part of the reader (Garner, 1990), as well as task persistence (Gersten, Fuchs, Williams, & Baker, 2001). Thus, strategic weaknesses in poor readers sometimes may reflect a tendency to give up easily when confronted with challenging reading tasks, not a true inability to develop or use strategic knowledge.

Patterns Related to SCD

Nonstrategic Comprehenders. Like delayed word readers, nonstrategic comprehenders also go astray in the phase of automatic word recognition, but for different reasons. Delayed word readers have a delay in acquiring word-recognition skills that has secondary effects on their acquisition of strategic comprehension skills; however, their oral language abilities are at least age appropriate. In contrast, nonstrategic comprehenders make normal progress in the early phases of reading development involving word recognition but fail to acquire reading comprehension abilities, such as strategic knowledge, for reasons other than a word-recognition or phonological problem. These reasons could include not only broad oral language weaknesses or working memory difficulties but also inadequate comprehension instruction, impoverished reading experiences, and lack of engagement. Nonstrategic comprehenders fail to develop routine use of reading comprehension strategies and thus are very impaired with regard to strategy use and comprehension.

Suboptimal Comprehenders. Like nonstrategic comprehenders, suboptimal comprehenders have a profile involving SCD. However, they go astray somewhat later in the process of reading development, in the phase of strategic reading, and primarily lack higher order comprehension abilities. Although they have the ability to use at least some comprehension strategies, suboptimal comprehenders may lack higher level strategies. Thus, the two patterns of SCD differ primarily in onset and degree of reading-comprehension impairment, with suboptimal comprehenders less impaired than nonstrategic comprehenders. However, at advanced levels of schooling, such as high school and college, suboptimal reading may still create serious difficulties.

Patterns Related to MRD

Students with MRD have sometimes been called "garden-variety poor readers" (e.g., Hoover & Gough, 1990; Spear-Swerling, 2004a); here I use the term *mixed reading difficulties* after Catts et al. (2005) to convey reading problems involving both word-recognition and core comprehension abilities. As in the case of SCD, these problems with core comprehension abilities often involve oral language comprehension (Catts et al., 2005, 2006; Nation, 2005), although weaknesses in other abilities, such as working memory or the use of text comprehension strategies, could also be involved. Like children with SWRD, those with MRD have trouble in the early phases of reading development because of poor word recognition and phonological weaknesses. In the early grades, the word-recognition difficulties of students with MRD may be more obvious than their comprehension problems because the comprehension demands of beginning texts are relatively low (Chall, Jacobs, & Baldwin, 1990) and because reading comprehension cannot even come into play without a basic level of word recognition. However, students with MRD have trouble with reading comprehension even after remediation of their word-recognition skills because their poor reading comprehension relates only partially to weak word recognition.

In contrast to children with SWRD, who generally do well with material presented verbally (e.g., during class discussions of material read aloud by the teacher), children with MRD may have comprehension difficulties in listening as well as in reading. They may appear to respond to intervention targeting word recognition in the early grades, only to fall behind again in the later grades. These students have especially complex intervention needs involving both word-recognition and core comprehension abilities. As shown in Table 1, these specific needs depend on the pattern of word-recognition difficulties (i.e., nonalphabetic, inaccurate, nonautomatic, or delayed) and the core comprehension abilities which are lacking (e.g., vocabulary, knowledge of comprehension strategies, inferencing). In terms of the map metaphor shown in Figure 1, students with MRD can be conceptualized as going off track at more than one phase of reading development, initially in one of the early phases involving word recognition and later on in one of the more advanced phases of reading.

Possible Shifts in Reading Profiles and Patterns

Reading profiles and patterns have the potential to shift over time. A variety of influences may contribute to changes in a student's profile of reading difficulties, including developmental changes and increasing grade expectations in reading. For example, Catts et al. (2006) found considerable stability in poor readers' underlying profiles of phonological word-reading versus oral language comprehension abilities from kindergarten to eighth grade. However, for students with SCD, reading comprehension difficulties as measured by the Gray Oral Reading Test were considerably less pronounced in second grade than in eighth grade, perhaps because of developmental changes in the relative importance of word reading versus language comprehension to reading comprehension across grades. Similarly, Chall et al. (1990) followed a group of low-SES youngsters with SCD whose vocabulary weaknesses became apparent in fourth grade but did not significantly influence reading comprehension until about sixth or seventh grade, with a progressive deterioration in reading comprehension thereafter. These and other studies support the idea that many students with SCD have subtle language problems from the early grades, but those language weaknesses have a larger impact on reading comprehension as the students progress into later grades.

Interestingly, Chall et al. (1990) found that a deceleration in vocabulary scores also was associated with a deceleration in word recognition and spelling scores in the later grades, and Compton et al. (2012) found that fifth-grade students identified with SWRD tended to have relative weaknesses in working memory and oral language. Thus, as students advance into later levels of schooling where decoding of multisyllabic words is important, oral language and working memory problems may begin to have an impact on word reading as well as reading comprehension.

Another potential influence on struggling readers' profiles involves certain "side effects" of the initial reading difficulty itself. Stanovich (1986) termed these *Matthew effects* after the Biblical phrase about the rich getting richer and the poor getting poorer. For example, children who struggle in reading tend to get much less practice reading than do good readers, both in and out of school. Because reading contributes to the development of important linguistic and cognitive abilities, individual differences in learning to read may have broad effects on background knowledge and language over time. In fact, Stanovich (1991) suggested that some children with SWRD eventually may develop an MRD profile, as their originally circumscribed word-recognition difficulties have a spreading effect on other areas of language and knowledge, although some studies have not found this spreading effect (e.g., Scarborough & Parker, 2003).

One obvious influence on patterns of reading difficulties involves instruction and intervention. Research on RTI models has demonstrated that especially in the area of word-level reading skills, research-based instruction and interventions can ameliorate, or even prevent entirely, some reading difficulties. Thus, a child with SWRD in the early grades, including one with an inherited vulnerability to RD, might become a normally achieving reader if provided with prompt, appropriate intervention; or, a student with SWRD and mild language weaknesses might respond to effective phonics intervention in the primary grades but go on to evidence an SCD profile in the later grades.

An Interactive Perspective on Reading Development and Disabilities

The road map model involves an interactive perspective on reading development and reading disability (Spear-Swerling & Sternberg, 1994, 1996) that is very consistent with the views of a number of other investigators (e.g., Lipson & Wixson, 1986; Ruddell & Unrau, 1994; Valencia, 2011). The model conceptualizes both good and poor reading as involving an interaction between children's intrinsic characteristics and extrinsic factors such as instruction, experience, and home environment. Intrinsic characteristics include not only children's reading-related abilities but also other important intrinsic influences on reading outcomes, such as frustration tolerance and other abilities involved in self-regulation (Smith, Borkowski, & Whitman, 2008).

Although I have described the various profiles and patterns of reading difficulties in terms of deviations from the path of typical reading development, children with reading difficulties differ from typical younger readers in some important respects. For instance, students with SWRD may compensate for deficient phonological skills in ways uncharacteristic of younger, normally achieving children matched to them on word-recognition level (Greenberg, Ehri, & Perin, 2002), and like other struggling readers, they certainly have a host of negative experiences with reading, such as repeated failure, not typical of younger good readers. The road map metaphor and the right-hand box in Figure 1 labeled "negative consequences of reading failure" attempt to capture these distinctions between students with reading difficulties and normally achieving but younger readers.

Educational Implications of the Road Map Model

Planning Intervention

The use of poor reader profiles, as well as the specific patterns of reading difficulties within each profile explained above, can be very helpful in planning intervention. Students with poor reading comprehension related to SWRD require a different kind of intervention than do those whose difficulty involves SCD. Furthermore, inaccurate word readers have somewhat different instructional needs than do nonautomatic word readers. Both inaccurate and nonautomatic readers usually require fluency building, but inaccurate word readers require basic phonics intervention, whereas nonautomatic readers—if they need remediation of word accuracy at all—require a focus on structural analysis and decoding of multisyllabic words. Determining the underlying profile and pattern associated with poor reading is an important first step to designing appropriate intervention.

As discussed by Valencia (2011), profiles and patterns provide helpful initial information about struggling readers' overall strengths and weaknesses in key reading-related abilities; however, for most struggling readers, additional diagnostic assessments will be necessary for planning instruction. For instance, two inaccurate word readers might be functioning at different levels in terms of specific decoding skills; two nonstrategic comprehenders might vary substantially in important comprehension abilities such as vocabulary or use of specific comprehension strategies. Teachers should supplement information about profiles and patterns with more fine-grained analysis of students' instructional needs, especially in their areas of difficulty.

Early Identification and Prevention of Reading Problems

Knowledge about the phases of typical reading development can help educators design effective core instruction by anticipating both current and future demands children have to meet in reading; for at-risk students, information about common profiles and patterns of reading difficulties can assist early identification efforts. For example, many students with SCD or MRD have subtle language weaknesses easily overlooked early on but exerting a bigger impact on reading comprehension in the upper grades, when expectations for comprehension become more demanding. In the primary grades, along with assessment of children's phonological skills, assessment of other language abilities such as vocabulary and listening comprehension might enable more timely intervention and even prevention of future problems in reading comprehension in some children (Scarborough, 2005). Furthermore, given the common role of vocabulary weaknesses in the reading problems of low-SES children and English learners (e.g., Lesaux & Kieffer, 2010), an increased emphasis on vocabulary development in schools serving these populations in the primary grades might help prevent later reading difficulties in many children (Biemiller, 1999). In addition, because a history of preschool language delay tends to presage reading problems (Catts et al., 2012; Scarborough, 2005), educators should consider students' developmental language history in screening for reading difficulties, both in the primary grades and at later levels of schooling.

Using Profiles and Patterns in Identification of RD

Simply evidencing a particular profile or pattern of reading difficulties does not mean that a student has RD. To be identified with RD, students must meet other criteria besides low reading achievement; in particular, their reading difficulties cannot primarily be due to another disability, lack of instruction, or lack of opportunity to learn. The logic behind RTI approaches to identification of RD is that the provision of research-based interventions helps rule out instructional factors and inadequate opportunity to learn as causes of students' reading problems. Poor implementations of RTI can certainly undermine this logic. Nonetheless, RTI approaches address the need to consider instructional factors in identification of RD much more directly than have most previous identification practices, including the IQ–achievement discrepancy approach.

IQ–achievement discrepancy criteria tend to select for the SWRD pattern of reading difficulties, largely because of the relationship between verbal IQ and oral language abilities, especially vocabulary. Students with a large gap between their

IQs and their reading achievement are likely to have problems focused on word recognition not on language comprehension (Fletcher et al., 2007). However, with the use of RTI, students with a variety of reading profiles, including MRD and SCD as well as SWRD, could be eligible for RD services if they demonstrate inadequate response to research-based interventions in their areas of difficulty and meet exclusionary criteria. Thus, states eliminating the discrepancy model in favor of RTI criteria may identify a broader range of reading problems in the category of RD than they have identified in the past.

Exclusionary criteria exclude from the category of RD reading problems associated primarily with other disabilities, such as intellectual disabilities, as well as reading problems associated mainly with lack of instruction or lack of opportunity to learn. Exclusion of intellectual disabilities does not require routine IQ testing because students with intellectual disabilities have significant impairments in adaptive behavior—self-help and social skills—in addition to low IQ scores (Fletcher et al., 2007). Therefore, only students with limitations in adaptive behavior, not all students undergoing evaluation for RD, would require IQ tests to rule out intellectual disabilities.

The use of RTI approaches to identify RD will likely make application of exclusionary criteria more complex for educators than in past approaches to identification because of the wide variety of abilities that serve comprehension as well as the many types of disabilities associated with poor comprehension. For instance, students with autism spectrum disorders often show a profile of SCD in reading (Huemer & Mann, 2010). However, these students have some unique intervention needs, such as those involving pragmatic language and social functioning, that differ from those of students with language-based RD. Likewise, SCD is a common profile of adolescent English learners and students from low-SES backgrounds (Lesaux & Kieffer, 2010). Most of these previously mentioned students would not be conceptualized as having RD because they would not meet exclusionary criteria, although many would likely benefit from the research-based interventions provided via RTI approaches.

Application of exclusionary criteria sometimes requires consideration of students' primary versus secondary problems. For example, an English learner could be identified with RD if it were determined that the student's primary problem was a learning difficulty and not lack of exposure to English—say, as indicated by the student having similar language and reading problems in the native language as in English. Accurately distinguishing between primary and secondary difficulties can be challenging but is important so students with genuine RD, such as English learners or low-SES students with RD, are not wrongly excluded from special education services.

Some Challenges of Using RTI Criteria to Identify RD

Inconsistent Identification Practices

Under IDEA 2004, identification practices for RD will often be inconsistent across schools, given the fact that many states have chosen to leave decision making about overall criteria for LD to local districts (Zirkel & Thomas, 2010). There is some logic to this choice; large-scale implementation of RTI is recent, and without evidence about the best ways to implement many specific details of RTI, states understandably are reluctant to be prescriptive. Nevertheless, inconsistent identification practices for LD have been a problem in the past (Moats & Lyon, 1993), and the use of RTI is unlikely to improve this situation in the near future.

Challenges Involving Measurement and Assessment

Universal screening and progress monitoring are fundamental to RTI approaches. For children with word-recognition and fluency difficulties, there are some very useful screening and progress-monitoring measures, including assessments of out-of-context word decoding and oral passage reading fluency. However, determination of intervention responsiveness and identification of RD may vary depending on the measures selected. In their study of first graders receiving a standard protocol intervention, Denton et al. (2010) identified 91% as showing adequate response to intervention based on word-reading accuracy criteria but only 48% based on oral reading fluency criteria (words read correctly per minute in first-grade text). Another study employing the same intervention (Mathes et al., 2005) found a similar pattern of results, although in this study a higher percentage of intervention responders (77%) met the oral reading fluency benchmark. Variations in choices of progress-monitoring tools will tend to exacerbate the inconsistencies in identification practices mentioned above.

In the area of comprehension, measurement issues are especially complex. Oral reading fluency measures, particularly those involving only a words-correct-per-minute benchmark, tend to miss struggling readers with a profile of SCD (Riedel, 2007; Valencia et al., 2010). The use of additional screening measures, such as oral vocabulary or passage comprehension, could improve early identification of these students. Some schools may already have reading comprehension scores available, such as state-mandated assessment data, for use in initial screening, especially beyond the early grades. However, another vital issue involves the fact that judgments of reading comprehension performance can vary substantially for individual children depending on the measure of reading comprehension. All reading comprehension measures tap both word-recognition and oral language comprehension abilities, but the extent to which specific tests tap these abilities, and hence the poor reader profile they most often identify, varies with the characteristics of the test. For instance, reading comprehension tests that employ a cloze or maze format tend to assess word recognition relatively more heavily than they assess oral language comprehension, whereas tests that require students to read passages and answer questions about them tend to show the opposite pattern (Keenan, Betjemann, & Olson, 2008; Nation & Snowling, 1997; Spear-Swerling, 2004b). The former tests, therefore, are somewhat more likely to identify poor readers with SWRD and the latter those with SCD. Many other features of reading comprehension tests are also important in relation to individual students' performance (see, e.g., Cutting & Scarborough, 2006; Jenkins, Johnson, & Hileman, 2004; Keenan & Betjemann, 2006). Educators must consider the nature of the comprehension measure when interpreting individual students' reading comprehension performance. They also should interpret performance on formal tests in relation to everyday classroom work because many standardized reading comprehension tests do not tap the complex comprehension abilities expected of students at upper grade levels (Allington & McGill-Franzen, 2008).

Challenges Involving Intervention

In using RTI criteria to identify RD, much hinges on the quality of interventions. Inappropriate interventions not only may fail in effectiveness and waste resources but also will have little value in helping to rule out instructional or experiential factors in the difficulties of struggling readers under consideration for special education. Although there is considerable research evidence on appropriate interventions for students with SWRD, evidence is more limited for those with comprehension-based reading difficulties, especially at upper grade levels. More research is needed on the different components of comprehension (e.g., vocabulary, listening comprehension, strategic knowledge) and on how different types of comprehension weaknesses might respond to different approaches to comprehension instruction. Further study of the efficacy of interventions aimed specifically at older poor readers is essential because there is substantial agreement that even the most effective early intervention programs will not prevent reading difficulties in all children and because some serious reading problems do not emerge until the middle grades or later.

Not only effective methods of intervention but also knowledgeable teachers are important to good reading outcomes (Piasta, Connor, Fishman, & Morrison, 2009). Information about common reading profiles and patterns of difficulties can be useful to all teachers of reading, but making use of this information entails a substantial knowledge base about reading development and individual differences that affect reading, as well as about how to assess and teach a wide range of reading-related abilities to diverse learners. Currently both general and special educators often lack this kind of knowledge (Spear-Swerling, 2008; Spear-Swerling & Cheesman, 2012), so implementing RTI effectively in many schools will require substantial professional development efforts.

Conclusions and Future Directions

Despite the kinds of challenges outlined above, the use of RTI criteria to identify RD is a major advance over traditional approaches to LD identification based on the IQ–achievement discrepancy model. If Jamie, the fourth grader discussed in the opening to this chapter, had attended a school with an RTI model, educators would likely have identified and addressed his reading difficulties much earlier, before he fell so far behind. His teachers probably would have employed assessments with better capacity to inform his interventions and less likelihood of doing harm because of inappropriate inferences based on his IQ score. Furthermore, RTI criteria for identifying RD would have focused Jamie's teachers, and other adults trying to help him, on educationally meaningful questions, even if not all of those questions currently have clear or easy answers.

Implementing RTI involves many challenges for schools beyond those discussed here. There certainly is a need for further research in many areas, including the most effective approaches to measurement of progress for readers of different profiles and ages; assessment of reading comprehension; interventions for comprehension, including different components of comprehension; and preservice preparation and professional development of teachers. However, RTI criteria avoid many past problems with identification of RD via the IQ–achievement discrepancy model, such as failure to identify at-risk readers early, misidentifying as disabled poor readers whose problems are largely experiential or instructional in nature, limited educational relevance, and myriad problems associated with the routine use of IQ tests. In conjunction with RTI, an analysis of common profiles and patterns of reading difficulties is highly relevant to prevention of reading difficulties, as well as to early identification and planning intervention for students with reading problems. Moreover, such an approach is useful not only for students with RD but for other poor readers as well.

QUESTIONS FOR REFLECTION

1. What are the advantages of using RTI criteria to identify reading disabilities rather than the IQ–achievement discrepancy model?
2. In what ways are the core features of reading disabilities accounted for through RTI?
3. In what ways do the common cognitive profiles and patterns of reading difficulties that Spear-Swerling provides account for the various challenges that struggling readers face?
4. In what ways can the common cognitive profiles and patterns of reading difficulties be used to identify reading disabilities?

REFERENCES

Aaron, P.G., Joshi, M., Gooden, R., & Bentum, K. (2008). Diagnosis and treatment of reading disabilities based on the component model of reading: An alternative to the discrepancy model of LD. *Journal of Learning Disabilities*, *41*(1), 67–84. doi:10.1177/0022219407310838

Adams, M.J. (1990). *Beginning to read: Thinking and learning about print*. Cambridge, MA: MIT Press.

Allington, R.L., & McGill-Franzen, A. (2008). Comprehension difficulties among struggling readers. In S.E. Israel & G.G. Duffy (Eds.), *Handbook of research on reading comprehension* (pp. 551–568). New York: Routledge.

Benjamin, R.G., & Schwanenflugel, P.J. (2010). Text complexity and oral reading prosody in young readers. *Reading Research Quarterly*, *45*(4), 388–404. doi:10.1598/RRQ.45.4.2

Biemiller, A. (1999). *Language and reading success*. Cambridge, MA: Brookline.

Blachman, B.A., Schatschneider, C., Fletcher, J.M., Francis, D.J., Clonan, S.M., Shaywitz, B.A., et al. (2004). Effects of intensive reading remediation for second and third graders. *Journal of Educational Psychology, 96*(3), 444–461. doi:10.1037/0022-0663.96.3.444

Byrne, B., Samuelsson, S., Wadsworth, S., Hulslander, J., Corley, R., DeFries, J.C., et al. (2007). Longitudinal twin study of early literacy development: Preschool through grade 1. *Reading and Writing, 20*(1/2), 77–102. doi: 10.1007/s11145-006-9019-9

Cain, K., Oakhill, J.V., & Bryant, P.E. (2004). Children's reading comprehension ability: Concurrent prediction by working memory, verbal ability, and component skills. *Journal of Educational Psychology, 96*(1), 31–42. doi:10.1037/0022-0663.96.1.31

Carlisle, J.F. (2010). Effects of instruction in morphological awareness on literacy achievement: An integrative review. *Reading Research Quarterly, 45*(4), 464–487. doi:10.1598/RRQ.45.4.5

Catts, H.W., Adlof, S.M., & Weismer, S.E. (2006). Language deficits in poor comprehenders: A case for the simple view of reading. *Journal of Speech, Language, and Hearing Research, 49*(2), 278–293.

Catts, H.W., Compton, D.L., Tomblin, J.B., & Bridges, M.S. (2012). Prevalence and nature of late-emerging poor readers. *Journal of Educational Psychology, 104*(2), 166–181.

Catts, H.W., Hogan, T.P., & Adlof, S.M. (2005). Developmental changes in reading and reading disabilities. In H.W. Catts & A. Kamhi (Eds.), *The connections between language and reading disabilities* (pp. 25–40). Mahwah, NJ: Erlbaum.

Chall, J. (1983). *Stages of reading development*. New York: McGraw-Hill.

Chall, J., Jacobs, V.A., & Baldwin, L.E. (1990). *The reading crisis: Why poor children fall behind*. Cambridge, MA: Harvard University Press.

Compton, D.L., Fuchs, L.S., Fuchs, D., Lambert, W., & Hamlett, C. (2012). The cognitive and academic profiles of reading and mathematics learning disabilities. *Journal of Learning Disabilities, 45*(1), 79–95.

Cortiella, C. (2009). *The state of learning disabilities*. New York: National Center for Learning Disabilities.

Cunningham, A.E., & Stanovich, K.E. (1991). Tracking the unique effects of print exposure in children: Associations with vocabulary, general knowledge, and spelling. *Journal of Educational Psychology, 83*(2), 264–274. doi:10.1037/0022-0663.83.2.264

Cutting, L.E., & Scarborough, H.S. (2006). Prediction of reading comprehension: Relative contributions of word recognition, language proficiency, and other cognitive skills can depend on how comprehension is measured. *Scientific Studies of Reading, 10*(3), 277–299. doi:10.1207/s1532799xssr1003_5

Daneman, M., & Carpenter, P.A. (1980). Individual differences in working memory and reading. *Journal of Verbal Learning and Verbal Behavior, 19*, 450–466.

Denton, C.A., Fletcher, J.M., Anthony, J.L., & Francis, D.J. (2006). An evaluation of intensive intervention for students with persistent reading difficulties. *Journal of Learning Disabilities, 39*(5), 447–466. doi:10.1177/00222194060390050601

Denton, C.A., Nimon, K., Mathes, P.G., Swanson, E.A., Kethley, C., Kurz, T.B., et al. (2010). Effectiveness of a supplemental early reading intervention scaled up in multiple schools. *Exceptional Children, 76*(4), 394–416.

Ehri, L.C. (1991). Learning to read and spell words. In L. Rieben & C.A. Perfetti (Eds.), *Learning to read: Basic research and its implications* (pp. 57–73). Mahwah, NJ: Erlbaum.

Ehri, L.C. (2005). Learning to read words: Theory, findings, and issues. *Scientific Studies of Reading, 9*(2), 167–188. doi:10.1207/s1532799xssr0902_4

Fletcher, J.M., Lyon, G.R., Fuchs, L.S., & Barnes, M.A. (2007). *Learning disabilities: From identification to intervention*. New York: Guilford.

Fuchs, D., Fuchs, L.S., & Stecker, P.M. (2010). The "blurring" of special education in a new continuum of general education placements and services. *Exceptional Children, 76*(3), 301–324.

Fuchs, L.S., Fuchs, D., Hosp, M., & Jenkins, J.R. (2001). Oral reading fluency as an indicator of reading competence: A theoretical, empirical, and historical analysis. *Scientific Studies of Reading, 5*(3), 239–256. doi:10.1207/S1532799XSSR0503_3

Garner, R. (1990). When children and adults do not use learning strategies: Toward a theory of settings. *Review of Educational Research, 60*(4), 517–529.

Gersten, R., Fuchs, L.S., Williams, J.P., & Baker, S. (2001). Teaching reading-comprehension strategies to students with learning disabilities: A review of research. *Review of Educational Research, 71*(2), 279–320. doi:10.3102/00346543071002279

Greenberg, D., Ehri, L.C., & Perin, D. (2002). Do adult literacy students make the same word-reading and spelling errors as children matched for word-reading age? *Scientific Studies of Reading, 6*(3), 221–243. doi:10.1207/S1532799XSSR0603_2

Hoover, W.A., & Gough, P.B. (1990). The simple view of reading. *Reading and Writing, 2*(2), 127–160. doi:10.1007/BF00401799

Huemer, S.V., & Mann, V. (2010). A comprehensive profile of decoding and comprehension in autism spectrum disorders. *Journal of Autism and Developmental Disorders, 40*(4), 485–493. doi:10.1007/s10803-009-0892-3

Jenkins, J.R., Johnson, E., & Hileman, J. (2004). When is reading also writing: Sources of individual differences on the new reading performance assessments. *Scientific Studies of Reading, 8*(2), 125–151. doi:10.1207/s1532799xssr0802_2

Keenan, J.M., & Betjemann, R.S. (2006). Comprehending the Gray Oral Reading Test without reading it: Why comprehension tests should not include passage-independent items. *Scientific Studies of Reading, 10*(4), 363–380. doi:10.1207/s1532799xssr1004_2

Keenan, J.M., Betjemann, R.S., & Olson, R.K. (2008). Reading comprehension tests vary in the skills they assess: Differential dependence on decoding and oral comprehension. *Scientific Studies of Reading, 12*(3), 281–300. doi:10.1080/10888430802132279

Kirby, J.R., Georgiou, G.K., Martinussen, R., & Parrila, R. (2010). Naming speed and reading: From prediction to instruction. *Reading Research Quarterly, 45*(3), 341–362. doi:10.1598/RRQ.45.3.4

Kuhn, M.R., Schwanenflugel, P.J., & Meisinger, E.B. (2010). Aligning theory and assessment of reading fluency: Automaticity, prosody, and definitions of fluency. *Reading Research Quarterly, 45*(2), 230–251. doi:10.1598/RRQ.45.2.4

Leach, J.M., Scarborough, H.S., & Rescorla, L. (2003). Late-emerging reading disabilities. *Journal of Educational Psychology, 95*(2), 211–224. doi:10.1037/0022-0663.95.2.211

Lesaux, N.K., & Kieffer, M.J. (2010). Exploring sources of reading comprehension difficulties among language minority learners and their classmates in early adolescence. *American Educational Research Journal, 47*(3), 596–632. doi:10.3102/0002831209355469

Lipka, O., Lesaux, N., & Siegel, L. (2006). Retrospective analyses of the reading development of grade 4 students with reading disabilities: Risk status and profiles over 5 years. *Journal of Learning Disabilities, 39*(4), 364–378.

Lipson, M.Y., & Wixson, K.K. (1986). Reading disability research: An interactionist perspective. *Review of Educational Research, 56*(1), 111–136.

Lyon, G.R., Shaywitz, S.E., & Shaywitz, B.A. (2003). A definition of dyslexia. *Annals of Dyslexia, 53*(1), 1–14. doi:10.1007/s11881-003-0001-9

Mathes, P.G., Denton, C.A., Fletcher, J.M., Anthony, J.L., Francis, D.J., & Schatschneider, C. (2005). The effects of theoretically different instruction and student characteristics on the skills of struggling readers. *Reading Research Quarterly, 40*(2), 148–182. doi:10.1598/RRQ.40.2.2

Moats, L.C., & Lyon, G.R. (1993). Learning disabilities in the United States: Advocacy, science, and the future of the field. *Journal of Learning Disabilities, 26*(5), 282–294. doi:10.1177/002221949302600501

Nation, K. (2005). Children's reading comprehension difficulties. In M.J. Snowling & C. Hulme (Eds.), *The science of reading: A handbook* (pp. 248–265). Oxford, UK: Blackwell. doi:10.1002/9780470757642.ch14

Nation, K., & Snowling, M. (1997). Assessing reading difficulties: The validity and utility of current measures of reading skill. *The British Journal of Educational Psychology, 67*(3), 359–370. doi:10.1111/j.2044-8279.1997.tb01250.x

Olson, R.K., Keenan, J.M., Byrne, B., Samuelsson, S., Coventry, W., Corley, R., et al. (2011). Genetic and environmental influences on vocabulary and reading development. *Scientific Studies of Reading, 15*(1), 26–46. doi:10.1080/10888438.2011.536128

Perfetti, C.A. (1985). *Reading ability*. New York: Oxford University Press.

Piasta, S.B., Connor, C.M., Fishman, B.J., & Morrison, F.J. (2009). Teachers' knowledge of literacy concepts, classroom practices, and student reading growth. *Scientific Studies of Reading, 13*(3), 224–248. doi:10.1080/10888430902851364

Riedel, B.W. (2007). The relation between DIBELS, reading comprehension, and vocabulary in urban first-grade students. *Reading Research Quarterly, 42*(4), 546–567. doi:10.1598/RRQ.42.4.5

Ruddell, R.B., & Unrau, N.J. (1994). Reading as a meaning-construction process: The reader, the text, and the teacher. In R.B. Ruddell, M.R. Ruddell, & H. Singer (Eds.), *Theoretical models and processes of reading* (4th ed., pp. 996–1056). Newark, DE: International Reading Association.

Rupley, W.H., Willson, V.L., & Nichols, W.D. (1998). Exploration of the developmental components contributing to elementary school children's reading comprehension. *Scientific Studies of Reading, 2*(2), 143–158. doi:10.1207/s1532799xssr0202_3

Scarborough, H.S. (2005). Developmental relationships between language and reading: Reconciling a beautiful hypothesis with some ugly facts. In H.W. Catts & A. Kamhi (Eds.), *The connections between language and reading disabilities* (pp. 3–24). Mahwah, NJ: Erlbaum.

Scarborough, H.S., & Brady, S.A. (2002). Toward a common terminology for talking about speech and reading: A glossary of the "*phon*" words and some related terms. *Journal of Literacy Research, 34*(3), 299–336. doi:10.1207/s15548430jlr3403_3

Scarborough, H.S., & Parker, J.D. (2003). Matthew effects in children with learning disabilities: Development of reading, IQ, and psychosocial problems from grade 2 to grade 8. *Annals of Dyslexia, 53*(1), 47–71. doi:10.1007/s11881-003-0004-6

Shankweiler, D., Crain, S., Brady, S., & Macaruso, P. (1992). Identifying the causes of reading disability. In P.B. Gough, L.C. Ehri, & R. Treiman (Eds.), *Reading acquisition* (pp. 275–305). Hillsdale, NJ: Erlbaum.

Siegel, L.S. (1988). Evidence that IQ scores are irrelevant to the definition and analysis of reading disability. *Canadian Journal of Psychology, 42*(2), 201–215. doi:10.1037/h0084184

Simmons, D.C., Coyne, M.D., Hagan-Burke, S., Kwok, O., Simmons, L., Johnson, C., et al. (2011). Effects of supplemental reading interventions in authentic contexts: A comparison of kindergartners' response. *Exceptional Children, 77*(2), 207–228.

Smith, L.E., Borkowski, J.G., & Whitman, T.L. (2008). From reading readiness to reading competence: The role of self-regulation in at-risk children. *Scientific Studies of Reading, 12*(2), 131–152. doi:10.1080/10888430801917167

Spear-Swerling, L. (2004a). A road map for understanding reading disability and other reading problems: Origins, intervention, and prevention. In R.B. Ruddell & N.J. Unrau (Eds.), *Theoretical models and processes of reading* (Vol. 5, pp. 517–573). Newark, DE: International Reading Association. doi:10.1598/0872075028.18

Spear-Swerling, L. (2004b). Fourth-graders' performance on a state-mandated assessment involving two different measures of reading comprehension. *Reading Psychology*, 25(2), 121–148. doi:10.1080/02702710490435727

Spear-Swerling, L. (2008). Response to intervention and teacher preparation. In E. Grigorenko (Ed.), *Educating individuals with disabilities: IDEA 2004 and beyond* (pp. 273–294). New York: Springer.

Spear-Swerling, L., & Cheesman, E. (2012). Teachers' knowledge base for implementing response-to-intervention models in reading. *Reading & Writing*, 25(7), 1691–1723. doi:10.1007/s11145-011-9338-3

Spear-Swerling, L., & Sternberg, R.J. (1994). The road not taken: An integrative theoretical model of reading disability. *Journal of Learning Disabilities*, 27(2), 91–103, 122. doi:10.1177/002221949402700204

Spear-Swerling, L., & Sternberg, R.J. (1996). *Off track: When poor readers become "learning disabled."* Boulder, CO: Westview.

Speece, D.L., Case, L.P., & Molloy, D.W. (2003). Responsiveness to general education instruction as the first gate to learning disabilities identification. *Learning Disabilities Research & Practice*, 18(3), 147–156. doi:10.1111/1540-5826.00071

Stanovich, K.E. (1986). Matthew effects in reading: Some consequences of individual differences in the acquisition of literacy. *Reading Research Quarterly*, 21(4), 360–406. doi:10.1598/RRQ.21.4.1

Stanovich, K.E. (1991). Discrepancy definitions of reading disability: Has intelligence led us astray? *Reading Research Quarterly*, 26(1), 7–29. doi:10.2307/747729

Stanovich, K.E. (2000). *Progress in understanding reading: Scientific foundations and new frontiers.* New York: Guilford.

Stanovich, K.E., & Siegel, L.S. (1994). Phenotypic performance profile of children with reading disabilities: A regression-based test of the phonological-core variable-difference model. *Journal of Educational Psychology*, 86(1), 24–53. doi:10.1037/0022-0663.86.1.24

Torgesen, J.K., Alexander, A., Wagner, R.K., Rashotte, C., Voeller, K., & Conway, T. (2001). Intensive remedial instruction for children with severe reading disabilities: Immediate and long-term outcomes from two instructional approaches. *Journal of Learning Disabilities*, 34(1), 33–58. doi:10.1177/002221940103400104

Valencia, S.W. (2011). Reader profiles and reading disabilities. In R.L. Allington & A. McGill-Franzen (Eds.), *Handbook of research on reading disabilities* (pp. 25–35). New York: Routledge.

Valencia, S.W., Smith, A.T., Reece, A.M., Li, M., Wixson, K.K., & Newman, H. (2010). Oral reading fluency assessment: Issues of construct, criterion, and consequential validity. *Reading Research Quarterly*, 45(3), 270–291. doi:10.1598/RRQ.45.3.1

Vellutino, F.R., & Scanlon, D.M. (2002). Emergent literacy skills, early instruction, and individual differences as determinants of difficulties in learning to read: The case for early intervention. In S.B. Neuman & D.K. Dickinson (Eds.), *Handbook of early literacy research* (pp. 295–321). New York: Guilford.

Vellutino, F.R., Tunmer, W.E., Jaccard, J.J., & Chen, R. (2007). Components of reading ability: Multivariate evidence for a convergent skills model of reading development. *Scientific Studies of Reading*, 11(1), 3–32.

Wolf, M., & Bowers, P.G. (1999). The double-deficit hypothesis for the developmental dyslexias. *Journal of Educational Psychology*, 91(3), 415–438. doi:10.1037/0022-0663.91.3.415

Zirkel, P.A. (2011). What does the law say? *Teaching Exceptional Children*, 43(3), 65–67.

Zirkel, P.A., & Thomas, L.B. (2010). State laws and guidelines for implementing RTI. *Teaching Exceptional Children*, 43(1), 60–73.

CHAPTER 17

Language Pathways Into the Community of Minds

Katherine Nelson, City University of New York

In this chapter I argue that adherence to the formulation "theory of mind" has narrowed the scope of attention to developments that contribute to children's ability to understand social and psychological phenomena. Developments in infancy and early childhood, such as shared attention and imitation, that are generally seen as precursors or predispositions to later theory of mind are, in the present view, better conceived as general characteristics of early development that have wide-ranging influences on all areas of psychological growth. At the same time, areas of competence, such as general reasoning, that are considered outside the "domain" of theory of mind can be shown to be crucial to its achievement, as it is usually evaluated in terms of the understanding of false belief. The resulting focus, I argue, has led theorists down a path that obscures the true importance of developments in early childhood, of which performance on theory-of-mind tasks is but one achievement. Further, I argue that language is the most important general function that leads to higher-order cognitive processes, including the processes involved in theory of mind, and that these developments begin to have their effects during the preschool years.

In brief, theory of mind as usually considered is too narrowly construed, while those influences that lead to success on theory-of-mind measures are more general across development in different domains of social and general cognition. This argument has implications for domain theories in general, as well as for modularity and theory theories in the theory-of-mind area. Having construed theory of mind as a separate cognitive domain to begin with, researchers became vulnerable to claims of modules, and of domain-specific theories as explanations of its development. Meanwhile, aspects of development that are not domain-defined, including memory, language, inference, reasoning, concept formation, knowledge acquisition, and imagination, were considered ancillary "performance" factors. Most important, social experiences, including attachment, play, and conversation, have tended to be looked on as modulating factors that influence but do not determine the acquisition of theory of mind.

In addition, a novel developmental mechanism, implicit theory construction or theory revision, has been invented to explain development within this domain

This chapter is reprinted from *Why Language Matters for Theory of Mind* (pp. 26–49), edited by J.W. Astington and J.A. Baird, 2005, New York: Oxford University Press.

and has been extended to other areas of knowledge acquisition. Yet there has been no specification as to how an implicit theory could be constructed in infancy or early childhood or how it might relate to explicit theory construction or explicit knowledge in general. Some writers seem to take implicit theory construction to be essentially the same as general conceptual processes (and therefore a harmless usage), but others (Gopnik & Wellman, 1994; Wellman, 1988; Wellman & Gelman, 1992) make the larger claim that a theory, implicit or explicit, is coherent within a domain, is characterized by causal relations between its concepts, and is subject to revision in light of new data.

The theory approach has led to the description of a succeeding series of different theories that infants and young children are alleged to construct during the first 5 years of life, as illustrated in Figure 1. Note that in this figure the data lie outside the theory, reflecting the presumption of an abstract epistemic structure separate from its experiential source. The guiding assumption seems to be that from birth (if not before), children have the same cognitive resources as ourselves (i.e., educated adults) for gathering and organizing data in the domain of psychological and social functioning and for forming and testing hypotheses—derived from causally connected theoretical structures—about these matters. I believe that this assumption is unwarranted and that it prevents researchers from entertaining both the breadth and the limitations of young children's knowledge sources in experience, as well as the breadth and limitations of their cognitive resources.

Theoretical approaches to this area other than the dominant "theory theory" propose various precursor abilities (e.g., attachment, pretense, executive function, meta-representation) as leading more or less directly, alone or in combination, to a successful achievement of theory of mind (Fonagy & Target, 1997; Frye, 1999; Leslie, 1987; Perner, 1991). Although this way of viewing the matter (illustrated in Figure 2) has value in relating these earlier developments to the later understanding of false belief, the causal directions implied are theoretically and empirically vulnerable. It is not that any of these abilities are irrelevant to theory of mind; rather, it is the additivity assumption and the direct causal relation assumption that are in question here. All that has yet been shown is that some of these may be prerequisites to theory of mind; it has not been determined that they have a direct

Figure 1. The Theory View

$ToM_1 \xrightarrow{\text{Data}} ToM_2 \xrightarrow{\text{Data}} ToM_3 \xrightarrow{\text{Data}}$ REAL ToM

Figure 2. The Generic Development View

(Intersubjectivity) + (Self) + (Imagination) + (Executive Function) + (Conversation)

$\longrightarrow$ ToM

causal relation to its achievement. And, indeed, even the evidence that they are necessary if not sufficient is not really there.

The only ability that has clearly been shown to be directly related to theory-of-mind competence is language, in that children without language or with impoverished language do not achieve theory of mind, and neither do nonhuman primates that lack language.

In this chapter, I argue that the area under examination needs rethinking to bring it into its proper relation to the overall course of social and cognitive development during the crucial preschool years, and to the preceding as well as succeeding developments to which it has been related, theoretically or empirically. I believe that what is required is a developmental systems approach (Oyama, 1985) that indicates the interactions among the many and various social and cognitive processes as they develop. The most important development, the one with maximum impact on all social and cognitive functioning, is the acquisition of complex language—including semantics and syntax—and its use as a representational system in conveying and reflecting on knowledge, imaginative constructions, reminiscence, explanations, and other social and cultural, as well as cognitive, functions.

The metaphor that I propose to replace the theory metaphor ensconced in current terminology is the *Community of Minds*, and the developmental process I propose is that of *entering into the community of minds*, a process made possible through the use, comprehension, and production of language. In the first section I describe the construct of the community and its advantage over the theory construct. This conception was introduced in a paper by Nelson, Henseler, and Plesa (2000) and elaborated in Nelson et al. (2003). The second section of the chapter describes how the child proceeds, on the basis of general developmental processes but only with the aid of language, to begin to enter this community.

The Community of Minds

Assuming that during their first 10 years children are developing toward membership in a human community of minds broadens the concept of "theory of mind" from something that children invent for themselves (but that just happens to agree with everyone else's theory) to a cultural conception of what it is to be human within a human community. Importantly, the metaphor emphasizes two facets of this development: the concept of minds and the idea of community.

First, what is at stake is understanding—and thus basing predictions and explanations on—*minds* in the plural. Rather than putting the emphasis on the universal Mind, the emphasis is on minds that interact with and also differ from one another, as well as having certain similarities of structure and content. Ultimately, understanding differences among minds requires understanding the sources of differences among people—their backgrounds, personalities, relationships, and histories.

The main reason for "reading" minds is to interpret the difference between others' and one's own state of mind. Indeed, this is the first step toward entry into the community, and it begins as the child is exposed to what other people think in contrast to what the child thinks, which becomes possible through language in the early childhood years. At the beginning of life, a child has neither the concept of "mind" nor, therefore, any basis on which to believe that the contents of another's mind are any different from the child's own.

The second important emphasis in the metaphor is on the *community*. In work on theory of mind, typically the problem is posed as one of understanding the beliefs of other individuals on the basis of their actions or interpreting their actions on the basis of their beliefs. This is surely a useful component of social life, but the truly important understanding is far broader: it involves the myriad sources of beliefs, reasons for doubting beliefs, beliefs that are broadly held, beliefs that are held to be wrong, or that are held to be the truth, or that are held to be immoral. These are often matters of testimony (as Harris, 2000, 2001, has been investigating); they are the stuff of the knowledge and beliefs of the cultural community. These are where the minds interact and come to agreement and disagreement, and where matters of possibly great significance may result, for example, in the case of religious beliefs that bring one community into conflict with another.

As an example that has been used in theory-of-mind research, deception—lying—must be understood in its relation to cultural understandings and rules (Chandler, Fritz, & Hala, 1989; Polak & Harris, 1999; Sinclair, 1996). If it is just a question of my telling you that there are no more cookies so that I can sneak the last one into my room and eat it by myself, this may be seen as only a selfish way of achieving a personal goal. But in the context of the scarcity of food within a family or community, the lie takes on much greater significance. This is why parents, following the moral dictates of the community, place great stress on not telling lies; any lie in itself might be harmless, but the habit of lying is harmful to both the person and the community. Still, the 3-year-old who has just discovered the possibility of deception, the possibility that she may act one way and represent the opposite in language, has made a momentous discovery, one that is certainly related to achieving the conventional stage of theory of mind. Yet, in the Community of Minds this is held to be an unacceptable, even immoral, sometimes illegal, act, one that the child must learn to avoid. In the Community of Minds, that is, morality is not a domain separate from Mind, but it is foremost a domain of action and one that must be monitored. Morality itself, of course, is a matter of cultural, and linguistic, definitions, although there are clearly cultural universals, as well as cultural differences, in this area.

The Community of Minds depends inextricably on the capacity to talk about matters of interest to the members of the community, that is, to talk about things that are on members' minds. These may be matters of social relationships (gossip), political affairs, education, the natural world (weather, environmental disasters), economic affairs, literature and art, games and drama, reminiscences about the past, plans for the future, histories, myths, religious doctrine, moral principles, and other matters. In other words, the kinds of matters that are on people's minds in the community are as broad as life itself. In a literate world, some of the discussions of these matters are distributed through journals, newspapers, and books, as well as through electronic and audiovisual media.

Theory-of-mind theorists may protest that these are the various *contents* of belief, not the construct of belief itself (which it is alleged is what the child must attain). But it is precisely the fact that belief is always *about* something that is important; it is not a thing in itself. Children must come to understand the *contents* of belief, not primarily the concept of belief.[1] They acquire knowledge of procedures and actions that lead them to reason about whether someone could or does know about something that differs from one's own state of knowledge about that thing. It is this differentiation of another's states of knowledge from one's own that is the key to success on theory of mind, but the differentiation can only be made on the grounds of particular contents, not on the grounds of belief itself. Making these differentiations is a critical step in development, not only for discerning false belief in theory-of-mind tasks, and I return to discuss it later in the section on entering the Community of Minds.

Many theorists have attempted to place theory of mind in the context of specific human capacities evolved through natural evolutionary processes. For some, this involves a special brain module (e.g., Leslie, 1987), but others see it as a more general ability to deal with the demands of the social world, where social exchange requires vigilance against cheating, for example (Byrne & Whiten, 1988). These ideas are based in the widely accepted proposal that primates in general and humans in particular evolved large brains in response to the complexities of the relations involved in social groups. This is a reasonable assumption, based on the available evidence. However, it primarily accounts for one-to-one, face-to-face interactions and relations. What is specific to human life space is the proliferation of huge collections of individuals across space and time, and the cultural institutions and communicative systems, including language, devised to deal with these conditions. One-on-one relations may be typical of some family situations, but, in general, certainly in modern societies, social interactions involve collaborative and competitive groups of individuals, usually organized into institutions, such as religions, educational systems, economic systems, government systems, and so on within smaller and larger conglomerations.

The point here is that what has been studied in terms of theory of mind is a tiny step into generalizing one-on-one social understanding from the well-known intimate relations within the family to the same kind of relations among unfamiliar others. One might assume that once this kind of generalization is made, the way is open to begin to participate more competently in the concerns of the wider community. But it is possible that the particular one-to-one understanding involved in false belief is not a prerequisite but an outcome of understanding the concerns of the larger community. Conversations about the past between parents and children during the third and fourth years often concern issues of emotions and moral actions (Fivush, 1993, 1994). Parent–child conversations during bookreading also frequently include the interpretation of mental states of story characters. Such discussions may explicitly present the contrast between one character's beliefs and another's and may incorporate the norms of the community with respect to issues such as acting on one's desires and emotions.

These and other concerns of the community are displayed in communal narratives. Many theorists have suggested that language emerged during the prehistory of our species to support narratives, both gossip, talking about other people's stories (Dunbar, 1996), and myth, explaining matters of concern to the whole community (Donald, 1991). In both cases, such narratives incorporate the concerns with motivation, causation, and social distinctions that are embedded in theory of mind. In addition, they incorporate notions of temporality, the representation and manipulation of which is a unique aspect of human society. Complex, historically conscious societies construct elaborate structures for understanding time and its relation to the present. The young child has no access to these ways of thinking of time, but in the course of listening to the community's stories and conversing with its adults, the child finds that they come into focus in much the same way as constructs of mental states (Nelson, 1989, 1996). In the process, the child gains access to the concerns of the Community of Minds.

How to Enter the Community of Minds

The key to the door that opens into the Community of Minds lies in differentiating one's own private view of the world from that of others and joining in the common but variable mind-space there. The key question, then, is "How does that differentiation come about, in particular and in general?" Even as adults, we often assume that other people with whom we are communicating share our beliefs and background knowledge; we are often surprised to find that they do not. The very young child is different only in assuming that everyone has the same knowledge. Usually the way we discover that others' knowledge differs from ours is that they tell us. The core of the claim made here is that the young child learns the same way and thus gradually learns the general principle that people differ; the child also learns to track such differences when there are salient clues to be followed (as in theory-of-mind tasks).

In a complex, modern culture, children are bathed in verbal stuff from the beginning of life and begin to learn how to use pieces of the prevailing language between 1 and 2 years, but it is a few years more before they begin to tune into much of it or to begin to take part in its "mind exchange" system. Members of the community have special ways of talking about the activities of people in the community. They attribute thoughts to others ("he thinks it's a good idea to get out of the stock market now"), claim knowledge ("I know she's in town because I talked to her on the phone yesterday"), state beliefs ("I'm pretty sure it's going to be a long war"), and use mental-state language for many other purposes as well: "We're planning to go to the game on Saturday"; "I guess..."; "Remember when..."; "Imagine that...."

To become a member of the community and enter into its "mind exchange system," children must learn the language of the mind. This is one of the prerequisites that language fulfills. But it is not the only one. Children must be able to understand not only that "think" and "know" and "remember" and so on refer to mental states but also that the propositions that follow these words represent the mental contents of the other (de Villiers & Pyers, 1997). They must become capable of turning someone else's statement about belief into their own mental representation of what the other believes. That is, they must be able to use language as a representational system. These are difficult accomplishments that require several years of experience with language in use.

Beginning Outside the Community

For the first several years of the child's life, all "knowledge" is strictly a private matter; that is, although it is acquired within a social world, its sources are those of individual perceptual mechanisms, primarily vision, supplemented by memory for individual experience, inference mechanisms, and constructive conceptual processes. It is not that the infant is a passive observer; infants actively explore as much as they are enabled to do by motor ability and parental restraints. But they are limited in their information-gathering to what their own perceptual and cognitive powers can glean. This proposition holds regardless of whether one assumes that infants have "built-in" knowledge of systems such as language, the physical world, or theory of mind and how that knowledge may be structured. Such "knowledge," to the extent that it exists and is available to all infants, is nonetheless private to each. It also holds despite the fact that the infant exists in a social world, is in intimate contact with others there, and has ways of communicating, sharing feelings through touch, facial and vocal expressions, and so on. The infant, however, has no way of either giving or receiving information about how she views the world, what she believes about its people, objects, and events, or other matters. Adults around the infant may attempt to read her mind and may even be successful in predicting what she wants and how she feels. But this is a chancy business on both sides.

During the second and third years, the child is able to use some active external mechanisms—imitation and play—to supplement those of observation and manipulation, but the interpretation of the meaning of what she experiences remains a private matter. We can think of the child as using observation to painstakingly construct a mental model of the world around her, but a model all from a single perspective, her own. The difference between this "baby model" and the parent's model is even greater than casual reflection might suggest. The world of the parents is an interpreted one; that is, it is a world of cultural scenes, situations, and artifacts, whose meaning is transparent to the adult, from the very structure and furnishing of the child's home and the appropriate clothing for an infant or child in the resident culture, to the significance of the toys that the child is given and the rituals, such as meals and bedtime, that the child is engaged in. The child's model of the world includes these things, but with only the personal, idiosyncratic meaning that personal babyish experience bestows upon them, in particular their relevance and function for the self.

As the child comes to learn words and receive verbal messages, the perspective of another may come into play. When Mother shouts NO! as the toddler reaches toward the electric socket, the child understands that the adult is opposing her own perspective on the activity. At first, as Fonagy and Target (1997) have argued, the way in which this perspective is perceived by the child may be emotionally disturbing, because, from the private mind view, there is only one reality, that of one's own experience. A mother's emotional reaction to one's actions may be especially frightening because it is merged with one's own disposition and action.

It is important, as Fonagy and Target emphasize, that the child can begin to distinguish the parent's desires and emotions from her own, and beginning language helps in achieving this distinction between the self and the significant other. In turn, this insight may be the beginning of seeing others as having goals different from one's own. Such a dual perspective does not require a two-mind view because the two goals or intentions are part of the representation of the single ongoing situation or scene. Perceiving another's goals does not imply conceiving of another's mind, nor does it imply imagining mother's beliefs as different from one's own. It does not, that is, require meta-representation that is capable of tracking one representation in contrast to another. The conflicting goals are simply part of the same ongoing event. The child would have to get behind the goals to see why Mother is forbidding the child's intended actions in order to put the conflict on a mental rather than a behavioral plane.[2]

Becoming a Participant

In contrast to this view, the beginning of theory of mind is widely held to lie in the achievement of intersubjectivity in infancy, signaling the onset of a concept of intentionality of self and other (e.g., Tomasello, 1999). The milestones in infant development that provide the evidence for this attribution, in particular evidence of shared attention, and their significance for the ensuing phase of first language acquisition, are without doubt of real importance to the developments we are concerned with. However, I doubt that there is a direct route from such primitive intersubjectivity to a full-blown theory of mind. Rather, interaction in joint activities, involving the focus of other and self on the same object, for example, contributes directly to the successful achievements in motoric, communicative, and exploratory activities of the 10- to 12-month period of development. It allows sharing activities with another and taking different roles within the activity, as in feeding. It also allows the child to have a sense of sharing perception and action, while at the same time differentiating the self from the shared. It fosters the move toward associating the sounds of language with shared attention to objects and actions within those activities. It does not, however, require a concept of mind or minds. There is no evidence that children are cognitively tracking anything but the actions of self and other. The same can be said of the reciprocal imitation that is frequently observed (and studied) at this time (Meltzoff & Gopnik, 1993).

As for the somewhat later evidence of interpretation of another's *intention* in action, or in applying words to objects, as in Meltzoff's or Tomasello's work

(Meltzoff & Moore, 1999; Tomasello, 1999), the child's interpretation requires an implicit understanding of means–ends connections in others' as well as one's own actions but does not require attributing mental activity to another. It does not require that the child attribute to the other *thoughts* about a goal.

It is important to be clear here. These developments—shared attention, attributed intentionality, word learning—are important prerequisites for moving toward participation in the Community of Minds. But they are not yet evidence of participating in this community. The theoretical error arises, in my opinion, when they are treated as evidence of children's having some sort of theory of mind, although not yet a successful theory (Baron-Cohen, 2000; Gopnik, Capps, & Meltzoff, 2000). These theories, in different ways, project the same cognitive structures and functions in the infant as are assumed to exist in the older child or adult; thus, the descriptions of the child's accomplishments at 2 years are formulated in the favored cognitive science language of "theory of mind," although that theory lies in the distant future. I refer to this as the "analytic fallacy," whereby the characteristics of a completed structure are attributed to the system in development, for which the components may be quite different (Nelson, 1979, 1996). The general point is that disagreements here rest on interpretations from initial assumptions, not on any empirical evidence for intentional understanding.

In contrast, the claim here is that the understandings and practices of the infant and toddler period serve as background knowledge that enables the child to take part in the ongoing activities of that period, in particular, to learn basic language and thus to move on to the next point in the developmental sequence, when talk about causes and sequences with parents and others leads to encounters with the abstractions of mind talk. The teleology here of "moving on" is not in the child; the focus of the child is on the present, not on learning for the future. In sum, the existence of continuity in development does not justify the attribution of a nascent theory even before the alleged achievement of theory of mind.

Learning the Talk

Representing mental states and actions in language[3] requires abstraction from the real world of experience. This is not to say that mental states have no reality; but it is to say that they are abstract constructs designed to account for what we do mentally, to divide the domain of what we call cognition into convenient pieces for discussion. Like all bits of language, they take their meaning from the agreement within the community that they carve up and express a portion of reality in appropriate ways. For example, we can all commonly agree that we have memories and thus understand one another when a person says, "I remember X." But, going further, to divide up the domain of memory is far more controversial, even with scientific research to back up the divisions, as theoretical disagreements can attest (e.g., Schacter, 1992; Tulving, 1983). The point here is that to enter the Community of Minds, the child must learn the language of abstractions, where referents are matters of communal agreement on shared concepts, not material parts of the observable world. The language of the mind is of course only one aspect of the abstract and complex language of the community.

Considerable research is available on children's acquisition of the lexicon of mental states, especially words for beliefs (*think*, *know*, *guess*) but also words for perception (*see*, *hear*) and emotion (*happy*, *sad*, *angry*). Although the mental-state lexicon is far more extensive and dynamic than current studies generally reflect, the data available have indicated important conclusions about children's mastery of the focal terms (Bartsch & Wellman, 1995; Bretherton & Beeghly, 1982; Furrow, Moore, Davidge, & Chiasson, 1992; Johnson & Maratsos, 1977; Moore, Bryant, & Furrow, 1989; Shaw, 1999). First, children begin to use a variety of mental-state terms as early as 2 years, especially emotional and perceptual terms. Second, at 3 years, most children studied produce the focal cognitive terms *think* and *know* in the course of everyday conversations, at least occasionally. Third, it is not until about 4 years that children appear to use these terms to indicate specific mental states, distinguishing between the meanings of *think* and *know* on the basis of certainty. Fourth, it is not until the early school years that tests of comprehension show clear discrimination among the terms *think*, *know*, and *guess*. And even in the late elementary years, children do not demonstrate understanding of the full range of distinctive meanings of *know* (Booth & Hall, 1995).

This body of research has important implications for children's understanding of cultural concepts of mind that derive from our knowledge of semantics and the process of acquiring abstract word meanings. Many researchers assume that if the child responds appropriately to *think*, for example, in a test situation, that child understands the concept symbolized by the word. There are two problems with this assumption. First, the concepts behind these mental-state terms are invariably complex, with loosely associated meanings and uses, only some of which refer to mental states. They are used in conversation by adults in a variety of ways and contexts. Further, children begin to use the terms in restricted conversational contexts modeled on one or a few adult uses (Shaw, 1999). Second, the acquisition of meaning of abstract terms such as mental-state words is best conceptualized in terms of acquiring meaning from use (Montgomery, 2002; Nelson & Shaw, 2002). This is a gradual process that begins with appropriate uses in contexts where they have been used by adults, but the use by the child is "without meaning"—it is simply pragmatic. Subsequently, this use is extended to other contexts, and other uses by adults flag the attention of the child, who then gradually builds up an inferential understanding of what the term implies. Evidence for this process comes not only from recent research on the acquisition of mental-state terms but also research on other terms, such as temporal and causal relations, that do not have concrete referents (Levy & Nelson, 1994). (For recent evidence of the causal relation between mothers' use of mental-state terms, children's later uses, and their performance on theory-of-mind tasks, see Ruffman, Slade, & Crowe, 2002).

We can conclude that children are attentive to the language of the mind from about 2 to 3 years but that its meanings are obscure at the outset and only gradually become clarified and distinctive. As Dunn (1988) has pointed out, children begin to be curious about people's intentions and emotions and to talk about them with family members from the age of 2 years or so. However, the fact that they talk about these matters, using the words of the mental, does not indicate that they have a concept of mind, much less a *theory* of mind, or even that they have concepts of thinking and knowing. These attributions are, I believe, overinterpretations of the data, based on the simplistic idea that children's language transparently expresses their thoughts and feelings.

The most plausible alternative interpretation is that children are eager to interact with others, others who talk about mental states, thus leading children to the topic. Woolfe, Want, and Siegel (2002) reported an important study of deaf children's delayed acquisition of theory of mind. They compared early sign language learners, who were children of deaf parents, with later sign learners, children of hearing and speaking parents, on pictorial theory-of-mind tasks. Early signers outperformed later signers, and the authors conclude that the critical explanatory factor was social understanding mediated by early experience in conversation. This conclusion is highly consistent with the argument put forth here. That children are interested in talking about what lies behind actions, or why people attribute motives to others, and that they acquire some of the terminology for doing so, is an indication that they have entered a pathway that leads into the larger community of minds. However, it does not mean that they have arrived at that destination.

The following conversation between a 3½-year-old child and her mother, from Shaw's (1999) study of mental-state terms, provides insight into some of the gaps between words and concepts in the process of their acquisition.

Child K, 42 months, Meal Context, with Mother M

K: You know something?

M: What?

(Pause)

K: Let me think

(Pause)

K: What's her name again?

M: What?

K: What's her name again?

M: Who?

K: That girl

M: Who?

K: Don't you remember her?

K: You've seen her before

M: No

K: Yes

M: Where is she?

K: I don't know

M: Oh

K: I don't know her name

K: Somebody has a rocket

K: That can turn into a big rocket

M: Yeah?

K: (nods)

M: Who is this person?

K: I don't know her

M: Where'd you meet her?

K: At our house!

M: At our house?

M: Somebody with a rocket came to our house?

K: Uh huh

M: Was I home for this?

K: (shakes head)

M: No

M: So how would I know who this is?

M: How do you know she had a rocket?

K: Cause she told us

M: Oh, okay

M: Was this Katie?

K: (nods)

M: Oh, okay

Notice that this conversation is about something the child remembers but of which the mother has no knowledge. The child (K) opens the dialogue by asking, "You know something?" This is a purely pragmatic conversational device. She then continues, "let me think"; again, this is a familiar conversational device. She then asks her mother what the name of someone is, and the following turns are efforts to jog the mother's memory, including K's assumption that her mother should know the girl because she's seen her before, which is of course a good clue to knowledge. However, her mother has no clue as to which girl among many she's seen that K has in mind. Then follows the revelation that this person had a rocket "at our house." After four more turns, K acknowledges that mother wasn't home when the rocket episode occurred, and Mother asks, "so how would I know who this is?" In what follows after an irrelevant bit of talk, K acknowledges that she knew about the rocket because the girl told her, again relevant evidence of knowledge. On some basis obscure to us, Mother now "reads K's mind" and guesses the name of the child.

We know from this transcript that K has a reasonably extensive lexicon of cognitive mental-state terms: *know*, *remember*, and *think*. But it is also clear that she has not quite put together how shared knowledge comes into being. She knows that she cannot remember the name and that her mother knows the name, but, in trying to jog her mother's memory, she mentions an episode that the mother could not know about because she was not there. The bottom line here is that knowing about knowing is highly complex and that children who facilely use the language of the mind may have a very incomplete grasp of how real-world experience maps onto the abstract theoretical structure of the concepts they are invoking with their language.

The most important point revealed in this excerpt is that the conversation itself provides evidence for the child about the missing pieces of her concepts of knowing, as the mother feeds back her own ignorance of what the child is trying to uncover. The child is confused about the private and public status of experience-based knowledge, and her mother points this out quite clearly. Indeed, learning the meanings of words for talking about mind-stuff depends entirely on listening to the talk of others on these topics. For this reason, the practice of comprehension—listening, attending, and interpreting—is even more important for the child in this process than expressing one's own thoughts, although the latter is helpful in guiding adults in how to take advantage of the state of the child's knowledge. This point is considered further in the next section.

Representing in Language

Although learning the right words and how they are used in talking about mental processes is helpful in following mind talk, the most important achievement in language for entering the cultural community of minds is facility with language as a representational medium. This point seems to be where misconceptions of the significance of language to theory of mind are most pervasive, and it therefore requires elaboration. Several studies carried out at the City University of New York (CUNY) by my former students have contributed to our understanding of this development, which I will be drawing on in the discussion of representational language. I first want to clarify what we mean by representational language.

Most uses of language by the child up to about 2½ years, during the time when basic vocabulary and simple grammar are being acquired, are highly pragmatic, about the here and now, focused mostly on the interpersonal functions of speech, not on the mathetic, ideational, or cognitive functions. But despite the relative poverty of the 2-year-old's productive and receptive language, parents (at least middle-class Western parents) typically begin addressing fairly complex ideas, descriptions, and explanations in extended passages of speech to their children when they are as young as 18 months to 2 years. Such talk may include reference to sources of knowledge (such as seeing and hearing about), to the differentiation of one's own and other's knowledge and experience (as in the excerpt from K's dialogue), or the distinction between imagined action and real action, and other matters of testimony (Harris, 2001).

These practices have been studied especially in relation to parents' talk about the past in studies of children's emerging memory for experienced events (see Nelson & Fivush, 2004). Two-year-olds typically contribute one or a few words, perhaps a single observed fact, to these conversations, but they often listen attentively as mothers spin out a remembered episode through questions and elaborations (Reese, 2000). What is going on here? The listeners (and not all children are attentive listeners) are entering into the practice of listening, attending, and interpreting extended speech—episodes of the use of language as a representing medium. The words and sentences ideally evoke for both speaker and hearer an event from a different time and place. What is represented may be a remembered real occasion of an interesting experience, an imagined unreality in play, a fictional story, an explanation of a museum exhibit, or any other topic that the parent thinks the child is or should be interested in. In these extended passages, parents, of course, use complex grammatical constructions, abstract words, references to things, places, people, and events that the child has no other knowledge about, and so on. This is the language of the cultural world, the educational world, and the Community of Minds, where learning, knowing, and remembering are as important as, perhaps more important than, predictions and explanations about other people's actions. And, of course, pretense and stories are organized around the very matters that theory of mind measures—what people want, plan, think, and know in relation to what they do, and their emotional states in response to the outcomes of actions.

Bruner (1986) emphasized the distinction between two kinds of thought: paradigmatic and narrative, a distinction that has proved to be useful in analyzing how parents and children talk about events (Nelson, 1996; Tessler & Nelson, 1994). Bruner further pointed out that narrative is composed not only of a sequence of actions but also of intentions and goals, what he calls the landscape of consciousness, in contrast to the landscape of action. The landscape of consciousness is concerned with beliefs and thoughts, possibilities, temporality, motives (e.g., love, revenge, jealousy), emotions (e.g., surprise, outrage, happiness, disappointment), plans, goals, deception, and so on—in other words, the meanings behind the actions, meanings that might be in the minds of one actor but not another.

Over the past 20 years or so, the study of narrative thinking, understanding, and production by children as well as adults has become a focal topic among many developmental psychologists (e.g., Bamberg, 1997). Analyses of children's spontaneous narratives (Miller, Potts, Fung, Hoogstra, & Mintz, 1990; Nelson, 1989), elicited narratives (Fivush, 1994; Plesa, 2001) and story recall (Henseler, 2000) converge on the conclusion that prior to about 5 years of age, children include very little of the landscape of consciousness in their narrative productions, relying instead on the landscape of action, although they usually can report more of the motivations and emotions when prompted and when asked to recall a story that has been read to them. Despite extensive practice at story listening over the years from 3 to 5, most children seem to find the action in their own narratives of "what happened" to them, or in a made-up story, to be self-explanatory and to need little explanation in terms of mindfulness. Even 6-year-olds, when asked to recall the narrative after watching a video based on a version of the Maxi task story in which the motives for moving the desirable object were ambiguous, provided a simple action sequence and did not explain the action in terms of motivations, beliefs, desires, or emotions (Plesa, 2001).

At CUNY, we have become alerted to the possible significance of receptive language competence through finding that receptive language, as measured by standardized tests, related more highly than expressive language to verbal memory for an event, story understanding, narrative productions, and, according to some studies, theory-of-mind tasks. In a study of episodic memory in 3- and 4-year-olds, Walkenfeld (2000) used a clinical evaluation of language, the TELD, which includes measures of expressive and receptive components, to evaluate the relation between language and recall of a complex novel event after a 6-week delay. The study compared the effects of verbal reinstatement midway through the delay period with those of re-enactment of the event and of no interim re-experience. The difference between groups mildly favored the verbal reinstatement condition, but the main story was the influence of language ability on performance. Receptive language, entered as a control variable, was highly significant, overriding group differences. In regression analyses, age was not predictive of recall when entered with language, and receptive rather than expressive language was a significant predictor of both recall and narrative coherence. Episodic or autobiographical memory for a complex event demands connected and extended representations, involving temporal and causal connections, and attributions of personal involvement and actions. These are also the kinds of representations that are required in theory-of-mind studies, although the typical events used in such studies are shorter and less personally involving than events used in memory studies.

Listening to stories requires mastery of the representational language of narrative even more than does episodic memory in that psychological causal factors are usually involved and are either implicit or made explicit through descriptive and explanatory language. Listening to stories is therefore an important passage along the road to the Community of Minds. Indeed, in listening to stories, the child must become expert at hearing and retaining a passage of speech long enough to interpret its meaning as a whole and then to connect it to succeeding passages to understand a whole episode. In other words, story understanding requires the use of language as an *internal* personal representation, one derived from the external presentation. Further, the story is about something that is removed from the here and now, and from the child's own experience, possibly about something that is totally unreal, a product of the imagination of the author. This requires the child to represent in mind a reality that is at odds with the known and present reality.

Our assumption is that mental representations of this kind are not possible without the use of representational language and that therefore children's relative degree of language skill, as measured by standard tests, should be related to their understanding of story themes and characters. As expected, Fontaine's

(2002) study of 4- and 5-year-olds' story understanding and representation with different story genres (fantasy and reality) found that receptive language was a significant predictor for both story understanding and understanding of the relation of fantasy and reality in stories. Henseler's (2000) study required 3- to 5-year-old children to produce a memory narrative of an experience of playing a game with another child. Children were also given a story recall task, a theory-of-mind task, and a standard language development test. Again, receptive language was found to significantly predict narrative productions, game recounting, and story recall. Total language scores, and not age, predicted theory-of-mind performance. Several additional findings bear on theory-of-mind issues. First, no child, even at 5 years, included references to mental states in recounting the game, although during the game the experimenter had used mental-state language extensively (e.g., what do you *think* is in the box?). This is consistent with previous findings that it is not until middle childhood that children usually include mental states in spontaneous narratives. Some children did include mental-state terms in their recall of the story, however, including variants of the terms used by the author; use of mental terms in this context was associated with age, rather than language scores.

In each of these studies, strong relations between receptive language and measures of story understanding and narrative productions were found, despite the fact that all of the data relied on the child's expressive language skills. This discrepancy implies that the variation in comprehension of linguistic representations among children of similar ages accounts for differences in their ability to remember, reason about, or understand complex relations between the matters presented in this form. Put this way, the conclusion appears obvious—language is necessary to perform on language-dependent tasks, such as theory of mind, that rely on verbally presented stories, recall, and answering questions as data. As suggested throughout this chapter, however, I am claiming that the relation is stronger than that and that higher-level cognitive skills require the ability to operate with linguistic representations.

Why might there be a particular relation between receptive language and the achievement of higher levels of the cognitive functions of language? On reflection, it is obvious that the basic requirement of engaging in those higher levels is the ability to represent alternative possibilities; two different states of the world (e.g., the past and the present); two different understandings or experiences, one's own and another's; two different beliefs; an imagined state and a real state. The suggestion here is that this duality of representations, enabling one to hold in mind two conflicting possibilities, becomes possible through the internalization of language as a cognitive representational tool. Initially, this move may come about through talk about the there and then, contrasting a language representation of the past with the present experience of reality, and discussions about past experience are common with children as young as 2 years (Fivush, 1994).

A further move is the contrast of two mental representations, as required in theory-of-mind tasks. In the theory-of-mind literature, these moves have been illustrated as "mind pictures" representing scenes where one person is thinking that another person is thinking (Perner, 1991; Wellman, 1990). Under the present analysis, such pictures are misleading; rather, internal linguistic representations enable the duality of beliefs to be entertained. The proposed sequence of development in brief is as follows: through relevant conversational experiences, the child is exposed to increasingly complex and extended uses of representational language and comes to master the skills, involving short-term memory and semantic interpretation—that are necessary for the comprehension of such linguistically formulated messages. Next, the child becomes capable of repeating to self or others what has been heard on the same or a later occasion. (This is reflected in tests of receptive language. It also appears in the repetition of stories or of other people's experiential reports.) Then the child may begin to use verbal representations both to compose stories or reminiscences (reflected in expressive language) and to serve as internal cognitive representations, enabling the duality of mental representations.

Children of 4 and 5 years have usually learned to "receive" information in story form and to remember it for future telling to a greater extent than they have learned to turn a memory of their own experience into a tale for the telling, including the mental states of the characters involved. Such an asymmetry may help in understanding how children enter into the Community of Minds. What we don't know is what the relation is between the memory for the story and its use in further cognitive operations. Researchers often assume that young children are very good at story understanding and recall, to the extent that they use these modes in research on theory-of-mind and other complex tasks. Such studies should at least include a measure of language competence to determine to what extent children's performance on the task of interest is in fact a product of their skill in story understanding. Certainly, receptive language ability is a factor in story recall and story understanding, as the studies summarized here have shown.

At the very least, good performance on tests of receptive language, even of receptive vocabulary, such as the PPVT, is an indication of extensive experience with talking with adults about complex topics in extended discourse formats. Given the assumption that such discussions are a potent source of information about the relation of mental states to people's actions, as well as many other matters of interest to the Community of Minds, the relation between receptive language and various cognitive tasks becomes very understandable.

Finally, it should be noted that, to the extent that experience with narratives in stories or conversations is found to be critical to children's achievement of theory of mind, the case for beginning with an understanding of the relation of mental states to action among people in stories, that is, people symbolically represented, becomes plausible. It is within a narrative that differential understandings and motivations are highlighted as crucial to understanding the goals and means to achieve them that constitute the plot of a story. This understanding then may

Figure 3. Pathways to the Community of Minds

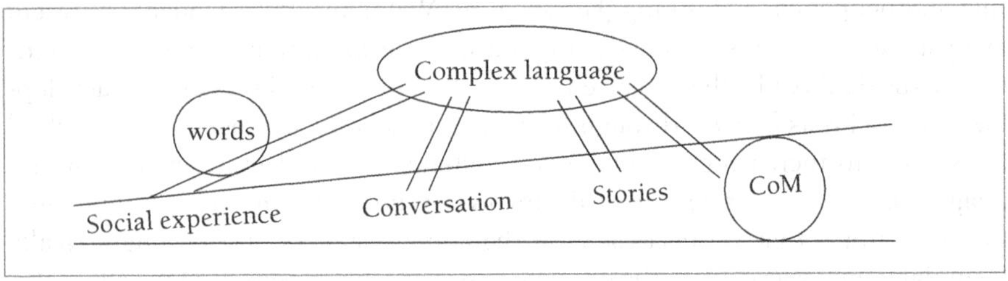

in turn be generalized to singular examples that the child meets on a one-to-one basis in everyday experiential contexts.

Paths Leading Into the Community of Minds

On the basis of the varying evidence and theoretical propositions presented here, I am proposing a different developmental scheme than those sketched earlier to illustrate the theory view (Figure 1) and the generic developmental view (Figure 2). Here (Figure 3), I envision the child moving along an experiential pathway, acquiring new skills, socializing with family members and others, and gradually developing insights into intentional action, reflecting on self, and then breaking through into language. What follows that breakthrough is not an immediate grasp of all that the Community of Minds has to offer, of course, but it significantly broadens experience, especially social experience and experience of the symbolically organized world and of abstract concepts not accessible except through language, such as the concept of mind. Equipped with complex, representational language, the child can participate in story listening, talk about her own experiences in the past and the future, and speculate with others about why things are the way they are, including why people do the things they do. This is the entry point into the Community of Minds, and the community enthusiastically welcomes all the children who enter there, ushering them forthwith into formal schooling, the acquisition of literacy, and complex cultural knowledge, including theories about the world.

Conclusion: Why Language Matters

Language matters because theory of mind is not an individual possession but part of a communally shared belief system about human goals, aspirations, motivations, knowledge systems, and value systems. The cognitive effects of linguistic communication are uniquely human and are set in place during the preschool years in normal development. Those who for one reason or another do not have these experiences (deaf children, autistic children) may linger on the outskirts of the community, able to participate only with difficulty. They may reason their way through certain tasks, but they do so using cognitive skills other than those of the normally developing 5-year-old.

Charles Taylor (1985, p. 263) said it very well: "there are three things that get done in language:

- making articulations, and hence bringing about explicit awareness;
- putting things in public space, thereby constituting public space;
- making the discriminations which are foundational to human concerns, and hence opening us to these concerns."

Although all of these are involved in the child's coming into the consciousness that language allows, it is the last, opening up to the concerns of the community, that I believe is most significant. It takes the child beyond his own private concerns and beliefs and opens up the possibility of understanding the concerns, and thereby the beliefs, of others in the Community of Minds.

QUESTIONS FOR REFLECTION

1. What is the significance of community in cognitive and linguistic development?
2. How do children gradually gain entrance into the community of minds?
3. What role does narrative talking and thinking play in language development?
4. What is the relation between receptive language and the achievement of higher levels of cognitive functions of language?

ACKNOWLEDGMENTS

I would like to acknowledge with grateful appreciation the invaluable contributions of Sylvie Goldman, Sarah Henseler, Daniela Plesa Skwerer, Nechama Presler, Lea Kessler Shaw, and Faye Fried Walkenfeld for the projects and ideas reported in this essay.

NOTES

[1] ToM theorists may argue that it is not possible to understand the contents without the concept of belief. I believe this may be based on a conflation of the language of belief with the concept of belief. The child may learn to use the terms "think" or "know" in complement constructions indicating his or her own state of belief without having the requisite insight that this construction refers to a generalized concept of a kind of mental attitude toward the contents. Consider the following exchange: Mother: "Where are your shoes?" Child: "I know! They're in the closet." Here the child is accessing a belief (where the shoes are) and using the expression "I know." Next: Mother looks in the closet and does not find them, then says: "I think they're in the kitchen—I remember seeing them there." Child: "I'll get them," moving to the kitchen. What in this exchange requires us to assume that the child has a concept of belief, although she both expresses her own belief and interprets the expression (I think) by Mother? The position I take is that the concept of belief may be constructed on the basis of experience of many such exchanges but does not require at the outset the existence of such a concept in order to first compare one's own belief with the conflicting statement of another's

belief state. Indeed, I find it hard to understand how a child could construct the concept of belief without the experience of using language that expresses such differences.

[2] Again, ToM theorists may argue otherwise, but consideration of animal conflicts suggests that simple differences in goals and intentions do not necessarily lead to entertaining the possibility of conflicting mental states. (See Byrne & Whiten, 1988, for discussion of similar issues in regard to other primates.)

[3] The assumption here is that there is no other way to represent them. The contrasting generally accepted assumption that concepts (representations) must be present prior to their appearance in language cannot be right for mental state and many other abstract concepts, as I implicitly argue in what follows.

REFERENCES

Bamberg, M. (Ed.), (1997). *Narrative development: Six approaches.* Mahwah, NJ: Erlbaum.

Baron-Cohen, S. (2000). Theory of mind and autism: a fifteen-year review. In S. Baron-Cohen, H. Tager-Flusberg, & D. J. Cohen (Eds.), *Understanding other minds: Perspectives from developmental cognitive neuroscience* (pp. 3–20). Oxford: Oxford University Press.

Bartsch, K., & Wellman, H. M. (1995). *Children talk about the mind.* New York: Oxford University Press.

Booth, J. R., & Hall, W. S. (1995). Development of the understanding of the polysemous meanings of the mental state verb *know. Cognitive Development, 10,* 529–550.

Bretherton, I., & Beeghly, M. (1982). Talking about internal states: The acquisition of an explicit theory of mind. *Developmental Psychology, 18,* 906–921.

Bruner, J. S. (1986). *Actual minds, possible worlds.* Cambridge, MA: Harvard University Press.

Byrne, R., & Whiten, A. (Eds.). (1988). *Machiavellian intelligence.* Oxford: Oxford University Press.

Chandler, M., Fritz, A., & Hala, S. (1989). Deception as a marker of 2-year-olds', 3-year-olds', and 4-year-olds' early theories of mind. *Child Development, 60,* 1263–1277.

de Villiers, J. G., & Pyers, J. (1997). Complementing cognition: The relationship between language and theory of mind. In E. Hughes, M. Hughes, & A. Greenhill (Eds.), *Proceedings of the 21st Annual Boston University Conference on Language Development* (pp. 136–147). Somerville, MA: Cascadilla Press.

Donald, M. (1991). *Origins of the modern mind.* Cambridge, MA: Harvard University Press.

Dunbar, R. (1996). *Grooming, gossip and the evolution of language.* Boston: Faber & Faber.

Dunn, J. (1988). *The beginnings of social understanding.* Cambridge, MA: Harvard University Press.

Fivush, R. (1993). Emotional content of parent-child conversations about the past. In C. A. Nelson (Ed.), *Memory and affect in development* (Vol. 26, pp. 39–77). Hillsdale, NJ: Erlbaum.

Fivush, R. (1994). Constructing narrative, emotion, and self in parent–child conversations about the past. In U. Neisser & R. Fivush (Eds.), *The remembering self: Construction and accuracy in the self-narrative* (pp. 136–157). New York: Cambridge University Press.

Fonagy, P., & Target, M. (1997). Attachment and reflective function: Their role in self-organization. *Development and Psychopathology, 9,* 679–700.

Fontaine, R. G. (2002). Children's understanding of story: The influence of genre, affect and language. Unpublished Ph.D. dissertation, City University of New York Graduate School, New York.

Frye, D. (1999). Development of intention: The relation of executive function to theory of mind. In P. D. Zelazo, J. W. Astington, & D. R. Olson (Eds.). *Developing theories of intention: Social understanding and self-control* (pp. 119–131). Mahwah, NJ: Erlbaum.

Furrow, D., Moore, C., Davidge, J., & Chiasson, L. (1992). Mental terms in mothers' and children's speech: Similarities and relationships. *Journal of Child Language, 19,* 617–632.

Gopnik, A., Capps, L., & Meltzoff, A. N. (2000). Early theories of mind: What the theory theory can tell us about autism. In S. Baron-Cohen, H. Tager-Flusberg, & D. J. Cohen (Eds.), *Understanding other minds: Perspectives from developmental cognitive neuroscience* (pp. 50–72). Oxford: Oxford University Press.

Gopnik, A., & Wellman, H. (1994). The theory theory. In L. A. Hirschfeld & S. A. Gelman (Eds.), *Mapping the mind* (pp. 257–293). New York: Cambridge University Press.

Harris, P. L. (2000). *The work of the imagination.* Oxford: Blackwell.

Harris, P. L. (2001). Thinking about the unknown. *Trends in Cognitive Science, 5,* 494–498.

Henseler, S. (2000). Young children's developing theory of mind: Person reference, psychological understanding and narrative skill. Unpublished Ph.D. dissertation, City University of New York Graduate Center, New York.

Johnson, C. N., & Maratsos, M. P. (1977). Early comprehension of mental verbs: Think and know. *Child Development, 48,* 1743–1747.

Leslie, A. M. (1987). Pretense and representation: The origins of "theory of mind." *Psychological Review, 94,* 412–426.

Levy, E., & Nelson, K. (1994). Words in discourse: A dialectical approach to the acquisition of meaning and use. *Journal of Child Language, 21*, 367–390.

Meltzoff, A. N., & Gopnik, A. (1993). The role of imitation in understanding persons and developing theories of mind. In S. Baron-Cohen, H. Tager-Flusberg, & D. J. Cohen (Eds.), *Understanding other minds: Perspectives from autism* (pp. 335–366). Oxford: Oxford University Press.

Meltzoff, A. N., & Moore, M. K. (1999). A new foundation for cognitive development in infancy: The birth of the representational infant. In E. K. Scholnick, K. Nelson, S. A. Gelman, & P. H. Miller (Eds.), *Conceptual development: Piaget's legacy* (pp. 53–78). Mahwah, NJ: Erlbaum.

Miller, P. J., Potts, R., Fung, H., Hoogstra, L., & Mintz, J. (1990). Narrative practices and the social construction of self in childhood. *American Ethnologist, 17*, 292–311.

Montgomery, D. E. (2002). Mental verbs and semantic development. *Journal of Cognition and Development, 3*, 357–384.

Moore, C., Bryant, D., & Furrow, D. (1989). Mental terms and the development of certainty. *Child Development, 60*, 167–171.

Nelson, K. (1979). Explorations in the development of a functional semantic system. In W. Collins (Ed.), *Children's language and communication: Minnesota symposium on child psychology* (Vol. 12, pp. 47–81). Hillsdale, NJ: Erlbaum.

Nelson, K. (Ed.). (1989). *Narratives from the crib*. Cambridge, MA: Harvard University Press.

Nelson, K. (1996). *Language in cognitive development: The emergence of the mediated mind*. New York: Cambridge University Press.

Nelson, K., & Fivush, R. (2004). The emergence of autobiographical memory: A social cultural developmental theory. *Psychological Review, 111*, 486–511.

Nelson, K., Henseler, S., & Plesa, D. (2000). Entering a community of minds: A Feminist perspective on theory of mind development. In P. Miller & E. S. Scholnick (Eds.), *Toward a Feminist Developmental Psychology* (pp. 61–83). New York: Routledge.

Nelson, K., Plesa, D., Goldman, S., Henseler, S., Presler, N., & Walkenfeld, F. F. (2003). Entering a community of minds: An experiential approach to "theory of mind." *Human Development, 46*, 24–46.

Nelson, K., & Shaw, L. K. (2002). Developing a socially shared symbolic system. In E. Amsel & J. Byrnes (Eds.), *Language, literacy and cognitive development: The development and consequences of symbolic communication* (pp. 27–58). Mahwah, NJ: Erlbaum.

Oyama, S. (1985). *The ontogeny of information: Developmental systems and evolution*. New York: Cambridge University Press.

Perner, J. (1991). *Understanding the representational mind*. Cambridge, MA: MIT Press.

Plesa, D. (2001). Children's early construals of subjectivity: Understanding the interpretive mind. Unpublished Ph.D. dissertation, City University of New York Graduate School, New York.

Polak, A. & Harris, P. L. (1999). Deception by young children following non-compliance. *Developmental Psychology, 35*, 561–568.

Reese, E. (2000, March). A model of the origins of autobiographical memory. Memory Research Theme Symposium: Memory development: Biological, cognitive and social perspectives. University of Dunedin, New Zealand.

Ruffman, T., Slade, L., & Crowe, E. (2002). The relation between children's and mothers' mental state language and theory-of-mind understanding. *Child Development, 73*, 734–751.

Schacter, D. L. (1992). Understanding implicit memory. *American Psychologist, 47*, 559–569.

Shaw, L. K. (1999). The development of the meanings of "think" and "know" through conversation. Unpublished Ph.D. dissertation, City University of New York Graduate Center, New York.

Sinclair, A. (1996). Young children's practical deceptions and their understanding of false belief. *New Ideas in Psychology, 14*, 157–173.

Taylor, C. (1985). *Philosophy and the human sciences: Philosophical papers*. (Vol. 1). Cambridge: Cambridge University Press.

Tessler, M., & Nelson, K. (1994). Making memories: The influence of joint encoding on later recall. *Consciousness and Cognition, 3*, 307–326.

Tomasello, M. (1999). Having intentions, understanding intentions, and understanding communicative intentions. In P. D. Zelazo, J. W. Astington, & D. R. Olson (Eds.), *Developing theories of intention: Social understanding and self-control* (pp. 63–76). Mahwah, NJ: Erlbaum.

Tulving, E. (1983). *Elements of episodic memory*. New York: Oxford University Press.

Walkenfeld, F. F. (2000). Reminder and language effects on preschoolers' memory reports: Do words speak louder than actions? Unpublished Ph.D. dissertation, City University of New York Graduate School, New York.

Wellman, H. M. (1988). First steps in the child's theorizing about the mind. In J. W. Astington, P. L. Harris, & D. R. Olson (Eds.), *Developing theories of mind* (pp. 64–92). New York: Cambridge University Press.

Wellman, H. M. (1990). *The child's theory of mind*. Cambridge, MA: MIT Press.

Wellman, H. M., & Gelman, S. A. (1992). Cognitive development: Foundational theories of core domains. *Annual Review of Psychology, 43*, 337–375.

Woolfe, T., Want, S. C., & Siegal, M. (2002). Signposts to development: Theory of mind in deaf children. *Child Development, 73*, 768–778.

CHAPTER 18

Vocabulary Processes

William E. Nagy, Seattle Pacific University

Judith A. Scott, University of California, Santa Cruz

This chapter is about vocabulary processes and, in particular, vocabulary acquisition processes. Our focus is on how school children add words to their reading and writing vocabularies and how they learn the meanings of new words.

There continues to be a strong, if not increasing, interest in vocabulary among reading researchers, according to extensive reviews of recent research provided by Beck and McKeown (1991) in Volume II of the *Handbook of Reading Research*, as well as by Baumann and Kameenui (1991) and Ruddell (1994). A similar concern for vocabulary among second-language researchers is evidenced by several recent books (e.g., Coady & Huckin, 1997; Schmitt & McCarthy, 1997). This interest in vocabulary stems in part from the long-standing recognition that vocabulary knowledge strongly influences reading comprehension (Davis, 1944; Anderson & Freebody, 1981). Among practitioners, on the other hand, interest in vocabulary has varied and is currently not especially high. For the last 2 years, the International Reading Association reported on a survey of "hot topics" in literacy research (Cassidy & Wenrich, 1997, 1998). In both years, vocabulary was rated as "cold," the bottom category. This low level of interest reflects an emphasis on instruction that is authentic, meaningful, and integrated, which stands in stark contrast to most traditional practices associated with vocabulary. To many, the word *vocabulary* may suggest a reductionist perspective in which words are learned by memorizing short definitions and sentences are understood in a strictly bottom-up fashion by putting together the meanings of individual words—a picture inconsistent with our current understanding of the reading process.

This piece counters a reductionist perspective on vocabulary in two ways. In the first section of the chapter we discuss the complexity of word knowledge. In the second section we discuss how children gain information about words from context, word parts, and definitions, noting the limitations as well as the potential of each of these sources, and emphasizing the role of metalinguistic awareness in vocabulary learning.

The Complexity of Word Knowledge

Any attempt to understand the processes by which children's vocabularies grow must be based on a recognition of the complexity of word knowledge. Five aspects

This chapter is reprinted from *Handbook of Reading Research* (Vol. 3, pp. 269–284), edited by M.L. Kamil, P.B. Mosenthal, P.D. Pearson, and R. Barr, 2000, Mahwah, NJ: Erlbaum.

of this complexity that have long been recognized by vocabulary researchers are: (a) incrementality—knowing a word is a matter of degrees, not all-or-nothing; (b) multidimensionality—word knowledge consists of several qualitatively different types of knowledge; (c) polysemy—words often have multiple meanings; (d) interrelatedness—one's knowledge of any given word is not independent of one's knowledge of other words; and (e) heterogeneity—what it means to know a word differs substantially depending on the kind of word. We consider these in turn.

Incrementality

Word learning is incremental—it takes place in many steps. In her classic research on early childhood language development, Eve Clark (1973, 1993) provided a detailed picture of how children's knowledge of word meanings is often initially incomplete but, over time, gradually approximates the adult understanding. Likewise, Susan Carey's (1978) seminal work on children's word learning distinguished between quick mapping (i.e., the initial establishment of a partial representation of a word meaning, sometimes on the basis of a single encounter) and extended mapping (i.e., the process of progressive refinement of word knowledge).

The incremental nature of word learning has sometimes been expressed in terms of a linear scale with several points. Dale (1965) proposed four stages: (1) never saw it before; (2) heard it but doesn't know what it means; (3) recognizes it in context as having something to do with...; and (4) knows it well. A recent variation by Paribakht and Wesche (1997) is similar, but adds a fifth point: (5) I can use this word in a sentence.

Although such scales are a great improvement over an all-or-nothing picture of word knowledge, and serve as a useful basis for more sensitive assessments of word knowledge (Paribakht & Wesche, 1997), they are not intended to imply that there are only four or five discrete levels of word knowledge. In a series of experiments, Durso and Shore (1991) found that college undergraduates were able to distinguish between correct and incorrect uses of words, at a rate significantly greater than chance, even for words that they had previously judged not to be real English words at all. These results suggest that even at the lowest levels of word knowledge, within Dale's stage 1, there are measurable differences in word knowledge. At the other end of the scale, in a series of studies of high-quality vocabulary instruction, Beck, McKeown, and their colleagues (Beck, Perfetti, & McKeown, 1982; McKeown, Beck, Omanson, & Perfetti, 1983; McKeown, Beck, Omanson, & Pople, 1985) found that up to 40 instructional encounters with a word (and high-quality instruction at that) do not bring students to a ceiling.

An incremental view of word learning helps explain how a great deal of vocabulary knowledge can be gained incidentally from context, even when individual encounters with words in context are not particularly informative (Schatz & Baldwin, 1986). Several studies have used tests representing multiple levels of word knowledge to measure the amount of word knowledge readers gain when encountering words in natural context (Nagy, Herman, & Anderson, 1985;

Schwanenflugel, Stahl, & McFalls, 1997; Stallman, 1991). If incidental learning from context could lead to only vague knowledge of words, one would expect the benefits of reading to be strongest for the most lenient criteria of word knowledge, and weaker or absent for more stringent criteria. However, in all three of these studies, the amount of word learning observed was not significantly different for different levels of word knowledge.

The research is clear in showing that word learning *can* be incremental—that one's knowledge of a word can grow on the basis of almost infinitesimally small steps. Less is known about the extent to which word learning is *necessarily* incremental—that is, what limits may exist on the amount or type of knowledge that a learner can gain about a word on the basis of any single encounter. Although good instruction is unquestionably more efficient than chance incidental encounters for learning a specific set of words, there is still good reason to believe that there are practical, if not theoretical, limits to how much an individual can learn about a word on any given occasion. Even four instructional encounters of high quality do not lead to a level of word knowledge adequate to measurably improve comprehension of text containing the instructed word (McKeown et al., 1985). Other research on word learning (e.g., Gildea, Miller, & Wurtenberg, 1990) suggests that there are significant limitations on learners' ability to integrate information from multiple sources on any given occasion.

Polysemy

Words often have more than one meaning, and the more frequent a word is in the language, the more meanings it is likely to have. The simple fact that a word can have two or more unrelated meanings (e.g., *bear* meaning animal and *bear* meaning carry) adds substantial cognitive complexity to the task of using a dictionary (Miller & Gildea, 1987). Even more troublesome, at least to the theoretician, is the fact that the multiple meanings of words range from being completely unrelated to being so close that the shade of meaning separating the two may exist only in the mind of a compulsive lexicographer (Anderson & Nagy, 1991). In fact, word meanings are inherently flexible, and always nuanced in some way by the context in which they occur (Green, 1989; Nagy, 1997). The meaning of a word one encounters must be inferred from context, even if the word is already familiar, as in the phrase "a soft distant symphony of rushing wind" (Polacco, 1996, p. 25). In many cases, the required inferences are easy and natural, but figurative language is certainly not without its pitfalls for students (Ortony, Reynolds, & Arter, 1978; Winner, Engel, & Gardner, 1980). If vocabulary instruction is to address this aspect of the complexity of word knowledge, students must not only be taught to choose effectively among the multiple meanings of a word offered in dictionaries, but to expect words to be used with novel shades of meanings.

Multidimensionality

Discussions of the incremental nature of word learning sometimes appear to assume that word knowledge can be expressed in terms of a single dimension. For some purposes, it may be useful to conceptualize word knowledge in terms of a continuum ranging from "none" to "complete." However, it has long been recognized that word knowledge consists of multiple dimensions (Calfee & Drum, 1986; Cronbach, 1942; Kameenui, Dixon, & Carnine, 1987; Richards, 1976). Nation (1990) offered eight aspects of word knowledge: knowledge of the word's spoken form, written form, grammatical behavior, collocational behavior (what other words does this word commonly occur with?), frequency, stylistic register, conceptual meaning, and associations with others words. Other versions of such a list (e.g., Laufer, 1998) distinguish among different types of relationships between words, such as morphological relationships (prefixation and suffixation) and semantic relationships (antonyms, synonyms), and further subcategorize meaning into referential (denotative) and affective (connotative). Graves (1986) distinguished different kinds of word learning tasks—learning new concepts, learning new labels for known concepts, and bringing words into students' productive vocabularies.

Various aspects of word knowledge might be reducible to a single continuum if one could show that there were strong implicational relations between them. However, it is unlikely that there are any absolute constraints governing the order in which different aspects of word knowledge are acquired. Everyday observation suggests that different facets of word knowledge are relatively independent: One student might know the definition for a word but not be able to use it properly in a sentence; another may use the word in seemingly appropriate ways and yet have a misunderstanding of its meaning. One person may recognize a word and yet have no understanding at all of what it means, whereas others (as was demonstrated by Durso and Shore, 1991) may not recall having ever seen a word before and yet have a partial understanding of its meaning.

In a recent study of learners of English as a second language, Schmitt (1998) found that one could not predict on the basis of one aspect of word knowledge what the learner's knowledge of another aspect would be. Thus, word knowledge must be characterized in terms of a number of different aspects which are at least partially independent. Furthermore, each of these is itself likely to be best characterized as a matter of degree.

Interrelatedness

Words are often taught and tested as if they were essentially isolated units of knowledge. Clearly such practice is inconsistent with a constructivist understanding of knowledge that emphasizes the importance of linking what is learned to familiar words and concepts. How well a person knows the meaning of *whale* depends in part on their understanding of *mammal*. A person who already knows the words *hot*, *cold*, and *cool* has already acquired some of the components of the word *warm*, even if the word *warm* has not yet been encountered.

The potential extent of interconnectedness in vocabulary knowledge is underscored by the Landauer and Dumais (1997) simulation of word learning from context. In their simulation, the input was 4.6 million words of text (in samples each about 150 words in length) from an electronic encyclopedia. A multidimensional vector was calculated for each word on the basis of its co-occurrence with other words in the sample texts. The simulation was evaluated by using the knowledge represented in these vectors to take a test of 80 items from the *Test of English as a Foreign Language* (TOEFL), a test commonly used to measure the English proficiency of international students studying in the United States. Interestingly, the Landauer and Dumais model got a score almost identical to the mean of a large sample of applicants to U.S. colleges from non-English-speaking countries.

One of the most striking findings of this study is the fact that as much as three fourths of the learning that resulted from the input of a segment of text was for words that were not even contained in that segment. At first glance, this finding seems counterintuitive. On the other hand, in the case of words obviously related in meaning, it is not difficult to understand how exposure to a text can contribute to one's knowledge of words not in the text. For example, reading a text about weaving might well increase one's understanding of the words *warp* and *woof* even if these words did not occur in the text. In the Landauer and Dumais (1997) simulation, computationally equivalent to a connectionist network, the information about any given word is represented throughout the entire network, and input about any single word can potentially change the configuration of relationships throughout the network. Although one must be cautious in extrapolating from this simulation to human learning, at very least it raises the possibility that the interconnectedness among words in human memory may be far greater than is commonly assumed, and certainly far greater than is represented in dictionary definitions.

Heterogeneity

Another type of complexity in word knowledge is the fact that what it means to know a word depends on what kind of word one is talking about. For example, knowing function words such as *the* or *if* is quite different from knowing terms such as *hypotenuse* or *ion*. The fact that the different dimensions of word knowledge are at least partially independent of each other also means that the same word can require different types of learning from different types of students, depending on what they already know about a word.

Implications of the Complexity of Word Knowledge

The complex picture of word knowledge we have outlined stands in sharp contrast to some of the traditional vocabulary instruction practices still being used in schools, although most of the points we have made have been acknowledged by vocabulary researchers for decades (e.g., Calfee & Drum, 1986; Cronbach, 1942; Richards, 1976). The knowledge that students have for many words is far more complex than could be attained through instruction that relies primarily on definitions. Not only are there too many words to teach them all to students one by one; there is too much to learn about each word to be covered by anything but exceptionally rich and multifaceted instruction. Hence, the complexity of word knowledge further bolsters the argument that much of students' vocabulary knowledge must be gained through means other than explicit vocabulary instruction. In those cases when students are dependent on instruction to learn a word, if they are to truly gain ownership of that word, the instruction must provide multiple and varied encounters with that word (Stahl & Fairbanks, 1986).

Although we believe it is important to recognize that only a small proportion of words that students learn can be covered in explicit vocabulary instruction, we want to stress an even more basic point: that knowing a word cannot be identified with knowing a definition. This point was argued at length by Anderson and Nagy (1991) in Volume II of the *Handbook of Reading Research*. Here we want to emphasize the point that word knowledge is primarily procedural rather than declarative, a matter of "knowing how" rather than "knowing that." Admittedly, there is a declarative component to at least some types of vocabulary knowledge. This seems especially true in the realm of technical or content-specific vocabulary; for example, if someone is not able to explain what *carbon dioxide* is, it is questionable that he or she knows the meaning of the word. On the other hand, for much nontechnical vocabulary, it may be more useful to conceptualize word knowledge as being primarily procedural. That is, knowing a word means being able to do things with it: To recognize it in connected speech or in print, to access its meaning, to pronounce it—and to be able to do these things within a fraction of a second. None of these processes is anything like remembering a verbal definition. In most cases, knowing a word is more like knowing how to use a tool than it is like being able to state a fact. Word knowledge is applied knowledge: A person who knows a word can recognize it, and use it, in novel contexts, and uses knowledge of the word, in combination with other types of knowledge, to construct a meaning for a text.

Metalinguistic Demands of Word Learning

In traditional vocabulary instruction, students spend much of their time learning definitions (Watts, 1995). Such instruction is inconsistent with current understandings of the learning process. In the previous section of this chapter, we have outlined the dimensions of word knowledge that are rarely conveyed adequately in definitions. Another problem with memorizing definitions is the passive nature of the role it assigns to students. Teaching students new words by giving them definitions is the antithesis of a constructivist approach to learning.

If students are to take an active role in word learning, and assume increasing responsibility for their own vocabulary growth, they need at least some information about the nature of word knowledge and the processes by which it is acquired. That is, they need metacognitive and metalinguistic ability in the realm of word learning. In this section of the chapter, we describe some of the specific types of metalinguistic abilities that contribute to word learning.

Metalinguistic ability is the ability to reflect on and manipulate the structural features of language (Tunmer, Herriman, & Nesdale, 1988). It can be understood as a subcategory of metacognition, that is, the awareness of and control over one's cognitive processes. Recently, much attention has been devoted to a particular kind of metalinguistic ability, phonemic awareness (i.e., the ability to reflect on and manipulate phonemes, the individual units of sound out of which spoken words are constructed). However, other types of metalinguistic awareness, such as morphological awareness and syntactic awareness, are also believed to play an important role in reading (Carlisle, 1995; Tunmer et al., 1988; Tunmer, Nesdale, & Wright, 1987; Warren-Leubecker, 1987; Willows & Ryan, 1986).

A number of vocabulary researchers (e.g., Anderson & Nagy, 1992; Baumann & Kameenui, 1991; Graves, 1986) have held up the idea of "word awareness" or "word consciousness" as an important goal of vocabulary instruction. However, the exact nature of such awareness has seldom been explicated. We believe that word awareness, like word knowledge, is a complex and multifaceted construct, and that there are many ways in which students' awareness of language impacts their word learning. Understanding the metalinguistic demands of the vocabulary-related tasks students encounter in school provides insight into the surprising difficulties students often experience with these tasks.

Metalinguistic Awareness and Word Parts

The importance of phonemic awareness has been highlighted in a growing body of research on learning to read. In an alphabetic language like English, in which letters generally map onto phonemes, it is crucial that children are able to segment spoken words into phonemes and learn the mappings between these phonemes and the letters that represent them.

Recently, however, the contribution of morphological awareness to reading has drawn the attention of some researchers. Morphemes are meaningful word parts; for example, the word *walks* can be divided into two morphemes, *walk* and *s*. In those places where English orthography deviates from the phonemic principle, it is often in the direction of giving consistent representations to morphemes. For example, *ed* is pronounced differently in the words *helped*, *poured*, and *pleaded*. The less regular relationship between spelling and sound allows for a more consistent link from spelling to meaning. Only by noticing the shared morpheme in *sign* and *signature* can one make any sense of the spelling of the former. The fact that many of the apparent irregularities in English spelling are motivated by morphological relationships suggests that awareness of these relationships may contribute to spelling and reading ability. And, in fact, it has been found that morphological awareness makes a significant contribution to reading ability, even when phonemic awareness has been taken into account (Carlisle, 1995; Carlisle & Nomanbhoy, 1993). Knowledge of morphology is likewise correlated with reading ability into high school (Nagy, Diakidoy, & Anderson, 1993).

It is hard to overstate the importance of morphology in vocabulary growth. Nagy and Anderson (1984) estimated that about 60% of the new words a student encounters in reading are analyzable into parts that give substantial help in figuring out their meaning. Anglin's (1993) study of children's vocabulary growth showed that between first and fifth grade, the number of root words known by children in his study increased by around 4,000 words. In the same time period, the number of derived (prefixed or suffixed) words known by students increases by about 14,000 words. There is a veritable explosion in children's knowledge of derived words, especially between third and fifth grades. As Anglin noted, the bulk of this increase appears to reflect morphological problem solving, that is, interpreting new words by breaking them down into their component morphemes.

There is reason to believe that effective use of morphology in word learning depends on metalinguistic sophistication that continues to develop through high school. Most children presumably achieve the basic morphological insight—that longer words can often be broken down into shorter words or pieces that give clues to their meanings—before fourth grade (Anglin, 1993; Tyler & Nagy, 1989). However, word structure in English is complex, and there is development in children's knowledge of word formation processes at least through high school (Nagy et al., 1993; Nagy & Scott, 1990; Tyler & Nagy, 1989).

English and Spanish share many cognates—word pairs such as English *tranquil* and Spanish *tranquilo* that are similar in spelling, pronunciation, and meaning. Recognizing such relationships must depend on abilities similar to those required to recognize morphological relationships in English. Many pairs of morphologically related words in English likewise involve changes in spelling and pronunciation as well as shifts in meaning—for example, *divide/division*, *sane/sanity*, *combine/combination*, *respond/responsible*. Hancin-Bhatt and Nagy (1994) found that Spanish–English bilingual students' ability to recognize such relations increased far more dramatically between fourth and eighth grade than did their vocabulary knowledge in either Spanish or English. These results suggest that the ability to see morphological relationships that are partially obscured by changes in spelling and pronunciation may depend on metalinguistic sensitivities that develop, or at least increase substantially, after fourth grade.

It should also be noted that some aspects of morphological knowledge are closely related to syntactic awareness. In particular, learning the meanings of derivational suffixes (e.g., *-tion*, *-ness*, *-ly*) requires reflecting on the syntactic role of the suffixed word in the sentence (see Nagy et al., 1993).

Not surprisingly, there are differences of opinion about the contribution of morphological knowledge to reading and vocabulary growth. Some (e.g., Nation, 1990) note the irregularities of English morphology (what does *casualty* have to do with *casual*, or *emergency* with *emerge*?) and suggest that students should only consider morphological clues after they have first used context to make a hypothesis about the meaning of a word. However, the vast majority of words composed of more than one morpheme are semantically transparent—that is, their meanings are largely predictable on the basis of the meanings of their parts (Nagy & Anderson, 1984). The fact that some words (like *casualty*) are irregular indicates, not that word parts are useless as clues, but that readers must be strategic and flexible in their use of potential sources of information about words.

Metalinguistic Awareness and Use of Context

Context and morphology (word parts) are the two major sources of information immediately available to a reader who comes across a new word. Effective use of context, like effective use of morphology, requires some level of metalinguistic awareness.

Tunmer and his colleagues (Gough & Tunmer, 1986; Tunmer, 1990; Tunmer et al., 1988) argued that syntactic awareness (i.e., the ability to reflect on and manipulate the order of words in a sentence) contributes to reading ability in at least two ways. First of all, developing one's reading vocabulary depends on both phonological recoding and context, because phonological recoding alone cannot always uniquely determine the pronunciation of a word; context is sometimes necessary to determine which of several possible sounds a letter may represent. Effective use of context is, in turn, hypothesized to rely on syntactic awareness. Second, syntactic awareness may help the reader monitor comprehension.

Gottardo, Stanovich, and Siegel (1996), on the other hand, claimed that syntactic awareness does not make an independent contribution to reading, above and beyond the contribution represented by short-term, phonological memory. That is, correlations between reading difficulty and deficient syntactic awareness may arise as epiphenomena of deficiencies in phonological processing (p. 563). Although not denying the importance of phonological processing in reading difficulties, we believe that several types of evidence suggest a direct link between syntactic awareness and reading comprehension.

First of all, syntactic awareness training has been shown to improve reading comprehension (Kennedy & Weener, 1974; Weaver, 1979). Likewise, training studies in the use of context (e.g., Buikema & Graves, 1993; Jenkins, Matlock, & Slocum, 1989; see Kuhn & Stahl, 1998, for a review) have resulted in increases in children's ability to learn words. The relative brevity of most such interventions makes it likely that the benefits reflect increased metalinguistic and metacognitive awareness rather than gains in short-term phonological memory.

Second, it could be argued that the verbal working memory task used by Gottardo et al. (1996) includes a component of metalinguistic awareness. Subjects were asked to make true–false judgments about simple statements (e.g., fish swim in the sky), and their score on these judgments was incorporated into the verbal working memory score. After listening to a set of sentences, they were asked to recall the final word of each sentence in the set. To do this, subjects must pay attention to the surface form of the sentence, rather than its meaning, a task that requires conscious attention to word order, that is, syntactic awareness.

Third, there is evidence that the contribution of syntactic awareness and other components of metalinguistic awareness to reading comprehension, relative to that of phonological awareness, increases with grade level (Roth, Speece, Cooper, & De la Paz, 1996).

The most convincing evidence that syntactic awareness contributes to effective use of context comes from examining the protocols of students attempting to infer the meanings of novel words from context. In Werner and Kaplan's (1952) classic study of inferring word meanings from context, children were given a series of sentences containing a nonsense word and asked to infer its meaning. Here are the responses from an 11-year-old boy (p. 16; the word *hudray* was intended to mean "grow" or "increase"):

> Sentence 1: If you eat well and sleep well you will hudray.
>
> Response: Feel good.
>
> Sentence 2: Mrs. Smith wanted to hudray her family.
>
> Response: Mrs. Smith wanted to make her family feel good.
>
> Sentence 3: Jane had to hudray the cloth so that the dress would fit Mary.
>
> Response: Jane makes the dress good to fit Mary so Mary feels good.

These responses show that this child is willing to ignore the syntactic structure of the sentences (especially sentence 3) in order to maintain his original hypothesis about the word's meaning. McKeown's (1985) study of high- and low-ability readers learning from context likewise included examples of responses that appear to reflect lack of attention to the syntactic role of the target word in the sentence.

Does use of context to learn the meanings of new words always require metalinguistic awareness? Presumably not; the rapid vocabulary acquisition of very young children takes place at an age when many aspects of metalinguistic awareness are not measurably present. However, a distinction must be made between incidental learning of word meanings from context and deriving word meanings. The latter process is usually examined by asking students to come up with, or select, an appropriate meaning for an unfamiliar word with the context available. Such a task is likely to be more metacognitively and metalinguistically demanding than incidental word learning. This may account for the fact that studies of truly incidental word learning have often found no significant effects of verbal ability (e.g., Nagy, Anderson, & Herman, 1987; Nagy et al., 1985; Stahl, 1989; Stallman, 1991), whereas studies of deriving word meaning have generally found large ability effects (e.g., Jenkins, Stein, & Wysocki, 1984; Daneman & Green, 1986; McKeown, 1985; Sternberg & Powell, 1983).

The research on learning words from context clearly documents the fact that chances of learning very much about a word from any single encounter with that word in natural context are very slim (Beck, McKeown, & McCaslin, 1983; Nagy et al., 1987; Schatz & Baldwin, 1986). It is extremely important for teachers to recognize that although context may be a "natural" means of word learning, it is not especially effective in the short run. Likewise, it is important for students to have realistic expectations about the amount of information they can gain from context. Training students on artificially helpful contexts may actually decrease their effectiveness at using the contextual clues available in natural text (Kranzer, 1988).

Metalinguistic Awareness and the Use of Definitions

The chief strength of definitions is that they provide explicit information about word meanings that is normally only implicit in context. If you want a student to know what a particular word means, explaining it is unquestionably more effective than waiting for the student to encounter it numerous times in context.

One of the chief weaknesses of definitions is their failure to provide information about usage that is accessible to school children. Miller and Gildea (1987) studied sentences children generated when given definitions of unfamiliar words, and concluded that this widely used task, although it reveals interesting things about children's processing of definitions, is pedagogically useless. Children's difficulty with this task may stem in part from the often convoluted language of definitions, but even clearly written definitions do not guarantee success. McKeown (1993) carefully revised definitions to make them both more accurate and more clear to students and found that the revised definitions were significantly superior to their original dictionary counterparts in terms of students' ability to apply knowledge of their meanings. There was also an effect on usage: Only 25% of the sentences generated from the original definitions were judged acceptable, whereas 50% of the sentences generated from the revised definitions were acceptable. This is a substantial increase, but it is also a striking demonstration of the fact that even definitions of very high quality are often inadequate as sources of information on usage.

Students sometimes have trouble extracting even a general idea of the meaning of a word from a definition (Scott & Nagy, 1997). Some of the difficulty may stem from lack of familiarity with the conventions of traditional definitions, but changing the format and style of definitions does not necessarily increase their usefulness to students (Fischer, 1990, 1994; Scott & Nagy, 1997). A bigger problem appears to be the metacognitive and metalinguistic demands of using definitions.

Scott and Nagy (1997), following up on Miller and Gildea's (1987) study, found that the difficulty experienced by children in interpreting definitions was primarily due to their failure to take the syntax, or structure, of definitions into account. Their errors could be best characterized as selecting a salient fragment of the definition as representing the meaning of the whole word.

There are two metalinguistic dimensions to these errors. One is a lack of sensitivity to syntactic structure. In analyzing think-aloud protocols of children attempting to integrate information from definitions with sentences containing the word defined, Scott (1991) found a common problem was failure to take part of speech into account. It wasn't clear whether the failure was in the analysis of the sentence, or in the analysis of the definition, but lack of attention to syntax was obviously a major factor.

Another aspect of metalinguistic awareness involved in children's understanding of definitions has to do with their concept of definition. Fischer's (1990; 1994) investigation of German high school students' use of bilingual dictionary definitions suggested that the students approached the task with the expectation of finding simple synonyms. It may be natural for students of a second language as similar to their first as English is to German to expect one-to-one mappings between words. Language instruction may contribute to such expectations. However, true synonyms are rare, both within and between languages.

The Concept of Word

We have just described some of the ways that metalinguistic awareness contributes to students' independent word learning—their use of word parts, context, and definitions. However, metalinguistic awareness contributes to vocabulary learning at an even more fundamental level. Almost any conceivable vocabulary activity requires children to talk and think about words and their meanings; that is, it presupposes the metalinguistic concept of word. This concept is more complex and more problematic than is commonly recognized. In fact, research on the acquisition of this concept suggests that, even in the middle elementary grades, it cannot be taken completely for granted.

Roberts (1992) documented the gradual nature of children's development of the concept of *word*. Five-year-old preschoolers have trouble dissociating a word from its referent; when asked which is the bigger word, *caterpillar* or *dog*, they will usually answer *dog*. In Roberts's study, even third-grade students were not all at ceiling in her measures of their understanding of the concept of word.

Bowey and Tunmer (1984) pointed out that there are three requirements for full awareness of the concept of word: (a) awareness of the word as a unit of language, (b) awareness of the word as an arbitrary phonological label, and (c) comprehension of the metalinguistic term *word*. In a review of research on metalinguistic awareness, Gombert (1992) argued that there is no clear evidence for the existence of these abilities before the age of 7 years (p. 80). Likewise, there is evidence that some of these requirements are not fully present in children up to the age of at least 10. Piaget (1926) claimed that children did not recognize words as a simple sign (i.e., as an arbitrary label) until the age of 9 or 10. Berthoud-Papandropolou (1980; cited in Gombert, 1992), investigating children's ability to segment sentences into words, concluded that children younger than 11 did not consistently reach 100% accuracy.

Understanding the Function of Vocabulary in Decontextualized Language

The language young children most commonly experience is contextualized—that is, it is language about, and embedded in, a shared context. In a face-to-face conversation, the speakers share a physical context, use gesture and intonation, and make many assumptions about shared knowledge, experiences, and beliefs. They are able to communicate effectively in words that would not necessarily be understood by someone who had access only to a transcript of the conversation. Written language—and especially language written for an audience not present and not personally known to the writer—tends to be decontextualized; that is, the success of the communication relies more heavily on the language itself, and less on shared knowledge or context (Snow, 1991, 1994). What contextualized language accomplishes through gesture, intonation, and allusions to shared knowledge and experiences, decontextualized language must accomplish primarily through precision in choice of words (Chafe & Danielewicz, 1987). This is one of the reasons why written language, which is typically decontextualized, tends to use a far richer vocabulary than oral language, which is typically contextualized (Hayes, 1988).

Not all oral language is contextualized. Storytellers use language to create a world distinct from the here-and-now context, in which the language alone carries most of the communicative burden. But many children, especially if they have not been read to very much, may come to school having had relatively little experience with decontextualized language. Not surprisingly, facility with decontextualized language is related to children's reading ability (Snow, 1991, 1994; Snow, Cancino, Gonzales, & Shriberg, 1989).

Because decontextualized language contains richer vocabulary, exposure to such language is important for children's vocabulary growth. However, we would like to suggest that children's vocabulary growth is benefited not just by exposure to decontextualized language, but by an appreciation of the role that vocabulary plays in such language. Precision of word choice is seldom crucial in everyday conversation, but it is the primary communicative tool of the writer. The motivation to learn the richer vocabulary of decontextualized language may depend on a student's feel for the difference between the communicative strategies of speakers and writers. Scott, working with a group of teacher-researchers, found that conscious attention to words and word choice helped students' writing, led to critical analysis of authors' writing, and changed the way teachers taught both reading and writing (Scott, Asselin, Henry, & Butler, 1997; Scott, Blackstone, Cross, Jones, Skobel, Wells, & Jensen, 1996; Scott, Butler, & Asselin, 1996; Scott & Wells, 1998). Research on the long-term impact of such instruction on students' vocabulary growth is still needed.

Conclusion

Any type of learning, if examined closely enough, looks so complex that one wonders how children can do it at all. In this chapter, we have tried to convey some of the complexity of the processes involved in vocabulary acquisition.

For many children, of course, vocabulary growth appears to proceed with astonishing ease and rapidity. Beck and McKeown (1991), comparing previously published figures, estimated that average children learn words at a rate of something like 2,500 to 3,000 words a year. More conservative accounts put the figure at 1,000 words a year (Goulden, Nation, & Read, 1990; D'Anna, Zechmeister, & Hall, 1991). We have argued elsewhere at length (Anderson & Nagy, 1992; Nagy, 1998) why we consider these latter estimates unrealistically low. Anglin (1993) conducted a major study of children's vocabulary growth between first and fifth grade that helped clarify the nature of the differences between conflicting estimates. Given a conservative definition of vocabulary—counting only root words—Anglin found a rate of growth identical to that reported by Goulden et al. (1990) and D'Anna et al. (1991). However, using a more inclusive concept of "psychologically basic vocabulary"—including, for example, idioms and derived words for which there was no evidence that children used morphological analysis—Anglin (1993) arrived at an estimate in the range suggested by Beck and McKeown (1991). In their commentary on Anglin's work, Miller and Wakefield (1993) argued that Anglin's figures should be doubled.

Regardless of exactly where the truth lies within this range of estimates, we are left with a paradox. At least some children learn 2,000 or more new words per year, most of these apart from explicit instruction. Is the complexity and difficulty of the vocabulary acquisition processes presented in this chapter illusory?

We believe not. The high rates of vocabulary growth seen in many children occur only through immersion in massive amounts of rich written and oral language. Students who need help most in the area of vocabulary—those whose home experience has not given them a substantial foundation in the vocabulary of literate and academic English—need to acquire words at a pace even faster than that of their peers, but by no means do they always find this process easy or automatic.

Vocabulary researchers concerned with second language learning have argued that "natural" vocabulary acquisition is simply not efficient enough to produce the desired rates of learning. Natural context is not an especially rich source of information about word meanings. If there are particular words one wants a student to learn, free reading is perhaps the least effective means available. However, presenting students with more concentrated information about words introduces another set of difficulties. We have outlined two major categories of such difficulties in this chapter. The first is the complexity of word meanings. Definitions, the traditional means of offering concentrated information about words to students, do not contain the quantity or quality of information that constitutes true word knowledge. Students can gain some word knowledge from definitions, but generally only if they are given other types of information about the word (e.g., examples of how it is used) and opportunities to apply this information in meaningful tasks (Stahl, 1986; Stahl & Fairbanks, 1986). Some types of words (e.g., verbs and abstract nouns) may be more difficult to learn from definitions than others (e.g., concrete nouns).

A second major type of difficulty is the metalinguistic sophistication that is presupposed by most vocabulary-related school tasks. Vocabulary activities at every grade level require metalinguistic abilities and awareness that cannot be taken for granted on the part of students. In the early elementary grades, even fundamental concepts about words as units of form and meaning are still in the process of being consolidated. Independent word learning strategies rely on metalinguistic knowledge that is still developing during the upper elementary grades.

A recent study on the development of phonemic awareness (Scarborough, Ehri, Olson, & Fowler, 1998) shows that this aspect of metalinguistic awareness, which impacts the earliest stages of formal reading instruction, does not appear to reach a ceiling among college students. Given the complex nature of word knowledge, we feel safe in predicting that the various aspects of metalinguistic awareness involved in word learning will not be fully present even in many adults.

We believe that the role of metalinguistic awareness in vocabulary growth offers a promising area for future research. Although there is substantial research support for the broad outlines of the picture of vocabulary processes that we have drawn in this chapter, there are also large areas of uncharted territory. Roberts's (1992) article on children's development of the concept of word is one of the few examples of research explicitly addressing the metalinguistic foundations of vocabulary learning in the literature on literacy research. No one, to our knowledge, has addressed the effects of varying levels of metalinguistic awareness on children's ability to profit from different types of vocabulary instruction or from different types of information about words. There is also need for research examining the effects of instruction that fosters word consciousness on students' vocabulary growth.

If students are to become active and independent learners in the area of vocabulary, they need to have some understanding of the territory that they are operating in. Such an understanding depends on explanations by teachers who themselves have some grasp of the complexity of word knowledge. Students' understanding of words and of the word learning process also depends on the type of vocabulary instruction they experience. A diet of synonyms and short glossary definitions runs the danger of failing to produce usable knowledge of those words, and creates simplistic beliefs that can interfere with future word learning. The quality of vocabulary instruction must therefore be judged, not just on whether it produces immediate gains in students' understanding of specific words, but also on whether it communicates an accurate picture of the nature of word knowledge and reasonable expectations about the word learning process.

QUESTIONS FOR REFLECTION

1. What are the potential dangers of a traditional mode of vocabulary instruction in which teachers assign definitions and students learn them?
2. How does morphological and syntactic awareness contribute to vocabulary growth?
3. How does decontextualized language improve children's vocabulary growth?

REFERENCES

Anderson, R. C., & Freebody, P. (1981). Vocabulary knowledge. In J. Guthrie (Ed.), *Comprehension and teaching: Research reviews* (pp. 77–117). Newark, DE: International Reading Association.

Anderson, R. C., & Nagy, W. (1991). Word meanings. In R. Barr, M. Kamil, P. Mosenthal, & P. D. Pearson (Eds.), *Handbook of reading research* (Vol. II, pp. 690–724). White Plains, NY: Longman.

Anderson, R. C., & Nagy, W. (1992). The vocabulary conundrum. *American Educator, 16*, 14–18, 44–47.

Anglin, J. M. (1993). Vocabulary development: A morphological analysis. *Monographs of the Society of Research in Child Development*, Serial No. 238, Vol. 58, No. 10.

Baumann, J. F., & Kameenui, E. J. (1991). Research on vocabulary: Ode to Voltaire. In J. Flood, J.

Jensen, D. Lapp, & J. Squire (Eds.), *Handbook of research on teaching the English language arts* (pp. 604–632). New York: Macmillan.
Beck, I., & McKeown, M. (1991). Conditions of vocabulary acquisition. In R. Barr, M. Kamil, P. Mosenthal, & P. D. Pearson (Eds.), *Handbook of reading research* (Vol. II, pp. 789–814). White Plains, NY: Longman.
Beck, I., McKeown, M., & McCaslin, E. (1983). All contexts are not created equal. *Elementary School Journal, 83*, 177–181.
Beck, I., Perfetti, C., & McKeown, M. (1982). Effects of long-term vocabulary instruction on lexical access and reading comprehension. *Journal of Educational Psychology, 74*, 506–521.
Bowey, J., & Tunmer, W. E. (1984). Development of children's understanding of the metalinguistic term word. *Journal of Educational Psychology, 76*(3), 500–512.
Buikema, J., & Graves, M. (1993). Teaching students to use context cues to infer word meanings. *Journal of Reading, 36*, 450–457.
Calfee, R. C., & Drum, P. (1986). Research on teaching reading. In M. C. Wittrock (Ed.), *Handbook of research on teaching* (pp. 804–849). New York: Macmillan.
Carey, S. (1978). The child as word learner. In M. Halle, J. Bresnan, & G. Miller (Eds.), *Linguistic theory and psychological reality* (pp. 264–293). Cambridge, MA: MIT Press.
Carlisle, J. (1995). Morphological awareness and early reading achievement. In L. Feldman (Ed.), *Morphological aspects of language processing* (pp. 189–209). Hillsdale, NJ: Lawrence Erlbaum Associates.
Carlisle, J., & Nomanbhoy, D. (1993). Phonological and morphological awareness in first graders. *Applied Psycholinguistics, 14*, 177–195.
Cassidy, J., & Wenrich, J. (1997). What's hot, what's not for 1997. *Reading Today, 14*(4), 34.
Cassidy, J., & Wenrich, J. (1998). What's hot, what's not for 1998. *Reading Today, 15*(4), 1, 28.
Chafe, W., & Danielewicz, J. (1987). Properties of spoken and written language. In R. Horowitz & S. J. Samuels (Eds.), *Comprehending oral and written language* (pp. 83–113). San Diego, CA: Academic Press.
Clark, E. V. (1973). What's in a word? On the child's acquisition of semantics in his first language. In T. E. Moore (Ed.), *Cognitive development and the acquisition of language* (pp. 65–110). New York: Academic Press.
Clark, E. V. (1993). *The lexicon in acquisition*. Cambridge: Cambridge University Press.
Coady, J., & Huckin, T. (1997). *Second language vocabulary acquisition*. Cambridge: Cambridge University Press.
Cronbach, L. J. (1942). An analysis of techniques for diagnostic vocabulary testing. *Journal of Educational Research, 36*, 206–217.
D'Anna, C. A., Zechmeister, E. B., & Hall, J. W. (1991). Toward a meaningful definition of vocabulary size. *Journal of Reading Behavior, 23*, 109–122.
Dale, E. (1965). Vocabulary measurement: Techniques and major findings. *Elementary English, 42*, 82–88.
Daneman, M., & Green, I. (1986). Individual differences in comprehending and producing words in context. *Journal of Memory and Language, 25*, 1–18.
Davis, F. B. (1944). Fundamental factors in reading comprehension. *Psychometrika, 9*, 185–197.
Durso, F. T., & Shore, W. J. (1991). Partial knowledge of word meanings. *Journal of Experimental Psychology: General, 120*, 190–202.
Fischer, U. (1990). *How students learn words from a dictionary and in context*. Unpublished doctoral dissertation, Princeton University.
Fischer, U. (1994). Learning words from context and dictionaries: An experimental comparison. *Applied Psycholinguistics, 15*, 551–574.
Gildea, P., Miller, G., & Wurtenberg, C. (1990). Contextual enrichment by videodisk. In D. Nix & R. Spiro (Eds.), *Cognition, education, and multimedia: Exploring ideas in high technology* (pp. 1–29). Hillsdale, NJ: Lawrence Erlbaum Associates.
Gombert, J. (1992). *Metalinguistic development*. Chicago, University of Chicago Press.
Gottardo, A., Stanovich, K., & Siegel, L. (1996). The relationships between phonological sensitivity, syntactic processing, and verbal working memory in the reading performance of third grade children. *Journal of Experimental Child Psychology, 63*, 563–582.
Gough, P., & Tunmer, W. E. (1986). Decoding, reading, and reading ability. *Remedial and Special Education, 7*, 6–10.
Goulden, R., Nation, P., & Read, J. (1990). How large can a receptive vocabulary be? *Applied Linguistics, 11*, 341–363.
Graves, M. F. (1986). Vocabulary learning and instruction. In E. Z. Rothkopf & L. C. Ehri (Eds.), *Review of research in education* (Vol. 13, pp. 49–89). Washington, DC: American Educational Research Association.
Green, G. M. (1989). *Pragmatics and natural language understanding*. Hillsdale, NJ: Lawrence Erlbaum Associates.
Hancin-Bhatt, B., & Nagy, W. (1994). Lexical transfer and second language morphological development. *Applied Psycholinguistics, 15*, 289–310.
Hayes, D. (1988). Speaking and writing: Distinct patterns of word choice. *Journal of Memory and Language, 27*, 572–585.
Jenkins, J. R., Matlock, B., & Slocum, T. A. (1989). Two approaches to vocabulary instruction: The teaching of individual word meanings and practice in deriving word meaning from context. *Reading Research Quarterly, 24*, 215–235.
Jenkins, J. R., Stein, M. L., & Wysocki, K. (1984). Learning vocabulary through reading. *American Educational Research Journal, 21*, 767–787.

Kameenui, E. J., Dixon, D. W., & Carnine, R. C. (1987). Issues in the design of vocabulary instruction. In M. G. McKeown & M. E. Curtis (Eds.), *The nature of vocabulary acquisition* (pp. 129–145). Hillsdale, NJ: Lawrence Erlbaum Associates.

Kennedy, D., & Weener, P. (1974). Visual and auditory training with the cloze procedure to improve reading and listening comprehension. *Reading Research Quarterly, 8*, 524–541.

Kranzer, K. G. (1988). *A study of the effects of instruction on incidental word learning and on the ability to derive word meaning from con text.* Unpublished doctoral dissertation, University of Delaware.

Kuhn, M., & Stahl, S. (1998). Teaching children to learn word meanings from context: A synthesis and some questions. *Journal of Literacy Research, 30*, 119–138.

Landauer, T., & Dumais, S. (1997). A solution to Plato's problem: The Latent Semantic Analysis theory of acquisition, induction, and representation of knowledge. *Psychological Review, 104*, 211–240.

Laufer, B. (1998). What's in a word that makes it hard or easy: Some intralexical factors that affect the learning of words. In N. Schmitt & M. McCarthy (Eds.), *Vocabulary: Description, acquisition and pedagogy* (pp. 140–155). Cambridge: Cambridge University Press.

McKeown, M. (1985). The acquisition of word meaning from context by children of high and low ability. *Reading Research Quarterly, 20*, 482–496.

McKeown, M. (1993). Creating definitions for young word learners. *Reading Research Quarterly, 28*, 16–33.

McKeown, M., Beck, I., Omanson, R., & Perfetti, C. (1983). The effects of long-term vocabulary instruction on reading comprehension: A replication. *Journal of Reading Behavior, 15*, 3–18.

McKeown, M., Beck, I., Omanson, R., & Pople, M. (1985). Some effects of the nature and frequency of vocabulary instruction on the knowledge and use of words. *Reading Research Quarterly, 20*, 522–535.

Miller, G., & Gildea, P. (1987). How children learn words. *Scientific American, 257*, 94–99.

Miller, G., & Wakefield, P. (1993). On Anglin's analysis of vocabulary growth. *Monographs of the Society for Research in Child Development*, Serial No. 238, Vol. 58, pp. 167–175.

Nagy, W. (1997). On the role of context in first- and second-language vocabulary learning. In N. Schmitt & M. McCarthy (Eds.), *Vocabulary: Description, acquisition and pedagogy* (pp. 64–83). Cambridge: Cambridge University Press.

Nagy, W., & Anderson, R. C. (1984). How many words are there in printed school English? *Reading Research Quarterly, 19*, 304–330.

Nagy, W., Anderson, R. C., & Herman, P. (1987). Learning word meanings from context during normal reading. *American Educational Research Journal, 24*, 237–270.

Nagy, W., Diakidoy, I., & Anderson, R. C. (1993). The acquisition of morphology: Learning the contribution of suffixes to the meanings of derivatives. *Journal of Reading Behavior, 25*, 155–170.

Nagy, W., García, G. E., Durgunoglu, A., & Hancin-Bhatt, B. (1993). Spanish-English bilingual students' use of cognates in English reading. *Journal of Reading Behavior, 25*, 241–259.

Nagy, W., Herman, P., & Anderson, R. (1985). Learning words from context. *Reading Research Quarterly, 20*, 233–253.

Nagy, W. E., & Scott, J. A. (1990). Word schemas: Expectations about the form and meaning of new words. *Cognition and Instruction, 7*, 105–127.

Nation, I. S. P. (1990). *Teaching and learning vocabulary.* New York: Newbury House.

Ortony, A., Reynolds, R., & Arter, J. (1978). Metaphor: Theoretical and empirical research. *Psychological Bulletin, 85*, 919–943.

Paribakht, T. S., & Wesche, M. (1997). Vocabulary enhancement activities and reading for meaning in second language vocabulary acquisition. In J. Coady & T. Huckin (Eds.), *Second language vocabulary acquisition* (pp. 174–200). Cambridge: Cambridge University Press.

Piaget, J. (1926). *The language and thought of the child* (M. Worden, Trans.). New York: Harcourt, Brace, & World.

Polacco, P. (1996). *I can hear the sun: A modern myth.* New York: Philomel.

Richards, J. (1976). The role of vocabulary teaching. *TESOL Quarterly, 10*, 77–89.

Roberts, B. (1992). The evolution of the young child's concept of word as a unit of spoken and written language. *Reading Research Quarterly, 27*, 124–138.

Roth, F., Speece, D., Cooper, D., & De la Paz, S. (1996). Unresolved mysteries: How do metalinguistic and narrative skills connect with early reading? *Journal of Special Education, 30*, 257–277.

Ruddell, M. R. (1994). Vocabulary knowledge and comprehension: A comprehension-process view of complex literary relationships. In R. Ruddell, M. R. Ruddell, & H. Singer (Eds.), *Theoretical models and processes of reading* (4th ed., pp. 414–447). Newark, DE: International Reading Association.

Scarborough, H., Ehri, L., Olson, R., & Fowler, A. (1998). The fate of phonemic awareness beyond the elementary school years. *Scientific Studies of Reading, 2*, 115–142.

Schatz, E. K., & Baldwin, R. S. (1986). Context clues are unreliable predictors of word meanings. *Reading Research Quarterly, 21*, 439–453.

Schmitt, N. (1998). Tracking the incremental acquisition of second language vocabulary: A longitudinal study. *Language Learning, 48*(2), 281–317.

Schmitt, N., & McCarthy, M. (Eds.). (1997). *Vocabulary: Description, acquisition, and pedagogy.* Cambridge: Cambridge University Press.

Schwanenflugel, P., Stahl, S., & McFalls, E. (1997). Partial word knowledge and vocabulary growth during reading comprehension. *Journal of Literacy Research, 29*, 531–553.

Scott, J. (1991). *Using definitions to understand new words*. Unpublished doctoral dissertation, University of Illinois at Urbana-Champaign.

Scott, J., Asselin, M., Henry, S., & Butler, C. (1997, June). *Making rich language visible: Reports from a multi-dimensional study on word learning*. Paper presented at the annual meeting of the Canadian Society for the Study of Education, Newfoundland.

Scott, J., Blackstone, T., Cross, S., Jones, A., Skobel, B., Wells, J., & Jensen, Y. (1996, May). *The power of language: Creating contexts which enrich children's understanding and use of words.* A micro-workshop presented at the 41st annual convention of the International Reading Association, New Orleans, LA.

Scott, J., Butler, C., & Asselin, M. (1996, December). *The effect of mediated assistance in word learning.* Paper presented at the 46th annual meeting of the National Reading Conference, Charleston, SC.

Scott, J., & Nagy, W. (1997). Understanding the definitions of unfamiliar verbs. *Reading Research Quarterly, 32*, 184–200.

Scott, J., & Wells, J. (1998). Readers take responsibility: Literature circles and the growth of critical thinking. In K. Beers & B. Samuels (Eds.), *Into focus: Middle school readers* (pp. 177–197). Norwood, MA: Christopher-Gordon.

Snow, C. (1991). The theoretical basis for relationships between language and literacy development. *Journal of Research in Childhood Education, 6*, 5–10.

Snow, C. (1994). What is so hard about learning to read? A pragmatic analysis. In J. Duchan, L. Hewitt, & R. Sonnenmeier (Eds.), *Pragmatics: From theory to practice* (pp. 164–184). Englewood Cliffs, NJ: Prentice Hall.

Snow, C., Cancino, H., Gonzales, P., & Shriberg, E. (1989). Giving formal definitions: An oral language correlate of school literacy. In D. Bloome (Ed.), *Literacy in classrooms* (pp. 233–249). Norwood, NJ: Ablex.

Stahl, S. (1986). Three principles of effective vocabulary instruction. *Journal of Reading, 29*, 662–668.

Stahl, S. (1989). Task variations and prior knowledge in learning word meanings from context. In S. McCormick & J. Zutell (Eds.), *Cognitive and social perspectives for literacy research and instruction. Thirty-eighth yearbook of the National Reading conference* (pp. 197–204). Chicago: National Reading Conference.

Stahl, S., & Fairbanks, M. (1986). The effects of vocabulary instruction: A model-based meta-analysis. *Review of Educational Research, 56*, 72–110.

Stallman, A. (1991). *Learning vocabulary from context: Effects of focusing attention on individual words during reading.* Unpublished doctoral dissertation, University of Illinois at Urbana-Champaign.

Sternberg, R., & Powell, J. S. (1983). Comprehending verbal comprehension. *American Psychologist, 38*, 878–893.

Tunmer, W. E. (1990). The role of language prediction skills in beginning reading. *New Zealand Journal of Educational Studies, 25*, 95–114.

Tunmer, W. E., Herriman, M., & Nesdale, A. (1988). Metalinguistic abilities and beginning reading. *Reading Research Quarterly, 23*, 134–158.

Tunmer, W. E., Nesdale, A. R., & Wright, A. D. (1987). Syntactic awareness and reading acquisition. *British Journal of Developmental Psychology, 5*, 25–34.

Tyler, A., & Nagy, W. (1989). The acquisition of English derivational morphology. *Journal of Verbal Learning and Verbal Behavior, 14*, 638–647.

Warren-Leubecker, A. (1987). Competence and performance factors in word order awareness and early reading. *Journal of Experimental Child Psychology, 43*(1), 62–80.

Watts, S. M. (1995). Vocabulary instruction during reading lessons in six classrooms. *Journal of Reading Behavior, 27*, 399–424.

Weaver, P. (1979). Improving reading instruction: Effects of sentence organization instruction. *Reading Research Quarterly, 15*, 127–146.

Werner, H., & Kaplan, E. (1952). The acquisition of word meanings: A developmental study. *Monographs of the Society of Research in Child Development*, Vol. 15, Serial 51(1).

Willows, D., & Ryan, E. B. (1986). The development of grammatical sensitivity and its relationship to early reading achievement. *Reading Research Quarterly, 21*, 253–266.

Winner, E., Engel, M., & Gardner, H. (1980). Misunderstanding metaphor: What's the problem? *Journal of Experimental Child Psychology, 30*, 22–32.

CHAPTER 19

Role of the Reader's Schema in Comprehension, Learning, and Memory

Richard C. Anderson, University of Illinois at Urbana-Champaign

The last several years have witnessed the articulation of a largely new theory of reading, a theory already accepted by the majority of scholars in the field. According to the theory, a reader's *schema*, or organized knowledge of the world, provides much of the basis for comprehending, learning, and remembering the ideas in stories and texts. In this chapter I attempt to explain schema theory, give illustrations of the supporting evidence, and suggest applications to classroom teaching and the design of instructional materials.

A Schema-Theoretic Interpretation of Comprehension

In schema-theoretic terms, a reader comprehends a message when he is able to bring to mind a schema that gives a good account of the objects and events described in the message. Ordinarily, comprehension proceeds so smoothly that we are unaware of the process of "cutting and fitting" a schema in order to achieve a satisfactory account of a message. It is instructive, therefore, to try to understand material that gives us pause, so that we can reflect upon our own minds at work. Consider the following sentence, drawn from the work of Bransford and McCarrell (1974):

> The notes were sour because the seam split.

Notice that all of the words are familiar and that the syntax is straightforward, yet the sentence does not "make sense" to most people. Now notice what happens when the additional clue, "bagpipe," is provided. At this point the sentence does make sense because one is able to interpret all the words in the sentence in terms of certain specific objects and events and their interrelations.

Let us examine another sentence:

> The big number 37 smashed the ball over the fence.

This sentence is easy to interpret. *Big Number 37* is a baseball player. The sense of *smash the ball* is to propel it rapidly by hitting it strongly with a bat. The fence is at the boundary of a playing field. The ball was hit hard enough that it flew over the fence.

This chapter is reprinted from *Learning to Read in American Schools: Basal Readers and Content Texts* (pp. 243–257), edited by R.C. Anderson, J. Osborn, & R.J. Tierney, 1984, Hillsdale, NJ: Erlbaum.

Suppose a person with absolutely no knowledge of baseball read the Big Number 37 sentence. Such a person could not easily construct an interpretation of the sentence, but with enough mental effort might be able to conceive of large numerals, perhaps made of metal, attached to the front of an apartment building. Further, the person might imagine that the numerals come loose and fall, striking a ball resting on top of, or lodged above, a fence, causing the ball to break. Most people regard this as an improbable interpretation, certainly one that never would have occurred to them, but they readily acknowledge that it is a "good" interpretation. What makes it good? The answer is that the interpretation is complete and consistent. It is complete in the sense that every element in the sentence is interpreted; there are no loose ends left unexplained. The interpretation is consistent in that no part of it does serious violence to knowledge about the physical and social world.

Both interpretations of the Big Number 37 sentence assume a real world. Criteria of consistency are relaxed in fictional worlds in which animals talk or men wearing capes leap tall buildings in a single bound. But there are conventions about what is possible in fictional worlds as well. The knowledgeable reader will be annoyed if these conventions are violated. The less knowledgeable reader simply will be confused.

It should not be imagined that there is some simple, literal level of comprehension of stories and texts that does not require coming up with a schema. This important point is illustrated in a classic study by Bransford and Johnson (1972) in which subjects read paragraphs, such as the following, written so that most people are unable to construct a schema that will account for the material:

> If the balloons popped the sound wouldn't be able to carry since everything would be too far away from the correct floor. A closed window would also prevent the sound from carrying, since most buildings tend to be well insulated. Since the whole operation depends upon a steady flow of electricity, a break in the middle of the wire would also cause problems. Of course, the fellow could shout, but the human voice is not loud enough to carry that far. An additional problem is that a string could break on the instrument. Then there could be no accompaniment to the message. It is clear that the best situation would involve less distance. Then there would be fewer potential problems. With face to face contact, the least number of things could go wrong. (p. 719)

Subjects rated this passage as very difficult to understand, and they were unable to remember much of it. In contrast, subjects shown the drawing on the left side of Figure 1 found the passage more comprehensible and were able to remember a great deal of it. Another group saw the drawing on the right in Figure 1. This group remembered no more than the group that did not receive a drawing. The experiment demonstrates that what is critical for comprehension is a schema accounting for the *relationships* among elements; it is not enough for the elements to be concrete and imageable.

Trick passages, such as the foregoing one about the communication problems of a modern day Romeo, are useful for illustrating what happens when a

Figure 1.

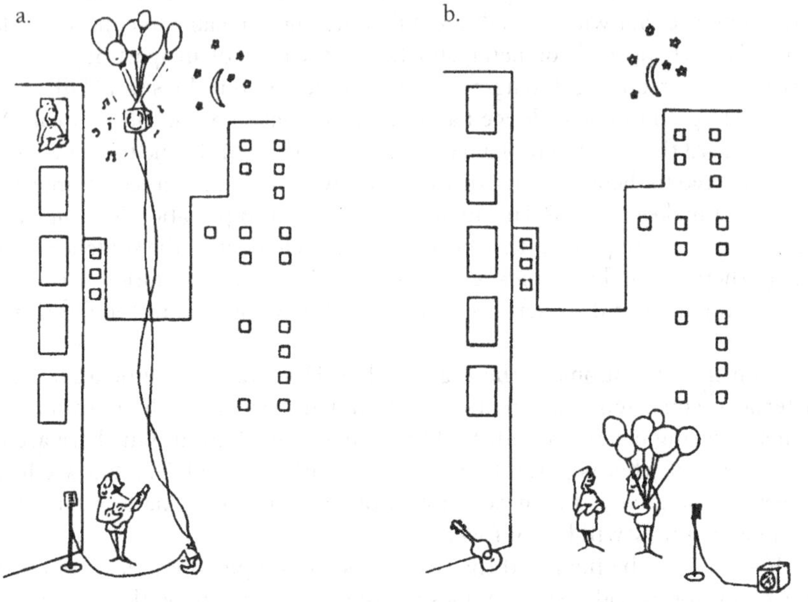

Illustrations from Bransford and Johnson (1972). Version "a" represents the appropriate context and version "b" represents the inappropriate context. See text for accompanying passage.

reader is completely unable to discover a schema that will fit a passage and, therefore, finds the passage entirely incomprehensible. More typical is the situation in which a reader knows something about a topic, but falls far short of being an expert. Chiesi, Spilich, and Voss (1979) asked people high and low in knowledge of baseball to read and recall a report of a half-inning from a fictitious baseball game. Knowledge of baseball had both qualitative and quantitative effects on performance. High-knowledge subjects were more likely to recall and embellish upon aspects of strategic significance to the game. Low-knowledge subjects, in contrast, were more likely to include information incidental to the play of the game.

Schema theory highlights the fact that often more than one interpretation of a text is possible. The schema that will be brought to bear on a text depends upon the reader's age, sex, race, religion, nationality, occupation—in short, it depends upon the reader's culture. This point was illustrated in an experiment completed by Anderson, Reynolds, Schallert, and Goetz (1977), who asked people to read the following passage:

> Tony slowly got up from the mat, planning his escape. He hesitated a moment and thought. Things were not going well. What bothered him most was being held,

> especially since the charge against him had been weak. He considered his present situation. The lock that held him was strong but he thought he could break it. He knew, however, that his timing would have to be perfect. Tony was aware that it was because of his early roughness that he had been penalized so severely—much too severely from his point of view. The situation was becoming frustrating; the pressure had been grinding on him for too long. He was being ridden unmercifully. Tony was getting angry now. He felt he was ready to make his move. He knew that his success or failure would depend on what he did in the next few seconds.

Most people think the foregoing passage is about a convict planning his escape from prison. A special group of people, however, see the passage an entirely different way; these are men who have been involved in the sport of wrestling. They think the passage is about a wrestler caught in the hold of an opponent. Notice how the interpretation of *lock* varies according to perspective. In the one case, it is a piece of hardware that holds a cell door shut; in the other it may be a sweaty arm around a neck. Males enrolled in a weight lifting class and females enrolled in a music education class read the foregoing passage and another passage that most people interpret as being about several people playing cards, but that can be interpreted as being about a rehearsal session of a woodwind ensemble. The results were as expected. Scores on a multiple choice test designed to reveal interpretations of the passages showing striking relationships to the subjects' background. Physical education students usually gave a wrestling interpretation to the prison/wrestling passage and a card playing interpretation to the card/music passage, whereas the reverse was true of the music education students. Similarly, when subjects were asked to recall the passages, theme-revealing distortions appeared, even though the instructions emphasized reproducing the exact words of the original text. For example, a physical education student stated, "Rocky was penalized early in the match for roughness or a dangerous hold," while a music education student wrote, "he was angry that he had been caught and arrested."

The thesis of this section is that comprehension is a matter of activating or constructing a schema that provides a coherent explanation of objects and events mentioned in a discourse. In sharp contrast is the conventional view that comprehension consists of aggregating the meanings of words to form the meanings of clauses, aggregating the meanings of clauses to form the meanings of sentences, aggregating the meanings of sentences to form the meanings of paragraphs, and so on. The illustrations in this section were intended to demonstrate the insufficiency of this conventional view. The meanings of the words cannot be "added up" to give the meaning of the whole. The click of comprehension occurs only when the reader evolves a schema that explains the whole message.

Schema-Based Processes in Learning and Remembering

According to schema theory, reading involves more or less simultaneous analysis at many different levels. The levels include graphophonemic, morphemic, semantic, syntactic, pragmatic, and interpretive. Reading is conceived to be an interactive process. This means that analysis does not proceed in a strict order from the visual information in letters to the overall interpretation of a text. Instead, as a person reads, an interpretation of what a segment of a text might mean is theorized to depend both on analysis of the print and on hypotheses in the person's mind. Processes that flow from the print are called "bottom-up" or "data driven" whereas processes that flow in the other direction are called "top-down" or "hypothesis driven," following Bobrow and Norman (1975). In the passage about Tony, who is either a wrestler or a prisoner, processing the word *lock* has the potential to activate either a piece-of-hardware meaning or a wrestling-hold meaning. The hypothesis the reader has already formulated about the text will tip the scales in the direction of one of the two meanings, usually without the reader's being aware that an alternative meaning is possible. Psychologists are at work developing detailed models of the mechanisms by which information from different levels of analysis is combined during reading (see Just & Carpenter, 1980; Rumelhart & McClelland, 1980).

The reader's schema affects both learning and remembering of the information and ideas in a text. Six functions of schemata that have been proposed (Anderson, 1978; Anderson & Pichert, 1978) are briefly explained.

A schema provides ideational scaffolding for assimilating text information. The idea is that a schema provides a niche, or slot, for certain text information. For instance, there is a slot for the main entree in a dining-at-a-fine-restaurant schema and a slot for the murder weapon in a who-done-it schema. Information that fits slots in the reader's schema is readily learned, perhaps with little mental effort.

A schema facilitates selective allocation of attention. A schema provides part of the basis for determining the important aspects of a text. It is hypothesized that skilled readers use importance as one basis for allocating cognitive resources—that is, for deciding where to pay close attention.

A schema enables inferential elaboration. No text is completely explicit. A reader's schema provides the basis for making inferences that go beyond the information literally stated in a text.

A schema allows orderly searches of memory. A schema can provide the reader with a guide to the types of information that need to be recalled. For instance, a person attempting to recall the food served at a fine meal can review the categories of food typically included in a fine meal: What was the appetizer? What was the soup? Was there a salad? And so on. In other words, by tracing through the schema used to structure the text, the reader is helped to gain access to the particular information learned when the text was read.

A schema facilitates editing and summarizing. Since a schema contains within itself criteria of importance, it enables the reader to produce summaries that include significant propositions and omit trivial ones.

A schema permits inferential reconstruction. When there are gaps in memory, a rememberer's schema, along with the specific text information that can be recalled, helps generate hypotheses about the missing information. For example, suppose a person cannot recall what beverage was served with a fine meal. If he can recall that the entree was fish, he will be able to infer that the beverage may have been white wine.

The foregoing are tentative hypotheses about the functions of a schema in text processing, conceived to provide the broadest possible interpretation of available data. Several of the hypotheses can be regarded as rivals—for instance, the ideational scaffolding hypothesis and the selective attention hypothesis—and it may be that not all of them will turn out to be viable. Researchers are now actively at work developing precise models of schema-based processes and subjecting these models to experimental test.

Evidence for Schema Theory

There is now a really good case that schemata incorporating knowledge of the world play an important role in language comprehension. We are beginning to see research on differentiated functions. In a few years it should be possible to speak in more detail about the specific processing mechanisms in which schemata are involved.

Many of the claims of schema theory are nicely illustrated in a cross-cultural experiment, completed by Steffensen, Joag-Dev, and Anderson (1979), in which Indians (natives of India) and Americans read letters about an Indian and an American wedding. Of course, every adult member of a society has a well-developed marriage schema. There are substantial differences between Indian and American cultures in the nature of marriages. As a consequence, large differences in comprehension, learning, and memory for the letters were expected.

Table 1 summarizes analyses of the recall of the letters by Indian and American subjects. The first row in the table indicates the amount of time subjects spent reading the letters. As can be seen, subjects spent less time reading what for them was the native passage. This was as expected since a familiar schema should speed up and expedite a reader's processing.

The second row in Table 1 presents the number of idea units recalled. The gist measure includes not only propositions recalled verbatim but also acceptable

Table 1. Mean Performance on Various Measures

	Nationality			
	Americans		Indians	
Measure	American Passage	Indian Passage	American Passage	Indian Passage
Time (seconds)	168	213	304	276
Gist recall	52.4	37.9	27.3	37.6
Elaborations	5.7	.1	.2	5.4
Distortions	.1	7.6	5.5	.3
Other overt errors	7.5	5.2	8.0	5.9
Omissions	76.2	76.6	95.5	83.3

(From Steffensen, Joag-Dev, and Anderson, 1979)

paraphrases. The finding was precisely as expected. Americans recalled more of the American text, whereas Indians recalled more of the Indian passage. Within current formulations of schema theory, there are a couple of reasons for predicting that people would learn and remember more of a text about a marriage in their own culture: A culturally appropriate schema may provide the ideational scaffolding that makes it easy to learn information that fits into that schema, or, it may be that the information, once learned, is more accessible because the schema is a structure that makes it easy to search memory.

The row labeled *Elaborations* in Table 1 contains the frequency of culturally appropriate extensions of the text. The next row, labeled *Distortions,* contains the frequency of culturally inappropriate modifications of the text. Ever since Bartlett's day, elaborations and distortions have provided the intuitively most compelling evidence for the role of schemata. Many fascinating instances appeared in the protocols collected in the present study. A section of the American passage upon which interesting cultural differences surfaced read as follows:

> Did you know that Pam was going to wear her grandmother's wedding dress? That gave her something that was old, and borrowed, too. It was made of lace over satin, with very large puff sleeves and looked absolutely charming on her.

One Indian had this to say about the American bride's dress: "She was looking alright except the dress was too old and out of fashion." Wearing an heirloom wedding dress is a completely acceptable aspect of the pageantry of the American marriage ceremony. This Indian appears to have completely missed this and has inferred that the dress was out of fashion, on the basis that Indians attach importance to displays of social status, manifested in such details as wearing an up-to-date, fashionable sari.

The gifts described in the Indian passage that were given to the groom's family by the bride's, the dowry, and the reference to the concern of the bride's family that a scooter might be requested were a source of confusion for our American subjects. First of all, the "agreement about the gifts to be given to the in-laws" was changed to "the exchange of gifts," a wording that suggests that gifts are flowing in two directions, not one. Another subject identified the gifts given to the in-laws as favors, which are often given in American weddings to the attendants by the bride and groom.

In another facet of the study, different groups of Indians and Americans read the letters and rated the significance of each of the propositions. It was expected that Americans would regard as important propositions conveying information about ritual and ceremony whereas Indians would see as important propositions dealing with financial and social status. Table 2 contains examples of text units that received contrasting ratings of importance from Indians and Americans. Schema theory predicts that text units that are important in the light of the schema are more likely to be learned and, once learned, are more likely to be remembered. This prediction was confirmed. Subjects did recall more text

Table 2. Examples of Idea Units of Contrasting Importance to Americans and Indians

American Passage		Indian Passage	
Idea Units More Important to Americans	**Idea Units More Important to Indians**	**Idea Units More Important to Americans**	**Idea Units More Important to Indians**
Then on Friday night *they had the rehearsal* at the church *and the rehearsal dinner,* which lasted until almost midnight. *All the attendants wore dresses that were specially designed to go with Pam's.* Her mother wore yellow, which looks great on her with her bleached hair, *and George's mother wore pale green.*	*She'll be lucky if she can even get her daughter married, the way things are going.* Her mother wore yellow, which looks great on her *with her bleached hair,* and George's mother wore pale green. Have you seen the diamond she has? *It must have cost George a fortune because it's almost two carats.*	Prema's husband had to wear a dhoti *for that ceremony and for the wedding the next day.* *There were only the usual essential rituals:* the curtain removal, the parents giving the daughter away, walking seven steps together, etc., *and plenty of smoke from the sacred fire.* There must have been about five hundred people *at the wedding feast. Since only fifty people could be seated at one time, it went on for a long time.*	*Prema's in-laws seem to be nice enough people.* They did not create any problem in the wedding, *even though Prema's husband is their only son.* *Since they did not ask for any dowry,* Prema's parents were a little worried about their asking for a scooter before the wedding, *but they didn't ask for one.* *Prema's parents were very sad when she left.*

Note. Important idea units are in italics.

information rated as important by their cultural cohorts, whether recalling what for them was the native or the foreign text.

Of course, it is one thing to show, as Steffensen, Joag-dev, and Anderson did, that readers from distinctly different national cultures give different interpretations to culturally sensitive materials, and quite another to find the same phenomenon among readers from different but overlapping subcultures within the same country. A critical issue is whether cultural variation within the United States could be a factor in differential reading comprehension. Minority children could have a handicap if stories, texts, and test items presuppose a cultural perspective that the children do not share. An initial exploration of this issue has been completed by Reynolds, Taylor, Steffensen, Shirey, and Anderson (1982), who wrote a passage around an episode involving "sounding." Sounding is an activity predominantly found in the black community in which the participants try to outdo each other in an exchange of insults (Labov, 1972). In two group studies, and one in which subjects were individually interviewed, black teenagers tended to see the episode as involving friendly give-and-take, whereas white teenagers interpreted it as an ugly confrontation, sometimes one involving physical violence. For example, when attempting to recall the incident, a black male wrote, "That everybody tried to get on the person side that joke were the best." A white male wrote, "Soon there was a riot. All the kids were fighting." This research established that when written material has an identifiable cultural loading there is a pronounced effect on comprehension. It remains to be seen how much school reading material is culturally loaded.

In the foregoing research, schemata were manipulated by selecting subjects with different backgrounds. Another approach for getting people to bring different schemata to bear is by selecting different passages. Anderson, Spiro, and Anderson (1978) wrote two closely comparable passages, one about dining at a fancy restaurant, the other about a trip to a supermarket. The same 18 items of food and beverage were mentioned in the two texts, in the same order, and attributed to the same characters. The first hypothesis was that subjects who received the restaurant passage would learn and recall more food and beverage information than subjects who received the supermarket passage. The reasoning was that a dining-at-a-fine-restaurant schema has a more constrained structure than a trip-to-a-supermarket schema. That is to say, fewer food and beverage items will fit the former schema; one could choose soda-pop and hot dogs at a supermarket, but these items would not be ordered at a fine restaurant. Moreover there are more cross-connections among items in a restaurant schema. For example, a steak will be accompanied by a baked potato, or maybe french fries. In two experiments, subjects who read the restaurant text recalled more food and beverage items than subjects who read the supermarket text.

The second prediction was that students who read the restaurant text would more often attribute the food and drink items to the correct characters. In a supermarket it does not matter, for instance, who throws the brussel sprouts into the shopping cart, but in a restaurant it does matter who orders which item. This prediction was confirmed in two experiments.

A third prediction was that order of recall of foods and beverages would correspond more closely to order of mention in the text for subjects who read the restaurant story. There is not, or need not be, a prescribed sequence for selecting items in a grocery store, but there is a characteristic order in which items are served in a restaurant. This hypothesis was supported in one experiment and the trend of the data favored it in a second.

Another technique for manipulating readers' schemata is by assigning them different perspectives. Pichert and Anderson (1977) asked people to pretend that they were either burglars or homebuyers before reading a story about what two boys did at one of the boys' homes while they were skipping school. The finding was that people learned more of the information important to their assigned perspective. For instance, burglars were more likely to learn that three 10-speed bikes were parked in the garage, whereas homebuyers were more likely to learn that the house had a leaky roof. Anderson and Pichert (1978; see also Anderson, Pichert, & Shirey, 1983) went on to show that the reader's perspective has independent effects on learning and recall. Subjects who switch perspectives and then recall the story for a second time recall additional, previously unrecalled, information important to their new perspective but unimportant to their original perspective. For example, a person who begins as a homebuyer may fail to remember that the story says the side door is kept unlocked, but may later remember this information when told to assume the role of a burglar. Subjects report that previously unrecalled information significant in the light of the new perspective "pops" into their heads.

Recent unpublished research in my laboratory, completed in collaboration with Ralph Reynolds and Paul Wilson, suggests selective allocation of attention to text elements that are important in the light of the reader's schema. We have employed two measures of attention. The first is the amount of time a subject spends reading schema-relevant sentences. The second is the response time to a probe presented during schema-relevant sentences. The probe is a tone sounded through earphones; the subject responds by pushing a button as fast as possible. The logic of the probe task is that if the mind is occupied with reading, there will be a slight delay in responding to the probe. Our results indicate that people assigned a burglar perspective, for instance, have slightly longer reading times and slightly longer probe times when reading burglar-relevant sentences. Comparable results have been obtained by other investigators (Cirilo & Foss, 1980; Haberlandt, Berian, & Sandson, 1980; Just & Carpenter, 1980).

Implications of Schema Theory for Design of Materials and Classroom Instruction

First, I urge publishers to include teaching suggestions in manuals designed to help children activate relevant knowledge before reading. Children do not spontaneously integrate what they are reading with what they already know (cf. Paris & Lindauer, 1976). This means that special attention should be paid to preparation for reading. Questions should be asked that remind children of relevant experiences of their own and orient them toward the problems faced by story characters.

Second, the teachers' manuals accompanying basal programs and content area texts ought to include suggestions for building prerequisite knowledge when it cannot be safely presupposed. According to schema theory, this practice should promote comprehension. There is direct evidence to support knowledge-building activities. Hayes and Tierney (1980) asked American high school students to read and recall newspaper reports of cricket matches. Performance improved sharply when the students received instruction on the nature of the game of cricket before reading the newspaper reports.

Third, I call for publishers to feature lesson activities that will lead children to meaningfully integrate what they already know with what is presented on the printed page. From the perspective of schema theory, prediction techniques such as the Directed Reading-Thinking Activity (Stauffer, 1969) can be recommended.

The DRTA would appear to cause readers to search their store of knowledge and integrate what they already know with what is stated. It must be acknowledged, however, that the empirical evidence for the efficacy of the DRTA is flimsy at present (Tierney & Cunningham, in press). Recently, Anderson, Mason, and Shirey (1983, Experiment 2) have illustrated that under optimum conditions strong benefits can be obtained using a prediction technique. A heterogeneous sample of third graders read sentences such as, "The stupid child ran into the street after the ball." Children in the prediction group read each sentence aloud and then indicated what might happen next. In the case of the sentence above, a frequent prediction was that the child might get hit by a car. A second group read the sentences aloud with an emphasis on accurate decoding. A third and a fourth group listened to the sentences and read them silently. The finding was that the prediction group recalled 72% of the sentences, whereas the average for the other three groups was 43%.

Fourth, I urge publishers to employ devices that will highlight the structure of text material. Schema theory inclines one to endorse the practice of providing advance organizers or structured overviews, along the lines proposed by Ausubel (1968) and Herber (1978). Ausubel, who can be regarded as one of the pioneer schema theorists, has stated that "the principal function of the organizer is to bridge the gap between what the learner already knows and what he needs to know before he can successfully learn the task at hand" (1968, p. 148). There have been dozens of empirical studies of advance organizers over the past 20 years. Thorough reviews of this bulky literature by Mayer (1979) and Luiten, Ames, and Ackerson (1980) point to the conclusion that organizers generally have a facilitative effect. Nevertheless, from within current formulations of schema theory, there is room for reservations about advance organizers. Notably, Ausubel's insistence (cf. 1968, pp. 148, 333) that organizers must be stated at a high level of generality, abstractness, and inclusiveness is puzzling. The problem is that general, abstract language often is difficult to understand. Children, in particular, are more easily reminded of what they know when concrete language is used. As Ausubel himself has acknowledged (e.g., 1968, p. 149), "To be useful...organizers themselves must obviously be learnable and must be stated in familiar terms."

A final implication of schema theory is that minority children may sometimes be counted as failing to comprehend school reading material because their schemata do not match those of the majority culture. Basal reading programs, content area texts, and standardized tests lean heavily on the conventional assumption that meaning is inherent in the words and structure of a text. When prior knowledge is required, it is assumed to be knowledge common to children from every subculture. When new ideas are introduced, these are assumed to be equally accessible to every child. Considering the strong effects that culture has on reading comprehension, the question that naturally arises is whether children from different subcultures can so confidently be assumed to bring a common schema to written material. To be sure, subcultures within this country do overlap. But is it safe simply to *assume* that when reading the same story, children from every subculture will have the same experience with the setting, ascribe the same goals and motives to characters, imagine the same sequence of actions, predict the same emotional reactions, or expect the same outcomes? This is a question that the research community and the school publishing industry ought to address with renewed vigor.

QUESTIONS FOR REFLECTION

1. Why is schema theory critical to understanding comprehension instruction?
2. What is the difference between top-down and bottom-up views of reading?
3. What challenges are created when stories, texts, and test items used in classrooms presuppose a cultural perspective that not all children share?

REFERENCES

Anderson, R.C. (1978). Schema-directed processes in language comprehension. In A. Lesgold, J. Pellegrino, S. Fokkema, & R. Glaser (Eds.), *Cognitive psychology and instruction*. New York: Plenum.

Anderson, R.C., Mason, J., & Shirey, L.L. (1983). *The reading group: An experimental investigation of a labyrinth* (Tech. Rep. No. 271). Champaign: University of Illinois, Center for the Study of Reading.

Anderson, R.C., & Pichert, J.W. (1978). Recall of previously unrecallable information following a shift in perspective. *Journal of Verbal Learning and Verbal Behavior, 17*, 1–12.

Anderson, R.C., Pichert, J.W., & Shirey, L.L. (1983). Effects of the reader's schema at different points in time. *Journal of Educational Psychology, 75*(2), 271–279.

Anderson, R.C., Reynolds, R.E., Schallert, D.L., & Goetz, E.T. (1977). Frameworks for comprehending discourse. *American Educational Research Journal, 14*, 367–382.

Anderson, R.C., Spiro, R.J., & Anderson, M.C. (1978). Schemata as scaffolding for the representation of information in connected discourse. *American Educational Research Journal, 15*, 433–440.

Ausubel, D.P. (1968). *Educational psychology: A cognitive view*. New York: Holt, Rinehart.

Bobrow, D.G., & Norman, D.A. (1975). Some principles of memory schemata. In D.G. Bobrow & A.M. Collins (Eds.), *Representation and understanding: Studies in cognitive science*. New York: Academic.

Bransford, J.D., & Johnson, M.K. (1972). Contextual prerequisites for understanding: Some investigations of comprehension and recall. *Journal of Verbal Learning and Verbal Behavior, 11*, 717–726.

Bransford, J.D., & McCarrell, N.S. (1974). A sketch of a cognitive approach to comprehension. In W.B. Weimer & D.S. Palermo (Eds.), *Cognition and the symbolic process*. Hillsdale, NJ: Erlbaum.

Chiesi, H.L., Spilich, G.J., & Voss, J.F. (1979). Acquisition of domain-related information in relation to high- and low-domain knowledge. *Journal of Verbal Learning and Verbal Behavior, 18*, 257–274.

Cirilo, R.K., & Foss, D.J. (1980). Text structure and reading time for sentences. *Journal of Verbal Learning and Verbal Behavior, 19*, 96–109.

Haberlandt, K., Berian, C., & Sandson, J. (1980). The episode schema in story processing. *Journal of Verbal Learning and Verbal Behavior, 19*, 635–650.

Hayes, D.A., & Tierney, R.J. (1980, October). *Increasing background knowledge through analogy: Its effects upon comprehension and learning* (Tech. Rep. No. 186). Urbana: University of Illinois, Center for the Study of Reading. (ERIC Document Reproduction Service No. ED195953)

Herber, H.L. (1978). *Teaching reading in content areas* (2nd ed.). Englewood Cliffs, NJ: Prentice Hall.

Just, M.A., & Carpenter, P.A. (1980). A theory of reading: From eye fixation to comprehension. *Psychological Review, 87*, 329–354.

Labov, W. (1972). *Language in the inner city: Studies in the black English vernacular*. Washington, DC: Center for Applied Linguistics.

Luiten, J., Ames, W., & Ackerson, G. (1980). A meta-analysis of the effects of advance organizers on learning and retention. *American Educational Research Journal, 17*, 211–218.

Mayer, R.E. (1979). Can advance organizers influence meaningful learning? *Review of Educational Research, 49*, 371–383.

Paris, S.G., & Lindauer, B.K. (1976). The role of inference in children's comprehension and memory. *Cognitive Psychology, 8*, 217–227.
Pichert, J.W., & Anderson, R.C. (1977). Taking different perspectives on a story. *Journal of Educational Psychology, 69*, 309–315.
Reynolds, R.E., Taylor, M.A., Steffensen, M.S., Shirey, L.L., & Anderson, R.C. (1982). Cultural schemata and reading comprehension. *Reading Research Quarterly, 17*(3), 353–366.
Rumelhart, D.E., & McClelland, J.L. (1980). *An interactive activation model of the effect of context in perception* (Part 2; CHIP Tech. Rep.). La Jolla, CA: University of California, Center for Human Information Processing.
Stauffer, R.G. (1969). *Teaching reading as a thinking process*. New York: Harper & Row.
Steffensen, M.S., Joag-Dev, C., & Anderson, R.C. (1979). A cross-cultural perspective on reading comprehension. *Reading Research Quarterly, 15*, 10–29.
Tierney, R.J., & Cunningham, J.W. (in press). Research on teaching reading comprehension. In P.D. Pearson, R. Barr, M.L. Kamil, & P. Mosenthal (Eds.), *Handbook of reading research*. New York: Longman.

CHAPTER 20

Schema Theory Revisited

Mary B. McVee, University at Buffalo, State University of New York

KaiLonnie Dunsmore, National Center for Literacy Education*

James R. Gavelek, University of Illinois at Chicago

The influence of the cognitive revolution on literacy research and practice over the past quarter of a century has been both profound and pervasive. This influence is, perhaps, seen most readily in relation to the development of schema theory and the role it has played in exploring and conceptualizing reading and writing (e.g., Anderson & Pearson, 1984; Tierney & Shanahan, 1991). Recently, however, we have witnessed the growing influence of various social conceptions of mind with their corresponding implications for understanding literacy processes. These have included Vygotsky's sociocultural theory (e.g., Cole, 1996; Gavelek & Raphael, 1996; Moll, 1990; Wertsch, 1991, 1998), various renderings of social constructivism (Au, 1998; Greene & Ackerman, 1995; Spivey, 1997), and discursive psychology (Gergen & Gergen, 1983; Harré & Gillett, 1994). Central to this recognition of the social is the important role of discourse processes in the development of mind and literacy (e.g., Gee, 1997a, 2000; Santa Barbara Discourse Group, 1994). As is often the case in pendulum sweeps that characterize educational inquiry, there is a danger of overcorrection. Either the social comes to be emphasized to the relative exclusion of the individual, or vice versa.

With this in mind, we examine recent contributions of social and cultural perspectives and how these might contribute to and change our current conceptions of schema theory. With its emphasis on individual, cognitive processes, schema theory and research conducted through that lens have helped researchers and teachers to understand how knowledge is organized and has helped shed light on the individual cognitive routines that children employ during the reading process. We examine schema theory because of its resilience in the field and because of its utility in helping teachers and researchers understand the role of an individual's prior knowledge in comprehension. Whereas schema theory foregrounds the role of individual cognitive processes, sociocultural theories, particularly the work of Vygotsky (1978, 1986) and scholars who use Vygotsky's work (e.g., Au, 1998; Cole, 1996; Gavelek & Raphael, 1996; Gee, 1992; Holland & Cole, 1995; Kozulin, Gindis, Ageyev, & Miller, 2003; Moll, 1990; Rogoff, 1993; Wells, 1999) have also provided significant insights into individuals' meaning-making processes by highlighting the role of language as mediational tool, the importance

This chapter is reprinted from *Review of Educational Research,* 75(4), 531–566. Copyright © 2005 by Sage. Reprinted with permission.

of social interactions, and the situatedness of language and social interactions within cultural and historical systems. We examine sociocultural perspectives because of their continuing influence and importance in the field and their ability to contribute to our understanding of the interplay between literate processes and the social and cultural lives of children as they carry out meaning-making activities. In undertaking such exploration, we seek to blur the boundaries that have traditionally separated schema theoretic perspectives and research from sociocultural perspectives and research, with the aim of rethinking the construct of schema.

As teachers and teacher educators, we believe that schema theory has been a powerful tool in helping us and in helping pre-service and in-service teachers understand reading comprehension. But the growing influence of sociocultural perspectives has also led to an additional tension. We have noted that researchers and authors of literacy and language arts textbooks continue to talk about schema theory as a useful model of *reading* comprehension, as distinct from current sociocultural lines of inquiry into *literacy* development and practice, because such inquiries emerged from different views of knowledge and knowledge construction. Although discussions of schema theory inevitably raise discussions of cultural knowledge, little work has been undertaken to bridge the gap between versions of schema as an in-the-head phenomenon and more recent sociocultural perspectives that treat schema as something that exists beyond the individual and within an individual's social and cultural communities. For example, how might we rethink schema in light of perspectives that argue that mind "extends beyond the skin" (Wertsch, 1991, p. 14), in that mind is discursively produced (e.g., Harré & Gillett, 1994; Harré & Stearns, 1995) and socially distributed (Gee, 1992, 1997b; Lave & Wenger, 1991; Rogoff & Lave, 1984)? In particular, what might we learn from sociocultural perspectives about the origins and development of schemas?

To begin exploring such questions, we first briefly consider why it is important at this juncture to revisit schema theory. Second, we identify what we believe are the salient features of schema theory, and we trace the origins of schema as a construct and as related to research in the literacy field. We argue that schema theorists have inadequately explored the issue of schema origination. The genetic question focusing on the origins and development of knowledge is a fundamental question essential to sociocultural examinations of learning (Wertsch, 1991), and a question that must be considered in reconciling social and individual perspectives. Third, we examine sociocultural perspectives to consider what they can contribute to our understandings of schema. By "sociocultural" we refer to the belief that thought has its genesis in social interaction (Vygotsky, 1978, 1986). Both externally focused, interpsychological tools, such as language and other sign systems, and internally focused, intrapsychological tools, such as thought, are created, shaped, and sustained in social and cultural contexts. Thus cognition does not exist as an isolated process within the individual but as a "bio-social-cultural process" that is both public and private (Cole, 1996, p. 136). Sociocultural perspectives explore the role of ideal and material tools and activities, noting that both are ensconced in cultural systems and thus are devoid of meaning outside particular contexts and activities. We believe that by more explicitly linking the construct of schema with explorations of ideal and material tools and activity, we can enrich our understandings of schema theory. We posit that such a linkage may also have the added benefit of enriching our understandings of sociocultural perspectives. To illustrate the ways that schema theory has helped us understand comprehension and learning, and to illustrate some of our concerns about schema theory as traditionally conceived, we provide an example of classroom practice. Throughout this article, we advance the notion of schemas[1] as transactional and embodied constructs to address the subject–object dualism that underlies traditional cognitive science approaches.

Why Revisit Schema Theory?

Building on What We Have Learned

Recently, there have been calls to accept what we have learned about literacy practices and instruction and to acknowledge how our past knowledge helps to inform our present endeavors. Raphael (2001) reminded literacy educators and researchers that there is a collective body of knowledge that has been identified and developed related to literacy practices. In identifying various phases of literacy research, Raphael urged literacy scholars to look across these practices and acknowledge the impressive body of knowledge and areas of consensus that exist in the field, in order to avoid a mistake that has often been made in educational research. She argued that, "instead of recognizing that with each passing decade, our field has learned more about how to teach literacy, about the complexity of the literacy processes, and about the ways in which literacy is instantiated and valued across time and cultures; we [have] essentially [fallen] into the trap of assuming that new knowledge somehow replaced or overshadowed previous practice" (Raphael, 2001, p. 9).

Others have also attempted to move the field toward consensus by pointing out some commonly accepted beliefs about literacy and literacy instruction (e.g., Dudley-Marling & Murphy, 1998; Pearson, 1996). Most of those who have identified an area for consensus have done so in relation to instructional practice. However, it is also important to revisit the particular theories and theoretical constructs on which such practices are predicated. Obviously, there are substantively different issues to draw upon when we foreground theory. The epistemological views tied to theory, for example, may not allow for consensus or agreement in the same manner as when we discuss methods of literacy learning and practice. Yet we believe there are some areas that are complementary but which are often seen as disparate and incommensurable, as was recently noted by Purcell-Gates, Jacobson, and Degener (2004) in their review of social and cognitive theories of literacy development. In addition, although scholars, notably Smagorinsky (2001), have begun articulating cultural theories of reading, we believe that additional explorations are needed.

As we were preparing this article, some of our colleagues asked us why we felt it was important to revisit schema theory. Some skeptics cite numerous studies couched in sociocultural perspectives and numerous reviews of research that seem to establish sociocultural perspectives as "the winner" in the clash of cognitive versus social paradigms. A review of the third volume of the *Handbook of Reading Research* (Kamil, Mosenthal, Pearson, & Barr, 2000) bears out the importance of social and cultural perspectives and their role in reading research (see, for example, Bean, 2000; Florio-Ruane & McVee, 2000; Gaffney & Anderson, 2000; Gee, 2000). Despite the fact that sociocultural perspectives have become increasingly prominent in conceptualizing educational research and practice (Hruby, 2001), we also believe that the concept of schema is a useful and powerful tool for understanding reading processes.

Schema as a Construct for Understanding Reading Processes

The extent to which the literacy field still relies on and values schema theory can be seen from the results of an analysis of current reading and language arts texts for pre-service and in-service teachers. In a review of 25 reading/language arts texts published between 1989 and 2004, we found that all of the texts introduced schema theory to help explain the reading process, especially comprehension. The widespread reliance on schema theory indicates that educators still believe schema theory is a valuable tool in helping pre-service and in-service teachers understand cognitive and individual aspects of reading. At the same time, most of these same reading and language arts texts introduce their readers to sociocultural theories, particularly the work of Vygotsky. Despite the heavy reliance overall on social perspectives, none of the texts that we reviewed foregrounded social and cultural factors in their discussion of schema. A few noted that schema theory implies a network of social and cultural relationships but did not develop that idea with reference to social theories of reading and language use (e.g., Graves, Juel, & Graves, 2004). Only two of the texts (Lipson & Wixson, 1997/2003; Weaver, 1994/2002) sought to explicitly conjoin the discussion of cognitive perspectives with social perspectives on learning.

It is possible that this compartmentalization exists, in part, because textbooks are created to present information in an efficient and fairly straightforward manner; or the compartmentalization may be due to the lag that often exists when theory and research are translated into practice. That schema theory is still widely cited in reading and language arts texts is more intriguing when we consider that in a review of articles on research and practice, Gaffney and Anderson (2000) found that the terms "schema" or "schema theory" have fallen into disuse in describing research and practice in published journals. Although the terms "schema" or "schemata" appeared frequently in research and practitioner journals in the 1980s, researchers in recent years have opted to use terms such as *existing knowledge, topic knowledge, prior knowledge,* and *previous knowledge.* Gaffney and Anderson took this shift in terms as an indication that schema theory is used in general ways, and they expressed surprise at the limited references to schema theory in research, given the impact of schema theory on reading research in the early to middle 1980s. Others have observed that using terms such as *background knowledge* or *prior knowledge* interchangeably with *schema* implies a consensus that does not exist (Sadoski, Paivio, & Goetz, 1991). This concern aside, the continued reliance on schema theory in textbooks as a means of describing cognitive reading processes to pre-service and in-service teachers supports Gaffney and Anderson's assertion that schema theory is still influencing our perceptions of reading and is believed to be a viable and valuable explanation for teachers. The point here is that the construct of schema is more than just a useful metaphor. The metaphor itself says something about how literacy researchers and educators have come to see reading processes, because "structural metaphors guide our thinking (Lakoff & Johnson, 1999) and, when incorporated into our models of cognition, stake out the parameters of our epistemologies" (Hruby, 2001, p. 48).

At the same time, the dearth of articles that directly explore similarities between schema and sociocultural perspectives leads us to believe that literacy researchers and educators have not yet thought through the relationship between schema theory and more recently adopted sociocultural perspectives. Although we conjecture that many of our colleagues in literacy will agree that schema theoretic perspectives and sociocultural perspectives are not as dichotomous as once believed (see Frawley, 1997), we know of no published work to date that explores whether and how schema theoretic perspectives may be reconciled with the social perspectives of mind and literacy espoused by sociocultural researchers.

Historical Review of Schema Theories

Early Use of "Schema": The Work of Kant, Bartlett, and Piaget

The concept of the schema can be traced to Plato and Aristotle (Marshall, 1995), but Kant (1929) is generally considered to be the first to talk about schemas as organizing structures that mediate how we see and interpret the world (Johnson, 1987). Schemas are "a sort of bias inherent in the mind" (Campbell, 1989, p. 90). For Kant a schema stood between or mediated the external world and internal mental structures; a schema was a lens that both shaped and was shaped by experience.

Bartlett (1932/1995) used the term schema and conducted experiments to explore schemas as cultural constructs in memory, and this is the work most widely cited by schema theorists working in the cognitive era (Saito, 1996). Bartlett's research and writing point to schemas as more than in-the-head phenomena and provide a basis for thinking of them as patterns that extend beyond the knower into the social and cultural world (Saito, 1996, 2000). In looking at Bartlett's work, it becomes clear that schema theory, at its inception, was not about in-the-head phenomena only. Middleton and Crook (1996) wrote of Bartlett (citing a 1961 republication of the same 1932/1995 book that we reference):

> Bartlett discussed schema as an "organized setting" and not as some uniform feature of the mind (Bartlett, 1932/1961, p. 200). Schemata in such a view (i.e., Bartlett's) are

not knowledge structures stored in the brains or minds of individuals for the interpretation of experience, but functional properties of adaptations between persons and their physical and social environments. (p. 202)

For Bartlett, schemas highlighted the reciprocity between culture and memory. Schemas were necessary to explain the constitutive role of culturally organized experience in individual sense making. This early use of the term suggested a transactional relationship between individual knowledge and cultural practice.

Contemporaries of Bartlett (e.g., Dewey, Bentley, and Rosenblatt) developed psychological and literary theories that explicitly used the concept of *transactionalism*. It is clear from Rosenblatt's (1989) definition of *transaction*, below, that the spirit of transactionalism was reflected in Bartlett's initial construction of the concept of schemas:

> Instead of separate, already defined entities acting on one another (an interaction), Dewey and Bentley (1949, p. 69) suggested that the term *transaction* be used to designate relationships in which each element conditions and is conditioned by the other in a mutually constituted situation. This view requires a break with entrenched habits of thinking. The old stimulus–response, subject–object, individual–social dualisms give way to a recognition that such relationships take place in a context that also enters into the event. *Human activities and relationships are seen as transactions in which the individual and the social, cultural, and natural elements interfuse.* (italics added; Rosenblatt, 1989, p. 154)

Schema was also the central mediational construct in Jean Piaget's (1952) structural theory of the origins and development of cognition. For Piaget, development was interpreted as an ongoing dialectic in which the individual either assimilates new experience consistent with existing schemas or changes (i.e., accommodates) schemas to fit his or her experience. What is more, Piaget emphasized the embodied nature of schema formation by calling attention to the importance of sensory–motor schemata in an individual's early development. But we find it interesting that, although Piaget shared the individualistic bias of cognitive scientists, the latter seem to have been little influenced by either the developmental or the embodied dimensions of Piaget's conceptions of schemas.

Central to our discussion in this article is the recognition that the early development and use of the schema construct had its origin in efforts to understand individual thought processes as inextricably embedded in cultural life. Individual knowledge schemas were transactionally linked to culturally organized experience.[2] In the analysis that follows, we argue that this connection was lost in later applications of schema to the reading process. In fact, after a close examination of Bartlett's work and some of his experiments, Beals (1998) wrote:

> Unfortunately, this view of schema as shaped by culture is not included in some current versions of schema theory. Although Bartlett is widely cited as the source of the term schema as a model for the organization of memory, the application of the concept to much cognitive science and psychological theory and research washes

out the "essentially social character" (p. 225) of schema to which Bartlett (1932) pointed. (p. 10)

We now turn toward exploration of modern conceptions and applications of schema in cognitive psychology, including some of the limitations of schema theoretic perspectives.

Schema Theoretic Perspectives in the 1970s and '80s

Contemporary conceptions of schema derive primarily from work conducted in cognitive science during the 1970s. As we begin our exploration of schema theory within cognitive psychology, several definitions may be helpful. Rumelhart and Ortony (1977) defined schemas as "data structures for representing the generic concepts stored in memory. They exist for generalized concepts underlying objects, situations, events, sequences of events, actions, and sequences of actions" (p. 101). Brewer and Nakamura (1984), in an attempt to address the role of schema in remembering knowledge and constructing new knowledge, wrote: "In brief, [schemas] are higher-order cognitive structures that have been hypothesized to underlie many aspects of human knowledge and skill. They serve a crucial role in providing an account of how old knowledge interacts with new knowledge in perception, language, thought, and memory" (p. 120). These definitions highlight several important features of schemas as noted by Rumelhart (1984):

- Schemas have variables.
- Schemas can be embedded, one within another.
- Schemas represent knowledge at all levels of abstraction.
- Schemas represent *knowledge* rather than definitions [italics in the original].
- Schemas are active processes.
- Schemas are recognition devices whose processing is aimed at the evaluation of their goodness of fit to the data being process. (Rumelhart, 1984, p. 169)

Although much of the early work on schema theory in the 1970s was published by cognitive scientists exploring knowledge construction through computer metaphors (e.g., Minsky, 1975; Schank & Abelson, 1975; Winograd, 1975), such theories were readily applied to the study of reading. Cognitive scientists studying story schemas provided a clear link between schema theory and reading research in comprehension by exploring story structure and recall (e.g., Mandler & Johnson, 1977; Rumelhart, 1975). Other scholars (e.g., Anderson, 1977, 1978; Anderson & Pearson, 1984; Bransford & Johnson, 1972, 1973), working primarily on investigations of reading comprehension, contributed significantly to the work on schemas and helped bring schema research into mainstream reading research.

Perhaps the best summary of schema theory and its importance for the reading field comes from Pearson (1992), who observed: "Anderson and Pearson's (1984) schema-theoretic account of reading comprehension typifies the cognitively oriented version of this [reading] model, with its twin emphases on prior knowledge (as a resource) and inference (as a process) in directing the construction of meaning" (p. 1075). Pearson's summary emphasizes the cognitive processes that are to some degree made visible by schema theory. Elsewhere, Anderson and Pearson explain that schema theory is "a model for representing how knowledge is stored in human memory" (1984, p. 259); and later, "the reader's schema is a structure that facilitates planful retrieval of text information from memory and permits reconstruction of elements that were not learned or have been forgotten" (p. 285).

Schema theory was a major force in the development of reading models and had an important influence on research, particularly in relation to reading comprehension and learning. It provided researchers and teachers with a model for representing knowledge and organizing experience. It also provided a window into how individuals might transfer and generate knowledge, for example, by explaining how a schema for a cup would help an individual understand other containers. Throughout the 1970s and early 1980s, scholars (e.g., Anderson, 1977, 1978; Pitchert & Anderson, 1977) conducted groundbreaking research in the role of schema in stories and the reading process. Scholars also wrote articles for teachers (e.g., Hacker, 1980; Pearson, 1982). By the mid-1980s, schema theory exerted enough influence that Anderson and Pearson noted, in their review in the second *Handbook of Reading Research,* that "schema-theoretic notions became the driving force behind empirical investigations of basic processes in reading" (p. 259). A review of research and practitioner journals gives credence to their claim. Research using schema theory was prevalent in literacy journals for the decade from 1978 to 1988 (Gaffney & Anderson, 2000).

Limitations of Schema Theory and Studies of Schema

Although schema theory obviously had an impact on the study of reading processes, the construct of schema and the theories describing schema activation and use had limitations that were noted by both proponents and critics. Early definitions of schema theory, for example, presented schemas as fixed, rigid structures (Schank & Abelson, 1977), but, as Kintsch (1998) noted, such rigid definitions were quickly revised to include more loosely defined structures. Despite this change, studies of schema tended to be limited in a number of ways. We provide a brief review of some of the criticisms of schema theory, using a study by Anderson, Reynolds, Schallert, and Goetz (1977) that has often been cited by reading researchers.

In this study, Anderson et al. presented music students and weightlifters with ambiguous passages and found that the students' experiences and knowledge influenced their interpretations of the passages. That is, the music students typically read the ambiguous passage (Appendix A) as a story about four friends getting together on the weekend to play music. Weightlifters reading the same passage tended to read it as a passage about playing cards. Concomitantly, the music students read another ambiguous passage as referring to a prison break, whereas the weight-lifters read it as referring to wrestling (Appendix B). One of the strengths of schema theory in this study and in others is that it provided a way of thinking about prior knowledge in text interpretation and how an individual's experience (e.g., as a weight-lifter or a flutist) would shape their interpretation of text. Most critics of schema theory accept and acknowledge the importance of schema in providing a means of describing and thinking about prior knowledge in text interpretation and how an individual's experience would shape his or her interpretation of text (see Carver, 1992, for an alternative viewpoint), but detractors raise numerous other criticisms, summarized below.

Many schema-related studies, including the one above, have relied on what Sadoski et al. (1991) refer to as "bizarre texts" (p. 469). Bizarre texts are ambiguous, containing few or no concrete referents. Such texts are useful in activating particular schemas as they relate to a person's experience or prior knowledge, but these ambiguous texts differ from naturally occurring texts, which contain specific referents even when they are challenging because of their content, specialized discourse, or reading level. Responses to bizarre texts tend to activate pre-existing default schemas and thus do not account for the more rich, complex, diversified types of knowledge that are stored when a person reads other texts or encounters other less constrained circumstances (Alba & Hasher, 1983; Nasajii, 2002). Because the ambiguous texts are specialized and involve particular comprehension processes, schema theory does little, argues Carver (1992), to explain the "normal, typical, or ordinary reading—called rauding" (p. 165). Studies such as the one with the musicians and wrestlers make clear the importance of a reader's personal background and surrounding contexts, but are further limited because they raise questions about how relevant and generalizable findings are for "the reading of naturally occurring texts" (Sadoski et al., p. 470; see also Alba & Hasher, 1983). Moreover, despite some notable exceptions, which we will address momentarily, most studies of schema are limited because of relying on experimental procedures rather than community-based or classroom-based settings and tasks.

To address a number of limitations of schema theoretic perspectives, some researchers have proposed alternative theories, often from an associationist or connectionist perspective. Sadoski and Paivio (2001) proposed Dual Coding Theory (DCT) as an alternative to schema theoretic perspectives. DCT focuses on areas related to verbal and nonverbal encoding and to the role of imagery in reading and writing. This attention to imagery is something that other researchers have not taken into account. Sadoski and Paivio eschew the use of the term schema as they contrast DCT with a number of perspectives on reading and writing that make use of the term schema. Kintsch (1998), on the other hand, continues to use the term, while noting its limitations as he proposes a "construction–integration (CI) model" (p. 94). Kintsch observes that schemas, as traditionally conceived of in connection with comprehension, have been seen largely as top-down processes that are tightly controlled, whereas a substantial amount of research indicates "the need for conceiving of comprehension as a more bottom-up, loosely structured process" (p. 94). Kintsch contrasts schemas, which he calls "fixed control structures" (p. 94), with comprehension, which he describes as "incredibly flexible and context-sensitive" (p. 94). His model incorporates schema but is broader and more complex than traditional schema theoretic perspectives.

Our review of the limitations of schema theory and alternative views is not meant to be exhaustive. Rather, we wish to point out some of the limitations and to note two, in particular, that are most relevant to the work we have taken up in this article. In addition to the rigidity of schemas as traditionally conceived, scholars have noted that issues of schema construction and activation are problematic. For example, research, such as that with the musicians and wrestlers described earlier, has focused on schema activation, not creation. This poses the problem of needing to "fill slots in schemata *ad infinitum*" (Nassaji, 2002, p. 445). In this article we do not address the issue of schemas endlessly deferred but are more interested in the question of the origins and development of schemas. In what do schemas have their origins? Traditional schema studies have done little to address this question.

In addressing this question, we are interested in the role of social and cultural factors. Although various definitions of schema and the numerous critiques of schema suggest attention to both individual and social contexts, cultural and social factors typically are acknowledged by schema theorists, and by many of their critics, as just another set of variables (Middelton & Crook, 1996).

We do not mean to suggest that researchers have not investigated schema and its relationship to culture. For example, in an international, cross-cultural study, Pritchard (1990) examined how cultural schemas influenced 11th-grade readers from the United States and from the Pacific island nation of Palau. Steffenson, Joag-Dev, and Anderson (1979) examined Indian and American university students' understandings as they read culturally familiar and unfamiliar passages about weddings. Yet few studies using schema theory have examined how various cultural groups within the United States interpret texts. A notable exception is preliminary research reported by Anderson (1994) that investigated how Black and White teenagers perceived passages involving "sounding," the good-natured exchange of insults in the Black community (see Reynolds, Taylor, Steffensen, Shirey, & Anderson, 1981, 1982; see also Lee, 1995). It is noteworthy that this particular investigation explored a community-based practice rather than a school text, and as Anderson notes, "It remains to be seen how much school reading material is culturally loaded" (p. 478). Anderson's comments alert us to the need to explore cultural and social factors not as background variables but as integral components of schema in their own right.

The Influence of Sociocultural Perspectives: Reading as Social, Contextualized Practice

Although schema theory helped researchers and theorists to think about the inner workings of the mind and how knowledge is stored in memory, changes, and is used in comprehending texts, the theory as taken up during the cognitive revolution largely marginalized the role of the individual's social and cultural life. Experience figured prominently in schema theory, but the version of culture implied by schema theoretic models, and by some alternative models, is vastly oversimplified when compared with the increasingly complex, and contested, views of culture that were emerging from anthropologists (e.g., Clifford, 1988; Clifford & Marcus, 1986), from cultural psychologists (Scribner & Cole, 1981), and from the work of educational anthropologists (e.g., Au, 1980; Heath, 1983; Watson-Gegeo & Boggs, 1977) who were exploring literacy processes during the 1970s and '80s.

A number of theoretical, methodological, and contextual factors converged during the 1970s and '80s to facilitate a greater consideration of social factors in literacy development. There were increasing concerns about issues of culture and language in educational settings and in relation to populations that had not achieved school success. These concerns emerged while Vygotsky's works were becoming more widely available in English (Moll, 2001). In addition, to explore issues of language and culture in teaching and learning, some researchers turned to ethnographic methodologies, creating a more interdisciplinary study of literacy. Writing about this shift in reading research, Florio-Ruane and McVee (2000) observed, "Researchers from a hybrid of traditions including anthropology and psychology have probed how literacy as both cultural tool and cultural practice is influenced by social and historical factors as well as the micro-politics of face to face interaction (e.g., Scribner & Cole, 1981; Moll, 1992)" (p. 158). Increasingly, researchers turned toward exploring the tools and signs related to literacy practices situated within particular contexts and activities. Within the United States, researchers also turned to the work of other Russian activity theorists and psychologists, particularly as their work was interpreted by American scholars (e.g., Cole, 1996; Moll, 1990; Scribner & Cole, 1981; Wertsch, 1985, 1991).[3]

Although research explicitly based on schema theory continued into the late 1980s and 1990s, it was from the mid-1970s through the early 1980s that the most theory and research were generated from schema theoretic perspectives and the findings most often actively applied to the study of reading processes. Pearson (1992) observed that although more research on basic reading processes was actually conducted in the 1980s, this work did not dominate then as it had in the 1970s. Among other causes, Pearson attributes this development to the increasing attention focused on the social and cultural factors related to literacy (e.g., Au, 1980; Au & Mason, 1981;Cazden, 1988; Heath, 1983; Moll & Diaz, 1987). As a result, research focused on models and theories of reading processes became "old news." Finally, and perhaps as an outgrowth of the focus on social and cultural factors, research on the basic reading process "was recaptured by the cognitive psychology community and tended to be reported in journals and edited volumes with more of a cognitive science focus" (Pearson, 1992, p. 1077). In fact, although many cognitive scientists have continued extending and elaborating their work, particularly through connectionist theory (e.g., Rumelhart, 1990, 1994; Ramsey, Stich, & Rumelhart, 1991), this later work has not yet had the same amount of influence on the literacy field as the main body of work developed earlier by cognitive scientists. Even theories that are specific in addressing the limitations of schema theory (e.g., Carver, 1992; Kintsch, 1998; Sadoski & Paivio, 2001), have met with limited uptake in relation to recent literacy research and practice in the broader literacy community.

As Pearson suggested, because cognitive accounts of reading processes failed to address the sociocultural dimensions of literacy that anthropologists and sociologists were uncovering, parallel lines of research emerged. It may be that these parallel lines simply mirrored the dualism between individual and social perspectives that characterized cognitive psychology. In his criticism of the cognitive revolution and the metaphor of mind as computer, Bruner (1990) wrote: "There could be no place for 'mind' in such a system—'mind' in the sense of intentional states like believing, desiring, intending, grasping a meaning" (p. 8). Computational models of mind, as presented by cognitive scientists, have represented individual knowledge as existing distinct from, and thus portable across, sociocultural contexts. Absent is the constitutive force of the social—that schemas are cultural historical constructions that emerge only within the individual through transactions with others.

Although many cite Bartlett or Kant as early proponents of the term schema, Anderson and Pearson (1984) wrote that "the full development of schema theory as a model for representing how knowledge is stored in human memory had to await the revolution in our conception of how humans process information spurred by the thinking of computer scientists doing simulations of human cognition (e.g., Minsky, 1975; Winograd, 1975)" (p. 259). The model of the mind as machine, as information processor, is largely accepted to be at odds with sociocultural perspectives, although there are several scholars who have written persuasively about what they learned from both perspectives (cf. Beals, 1998; Frawley, 1997). Clearly, there are some major differences between these paradigms. A view of mind predicated on an information-processing model is critically at odds with sociocultural perspectives that assert that the genesis of thought, language, and, therefore, development lies in social and cultural activity.[4] Social and cultural considerations are therefore *the* most critical and essential factors in schema acquisition. It is not enough to acknowledge the role of the social and cultural at the margins of cognition. Rather, as Wertsch (1991) has noted, we must explore how social and cultural tools and activity mediate learning and development. Thus the genesis of individual literacy knowledge is situated in the sociocultural milieu and is inextricably tied to the milieu's discourse practices, mediational tools, and cultural artifacts, which have both a material and an ideational character. Both ideal and material tools are always value-laden because they are shaped by relationships within and among people. People position these tools according to sociocultural norms governing the activity in the moment.

In the next section we discuss contributions that sociocultural perspectives can make to our understandings of schema, and we also suggest some ways that schema theory might help us to think about sociocultural perspectives. We raise issues related to the origins and development of schemas as mediated by material and ideational tools and by embodiment, and as cultural processes of social–individual origin that have both public and private dimensions.

Sociocultural Perspectives on Schema

Addressing the Genetic Question: The Origins and Development of Schemas

The cognitivism of most cognitive science approaches has generally been premised on a rationalist worldview that is inherently dualistic. In such a view, the active individual-as-knower is generally assumed to stand separate and apart from the world-as-known, such that the former is able to represent the latter through his or her schematic representations. In such a view, mind is hyper-rationalized, that is, an overemphasis is placed on cognitive structures and processes within the individual. In contrast, transactionalist perspectives—such as those held by Dewey and Bentley (1949), Gee (1992, 1997a, 1997b, 2000, 2004), Smagorinsky (2001), and Vygotsky (1978, 1986)—generally assume that the knower and the known, the person and the environment, including other individuals, are mutually constitutive of each other. This perspective carries profound implications for how we conceptualize the origins and development of representational constructs such as schema. Rather than perceiving schema or cognitive structures as in-the-head representations of something out there in the world, thus separating knower and known, the transactional nature of knowing acknowledges that the dualistic separation of subject and object is "not given and ready-made; [dualism] is an idea that belongs to the human history of mind and nature" (Varela, Thompson, & Rosh, 1991, p. 141).

In contrast to a transactional view, schema theory as developed in the 1970s and '80s posited that meaning was stored in mental structures, which in turn were activated and organized during the reading process. Reading became the unique arrangement of mental structures as elicited by any particular text, as opposed to being inextricably situated in the process of the interaction between texts and schema. Meanings in the head, though shaped by experience, were nonetheless viewed as having an existence independent of any particular embodied activity. Although this explains the relationship between past and present experience and the conventionalization of experience into scripts, frames, and roles that represent our understanding of what is and could be, it does not account for the origins and development of these mental structures.

Indeed, the genetic question is not one that was identified as a primary concern to schema theorists. The primary challenge for schema theorists, as Anderson and Pearson (1984) described it, was to give specificity to "the form and substance of schema" and to specify the processes that allowed for schema use (p. 259). Anderson and Pearson and others emphasize the application of schemas to reading processes with scant attention to the origins and development of schemas. In addition, schema development has been described as reorganization of existing mental structures; new schemas are created only by analogy or reconfiguration of old ones. Yet the origin of these schemas is not accounted for. As stated by Rochelle and Clancy (1992), "Researchers may ask, 'What is the raw material of reasoning?' (Koedinger & Anderson, 1990), but they tend to give one choice—varieties of representations. Schema models of learning involve perceptible features but deal only with a priori representations of experience (Schank & Abelson, 1977)" (p. 448). Thus they do not address the origins and processes by which schema develop.

Hatano (1993) has argued that as researchers have begun to study teaching and learning from a constructivist stance, as opposed to a transmission-oriented stance, they need to further refine their understanding of Vygotsky's theory to more fully "explain the sociogenesis of individual cognition from the constructivist point of view" (p. 164). One of the ways to do this is by investigating and describing the "material upon which constructive mental processes work" (Resnick, 1987, in Hatano, p. 164). Hatano urges scholars to specify in greater detail the "*nature* of the material and *how* it is worked on by an active mind" (italics added; p. 164). In other words, if researchers think about schemas from a sociocultural perspective, this involves rethinking both the *nature* of schemas (i.e., What are the salient features of schemas from a sociocultural perspective?) and their *use* (i.e., What are the mediational features of schemas? How do schemas function as mediational tools?). To further explore the cultural and environmental materials and their role in cognition implies exploring learning and cognition not as contained within an individual but as created in the interaction between material and activity.

Holland and Cole (1995) suggest that schemas represent the ideal—that is, conceptual—aspects of cognition, whereas discourse represents the material aspects. Both serve as artifacts—collective tools with histories and functions that are continually modified within social practices—to mediate human cognition. Understanding that cognitive activity in any single instance is mediated by the ideal as well as the material aspects of cultural artifacts affords opportunities to attend to the ways in which individual motivations and intentions and the rules governing social activity reflect the essentially dialogic nature of meaning making. Holland and Cole suggest that although schemas attend to the habitual forms of behavior, they "always must be woven to the particulars of a situation" (p. 480). Elsewhere, Cole (1996) explains that,

> defined in this manner, the properties of artifacts apply with equal force whether one is considering languages or more mundane forms of artifacts such as tables and knives which constitute material culture. What differentiates the word "table" from an actual table is the relative prominence of their material and ideal aspects and the kinds of coordinations they afford. No word exists apart from its material instantiation, whereas every table embodies an order imposed by thinking human beings. (p. 117)

Vygotsky also recognized that words are imbued with psychological sense and not just meaning as linguistically defined. "The sense of a word...is the sum of all the psychological events aroused in our consciousness by the word. It is a dynamic, fluid, complex whole, which has several zones of unequal stability. Meaning is only one of the zones of sense, the most stable and precise zone" (Vygotsky, 1986, p. 146). No single definition can ever capture the full sense of a word. Word meanings are indeterminate. It is only within the rules of the language game that meanings arise (Wittgenstein, 1961). This shifts the focus of our investigations and the unit of analysis away from the mental processes alone toward examination of activities or events. Of this shift Rogoff (1993) writes, "An important perspective that results from using the dynamic event/activity as unit of analysis is a shift from considering cognition as a collection of mental possessions (such as thoughts, schemas, memories, scripts, and plans) to regarding cognition as the active process of solving mental and other problems (e.g., by thinking, recounting, remembering, organizing, planning, and contemplating), generally in the service of intelligent action" (p. 124).

It is only by attending to the materiality of artifacts that we can explore the way cognitive processes are dependent on the social and physical practices that both enable and constrain the meaning potential. Many investigations of literacy (e.g., Heath, 1983; Moll, 1994; Purcell-Gates, 1995; Watson-Gegeo & Boggs, 1977) have demonstrated the ways that various speech communities offer students different (not less) ideational and material artifacts to mediate their understanding and experience of any text activity. These examples of work related to the discursive aspects of meaning making further problematize psychological explanations of schemas that treat culture as a variable within, rather than a constituent of, mental representations. They are also important because they draw our attention to the power contained in such tools, as particular tools can either facilitate or constrain our participation in particular activities. This is particularly relevant in educational arenas where the use of particular tools can lead to the labeling of some students as successful, even gifted, while others are labeled as at risk or struggling.

One example of the need to focus on both the material and ideal comes from Wertsch's (1998) interpretation of research conducted by Beck and colleagues (Beck & McKeown, 1994; Beck, McKeown, & Gromoll, 1989; Beck, McKeown, Sinatra, & Loxterman, 1991). These researchers argue that students could not make connections between events presented in the texts in a coherent way because the texts themselves were inadequate; that is, the history texts did not have textual coherence. The researchers also argued that teachers try to cover too much material. This in turn thwarts students' attempts to make connections. Wertsch interprets these studies by using narrative as a cultural tool that mediates students' understandings of the text and of history. He writes:

> In terms of mediated action, the point is that students had not mastered the cultural tool—namely, a historical narrative—and for this reason they could not take advantage of the affordances this cultural tool offered as they sought to carry out the form of mediated action involved in reproducing accounts of the American Revolution. These students knew too little in the sense that they had not mastered the narrative

form that consists of an ensemble of interrelationships organized into a single whole. (Wertsch, 1998, p.87)

Wertsch acknowledges that the students have mastered other narrative forms and understand them. What is different here is that the specific form, a historical narrative, has not been mastered.

This is similar to the problem cited by Bransford (1983): that packets of information in texts may appear unrelated to students. The great difficulty lies not in presenting students with more information but in providing for them a means to recognize and construct the relationships between various bits of information—that is, weaving the strands of information into a coherent schema that facilitates students' understandings of content. Wertsch makes a similar point when he writes that, "unless it is integrated into a coherent schema (i.e., a narrative, in the cases that I am considering), information is very hard to comprehend and retain" (1998, p. 86).

Schemas as Embodied

The effort to construct knowledge relationships is affected not only by the material and ideal tools that a learner has access to but also by the character of embodied learning and embodied interaction. In the following extended quotation, Johnson (cited in Varela, Thompson, & Rosch, 1991) explains:

> Meaning includes patterns of embodied experience and preconceptual structures of our sensibility (i.e., our mode of perception, or orienting ourselves, and of interacting with other objects, events, or persons). These embodied patterns do not remain private or peculiar to the person who experiences them. Our community helps us interpret and codify many of our felt patterns. They become shared cultural modes of experience and help to determine the nature of our meaningful, coherent understanding of our "world." (p. 150)

Johnson (1987) proposes a meaning for schemas that differs in an important way from that offered by cognitive scientists. In contrast to the symbolic or propositional nature of schemas conceptualized by cognitive scientists, Johnson maintains that embodied schemas are "constantly operating in our perception, bodily movement through space, and physical manipulation of objects" (p. 23). This perspective on the role of embodiment is further elaborated in Lakoff and Johnson's (1999) groundbreaking book *Philosophy in the Flesh: The Embodied Mind and Its Challenge to Western Thought.*

Such a view foregrounds the ways in which meaning is shaped not just by experience as recollected, by reified event structures, or by material and ideal artifacts, but also by *embodied* experience and the ways in which that embodied experience is shaped by others in our social community. In such a view, "cultural modes of experience" act as one means of mediating our perceptions of the world. In turn, cultural modes shape, and are shaped by, both the ideal and the material artifacts that we make use of.

There is growing attention to the embodiment of human cognition (e.g., Clark, 1997; Johnson, 1987), although attention to issues of embodiment is not new. William James (1890) wrote that "we sense our bodily selves as the seat of our thinking" (cited in Rosenblatt, 1989, p. 245), and thus he suggests that when we look at a tree stump and think of it as a chair, we reveal the relationship between our inner world and the external workings of it through a bodily form. Similarly, consider Lakoff and Johnson's (1980) assertion that not only is all language metaphorical, but our metaphors emerge through our physical activity in the world. They note that

> metaphors are grounded by virtue of systematic correlates with experience....We are not claiming that physical experience is in any way more basic than other kinds of experience, whether emotional, mental, cultural or whatever....Rather what we are claiming about grounding is that we typically conceptualize the nonphysical in terms of the physical—that is, we conceptualize the less clearly delineated in terms of the more clearly delineated." (italics in the original; p. 58)

A shortcoming of schema theory as traditionally conceived by cognitive science is that it implies an understanding of literacy as unconnected to embodied material experience. Recently, Gee (2004) made this point in writing about traditional views of cognition and learning, particularly learning to read:

> Learning does not work well when learners are forced to check their bodies at the schoolroom door like guns in the old West. School learning is often about disembodied minds learning outside any context of decisions and actions. When people learn something as a cultural process their bodies are involved because cultural learning always involves having specific experiences that facilitate learning, not just memorizing words.
>
> Traditionalists treat learning to read as if "read" was an intransitive verb. People just "read." But no one just reads; rather they read *something*. (italics in the original; Gee, 2004, p. 39)

Rather than the embodied, situated approach described by Gee, cognitive versions of schema theory privilege literacy, and to some extent language, as if it were divorced from use and practice.

Consider, for example, the way in which many experiments on schema have been carried out. Most have been conducted in laboratory settings with adults who have been asked to read one or perhaps several narrative passages related to already existing, or default, schemas (Nassaji, 2002). Although such investigations were necessary to define and explore schemas as constructs and to determine how schemas are activated and applied, they have also put forward a relatively narrow view of schema activation and construction that emphasizes the individual. In this sense, we might say that schema theoretic views have hyper-rationalized literacy processes, foregrounding the cognitive at the expense of the material. Yet language is a way of *doing* things in the world. The determination that a child is having difficulty comprehending some particular text well involves judgments about the values, norms, roles, and goals that position the child in a particular way with respect to a text. The discourse processes required in the moment are embedded in cultural histories not just of individuals but of kinship groups, social classes, and political ideologies. It is not merely words but social and cultural practices, opportunities, and interactions that must be provided. In addition, these experiences, opportunities, and interactions must allow for a child to engage with a range of mediational artifacts, both material and ideal, thus tying language to authentic material and cognitive practices and embodied activity. Schemas, as traditionally conceived of in relation to reading, were limited to in-the-head categories, in part, because they were removed from materiality connected to cultural context and processes.

The Origins and Development of Schemas as a Cultural Process

Cognition as cultural process implies a social conception of mind. Gee (1997b) characterized the social mind and its ability to interpret the world as a pattern recognizer:

> Because the world is infinitely full of potentially meaningful patterns and subpatterns in any domain, something must guide the learner in selecting the patterns and subpatterns to focus on. This something resides in the cultural models of the learner's sociocultural groups and the practices and settings in which they are rooted. Because the mind is a pattern recognizer and there are infinite ways to pattern features of the world, of necessity, although perhaps ironically, the mind is social (really, cultural) in the sense that sociocultural practice and settings guide the patterns in terms of which the learner thinks acts, talks values, and interacts. (p. 240)

Acting as a "pattern recognizer," the mind guides learners in accordance with perceived cultural patterns, not just in the head but in the world. Mind, in Gee's portrayal, reflects the embodied nature of knowing socially and culturally as one interacts with the world. Meaning is not just in the head or in the body, but in the world. That is, meaning does not exist in the form of words or even images, but within our relationships among and across experiences, actions, talk, people, and all sorts of culturally situated knowledge (Gee, 2004). As Gavelek and Raphael (1996) have observed, "through our interactions with more knowledgeable others, we acquire the culturally variable and historically changing higher psychological functions that make possible the intelligence unique to humankind. The higher psychological processes that define us as cultural beings thus emerge from, but are not reducible to, the elementary psychological processes that characterize us as biological beings" (p. 184).

Sociocultural theorists argue that schemas emerge from the social interactions between an individual and his environment. This is the same principle that operates in Vygotsky's general law of cultural development. Vygotsky (1978) wrote: "Every function in the child's cultural development appears twice: first, on the social level, and later, on the individual level; first *between* people (*interpsychological*), and then *inside* the child (*intrapsychological*)....All higher functions originate as actual relations between human individuals" (italics in the original;

p. 57). Vygotsky's general law of cultural development underscores the importance of the roles of both the social and the individual. The Vygotsky Space (see Figure 1), adapted from Harré (1984) by Gavelek and Raphael (1996), aids visualization of the myriad ways that the social and the individual come into play as knowledge is constructed and internalized. The model draws our attention to one of the basic principles of internalization as described by Robbins (2003): "The key aspect of internalization is the rooting or the process of ingrowth that leads to

Figure 1. The Vygotsky Space

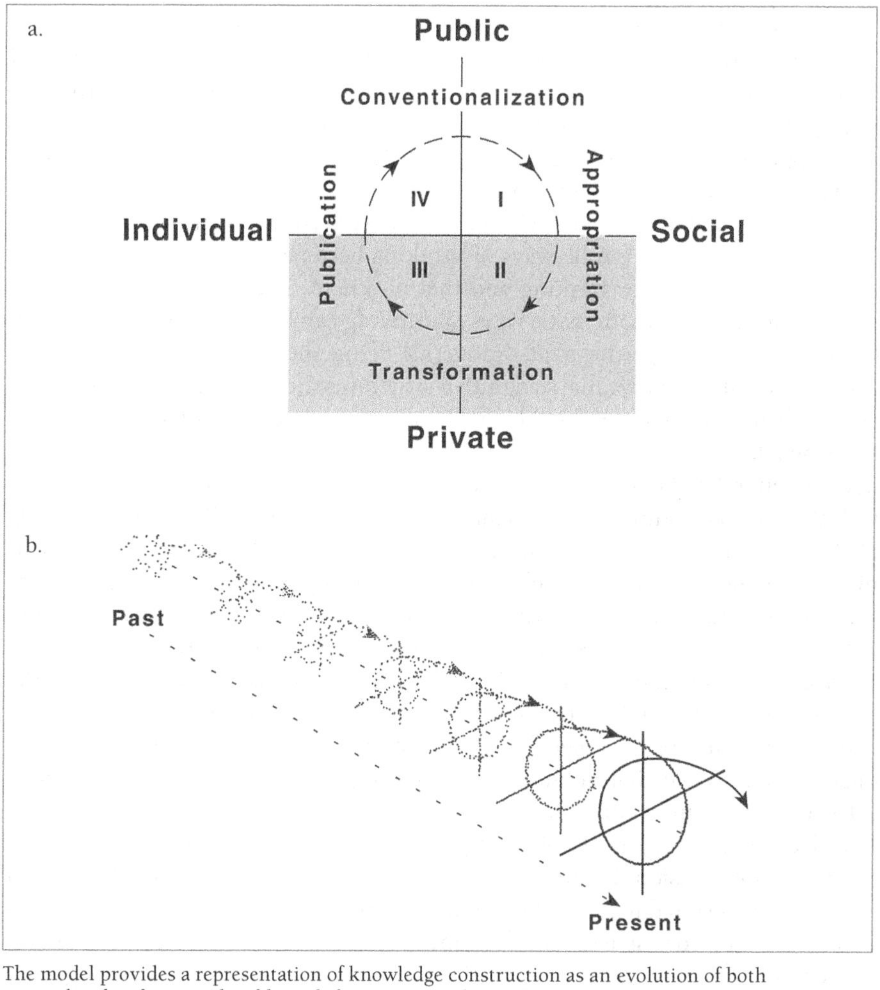

The model provides a representation of knowledge construction as an evolution of both internalized and externalized knowledge processes that include individual and social considerations. Adapted from the work of Harré (1984); the figure on which this adaptation is based originally appeared in Gavelek & Raphael (1996), p. 186. Copyright 1996 by the National Council of Teachers of English. Reprinted with permission.

personal transformation. Internalization is not understood as a reflection of the external, but rather a transformation of the external" (p. 31). The Vygotsky Space model provides opportunities for thinking about knowledge construction as an evolution of both internalized and externalized knowledge processes that include individual and social considerations.

The four quadrants of the Vygotsky space (Figure 1a) are formed by the intersection of two orthogonal dimensions, one public ←→ private dimension and a second social ←→ individual dimension (arrows indicate two-way interaction). Together these two dimensions create four "spaces": (1) public–social, (2) private–social, (3) private–individual, and (4) public–individual. The origins and development of a person's cognitive processes and structures proceed iteratively through Quadrants I through IV and are characterized by four corresponding transitions: (1) appropriation (Q_I–Q_{II}), in which an individual appropriates certain ways of thinking acquired discursively in interaction with others; (2) transformation (Q_{II}–Q_{III}), in which an individual transforms and takes ownership of these previously appropriated ways of thinking; (3) publication (Q_{III}–Q_{IV}), in which an individual goes public or makes observable through talk or actions, or both, his or her thinking that was previously private; and (4) conventionalization (Q_{IV}–Q_I), the process whereby these public ways of thinking become conventionalized as part of the individual's own thinking and that of others. The origins, development, and transformation of schematic ways of thinking can be understood as the iterative movement through these quadrants that define the Vygotsky space. Through this movement, an individual's cognitive structures (i.e., schemas) and processes emerge from, but are not reducible to, his or her interactions with others.

Consider, for example, fifth-grade students engaging in book clubs to learn new content related to literacy and social studies (e.g., how to discuss a book, historical fiction as a genre, developments leading to the U.S. Civil War, the meaning of "Confederate" and "Union"). In this context a student, Jason, has the opportunity to use public discourse, such as written book logs and talk about text, to engage in social knowledge construction with others in the public sphere (Q_I) and, at the same time, to use these tools (e.g., writing, discourse, reflection) to make connections through his thinking (Q_{II}–Q_{III}). Part and parcel of this process is the extent to which he is able to transform and apply what he has appropriated. In Q_{IV} and Q_I again, interpsychological engagement helps provide opportunities for the ongoing, iterative mediation and elaboration of Jason's knowledge. For example, if Jason is struggling to understand what he has read, discussing a text with more knowledgeable peers in a book club group may provide scaffolding to support Jason's comprehension. In this circumstance his learning is mediated by written language (the printed text), oral language (discussion), and numerous other tools both ideal (e.g., word sense, schemas) and material (e.g., discourse, paper). Social interactions facilitate Jason's internalization of various kinds of knowledge and provide the basis on which he and other students interact with that knowledge at an individual level (Q_{II} and Q_{III}). For example, through writing Jason may take a construct acquired in the public setting (e.g., writing reading logs as responses to text) and then transform it through private cognitive activity (i.e., by inventing a new reading log focused on the titles across various texts).

The point here is that it is not that the public interactions are more important than the cognitive processes, but rather that cognition is a culturally situated process involving mental problem solving in a particular context. Such a view contrasts with traditional perspectives of cognition, which portray cognition as a set of independent, decontextualized mental representations (Rogoff, 1993). This is congruent with what Gutiérrez, Baquendano-Lopez, and Tuner (1997) label the "third space." In such a space, "learning takes precedence over teaching; instruction is consciously local, contingent, situated, and strategic" (p. 372). In Jason's case, he is introduced to reading logs as a *convention* used by students and teachers in book club discussions (Q_I). Over time, he *appropriates* this particular convention, becoming familiar with multiple forms and functions of reading logs (Q_{II}). In introducing his own format for a reading log, he has *transformed* the idea originally presented to him (Q_{III}). Jason shares this new type of reading log with his teacher and classmates as a means of knowledge sharing or *publication* (Q_{IV}). His learning is based on a repertoire of socially situated skills and behaviors as well as on knowledge about language. In this context, Jason has the opportunity to act as both novice and expert.

The Vygotsky Space model represents the recursive nature of Jason's learning, but readers should note that the model is limited by its two-dimensional presentation. Figure 1b represents a three-dimensional model that highlights the recursive nature of knowledge construction and internalization. One of the limits of this model is that it still appears that each axis and quadrant must be activated in sequence while internalizing any concept. However, knowledge construction is obviously more complex than as portrayed in Figure 1a. For example, we might actually find situations where particular knowledge conventions are appropriated but not publicized (e.g., where a student can recognize and construct a mental character map but does not write the character map down or publicize his knowledge), or appropriated but not transformed (e.g., a student who always follows the model of reading logs supplied by the teacher). In addition, in Jason's case, the new knowledge that he has constructed about the writing convention of reading logs can be represented one way in the Vygotsky Space, whereas his understanding of other content knowledge (e.g., reasons for the Civil War) might be represented another way by using the Vygotsky Space model.

The Vygotsky Space portrays the continuum of knowledge construction through public ⟵⟶ private, social ⟵⟶ individual domains. In public cognitive activity, the teacher can assist students in making visible what are typically invisible, private processes. For example, Jason's teacher Mrs. Pardo could ask him to do a think aloud about his reading log to describe how he came up with the idea for a new reading log format and his purpose in doing so. However, her access to the private cognitive domain is limited. As noted by Gavelek and Raphael (1996), "When cognitive activity is private, the thinking can only be inferred—for example, by reading something a child has written (i.e., inferring, based on that public performance, what might have preceded it" (pp. 186–187).

In this regard, teachers do not have access to the intramental processes of concept formation but might infer them from work made public by the student. The Vygotsky Space, in Quadrants II and III, draws our attention to where sociocognitive processes go underground, within the individual. Two considerations are worth noting. The first is that there is no schism that exists between the public–private and external–internal realms, a consideration that Vygotsky himself has noted (1986). The second consideration is that Vygotsky described a multifaceted process for knowledge construction involving multiple phases and stages (1986, pp. 110–126).

As acknowledged above, we feel that schema theory can help literacy researchers attend to both the material and ideal in tool use. Holland and Cole (1995) acknowledged a similar contribution when they wrote:

> Taken together, the ideas of cultural schemas and cultural models appear to offer a congenial set of linkages between culture and mental structure. But, as ordinarily interpreted, the ideas of cultural model, schema, and script differ from our characterization of artifacts presented here in on a crucial respect: they are widely interpreted as ideal, conceptual, "in the head" phenomena, both by psychologists (e.g., Rumelhart, 1978; Schank & Abelson, 1977) and anthropologists (D'Andrade, 1984; Quinn & Holland, 1987). We insist that in practice cultural artifacts always have a material as well as an ideal aspect. (p. 480)

We see a second potential contribution of schema theory in helping sociocultural researchers to address unfinished explorations of scientific and spontaneous concepts (Vygotsky, 1986). Everyday concepts are those that are formed through our experience with the world—again, our embodied experience. The relationship between everyday concepts and scientific or systematic concepts, associated with higher-order thinking, has not been clearly established. Schema theory may be one means of more clearly understanding these constructs and their relationship as it draws our attention to private cognitive processes.

If we think of schema as embodied and not just in the head, then it becomes clear that patterns of enactment, ways of engaging the world, both shape our interpretation of cultural activity and are shaped by cultural activity. This requires very different ways of thinking about teaching and learning. Not only must teachers scaffold and model for students, but they must also be cognizant of the role of schemas as embodied social and cultural constructs that mediate students' learning. Here, a distinction needs to be made between schema as an organizational feature that the mind imposes on experience and schema as a mental representation that mediates activity. Teachers must provide meaningful contexts where students engage with cultural activities and materials (e.g., written and spoken language, texts, and questions) in ways that help students to understand and internalize patterns embodied in the cultural materials and activities that facilitate success in U.S. schools. At the same time, it is critical that teachers recognize the political nature of this reality. All cultural activity is imbued with and linked to power; therefore, schemas can assist a learner in accessing relevant knowledge, or culturally situated schemas may cause confusion or even precipitate resistance. Such is the political nature of schemas.

We now turn to an example from classroom practice to explore the various theoretical points introduced in the previous sections.

Using Schema Theory to Explore an Example of Classroom Practice

We have adapted the following description of a classroom interaction and one student's response to it from Brock (1997) and Brock and Raphael (2005), with the authors' permission. In the scene below, Brock (1997) described how Deng, a student of Hmong descent, responded to an activity related to the book *Maniac Magee* that Mrs. Weber and her class had been reading. Mrs. Weber used the book to foreground issues of racial prejudice and homelessness as part of a unit that explored race and racism in America. Along with reading *Maniac Magee,* students listened to Dr. Martin Luther King Jr.'s "I Have a Dream" speech and engaged in teacher-directed discussion related to the speech and in other discussions and activities to help them understand key concepts presented in the unit. During this unit students needed to draw on prior knowledge; students needed to construct or apply schemas to comprehend text and classroom activities. In this way, the vignette typifies many of the literate activities involving schema use in classroom settings. In the following excerpt, Mrs. Weber reads from a section of *Maniac Magee:*

> Maniac loved the colors of the East End, the people colors. For the life of him, he couldn't figure why these East Enders called themselves black. He kept looking and looking, and the colors he found were gingersnap and light fudge and dark fudge and acorn and butter rum and cinnamon and burnt orange. But never licorice, which, to him, was real black. (Spinelli, 1990, p. 51; quoted in Brock, p. 128)

Brock describes the classroom interaction and response to the passage:

> Mrs. Weber paused shortly after reading the above segment and said, "I want to stop there for a minute and I want to go back to the colors. That was a significant passage in that the author wants you to know that Maniac didn't see the ultimate of contrasts—black and white. He couldn't figure out why blacks called themselves black. He looked at skin tones and he said, "I see cinnamon." What do you think about when you think about cinnamon?" (Transcript, 5-22-95). The class discussed Spinelli's use of descriptive words for colors and how some of those words (e.g., cinnamon, acorn, etc.) made them feel. Then the teacher said, "I want you to put your hands out right here" (Transcript, 5-22-95).
>
> She told the children that she wanted to look at all the different shades of their hands.
>
> The children and the teacher moved off of their chairs into the center of the circle and began to hold out their hands. Because the class was ethnically diverse with African American, Hispanic, Caucasian, and Asian children, there was a stunning

array of different colored hands in the center of the circle. One child, Bill, said, "Oh cool, it goes from light to dark." Then the class discussed the colors of their own hands. They talked about butterscotch, cinnamon, flan, etc. Mrs. Weber talked about the beauty of variations and closed this discussion segment by suggesting, "I have the feeling that the author wants you to know that Maniac spends time looking at the person rather than at the skin tone" (Transcript, 5-22-95). (Brock, 1997, p. 129)

Because Brock had videotaped the session and later conducted a viewing session with Deng, we have a window into how he interpreted the above activity. Because Deng had been in the United States for only 2 years, Brock enlisted the help of Vue, a Hmong translator, to increase the likelihood that her questions and inquiries were understood and to ensure that she understood Deng's responses. As both Brock and the translator interacted with Deng in discussing the episode above, it became clear to them that Deng had not fully understood the teacher's purpose for the activity. He interpreted the teacher's request to look at the shades of hands in the circle as a literal task, to simply observe the colors of the students' hands. It also became clear that Deng did not fully understand the concept of racism. In contrast, Mrs. Weber, Vue, and Brock understood the figurative nature of Mrs. Weber's request. In addition, Brock noted that Vue, who had lived for 8 years in the United States, understood the nature of racism in the United States because he had experienced it in school (Brock, 1999, personal communication).

Before the scene described above, the class had engaged in both small and large group activities and discussions pertaining to racism over a period of weeks, which, according to cognitive perspectives of schema, should have assisted Deng in constructing or activating a schema for racism. Yet, as the interaction with Brock as researcher and Vue as translator made clear, Deng did not have a well-developed schema for racism. In fact, even after discussing the issue in Hmong with Vue, there was some doubt as to whether he fully understood the teacher's reasoning behind the hand activity at all. This is a case where it is possible to conclude that, because the teacher had included many activities and strategies for engaging with the concept of racism before the hand activity (opportunities for activating or constructing a schema), there was something "wrong with" or faulty in Deng's schema—a view predicated on a deficit model wherein the difficulty in learning is seen as an internal deficit of the student or his culture (Sleeter & Grant, 1988).

On the other hand, there are those who will legitimately point out that if the teacher had more knowledge of race relations in the Asian countries where Deng had lived, she might have been able to make more direct connections to his prior knowledge. However, we feel that this second alternative fails to adequately address the context and its participants. Such a perspective assumes that "in-the-head" knowledge that could be conveyed from teacher to student will address a problem that originates in a social milieu. Given the transactional nature of knowledge, Mrs. Weber's schema of race and racism both shapes and is shaped by her engagement with the world and by the social and cultural patterns that she perceives. Even if Mrs. Weber had read about or was knowledgeable about racism in Asia, she would have understood both the constructs of race and racism from an embodied perspective—as a Euro-American female in the context of U.S. society and cultural interactions. Although knowledge of Deng's experiences in other cultures could have been helpful, such knowledge is limited by the context, the participants, and the cultural and material activity encountered. That is to say, both Deng and his teacher's understandings are "distributed across other people and various symbols, tools, objects and technologies" (Gee, 2000, p. 198) rather than being simply contained in the mind. The example also draws our attention to the limitations of an approach to literacy instruction that posits that information about a student's culture or ethnicity is "the answer" to assisting that student in forming knowledge structures such as schema.

Deng's situation serves to illustrate the complexity of supporting comprehension for students, particularly those who are English language learners. In essence, Mrs. Weber was doing many of the "right things." She drew from a variety of texts and discussed them, albeit in teacher-directed fashion, with her students; and in the example cited here she called students' attention to their own skin colors. Yet, at the same time, Deng's teacher enacted a set of activities that replicated her own ideological relationship with the experiences and ideas represented in *Maniac Magee*. She presumed that in engaging in these activities, the students would reposition themselves with respect to the texts in ways that allowed their understandings to mirror her own—and these interactions were likely helpful to some children. The point here is that they were not sufficient for Deng. In this context, Deng lacked opportunities both for comprehensible input and opportunities for output. Brock notes that only in listening to Deng's own account and assisted by Vue as translator did she become aware that Deng was not understanding the story; he did not understand Mrs. Weber's earlier discussion of moral and ethical issues related to racism. Deng did not have an opportunity to construct knowledge about the text in other ways (e.g., small, dialogic, peer-led discussions) that might have provided alternative opportunities and tools for learning.

The difficulty for both Deng and his teacher lies in how to help Deng construct novel events and construct a new schema. "Many schema theorists," writes Bransford (1983), "have very little to say about the processes by which novel events are comprehended and new schemas are acquired" (p. 263). One of the problems, Bransford argues, is that relatively subtle differences in people's schemas can have dramatic differences on their interpretations. More important, Bransford notes that much of the research on schema theory uses pre-existing schemas to demonstrate schema change or adaptation rather than addressing the issue of schema construction in relation to a totally new topic.

Bransford uses the example of an airport schema and how to understand the relationship between the following two sentences: "Jane did not wear her silver jewelry because she was going somewhere. She was going to the airport." To fully comprehend the sentences, a reader must possess a complex understanding of airports and of airport security and how it works. In a classroom for students who may not possess such a schema, we might simply tell them that there are metal detectors or even show them pictures. However, Bransford asserts, this is highly problematic because in constructing a new schema, children often have difficulty in relating pieces of information to each other. He goes on to explain by using examples of children dealing with new information regarding Native American Indians. Because the content was unfamiliar to the children, they had a great deal of difficulty understanding their texts. Furthermore, and more important here, the children did not understand how to connect the various bits of information that were in the text. According to Bransford, a monumental problem to be overcome is how to assist learners in connecting packets of information—information that they perceive to be unconnected. We have argued that activating prior knowledge, making personal connections, and the like were not enough to scaffold Deng's learning. However, given his lack of understanding after all the activities that occurred in his classroom, it would not be far-fetched for us or for Deng's teacher to conclude that the problem is Deng's lack of an appropriate schema and to place the responsibility for misunderstanding on Deng.

We are fully aware that proponents of schema theory never intended or used schema theory to promote deficit models of education. Indeed, Bransford (1983) argues against deficit models when he writes, "Some children may appear to have poor comprehension and memory skills not because they have some inherent memory 'deficits,' but because they lack or fail to activate, the background knowledge that was presupposed by a message or text" (p. 260). We wish to be equally clear that our point here is not to discount the role of the teacher, for teachers are clearly important in assisting students in their learning, particularly in guiding learners to become aware of patterns (Gee, 2000). What we are prepared to argue is that, although connections to prior knowledge are critical, schema theory must also include specific attention to the role of cultural material and activity, and that teachers must attend to both.

Such a reformulation repositions schema as more than prior knowledge or topic knowledge. For example, although Mrs. Weber, Deng's teacher, was an experienced teacher who provided activities to support her students' learning in the unit on racism, closer analysis of Deng's classroom interactions reveal that he had little opportunity for dialogic engagement. Brock explains how, although the class engaged in group discussion of the text, these discussions almost always occurred in a whole-class setting and followed the typical IRE pattern, in which the teacher initiates a question, the children reply, and then the teacher evaluates their responses (Brock, 2005). Further analysis revealed that only a limited number of students participated in these "discussions." These interactions differed greatly from the dialogic type of engagement that occurred between Brock, Vue, and Deng as Deng viewed the class sessions on videotape. During the viewing sessions, it is clear that Deng's growing understanding of the classroom events was mediated by both the ideal and the material artifacts present—for example, by the presence of the videotapes, by Deng's control of the remote in stopping the tape, by his use of the opportunity to ask questions of Brock and Vue, and by the language use and opportunities afforded by the presence of Brock and Vue, the Hmong translator.

In relation to Deng, we agree with Brock that Deng lacked opportunities to learn within the classroom setting. The lack of opportunities to learn were related to teacher-directed activities and strategies used in the classroom and to the lack of opportunity for Deng to publicize the knowledge that he was internalizing, or failing to internalize. The lack of opportunity in the classroom was also related to the patterns of language and of cultural activity through which Deng's learning was mediated. These patterns were not contained in Deng's mind in script-like form but existed in the patterns that Deng saw in cultural activities and materials (Holland & Cole, 1995). Although schema theoretic perspectives draw our attention to Deng's prior experience or background knowledge and toward the teacher's efforts to support student learning by providing numerous activities or encounters with various texts involving racism, our perspective and understanding of Deng's experience is made far richer and more complex by closer consideration of sociocultural concerns, particularly the role of material and ideal artifacts. In addition, a sociocultural perspective draws our attention to how Deng was positioned by others and the political implications of such positioning. By giving Deng access to tools that would help him to articulate his understanding of class interactions (Vue as translator, a video, etc.), Brock positioned Deng as an active participant in constructing knowledge about his own learning. This shift changes the context and provides an opportunity for him to appropriate, transform, and make his knowledge public. This is, essentially, a political act, as it shifts Deng from a passive receptor of knowledge to an active participant in knowledge construction.

In summary, there are three ways that sociocultural perspectives help us to rethink Deng's classroom experiences or opportunities in ways that traditional schema theory, as conceived of by cognitive scientists, cannot. First, sociocultural perspectives draw our attention to the issues of the origin and development of Deng's schemas. This genetic question is essential in social conceptions of mind (Wertsch, 1991) and is an area of fundamental difference between social and individual perspectives of mind. This leads us to be mindful that Mrs. Weber and Deng are both filtering the construction of knowledge through cultural lenses and identities in both the private and public domain.

Second, in considering the origination and development of schemas, sociocultural perspectives draw our attention to the ways in which knower and known are not separate entities as premised in information processing models of mind. That is, in Deng's example, it is not simply the case that Mrs. Weber must assist in the transfer of knowledge "out there" in the world and in the text to Deng's mind. Rather, Deng as learner and knowledge of the text as known are mutually constitutive; knowing is a cultural process embodied within the cultural and social systems. Only a transactional view of schemas enables us to both acknowledge and explore the interdependence between the text, practices, and contexts within which the cognitive process occurs.

Third, a sociocultural perspective highlights the role of mediational tools, for example, activities such as language (both Hmong and English), and texts such as books, along with videotapes and conversations. These activities and tools involve both the material and the ideal artifacts with which Deng interacts. There is an interdependence of thought and language, and of speech and activity, in the immediate contexts within which any act of text comprehension occurs. Because thought, language, speech, and activity are interrelated and symbiotic, we are encouraged to view cognition as a cultural process rather than as only a collection of mental processes (Rogoff, 1993). Cultural processes of cognition occur in contexts that are historically and socially bound, and thus they are political entities. From this vantage point, the role of the teacher takes on even more profound dimensions and responsibilities because the teacher is more than just a more knowledgeable other. She becomes a mediating agent who facilitates, or who may fail to facilitate, the acquisition of knowledge and the use of particular cognitive tools within a culturally bound activity system, thus emphasizing teaching itself as a political act.

Implications for Future Inquiry

Throughout this article we have tried to articulate what it means to consider schemas from a sociocultural perspective. In summary, we remind our readers of three key points: (1) Schema and other cognitive processes or structures are embodied—that is, who we are as biological beings determines our sensorial interactions with the world and thus the nature of the representations we construct; (2) knowledge is situated in the transaction between world and individual; and (3) these transactions are mediated by culturally and socially enacted practices carried out through material and ideal artifacts.

The implications for future inquiry turn critically on what we take schemas to be, how they are formed, and the processes by which they develop and are transformed. We have seen that many researchers consider the schema construct to be ill-defined. Yet the construct has been remarkably generative of research and educational practices. We have also seen that the conception of the schema as offered by Bartlett was based on the assumption that we build our (schematic) understandings of the world on the basis of our embodied and socially mediated transactions with the world. These transactions with others are critical in the formation and continued development of mind. Our individual schematic understandings thus emerge from, but are not reducible to, our sociocultural transactions with others. In contrast, conceptions of schema theory proffered by cognitive science have assumed that there is a divide between the knower and the known, that schemas are formed within individuals, and that schema formation is a disembodied, in-the-head proposition.

What seems clear is that individuals engage in patterned ways of interacting with, understanding, and remembering their world. Whether one conceptualizes these transformations in individual thinking in terms of schemas, cognitive structures, or representations, the fact remains that schemas (or cognitive structures or representations) are transformed as a result of these transactions with the world through material and ideational means. What seems equally clear is that we have little understanding of how the schemas originate and develop or what role social and cultural factors play in these genetic processes. As noted above, sociocultural theory has the potential to elaborate and further enrich these fundamental insights concerning the genesis and development of schemas. Perhaps the most important conceptual question raised by this treatise concerns when a construct, or theory built around a construct, ceases to be the theory (or construct) that it was. Does an embodied, transactional, and culturally informed conception of the origins and development of schemas so radically alter the received understanding of the construct that it no longer resembles what was originally intended by cognitive scientists?

We raise this last question as more than a rhetorical exercise. To acknowledge the embodied, transactional, and cultural nature of schemas also requires acknowledging and addressing the inherently political nature of knowledge—something that we have alluded to but not fully explored. While traditional versions of the schema construct that were developed by cognitive science present knowledge construction through a value-neutral metaphor (e.g., schemas are knowledge organization structures like a file cabinet) other versions (e.g., Bruner, 1996; Ferdman, 1990; Gee, 2004; New London Group, 1996) suggest that knowledge construction, particularly in the form of literacy teaching, learning, and research, is political in nature; that is, it is imbued with beliefs, ideals, and values. New Literacies scholars point to the need to acknowledge and address the increasingly diverse cultural contexts and increasingly diverse digital contexts encountered by students (Gee, 2003, 2004; Lankshear & Knobel, 2003). Gee, for example, observes that those who will have access to power and social goods under new capitalism will be the "shape shifting portfolio people" (p. 105) who can rapidly adapt and use their knowledge acquired through the right "sorts of experiences, skills, and achievements...accrued...with the 'right' sort of people" (p. 106). In other words, those who have a broad repertoire of ideal and material tools and a great command of that repertoire will be able to use this knowledge to their advantage. Gee and others have noted that the increasingly multimodal nature of literacies makes it difficult to ignore the embodied nature of learning. At the same time that ever more complex types of tools are required, many minority children and many children who live in poverty, start school already at a disadvantage because many have not had the same exposure to academic discourse as their more affluent peers. Although all children come to school with pre-existing knowledge structures, in many cases the knowledge and learning processes that the children possess is not the same as, and may even conflict with, the types of knowledge and knowledge construction emphasized in school (Heath, 1983). Many scholars advocate making use of children's internal knowledge, promoting different types of knowledge as a strength rather than a deficit (Gutiérrez et al., 1997; Heath, 1983; Moll, 1994). In contrast to more complex and contextualized approaches to address issues of literacy and equity, neoliberal philosophies of schooling address equity through standards, testing, accountability, and a free market. Thus children who are already at a disadvantage are offered "the basics" and only the basics, when, in reality, they need much more to acquire the material and ideal tools to enable them to succeed in a rapidly changing environment.

As noted earlier, Gaffney and Anderson (2000) have observed that, in literacy research, schema theory has fallen by the wayside and is seldom used directly in explaining, exploring, or conceptualizing contemporary research. Whether the construct of schema can itself be redefined to factor in the political nature of embodied, transactional knowledge remains to be seen. When reading the critique of neoliberal agendas by New Literacies scholars, we are less than sanguine about this prospect, especially when we note that some time ago scholars encouraged researchers to widen their investigations of culture and cognition (e.g., Cole, 1996).

On the other hand, there are a number of literacy scholars who have called attention to new and emerging digital technologies, in particular, nonlinear texts. Many literacy scholars argue that such texts require new skills and strategies for reading (Reinking, McKenna, Labbo, & Kieffer, 1998). If so, traditional understandings of comprehension predicated on schema theory and the exploration of linear, print-based texts will likely be inadequate to explain the cognitive processes that a reader must engage when exploring texts in hypermedia environments such as the Internet. Some scholars have, in fact, noted that schemas, as rigid knowledge structures, are inadequate to explain the processes and outcomes prefigured by new technologies such as hyptertexts (e.g., Mishra, Spiro, & Feltovich, 1996; Spiro & Jehng, 1990; Spiro, Coulson, Feltovich, & Anderson, 1988). It may well be that the work of Spiro and his colleagues in cognitive flexibility theory is more applicable to new and emerging technologies than versions of schema theory as developed by cognitive scientists. Cognitive flexibility theory, with its exploration of learning in "ill-structured domains," may also be more compatible with the perspectives advocated by New Literacies scholars.

Throughout this essay, we have engaged in what Florio-Ruane (2002) calls "epistemological stocktaking," wherein we evaluate research and theories that we ascribe to and the practices that we carry out in our field of study (p. 207). It is in this tradition that we present this revisitation of schema. We propose our exploration of schemas as the beginning of a dialogue, in the hope that literacy researchers and educators will further explore the valuable contribution that schema theoretic perspectives have made to literacy research, practice, and theory. At the same time, we acknowledge limitations of the schema construct as traditionally conceived. We propose, in addition, that literacy researchers and educators engage in productive dialogue exploring how a transactional notion of schema might assist us, as teachers and researchers, as we continue to investigate language processes such as reading, writing, listening, and speaking in the increasingly diverse social and cultural settings of U.S. society.

QUESTIONS FOR REFLECTION

1. What differences are there between cognitive and sociocultural approaches to understanding literacy?
2. How do rationalist worldviews that see schema as in the head differ from transactionalist perspectives that challenge subject–object dualisms?
3. Why is it important to consider the origins of schema development?

NOTES

*When this chapter was written, Dunsmore was at Calvin College.

The authors would like to thank the three anonymous reviewers and Diane Barone, Fenice Boyd, Cynthia Brock, and Mary Rozendal for their feedback on numerous versions of this manuscript.

[1] In keeping with the recommendations of the *Publication Manual of the American Psychological Association* (5th ed.), we use the plural term "schemas" instead of the traditional term "schemata" throughout this article.

[2] Readers interested in the notion of transaction and cultural theories of reading may wish to consult Smagorinsky (2001). Smagorinsky does not revisit schema theoretic perspectives in his article, but his exploration of text generation and the role of tools and signs in the construction of meaning through what he calls the "transactional zone" (p. 140) is highly relevant to issues that we discuss in this article.

[3] For readers interested in the origins of sociocultural perspectives and activity theory, including interesting sociohistorical contexts, we suggest Blanck (1990); Robbins (2003); Rosa & Montero (1990); and Van der Veer & Valsiner (1991).

[4] Several published researchers have also written about this tension. Beals (1998) notes that, on first being introduced to a definition of schema while taking a graduate course, she found it relevant in explaining her own learning. However, as she continued reading about schema theory, she quickly became "disenchanted with its application to information processing theories and methods of teaching reading." Yet she also notes that schema is "a crucial idea in the study of development" (p. 11). Beals calls upon Bakhtin's work to draw "society into the individual mind, and the individual mind into society" (p. 11) and advocates a conception of schema that is closer to Bartlett's original version than to the later version articulated by cognitive scientists.

Another example comes from William Frawley, who describes, in *Vygotsky and Cognitive Science* (1997), how as a graduate student he studied both sociocultural and information-processing theories of language. In reflecting on that experience he notes: "The two views of the human—as device and a person—never seemed at odds to me. Thanks to the integrity of my teachers, they were never put at odds. That was reserved for the partisan and often dangerous world of the profession, where suggestions that the computational and the sociocultural mind not only went together but belonged together met with a few worried looks" (p. 1).

REFERENCES

Alba, J. W., & Hasher, L. (1983). Is memory schematic? *Psychological Bulletin, 93*(2), 203–231.

Anderson, R. C. (1977). The notion of schemata and the educational enterprise: General discussion of the conference. In R. C. Anderson & R. J. Spiro (Eds.), *Schooling and the acquisition of knowledge* (pp. 415–431). Hillsdale, NJ: Lawrence Erlbaum.

Anderson, R. C. (1978). Schema-directed processes in language comprehension. In A. Lesgold, J. Pelligrino, S. Fokkema, & R. Glaser (Eds.), *Cognitive psychology and education instruction*. New York: Plenum.

Anderson, R. C. (1994). Role of the reader's schema in comprehension, learning, and memory. In R. B. Ruddell, M. R. Ruddell, & H. Singer (Eds.), *Theoretical models and processes of reading* (4th ed., pp. 469–482). Newark, DE: International Reading Association.

Anderson, R. C., & Pearson, P. D. (1984). A schema-theoretic view of basic processes in reading comprehension. In P. D. Pearson (Ed.), *Handbook of reading research* (Vol. 1, pp. 255–291). New York: Longman.

Anderson, R. C., Reynolds, R. E., Schallert, D. L., & Goetz, E. T. (1977). Frameworks for comprehending discourse. *American Educational Research Journal, 14*(4), 367–381.

Au, K. H. (1980). Participation structures in a reading lesson with Hawaiian children: Analysis of a culturally appropriate instructional event. *Anthropology and Education Quarterly, 11*(2), 91–115.

Au, K. H. (1998). Social constructivism and the school literacy learning of students of diverse backgrounds. *Journal of Literacy Research, 30*(2), 297–319.

Au, K. H., & Mason, J. M. (1981). Social organizational factors in learning to read: The balance of rights hypothesis. *Reading Research Quarterly, 17*(1), 115–152.

Bartlett, F. C. (1995). *Remembering*. New York: Cambridge University Press. (Original work published 1932)

Beals, D. E. (1998). Reappropriating schema: Conceptions of development from Bartlett and Bakhtin. *Mind, Culture, and Activity 5*(1), 3–24.

Bean, T. W. (2000). Reading in the content areas: Social constructivist dimensions. In M. L. Kamil, P. B. Mosenthal, P. D. Pearson, & R. Barr (Eds.), *Handbook of reading research* (Vol. 3, pp. 629–644). Mahwah, NJ: Lawrence Erlbaum.

Beck, I. L., & McKeown, M. G. (1994). Outcomes of history instruction: Paste-up accounts. In M. Carretero and J. F. Voss (Eds.), *Cognitive and instructional processes in history and the social sciences* (pp. 237–256). Hillsdale, NJ: Lawrence Erlbaum.

Beck, I. L., McKeown, M. G., & Gromoll, E. W. (1989). Learning from social studies texts. *Cognition and Instruction, 6*(2), 99–158.

Beck, I. L., McKeown, M. G., Sinatra, G. M., & Loxterman, J. A. (1991). Revising social studies texts from a text-processing perspective: Evidence of improved comprehensibility. *Reading Research Quarterly, 26*(3), 251–276.

Blanck, G. (1990). Vygotsky: The man and his cause. In L. C. Moll (Ed.), *Vygotsky and education* (pp. 31–58). New York: Cambridge University Press.

Bransford, J. D. (1983). Schema activation and schema acquisition: Comments on Richard C. Anderson's remarks. In R. C. Anderson, J. Osborn, & R. C. Tierney (Eds.), *Learning to read in American schools* (pp. 259–272). Hillsdale, NJ: Lawrence Erlbaum.

Bransford, J. D., & Johnson, M. K. (1972). Contextual prerequisites for understanding: Some investigations of comprehension and recall. *Journal of Verbal Learning and Verbal Behavior, 11*, 717–726.

Bransford, J. D., & Johnson, M. K. (1973). Considerations of some problems of comprehension. In W. G. Chase (Ed.), *Visual information processing* (pp. 383–438). New York: Academic Press.

Brewer, W. F., & Nakamura, G. V. (1984). The nature and functions of schemas. In R. S. Wyer & T. K. Srull (Eds.), *Handbook of social cognition* (Vol. I, pp. 119–160). Hillsdale, NJ: Lawrence Erlbaum.

Brock, C. H. (1997). Exploring a second language learner's opportunities for literacy learning in a mainstream classroom: A collaborative case study analysis. Unpublished doctoral dissertation, Michigan State University, East Lansing.

Brock, C. H., & Raphael, T. E. (2005). *Windows to language, literacy, and culture: Insights from an English-language learner.* Newark, DE: International Reading Association.

Bruner, J. S. (1990). *Acts of meaning*. Cambridge, MA: Harvard University Press.

Bruner, J. S. (1996). *The culture of education*. Cambridge, MA: Harvard University Press.

Campbell, J. (1989). *The improbable machine: What the upheavals in artificial intelligence research reveal about how the mind really works*. New York: Simon & Schuster.

Carver, R. P. (1992). Effect of prediction activities, prior knowledge, and text type upon amount comprehended: Using rauding theory to critique schema theory research. *Reading Research Quarterly, 27*(2), 164–174.

Cazden, C. B. (1988). *Classroom discourse: The language of teaching and learning*. Portsmouth, NH: Heinemann.

Clark, A. (1997). *Being there: Putting, brain, body, and the world together again*. Cambridge, MA: MIT Press.

Clifford, J. (1988). *The predicament of culture*. Cambridge, MA: Harvard University Press.

Clifford, J., & Marcus, G. (Eds.). (1986). *Writing culture*. Berkeley: University of California.

Cole, M. (1996). *Cultural psychology: A once and future discipline*. Cambridge, MA: Belknap Press of Harvard University Press.

D'Andrade, R. (1984). Cultural meaning systems. In R. Shweder & R. LeVine (Eds.), *Culture theory: Essays on mind, self, and emotion* (pp. 88–119). Cambridge, UK: Cambridge University Press.

Dewey, J., & Bentley, A. F. (1949). *Knowing and the known*. Boston: Beacon Press.

Dudley-Marling, C., & Murphy, S. (1998). Editor's pages. *Language Arts, 76*(1), 8–9.

Ferdman, B. M. (1990). Literacy and cultural identity. *Harvard Educational Review, 60*, 181–203.

Florio-Ruane, S. (2002). More light: An argument for complexity in studies of teaching and teacher education. *Journal of Teacher Education, 53*(3), 205–215.

Florio-Ruane, S., & McVee, M. (2000). Ethnographic approaches to literacy research. In M. L. Kamil, P. B. Mosenthal, P. D. Pearson, & R. Barr (Eds.), *Handbook of reading research* (Vol. 3, pp. 153–162). Mahwah, NJ: Lawrence Erlbaum.

Frawley, W. (1997). *Vygotsky and cognitive science.* Cambridge, MA: Harvard University Press.

Gaffney, J. S., & Anderson, R. C (2000). Trends in reading research in the United States: Changing intellectual currents over three decades. In M. L. Kamil, P. B. Mosenthal, P. D. Pearson, & R. Barr (Eds.), *Handbook of reading research* (Vol. 3, pp. 53–74). Mahwah, NJ: Lawrence Erlbaum.

Gavelek, J. R., & Raphael, T. E. (1996). Changing talk about text: New roles for teachers and students. *Language Arts, 73*(3), 182–192.

Gee, J. P. (1992). *The social mind.* New York: Bergin & Garvey.

Gee, J. P. (1997a). Meanings in discourses: Coordinating and being coordinated. In S. Muspratt, A. Luke, & P. Freebody (Eds.), *Constructing critical literacies: Teaching and learning textual practice* (pp. 273–302). Cresskill, NJ: Hampton Press.

Gee, J. P. (1997b). Thinking, learning, and reading: The situated sociocultural mind. In D. Kirshner & J. A. Whitson (Eds.), *Situated cognition: Social, semiotic, and psychological perspectives* (pp. 235–259). Mahwah, NJ: Lawrence Erlbaum.

Gee, J. P. (2000). Discourse and sociocultural studies in reading. In M. L. Kamil, P. B. Mosenthal, P. D. Pearson, & R. Barr (Eds.), *Handbook of reading research* (Vol. 3, pp. 195–207). Mahwah, NJ: Lawrence Erlbaum.

Gee, J. P. (2003). *What video games have to teach us about learning and literacy.* New York: Palgrave.

Gee, J. P. (2004). *Situated language and learning.* New York: Routledge.

Gergen, K., & Gergen, M. (1983). Narratives of the self. In T. Sarbin & K. Scheibe (Eds.), Studies in social identity (pp. 254–273). New York: Praeger.

Graves, M. F., Juel, C., & Graves, B. B. (2004). *Teaching reading in the 21st century* (3rd ed.). Boston: Pearson Education.

Greene, S., & Ackerman, J. M. (1995). Expanding the constructivist metaphor: A rhetorical perspective on literacy research and practice. *Review of Educational Research, 65*(4), 383–420.

Gutiérrez, K., Baquendano-Lopez, P., & Turner, M. G. (1997). Putting language back into Language Arts: When the radical middle meets the Third Space. *Language Arts, 74*(5), 368–378.

Hacker, C. J. (1980). From schema theory to classroom practice. *Language Arts, 57*(8), 866–871.

Harré, R. (1984). *Personal being: A theory for individual psychology.* Cambridge, MA: Harvard University Press.

Harré, R., & Gillett, G. (1994). *The discursive mind.* Thousand Oaks, CA: Sage Publications.

Harré, R., & Stearns, P. (1995). *Discursive psychology in practice.* London: Sage Publications.

Hatano, G. (1993). Time to merge Vygotskian and constructivist conceptions of knowledge acquisition. In E. A. Forman, N. Minick, & C. Addison Stone (Eds.), *Contexts for learning: Sociocultural dynamics in children's development* (pp. 153–166). New York: Oxford University Press.

Heath, S. B. (1983). *Ways with words: Language, life, and work in communities and classrooms.* New York: Cambridge University Press.

Holland, D., & Cole, M. (1995). Between discourse and schema: Reformulating a cultural-historical approach to culture and mind. *Anthropology and Education Quarterly, 26*(4), 475–490.

Hruby, G. G. (2001). Sociological, postmodern, and new realism perspectives in social constructionism: Implications for literacy research. *Reading Research Quarterly, 36*(1), 48–62.

Johnson, M. (1987). *The body in the mind: The bodily basis of meaning, imagination, and reason.* Chicago: University of Chicago Press.

Kamil, M. L., Mosenthal, P. B., Pearson, P. D., & Barr, R. (2000). *Handbook of reading research* (Vol. 3). Mahwah, NJ: Lawrence Erlbaum.

Kant, I. (1929). *Critique of pure reason* (N. K. Smith, Trans.). New York: St. Martin's Press. (Original work published in 1781).

Kintsch, W. (1998). *Comprehension: A paradigm for cognition.* New York: Cambridge University Press.

Koedinger, K. R., & Anderson, J. R. (1990). Abstract planning and perceptual chunks: Elements of expertise in geometry. *Cognitive Science, 114*, 511–550.

Kozulin, A., Gindis, B., Ageyev, V. S., & Miller, S. M. (2003). *Vygotsky's educational theory in cultural context.* New York: Cambridge University Press.

Lakoff, G., & Johnson, M. (1980). *Metaphors we live by.* Chicago: University of Chicago Press.

Lakoff, G., & Johnson, M. (1999). *Philosophy in the flesh: The embodied mind and its challenge to Western thought.* New York: Basic Books.

Lankshear, C., & Knobel, M. (2003). *New literacies: Changing knowledge and classroom learning.* Philadelphia: Open University Press.

Lave, J., & Wenger, E. (1991). *Situated learning: Legitimate peripheral participation.* New York: Cambridge University Press.

Lee, C. D. (1995). A culturally based cognitive apprenticeship: Teaching African American high school students skills in literary interpretation. *Reading Research Quarterly, 30*(4), 608–630.

Lipson, M. Y., & Wixson, K. K. (1997). *Assessment and instruction of reading and writing disability: An interactive approach* (2nd ed.). New York: Longman.

Lipson, M. Y., & Wixson, K. K. (2003). *Assessment and instruction of reading and writing difficulty: An interactive approach* (3rd ed.). Boston: Pearson Education.

Mandler, J. M., & Johnson, N. S. (1977). Remembrance of things parsed: Story structure and recall. *Cognitive Psychology, 9,* 111–151.

Marshall, S. P. (1995). *Schemas in problem solving.* Cambridge, UK: Cambridge University Press.

Middleton, D., & Crook, C. (1996). Bartlett and socially ordered consciousness: A discursive perspective: Comments on Rosa. *Culture & Psychology, 2,* 379–396.

Minsky, M. (1975). A framework for representing knowledge. In P. H. Winston (Ed.), *The psychology of computer vision* (pp. 211–277). New York: McGraw Hill.

Mishra, P., Spiro, R. J., & Feltovich, P. J. (1996). Technology, representation, and cognition: The prefiguring of knowledge in cognitive flexibility hypertexts. In H. van Oostendorp & S. de Mul (Eds.), *Cognitive aspects of electronic text processing* (pp. 287–305). Norwood, NJ: Ablex.

Moll, L. C. (1990). *Vygotsky and education.* Cambridge, UK: Cambridge University Press.

Moll, L. C. (1992). Bilingual classroom studies and community analysis. *Educational Researcher, 21*(2), 20–24.

Moll, L. C. (1994). Literacy research in community and classrooms: A sociocultural approach. In R. B. Ruddell & H. Singer (Eds.), *Theoretical models and processes of reading* (4th ed., pp. 179–207). Newark, DE: International Reading Association.

Moll, L. C. (2001). Through the mediation of others: Vygotskian research on teaching. In V. Richardson (Ed.), *Handbook of research on teaching* (4th ed., pp. 111–129). Washington, DC: American Educational Research Association.

Moll, L. C., & Diaz, R. (1987). Teaching writing as communication: The use of ethnographic findings in classroom practice. In D. Bloome (Ed.), *Literacy and schooling* (pp. 195–221). Norwood, NJ: Ablex.

Nassaji, H. (2002). Schema theory and knowledge-based processes in second language reading comprehension: A need for alternative perspectives. *Language Learning, 52*(2), 439–481.

New London Group. (1996). A pedagogy of multiliteracies: Designing social futures. *Harvard Educational Review, 66*(1), 60–92.

Pearson, P. D. (1982). A primer for schema theory. *Volta Review, 84,* 25–34.

Pearson, P. D. (1992). Reading. In Marvin C. Alkin (Ed.), *The encyclopedia of educational research* (Vol. 3, pp. 1075–1085). American Educational Research Association.

Pearson, P. D. (1996). Reclaiming the center. In M. F. Graves, P. van den Broek, & B. M. Taylor (Eds.), *The first R: Every child's right to read* (pp. 259–274). New York: Teachers College Press.

Piaget, J. (1952). *The origins of intelligence in children* (Margaret Cook, Trans). New York: International Universities Press.

Pichert, J. W., & Anderson, R. C. (1977). Taking different perspectives on a story. *Journal of Educational Psychology, 69*(4), 309–315.

Pritchard, R. (1990). The effects of cultural schemata on reading processing strategies. *Reading Research Quarterly, 25*(4), 273–295.

Purcell-Gates, V. (1995). *Other people's words: The cycle of low literacy.* Cambridge, MA: Harvard University Press.

Purcell-Gates, V., Jacobson, E., & Degener, S. (2004). *Print literacy development: Uniting cognitive and social practice theories.* Cambridge, MA: Harvard University Press.

Quinn, N., & Holland, D. (1987). Culture and cognition. In D. Holland & N. Quinn (Eds.), *Cultural models in language and thought* (pp. 3–40). New York: Cambridge University Press.

Ramsey, W., Stich, S. P., & Rumelhart, D. E. (1991). *Philosophy and connectionist theory.* Hillsdale, NJ: Lawrence Erlbaum.

Raphael, T. E. (2001). Literacy teaching, literacy learning: Lessons from the Book Club Plus Project. In J. V. Hoffman, D. L. Schallert, C. M. Fairbanks, J. Worthy, & B. Maloch (Eds.), *50th Yearbook of the National Reading Conference* (pp. 1–20). Chicago: National Reading Conference.

Reinking, D., McKenna, M. C., Labbo, L. D., & Kieffer, R. D. (1998). *Handbook of literacy and technology.* Mahwah, NJ: Erlbaum.

Reynolds, R. E., Taylor, M. A., Steffensen, M. S., Shirey, L. L., & Anderson, R. C. (1981, April). *Cultural schemata and reading comprehension* (Tech. Rep. No. 201). Urbana, IL: University of Illinois, Center for the Study of Reading.

Reynolds, R. E., Taylor, M. A., Steffensen, M. S., Shirey, L. L., & Anderson, R. C. (1982). Cultural schemata and reading comprehension. *Reading Research Quarterly, 17*(3), 353–366.

Robbins, D. (2003). *Vygotsky's and A. A. Leontiev's semiotics and psycholinguistics: Applications for education, second language acquisition, and theories of language.* Westport, CT: Praeger.

Rogoff, B. (1993). Children's participation and participatory appropriation in sociocultural activity. In R. H. Wozniak & K. W. Fischer (Eds.), *Development in context: Acting and thinking in specific environments* (pp. 121–153). Hillsdale, NJ: Lawrence Erlbaum.

Rogoff, B., & Lave, J. (Eds.). (1984). *Everyday cognition: Its development in social context.* Cambridge, MA: Harvard University Press.

Rosa, A., & Montero, I. (1990). The historical context of Vygotsky's work: A sociohistorical approach. In L. C. Moll (Ed.), *Vygotsky and education* (pp. 59–88). New York: Cambridge University Press.

Roschelle, J., & Clancey, W. J. (1992). Learning as social and neural. *Educational Psychologist, 27*(4), 435–453.

Rosenblatt, L. M. (1989). Writing and reading transactional theory. In J. Mason (Ed.), *Reading and writing connections* (pp. 153–176). Boston: Allyn & Bacon.

Rumelhart, D. E. (1975). Notes on a schema for stories. In D. G. Bobrow & A. M. Collins (Eds.), *Representation and understanding: Studies in cognitive science* (pp. 211–236). New York: Academic Free Press.

Rumelhart, D. E. (1978). Schemata: The building blocks of cognition. In R. J. Spiro, B. C. Bruce, & W. F. Brewer (Eds.) *Theoretical issues in reading comprehension* (pp. 33–58). Hillsdale, NJ: Lawrence Erlbaum.

Rumelhart, D. E. (1984). Schemata and the cognitive system. In R. S. Wyer & T. K. Srull, *Handbook of social cognition* (pp. 161–188). Hillsdale, NJ: Lawrence Erlbaum.

Rumelhart, D. E. (1990). The architecture of mind: A connectionist approach. In M. I. Posner (Ed.), *Foundations of cognitive science* (pp. 133–159). Cambridge, MA: MIT Press.

Rumelhart, D. E. (1994). Toward an interactive model of reading. In R. B. Ruddell & M. Rapp (Eds.), *Theoretical models and processes of reading* (4th ed., pp. 864–894). Newark, DE: International Reading Association.

Rumelhart, D. E., & Ortney, A. (1977). The representation of knowledge in memory. In R. C. Anderson, R. J. Spiro, & W. E. Montague (Eds.), *Schooling and the acquisition of knowledge* (pp. 99–135). Hillsdale, NJ: Lawrence Erlbaum.

Sadoski, M., & Paivio, A. (2001). *Imagery and text: A dual coding theory of reading and writing.* Mahwah, NJ: Lawrence Erlbaum.

Sadoski, M., Paivio, A., & Goetz, E. T. (1991). A critique of schema theory in reading and a dual coding theory alternative. *Reading Research Quarterly, 26*(4), 463–484.

Saito, A. (1996). Social origins of cognition: Bartlett, evolutionary perspective and embodied mind approach. *Journal for the Theory of Social Behaviour, 26*(4), 399–421.

Saito, A. (Ed.). (2000). *Bartlett, culture and cognition.* London: Psychology Press.

Santa Barbara Discourse Group. (1994). Constructing literacy in classrooms: Literate action as social accomplishment. In R. B. Ruddell, M. R. Ruddell, & H. Singer (Eds.), *Theoretical models and processes of reading* (pp. 124–154). Newark, DE: International Reading Association.

Schank, R. C., & Abelson, R. (1977). *Scripts, plans, goals and understanding.* Hillsdale, NJ: Lawrence Erlbaum.

Scribner, S., & Cole, M. (1981). *The psychology of literacy.* Cambridge, MA: Harvard University Press.

Sleeter, C. E., & Grant, C. A. (1988). *Making choices for multicultural education.* New York: Merrill.

Smagorinsky, P. (2001). If meaning is constructed, what's it made from? Toward a cultural theory of reading. *Review of Educational Research, 71*(1), 133–169.

Spinelli, J. (1990). *Maniac Magee.* New York: Little, Brown.

Spiro, R. J., & Jehng, J. (1990). Cognitive flexibility and hypertext: Theory and technology for the nonlinear and multidimensional traversal of complex subject matter. In D. Nix & R. Spiro (Eds.), *Cognition, education, and multimedia: Exploring ideas in high technology* (pp. 165–205). Hillsdale, NJ: Lawrence Erlbaum.

Spiro, R. J., Coulson, R. L., Feltovich, P. J., & Anderson, D. K. (1988). Cognitive flexibility theory: Advanced knowledge acquisition in ill-structured domains. In *Proceedings of the 10th Annual Conference of the Cognitive Science Society* (pp. 375–383). Hillsdale, NJ: Lawrence Erlbaum.

Spivey, N. N. (1997). *The constructivist metaphor: Reading, writing, and the making of meaning.* New York: Academic Press.

Steffensen, M. S., Joag-dev, C., & Anderson, R. C. (1979). A cross-cultural perspective on reading comprehension. *Reading Research Quarterly, 15*(1), 10–29.

Tierney, R., & Shanahan, T. (1991). Research on the reading–writing relationship: Interactions, transactions, and outcomes. In R. Barr, M. Kamil, P. Mosenthal, & P. D. Pearson (Eds.), *Handbook of reading research* (Vol. 2, pp. 246–280). New York: Longman.

Van der Veer, R., & Valsiner, J. (1991). *Understanding Vygotsky: A quest for synthesis.* Oxford, UK: Basil Blackwell.

Varela, F. J., Thompson, E., & Rosch, E. (1991). *The embodied mind: Cognitive science and human experience.* Cambridge, MA: MIT Press.

Vygotsky, L. S. (1978). *Mind in society.* Cambridge: Harvard University Press.

Vygotsky, L. S. (1986). *Thought and language.* Cambridge: MIT Press.

Watson-Gegeo, K. A., & Boggs, S. T. (1977). From verbal play to talk story: The role of routine in speech events among Hawaiian children. In S. Ervin-Tripp & C. Mitchell-Kernan (Eds.), *Child discourse* (pp. 67–90). New York: Academic Press.

Weaver, C. (1994). *Reading process and practice* (2nd ed). Portsmouth, NH: Heinemann.

Weaver, C. (2002). *Reading process and practice* (3rd ed). Portsmouth, NH: Heinemann.

Wells, G. (1999). *Dialogic inquiry: Toward a sociocultural practice and theory of education.* Cambridge, UK: Cambridge University Press.

Wertsch, J. V. (1985). *Vygotsky and the social formation of mind.* Cambridge, MA: Harvard University Press.

Wertsch, J. V. (1991). *Voices of the mind: A sociocultural approach to mediated action.* Cambridge, MA: Harvard University Press.

Wertsch, J. V. (1998). *Mind as action.* New York: Oxford University Press.

Winograd, T. (1975). Frame representations and the declarative–procedural controversy. In D. G. Bobrow & A. M. Collins (Eds.), *Representation and understanding: Studies in cognitive science.* New York: Academic Press.

Wittgenstein, L. (1961). *Notebooks, 1914–1916.* New York: Harper.

APPENDIX A

Prison/Wrestling Passage

Rocky slowly got up from the mat, planning his escape. He hesitated a moment and thought. Things were not going well. What bothered him most was being held, especially since the charge against him had been weak. He considered his present situation. The lock that held him was strong, but he thought he could break it. He knew, however, that his timing would have to be perfect. Rocky was aware that it was because of his early roughness that he had been penalized so severely—much too severely from his point of view. The situation was becoming frustrating; the pressure had been grinding on him for too long. He was being ridden unmercifully. Rocky was getting angry now. He felt he was ready to make his move. He knew that his success or failure would depend on what he did in the next few seconds (Anderson, Reynolds, Schallert, & Goetz, 1977, p. 372).

APPENDIX B

Card/Music Passage

Every Saturday night, four good friends get together. When Jerry, Mike, and Pat arrived, Karen was sitting in her living room writing some notes. She quickly gathered the cards and stood up to greet her friends at the door. They followed her into the living room but as usual they couldn't agree on exactly what to play. Jerry eventually took a stand and set things up. Finally, they began to play. Karen's recorder filled the room with soft and pleasant music. Early in the evening, Mike noticed Pat's hand and the many diamonds. As the night progressed the tempo of play increased. Finally, a lull in the activities occurred. Taking advantage of this, Jerry pondered the arrangement in front of him. Mike interrupted Jerry's reverie and said, "Let's hear the score." They listened carefully and commented on their performance. When the comments were all heard, exhausted but happy, Karen's friends went home (Anderson, Reynolds, Schallert, & Goetz, 1977, p. 372).

CHAPTER 21

To Err Is Human: Learning About Language Processes by Analyzing Miscues

Yetta M. Goodman and Kenneth S. Goodman,
University of Arizona

Everything people do, they do imperfectly. This is not a flaw but an asset. If we always performed perfectly, we could not maintain the tentativeness and flexibility that characterize human learning and the ways we interact with our environment and with one another. This model of imperfection causes us as researchers not to worry about why people fall short of perfection; rather, we are concerned with why people do what they do and with what we can learn about language processes from observing such phenomena.

The power of language users to fill knowledge gaps with missing elements, to infer unstated meanings and underlying structures, and to deal with novel experiences, novel thoughts, and novel emotions derives from the ability to predict, to guess, to make choices, to take risks, to go beyond observable data. We must have the capability of being wrong lest the limits on our functioning be too narrowly constrained. Unlike the computer, people do not exhibit specifically programmed, totally dependable responses time after time. We are tentative, we act impulsively, we make mistakes, and we tolerate our own deviations and the mistakes of others.

If you doubt that perfection in human behavior is the exception rather than the norm, consider how intensely a performer of any kind—athlete, actor, musician, writer, reader—must practice to achieve anything approaching error-free performance. If you doubt our view of how people deal with mistakes, think about the proofreader who skips over errors in a text or the native North Americans who deliberately insert flaws in handicrafts to remind themselves that the crafts are the work of human hands.

Miscues: Unexpected Responses

For more than 25 years we have studied the reading process by analyzing the miscues (or unexpected responses) of children and adults orally reading written texts. Ken Goodman coined this use of the word *miscue* because of the negative connotation and history of the term *error*. The term *miscue* reveals that miscues are unexpected responses cued by readers' linguistic or conceptual cognitive structures.

This chapter is reprinted from *Theoretical Models and Processes of Reading* (4th ed., pp. 104–123), edited by R.B. Ruddell, M.R. Ruddell, and H. Singer, 1994, Newark, DE: International Reading Association.

We started with the assumption that everything that happens during reading is caused, that a person's unexpected responses are produced in the same way and from the same knowledge, experience, and intellectual processes as expected responses. Reading aloud involves continuous oral response by the reader, which allows for comparisons between expected and observed responses. Such comparisons reveal the reader's knowledge, experience, and intellectual processes. Oral readers are engaged in comprehending written language while they produce oral responses. Because an oral response is generated while meaning is being constructed, it not only is a form of linguistic performance but also provides a powerful means of examining readers' process and underlying competence.

Miscue analysis requires several conditions. The written material must be new to the readers and complete with a beginning, middle, and end. The text needs to be long and challenging enough to produce sufficient numbers of miscues for patterns to appear. In addition, readers receive no help and are not interrupted. At most, if readers hesitate for more than 30 seconds, they are urged to guess, and only if hesitation continues are they told to keep reading even if it means skipping a word or phrase. Except that it takes place orally and not silently, the reading during miscue analysis requires as normal a situation as possible.

Depending on the purpose of miscue analysis research, readers often have been provided with more than one reading task. Various fiction and nonfiction reading materials have been used, including stories and articles from basal readers, textbooks, trade books, and magazines. Readers have been drawn from elementary, secondary, and adult populations and from a wide range of proficiency and racial, linguistic, and national backgrounds. Studies have been conducted in many languages other than English and in various writing systems (Goodman, Brown, & Marek, 1993).

Betsy's oral reading of the folktale "The Man Who Kept House" (from McInnes, Gerrard, & Ryckman, 1964, pp. 282–283) is used throughout for examples (Goodman, Watson, & Burke, 1987). The story has 68 sentences, 711 words. Betsy, a 9-year-old from Toronto, was selected by her teacher as representative of students with reading difficulties. Betsy read the story hesitantly, although in most places she read with appropriate expression. Below are the first 14 sentences (s1–s14) from the story, with the actual printed text on the left and the transcript of Betsy's oral reading on the right.

	Text	*Transcript*
s1	Once upon a time there was a woodman who thought that no one worked as hard as he did.	Once upon a time there was a woodman. He threw...who thought that no one worked as hard as he did.
s2	One evening when he came home from work, he said to his wife, "What do you do all day while I am away cutting wood?"	One evening when he...when he came home from work, he said to his wife, "I want you do all day...what do you do all day when I am always cutting wood?"

s3	"I keep house," replied the wife, "and keeping house is hard work."	"I keep...I keep house," replied the wife, "and keeping...and keeping...and keeping house is and work."
s4	"Hard work!" said the husband.	"Hard work!" said the husband.
s5	"You don't know what hard work is!	"You don't know what hard work is!
s6	You should try cutting wood!"	You should try cutting wood!"
s7	"I'd be glad to," said the wife.	"I'll be glad to," said the wife.
s8	"Why don't you do my work some day?	"Why don't you.... Why don't you do my work so...some day?
s9	I'll stay home and keep house," said the woodman.	I'll start house and keeping house," said the woodman.
s10	"If you stay home to do my work, you'll have to make butter, carry water from the well, wash the clothes, clean the house, and look after the baby," said the wife.	"If you start house.... If you start home to do my work, well you'll have to make bread, carry...carry water from the well, wash the clothes, clean the house, and look after the baby," said the wife.
s11	"I can do all that," replied the husband.	"I can do that.... I can do all that," replied the husband.
s12	"We'll do it tomorrow!"	"Well you do it tomorrow!"
s13	So the next morning the wife went off to the forest.	So the next day the wife went off to the forest.
s14	The husband stayed home and began to do his wife's job.	The husband stayed home and began to do his work.

Betsy's performance reveals her language knowledge. These examples are not unusual; what Betsy does is done by other readers. She processes graphophonic information: Most of her miscues show a graphic and phonic relationship between the expected and the observed response. She processes syntactic information: She substitutes noun for noun, verb for verb, noun phrase for noun phrase, verb phrase for verb phrase. She transforms phrases, clauses, and sentences: She omits an intensifier, changes a dependent clause to an independent clause, shifts a *wh* question sentence to a declarative sentence. She draws on her conceptual and linguistic background and struggles toward meaning by regressing, correcting, and reprocessing as necessary. She predicts appropriate structures and monitors her own success based on the degree to which she is making sense. She develops and uses psychosociolinguistic strategies as she reads. There is nothing random about her miscues.

Reading Miscues and Comprehension

Because we understand that the brain is the organ of human information processing, that it is not a prisoner of the senses but controls the sensory organs and selectively uses their input, we should not be surprised that what is said in oral reading is not what the eye has seen but what the brain has generated for the mouth to report. The text is what the brain responds to; the oral output reflects the underlying competence and the psychosociolinguistic processes that have generated it. When expected and observed responses match, we get little insight into this process. When they do not match and a miscue results, researchers have a window on the reading process.

We have come to believe that the strategies readers use when miscues occur are the same as when there are no miscues. Except for s3, s8, and s9, all of Betsy's miscues produced fully acceptable sentences or were self-corrected. By analyzing whether miscues are semantically acceptable with regard to the whole text or are acceptable only with regard to the prior portion of text, it is possible to infer the strategies readers actively engage in. s2 provides a powerful example. Betsy reads, *I want you do all day*, hesitates, reads slowly, and eventually—after a 23-second pause—reconsiders, probably rereads silently, and self-corrects the initial clause in this sentence. The verb *said* in the sentence portion prior to her miscue and her knowledge about what husbands might say when they come home from work allowed her to predict *I want you....* After she self-corrects the first part of the dialogue, she reads, *when I am always cutting wood* for *while I am away cutting wood* with confidence and continues her reading. These two substitution miscues (*when* for *while* and *always* for *away*) produce a clause that fits with the meaning of the rest of the story. The more proficient the reader, the greater the proportion of semantically acceptable miscues or miscues acceptable with the prior portion of the text that are self-corrected (Goodman & Burke, 1973).

In s12 Betsy produces, *Well you do it tomorrow* instead of *We'll do it tomorrow.* Although it seems that Betsy simply substitutes *well* for *we'll* and inserts *you*, the miscues are shown to be more complex when we examine how the phrase and clauses are affected by the miscues. Betsy substitutes an interjection prior to the subject *you* to substitute for the noun and the beginning of the verb phrase represented by the contraction *we'll.* In addition, Betsy shifts intonation to indicate that the wife rather than the husband is talking. Apparently Betsy predicted that the wife was going to speak to maintain the pattern of husband–wife conversation that is established by the author in the previous sections (s2 and s11). Although the author's intended meaning is changed, the sentence is semantically acceptable within the story.

A reader's predicting and confirming strategies are evident in miscues that are acceptable with the text portion prior to the miscues. Such miscues often occur at pivotal points in sentences, such as junctures between clauses or phrases. At such points the author may select from a variety of linguistic structures to compose the text; the reader has similar options but may predict a structure that is different than the author's. Consider these examples from Betsy's reading:

	Text	*Transcript*
s38	"I'll light a fire in the fireplace and the porridge will be ready in a few minutes.	"I'll light a fire in the fireplace and I'll... and the porridge will be ready in a flash...a few minutes."
s48	Then he was afraid that she would fall off.	Then he was afraid that the...that she would fall off.

Betsy's predictions of *I'll* instead of *the* in the second clause of the first example is logical. Because *and* often connects two parallel items, it is not an unreasonable prediction that the second clause will begin with the subject of the first. However, when *I'll* does not fit with the second clause, Betsy confidently disconfirms her prediction and immediately self-corrects. The miscue substitution of *the* for *she* in the second example is also at a pivotal point in the sentence. Whenever an author uses a pronoun to refer to a previously stated noun phrase, a reader may revert to the original noun phrase. The reverse phenomenon also occurs. When the author chooses a noun for which the referent has been established earlier, the reader may use that pronoun. Choosing a noun for which the referent has been established earlier, the reader may use that pronoun. Betsy was probably predicting *the cow* which *she* refers to. These miscues clearly show that Betsy is an active language user as she reads. Ken Goodman has done studies on the control readers have over determiners and pronouns in relation to the cohesion of text (Goodman, 1983; Goodman & Gespass, 1983).

The idea that miscues often occur at specific pivotal points in any text is important enough to provide an example from another reader. An Appalachian reader, while reading the phrase "By the time I got out and over to where they were," inserted *of the water* between *out* and *and*. In the previous paragraph the male character is in the water. The author and the reader have similar options at this point in the grammatical structure. The prepositional phrase *of the water* is understood by the reader though not stated by the author and therefore may be omitted or inserted without changing the meaning. In this case, the reader makes explicit what the author left implicit.

Miscues that result in semantically acceptable structures are confirmed as acceptable to readers and, therefore, are less likely to be corrected than those that are not acceptable or acceptable only with the immediately preceding text. Miscues at pivotal points in the text are often acceptable with regard to the preceding text. Of the 10 semantically acceptable miscues that Betsy produced in the first excerpt, she corrected only one (*all* in s11). However, of the six miscues that were acceptable only with the prior portion of the text, she corrected four. Such correction strategies tend to occur when the reader believes they are most needed—when a prediction has been disconfirmed by subsequent language cues.

Insights are gained into the reader's construction of meaning and the process of comprehension when we ask questions such as "Why did the reader make this miscue? Does it make sense in the context of this story or article?" Through such examination, it is possible to see the pattern of comprehending strategies a reader engages in.

We contrast comprehending—what the reader does to understand during the reading of a text—with comprehension—what the reader understands at the end of the reading. Open-ended retellings that always follow the reading during miscue analysis are an index of comprehension. They add to the profile of comprehending, which shows the reader's concern for meaning as expressed through the reading miscues. Retellings also provide an opportunity for the researcher or teacher to gain insight into how concepts and language are actively used and developed throughout a reading event.

Although the concept of retelling is common to present-day research, in the early 1960s when we first used this concept, many questioned the term and the appropriateness of its use in reading research. Rather than asking direct questions that would give cues to the reader about what is significant in the story, we asked for unaided retelling. Information on the readers' understanding of the text emerges from the organization they use in retelling the story, from whether they use the author's language or their own, and from the conceptions or misconceptions they reveal. Here is the first segment of Betsy's retelling:

> Um...it was about this woodman and um...when he...he thought that he um...he had harder work to do than his wife. So he went home and he told his wife, "What have you been doing all day." And then his wife told him. And then, um...and then, he thought that it was easy work. And...so...so his wife, so his wife, so she um...so the wife said, "Well so you have to keep," no...the husband says that you have to go to the woods and cut...and have to go out in the forest and cut wood and I'll stay home. And the next day they did that.

By comparing our interpretation of the story with Betsy's retelling and her miscues, we are able to analyze how much learning has occurred during Betsy and the author's transaction. For example, although the story frequently uses *woodman* and *to cut wood, forest*, the noun used to refer to setting, is used twice. Not only does Betsy provide evidence in her retelling that she knows that *woods* and *forest* are synonymous, she also indicates that she knows the author's choice is *forest*. The maze she works through suggests her search for the author's language. Her oral language mazes are evidence of her intentions and self-correction patterns. Betsy seems to believe that the teacher is looking for the author's language rather than her own. Additional evidence of Betsy's concern to reproduce the author's language is seen in her use of *woodman* and *husband*. In the story, the woodman is referred to as *woodman* and *husband* eight times each and as *man* four times; the wife is referred to only as *wife*. Otherwise pronouns are used to refer to the husband and wife. In the retelling, Betsy uses *husband* and *woodman* six times and *man* only once; she called the wife only *wife*. Betsy always uses appropriate pronouns in referring to the husband and wife. However, when *cow* was the referent, she substituted *he* for *she* twice. (What does Betsy know about the sex of cattle?)

The linguistic and conceptual schematic background a reader brings to reading not only shows in miscues but is implicit in the developing conceptions or misconceptions revealed through the reader's retelling. Betsy adds to her conceptual base and builds her control of language as she reads this story, but her ability to do both is limited by what she brings to the task. In the story, the husband has to make butter in a churn. Betsy makes miscues whenever butter-making is mentioned. For example, in s10 she substituted *bread* for *butter*. (Breadmaking is much more common than butter-making as a home activity for North American children.) The next time *butter* appears, in s15, she reads it as expected. However, in s18, *Soon the cream will turn into butter*, Betsy reads *buttermilk* for *butter*. Other references to butter-making include the words *churn* or *cream*. Betsy reads *cream* as expected each time it appears in the text but produces miscues for *churn*. She pauses about 10 seconds at the first appearance of *churn* and finally says it with exaggerated articulation. However, the next two times *churn* appears, Betsy reads *cream*.

	Text	*Transcript*
s25	...he saw a big pig inside, with its nose in the churn.	...he saw a big pig inside, with its nose in the cream.
s28	It bumped into the churn, knocking it over.	It jumped...it bumped into the cream, knocking it over.
s29	The cream splashed all over the room.	The cream shado [nonword miscue]... splashed all over the room.

In the retelling Betsy provides evidence that her miscues are conceptually based and not mere confusions:

> And the husband was sitting down and he poured some buttermilk and um...in a jar. And, and he was making buttermilk, and then he um...heard the baby crying. So he looked all around in the room and um.... And then he saw a big, a big, um...pig. Um... he saw a big pig inside the house. So, he told him to get out and he, the pig, started racing around and um...he di...he um...bumped into the buttermilk and then the buttermilk fell down and then the pig, um...went out.

Betsy, who is growing up in a metropolis, knows little about how butter is made in churns. She knows that there is a relationship between cream and butter, although she does not know the details of that relationship. According to her teacher, she has also taken part in a traditional primary school activity in which sweet cream is poured into a jar, closed up, and shaken until butter and buttermilk are produced. Although Betsy's miscues and retelling suggest that she has only some knowledge about butter-making, the concept is peripheral to comprehending the story. All that she needs to know is that butter-making is one of the wife's many chores that can cause the woodman trouble.

For a long time, teachers have been confused about how a reader can know something in one context but not know it in another. Such confusion comes from the belief that reading is word recognition; on the contrary, words in different syntactic and semantic contexts become different entities for readers, and Betsy's response to the structure *keep house* is good evidence for this. In s3, where the clauses *I keep house* and *and keeping house* occur the first time, Betsy reads the expected responses but repeats each several times before getting the words right, suggesting that she is grappling with their meanings. In s9 she reads *start house and keeping house* for *stay home and keep house*, and she reads the first phrase in s10 as *If you start home to do my work*. The structure *keep house* is a complex one. To a 9-year-old, *keep* is a verb that means being able to hold on to or take care of something small. *Keeping house* is no longer a common idiom in American or

Canadian English. *Stay home* adds complexity to *keep house*. Used with different verbs and different function words, *home* and *house* are sometimes synonyms and sometimes not. The transitive and intransitive nature of *keep* and *stay* as well as the infinitive structure *to keep* and *to stay* add to the complexity of the verb phrases.

In her search for meaning and her transaction with the published text, Betsy continues to develop strategies to handle these complex problems. In s14 she produces *stayed home*; however, in s35 she encounters *keeping house* again and reads, *perhaps keeping house...home and...is...hard work*. She is exploring the concept and grammaticality of *keeping house*. She first reads the expected response and then abandons it. In the story *home* appears seven times and *house* 10 times. Betsy reads them correctly in every context except in the patterns *staying home* and *keeping house*. Yet as she continues to work on these phrases throughout her reading she finally is able to handle the structures and either self-corrects successfully or produces a semantically acceptable sentence. Thus Betsy's miscues and retelling reveal the dynamic transaction between a reader and written language.

Through careful observation and evaluation, miscue analysis provides evidence of the ways in which the published text teaches the reader (Meek, 1988). Through continuous transactions with the text, Betsy develops as a reader. Our analysis also provides evidence for the published text as a mediator. Betsy is in a continuing zone of proximal development as she works at making sense of this text (Vygotsky, 1934/1978). Because the text is a complete one it mediates Betsy's development.

The Reader: An Intuitive Grammarian

Reading is not simply knowing sounds, words, sentences, and the abstract parts of language that can be studied by linguists. Reading, like listening, consists of processing language and constructing meaning. The reader brings a great deal of information to this complex and active process. A large body of research has been concerned with meaning construction and the understanding of reading processes and has provided supporting evidence to many of the principles we have revealed through miscue analysis. However, there is still too little attention paid to the ability of readers to make use of their knowledge of the syntax of their language as they read.

Readers sometimes cope with texts that they do not understand well by manipulating the language. Their miscues demonstrate this. The work of both Chomsky and Halliday has helped us understand the syntactic transformations that occur as readers transact with texts. Such manipulations are often seen when readers correctly answer questions about material they do not understand. For example, we ask readers to read an article entitled "Downhole Heave Compensator" (Kirk, 1974). Most readers claim little comprehension, but they can answer the question "What were the two things destroying the underreamers?" by finding the statement in the text that reads, "We were trying to keep drillships and semisubmersibles from wiping out our underreamers" (p. 88). It is because of such ability to manipulate the syntax of questions that we decided to use open-ended retellings for miscue analysis.

In miscue analysis research, we examine the syntactic nature of the miscues, the points in the text where miscues occur, and the syntactic acceptability of sentences that include miscues. Readers often produce sentences that are syntactically, but not semantically, acceptable. In s10 Betsy finally reads, *If you start home to do my work* for the text phrase *If you stay home to do my work*. Her reading of this phrase is syntactically acceptable in the story but unacceptable semantically because it is important to the story line that the woodman stay home.

We became aware that readers were able to maintain the grammaticality of sentences even if the meaning was not maintained when we examined the phenomenon of nonwords. Such nonsense words give us insight into English-speaking readers' grammatical awareness because sentences with nonwords often retain the grammatical features of English although they lose English meaning. Betsy produces only 2 nonword miscues among the 75 miscues she produces. In s58 Betsy reads, *As for the cow, she hang between the roof and the gorun* instead of the expected response *She hung between the roof and the ground*. She repeats *and the* prior to *ground* three times and pauses for about 10 seconds between each repetition. She seems to be aware that the word *ground* is not a familiar one in this context, but she maintains a noun intonation for the nonword. This allows her to maintain the grammatical sense of the sentence so that later in the story when the text reads *the cow fell to the ground*, she reads it as expected without hesitation.

Use of intonation also provides evidence for the grammatical similarity between the nonword and the text word. Miscues on the different forms of *to* (as the initial part of an infinitive or as a preposition), *two*, and *too* are easy to clarify by paying attention to intonation patterns. Nonwords most often retain similarities not only in number of syllables, word length, and spelling but also in bound morphemes—the smallest units that carry meaning or grammatical information within a word but cannot stand alone (for example, the *ed* in *carried*). In one of our research studies (Goodman & Burke, 1973), a group of sixth graders read a story that included the following: "Clearly and distinctively Andrew said 'philosophical'" and "A distinct quiver in his voice." The nonword substitutions for each were different depending on the grammatical function of the word. For *distinctly* readers read nonwords that sounded like *distikily, distintly*, and *definely*, while for *distinct* they read *dristic, distink, distet*.

There is abundant evidence in miscues of readers' strong awareness of bound morphemic rules. Our data on readers' word-for-word substitutions, whether nonwords or real words, show that, on average, 80% of the observed responses retain the morphemic markings of the text. For example, if the text word is a non-inflected form of a verb, the reader will tend to substitute that form; if the word has a prefix, the reader's substitution will tend to include a prefix. Derivational suffixes will be replaced by derivational suffixes, contractional suffixes by contractional suffixes.

Maintaining the syntactic acceptability of the text allows readers to continue reading and at the same time to maintain the cohesion and coherence of the text. Only a small portion of Betsy's substitution miscues do not retain the same grammatical function as the text word. Analysis of the word-for-word substitutions of fourth and sixth graders showed that their miscues retained the identical grammatical function over 73% of the time for nouns and verbs (Goodman & Burke, 1973). Function words were the same 67% or more of the time, while noun modifiers were retained approximately 60% of the time. In addition, an examination of what kinds of grammatical function were used for substitution when they were not identical indicated that nouns, noun modifiers, and function words are substituted for one another to a much greater degree than they are for verbs. Again this suggests the power of grammaticality on reading. Of 501 substitution miscues produced by fourth graders, only 3 times was a noun substituted for a verb modifier, and sixth graders made such a substitution only once in 424 miscues.

Evidence from miscues occurring at the beginning of sentences also adds insight into readers' awareness of the grammatical constraints of language. Generally, in prose for children few sentences begin with prepositions, intensifiers, adjectives, or singular common nouns without a preceding determiner. When readers produce miscues on the beginning words of sentences that do not retain the grammatical function of the text, we could not find one miscue that represented any of these unexpected grammatical forms. (One day we will do an article called "Miscues Readers Don't Make." Some of the strongest evidence comes from all the things readers could do that they do not.) These patterns are so strong that we have been able to detect manufactured examples in some professional texts. The authors have offered examples of errors readers do not make.

Readers' miscues that cross sentence boundaries also provide insight into the readers' grammatical sophistication. It is not uncommon to hear teachers complain that readers read past periods. Closer examination of this phenomenon suggests that when readers do this they are usually making a logical prediction that is based on a linguistic alternative. Although Betsy does this a few times, we will use an example from a story we used with fourth graders: *He still thought it more fun to pretend to be a great scientist, mixing the strange and the unknown* (Goodman & Goodman, 1978). Many readers predict that *strange* and *unknown* are adjectives and intone the sentence accordingly. This means that their voices are left up in the air, so to speak, in anticipation of a noun. The more proficient readers in the study regress at this point and self-correct by shifting to an end-of-the-sentence intonation pattern. Less proficient readers either do not correct at all and continue reading sounding surprised or try to regress without producing the appropriate intonation pattern.

Interrelations of All the Cueing Systems

Reading involves the interrelationship of all the language systems. All readers use graphic information to various degrees. Our research (Goodman & Burke, 1973) demonstrates that the least proficient readers we studied in the 6th, 8th, and 10th grades use graphic information more than the most proficient readers. Readers also produce substitution miscues similar to the phonemic patterns of text words. An examination of Betsy's word substitution miscues reveals that she pays more attention to the look-alike quality of the words than to their sound-alike quality. Although attention to graphic features occurs more frequently than attention to the phonemic patterns, readers use both systems to show that they call on their knowledge of the graphophonic system. Yet the use of these systems cannot explain why Betsy would produce a substitution such as *day* for *morning* or *job* for *work* (s13 and s14). She is clearly showing her use of the syntactic system and her ability to retain the grammatical function and morphemic constraints of the expected response. But the graphophonic and syntactic systems together do not explain why Betsy could seemingly understand words such as *house*, *home*, *ground*, and *cream* in certain contexts but not in others. To understand these aspects of reading, one must examine the interrelationship of all the cueing systems.

The integration of all the language systems (grammatical, graphophonic, semantic, and pragmatic) are necessary in order for reading to take place. Miscue analysis provides evidence that readers integrate cueing systems from the earliest initial attempts at reading. Readers sample and make judgments about which cues from each system will provide the most useful information in making predictions that will get them to meaning. All the miscue examples we have cited point to the notion that readers monitor their reading and ask themselves, "Does this sound like language?" (syntactically acceptable) and "Does this make sense in this story?" (semantically acceptable). Finally, if they have to return to the text to check things, they look more closely at the print using their graphophonic knowledge to confirm and self-correct as they read.

As readers make use of their knowledge of all the language cues, they predict, make inferences, select significant features, confirm, and constantly work toward constructing a meaningful text. Not only are they constructing meaning, they are constructing themselves as readers.

Schema-Forming and Schema-Driven Miscues

Our analysis of oral reading miscues began with the foundational assumption that reading is a language process parallel to listening. Everything we have observed among readers from beginners to those with great proficiency supports the validity of this assumption. The analysis of miscues, in turn, has been the basis for the development of a theory and model of the reading process.

What we have learned about miscues in reading has been applied to aspects of language such as spelling, composition, response to literature, and oral language development. Such research, liberated from the "perfection misconception," has demonstrated the linguistic creativity of humans. Errors children make as they develop oral language have provided insight not only into how the young learn language but into the nature of language—how it develops, grows, and changes (Brown, 1973). Children also invent schemata about the nature of written language as they become writers (Ferreiro & Teberosky, 1982; Goodman

& Wilde, 1992). Invented punctuation and spelling are especially good examples of the ways in which children learn to control the relationship between the sound system of their dialects and the conventions of the writing system (Read, 1986; Wilde, 1992). Adults develop the craft of writing through making miscues (Shaughnessy, 1977). Rosenblatt (1978) has long argued for a transactional view of reader response to literature in which all response is seen as a transaction between reader and text which of necessity results in variation among readers as they proceed toward interpretation, evaluation, and criticism. The readers' schemata are vital to the transactions.

What we have learned from the study of oral reading miscues and what we have seen in research on other language processes can help to explain the generation of miscues. The concept of schema is helpful to explore how miscues are necessary to language learning. A schema, as we define the term, is an organized cognitive structure of related knowledge, ideas, emotions, and actions that has been internalized and that guides and controls a person's use of subsequent information and response to experience.

Humans have schemata for everything they know and do. We have linguistic schemata (which we call rules) by which we produce and comprehend language. For example, we know when to expect or produce questions and when a question requires an answer. We have schemata for what language does and how it works. With such schemata, we use language to control the behavior of others. We have conceptual schemata for our ideas, concepts, and knowledge of the world. We may reject a Picasso portrait because it does not meet our expectation or schema of the human face.

Our work has led us to believe that humans also develop overarching schemata for creating new schemata and modifying old ones. These we might call schemata for new schema formation. Chomsky's (1965) concept that the generation of language is controlled by a finite set of transformational rules is a case of a schema for schema formation. The rules determine and limit what syntactic patterns may be accepted as grammatical in a language; these same rules also make it possible for speakers to create new sentences that have never been heard before but will be comprehensible to others.

Conceptual schemata work much the same way, and they are also controlled by overarching schemata. That explains why we often use analogy and metaphor in making connections to well-known words and ideas when we talk about new experiences. An example is the use of the term *docking* for space travel. Conceptual and linguistic schemata are at work simultaneously. The schemata must all be in harmony. If more than one complexity occurs, the result is compounding; the possibility of miscues increases disproportionately.

The earlier discussion about Betsy's miscues relating to the concepts of *to stay home* and *to keep house* is a good example. Her complete retelling after reading indicates good understanding of these concepts. In order to build this kind of understanding, Betsy has to work hard during her reading. She relates her own limited knowledge of staying home and keeping house to the meanings she is constructing in transaction with the author. She has to develop control over the syntactic and conceptional complexity of *stay home* and *keep house* and add to her understanding of the relationship of *home* and *house*. She keeps selectively using the available graphophonic cues to produce both expected and unexpected responses. It is important to understand the complexity of thinking that Betsy has to use and that her miscues reflect. Much of children's language learning can be explained in terms of developing control over language schemata. With growing linguistic and conceptual schemata, children use language to predict, process, and monitor expression and comprehension.

Now let's reconsider a concept from miscue analysis: Miscues are produced by the same process and in response to the same cues as expected responses. Putting that together with what we have just said about schema formation and use, we can consider miscues from the perspective of two schema processes: *schema-forming* or *schema-driven* miscues. And because schemata can be forming while we use our existing schemata, both processes can go on at the same time.

Piaget's (1977) concepts of assimilation and accommodation are pertinent here. A schema-forming miscue may be seen as a struggle toward accommodation, while a schema-driven miscue shows assimilation at work. Further, the effect of the miscue on subsequent language processing or intent may result in a disequilibrium, which may lead to reprocessing—that is, self-correction. Schemata may need to be abandoned, modified, or reformed as miscues are corrected.

A *schema-forming* miscue reflects the developmental process of building the rule systems of language and concepts, learning to apply those language rule systems, and delimiting them. For example, Susie responds to the printed name Corn Flakes on a box of cereal by pointing to each line of print successfully while drawing out the word *ceeerrreeeeuuuull* until she finishes moving her finger. Although she has not yet developed the concept that English print is alphabetic, she shows through her unexpected response that she is developing a schema concerning a relationship between the length of print and the length of oral utterance.

The young child's development of the rules of past tense, number, and gender are reflected in the miscues children make in oral language (Brown, 1973). Rebecca, age 3, provides a good example when she says to her aunt, who is waiting to read her a story, "I'll come and get you in a few whiles." She shows her control of the schema for pluralization (*few* take a plural) but she has taken *while*, which functions as a noun in the idiom *wait a little while* and has made it a count noun (*a few whiles*).

In the view of some scholars, a subject's production of language is dependent on whether the subject is dealing with old or new information. A schema-forming miscue is likely to involve new information, either linguistic or conceptual, which may not be easily assimilated. A schema-driven miscue may involve either old (given) information or new information in a predictable context. Furthermore, the schema, as well as the information, may be old or new.

A *schema-driven* miscue is one that results from the use of existing schemata to produce or comprehend language. In our research the concept of prediction has become important. Texts are hard or easy in proportion to how predictable they are for readers. They may use their existing schema to predict and comprehend, but sometimes the organization of the knowledge—that is, the schema on which the predictions are made—is so strong that it overrides the text and miscues occur. In the initial paragraph of a story that many adolescents and adults have read for us, the phrase *the headlamps of the car* occurs. The majority read *headlights* rather than *headlamps*. Many of those who do read *headlamps* indicate that they expected *headlights* and had to reread to accept *headlamps*.

Language variations also show evidence of schema-driven miscues. We shift dialects and registers when we move from formal written language to more informal styles or from one regional dialect to another. Tommy was overheard saying to his mother, a Texan, "Mom, Dad wants to know where the bucket is" and then to his father, a Midwesterner, "Here's the pail, Dad." Tommy had learned to switch codes depending on the situation, and his schema-driven responses were appropriate to each parent. Understanding that dialect miscues are driven by schema may help teachers and researchers see them in proper perspective. A rural African American fourth grader in Port Gibson, Mississippi, was reading a story that included the line *the ducks walked in single file*. At this point in the story, mother duck was leading her babies in a proud and haughty manner. The child reading that line produced *the ducks walk signifying*.

The malapropisms that we all exhibit are also evidence of schema-driven miscues at work. We try to use schemata for word formation beyond word-formation limits. These result in miscues in listening as well as speaking. Television's Archie Bunker was upset because of the *alteration* he had had with a boisterous customer. We cannot help relating the concept of schema-driven miscues to Tannen's (1990) work on conversations between men and women and among different ethnic groups. "I make sense of seemingly senseless misunderstandings that haunt our relationships and show that a man and a woman can interpret the same conversation differently, even when there is no apparent misunderstanding," she writes (p. 13). By understanding the reasons that underlie our misunderstandings perhaps we can form schemata that will help us "prevent or relieve some of the frustration" (p. 13).

In many cases it is not easy to separate miscues into schema-forming or schema-driven processes because they often occur simultaneously. At any particular point in time, it is fairly easy to explain the schemata that drive the miscues that occur. Schema formation, on the other hand, is less likely to occur at a single point and be easily discernible in a single miscue. The study of children's writing development allows us one way to observe the process of schema formation. It also reveals how both schema-forming and schema-driven miscues can occur in concert. An example from a story that Jennifer wrote in the first grade illustrates invented spelling that is driven by her linguistic schemata. Jennifer produced past-tense verbs about 20 times. Each reflected her invented phonic rules (and her awareness of the phonological rules of her own speech) because each had the letter *d* or *t* at the end, representing the appropriate phoneme. These spelling miscues included *rapt* (wrapped) and *yeld* (yelled). Her phonic schemata at this point led her to invent consistent spellings of single letters for single sounds. But a year later her spelling represented an awareness of the interrelationship of both the morphophonemic rules (past tense taking one of three forms depending on the preceding consonants) and the orthographic rule that spelling is not determined by sound in a simple one-to-one manner. Of 28 regular past-tense verbs in a story she wrote in the second grade, 25 were spelled conventionally. Jennifer was in a classroom where a lot of writing was encouraged but there was no direct teaching of spelling. During this year, she continually reformed her schemata and moved toward socially conventional ones.

Readers' miscues often can be driven by conceptual schemata, but at the same time readers can be forming new schemata. This is often revealed through the retelling as well as the miscues. In our research, we have had children read a story that has a significant concept represented by an unfamiliar but high-frequency word. One such word was *typical*. Although the children who read this story often reproduced oral substitutions for *typical* in the text (such as *tropical*, *type-ical*, and *topical*), they usually were able to explain the meaning of the word as it developed in the reading of the text. One Texas youngster said, "Oh, yeah, *tropical* means ordinary, just like all kinds of other babies. But, you know, it could also be a big storm."

Sometimes a new word represents a concept well known to the reader. In this case the reader must assimilate the new term to the old concept. Bilingual students often face this when they begin to read in a second language. We studied Arabic immigrant students who produced miscues on the word *plow* in a story they were reading, substituting *palow, pull, pole, polo, plew*, and *blow*, among other words and nonwords (Goodman & Goodman, 1978). However, they all were able to provide evidence that they had a "plowing" schema. One reader's example is representative:

> Well, it's a thing with two handles and something pointing down. You got to pull it. But they don't push it with a camel. They push it with a cow. When the cow moves, the one who's pushing it got to go push on it so it goes deeper in the underground.

In such a context we see both schema-driving and schema-forming processes taking place in a dynamic way. These fourth-grade Arabic readers are new to English. They use their developing knowledge of English to produce unexpected responses to the word *plow* and their knowledge about plowing to show understanding of the concept (schema-driven). At the same time, they add new knowledge as they encounter the English word for the concept (schema-forming). The example also indicates that the reader rejected the story element that a camel was used to pull a plow as implausible because of his conceptual schema.

We hope that our discussion of the role miscues play in language learning communicates to teachers and researchers that miscues are the positive effects of linguistic and conceptual processes rather than the failure to communicate or comprehend. If a language user loses meaning, she or he is likely to produce a miscue. If the language user chooses a syntactic schema different from the author's, a miscue will likely result. If a reader or listener interprets in a way different from the meaning intended by the speaker or author, a miscue will result. Miscues reflect readers' abilities to liberate themselves from detailed attention to print as they leap toward meaning. Readers make use of their linguistic and conceptual schemata to reverse, substitute, insert, omit, rearrange, paraphrase, and transform. They do this not only with letters and single words, but with two-word sequences, phrases, clauses, and sentences. Their own experiences, values, conceptual structures, expectations, dialects, and lifestyles are integral to the process. The meanings they construct can never be a simple reconstruction of the author's conceptual structures because they are dependent on the reader's schemata.

Risk-taking has been recognized as a significant aspect of both language learning and proficient language use. In risk-taking there is a necessary balance between tentativeness and self-confidence. Miscues reflect the degree to which existing schemata fit the existing circumstance and the level of confidence of the language user. In speaking a second language, speakers often show great tentativeness, consciously groping for control of developing schemata. As their confidence grows so does their risk-taking, and their miscues show the influence either of schemata for the first language (schema-driven) or of their developing schemata for the second language (schema-forming). An example of the former cautious type is this sentence from a native Spanish-speaking adult who is asking his English teacher for advice: "Ms. Buck, please, I hope I do not molest you." This oral miscue is driven by the speaker's schema for the Spanish *molestar* (to bother). In her response to the student, the teacher will provide information that will help the student form a schema to provide semantic limits for the English *molest*.

Oral and Silent Reading

We need to say a word about the relationship between oral and silent reading because much of miscue analysis research uses oral reading. The basic mode of reading is silent. Oral reading is special because it requires production of an oral representation concurrently with comprehending. The functions of oral reading are limited. It is a performing art used by teachers, entertainers, politicians, and religious leaders. We have already explained why we use oral reading in miscue analysis. But a basic question remains: Are oral and silent reading similar enough to justify generalizing from studies of oral reading miscues to theories and models of silent reading?

In our view, a single process underlies all reading. The language cueing systems and the strategies of oral and silent reading are essentially the same. The miscues we find in oral reading occur in silent reading as well. We have some research evidence of that. Studies of nonidentical fillers of cloze blanks (responses that do not match the deleted words) show remarkable correspondence to oral reading miscues and indicate that the processes of oral and silent reading are much the same (Anderson, 1982; Cambourne & Rousch, 1979; Chapman, 1981).

Still, there are dissimilarities between oral and silent reading. First, oral reading is limited to the speed at which speech can be produced; therefore, it need not be as efficient as rapid silent reading. Next, superficial misarticulations such as *hangaber* for *hamburger* occur in oral reading but are not part of silent reading. Also, oral readers, conscious of their audience, read passages differently from when they read silently. Examples are production of nonword substitutions, persistence with several attempts at problem spots, overt regression to correct miscues already mentally corrected, and deliberate adjustments in ensuing text to cover miscues so that listeners will not notice them. Furthermore, oral readers may take fewer risks than silent readers. This can be seen in the deliberate omission of unfamiliar words, reluctance to attempt correction even though meaning is disrupted, and avoidance of overtly making corrections that have taken place silently to avoid calling attention to miscues. Finally, relatively proficient readers, particularly adults, may become so concerned with superficial fluency that they short-circuit the basic concern for meaning. Professional oral readers (newscasters, for example) seem to suffer from this malady. With these reservations noted, we believe that making sense is the same in oral and silent reading; in construction of meaning, miscues must occur in both.

Parts and Wholes

Too much research on language and language learning is still concerned with isolated sounds, letters, word parts, words, and even sentences. Such fragmentation, although it simplifies research design and the complexity of the phenomena under study, seriously distorts processes, tasks, cue values, interactions, and realities. Many years ago, Kintsch (1974) wrote as follows:

> Psycholinguistics is changing in character.... The 1950s were still dominated by the nonsense syllables...the 1960s were characterized by the use of word lists, while the present decade is witnessing a shift to even more complex learning materials. At present, we have reached the point where lists of sentences are being substituted for word lists in studies of recall recognition. Hopefully, this will not be the endpoint of this development, and we shall soon see psychologists handle effectively the problems posed by the analysis of connected text. (p. 2)

Through miscue analysis we have learned that, other things being equal, short language sequences are harder to comprehend than are long ones. Sentences are easier than words, paragraphs easier than sentences, pages easier than paragraphs, and stories easier than pages. We see two reasons for this. First, it takes some familiarity with the style and general semantic thrust of a text's language for the reader to make successful predictions. Style is largely a matter of an author's syntactic preferences; the semantic context develops over the entire text. Short texts provide limited cues for readers to build a sense of either style or meaning. Second, the disruptive effect of particular miscues on meaning is much greater in short texts. Longer texts offer redundant opportunities to recover and self-correct. This suggests why findings from studies of words, sentences, and short passages produce different results from those that involve whole texts. It also raises a major question about using standardized tests, which employ words, phrases, sentences, and short texts to assess reading proficiency.

Sooner or later all attempts to understand language—its development and its function as the medium of human communication—must confront linguistic reality. Theories, models, grammars, and research paradigms must predict and explain what people do when they use language and what makes it possible for them to do so. Researchers have contrived ingenious ways to make a small bit of linguistic or psycholinguistic reality available for examination. But then what they see is often out of focus, distorted by the design. Miscue analysis research makes fully available the reality of the miscues language users produce as they participate in real speech and literacy events. Huey (1908) said,

> And so to completely analyze what we do when we read would almost be the acme of a psychologist's achievements, for it would be to describe very many of the most intricate workings of the human mind, as well as to unravel the tangled story of the most remarkable specific performance that civilization has learned in all its history. (p. 6)

To this we add that miscues are the windows on language processes at work.

QUESTIONS FOR REFLECTION

1. How do miscues provide insights into the reading process?
2. What information do unaided retellings provide that direct questions do not?
3. How is it that children can recognize specific words in one context and not recognize them in another?
4. How can the difference between schema-forming and schema-driven miscues be of value in understanding the way in which children process text?

NOTE

This chapter is based on and updated from "Learning About Psycholinguistic Processes by Analyzing Oral Reading," *Harvard Educational Review*, 47(3), 317–333; and "To Err Is Human," *New York University Education Quarterly*, *12*(4), 14–19.

REFERENCES

Anderson, J. (1982, July). *The writer, the reader, the text.* Paper presented at the 19th annual UKRA Reading Conference, Newcastle-upon-Tyne, United Kingdom.

Brown, R. (1973). *A first language: The early stages.* Cambridge, MA: Harvard University Press.

Cambourne, B., & Rousch, P. (1979). *A psycholinguistic model of the reading process as it relates to proficient, average, and low-ability readers* (Tech. Rep.). Wagga Wagga, NSW, Australia: Riverina College of Advanced Education, Charles Sturt University.

Chapman, J.L. (1981). The reader and the text. In J.L. Chapman (Ed.), *The reader and the text*. London: Heinemann.
Chomsky, N. (1965). *Aspects of the theory of syntax*. Cambridge, MA: MIT Press.
Ferreiro, E., & Teberosky, A. (1982). *Literacy before schooling*. Portsmouth, NH: Heinemann.
Goodman, K.S. (1983, July). *Text features as they relate to miscues: Determiners* (Occasional Paper No. 8). Tucson: Program in Language and Literacy, College of Education, University of Arizona.
Goodman, K.S., Brown, J., & Marek, A. (1993). *Annotated chronological bibliography of miscue analysis* (Occasional Paper No. 16). Tucson: Program in Language and Literacy, College of Education, University of Arizona.
Goodman, K.S., & Burke, C.L. (1973, April). *Theoretically based studies of patterns of miscues in oral reading performance* (Project No. 9-0375). Washington, DC: U.S. Office of Education.
Goodman, K.S., & Gespass, S. (1983, March). *Text features as they relate to miscues: Pronouns* (Occasional Paper No. 7). Tucson: Program in Language and Literacy, College of Education, University of Arizona.
Goodman, K.S., & Goodman, Y.M. (1978). *Reading of American children whose language is a stable rural dialect of English or a language other than English* (Final Report, Project NIE-C-00-3-0087). Washington DC: U.S. Department of Health, Education and Welfare, National Institute of Education.
Goodman, Y.M., Watson, D., & Burke, C. (1987). *Reading miscue inventory: Alternative procedures*. Katonah, NY: Richard C. Owen.
Goodman, Y.M., & Wilde, S. (1992). *Literacy events in a community of young writers*. New York: Teachers College Press.
Huey, E.B. (1908). *The psychology and pedagogy of reading*. New York: Macmillan.
Kintsch, W. (1974). *The representation of meaning in memory*. Hillsdale, NJ: Erlbaum.
Kirk, S. (1974, June). Downhole heave compensator: A tool designed by hindsight. *Drilling-DCW*, 88.
McInnes, J., Gerrard, M., & Ryckman, J. (Series Eds.). (1964). *Magic and make believe* (Basal Program). Don Mills, ON: Thomas Nelson.
Meek, M. (1988). *How texts teach what readers learn*. Exeter, UK: Thimble.
Piaget, J. (1977). *The development of thought: Equilibration of cognitive structures*. New York: Viking.
Read, C. (1986). *Children's creative spelling*. London: Routledge & Kegan Paul.
Rosenblatt, L. (1978). *The reader, the text, the poem: The transactional theory of the literary work*. Carbondale: Southern Illinois University Press.
Shaughnessy, M.P. (1977). *Errors and expectations: A guide for the teacher of basic writing*. New York: Oxford University Press.
Tannen, D. (1990). *You just don't understand: Women and men in conversation*. New York: Morrow.
Vygotsky, L.S. (1978). *Mind in society: The development of higher psychological processes* (M. Cole, V. John-Steiner, S. Scribner, & E. Souberman, Eds. & Trans.). Cambridge, MA: Harvard University Press. (Original work published 1934)
Wilde, S. (1992). *You kan red this! Spelling and punctuation for whole language classrooms, K–6*. Portsmouth, NH: Heinemann.

CHAPTER 22

Cognitive Flexibility Theory: Advanced Knowledge Acquisition in Ill-Structured Domains

Rand J. Spiro, Michigan State University*

Richard L. Coulson, Southern Illinois University School of Medicine*

Paul J. Feltovich, Florida Institute for Human and Machine Cognition*

Daniel K. Anderson, Sharecare*

Advanced knowledge acquisition in a subject area is different in many important ways from introductory learning (and from expertise). In this paper we discuss some of the special characteristics of advanced learning of complex conceptual material. We note how these characteristics are often at odds with the goals and tactics of introductory instruction and with psychological biases in learning. We allude to our research in biomedical cognition that has revealed a substantial incidence of misconception attributable to various forms of oversimplification, and we outline the factors that contribute to suboptimal learning at the advanced stage. We then sketch a theoretical orientation for more successful advanced knowledge acquisition in ill-structured domains, cognitive flexibility theory. This orientation emphasizes the use of multiple mental and pedagogical representations; the promotion of multiple alternative systems of linkage among knowledge elements; the promotion of schema assembly (as opposed to the retrieval of prepackaged schemata); the centrality of "cases of application" as a vehicle for engendering functional conceptual understanding; and the need for participatory learning, tutorial guidance, and adjunct support for aiding the management of complexity. A computer hypertext approach that implements cognitive flexibility theory is discussed.

The Goals of Advanced Knowledge Acquisition

In our work we have been interested in "advanced knowledge acquisition"—learning beyond the introductory stage for a subject area but before the achievement of practiced expertise that comes with massive experience. This often neglected intermediate stage is important because the aims and means of advanced knowledge

This chapter is reprinted from *Tenth Annual Conference of the Cognitive Science Society Proceedings* (pp. 640–653), edited by V. Patel, Hillsdale, NJ: Erlbaum.

acquisition are different from those of introductory learning. In introductory learning the goal is often mere exposure to content and the establishment of a general orientation to a field; objectives of assessment are likewise confined to the simple effects of exposure (e.g., recognition and recall). At some point in learning about a knowledge domain, the goal must change; at some point, students must "get it right." This is the stage of advanced knowledge acquisition (Feltovich, Spiro, & Coulson, 1989; Spiro, Feltovich, Coulson, & Anderson, 1989; Spiro et al., 1987): The learner must *attain a deeper understanding of content material, reason with it, and apply it flexibly in diverse contexts.* Obstacles to advanced knowledge acquisition include conceptual complexity and the increasing ill-structuredness that comes into play with more advanced approaches to a subject area. By *ill-structuredness* we mean that many concepts (interacting contextually) are pertinent in the typical case of knowledge application, and that their patterns of combination are inconsistent across case applications of the same nominal type. (See Spiro et al., 1987, for a more detailed treatment of the nature and consequences of ill-structuredness.)

The methods of education in introductory and advanced learning seem, in many ways, to be at odds. For example, compartmentalizing knowledge, presenting clear instances (and not the many pertinent exceptions), and employing reproductive memory criteria are often in conflict with the realities of advanced learning—knowledge, which is intertwined and dependent, has significant context-dependent variations and requires the ability to respond flexibly to "messy" application situations. These discrepancies in aims and tactics (along with many others that we have observed) raise the possibility that introductory learning, even when it is "successful," lays foundations in knowledge and in an approach to learning that interfere with advanced acquisition. As we have seen repeatedly demonstrated, that possibility is an actuality (Coulson, Feltovich, & Spiro, 1986; Feltovich et al., 1989; Spiro et al., 1987; Spiro et al., 1989).

Deficiencies in Advanced Knowledge Acquisition

Medical school is an archetype of an advanced knowledge acquisition setting (Feltovich et al., 1989). Medical students have already had introductory exposure to many of the subject areas of biological science that they go on to study in medical school, but they are certainly not yet expert. Furthermore, the goals of medical education are clearly those of advanced knowledge acquisition. Important aspects of conceptual complexity must now be mastered (superficial familiarity with key concepts is no longer sufficient), and the ability to apply knowledge from formal instruction to real-world cases is certainly something that is expected of those studying to be physicians.

In our laboratory we have been studying medical students' learning, understanding, and application of important but difficult biomedical science concepts. This effort has revealed widely held systematic misconceptions among students, despite their having been exposed to appropriate information (Coulson et al., 1986; Feltovich et al., 1989; Spiro et al., 1987; Spiro et al., 1989). Stubborn misconceptions, notwithstanding usual classroom efforts at instruction, have been found for difficult concepts in other areas as well (e.g., physics: Champagne, Gunstone, & Klopfer, 1985; White, 1984).

The biomedical misconceptions that we have identified are of various kinds (Feltovich et al., 1989; Spiro et al., 1989). These include *contentive* errors, often involving overgeneralization—for example, areas of subject matter are seen as being more similar than they really are. Errors attributable to dysfunctional biases in *mental representation* are also observed—for example, dynamic processes are often represented more statically. *Prefigurative "world views"* that underlie learners' understanding processes also cause problems—for example, the presupposition that the world works in such a way that "parts add up to wholes" leads students to decompose complex processes into components that are treated (mistakenly) as independent. Furthermore, at all these levels misconceptions interact in *reciprocally supportive* ways and combine to yield higher-order misconceptions (Coulson et al., 1986; Feltovich et al., 1989). Failures of understanding *compound* themselves, building up durable chains of larger-scale misconception.

Reductive Biases: The Pervasive Role of Oversimplification in the Development of Misconceptions

A predominant share of the misconceptions (and networks of misconception) that we have identified reflect one or another kind of *oversimplification* of complex material—associated with learners' earlier experiences with introductory learning, and even influenced by many experiences with advanced learning. Misconceptions of advanced material result both from interference from earlier, simplified treatments of that material and from a prevailing mode of approaching the learning process in general that fosters simplificational strategies and leaves learners without an appropriate cognitive repertoire for the processing of complexity (Feltovich et al., 1989; Spiro et al., 1987; Spiro et al., 1989).

We have termed the general tendency to reduce important aspects of complexity the *reductive bias*. Several forms of the bias have been identified, selected examples of which follow (see Coulson et al., 1986; Feltovich et al., 1989; Spiro et al., 1989, for *examples of biomedical misconceptions* corresponding to the types of reductive bias listed).

1. Oversimplification of complex and irregular structure. Superficial similarities among related phenomena are treated as unifying characteristics. Interacting components are treated as independent. Incomplete conceptual accounts are presented (or accepted by the learner) as being comprehensive. Instances that are referred to as belonging to the same generic category are treated in a uniform manner despite their being highly diverse. The irregular is treated as regular, the nonroutine as routine, the disorderly as orderly, the continuous as discrete, the dynamic as static, the multidimensional as unidimensional. (This first reductive bias is the most general one, encompassing many of the specific ones listed below.)

2. Overreliance on a single basis for mental representation. A single, encompassing, representational logic is applied to complex concepts and phenomena that are inadequately covered by that logic—for example, understanding of a new concept is reduced to the features of a (partially) analogous concept. New, highly divergent examples are understood by exclusive reference to a single prototype. A single schema or theory is proffered and preferred, despite the fact that its coverage is significantly incomplete. Complexly multifaceted content has its understanding narrowed to just those aspects covered by a single organizational scheme. And so on.

3. Overreliance on "top down" processing. Understanding and decision-making in knowledge application situations (i.e., cases) rely too exclusively on generic abstractions (i.e., concepts, theories, etc.); detailed knowledge of *case* structure is not used enough (i.e., knowledge of "how cases go," as well as reasoning from specific case precedents).

4. Context-independent conceptual representation. The contexts in which a concept is relevant are treated as having overly uniform characteristics. This promotes the representation of conceptual knowledge in a manner too abstract for effective application (i.e., without sufficient regard for the specifics of application in context). Concepts are insufficiently tailored to their uses; concepts are not recognized as relevant when, in fact, they are; and concepts are mistakenly judged to be relevant in contexts where they are not.

5. Overreliance on precompiled knowledge structures. *Fixed* protocols or rigidly *prepackaged* schemata are presented to learners and used by them as recipes for what to do in new cases.

6. Rigid compartmentalization of knowledge components. Components of knowledge that are in fact interdependent are treated as being separable from each other. Learners develop mistaken beliefs in the independence of the components. Relatedly, where knowledge components do function independently, it may nevertheless be the case that conveying relationships between their conceptual structures would aid understanding; these connections are not drawn. When components are interrelated, there is a tendency to use just one linkage scheme, thereby underrepresenting the richness of interconnection in the system and promoting narrow, doctrinaire viewpoints (see the problem of single representations).

7. Passive transmission of knowledge. Knowledge is preemptively encoded under a scheme determined by external authority (e.g., a textbook) or a scheme that facilitates delivery and use. Knowledge is "handed" to the learner. The preemptive encoding is passively received by the learner, and useful benefits that result from personalized knowledge representations, derivable from active exploration and involvement in the subject area, do not develop. When active, participatory learning is encouraged, adequate support for the management of increased indeterminacy and cognitive load is not provided (e.g., mentor guidance, memory aids, etc.).

The next section will outline our theoretical approach to *remedying* the problems of advanced knowledge acquisition caused by these reductive biases.

Cognitive Flexibility Theory: Themes of Advanced Knowledge Acquisition

Where has our research on the *problems* of advanced knowledge acquisition led us? To an overall theoretical orientation that in many ways derives its fundamental themes from the specific nature of those learning problems, as the problems relate to the characteristics of ill-structured domains and the special goals of advanced knowledge acquisition (i.e., mastery of conceptual complexity and knowledge application/transfer).

In this section we provide a brief discussion of our most fundamental, theoretically motivated remedies for the problems of advanced knowledge acquisition. The following themes constitute different facets of what we call *cognitive flexibility* (Spiro et al., 1987). The themes are, in a sense, *conditions* for developing mastery of complexity and knowledge transferability. Each of the headlined theoretical commitments has received some form of implementation, either in our experiments or in our theory-based computer hypertext systems (including one prototype that implements the theory's principles of advanced knowledge acquisition in cardiovascular medicine, the Cardioworld Explorer). Given the extreme limitations of space, the themes are discussed schematically and in the abstract; detailed development of theoretical rationales, examples of our concrete instantiations of the themes (in the biomedical domain and others that we have studied), and patterns of empirical support for our claims can be found in our cited papers.

1. Avoidance of oversimplification and overregularization. Because of the strong bias toward oversimplification that we have observed, it is clear that advanced knowledge acquisition must place a high premium on making salient those ways that knowledge is not as simple and orderly as it might first seem in introductory treatments. Where the problem is so often a presumption of simplicity and regularity, the remedy is to take special measures to *demonstrate complexities and irregularities*. It is important to lay bare the limitations of initial, first-pass understandings, to highlight exceptions, to show how the superficially similar is dissimilar and how superficial unities are broken. Where conceptual error frequently occurs from atomistic decomposition of complexly interacting information followed by misguided attempts at "additive" reassembly of the decomposed elements, the remedy is to take pains to *highlight component interactions*, to clearly demonstrate the intricate patterns of *conceptual combination*.

This is a very general theme, encompassing many of the others that follow in this list. Cognitive flexibility involves the *selective* use of knowledge to *adaptively fit* the needs of understanding and decision making in a particular situation; the potential for maximally adaptive *knowledge assembly* depends on having available as full a representation of complexity to draw upon as possible.

2. Multiple representations. Single representations (e.g., a single schema, organizational logic, line of argument, prototype, analogy, etc.) will miss important facets of complex concepts. Cognitive flexibility is dependent on having a diversified repertoire of ways of thinking about a conceptual topic. Knowledge that will have to be used in many ways has to be learned, represented, and tried out (in application) in many ways.

The use of multiple representations is important at different levels. For example, we have found multiple analogies to be very useful in understanding complex individual concepts (Spiro et al., 1989; see the example below of force production by muscle fibers; see also Collins & Gentner, 1987; White & Frederiksen, 1987). However, the importance of multiple representations may be even more important for larger units of analysis. For example, we have found that students' understandings of the entire domain of biomedical knowledge are adversely affected by the tendency to use just one way of modeling the various phenomena they encounter, one that comes from the *metaphor of the machine*. This one "lens" leads them to take for granted certain issues related to the nature of explanations, the structure of mental models of functional systems, and so on. These students develop understandings that do not capture important aspects of the biomedical domain (e.g., inherently organic processes). Their understandings would be more complete if they were to augment the selective view that results from their mechanistic bias with other understandings that selectively emerge from the unique aspects of other cognitive "lenses"—for example, from *organicist* metaphors (Feltovich et al., 1989).

The need for multiple representations applies not only to complex concepts, but to cases as well. In an ill-structured domain, cases (examples, occurrences, events—occasions of use of conceptual knowledge) tend to be complex and highly variable one to the next. The complexity of cases requires that they be represented from multiple theoretical/conceptual perspectives; if cases are treated narrowly by characterizing them using a too limited subset of their relevant perspectives, the ability to process future cases will be limited. First, there will be an assumption that cases are simpler than they in fact are, and attempts to deal with new cases will prematurely conclude after they are only *partially* analyzed. Second, there will be insufficient preparedness to deal with the specific patterns of interaction of theoretical/conceptual perspectives within cases. Third, to the extent that performance in future cases will require reasoning from sets of precedent cases (which is always a greater need in ill-structured domains), the likelihood of having case representations available in prior knowledge which are maximally apt in their relation to some new case is lessened to the extent that cases are narrowly represented in memory. This is especially so when there is substantial across-case dissimilarity; the relative novelty of a new case in an ill-structured domain will require more elaborate efforts to find appropriate precedents—the wider the variety that is available, the better the chances of finding a fit.

An example of multiple representations: Integrated multiple analogies for complex concepts. As we have said, our studies of medical students have indicated that one of the most serious contributors to the problems of advanced knowledge acquisition is the use of a single knowledge representation. Complex concepts can rarely be adequately represented using a single schema, theoretical perspective, line of exposition, and so on. Nevertheless, in practice, complex concepts frequently are represented in some single fashion, with substantial consequences.

Our remedy has been to approach learning in all the domains that we have studied with the goal of promoting *multiple representations* (e.g., multiple precedent cases for a new case; multiple organizational schemes for representing the same content material in our computer hypertexts; etc.). Here we will briefly consider just the case of analogy. We have discovered a large number of misconceptions that result from the overextended application of analogies (Spiro et al., 1989). To combat the negative effects of a powerful and seductive single analogy, we employ *sets of integrated multiple analogies*. Whenever a source concept in an analogy is missing important aspects of a target concept or the source concept is in some way misleading about the target concept, we introduce *another* analogy to counteract those specific negative effects of the earlier analogy.

So, where we find that misconceptions about the nature of force production by muscle fibers often develop because of a common analogy to the operation of rowing crews (sarcomere "arms" and "oars" both generate force by a kind of "pulling"), other analogies are introduced to mitigate the negative effects of the limited rowing-crew analogy (Spiro et al., 1989). An analogy to turnbuckles corrects misleading notions about the nature of relative movement and the gross structures within the muscle. An analogy to "finger handcuffs" covers important information missing in the rowing-crew analogy about limits of fiber length (the elastin covering on muscle fiber bundles constricts at long lengths, stopping extension in a manner similar to the cross-hatched finger cuffs when you try to pull a finger out of each end). And so on. A composite imaging technique that helps the user integrate the multiple analogies, so that the correct aspects of each analogy can be selectively instantiated in relevant contexts of use of the target concept, has also been developed. The procedure facilitates the learning of a concept (through the pedagogical benefits of analogy), while maintaining the integrity of the concept's complexities (by using multiple analogies to cover the concept's multifacetedness and to vitiate the force of incorrect aspects of any single analogy) (see also Burnstein, 1983).

Theory-based hypertext systems to implement the themes of advanced knowledge acquisition in ill-structured domains: The importance of revisiting and rearranging in the development of multiple representations. Much of the work on computer hypertext systems has been driven by the power of the technology rather than by a coherent view of the cognitive psychology of nonlinear and multidimensional learning and instruction. In contrast, our hypertext approaches have a basis in cognitive theory—they derive from the themes of cognitive flexibility theory. And their realm of operation is specified; they are especially targeted at advanced knowledge acquisition in ill-structured domains. (There is no point in imposing the extra cognitive load of nonlinearity and multidimensionality if the domain being studied is simple and well structured or if the goals of learning are the more easily attainable ones of introductory treatments). We will briefly characterize our approach to implementing cognitive flexibility theory in computer hypertext systems.

Our hypertext systems build multiple representations in a manner that can be understood using a metaphor of landscape exploration. Deep understanding of a complex landscape will not be obtained from a single traversal. Similarly for a *conceptual* landscape. Rather, *the landscape must be criss-crossed in many directions* to master its complexity and to avoid having the fullness of the domain attenuated (Spiro et al., 1987; Wittgenstein, 1953). The same sites in a landscape (the same cases or concepts in a knowledge domain) should be *revisited* from different directions, thought about from different perspectives, and so on. There is a limit to how much understanding of a complex entity can be achieved in a single treatment, in a single context, for a single purpose. By *repeating* the presentation of the same complex case or concept information in *new contexts*, additional aspects of the multifacetedness of these "landscape sites" are brought out, enabling the kind of rich representations necessary in a complex and ill-structured domain. Thus, cognitive flexibility is fostered by a flexible approach to learning and instruction. The same content material is covered in different ways at different times in order to demonstrate the potential flexibility of use inherent in that content (Spiro & Jehng, 1990; Spiro et al., 1987).

3. **Centrality of cases.** The more ill structured the domain, the poorer the guidance for knowledge *application* that top-down structures will generally provide. That is, the way abstract concepts (theories, general principles, etc.) should be used to facilitate understanding and to dictate action in naturally occurring cases becomes increasingly indeterminate in ill-structured domains. The application of knowledge to cases in an ill-structured domain (i.e., a domain in which cases are individually multidimensional and irregularly related one to the next) cannot be prescribed in advance by general principles. This is because, in ill-structured domains, there is great variability from case to case regarding which conceptual elements will be relevant and in what pattern of combination. In an ill-structured domain, general principles will not capture enough of the structured dynamics of cases; increased flexibility in responding to highly diverse new cases comes increasingly from reliance on reasoning from precedent cases.

Thus, examples/cases cannot be assigned the ancillary status of merely illustrating abstract principles (and then being discardable); the cases are key—examples are necessary and not just nice (Feltovich et al., 1989; Spiro & Jehng, 1990; Spiro et al., 1987).

4. **Conceptual knowledge as knowledge in use.** Not only is it more difficult to count on top-down prescriptions for performance in new cases in an ill-structured domain (i.e., abstract concepts/theories inadequately determine responses to new cases), but there is also considerable indeterminateness in defining conditions for *accessing* conceptual structures in the first place, to engage the guidance the conceptual structures *do* offer. It is not that abstract knowledge has no role in ill-structured domains but that its role is highly intertwined with that of case-centered reasoning. Put another way, in an ill-structured domain

there will be greatly increased variability across cases in the way the same concept is used or applied. Thus it is harder to get from features of cases to the concepts that might need to be applied to those cases. And it is harder to apply a concept, once assessed, if it has many different kinds of uses across cases—concepts must be *tailored* to their application contexts. The Wittgensteinian dictum that meaning is determined by use clearly applies in ill-structured domains. If a concept's meaning in use cannot be determined universally across cases (as in an ill-structured domain), then one must pay much more attention to the details of how the concept is used—*knowledge in practice*, rather than in the abstract (Spiro & Jehng, 1990; Spiro et al., 1987; Wittgenstein, 1953).

In medical training, this issue of *variability and combination in concept instantiation* has an obvious implication for the traditional difficulty of integrating the biomedical basic science parts of the curriculum with the clinical parts. Physicians' practice would be improved if in problematic situations they could apply the interacting basic biomedical science concepts that underlie the clinical situation that is posing the problem. However, it is very difficult for medical students to learn how to get to the basic science concepts from clinical presenting features, partly because of the great variability across clinical cases in the way those concepts get instantiated. A key feature of our Cardioworld Explorer hypertext is that it permits the learner to selectively examine the full range of uses of any selected basic science concept (or any selected combination of concepts) across cases with differing clinical features, teaching the patterns of concept application and thus facilitating *access* to conceptual information in clinical contexts (as well as fostering an understanding of the different ways that a given concept has to be tailored to be clinically relevant).

Again, in an ill-structured domain the meaning of a concept is intimately connected to its patterns of use. When the uses (instances, cases) of the same concept have a complex and irregular distribution (i.e., the domain is ill structured), adequate prepackaged prescriptions for proper activation of the concept cannot be provided (i.e., *concept instantiation is nonroutine*). Instead, greater weight (than in a well-structured domain) must be given to activating concepts in a new case by examination of family resemblances across the features of *past cases* that have been called (labeled as instances of) that concept.

5. Schema assembly (from rigidity to flexibility). In an ill-structured domain, emphasis must be shifted from *retrieval* of intact, rigid, precompiled knowledge structures to *assembly* of knowledge from different conceptual and precedent case sources to adaptively fit the situation at hand (Spiro, 1980; Spiro et al., 1987). This follows, again, from characteristics of ill-structured domains. Since ill-structuredness implies kinds of complexity and irregularity that militate against the use of knowledge structures that assume routinizability across cases, the role of intact schema retrieval must be diminished—greater across-case differences cause a necessary decline in the ability of any large, single precompilation to fit a wide variety of cases. In complex and ill-structured domains, one cannot have a prepackaged schema for everything. As ill-structuredness increases, the use of *rigid* knowledge structures (i.e., the same precompiled knowledge structure used for many cases) must be replaced by *flexible*, recombinable knowledge structures. For any particular case, many *small* precompiled knowledge structures will need to be used. And there will be relatively little repetition of patterns across case-specific assemblies of these smaller pieces of precompiled knowledge. Accordingly, in knowledge acquisition for cognitive flexibility, the "storage of fixed knowledge is devalued in favor of the *mobilization of potential knowledge*" (Spiro et al., 1987; see also Schank, 1982).

6. Noncompartmentalization of concepts and cases (multiple interconnectedness). Because of the complex and irregular way that abstract conceptual features weave through cases/examples in ill-structured domains, knowledge cannot be neatly compartmentalized. In order to enable the situation-dependent, adaptive schema assembly from disparate knowledge sources that characterizes cognitive flexibility, those multiple sources must be highly interconnected. Concepts cannot be treated as separate "chapters." Retroactive assembly of independently taught, and noninterrelated, constituent conceptual aspects too often fails. Also, although cases have to be focused on separately so that the complexity of case structure is conveyed, they should not be taught in *just* that way—connections across cases must also be established. Rather than relegating concepts or cases to separate compartments, chapters, and so on, our systems strive for *multiple interconnectedness (of cases and concepts) along multiple conceptual and clinical dimensions*.

Our approach to fostering multiple interconnectedness of knowledge representations in our hypertexts is to code case segments with a multidimensional vector indicating the relevance of a variety of thematic/conceptual dimensions to that case segment (Spiro & Jehng, 1990). (Positive values in the vector also point to commentary, providing expert guidance about the nature of the conceptual dimension's instantiation in that particular case segment; this helps with the problem of teaching conceptual knowledge in use, discussed earlier). Then, as the hypertext program guides the learner in criss-crossing the domain's "landscape" by exploring patterns of overlap in the vectors for different case segments, knowledge representations are built up in which parts of cases are connected with many parts of other cases, along many conceptual/theoretical dimensions of case-segment similarity. In that way, many alternative paths are established to get from one part of the overall knowledge base to any other part of the knowledge base that aspects of some future case may signal as relevant. Thus, the potential for flexible, situation-adaptive schema assembly is fostered (along with such other virtues as the establishment of multiple routes for memory access to any node in the system).

So, for example, in the Cardioworld Explorer, segments of clinical cases are encoded with a vector of clinical and basic biomedical science themes that are relevant to each segment. The system can then establish connections between a segment of one case and segments of many other cases, along the various (conceptual and clinical) thematic dimensions represented in the vector. In case-based instruction, it is often true that there are important, instructive relationships between an aspect of one case and aspects of others. Such relationships are rarely brought out. Our hypertext systems capture these many lessons that are missed in strict case-by-case (or problem-by-problem) instruction. In an ill-structured domain, facilitating retrieval of multiple (partial) precedents is important, because understanding what to do in a given case context will usually require reference to more than any single prototype—the case in question will be "kind of like this earlier one, kind of like that one," and so on. Also, understanding of the case in question will require that various concepts be brought to bear and integrated; this, too, is facilitated by the multiple conceptual coding scheme employed in our systems.

There are several other benefits of the multiple-conceptual coding of multiple case segments. A power/efficiency advantage is that it allows the hypertexts to automatically generate large numbers of lessons (many "landscape criss-crossings"). If, for example, each of 20 cases is divided into an average of 10 case segments, each with a value of 15 relevant thematic dimensions, there is a manyfold increase in the number of possible automatizable instructional comparisons and contrasts that results from having 200 case segments (instead of 20 full cases) intertwined by relationships in the 15-slot vector.

Also, the use of case segments prevents the subsumption to a "common denominator" that occurs when larger structural units are used; an interesting local element of a case will tend to get lost if it has features that are not present in other parts of the case (when the monolithic case is the structural unit). Using small case segments (minicases) helps retain the *plurality* of situations.

There is another virtue of the division into case segments and the multidimensional coding of the segments that relates to keeping case understanding from being overly simplified. In an ill-structured knowledge domain, by definition, there is sufficient variability across cases (due in part to the interaction of the many factors that make up complex cases) that the set of cases that might be nominally grouped together under some schema or classification will be greatly variable in their particulars. A case, instead of being represented as one kind of thing conveying one kind of "lesson," is instead clearly shown to the learner to be *many things*. Cases of the same nominal type have different segments or scenes that are demonstrated not to be the same, and each of the segments is shown to have multiple significances. Therefore, the common temptation to nest cases uniquely under a single superordinate conceptual category will be resisted, making it less likely that the complex relationships among cases in a domain will be artificially regularized. In an ill-structured domain, cases are related to many different concepts of the domain, and it promotes dysfunctional simplification to nest or "slot" cases hierarchically under single conceptual categories (e.g., "The following cases are examples of x [only]"). When there is considerable across-case variability, as there will be in an ill-structured domain, cognitive flexibility requires that case information be coded conceptually for the many different kinds of use that new situations may require.

The thematic coding scheme and the landscape criss-crossing system of instruction result in a weblike multiple interconnectedness on multiple dimensions that is not subject to the limitations of instruction characterized by a single organizational slant. Instead of a single text with a single organizational scheme and a single sequencing of comparisons and contrasts, our hypertexts allow the same information to be automatically reconfigured according to a huge number of possible organizational schemes determined by using subsets of the multiple thematic coding space; our hypertexts enable the *virtually limitless automatic generation of new text configurations*. Because of the richness of ill-structured domains such as biomedical science, each of these text configurations teaches some case- (experience-) grounded lessons that would not have been taught (or easily seen if taught) from another text's organizational perspective. Such additional experiences and perspectives are always helpful in a complex domain—a physician never learns all that it would be helpful to learn (which is why additional experience is always valued in a physician). Hypertext systems like the Cardioworld Explorer systematically *consolidate the process of acquiring experience*.

Yet another virtue of the multiple interconnectedness along multiple dimensions of the representations that our systems build has to do with the problem of reciprocal-misconception compounding that we have observed in our studies of medical students and physicians (Coulson et al., 1986; Feltovich et al., 1989). Misconceptions bolster each other and combine to form seductively entrenched *networks of misconception*. Our approach helps forestall the development of misconception networks by developing a kind of *positive reciprocation*. Because *correctly conceived representations with a high degree of multiple interconnectedness are established*, the fresh entry of fallacious knowledge at any node in the weblike network will fire off so many connections that it would be likely to activate some *misconception-disabling correct knowledge*. Before you can go too far wrong, you are likely to touch something that sets you right.

7. Active participation, tutorial guidance, and adjunct support for the management of complexity. In an ill-structured domain, knowledge cannot just be handed to the learner. A priori codifications of knowledge are likely to misrepresent. (That is part of what ill-structuredness means). Hence the importance, increasingly widely recognized today, of active learner involvement in knowledge acquisition, accompanied by opportunistic guidance by expert mentors (which can be incorporated in a computer program—it does not have to be live, one-to-one guidance). Furthermore, aids must be provided to help the learner manage the added complexity that comes with ill structure. Our hypertext programs allow learners to explore complex conceptual landscapes in many directions with expert guidance and various kinds of cognitive support (e.g., integrated visual displays). When there are limits to the *explicit* transmission of knowledge, learners will need special kinds of help in figuring things out for themselves (see Barrows & Tamblyn, 1980; Collins, Brown, & Newman, 1989; Spiro et el., 1987).

Recapitulation: A Shift From Single to Multiple Representations and From Generic Schema Retrieval to Situation-Specific Knowledge Assembly

In general, we argue that the goals of advanced knowledge acquisition in complex and ill-structured domains can best be attained (and the problems we have identified avoided) by the development of mental representations that support cognitive flexibility. Central to the cultivation of *cognitive flexibility* are approaches to learning, instruction, and knowledge representation that (a) allow an important role for *multiple representations*, (b) view learning as the multidirectional and multiperspectival "criss-crossing" of cases and concepts that make up complex domains' "landscapes" (with resulting interconnectedness along multiple dimensions), and (c) foster the ability to assemble diverse knowledge sources to adaptively fit the needs of a particular knowledge application situation (rather than the search for a precompiled schema that fits the situation). We suggest that theory-based computer hypertext systems can implement the goals and strategies of cognitive flexibility theory, engendering multiple cognitive representations that capture the real-world complexities of the kinds of cases to which abstract conceptual knowledge must be applied.

QUESTIONS FOR REFLECTION

1. How can teachers "take special measures to demonstrate complexities and irregularities"?
2. Whereas the authors of this chapter describe the use of case studies for medical school education, how might case studies be used in elementary school teaching?
3. How do the authors argue for a different view of schema theory?
4. Because most content knowledge is presented to students as chapters or topics, what can a teacher do to enhance students' capacity for knowledge use in ill-structured domains?

ACKNOWLEDGMENTS

The research reported in this paper was supported by grants from the Army Research Institute (MDA903-86-K-0443), the Office of Naval Research (N00014-88-K-0286, N00014-87-G-0165, N00014-88-K-0077), the Josiah Macy Foundation (B852001), and the Office of Educational Research and Improvement (OEG 0087-C1001). The publication does not necessarily reflect the views of the agencies supporting the research.

The authors would like to acknowledge the contributions of Jane Adami and Joan Feltovich to various aspects of this research.

NOTE

*When this chapter was written, Spiro was at the University of Illinois at Urbana-Champaign, and Coulson, Feltovich, and Anderson were at the Southern Illinois University School of Medicine.

REFERENCES

Barrows, H.S., & Tamblyn, R.M. (1980). *Problem-based learning.* New York: Springer.

Burnstein, M. (1983). Concept formation by incremental analogical reasoning and debugging. *Proceedings of the International Machine Learning Workshop*, Champaign, IL.

Champagne, A.B., Gunstone, R.F., & Klopfer, L.E. (1985). Effecting changes in cognitive structures among physics students. In L.H. West & A.L. Pines (Eds.), *Cognitive structure and conceptual change.* Orlando, FL: Academic.

Collins, A., Brown, J.S., & Newman, S.E. (1989). Cognitive apprenticeship: Teaching the crafts of reading, writing, and mathematics. In L.B. Resnick (Ed.), *Knowing, learning, and instruction: Essays in honor of Robert Glaser.* Hillsdale, NJ: Erlbaum.

Collins, A., & Gentner, D. (1987). How people construct mental models. In D. Holland & S. Quinn (Eds.), *Cultural models in thought and language.* Cambridge, UK: Cambridge University Press.

Coulson, R.L., Feltovich, P.J., & Spiro, R.J. (1986). *Foundations of a misunderstanding of the ultrastructural basis of myocardial failure: A reciprocating network of over-simplifications* (Tech. Rep. No. 1). Springfield: Southern Illinois University School of Medicine, Conceptual Knowledge Research Project.

Feltovich, P.J., Spiro, R.J., & Coulson, R.L. (1989). The nature of conceptual understanding in biomedicine: The deep structure of complex ideas and the development of misconceptions. In D.A. Evans & V.L. Patel (Eds.), *The cognitive sciences in medicine: Biomedical modeling.* Cambridge, MA: MIT Press.

Schank, R.C. (1982). *Dynamic memory: A theory of reminding and learning in computers and people.* Cambridge, UK: Cambridge University Press.

Spiro, R.J. (1980). Accommodative reconstruction in prose recall. *Journal of Verbal Learning and Verbal Behavior, 19*, 84–95.

Spiro, R.J., Feltovich, P.J., Coulson, R.L., & Anderson, D.K. (1989). Multiple analogies for complex concepts: Antidotes for analogy-induced misconception in advanced knowledge acquisition. In S. Vosniadou & A. Ortony (Eds.), *Similarity and analogical reasoning.* Cambridge, UK: Cambridge University Press.

Spiro, R.J., & Jehng, J.C. (1990). Cognitive flexibility and hypertext: Theory and technology for the nonlinear and multidimensional traversal of complex subject matter. In D. Nix & R.J. Spiro (Eds.), *Cognition, education, and multimedia: Exploring ideas in high technology.* Hillsdale, NJ: Erlbaum.

Spiro, R.J., Vispoel, W.L., Schmitz, J., Samarapungavan, A., & Boerger, A. (1987). Knowledge acquisition for application: Cognitive flexibility and transfer in complex content domains. In B.C. Britton & S. Glynn (Eds.), *Executive control processes in reading.* Hillsdale, NJ: Erlbaum.

White, B.Y. (1984). Designing computer games to help physics students understand Newton's law of motion. *Cognition and Instruction, 1*, 69–108.

White, B.Y., & Frederiksen, J.R. (1987, November). *Causal model progressions as a foundation for intelligent learning environments* (BBN Rep. No. 6686). Cambridge, MA: Bolt Beranek & Newman.

Wittgenstein, L. (1953). *Philosophical investigations.* New York: Macmillan.

CHAPTER 23

Educational Neuroscience for Reading Researchers

George G. Hruby, University of Kentucky

Usha Goswami, University of Cambridge

For the past 30 years, research on the brain has advanced impressively. This work, from fields known collectively as the neurosciences, has expanded our understanding of the neural chemistry, physiology, and growth processes that support behavior, cognition, language, emotion, sociality, and their development. It has also cast considerable light on the nature of individual differences and relatable disabilities, from genetic to behavioral levels of analysis. As these areas of research have expanded, attempts to relate insights from the neurosciences to education have been numerous, although the quality of these attempts have been variable and often, perhaps, premature or overexuberant, as many have commented (e.g., Bruer, 1997; Goswami, 2006; Hirsh-Pasek et al., 2007; Willis, 2007). Nonetheless, of all the areas addressed by the emerging field of educational neuroscience, Varma, McCandliss, and Schwartz (2008) have suggested that the neuroscience of reading processes has proven the most impressive in its sophistication.

In this review of the neuroscience literature on reading, we briefly describe the current state of the science regarding neural correlates of acknowledged and potential reading processes and reading development. Specifically, we briefly review the neural correlates of decoding and language comprehension and relate such findings to current models of reading, reading instruction, and reading disability. We then discuss what neuroscience research might mean for researchers and practitioners in education. We conclude by suggesting that the field has a clear need for literacy education scholars who are knowledgeable about the developmental and life sciences—individuals who could make use of insights from disciplines such as neuroscience to help inform reading theory, policy, and research.

Although our theme is the relationship of brain research to reading education, we do not devote extended paragraphs here to the research methods used in neuroscience, except as this may be necessary to clarify issues for scholars of literacy. This more technical information is interesting in its own right, of course, but it is readily available in previously published reviews and introductory texts (e.g., Gazzaniga, 2010; Hruby, 2009; Huettel, Song, & McCarthy, 2009; Luck, 2005; Mody, 2004; Willis, 2007). We allude to these details where helpful. (Refer to Table 1 for a helpful glossary of terms used throughout this article.) As in all

This chapter is adapted from "Neuroscience and Reading: A Review for Reading Education Researchers," *Reading Research Quarterly*, 46(2), 156–172.

Table 1. Glossary

Terms	Definition
	Orientation
anterior	Portion of a brain area most toward the front of the brain (e.g., anterior temporal = the area of the temporal lobe most toward the front of the head)
bilateral	On both sides of the brain in relatively the same hemispheric location
central	Toward the center of the brain
dorsal	Toward the top or top back of the brain
inferior	Portion of a brain area most toward the bottom of the brain
posterior	Portion of a brain area most toward the back of the brain
superior	Portion of a brain area most toward the top of the brain
ventral	Toward the underside of the brain
	Anatomical
amygdala	Almond-shaped area near the hippocampus for rapid identification of danger associations; regulates fear response
cerebellum	Bunlike lobe beneath the occipital cortex; processes automatic or repetitive motor movements
cerebrum	Sitting atop the brain stem; the most evolutionarily advanced of the major brain divisions; folded into gyri and sulci
cingulate cortex; anterior/posterior	Located in the middle of the cortex; processes input from the thalamus and neocortical areas; part of the limbic system regulating memory, emotion, and executive function
cortex, cortical, cerebral cortex	The folded sheet of neural tissue outermost to the cerebrum
encephalon	All the higher areas of the nervous system contained within the skull; the brain
frontal cortex/lobe	Forwardmost of the four major lobes of the cortex; associated with executive function, decision making, planning, building novel situation models, analyzing structure, motor associations, and motor control
gyrus (pl. *gyri*)	A ridge on the brain surface formed by the folding of brain tissue in the cortex
hemisphere	Halves of the neocortex; left and right
hippocampus	Part of the limbic system situated below the brain; somewhat wishbone shaped and extending into both hemispheres beneath the temporal lobes; related to memory formation and retrieval
lobe	A major anatomical region of the brain
neocortex	Outermost layers of the cerebral cortex
occipital cortex/lobe	Posteriormost cortical lobe; processes visual input
orbitofrontal cortex/ lobe	Area of the prefrontal lobe directly over the eye sockets; associated with decision making, emotional control, and reward monitoring *(continued)*

Table 1. Glossary (*Continued*)

Terms	Definition
	Anatomical (continued)
parietal cortex/lobe	Posterior area of the brain between the sensory-motor and occipital lobes; integrates various sensory modalities from both the sensory cortex and occipital lobe; processes spatial relationship and coordinates of the body, maps, and so forth (generally in the right hemisphere), and symbolic functions in language and math; cross-modal associations allowing for categorization and categorical interrelationship
prefrontal cortex/ lobe	Anterior area of the frontal lobe; associated with social behaviors, personality, and complex cognitive processes such as planning
sensory-motor cortex	Saddling across the middle of the cerebral cortex; the posterior strip devoted to sensory input, the anterior strip devoted to motor movements; arranged somatotopically (i.e., located in an anatomically coherent sequence; e.g., motor area for the hand is near the motor area for the arm not the feet)
sulcus (pl. *sulci*)	The fissures between gyri on the brain surface
temporal cortex/lobe	Located in the vicinity of the temple, just over and anterior to the ears, on either side of the brain; processes auditory input, word forms, word meanings, sign meanings, and faces and is related to episodic and declarative memory as well as long-term memory thanks to its proximity to the hippocampus
	Methods of Brain Study
EEG	Electroencephalography; measuring activity of the brain through fluctuations in electrical charge at the surface of the scalp
encephalographic	Measuring activity in the brain through monitoring of electromagnetic fluctuations at the surface of the scalp
fMRI	Functional magnetic resonance imaging; color-coded indications of differences in blood flow (or other correlates, e.g., glucose or oxygen) between two conditions mapped onto an MRI image of the brain; because neurons require glucose and oxygen to function, the more glucose and oxygen taken up in an area of the brain, the greater the activity presumed to occur in the area
hemodynamic	Literally, blood flow; tracks blood flow in the brain, glucose concentrations, oxygen concentrations, or radioactive isotopes injected into the blood stream
MEG	Magnetoencephalography; measuring activity of the brain through fluctuations in magnetic charge at the surface of the scalp
MRI	Magnetic resonance imaging; imaging brain structure through detected differences in water density using magnetic current to align the water molecules in the brain
PET	Positron emission tomography; images the brain with radioactive isotopes, typically of glucose, which are taken up by brain cells when they are active, indicating areas of the brain that are relatively more active than others

experimental science, the findings and innovative techniques employed by neuroscience are still developing and are regularly subject to revision and critique, a point we elaborate on in this review.

Nevertheless, integrating findings from neuroscience research with other research perspectives on literacy offers exciting opportunities for education (Szűcs & Goswami, 2007; Willingham & Lloyd, 2007). Even though it is currently premature to make grand claims for the value of neuroscience research for application in literacy education practice, research, or policy, it is already clear that promising advances are being made. To give an example, the auditory neuroscience of basic speech processing is transforming our understanding of how the speech signal is coded neurally, foregrounding the importance of syllables and speech rhythm over phonemes (see Goswami & Szűcs, 2011). Such basic research has implications for educational debates about teaching phonics and the educational value of oral language instruction, nursery rhymes, and poetry for reading acquisition. As another example, it will soon be possible to explore the impact of learning metrical poetry on the neural structures that are active during speech processing (see Goswami & Szűcs, 2011). Hence, basic research in neuroscience may enable the development of a complementary evidence base to social and cultural perspectives for emphasizing oral language activities in early literacy programs.

Neural Correlates of Reading: An Overview

Studies of neural activation during reading can show us where and when reading processes occur in the brain. Neural imaging does not indicate that there are areas of the brain dedicated from birth to those reading processes; rather, most imaging indicates the anatomical result of development in response to successful instructional experiences. Thus, when brain images of struggling readers or nonreaders show different patterns of neural activation compared with competent readers, we cannot immediately determine from these data alone whether the difference is neurological/genetic or environmental/instructional. A reader with a genetically based neurological malformation preventing typical reading development may show the same atypical activation as a reader who did not receive quality reading instruction, a reader who received quality instruction but who was not developmentally ready for it, a reader who has linguistic and cognitive deficiencies because of limited early childhood language experiences, or a reader who has emotional problems because of an abusive home environment disruptive of his or her schooling. A brain chart, therefore, is not prima facie evidence for an innate deficiency.

The two most noted areas of brain research relatable to reading are correlational imaging studies that localize functional brain activity anatomically and correlational studies of neural activity that localize it in the time course of a reading event. A host of investigative technologies have been brought to bear in this work, and devising valid research designs is an ongoing challenge, as the sophistication of the facilitating technologies continues to advance rapidly. The results, too, are often highly variable and conflicting (Ross, 2010), and literacy educators should not get too caught up in the neophrenology—or less optimistically, "blobology" (Lieberman, 2006, p. 173)—wherein areas of dedicated function are mapped to precise locations in the brain.

More promising, brain imaging research may help alert us to disparities among the categories of reading subprocess demonstrated in the neurological research and those variously employed in models of reading (see examples in Ruddell & Unrau, 2004). As an example, a commonly employed phrase such as "sounding out the text" might suggest a singular text-to-sound decoding mechanism localized to a single brain area. However, brain-imaging studies have demonstrated several quite distinct areas of the brain that are active during sounding out (e.g., sensory visual processing of letters and visual word forms, perceptual processing of speech sounds, speech motor processing, spatial orientation). That being noted, we cannot yet dependably match specific brain areas to categories of function that may be impaired in a struggling decoder (e.g., visual crowding of letters). Similarly, many areas of the brain are devoted to the processing of word meaning, syntax, and sentence-level semantics. Yet, imaging techniques are not at the point where we can identify a particular area as a potential locus of confound for a struggling comprehender.

At first, it might not be clear why anyone would even wish to do so. As a practical matter, there is no reason to employ multimillion-dollar brain-imaging technology as a literacy assessment when much simpler and affordable behavioral assessments, coherently constructed and reasonably well tested for reliability and validity, are readily available. As a pedagogical matter, the ultimate objective of reading instruction is not to mediate brain activity or anatomy for its own sake but to facilitate the development of functional and assessable reading behaviors and remediate severe instances of dysfunction. Another objective is to foster an appreciation in students for the value of rewarding reading experiences, both individual and shared.

Conversely, the neuroscience research on reading and language processes suggests more generally that certain categories of function correlate with unique, if varied, activation of human brains. Models of decoding, comprehension, or reading that overlook any of these subprocesses, or stress some at the expense of others, may run the risk of failing to address the individual needs of developing or struggling readers, as some behavioral research already has suggested. We argue that the broader theoretical implications of neuroscience for understanding the vagaries and variability of literacy learning and development may prove of greater value for literacy education scholars than the still uncertain anatomical loci and biochemical processes of the brain.

Additionally, future work in educational neuroscience could lead to biomarkers for flagging future developmental and instructional difficulties in certain children, which could be helpful for providing those children with closer behavioral assessments and early interventions (Beddington et al., 2008; Goswami, 2009). However, as with any clinical assessment, guarding against false positives and premature tracking will be crucial for credibility. Early childhood is a notoriously pliant time, neurologically as well as behaviorally. Although the promise of biomarkers to confirm less precise behavioral assessments of cognitive or developmental difficulties is great, neuroscience is not yet at the point where it can help educators pick out particular subprocesses for intensive remediation of a struggling child. Given the immense functional variation of human brains and human beings, it is uncertain that it will ever do so in any but an ancillary fashion.

The anatomical localization of reading processes outlined in this review is based largely on hemodynamic correlation studies (i.e., studies of blood flow, glucose, or oxygen uptake in the brain) as biochemical correlates of neural activation, employing methods such as functional magnetic resonance imaging (fMRI) or positron emission tomography (PET). These studies do not, as is often misconstrued, provide a photograph of an individual brain in action. The colorful images are, in fact, statistical charts, indicating the difference between an experimental and a comparison condition averaged over a group of participants and trials. Because of the necessary use of subtractive methods between active conditions, the neural localization indicated in the charts are as much the result of the comparison condition chosen as the target condition being investigated (Caplan, 2004). In other words, the indicated result is the averaged difference between the two conditions, indicating the activity of the target condition relative to the activity of a selected comparison condition. Change the comparison condition, and you may well change the area of activation for a target behavior (e.g., Price & Mechelli, 2005).

Although results may indicate necessary areas of neural activation that exceed a particular, if conventional, signal–noise threshold, brain images do not provide a guide as to what would be comprehensively sufficient for a cognitive or behavioral function. Indications of localized activity may also indicate the particular degree of difficulty or familiarity of a task, which will vary between subjects and over trials, rather than the average baseline activity necessary for it, and the potential for meaningless positives is greater than appreciated by the nonspecialist (Bennett, Wolford, & Miller, 2009; Brown, 2007; Oakes et al., 2007). Finally, localized correlates of neural activity may indicate convergence zones for networks of necessary activation that may extend across the brain (Patterson, Nestor, & Rogers, 2007), which may be particularly true of complex or higher order tasks (Bennett & Miller, 2010). For instance, the simpler subprocesses involved in decoding are relatively easy to map to particular locations (e.g., visual processing in the occipital lobe) and, as a result, can be mapped as trajectories of typical sequence, of which some have argued there are two: a dorsal for sounding out and a ventral for word form (Dehaene, 2009). By contrast, the more complex subprocesses in readers' meaning construction seem to tap areas that process word meaning, syntax, semantics, text and narrative structure, tone, prior knowledge, emotion, and more in a multidirectional fashion and with great variability between subjects and readings (Boulenger, Hauk, & Pulvermüller, 2009; Hagoort, Hald, Bastiaansen, & Petersson, 2004; Patterson et al., 2007).

Lesion studies of stroke and accident victims, brain stimulation studies (e.g., transcranial magnetic stimulation), direct electrode assay studies, and imaging of functionally dedicated neural tracts (e.g., single photon emission computed tomography) have added to this anatomical data with ever greater detail and sophistication. However, hemodynamic studies typically span the neural activity of two to three seconds, which is an enormous amount of time for neural activity. For this reason, studies of direct electrical activity, known as event-related potential (ERP) studies, may be of more interest to reading process theorists because they provide a more precise tracking of when in the time course of a reading certain correlates of reading subprocess occur. These studies, tracking either neural action potentials (i.e., cascades of membrane depolarization running the length of thousands of neurons at a go; e.g., electroencephalography [EEG], direct electrode assays) or the fluctuation of electromagnetic radiation at different points across the scalp (e.g., magnetoencephalography [MEG]) can distinguish the timing of events with millisecond precision. Newer MEG techniques are also much more precise in terms of anatomical location, although many technical and interpretive challenges still persist. As with the anatomical data, the hope is that this time-course data may eventually enable the identification and location of distinct subprocesses in reading.

The following review of the neural correlates of reading is quite condensed. The research base in this area is not only relatively large but also relatively new, highly varied, and growing exponentially (Cabeza & Nyberg, 2000). Replication and meta-analysis are limited. We have therefore restricted our review to studies and findings illustrative of less controversial claims, with only occasional notation of exciting but uncertain evidence.

Decoding Processes in the Brain

What does the brain do when engaged in decoding or decoding-related processes? The simplest way to approach this question is to review imaging studies in which participants are given either real or nonsense words (i.e., unfamiliar letter strings that can be decoded; e.g., *tegwop*) and asked to read them. Early studies compared brain activation during single-word reading, using fMRI or PET with brain activation in a resting condition with eyes closed. For example, Rumsey et al. (1997) used this experimental design with skilled adult readers and PET, whereas Brunswick, McCrory, Price, Frith, and Frith (1999) used this experimental design with skilled adult readers and fMRI. As might be expected, a very large number of brain areas are activated in such experimental designs. There is extensive activation bilaterally (i.e., in both hemispheres) in brain areas related to audition, vision, spatial and cross-modal processing, and spoken-language areas (e.g., posterior superior temporal cortex, occipitotemporal cortex, temporal and parietal areas, frontal cortex). Experiments using EEG that have contrasted real words and nonsense words, thereby keeping the visual–spatial demands associated with text processing constant and varying only whether the decoding target is a lexical word form, have shown that the brain responds differently to real versus nonsense words within one fifth of a second. This implies that lexical access (i.e., contact between the visual word form and its meaning) occurs very rapidly during reading. The speed of this differentiation has been shown to be similar for both children and adults across languages, suggesting that the time course of visual word recognition is very rapid (160–180 ms; see Csépe, Szücs, & Honbolygó, 2003; Sauseng, Bergmann, & Wimmer, 2004).

Implicit Reading Tasks. Comparing brain activity during visual identification of words with a subject's having his or her eyes closed cannot tell us anything specific about reading or its development, which has led the field to develop the implicit reading task. Implicit reading tasks try to dissociate reading, as the making of meaning from strings of printed symbols, from the associated requirements of processing visual sequences of such symbols. The implicit reading task uses false fonts (i.e., meaningless hieroglyphic-type symbols matched to letters for visual features like the ascenders in the letters *b, d, k*) and asks participants to pick out target visual features, such as ascenders. Brain activity for this visual search task is then compared with the same task based on words (i.e., picking the number of ascenders in a word such as *bubble*). In adults, such fMRI and PET studies (e.g., Price et al., 2003) have shown activation that is usually left-lateralized and focused on the occipitotemporal and posterior superior temporal cortices (see Figure 1; Price & McCrory, 2005). These left-hemisphere areas have hence been described as the core areas for letter identification in word reading. These areas are also active during spoken-language tasks (in the left superior temporal cortex) and visual tasks involving spoken language, such as picture naming (in the left occipitotemporal cortex).

Studies of children have generally supported the claim that a left-lateralized set of occipital and temporal areas are core to the word reading network. For example, Eden and colleagues used fMRI and the false-font task to compare brain activation during implicit reading in children and college students ages 7–22 years (Turkeltaub, Gareau, Flowers, Zeffiro, & Eden, 2003). First, the experimenters established that the 7-year-olds could perform the false-font task as competently as the college students, which was important, as the researchers hoped to attribute any changes in reading-related neural activity to developmental differences rather than differences in expertise. Comparisons of children with adults for word reading are always confounded by the inevitably greater familiarity that adults have with written words. Adults have read more words than children have, and this experiential factor will be reflected in brain activation; the same difference in word reading experience affects comparisons between children with and without dyslexia. Turkeltaub et al. reported that adults performing the implicit reading task activated the usual left-lateralized sites, including the left posterior temporal and left inferior frontal cortices.

However, when they restricted their analyses to children below 9 years of age, the main area engaged was the left posterior superior temporal cortex. This neural area is also active when participants perform phonological tasks in the

Figure 1. Cortical Areas Activated During the Reading of Single Words

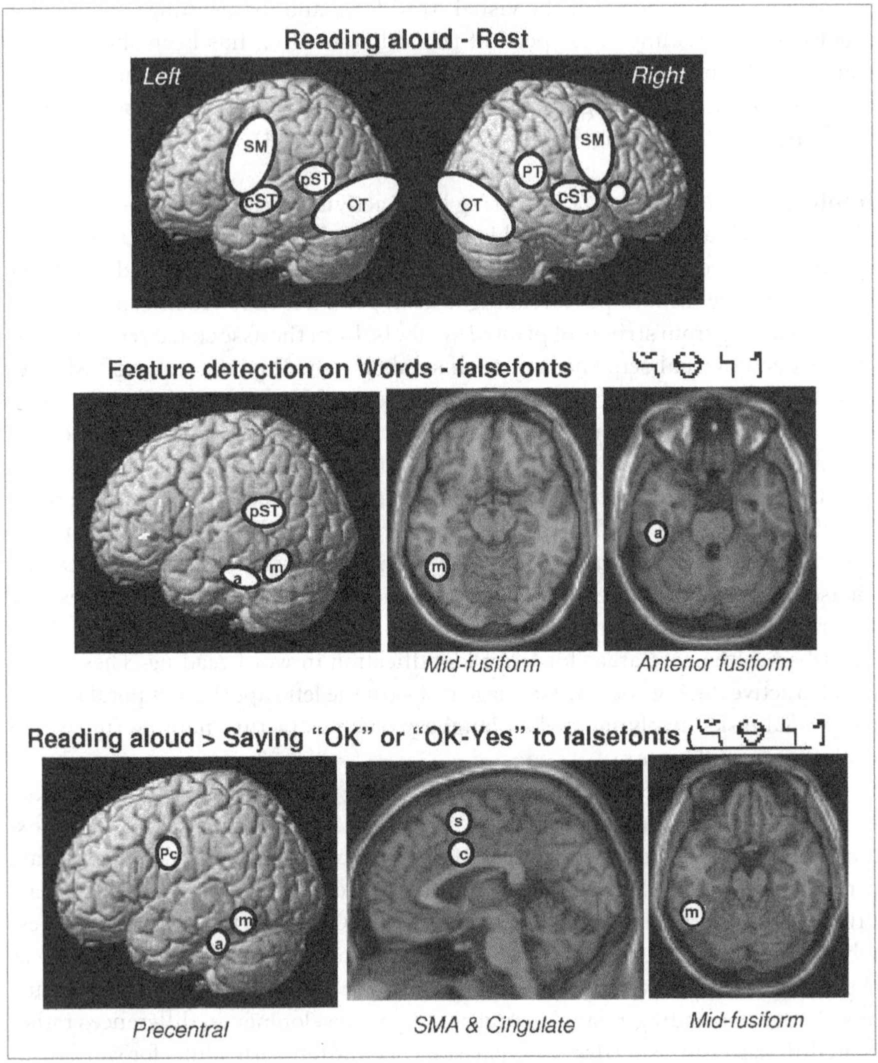

Note. cST = central superior temporal cortex. OT = occipitotemporal cortex. pST = posterior superior temporal cortex. PT = posterior temporal cortex. SM = sensory-motor cortex. From "Functional Brain Imaging Studies of Skilled Reading and Developmental Dyslexia," by C.J. Price and E. McCrory, 2005, in M.J. Snowling and C. Hulme (Eds.), *The Science of Reading: A Handbook*, Malden, MA: Blackwell, p. 483.

scanner, such as rhyme judgment. Turkeltaub et al. (2003) thus suggested that activity in this area could be the neural correlate of grapheme–phoneme translation. When they looked at changes in activation with age, they found that activity in left temporal and frontal areas increased, while activity previously observed in right posterior areas declined. This pattern was interpreted as showing that reading-related activity becomes more left-lateralized with development.

The Visual Word Form Area. The left occipitotemporal cortex is involved in object recognition and is an area of interest in research on decoding because it has been suggested to house a word form area. This area is in essence a part of the visual cortex specialized for recognizing print, although there is some debate about this (see Démonet, Thierry, & Cardebat, 2005; Price & Devlin, 2003; Price & Mechelli, 2005). Labeled the visual word form area (VWFA), this neural region shows activity whenever printed words are shown to the adult brain, even if the words are only shown in the left visual field, which means that they first activate visual areas in the right hemisphere (see Cohen & Dehaene, 2004). The VWFA is also active when children are shown printed words.

However, expertise clearly plays a role in brain activation, as the VWFA becomes more active as children get older and become better readers (Pugh, 2006). Pugh and others have suggested that the amount of activity in the VWFA is the best neural correlate that we have of reading expertise. However, the VWFA is also active when one is shown nonsense words, which suggests that it is not purely an area responsive to word forms. Rather, it appears responsive to any sequence of printed letters. Nevertheless, activity in the VWFA increases when orthographic strings are more familiar, such that nonsense words that contain large fragments of real words elicit greater brain activity. Again, this supports a role for expertise in print–sound connections in modulating this brain activation, and as might be expected, the VWFA shows reduced activation in developmental dyslexia (e.g., B.A. Shaywitz et al., 2002).

Recently, a number of developmental studies have analyzed how neural activity in the VWFA tunes itself to print and becomes specialized for letter strings that are real words. In a study conducted in Switzerland, Maurer, Brandeis, and their colleagues (e.g., Maurer, Brem, Bucher, & Brandeis, 2005; Maurer et al., 2007) followed longitudinally, from the very beginning of learning to read in German, a sample of children who either were at risk for developmental dyslexia or had no risk for it in terms of family history. The researchers used EEG to measure millisecond-level changes in the electrical activity associated with the recognition of word forms. The task was to detect the repetition of either real words or meaningless symbol strings. As noted earlier, the brain registers a difference in activity to words versus nonsense words by about 160–180 milliseconds after the letter string is presented, hence the N170 (i.e., a negative deflection in brain electrical activity approximately 170 ms after stimulus onset) was the main measure of word-specific neural processing. Brain activity was recorded in kindergarten, before the children had received any instruction in reading, and again in second grade. Before any reading instruction had commenced, the children did not show an N170 to printed words, despite having considerable knowledge about individual letters. After approximately 1.5 years of reading instruction, the typically developing children showed a reliable N170 to words, described by the authors as evidence for a coarse tuning to print. The children at risk for dyslexia showed no significant differences in their brain activation compared with control children during the kindergarten measurements, but they did show a significantly reduced N170 to word forms in second grade. This response was reduced rather than absent. Maurer et al. (2007) suggested that the reduced N170 response was a clear neural correlate of a visual word-processing deficit.

Integrating Letters and Sounds. Since we know from behavioral work that visual word recognition is not a purely visual task, imaging studies showing neural activation when letters are associated with speech sounds are also required to interpret this word–symbol string difference. Blomert, Blau, and their colleagues have been carrying out a series of such studies using fMRI with adults who read in Dutch. For example, Blau, Van Atteveldt, Formisano, Goebel, and Blomert (2008) asked participants to decide whether they heard the vowel sound /a/ or /e/ in a forced-choice auditory task using degraded stimuli to avoid ceiling effects. Participants either heard just the speech sounds or heard the speech sounds in the presence of visually presented letters. The letters were either congruent (e.g., letter *A* for sound /a/) or incongruent (e.g., letter *A* for sound /e/).

Participants were significantly better at recognizing the target speech sound in the auditory–visual condition compared with the auditory-alone condition for the congruent letters and significantly worse for the incongruent letters. The fMRI data showed that brain activity in the auditory–visual condition differed in speech recognition areas of the brain and not in occipital areas, such as the VWFA. When the letters were congruent with the speech sounds, activity increased, and when the letters were incongruent with the speech sounds, activity decreased. However, an area very close to the VWFA was also modulated by auditory–visual congruency. Thus, although this study demonstrated that visual letters have a clear effect on the neural activity in areas classically active during speech processing, it did not demonstrate changes in neural activity in areas classically active during word decoding, but rather in closely associated areas.

Similar studies with children would be of interest in helping to pinpoint where, or perhaps when and where, neural activity correlated with letter–sound integration is situated. Meanwhile, Blau and colleagues have used the same task with adults with dyslexia and shown that incongruent letter–sound pairs (e.g., *A* and /e/) do not suppress neural activity in these speech-processing areas compared with the auditory-alone condition. The adults with dyslexia showed an enhancement in processing for the congruent condition (i.e., *A* and /a/), however, although it was weaker than in controls. Therefore, imaging data have shown similar neural processing in this task in typically reading adults and adults with dyslexia when letters and sounds are congruent, with decreased activity accompanying decreased decoding skill. Letter–sound integration as indexed by this particular neural correlate is, however, different in dyslexia, such that when letters and sounds do not match (e.g., *A* and /e/), incongruency does not change activity in this brain region for adults with dyslexia. This might be expected given the behavioral phenotype, but it is nonetheless interesting.

Time Course of Activation During Decoding. The neuroimaging studies discussed so far have shown systematic correlations between visual and auditory brain areas and word decoding, which will not be surprising to educators. However, one area in which neuroimaging has the potential to go beyond the correlations expected from behavioral studies is the measurement of the time course of activation. The sequence in which different brain areas become activated during reading is of interest, given different developmental models of how decoding skills become established. Such sequential information enables a test of developmental stage theories, such as the assumption that there is an early logographic stage in visual word recognition (Frith, 1985). In the logographic stage, it is assumed that holistic visual stimuli are associated with whole spoken words in the same way as familiar symbols like £ and $ are associated with the spoken words *pound* and *dollar.* If children can really go directly from print to meaning without recoding the print into sound first, then we might expect that neural structures active when viewing text and understanding meaning should show activation in very young readers, whereas neural structures that are active during phonological recoding should not.

Although imaging methods can track the time course of the activation of different neural structures, such methods are not easy to use with children, and relevant studies are currently rare. One technique, magnetic source imaging (MSI), depends on a combination of MEG and MRI (Simos et al., 2005). MEG measures the tiny magnetic fields generated by the electrical activity in the brain, rather than the electrical activity itself, and combines this information with MRI scans to localize the activity. The magnetic fields are tiny, estimated to be 1 billion times smaller than the magnetic field generated by the electricity in a lightbulb, and the technique is very expensive. Nevertheless, Simos and colleagues were able to conduct a longitudinal MSI study of 33 English-speaking children, measuring brain activity at the end of kindergarten and again at the end of first grade. The children completed a letter–sound task (i.e., the child saw a letter and had to provide its sound) and a simple nonsense-word reading task based on easy items with many analogies (e.g., *lan*).

A total of 33 children were studied, and half the group (16 children) were thought to be at risk of developmental dyslexia. This high-risk group showed significantly delayed neural activity in response to both letters and nonsense words in kindergarten in the occipitotemporal region, showing activation on average after 320 milliseconds compared with 210 milliseconds for children who were not at risk. The high-risk group also showed atypical activation in the left inferior frontal gyrus when performing the letter–sound task. For the high-risk children, the onset of neural activity in this region actually increased, from 603 milliseconds in kindergarten to 786 milliseconds in first grade. The typically developing children did not show this processing time increase. Comparing the onset of activity of the three core neural networks for reading, Simos et al. (2005) reported that low-risk children showed early activity in left occipitotemporal regions, followed by activity in temporoparietal regions, predominantly in the left hemisphere, and then bilateral activity in inferior frontal regions, which were also active during the production of speech. In contrast, high-risk children showed little differentiation in terms of the time course of activation between the occipitotemporal and temporoparietal regions. Nevertheless, temporoparietal activation is usually correlated with recoding print to sound, questioning the necessity of an early logographic stage in the development of decoding skills.

Analyses of Brain Structures. Another method for exploring how different neural areas are related during word decoding is to analyze structural differences in the neural areas known to be important for reading words. One available method, diffusion tensor imaging (DTI), can be used to measure white matter tracts, the "information highways" of the brain; white matter is the axons connecting different neurons in the brain and appears white because of the fatty myelin sheaths that speed up electrical signal transmission along the axons. In DTI, the diffusion of water in brain tissue is measured, enabling axonal fibers to be tracked because water diffuses more readily along the orientation of these fibers than in other directions.

Niogi and McCandliss (2006) used DTI to study white matter tracts in 31 children ages 6–10 years, 11 of whom were reading impaired. The children were also given standardized measures of reading, such as the Woodcock–Johnson word identification and word attack subscales. White matter integrity (i.e., axonal coherence and density) in two regions of the left temporoparietal cortex, the superior corona radiata in the left temporal lobe and the centrum semiovale, was correlated with performance in the word identification task. Therefore, the microstructure of white matter in these regions was correlated with individual differences in word reading. There was no similar correlation for homologous areas in the right hemisphere, and the relationships remained significant even after controlling for working memory, age, and nonverbal IQ in multiple regression equations.

Longitudinal investigation of the development of the microstructure of these areas could throw light on which developmental factors promote this structure–function relationship. Although such studies are not yet in the literature, we will mention one recent connectivity study notable for its ingenuity, which also illustrates how correlations, even correlations between brain structure rather than function (i.e., neural activity), are very far at present from throwing light on developmental mechanisms.

Carreiras et al. (2009) compared Colombian "guerrillas" (p. 983) reintegrating into Colombian society and belatedly learning to read as adults (i.e., late literates) with carefully matched adult illiterates, who had never learned to read in spite of having grown up in more typical social contexts, as well as typically reading adults (i.e., early literates). In this study, the structural brain differences shown using MRI and DTI between the late literates relative to the illiterates contradicted the classical version of the neural model of word reading, which assumes that information flows from the visual areas of the brain to the speech-related areas when visual word forms are encountered. Instead, the authors found that the angular gyrus, a classical spoken-language area, modulated dorsal occipital activity (i.e., the activation patterns suggested that spoken language areas controlled the amount of activation in visual areas). Carreiras and colleagues suggested that the oft-reported reduction in gray matter in the left temporoparietal areas in developmental dyslexia and associated reduced neural activity may be completely linked to reading expertise and have nothing to do functionally with having developmental dyslexia.

Synthesis. At present, there are still relatively few neuroimaging studies of word decoding by typically developing children. There are more studies of word decoding by children with dyslexia, but these have only been mentioned in passing here, as there are many difficulties in linking neural activation levels in these children with word reading per se. Nevertheless, there are some very consistent patterns of correlation in the neuroimaging studies of decoding that are available. Word processing appears to correlate with left-hemisphere activity. There is more neural activation in the left temporoparietal and occipitotemporal areas as reading skill increases.

The studies discussed earlier suggest that these correlations depend both on developing visual expertise (i.e., experience with the special visual stimuli that are words) and developing skills in letter–sound integration. When children have to read words aloud, there is also left-lateralized activity in the frontal areas of the brain that are associated with speech production and possibly articulatory codes, even when speech is not overtly produced in the scanner. None of these studies can as yet give us insights into developmental causal mechanisms. Nevertheless, the careful documentation of the neural networks that are active during decoding, their connectivity, and the time sequence of their activation are important first steps in using neuroimaging techniques to ask educationally relevant questions.

Language Comprehension Processes in the Brain

To date, most efforts at educational neuroscience matching neuroscience research to reading education have focused on brain processes and structures related to decoding instruction and its impairments, as in dyslexia (e.g., Hudson, High, & Otaiba, 2007; S. Shaywitz, 2003). This contrasts greatly with the nature of scholarship on reading and literacy education in general, including on reading disabilities, in which an emphasis on comprehension, as well as learner motivation, sociocultural context, identity, and other factors, is well developed (e.g., Israel & Duffy, 2009; Kamil, Pearson, Moje, & Afflerbach, 2010; McGill-Franzen & Allington, 2011). For the larger reading education field, then, educational neuroscience literature reviews that omit available research on language comprehension and other global processes fail to address many issues typically treated in literacy scholarship. More important, they fail to paint a comprehensive picture of the neuroscience research on reading as well. Attention to how comprehension is understood by neurolinguists demonstrates the possible value of this work.

Aside from vocabulary knowledge and cognitive strategies for content understanding, what reading education scholars and teacher educators presume language comprehension to entail is less than clear. Where the term *comprehension* is not circularly defined as understanding or meaning making, it is typically defined by the nature of what researchers can dependably measure. In essence, comprehension becomes what comprehension tests test, but the underlying subprocesses that present difficulties for struggling comprehenders/readers are often poorly articulated (cf. Lesaux & Kieffer, 2010). Syntax and semantics are alluded to irregularly and with great definitional variation (e.g., National Governors Association Center for Best Practices & Council of Chief State School Officers [NGA & CCSSO], 2010a).

English language arts instruction, in addition to word study, typically emphasizes instruction in the rules of grammar as well as style and, to a lesser extent, the nature of genre, tone, and discourse. Yet, the tracking of sentence- and paragraph-level semantic analysis, apart from syntax, is weak to nonexistent in most reading assessments (e.g., NGA & CCSSO, 2010b) and even in scholarship on the importance of language ability in literacy (e.g., Dickinson, Golinkoff, & Hirsh-Pasek, 2010). Attention by reading researchers and teacher educators to how neuroscientists parse the floating signifier of language comprehension may provide an alternative and possibly fuller map of necessary comprehension subprocesses. We group these here in terms of (a) word meaning processes, (b) syntactic and sentence-level meaning processes (semantics), (c) emotional signification, and (d) higher order cognitive and text feature processes.

What's in a Word? In the neurolinguistic research base, comprehension is presumed to begin with relating an identified word form to its possible meanings through association as an item of vocabulary. As a result, research on word form recognition, morphological analysis, and word meaning, or semantics at the single-word level, is abundant (see the review in Osterhout, Kim, & Kuperberg, 2006). As already noted, word form identification may correlate with activity in the left inferior occipitotemporal area along the fusiform gyrus.

Word meaning has been commonly correlated with activation in the left medial, superior, and superior posterior temporal areas. In the early work along these lines, it was prematurely claimed that particular categories and classes of word meanings could be located in distinct areas of the left temporal lobe. With each new category studied (e.g., tools, machines, buildings, domestic animals, farm animals, wild animals), strong claims were made for distinct areas of activation. There seemed to be no end to the possible categorical distinctions that could be mapped, assuring a steady stream of such studies. However, eventual follow-up work found a lack of replication for these findings, indicating (a) individual but perfectly functional differences in localization, (b) a lack of clarity about what *encoding in the brain* might mean, and (c) overconfidence in the reliability of the early imaging techniques (Heim, 2005). Periodic improvements in imaging precision have inspired similar claims regarding word localization in the temporal lobe and elsewhere, but unless well replicated, they should be taken with caution (Ross, 2010).

More current work has suggested that areas across the brain dedicated to basic sensory, motor, emotional, analytic, or social processing converge in the left temporal lobe for word meanings (Frishkoff, Perfetti, & Westbury, 2009; Patterson et al., 2007). For instance, verbs that indicate physical actions activate areas in the motor or premotor cortex that link to categorical identification and word representation convergence zones in the left inferior anterior temporal area (Willems, Hagoort, & Casasanto, 2010).

The relationship of word identification ability to comprehension is now well known, but the relationship of word identification to subprocesses for identifying association patterns of spelling, sound, and meaning is ongoing. Building on Perfetti's lexical quality hypothesis (Perfetti & Hart, 2002), which asserts that the richness or abundance of semantic associations with a word is a correlate of comprehension of the text, Balass, Nelson, and Perfetti (2010) asked participants in an ERP study to make meaning judgments about newly learned, familiar, and unlearned words. This was done in three different conditions: (1) orthography to meaning (i.e., no phonology), wherein the participants were required to learn the spelling and meaning of rare words; (2) orthography to phonology (i.e., no meaning), wherein participants were required to learn the spelling and pronunciation of rare words; and (3) phonology to meaning (i.e., no orthography), wherein participants were required to learn the pronunciation and meaning of rare words. After being tested to demonstrate their knowledge of these new words, subjects were given a semantic-relatedness judgment task, matching related and nonrelated words, for rare words, known words, and unknown words not included in the previous learning task. ERP measurements were taken to determine novelty effects (P600) and meaning effects (N400).

The results suggested that the degree of word knowledge, specifically phonological, orthographic, and semantic knowledge, developed at the time of word learning influenced subsequent recognition of the word in new contexts, a finding with implications for vocabulary instruction. Although there were no comprehension differences in the behavioral data, the ERP data found the orthography–meaning condition produced a more powerful recognition effect than the orthography–phonology and phonology–meaning conditions. This is significant for vocabulary learning because incremental knowledge development about a word over time, primarily through print encounters, relies on recognizing past encounters with the word in print.

To study the role of morphological processing of words, Bozic, Marslen-Wilson, Stamatakis, Davis, and Tyler (2007) used fMRI to examine areas of activation by contrasting priming of word pairs that shared either an opaque morphological relationship (e.g., *archer, arch*) or a transparent morphological relationship (e.g., *bravely, brave*) with meaning-only (e.g., *stop, halt*), form-only (e.g., *catalog, cat*), and identity-priming (e.g., *cat, cat*) word pairs. The results suggested that morphological analysis is a subprocess involving left frontal areas of the brain distinct from word form recognition or word meaning identification processes located elsewhere. This finding may be of potential significance for educational research on vocabulary instruction considering the role of morphological analysis in word identification. Interestingly, this area of the brain is also activated in syntactic processing of sentences, a process known to often rely on morphemic indicators of grammatical relationship.

Occasionally, words must be parsed in terms of their syntactic or semantic function before they can be definitively identified or sounded out correctly as words (e.g., the noun or verb form of *progress*, the present or past tense verb form of *read*). Reading researchers already know that word processing is highly adaptive on behalf of comprehension satisfaction, and strict linearity of processing is absent, even at the word form level. Neuroscience studies have confirmed that syntactic and semantic processes can have a top-down effect on word meaning processes, and this effect may play a variable role even for words that are not ambiguous (Kuperberg, 2007). These results indicate that models of language that assume language meaning derives only from word meanings linked with grammatical markers are inadequate for representing authentic language processing (Boulenger et al., 2009; Friederici & Weissenborn, 2007; Hagoort & van Berkum, 2007; Rimrodt et al., 2009).

Syntax and Semantics. Research on vocabulary has been complemented by a substantial body of studies on syntactic processing (i.e., identification of grammatical function, grammatical interrelationship of words in a clause or sentence) and semantic processing (i.e., identification of indicative intention of words, phrases, and idioms, and their intentional relationship at a clausal, sentence, or passage level). The anatomical areas and time-course involvement of these two general domains appear distinct yet overlapping, and much more work on these processes can be expected. It could be that the traditional distinction between these domains is not easily disentangled at the level of neural function.

Typically, syntactic or semantic anomalies are used in comparisons to distinguish the relevant neural correlates. For instance, semantically anomalous sentences (e.g., "When peanuts fall in love...") elicit an exaggerated N400 signature, a peaking of negative charge approximately 400 milliseconds after the lexical anomaly, in the central parietal region (van Berkum, Hagoort, & Brown, 1999; see the review in Kutas, Van Petten, & Kluender, 2006). By contrast, anomalous syntactic structure elicits an abnormal early positive charge in the left anterior region, followed by an exaggerated P600 signature, a peaking of positive charge 600 milliseconds after onset, either in the central parietal region (Friederici & Kotz, 2003; Friederici, von Cramon, & Kotz, 1999), as with the N400, or in more anterior (i.e., frontal) areas of the brain (Osterhout et al., 2006). These unique time-course signatures suggest that semantic and syntactic processing of anomalies are neurologically distinct operations. The research further suggests that semantic and syntactic processing of correct or typical sentences is similarly timed (Kaan, Harris, Gibson, & Holcomb, 2000). In other words, ERP studies indicate that on a word-by-word basis, early brain activation is for word and morphosyntactic identification, followed at the N400 by semantic identification and at the P600 by a sentence-level syntactic recheck (Friederici & Kotz, 2003).

Such findings can support linear theories of syntactic processing (e.g., Friederici, 2002), although alternative distributed processing theories have been suggested (e.g., Hagoort, 2003) and supported by studies (Cooke et al., 2006; Hald, Bastiaansen, & Hagoort, 2006). Other studies suggest that traditional notions of syntax and semantics are ill matched to the processing indicated by ERP evidence, and alternative explanations of meaning elaboration are required to make sense of the data (Kuperberg, 2007). In spite of the uncertainties, timing of process is clearly of importance (Perfetti & Bolger, 2004), and when matched to more spatially precise imaging techniques, such as the newer MEG or fMRI techniques, ERP methods may give a more reliable indication of the order and structure of synactic and semantic processing of texts during comprehension (Heim, 2005).

Turning to the hemodynamic research (e.g., fMRI, PET), syntactic processes have been found to dependably associate with activity in the left frontal gyrus, or Broca's area (Sakai, Noguchi, Takeuchi, & Watanabe, 2002). Semantic processes are more variably located, depending on whether they are at the word level (posterior superior temporal and temporoparietal; e.g., Wernicke's area and related basal language areas, such as the supramarginal gyrus and temporal sulcus, as well as in left inferior frontal areas, at least for articulatory rehearsal; Rogalsky, Matchin, & Hickok, 2008), sentence level (left inferior frontal areas proximal to Broca's area), or text/discourse level (more distributed and bilateral frontal and parietal areas depending on task complexity or degree of abstraction; Binder, Desai, Graves, & Conant, 2009).

These areas of dedicated activation in response to syntactic and semantic demands develop over time in individually variable ways, possibly as a result of differing experience. Berl and colleagues (2010) used fMRI to study the effects of task, age, neuropsychological skill, and posttask performance in the reading versus listening of developmentally appropriate paragraph-length texts by subjects ranging from early childhood through preadolescence. The researchers found a consistent activation across ages and modality (i.e., reading, listening) in the left superior temporal sulcus, dubbing it the "comprehension cortex" (p. 115) because of its involvement in lexical-level syntactic and semantic tasks.

However, they also noted developmental differences in text-comprehension processing, with younger children demonstrating a more diffusely distributed activation pattern that included the right temporal pole and right cerebellum. Older children and adolescents showed increased activation in the left inferior frontal cortex while listening to stories, suggesting an increased recruitment of this area for more structurally complex texts, and this activation correlated positively with comprehension results. Reading was shown to require activation across a greater number of cortical areas than listening was (see Figure 2; Berl et al., 2010), including the right temporal and right inferior frontal lobes, possibly suggesting that children require this additional activation to construct meaning from the

Figure 2. Cortical Areas Active in Listening Comprehension Versus Reading Comprehension in 4–12-Year-Old Children

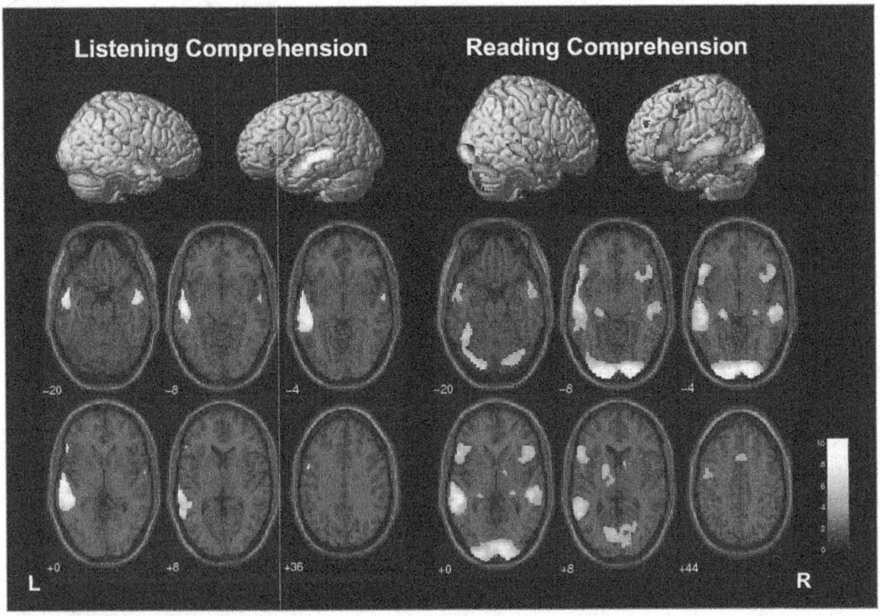

Note. There was greater activation in the reading condition because of visual, letter-identification, and word form processing, but also possible verbal rehearsal and/or more syntactic–semantic processing. The comparison indicates a common language comprehension cluster in the superior to medial left temporal cortex similar to that found in adults. From "Functional Anatomy of Listening and Reading Comprehension During Development," by M.M. Berl, E.S. Duke, J. Mayo, L.R. Rosenberger, E.N. Moore, J. VanMeter, et al., 2010, *Brain and Language, 114*(2), p. 120.

more difficult semantic structures typical of written texts compared with the age-typical semantic structures of children's oral language (cf. Yeatman, Ben-Shachar, Glover, & Feldman, 2010).

The Role of Emotion in Meaning. Emotional valance seems intuitively to be integral in tracking the meaning and/or meaningfulness of language and what it represents, and the neurolinguistic literature supports this (Ferstl, Rinck, & von Cramon, 2005; Havas, Glenberg, & Rinck, 2007), with corresponding neural activity found in the anterior temporal and inferior prefrontal areas adjacent to the orbitofrontal cortex. These cortical areas are known to develop early in childhood for affect regulation and socioemotional response (for introductions to social neuroscience of early childhood, see Cozolino, 2006; Schore, 1994). They connect to subcortical areas in the basal ganglia that comodulate the endocrine system, and thereby the individual's emotional state, and are closely tied, both neurologically and hormonally, to subcortical areas involved in memory formation and its reconstruction, such as in the hypothalamus, anterior cingulate, and amygdala. There is also a fair degree of overlap between areas of the brain active during both emotional control and semantic memory (Binney, Embleton, Jefferies, Parker, & Ralph, 2010).

It should be acknowledged that the neurological basis for the relationship of emotion and sociality to language comprehension development is not yet well understood theoretically (cf. Immordino-Yang & Damasio, 2007). Nonetheless, these subcortical areas, and loci in the orbitofrontal and anterior temporal cortices, may prove a crucial link between language and meaning and could provide another front in the growing appreciation for the importance of early childhood social, emotional, and language development for subsequent literacy achievement (Beaucousin et al., 2007; Kuhl & Rivera-Gaxiola, 2008), as well as for the emotional quality of classroom environments.

Higher Order Cognitive and Discourse-Level Processes in Reading. Research is accumulating on the neural correlates of text genre identification, action tracking, processing of expository and narrative text structures, determining the appropriateness of tone or trope (e.g., irony, metaphor), identification and processing of idiom, and the use of appropriate discourse forms (for an intriguing review of some of these processes, see Perfetti & Frishkoff, 2008). For instance, the importance of basic cognitive functions, such as inference in relating textual information to prior world knowledge, is treated at some length (Friese, Rutschmann, Raabe, & Schmalhofer, 2008; Mason & Just, 2011). Executive skills in text tracking (Sesma, Mahone, Levine, Eason, & Cutting, 2009) and reader's analysis of metaphor (Mashal, Faust, Hendler, & Jung-Beeman, 2009) are additional examples of such work.

Making sense of decoded text symbols affords less of the contextual information provided during auditory processing of speech from, for instance, the visual tracking of facial movements to help identify ambiguous phonemes, as in the McGurk effect (Beauchamp, Nath, & Pasalar, 2010), or integrating the semantic content of hand gestures (Dick, Goldin-Meadow, Hasson, Skipper, & Small, 2009). Higher order context effects, such as those associated with linguistic environment, appear to have a developmental, not just functional, effect on language comprehension processes, particularly regarding syntax and higher order semantics and idioms (Raizada, Richards, Meltzoff, & Kuhl, 2008). All of these issues will likely become important as educational neuroscience further explores the effects of home and classroom discourse participation on language development.

Neuroscience research on the processing of text content in terms of subjects' prior knowledge is in its infancy; as an example of this research, Speer, Reynolds, Swallow, and Zacks (2009) have suggested that processing scenes and actions described in narrative texts involves sensory and motor processing areas of the brain. The importance of prior knowledge for text comprehension is well documented, with a distinction being made between declarative and procedural knowledge and between prior knowledge of the world and prior knowledge specific to language (e.g., prior knowledge of vocabulary, prior knowledge of dialect- and discourse-specific syntactic and semantic patterns, prior knowledge of domain-specific discourses and genres). There is the possibility that insofar as this prior knowledge of language or even of social protocols is the result of overlearned and thus automatized pattern recognition (e.g., syntactic and idiomatic pattern recognition), it would be more appropriately categorized as a form of developed skill rather than as explicit knowledge. (Rule application models of language processing blur this distinction.) Still, the difference between prior knowledge that is specific to language comprehension rather than content comprehension is worth noting.

Also worth noting is the distinction between the tapping of developed processing skills and long-term memory with working memory's role in the construction of situation models from text. The construction of summary memories of a passage for retelling, for instance, requires the compression of details on the basis of significance. Lillywhite and colleagues (2010) used fMRI to contrast subjects' processing of passages read to them repeatedly and found a marked difference in neural activation between the first and subsequent hearing of the texts. The neural activation between the iterations of the passages extended from chiefly auditory and language comprehension areas in the initial reading to include areas in the frontal, parietal, and subcortical areas during subsequent readings, suggesting areas for modeling, memory, and recognition processes beyond basic language comprehension processes. When the analyses were extended to subjects' retelling or summarizing of the text, a strong correlation was discovered with activity in the right parietal cortex, suggesting its role in discourse representation.

Such discourse processing research may be of interest to reading professionals. However, it is rarely the case that the term *discourse* in neurolinguistics means what it does in psycho- or sociolinguistics (e.g., Gee, 2008), sources that have been highly influential in reading education scholarship. For the relevant neurolinguistic research, discourse is simply extended, usually narrative, text, with all of the micro- and macrostructural elements of such texts intact (e.g., Lillywhite et al., 2010). The point of such research is to determine the neural activity that correlates with the processing of such features and, as a result, determine whether structure-related categories of mental process have a tangible neural signature.

For instance, Yarkoni, Speer, and Zacks (2008) used fMRI to distinguish sentence-level comprehension processing from passage-level comprehension processing. Presuming that the reading of a narrative requires the building of mental representations of the narrative, which are then employed constructively to process subsequent narrative elements, they tracked the reading of cohesive narratives contrasted to paragraphs comprised of unrelated sentences. They found that similar areas of the brain were involved for comprehending the content of sentences, but distinct areas were tapped for the processing of the situation model, with the posterior parietal cortex implicated in the construction of such models, and anterior temporal areas implicated in their maintenance. Taking a different approach, Whitney and colleagues (2009) explored the distributed neural network underlying story comprehension. They contrasted the processing of sentence boundaries with content-substantive narrative shifts and were thereby able to demonstrate the role of the medial parietal cortex in narrative structure comprehension, and the apparent role of the precuneus and posterior cingulate in updating story representations. The role of the precuneus, tucked into the medial parietal fissure, for higher order processing is particularly intriguing, given its potential contribution to self-awareness and self-monitoring (Cavanna & Trimble, 2006).

As literacy scholars have long appreciated, reading is more than just the mental processes inside the head of a reader. Social, linguistic, and cultural factors all play a role both during a reading event and in reading development over time. Current developmental science has suggested that these contextual factors do not just happen to a reader but are aspects of a developing child's social and cultural environment, a symbolic landscape that the child learns to appropriate, represent, and negotiate in a generally functional and eventually strategic fashion (see the reviews in Eisenberg, 2006). Insofar as a reader perceives and responds, mentally or behaviorally, to representational elements of his or her sociocultural landscape, there will be correlated neurological activity and development to study (e.g., monitoring the intentions of others as distinguishable from physical causality; Mason & Just, 2011). The neurological correlates of such perceptions and responses are the focus of study for researchers in developmental cognitive neuroscience, the neuroscience of affect regulation, personality neuroscience, and social neuroscience.

Synthesis. The anatomical areas of the brain that correlate with the foundational language comprehension functions (i.e., vocabulary, syntax, semantics) are generally more active in the left hemisphere of the neocortex, although homologous areas in the right hemisphere are typically activated as well, especially for reading, possibly for related but distinct discourse processing or textual representations (Ferstl, Neumann, Bogler, & von Cramon, 2008). Higher order comprehension processes and strategic analysis involve a much more distributed set of brain loci.

The ERP time-course studies of syntactic and semantic processing during text comprehension in competent adult readers have indicated that syntactic processing begins in the left frontal and anterior temporal lobes with phrase-structure monitoring at approximately 150–250 milliseconds (Segalowitz & Zheng, 2009); expanding to verb–subject or syntactic/thematic processing around 300–350 milliseconds in the left inferior gyrus; an assessment of the semantic intention within the sentence at approximately 400 milliseconds (Marinkovic et al., 2003); and culminating, especially in cases of more complex syntactic structures, with a syntactic recheck or incongruity/novelty effect, peaking at approximately 600 milliseconds (Hagoort, 2003). Integration of syntactic and semantic processes occur at approximately 400–600 milliseconds (Friederici & Weissenborn, 2007). More global-level processing of text features occur subsequently. Although anatomical localization of these events in time-course studies does not always precisely match that suggested by functional anatomical studies, both types of studies are in agreement regarding the distinctive nature of word meaning, syntax, and semantic processes.

The neuroscience work on comprehension is far more variable than that on decoding processes in part because it ranges over a more extended and theoretically variable set of subprocesses. There is great theoretical uncertainty about the role these subprocesses play in text comprehension, and clearly the role would vary depending on the nature of the text, the culturally specific representational system employed, the purpose and context of the reading, and the ability and educational level of the reader. The same challenges to reliability posed to reading inventories at higher grade levels is at work here as well. For these reasons, constructing more ecologically valid studies of brain activation during comprehension would be helpful. In the future, this research may require a more substantial contribution from educational researchers than they have provided in the past.

Issues in the Educational Neuroscience of Reading

Methodological Issues in Neuroscience Research. Recent technological advances in the neurosciences have been rapid, and the number of cognitive neuroscience studies has expanded exponentially (Cabeza & Nyberg, 2000). Nevertheless, the majority of imaging findings are less than a decade old and are thus unreplicated. Meta-analyses are scarce (Maisog, Einbinder, Flowers, Turkeltaub, & Eden, 2008). Because of the novelty of the technological advances, many brain-imaging studies are often as much about a method's appropriate use, research design, and implementation as they are about the object of investigation, which has made for some engaging debates within the neuroscience literature. At first blush, reading education researchers may find these debates impenetrably technical.

Yet, most of the critique revolves around the fundamentals of research design and the logic of interpretation, issues with which well-prepared literacy researchers are familiar. Debates about such conceptual fundamentals as the difference between necessary and sufficient conditions, between correlation and causation, between reliability and validity, between constrained and unconstrained variables, and the use of circular reasoning and other fallacies in research design and interpretation have all made appearances in the history of reading research. Literacy researchers will find these familiar motifs evident in the critical neuroscience literature as well.

Among the technical and interpretive concerns recently treated, Vul, Harris, Winkielman, and Pashler (2009) noted that correlations in brain-imaging studies may have been seriously overstated. Bennett, Baird, Miller, and Wolford (2009) noted that the reliability of brain–behavior correlates varies widely depending on the type of behavior being correlated, and they reviewed many of the challenges that remain regarding reliability in brain-imaging studies. One possible issue has been inadequate attention to the need for multiple-comparisons correction, given the extensive number of calculations between conditions required in neuroimaging techniques (Bennett, Baird, et al., 2009). Other methodological issues have been suggested as well (see Brown, 2007; Oakes et al., 2007). All of this should caution educators and educational researchers from taking any particular brain study finding at face value, particularly when disseminated through the popular media, let alone as a definitive form of evidence for a reading program, method, policy, or theory.

Conceptual Frameworks for Bridging Neuroscience and Reading Research. At present, there is an emerging interdisciplinary neurocognitive perspective that is seeking to integrate brain, cognitive, social, and cultural perspectives on learning and activity (Fischer, Bernstein, & Immordino-Yang, 2007; Hall, Goswami, Harrison, Ellis, & Soler, 2010; Varma et al., 2008). Neuroscience research, research on educational processes, and research on learning can be mutually informing. For example, recent advances in neuroscience link directly to long-standing models in cognitive educational psychology, enabling the rigorous analysis of such models from a new evidence base. Unfortunately, this computational-brain framework is the one most often garbled in the popular media and brain-based education materials.

At the same time, an alternative theoretical framework is emerging that is organic rather than mechanistic, biological rather than representational, built on the motif of learning as growth (not merely conceptual growth but actual neurophysiological development), and powered by the bioecological dynamics of organisms as agents growing functionally in response to their ecological contingencies, environments to which they adapt through behavioral, developmental, epigenetic, and even evolutionary processes (e.g., Mareschal et al., 2007). An awareness of complex dynamical effects over time and across scales of analysis is certainly relevant to research in literacy education, particularly to research on sociocultural factors and on situated cognition.

Other theoretical frameworks are also possible (see Meltzoff, Kuhl, Movellan, & Sejnowski, 2009). Given the relatively advanced state of educational neuroscience on reading, literacy education seems to be an ideal field within which to forge and field-test new theoretical frameworks informed by, and coherent with, research in the neurosciences (Hruby, 2009). Such work could have significant implications for educational policy, theory, and practice.

Topical Focus and Level of Analysis. Remembering that research is about what it is about and not something else is almost too obvious to elaborate on, yet this fundamental observation has already been underscored by cognitive and neuroscience researchers alike (e.g., Bruer, 1997; Hirsh-Pasek et al., 2007). If we require research-based evidence on effective classroom practices, we should first attend to the copious research on effective classroom practices. If we are dissatisfied with this research, or the implications of its findings, we ought to attempt to improve on it. There is a kind of natural hierarchy to what kind of research is most relevant to a problem, and research on the problem itself should come first. Cognitive and social aspects of learning should probably come next, with cognitive neuroscience and educational neuroscience playing a more distant role. Yet, crucially, all of these research perspectives will eventually be important in achieving a full understanding of, for instance, the efficacy of classroom practices. All of these different levels of analysis and explanation have mutually supportive roles to play in an integrated understanding of how to improve classroom practices for literacy development. Reduction of cause to a single level of analysis when researching the complex nature of bioecological systems is unwarrantable and unlikely to be helpful for finding connections to efficacious educational practice.

The reading education research base, taken at large, indicates that the answer to the simplistic question, What works?, is it depends—on student variability, teacher efficacy, material resources, curricular objectives, and numerous other contextual factors. As experienced teachers know, no method will work for everyone in a given class, and nothing works for anyone all the time. Given that, the question should probably be rephrased as, What works for particular kinds of students, under particular circumstances, to particular ends, with particular dependability? Reading researchers have developed many useful methods and theoretical frameworks for investigating elements of this larger question. Yet, neuroscience also offers us methods for studying these questions within an educational context. Neuroscientists are trying to achieve an understanding of how learning occurs at neurosystemic, neurocytological, neurochemical, and neurogenomic levels of analyses. At these levels of analysis, learning will depend on physiological processes that may come to be phrased as general laws of learning. As we discover what these processes are, we can then use them to examine learning at the physiological level in response to various contexts and situations of learning. It is critical to be aware that neuroscience will not replace understandings arising from social science. Rather, neuroscience can complement the understandings derived from educational research and reinforce and refine our understanding of the processes involved in discourse comprehension and its development.

Research from ancillary domains, when coherently theorized as pertinent to classroom evidence, can be very illuminating and help us expand or reframe our thinking, as the history of reading education research has suggested (Alexander & Fox, 2004). As more is understood about the neurological processes and development that correlate with reading and its instruction, educational neuroscience on reading processes will likely begin to influence our theoretical constructs about reading education across the life span and, thereby, inform public discourse and policy formation. It therefore would be helpful if reading education scholars developed expertise in the research, philosophy, and limitations of neuroscience, and the developmental sciences more broadly, to help inform the public debate.

Biology and Complexity

Current life science has provided us with a much more complex understanding of developmental processes than popular views of genetic determinism may suggest. Physiological and genetic propensities are realized through interaction with an environment, be it nucleic, biochemical, cytological, systemic, organic, social, or symbolic (Gottlieb, 2007). Given the severely limited number of genes in the human genome that distinguish us from other species, much of the necessary information for behavior and learning is not actually encoded in the genome but off-loaded in the environment in which the genome has historically and developmentally functioned; the same also may be true of the putative need for the knowledge representations required for adaptive behavior (Clancey, 1997; Hendriks-Jansen, 1996).

This insight lies at the heart of the promise of neuroscience for literacy education. Literacy educators are creating the contexts within which children's brains develop, enabling them to perform increasingly demanding reading tasks and develop capacities for comprehension, understanding, and lifelong learning across many situations and domains. Reading and literacy development involve relationships among social, cultural, biological, cognitive, and developmental processes. The need to incorporate all research perspectives in constructing optimal policy and pedagogy means that the impact of bringing neuroscience into the traditions in reading education and literacy research may be profound.

Final Comments

In this review of the neuroscience research related to reading and literacy, we briefly reviewed findings on neurological correlates of decoding and comprehension, as well as some higher order processes in reading. We also elaborated on several issues regarding neuroscience methodology and theoretical framing for bringing neuroscience and literacy education research into an interdisciplinary conversation. We discussed some general cautions and mistaken assumptions.

As we hope we have made clear, the potential of neuroscience to help expand our understanding of reading processes, their development, and their occasional dysfunction is profound. We hope that our review of the research provides a helpful overview of the terrain and the issues confronting any attempt at an interdisciplinary conversation between literacy education research and neuroscience research. A successful interdisciplinary conversation could helpfully address many questions about literacy and its instruction and development. Until such time as knowledgeable literacy education scholars prepare themselves to engage in such a conversation, the full promise of the biological sciences for analyzing educational issues will remain obscure.

QUESTIONS FOR REFLECTION

1. What implications of brain-imaging research are promising for literacy educators?
2. How is the theorized brain activity different for decoding processes and for meaning-construction processes?
3. What are implications of the finding that letter–sound congruence results in higher levels of brain activity than does sound alone?
4. Why is comprehension so difficult to measure through brain activity scanning?

NOTES

Goswami, supported by the Medical Research Council (Grant G0400574) and a major research fellowship from the Leverhulme Trust, took the lead on the decoding processes section of this article. The authors thank Carl Frederiksen, Chuck Perfetti, and the *Reading Research Quarterly* editors for helpful comments and advice.

REFERENCES

Alexander, P.A., & Fox, E. (2004). A historical perspective on reading research and practice. In R.B. Ruddell & N.J. Unrau (Eds.), *Theoretical models and processes of reading* (5th ed., pp. 33–68). Newark, DE: International Reading Association. doi:10.1598/0872075028.2

Balass, M., Nelson, J.R., & Perfetti, C.A. (2010). Word learning: An ERP investigation of word experience effects on recognition and word processing. *Contemporary Educational Psychology*, *35*(2), 126–140. doi:10.1016/j.cedpsych.2010.04.001

Beauchamp, M.S., Nath, A.R., & Pasalar, S. (2010). fMRI-guided transcranial magnetic stimulation reveals that the superior temporal sulcus is a cortical locus of the McGurk effect. *The Journal of Neuroscience*, *30*(7), 2414–2417. doi:10.1523/JNEUROSCI.4865-09.2010

Beaucousin, V., Lacheret, A., Turbelin, M., Morel, M., Mazoyer, B., & Tzourio-Mazoyer, N. (2007). FMRI study of emotional speech comprehension. *Cerebral Cortex*, *17*(2), 339–352. doi:10.1093/cercor/bhj151

Beddington, J., Cooper, C.L., Field, J., Goswami, U., Huppert, F.A., Jenkins, R., et al. (2008). The mental wealth of nations. *Nature*, *455*(7216), 1057–1060. doi:10.1038/4551057a

Bennett, C.M., Baird, A.A., Miller, M.B., & Wolford, G.L. (2009). Neural correlates of interspecies perspective taking in the post-mortem Atlantic salmon: An argument for multiple comparisons correction. *Prefrontal.org*. Retrieved November 26, 2010, from prefrontal.org/files/posters/Bennett-Salmon-2009.pdf

Bennett, C.M., & Miller, M.B. (2010). How reliable are the results from functional magnetic resonance imaging? *Annals of the New York Academy of Sciences*, *1191*, 133–155. doi:10.1111/j.1749–6632.2010.05446.x

Bennett, C.M., Wolford, G.L., & Miller, M.B. (2009). The principled control of false positives in neuroimaging. *Social Cognitive and Affective Neuroscience*, *4*(4), 417–422. doi:10.1093/scan/nsp053

Berl, M.M., Duke, E.S., Mayo, J., Rosenberger, L.R., Moore, E.N., VanMeter, J., et al. (2010). Functional anatomy of listening and reading comprehension during development. *Brain and Language*, *114*(2), 115–125. doi:10.1016/j.bandl.2010.06.002

Binder, J.R., Desai, R.H., Graves, W.W., & Conant, L.L. (2009). Where is the semantic system? A critical review and meta-analysis of 120 functional neuroimaging studies. *Cerebral Cortex*, *19*(12), 2767–2796. doi:10.1093/cercor/bhp055

Binney, R.J., Embleton, K.V., Jefferies, E., Parker, G.J.M., & Ralph, M.A.L. (2010). The ventral and inferolateral aspects of the anterior temporal lobe are crucial in semantic memory: Evidence from a novel direct comparison of distortion-corrected fMRI, rTMS, and semantic dementia. *Cerebral Cortex*, *20*(11), 2728–2738. doi:10.1093/cercor/bhq019

Blau, V., Van Atteveldt, N., Formisano, E., Goebel, R., & Blomert, L. (2008). Task-irrelevant visual letters interact with the processing of speech sounds in heteromodal and unimodal cortex. *European Journal of Neuroscience*, *28*(3), 500–509. doi:10.1111/j.1460–9568.2008.06350.x

Boulenger, V., Hauk, O., & Pulvermüller, F. (2009). Grasping ideas with the motor system: Semantic somatotopy in idiom comprehension. *Cerebral Cortex*, *19*(8), 1905–1914. doi:10.1093/cercor/bhn217

Bozic, M., Marslen-Wilson, W.D., Stamatakis, E.A., Davis, M.H., & Tyler, L.K. (2007). Differentiating morphology, form, and meaning: Neural correlates of morphological complexity. *Journal of Cognitive Neuroscience*, *19*(9), 1464–1475. doi:10.1162/jocn.2007.19.9.1464

Brown, G.G. (2007). Functional magnetic resonance imaging in clinical practice: Look before you leap. *Neuropsychology Review*, *17*(2), 103–106. doi:10.1007/s11065-007-9027-9

Bruer, J.T. (1997). Education and the brain: A bridge too far. *Educational Researcher*, *26*(8), 4–16.

Brunswick, N., McCrory, E., Price, C.J., Frith, C.D., & Frith, U. (1999). Explicit and implicit processing of words and pseudowords by adult developmental dyslexics: A search for Wernicke's Wortschatz. *Brain*, *122*(10), 1901–1917. doi:10.1093/brain/122.10.1901

Cabeza, R., & Nyberg, L. (2000). Imaging cognition II: An empirical review of 275 PET and fMRI studies. *Journal of Cognitive Neuroscience*, *12*(1), 1–47. doi:10.1162/08989290051137585

Caplan, D. (2004). Functional neuroimaging studies of written sentence comprehension. *Scientific Studies of Reading*, *8*(3), 225–240. doi:10.1207/s1532799xssr0803_3

Carreiras, M., Seghier, M.L., Baquero, S., Estévez, A., Lozano, A., Devlin, J.T., et al. (2009). An anatomical signature for literacy. *Nature*, *461*(7266), 983–986. doi:10.1038/nature08461

Cavanna, A.E., & Trimble, M.R. (2006). The precuneus: A review of its functional anatomy and behavioural correlates. *Brain, 129*(3), 564–583. doi:10.1093/brain/awl004
Clancey, W.J. (1997). *Situated cognition: On human knowledge and computer representations*. New York: Cambridge University Press.
Cohen, L., & Dehaene, S. (2004). Specialization within the ventral stream: The case for the visual word form area. *NeuroImage, 22*(1), 466–476. doi:10.1016/j.neuroimage.2003.12.049
Cooke, A., Grossman, M., DeVita, C., Gonzalez-Atavales, J., Moore, P., Chen, W., et al. (2006). Large-scale neural network for sentence processing. *Brain and Language, 96*(1), 14–36. doi:10.1016/j.bandl.2005.07.072
Cozolino, L. (2006). *The neuroscience of human relationships: Attachment and the developing social brain*. New York: W.W. Norton.
Csépe, V., Szücs, D., & Honbolygó, F. (2003). Number-word reading as challenging task in dyslexia? An ERP study. *International Journal of Psychophysiology, 51*(1), 69–83. doi:10.1016/S0167-8760(03)00154-5
Dehaene, S. (2009). *Reading in the brain: The science and evolution of a human invention*. New York: Penguin.
Démonet, J.-F., Thierry, G., & Cardebat, D. (2005). Renewal of the neurophysiology of language: Functional neuroimaging. *Physiological Reviews, 85*(1), 49–95. doi:10.1152/physrev.00049.2003
Dick, A.S., Goldin-Meadow, S., Hasson, U., Skipper, J.I., & Small, S.L. (2009). Co-speech gestures influence neural activity in brain regions associated with processing semantic information. *Human Brain Mapping, 30*(11), 3509–3526. doi:10.1002/hbm.20774
Dickinson, D.K., Golinkoff, R.M., & Hirsh-Pasek, K. (2010). Speaking out for language: Why language is central to reading development. *Educational Researcher, 39*(4), 305–310. doi:10.3102/0013189X10370204
Eisenberg, N. (Vol. Ed.). (2006). *Handbook of child psychology: Vol. 3. Social, emotional, and personality development* (6th ed.). New York: John Wiley & Sons.
Ferstl, E.C., Neumann, J., Bogler, C., & von Cramon, D.Y. (2008). The extended language network: A meta-analysis of neuroimaging studies on text comprehension. *Human Brain Mapping, 29*(5), 581–593. doi:10.1002/hbm.20422
Ferstl, E.C., Rinck, M., & von Cramon, D.Y. (2005). Emotional and temporal aspects of situation model processing during text comprehension: An event-related fMRI study. *Journal of Cognitive Neuroscience, 17*(5), 724–739. doi:10.1162/0898929053747658
Fischer, K.W., Bernstein, J.H., & Immordino-Yang, M.H. (Eds.). (2007). *Mind, brain and education in reading disorders*. New York: Cambridge University Press.
Friederici, A.D. (2002). Towards a neural basis of auditory sentence processing. *Trends in Cognitive Sciences, 6*(2), 78–84. doi:10.1016/S1364-6613(00)01839-8
Friederici, A.D., & Kotz, S.A. (2003). The brain basis of syntactic processes: Functional imaging and lesion studies. *NeuroImage, 20*(Suppl. 1), S8–S17. doi:10.1016/j.neuroimage.2003.09.003
Friederici, A.D., von Cramon, D.Y., & Kotz, S.A. (1999). Language related brain potentials in patients with cortical and subcortical left hemisphere lesions. *Brain, 122*(6), 1033–1047. doi:10.1093/brain/122.6.1033
Friederici, A.D., & Weissenborn, J. (2007). Mapping sentence form onto meaning: The syntax–semantic interface. *Brain Research, 1146*, 50–58. doi:10.1016/j.brainres.2006.08.038.
Friese, U., Rutschmann, R., Raabe, M., & Schmalhofer, F. (2008). Neural indicators of inference processes in text comprehension: An event-related functional magnetic resonance imaging study. *Journal of Cognitive Neuroscience, 20*(11), 2110–2124. doi:10.1162/jocn.2008.20141
Frishkoff, G.A., Perfetti, C.A., & Westbury, C. (2009). ERP measures of partial semantic knowledge: Left temporal indices of skill differences and lexical quality. *Biological Psychology, 80*(1), 130–147. doi:10.1016/j.biopsycho.2008.04.017
Frith, U. (1985). Beneath the surface of developmental dyslexia. In K.E. Patterson, J.C. Marshall, & M. Coltheart (Eds.), *Surface dyslexia: Neuropsychological and cognitive studies of phonological reading* (pp. 301–330). Hillsdale, NJ: Erlbaum.
Gazzaniga, M.S. (Ed.). (2010). *The cognitive neurosciences* (4th ed.). Cambridge, MA: MIT Press.
Gee, J.P. (2008). *Social linguistics and literacies: Ideology in discourses* (3rd ed.). New York: Routledge.
Goswami, U. (2006). Neuroscience and education: From research to practice? *Nature Reviews Neuroscience, 7*(5), 406–413. doi:10.1038/nrn1907
Goswami, U. (2009). Mind, brain, and literacy: Biomarkers as usable knowledge for education. *Mind, Brain, and Education, 3*(3), 176–184. doi:10.1111/j.1751-228X.2009.01068.x
Goswami, U., & Szücs, D. (2011). Educational neuroscience: Developmental mechanisms towards a conceptual framework. *NeuroImage, 57*(3), 651–658.
Gottlieb, G. (2007). Developmental neurobehavioral genetics: Development as explanation. In B.C. Jones & P. Mormède (Eds.), *Neurobehavioral genetics: Methods and applications* (2nd ed., pp. 17–27). Boca Raton, FL: CRC.
Hagoort, P. (2003). Interplay between syntax and semantics during sentence comprehension: ERP effects of combining syntactic and semantic violations. *Journal of Cognitive Neuroscience, 15*(6), 883–899. doi:10.1162/089892903322370807
Hagoort, P., Hald, L., Bastiaansen, M., & Petersson, K.M. (2004). Integration of word meaning and world knowledge in language comprehension. *Science, 304*(5669), 438–441. doi:10.1126/science.1095455

Hagoort, P., & van Berkum, J. (2007). Beyond the sentence given. *Philosophical Transactions of the Royal Society B: Biological Sciences*, *362*(1481), 801–811. doi:10.1098/rstb.2007.2089

Hald, L.A., Bastiaansen, M.C., & Hagoort, P. (2006). EEG theta and gamma responses to semantic violations in online sentence processing. *Brain and Language*, *96*(1), 90–105. doi:10.1016/j.bandl.2005.06.007

Hall, K., Goswami, U., Harrison, C., Ellis, S., & Soler, J. (Eds.). (2010). *Interdisciplinary perspectives on learning to read: Culture, cognition and pedagogy*. New York: Routledge.

Havas, D.A., Glenberg, A.M., & Rinck, M. (2007). Emotion simulation during language comprehension. *Psychonomic Bulletin & Review*, *14*(3), 436–441. doi:10.3758/BF03194085

Heim, S. (2005). The structure and dynamics of normal language processing: Insights from neuroimaging. *Acta Neurobiologiae Experimentalis*, *65*(1), 95–116.

Hendriks-Jansen, H. (1996). *Catching ourselves in the act: Situated activity, interactive emergence, evolution, and human thought*. Cambridge, MA: MIT Press.

Hirsh-Pasek, K., Bruer, J., Kuhl, P., Goldin-Meadow, S., Stern, E., Galles, N.S., et al. (2007). *The Santiago declaration*. Retrieved November 26, 2010, from www.jsmf.org/santiagodeclaration/

Hruby, G.G. (2009). Grounding reading comprehension theory in the neuroscience literatures. In S.E. Israel & G.G. Duffy (Eds.), *Handbook of research on reading comprehension* (pp. 189–223). New York: Routledge.

Hudson, R.F., High, L., & Otaiba, S.A. (2007). Dyslexia and the brain: What does current research tell us? *The Reading Teacher*, *60*(6), 506–515. doi:10.1598/RT.60.6.1

Huettel, S.A., Song, A.W., & McCarthy, G. (2009). *Functional magnetic resonance imaging* (2nd ed.). Sunderland, MA: Sinauer.

Immordino-Yang, M.H., & Damasio, A. (2007). We feel, therefore we learn: The relevance of affective and social neuroscience to education. *Mind, Brain, and Education*, *1*(1), 3–10. doi:10.1111/j.1751-228X.2007.00004.x

Israel, S.E., & Duffy, G.G. (Eds.). (2009). *Handbook of research on reading comprehension*. New York: Routledge.

Kaan, E., Harris, A., Gibson, E., & Holcomb, P. (2000). The P600 as an index of syntactic integration difficulty. *Language and Cognitive Processes*, *15*(2), 159–201. doi:10.1080/016909600386084

Kamil, M.L., Pearson, P.D., Moje, E.B., & Afflerbach, P.P. (Eds.). (2010). *Handbook of reading research* (Vol. 4). New York: Routledge.

Kuhl, P., & Rivera-Gaxiola, M. (2008). Neural substrates of language acquisition. *Annual Review of Neuroscience*, *31*, 511–534. doi:10.1146/annurev.neuro.30.051606.094321

Kuperberg, G.R. (2007). Neural mechanisms of language comprehension: Challenges to syntax. *Brain Research*, *1146*, 23–49. doi:10.1016/j.brainres.2006.12.063

Kutas, M., Van Petten, C.K., & Kluender, R. (2006). Psycholinguistics electrified II (1994–2005). In M.J. Traxler & M.A. Gernsbacher (Eds.), *Handbook of psycholinguistics* (2nd ed., pp. 659–724). Burlington, MA: Academic. doi:10.1016/B978-012369374-7/50018-3

Lesaux, N.K., & Kieffer, M.J. (2010). Exploring sources of reading comprehension difficulties among language minority learners and their classmates in early adolescence. *American Educational Research Journal*, *47*(3), 596–632. doi:10.3102/0002831209355469

Lieberman, P. (2006). *Toward an evolutionary biology of language*. Cambridge, MA: Belknap.

Lillywhite, L.M., Saling, M.M., Demutska, A., Masterton, R., Farquharson, S., & Jackson, G.D. (2010). The neural architecture of discourse compression. *Neuropsychologia*, *48*(4), 873–879. doi:10.1016/j.neuropsychologia.2009.11.004

Luck, S.J. (2005). *An introduction to the event-related potential technique*. Cambridge, MA: MIT Press.

Maisog, J.M., Einbinder, E.R., Flowers, D.L., Turkeltaub, P.E., & Eden, G.F. (2008). A meta-analysis of functional neuroimaging studies of dyslexia. *Annals of the New York Academy of Sciences*, *1145*, 237–259. doi:10.1196/annals.1416.024

Mareschal, D., Johnson, M.H., Sirois, S., Spratling, M.W., Thomas, M.S.C., & Westermann, G. (2007). Neuroconstructivism: *Vol. 1. How the brain constructs cognition*. New York: Oxford University Press.

Marinkovic, K., Dhond, R.P., Dale, A.M., Glessner, M., Carr, V., & Halgren, E. (2003). Spatiotemporal dynamics of modality-specific and supramodal word processing. *Neuron*, *38*(3), 487–497. doi:10.1016/S0896-6273(03)00197-1

Mashal, N., Faust, M., Hendler, T., & Jung-Beeman, M. (2009). An fMRI study of processing novel metaphoric sentences. *Laterality: Asymmetries of Body, Brain and Cognition*, *14*(1), 30–54.

Mason, R.A., & Just, M.A. (2011). Differentiable cortical networks for inferences concerning people's intentions versus physical causality. *Human Brain Mapping*, *32*(2), 313–329. doi:10.1002/hbm.21021

Maurer, U., Brem, S., Bucher, K., & Brandeis, D. (2005). Emerging neurophysiological specialization for letter strings. *Journal of Cognitive Neuroscience*, *17*(10), 1532–1552. doi:10.1162/089892905774597218

Maurer, U., Brem, S., Bucher, K., Kranz, F., Benz, R., Steinhausen, H., et al. (2007). Impaired tuning of a fast occipito-temporal response for print in dyslexic children learning to read. *Brain*, *130*(12), 3200–3210. doi:10.1093/brain/awm193

McGill-Franzen, A., & Allington, R.L. (Eds.). (2011). *Handbook of reading disability research*. New York: Routledge.

Meltzoff, A.N., Kuhl, P.K., Movellan, J., & Sejnowski, T.J. (2009). Foundations for a new

science of learning. *Science, 325*(5938), 284–288. doi:10.1126/science.1175626
Mody, M. (2004). Neurobiological correlates of language and reading impairments. In C.A. Stone, E.R. Silliman, B.J. Ehren, & K. Apel (Eds.), *Handbook of language and literacy: Development and disorders* (pp. 49–72). New York: Guilford.
National Governors Association Center for Best Practices & Council of Chief State School Officers. (2010a). *Common core state standards for English language arts and literacy in history/social studies, science, and technical subjects.* Retrieved June 1, 2010, from www.corestandards.org/assets/CCSSI_ELA%20Standards.pdf
National Governors Association Center for Best Practices & Council of Chief State School Officers. (2010b). *Common core state standards for English language arts and literacy in history/social studies, science, and technical subjects: Appendix B: Text exemplars and sample performance tasks.* Retrieved June 1, 2010, from www.corestandards.org/assets/Appendix_B.pdf
Niogi, S.N., & McCandliss, B.D. (2006). Left lateralized white matter microstructure accounts for individual differences in reading ability and disability. *Neuropsychologia, 44*(11), 2178–2188. doi:10.1016/j.neuropsychologia.2006.01.011
Oakes, T.R., Fox, A.S., Johnstone, T., Chung, M.K., Kalin, N., & Davidson, R.J. (2007). Integrating VBM into the general linear model with voxelwise anatomical covariates. *NeuroImage, 34*(2), 500–508. doi:10.1016/j.neuroimage.2006.10.007
Osterhout, L., Kim, A., & Kuperberg, G. (2006). *The neurobiology of sentence comprehension.* Unpublished manuscript, University of Washington, Seattle; Tufts University, Medford, MA; Massachusetts General Hospital, Boston. Retrieved May 9, 2009, from psych.colorado.edu/~aakim/osterhout_handbook_of_psycholinguistics_chapter_v2.pdf
Patterson, K., Nestor, P.J., & Rogers, T.T. (2007). Where do you know what you know? The representation of semantic knowledge in the human brain. *Nature Reviews Neuroscience, 8,* 976–987. doi:10.1038/nrn2277
Perfetti, C.A., & Bolger, D.J. (2004). The brain might read that way. *Scientific Studies of Reading, 8*(3), 293–304. doi:10.1207/s1532799xssr0803_7
Perfetti, C.A., & Frishkoff, G.A. (2008). The neural bases of text and discourse processing. In B. Stemmer & H.A. Whitaker (Eds.), *Handbook of the neuroscience of language* (pp. 165–174). Burlington, MA: Academic. doi:10.1016/B978-0-08-045352-1.00016-1
Perfetti, C.A., & Hart, L. (2002). The lexical quality hypothesis. In L. Verhoeven, C. Elbro, & P. Reitsma (Eds.), *Precursors of functional literacy* (pp. 189–213). Philadelphia: John Benjamins.
Price, C.J., & Devlin, J.T. (2003). The myth of the visual word form area. *NeuroImage, 19*(3), 473–481. doi:10.1016/S1053–8119(03)00084–3
Price, C.J., Gorno-Tempini, M.L., Graham, K.S., Biggio, N., Mechelli, A., Patterson, K., et al. (2003). Normal and pathological reading: Converging data from lesion and imaging studies. *NeuroImage, 20*(Suppl. 1), S30–S41. doi:10.1016/j.neuroimage.2003.09.012
Price, C.J., & McCrory, E. (2005). Functional brain imaging studies of skilled reading and developmental dyslexia. In M.J. Snowling & C. Hulme (Eds.), *The science of reading: A handbook* (pp. 473–496). Malden, MA: Blackwell. doi:10.1002/9780470757642.ch25
Price, C.J., & Mechelli, A. (2005). Reading and reading disturbance. *Current Opinion in Neurobiology, 15*(2), 231–238. doi:10.1016/j.conb.2005.03.003
Pugh, K. (2006). A neurocognitive overview of reading acquisition and dyslexia across languages. *Developmental Science, 9*(5), 448–450. doi:10.1111/j.1467-7687.2006.00528.x
Raizada, R.D.S., Richards, T.L., Meltzoff, A., & Kuhl, P.K. (2008). Socioeconomic status predicts hemispheric specialisation of the left inferior frontal gyrus in young children. *NeuroImage, 40*(3), 1392–1401. doi:10.1016/j.neuroimage.2008.01.021
Rimrodt, S.L., Clements-Stephens, A.M., Pugh, K.R., Cortney, S.M., Gaur, P., Pekar, J.J., et al. (2009). Functional MRI of sentence comprehension in children with dyslexia: Beyond word recognition. *Cerebral Cortex, 19*(2), 402–413. doi:10.1093/cercor/bhn092
Rogalsky, C., Matchin, W., & Hickok, G. (2008). Broca's area, sentence comprehension, and working memory: An fMRI study. *Frontiers in Human Neuroscience, 2.* doi:10.3389/neuro.09.014.2008
Ross, E.D. (2010). Cerebral localization of functions and the neurology of language: Fact versus fiction or is it something else? *The Neuroscientist, 16*(3), 222–243. doi:10.1177/1073858409349899
Ruddell, R.B., & Unrau, N.J. (Eds.). (2004). *Theoretical models and processes of reading* (5th ed.). Newark, DE: International Reading Association.
Rumsey, J.M., Horwitz, B., Donohue, B.C., Nace, K., Maisog, J.M., & Andreason, P. (1997). Phonological and orthographic components of word recognition: A PET-rCBF study. *Brain, 120*(5), 739–759. doi:10.1093/brain/120.5.739
Sakai, K.L., Noguchi, Y., Takeuchi, T., & Watanabe, E. (2002). Selective priming of syntactic processing by event-related transcranial magnetic stimulation of Broca's area. *Neuron, 35*(6), 1177–1182. doi:10.1016/S0896-6273(02)00873-5
Sauseng, P., Bergmann, J., & Wimmer, H. (2004). When does the brain register deviances from standard word spellings? An ERP study. *Cognitive Brain Research, 20*(3), 529–532. doi:10.1016/j.cogbrainres.2004.04.008
Schore, A.N. (1994). *Affect regulation and the origin of the self: The neurobiology of emotional development.* Hillsdale, NJ: Erlbaum.
Segalowitz, S.J., & Zheng, X. (2009). An ERP study of category priming: Evidence of early lexical

semantic access. *Biological Psychology, 80*(1), 122–129. doi:10.1016/j.biopsycho.2008.04.009

Sesma, H.W., Mahone, E.M., Levine, T., Eason, S.H., & Cutting, L.E. (2009). The contribution of executive skills to reading comprehension. *Child Neuropsychology, 15*(3), 232–246. doi:10.1080/09297040802220029

Shaywitz, B.A., Shaywitz, S.E., Pugh, K.R., Mencl, W.E., Fulbright, R.K., Skudlarski, P., et al. (2002). Disruption of posterior brain systems for reading in children with developmental dyslexia. *Biological Psychiatry, 52*(2), 101–110. doi:10.1016/S0006–3223(02)01365–3

Shaywitz, S. (2003). *Overcoming dyslexia: A new and complete science-based program for reading problems at any level.* New York: Alfred A. Knopf.

Simos, P.G., Fletcher, J.M., Sarkari, S., Billingsley, R.L., Francis, D.J., Castillo, E.M., et al. (2005). Early development of neurophysiological processes involved in normal reading and reading disability: A magnetic source imaging study. *Neuropsychology, 19*(6), 787–798. doi:10.1037/0894-4105.19.6.787

Speer, N.K., Reynolds, J.R., Swallow, K.M., & Zacks, J.M. (2009). Reading stories activates neural representations of visual and motor experiences. *Psychological Science, 20*(8), 989–999. doi:10.1111/j.1467–9280.2009.02397.x

Szücs, D., & Goswami, U. (2007). Educational neuroscience: Defining a new discipline for the study of mental representations. *Mind, Brain, and Education, 1*(3), 114–127. doi:10.1111/j.1751-228X.2007.00012.x

Turkeltaub, P.E., Gareau, L., Flowers, D.L., Zeffiro, T.A., & Eden, G.F. (2003). Development of neural mechanisms for reading. *Nature Neuroscience, 6*(7), 767–773. doi:10.1038/nn1065.

van Berkum, J., Hagoort, P., & Brown, C. (1999). Semantic integration in sentences and discourse: Evidence from the N400. *Journal of Cognitive Neuroscience, 11*(6), 657–671. doi:10.1162/089892999563724

Varma, S., McCandliss, B.D., & Schwartz, D.L. (2008). Scientific and pragmatic challenges for bridging education and neuroscience. *Educational Researcher, 37*(3), 140–152. doi:10.3102/0013189X08317687

Vul, E., Harris, C., Winkielman, P., & Pashler, H. (2009). Puzzlingly high correlations in fMRI studies of emotion, personality, and social cognition. *Perspectives on Psychological Science, 4*(3), 274–290. doi:10.1111/j.1745-6924.2009.01125.x

Whitney, C., Huber, W., Klann, J., Weis, S., Krach, S., & Kircher, T. (2009). Neural correlates of narrative shifts during auditory story comprehension. *NeuroImage, 47*(1), 360–366. doi:10.1016/j.neuroimage.2009.04.037

Willems, R.M., Hagoort, P., & Casasanto, D. (2010). Body-specific representations of action verbs: Neural evidence from right- and left-handers. *Psychological Science, 21*(1), 67–74. doi:10.1177/0956797609354072

Willingham, D.T., & Lloyd, J.W. (2007). How educational theories can use neuroscientific data. *Mind, Brain, and Education, 1*(3), 140–149. doi:10.1111/j.1751-228X.2007.00014.x

Willis, J. (2007). Which brain research can educators trust? *Phi Delta Kappan, 88*(9), 697–699.

Yarkoni, T., Speer, N.K., & Zacks, J.M. (2008). Neural substrates of narrative comprehension and memory. *NeuroImage, 41*(4), 1408–1425. doi:10.1016/j.neuroimage.2008.03.062

Yeatman, J.D., Ben-Shachar, M., Glover, G.H., & Feldman, H.M. (2010). Individual differences in auditory sentence comprehension in children: An exploratory event-related functional magnet resonance imaging investigation. *Brain and Language, 114*(2), 72–79. doi:10.1016/j.bandl.2009.11.006

CHAPTER 24

Effects of Motivational and Cognitive Variables on Reading Comprehension

Ana Taboada, George Mason University

Stephen M. Tonks, Northern Illinois University

Allan Wigfield and John T. Guthrie, University of Maryland, College Park

Introduction

Reading instructional programs increasingly focus on comprehension skills as children matriculate through school. Researchers and practitioners (Alexander & Jetton, 2000; Kintsch, 1998) have acknowledged the importance of students' reading comprehension skills to success in a variety of school subject areas as well as other achievement outcomes. Given its importance to children's school success, researchers are investigating what predicts the growth of reading comprehension skills. Studies have shown that both motivational (Chapman & Tunmer, 1995; Guthrie, Wigfield, Metsala, & Cox, 1999; Guthrie et al., 2006) and cognitive variables (e.g., Pressley & Harris, 2006) predict reading comprehension and other achievement outcomes. However, most studies, to date, have looked either at the relation of motivation variables to reading comprehension or the relation of cognitive variables to reading comprehension. Few works have examined how both sets of variables predict reading comprehension when controlling for the other set of variables. The overall purpose of this study was to examine how both motivational and cognitive variables predict late elementary school-aged children's reading comprehension.

Motivation researchers have discussed how motivational and cognitive processes interact, and how each affects achievement outcomes (Pintrich, 2003; Pintrich, Marx, & Boyle, 1993; Wigfield, Eccles, Schiefele, Roeser, & Davis-Kean, 2006). In particular, such research has focused on how motivation provides an activating, energizing role for cognitive processes, which in turn can impact achievement (Pintrich; Wigfield et al., 2006). For example, Wigfield et al. reviewed work showing that motivational variables such as self-efficacy and intrinsic motivation predict students' achievement in different areas such as reading ability, math, language arts, sports, and occupational choice. However, Pintrich noted that there is little specific information in the literature about the strength of these activating processes or how they operate. For instance, it is likely, that there are multiple motivational pathways for the energization of students' behaviors

This chapter is reprinted from *Reading and Writing*, 22(1), 85–106. Copyright © 2009 by Springer. Reprinted with permission.

such that some students may be motivated by their self-efficacy beliefs, whereas others may activate cognitive processes through personal interests or contextual factors. Research that examines the different ways that motivation relates to various cognitive processes speaks of the need for integrated models of motivation and cognition that has been emphasized in the motivation field (Pintrich).

In the field of reading motivation, in particular, several researchers have examined the relations among motivation variables and literacy skills. For example, research has found relationships of young children's reading self-concept (assessed as students' perceptions of reading competence, the difficulty of reading, and their attitude towards reading) with word recognition and reading comprehension skills (Chapman & Tunmer; 1995; Chapman, Tunmer, & Prochnow, 2000). Findings showed that children who reported negative reading self-concepts performed more poorly on reading-related tasks than did children with positive reading self-concepts (Chapman et al.).

In her study with first through fourth graders, Gottfried (1990) showed that reading comprehension positively correlated with intrinsic motivation for reading. Research with gifted populations has also shown that students with exceptionally high academic intrinsic motivation performed better on various reading measures from the elementary through the high school grades (Gottfried, Cook, Gottfried, & Morris, 2005). Also, late-elementary school students' task-mastery goals have been found to be associated with their use of active (as opposed to superficial) learning strategies in literacy tasks (Meece & Miller, 1999, 2001), and students' intrinsic motivation has been associated with high-level, complex literacy tasks (Turner, 1995) and reading amount and text comprehension (Guthrie et al., 1999).

In addition, research has established that specific dimensions of reading motivation (such as involvement and curiosity) and reading comprehension are correlated (Baker & Wigfield, 1999; Wang & Guthrie, 2004). This research has contributed by identifying the multiple dimensions of motivation, as well as demonstrating the specificity of motivation within the domain of reading (Guthrie et al., 1999; Wigfield, Guthrie, Tonks, & Perencevich, 2004). However, little work has been done that examines simultaneously the role of both cognitive and motivational variables on reading comprehension. Further, there is even less work that addresses the role that both cognitive and motivation predictors play in the *growth* of reading comprehension (Guthrie et al., 2007). Given these limitations in previous literature, in this study we examine possible ways in which cognitive and motivational variables operate in relation to reading comprehension and its growth. We turn next to specific dimensions of motivation and how they relate to reading comprehension.

Dimensions of Reading Motivation

Achievement motivation and motivation in specific domains such as reading are construed as multidimensional phenomena (e.g., Eccles & Wigfield, 2002; Schiefele, 1999; Wang & Guthrie, 2004; Wigfield & Guthrie, 1997). Factor analysis has distinguished at least nine components of reading motivation (Baker

& Wigfield, 1999; Wigfield & Guthrie, 1997): (a) interest, (b) preference for challenge, (c) involvement, (d) self-efficacy, (e) competition, (f) recognition, (g) grades, (h) social interaction, and (i) work avoidance. Furthermore, motivations that are more internal, such as interest or curiosity, preference for challenge, and involvement have been distinguished as separate constructs in structural equation modeling from more external motivations such as grades and recognition and have been found to be strongly associated with reading comprehension not only in Caucasian students, but also in minority students and other cultures (Unrau & Schlackman, 2006; Wang & Guthrie, 2004).

In this study, we focused on five related dimensions of reading motivation and argue that they constitute a construct called *internal motivation for reading.* These five dimensions of motivation are: (a) perceived control, (b) interest, (c) self-efficacy, (d) involvement, and (e) social collaboration. We focus on internal motivation, rather than external, because individuals who are internally motivated show greater perseverance and sustained effort in their activities (Ryan & Deci, 2000). We focus on these five dimensions because prior research has determined their contributions to reading comprehension and literacy skills. In addition, empirical evidence has shown the interrelatedness of these five dimensions. For instance, Guthrie et al. (2007) examined these constructs with fifth-graders and found that correlations among them were statistically significant at two time points in the school year, indicating that they are indeed related to each other. These moderate correlations indicate that these dimensions of motivation are independent, while still related. In view of the interrelationships among these constructs we characterize these dimensions of motivation as representing the construct of internal motivation for reading. We describe internal motivation as strongly related to intrinsic motivation because it comes from within the individual and it moves the individual to pursue an activity for its own sake rather than for external reasons (Ryan & Deci, 2000). However, we also view internal motivation for reading as slightly different from intrinsic motivation because of the presence of self-efficacy as a distinct, and well-researched independent construct that relates to intrinsic motivation but it is still separate from it (Bandura, 1997). Lastly, we find support for the cohesiveness of internal motivation for reading on the empirical evidence that has repeatedly shown relationships between the different dimensions that comprise our measure of internal motivation and reading comprehension at different ages. We discuss each of the dimensions of internal motivation next.

Perceived Control. Perceived control over reading refers to students' choices and perceptions of their own control over their reading-related activities (Guthrie et al., 2007). Skinner and Greene (2008, in press) describe perceived control as individuals' interpretations of the control they have over their experiences and the expectations that the self can produce desired and prevent undesired outcomes. Perceived control is often operationalized in classrooms as student choice.

Perceived control and choice are associated positively with achievement in reading (Skinner, Wellborn, & Connell, 1990; Sweet, Guthrie, & Ng, 1998).

Interest. Interest has been defined as a "relatively stable evaluative orientation toward a certain domain" (Schiefele, 1999, p. 258) and described as a personal investment in an activity (Alexander & Murphy, 1998). Student interest has been shown to correlate with cognitive processes such as deeper text processing of text learning when other factors such as text length, text genre, background knowledge, and text difficulty were statistically controlled. Interest has also been found to correlate more highly with deep-level learning than with surface-level learning from texts (Schiefele, 1996; Schiefele & Krapp, 1996).

Involvement. Involvement can be defined as a descriptor of internal motivation that refers to the feeling of being absorbed in reading activities and spending significant amounts of time reading. Involvement and interest are highly related but they are still separable from each other. Devotion of time to an activity or a task denotes the individual's involvement in it. Students who are highly involved in reading seem to create the opportunities that will support long periods of sustained reading such as organizing their activities and planning for reading time (Wigfield & Guthrie, 1997).

Self-Efficacy. In both, the general motivation literature and the literature on reading motivation, one central dimension is beliefs about one's ability, or self-efficacy. Self-efficacy refers to individuals' judgments and perceptions about whether they are capable of doing well and accomplishing a task (Bandura, 1997). Reading self-efficacy refers to individuals' judgments or self-evaluations about their ability to do well on reading activities such as reading a book, or reading a passage (Chapman et al., 2000; Schunk & Pajares, 2002; Wigfield et al., 2006). Reading self-efficacy has been found to correlate positively with different measures of reading, such as reading comprehension (Schunk & Rice, 1993), breadth of reading and amount of reading outside of school (Wigfield & Guthrie, 1997).

Social Collaboration. Social collaboration in reading has also been studied within the motivation literature (e.g., Wigfield & Guthrie, 1997). It consists of productive social interactions among learners in relation to literacy tasks such as literature circles (Almasi, 1995), or idea circles where students share conceptual ideas from different informational texts (Guthrie & McCann, 1997). Collaboration among students in reading has been correlated with dimensions of intrinsic motivation such as curiosity and reading involvement, as well as amount and breadth of reading (Wigfield & Guthrie).

Teachers' Perceptions of Student Motivation. We used teacher ratings of the different dimensions of students' motivation as our indicator of motivation, creating an overall student internal motivation score from these ratings. One of the reasons we used teacher ratings (perceptions) of students' motivation rather than student self-report was to avoid the inherent problems of social desirability of responses to self-report measures. We also wanted to build on previous research which has used teachers' observations or teachers' ratings of students' behaviors to measure motivation. For example, Onatsu-Arvilommi and Nurmi (2000) showed reciprocal relations between teachers' ratings of students' behaviors of perseverance on task and persistence for challenging tasks and the reading skills of 6 and 7 year-olds. Further, these investigators found that teachers' ratings of students' motivations predicted reading skills at a later point even after earlier levels of reading skills, overall cognitive competence, and reading-related specific competence were controlled for. More recent studies have also supported the validity of teachers' perceptions of motivation for older, later-elementary school aged children. Specifically, external observers' ratings of student internal motivation on the constructs of perceived control (choice), interest, involvement, social collaboration, and self-efficacy correlated significantly with teacher's ratings of students' internal motivation on the same constructs (Guthrie et al., 2007).

Activating Background Knowledge, Questioning, and Reading Comprehension

Reading comprehension is an activity that demands high cognitive resources (Duke & Pearson, 2002). Among these cognitive resources, the role of reading strategies in supporting reading comprehension has been documented extensively. Research has repeatedly indicated that strategy instruction increases text comprehension (Duke & Pearson; National Reading Panel, 2000; Palincsar & Brown, 1984; Pearson & Fielding, 1991; Pressley, 2000; Pressley, Wharton-McDonald, Mistretta-Hampston, & Echevarria, 1998) and it has also highlighted the predictive power of reading strategies on reading comprehension (see Pressley & Harris, 2006 for a review). In this study we focus on two specific cognitive reading strategies: activating background knowledge and student questioning in relation to text.

Background knowledge has been consistently identified as having a significant role in forming an organized, coherent mental representation of text (e.g., Kintsch, 1998, McNamara, 2001; Salmerón, Kintsch, & Cañas, 2006; van den Broek, Rapp, & Kendeou, 2005). Seminal studies indicated that comprehension is strongly influenced by the degree of overlap between the reader's background knowledge and the text content (e.g., Brown, Palincsar, & Ambruster, 1984). Later cognitive research has explored more specific roles that background knowledge plays in reading comprehension such as its interaction with text coherence for traditional printed texts and for hypertexts (McNamara, 2001; McNamara, Kintsch, Songer, & Kintsch, 1996; Salmerón et al., 2006).

Student questioning is defined as self-generated questions in relation to a text, topic, or domain (Taboada & Guthrie, 2004) and has been characterized as a self-regulatory strategy that fosters reading comprehension (Collins, Brown, & Newman, 1990; Palincsar & Brown, 1984). Research on student questioning has shown that teaching students questioning strategies, such as distinguishing between good questions from poor questions (Cohen, 1983), asking main idea versus detailed questions (Dreher & Gambrell, 1985; Palincsar & Brown, 1984; Wong & Jones, 1982), or asking questions in relation to different expository text structures (Feldt, Feldt, & Kilburg, 2002) is linked to improved reading comprehension. These instructional effects of student questioning on reading comprehension have been shown in students across the age span from third grade through college (Cohen, 1983; King & Rosenshine, 1993; Nolte & Singer, 1985; Raphael & Pearson, 1985; Scardamalia & Bereiter, 1992; Singer & Donlan, 1982; Taylor & Frye, 1992). In their extensive review of instructional studies on question generation, Rosenshine, Meister, & Chapman (1996) concluded that the majority of the authors attributed the benefits of questioning on comprehension to the fact that questioning fosters active processing of text and comprehension-monitoring. More recent work has proposed that when it comes to expository texts, students' questions enhance reading comprehension to the extent that their questions support the conceptual knowledge structure of the text (Taboada & Guthrie, 2006).

The Present Study

Even though questioning and background knowledge-activation have been studied repeatedly as cognitive variables in relation to reading comprehension, and, by the same token, several dimensions of motivation have been examined in relation to reading comprehension, these cognitive and motivational variables have not been studied simultaneously in relation to text comprehension. Given the prominent role of each of these variables, the aim of this study was to examine the relative predictive power of internal motivation, background knowledge activation, and student text-based questioning on the outcomes of reading comprehension and reading comprehension growth.

We expected that student internal motivation, and student use of cognitive strategies will independently contribute to variance in reading comprehension and reading comprehension growth. Our expectation was based on cognitive accounts of reading comprehension that highlight the role of cognitive processes in reading comprehension and on accounts of the significant role that motivation plays in reading comprehension. According to leading theorists, the goal of reading comprehension is to form an organized, coherent mental representation that is similar to the structure of the text that is being read (Gernsbacher, Varner, & Faust, 1990; Kintsch, 1998). The use of reading strategies such as background knowledge activation and student questioning contributes to the building of such a coherent mental text-representation. Further, extensive research has emphasized the positive effects that students' use of cognitive reading strategies have on reading comprehension (e.g., Duke & Pearson, 2002; Pressley & Harris, 2006; Taboada & Guthrie, 2006). Similarly and as previously stated, motivation for reading has been repeatedly related to reading comprehension and other reading achievement outcomes (e.g., see Wigfield et al. 2006 for a review).

We addressed the following two research questions:

1. Do motivation, background knowledge, and student questioning each make significant independent contributions to the variance in reading comprehension performance?
2. Do motivation, background knowledge, and student questioning each make significant independent contributions to the variance in reading comprehension growth?

Method

Participants

Fourth-grade students (N = 205) from four schools in a small mid-Atlantic city school district participated with parental permission. Table 1 shows descriptive statistics for the sample. In regards to ethnicity, our sample was somewhat more diverse than the school district as a whole, where the proportions are as follows: 8% African American, 2% Asian, 87% Caucasian, 2% Hispanic, and 1% other. With regard to students' socioeconomic status, approximately 20% qualified for free and reduced-price meals; the district-wide average was 13%.

Measures

Five measures were used in this study: (a) background knowledge, (b) student questioning, (c) multiple-text reading comprehension, (d) Gates-MacGinitie Reading Test, and (e) internal motivation. The first three measures, (a), (b), and (c) were accompanied by a researcher-designed reading packet. We administered three alternative forms of the reading packet, each with a different theme: Oceans and Forests (Form A), Ponds and Deserts (Form B), or Rivers and Grasslands (Form C). The three reading packets were parallel in content difficulty, text structure, text difficulty, length per section, number of relevant sections and distracters, and number and type of illustrations (e.g., biome versus animal illustrations). Each 75-page reading packet contained 22 sections. Reading packets contained an equal number of easy (Grades 2–3) and difficult (Grades 4–6) texts, representing

Table 1. Demographic Data of the Sample

	Students	Percent
Total N	205	100.0
Sex		
Girls	108	52.7
Boys	97	47.3
Ethnicity		
African American	35	17.1
Asian	8	3.9
Caucasian	138	67.3
Hispanic	15	7.3
Other/missing	9	4.4

nine ecological concepts and defining information on the biomes. Texts were compiled from life science trade books and they all covered the content of ecological knowledge within life science. To ensure counterbalanced administration of text packets, students within classrooms were randomly assigned one of the three reading packets so that an equal number of students within each classroom received each packet.

The two reading comprehension measures, multiple-text reading comprehension and the Gates-MacGinitie reading comprehension test were administered in September and December of the school year (Times 1 and 2). Data for the measures of background knowledge, student questioning, and internal motivation were collected in December only (Time 2) so as to examine the association of these variables with reading comprehension growth. Teachers administered assessments in their classrooms during four 60-minute periods. Each measure is described next.

Activation of Background Knowledge. The measure assessed students' activation of background knowledge on a given pair of biomes (e.g., ponds and deserts, rivers and grasslands, or oceans and forests) before reading about the topic. Students wrote what they knew about plant and animal life in their assigned biome in response to a general prompt to elicit their knowledge in the topic. This was a 15-minute, open-ended writing activity. Responses were coded using a six-level rubric (see Appendix A for the complete version of the rubric). Levels in the rubric were hierarchically organized from lower to higher levels, with lower levels including minimal or inaccurate information and higher levels including more accurate information organized in relation to a set of nine, pre-defined ecological concepts (e.g., respiration, feeding, locomotion, communication, defense, reproduction etc.). For example, at Level 1 students wrote minimal statements with very few characteristics of a biome or an organism living in the biome. These statements included neither the central ecological concepts nor definitions of the biomes. In the intermediate levels (Levels 2 and 3) students included characteristics of one or more biomes, or they presented several organisms correctly classified to one or both biomes. However, at these levels definitions and ecological concepts were not always present. At higher levels (Levels 4 and 5) students included some knowledge of ecological concepts, and relationships among different organisms and their biomes. The highest level (Level 6) was characterized by background knowledge statements that were sufficiently elaborated to denote knowledge of interrelationships among several organisms and their habitats and biomes (see Appendix A for examples of each level). Interrater agreement for 26 responses on this measure was 100% adjacent and 77% exact. A third rater resolved differences.

Student Questioning. Student questioning assessed students' self-generated questions in relation to text. After browsing the reading packet for a few minutes, students had 20 minutes to write questions about their assigned biomes and the animals and plants living in them. Questions were coded based on a four-level rubric (see Appendix B, Questioning Rubric). Question levels varied in terms of the complexity and elaboration of the requested answer. Lower level questions (Level 1) required factual or yes/no answers. Level 2 questions requested information about ecological concepts, thus they elicited at least a simple explanation about a central concept. Level 3 questions were also conceptual in their requests, but were characterized by expressing some background knowledge in the question itself. The highest question level (Level 4) consisted of questions asking about relationships among ecological concepts for a given organism or for specific relationships among organisms and their biomes or habitats.

Students wrote 0–10 questions and were given a rubric score of 1–4 for each question and a score of zero if they wrote no questions. On the basis of 10 possible questions, a student's score could range from 0–40. The mean score for each student was used for data analysis. Interrater agreement on 100 questions for 25 students was 100% for adjacent and 90% for exact coding.

Multiple-Text Reading Comprehension. This measure of comprehension assessed knowledge built from text. In an open-ended, constructed-response task, students wrote what they knew after reading the packet and taking notes on its content. They were given 30 minutes to respond to text and express their knowledge, with two statements of encouragement after 7 and 13 minutes. Written responses were coded based on the same six-level rubric that was used for the measure of background knowledge (see Appendix A). Knowledge built from text was assessed by examining organization of information in response to key concepts and supporting facts. Thus, lower levels of reading comprehension included knowledge statements with few and non-essential characteristics of biomes and organisms living in them. Whereas, higher levels of reading comprehension included biome definitions and ecological concepts with specific supporting facts organized in a coherent statement. Interrater agreement for 20 responses was 100% for adjacent and 80% for exact coding. A third rater resolved differences.

Gates-MacGinitie Reading Test. Alternative forms of the Gates-MacGinitie Reading Test, Comprehension subtest (Level 4) were administered in a 50-minute period and the extended scale score was used for data analysis. The Comprehension subtest consists of fiction and nonfiction passages from various content areas for which students answer multiple choice questions. Some of the questions require answers to information that is explicitly stated in the passage, whereas others require constructing answers based on implicit information. Across-time reliability (September to December) was $r\ (205) = .75$, $p < .001$.

Internal Motivation. The internal motivation measure used in this study consisted of five items that measured the five dimensions of internal motivation described earlier. Teachers answered five items about each student in their class. The purpose of the internal motivation measure was to assess the extent to which each student was a motivated reader within the classroom, according to the teacher's perception. Teachers rated the students in their classrooms on the following items: (a) reads favorite topics and authors (interest); (b) thinks deeply about the content of texts (involvement); (c) is a confident reader (self-efficacy); (d) enjoys discussing books with peers (social collaboration); and (e) often reads independently (perceived control in reading). Teachers rated their students in a 20-minute session, after repeated observations of students' behaviors and attitudes towards reading and reading activities. The response format was Not True (1) to Very True (5) and students received a score between 5 and 25. Cronbach's alpha reliability of all items was .90 for this sample ($N = 205$), which indicates very high reliability.

Results

The means and standard deviations of all the variables are reported in Table 2, while Table 3 reports correlations among the variables. Note that the two reading comprehension measures, the Gates-MacGinitie (GM) and the multiple-text reading comprehension (MTC), were administered at Times 1 and 2. Data for the

Table 2. Means and Standard Deviations of Variables Used in Multiple Regressions

Variable	*M*	*SD*
Gates-MacGinitie Time 1	486.75	47.37
Gates-MacGinitie Time 2	501.93	44.54
Mult Text Comp Time 1	2.85	1.14
Mult Text Comp Time 2	3.33	1.28
Background Knowledge	2.47	.85
Motivation	19.39	4.79
Questioning	1.46	.54

Notes: $n = 205$
Mult Text Comp = Multiple-Text Reading Comprehension

Table 3. Correlations Among Measures of Reading Comprehension, Background Knowledge, Motivation and Questioning

	1	2	3	4	5	6
1. Gates-MacGinitie Time 1	–					
2. Gates-MacGinitie Time 2	.75**	–				
3. Mult Text Comp Time 1	.49**	.39**	–			
4. Mult Text Comp Time 2	.46**	.50**	.41**	–		
5. Background Knowledge	.34**	.39**	.31**	.41**	–	
6. Motivation	.51**	.49**	.38**	.42**	.35**	–
7. Questioning	.36**	.40**	.21*	.27**	.27**	.20*

Notes: $n = 205$
Mult Text Comp = Multiple-Text Reading Comprehension
* $p < .01$, two-tailed
** $p < .001$, two-tailed

remaining variables were collected at Time 2. To examine our research questions, we conducted a series of multiple regression analyses, the dependent variable being reading comprehension at Time 2 (either GM or MTC) and the independent variables being motivation, background knowledge and questioning.

Predictors of Reading Comprehension Performance

Our first research question asks whether motivation, background knowledge, and student questioning accounted for significant variance in reading comprehension performance independent of one another, that is, when the other two variables were statistically controlled. To address this question, we performed six regressions (three using GM Time 2 and three using MTC Time 2) in order to enter each independent variable as the third step. All together, the three variables explained 36.3% of the variance in GM and 26.9% in MTC. When entered in the third step of the regression equation, each variable contributed a statistically significant amount of variance in both GM and MTC (Table 4). These analyses support an affirmative answer to our first research question: Each of these variables added significantly to the variance in each of two measures of reading comprehension after controlling for the other two variables in the regression equation.

Predictors of Reading Comprehension Growth

Our second research question asks whether motivation, background knowledge and questioning explained variance in reading comprehension growth. We operationalized growth by entering Time 1 reading comprehension into the regression prior to the other three independent variables. Such a test provides an extremely strong statistical control in that a large portion of the variance in the dependent variable is explained by the variable of prior reading comprehension in the first step of the regression equation. This procedure has been used in previous research (Allen, Cipielewski, & Stanovich, 1992; Onatsu-Arvilommi & Nurmi,

Table 4. Regression Statistics for Motivation, Background Knowledge, and Questioning When Entered as Third Step in Six Separate Multiple Regressions

Dependent Variable	ΔR^2	Final Beta
Gates-MacGinitie Time 2		
Motivation	.118	.37***
Background knowledge	.027	.18**
Questioning	.074	.28***
Multiple-Text Reading Comprehension Time 2		
Motivation	.076	.30***
Background knowledge	.059	.27***
Questioning	.018	.14*

Notes: The first and second steps of each equation were the two independent variables not used in the third step (Motivation, Background Knowledge, or Questioning)
* $p < .05$, ** $p < .01$, *** $p < .001$

Table 5. Regression Statistics for Motivation, Background Knowledge, and Questioning When Entered as Fourth Step in Six Separate Multiple Regressions

Dependent Variable	ΔR^2	Final Beta
Gates-MacGinitie Time 2[a]		
Motivation	.009	.11*
Background knowledge	.008	.10*
Questioning	.016	.14**
Multiple-Text Reading Comprehension Time 2[b]		
Motivation	.040	.23**
Background knowledge	.041	.23**
Questioning	.012	.12[†]

Notes: [a] The first step was Gates-MacGinitie Time 1; [b] The first step was Multiple-Text Reading Comprehension Time 1; The second and third steps of each regression were the two independent variables not used in the fourth step (Motivation, Background Knowledge, or Questioning)
[†] $p = .06$, * $p < .05$, ** $p < .01$, *** $p < .001$

2000). It is based on the assumption that when a measure of reading achievement administered at an earlier date (in this case Time 1), acts as a control for a measure of reading achievement administered at a later date (in this case Time 2), then a third variable that was associated with the later measure of reading achievement can be said to be a predictor of *growth* in reading comprehension.

Results indicated that GM Time 1 accounted for 56.1% of the variance of GM Time 2 and MTC Time 1 accounted for 16.8% of the variance in MTC Time 2. After entering Time 1 reading comprehension, background knowledge and questioning, motivation still added significantly to the variance in reading comprehension growth when measured with GM and with MTC (Table 5). Similarly, when background knowledge was entered last in the regression equation, it added significantly to growth in both measures of reading comprehension (Table 5). Lastly, when entered last, questioning contributed significantly to growth in GM, although its contribution to growth in MTC was weaker (Table 5).

Discussion

In recent years, motivational researchers have called for research that helps the field understand how motivational constructs relate to various cognitive processes, in such a way that more integrated models of motivation and cognition emerge (e.g., Pintrich, 2003). The present study contributes to extant work on the relations of motivational and cognitive processes to reading comprehension by showing how motivational and cognitive variables independently predict reading comprehension. Results support the notion that even with strong statistical controls, internal motivation, as well as the cognitive variables of background knowledge and student questioning, make significant and independent contributions to variance in two separate measures of reading comprehension. In addition, each of the predictor variables contributed significantly to *growth* in reading comprehension with the effects of previous comprehension controlled.

Thus, this study contributes to extant literature in two main ways. First, results from this study allow examining the specific contributions of internal motivation to reading comprehension, when the contributions of two important cognitive processes or strategies are simultaneously taken into account. To our knowledge this study constitutes a first attempt in this regard. Recent investigations have delved more deeply into whether specific dimensions of reading motivation contribute to growth in reading comprehension (Guthrie et al., 2007). Findings have indicated that indeed motivational constructs such as student choice, involvement, and interest predicted reading comprehension growth after controlling for students' initial reading comprehension. However, no other cognitive variables have been taken into account in these analyses. Thus, as noted by these authors in past investigations (e.g., Guthrie et al., 1999) there is an absence of studies measuring reading strategies independently of text comprehension itself, *and* measuring the simultaneous contribution of these variables and of internal motivation to reading comprehension and its growth.

We propose that it is not the predominance of cognitive processes over internal motivation or of internal motivation over cognitive processes that explain the contribution of these variables to reading comprehension. Rather, our data support the view that background knowledge, student questioning, and students' internal motivations make independent contributions to students' reading comprehension. We view these independent contributions as indicators of the importance of each of these variables in relation to reading comprehension. However, and in accordance with many theories of motivation (see Pintrich, 2003; Wigfield et al., 2006), we see internal motivation as the energizer of these linkages helping students to engage their cognitive processes and strategy use, which leads to growth in comprehension. We suggest that an internally motivated reader will be more devoted to reading and thus comprehend better. In other words, if internal motivation for reading is present and fostered in students, the cognitive processes of background knowledge activation and student questioning become more fluent, enhancing students' text comprehension. Internally motivated readers have a desire to comprehend text. This desire to understand energizes the use of reading strategies by causing the reader to be metacognitive, whether it is by asking a question, forming a summary of what has been read, or activating background knowledge to build a fuller text representation.

How are the two specific reading strategies examined in our study (i.e., activation of background knowledge and student questioning) energized by a reader's internal motivation? With respect to readers' activation of background knowledge, it is plausible that internally motivated students are better able to remember what they are reading and better at building stronger and more stable knowledge representations. Then, with further reading, internally motivated readers may be better able to connect text to their background knowledge and continue to build fuller and richer text representations.

With respect to readers' questioning, this is a reading strategy that by its characteristics denotes not only cognitive, but also motivational attributes of a reader. From a motivational standpoint, a reader who asks a relatively large number of high-quality questions conveys her curiosity, inquisitiveness, and interest in the topic and the text at hand. Research in student questioning has described this curiosity as the active, initiative-driven predisposition of learners who pose a substantial number of questions (e.g., Collins, Brown, & Newman, 1990; Graesser, McMahen, & Johnson, 1994) but this research has not necessarily linked these dimensions of questioning to specific motivational constructs. We believe such linkages can be made. For example, student self-generated questions express their interest in relation to the topic they are about to read; when given the opportunity to ask their own questions in relation to text students are empowered to (a) set their own goals for reading and (b) select and process certain types of information in preference to others, a characteristic central to the notion of interest (Hidi, 1990). Student questions also encompass possibilities for perceived-control and autonomy. By writing their own questions students become aware that they are not merely responding to the teacher's or test maker's questions, but rather they have an opportunity to decide what is of relevance in their reading and then pursue this relevant information by seeking answers to their questions. Lastly, student-generated questions can also embody opportunities for self-efficacy development, especially when students are taught to differentiate among question types or levels and are provided with opportunities to compare their current performances with past performances in generating questions and note their progress in the use of the strategy.

The second major contribution of this study to the literature rests on its instructional implications. Given that the results of this study showed that both cognitive reading strategies and internal motivation contribute independently to students' reading comprehension and its growth, educators and practitioners need to take into account the significance that both of these practices have for reading comprehension instruction. The benefits of cognitive strategies for reading comprehension have been well established (e.g., Duke & Pearson, 2002; National Reading Panel, 2000; Pressley & Harris, 2006). However, educators need also to consider how reading strategies can be taught and fostered in the light of supporting students' internal motivation for reading. In other words, students need opportunities to use reading strategies in a classroom context where internal motivation is equally supported through concrete practices. For example, summarizing a text or asking questions in relation to a text that is disconnected from students' backgrounds or for which students do not have a broader context to relate the content to (e.g., completely disconnected from units that students are learning in social studies or science) will not be as successful as providing students with texts that relate to their backgrounds, or with texts for which students can make connections to ideas learned in science or social studies (Guthrie et al., 2004, 2006). If teachers can incorporate principles that support building different aspects of internal motivation for reading they most probably have higher chances of having students use reading strategies successfully, and in turn, become better comprehenders (Guthrie et al., 2004, 2006). Further, these dimensions of motivation have been discussed extensively in terms of classroom practices that can be supported and developed by teachers in classrooms across the age span (see Stipek, 1996; Perry, Turner, & Meyer, 2006). The contributions of both cognitive and motivational factors to reading comprehension and its growth, evident in the results of this study, serve to emphasize that both are equally important in the development of students' reading comprehension and neither should be neglected in classroom instruction.

Limitations and Considerations for Future Research

The present study has some limitations that should be acknowledged. First, because the study is correlational it does not provide information about the processes involved in the observed relations of internal motivation, cognitive processes, and reading comprehension. From this study we gleaned some information about the strength of these relations and also that motivational and cognitive variables both predict comprehension, but data from this study only allows us to hypothesize about possible explanations for the relationships among these variables. Second, only two reading strategies were used in these analyses, thus future research should examine other cognitive variables in these categories. Similarly, a composite internal motivation variable was used in these analyses. In future work it would be interesting to examine the separate dimensions of internal motivation. Finally, we studied the relations of reading motivation, cognitive processes, and reading comprehension in fourth-grade students. Future studies should examine these relations developmentally, to see when they begin to emerge and whether they get stronger as children get older.

Based on these limitations and emerging trends in the field of reading motivation we consider three avenues for future research. First, we suggest that researchers should begin studying *how* motivation, cognitive processes, and reading comprehension relate. This could be done through interview studies to ascertain individuals' understandings of how their motivation relates to their cognitive effort, and reading strategies in particular. Such studies could ask students directly about their perceptions of these relations. Gaining a better understanding of the processes involved in such relations will help educators develop more effective interventions to enhance both the motivation for reading and the use of cognitive reading strategies.

Second, in this paper, we discussed ways in which motivation energizes or activates cognitive processes. Both Guthrie et al. (2004) and Pintrich (2003) suggested that cognitive processes also might influence motivation. For instance, when given an activity or task in school, students' background knowledge with respect to that activity may activate motivational processes and beliefs, such as their self-efficacy or interest. If they know a lot about the activity, they may feel more efficacious about taking on a new activity in this area, and also, may be more interested in it. Guthrie and colleagues suggested that when the students participate in reading activities which provide strong content goals and contain rich topical content, students become more motivated to engage in and to gain knowledge from these activities. Thus, future research should examine the reciprocal ways in which cognitive and motivational processes interact.

Third, our data suggest that motivation contributed to reading comprehension independently from students' background knowledge and their questioning in reading. This implies that the motivation effect was not attributable to these two powerful cognitive processes. Thus, as our data indicates, motivation may be an affective construct that directly influences reading comprehension. However, it remains possible that the motivation effect is mediated by a cognitive variable that was not measured in this study and that needs to be tested through the use of path analyses or other statistical procedures that were not used in the present study. For example, inferencing is a powerful memory-based process that was not measured, nor was comprehension monitoring, a metacognitive process. Either of these could mediate the effect of motivation on comprehension. Thus, although motivation appears to contribute independently from two cognitive processes (background knowledge and questioning strategy) there are additional cognitive variables that should be tested as potential mediators of the effect of motivation on reading comprehension.

QUESTIONS FOR REFLECTION

1. Why is it important to study motivation in specific disciplinary domains?
2. How might internal motivation for reading stimulate cognitive strategy usage for students?
3. What types of practices can teachers employ to engage internal motivation and cognitive strategy usage?
4. In what way do the findings in this study support earlier work that argues for including motivation as a factor in studies of reading comprehension?

ACKNOWLEDGEMENTS

The work reported herein was supported by the Interagency Educational Research Initiative (IERI) (Award #0089225) as administered by the National Science Foundation. The findings and opinions expressed here do not necessarily reflect the position or policies of the Interagency Educational Research Initiative, the National Science Foundation, or the University of Maryland. The authors of this manuscript thank Eileen Kramer and Vanessa Rutherford for their assistance in preparing this document.

REFERENCES

Alexander, P. A., & Jetton, T. L. (2000). Learning from text: A multidimensional and developmental perspective. In M. L. Kamil, P. B. Mosenthal, P. D. Pearson, & R. Barr (Eds.), *Handbook of reading research* (Vol. 3, pp. 285–310). Mahwah, NJ: Erlbaum.

Alexander, P. A., & Murphy, P. K. (1998). Profiling the differences in students' knowledge, interest, and strategic processing. *Journal of Educational Psychology*, *90*, 435–447.

Allen, L., Cipielewski, J., & Stanovich, K. (1992). Multiple indicators of children's reading habits and attitudes: construct validity and cognitive correlates. *Journal of Educational Psychology, 84*, 489–503.

Almasi, J. (1995). The nature of fourth graders' sociocognitive conflicts in peer-led and teacher-led discussions of literature. *Reading Research Quarterly, 30*, 314–351.

Baker, L., & Wigfield, A. (1999). Dimensions of children's motivation for reading and their relationships to reading activity and reading achievement. *Reading Research Quarterly, 34*, 452–477.

Bandura, A. (1997). *Self-efficacy: The exercise of control.* New York: W. H. Freeman.

Brown, A., Palincsar, A. S., & Ambruster, B. (1984). Inducing comprehension-fostering activities in interactive learning situations. In H. Mandl, N. Stein, & T. Trabasso (Eds.), *Learning and comprehension of texts* (pp. 255–287). Hillsdale, NJ: Erlbaum.

Chapman, J. W., & Tunmer, W. E. (1995). Development of young children's reading self-concepts: An examination of emerging subcomponents and their relationship with reading achievement. *Journal of Educational Psychology, 87*, 154–167.

Chapman, J. W., Tunmer, W. E., & Prochnow, J. E. (2000). Early reading-related skills and performance, reading self-concept, and the development of academic self-concept: A longitudinal study. *Journal of Educational Psychology, 92*, 703–708.

Cohen, R. (1983). Self-generated questions as an aid to reading comprehension. *The Reading Teacher, 36*, 770–775.

Collins, A., Brown, J. S., & Newman, S. E. (1990). Cognitive apprenticeship: Teaching the crafts of reading, writing, and mathematics. In L. Resnick (Ed.), *Knowing, learning, and instruction: Essays in honor of Robert Glaser* (pp. 453–494). Hillsdale, NJ: Lawrence Erlbaum Associates.

Dreher, M. J., & Gambrell, L. B. (1985). Teaching children to use a self-questioning strategy for studying expository prose. *Reading Improvement, 22*, 2–7.

Duke, N. K., & Pearson, P. D. (2002). Effective practices for developing reading comprehension. In A. E. Farstrup & S. J. Samuels (Eds.), *What research has to say about reading instruction* (3rd ed., pp. 205–242). Newark, DE: International Reading Association.

Eccles, J. S., & Wigfield, A. (2002). Motivational beliefs, values, and goals. *Annual Review of Psychology, 53*, 109–132.

Feldt, R. C., Feldt, R. A., & Kilburg, K. (2002). Acquisition, maintenance, and transfer of a questioning strategy in second-and third-grade students to learn from science textbooks. *Reading Psychology, 23*, 181–198.

Gernsbacher, M. A., Varner, K. R., & Faust, M. E. (1990). Investigating differences in general comprehension skill. Journal of Experimental Psychology: *Learning, Memory, and Cognition, 16*, 430–445.

Gottfried, A. E. (1990). Academic intrinsic motivation in young elementary school children. *Journal of Educational Psychology, 82*, 525–538.

Gottfried, A. W., Cook, C. R., Gottfried, A. E., & Morris, P. E. (2005). Educational characteristics of adolescents with gifted academic intrinsic motivation: A longitudinal investigation from school entry through early adulthood. *Gifted Child Quarterly, 49*, 172–186.

Graesser, A. C., McMahen, C. L., & Johnson, B. K. (1994). Question asking and answering. In M. A. Gernsbacher (Ed.), *Handbook of psycholinguistics* (pp. 517–538). San Diego, CA: Academic Press.

Guthrie, J. T., Hoa, A. L. W., Wigfield, A., Tonks, S. M., Humenick, N. M., & Littles, E. (2007). Reading motivation and reading comprehension growth in the later elementary years. *Contemporary Educational Psychology, 32*, 282–313.

Guthrie, J. T., & McCann, A. D. (1997). Characteristics of classrooms that promote motivations and strategies for learning. In J. T. Guthrie & W. Wigfield (Eds.), *Reading engagement: Motivating readers through integrated instruction* (pp. 128–148). Newark, DE: International Reading Association.

Guthrie, J. T., Wigfield, A., Barbosa, P., Perencevich, K. C., Taboada, A., Davis, M., et al. (2004). Increasing reading comprehension and engagement through concept-oriented reading instruction. *Journal of Educational Psychology, 96*(3), 1–21.

Guthrie, J. T., Wigfield, A., Humenick, N. M., Perencevich, K. C., Taboada, A., & Barbosa, P. (2006). Influences of stimulating tasks on reading motivation and comprehension. *Journal of Educational Research, 99*, 232–245.

Guthrie, J. T., Wigfield, A., Metsala, J. L., & Cox, K. E. (1999). Motivational and cognitive predictors of text comprehension and reading amount. *Scientific Studies of Reading, 3*, 231–256.

Hidi, S. (1990). Interest and its contribution as a mental resource for learning. *Review of Educational Research, 60*, 549–571.

King, A., & Rosenshine, B. (1993). Effects of guided cooperative questioning on children's knowledge construction. *Journal of Experimental Education, 61*, 127–148.

Kintsch, W. (1998). *Comprehension: A paradigm for cognition.* New York: Cambridge University Press.

Meece, J. L., & Miller, S. D. (1999). A longitudinal analysis of elementary school students' achievement goals in literacy activities. *Contemporary Educational Psychology, 26*, 454–480.

Meece, J. L., & Miller, S. D. (2001). Changes in elementary school children's achievement goals for reading and writing: Results of a longitudinal and an intervention study. *Scientific Studies of Reading, 3*, 207–229.

McNamara, D. S. (2001). Reading both high-coherence and low-coherence texts: Effects of text sequence and prior knowledge. *Canadian Journal of Experimental Psychology, 55*, 51–62.

McNamara, D. S., Kintsch, E., Songer, N. B., & Kintsch, W. (1996). Text coherence, background knowledge and levels of understanding in learning from text. *Cognition & Instruction, 14*, 1–44.

National Reading Panel. (2000). *Teaching children to read: An evidence-based assessment of the scientific research literature on reading and its implications for reading instruction*. Washington, DC: National Institute of Child Health and Human Development (Tech. Rep. No. 00-4769).

Nolte, R. Y., & Singer, H. (1985). Active comprehension: Teaching a process of reading comprehension and its effects on reading achievement. *Reading Teacher, 39*, 24–31.

Onatsu-Arvilommi, T., & Nurmi, J. (2000). The role of task-avoidant and task-focused behavior in the development of reading and mathematical skills during the first school year: a cross-lagged longitudinal study. *Journal of Educational Psychology*, 2, 478–491.

Palincsar, A. S., & Brown, A. L. (1984). Reciprocal teaching of comprehension-fostering and comprehension-monitoring activities. *Cognition and Instruction*, 2, 117–175.

Pearson, P. D., & Fielding, L. (1991). Comprehension instruction. In R. Barr, M. L. Kamil, P. Mosenthal, & P. D. Pearson (Eds.), *Handbook of reading research* (pp. 815–860). White Plains, NY: Longman.

Perry, N. E., Turner, J. C., & Meyer, D. K. (2006). Classroom contexts for motivating learners. In P. Alexander & P. Winnie (Eds.), *Handbook of educational psychology* (2nd ed., pp. 327–348). Mahwah, NJ: Lawrence Erlbaum Associates.

Pintrich, P. R. (2003). A motivational science perspective on the role of student motivation in learning and teaching contexts. *Journal of Educational Psychology, 95*, 667–686.

Pintrich, P. R., Marx, R. W., & Boyle, R. A. (1993). Beyond cold conceptual change: The role of motivational beliefs and classroom contextual factors in the process of conceptual change. *Review of Educational Research, 63*, 167–199.

Pressley, M. (2000). What should comprehension instruction be the instruction of? In M. L. Kamil, P. B. Mosenthal, & P. D. Pearson (Eds.), *Handbook of reading research* (pp. 545–561). Mahwah, NJ: Erlbaum.

Pressley, M., Wharton-McDonald, R., Mistretta-Hampton, J. M., & Echevarria, M. (1998). The nature of literacy instruction in ten grade 4/5 classrooms in upstate New York. *Scientific Studies of Reading*, 2, 159–194.

Pressley, G. M., & Harris, K. H. (2006). Cognitive strategies instruction: From basic research to classroom instruction. In P. A. Alexander & P. H. Winne (Eds.), *Handbook of educational psychology* (2nd ed., pp. 265–286). Mahwah, NJ: Erlbaum.

Raphael, T. E., & Pearson, P. D. (1985). Increasing students' awareness of sources of information for answering questions. *American Educational Research Journal*, 22, 217–235.

Rosenshine, B., Meister, C., & Chapman, S. (1996). Teaching students to generate questions: A review of the intervention studies. *Review of Educational Research, 66*, 181–122.

Ryan, R. M., & Deci, E. L. (2000). Intrinsic and extrinsic motivations: Classic definitions and new directions. *Contemporary Educational Psychology, 25*, 54–67.

Salmerón, L., Kintsch, W., & Cañas, J. J. (2006). Reading strategies and prior knowledge in learning from hypertext. *Memory and Cognition, 34*, 1157–1171.

Scardamalia, M., & Bereiter, C. (1992). Text-based and knowledge-based questioning by children. *Cognition and Instruction, 9*, 177–199.

Schiefele, U. (1996). Topic interest, text representation, and quality of experience. *Contemporary Educational Psychology, 21*, 3–18.

Schiefele, U. (1999). Interest and learning from text. *Scientific Studies of Reading*, 3, 257–279.

Schiefele, U., & Krapp, A. (1996). Topic interest and free recall of expository test. *Learning and Individual Differences, 8*, 141–160.

Schunk, D. H., & Pajares, F. (2002). The development of academic self-efficacy. In A. Wigfield & J. S. Eccles (Eds.), *Development of achievement motivation* (pp. 16–32). San Diego, CA: Academic Press.

Schunk, D. H., & Rice, J. M. (1993). Strategy fading and progress feedback: Effects on self-efficacy and comprehension among students receiving remedial reading services. *Journal of Special Education, 27*, 257–276.

Singer, H., & Donlan, D. (1982). Active comprehension: Problem-solving schema with question generation for comprehension of complex short stories. *Reading Research Quarterly, 17*, 166–186.

Skinner, E., & Greene, T. (2008). Perceived control: Engagement, coping, and development. In T. L. Good (Ed.), *21st Century education: A reference handbook*. Newbury Park: Sage Publications (in press).

Skinner, E. A., Wellborn, J. G., & Connell, J. P. (1990). What it takes to do well in school and whether I've got it: A process model of perceived control and children's engagement and achievement in school. *Journal of Educational Psychology, 82*, 22–32.

Stipek, D. J. (1996). Motivation and instruction. In D. Berliner & R. Calfee (Eds.), *Handbook of educational psychology*. New York: Macmillan.

Sweet, A. P., Guthrie, J. T., & Ng, M. M. (1998). Teacher perceptions and student reading motivation. *Journal of Educational Psychology, 90*, 210–223.

Taboada, A., & Guthrie, J. T. (2004). Growth of cognitive strategies for reading comprehension. In J. T. Guthrie, A. Wigfield, & K. C. Perencevich (Eds.), *Motivating reading comprehension:*

Concept-oriented reading instruction (pp. 273–306). Mahwah, NJ: Erlbaum.

Taboada, A., & Guthrie, J. T. (2006). Contributions of student questioning and prior knowledge to construction of knowledge from reading information text. *Journal of Literacy Research, 38,* 1–35.

Taylor, B. M., & Frye, B. J. (1992). Comprehension strategy instruction in the intermediate grades. *Reading Research and Instruction, 32,* 39–48.

Turner, J. (1995). The influence of classroom contexts on young children's motivation for literacy. *Reading Research Quarterly, 30,* 410–441.

Unrau, N., & Schlackman, J. (2006). Motivation and its relation to reading achievement in an urban middle school. *Journal of Educational Research, 100,* 81–101.

van den Broek, P., Rapp, D. N., & Kendeou, P. (2005). Integrating memory-based and constructionist processes in accounts of reading comprehension. *Discourse Processes, 39,* 299–316.

Wang, J. H. Y., & Guthrie, J. T. (2004). Modeling the effects of intrinsic motivation, extrinsic motivation, amount of reading and past reading achievement on text comprehension between U.S. and Chinese students. *Reading Research Quarterly, 39,* 162–186.

Wigfield, A., Eccles, J. S., Schiefele, U., Roeser, R., & Davis-Kean, P. (2006). Development of achievement motivation. In W. Damon (Series Ed.) and N. Eisenberg (Volume Ed.), *Handbook of child psychology* (6th ed., Vol. 3, pp. 933–1002). New York: Wiley.

Wigfield, A., & Guthrie, J. T. (1997). Relations of children's motivation for reading to the amount and breadth of their reading. *Journal of Educational Psychology, 89,* 420–432.

Wigfield, A., Guthrie, J. T., Tonks, S., & Perencevich, K. (2004). Children's motivation for reading: Domain specificity and instructional influences. *Journal of Educational Research, 97,* 299–309.

Wong, B. Y., & Jones, W. (1982). Increasing metacomprehension in learning disabled and normally achieving students through self-questioning training. *Learning Disability Quarterly, 5,* 228–240.

APPENDIX A

Conceptual Knowledge Rubric

Background Knowledge and Multiple-Text Reading Comprehension Assessment

Level 1: Facts and associations—simple.

Students present a few characteristics of a biome or an organism.

Example: In grasslands are lions, tigers, zebras.

Level 2: Facts and associations—extended.

Students correctly classify several organisms, often in lists, with limited definitions.

Example: Animals live in a desert. They like to live there because it's nice and warm. Ducks like to drink water in the pond. They are different because one of them is wet and the other dry. Snake and bears, birds, live in the deserts. They help each other live by giving the animals water and some food that's what the mothers do.

Level 3: Concepts and evidence—simple.

Students present well-formed definitions of biomes with many organisms correctly classified, accompanied by one or two simple concepts with minimal supporting evidence.

Example: Deserts are different than ponds because deserts have a little bit of water and ponds have a lot of water. The animals that live in a pond are snakes, fish, bugs, ducks, and plants. The plants that live in a pond are grass and seaweed. The animals and plants that live in a desert are rattlesnakes, foxes, rabbits, owls, woodpeckers. The plants that live in a desert are cactus, little grass, small trees. Some of the animals eat plants. The plants eat the food in the soil and the little rain. The animals help the plants live by when the animals step on the ground it makes it a little soft and it is easy for the plants to grow. The plants help the animals by bringing some animals close so other animals can catch them and eat them. The animals also help the plant when some of the bugs that drink the plants nectar carry things from one plant to another.

Level 4: Concepts and evidence—extended.
Students display several concepts of survival illustrated by specific organisms with their physical characteristics and behavioral patterns.

Example: Some snakes, which live in the desert, squeeze their prey to death and then eat them. This is called a deadly hug. Bright markings on some snakes are warnings to stay away. In the desert two male jackrabbits fight for a female. Some deserts are actually cold and rocky. Both deserts' hot or cold, it barely ever rain and if it does it comes down so fast and so hard it just runs off and does not sink into the ground.

Level 5: Patterns of relationships—simple.
Students convey knowledge of relationships among concepts of survival supported by descriptions of multiple organisms and their habitats.

Example: A river is different from grassland because a river is body of water and grassland is land. A river is fast flowing. Grasshoppers live in grasslands. A grasshopper called a locust lays its egg in a thin case. One case could carry 100 eggs. The largest herbivores in the grassland are an elephant. In the African savanna meat-eats prey on grazing animals, such as zebra. Many animals live in grasslands. The river is a home to many animals. In just a drop of river water millions of animals can be living in it. Many fish live in the river. Many birds fly above the grasslands and rivers. A river is called freshwater because it has no salt in it.

Level 6: Patterns of relationships—extended.
Students show complex relationships among concepts of survival emphasizing interdependence among organisms.

Example: River and grassland are alike and different. Rivers have lots of aquatic animals. Grasslands have mammals and birds. Rivers don't have many plants but grassland have trees and lots of grass. Rivers have lots of animal like fish trout and stickle backs. They also have insects and mammals, like the giant water bug and river otters. Grasslands usually have lions, zebras, giraffes, antelope, gazelles, and birds. In rivers the food chain starts with a snail. Insects and small animals eat the snail. Then fish eat the small animals and insects. Then bigger animals like the heron and bears eat the fish. Snails also eat algae with grows form the sun. In the grass lands the sun grown the grass. Animals like gazelle, antelope, and zebra eat the grass. Then animals like lions eat them. This is called a food chain of what eats what. In a way the animals are helping each other live. Animals have special things for uses. Otters have closable noses and ears. Gills let fish breath under water. Some fish lay thousands of egg because lot of animals like eating fish eggs. Some animals have camouflage. Swallow tail butter fly larva look like bird droppings. That is what I know and about grasslands rivers.

APPENDIX B

Questioning Rubric

Level 1: Factual information

Questions are simple in form and request a simple answer, such as a single fact. Questions are a request for a factual proposition. They are based on naïve concepts about the world rather than disciplined understanding of the subject matter Questions refer to relatively trivial, non-defining characteristics of organisms (plants and animals), ecological concepts or biomes.

Examples: How big are bats? Do sharks eat trash? How much do bears weigh? Are there crabs in a river? How old do orangutans get? How big are grasslands? How many rivers are there in the world?

Level 2: Simple description

Questions are a request for a global statement about an ecological concept or an important aspect of survival. Questions may also request general information that denotes a link between the biome and organisms that live in it. The question may be simple, yet the answer may contain multiple facts and generalizations. The answer may be a moderately complex description or an explanation of an animal's behavior or physical characteristics. An answer may also be a set of distinctions necessary to account for all the forms of species.

Examples: How do sharks have babies? How do birds fly? How do bats protect themselves? What kinds of sharks are in the ocean? What kind of waters do sharks live in? How far do polar bears swim in the ocean?

Level 3: Complex explanation

Questions are a request for an elaborated explanation about a specific aspect of an ecological concept with accompanying evidence. The question probes the ecological concept by using knowledge about survival or animal biological characteristics. Questions may also request information that denote a link between the biome and organisms that live in it. Questions use defining features of biomes to probe for the influence those attributes have on life in the biome. The question is complex and the expected answer requires elaborated propositions, general principles and supporting evidence about ecological concepts.

Examples: Why do sharks sink when they stop swimming? Why do sharks eat things that bleed? How do polar bears keep warm in their den? Why do sharks have 3 rows of teeth? Why is the polar bear's summer coat a different color? Do fruit-eating bats have really good eyes? Do owls that live in the desert hunt at night? Why do Elf Owls make their homes in cactuses?

Level 4: Pattern of relationships

Questions display science knowledge coherently expressed to probe the interrelationship of concepts, the interaction with the biome or interdependencies of organisms. Questions are a request for principled understanding with evidence for complex interactions among multiple concepts and possibly across biomes. Knowledge is used to form a focused inquiry into a specific aspect of a biological concept and an organism's interaction with its' biome. Answers may consist of a complex network of two or more concepts.

Examples: Do snakes use their fangs to kill their enemies as well as poison their prey? Do polar bears hunt seals to eat or feed their babies? Why do salmon go to the sea to mate and lay eggs in the river? How do animals and plants in the desert help each other? How are grassland animals and river animals the same and different? Is the polar bear at the top of the food chain?

CHAPTER 25

Toward a More Anatomically Complete Model of Literacy Instruction: A Focus on African American Male Adolescents and Texts

Alfred W. Tatum, University of Illinois at Chicago

According to many standardized assessments, educators in the U.S. continually fail to advance the literacy development and academic achievement of African American male adolescents, particularly the ones who live and go to schools in high-poverty communities. There is an absence of interdisciplinary depth, theoretical grounding, and focus on responsive pedagogy required to provide effective literacy instruction for these young men. For example, when policymakers plan literacy reforms, they often do not consider research on resilience (Henderson & Milstein, 2003; Werner & Smith, 1992), life outcome perspectives (Mizell, 1999), the relationship between masculinity and schooling (Gilbert & Gilbert, 1998; Young, 2000), the relationship between neighborhood quality and schooling (Ceballo, McLoyd, & Toyokawa, 2004), and how social processes of race, class, and gender are interwoven with literacy (Greene & Abt-Perkins, 2003; Lesko, 2000; Swanson, Cunningham, & Spencer, 2003). In efforts to reverse trends of poor reading outcomes among this group, the multiple in-school and out-of-school contexts that African American male adolescents have to negotiate are often ignored when developing or adopting instructional plans, selecting curricula, or examining students' placement in low-level or remedial courses.

My experience over the past fourteen years as a teacher, researcher, and professional developer in middle and high schools leads me to assert that many school leaders are not openly and critically discussing issues of race, language, gender, social class, and adolescent literacy. Discussion of race and social class creates tension in schools, and is often devoid of the critical analysis such a dialogue deserves. I am often asked to explain why I feel the need to write about African American adolescent males when the data are clear about their dismal reading achievement and the deleterious outcomes these young men experience in school and society. It is because there is an urgent need to address both the literacy needs and life outcomes of African American male adolescents in order to improve the conditions of these young men in school and society. It has become perfunctory to describe African American males using high school dropout,

This chapter is reprinted from *Harvard Educational Review*, 78(1), 155–180.

incarceration, and unemployment statistics, without also providing the necessary careful analysis done by social scientists and educators to unearth the root causes of these outcomes (Roderick, 1994). Questions related to educational malfeasance toward poor adolescents, particularly African American males, are not asked, and our educational discourse suffers as a result.

In this article, I describe the need for a more anatomically complete model of literacy instruction for African American male adolescents. After describing the model, I explain how the adolescent literacy crisis and its framing can potentially interrupt the implementation of such a model for young men of color. The last section of the article focuses on a qualitative case study with a sixteen-year-old African American male and highlights the centrality of meaningful texts to any literacy model that aims to advance the literacy development of African American male adolescents.

By expressly focusing on African American males in this article, I do not intend to undermine the significance of addressing the literacy needs of *all* adolescents in the United States, where an adolescent literacy crisis has been identified (Biancarosa & Snow, 2006). A false polarization is often evoked when efforts are aimed specifically to address the literacy needs of African American male adolescents. It is often intimated that a concentrated focus on African American males suggests that the literacy needs of African American adolescent girls or other adolescents are less important or do not require the same attention. This is simply not the case. It is the case, however, that literacy reform efforts aimed at improving African American male adolescents' reading achievement and life outcomes have been woefully inadequate and have underestimated the depth of their literacy needs in both racially segregated and racially integrated schools. Therefore, I have been working for the past eight years to develop a model for advancing the literacy development of African American male adolescents. Though the model is theoretically grounded in the literacy needs of these young men, it does not exclude other populations and may even be useful in promoting the literacy development of all students.

My work began as an eighth-grade social studies teacher on Chicago's South Side, working with struggling adolescent readers. In trying to improve their reading achievement, I was confronted with myriad challenges, including students' accumulation of failure, poor concepts of reading, and lack of self-efficacy stemming from years of ineffective instruction. Offsetting the resistance toward reading among my African American male students was particularly challenging. Four of the eighth-grade boys I taught during my third year of teaching simply refused to read. I began to engage their voices as a teacher-researcher to find ways to break down the barriers that disenfranchised these boys, who had been assigned to a low-level reading track (Tatum, 2000). Over time, I realized that the four major barriers to their engagement with reading were the fear of being publicly embarrassed if they failed in front of their peers, their limited vocabulary knowledge, the lack of attention their former teachers placed on reading books and engaging with texts, and their perceptions that teachers expected them to fail.

Since that time, I have conducted two qualitative case studies exploring the root causes of reluctance among some African American male adolescents. The first was a case study of a professional development initiative aimed at identifying the aspects of professional development that teachers found most useful for advancing the literacy development of seventh- and eighth-grade African American students (Tatum, 2002, 2003). The second was a case study of an African American teenage male, in which I sought to identify texts and textual characteristics he found effective for becoming a better reader and shaping his own identity (Tatum, in press). Some aspects of the latter study are described in this article. Currently, I am in my nineteenth month of working to help close the reading achievement gap in a large, racially integrated high school where the African American males are among the lowest-performing readers and have not made Adequate Yearly Progress under No Child Left Behind in the past five years. Additionally, my own status as an African American male who was educated in several of Chicago's inner-city schools in high-poverty neighborhoods, and who later became a teacher and reading specialist in similar communities, informs the call I make to move toward a more anatomically complete model of literacy instruction for adolescents (Tatum, 2003, 2005).

The more anatomically complete model of literacy instruction that I propose integrates effective instructional practices informed by the extant reading research on adolescent literacy (Alvermann, Hinchman, Moore, Phelps, & Waff, 2006; Biancarosa & Snow, 2006; Jetton & Dole, 2004; Rush, Eakle, & Berger; 2007), by research on African American males (Fashola, 2005; Polite & Davis, 1999), and by research on boys and literacy (Brozo, 2002; Smith & Wilhelm, 2002). My model also gives attention to multiple conceptualizations of literacies and identities, some of which are situated within power structures such as class, gender, and race (Collins & Blot, 2003; Street, 1995). Finally, it aims to support teachers in structuring their students' day-to-day activities in a way that maximizes their engagement with meaningful, relevant texts.

As displayed in Figure 1, the model I am advancing has multiple theoretical, instructional, and professional development strands. *Theoretical strands* constitute the head of the model and focus on defining the role of literacy instruction for adolescents in their present-day contexts, creating curriculum orientations that empower them, and using a culturally responsive approach to literacy teaching. Each of these strands is glaringly omitted in many school literacy reform efforts. The *instructional strands* comprise the body of the model and focus on research-based reading practices. The *professional development strands* serve as the legs of the model and focus on in-school teacher professional development and teacher preparation.

At present, most literacy reform efforts focus primarily on the instructional strands (body), and thus constitute what I refer to as an anatomically *incomplete* model of literacy instruction. For example, Chicago Public Schools, the third-largest school district in the United States, uses a literacy reform framework that focuses primarily on word study, fluency, comprehension, and writing. Yet

Figure 1. A More Anatomically Complete Model of Literacy Instruction

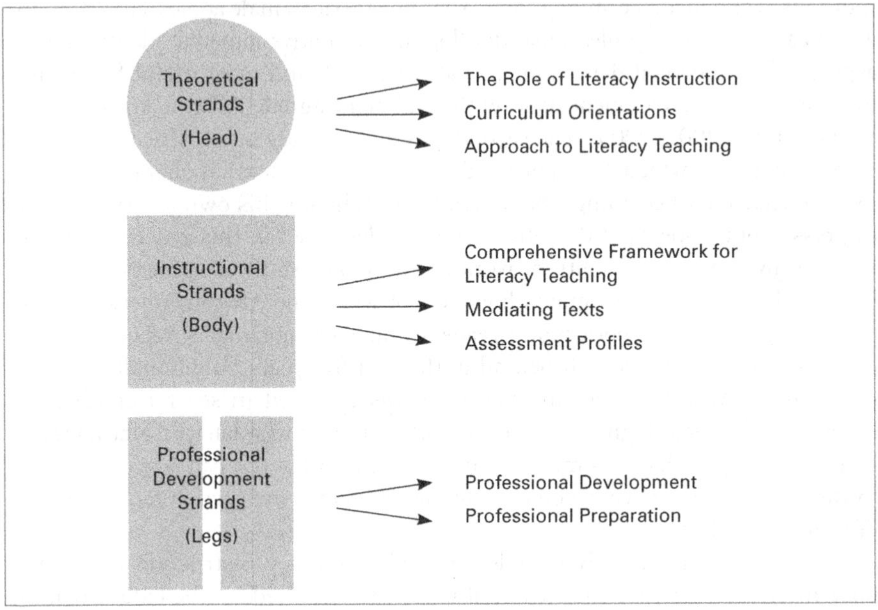

according to recent National Assessment of Educational Progress (NAEP) data, only 17 percent of Chicago's eighth-grade students scored at a proficient level in reading, performing better than only three large urban districts in the United States. While reading strategies offer much-needed support for struggling adolescent readers (Heller & Greenleaf, 2007), the corpus of these strategies aimed at improving the reading achievement of African American adolescent males remains insufficient.

Many teachers who have a strong foundational knowledge for teaching reading still experience difficulty teaching African American male adolescents who attend schools in high-poverty communities. During an e-mail exchange, a veteran educator informed me that she had more than twenty-five years of experience teaching reading strategies but found she was ineffective with the African American ninth-grade males in her classes. She acknowledged that she did not have sufficient competence with other components of literacy instruction, which I refer to here as "vital signs," that could contribute to her effectiveness with African American male adolescents.

Multiple Vital Signs of Literacy Instruction

A more anatomically complete model of literacy instruction pays attention to four categories of literacy vital signs—vital signs of *reading*, vital signs of *readers*, vital signs of *reading instruction*, and vital signs of *educators*—all essential elements for improving students' reading achievement. The vital signs refer to aspects of instruction that should be cultivated in classrooms and tailored to the characteristics of educators and students. As shown in Table 1, the vital signs categories correspond to four parallel gaps affecting students' literacy-related outcomes: a reading achievement gap, a relationship gap, a rigor gap, and a responsiveness gap.

The vital signs of *reading* provide the necessary working tools (e.g., decoding, self-questioning and comprehension-monitoring techniques, summarizing, and other strategies) that students need to handle texts independently, and they constitute a necessary minimum set of tools for all literacy efforts. Attending to the vital signs of reading by focusing on students' reading skills is important in addressing the reading achievement gap. The vital signs of *readers* direct educators' attention to students' lived experiences, both in school and outside of school, and are useful for considering ways to improve the human condition. When educators attend to the vital signs of readers—the everyday lives of the students they teach—they begin to build supportive relationships with their students and thereby address the relationship gap.

The third set of vital signs, those of *reading instruction*, are intimately related to rescuing and refining the significance of literacy teaching for adolescents in this current era of accountability. In other words, they are useful for conceptualizing the rationale for literacy teaching and enhancing academic rigor in the classroom. Attention to the vital signs of reading instruction should cause educators to reflect on texts, quality instructional supports, assessments, and the potential uses of technology in an attempt to shape rigorous learning experiences for adolescents.

Table 1. Multiple Vital Signs of Literacy Instruction

	Reading	Readers	Reading Instruction	Educators
Rationale	Providing the working tools (What)	Improving the human condition (Why)	Refining the significance of literacy teaching (How)	Interacting with students, not scorecards of achievement (Who)
Vital signs	Word knowledge Fluency Strategy knowledge Writing Language proficiency	Home life Culture Environment Language Economics	Quality instructional support Text Context Assessment Technology	Competence Caring Commitment Culpability
Aims to correct	Reading achievement gap	Relationship gap	Rigor gap	Responsiveness gap

The vital signs of *educators* are related to shaping educational contexts characterized by caring, commitment, competence, and culpability. Adolescents benefit when they know that they belong in the learning environment, when they experience psychosocial membership, and when they feel they are in the presence of an adult advocate who is not going to give up on them (Goodenow, 1993; Price, 2000). In this sense, attention to the vital signs of educators is a critical step toward addressing the responsiveness gap. Moving toward a more anatomically complete model of literacy instruction that pays attention to these vital signs requires an understanding of the current adolescent literacy crisis and how African American adolescent males are situated within it.

Overview of the Adolescent Literacy Crisis

The term *adolescent literacy crisis* is the current descriptor used in the United States to encapsulate the more than two-thirds of all eighth- through twelfth-grade students who are reading below a proficient level. Reading achievement is clearly marked along economic, ethnic, and gender lines. The confluence of historical antecedents, social class, community membership, language, race, ethnicity, and gender; their interplay with institutional structures (e.g., schools and government); and the shaping of these institutional structures by educators and policymakers have contributed to a crisis in literacy education that is difficult to unravel. Although this crisis begins to take form in the earlier grades, it becomes more pronounced during adolescence and contributes to the fact that more than 7,000 U.S. students drop out of high school each school day (Alliance for Excellent Education, 2006).

The landscape of adolescent literacy development and proposed solutions to the adolescent literacy crisis in the United States are influenced by, at minimum, seven elements (see Table 2). The market economy, advances in technology, and globalization have a gripping influence on the politicized discourse about adolescent literacy. The roles of reading and writing for adolescents, particularly high school students, are viewed in direct relationship with the economy. According to a recent report by the National Center on Education and the Economy (2006):

> This is a world in which a very high level of preparation of reading, writing, speaking, mathematics, science, literature, history, and the arts will be an indispensable foundation for everything that comes after for most members of the workforce. It is a world in which comfort with ideas and abstractions is the passport to a good job, in which creativity and innovation are the key to a good life, in which levels of education—a very different kind of education than most of us have had—are going to be the only security there is. (p. 6)

Although an economic focus and attention to twenty-first-century literacy skills have become paramount in the national dialogue, we lack a clear definition of literacy instruction for adolescents in the United States that will translate into successful classroom practice. Without this clear definition, overwhelming and embarrassing inconsistency in literacy instruction occurs and can be expected to

Table 2. Seven Critical Elements Shaping the Landscape of Literacy Instruction in the United States

Accountability NCLB AYP NAEP	Accountability has a gripping influence on the national dialogue about adolescent literacy. Discussions and literacy reform efforts are framed by No Child Left Behind, Adequate Yearly Progress, and National Assessment of Educational Progress outcomes.
Standards Professional organizations States Content areas	Professional organizations such as the International Reading Association and the U.S. states have developed standards to shape literacy practices. These standards are often found in lesson plans and are made visible in classrooms during instruction, as mandated by school and/or district administrators.
Teacher preparation and teacher professional development	Teacher education programs are increasingly held accountable for poor adolescent literacy, while at the same time there has been a proliferation of teacher professional development focused on literacy instruction across the United States. Increasingly, there are more literacy coaches assigned to middle schools and high schools to support struggling readers.
Gap focus Reading achievement gap Racial achievement gap Opportunity gap Preparation gap	Closing the reading achievement gap between White students and students of color has been discussed for the past forty years. Increasingly, schools are gauging their success by their ability to close the reading achievement gap. The gap is often discussed in terms of race, opportunity, or preparation.
Diversity Shifting demographics English-language learners (ELLs)	Schools are experiencing major shifts in their demographics: Urban areas become destabilized as students move to surrounding suburban school districts, and increased numbers of immigrants to the United States have led to a dramatic increase in the number of ELLs in America's classrooms.
Social class Poverty Parenting	Reading data are aggregated to examine the performance of students from homes with low socioeconomic status. Research also looks at the effect of parents' levels of education on students' literacy.
Race Impact Dialogue	Although the dialogue is not robust in literacy reform efforts, there is a racialized component to the gap in reading achievement. There is a reading achievement gap between middle-income African Americans and middle-income Whites.

continue across schools. Literacy experiences and the ways that literacy instruction is conceptualized and practiced are characteristically different for adolescents attending schools in economically depressed environments and for adolescents who come from affluent homes and attend schools in affluent neighborhoods. The same differences exist in mixed-income school environments in which students' literacy experiences and academic schedules are governed by reading achievement data. Arguably, shortsighted or quick-fix solutions to the adolescent literacy crisis will continue to result in different literacy experiences and life-outcome trajectories for adolescents on opposite ends of the economic continuum.

Situating the African American Adolescent Male in the Crisis

The focus on economic projections oversimplifies the role of literacy education in the lives of African American males, who constitute 7 percent of the school-aged population. First, an economic focus fails to account for the day-to-day realities of African American males, particularly the young men living in high-poverty communities where long-term economic projections are overshadowed by immediate concerns like violence, classism, and poor schooling—conditions that cause many of them to feel dehumanized and devalued. Literacy education has to have a strong gravitational pull for African American male adolescents in their present-day contexts. Externally driven rationales for literacy instruction rooted in macrosociological concerns—such as taking on the challenges of life in a global economy, or stabilizing communities that are imploding because of concentrated poverty—fail to interrupt students' existing "maladaptive solutions" (Spencer, 1999).

Unfortunately, the African American male presence in reading research is dismal (Lindo, 2006). Up to this point, studies involving African American males have focused on factors that characterize these young men as *at-risk*. These studies have also ignored their racialized and gendered identities and have focused on comparing their academic outcomes to those of other students (Davis, 2001; Gilbert & Gilbert, 1998; Price, 2000). A meta-analysis is needed that examines how instructional practices, texts, and classroom contexts can be shaped to advance the literacy development of African American male adolescents, particularly the ones who experience difficulty with school-based reading (Tatum & Fisher, in press). The current absence of adequate research is contributing to policy, curricular, and pedagogical misalignments that are not effective for these young men. The lack of research on African American male adolescents contributes to three major issues:

1. Many educators are failing to increase African American male adolescents' engagement with texts, and subsequently, their overall reading achievement scores.
2. Specific texts and text characteristics that engage African American adolescent males are strikingly absent from the curriculum (Tatum, 2006).

3. Educators find it difficult to use texts to counter in-school and out-of-school context-related issues that heighten the vulnerability level of African American males.

The goals of literacy for African American male adolescents remain trapped in an achievement-score quagmire. At the same time, solutions to the adolescent literacy crisis are grounded in economic referents, such as the market economy and the need for future workers. These foci have unintended, negative consequences for schools' efforts to promote the literacy of African American male adolescents. First, they position adolescent literacy development as an in-school phenomenon related to standardized scores. Secondly, the crisis, as it is currently framed, affects the definition of adolescent literacy. A limited view of the crisis results in observable practical and theoretical vacillations among educators, policymakers, and educational publishers. The search for solutions to the adolescent literacy crisis remains scattered; teachers of adolescents lack clarity about what competencies outside their disciplines they need to develop; and the support provided by professional developers remains as varied as the professional developers themselves. The lives of many adolescents, particularly adolescent males of color, are treated as expendable, both within and outside of schools.

In subsequent sections of this article, I draw from a qualitative case study I conducted that supports my proposed model of a more anatomically complete model of literacy instruction. This study examined how choosing the right texts is central to advancing the literacy development of African American male adolescents. By illustrating the importance of engaging African American adolescent males with texts they find meaningful, the case study affirms the need for a more anatomically complete model of literacy instruction in schools.

African American Males and Texts

The impact of texts on the lives of African American adolescent males cannot be underestimated. Historically, texts have been central to the literacy development of African American males, with eminently clear connections among reading, writing, speaking, and actions (Tatum, 2005). Historical accounts of the lives of African American men are laden with references to enabling texts. An *enabling text*, as I define it, is one that moves beyond a solely cognitive focus—such as skill and strategy development—to include a social, cultural, political, spiritual, or economic focus. I was able to identify such texts by examining biographical and autobiographical documents written by Black male archetypes from the past century.

As part of my examination, I constructed textual lineages (Tatum, 2007) of Black male archetypes' literary experiences. *Textual lineages* are diagrams of texts that individuals found meaningful and significant, as evidenced by documents they have written. I constructed the lineages by placing the first pivotal text the archetypes identified at the top of the diagram. I then recorded other texts in the order they were discussed in the individuals' biographical and autobiographical narratives. For example, Eldridge Cleaver, who wrote the memoir *Soul on Ice* (1968), shared "how he devoured [the book, *Negroes with Guns* by Robert Williams] and let a few friends read it, before the [prison] library dug it and put it on the blacklist" (p. 71) (see Figure 2). He described other texts as "books that one wants to read—so bad that it [causes] a taste [in] the mouth" that only the books can satisfy (p. 70). Cleaver also complained that he could not get his hands on texts that were satisfactory to a man trying to function in the society and time in which he lived.

Subsequent to constructing the textual lineages of more than thirty Black male archetypes—among them Nat Turner, Frederick Douglass, Malcolm X, Huey Newton, and Tupac Shakur—I constructed my own textual lineage using texts that were significant to me in middle and high school (see Figure 3). I also

Figure 2. Eldridge Cleaver's Textual Lineage, Constructed From Reading Cleaver's *Soul on Ice* (1968)

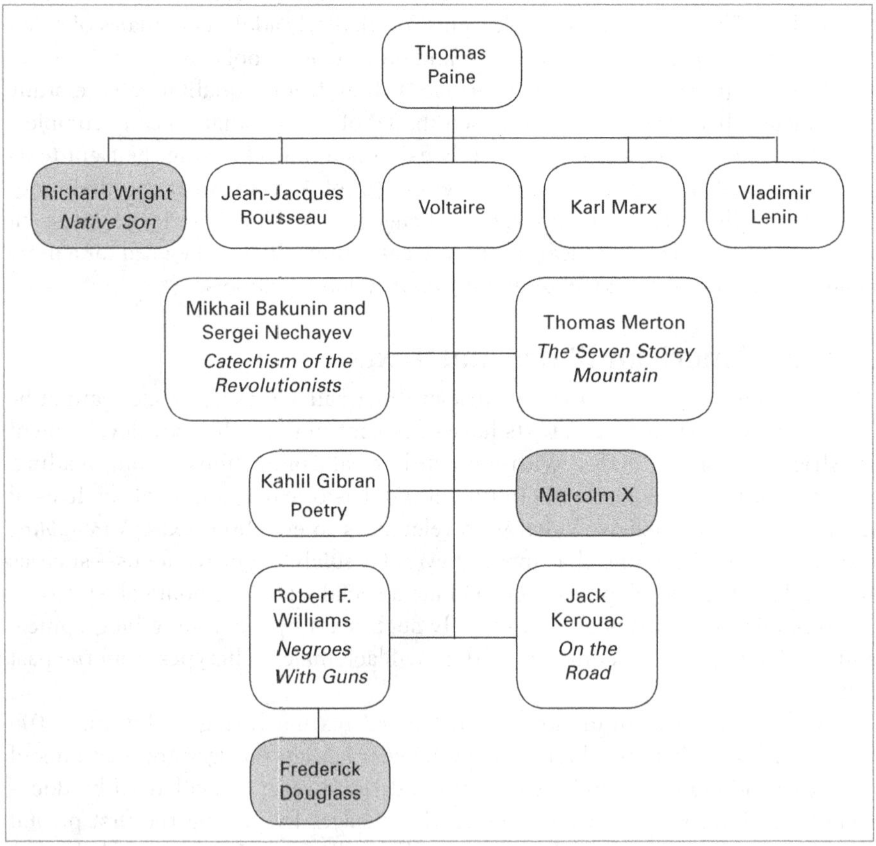

(The shaded boxes denote texts that recur in the textual lineages of African American males from the 1960s onward.)

Figure 3. Tatum's Textual Lineage From Middle and High School

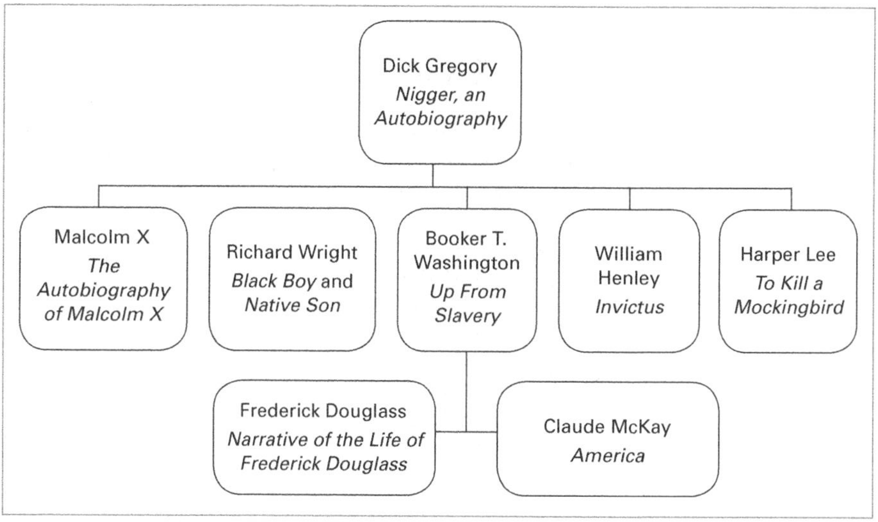

collected 243 textual lineages from African American males in middle and high schools in an attempt to identify the characteristics of texts they found meaningful and significant, and to compare these characteristics to those identified in the examination of the textual lineages of Black male archetypes and myself (Tatum, in progress). Early analysis suggests that there are four characteristics of texts that African American males find meaningful and significant:

1. They contribute to a healthy psyche.
2. They focus on a collective struggle.
3. They provide a road map for being, doing, and acting.
4. They provide modern awareness of the real world. (Tatum, 2007)

Unfortunately, many African American male adolescents who struggle with reading are unable to identify texts that they find significant. As evidenced by the blank lineage submitted by an eighth-grade boy in an urban middle school (see Figure 4), these young men often lack a growing textual lineage. Instead, they generally encounter texts that are *disabling*—texts that reinforce their perception of being struggling readers. While disabling texts ignore students' local contexts and their desire as adolescents for self-definition, *enabling* texts and their characteristics are central to a more anatomically complete model of literacy instruction. To investigate how an adolescent encounters and thinks about such texts, I designed the case study described in the section that follows.

Figure 4. Textual Lineage of an Eighth-Grade Boy Attending an Urban Middle School

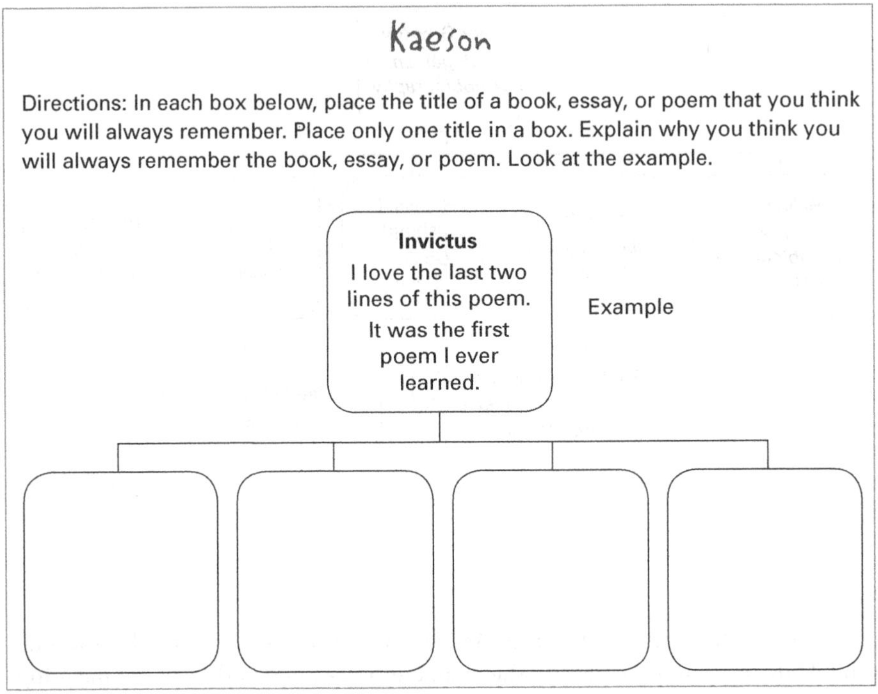

A Qualitative Case Study

In an attempt to identify characteristics of texts and ways to effectively mediate texts with African American male adolescents, I designed a ten-month, in-depth qualitative case study (Merriam, 1998) to identify and describe the aspects of texts that Quincy, the pseudonym of a sixteen-year-old African American male, found most useful for improving his reading and shaping his identity. Quincy's mother approached me through a mutual friend and asked me to help save her son's life. The mother feared that Quincy, who was retained three times in a K–8 school because of his failure to meet the minimum reading score for promotion to high school, would be dead or incarcerated in three years if he did not become a better reader.

The study was framed by a phenomenological variant of ecological systems theory (Spencer, Dupree, & Hartmann, 1997) that takes into account structural and contextual barriers to identity formation and the implication of these barriers for psychosocial processes such as self-appraisal. This theoretical framework was useful because Quincy's view of himself and of how others viewed him seemed to be interrupting his literacy development, and structural and contextual barriers to his identity formation could not be ignored. At the time of the study, Quincy lived in one of Chicago's inner-city neighborhoods, which he described in the following way:

> I know the West Side of Chicago is ghetto...On my little three block[s], Mona, Mavis, and Monte, where I stay at, there may be a lot of kids, but all blocks got drugs on them....It's like a drug house or something. In that three-block area you see cars, everything, police cars comin' through twenty-four seven.

Along with having to withstand the negative community contexts, Quincy was also struggling to overcome some the psychological overload thrust upon him by his family, as evidenced by his sharing the comment, "They all think I am dumb." His family members' views became more pronounced after Quincy dropped out of school during the middle of his freshman year.

Additionally, Quincy suffered from an underexposure to reading materials in school and at home. He had never read anything that affected him and he had never read a complete book. Essentially, he was striving for identity without the benefit of having read texts that could potentially inform his identity development. During our first interview, he shared, "To say the truth, I ain't read a book." He then informed me that his teachers did not assign books at school.

Data Collection

The study was designed to gather Quincy's views on how texts (i.e., poems, essays, speeches, books, and news clippings) affected the way he viewed himself as he negotiated his home and community contexts. I attempted to identify texts that would provide Quincy with capital to become resilient amid some of his negative environmental conditions. Consistent with the anatomically complete model in which an understanding of a student's context drives instructional decisions, I planned to use these texts to provide explicit reading skill and strategy instruction. Quincy consented to participate in the study by agreeing to do the following:

1. Read books, articles, newspaper clippings, and speeches I recommended. He was given the final decision about the material he chose to read.
2. Participate in twenty 90-minute audio-taped discussions about the reading materials that took place every other Saturday morning at a bookstore or library near his home.
3. Write reflections in a journal during the last ten minutes of each discussion.
4. Participate in four 30-minute interviews to reflect on the discussions. The interviews were scheduled at ten-week intervals.

Data Analysis

I analyzed discussion and interview transcripts line by line in order to name and identify characteristics of texts or in-school and out-of-school variables that affected Quincy's engagement with texts. I generated codes or used *in vivo* codes (Strauss & Corbin, 1998) after each discussion. I attached researcher's memos to the codes to add attributes or question their potential multiple meanings, to develop a more specific focus, and to prepare questions to ask the case-study participant in subsequent discussions (Glesne & Peshkin, 1992). I then grouped the codes based on their ability to describe the case-study participant's perspectives about texts and text types he found most useful for addressing his literacy needs, as well as variables that interrupted his engagement with texts. Using an approach similar to that of Ivey (1999), I triangulated data across sessions by rereading the transcripts from our previous discussions, along with the participant's written reflections, before reading new transcripts and reflections. I also shared my thinking with Quincy during each session to resolve any misunderstandings I might have held about the data. For example, I would ask him if I was representing his thoughts clearly.

Results

During the study, Quincy read or attempted to read four books, two speeches, two poems, and excerpts from two books (see Table 3). His text-related discussions provide valuable insights for shaping educational contexts and selecting and mediating text with an African American male adolescent who struggles with reading. Three major themes emerged in the study: perceived supports, meaningful engagement with texts, and self-organizing processes.

Perceived Supports

During the first interview I conducted with Quincy, we discussed teachers' perceptions of African American males. I wanted to know how he believed others viewed him. Excerpts from our conversation are included below:

Table 3. Texts Quincy Read During the Case Study

Books	"*Yo, Little Brother . . .*" (Davis & Jackson, 1998) *Handbook for Boys: A Novel* (Myers, 2002) *Monster* (Myers, 1999) *Willie Lynch: Why African Americans Have So Many Issues* (Sims, 2002)
Poems	"Does the World Care if I Exist" (Tatum, 2005) "Life through My Eyes" (Shakur, 1999)
Speeches	Bill Cosby's (2004) Address to the NAACP on the Fiftieth Anniversary of *Brown v. Board of Education* Martin Luther King Jr.'s (1963) "I Have a Dream"
Excerpts	"Letter to My Nephew" from James Baldwin (1963), *The Fire Next Time* "Black Power" from Martin Luther King Jr. (1967), *Where Do We Go from Here: Chaos or Community?*

Tatum: When you come in contact with people who are not African American, how do you think they perceive you?

Quincy: ...I was in school with all Whites; they treated me the same way they treated all the other people. So basically, I don't see nothing wrong. I think they do a good job.

Tatum: So you would agree that they do not have a negative perception of you?

Quincy: No, only thing that is wrong, they just didn't know how to handle the African American kids.

Tatum: Are you talking about the teachers?

Quincy: Yeah...They are, like, scared or something. I don't know what it is, but I think African American teachers know what to do. They look at our work and they see our grades and tell us what we need to do, unlike other teachers. They give us afterschool help, give us help on this and this and this, give us some private time, and help you out. The other teachers, they do a good job too, but they're not like African American teachers. My point: African American teachers—when we act up, they know how we are, they know what it is, and the other teachers, they be quick to send you out for a quick descent to the principal and get suspended for something.

Tatum: Do you have specific examples?

Quincy: I don't know what it was, but I kept asking the teacher for help, and she's like, you're doing good in this class; you don't need help. And I told her all I need help is with one problem, and you can go finish whatever you were doing. And she thought I was really being smart, and she sent me out. And the rest of the class tried to get me out of trouble, but she made a big deal and I got suspended for it.

Tatum: You said something interesting to me. You said that some teachers don't know how to handle African American kids; some of them might be scared. Talk about that a little more.

Quincy: 'Cause they just think we're worthless. They think we are just going to give up. We won't do what we need to do right. They try to help us, but they won't constantly help us to get us on track. Like the rest of the class, we fall behind, but they don't take the time when they can get the class started on work. They just go on grades and try to get their stuff together, but they just need to come over and give us a little sermon. But they just don't do that.

Quincy perceived that the support of classroom teachers was lacking, and assessed this lack of support as a form of rejection stemming from teachers' perceptions of African American students as worthless. A month into the study, he continued to describe the lack of support, this time in the midst of a reading event, as we discussed the text, "*Yo, Little Brother...*" (Davis & Jackson, 1998), a book he found favorable. He made the following comments about the book:

> I don't know what made me read it, but I was, like, totally involved in what he's saying, what the guy was saying. To tell you the truth, I read this book in one day. I ain't started it until that Monday, and I sat down 'cause I wasn't going to read it at first, but I sat down, and said, let me read this book. So as I flip over the pages and I start out reading, I'm like, I like this book for a reason, so I'm going to try to read, and then I seen this say "Street Smarts" right at the top. I know I know a lot about the street, so I just read to see what they was talking about. Then some of the things they was saying was true...As I was going along I wanted to stop, but I couldn't. I was like, I started it, and I ain't going to sleep 'til about six in the morning. That's how into it I was, and I didn't know I could get into a book like that. To tell you the truth, I forgot I was reading...This is a good book, it help you out a lot.

I wanted Quincy to compare this text to the types of materials he read in school, and to determine if he would prefer to read more of such texts in school. Excerpts from the interview are shown below:

Tatum: Do you read these types of materials in school?

Quincy: No, I do not.

Tatum: Do you think you should be reading these types of materials in school?

Quincy: ...I think it would be a waste of time.

Tatum: To read something like this?

Quincy: Yes, even though it would help a lot of people.

Tatum: It helps a lot of people, but it would be a waste of time. Help me through this confusion.

Quincy: It is something that we should be reading in school, but the teachers would read it and use it like a story. They ain't going to explain what it means. They going to give us things to write about it and all, but they ain't going to really explain it like the book is. The kids that don't understand what they see in here, they ain't going to really know what they are talking about. If they are going to start a book like this, they gotta let them know what [it] means. Especially what [it] means.

Quincy's comments suggest that the text he found meaningful outside of school would be less valuable if it became part of the school curriculum, because he believed teachers would fail to discuss its significance. This is one of the shortcomings that result from not using a more anatomically complete model of literacy instruction that brings attention to instructional and theoretical strands, which can inform how we discuss texts with adolescents. Quincy's remarks suggest that in his school, such texts would be mediated in ways that pay attention to the vital signs of *reading* (e.g., school-based writing assignments, assessment questions) but ignore the vital signs of *readers* and *reading instruction*—namely, shaping classroom contexts to pay attention to students' lived experiences and providing opportunities for meaningful engagement with texts.

Meaningful Engagement With Texts

Commenting again on "*Yo, Little Brother...*" (Davis & Jackson, 1998), the book Quincy read prior to our second meeting, he explained why certain pages of the text resonated with him. After reading in the book about Driving While Black (DWB), he used the text to make sense of a DWB experience he had had while en route to a luncheon:

Tatum: Why do you think those pages of the text stood out to you?

Quincy: Because my friend's dad drove me and two other guys, and we all were Black in the car, and we really weren't doing nothing. We were going the speed limit and all, and as he was driving, the police pulled him over and all of us. He made us get out of the car, thinking we had drugs and stuff on us, even though we all had suits on. He searched us, then he searched the car, and the guy asked the officer why it was he was stopped. And then I heard this with my own ears, he was like "DWB," but I don't know what that means.

Tatum: Who said DWB?

Quincy: The officer.

Tatum: Was he White or Black?

Quincy: I think he was White. I don't really remember. When he said that, I really didn't know what he means until I read this. When I thought about it, DWB, I don't know how it popped back to [the day of] my luncheon, but then I realized what DWB was.

Quincy's year-old personal experience with police misconduct resurfaced after reading the text, which ultimately helped him make sense of an incident that had embarrassed him. Describing how he felt about being stopped and searched by the police, he said, "I was a little embarrassed, to tell the truth. I was on my way to a luncheon and I didn't want to get messed up or nothing. I wanted to stay clean all the way there." This dehumanizing and devaluing of the African American male adolescent is often overlooked by literacy models that are solely grounded in cognitive reading processes. By failing to consider these societal ills, such models may inadvertently undermine African American males' meaningful engagement with texts.

The types of texts students are asked to read, the structure of the texts, and students' limited reading skills also interrupt meaningful engagement with texts. This was evident in Quincy's failure to complete the text, *Willie Lynch: Why African Americans Have So Many Issues* (Sims, 2002), which he selected to read between our second and third sessions. He was unable to get past the first two pages. I discovered that he had been trying to read the preface of the book, which I had not anticipated:

Tatum: I gave you five different titles to choose from the last time. Why did you select this text?

Quincy: Because I wanted to see what he was talking about.

Tatum: What stood out to you as you read the text?

Quincy: I really didn't get into it. I started reading the first two pages. I just wanted to understand.

Tatum: Talk about that a little more.

Quincy: I started reading, and as I was reading, I just couldn't get into this book.

Tatum: Can you explain why it did not hold your attention?

Quincy: Man, I just didn't get into it. I tried reading it a couple more times. Maybe it was just, maybe it was just the [preface].

Tatum: Did you move beyond the preface? Do you know the purpose of the preface?

Quincy: No.

Quincy could not get into the book "'cause every time [he] took a break [he] gotta read over what [he] read." To continue the session, I read part of the text with Quincy and provided him with strategies for decoding the text and monitoring his comprehension, areas I had assessed to be his weaknesses. He became engaged with the text during the session:

Tatum: I want you to read page forty-six.

Quincy: "Year after year we allow our boys to attend inferior public schools and then we wonder why they don't like school. African American boys don't like school because school educators, administrators and the American educational system do not like African American boys."

Tatum: Do you think this is true?

Quincy: No.

Tatum: Why aren't you going to one of the highest-achieving schools?

Quincy: Because... (long pause)

Tatum: Do you feel that you are receiving an inferior education as opposed to a superior education?

Quincy: Not really.

Tatum: Talk about that.

Quincy: They are teaching us some things, but they ain't teaching us the best they could.

This session suggests a very important caveat to consider when mediating texts with struggling adolescent readers. The content of the text alone may not be sufficient to move them toward engagement. Instructional supports that include explicit strategy instruction and ways of finding an entry point or entry passage to the text may be necessary to get adolescents engaged. In this conversation, I asked Quincy questions about his own educational experiences in order to make the argument in the text more concrete. Quincy became more engaged when these supports were provided. For instance, in this conversation, he challenged and then expanded upon the author's assertions. I look back at this session and this text as the tipping point when Quincy starting viewing texts as a tool to think about his own life. He stated at the end of this session and the subsequent sessions, "I got to get it right. I got to get my life right."

Self-Organizing Processes

Quincy's engagement with texts had increased by the sixteenth week of the case study. By this time, he had reenrolled in an alternative high school after sitting out for several months. In our meetings, he began to ask more questions about the texts and engage in more reflection, whereas at the beginning of the study, he would simply identify parts of the texts that stood out to him and read those parts during our time together. I often initiated those discussions by asking Quincy questions to help him gather his thoughts about the readings. During our seventh session, however, Quincy initiated the discussion with a question based on his reading of the poem, "Does the World Care if I Exist" (Tatum, 2005), which is excerpted here:

> Does the world care if I exist?
> Or, am I just America's problem?
> Don't they know I am dying like no other?
> No, they just fear me, they can't hear me
> Hell, you can't even teach me how to read—Mr. and Mrs. Teacher
> Then you flunk me, and blame it on me
> Some of it's my fault
> Probably some of my momma's fault as well
> But you're at fault, too
> I don't want your pity or your crying
> Teach me how to man-up, and be a man
> Help me to stop dying
> If you don't this nation will continue to spill over with the black man's blood
> You'll have to build more jails.
> It is now your time to act
> If you don't act
> I now believe that, *America does not care if I exist,* is a fact.
> No more peace until we all get a piece (American pie)
> Damn, my time expired. I'm gone... (p. 7)

As we entered the library to have our discussion about the poem, he asked, "I wanna know what made you, like, write. What made you describe that type of boy?" Excerpts from the interview follow:

Tatum: I wanted to write to help people understand that a lot of African American males do not believe the world cares if they exist. Also, this poem reflects my own childhood and the experiences of a lot of other young men that grew up on the South Side of Chicago. This is how I saw a lot of the young brothers I grew up with...What was it about the poem that led you to that question? Is there something that stood out to you?

Quincy: I don't know, 'cause it's like, in the beginning, I read the title and it was like, did the world care if I exist? What I see now is, like, when African Americans go to jail, they don't care if they exist, basically. If they really cared, they would do more positive things to help them not go to jail. And like in the middle or the end, wherever it was, when he was like, "you would have to build more jails because of the"—like, I don't know what he means by the "Black male's blood," or what that means.

Tatum: It's saying that this nation will continue to spill over with the Black male's blood. That means you will find more African American men murdering African American men. The blood of African American men will fill America's streets if we don't do something different to address their multiple needs.

Quincy: OK. There was another part I liked. They talking about the teachers in the school. He was saying, like, part of it was his fault, his parents' fault, and the teachers' fault. That is how he worked his way out of it, 'cause he has got to do the work his self, he can't just depend on nobody else. It is [the] majority of the teachers' fault, because, like, they teach us what they supposed to teach; they don't teach anything that is going to help the students.

Tatum: Help me understand what you mean.

Quincy: OK, what I mean by that is, like a list of assignments—it is just like you get assigned a list of assignments that you want the class to learn, but it ain't like what the class *needs* to learn.

Tatum: What are some things that students need to learn?

Quincy: Since I have been going to school lately, it is like the teachers don't even care. It's like they just teach the things just thrown on grade level just to get out of class. Go to the next shelf, make sure you get the grades. Like teaching stuff you already know. Why don't they just go to something new? Sometimes it is just good to work hard; you know what I am saying? If you give us some easy work when we know we are going to finish that in less than a minute, give us something that we have got to sit down and think about.

Tatum: Is that happening in your new school?

Quincy: Don't laugh; this might be funny, but don't laugh. My teacher teaching us literature, right, but he doing measurements and stuff. Ain't literature something like reading? We didn't even have no books. The only thing we got books for is the science.

This poem led Quincy to examine his existence in the alternative high school setting, and further, it led to a meaningful exchange of ideas between us, initiated by Quincy's questions. He questioned curriculum orientations and analyzed the plight of African American males and their shared culpability in their social demise. Quincy did not understand why teachers refused to challenge him and his African American classmates. Sadly, the time that was allocated for literature instruction was co-opted by math because of the absence of other texts. He asked me not to laugh, but I think his warning would have been more targeted if he had told me not to explode with anger or cry.

Quincy continued to ask questions about the texts during our discussions. In our last session together, he read the following excerpt from Martin Luther King Jr.'s discussion of Black power (Hord & Lee, 1995):

> But we are also Americans. Abused and scorned though we may be, our destiny is tied up with the destiny of America. The Negro must face the fact that America is now his home, a home that he helped to build through blood, sweat, and tears. Since we are Americans the solution to our problem will not come through seeking to build a separate black nation within a nation, but by finding that creative minority of the concerned from the ofttimes apathetic majority, and together moving toward that colorless power that we all need for security and justice. (p. 295)

The last text-based question Quincy asked me was, "What did he mean by 'creative minority'?" After sharing my thoughts on the phrase "creative minority," I asked him why he had asked the question. Quincy said, "I just wanted to understand it." He began to seek understanding from texts as he thought about his own life. He found that the texts and our discussions of them led him to some self-correcting processes, such as reenrolling in school after dropping out and forming a better relationship with his mother (Tatum, in press).

Early in the study, Quincy shared his belief that he was poorly served by his literacy experiences in school because teachers failed to "read" him. When I asked him how teachers could read him without living his experiences, he offered:

> It like the same thing Tupac (Shakur, 1999) is saying in "life in his eyes." I mean, you gotta see what you see in your eyes, what you see every day. It's like a good book or something. You reading it at home and you think somebody else might like it. You ask them to read the title. If you tell a student that you really liked a book and it was good, they gonna notice it and give it a chance, the first couple of pages, or chapter or something. They don't like it; they will let you know...You can hear conversations sometimes. What they are going through...I ain't doubting teachers don't care; they care. If they didn't care, they wouldn't be there, but it just that they are doing what they want to do. They doing what they think they need to teach; they ain't doing what the students need. They ain't reading us.

In his final comments, Quincy referred to Tupac's (Shakur, 1999) poem, "Life through My Eyes," a text we read and discussed during the study. In it, Tupac states,

> Fun and games R few but treasured like gold 2 me,
> cuz I realize that I must return 2 my spot in poverty.
> But mock my words when I say my heart will not exist
> unless my destiny comes through and puts an end 2 all of this. (p. 11)

Quincy dropped out of the study after his mother kicked him out of the house and told him to move in with his father, who had recently been released from prison. The potential to use literacy instruction and texts to empower this African American male adolescent was not realized. Sadly, his recent reentry into high school had done nothing to jumpstart that potential, and, in fact, seemed to squander it.

During the study, Quincy was slowly becoming more convinced about the power of texts, particularly the enabling texts he selected from the choices I provided. When he reenrolled in the alternative high school, he expected to be able to read these kinds of texts in school, but he discovered that the same old material he had been provided before he had dropped out was still the standard fare. Quincy believed me as I discussed how texts could help him shape a positive life trajectory. He also discovered something about himself as he read the material—texts that I hope will become a part of his textual lineage.

The stakes are much higher for Quincy now. He has a son and another child on the way—two kids who will be raised by a father who has yet to receive a high school diploma.

Concluding Thoughts

In this article, I discussed the need for a more anatomically complete model of literacy for African American male adolescents, particularly the ones living under the weight of a widening gulf of social, economic, and educational disparity. I assert that literacy instruction can serve as a mechanism to shape a more egalitarian, just society by paying attention to the varied needs of adolescents now living in high-poverty communities. It is naive to believe, or mendacious to suggest, that the broader societal aims that should be associated with literacy instruction can be reached by focusing on research-based skills and strategies alone. There are multiple tangible and intangible influences on adolescent literacy development. In-school factors and out-of-school factors function in concert with students' external and internal resources, and they all combine to impact their literacy development.

Educators and policymakers must assiduously question how policy, pedagogical practices, and research will benefit and advance the literacy development of both the poorest and the most privileged adolescents in this nation. The economically privileged and economically disadvantaged adolescents of today will be bound together to solve the nation's political, social, and educational problems. Literacy development has to be conceptualized in such a way that it addresses the needs of *all* adolescents, including African American male adolescents. It also has to be conceptualized to preserve American democracy and the American economy, which are now threatened by the large number of high school dropouts who will not be able to find sustainable employment or participate in the political process.

There is a need to include the voices of African American adolescent males in literacy research. While qualitative research provides powerful data, large-scale research studies are needed to specifically examine the literacy development of African American adolescent males. This can be accomplished by conducting carefully controlled studies in schools where we find African American adolescent males who struggle with reading. The results of these studies can then be combined with the best practices found in descriptive and qualitative studies. This approach will potentially guard against essentializing African American male adolescents' literacy experiences in the United States.

Additionally, more attention needs to be given to text types, characteristics of texts, and the role of texts in advancing the literacy development of African American males. There is ample historical precedent for the role of texts in shaping the lives of African American males in the United States. Educators often overlook this precedent when making curricular decisions purportedly designed to improve the reading outcomes of African American males.

It may be helpful to adopt a life course perspective (Mizell, 1999) that aligns neatly with cultural-ecological theories addressing out-of-school and in-school contexts, students' identities, and the structural barriers that exist in a highly stratified class-based and race-based society. But taking on such a perspective requires a broader conceptualization of literacy instruction for African American male adolescents, who can be both resilient and vulnerable at the same time. I suggest that educators and school reformers adopt a more anatomically complete model of literacy instruction that integrates theoretical, instructional, and professional development strands—head, body, and legs, respectively—as a comprehensive approach to advancing the literacy development of African American male adolescents. Moving toward a more anatomically complete model of literacy development can expand the lens of the adolescent literacy field, inform and shape the direction of educational research, and advance the literacy development of African American male adolescents in ways that will benefit them in school and society.

REFERENCES

Alliance for Excellent Education. (2006). *Who's counted? Who's counting? Understanding high school graduation rates*. Washington, DC: Author.

Alvermann, D. E., Hinchman, K. A., Moore, D. W., Phelps, S. F., & Waff, D. R. (Eds.) (2006). *Reconceptualizing the literacies in adolescents' lives* (2nd ed.). Mahwah, NJ: Erlbaum.

Baldwin, J. (1963). *The fire next time*. New York: Dial Press.

Biancarosa, C., & Snow, C. E. (2006). *Reading next—A vision for action and research in middle and high school literacy: A report to Carnegie Corporation of New York* (2nd ed.). Washington, DC: Alliance for Excellent Education.

Brozo, W. (2002). *To be a boy, to be a reader: Engaging teen and preteen boys in active literacy*. Newark, DE: International Reading Association.

Ceballo, R., McLoyd, V., & Toyokawa, T. (2004). The influence of neighborhood quality on adolescents' educational values and school effort. *Journal of Adolescent Research, 19*(6), 716–739.

Cleaver, E. (1968). *Soul on ice*. New York: Dell.

Collins, J., & Blot, R. K. (2003). *Literacy and literacies: Texts, power, and identity*. Cambridge, England: Cambridge University Press.

Cosby, W. (2004, 17 May). Address at the NAACP's commemoration of the fiftieth anniversary of *Brown v. Board of Education*. Retrieved December

7, 2007, from http://www.americanrhetoric.com/speeches/billcosbypoundcakespeech.htm
Davis, A., & Jackson, J. (1998). *"Yo, little brother...": Basic rules of survival for young African American males.* Chicago: African American Images.
Davis, J. (2001). Transgressing the masculine: African American boys and the failure of schools. In W. Martino & B. Meyenn (Eds.), *What about the boys?* (pp. 140–153). Philadelphia, PA: Open University Press.
Fashola, O. S. (Ed.). (2005). *Educating African American males: Voices from the field.* Thousand Oaks, CA: Corwin Press.
Gilbert, R., & Gilbert, P. (1998). *Masculinity goes to school.* New York: Routledge.
Glesne, C., & Peshkin, A. (1992). *Becoming qualitative researchers: An introduction.* White Plains, NY: Longman.
Goodenow, C. (1993). The psychological sense of school membership among adolescents: Scale development and educational correlates. *Psychology in the Schools, 30,* 79–91.
Greene, S., & Abt-Perkins, D. (2003). *Making race visible: Literacy research for cultural understanding.* New York: Teachers College Press.
Heller, R., & Greenleaf, C. (2007). *Literacy instruction in the content areas: Getting to the core of middle and high school improvement.* Washington, DC: Alliance for Excellent Education.
Henderson, N., & Milstein, M. (2003). *Resiliency in schools: Making it happen for students and educators.* Thousand Oaks, CA: Corwin Press.
Hord, F. L., & Lee, J. S. (Eds.). (1995). *I am because we are: Readings in Black philosophy.* Amherst: University of Massachusetts Press.
Ivey, G. (1999). A multicase study in the middle school: Complexities among young adolescent readers. *Reading Research Quarterly, 34*(2), 172–192.
Jetton, T., & Dole, J. (Eds.). (2004). *Adolescent literacy research and practice.* New York: Guilford.
King, M. L., Jr. (1963, Aug. 28). I have a dream. Retrieved December 7, 2007, from http://www.americanrhetoric.com/speeches/mlkihaveadream.htm
King, M. L., Jr. (1967). *Where do we go from here: Chaos or community?* Boston, MA: Beacon.
Lesko, N. (2000). *Masculinities at school.* Thousand Oaks, CA: Sage.
Lindo, E. (2006). The African American presence in reading intervention experiments. *Remedial and Special Education, 27*(3), 148–153.
Merriam, S. (1998). *Qualitative research and case study applications in education.* San Francisco, CA: Jossey-Bass.
Mizell, C. A. (1999). Life course influences of African American men's depression: Adolescent parental composition, self-concept, and adult earnings. *Journal of African American Studies, 29*(4), 467–490.
Myers, W. D. (1999). *Monster.* New York: HarperCollins.
Myers, W. D. (2002). *Handbook for boys: A novel.* New York: Amistad.
National Center on Education and the Economy. (2006). *Tough choices or tough times: The report of the New Commission on the Skills of the American Workforce.* San Francisco: Jossey-Bass.
Polite, V., & Davis, J. (Eds.). (1999). *African American males in school and society: Practices and policies for effective education.* New York: Teachers College Press.
Price, J. (2000). Peer (dis)connections, school, and African American masculinities. In N. Lesko (Ed.), *Masculinities at school* (pp. 127–159). Thousand Oaks, CA: Sage.
Roderick, M. (1994). Grade retention and school dropout: Investigating the association. *American Educational Research Journal, 31*(4), 729–759.
Rush, L., Eakle, J., & Berger, A. (Eds.). (2007). *Secondary school literacy: What research reveals for classroom practice.* Urbana, IL: National Council of Teachers of English.
Shakur, T. (1999). *The rose that grew from the concrete.* New York: Pocket Books.
Sims, M. (2002). *Willie Lynch: Why African Americans have so many issues.* Chicago: Author.
Smith, M., & Wilhelm, J. (2002). *"Reading don't fix no Chevys": Literacy in the lives of young men.* Portsmouth, NH: Heinemann.
Spencer, M. B. (1999). Social and cultural influences on school adjustment: The application of an identity-focused cultural ecological perspective. *Educational Psychologist, 34*(1), 43–57.
Spencer, M. B., Dupree, D., & Hartmann, T. (1997). A phenomenological variant of ecological systems theory (PVEST): A self-organization perspective in context. *Development and Psychopathology, 9*(4), 817–833.
Strauss, A., & Corbin, J. (1998). *Basics of qualitative research: Grounded theory procedures and techniques* (2nd ed.). Newbury Park, CA: Sage.
Street, B. (1995). *Social literacies: Critical approaches to literacy in development, ethnography and education.* London: Longman.
Swanson, D., Cunningham, M., & Spencer, M. B. (2003). Black males' structural conditions, achievement patterns, normative needs, and "opportunities." *Urban Education, 38*(5), 608–633.
Tatum, A. W. (2000). Breaking down barriers that disenfranchise African American adolescents in low-level reading tracks. *Journal of Adolescent & Adult Literacy, 44,* 52–64.
Tatum, A. W. (2002). Professional development for teachers of African American adolescents. *Illinois Reading Council Journal, 30*(1), 42–52.
Tatum, A. W. (2003). *Advancing the literacies of African American adolescents: A case study of professional development.* Unpublished doctoral dissertation, University of Illinois at Chicago.
Tatum, A. W. (2005). *Teaching reading to African American adolescent males: Closing the achievement gap.* Portland, ME: Stenhouse.

Tatum, A. W. (2006). Engaging African American males in reading. *Educational Leadership, 63*(5), 44–49.

Tatum, A. W. (2007). Building the textual lineages of African American male adolescents. In K. Beers, R. Probst, and L. Rief (Eds.), *Adolescent literacy: Turning promise into practice* (pp. 81–85). Portsmouth, NH: Heinemann.

Tatum, A. W. (in press). African American males at risk: A researcher's study of endangered males and literature that works. In S. Lehr (Ed.), *Shattering the looking glass: Issues, controversy, and trends in children's literature.* Norwood, MA: Christopher Gordon.

Tatum, A. W. (in progress). *Rebuilding the textual lineages of African American male adolescents.* Portsmouth, NH: Heinemann.

Tatum, A. W., & Fisher, T. A. (in press). Nurturing resilience among adolescent readers. In S. Lenski and J. Lewis (Eds.), *Addressing the needs of struggling middle level and high school readers.* New York: Guilford.

Werner, E. E., & Smith, R. S. (1992). *Overcoming the odds: High-risk children from birth to adulthood.* New York: Cornell University Press.

Young, J. P. (2000). Boy talk: Critical literacy and masculinities. *Reading Research Quarterly, 35*(3), 312–337.

CHAPTER 26

Marie M. Clay's Theoretical Perspective: A Literacy Processing Theory

Mary Anne Doyle, University of Connecticut

Marie M. Clay was a clinical child psychologist who chose to study young learners during their initial, formative years of literacy acquisition. Applying the perspectives and practices of developmental psychology (Clay, 2001), she sought to document behavioral changes in children's literacy development by capturing performance in reading and writing tasks collected over time. She therefore designed studies to gather empirical evidence collected in controlled conditions, and she grounded her tentative theories in the resulting data (Clay, 1998).

Clay's initial work was motivated by questions resulting from the correlations found between learners' literacy performance in the first year of school and their rankings among peers in subsequent years. Specifically, she found that those with very limited progress in reading and writing at the end of their first year of instruction remained among the lowest performing students year after year. To address this challenge and create instructional opportunities to change predictions of failure, Clay chose to initiate her work by pursuing clarification of optimal literacy development among young learners, that is, securing descriptions of the literacy progress of successful children.

Applying the perspectives and practices of developmental psychology (Clay, 1991a), she documented changes in children's literacy development by capturing behavioral performance in reading and writing tasks collected longitudinally. There were no existing accounts of learners engaged in their earliest school-based encounters with literacy; therefore, she set out to document what occurs, which she referred to as a legitimate first step (Clay, 2001). Although delineation of behaviors changing over time was her first objective, related goals, aligned with her developmental orientation, were explanations of observed changes and consideration of how to modify learning conditions to optimize development for all individuals (Clay, 2004). For struggling learners, she described this as "leading children back...to a more secure developmental track, that is, to the *recovery of a more normal trajectory*" (Clay, 1998, pp. 288–289), which brought her to the study of intervention.

Resulting from her earliest investigations of literacy, Clay (2001) embraced a complex theory of literacy and defined reading as a message-getting, problem-solving activity, which increases in power and flexibility the more it is practised. It is complex because within the directional constraints of written language, verbal and perceptual behaviours are purposefully directed in some integrated way to the problem of extracting sequences of information from texts to yield meaningful and specific communications. (p. 1)

Her quest for theoretical explanations focused on building understandings of both the specific perceptual and cognitive behaviors involved in reading and writing and explanations of the integration of complex in-the-head processes. Thus, explanations of progress involved descriptions of working systems, that is, the perceptual and cognitive working systems directed to complete reading and writing tasks.

The acquisition of literacy processing "begins when a child is expected to compose and write a simple message or read a simple continuous text" (Clay, 2001, p. 97), for it is in processing complete messages that the working systems for literacy are engaged and developed. She therefore focused on learners reading continuous texts and composing and writing personal messages.

Initially, Clay focused on discovering the emerging and changing literacy behaviors of children who were found to be proficient readers and writers for their age cohort. She sought to base her inferences on patterns of development in the behaviors of those children exhibiting expected changes in reading and writing over their first year of school. An additional benefit of detailed accounts of optimal development was understandings of "when and how to begin teaching, of the changes that may be expected over time, of the track that most children take, of the variability to be expected, and of different developmental paths" (Clay, 1998, p. 255).

Clay considered the pre-school, developmental histories of children to be unique, individual, and replete with complex learning tasks. Children construct their own understandings as a result of opportunities to learn, they do not shy away from complexity, and they bring their unique stores of knowledge with them to school. At 5 years of age, each school entrant has extensive knowledge of oral language even though their oral language acquisition is incomplete. Their oral language proficiency, their vocabulary knowledge, their knowledge of their worlds, and their pre-school experiences with literacy are available when formal literacy instruction begins and they initiate construction of complex processing systems.

The following discussion reviews Clay's discoveries resulting from her meticulous efforts to describe changes observed in children's literacy processing during early acquisition, the theoretical perspective resulting from her quest to explain observed changes, and actions relative to promoting optimal development for young learners in need of a more secure developmental track.

Research Efforts: Documenting Changes Observed in Literacy Processing

Clay began her quest to document change in observable literacy behaviors with an atheoretical, no-hypothesis stance to data collection (Clay, 1982). Unsatisfied with existing explanations of reading acquisition, she sought new understandings through scientific methodology involving both qualitative and quantitative procedures. Her initial goal was to record children's behaviors sequentially "using reliable, systematic sampling and observation techniques" (Jones & Smith-Burke, 1999, p. 262).

Clay's methodology deviated from prevalent approaches that tended to quantify the effects of instruction by examining learners' pre- and postinstructional performance. In opposition to quantifying the effects of instruction (or teaching), Clay's interest was the delineation of qualitative changes in children's learning. She focused on the study of observable behaviors in how children work in reading and writing continuous texts (i.e., literacy processing) and interpreted changes as signals of change in psychological processes, such as perceiving, linking, and decision making. She referred to her perspective as a literacy processing view of progress in literacy acquisition and determined that the resulting descriptions of change offered an alternative view of progress—alternative to the more common use of pre- and posttests and statistical computations to set expectations (of both curricular goals and student achievement) and to evaluate results (Clay, 2001). Her focus included examining what young readers do as they encounter and problem solve increasingly difficult tasks. Therefore, by studying learners over time through the documentation of observed behaviors, she sought to clarify the sequence of changes in ways children process information and the emergence of competencies for effective reading and writing.

To conduct her research, she developed and applied an unusual lens, defined by her as any observational tool or research methodology that gathers "detailed data on changes in literacy processing over short intervals of time from subjects engaged in reading or writing continuous texts" (Clay, 2001, p. 16). Clay's running record of reading provides an example of an observational tool for collecting sequential, detailed accounts of what occurs as a child reads continuous text.

Clay's (1982) seminal research of 100 New Zealand children entering school at the age of 5.0 was a longitudinal study involving both weekly, systematic observations of individuals' writing and reading behaviors collected within natural settings and a test battery administered at three points over each child's first year of school. Clay conducted her study in classrooms where children were engaged in writing personal messages and reading storybooks daily within weeks of entering school. Although the participants were from different classrooms and schools, Clay determined that the common curriculum guidelines created instructional consistency across settings. Teachers did not delay opportunities for authentic literacy tasks, nor did they follow a prescriptive curriculum requiring proficiency with prerequisite skills prior to engaging children in reading and writing stories. Teachers expected children to work as independently as possible, and their expectations matched children's competencies. Thus, initial writing samples were often drawings with labeling provided by an adult. Although none of her participants could read at entry to school, all were introduced to short story books written in a familiar language within their first seven weeks of school.

When children reached the end of their first year of instruction and were tested with standardized instruments, Clay used the results to create four groups of varying levels of proficiency: high, high average, low average, and low. Comparing the performance within and between groups, Clay (1966) discovered that children were significantly different in their literacy learning. The results revealed multifactored ways in which children "constructed complex literacy processing systems for both reading and writing" (Clay, 2001, p. 288). Her documented map of literacy behaviors allowed her to describe literacy learning in the process of change, which gave Clay the genesis of her literacy processing theory.

This study prompted ongoing research conducted by Clay and her colleagues to pursue and confirm understandings and to test alternative hypotheses. The foci of her extensive body of research include the reading behaviors of children in their third year of instruction, syntactic analyses of reading errors, self-correction behavior, writing development, oral language performance, language proficiency of bilingual children, analysis of linguistic variables in oral reading (juncture, pitch, stress), concepts about print, visual perception, prevention, and early intervention (see Clay, 1982, 2001).

Research Findings: Documented Changes in Literacy Behaviors Over Time

Clay observed that the young learners she followed often read their first books using low-level strategies, or primitive working systems, acquired from experiences with talking, writing, and listening to stories prior to entering school. For example, some appeared to rely on their auditory memory of predictable sentences or stories. Many were aware of concepts of books, including awareness of the connections between pictures and text and anticipating and using a repeated sentence pattern. Their prereading behaviors indicated that they were attending to many aspects of literacy as

- they responded to print with a series of utterances
- they checked with pictures for agreement
- they matched pointing and word utterance on 50 percent of the text
- they increased attention to words using the spaces between words to guide them
- they located one or more words on request (Clay, 2001, p. 59)

Although such early processing behaviors (low-level strategies for reading) are not effective, they were found by Clay to be an adequate, initial starting place as they evolved into behaviors revealing more complex working systems and accurate and efficient responses as a result of instruction. Clay (1982) confirmed that the development and learning that led to more appropriate literacy processing behaviors resulted from ongoing exposure to stories (i.e., continuous texts). There was no advantage to delaying text reading and personal writing opportunities for 5-year-old children. In contrast, experience in continuous texts revealed important advantages.

Clay (1966, 1982) reported observing changes in a range of behaviors in each of four areas as learners exhibited more proficient reading behaviors. These four areas are (1) the directional constraints on movement (i.e., consistent left to right movement across words and lines of text), (2) visual perception of print (i.e., awareness of letter and word forms), (3) constructing appropriate types of speech responses (i.e., appropriate speech or syntax), and (4) the matching of spoken word units to written word units (i.e., synchronized one-to-one matching; Clay, 1982).

Clay determined that the earliest, teacher-scaffolded reading and writing activities supported essential learning neglected by most literacy theories. This includes the appropriate directional schema for attending to print and the movement patterns for processing text. "Directional behaviors manage the order in which readers and writers attend to anything in print. Gaining control of them is a foundational step in literacy as oral language is matched to written language" (Clay, 2001, p. 118). Establishing consistency in directing visual attention to print so lines of text, words, letters, and clusters of letters within words are scanned left to right in sequence is challenging and requires time. Evidence resulting from a study of quadruplets revealed both a time span of six months and clear, individual differences among children in the time needed to secure appropriate directional scanning of text (Clay, 1974, 2001).

Where to look, what to look for, and how to fixate and move the eyes across print are among the first things learned by novice readers. For the beginning reader/writer, this learning involves coordinating the body, hand, and eye movements needed for literacy processing, and thus, motor behaviors create an early working system for processing text. Gradually, directional order and one-to-one matching of speech with print become established routines requiring no conscious attention. This learning is one of the advantages of immersing beginning readers in the reading and writing of continuous texts.

In regard to visual perception of print, Clay found the richest depictions of the learner's awareness of letter and word forms in the writing products of her proficient learners. The following is a brief depiction of this learning of the features of print and the relationship between letters and words. Children gradually shifted from creating messages by drawing and writing to recording written messages without drawings; they exhibited awareness that writing consists of letters, a string of letters comprise a word, a word is a specific sequence of letters, and the sequence of letters relates to the spoken form of the word (Clay, 1998). The child's knowledge of letters and sound–symbol relationships is neither extensive nor complete at this point, and gaining control of this information is a major task. However, awareness and initial understandings create supportive visual knowledge for early reading that will continue to expand as a result of ongoing reading and writing experiences.

With only a few known items of visual knowledge (several letters and words), the proficient readers appeared to expand their literacy processing by increased applications of their newly acquired information. Analyses of their oral reading errors revealed searching and monitoring behaviors on the basis of visual information, often only an initial letter. The important processing advance was the child's increased receptiveness to visual information and ability to pull a new kind of information in print knowledge together with other knowledge sources (i.e., syntactic information) to read a message (Clay, 2001, p. 64).

Clay determined that early writing experiences served as a significant source of new learning that contributed to the child's construction of more effective working systems for processing literacy. Children in her studies were learning to read and write concurrently, which created benefits supporting the acquisition of foundational knowledge and the inner control of literacy processing. By writing a single sentence, the learner coordinates a range of behaviors: movement patterns required for dealing with print, ordering written language in appropriate sequences, visual scanning of letters and words, and the analysis of sounds in words. The learner attends to features of letters, learns new letters and some words, and begins to link sounds with letters. Writing experiences help build the working systems needed to search for information in print, strategies used to combine and check information, an awareness of how to construct a message, and awareness of the sources of knowledge available in written language (Clay, 2001, p. 17). These represent key, foundational aspects shared by writing and reading.

Based on her study of writing development over time, Clay (1975) observed that in the writing context, young writers

> do not learn about language on any one level of organization before they manipulate units at higher levels. When they know a few letters they can produce several words, and with several words they can make a variety of sentences. (p. 19)

Their attention to letters, sounds, and words serves their efforts to record personal messages, and they manage the complexity of the full range of information sources to complete their intentions. Clay (1982) noted that although their initial understandings are perhaps intuitive, her observations and evidence suggest that children learn on all levels of the language hierarchy at once, and it is the "rich intermingling of language learning across levels which probably accounts in some way for the fast progress which the best children can make" (Clay, 1975, p. 19). This represents the reciprocity between writing and reading that is so beneficial to the learner's construction of early literacy systems and acquisition of language knowledge that extends processing in both reading and writing.

Interestingly, Clay (1982) found no developmental sequence apparent in her records of proficient readers' emerging and changing behaviors in reading and writing. Individual children exhibited unique developmental histories, including "by-passing many of the steps which another child may follow" (Clay, 1982, p. 14). This discovery confirmed that individual learners take different paths to proficient reading and writing development (Clay, 1998, 2001). However, records also revealed that some children had difficulties with various aspects of the four early areas of development, and others persisted with inappropriate responses to reading and writing, such as a consistent right to left approach to print or inventing stories when asked to read (Clay, 1982).

In regard to changes documented in the readers' awareness of foundational literacy behaviors, records of reading behaviors revealed increasing awareness of the following:

- where to attend
- where to search
- what information to use
- what to relate information to
- how to monitor its acceptability
- what to do in the face of a dissonant result (Clay, 2001, p. 104)

As children gained awareness and their behaviors suggested more proficient working systems, they began to integrate information from two or more sources (e.g., from visual and syntactic information sources) more consistently to match what they said to the print. These behaviors were early forms of efficient reading behaviors that "became purposefully directed in some primitively integrated way to the problem of extracting a sequence of cues from text" (Clay, 2001, p. 60). These behaviors were interpreted by the teachers in Clay's study as indicative of the learners' preparedness for their first formal instructional texts.

One pattern of behavior appearing in Clay's original data was the unprompted, spontaneous self-correction of reading errors by young learners. Self-corrections were observed in the earliest readings of stories and first appeared when the child noted that his or her speech (oral reading of words) did not correspond to (match) the locating movements for the printed words on the page (often involving finger pointing). Based on monitoring appropriate movement patterns for reading, the reader revised, or corrected, his reading. This early behavior indicates a learner's willingness to choose between alternatives in order to read a precise message and maintain a fit between the language and visual information, two sources of information for text reading (Clay, 1991b, 2001).

As her proficient readers advanced in text reading levels, Clay (1991b, 2001) found that self-correction behaviors revealed that readers could search and check more and more detail in print to both correct and confirm their reading, which involved the range of information sources: visual information, including letter forms and letter–sound relationships; syntax; and semantic information. Clay (1982, 1991b, 2001) proposed that self-correction and the problem solving it entails is tutorial for the reader who is reinforced internally for his or her monitoring, searching, generating, choosing, and evaluating. Thus, Clay (2001) suggested that a learner's "willingness to choose between alternatives leads to a search for more information and this can potentially take processing to new levels of complexity" (p. 120).

There were two additional discoveries regarding self-correction behavior. First, a high level of reading accuracy (90%) is required for proficient self-correction behavior, and there is a clear progression in the amount of rereading completed by readers engaged in self-correcting. Records revealed that rereading is initially done from the very beginning of a sentence or a line of text and progresses to the rereading of a phrase, then rereading of a word, then an initial letter. Clay (2001) reported that this sequence, a pattern found to be identical in the records of high and low progress readers, provides a way to judge progress and observe change in the reader's literacy processing over time.

At the point when proficient learners transitioned into formal instruction, Clay's (2001) records of behaviors revealed the following:

- They could not read, but they identified the words in the text with 80% accuracy.
- They selected words one after the other to construct viable sentences.
- They could reject a response and try a different one.
- They began to self-correct.
- They knew a few words in reading and/or writing.
- They could bring two kinds of behaviors together (e.g., verbal and pointing behavior).
- They often stressed the separation (juncture) between words.

Gradually, readers demonstrated the ability to construct what a line of text might say, locate the sequence of information to attend to, and detect, or monitor, mismatches between their seeing and saying (Clay, 2001).

As these beginning readers worked with different kinds of information, their processing was labored, observable, and sequential. The transitions and development that Clay observed were replicated by Nalder (as cited in Clay, 2001) and delineated as follows:

- (Readers) begin to try to use the language of the book, to match what they say line by line and (later) word by word with some attention to occasional visual cues in known words. Language composed by the child supports any processing but can override the printed text.
- Another change is detected when the reader uses the language of the book, matched word to word, and definitely attends to some visual information. There is a lot of searching, checking and self-correcting with appropriate appeals for help and some omissions.
- Within about six months, fluent accurate reading is achieved by many with some successful solving, and two or more sources of information are used for one decision.
- After six months at school, proficient readers can be independent when handling the challenges in appropriately selected easy texts, using several sources of information (semantic, syntactic, visual, or sounds in sequence), and knowing how to check one kind of information against another.

Therefore, as a result of instruction in continuous text, "a quite simple set of responses became controlled, accurate and co-ordinated" (Clay, 2001, p. 59). In effect, these behaviors were early forms of efficient reading behaviors that

> became purposefully directed in some primitively integrated way to the problem of extracting a sequence of cues from text. Children were attending to letters, and words, and the sounds of letters in reading and writing, and they monitored these activities while enjoying the story they were composing in either reading or writing. (Clay, 2001, p. 60)

Clay had documented the early emergence of foundational processing and ongoing changes in her readers' literacy processing systems. She found that from the beginning, proficient readers use language and visual and motor information so "what on the surface looks like simple word-by-word reading...involves children in linking many things they know from different sources (visual, auditory/phonological, movement, speaking/articulating, and knowledge of the language)" (Clay, 2001, p. 79) to read a precise message. In effect, the reader making good progress constructs a literacy processing system that involves all language knowledge sources, including story structure, language structure, words and word structure, letters, and the features and sounds of letters.

Over time, the records of oral reading by proficient, beginning readers revealed increasing attention to and success with the visual information in text (e.g., initial letters, letter clusters, word parts, words) while maintaining appropriate syntactic and semantic utterances for the given context. In the beginning reader, each knowledge source is limited, and proficient development results from ongoing instruction in both reading and writing contexts. Much of the new learning entails visual perception and the acquisition of a large set of items (e.g., letters, letter clusters, words) acquired over time. However, in both reading and writing contexts, Clay's young learners engaged in literacy activities successfully by being allowed to draw on their existing language knowledge while being introduced to new learning. Clay (1982) found this to be true of a diverse set of learners, even bilingual children whose command of the English language of instruction was limited.

Proficient readers used their knowledge of oral language from the beginning. Their oral language provided a reliable source of information for predicting messages and for detecting reading errors. Gradually, the readers' awareness of semantic and syntactic information in text was enhanced by visual perceptual learning, including the learning of letters, letter–sound associations, words, and the use of word parts and syllables. Over time, semantic and syntactic information sources continued to expand, and important learning also proceeded "in the direction of more and more receptiveness to visual perception cues which must eventually dominate the process" (Clay, 1982, p. 28). Reading is a visual task, and the learner's increased, detailed control of visual information is an essential part of early reading acquisition (Clay, 2001).

In addition to the observed changes over time in a proficient reader's awareness of and increasing knowledge of the range of sources of language information in text, Clay's (2001) evidence also revealed how the early, primitive literacy processing expanded into more efficient decision-making. She discovered that proficient readers were constructing a network of strategic behaviors, action systems, or cell assemblies for processing text—cognitive terms useful in describing "what readers do as they work sequentially on the information sources in print to get the author's message" (Clay, 2001, p. 198). The readers had learned how to search and check information, how to go back to search again, and how to monitor their reading and confirm their decision making. The types of strategic behaviors they applied include the following:

- controlling serial order according to the directional rules for the script being read, across lines and within words
- using what you know about in reading to help writing and vice versa
- problem-solving with more than one kind of information
- actively searching for various types of information in print
- using visual information
- using language information
- drawing on stored information
- using phonological information
- working on categories, rules or probabilities about features in print
- using strategies which maintain fluency
- using strategies which problem-solve new features of printed words and meanings
- using strategies which detect and correct error (Clay, 2001, p. 199)

To explore the reading of proficient readers after three years of instruction, children's oral reading behaviors were gathered in a number of studies conducted by Clay and colleagues (see Clay, 1982). Clay's summary of this observational data revealed successful readers working sequentially across text, giving detailed attention to the range of information sources. They read accurately at a good pace, solved new or difficult words independently, and detected and self-corrected many of their errors.

Analyses of oral reading errors showed that on many occasions, the word read, although wrong, was typically influenced by syntax, meaning, letter knowledge, and letter–sound relationships. When an error occurred and was uncorrected, the substituted word corresponded to the text word on all four types of information, suggesting that good readers could be using subword, word, syntactic, and semantic information jointly when approaching unfamiliar words to read with accuracy. Self-corrections implied a mismatch between the information used in the substitution and other information sources available to and monitored by the reader. In addition to noting that these readers attended to multiple sources of language information, Clay (2001) also discovered that when the proficient readers in this age group engaged in analyzing text, they initiated their problem solving from any one of the information sources. In summarizing her observations, Clay (1982) suggested that the processing behaviors of these readers approximated the behaviors of a mature reader.

Summary of the Research

This overview of the documented findings of studies conducted by Clay with follow-up investigations by her colleagues confirms that literacy processing behaviors of young learners engaged in reading and writing continuous text change over time. Beginning, novice readers/writers apply low-level strategies in their earliest attempts to read and write as they approach literacy tasks with vague, rudimentary understandings. They gain proficiency as a result of opportunities to engage in reading and writing continuous texts with supportive instruction. They acquire more knowledge to support their processing, and over time their behaviors indicate acquisition of a more efficient and effective inner processing system, a complex network of working systems for processing text.

The patterns of behaviors observed in the records of children over multiple early studies, and ultimately over years of research with thousands of learners in her early intervention, led Clay to two theoretical considerations. She had discovered a transformative model of literacy acquisition, explaining changes in processing systems from primitive to more expert over the first year of school, and she had evidence on which to base a literacy processing theory.

Theoretical Perspective: Literacy Processing Theory

Resulting from her earliest investigations, Clay embraced a complex theory of literacy and defined reading, as we saw in the first section of this chapter. Her quest for theoretical explanations focused on building understandings of both the specific perceptual and cognitive behaviors involved in reading and writing and explanations of the integration of complex in-the-head processes. Thus, explanations of progress involved descriptions of the emergence of a network of complex neural processing systems, that is, the perceptual and cognitive working systems directed to complete reading and writing tasks.

Literacy processing is a reader's decision making about what a text says. It involves

> many working systems in the brain which search for and pick up verbal and perceptual information governed by directional rules; other systems which work on that information and make decisions; other systems which monitor and verify those decisions; and systems which produce responses. (Clay, 2001, p. 1)

These working systems are neural networks, perceptual and cognitive systems, which are constructed by the learner as a result of engagement in reading continuous texts to discern meaningful messages. For the proficient reader after one year of instruction, these working systems have the capacity to function as self-extending systems, allowing the learner to expand his or her competencies in acts of processing texts of increasing demands.

Readers operate on multiple sources of information to read for meaning, and Clay found this processing reflective of Rumelhart's (1994; see Chapter 29 this volume) interactive theory of reading. Rumelhart's theory posits that all knowledge sources are decision-making sources, and the reader's perceptions during reading are the product of interactions among all levels of the language hierarchy. For Rumelhart, this involves hypothesis generating and evaluating during the act of reading as tentative decisions about the message are made and then confirmed or revised on the basis of perceiving more and more information. For example, decisions regarding perceptions of letter features, letter sounds, letter clusters, and words are evaluated and confirmed or revised in conjunction with decisions regarding syntactic information, at either a phrase or clause level, and decisions on the basis of semantic information, which is more general knowledge of the topic or genre. Thus, the reader attends to all available sources of information in text (visual, syntactic, semantic), and "the reading process is the product of the simultaneous joint application of all the knowledge sources" (Chapter 29 this volume, p. 732).

The reader's knowledge of the language information sources in text support his or her complex processing systems, that is, the decision making that serves reading for meaning. The reader's working systems consider, scan, and integrate information from all levels of the language hierarchy when processing text, and therefore, giving more value to any level of the linguist's hierarchy of language information is unproductive and may be misleading. It is agreement across information sources that confirms a good decision and incongruity that signals the need for more searching, confirming, and perhaps correcting. To add understanding of the perceptual and cognitive working systems, Clay (2001) referenced Singer's concept of assembling the working systems for a specific task, a theory that allows "more scope for knowledge sources and neurological networks to be used flexibly and effectively by readers" (p. 101).

According to Singer (1994), readers who have acquired the necessary working systems are able to mobilize rapidly and flexibly a hierarchical organization of subsystems in which a minimum of mental energy and attention are devoted to input systems (perceptual systems involved in the perception of stimuli, including visual information) and a maximum is expended on mediation and output systems (cognitive systems involved in interpreting, inferring, integrating, and responding). Thus, when reading is proceeding in a fluent, proficient manner, the perceptual working systems operate without conscious attention, allowing the reader to focus attention on thinking about and responding to meaning, which engages the cognitive systems.

This processing suggests that the reader is employing working systems to search and monitor information sources supportive of his construction of meaning with ease. In terms of visual information specifically, this means that the information is located and scanned proficiently and recognized instantly. However, when a reader detects any disruption of meaning, the reader will shift attention to problem solve the dissonance by attending more closely to information sources supportive in refining his or her decision making. In beginning readers, this often involves analyzing visual information to identify words by focusing on the features and sounds of letters, or clusters of letters. As the young reader acquires more knowledge of each information source in text and "comes to know how and when each kind of information can help with decisions" (Clay, 2001, p. 111), the reader becomes more efficient in shifting to problem solving and resolving any issue quickly without loss of meaning.

Cognition and perception (and the related working systems) function on a problem-solving continuum (Bruner, 1957, 1974; Clay, 1991b, 2001), and shifts of conscious attention and problem-solving behaviors occur in ever-changing sequences. In effect, the reader adapts a range of complex processes flexibly "to the demands of a specific literacy task by assembling a temporary system from among those available to deal with the literacy task at hand" (Clay, 2001, p. 101).

Singer (1994) described readers mobilizing "cell assemblies in the brain and organizing them into different working systems according to moment-to-moment changes in the tasks or purposes of the reader" (Clay, 2001, p. 112). This suggests the individualized nature of both the emerging literacy processing systems of young readers and the ongoing, ever-changing assemblies of working systems supporting proficient reading. Clay (1998, 2001) and Singer both concluded that there could be more than one route to successful reading: "Individuals may attain the same level of achievement but by means of different compilations of working systems" (Clay, 2001, p. 113). Reading and learning to read vary in many ways across individuals.

The neural networks for literacy do not exist before the child engages in reading and writing continuous texts. Yet, as teachers provide children opportunities to write and to read a gradient of texts with increments of increasing challenges, learners have new opportunities to work at higher levels of complexity. This creates the problem-solving experiences that extend the efficiency of the neural processing systems.

Clay's literacy processing theory, a theory of assembling a complex network of perceptual and cognitive working systems for reading or writing continuous texts, is based on her observational research. Her meticulous documentation and study of patterns of behaviors collected over time revealed key discoveries. These include the "critical factor of individual differences" (Clay, 2001, p. 137) substantiating different paths to proficient literacy acquisition among young learners; the reciprocity of reading and writing; the transformational nature of literacy acquisition, that is, change over time in processing behaviors as learners acquire more knowledge and initial primitive strategies become more like that of a mature reader; and the initial evidence of a learner's self-extending system, "the strategic power to use what is known in the service of problem-solving the unknown" (Clay, 2001, p. 129). In effect, learners acquire a neural network of complex working systems that learns to extend itself.

While aspects of both Singer and Rumelhart's models of reading resonated with Clay's observations, she found that because neither theorist had addressed the early formative period of literacy acquisition, their explanations were incomplete. Clay's (2001) theory offers literacy awareness and orientation to print as essential aspects of early literacy learning:

> Children have to adapt their preschool working systems to make them work on the written code, learn some new skills, lay down the foundational knowledge sources and learn how knowledge from very different sources can be found, assembled, and integrated. (Clay, 2001, p. 137)

The key concepts include knowing the following:

- how to assemble stories
- that print can be written
- that attention must follow the rules of direction
- that symbols have only one orientation
- how to switch attention out to the page and back into the head
- how to work with complex information and come to decisions (Clay, 2001, p. 137)

In summary, Clay's meticulous documentation of observed literacy behaviors collected over time revealed changes in children's literacy processing during early acquisition and led her to a complex literacy processing theory, which she described as follows:

> In a complex model of interacting competencies in reading and writing the reader can potentially draw from all his or her current understanding, and all his or her language competencies, and visual information, and phonological information and knowledge of printing conventions, in ways which *extend both the searching and linking processes as well as the item knowledge repertoires.* Learners pull together necessary information from print in simple ways at first..., but as opportunities to read and write accumulate over time the learner becomes able to quickly and momentarily construct a somewhat complex operating system which might solve the problem. (Clay, 2001, p. 224)

It was her perspective that this complex processing theory was critically important in creating powerful learning opportunities for any child struggling with early literacy.

Instructional Implications of a Complex Literacy Theory

As Clay's research focus evolved to investigating instructional assistance for young readers/writers struggling with literacy acquisition, she approached challenging issues with a developmental perspective and her emerging, theoretical explanations of change over time in literacy processing behaviors. Her goal was an intervention designed to allow optimal literacy development that would result in proficient performance in reading and writing and prevent subsequent failures. On the basis of her theoretical perspective, it is apparent that such complex learning results from "a curriculum of psychological processes (perceptual and cognitive) necessary for working with written language" (Clay, 2005a, p. 18). Specific goals are to accelerate the pace of learning, lift each child's level of achievement, and build a secure foundation for subsequent literacy learning (Clay, 2001).

Intervening early in the child's educational experience was paramount to Clay, as she had determined that the developing competencies of low-progress children differed from those of proficient learners from the initial, earliest opportunities to read and write (Clay, 1966, 1982). Low-progress students were observed to initiate literacy learning with ineffective behaviors, and their processing did not improve during their first year of instruction. Consequently, Clay (1987) realized that the gap existing between proficient and low-progress children in the first year of school widened over time. For these children, classroom programs did not meet their individual needs, and the most deleterious outcome of such instruction, inadequate for any of a wide range of reasons, is a child who has learned to be leaning disabled (Clay, 1987; Vellutino, 2010). For both Clay and Vellutino, this means that children may appear learning disabled as a result of instructional and experiential deficits, not as a result of cognitive deficits. Early intervention is key to averting ongoing difficulties and confusion and to bringing children quickly to levels of proficiency that allow them to profit from classroom literacy programs.

An important aspect of designing instruction to meet individual needs was Clay's rejection of any single cause of literacy difficulties. Multiple causes, idiosyncratic to individual learners, require individual programs of instruction delivered in one-on-one settings. This allows the greatest scope for adjusting instruction to "find ways around a child's limitations in some functions, and which could break a cycle of interacting deficits, whatever those limitations might be" (Clay, 2001, p. 220). One-on-one instructional settings allow the teacher to focus intently on the learner's response repertoire, respond immediately with the most appropriate, contingent support, and adjust instruction as needed. This is the important experience needed by the child who is having severe difficulty in acquiring literacy.

Clay based the goals of her early, individually delivered intervention on her study of proficient readers and focused on how to help struggling learners acquire complex neural networks for processing text. Active learners construct theories of reading and writing that emerge from primitive beginnings and transform as a result of instruction and experience into more mature behaviors. Instruction must support the child's construction of working systems that use all sources of language knowledge to read and write texts and become able to expand and improve as a result of ongoing challenge in texts of increasing complexity. Self-improvement results from the independent learning created by effective linking, evaluating, and decision making, which constitutes the self-extending system. Such independence in reading and writing is encouraged by teachers who scaffold the learner (Vygotsky, 1962) and ultimately act as a resource as the child "pursues a large amount of the activity by himself, pushing the boundaries of his own capacities" (Clay, 1991b, p. 255). Because the self-extending system creates a bootstrapping effect (Stanovich, 1986), Clay (2001) likened it to what Stanovich labeled the positive Matthew effect; she attributed this effect to the complexity of interacting neural networks.

Complex learning results from instruction that starts with a child's strengths and builds on his or her existing, perhaps primitive, processing systems (Clay, 1998, 2005a). Teachers accomplish this by drawing on the child's competent systems while supporting new tentative responding until new strengths are established (Clay, 2001). As a result, the child experiences success, feels in control of his or her learning, and gains awareness of new features of text and/or new ways of responding (Clay, 1998). Teachers make use of each individual's existing response repertoire; therefore, each child's series of lessons is unique, and different paths to efficient processing are expected and supported (Clay, 1998).

Clay (2005a) identified two key hypotheses that informed her intervention plan. The first is that the child's instruction should be based on the teacher's continuous, detailed observations of literacy behaviors. Thus, the reflective teacher considers her observations of the child's problem-solving strategies in writing and in reading daily (using running records). The child's new discoveries, partially correct responses, and self-correction behaviors inform instructional decisions, which often occurs on a moment-to-moment basis. The second hypothesis is that the reciprocal relationship between reading and writing creates powerful opportunities for the learner's competencies in one area to support learning in the second.

More specifically, Clay (2001) discerned that the similar aspects shared by reading and writing include the following:

> 1) the stores of knowledge about letters, sounds and words which they can draw upon, 2) the ways in which known oral language contributes to print activities, 3) some similar processes that learners use to search for the information they need to solve new problems, and 4) ways in which they pull together or integrate different types of information common to both activities. (p. 33)

More specific examples of processes common to both reading and writing activities include the following:

- controlling serial order
- problem-solving with more than one kind of information
- drawing on stored information and acting on it
- using visual information
- using phonological information
- using the meaning of what was composed
- using the vocabulary and structure of what was composed

- searching, checking and correcting
- categorizing, using rules, and estimating probabilities of occurrence (Clay, 2001, p. 32)

Clay's (2005b) instructional plan for daily lessons includes reading texts of easy and instructional levels, writing personal stories, and using brief decontextualized activities to support learning items such as letters and words, which are encountered in and linked to reading and writing activities. The texts for reading are not controlled or contrived; they are selected to give the young reader access to all levels of the language hierarchy as working systems for perceiving, integrating, and evaluating information sources—strengthened only as a result of reading continuous, meaningful texts.

In describing the instruction that reflects important theoretical constructs, Clay (2001) emphasized the following:

- The teacher would support the development of literacy processing by astute selection of tasks, judicious sharing of tasks, and by varying the time, difficulty, content, interest and methods of instruction, and type and amount of conversation within the standard lesson activities.
- The teacher would foster and support active constructive problem-solving, self-monitoring, and self correction from the first lesson, helping learners to understand that they must take over the expansion of their own competencies. To do this the teacher would focus on process variables (how to get and use information) rather than on mere correctness and habitual responses, and would temporarily value responses that were partially correct for what ever they contributed toward correctness.
- The teacher would set the level of task difficulty to ensure high rates of correct responding plus appropriate challenge so that the active processing system could learn from its own attempts to go beyond current knowledge. (p. 225)

Clay (2009) approached the challenges in helping low-progress learners recover a more normal trajectory of literacy performance by asking, what is possible? This led to years of exploration and theory refinement, lesson design, and extensive research of instructional approaches, teacher effectiveness, and children's progress. The result of her development and design efforts was an early intervention known internationally as Reading Recovery, an intervention she also referred to as Reading and Writing Recovery (Clay, 2001). Reading Recovery is currently available to children experiencing the most difficulty in reading and writing following one year of schooling in educational systems around the world.

In the early development phase of her intervention,

> Clay used a grounded theory approach: She used observations of children and teachers to develop theory, she used theory to guide selection of methods, she applied the methods to practice in a systematic way, and she used detailed observations and records to confirm or revise theory and procedures. (Jones & Smith-Burke, 1999, p. 271)

Clay (2009) conducted studies to explore questions regarding teaching procedures, teacher-training possibilities, implementation issues, decisions about when to end a child's series of lessons, and sustained effects for participants one year as well as three years following the intervention (Jones & Smith-Burke, 1999). In this way, working with teachers and testing the intervention in schools, Clay was able to confirm instructional decisions and discern important training and implementation issues.

Professional development and implementation issues received extensive attention as Clay was asked to scale up Reading Recovery, and she approached all challenges with tentativeness, flexibility, and a problem-solving attitude (Clay, 2001). Always supportive of classroom teachers, she designed a trainer-of-trainer model of professional preparation and found teachers astute learners of her complex literacy theory and instructional procedures. She was masterful in addressing implementation issues, and as educators from other countries and in languages other than English worked with her to adopt and implement Reading Recovery, she was sensitive to cultural and educational differences. "Using a process of accommodation, she found adaptive ways to implement Reading Recovery without lessening the high standards that lead to optimal results for both teachers and children" (Doyle, 2009, pp. 292–293).

The success of these efforts is assessed in evaluation studies replicated by each country with a national implementation, and the resulting data, collected and analyzed for each participating child, are reported annually (see Watson & Askew, 2009, for full descriptions). These reports confirm that Reading Recovery has been successful in accelerating learning and securing a firm literacy foundation for children in diverse settings and in multiple languages, including English, Spanish, and French.

Clay (2001) has attributed the success of Reading Recovery to five key aspects, including the specific guidelines for program delivery, the training that prepares teachers to be astute decision makers, a theory of constructive learning, a complex theory of literacy learning, and lesson components that support perceptual and cognitive processing. These components suggest that she based her early intervention on considerations of behaviors observed in proficient learners over time and instructional modifications needed to optimize literacy development for struggling learners.

Summary

This discussion has presented a review of Marie M. Clay's complex literacy processing theory, her theoretical perspective of literacy learning, and implications of her theory for her design of an intervention for children struggling with early literacy. From these efforts, via a grounded theory process, Clay solidified her literacy processing theory of reading and writing continuous texts, explaining how literacy learning is transformed in a series of changes from simple to more complex processes. Her studies afforded examination of behavioral evidence revealing the nature of the learner's construction of literacy processing abilities over time. In addition, noting that new entrants bring vastly different personal repertories of experience and knowledge to school, she documented how unique, or individual, their paths to literacy might be.

Clay's analyses of early literacy behaviors led to what she called a literacy processing theory, a theory of assembling perceptual and cognitive working systems capable of completing increasingly complex tasks (Clay, 2001). She considered Rumelhart's (Chapter 29 this volume) information processing theory helpful for considering the integration of language information sources, and she was informed by the theoretical discussions of Holmes (1953, 1960/1970) and Singer (1994). However, Clay also realized that theorists had not considered the challenges and learning associated with initial literacy acquisition. Her observational research led her to important discoveries, and her resulting theory is a multifaceted theory of beginning reading and writing, accounting for the early, foundational learning necessary for acquiring complex cognitive processing.

When Clay initiated her observational research, her methodology differed from the existing practices to quantify learner performance. Her interest was to delineate qualitative changes in children's learning. She created new assessment tools, considered an unusual lens for documenting behaviors sequentially, and collected data longitudinally. Therefore, her focus and approach parallel the microgenetic analyses of learning, as described by Siegler (2006), currently applied by developmental psychologists, and discussed in relation to Clay's literacy processing perspective by Schwartz and Gallant (2011).

Microgenetic analyses involve the scientific exploration of the genesis, or very beginnings, of learners' strategic behaviors, how children's learning occurs, and how it changes over time. Specifically, the methods of study include observations that span the period of rapidly changing competencies by securing a density of observations—a high amount of observations in relation to the rate of change. The resulting observations of learners engaged in specific tasks are analyzed intensively with the goal of inferring in-the-head processes (see Siegler, 2006). Clay's studies (1966, 1974, 1975, 1982, 2001) of changes over time in the reading and writing behaviors of novice learners not only provide the first, rich model of this scientific approach to the study of early literacy but also reveal the importance and power of alternative approaches to understanding complex literacy learning.

Clay was astute at transitioning her theory to practice, making a remarkable difference for children, teachers, and schools. Again, she applied scientific rigor to test all aspects of her assessment instruments, the instructional practices designed to support the learner's construction of perceptual/cognitive working systems, teachers' professional development, and effective implementations of early intervention in a wide range of differing school systems. The success of her Reading Recovery early intervention, substantiated internationally by ongoing analyses of student data, attests to the robustness of her theoretical perspectives of literacy acquisition, children's learning, professional development, and systemic design.

Additional indicators of effectiveness are found in evaluations conducted by non–Reading Recovery entities. The National Center on Response to Intervention in the United States has endorsed her assessment tool, *An Observation Survey of Early Literacy Achievement* (Clay, 2006), and the What Works Clearinghouse (2008a, 2008b) has substantiated the scientific evidence resulting from multiple researchers' investigations of instructional effects. Reading Recovery is currently recognized as a powerful, scientifically based Response to Intervention, and in fact, Clay's contribution to the movement is considered seminal (Vellutino, 2010). Vellutino has acknowledged that "Marie Clay was actually the first reading researcher to use RTI to identify children who might be afflicted by organically based reading difficulties" (p. 7) as opposed to limitations resulting from experiential or instructional deficits which Reading Recovery instruction addresses.

Clay (2001) has written that she used theory as a tool to explain the changes in literacy behaviors discovered in the reading and writing processes that she documented so astutely. Always tentative, she described herself as living in a "perpetual state of enquiry" (Clay, 2001, p. 3) and sought refinement of her perspectives through her ongoing search for answers to important, new questions. Her quest for explanations and her actions relative to promoting the optimal development of learning potential among young learners are profound contributions to the literacy community and millions of children around the world.

QUESTIONS FOR REFLECTION

1. What implications for instruction arise from Clay's finding that there is no single consistent developmental sequence that exists for all young readers and writers?
2. How can an early-literacy teacher use Clay's findings and theories to structure effective interventions for each child?
3. Why is it important, according to Clay, to integrate reading and writing activities for emergent readers?

REFERENCES

Bruner, J.S. (1957). On perceptual readiness. *Psychological Review, 64*(2), 123–152. doi:10.1037/h0043805

Bruner, J.S. (1974). The organisation of early skilled action. In M.P.M. Richards (Ed.), *The integration of a child into a social world* (pp. 167–184). London: Cambridge University Press.

Clay, M.M. (1966). *Emergent reading behaviour.* Unpublished doctoral dissertation. University of Auckland, New Zealand.

Clay, M.M. (1974). The spatial characteristics of the open book. *Visible Language, 8*(3), 275–282.

Clay, M.M. (1975). *What did I write? Beginning writing behaviour.* Auckland, NZ: Heinemann.

Clay, M.M. (1982). *Observing young readers: Selected papers.* Exeter, NH: Heinemann.

Clay, M.M. (1987). Learning to be learning disabled. *New Zealand Journal of Educational Studies, 22*(2), 155–173.

Clay, M.M. (1991a). Child development. In J. Flood, J. Jensen, D. Lapp, & J.R. Squire (Eds.), *Handbook of research on teaching the English language arts* (pp. 40–45). Newark: DE: International Reading

Association; Urbana, IL: National Council of Teachers of English.
Clay, M.M. (1991b). *Becoming literate: The construction of inner control.* Portsmouth, NH: Heinemann.
Clay, M.M. (1998). *By different paths to common outcomes.* York, ME: Stenhouse.
Clay, M.M. (2001). *Change over time in children's literacy development.* Portsmouth, NH: Heinemann.
Clay, M.M. (2004). Simply by sailing in a new direction you could enlarge the world. In J. Worthy, B. Maloch, J.V. Hoffman, D.L. Schallert, & C.M. Fairbanks (Eds.), *Fifty-third yearbook of the National Reading Conference* (pp. 60–66). Oak Creek, WI: National Reading Conference.
Clay, M.M. (2005a). *Literacy lessons designed for individuals: Part one: Why? when? and how?* Portsmouth, NH: Heinemann.
Clay, M.M. (2005b). *Literacy lessons designed for individuals: Part two: Teaching procedures.* Portsmouth, NH: Heinemann.
Clay, M.M. (2006). *An observation survey of early literacy achievement* (Rev. 2nd ed.). Portsmouth, NH: Heinemann.
Clay, M.M. (2009). The Reading Recovery research reports. In B. Watson & B. Askew (Eds.), *Boundless horizons: Marie Clay's search for the possible in children's literacy* (pp. 37–100). Rosedale, New Zealand: Pearson Education.
Doyle, M.A. (2009). A dynamic future. In B. Watson & B. Askew (Eds.), *Boundless horizons: Marie Clay's search for the possible in children's literacy* (pp. 287–308). Rosedale, New Zealand: Pearson Education.
Holmes, J.A. (1953). *The substrata-factor theory of reading.* Berkeley, CA: California.
Holmes, J.A. (1970). The substrata-factor theory of reading: Some experimental evidence. In H. Singer & R.B. Ruddell (Eds.), *Theoretical models and processes of reading* (pp. 187–197). Newark, DE: International Reading Association. (Reprinted from *New frontiers in reading*, by J.A. Figurel, Ed., 1960, New York: Scholastic)
Jones, N.K., & Smith-Burke, M.T. (1999). Forging an interactive relationship among research, theory, and practice: Clay's research design and methodology. In J.S. Gaffney & B.J. Askew (Eds.), *Stirring the waters: The influence of Marie Clay* (pp. 261–285). Portsmouth, NH: Heinemann.
Rumelhart, D.E. (1994). Toward an interactive model of reading. In R.B. Ruddell, M.R. Ruddell, & H. Singer (Eds.), *Theoretical models and processes of reading* (4th ed., pp. 864–894). Newark, DE: International Reading Association.
Schwartz, R.M., & Gallant, P.A. (2011). The role of self-monitoring in initial word-recognition learning. In C. Wyatt-Smith, J. Elkins, & S. Gunn (Eds.), *Multiple perspectives on difficulties in learning literacy and numeracy* (pp. 235–253). New York: Springer. doi:10.1007/978-1-4020-8864-3_11
Siegler, R.S. (2006). Microgenetic analyses of learning. In W. Damon, R.M. Lerner (Series Eds.), D. Kuhn, & R.S. Siegler (Vol. Eds.), *Handbook of child psychology: Vol. 2. Cognition, perception, and language* (6th ed., pp. 464–510). Hoboken, NJ: Wiley.
Singer, H. (1994). The substrata-factor theory of reading. In R.B. Ruddell, M.R. Ruddell, & H. Singer (Eds.), *Theoretical models and processes of reading* (4th ed., pp. 895–927). Newark, DE: International Reading Association.
Stanovich, K.E. (1986). Matthew effects in reading: Some consequences of individual differences in the acquisition of literacy. *Reading Research Quarterly, 21*(4), 360–407. doi:10.1598/RRQ.21.4.1
Vellutino, F.R. (2010). Learning to be learning disabled: Marie Clay's seminal contribution to the Response to Intervention approach to identifying specific reading disability. *The Journal of Reading Recovery, 10*(1), 5–23.
Vygotsky, L.S. (1962). *Thought and language* (E. Hanfmann & G. Vakar, Eds. & Trans.). Cambridge, MA: MIT Press. doi:10.1037/11193-000
Watson, B., & Askew, B. (Eds.). (2009). *Boundless horizons: Marie Clay's search for the possible in children's literacy.* Rosedale, New Zealand: Pearson Education.
What Works Clearinghouse. (2008a). *Reading Recovery* (WWC Intervention Report). Washington, DC: Institute of Education Sciences, U.S. Department of Education. Retrieved May 15, 2012, from ies.ed.gov/ncee/wwc/reports/beginning_reading/reading_recovery/
What Works Clearinghouse. (2008b). *Reading Recovery appendix* (WWC Intervention Report). Washington, DC: Institute of Education Sciences, U.S. Department of Education. Retrieved May 15, 2012, from ies.ed.gov/ncee/wwc/reports/beginning_reading/reading_recovery/

Instructing Comprehension-Fostering Activities in Interactive Learning Situations

Ann L. Brown, University of California, Berkeley*
Annemarie Sullivan Palincsar, University of Michigan*
Bonnie B. Armbruster, University of Illinois at Urbana-Champaign

Introduction

"Pupils don't learn to comprehend by osmosis" (Cushenbery, 1969). As with any definite statement concerning the acquisition of reading skills, this could be a controversial position, but a main theme of this chapter is that, at least for a sizable number of children, the statement is true. It is also argued that children who need extensive instruction in comprehending written materials most are least likely to receive it. The latter part of the chapter describes cognitive-skills training studies that have provided extensive practice in comprehension-fostering activities and have resulted in substantial improvements in students' ability to learn from texts.

Resnick (1979) has argued that there are two main biases in reading instruction, namely direct instruction of decoding and informal teaching of comprehension. Those who advocate a heavy emphasis on decoding mechanisms in early reading also tend toward the direct-instruction approach, whereas those who emphasize early attention to language processing, language arts, or comprehension tend also to espouse learner-directed, informal instructional approaches. As Resnick also argued, there is no reason in principle why one cannot have direct instruction in comprehension or (a little harder to envisage) informal instruction in decoding. In this chapter, concern is with one of the underpopulated cells, relatively direct or explicit instruction in comprehension. Of particular concern is the explicit instruction of comprehension-fostering skills with children at risk for academic failure precisely because they experience unusual difficulties in this arena.

Prereading Experiences

Preschool Reading Dyads

Learning to read does not begin when the child enters school; the child brings a history of preschool learning experiences that, to a greater or lesser extent, have prepared the way for a smooth transition. Some of these experiences could clearly

This chapter is reprinted from *Learning and Comprehension of Text* (pp. 255–286), edited by H. Mandl, N.L. Stein, and T. Trabasso.

be classified as prereading activities; others are more general learning practices with some relevance to reading. Many of these early experiences have taken place in social settings that share pertinent features with common school learning activities. Some children have considerable preschool experience in interactions that are very similar to school reading groups; others have not.

Certain parent–child interactions are ideal practicing grounds for subsequent teacher–child activities that will be of central importance in the early grades. Social settings such as these, where the child interacts with experts in a problem-solving domain, are settings where a great deal of learning occurs in and out of school. Indeed, some would argue that the majority of learning is shaped by social processes (Laboratory of Comparative Human Cognition, in press; Vygotsky, 1934/1978). From this perspective it is claimed that children first experience a particular set of problem-solving activities in the presence of others and only gradually come to perform these functions for themselves. First, the adult (parent, teacher, etc.) guides the child's activity, doing much of the cognitive work herself, but gradually the adult and child come to share the cognitive functions with the child taking initiative and the adult correcting and guiding where the child falters. Finally, the adult allows the child to take over the major thinking role and adopts the stance of a supportive and sympathetic audience.

This developmental progress from social to individual cognitive processing (other regulation to self-regulation) is nicely illustrated in parent–child learning dyads such as those reported by Wertsch (1978). Of particular interest to the argument here are the interactions of mothers and children as they engage in picture book "reading."

At least in middle class homes, a stable locus of parent–child interactions is the picture book task. Ninio and Bruner (1978) observed one mother–infant dyad longitudinally, starting when the child was only 8 months old and terminating (unfortunately) when he was 18 months old. From the very beginning, their interaction can best be described as a dialogue with the timing of mother's and child's behavior following an almost complete alternation pattern strikingly similar to the turn-taking conventions observed in dialogue. The mother initially is very much in command and seduces the child into the ritual dialogue for picture book reading by accepting any response from the baby as appropriate for his turn in the conversation. Indeed, Ninio and Bruner point out that the mother accepts an astonishing variety of responses as acceptable turn-taking behavior interpreting anything as having a "specific, intelligible content." The "imputation of intent and content" to the child's activities constitutes "an important mechanism by which the child is advanced to more adult-like communicative behavior" (Ninio & Bruner, 1978, p. 8).

A dramatic shift in responsibility comes when the child begins to label pictures for himself. Now the mother acts as if she believes the child has uttered words rather than babble. As the mother's theory of the child changes, so does her part in the dialogue. At first she appears to be content with any vocalization, but as soon as actual words can be produced the mother steps up her demands and asks for a label with the query "What's that?" The mother seems to increase her level of expectation, first "coaxing the child to substitute a vocalization for a non-vocal sign and later a well-formed word for a babbled vocalization." Initially, the mother does all the labeling because she assumes that the child cannot. According to Ninio and Bruner (1978),

> Later, the mother starts a cycle with a label *ONLY* if she thinks that the child will not label the picture himself, either because he does not yet know the correct word or he is not attentive enough to make the effort at labeling. If circumstances seem more favorable for labeling to occur, she will usually start the cycle with a "*What's that?*" question. (p. 14)

Responsibility for labeling is transferred from the mother to the child in response to his increasing store of knowledge, finely monitored by the mother. During the course of the study, the mother constantly updated her inventory of the words the child had previously understood and repeatedly attempted to make contact with his growing knowledge base. For example:

1. You haven't seen one of those; that's a goose.
2. You don't really know what those are, do you? They are mittens; wrong time of year for those.
3. It's a dog; I know you know that one.
4. We'll find you something you know very well.
5. Come on, you've learned "bricks."

DeLoache (1983) has repeated many of these observations in a cross-sectional study of mothers reading to their children. The children ranged from 17–38 months. The mothers of the youngest children point to the objects and label them, sometimes providing some additional information. In the middle age group, the children are much more active. Their mothers ask them to point to and label objects and to provide other information about the picture. These children often spontaneously provide labels ("There's a horsie") or ask the mothers for labels ("What's this?"). In the oldest group studied, more complex stories were introduced, and the mothers do much more than simply label objects. They talk about the relation among the objects in the picture and relate them to the child's experience—e.g., "That's right, that's a bee hive. Do you know what bees make? They make honey. They get nectar from flowers and use it to make honey, and then they put the honey in the bee hive." When the child can recognize the pictures and knows something about them, the mother uses the material to provide the child with a great deal of background information only loosely related to the actual pictures. It is not simply that the amount of help changes as the child becomes more competent, but the quality of help is finely geared to the child's current level.

In both the Ninio and Bruner and DeLoache dyads, the mother is seen functioning repeatedly in the child's "region of sensitivity to instruction" (Wood & Middleton, 1975) or "zone of proximal development" (Vygotsky, 1934/1978). As the child advances so does the level of collaboration demanded by the mother. The mother systematically shapes their joint experiences in such a way that the child will be drawn into taking more and more responsibility for the dyad's work. In so doing, the mother not only provides an optimal learning environment, she also models appropriate comprehension-fostering activities such as elaboration, activating appropriate background knowledge, and questioning strategies. These crucial activities are thereby made *overt* and *explicit*.

Inadequate Early Mediated Learning

It has been argued that parent–child interactions such as the social reading experiences just described are important preparations for early school success. It has also been argued that a severe lack of interactive experiences is a primary source of academic retardation. A leading advocate of this position is Feuerstein (1979, 1980), who argues that cognitive growth is very heavily dependent on the quality of *mediated learning* that the child experiences. According to Feuerstein (1979), "Mediated learning is the training given to the human organism by an experienced adult who frames, selects, focuses, and feeds back an environmental experience in such a way as to create appropriate learning sets" (p. 6). These mediated-learning experiences are an essential aspect of development beginning when the parent selects significant objects for the infant to focus on and proceeding throughout development with the adult systematically shaping the child's learning experiences. Feuerstein believes that this is the principal means by which children develop the cognitive operations necessary for learning independently. By interacting with an adult, who models and guides problem-solving activities and structures learning environments, children gradually come to adopt structuring and regulating activities of their own. It is argued that cognitive skills, including those of comprehension fostering and monitoring, develop normally via a process whereby the adult models and prompts their use and the children gradually adopt such activities as part of their own repertoire.

Feuerstein believes that the principal reason for the poor academic performance of many disadvantaged students is the lack of consistent instruction by parental models in their earlier developmental histories because of parental apathy, ignorance, or overcommitment. Quite simply, parents in disadvantaged homes were often themselves disadvantaged children and cannot be expected to teach what they perhaps do not know; large family size and the need for a working mother do not leave a great deal of time for Socratic dialogue games. In addition, interactive styles of continually questioning and extending the limits of knowledge that are typical of middle-class social-interaction patterns (Ninio & Bruner, 1978) may even be alien to some cultures (Au, 1979; Bernstein, 1971).

Mediated-learning activities, however, are exactly what occur in schools, and the middle-class child comes well prepared to take part in these rituals. Not only does the disadvantaged child lack sufficient prior exposure, but there is evidence that teachers give less experience in this learning mode to those who, because of their lack of prior experience, need it most.

School Reading Experiences

Teachers as Models of Reading Strategies

Ideally when the child reaches school, teachers take over some of the mediating functions, acting as models and promoters of comprehension-fostering activities. In schools, effective teachers are those who engage in continued prompts to get children to plan and monitor their own reading activities. Effective teachers model many forms of critical thinking for their students (Collins & Stevens, 1982). Thus, Collins and Smith's (1982) recent call for teachers to model comprehension-monitoring activities is timely but not novel. In a recent review of the literature, Bird (1980) traces the history of this idea and points out that it is a recurrent theme in the reading-education literature. For example, Lorge (1957) stressed that the teacher should model active-comprehension processes and direct the child's attention to the thinking and reasoning processes that he or she engages in while reading for meaning. Smith (1961) also called for teachers to ask questions that stimulate the drawing of inferences, the making of predictions and of comparisons, and the use of cause and effect reasoning. This theme was repeated by King (1967) and Gantt (1970), who described programs of teacher-directed questioning by which children are led through the sequence of thinking necessary to understand the passage. Similarly, Schwartz and Scheff (1975) suggested that teachers encourage active reading by demonstrating their own curiosity, posing questions, reasoning, predicting, and verifying inferences and conclusions.

Good teachers do this, of course. Even teachers who refrain from such activities in reading group do demonstrate them in, for example, reading a story to the whole class (Griffin, 1977). In their discussion of why teachers are easier to understand than texts, Schallert and Kleiman (1979) identified four main activities that teachers use to help children understand. They tailor the message to the child's level, activate relevant background knowledge, focus student attention on main points, and force comprehension monitoring by probing and question-asking aimed at testing the degree of understanding.

The main theme of all this work is that the ideal teacher functions as a model of comprehension-fostering and -monitoring activities largely by activating relevant knowledge and questioning basic assumptions. These are the essential features of the teaching style referred to variously as Socratic, case, or inquiry methods. Collins and Stevens (1982) have examined a variety of teachers and developed a taxonomy of tactics that are commonly used by outstanding teachers, notably the "entrapment ploys" of counterexamples and invidious generalizations, the "extension ploys" that force students to apply their new-found knowledge broadly, and the "debugging ploys" that force students to correct their misconceptions (Collins & Stevens, 1982).

Collins and Stevens point out that a main goal of such dialogues is not to convey the content of a particular domain. If this were the aim, the method would be inefficient due to the low rate of information transfer; more points can be conveyed in a lecture than can be discussed in a Socratic dialogue. If the method is successful, it is because it teaches students to think scientifically, to make predictions, to question and evaluate. An effective aid to knowledge building and revision is the ploy of forcing learners to make their theories explicit and to defend them to others.

In order for these activities of questioning, predicting, hypothesis generation, testing, and revision to be of service to the child, it is necessary that they are transferred from the teacher to the child in such a way that they form part of the learner's battery of comprehension-fostering skills. A common problem with all these approaches, as pointed out by Jenkinson (1969) and Gall (1970), is that they presuppose that children witnessing these activities will come to employ them on their own. This is the problem of *internalization*, how the child comes to use personally activities that were originally social (Vygotsky, 1934/1978). We return to this point later.

Reading Groups and Reading Status

Not all children are exposed to gifted teachers, and even the same teachers may offer different learning environments to those viewed as good or poor readers (Brown, Palincsar, & Purcell, in press). The selection of a curriculum is itself the selection of a particular reading environment. Bartlett (1979) claimed that disadvantaged children are most likely to be exposed to early-reading programs with a heavy emphasis on decoding such as Distar, whereas middle-class children receive earlier exposure to programs that emphasize comprehension such as Open Court. Bartlett goes on to compare the types of questions featured prominently in Distar exercises to those recommended by Open Court. In general, the Distar questions tend to focus on locating and remembering specific information, whereas the Open Court questions promote reflection upon and the questioning of the meaning of the text. Hence, a different type of instruction is aimed at children who enter school differentially prepared for the experience.

Even if the curriculum and classroom placement do not differ, there remains evidence that the reading environment is not equal for all children. For example, detailed observations of reading groups (Allington, 1980; Au, 1980; Cazden, 1979; Collins, 1980; McDermott, 1978) have shown that good and poor readers are not treated equally. Good readers are questioned about the meaning behind what they are reading, and they are asked to evaluate and criticize material frequently. A considerable amount of time in the good reading group is "on task"; i.e., reading-related activities occur, and a sizable amount of the group activities are of an optimal "comprehension-fostering" type. In the good reading group, the teacher adopts the procedure of asking every child to read in turn; but in the poorer reading group, turn taking is at the teacher's request, and the really poor readers are not called upon to perform to save everyone embarrassment (McDermott, 1978). Precious little time in the poor reading group is spent doing comprehension-fostering activities; the lion's share of activities involve the establishment of such rituals as turn taking and hand raising. When and if they are required to read, poor readers receive primarily drill in pronunciation and decoding. Rarely are they given practice in qualifying and evaluating their comprehension (Allington,

1980; Collins, 1980). A case could even be made that the poorest readers receive little formal reading comprehension instruction in these groups (McDermott, 1978)!

Children who come to school inadequately prepared for reading, for whatever reason, tend to end up in the bottom reading groups and are, therefore, exposed to different reading experiences. The emphasis is clearly on decoding and not on comprehension. If as a result of their initial failure and subsequent treatment these children are singled out for special education, they run the risk of an intensive version of this same treatment; for special education in reading problems has an even heavier emphasis on decoding skills at the expense of reading-comprehension instruction.

A strong emphasis on direct instruction in basic skills permeates resource rooms and special education classrooms, perhaps an understandable reaction to the "lack" of these skills demonstrated by the students. Special education classes are more likely to provide step-by-step instruction for students in basic skills (decoding, etc.) and rarely allow the students to figure out meanings or question their assumptions. Heavily programmed and guided learning of this type may be a practical and efficient means of getting less successful students to perform better on a particular task, i.e., word recognition. But it is the teacher, not the child, who is making all the learning decisions. Such experience is less likely to be the appropriate procedure for promoting insightful learning. Students may learn something about a particular task, but they are less likely to learn how to learn from reading (Brown, 1982).

Of course we are not arguing against the practice of direct instruction in decoding per se. As Resnick (1979) has pointed out, there is a great deal of evidence to support the success of reading programs that favor early direct instruction of decoding. We do argue, however, that instruction in comprehension can and should be offered in addition (Tharp, 1982), because the current state of affairs is that poor readers, particularly those labeled as learning disabled or mildly retarded, are unlikely in the present system to develop adequate reading-comprehension skills. Decoding is mastered eventually but reading-comprehension scores remain low and possibly permanently and severely depressed. Many factors may be responsible for this typical pattern, but one that is rarely addressed is the simple explanation of practice. Practice makes possible; if so, perhaps we should not be surprised to find a cumulative deficit in comprehension skills in those who are systematically denied extensive experience in comprehension-fostering activities.

In summary, following repeated experience with experts (parents, caretakers, teachers, etc.) who situate, elaborate, evaluate, and extend the limits of their experience, many students develop a battery of school-relevant autocritical skills (Binet, 1909; Brown, in press) that include comprehension-fostering activities ideally tailored for reading. These skills are essential acquisitions, if students are to learn how to learn independently. If for some reason the child is deprived of a constant history of such interaction in and out of school, the development of an adequate battery of self-regulatory skills for performing independently on academic tasks may be impeded.

Given this argument, an appropriate training experience would be to attempt to mimic naturally occurring interactive-learning settings as a context for instruction. In a subsequent section, a series of experiments is reviewed that may have promise for improving comprehension skills precisely because they attempt to help children adopt for themselves questioning and monitoring activities that they experience initially in interactive settings.

Comprehension-Fostering Activities

Before proceeding to a discussion of instruction, an attempt is made to be somewhat more explicit about the nature of the comprehension processes involved in effective reading. We concentrate on those that promote comprehension and lead to effective comprehension monitoring, i.e., activities engaged in by readers to ensure that comprehension is proceeding smoothly. Although far from a detailed task analysis of reading comprehension, there are several overlapping skills that have been mentioned repeatedly as prime comprehension-fostering activities in a variety of recent theoretical treatments (Baker & Brown, 1984a, 1984b; Brown, 1980; Collins & Smith, 1982; Dansereau, 1980; Markman, 1981). These activities include

1. clarifying the purposes of reading, i.e., understanding the task demands, both explicit and implicit;
2. activating relevant background knowledge;
3. allocating attention so that concentration can be focused on the major content at the expense of trivia;
4. critical evaluation of content for internal consistency and compatibility with prior knowledge and common sense;
5. monitoring ongoing activities to see if comprehension is occurring by engaging in such activities as periodic review and self-interrogation; and
6. drawing and testing inferences of many kinds, including interpretations, predictions, and conclusions.

All of these activities appear as academic tasks in their own right; for example, it is a common practice to call on children to concentrate on the main idea, to think critically about the content of what they are reading, to summarize or answer questions on a passage. But, in addition, these activities, if engaged in while reading, serve to enhance comprehension and afford an opportunity for the student to check whether it is occurring. That is, they can be both *comprehension-fostering* and *comprehension-monitoring* activities if properly used. Self-directed summarization is an excellent comprehension-fostering and -monitoring technique (Brown & Day, 1983; Brown, Day, & Jones, 1983; Day, 1980; Linden & Wittrock, 1981). Monitoring one's progress while reading, to test whether one can pinpoint and retain important material, provides a check that comprehension is progressing smoothly. If the reader cannot produce an adequate synopsis of what is being read, this is a clear sign that comprehension is *not* proceeding smoothly and that remedial action is called for.

Similarly, self-directed questioning concerning the meaning of text content leads students to a more active monitoring of their own comprehension (André & Anderson, 1978/1979). Thus, closing one's eyes (metaphorically) and attempting to state the gist of what one has read and asking questions of an *interpretive* and *predictive* nature (Collins & Smith, 1982) are activities that both improve comprehension and permit students to monitor their own understanding. These are also the kinds of active and aggressive interactions with texts that poor readers do not engage in readily; the need for explicit instruction in comprehension-enhancing activities is particularly acute for the slow-learning student (Brown & Palincsar, 1982).

Instructing Reading Comprehension

Teaching Settings and Reading Strategies

In this section a series of successful training studies is described which attempt to combine a knowledge of effective teaching settings and appropriate learning activities in order to improve comprehension (Palincsar & Brown, 1983). We have argued that many students lack sufficient practice in interactive-learning situations where comprehension-fostering activities are modeled and promoted. If this were true, then an obvious compensatory strategy would be to design instruction where practice in the essential skills is embedded within an interactive-learning situation that mimics the idealized mother–child, teacher–child dialogues previously described.

The particular skills selected for training were *summarizing* (self-review), *questioning*, *clarifying*, and *predicting*. There is a large literature connected with each activity. A considerable amount is known about the use or nonuse of the activities in isolation, especially in response to direct instruction. But considerably less is known about the spontaneous orchestration of a battery of such activities in the face of different forms of comprehension failure. For example, high school and junior college students have a great deal of trouble writing adequate synopses of texts (Brown & Day, 1983), although well-designed training can improve these skills (Day, 1980). Very little is known, however, about the use of self-directed paraphrasing as a method of periodic review or as a means of monitoring comprehension when the text gets difficult. Also, young and poor readers have difficulty evaluating texts for clarity, internal consistency, or compatibility with known facts (Markman, 1981), and training helps here too (Markman & Gorin, 1981). But again, little is known about where and when and with what actual processes the reader will engage in such monitoring spontaneously. Similarly, students often fail to generate questions and can be trained to perform better on these skills in isolation (André & Anderson, 1978/1979), but little is known about the spontaneous use of questioning as part of a concerted, personally designed, and coordinated plan of attack in the face of comprehensive difficulties. Therefore, in this series of studies the four activities of self-directed summarizing (review), questioning, clarifying, and predicting are combined in a package of activities with the general aim of enhancing understanding. Each "separate" activity, however, was used in response to a concrete problem of text comprehension. Clarifying occurred only if there were confusions either in the text (unclear referent, etc.) or in the student's interpretation of the text. Summarizing was modeled as an activity of self-review; it was engaged in in order to state to the group what had just happened in the text and as a test that the content had been understood. If an adequate synopsis could not be reached, this fact was regarded *not* as a failure to perform a particular decontextualized skill but as an important source of information that comprehension was not proceeding as it should and remedial action (such as rereading or clarifying) was needed. Questioning, similarly, was not practiced as a teacher-directed isolated activity, but as a concrete task—what question would a teacher or test ask about that section of the text. Students reacted very positively to this concrete detective work, rather than the more typical isolated skills-training approach as we will see.

We embedded these activities within a training procedure that was very similar to the interactive mother–child, teacher–student dyads described earlier. The procedure was also similar to that of reciprocal questioning. Manzo (1969) introduced a variant of this with his ReQuest procedure. Teachers and small groups of remedial-reading students took turns asking themselves questions about what they were reading. Questions followed every sentence, a procedure that would not encourage synthesis across larger segments of text. And the types of questions modeled and generated were not necessarily optimal. For example, one teacher modeled the question, "What was the third word in the first sentence?" Even so, Manzo reported significant improvement in standardized reading-comprehension scores. Frase and Schwartz (1975) also had college students taking turns generating or answering questions. Regardless of which role the students assumed, they performed better than when engaged in silent reading. Even though training was not extensive and again there was no attempt to ensure adequate quality of questions, the intervention produced a modest but reliable effect. Given these promising precursors, a reciprocal teaching method was adopted where, in addition to question generation, the activities of reciprocal paraphrasing, clarifying, and predicting were added.

Instructing Comprehension-Fostering by Reciprocal Teaching

So far three studies have been completed (Palincsar & Brown, 1983). The first two are laboratory studies with an experimenter (Palincsar) interacting with individual children or with pairs of students. The third study was conducted in the classroom by regular classroom teachers. The students in all three studies were seventh graders with average decoding skills but seriously deficient comprehension scores.[1]

Study 1. In Study 1, four students served as subjects in an extensive training experiment (for full details see Palincsar & Brown, 1983). Each subject served as his or her own control. After completing the decoding and comprehension tests that made them eligible for the study, the students received a period of baseline assessment, on each day of which they read a 500-word expository passage and then attempted to answer 10 comprehension questions independently. This baseline procedure of reading and answering questions on a novel assessment passage each day was also followed during maintenance and long-term follow-up periods. During training periods the students also read and answered questions on a novel assessment passage, but the assessment stage was preceded by interactive training sessions on still different passages. All data reported are percent correct from the daily independent-assessment test, *not* from the interacted-upon texts.

There were 6–8 days of initial baseline, 10 days of reciprocal teaching, followed by 6 days of maintenance and then a further 3 days of reciprocal teaching. Six months later, the students were retested for 8 days—4 days of untreated maintenance followed by 2 days where reciprocal teaching was reintroduced, which was followed in turn by a final 2 days of maintenance.[2]

During the reciprocal-teaching intervention, the investigator and the student engaged in an interactive-learning game that involved taking turns in leading a dialogue concerning each segment of text. If the passage was new, the investigator called the student's attention to the title, asked for predictions based upon the title, and discussed the relationship of the passage to prior knowledge. For example, if the passage were entitled *Ship of the Desert*, the investigator and student would speculate about what the passage might concern and would review what they knew about the characteristics of the desert. If the passage were partially completed, the investigator would ask the student to recall and state the topic of the text and several important points already covered in the passage.

The investigator then assigned a segment of the passage to be read (usually a paragraph) and either indicated that it was her turn to be the teacher or assigned the student to teach that segment. The investigator and student then read the assigned segment silently. After reading the text, the teacher for that segment summarized the content, discussed and clarified any difficulties, asked a question that a teacher or test might ask on the segment, and finally made a prediction about future content. All of these activities were embedded in as natural a dialogue as possible with the teacher and student giving feedback to each other.

Throughout the interventions, the students were explicitly told that these activities were general strategies to help them understand better as they read and that they should try to do something like this when they read silently. It was pointed out that being able to say in your own words what one has just read and being able to guess that the questions will be on a test are sure ways of testing oneself to see if one has understood.

At first the students had difficulty taking their part in the dialogue, experiencing particular difficulties with summarizing and formulating questions. The adult teacher helped with a variety of prompting techniques such as "What question did you think a teacher might ask?"; "Remember, a summary is a shortened version; it doesn't include detail"; "If you're having a hard time summarizing, why don't you think of a question first?"

The adult teacher also provided praise and feedback specific to the student's participation: "You asked that question well; it was very clear what information you wanted"; "Excellent prediction; let's see if you're right"; "That was interesting information. It was information that I would call detail in the passage. Can you find the most important information?" After this type of feedback, the adult teacher modeled any activity that continued to need improvement: "A question I would have asked would be..."; "I would summarize by saying..."; "Did you find this statement unclear?"

Initially, then, the experimenter modeled appropriate activities, but the students had great difficulty assuming the role of dialogue leader when their turn came. The experimenter was sometimes forced to resort to constructing paraphrases and questions for the student to mimic. In this initial phase, the experimenter was modeling effective comprehension-monitoring strategies, but the student was a relatively passive observer.

In the intermediate phase, the students became much more capable of playing their role as dialogue leader and by the end of 10 sessions were providing paraphrases and questions of some sophistication. For example, in the initial sessions, 46% of questions produced by the students were judged as nonquestions or as needing clarification. By the end of the sessions only 2% of responses were judged as either needing clarification or nonquestions. Unclear questions drop out and are replaced over time with questions focusing on the main idea of each text segment. Examples of questions judged to be needing clarification, main idea, and detail are shown in Table 1.

A similar improvement was found for summary statements. At the beginning of the session, only 11% of summary statements captured main ideas, whereas at the end 60% of the statements were so classified. Examples of summary statements are shown in Table 2.

With repeated interaction with a model performing appropriate questioning and paraphrasing activities, the students became able to perform these functions on their own. Over time the students' questions became more like the tutor's, being classified as *inventions*, that is, questions and summaries of gist in one's own words, rather than selections, repetitions of words actually occurring in the text (Brown & Day, 1983). For example, an early occurring form of question would be to take verbatim from the text "plans are being made to use nuclear power" and append the question with the inflection "for what?" Later forms of questioning were more likely to be paraphrases of the gist in the students' own words. For example, reading a passage about fossils, one student posed the following question: "When an animal dies, certain parts decay, but what parts are saved?" This question was constructed by integrating information presented across several sentences. Given the steady improvement on the privately read texts, it would appear that students internalize these activities as part of their own repertoire of

Table 1. Examples of Student-Generated Questions During Reciprocal Teaching

Main-Idea Questions
Why don't people live in the desert? Why are the grasslands of Australia ideal for grazing? What does the light on the fish do? What did these people [the Chinese] invent? Plans are being made to use nuclear power for what? What are three main problems with all submarines? Is there just one kind of explosive? What are one of the three things people used explosives for? What are the Philippine officials going to do for the people?
Questions Pertaining to Detail
How far south do the maple trees grow? What color is the guards' uniforms? How many years did it take to build the Great Wall? What are chopsticks made out of? Tell me where the cats hide? What was the balloon material made of? What (on the fish) overlaps like shingles on a roof? How far can flying fish leap? What is the temperature along the southern shores of Australia?
Questions Requiring Clarification (and Suggested Appropriate Questions Regarding the Same Material and Ideas)
What was, uh, some kings were, uh, about the kings? (Why is it that kings did not always make the best judges?) What were some of the people? (What kinds of people can serve on a jury?) What was the Manaus built for? Wait a minute. What was the Manaus built for, what certain kinds of thing? Wait a minute. OK. What was the Manaus tree built for? (Why was the city of Manaus built?) What does it keep the ground? (What effect does snow have on the ground?) What are the Chinese people doing today, like.... What are they doing? (Why are the Chinese people rewriting their alphabet today?) There's you know, like, a few answers in here and one of my questions is, uh, anything that burns and explodes can be fast enough to.... See, they got names in here. OK? (Name some explosives.) In Africa, India, and the Southern Islands where the sun shines what happens to the people? You know, like...? (Why do people who live in Africa, India, and the Southern Islands have dark skin?)

comprehension-fostering skills. In support of this statement are the data from peer tutoring sessions taken at the termination of the study. Trained tutees faced with naive peers did attempt to model main idea paraphrase and questions (Palincsar & Brown, work in progress).

In addition to the qualitative changes in the students' dialogues, there was a gratifying improvement in the level of performance on the daily assessment

Table 2. Examples of Student-Generated Summary Statements During Reciprocal Teaching

Main-Idea Statements
It says if a man does his job real good, then he will do better in his next life. I learned that they have different kinds of Gods, not just Brahman, every family has their own. It tells us about the two kinds of camels, what they are like and where they live. My summary is that the part of the earth that we live on and see and know is the top layer, the crust. This paragraph talks about what happens when people perspire or sweat. They lose a large amount of salt and they get weakness.
Detail Statements
It is a pair of fins which look like legs. The sea horse always swims head up. There were large lizards and four eyed fish and 30 foot dandelion. What I learned is that a submarine went around the world in 84 days. I learned that Cousteau's first artificial island was in the North Sea. Professor Charles went 27 miles and rose 2000 feet in his balloon. They [the aborigines] don't wear much clothes on. They [Egyptians] made bread a long time ago.
Incomplete Statements and Corresponding Text Segment
They talk about it was the richest island; but it didn't have something, OK, it was the richest island but didn't have everything. They didn't have something. (Although this was a very rich land, no people lived there.) If you pick a cherry branch in the winter you will have luck hoping they will bloom early. (If you pick a cherry branch in the winter, you will have no luck with it blooming.) And uranium can be making explosion that equals a skyscraper. (A small amount of uranium can cause an explosion as great as a skyscraper full of dynamite.)
Examples of Student-Generated Critical/Evaluative Comments
"Boy, the paragraph sure is a mess. It is all over the place." "I don't see how they can say 'heat lightning occurs on hot summer days.' How could you see it?" "It says here 'cloud to cloud' then 'cloud to earth.' Wouldn't that be the same thing?" "The word *meter* throws me off in this sentence." "What's the difference between soap and detergent anyway?" "At first I didn't get this because I thought the word *pumping* was *bumping*." "I don't know what *omitting* is." "I have one, what do they mean by 'far away dreams'?"

question-answering score. The students averaged 15% correct during baseline. After the introduction of the reciprocal teaching, the students reached accuracy levels of 80–90% correct. This level was durable across both the maintenance and brief reintroduction of the intervention. After the 6-month delay, the students averaged 60% correct without help, significant savings over their original level of 15%. After only 1 day of renewed reciprocal teaching, the performance of 2 students returned to 80% and for the remaining students it reached 90% correct; again, the levels were maintained when the intervention was removed. Remember that these scores were obtained on the *privately read* assessment passages, i.e., different texts that the students read independently after their interaction with the instructor. What was learned during the instructional sequence was used independently by the learners.

Generalization to classroom settings. Throughout the study, a series of 5 probes was made in the social studies classroom setting to see if the students would show any improvement on the identical task of answering 10 comprehension questions on a test. The students were not told that these tests, administered by the classroom teacher, had anything to do with the intervention. All seventh graders took the social studies test as part of their regular classroom activity. The experimental students began the study below the 15th percentile on this task compared with the remaining seventh graders in their school. Performance fluctuated widely, which was not surprising as little was done to promote generalization to the classroom; e.g., the classroom teaching did not encourage the use of strategies and the students received no feedback regarding classroom performance. However, the following mean gains in percentile ranks were obtained between the baseline and final probes: Student 1 = 20, Student 2 = 46, Student 3 = 4, and Student 4 = 34.

In summary, students in Study 1 showed a dramatic improvement in their ability to answer comprehension questions on independently read texts. This improvement was durable in the resource room setting and showed some tendency to generalize to the classroom setting. In addition, qualitative improvement in the students' dialogues reflected their increasing tendency to concentrate on questions and summaries of the main idea. The reciprocal-teaching procedure was a powerful intervention for improving comprehension.

Study 2. Encouraged by the success of the initial study, it was decided to replicate the main features of the successful reciprocal-teaching procedure with 6 additional students, in 3 groups of 2. In addition to group size, the second study also differed from the first in that (1) a criterion level of 75% correct on 4 out of 5 consecutive days was established; (2) students received explicit (graphed) knowledge of results; and (3) tests of transfer were included.

The tests of transfer were selected because it was believed that they tapped the skills taught during the reciprocal teaching and, pragmatically, because a considerable body of prior work has established "normal" levels of performance for seventh graders. Two of the four transfer tests were measures of the two most frequently engaged in activities during the reciprocal-teaching sessions, *summarizing* (Brown & Day, 1983) and *predicting questions* that might be asked concerning each segment of text. In addition, two other tests were used as measures of general comprehension monitoring, *error detection* (Harris, Kruithof, Terwogt,

& Visser, 1981; Markman, 1981) and *rating importance of segments of narratives* (Brown & Smiley, 1977).

There were 4 phases to the study. As in Study 1, each student was given a daily assessment passage on which he or she answered 10 comprehension questions, and this was all that occurred on baseline and maintenance days. On intervention days, the assessment passage was preceded by the reciprocal-teaching intervention, identical to that described in Study 1. The phases of Study 2 were as follows:

1. *Variable baseline* consisting of 4 days for Group 1, 6 days for Group 2, and 8 days for Group 3
2. *Reciprocal-teaching intervention* consisting of approximately 20 days
3. *Maintenance* consisting of 5 days of testing at the termination of training
4. *Long-term follow-up* that took place 8 weeks later (3 days)

All students were appraised of their progress on a daily basis. They were shown graphs depicting the percentage correct for the previous day's assessment.

The data from the daily assessment passages are shown in Figure 1. The 6 students of Study 2 had baseline accuracy not exceeding 40% correct. They proceeded to make stepwise progression toward means in excess of 75%. Four of the six students reached a stable level of 80% for 5 successive days, taking 12, 11, 11, and 15 days respectively to do it (Students 1, 3, 4, and 6). Student 5 reached criterion of 75% correct in 12 days. Student 2 was the only "failure"; she progressed from a baseline of 12% correct and reached a steady level of 50% correct in 12 days, a significant improvement, but she never approached the criterion level of the remaining 5 students. All students maintained their improved level of performance on both short- and long-term maintenance tests.

A similar improvement in the quality of the dialogues over time was found in Study 1 and Study 2 (see Palincsar & Brown, 1983, for details). At the outset, students required more assistance with the dialogue, asked more unclear and detailed questions, and made more incomplete/incorrect or detailed summaries than they did on the last intervention day. Both main-idea questions and paraphrases increased significantly over time.

Students improved at differential rates. For example, Student 6, a minority student whose Slossen test indicated an IQ of 70, made steady but slow progress as indicated by the dialogue shown in Table 3. The data are taken from Days 1 to 15, the day on which he reached criterion. From a very slow start, this student did achieve an acceptable level of performance both on the dialogues and on his daily assessment passages.

Generalization probes taken in the classroom setting resulted in variable performance but did show clear evidence of improvement. Probes were taken in two settings, social studies and science. At baseline on the social studies probe the range of percentile rankings was .9–43, with four students at or below the 5th percentile. The percentile rankings were typically higher in science with a

Figure 1. An Example of the Daily Data From Individual Subjects During Baseline, Intervention, Maintenance, and Long-Term Follow-Up

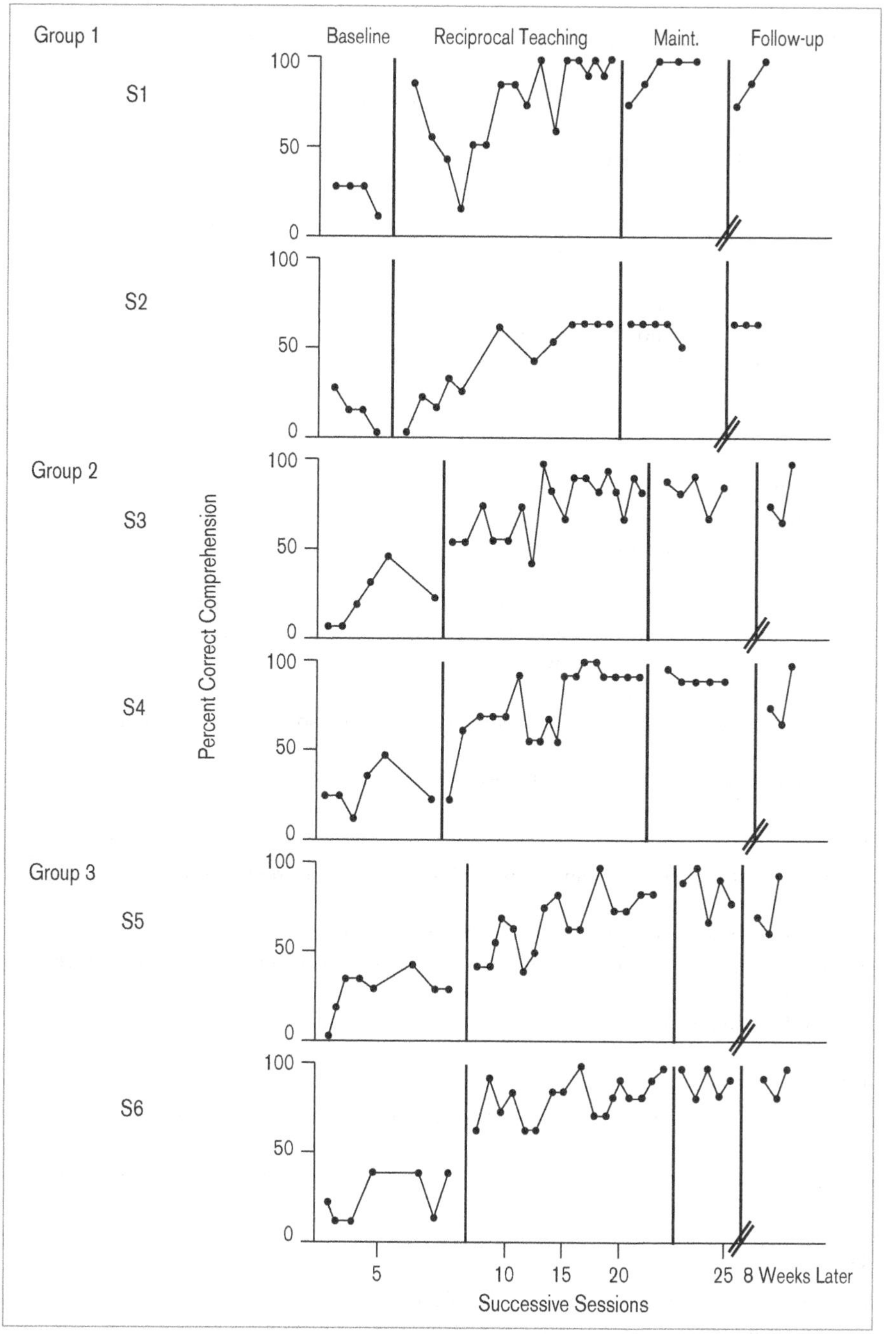

These data are taken from the six experimental subjects of Palincsar and Brown (1983), Study 2.

Table 3. The Acquisition of Question-Asking by One Seventh-Grade Student

Day 1
S: What is found in the southeastern snakes, also the copperhead, rattlesnakes, vipers—they have. I'm not doing this right. T: All right. Do you want to know about the pit vipers? S: Yeah. T: What would be a good question about the pit vipers that starts with the word *why*? S: (no response) T: How about, "Why are the snakes called pit vipers?" S: Why do they want to know that they are called pit vipers? T: Try it again. S: Why do they, pit vipers in a pit? T: How about, "Why do they call the snakes pit vipers?" S: Why do they call the snakes pit vipers? T: There you go! Good for you.
Day 4
S: (no question) T: What's this paragraph about? S: Spinner's mate. How do spinner's mate.... T: That's good. Keep going. S: How do spinner's mate is small than.... How am I going to say that? T: Take your time with it. You want to ask a question about spinner's mate and what he does, beginning with the word *how*. S: How do they spend most of his time sitting? T: You're very close. The question would be, "How does spinner's mate spent most of his time?" Now you ask it. S: How does spinner's mate spend most of his time?
Day 7
S: How does the pressure from below push the mass of hot rock against the opening? Is that it? T: Not quite. Start your question with "What happens when?" S: What happens when the pressure from below pushes the mass of rock against the opening? T: Good for you! Good job.
Day 11
S: What is the most interesting of the insect-eating plants, and where do the plants live at? T: Two excellent questions! They are both clear and important questions. Ask us one at a time now.
Day 15
S: Why do scientists come to the south pole to study? T: Excellent question. This is what this paragraph is all about.

range of 2–47, four students scoring at or below the 25th percentile. Although performance on these probes was variable, the total mean change in percentile rankings (combined across settings and phases) were Student 1, 47; Student 2, –.5; Student 3, 26; Student 4, 35.5; Student 5, 40.6; and Student 6, 36. Excluding Student 2, at the conclusion of the study, the range of subjects' mean percentile ranks was 49–76. All students, except Student 2, demonstrated considerable generalization to the classroom setting. Student 2 was also the only student who did not reach criterion during the intervention.

Transfer tests were conducted in a pre- and posttest format. It would be impossible to go into all the details of the transfer probes here (see Palincsar & Brown, 1983, for details). Briefly, three of the four tests showed a significant improvement: writing summaries, designing questions to be asked on a test, and error detection using the Harris et al. (1981) procedure. The students did not improve on the Brown and Smiley (1977) task of rating narratives for variations in importance, although they did improve in their ability to select important elements in their summary writing.[3]

To give only the flavor of the transfer results, we consider one test, the question-prediction task. The ability to generate important and clear questions was a skill that received considerable focus during training. A transfer measure was included to assess the accuracy with which students could identify and construct "teacher-like" questions. The students were given 4 randomly assigned passages, 2 prior and 2 following the study. Students were asked to predict and write 10 questions a classroom teacher might ask if testing the student's knowledge of the passage.

The pre- and posttest scores are shown in Figure 2 for the students of Studies 2 and 3 and also for an untreated control group. The comparison group on the right of the figure represents the level set by average seventh-grade readers on this task. Training brought the level of performance up to that set by the normal comparison group. The graph is designed to illustrate where the improvement was found. Trained students improved in the overall quality of their questions, in the match between their questions and those actually generated by teachers, in their ability to paraphrase rather than lift questions directly from the text, and in their ability to concentrate on the main ideas.

In summary, the main findings of Study 2 were that students diagnosed as experiencing particular problems with reading comprehension improved considerably as a result of taking part in the reciprocal-teaching sessions. All students reached asymptote within 15 days, and for 5 of the 6 the level was at 70–80% correct, comparable to accuracy attained by 13 good comprehenders who acted as control subjects. Only Student 2 failed to reach the normal level, but she did improve from 12% to 50% and maintained that level well. Indeed, all of the students maintained their asymptotic level for at least 8 weeks.

In addition to this dramatic increase on the daily comprehension measures, the students improved their percentile ranking in the classroom, gaining an average of 37 percentile points. The quantitative improvement in the ability to

Figure 2. An Example of the Transfer Effects Found in Palincsar and Brown (1983), Studies 2 and 3

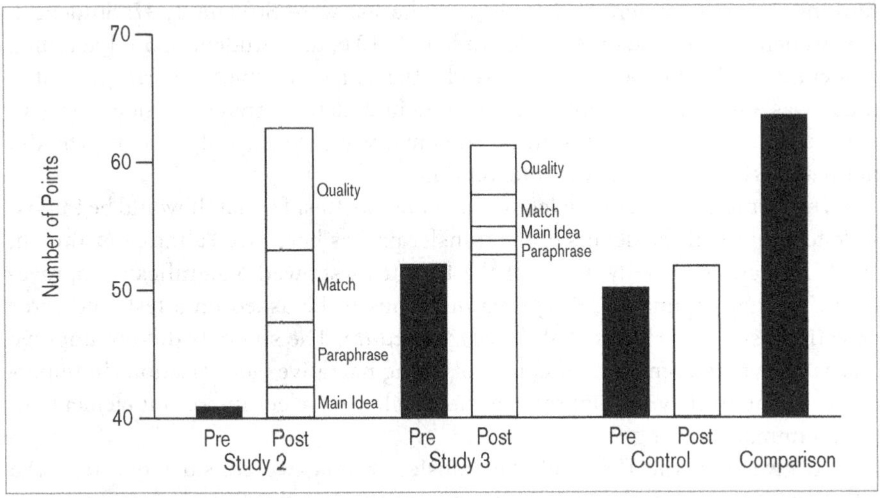

These data are taken from the Question-Prediction Task. The degree and type of posttest improvement of the experimental subjects are detailed.

answer comprehension questions on texts read in a variety of settings was accompanied by a qualitative improvement in the students' dialogues. Main-idea statements and summaries came to predominate, and unclear, incomplete, or detail responses dropped out.

There was also encouraging evidence of transfer to new tasks. Reliable improvement was found in the ability to use condensation rules for summarizing, in the ability to predict questions that a teacher might ask concerning a text segment, and in the ability to detect incongruous sentences embedded in prose passages.

Study 3. Given the success of Studies 1 and 2, another replication was attempted, but this time the teacher would be a "real" teacher, not an investigator, and the instruction would take place in naturally occurring groups within the school setting. In Study 3, four groups of students were considered, two classroom reading groups for the poorest readers and two reading groups that met regularly in a resource room. The group size ranged from 4 to 7 students. In all other respects the study was a replica of Study 2.

The teachers received three training sessions. In the first, they were introduced to the rationale behind the reciprocal-teaching intervention and were shown the results of Study 1. They also viewed a videotape of the investigator employing the technique with a group of students.

In the second training session, the teacher and the investigator practiced the procedures privately with the investigator modeling both the teacher's role and behaviors that might be expected from students. Difficulties that could arise were anticipated and discussed, such as situations where a student is unable to generate a question or where a student summarizes by reiterating the whole paragraph in detail. Remedial steps were demonstrated.

In the final session, the teacher and the investigator met with a group of seventh graders who were not taking part in the study and practiced the procedure. The investigator modeled how the procedure would be introduced to the students, and modeled the four main activities and the process of feedback. The teachers then assumed responsibility for the group, and as the practice session transpired, the teacher and investigator discussed the proceedings with each other. In addition, the teachers were left with several pages of directions regarding the introduction and daily format of the training sessions. The investigator also checked weekly on the teacher-directed sessions to see if the intervention was being conducted properly. These visits provided further opportunity for discussion and resolution of any difficulties encountered. The students were shown their progress charts on a daily basis during baseline, maintenance, and long-term follow-up, and on a weekly basis during intervention, and their improvement was discussed with them. All reciprocal-teaching sessions were tape-recorded.

The four groups of subjects were subjected to different amounts of baseline (4–10 days); otherwise, they were treated identically. Individually, the students performed in a manner similar to that found in Study 2 (see Palincsar & Brown, 1983, for full details). All of the subjects in Groups 1–3 individually reached criterion within 15 days. In Group 4, all students reached criterion in 5 days. If one considers the group means, two groups reached criterion in 13 days (Groups 1 and 2), one in 9 days (Group 3), and one in 5 days (Group 4). It is interesting to note that in Group 4, 2 of the 4 students were performing quite well on the first day. The resultant group in some sense consisted of three models, the teacher and the 2 good students, and 2 tutees, the remaining 2 poor students. In this favorable milieu, the poor students rapidly improved, and the entire group reached criterion in 5 days, versus a mean of 12 days for the other groups. Such findings if replicated could have important implications for decisions concerning the composition of the "optimal" reading group. All improvements were maintained over both short- and long-term follow-up sessions.

Quality of dialogue. An improvement in quality of dialogue was found as in Studies 1 and 2 but was less dramatic in Study 3. In the group settings, the teachers decided to call upon the "better students" in the initial sessions and then gradually to introduce the poorer students into the dialogue as they felt they could handle the responsibility, a natural procedure for experienced teachers. This resulted in a level of student responses that was higher initially and did not improve as dramatically over sessions. The trend was still the same, however, with incomplete or unclear questions decreasing from 20% to 4% and main-idea questions increasing from 57% to 70% across the sessions. Similarly, main-idea summaries increased from 68% to 85% of the total produced by the groups.

Transfer Tests

The same pattern of transfer performance occurred in Studies 2 and 3. Reliable improvements were found on three of the four tests: writing summaries, predicting questions, and error detecting. Again training brought the level of performance up to that set by normal seventh-grade readers.

The Palincsar and Brown series of studies can be regarded as successful for six main reasons:

1. The effect was large and reliable; of the 10 subjects included in Studies 1 and 2, 9 improved to the level set by good comprehenders, and all of the subjects in Study 3 met this level.
2. The effect was durable; maintenance probes showed no drop in the level of performance for up to an 8-week period (Studies 2 and 3). Although there was a decline after 6 months (levels dropping from 70–80% to 50–60%), only one session with the reciprocal-teaching procedure was sufficient to raise performance back to the short-term maintenance level (Study 1).
3. The effect generalized to the classroom setting; of the 10 students taking part in Studies 1 and 2, 9 showed a clear pattern of improvement, averaging a 36 percentile-rank increase, thus bringing them up to at least the average level for their age mates. Given the difficulty reported in obtaining generalization of trained skills across setting (Brown & Campione, 1978; Meichenbaum & Asarnow, 1978), this is an impressive finding.
4. Training resulted in reliable transfer to dissimilar tasks; summarizing, predicting questions, and detecting incongruities all improved. Again this is an impressive finding given prior difficulty with obtaining transfer of cognitive-skills training (Brown & Campione, 1978; Brown, Campione, & Day, 1981).
5. Sizable improvements in standardized comprehension scores were recorded for the majority of subjects.
6. The intervention was no less successful in natural group settings conducted by teachers than it was in the laboratory when conducted by the experimenter.

Training Studies and the Problem of Multiple Determinants

Let us consider some possible reasons for the success of the Palincsar and Brown studies when so many other attempts have failed to find durability, generalization, and transfer of the effects of training. First, the training was extensive. Second, the activities trained were well specified theoretically, and well established empirically as particularly problematic for poor readers. Third, the training was specifically tailored to the needs of these particular students, good decoders but passive comprehenders. Fourth, the skills themselves could reasonably be expected to be trans-situational. Such ubiquitous activities of self-review and self-interrogation are pertinent in a wide variety of knowledge-acquisition tasks.

In addition, a great deal of attention was paid to "metacognitive" variables (Baker & Brown, 1984a): The subjects were fully informed about the reasons why these activities were important; the subjects were given explicit information concerning the generality of the activities and their range of utility; the subjects were trained in self-regulatory activities including the checking and monitoring of their own comprehension; and the skills themselves were general comprehension-monitoring activities applicable in a wide variety of reading/studying tasks.

The reciprocal-teaching mode itself could be responsible for the improvement. The interactive format permits extensive modeling of the target activities in a reasonably natural setting. It also forces the students to participate at whatever level they can so that the teacher can evaluate current states and provide appropriate feedback and assistance (refer to Table 3).

Listing all the good points about the Palincsar and Brown studies leads us to the obvious problem of interpretation. The studies are multiply confounded, and this is true to some extent of all the successful cognitive-training studies to date (Chipman, Segal, & Glaser, in press). For example, would a single activity rather than the package of paraphrasing, questioning, predicting, and clarifying have been successful? Component analyses studies currently underway in our laboratory suggest that whereas all of the activities engaged in individually result in improvement, the summary component is the most powerful. The combined package, however, is the most effective intervention.

Similarly, the addition of the metacognitive setting variables may or may not be essential and such variables permit of degrees. For example, in a Ph.D. thesis conducted in our laboratory, Day (1980) trained junior college students to apply basic rules of summarization and to check that they were using the rules appropriately. The subjects were remedial students who, although of normal reading ability, were diagnosed as having writing problems. There were three main instructional conditions that varied in how explicit the training was:

1. *Self-management*: The students were given general encouragement to write a good summary, to capture the main ideas, to dispense with trivia and all unnecessary words—but they were not told rules for achieving this end.
2. *Rules*: The students were given explicit instructions and modeling in the use of the rules of deletion, selection, invention, etc.
3. *Control of the rules*: The third and most explicit training condition involved training in the rules and additional explicit training in the control of these rules; i.e., the students were shown how to check that they had a topic sentence for each paragraph, how to check that all redundancies had been deleted, all trivia erased, etc., and how to check that any lists of items had been replaced with superordinates, etc.

An example of the results is shown in Figure 3, where the data from one of the rules, selection, are shown. The degree of posttest improvement was significantly related to the explicitness of training. Merely telling students to stay on task,

Figure 3. An Example of the Type of Improvement Found as a Result of the Explicitness of Training

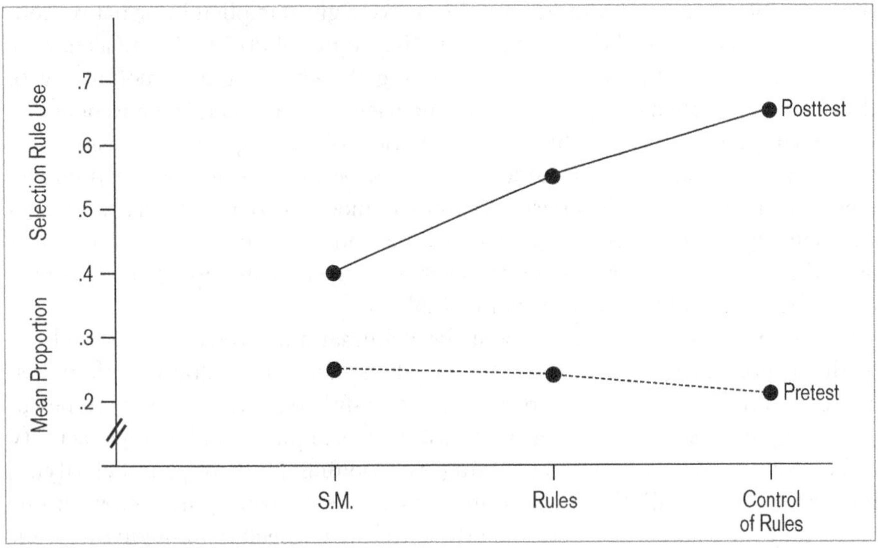

These data are taken from Day (1980) and depict the pre- and posttest results on the selection rule of summarization.

be economical, concentrate on main ideas, i.e., the self-management condition, produced significantly less improvement than did direct instruction in using the specific rules, which in turn was less successful than a combined package that involved both practice using the task-appropriate rules *and* direct instruction in monitoring and overseeing their application. In this context it should be noted that in the Palincsar and Brown studies, the students not only received modeling of the appropriate comprehension-fostering activities, they were also explicitly and repeatedly directed to use these activities while reading on their own.

There is growing evidence that the most successful cognitive-skills training packages will include three components: (1) *skills* training, practice in the use of the task-appropriate cognitive skills; (2) *self-control* training, direct instruction in how to orchestrate, oversee, and monitor the effective use of the skills; and (3) *awareness* training, information concerning the reasons why such strategy use improves performance and detailed instruction in when and where the strategies should be used. For practical reasons, interventions should include all these factors (Brown & Palincsar, 1982), but for theoretical reasons, we need to conduct component analyses of the separate effect of all three forms of metacognitive settings (Brown, Bransford, Ferrara, & Campione, 1983).

The reciprocal-teaching package is also multiply confounded. Would modeling alone, feedback alone, or just explicit instruction be as effective? Such component analyses studies are currently underway in our laboratory. Preliminary evidence again favors the combined package (see also Bird, 1980), but more data are needed.

From a practical standpoint, the results of the required component analyses would be helpful in permitting the streamlining of the training packages into efficient and economical units. From a theoretical perspective, we need considerable further research before we can attribute the success of the intervention appropriately. Of course, it could be that multiply confounded interventions are needed because successful reading comprehension is a multiply determined outcome; i.e., effective comprehension rests on the interaction of a number of "separate" activities. Given the typically limited outcome of restricted cognitive-skills training studies (Brown, Campione, & Day, 1981), we advocate the procedure of *first* obtaining an educationally relevant, sizable, durable, and generalized effect of training and then conducting the necessary investigations to determine the subcomponents that are primarily responsible for the improvement.

The Theoretical and Practical Status of Training Studies

Until the mid-1970s, the prognosis of worthwhile educational gains from cognitive-skills training studies was poor. Although some success had been achieved in obtaining improvement on a particular skill in isolation, this improvement was often slight and fleeting, and there was very little evidence of transfer. Maintenance over time, generalization across settings, and transfer within conceptual domains were rarely found. The more difficulties the learner experienced initially, the more fleeting and bounded were the effects of training (Brown & Campione, 1978, 1981; Meichenbaum & Asarnow, 1978). But the picture has changed in the last few years; the success of the Palincsar and Brown studies is not an isolated phenomenon (Chipman, Segal, & Glaser, in press). The current outlook is quite optimistic. From a practical point of view, it is clear that we can train instructionally relevant cognitive skills even with subjects who would be regarded as recalcitrant. This training can be carried out under the pressure of normal classroom settings, and it does result in worthwhile and reliable improvements in the Palincsar and Brown studies, bringing students from the very bottom of the distribution of their age peers to the average set by their normal reading classmates. The necessary research needed now consists of extensions across skills and settings and of "clean-up" operations that would permit us to test the limits of these exciting findings and streamline our instructional packages. Cognitive skills can be trained, and such training can be durable and generalizable.

From a theoretical standpoint, training studies are not just exercises in cognitive engineering with immediate applicability to school settings. They are also direct tests of theory involving degrees of experimental manipulation and control in an area where a great deal of data consist of simple one-shot developmental demonstrations (see chapter 9 of *Learning and Comprehension of Text,* 1984, for a detailed discussion of this argument). A great deal of development research is correlational in nature, and there are problems with interpreting such results. To give an example from our own work, in many studies we consider the performance of students who do or do not spontaneously adopt an appropriate text-processing strategy, and this is often the major variable carrying a developmental trend. For example, 5th and 7th graders who make adequate rough drafts when paraphrasing (Brown, Day, & Jones, 1983) or spontaneously underline or take notes of important text elements and so on (Brown & Smiley, 1978) perform as well as the majority of 12th graders, whereas 12th graders who fail to employ these activities perform more like 5th graders. This pattern suggests that it is the strategy that leads to efficiency, and developmental trends showing improvements with age are created by the increased proportion of strategic subjects. This is a reasonable interpretation, but as the data are primarily correlational, the interpretation is not that simple. It could be that the young, spontaneous strategy users are the more efficient children in general and would perform better than their peers on any task and on the particular task in question without the use of strategies. Even partialling out ability factors such as IQ or reading scores does not totally bypass this problem.

The training study is then an important tool for providing convergent evidence of the importance of the strategy under consideration. First, the theorist speculates about the underlying processes involved in reading comprehension. Next is the correlational step; students who read well are also found to perform well on the identified underlying processes, whereas poor readers experience particular difficulty on just these activities (Armbruster, Echols, & Brown, 1982; Baker & Brown, 1984a, 1984b; Brown & Palincsar, 1982). Finally, students who are not using the strategy are given training designed to induce the use of processes theoretically specified as key activities underlying efficiency. Others are not. If the theory is correct (and training adequate) and these are the underlying effective processes, trained students' performances should become more like those of spontaneous users. There are nontrivial problems with interpreting the outcomes of training studies (Brown & Campione, 1978, 1981), but they do provide an important manipulative tool to aid theory development. Thus from the point of view of both theory development and successful cognitive instruction, training studies such as those reported here are valuable tools for enhancing our understanding of the mechanism of reading comprehension.

QUESTIONS FOR REFLECTION

1. What processes did the authors of reciprocal teaching go through to create the strategy?
2. Why is it difficult to isolate one specific strategy or instructional tool that will help poor readers become better at comprehension?
3. How did the authors confirm the efficacy of reciprocal teaching?
4. What might be the challenges of replicating the elements of the authors' training studies in your own classroom?

ACKNOWLEDGMENT

The preparation of this manuscript was supported in part by Grants HD06864 and HD05951 from the National Institute of Child Health and Human Development and in part by NIE-C-400-76-0116 from the National Institute of Education.

NOTES

*When this chapter was written, Brown and Palincsar were at the University of Illinois at Urbana-Champaign.

[1] The students were of low-normal intelligence (mean IQ 84) and low socioeconomic status. Their decoding was judged adequate as they could read grade-appropriate texts at a rate of 80–100 wpm with no more than 2 errors per minute. Their standardized reading comprehension scores averaged 3 years delayed.

[2] In Study 1, another group of students received a second intervention, locating information (see Palincsar & Brown, 1983, for details), where they were trained to answer comprehension questions by using the text intelligently. These students did improve from their starting level of 15% to approximately 50%, but they never reached the level of the reciprocal-teaching group, and they failed to maintain this level over time.

[3] In Studies 2 and 3, there were treated and untreated control groups consisting of students matched with the experimental subjects for decoding and comprehension scores, as well as IQ, standardized tests, and class placement. These students demonstrated no significant change on their performance on the baseline, maintenance, and follow-up stages of the study. Neither did they improve their performance on any of the tests of generalization (to the classroom) or transfer (across laboratory tasks). For full details on the control groups included in Studies 1 to 3, see Palincsar and Brown (1983).

REFERENCES

Allington, R. (1980). Teacher interruption behavior during primary-grade oral reading. *Journal of Educational Psychology, 72*(3), 371–377.

André, M.D.A., & Anderson, T.H. (1978/1979). The development and evaluation of a self-questioning study technique. *Reading Research Quarterly, 14*, 605–623.

Armbruster, B.B., Echols, C.H., & Brown, A.L. (1982). The role of metacognition in reading to learn: A developmental perspective. *Volta Review, 84*(5), 45–56.

Au, K.H. (1979). Using the Experience-Text-Relationship method with minority children. *The Reading Teacher, 32*(6), 677–679.

Au, K.H. (1980). *A test of the social organizational hypothesis: Relationships between participation structures and learning to read.* Unpublished doctoral dissertation, University of Illinois, Urbana-Champaign.

Baker, L., & Brown, A.L. (1984a). Cognitive monitoring in reading. In J. Flood (Ed.), *Understanding reading comprehension* (pp. 21–44). Newark, DE: International Reading Association.

Baker, L., & Brown, A.L. (1984b). Metacognition and the reading process. In P.D. Pearson, R. Barr, M.L. Kamil, & P. Mosenthal (Eds.), *Handbook of reading research* (pp. 353–394). New York: Longman.

Bartlett, E.J. (1979). Curriculum, concepts of literacy and social class. In L.B. Resnick & P.A. Weaver (Eds.), *Theory and practice of early reading* (Vol. 2). Hillsdale, NJ: Erlbaum.

Bernstein, B. (1971). *Class codes and control* (Vol. 1). London: Routledge & Kegan Paul.

Binet, A. (1909). *Les idées modernes sur les infants.* Paris: Flammarion.

Bird, M. (1980). *Reading comprehension strategies: A direct teaching approach.* Unpublished doctoral dissertation, University of Toronto, Ontario, Canada.

Brown, A.L. (1980). Metacognitive development and reading. In R.J. Spiro, B. Bruce, & W. Brewer (Eds.), *Theoretical issues in reading comprehension.* Hillsdale, NJ: Erlbaum.

Brown, A.L. (1982). Learning how to learn from reading. In J.A. Langer & M.T. Smith-Burke (Eds.), *Reader meets author/bridging the gap: A psycholinguistic and social linguistic perspective.* Newark, DE: International Reading Association.

Brown, A.L. (in press). Mental orthopedics: A conversation with Alfred Binet. In S. Chipman, J. Segal, & R. Glaser (Eds.), *Thinking and learning skills: Research and open questions* (Vol. 2). Hillsdale, NJ: Erlbaum.

Brown, A.L., Bransford, J.D., Ferrara, R.A., & Campione, J.C. (1983). Learning, remembering, and understanding. In J.H. Flavell & E.M. Markman (Eds.), *Carmichael's manual of child psychology* (Vol. 1). New York: Wiley.

Brown, A.L., & Campione, J.C. (1978). Permissible inferences from cognitive training studies in developmental research. In W.S. Hall & M. Cole (Eds.), *Quarterly Newsletter of the Institute for Comparative Human Behavior, 2*(3), 46–53.

Brown, A.L., & Campione, J.C. (1981). Inducing flexible thinking: A problem of access. In M. Friedman, J.P. Das, & N. O'Connor (Eds.), *Intelligence and learning*. New York: Plenum.

Brown, A.L., Campione, J.C., & Day, J.D. (1981). Learning to learn: On training students to learn from texts. *Educational Researcher, 10*(2), 14–21.

Brown, A.L., & Day, J.D. (1983). Macro-rules for summarizing texts: The development of expertise. *Journal of Verbal Learning and Verbal Behavior, 22*, 1–14.

Brown, A.L., Day, J.D., & Jones, R.S. (1983). The development of plans for summarizing texts. *Child Development, 54*, 968–979.

Brown, A.L., & Palincsar, A.S. (1982). Inducing strategic learning from texts by means of informed, self-control training. *Topics in Learning and Learning Disabilities, 2*(1), 1–17.

Brown, A.L., Palincsar, A.S., & Purcell, L. (in press). Poor readers: Teach, don't label. In U. Neisser (Ed.), *The school achievement of minority children: New perspectives*. Hillsdale, NJ: Erlbaum.

Brown, A.L., & Smiley, S.S. (1977). Rating the importance of structural units of prose passages: A problem of metacognitive development. *Child Development, 48*, 1–8.

Brown, A.L., & Smiley, S.S. (1978). The development of strategies for studying texts. *Child Development, 49*, 1076–1088.

Cazden, C.B. (1979). Learning to reading in classroom interaction. In L.B. Resnick & P.A. Weaver (Eds.), *Theory and practice of early reading* (Vol. 3). Hillsdale, NJ: Erlbaum.

Chipman, S., Segal, J., & Glaser, R. (Eds.). (in press). *Thinking and learning skills: Research and open questions* (Vol. 2). Hillsdale, NJ: Erlbaum.

Collins, A.M., & Smith, E.E. (1982). Teaching the process of reading comprehension. In D.K. Detterman & R.J. Sternberg (Eds.), *How and how much can intelligence be increased*. Norwood, NJ: Ablex.

Collins, A.M., & Stevens, A. (1982). Goals and strategies of inquiry teachers. In R. Glaser (Ed.), *Advances in instructional psychology* (Vol. 2). Hillsdale, NJ: Erlbaum.

Collins, J. (1980). Differential treatment in reading groups. In J. Cook-Gumperz (Ed.), *Educational discourse*. London: Heinemann.

Cushenbery, D.C. (1969). Building effective comprehension skills. In J.A. Figurel (Ed.), *Reading and realism* (Proceedings of the 13th Annual Convention of the International Reading Association). Newark, DE: International Reading Association.

Dansereau, D.F. (1980, October). *Learning strategy research*. Paper presented at NIELRDC Conference on Thinking and Learning Skills, Pittsburgh, PA.

Day, J.D. (1980). *Training summarization skills: A comparison of teaching methods*. Unpublished doctoral dissertation, University of Illinois, Urbana-Champaign.

DeLoache, J.S. (1983, April). *Mother-child picture book reading as a context for memory training*. Paper presented at the Society for Research in Child Development Meeting, Detroit, MI.

Feuerstein, R. (1979). *The dynamic assessment of retarded performers: The learning-potential assessment device, theory, instruments, and techniques*. Baltimore: University Park Press.

Feuerstein, R. (1980). *Instrumental enrichment: An intervention program for cognitive modifiability*. Baltimore: University Park Press.

Frase, L.T., & Schwartz, B.J. (1975). Effect of question production and answering on prose recall. *Journal of Educational Psychology, 67*, 628–635.

Gall, M.D. (1970). The use of questions in teaching. *Review of Educational Research, 40*, 707–720.

Gantt, W.N. (1970). Questions for thinking: A teaching strategy that makes a difference for disadvantaged learners. *The Reading Teacher, 24*, 12–16, 22.

Griffin, P. (1977). How and when does reading occur in the classroom? *Theory Into Practice, 16*, 376–383.

Harris, P.L., Kruithof, A., Terwogt, M.M., & Visser, P. (1981). Children's detection and awareness of textual anomaly. *Journal of Experimental Child Psychology, 31*, 212–230.

Jenkinson, M.D. (1969). Cognitive processes in reading: Implications for further research and classroom practice. In J.A. Figurel (Ed.), *Reading and realism* (Proceedings of the 13th Annual Convention of the International Reading Association). Newark, DE: International Reading Association.

King, M.L. (1967). New developments in the evaluation of critical reading. *Forging ahead in reading* (International Reading Association Proceedings, 12), 179–185.

Laboratory of Comparative Human Cognition. (in press). The zone of proximal development: Where culture and cognition create one another. In J.V. Wertsch (Ed.), *Culture, communication, and cognition: Vygotskian perspectives*. New York: Cambridge University Press.

Linden, M., & Wittrock, M.C. (1981). The teaching of reading comprehension according to the model of generative learning. *Reading Research Quarterly, 16*, 44–57.

Lorge, I. (1957). Reading, thinking, and learning. *International Reading Association Proceedings, 2*, 15–18.

Manzo, A.V. (1969). The ReQuest procedure. *Journal of Reading, 13*, 123–126, 163–164.

Markman, E.M. (1981). Comprehension monitoring. In W.P. Dickson (Ed.), *Children's oral communication skills*. New York: Academic.

Markman, E.M., & Gorin, L. (1981). Children's ability to adjust their standards for evaluating comprehension. *Journal of Educational Psychology*, *83*(3), 320–325.

McDermott, R.P. (1978). Kids make sense: An ethnographic account of the interactional management of success and failures in one first-grade classroom (Doctoral dissertation, Stanford University, 1976). *Dissertation Abstracts International*, *38*, 1505A.

Meichenbaum, D., & Asarnow, J. (1978). Cognitive-behavioral modification and metacognitive development: Implications for the classroom. In P. Kendall & S. Hollon (Eds.), *Cognitive-behavioral interventions: Theory, research, and procedure*. New York: Academic.

Ninio, A., & Bruner, J.S. (1978). The achievement and antecedents of labeling. *Journal of Child Language*, *5*, 1–15.

Palincsar, A.S., & Brown, A.L. (1983). *Reciprocal teaching of comprehension-monitoring activities* (Tech. Rep. No. 269). Champaign: University of Illinois, Center for the Study of Reading.

Resnick, L.B. (1979). Theories and prescriptions for early reading instruction. In L.B. Resnick & P.A. Weaver (Eds.), *Theory and practice of early reading* (Vol. 2). Hillsdale, NJ: Erlbaum.

Schallert, D.L., & Kleiman, G.M. (1979, June). *Some reasons why the teacher is easier to understand than the text book* (Reading Education Rep. No. 9). Champaign: University of Illinois, Center for the Study of Reading. (Eric Document Reproduction Service No. ED172189)

Schwartz, E., & Scheff, A. (1975). Student involvement in questioning for comprehension. *The Reading Teacher*, *29*, 150–154.

Smith, N.B. (1961). The good reader thinks critically. *The Reading Teacher*, *15*, 162–171.

Tharp, R.G. (1982). The effective instruction of comprehension: Results and description of the Kamehameha Early Education Program. *Reading Research Quarterly*, *17*, 503–527.

Vygotsky, L.S. (1978). *Mind in society: The development of higher psychological processes* (M. Cole, V. John-Steiner, S. Scribner, & E. Souberman, Eds. & Trans.). Cambridge, MA: Harvard University Press. (Original work published 1934)

Wertsch, J.V. (1978). Adult–child interaction and the roots of metacognition. *The Quarterly Newsletter of the Institute for Comparative Human Development*, *2*(1), 15–18.

Wood, D., & Middleton, D. (1975). A study of assisted problem-solving. *British Journal of Psychology*, *66*(2), 181–191.

Postscript on Reciprocal Teaching

Annemarie Sullivan Palincsar

I am thankful to the editors for this opportunity to include a sequel to the chapter "Instructing Comprehension-Fostering Activities in Interactive Learning Situations." Whereas the original chapter was comprehensive in its attention to comprehension instruction, this postscript focuses on reciprocal teaching (RT), specifically on the evolution of the intervention itself, as well as the evolution of research on RT. Finally, I speak to the evolution of the field with respect to comprehension instruction, as informed by research on RT.

There are two transformations in the design and use of RT that seem noteworthy. One was the introduction of thematically related passages as the grist for the dialogues. The initial studies of RT employed grade-appropriate texts that addressed a broad array of (fairly random) unrelated topics; the limitation of this choice was that it did not promote the use of the dialogues for knowledge building over time. In contrast, in a line of inquiry conducted with first-grade students in which RT was used to teach listening comprehension, we wrote texts that presented simple science concepts related to animal survival: protection from elements, natural pest control, adaptation and extinction, camouflage, and mimicry. For example, the theme "protection against elements" included passages about porcupines, turtles, and armadillos. Furthermore, the teacher was urged to first determine whether the students would spontaneously focus on the content of the theme in their discussion of the passage. If the students failed to do so, the teacher was encouraged to make the theme explicit (Palincsar & Brown, 1988; Palincsar, Stevens, & Gavelek, 1989).

The results of the listening comprehension assessments that we administered were that the students in the RT group scored 70% correct after 20 days of discussions, whereas the students in the comparison condition, who listened to each story but did not have the benefit of discussion, scored 40% correct on these measures. Furthermore, the students in the experimental group were significantly more successful at identifying the gist of passages and recognizing and applying analogical information in the test passages to novel passages (Palincsar, Brown, & Campione, 1993).

A second curricular modification was the inclusion of RT as one participation structure within Brown and Campione's (1994, 1996) "fostering a community of learners" research. In these classrooms, students were prepared to use RT dialogues in the same fashion that students in earlier research were prepared, but RT was then incorporated in a much larger and more ambitious curriculum: Student groups would become experts regarding particular topics (e.g., interdependence in an ecosystem), and the students used RT dialogues in the course of conducting their research and sharing their research with others. Both of these curricular adaptations are significant with respect to what they communicate about the ultimate goal of RT dialogues, a goal that will be revisited shortly in this postscript.

The earliest characterizations of RT indicated that there were three essential components to understanding and replicating RT: the four strategies that were complementary and designed to accomplish different work in the context of constructing the meaning of text, the teacher–student/student–student dialogue that was key to the collaborative construction of meaning, and the roles of the teacher in the dialogues. These roles were characterized as multifaceted and included diagnosing difficulties arising in understanding the text, and adjusting support to enact the strategies as needed. Ideally, as teachers model these roles, students will begin to assume greater responsibility for assuming these roles themselves. Studies that followed the initial studies of RT were designed to investigate the interaction of these three components. For example, Palincsar (1986) reported analyses of teacher–student dialogues, examining groups of first graders and their teachers, all of whom were using RT with the same texts but with more and less success. Features characterizing the teachers' practices in the more successful groups included requesting that students elaborate on their ideas, restoring direction to the discussion when it began to meander, and reworking students' contributions so they were integrated into the discussion.

Perhaps as a function of how deceptively simple RT looks on the outside, certainly as a function of not having sufficient supports for dissemination, and perhaps as a function of being a significant departure from typical classroom practice, as RT was disseminated, it fell prey to what Haertel (1986) has called a series of "lethal mutations" (p. 52). Perhaps because they are the easiest part of the instruction to get a handle on—certainly in contrast to the discourse in which they were embedded—the four strategies appear to have taken on a life of their own; they appear in standards, in reading texts, in worksheets, and in language arts series. A quick Internet search reveals many examples of videos in which groups purport to be engaged in RT dialogues, but there is nothing dialogic about the instruction. Typically, what is demonstrated is practice in the use of the four strategies, with little evidence that the group is using the strategies to construct a coherent representation of the ideas in the text.

Spurred by this "lethal mutations" phenomenon and seeking a more powerful way to accurately communicate the characteristics of RT, Palincsar and Spiro collaborated on the design of a Web-based hypermedia environment, which Spiro calls an Experience Acceleration Support Environment, or EASE system (Spiro & Jehng, 1990). We named our EASE system Teaching Text, Making Meaning (TTMM; see edrl.educ.msu.edu/CompStrat/login.asp, username: demo, password: demo). TTMM was developed through an iterative coding process in which we analyzed 35 hours of reading comprehension instruction dialogues with upper elementary students; the 35 hours were converted to 188 short video clips grouped into categories, which we refer to as themes. The 10 themes (e.g., building a learning community, modeling expert reading, using text characteristics) are further divided into specific topics. For example, the "using text characteristics" theme includes clips about genre, text structure, and text features (e.g., illustrations). The 10 themes and their associated topics were selected because they address the issues that teachers face as they plan, enact, and evaluate text-based discussions. For example, the "using text characteristics" theme illustrates how a teacher might make use of an illustration in the text to support students' understanding of the content. Linked to a number of the instructional clips are related interviews in which the teachers reflect on the instructional moment featured in each clip, such as evaluating their practice, describing tensions in the instruction, or identifying alternative decisions entertained in the moment.

The navigability of an EASE system raises interesting questions about communicating about teaching, specifically about the teaching of reading comprehension. The video clips are not primarily organized around a particular instructional approach; rather, they are organized around moments of teaching and learning. Assembling this environment challenged us to think about useful grain sizes for parsing the work of teaching and the development of competence as text comprehenders. The hypermedia tool gives teachers the ability to navigate the system as a function of their own needs and interests; furthermore, they can use the system to engage in inquiry, essentially bringing their own question(s) to the data, which, in this case, are the video clips. Analyses of teachers engaged in use of the system reveals evidence of increased sensitivity to context and a greater appreciation for the nuanced nature of the application of practices such as scaffolding. For example, teachers were observed shifting over time from searching for a singular and prescriptive definition of scaffolding to a more situation-sensitive analysis of the forms and purposes for scaffolding (Palincsar et al., 2007).

In addition to the research conducted by its developers, RT has a broad research base that has been built by others (Rosenshine & Meister, 1994). Although originally designed for use with elementary students scoring at or below the 35th percentile on standardized reading measures, RT has been implemented and found effective in a variety of contexts and for a variety of readers. The approach has been effective in teaching students with mild disabilities in resource (Marston, 1995) and inclusive settings (Lederer, 2000), deaf and hard-of-hearing students (Al-Hilawani, 2003), high school students (Alfassi, 1998; Westera & Moore, 1995), bilingual students in the United States (Padrón, 1992), and international students who are learning English as a second language (Fung, Wilkinson, & Moore, 2003).

Of course, RT is only one of many instructional approaches that have been advanced by the literacy community to improve reading comprehension. It is, therefore, disappointing that descriptive studies reveal that comprehension instruction continues to be enacted infrequently (Connor, Morrison, & Petrella, 2004; Taylor, Pearson, Clark, & Walpole, 2000) and inadequately (Dewitz, Jones, & Leahy, 2009). Furthermore, despite decades of research testifying to the effectiveness of teaching readers to be self-regulating or strategic in their reading of text, strategy instruction itself has come under attack by members of the literacy community (e.g., McKeown, Beck, & Blake, 2009; Wilkinson & Son, 2011). As the history of RT testifies, strategy instruction becomes vulnerable when the rigid or isolated teaching of strategies becomes the goal of instruction, rather than the flexible and opportunistic application of strategies to sense making with text. The cumulative research on RT suggests that features of powerful comprehension instruction include the use of related texts that allow students to experience the process of deepening their understanding across texts; the teaching of strategies as a repertoire of thinking tools that should be used in opportunistic ways, as determined by the demands of the text and the goals of the reader; and the explicit teaching of strategies in the service of advancing knowledge building.

REFERENCES

Alfassi, M. (1998). Reading for meaning: The efficacy of reciprocal teaching in fostering reading comprehension in high school students in remedial reading classes. *American Educational Research Journal*, *35*(2), 309–332.

Al-Hilawani, Y.A. (2003). Clinical examination of three methods of teaching reading comprehension to deaf and hard-of-hearing students: From research to classroom applications. *Journal of Deaf Studies and Deaf Education*, *8*(2), 146–156. doi:10.1093/deafed/eng001

Brown, A.L., & Campione, J.C. (1994). Guided discovery in a community of learners. In K. McGilly (Ed.), *Classroom lessons: Integrating cognitive theory and classroom practice* (pp. 229–270). Cambridge, MA: MIT Press.

Brown, A.L., & Campione, J.C. (1996). Psychological theory and the design of innovative learning environments: On procedures, principles, and systems. In L. Schauble & R. Glaser (Eds.), *Innovations in learning: New environments for education* (pp. 289–325). Mahwah, NJ: Erlbaum.

Connor, C.M., Morrison, F.J., & Petrella, J.N. (2004). Effective reading comprehension instruction: Examining child × instruction interactions. *Journal of Educational Psychology*, *96*(4), 682–698. doi:10.1037/0022-0663.96.4.682

Dewitz, P., Jones, J., & Leahy, S. (2009). Comprehension strategy instruction in core reading programs. *Reading Research Quarterly*, *44*(2), 102–126. doi:10.1598/RRQ.44.2.1

Fung, I.Y.Y., Wilkinson, I.A.G., & Moore, D.W. (2003). L1-assisted reciprocal teaching to improve ESL students' comprehension of English expository text. *Learning and Instruction*, *13*(1), 1–31. doi:10.1016/S0959-4752(01)00033-0

Haertel, E. (1986). The valid use of student performance measures for teacher evaluation. *Educational Evaluation and Policy Analysis*, *8*(1), 45–60.
Lederer, J.M. (2000). Reciprocal teaching of social studies in inclusive elementary classrooms. *Journal of Learning Disabilities*, *33*(1), 91–106. doi:10.1177/002221940003300112
Marston, D. (1995). Comparison of reading intervention approaches for students with mild disabilities. *Exceptional Children*, *62*(1), 20–37.
McKeown, M.G., Beck, I.L., & Blake, R.G.K. (2009). Rethinking reading comprehension instruction: A comparison of instruction for strategies and content approaches. *Reading Research Quarterly*, *44*(3), 218–253. doi:10.1598/RRQ.44.3.1
Padrón, Y.N. (1992). The effect of strategy instruction on bilingual students' cognitive strategy use in reading. *Bilingual Research Journal*, *16*(3/4), 35–51. doi:10.1080/15235882.1992.10162636
Palincsar, A.S. (1986). The role of dialogue in providing scaffolded instruction. *Educational Psychologist*, *21*(1/2), 73–98.
Palincsar, A.S., & Brown, A.L. (1988). Teaching and practicing thinking skills to promote comprehension in the context of group problem solving. *Remedial and Special Education*, *9*(1), 53–59. doi:10.1177/074193258800900110
Palincsar, A.S., Brown, A.L., & Campione, J.C. (1993). First-grade dialogues for knowledge acquisition and use. In E.A. Forman, N. Minick, & C.A. Stone (Eds.), *Contexts for learning: Sociocultural dynamics in children's development* (pp. 43–57). New York: Oxford University Press.
Palincsar, A.S., Spiro, R.J., Kucan, L., Magnusson, S.J., Collins, B., Hapgood, S., et al. (2007). Designing a hypermedia environment to support comprehension instruction. In D.S. McNamara (Ed.), *Reading comprehension strategies: Theories, interventions, and technologies* (pp. 441–462). Mahwah, NJ: Erlbaum.
Palincsar, A.S., Stevens, D.D., & Gavelek, J.R. (1989). Collaborating with teachers in the interest of student collaboration. *International Journal of Educational Research*, *13*(1), 41–53. doi:10.1016/0883-0355(89)90015-3
Rosenshine, B., & Meister, C. (1994). Reciprocal teaching: A review of the research. *Review of Educational Research*, *64*(4), 479–530.
Spiro, R.J., & Jehng, J. (1990). Cognitive flexibility and hypertext: Theory and technology for the nonlinear and multidimensional traversal of complex subject matter. In D. Nix & R.J. Spiro (Eds.), *Cognition, education, and multimedia: Exploring ideas in high technology* (pp. 163–205). Hillsdale, NJ: Erlbaum.
Taylor, B.M., Pearson, P.D., Clark, K., & Walpole, S. (2000). Effective schools and accomplished teachers: Lessons about primary-grade reading instruction in low-income schools. *The Elementary School Journal*, *101*(2), 121–165. doi:10.1086/499662
Westera, J., & Moore, D.W. (1995). Reciprocal teaching of reading comprehension in a New Zealand high school. *Psychology in the Schools*, *32*(3), 225–232. doi:10.1002/1520-6807(199507)32:3<225::AID-PITS2310320310>3.0.CO;2-F
Wilkinson, I.A.G., & Son, E.H. (2011). A dialogic turn in research on learning and teaching to comprehend. In M.L. Kamil, P.D. Pearson, E.B. Moje, & P.P. Afflerbach (Eds.), *Handbook of reading research* (Vol. 4, pp. 359–387). New York: Routledge.

Models of Reading and Writing Processes

What's in a Model of Literacy Processes?

The word *model* can have many meanings and manifestations, as explained in Chapter 2. In this section, models are viewed as metaphors that help us visualize and understand research and theories that explain components of the reading process. Ranging from the basic to the highly sophisticated, models of reading render specific features of the reading process, such as word recognition, or depict more globally an integrated and interacting network of specific components, all of which contribute to the mind-making meaning from a text. Similarly, a model of writing helps us see how writing processes function and interact as writers create texts.

We can begin to see a reader's mind at work with the help of models. They enable us to understand how texts are constructed when a reader reads or a writer writes. Each component depicted in a model, as well as the interaction of components, is based on extensive research and theory that inform the design of a model of reading or writing. Most designers of models draw from their own theory base and research as well as that of others to construct a model. A careful synthesis of components and their functions often provides an explanation of processes that otherwise are difficult, if not impossible, to observe and understand.

Whereas some literacy models show complex, interacting systems contributing to comprehension during reading or the construction of text during writing, other models focus on only one component. In either case, our limited capacity to observe, measure, collect information, and describe processes precisely limits the accuracy of a reading model. Furthermore, models of reading, like a snapshot, often depict a moment in time described in ordinary language processed linearly, whereas reading is a continuous, recursive, and multileveled process.

The Benefits of Reading Models

Everyone who teaches reading has some model of the reading process that influences, perhaps unconsciously, their instructional decision making. We know that teachers' understanding the reading process more fully and explicitly contributes to improvements in instructional practice and deeper knowledge of their students' learning (Beck, 1989). Models provide educators with a deeper understanding of reading processes, where breakdowns in comprehension can occur, and what strategies could improve reading processes.

First, with respect to understanding reading, a model integrates research findings, makes theory graphic, and provides an explanation of how reading takes place in accord with what we currently know. Whereas taking apart a car's engine helps us see how it works and so discover how to repair it, dismantling the reading process presents us with a very different problem. Although reading is a highly complex and hidden process with no pistons, valves, or crankshafts to pull out for observation, we have a substantial amount of research and theoretical knowledge about it. What we know enables us to construct a model to visualize this mysterious, invisible process. Furthermore, once we have begun to make more visible our understanding of reading through models, we tend to move those models toward greater sophistication.

Second, a model of reading helps us detect where breakdowns in comprehension could occur. A model helps us visualize what components may fail to contribute to smooth meaning making while reading. For example, weak or slow word recognition can cause poor comprehension. In short, models help us understand what contributes to a struggling reader's troubles.

Third, a model provides clues about instructional approaches and intervention strategies that could help readers at different stages in reading development. Although using a reading model to develop prescription-based instruction is a risky practice, we can use models as resources for good hints. A well-designed model based in solid research can create more opportunities to envision instructional interventions.

From Research to Model

Models of reading and writing picture mental events based on extensive research. Much of the research and theory reported in this and earlier editions of *Theoretical Models and Processes of Reading* has contributed to the models that appear here.

The discovery of many intertextual connections awaits readers who have already explored the chapters on research from earlier parts of this book from which the models arise. Among potential interconnections are the following:

- Eras of reading research identified and described by Alexander and Fox (Chapter 1)
- Language processes, such as the windows into reading that miscue analysis provides (Goodman & Goodman, Chapter 21) or the window into writing that the close observation of young children in classrooms enables (Dyson & Genishi, Chapter 6)
- The social and cultural contexts of literacy, such as reading from a sociocognitive perspective (Gee, Chapter 4), the dynamics of peer interaction (Forman & Cazden, Chapter 7), or the effects of linking critical discussion of student achievement to research on effective comprehension practices to meet specific student needs (Lai, McNaughton, Amituanai-Toloa, Turner, & Hsiao, Chapter 11)

- Literacy development during early childhood and implications for early literacy instruction (Lonigan & Shanahan, Chapter 13), the development of word recognition (Ehri & McCormick, Chapter 12), and the development of fluency (Kuhn & Stahl, Chapter 15)
- Comprehension and comprehension theories and strategies, such as vocabulary development (Nagy & Scott, Chapter 18) and research on schema theory (Anderson, Chapter 19; McVee, Dunsmore, & Gavelek, Chapter 20; Spiro, Coulson, Feltovich, & Anderson, Chapter 22)
- Motivation and engagement, such as methods of literacy instruction with relevant texts that help young men of color respond to their lived contexts (Tatum, Chapter 25), and the effects of motivation, background knowledge, and cognitive strategy use on children's reading comprehension (Taboada, Tonks, Wigfield, & Guthrie, Chapter 24)
- Instructional effects on literacy development appearing in research that Clay conducted and that contributed to an early intervention known as Reading Recovery (Doyle, Chapter 26) and in research on comprehension and strategy instruction that led to reciprocal teaching (Brown, Palincsar, & Armbruster, Chapter 27)

Many of the models presented in this section rely on these and other research studies, theories that evolved from them, and hypotheses about how features focused on in one study may interact with features of another. For example, hypotheses based on schema theory provided several model builders with an explanation of how background knowledge may affect the reading process.

Theory and Research Generate Waves of Theoretical Models

Several sources of theory and research have fed the development of models for reading and writing. One of the major sources of knowledge-generating models developed since the 1970s has been fed by information emerging from research in cognitive psychology. From research on the mind's cognitive processes, especially studies that related directly to processing information and texts, designers have created several waves of cognitive processing models, some of which have crested and diminished in influence while others have remained highly influential. Some waves contained only one or two models. Other waves included many models, with earlier models influencing the design of subsequent models within that wave. The waves begin with bottom-up models, followed by top-down models, and progress to interactive or bottom-up/top-down designs (Rumelhart, Chapter 29; Samuels, Chapter 28). The wave of interactive models was, in turn, followed by important extensions and elaborations (Hannon, Chapter 33; Just & Carpenter, Chapter 30; Kintsch, Chapter 32).

Research and theory in other domains have fed several wave-generating knowledge resources. These include Sadoski and Paivio's dual coding theory (DCT;

Chapter 34) and Rosenblatt's transactional theory (Chapter 35). From research examining relationships between reading and writing from both a discourse and cognitive perspective, Parodi (Chapter 36) found significant coefficients between reading and writing on several psycholinguistic levels that could contribute to a model depicting their interrelatedness. Furthermore, advances in statistical methods and their application to the testing of theoretical models of reading are manifested in the use of structural equation models (Cromley & Azevedo, 2007: Cromley, Snyder-Hogan, & Luciw-Dubas, 2010; Hannon, Chapter 33).

The last wave of cognitive processing models addressed in this volume embeds an interactive model within the social context of the classroom, where interpretations of texts by students and teacher are shared and meanings negotiated (Ruddell & Unrau, Chapter 38). Each of these waves above is described in more detail in the following paragraphs.

Bottom-Up (Wave 1)

Gough's (1972) "one second of reading" model depicts a process that began with low-level sensory representations (letter input) and proceeded through phonemic and lexical-level representation to deeper structural representation. The flow of information is completely bottom-up with no higher level process, such as information held in long-term memory, affecting lower level representations. In "One Second of Reading: Postscript," Gough (1985) acknowledged the problems inherent in his model.

Top-Down (Wave 2)

The next (or second) wave of models focused on what readers remembered after reading a text, and the discovery that text memory was systematic. The questions guiding the design of that generation were, What do readers remember about the text they read, and what do those memories tell us about the nature of the memory representations resulting from reading? The theories arising from this wave focused on top-down memory influences, especially that of text structure. Story grammars (Stein & Glenn, 1979), script theory (Schank & Abelson, 1977), and hierarchical theories based on text structure (Meyer, 1975; Meyer & Poon, 2001) arose as answers to the questions guiding these researchers.

Top-Down (Wave 3)

Nearly synchronous with the second wave of theories was a third wave focused on a broader view of what readers bring to a text. Note that the second wave text structure–recall theories described earlier focus only on the connection between the background knowledge that a reader brings to a text and the reader's comprehension of the text (Pearson & Stephens, 1992). The provocative, third wave question became, What influence does a reader's background knowledge have on the meanings constructed when reading? Schema theory (Anderson, Chapter 19; McVee et al., Chapter 20) arose from efforts to answer that question, and the answer constituted a new third wave of reading theory. Schema theory lies at the core of many models of reading, including several presented in this section.

Bottom-Up/Top-Down (Wave 4)

A fourth wave of models emerging mostly in the early 1980s favored a focus on a bottom-up plus top-down interaction that shaped comprehension. The question for these researchers was, What do readers do as they move through a text? These fourth wave models took into account readers' efforts to construct coherent text representations with respect to that text's referential and causal structure. Different manifestations of the fourth wave appear in Samuels's automatic information-processing model (Chapter 28), Rumelhart's interactive model (Chapter 29), Just and Carpenter's model that accounts for eye fixations (Chapter 30), Adams's processor model (Chapter 31), Kintsch's construction–integration model (Chapter 32), and Hannon's cognitive components-resource model (Chapter 33). Many of these model designers influenced one another, as is the case with Just and Carpenter's influence on Adams's model, and Kintsch's influence on Hannon's model.

Bottom-Up/Top-Down + Sociocultural Context (Wave 5)

A fifth wave of model building puts the reader with a text in a social and cultural context. That context may be one that shapes and defines the reader (Gee, Chapter 4) or influences responses to texts (Alvermann, Young, Green, & Wisenbaker, 1999). Ruddell and Unrau (Chapter 38) present a sociocognitive model of reading in which meanings are constructed during a socioculturally contextualized bottom-up/top-down reading process. Readers interpret and negotiate meanings not only for linguistically based texts but also for tasks, sources of authority, and sociocultural factors.

Resources Stimulating Additional Model Development

Several other resources have stimulated the creation of models of reading, writing, and the relationships between them. Those models include ones grounded in dual coding theory, transactional theory, research on reading–writing connections, and rhetoric.

As a theory of general cognition first developed to explain verbal and nonverbal influences on memory, DCT was extended by Sadoski and Paivio (Chapter 34) into the realm of literacy and reading comprehension. The authors draw on DCT to explain decoding, comprehension, and readers' responses to texts. Their DCT model, rich in explanatory power, provides an alternative to reading models based primarily on verbal processes, such as schema theory. Authors of the DCT model have also demonstrated how DCT can explain written composition (Sadoski & Paivio, 2001).

From an array of disciplinary perspectives, including philosophy, comparative literature, aesthetics, linguistics, and sociology, which formed early in the 20th century, Rosenblatt (Chapter 35) developed a transactional theory and model of both reading and writing. Her model differs in significant ways from cognitive processing models of reading and can be viewed as a wave unto itself. Rather than thinking of reading as a separate reader taking in a separate text, Rosenblatt views the reader and text as two aspects of a dynamic process. Readers do not get meaning from the text because meaning does not reside in the text; meaning issues from the transaction between the reader and the text. Readers, while transacting with a text, form a structure of the text's elements that becomes an object of thought, what she calls the evocation. Readers then respond to emerging evocations while reading and form interpretations that report, analyze, and explain those evocations. Furthermore, according to Rosenblatt's transactional model, readers adopt a stance toward a text on an efferent–aesthetic continuum. Readers adopt an efferent stance when their purpose for reading is to extract and retain information from a reading event. They adopt an aesthetic stance when their purpose for reading is to engage in a lived-through experience. These two stances are sometimes incorrectly identified as binaries; however, according to Rosenblatt, both stances are manifest in every reading on an efferent–aesthetic continuum.

Growing concerns internationally about the limited ability of students to read and write persuasive or argumentative texts have given impetus to research on reading and writing processes during interaction with argumentative texts and to the development of intervention programs to improve students' strategic and critical approaches to more complex texts. For example, in Chile, Parodi (Chapter 36) investigated the relationships between comprehension and the production of argumentative texts. His findings suggest how a network of reading–writing connections could contribute to the development of more effective classroom instruction and promote students' mastery of reading and writing argumentative texts. Increasing concerns in the United States over the large and often increasing numbers of college students arriving for their freshman classes underprepared to read and write expository prose (ACT, 2005; Intersegmental Committee of the Academic Senates..., 2002; Joftus, 2002) spurred the development of intervention programs to better prepare students for the rigors of college reading and writing. Many of these interventions were implemented at the college level in the form of remedial courses, but a newer form of intervention at the high school level has been developed and implemented in California. Called the Expository Reading and Writing Course, the program is based on a template that serves as a model for the development of instructional modules based on engaging and challenging texts. Students learn to read rhetorically, connect reading to writing, and write rhetorically as they progress through a series of modules that focus on various topics and themes.

With advances in technology and new methods to study reading processes, such as functional magnetic resonance imagery, new sources of knowledge are beginning to contribute to our understanding of how the brain functions while reading (Hruby & Goswami, Chapter 23). Still over the horizon, future models of reading may be useful in identifying brain patterns of highly effective and skilled readers as well as those of readers who are experiencing delays or difficulties.

We are clearly on a threshold of discoveries that may add enormously to our understanding of reading processes, to the formulation of new theories, and to the creation of innovative models.

RECOMMENDED READINGS

De La Paz, S., Swanson, P.N., & Graham, S. (1998). The contribution of executive control to the revising by students with writing and learning difficulties. *Journal of Educational Psychology, 90*(3), 448–460.

Graesser, A.C., Swamer, S.S., Baggett, W.B., & Sell, M.A. (1996). New models of deep comprehension. In B.K. Britton & A.C. Graesser (Eds.), *Models of understanding text* (pp. 1–32). Mahwah, NJ: Erlbaum.

Holmes, J.A. (1970). The substrata-factor theory of reading: Some experimental evidence. In H. Singer & R.B. Ruddell (Eds.), *Theoretical models and processes of reading* (pp. 187–197). Newark, DE: International Reading Association. (Reprinted from *New frontiers in reading*, by J.A. Figurel, Ed., 1960, New York: Scholastic)

Singer, H. (1985). The substrata-factor theory of reading. In H. Singer & R.B. Ruddell (Eds.), *Theoretical models and processes of reading* (3rd ed., pp. 630–660). Newark, DE: International Reading Association.

Van Meter, P. (2001). Drawing construction as a strategy for learning from text. *Journal of Educational Psychology, 93*(1), 129–140.

REFERENCES

ACT. (2005). *Crisis at the core: Preparing all students for college and work.* Iowa City, IA: Author. Retrieved October 15, 2012, from www.act.org/research/policymakers/pdf/crisis_report.pdf

Alvermann, D.E., Young, J.P., Green, C., & Wisenbaker, J.M. (1999). Adolescents' perceptions and negotiations of literacy practices in after-school read and talk clubs. *American Educational Research Journal, 36*(2), 221–264.

Beck, I.L. (1989). Improving practice through understanding reading. In L.B. Resnick & L.E. Klopfer (Eds.), *Toward the thinking curriculum: Current cognitive research* (pp. 40–58). Alexandria, VA: Association for Supervision and Curriculum Development.

Cromley, J.G., & Azevedo, R. (2007). Testing and refining the direct and inferential mediation model of reading comprehension. *Journal of Educational Psychology, 99*(2), 311–325.

Cromley, J.G., Snyder-Hogan, L.E., & Luciw-Dubas, U.A. (2010). Reading comprehension of scientific texts: A domain-specific test of the direct and inferential mediation model of reading comprehension. *Journal of Educational Psychology, 102*(3), 687–700.

Gough, P.B. (1972). One second of reading. In J.F. Kavanagh & I.G. Mattingly (Eds.), *Language by ear and by eye: The relationships between speech and reading* (pp. 331–358). Cambridge, MA: MIT Press.

Gough, P.B. (1985). One second of reading: Postscript. In H. Singer & R.B. Ruddell (Eds.), *Theoretical models and processes of reading* (3rd ed., pp. 687–688). Newark, DE: International Reading Association.

Intersegmental Committee of the Academic Senates of the California Community Colleges, the California State University, and the University of California. (2002). *Academic literacy: A statement of competencies expected of students entering California's public colleges and universities.* Sacramento: Author.

Joftus, S. (2002). *Every child a graduate: A framework for an excellent education for all middle and high school students.* Washington, DC: Alliance for Excellent Education.

Meyer, B.J.F. (1975). *The organization of prose and its effects on memory.* Amsterdam: North-Holland.

Meyer, B.J.F., & Poon, L.W. (2001). Effects of structure strategy training and signaling on recall of text. *Journal of Educational Psychology, 93*(1), 141–159.

Pearson, P.D., & Stephens, D. (1992). Learning about literacy: A 30-year journey. In C. Gordon, G.D. Labercane, & W.R. McEachern (Eds.), *Elementary reading instruction: Process and practice* (pp. 4–18). Lexington, MA: Ginn.

Sadoski, M., & Paivio, A. (2001). *Imagery and text: A dual coding theory of reading and writing.* Mahwah, NJ: Erlbaum.

Schank, R.C., & Abelson, R.P. (1977). *Scripts, plans, goals, and understanding: An inquiry into human knowledge structures.* Hillsdale, NJ: Erlbaum.

Stein, N.L., & Glenn, C.G. (1979). An analysis of story comprehension in elementary school children. In Freedle, R.O. (Ed.), *New directions in discourse processing* (pp. 53–120). Norwood, NJ: Ablex.

CHAPTER 28

Toward a Theory of Automatic Information Processing in Reading, Revisited

S. Jay Samuels, University of Minnesota

The LaBerge–Samuels (1974) model of automatic information processing in reading is now two decades old and has had a long and useful life. In reading methods textbooks, it is the most widely quoted of all the reading theories (Blanchard, Rottenberg, & Jones, 1989). When the model was in its infancy, it attracted the interest of teachers and researchers because it used the concept of automaticity to explain why fluent readers are able to decode and understand text with ease while beginning readers have difficulty. Later the model provided the conceptual groundwork for repeated reading (Samuels, 1979), a method for helping beginning readers become automatic decoders. Researchers have also realized that the concept of automaticity can be extended to any skill in reading. Most recently, it has spurred cognitive psychologists to offer new explanations concerning what happens when one develops a skill to the automatic level. In fact, Logan (1988a) believes the new explanations of automaticity are so important that he stated as follows:

> There is a battle raging in the ivory tower over the concept of automaticity. One faction represents "the old guard," the modal view of the field, and construes automaticity as a way to overcome resource limitations. The other function is revolutionary (or sees itself as such) and construes automaticity as a memory phenomenon reflecting the consequences of running a large database through an efficient retrieval process. The battle may turn out to be a tempest in a teapot, affecting no more than academic promotion and tenure.

In this piece about automaticity theory, I will attempt to do two things:

1. describe automaticity theory and its practical applications; and
2. explain some of the new ideas about automaticity.

The LaBerge–Samuels Model of Automatic Information Processing

A good theoretical model has three characteristics: It summarizes a considerable amount of information discovered in the past; it helps explain and make more understandable what is happening in the present; and it allows one to make

This chapter is reprinted from *Theoretical Models and Processes of Reading* (4th ed., pp. 816–837), edited by R.B. Ruddell, M.R. Ruddell, & H. Singer, Newark, DE: International Reading Association.

predictions about the future. From a scientific viewpoint, the ability to make predictions is most important because the accuracy of the predictions is what allows one to test the model's validity. When the test results fail to support the predictions, then the model has to be revised. The LaBerge–Samuels automaticity model has these three characteristics of summarizing the past, explaining the present, and predicting the future. Many aspects of the model—such as its description of how the eye processes print—were taken from past research on visual processing. Further, the model brings together research findings from a variety of areas in an attempt to explain the present. For example, it explains the crucial differences between beginning and fluent reading so that one can understand why beginning readers have so much difficulty understanding what they read. And finally, over the years a number of tests and revisions have been made of the model.

Attention

The LaBerge–Samuels model attempts to identify components in the information-processing system, trace the routes that information takes as it passes through the system, and identify changes in the form of the information as it moves from the surface of the page into the deeper semantic-linguistic centers of the brain. At the heart of the model is *attention.* Attention has two components, internal and external. To the layperson, the external aspects of attention are the more familiar. When a classroom teacher says that a student does not pay attention and therefore is not living up to his or her potential, it is external attention that is being described. Other manifestations of external attention have to do with what may be called *orienting behavior*, the directing of one's sensory organs (such as eyes and ears) in such a way as to maximize information input. If an observer can watch the behavior of another and determine whether that person is paying attention (as a teacher often does), it is the level of external attention that is being determined.

External attention has important implications for learning in general and for learning to read in particular. In fact, most psychologists would agree that it is a prerequisite, that without the external and internal components of attention there can be no learning. Classroom observation has thrown some light on the relationship between external attention and reading. A fairly well-documented finding is that during elementary school years, girls surpass boys in reading achievement. Is this superiority the result of some maturational genetic sex-linked advantage or of cultural forces at work in the classroom? One line of research showed that when boys were put in booths that resemble airplane cockpits for a reading hour, they learned more from texts than did girls, this suggesting a cultural rather than genetic advantage. These booths are not only exciting to boys but also help them focus their attention on the reading by reducing extraneous sources of stimulation. Another line of classroom research found that girls were significantly more attentive during the reading hour than were boys; these same girls were also superior readers. In this classroom study, as external signs of attention (such as looking in books and working on reading assignments) increased in both boys and girls, so did reading scores (Samuels & Turnure, 1974).

Although external aspects of attention are important to learning and comprehension, the internal aspects are even more crucial and represent the core component of the LaBerge–Samuels model. External aspects of attention such as orientation of sensory receptors indicate that internal processing of information is taking place; when a person's eyes are glued to a book, we assume he or she is internally processing the information on the page and trying to construct meaning from it. The internal characteristics of attention are far more difficult to describe. Imagine a laboratory in which an experimental subject is given earphones and told that a male voice will be heard in one ear and a female voice in the other. Our subject is told to remember the information given by the female voice and has no difficulty performing this task. Even if we increase the task difficulty by alternating the ear in which the female voice is transmitted, our subject can successfully direct attention to the appropriate voice. This selection of the appropriate voice to listen to is an example of internal control of attention.

The same ability to process and recall auditory information occurs in natural, real-life settings. Cocktail parties are frequently crowded situations in which many people move about and talk to one another. Imagine talking to a friend at a cocktail party. Both the external and internal components of attention are directed at your friend. Suddenly, from behind, you hear part of an interesting conversation you want to hear more of. Without turning your head away from your friend or giving any outward sign to either your friend or the person behind you, you begin to take in as much of two conversations as you can. This ability to take in parts of several conversations at will by switching attention back and forth without anyone's knowledge has come to be called the "cocktail party phenomenon."

Internal attention has three characteristics, as follows:

1. *Alertness.* Alertness simply refers to the active attempt to come in contact with sources of information. Alertness also can be thought of in terms of vigilance.
2. *Selectivity.* Our environment is such that at any moment under ordinary circumstances, our sensory organs—eyes, ears, nose, skin, tongue—can be bombarded with multiple, competing stimuli. As you read this line, are you aware that the lines above and below are also on your retina? We are generally unaware of this, and the process of selective attention enables us to choose which line we will process. Similarly, when we go to a party, several conversations usually compete for our attention, yet we are able to select which one we will process at any given moment. Following is a passage that shows how selective attention operates in the visual mode. It contains two different ideas—one written in uppercase and the other in lowercase letters. Read only the text in uppercase letters and be prepared to answer the question at the end:

   WHY the YOU purpose SHOULD of GET the THE investigation SHAFT was A to SHAFT test IS the THE focal MOST attention EFFICIENT hypothesis

WAY this TO hypothesis DELIVER suggests POWER that FROM when THE a ENGINE picture TO and THE a REAR word WHEEL are IT presented WILL together NOT the SPRAY student YOU will WITH focus OIL on NOR that WILL part IT of BREAK the AS stimulus EASILY which AS most A readily CHAIN elicits IN a FACT correct A response SHAFT a IS poor ALMOST reader INDESTRUCTIBLE finds AND the BECAUSE picture IT easier IS to ENCLOSED use IN than A the BATH word OF and OIL attends IT to IS the ALMOST picture SILENT

What are the advantages of a drive shaft?

Most people who read this passage have no difficulty selecting the message on which to place their attention. Furthermore, the passage on drive shafts usually is read with a high level of literal comprehension.

3. *Limited capacity.* The human mind, like the fastest computer, has limited capacity to process information. With the human mind, the limitation comes from the limited amount of attention available for information processing. Attention may be thought of as the effort or energy used to process information. When we are learning a complicated skill, the demands of learning that skill use up all our attention resources and we find we can pay attention to only one task at a time. For example, beginning drivers often find that while driving, they dislike experiencing any competing demands on their attention, such as conversation with a passenger. With extensive practice, the attention demands of driving decrease sufficiently so drivers can process multiple sources of information at the same time. Experienced drivers can simultaneously operate the car, engage in conversation, and enjoy music.

One way to think of automaticity is that it represents the ability to perform a task with little attention. The critical test of automaticity is that the task, which at the beginning stage of learning could be performed only by itself, now can be performed along with one or more other tasks. What is the mechanism that allows this transformation from beginner to expert? This question will be addressed in the final section of this piece.

To summarize, attention can be divided into two broad categories, one having to do with external and the other with internal components. The external aspects of attention are directly observable and are generally related to the orientation of one's sensory organs; the internal aspects of attention—alertness, selectivity, and limited capacity—are not directly observable. How do these concepts relate to reading?

Decoding. Internal components of attention are central to the theory of automatic information processing in reading. It is assumed in the theory—as well as by many who study reading—that getting meaning from printed words involves a two-step process: First, the printed words must be decoded; second, the decoded words must be comprehended. *Decoding* in relation to reading is the process of translating printed words into spoken words. It is not necessary for the "spoken words" actually to be uttered aloud.

Comprehension. Even though definitive explanations of the mechanisms underlying comprehension are currently unavailable, it seems reasonably clear that research will find that attention is required for processing an unfamiliar passage for its meaning. With all the practice experienced readers get at processing for meaning, one may wonder why skill development in this area does not reach the point of automaticity. Granted, when a competent adult reader encounters highly familiar words (such as *cat*, *kitchen*, *wheel*, or *milk*) in print, their meaning is in all probability immediately available without the need of attention. The ability to get the meaning of each word in a sentence, however, is not the same as the ability to comprehend a sentence. In comprehending a sentence, one must be able to interrelate and combine the separate meanings of each of its words. From this point of view, comprehension is a constructive process of synthesis and putting word meanings together in special ways, much as individual bricks are combined in the construction of a house. Whereas one may go from print to the meanings of individual words automatically, the acts of integrating, relating, and combining these meanings in the unique ways demanded by sentences are required for comprehension. Even in a passage as simple as "The dog is in the house," attention is necessary to determine, for example, the relationship of the dog to the house. Is the dog on, in, under, or next to the house? An understanding of "The grandmother spanked her grandchild" requires knowledge of what the action is, who the agent is, and who the object of the action is. To understand the relationship of grandmother to grandchild requires complex analysis of such features as how many generations separate the two.

If even simple sentences require a reader's attention in order to determine the relationships that exist among their parts, imagine what happens when more complex sentences on more complex topics are read. When one superimposes the added burdens on attention and memory that occur when a poor reader—who is still using attention to decode—encounters a difficult passage, there is little wonder that comprehension seems to suffer.

Attention Switching in Reading. For many students, learning to read is a difficult task requiring considerable attention. If each student had unlimited quantities of attention to focus on the task there would be no problem, but this is not the case. When a student encounters a task requiring more attention than is available, he or she is faced with a problem. The beginning reader must use attention in order to get the decoding done. Herein lies the dilemma: If the reader's attention is on decoding and if attention can be directed at only one process at a time, the comprehension task is not getting done. Since the end product of reading should be comprehension, the beginning reader is faced with a formidable problem.

Figure 1A shows how beginning readers process text. Because the attention demands of decoding and comprehension exceed their attention capacity, these

Figure 1. Attention and Reading

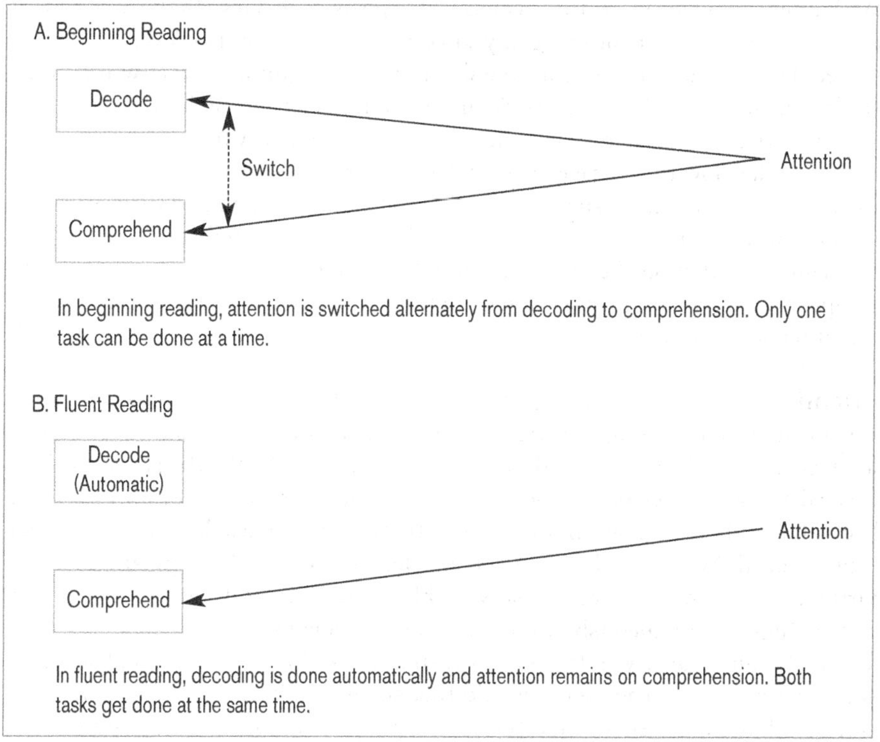

readers put their attention on the decoding task and then switch attention to comprehension to understand what they have decoded. The process is similar to what happens at a cocktail party when one tries to take in several conversations by switching attention back and forth among them. A beginning reader often reads a passage several times: first to decode from symbol to spoken words (this puts considerable strain on attention and memory systems) and subsequently to comprehend.

Although the beginning reader *is* able to comprehend by switching attention back and forth in this way, the process is slow, laborious, and frustrating. For those of you who doubt this, can you recall or imagine the difficulty of trying to comprehend a foreign language not yet mastered? To determine meaning, you first have to translate the foreign words and then you must comprehend what has been translated.

In many ways the problem facing the beginning reader is similar to that facing the beginning driver who is trying to drive a car and listen to a passenger's conversation. The beginning driver places attention on the mechanical aspects of driving, such as steering; controlling the accelerator, brake, clutch, and gears;

signaling turns; and other operations involved in getting to a destination safely. With attention focused on the mechanical aspects of driving, the driver finds it difficult to process for meaning any ongoing conversation. However, with continued driving practice over considerable time, the beginning driver will become skilled, and a skilled driver can perform the routine mechanical functions of driving with little attention. In fact, skilled drivers who regularly travel the same route often wonder how they arrive at their destination. These drivers are performing the routine, mechanical aspects of driving without attention, and their attention is thus left free to process conversation or think private thoughts.

Thus far, what has been explained is how the beginning reader manages to comprehend by means of attention switching. What is left to explain is how the fluent reader gets the job done.

Attention in Fluent Reading. I recently asked a skilled typist to type what was printed in a newspaper article. My instructions were that she should strive for accuracy and keep up a modest, steady typing pace. While the typist worked, I asked her a number of questions, to which she responded appropriately. Our back-and-forth conversation went on without any noticeable decrease in her typing speed. When she finished the article, we proofed the copy and found it virtually free of errors. The typist was able to perform both tasks—typing and conversing—simultaneously. In a somewhat analogous experimental situation, a skilled piano player was fitted with earphones and given music she had never seen before to sight-read. She was told that she would hear a voice speaking in a conversational manner through the earphones and that she was to repeat aloud what she heard while she played the piece. (In a laboratory procedure, repeating aloud what one hears is called "shadowing.") In order to be sure that the proper notes were played and the correct words were repeated, a tape recorder was set up. When the procedure was completed, we found that the piano player was able to faithfully perform both tasks simultaneously.

There are certain similarities in the experiments. First, in both cases incoming information—visual and aural—had to be processed. Second, the information that came in by ear for the typist (listening to what I said, processing it, and forming an answer) and for the piano player (listening to meaningful speech and then repeating it) required attention so that the subsequent task could be performed. A third similarity is that attention is required at the beginning stages of skill development in both typing and piano playing, but as fluency develops, both tasks can be performed with significantly less attention. Herein lies the answer to the question as to how two tasks, each of which ordinarily requires the services of attention, can be performed simultaneously: As a person develops skill at the task, the skill can be performed with less attention. For example, some years ago I visited a friend who was studying to be a surgeon. To practice his surgical knot tying, he had a small board fitted with tiny pegs on which he would hook the threads and tie the knots. In the beginning stages of skill development, while his fingers were slowly working on the knots, he focused his eyes on his fingers to guide the movements. Any attempt on my part to talk was met with his request to hold off on conversation; he said he could not concentrate on knot tying and talk at the same time. It would appear that his attention was being directed at the knot tying, thus preventing him from processing conversation. After years of practice on the knot-tying board, my friend was able to tie the knots while watching television and conversing.

Automaticity. When a task that formerly required attention for its performance can be performed without attention, the task is being done automatically. Automaticity in information processing, then, simply means that information is processed with little attention. One way to determine if a person is performing a process automatically is to give him or her two tasks to perform at the same time. If the tasks can be performed simultaneously, at least one of them is being done automatically.

With the concept of automaticity in mind, it is now a simple matter to describe how the fluent reader is able to perform the two-step decoding–comprehension process in reading. The decoding is done automatically—and thus attention is available for getting meaning from the printed words. This is shown in Figure 1B.

There are times, however, when skilled readers turn their attention away from getting meaning from the printed words. One such situation arises when unusual words—such as foreign words or scientific terminology—are encountered. The reader must then put attention on decoding in order to translate these verbal symbols. Another such situation occurs when a skilled reader is proofreading. As most experienced writers know, it is a poor idea to read for meaning while trying to locate errors. Proofreading is done most efficiently when one's attention is directed away from meaning and put on possible errors in the text.

Other Components in the LaBerge–Samuels Model

Most information-processing models indicate the components involved and the direction of flow of information through the system. However, these linear models tend to suggest that there is only one way to process information. As any skilled reader who has thought about reading processes knows, there are a variety of ways to read. The LaBerge–Samuels model shows the variety of routes used in going from print to meaning.

Figure 2 shows the LaBerge–Samuels information-processing model with its components. The first component is visual memory (VM), where the visual information from the text is processed. Next, there is phonological memory (PM) where the auditory representations of the visual codes are processed. Because all information arrives in some context, episodic memory (EM) records contextual details pertaining to time and place. In order to process information, attention is required; this is shown as A. Finally, there is semantic memory (SM), where knowledge of all kinds is stored. In order to account for processing of a word through use of the visual information on the page (bottom-up processing) as well as the knowledge stored in semantic memory (top-down processing), the model must allow for an

Figure 2. The LaBerge–Samuels Model

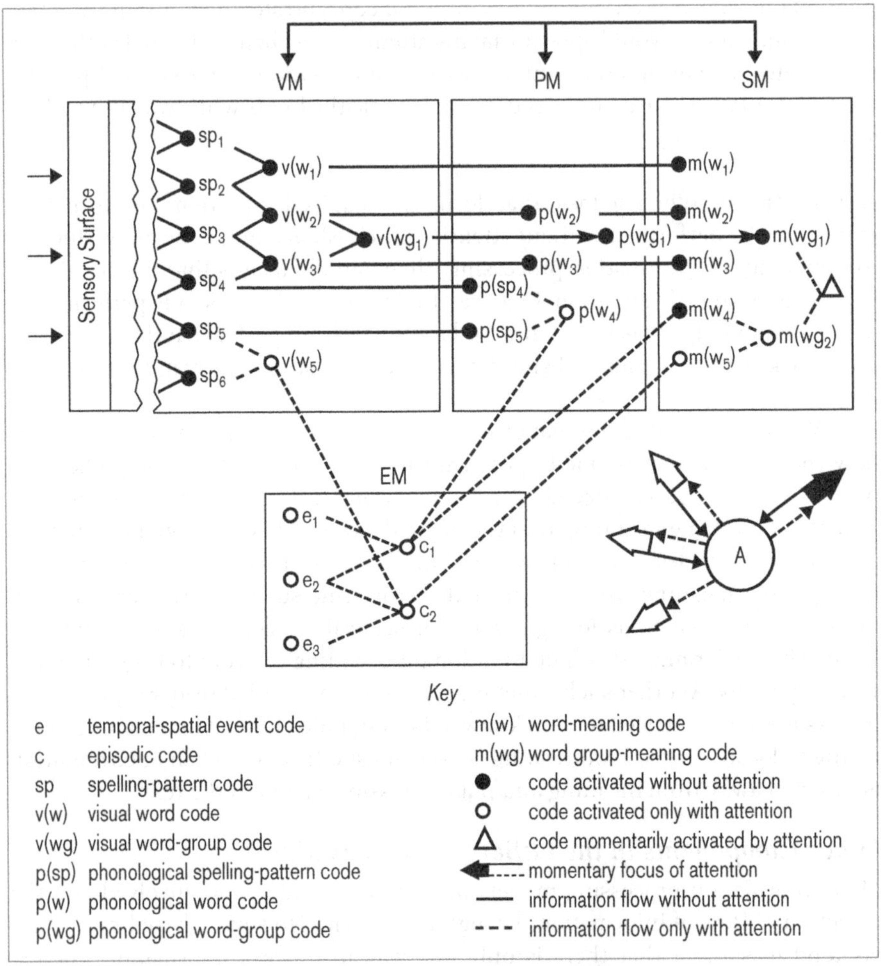

interaction of visual information and knowledge as a basis for word recognition. While some who study our model think of it as bottom up, the feedback loops from semantic memory to phonological memory to visual memory account for top-down processing. For example, if one sees "Father cut the g _ _ _ _ _," the context would suggest the target word is *grass*.

Visual Memory. As seen in Figure 3, visual memory is the first component, or processing stage, in the model. Incoming information from the words in print first strikes the sensory surface of the eye, where detectors process features such as lines, curves, angles, intersections, and relational features.

Figure 3. Model of Visual Memory

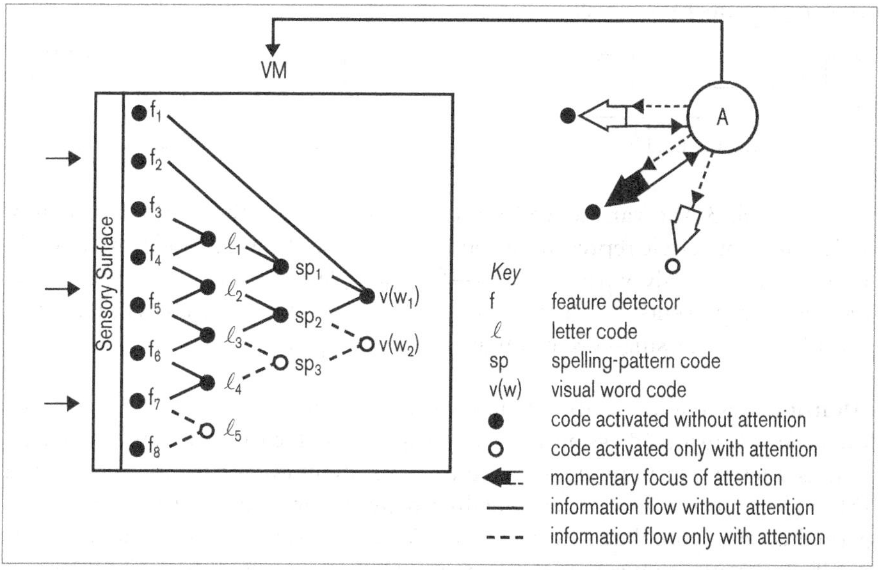

For example, what feature does one use to recognize the letter *b*? By analysis, one can separate *b* into a vertical line and a circle. But this is entirely unsatisfactory as a method for identifying a letter because *d*, *p*, and *g* share these components. By adding relational features, such as up or down and left or right, we arrive at a set of features uniquely descriptive of *b*—the circle is to the right and at the bottom of the vertical. By contrast, the letter *p* would be described as having the circle to the right and at the top of the vertical. Thus each letter can be described by a set of unique features.

To continue with this explanation of how a perceptual code is learned, as one goes from left to right in the hierarchical model of VM, one notes that different kinds of information get processed. The model shows how the visual information is analyzed by detectors into features, which at the next level are combined to form letters. At the next level in the model, letter combinations such as *sh*, *th*, *bl*, *-ing*, and *anti-* may be combined to form spelling patterns, and the spelling patterns feed into word codes. The use of the term *codes* in the model refers to the form in which information is represented. Thus there may be letter codes, spelling-pattern codes, and word codes.

There are two additional features in this model of VM, labeled f_1 and f_2. Unlike the other features that lead into letters, f_1 and f_2 indicate that features other than letters may be used in the identification of a word. For example, word configuration and length may be used in combination with other sources of textual information in word recognition. Assume that the words we wish to identify are *hippopotamus*, *dog*, and *cat*. It is a simple task to determine which configuration below represents each word:

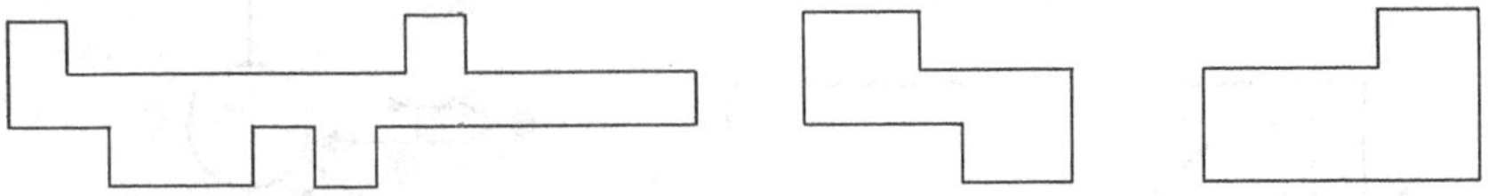

In Figure 3, the various codes are represented by either a filled or empty circle. An empty circle represents a code that is not well learned and consequently can be activated only with attention—for example, codes ℓ_5, sp_3, and $v(w_2)$. A filled circle represents a well-learned code that does not require attention for its activation or processing—for example, codes ℓ_1, sp_1, and $v(w_1)$.

Attention. In Figure 2, the attention center is symbolized by A in a circle. Attention is considered essential in the early stages of learning a perceptual code such as a letter. An individual is free to focus attention at various levels of the VM model—on features, letters, spelling patterns, or whole words. When well-learned codes, symbolized by a filled circle, are activated by stimulation, attention from the attention center is not required for processing. When stimulation of poorly learned codes, symbolized by an empty circle, occurs, attention is required for processing. With continued activation and processing of these poorly learned codes, an individual develops a level of skill such that attention is no longer required for their processing.

It is important to make a distinction between accuracy and automaticity. A student may be accurate without being automatic. At the accurate levels of skill development, attention is required. When asked if two letters are the same, the student may use attention to scan the features to determine the correct answer; with practice, the student will reach automaticity and be able to come up with the correct answer with little attention. In most classrooms the tests that are administered measure response accuracy. We need good tests that measure automatic levels of skill development. Fortunately, there are a number of indicators of automaticity teachers can use. Generally, if a student is automatic, there is a high level of accuracy combined with speed. With reading aloud, for example, automaticity may be indicated by the amount of expression in the student's voice. When a student is familiar with the task of oral reading and decodes automatically, he or she will generally read with expression and comprehend and recall what has been read. Nonautomatic decoders, when asked to read orally, usually read without expression and have difficulty comprehending and recalling what they have read.

Before leaving the hierarchical model of visual memory, it would be useful to outline the probable course of learning to identify a letter. This learning is conceptualized as a two-step process. As explained previously, the first step is to analyze and select the relevant features of the letter. To a large extent, this task of searching for features is similar to the initial stages of a concept-learning task, in which one must identify the relevant attributes of the concept. Generally, the rate at which children are able to identify the features of letters is quite slow. However, with practice they develop improved strategies, and the rate at which they can identify features increases. In order to help new readers select the appropriate features, it is important to have them make same–different judgments among visually similar letters in groups—for example, *huvn*, *mnuv*, *coeu*, *klth*, and *xvzw*. In the next stage of perceptual learning, students must combine these separate features into a single letter code, a process that at first requires attention. With practice, students will unitize the separate features into a single letter code; skilled readers, for example, see *b* and not "l" plus "o." With extended practice at letter identification, students' unitization of the features occurs without attention.

Phonological Memory. Input into the phonological memory (PM) system comes from a variety of sources: visual memory, episodic memory, feedback from semantic memory, and articulatory responses, as well as from direct external acoustic stimulation. Some of these sources of input are shown in Figure 2. It is assumed that the phonological memory system contains units that are related to acoustic and articulatory inputs. Although acoustic input seems logical enough, one might wonder why there would be articulatory input in a phonological system. There is evidence that the kinds of articulatory-muscle responses made in producing a sound may also be involved in perceiving that sound (Liberman et al., 1967). Thus acoustic input from stimulation external to the individual and articulatory input from stimulation internal to the individual are thought to be part of the phonological memory system.

With the rich variety of input flowing into PM, one might be tempted to describe how that input is organized. However, doing so might seriously reduce the effectiveness of the model by attempting to have it explain too much or be overly comprehensive. Therefore, only the organization of acoustic units will be described here. The acoustic units in PM are features, phonemes, syllables, and words. These units in PM are counterparts of the features, letters, spelling patterns, and words found in visual memory. Just as the units in visual memory are arranged in a hierarchy, so too are the units in phonological memory.

Acoustic features are represented by contrasts, such as /pa/–/ga/–/ta/. These differences are represented in the location where the consonant sound is made. The first sound is made with the lips, the second at the back of the throat, and the third at the roof of the mouth. (It is interesting to note that in attempting to describe features we hear, we resort to identifying the place of articulation.) Another difference is the manner in which the sounds are produced. For example, when saying /pa/–/ma/, one observes that both sounds are produced with the lips but that only in the first sound is breath expelled.

The model of visual memory indicates that a letter consists of a set of visual features that uniquely describes it. Similarly, in the model of phonological memory, a phoneme consists of a set of uniquely descriptive acoustic features. A phoneme may be thought of as a sound unit that indicates a change in word meaning, such as the difference between /m/, /p/, and /f/ as in *man*, *pan*, *fan*, or the

/s/ sound in *cat–cats*. Each of these phonemes signals a change in word meaning. Despite the enormous variety of words found in the English language, approximately 44 phonemes are sufficient to produce the rich variety of words we use.

Similarities Between Visual and Phonological Memory. I described the hierarchy in visual memory as moving from features to letters to spelling patterns and finally to words. The hierarchy in the phonological memory system moves from features to phonemes to syllables and finally to words. In both visual and phonological memory, information processing may move from features up to words or from words down to features. When going from a whole word to features, a decomposition into parts takes place; teachers often call this process "analysis." For example, when a teacher asks students to listen for the difference between /sat/ and /sad/, the process requires a top-down analysis from whole to parts. On the other hand, when students sound out a new word letter-by-letter and blend the sounds to form a word, they are engaging in a bottom-up process of synthesizing a word from its parts to a whole.

Episodic Memory. Episodic memory (EM) is responsible for putting a time, place, and context tag on events and knowledge. When an individual recalls the details of an event that happened in the past, it is episodic memory that is called on. Thus, the organization of knowledge and events in EM may be listed in categories under the *wh* words, such as *when* (time), *where* (place), and *who* (persons). For example, an individual may receive lessons (an event) on how to drive a car. This event may be recalled with details, such as *who* was the instructor, *when* did the instruction occur, and *what* type of vehicle was used. The abstract knowledge of how to drive is the essential information that is retained. This knowledge is stored in semantic memory, while the associated details surrounding the instruction remain in episodic memory where they may eventually be "lost" in time. For example, I have retained the abstract knowledge of how to add, subtract, multiply, and divide, which I learned long ago, but not the names of the teachers who taught me nor of the students who sat next to me.

Semantic Memory and Comprehension. The final component in the automaticity model is semantic memory. It is here that individual word meanings are produced, and it is also here that the comprehension of written messages occurs. Earlier in this article, I distinguished between the attentional processes involved in getting the meaning of a word and comprehending a written passage. When familiar words are decoded by skilled readers, the word meanings may be assessed automatically, without attention. On the other hand, under most conditions comprehension does not occur automatically and therefore requires attention.

In order to get at the underlying meaning in a sentence, attention comes into play in a number of ways during the comprehension process. It is used to organize the words in a sentence into grammatical units, and it is used to determine the relationships in meanings that exist within and between grammatical units. For example, as verbal concepts, the meanings of *fierce* and *dog* may exist separately. When, however, the noun phrase "the fierce dog" is encountered, it has one meaning, and it is in semantic memory that the blending of these two verbal concepts occurs. This example simply illustrates how attention might be used to determine the relationships in meaning within a grammatical unit.

The Role of Attention in Comprehension

Let us now examine how a sentence such as "The fierce dog bit the tall man" is processed for comprehension. (Because the focus of this article is not comprehension, however, the description will be sketchy in the extreme.) When decoding familiar words such as those found in this sentence, a skilled reader assesses the meaning of each word directly, without attention; this is indicated in Figure 4 by the solid lines from V(W1) to M(W1), for example. However, in order for the reader

Figure 4. How Attention Is Used to Construct the Meaning of a Sentence

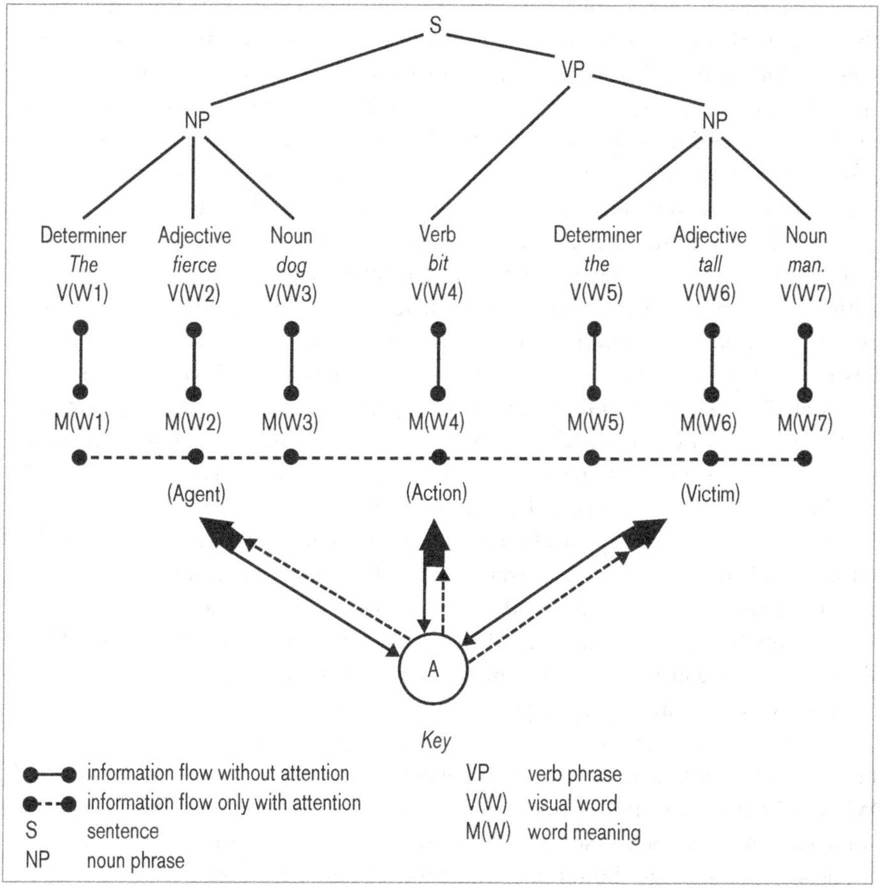

to understand the meaning of the sentence as a whole, the individual word must be grouped into units such as the noun phrase (NP) and verb phrase (VP), and this requires attention. By breaking this sentence into its grammatical units (see Figure 4), the reader determines the agent, the action, and the victim. However, the comprehension process still is not complete. The reader also must decide on the meaning of the sentence as a whole. This combining of meanings is viewed as an active, constructive process that requires attention for its completion.

Automaticity and Comprehension: Application to Schema Theory

When our model was first published, we thought of automaticity in a very limited way. In time, however, we realized that the concept would be extended to include virtually every aspect of reading comprehension—from the metacognitive self-monitoring of comprehension to the actual process of comprehension itself.

While the comprehension process usually is costly in terms of demands on attention, there are subelements within the process that can become automatic. This can be illustrated in relation to schema theory, at present one of the dominant theories of text comprehension. A schema is a personal knowledge base about categories such as restaurants, schools, transportation, and so on. A school schema, for example, would contain information about objects, activities, rules, and concepts that relate to schools. One should not think of a schema as a concept; a schema is broad in scope and consists of bundles of related concepts, whereas a concept is narrow and specific. Because of the breadth of knowledge encapsulated in a schema, it is an ideal instrument to use in understanding a text.

In order to comprehend what we read, we have to relate the information in the text to the knowledge stored in the schemata in our heads. The speed with which we gain access to the knowledge stored in schemata as we read is an important factor in reading fluency known as the "speed of lexical access." It has been established that poor readers generally have slow lexical access speed (Samuels & Naslund, 1994). An analogy may help explain this concept. Imagine that a dictionary of words and their meanings is stored in your semantic memory. When you know a word's spelling, its meaning can be discovered by locating the word's entry in the dictionary. The speed with which you can look up the word in your mental dictionary can be taken as one aspect of lexical access speed. A rather simple technique can illustrate another aspect of lexical access speed. Take a sheet of paper and draw on it 30 easily named common objects such as a tree, shoe, comb, hat, pencil, and so on. Have students name the objects as quickly as they can while you record their times. There is usually a significant correlation between speed of naming, an aspect of lexical access, and reading achievement.

Although it is known that speed of lexical access is associated with comprehension, it has not been established what accounts for differences in access speed. What is being suggested is that the comprehension difficulties experienced by some students may be caused by the fact that the concepts and knowledge stored in the schemata cannot be rapidly and automatically accessed.

The role of schema-based prior knowledge in acquiring comprehension skills is an important issue. Automatic word-decoding skills and prior knowledge of a text's content may interact and strongly affect success in comprehension. It has been observed that skilled readers can efficiently process texts covering unfamiliar materials almost or just as easily as familiar materials, whereas some less skilled readers demonstrate differential success in processing and recalling information from text. Schneider, Körkel, and Weinert (1988) showed such differential performance with materials that were either familiar or unfamiliar to skilled and less-skilled children in a German elementary school. They found that children who knew a great deal about soccer efficiently and accurately comprehended and recalled texts about soccer, regardless of their general mental aptitude (measured with IQ-type tests). In addition, children who had extensive knowledge about soccer but low general mental aptitude recalled significantly more details from soccer texts than did children who had little soccer knowledge and either high or low aptitude. It would appear that a strong relationship exists between reading performance and prior knowledge. When judging the degree of automaticity in readers' decoding skills based on their comprehension and recall of text, familiarity with the subject matter must therefore be taken into account.

This contextual effect in reading also may result from readers' acquisition of internal lexicons and vocabulary through repeated experience. These lexicons may be thought of as particular organizations of vocabulary, with many overlapping entries between lexical categories. A German child who lives for soccer has a soccer lexicon that can be activated more easily and rapidly than could be the soccer lexicon of an American child who lives for baseball. In other words, speed of access is faster for the vocabulary we are most familiar with. Prior knowledge and the lexicon associated with that knowledge can interact with the decoding of words in texts on familiar topics. The process of retrieving lexical information may enhance readers' matching of phoneme combinations with appropriate context-related words. For example, a child who is familiar with soccer might decode a soccer-related word never read before faster than could a child who is unfamiliar with soccer, even if both children are inefficient decoders. The child familiar with the sport may need only to sound out the first few phonemes of *penalty*, for example, to access this word and conclude that it is an appropriate choice to precede the more familiar word *kick*; the child with little knowledge about soccer may struggle with the sounds of *penalty* and not be able to access the meaning of this word very readily. Thus lexical access and knowledge of a subject can compensate somewhat for poor decoding skills.

Optional Word-Recognition Processing Strategies

I have described each of the components of the model of automatic information processing in reading, and in an earlier section I described the different ways to recognize a word. In this section, I will summarize the various options available for processing a word. Referring back to Figure 2, we can trace the information flow for the various options, starting from the top and proceeding downward.

(Rather than present the processing options in great detail, I will simply suggest general ways that meaning can be obtained.) Only the symbols in visual memory will be given here. To follow the description, simply start with visual memory and move along the lines in the figure from left to right.

Option 1. The visual word $v(w_1)$ is automatically decoded, and the word meaning $m(w_1)$ is available automatically. This occurs when a skilled reader reads a common word such as *dog* or *car.*

Option 2. The visual $v(w_2)$ is automatically decoded. In turn, the phonological code for the word $p(w_2)$ is automatically activated, which in turn automatically activates the word meaning $m(w_2)$. This occurs when a skilled reader encounters a common word but subvocalizes it.

Option 3. Two different visual words in a visual word group $v(wg_1)$—such as *ice cream*—are decoded automatically. In turn, the phonological code $p(wg_1)$ for the word group is activated automatically. Next, the meaning of the word group $m(wg_1)$ is made available automatically in semantic memory.

Option 4. A visual word such as *digraph* is coded automatically into two spelling patterns—*di* and *graph*—represented by sp_4 and sp_5. Next, the phonological code for these spelling patterns is activated automatically. However, from this point on, attention is used to blend the two spelling patterns into one word, to excite the episodic code, and to access the meaning code for the word. This course of events would occur with a skilled reader who has no difficulty with decoding but is somewhat uncertain about the technical definition of *digraph.*

Option 5. A highly unfamiliar visual word is coded with attention into $v(w_5)$ Attention is used to activate the episodic code, the phonological code, and the meaning code. This sequence of events might occur with a foreign name that is difficult to pronounce easily.

Option 6. There is another route to word meaning that is now shown on the model as depicted in Figure 2. A reader can visually recognize the word as a holistic unit without constructing it from the spelling of individual letters, and then go directly to meaning in semantic memory. A study by Samuels, LaBerge, and Bremer (1978) demonstrated that students who were not automatic decoders did letter-by-letter word recognition, while students who were automatic decoders recognized words as holistic units.

Feedback From Semantic Memory

Before leaving the model of automatic information processing in Figure 2, take note of the arrow leading from semantic memory to visual and phonological memory. This arrow indicates an important function and represents a marked departure from the original automaticity model. The present automaticity model has feedback loops, because what happens in semantic memory may influence processes that occur earlier.

Implications of the Automaticity Model for Diagnosis of Reading Problems and Instruction

Earlier, I mentioned the practicality of a good theory. In this section, a few of the practical implications of the LaBerge–Samuels model are explored.

The automaticity theory helps diagnose certain kinds of common reading problems. Teachers have observed that some students can recognize words accurately but not comprehend them with ease. Teachers call this problem "barking at print." Automaticity theory suggests that one possible reason for the students' problem is that the decoding requires so much attention that it interferes with comprehension. Another common problem is seen when skilled readers, often college students, claim that even though they read the text with care, they cannot remember what they have read. Because the students are skilled readers, the decoding of the words on the page can take place with little attention, thus leaving attention free to be directed elsewhere. Automaticity theory suggests that instead of focusing on deriving meaning from the text and understanding and recalling the author's viewpoints, the students' attention perhaps wanders to matters entirely unrelated to the text.

These problems require quite different remedies. For students whose attention is on decoding rather than comprehension, one solution is to provide texts that are easier to read. Another solution is to suggest that they read the text several times until the meaning becomes clear. This practice is often followed in beginning stages of reading. The first time or two, students read the text, emphasizing decoding; once they are able to decode the words, the students switch their attention to meaning. A third solution lies in the realization that more than accuracy is needed for students to become skilled readers. Readers must go beyond accuracy to reach automaticity. In human activities that require high levels of proficiency, a considerable amount of time must be spent in practicing the skills leading to mastery. Only by spending a great deal of time reading will students develop beyond the level of mere accuracy. Practice may be on important subskills in reading, but it also must include time spent on reading easy, interesting, and meaningful material. At one time, teachers felt guilty about having students spend time on a task at which they had exhibited some minimal level of proficiency; they were afraid of being accused of giving the students busywork. However, since reaching automaticity in reading requires practice, teachers should know that what may appear to be busywork to some is actually "automaticity training."

For students who are skilled readers but have difficulty remembering what they read, it is often helpful to explain that poor recall is due not to a memory deficit but to lack of attention directed on processing the text. Although the mere explanation of the nature of the problem is often helpful to students, additional aid is frequently needed. To help students focus attention on text meaning, they should be taught how to engage in self-testing. Asking themselves, What ideas were expressed on this page? at the end of each page helps students in the areas of comprehension and recall.

The Method of Repeated Readings

An interesting area of inquiry is what can be learned about how to teach reading from areas of human activity that require extraordinarily high levels of skill development, such as music and sports. Both of these areas have training methods that differ from those generally used in reading. In music, for example, the teacher may assign one or two pieces of music and tell the beginning student to practice these pieces for a week. The student's goal is to play the pieces accurately and with fluency, so he practices the same pieces over and over, trying to reduce errors and to blend the notes into a smooth rendition.

A somewhat different situation exists in beginning reading. Although the goals in both music and reading are accuracy and fluency, the beginning reader is seldom encouraged to read and reread a passage until these goals are achieved. Instead, teachers tend to move many students rapidly through the pages in the text before any degree of mastery has been reached. For several years I have been using a technique I call "the method of repeated readings" (Samuels, 1979) with enough resulting improvement in students' comprehension and reading speed to justify suggesting it here. It is used in conjunction with whatever the ongoing method of teaching reading happens to be. Of course, many teachers will probably want to alter this method of repeated readings somewhat to fit particular classroom needs. The technique is as follows:

1. The student selects a passage that is neither so hard that he or she cannot read any of the words nor so easy that all of the words can be read with high accuracy and speed. The selection can be a passage as short as 50 words or as long as 500 words, depending on the reader's skill.
2. The helper—a teacher, teacher's aide, parent, or student tutor—makes a chart for recording word-recognition errors and speed.
3. The student reads the selection aloud to the helper, who counts the number of errors and records the reading time in seconds. These data on errors and speed are put on the chart for each testing.
4. The student rereads the selection independently until called to read aloud again by the helper. It may be necessary to write the words the student cannot read on a sheet of paper and have him or her study them in addition to rereading the selection.
5. The testing–reading cycle is repeated until the student can read the selection with some degree of fluency. It is *not* important to eliminate all word-recognition errors, but it is important to have the student read the selection with fluency. When this goal is reached, a new selection is chosen and the process is repeated. The charts provide feedback to the student to indicate rate of progress.

A useful modification of this technique is to have the helper make a tape recording of the story. While listening to the story on the tape, the student can read along silently. As soon as possible, the student then practices rereading the story silently without the tape recorder. Thus there is a progression from reading with auditory support to reading without support. The practice is continued until the student can read the selection aloud with fluency.

Recent Criticism of the LaBerge–Samuels Automaticity Theory

Publications by Logan (1988a, 1988b) and Stanovich (1990) have called into question some of the basic principles underlying the automaticity theory as put forth by LaBerge and Samuels (1974). As explained earlier in this article, the essence of automaticity theory is that cognitive tasks such as reading expend attentional resources, of which there are only a limited supply available at any instant. Through training and practice, the attentional demands of a particular task decrease to the point where the task is performed automatically and can be completed simultaneously with other tasks. Logan and Stanovich suggest instead that automaticity may be acquired without invoking concepts of resource limitations and attention. What they offer is a view of automaticity as a memory phenomenon:

> The theory assumes that novices begin with a general algorithm that is sufficient to perform the task. As they gain experience, they learn specific solutions to specific problems, which they retrieve when they encounter the same problem again. Then, they can respond with the solution retried from memory or the one computed by the algorithm. At some point, they may gain enough experience to respond with a solution from memory on every trial and abandon the algorithm entirely. At that point, their performance is automatic. Automatization reflects a transition from algorithm-based performance to memory-based performance. (Logan, 1988b)

In this view, there are two routes to a correct response: One is an automatic, direct, and rapid memory retrieval that comes only after a long training period, while the other uses an algorithm acquired during the early stages of learning. At the simplest level, the beginning reader who laboriously sounds out a word is using an algorithm, whereas the reader who has had extended practice can recognize the same word rapidly and automatically as a memory phenomenon.

Anderson (1982) has suggested a model of memory and learning that incorporates ideas about effortful early learning and effortless skilled learning. These ideas are similar to those put forth by Logan and Stanovich. Anderson proposes three phases in learning a skill. During the first or "declarative knowledge" phase, the knowledge is encoded in separate compartments, and execution of the skill requires considerable effort. (One may assume that during the first phase, the execution of the skill is as through an algorithm.) In the second or "compilation" phase, the knowledge is aggregated into larger units. In the third or "procedural knowledge" phase, the knowledge is compiled in large enough units that it allows the task to be performed with little effort from an easily accessed memory. These alternate views of automaticity are a useful addition to work in the field because they explain the mechanism by which attention can be withdrawn from a problem. This does not necessarily make the concept of limited attentional resources a less useful construct, however, since one may assume that when a task has been encapsulated or memorized, less attention is required for its execution.

In closing this article, I am reminded of the story about the college student who went home from school and was asked, "What did you study this term?" The student replied that he had studied theoretical models of reading. "And what did you learn about theoretical models?" the student was asked. "More than I ever wanted to know," he replied. My hope is that this has not been the case for you.

QUESTIONS FOR REFLECTION

1. What role does attention play in reading comprehension?
2. What is the significance of the four types of memory (visual, phonological, episodic, and semantic) in the LeBerge–Samuels model?
3. How does schema theory help explain automaticity?
4. How can a teacher determine automaticity in a student's reading?
5. Criticism of the LaBerge–Samuels model centers on memory versus attention. What is the central concern of critics, and what is your opinion of this disagreement?

REFERENCES

Anderson, J.R. (1982). *Cognitive skills and their acquisition*. Hillsdale, NJ: Erlbaum.

Blanchard, J., Rottenberg, C., & Jones, J. (1989). *Foundational literature in elementary reading methodology textbooks*. Tempe: Arizona State University, College of Education.

LaBerge, D., & Samuels, S.J. (1974). Toward a theory of automatic information processing in reading. *Cognitive Psychology*, 6, 293–323.

Liberman, A.M., Cooper, F., Shankweiler, D., & Studdert-Kennedy, M. (1967). Perception of the speech code. *Psychological Review*, *74*, 431–461.

Logan, G. (1988a). Automaticity, resources, and memory: Theoretical controversies and practical implications. *Human Factors*, *30*, 583–598.

Logan, G. (1988b). Toward an instance theory of automatization. *Psychological Review*, 95, 492–527.

Samuels, S.J. (1979). The method of repeated reading. *The Reading Teacher*, 32, 403–408.

Samuels, S.J., LaBerge, D., & Bremer, C. (1978). Units of word recognition: Evidence for developmental changes. *Journal of Verbal Learning and Verbal Behavior*, *17*, 715–720.

Samuels, S.J., & Naslund, J.C. (1994). Individual differences in reading: The case for lexical access. *Reading and Writing Quarterly*, *10*(4), 285–296.

Samuels, S.J., & Turnure, J. (1974). Attention and reading achievement in first grade boys and girls. *Journal of Educational Psychology*, 66, 29–32.

Schneider, W., Körkel, J., & Weinert, F.E. (1988, July). *Expert knowledge, general abilities, and text processing*. Paper presented at the Workshop on Interactions Among Aptitudes, Strategies, and Knowledge in Cognitive Performance, Munich, Germany.

Stanovich, K. (1990). Concepts in developmental theories of reading skill: Cognitive resources, automaticity, and modularity. *Developmental Review*, *10*, 72–100.

CHAPTER 29

Toward an Interactive Model of Reading

David E. Rumelhart, Stanford University*

Reading is the process of understanding written language. It begins with a flutter of patterns on the retina and ends (when successful) with a definite idea about the author's intended message. Thus, reading is at once a "perceptual" and a "cognitive" process. It is a process that bridges and blurs these two traditional distinctions. Moreover, a skilled reader must be able to make use of sensory, syntactic, semantic, and pragmatic information to accomplish his task. These various sources of information appear to interact in many complex ways during the process of reading. A theorist faced with the task of accounting for reading must devise a formalism rich enough to represent all of these different kinds of information and their interactions.

The study of reading was a central concern of early psychologists (see Huey, 1908). Now, after years of dormancy, reading has again become a central concern for many psychologists. It would seem that the advent of the information-processing approach to psychology has given both experimentalists and theorists paradigms within which to study the reading process. The formalisms of information processing, the flowcharts, notions of information flow, and so forth have served as useful vehicles for the development of first approximation models of the reading process. Unfortunately, the most familiar information-processing formalisms apply most naturally to models assuming a series of noninteracting stages of processing or (at best) a set of independent parallel processing units. There are many results in the reading literature that appear to call for highly interactive parallel processing units. It is my suspicion that the serial, noninteracting models have been developed not so much because of an abiding belief that interactions do not take place, but rather because the appropriate formalisms have not been available. It is the purpose of this chapter to adapt a formalism developed in the context of parallel computation to the specification of a model for reading and then show that such a model can account in a convenient way for those aspects of reading that appear puzzling in the context of more linear stage-oriented models. No claim is made about the adequacy of the particular model developed. The primary claim is that this richer formalism will allow for the specification of more detailed models. These will be able to characterize aspects of the reading process that are difficult or impossible to characterize within the more familiar information-processing formulations.

First, I will review two recent models of the reading process. Then, I will discuss some of the empirical evidence that is not conveniently accounted for

This chapter is reprinted from *Theoretical Models and Processes of Reading* (3rd ed., pp. 722–750), edited by H. Singer & R.B. Ruddell, Newark, DE: International Reading Association.

by these models or their natural extensions. Finally, I will develop a reading model that makes use of a formalism allowing highly interactive parallel processing units and then show that this model offers a reasonable account of the Problematic Results section.

Current Models of Reading

Gough's Model

Gough (1972) has proposed a model of reading that is remarkable in the degree to which it attempts to give a complete information-processing account of the reading process. Gough attempts to pin down as completely as possible the events that occur during the first second of reading. A schematic diagram representing the flow of information during the reading process is shown in Figure 1. According to Gough's model, graphemic information enters the visual system and is registered in an *icon*, which holds it briefly while it is scanned and operated on by a *pattern-recognition* device. This device identifies the letters of the input string. These letters are then read into a *character register*, which holds them while a *decoder* (with the aid of a *code book*) converts the character strings into their underlying *phonemic* representation. The phonemic representation of the original character strings serves as input to a *librarian*, which matches up these phonemic strings against the *lexicon* and feeds the resulting lexical entries into *primary memory*. The four or five lexical items held in primary memory at any one time serve as input to a magical system (dubbed *Merlin*), which somehow applies its knowledge of the syntax and semantics to determine the deep structure (or perhaps the meaning?) of the input. This deep structure is then forwarded to its final memory register TPWSGWTAU (the place where sentences go when they are understood). When all inputs of the text have found their final resting place in TPWSGWTAU, the text has been read and the reading is complete.

I do not want to discuss the merits or demerits of Gough's particular model at this point. Instead, I point to the general form of the model. For Gough, reading consists of a sequentially ordered set of transformations. The input signal is first registered in the icon and then transformed from a character-level representation to phonemic representation, then lexical-level representation, and finally to deep structural representation. Thus, the input is sequentially transformed from low-level sensory information into ever higher-level encodings. Note, however, that the information flow is totally "bottom up." That is, the information is initiated with the sensory signal, and no higher level of processing can affect any lower level. The reading process is strict letter-by-letter, word-by-word analysis of the input string. There is no provision for interaction within the system. The processing at any level can directly affect only the immediately higher level.

LaBerge–Samuels Model

In another paper, LaBerge and Samuels (1974) have developed an equally detailed (although somewhat more perceptually oriented) model of the reading process.

Figure 1. Gough's Reading Model

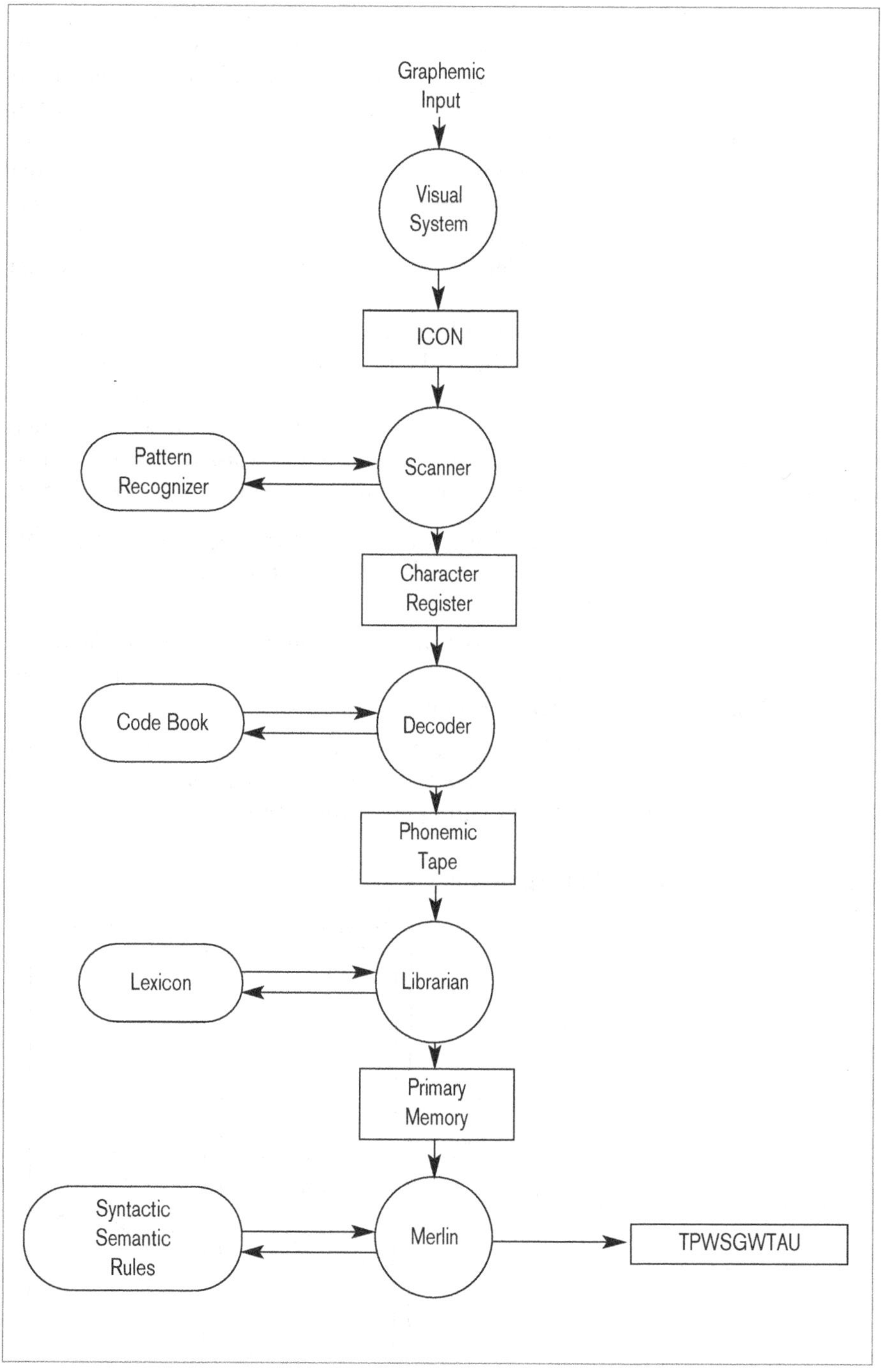

After Gough, 1972.

Figure 2 gives a schematic representation of their model. The basic model consists of three memory systems holding three different representations of the input string. The Visual Memory System holds visually based representations of the features, letters, spelling groups, words, and word clusters. The Phonological Memory System holds phonological representations of spelling groups, words, and word groups. Finally, the Semantic Memory System holds the semantic representation of the words, word groups, and sentences that are read. The reading process begins with the registration of the visual signal on the sensory surface. The information is then analyzed by a set of specialized *feature detectors* that extract information about lines, angles, intersections, and so on, from the physical stimulus. Most of these feature detectors, f_1, feed directly into letter codes, l_1. Thus, the activation of letter codes results naturally from the convergence of a set of feature detectors. These letter codes feed into spelling-pattern codes, sp_1, which in turn feed into visual word codes, $v(w_1)$. Some features (e.g., f_2) map directly into spelling pattern codes and others (f_1) directly into visual word codes. Such features are sensitive to the overall configuration of the words and spelling patterns. There are a number of routes whereby words can be mapped into meanings.

1. Visual word codes can feed directly into word-meaning codes, $m(w_1)$. This route would be necessary for the discrimination of such homophonous word pairs as *pear* and *pair* or *chute* and *shoot.*
2. The visual word codes can pass through a phonological word code, $p(w_1)$, and then into a word-meaning code. This is perhaps the ordinary route of analysis within the LaBerge–Samuels model.
3. The model also allows for word groups, such as *time out*, to be analyzed into visual word-group codes, $v(wg_1)$, from these into phonetic word-group codes, $p(wg_1)$, and finally into group meanings, $m(wg_1)$.

Figure 2. Reading in the LaBerge–Samuels Model

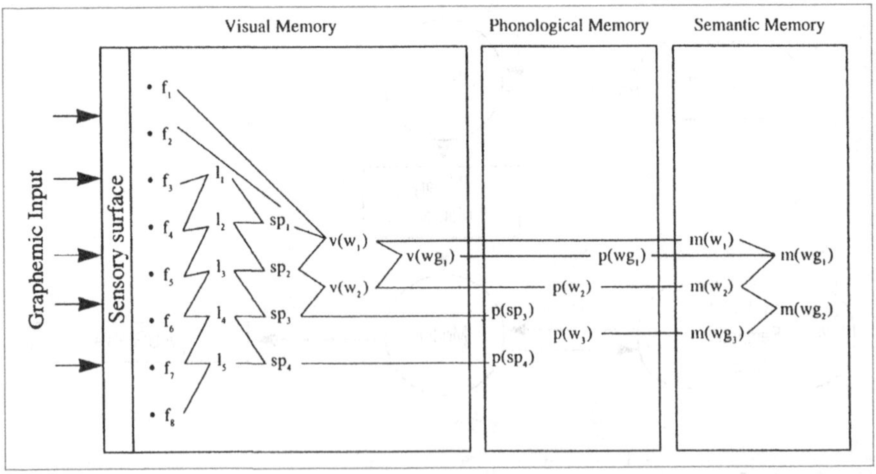

After LaBerge and Samuels, 1974.

4. When a word has not been learned as a visual stimulus, information can be translated directly from visual spelling patterns into phonological spelling patterns, $p(sp_1)$, from these into phonological word codes, and finally into word-meaning codes. In addition, word-meaning codes feed into word-group–meaning codes.

Ultimately, when the entire set of inputs has been presented, a set of word-group meanings will emerge and the reader will be said to have understood the input.[1]

Again, I do not want to discuss the particular merits or demerits of the LaBerge–Samuels model. Rather, I again point out the general form of the model and suggest that it takes that form, at least to some extent, because of the formalisms used to represent the ideas. The LaBerge–Samuels model, like the Gough model, is a strictly bottom-up process.[2] Although there are alternative routes, the basic sequence is from features to letters, to spelling patterns, to visual word representations, to phonological word representations, to word meanings, to word-group meanings—a series of stages, each corresponding to a level of analysis in which no higher level can in any way modify or change the analysis at a lower level. The LaBerge–Samuels model (unlike the Gough model) does allow certain stages to be bypassed. This allows multiple paths of analysis and alleviates some of the empirical problems of the Gough model. Nevertheless, there are a number of results in the literature that are difficult to account for with either model. I turn now to a discussion of a number of these problems.

Problematic Results

All of the results discussed in this section have one characteristic in common. In each case it appears that the apprehension of information at one level of analysis is partially determined by higher levels of analysis. By and large, such results are very difficult to incorporate in a processing model that assumes that information flows strictly from lower to higher levels. I will begin with a discussion of the effects of orthographic structure on the perception of letters, proceed to a discussion of the effects of syntax on word perception, then to the effects of semantics on word and syntax perception, and finally to the effects of general pragmatic factors on the perception of meanings.[3]

The Perceptions of Letters Often Depend on the Surrounding Letters

The literature on reading abounds with evidence on this point. Perhaps the most difficult of these results for a purely bottom-up model to account for are the well-known context effects illustrated in Figure 3 (after Nash-Weber, 1975). Here we see an ambiguous symbol, 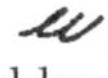, which is interpreted as a *w* in one context and interpreted as an *e* followed by a *v* in another context. It would appear that our interpretation of the sentence has determined our perception of the ambiguous symbol.

The problem with results such as these stems from the fact that we appear to have "word-level" or "phrase-level" perceptions determining our perceptions at

Figure 3. The Dependence of Letter Perception on Context

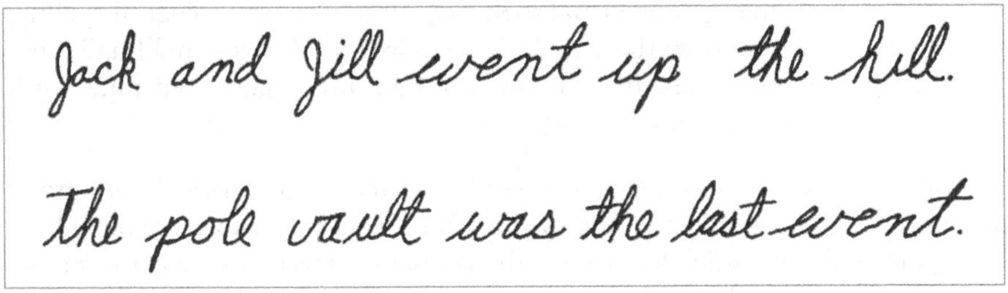

After Nash-Weber, 1975.

the letter level, a higher-level perception affecting a lower-level one. These results can be accounted for by bottom-up models, but only at some cost. No final decision can be made at the letter level. Either a set of alternative possibilities must be passed on, or the direct feature information must be sent to the higher levels. In either of these cases, the notion that letter perception precedes word perception becomes suspect. Word and letter perception occur simultaneously.

Perhaps the strongest objection to a demonstration such as this one is that it is unusual to find such ambiguous letters and that the norm involves characters that are perfectly discriminable. Although this may be true of printed text, it is not true of handwriting. Characters often can be interpreted only with reference to their context. Yet I would not want to argue that the reading process is essentially different for handwritten than for printed material.

There are many other results that appear to call for this same conclusion. For example, more letters can be apprehended per unit time when a word is presented than when a string of unrelated letters is presented (Huey, 1908/1968). A letter string formed either by deleting a letter of a word or replacing one or two of the letters of the word is often clearly perceived as the original word (Pillsbury, 1897). Even when great care is taken to control for guessing, a letter is more accurately perceived when it is part of a word than when it is among a set of unrelated letters (Reicher, 1969). All of these results appear to argue strongly that letter perceptions are facilitated by being in words. Word-level perceptions affect letter-level perceptions. Here again, the only way that the types of models under consideration can account for these effects is to suppose that partial letter information is somehow preserved and the additional constraints of the word level are brought to bear on the partial letter information.

It is of some interest that these effects can be observed in letter strings that are not words but that are similar to words in important ways. For example, the more the sequential transition probabilities among letters in a string approximate those of English, the more letters can be perceived per unit time (Miller, Bruner, & Postman, 1954). Similarly, even when guessing is controlled (as in the Reicher, 1969, experiment), letters embedded in orthographically regular strings are more accurately perceived than those embedded among orthographically irregular strings (McClelland & Johnston, 1977). Thus, not only is a letter embedded in a word easier to see, but also merely being a part of an orthographically well-formed string aids perception virtually as much. This suggests that orthographic knowledge plays a role nearly as strong as lexical knowledge in the perception of letter strings.

Not only does orthographic structure have a positive effect on the perception of letters embedded in an orthographically regular string, but also our apprehension of orthographically irregular strings often is distorted to allow us to perceive the string as being orthographically regular. This point is nicely illustrated in a recent experiment carried out in our laboratory by Albert Stevens. In this experiment, subjects were presented with letter strings consisting of two consonants (i.e., an initial consonant cluster designated CC_i) followed by two vowels (a vowel cluster, designated VC) followed by two more consonants (a final consonant cluster, CC_f). The initial consonant cluster was constructed from pairs of consonants that can occur at the beginning of English words in only one order (e.g., English words can begin with *pr* but not *rp*). Similarly the vowel clusters used occur as diphthongs in English in one order but not in the other (e.g., *ai* but not *ia*). The final consonant clusters were similarly chosen so that they occur at the end of English words in one order but not the other (e.g., *ck* but not *kc*). Strings were then constructed in which each letter cluster was either in its legal or illegal order. Table 1 illustrates several examples of the various types of letter strings.

Subjects were given tachistoscopic presentations of the various letter strings and asked to name the letters they observed. Of particular interest are the times when they were presented illegal strings but made them legal by transposing the letter pair in their reports. Figure 4 illustrates the comparison of interest. The figure compares the percentage of times an illegally ordered letter cluster is transposed into a legal cluster with the number of times a legal letter cluster is transposed into an illegal one. The results show that although initial consonant clusters are never transposed, illegal vowel clusters are transposed almost 25% of the time as compared to only about 3% transposition for the legal vowel clusters. Similarly, final consonant clusters are transposed almost 14% of the time when they are illegal, but only about 3% of the time when they are legal. These results show clearly the effect that orthographic structure has on our perception of letter strings. The perception of a certain letter in a certain position depends on what we perceive in adjacent

Table 1. Examples of Legal and Illegal Letter Strings

	CC_i			
	Legal VC		Illegal VC	
CC_f	Legal	Illegal	Legal	Illegal
Legal	praick	priack	rpaick	rpiack
	stourt	stuort	tsourt	tsuort
Illegal	praikc	priakc	rpaikc	rpiakc
	stoutr	stuotr	tsoutr	tsuotr

Figure 4. Transpositions as a Function of Letter Location

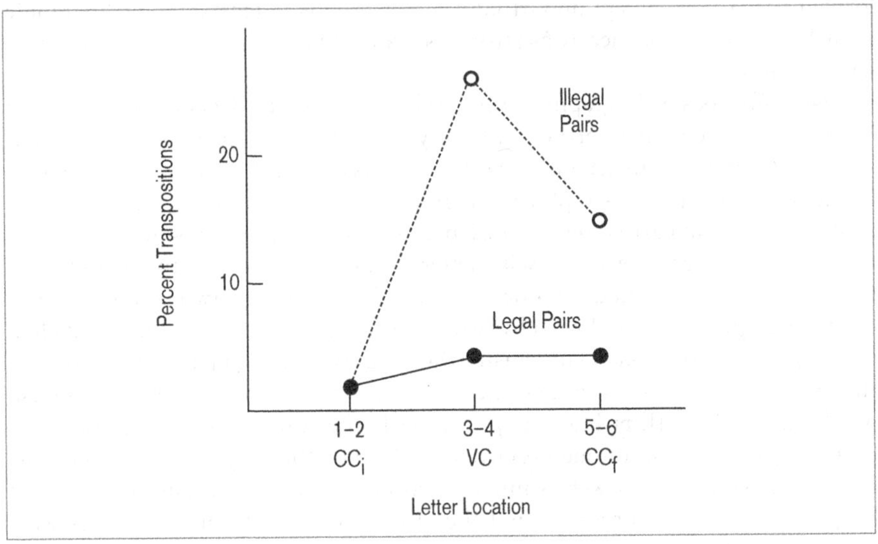

positions as well as on the sensory evidence we have available about that position in the string.

To summarize, then, it appears that no model that supposes that we first perceive the letters in a stimulus and then put them together into higher-order units can be correct. However, models such as the Gough model and the LaBerge–Samuels model can survive such results if they assume that partial information is somehow forwarded to the higher levels of analysis and that the final decision as to which letters were present is delayed until this further processing has been accomplished.

Whereas it is not too difficult to see how, say, the LaBerge–Samuels model could account for the effects of orthographic structure on letter perception, it is somewhat more difficult to see how the effects of syntax and semantics can be mediated within such a model. I now turn to evidence for syntactic effects in reading.

Our Perception of Words Depends on the Syntactic Environment in Which We Encounter the Words

Perhaps the best evidence for syntactic effects on the level of word perception comes from an analysis of oral reading errors. The most common error in oral reading is the substitution error—when an incorrect word is simply substituted for the correct one. If syntax had no effect on word perception, we would expect that reading errors should be determined by visual similarity and not by part of speech. However, there is a strong tendency for a reading error to be of the same part of speech as the word for which it was substituted. Thus, for example, Kolers (1970) reported that nearly 70% of the substitution errors made by adult readers on geometrically transformed text were of the same part of speech as the correct word. By chance, one would expect only about 18% of the errors should be of the correct part of speech.

In another study, Weber (1970) analyzed reading errors by first graders and found that over 90% of the errors made were grammatically consistent with the sentence to the point of the error. Although it is not clear what percentage to expect under assumptions of random guessing, it is obviously much lower than 90% in most texts. One might argue that these results and those of Kolers occur because words in the same syntactic class are more similar to each other than they are to words outside that class. It is interesting to note in this regard that in the Weber study, the ungrammatical errors were significantly more similar to the correct word than were the grammatical words—at least an indication that this is a syntactic effect and not a visual one.

In another experiment, carried out by Stevens and Rumelhart (1975) with adult readers, an oral reading task showed that about 98% of the substitution errors that were recognizable as words were grammatical. Moreover, nearly 80% of the time the substituted words were of the same syntactic class as the class most frequently predicted at that part in a cloze experiment. Once again, it appears that we have a case of grammatical knowledge helping to determine the word read.

In addition, in an important experiment, Miller and Isard (1963) compared perceptibility of spoken words under conditions in which normal syntactic structure was violated with the case in which syntactic structure was intact. They found that many more words could be reported when the sentences were syntactically normal. Although I do not know of a similar study with written materials, it is doubtless that similar results would occur—another case of a higher level of processing determining the perceptibility of units at a lower level.

It is difficult to see exactly how the models under discussion would deal with results such as these. In the Gough model, syntactic processing occurs only very late in the processing sequence—after information has entered short-term memory. It seems unlikely that he would want to assume that partial information is preserved that far in the process. It is not clear just where syntax should be put in the LaBerge–Samuels model. It is particularly difficult to represent productive syntactic rules of the sort linguists suggest in the LaBerge–Samuels formalism. As I will discuss, it would appear to be essential to be able to represent systems of rules to account for such results.

Our Perception of Words Depends on the Semantic Environment in Which We Encounter the Words

It is even more difficult to incorporate a mechanism for semantic effects on the word-recognition process into a purely bottom-up model than it is to incorporate a mechanism for syntactic effects. There have recently been a number of studies that provide very nice demonstrations of semantic effects on word recognition.

In a series of experiments, Meyer, Schvaneveldt, and Ruddy (Meyer & Schvaneveldt, 1971; Meyer, Schvaneveldt, & Ruddy, 1972, 1974; Ruddy, Meyer, &

Schvaneveldt, 1973; Schvaneveldt & Meyer, 1973) have reported convincing evidence of semantic effects on word recognition. The basic procedure in these experiments involved measuring reaction times to come to a lexical decision about a pair of words. The basic result is that the decision can be made much faster when the pair of words are semantically related (such as *bread–butter* or *doctor–nurse*) than when they are unrelated (such as *bread–doctor* and *nurse–butter*). The most plausible account of these results would seem to be that the process of perceiving the first word somehow allows us to process the second word more quickly just in case it is a semantically related word. Thus, we again have the processing at the semantic level modifying our processing at the word level.

In a series of experiments recently carried out in our laboratory, Graboi (1974) demonstrated this same general effect using quite a different method. In one of his experiments Graboi employed a variation of Neisser's search procedure. First, subjects were trained to search for occurrence of any one of five target words among a list of semantically unrelated nontargets. Half of the subjects searched for any one of the words labeled Experimental Target Set (see Table 2) scattered among lists constructed from the Unassociated Nontargets. The other half of the subjects searched for the words labeled *Control Target Set* against the same background. Notice that neither target set is semantically related to the nontarget background in which it is searched for. After 14 hours of training, the experimental group was searching their lists at a rate of 182.2 milliseconds (msec)

Table 2. Alternative Stimuli in the Target and Nontarget Sets

	A. Associated Nontargets	
Experimental	WORM CHICK NESTS ROBIN CHIRP WINGS FLY	Control
Target Set	EAGLE PARROT SONG BLACK GRAY PURPLE	Target Set
	BROWN GOLD BLUE RED YELLOW GREEN PAINT	
	SAVE SPEND COINS DIME BANK SILVER DOLLAR	
	CASH PENNY PEARL BOOKS SCHOOL READ	
	CLASS WRITE TEACH EXAM NOTES GRADE	
	STUDY ORANGE NUTS GRAPE SWEET PLUM	
BIRD:	APPLE PEACH PEAR FRESH LEMON	:ROCK
COLOR:		:CHAIR
MONEY:	B. Unassociated Nontargets	:HOUSE
LEARN:	HUG PEN SLEEP NIGHT BRIDGE STAPLE LAMP	:SPORT
FRUIT:	RULER LEADER ROAR SUNNY PLACE CORNER	:CLOUD
	ALBUM ABOUT RATE WEEK POINT SWITCH	
	ANKLE TOWN DIAL SPOON TOWEL SHEET STOVE	
	CRUST BRUSH GLASS ROAD WHICH AFTER	
	PASS STORY SIGN CHURCH MURAL PHONE	
	BOOTH CARD STREET MOTOR RADIO KNOB	
	PLUG DRIVE LINE TASK PRINT SHIFT	

per word. The control group scanned at a rate of 180.0 msec per word. At the 15th hour of practice, the background lists were changed. Both groups now searched for their targets against the Associated Nontarget background. Now the experimental group was searching for its targets against a background of nontargets, all semantically associated with the target set. The control group also was switched, but the Associated Nontargets were not semantically related to the control target set. After the change, we found that the control group scanned against the new background at about the same rate as they scanned the old one—179 msec per word scanned. The experimental group, however, scanning through words semantically related to the target set, was slowed to a rate of 197.4 msec per word.

One might suppose that the subjects in the experimental group were just surprised to see related words in the background and a few long pauses accounted for the entire difference. However, on this account one would expect the difference soon to disappear. But this did not happen. Through 5 additional hours of searching (they searched through 2,000 words during a 1-hour session), the difference between the control and experimental subjects remained at about 20 msec per word. It would thus appear that, even when searching for particular words, our expectations are based on meaning as well as visual form.

Using still another experimental procedure, Tulving and Gold (1963) and Tulving, Mandler, and Baumal (1964) both found that the prior presentation of a sentence context lowers the threshold at which a tachistoscopically presented word can be recognized.

Again we have a case of a higher level of processing (meaning) apparently affecting our ability to process at a lower level (the word level). Notice, moreover, that semantic relatedness can either make our processing more efficient (as with the Meyer et al., 1974, and Tulving and Gold, 1963, experiments), or it can interfere with our processing (as with the Graboi, 1974, experiment). It is again difficult to see how a strictly bottom-up, stage-by-stage processing model can account for results such as these.

Our Perception of Syntax Depends on the Semantic Context in Which the String Appears

Although neither Gough nor LaBerge and Samuels have attempted to specify their models much beyond the level of words, a complete model of reading must, of course, account for the way semantics affects our apprehension of the syntax of a sentence we are reading. Experiments at this level are few and far between, but there are numerous examples that seem rather compelling on this general point.

Perhaps the most commonly observed effect of this sort involves the semantic disambiguation of syntactically ambiguous sentences. Consider the following sentences:

(1) a. They are eating apples.

b. The children are eating apples.

c. The juicy red ones are eating apples.

At the syntactic level, all three sentences allow for at least two readings:

1. The reading in which the thing referred to by the first noun phrase is performing the act of eating some apples.
2. The reading in which the thing referred to by the first noun phrase is said to be a member of the class of "eating apples."

However, at a semantic level only the first one remains ambiguous—even it would be disambiguated if we had some notion as to the referent of *they*.

Schank (1973) has given a number of similar examples. Consider, for example, the following sentences:

(2) a. I saw the Grand Canyon flying to New York.

b. I saw the Grand Canyon *while I was* flying to New York.

c. I saw the Grand Canyon *which was* flying to New York.

Most readers immediately interpret Sentence (2a) as meaning the same as (2b) rather than Sentence (2c) simply on the grounds that it is semantically anomalous to imagine the Grand Canyon actually flying. On the other hand, Sentence (3a) is ordinarily interpreted to mean the same as Sentence (3c) rather than Sentence (3b):

(3) a. I saw the cattle grazing in the field.

b. I saw the cattle *while I was* grazing in the field.

c. I saw the cattle *that were* grazing in the field.

In Examples (1), (2), and (3), semantics play the determining role as to which surface structure we apprehend. Thus, just as orthographic structure affects our ability to perceive letters and syntax, and semantics affects our perception of words, so too does semantics affect our apprehension of syntax.

Our Interpretation of the Meaning of What We Read Depends on the General Context in Which We Encounter the Text

Just as the appropriate interpretation of our ambiguous symbol, , was determined by the sentence in which it was embedded, so too it often happens that the *meaning* of a word is dependent on the words surrounding it. Consider, for example, the following sentences:

(4) a. The statistician could be certain that the difference was significant *since all of the figures on the right-hand side of the table were larger than any of those on the left.*

b. The craftsman was certainly justified in charging more for the carvings on the right *since all of the figures on the right-hand side of the table were larger than any of those on the left.*

Here our interpretation of the second clause is thus quite different depending on the nature of the first clause. In Sentence (4a) for example, the term *figure* is readily interpreted as being a number, the term *table* a place for writing numbers, and the relation *larger* can properly be interpreted to mean >. In Sentence (4b) on the other hand, the term *figure* presumably refers to a small statue, the term *table* refers to a physical object with a flat top used for setting things on, and the relation *larger* clearly means something like *of greater volume*. Here we have a case in which no determination about the meaning of these individual words can be made without consideration of the entire sentence. Thus, no decision can be made about the meaning of a word without consideration of the meaning of the entire sentence in which the word appears.

Not only is the interpretation of individual words dependent on the sentential context in which they are found, but the meaning of entire sentences is dependent on the general context in which they appear. The following example from Bransford and Johnson (1973) is a case in point:

(5)

> Watching a Peace March From the 40th Floor
>
> The view was breathtaking. From the window one could see the crowd below. Everything looked extremely small from such a distance, but the colorful costumes could still be seen. Everyone seemed to be moving in the same direction in an orderly fashion and there seemed to be little children as well as adults. The landing was gentle, and luckily the atmosphere was such that no special suits had to be worn. At first there was a great deal of activity. Later, when the speeches started, the crowd quieted down. The man with the television camera took many shots of the setting and the crowd. Everyone was very friendly and seemed glad when the music started. (p. 412)

In this passage, the sentence beginning "The landing was gentle..." appears to make no sense. No clear meaning can be assigned to it in this context. As such, when subjects were given the passage and later asked to recall it, very few subjects remembered the anomalous sentence. On the other hand, when the passage was titled "A Space Trip to an Inhabited Planet" the entire passage was given quite a different interpretation. In this case, the anomalous sentence fits into the general interpretation of the paragraph very well. Subjects given the "Space Trip" title recalled the critical sentence three times as often as those given the "Peace March" title. Many other examples could be given. The dependence of meaning on context would appear to be the norm rather than the exception in reading.

To summarize, these results taken together appear to support the view that our apprehension of information at one level of analysis often can depend on our apprehension of information at a higher level. How can this be? Surely we cannot first perceive the meaning of what we read and only later discover what the sentences, words, or letters were that mediated the meaning. To paraphrase a remark attributed to Gough (as cited in Brewer, 1972), it is difficult to "see how the syntax [or semantics, for that matter] can go out and mess around with the print"

(p. 360). The problem, I believe, arises from the linear stage formalism that has served so well. The answer, I suspect, comes by presuming that all these knowledge sources apply simultaneously and that our perceptions are the product of the simultaneous interactions among all of them.

An Interactive Model

Perhaps the most natural information-processing representation of the theoretical ideas suggested in the previous section is illustrated in Figure 5. The figure illustrates the assumption that graphemic information enters the system and is registered in a visual information store (VIS). A feature extraction device is then assumed to operate on this information, extracting the critical features from the VIS. These features serve as the sensory input to a pattern synthesizer. In addition to this sensory information, the pattern synthesizer has available nonsensory information about the orthographic structure of the language (including information about the probability of various strings of characters), information about lexical items in the language, information about the syntactic possibilities (and probabilities), information about the semantics of the language, and information about the current contextual situation (pragmatic information). The pattern synthesizer, then, uses all of this information to produce a "most probable interpretation" of the graphemic input. Thus, all of the various sources of knowledge, both sensory and nonsensory, come together at one place, and the reading process is the product of the simultaneous joint application of all the knowledge sources.

Although the model previously outlined may, in fact, be an accurate representation of the reading process, it is of very little help as a model of reading. It is one thing to suggest that all of these different information sources interact (as many writers have) but quite another to specify a psychologically plausible

Figure 5. A Stage Representation of an Interactive Model of Reading

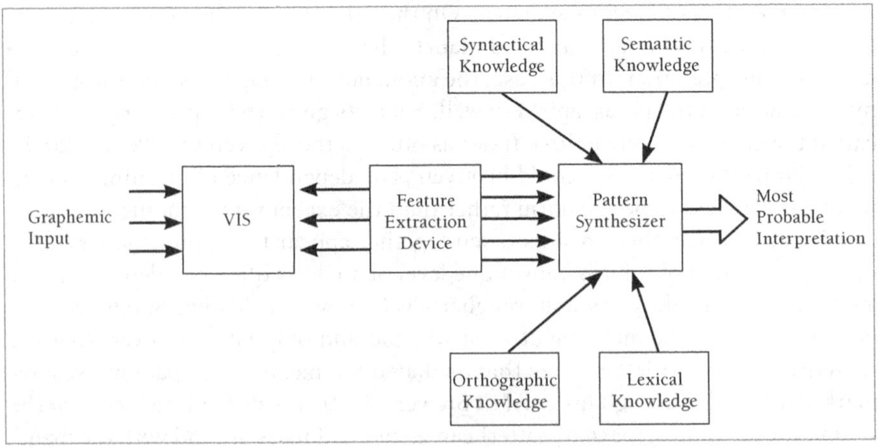

hypothesis about how they interact. Thus, it is clear why serious theorists who have attempted to develop detailed models of the reading process (e.g., Gough, 1972; LaBerge & Samuels, 1974) have stayed away from a formulation of the sort illustrated in Figure 5. All that is interesting in the model takes place in the box labeled *Pattern Synthesizer.* The flowchart does little more than list the relevant variables. We need a representation for the operation of the pattern synthesizer itself. To represent that, we must develop a means of representing the operation of a set of parallel interacting processes.

Flowcharts are best suited to represent the simple serial flow of information. They are badly suited for the representation of a set of parallel, highly interactive processes. However, with the advent of the parallel computer (at least as a conceptual device), computer scientists have begun to develop formalisms for the representation of parallel processes. It is interesting that the major problem in each case seems to have been the representation of the lines of communication among the otherwise independent processes.

Of the several different systems of communication that have been proposed, two were developed in the context of language processing by computer and seem to be most promising as a formalism for the development of a reading model. One of these was developed by Kaplan (1973) and is called the General Syntactic Processor (GSP). The second was developed by Reddy and his associates at Carnegie Mellon University (see Lesser, Fennell, Erman, & Reddy, 1974) as an environment for a speech understanding program. This system is called HEARSAY II. These two systems have a good deal in common and solve the communication problem in much the same way—namely, both systems consist of sets of totally independent asynchronous processes that communicate by means of a global, highly structured data storage device. In Kaplan's system the communication center is called a *chart*; in the HEARSAY system it is called a *blackboard*. I use the more neutral term *message center* in my development below. This development is most closely related to the HEARSAY system and could well be considered as an application of the HEARSAY model to reading. However, I also draw from aspects of GSP, and the model as I develop it has the Rumelhart and Siple (1974) model of word recognition as a special case.

Following HEARSAY, the model can be characterized as consisting of a set of independent *knowledge sources.* (These knowledge sources correspond to the sources of input to the pattern synthesizer in Figure 5.) Each knowledge source contains specialized knowledge about some aspect of the reading process. The message center keeps a running list of hypotheses about the nature of the input string. Each knowledge source constantly scans the message center for the appearance of hypotheses relevant to its own sphere of knowledge. Whenever such a hypothesis enters the message center, the knowledge source in question evaluates the hypothesis in light of its own specialized knowledge. As a result of its analysis, the hypothesis may be confirmed, the hypothesis may be disconfirmed and removed from the message center, or a new hypothesis can be added to the message center. This process continues until some decision can be reached. At that point the most probable hypothesis is determined to be the correct one. To facilitate the process, the message center is highly structured so that the knowledge sources know exactly where to find relevant hypotheses and so that dependencies among hypotheses are easily determined.

The Message Center

The message center can be represented as a three-dimensional space: one dimension representing the position along the line of text, one dimension representing the level of the hypothesis (word level, letter level, phrase level, etc.), and one dimension representing alternative hypotheses at the same level. Associated with each hypothesis is a running estimate of the probability that it is the correct hypothesis. Moreover, hypotheses at each level may have pointers to hypotheses at higher or lower levels on which they are dependent. Thus, for example, the hypothesis that the first word in a string is the word *the* is supported by the hypothesis that the first letter of the string is *t* and supports the hypothesis that the string begins with a noun phrase.

Figure 6 illustrates a two-dimensional slice of the message center at some point during the reading of the phrase *the car.*

Figure 6. A Two-Dimensional Slice of the Message Center

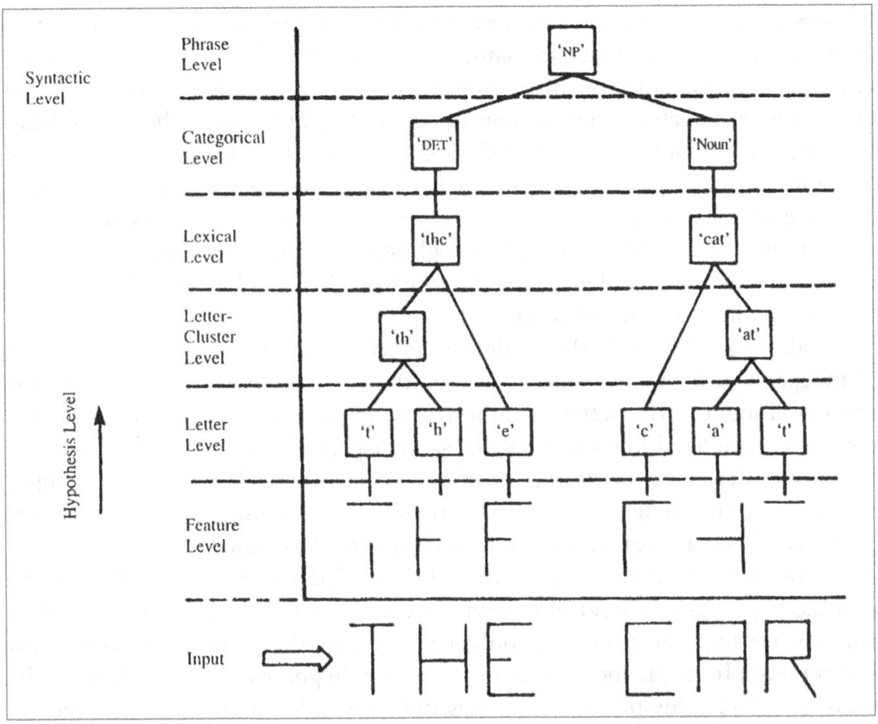

The figure illustrates hypotheses at five different levels (feature level, letter level, letter-cluster level, lexical level, and syntactic level). The diagram is only a two-dimensional slice inasmuch as no alternative hypotheses are illustrated. In practice, of course, many alternative hypotheses would be considered and evaluated in the course of reading this phrase. It should be pointed out that the tree-like structure should not be taken to mean that the tree was constructed either from a purely bottom-up process (starting with the features, then hypothesizing the letters, then the letter clusters, etc.), nor from a purely top-down analysis (starting with a view that we have a noun phrase and that noun phrases are made up of determiners followed by nouns, etc.). Rather, the hypotheses can be generated at any level. If it is likely that a line begins with a noun phrase, then we postulate a noun phrase and look for evidence. If we see features that suggest a *t* as the first letter, we postulate a *t* in the first position and continue processing. If we later have to reject either or both of these hypotheses, little is lost. The system makes the best guesses and checks out their implications. If these guesses are wrong, it will take a bit longer, but the system will eventually find some hypotheses at some level that it can accept.

An Example. To illustrate the operation of the system, consider the following experimental procedure. A subject is presented with a picture (e.g., Figure 7) and

Figure 7. A Scene

Figure provided by Jean Mandler.

allowed to view it for a few seconds. Then he is given a tachistoscopic presentation of a noun phrase that he knows will refer to one of the objects in the picture. His job is to decide which object was referred to. This experimental procedure is designed to simulate the process of reading a phrase for meaning. (An experimental procedure of this sort is currently under development in our laboratory.) I will illustrate the current model by showing the changes we might expect in the message center as the phrase THE CAR is read after viewing Figure 7.

Figure 8 shows the message center at an early point in the processing of this phrase. The subject knows from the instructions of the experiment that the

Figure 8. The Message Center Shortly After Processing Has Begun on THE CAR

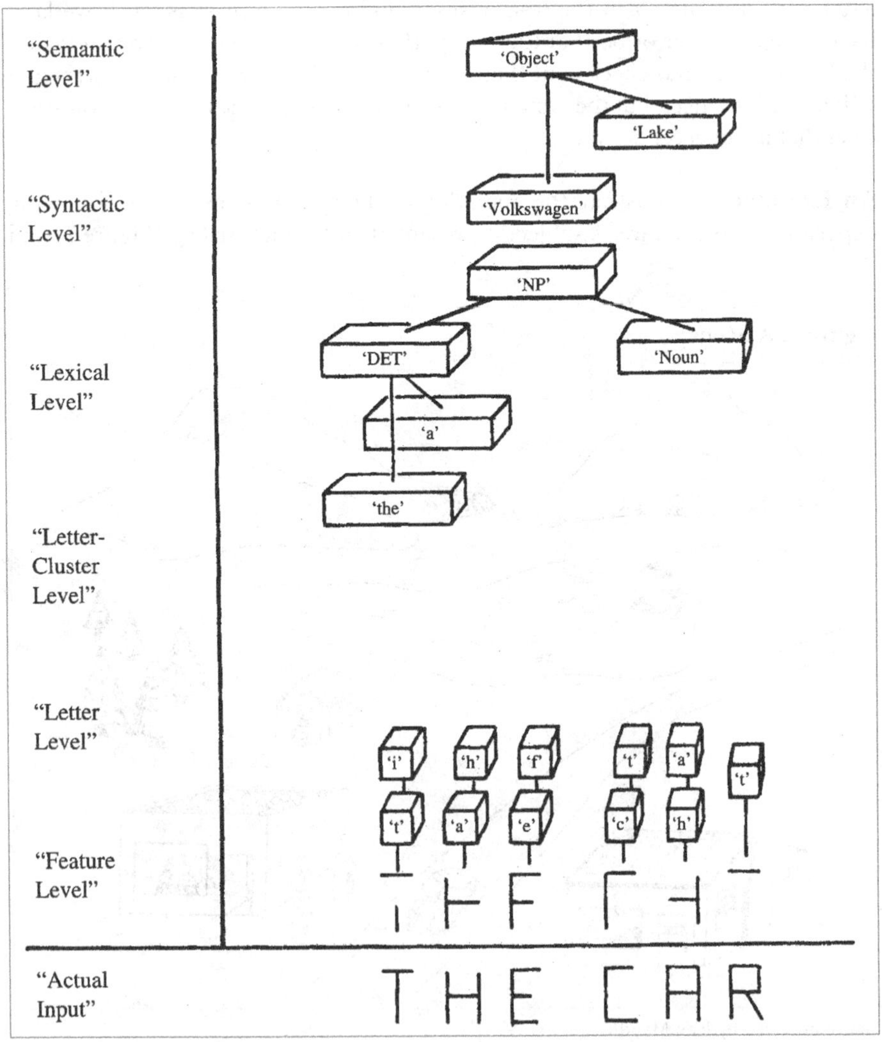

phrase will refer to some object in the picture. Thus, the semantic-level "object" hypothesis can be entered and assigned a high likelihood value from the start. Moreover, through looking at the picture and perceiving certain aspects of it as salient, the subject will develop expectations as to the probable referent of the phrase. In this case, I have assumed that the subject set up special expectations for a phrase referring to *the lake* or to *the Volkswagen*.

Similarly, at the syntactic level, the subject can be quite certain that the input will form a noun phrase. Thus, the hypothesis "NP" is entered into the message center and assigned a high value. Noun phrases have a rather characteristic structure. About 25% of the time they begin with a determiner (DET). Thus, in the example, I have assumed that the hypothesis that the first word was a determiner was entered. Similarly, we can expect the second word of a noun phrase to be a noun about 20% of the time. Thus, I have entered the hypothesis that the second word is a noun. Now, in the case where the first word is a determiner, we could expect it to be the word *the* about 60% of the time and the word *a* about 20%. Thus, I have assumed that these two hypotheses have also been entered.

As all these hypotheses are being entered in top-down fashion, hypotheses at the letter level also are being entered bottom-up on the basis of featural information. In the example, I have assumed that for each of the first five letter positions the two most promising letter possibilities were entered as hypotheses. For the sixth letter position, which contains very little featural information, I have assumed that only its most likely letter hypothesis has been entered.

Figure 9 illustrates the state of the message center at a later point in the processing. In the meantime, the lexical hypothesis "a" has led to a letter hypothesis that was then tested against the featural information and rejected. The hypothesization of an initial "t" has led to the hypothesization of an initial "th" at the letter cluster level—a hypothesis that is given added validity by the possible "h" in the second position. The lexical-level hypothesis of the word "the" also has led to the hypothesization of the letter cluster "th" followed by the letter "e." The prior existence of these hypotheses generated from the bottom up has led to a mutual strengthening of all of the hypotheses in question and a resultant weakening of the alternative letter hypotheses at the first three letter positions.

While this processing was taking place, lexical hypotheses were generated from the semantic level as possible nouns. In this instance I have assumed that the semantic hypothesis "lake" has led to the lexical hypothesis that the word *lake* was in the string and that the semantic hypothesis "Volkswagen" has led to the lexical hypothesis "Volkswagen" and to the lexical hypothesis "car." Meanwhile, the letter hypotheses have led to alternative letter-cluster hypotheses "ch" and "at."

Figure 10 illustrates the state of the message center at a still later point in the processing of the input. By this point, the hypothesis that the first word is *the* has reached a sufficient value that further processing has ceased. No new hypotheses have been generated about the first word. On the other hand, lexical hypotheses on the second word have proliferated. The existence of the letter hypothesis "c" followed by the letter-cluster hypothesis "at" has led to a hypothesization of the

Figure 9. The Message Center Slightly Later in the Processing Sequence

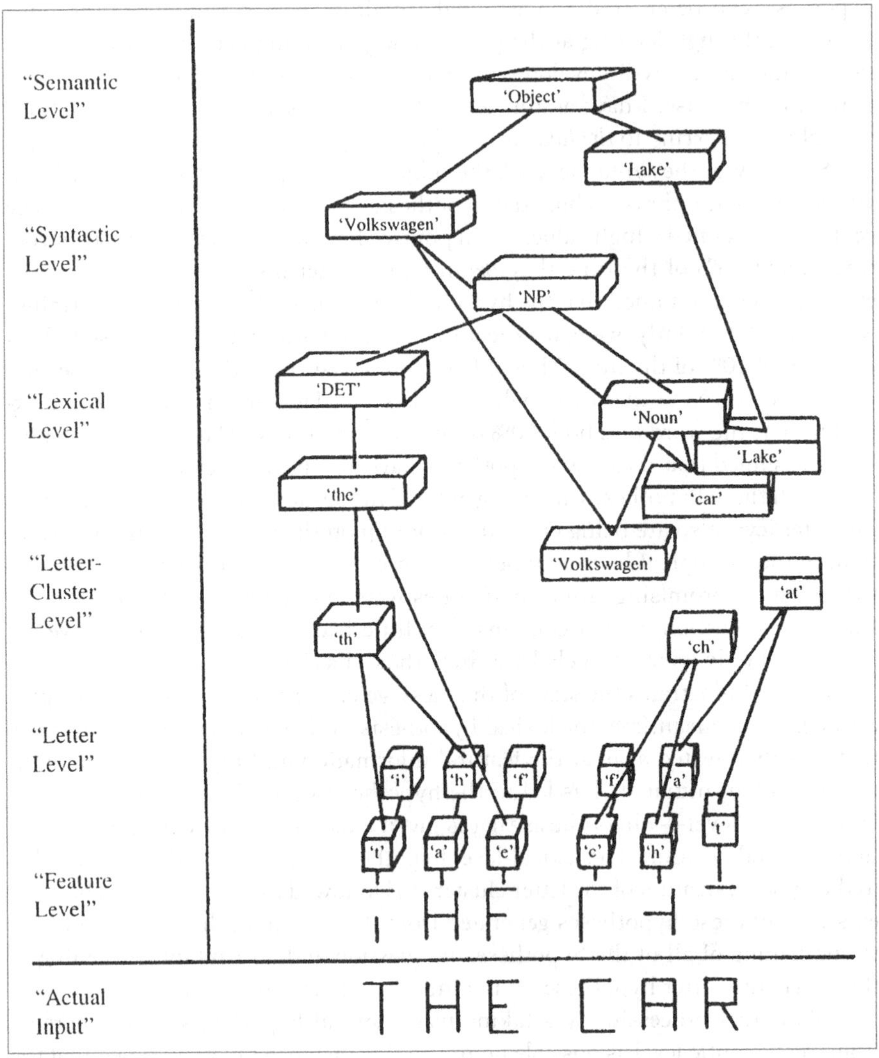

lexical item "cat." Similarly, the letter hypothesis "f" followed by "at" has led to hypothesizing the lexical item "fat." The lexical hypothesis "cat" is consistent with the "noun" hypothesis, thus strengthening the view that the second word is a noun. At the same time, the lexical hypotheses "lake," "Volkswagen," and "car" either have strengthened existing letter hypotheses or have caused new ones to be generated. Notice, in particular, that the prior existence of the letter hypotheses "c" and "a" strengthened the semantically derived lexical hypothesis "car," which in turn strengthened the letter hypothesis "r"—even though the letter hypothesis

Figure 10. The Message Center Well Into the Processing Sequence

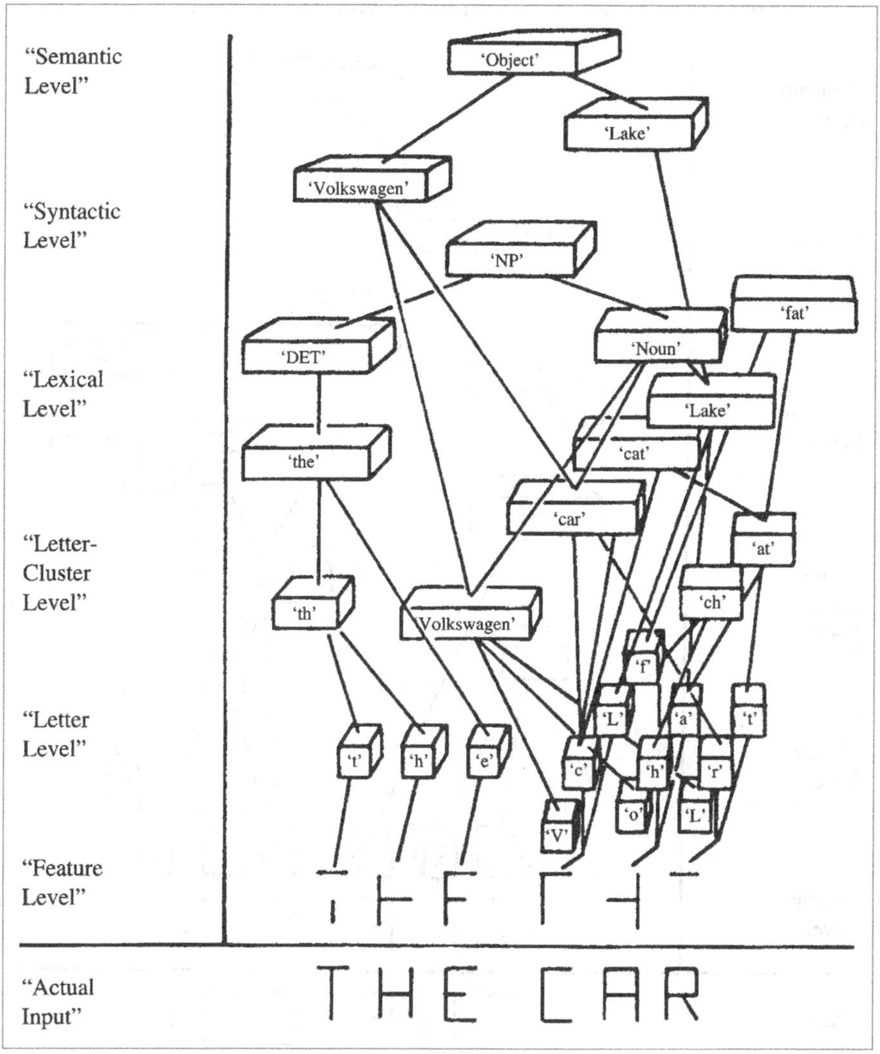

"r" has not yet been evaluated in light of the featural information in the final position.

Finally, Figure 11 illustrates a state of processing after the letter hypotheses have been tested against the featural information. At this point only three lexical hypotheses for the second word remain—"fat," "cat," and "car." The lexical hypothesis "fat" has led to the syntactic hypothesis that the second word is an adjective (ADJ), and the lexical hypothesis "cat" has led to the semantic-level hypothesis that there should be a cat in the picture. Meanwhile, the semantic

Figure 11. The Message Center Near the End of Processing: At This Point the Semantics of the Input Have Been Pretty Well Determined

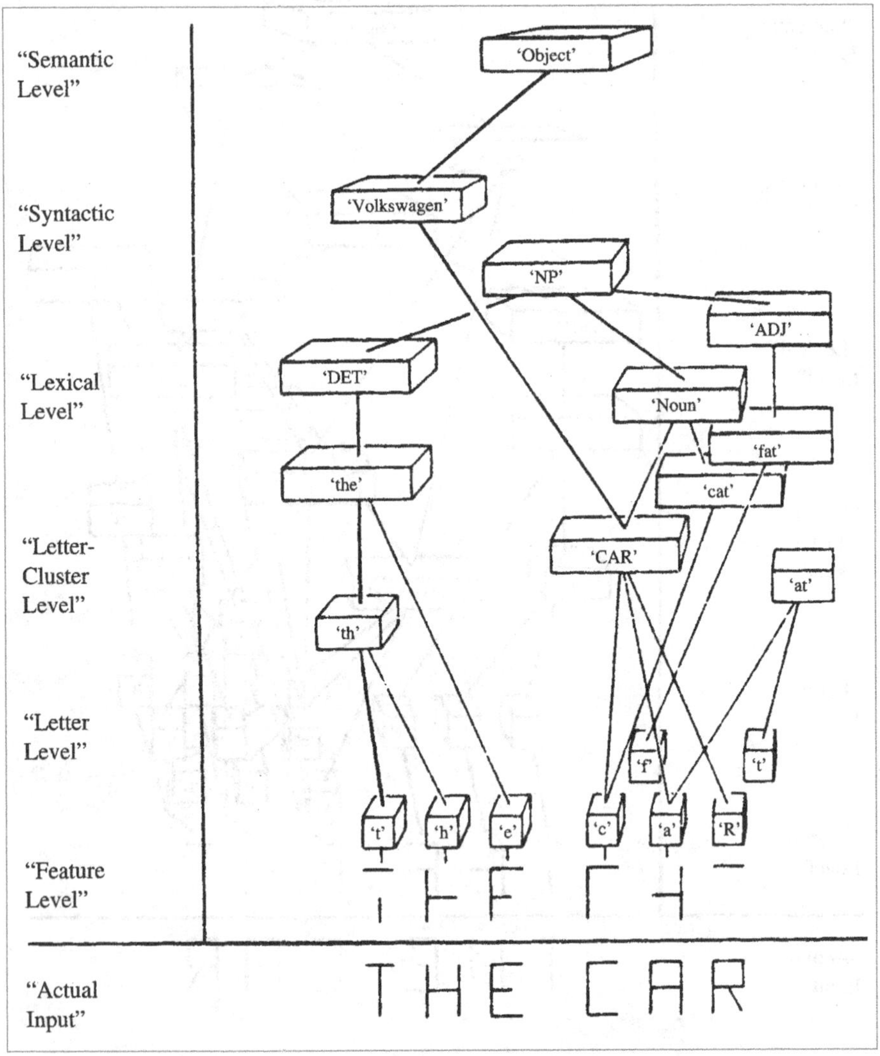

hypothesis "Volkswagen" has been strengthened by the finding that the final featural information is consistent with the hypothesis that the last letter is an *r*. At this point the semantic hypothesis "Volkswagen" is probably high enough to lead to a response. If not, a test of the semantic hypothesis "cat" will lead to the rejection of that hypothesis and the consequent strengthening of the "Volkswagen" hypothesis and thus the lexical hypothesis "car" and the letter-level hypotheses "c," "a," and "r."

It should be clear from this example how, in principle at least, one could build a model of reading that actually would employ constraints from all levels concurrently in the process of constructing an interpretation of an input string. Of course, this example is a long way from the specification of such a model. All I have illustrated here is the nature of the message center and how it is structured to facilitate communication among processes acting at various levels. Before a concrete model of reading can be specified, the nature of the various knowledge sources must be specified as well. I now turn to a brief discussion of the separation of the various knowledge sources.

The Knowledge Sources

I do not yet have a detailed model of the operation of all the knowledge sources. However, I do have ideas about a number of them and will now discuss them.

1. *Featural knowledge.* At this level, I am assuming that features are extracted according to the assumptions of the Rumelhart and Siple (1974) model. Moreover, I am assuming that these critical features are the basic level of processing. In a tachistoscopic experiment, all decisions must be made with respect to the set of features extracted during and shortly after the exposure. In freereading situations, the reader can go back and get more featural information if no hypothesis gets a sufficiently high rating or if some hypothesis does get a high rating at one point and is later rejected. Such occasions probably account for regressions in eye movements.

2. *Letter-level knowledge.* This knowledge source scans the feature inputs, and whenever it finds a close match to a known letter, it posits a letter hypothesis. In addition, whenever a letter hypothesis appears from a higher level, this knowledge source evaluates that hypothesis against the feature information. In addition to information about letters in various fonts, the letter-level knowledge source presumably takes into account the probabilities of letters in the language. Thus, relatively more featural evidence would be necessary to postulate a "z" or "q" than an "e" or a "t."

3. *Letter-cluster knowledge.* This knowledge source scans the incoming letter-level hypotheses, looking for letter sequences that are likely and form units in the language or for single letters that are frequently followed or preceded by another letter (e.g., as *q* is frequently followed by *u*). In either case a letter cluster is postulated. In the latter case a letter-level hypothesis is also introduced. (That is, if a *q* is found, a *qu* is postulated at the letter-cluster level and a *u* is postulated at the letter level.) The value associated with any of these hypotheses depends on the values of the letter-level information on which it is based and on the frequency of such clusters in the language. In addition, the letter-cluster knowledge source looks for the introduction of letter-cluster hypotheses from the lexical level. Whenever it finds these it evaluates them by proposing the appropriate letter-level hypotheses. For this knowledge source, as with all others, the most probable hypotheses that are unsupported from the following or that support no higher-level hypotheses are evaluated first.

4. *Lexical-level knowledge.* The lexical-level knowledge source operates in exactly the same way as the other knowledge sources. It scans the letter-cluster and letter hypotheses for letter sequences that form lexical items or that are close to lexical items. When it finds such information, it posits the appropriate lexical-level hypotheses and any additional letter-cluster or letter-level hypotheses. When evaluating the goodness of any hypothesis, it takes into account the goodness of the evidence on which it is based and the a priori frequency of that item in the language. In addition, whenever a lexical item is postulated from either the semantic or syntactic levels, this knowledge source evaluates that hypothesis by postulating those letter-cluster and letter hypotheses that are not yet present. Those letter and letter-cluster hypotheses that are present are strengthened due to the convergence of lines of evidence. Other alternatives without such convergent information are relatively weakened.

5. *Syntactic knowledge.* Like all the other knowledge sources, this knowledge source is designed to operate in both a bottom-up and top-down mode. Thus, whenever a lexical hypothesis is suggested, one or more syntactic category hypotheses are entered into the message center. In general, not all syntactic category hypotheses consistent with the lexical form would be expected. Instead, those categories that are most probable, given that lexical item, would be entered first. Similarly, sequences of lexical category hypotheses would be scanned, looking for phrase possibilities, and so on. At the same time, the syntactic knowledge source would have the capacity to operate in a top-down fashion. Thus, for example, whenever a noun-phrase hypothesis were entered, the syntactic knowledge source would establish, say, a determiner, syntactic category hypothesis that in turn might initiate lexical-level hypotheses of determiner words such as *a* and *the*. Following Kaplan's (1973) GSP, I assume that this top-down portion of the syntactic knowledge source would be well represented by an Augmented Transition Network (ATN) parser. (See Stevens and Rumelhart, 1975, for an application of an ATN to reading data.) Like all other levels, the syntactic hypotheses are given values dependent on the goodness of the evidence (or prior probabilities) of the hypotheses on which they are based. Moreover, a convergence of top-down and bottom-up hypotheses strengthens both.

6. *Semantic-level knowledge.* This is perhaps the most difficult level to characterize. Nevertheless, I assume that its operation is essentially the same as the others. Whenever strong lexical hypotheses occur, this knowledge source must have the ability to look for semantic-level correlates to evaluate the plausibility of the hypothesis (at both the lexical and syntactic levels). Moreover, it must be able to develop hypotheses about the content of the input and generate lexical-level hypotheses as possible representations of this. The experimental procedure discussed in the previous section was designed as an attempt to reduce the complexity of the semantic component by supposing a relatively simple referential semantics.

Still, of course, after having outlined the functional characteristics of the various knowledge sources, I am still far from the quantitative model I have in mind.

However, it would appear that a HEARSAY-type model such as this offers promise as a framework for the development of serious models of reading that nevertheless assumes a highly interactive parallel processing system.

A Mathematical Model of Hypothesis Evaluation

In this section I will specify in somewhat more detail the nature of the hypothesis-evaluation process I envision. Figure 12 illustrates a simplified version of the message center from the primary example. This figure differs somewhat in format from the previous figures of this type in order to make clearer the sequential dependencies among hypotheses at the same level. Thus, the fact that an "NP" consists of a "DET" and "NOUN" and that the word *cat* consists of *c* + *a* + *t* is illustrated by the arrows connecting those constituents at the same level. Moreover, the dependency arrows have been drawn to only the left-hand member of such hypothesis sequences. In a sense, as we shall see below, the left-hand member is representing the entire sequence of hypotheses.

There are four different types of dependency relationships among hypotheses in this model. These types are illustrated in the figure. First, a hypothesis may

Figure 12. An Illustration of the Relations Among the Hypotheses in the Message Center

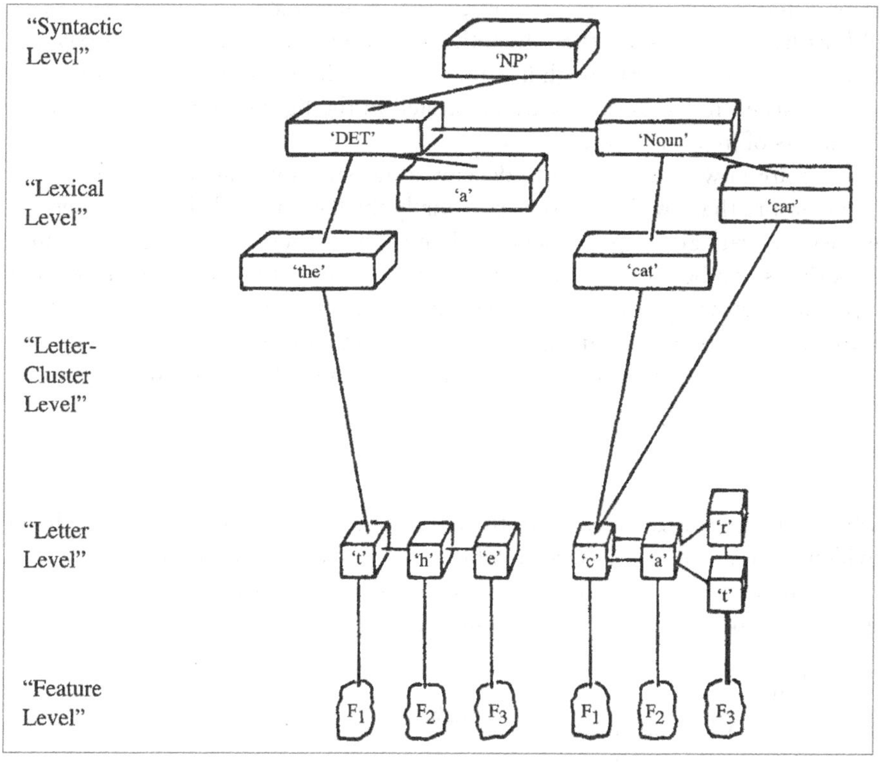

have one or more *daughter* hypotheses. A daughter hypothesis is one at a lower level that is connected directly to a higher-level hypothesis. In the figure, the hypothesis "DET" has two daughter hypotheses: "the" and "a." The hypothesis "the" has a single daughter, "t." A hypothesis may have any number of daughters. Each daughter is an alternative way in which the higher hypothesis can be realized. Thus, "the" and "a" are alternative ways in which "DET" can be realized. For any hypothesis, h_i, I shall use the symbol D_i to designate its set of daughters.

The reciprocal relationship to daughter is *parent*. Any hypothesis may have one or more parent hypotheses. A parent hypothesis is one to which a hypothesis can lend direct support. Thus, in the figure, "NOUN" is a parent of both "car" and "cat." Similarly, the letter hypothesis "c" has two different parents, "car" and "cat." Only hypotheses that are at the left-most position of a sequence of hypotheses may have parents. Thus, the hypothesis "NOUN" has no parent. For each hypothesis, h_i, I shall designate the set of parents P_i.

In addition to parents and daughters, hypotheses may have *sisters*. Sisters are hypotheses in a sequence that either follow or precede a particular hypothesis at the same level. Sisters are not alternatives but are consistent possibilities of the same level. There are two sorts of sister hypotheses: *right sisters* and *left sisters*. Right sisters are hypotheses that follow a given hypothesis in a sequence of hypotheses. Thus, "NOUN" would be a right sister of "DET," and "r" and "t" are right sisters of the letter-level hypothesis "a." I designate the set of right sisters of h_i as R_i. Left sisters are those hypotheses that precede a given hypothesis in a string of hypotheses. Although it is possible for a hypothesis to have more than one left sister, no cases of this are illustrated in the figure. I designate the set of left sisters of hypothesis h_i as L_i.

We are now in a position to develop a measure for evaluating hypotheses. The measure that I will propose is essentially the Baysian probability that the hypothesis is true given the evidence at hand. The evidence favoring a particular hypothesis can be broken down into two parts: contextual evidence, dependent only on sister and parent hypotheses; and direct evidence, dependent solely on the evidence derived from daughter hypotheses and, ultimately, featural evidence. Equation (1) illustrates the assumed multiplicative relationship between these two kinds of evidence:

(1) $$s_i = v_i \cdot \beta_i^4$$

where s_i is the overall strength of the hypothesis h_i, v_i is a measure of the direct evidence for h_i, and β_i is a measure of the contextual evidence for h_i. Now we can define the values of v_i and β_i in terms of the parents and sisters of h_i. Equation (2) gives the value of the contextual strength of h_i:

(2) $$\beta_i = \begin{cases} \Pr(h_i) & P_i = L_i = \varphi \\ \Sigma_{s_k} \cdot \dfrac{\Pr(h_i|h_k)}{v_i} & \text{otherwise,} \end{cases}$$

where the sum is over all $h_k \in P_i$ or L_i. Thus, when h_i has no parents or left sisters, its contextual strength is given by its a priori probability. Otherwise, its contextual strength is given by the sum, over all of its left sisters and parents of the strength of the left sister or parent, h_k, times the conditional probability of the hypothesis given h_k. The sum is then divided by its own direct strength so that its direct strength will not contribute to its contextual strength (because as we shall see, its own direct strength contributes to the strength of its parents and left sisters and is represented multiplicatively in s_k).

Direct evidence for a hypothesis comes only from its daughters. Equation (3) gives the direct evidence for a hypothesis as a function of a value associated with its daughters:

(3) $$v_i = \begin{cases} \Sigma C_{ik} \cdot \Pr(h_k|h_i) & D_i \neq \varphi \\ 1 & \text{otherwise,} \end{cases}$$

where the sum is over all $h_k \in D_i$, and where C_{ik} is the *cumulative evidence* for hypothesis h_i associated with the sequence of hypotheses whose left-most member is the daughter h_k. Thus, in the diagram, the direct evidence for "car" is determined jointly by the direct evidence for "c," for "a," and for "r." The value of C_{ik} is given by the following equation:

(4) $$C_{i,k} = \begin{cases} v_k & R_k = \varphi \\ \sum_j v_k \cdot C_{i,j} \cdot \Pr(h_j|h_i, h_k) & \text{otherwise,} \end{cases}$$

where the sum is over all $h_j \in R_k$. Thus, the cumulative evidence for hypothesis h_i associated with hypothesis h_k is determined by the product of the direct evidence for h_k and the cumulative evidence for its right sister. If its probable right sisters are very strong, then the cumulative evidence is very strong and thus offers good support to its parent. Otherwise, it offers support against its parent.

Finally, we must give special attention to the first-level hypotheses associated with featural-level inputs. For any letter hypothesis h_i, featural-level inputs have cumulative values of C_{iF} given by:

(5) $$C_{i,F} = [\Pr(F)]^{-1}$$

where F is the set of features observed in that location. This, in effect, is a normalizer designed to keep the strengths in the 0 to 1 range.

The equations (1) to (5) define a system of evaluation that makes near optimal use of the information available at any given point in time. Whenever a new hypothesis is postulated and a new connection is drawn, new values must be computed for the entire set of hypotheses. Resources can be allotted to the knowledge sources based upon their momentary evaluations. Effort can be focused on generating hypotheses from the top down whenever we have hypotheses with strong contextual strengths and few daughter hypotheses. Effort can be focused on the generation of hypotheses from the bottom up whenever there is strong direct evidence and few parents. Moreover, the strength values can be signals to stop processing and accept a hypothesis. When some criterion strength value is obtained, a hypothesis can be accepted and no further processing need be required. Then resources can be siphoned to other more critical areas.

Of course, specifying equations such as these does not fully specify our model. We must specify all of the knowledge sources and how they postulate hypotheses. They do, I feel, illustrate that the model under consideration can be quantified and can generate specific predictions—in spite of the enormous complexity of a highly interactive system.

QUESTIONS FOR REFLECTION

1. Why does Rumelhart disagree with linear models of reading processing that suggest letter perception precedes word or syntactic recognition?
2. How does Rumelhart use the concept of hypothesis testing to explain his theory of message center processing?
3. Rumelhart proposed that bottom-up models do not fully describe the influence of higher level processing on lower level perceptions. What is his evidence for this proposition?
4. Why did Rumelhart consider his model interactive rather than bottom-up or top-down?

ACKNOWLEDGMENT

Research support was provided by grant NS 07454 from the National Institute of Health.

NOTES

*When this chapter was written, Rumelhart was at the University of California, San Diego.

[1] LaBerge and Samuels were particularly interested in the role of attention and the notion of automaticity in reading. I also have omitted discussion of episodic memory because neither one of these aspects of their model is relevant to my point here.

[2] Actually, the aforementioned attention mechanism of the LaBerge–Samuels model offers *some* top-down capacity. However, within their model it is limited and serves to speed up certain weak bottom-up paths.

[3] I use the term *perception* rather freely here. In general, it is my opinion that the distinction between the perceptual and conceptual aspects of reading is not that useful. As I will suggest later, there appears to be a continuity between what has been called perception and what has been called comprehension. My use of the term *perception* in the present context is simply the use of the one term to cover the entire process.

[4] This is the same relationship between these two sorts of evidence assumed by Luce (1959) and which is incorporated into the Rumelhart and Siple (1974) model for word recognition.

REFERENCES

Bransford, J.D., & Johnson, M.K. (1973). Considerations of some problems of comprehension. In W.G. Chase (Ed.), *Visual information processing*. New York: Academic.

Brewer, W.F. (1972). Is reading a letter-by-letter process? In J.F. Kavanagh & I.G. Mattingly (Eds.), *Language by ear and by eye: The relationships between speech and reading*. Cambridge, MA: MIT Press.

Gough, P.B. (1972). One second of reading. In J.F. Kavanagh & I.G. Mattingly (Eds.), *Language by ear and by eye: The relationships between speech and reading*. Cambridge, MA: MIT Press.

Graboi, D. (1974). *Physical shape, practice and meaning in visual search*. Unpublished doctoral dissertation, University of California, San Diego.

Huey, E.B. (1968). *The psychology and pedagogy of reading*. Cambridge, MA: MIT Press. (Original work published 1908)

Kaplan, R.M. (1973). A general syntactic processor. In R. Rustin (Ed.), *Natural language processing*. New York: Algorithmics.

Kolers, P.A. (1970). Three stages in reading. In H. Levin & J.T. Williams (Eds.), *Basic studies in reading*. New York: Basic.

LaBerge, D., & Samuels, S.J. (1974). Toward a theory of automatic information processing in reading. *Cognitive Psychology, 6*, 293–323.

Lesser, V.R., Fennell, R.D., Erman, L.D., & Reddy, D.R. (1974). *Organization of the HEARSAY II speech understanding system* (Working Papers in Speech Recognition III). Pittsburgh, PA: Carnegie Mellon University.

Luce, R.D. (1959). *Individual choice behavior*. New York: Wiley.

McClelland, J.L., & Johnston, J.C. (1977). The role of familiar units in perception of words and nonwords. *Perception and Psychophysics, 22*, 249–261.

Meyer, D.E., & Schvaneveldt, R.W. (1971). Facilitation in recognizing pairs of words: Evidence of a dependence between retrieval operations. *Journal of Experimental Psychology, 90*, 227–234.

Meyer, D.E., Schvaneveldt, R.W., & Ruddy, M.G. (1972, November). *Activation of lexical memory*. Paper presented at the meeting of the Psychonomic Society, St. Louis, MO.

Meyer, D.E., Schvaneveldt, R.W., & Ruddy, M.G. (1974). Functions of phonemic and graphemic codes in visual word recognition. *Memory and Cognition*, 2, 309–321.

Miller, G.A., Bruner, J.S., & Postman, L. (1954). Familiarity of letter sequences and tachistoscopic identification. *Journal of Genetic Psychology, 50*, 129–139.

Miller, G.A., & Isard, S. (1963). Some perceptual consequences of linguistic rules. *Journal of Verbal Learning and Verbal Behavior, 2*, 217–228.

Nash-Weber, B. (1975). The role of semantics in automatic speech understanding. In D.B. Bobrow & A. Collins (Eds.), *Representation and understanding*. New York: Academic.

Pillsbury, W.B. (1897). A study in apperception. *American Journal of Psychology, 8*, 315–393.

Reicher, G.M. (1969). Perceptual recognition as a function of meaningfulness of stimulus material. *Journal of Experimental Psychology, 81*, 274–280.

Ruddy, M.G., Meyer, D.E., & Schvaneveldt, R.W. (1973, May). *Context effects on phonemic encoding in visual word recognition*. Paper presented at the meeting of the Midwestern Psychological Association, Chicago, IL.

Rumelhart, D.E., & Siple, P. (1974). Process of recognizing tachistoscopically presented words. *Psychological Review, 81*, 99–118.

Schank, R.C. (1973). Identification of conceptualizations underlying natural language. In R.C. Schank & K.M. Colby (Eds.), *Computer models of thought and language*. San Francisco: Freeman.

Schvaneveldt, R.W., & Meyer, D.E. (1973). Retrieval and comparison processes in semantic memory. In S. Kornblum (Ed.), *Attention and performance IV*. New York: Academic.

Stevens, A.L., & Rumelhart, D.E. (1975). Errors in reading: Analysis using an augmented network model of grammar. In D.A. Norman, D.E. Rumelhart, & the LNR Research Group, *Explorations in cognition*. San Francisco: Freeman.

Tulving, E., & Gold, C. (1963). Stimulus information and contextual information as determinants of tachistoscopic recognition of words. *Journal of Experimental Psychology, 66*, 319–327.

Tulving, E., Mandler, G., & Baumal, R. (1964). Interaction of two sources of information in tachistoscopic word recognition. *Canadian Journal of Psychology, 18*, 62–71.

Weber, R.M. (1970). First graders' use of grammatical context in reading. In H. Levin & J.T. Williams (Eds.), *Basic studies in reading*. New York: Basic.

CHAPTER 30

A Theory of Reading: From Eye Fixations to Comprehension

Marcel Adam Just and Patricia A. Carpenter, Carnegie Mellon University

Although readers go through many of the same processes as listeners, there is one striking difference between reading and listening comprehension—a reader can control the rate of input. Unlike a listener, a reader can skip over portions of the text, reread sections, or pause on a particular word. A reader can take in information at a pace that matches the internal comprehension processes. By examining where a reader pauses, it is possible to learn about the comprehension processes themselves. Using this approach, a process model of reading comprehension is developed that accounts for the gaze durations of college students reading scientific passages.

The following display presents an excerpt from the data to illustrate some characteristics of eye fixations that motivate the model. This display presents a protocol of a college student reading the first two sentences of a passage about the properties of flywheels. The reader averages about 200 words per minute on the scientific texts. In this study, the reader was told to read a paragraph with understanding and then recall its content. Consecutive fixations on the same word have been aggregated into units called *gazes*. The gazes within each sentence have been sequentially numbered above the fixated word with the gaze durations (in msec) indicated below the sequence number.

```
   1       2   3    4     5          6          7        8       9     1
 1566    267 400   83   267        617        767      450     450   400
Flywheels are one of the oldest mechanical devices known to man. Every

2          3         5   4   6    7        8              9         10    11
616       517      684 250 317  617     1116            367       467   483
internal-combustion engine contains a small flywheel that converts the jerky motion

   12               13    14    15   16   17        18   19   20   21
  450              383   284   383  317  283       533   50  366  566
of the pistons into the smooth flow of energy that powers the drive shaft.
```

One important aspect of the protocol is that almost every content word is fixated at least once. There is a common misconception that readers do not fixate every word, but only some small proportion of the text, perhaps one out of every

This chapter is reprinted from *Psychological Review*, 87(4), 329–354. Copyright © 1980 by the American Psychological Association. Reprinted with permission.

two or three words. However, the data to be presented in this article (and most of our other data collected in reading experiments) show that during ordinary reading, almost all content words are fixated. This applies not only to scientific text but also to narratives written for adult readers. The current data are not novel in this regard. The eye fixation studies from the first part of the century point to the same conclusion (Buswell, 1937, chap. 4; Dearborn, 1906, chap. 4; Judd & Buswell, 1922, chap. 2). When readers are given a text that is appropriate for their age level, they average 1.2 words per fixation. The words that are not always fixated tend to be short function words, such as *the*, *of*, and *a*. The number of words per fixation is even lower if the text is especially difficult or if the reader is poorly educated. Of course, this is not the case when adults are given simple texts, such as children's stories; under such circumstances, these same studies show an increase to an average of two words per fixation. Similarly, readers skip more words if they are speed-reading or skimming (Taylor, 1962). These old results and the current results are consistent with the report of McConkie and Rayner (1975; Rayner, 1978) that readers generally cannot determine the meaning of a word that is in peripheral vision. These results have important implications for the present model; since most words of a text are fixated, we can try to account for the total duration of comprehension in terms of the gaze duration on each word.

The protocol also shows that the gaze duration varies considerably from word to word. There is a misconception that individual fixations are all about 250 msec in duration. But this is not true; there is a large variation in the duration of individual fixations as well as the total gaze duration on individual words. As the preceding display shows, some gaze durations are very long, such as the gaze on the word *Flywheels*. The model proposes that gaze durations reflect the time to execute comprehension processes. In this case the longer fixations are attributed to longer processing caused by the word's infrequency and its thematic importance. Also, the fixations at the end of each sentence tend to be long. For example, this reader had gaze durations of 450 and 566 msec on each of the last words of the first two sentences. The sentence-terminal pauses will be shown to reflect an integrative process that is evoked at the ends of sentences.

The link between eye fixation data and the theory rests on two assumptions. The first, called the immediacy assumption, is that a reader tries to interpret each content word of a text as it is encountered, even at the expense of making guesses that sometimes turn out to be wrong. Interpretation refers to processing at several levels such as encoding the word, choosing one meaning of it, assigning it to its referent, and determining its status in the sentence and in the discourse. The immediacy assumption posits that the interpretations at all levels of processing are not deferred; they occur as soon as possible, a qualification that will be clarified later.

The second assumption, the eye–mind assumption, is that the eye remains fixated on a word as long as the word is being processed. So the time it takes to process a newly fixated word is directly indicated by the gaze duration. Of course, comprehending that word often involves the use of information from preceding parts of the text, without any backward fixations. So the concepts corresponding to two different words may be compared to each other, for example, whereas only the more recently encountered word is fixated. The eye–mind assumption can be contrasted with an alternative view that data acquired from several successive eye fixations are internally buffered before being semantically processed (Bouma & deVoogd, 1974). This alternative view was proposed to explain a reading task in which the phrases of a text were successively presented in the same location. However, the situation was unusual in two ways. First, there were no eye movements involved, so the normal reading processes may not have been used. Second, and more telling, readers could not perform a simple comprehension test after seeing the text this way. By contrast, several studies of more natural situations support the eye–mind assumption that readers pause on words that require more processing (Just & Carpenter, 1978; Carpenter & Daneman, 1980). The eye–mind assumption posits that there is no appreciable lag between what is being fixated and what is being processed. This assumption has also been explored in spatial problem-solving tasks and has been supported in that domain as well as in reading (Just & Carpenter, 1976). The immediacy and eye–mind assumptions are used to interpret gaze duration data in the development of the reading model.

The article has four major sections. The first briefly describes a theoretical framework for the processes and structures in reading. The second section describes the reading task and eye fixation results accounted for by the model. The third section presents the model itself, with subsections describing each component process of the model. The fourth section discusses some implications of the theory for language comprehension and relates this theory of reading to other approaches.

Theoretical Framework

Reading can be construed as the coordinated execution of a number of processing stages such as word encoding, lexical access, assigning semantic roles, and relating the information in a given sentence to previous sentences and previous knowledge. Some of the major stages of the proposed model are depicted schematically in Figure 1. The diagram depicts both processes and structures. The stages of reading in the left-hand column are shown in their usual sequence of execution. The long-term memory on the right-hand side is the storehouse of knowledge, including the procedural knowledge used in executing the stages on the left. The working memory in the middle mediates the long-term memory and the comprehension processes. Although it is easy to informally agree on the general involvement of these processes in reading, it is more difficult to specify the characteristics of the processes, their interrelations, and their effects on reading performance.

The nature of comprehension processes depends on a larger issue, namely the architecture of the processing system in which they are embedded. Although the human architecture is very far from being known, production systems have been suggested as a possible framework because they have several properties that might plausibly be shared by the human system. Detailed discussions of production systems as models of the human architecture are presented elsewhere

Figure 1. A Schematic Diagram of the Major Processes and Structures in Reading Comprehension

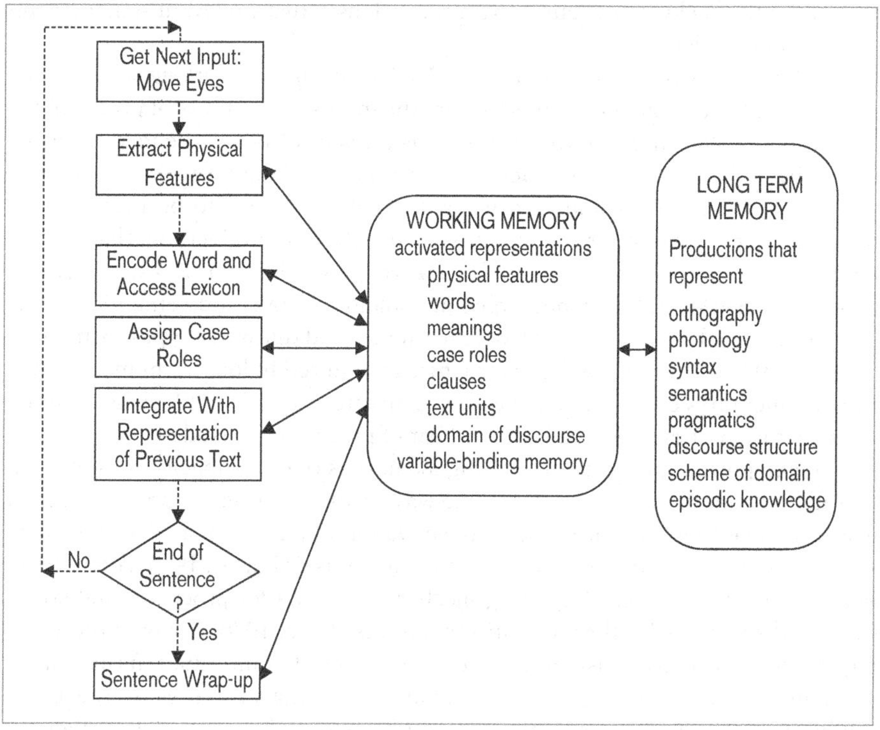

Solid lines denote data-flow paths, and dashed lines indicate canonical flow of control.

(Anderson, 1976; Newell, 1973, 1980). The following three major properties are of particular relevance here.

1. *Structural and procedural knowledge is stored in the form of condition–action rules, such that a given stimulus condition produces a given action.* The productions "fire" one after the other (serially), and it is this serial processing that consumes time in comprehension and other forms of thought. In addition to the serial productions, there are also fast, automatic productions that produce spreading activation among associated concepts (Anderson, 1976; Collins & Loftus, 1975). These automatic productions operate in parallel to the serial productions and in parallel to each other (Newell, 1980). These productions are fast and automatic because they operate only on constants; that is, they directly associate an action with a particular condition (such as activating the concept *dog* on detecting *cat*). By contrast, serial productions are slow because they operate on variables as well as constants; they associate an action with a class of conditions. A serial production can fire only after the particular condition instance is bound to the variable specified in the production. It may be the binding of variables that consumes

time and capacity (Newell, 1980). This architectural feature of two kinds of productions permits serial comprehension processes to operate in the foreground, whereas in the background, automatic productions activate relevant semantic and episodic knowledge.

2. *Productions operate on the symbols in a limited-capacity working memory.* The symbols are the activated concepts that are the inputs and outputs of productions. Items are inserted into working memory as a result of being encoded from the text or being inserted by a production. Retrieval from long-term memory occurs when a production fires and activates a concept, causing it to be inserted into working memory. Long-term memory is a collection of productions that are the repositories of both procedural and declarative knowledge. In the case of reading, this knowledge includes orthography, phonology, syntax, and semantics of the language, as well as schemas for particular topics and discourse types (Schank & Abelson, 1977). A new knowledge structure is acquired in long-term memory if a new production is created to encode that structure (Newell, 1980). This occurs if the structure participates in a large number of processing episodes.

One important property of working memory is that its capacity is limited, so that information is sometimes lost. One way in which capacity can be exceeded (causing forgetting) is that the level of activation of an item may decay to some subthreshold level through disuse over time (Collins & Loftus, 1975; Hitch, 1978; Reitman, 1974). A second forgetting mechanism allows for processes and structures to displace each other, within some limits (Case, 1978). Heavy processing requirements in a given task may decrease the amount of information that can be maintained, perhaps by generating too many competing structures or by actively inhibiting the maintenance of preceding information. There is recent evidence to suggest that working memory capacity (as opposed to passive memory span) is strongly correlated with individual differences in reading comprehension performance, presumably because readers with greater capacity can integrate more elements of the text at a given time (Daneman & Carpenter, in press).

3. *Production systems have a mechanism for adaptive sequencing of processes.* The items in working memory at a given time enable a given production to fire and insert new items, which in turn enable another production, and so on. In this way, the intermediate results of the comprehension process that are placed in working memory can influence or sequence subsequent processing. There is no need for a superordinate controlling program to sequence the mental actions.

The self-sequencing nature of productions is compatible with the model depicted in Figure 1. The composition of each stage is simply a collection of productions that share a common higher level goal. The productions within a stage have similar enabling conditions and produce actions that serve as conditions for other productions in the same stage. The productions within a stage need not be bound to each other in any other way. Thus the ordering of stages with a production system is accomplished not by direct control transfer mechanisms but an indirect self-sequencing accomplished by one production helping to create the conditions that enable the "next" production to fire.

This architecture permits stages to be executed not only in canonical orders but also in noncanonical orders. There are occasions when some stages of reading seem to be partially or entirely skipped; some stages seem to be executed out of sequence, and some "later" stages sometimes seem to be able to influence "earlier" stages (Levy, in press). Stages can be executed earlier than normal if their enabling conditions exist earlier than normal. For example, if a context strongly primes a case role, then the case assignment could precede the lexical access of a word. Having read *John pounded the nail with a* _____, a reader can assign the last word to the instrumental case on the basis of cues provided by the words *pound* and *nail*, before encoding *hammer*. This organization can permit "context effects" in comprehension, where a strong preceding context shortens reading time on a given word or clause. This might occur if a processing stage that is normally intermediate between two others is partially or entirely eliminated. It could be eliminated if the preceding stage plus the context provided sufficient enabling conditions for the later stage. Analogously, a misleading context could lengthen comprehension time by providing elements that enable conflicting processes.

The production system organization can also explain how "later" stages can influence "earlier" stages, so that higher level schemas can affect word encoding, for example. If the productions of the normally later stage are enabled earlier than usual, then their outputs can serve as inputs to the normally earlier stage. The ordering of stages does not have to be entirely reversed to obtain this top-down influence. It may be sufficient for just a portion of the productions of the "later" stage to fire in order to influence the "earlier" stage.

In this view of processing stages, several stages can be executed contemporaneously in the sense that firings of productions of two or more stages may be interleaved. Consequently, data and control can be transferred back and forth among different stages, somewhat similarly to computer programs organized into coroutines. Coroutines are two or more subprograms that have equal status (i.e., there is no master–slave relationship). When one coroutine obtains control, it executes until it detects a condition indicating it should relinquish control, and then another coroutine executes, and so on. One interesting difference between coroutines and the production system model is that coroutines generally transfer data between each other only along specified paths, used especially for this purpose. By contrast, productions "transfer" data by placing it in the working memory, so that all processes have access to it. In this sense, the working memory serves as a message center, and communication among stages is by means of the items in working memory. This is distinct from one stage feeding its output directly to another stage.

Research

Texts

This section describes the texts that were used in the reading research because their properties, both local and global, have a large influence on the processing.

The global organization of a narrative text has been shown to influence how a reader recalls the text (Kintsch & van Dijk, 1978; Mandler & Johnson, 1977; Meyer, 1975; Rumelhart, 1977b; Thorndyke, 1977). The experiment reported next shows that the organization has at least part of its effect when the text is being read. Scientific texts were selected from *Newsweek* and *Time* because their content and style are typical of what students read to learn about technical topics. The passages discussed a variety of topics that were generally unfamiliar to the readers in the study. When readers were asked to rate their familiarity with the topic of each passage on a 5-point scale, the modal rating was at the "entirely unfamiliar" end of the scale. There were 15 passages, averaging 132 words each. Although the texts are moderately well written, they are on the borderline between "fairly difficult" and "difficult" on Flesch's (1951) readability scale, with 17 words per sentence and 1.6 syllables per word. The following is an example of one of the passages:

> Flywheels are one of the oldest mechanical devices known to man. Every internal-combustion engine contains a small flywheel that converts the jerky motion of the pistons into the smooth flow of energy that powers the drive shaft. The greater the mass of a flywheel and the faster it spins, the more energy can be stored in it. But its maximum spinning speed is limited by the strength of the material it is made from. If it spins too fast for its mass, any flywheel will fly apart. One type of flywheel consists of round sandwiches of fiberglass and rubber providing the maximum possible storage of energy when the wheel is confined in a small space as in an automobile. Another type, the "superflywheel," consists of a series of rimless spokes. This flywheel stores the maximum energy when space is unlimited.

The content of the passages was analyzed by segmenting the text into idea units and categorizing these units by means of a simple text grammar. First, all of the 15 passages were segmented into text units called *sectors*, producing 274 sectors. The average sector length was seven words. Each sector was judged to be a single meaningful piece of information, whether it consisted of a word, phrase, clause, or sentence. The general criteria for segmentation into sectors were similar to those used by Meyer and McConkie (1973), who related such text units to recall performance.

A simplified grammar was developed to categorize the sectors of the texts. The grammar (shown schematically in Figure 2) classifies the text units into a structure that is quasi-hierarchical. This abbreviated grammar captures most of the regularities in our short passages (see Vesonder, 1979, for a more complete grammar for longer scientific passages). The initial sentences generally introduced a topic—a scientific development or event. The beginnings of the passage sometimes gave details of the time, place, and people involved with the discovery. Familiar concepts were simply named, whereas unusual concepts were accompanied by an explicit definition. The main topic itself was developed through specific examples or through subtopics that were then expanded with further descriptions, explanations, and concrete examples. Consequences, usually toward the end of the passage, stated the importance of the event for other applications. Table 1 shows how each text unit or sector in the "Flywheel" passage was classified

Figure 2. A Schematic Diagram of the Major Text-Grammatical Categories of Information in the Scientific Paragraphs

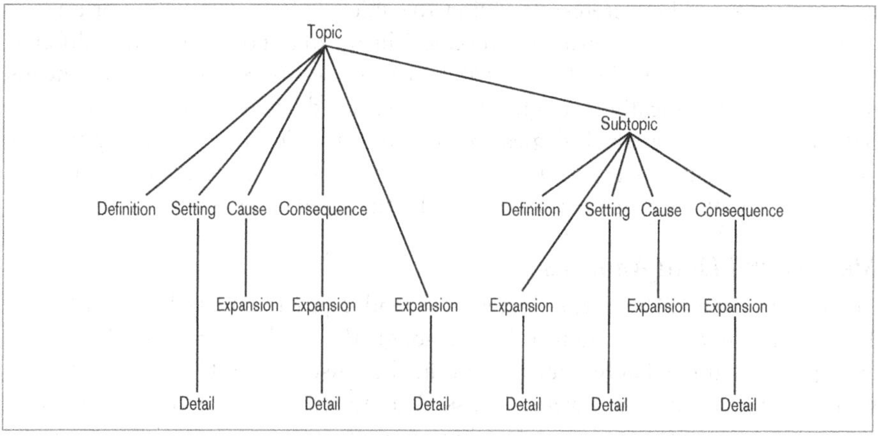

Table 1. A Classification of the "Flywheel" Passage Into Text-Grammatical Categories

Category	Sector
Topic	Flywheels are one of the oldest mechanical devices
Topic	known to man
Expansion	Every internal-combustion engine contains a small flywheel
Expansion	that converts the jerky motion of the pistons into the smooth flow of energy
Expansion	that powers the drive shaft
Cause	The greater the mass of a flywheel and the faster it spins,
Consequence	the more energy can be stored in it.
Subtopic	But its maximum spinning speed is limited by the strength of the material
Subtopic	it is made from.
Expansion	If it spins too fast for its mass,
Expansion	any flywheel will fly apart.
Definition	One type of flywheel consists of round sandwiches of fiberglass and rubber
Expansion	providing the maximum possible storage of energy
Expansion	when the wheel is confined in a small space
Detail	as in an automobile.
Definition	Another type, the "superflywheel," consists of a series of rimless spokes.
Expansion	This flywheel stores the maximum energy
Detail	when space is unlimited.

according to these categories. Each of the 274 sectors was assigned to one of the five levels of the grammar by one of the authors. The levels of the grammar were further confirmed by a pretest involving 16 subjects who rated the importance of each sector in its passage on a 7-point scale. The mean importance ratings differed reliably among the five levels $F(4, 270) = 40.04$, $p < .01$. Specifically, the means decreased monotonically through the five postulated levels. Hence, the grammar potentially has some psychological reality, and its relevance to reading will be demonstrated with the eye fixation data. The next section presents the data collection and analysis procedures, followed by the model and results.

Method and Data Analysis

The readers were 14 undergraduates who read 2 practice texts followed by the 15 scientific texts in random order. Although the readers were asked to recall each passage immediately after reading it, they also were told to read naturally without memorizing. They were also asked not to reread the passage or parts of it. The texts were presented on a television monitor using uppercase and lowercase letters and a conventional paragraph layout. To initiate the reading of a passage, the reader had to look at a fixation point (located where the first word of the paragraph would later appear) and press a "ready" button. If the reader's point of regard (as measured by the eye tracker) was within 1° of the fixation point, then exactly 500 msec later the passage appeared in its entirety on the screen. The passage appeared instantaneously (i.e., within one video frame) and remained there until the reader signaled that he had finished reading by pushing a response button.

The reader's pupil and corneal reflections were monitored relatively unobtrusively by a television camera that was 75 cm away. The monitoring system, manufactured by Applied Science Laboratories, computed the reader's point of regard (as opposed to eye or head position) every 16.7 msec. The accuracy of the tracker was verified before and after each passage was read by having the reader look at a fixation point and determining whether the obtained point of regard was within 1° of that point. This procedure indicated that accuracy was maintained during the reading of 195 of the 210 experimental passages in the entire experiment; the data from the 15 inaccurate trials were discarded.

Data reduction procedures converted the 60 observations per sec into fixations and then into gazes on each word. While the data were being acquired, a new "fixation" was scored as having occurred if the point of regard changed by more than 1° (the size of a three-letter syllable). The durations of blinks that were preceded and followed by fixations on the same location were attributed to the reading time on that location. Another program aggregated consecutive fixations on the same word into gazes and computed the duration of gaze on each of the 1,936 words in the 15 passages. Fixations on interword spaces were attributed to the word on the right because the perceptual span is centered to the right of the point of regard, at least for readers of left-to-right languages (McConkie & Rayner, 1976; Schiepers, 1980). The durations of saccades, blinks that occurred between words, regressions, and rereading were not included in the data analysis. Because of the instructions not to reread, these categories account for relatively little of the total reading time, approximately 12% in all. The mean duration of gaze on each word was computed by averaging over readers; these 1,936 mean gaze durations constitute the main dependent measure of interest.

The model presents a number of factors that influence various reading processes; some factors have their effect on individual words and some on larger units, such as clauses. The data were fit to the model with a multiple linear regression in which the independent variables were the factors postulated to affect reading time, and the dependent variable was the mean gaze duration on each word. Since the model also applies at the level of clauses and phrases, a second regression analysis was done at the phrase/clause level. The independent variables for the latter analysis were the factors postulated to affect reading time at the clause level, and the independent variable was the mean gaze duration on each of the 274 sectors described previously.

The psychological interpretation of the independent variables in the two regression analyses will be described in detail in the sections that follow. The equation for the analysis of the gaze duration on individual words was

$$GW_i = \Sigma a_m X_{im} + \epsilon_i,$$

where GW_i is the gaze duration on a word i, a_m is the regression weight in msec for independent variable X_m, and X_{im} are the independent variables that code the following seven properties of word i: (a) length, (b) the logarithm of its normative frequency, (c) whether the word occurs at the beginning of a line of text, (d) whether it is a novel word to the reader, (e) its case grammatical role (one of 11 possibilities), (f) whether it is the last word in a sentence, (g) whether it is the last word in a paragraph.

The equation for the analysis of the gaze duration on individual sectors was

$$GS_j = b_0 + \Sigma b_n Z_{jn} + \epsilon_j$$

where GS_j is the gaze duration on sector j, and b_n is the regression weight in msec for independent variable Z_n. The Z_{jn} are the independent variables that code the following eight properties of sector j: (a) its text grammatical level, multiplied by the number of content words; (b) length; (c) the sum of the logarithms of the frequencies of its component words; (d) the number of line-initial words it contains; (e) the number of novel words it contains; (f) the sum of the case role regression weights of its component words; (g) whether it is the last sector in a sentence; (h) whether it is the last sector in a paragraph.

Results

The mean gaze duration on each word (239 msec) indicated reading rates that are typical for texts of this difficulty. If the 239 msec per word is incremented by 12% to allow for saccades, blinks, and occasional rereading, the reading rate is

225 words per min. The standard deviation of the 239-msec gaze mean was 168 msec, indicating considerable variability in gaze duration from word to word. The results of the regression analyses are shown in Table 2. The table is divided into three sections, corresponding to the three major processing stages postulated by the model, encoding and lexical access, case role assignment, and interclause integration. The regression weights shown in Table 2 for the word-by-word analysis (above the double line) are derived from a regression equation involving 17 independent variables (11 of which are the case role indicator variables). The standard error of estimate of this model was 88 msec, and the R^2 value was .72. The results of the interclause integration stage make use of both the word-by-word analysis and the sector-by-sector analysis. (The latter analysis will be explained in more detail in the section on interclause integration.) Since the gaze durations

Table 2. Application of the Regression Model to the Gaze Duration on Each Word (Above Double Line) and to Each Sector (Below Double Line)

Processing Stage	Factor	Regression Weight (msec)
Encoding and lexical access	No. of syllables	52**
	Log frequency	53**
	Beginning of line	30**
	Novel word	802**
Case role assignment	Agent (86)	51**
	Instrument (110)	53**
	Direct or indirect object (174)	25*
	Adverb/manner (35)	29
	Place or time (64)	23
	Possessive (genitive) (39)	16
	Verb (368)	33**
	State/adjective (451)	44**
	Rhetorical word (15)	70**
	Determiner (243)	26**
	Connective (351)	9
Interclause integration	Last word in sentence	71**
	Last word in paragraph	157**
	Integration time per content word from regression analysis of data aggregated into sectors	
	Topic (22)	72**
	Definition/cause/consequence (23)	94**
	Subtopic (48)	78**
	Expansion (68)	73**
	Detail (113)	60**

Note. Frequency of occurrence of cast roles is in parentheses.
* $t = p < .05$; ** $t = p < .01$.

on successive words and phrases are time-series data, it is interesting to note that there was no reliable positive serial correlation among the residuals in the word-by-word regression or the sector-by-sector regression.

The Reading Model

The next five subsections describe the major stages shown in Figure 1: get next input, word encoding and lexical access, case role assignment, interclause integration, and sentence wrap-up. Each subsection describes the processes in that stage together with the factors that affect the duration of those processes, and hence the gaze durations.

Get Next Input

This is the first stage of a cycle that finds information, encodes it, and processes it. When the perceptual and semantic stages have done all of the requisite processing on a particular word, the eye is directed to land in a new place where it continues to rest until the requisite processing is done, and so forth. The specification of what constitutes "all of the requisite processing" is contained in a list of conditions that must be satisfied before the reader terminates the gaze on the current word and fixates the next one. These conditions include a specification of the goals of normal reading. For instance, one condition may be that a meaning of the word be accessed, and another condition may be that a case role be assigned. These conditions can also reflect more specific reading goals. A reader who is trying to memorize a text may have as a condition that the word or phrase be transferred to long-term memory. By setting the conditions appropriately, the reader can adjust his processes to the situation at hand. When the goal conditions for processing a word are satisfied, the resulting action is get next input.

The command to get next input usually results in a saccade to the next part of the text, one or two words forward. The process that selects the placement of the next forward fixation does not have to be very complex or intelligent. The choice of where to place the next forward fixation appears to depend primarily on the length of the next word or two to the right of the current fixation (McConkie & Rayner, 1975). The length information, which is encoded parafoveally, is then used to program a rightward saccade. However, if only the right margin is visible in the parafovea, then the eye is directed to the first word of the next line, producing a return sweep. In this case the information in peripheral vision is not adequate for accurate targeting. The return sweep is typically too short; the eye often lands on the second word of the new line for a brief amount of time (50 or 75 msec) and then makes a corrective saccade leftward to the first word of the line (Bayle, 1942). On occasion, a comprehension stage may require a review of previously read text to reencode it or process it to deeper levels. In those cases, the get next input stage results in a regressive saccade to the relevant portion of the text.

The duration of the get next input stage is short, consisting of the time for a neural signal to be transmitted to the eye muscles. In monkeys, this takes about 30 msec (Robinson, 1972). This duration must not be confused with the typical

150- to 200-msec latency of a saccade to a visual stimulus that has spatial or temporal uncertainty (Westheimer, 1954). These latencies include stimulus detection, interpretation, and selection of the next fixation target. In normal reading, there is very little uncertainty about direction of the next saccade (it is almost always rightward for forward fixations, except for the return sweeps), nor is there much uncertainty about distance. On the average, the saccade distance may be simply the mean center-to-center distance between words, a distance that does not vary much, relative to the physically possible variation in eye movements. Thus it is reasonable to suppose that the preprogramming time is very short here, consisting usually of a "go" signal and the time it takes that signal to be translated into a motor movement, about 30 msec (Robinson, 1972). The actual movements, the saccades, constitute about 5%–10% of the total reading time. Recent analyses suggest that the saccade itself may destroy the visual persistence of the information from the preceding fixation so that it does not mask the input from the new fixation (Breitmeyer, 1980). Consequently, it is reasonable to assume that stimulus encoding can commence soon after the eye arrives at a new location.

Word Encoding and Lexical Access

The reading process involves encoding a word into an internal semantic format. It is assumed that prior to this encoding, the transduction from the printed word to the visual features has already taken place, and that the features have been deposited into the working memory. Perceptual encoding productions use the visual features as conditions; their action is to activate the representation of the word. Once the representation of the word has been sufficiently activated, its corresponding concept is accessed and inserted into working memory. The concept serves as a pointer to a more complete representation of the meaning, which consists of a small semantic network realized as a set of productions. The major nodes of the network are the possible meanings of the word, the semantic and syntactic properties of the meanings, and information about the contexts in which they usually occur (see Rieger, 1979, for a related proposal). The word meanings are represented as abstract predicates, defined by their relations to other predicates.

The productions that encode a word generally trigger on orthographically based subword units such as syllables (Mewhort & Beal, 1977; Spoehr & Smith, 1973; Taft, 1979). However, there are times when alternative codes, including orthographic, phonological, and whole-word codes, are used (Baron, 1977; Kleiman, 1975; LaBerge & Samuels, 1974). Since the syllablelike encoding is believed to be the dominant mode, the data were analyzed in terms of the number of syllables in each word. Encoding time increased by 52 msec for each syllable, as shown in Table 2.

The mechanism underlying lexical access is the activation of a word's meaning representation by various sources. There are three ways that a concept's level of activation can be temporarily increased above its base level. One activation mechanism is perceptual encoding; the encoded representation of a word can activate its meaning. A second source is the parallel productions that produce spreading activation through the semantic and episodic knowledge base of the reader. The third source is activation by the serial productions that do the major computations in all of the stages of processing. When a concept has been activated above some threshold by one or more of these sources, a pointer to its meaning is inserted into working memory. The activation level gradually decays to a subthreshold level unless some process reactivates it. If the word soon reoccurs in the text while the concept is still activated, lexical access will be facilitated because the activation level will still be close to threshold. When the activation level does decrease, it decreases to an asymptote slightly higher than the old base level. In this way, the system can learn from both local and long-term word repetitions. Frequently used words will have a high base level of activation, and consequently will require relatively less additional activation to retrieve them. Thus, frequent words should take less time to access than infrequent words (Morton, 1969). Similarly, the various possible interpretations of each word will have different base activation levels, such that the more common interpretations have higher base activation levels. For example, although the word *does* has at least two very different meanings, the "third-person-singular verb" interpretation would have a higher base activation because it is more common than the "female deer" interpretation (Carpenter & Daneman, 1980). The more common interpretation would then be accessed faster, since less additional activation would be required to bring the activation level to threshold. This model of lexical access can account for word frequency effects, priming effects, and repetition effects in reading.

The gaze duration showed both frequency and repetition effects. Frequency was analyzed by relating gaze duration to the logarithm of the normative frequency of each word, based on the Kučera and Francis (1967) norms. It was expected that gaze duration would decrease with the logarithm of the word's frequency; that is, small differences among infrequent words would be as important as much larger differences among frequent words (Mitchell & Green, 1978). For algebraic convenience, the normative frequencies were increased by one (to eliminate the problem of taking the logarithm of zero), and the logarithm was computed and then subtracted from 4.85, the logarithm of the frequency of the most frequent English word. The analysis indicated a clear relation between this measure of frequency and gaze duration. As shown in Table 2, gaze duration increased by 53 msec for each log unit of decrease in word frequency. A moderately frequent word like *water* (with a frequency of 442) was accessed 140 msec faster than a word that did not appear in the norms.

At one extreme of the frequency dimension are words that a reader has never encountered before. In scientific passages, the novel words tend to be technical terms. To read these words, a reader cannot depend on contacting some prior perceptual and semantic representation; neither exists. The reader must construct some perceptual representation (perhaps phonological as well as orthographic), associate this with the semantic and syntactic properties of the concept that can be inferred from the passage, and then possibly construct a lexical entry. These processes seem to take a great deal more time than ordinary encoding and access processes. Two judges identified seven words in the texts (that had zero frequency) as probably entirely novel to the readers. Novelty was coded as an indicator variable, and it was found that these words took an additional 802 msec on average to process, as shown in Table 2. However, there was considerable variability among the words; their gaze durations ranged from 913 msec (for *staphylococci*) to 2,431 msec (for *thermoluminescence*).

Once a word has been encoded and accessed once, it should be easier to access it when it occurs again. Other research has suggested that frequency and repetition have their primary effect on lexical access rather than encoding (Dixon & Rothkopf, 1979; Glanzer & Ehrenreich, 1979; Scarborough, Cortese, & Scarborough, 1977), although the possibility of some small effects on the encoding process does exist. According to the model, repetition effects should occur in reading because the first time a word meaning is accessed, it should temporarily achieve a higher activation level similar to the level of a more frequent word. This mechanism particularly predicts repetition effects for infrequent words, whose activation levels are low to start with, but not for the highly frequent words that occur in natural text. Generally, repetition effects are larger for low-frequency words (Scarborough et al., 1977). "Low frequency" in the Scarborough study was defined as less than 28 occurrences per million, the boundary of 28 emerging from a median split of the frequencies of their stimuli. So the analysis of repetition effects was limited to words with frequencies of 25 occurrences per million or less. There were 346 such instances in the text; 251 were initial occurrences and 95 were repetitions. The repetitions were words with the same morphological stem, disregarding affixes. An analysis of covariance on this subset of the data examined the effects of repetitions covarying out the number of syllables. The adjusted mean gaze durations were 49 msec longer on the initial appearance of these words than on the subsequent appearances, $t(343) = 2.21$, $p < .03$. Most of this effect (43 msec) was obtained on the second appearance of a word. These results indicate that once an infrequent word appears in a text, processing time on that word is decreased on subsequent appearances.

Lexical access is complicated by the fact that some words have more than one meaning, so the appropriate interpretation must be selected, or at least guessed at. When a polysemous word is accessed, the word representation that is retrieved is a pointer to a semantic network that includes the multiple representations. The interpretation that is selected is the one with the highest activation level, and several factors can affect the activation. First, some interpretations start off with a higher activation level; for instance, the "third-person-singular" interpretation of *does* has a higher base activation level than the "deer" interpretation. Second, the automatic productions that produce spreading activation can contribute selectively to the activation level of one particular interpretation. The spreading activation can emanate from the preceding semantic and syntactic context, from the reader's knowledge of the domain, and from knowledge of the discourse style. Third, the output of other stages operating on the same word may activate a particular interpretation. For example, although *hammer* can be interpreted as a noun or a verb, a sentence context that suggests an instrument to the case role assignment stage (e.g., *John hit the nail with a* _____) may help activate the noun interpretation. Fourth, when a word with many highly related meanings occurs in an impoverished context, there may be no single interpretation with higher activation than the others, and the superordinate concept may be the selected interpretation of the word. This probably occurs for words that have many closely related interpretations, such as *get* and *take*.

The selection of only one interpretation of each word, posited by the immediacy assumption, provides a measure of cognitive economy. Selecting just one interpretation allows the activation of the unselected interpretations to decay, preventing them from activating their associates. Thus, the contextual effects would remain focused in the appropriate semantic domain. This permits a limited-capacity working memory to cope with the information flow in a spreading activation environment that may activate many interpretations and associations for any lexical item. This method of processing also avoids the combinatorial explosion that results from entertaining more than one interpretation for several successive words.

This aspect of the model is consistent with some recent results on lexical access that indicate that although multiple meanings of a word are initially activated, only one meaning remains activated after a few hundred milliseconds. In one experiment, the subjects simultaneously listened to a sentence and pronounced a visually presented word. When an ambiguous word (*rose*) was presented auditorally in a syntactic context (e.g., *They all rose*), the speed of pronouncing a simultaneous visual probe related to either meaning (stood or flower) was faster than in a control condition (Tanenhaus, Leiman, & Seidenberg, 1979). In another experiment, the subjects listened to a sentence and performed a lexical decision task on visually presented stimuli. When an ambiguous word (*bug*) was presented in a semantic context (*John saw several spiders, roaches, and bugs*), the speed of a simultaneous lexical decision related to either meaning (insect or spy) was faster than a control (Swinney, 1979). In both studies, the facilitation of the inappropriate meaning was obtained only within a few hundred milliseconds of the occurrence of the ambiguous word. If the probe was delayed longer, the inappropriate interpretation was no faster than the control. These results suggest that both meanings are available when an ambiguous word is being accessed, but the inappropriate meaning is lost from working memory after a short time.

As the interpretation of the text is constructed, a corresponding representation of the extensive meaning—the things being talked about—is also being built. If the referents of the words in a passage cannot be determined, the text will be more difficult to understand. One example of this problem is highlighted in a passage from Bransford and Johnson (1973) concerning a procedure that involved arranging "things into groups. Of course, one may be sufficient depending on how much there is...." (p. 400). Subjects who were not given the title *Washing Clothes* thought the story was incomprehensible. The referential representation helps the reader disambiguate referents, infer relations, and integrate the text.

The immediacy assumption posits that an attempt to relate each content word to its referent occurs as soon as possible. Sometimes this can be done when the word is first fixated, but sometimes more information is required. For example, although the semantic interpretation of a relative adjective like *large* can be computed immediately, the extensive meaning depends on the word it modifies (e.g., *large insect* vs. *large building*). The referent of the entire noun phrase can be computed only after both words are processed. The immediacy assumption does not state that the relating is done immediately on each content word, but rather that it occurs as soon as possible. This is an important distinction that will be made again in the discussion on integrative processes.

Assigning Case Roles

Comprehension involves determining the relations among words, the relations among clauses, and the relations among whole units of text. This section describes the first of these processes, that of determining the relations among the words in a clause (or in Schank's, 1972, terms, determining the dependencies among the concepts). These relations can be categorized into semantic cases, such as agent, recipient, location, time, manner, instrument, action, or state (Chafe, 1970; Fillmore, 1968). The case role assignment process usually takes as input a representation of the fixated word, including information about its possible case roles and syntactic properties. For example, hammers tend to be instruments rather than locations or recipients, and information about a word's usual case role can be an important contributor to the assignment process. But this normative information generally is not sufficient to assign its case role in a particular clause. Consequently, the assignment process relies on heuristics that use the word meaning together with information about the prior semantic and syntactic context, as well as language-based inferences. The output of the process is a representation of the word's semantic role with respect to the other constituents in its clause.

Just as certain meanings suggest particular case roles, so, too, can the context prime a particular case role. Consider the sentence *John was interrogated by the* _____. The semantic and syntactic cues suggest that the missing word will be an agent, such as *detective*. The strength of the context becomes evident if the primed case does not occur, for example, *John was interrogated by the window*. The prior semantic context can precede the affected case assignment by more than a few words. In the sentences *The lawyer wanted to know where in the room John had been interrogated* and *Mary told him that John was interrogated by the window*, the thematic focus of the first sentence on a location alters the interpretation of *by* and facilitates a locative case role assignment for *window*.

The specific heuristics that are used in case role assignment have received some attention (see Clark & Clark, 1977, for some examples). Many proposals contain the suggestion that readers use the verb as a pivotal source of information to establish the necessary and possible case roles and then fit the noun phrases into those slots (Schank, 1972). But the immediacy assumption posits that the case role assignment for an item preceding the verb is not postponed in anticipation of the verb. Similar to the lexical access stage, the case assignment stage makes a best guess about a word's case when the word is fixated, rather than making the decision contingent on subsequent words. So, the model would not accord any special status to verbs. Another suggested heuristic (that children appear to use) is to assign a sequence consisting of animate noun–verb–noun to the case roles of agent–action–object (Bever, 1970). Like all heuristics, this one sometimes fails, so young children sometimes misinterpret passive sentences (Fraser, Bellugi, & Brown, 1963). This heuristic may be employed by adults, but in a modified version that conforms to the immediacy assumption. Rather than waiting for the three major constituents before assigning case roles, the reader should assign an animate noun to the agent role as soon as it is encountered, in the absence of contrary prior context.

The immediate assignment of a case role implies that readers will sometimes make errors and have to revise previous decisions. For example, an adult who assigns the role of agent to an animate noun and then encounters a passive verb will have to revise the agent assignment. (Presumably, young children do not make this revision.) The immediacy of the case assignment process is evident in the reading of sentences such as *Mary loves Jonathan....* The immediacy assumption suggests that a reader would assign to *Jonathan* the role of recipient; this would in turn result in an incorrect assignment if the sentence continued *Mary loves Jonathan apples.*

Because case roles are assigned within clauses, the assignment process must include a segmentation procedure to determine clause boundaries within sentences. Sentences can sometimes be segmented into clauses on the basis of explicit markers, such as a subordinating conjunction (e.g., *because, when*). More often, the reader cannot tell with certainty where one clause ends and another starts until beyond the clause boundary (or potential boundary). A general strategy for dealing with such cases has been suggested, namely to assign a word to the clause being processed, if possible (Frazier & Fodor, 1978). For example, the word *soil* in the sentence *When farmers are plowing the soil...* can continue the initial clause (*When farmers are plowing the soil, it is most fertile*) or start a new one (*When farmers are plowing the soil is most fertile*). The suggested strategy is to continue the initial clause until contrary information is encountered. Interestingly, the strategy discussed by Frazier and Fodor (1978) presupposes the immediacy assumption; the segmentation decision arises because case roles are assigned as soon as the words are encountered.

There is no direct mapping between particular case roles and the duration of the assignment process. For example, there is no a priori reason to expect that assignment of instruments takes more or less time than locations. The time for a particular assignment might depend more on the context and properties of the word than on the particular case role being assigned. Detailed specification of the process is not within the scope of this article; it probably requires a large-scale simulation model to examine the complex interactions of different levels of processing. Nevertheless, we examined whether, all things being equal, different case role assignments tend to take different amounts of time.

The analysis included the usual case roles just noted (Fillmore, 1968), as well as other categories such as determiners and adjectives that are not cases but still play a part in the parsing and assignment process. Each word was classified into 1 of 11 categories: verb, agent, instrument, indirect or direct object, location or time, adverb, adjective or state, connective (preposition or conjunction), possessive, determiner, and rhetorical word (such as *well*). Some cases were pooled (such as location and time) because they were relatively infrequent in the text and because they have some conceptual similarity. The case roles were coded as indicator variables and were all entered into the regression with the intercept forced to zero.

The results of the case role assignment analysis, shown in Table 2, indicate that there are some variations among the cases. As expected, verbs did not take particularly long (33 msec), and in fact, although the time was significantly different from 0, it was not greater than the agent or instrument cases (51 msec and 53 msec, respectively). Four cases had parameters that were not significantly different from 0, connectives (9 msec), adverb/manner (29 msec), place or time (23 msec), and possessives (16 msec). These parameters could reflect some properties of particular word classes, in addition to parsing and case role assignment processes. For example, if a connective (e.g., *and* or *but*) simply takes less time to access than other words, the advantage should appear in this parameter. However, the parameters are not due solely to length or frequency, since these variables make a separate contribution to the regression equation. Although this analysis does not examine any of the contextual effects thought to be of some importance in the case assignment process, it does indicate roughly the relative amount of time spent assigning various categories of words to their case roles in a clause. Later theories will have to account for the precise pattern of case assignment durations in terms of specific operations that use prior context and word meanings to assign the various cases.

Interclause Integration

Clauses and sentences must be related to each other by the reader to capture the coherence in the text. As each new clause or sentence is encountered, it must be integrated with the previous information acquired from the text or with the knowledge retrieved from the reader's long-term memory. Integrating the new sentence with the old information consists of representing the relations between the new and the old structures.

Several search strategies may be used to locate old information that is related to the new information. One strategy is to check if the new information is related to the other information that is already in working memory either because it has been repeatedly referred to or because it is recent (Carpenter & Just, 1977a; Kintsch & van Dijk, 1978). Using this strategy implies that adjacency between clauses and sentences will cause a search for a possible relation. For instance, the adjacent sentences *Mary hurt herself* and *John laughed* seem related (John must be a cad) even though there is no explicit mention of the relation. This strategy also entails trying to relate new information to a topic that is active in working memory. This is a good strategy, since information in a passage should be related to the topic.

A second strategy is to search for specific connections based on cues in the new sentence itself. Sentences often contain old information as well as new. Sometimes the old information is explicitly marked (as in cleft constructions and relative clauses), but often it is simply some argument repeated from the prior text. The reader can use this old information to search his or her long-term text representation and referential representation for potential points of attachment between the new information and the old (Haviland & Clark, 1974). This second strategy may take more time than the first. In fact, it takes longer to read a sentence that refers to information introduced several sentences earlier than one that refers to recently introduced information (Carpenter & Just, 1977a).

There are two main points at which integration can occur. First, as each ensuing word of the text is encountered, there is an attempt to relate it to previous information (Just & Carpenter, 1978). Second, a running representation of the clause is maintained, with an updating as each word of the clause is read. This running clause representation consists of the configuration of clause elements arranged according to their case relations. This second type of integration involves an attempt to relate the running clause representation to previous information at each update. Integration occurs whenever a linking relation can be computed. Consider the sentence *Although he spoke softly, yesterday's speaker could hear the little boy's question*. The point of this example is not so much that the initial integration of *he* and *speaker* is incorrect, but that the integration is attempted at the earliest opportunity. This model implies that integration time may be distributed over fixations on different parts of a clause. Moreover, the duration of the process may depend on the number of concepts in the clause; as these increase, the number of potential points of contact between the new clause and previous information will increase. There is also evidence for integration triggered by the end of the sentence; this process is discussed next in more detail.

Integration results in the creation of a new structure. The symbol representing that structure is a pointer to the integrated concepts, and this superordinate symbol is then available for further processing. In this way, integration can chunk the incoming text and allows a limited working memory to deal with large segments of prose. The macrorules proposed by Kintsch and van Dijk (1978) can be construed as productions that integrate.

Integration can also lead to forgetting in working memory. As each new chunk is formed, there is a possibility that it will displace some previous information from working memory. Particularly vulnerable are items that are only marginally activated, usually because they were processed much earlier and have not recently participated in a production. For instance, the representation of a clause will decay if it was processed early in a text and was not related to subsequent information. This mechanism can also clear working memory of "lower level" representations that are no longer necessary. For example, the verbatim representation of a previously read sentence may be displaced by the processes that integrated the sentence with other information (Jarvella, 1971). By contrast, the semantic elements that participate in an integration production obtain an increased activation level. This increases the probability that they will become a permanent part of long-term memory.

The main types of interclause relations in the scientific passages correspond to the text-grammatical categories described previously, such as definitions, causes, consequences, examples, and so forth. Text roles that are usually more important to the text and to the reader's goals, such as topics or definitions, are integrated differently than less important units, such as details. The more central units will initiate more retrievals of relevant previous knowledge of the domain (schematic knowledge) and retrievals of information acquired from the text but no longer resident in the working memory. In addition, more relations will be computed between the semantically central propositions and previous information because centrality inherently entails relations with many other units. By contrast, details are often less important to the reader's goals and to the text. Moreover, when a detail is to be integrated, the process is simpler because details are often concrete instantiations of an immediately preceding statement (at least in these scientific texts), so they can be quickly appended to information still present in the working memory. Thus, higher level units will take more time to integrate because their integration is usually essential to the reader's goals, and because integration of higher units involves more relations to be computed and more retrievals to be made.

The nature of the link relating two structures may be explicitly denoted either in the text (with connectives like *because*, *therefore*, and *for instance*) or it may have to be inferred on the basis of schematic knowledge of the domain. For example, the causal relation between the sentences *Cynthia fell off the rocking horse* and *She cried bitter tears* is inferred from the reader's knowledge about the temporal and causal relation between falling and hurting oneself (Charniak, 1972).

The model predicts that the gaze duration on a sector depends on its text-grammatical role and on the number of concepts it contains. Because integration can occur at many points in a sector, the gaze duration associated with integration cannot be localized to a particular word. Thus, to do the clause level of analysis, the gaze durations on the individual words of a sector were cumulated, producing a total of 274 sector gaze durations as the dependent variable. The independent variables were the aggregates of the word-level variables, except for case roles. The independent variable that coded the case-role effect for a sector was the sum of the case-coefficients (obtained from the word-by-word regression analysis) for each of the words in the sector. A new independent variable coded the text-grammatical role of a sector and its number of content words; it was the interaction of the indicator variables that represented the five text-grammatical levels and the number of content words in the sector, with content words defined as in Hockett (1958).

The results indicate that the integration time for a given sector depends on its text-grammatical role. The portion of Table 2 below the double line shows the integration time per content word for each type of sector. Generally, more important or central sectors take longer to integrate. The model describes this effect in terms of the integrative processes initiated by the semantics of the different types of information and their relevance to the reader's goals. An analysis of covariance examined the effect of text roles covarying out the number of syllables. The adjusted mean gaze durations differed reliably, $F(4, 268) = 8.82$, $p < .01$; paired comparisons indicated that details took significantly less time than all other roles, and expansions took significantly less time than topics and definitions/causes/consequences (all *p*s $< .01$). These results quantitatively and qualitatively replicate those reported previously for a slightly different paradigm (Carpenter & Just, in press). The previously obtained coefficients for the five text-grammatical categories were 65, 106, 81, 76, and 47 msec per content word, respectively, corresponding to the newly obtained 72, 94, 78, 73, and 60. The model accounts very well for the sector-level data. The R^2 value was .94, and the standard error of estimate was 234. The mean gaze duration on a sector was 1,690 msec, with a standard deviation of 902 msec, and the mean sector length was 4.9 words.[1]

One cost of immediate interpretation, case role assignment, and integration is that some decisions will prove to be incorrect. There must be mechanisms to detect and recover from such errors. The detection of a misinterpretation often occurs when new information to be integrated is inconsistent with previous information. Thus, misinterpretation detection may be construed as inconsistency detection. For example, the sentence *There were tears in her brown dress* causes errors initially because the most frequent interpretation of *tears* is not the appropriate one here, and the initial interpretation is incompatible with *dress*. The eye fixations of subjects reading such garden path sentences clearly indicate that readers do detect inconsistencies, typically at the point at which the inconsistency is first evident (Carpenter & Daneman, 1980). At that point, they use a number of error-recovery heuristics that enable them to reinterpret the text. They do not start reinterpreting the sentence from its beginning. The heuristics point them to the locus of the probable error. Readers start the backtracking with the word that first reveals the inconsistency, in this case, *dress*. If that word cannot be reinterpreted, they make regressions to the site of other words that were initially difficult to interpret, such as ambiguous words on which a best guess about word meaning had to be made. The ability to return directly to the locus of the misinterpretation and to recover from an error makes the immediacy strategy feasible.

Sentence Wrap-Up

A special computational episode occurs when a reader reaches the end of a sentence. This episode, called sentence wrap-up, is not a stage of processing defined by its function, but rather by virtue of being executed when the reader reaches the end of a sentence. The processes that occur during sentence wrap-up involve a search for referents that have not been assigned, the construction of interclause relations (with the aid of inferences, if necessary), and an attempt to handle any inconsistencies that could not be resolved within the sentence.

The ends of sentences have two important properties that make them especially good places for integration. First, within-sentence ambiguities are usually clarified by the end of the sentence. For example, if a sentence introduces a new object or person whose identity cannot be inferred from the preceding context, some cue to their identity is generally given by the end of the sentence. For that reason, if readers cannot immediately determine the referent of a particular word, then they can expect to be told the referent or given enough information to infer it by the end of the sentence. Indeed, readers do use the ends of sentences to process inconsistencies that they cannot resolve within the sentence (Carpenter & Daneman, 1980). The second property is that the end of a sentence unambiguously signals the end of one thought and the beginning of a new one. It can be contrasted with weaker cues that signal within-sentence clause boundaries such as commas, relative pronouns, and conjunctions that can signal other things besides the end of a clause. Since ends of sentences are unambiguous, they have the same role across sentences, and they may be processed more uniformly than the cues to within-sentence clause boundaries.

There is ample empirical support for the integrative processing at the ends of sentences. Previous eye fixation studies show that when a lexically based inference must be made to relate a new sentence to some previous portion of the text, there is a strong tendency to pause at the lexical item in question and at the end of the sentence that contains it (Just & Carpenter, 1978). Readers were given paragraphs containing pairs of related sentences; the first noun in the second sentence was the agent or instrument of the verb in the first sentence:

(1a) *It was dark and stormy the night the millionaire was murdered.*

(1b) *The killer left no clues for the police to trace.*

In another condition, the integrating inference was less direct:

(2a) *It was dark and stormy the night the millionaire died.*

(2b) *The killer left no clues for the police to trace.*

It took about 500 msec longer to process Sentence 2b than 1b, presumably due to the more difficult inference linking *killer* to *die*. There were two main places in which the readers paused for those 500 msec, indicating the points at which the inference was being computed. One point was on the word *killer*, and the other was on the end of the sentence containing *killer*. Another eye fixation study showed that integration linking a pronoun to its antecedent can occur either when the pronoun is first encountered or at the end of the sentence containing the pronoun (Carpenter & Just, 1977b).

Reading-time studies also have shown that there is extra processing at the end of a sentence. When subjects self-pace the word-by-word or phrase-by-phrase presentation of a text, they tend to pause longer at the word or phrase that terminates a sentence (Aaronson & Scarborough, 1976; Mitchell & Green, 1978). The pause has been attributed to contextual integration processes, similar to the proposed interclause integration process here. Yet another source of evidence for sentence wrap-up processes is that verbatim memory for recently comprehended text declines after a sentence boundary (Jarvella, 1971; Perfetti & Lesgold, 1977). The model attributes the decline to the interference between sentence wrap-up processes and the maintenance of verbatim information in working memory. Finally, another reason to expect sentence wrap-up processes is that we have observed pauses at sentence terminations in an eye fixation study similar to the one reported here (Carpenter & Just, in press). However, the current study provides stronger evidence because the text was presented all at once.

The results indicate that readers did pause longer on the last word in a sentence. As Table 2 shows, the duration of the sentence wrap-up period is 71 msec.

It is possible that wrap-up episodes could occur at the ends of text units smaller or larger than a sentence. For example, the data of Aaronson and Scarborough (1976) suggest that there are sometimes wrap-up processes at the ends of clauses. It is also possible that wrap-up could occur under some circumstances at the ends of paragraphs. The decision of when and if to do a wrap-up may be controlled by the desired depth of processing. For example, skimming may require wrap-up only at paragraph terminations, whereas understanding a legal contract may require wrap-up at clause boundaries. In fact, the clause-boundary effects obtained by Aaronson and Scarborough are sensitive to the subjects' reading goals. The current analysis indicated that the final word in the paragraph might also be a wrap-up point; it received an additional 157 msec of fixation. However, since readers also pressed a button to indicate that they had finished reading the passage, this parameter might be influenced by their motor response.

Finally, the model included one other factor that involves a physical property of reading, namely the return sweep of the eyes from the right-hand side of one line of text to the left-hand side of the next line. Return sweeps are often inaccurate, landing to the right of the first word in a line. The inaccuracy is often corrected by a leftward saccade to the first word. As a result of this error and recovery, the first word on a line eventually receives an increased gaze duration, relative to a line-medial word. Almost all readers we have studied display the undershoot, but there are considerable individual differences in whether they compensate for it by making an extra leftward fixation to the first word. In fact, some researchers have associated these corrective leftward movements with poor readers (Bayle, 1942). To test for increased gaze durations on line-initial words, an indicator variable coded whether a word was the first one on a line. As Table 2 shows, these words received an additional 30 msec of fixation.

Fit of the Model

To see how well the model accounts for the data, one can informally compare how closely the estimated gaze durations match the observed gaze durations. The display that follows shows the estimated (in italics) and observed (in msec) gaze durations for two sentences from the "Flywheel" passage. The estimated durations can be computed by an appropriate combination of the weights given in Table 2. These estimates take into account the processes of encoding, lexical access, case-role assignment, sentence wrap-up, and the beginning of the line effect; they do not include integration time for text roles, since there is no way to distribute this time on a word-by-word basis. In spite of this, the match is satisfactory, and as mentioned earlier, the standard error of estimate was 88 msec overall.

169 215 165 295 290 73 196 504 29 482 0 328
165 236 75 409 304 75 249 438 75 413 80 338
...One type of flywheel consists of round sandwiches of fiberglass and rubber

431 51 369 326 308 22 272 253 128 199 69 336 32 41
349 78 354 318 297 75 378 138 77 239 128 326 87 102
providing the maximum possible storage of energy when the wheel is confined in a

267 197 70 164 195 340 323 182 72 626 276 46 21
206 209 112 87 127 465 334 236 77 513 304 75 102
small space as in an automobile. Another type, the "superflywheel," consists of a

346 60 467 519
289 75 361 319
series of rimless spokes...

Table 3 presents an analogous comparison from the sector-by-sector analysis; this includes integration time. Again, the estimates from the model match the observed data quite well. The standard error of estimate was 234 msec overall.

Another way to evaluate the goodness of fit is to compare the regression results to those of another model that lacks most of the theoretically interesting independent variables and contains only the variable that codes the number of syllables. For the word-by-word analysis, this rudimentary model produces an R^2 of .46, compared to .72 for the complete model. For the sector-by-sector analysis, the rudimentary model accounts for a large portion of the variance between the gaze durations on sectors ($R^2 = .87$). This is not surprising, since there is considerable variation in their lengths. The complete sector-by-sector model accounts for 94% of the variance, or 54% of the variance unaccounted for by the reduced model.

The regression equations were also fit to the gaze durations of each of the 14 readers individually. The subjects varied in their reading skill, with self-reported Scholastic Aptitude Test scores ranging from 410 to 660, which were correlated with their reading speeds in the experiment, ranging from 186 words per min. to 377 words per min. $r(12) = .54$, $p < .05$. The mean R^2 of the 14 readers was .36 on the word-by-word analysis and .75 on the sector-by-sector analysis. This indicates

Table 3. Observed and Estimated Gaze Durations (msec) on Each Sector of the "Flywheel" Passage, According to the Sector-by-Sector Regression Analysis of the Group Data

Sector	Observed	Estimated
Flywheels are one of the oldest mechanical devices	1,921	1,999
known to man.	478	680
Every internal-combustion engine contains a small flywheel	2,316	2,398
that converts the jerky motion of the pistons into the smooth flow of energy	2,477	2,807
that powers the drive shaft.	1,056	1,264
The greater the mass of a flywheel and the faster it spins,	2,143	2,304
the more energy can be stored in it.	1,270	1,536
But its maximum spinning speed is limited by the strength of the material	2,440	2,553
it is made from.	615	780
If it spins too fast for its mass,	1,414	1,502
any flywheel will fly apart.	1,200	1,304
One type of flywheel consists of round sandwiches of fiberglass and rubber	2,746	3,064
providing the maximum possible storage of energy	1,799	1,870
when the wheel is confined in a small space	1,522	1,448
as in an automobile.	769	718
Another type, the "superflywheel," consists of a series of rimless spokes.	2,938	2,830
This flywheel stores the maximum energy	1,416	1,596
when space is unlimited.	1,289	1,252

substantial noise in each reader's word-by-word data. Some of the regression weights of the readers indicated considerable individual differences with respect to certain processes. For example, 4 of the 14 readers spent no extra time on the last word of a sentence. Another parameter of great variability among readers was the extra time spent on novel words, which ranged from 94 msec to 1,490 msec.

Although the sector-by-sector regression analysis uses an independent variable (the sum of the case role coefficients) that is estimated from the same data, this procedure does not do violence to the results. To estimate the effect of this procedure, the 14 subjects were divided randomly into two subgroups, and the case-role coefficients were obtained for each subgroup in a word-by-word analysis. Then these coefficients were aggregated and used as independent variables in a sector-by-sector analysis, such that one subgroup's coefficients were used in the analysis of the other subgroup's sector gaze durations. The results indicated no difference of any importance between the two subanalyses, and generally confirmed that using the case role coefficients from the word analysis in the sector analysis was an acceptable procedure.

Some of the variables that were reliable in the word-by-word analysis were not reliable in the sector analysis. For example, sectors that included a line-initial word did not have reliably longer durations, and sectors that included the end of a sentence took 57 msec longer, but the reliability of the effect was marginal ($p < .08$). The sum of the logarithms of the frequencies of the words in a sector did not reliably affect gaze duration on the sector. These differences between the two levels of analysis indicate that some effects that are word specific are not reliable or large enough to be detected when the data are aggregated over groups of words. Nevertheless, some of these effects can be detected at the sector level if the appropriate analysis is done. For example, the reason that the frequency effect was not reliable is that the aggregation of the logarithms smooths over the differences between infrequent words and frequent words. A regression analysis of the sector data shows a reliable word frequency effect if the independent variable encodes the number of infrequent words (arbitrarily defined as less than 25 in Kučera & Francis, 1967) occurring for the first time. This latter analysis indicates 82-msec extra spent for each infrequent word, and has an R^2 of .94. (Carpenter & Just, in press, reported a 51-msec effect for this variable.)

Recall Performance

The recall of a given part of a text should depend in part on what happens to the information as it is read. A clause that is thoroughly integrated with the representation of the text should tend to be stored in long-term memory, and therefore should be recalled better. There are two factors that determine how well a clause will be integrated. First, those sectors on which more integration time has been spent, like topics and definitions, should be recalled better. As predicted the integration parameter for a text role (i.e., the five weights at the bottom of Table 2) reliably affected the probability that a sector would be recalled, $t(271) = 2.01$, $p < .05$. A second factor affecting integration is the number of times an argument of a clause is referred to in the text; each repetition involving that argument may initiate another integration episode that increases its chances of being recalled (Kintsch & van Dijk, 1978). A rough index of this kind of repetition was obtained by counting the number of times the arguments of each sector were repeated in subsequent sectors. The frequency of reference to the arguments did increase the probability of recalling a sector, $t(271) = 5.90$, $p < .01$.

The recall measure just reported was the proportion of the 14 subjects that recalled each of the 274 sectors. Two independent judges assigned 100%, 50%, or 0% credit for the recall of each sector, depending on whether it had been fully, partially, or not at all correctly recalled. Synonyms and paraphrases were given full credit if they were close to the gist of the sector. If only a part of a sector was recalled, then partial credit was given. The two judges were in full agreement about 80% of the time and in partial agreement (i.e., within 50%) on 94% of the judgments; disagreements were resolved by a third judge.

Text units that were higher in the text grammar were generally recalled better, $F(4, 269) = 5.67$, $p < .01$. There was a monotonic increase in the probability of recall as a function of a sector's level in the text grammar. Recall probabilities were lowest for details (.31), then increased for expansions (.34), subtopics (.39), definitions/causes/consequences (.41), and topics (.53). This replicates previous text-role effects observed with other types of texts (Meyer, 1975; Thorndyke, 1977). The model partially explains this result in terms of the processes that occur during comprehension. In addition, retrieval processes may play a role in this effect. For example, there may be many retrieval paths from less important concepts that lead to topics, but not vice versa. Also, a complete model of recall will have to consider how the recall of particular facts is affected by the reader's previous knowledge. Although the passages were generally unfamiliar, particular facts surely differed in their familiarity, and this could have a powerful effect on recall (Spilich, Vesonder, Chiesi, & Voss, 1979). Finally, there could be response output effects in recall. In summary, the results show that a model of the comprehension processes can be used to partially account for recall performance. To totally explain recall will require a precise account of the role of prior long-term knowledge and the role of retrieval and reconstruction processes in recall.

Discussion

This section discusses three aspects of the theory: first, the implications of the immediacy assumption for language processing in general; second, how variation in reading modes can be handled by the theory; and third, the relation of the current theory to other theories of reading.

The Immediacy Assumption

The model's ability to account for fixation durations in terms of the processes that operate on words provides some validation for the immediacy and eye–mind assumptions. Readers interpret a word while they are fixating it, and they continue to fixate it until they have processed it as far as they can. As mentioned before, this kind of processing eliminates the difficulties caused by the potential ambiguity in language. It avoids the memory load and computational explosion that would result if a reader kept track of several possible meanings, case roles, and referents for each word and computed the final interpretation at the end of a clause or a sentence. This architectural feature also allows a limited-capacity processor to operate on a large semantic network without being bombarded by irrelevant associations. After a single interpretation has been selected, the activation of the unselected meanings can be dampened to their base levels so that they will not activate their semantic associates any further. This minimizes the chances that the reader will be conceptually driven in many directions at the same time.

The cost of this kind of processing is fairly low because the early decisions usually are correct. This is accomplished by taking a large amount of information into account in reaching a decision. The processes have specific heuristics to combine semantic, syntactic, and discourse information. Equally important, the processes operate on a data base that is strongly biased in favor of the common uses of words and phrases, but one that also reflects the effects of local context. The cost is also low because the reader can recover from errors. It would be devastating if there were no way to modify an incorrect interpretation at some later point. However, there are error-recovery heuristics that seem fairly efficient, although the precise mechanisms are only now being explored (Carpenter & Daneman, 1980).

The fact that a reader's heuristics for interpreting the text are good explains why the garden path phenomenon is not the predominant experience in comprehension; it only happens occasionally. Perhaps the most common, everyday garden path experiences occur when reading newspaper headlines; for example, *Carter Views Discussed* and *Judge Admits Two Reporters.* The incorrect initial interpretations occur because headlines are stripped of the syntactic and contextual cues that guide the processing of normal text. Similarly, many jokes and puns explicitly rely on the contrast between two interpretations of an ambiguous word or phrase (Schultz & Horibe, 1974). Even garden path sentences sometimes seem funny. The humor in all of these cases resides in the incongruity between the initial interpretation and the ultimate one. Garden path sentences are also infrequent because writers usually try to avoid ambiguities that might encourage or allow incorrect interpretations. These kinds of sentences are useful tools for studying comprehension because they indicate where the usual comprehension strategies fail. But the fact that they are not frequent indicates that a reader's heuristics usually are sufficient.

Variation in Reading

There is no single mode of reading. Reading varies as a function of who is reading, what they are reading, and why they are reading it. The proposed model for the reading of scientific texts in this task is only one point in a multidimensional space of reading models. However, such variation can be accommodated within the framework presented in this article.

The reader's goals are perhaps the most important determinant of the reading process. A reader who skims a passage for the main point reads differently than someone who is trying to memorize a passage, or another person who is reading for entertainment. Goals can be represented in several aspects of the theory, but the main way is to require that each goal is satisfied or at least attempted before proceeding on to the next word, clause, or sentence. These goals correspond to the major products of each stage of comprehension and to the specific demands of a particular task. For example, an obvious goal associated with lexical access might be that one interpretation is selected. An added goal associated with the task of memorizing a passage may require rehearsing phrases or constructing explicit mnemonics before going on to the next phrase or sentence. But goals can be deleted as well as added. A speed-reader may well eliminate goals for syntactic coherence, because the strategy of skipping over many words will destroy the syntax. Variations in goals can be detected with the current theory and analytic techniques. For example, it is possible to determine how much time is spent integrating different kinds of text roles in different tasks. When readers anticipate a recognition comprehension test, rather than recall, they spend less time integrating details (Carpenter & Just, in press).

Reading also depends on the text, the topic, and the reader's familiarity with both. A well-written paragraph on a familiar topic will be easier to process at all stages of comprehension. The lexical items will be easier to encode, the concepts will be more easily accessed, the case and text roles will be easier to infer, and the interrelations will be easier to represent. All of these dimensions of variation can be accommodated, measured, and evaluated within the theoretical framework. Moreover, any adequate theory must be sufficiently flexible to encompass such variation.

Even reading of the same text under the same circumstances will vary from person to person. There are several plausible sources of individual differences in the theory. One interesting source is the operational capacity of the working memory. Readers with a large working memory should be able to retain more of the text in the memory while processing new text, so their integration of the information may be more thorough. A promising first exploration of this hypothesis has found a very strong correlation between working memory capacity and various aspects of reading comprehension tests (Daneman & Carpenter, in press). By contrast, traditional measures of passive short-term memory capacity do not have a strong correlation with reading comprehension. Operational capacity may depend on the automaticity of basic reading processes such as encoding and lexical access. Poor readers may devote more time and attention to these processes (Hunt, Lunneborg, & Lewis, 1975; Perfetti & Lesgold, 1977) and consequently have less capacity for maintaining previous information and integrating the new information (Case, 1978).

Theories of Reading

Previous theories of reading have varied in their choice of dependent measures, the levels of information represented in the theory, and the implementation of top-down effects. It is useful to consider how the current theory compares to these alternative proposals along these three dimensions.

One important feature of the current theory is its attempt to account for reading time on individual words, clauses, and sentences. This approach can be distinguished from research that is more centrally concerned with recall, question answering, and summarizing (e.g., Rumelhart, 1977b). The dependent measure is not an incidental aspect of a theory; it has important implications for which issues the theory addresses. The present focus on processing time has resulted in a theory that accounts for the moment-by-moment, real-time characteristics of reading. By contrast, the theory pays less attention to retrieval and reconstruction, two later occurring processes that are important to an account of summarization.

Another feature of the theory is the attempt to account for performance at several levels of processing. Previous theories have tended to neglect certain stages.

For example, the reading models of LaBerge and Samuels (1974) and Gough (1972) focus on the word-encoding processes, whereas the model of Kintsch and van Dijk (1978) focuses on integration. This is not to say that these models do not acknowledge other aspects of processing, but simply that they describe detailed mechanisms for one aspect of reading and no comparable mechanisms for other stages. The current theory has attempted to span the stages of reading by describing mechanisms for the word-encoding and lexical-access stages, as well as the parsing and text integration stages. Moreover, it has attempted to describe some formal similarities by placing them all within the architecture of a production system.

A final but important distinction among reading theories is the manner in which they accommodate top-down and bottom-up factors in reading (see Rumelhart, 1977a). Some reading theories, particularly those addressed to word encoding, omit mechanisms to account for top-down or contextual effects (e.g., Gough, 1972). At the other extreme, there have been some theories that appear to place a major burden of comprehension on contextual effects. Some of these are recent schema-based theories of language comprehension (Schank & Abelson, 1977). Others are the older top-down models, developed out of analysis-by-synthesis theory; these models suggested that readers form explicit predictions about the next word and fixate it merely to confirm the hypothesis (Goodman & Niles, 1970). The current model falls somewhere between the extremes. It allows for contextual influences and for the interaction among comprehension processes. Knowledge about a topic, syntactic constraints, and semantic associates can all play a role in activating and selecting the appropriate concepts. However, the printed words themselves are usually the best information source that the reader has, and they can seldom be entirely replaced by guesses from the preceding context. Thus the top-down processes can influence the bottom-up ones, but their role is to participate in selecting interpretations rather than to dominate the bottom-up processes. Finally, the production system architecture permits a degree of coordination among different processes, so that any stage can be influenced by any cotemporaneously or previously executed stage.

Future Directions

The current theory suggests two major avenues of reading research. One direction is to construct computer simulations that are driven by reading performance data. The postulated human heuristics can be implemented in a computer program to examine the resulting complex interactions among knowledge sources. Reading-time data may be sufficiently constraining to select among various alternative heuristics. We are currently implementing aspects of the model presented here as a production system in collaboration with a colleague, Robert Thibadeau, to develop greater specification and more stringent tests of the model.

Although the production system framework is not essential for the interpretation of the empirical results in the present study, it has other benefits. First, it provides an architecture that can accommodate the flexibility and interaction that has been observed among the processes in reading and still express typical or canonical processing. Even though this theoretical framework is minimally specified, it seems sensible to start at this point and allow successive generations of data to constrain it, as Newell (1980) suggests. Finally, when expressed as a computer simulation, the model retains correspondence to postulated human processes and structures. Collections of serial productions may correspond to heuristic processes employed in comprehension. The firing of parallel productions can be identified with spreading activation in long-term memory. The production system's working memory can be identified with the reader's working memory. Thus, the production system can be viewed as a useful theoretical vehicle, or excess baggage, depending on one's intended destination.

The second avenue includes further empirical research on the real-time characteristics of reading. Eye movement and reading-time methodologies can reveal reading characteristics with other types of texts, tasks, and readers. The useful property of these methodologies is that they can measure reading time on successive units of text. One method is to present the successive words of a sentence one at a time, allowing the reader to control the interword interval (Aaronson & Scarborough, 1976). This procedure is only one end of a continuum defined by what units are presented. Rather than single words, they could be phrases, clauses, sentences, or entire passages (Carpenter & Just, 1977a; Mitchell & Green, 1978; Kieras, 1979). In this way, it will be possible to gain more information about human performance characteristics and then use these data to develop a more complete theory of reading.

ACKNOWLEDGMENTS

The research was supported in part by Grant G-79-0119 from the National Institute of Education and Grant MH-29617 from the National Institute of Mental Health.

We thank Allen Newell and Robert Thibadeau for their very helpful discussions.

The order of authorship was decided by the toss of a coin.

QUESTIONS FOR REFLECTION

1. How does working-memory capacity influence reading comprehension?
2. How does the purpose for reading influence the input stage of Just and Carpenter's reading model?
3. How could a teacher use Just and Carpenter's theory about lexical-access processes to help a child with poor reading skills?

NOTE

[1] It might be argued that the variables coding the text-grammatical roles ought to be independent of the number of content words. One might argue that a definition, for example, takes a fixed amount of time to integrate, regardless of the number of content words it contains.

Although the model predicts a length-sensitive duration, the analysis can also be done with five simple indicator variables to encode the five levels of the grammar. This analysis produced a fit that was almost as good ($R^2 = .93$). The weights (assuming a zero intercept) were 250, 341, 257, 214, and 118 msec for the five categories, from topics to details. Although this alternative is not ruled out by the data, we will continue to retain the view that integration time depends on the number of content words involved.

REFERENCES

Aaronson D., & Scarborough, H.S. (1976). Performance theories for sentence coding: Some quantitative evidence. *Journal of Experimental Psychology: Human Perception and Performance, 2*, 56–70.

Anderson, J.R. (1976). *Language, memory, and thought*. Hillsdale, NJ: Erlbaum.

Baron, J. (1977). Mechanisms for pronouncing printed words: Use and acquisition. In D. LaBerge & S.J. Samuels (Eds.), *Basic processes in reading: Perception and comprehension*. Hillsdale, NJ: Erlbaum.

Bayle, E. (1942). The nature and causes of regressive movements in reading. *Journal of Experimental Education, 11*, 16–36.

Bever, T.G. (1970). The cognitive basis for linguistic structures. In J.R. Hayes (Ed.), *Cognition and the development of language*. New York: Wiley.

Bouma H., & deVoogd, A.H. (1974). On the control of eye saccades in reading. *Vision Research, 14*, 273–284.

Bransford, J.D., & Johnson, M.K. (1973). Considerations of some problems of comprehension. In W.G. Chase (Ed.), *Visual information processing*. New York: Academic Press.

Breitmeyer, B.G. (1980). Unmasking visual masking: A look at the "why" behind the veil of "how." *Psychological Review, 87*, 52–69.

Buswell, G.T. (1937). *How adults read* (Supplementary Educational Monograph 45). Chicago: University of Chicago Press.

Carpenter, P.A., & Daneman, M. (1980). *Lexical access and error recovery in reading: A model based on eye fixations*. Unpublished manuscript, Carnegie Mellon University, Pittsburgh, PA.

Carpenter, P.A., & Just, M.A. (1977a). Integrative processes in comprehension. In D. LaBerge & S.J. Samuels (Eds.), *Basic processes in reading: Perception and comprehension*. Hillsdale, NJ: Erlbaum.

Carpenter, P.A., & Just, M.A. (1977b). Reading comprehension as eyes see it. In M.A. Just & P.A. Carpenter (Eds.), *Cognitive processes in comprehension*. Hillsdale, NJ: Erlbaum.

Carpenter, P.A., & Just, M.A. (in press). Cognitive processes in reading: Models based on readers' eye fixations. In A.M. Lesgold & C.A. Perfetti (Eds.), *Interactive processes in reading*. Hillsdale, NJ: Erlbaum.

Case, R. (1978). Intellectual development from birth to adulthood: A neo-Piagetian interpretation. In R. Siegler (Ed.), *Children's thinking: What develops?* Hillsdale, NJ: Erlbaum.

Chafe, W.L. (1970). *Meaning and the structure of language*. Chicago: University of Chicago Press.

Charniak, E. (1972). *Toward a model of children's story comprehension* (Tech. Rep. No. 266). Cambridge, MA: MIT Artificial Intelligence Laboratory.

Clark, H.H., & Clark, E.V. (1977). *Psychology and language*. New York: Harcourt Brace Jovanovich.

Collins, A.M., & Loftus, E.F. (1975). A spreading activation theory of semantic processing. *Psychological Review, 82*, 407–428.

Daneman, M., & Carpenter, P.A. (in press). Individual differences in working memory and reading. *Journal of Verbal Learning and Verbal Behavior, 19*, 450–466.

Dearborn, W. (1906). *The psychology of reading* (Columbia University contributions to philosophy and psychology). New York: Science Press.

Dixon, P., & Rothkopf, E.Z. (1979). Word repetition, lexical access, and the process of searching words and sentences. *Journal of Verbal Learning and Verbal Behavior, 18*, 629–644.

Fillmore, C.J. (1968). The case for case. In E. Bach & R.T. Harms (Eds.), *Universals in linguistic theory*. New York: Holt, Rinehart & Winston.

Flesch, R.F. (1951). *How to test readability*. New York: Harper.

Fraser, C., Bellugi, U., & Brown, R. (1963). Control of grammar in imitation, comprehension, and production. *Journal of Verbal Learning and Verbal Behavior, 2*, 121–135.

Frazier, L., & Fodor, J. (1978). The sausage machine: A new two-stage parsing model. *Cognition, 6*, 291–325.

Glanzer, M., & Ehrenreich, S.L. (1979). Structure and search for the internal lexicon. *Journal of Verbal Learning and Verbal Behavior, 18*, 381–398.

Goodman, K.S., & Niles, O.S. (1970). *Reading process and program*. Urbana, IL: National Council of Teachers of English.

Gough, P.B. (1972). One second of reading. In J.F. Kavanagh & I.G. Mattingly (Eds.), *Language by eye and ear*. Cambridge, MA: MIT Press.

Haviland, S.E., & Clark, H.H. (1974). What's new? Acquiring new information as a process in comprehension. *Journal of Verbal Learning and Verbal Behavior, 13*, 512–521.

Hitch, G.J. (1978). The role of short-term working memory in mental arithmetic. *Cognitive Psychology, 10*, 302–323.

Hockett, C.F. (1958). *A course in modern linguistics*. New York: Macmillan.

Hunt, E., Lunneborg, C., & Lewis, J. (1975). What does it mean to be high verbal? *Cognitive Psychology*, *2*, 194–227.

Jarvella, R.J. (1971). Syntactic processing of connected speech. *Journal of Verbal Learning and Verbal Behavior*, *10*, 409–416.

Judd, C.H., & Buswell, G.T. (1922). *Silent reading: A study of the various types* (Supplementary Educational Monograph 23). Chicago: University of Chicago Press.

Just, M.A., & Carpenter, P.A. (1976). Eye fixations and cognitive processes. *Cognitive Psychology*, *8*, 441–480.

Just, M.A., & Carpenter, P.A. (1978). Inference processes during reading: Reflections from eye fixations. In J.W. Senders, D.F. Fisher, & R.A. Monty (Eds.), *Eye movements and the higher psychological functions*. Hillsdale, NJ: Erlbaum.

Kieras, D.E. (1979). *Modelling reading times in different reading tasks with a simulation model of comprehension* (Tech. Rep. No. 2). Tucson: University of Arizona.

Kintsch, W., & van Dijk, T.A. (1978). Toward a model of text comprehension and production. *Psychological Review*, *85*, 363–394.

Kleiman, G.M. (1975). Speech recoding in reading. *Journal of Verbal Learning and Verbal Behavior*, *14*, 323–339.

Kučera, H., & Francis, W.N. (1967). *Computational analysis of present-day American English*. Providence, RI: Brown University Press.

LaBerge, D., & Samuels, S.J. (1974). Toward a theory of automatic information processing in reading. *Cognitive Psychology*, *6*, 293–323.

Levy, B.A. (in press). Interactive processes during reading. In A.M. Lesgold & C.A. Perfetti (Eds.), *Interactive processes in reading*. Hillsdale, NJ: Erlbaum.

Mandler, J.M., & Johnson, N.S. (1977). Remembrance of things parsed: Story structure and recall. *Cognitive Psychology*, *9*, 111–151.

McConkie, G.W., & Rayner, K. (1975). The span of the effective stimulus during a fixation in reading. *Perception & Psychophysics*, *17*, 578–586.

McConkie, G.W., & Rayner, K. (1976). Asymmetry of the perceptual span in reading. *Bulletin of the Psychonomic Society*, *8*, 365–368.

Mewhort, D., & Beal, A.L. (1977). Mechanisms of word identification. *Journal of Experimental Psychology: Human Perception and Performance*, *3*, 629–640.

Meyer, B. (1975). *The organization of prose and its effect on recall*. Amsterdam: North-Holland.

Meyer, B., & McConkie, G.W. (1973). What is recalled after hearing a passage? *Journal of Educational Psychology*, *65*, 109–117.

Mitchell, D.C., & Green, D.W. (1978). The effects of context and content on immediate processing in reading. *Quarterly Journal of Experimental Psychology*, *30*, 609–636.

Morton, J. (1969). Interaction of information in word recognition. *Psychological Review*, *76*, 165–178.

Newell, A. (1973). Production systems: Models of control structures. In W.G. Chase (Ed.), *Visual information processing*. New York: Academic Press.

Newell, A. (1980). Harpy, production systems and human cognition. In R. Cole (Ed.), *Perception and production of fluent speech*. Hillsdale. NJ: Erlbaum.

Perfetti, C.A., & Lesgold, A.M. (1977). Discourse comprehension and sources of individual differences. In M.A. Just & P.A. Carpenter (Eds.), *Cognitive processes in comprehension*. Hillsdale, NJ: Erlbaum.

Rayner, K. (1978). Eye movements in reading and information processing. *Psychological Bulletin*, *85*, 618–660.

Reitman, J.S. (1974). Without surreptitious rehearsal, information in short-term memory decays. *Journal of Verbal Learning and Verbal Behavior*, *13*, 365–377.

Rieger, C.J. (1979). Five aspects of a full-scale story comprehension model. In N.V. Findler (Ed.), *Associative networks*. New York: Academic Press.

Robinson, D.A. (1972). Eye movements evoked by collicular stimulation in the alert monkey. *Vision Research*, *12*, 1795–1808.

Rumelhart, D.E. (1977a). Toward an interactive model of reading. In S. Dornic (Ed.), *Attention and performance VI*. Hillsdale, NJ: Erlbaum.

Rumelhart, D.E. (1977b). Understanding and summarizing brief stories. In D. LaBerge & S.J. Samuels (Eds.), *Basic processes in reading: Perception and comprehension*. Hillsdale, NJ: Erlbaum.

Scarborough, D.L., Cortese, C., & Scarborough, H.S. (1977). Frequency and repetition effects in lexical memory. *Journal of Experimental Psychology: Human Perception and Performance*, *3*, 1–17.

Schank, R.C. (1972). Conceptual dependency: A theory of natural language understanding. *Cognitive Psychology*, *3*, 552–631.

Schank, R.C., & Abelson, R.P. (1977). *Scripts, plans, goals, and understanding: An inquiry into human knowledge structures*. Hillsdale, NJ: Erlbaum.

Schiepers, C. (1980). Response latency and accuracy in visual word recognition. *Perception & Psychophysics*, *27*, 71–81.

Shultz, T., & Horibe, F. (1974). Development of the appreciation of verbal jokes. *Developmental Psychology*, *10*, 13–20.

Spilich, G.J., Vesonder, G.T., Chiesi, H.L., & Voss, J.F. (1979). Text processing of domain-related information for individuals with high and low domain knowledge. *Journal of Verbal Learning and Verbal Behavior*, *18*, 275–290.

Spoehr, K.T., & Smith, E. (1973). The role of syllables in perceptual processing. *Cognitive Psychology*, *5*, 71–89.

Swinney, D.A. (1979). Lexical access during sentence comprehension: (Re)consideration of context effects. *Journal of Verbal Learning and Verbal Behavior, 18*, 645–659.

Taft, M. (1979). Recognition of affixed words and the word frequency effect. *Memory & Cognition, 7*, 263–272.

Tanenhaus, M.K., Leiman, J.M., & Seidenberg, M.S. (1979). Evidence for multiple stages in the processing of ambiguous words in syntactic contexts. *Journal of Verbal Learning and Verbal Behavior, 18*, 427–440.

Taylor, S.E. (1962). *An evaluation of forty-one trainees who had recently completed the "reading dynamics" program* (11th yearbook of the National Reading Conference, pp. 41–55).

Thorndyke, P.W. (1977). Cognitive structures in comprehension and memory of narrative discourse. *Cognitive Psychology, 9*, 77–110.

Vesonder, G.T. (1979). *The role of knowledge in the processing of experimental reports.* Unpublished doctoral dissertation, University of Pittsburgh, Pittsburgh, PA.

Westheimer, G.H. (1954). Eye movement responses to a horizontally moving visual stimulus. *Archives of Ophthalmology, 52*, 932–943.

CHAPTER 31

Modeling the Connections Between Word Recognition and Reading

Marilyn Jager Adams, Brown University*

Skillful reading is the product of an amazingly complex array of knowledge and abilities. How is it, then, that so much of the scientific literature on reading is centered on word recognition? One answer is that the field has lacked the scientific sophistication to go much beyond words; another, however, is that until we truly began to understand the relation of words to the rest of the reading process, we were hard pressed to move on.

True, the ability to recognize words is but a tiny component of the larger literacy challenge. Also true, the knowledge and activities involved in visually recognizing individual printed words are useless in and of themselves. And equally true, word recognition is only valuable and, in a strong sense, only possible as it is received and guided by the larger activities of language comprehension and thought.

On the other hand, unless the processes involved in individual-word recognition operate properly, nothing else in the system can either. The purpose of this article is to explore the relationship between word recognition and literacy. It is, moreover, to show how scientific efforts to understand these relationships have brought us ever closer to a larger understanding of the nature of reading.

The Operation of the Reading System

To clarify the relation of word-recognition processes to the rest of the system, an analogy might be useful. Let's say that the system that supports our ability to read is a car. Within this analogy, print is gas. The engine and the mechanics of the car are the perceptual and conceptual machinery that make the system run.

It is obvious that print is essential to reading—no gas, no driving. But print alone is not enough to make the reading car go. Reading cannot begin without the spark of visual recognition. And just as cars are designed with more than one spark plug, so the reading system is designed to take in the physically separable pieces of print not one at a time, but in intricately coordinated concert. Like the crankshaft in a car, the reader's learned associations among letters and words keep the reading car rolling despite problems that might arise: The occasional letter that is misperceived or even illegible does not stop the reading machine any

This chapter is reprinted from *Theoretical Models and Processes of Reading* (4th ed., pp. 838–863), edited by R.B. Ruddell, M.R. Ruddell, and H. Singer, Newark, DE: International Reading Association. Copyright © 1994 by the International Reading Association. (Adapted from "What Skillful Readers Know," in *Beginning to Read: Thinking and Learning About Print, a Summary*, 1990, Champaign: Center for the Study of Reading, University of Illinois at Urbana-Champaign.)

more than the occasional misfire of a spark plug or impurity in the gas will stop a car. Even so, the engine is only indirectly responsible for making the car go. The engine turns gas to kinetic energy, and the energy turns the wheels. Similarly, the perceptual system turns print to mental energy, such that it can be understood.

Obviously a car *couldn't* be driven without gas, without spark plugs, without a crankshaft, and without a differential and wheels. But it is also important to recognize that a car *wouldn't* be driven if it didn't run well. Imagine that you had to push a button every time you wanted a spark plug to fire. Imagine that the car would only go a couple of miles per hour or that it stalled unpredictably every few moments. You would very likely choose not to drive at all. These problems are analogous to the difficulties that must befall the reader who cannot transform print to language and meaning with reasonable speed and ease. In particular, if a child's word-recognition skills are sufficiently poor, the time and effort involved in reading may well overwhelm its hoped-for rewards. If so, the child is likely to choose not to read at all. And here is the tragedy: To the extent that children do not read, they forfeit the practice and experience needed to make reading easier and more profitable. To the extent that children do not read, they can only continue to have difficulty reading, to fall farther and farther behind their peers in both reading and the conceptual returns it offers (see, especially, Stanovich, 1986, 1993).

Clearly, without gas and without an engine and mechanics in adequate working order, the car will not go. Suppose, however, that your reading system has plenty of print to consume and a fine mechanical system. Are you on your way? No. First you have to want to go somewhere, and you have to have some idea of how to get there. As you travel, you must monitor and control your path. Periodically, you must assess your whereabouts and progress with respect to your final destination. At the same time, you must attend to the local details of the road and control your car through them. Indeed, the amount of active attention you will have to devote to your immediate progress will necessarily depend on such variables as the navigability of the route—how far you can see ahead and whether the way is bumpy, winding, congested, or unpredictable—and its familiarity.

Similarly, if texts are difficult in wording or structure or unfamiliar in concept, they require the active attention of the reader. But the more one must direct attention to local difficulties of reading, the less attention one has available to support larger understanding. Only to the extent that the ability to recognize and capture the meaning of print is rapid, effortless, and automatic can the reader have available the cognitive energy and resources on which true comprehension depends. Only to that extent can the reader have the perspective and capacity to reflect upon the journey.

As it happens, *everybody* wants to go somewhere. Everybody wants the stimulation of new challenges and the sense of growth and accomplishment that comes with conquering them. Understandably, if reading seems tedious or unproductive, children will seek other ways to spend their time; indeed, they may avoid it altogether. In a recent survey of fourth graders, 40% of the poor readers claimed that they would rather clean their rooms than read. One child stated, "I'd rather clean the mold around the bathtub than read" (Juel, 1988).

Fortunately, for purposes of schooling, most young children will go almost anywhere they are led—so long as they are neither frustrated nor bored. But even as this eases our task as reading educators, it greatly increases our responsibility. It is up to us to lead our children in the right direction.

And it is here that the car analogy breaks down. So apt for describing the operation of the system, it is wholly inappropriate for modeling its acquisition. Building a car is a modular, hierarchical activity. From the bottom up, the discrete and countable parts of the car's subsystems are fastened together; then, one by one, from the inside out and only as each is completed, the subsystems are connected to one another. In contrast, the parts of the reading system are not discrete. We cannot proceed by completing each one in isolation and then fastening it to another. Rather, the parts of the reading system must grow together. They must grow to and from one another.

For the connections and even the connected parts to develop properly, they must be linked in the very course of their acquisition. And this dependency works in both directions. We cannot properly develop the higher order processes without due attention to the lower; nor can we focus on the lower order processes without constantly clarifying and exercising their connections to the higher.

The great challenge for reading educators, therefore, is one of understanding the parts of the system and their interrelations. In this article, I will focus on current models of skillful readers. What special kinds of knowledge do skillful readers have? How is it organized, and what are the processes that bring it into play? And how does our evolving understanding of skillful readers help us understand the learning process and its difficulties?

What Do Skillful Readers Do?

Perhaps the single most striking characteristic of skillful readers is the speed and effortlessness with which they breeze through text. The rate at which they read typically exceeds five words per second (Rayner & Pollatsek, 1987). Indeed, they appear to recognize whole words at a glance, gleaning their appropriate meaning at once (Cattell, 1885). How do they do so?

Some Questions

Do skillful readers, in fact, recognize words as wholes? In recognizing an individual word, do readers depend on its overall pattern or shape rather than any closer analysis of the letters within it? If so, then doesn't it seem counterproductive to train children to focus on the letter-by-letter spellings of words?

Do skillful readers access the *meaning* of a word directly from seeing it? If so, then doesn't it seem counterproductive to teach children to sound words out?

Do skillful readers use context to anticipate upcoming words so as to reduce the visual detail they need from the text? If so, then in place of rigorous decoding instruction, wouldn't it be better to teach children to use context together with such minimal distinguishing cues of words as first letters and overall length?

Do skillful readers use context to anticipate the words they will see, such that their comprehension consists as much of confirming as of interpreting their meanings? If so, then shouldn't a central focus of beginning reading instruction be one of discouraging children's tendency to pore over the separate words in text and of strengthening their ability to guess the words instead?

Some Answers From Research

Each of these notions has been seriously entertained by researchers at one time or another, and the instructional implications of each are realized prominently in many curricula and classroom practices. Under scrutiny, however, each of these notions has been proved incorrect. More than that, each has been proved incorrect in ways that strongly argue against their instructional translations.

As it turns out, research has long shown that skillful readers are relatively indifferent to the shapes of the words they read (see Woodworth, 1938). Even when the letters that make them up are randomly sampled from a variety of type styles and sizes in both uppercase and lowercase fonts, skillful readers seem to recognize familiar words as wholes (Adams, 1979a). At the same time, skillful readers visually process virtually every letter of every word as they read; this is true whether they are reading isolated words or meaningful, connected text—and, surprise of surprises, it is even true when they are reading cursive handwriting (De Zuniga, Humphreys, & Evett, 1991). To be sure, skillful readers rarely think about individual letters or words as they read. At a conscious level, they may not even notice flagrant misspellings or misprints. But, conscious or not, studies show that letter recognition is integral to the reading process and that even the slightest misprint, tucked deep within a long and highly predictable word, tends to be detected by the visual systems of skillful readers; detection is signaled by readers' eyes flicking back to the misprint to make sure the type was seen correctly (McConkie & Zola, 1981).

Research also negates the notion that skillful readers use contextual guidance to preselect the meanings of the words they will read. Consider the following sentences:

> They all rose.
>
> John saw several spiders, roaches, and bugs.

The last word of each of these sentences is, in itself, ambiguous—but would you have noticed if that hadn't been pointed out? Although it feels as though context preselects the appropriate meanings of such words, that is not exactly what happens. Research demonstrates that all the meanings of an ambiguous word are aroused in the course of perception. Very shortly (within tenths of a second) thereafter—too quickly for us to become aware of the confusion—context selects the most appropriate meaning from among the alternatives. (For a review of research in this area, see Seidenberg et al., 1982.)

Finally, research proves that skillful readers habitually translate spellings to sounds as they read (see Barron, 1981a, 1981b; Patterson & Coltheart, 1987). But why? If visually familiar words do indeed activate their meanings directly for readers—and they do—then of what conceivable value are such phonological translations? The answer to this question has come only through many years of work and many research studies: Such spelling-to-sound translations are vital to both fluent reading and its acquisition. To see why, we must look more deeply into the reading system.

Modeling the Reading System: Four Processors

The purpose of models is to combine findings from many studies into a single, coherent system. Because a usefully detailed model lays bare those spots where assumptions are not supported by research, it is an extremely valuable scientific tool. In particular, where the model's pieces seem to fit in more than one way or not to fit at all, the researcher must conclude that some assumption is awry or that some important consideration has been overlooked. Gradually through the cyclical process of modeling, assessing, and gathering new data, researchers gain an ever more refined and complete image of the parts of a system and how they must work together.

By developing more comprehensive models of the nature of the reading system and the interrelations of its parts, researchers have strived to understand the reading process as a whole. Anchored in psychological research and built through laboratory studies and simulations, contemporary models of reading are complex. However, it is because they have been developed with such analytic care that their instructional implications carry special weight.

Indeed, because they move beyond the boundaries of our field to exploit advances in logical, mathematical, and computational sciences, recent models appear provocatively capable of mimicking the processes of reading and learning to read. These newer models, alternatively known as connectionist, neural net, or parallel distributed processing (PDP) models, are built on the assumption that learning progresses as the learner comes to respond to the relationships among patterns or events. It is, for example, the overlearned relations among its sides that enables recognition of a triangle, just as it is the overlearned relations among its letters that enables recognition of a word. Similarly, it is the relations among the pitch, timing, and quality of its notes that evoke interest in a piece of music, just as it is the relations among the meanings of its words that give texture and meaning to a sentence. (For a description of the logic and dynamics of these models, see Rumelhart & McClelland, 1986; for an exploration of their pertinence to reading, see Adams, 1990, and Seidenberg & McClelland, 1989; for a discussion of their general importance and potential, see Bereiter, 1991.)

The power of these models derives from the fact that they are neither top down nor bottom up in nature. Instead, all relevant processes they include are simultaneously active and interactive; all simultaneously issue and accommodate information to and from one another. The key to these models, in other words, is not the dominance of one set of processes over the others, but the coordination and cooperation of all as shaped by the reader's own prior knowledge and experience.

As adapted to the reading situation, the grand logic of these models is schematized in Figure 1 (see Adams, 1990, for a fuller description and discussion). Within each of the "processors," knowledge is represented by many simpler units that have become linked to, connected with, or associated with one another through experience. The oval labeled "orthographic processor," for example, represents the reader's knowledge of the visual images of words. Within it, individual letters are represented as interconnected bundles of more elementary visual features, while printed words are represented as interconnected sets of letters. Similarly, the meanings of a familiar word are represented in the meaning processor as bundles of simpler meaning elements, just as its pronunciation is represented in the phonological processor as a complex of elementary speech sounds.

I introduced the term "processors" in quotation marks so as to emphasize that it is mostly for descriptive convenience that the different types have been separated one from another. The associations among pieces of knowledge depend not on the "processor" in which each resides, but on the ways in which they have become interrelated or connected through experience. Indeed, the links among any set of representational units are nothing more than a cumulative record of the ways in which those units have been related to one another in a person's

Figure 1. Modeling the Reading System: Four Processors

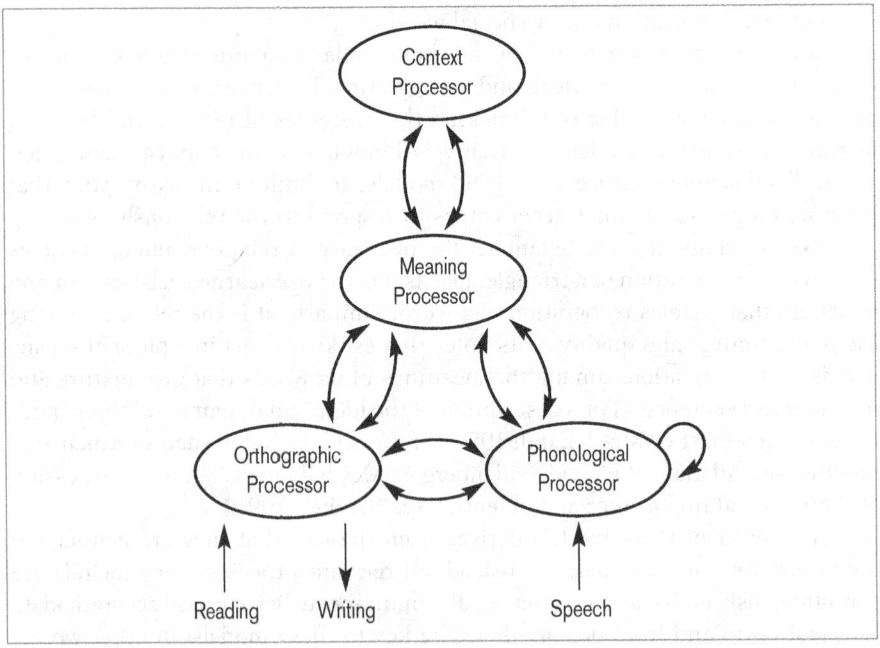

experience. The more frequently a pattern of activity has been brought to mind, the stronger and more complete will be the bonds that hold it together. Ultimately it is these bonds, these interrelations—as they pass excitation and inhibition among the elements that they link together—that are responsible for the fluency of the reader and the seeming coherence of the text.

For the skillful reader, as the letters of a word in fixation are recognized, they activate the spelling patterns, pronunciations, and meanings with which they are compatible. At the same time, using its larger knowledge of the text, the context processor swings its own bias among rival candidates so as to maintain the coherence of the message. Meanwhile, as each processor homes in on the word's identity, it relays its progress back to the others such that wherever hypotheses agree among processors, their resolution is speeded and strengthened.

In this way, speed and fluency are seen as an emergent property of the mature reading system. With recognition initiated by the print on the page and hastened by the connectivity both within and between the processors, skillful readers access the spelling, sound, meaning, and contextual role of a familiar word almost automatically and simultaneously. But note: Speed and fluency are not just an outgrowth of skillful reading; they are necessary for its happening. To understand better the knowledge and processes involved, let us examine each of the processors in turn.

The Orthographic Processor

To be fluent and productive, reading depends no more on recognizing words than on astute and flexible consideration of the linguistic and conceptual contexts in which they occur. Indeed, the whole point of the model outlined above is that, in skillful reading, the mind works interactively and in parallel with as many cues and clues as it can recognize as relevant.

Nevertheless, as illustrated in Figure 1, the orthographic processor alone receives information directly from the printed page. By implication, the letters and words of text constitute the basic perceptual data of reading, and this is as it should be. After all, the words on the page are authors' principal means of conveying their message. It will not do for readers to ignore them, nor will guessing suffice: Even skillful adults are unable to guess correctly more than 25% of the time (Gough, Alford, & Holley-Wilcox, 1981).

For skillful readers, meaningful text is read through what is essentially (in English) a left-to-right, line-by-line, word-by-word process. In general, skillful readers visually process virtually each letter of every word they read, translating print to speech as they go. They do so whether they are reading isolated words or meaningful, connected text. They do so regardless of the ease or difficulty of the text, regardless of its semantic, syntactic, or orthographic predictability. There may be no more broadly or diversely replicated set of findings in modern cognitive psychology than those that show that skillful readers visually process nearly every letter and word of text as they read. (For reviews, see Adams, 1990; Patterson & Coltheart, 1987.)

Eye movement research informs us that our eyes do not move smoothly through the lines of text while we read. Instead, they leap from word to word, fixating briefly toward the center of each and then jumping to the next. Occasionally, readers do skip a word, but almost never more than one. Further, the words that are skipped tend rather exclusively to be short function words such as *of*, *a*, and *to*. Many function words and the vast majority of content words receive readers' direct gaze. (For a review, see Just & Carpenter, 1987.)

With normal print, the eye can clearly resolve up to three or so letters to the left of its fixation point and about twice that many to the right during each fixation. With these letters as its basic data, the system goes to work. To see how it proceeds, let us consider two examples. First, suppose the reader's eye lands on the word *the*. Because *the* is a frequently occurring and familiar word, all of its letters should be strongly interconnected within the reader's orthographic memory. As the reader looks at the word, the units corresponding to each of the letters receive visual stimulation from the page. Because the units are so strongly interconnected in the reader's memory, each will pass stimulation to the others, causing all to be recognized nearly at once and to hang together in the reader's mind as a familiar, cohesive spelling pattern.

Now suppose instead that the eye lands upon the nonword *tqe*. Because this string of letters is so similar to the word *the*, the reader's orthographic memory will attempt to process it in the same way. That is, the *t* and *e* units will pass stimulation to each other; they also will pass stimulation to the *h* unit. This time, however, because the *h* receives no direct visual stimulation, it cannot pass any back. At the same time, because *q* is almost always followed by *u* in English, the *q* unit will pass its stimulation to the unit for the absent *u*. As the directly stimulated letter units send their activation inappropriately around the letter network, they end up hurting rather than helping one another's progress. Eventually the direct visual stimulation from the page will bring each of the presented letters to peak stimulation, and the reader will see the string as printed: *tqe*. However, the perception of each letter will have taken longer and will have gelled independently of the others (McClelland & Rumelhart, 1981).

Through experience, the associative network comes to respond not just to next-door neighbors but also to the larger sequences and patterns of letters that represent whole, familiar words. And eventually, through its overlapping representation of many, many different words, it becomes responsive to common spelling patterns independently of the particular words in which they occur. Ultimately, it is the learned associations between and among individual letters that are responsible for the easy, holistic manner in which skillful readers respond to printed words. It is because of them that familiar words and spelling patterns are easier to read than the sum of their parts.

Yet the interletter associations provide other services that are of equal importance to the reader. These services include processing letter order and breaking words into syllables.

Processing Letter Order. Although the visual system is remarkably efficient at extracting information necessary for letter identification, it is quite sloppy about processing letter order. This is a physical limitation, affecting skillful readers as much as unskilled ones (Estes, 1977). Nevertheless, skillful readers almost never make mistakes in reporting the order of the letters in words they read; poor readers, in contrast, may often do so. Although letter-order difficulties were once taken as symptomatic of a basic perceptual deficit, that explanation has been proven incorrect (Liberman et al., 1971). Such difficulties seem instead to reflect insufficient orthographic learning. Specifically, among skillful readers, knowledge about the likely ordering of a string of letters is captured in the learned associations between them. In the very course of perception, therefore, this knowledge serves to corroborate the sensory system's noisy transmission of letter order. In keeping with this view, good readers rarely err in reporting the order of the letters in either real words or regularly spelled nonwords (such as *bome* or *mave*). Yet when faced with orthographically irregular strings such as *gtsi* or *ynrh*, they make just as many ordering errors as do poor readers—even more if they were *expecting* to see a regularly spelled string (Adams, 1979b).

There are several ways in which readers can conquer the letter-order problem even without well-developed interletter associations. One is to stick with print that is sufficiently large and spaced out so that no two letters will share the same physical input channel; no doubt this is the underlying reason for our time-honored practice of setting primers in large type. Another is for readers to increase the number or duration of their fixations on each word. In keeping with this, note that prolonged and repeated fixations on words are characteristic of young and disabled readers (Just & Carpenter, 1987). In the long run, however, the only efficient and reliable way around this difficulty is for readers to learn more about likely and unlikely sequences of letters in the words of their language. Eventually, this knowledge will come to compensate for the visual system's inherent difficulty with letter order.

Breaking Words Into Syllables. Struggle as they might, poor readers characteristically block on long, polysyllabic words—even when those words are familiar within their oral vocabulary. In contrast, skillful readers rarely experience such difficulty. As an example, try reading the following: *trypsinogen, anfractuosity, prolegomenous, interfascicular.* Although none of these words may be familiar to you, chances are that your attempts to read them were relatively forthcoming as well as correct, or nearly so. Moreover, if you listened carefully to your reading performance, you may have heard yourself producing them in a manner much closer to syllable by syllable than holistically or letter by letter.

It turns out that skillful readers' ability to read long words depends inseparably on their ability to break the words into syllables (Mewhort & Campbell, 1981), and this is true for familiar as well as unfamiliar words. Laboratory studies prove that skillful readers break words into syllables automatically and in the very course of perceiving their letters. The means by which skillful readers do this is again rooted in their overlearned knowledge about likely and unlikely sequences of letters. More specifically, for any language that is basically alphabetic, strings of speech sounds that can be co-articulated tend to be represented by frequent sequences of letters, while those that cannot, are not. As an example, the spoken sequence /dr____/ is a frequent and pronounceable form in English—as in *drag, dress, drip,* and *drove*—while /dn___/ is not. Consistent with this, the letter sequence *dr*___ is 40 times more likely to occur in print than the sequence *dn*___ (Mayzner & Tresselt, 1965). Through the learned associations in the reader's letter-recognition network, the letters *d* and *r* will automatically boost each other's perceptibility when seen in print, while the letters *d* and *n* will not.

The importance of this difference is that, although unlikely letter sequences such as *dn* cannot occur within the same syllable, they can and do occur at syllable boundaries (for example, *midnight, baldness, kidnap, Sidney*). As the reader processes such words, the likely combinations of letters promote and attract one another, emerging perceptually as a cohesive spelling pattern. At the same time, however, the unlikely pairs inhibit and repel each other, thus pushing separate syllables apart. As a result, the perceived letters are tightly bound to one another within syllables but somewhat detached at the boundaries between syllables. In this way, polysyllabic words are perceived as sequences of spelling patterns corresponding to syllabic units.

At this point, a word of caution is warranted. The knowledge underlying automatic syllabification skills cannot be directly instilled. To ask children to study unlikely letter pairs would be counterproductive: It would serve to increase the strength of the associations between such letters in memory, which is just the opposite of what is needed. Beyond that, one cannot hope to specify spelling patterns corresponding to syllabic units or their boundaries independent of the larger orthographic context in which they occur. That is, one cannot take any given letter string—say, *par*—and proclaim it to be a syllabic unit. Sometimes it will be (*par-tial, par-take*), and sometimes it will not (*part-ly, pa-rade*). In syllabifying words, the orthographic processor responds to the relative strengths of the interletter associations (Adams, 1981; Seidenberg, 1987). Using knowledge of simple letter sequences as well as larger letter patterns (for example, *fa-ther* versus *fat-head*), it breaks a word into syllables not at predesignated junctures but at the weakest link between letters. It can do so only to the extent that the reader has acquired a broad and deep knowledge of orthography. Meanwhile, there is much to recommend that oft-used technique of helping children penetrate those troublesome long words by uncovering them syllable by syllable as they read.

Helping Beginners. Before leaving this section, it is worth reflecting that all the orthographic processor's magic presumes a deep and ready knowledge of the letterwise spellings of words. Quick, holistic word recognition, comfort with grown-up-sized print, automatic syllabification, morphemic sensitivity—all of these depend on such knowledge. At the same time, research indicates that difficulties at the level of letter and word recognition are the single most pervasive and debilitating cause of reading disability (Perfetti, 1985; Stanovich, 1986; Vellutino, 1991; Vernon, 1971).

Fortunately, theory and research also affirm that human memory is well designed for learning about such relations among letters—but only if it is induced to attend to them in the course of perception. Here, then, is a problem. In general, children seem disposed to view words not as ordered and analyzable strings of letters but holistically, rather like pictures (Byrne, 1992; Masonheimer, Drum, & Ehri, 1984). Indeed, given a good visual memory, children have shown themselves able to recognize several thousand words through this approach (Juel, 1991). But can they learn 50,000? And when they find they cannot, how difficult—cognitively and emotionally—will it be to effect repairs?

Beginning reading is quite difficult for some children. One of the reasons is surely that the knowledge to respond instantly, effortlessly, and accurately to frequent words and spelling patterns involves an impressive amount of perceptual learning. Regardless of intelligence, effort, rearing, or desire, this learning settles in more quickly for some children than for others. There are many ways to support this learning—including writing, spelling, and phonics instruction; patience; encouragement; and lots of beneath-frustration-level reading and rereading. However, research argues firmly that there is no substitute for it.

The Context Processor

The context processor is in charge of constructing a coherent, ongoing interpretation of the text. In particular, it is responsible for priming and selecting word meanings that are appropriate to the text. This is important not just for blatantly ambiguous words (such as soccer *ball* versus inaugural *ball*) but, to a lesser extent, for almost any word.

As an example, consider the word *Wyoming*. Those of us in the United States might consider *Wyoming* to have a unique and stable meaning as a proper noun. Nevertheless, its mention brings very different images to mind in a discussion of presidential campaign strategies and electoral college votes than it does in a discussion of beautiful national parks. In fact, both of these images—and many more besides—are part of the total array of meaning that each of us associates with the word *Wyoming*. We are able to follow discussions of Wyoming with understanding because the context processor selectively emphasizes those aspects of a word's total meaning that are relevant to its ongoing interpretation.

In theory, the context processor works by sending its own stimulation to the meanings that it expects. This extra stimulation boosts the contextually appropriate dimensions of a word's meaning, causing them to dominate the reader's interpretation of the text. Yet even while the context processor facilitates the reader's awareness of appropriate words and meanings, it does not prevent stimulation of inappropriate ones. To use an earlier example, given a sentence such as "John saw several spiders, roaches, and bugs," people very briefly show signs (but not conscious awareness) of having interpreted the last word to mean both "insects" and "spying devices" (Seidenberg et al., 1982). Alternatively, given a sentence such as "At the farmstand, we got tomatoes, squash, and corn on the ___," the reader may quite automatically—thanks to the context processor—expect the word *cob*. But if the complete sentence turns out, instead, to read, "At the farmstand, we got tomatoes, squash, and corn on the car," that expectation would be quickly overridden. And, nearly as quickly, the context processor would also revise the reader's understanding of the situation so it meets the text.

For skillful readers, the role of context is not to displace or supplant the information on the page; it is, instead, to help the reader make the most of that information, as quickly and efficiently as possible. To that end, it is necessarily the author's words that must take precedence. Consistent with this, study after study has shown that context significantly affects the speed or accuracy with which skillful readers perceive familiar words *only* when the experimenter has done something to slow or disrupt the orthographic processing of the word (see, e.g., Stanovich, 1980, 1984).

Provided that a text is not too difficult, beginners, like skillful readers, are naturally attuned to its linguistic and semantic flow as they read. Further, as long as the stories are simple and until the processes involved in visual word recognition are fairly well developed, many readers find that they often can guess the identity of a word as accurately and more easily than they can decode it. For these reasons, it has been found that among young and disabled readers, word-recognition performance is especially sensitive to context and contextually appropriate substitution errors are frequent (see, e.g., Biemiller, 1970; Weber, 1970).

Although such sensitivity to context can only be a good sign, its dominance is a symptom that orthographic processing is proceeding neither quickly nor completely enough to do its job. But, one might ask, is this reason for concern? If the children are grasping the meaning of the text well enough to fill in the blanks, then clearly they are reading thoughtfully and strategically. If so, is there any reason to intervene?

As you ponder these questions, I ask you to add the following consideration. As the purpose of classroom texts shifts from one of learning to read to one of reading to learn, children will increasingly encounter words they do not recognize in contexts that do not help. Very often, however, it will be precisely these unknown words—*isosceles*, *circumference*, *photosynthesis*, *Antarctica*, *equator*—that are most central to the point of the lesson.

Research shows that as children move a little further into the reading process—usually toward the end of first grade or the beginning of second—they often turn what seems disproportionate attention to the individual words on the page. Suddenly, they start reading *there* for *three*, *was* for *saw*, and *from* for *form*; the effort they invest in reading a word seems unrelieved by the most obvious of contextual cues; their misreadings, while graphically related to the print on the page, may often be wholly inappropriate in context; and they may develop a tendency to stare at difficult words without responding at all.

For different children, these tendencies may be more or less pronounced and may persist for longer or shorter periods. Nevertheless, as Downing (1979) explains, these tendencies reflect a necessary and highly functional phase in the acquisition of any complex skill. The only way for the visual system to learn about the spellings of words is by devoting attention to them. As the spellings of more and more words are internalized, decoding will become more and more automatic, and only when it becomes automatic can it properly work in concert, rather than in competition, with contextual processing. Meanwhile, the instructional challenge is not to quash this phase but to help children through it as efficiently, effectively, and supportively as possible. To this end, there may be no better means than encouraging a lot of reading and rereading of interesting and beneath-frustration-level text.

The Meaning Processor

The inner workings of the meaning processor appear similar to those of the orthographic processor. In particular, the units in the meaning processor apparently do not correspond to whole, familiar words. Instead, just as the spellings of familiar words are represented in the orthographic processor as interassociated sets of letters, their meanings are represented in the meaning processor as interassociated sets of more primitive meaning elements. It is this piecemeal nature of word meanings that allows us to focus on one aspect or another of a word's full meaning as appropriate in context. In addition, it enables us to acquire the meaning of new words gradually by encountering them in context.

Learning New Word Meanings From Context. Suppose that, while reading a story, a child encounters a word that he or she has neither seen nor heard before. As usual, the spelling and pronunciation of this word will be shipped automatically to the meaning processor, but because the word is entirely unfamiliar, it cannot in itself evoke any particular meaning. Instead, when the word reaches the meaning processor, all it will find is the pattern of activation provoked by the context processor. This pattern may be more or less diffuse, depending on how tightly the context has anticipated the unknown word. Nevertheless, when the orthographic pattern meets these activated meaning units, a bond will begin to form between them.

The impact of such an incidental learning experience is expected to be small: Context is rarely pointed enough to predict the precise meaning of a word. On the other hand, it's a start. When the same word is encountered again, it will meet whatever was learned from the prior context plus the meaning set off by the new context. Wherever the meaning units of the old and new contexts overlap, they will become more strongly associated with one another and with the orthographic and phonological representations of the word. Given a number of encounters with this word over a variety of different contexts, the units that are reinforced most often will be those that belong to the meaning of the word itself. In this way, the word may eventually be learned well enough to contribute independently and appropriately to the meaning of a text, if not to allow the child to generate a well-articulated dictionary definition.

Although important, such learning from context is inherently gradual and imprecise. The likelihood that a child will learn the meaning of a word from a single exposure in meaningful context ranges from 5% to 20% (Nagy, Anderson, & Herman, 1987). By implication, the extent of such incidental vocabulary acquisition depends strongly on the amount a child reads. The average fifth grader is estimated to read about 1 million words of text per year: 650,000 out of school and the rest in school (Nagy, Herman, & Anderson, 1985). Of these words, roughly 16,000 to 24,000 will be unknown (Anderson & Freebody, 1983). Conservatively assuming a 5% chance of learning each, the result is a vocabulary increase of 800 to 1,200 new words each year through reading. Learning from context accordingly accounts for a substantial fraction of the 3,000 new words that children are, on average, expected to master each year (Miller & Gildea, 1987).

This research sheds light on some of the most striking differences observed in children's conceptual growth. The estimates above are based on the average reader. Some children read millions and millions of words of text each year; their vocabularies are expected to be strong. At the same time, others read practically nothing at all outside of school. Overall, Nagy, Anderson, and Herman (1987) estimate that the 90th percentile student reads about *200 times* more text per year than the 10th percentile student does. Learning begets learning. The amount that children read influences not only their vocabulary growth but also the conceptual and linguistic knowledge that enables that growth and makes it useful.

Direct Vocabulary Instruction. Beyond such learning through reading, direct vocabulary instruction has been shown to result in a general increase in both word knowledge and reading comprehension (Stahl & Fairbanks, 1986). To be most effective, such instruction should include a number of examples of the word's usage in context in addition to definitional information. Research has shown that in direct vocabulary instruction as in incidental learning, the number of times children encounter a word is a strong predictor of how well they learn it. But almost as important as the number of encounters is the richness and variety of the contexts in which the word appears. Of particular interest is the finding that through rich and diverse experiences with a word, children appear to gain a special advantage in understanding its connotations or submeanings in specific contexts and in exploiting its extended meaning in text comprehension (McKeown et al., 1985).

Prefixes, Suffixes, and Roots. The direct link between the orthographic and meaning processors may also be responsible for skillful readers' perceptual sensitivity to the roots and affixes of polysyllabic words (see Fowler, Napps, & Feldman, 1985; Manelis & Tharp, 1977; Taft, 1985; Tyler & Nagy, 1987). Moreover, this link prompts the idea that teaching children about derivational morphologies might be a useful step toward both spelling and vocabulary development.

For example, once one sees that *concurrent* consists of "with" (*con-*) plus *current*, the word is no longer a spelling problem; it must have two *rs* as in *current*, and it can't end in *-ant* or it would mean *with a raisin*. Conversely, knowing the meanings of common roots may qualitatively and profitably change one's understanding of other words in their derivational family. Thus, learning that *fid* means "trust" or "faith" may significantly alter and connect one's understanding of words like *confidence*, *fidelity*, *fiduciary*, and *bona fide*; discovering that *path* means "suffering" may alter and connect one's understanding of words like *sympathy*, *psychopath*, and *pathologist*. Moreover, a well-developed sensitivity to morphological clues may be useful for inferring the meanings of new words.

All such advantages notwithstanding, research demonstrates that adult readers of English are surprisingly oblivious to the morphological structure of words (Kaye & Sternberg, 1982), and efforts specifically intended to teach children about the derivational morphologies of words have yielded mixed results (Johnson & Baumann, 1984; Otterman, 1955). Although such lessons have been shown to increase children's proficiency with both the spellings and meanings of the words studied, they have produced little increase in their ability to interpret new derivationally complex words.

In the end, it may be that such morphologically based insights never come automatically but only through deliberate search. Perhaps the wordsmith's advantage is principally strategic; he or she has learned to examine each new word for familiar parts and to think about their implications with respect to the word's usage and meaning. If so, then perhaps the objectives of our lessons on derivationally complex words should be rethought. Perhaps instead of teaching children about any particular sets of roots or affixes, our objective should be one of developing children's *awareness* of word structure and their inclination to look for and think about such relations in new words.

As an inspiring example of the promise of this approach, I refer you to a monograph by O'Rourke (1974). As O'Rourke led his students to make a habit of seeking, comparing, contrasting, and categorizing the meanings and spellings of complex words, their measurable vocabulary scores increased quite dramatically. In addition, showing that these lessons had affected not just their knowledge of particular words but also their thinking about them, the children tended to create new words to suit their expressive needs while writing—for example, *jector* (hurler), *tracted* (pulled, hauled), *audict* (someone who likes to hear records), *intraction* (pulling from within), *solarscope* (sun viewer), *phonomatic* (something that makes sounds by itself), *astrometer* (a device that measures stars). While some of these words are endearingly funny, others are soberingly legitimate.

In any case, it may also be wise to recognize that word roots and syllabic units rarely coincide. In terms of syllables, for example, the word *information* may be parsed into *in-for-ma-tion*; in terms of morphemes, it is *in-form-ation*. Research has demonstrated that the spelling patterns to which children are asked to attend during instruction significantly influence the patterns to which they do attend during word recognition (Juel & Roper/Schneider, 1985). Research also indicates that, for purposes of facilitating word recognition, it is familiarity with patterns that occur in a large variety of words that is most helpful (Juel, 1983). Thus, while appreciation of the *form* in *information* might shed light on its deeper meaning, familiarity with the *for* will help a reader read more words. The suggestion is that even when and if the worth of lessons on derivational morphology is firmly demonstrated, such instruction may nevertheless be best postponed until later years of schooling.

In summary, the most important point of this section is that meaningful experiences with words are important to the acquisition of the words' usage and interpretation as well as their orthography. The best way to foster children's visual vocabulary—as well as their larger literacy growth—is to have them read as frequently, broadly, and thoughtfully as possible. It is not merely that such reading results in vocabulary growth but that, more important, it affords children the conceptual and linguistic experience that at once enable that growth and make it worthwhile.

The Phonological Processor

Intuition suggests that visually familiar words can be recognized immediately and directly by sight, with no need for sounding out at any level. Consistent with this, research affirms that skillful readers do not depend on phonological translations for recognizing familiar words (see Spoehr, 1981). On the other hand, skillful readers automatically and rather irrepressibly seem to produce such translations anyway (Perfetti, Bell, & Delaney, 1988; Tannenhaus, Flanigan, & Seidenberg, 1980; VanOrden, 1991). Far from being unnecessary, the phonological loop provides invaluable support to the reader. First, it provides a redundant processing route—a back-up system—for the orthographic processor. Second, it provides critical support for the comprehension process as it effectively increases the reader's running memory for text. Without the added assistance of the phonological processor, even the most skillful readers would find themselves faltering for fluency and comprehension except with the easiest text.

As with the other processors, the phonological processor is seen to contain a complex network of units. The auditory image of any particular word, syllable, or phoneme corresponds to the activation of a particular, interconnected set of those units (McClelland & Elman, 1986). Figure 1 shows how readers' phonological knowledge and processes are related to the rest of the reading system. Note especially how the phonological processor is connected in both directions to the orthographic processor and the meaning processor. The arrow that runs from the orthographic to the phonological processor indicates that, even as the orthographic processor begins to resolve the image of a string of letters, it relays stimulation to corresponding units in the phonological processor. Meanwhile, the activation of a word's pronunciation will, in turn, pass stimulation to its meaning, as symbolized by the arrow running from the phonological to the meaning processor. In this way, the connections through the phonological processor provide a means for identifying words that, although visually unfamiliar, are in the reader's speaking or listening vocabulary. Yet that is only their most immediate and obvious advantage.

To the extent that any word is both orally and visually familiar, this process ensures that the meaning processor will receive activation from *both* the phonological and the orthographic processor. As these contributions support and interact with one another, they serve to ease and speed recognition of the word. Further, as the response of the meaning processor is strengthened and focused, so too is the activation that it passes back to the other processors—and the stronger the feedback, the greater the learning. Thus, the contributions of the phonological processor act to hasten and consolidate the direct connections between all the processors, and that includes the *direct* connections between sight and meaning.

The connections running from the phonological processor back to the orthographic processor are equally important in supporting visual learning. Specifically, where the efforts of the orthographic processor arouse pronounceable responses in the phonological processor, the phonological processor will reciprocally send excitation right back. In this way, the feedback from the phonological processor provokes the orthographic processor to attend to letters that might otherwise be overlooked, even while helping it glue the whole, correctly ordered string together. The prior knowledge and constraints offered by the phonological processor play an indispensable role in helping young readers organize, consolidate, and remember spelling patterns visually.

Finally, note that there is also an arrow running from the meaning processor to the phonological processor in Figure 1. Because of this connection, the activation of a word's meaning will send stimulation to the phonological units corresponding to its pronunciation. The reader's tendency to translate print to speech is thus doubly stimulated, both from the word's spelling and from its meaning. This is one reason that phonological translation of print is so automatic—and beyond that, it completes the circularity and feedback of the system in both directions. It is this circularity and feedback that ultimately underlies the automaticity of the word-recognition system. Because of this circularity, the responses of all the processors speed and support one another wherever they are consistent; wherever they are inconsistent, they are automatically corrected or flagged for special attention.

The phonological processor has two other features that set it apart from the others. First, like the orthographic processor, the phonological processor accepts information from the outside, although the information it accepts is speech. (The orthographic processor remains the only one to receive information directly from the printed page.) Second—and this turns out to be an important asset in reading—the knowledge represented within the phonological processor can be activated at will. We can speak, subvocalize, or otherwise generate speech images whenever we wish.

Phonological Translation and Fluent Word Recognition. As shown in Figure 1 and supported by our intuitions, phonological translation is not always necessary for word recognition. As reflected by the direct connections between the orthographic and meaning processors, visually familiar words can be recognized and understood with no need of phonological translation. Yet a word can map instantly, effortlessly, and accurately from sight to meaning only to the extent that its unique, ordered sequence of letters has been visually learned and overlearned through experience. The problem is that printed words vary enormously in their frequency and, therefore, in their visual familiarity to a reader.

Analyses of the everyday reading matter of adults reveal that the vast majority of print consists of relatively few, very frequently occurring words (Kučera & Francis, 1967). Because each of these words is highly familiar to the skilled reader, each is recognized quickly and easily. However, these oft-repeated words account for but a small fraction of the number of different words readers encounter. The vast majority of distinct words in print are relatively infrequent—occurring less than once in every million words of running text. Because these words are so rarely seen, the reader's visual familiarity with most of them must be relatively weak and incomplete—often too weak and incomplete to support the perceptual speed and automaticity on which comprehension depends.

Word counts of children's reading materials reveal a similar pattern. Fifty percent of the print they are likely to see, in school and out, is accounted for by only 109 different words, 90% by only 5,000 different words (Carroll, Davies, & Richman, 1971). It is reasonable to suppose that not too far into their schooling, most children will be quick to recognize most of these words by sight. But how are they to cope with the tens of thousands of other words they see? It will not do to skip such words or guess at their identities. Although the coherence of a text depends strongly on its frequent words—*it*, *that*, *this*, *and*, *because*, *when*, *while*, and so on—the information in a text depends on its less frequent words—*doctor*, *fever*, *infection*, *medicine*, *penicillin*, *Alexander Fleming*, *melon*, *mold*, *poison*, *bacteria*, *antibiotic*, *protect*, *germs*, and *disease*, for example. For skillful readers, automatic phonological translations provide a back-up system for recognizing visually less familiar words. As a consequence of the alphabetic principle, syllables are represented by frequent spelling patterns. For the skillful reader, therefore, even if a word as a whole is not visually familiar, fragments of its spelling most certainly will be. Because of the reader's spelling–sound associations, these spelling patterns will be translated automatically to their phonological equivalents. If the word is in the reader's speaking or listening vocabulary, its pronunciation will in turn evoke its meaning. In this way, even the occasional never-before-seen word may be read and understood with little or no outward sign or feeling of difficulty.

The automaticity of skillful readers' spelling-to-sound translations ensures that those many words of marginal visual familiarity will be recognized with the ease and speed required for fluent reading comprehension. Further, as the phonological translations serve to turn on both the word's meaning and its spelling, each encounter with the word strengthens direct spelling-to-meaning connections.

Phonological Translation and Comprehension. As it turns out, the value of automatic phonological translations extends beyond their service to the word-recognition process. Specifically, the language comprehension system is designed to work with whole, cohesive grammatical units—whole phrases' or sentences' worth of words—at once. Whether in listening or reading, the process through which it does so is much the same (Jarvella, 1971; Kleiman, 1975). In either case, the words of a message are presented and perceived one by one. And although they are tentatively interpreted on the fly, they are fully digested only afterward, when the clause or sentence is complete. In mystical deference to this process, speakers drop their pitch and pause at the end of every sentence; by dropping their pitch, they let their listeners know that it's time to interpret, and by pausing, they afford their listeners time to do so. Mimicking this rhythm, skillful readers are found to march their eyes through all the words of a sentence from beginning to end, and when they reach the period, they pause and think (Just & Carpenter, 1987).

Again, it is during these end-of-sentence pauses that listeners or readers actively construct and reflect on their interpretations, that they work out the collective meaning of the chain of words in memory and that meaning's contribution to their overall understanding of the conversation or text. Yet in order for this interpretive process to succeed, the whole clause or sentence must still exist, more or less intact, in the listener's or reader's memory when she or he is ready to work on it. So what does this have to do with phonological translations? A lot. Whereas the visual system is designed for encoding spatial patterns and transitions, the auditory system is designed for remembering ordered temporal patterns of information. Thus, by thinking or speaking the words to themselves, skillful readers effectively extend the longevity and holding capacity of their verbatim memory. Preventing skillful readers from subvocalizing does not impair their ability to interpret single, familiar words or simple sentences; on the other hand, it severely disrupts their ability to remember or comprehend long or complex sentences (Baddeley, 1979; Levy, 1977, 1978; Waters, Caplan, & Hildebrandt, 1987). In keeping with this, you may notice that your own tendency to subvocalize becomes more noticeable when you are trying to read sentences that are especially long and difficult.

Even though this particular advantage of phonological translation has nothing to do with word identification per se, it points up one more reason the speed and effortlessness of the word-recognition process is so important. Auditory memory is highly sensitive to the pace with which information arrives (Dempster, 1981). If it takes a child too long to identify successive words, the beginning of the sentence will fade from memory before the end has been registered. Further, where a child is actively engaged in sounding out individual letters and syllables, the phonological processor is necessarily unavailable for retaining the wording of clauses. (For a discussion of the trade-offs between processing and storage demands in the reading situation, see Daneman & Tardif, 1987; Perfetti, 1985.)

Phonological Translations: A Once-Over. In sum, phonological translations are subservient to both reading and learning to read in a number of different ways. Most obviously, the capacity for phonological translations underlies the ability to "sound out" new words. Less obvious but of equal importance, where the sounding out process is reasonably fast and efficient, it serves powerfully to hasten the word's visual acquisition. Moreover, the benefits of this basic ability are no less valuable for mature readers than they are for beginners. In particular, it ensures that those many, many words of known meaning but limited visual familiarity can be recognized with the ease and speed required for reading with fluency and comprehension.

In this vein, it is worth noting that of the thousands upon thousands of different words that a skillful reader is expected to know, the vast majority are encountered very rarely. The person with an average daily diet of print would be lucky to have seen many of these words even once in a whole year's worth of reading. How many of these words would you lose, how many would fade away or blur together, if you depended on the strength and completeness of your visual memory alone? Finally, research shows that long and complex sentences cannot be understood without the mnemonic support gained through phonological translation.

The capacity for rapid, easy phonological translation has sometimes been dismissed as superfluous, optional, or even as a misguided or dysfunctional diversion of effort. Against these notions, insensitivity to the sounds of speech and difficulties in relating them to letters and spellings are found to be the single most frequent hole in the reading and language abilities of disabled readers of all ages (for reviews, see, e.g., Brady & Shankweiler, 1991; Carr & Levy, 1990; Stanovich, 1986). When given special instruction on breaking words into sounds and relating sounds to spellings, such readers generally do improve—sometimes dramatically (Blachman, 1987; Williams, 1979, 1980). Despite such help, however, Bruck (1992) has shown that, for many dyslexics, a core difficulty with spellings and sounds persists even into adulthood—and alongside, their reading continues to be slow and effortful.

In principle, the letters of an alphabetic script represent the phonemes of its language. Because of this, learning about spelling–sound relationships in a way that is useful for reading depends on phonemic awareness—that is, it depends on a conscious recognition that the sounds of words can be represented by a relatively small set of articulatory gestures, the phonemes.

Phonemic awareness is not natural. Instead, the ease with which people can gain conscious access to their phonological knowledge ranges broadly and appears to be determined, in part, by heredity (Olson et al., 1990). It is because of its difficulty for so many children that solid attention to the development of phonemic awareness is so vital a component of the preschool and primary classroom. Moreover, the pressing issue for the field of dyslexia at this time is the extent to which the elusiveness of its cure derives from the difficulties of trying to turn off or displace an overlearned but self-limiting mode of perceiving text. To what extent would the syndrome go away if we could ensure that all children got off to the right start?

Summary

Relative to the overall literacy challenge, learning to recognize words really is a very small component. Yet it is also wholly necessary. In the end, the print on the page constitutes the basic perceptual data of reading. Rather than diverting efforts in search of meaning, the reader's letter- and word-wise processes supply the text-based information on which comprehension depends. As fluent readers move quickly and easily through the print, literal comprehension automatically unfolds apace.

But neither is literal comprehension the goal of reading. The full interpretation of a complex text may require retrieval of particular facts or events that were presented many pages earlier. It may also require consideration of knowledge and construction of arguments that are entirely extraneous to the text. And it certainly requires the critical and inferential activities necessary for putting such information together.

To be sure, it is this level of interpretation that we think of as true understanding. Yet interpretation at this level is not automatic; it requires active attention and can only be as fruitful as the effort and quality of thought that readers invest in it. But the effort and thought that readers can invest depends, in turn, on the ease and completeness with which they have executed the levels that support it. Deep and ready working knowledge of letters, spelling patterns, and words, and of the phonological translations of all three, are of inescapable importance to both skillful reading and its acquisition—not because they are the be-all or the end-all of the reading process, but because they enable it.

QUESTIONS FOR REFLECTION

1. How does the model that Adams developed help us understand why poor readers block on long, polysyllabic words?
2. In the introduction to her model, Adams poses the question, "Do skillful readers use context to anticipate upcoming words so as to reduce the visual detail they need from the text?" (p. 785). How does her model answer that question?
3. Do you agree or disagree with the importance that Adams gives to phonological translation in her model? Explain your position in the context of her model and your understanding of phonological processing.
4. Why do you think Adams decided to present a description of her model's four processors in the order she presents them?

NOTE

*When this chapter was written, Adams was at Bolt Beranek and Newman.

REFERENCES

Adams, M.J. (1979a). Models of word recognition. *Cognitive Psychology, 11*, 133–176.

Adams, M.J. (1979b). Some differences between good and poor readers. In M.L. Kamil & A.J. Moe (Eds.), *Reading research: Studies and applications* (pp. 140–144). Clemson, SC: National Reading Conference.

Adams, M.J. (1981). What good is orthographic redundancy? In O.J.L. Tzeng & H. Singer (Eds.), *Perception of print* (pp. 197–221). Hillsdale, NJ: Erlbaum.

Adams, M.J. (1990). *Beginning to read: Thinking and learning about print*. Cambridge, MA: MIT Press.

Anderson, R.C., & Freebody, P. (1983). Reading comprehension and the assessment and acquisition of word knowledge. In B. Hutson (Ed.), *Advances in reading/language research* (pp. 231–256). Greenwich, CT: JAI Press.

Baddeley, A.D. (1979). Working memory and reading. In P. Kolers, E. Wrolstad, & H. Bouma (Eds.), *Processing of visible language* (Vol. 1). New York: Plenum.

Barron, R.W. (1981a). Development of visual word recognition: A review. In G.E. MacKinnon & T.G. Waller (Eds.), *Reading research: Advances in theory and practice* (Vol. 3, pp. 119–158). New York: Academic.

Barron, R.W. (1981b). Reading skill and reading strategies. In A.M. Lesgold & C.A. Perfetti (Eds.), *Interactive processes in reading* (pp. 299–328). Hillsdale, NJ: Erlbaum.

Bereiter, C. (1991). Implications of connectionism for thinking about rules. *Educational Researcher, 20*(3), 10–16.

Biemiller, A. (1970). The development of the use of graphic and contextual information as children learn to read. *Reading Research Quarterly*, 6, 75–96.

Blachman, B.A. (1987). An alternative classroom reading program for learning disabled and other low-achieving children. In W. Ellis (Ed.), *Intimacy with language: A forgotten basic in teacher education* (pp. 49–55). Baltimore: Orton Dyslexia Society.

Brady, S.A., & Shankweiler, D.P. (1991). *Phonological processes in literacy*. Hillsdale, NJ: Erlbaum.

Bruck, M. (1992). Persistence of dyslexics' phonological awareness deficits. *Developmental Psychology*, 28, 874–886.

Byrne, B. (1992). Studies in the acquisition procedure for reading: Rationale, hypotheses, and data. In P.B. Gough, L.C. Ehri, & R. Treiman (Eds.), *Reading acquisition* (pp. 1–34). Hillsdale, NJ: Erlbaum.

Carr, T.H., & Levy, B.A. (1990). *Reading and its development*. Hillsdale, NJ: Erlbaum.

Carroll, J.B., Davies, P., & Richman, B. (1971). *Word frequency book*. Boston: Houghton Mifflin.

Cattell, J.M. (1885). Über die Zeit der Erkennung und Benennung von Schriftzeichen, Bildern und Farben [The time it takes to recognize and name letters, pictures, and colors]. *Philosophische Studien*, 2, 635–650.

Daneman, M., & Tardif, T. (1987). Working memory and reading skill re-examined. In M. Coltheart (Ed.), *Attention and performance XII: The psychology of reading* (pp. 491–508). Hillsdale, NJ: Erlbaum.

Dempster, F.N. (1981). Memory span: Sources of individual and developmental differences. *Psychological Bulletin*, 89, 63–100.

De Zuniga, C.M., Humphreys, G.W., & Evett, L.J. (1991). Additive and interactive effects of repetition, degradation, and word frequency in the reading of handwriting. In D. Besner & G.W. Humphreys (Eds.), *Basic processes in reading* (pp. 10–33). Hillsdale, NJ: Erlbaum.

Downing, J. (1979). *Reading and reasoning*. New York: Springer-Verlag.

Estes, W.K. (1977). On the interaction of perception and memory in reading. In D. LaBerge & S.J. Samuels (Eds.), *Basic processes in reading* (pp. 1–25). Hillsdale, NJ: Erlbaum.

Fowler, C.A., Napps, S., & Feldman, L. (1985). Relations among regular and irregular morphologically related words in the lexicon as revealed by repetition priming. *Journal of Experimental Psychology: Learning, Memory, and Cognition, 10*, 241–255.

Gough, P.B., Alford, J.A., & Holley-Wilcox, P. (1981). Words and contexts. In O.J.L. Tzeng & H. Singer (Eds.), *Perception of print* (pp. 85–102). Hillsdale, NJ: Erlbaum.

Jarvella, R. (1971). Syntactic processing of connected speech. *Journal of Verbal Learning and Verbal Behavior, 10*, 409–416.

Johnson, D.D., & Baumann, J.F. (1984). Word identification. In P.D. Pearson, R. Barr, M.L. Kamil, & P. Mosenthal (Eds.), *Handbook of reading research* (pp. 583–608). New York: Longman.

Juel, C. (1983). The development and use of mediated word identification. *Reading Research Quarterly, 18*, 306–327.

Juel, C. (1988). Learning to read and write: A longitudinal study of fifty-four children from first through fourth grade. *Journal of Educational Psychology, 80*, 437–447.

Juel, C. (1991). Beginning reading. In R. Barr, M.L. Kamil, P. Mosenthal, & P.D. Pearson (Eds.), *Handbook of reading research* (Vol. 2, pp. 759–788). White Plains, NY: Longman.

Juel, C., & Roper/Schneider, D. (1985). The influence of basal readers on first grade reading. *Reading Research Quarterly, 20*, 134–152.

Just, M.A., & Carpenter, P.A. (1987). *The psychology of reading and language comprehension*. Boston: Allyn & Bacon.

Kaye, D.B., & Sternberg, R.J. (1982). *The development of lexical decomposition ability*. Unpublished manuscript, Yale University, New Haven, CT.

Kleiman, G.M. (1975). Speech recoding in reading. *Journal of Verbal Learning and Verbal Behavior, 14*, 323–339.

Kučera, H., & Francis, W.N. (1967). *Computational analysis of present-day American English.* Providence, RI: Brown University Press.

Levy, B.A. (1977). Reading: Speech and meaning processes. *Journal of Verbal Learning and Verbal Behavior, 16*, 623–628.

Levy, B.A. (1978). Speech processes during reading. In A.M. Lesgold, S.W. Pellegrino, S.W. Fokkema, & R. Glaser (Eds.), *Cognitive psychology and instruction.* New York: Plenum.

Liberman, I.Y., Shankweiler, D., Orlando, C., Harris, K.S., & Berti, F.B. (1971). Letter confusions and reversals of sequence in the beginning reader: Implications for Orton's theory of developmental dyslexia. *Cortex, 7*, 127–142.

Manelis, L., & Tharp, D. (1977). The processing of affixed words. *Memory and Cognition, 5*, 690–695.

Masonheimer, P.E., Drum, P.A., & Ehri, L.C. (1984). Does environmental print identification lead children into word reading? *Journal of Reading Behavior, 16*, 257–271.

Mayzner, M.S., & Tresselt, M.E. (1965). Tables of single-letter and digram frequency-counts for various word-length and letter position combinations. *Psychonomic Monograph Supplements, 1*, 13–32.

McClelland, J.L., & Elman, J.L. (1986). The TRACE model of speech perception. *Cognitive Psychology, 18*, 1–86.

McClelland, J.L., & Rumelhart, D.E. (1981). An interactive activation model of context effects in letter perception: Part 1, an account of basic findings. *Psychological Review, 88*, 373–407.

McConkie, G.W., & Zola, D. (1981). Language constraints and the functional stimulus in reading. In A.M. Lesgold & C.A. Perfetti (Eds.), *Interactive processes in reading* (pp. 155–175). Hillsdale, NJ: Erlbaum.

McKeown, M.G., Beck, I.L., Omanson, R.C., & Pople, M.T. (1985). Some effects of the nature and frequency of vocabulary instruction on the knowledge and use of words. *Reading Research Quarterly, 20*, 522–535.

Mewhort, D.J.K., & Campbell, A.J. (1981). Toward a model of skilled reading: An analysis of performance in tachistoscopic tasks. In G.E. MacKinnon & T.G. Waller (Eds.), *Reading research: Advances in theory and practice* (Vol. 3, pp. 39–118). New York: Academic.

Miller, G.A., & Gildea, P.M. (1987): How children learn words. *Scientific American, 257*(3), 94–99.

Nagy, W.E., Anderson, R.C., & Herman, P.A. (1987). Learning word meanings from context during normal reading. *American Educational Research Journal, 24*, 237–270.

Nagy, W.E., Herman, P.A., & Anderson, R.C. (1985). Learning words from context. *Reading Research Quarterly, 20*, 233–253.

Olson, R., Wise, B., Conners, F., & Rack, J. (1990). Organization, heritability, and remediation of component word recognition and language skills in disabled readers. In T.H. Carr & B.A. Levy (Eds.), *Reading and its development* (pp. 261–322). Hillsdale, NJ: Erlbaum.

O'Rourke, J.P. (1974). *Toward a science of vocabulary development.* The Hague, the Netherlands: Mouton.

Otterman, L.M. (1955). The value of teaching prefixes and word-roots. *Journal of Educational Research, 48*, 611–616.

Patterson, K.E., & Coltheart, V. (1987). Phonological processes in reading: A tutorial review. In M. Coltheart (Ed.), *Attention and performance XII: The psychology of reading.* Hillsdale, NJ: Erlbaum.

Perfetti, C.A. (1985). *Reading ability.* New York: Oxford University Press.

Perfetti, C.A., Bell, L.C., & Delaney, S.M. (1988). Automatic (prelexical) phonetic activation in silent word reading: Evidence from backward masking. *Journal of Memory and Language, 27*, 1–22.

Rayner, K., & Pollatsek, A. (1987). Eye movements in reading: A tutorial review. In M. Coltheart (Ed.), *Attention and performance XII: The psychology of reading* (pp. 327–362). Hillsdale, NJ: Erlbaum.

Rumelhart, D.E., & McClelland, J.L. (1986). On learning the past tenses of English verbs. In J.L. McClelland & D.E. Rumelhart (Eds.), *Parallel distributed processing, Vol. 2: Psychological and biological models* (pp. 216–271). Cambridge, MA: MIT Press.

Seidenberg, M.S. (1987). Sublexical structures in visual word recognition: Access units or orthographic redundancy. In M. Coltheart (Ed.), *Attention and performance XII: The psychology of reading* (pp. 245–263). Hillsdale, NJ: Erlbaum.

Seidenberg, M.S., & McClelland, J.L. (1989). A distributed, developmental model of word recognition and naming. *Psychological Review, 96*, 523–568.

Seidenberg, M.S., Tannenhaus, M.K., Leiman, J.M., & Bienkowski, M. (1982). Automatic access of the meanings of ambiguous words in context: Some limitations of knowledge-based processing. *Cognitive Psychology, 14*, 489–537.

Spoehr, K.T. (1981). Word recognition in speech and reading: Toward a theory of language processing. In P.D. Eimas & J.L. Miller (Eds.), *Perspectives on the study of speech.* Hillsdale, NJ: Erlbaum.

Stahl, S.A., & Fairbanks, M.M. (1986). The effects of vocabulary instruction: A model-based meta-analysis. *Review of Educational Research, 56*(1), 72–110.

Stanovich, K.E. (1980). Toward an interactive-compensatory model of individual differences in the development of reading fluency. *Reading Research Quarterly, 16*, 32–71.

Stanovich, K.E. (1984). The interactive-compensatory model of reading: A confluence of developmental, experimental, and educational psychology. *Remedial and Special Education, 5,* 11–19.

Stanovich, K.E. (1986). Matthew effects in reading: Some consequences of individual differences in the acquisition of literacy. *Reading Research Quarterly, 21,* 360–406.

Stanovich, K.E. (1993). Does reading make you smarter? Literacy and the development of verbal intelligence. In H. Reese (Ed.), *Advances in child development and behavior* (Vol. 24). New York: Academic.

Taft, M. (1985). The decoding of words in lexical access: A review of the morphographic approach. In D. Besner, T.G. Waller, & G.E. MacKinnon (Eds.), *Reading research: Advances in theory and practice* (Vol. 5). New York: Academic.

Tannenhaus, M.K., Flanigan, H., & Seidenberg, M.S. (1980). Orthographic and phonological code activation in auditory and visual word recognition. *Memory and Cognition, 8,* 513–520.

Tyler, A., & Nagy, W.E. (1987). *Use of derivational morphology during reading.* Unpublished manuscript, University of Illinois, Champaign.

VanOrden, G.C. (1991). Phonologic mediation is fundamental to reading. In D. Besner & G.W. Humphreys (Eds.), *Basic processes in reading* (pp. 77–103). Hillsdale, NJ: Erlbaum.

Vellutino, F.R. (1991). Introduction to three studies on reading acquisition: Convergent findings on theoretical foundations of code-oriented versus whole-language approaches to reading instruction. *Journal of Educational Psychology, 83,* 437–443.

Vernon, M.D. (1971). *Reading and its difficulties.* Cambridge, UK: Cambridge University Press.

Waters, G., Caplan, D., & Hildebrandt, N. (1987). Working memory and written sentence comprehension. In M. Coltheart (Ed.), *Attention and performance XII: The psychology of reading* (pp. 531–555). Hillsdale, NJ: Erlbaum.

Weber, R.M. (1970). First graders' use of grammatical context in reading. In H. Levin & J.P. Williams (Eds.), *Basic studies on reading* (pp. 147–163). New York: Basic.

Williams, J.P. (1979). The ABD's of reading: A program for the learning disabled. In L.A. Resnick & P.A. Weaver (Eds.), *Theory and practice of early reading* (Vol. 3, pp. 227–259). Hillsdale, NJ: Erlbaum.

Williams, J.P. (1980). Teaching decoding with a special emphasis on phoneme analysis and phoneme blending. *Journal of Educational Psychology, 72,* 1–15.

Woodworth, R.A. (1938). *Experimental psychology.* New York: Henry Holt.

CHAPTER 32

Revisiting the Construction–Integration Model of Text Comprehension and Its Implications for Instruction

Walter Kintsch, University of Colorado at Boulder

Comprehension: A Paradigm for Cognition

Understanding and *comprehension* are everyday terms—useful but imprecise. We know what we mean when we say we understand a text, but understanding is difficult to define precisely: It is not necessary that we repeat the text verbatim, but we ought to be able to come up with the gist; it is not necessary that we think of every implication of what we have read, but we do not understand it if we miss the most obvious ones; it is not necessary that we answer every question that could be asked, but we cannot miss them all. In the laboratory as well as in the classroom, this problem is solved by fiat operationally. We are willing to say that someone understands a text if he or she passes whatever test we have decided on: provide a summary, answer questions, verify inferences, and so forth. Not all of these operational definitions of understanding are equivalent, nor are they appropriate for all purposes. Much of the discussion in this piece aims at clarifying this situation empirically by showing what works where and for what purposes and theoretically by providing a framework that allows us to describe the different flavors of comprehension processes and outcomes.

There is, however, also a more technical use of the term *comprehension* that concerns us here. It is the sense in which comprehension is used in the phrase *comprehension as a paradigm for cognition.* Cognition ranges from perception on the one hand to analytic thought on the other. Typically, the processes of perception and thinking are conceptualized in different ways. Perception is usually considered as some sort of constraint satisfaction process, where the organism must make sense of a wide variety of sensory inputs involving several modalities, such as solving a puzzle in which the pieces could be assembled in several different ways; the best way is the one that violates the least number of constraints. Thinking or problem solving, in contrast, is a matter of planning, of generating search spaces and using means–end strategies to find a solution path. Reading comprehension shares aspects with both. On the one hand, one normally just reads and understands, much like we understand when we look at a visual scene, without elaborate planning and

This chapter is adapted from "The Construction–Integration Model of Text Comprehension and Its Implications for Instruction," *Theoretical Models and Processes of Reading* (5th ed., pp. 1270–1328), edited by R.B. Ruddell and N.J. Unrau, 2004, Newark, DE: International Reading Association.

effortful problem solving. On the other hand, when this normal process breaks down, the reader (or perceiver) becomes a problem solver who must figure out what it is he or she reads (or sees). Comprehension in this technical sense is automatic meaning construction via constraint satisfaction, without purposeful, conscious effort. Normal reading involves automatic comprehension, as well as conscious problem solving whenever the pieces of the puzzle do not fit together as they should.

The theory of text comprehension outlined here is a comprehension model in the sense discussed, but it leaves room for problem solving and planning when that becomes necessary to complement normal reading. This is a matter with considerable educational implications because instruction by its very nature pushes readers beyond what they already know and are comfortable with, requiring active, effortful, resource-demanding problem-solving activities that are difficult to maintain and direct.

Cognition and Representation

Theorists interested in text comprehension talk about the outcome of comprehension in terms of mental representations. Considered most broadly, in the present context, a mental representation is some change in the way the mind views the world as a result of reading a text, that is, some sort of trace of the text read, including indirect effects, cognitive as well as affective ones—perhaps a tendency to act in a certain way or to feel good or bad about something. There is little agreement about mental representations (or the lack thereof) among cognitive scientists at this point, and it would be impossible to do justice to the complex literature in a brief review. But there are a few points that are directly relevant to text comprehension and that are not overly controversial.

The mind represents different aspects of the world. It is convenient to talk about these as different types or levels of representation. In a reading context, the levels that concern us most directly are perceptual, verbal, and semantic representations. Perceptual representations may be images of how the words looked on the page or how they sounded when spoken by a particular person. They also may be, however, images of the scene described by the text, constructed by the reader. Verbal or linguistic representations are about the words, sentences, and discourses themselves. Semantic representations refer to the ideas expressed by the words. Obviously, these levels are not cleanly separable. A word has perceptual characteristics as well as meaning, but when we talk about how a word is perceived and remembered, it is useful to keep these different aspects separate because they behave differently. Similar visual forms are confused with each other, as are similar phonemes, but words are more often confused on the basis of semantic similarity; decoding is strongly influenced by word length and word frequency, but semantic relations and conceptual structure are more important for comprehension. Hence, psychologists, as well as educators, do well to differentiate between the various levels of mental representations.

There is one more reason for the distinction among levels of representation. Theorists and model builders can deal quite well with verbal and semantic representations, but so far they have not developed the tools to deal effectively with imagery. Various systems are in use to represent the meaning of words. Feature systems are used widely; for instance, *bachelor* has the features *male* and *unmarried*, plus some others. Alternatively, word meanings are represented by their position in a semantic structure: *Shark* is defined as a member of the category *fish*, with special properties, such as *dangerous*. Or one can define word meanings by their position in a semantic space: *Lion* might be characterized by high values on the dimensions *size* and *ferocity*, whereas *mouse* would have low values. High-dimensional, abstract semantic spaces are especially effective for representing the meaning of words. Propositions are idea units, combining more than one word in a schematic form: *The hiker watches the elk with his binoculars* is a conceptual unit that relates, by means of the predicate *watches*, an agent, object, and an instrument in a meaningful, conventional way. Propositions thus allow the theorist to represent the meaning of sentences, independent of their syntactic structure (e.g., a sentence in passive or active voice would be represented by the same proposition). Furthermore, propositions can be combined to form representations of whole texts, as described in more detail below. The structure of these text representations is of great significance because it allows the theorist to distinguish important ideas from mere detail, and it predicts how a text is comprehended and remembered.

Propositional structures are useful to represent the meaning of a text because they tend to mimic the properties of how people represent the meaning of a text. As yet we do not have comparable systems to represent mental images. Pictures will not do, for much the same reason that a text is not well represented by the actual words used: The picture does not make explicit the psychologically important aspects of an image. In the auditory domain, phonemic features capture quite well the salient aspects of how people perceive and remember the sounds of a language. However, visual feature systems have been only partially successful and have limited use. Although propositions provide the theorist with a convenient and workable representation for the meaning of texts, at present there really is no language that we can use to represent the salient features of complex mental images. This deficiency is a major reason why much of the research on text comprehension has focused on the verbal aspects, neglecting the role of mental imagery for all its acknowledged significance. We shall, however, point out that significance wherever possible.

Levels of Text Representation

Texts consist of words organized into sentences, paragraphs, and higher order discourse units such as sections or chapters. The mental representation a reader forms thereof often is called the *surface-level memory*—the memory for the actual words and phrases of the text. Surface memory is typically short-lived, especially for instructional texts, where it does not matter much exactly how something is said (Sachs, 1967). Where that matters, as in a poem, joke, or argument, exact wording can be remembered very well, however (W. Kintsch & Bates, 1977).

For many purposes, we are not concerned with exact wording but with the message conveyed. Thus, it is useful to distinguish a semantic level of text representation—the ideas expressed by the text. We shall call this the *propositional level* of representation because propositions are one way of specifying what constitutes an idea in a text.

For the present purposes,[1] we define *atomic proposition* as a linguistic unit consisting of a relational term (or predicate) and one or more arguments (which may be concepts or other propositions). Some examples of phrases and their corresponding atomic propositions are as follows:

(1) *Little boy* or *The boy is little* → [LITTLE, BOY]

(2) *The boy chopped the wood* → [CHOP, BOY, WOOD]

Note that this representation does not represent all information in a sentence (e.g., the past tense in (2), which is not important enough in many situations in which such propositional representations are used).

A *complex proposition* is a network of atomic propositions corresponding to a (simple) sentence. Propositions are linked in a network either because they are related referentially, as in (3), or because of propositional embedding (in (4) the arguments of the proposition are themselves atomic propositions).

(3) *The little boy chopped wood* → [CHOP, BOY, WOOD] — [LITTLE, BOY]

(4) *Although the boy was little, he chopped the wood* →

[ALTHOUGH] —— [LITTLE, BOY]

[CHOP, BOY, WOOD]

Links may be based on other-than-referential overlap among propositions, for example, on the basis of a causal relationship, as in the following sentence:

(5) *The little boy was tired from chopping wood* →

[TIRED, BOY] —— [LITTLE, BOY]

[CHOP, BOY, WOOD]

This form of propositional representation is intentionally crude; its purpose is not to represent the meaning of a text in all its considerable complexity but to make it possible to count idea units in a text in a reasonably principled way (W. Kintsch, 1974; van Dijk & Kintsch, 1983). Both for the purpose of psychological research on text and instructional design, the number of idea units as defined here and their interrelationship are major variables of interest. Usually, we are not interested in how many words someone remembers but in how many and which ideas are remembered. What makes reading difficult is determined not only by sentence length and the familiarity of the words used but also by the number of ideas expressed, their coherence, and their structure (W. Kintsch, 1974). Propositional analysis, therefore, has become a valuable research tool (although it is not a teaching tool). Unfortunately, because it depends on hand coding, it is extremely laborious and not fully objective (a current guide is W. Kintsch, 1998, Chap. 3.1.1).

The syntactic information in a sentence largely determines the structure of the propositional network. For instance, the main verb of a sentence is taken to form the superordinate proposition, and modifiers are subordinated to it, as in (3). However, there is more structure in a discourse than the sentence syntax. Discourses are organized globally, often according to conventional rhetorical formats. Thus, the simplest stories are of the form setting–complication–resolution; instructional texts may employ various structures such as a compare-and-contrast schema or a generalization-plus-examples schema. To distinguish this discourse-level structure from the sentence-level structure, the terms *macrostructure* and *microstructure* are used. The microstructure of a text is the network of propositions that represents the meaning of the text. One can think of it as a translation from the actual words used into an idea-level format. The macrostructure is the global organization of these ideas into higher order units. Thus, a story may have many propositions linked in a complex network, but at the macrostructure level, these propositions are grouped into the conventional sections: setting, complication, and resolution. However, a writer also could have chosen a different way of telling his story, for example, starting with the resolution and then filling in the setting and complication in the form of a flashback. That approach yields a very different macrostructure, while the microstructure might not be changed very much.

Microstructure and macrostructure together form the *textbase*, the semantic underpinning of a text. However, for purposes of psychological research on text comprehension, as well as for understanding educational practice, it is important to distinguish a further level of text representation, the *situation model*. The situation model represents the information provided by the text, independent of the particular manner in which it was expressed in the text, and integrated with background information from the reader's prior knowledge. What sort of situation model readers construct depends very much on their goals in reading the text as well as the amount of relevant prior knowledge they have. Thus, cooperative and attentive readers will more or less form the same textbase micro- and macrostructures, as invited by the author of the text. But depending on readers' interests, purposes, and background knowledge, they may form widely different situation models. In instruction, it is usually the situation model that the student forms from reading a text that is of interest; the teacher does not care whether the student can recite the text but whether the student understood it correctly and, for future use, was able to integrate the textual information with whatever background knowledge there was.

Situation models are not necessarily verbal. Texts are verbal, and textbases are propositional structures, but to model the situation described by a text, people often resort to imagery. Mental images of maps, diagrams, and pictures are integrated with verbal information in ways not well understood by researchers.

Individual preferences in this regard further limit the ability to predict just what sort of a situation model a reader will form from a text.

It is important to ask not only whether a good, correct situation model has been formed by a reader reading a text but also whether this new model has been integrated with the reader's prior knowledge. It is quite possible that readers may construct adequate textbases but fail to link them with other relevant portions of their prior knowledge. The result is encapsulated knowledge. If readers are reminded of the text from which they have acquired this knowledge, they can remember it and successfully use this knowledge, but it is not part of their generally available knowledge base. Encapsulated knowledge can be retrieved only via the specific episodic text memory; it is not available on occasions when such knowledge may be useful but the episodic retrieval cues are lacking. Thus, students can do their calculus problems at the ends of the chapters in their textbooks and even on final exams, but they have no idea what to do when they are supposed to use their knowledge in an engineering class. To make knowledge acquired from texts usable in novel situations, it must be actively linked to semantic retrieval cues, which is not an automatic process but one that requires strategic action and effort on the part of the reader/learner.

Example: Levels of Representation

"Connected" is a story of about 2,500 words written with the purpose of teaching novice students some basic facts about electricity that are embedded in the story in the form of explanations provided by a father to his daughter, who is trying to solve a puzzle requiring knowledge of these facts. The story has four subheadings: "An important event," "Life on the farm," "How does electricity work?," and "Solving the mystery."

The surface memory for this text refers to whatever sentences and sentence fragments from this text are still available in the reader's memory, and it need not concern us further here.

The macrostructure of the text is shown in Table 1. It is basically a high-level summary, organized according to the classical story schema. It only roughly corresponds to the subheadings of the actual text: The setting comprises the first section and part of the second, the complication corresponds to part of the second and the third sections, and the resolution matches the final section.

An example of the microstructure for this text is given for one brief paragraph in Table 2. The first sentence is represented as two complex propositions, C1 and C2, each consisting of three atomic propositions. C1 and C2 are linked by P4 (i.e., the sentence connective *while*). The third and fourth sentences of the paragraph are each represented by a complex proposition, C3 and C4. Note that anaphoric inferences are necessary here: The *she* of the text has to be identified as *Katie*. To understand, a further inference is required: The *appliances* in the last sentence must be identified with the *electric iron*, the *electric lamp*, and the *electric sewing machine* mentioned earlier. For an adult reader, this is an automatic inference, made unconsciously and effortlessly. For a child, however, who does not

Table 1. The Macrostructure of the Story "Connected"

Setting *Location*: on a farm *Time*: old days *Actors*: Katie, Tom, and their parents
Electricity is coming to town. The children wonder what sort of appliance their parents are going to buy.
Complication Their father asks them to guess what electricity-using appliance they will get first. Katie finds out how electricity works and what it is used for. She finds out that the appliance is not to produce either heat or motion.
Resolution Because there are two wires on the electric line being installed, the first appliance their parents buy will be a telephone.

Table 2. The Microstructure for One Paragraph

In town, her father filled the Model T's gas tank, while Katie bought a sewing machine belt and browsed in the general store. She saw an electric iron, electric lamps, and a sewing machine that no one had to pedal. She realized there were **appliances** *that made heat and light and those that moved.*

C1	P1	[IN, TOWN, P2]
	P2	[FILL, FATHER, GAS-TANK]
	P3	[HAS-PART, MODEL-T, GAS-TANK]
	P4	[WHILE, P2, P5, P7]
C2	P5	[BUY, KATIE, BELT]
	P6	[HAS-PART, SEWING-MACHINE, BELT]
	P7	[BROWSE, KATIE, GENERAL-STORE]
C3	P8	[SEE, **KATIE**, IRON, LAMPS, SEWING-MACHINE]
	P9	[ELECTRIC, IRON]
	P10	[ELECTRIC, LAMPS]
	P11	[NOT-HAVE, SEWING-MACHINE, PEDAL]
C4	P12	[REALIZE, **KATIE**, P13, P14]
	P13	[MAKE, APPLIANCE, HEAT, LIGHT]
	P14	[MOVE, APPLIANCE]
	INF	[IS, **APPLIANCES**, P9, P10, P11]

Note. For explanation, see page 812. C = a complex proposition. P = an atomic proposition.

really know what an appliance is, this may be a major stumbling block, requiring the reader to regress and figure out that the *appliances* are the *lamp* (which makes *light*), the *iron* (which makes *heat*), and the *sewing machine* (whose parts *moved*). What is necessary here is a conscious, strategic process of meaning construction, which is effortful and resource demanding. The reader who avoids this effort still can form a coherent textbase—Katie realizes that appliances make heat and so on—but will be unable to construct an adequate situation model without knowing what *appliances* refers to.

What sort of situation model might a student construct upon reading this story? The student's reading goal is to learn about electricity. Hence, the situation model we are interested in concerns what the student has learned about electricity; the story is merely there to keep up the students' interest. Skillfully interwoven into our story is a puzzle, the "mystery" Katie must solve for which one needs to know certain elementary facts about electricity. The students are not faced with a list of dry facts about electricity but with information that is significant for the puzzle they—and Katie—are trying to solve. Table 3 lists these facts as the situation model a successful reader will form and link to whatever he or she already knows about electricity.

To construct Table 3, hypothetical prior knowledge for a typical reader has been assumed; any real reader may not know exactly what is listed. What is important is that the readers retrieve such pieces of prior knowledge at the right moment when reading this story so they can become associated with the new information provided by the text. Thus, suppose a reader already knows that electricity is needed for ironing; now he or she learns that the electric energy generates heat in the process of ironing, and if this new bit of information is linked with what is already known, it successfully becomes a part of the reader's knowledge base, not just an item of information remembered in the context of that particular text.

Surface structure, textbase, and situation model are levels of the mental representation of texts. We next turn to the question of how these representations are constructed.

Table 3. The Situation Model

Prior Knowledge	Information Provided by the Text
Electricity needs **wires**.	Electricity comes to you via **wires** (you do not have to **get it like wood to burn in the stove**).
You have to **bring wood in for the stove**.	Electricity is generated from coal or water. Static electricity produces sparks and lightning. Electric current is a form of energy (like water power).
Electricity is needed for **lamps**, **ironing**, **sewing machines**, and **telephones**.	Electric energy is used to make **light** (by heating up the filament in a bulb). make heat (such as for **ironing**). make motion (such as in a **sewing machine** or record player). talk on the **telephone** (which needs extra wire and was invented by Bell).

Note. Links are formed between corresponding items printed in bold.

The Process of Comprehension: Construction and Integration

Most of the research on reading deals with the decoding problem: How do readers translate the written text into words and sentences? In other words, how is the surface representation generated from a written text? This is, of course, an extremely important question with complex answers, but it is not the question that will be addressed here. Instead, we shall assume this level of representation as given and look at the formation of the textbase and the situation model.

Microstructure

Given a text—a structured string of sentences—how are the corresponding idea units derived, and how are they organized? For the most part, the language provides good cues as to the underlying ideas: *The goat ate the grass* unproblematically translates into [EAT, GOAT, GRASS]. However, language is full of ambiguities. We understand both of the following sentences:

(6) *The grade was too steep.*

(7) *His grade was an A.*

And we know who *she* and *he* are in these two sentences:

(8) *The nurse scolded the woman because she had not taken her medicine.*

(9) *The hiker saw the grizzly bear. He was afraid.*

There are two kinds of explanations of how people deal with such ambiguities, top-down theories and bottom-up theories. According to the top-down view, a schema filters out incorrect interpretations: We know we are talking about a hill, or a student, and hence assign the right meaning to *grade*; the nurse–patient schema dictates the referent for *she*; and the grizzly bear schema specifies who has to be afraid. Schema theory is very powerful (e.g., Schank & Abelson, 1977), and schema effects in perception and comprehension are well documented. Nevertheless, schema-as-filter theories of comprehension cannot fully account for comprehension processes and have been replaced by theories that assign a more decisive role to bottom-up processes, such as the construction–integration (CI) model (W. Kintsch, 1988, 1998). Instead of trying to construct only the correct meaning of a sentence, the CI model generates several plausible meanings in parallel and only later, when a rich context is available, sorts out which construction is the right one. This sorting out is done by means of an integration or constraint satisfaction process that suppresses those constructions that do not fit in well with the context and strengthens those that do. Specifically, activation is spread around in the propositional network that has been constructed, including the contradictory elements; the activation eventually settles on those nodes of the network that hang together, while outliers and isolated nodes become deactivated. Thus, in (6) and (7), propositions will be constructed initially involving both meanings of *grade*, but the incorrect meaning will become deactivated during the integration phase. For the anaphora identification in (8), the construction process yields

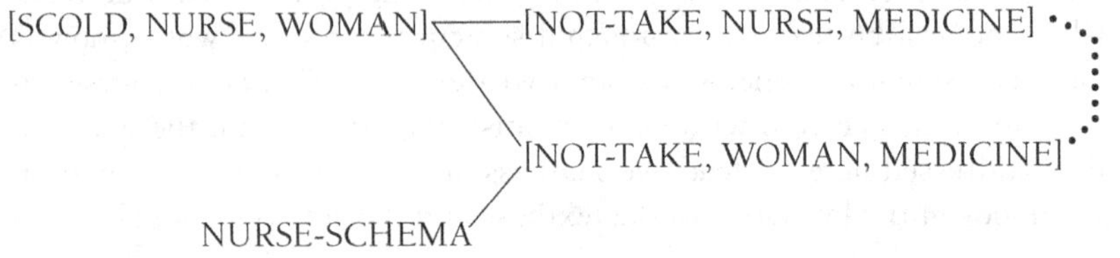

where the dotted line indicates an inhibitory link. In the integration process, the correct proposition will win out because it is connected to prior knowledge about nurses and patients (here labeled the NURSE-SCHEMA). Thus, schemata play a role in the CI model, too, not as filters that control construction but as context that influences the integration process. The inference in (9) is handled similarly: In the construction phase, the model is not sure whether the *hiker* or the *bear* is afraid, but prior knowledge settles that question during the integration phase. Thus, the CI model uses a bottom-up construction phase in which contradictory assumptions are explored, resulting in an incoherent network that needs to be cleaned up in the integration phase. The computational advantage of such a dual process is that the construction rules do not have to be very smart because errors can be corrected in the integration phase. Psychological data that suggest that human comprehension processes employ a similar scheme are discussed in a subsequent section on word identification.

To illustrate the construction of a microstructure, let us return to the "Connected" story discussed earlier. The list of propositions in Table 2 corresponds to the network shown in Figure 1. The links in Figure 1 are based on referential overlap between propositions. Two obligatory inferences are required to identify the pronouns for P8 and P12.

The final activation values for the network in Figure 1, once the process of spreading activation has stabilized, are shown in Figure 2. Figure 2 implies that after reading this paragraph, the strongest information in memory should be that Katie bought a belt, browsed in the general store, and saw an electric iron, electric lamps, and a sewing machine. On a recall test, those should be the items most frequently recalled. A large number of studies have borne out such recall predictions (e.g., W. Kintsch, 1974).

Also shown in Figure 2 are the strength values obtained if the reader makes the optional inference [IS-APPLIANCE, IRON, LAMP, SEWING-MACHINE]. This inference changes the picture a great deal by emphasizing the relationship between the (complex) propositions corresponding to the last two sentences of the text. It will be remembered that this was an instructional text supposed to teach about electricity. Note that without this "deep" processing (the inference about appliances), the present paragraph would not contribute much to the goal of learning physics.

Figure 1. The CI Network for a Paragraph From the "Connected" Story (Corresponds to the Proposition List in Table 2)

IN-TOWN	c0	0.1806	(P1)
FILL-GASTANK	c0	0.5027	(P2)
OF-MODEL-T	c0	0.1806	(P3)
WHILE	c0	0.8604	(P4)
BUY-BELT	c0	0.2852	(P5)
FOR-SEWING-MACHINE	c0	0.3566	(P6)
BROWSE-STORE	c0	0.9063	(P7)
SEE	c0	1.0000	(P8)
ELECTRIC-IRON	c0	0.4474	(P9)
ELECTRIC-LAMP	c0	0.4474	(P10)
SEWING-MACH-WITHOUT	c0	0.4474	(P11)
REALIZE	c0	0.8809	(P12)
APPLIANCE-MAKE-LIGHT	c0	0.4474	(P13)
APPLIANCE-MAKE-MOVE	c0	0.4474	(P14)
FATHER	c0	0.1806	(V1)
KATIE	c0	0.7863	(V2)
IS-APPLIANCE	c0	1.0000	(S1)

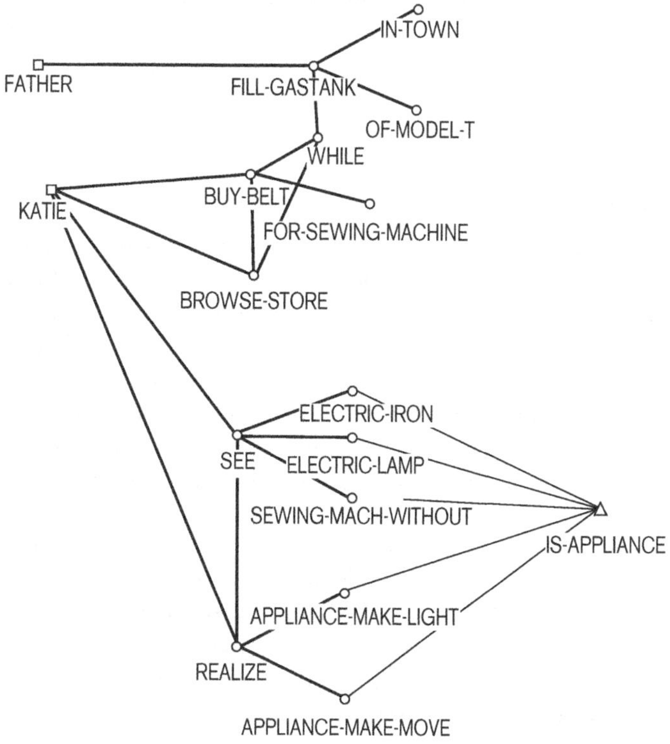

Figure 2. The Result of the Integration Process for the Network in Figure 1, Without the Inference (IS-APPLIANCE) and With It (Darker Bars)

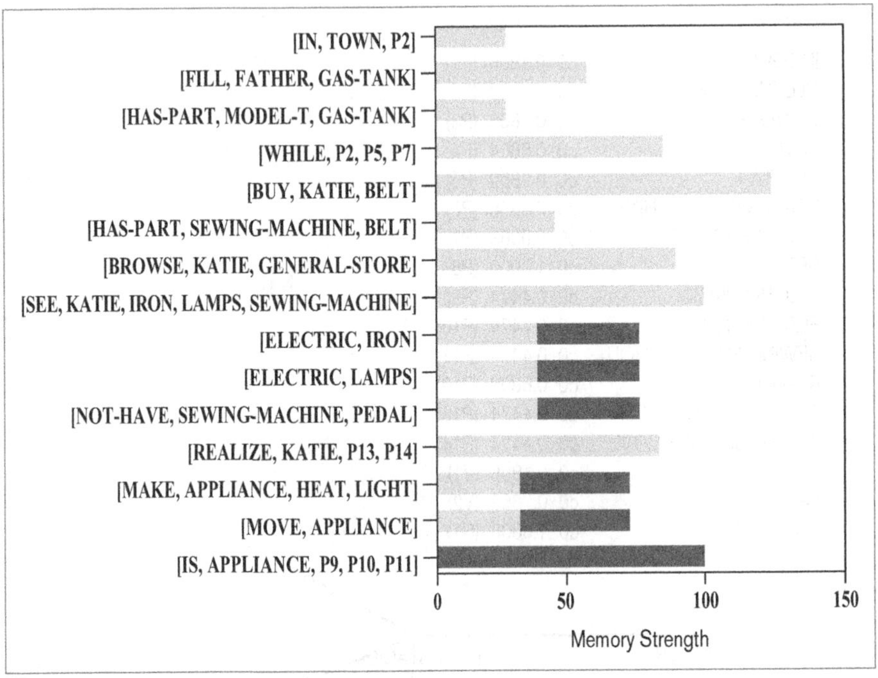

Macrostructure

Generally (except for the case of very brief texts), understanding a text requires formulating a mental representation of its macrostructure. Just what role a proposition plays in a text depends on its function in the overall structure: It may be part of the gist of an essay, or it may be an expendable detail; it may be a crucial link in the causal chain of a story, or it may be irrelevant to the main story line. To capture this kind of intuition, van Dijk (1980) has introduced the concept of a macrostructure. The macrostructure of a text consists of those propositions that are globally relevant, that form its gist in everyday language. Macrostructures are frequently but not necessarily schematic; that is, they are based on conventional rhetorical forms. Thus, narratives have a conventional structure in our culture; essays may be in the form of arguments, or definitions-plus-illustrations, and so on (see van Dijk & Kintsch, 1983, Chap. 2.9, for a detailed discussion). Van Dijk (1980) has enumerated three rules that describe the formation of macrostructures: (1) *selection* of macrorelevant propositions (and correspondingly the deletion of propositions that are not macrorelevant); (2) *generalization*, that is, substitution of a superordinate proposition for subordinate propositions; and (3) *construction*, the substitution of a general proposition describing a whole sequence of interrelated propositions. Given a text and a set of macropropositions, these rules can be used to show how the macropropositions were derived from the text. However, these rules are post hoc: They describe how macropropositions were derived after the fact, but they are not rules that allow us to generate macropropositions from a text. They do not tell us what is to be deleted or what is to be generalized. In order to use these rules, one must already know what is macrorelevant, what can be subsumed under a construction, and so on. In other words, the macrorules are incomplete because they do not include the conditions for their application. This shortcoming has seriously limited the modeling of macrostructures, which is unfortunate because macrostructures play such an important role in comprehension (e.g., W. Kintsch & van Dijk, 1978).

A logical analysis of the relations linking linguistic units that overcomes some of the limitations of macrorules has been suggested by Le (2002), who distinguishes three types of relations among text units: (1) coordination (either in the form of elaboration or parallelism), (2) subordination, and (3) superordination. After one specifies the relations among text units (sentences or complex propositions), hierarchical structures at levels higher than the sentence can be generated that allow the identification of macropropositions. To illustrate Le's procedure, consider the brief paragraph analyzed in Table 2 that consists of four complex propositions, C1–C4. As shown in Table 4, C1 is subordinated to C2; C2 and C3 are coordinated, C3 being an elaboration of C2. C4 is logically superordinated to C3 because it expresses a generalization based on C3. Thus, Le's analysis identifies C4—the complex proposition at the highest level in the paragraph hierarchy—as the macroproposition for that paragraph.

A different approach to the generation of macrostructures has been taken by W. Kintsch (2002). It is not based on a logical analysis of the relations among text units, but rather on the centrality of the content of the (complex) propositions. Latent Semantic Analysis (LSA; Landauer, McNamara, Dennis, & Kintsch, 2007)

Table 4. Determining the Macroproposition for a Paragraph

C1	*In town, her father filled the Model T's gas tank,*
C2	*while Katie bought a sewing machine belt and browsed in the general store.*
C3	*She saw an electric iron, electric lamps, and a sewing machine that no one had to pedal.*
C4	*She realized there were appliances that made heat and light and those that moved.*

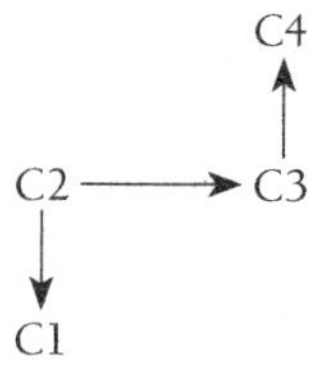

allows one to measure the similarity of the content of sentences. The sentence in a paragraph that is most similar to all the other sentences in that paragraph is a good candidate for a macroproposition because it is the most central one. In Table 4, C3 correlates most strongly with the other sentences, as measured by LSA, and hence should be considered as the macroproposition for this paragraph. Note that this is a different result than the one obtained from Le's (2002) logical analysis. There is no reason why two so totally different methods should yield identical results; large-scale empirical tests of which predictions correspond best with human judgments have not yet been reported. Note also that in terms of the activation values for complex propositions as shown in Figure 2, the most strongly activated complex proposition is C2. (Activation values for complex propositions are obtained by adding the activation values of their constituent atomic propositions.)

It has long been known that gist-level—that is, macrostructure—processes play a decisive role in the comprehension and memory of long texts. That much was shown by W. Kintsch and van Dijk in their 1978 paper. Modeling the generation of macrostructures, however, is still in its infancy, as the earlier discussion illustrates. Worse, there are basic limitations to the approaches of Le (2002) and W. Kintsch (2002): Both models can only select from the propositions in a text, whereas macropropositions often must be constructed by the reader. Macropropositions frequently are inferences that are not stated explicitly in the text. Computational models specifying how new macropropositions are generated do not yet exist. This is an important area for future research, as is the research on the formation of situation models, which is in a similarly underdeveloped state.

Situation Models

The problems faced by the researcher trying to model the formation of situation models are formidable. Textbases at the micro- and macrolevel are tightly constrained by the nature of the text, which a faithful reader must respect. The text, however, is only one factor in the situation model: The reader's goals, interests, beliefs, and prior knowledge also must be taken into account. Generally, these are only incompletely known. Furthermore, even the form that a situation model takes is not fully constrained: Situation models may be imagery based, in which case the propositional formalism currently used by most models fails us. Nevertheless, in well-defined contexts, modeling situation models is quite feasible and will surely be the focus of research on text comprehension in the next decade.[2]

How one might approach this task has been demonstrated by Schmalhofer, McDaniel, and Keefe (2002). The CI model simulates the construction of a textbase: A network of propositions derived from the text is constructed and integrated via a spreading activation constraint satisfaction process. Schmalhofer et al. added two other networks to the propositional network: (1) a surface level, where the nodes are linguistic structures and words; and (2) a situation representation, where the nodes are schemata. Nodes are interconnected at each level, but importantly, there are also links between levels, so a sentence in the surface structure is connected to the corresponding proposition in the textbase, which in turn is connected to the appropriate schema at the situation model level. Schmalhofer et al. illustrate their model with an example that is reproduced here in simplified form in Figure 3. The text is a story about a movie stunt that results in a fatal accident. For the surface level of analysis, one sentence is shown, with word units L9 to L12 and syntactic units S8 and S9; of course, all this is part of a much larger network with rich interconnections not shown here. The units at the surface level are connected not only to each other but also to the propositional units at the textbase level. The propositions of the textbase are linked, in turn, to the situation model units, which here are schemata. The STUNT-SCHEMA has been partly filled in with information from previous portions of the text, but it is updated now with current information from the sentence being processed: An action and a result slot are filled in. When activation is spread in such a triple network, it is

Figure 3. Surface Structure, Textbase, and Situation Model

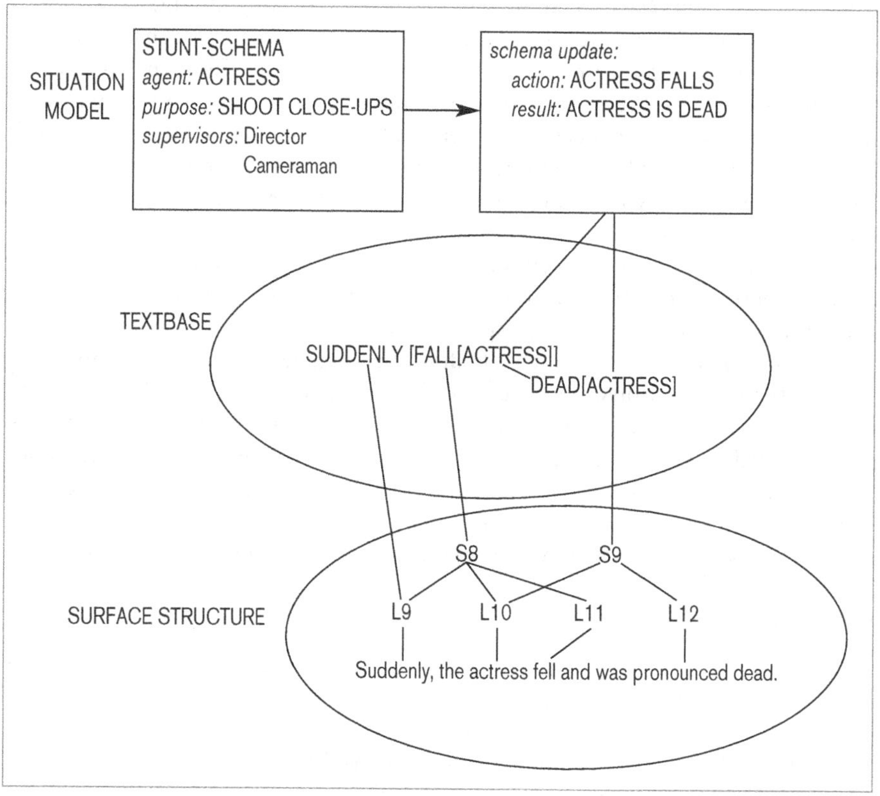

Note. L = word units. S = syntactic units. Based on "A Unified Model for Predictive and Bridging Inferences," by F. Schmalhofer, M.A. McDaniel, and D. Keefe, 2002, *Discourse Processes*, *33*(2), 105–132.

the structure present at each level of analysis that determines which nodes get activated, and complex interactions between levels also occur. This has important consequences, especially for the maintenance of inferences, as Schmalhofer et al. show. A model such as this explains how inferences at the situation model level can become integral parts of text memory, solidly and permanently anchored in the text structure.

The approach to modeling situation models pioneered by Schmalhofer et al. (2002) is a very promising one. Still, there are some limitations: The researchers selected their story in such a way that schema units were appropriate to represent the situation model. Not all situation models can be represented by schemata, however, and a more general approach is required. What needs to be represented in a situation model is at least partially understood (Graesser, Millis, & Zwaan, 1997; Zwaan & Radvansky, 1998). This is an active research area today (Louwerse, 2002; Tapiero, 2007; Todaro, Millis, & Dandotkar, 2010), with the goal of developing and evaluating situation models for complex narratives and especially declarative texts, such as chapters from a science text, at the same level of detail and explicitness as Schmalhofer et al. have done for simple stories. If we understand better what students have to do, we shall be better able to guide and help them.

To summarize the research on the processes of text comprehension, we can say that we have a good understanding of how people go from the words and sentences of a text to the underlying ideas and how the text structure determines the organization of these ideas into a coherent textbase, at least at the local level. Less is known about global organization, or how readers form macrostructures, and even less is known about how situation models are constructed through the interplay among texts, background knowledge, and reader goals. However, promising beginnings have been made in these areas, and rapid progress can be expected now that reading researchers are placing more emphasis on comprehension rather than on the decoding aspects of reading.

The first part of this chapter has described a general theory of comprehension. In the next sections, the focus will be on the application of that theory to important research topics in the area of discourse comprehension: how words are identified in a discourse context, the representation of knowledge, the construction of macrostructures and situation models, and the role of inferences and working memory. Of particular interest are the implications of these research results for instruction, which will be emphasized throughout this discussion.

Word Identification

A great deal of research has gone into determining how the letter shapes on a page are turned into meaningful words. The results of this work will not be reviewed here because they have been discussed in other chapters of this volume (see Ehri & McCormick, Chapter 12; Kuhn & Stahl, Chapter 15; Nagy & Scott, Chapter 18). Instead, a body of research will be introduced here that complements this research in that it is concerned with the question of how readers arrive at the correct sense or meaning of a word[3] when they encounter it in a discourse context. To give a concrete example of what the issue is here, consider the following sentences:

(10) *A beautiful sight in downtown Denver is the mint.*

(11) *A fragrant tea is made with mint.*

How do we know that *mint* is a building in the first sentence but the leaves of a plant in the second? *Mint* is a homonym in English, that is, a word with more than one meaning, and readers obviously and effortlessly find the right meaning when they read (10) and (11). Similarly, when words with only a single meaning are used in different senses, readers readily perceive what is meant:

(12) *The fox ran faster than the hedgehog.*

(13) *The chancellor's decree ran into strong opposition.*

One explanation of how readers identify word meanings in context assumes that all word meanings and word senses are listed in a mental lexicon and that readers must select the right meaning or sense for the given context. There are at least two ways in which this selection could occur:

1. The schema acts as a filter. Suppose that each word meaning/sense in the mental lexicon is associated with a specific context. Thus, *mint* in (10) is associated with *a building-in-which-coins-are-manufactured* schema; reading (10) activates this schema, and the schema selects the proper sense of *mint* from the list of available senses. This is a top-down model, where the schema acts like a filter, admitting only the schema-relevant meaning and not admitting irrelevant meanings. Models of this type have been proposed by, among others, Schank and Abelson (1977).
2. The context suppresses inappropriate meanings. According to this model, all meanings/senses of a word are activated when reading it, but inappropriate meanings are suppressed by the context because they do not fit the contextual constraints. When reading (10), all versions of *mint* in the mental lexicon would be activated initially, but only one—the one associated with *building*, *downtown*, and *Denver*—would be consistent with the sentence context and would survive. Models of this type have been proposed by, among others, Swinney (1979).

Fortunately, it is possible to decide among these alternatives experimentally. Till, Mross, and Kintsch (1988) have reported a relevant experiment using the "lexical decision" method. In this experiment, participants read sentences such as (10) and were then asked to decide as quickly as possible whether a briefly presented string of letters was an English word. Four types of test items were used (each participant saw only one of these):

1. A nonword string (e.g., *baher*) for which the correct response was no
2. An associate of the target word that was contextually appropriate (e.g., *money*)

3. An associate of the target word that was contextually inappropriate (e.g., *tea*)

4. An unrelated control word (e.g., *baker*)

The correct response for the last three items was yes, but interesting differences in response speed were observed. When the test item was presented immediately after the sentence, response times for associated items were significantly shorter than response times to unrelated control items, whether or not the association was contextually appropriate. That is, *mint* in (10) primed both *money* and *tea*. When the test item was presented with a 350-millisecond (msec) delay after the sentence, the response time for the contextually appropriate associate was shorter than the response time for either the control word or the inappropriate associate. That is, 350 msec after reading (10), only *money* was primed, not *tea*.

The Till et al. (1988) data clearly contradict the schema-as-filter model and support a model that posits a bottom-up activation of all word meanings, followed by a contextual constraint satisfaction process that deactivates inappropriate meaning. Indeed, these data were one of the original inspirations for the CI model (W. Kintsch, 1988). Today there exists a very large and complex literature on this subject, which cannot be reviewed here (see, e.g., Rayner, Pacht, & Duffy, 1994). Results depend on various boundary conditions, but on the whole, they effectively rule out the schema-as-filter model. It appears that, generally, multiple meanings and senses of a word are activated initially but that context-inappropriate meanings and senses are suppressed rapidly.

It is difficult to imagine, however, how such a meaning selection model could work. Just what are the cues that allow the selection of the right meaning or sense among so many alternatives? Furthermore, just what are the alternatives in the mental lexicon? How do we decide how many meanings or senses a word has? People learn to use words in ever-novel ways. Can a mental lexicon in which every use must somehow be explicitly defined do justice to this complexity? What if the different word meanings and senses are not predefined in a mental lexicon but emerge in context? How could such a generative lexicon be constructed? One attempt to do so invokes the idea of semantic elements that can be combined to form all meanings, much like the 100+ chemical elements can be combined to form all the manifold substances in the universe. This approach has not been successful, however, because no one has been able to come up with a principled list of semantic elements or the rule system that would allow us to construct all meanings from the combination of these elements. An alternative approach that appears promising to achievement of the goal of a generative lexicon is based on some recent developments in statistical semantics.

Macrostructures and Summaries

Macrostructures are mental representations of text at a global level. They may simply mirror the structure of the text from which they were derived, or they may reflect, to varying degrees, the comprehender's own prior knowledge structure that has been imposed on the text in the creation of a situation model.

Macrostructures as envisaged by van Dijk (1980) and discussed in van Dijk and Kintsch (1983) are hierarchies of propositions. Macropropositions put into words are summary statements at different levels of generality. They subsume what the different sections of a text are about. They are derived from the text by the operations of selection, generalization, and construction, but propositional macrostructures cannot be computed automatically from a text. The macrorules merely help us explain what can be done, but they are not algorithms or computational procedures that generate macropropositions from a text automatically. A computationally more feasible—but in other ways more limited—alternative for the representation of macrostructures is provided by LSA (Landauer et al., 2007). LSA serves as a model of how human verbal knowledge is represented and is of considerable benefit for modeling the use of knowledge in comprehension. Instead of representing the meaning of a sentence by a proposition, the meaning can be represented as a vector in an existing high-dimensional semantic space. For some purposes, such a representation is all that is needed. For example, one can compare new texts, such as summaries students write, with these macrovectors; one can compute the importance or typicality of sentences from the text, and so on.

For other purposes, verbal statements corresponding to macropropositions are needed. W. Kintsch (2002) has described how LSA can be used to select topic sentences from a text and to generate a summary by concatenating these topic sentences. There is more to a summary than just selecting topic sentences, but it is instructive to see what can be achieved in that way—and what is still missing. The text analyzed by Kintsch is a chapter titled "Wind Energy," taken from a junior high school science textbook. It is 960 words long and divided by its author into six sections, each with its own subtitles. Thus, the author indicates the intended macrostructure and even provides appropriate macropropositions, in the form of six subtitles. Macrorules can be used to explain where these subtitles come from. Consider the following paragraph (the second subsection of the chapter):

(14) *The history of windmills*

> *Since ancient times, people have harnessed the wind's energy. Over 5,000 years ago, the ancient Egyptians used the wind to sail ships on the Nile River. Later, people built windmills to grind wheat and other grains. The early windmills looked like paddle wheels. Centuries later, the people in Holland improved the windmill. They gave it propeller-type blades. Holland is still famous for its windmills. In this country, the colonists used windmills to grind wheat and corn, to pump water, and to cut wood at sawmills. Today people still sometimes use windmills to grind grain and pump water, but they also use new wind machines to make electricity.*

The macrorule of construction can be used to compress sentences 2–4 into

> *People used wind energy in Egypt.*

Similarly, the other sentences of the paragraph can be reduced to

People used windmills in Holland.
People used windmills in the colonies.
People use windmills today.

These sentences can be transformed by the macrorule of generalization into

(15) *People used windmills throughout history.*

or

(16) *The history of windmills.*[4]

Thus, macrorules allow us to postdict, or explain, what the author did. But the application of these rules depends on our intuitions about the text and our knowledge about it. By themselves, these rules cannot compute anything.

LSA provides a computational mechanism that can compute macrostructures of a kind. For instance, we can compute a vector in LSA space that is the centroid of all the words in paragraph (14). Such a vector may seem to be totally useless—it is, after all, a list of 300 uninterpretable numbers—but that is not so. It can be quite useful, for instance, to decide how appropriate a proposed subtitle is. The cosine between the paragraph vector and the proposed subtitle is a measure of how close the subtitle is to the paragraph as a whole. For instance, (15) and (16) have rather similar cosines with the paragraph: .39 and .48, respectively—high enough to indicate that they are both acceptable summary statements. But suppose we had chosen an ill-considered subtitle for the paragraph such as "Holland is still famous," or something totally inappropriate such as "Rain douses forest fires." The cosine measure would have allowed us to reject these choices (the cosine is .26 in the first case and only .05 in the second—both much lower than the cosines for (15) and (16)).

There are other uses for vector representation of a macrostructure, too. For instance, we can compute how closely related the sections of a text are to each other. This kind of information can be of interest in various ways. If two sections of a text are very closely related, one might consider combining them. Or if two similar sections are separated by a dissimilar one in the text, one might consider reordering the sections of the text. We also can obtain a measure of how important a section is to the overall text. One way to do this is to compute the cosine between the whole text and each section.

To generate the full range of macropropositions is beyond the scope of LSA; operations such as generalization and construction are not readily modeled within this framework. But we can generate a degenerate macrostructure using only the selection operation. For each section, we can find the most typical sentence in the section. For this purpose, we define *most typical* as the sentence with the highest average cosine to all the other sentences in the section. This will not always yield the best result because the ideal macroproposition may involve generalization or construction, but it will serve as a reasonable approximation.

Thus, some progress can be made toward a computational model of macrostructure generation. LSA allows us to generate an abstract vector representation of the macrostructure of a text (at least in those cases where the subsections of the text are clearly indicated, as in the example above). Furthermore, procedures can be devised to select the most typical sentence for each section of a text. However, that does not make a summary yet, and the operations for reducing the selected typical sentence to an essential phrase or fragment depend on more analytic procedures that go beyond LSA.

There are other, more practical uses of LSA's ability to represent the content of a text mathematically and compare it with other texts. For instance, we can express the summary written by a student as a vector and compare it with the vector of the to-be-summarized text. If the cosine between summary and text is high, the summary has much the same content as the original text. However, if the cosine is low, the summary does not reflect the content of the original text. A system, called *Summary Street*, that employs this method to help students write better summaries has been used with considerable success in some classrooms (E. Kintsch et al., 2000; E. Kintsch, Caccamise, Franzke, Johnson, & Dooley, 2007). For instance, students in sixth-grade classes were routinely asked to write summaries of chapters of their science textbooks. The teachers assigned a text to be summarized, say, on energy sources (coal, wind, petroleum, etc.) or Meso-American civilizations (Incan, Mayan, or Aztec). Each text is usually composed of four or five sections, and the teachers wanted the content of each section to be covered in the summary. Furthermore, the teachers required the summary to be of a certain length, say, between 150 and 200 words. The students write their summaries on an interface that is much like a standard word processor and send them to the LSA system for analysis via the Web. The feedback is received almost immediately and involves a number of steps.

Content feedback indicates whether all sections of the text have been covered in the summary. For this purpose, the cosine between the student's summary and each of the sections of a text are computed. If a cosine is below a certain threshold value, the student is told that this section is not adequately covered in the summary. The student then has the option to look at the appropriate section of the text on the computer screen and add some material about this section to the summary. If the threshold is exceeded for all sections, the student is told that he or she has now covered all parts of the text. Because the length of the summaries is restricted to avoid extensive copying from the source texts, students are told how long their summaries are so far and which of their sentences may be redundant or irrelevant.

Summary Street has been shown to be effective in helping students write better summaries. When summary writing was compared with and without system feedback (Wade-Stein & Kintsch, 2004), the analysis showed that students were willing to work harder and longer when given feedback. Indeed, their time on task more than doubled. Summaries written with content feedback received higher grades from the teachers. This was the case for difficult summaries, for which grades more than doubled, whereas for texts that were easy to summarize anyway, the use of the system had no significant effect. Finally, a transfer effect was observed. Students who had written summaries with the help of the system wrote better summaries a week later even when they no longer had access to the feedback the system provided. They had learned something about how summaries should be written.

Summary Street has been used by thousands of students in several hundred middle school classrooms with considerable success: Students who actually used the program at least four or five times during a year actually learned how to write summaries (E. Kintsch et al., 2007). Today, the WriteToLearn software marketed by Pearson Education incorporates a version of *Summary Street*.

Inferences and Situation Models[5]

Text comprehension always goes beyond the text. The mental representations that readers construct—their understanding of the text—depend as much on what readers bring to the text, such as their goals, interests, and prior experience, as on the text itself. Readers must make inferences to construct situation models. But not all inferences in comprehension are alike.

Classification of Inferences

A distinction should be made between problem-solving processes on the one hand, where there are premises from which some conclusion is drawn (not necessarily by the rules of logic)—which may be justly called inferences—and knowledge-retrieval processes on the other hand, where a gap in the text is bridged by some piece of preexisting knowledge that has been retrieved (W. Kintsch, 1998). Both inferences proper and knowledge retrieval may be either automatic (and usually unconscious) or controlled (and usually conscious and strategic). This classification results in the 2-by-2 table shown in Table 5.

Table 5. A Classification System for Inferences in Text Comprehension

	Retrieval	Generation
	A	C
Automatic processes	Bridging inferences Associative elaborations	Transitive inferences in a familiar domain
	B	D
Controlled processes	Search for bridging knowledge	Logical inferences

Note. Based on *Comprehension: A Paradigm for Cognition*, by W. Kintsch, 1998. New York: Cambridge University Press.

Retrieval adds preexisting information to a text from long-term memory. Generation, in contrast, produces new information by deriving it from information in the text by some inference procedure. Thus, while the term *inference* is suitable for information-generation processes, it is a misnomer for retrieval processes.

A prototypical example for cell A, the automatic retrieval process that enriches the information in a text, would be the activation of *with a hammer* by *John nailed down a board*, or *cars have doors* by *A car stopped. The door opened.* In both cases sufficient retrieval cues for the information retrieved exist in short-term memory. These cues are linked with pertinent information in long-term memory. Such knowledge use is automatic and rapid, and it places no demands on cognitive resources.

There are two theories that describe automatic knowledge retrieval. One is the long-term working memory theory of Ericsson and Kintsch (1995), which is described in more detail in the next section of this chapter. According to the long-term working memory theory, for well-practiced associations, retrieval cues in short-term memory are linked to contents in long-term memory, which thereby become directly available, thus expanding the capacity of working memory. An alternative model for this kind of knowledge retrieval is the resonance theory of Myers (Myers, O'Brien, Albrecht, & Mason, 1994). According to this model, cues in short-term memory produce a resonance in long-term memory, so the resonating items become available for further processing in working memory. Thus, either via retrieval structures or resonance, relevant, strongly related items in long-term memory become potential parts of working memory, creating a long-term working memory that is much richer than the severely capacity-restricted short-term working memory. Indeed, it is only this long-term working memory that makes discourse comprehension (or, indeed, any other expert performance) possible. Smooth, efficient functioning would be impossible if we had no way of expanding working-memory capacity beyond the rigid limits of short-term memory.

In cell B of Table 5 are cases where automatic retrieval is not possible. That is, the cues present in short-term memory do not retrieve relevant information that bridge whatever gap exists in the text. An extended search of memory is required to yield the needed information. A memory search is a strategic, controlled, resource-demanding process in which the cues available in short-term memory are used to retrieve other likely cues from long-term memory that, in turn, are capable of retrieving what is needed. Consider the following sentences:

(17) *Danny wanted a new bike. He worked as a waiter.*

Purely automatic, associative elaboration might not retrieve the causal chain from *want-bike* to *buy-bike* to *money* to *work*. However, a directed search for causal connections between the two sentences would easily generate these by-no-means-obscure links. In all probability, genre-specific strategies exist to guide such search processes. In a story, one would look for causal links. In a legal argument, one routinely looks for contradictions. In an algebraic word problem, algebraic formulas guide the search. The difficulty of such procedures, and the resource demands they make, vary widely.

Retrieval processes merely access information available in long-term memory, either automatically or by a resource-demanding search. Generation processes actually compute new information on the basis of the text and relevant background information in long-term memory. They, too, may be either automatic or controlled.

Some generation procedures are fully automatic (cell C of Table 5). For instance, given the sentence

(18) *Three turtles rested on a floating log, and a fish swam beneath them.*

the statement *The turtles are above the fish* is immediately available to a reader. Indeed, readers often are unable to distinguish whether they were explicitly told this information (e.g., Bransford, Barclay, & Franks, 1972). Note, however, that this is not merely a question of knowledge retrieval as in *doors are parts of cars*: The statement *the turtles are above the fish* is not something that already exists in long-term memory and is now retrieved, but it is generated during the comprehension process. The reason why it is so highly available in the reader's working memory is, presumably, that the fish-log-and-turtle scene is encoded as an image, and this mental image constitutes a highly effective retrieval structure that provides ready access to all its parts—not just the verbal expression used in its construction.

The information that allows the reader to infer that the turtles are above the fish is, presumably, in the form of a spatial image. It is given directly by the image that serves as the situation model representation of the sentence in question. Indeed, at this level of representation, there is no difference between explicit and implicit statements. A difference only exists at the level of the textbase and surface representation, which, however, may not always be effective (as in the experiments of Bransford et al., 1972, in which subjects could not distinguish between explicit and implicit statements, given study and test sentences as in the example discussed here).

However, what happens in cell C of Table 5 should hardly be called an inference either. It is simply a case, in which due to the analog nature of the mental representation involved, more information is generated in forming a situation model than was explicit in the text. The term *inference* really should be reserved for cell D of Table 5. This is the domain of deductive reasoning. It is a domain that extends far beyond text comprehension, although deductive reasoning undoubtedly plays an important role in text comprehension, too. Explicit reasoning comes into play when comprehension proper breaks down. When the network does not integrate, and the gaps in the text cannot be bridged any other way, then reasoning is called for as the ultimate repair procedure.

Inferences (real inferences, as in cell D) require specific inference procedures. What these inference operations are is a matter of considerable controversy in psychology—whether inference proceeds by rule (Rips, 1994) or mental model (Johnson-Laird, Byrne, & Schaeken, 1992). Inferences in domains where the basic representation is an action or perceptual representation, that is, analog rather than linguistic or abstract, probably involve operations on mental models. Inferences in truly symbolic, abstract domains may be by rule. Inferences in the linguistic domain, where the representation is at the narrative level, may be based on mental models but also could involve purely verbal inference rules.

Inference Generation During Discourse Comprehension

The literature on "inferences" in discourse comprehension is for the most part not concerned with cell D of Table 5. Indeed, it is heavily concentrated on cell A, the processes that are the least inferencelike, according to the argument presented here. A major focus of the recent research has been on the question of to what extent inferences are made during normal comprehension. On the one hand, it is clear that if the readers of a story are asked to make inferences and are given sufficient time and incentive, there is almost no limit to what they will produce (Graesser, 1981). On the other hand, there is good evidence that much of the time, and in particular in many psychology experiments, readers are lazy and get away with a minimum of work (e.g., Foertsch & Gernsbacher, 1994). McKoon and Ratcliff (1992, 1995) have elaborated the latter position as the *minimalist hypothesis*, which holds that the only inferences readers normally make are bridging inferences required for the maintenance of local coherence, and knowledge elaboration where there are strong preexisting, multiple associations. Many text researchers (e.g., Graesser & Kreuz, 1993; Graesser, Singer, & Trabasso, 1994; Singer, Graesser, & Trabasso, 1994), however, feel that this minimalist position underestimates the amount of inference making that occurs during normal reading and would at the least add inferences that are necessary for global coherence to the list (superordinate goal inferences, thematic inferences, and character emotional reactions). While this controversy has contributed a great deal to our understanding of the role of inferences in text comprehension, it also has shown that the question concerning which inferences are necessary for and are normally made during text comprehension has no simple answer. Text characteristics (much of the research is based on stories, mostly ministories), task demands, and individual differences among readers create a complex, though orderly, picture.

Trabasso and Suh (1993) have combined discourse analysis, talk-aloud procedures, and experimental measures, such as recognition priming, reading times, coherence ratings, and story recall, to show that their readers made causal inferences in reading a story and that these inferences could be predicted by their analysis.

In an illuminating series of studies, O'Brien and his colleagues have shown that causal inferences in story understanding should best be regarded as a passive operation that makes available background and causal antecedents via a resonance-like mechanism (or what I would call a retrieval structure). Such a process contributes to the coherence of the text representation (Garrod, O'Brien, Morris, & Rayner, 1990) but is not predictive. Readers refrain from prediction unless there is absolutely no chance of being discomfirmed (O'Brien, Shank, Myers, & Rayner, 1988). Global automatic goal inferences occur only under limited conditions (Albrecht, O'Brien, Mason, & Myers, 1995), probably because such inferences are as risky as predictions: They are frequently discomfirmed as the later text reveals a different goal. When global goal inferences occur, resonance describes what happens better than the notion of inference. Through resonance, related parts of a text are connected because of preexisting retrieval structures. In contrast, the construction of a full mental model with rich causal connections appears rather as a nonautomatic, controlled process (Albrecht & O'Brien, 1995; O'Brien, 1995).

How much time and resources the reader has strongly determines the amount of inference making that occurs. Magliano, Baggett, Johnson, and Graesser (1993), using a lexical decision task, found that causal antecedent inferences were not made when texts were presented rapidly at a 250-msec rate, but they were made when the presentation rate was 400 msec. Long, Golding, and Graesser (1992) found that superordinate goal inferences linking various episodes of a story (but not subordinated goal inferences) were made by readers when they were given a lot of time. However, with a rapid presentation rate, only good comprehenders made such inferences, while there was no evidence for goal inferences by poor comprehenders (Long & Golding, 1993).

Readers are much more likely to make antecedent causal inferences than consequent causal inferences (e.g., Magliano et al., 1993). For instance, readers of *The clouds gathered quickly, and it became ominously dark. The downpour only lasted 10 minutes* infer the causal antecedent *the clouds caused the rain*. But given *The clouds gathered quickly, and it became ominously dark*, they do not infer the consequent *the clouds caused rain*. This finding that antecedent, but not consequent causal, inferences are made in text comprehension is readily accounted for by the CI model. Suppose a text describes a situation that is a common cause of some event and then asserts that this event occurred, without mentioning an explicit causal connection between the antecedent and the event. Preexisting retrieval structures causally link the antecedent and the event in the reader's memory, and the causal link will be activated and is likely to become a permanent part of the reader's episodic text memory because it connects two highly activated nodes in the memory structure.

The situation is different for the consequent inferences. The same retrieval structures that made available the causal antecedent will make available the causal consequent, too. But at that point in the reading process, the consequent is a dangling node in the episodic text structure because it is connected to nothing else in the network but the antecedent. Therefore, the consequent will not receive much activation in the integration process and will be excluded from episodic memory. Thus, *The clouds gathered quickly, and it became ominously dark* might make available *the clouds caused rain*, but if nothing else in the text connects to *rain*, this node will become quickly deactivated in the network. When in a later processing cycle other information becomes available that could have linked with *rain*, that node is most likely lost from working memory. Hence, although the retrieval structures in the reader's long-term memory make available both antecedent and consequent information, only the former is likely to survive the integration process and become a stable component of the reader's text memory.

Time Course for Constructing Knowledge-Based Inferences

Of considerable interest is the time course of constructing knowledge-based inferences in text comprehension. We know that it takes about 300–350 msec for word meanings to become fixed in a discourse context. Inferences require more time. In Till et al. (1988), no evidence for topic inferences was obtained at a stimulus onset asynchrony (SOA; the time interval between the presentation of the target word and the test word) of 500 msec, but topic inferences were clearly made at an SOA of 1,000 msec (there were no data points in between). In contrast, Magliano et al. (1993) found that antecedent causal inferences required an SOA of only 400 msec. Long, Oppy, and Seely (1994), in a study modeled after Till et al.'s, have used SOAs of 200, 300, 400, 500, 750, and 1,000 msec. Associative effects are already fully apparent in their data at 300 msec. Topic effects develop gradually: They are already apparent at 500 msec but increase in strength up to 750 msec. Because different materials and conditions were used in all these studies, the differences in the results are not surprising. It seems that sentence-level inferences require from 400 to 750 msec, depending on experimental conditions. Thus, sentence meanings take roughly twice as long as word meanings to fixate.

The Construction of Situation Models

Much recent research has been concerned with the construction of situation models (e.g., Glenberg, Kruley, & Langston, 1994; Glenberg & Langston, 1992; Graesser & Zwaan, 1995; Mani & Johnson-Laird, 1982; Tapiero, 2007; Todaro et al., 2010; Trabasso & Suh, 1993; Zwaan, Magliano, & Graesser, 1995). There is no single type of situation model and not a single process for the construction of such models. Situation models are a form of "inference" by definition, and Table 5 is as relevant for situation models as it is for any other "inference" in discourse comprehension. That is, situation models may vary widely in their character. In the simplest case, their construction is automatic. Relevant information is furnished by existing retrieval structures, as in the examples given for cell A in Table 5. Or it may be available simply as a consequence of a particular form of representation, such as imagery. Such situation model inferences do not add new propositions to the memory representation of the text but simply make available information in long-term memory via retrieval structures, or information that is implicit in the mental representation, such as an image (see Fincher-Kiefer, 1993, and Perfetti, 1993, for similar suggestions). On the contrary, situation models can be much more complex and result from extended, resource-demanding, controlled processes. All kinds of representations and constructions may be involved. The process may be shared by a social group or even by a whole culture and extend over prolonged periods of time. Text interpretation is not something that is confined to the laboratory.

Spatial and temporal information are usually important components of a situation model. Perrig and Kintsch (1985) had subjects read descriptions of the spatial layout of a small town. The same town was described in two ways, first by providing route descriptions (*after the church, turn right on Main Street to go to the courthouse*) and second by means of survey descriptions (*the courthouse is north of the church on Main Street*). Subjects were tested both for their ability to recall and recognize the text they had read and to make novel spatial inferences on the basis of that text. The results of their first experiment dramatically illustrated the textbase–situation model distinction: Subjects' recall was excellent and sentence recognition nearly perfect—but their ability to verify inferences was similar to results of random choices. In a second experiment, with a simpler town and more study time, subjects successfully constructed a spatial situation model. They performed well on recall and recognition as well as on inference tasks. Interestingly, the kind of situation model differed, depending on the text they had read: Route texts led to route models, and survey texts led to survey models. When the inference question was in the same form as the text a subject had read, performance was better than when the text was a route description and the question in the survey format, or vice versa. The Perrig and Kintsch study shows that situation models are by no means automatic consequences of good textbases and that there may be different types of situation models. Which one is best depends on the reader's purpose.

A study by van der Meer, Beyer, Heinze, and Badel (2002) explored the construction of temporal situation models by presenting events in their chronological order (*fall down–get up*) or in reverse order (*fall down–slip*). Overall, chronologically related information was accessed faster compared with reverse-ordered sentences, but processing time made a crucial difference. When there was not enough processing time, neither chronological nor reverse information was integrated into the situation model. When there was a great deal of time for elaboration, both were integrated. In the intermediate condition, however, chronologically ordered events were integrated into the situation model, whereas reverse, past-oriented events were not. Thus, what sort of inferences people make and how elaborate a situation model they construct depend crucially on the amount of processing. If there is time and they are motivated, people will construct rich situation models—but that is a controlled, effortful process, not the kind of automatic knowledge activation discussed earlier.

Research on Reading Comprehension and the Teaching of Reading Comprehension

Research on reading has been an active field in the last few decades. Relatively large sums of money have been made available by federal agencies such as the National Institute of Mental Health to support this field. However, the focus of this research effort has been squarely on early reading instruction—on the study of decoding processes, rather than comprehension. To focus research on decoding was a perfectly defensible and successful strategy: We now have a fairly good understanding of the cognitive bases of decoding processes in reading and about reading instruction in the early grades. Surely, there remain problems to be resolved, but there exists an underlying consensus today about early reading instruction in the United States, as exemplified by the National Research Council's report *Preventing Reading Difficulties in Young Children* (Snow, Burns, & Griffin, 1998). Educators know what to do, even if getting it done in schools on a national scale is still another matter.

There also is agreement among reading researchers today that research on reading comprehension lags far behind research on decoding processes and early reading instruction and that it is time to shift the research focus onto reading comprehension beyond the early years. Recent assessments of research needs by the RAND Reading Study Group (2002) and the Strategic Education Research Partnership report of the National Research Council's Panel on Learning and Instruction (Donovan, Wigdor, & Snow, 2003) agree on the need for a better understanding of the processes of text comprehension as well as instructional methods to improve comprehension.

My goal in this chapter has been to show that there exists a solid basis for further research in reading comprehension. We do not have to start from zero; there is a sparse but solid database, as well as a theoretical framework, that can serve at least as a good starting point for further research on reading comprehension. Throughout this chapter, open research questions have been pointed out, most pressingly about the formation of situation models and the modeling of macrostructures. There is much to be learned, but we also have already learned quite a bit about comprehension. This chapter was not intended as a general review of research on comprehension, but rather as a description of one particular research program and theoretical approach. A broader discussion would certainly have provided further evidence of the considerable progress made in the study of reading comprehension in recent years.

In the meantime, the way we read is changing: Web-based materials have become more and more important. Thus, comprehension research must deal with hypertext and multimedia because students today depend on these sources for information and learning. How comprehension theory can be expanded to incorporate these modern developments has been discussed by Butcher and Kintsch (2013).

The explicit goal of the comprehension research presented here is to inform instructional practice. As yet, this link is weak because there are so many unanswered questions and limited, conditional answers, but there is no reason to suppose that a focused research effort in this area would not yield results that achieve this goal.

Theories of discourse comprehension such as the one presented here are based on data from proficient readers. Indeed, these readers, as long as they read familiar material, can be considered to be comprehension experts. Comprehension for them is fluent, automatic, and easy. Well-established knowledge structures and skills are the basis for this automaticity. The goal of instruction is to help students become such expert readers. Paradoxically, however, comprehension instruction requires students to behave in very different ways than experienced readers do. Because for student readers comprehension is not the automatic, fluent process that it is for mature readers, students need to engage in active problem solving, knowledge construction, self-explanation, and monitoring—activities very different from the automatic, fluent comprehension of experts. For the expert reader, comprehension is easy; to become an expert, comprehension must be hard work. Research on comprehension, therefore, has two quite distinct goals: (1) to describe expert comprehension with all its components and (2) to determine the training sequence that leads to this expert performance. What the student needs to do in training is quite different from how the expert operates. This is not a problem peculiar to comprehension training. Take, for example, ski instruction. Watching the instructor glide down a steep slope with elegant turns is not helpful to the novice skier. The novice must learn by doing things quite differently, and with much more effort, and the instructor must gradually, via a carefully thought-out training sequence, bring the novice to the point where he can begin skiing like an expert, that is, when he is no longer a novice. Thus, if it is to be relevant for instruction, comprehension theory must pay attention not only to the final automatic comprehension that characterizes expert readers in familiar domains but also to the strategies that support comprehension for the beginner, or for the expert who is faced with materials outside his or her domain of expertise (W. Kintsch, 2009).

Assessment plays a central role in gaining expertise in reading comprehension. This chapter has stressed how nontrivial comprehension assessment is. The levels of comprehension range from the superficial to the deep, from surface features to the textbase to the situation model. Assessing comprehension at these different levels is tricky because quite different tests are required. To teach comprehension, we need a thorough understanding of the different aspects of comprehension and the tests that assess comprehension at these different levels. Richer comprehension tests need to be developed and evaluated that adequately assess the different aspects of comprehension. Furthermore, not only must teachers be able to tell how well students understood something, but the students themselves also must have tools to assess their comprehension or lack thereof. People are notoriously bad at this task, and one of the goals of comprehension research must be to find better, and more practical, ways to assess comprehension.

Research on comprehension will probably see a big boost in the next decades. To fulfill its potential, it will have to find the right balance between observation, experiment, and theory. Careful studies of the basic cognitive processes in comprehension are needed, together with research on instructional practices and tools that support effective comprehension. Our goal should be a comprehensive theory of comprehension that allows us to understand how people, novices as well as experts, will react in novel situations. We cannot always perform a new experiment for every new question; instead, we need a broad theoretical framework that provides reasonably good answers to these questions. Educational researchers need a reliable theory to navigate by, much as engineers do in other fields, when they only occasionally resort to experiment because they know they can rely on their computations, except for special problems.

QUESTIONS FOR REFLECTION

1. How is reading comprehension an effective model or paradigm for problem solving?
2. What role does proposition construction play in comprehension?
3. What influences are there on readers' construction of situation models during reading of text?
4. How does Kintsch explain the difference between aspects of comprehension according to top-down schema theory and bottom-up construction–integration theory?
5. How does Kintsch describe the possible uses of Latent Semantic Analysis to improve reader comprehension?

NOTES

[1] The term *proposition* was borrowed from logic, where it is used quite differently.

[2] The distinction between textbase and situation model is made for the convenience of the theorist; mental representation integrates aspects of both.

[3] Different word *meanings* are unrelated, as in *bank-(of river)* and *bank-(financial institution)*; different word senses are related, as in *chill-(bodily coldness with shivering)* and *chill-(moderate coldness)*.

[4] For comparison, the autosummary computed by MS Word is "Later, people built windmills to grind wheat and other grains."

[5] Based in part on W. Kintsch (1998, Chap. 6).

REFERENCES

Albrecht, J.E., & O'Brien, E.J. (1995). Goal processing and the maintenance of global coherence. In R.F. Lorch & E.J. O'Brien (Eds.), *Sources of coherence in reading* (pp. 263–278). Hillsdale, NJ: Erlbaum.

Albrecht, J.E., O'Brien, E.J., Mason, R.A., & Myers, J.L. (1995). The role of perspective in the accessibility of goals during reading. *Journal of Experimental Psychology: Learning, Memory, and Cognition*, *21*, 364–372.

Bransford, J.D., Barclay, J.R., & Franks, J.J. (1972). Sentence memory: A constructive versus interpretive approach. *Cognitive Psychology*, *3*, 193–209.

Butcher, K.R., & Kintsch, W. (2013). Text comprehension and discourse processing. In I.B. Weiner (Series Ed.), A.F. Healy, & R.W. Proctor (Vol. Eds.), *Experimental psychology: Vol. 4. Handbook of psychology* (2nd ed., pp. 578–604). Hoboken, NJ: John Wiley & Sons.

Donovan, M.S., Wigdor, A.K., & Snow, C.E. (Eds.). (2003). *Strategic Education Research Partnership*. Washington, DC: National Academy Press.

Ericsson, K.A., & Kintsch, W. (1995). Long-term working memory. *Psychological Review, 102*(2), 211–245.

Fincher-Kiefer, R.H. (1993). The role of predictive inferences in situation model construction. *Discourse Processes, 16*(1), 99–124.

Foertsch, J., & Gernsbacher, M.A. (1994). In search of complete comprehension: Getting "minimalists" to work. *Discourse Processes, 18*(3), 271–296.

Garrod, S., O'Brien, E.J., Morris, R.K., & Rayner, K. (1990). Elaborative inferencing as an active or passive process. *Journal of Experimental Psychology: Learning, Memory, and Cognition, 16*, 250–257.

Glenberg, A.M., Kruley, P., & Langston, W.E. (1994). Analogical processes in comprehension: Simulation of a mental model. In M.A. Gernsbacher (Ed.), *Handbook of psycholinguistics* (pp. 609–640). San Diego, CA: Academic.

Glenberg, A.M., & Langston, W.E. (1992). Comprehension of illustrated text: Pictures help to build mental models. *Journal of Memory and Language, 31*(2), 129–151.

Graesser, A.C. (1981). *Prose comprehension beyond the word*. New York: Springer.

Graesser, A.C., & Kreuz, R.J. (1993). A theory of inference generation during text comprehension. *Discourse Processes, 16*(1/2), 145–160.

Graesser, A.C., Millis, K.K., & Zwaan, R.A. (1997). Discourse comprehension. *Annual Review of Psychology, 48*, 163–189.

Graesser, A.C., Singer, M., & Trabasso, T. (1994). Constructing inferences during narrative text comprehension. *Psychological Review, 101*(3), 371–395.

Graesser, A.C., & Zwaan, R.A. (1995). Inference generation and the construction of situation models. In C.A. Weaver, S. Mannes, & C.R. Fletcher (Eds.), *Discourse comprehension: Essays in honor of Walter Kintsch* (pp. 117–139). Hillsdale, NJ: Erlbaum.

Johnson-Laird, P.N., Byrne, R.M.J., & Schaeken, W. (1992). Propositional reasoning by model. *Psychological Review, 99*(3), 418–439.

Kintsch, E., Caccamise, D., Franzke, M., Johnson, N., & Dooley, S. (2007). Summary Street®: Computer-guided summary writing. In T.K. Landauer, D.S. McNamara, S. Dennis, & W. Kintsch (Eds.), *Handbook of Latent Semantic Analysis* (pp. 263–277). Mahwah, NJ: Erlbaum.

Kintsch, E., Steinhart, D., Stahl, G., Matthews, C., Lamb, R., & LSA Research Group. (2000). Developing summarization skills through the use of LSA-backed feedback. *Interactive Learning Environments, 8*(2), 87–109.

Kintsch, W. (1974). *The representation of meaning in memory*. Hillsdale, NJ: Erlbaum.

Kintsch, W. (1988). The role of knowledge in discourse comprehension: A construction–integration model. *Psychological Review, 95*(2), 163–182.

Kintsch, W. (1998). *Comprehension: A paradigm for cognition*. New York: Cambridge University Press.

Kintsch, W. (2002). On the notion of theme and topic in psychological process models of text comprehension. In M. Louwerse & W. van Peer (Eds.), *Thematics: Interdisciplinary studies* (pp. 157–170). Amsterdam: John Benjamins.

Kintsch, W. (2009). Learning and constructivism. In S. Tobias & T.M. Duffy (Eds.), *Constructivist instruction: Success or failure?* (pp. 223–241). New York: Routledge.

Kintsch, W., & Bates, E. (1977). Recognition memory for statements from a classroom lecture. *Journal of Experimental Psychology: Human Learning and Memory, 3*, 150–159.

Kintsch, W., & van Dijk, T.A. (1978). Towards a model of text comprehension and production. *Psychological Review, 85*, 363–394.

Landauer, T.K., McNamara, D.S., Dennis, S., & Kintsch, W. (Eds.). (2007). *Handbook of Latent Semantic Analysis*. Mahwah, NJ: Erlbaum.

Le, E. (2002). Themes and hierarchical structures of written text. In M. Louwerse & W. van Peer (Eds.), *Thematics: Interdisciplinary studies* (pp. 171–188). Amsterdam: John Benjamins.

Long, D.L., & Golding, J.M. (1993). Superordinate goal inferences: Are they automatically generated during reading? *Discourse Processes, 16*(1/2), 55–73.

Long, D.L., Golding, J.M., & Graesser, A.C. (1992). A test of the on-line status of goal-related inferences. *Journal of Memory and Language, 31*, 634–647.

Long, D.L., Oppy, B.J., & Seely, M.R. (1994). Individual differences in the time course of differential processing. *Journal of Experimental Psychology: Learning, Memory, and Cognition, 20*, 1456–1470.

Louwerse, M. (2002). Computational retrieval of texts. In M. Louwerse & W. van Peer (Eds.), *Thematics: Interdisciplinary studies* (pp. 189–216). Amsterdam: John Benjamins.

Magliano, J.P., Baggett, W.B., Johnson, B.K., & Graesser, A.C. (1993). The time course of generating causal antecedent and causal consequence inferences. *Discourse Processes, 16*(1/2), 35–53.

Mani, K., & Johnson-Laird, P.N. (1982). The mental representation of spatial descriptions. *Memory & Cognition, 10*(2), 181–187.

McKoon, G., & Ratcliff, R. (1992). Inference during reading. *Psychological Review, 99*(3), 440–466.

McKoon, G., & Ratcliff, R. (1995). The minimalist hypothesis: Directions for research. In C.A. Weaver, S. Mannes, & C.R. Fletcher (Eds.), *Discourse comprehension: Essays in honor of Walter Kintsch* (pp. 97–116). Hillsdale, NJ: Erlbaum.

Myers, J.L., O'Brien, E.J., Albrecht, J.E., & Mason, R.A. (1994). Maintaining global coherence during reading. *Journal of Experimental Psychology: Learning, Memory, and Cognition, 20*, 876–886.

O'Brien, E.J. (1995). Automatic components of discourse comprehension. In R.F. Lorch & E.J. O'Brien (Eds.), *Sources of coherence in reading* (pp. 159–176). Hillsdale, NJ: Erlbaum.

O'Brien, E.J., Shank, D.M., Myers, J.L., & Rayner, K. (1988). Elaborative inferences during reading: Do they occur on-line? *Journal of Experimental Psychology: Learning, Memory, and Cognition, 14*(3), 410–420.

Perfetti, C.A. (1993). Why inferences might be restricted. *Discourse Processes, 16*(1/2), 181–192.

Perrig, W., & Kintsch, W. (1985). Propositional and situational representations of text. *Journal of Memory and Language, 24*, 503–518.

RAND Reading Study Group. (2002). *Reading for understanding: Toward an R&D program in reading comprehension.* Santa Monica, CA: RAND.

Rayner, K., Pacht, J.M., & Duffy, S.A. (1994). Effects of prior encounter and global discourse bias on the processing of lexically ambiguous words: Evidence from eye fixations. *Journal of Memory and Language, 33*, 527–544.

Rips, L.J. (1994). *The psychology of proof: Deductive reasoning in human thinking.* Cambridge, MA: MIT Press.

Sachs, J.S. (1967). Recognition memory for syntactic and semantic aspects of connected discourse. *Perception and Psychophysics, 2*, 437–442.

Schank, R.C., & Abelson, R.P. (1977). *Scripts, plans, goals, and understanding: An inquiry into human knowledge structures.* Hillsdale, NJ: Erlbaum.

Schmalhofer, F., McDaniel, M.A., & Keefe, D. (2002). A unified model for predictive and bridging inferences. *Discourse Processes, 33*(2), 105–132.

Singer, M., Graesser, A.C., & Trabasso, T. (1994). Minimal or global inference during reading. *Journal of Memory and Language, 33*, 421–441.

Snow, C.E., Burns, M.S., & Griffin, P. (Eds.). (1998). *Preventing reading difficulties in young children.* Washington, DC: National Academy Press.

Swinney, D.A. (1979). Lexical access during sentence comprehension: (Re)consideration of context effects. *Journal of Verbal Learning and Verbal Behavior, 18*, 645–659.

Tapiero, I. (2007). *Situation models and levels of coherence: Toward a definition of comprehension.* Mahwah, NJ: Erlbaum.

Till, R.E., Mross, E.F., & Kintsch, W. (1988). Time course of priming for associate and inference words in a discourse context. *Memory & Cognition, 16*(4), 283–298.

Todaro, S., Millis, K., & Dandotkar, S. (2010). The impact of semantic and causal relatedness and reading skill on standards of coherence. *Discourse Processes, 47*(5), 421–446.

Trabasso, T., & Suh, S. (1993). Understanding text: Achieving explanatory coherence through online inferences and mental operations in working memory. *Discourse Processes, 16*(1/2), 3–34.

van der Meer, E., Beyer, R., Heinze, B., & Badel, I. (2002). Temporal order relations in language comprehension. *Journal of Experimental Psychology: Learning, Memory, and Cognition, 28*(4), 770–779.

van Dijk, T.A. (1980). *Macrostructures: An interdisciplinary study of global structures in discourse, interaction, and cognition.* Hillsdale, NJ: Erlbaum.

van Dijk, T.A., & Kintsch, W. (1983). *Strategies of discourse comprehension.* New York: Academic Press.

Wade-Stein, D., & Kintsch, E. (2004). Summary Street: Interactive computer support for writing. *Cognition and Instruction, 22*(3), 333–362.

Zwaan, R.A., Magliano, J.P., & Graesser, A.C. (1995). Dimensions of situation model construction in narrative comprehension. *Journal of Experimental Psychology: Learning, Memory, and Cognition, 21*, 386–397.

Zwaan, R.A., & Radvansky, G.A. (1998). Situation models in language comprehension and memory. *Psychological Bulletin, 123*(2), 162–185.

CHAPTER 33

Understanding the Relative Contributions of Lower-Level Word Processes, Higher-Level Processes, and Working Memory to Reading Comprehension Performance in Proficient Adult Readers

Brenda Hannon, Texas A&M University–Kingsville*

There is considerable evidence concerning the contributions of lower-level word processes, higher-level processes, and working memory to individual differences in reading comprehension performance. However, because the bulk of the research has focused on a single source of individual differences in isolation, little is known about the relationships among these sources (Cornoldi, De Beni, & Pazzaglia, 1996; McNamara & Magliano, 2009; Perfetti, Landi, & Oakhill, 2005) or whether one or all of them make separate and important contributions to reading comprehension (Cornoldi et al., 1996). Furthermore, although most theories of reading comprehension provide details about the nature of mental representations of text, they frequently fail to account for complex relationships among the sources of individual differences that both form these mental representations and predict reading comprehension performance (McNamara & Magliano, 2009). The present study addresses these shortcomings by using structural equation models (SEMs) to examine the relationships among sources of individual differences in reading comprehension for proficient adult readers. Specifically, the principal SEM tested in this study, which is called the cognitive components-resource model of reading comprehension (CC-R model), proposes a set of relationships among (a) lower-level processes that decode words, (b) higher-level processes that extract explicit and implicit information from text and integrate text-based information with prior knowledge, and (c) limited cognitive resources that are shared by many processes (i.e., working memory).[1]

Background

Most studies of reading comprehension have investigated the contribution of a single source of individual differences to reading comprehension performance in isolation (Hannon & Daneman, 2001a). However, the actual source under investigation

This chapter is reprinted from *Reading Research Quarterly*, 47(2), pp. 125–152.

has often varied from study to study, and there is little agreement among theories as to which source contributes the most to reading comprehension (Hannon & Daneman, 2001a). According to the simple view of reading (e.g., Gough, Hoover, & Peterson, 1996; Hoover & Gough, 1990; Tunmer, 2008) and two popular developmental theories of reading comprehension acquisition, the verbal efficiency (e.g., Perfetti, 1985, 1997) and automaticity theories (e.g., LaBerge & Samuels, 1974), word fluency (i.e., speed at accessing the meanings of words) is an important contributor to reading comprehension performance. In support of this assumption are a number of studies, including those assessing normal adult readers that show accuracies/efficiencies of lower-level word processes vary as a function of reading comprehension skill. For instance, studies that have classified adult readers as skilled or less skilled by using a mean split of performance on a measure of reading comprehension have shown that skilled adult readers are more efficient than less skilled adult readers at recognizing printed words (e.g., Bell & Perfetti, 1994). Skilled adult readers are also faster and more accurate at deriving phonology from print (e.g., Cunningham, Stanovich, & Wilson, 1990) and faster at accessing word meanings (e.g., Chabot, Zehr, Prinzo, & Petros, 1984). Indeed, for adult readers, the correlations between lower-level word processes and reading comprehension can be as high as 0.55 (Cunningham et al., 1990; see also Holmes, 2009).

According to other theories, higher-level processes that extract explicit and implicit information from text and integrate this text-based information with prior knowledge are the major source of individual differences in reading comprehension for adult readers (Graesser, Singer, & Trabasso, 1994; Hannon & Daneman, 2001a, 2009; Kintsch, 1998). In fact, studies assessing proficient adult readers have shown that higher-level processes account for as much as 34–60% of the variance in performance on standardized measures of reading comprehension (e.g., Hannon & Daneman, 2001a). Compared with less skilled adult readers, skilled adult readers are better at using their prior knowledge to connect or bridge ideas in a text (Singer & Ritchot, 1996), are better at inferring themes spontaneously as they read (Hannon & Daneman, 1998; Long, Oppy, & Seely, 1994), and are more likely to compute the antecedent referent of a pronoun (Long & De Ley, 2000). Adult skilled readers are also better than less skilled adult readers at remembering new explicit information presented in a text (Masson & Miller, 1983), are more likely to make correct text-based inferences (Long, Oppy, & Seely, 1997), and are better than less skilled adult readers at accessing semantic information from long-term memory (Hannon & Daneman, 2001a). For example, skilled adult readers are better at accessing facts, such as *an elephant is larger than a dog*, or *an ostrich is larger than a robin* (e.g., Hannon & Daneman, 2001a, 2001b, 2006, 2009).

Still other theories promote working memory, a limited resource shared by many cognitive processes, as a major source of individual differences in adult reading comprehension. According to the working memory theories proposed by Daneman and Carpenter (1980) and Just and Carpenter (1992), less-skilled readers are at a disadvantage with all of the processes that require the successive integration of information in a text because they have less working memory capacity to keep the earlier information active (see also Hannon & Daneman, 2001a). Indeed, a meta-analysis of the working memory literature shows that working memory measures that include both processing (e.g., sentence verification) and storage components (e.g., remembering last words of sentences), such as the reading span and operation span, account for 17% of the variance in performance on general or global measures of reading comprehension and 27% of the variance in performance on specific measures of reading comprehension (Daneman & Merikle, 1996).

In contrast to the single-source approach for identifying important sources of individual differences in reading comprehension is the multiple-source approach. Britton, Stimson, Stennett, and Gülgöz (1998), for instance, examined the relative contributions of inferential processing, domain knowledge, metacognition, and working memory to learning from text in adult readers. Similar multivariate studies have been conducted with prereaders (Hannon & Frias, 2012), children (Cain, Oakhill, & Bryant, 2004), adolescents (Cromley & Azevedo, 2007), and seniors (Hannon & Daneman, 2009). Yet, there still has been little to no research about the relationships among lower-level word processes, higher-level processes, and working memory because few studies have examined these three sources simultaneously. Furthermore, there has been little research examining their relative contributions to reading comprehension performance in proficient adult readers. For instance, although Baddeley, Logie, Nimmo-Smith, and Brereton (1985) showed that lower-level word processes and working memory each make separate and significant contributions to reading comprehension performance in adult readers, Daneman and Hannon (2007) showed that working memory contributed little to reading comprehension performance for adults once the variances for higher-level processes were partialed out. Findings such as these suggest that when the contributions of lower-level processes, higher-level processes, and working memory are compared simultaneously, only lower- and higher-level processes make significant contributions. This latter possibility remains untested.

Furthermore, although many theories of reading comprehension acknowledge that lower-level word processes provide some of the information used by higher-level processes during comprehension, there are few theoretical assumptions pertaining to how these two sources of individual differences might interact. Indeed, based on a comparison of seven theories of reading comprehension (i.e., the construction–integration, structure-building, resonance, event-indexing, causal network, constructionist theory, and landscape models), McNamara and Magliano (2009) concluded that although most models of reading comprehension provide details and assumptions about the nature of mental representations of the text, they fail to account for complex relationships among lower-level word processes, higher-level processes, and characteristics of the reader. This finding is surprising given that measures of lower-level word processes, higher-level processes, and working memory routinely account for large amounts of variance in performance on measures of adult reading comprehension. Thus, the present study informs a number of important theories of reading comprehension ability by examining relationships among these three sources of individual differences.

The CC-R Model

The CC-R model is a SEM that was developed to examine the relationships among three sources of individual differences that contribute to reading comprehension performance: lower-level word processes, higher-level processes, and working memory. Other popular models of comprehension, such as the construction–integration model (e.g., Kintsch, 1988, 1994, 1998), also include some or all of these sources as predictors, although as mentioned earlier, these models fail to provide assumptions about how these processes might interact. Furthermore, the simple view of reading (e.g., Gough et al., 1996; Tunmer, 2008) includes word decoding and comprehension (as measured by tests of listening comprehension), the learning from text model (e.g., Britton et al., 1998) includes inferential processes and working memory, and the direct and mediation model of reading comprehension for adolescents (e.g., Cromley & Azevedo, 2007) includes inferential processes and lower-level word processes. This section covers a description of the CC-R model, explanations of its assumptions in the context of some reading comprehension theories, and a review of the literature supporting the relationships among its components. Although most of the supporting literature involves normal adult readers, developmental literature is also described in instances where the literature is limited.

Description of the CC-R Model

In the CC-R model, adult reading comprehension performance is presumed to result from a set of relationships among lower-level word processes, higher-level processes (i.e., text memory, text inferencing, knowledge access, knowledge integration), and resources (e.g., working memory, speed). This model hypothesizes that knowledge integration directly influences reading comprehension. That is, being able to integrate prior knowledge with new text-based information facilitates text comprehension. As a person reads, inchoate ideas are embellished with prior knowledge, text coherence is maintained by bridging two text-based ideas with prior knowledge, story outcomes are predicted because of schemas, global themes are inferred, and comparisons are made between new information in the text and prior knowledge in long-term memory.

Additionally, the CC-R model hypothesizes that knowledge integration is directly influenced by processes that access prior knowledge from long-term memory (i.e., knowledge access) and encode new text-based information (i.e., text memory, text inferencing). For example, to make the knowledge-based inference that the cigarette started the fire, a reader must use (a) text memory processes to encode the text-based information (i.e., *A cigarette was carelessly discarded. The fire destroyed many acres of forest.*) and (b) knowledge access processes to access his or her long-term semantic memory for the fact that *cigarettes start fires* to (c) integrate the text-based information with the information from semantic memory. If either his or her text memory or the knowledge access processes fail, knowledge integration will also fail. However, knowledge access and text-based processes (i.e., text memory, text inferencing) only indirectly influence reading comprehension because their influences are mediated by knowledge integration (i.e., knowledge access, text-based processes → knowledge integration → reading comprehension).

For the purposes of the present study, text-based processes are operationalized as those processes that are used to learn new ideas explicitly or implicitly presented in a text; text-based processes do not include those processes that decode/identify individual words. For example, in the following paragraph:

> The plane flew over the house. The house was in Saskatoon. The plane landed in a field.

text memory process(es) are used to learn the explicit facts (e.g., *The plane flew over the house; the plane landed in a field.*), whereas text inferencing process(es) are used to learn the implicit facts (e.g., *The plane flew over Saskatoon.*). In contrast, knowledge access processes that are used to recall semantic information from long-term memory (e.g., *Planes can fly; planes can land in fields.*) are not used to learn explicit and implicit text-based information.

Finally, working memory, a resource shared by many cognitive processes (Daneman & Hannon, 2007), is also hypothesized to directly influence knowledge integration. However, because the CC-R model defines working memory as a limited cognitive resource, its influence on reading comprehension is largely indirect, mediated by those processes that draw on working memory, such as knowledge integration, and directly influence reading comprehension performance (i.e., working memory → knowledge integration → reading comprehension).

Further, the CC-R model hypothesizes that speed at reading, deciding, and/or processing sentences directly influences reading comprehension. For the purposes of this article, this speed measure is called sentence processing speed or just speed. Comprehending text is information laden, and consequently, speed at sentence processing influences comprehension inasmuch as slow and inefficient sentence processing can delay overall information processing, which in turn might result in information loss. In addition, the CC-R model hypothesizes that lower-level word processes, specifically speed at processing words (i.e., word fluency), directly influence reading comprehension. Like sentence processing speed, word fluency influences reading comprehension inasmuch as quick, efficient, and more accurate word processing decreases passage reading time, which in turn increases question answering time (see Bell & Perfetti, 1994, for more on the importance of word fluency in adult reading). Word fluency also has an indirect influence on reading comprehension because word fluency directly influences sentence processing speed, and sentence processing speed directly influences reading comprehension (i.e., word fluency → speed → reading comprehension). This latter direct influence on sentence processing speed is expected because speed at accessing the meanings of words (i.e., word fluency) is a component of sentence processing speed.

Assumptions of the CC-R Model

Assumption 1: Word-Level and Higher-Level Cognitive Processes Are Separate Constructs in Adult Readers. The quality/efficiency of an adult reader's lower-level word processes that are used for decoding and recognizing words are separate from his or her higher-level cognitive processes that are used for learning and integrating text with prior knowledge (and vice versa). Although little to no adult research has examined the relationship between lower- and higher-level processes, there are a number of developmental studies that have shown nonsignificant relationships between measures of these two sources of individual differences (e.g., Aaron, Frantz, & Manges, 1990; August, Francis, Hsu, & Snow, 2006; Cain et al., 2004; Crain, 1989; Frith & Snowling, 1983; Oakhill, Cain, & Bryant, 2003). For instance, August et al. (2006) showed that measures assessing lower-level letter-word identification/pronunciation processes and the higher-level processes of text memory, text inferencing, and knowledge integration were, at best, weakly related in 5–8-year-olds. Similarly, Oakhill et al. (2003) showed that measures assessing word reading and knowledge integration were dissociable in 7–9-year-olds.

Assumption 2: There Are Multiple Higher-Level Cognitive Processes. Unlike the simple view of reading (Gough et al., 1996), which assumes that comprehension is a unitary component that is assessed with measures of listening comprehension, the CC-R model assumes that comprehension is a collection of higher-level processes (i.e., text memory, text inferencing, knowledge access, knowledge integration) that form a specific pattern of relationships. That is, text-based processes that are used to encode/learn new facts presented in a text (i.e., text memory, text inferencing) are highly related to one another but are weakly related to processes that access prior knowledge. Conversely, knowledge integration processes, which rely on new text-based information and existing information from prior knowledge, are related to both the text-based and knowledge access processes. Because the CC-R model identifies the types of higher-level processes that are used when comprehending text, it can be said that the CC-R model informs the simple view of reading by revealing that the comprehension component consists of multiple identifiable higher-level processes.

Assumption 3: Readers Form a Single Mental Representation of a Text That Varies in Quality From Reader to Reader. As readers are reading text, they form a single mental representation. However, because the qualities of lower- and higher-level processes and the amount of working memory resources used to construct this representation vary from reader to reader, the quality of the mental representation also varies from reader to reader.[2] For instance, a mental representation of a text may be fragmented because a reader failed to use text inferencing or bridging inference processes to connect ideas in the text.

Assumption 4: For Adults, Lower-Level Word Processes Neither Consume Working Memory Resources nor Influence Higher-Level Processes. In the CC-R model, lower-level word processes neither consume limited cognitive resources nor indirectly influence the performance of higher-level processes. That is, because the lower-level word processes of proficient adult readers are substantially quicker and more efficient than those of beginning or struggling readers, the word processes of even the slowest adult reader are fast enough that they do not consume working memory resources that are necessary for executing higher-level processes. In support of this assumption are correlational studies which have shown, at best, minimal relationships between measures assessing lower-level word processes and working memory in proficient adult readers (e.g., Baddeley et al., 1985; Dixon, LeFevre, & Twilley, 1988).[3]

Assumption 5: Working Memory Exerts Little to No Direct Influence on Reading Comprehension Performance. According to the CC-R model, working memory has little to no direct influence on reading comprehension for proficient adult readers. Rather, its influence is largely indirect—mediated via higher-level processes (i.e., working memory → higher-level processes → reading comprehension). In support of this assumption are Britton et al.'s (1998) SEM findings. In their study, a SEM that included a path from working memory to higher-level processes but excluded a direct path from working memory to reading comprehension explained the data better than did a SEM that included both of these paths. Additionally, Daneman and Hannon (2007) showed that working memory accounted for little of the variance in adult reading comprehension performance once the variance for higher-level processes was partialed out (see Hannon & Daneman, 2009, for similar findings with older adults).

Literature Supporting the Paths in the CC-R Model

Figure 1 depicts the path diagram for the CC-R model. Each unidirectional arrow represents a direct path and its direction of influence; for example, the path from working memory to knowledge integration in Figure 1 signifies working memory's direct influence on knowledge integration. The absence of a path indicates no direct influence. The path numbers are for organizing the supporting literature, which includes brief theoretical explanations where appropriate and, where possible, a variety of different studies (e.g., correlational, regression, SEM).

Path 1: The Influence of Knowledge Integration on Reading Comprehension. Most reading comprehension models (e.g., construction–integration, learning from text, constructionist) include knowledge-based inferences that are used to integrate information from prior knowledge with information from the text. Readers can generate a wide variety of knowledge-based inferences, such as causal antecedent, thematic, and predictive (Graesser et al., 1994), but only a subset is routinely generated during reading comprehension (Graesser et al., 1994; Singer, Graesser, & Trabasso, 1994). Further, frequency of inference

Figure 1. Path Diagram of the Cognitive Components and Resource Model of Reading Comprehension

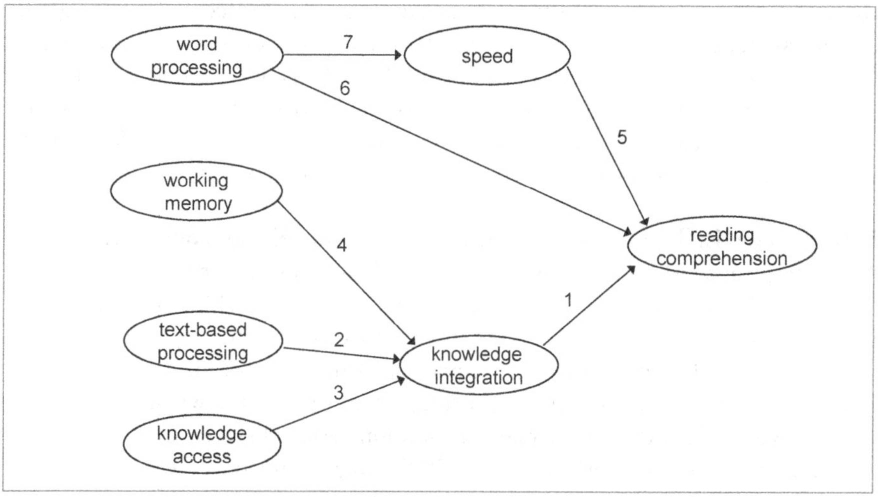

Note. A unique number represents each separate path.

generation is related to reading comprehension skill. Long et al. (1994), for instance, showed that skilled adult readers (as determined by performance on a comprehension measure) are more likely than less skilled adult readers to generate inferences about themes of short passages. Murray and Burke (2003) showed that skilled adult readers are more likely than moderately or less skilled adult readers to generate predictive inferences automatically as they read. Still other researchers have shown that skilled adult readers are more likely to use prior knowledge to bridge ideas in a text to make otherwise incoherent text coherent (Halldorson & Singer, 2002; Keenan & Kintsch, 1974; Singer, Halldorson, Lear, & Andrusiak, 1992). For more examples, see Schmalhofer, McDaniel, and Keefe (2002) and Zhang and Hoosain (2001); for a minimalist view on inferences, see McKoon and Ratcliff (1992).

Paths 2 and 3: The Influences of Text-Based Processing and Knowledge Access on Knowledge Integration. To date, few studies have shown that both text-based (i.e., text memory, text inferencing) and knowledge access processes influence knowledge integration. Potts and Peterson (1985), for instance, showed that the ability to integrate prior knowledge with new text-based information (i.e., knowledge integration) correlated with both the ability to learn explicit and implicit text-based information (i.e., text memory, text inferencing) and the ability to access information from prior knowledge (i.e., knowledge access). Hannon and Daneman (2006) replicated Potts and Peterson's pattern of correlations using SEMs, and August et al. (2006) replicated their pattern using a variant of Hannon and Daneman's measure and beginning readers. In addition, using think-aloud protocols, Magliano, Trabasso, and Graesser (1999) showed that their "readers relied more on world knowledge as a basis for explaining [the text] when the prior context did not provide the sufficient causal conditions for [comprehending] the current sentence" (p. 626). In other words, their readers used both information from the text (i.e., the current sentence) and knowledge from long-term memory (i.e., world knowledge) to generate knowledge-based inferences. This research also suggested that text-based processes (e.g., text inferencing) are different from knowledge-based processes (e.g., knowledge-based inferencing).

Path 4: The Influence of Working Memory on Knowledge Integration. According to working memory theories of reading comprehension ability (Daneman & Carpenter, 1980; Just & Carpenter, 1992), working memory capacity is a limited resource that readers draw on to execute higher-level processes such as knowledge integration. In support of this assumption are studies that have shown relationships between working memory and knowledge integration (e.g., Calvo, 2001, 2005; Daneman & Hannon, 2007; Estevez & Calvo, 2000; Singer, Andrusiak, Reisdorf, & Black, 1992). Singer, Andrusiak, et al. (1992), for example, showed that readers with larger working memories are better at executing bridging inferences than readers with smaller working memories are. Using SEMs, Britton et al. (1998) showed that knowledge integration draws on working memory. Similar results have been found in studies using eye-tracking technology (e.g., Calvo, 2001), older adults (e.g., Hannon & Daneman, 2009), children (e.g., Cain et al., 2004), and prereaders (e.g., Hannon & Frias, 2012).

Path 5: The Influence of Speed on Comprehension. According to Hannon and Daneman (2001a), an adult reader's speed at reading, deciding, and responding to test statements predicts reading comprehension performance. Indeed, these authors showed that their speed measure correlated quite well with reading comprehension performance inasmuch as faster adult readers, who had lower reaction times, tended to have higher comprehension scores, ranging from $r = -0.46$ to -0.28. This speed–comprehension correlation persists even when the passages are taken from the Verbal Scholastic Aptitude Test (e.g., Hannon & Daneman, 2006) or the population of interest is older adults (e.g., Hannon & Daneman, 2009). Similarly, Bell and Perfetti (1994), Baddeley et al. (1985), and Dixon et al. (1988) showed that reading time for passages accounted for small but significant amounts of variance in reading comprehension performance in adult readers (see Klauda & Guthrie, 2008, for more about the relationships among syntactic sentence fluency, semantic sentence fluency, and reading comprehension in adolescents; see also Lomax & McGee, 1987, who showed that the reading speed–reading comprehension relationship is indirect for pre- and beginning readers because it is mediated via lower-level word processes).

Path 6: The Influence of Word Processing on Reading Comprehension. The relationships between lower-level word processes and reading comprehension are well documented even with proficient adult readers (e.g., Baddeley et al.,

1985; Bell & Perfetti, 1994; Cunningham et al., 1990; Dixon et al., 1988; Holmes, 2009; Landi, 2010). Bell and Perfetti, for instance, showed that speed at reading lists of high-frequency words, low-frequency words, and pseudowords accounted for as much as 21% of the variance in adult reading comprehension. Cunningham et al. observed that speed at pronouncing pseudowords (e.g., *danter, comt*) accounted for 30.2% of the variance in adult reading comprehension. Baddeley et al. showed that speed at classifying words, nonwords, and homophones accounted for as much as 25% of variance in adult reading comprehension. Similar findings have also been found in the developmental literature (e.g., August et al., 2006; Jenkins et al., 2003; Kendeou, van den Broek, White, & Lynch, 2009; Klauda & Guthrie, 2008). However, findings from a meta-analysis by Gough et al. (1996) suggest that the influences that lower-level word processes exert on reading comprehension decrease with increases in age.

Path 7: The Influence of Word Processing on Speed. There is limited information about the relationship between word processing and speed of sentence processing because studies have only recently begun to examine their simultaneous contributions to reading comprehension. Further, most of these studies assessed children rather than adults. Nevertheless, the findings suggest a positive relationship between these two constructs. Jenkins et al. (2003), for example, observed a positive correlation between measures of word processing speed (i.e., seconds per word read correctly from a list) and sentence fluency (i.e., seconds per word read correctly from a passage) in a group of fourth graders (cf. Lomax & McGee, 1987, who showed that reading speed has a reciprocal relationship with word processing in pre- and beginning readers.). Similarly, Klauda and Guthrie (2008) observed strong correlations between measures of word processing (i.e., how quickly each word in a list is identified) and syntactic processing (i.e., accuracy and speed in processing phrase/sentence units of a text) in a group of fifth graders. Finally, using a group of proficient adult readers, Jackson (2005) observed a small but significant positive correlation (average $r = 0.29$) between multiple measures of word decoding (e.g., letter-word identification, pseudoword reading) and speed of sentence processing (e.g., reading rate, reading sentences, judging truthfulness; see also Dixon et al., 1988, who observed a small but significant correlation of $r = 0.21$ between similar measures in proficient adult readers).

Summary and Present Study

This study uses SEMs to assess the relationships among three sources of individual differences in adult reading comprehension. More specifically, the CC-R model examines the relationships among (a) lower-level processes that decode words, (b) higher-level processes that extract explicit and implicit information from text and integrate text-based information with prior knowledge, and (c) limited cognitive resources that are shared by many processes (i.e., working memory). To accomplish this goal, proficient adult readers (i.e., university students) completed a battery of tasks that assessed reading comprehension and theory-relevant sources of individual differences. Performance on these tasks served as the observed variables for SEMs that assessed the CC-R model and most of its assumptions.

All the measures in the present study are frequently used and/or have good psychometric properties. For example, the two measures of general or global reading comprehension were versions of the frequently used Nelson-Denny Reading Test. Each version was administered as a timed test. Timed tests are often used by educators to evaluate student performance (e.g., SAT-V, GRE) and by researchers to assess reading comprehension skill (e.g., Bell & Perfetti, 1994; Long et al., 1994). Indeed, studies have shown that standard administrations of the Nelson-Denny have very good correlations with other measures of global reading comprehension, such as the passages taken from the SAT-V (e.g., Daneman & Hannon, 2001; Hannon & Daneman, 2006).

The measures of lower-level word processes were Bell and Perfetti's (1994) orthographic and phonemic lexical decision tasks. In the orthographic task, readers select which of two letter strings is a word (e.g., *date dait*), whereas in the phonemic task, they select which of two letter strings sounds like a word (e.g., *heer heem*). Bell and Perfetti described the latter task as phonemic because decisions are based on pronunciation of pseudowords, whereas they described the first task as orthographic because decisions are based on spelling. Because the orthographic and phonemic tasks are free of contextual words that aid word identification processes, both tasks are considered good and relatively pure measures of word decoding (e.g., Perfetti, Marron, & Foltz, 1996).

Higher-level processes were assessed using Hannon and Daneman's (2001a) component processes task (CPT). The CPT estimates a reader's ability to recall text, make text-based inferences, and access and integrate prior knowledge with text-based information. The CPT accounts for 34–60% of the variance in performance on measures of reading comprehension and is better at predicting reading comprehension than measures of working memory or vocabulary. Each component has a high degree of construct validity and reliability; Cronbach's αs are typically 0.86–0.88 (Hannon & Daneman, 2001a). The internal structure of the CPT has also been validated using SEMs, factor analysis, and correlations (e.g., Hannon & Daneman, 2001a, 2006, 2009). Finally, the reading and operation spans (Daneman & Carpenter, 1980; Turner & Engle, 1989) assessed working memory. Both tasks are considered to be good measures of working memory that consistently account for variance in reading comprehension (Daneman & Merikle, 1996).

Method

Participants

The participants were 150 University of Texas at San Antonio students who were 18–25 years of age and received $35 for their participation. All students were prescreened to ensure that they were free of any known learning disability and that they were monolingual, native English speakers who spoke few words in another language. Thirty-two participants were male, 116 were female, and there was no information about the remaining two participants.

Measures of Reading Comprehension Ability

Students completed two of the four forms (i.e., E, F, G, H) of a standardized measure of general or global reading comprehension called the Nelson-Denny. Each form of the Nelson-Denny consists of seven or eight short passages and 36–38 multiple-choice questions. Each passage is approximately 260 words in length and assesses comprehension of a wide range of topics. For example, biographical topics include artists and philosophers (e.g., Browning, Caravaggio, Shelly, Homer, Keats, Jung), inventors (e.g., Fuller, Washington Carver) and conquerors (e.g., Napoleon). Explanation-based topics include science (e.g., atomic energy, mold, bacteria, hydrochloric acid, insect communication, compounds), business (e.g., marketing, governments, economics, schools), and professions (e.g., soil conservationists, hydrographers). Scores on the Nelson-Denny correlate well with scores on the SAT-V reading passages: $r = 0.55$ to 0.74 (e.g., Daneman & Hannon, 2001; Hannon & Daneman, 2006).

Forms E, F, G, and H were divided into two sets; set 1 contained forms E and H, and set 2 contained forms F and G. These pairings occurred because pretesting revealed that form E was the most difficult and form H was the easiest. Seventy-four students completed set 1, and 76 students completed set 2.[4] Because a student's performance can vary from session to session, it was deemed prudent to assess reading comprehension in each session. More important, from a psychometric perspective, an aggregate of multiple measures for a single construct is always better than a single measure (e.g., Lubinski, 2004). Students assigned to set 1 completed form E in session 1 and form H in session 2, and students assigned to set 2 completed form F in session 1 and form G in session 2.

During all administrations, students could refer to the passages as they answered the questions. In session 1, they had 20 minutes to complete either form E or F, and in session 2, they had 15 minutes to complete either form G or H. The alternate-form reliabilities for forms E and F and forms G and H are 0.77 and 0.81, respectively. Forms G and H were administered as 15-minute tests because pilot testing revealed that these forms were prone to ceiling effects when they were administered as 20-minute tests. Because students completed either form E or F in session 1 and either form G or H in session 2, the scores of form F were transformed to fit the scale for form E, and the scores for form G were transformed to fit the scale for form H. The transformation procedure involved converting the raw scores for forms F and G into z-scores and then converting these z-scores into raw scores for the appropriate form. These transformations were necessary because subsequent analyses treated the two reading comprehension forms in session 1 as the same measure and the two reading comprehension forms in session 2 as the same measure. However, because neither of the two forms within the same session had the same mean and distribution, one form needed to be transformed to the distribution of the other form.

Finally, to verify that the aggregate of the reading comprehension forms in set 1 (i.e., forms E and H) were psychometrically equivalent to the aggregate of the reading comprehension forms in set 2 (i.e., forms F and G), I completed an invariant factor analysis, which compared the measurement models for each set of reading comprehension measures. I also statistically compared the zero-order correlations for the data from set 1 with the zero-order correlations for the data from set 2. Because the invariant factor analysis tests the measurement model, it includes all the relevant measures for each construct (see the measurement model for the CC-R model in Figure 2). The idea behind this analysis is that if it indicates that the two measurement models are equivalent, then the psychometric measurement of the two sets of reading comprehension measures are also equivalent. The results of the invariant factor analysis revealed no difference between the measurement models for sets 1 and 2: $\chi^2(6) = 10.10$, $p = .12$. In other words, according to this multivariate analysis, the reading comprehension measures in sets 1 and 2 are psychometrically equivalent. Furthermore, as Appendix A shows, there were no significant differences between the zero-order correlations associated with set 1's reading comprehension forms and the zero-order correlations associated with set 2's reading comprehension forms. In other words, the univariate *z*-tests support the findings of the multivariate test, the invariant factor analysis.

Figure 2. Path Diagram of the Measurement Model for the Cognitive Components and Resource Model of Reading Comprehension

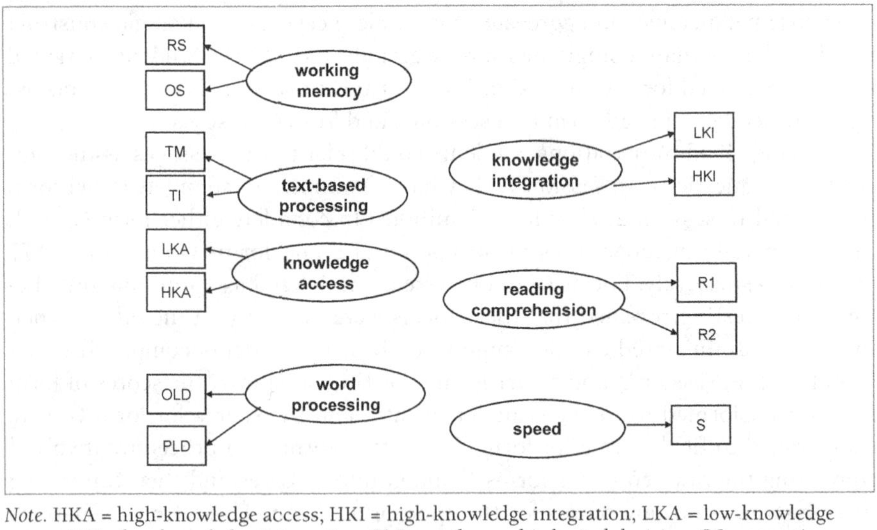

Note. HKA = high-knowledge access; HKI = high-knowledge integration; LKA = low-knowledge access; LKI = low-knowledge integration; OLD = orthographic lexical decision; OS = operation span; PLD = phonemic lexical decision; R1 = reading comprehension measure from session 1; R2 = reading comprehension measure from session 2; RS = reading span; S = speed; TI = text inferencing; TM = text memory.

Measures of Lower-Level Word Processing

The phonemic and orthographic lexical decision tasks were variants of tasks used by Bell and Perfetti (1994) and Olson, Kliegl, and Davidson (1983). In the phonemic task, students decide which of two pseudowords can be pronounced as a real word (e.g., *bair boir*), whereas in the orthographic task, they decide which of two letter strings is a real word (e.g., *bear bair*). In each task, students viewed two letter strings positioned in the middle of a computer screen (e.g., *frute frait*) and then pressed a key marked L (left) or R (right) to represent their decision. Students completed four practice trials and then two blocks of 48 trials each. Average reaction times for correct responses were the dependent measures. The total time needed to complete the phonemic task was about 10–15 minutes, whereas for the orthographic task, it was about 8–10 minutes. Appendix B includes additional examples of stimuli.

Measures of High-Level Component Processes: Text Memory, Text Inferencing, Low- and High-Knowledge Access, Low- and High-Knowledge Integration, and Speed

Text memory, text inferencing, knowledge access, knowledge integration, and speed were assessed using a variant of the CPT (Hannon & Daneman, 2001a). The CPT consists of seven short paragraphs that describe relations among two real and three artificial terms. For example,

> A WEMP resembles a WHALE but is larger and weighs more.
>
> A whiskered TILN resembles a PIRANHA but is smaller and weighs more.
>
> A LORK resembles a TILN but is smaller, weighs more and is kept as a pet.

Linear orderings (i.e., size: wemp > whale > piranha > tiln > lork) can be constructed by combining the relations described in a paragraph with world knowledge accessed from prior knowledge (i.e., *A whale is larger than a piranha.*). For more about the paragraphs and their presentation, see Hannon and Daneman (2001a, 2001b, 2006, 2009).

Test statements followed each paragraph, half of which were true and half false. In total, there were 240 accompanying statements. Explicit paragraph information was assessed by 84 text memory statements (e.g., "A WEMP is larger than a WHALE."), whereas implicit paragraph information was assessed by 36 text inferencing statements (e.g., "A PIRANHA is larger than a LORK."); neither of these statement types required prior knowledge. In contrast, the knowledge access statements measured access to prior knowledge, and no text-based information was required. There were 36 low-knowledge access statements (e.g., "A WHALE is larger than a GOLDFISH.") and 24 high-knowledge access statements (e.g., "SHARKS are typically vicious, whereas WHALES are not."). Low-knowledge access statements included a feature (e.g., larger than) and a real term from the paragraph (e.g., *WHALE*), whereas high-knowledge access statements included just a real term from the paragraph (e.g., *WHALES*). By including a feature and a term not presented in the paragraph, the high-knowledge access statements required more sophisticated access to and reasoning about the relations between the real terms than did the low-knowledge access statements.

The two types of knowledge-integration measures required accessing prior knowledge and integrating it with text-based information. There were 24 low-knowledge integration statements (e.g., "A WHALE is larger than a TILN.") and 36 high-knowledge integration statements (e.g., "Like SHARKS, WEMPS do not typically fit in a fish tank."). These two types of statements varied in complexity; low-knowledge integration statements required integrating a prior knowledge fact (e.g., whales are larger than piranha) with a text fact (e.g., "A TILN is smaller than a PIRANHA."), whereas high-knowledge integration statements required integrating a prior knowledge fact (e.g., a shark does not fit in a fish tank) with a fact that was implied in the text (e.g., a WEMP resembles a WHALE, and because whales do not fit in a fish tank, a WEMP cannot fit in a fish tank; see Appendix C for another example). Accuracy (i.e., number correct) was the primary dependent measure for each statement type.

Finally, speed was assessed using Hannon and Daneman's (2001a) procedure. That is, a speed measure for each higher-level process (e.g., text memory, low-knowledge access) was calculated by averaging the reaction time for statements answered correctly (see Jackson, 2005, who also used sentence judgments to assess speed).[5] Next, the correlations among the speed measures were inspected to verify that they were all indeed highly correlated with one another. Finally, the correlations between the speed and accuracy measures were inspected to verify that each speed measure was, at best, weakly correlated with its respective accuracy measure. For example, the correlation between the speed and accuracy measures for text memory was inspected to verify that it was weakly correlated. The results revealed that all the speed measures were highly correlated with each other ($r = 0.64$ to 0.79) but were, at best, weakly correlated with their respective accuracy measures ($r = -0.18$ to 0.01). These two patterns of correlations suggest that the speed measures are likely tapping a common factor and that this factor is different from those constructs assessed with the accuracy measures. Because all the statements represent a common factor, speed was calculated by averaging the reaction times for correct responses on all types of statements.

The instructions directed students to use their world knowledge while performing the task. They pressed the + key for the first sentence of a paragraph and then, after reading this sentence, pressed the + key for the next sentence. At this point, the first sentence disappeared, and the second sentence appeared. After reading all three sentences in this manner, test statements appeared randomly, one at a time, in the middle of the computer screen. If a student failed to respond to a test statement within a 12-second window, that test statement disappeared, and the next one appeared. All response failures were classified as errors. The total administration time was approximately 20–30 minutes.

Measures of Working Memory

Students completed two measures of working memory, reading span (Daneman & Carpenter, 1980) and operation span (Turner & Engle, 1989). Because the reading and operation span tasks are described in full elsewhere (e.g., Daneman & Hannon, 2001, 2007; Turner & Engle, 1989), they are only briefly described here. In the reading span task, students read aloud a set of unrelated sentences, made a sensibility judgment about each sentence, and then at the end of a set, recalled the last word of each sentence. For example, in a two-sentence set, students may have read "An eerie breeze chilled the warm, humid air. The umbrella grabbed its bat and stepped up to the plate." Students should have responded yes after reading aloud the first sentence and no after reading aloud the second sentence. At the end of the set, they would recall *air* and *plate*.

In the operation span task, students read aloud a set of math equations followed by words, made judgments about the truthfulness of each math equation, and then at the end of a set, recalled the words accompanying each equation. For example, students may have read "$(1 \times 2) - 1 = 5$ judge; $(8/4) + 6 = 8$ husband." They should have responded no after reading the first equation and word, responded yes after reading the second equation and word, and then at the end of the set, recalled *judge* and *husband*. Reading and operation span were the total number of words out of 100 that a student could recall. The total administration time for the reading span task was about 25 minutes, whereas the total administration time for the operation span task was about 15–20 minutes.

Design and Procedure

In session 1, small groups of students (i.e., one to three) were administered the following tasks in the following order: the CPT (Hannon & Daneman, 2001a), a form of the Nelson-Denny, and the phonemic and orthographic lexical decision tasks (Bell & Perfetti, 1994). In session 2, each student was administered the following tasks in the following order: Daneman and Carpenter's (1980) reading span task, another form of the Nelson-Denny, and Turner and Engle's (1989) operation span task. The tasks in session 2 were administered individually because the two span measures required a student to speak aloud.

Data Analysis–SEM Fitting

LISREL 8.52 (Jöreskog & Sörbom, 2002) and maximum likelihood estimation were used to estimate the fits of the SEMs to the raw data. Fits were assessed for both the measurement and structural models.

Measurement Model. Each latent variable included at least two observed variables except speed, which included a single observed variable (see Britton et al., 1998, for a similar situation). As per the recommendations of Schumacker and Lomax (1996) and Jöreskog and Sörbom (1993), the reliability of the sole observed variable for the latent variable speed was specified; specifically, for the measurement model and all other subsequent models, it was set to 0.85. Figure 2 depicts the measurement model.

Structural Model. As Figure 3 shows, the CC-R model has seven direct paths: (1) knowledge integration to reading comprehension, (2) speed to reading comprehension, (3) word processing to reading comprehension, (4) text-based processing to knowledge integration, (5) knowledge access to knowledge integration, (6) working memory to knowledge integration, and (7) word processing to speed. For all models, paths leading from one latent variable to another exert direct influence when their coefficients are significantly different from 0. from word processing to reading comprehension and the path leading from speed to reading comprehension would be negative because faster readers, who have lower reaction times, would tend to have higher comprehension scores. It was also expected that these path coefficients would be negative in the alternative models that were used to assess assumptions 4 and 5 of the CC-R model.

Comparisons With Other Models. As recommended by Jöreskog and Sörbom (2002), the CC-R model was compared with baseline and alternative models. Comparisons to baseline models are important because they assess the CC-R model's fit of the data relative to the best and poorest fitting models. Comparisons to alternative models are important because they assess the veracity of the assumptions of the CC-R model. Assumptions 1, 2, 4, and 5 of the CC-R model were tested; assumption 3 was not testable using the existing experimental design.

Figure 3. Structural Equation Model of the Cognitive Components and Resource Model of Reading Comprehension With Significant Path Coefficients

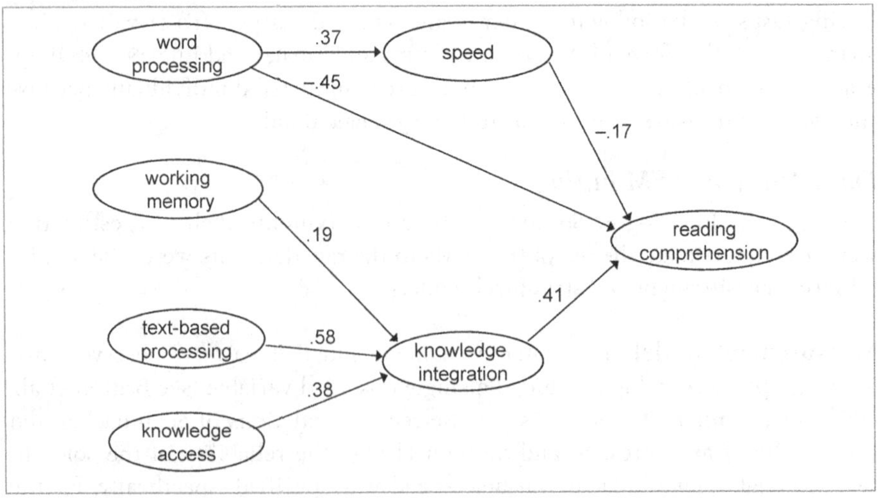

Two types of comparisons were made between the CC-R and baseline/alternative models. Comparison 1 assessed the fit indexes that are described later. Model(s) with fit indexes outside acceptable limits were deemed to be less successful. Comparison 2 statistically compared the CC-R model to the baseline/alternative models using a χ^2-difference test. In a χ^2-difference test, the χ^2 value for the baseline/alternative model is subtracted from the χ^2 value for the CC-R model. The remaining difference is then assessed using a χ^2 table and the net number of degrees of freedom (i.e., df for CC-R model – df for baseline/alternative model). If the χ^2 difference is significant, then one model is significantly better at explaining the data than the other. It is important to note that of these two comparisons, comparison 2 is the most important.

The CC-R model was first compared with the upper and lower boundary baseline models, which were models that represented the best (i.e., upper boundary) and poorest (i.e., lower boundary) fits for the existing data. At the upper boundary was the measurement model. This model provided the best fit to the data because no explicit relations were defined among the latent variables. At the lower boundary was the lower bound null model. This model was similar to the measurement model except that its latent variables were constrained to be uncorrelated. In other words, this model assumed no relations among the latent variables and, therefore, represented the poorest fit to the data. Ideally, the theoretical model of interest (i.e., the CC-R model) should be significantly better at explaining the data than the lower bound model.

Besides the baseline models, alternative models were included to test some of the assumptions of the CC-R model. For assumption 1, which states that word- and higher-level processes are separate constructs, comparisons were made between two SEMs: (1) an independent SEM that included separate latent variables for word- and higher-level processes and (2) a nonindependent SEM that did not include separate latent variables for word- and higher-level processes. Both of these SEMs were similar to the measurement model except that the independent SEM had four latent variables (i.e., word processing, text-based processing, knowledge access, knowledge integration), whereas the nonindependent SEM had three latent variables (i.e., text-based processing, knowledge access, knowledge integration). In both SEMs, the latent variables were measured with the same observed variables used in the measurement model except that in the nonindependent SEM, each latent variable also included the two observed variables that assessed word processing (i.e., the orthographic and phonemic lexical decision tasks). If lower-level word processes and higher-level processes are separate constructs, then the independent SEM would be significantly better at explaining the data than the nonindependent SEM would. Conversely, if lower-level word processes and higher-level processes are not separate constructs (i.e., a violation of assumption 1), then the nonindependent SEM would be significantly better at explaining the data.

For assumption 2, which states that there are multiple higher-level processes, comparisons were made between (a) a multifactor SEM that included separate latent variables for each of the higher-level processes and (b) a single-factor SEM that included a single latent variable that represented all of the higher-level processes. The multifactor SEM included three latent variables: text-based processing, knowledge access, and knowledge integration; the latent variables were measured with the same observed variables that were used in the measurement model. The single-factor SEM included a single latent variable that was measured with the six observed variables that measured the higher-level processes (i.e., text memory, text inferencing, low-knowledge integration, high-knowledge integration, low-knowledge access, high-knowledge access). If there are multiple higher-level processes, then the multifactor SEM should be significantly better at explaining the data than the single-factor SEM is. Conversely, if there is only a single higher-level process (i.e., a violation of assumption 2), then the single-factor SEM should be significantly better at explaining the data.

For part 1 of assumption 4, which states that lower-level word processes do not directly consume working memory resources, comparisons were made between two nearly identical SEMs: (1) the CC-R model, which does not include a path leading from word processes to working memory; and (2) the CC-R1-WM model, a variant of the CC-R model that includes a path leading from word processing to working memory. As Figure 4 shows, the CC-R1-WM model is identical to the CC-R model except that the CC-R1-WM model includes a direct path leading from word processing to working memory. It was expected that the coefficient for the path leading from word processing to working memory (i.e., the new path) would be negative because faster readers, who have lower reaction times, would tend to have higher working memory scores. If word processing directly influences working memory (i.e., a violation of assumption 4), then the CC-R1-WM model should be better at explaining the data than the CC-R model is. Conversely, if word processing does not directly influence working memory, then the CC-R model should be better at explaining the data than the CC-R1-WM model is.

For part 2 of assumption 4, which states that lower-level word processes do not directly influence higher-level processes, comparisons were made between two nearly identical SEMs: (1) the CC-R model, which does not include a path leading from lower-level word processes to higher-level processes; and (2) the CC-R1-WP model, a variant of the CC-R model that includes paths leading from word processing to the higher-level processes of text-based processing, knowledge access, and knowledge integration. As Figure 5 shows, the CC-R1-WP model is identical to the CC-R model except that the CC-R1-WP model includes direct paths leading from word processing to text-based processing, from word processing to knowledge access, and from word processing to knowledge integration. It was expected that the coefficients for the paths leading from word processing to text-based processing, knowledge access, knowledge integration (i.e., the new paths) would be negative. These negative coefficients mean that faster readers, who have lower reaction times, would tend to have higher text processing, knowledge access, and knowledge integration scores. If word processing directly influences higher-level processes (i.e., a violation of assumption 4), then the CC-R1-WP

Figure 4. Structural Equation Model of the CC-R1-WM Model With Path Coefficients

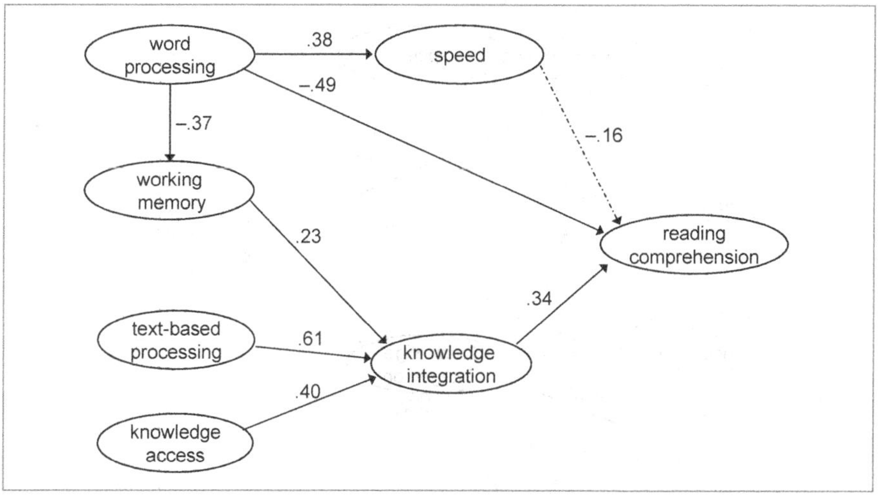

Note. Solid lines represent significant path coefficients, whereas the broken line represents nonsignificant structure coefficients. This structural equation model is identical to the cognitive components and resource model of reading comprehension (CC-R model) except for the addition of a path leading from word processing to working memory.

Figure 5. Structural Equation Model of the CC-R1-WP Model With Path Coefficients

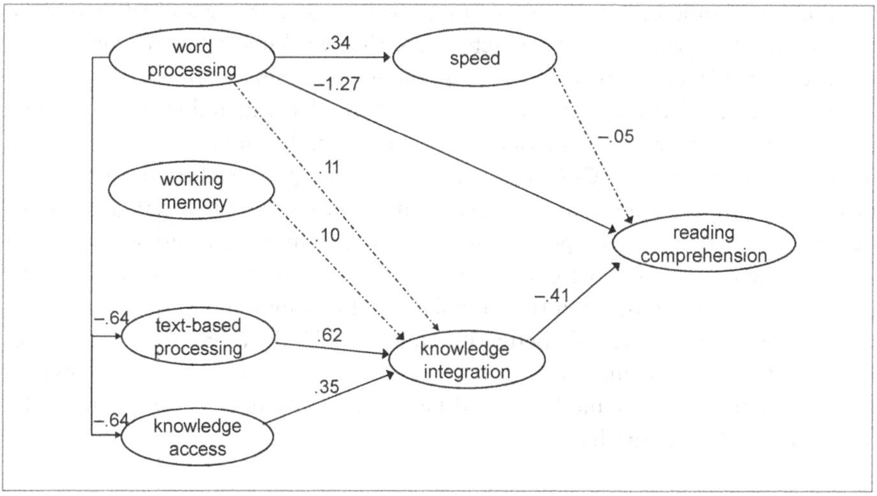

Note. Solid lines represent significant path coefficients, whereas broken lines represent nonsignificant structure coefficients. This structural equation model is identical to the cognitive components and resource model of reading comprehension (CC-R model) except for the addition of paths leading from word processing to the higher-level processes of text-based processing, knowledge access, and knowledge integration.

Figure 6. Structural Equation Model of the CC-R2 Model With Path Coefficients

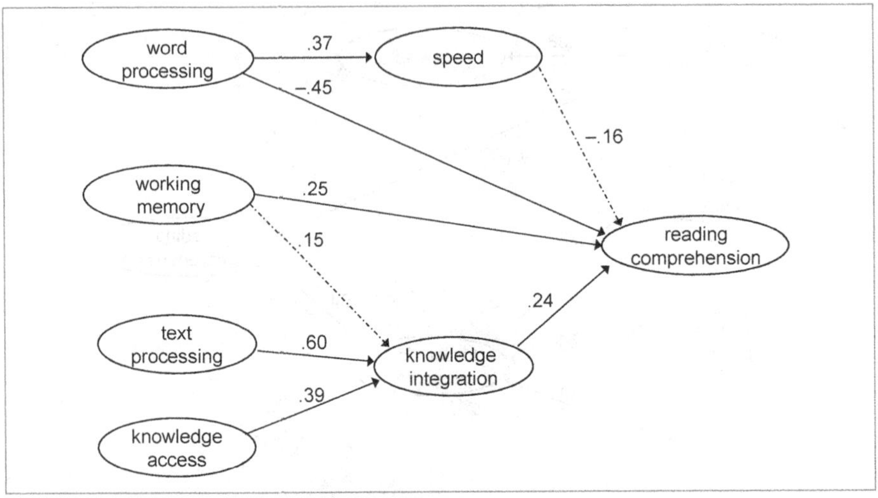

Note. Solid lines represent significant path coefficients, whereas broken lines represent nonsignificant structure coefficients. This structural equation model is identical to the cognitive components and resource model of reading comprehension (CC-R model) except for the addition of a path leading from working memory to reading comprehension.

model should be better at explaining the data than the CC-R model is. Conversely, if word processing does not directly influence higher-level processes, then the CC-R model should be better at explaining the data than the CC-R1-WP model is.

Finally, for assumption 5, which states that working memory exerts little to no direct influence on reading comprehension, comparisons were made between two nearly identical SEMs: (1) the CC-R model, which does not include a path leading from working memory to reading comprehension; and (2) the CC-R2 model, a variant of the CC-R model that includes a path leading from working memory to reading comprehension. As Figure 6 shows, the CC-R2 model is identical to the CC-R model except that the CC-R2 model includes a path leading from working memory to reading comprehension. If working memory directly influences reading comprehension (i.e., a violation of assumption 5), then the CC-R2 model should be significantly better at explaining the data than the CC-R model is. In contrast, if working memory does not directly influence reading comprehension, then the CC-R model should be significantly better at explaining the data than the CC-R2 model is.

Fit Indexes

Following Hoyle and Panter's (1995) recommendations, model fit was evaluated using a collection of fit indexes. The absolute fit indexes were the traditional χ^2 test of exact model fit, the χ^2 test of close model fit (Browne & Cudeck, 1993), the goodness-of-fit index (GFI), the adjusted GFI (AGFI; Jöreskog & Sörbom, 1981), the root mean square error of approximation (RMSEA; Steiger & Lind, 1980), and the 90% confidence intervals for the RMSEA. The incremental fit statistic was the comparative fit index (CFI; Bentler, 1989). For the χ^2 test of exact fit (i.e., *p* exact), the hypothesis being tested assumes an exact model f it that is acceptable. Thus, a good-fitting model is indicated by nonsignificant χ^2 results, and the greater the *p* value, the better the fit. For the χ^2 test of close fit (i.e., *p* close), the hypothesis is for the alternative model, which states that RMSEA is >0.05. If the value for *p* close is >.05, then it is concluded that the model fit is close (Kline, 2011). For the AGFI and GFI, the guideline is that good-fitting models have values of ≥0.90; for the CFI, the value was set to ≥0.95 (Russell, 2002). Conversely, for the RMSEA statistic, the guideline is that values of ≤0.05 indicate a good-fitting model (Steiger, 1989). For other views on the criteria for good model fit indexes, see Fan, Thompson, and Wang (1999), Fan and Sivo (2005), Hu and Bentler (1999), and Marsh, Hau, and Wen (2004).

Results

The results include four sections. Section 1 reports the results of the data screening, section 2 reports the preliminary descriptive statistics including the correlational analysis, and section 3 reports the measurement model. Finally, section 4 reports the results of the CC-R SEM, comparisons of the CC-R model with the baseline models, and the statistical tests of four of the assumptions of the CC-R model.

Data Screening

SAS and PRELIS were used to screen the data for the following: (i) outliers (univariate statistics: studentized residual, DFITTS, DFBETAS, Cook's D; multivariate statistic: Mahalanobis distance values; Tabachnick & Fidell, 2007); (ii) values that exerted excessive leverage (leverage statistic, *h*, also known as the hat value); (iii) linearity (bivariate scatterplots); (iv) normality (univariate: normality probability plots; multivariate: Mardia's statistic; West, Finch, & Curran, 1995); and (v) multicollinearity (tolerance test via regression analysis).

Preliminary regression analyses, which included all of the measures as predictors, revealed that one outlier exerted considerable leverage (i.e., studentized residual, DFITTS, DFBETAS, and the leverage statistic, *h*, all above acceptable limits). The outlier was removed, and all data screening was repeated on the data for the remaining 149 students. The results revealed that all univariate and multivariate screening statistics were within acceptable limits. Most notably, all Mahalanobis distance scores were well below the limit (indicating no multivariate outliers); Mardia's statistic was 1.014, which is well below the critical 1.96 limit (i.e., there was multivariate normality); and tolerance values were all above the 0.20 limit (indicating very little multicollinearity).[6]

Preliminary Descriptive Statistics

Descriptive statistics, correlations, and Cronbach's αs for the measures are reported in Table 1. As the table shows, all the measures had excellent reliability, with standardized Cronbach's αs ranging from 0.83 to 0.97. In addition, the correlations provide some preliminary support for some of the assumptions of the CC-R model. For example, the measures of word processing and working memory were uncorrelated ($r = -0.16$ to 0.01)—a finding that is consistent with the assumption that word processing does not consume limited working memory resources. The two measures of word processing and six measures of higher-level processes were, at best, weakly correlated ($r = -0.30$ to -0.04)—a finding that is consistent with the assumption that lower-level word processes and higher-level processes are separate constructs. The measure of speed was, at best, weakly correlated with the accuracy measures for the higher-level processes ($r = -0.17$ to -0.06)—a finding that suggests that speed is indeed a separate construct from text memory, text inferencing, knowledge access, and knowledge integration. Finally, there was a great deal of similarity between the correlations for the reading comprehension measure in session 1 and the correlations for the reading comprehension measure in session 2—a finding that suggests that these two measures are equivalent.

Of course, it is important to remember that correlations are limited in the amount of information they can convey. Although they provide some insight into what happens with two variables, they do not provide any insight into what happens when three or more variables are considered simultaneously. For this reason, the correlations should be considered as preliminary information for the SEMs.

Measurement Model

As shown in the last row of Table 1, all the factor loadings for the measurement model were significant (ranging from 0.62 to 0.97). Further, all of the fit indexes reported in Table 2 suggest that the measurement model fits the data well. Thus, based on these two criteria, it appears that each observed variable is suitable for measuring its respective latent variable. That is, the observed variables text memory and text inferencing are suitable for measuring the latent variable text-based processing, the observed variables low- and high-knowledge integration are suitable for measuring the latent variable knowledge integration, and so forth.

The CC-R Model

Fit of the CC-R Model. Figure 3 depicts the path diagram for the CC-R model. To reiterate, for all SEMs, the numbers on the paths are path coefficients, which can be used to gauge the size of a relationship between the latent variables. Solid lines represent relationships with coefficients significantly different from 0, whereas dashed lines represent relationships with coefficients not significantly different from 0. As Figure 3 shows, all the path coefficients for the CC-R model were significant. Further, the pattern of relationships among the latent variables for text-based processing, knowledge access, and knowledge integration confirmed the pattern observed by Hannon and Daneman (2006). That is, knowledge

Table 1. Correlations, Descriptive Statistics, Cronbach's αs, and Factor Loadings for Measures of Lower-Level Word Processes, Higher-Level Processes, Working Memory, and Reading Comprehension (n = 149)

	1	2	3	4	5	6	7	8	9	10	11	12	13
1. Reading comprehension 1	—	0.69	−0.43	−0.39	0.34	0.32	0.33	0.44	0.28	0.25	−0.29	0.27	0.41
2. Reading comprehension 2		—	−0.33	−0.36	0.37	0.37	0.34	0.43	0.24	0.25	−0.37	0.26	0.39
3. Orthographic lexical decision			—	0.53	−0.30	−0.21	−0.18	−0.24	−0.12	−0.16	0.28	−0.11	−0.16
4. Phonemic lexical decision				—	−0.11	−0.06	−0.13	−0.15	−0.21	−0.04	0.22	0.01	−0.15
5. Text memory					—	0.86	0.63	0.71	0.29	0.33	−0.07	0.34	0.44
6. Text inferencing						—	0.56	0.66	0.24	0.29	−0.06	0.36	0.48
7. Low-knowledge integration							—	0.62	0.41	0.40	−0.13	0.36	0.36
8. High-knowledge integration								—	0.34	0.37	−0.17	0.39	0.47
9. Low-knowledge access									—	0.40	−0.17	0.12	0.22
10. High-knowledge access										—	−0.15	0.17	0.23
11. Speed											—	−0.05	−0.21
12. Operation span												—	0.58
13. Reading span													
Mean	24.30	27.54	1,147.20	3,390.90	68.03	26.56	20.53	27.34	33.70	22.37	3,871.10	68.89	56.90
Standard deviation	5.25	5.33	221.28	1,085.80	11.32	5.20	2.78	4.95	2.10	1.70	662.93	12.79	11.17
Skewness	−0.37	−0.10	1.13	1.09	−0.82	−0.59	−0.71	−0.31	−1.27	−1.14	0.13	0.48	0.01
Kurtosis	−0.53	−0.55	1.42	1.32	−0.90	−0.44	−0.29	−0.70	1.75	1.46	−0.77	−0.25	−0.06
Lowest score	11.00	15.00	721.84	1,882.80	38.00	13.00	12.00	15.00	22.00	15.00	2,469.33	37.00	35.00
Highest score	34.00	37.00	1,964.00	7,074.72	83.00	36.00	24.00	36.00	36.00	24.00	5,477.81	94.00	90.00
Maximum score	36.00	38.00	—	—	84.00	36.00	24.00	36.00	36.00	24.00	—	100.00	100.00
Cronbach's α	.84	.89	.90	.86	.95	.91	.90	.94	.91	.83	.95	.92	.85
Factor loading	0.85	0.80	0.78	0.68	0.96	0.89	0.74	0.83	0.62	0.64	0.97	0.87	0.66

Note. For $r \geq 0.161$, $p < .05$. The measures of word processing are items 3 and 4. The measures of higher-level processes are items 5–11. The factor loadings reported are for the measurement model.

Table 2. Fit Statistics for Models of Reading Comprehension (n = 149)

Competing Models	χ^2	df	$\Delta\chi^2$	Δdf	p Exact	p Close	GFI	AGFI	RMSEA	CI_{90} for RMSEA	CFI
Measurement	48.24	45			.34	.86	0.95	0.90	0.022	0.000–0.061	1.00
CC-R	59.23	53	10.99	8	.26	.84	0.94	0.90	0.028	0.000–0.061	0.99
Lower bound null[a]	465.84	66	406.61*	13	.00	.00	0.67	0.55	0.200	0.190–0.220	0.76
Independent	16.81	14			.27	.59	0.97	0.93	0.032	0.000–0.092	1.00
Nonindependent[b]	53.54	15	36.73*	1	.00	.00	0.92	0.80	0.132	0.095–0.170	0.93
Multifactor	4.36	6			.63	.80	0.92	0.97	0.000	0.000–0.089	1.00
Single-factor[c]	54.53	9	50.17*	3	.00	.00	0.89	0.74	0.185	0.140–0.230	0.94
CC-R1-WM[a]	86.70	55	27.47*	2	.00	.20	0.92	0.86	0.062	0.036–0.087	0.97
CC-R1-WP[a]	99.21	55	39.98*	2	.00	.05	0.91	0.85	0.074	0.050–0.097	0.96
CC-R2[a]	54.27	52	4.96*	1	.39	.90	0.95	0.91	0.017	0.000–0.056	1.00
CC-R2+IWM[d]	57.17	53	3.10	1	.32	.88	0.94	0.90	0.023	0.000–0.058	0.99
			2.06	0							

Note. CC-R model = cognitive components and resource model of reading comprehension. CC-R1-WM = the CC-R model plus a path leading from word processing to working memory. CC-R1-WP = the CC-R model plus paths leading from word processing to the higher-level processes of text-based processing, knowledge access, and knowledge integration. CC-R2 = the CC-R model plus a path leading from working memory to reading comprehension. CC-R2+IWM = the CC-R2 model minus the path leading from working memory to knowledge integration. CI_{90} = 90% confidence interval for RMSEA.

[a]With the exception of the CC-R model, $\Delta\chi^2$ represents the difference in χ^2 between the model of interest and the CC-R model. The $\Delta\chi^2$ and Δdf for the CC-R model represent the difference between the CC-R model and the measurement model.

[b]$\Delta\chi^2$ is between the independent and nonindependent models.

[c]$\Delta\chi^2$ is between the multiple- and single-factor models.

[d]The first $\Delta\chi^2$ is the difference between the CC-R2 and the CC-R2+IWM, and the second $\Delta\chi^2$ is the difference between the CC-R and the CC-R2+IWM; p exact tests for discrepancies between the data and the model (Kline, 2011), and p close tests the alternative model that the RMSEA is >0.05. If the value for p close is >0.05, then it is concluded that the fit of the model is close (Kline, 2011).

*A significant difference from the model at $p < .05$.

Table 3. **Direct, Indirect, and Total Effects of Predictors on Reading Comprehension Performance for the CC-R and CC-R2 Models ($n = 149$)**

Variable	Direct	Indirect	Total
CC-R model			
Knowledge integration	0.410	—	0.410
Speed	−0.170	—	−0.170
Word processing	−0.450	−0.063	−0.513
Working memory	—	0.078	0.078
Text-based processing	—	0.238	0.238
Knowledge access	—	0.156	0.156
CC-R2 model			
Knowledge integration	0.240	—	0.240
Speed	−0.160	—	−0.160
Word processing	−0.450	−0.056	−0.506
Working memory	0.250	0.036	0.286
Text-based processing	—	0.144	0.144
Knowledge access	—	0.094	0.094

Note. $p < .05$ for all values. The CC-R2 model is identical to the cognitive components and resource model of reading comprehension (CC-R) model except for the addition of a direct path from working memory to reading comprehension (see Figure 6).

integration was directly influenced by both text-based processing and knowledge access. In addition, as Table 2 shows, all the fit indexes for the CC-R model fell well within acceptable limits. Thus, based on these criteria, it appears that the CC-R model is a good model for explaining the existing data.

To determine the relative contribution of each source of individual differences to reading comprehension performance, the direct, indirect, and total effects were calculated for each latent variable. As Table 3 shows, higher-level processes and word processing exerted considerably more influence on reading comprehension performance than did working memory (−0.513 to 0.156 versus 0.078, respectively). Indeed, when combined, higher-level processes had the largest total effect (0.410 + 0.238 + 0.156 = 0.804) relative to speed of word processing (−0.513), speed (−0.170), and working memory (0.078).

Comparisons With Baseline Models. To reiterate, baseline models are used to gauge how well the theoretical model fits the data. The first comparison was between the CC-R model and the upper boundary model, the measurement model. As shown in Table 2, these two models were equivalent: χ^2-difference(8) = 10.99, $p = .202$. This finding suggests that the CC-R model is as good as the upper boundary model for explaining the existing data. The second comparison was between the CC-R and lower bound models. As Table 2 shows, none of the fit indexes for the lower bound model were within acceptable limits; as mentioned earlier, this was expected. Further, the χ^2-difference test between the two models was significant: χ^2-difference(13) = 406.61, $p < .001$. This latter finding suggests that the

CC-R model is a significantly better model for explaining the existing data than is the lower bound null model.

Testing Assumption 1. To test the assumption that word- and higher-level processes are separate constructs, comparisons were made between (a) an independent SEM that included separate latent variables for word- and higher-level processes and (b) a nonindependent SEM that did not include separate latent variables for word- and higher-level processes. Table 2 shows the fit indexes for the independent and nonindependent SEMs. As the table shows, all of the fit indexes for the independent SEM were within acceptable limits. In contrast, some of the fit indexes for the nonindependent SEM, such as the *p*-exact, *p*-close, AGFI, and RMSEA indexes, were outside acceptable limits. Further, the χ^2-difference test suggested that the independent SEM was significantly better at explaining the data than the nonindependent SEM was: χ^2-difference(1) = 36.73, $p < .001$. In other words, these findings support the CC-R model's assumption that lower-level word processes and higher-level processes are separate constructs.

Testing Assumption 2. To test the assumption that there are multiple higher-level processes, comparisons were made between (a) a multifactor SEM that included separate latent variables for each of the major higher-level processes and (b) a single-factor SEM that included a single latent variable that represented all of the higher-level processes. Table 2 shows the fit indexes for the multiple- and single-factor SEMs. As the table shows, all of the fit indexes for the multifactor SEM were within acceptable limits. In contrast, some of the fit indexes for the single-factor SEM, such as the *p*-exact, *p*-close, AGFI, and RMSEA indexes, were outside acceptable limits. Further, the χ^2-difference test between the multiple- and single-factor SEMs suggested that the multifactor SEM was significantly better at explaining the data than a single-factor SEM was: χ^2-difference(3) = 50.17, $p < .001$. In other words, these findings support the CC-R model's assumption that there are multiple higher-level processes.

Testing Assumption 4. To test the assumption that lower-level word processes have no influence on working memory, comparisons were made between (a) the CC-R model, which does not include a direct path leading from lower-level word processes to working memory, and (b) the CC-R1-WM model, which is identical to the CC-R model except that the CC-R1-WM model includes a direct path leading from lower-level word processes to working memory. As shown in Table 2, some of the fit indexes for the CC-R1-WM model (e.g., *p*-exact, RMSEA) were poor, especially when they were compared with those of the CC-R model. Also, the χ^2-difference test suggested that the CC-R1-WM model had a poorer fit to the data than the CC-R model did: χ^2-difference(2) = 27.47, $p < .001$. Thus, taken as a whole, these findings suggest that a model that excludes a path from word processing to working memory (i.e., the CC-R model) explains the data better than does a model that includes this path (i.e., the CC-R1-WM model). In other words, these findings support the CC-R model's assumption that lower-level word processes do not consume limited working memory resources.

To test the assumption that lower-level word processes do not influence higher-level processes, comparisons were made between (a) the CC-R model, which does not include a direct path leading from lower-level word processes to higher-level processes, and (b) the CC-R1-WP model, which is identical to the CC-R model except that the CC-R1-WP model includes direct paths leading from lower-level word processes to text-based processing, from lower-level word processes to knowledge access, and from lower-level word processes to knowledge integration. As shown in Table 2, some of the fit indexes for the CC-R1-WP model (e.g., *p*-exact, RMSEA) were poor, especially when they were compared with those of the CC-R model. Also, the χ^2-difference test suggested that the CC-R1-WP model had a poorer fit to the data than the CC-R model did: χ^2-difference(2) = 39.98, $p < .001$. Thus, taken as a whole, these findings suggest that a model that excludes paths leading from word processing to the higher-level processes (i.e., the CC-R model) explains the data better than does a model that includes these paths (i.e., the CC-R1-WP model). In other words, these findings support the CC-R model's assumption that lower-level word processes do not influence higher-level processes.

Testing Assumption 5. To test whether working memory has little to no direct influence on reading comprehension, comparisons were made between two nearly identical models: (1) the CC-R model, which does not include a direct path leading from working memory to reading comprehension, and (2) the CC-R2 model, which is identical to the CC-R model except that the CC-R2 model includes a direct path leading from working memory to reading comprehension. As shown in Table 2, all of the fit indexes for the CC-R2 model were significant. Moreover, the values for the fit indexes were as good as, and in some instances better than, those for the CC-R model. In addition, the χ^2-difference test suggested that the CC-R2 model fit the data better than the CC-R model did: χ^2-difference(1) = 4.96, $p = .026$. Taken as a whole, these findings suggest that a model that includes both direct and indirect paths from working memory to reading comprehension (i.e., the CC-R2 model) explains the data better than does a model that excludes the direct path (i.e., the CC-R model). In other words, these findings do not support the assumption that working memory exerts only an indirect influence on reading comprehension. Table 3 shows the specific values for these influences.

To reconcile the difference between this finding and previous research that has shown that working memory contributes little to reading comprehension performance once the variance attributed to higher-level processes is accounted for (Daneman & Hannon, 2007; Hannon & Daneman, 2001a), the amount of variance in reading comprehension that was accounted for by the CC-R versus CC-R2 models was examined. The LISREL output revealed that the CC-R and CC-R2 models accounted for 60% and 62% of the variance, respectively. This small 2.0% difference is consistent with earlier research that has shown that working memory accounts for little additional variance in reading comprehension performance once higher-level processes are accounted for (e.g., Daneman & Hannon, 2007). In addition, in conjunction with the earlier finding of the present study, although the CC-R2 model provides a better fit to the data, this better fit accounts for only 2.0% additional variance in reading comprehension performance.

Given that the results suggest that the CC-R2 model is better than the CC-R model at explaining the data, the CC-R2 model was compared with a new SEM that includes just a direct influence between working memory and reading comprehension. This new SEM is called the CC-R2+IWM (CC-R2 plus independent working memory model). As shown in Figure 7, the CC-R2+IWM model is identical to the CC-R2 model except that the CC-R2+IWM model excludes the nonsignificant path leading from working memory to knowledge integration. The exclusion of this path makes working memory's influence on reading comprehension performance completely direct and independent of higher-level processes. If so, then the CC-R2+IWM model should be better at explaining the data than does the CC-R model, which includes an indirect path. The CC-R2+IWM model should also be as good as, or perhaps even better than, the CC-R2 model, which includes both direct and indirect paths.

As shown in Table 2, all of the fit indexes for the CC-R2+IWM model were within acceptable limits. However, a subsequent χ^2-difference test revealed no significant difference between the CC-R2+IWM and CC-R models, even though the χ^2-difference test approached significance in favor of the CC-R2 model:

Figure 7. SEM of CC-R2+IWM Model With Path Coefficients

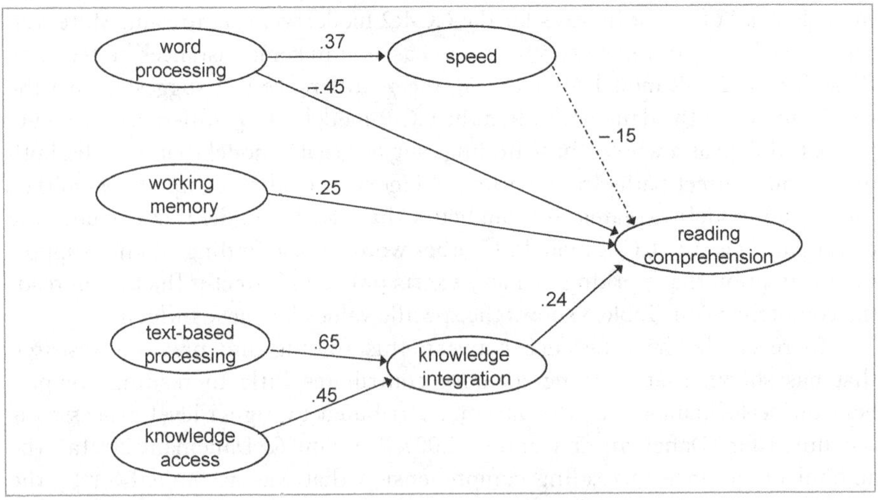

Note. Solid lines represent significant path coefficients, whereas the broken line represents nonsignificant structure coefficients. This SEM is identical to the cognitive components and resource model of reading comprehension (CC-R model) except for the addition of a path leading from working memory to reading comprehension (CC-R2 model) and the exclusion of the path leading from working memory to knowledge integration.

χ^2-difference(1) = 3.10, p = .078. Based on this latter finding and the earlier finding that the CC-R2 model is better at explaining the existing data than the CC-R model is, it appears that the CC-R2 model is the best model for explaining the relationship between working memory and reading comprehension performance. That is, rather than have an indirect (i.e., CC-R model) or direct (i.e., CC-R2+IWM model) influence on reading comprehension performance, the present findings suggest that working memory has both direct and indirect influences (i.e., CC-R2 model).

Discussion

Although it is generally accepted that comprehension is not simply the sum of its processes (Kintsch & Rawson, 2005), little is known about how many of its processes interact (Cornoldi et al., 1996; Perfetti et al., 2005) or whether one or all of them make separate and important contributions to reading comprehension performance (Perfetti et al., 1996). This lack of knowledge is quite surprising given that it has strong implications for major theories of comprehension that include lower-level word processes, higher-level cognitive processes, and working memory capacity. The present study addresses these limitations by developing and testing a SEM called the CC-R model—a model of reading comprehension that proposes a set of relationships among lower-level processes, higher-level processes, and working memory.

The results show that a variant of the CC-R model, namely the CC-R2 model, explains the present data well. That is, the CC-R2 model is suitable for both understanding the relationships among lower-level word processes, higher-level processes, and working memory and for predicting performance on standardized measures of adult reading comprehension. Next is a detailed discussion of the results, their theoretical and practical implications, and their limitations.

Relationships Among Lower-Level Processes, Higher-Level Processes, and Working Memory

With respect to lower-level word processing (i.e., word fluency), higher-level processes, and working memory, the present study reveals a number of findings that fill gaps in the literature. First, the zero-order correlations suggest little to no relationship between lower-level word processes and working memory, a finding that suggests that lower-level processes and working memory are separate constructs. Further, a comparison between two SEMs showed that the CC-R model, which excludes a path from word processing to working memory, is superior to the CC-R1-WM model, which includes that path. Thus, taken as a whole, these findings support previous research that has shown that lower-level word processes exert little influence on working memory in adults (e.g., Baddeley et al., 1985; Dixon et al., 1988). The new contribution of this specific finding is the use of a SEM as well as the use of multiple measures of word processes and working memory simultaneously.

Of course, one could argue that the reason why the word processing–working memory relationship is absent is because not all of the tasks were measuring nonverbal information. That is, perhaps differences in the types of information being processed in the measures of word processes (i.e., verbal) versus the operation span task (i.e., math + verbal) eliminated the possibility of a strong relationship between word processing and working memory. Although this possibility has merit, it seems unlikely because scores on the same verbal word processing measures failed to correlate with scores on the reading span task (a verbal measure of working memory) and the CPT (a verbal measure of multiple higher-level processes). Thus, when one considers this pattern of results, it seems that differences in the types of information being processed fails to explain the lack of a word processing–working memory relationship.

A second finding is there are, at best, weak relationships between measures of lower-level word processing and higher-level processes. Indeed, both the zero-order correlations and the comparisons between the SEMs testing assumptions 1 and 4 support this finding. The present results are some of the first to provide evidence of the idea that lower- and higher-level processes might be separate constructs in an adult population. The results are also consistent with the modest pattern of relationships that Cain et al. (2004) and August et al. (2006) observed with children and that Hannon and Frias (2012) observed with prereaders who were 4 and 5 years old.

A third finding is the weak relationship between word processing and speed. Although the tasks for both constructs measured reaction time (i.e., the word fluency task measured speed at deciding which string of letters is a word; the speed task measured speed at processing CPT test statements), and word processing directly influenced speed (i.e., word processing speed), both constructs separately predicted reading comprehension performance. This latter finding parallels findings from recent developmental research (e.g., Jenkins et al., 2003; Klauda & Guthrie, 2008) inasmuch as it suggests that word decoding and speed are not a unitary construct. From a theoretical perspective, this finding adds an interesting twist to the cognitive slowing hypothesis prominent in the aging literature because according to this hypothesis, speed is a unidimensional construct rather than a multidimensional one.

A fourth finding is that the higher-level processes form a very specific pattern of relationships. For example, the zero-order correlations suggest that text-based processes that are used to encode/learn new facts presented in a text (e.g., text memory, text inferencing) are highly related to one another but are, at best, weakly related to processes that access prior knowledge from long-term memory. Conversely, knowledge integration processes, which rely on new text-based information and existing information from prior knowledge, are related to both the text-based and knowledge access processes. Further, a comparison between two SEMs showed that a multifactor model, which depicted higher-level processes forming a specific pattern of separate factors, was superior to a single-factor model, which specified that higher-level processes form a single factor. Thus, taken as a whole, these findings support the idea that there are multiple higher-level processes (i.e., assumption 2). The findings also provide a framework for future research that might assess how other processes or resources, not assessed in the present study, might interact with the higher-level processes that were assessed in the present study.

In addition, these findings inform the simple view of reading (e.g., Gough et al., 1996), a very popular conceptualization of reading comprehension that defines reading comprehension as a multiplicative function of two separate clusters of abilities: word decoding × language comprehension (i.e., $R = D \times C$). Consistent with the simple view of reading, the present study supports the notion that lower-level word processes are separate or independent of higher-level processes that are used for comprehension. Conversely, the simple view of reading defines comprehension as a single unitary factor/process, whereas the present study suggests that there are multiple higher-level processes used for comprehension that form a very specific pattern of relationships. Furthermore, the results suggest that whereas some of these higher-level processes are related to one another (e.g., text processing with knowledge integration, knowledge access with knowledge integration), others are, at best, weakly related (e.g., text processing and knowledge access).

Finally, the present findings inform a number of theories of reading comprehension. As mentioned earlier, theories of reading comprehension have primarily focused on understanding and explaining the nature of mental representations of text rather than complex relationships among lower-level word processes, higher-level processes, and characteristics of the reader (McNamara & Magliano, 2009). The present study informs these theories by (a) proposing a set of relationships between lower- and higher-level processes, (b) showing that an individual-differences approach is suitable for assessing the relationships between lower- and higher-level processes, and (c) showing that SEMs are a viable statistical tool for assessing models of reading comprehension. In other words, the present study provides a foundation for future research to test and compare theories of reading comprehension, to assess the relationships among lower- and higher-level processes and other sources of individual differences, and to assess the relative predictive powers of sources of individual differences with various genres of text.

Predicting Performance on Measures of Adult Reading Comprehension

With regards to predicting performance on standardized measures of reading comprehension in adults, the present study shows that lower-level word processes, higher-level processes, and working memory each account for significant amounts of variance in reading comprehension performance. Indeed, as Table 3 shows, the effects for these three sources of individual differences are all significant. Also, the CC-R and CC-R2 models account for 60% and 62% of the variance in reading comprehension performance, respectively.

Notwithstanding, the results assessing the veracity of the assumptions of the CC-R model fail to support the assumption that working memory only indirectly influences reading comprehension. Rather, they reveal a more complicated relationship. Consistent with assumption 5, a SEM that includes both direct and indirect working memory–reading comprehension relationships (i.e., CC-R2 model) accounts for only 2% more variance in reading comprehension performance than does the CC-R model, a SEM that includes only an indirect working memory–reading comprehension relationship. In other words, the addition of the direct relationship accounted for little additional variance in reading comprehension performance, a finding that also replicates previous regression analysis research (e.g., Daneman & Hannon, 2007; Hannon & Daneman, 2001a). Conversely, inconsistent with assumption 5, a SEM that includes both direct and indirect working memory–reading comprehension relationships (i.e., CC-R2 model) is a better fit for the existing data than the CC-R model is. In other words, a variant of the CC-R model—the CC-R2 model—is significantly better than the CC-R model at explaining the existing data.

It should be noted, however, that this latter finding fails to replicate previous SEM research that has shown that working memory exerts only an indirect influence on reading comprehension (e.g., Britton et al., 1998). In other words, previous research supported assumption 5 of the CC-R model. Of course, there are numerous differences between the measures used by Britton et al. and those of the present study. Nevertheless, given that the CC-R2 model accounts for only 2% additional variance in reading comprehension performance over and above the original CC-R model, it is recommended that future research examine the working memory–reading comprehension relationship(s) using different measures of working memory and higher-level processes.

Additional Findings and Other Contributions

There are also other findings that are not the primary focus of the present study but still warrant discussion. For example, methodologically speaking, the present study goes well beyond previous research in at least three important ways. First, for most of the sources of individual differences, multiple measures were included as opposed to a single measure. This approach increases the probability that the present results will generalize to other studies. Also, by examining multiple sources of individual differences simultaneously, the present study reveals the relationships among the sources. Specifically, word processing appears to be a separate construct from higher-level processes and working memory, whereas the higher-level process of knowledge integration draws on working memory resources.

Further, the tasks measuring the sources of individual differences differed from the reading comprehension measures in a number of ways. For instance, whereas the reading comprehension measures assessed reading comprehension via multiple-choice questions, the measures for the sources assessed their respective constructs via lexical decisions (i.e., word processing), true/false statements (i.e., higher-level processes), and free recall (i.e., working memory). Whereas the reading comprehension measures assessed reading comprehension via number of correct answers, the measures for word processing assessed word processes via reaction time. Finally, whereas the reading comprehension measures allowed readers to refer back to the passages, the measures for the higher-level processes and working memory had greater memory demands inasmuch as both tasks required readers to retain information in memory and then recall it.

Also, it is important to acknowledge the utility of the CPT. Measures with strong psychometric properties are invaluable for assessing cognitive constructs delineated by theories of comprehension processing in cognitive science (e.g., Pellegrino, Baxter, & Glaser, 1999; Pellegrino & Glaser, 1979). Unfortunately, prior to the CPT, there were few measures assessing higher-level processes with good psychometric properties. Consequently, research was hampered because researchers were unable to assess the relative contributions of lower-level word processes, higher-level processes, and working memory to performances on measures of reading or listening comprehension. Researchers were also unable to assess or compare theoretical models of comprehension. The findings of the present study suggest that with measures like the CPT, researchers can advance knowledge about higher-level processes, their relationships with one another, their relationships with other important constructs such as lower-level word processes and working memory, and their predictive powers with respect to important constructs such as reading comprehension, listening comprehension, and fluid intelligence.

Also of practical interest is the finding that performance on a standardized measure of adult general or global reading comprehension consists of many separate sources of individual differences. This finding is of interest to educators because it implies that no single source is likely to be the cause of poor comprehension. Indeed, the results of the present study add to a growing developmental literature that suggests that poor comprehension might be attributed to one or many sources of individual differences—poor word decoding, weak knowledge integration, and/or small working memory capacities (e.g., Cain et al., 2004; Oakhill et al., 2003)—and each of these sources of individual differences might require a different intervention.

Finally, of theoretical interest is the finding that high-knowledge integration is an important source of individual differences in adult reading comprehension. This finding is consistent with recent research that has advocated integration of text-based information with prior knowledge as an important process in reading comprehension (Britton et al., 1998; Hannon & Daneman, 2001a, 2006, 2009). This finding also supports theories of reading comprehension that advocate building text structures (Gernsbacher, 1990), extending working memory by integrating prior knowledge with text-based information (Ericsson & Kintsch, 1995), and models of learning from instructional text (Britton et al., 1998).

Limitations

Although the present study has a number of theoretical and practical implications, the present study is only a beginning, as other factors, such as test administration, might influence the relative predictive powers of lower-level word processes, higher-level processes, and working memory for reading comprehension performance.[7] Consider, for example, preestablished time restrictions frequently imposed during administrations of reading comprehension measures. In the present study, standardized reading comprehension measures with time restrictions were selected because timed tests are often used by educators to evaluate students (e.g., SAT-V, GRE) and by researchers to assess adult reading comprehension skill (e.g., Bell & Perfetti, 1994; Cunningham et al., 1990; Daneman & Hannon, 2001; Dixon et al., 1988; Hannon & Daneman, 1998, 2006; Holmes, 2009; Landi, 2010; Long et al., 1994; Masson & Miller, 1983). By selecting this type of test, however, it is possible that the predictive powers of the speed measures (i.e., word processing, speed) were simply an artifact of the imposed time limits of the reading comprehension measures.

Although this might be a factor, other studies have suggested that the speed–reading comprehension correlation is not simply an artifact of speed = a speeded or timed measure. For example, Hannon and Daneman (2001a) found that speed correlated with scores on untimed measures of vocabulary knowledge (i.e., Mill Hill Vocabulary Scale) and vocabulary acquisition yet failed to correlate with scores on timed measures of verbal analogies and bridging inferences. Similarly, Klauda and Guthrie (2008) observed that scores on a measure of passage processing speed correlated with scores on an untimed measure of inference generation. Although this is a question for future research, perhaps speed of processing sentences/responding to test statements is more a general or global factor that influences many types of cognitive constructs (see Verhaeghen et al., 1993, for a similar argument in the aging literature). Finally, regardless of the explanation, the present findings show that speed is highly predictive of scores on a frequently administered, standardized test of reading comprehension.

A second factor that might affect the relative predictive powers of the sources of individual differences for reading comprehension is whether the test of reading comprehension permits referrals back to the passages. Frequently used measures of reading comprehension ability, such as the Nelson-Denny and SAT-V, allow referrals to passages as students answer the questions; in fact, the SAT-V includes passage line numbers to assist with referrals. By allowing referrals, however, it is possible that students rely more heavily on test-taking strategies rather than cognitive processes and resources that are used for learning and integrating text. Indeed, studies have shown that some students will simply scan passages for answers to questions rather than monitor their performance or integrate a passage into a coherent text representation (e.g., Farr, Pritchard, & Smitten, 1990). Studies have also shown that passage availability during question answering can greatly influence the predictive powers of domain knowledge about the passages (e.g., Ozuru, Best, Bell, Witherspoon, & McNamara, 2007). Again, these findings do not diminish the findings of the present study but do suggest the interesting possibility that perhaps some cognitive processes and resources, such as high-knowledge integration and working memory, might be more predictive of reading comprehension when passages are absent during test taking. Conversely, other processes, such as lower-level word processes, might become less predictive (see Andreassen & Bråten, 2010, for evidence of these latter two possibilities with fifth-grade students).

A third factor that might influence the relative predictive powers of the sources of individual differences for reading comprehension is the type of text, narrative versus expository. The reading comprehension measures administered in the present study consisted of short, expository texts. Although this type of text is representative of the texts that students frequently encounter, expository texts differ substantially from narrative texts, particularly in their potential for using existing knowledge, schemas, and scripts. Whereas narrative texts share conversational characteristics that occur frequently in everyday conversations (e.g., contextual situations, temporal/causal sequences), expository texts share characteristics with lectures and factual oral documentaries that occur less frequently (Graesser et al., 1994). Narrative texts often include familiar content (e.g., eating a meal), which makes it easier to draw on existing knowledge and schemas. In contrast, expository texts often include unfamiliar content (Graesser et al., 1994; Singer, Harkness, & Stewart, 1997), which reduces the potential for drawing on existing knowledge and schemas.

Because the present study used standardized reading comprehension measures composed of expository texts and because expository and narrative texts differ in their potential for using prior knowledge and schemas, it is possible that the predictive powers of the sources of individual differences differ for these two types of texts. For example, perhaps lower-level word processes will be less predictive of comprehension of narrative texts than expository texts would be because the common conversational characteristics inherent in narrative texts might place fewer demands on accessing word meanings. In contrast, knowledge access might be more predictive of comprehension of narratives because it measures access to prior knowledge, a resource that is more important for reading narrative texts rather than expository ones.

A fourth factor that might influence the relative predictive powers of the sources of individual differences is the use of the Nelson-Denny as the only measure of reading comprehension. At present, there are conflicting views about the extent to which the Nelson-Denny might be assessing elemental processes (e.g., text memory) versus more sophisticated processes (e.g., knowledge integration). On the one hand, researchers have pointed out that a large percentage of the multiple-choice questions in form F of the Nelson-Denny assess elemental facts rather than knowledge acquired from more sophisticated inferences and concepts typically found in the global context or situation model (Magliano, Millis, Ozuru, & McNamara, 2007). On the other hand, researchers have shown that even if multiple-choice questions are assessing knowledge for basic elemental facts, the cognitive processes that these questions assess are not necessarily basic elemental processes. Rather, the questions may be assessing more sophisticated processes. For example, Hannon and Daneman (2001a) showed that multiple-choice questions assessing elemental detail facts explicitly mentioned in historical and biographical passages were better at assessing sophisticated processes (e.g., knowledge integration) than elementary text-based processes (e.g., text memory). In other words, questions assessing basic elemental facts did not assess only elemental processes.

Finally, critics have argued that measures like the Nelson-Denny are more off-line measures of comprehension rather than online ones (e.g., Magliano et al., 2007; Magliano, Millis, the RSAT Development Team, Levinstein, & Boonthum, 2011). For this reason, researchers are currently developing new reading comprehension tools, such as the Reading Strategy Assessment Tool (RSAT; Magliano et al., 2011), that are designed to assess comprehension processes as they unfold online.

Besides considering factors that might influence the relative predictive powers of the sources of individual differences used in the present study, there are other cognitive resources, processes, and strategies that are predictive of reading comprehension that were not studied. For instance, absent were measures of prior knowledge and the metacognitive skill of sensing breaks in a passage—two other known predictors of reading comprehension and learning performance (Britton et al., 1998). Although these omissions do not invalidate the present results, questions remain as to how these other factors might predict reading comprehension performance relative to the three sources of individual differences found in the CC-R and CC-R2 models.

Another limitation is that the present study's experimental design does not permit assessment of the veracity of assumption 3, which states that readers form a single representation that varies in quality from reader to reader. Although not assessing assumption 3 does not diminish the present results, it would be interesting to test this assumption. On the one hand, it seems to make sense because one would expect the better cognitive processes of the skilled readers to form a more complete representation. On the other hand, recent neural research suggested that the picture might not be so simple because skilled and less skilled adult readers represent discourse differently across the two hemispheres (e.g., Prat, Long, & Baynes, 2007). Unlike their less skilled counterparts, skilled readers show a more left-lateralized pattern of discourse representation, including exclusive sensitivity to propositional and topic relations in the left hemisphere (Prat et al., 2007). In contrast, less-skilled readers show a more mixed-hemispheric pattern of discourse representation, whereas their sensitivity to topic relations is exclusive to the right hemisphere (Prat et al., 2007).

Another potential limitation is that perhaps the strong correlations between measures of lower-level word processes and reading comprehension and the strong correlations between measures of higher-level processes and reading comprehension were because all of these measures assessed verbal information. Although this limitation exists and its extent should be explored in future research, it is important to remember that it does not reduce the differences in the relative influences that lower-level word processes versus higher-level processes make on reading comprehension performance. Nor does this limitation explain the minimal relationship between lower- and higher-level processes.

Yet another limitation is that the latent variable speed had only one observed variable. As mentioned earlier, this is an acceptable practice, although it is not recommended (Jöreskog & Sörbom, 1993). By using a single observed measure of a latent variable, it is assumed that the observed variable is a perfect measure of the latent variable. It is for this reason that Schumacker and Lomax (1996) and Jöreskog and Sörbom (1993) recommended that the reliability of the observed variable be set, which was the procedure used in the present study. Further, it should be noted that using only one or two observed variables for each latent variable is also a limitation; using three observed variables is preferable. For this reason, future research should explore the CC-R and CC-R2 models with more than two observed variables representing the latent variables.

Finally, it should be noted that unlike the construction–integration model (Kintsch, 1998), which explains different types of comprehension for a number of different populations, the present findings provide evidence only that the CC-R model and its variant, the CC-R2 model, are good SEMs for explaining reading comprehension in a rather circumscribed population of adult readers, namely university students. Future research should test whether these models are suitable for predicting other types of comprehension (e.g., listening) and whether they generalize to other populations, such as a community sample of adult readers, adolescents, or beginning readers.

Conclusion

The present study used SEMs to examine the relationships among three sources of individual differences in adult reading comprehension: lower-level word processes, higher-level processes, and working memory. Using a population of proficient adult readers, the results show that a variant of the CC-R model, the CC-R2 model, is suitable for both understanding the relations among the sources of individual differences and predicting performance on standardized measures of reading comprehension. Indeed, the CC-R2 model accounted for 62% of the variance in reading comprehension performance. Of course, the present findings are limited to the measures used in the present study, and future research should examine whether they generalize to other measures. In addition, future research should explore the relationships among lower-level word processes, higher-level processes, and working memory using other types of methodology. For example, the assumptions of the CC-R and CC-R2 models could be tested experimentally or in real time using computer models. Finally, future research should assess whether the CC-R and CC-R2 models prevail across the life span.

QUESTIONS FOR REFLECTION

1. How do the assumptions of the cognitive components-resource model of reading comprehension (CC-R2) compare with Kintsch's construction–integration model?
2. What implications for instruction might surface as a result of Hannon's theory that word-level and higher-level cognitive processes are different in adult readers and young children?
3. How does the CC-R2 model as described by the author provide direction for your teaching of young readers?
4. How do the findings of this study counter the "simple view of reading" that views comprehension as a multiplicative function of word decoding and language comprehension ($R = D \times C$)?

NOTES

*When this chapter was written, Hannon was at the University of Saskatchewan.

I would like to thank Joe Magliano for his very helpful comments. I also thank Jill Argus for helping with data collection and Corey Vogel for helping with data scoring.

[1] There are many ways to classify cognitive processes and resources. For the purposes of the present study, I classify cognitive processes and resources in terms of a hierarchy. More specifically, those processes that are used to pronounce sounds and decode/identify words are classified as lower-level word processes. Those processes that are used to process larger units of information, such as ideas or propositions, are classified as higher-level processes.

[2] In many respects, this process account of the text representation is analogous to the process account of memory. That is, rather than propose a host of different types of memory that are presumably stored in different locations in our brains, memory researchers are starting to explain different types of memory in terms of different cognitive processes acting on the same memories (see Haberlandt, 1999, for more on this point).

[3] The major assumption of the automaticity and verbal efficiency theories is the opposite of assumption 4 of the CC-R model (LaBerge & Samuels, 1974; Perfetti, 1985). According to these developmental theories, word processes directly influence working memory because their efficiency influences the amount of working memory available for executing higher-level processes (Jenkins, Fuchs, van den Broek, Espin, & Deno, 2003). Slower word processes consume many working memory resources that are needed for executing higher-level processes, whereas faster word processes consume few working memory resources. Of course, the former two theories describe the acquisition of reading in beginning readers, whereas the CC-R model describes the processes of reading in proficient adult readers. For this reason, the automaticity and verbal efficiency theories might be a more appropriate model for beginning readers, whereas the CC-R model might be more appropriate for adults.

[4] In retrospect, it was unwise to counterbalance the forms of the Nelson-Denny because it potentially increases error and reduces power. However, the alternate form reliabilities for the Nelson-Denny are high (0.77 or higher), which suggests that the forms are interchangeable. Further, the subsequent analysis shows that the counterbalancing had a minimal

influence (see Engle, Tuholski, Laughlin, & Conway, 1999, who also made a similar error with counterbalancing).

[5] Although speed is a composite score of the reaction time for the test statements for the higher-level processes, speed is not really a higher-level process, nor can it be considered a lower-level word process. Rather, consistent with Verhaeghen, Marcoen, and Goossens (1993), speed should perhaps be classified as a general or more global factor/resource that may or may not influence other resources (e.g., working memory) or specific processes (e.g., lower-level word processes, text memory, text inferencing, knowledge access, knowledge integration).

[6] As noted by one of the reviewers, maximum likelihood estimation is very sensitive to non-normal data (see also Fan et al., 1999). For this reason, the reviewer suggested examining the statistics for univariate skew and kurtosis. The results of this analysis revealed that the skew and kurtosis for the low-knowledge access measure exceeded the maximum allowable limits for normality for skew and kurtosis (i.e., +/–1.5 for skew, +/–3.0 for kurtosis). A closer inspection of the data for this measure revealed that three data points were below the –3.0 standard deviation limit for univariate outliers. Based on the recommendations of Kline (2011), these three data points were replaced with values that were equivalent to the mean minus three standard deviations. Table 1 shows the new, recalculated descriptive statistics for the low-knowledge access measure. As this table shows, all the descriptive statistics for this measure are within normal limits. All subsequent data analysis (i.e., correlations, factor analysis, SEMs) are based on this transformed data.

[7] Factors affecting the relative influences of lower-level word processes, higher-level processes, and working memory apply to all theories of reading comprehension, not just the CC-R model.

REFERENCES

Aaron, P.G., Frantz, S.S., & Manges, A.R. (1990). Dissociation between comprehension and pronunciation in dyslexic and hyperlexic children. *Reading and Writing, 2*(3), 243–264. doi:10.1007/BF00257974

Andreassen, R., & Bråten, I. (2010). Examining the prediction of reading comprehension on different multiple-choice tests. *Journal of Research in Reading, 33*(3), 263–283. doi:10.1111/j.1467-9817.2009.01413.x

August, D., Francis, D.J., Hsu, H.A., & Snow, C.E. (2006). Assessing reading comprehension in bilinguals. *The Elementary School Journal, 107*(2), 221–238. doi:10.1086/510656

Baddeley, A., Logie, R., Nimmo-Smith, I., & Brereton, N. (1985). Components of fluent reading. *Journal of Memory and Language, 24*(1), 119–131. doi:10.1016/0749-596X(85)90019-1

Bell, L.C., & Perfetti, C.A. (1994). Reading skill: Some adult comparisons. *Journal of Educational Psychology, 86*(2), 244–255. doi:10.1037/0022-0663.86.2.244

Bentler, P.M. (1989). *EQS structural equations program manual.* Los Angeles: BMDP Statistical Software.

Britton, B.K., Stimson, M., Stennett, B., & Gülgöz, S. (1998). Learning from instructional text: Test of an individual-differences model. *Journal of Educational Psychology, 90*(3), 476–491. doi:10.1037/0022-0663.90.3.476

Browne, M.W., & Cudeck, R. (1993). Alternative ways of assessing model fit. In K.A. Bollen & J.S. Long (Eds.), *Testing structural equation models* (pp. 136–162). Newbury Park, CA: Sage.

Cain, K., Oakhill, J., & Bryant, P. (2004). Children's reading comprehension ability: Concurrent prediction by working memory, verbal ability and component skill. *Journal of Educational Psychology, 96*(1), 31–42. doi:10.1037/0022-0663.96.1.31

Calvo, M.G. (2001). Working memory and inferences: Evidence from eye fixations during reading. *Memory, 9*(4), 365–381. doi:10.1080/09658210143000083

Calvo, M.G. (2005). Relative contribution of vocabulary knowledge and working memory span to elaborative inferences in reading. *Learning and Individual Differences, 15*(1), 53–65. doi:10.1016/j.lindif.2004.07.002

Chabot, R.J., Zehr, H.D., Prinzo, O.V., & Petros, T.V. (1984). The speed of word recognition subprocesses and reading achievement in college students. *Reading Research Quarterly, 19*(2), 147–161. doi:10.2307/747359

Cornoldi, C., De Beni, R., & Pazzaglia, F. (1996). Profiles of reading comprehension difficulties: An analysis of single cases. In C. Cornoldi & J. Oakhill (Eds.), *Reading comprehension difficulties: Processes and intervention* (pp. 113–136). Mahwah, NJ: Erlbaum.

Crain, S. (1989). Why poor readers misunderstand spoken sentences. In D. Shankweiler & I.Y. Liberman (Eds.), *Phonology and reading disability: Solving the reading puzzle* (International Academy for Research in Learning Disabilities Monograph No. 6, pp. 133–166). Ann Arbor: University of Michigan Press.

Cromley, J.G., & Azevedo, R. (2007). Testing and refining the direct and inferential mediation model of reading comprehension. *Journal of Educational Psychology, 99*(2), 311–325. doi:10.1037/0022-0663.99.2.311

Cunningham, A.E., Stanovich, K.E., & Wilson, M.R. (1990). Cognitive variation in adult college students differing in reading ability. In T.H. Carr & B.A. Levy (Eds.), *Reading and its development: Component skills approaches* (pp. 129–159). San Diego, CA: Academic.

Daneman, M., & Carpenter, P.A. (1980). Individual differences in working memory and reading. *Journal of Verbal Learning and Verbal Behavior, 19*(4), 450–466. doi:10.1016/S0022-5371(80)90312-6

Daneman, M., & Hannon, B. (2001). Using working memory theory to investigate the construct validity of multiple-choice reading comprehension tests such as the SAT. *Journal of Experimental Psychology: General, 130*(2), 208–223. doi:10.1037/0096-3445.130.2.208

Daneman, M., & Hannon, B. (2007). What do working memory span tasks like reading span really measure? In N. Osaka, R.H. Logie, & M. D'Esposito (Eds.), *The cognitive neuroscience of working memory* (pp. 21–42). New York: Oxford University Press.

Daneman, M., & Merikle, P.M. (1996). Working memory and language comprehension: A meta-analysis. *Psychonomic Bulletin & Review, 3*(4), 422–433. doi:10.3758/BF03214546

Dixon, P., LeFevre, J., & Twilley, L.C. (1988). Word knowledge and working memory as predictors of reading skill. *Journal of Educational Psychology, 80*(4), 465–472. doi:10.1037/0022-0663.80.4.465

Engle, R.W., Tuholski, S.W., Laughlin, J.E., & Conway, A.R. (1999). Working memory, short-term memory, and general fluid intelligence: A latent-variable approach. *Journal of Experimental Psychology: General, 128*(3), 309–331.

Ericsson, K.A., & Kintsch, W. (1995). Long-term working memory. *Psychological Review, 102*(2), 211–245. doi:10.1037/0033-295X.102.2.211

Estevez, A., & Calvo, M.G. (2000). Working memory capacity and time course of predictive inferences. *Memory, 8*(1), 51–61. doi:10.1080/096582100387704

Fan, X., & Sivo, S.A. (2005). Sensitivity of fit indexes to misspecified structural or measurement model components: Rationale of two-index strategy revisited. *Structural Equation Modeling, 12*(3), 343–367. doi:10.1207/s15328007sem1203_1

Fan, X., Thompson, B., & Wang, L. (1999). Effects of sample size, estimation methods, and model specification on structural equation modeling fit indexes. *Structural Equation Modeling, 6*(1), 56–83. doi:10.1080/10705519909540119

Farr, R., Pritchard, R., & Smitten, B. (1990). A description of what happens when an examinee takes a multiple-choice reading comprehension test. *Journal of Educational Measurement, 27*(3), 209–226. doi:10.1111/j.1745-3984.1990.tb00744.x

Frith, U., & Snowling, M. (1983). Reading for meaning and reading for sound in autistic and dyslexic children. *British Journal of Developmental Psychology, 1*(4), 329–342. doi:10.1111/j.2044-835X.1983.tb00906.x

Gernsbacher, M.A. (1990). *Language comprehension as structure building.* Hillsdale, NJ: Erlbaum.

Gough, P.B., Hoover, W.A., & Peterson, C.L. (1996). Some observations on a simple view of reading. In C. Cornoldi & J. Oakhill (Eds.), *Reading comprehension difficulties: Processes and intervention* (pp. 1–13). Mahwah, NJ: Erlbaum.

Graesser, A.C., Singer, M., & Trabasso, T. (1994). Constructing inferences during narrative text comprehension. *Psychological Review, 101*(3), 371–395. doi:10.1037/0033-295X.101.3.371

Haberlandt, K. (1999). *Human memory: Exploration and application.* Boston: Allyn & Bacon.

Halldorson, M., & Singer, M. (2002). Inference processes: Integrating relevant knowledge and text information. *Discourse Processes, 34*(2), 145–161. doi:10.1207/S15326950DP3402_2

Hannon, B., & Daneman, M. (1998). Facilitating knowledge-based inferences in less-skilled readers. *Contemporary Educational Psychology, 23*(2), 149–172. doi:10.1006/ceps.1997.0968

Hannon, B., & Daneman, M. (2001a). A new tool for measuring and understanding individual differences in the component processes of reading comprehension. *Journal of Educational Psychology, 93*(1), 103–128. doi:10.1037/0022-0663.93.1.103

Hannon, B., & Daneman, M. (2001b). Susceptibility to semantic illusions: An individual-differences perspective. *Memory & Cognition, 29*(3), 449–461. doi:10.3758/BF03196396

Hannon, B., & Daneman, M. (2006). What do tests of reading comprehension ability such as the VSAT really measure? A Componential analysis. In A.V. Mittel (Ed.), *Focus on educational psychology* (pp. 105–146). New York: Nova Science.

Hannon, B., & Daneman, M. (2009). Age-related changes in reading comprehension: An individual-differences perspective. *Experimental Aging Research, 35*(4), 432–456. doi:10.1080/03610730903175808

Hannon, B., & Frias, S. (2012). *A new measure for assessing the contributions of higher-level component processes to language comprehension in prereaders.* Manuscript submitted for publication.

Holmes, V.M. (2009). Bot tom-up processing and reading comprehension in experienced adult readers. *Journal of Research in Reading, 32*(3), 309–326. doi:10.1111/j.1467-9817.2009.01396.x

Hoover, W.A., & Gough, P.B. (1990). The simple view of reading. *Reading and Writing*, *2*(2), 127–160.

Hoyle, R.H., & Panter, A.T. (1995). Writing about structural equation models. In R.H. Hoyle (Ed.), *Structural equation modeling: Concepts, issues and applications* (pp. 158–176). Thousand Oaks, CA: Sage.

Hu, L., & Bentler, P.M. (1999). Cutoff criteria for fit indexes in covariance structure analysis: Conventional criteria versus new alternatives. *Structural Equation Modeling*, *6*(1), 1–55. doi:10.1080/10705519909540118

Jackson, N.E. (2005). Are university students' component reading skills related to their text comprehension and academic achievement? *Learning and Individual Differences*, *15*(2), 113–139. doi:10.1016/j.lindif.2004.11.001

Jenkins, J.R., Fuchs, L.S., van den Broek, P., Espin, C., & Deno, S.L. (2003). Sources of individual differences in reading comprehension and reading fluency. *Journal of Educational Psychology*, *95*(4), 719–729. doi:10.1037/0022-0663.95.4.719

Jöreskog, K.G., & Sörbom, D. (1981). *LISREL V: Analysis of linear structural relationships by the method of maximum likelihood and least squares methods*. Chicago: National Education Resources.

Jöreskog, K.G., & Sörbom, D. (1993). *LISREL 8: Structural equation modeling with the SIMPLIS command language*. Chicago: Scientific Software International.

Jöreskog, K.G., & Sörbom, D. (2002). *LISREL 8: Structural equation modeling with the SIMPLIS command language* (Rev. ed.). Chicago: Scientific Software International.

Just, M.A., & Carpenter, P.A. (1992). A capacity theory of comprehension: Individual differences in working memory. *Psychological Review*, *99*(1), 122–149. doi:10.1037/0033-295X.99.1.122

Keenan, J.M., & Kintsch, W. (1974). Memory for information inferred during reading. In W. Kintsch (Ed.), *The representation of meaning in memory* (pp. 153–178). Hillsdale, NJ: Erlbaum.

Kendeou, P., van den Broek, P., White, M.J., & Lynch, J.S. (2009). Predicting reading comprehension in early elementary school: The independent contributions of oral language and decoding skills. *Journal of Educational Psychology*, *101*(4), 765–778. doi:10.1037/a0015956

Kintsch, W. (1988). The role of knowledge in discourse comprehension: A construction–integration model. *Psychological Review*, *95*(2), 163–182. doi:10.1037/0033-295X.95.2.163

Kintsch, W. (1994). Text comprehension, memory, and learning. *American Psychologist*, *49*(4), 294–303.

Kintsch, W. (1998). *Comprehension: A paradigm for cognition*. New York: Cambridge University Press.

Kintsch, W., & Rawson, K.A. (2005). Comprehension. In M.J. Snowling & C. Hulme (Eds.), *The science of reading: A handbook* (pp. 209–226). Malden, MA: Blackwell. doi:10.1002/9780470757642.ch12

Klauda, S.L., & Guthrie, J.T. (2008). Relationships of three components of reading fluency to reading comprehension. *Journal of Educational Psychology*, *100*(2), 310–321. doi:10.1037/0022-0663.100.2.310

Kline, R.B. (2011). *Principles and practice of structural equation modeling* (3rd ed.). New York: Guilford.

LaBerge, D., & Samuels, S.J. (1974). Toward a theory of automatic information processing in reading. *Cognitive Psychology*, *6*(2), 293–323. doi:10.1016/0010-0285(74)90015-2

Landi, N. (2010). An examination of the relationship between reading comprehension, higher-level and lower-level reading subskills in adults. *Reading and Writing*, *23*(6), 701–717. doi:10.1007/s11145-009-9180-z

Lomax, R.G., & McGee, L.M. (1987). Young children's concepts about print and reading: Toward a model of word reading acquisition. *Reading Research Quarterly*, *22*(2), 237–256. doi:10.2307/747667

Long, D.L., & De Ley, L. (2000). Implicit causality and discourse focus: The interaction of text and reader characteristics in pronoun resolution. *Journal of Memory and Language*, *42*(4), 545–570. doi:10.1006/jmla.1999.2695

Long, D.L., Oppy, B.J., & Seely, M.R. (1994). Individual differences in the time course of inferential processing. *Journal of Experimental Psychology: Learning, Memory, and Cognition*, *20*(6), 1456–1470. doi:10.1037/0278-7393.20.6.1456

Long, D.L., Oppy, B.J., & Seely, M.R. (1997). Individual differences in readers' sentence- and text-level representations. *Journal of Memory and Language*, *36*(1), 129–145. doi:10.1006/jmla.1996.2485

Lubinski, D. (2004). Introduction to the special section on cognitive abilities: 100 years after Spearman's (1904) "'General intelligence,' objectively determined and measured." *Journal of Personality and Social Psychology*, *86*(1), 96–111. doi:10.1037/0022-3514.86.1.96

Magliano, J.P., Millis, K., Ozuru, Y., & McNamara, D.S. (2007). A multidimensional framework to evaluate reading assessment tools. In D.S. McNamara (Ed.), *Reading comprehension strategies: Theories, interventions, and technologies* (pp. 107–136). Mahwah, NJ: Erlbaum.

Magliano, J.P., Millis, K.K., the RSAT Development Team, Levinstein, I., & Boonthum, C. (2011). Assessing comprehension during reading with the Reading Strategy Assessment Tool (RSAT). *Metacognition and Learning*, *6*(2), 131–154. doi:10.1007/s11409-010-9064-2

Magliano, J.P., Trabasso, T., & Graesser, A.C. (1999). Strategic processing during comprehension. *Journal of Educational Psychology*, *91*(4), 615–629. doi:10.1037/0022-0663.91.4.615

Marsh, H.W., Hau, K., & Wen, Z. (2004). In search of golden rules: Comment on hypothesis-testing approaches to setting cutoff values for fit indexes and dangers in overgeneralizing Hu and Bentler's (1999) findings. *Structural Equation Modeling, 11*(3), 320–341. doi:10.1207/s15328007sem1103_2

Masson, M.E., & Miller, J.A. (1983). Working memory and individual differences in comprehension and memory of text. *Journal of Educational Psychology, 75*(2), 314–318. doi:10.1037/0022-0663.75.2.314

McKoon, G., & Ratcliff, R. (1992). Inferences during reading. *Psychological Review, 99*(3), 440–466. doi:10.1037/0033-295X.99.3.440

McNamara, D.S., & Magliano, J.P. (2009). Toward a comprehensive model of comprehension. In B. Ross (Ed.), *The psychology of learning and motivation* (Vol. 51, pp. 297–384). New York: Elsevier Science. doi:10.1016/S0079-7421(09)51009-2

Murray, J.D., & Burke, K.A. (2003). Activation and encoding of predictive inferences: The role of reading skill. *Discourse Processes, 35*(2), 81–102. doi:10.1207/S15326950DP3502_1

Oakhill, J.V., Cain, K., & Bryant, P.E. (2003). The dissociation of word reading and text comprehension: Evidence from component skills. *Language and Cognitive Processes, 18*(4), 443–468. doi:10.1080/01690960344000008

Olson, R.K., Kliegl, R., & Davidson, B.J. (1983). Dyslexia and normal readers' eye movements. *Journal of Experimental Psychology: Human Perception and Performance, 9*(5), 816–825. doi:10.1037/0096-1523.9.5.816

Ozuru, Y., Best, R., Bell, C., Witherspoon, A., & McNamara, D.S. (2007). Influence of question format and text availability on the assessment of expository text comprehension. *Cognition and Instruction, 25*(4), 399–438. doi:10.1080/07370000701632371

Pellegrino, J.W., Baxter, G.P., & Glaser, R. (1999). Addressing the "two disciplines" problem: Linking theories of cognition and learning with assessment and instructional practice. *Review of Research in Education, 24*(1), 307–353. doi:10.3102/0091732X024001307

Pellegrino, J.W., & Glaser, R. (1979). Cognitive correlates and components in the analysis of individual differences. *Intelligence, 3*(3), 187–215. doi:10.1016/0160-2896(79)90017-5

Perfetti, C.A. (1985). *Reading ability*. New York: Oxford University Press.

Perfetti, C.A. (1997). Sentences, individual differences, and multiple texts: Three issues in text comprehension. *Discourse Processes, 23*(3), 337–355. doi:10.1080/01638539709544996

Perfetti, C.A., Landi, N., & Oakhill, J. (2005). The acquisition of reading comprehension skill. In M.J. Snowling & C. Hulme (Eds.), *The science of reading: A handbook* (pp. 227–247). Malden, MA: Blackwell. doi:10.1002/9780470757642.ch13

Perfetti, C.A., Marron, M.A., & Foltz, P.W. (1996). Sources of comprehension failure: Theoretical perspectives and case studies. In C. Cornoldi & J. Oakhill (Eds.), *Reading comprehension difficulties: Processes and intervention* (pp. 137–166). Mahwah, NJ: Erlbaum.

Potts, G.R., & Peterson, S.B. (1985). Incorporation versus compartmentalization in memory for discourse. *Journal of Memory and Language, 24*(1), 107–118. doi:10.1016/0749-596X(85)90018-X

Prat, C.S., Long, D.L., & Baynes, K. (2007). The representation of discourse in the two hemispheres: An individual differences investigation. *Brain and Language, 100*(3), 283–294. doi:10.1016/j.bandl.2006.11.002

Russell, D.W. (2002). In search of underlying dimensions: The use (and abuse) of factor analysis. *Personality and Social Psychology Bulletin, 28*(12), 1629–1646. doi:10.1177/014616702237645

Schmalhofer, F., McDaniel, M.A., & Keefe, D. (2002). A unified model for predictive and bridging inferences. *Discourse Processes, 33*(2), 105–132. doi:10.1207/S15326950DP3302_01

Schumacker, R.E., & Lomax, R.G. (1996). *A beginner's guide to structural equation modeling*. Mahwah, NJ: Erlbaum.

Singer, M., Andrusiak, P., Reisdorf, P., & Black, N.L. (1992). Individual differences in bridging inference processes. *Memory & Cognition, 20*(5), 539–548. doi:10.3758/BF03199586

Singer, M., Graesser, A.C., & Trabasso, T. (1994). Minimal or global inference during reading. *Journal of Memory and Language, 33*(4), 421–441. doi:10.1006/jmla.1994.1020

Singer, M., Halldorson, M., Lear, J.C., & Andrusiak, P. (1992). Validation of causal bridging inferences in discourse understanding. *Journal of Memory and Language, 31*(4), 507–524. doi:10.1016/0749-596X(92)90026-T

Singer, M., Harkness, D., & Stewart, S.T. (1997). Constructing inferences in expository text comprehension. *Discourse Processes, 24*(2/3), 199–228. doi:10.1080/01638539709545013

Singer, M., & Ritchot, K.F.M. (1996). The role of working memory capacity and knowledge access in text inference processing. *Memory & Cognition, 24*(6), 733–743. doi:10.3758/BF03201098

Steiger, J.H. (1989). *EzPATH: Causal modeling, a supplementary module for SYSTAT and SYGRAPH, PC/MS-DOS*. Evanston, IL: SYSTAT.

Steiger, J.H., & Lind, J.C. (1980, May). *Statistically based tests for the number of common factors*. Paper presented at the annual meeting of the Psychometric Society, Iowa City, IA.

Tabachnick, B.G., & Fidell, L.S. (2007). *Using multivariate statistics* (5th ed.). New York: Allyn & Bacon.

Tunmer, W.E. (2008). Recent developments in reading intervention research: Introduction to the special issue. *Reading and Writing, 21*(4), 299–316. doi:10.1007/s11145-007-9108-4

Turner, M.L., & Engle, R.W. (1989). Is working memory capacity task dependent? *Journal of Memory and Language, 28*(2), 127–154. doi:10.1016/0749-596X(89)90040-5

Verhaeghen, P., Marcoen, A., & Goossens, L. (1993). Facts and fiction about memory aging: A quantitative integration of research findings. *The Journal of Gerontology, 48*(4), P157–P171.

West, S.G., Finch, J.F., & Curran, P.J. (1995). Structural equation models with non-normal variables: Problems and remedies. In R.H. Hoyle (Ed.), *Structural equation modeling: Concepts, issues, and applications* (pp. 56–75). Thousand Oaks, CA: Sage.

Zhang, H., & Hoosain, R. (2001). The influence of narrative text characteristics on thematic inference during reading. *Journal of Research in Reading, 24*(2), 173–186. doi:10.1111/1467-9817.00140

APPENDIX A

Z-Tests Assessing the Relative Contributions of Each Predictor to Performance on the Nelson-Denny Forms Used in Set 1 Versus Performance on the Nelson-Denny Forms Used in Set 2

As noted in the Methods section, students completed two forms of the Nelson-Denny, either set 1 (forms E and H) or set 2 (forms F and G). To test whether the zero-order correlations between scores on the predictors and the reading comprehension forms are equivalent, I completed a number of *z*-tests. These *z*-tests were computed between forms that were matched in the same session. That is, comparisons were made between form E and form F and between form H and form G for each of the predictors. For instance, a *z*-test assessed whether the correlation between scores on text memory and form E (i.e., set 1, session 1) was equivalent to the correlation between scores on text memory and form F (i.e., set 2, session 1); a *z*-test assessed whether the correlation between scores on text memory and form H (i.e., set 1, session 2) was equivalent to the correlation between scores on text memory and form G (i.e., set 2, session 2); and so forth. None of the *z*-tests was significant. For example, for the largest $z = -1.28$, $p > .10$.

Predictor	*z*-Score Between Forms E and F	*z*-Score Between Forms H and G
Text memory	−0.40	−0.10
Text inferencing	0.07	−0.38
Low-knowledge integration	−1.19	0.88
High-knowledge integration	−0.29	−0.33
Low-knowledge access	−0.03	−0.07
High-knowledge access	0.29	−0.35
Speed	0.10	−0.10
Reading span	1.16	1.17
Operation span	0.3	1.03
Orthographic task	−1.10	0.91
Phonemic task	−1.28	0.93

APPENDIX B

Examples of Stimuli Used in the Phonemic and Orthographic Lexical Decision Tasks

Phonemic	Orthographic
daiw dair	date dait
heer heem	chear cheer
paz pai	rare rair
yeat yeer	fite fight
voat voam	meek meak
faid foid	prair prayer
stawe stane	yearn yurn
myde syde	kurl curl
spair spaor	mate mait
hoap hoate	furst first

APPENDIX C

Sample Paragraphs and Questions From the Component Processes Task*

Vehicle Item

Paragraph

A NORT resembles a JET but is faster and weighs more.

A BERL resembles a CAR but is slower and weighs more.

A SAMP resembles a BERL but is slower and weighs more.

Features/Relations

speed NORT > JET > CAR > BERL > SAMP

weight NORT > JET > CAR > SAMP > BERL > CAR

Test Statements

Text Memory

A NORT is faster than a JET. (true)

A JET is faster than a NORT. (false)

Text Inferencing

A SAMP is slower than a CAR. (true)

A CAR is slower than a SAMP. (false)

Low-Knowledge Access

A JET is faster than a CAR. (true)

A CAR is faster than a JET. (false)

High-Knowledge Access

A JET has a pilot, whereas a MOTORCYCLE doesn't. (true)

A JET has a driver, whereas a MOTORCYCLE doesn't. (false)

Low-Knowledge Integration

A NORT is faster than a CAR. (true)

A CAR is faster than a NORT. (false)

High-Knowledge Integration

Like ROCKETS, NORTS travel in the air. (true)

Like MOTORCYCLES, NORTS travel across the land. (false)

Like MOTORCYCLES, BERLS travel across the land. (true)

Like ROCKETS, BERLS travel in the air. (false)

Speed

Average reaction time for all correctly answered test statements.

*From "Susceptibility to Semantic Illusions: An Individual-Differences Perspective," by B. Hannon and M. Daneman, 2001, *Memory & Cognition*, 29(3), p. 453. Copyright 2001 by the Psychonomic Society. Adapted with permission.

CHAPTER 34

A Dual Coding Theoretical Model of Reading

Mark Sadoski, Texas A&M University

Allan Paivio, University of Western Ontario

Dual Coding Theory (DCT) is an established theory of general cognition that has been directly applied to literacy. This theory was originally developed to account for verbal and nonverbal influences on memory, and it has been extended to many other areas of cognition through a systematic program of research over many years (Paivio, 1971, 1986, 1991). DCT has been extended to literacy as an account of reading comprehension (Sadoski & Paivio, 1994; Sadoski, Paivio, & Goetz, 1991), as an account of written composition (Sadoski, 1992), and as a unified theory of reading and writing (Sadoski & Paivio, 2001). For the fullest understanding of the theory, these references and the specific studies they cite should be consulted. This article briefly discusses the DCT account of certain basic processes in reading, including decoding, comprehension, and response.

The value of explaining reading under the aegis of a theory of general cognition is compelling. Reading is a cognitive act, but there is nothing about reading that does not occur in other cognitive acts that do not involve reading. We perceive, recognize, interpret, comprehend, appreciate, and remember information that is not in text form as well as information that is in text form. Cognition in reading is a special case of general cognition that involves written language. Theories specific to reading must eventually conform to broader theories of general cognition for scientific progress to advance. DCT provides one vehicle for that advancement.

Another value offered by DCT is that it provides a combined account of decoding, comprehension, and response. Theories of reading often focus on one or another of these aspects of reading but not all. As we shall see, the same basic DCT principles apply to grapheme–phoneme correspondences, word meaning, grammar, the construction of mental models of text episodes, and even imaginative responses to text. In this article, we will briefly explain the theory's basic assumptions; provide accounts of decoding, comprehension, and response; compare and contrast DCT with other theories of reading; and discuss its implications for research and practice.

This chapter is reprinted from *Theoretical Models and Processes of Reading* (5th ed., pp. 1329–1362), edited by R.B. Ruddell and N.J. Unrau, Newark, DE: International Reading Association.

Basic Assumptions

A basic premise of DCT is that all mental representations retain some of the concrete qualities of the external experiences from which they derive. These experiences can be linguistic or nonlinguistic. Their differing characteristics develop into two separate mental systems or codes: one specialized for representing and processing language (the verbal code) and one for processing nonlinguistic objects and events (the nonverbal code). The latter is frequently referred to as the imagery system or code because its functions include the generation, analysis, and transformation of mental images. Each code has its own characteristic units and hierarchical organization. Together, the two codes account for knowledge of language and knowledge of the world.

The two mental codes and our five senses are orthogonal in DCT. This means that the two codes each have subsets of mental representations that are qualitatively different because of the different sensory experiences from which they originated. Because sensory systems are linked to motor response systems in perception (e.g., eye movements, listening attitudes, active touch), these subsets have sensorimotor qualities. We develop visual representations in the verbal code for language units we have seen, such as letters, words, or phrases (e.g., *baseball bat*). But we also develop visual representations in the nonverbal code for nonlinguistic forms that we have seen, such as common objects or scenes (e.g., a wooden or aluminum baseball bat). Likewise, we develop auditory representations in the verbal code for speech units we have heard, such as phonemes and their combinations (e.g., the phoneme /b/, the rime /-at/, the word /bat/), and auditory representations in the nonverbal code for nonlinguistic environmental sounds we have heard (e.g., the crack of a wooden bat or the clink of an aluminum bat hitting a ball). Likewise, we develop haptic (i.e., kinesthetic or tactile) representations in the verbal code for linguistic motor acts (e.g., pronouncing /b/ or writing the letter *b* or touching the Braille sign for *b*), and we develop haptic representations in the nonverbal code for the active "feel" of objects, textures, and movements (e.g., the heft and swing of a baseball bat). We do not represent language in the chemical sense modalities (smell and taste), but we have nonverbal representations for them (e.g., the smell and taste of a juicy hot dog at a baseball game). Images in these modalities are typically less vivid for most people. (Table 1 provides a diagram of this orthogonal relationship.) To these modalities might be added affect—emotional feelings and reactions. These are nonverbal by definition, although we have many names for emotional states. We also have imagery for such states, and it forms an important component of meaning. We might imagine the excitement of an enthusiastic fan at a baseball game, for example.

Understanding these "codes and modes" is basic to understanding the DCT interpretation of reading. The overall system can be imagined as a set of modality- and code-specific subsystems that are laced with interconnections. These subsystems are independent and appear to be specialized in certain, sometimes multiple, areas of the brain. For example, some persons with alexia cannot read the phrase *baseball bat* but can recognize the phrase when it is spoken and

Table 1. Orthogonal Relationship Between Mental Codes and Sense Modalities

	Mental Codes	
Sense Modality	**Verbal**	**Nonverbal**
Visual	Visual language (writing)	Visual objects
Auditory	Auditory language (speech)	Environmental sounds
Haptic	Braille, handwriting	"Feel" of objects
Gustatory	—	Taste memories
Olfactory	—	Smell memories

Empty cells indicate the absence of verbal representations in these modalities.

even write it, providing evidence of independent, modality-specific representations within the verbal code. Some persons with anomia can recognize a baseball bat but not be able to name it, providing evidence of a general independence between nonverbal and verbal codes. For relevant neuropsychological evidence see Paivio (1986, 1991) and West, O'Rourke, and Holcomb (1998). Sacks (2002) provides a readable case study of neuropathology affecting only certain aspects of reading. A misunderstanding of the distinction between mental codes and sensory modalities has sometimes led to the inaccurate characterization of DCT as being about the verbal and visual codes. The correct distinctions are between verbal and nonverbal (imagery) codes, and between the visual modality and the other sensory modalities.

A common manifestation of the modular nature of our representational subsystems is seen in the phenomenon of modality-specific interference, the limited ability to do two things in the same modality at once. For example, it is difficult to listen to two conversations at once—our verbal, auditory capacity is quickly overcome and we must "shuttle" between the two. This ability has been called the "cocktail-party phenomenon" (Harris & Hodges, 1995, p. 33). In reading, it is somewhat difficult to visually process the print and extensively visualize its semantic content at the same time, particularly for the unskilled reader. Either the reader tends to slow down or the number of oral reading miscues increases (Denis, 1982; Eddy & Glass, 1981; Hodes, 1994; Sadoski, 1983, 1985). More discussion of this phenomenon and its implications will appear later. Next, we will discuss the basic units that compose each system, their organization in each system, and the kinds of interconnections and processing operations that occur to them.

Basic Units

Cognitive theories usually specify basic units or "building blocks" of cognition. The basic units in the verbal system are *logogens*, and the basic units in the nonverbal system are *imagens*. These terms are merely jargon for the way the brain represents different types of information, but DCT assumes that they are concrete, as opposed to being abstract and amodal. The terms are not meant to imply static units. Although memory representations have some permanence, they are better thought of as evolving and flexible, such as the way our vocabulary knowledge is constantly enriched by experiencing words in different contexts or the way images are often of novel scenes comprised of familiar elements.

A logogen is anything learned as a unit of language in some sense modality. Language units vary in size, although some sizes are more familiar than others (e.g., words). Hence, we have visual logogens for written letters, words, and phrases; auditory logogens for phonemes and word and phrase pronunciations; and haptic logogens for pronouncing, writing, or signing these language units. In speech, phonemic logogens may be represented in closely associated auditory–motor form. That is, a phoneme may be represented as a physical articulation of the speech organs as well as an auditory sound (Liberman & Mattingly, 1985).

Logogens are derived from the perception of language and influence its perception. A charming example is the child learning to say the alphabet who perceives the spoken sequence "l, m, n, o" as "elemeno." The letter-name sequence initially is perceived as one auditory–motor unit; with more learning it will be perceived as four separate units. Similarly, words can be learned before their individual letters or phonemes are learned, and words can be identified as rapidly, or more rapidly, than their individual letters or phonemes after they are learned.

Imagens are modality specific and vary in size as well, and they tend to be perceived in nested sets. That is, mental images are often embedded in larger mental images. Hence, we can visually imagine a baseball bat, the bat in the hands of a batter, and the batter at home plate in a crowded stadium. In the auditory modality, we can imagine the crack of the bat, or the crack of the bat over the noise of the crowd. These perceptions may be associated into an auditory–visual mental episode that may be transformed into a sequence of the bat being swung, the crack of the bat and roar of the crowd, and the batter running to base as the ball speeds away. That is, while the imagens remain modality specific, they can be incorporated into a larger mental structure that reflects the multisensory nature of physical reality.

Both types of representations can be activated in various ways. Logogens can be activated by direct sensory input such as seeing printed language, or imagens can be activated by seeing familiar objects. However, both types of mental representation can be activated indirectly, as when we spontaneously form images to words or name objects. Both internal and external contexts also can prime language or imagery. Seeing the word *baseball* can indirectly activate an internal, associated neighborhood of logogens such as *bat*, *glove*, *game*, *cap*, and so on. All these words could in turn activate related imagens. External contexts would serve to limit the activated set to the most relevant members. Therefore, both bottom-up and top-down inputs can activate mental representations in interactive ways. When enough input is received from any one source or a combination of sources, the representation is activated. What constitutes enough activation is a matter of the strength of the inputs or how often or how recently a representation has been excited. Many of these assumptions are common to most network theories of cognition, but DCT is unique in its emphasis on the modality-specific verbal and nonverbal distinctions in mental representation. More discussion of processing operations follows the next section.

Unit- and System-Level Organization

Logogens and the verbal system into which they are organized are characterized by sequential constraints. In all languages, units are combined into certain conventional sequences at all levels. Hence, the letters *b*, *a*, and *t* are sequenced as *bat* or *tab* but not *bta*; the words *a*, *baseball*, and *bat* are sequenced as *a baseball bat* or *bat a baseball* but not *baseball a bat*, and so on. A hierarchy characterizes the verbal system such that smaller units can be synthesized sequentially into larger units (e.g., letters to words) or larger units can be analyzed sequentially into smaller units (e.g., words to letters). However, units at each level retain a degree of independence such that a spoken word, for example, can be recognized without necessarily analyzing its phonemic structure. The developmental basis of this organization is thought to be the temporally sequential nature of speech or the linear nature of print that we experience in encounters with language. A common example is that it is easier to spell a long word forward than backward from memory; the logogen is constrained by our left-to-right conventional experience (the principle is reversed in languages that are read and written right to left).

The hierarchical organization of the nonverbal system is qualitatively different. Imagens are represented and organized in a more continuous, integrated way and cannot be separated as easily into discrete elements comparable to phonemes, letters, or words. The developmental basis for this system is the generally more holistic nature of nonverbal perceptions that occur as clusters of units available simultaneously in different senses. An example is the baseball episode given earlier. We can synthesize images of smaller units (a baseball bat) into embedded or nested units (a bat in the hands of a batter) to still larger sets (the batter in a stadium with a roaring crowd), or we can analyze the scene in reverse. In the visual modality, this often takes a cinematic form in which we "zoom" in or out or "cut" to a wide angle or a close-up. Dynamic, multimodal imagery sequences also can be represented, as the episode of the batter hitting the ball with a loud crack and running to first base as the crowd roars.

Therefore, both the verbal and nonverbal systems have modality-specific units of various size that are organized hierarchically, but the respective units and their hierarchies are qualitatively different. Logogens and their verbal hierarchy are heavily sequentially constrained, whereas imagens and their nonverbal hierarchy are more holistic and simultaneous. This combination provides great flexibility to cognition.

Processing Operations

Three distinct dimensions, or "levels," of processing are theorized in DCT: (1) representational processing, (2) associative processing, and (3) referential processing. The levels metaphor is only partly useful because associative and referential processing can be seen as spreading activation at the same "level" but involving different codes. In DCT, processing involves both the degree and kind of elaboration.

Representational processing is the initial activation of logogens or imagens. This level is analogous to simply recognizing something as familiar and does not necessarily imply meaningful comprehension. The activation of a representation depends on the stimulus situation and individual differences. In reading text, the stimulus would be the text characteristics, and individual differences would include reading ability, background knowledge, instructions, and so on. Therefore, the activation of a visual logogen for a printed word would involve the legibility of the printed form, the reader's familiarity with the word's visual features and configuration, and any priming effects of context. If the visually recognized word also were familiar from speech, its associated auditory–motor phonological logogen usually would be activated rapidly in turn (e.g., *baseball*). All this would be carried out in milliseconds and perhaps without conscious attention. If the visual word were not familiar, visual and phonological logogens at lower levels, such as letter combinations, would be activated, requiring more time and attention (e.g., *base—ball*). This degree of activation may implicate higher-order processes in the word's recognition, as will be seen later. On the other hand, whole familiar phrases can be recognized and named at a glance by the skilled reader (e.g., *baseball bat*).

Associative processing involves spreading activation within a code that is typically associated with meaningful comprehension. The association between a visual word logogen and an auditory–motor word logogen (i.e., phonological recoding) is an example of associative processing that does not necessarily involve meaning and is usually relegated to the representational level. However, the phonological recoding of a visual word may involve its comprehension in some cases. Heteronyms have one spelling but different meanings and respective pronunciations, and their phonological recoding depends on which meaning is implied by context (e.g., *bass* drum, largemouth *bass*). Unfamiliar and graphophonemically irregular words may implicate meaning as well because representational processing is slowed.

Meaningful associative processing within the verbal code involves the activation of logogens of at least the morpheme level by previously activated logogens. For example, the word *single* has many verbal associations, but only a subset will be activated in a given context. In a baseball game, the word *single* would activate verbal associations such as *hit*, *first base*, *advance a runner*, and so on. In other contexts, the word *single* could activate very different verbal associates such as *one-dollar bill*, *unmarried*, *hotel room*, and so on. Meaning is both constrained and elaborated by the set of verbal associates activated.

Referential processing involves the spreading of activation between the codes that is associated with meaningful comprehension. In reading, this means that activated logogens in turn activate imagens in the same way they activate other logogens. The phrase *baseball bat* can activate mental images of a wooden or aluminum baseball bat; *single* can activate an entire dynamic, nested set of images of a batter hitting a baseball and running to first base in a stadium. That is, there is not a one-to-one referential correspondence between logogens and imagens. Some logogens might referentially activate few imagens, while other logogens might activate many. Some logogens might activate no imagens at all. This is particularly true of language that is highly abstract; it is difficult to form images of *basic idea*, for example. Without the context of a concrete situation, such phrases lack any referential meaning and can be defined only verbally. This implies that concrete language generally should be better understood, a consistent finding in research.

Once activated logogens spread their activation referentially to one or more imagens in the nonverbal system, associative processing may occur within that system and, in turn, refer back to the verbal system. For example, the set of imagens referentially activated by the logogen *single* might be associatively elaborated in the nonverbal system to include a batter running to first base in a crowded stadium of cheering fans. These imagens might, in return, referentially activate logogens such as *stadium*, *crowd*, or *cheers*. In this way, spreading activation between and within codes defines and elaborates the meaning of language. Further, it supplies inferred information to the interpretation. Mental imagery plays an invaluable role in adding concrete sensory substance to the meaning; taken literally, this is what "making sense" in reading is all about.

Figure 1 shows a theoretical model of these units and processes. Verbal and nonverbal stimuli are perceived by the sensory systems, and logogens and imagens are activated. The verbal system is illustrated as a hierarchical, sequenced arrangement of logogens. These units are modality specific and occur in different sizes so that smaller logogens may be representations for graphemes or phonemes, larger logogens may be visual words or their auditory–motor pronunciations, and so on. The associative relationships illustrated by the arrows are of many kinds: graphophonemic associations (*b*-/b/), compound word associations (e.g., *baseball*), common sequences (e.g., *first, second, third, home*), hierarchical associations (e.g., *organized activities, sports, baseball*), synonym or antonym associations (e.g., *batter–hitter*; *safe–out*), and so on. The nonverbal system is illustrated as a series of overlapping and nested sets of imagens (e.g., a baseball bat being swung by a batter in a crowded stadium of cheering fans) or other imagens not associated with a given set. Referential connections are illustrated as arrows running between the coding systems. Verbal and nonverbal responses are shown as output of the respective systems.

Figure 1 illustrates some of the most basic assumptions of DCT, but the illustration is necessarily simple. In actuality, a model for reading even a simple text would be interlaced with connections and abuzz with activity. Further discussion can be found in Sadoski and Paivio (2001).

Figure 1. General Model of Dual Coding Theory

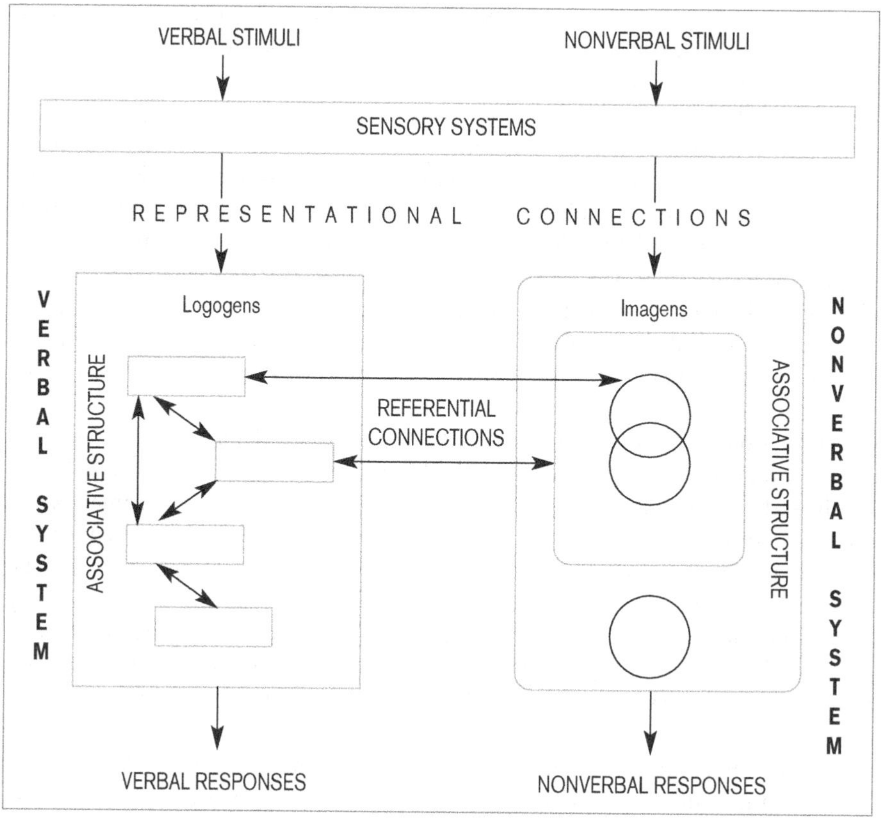

Explaining the Reading Process

The discussion in the preceding section provided an overview of the basic assumptions of DCT in reading-relevant terms. The reading process can be better explained through an extended example that involves decoding, comprehension, and response in reading a simple sentence. We will deviate briefly to elaborate on decoding, comprehension, and response in turn. We use a single sentence here, but the reader should keep in mind that such sentences are more realistically read in much richer, extended contexts.

Consider the skilled reading and in-depth comprehension of the sentence *The batter singled to center in the first.* The process begins as the eyes fixate on the printed forms, probably *The batter* in the first fixation (eye movement studies indicate an average span of about nine characters per fixation). Visual logogens for the familiar words *The* and *batter* are activated at the representational level and immediately associated with their auditory–motor logogens. *The batter* may be experienced as inner speech, recoded in phonological form. Perhaps equally quickly, the words are syntactically associated as a simple noun phrase. Spreading activation to semantic associations also occurs rapidly, with the different associates of *batter* activated as options. Common verbal associates of *batter* could be *baseball player, cake mixture*, or *strike repeatedly*, and nonverbal referential connections could be images of the same. However, in the present context the word *batter* has been used in connection with other baseball terms, and context effects would prime the former option and inhibit the latter ones. Also, *The* preceding *batter* signals a noun usage of *batter*, syntactically inhibiting the verb option *strike repeatedly*. Within perhaps 500 milliseconds (an estimate from electroencephalographic studies), the words *The batter* are phonologically recoded and provisionally comprehended in both verbal and nonverbal form as a baseball player at bat.

A word is needed here about decoding. In reading, this term is theoretically imprecise. The term *recoding* often is preferred because it indicates converting the printed form to the spoken form without necessarily comprehending, as the general definition of decoding implies (i.e., to decode a message). Conformably, DCT assumes that in reading, the activation of logogens at the representational level involves their phonological associations but not necessarily their semantic associates and referents. For highly familiar words this happens without conscious effort, hence the term *automatic*. Very familiar phrases such as *The batter* may be recoded as a single unit similar to *hot dog*. However, less-familiar, phonologically ambiguous, or graphophonemically irregular words may require more grapheme–phoneme-level processing, more conscious effort, and possibly some semantic and syntactic processing. Thus, DCT accommodates multiple-route models of phonology in word reading (e.g., Coltheart, Curtis, Atkins, & Haller, 1993).

Returning to our example, the next fixation falls on the word *singled*, perhaps already noticed in the parafovea of the first fixation. This word appears after the noun phrase and is marked as a verb by the *-ed* suffix. Associative processing syntactically connects *The batter* with *singled*, and the familiar subject–verb syntactic pattern is recognized.

A word is needed here about grammar. Extensive grammatical parsing is not often conscious, and it may be less complex than is commonly assumed. The verb here may be comprehended simply as a modifier of the noun phrase. That is, a mental model of the sentence thus far may be forming in which the batter is imagined in action, hitting the ball and running to first base. This emerging mental model takes the form of a verbal–nonverbal, syntactic and semantic episode in short-term memory. For those readers less familiar with baseball terms, the word *singled* may need to be syntactically paraphrased to *hit a single* for clarification, but the result would be the same. In this sense, grammar need not involve abstract deep-structure propositions or transformational rules. Simple word sequences that evoke a comprehensible image can account for much. This is the DCT view of deep structure; more will be discussed later.

The next fixation includes *to center*. The various associates and referents of *to center* (e.g., *between left field and right field, to balance*) are part of the spreading activation, with context inhibiting less-appropriate ones. Again, a less-familiar reader may verbally elaborate this elliptical phrase into *to center field*. The words *The batter singled to center (field)* may then be syntactically parsed as the familiar subject–verb–modifier pattern, recoded phonologically as inner speech, and imagined to now include the ball speeding to the middle outfield as the batter runs to first base.

The final fixation falls on *in the first*. Familiar verbal elaborations of *in the first*, such as *in the first inning* or *in the first place*, may be associatively activated, with context inhibiting the latter. The phrase will be recognized as a modifier by association with the syntax established so far and the entire sentence parsed and cumulatively recoded as inner speech. However, *in the first* probably would add little to the imaginal mental model of the episode except possible time cues such as the fresh uniforms and unscuffed baselines of the early innings of a baseball game. However, it might involve another nonverbal aspect of comprehension—an affective response. More on this topic will be discussed later.

As described so far, the processing of the simple sentence *The batter singled to center in the first* would take about two seconds at a typical reading rate of 250 wpm (longer for readers unfamiliar with baseball). For a skilled reader reading for full comprehension and recall, the result probably would include the sentence recoded as inner speech and comprehended as a verbal–nonverbal mental model of the episode. Note that neither is necessarily experienced consciously, or perhaps only barely so, and both may be rehearsed in memory after the last fixation. These responses differ with readers and situations. However, considerable experimental data, including neuropsychological data, support this scenario (Lucas, 1999; West et al., 1998).

A word is needed here about meaning, comprehension, and mental models. As noted in the present example, the text would be mentally represented in two codes and in at least two different modalities: (1) an auditory–motor representation probably experienced as inner speech and (2) a visuo-spatial representation probably experienced as mental imagery. Both might be elaborated in various ways. As noted, the word *center* may be mentally elaborated to *center field*, and *in the first* may be elaborated to *in the first inning*. Beyond this, verbal elaboration may take the form of a related set of activated associations in the verbal system such as *baseball, pitcher, swing, hit, fly, grounder, outfield, run, first base, safe, stadium, crowd*, and so on. The imagery representation might be in modalities other than the visual, depending on the degree of elaboration. A more fully elaborated image might include the crack of the bat and the roar of the crowd, for example. Associative connections and referential connections between the verbal associates and the nonverbal associates form an internally consistent network that is the basis of meaning, comprehension, and the mental model.

Meaning in this instance consists of this coherent network of activated verbal and nonverbal representations. The richer the elaboration of activated mental representations and their defining interconnections, the more "meaningful" our response. *Comprehension* is the relative equilibrium in the network. The set of verbal associations and the set of nonverbal associations correspond to and restrict each other sufficiently well to produce closure rather than a random-search activation without coherence. The term *mental model*, as used here, applies to the total verbal–nonverbal correspondence aggregate. The mental model is the restricted set of activated representations and the associative and referential connections between them. The term does not imply any theoretical construct beyond what already has been explained. A mental model in DCT is not an abstraction; the modality-specific units activated and connected retain some of their original sensory properties, similar to pebbles in an aggregate or particles in a suspension.

However, the discussion of our example does not end here. Consider the inferences that may occur as a mental model is formed for the sentence *The batter singled to center in the first*. The sentence does not specify if the hit was a fly ball or ground ball. It does not specify if the game was a professional baseball game or a Little League game. It does not specify if the stadium was opened or closed or if there was a stadium and spectators at all. It does not specify if the game was at night or during the day. Yet our mental models are often specific on such points. Many of these inferences can be attributed to mental imagery—imagining in concrete specifics the general situation described by the language. Imagery forms an invaluable companion to language in fleshing out language's skeleton.

None of these inferences is obligatory; all are probabilistic in varying degree. Readers read with varying degrees of depth and elaboration based on purposes and individual differences. Comprehension is not an all-or-none process; it occurs in degrees from simple recognition to strategic elaboration. In many cases our comprehension is superficial because there is no time, need, or inclination to elaborate as deeply as we might. In other cases, our comprehension is deeper, richer, and more precise.

This leads us back to the subject of response. In many ways, this term implies the formation of a mental model, a coherent and elaborate rendition of the text. A reader may fully experience even a simple text such as *The batter singled to center in the first* by imagining the event as described. In a still more elaborate response, one might "feel" oneself as the batter, haptically sensing the heft of the bat and the jolt as it connects. But response often implies more than sensory imagery or a mental model. We noted earlier that the phrase *in the first* adds a time cue to the sentence. This simple time cue may evoke an evaluative and mildly affective response. A single *in the first* is not as critical as a single *in the bottom of the ninth with the game tied*. That is, there is a different emotional significance to the two time settings. This introduces a nonverbal, emotional–evaluative dimension to the response. In full and complete narrative texts, such as stories, such emotional responses are an important aspect of experiencing the text (e.g., Sadoski, Goetz, & Kangiser, 1988).

In other contexts, response may take a more logical or rational form. Analyzing an exposition or an argument may introduce a verbal monitoring of the text experienced in inner expressions such as "I don't get this," "Now I see," or "But you haven't considered...." Our critical and evaluative powers also are exercised here, and the experience also may be emotional. We are impressed with a well-argued position with which we are forced to agree. We are disappointed by sloganeering that dismisses a difficult problem with a one-syllable solution. In its fullest sense, response involves the reader as a part of the authoring, a partner who stands toe-to-toe with the author and answers back. This may take the reading beyond what the text language may have included or what the author may have ever intended.

A question sometimes raised about DCT is how readers comprehend and respond to highly abstract language. The answer is that the encoding of abstract language is primarily a matter of verbal associations. Consider the abstract sentence *The basic idea remained vague.* As with a more concrete sentence, this sentence can be phonologically recoded, grammatically parsed, and associated with other language units (e.g., *basic idea* = *main thought*, *remained vague* = *stayed unclear*). But beyond such mental parsing and paraphrasing, there is little substance to the sentence. Without a concrete contextual referent to concretize the abstract, it remains a verbalism with unrealized potential. Such sentences may be integrated as verbal units and achieve a degree of meaning at the associative level, but their fuller meaning and response awaits a more concrete context.

Empirical Evidence

The constellation of predictions derived from the DCT model of reading has been only partially developed and tested, but relevant evidence is available on several research fronts. Next, we will review certain empirical evidence in the areas of decoding, comprehension, and response.

Decoding

Printed words usually are recoded promptly into an auditory–motor (phonemic) form. In DCT, this involves activation of verbal–associative connections between visual logogens and auditory–motor logogens. As discussed previously, these connections generally are assumed to occur at the representational level because they usually can be achieved before a syntactic or semantic interpretation is generated. However, this does involve associative processing, and the time required for this processing will presumably vary with word familiarity, grapheme–phoneme consistency, and other factors. Therefore, spreading activation could theoretically reach and activate still other representations during this time. These representations include imagens, possibly implicating imagery as a semantic factor in word recognition.

In fact, word imageability is one of the best predictors of oral reading performance in beginning reading or in certain acquired disorders of reading. Beginning readers read concrete, imageable words more accurately than abstract words, with these effects more prominent for poor readers (Coltheart, Laxon, & Keating, 1988; Jorm, 1977; Juel & Holmes, 1981). Neurological patients with severe phonological deficits, whose reading ability is assumed to rely mainly on direct access from orthography to semantic interpretations, often are markedly more successful in reading concrete, imageable words than abstract words (e.g., Coltheart, Patterson, & Marshall, 1980; Funnell & Allport, 1987; Plaut & Shallice, 1993). This evidence is supportive of multiple-route models of the oral reading of words (Coltheart, Rastle, Perry, Langdon, & Ziegler, 2001).

If a word's concreteness can influence the process of naming it, this influence might be seen mainly on words in which orthographic-to-phonological recoding is slowed by their low-frequency, their irregular spelling–sound correspondences, or both. Strain, Patterson, and Seidenberg (1995) tested this prediction. They found that, controlling for word familiarity and linguistic variables (i.e., initial phoneme, word length, positional bigram frequency), adults were slower and more error prone when naming abstract irregular words (e.g., *scarce*) than when naming abstract regular words (e.g., *scribe*) or imageable irregular words (e.g., *sword*). That is, irregular concrete words were named sooner and more accurately than irregular abstract words because the spelling–sound processing time was sufficient to allow for the activation of corresponding imagens. However, when the words were regular, the associations between spelling and naming were rapidly achieved whether the words were concrete or abstract, so the activation of imagens for the concrete words did not have time to produce a similar effect in naming. Overall, they found that imageability especially facilitated the naming of low-frequency irregular words.

This study has been subject to considerable replication and scrutiny. It was replicated and extended by Strain and Herdman (1999), who found the same interaction between frequency, regularity, and imageability in word naming. They found an even stronger effect for imageability in the naming of low-frequency regular words, although this was still less than for low-frequency irregular words. They also found that the more skilled in decoding participants were, the less strongly imageability influenced word naming, although the effect was still present even for highly skilled decoders. Overall, Strain and Herdman interpreted their findings to mean that imageability plays a role in naming words when the connections between orthography and phonology are weak, whether this is due to irregular spelling–sound correspondences or low decoding skill.

Monaghan and Ellis (2002) replicated the original study and again found the interaction between regularity and imageability. However, they attributed it to age of acquisition of the word because when this variable was covaried the interaction was nonsignificant. They argued that irregular words and low-frequency words would be acquired later and this would largely account for the effect. However, Strain, Patterson, and Seidenberg (2002) questioned the use of age of acquisition because when they reanalyzed their original data with age of acquisition as a covariate the interaction of regularity and imageability persisted. Furthermore, they presented new data confirming the interaction when age of acquisition was controlled. Ellis and Monaghan (2002) rejoined on methodological grounds but presented no new data. Overall, these results suggest a persistent but qualified interaction between imageability and regularity in word naming.

The theoretical point becomes clearer in different orthographies. Printed languages differ in the degree to which they represent spoken language. In Persian, words are sometimes written with consonant letters only (opaque words) and sometimes with full vowels (transparent words). The opaque words, therefore, present more decoding difficulties. A significant imageability effect was found by Baluch and Besner (2001) in naming both high- and low-frequency opaque words in Persian, while the effect was not present for matched transparent words. These findings have been extended to Turkish, a perfectly transparent orthography in which each of its 29 letters corresponds to only one spoken sound invariantly and independent of context. Raman, Baluch, and Besner (1997) found no significant effects of imageability on word naming of Turkish high- and low-frequency words, consistent with the prediction. However, Raman and Baluch (2001) additionally investigated reading skill and found that skilled readers in Turkish named imageable, low-frequency words faster than matched abstract low-frequency words, similar to what Strain and Herdman (1999) found in English and also consistent with prediction. Less-skilled readers did not name imageable, low-frequency words faster than matched abstract, low-frequency words, a result different from Strain and Herdman, but this was attributed to differences in reading Turkish and English. Janyan and Andonova (2003) still found independent effects of imageability and frequency in naming words in Bulgarian, an orthography with more graphophonemic consistency than English but less than Turkish. Furthermore, these researchers found that imageability was more associated with right-hemispheric brain activation, consistent with a neuropsychological account of encoding differences.

In sum, these studies indicate that imageability plays a role in naming words when the connections between orthography and phonology are labored, whether this is due to irregular spelling–sound correspondences or low word frequency (i.e., unfamiliarity). The effect of decoding skill also interacts with these factors differently in different orthographies. These results are theoretically consistent with the interactive DCT model of reading presented previously, as well as with multiple-route decoding models.

Specifically, visual logogens activated by printed concrete words spread their activation to both auditory–motor naming logogens and imagens for referential meaning. The activated imagens can contribute significantly to the activation of the naming logogens when the route between the visual logogens and the naming logogens is slow. The effect is predictably differential across orthographies, a script-specific phenomenon. The effect is also complex, predicting at least a triple interaction. As Strain et al. (2002) conclude, "almost all of the factors in the domain of word familiarity and meaningfulness are correlated with one another, and it is a brave experimenter who attempts to establish the prominence of one while denying any impact for the others" (p. 212; cf. Venezky & Massaro, 1987). Multiple factors influence word decoding, of which imageability is one, under theoretically predictable conditions. These observations are compatible with DCT but incompatible with theories that posit modality-independent word units, concept nodes, or abstract propositions. Moreover, these observations have implications for sight-vocabulary learning as discussed later.

Comprehension

In DCT, a key factor in reading comprehension is language concreteness. This is mainly because concrete language can referentially activate mental images as well as associatively activate mental language, whereas abstract language has relatively less access to the imagery code. Hence, concrete language, such as *baseball bat*, should be easier to understand than abstract language, such as *basic idea*, because concrete language can be dually encoded. In DCT, the two codes are assumed to be independent and additive in their effects, predicting that concrete language should be nearly twice as comprehensible and memorable as abstract language, other factors being equal. The empirical record over the last 30 years has shown just this. Concrete words, phrases, sentences, paragraphs, and longer texts have been consistently shown to be more than twice as comprehensible and memorable as abstract language units matched for readability, familiarity, and other variables. The evidence relevant to reading has been reviewed extensively (Sadoski & Paivio, 2001). Here we will focus on how predictions made by DCT in the area of comprehension and recall have prevailed in experimental tests against the predictions of other theories.

A case in point involves the competing predictions of DCT and context availability theory (Kieras, 1978). Rather than assuming separate verbal and nonverbal codes, context availability theory assumes that all language, whether abstract or concrete, is comprehended and remembered by incorporation into a network of abstract, amodal propositions. Moreover, this theory assumes that concrete language is easier to comprehend and remember because it can be associated more readily with other propositions in the network—it simply has more connections. But this advantage can be offset when abstract language deals with highly familiar information or when abstract language is presented in a supportive context because the connections are then enhanced for the reader. The differing assumptions of DCT and the context availability model present a situation all too rare in reading research: two rival theories that are sufficiently well articulated to make testable predictions that are contradictory.

A test of these competing predictions was performed by Sadoski, Goetz, and Avila (1995). They used four factual paragraphs about historical figures (Michelangelo and James Madison) that were matched for number of sentences, words, and syllables; sentence length; information density; text cohesion; and rated comprehensibility. In one set, two paragraphs were rated equal in familiarity, but one paragraph was rated more concrete than the other. In this case, DCT predicted that the concrete paragraph should be recalled better than the abstract paragraph because of the additional integrating medium provided by imagery, whereas the context availability model predicted that they should be recalled equally because the abstract language was equally familiar and presented in context. In the other set, the paragraphs differed in both familiarity and concreteness, with the abstract paragraph being the more familiar of the two. In this case, DCT predicted that the familiar abstract paragraph should be recalled about as well as the unfamiliar concrete paragraph (i.e., the advantage of concreteness would be offset by lower familiarity), whereas the context availability model predicted that the abstract paragraph would be recalled better than the concrete paragraph (i.e., the disadvantage of abstractness would be offset by higher familiarity).

In the case in which the concrete and abstract paragraphs were equally familiar, study participants recalled the concrete paragraph nearly twice as well. In the case in which the abstract paragraph was more familiar, study participants recalled the paragraphs equally well. These results were consistent with DCT but inconsistent with context availability theory. Other experimental findings using different methods and materials have confirmed these results (e.g., Holcomb, Kounios, Anderson, & West, 1999; Kounios & Holcomb, 1994; Nelson & Schreiber, 1992; Sadoski, Goetz, & Fritz, 1993; Sadoski, Goetz, & Rodriguez, 2000).

Another case of competing predictions between DCT and another theory involved the relational–distinctiveness model of Marschark and Hunt (1989) in explaining the integration of abstract text. Abstract sentences, such as *The basic idea remained vague*, sometimes can be encoded as integrated verbal units as well as concrete sentences, even though concrete sentences enjoy more comprehensible and memorable content. These questions about the DCT explanation of the integration and recall of abstract text were first raised by Marschark and Paivio (1977). The authors studied the cued recall of concrete and abstract sentences and found that, whereas recall was higher for concrete sentences, the two types of sentences did not differ in the extent to which recall was integrated as measured by the retrieval effectiveness of verbal cues that were related to the whole sentence or to only one content word in the sentence. The higher recall for concrete sentences was consistent with the DCT assumption that dually encoded information is more memorable, but the equal integration effect was inconsistent with the assumption that imagery is a superior integrating medium.

Marschark and Paivio (1977) concluded that dual coding accounted for the higher recall of concrete sentences but that some other explanation was needed to explain the equivalent integration effects. Verbal associative processes were a likely DCT candidate because these processes apply equally to concrete and abstract language. An alternative theory was posed by Marschark and Hunt (1989). This theory assumed that distinctiveness and relatedness are different forms of mental processing that act as partners. Mental imagery evoked by concrete language increases the distinction from or contrast of concrete language to abstract language rather than providing a separate memory code, but this distinctiveness is dependent on an established relationship between the language units. Hence, this theory, like context availability theory, predicts that familiar, contextually associated abstract language should be integrated as well as concrete language.

A resolution to the issue was obtained by Paivio, Walsh, and Bons (1994). Their experimental results showed that strong verbal associations are *necessary* to produce integration of abstract word pairs, whereas imagery is *sufficient* to produce integration of concrete word pairs even when verbal associations are not present. The results were not consistent with the relational–distinctiveness view because integration still occurred for concrete word pairs where the pair members were not related. These findings provide a DCT explanation for the integration of abstract language, but they further offer a possible explanation for the integration of even weakly related concrete language.

For example, consider again the abstract sentence *The basic idea remained vague* and the concrete sentence *The batter singled to center in the first*. The former sentence might be integrated grammatically because the predicate adjective *vague* links directly back to the subject noun *idea*; the modifier is part of the sentence kernel and binds the subject and the predicate closely together. In the latter sentence, the kernel is *The batter singled*; this is followed by two independent modifying phrases in a loose construction. This sentence might be integrated more through its imagery, with *singled to center* and *in the first* adding imaginal and verbal elaboration as discussed previously. Stated differently, the integrative mental model of the abstract sentence may be more verbal–associative, and the integrative mental model of the concrete sentence may be more nonverbal–imaginal. Hence, both concrete and abstract sentences might be encoded as integrated units but for theoretically different reasons. However, this interpretation is speculative, and further research is needed.

In sum, DCT can provide a coherent account of the critical role played by language concreteness in reading comprehension. The evidence cited poses problems for theories that propose that all language is mentally encoded in abstract, propositional form. Furthermore, DCT can provide experimental predictions about the comprehension and recall of concrete and abstract text, and about the integration of both concrete and abstract text, in a theoretically consistent and parsimonious way.

Response

Mental imagery and its correlate, emotional response, are vital to aesthetic response to text. Imaginative and affective processes are how a text is "realized," "lived through," or "brought to life." As discussed earlier, some aspects of response may be contemporaneous with the formation of a mental model of the text, so that the distinction between comprehension and response is somewhat fuzzy. Response can take more objective forms as well, such as critical evaluation against some standard as in rating the importance of a text segment relative to the whole.

The empirical evidence for the relationship between imaginative and affective processes in responding to text was reviewed by Goetz and Sadoski (1996). A program of research carried out over 10 years revealed that imagery and affective response to text can be measured reliably and validly using conventional methods. Both the strength of response, as measured by quantitative ratings, and the nature of response, as measured by qualitative reports, were investigated in this research program.

The core of this research program was a set of complementary studies using literary short stories. In one study (Sadoski & Goetz, 1985), participants read and later rated each paragraph in an adventure story for either the degree of imagery experienced, the degree of emotional response experienced, or the relative importance to the story as a whole. The alpha reliabilities of these ratings, for this story as well as other similar stories, were regularly found to exceed .90 (Goetz, Sadoski, Stowe, Fetsco, & Kemp, 1993; Sadoski et al., 1988). In all these studies, imagery ratings, affect ratings, and importance ratings were moderately to strongly correlated with each other in an overall response aggregate. The correlation between imagery ratings and affect ratings persisted even after controlling for paragraph length and the importance ratings. However, the relationship between either imagery ratings or affect ratings and importance ratings was considerably attenuated when the effects of paragraph length and the remaining rating were partialed. This means that imagery and affective response can generally be seen as a related but qualitatively different form of response from evaluating importance.

Qualitative reports were the focus of another related study (Sadoski, Goetz, Olivarez, Lee, & Roberts, 1990). Using the same story as Sadoski and Goetz (1985), participants read and then produced written recalls and imagery reports. With the most extensive coding system for imagery reports yet devised, imagery was coded into categories such as (a) directly related to a paragraph, (b) a synthesis of information from two or more paragraphs, (c) distortion of story information, (d) an importation consistent with the story, or (e) an importation inconsistent with the story. The imagery reports also were categorized according to modality (e.g., visual, auditory, tactile, affective). Recall protocols were similarly coded in categories including (a) gist, (b) synthesis from across text units, (c) distortion, (d) an importation consistent with the story, or (e) an importation inconsistent with the story. Reliability between independent raters ranged from .84 to .95 for all codings. A factor analysis of the imagery and recall categories revealed four underlying factors, dominated respectively by visual imagery, affective imagery (i.e., imagining the feelings of the characters), imported imagery consistent with the story, and distortion recall. Verbal recall categories loaded on these factors as well but were consistently lower. Hence, story response could be seen as primarily experienced in the form of mental imagery and affect and somewhat less in the form of verbal recall.

A subsequent study used the ratings from Sadoski and Goetz (1985) as predictors of the imagery reports of Sadoski et al. (1990). Goetz, Sadoski, and Olivarez (1991) employed hierarchical regression analyses that first removed between-subjects variance and variance due to surface-level text factors and found that the paragraph-level imagery ratings of the first group of readers were highly significant predictors of the respective paragraph-level imagery reports of the second, independent group of readers. Another finding using the same methodology was that importance ratings and surface-level text factors were better predictors of verbal recalls than of imagery ratings. Hence, the evaluation of importance can again be seen as qualitatively different from imaginative response, although they remain correlated in the overall response.

In sum, this program of research has shown that imaginative responses are central to reading literary stories and that they can be defined, measured, and interpreted reliably and validly using conventional research methods. Imagery and emotional response are moderately to strongly correlated in story response. Further, they are both related to more objective, text-based responses such as evaluations of plot importance. As Sadoski et al. (1988) note, "these three response types often occurred simultaneously, in what may be an overall response comprising both comprehension of plot salience, and vicarious, emotionally infused, and fully perceived experiences of story events" (p. 333). Together, these response types form an overall response that involves both the intellect and the emotions.

Comparison Between DCT and Other Theories of Reading

In an earlier section we compared DCT with context availability theory and distinctiveness–relational processing theory in making predictions about reading. DCT also has been extensively compared with schema theory as an explanation of reading comprehension (Sadoski & Paivio, 1994, 2001; Sadoski et al., 1991). Further, DCT has also been compared extensively with the theories of Rumelhart (1977) and Kintsch (1988) (see Sadoski and Paivio, 2001). An updated version of Kintsch's theory (Kintsch, 1998) also has been addressed from a DCT perspective (Sadoski, 1999). We will summarize and comment on those comparisons here.

These theories of reading have much in common with DCT. A major similarity is that they all are interactive theories in which reading is served by bottom-up and top-down processes working in combination. All these theories are similar in assuming a prominent place for prior knowledge structures in reading. Another similarity is that they allow, to different degrees, for the representation of knowledge in more than one form.

However, a basic distinction between DCT and these other theories is that they assume that most knowledge in memory is abstract and amodal, existing in a state that has no objective reality and is associated with no sensory modality. How any knowledge that is not innate becomes divorced from sensory input is an important theoretical and epistemological question that has not been well explained. These theories propose no apparent answer to this question; rather, they simply assume the existence of abstract, amodal knowledge. One apparent reason for this is so that these theories can be modeled by artificial intelligence and subjected to computer simulations.

Rumelhart's (1977) parallel distributed processing model is one example. The parallel sources of knowledge in this theory are letter-feature knowledge, letter knowledge, letter-cluster knowledge, lexical knowledge, syntactic knowledge, and semantic knowledge. The forms that these different knowledge sources take are not specified, but examples provided suggest that they are ultimately all in an identically computational form. For example, a series of equations is presented in Rumelhart (1977) that determines the Baysian probability of testing a set of multilevel hypotheses for the recognition and comprehension of a phrase against letter-feature data. Several computer programs are cited for the source of these formalisms including Kaplan's (1973) General Syntactic Parser and the HEARSAY speech recognition program (Lesser, Fennel, Erman, & Reddy, 1975). That is, whatever the source of the original input (e.g., visual features of letters), all information is theoretically converted to, and processed in, a common computational form. As a result, this theory does not discuss the roles of phonological recoding, inner speech, or mental imagery in any form. This would call for at least some differences in internal representation modalities. Rumelhart's (1977) model has since evolved into a connectionist theory that similarly assumes abstract, computational representations (cf. Rumelhart & McClelland, 1986).

Kintsch's (1998) Construction–Integration model is another example. This model assumes three codes or forms of knowledge representation: (1) verbatim information, (2) the propositional textbase, and (3) the mental model. Verbatim information is surface structure information, including specific words and syntactic arrangements. The propositional code is an abstract, deep structure code formed when abstract proposition-schemata are instantiated with surface structure information and the surface structure is quickly lost. Individual propositions are then connected into a propositional textbase. The mental model is either a well-integrated propositional textbase or a mental image of a situation that is somehow derived from the textbase. Hence, this theory can be seen as a triple-coding theory that assumes that verbal language and mental imagery may be inputs and outputs but the central processing unit is propositional in nature. Hence, it is primarily a single-code theory (see Sadoski, 1999, for more discussion).

Recent modifications of this theory have made it still more amenable to computer programming. Rather than thinking of concepts or propositions as abstract nodes in a knowledge network, the theory now treats propositions as vectors of numbers in a multidimensional statistical space, with each number indicating the strength with which the proposition is linked to another proposition (i.e., Latent Semantic Analysis). This brings the theory closer to DCT on the one hand because associational strength between individual mental representations is critical, but further away on the other hand because the entire system is based in computational formalism. As with Rumelhart (1977), this theory does not discuss the role of phonological recoding or inner speech, and it treats mental imagery as an afterthought.

Whether the formalisms of artificial intelligence as posed by these theories are useful in advancing our understanding of cognition in reading remains to be seen. Computer-implemented models that coincide with human data are interesting exercises, but the name of the game in theory is to know why. Such exercises run the risk of reification—the fallacy of explaining something and then treating the explanation as real rather than the thing being explained. In any event, it is useful to remember that abstractions, such as schemata, propositions, and abstract concept nodes, are difficult to operationalize and empirically test with human data. Their interpretive power lies largely in the assumption that they exist in the first place, mentally analogous to computer programs. As an alternative, DCT relies on constructs that may be experienced consciously to some degree and for which plausible human assessments can be devised: natural language, mental imagery, and their associations.

Directions for Further Research

Although it is one of the better-established theories of general cognition, DCT is a relative newcomer to the scene of reading theory. Despite a strong empirical record over the last several decades in accounting for verbal behavior, much more research is needed. In this section, we will pose certain issues deserving of further research in decoding, comprehension, and response.

Decoding

Considerable evidence now exists that the concreteness or imageability of written language is a factor in its phonological recoding. This evidence is consistent with the interactive nature of reading, where top-down semantic and syntactic factors and bottom-up decoding factors interact at all levels. This evidence also reinforces the assertion that there may be more to the phenomena of phonological recoding and inner speech than providing us with a strategy for lexical access—meaning may precede phonology more than we realize. While much phonological recoding may occur at a deep, cortical level, its more conscious manifestation is inner speech.

Despite the pervasiveness of inner speech in reading, too little is known about this phenomenon. Huey (1908/1968) devotes a chapter to it, regarding inner speech as a ubiquitous short-term memory phenomenon. In a landmark study in which subvocalization was measured by surgically inserting electrodes into the speech musculature, Edfeldt (1960) found that (a) all readers appear to engage in inner speech to varying degrees, especially as reading becomes increasingly difficult; (b) inner speech has no detrimental effect on reading; and (c) good readers engage in less inner speech than poor readers. Both Huey and Edfeldt point out that inner speech is not inevitable in reading. Later research reviews by Gibson and Levin (1975) and Rayner and Pollatsek (1989) arrived at the same general conclusions: Inner speech seems to be a useful but not obligatory vehicle for recoding text in short-term memory in order to parse sentences, associate words contextually, and inwardly express a spoken interpretation.

But these explanations raise unanswered questions. If inner speech is not strictly necessary, why not simply an "inner semantics" that operates directly on print input, at least for good readers past the early developmental stages of reading? Speed reading courses have long advocated "breaking the sound barrier" and reading purely visually to increase rate and improve comprehension and retention (Frank, 1994). However, Carver (1982) empirically determined that for skilled readers the optimal rate of comprehending prose while reading was identical to the optimal rate of comprehending prose while listening. This rate was about 300 wpm—about the maximum rate at which speech can be produced comfortably. What accounts for the pervasiveness of inner speech, its increase as text difficulty increases, and its convergence with rate of comprehension if it is unnecessary?

The DCT approach to these issues might pose inner speech as mental imagery in the auditory–motor modality being used to retain the surface form of a sentence while higher-order comprehension processes occur. Recoding printed language from the visual modality to auditory–motor form is needed because the visual modality can be overloaded if it has to simultaneously (a) hold sentence segments already seen in visual memory, (b) process upcoming print, and (c) construct visual mental images as needed or preferred. Earlier in the article we discussed the concept of modality-specific interference, the difficulty of trying to perform different tasks in the same sensory modality. The principle may apply strongly here: There is too much activity in reading for the visual pathways in the brain to handle alone. Recoding to the auditory–motor modality allows nonvisual rehearsal and speech-like parsing to occur while new text is visually processed and a semantic interpretation, including visual images, is constructed. Of course, inner speech may serve other functions as well, such as strategically "sounding out" unfamiliar words or "hearing" vocal phrasings, intonations, or other forms of expressive interpretation. It also may serve as an internal surrogate for the original and most common form of comprehended language, oral speech.

In short, inner speech may serve a needed rehearsal function in an alternative modality without which reading could not optimally occur. Educationally, this implies that inner speech should be encouraged and taught when, in fact, many instructional programs have been introduced to eliminate it. Theoretically, this implies still more problems for propositional theories. If the surface form of the text is immediately converted to abstract, amodal propositions and the surface structure lost, what theoretical purpose could inner speech possibly serve and why should it be so common?

Comprehension

An issue in need of renewed research from the viewpoint of all cognitive theories is that of the nature of grammar and its role in comprehending text. Over the years, grammars of various kinds have been formulated, including traditional grammar, structural grammar, case grammar, and transformational grammar. The similarities and differences between these grammars are more complex than is usually assumed. Chomsky's (1957) transformational grammar, which shared much with traditional grammar and was contrasted with the descriptive patterns of structural grammar, enjoyed considerable popularity during the second half of the 20th century. However, its explanation of sentence comprehension has become heavily strained and has not met with empirical support.

According to the transformational view, all mental activity is rule governed and verbal. Complex sentences are mentally broken down into their deep-structure kernels and understood in terms of transformational rules that are basically innate and universal. Therefore, sentence comprehension is a function of transformational complexity, or the number and nature of transformations that separate a sentence from its underlying structure. However, empirical research has found that after controlling for sentence length and implied changes in meaning, transformations had little effect on processing time (reviewed in Williams, 1998). That is, neither deep structures nor transformations appeared to have any psychological reality. However, studies of sentence transformation consistently showed that word meaning plays a crucial role in comprehension, even overriding syntactic information at times (reviewed in Paivio, 1971). Paivio suggests that imagery might play a substantial role in sentence grammar, particularly in the case of concrete sentences.

Semantic word attributes invited attention to case grammars. These grammars described sentences as relationships between cases such as agent, object, instrument, and so on (e.g., Fillmore, 1968). Early versions of these grammars, modified by developments in artificial intelligence and by some psychological evidence, were used as the basis of various propositional approaches to cognition and language (e.g., Kintsch, 1998). However, Fillmore (1976, 1984) revised his case grammar theory by putting special emphasis on the perceptual, or imagined, scenes and perspectives to which sentences refer. Case grammar with these modifications met with more empirical support than transformational grammar. For example, Black, Turner, and Bower (1979) had subjects read sentences with a single vantage point, such as *Terry finished working in the yard and went into the house,* and sentences with a changing vantage point, such as *Terry finished working in the yard and came into the house.* Sentences with changing vantage points took longer to comprehend, were rated harder to understand, and were likely to be recalled from a single vantage point. Such evidence provides more support for the view that both verbal and nonverbal processes are involved in grammar and comprehension.

More recent developments are still more consistent with the DCT view. Connectionist views have produced a form of grammar called *cognitive grammar* (Langacker, 1987, 1991). Cognitive grammar simplifies the field by rejecting the rule-governed model of mind and language and replacing it with an associational model. In this model, networks of association evolve with the experience of the individual, including linguistic associations. No innate or intrinsic rules are involved; language is governed by patterns of regularity that develop from childhood. The number of common syntactic patterns in a language is relatively small (e.g., the subject–verb–object pattern in English). All sentences are variations on a few patterns that may be represented as exemplars and varied by analogy. Descriptive, structural grammar is best suited to this explanation of grammar, and word meaning plays a more important role.

More significant from the DCT point of view, cognition is not seen as essentially verbal. Cognitive grammar assumes that mental representations can be imagistic. Language processing is a matter of matching words with mental representations and mental models of reality that may be in the form of imagery. Imagery is therefore an important substratum of language in the form of experience-based knowledge of the world to which language refers, rather than a propositional deep structure with innate origins.

In sum, cognitive grammar offers an elegant, empirically verifiable approach that capitalizes on verbal and nonverbal mental representations and syntactic patterns that are experienced readily and do not require the burdensome and unverified assumptions of transformational grammar. The consistency of DCT with these explanations is strong, and future research in this area holds promise for understanding the nature and role of grammar in reading.

Response

Considerable progress has been made in linking theories of literary interpretation to scientific theories of cognition with empirical verification, a situation little entertained as recently as 25 years ago (Kruez & MacNealy, 1996). Indeed, the study of reader response to literature has become one of the more popular subjects in reading research. Mental imagery and affect obviously are crucial to literary response because the sensuous realization of setting, episode, character, and conflict is central to the "lived through" experience of a literary text. If evidence is needed to support this point, Miall and Kuiken (1995) factor analyzed a questionnaire of 68 items covering a broad spectrum of literary responses and found factors for imagery and empathy. They grouped these into a higher-order factor they called *experiencing*, the dimension of being absorbed in a literary work. Conformably, much research from the DCT perspective has shown that imagery and emotional response are persistently related in responding to literature. This research was reviewed by Goetz and Sadoski (1996) and was summarized earlier.

An issue that deserves attention is the challenge posed by this research for some reader-response theories. Rosenblatt's (1994, see Chapter 35 this volume) transactional theory has enjoyed considerable attention in recent years as an explanation for the way readers approach texts with different stances in mind. Specifically, this theory proposes that the reading transaction exists on a continuum between efferent reading and aesthetic reading. In the efferent stance, the reader is mainly concerned with information to be extracted and retained after the reading event. In the aesthetic stance, the reader is mainly concerned with the evocation of sensations, images, and scenes as they unfold in the moment. The reader may vary stances so that, for example, poetry could be read as a source of historical information, or a historical exposition could be read to imagine the sights, sounds, and emotions of the historical events. Moreover, readers can slide along the continuum from moment to moment within a reading so that no reading is probably ever purely efferent or aesthetic.

The challenge involved is that considerable evidence shows that what is most imaged and felt in a reading is what is most retained over the long term. For example, Sadoski and Quast (1990) had their participants read and then rate the paragraphs in three feature journalism stories for the imagery experienced, the emotions experienced, or the importance to the story as a whole. Readers were assigned to read the articles as they would normally read an article about current events and people, not for testing. Sixteen days later, the readers were given a surprise recall task: They were asked to write down whatever they most remembered about the stories. What was recalled was overwhelmingly associated with the emotions and imagery experienced during the reading as determined by the readers' own statements and earlier ratings. What was rated as important was recalled poorly. That is, what was retained long after the reading event was the subjective, aesthetic experience.

This result seems inconsistent with the postulation of an efferent–aesthetic continuum. If this continuum works as a true continuum, it follows that as the reader moves toward one pole, he or she must move away from the other. If efferent reading is determined by what is retained, then the aesthetic aspects of the reading, including images and emotions, should have been recalled poorly, and information seen as important should have been recalled better. But these results indicate that what was carried away from the reading was aesthetic. That is, the transactional theory of reader response does not appear to sufficiently take into account the nature of memory for what is read, whatever the reader's stance may be. We do not necessarily remember what we read for information unless we make efforts to memorize or otherwise record the information. Mental imagery and its frequent correlate, emotional response, can be evoked even when reading for superficial information. For example, Sadoski et al. (1990) found that students who were assigned to read to find typographical errors intentionally inserted in the text of a literary story reported as much imagery and affect as students assigned to read the story normally for pleasure. In short, stance may be less consequential than is assumed; a good story is captivating even if we intend to read for other purposes.

Directions for Practice

DCT provides rich implications for instruction in decoding, comprehension, and response. A growing body of empirical support for DCT principles in each of these areas of teaching reading has been identified and synthesized, and more research is forthcoming. We will briefly review highlights.

Decoding

Recently, decodable texts have been used extensively in beginning reading. Decodable texts use a high proportion of graphophonemically regular words that are intended to assist students in learning to decode and gain a sight vocabulary. However, word imageability also has been found to strongly affect sight-word learning. That is, decodability may not be enough.

Hargis and Gickling (1978) taught kindergartners a set of concrete sight words and a set of abstract sight words that were matched for length and frequency. All the words were familiar words that were initially unknown to the children by sight. During training, the children (a) were shown the words on flash cards, (b) heard each word pronounced, (c) heard each word used in a sentence, (d) used the word in a sentence of their own, and (e) repeated the word. Two days later, more than three times as many concrete words were named correctly. Ten days later, more than four times as many concrete words were named correctly. These results were later replicated with both kindergartners of normal ability and older mentally retarded children (Gickling, Hargis, & Alexander, 1981).

Kolker and Terwilliger (1981) also taught first- and second-grade children concrete and abstract sight words. The words were initially unknown by sight but were familiar in speech. The words were presented for one second on a flash card and pronounced for the child. The child then repeated the words, and corrections were provided as necessary. This continued until a learning criterion was reached. The first graders took about 60% more trials to learn to correctly name the abstract words than the concrete words. The difference for the second graders was less (about 8% more trials for abstract words) but still statistically significant. Terwilliger and Kolker (1982) replicated their results while manipulating word confusability (i.e., same or different initial consonants). Similar results were obtained with kindergartners and beginning first graders by van der Veur (1975) and Wolpert (1972).

Hargis, Terhaar-Yonkers, Williams, and Reed (1988) extended this research to middle-grade children with reading problems. In addition to manipulating word concreteness, the experiment included manipulations for word decodability and word presentation in story context or in isolation. Results determined that (a) concrete words were learned about 12% faster than abstract words, (b) words presented in story contexts were learned about 12% faster than words presented in isolation, and (c) decodable words were learned about 6% faster than nondecodable words. An interaction between these factors indicated that abstract words presented in isolation took the longest to learn regardless of decodability, whereas concrete, decodable words were learned fastest regardless of context.

The results of these studies are very consistent with DCT and suggest that beginning reading materials and lessons emphasize concreteness as well as decodability and context in learning sight vocabulary. Overall, concrete words are learned faster even without the benefit of context, especially if decodable. Abstract words that vary in decodability are learned more slowly and are learned better in context. These results are compatible with similar findings regarding word recognition by adults, as discussed earlier (e.g., Strain & Herdman, 1999; Strain et al., 1995, 2002).

Comprehension

Throughout history, DCT principles have been extensively applied—often intuitively—to teaching reading comprehension. Sadoski and Paivio (2001) reviewed the history of teaching text comprehension from ancient to modern times and found an alternation between emphasis on the abstract and the verbal (e.g., outlines, epitomes) and the concrete and the imaginal (e.g., object lessons, imagery training). Clark and Paivio (1991) reviewed decades of empirical studies relevant to DCT in education and determined that mental imagery, concreteness, and verbal associative processes play major roles in the representation and comprehension of knowledge, learning and memory of school material, effective instruction, individual differences, and motivation. Ruddell (1997), in his summary of his research program on influential teachers of reading, found that such teachers used highly effective strategies, including the use of concrete examples, their extension to more abstract examples, and the analysis of abstract concepts in concrete terms.

The use of induced mental imagery to enhance student understanding and learning has gained an increasing record of acceptance (see reviews by Gambrell & Koskinen, 2002; Sadoski & Paivio, 2001). The general conclusion of both of these reviews is that instructions to form mental images significantly enhance the reading comprehension and memory of both children and adults in various ways. Numerous studies have shown, for example, that elementary-grade students know how to induce mental imagery and that only brief training and teacher scaffolding are necessary for most children to effectively use mental imagery as a reading comprehension strategy.

For example, Gambrell (1982) had first and third graders read short stories in sections. Before each section, the experimental group was told to make pictures in their minds to help remember, whereas the control group was told to think about what they read in order to remember. After reading each section, the participants were asked a prediction question, "What do you think is going to happen next?" Their responses were scored for factual accuracy and the number of accurate predictions. Third graders in the imagery group reported twice as many facts and made twice as many accurate predictions as the control group members. First graders in the imagery group also tended to outperform control group members on both measures, but the differences were not statistically significant. This study indicates that even with minimal inducement, children can use mental imagery to comprehend factual material and make accurate inferential predictions.

Mental imagery also has been used as a remediation technique for poor comprehenders. One example is a technique developed by Bell (1986) that is based on DCT principles. Instruction involves requiring students to form images in increasing detail to progressively larger units of language, including words, phrases, sentences, and texts. This technique was experimentally tested against reciprocal teaching as a comprehension development strategy (clarify, summarize, question, and predict) and a no-strategy control condition (Johnson-Glenberg, 2000). A variety of comprehension measures were used, including prediction, recall, explicit questions, implicit questions, and a standardized reading comprehension test. While many of the between-group contrasts did not significantly differ, both experimental treatments outperformed the control condition on answering implicit questions. The reciprocal teaching group outperformed the imagery training group only on answering explicit questions. The researcher concluded that both forms of strategy training were generally valuable in improving the comprehension of students with problems in this area. Further research in this area would be useful.

Response

Teaching reader response is an area fraught with controversy. Miall (1996), based on his extensive research into reader response, questions whether response can or should be taught at all. He bemoans the status of teaching literary response in many classrooms:

> I am aware of literature classes in schools and universities that, although often well-intentioned, are laying waste to students' experiences of literature. Like the loggers in one of our northern forests, there are teachers in too many classes whose work succeeds only in clear cutting every shoot of literary interest, leaving hardly a stump behind, mainly for the sake of that giant pulp mill, the testing and examining of students. (pp. 463–464)

There is no easy solution to this problem. Images and feelings are deeply personal, and instruction in *what* to imagine and feel is surely less appropriate *than* to imagine and feel. The basis of an effective literary education is in nurturing response but also in disciplining it so that it is not simply a flight of the imagination or an exercise in the affective fallacy. Finding a way to do this is a pressing problem for researchers and educators. One educationally valid method from a reading viewpoint might involve the avoidance of didactically explaining the effects of a literary work, instead investigating how authors achieve whatever effects they cause in readers.

Sadoski (2002) discusses how DCT principles might explain the way poets use imagery and language in collaboration or contention to obtain effects on readers. Several commonly taught poems are presented, showing that the mental images evoked by the poem are sometimes in contrast with the language of the poem. For example, John Masefield's poem "Sea Fever" (Masefield, 1951) deals with a sailor's yearning to go back to sea, although the reasons for not doing so are unclear. Images are evoked of tall sailing ships, the kick of the wheel, the song of the wind, and the clouds flying by. But the rhythm of the poem alternates between rollicking, fast-paced lines and slower, languorous lines. The images are all of freedom, but the lines constrain the reader every time the poem gets going again. The language, therefore, is inconsistent with the images evoked, and the contrast is provocative. Does this mean that the sailor is somehow incapacitated and either spiritually or physically unable to go back to sea? No explicit meaning can be assigned because it is all inferred and ambiguous. Rather, the effects caused in the readers are discussed in a disciplined way without acceptance or rejection. This approach may be more appropriate for some poems than others, but as a general approach, the scrutiny of the effects produced by language and imagery in collaboration or in contrast may be one useful solution to how to best deal with reader response in education.

Conclusion

DCT is a theory of general cognition that addresses reading in all its psychological aspects. Few theories offer this scope and have achieved its broad base of empirical support. Comprehensive cognitive theories of reading with established programs of scientific testing are young, little more than 30 years old. They may be compared to the first comprehensive theory of gravitation that dates back more than 300 years or to the first comprehensive theory of evolution that dates back nearly 150 years. New theories are subject to change as evidence accumulates, and they can be expected to make few clear and unambiguous predictions (a statement that applies to all the theories in this volume). However, DCT specifies to a considerable extent constructs of mind that have been of interest since ancient times and will undoubtedly continue to be of interest in the future. Both language and mental imagery in its various forms are among these constructs. The predictions of DCT have held up favorably against other theories to date, and its future in advancing the knowledge of reading is promising.

QUESTIONS FOR REFLECTION

1. How do verbal and nonverbal processes influence and support each other during reading?
2. To what effect can a reading teacher use DCT to support struggling readers?
3. How does response theory in DCT compare with Rosenblatt's transactional theory of reader response?

REFERENCES

Baluch, B., & Besner, D. (2001). Basic processes in reading: Semantics affects speeded naming of high frequency words in an alphabetic script. *Canadian Journal of Experimental Psychology, 55*(1), 63–69.

Bell, N. (1986). *Visualizing and verbalizing for language comprehension and thinking.* Paso Robles, CA: Academy of Reading Publications.

Black, J.B., Turner, T.J., & Bower, G.H. (1979). Spatial reference points in language comprehension. *Journal of Verbal Learning and Verbal Behavior, 18*, 187–198.

Carver, R.P. (1982). Optimal rate of reading prose. *Reading Research Quarterly, 18*, 56–88.

Chomsky, N. (1957). *Syntactic structures.* The Hague, the Netherlands: Mouton.

Clark, J.M., & Paivio, A. (1991). Dual coding theory and education. *Educational Psychology Review, 3*, 149–210.

Coltheart, M., Curtis, B., Atkins, P., & Haller, M. (1993). Models of reading aloud: Dual-route and parallel-distributed-processing approaches. *Psychological Review, 100*, 589–608.

Coltheart, M., Laxton, V.J., & Keating, C. (1988). Effects of word imageability and age of acquisition on children's reading. *British Journal of Psychology, 79*, 1–12.

Coltheart, M., Patterson, K., & Marshall, J.C. (Eds.). (1980). *Deep dyslexia.* London: Routledge & Kegan Paul.

Coltheart, M., Rastle, K., Perry, C., Langdon, R., & Ziegler, J. (2001). DRC: A dual route cascaded model of visual word recognition and reading aloud. *Psychological Review, 108*(1), 204–256.

Denis, M. (1982). Imaging while reading text: A study of individual differences. *Memory & Cognition, 10*, 540–545.

Eddy, J.K., & Glass, A.L. (1981). Reading and listening to high and low imagery sentences. *Journal of Verbal Learning and Verbal Behavior, 20*(3), 333–345.

Edfeldt, A.W. (1960). *Silent speech and silent reading.* Chicago: University of Chicago Press.

Ellis, A.W., & Monaghan, J. (2002). Reply to Strain, Patterson, and Seidenberg (2002). *Journal of Experimental Psychology: Learning, Memory, and Cognition, 28*, 215–220.

Fillmore, C.J. (1968). The case for case. In E. Bach & R.T. Harms (Eds.), *Universals in linguistic theory* (pp. 1–88). New York: Holt, Rinehart & Winston.

Fillmore, C.J. (1976). The case for case reopened. In P. Cole (Ed.), *Syntax and semantics: Grammatical relations* (pp. 59–81). New York: Academic Press.

Fillmore, C.J. (1984). Lexical semantics and text semantics. In J.E. Copeland (Ed.), *New directions in linguistics and semiotics* (pp. 123–147). College Station: Texas A&M University Press.

Frank, S.D. (1994). *The Evelyn Wood seven-day speed reading and learning program*. New York: Barnes & Noble.

Funnell, E., & Allport, A. (1987). Non-linguistic cognition and word meanings: Neuropsychological exploration of common mechanisms. In A.A. Allport, D.G. MacKay, W. Prinz, & E. Scheerer (Eds.), *Language perception and production: Relationships between listening, speaking, reading, and writing* (pp. 367–400). New York: Academic Press.

Gambrell, L.B. (1982). Induced mental imagery and the text prediction performance of first and third graders. In J.A. Niles & L.A. Harris (Eds.), *New inquiries in reading research and instruction* (31st yearbook of the National Reading Conference, pp. 131–135). Rochester, NY: National Reading Conference.

Gambrell, L.B., & Koskinen, P.S. (2002). Imagery: A strategy for enhancing comprehension. In C.C. Block & M. Pressley (Eds.), *Comprehension instruction: Research-based best practices*. New York: Guilford.

Gibson, E.J., & Levin, H. (1975). *The psychology of reading*. Cambridge, MA: MIT Press.

Gickling, E.E., Hargis, C.H., & Alexander, D.R. (1981). The function of imagery in sight word recognition among retarded and nonretarded children. *Education and Training of the Mentally Retarded, 16*(4), 259–263.

Goetz, E.T., & Sadoski, M. (1996). Imaginative processes in literary comprehension. In R.J. Kreuz & M.S. MacNealy (Eds.), *Empirical approaches to literature and aesthetics* (pp. 221–240). Norwood, NJ: Ablex.

Goetz, E.T., Sadoski, M., & Olivarez, A., Jr. (1991). Getting a reading on reader response: Relationships between imagery, affect, and importance ratings, recall and imagery reports. *Reading Psychology, 12*(1), 13–26.

Goetz, E.T., Sadoski, M., Stowe, M.L., Fetsco, T.G., & Kemp, S.G. (1993). Imagery and emotional response in reading literary text. *Poetics, 22*, 35–49.

Hargis, C.H., & Gickling, E.E. (1978). The function of imagery in word recognition development. *The Reading Teacher, 31*, 870–874.

Hargis, C.H., Terhaar-Yonkers, M., Williams, P.C., & Reed, M.T. (1988). Repetition requirements for word recognition. *Journal of Reading, 31*, 320–327.

Harris, T.L., & Hodges, R.E. (1995). *The literacy dictionary: The vocabulary of reading and writing*. Newark, DE: International Reading Association.

Hodes, C.L. (1994). The role of visual mental imagery in the speed-accuracy tradeoff: A preliminary investigation. *Journal of Educational Technology Systems, 23*(1), 53–61.

Holcomb, P.J., Kounios, J., Anderson, J.E., & West, W.C. (1999). Dual-coding, context-availability, and concreteness effects in sentence comprehension: An electrophysiological investigation. *Journal of Experimental Psychology: Learning, Memory, and Cognition, 25*(3), 721–742.

Huey, E.B. (1968). *The psychology and pedagogy of reading*. Cambridge, MA: MIT Press. (Original work published 1908)

Janyan, A., & Andonova, E. (2003). Visual field differences in word naming. In F. Schmalhofer, R.M. Young, & G. Katz (Eds.), *Proceedings of Eurocogsci 03* (pp. 187–192). Mahwah, NJ: Erlbaum.

Johnson-Glenberg, M.C. (2000). Training reading comprehension in adequate decoders/poor comprehenders: Verbal versus visual strategies. *Journal of Educational Psychology, 92*(4), 772–782.

Jorm, A.F. (1977). Effect of word imagery on reading performance as a function of reader ability. *Journal of Educational Psychology, 69*(1), 46–54.

Juel, C., & Holmes, B. (1981). Oral and silent reading of sentences. *Reading Research Quarterly, 16*, 545–568.

Kaplan, R.M. (1973). A general syntactic processor. In R. Rustin (Ed.), *Natural language processing* (Courant Computer Science, Symposium 8). New York: Algorithmics.

Kieras, D. (1978). Beyond pictures and words: Alternative information-processing models for imagery effects in verbal memory. *Psychological Bulletin, 85*, 532–554.

Kintsch, W. (1988). The role of knowledge in discourse comprehension: A construction–integration model. *Psychological Review, 95*(2), 163–182.

Kintsch, W. (1998). *Comprehension: A paradigm for cognition*. Cambridge, UK: Cambridge University Press.

Kolker, B., & Terwilliger, P.N. (1981). Sight vocabulary learning of first and second graders. *Reading World, 20*(4), 251–258.

Kounios, J., & Holcomb, P.J. (1994). Concreteness effects in semantic processing: ERP evidence supporting dual-coding theory. *Journal of Experimental Psychology: Learning, Memory, and Cognition, 20*, 804–823.

Kreuz, R.J., & MacNealy, M.S. (Eds.). (1996). *Empirical approaches to literature and aesthetics*. Norwood, NJ: Ablex.

Langacker, R.W. (1987). *Foundations of cognitive grammar: Vol. I, Theoretical prerequisites*. Stanford, CA: Stanford University Press.

Langacker, R.W. (1991). *Concept, image, and symbol: The cognitive basis of grammar.* New York: du Gruyter.

Lesser, V.R., Fennell, R.D., Erman, L.D., & Reddy, D.R. (1975). Organization of the HEARSAY-II speech understanding system. *IEEE Transactions on Acoustics, Speech, and Signal Processing, 23*(1), 11–23.

Liberman, A.M., & Mattingly, I.G. (1985). The motor theory of speech perception revisited. *Cognition, 21*(1), 1–36.

Lucas, M. (1999). Context effects in lexical access: A meta-analysis. *Memory & Cognition, 27*, 385–398.

Marschark, M., & Hunt, R.R. (1989). A reexamination of the role of imagery in learning and memory. *Journal of Experimental Psychology: Learning, Memory, and Cognition, 15*(4), 710–720.

Marschark, M., & Paivio, A. (1977). Integrative processing of concrete and abstract sentences. *Journal of Verbal Learning and Verbal Behavior, 16*, 217–231.

Masefield, J. (1951). *Poems.* New York: Macmillan.

Miall, D.S. (1996). Empowering the reader: Literary response and classroom learning. In R.J. Kreuz & M.S. MacNealy (Eds.), *Empirical approaches to literature and aesthetics* (pp. 463–478). Norwood, NJ: Ablex.

Miall, D.S., & Kuiken, D. (1995). Aspects of literary response: A new questionnaire. *Research in the Teaching of English, 29*(1), 37–58.

Monaghan, J., & Ellis, A.W. (2002). What exactly interacts with spelling-sound consistency in word naming? *Journal of Experimental Psychology: Learning, Memory, and Cognition, 28*, 183–206.

Nelson, D.L., & Schreiber, T.A. (1992). Word concreteness and word structure as independent determinants of recall. *Journal of Memory and Language, 31*, 237–260.

Paivio, A. (1971). *Imagery and verbal processes.* New York: Holt, Rinehart, and Winston.

Paivio, A. (1986). *Mental representations: A dual coding approach.* New York: Oxford University Press.

Paivio, A. (1991). Dual coding theory: Retrospect and current status. *Canadian Journal of Psychology, 45*, 255–287.

Paivio, A., Walsh, M., & Bons, T. (1994). Concreteness effects in memory: When and why? *Journal of Experimental Psychology: Learning, Memory, and Cognition, 20*, 1196–1204.

Plaut, D.C., & Shallice, T. (1993). Deep dyslexia: A case study of connectionist neuropsychology. *Cognitive Neuropsychology, 10*, 377–500.

Raman, I., & Baluch, B. (2001). Semantic effects as a function of reading skill in word naming of a transparent orthography. *Reading and Writing, 14*(7/8), 599–614.

Raman, I., Baluch, B., & Besner, D. (1997). *Imageability and frequency effects on visual word recognition: Evidence from a transparent orthography.* Paper presented at the Fifth European Congress of Psychology, Dublin, Ireland.

Rayner, K., & Pollatsek, A. (1989). *The psychology of reading.* Englewood Cliffs, NJ: Prentice Hall.

Rosenblatt, L.M. (1994). The transactional theory of reading and writing. In R.B. Ruddell, M.R. Ruddell, & H. Singer (Eds.), *Theoretical models and processes of reading* (4th ed., pp. 1057–1092). Newark, DE: International Reading Association.

Ruddell, R.B. (1997). Researching the influential literacy teacher: Characteristics, beliefs, strategies, and new research directions. In C.K. Kinzer, K.A. Hinchman, & D.J. Leu (Eds.), *Inquiries in literacy theory and practice* (46th yearbook of the National Reading Conference, pp. 37–53). Chicago: National Reading Conference.

Rumelhart, D.E. (1977). Toward an interactive model of reading. In S. Dornic (Ed.), *Attention and performance* (pp. 573–603). New York: Academic Press.

Rumelhart, D.E., & McClelland, J.L. (1986). *Parallel distributed processing.* Cambridge, MA: MIT Press.

Sacks, O. (2002, October 7). The case of Anna H. *The New Yorker*, 62–73.

Sadoski, M. (1983). An exploratory study of the relationships between reported imagery and the comprehension and recall of a story. *Reading Research Quarterly, 19*, 110–123.

Sadoski, M. (1985). The natural use of imagery in story comprehension and recall: Replication and extension. *Reading Research Quarterly, 20*, 658–667.

Sadoski, M. (1992). Imagination, cognition, and persona. *Rhetoric Review, 10*, 266–278.

Sadoski, M. (1999). Comprehending comprehension [Essay review of the book *Comprehension: A paradigm for cognition*]. *Reading Research Quarterly, 34*, 493–500.

Sadoski, M. (2002). Dual coding theory and reading poetic text. *Journal of the Imagination in Language Learning and Teaching, 7*, 78–83.

Sadoski, M., & Goetz, E.T. (1985). Relationships between affect, imagery, and importance ratings for segments of a story. In J.A. Niles & R. Lalik (Eds.), *Issues in literacy: A research perspective* (34th yearbook of the National Reading Conference, pp. 180–185). Washington, DC: National Reading Conference.

Sadoski, M., Goetz, E.T., & Avila, E. (1995). Concreteness effects in text recall: Dual coding or context availability? *Reading Research Quarterly, 30*, 278–288.

Sadoski, M., Goetz, E.T., & Fritz, J. (1993). Impact of concreteness on comprehensibility, interest, and memory for text: Implications for dual coding theory and text design. *Journal of Educational Psychology, 85*, 291–304.

Sadoski, M., Goetz, E.T., & Kangiser, S. (1988). Imagination in story response: Relationships between imagery, affect, and structural importance. *Reading Research Quarterly, 23*, 320–336.

Sadoski, M., Goetz, E.T., Olivarez, A., Lee, S., & Roberts, N.M. (1990). Imagination in story reading: The role of imagery, verbal recall,

story analysis, and processing levels. *Journal of Reading Behavior, 22*, 55–70.
Sadoski, M., Goetz, E.T., & Rodriguez, M. (2000). Engaging texts: Effects of concreteness on comprehensibility, interest, and recall in four text types. *Journal of Educational Psychology, 92*, 85–95.
Sadoski, M., & Paivio, A. (1994). A dual coding view of imagery and verbal processes in reading comprehension. In R.B. Ruddell, M.R. Ruddell, & H. Singer (Eds.), *Theoretical models and processes of reading* (4th ed., pp. 582–601). Newark, DE: International Reading Association.
Sadoski, M., & Paivio, A. (2001). *Imagery and text: A dual coding theory of reading and writing.* Mahwah, NJ: Erlbaum.
Sadoski, M., Paivio, A., & Goetz, E.T. (1991). A critique of schema theory in reading and a dual coding alternative. *Reading Research Quarterly, 26*, 463–484.
Sadoski, M., & Quast, Z. (1990). Reader response and long-term recall for journalistic text: The roles of imagery, affect, and importance. *Reading Research Quarterly, 25*, 256–272.
Strain, E., & Herdman, C.M. (1999). Imageability effects in word naming: An individual differences analysis. *Canadian Journal of Experimental Psychology, 53*, 347–359.
Strain, E., Patterson, K., & Seidenberg, M.S. (1995). Semantic effects in single-word naming. *Journal of Experimental Psychology: Learning, Memory, and Cognition, 21*, 1140–1154.
Strain, E., Patterson, K., & Seidenberg, M.S. (2002). Theories of word naming interact with spelling–sound consistency. *Journal of Experimental Psychology: Learning, Memory, and Cognition, 28*, 207–214.
Terwilliger, P.N., & Kolker, B.S. (1982). The effects of learning confusable words on subsequent learning of high or low imagery words. *Reading World, 21*, 286–292.
van der Veur, B.W. (1975). Imagery rating of 1,000 frequently used words. *Journal of Educational Psychology, 67*, 44–56.
Venezky, R.L., & Massaro, D.W. (1987). Orthographic structure and spelling-sound regularity in reading English words. In A.A. Allport, D.G. MacKay, W. Prinz, & E. Scheerer (Eds.), *Language perception and production: Relationships between listening, speaking, reading, and writing* (pp. 159–179). New York: Academic Press.
West, W.C., O'Rourke, T.B., & Holcomb, P.J. (1998). Event-related brain potentials and language comprehension: A cognitive neuroscience approach to the study of intellectual functioning. In S. Soraci & W.J. McIlvane (Eds.), *Perspectives on fundamental processes in intellectual functioning* (pp. 131–168). Stamford, CT: Ablex.
Williams, J.D. (1998). *Preparing to teach writing: Research, theory, and practice* (2nd ed.). Mahwah, NJ: Erlbaum.
Wolpert, E.M. (1972). Length, imagery values, and word recognition. *The Reading Teacher, 26*, 180–186.

Dual Coding Theory and Literacy: Update

The decade since our chapter appeared in the last edition of this volume has been a propitious time for Dual Coding Theory (DCT). We have elaborated those developments in Sadoski and Paivio (2013), and we highlight a few selected developments here.

Toward a Unified Theory of Literacy

We maintain that DCT is the most viable current candidate to unify the cognitive aspects of literacy theory (Sadoski & Paivio, 2007). A long-standing problem in literacy is that theories of limited aspects of reading and writing have developed separately, so theories of decoding, comprehension, response, and composing remain a patchwork. Scientifically, this situation is unsustainable: The goal of all scientific explanation is unified, comprehensive theories. DCT is an established theory of cognition that provides one unifying framework for literacy, although all scientific theories are tentative and evolving.

A case in point is DCT's subsumption of the venerable model of LaBerge and Samuels (1974, updated by Samuels as Chapter 28 this volume; hereafter the LS model). Noting that DCT had mainly emphasized reading comprehension, Sadoski and Paivio (2007) stated that the decoding aspects of the LS model "would be readily encompassed by DCT" (p. 350). Samuels (2006) suggested a complementary need: "Although our model shows how the information from the page is processed and moved along to comprehension, the model has almost nothing to say about the comprehension process" (pp. 334–335).

Sadoski, McTigue, and Paivio (2012; also see Sadoski & Paivio, 2013, Chapter 7) detailed how DCT subsumed everything in the LS model and merged it with the established DCT account of comprehension. Moreover, the subsumed model explained research that the LS model could not explain alone. We summarize next; for details, see the references.

A basic principle of DCT is that all mental representations are embodied and modality specific (e.g., visual, auditory) as opposed to abstract and amodal. Another DCT principle is that these representations are formed into two codes: the verbal code specialized for language and the nonverbal code specialized for world knowledge in the form of sensory images. The LS model partially conformed to the first principle in positing two modality-specific memory stores: visual memory and phonological memory (Samuels, Chapter 28 this volume). Visual memory accounted for visual recognition of letters and written words, and phonological memory for their spoken counterparts. However, two other memory stores—semantic memory and episodic memory—were represented by abstract, amodal word-meaning codes and temporal-spatial event codes. This is inconsistent with DCT, which posits all memory as modality specific.

The DCT model of the reading process (see Sadoski et al., 2012, Figure 4; Sadoski & Paivio, 2013, Figure 7.1) replaced these abstract codes with modality-specific encodings in a network of probabilistic connections between verbal and nonverbal representations that accounts for both decoding and comprehension (for the DCT account of comprehension, see Sadoski & Paivio, 2001, 2013, and our reprinted chapter on the preceding pages of this volume). That is, both decoding and comprehension could now be explained by a common theory—an incremental step toward a unified account of decoding and comprehension.

However, the DCT model explains research results that are daunting for the LS model alone. A case in point is sight vocabulary learning. Decades of studies have found that concrete, image-evoking words are learned much more readily than matched abstract words (Sadoski, 2005; Sadoski et al., 2012). The dual encoding of concrete words (i.e., verbal–nonverbal) can account for these results, but abstract word-meaning codes offer no ready explanation.

Embodied Cognition and Social Cognition

The last decade has also seen a movement in cognitive theory away from abstract, amodal forms of knowledge toward an embodied view. Embodied cognition has been well summarized by Thelen, Schöner, Scheier, and Smith (2001):

> To say that cognition is embodied means that it arises from bodily interactions with the world. From this point of view, cognition depends on the kinds of experiences that come from having a body with particular perceptual and motor capacities that are inseparably linked and that together form the matrix within which memory, emotion, language, and all other aspects of life are meshed. (p. 1)

From this perspective, all knowledge is inherently embodied—rooted in sensory experience. Embodied theories have been proposed by many (e.g., Barsalou, 1999; Glenberg, 1997; Lakoff & Johnson, 1999). Zwaan (2004) proposed an embodied, immersed experiencer theory of reading comprehension, citing DCT as one influence.

Embodied tenets have always been central to DCT (Paivio, 1971/1979, 1986, 2007; Sadoski & Paivio, 2001, 2013; Sadoski, Paivio, & Goetz, 1991). However, DCT differs from other embodied theories in its assumption of verbal and nonverbal codes. Both codes are modality specific (i.e., embodied) but differ with the nature of the information they evolved to handle. The verbal code is more sequentially constrained, whereas the nonverbal code is more synchronous. For example, spoken or written information describing an object in language occurs in a linear sequence, but the same information in a picture of the object occurs simultaneously.

Embodied theories can be contrasted with theories postulating abstract, amodal structures, such as schema theory (Anderson, Chapter 19 this volume). Schemata are abstract and amodal by definition (abstracted from sensory experience in some disembodied form), a condition rendering them difficult to empirically test (Alba & Hasher, 1983; Sadoski et al., 1991). Whether such theories can deal with increasing behavioral and neuropsychological evidence for embodied cognition is questionable. Efforts to recast schema theory in more embodied terms (e.g., McVee, Dunsmore, & Gavelek, Chapter 20 this volume) have been critiqued (Gredler, 2007; Krasny, Sadoski, & Paivio, 2007). While not agreeing with all of our critique, McVee, Gavelek, and Dunsmore (2007) acknowledged the limitations of the schema concept:

> Throughout our article (McVee et al., 2005), we stress this metaphorical and heuristic nature of the schema construct and its contested and variable interpretations. We noted that "perhaps the most important conceptual question...concerns when a construct, or a theory built around a construct, ceases to be the theory (or construct) that it was" (p. 566). The schema has been interpreted varyingly and may well have morphed into a construct with limitations that exceed its heuristic value. (p. 246)

However, embodied theories intrinsically engage sociocognitive and sociocultural cognition because we live in a world of social experience. Vygotsky's theories are often used in explaining these aspects of literacy (e.g., Forman &

Cazden, Chapter 7 this volume; McVee et al., Chapter 20 this volume). Whatever sociocultural value these theories may offer, a Vygotskian view of cognition is untenable because it maintains that all thought takes the form of inner speech, a position similar to his radical behaviorist contemporaries in the early 20th century. DCT maintains that thought takes the form of nonverbal mental images as well as inner speech. DCT also intrinsically involves social influences in constructing mental representations and even the self.

The constructivist philosophy of the pragmatists, especially George Herbert Mead (1934), is more consonant with DCT. Mead, a founder of social psychology, maintained prominent roles for both language and mental imagery in thought, action, communication, and the development of the self in a social world. He coined the term *generalized other*, our verbal and nonverbal developmental knowledge of "the organized community or social group which gives to the individual his unity of self" (p. 154). Because DCT emphasizes embodied experience in a social world, DCT maintains that we become social beings by definition. For a discussion of Mead's views in relation to DCT in literacy, see Sadoski (1992). For a broader discussion of the DCT perspective on the role of social interactions in forming the mind and the self, see Paivio (2007).

Neuropsychological Support

DCT predictions have a particularly strong record of neuropsychological confirmation (see Paivio, 2007, 2008; Sadoski & Paivio, 2013, Chap. 6). As noted earlier, differences in processing concrete and abstract language are central to DCT and provide a crucible for neuropsychological tests. Findings consistently indicate that both concrete and abstract language activate brain areas associated with language, but concrete language additionally activates areas associated with mental imagery.

For example, Dhond, Witzel, Dale, and Halgren (2007) used magnetoencephalography (similar to electroencephalography) to measure brain responses in judging whether words were concrete or abstract. They concluded that abstract words in particular "may be initially understood using a left lateralized fronto-temporal verbal-linguistic system that for concrete words is supplemented after a short delay by a right parietal and medial occipital imagistic network" (p. 355). Similarly, a differential pattern of brain area activation occurs in reading concrete and abstract sentences (e.g., Bergen, Lindsay, Matlock, & Narayanan, 2007; Holcomb, Kounios, Anderson, & West, 1999).

In a pair of seminal studies, Sadoski (1983, 1985) found that people report an image of the climax of a short story more than any other story part. Furthermore, such an image is associated with integrated story recall and emotional response. Xu, Kemeny, Park, Frattali, and Braun (2005) used functional magnetic resonance imaging to track brain activity during the reading of Aesop's fables. Consistent with Sadoski's results, they found that brain activation in the early stages was mainly, but not completely, in the left perisylvian language areas associated with word and sentence processing. However, as the story progressed and climaxed, an array of extralinguistic centers was activated, including the right perisylvian area, angular gyrus, and superior temporal sulcus—areas associated with mental imagery, multimodal integration, and emotional responses.

DCT continues to advance in explaining how both language and mental imagery are unified in literacy. DCT's principles are consistently supported in theory, research, and practice in the 21st century. The decades ahead should be interesting indeed.

REFERENCES

Alba, J.W., & Hasher, L. (1983). Is memory schematic? *Psychological Bulletin, 93*(2), 203–231. doi:10.1037/0033-2909.93.2.203

Barsalou, L.W. (1999). Perceptual symbol systems. *Behavioral and Brain Sciences, 22*(4), 577–609.

Bergen, B.K., Lindsay, S., Matlock, T., & Narayanan, S. (2007). Spatial and linguistic aspects of visual imagery in sentence comprehension. *Cognitive Science, 31*(5), 733–764. doi:10.1080/03640210701530748

Dhond, R.P., Witzel, T., Dale, A.M., & Halgren, E. (2007). Spatiotemporal cortical dynamics underlying abstract and concrete word reading. *Human Brain Mapping, 28*(4), 355–362. doi:10.1002/hbm.20282

Glenberg, A.M. (1997). What memory is for: Creating meaning in the service of action. *Behavioral and Brain Sciences, 20*(1), 1–19.

Gredler, M.E. (2007). Of cabbages and kings: Concepts and inferences curiously attributed to Lev Vygotsky (Commentary on McVee, Dunsmore, and Gavelek, 2005). *Review of Educational Research, 77*(2), 233–238. doi:10.3102/0034654306298270

Holcomb, P.J., Kounios, J., Anderson, J.E., & West, W.C. (1999). Dual-coding, context-availability, and concreteness effects in sentence comprehension: An electrophysiological investigation. *Journal of Experimental Psychology: Learning, Memory, and Cognition, 25*(3), 721–742. doi:10.1037/0278-7393.25.3.721

Krasny, K.A., Sadoski, M., & Paivio, A. (2007). Unwarranted return: A response to McVee, Dunsmore, and Gavelek's (2005) "Schema Theory Revisited." *Review of Educational Research, 77*(2), 239–244. doi:10.3102/003465430301958

LaBerge, D., & Samuels, S.J. (1974). Toward a theory of automatic information processing in reading. *Cognitive Psychology, 6*(2), 293–323. doi:10.1016/0010-0285(74)90015-2

Lakoff, G., & Johnson, M. (1999). *Philosophy in the flesh: The embodied mind and its challenge to Western thought.* New York: Basic.

McVee, M.B., Gavelek, J.R., & Dunsmore, K.L. (2007). Considerations of the social, individual, and embodied: A response to comments on "Schema Theory Revisited." *Review of Educational Research, 77*(2), 245–248. doi:10.3102/003465430301677

Mead, G.H. (1934). *Mind, self, and society: From the standpoint of a social behaviorist* (C.W. Morris, Ed.). Chicago: University of Chicago Press.

Paivio, A. (1979). *Imagery and verbal processes.* Hillsdale, NJ: Erlbaum. (Original work published 1971)

Paivio, A. (1986). *Mental representations: A dual coding approach.* New York: Oxford University Press.

Paivio, A. (2007). *Mind and its evolution: A dual coding theoretical approach.* Mahwah, NJ: Erlbaum.

Paivio, A. (2008). Looking at reading comprehension through the lens of neuroscience. In C.C. Block & S.R. Paris (Eds.), *Comprehension instruction: Research-based best practices* (pp. 101–113). New York: Guilford.

Sadoski, M. (1983). An exploratory study of the relationships between reported imagery and the comprehension and recall of a story. *Reading Research Quarterly, 19*(1), 110–123. doi:10.2307/747341

Sadoski, M. (1985). The natural use of imagery in story comprehension and recall: Replication and extension. *Reading Research Quarterly, 20*(5), 658–667. doi:10.2307/747949

Sadoski, M. (1992). Imagination, cognition, and persona. *Rhetoric Review, 10*(2), 266–278. doi:10.1080/07350199209388971

Sadoski, M. (2005). A dual coding view of vocabulary learning. *Reading & Writing Quarterly, 21*(3), 221–238. doi:10.1080/10573560590949359

Sadoski, M., McTigue, E.M., & Paivio, A. (2012). A dual coding theoretical model of decoding in reading: Subsuming the LaBerge and Samuels model. *Reading Psychology, 33*(5), 465–496. doi:10.1080/02702711.2011.557330

Sadoski, M., & Paivio, A. (2001). *Imagery and text: A dual coding theory of reading and writing.* Mahwah, NJ: Erlbaum.

Sadoski, M., & Paivio, A. (2007). Toward a unified theory of reading. *Scientific Studies of Reading, 11*(4), 337–356. doi:10.1080/10888430701530714

Sadoski, M., & Paivio, A. (2013). *Imagery and text: A dual coding theory of reading and writing* (2nd ed.). New York: Routledge.

Sadoski, M., Paivio, A., & Goetz, E.T. (1991). A critique of schema theory in reading and a dual coding alternative. *Reading Research Quarterly, 26*(4), 463–484. doi:10.2307/747898

Samuels, S.J. (2006). Looking backward: Reflections on a career in reading. *Journal of Literacy Research*, *38*(3), 327–344.
Thelen, E., Schöner, G., Scheier, C., & Smith, L.B. (2001). The dynamics of embodiment: A field theory of infant perseverative reaching. *Behavioral and Brain Sciences*, *24*(1), 1–34. doi:10.1017/S0140525X01003910
Xu, J., Kemeny, S., Park, G., Frattali, C., & Braun, A. (2005). Language in context: Emergent features of word, sentence, and narrative comprehension. *NeuroImage*, *25*(3), 1002–1015. doi:10.1016/j.neuroimage.2004.12.013
Zwaan, R.A. (2004). The immersed experiencer: Toward an embodied theory of language comprehension. In B.H. Ross (Ed.), *The psychology of learning and motivation* (Vol. 44, pp. 35–62). San Diego, CA: Elsevier Academic. doi:10.1016/S0079-7421(03)44002-4

The Transactional Theory of Reading and Writing

Louise M. Rosenblatt, New York University

> Terms such as *the reader* are somewhat misleading, though convenient, fictions. There is no such thing as a generic reader or a generic literary work; there are in reality only the potential millions of individual readers of individual literary works.... The reading of any work of literature is, of necessity, an individual and unique occurrence involving the mind and emotions of some particular reader. (Rosenblatt, 1938/1983)

That statement, first published in *Literature as Exploration* in 1938, seems especially important to reiterate at the beginning of a presentation of a "theoretical model" of the reading process. A theoretical model by definition is an abstraction, or a generalized pattern devised in order to think about a subject. Hence, it is essential to recognize that, as I concluded, we may generalize about similarities among such events, but we cannot evade the realization that there are actually only innumerable separate transactions between readers and texts.

As I sought to understand how we make the meanings called novels, poems, or plays, I discovered that I had developed a theoretical model that covers all modes of reading. Ten years of teaching courses in literature and composition had preceded the writing of that statement. This had made possible observation of readers encountering a wide range of "literary" and "nonliterary" texts, discussing them, keeping journals while reading them, and writing spontaneous reactions and reflective essays. And decades more of such observation preceded the publication of *The Reader, the Text, the Poem* (Rosenblatt, 1978), the fullest presentation of the theory and its implications for criticism.

Thus, the theory emerges from a process highly appropriate to the pragmatist philosophy it embodies. The problem arose in the context of a practical classroom situation. Observations of relevant episodes led to the hypotheses that constitute the theory of the reading process, and these have in turn been applied, tested, confirmed, or revised in the light of further observation.

Fortunately, while specializing in English and comparative literature, I was in touch with the thinking on the forefront of various disciplines. The interpretation of these observations of readers' reading drew on a number of different perspectives—literary and social history, philosophy, aesthetics, linguistics, psychology,

This chapter is reprinted from *Theoretical Models and Processes of Reading* (4th ed., pp. 1057–1092), edited by R.B. Ruddell, M.R. Ruddell, & H. Singer, Newark, DE: International Reading Association.

and sociology. Training in anthropology provided an especially important point of view. Ideas were developed that in some instances have only recently become established. It seems necessary, therefore, to begin by setting forth some of the basic assumptions and concepts that undergird the transactional theory of the reading process. This in turn will involve presentation of the transactional view of the writing process and the relationship between author and reader.

The Transactional Paradigm

Transaction

The terms *transaction* and *transactional* are consonant with a philosophic position increasingly accepted in the 20th century. A new paradigm in science (Kuhn, 1970) has required a change in our habits of thinking about our relationship to the world around us. For 300 years, Descartes' dualistic view of the self as distinct from nature sufficed, for example, for the Newtonian paradigm in physics. The self, or "subject," was separate from the "object" perceived. "Objective" facts, completely free of subjectivity, were sought, and a direct, immediate perception of "reality" was deemed possible. Einstein's theory and the developments in subatomic physics revealed the need to acknowledge that, as Neils Bohr (1959) explained, the observer is part of the observation—human beings are part of nature. Even the physicists' facts depend to some extent on the interests, hypotheses, and technologies of the observer. The human organism, it became apparent, is ultimately the mediator in any perception of the world or any sense of "reality."

John Dewey's pragmatist epistemology fitted the new paradigm. Hence, Dewey joined with Arthur F. Bentley to work out a new terminology in *Knowing and the Known* (1949). They believed the term *interaction* was too much associated with the old positivistic paradigm, with each element or unit being predefined as separate, as "thing balanced against thing," and their "interaction" studied. Instead, they chose *transaction* to imply "unfractured observation" of the whole situation. Systems of description and naming "are employed to deal with aspects and phases of action, without final attribution to 'elements' or presumptively detachable or independent 'entities,' 'essences,' or 'realities'" (p. 108). The knower, the knowing, and the known are seen as aspects of "one process." Each element conditions and is conditioned by the other in a mutually constituted situation (cf. Rosenblatt, 1985b).

The new paradigm requires a break with entrenched habits of thinking. The old stimulus–response, subject–object, individual–social dualisms give way to recognition of transactional relationships. The human being is seen as part of nature, continuously in transaction with an environment—each one conditions the other. The transactional mode of thinking has perhaps been most clearly assimilated in ecology. Human activities and relationships are seen as transactions in which the individual and social elements fuse with cultural and natural elements. Many current philosophy writers may differ on metaphysical implications but find it necessary to come to terms with the new paradigm.[1]

Language

The transactional concept has profound implications for understanding language. Traditionally, language has been viewed as primarily a self-contained system or code, a set of arbitrary rules and conventions that is manipulated as a tool by speakers and writers or imprints itself on the minds of listeners and readers. Even when the transactional approach has been accepted, this deeply ingrained way of thinking continues to function, tacitly or explicitly, in much theory, research, and teaching involving texts.[2]

The view of language basic to the transactional model of reading owes much to the philosopher John Dewey but even more to his contemporary Charles Sanders Peirce, who is recognized as the U.S. founder of the field of semiotics or semiology, the study of verbal and nonverbal signs. Peirce provided concepts that differentiate the transactional view of language and reading from structuralist and poststructuralist (especially deconstructionist) theories. These reflect the influence of another great semiotician, the French linguist Ferdinand de Saussure (Culler, 1982).

Saussure (1972) differentiated actual speech (*parole*) from the abstractions of the linguists (*langue*), but he stressed the arbitrary nature of signs and minimized the referential aspect. Even more important was his dyadic formulation of the relationship between "signifier and signified," or between words and concept. These emphases fostered a view of language as an autonomous, self-contained system (Rosenblatt, 1993).

In contrast, Peirce (1933, 1935) offered a triadic formulation. "A sign," Peirce wrote, "is in conjoint relation to the thing denoted and to the mind...." The "sign is related to its object only in consequence of a mental association, and depends on habit" (Vol. 3, p. 360). The triad constitutes a symbol. Peirce repeatedly refers to the human context of meaning. Because he evidently did not want to reinforce the notion of "mind" as an entity, he typically phrased the "conjoint" linkage as among sign, object, and "interpretant," which should be understood as a mental operation rather than an entity (Vol. 6, p. 347). Peirce's triadic model firmly grounds language in the transactions of individual human beings with their world.

Recent descriptions of the working of the brain by neurologists and other scientists seem very Peircean. Although they are dealing with a level not essential to our theoretical purposes, they provide an interesting reinforcement. "Many leading scientists, including Dr. Francis Crick, think that the brain creates unified circuits by oscillating distant components at a shared frequency" (Appenzeller, 1990, pp. 6–7). Neurologists speak of "a third-party convergence zone [which seems to be a neurological term for Peirce's interpretant] that mediates between word and concept convergence zones" (Damasio, 1989, pp. 123–132). Studies of children's acquisition of language support the Peircean triad, concluding that a vocalization or sign becomes a word, a verbal symbol, when the sign and its object or referent are linked with the same "organismic state" (Werner & Kaplan, 1962, p. 18).

Though language is usually defined as a socially generated system of communication—the very bloodstream of any society—the triadic concept reminds us that language is always internalized by a human being transacting with a particular environment. Vygotsky's recognition of the social context did not prevent his affirming the individual's role: The "sense of a word" is

> the sum of all the psychological events aroused in our consciousness by the word. It is a dynamic, fluid, complex whole, which has several zones of unequal stability. Meaning [i.e., reference] is only one of the zones of sense, the most stable and precise zone. A word acquires its sense from the context in which it appears; in different contexts, it changes its sense. (1962, p. 46)

Vygotsky postulated "the existence of a dynamic system of meaning, in which the affective and the intellectual unite." The earliest utterances of children evidently represent a fusion of "processes which later will branch off into referential, emotive, and associative part processes" (Rommetveit, 1968, pp. 147, 167). The child learns to sort out the various aspects of "sense" associated with a sign, decontextualize it, and recognize the public aspect of language, the collective language system. This does not, however, eliminate the other dimensions of sense. A language act cannot be thought of as totally affective or cognitive, or as totally public or private (Bates, 1979, pp. 65–66).

Bates provides the useful metaphor of an iceberg for the total sense of a word to its user: The visible tip represents what I term the public aspect of meaning, resting on the submerged base of private meaning. *Public* designates usages or meanings that dictionaries list. Multiple meanings indicated for the same word reflect the fact that the same sign takes on different meanings at different times and in different linguistic or different personal, cultural, or social contexts. In short, *public* refers to usages that some groups of people have developed and that the individual shares.

Note that *public* and *private* are not synonymous with *cognitive* and *affective*. Words may have publicly shared affective connotations. The individual's private associations with a word may or may not agree with its connotations for the group, although these connotations must also be individually acquired. Words necessarily involve for each person a mix of both public and private elements, the base as well as the tip of the semantic iceberg.

For the individual, then, the language is that part, or set of features, of the public system that has been internalized through that person's experiences with words in life situations. "Lexical concepts must be shared by speakers of a common language...yet there is room for considerable individual difference in the details of any concept" (Miller & Johnson-Laird, 1976, p. 700). The residue of the individual's past transactions—in particular, natural and social contexts—constitutes what can be termed a linguistic–experiential reservoir. William James especially suggests the presence of such a cumulative experiential aura of language.

Embodying funded assumptions, attitudes, and expectations about language and about the world, this inner capital is all that each of us has to draw on in speaking, listening, writing, or reading. We "make sense" of a new situation or transaction and make new meanings by applying, reorganizing, revising, or extending public and private elements selected from our personal linguistic–experiential reservoirs.

Linguistic Transactions

Face-to-face communication—such as a conversation in which a speaker is explaining something to another person—can provide a simplified example of the transactional nature of all linguistic activities. A conversation is a temporal activity, a back-and-forth process. Each person has come to the transaction with an individual history, manifested in what has been termed a linguistic–experiential reservoir. The verbal signs are the vibrations in the air caused by a speaker. Both speaker and addressee contribute throughout to the spoken text (even if the listener remains silent) and to the interpretations that it calls forth as it progresses. Each must construct some sense of the other person. Each draws on a particular linguistic–experiential reservoir. The specific situation, which may be social and personal, and the setting and occasion for the conversation in themselves provide clues or limitations as to the general subject or framework and hence to the references and implications of the verbal signs. The speaker and addressee both produce further delimiting cues through facial expressions, tones of voice, and gestures. In addition to such nonverbal indications of an ongoing mutual interpretation of the text, the listener may offer questions and comments. The speaker thus is constantly being helped to gauge and to confirm, revise, or expand the text. Hence, the text is shaped transactionally by both speaker and addressee.

The opening words of a conversation, far from being static, by the end of the interchange may have taken on a different meaning. And the attitudes, the state of mind, even the manifest personality traits, may have undergone change. Moreover, the spoken text may be interpreted differently by each of the conversationalists.

But how can we apply the conversation model of transaction to the relationship between writers and readers, when so many of the elements that contribute to the spoken transaction are missing—physical presence, timing, actual setting, nonverbal behaviors, tones of voice, and so on? The signs on the page are all that the writer and the reader have to make up for the absence of these other elements. The reader focuses attention on and transacts with an element in the environment, namely the signs on the page, the text.

Despite all the important differences noted above, speech, writing, and reading share the same basic process—transacting through a text. In any linguistic event, speakers and listeners and writers and readers have only their linguistic–experiential reservoirs as the basis for interpretation. Any interpretations or new meanings are restructurings or extensions of the stock of experiences of language, spoken and written, brought to the task. In Peircean terms, past linkages of sign, object, and interpretant must provide the basis for new linkages, or new structures of meaning. Instead of an interaction, such as billiard balls colliding, there has been a transaction, thought of rather in terms of reverberations, rapid oscillations, blendings, and mutual conditionings.

Selective Attention

William James's concept of "selective attention" provides an important insight into this process. During the first half of this century, a combination of behaviorism and positivism led to neglect of the concept, but since the 1970s psychologists have reasserted its importance (Blumenthal, 1977; Myers, 1986). James (1890) tells us that we are constantly engaged in a "choosing activity," which he terms "selective attention" (Vol. I, p. 284). We are constantly selecting out of the stream, or field, of consciousness "by the reinforcing and inhibiting agency of attention" (Vol. I, p. 288). This activity is sometimes termed "the cocktail party phenomenon": In a crowded room where many conversations are in progress, we focus our attention on only one of them at a time, and the others become a background hum. We can turn our selective attention toward a broader or narrower area of the field. Thus, while language activity implies an intermingled kinesthetic, cognitive, affective, associational matrix, what is pushed into the background or suppressed and what is brought into awareness and organized into meaning depend on where selective attention is focused.

The transactional concept will prevent our falling into the error of envisaging selective attention as a mechanical choosing among an array of fixed entities rather than as a dynamic centering on areas or aspects of the contents of consciousness. The linguistic reservoir should not be seen as encompassing verbal signs linked to fixed meanings, but as a fluid pool of potential triadic symbolizations. Such residual linkages of sign, signifier, and organic state, it will be seen, become actual symbolizations as selective attention functions under the shaping influence of particular times and circumstances.

In the linguistic event, any process will be affected also by the physical and emotional state of the individual, for example, by fatigue or stress. Attention may be controlled or wandering, intense or superficial. In the discussion that follows, it will be assumed that such factors enter into the transaction and affect the quality of the process under consideration.

The paradoxical situation is that the reader has only the black marks on the page as the means of arriving at a meaning—and that meaning can be constructed only by drawing on the reader's own personal linguistic and life experiences. Because a text must be produced by a writer before it can be read, logic might seem to dictate beginning with a discussion of the writing process. It is true that the writer seeks to express something, but the purpose is to communicate with a reader (even if it is only the writer wishing to preserve some thought or experience for future reference). Typically, the text is intended for others. Some sense of a reader or at least of the fact that the text will function in a reading process is thus implicit in the writing process. Hence, I shall discuss the reading process first, then the writing process. Then, I shall broach the problems of communication and validity of interpretation before considering implications for teaching and research.

The Reading Process

Transacting With the Text

The concepts of transaction, the transactional nature of language, and selective attention now can be applied to analysis of the reading process. Every reading act is an event, or a transaction involving a particular reader and a particular pattern of signs, a text, and occurring at a particular time in a particular context. Instead of two fixed entities acting on one another, the reader and the text are two aspects of a total dynamic situation. The "meaning" does not reside ready-made "in" the text or "in" the reader but happens or comes into being during the transaction between reader and text.

The term *text* in this analysis denotes, then, a set of signs capable of being interpreted as verbal symbols. Far from already possessing a meaning that can be imposed on all readers, the text actually remains simply marks on paper, an object in the environment, until some reader transacts with it. The term *reader* implies a transaction with a text; the term *text* implies a transaction with a reader. "Meaning" is what happens during the transaction—hence the fallacy of thinking of them as separate and distinct entities instead of factors in a total situation.

The notion that the marks in themselves possess meaning is hard to dispel. For example, *pain* for a French reader will link up with the concept of bread and for an English reader with the concept of bodily or mental suffering. A sentence that Noam Chomsky (1968, p. 27) made famous can help us realize that not even the syntax is inherent in the signs of the text but depends on the results of particular transactions: *Flying planes can be dangerous.*

Actually, only after we have selected a meaning can we infer a syntax from it. Usually, factors entering into the total transaction, such as the context and reader's purpose, will determine the reader's choice of meaning. Even if the reader recognizes the alternative syntactic possibilities, these factors still prevail. This casts doubt on the belief that the syntactical level, because it is lower or less complex, necessarily always precedes the semantic in the reading process. The transactional situation suggests that meaning implies syntax and that a reciprocal process is going on in which the broader aspects guiding choices are actively involved.

Here we see the difference between the physical text, defined as a pattern of signs, and what is usually called "the text," a syntactically patterned set of verbal symbols. This actually comes into being during the transaction with the signs on the page.

When we see a set of such marks on a page, we believe that it should give rise to some more or less coherent meaning. We bring our funded experience to bear. Multiple inner alternatives resonate to the signs. Not only the triadic linkages with the signs but also certain organismic states, or certain ranges of feeling, are stirred up in the linguistic–experiential reservoir. From these activated areas, selective attention—conditioned, as we have seen, by multiple physical, personal, social, and cultural factors entering into the situation—picks out elements that will be organized and synthesized into what constitutes "meaning." Choices have in effect probably been made simultaneously, as the various "levels" transact, conditioning one another, so to speak.

Reading is, to use James's phrase, a "choosing activity." From the very beginning, and often even before, some expectation, some tentative feeling, idea, or purpose, no matter how vague at first, starts the reading process and develops into the constantly self-revising impulse that guides selection, synthesis, and organization. The linguistic–experiential reservoir reflects the reader's cultural, social, and personal history. Past experience with language and with texts provides expectations. Other factors are the reader's present situation and interests. Perusing the unfolding text in the light of past syntactic and semantic experience, the reader seeks cues on which to base expectations about what is forthcoming. The text as a verbal pattern, we have seen, is part of what is being constructed. Possibilities open up concerning the general kind of meaning that may be developing, affecting choices in diction, syntax, and linguistic and literary conventions.

As the reader's eyes move along the page, the newly evoked symbolizations are tested for whether they can be fitted into the tentative meanings already constructed for the preceding portion of the text. Each additional choice will signal certain options and exclude others, so that even as the meaning evolves, the selecting, synthesizing impulse is itself constantly shaped and tested. If the marks on the page evoke elements that cannot be assimilated into the emerging synthesis, the guiding principle or framework is revised; if necessary, it is discarded and a complete rereading occurs. New tentative guidelines, new bases for a hypothetical structure, may then present themselves. Reader and text are involved in a complex, nonlinear, recursive, self-correcting transaction. The arousal and fulfillment—or frustration and revision—of expectations contribute to the construction of a cumulative meaning. From a to-and-fro interplay between reader, text, and context emerges a synthesis or organization, more or less coherent and complete. This meaning, this "evocation," is felt to correspond to the text.

Precisely because for experienced readers so much of the reading process is, or should be, automatic, aspects of the reading process tend to be described in impersonal, mechanistic terms. Psychologists are rightfully concerned with learning as much as possible about what goes on between the reader's first visual contact with the marks on the page and the completion of what is considered an interpretation of them. A number of different levels, systems, and strategies have been analytically designated, and research has been directed at clarifying their nature. These can be useful, but from a transactional point of view, it is important to recognize their potentialities and their limitations. A mechanistic analogy or metaphor lends itself especially to analyses of literal reading of simple texts. Results need to be cautiously interpreted. Recognizing the essential nature of both reader and text, the transactional theory requires an underlying metaphor of organic activity and reciprocity.

The optical studies of Adelbert Ames (1955) and the Ames–Cantril "transactional psychology" (Cantril & Livingston, 1963), which also derived its name from Dewey and Bentley's *Knowing and the Known* (1949), deserve first mention in this regard. These experiments demonstrated that perception depends much on the viewer's selection and organization of visual cues according to past experience, expectations, needs, and interests. The perception may be revised through continued transactions between the perceiver and the perceived object.

F.C. Bartlett's theory of *Remembering* (1932; which I regret having discovered even later than did his fellow scientists) and his term *schema* are often called on to explain psychological processes even broader than his special field. It is not clear, however, that those who so readily invoke his schema concept are heeding his fears about a narrow, static usage of the term. Rejecting the image of a warehouse of unchanging items as the metaphor for schemata, he emphasized rather "active, developing patterns"—"constituents of living, momentary settings belonging to the organism" (Bartlett, 1932, p. 201). His description of the "constructive character of remembering," his rejection of a simple mechanical linear process, and his concepts of the development and continuing revision of schemata all have parallels in the transactional theory of linguistic events. His recognition of the influence of both the interests of the individual and the social context on all levels of the process also seems decidedly transactional.

The Reader's Stance

The broad outline of the reading process sketched thus far requires further elaboration. An important distinction must be made between the operations that produce the meaning, say, of a scientific report and the operations that evoke a literary work of art. Neither contemporary reading theory nor literary theory has done justice to such readings, nor to the fact that they are to be understood as representing a continuum rather than an opposition. The tendency generally has been to assume that such a distinction depends entirely on the texts involved. The character of the "work" has been held to inhere entirely in the text. But we cannot look simply at the text and predict the nature of the work. We cannot assume, for instance, that a poem rather than an argument about fences will be evoked from the text of Frost's *Mending Wall* or that a novel rather than sociological facts about Victorian England will be evoked from Dickens's *Great Expectations*. Advertisements and newspaper reports have been read as poems. Each alternative represents a different kind of selective activity, a different kind of relationship, between the reader and the text.

Essential to any reading is the reader's adoption, conscious or unconscious, of what I have termed a *stance* guiding the "choosing activity" in the stream of consciousness. Recall that any linguistic event carries both public and private aspects. As the transaction with the printed text stirs up elements of the linguistic–experiential reservoir, the reader adopts a selective attitude or stance, bringing certain aspects into the center of attention and pushing others into the fringes of consciousness. A stance reflects the reader's purpose. The situation, the purpose, and the linguistic–experiential equipment of the reader, as well as the signs on the page, enter into the transaction and affect the extent to which public and private meanings and associations will be attended to.

The Efferent–Aesthetic Continuum

The reading event must fall somewhere in a continuum, determined by whether the reader adopts what I term a *predominantly aesthetic* stance or a *predominantly efferent* stance. A particular stance determines the proportion or mix of public and private elements of sense that fall within the scope of the reader's selective attention. Or, to recall Bates's metaphor, a stance results from the degree and scope of attention paid respectively to the tip and to the base of the iceberg. Such differences can be represented only by a continuum, which I term the *efferent–aesthetic continuum*.

The Efferent Stance

The term *efferent* (from the Latin *efferre*, to carry away) designates the kind of reading in which attention is centered predominantly on what is to be extracted and retained after the reading event. An extreme example is a man who has accidentally swallowed a poisonous liquid and is rapidly reading the label on the bottle to learn the antidote. Here, surely, we see an illustration of James's point about selective attention and our capacity to push into the periphery of awareness or ignore those elements that do not serve our present interests. The man's attention is focused on learning what is to be done as soon as the reading ends. He concentrates on what the words point to, ignoring anything other than their barest public referents, constructing as quickly as possible the directions for future action. These structured ideas are the evocation felt to correspond to the text.

Reading a newspaper, textbook, or legal brief would usually provide a similar, though less extreme, instance of the predominantly efferent stance. In efferent reading, then, we focus attention mainly on the public "tip of the iceberg" of sense. Meaning results from abstracting out and analytically structuring the ideas, information, directions, or conclusions to be retained, used, or acted on after the reading event.

The Aesthetic Stance

The predominantly aesthetic stance covers the other half of the continuum. In this kind of reading, the reader adopts an attitude of readiness to focus attention on what is being lived through during the reading event. The term *aesthetic* was chosen because its Greek source suggested perception through the senses, feelings, and intuitions. Welcomed into awareness are not only the public referents of the verbal signs but also the private part of the "iceberg" of meaning: the sensations, images, feelings, and ideas that are the residue of past psychological events involving those words and their referents. Attention may include the sounds and rhythms of the words themselves, heard in "the inner ear" as the signs are perceived.

The aesthetic reader pays attention to—savors—the qualities of the feelings, ideas, situations, scenes, personalities, and emotions that are called forth and participates in the tensions, conflicts, and resolutions of the images, ideas, and scenes as they unfold. The lived-through meaning is felt to correspond to the text. This meaning, shaped and experienced during the aesthetic transaction, constitutes "the literary work," the poem, story, or play. This "evocation," and not the text, is the object of the reader's "response" and "interpretation," both during and after the reading event.

Confusion about the matter of stance results from the entrenched habit of thinking of the *text* as efferent or aesthetic, expository or poetic, literary or nonliterary, and so on. Those who apply these terms to texts should realize that they actually are reporting their interpretation of the writer's intention as to what kind of reading the text should be given. The reader is free, however, to adopt either predominant stance toward any text. *Efferent* and *aesthetic* apply, then, to the writer's and the reader's selective attitude toward their own streams of consciousness during their respective linguistic events.

To recognize the essential nature of stance does not minimize the importance of the text in the transaction. Various verbal elements—metaphor, stylistic conventions or divergence from linguistic or semantic norms, even certain kinds of content—have been said to constitute the "poeticity" or "literariness" of a text. Such verbal elements, actually, do often serve as cues to the experienced reader to adopt an aesthetic stance. Yet it is possible to cite acknowledged literary works that lack one or all of these elements. Neither reading theorists nor literary theorists have given due credit to the fact that none of these or any other arrangements of words could make their "literary" or "poetic" contribution without the reader's prior shift of attention toward mainly the qualitative or experiential contents of consciousness, namely, the aesthetic stance.

The Continuum

The metaphorical nature of the term *the stream of consciousness* can be called on further to clarify the efferent–aesthetic continuum. We can image consciousness as a stream flowing through the darkness. Stance, then, can be represented as a mechanism lighting up—directing the attention to—different parts of the stream, selecting out objects that have floated to the surface in those areas and leaving the rest in shadow. Stance, in other words, provides the guiding orientation toward activating particular areas and elements of consciousness, that is, particular proportions of public and private aspects of meaning, leaving the rest at the dim periphery of attention. Some such play of attention over the contents of what emerges into consciousness must be involved in the reader's multifold choices from the linguistic–experiential reservoir.

Efferent and aesthetic reflect the two main ways of looking at the world, often summed up as "scientific" and "artistic." My redundant usage of "predominantly" aesthetic or efferent underlines rejection of the traditional, binary, either–or tendency to see them as in opposition. The efferent stance pays more attention to the cognitive, the referential, the factual, the analytic, the logical, the quantitative aspects of meaning. And the aesthetic stance pays more attention to the sensuous, the affective, the emotive, the qualitative. But nowhere can we find on the one hand the purely public and on the other hand the purely private. Both of these aspects of meaning are attended to in different proportions in any linguistic event. One of the earliest and most important steps in any reading event, therefore, is the selection of either a predominantly efferent or a predominantly aesthetic stance toward the transaction with a text. Figure 1 indicates different readings by the same reader of the same text at different points on the efferent–aesthetic continuum. Other readers would probably produce readings that fall at other points on the continuum.

Figure 1. The Efferent–Aesthetic Continuum

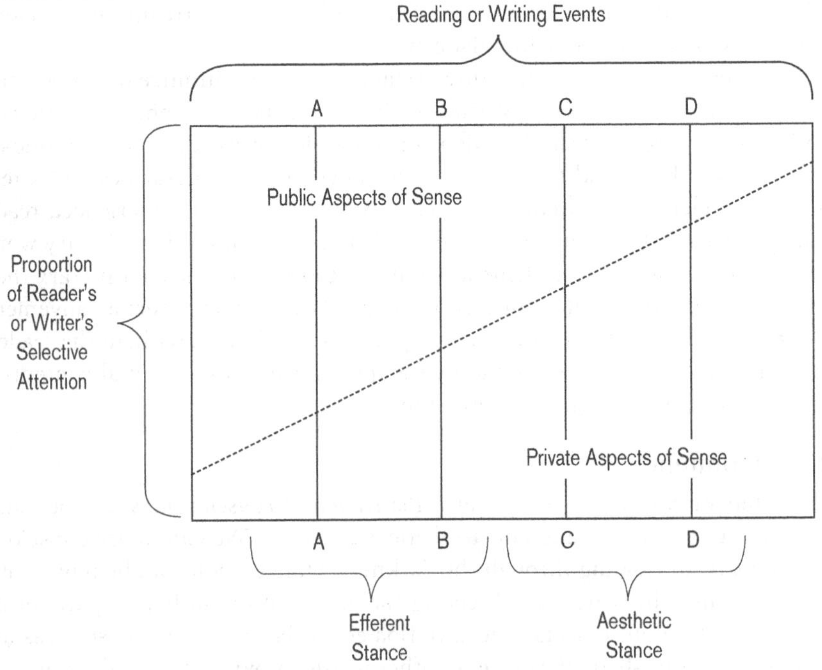

Any linguistic activity has both public (lexical, analytic, abstracting) and private (experiential, affective, associational) components. Stance is determined by the proportion of each component admitted into the scope of selective attention. The efferent stance draws mainly on the public aspect of sense; the aesthetic stance includes proportionally more of the experiential, private aspect.

Reading or writing events A and B fall into the efferent part of the continuum, with B admitting more private elements. Reading or writing events C and D both represent the aesthetic stance, with C according a higher proportion of attention to the public aspects of sense.

Although many readings may fall near the extremes, many others, perhaps most, may fall nearer the center of the continuum. Where both parts of the iceberg of meaning are more evenly balanced, confusion as to dominant stance is more likely and more counterproductive. It is possible to read efferently and assume one has evoked a poem, or to read aesthetically and assume one is arriving at logical conclusions to an argument.

Also, it is necessary to emphasize that a predominant stance does not rule out fluctuations. Within a particular aesthetic reading, attention may at times turn from the experiential synthesis to efferent analysis, as the reader recognizes some technical strategy or passes a critical judgment. Similarly, in an efferent reading, a general idea may be illustrated or reinforced by an aesthetically lived-through illustration or example. Despite the mix of private and public aspects of meaning in each stance, the two dominant stances are clearly distinguishable. No two readings, even by the same person, are identical. Still, someone else can read a text efferently and paraphrase it for us in such a way as to satisfy our efferent purpose. But no one else can read aesthetically—that is, experience the evocation of—a literary work of art for us.

Because each reading is an event in particular circumstances, the same text may be read either efferently or aesthetically. The experienced reader usually approaches a text alert to cues offered by the text and, unless another purpose intervenes, automatically adopts the appropriate predominant stance. Sometimes the title suffices as a cue. Probably one of the most obvious cues is the arrangement of broad margins and uneven lines that signals that the reader should adopt the aesthetic stance and undertake to make a poem. The opening lines of any text are especially important from this point of view, for their signaling of tone, attitude, and conventional indications of stance to be adopted.

Of course, the reader may overlook or misconstrue the cues, or they may be confusing. And the reader's own purpose, or schooling that indoctrinates the same undifferentiated approach to all texts, may dictate a different stance from the one the writer intended. For example, the student reading *A Tale of Two Cities* who knows that there will be a test on facts about characters and plot may be led to adopt a predominantly efferent stance, screening out all but the factual data. Similarly, readings of an article on zoology could range from analytic abstracting of factual content to an aesthetic savoring of the ordered structure of ideas, the rhythm of the sentences, and the images of animal life brought into consciousness.

Evocation, Response, Interpretation

The tendency to reify words is frequently represented by discussions centering on a title, say, *Invisible Man* or *The Bill of Rights*. These titles may refer to the text, as we have been using the word, that is, to the pattern of inscribed signs to be found in physical written or printed form. More often, however, the intended reference is to "the work." But the work—ideas and experiences linked with the text—can be found only in individual readers' reflections on the reading event, the evocation and responses to it during and after the reading event.

Evocation

Thus far, we have focused on the aspects of the reading process centered on organizing a structure of elements of consciousness construed as the meaning of the text. I term this *the evocation* to cover both efferent and aesthetic transactions. The evocation, the work, is not a physical "object," but, given another sense of that word, the evocation can be an object of thought.

The Second Stream of Response

We must recognize during the reading event a concurrent stream of reactions to, and transactions with, the emerging evocation. Even as we are generating the evocation, we are reacting to it; this may in turn affect our choices as we proceed with the reading. Such responses may be momentary, peripheral, or felt simply as a general state, for example, an ambiance of acceptance or perhaps of confirmation of ideas and attitudes brought to the reading. Sometimes something unexpected or contrary to prior knowledge or assumptions may trigger conscious reflection. Something not prepared for by the preceding organization of elements may cause a rereading. The attention may shift from the evocation to the formal or technical traits of the text. The range of potential reactions and the gamut of degrees of intensity and articulateness depend on the interplay among the character of the signs on the page (the text), what the individual reader brings to it, and the circumstances of the transaction.

The various strands of response, especially in the middle ranges of the efferent–aesthetic continuum, are sometimes simultaneous, interacting, and interwoven. They may seem actually woven into the texture of the evocation itself. Hence, one of the problems of critical reading is differentiation of the evocation corresponding to the text from the concurrent responses, which may be projections from the reader's a priori assumptions. Drawing the line between them is easier in theory than in the practice of any actual reading. The reader needs to learn to handle such elements of the reading experience. The problem takes on different forms in efferent and aesthetic reading.

Expressed Response

"Response" to the evocation often is designed as subsequent to the reading event. Actually, the basis is laid during the reading, in the concurrent second stream of reactions. The reader may recapture the general effect of this after the event and may seek to express it and to recall what in the evocation led to the response. Reflection on "the meaning" of even a simple text involves the recall, the reactivation of some aspects of the process carried on during the reading. "Interpretation" tends to be a continuation of this effort to clarify the evocation.

The account of the reading process thus far has indicated an organizing, synthesizing activity, the creation of tentative meanings, and their modification as new elements enter into the focus of attention. In some instances, the reader at some point simply registers a sense of having completed a sequential activity and moves on to other concerns. Sometimes a sense of the whole structure crystallizes by the close of the reading.

Expressed Interpretation

Actually, the process of interpretation that includes arriving at a sense of the whole has not been given enough attention in theories of reading, perhaps because reading research has typically dealt with simple reading events. For the term *interpret*, dictionaries list, among others, several relevant meanings. One is "to set forth the meaning of; to elucidate, to explain." Another is "to construe, or understand in a particular way." A third is "to bring out the meaning of by performance (as in music)." These tend to reflect the traditional notion of "the meaning" as inherent in the text.

The transactional theory requires that we draw on all three of these usages to cover the way in which the term should be applied to the reading process. The evocation of meaning in transaction with a text is indeed interpretation in the sense of performance, and transactional theory merges this with the idea of interpretation as individual construal. The evocation then becomes the object of interpretation in the sense of elucidating or explaining. The expressed interpretation draws on all these aspects of the total transaction.

Interpretation can be understood as the effort to report, analyze, and explain the evocation. The reader recalls the sensed, felt, thought evocation while at the same time applying some frame of reference or method of abstracting in order to characterize it, to find the assumptions or organizing ideas that relate the parts to the whole. The second stream of reactions will be recalled, and the reasons for them sought, in the evoked work or in prior assumptions and knowledge. The evocation and the concurrent streams of reaction may be related through stressing, for example, the logic of the structure of ideas in an efferent evocation or the assumptions about people or society underlying the lived-through experience of the aesthetic reading.

Usually, interpretation is expressed in the efferent mode, stressing underlying general ideas that link the signs of the text. Interpretation can take an aesthetic form, however, such as a poem, a painting, music, dramatization, or dance.

Interpretation brings with it the question of whether the reader has produced a meaning that is consonant with the author's probable intention. Here we find ourselves moving from the reader–text transaction to the relationship between author and reader. The process that produces the text will be considered before dealing with such matters as communication, validity of interpretation, and the implications of the transactional theory for teaching and research.

The Writing Process

The Writing Transaction

Writers facing a blank page, like readers approaching a text, have only their individual linguistic capital to draw on. For the writer, too, the residue of past experiences of language in particular situations provides the material from which the text will be constructed. As with the reader, any new meanings are restructurings or extensions of the stock of experiences the writer brings to the task. There is a continuing to-and-fro or transactional process as the writer looks at the page and adds to the text in the light of what has been written thus far.

An important difference between readers and writers should not be minimized, however. In the triadic sign–object–interpretant relationship, the reader has the physical pattern of signs to which to relate the symbolizations. The writer facing a blank page may start with only an organismic state, vague feelings and ideas that require further triadic definition before a symbolic configuration—a verbal text—can take shape.

Writing is always an event in time, occurring at a particular moment in the writer's biography, in particular circumstances, under particular external as well as internal pressures. In short, the writer is always transacting with a personal, social, and cultural environment. Thus, the writing process must be seen as always embodying both personal and social, or individual and environmental, factors.

Given the Peircean triadic view of the verbal symbol, the more accessible the fund of organismically linked words and referents, the more fluent the writing. This helps us place in perspective an activity such as free writing. Instead of treating it as a prescriptive "stage" of the writing process, as some seem to do, it should be seen as a technique for tapping the linguistic reservoir without being hampered by anxieties about acceptability of subject, sequence, or mechanics. Especially for those inhibited by unfortunate past writing experiences, this can be liberating, a warm-up exercise for starting the juices flowing, so to speak, and permitting elements of the experiential stream, verbal components of memory, and present concerns to rise to consciousness. The essential point is that the individual linguistic reservoir must be activated.

No matter how free and uninhibited the writing may be, the stream of images, ideas, memories, and words is not entirely random; William James reminds us that the "choosing activity" of selective attention operates to some degree. Like the reader, the writer needs to bring the selective process actively into play, to move toward a sense of some tentative focus for choice and synthesis (Emig, 1983).

This directedness will be fostered by the writer's awareness of the transactional situation: the context that initiates the need to write and the potential reader or readers to whom the text will presumably be addressed. Often in trial-and-error fashion, and through various freely flowing drafts, the writer's sensitivity to such factors translates itself into an increasingly clear impulse that guides selective attention and integration. For the experienced writer, the habit of such awareness, monitoring the multifold decisions or choices that make up the writing event, is more important than any explicit preliminary statement of goals or purpose.

The Writer's Stance

The concept of stance presented earlier in relation to reading is equally important for writing. A major aspect of the delimitation of purpose in writing is the adoption of a stance that falls at some point in the efferent–aesthetic continuum. The attitude toward what is activated in the linguistic–experiential reservoir manifests itself in the range and character of the verbal symbols that will "come to mind," and to which the writer will apply selective attention. The dominant stance determines the proportion of public and private aspects of sense that will be included in the scope of the writer's attention (see Figure 1).

In actual life, the selection of a predominant stance is not arbitrary but is a function of the circumstances, the writer's motives, the subject, and the relation between writer and prospective reader or readers. For example, someone who had been involved in an automobile collision would need to adopt very different stances in writing an account of the event for an insurance company and in describing it in a letter to a friend. The first would activate an efferent selective process, bringing into the center of consciousness and onto the page the public aspects, such as statements that could be verified by witnesses or by investigation of the terrain. In the letter to the friend, the purpose would be to share an experience. An aesthetic stance would bring within the scope of the writer's attention the same basic facts, together with feelings, sensations, tensions, images, and sounds lived through during this brush with death. The selective process would favor words that matched the writer's inner sense of the felt event and that also would activate in the prospective reader symbolic linkages evoking a similar experience. Given different purposes, other accounts might fall at other points of the efferent–aesthetic continuum.

Purpose or intention should emerge from, or be capable of constructively engaging, the writer's actual experiential and linguistic resources. Past experience need not be the limit of the writer's scope, but the writer faced with a blank page needs "live" ideas—that is, ideas having a strongly energizing linkage with the linguistic–experiential reservoir. Purposes or ideas that lack the capacity to connect with the writer's funded experience and present concerns cannot fully activate the linguistic reservoir and provide an impetus to thinking and writing.

A personally grounded purpose develops and impels movement forward. Live ideas growing out of situations, activities, discussions, problems, or needs provide the basis for an actively selective and synthesizing process of making meaning. The quickened fund of images, ideas, emotions, attitudes, and tendencies to act offers the means of making new connections, for discovering new facets of the world of objects and events, in short, for thinking and writing creatively.

Writing About Texts

When a reader describes, responds to, or interprets a work—that is, speaks or writes about a transaction with a text—a new text is being produced. The implications of this fact in terms of process should be more fully understood. When the reader becomes a writer about a work, the starting point is no longer the physical text, the marks on the page, but the meaning or the state of mind felt to correspond to that text. The reader may return to the original text to recapture how it entered into the transaction but must "find words" for explaining the evocation and the interpretation.

The reader-turned-writer must once again face the problem of choice of stance. In general, the choice seems to be the efferent stance. The purpose is mainly to explain, analyze, summarize, and categorize the evocation. This is usually true even when the reading has been predominantly aesthetic and a literary work of art is being discussed. However, the aesthetic stance might be adopted in order to communicate an experience expressing the response or the interpretation. An efferent reading of, for example, the U.S. Declaration of Independence might lead to a poem or a story. An aesthetic reading of the text of a poem might also lead, not to an efferently written critical essay, but to another poem, a painting, or a musical composition.

The translator of a poem is a clear example of the reader-turned-writer, being first a reader who evokes an experience through a transaction in one language and then a writer who seeks to express that experience through a writing transaction in another language. The experiential qualities generated in a transaction with one language must now be communicated to—evoked by—readers who have a different linguistic–experiential reservoir, acquired in a different culture.

Authorial Reading

Thus far, we have been developing parallels between the ways in which readers and writers select and synthesize elements from the personal linguistic reservoir, adopt stances that guide selective attention, and build a developing selective purpose. Emphasis has fallen mainly on similarities in composing structures of meaning related to texts. If readers are in that sense also writers, it is equally—and perhaps more obviously—true that writers must also be readers. At this point, however, some differences within the parallelisms begin to appear.

The writer, it is generally recognized, is the first reader of the text. Note an obvious, though neglected, difference: While readers transact with a writer's finished text, writers first read the text as it is being inscribed. Because both reading and writing are recursive processes carried on over a period of time, their very real similarities have masked a basic difference. The writer will often reread the total finished text, but, perhaps more important, the writer first reads and carries on a spiral, transactional relationship with the very text emerging on the page. This is a different kind of reading. It is authorial—a writer's reading. It should be seen as an integral part of the composing process. In fact, it is necessary to see that writing, or composing, a text involves *two* kinds of authorial reading, which I term *expression oriented* and *reception oriented.*

Expression-Oriented Authorial Reading

As a reader's eyes move along a printed text, the reader develops an organizing principle or framework. The newly evoked symbolizations are tested for whether they can be fitted into the tentative meanings already constructed for the preceding portion of the text. If the new signs create a problem, this may lead to a revision of the framework or even to a complete rereading of the text and restructuring of the attributed meaning.

The writer, like readers of another's text, peruses the succession of verbal signs being inscribed on the page to see whether the new words fit the preceding text. But this is a different, expression-oriented reading, which should be seen as an integral part of the composing process. As the new words appear on the page, they must be tested, not simply for how they make sense with the preceding text but also against an inner gauge—the intention, or purpose. The emerging meaning, even if it makes sense, must be judged as to whether it serves or hinders the purpose, however nebulous and inarticulate, that is the motive power in the writing. Expression-oriented authorial reading leads to revision even during the earlier phases of the writing process.

The Inner Gauge

Most writers will recall a situation that may illustrate the operation of an "inner gauge." A word comes to mind or flows from the pen and, even if it makes sense, is felt not to be right. One word after another may be brought into consciousness and still not satisfy. Sometimes the writer understands what is wrong with the word on the page—perhaps that it is ambiguous or does not suit the tone. But often the writer cannot articulate the reason for dissatisfaction. The tension simply disappears when "the right word" presents itself. When it does, a match between inner state and verbal sign has happened.

Such an episode manifests the process of testing against an inner touchstone. The French writer Gustave Flaubert with his search for *le mot juste*, the exact word, offers the analogy of the violinist who tries to make his fingers "reproduce precisely those sounds of which he has the inward sense" (1926, pp. 11, 47). The inner gauge may be an organic state, a mood, an idea, perhaps even a consciously constituted set of guidelines.

For the experienced writer, this kind of completely inner-oriented reading, which is integral to the composing process, depends on and nourishes an increasingly clear though often tacit sense of purpose, whether efferent or aesthetic. The writer tries to satisfy a personal conception while also refining it. Such transactional reading and revision can go on throughout the writing event. There are indeed times when this is the *only* reading component—when one writes for oneself alone, to express or record an experience in a diary or journal, or perhaps to analyze a situation or the pros and cons of a decision.

Reception-Oriented Authorial Reading

Usually, however, writing is felt to be part of a potential transaction with other readers. At some point, the writer dissociates from the text and reads it through the eyes of potential readers; the writer tries to judge the meaning *they* would make in transaction with that pattern of signs. But the writer does not simply adopt the "eyes" of the potential reader. Again, a twofold operation is involved. The emerging text is read to sense what others might make of it. But this hypothetical interpretation must also be checked against the writer's own inner sense of purpose.

The tendency has been to focus on writing with an eye on the anticipated reader. My concern is to show the interplay between the two kinds of authorial reading and the need, consciously or automatically, to decide the degree of emphasis on one or the other. The problem always is to find verbal signs likely to activate linkages in prospective readers' linguistic reservoirs matching those of the writer. A poet may be faced with the choice between a personally savored exotic metaphor and one more likely to be within the experience of prospective readers. Or a science writer may have to decide whether highly detailed precision may be too complex for the general reader.

Writers must already have some hold on the first, expression-oriented kind of inner awareness if they are to benefit from the second reading-through-the-eyes-of-others. The first becomes a criterion for the second. The experienced writer will probably engage in a synthesis, or rapid alternation, of the two kinds of authorial reading to guide the selective attention that filters out the verbal elements coming to mind. When communication is the aim, revision should be based on such double criteria in the rereading of the text.

Communication Between Author and Readers

The reader's to-and-fro process of building an interpretation becomes a form of transaction with an author persona sensed through and behind the text. The implied relationship is sometimes even termed "a contract" with the author. The closer their linguistic–experiential equipment, the more likely the reader's interpretation will fulfill the writer's intention. Sharing at least versions of the same language is so basic that it often is simply assumed. Other positive factors affecting communication are contemporary membership in the same social and cultural group, the same educational level, and membership in the same discourse community, such as academic, legal, athletic, literary, scientific, or theological. Given such similarities, the reader is more likely to bring to the text the prior knowledge, acquaintance with linguistic and literary conventions, and assumptions about social situations required for understanding implications or allusions and noting nuances of tone and thought.

Yet, because each individual's experience is unique, differences due to social, ethnic, educational, and personal factors exist, even with contemporaries. The reading of works written in another period bespeaks an inevitable difference in linguistic, social, or cultural context. Here, especially, readers may agree on interpretations without necessarily assuming that their evocations from the text fit the author's intention (Rosenblatt, 1978, p. 109ff).

Differences as to the author's intention often lead to consultation of extratextual sources. For works of the past especially, scholars call on systematic methods of philological, biographical, and historical research to discover the personal, social, and literary forces that shaped the writer's intention. The contemporary reception of the work also provides clues. Such evidence, even if it includes an author's stated intention, still yields hypothetical results and cannot dictate our interpretation. We must still read the text to decide whether it supports the hypothetical intention. The reader is constantly faced with the responsibility of deciding whether an interpretation is acceptable. The question of validity of interpretation must be faced before considering implications for teaching and research.

Validity of Interpretation

The problem of validity of interpretation has not received much attention in reading theory or educational methodology. Despite the extraordinary extent of the reliance on testing in our schools, there seems to be little interest in clarifying the criteria that enter into evaluation of "comprehension." Actual practice in the teaching of reading and in the instruments for testing of reading ability has evidently been tacitly based on, or at least has indoctrinated, the traditional assumption that there is a single determinate "correct" meaning attributable to each text. The stance factor, the efferent–aesthetic continuum, has especially been neglected; operationally, the emphasis has been on the efferent, even when "literature" was involved.

The polysemous character of language invalidates any simplistic approach to meaning, creating the problem of the relationship between the reader's interpretation and the author's intention. The impossibility of finding a single absolute meaning for a text or of expecting any interpretation absolutely to reflect the writer's intention is becoming generally recognized by contemporary theorists. "Intention" itself is not absolutely definable or delimitable even by the writer. The word *absolute*, the notion of a single "correct" meaning inherent "in" the text, is the stumbling block. The same text takes on different meanings in transactions with different readers or even with the same reader in different contexts or times.

Warranted Assertibility

The problem of the validity of any interpretation is part of the broader philosophical problem cited at the beginning of this chapter. Perception of the world is always through the medium of individual human beings transacting with their worlds. In recent decades, some literary theorists, deriving their arguments from poststructuralist Continental writers and taking a Saussurean view of language as an autonomous system, have arrived at an extreme relativist position. They have developed a reading method that assumes all texts can be "deconstructed" to reveal inner contradictions. Moreover, the language system and literary conventions are said to completely dominate author and reader, and agreement concerning interpretation simply reflects the particular "interpretive community" in which we find ourselves (Fish, 1980; Rosenblatt, 1991).

Such extreme relativism is not, however, a necessary conclusion from the premise that absolutely determinate meaning is impossible. By agreeing on criteria of evaluation of interpretations, we can accept the possibility of alternative interpretations yet decide that some are more acceptable than others.

John Dewey, accepting the nonfoundationalist epistemological premises and foregoing the quest for absolutes, solved the scientists' problem by his idea of "warranted assertibility" as the end of controlled inquiry (1938, pp. 9, 345). Given shared criteria concerning methods of investigation and kinds of evidence, there can be agreement concerning the decision as to what is a sound interpretation of the evidence, or "a warranted assertion." This is not set forth as permanent, absolute truth, but leaves open the possibility that alternative explanations for the same facts may be found, that new evidence may be discovered, or that different criteria or paradigms may be developed.

Although Dewey used primarily scientific interpretation or knowledge of the world based on scientific methods to illustrate warranted assertibility, he saw the concept as encompassing the arts and all human concerns. It can be applied to the problem of all linguistic interpretation (Rosenblatt, 1978, Chap. 7; 1983, p. 151ff). Given a shared cultural milieu and shared criteria of validity of interpretation, we can, without claiming to have the single "correct" meaning of a text, agree on an interpretation. Especially in aesthetic reading, we may find that alternative interpretations meet our minimum criteria, and we can still be free to consider some interpretations superior to others.

In contrast to the notion of readers locked into a narrow "interpretive community," the emphasis on making underlying or tacit criteria explicit provides the basis not only for agreement but also for understanding tacit sources of disagreement. This creates the possibility of change in interpretation, acceptance of alternative sets of criteria, or revision of criteria. Such self-awareness on the part of readers can foster communication across social, cultural, and historical differences between author and readers, as well as among readers (Rosenblatt, 1983).

In short, the concept of warranted assertibility, or shared criteria of validity of interpretation in a particular social context, recognizes that some readings may satisfy the criteria more fully than others. Basic criteria might be (1) that the context and purpose of the reading event, or the total transaction, be considered; (2) that the interpretation not be contradicted by, or not fail to cover, the full text, the signs on the page; and (3) that the interpretation not project meanings which cannot be related to signs on the page. Beyond these items arise criteria for interpretation and evaluation growing out of the whole structure of shared cultural, social, linguistic, and rhetorical assumptions.

Thus, we can be open to alternative readings of the text of *Hamlet*, but we also can consider some readings as superior to others according to certain explicit criteria, for example, complexity of intellectual and affective elements and nature of implicit value system. Such considerations permit comparison and "negotiation" among different readers of the same text as well as clarification of differences in assumptions concerning what constitutes a valid interpretation (Rosenblatt, 1978, 1983). On the efferent side of the continuum, current discussions of alternative criteria for interpretation of the U.S. Constitution provide another complex example.

Criteria for the Efferent–Aesthetic Continuum

Precisely because, as Figure 1 indicates, both public and private elements are present in all reading, the criteria of validity of interpretation differ for readings at various points on the efferent–aesthetic continuum. Because the predominantly efferent interpretation must be publicly verifiable or justifiable, the criteria of validity rest primarily on the public, referential aspects of meaning and require that any affective and associational aspects not dominate. The criteria for the predominantly aesthetic reading call for attention to the referential, cognitive aspects, but only as they are interwoven and colored by the private, affective, or experiential aspects generated by the author's patterns of signs. Especially in the middle ranges of the efferent–aesthetic continuum, it becomes important for writers to provide clear indications as to stance and for readers to be sensitive to the writer's purpose and the need to apply relevant criteria.

"Literary" Aspects of Efferent Reading

In recent decades, in one scientific field after another, the opposition between scientific and "literary" writing has been found to be illusory. Writers in the natural and social sciences have become aware of the extent to which they engage in semantic and syntactic practices that have usually been considered "literary" and that they, too, have been using narrative, metaphor, and other rhetorical devices. Examples are the importance of metaphor in writings about economics or the idea that the historian writes narrative and that he can never be completely objective in selecting his facts. Sensitivity to sexist and racist tropes has increased awareness of the extent to which metaphor permeates all kinds of texts and, indeed, all language. Sometimes the efferent–aesthetic distinction seems to be completely erased (for example, the historian is sometimes said to write "fiction").

It becomes necessary to recall that the stance reflecting the aesthetic or efferent purpose, not the syntactic and semantic devices alone, determines the appropriate criteria. For example, in a treatise on economics or a history of the frontier, the criteria of validity of interpretation appropriate to their disciplines, which involve primarily verifiability and logic, would still apply. When an economist remarks that "the scientists had better devise good metaphors and tell good stories" (McCloskey, 1985), the concept of a dominant stance becomes all the more essential. The criteria for "good" should be not only how vivid and appealing the stories are but also how they gibe with logic and facts and what value systems are implied.

The relevance of the efferent–aesthetic continuum (Figure 1) may be illustrated by the example of metaphor: The scientist speaks of the "wave" theory of light, and we focus on the technical concept at the extreme efferent end of the continuum. Shakespeare writes, "Like as the wave makes toward the pebbled shore / So do our minutes hasten to their end," and our aesthetic attention to the feeling of inevitability of the succeeding waves enhances the feeling of the inevitability of the passage of time in our lives. A political analysis suggested surrendering to the inevitability of fascism by calling it "the wave of the future.... There is no fighting it" (Lindbergh, 1940, p. 934). Despite the vividness of the metaphor, efferent attention should have remained dominant, applying the efferent criterion. Did logic and factual evidence support the persuasive appeal?

Implications for Teaching

Reading and Writing: Parallelisms and Differences

Parallelisms between reading and writing processes have raised questions concerning their connections, especially in the classroom. The reading and writing processes both overlap and differ. Both reader and writer engage in constituting symbolic structures of meaning in a to-and-fro, spiral transaction with the text. They follow similar patterns of thinking and call on similar linguistic habits. Both processes depend on the individual's past experiences with language in particular life situations. Both reader and writer therefore are drawing on past linkages of signs, signifiers, and organic states in order to create new symbolizations, new linkages, and new organic states. Both reader and writer develop a framework, principle, or purpose, however nebulous or explicit, that guides the selective attention and the synthesizing, organizing activities that constitute meaning. Moreover, every reading and writing act can be understood as falling somewhere on the efferent–aesthetic continuum and as being predominantly efferent or aesthetic.

The parallels should not mask the basic differences—the transaction that starts with a text produced by someone else is not the same as a transaction that starts with the individual facing a blank page. To an observer, two people perusing a typed page may seem to be doing the same thing (namely, "reading"). But if one of them is in the process of writing that text, different activities will be going on. The writer will be engaged in either expression-oriented or reception-oriented authorial reading. Moreover, because both reading and writing are rooted in mutually conditioning transactions between individuals and their particular environments, a person may have very different experiences with the two activities, may differ in attitudes toward them, and may be more proficient in one or the other. Writing and reading are sufficiently different to defeat the assumption that they are mirror images: The reader does not simply reenact the author's process. Hence, it cannot be assumed that the teaching of one activity automatically improves the student's competence in the other.

Still, the parallels in the reading and writing processes described above and the nature of the transaction between author and reader make it reasonable to expect that the teaching of one can affect the student's operations in the other. Reading, essential to anyone for intellectual and emotional enrichment, provides the writer with a sense of the potentialities of language. Writing deepens the reader's understanding of the importance of paying attention to diction, syntactic positions, emphasis, imagery, and conventions of genre. The fact that the sign–interpretant–object triad is, as Peirce said, dependent on habit indicates an even more important level of influence. Cross-fertilization will result from reinforcement of linguistic habits and thinking patterns resulting from shared transactional processes of purposive selective attention and synthesis. How fruitful the interplay between the individual student's writing and reading will be depends largely on the nature of the teaching and the educational context.

The Total Context

Here we return to our basic concept that human beings are always in transaction and in a reciprocal relationship with an environment, a context, a total situation. The classroom environment, or the atmosphere created by the teacher and students transacting with one another and the school setting, broadens out to include the whole institutional, social, and cultural context. These aspects of the transaction are crucial in thinking about education and especially the "literacy problem." Because each individual's linguistic–experiential reservoir is the residue of past transactions with the environment, such factors condition the sense of possibilities, or the potential organizing frameworks or schema and the knowledge and assumptions about the world, society, human nature, that each brings to the transactions. Socioeconomic and ethnic factors, for example, influence patterns of behavior, ways of carrying out tasks, even understanding of such concepts as "story" (Heath, 1983). Such elements also affect the individual's attitude toward self, toward the reading or writing activity, and toward the purpose for which it is being carried on.[3]

The transactional concept of the text always in relation either to author or reader in specific situations makes it untenable to treat the text as an isolated entity or to overemphasize either author or reader. Recognizing that language is not a self-contained system or static code on the one hand avoids the traditional obsession with the product—with skills, techniques, and conventions, essential though they are—and, on the other, prevents a pendulum swing to overemphasis on process or on the personal aspects.

Treatment of either reading or writing as a dissociated set of skills (though both require skills) or as primarily the acquisition of codes and conventions (though both involve them) inhibits sensitivity to the organic linkages of verbal signs and their objects. Manipulating syntactic units without a sense of a context that connects them into a meaningful relationship may in the long run be counterproductive.

Nor can the transactional view of the reading and writing processes be turned into a set of stages to be rigidly followed. The writer's drafts and final texts—or the reader's tentative interpretations, final evocation, and reflections—should be viewed as stopping points in a journey, as the outward and visible signs of a continuing process in the passage from one point to the other. A "good" product, whether a well-written paper or a sound textual interpretation, should not be an end in itself—a terminus—but should be the result of a process that builds the strengths for further journeys or, to change the metaphor, for further growth. "Product" and "process" become interlocking concerns in nurturing growth.

Hence, the teaching of reading and writing at any developmental level should have as its first concern the creation of environments and activities in which students are motivated and encouraged to draw on their own resources to make "live" meanings. With this as the fundamental criterion, emphasis falls on strengthening the basic processes that we have seen to be shared by reading and writing. The teaching of one can then reinforce linguistic habits and semantic approaches useful in the other. Such teaching, concerned with the ability of the individual to generate meaning, will permit constructive cross-fertilization of the reading and writing (and speech) processes.

Enriching the individual's linguistic–experiential reservoir becomes an underlying educational aim broader than the particular concern with either reading or writing. Especially in the early years, the linkage between verbal sign and experiential base is essential. The danger is that many current teaching practices may counteract the very processes presumably being taught. The organization of instruction, the atmosphere in the classroom, the kinds of questions asked, the ways of phrasing assignments, and the types of tests administered should be scrutinized from this point of view.

The importance of a sense of purpose, of a guiding principle of selection and organization in both writing and reading, is being increasingly recognized. The creation of contexts that permit purposive writing and reading can enable the student to build on past experience of life and language, to adopt the appropriate stance for selective attention, and to develop inner gauges or frameworks for choice and synthesis that produce new structures of live meaning.

Collaborative Interchange

In a favorable educational environment, speech is a vital ingredient of transactional pedagogy. Its importance in the individual's acquisition of a linguistic–experiential capital is clear. It can be an extremely important medium in the classroom. Dialogue between teacher and students and interchange among students can foster growth and cross-fertilization in both the reading and writing processes. Such discussion can help students develop insights concerning transactions with texts as well as metalinguistic understanding of skills and conventions in meaningful contexts.

Students' achievement of insight into their own reading and writing processes can be seen as the long-term justification for various curricular and teaching strategies. For example, writers at all levels can be helped to understand their transactional relationship to their readers by peer reading and discussion of texts. Their fellow students' questions, varied interpretations, and misunderstandings dramatize the necessity of the writer's providing verbal signs that will help readers gain required facts, share relevant sensations or attitudes, or make logical transitions. Such insights make possible the second, reader-oriented authorial reading.

Similarly, group interchange about readers' evocations from texts, whether of their peers or adult authors, can in general be a powerful means of stimulating growth in reading ability and critical acumen. Readers become aware of the need to pay attention to the author's words in order to avoid preconceptions and misinterpretations. When students share responses to transactions with the same text, they can learn how their evocations from the same signs differ, can return to the text to discover their own habits of selection and synthesis, and can become aware of, and critical of, their own processes as readers. Interchange about the problems of interpretation that a particular group of readers encounters and a collaborative movement toward self-critical interpretation of the text can lead to the development of critical concepts and interpretive criteria. Such metalinguistic awareness is valuable to students as both readers and writers.

The teacher in such a classroom is no longer simply a conveyor of ready-made teaching materials and recorder of results of ready-made tests or a dispenser of ready-made interpretations. Teaching becomes constructive, facilitating interchange, helping students make their spontaneous responses the basis for raising questions and growing in the ability to handle increasingly complex reading transactions (Rosenblatt, 1983).[4]

The Student's Efferent–Aesthetic Repertory

The efferent–aesthetic continuum, or the two basic ways of looking at the world, should be part of the student's repertory from the earliest years. Because both stances involve cognitive and affective as well as public and private elements, students need to learn to differentiate the circumstances that call for one or the other stance. Unfortunately, much current practice is counterproductive, either failing to encourage a definite stance or implicitly requiring an inappropriate one. Favorite illustrations are the third-grade workbook that prefaced its first poem with the question "What facts does this poem teach you?," and the boy who complained that he wanted information about dinosaurs, but his teacher only gave him "storybooks." Small wonder that graduates of our schools (and colleges) often read poems and novels efferently or respond to political statements and advertisements with an aesthetic stance.

Despite the overemphasis on the efferent in our schools, failure to understand the matter of the public–private "mix" has prevented successful teaching even of efferent reading and writing. Teaching practices and curricula, from the very beginning, should include both efferent and aesthetic linguistic activity and should build a sense of the different purposes involved. Instruction should foster the habits of selective attention and synthesis that draw on relevant elements in the semantic reservoir and should nourish the ability to handle the mix of private and public aspects appropriate to a particular transaction.

Especially in the early years, this should be done largely indirectly, through, for example, choice of texts, contexts for generating writing and reading, or implications concerning stance in the questions asked. In this way, texts can serve dynamically as sources from which to assimilate a sense of the potentialities of the English sentence and an awareness of strategies for organizing meaning and expressing feeling. Emphasis on analysis of the evocations, or terminology for categorizing and describing them have no value if they overshadow or substitute for the evoked work. Such activities acquire meaning and value when, for example, they answer a writer's own problems in expression or explain for a reader the role of the author's verbal strategies in producing a certain felt response.

The developmental sequence suggested here is especially important in aesthetic reading. Much teaching of poetry at every level, including high school and college, at present takes on a continuously repeated remedial character because of the continued confusion about stance through emphasis on efferent analysis of the "literary" work. Students need to be helped to have unimpeded aesthetic experiences. Very young children's delight in the sound and rhythms of words, their interest in stories, and their ability to move easily from verbal to other modes of expression too often fade. They need to be helped to hold on to the experiential aspect. When this can be taken for granted, efferent, analytical discussions of form or background will not be substitutes for the literary work but become a means of enhancing it. Discussion then can become the basis for assimilating criteria of sound interpretation and evaluation appropriate to the various points on the continuum and to the student's developmental status.

Implications for Research

Research based on the transactional model has a long history (Applebee, 1974; Farrell & Squire, 1990). Until fairly recently, it has generated research mainly by those concerned with the teaching of literature in high schools and colleges, rather than by those concerned with reading per se in the elementary school (Beach & Hynds, 1990; Flood et al., 1991; Purves & Beach, 1972). It is not possible here to survey this already considerable body of research, much of it exploring aspects of response to literature; nor does space allow discussion of recent volumes dealing with applications of transactional theory in elementary school, high school, and college (Clifford, 1991; Cox & Many, 1992; Hungerford, Holland, & Ernst, 1993; Karolides, 1992). I shall instead suggest some general considerations concerning research topics and theoretical and methodological pitfalls.

The transactional model of reading, writing, and teaching that has been presented constitutes, in a sense, a body of hypotheses to be investigated. The shift it represents from the Cartesian to the post-Einsteinian paradigm calls for removal of the limitations on research imposed by the dominance of positivistic behaviorism. Instead of mainly treating reading as a compendium of separate skills or as an isolated autonomous activity, research on any aspect should center on the human being speaking, writing, reading, and continuously transacting with a specific environment in its broadening circles of context. And as Bartlett (1932) reminds us, any secondary theoretical frameworks, such as schemata or strategies, are not stable entities but configurations in a dynamic, changing process. Although the focus here will be on reading research, the interrelationship among the linguistic modes, especially reading and writing, broadens the potential scope of problems mentioned.

The view of language as a dynamic system of meaning in which the affective and the cognitive unite raises questions about the emphasis of past research. Researchers' preoccupation with the efferent is exemplified by their focus on Piaget's work on the child's development of mathematical and logical concepts and the continuing neglect of the affective by behaviorist, cognitive, and artificial intelligence psychologists. This is slowly being counterbalanced by growing interest in the affective and the qualitative (e.g., Deese, 1973; Eisner & Peshkin, 1990; Izard, 1977). We need to understand more fully the child's growth in capacity for selective attention to, and synthesis of, the various components of meaning.

Research in reading should draw on a number of interrelated disciplines, such as physiology, sociology, and anthropology, and should converge with the general study of human development. The transactional theory especially raises questions that involve such broad connections. Also, the diverse subcultures and ethnic backgrounds represented by the student population and the many strands that contribute to a democratic culture present a wide range of questions for research about reading, teaching, and curriculum.

Developmental Processes

The adult capacity to engage in the tremendously complex process of reading depends ultimately on the individual's long developmental process, starting with "learning how to mean" (Halliday, 1975; Rosenblatt, 1985b). How does the child move from the earliest, undifferentiated state of the world to "the referential, emotive, and associative part processes" (Rommetveit, 1968, p. 167)? Developmental research can throw light on the relation of cognitive and emotional aspects in the growth of the ability to evoke meaning in transactions with texts.

Research is needed to accumulate systematic understanding of the positive environmental and educational factors that do justice to the essential nature of both efferent and aesthetic linguistic behavior, and to the role of the affective or private aspects of meaning in both stances. How can children's sensorimotor explorations of their worlds be reinforced, their sensitivity to the sounds and qualitative overtones of language be maintained? In short, what can foster their capacity to apprehend in order to comprehend, or construct, the poem, story, or play? Much also remains to be understood about development of the ability to infer, or make logical connections, or, in short, to read efferently and critically.

How early in the child's development should the context of the transaction with the text create a purpose for one or the other dominant stance, or help the reader learn to adopt a stance appropriate to the situation? At different developmental stages, what should be the role or roles of reflection on the reading experience through spoken comments, writing, and the use of other media?

An overarching question is this: How can skills be assimilated in a context that fosters understanding of their relevance to the production of meaning? How can the young reader acquire the knowledge, intellectual frameworks, and sense of values that provide the connecting links for turning discrete verbal signs into meaningful constructs? The traditional methods of teaching and testing recognize the important functions of the symbolic system, the alphabetic and phonological elements (the "code"), and linguistic conventions by fragmenting processes into small quantifiable units. These are quantitatively and hence economically assessable. But do such methods set up habits and attitudes toward the written word that inhibit the process of inferring meaning, or organizing and synthesizing, that enters into even simple reading tasks? How can we prepare the way for increasingly rich and demanding transactions with texts?

Performance

Assessment of performance level is usually required as a means of assuring the accountability of the school. Whether standardized tests accurately measure the student's ability is currently being called into question. Research on correlation of reading ability with factors such as age, gender, ethnic and socioeconomic background, and so on has confirmed the expectation that they are active factors. However, such research reports a state of affairs that is interpreted according to varying assumptions, not all conducive to the development of mature readers and writers. The transactional emphasis on the total context of the reading act reinforces the democratic concern with literacy and supports the call for vigorous political and social reform of negative environmental factors. At the same time teachers must recognize that the application of quantitatively based group labels to individual students may unfairly create erroneous expectations that become self-fulfilling prophecies.

Teaching Methods

In the current transition away from traditional teaching methods, there is the danger that inappropriate research designs may be invoked to evaluate particular teaching methods. What criteria of successful teaching and what assumptions about the nature of linguistic processes underlie the research design and the methods of measurement? Any interpretations of results should take into account the various considerations concerning reader, text, and context set forth in the transactional model.

Results of research assessing different teaching methods raise an important question: Did the actual teaching conform to the formulaic labels attached to the methods being compared? The vagueness of a term such as *reader-response method* can illustrate the importance of more precise understanding of the actual teaching processes being tested in a particular piece of research. The same term has been applied to teachers who, after eliciting student responses to a story, fall back on habitual methods of demonstrating the "correct" interpretation and to teachers who make the responses the beginning of a process of helping students grow in their ability to arrive at sound, self-critical interpretations.

Much remains to be done to develop operational descriptions of the approaches being compared. Studies are needed of how teachers lead, or facilitate, without dominating or dictating. Ethnographic study of classroom dynamics, records of interchange among teacher and students, videotapes of classrooms, and analyses of text give substance to test results.

Response

Students' empirical responses to a text (mainly written protocols) form the basis of much of the research on methods generally referred to as reader response or transactional. (The term *response* should be understood to cover multiple activities.) Protocols provide indirect evidence about the students' evocation, the work as experienced, and reactions to it. Such research requires a coherent system of analysis of students' written or oral reports. What evidence, for example, is there that the reading of a story has been predominantly aesthetic?

The problem of empirical assessment of the student's aesthetic reading of a text offers particular difficulties, especially because no single "correct" interpretation or evaluation is posited. This requires setting up criteria of interpretation that reflect not only the presence of personal feelings and associations, which are only one component, but also their relationship to the other cognitive and attitudinal components. In short, the assessment must be based on clearly articulated criteria as to signs of growing maturity in handling personal response, relating to the evoked text, and use of personal and intertextual experience vis-à-vis the responses of others.

In order to provide a basis for statistical correlation, content analysis of protocols has been used largely to determine the components or aspects of response. The purpose is to distinguish personal feelings and attitudes from, for example, efferent, analytic references to the sonnet form. This requires a systematic set of categories, such as *The Elements of Writing About a Literary Work* (Purves & Rippere, 1968), which has provided a common basis for a large number of studies. As the emphasis on process has increased, refinements or alternatives have been devised. The need is to provide for study of the relationship among the various aspects of response, or the processes of selecting and synthesizing activities by which readers arrive at evocations and interpretations (Rosenblatt, 1985a). Qualitative methods of research at least should supplement, or perhaps should become the foundation for, any quantitative methods of assessing transactions with the written word.

Experimental designs that seek to deal with the development of the ability to handle some aspect of literary art should avoid methodologies and experimental tasks that instead serve to test efferent metalinguistic capacities. For example, levels of ability to elucidate metaphor or to retell stories may not reflect children's actual sensing or experiencing of metaphors or stories so much as their capacity to efferently abstract or categorize (Verbrugge, 1979).

The dependence on single instances of reading in assessing an individual's abilities is currently being called into question. The previous reminder that we are dealing with points in a continuing and changing developmental process is especially relevant. Habits are acquired and change slowly; it may be found that the effects of a change, for example, from traditional to response methods of teaching literature, cannot be assessed without allowing for a period of transition from earlier approaches and the continuation of the new approaches over time.

Basal readers have in the past offered especially clear examples of questions and exercises tacitly calling for an efferent stance toward texts labeled stories and poems. There has been little to help students assimilate and make automatic the aesthetic mode of relating to a text. Here, preparations for reading, the teacher's questions both before and after reading, and the mode of assessment, which powerfully influences teaching, should be scrutinized.

Studies that seek to generalize about the development of abilities by simultaneous testing of the different age levels have the problem of taking into account the factor of schooling. To what extent do changes in children's ability to retell or comment on the grammar of a story reflect schooling in the appropriate way to talk about a story? Similarly, to what extent are reported changing literary interests in the middle years not a reflection of personality changes but of too narrow definitions of *literary*?

Research Methodologies

The preceding discussion has centered on suggesting problems for research implied by the transactional model. Research methods or designs have been mentioned mainly in reference to their potentialities and limitations for providing kinds of information needed and to criteria for interpretation of data. Quantitatively based generalizations about groups are usually called for, but currently there is interest in clarifying the potentialities and limitations of both quantitative and qualitative research. Empirical experimental designs are being supplemented or checked by other research approaches, such as the case study (Birnbaum & Emig, 1991), the use of journals, interviews during or after the linguistic event, portfolios, and recordings in various media. Because the single episode test has various limitations, research in which researcher and teacher collaborate, or carefully planned research carried on by the teacher, provides the opportunity for extended studies. The transactional model especially indicates the value of ethnographic or naturalistic research because it deals with problems in the context of the ongoing life of individuals and groups in a particular cultural, social, and educational environment (Kantor, Kirby, & Goetz, 1981; Zaharlick & Green, 1991). The developmental emphasis also supports the call for longitudinal studies (Tierney, 1991). Interdisciplinary collaboration, desirable at any time, seems especially so for longitudinal studies. Research will need to be sufficiently complex, varied, and interlocking to do justice to the fact that reading is at once an intensely individual and an intensely social activity, an activity that from the earliest years involves the whole spectrum of ways of looking at the world.

QUESTIONS FOR REFLECTION

1. Why does Rosenblatt say that it is difficult to arrive at a theory of reading?
2. According to Rosenblatt, how does stance affect reader response?
3. How can a teacher use Rosenblatt's transactional theory to enhance students' reading experiences in the classroom?

ACKNOWLEDGMENTS

I want to thank June Carroll Birnbaum and Roselmina Indrisano for reading this manuscript, and Nicholas Karolides and Sandra Murphy for reading earlier versions.

NOTES

[1] The 1949 volume marks Dewey's choice of *transaction* to designate a concept present in his work since 1896. My own use of the term after 1950 applied to an approach developed from 1938 on.

[2] By 1981, *transactional theory*, *efferent stance*, and *aesthetic stance* were sufficiently current to be listed and were attributed to me in *A Dictionary of Reading and Related Terms* (Harris & Hodges, 1981). But the often confused usage of the terms led me to write "Viewpoints: Transaction Versus Interaction—A Terminological Rescue Operation" (1985).

[3] The transactional model of reading presented here covers the whole range of similarities and differences among readers and between author and reader. Always in the transaction between reader and text, activation of the reader's linguistic–experiential reservoir must be the basis for the construction of new meanings and new experiences; hence, the applicability to bilingual instruction and the reading of texts produced in other cultures.

[4] *Literature as Exploration* emphasizes the instructional process that can be built on the basis of personal evocation and response. Illustrations of classroom discussions and chapters such as "Broadening the Framework," "Some Basic Social Concepts," and "Emotion and Reason" indicate how the teacher can democratically moderate discussion and help students toward growth not only in ability to handle increasingly complex texts but also in personal, social, and cultural understanding.

REFERENCES

Ames, A. (1955). *The nature of our perceptions, prehensions and behavior*. Princeton, NJ: Princeton University Press.

Appenzeller, T. (1990, November/December). Undivided attention. *The Sciences*.

Applebee, A.N. (1974). *Tradition and reform in the teaching of English*. Urbana, IL: National Council of Teachers of English.

Bartlett, F.C. (1932). *Remembering: A study in experimental and social psychology*. London: Cambridge University Press.

Bates, E. (1979). *The emergence of symbols*. New York: Academic.

Beach, R., & Hynds, S. (1990). Research on response to literature. In E. Farrell & J.R. Squire (Eds.), *Transactions with literature* (pp. 131–205). Urbana, IL: National Council of Teachers of English.

Birnbaum, J., & Emig, J. (1991). Case study. In J. Flood, J.M. Jensen, D. Lapp, & J.R. Squire (Eds.), *Handbook of research on teaching the English language arts* (pp. 195–204). New York: Macmillan.

Blumenthal, A.L. (1977). *The process of cognition*. Englewood Cliffs, NJ: Prentice Hall.

Bohr, N. (1959). Discussion with Einstein. In P.A. Schilpp (Ed.), *Albert Einstein, Philosopher-Scientist* (p. 210). New York: HarperCollins.

Cantril, H., & Livingston, W.K. (1963). The concept of transaction in psychology and neurology. *Journal of Individual Psychology, 19*, 3–16.

Chomsky, N. (1968). *Language and mind*. New York: Harcourt Brace.

Clifford, J. (Ed.). (1991). *The experience of reading: Louise Rosenblatt and reader response theory*. Portsmouth, NH: Boynton/_Cook.

Cox, C., & Many, J.E. (Eds.). (1992). *Reader's stance and literary understanding*. Norwood, NJ: Ablex.

Culler, J. (1982). *On deconstruction*. Ithaca, NY: Cornell University Press.

Damasio, A.R. (1989). The brain binds entities by multilingual activities for convergence zones. *Neural Computation, 1*.

Deese, J. (1973). Cognitive structure and affect in language. In P. Pliner & T. Alloway (Eds.), *Communication and affect*. New York: Academic.

Dewey, J. (1938). *Logic: The theory of inquiry*. New York: Henry Holt.

Dewey, J., & Bentley, A.F. (1949). *Knowing and the known*. Boston: Beacon.

Eisner, E.W., & Peshkin, A. (1990). *Qualitative inquiry in education: The continuing debate*. New York: Teachers College Press.

Emig, J. (1983). *The web of meaning*. Portsmouth, NH: Boynton/Cook.

Farrell, E., & Squire, J.R. (Eds.). (1990). *Transactions with literature.* Urbana, IL: National Council of Teachers of English.
Fish, S. (1980). *Is there a text in this class?* Cambridge, MA: Harvard University Press.
Flaubert, G. (1926). *Correspondance* (Vol. 2). Paris: Louis Conard.
Flood, J., Jensen, J.M., Lapp, D., & Squire, J.R. (Eds.). (1991). *Handbook of research on teaching the English language arts.* New York: Macmillan.
Halliday, M.A.K. (1975). *Learning how to mean.* New York: Elsevier.
Harris, T.L., & Hodges, R.E. (Eds.). (1981). *A dictionary of reading and related terms.* Newark, DE: International Reading Association.
Heath, S.B. (1983). *Ways with words: Language, life, and work in communities and classrooms.* Cambridge, UK: Cambridge University Press.
Hungerford, R., Holland, K., & Ernst, S. (Eds.). (1993). *Journeying: Children responding to literature.* Portsmouth, NH: Heinemann.
Izard, C.E. (1977). *Human emotions.* New York: Plenum.
James, W. (1890). *The principles of psychology* (2 vols.). New York: Henry Holt.
Kantor, K.J., Kirby, D.R., & Goetz, J.P. (1981). Research in context: Ethnographic studies in English education. *Research in the Teaching of English, 15*(4), 293–309.
Karolides, N.J. (Ed.). (1992). *Reader response in the classroom: Evoking and interpreting meaning in literature.* White Plains, NY: Longman.
Kuhn, T. (1970). *The structure of scientific revolutions* (2nd ed.). Chicago: University of Chicago Press.
Lindbergh, A.M. (1940). *The wave of the future.* New York: Harcourt Brace.
McCloskey, D. (1985). *The rhetoric of economics.* Madison: University of Wisconsin Press.
Miller, G.A., & Johnson-Laird, P.N. (1976). *Language and perception.* Cambridge, MA: Harvard University Press.
Myers, G. (1986). *William James: His life and thought.* New Haven, CT: Yale University Press.
Peirce, C.S. (1933, 1935). *Collected papers* (Vol. 3, Vol. 6) (P. Weiss & C. Hartshorne, Eds.). Cambridge, MA: Harvard University Press.
Purves, A.C., & Beach, R. (1972). *Literature and the reader: Research in response to literature.* Urbana, IL: National Council of Teachers of English.
Purves, A.C., & Rippere, V. (1968). *Elements of writing about a literary work: A study of response to literature.* Urbana, IL: National Council of Teachers of English.
Rommetveit, R. (1968). *Words, meanings, and messages.* New York: Academic.
Rosenblatt, L.M. (1978). *The reader, the text, the poem: The transactional theory of the literary work.* Carbondale: Southern Illinois University Press.
Rosenblatt, L.M. (1983). *Literature as exploration* (4th ed.). New York: Modern Language Association. (Original work published 1938)
Rosenblatt, L.M. (1985a). The transactional theory of the literary work: Implications for research. In C. Cooper (Ed.), *Researching response to literature and the teaching of literature.* Norwood, NJ: Ablex.
Rosenblatt, L.M. (1985b). Viewpoints: Transaction versus interaction—A terminological rescue operation. *Research in the Teaching of English, 19,* 96–107.
Rosenblatt, L.M. (1991). Literary theory. In J. Flood, J.M. Jensen, D. Lapp, & J.R. Squire (Eds.), *Handbook of research on teaching the English language arts* (pp. 57–62). New York: Macmillan.
Rosenblatt, L.M. (1993). The transactional theory: Against dualisms. *College English, 55*(4), 377–386.
Saussure, F. (1972). *Cours de linguistique générale.* Paris: Payot.
Tierney, R.J. (1991). Studies of reading and writing growth: Longitudinal research on literacy development. In J. Flood, J.M. Jensen, D. Lapp, & J.R. Squire (Eds.), *Handbook of research on teaching the English language arts* (pp. 176–194). New York: Macmillan.
Verbrugge, R.R. (1979). The primacy of metaphor in development. In E. Winner & H. Gardner (Eds.), *Fact, fiction, and fantasy in childhood.* San Francisco: Jossey-Bass.
Vygotsky, L.S. (1962). *Thought and language* (F. Hanmann & G. Vakar, Eds. & Trans.). Cambridge, MA: MIT Press.
Werner, H., & Kaplan, B. (1962). *Symbol formation.* New York: Wiley.
Zaharlick, A., & Green, J. (1991). Ethnographic research. In J. Flood, J.M. Jensen, D. Lapp, & J.R. Squire (Eds.), *Handbook of research on teaching the English language arts* (pp. 205–223). New York: Macmillan.

CHAPTER 36

Reading–Writing Connections: Discourse-Oriented Research

Giovanni Parodi, Pontificia Universidad Católica de Valparaíso

Introduction

The concern for the study of reading and writing has boomed in the last 10 or 15 years. Now that the revolution has come full cycle in cognitive sciences and discourse processing, no one doubts that adults must develop reflective and critical thinking that enables them to interact in an environment with increasing communicative demands. It is no news, however, that the discourse comprehension and production levels students show are below expected standards. Extensive research accounts for their underachievement, but many questions are yet to be answered, despite efforts made by researchers in the field (Brem, Russell, & Weems, 2001; Felton & Kuhn, 2001; Graesser, Gernsbacher, & Goldman, 1997; Graesser, Swamer, Baggett, & Sell, 1996; Parodi, 2002, 2003, 2005a, b; Peronard, Gómez, Parodi, & Núñez, 1998).

A quick review of the literature reveals researchers have only recently examined the relationships between processes involved in the comprehension and production of written texts. The high-level cognitive processes have been treated by various disciplines and interdisciplines as two separate, independent fields of study. Therefore, a new research area is emerging that systematically investigates comprehension and writing from the same discourse and cognitive perspective aiming at shedding light on their connections (Boscolo & Cisotto, 1999; Eisterhold, 1991; Parodi 1998, 2003; Sadoski & Paivio, 1994, 2001; Spivey, 1997; Van Dijk, 1985; Van Dijk & Kintsch, 1983).

The purpose of the present study is to explore the text reading–writing relations from a discourse and cognitive perspective adopting a naturalistic approach (Graesser, Magliano, & Haberlandt, 1994a; Kent, 1999; Parodi, 2003; Van Oostendorp & Zwaan, 1994; Weisser & Dobrin, 2001). Research on these relationships should eventually move beyond correlational studies (Parodi, 2003; Tierney & Shanahan, 1991), yet there is still a lack of investigation that compares measures from a text linguistics perspective. While our study is correlational, it nevertheless examines text variables. Moreover, our focus on argumentative text moves beyond the prevailing emphasis on narrative discourse.

The present study has three objectives. They are (1) to advance the study of connections by documenting a table of indexes from a psycholinguistic perspec-

This chapter is reprinted from *Reading and Writing*, 2007, *20*(3), 225–250.

tive; (2) to obtain contrastive data on performance measures for argumentative discourse comprehension and production; and (3) to determine correlations between reading and writing processes at different text levels (local versus global coherence and superstructural organization). We assume there are similarities between reading and writing, but we want to compare them systematically and analytically. Two main conclusions emerge. First, significant correlations are found between reading and writing. Second, the strongest links are detected at the level of local cohesion and the microstructural level. Since reading and writing argumentative texts are some of the most difficult tasks students face in academic life, we assume participants have problems in comprehending and producing this written organizational superstructure (thesis, arguments, and conclusion).

In order to achieve these objectives, we designed four tests: two comprehension tests and two writing tasks, as will be described later. The tests were administered to a group of 439 eighth graders attending subsidized schools in Valparaíso, Chile.

Theoretical Scope

Connections Between Textual Comprehension and Textual Production

The literature on reading–writing connections is scant, particularly among the publications available before the late 70s. Irwin (1992) and Tierney (1992) agree that the first published work on this line dates back to 1929 and that the 80s and the 90s were the decades when the reader/writer relation and cognitive processes were of major concern. According to these authors, no attempt at linking comprehension and written production was made before the 90s. Reading was essentially conceived as a receptive skill, while writing was a productive one, so they were taught independently. Stotsky (1983) presented a variety of correlational studies of comprehension and production, paying special attention to those carried out between 1965 and 1977. Most of these efforts correlate comprehension achievements with writing ability, and most of them reveal highly significant correlations. Subsequently, Shanahan (1984) and then Shanahan and Lomax (1986) detected positive correlations among various factors, which associated comprehension and production.

Tierney and Shanahan (1991) reviewed the state of research on reading–writing connections, including many aspects that had been neglected up to that time. The outcomes of several investigations were documented and critically examined, including educational implications. Their efforts to account for progress on the subject, from their perspective, reveal the limitations affecting the development both of theories and research to date. According to Irwin (1992), 83% of the research in this area until 1984 was classified as educational and were mainly experimental. Most efforts focused on instructional models with no incorporation of basic theoretical models (Eckhoff, 1983; Harp & Brewer, 1991; Hass, 1989; Heller, 1995; Sager, 1989). A very limited number of these studies included textual variables, most of them concentrating only on narrative texts.

From our perspective, most of these investigations have a number of problems. As a result of influential theories at particular historical moments, the underlying models in many cases were under strong structuralist influence that limited them to word and sentence units. Consequently, the instruments used to assess comprehension did not tap comprehension of a text, but instead typically tapped literal reproduction of the information (shallow level questions) or/and fluent reading aloud and recognition of particular syntax patterns (cloze test). The tests that measured production focused mainly on formal aspects rather than on substantive referential content; that is, the tests paid particular attention to spelling, use of assorted vocabulary items and diversity of syntax structures. They did not take into consideration other aspects, such as the implied audiences, the writer's role, the subject matters, and rhetorical composition (Ede & Lundford, 1988; Kucer, 2001; Langer, 2002; Spivey, 1997).

Investigations on reading–writing connections have not been guided by a consensual framework or unified theory of language processing. Therefore, the standards used to correlate reading and writing were not necessarily comparable and did not share a common ground of similarity. It is important to point out that the concepts of discourse, comprehension, and production have evolved dramatically during the last few years. Modern concepts of written discourse assign a central role to mental processes and the role of the reader/writer's previous knowledge (de Beaugrande, 1997; Gómez, 1994; Nystrand, 1987; Van Dijk, 1985). The main obstacles are: (a) problems with the theoretical definitions or theories underlying reading and writing, and (b) problems with the measures that are being compared when they do not focus on the same psycholinguistic construct.

This new emerging line of research maintains that reading and writing are related processes, and that there are insightful frameworks that relate the two activities. Examples of these are the investigations conducted by Spivey (1990, 1997) and by Sadoski and Paivio (1994, 2001). Spivey (1990) argues that if a written text is produced from particular sources, then the reader becomes a writer because the source text is transformed into a new text. That is to say, the writer, while using other texts in the creation of a new one, employs constructive operations of organization, selection, and connection to elaborate meaning. Spivey (1997) explored a discourse approach from the point of view of discourse analysis, semiotics, post-structuralism, and deconstructivism. Sadoski and Paivio (1994) were initially concerned with reading and were in search for a unified theory of literacy, so they proposed a dual coding theory for reading and writing. Sadoski and Paivio (2001) developed a systematic theoretical approach that covered the processes of comprehension and production and their different components, stressing the importance of integrating verbal and non-verbal cognition. Sadoski and Paivio justified (step-by-step) the central and integrated role of linguistics and mental imagery by articulating a unified theory for reading and writing with non-linguistic knowledge and imagery components (*Dual Coding Theory*).

Models of the Reading–Writing Connection

As discussed earlier, there are few doubts today whether discourse comprehension and production are related (Belanger, 1987; Eisterhold, 1991; Irwin & Doyle, 1992; Kucer, 1985, 2001; Langer, 1986, 2002; Parodi, 2003; Reuter, 1995; Sadoski & Paivio, 1994, 2001; Spivey, 1997). However, there is a central focus on the status of possible connections. Eisterhold (1991) postulates three interrelated hypotheses, which independently account for discourse connections. According to Eisterhold, these hypotheses reflect the direction of transfer from one discourse mode to the other. The differences between the models address the way cognitive processes and linguistic mechanisms are related to transfer between comprehension and production.

The bidirectional hypothesis starts from the assumption that reading and writing might be interactive in some levels, but independent in others. This model presents the relations between comprehension and production as a constellation of interrelated processes that use a substratum of common knowledge, without overloading the individual's cognitive system. What a person learns at one developmental stage of one domain may be qualitatively different from what he/she learns at another. So it is important to accept the existence of multiple relations between both domains, as well as the possibility that ontogenetic changes occur. Eisterhold (1991) contends that the bidirectional model is the most complex, but also the most complete. Moreover, Eisterhold postulates separate subsystems as well as particular underlying strategies that are common to both domains.

The bidirectional hypothesis is compatible with Van Dijk and Kintsch's (1983) idea that the reading–writing connections would save resources for the reader/writer's cognitive system. In essence, the possibility of having common basic strategies would allow a more economical distribution of the resources in discourse processing. Fitzgerald and Shanahan (2000) proposed a developmental model in which reading and writing are related differently as they change with growth. Figure 1 illustrates the ways in which the various components interact.

Substantial reflections on reading–writing connection were carried out in the sociohistorical constructivist paradigm (Greene & Ackerman, 1995; Irwin & Doyle, 1992; Kucer, 2001; Nystrand, 1990; Sadoski & Paivio, 2001; Spivey, 1997). The socioconstructivist assumption indirectly supports the relation proposed here that integrates reading and writing processes in a bidirectional model. They share a basic cognitive substratum, whose effective domain would have an impact on a qualitative improvement on the subjects' thinking processes.

Toward a Discourse Model of Comprehension/Production

The present study adopts a comprehensive theory proposed by Van Dijk and Kintsch (1983) to guide data collection analyses and to compare reading and writing processes from a bidirectional perspective. The perspective is compatible with the author's latest studies (Parodi, 1998, 2003) as well as various other recent contributions (Boscolo & Cisotto, 1999; Kucer, 2001; Nelson & Calfee, 1998; Reuter, 1995).

Figure 1. Diagram of a Bidirectional Model

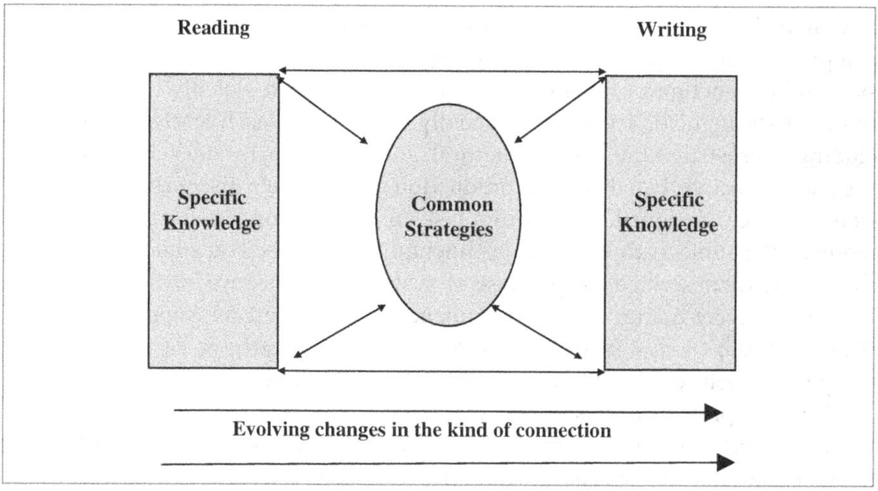

In Van Dijk and Kintsch (1983) the processes start as strategic ones, based on situational models. Van Dijk (1985, 1990, 1999, 2002) argues that an interdisiciplinary approach is needed to establish an explicit relation between discourse, cognition and social situations. Such a model should contain information about:

(1) A cognitive theory of strategic processing of information which assumes the strategic nature of comprehension and discourse production are flexible processes, having multiple levels functioning in tandem with one another.

(2) A sociocognitive theory of discourse, which extends the strategic model of processing, including the role of beliefs and attitudes in discourse processing.

Listing its basic components will suffice here:

(1) Model of context

(2) Control system

(3) Semantic comprehension/production

(4) Macrocomprehension/production

(5) Microcomprehension/production

A detailed explanation of each of these components as well as the strategic levels can be found in Van Dijk and Kintsch (1983) and Van Dijk (1980, 1985, 1990), complemented by Kintsch (1998), one of his most recent contributions.

Methods

The main focus of this research was to assess correlations between discourse comprehension and production. We computed correlations between comprehension and production of the students' achievements both globally (general mean scores at all linguistic levels) and partially (considering each level separately, including microstructural, macrostructural, and superstructural levels). To achieve the main objective, two discourse production tests and two discourse comprehension tests were designed. The written tasks of the writing tests (see Appendix 1) required the subjects to write an argumentative text based on some instructions that explicitly described the purpose of writing, the objective of the task or text type, the subject matter topic, the audience implied, and the supposed register (Camps, 1995; Camps & Millian, 2000; Coirier, Gaonac'h, & Passerault, 1996; Cooper & Odell, 1977, 1998; Ede & Lundford, 1988; Ruth & Murphy, 1988).

The comprehension tests (see Appendix 2) required students to read argumentative texts and answer nine open questions. The questions forced the readers to make some specific text-based inferences that were related to appropriate world knowledge and particular subprocesses under study (Graesser & Bower, 1992; Myers, Brown, & McGonigle, 1986; Parodi, 1989, 1990; Rickheit & Strohner, 1985). Both writing and reading tests focused on topics that had been previously discussed with the teachers of each class. Additionally, the students were given an interest test to select the topics they would like to read and write about (Vergara, 1999).

In an effort to avoid interference of any kind between the collection of samples for reading and writing, we organized all the sessions with substantial intervals between the four tests. One week intervened between reading tests and 10 days between the last administration of the reading test and the first writing test. The tests were administered by Spanish language teachers on different days of different weeks, and the tasks were considered as part of their daily school activities. The purpose of this methodology was to produce the minumun amount of interference with the normal school processes of constructing meaning through written discourse. The writing and reading processes were cognitively situated, public (Kent, 1999; Olson, 1999), and ecologically valid (Weisser & Dobrin, 2001).

Table 1 presents the kinds of questions included in the comprehension tests and the parameters evaluated on the written productions obtained. As is evident, one of the most important criteria was to assess similar factors in each process to ensure that the information being analyzed and compared was similar on psycholinguistic grounds and amenable to statistical comparison.

Table 1 tests are, in our opinion, one of the significant contributions of this study to the field of psycholinguistics. Since we have not found in the literature specific data to help us elaborate and evaluate reading and writing tests based on a clear text linguistics basis, we had to create guidelines that could be easily compared (see Appendix 3). An effort has been made to connect theory (Van Dijk & Kintsch, 1983; Van Dijk, 1980, 1985; Kintsch, 1998) to inferred empirical patterns that can be usefully compared on the same ground. As can be easily deduced from

Table 1. Guideline for Evaluating Reading and Writing Argumentative Discourse

Level	Comprehension	Production
Microstructure (local coherence relations)	(a) Inferred nominal correference (b) Inferred nominal ellipsis (c) Inferred cause–effect relations	(a) Maintained nominal correference (b) Maintained nominal ellipsis (c) Maintained cause–effect relations
Macrostructure (global coherence relations)	(a) Inferred main topic (b) Inferred macroproposition 1 (c) Inferred macroproposition 2	(a) Main topic development (b) Macroproposition 1 organization (c) Macroproposition 2 organization
Superstructure (text type canonical relations)	(a) Inferred thesis (b) Inferred arguments (c) Inferred conclusion	(a) Explicit adequate thesis (b) Adequate and coherent arguments (c) Adequate and coherent conclusion

Table 1, the main distinction in three discourse levels (micro coherence, macro coherence, and superstructural organization) is taken from our theoretical framework: Van Dijk (1980, 1985, 1990) and Van Dijk and Kintsch (1983).

In each of these processing textual levels, subdivisions have been made in order to obtain a display of subprocesses that may account for some of the most important variables involved. In comprehension tests, inferential questions were elaborated based on information in the text; for example, referential items were selected because they are known to provide crucial inferences required to comprehend a text (Gernsbacher, 1990; Graesser et al., 1994a; Peronard et al., 1998). In reading comprehension, a noun and a pronoun need to be linked together through an inference process in order to build local coherence (e.g., "Peter" and "he"); this was called *Inferred nominal co-reference*. In relation to the writing tests, in Spanish written discourse structure, a subject form is not repeated after an initial clarification because the verb shows agreement in person and number; so an elliptical noun or pronoun is required (e.g., The man is here. *Needs* help). This was called *Maintained nominal ellipsis*.

When we constructed the tests, we considered evidence showing that most Chilean eighth graders tend to produce two main arguments when writing argumentative texts (Parodi, 2000; Parodi & Núñez, 1998, 1999). Similarly, there was evidence that most texts selected by teachers for sixth and eighth graders had two macropropositions. These data were used when deciding what to include in the guideline (see Appendix 3) for designing and evaluating argumentative written discourse (Parodi, 1992, 1998, 2003, 2005a, b).

The selected sample of 439 students of both sexes was taken from 10 eighth grade courses of subsidized schools in Valparaíso, Chile. These schools are partly private and partly state funded and, in socio-economic terms, their students can be considered low middle class. Systematic compulsory education in Chile comprises 12 years: eight primary grades and four secondary grades. The child must be 7 years old at the beginning of the first grade, so our group students were approximately 13 years of age.

Analysis and Interpretation of the Results

Both the design and production of valid and reliable instruments to assess discourse comprehension and production must go through a number of major stages at evaluation to ascertain its validity (Crombach, 1988; Hedges, 1988). We adopted a triangulation method as a way to achieve these goals. Four experts judged the items based on the assessment guidelines, thus avoiding the distortion that a single evaluator might have caused. The experts read the tests and gave answers on a special sheet, with Likert scales, with different topics on each part of the tests. As a result of those analyses, a composite average (content validity and interraters reliability of) over 80% was reached. When the information obtained from the application of all the tests was processed, the statistical data analysis revealed that the difficulty of the comprehension test was 59.9%, whereas the difficulty of the production test was 60.3%. These are very good psychometric results for item difficulty. As far as the discrimination of the instrument is concerned, the comprehension test yielded 100%, and the production test 89%. The power of separation or internal differences between extreme scores was excellent in comprehension and optimal in production. The greater the difference between extreme scores, the better dispersion indexes in psychometric model adjusted to conventional formal instruction in Spanish.

Finally, the reliability coefficient of the comprehension test was 0.89 whereas the production test was 0.82, measured by an estimation of the KR20 (KR21) formula (Hair, Anderson, Tatham, & Black, 1999). These data support the claim that the tests were well designed and consistently measured what they were supposed to cover throughly. Results were valid and reliable according to psychometric criteria.

Results and Discussion

Performance Results

As a way to visualize performance per skill, Figure 2 shows some of the results from the general achievement at three discourse levels.

These percentages are remarkable in that they show internal congruence and comparative homogeneity. In observing these figures from a horizontal perspective, that is, per skill, the first thing that draws our attention is a progressive drop in achievement as the textual structure becomes more abstract, both in comprehension and production. In other words, the subjects have higher comprehension/production skills at local coherence level as opposed to macrostrategic skills. In

Figure 2. Achievement According to Structural Level

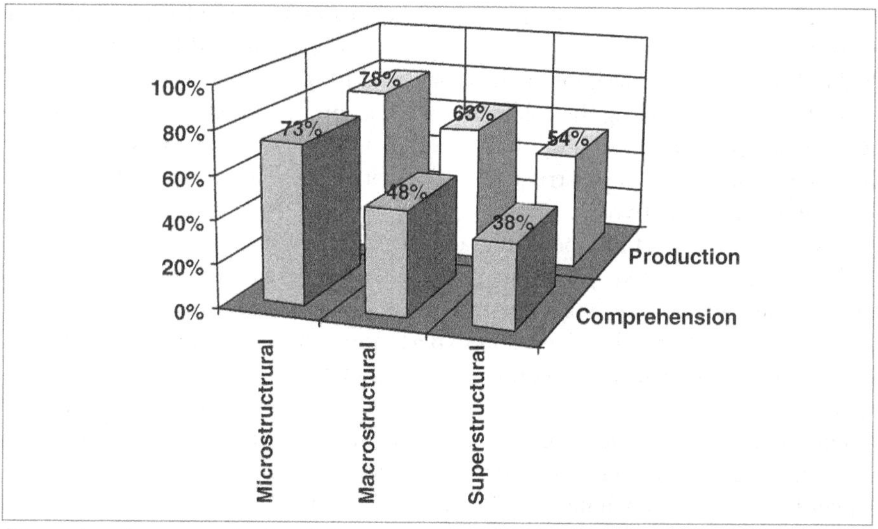

(Figures have been normalized to 100)

this light, the demands required by the argumentative structure stand out as the weakest level in these subjects, and greater difficulties can be seen in the command of discourse categories involved in the comprehension/production of the argumentative texts. According to these data, our hypothesis is confirmed: local coherence gets the highest scores and the organization structure of argumentation is one of the major difficulties for students, both in reading and writing. An explanation for this behavior can be found in that students this age are better at short-term memory challenges and their inferential processes work much better at relating information close together than information separated by several paragraphs or information that must be reduced and thoroughly processed in the light of a global idea. On the other hand, narrative discourse is still being overused in the school system, so students are not well trained in spoken or written argumentation, not only in Chile but in many other countries (Brem et al., 2001; Felton & Kuhn, 2001; Golder & Coirier, 1994; Parodi, 2003, 2005b; Peronard et al., 1998; Sánchez & Álvarez, 1999).

The comparative analysis of the percentages between the two skills shows an interesting progressive drop, which in turn, reveals great cross-sectional homogeneity between discourse comprehension and production. This illustrates the potential relations between the two higher cognitive processes being compared. A progressive relation of difficulty in each area of the analyzed discourse structure can be detected, and this gives evidence of a similar difference between each structural level, both in comprehension and production.

Based on a non-systematic qualitative analysis of the data collected, that is, on some random answers obtained from the comprehension and production tests, it is possible to suggest that the strategies most widely used by the students lead them to the production/comprehension of the written text as a list of ideas, with no organization or hierarchy. This can be seen in the apparent difficulty students had in inferring transparagraphic relations, that is, macrostructural links, which contribute to establishing the coherence of the in-progress text (writing) or of the text already produced (reading). It is also evident in the difficulty to work following an argumentative superstructural (schematic) plan, which should guide the writing or reading activities.

An explanation of this behavior, according to the theory guiding this study, is that students do not keep information in their short-term memory active, therefore, as they write, they forget the recently generated ideas and jump from one idea to the next. Normally, these non-expert writers have not been able to automatize the more superficial procedures, such as punctuation or insertion of connectors or accents, which leads to excessive concentration on those aspects, and less attention paid to the generation, organization and revision of their written ideas. Conversely, expert writers seem to maintain written and unwritten information longer in their short-term memory during the writing process.

From a discourse comprehension perspective, the same comparison can be established among the answers given by different comprehenders. Poor readers do not retain the incoming information in their short-term memory. Given their limited memory capacity and their inability to construct a reduced, coherent interpretation (macrostrategies), they forget the previous information to let the new information come in. Just like poor writers, poor readers focus their attention on very particular ideas and characterize them as macropropositions, without recognizing the superstructural categories of the texts. In turn, good readers, because of their better strategies and memory capacity, do construct a coherent interpretation of the information coming into their memory and can organize and reduce the information. Therefore, they can construct a situational model that helps interpret the text globally.

Correlational Statistics

Results between discourse comprehension and production showed an overall positive correlation (0.72). That is to say, there was 51.8% of intersection (commonality) between both variables. The detailed analyses of these figures led to determining that the relations between comprehension and production on the microstructural (0.57), macrostructural (0.68), and superstructural (0.79) levels were highly positive and significantly different from zero. All of this indicates that, in considering the final numbers, 51.8% commonality reveals a quite extensive intersecting area between comprehension and production from the cognitive/textual perspective, as far as written argumentative discourse is concerned.

In facing these results, a number of questions arise. First, what correlates these tests substantially? And, what is the underlying common factor?

One answer can be found in the bidirectional theory. Given the positive and significant correlations on all levels of comprehension/production, there must be a set of strategies in common, that is, procedural knowledge constituting the support of the textual comprehension and production mechanisms. Or, in the sense of Reuter (1995), there must be a general macrocompetence sustaining writing and reading, though such knowledge may vary throughout the subjects' development. In other words, the present findings suggest both a basic general common competence and the possibility of having mode-specific, diversified discourse competences. This reveals the possibility of exploring a more eclectic theoretical perspective of the mind such as the one proposed by Karmiloff-Smith (1992) in her representational redescription theory (RR). She suggests an approach in which a Piagetian constructivism and a general-based domain emphasis is combined with nativism and a Fodorian modularist view. In this new approach, Karmiloff-Smith proposes that the human cognitive development does not operate through stages but states, in opposition to classical Piaget perspective. The RR model focuses on ontogenetic progressive modularization process; this means that the child starts with general knowledge that progressively gets specialized in relatively independent modules. It could be that, therefore, reading and writing skills evolve from a general domain approach and move progressively towards a more modularist perspective as the human being develops. Of course, all this would favor a hybrid model of reading and writing in search for a general cognitive paradigm (Karmiloff-Smith, 1992; Kintsch, 1998) with a combination of symbolic and connectionist representations. Hybrid models such as this seem to be very useful nowadays, but face a lot of problems not clearly and properly addressed because the combination of these two kinds of cognitive representations (*propositions and connectionist neural nodes*) are not utterly unveiled (Parodi, 2002, 2003). This issue goes beyond the scope of this article, but it is nevertheless a major concern in the frameworks related to this line of research.

It is important to emphasize the difficulty in determining common strategies. Spivey (1997) and Sadoski and Paivio (2001) presented data on some common strategies, but they are so general that we believe their usefulness is very restricted and do not seem to help much in defining the possible psycholinguistic links. Also, Kucer (1985, 2001) has contributed some other common strategies for reading and writing (e.g., previous knowledge activation, discourse genre organization); again, the generality of the propositions imply that determining more specific common strategies might be a difficult task, based on the present available methods.

Another answer to the aforementioned questions could be found in the three levels of cognitive representation (*surface code, textbase, and situation model*) proposed by Van Dijk and Kintsch (1983) and Kintsch (1988, 1998). We agree with Graesser, Singer, and Trabasso (1994b) in that these are non-controversial components widely accepted by researchers in discourse processing. The data collected here helps us propose that students tend to process deeper reading–writing connections when constructing situational models, but it is possible students use less similar strategies in constructing surface code (i.e., the exact wording and syntax) and textbase (explicit text propositions plus inferences needed for text cohesion and coherence). The situation-model construction skills, which are at a more complex representation level, require an integration of information from different sources and an active elaboration of previous knowledge in episodic memory, one the students this age seems to lack of.

This line of explanation, based on the cognitive levels of representation, could be very useful and productive. Unfortunately, most research is focused on reading comprehension (Madden & Zwaan, 2003; Zwaan & Radvansky, 1998), but not much investigation has concentrated in the importance of situation models for writing skills. Again, as mentioned in the introduction, reading and writing seem to be moving along different roads.

The central argument, therefore, is that connections show the highest positive and significant correlation on processes that start as strategic ones, based mainly on situational models, and not closer to the surface codification. Van Dijk and Kintsch (1983) and Van Dijk (1985, 1990, 1999, 2002) would argue that an approach that establishes explicit relation between discourse, cognition and social situations should be better. So, having a high reading–writing connection correlation at argumentative superstructure, based on comparable tests and scores, is a step beyond the past research that had focused mainly on sentence structure and on narrative texts. Of course, the nature of the specific and more global strategies remains unknown or at a general cognitive level.

Finally, the educational implications of this data for classroom activities suggest that language teachers should exploit the potentiality of teaching and practicing reading and writing together, starting from local cohesion resources to different text organizations. One of the key concepts should be to begin with the text and not with the words or phrases: the semantic unit must be perceived as a whole from the beginning. It may also be suggested to focus on general cognitive processes such as remembering previous knowledge about language or activating general world knowledge (Kucer, 1985, 2001). Too much concentration on one process and/or strong separation between them may lead to encapsulated knowledge that cannot be used indistinctly, and this seems to go against the principle of saving cognitive energy.

Conclusion

The empirical evidence provided helps us conclude that our research hypothesis are confirmed and that the assumptions are correct: microstructuctural relations (the ones studied here) are the easiest relations comprehended and produced by this group of students; at the same time, argumentative text organization (superstructure) is not easy to manage by the 439 eighth graders. The highest positive and significant correlations are found in argumentative superstructure; this means that the strongest connections are detected in the schematic text structure. So, based in these results, we can offer new information on favor of the reading–writing relations, supported by comparable guidelines on argumentative discourse. The positive correlations between comprehension and production with an important degree of commonality are proofs of it. This means that the bidirectional hypothesis is confirmed as an interesting explanation of the results under analysis. At the same time, the analysis of our data leads us to confirm the existence of common basic strategies used by these 439 eighth graders when accomplishing writing and reading tasks, although more specific resources for each of the skills should be explored and detected.

These data contribute some empirical evidence collected from tests designed on similar discourse psycholinguistic grounds from text-oriented perspective. This information gives support to our initial questions that inquired about the potential existence of a general common cognitive system for both skills, though not denying the existence of some other more specific subsystems. This implies that the processes involved in both activities share some common knowledge-based strategies, yet to be determined in future research.

As pointed out at the beginning of this article, although we are certain we must move from correlational studies into more qualitative ones, the data collected has some degree of originality because it advances into the argumentative discourse and the parameters employed are more amenable to comparison. Of course, research should be conducted with empirical experiments on a multidimentional design, i.e., having proposed more than one line of data to help develop the objectives and support the information collected from one source of data or as this was called by Graesser et al. (1994b) the "three-pronged method." There have been some lively debates over the proper measures and experimental designs that test whether or not reading and writing processes can be explored and compared from the same empirical and theoretical approach. However, in this article, we do not dissect the methodological problems with each of the existing measures and tasks. There does not appear to be a perfect measure and task; there are merely trade-offs, with each enjoying some benefits and some shortcomings. The decisions made for this research are based on empirical studies that, in our opinion, have minimal methodological problems and are supported by previous experimental research.

In relation to the students' achievement levels, it is important to emphasize the fact that, not only in Chile but also in several other Latin American countries as well as Spain and the United States, teaching practices currently in use do not seem to lead to the expected levels of language performance. The efforts being made to remove students from the social and cultural isolation in which they are immersed have shown little impact until now (Arnoux, Nogueira, & Silvestri, 2002; Felton & Kuhn, 2001; Golder & Coirier, 1994; Parodi, 2001, 2003, 2005a, b; Peronard et al., 1998; Sánchez & Álvarez, 1999). An educational reform is underway in Chile and in many other countries, and it would be desirable to take some adequate steps towards the consideration of discourse practices as the nucleus of the construction of meaning. Argumentation should be the focus of much investigation and the development of better teaching strategies. Also, the discourse approach in education should bring greater freedom in the access to knowledge and society.

QUESTIONS FOR REFLECTION

1. From a cognitive science perspective, why is it important to blend the instruction of reading and writing?
2. What is your position on the author's argument that the reading and writing of narrative text is overused in schools?
3. How might the adoption of Parodi's recommendation for teaching discourse be of use in advancing the cause of social justice?

ACKNOWLEDGEMENT

This work was supported by FONDECYT Research Grant No. 1980/311.

REFERENCES

Arnoux, E., Nogueira, S., & Silvestri, A. (2002). La construcción de representaciones enunciativas: El reconocimiento de voces en la comprensión de textos polifónicos [The construction of representations: Voice recognition in reading poliphonic texts]. *Revista Signos [Signs Journal]*, *35*, 129–148.

Belanger, J. (1987). Theory and research into reading and writing connections: A critical review. *Reading-Canada Lecture*, *5*, 10–21.

Boscolo, P., & Cisotto, L. (1999). On narrative reading–writing relationships: How young writers construe the reader's need for inferences. In S. Goldman, A. Graesser & P. Broekvan den (Eds.), *Narrative comprehension, causality, and coherence. Essays in honor of Tom Trabasso* (pp. 161–178). Mahwah, NJ: Lawrence Erlbaum.

Brem, S., Russell, J., & Weems, L. (2001). Science on the web: Students' evaluations of scientific arguments. *Discourse Processes*, *32*, 191–213.

Camps, A. (1995). Aprender a escribir textos argumentativos: Características dialógicas de la argumentación escrita [Learning to write argumentative texts: Dialogic characteristics in composing argumentation]. Infancia y Aprendizaje [Childhood and learning], 25, 51–63.

Camps, A., & Millian, M. (2000). *Metalinguistic activity in learning to write*. Amsterdam: Amsterdan University Press.

Coirier, P., Gaonac'h, D., & Passerault, J. (1996). *Psycholinguistique textuelle [Text psycholinguistics]*. Paris: Hachette.

Cooper, L., & Odell, R. (1977). *Evaluating writing: Describing, measuring, judging*. Urbana, IL: NCTE.

Cooper, L., & Odell, R. (1998). *Evaluating writing: The role of teacher's knowledge about text, learning & culture*. Urbana, IL: NCTE.

Crombach, L. (1988). Five perspectives on validity argument. In H. Wainer & H. Braun (Eds.), *Test validity* (pp. 3–19). Hillsdale, NJ: Lawrence Erlbaum.

de Beaugrande, R. (1997). *New foundations for a science of text and discourse: Cognition, communication, and the freedom of access to knowledge and society*. Norwood, NJ: Ablex.

Eckhoff, S. (1983). How reading affects children's writing. *Language Arts*, *60*, 234–256.

Ede, L., & Lundford, A. (1988). Audience addressed/audience invoked: The role of audience in composition theory and pedagogy. In G. Tate & E. Corbett (Eds.), *The writing teacher's sourcebook* (pp. 248–259). New York: Oxford University Press.

Eisterhold, J. (1991). Reading–writing connections: Toward a description for second language learners. In B. Kroll (Ed.), *Second language writing: Research insights for the classroom* (pp. 88–101). Cambridge: Cambridge University Press.

Felton, M., & Kuhn, D. (2001). The development of argumentative discourse skill. *Discourse Processes*, *32*, 135–153.

Fitzgerald, J., & Shanahan, T. (2000). Reading and writing relations and their development. *Educational Psychologist*, *35*, 39–50.

Gernsbacher, M. (1990). *Language comprehension as structure building*. Hillsdale, NJ: Lawrence Erlbaum.

Golder, C., & Coirier, P. (1994). Argumentative text writing: Developmental trends. *Discourse Processes*, *18*, 187–210.

Gómez, L. (1994). La dimensión social de la comprensión textual [Social dimension of textual comprehension]. *Revista Signos [Signs Journal]*, *27*, 35–46.

Graesser, A., & Bower, G. (1992). *Inferences and text comprehension*. Hillsdale, NJ: Lawrence Erlbaum.

Graesser, A., Gernsbacher, M., & Goldman, S. (1997). Cognition. In T. Van Dijk (Ed.), *Discourse as structure and process. Discourse studies: A multidisciplinary introduction* (pp. 7–27). Vol. 1 London: SAGE.

Graesser, A., Magliano, J., & Haberlandt, K. (1994a). Psychological studies of naturalistic text. In H. Van Oostendorp & R. Zwaan (Eds.), *Naturalistic text comprehension* (pp. 9–33). Norwood, NJ: Ablex.

Graesser, A., Singer, M., & Trabasso, T. (1994b). Constructing inferences during narrative text comprehension. *Psychological Review, 101*, 371–395.

Graesser, A., Swamer, S., Baggett, W., & Sell, M. (1996). New models of deep comprehension. In B. Britton & A. Graesser (Eds.), *Models of understanding text* (pp. 5–27). Mahwah, NJ: Lawrence Erlbaum.

Greene, S., & Ackerman, J. (1995). Expanding the constructivist metaphor: A rethorical perspective on literacy research and practice. *Review of Educational Research, 65*, 383–420.

Hair, J., Anderson, R., Tatham, J., & Black, W. (1999). *Multivariate data analysis*. New York: Prentice Hall.

Harp, B., & Brewer, J. (1991). *Reading and writing: Teaching for the connections*. Orlando, FL: Harcourt Brace Yovanovich.

Hass, A. (1989). *Collaboration through writing and reading*. Urbana, IL: NCTE.

Hedges, L. (1988). The meta-analysis of test validity studies: Some new approaches. In H. Wainer & H. Braun (Eds.), *Test validity* (pp. 191–213). Hillsdale, NJ: Lawrence Erlbaum.

Heller, M. (1995). *Reading–writing connections: From theory to practice*. London: Longman.

Irwin, J. (1992). Research in reading/writing from 1900 to 1984. In J. Irwin & M. Doyle (Eds.), *Reading/writing connections: Learning from research* (pp. 308–333). Newark, DE: IRA.

Irwin, J., & Doyle, M. (Eds.) (1992). *Reading/writing connections: Learning from research*. Newark, Delaware: IRA.

Karmiloff-Smith, A. (1992). *Beyond modulary: A developmental perspective on cognitive science*. Cambridge, MA: MIT Press.

Kent, T. (Ed.) (1999). *Post-process theory. Beyond the writing-process paradigm*. Carbondale, IL: Southern Illinois University Press.

Kintsch, W. (1988). The role of knowledge in discourse comprehension: A construction–integration model. *Psychological Review, 95*, 163–182.

Kintsch, W. (1998). *Comprehension: A paradigm for cognition*. Cambridge: Cambridge University Press.

Kucer, S. (1985). The making of meaning: Reading and writing as parallel processes. *Written Communication, 2*, 317–356.

Kucer, S. (2001). *Dimensions of literacy. A conceptual base for teaching reading and writing in school settings*. Mahwah, NJ: Lawrence Erlbaum.

Langer, J. (1986). *Children reading and writing. Structures and strategies*. Norwood, NJ: Ablex Publishing.

Langer, J. (2002). *Effective literacy instruction. Building successful reading and writing programs*. Urbana, IL: NCTE.

Madden, C., & Zwaan, R. (2003). How does verb aspect constrain event representation?. *Memory & Cognition, 31*, 663–672.

Myers, T., Brown, K., & McGonigle, B. (1986). *Reasoning and discourse processes*. London: Academic Press.

Nelson, N., & Calfee, R. (1998). The reading–writing connections viewed historically. In N. Nelson & R. Calfee (Eds.), *The reading–writing connection* (pp. 1–52). Chicago, IL: The University of Chicago Press.

Nystrand, M. (1987). The role of context in written communication. In R. Horowitz & J. Samuels (Eds.), *Comprehending oral and written language* (pp. 197–212). New York: Academic Press.

Nystrand, M. (1990). Sharing words: The effects of readers on developing writers. *Written Communication, 7*, 3–24.

Olson, G. (1999). Toward a post-process composition: Abandoning the rhetoric of assertion. In T. Kent (Ed.), *Post-process theory. Beyond the writing-process paradigm* (pp. 7–15). Carbondale, IL: Southern Illinois University Press.

Parodi, G. (1989). La inferencia una aproximación al concepto [Inferences: Approaching the concept]. In: *Proceedings 8th congress of the Chilean society of linguistics* (pp. 211–220). Santiago de Chile.

Parodi, G. (1990). Los procesos inferenciales en la comprensión de textos escritos [Inferential processes in reading comprehension]. Pontificia Universidad Católica de Valparaíso. (Unpublished Masters dissertation).

Parodi, G. (1992). Estructura textual y estrategias lectoras [Text structure and reading strategies]. *Lenguas Modernas [Modern Languages], 19*, 89–98.

Parodi, G. (1998). Conexiones entre comprensión y producción de textos escritos: Estudio exploratorio en alumnos de educación básica [Reading–writing connections: Exploratory study with elementary schools students]. *Revista Lingüística en el Aula [Journal of Classroom Linguistics], 2*, 7–18.

Parodi, G. (2000). La evaluación de a producción de textos escritos argumentativos: Una alternativa cognitivo discursiva [Evaluating written argumentative texts: A discourse and cognitive alternative]. *Revista Signos [Signs Journal], 33*, 151–167.

Parodi, G. (2001). Comprensión y producción del discurso escrito: Estudio empírico en escolares chilenos [Reading and writing texts: Research with Chilean students]. *Revista Iberoamericana de Discurso y Sociedad [Iberoamerican Journal of Discourse and Society], 3*, 75–101.

Parodi, G. (2002). Comprensión lingüística: ¿Hacia dónde vamos desde donde estamos? [Reading comprehension: Where do we go from where we are?]. In: G. Parodi (Ed.), *Lingüística e interdisciplinariedad: Desafíos del nuevo milenio. Ensayos en honor a Marianne Peronard [Linguistics and interdisciplinarity: Challenges of the new millennium. Essays in honor of Marianne Peronard]* (pp. 44–67). Valparaíso: Editorial Universitaria de Valparaíso.

Parodi, G. (2003). *Relaciones entre lectura y escritura: Una perspectiva cognitiva discursiva [Relationships between reading and writing: Discursive and cognitive perspectives]*. Valparaíso: Editorial Universitaria de Valparaíso.

Parodi, G. (2005a). *Comprensión de textos escritos [Comprehension of written discourse]*. Buenos, Aires: EUDEBA.

Parodi, G. (Ed.) (2005b). *Discurso especializado e instituciones formadoras [Specialized discourse and academic institutions]*. Valparaíso: Editorial Universitaria de Valparaíso.

Parodi, G., & Núñez, P. (1998). El desarrollo de estrategias de lectura comprensiva: Una aplicación experimental del "Programa L y C: Leer y Comprender" [Reading strategies development: An experience with "Programa L y C: Leer y Comprender"]. In: M. Peronard, L. Gómez, G. Parodi, & P. Núñez (Eds.), *Comprensión de textos escritos: De la teoría a la sala de clases [Reading comprehension: From theory to practice]* (pp. 249–264). Santiago de Chile: Editorial Andrés Bello.

Parodi, G., & Núñez, P. (1999). En búsqueda de un modelo cognitivo/textual para la evaluación del texto escrito [In search of a model for the evaluation of written texts]. In: M. C. Martínez (Ed.), *Comprensión y producción de textos académicos: Expositivos y argumentativos [Reading and writing academic texts: Expositive and argumentative genres]* (pp. 81–115). Cali, Colombia: Universidad del Valle.

Peronard, M., Gómez, L., Parodi, G., & Núñez, P. (1998). *Comprensión de textos escritos: De la teoría a la sala de clases [Reading comprehension: From theory to practice]*. Santiago de Chile: Editorial Andrés Bello.

Reuter, Y. (1995). Les relations lecture-écriture dans le champ didactique [The reading–writing relationtionship in methodological applications]. *Pratiques [Practices]*, *86*, 5–23.

Rickheit, G., & Strohner, H. (1985). *Inferences in text processing*. Amsterdam, Netherlands: Elsevier Science Publications.

Ruth, L., & Murphy, S. (1988). *Designing writing tasks for the assessment of writing*. Norwood, NJ: Ablex.

Sadoski, M., & Paivio, A. (1994). A dual coding view of imagery and verbal processes in reading comprehension. In R. Ruddell, M. Rudell & H. Singer (Eds.), *Theoretical models and processes of reading* (pp. 582–601). Newark, DE: IRA.

Sadoski, M., & Paivio, A. (2001). Imagery and text: A dual coding theory of reading and writing. Mahwah, NJ: Lawrence Erlbaum.

Sager, M. (1989). Exploiting the reading–writing connection to engage students in text. *Journal of Reading*, *33*, 24–39.

Sánchez, I., & Álvarez, N. (1999). El discurso argumentativo de los escolares venezolanos: ¿Evolución o estancamiento? [Argumentative discourse in Venezuelan school students: Development or stagnation?]. Paper presented at the 3rd International Congress of Discourse Analysis (ALED): Santiago de Chile.

Shanahan, T. (1984). Nature of the reading–writing relation: An exploratory multivariate analysis. *Journal of Educational Psychology*, *76*, 466–477.

Shanahan, T., & Lomax, R. (1986). An analysis and comparison of theoretical models of the reading–writing relationship. *Journal of Educational Psychology*, *78*, 116–123.

Spivey, N. (1990). Transforming texts: Constructing processes in reading and writing. *Written Communication*, *7*, 256–290.

Spivey, N. (1997). *The constructivist metaphor: Reading, writing and the making of meaning*. San Diego, CA: Academic Press.

Stotsky, S. (1983). Research on reading/writing relationships: A synthesis and suggested directions. *Language Arts*, *60*, 627–642.

Tierney, R. (1992). Ongoing research and new directions. In J. Irwin & M. Doyle (Eds.), *Reading/writing connections: Learning from research* (pp. 246–259). Newark, DE: IRA.

Tierney, R., & Shanahan, T. (1991). Research on the reading–writing relationship: Interactions, transactions, and outcomes. In R. Barr, M. Kamil, P. Mosenthal & D. Pearson (Eds.), *Handbook of reading research* (pp. 246–280). Vol. II Mahwah, NJ: Lawrence Erlbaum.

Van Dijk, T. (1980). *Macrostructures*. Hilldale, NJ: Lawrence Erlbaum.

Van Dijk, T. (1985). Cognitive situation models in discourse production: The expression of ethnic situations in prejudiced discourse. In P. Forgas (Ed.), *Language and social situations* (pp. 61–79). New York: Springer Verlag.

Van Dijk, T. (1990). Social cognition and discourse. In H. Giles & W. P. Robinson (Eds.), *Handbook of language and social psychology* (pp. 145–167). New York: John Wiley & Sons.

Van Dijk, T. (1999). ¿Un estudio lingüístico de la ideología? [A linguistic study of ideology?]. In: G. Parodi (Ed.), *Discurso, cognición y educación. Ensayos en honor a Luis A. Gómez Macker [Discourse, cognition, and education. Essays in honor of Luis A. Gómez Macker]* (pp. 27–42). Valparaíso: Editorial Universitaria de Valparaíso.

Van Dijk, T. (2002). Tipos de conocimiento en el procesamiento del discurso [Knowledge types in discourse processing]. In: G. Parodi (Ed.), *Lingüística e interdisciplinariedad: Desafíos del nuevo milenio. Ensayos en honor a Marianne*

Peronard [Linguistics and interdisciplinarity: Challenges of the new millennium. Essays in honor of Marianne Peronard] (pp. 30–43). Valparaíso: Editorial Universitaria de Valparaíso.

Van Dijk, T., & Kintsch, W. (1983). *Strategies of discourse comprehension*. New York: Academic Press.

Van Oostendorp, H., & Zwaan, R. (1994). Introduction: Naturalistic texts and naturalistic tasks. In H. Van Oostendorp & R. Zwaan (Eds.), *Naturalistic text comprehension* (pp. 1–8). Norwood, NJ: Ablex Publishing.

Vergara, M. (1999). Diseño y aplicación de encuestas de intereses en temas para lectura y escritura [Design and administration of reading and writing tests of interests]. In: G. Parodi (Ed.), *Conexiones entre comprensión y producción de textos escritos en alumnos de educación básica [Reading-writing connections in elementary school students]* (pp. 47–71). Valparaíso: Pontificia Universidad Católica de Valparaíso.

Weisser, C., & Dobrin, S. (2001). *Ecocomposition: Theoretical and pedagogical approaches*. Albany, NY: State University of New York Press.

Zwaan, R., & Radvansky, G. (1998). Situation models in language comprehension and memory. *Psychological Bulletin*, *123*, 162–185.

APPENDIX 1

Writing Task

Taller de Escritura 1

Nombre: ....

Colegio: ....

Curso: 8° año básico Sexo: ....

En la actividad que viene a continuación, te invitamos a escribir un texto en el que te pedimos hacer tu mejor esfuerzo. Desde ya, agradecemos tu cooperación.

Actividad

Los directores de los canales de televisión han decidido que:

"Se eliminaran todos los programas acerca de deportes peligrosos".

Tú has sido elegido para comentar acerca de esta decisión en la nueva **Revista del Colegio**. Esta revista sera enviada a los directores de los canales de televisión.

Usa estas dos hojas para redactar tu artículo a ser publicado muy pronto.

Tiempo asignado: 45 minutos aproximadamente.

APPENDIX 1

Writing Task (Translation)

Writing Workshop 1

Name: ....

School: ....

Level: 8th grade

In this activity, we invite you to write a text in which you are asked to do your best effort. We appreciate your cooperation.

Activity

TV channels directors have decided that:

"All dangerous TV sport programs will be not be included any more".

You have been chosen to comment on this statement and write and essay for the new school journal. This issue will be sent to TV channels directors.

You can use these two sheets of paper to write your text.

You are given 45 minutes for this task.

APPENDIX 2

Reading Test and Inferential Questions

Sabías Tú Que...

(1) Desde la antigüedad, al hombre le ha gustado contemplar la belleza del mundo que lo rodea y gozar con los colores, formas y movimientos de todos los elementos de la naturaleza. Su mente inquieta lo ha llevado no sólo a observar el mundo, sino también a estudiarlo científicamente a través de diversos medios a los que puede recurrir. Sin duda, entre los múltiples avances científicos, los instrumentos que registran imágenes son algunos de los inventos que más han contribuido al desarrollo de la ciencia.

(2) Pocas personas han pensado en la importancia de los instrumentos que registran imágenes. Sin embargo, resulta interesante pensar en los beneficios que trae consigo esta actividad. Durante años, las personas morían de lo que, al parecer, era un dolor de estómago. Actualmente, muchos enfermos pueden mejorar gracias a que la ecotomografía, permite examinar el estómago del paciente. También es posible detectar tumores cerebrales con aparatos tan valiosos como el escáner. Además, hoy es posible controlar las etapas del embarazo y comprobar el crecimiento del feto con instrumentos especiales. Se puede decir que los instrumentos para registrar imágenes han contribuido a detectar a tiempo problemas relacionados con la salud.

(3) Para estudiar el interior del cuerpo humano, los científicos inventaron la ecografía, lo que resultó ser un aporte esencial para los ginecólogos. Estos últimos están interesados en el crecimiento del feto. Este procedimiento entrega datos precisos del desarrollo del ser que está por nacer. E incluso, durante el embarazo, permite obtener información acerca de la maduración del aparato respiratorio, que resulta fundamental para que el cuerpo humano funcione. La inmadurez del sistema de respiración impide que el recién nacido pueda sobrevivir. Durante mucho tiempo no se supo cómo resolver este problema. Hoy en día, los médicos mantienen al bebé en incubadoras por el tiempo que sea necesario.

(4) Por otra parte, se puede mencionar otra contribución de los instrumentos que captan imágenes. Por medio de ellos se ha podido registrar el movimiento de los astros en el espacio, a menos que las condiciones atmosféricas no sean las mejores. Como ocurrió, por ejemplo, con el eclipse del año 1998. Los astrónomos se concentraron en el norte de Chile para observar mejor este fenómeno, debido a la claridad de su cielo.

(5) Los científicos dedican gran parte de su tiempo a describir el universo. G. Dupont ha realizado uno de los avances más interesantes en el área. Este científico demostró que se podía fotografiar una sola imagen del universo con la ubicación de miles de estrellas. Debido a este descubrimiento, los investigadores franceses han podido observar algunos astros tal como se ordenan en el universo. Esta tarea es una de las metas que se ha planteado la astronomía.

Sin el uso de la fotografía, se habrían demorado meses en ubicar estas estrellas en un solo mapa.

(6) Sin importar las técnicas empleadas, es indudable que los instrumentos que registran imágenes han permitido el avance científico en diversas áreas. Se puede esperar que en un futuro cercano, el hombre sea capaz de inventar instrumentos con un nivel tecnológico cada vez más especializados. Estos avances permitirán a los investigadores descubrir cosas insospechadas hasta ahora.

Open Questions:

1. De acuerdo con el texto, ¿quéprocedimiento entrega datos precisos del desarrollo del ser que está por nacer?
2. ¿Cuál es la idea principal del párrafo 4?
3. Según el texto, ¿qué desea probar el autor?
4. Señala las razones más importantes que da el autor para probar la respuesta anterior.
5. De acuerdo con el texto, ¿por qué los médicos mantienen al recién nacido en incubadoras?
6. ¿Cuál es la idea principal del párrafo 2?
7. De acuerdo con el texto, ¿a qué conclusión llega el autor?
8. Según el texto, ¿quiénes se habrían demorado meses en ubicar todas las estrellas en un mismo mapa?
9. Escribe un resumen del texto en tres líneas.

APPENDIX 2

Reading Test and Inferential Questions (Translation)

Do you know that...?

(1) From old times, man liked to look at the beauty of the world that surrounds him and enjoy the colors, forms and movement of the nature elements. His wondering mind has taken him not only to observe the world but also to study it scientifically through different devices. Of course, devices that help capture images are some of the most incredible scientific advances and they have contributed much to science development.

(2) Few people have thought about the importance of the devices to register images. However, it is interesting to consider the benefits that they bring with them. During years, people died due to what thought stomach pain. Nowadays,

many ill people can get better thanks to echotomographies that allow doctors to examine the patient's stomach. Also, it is possible to detect brain tumors with devices such as scanners. Besides, it is possible to control the baby growing in the mother's womb and to exam the baby's healthy growing up. It is possible to say that these special devices to capture images have contributed immensely to detect on time health problems.

(3) To study the inner part of the human body, scientists invented the echography, which turned out to be a tremendous help for doctors. They are very much interested in the healthy growing of the fetus. This procedure gives the doctor precise information of the baby. During pregnancy, it helps get information about the maturity of the baby's breathing system, which is fundamental to keep the human body working properly. The breathing system immaturity is a major cause of death among babies. During a long time, there were no answer to solve this problem; nowadays, doctors keep immature babies in special devices until they are big enough to survive.

(4) On the other hand, it is also possible to mention another contribution of the devices that captures images. Using them properly, far away stars have been studied in detail, given the adequate weather conditions. For example, during the year 1998 scientists gathered together in the South of Chile to observe an eclipse, due to the special and clear sky of this region.

(5) Scientists spend a lot of time describing the universe. G. Dupont has produced one of the most interesting advances in this area of research. This scientist demonstrated that he could get with only one photograph of the universe the position of a lot of stars. Due to these findings, French researchers have been able to observe some stars in the right order in the universe. This step is only one of the many tasks that astronomy is interested in. Without the use of photographs, it would have taken lots of months to find the right place of some stars in just one map of the universe.

(6) No matter what kind of technique could be used to get images, it is undoubtedly true that without these devices the scientific advance would have not been the same in many research areas. It can be expected that in a near future man will be able to invent technological devices each time more specialized. These advances will help researchers discover unexpected unthinkable things.

Open Questions:

1. According to the text, which procedure does give precise data about the evolution of the baby?
2. Which is the main idea of paragraph 4?
3. According to the text, which is the author's purpose?
4. Explain the most important reasons given by the author to prove his thesis.
5. Why do doctors keep babies in special machines after having been delivered?

6. Which is the main idea of paragraph 2?
7. According to the text, which is the author's conclusion?
8. Based on your reading, who would have taken months in searching stars in the same map?
9. Write a summary of the text in three lines.

APPENDIX 3

Scoring Guideline for Argumentative Discourse (Reading and Writing)

Level	Scoring		Total	
Microstructural				
Nominal co-reference	1	3	5	5
Nominal ellipsis	1	3	5	5
Cause–effect relation	1	3	5	5
Macrostructural				
Macroproposition 1	1	5	9	9
Macroproposition 2	1	5	9	9
Topic	1	5	9	9
Superstructural				
Thesis	1	5	9	9
Arguments	1	5	9	9
Conclusion	1	5	9	9
Total Test	69			

Explanation: The scoring numbers were organized according to the weight we wanted to give to each psycholinguistic skill involved. Therefore, local coherence was given a maximum of 5 points for each feature (total 15). Macrostructural and superstructural levels, because of their higher importance in discourse processing, were given a maximum of 9 points (total 27). The numbers 3 or 5 in the medium scale were given when the expected process was not wrong but the answer was incomplete or the text produced was partly cohesive or coherent at the required level.

CHAPTER 37

Enacting Rhetorical Literacies: The Expository Reading and Writing Curriculum in Theory and Practice

Mira-Lisa Katz, Sonoma State University
Nancy Brynelson, California State University
John R. Edlund, California State Polytechnic University, Pomona

All true readings are subversive, against the grain, as Alice, a sane reader, discovered in the Looking-Glass world of mad name givers. The Duchess calls mustard a "mineral"; the Cheshire Cat purrs and calls it "growling"; a Canadian prime minister tears up the railway and calls it "progress"; a Swiss businessman traffics in loot and calls it "commerce"; an Argentinean president shelters murderers and calls it "amnesty." Against such misnomers readers can open the pages of their books. In such cases of willful madness, reading helps us maintain coherence in the chaos. Not to eliminate it, not to enclose experience within conventional verbal structures, but to allow chaos to progress creatively on its own vertiginous way. Not to trust the glittering surface of words but to burrow into the darkness.

Alberto Manguel (2010, p. 8)

This chapter analytically describes a promising high school English course, the Expository Reading and Writing Curriculum (ERWC), that effectively integrates multiple theories from the fields of reading comprehension, rhetoric, literacy, and composition to foster college readiness, academic literacy development, and literate identity formation at the high school level. Following a discussion of the policy context that spawned this statewide educational initiative in California, authors describe the curriculum, discuss significant theoretical influences, and explain how the ERWC puts these theories into practice in diverse instructional contexts. The chapter subsequently explains how the ERWC establishes a classroom environment in which the opinions of both students and teachers are actively sought and respected; provides strategic instructional scaffolding that enables students at varying levels of proficiency to more effectively read, think critically about, and compose sophisticated expository texts; integrates literacy pedagogies with concepts and practices from Aristotelian rhetoric to promote principled debates about ideas and texts that both students and teachers find highly engaging; and flexibly supports teachers' development of generative pedagogies that enable students to acquire high-level rhetorical literacies. Blending effective practices based on research in reading comprehension, rhetoric, literacy, and composition, the ERWC supports the development of young people's academic identities and civic literacies and strengthens teachers' capacities to further cultivate the deeply literate habits of mind that students need to be successful in college, career, and community.

Policy Context

In 2009, President Barack Obama announced the American Graduation Initiative and its goal of achieving "the highest proportion of college graduates in the world" by 2020 (Office of the Press Secretary, 2009, para. 3). Although calls for increased rates of college completion are louder today than ever before (Bill & Melinda Gates Foundation, 2010; J.M. Lee, Edwards, Menson, & Rawls, 2011; Lumina Foundation, 2010; National Governors Association [NGA], 2010; NGA & Council of Chief State School Officers [CCSSO], 2010c; U.S. Department of Education, 2011), they are hardly new, and the factors contributing to the lack of college completion have been well documented over time (Adelman, 1999, 2006; Lewis & Farris, 1996; Mansfield & Farris, 1991; Parsad & Lewis, 2003). The debate regarding the purpose of higher education and the role of remedial education within it—quality versus equity—began after World War II and the G.I. Bill, rose a second time in response to Sputnik, and escalated yet again in the 1970s after the Vietnam War and the Civil Rights movement (Parker, Bustillos, & Behringer, 2010), as higher education experienced increasing shifts in student demographics. The current debate regarding remediation has shifted yet again; now the choice is access versus efficiency due to the enormous costs of remediation.[1] The view that remedial programs are largely ineffective (based on college completion rates) heads the list of reasons why remediation during college should be prevented and eliminated (Alliance for Excellent Education, 2006, 2011c; Strong American Schools, 2008).

As readers of this volume are well aware, critiques of elementary and secondary education in general, and literacy education in particular, were brought into sharp focus with the publication of *A Nation at Risk: The Imperative for Educational Reform* (National Commission on Excellence in Education, 1983) and *Becoming a Nation of Readers: The Report of the Commission on Reading* (Anderson, Hiebert, Scott, & Wilkinson, 1984) and with the results of the 1994 National Assessment of Educational Progress in reading (Williams, Reese, Campbell, Mazzeo, & Phillips, 1995). Initially, the concern regarding the decline in levels of reading proficiency centered on the early elementary grades; attention turned, however, from the wars surrounding beginning reading to the crisis of adolescent literacy in the 2000s (ACT, 2006; Biancarosa & Snow, 2006; Committee to Improve Reading and Writing in Middle and High Schools, 2009; Kamil, 2003; Kamil et al., 2008; NASBE Study Group on Middle and High School Literacy, 2005; National Commission on Writing in America's Schools and Colleges, 2003; Torgesen et al., 2007) and the disconnect between high school curricula and college expectations (ACT, 2005; American Diploma Project, 2004; Conley, 2003; Intersegmental Committee of the Academic Senates of the California Community Colleges, the California State University, and the University of California [ICAS], 2002; Joftus, 2002; Kirst, 2004).

It was within this policy context that the board of trustees of the California State University (CSU) enacted Executive Order 665 in 1997, establishing criteria for determining proficiency in mathematics and English and the consequences for failing to meet the criteria. The board also established a goal for 90% of the CSU's incoming students to be proficient according to the 1997 criteria in both mathematics and English by 2007. Several years into the policy, it became clear that achieving the goal of 90% proficient was not realistic (Mills, 2004). Consistent with the move to align high school and college curricula, the CSU embarked on an initiative to align the K–16 assessment systems so students could be identified as ready or not ready for college-level courses in mathematics and English much earlier in their school careers, making college readiness something they could pursue while still in high school. The CSU's Early Assessment Program was established in 2002 in collaboration with the California Department of Education and the California State Board of Education to accomplish this goal. The Early Assessment Program consists of five components: the test administered in 11th grade in conjunction with the mandated California Standards Test; high school preparation in English and mathematics; teacher and administrator professional development; parent and family communication; and preservice teacher preparation. Starting in 2004, students who were identified as ready for college-level courses were exempted from the requirement to take placement tests in English and/or mathematics and were moved directly into credit-bearing coursework upon enrollment in the CSU. Students who were identified as not ready for college-level courses were encouraged to do additional preparation during their senior year of high school.

The ERWC Curriculum

In response to the call for additional preparation, a task force comprised of CSU and high school educators collaborated to create the ERWC. Designed to prepare college-bound seniors for the literacy demands of higher education and civic life, the ERWC guides students through a sequence of 14 rigorous instructional units organized into a yearlong, rhetoric-based course that develops advanced proficiency in expository, analytical, and persuasive reading and writing. The course helps students read, comprehend, respond to, talk, and write about nonfiction and literary texts and provides instruction in research methods and documentation conventions. Through long-term, deep engagement with texts from varied genres throughout the course, students increase their awareness of and ability to employ the rhetorical strategies and stylistic devices of published authors. They read closely to examine the relationship between an author's argument or theme and the audience and purpose; to analyze the impact of linguistic and rhetorical devices; and to examine the social, political, philosophical, and ideological assumptions that underlie each text. Students who successfully complete the course can effectively use these strategic approaches independently when reading unfamiliar texts and writing in response to them.

Throughout the course, students explore and analyze a wide range of texts, including contemporary essays, newspaper and magazine articles, editorials, reports, memos, biographies, online materials, and assorted public documents, as well as other nonfiction and fiction texts. Written assignments, formative assessments, and holistic scoring guides constitute part of each of the 14 instructional units or modules (most are based on multiple texts) organized across two semesters. Each module is built around a high-interest topic discussed from multiple perspectives, sometimes across genres. All modules include instruction in critical reading, metacognitive and rhetorical analyses, vocabulary, grammar, research methods, documentation conventions, and analytical writing based on information learned from, and in response to, the assigned texts.

A balanced and comprehensive 12th-grade English language arts course (see Figure 1), the ERWC performs two different but strategically related functions:

1. It prepares college-bound students to take on the methodical academic reading and writing practices expected by college faculty across the disciplines.
2. It prepares teachers to more advantageously support their high school students' development of the textual practices that they will need to succeed in college and beyond while meeting California's recently adopted Common Core State Standards (CCSS) for teaching informational texts and rhetorical analysis.

In addition to helping students develop the literacies and competencies expected in postsecondary contexts (as outlined by ICAS, 2002), the ERWC materials are designed to embody the following key principles of an effective expository reading and writing curriculum:

- The integration of interactive reading and writing processes
- A rhetorical approach to texts that fosters critical thinking
- Materials and themes that engage students and provide a foundation for principled debate and argument
- Classroom activities, language routines, and interactional patterns designed to model and foster successful practices of fluent readers and writers
- Research-based methodologies with a consistent relationship between theory and practice
- Built-in flexibility to allow teachers to respond to varied students' needs and diverse instructional contexts
- Alignment with California's CCSS for English language arts (California Department of Education, 2010)

Figure 1. Expository Reading and Writing Curriculum Matrix of Modules

Module Order	Module Summary & Final Writing Assignment	Texts
1. Fast Food: Who's to Blame?	Based on four newspaper articles and several letters to the editor, this module engages students in analyzing various perspectives on who is to blame for the rise in childhood obesity. Final Writing: timed writing, rhetorical evaluation of the letters to the editor, or text-based argumentative essay.	• Barboza, David. "If You Pitch It, They Will Eat." *New York Times* 3 Aug. 2003, late ed., sec. 3: 1. • Brownlee, Shannon. "It's Portion Distortion That Makes America Fat." *Sacramento Bee* 5 Jan. 2003: E1+. • Weintraub, Daniel. "The Battle Against Fast Food Begins in the Home." *Sacramento Bee* 17 Dec. 2002: B7. • Zinczenko, David. "Don't Blame the Eater." *New York Times* 23 Nov. 2002, late ed.: A19.
2. Going for the Look	After analyzing an article on the lawsuit accusing Abercrombie & Fitch of discriminatory hiring practices, *Going for the Look* concludes with a timed writing or an argumentative essay.	• Greenhouse, Steven. "Going for the Look, but Risking Discrimination." *New York Times* 13 July 2003, sec. 1: 12.
3. The Rhetoric of the Op-Ed Page: Ethos, Logos, and Pathos	This module introduces the Aristotelian concepts of ethos, logos, and pathos and applies them to a rhetorical analysis of an op-ed piece by Jeremy Rifkin. The culminating writing assignment is a letter to the editor responding to the Rifkin piece.	• Edlund, John. "Three Ways to Persuade." *Expository Reading and Writing Course: Semester One*. Long Beach: CA State UP, 2008. (29–32) • Rifkin, Jeremy. "A Change of Heart About Animals." *Los Angeles Times* 1 Sept. 2003: B15.
4. The Value of Life	*The Value of Life* asks students to synthesize and critically respond to four pieces: Hamlet's "To be, or not to be" soliloquy; an excerpt from Lance Armstrong's *It's Not About the Bike*; an article by Amanda Ripley on the aftermath of 9/11; and a life insurance tool, the Human Life Value Calculator. The unit concludes with an academic essay responding to all sources.	• Armstrong, Lance, with Sally Jenkins. *It's Not About the Bike: My Journey Back to Life*. New York: Putnam, 2000. (1–5) • Life and Health Insurance Foundation for Education. "The Human Life Value Calculator." • Ripley, Amanda. "What Is a Life Worth?" *Time* 11 Feb. 2002: 22–27. • Shakespeare, William. Hamlet, Act III, Sc. 1, Hamlet's "To be, or not to be" soliloquy.
5. Racial Profiling	After reading an argumentative essay by Bob Herbert on racial profiling, students write their own argumentative piece on a similar topic.	• Herbert, Bob. "In America; Hounding the Innocent." *New York Times* 13 July 1999, late ed., sec. 4: 17.

Module Order	Module Summary & Final Writing Assignment	Texts
6. Juvenile Justice	Drawing on four newspaper articles about whether juveniles who commit serious crimes should be tried and sentenced as adults, *Juvenile Justice* asks students to evaluate authors' rhetorical stances and synthesize their arguments in a text-based academic essay.	• Krikorian, Greg. "Many Kids Called Unfit for Adult Trial." *Sacramento Bee* 3 Mar. 2003: A6. • Liptak, Adam. "Ruling is Awaited on Death Penalty for Young Killers." *New York Times* 4 Jan. 2005, late ed.: A1+. • Lundstrom, Marjie. "Kids Are Kids—Until They Commit Crimes." *Sacramento Bee* 1 Mar. 2001: A3. • Thompson, Paul. "Startling Finds on Teenage Brains." *Sacramento Bee* 25 May 2001: B7.
7. The Last Meow	Focusing on a reflective essay about recent developments in veterinary medicine, *The Last Meow* asks students to infer the writer's argument and then compose a piece in one of the following genres: persuasive or academic summary, letter to the editor, I-Search or research paper, or other options.	• Bilger, Burkhard. "The Last Meow." *New Yorker* 8 Sept. 2003: 46–53.
8. Into the Wild	Based on *Into the Wild*, a full-length non-fiction work by Jon Krakauer (1996), this module offers students extended opportunities to think deeply about human motivation and maturation and includes excerpts from the American Transcendentalists and Russian novelists who influenced the main character's thinking. Students conclude with a text-based academic essay on one of a number of themes.	• Krakauer, Jon. *Into the Wild*. New York: Doubleday, 1996.
9. Bring a Text to Class	Introducing the second semester of the ERWC, *Bring a Text to Class* builds on out-of school texts, broadly conceived, that students bring in to share. The module enables students to make their textual expertise explicit and connects out-of-school and in-school reading. Students conclude by reflecting on classmates' chosen texts and reflecting metacognitively on their own reading practices.	• "Hip-Hop Becoming Worldwide Language for Youth Resistance." *USA Today Magazine* Sept. 2000: 7.

(continued)

Figure 1. Expository Reading and Writing Curriculum Matrix of Modules (*Continued*)

Module Order	Module Summary & Final Writing Assignment	Texts
10. Language, Gender, and Culture	Drawing on readings in literature and sociolinguistics, *Language, Gender, and Culture* invites students to explore how language conveys cultural values and gender-based communication styles. Students conclude with a text-based academic essay.	• Ehrlich, Gretel. "About Men." *The Solace of Open Spaces*. New York: Penguin, 1985. 49–53. • Kingston, Maxine Hong. *The Woman Warrior: Memoirs of a Childhood Among Ghosts*. New York: Random House, 1976. 165–82. • Tannen, Deborah. "His Politeness Is Her Powerlessness." *You Just Don't Understand: Women and Men in Conversation*. New York: William Morrow/HarperCollins, 1990. 203–05.
11. Left Hand of Darkness	*The Left Hand of Darkness* is a multi-genre science fiction novel that includes field reports, folktales, and other genre-bending texts. Students extend the rhetorical techniques of the ERWC to a full-length literary work and conclude with a text-based academic essay.	• Le Guin, Ursula K. *The Left Hand of Darkness*. New York: Penguin, 1969.
12. The Politics of Food	*The Politics of Food* is based on two articles that ask readers to consider connections between science, agriculture, and politics as they relate to human health and well-being. Students conclude the module with a text-based academic essay.	• Berry, Wendell. "The Pleasures of Eating." *What Are People For? Essays*. New York: North Point/Farrar, Straus and Giroux, 1990. 145–52. • Pollan, Michael. "When a Crop Becomes King." *New York Times* 19 July 2002, late ed.: A17.
13. Justice: Childhood Love Lessons	Based on an argumentative essay by bell hooks, *Childhood Love Lessons* examines the relationship between parental discipline and expressions of love. Students respond with a persuasive essay.	• hooks, bell. "Justice: Childhood Love Lessons." *All About Love: New Visions*. New York: William Morrow, 2000. 17–30.
14. Bullying at School: Research Project	In *Bullying at School*, students read widely from refereed journal articles and conduct primary and secondary research on their own, deepening their understanding of how to find, evaluate, and document sources. The unit concludes with students writing a School Code of Conduct on bullying.	• In addition to a number of other texts, articles from the following journals constitute the reading: *ERIC Digests*; *Curriculum Review*; *Current Health*; *Our Children*; *Time*; *Intervention in School and Clinic*; *Journal of the American Medical Association*; *Education World*; *Educational Leadership*; *Educational Research*.

These principles (California State University, 2008, p. xi) are instantiated in the ERWC's assignment template (a patterned process through which each of the curricular units is flexibly structured), which outlines the important moves that students make as they read and interact with texts, connect the texts they read to the writing they plan to do, and talk and write about the ideas and issues contained in and inspired by the texts. Throughout the instructional process, students read and revisit readings with different purposes. They discuss and write about the texts and their own thinking numerous times—each time with a different purpose. As a result of this relentless focus on the text, students construct deep understandings of what the texts say, mean, and do, and are subsequently able to use those understandings to craft and support their own arguments in both speaking and writing (see Figure 2). Throughout the ERWC course, the texts students read become progressively more complex, and what students do with texts, in terms of both reading and writing, becomes increasingly challenging.

The notion of text complexity has garnered national attention of late. In the national CCSS, text complexity is determined according to three factors:

> Qualitative evaluation of the text: Levels of meaning, structure, language conventionality and clarity, and knowledge demands
>
> Quantitative evaluation of the text: Readability measures and other scores of text complexity
>
> Matching reader to text and task: Reader variables (such as motivation, knowledge, and experiences) and task variables (such as purpose and the complexity generated by the task assigned and the questions posed) (NGA & CCSSO, 2010a, p. 12)

In addition to increasing comprehension demands over time, the ERWC's rhetorical approach engages students in extended and challenging composing processes. Although a given text may be fairly simple to read (at the levels of quantitative and possibly qualitative complexity, as defined earlier), what one does with a text may involve multiple and nuanced analyses. In conjunction with varied analytical reading, writing that involves negotiating and weaving together the voices of others and crafting one's own stance in response to multiple texts constitutes equally complex textual work.

Such notions of text and task complexity have recently converged in the context of conversations about the emphasis on argument in the new CCSS for writing. Literacy educator Gerald Graff asserts, "The university is largely an 'argument culture,'...therefore, K–12 schools should 'teach the conflicts' so that students are adept at understanding and engaging in argument (both oral and written) when they enter college" (NGA & CCSSO, 2010b, p. 24). In some circles in education (where rhetoric is not, perhaps, as commonly understood), we have observed that the term *argument* is sometimes used to refer only to logos. Although some educators around the nation have voiced concern about the emphasis on logical argument (logos) the ERWC teaches all three categories of appeals, or forms of persuasion that constitute Aristotelian rhetoric: ethos, the presentation of the character and authority of the speaker; logos, the use of words and arguments;

Figure 2. Expository Reading and Writing Curriculum Assignment Template Overview

<table>
<tr><td colspan="2">Reading Rhetorically
To “read rhetorically” means to focus not only on what the text says, but also on the purposes it serves, the intentions of the author, and the effects on the audience. This section is designed to scaffold the practices of fluent academic readers for students who are developing as academic readers, writers, and thinkers.</td></tr>
<tr><td>Prereading
• Getting Ready to Read
• Exploring Key Concepts
• Surveying the Text
• Making Predictions and Asking Questions
• Understanding Key Vocabulary</td><td>Prereading describes the processes that readers use as they prepare to read a new text. It involves surveying the text and considering what they know about the topic and the text itself, including its purpose, content, author, form, and language. This process helps readers to develop a rationale for reading, anticipate what the text will discuss, and establish a framework for understanding the text when reading begins.</td></tr>
<tr><td>Reading
• Reading for Understanding
• Considering the Structure of the Text
• Noticing Language
• Annotating and Questioning the Text
• Analyzing Stylistic Choices</td><td>The reading process involves using the knowledge developed during prereading to understand the text and to confirm, refine, or refute the predictions that the reader has made about the text. This section begins by asking students to read “with the grain,” also called “playing the believing game.” Once they have established their understanding of the text, they then read “against the grain,” also called “playing the doubting game.” Both processes help students comprehend a text more deeply.</td></tr>
<tr><td>Postreading
• Summarizing and Responding
• Thinking Critically
• Reflecting on Your Reading Process</td><td>Postreading describes the process that readers follow once they have read and reread the text. It can involve restating the central ideas of the text and responding to them from a personal perspective, but it also often includes questioning the text and noting its rhetorical strategies, evaluating its arguments and evidence, and considering how it fits into the larger conversation about the topic.</td></tr>
<tr><td colspan="2">Connecting Reading to Writing
Although the writing process can be divided into stages, writing—like reading—is essentially a recursive process that continually revisits previous moments. Up until this point students have been “writing to learn” by using writing for taking notes, making marginal notations, mapping the text, making predictions, and asking questions. At this point they are ready to build on the ongoing dialogue they have had with sources, peers, and teachers, producing their own texts by using the words, ideas, and arguments that have been raised in readings and class discussion. In this transitional moment, their reading will inform, inspire, and guide their writing as they shift from being an audience for the writing of others to addressing their own audience as writers themselves.</td></tr>
</table>

Discovering What You Think • Considering the Writing Task • Taking a Stance • Gathering Evidence to Support Your Claims • Getting Ready to Write	Allowing time for students to consider and process what they have read helps them establish a connection to the writing assignment. It promotes information gathering and idea generation as students begin to craft a response to a writing task. This transition from reading to writing provides opportunities for students to analyze information gathered during reading, assess its value, and begin to imagine the trajectory their own argument might take as they develop their thinking and attempt to convince readers of their stance.
Writing Rhetorically Thinking of writing as a rhetorical activity invites students to consider the importance of audience, purpose, ethos, situation, message, and genre as they write to affect readers in particular ways. The rhetorical approach calls on them to consider the circumstances that inform a particular occasion for writing before deciding on an argument and how it might give shape to their writing. Thus writing rhetorically emphasizes contextualized thinking, sense making, and persuasion as prerequisites for considerations about form or genre. At this point as students begin to compose a first draft, they are about to make an active contribution to the conversation among voices and between texts with which they have been interacting while reading. It can be helpful to think of the writing at this stage is "reading-based" in that it synthesizes the viewpoints and information of various sources for the writer's own purposes.	
Entering the Conversation • Composing a Draft • Considering Structure • Using the Words of Others (and Avoiding Plagiarism) • Negotiating Voices	Writing can be a way of discovering what we think and working through our personal concerns (as described above in "Discovering What You Think"), for example in diaries and journals, but most often we write to express our ideas to others; writing is communication. In addition to forms of print and electronic media, such as letters, newspaper articles, memos, posters, reports, online forums, and websites, writing broadly conceived also includes texting, emailing, posting to a blog or submitting a message to a discussion board, tweeting, or using social media sites like Facebook. All of these forms of writing, as well as the more formal academic essay privileged in schools and universities, involve writers in entering an ongoing conversation in order to communicate thoughts, ideas, and arguments.
Revising and Editing • Revising Rhetorically • Considering Stylistic Choices • Editing the Draft • Responding to Feedback • Reflecting on Your Writing Process	Most students equate revising with editing, but more advanced writers understand that revision involves "re-evaluating" the concepts of the paper: the use of information, the arrangement and structure of arguments, and the development and significance of ideas. Revision—as both a reading activity and a writing activity—is based on an assessment of how well the writing has communicated the writer's intentions—the argument or ideas of the text. Revising for rhetorical effectiveness invites writers to address issues of content and structure before addressing sentence-level concerns such as word choice and grammatical accuracy.

and pathos, the appeal to the emotions of the audience. Logos may be privileged in academic circles in general, and in the Common Core in particular, but the ERWC goes beyond the CCSS, apprenticing students to ways of analyzing the texts they read by using rhetoric and then applying those understandings to their writing. Because single texts often use multiple forms of persuasion, text analysis in the ERWC requires that students have a broad knowledge of rhetorical appeals. Although the ERWC embraces the CCSS in terms of teaching students to write effective logical arguments (as evidenced by the elements of the assignment template "Taking a Stance" and "Gathering Evidence to Support Your Claims"), the ERWC goes beyond the CCSS to include a broader range of stances and appeals that students may need to generate as writers themselves.

However, if students participating in the ERWC analyze and produce the kinds of texts envisioned by the curriculum, they will have gone well beyond the Common Core, and as well they should because they will need such skills and habits of mind to participate fully not only in college and career but also in many spheres beyond them. As the CCSS aptly assert:

> The value of effective argument extends well beyond the classroom or workplace.... As Richard Fulkerson (1996) puts it in *Teaching the Argument in Writing*, the proper context for thinking about argument is one "in which the goal is not victory but a good decision, one in which all arguers are at risk of needing to alter their views, one in which a participant takes seriously and fairly the views different from his or her own" (pp. 16–17). Such capacities are broadly important for the literate, educated person living in the diverse, information-rich environment of the twenty-first century. (NGA & CCSSO, 2010b, p. 25)

Disseminated via professional development jointly sponsored by the CSU system and county offices of education throughout California, to date more than 8,000 educators have participated in the 20-hour ERWC professional development program (usually spread over four days across a period of several months) to learn about the course, receive free copies of the curriculum, and join the statewide ERWC Online Community, an online forum that supports ERWC teachers and teacher educators throughout the state. The arc of professional learning for most teachers begins with use of ERWC modules integrated within their existing literature-based curriculum; as they teach more of the curriculum and witness the impact it has on their students' reading and writing, many teachers move into advocacy roles, working to persuade their school administrators to offer the ERWC as a dedicated 12th-grade English course. Approved by the University of California and the CSU as a yearlong college-preparatory English course in 2006, the ERWC has been formally adopted by over 500 California high schools. Originally aligned with California's English–language arts content standards (California Department of Education, 1998) and currently aligned with the recently adopted CCSS (California Department of Education, 2010), the ERWC lends itself to flexible use: Teachers can shape it to meet varied students' needs in diverse instructional contexts.

The policy context today is not very different from when the project began, except that a new urgency has crept into the dialogue as international comparisons of academic performance reveal ever-worsening rankings for U.S. students (Organisation for Economic Co-operation and Development, 2010). Calls for international benchmarking from the Education Commission of the States and many of the organizations cited earlier urge educators to do a better job of preparing students not just for college but also for global competition (Education Commission of the States, 2008; Thompson, 2009). The Alliance for Excellent Education (2011b) asserts, "now more than ever, the nation's education system is being challenged by a technology-driven global economy that requires a skilled and deeply literate workforce" (p. 1).

The CCSS are a response to the call for increased competitiveness and the desire for more consistent and coherent assessment data nationwide. The CCSS place an even greater emphasis on reading and writing complex informational text and argumentation than do the 1997 California English–language arts content standards (NGA & CCSSO, 2010c). Because of its focus on expository text and rhetoric, the ERWC aligns well with the new standards and is viewed by many as a model of effective and engaging curriculum that has the advantage of also addressing the CCSS (A.R. Vaughn, personal communication, October 26, 2011). Moreover, current teachers of the ERWC have been identified as potential leaders in the transition to California's CCSS (N.S. Brownell, personal communication, November 3, 2011).

The ERWC was designed to help students develop the literate dispositions and habits of mind necessary for academic success by building task persistence and competence through engaging topics and research-based instructional methodologies (Alvermann & Moore, 1991; Langer, 1995, 2000; Nystrand, 1997). Coupled with the focus on rhetoric and critical thinking—the real work of adults in college, careers, and communities—the ERWC enables students to develop agency in academic contexts, cultivate identities as potentially successful college-going students, and become active participants in the varied literacies woven throughout all facets of life.

Integrating the Teaching of Reading and Writing: A Brief History

Although we have known for some time that reading and writing are best taught together (Duke, Pearson, Strachan, & Billman, 2011; Shanahan, 2006; Tierney & Shanahan, 1991), the effective integration of reading and writing instruction remains largely a recommendation rather than an artful practice, while historically, many models of literacy have foregrounded the teaching of either reading (Anderson & Pearson, 1984; Kintsch, 2004; Rosenblatt, 1978/1994; Ruddell & Unrau, 2004) or writing (Flower & Hayes, 1981). The ERWC fully integrates reading and writing through sustained and recursive blending of comprehension, rhetoric, literacy, and composition processes and practices (Pressley, 2000, 2002; Wilkinson & Son, 2011).

Between the 1960s and 1980s, researchers began exploring the beneficial consequences of integrating the teaching of reading and writing (see Tierney & Shanahan, 1991, for an extensive review of the early work in this area). Very early studies (Loban, 1963, 1964, as cited in Tierney & Shanahan, 1991) have suggested that proficient writers read well, whereas less proficient writers are less successful at reading; however, later research (e.g., Martin, as cited in Tierney & Shanahan, 1991; Tierney, 1983, as cited in Tierney & Shanahan, 1991) have suggested that previous claims were overstated and somewhat misleading (Tierney & Shanahan, 1991). Shanahan and Lomax argued in 1986 that "reading influences writing, *and* writing influences reading," which suggests "that reading and writing should be taught in ways that maximize the possibility of using information drawn from both reading and writing. (p. 208)" (as quoted in Tierney & Shanahan, p. 249). Although such thinking is no longer new, blending rhetorically based reading and writing as the ERWC does in service of fostering deep academic learning and literacy embodies instantiations and combinations of reading and writing pedagogies that are novel.

Since the 1980s, there has been considerable interest in the similarities "between the cognitive *processes* underlying reading and writing" (Tierney & Shanahan, 1991, p. 250). Summaries of this research appear elsewhere (Langer & Flihan, 2000; Tierney & Shanahan, 1991), but for the purposes of the present review, Wittrock's 1984 claim remains noteworthy: "Reading and writing are generative cognitive processes in which readers and writers 'create meanings by building relations between the text and what they know, believe, and experience' (p. 77)" (as quoted in Tierney & Shanahan, 1991, p. 251). Other researchers suggest that reading and writing—both creative acts of composing—share underlying processes, such as goal setting, projection, perspective taking, and review (Tierney & Pearson, as cited in Tierney & Shanahan, 1991, p. 251). Kucer's (1985, 2009) research additionally highlights the salience of context and background knowledge in the production of textual worlds—a critically important idea that has been expanded on by other researchers.

Although process-oriented studies in recent decades have done much to enhance our understanding of the similarities and differences between reading and writing processes, and indeed, they confirm the benefits of integrated reading and writing instruction, studies to date have not yet gone far enough in helping us understand "the transactional nature of reading and writing, of intertextuality, of how interpersonal factors influence meaning-making" (Tierney & Shanahan, 1991, p. 255), nor has most research to date helped us understand the complex interpersonal factors that influence meaning making, or negotiations of voice, self, and other in the context of academic reading and writing. Also of importance to understanding the ERWC is the research on readers' and writers' transactions with texts (e.g., RAND Reading Study Group, 2002; Smith, 1983, 1984).

> To read and write, as Augustine and Winterowd (1986); Beach and Liebman-Kleine (1986); Bruce (1980); Tierney, LaZansky, Raphael, and Cohen (1987); Pratt (1977); Pearson and Tierney (1984); and Shanklin (1981) have suggested, requires authors

> who expect meaning-making on the part of readers *and* readers who do the meaning-making. Writers, as they produce text, consider their readers—or at least the transactions in which readers are likely to engage....[W]riters try to address and satisfy what they project as the response of the reader to that speech act that underlies the surface structure of the communication....Readers, as they read text, respond to what they perceive writers are trying to get them to think of, as well as what readers themselves perceive they need to do. (Tierney & Shanahan, 1991, p. 259)

Shanahan's (2006) review of research conducted between 1985 and 2000 claims that "reading and writing are dependent upon common cognitive substrata of abilities (e.g., visual, phonological, and semantic systems or short- and long-term memory), and anything that improves these abilities may have implications for both reading and writing development" (p. 174). Building on his research with Fitzgerald (Fitzgerald & Shanahan, as cited in Shanahan, 2006), he suggests that "readers and writers rely on four common knowledge bases" (p. 174): domain or content knowledge; metaknowledge; knowledge of specific features of writing (from phonemic, orthographic, and morphological to lexical, syntactic, and discursive); and procedural knowledge. Citing research spanning a century (from Dejerine's pioneering work in the 1890s on word blindness and agraphia to neuroscientific research from the late 1990s and early 2000s), Shanahan notes the importance of the "overlapping but separable nature of reading and writing at a neurological level" (p. 177).

This overlap, it turns out, is at the root of the two basic reasons it is beneficial to integrate reading and writing instructionally: The first has to do with what is shared across reading and writing domains, and the second has to do with what is different about them. Shanahan (2006) explains,

> One learning theory holds that learning is achieved through examining and reexamining information from a variety of cognitive perspectives (McGinley & Tierney, 1989)....Within this theory, each reconsideration of information [whether via reading or writing] is deepened, not from repetition (that is a memory issue), but from thinking about the information in a new way. Since reading and writing have a somewhat different cognitive footprint,...it is possible that reading and writing can provide these separate vantages for learning. (p. 177)

This explains why it is not enough to teach both reading and writing in the same class (as has so often been done during the past three decades in the name of 'integrating reading and writing'). "Research suggests that individuals combine reading and writing in different ways for various [real-world] tasks" (p. 177). Their usage must be truly woven together in ways that resonate deeply with authentic uses of reading and writing in the worlds of school, work, and civic life.

How we employ texts at school, at work, and in our communities determines, reflects, and supports the varied social and cultural purposes for which they are used. Shanahan (2006) concludes that a "rich empirical research base" demonstrates how

> reading and writing depend upon a common base of cognitive processes and knowledge, and we have a particularly fertile understanding of what kinds of linguistic knowledge are shared between reading and writing, how the patterns of this knowledge sharing change with development, and how reading and writing influence each other. These studies have revealed even closer relations between reading and writing than those previously found and have extended our understanding of the bidirectionality of these relations....
>
> Studies have shown that it is possible to teach reading so that it improves writing and to teach writing so that it improves reading, but we do not know how to do this consistently. (p. 179)

We suggest that the ERWC—which is both a curriculum and a method that puts rhetorical, sociocultural, composition, and comprehension theories of language and learning simultaneously into practice—is moving in this promising direction.

Comprehension: Where Reading Research Has Taken Us

Chronicling the development of over 50 years of reading research, Pearson (2011a) states that "most models of reading have tried to explain how reader factors, text factors and context factors interact when readers make meaning" (slide 25). Citing Richards, Pearson suggests that the scholarship of the mid-20th century, although focused on "new criticism" in literature (during the 1940s and 1950s), tended in the 1960s to follow bottom-up cognitive models, which he notes were very "text-centric" (slide 26). In the 1970s, cognitive models became more schema-based, "and the reader response models (Rosenblatt) of the 80s focused more on reader factors—knowledge or interpretation mattered most" (Pearson, 2011a, slide 28). The sociocultural models of the 1990s widened the scope of study to include social, socioeconomic, and cultural influences alongside purpose, situation, and the ways values of discourse communities inevitably collide in the context of literacy teaching and learning.

Tracing a parallel trajectory of scholarship on comprehension strategies instruction since the 1970s, Wilkinson and Son (2011) outline four waves of reading research (following the three described by Pressley). In the 1970s and early 1980s, research "focused on the effects of teaching students individual comprehension strategies" (p. 362). Although specific strategies (e.g., activating background knowledge, questioning, summarizing, picturing the text) proved effective, the second wave of research in the 1980s focused on multiple-strategies instruction (e.g., reciprocal teaching).

> During the second wave, the direct explanation approach to strategy instruction came to the fore (Duffy, et al., 1987). Teachers explained to students...how to use a small repertoire of strategies, modeled the use of the strategies, and engaged students in guided and independent practice of the strategies. (p. 362)

Studies of this approach yielded "fairly robust benefits for students' comprehension" (p. 362).

The third wave of research, Wilkinson and Son (2011) suggest, "focused on a more flexible approach...called 'transactional strategies instruction' (TSI), so called because it emphasized transactions between readers and text, transactions among participants (students and teacher), and joint construction of understanding" (p. 363). In TSI, there is more emphasis on conversation among students—"on dialogue, on giving students more control over their own learning, and on collaborative inquiry as a mean [*sic*] of constructing knowledge and understanding" (p. 367). Based on the evolution of this research, there is now "no doubt that instruction in small repertoires of comprehension strategies, when implemented well, produces robust effects on measures of comprehension, including standardized tests (e.g., Anderson, 1992; Brown et al., 1996; Collins, 1991)" (p. 364).

In their review of comprehension strategies instruction, Wilkinson and Son (2011) describe the final and fourth wave as dialogic. Central to such

> approaches is the juxtaposition of relative perspectives or discourses that gives rise to tension and sometimes conflict among different voices. From a dialogic perspective, it is from the interaction and struggle among different, even competing, voices that meaning and understanding emerge. (p. 367)

Programs that fall within this fourth wave include Concept-Oriented Reading Instruction (CORI), in-depth expanded applications of science, and Reading Apprenticeship (Greenleaf, Schoenbach, Cziko, & Mueller, 2001; Schoenbach & Greenleaf, 2009; Schoenbach, Greenleaf, Cziko, & Hurwitz, 1999). What these programs share is a focus on teaching comprehension within specific subject areas. Of particular note is the ability of programs like Reading Apprenticeship to help educators teach reading comprehension in middle and high school contexts where subject matter demands are more complex.

Unsurprisingly, classroom discussion plays a critical role in promoting comprehension. Although this idea is not new, its implementation is now based on more robust research and theory from sociocognitive, sociocultural, and other approaches to teaching and learning.

> From a sociocognitive perspective, discussion enables students to make public their perspectives on issues arising from the text, consider alternative perspectives proposed by peers, and attempt to reconcile conflicts among opposing points of view (Almasi, 1995). From a sociocultural perspective, discussion enables students to co-construct knowledge and understandings about the text and internalize ways of thinking that foster the knowledge, skills, and dispositions needed to transfer to the reading of new texts (Wells, 2007). And from a dialogic perspective, the tension and conflict between relative perspectives and competing voices in discussion about a text helps shape the discourse and students' comprehension (Nystrand, 2006). (Wilkinson & Son, 2011, p. 369)

As we might expect, the quality and types of talk matter; open discussion, authentic questions, and uptake of learners' ideas "in the context of academically challenging tasks" correlate positively with students' reading comprehension and academic performance (p. 370). Citing research by Anderson and colleagues, Wilkinson and Son (2011) posit that learning to make rhetorical moves in conversation (taking a position on an issue and using evidence to support it) transfers from group discussion to "written argumentation performed individually and independently" (p. 372). Intertextuality (cf. Lemke, 1992)—learning to make sense of multiple texts in conversations with one another—"might be regarded as the sine qua non of dialogic approaches to teaching comprehension" (Wilkinson and Son, 2011, p. 374). The bottom line is that high-quality discussion creates authentic opportunities "for students to develop the automatic, fluid articulation of strategies necessary for generative and flexible comprehension" (p. 376).

Enacting Rhetorical Literacies

A particularly critical element of the ERWC—the integration of Aristotelian rhetoric—is not considered fully enough (if at all) in the many studies cited earlier, nor is it considered more generally in most research on literacy and reading comprehension. We believe a greater focus on the rhetorical dimension could greatly enhance young people's academic literacies as well as their abilities to successfully engage in meaningful and principled civic debate. Originally inspired by Bean, Chappell, and Gillam (2004), the ERWC authors view both reading and writing as rhetorical processes. Essentially a dialogic approach to literacy (Bakhtin, 1981; Vygotsky, 1978; Wilkinson & Son, 2011), the ERWC is well positioned within Wilkinson and Son's fourth wave of dialogic research on comprehension instruction for its use of discussion, argumentation, and intertextuality (discussed in more detail in the next section). Also congruent with theories of engagement and motivation (Ainley, 2006; Bandura, 1997; Csikszentmihalyi, 1990, 1997; Deci, 1980; Hidi & Harackiewicz, 2000; Pajares, 2003; Reed, Schallert, Beth, & Woodruff, 2004; Ryan & Deci, 2000, 2002; Schunk, 2003), the ERWC echoes the key structures in CORI, including "1) goals for learning; 2) autonomy support; 3) social collaboration; 4) strategy instruction; 5) interesting texts; and 6) real-world interaction" (Swan, 2004, p. 285; see also Guthrie, McRae, & Klauda, 2007; Guthrie, Wigfield, Barbosa, et al., 2004; Guthrie, Wigfield, & Klauda, 2012; Guthrie, Wigfield, & Perencevich, 2004). The rhetorical literacies enacted through the ERWC promote textual and conversational processes and dispositions that aid comprehension, engagement, and transfer.

Such dialogical back-and-forth—what Bakhtin calls the reciprocal relationship between speaker and listener—is central to the rhetorical approach of the ERWC. As Bakhtin suggests, "a word is territory *shared* by both addresser and addressee, by the speaker and his interlocutor. (pp. 85–86)" (as quoted in Tierney & Shanahan, 1991, p. 259). Texts made up of words amplify this fundamental relationship. Drawing on Bakhtin's ideas, Nystrand (1986) describes what he calls the reciprocity principle, by which readers and writers orient their actions to others based on social rules of conduct. As readers and writers become more familiar with such rules and as habits of mind develop, the expectations for reciprocity in discourse shape ongoing dialogue. While the ERWC draws on concepts and research from the fields of composition, reading theory, and pedagogy as well as literacy studies, we posit that one of the most powerful dimensions of the ERWC curriculum is the strategic blending of Aristotelian rhetoric with research-based approaches to secondary and postsecondary literacies—in particular, the teaching of reading and composition.

Aristotle's practical and teachable system is an integral part of the ERWC reading process. For each reading, students are asked questions related to ethos about who the writer is, what authority the writer has to talk about the subject, what biases (social, cultural, political) the writer might have, and how the writer presents him- or herself. They are also asked pathos-related questions about how the writer is engaging their emotions and whether these strategies influence their response to the arguments of the piece. These questions inspire modes of response that are crucial to an academic assessment of the worth of a text: Is it logical, rational, reliable, and credible? They also teach students that authors deploy rhetorical and linguistic strategies designed to persuade readers and that they are the object of these strategies. These realizations cause students to feel that they have some power over the text, as they begin to see the rhetorical machinery in action, and to feel that they are personally part of the conversation. These dual effects increase students' engagement with the reading and, subsequently, with the writing.

Although the ERWC is deeply influenced by Aristotle, like some of the other fourth-wave dialogic approaches (Wilkinson & Son, 2011), it is also informed by concepts from Bakhtin (1981). His basic unit of analysis for understanding discourse is the utterance. He says, "Any utterance—the finished, written utterance not excepted—makes response to something and is calculated to be responded to in turn. It is but one link in a continuous chain of speech performances" (p. 35).

From this viewpoint, with anything we hear or read, the first act is a response; we agree, we disagree, we take offense, or we are puzzled, baffled, incredulous, or stunned. For Bakhtin (1981), understanding and response are one:

> In the actual life of speech, every concrete act of understanding is active: it assimilates the word to be understood into its own conceptual system filled with specific objects and emotional expressions, and is indissolubly merged with the response, with a motivated agreement or disagreement....Understanding comes to fruition only in the response. Understanding and response are dialectically merged and mutually condition each another; one is impossible without the other. (p. 282)

In most current models of reading comprehension, such as Kintsch's (2004), the reader processes the semantic, syntactical, and grammatical relationships in the text to form a textbase that interacts with prior knowledge (the knowledge base) to create a situational model of the meaning of the text. Such models are concerned primarily with how readers make meaning from text (rather than with the purposes of the author, the designs of the author on the reader, the reasons the reader has for reading a text, or what actions the reader may be inspired to take after reading). However, if we replace "knowledge base" with "conceptual system" (and Bakhtin would probably say "ideological system"), we get closer to what Bakhtin (1981) is getting at here. The knowledge base is not neutral; some meanings can be integrated more easily than others. Thus, there is always a response, a motivated agreement or disagreement. The ERWC curriculum deploys strategies for making meaning out of the text but importantly, we think, goes beyond the text and knowledge base to create a contextualized or situational model that includes rhetorical concerns.

Rhetoric, in fact, can be seen as strategies for influencing the way a text is received, what Bakhtin (1981) calls the response. For rhetorical models to work, however, an author or author concept must exist. We argue that blending rhetoric with reading comprehension strategies enhances students' abilities to accomplish one of the most distinctive features of academic discourse: the weaving together of others' words for the writer's own purposes. As students make the shift from readers to writers, they will need to quote, paraphrase, and summarize their sources. Bakhtin's notions about language are also useful for understanding and theorizing this process.

In "Discourse in the Novel," Bakhtin (1981) introduces the concept of double-voiced discourse, or heteroglossia. He defines *heteroglossia* as "*another's speech in another's language*, serving to express authorial intentions but in a refracted way" (p. 324). In other words, the novelist takes words and phrases from different social strata in society and puts them in the mouths of characters, where they resonate with the voices of the actual people who spoke them—the voice of the character, the voice of the narrator, and the voice of the author—each voice meaning something different. For Bakhtin, heteroglossia is a linguistic given; it constitutes the basic building material of the novel. The ERWC likewise treats academic texts as heteroglossic responses to other texts, other voices.

From a Bakhtinian point of view, an academic paper can be seen as a documented heteroglossic utterance. The ERWC teaches strategies that rhetorical writers use to control the effects of heteroglossia, to arrange the multiple voices into a unified choir. The student writer must indicate a stance toward each text that he or she uses in the piece and orchestrate how the different texts relate to one another. All of these practices of representing texts and voices are commonplace in academic writing, part of the appropriation and assimilation of the words and ideas of others. Building these kinds of textual dispositions, the ERWC enables students to enact rhetorical literacies with a sense of agency and engagement.

The Fifth Wave: Achieving Deeper Learning Through Rhetorical Literacies

To recap the research on comprehension strategies instruction as outlined earlier and elsewhere, Wilkinson and Son's (2011) first wave focused on single-strategy instruction, the second wave centered on multiple-strategies instruction, the third wave fostered transactional strategies instruction (the right tool at the right time), and the fourth wave attended additionally to the dialogue about—and with—texts and their authors. Pearson (2011b) proposes a fifth wave, "Something in between explicit lessons, opportunistic teaching, and mini-lessons" (slide 70). This imagined fifth wave of instruction uses authentic examples, a good deal of group problem solving, and genuine puzzling examples to help students distinguish between "Nike Reading: Just do it!" and "Sherlock Holmes Reading: Deliberate puzzle resolution, Reading Like a Detective" (slide 70). The goal is what the Alliance for Excellent Education (2011a, 2011b) calls deeper learning, which combines critical thinking and critical literacy. The first comes out of the "Liberal Humanist Tradition of Rhetoric and Argumentation," and the second emerges from a blend of "post-modern traditions, all of which begin with the assumption that language is inherently political, never neutral, [and] laden with purpose, intention, and action" (Pearson, 2011b, slide 132). The ERWC embodies this convergence, going beyond what text *says*, to help students examine not only what it *means* and *does* but also how it *achieves effects on readers*—that is, how an author wields language rhetorically and structurally to accomplish and convey meaning and intention or action. With regard to enhancing students' reading abilities, Pearson (2011b) suggests that we can improve students' comprehension when:

- We engage students in rich *discussions* that allow [them] to integrate knowledge, experience, strategies, and textual insights
- We recognize that talk is our most important vehicle for gaining a rich and highly differentiated/integrated vocabulary/conceptual knowledge base
- We engage kids in reading a variety of texts that vary in challenge, genre, and discipline
- We teach strategies and routines explicitly and in as contextualized a manner as we can muster!
- We provide lots of opportunities for just plain reading
- We aim for critical analysis of ideas:
  - From what the text Says → Means → Does
- We provide teachers with *real support* in PD (slide 136)

It is this rich and complex blending of reading comprehension, literacy, and rhetorical and composition processes and practices that constitutes rhetorical literacies.

Enhancing Reading Comprehension and Academic Literacies Through Discussion

Extending the tradition of research conducted since the 1970s and 1980s, Applebee, Langer, Nystrand, and Gamoran (2003) summarize 64 studies (from the fields of anthropology, linguistics, psychology, literary theory, and English education) documenting the effects of discussion on literacy performance in middle and high school English classes. These authors review the work of a variety of scholars who

> have argued that high-quality discussion and exploration of ideas—not just the presentation of high-quality content by the teacher or text—are central to the developing understandings of readers and writers (Alvermann et al., 1996; Eeds & Wells, 1989; Gambrell & Almasi, 1996; Guthrie, Schafer, Wang, & Afflerbach, 1995). (p. 688)

Applebee et al. assert that "students whose classroom literacy experiences emphasize discussion-based approaches in the context of high academic demands internalize the knowledge and skills necessary to engage in challenging literacy tasks on their own" (p. 685). Although their study looks more broadly at the effects of discussion-based approaches on literacy development, Applebee et al. found that "the approaches that contributed most to student performance on...complex literacy tasks...were those that used discussion to develop comprehensive understanding, encouraging exploration and multiple perspectives rather than focusing on correct interpretations and predetermined conclusions" (p. 722). They note that typically, research on comprehension strategy instruction "has focused on an array of specific techniques for structuring discussion and embedding comprehension strategies" (p. 722). In contrast, their measures of discussion-based activities focused,

> [m]ore generally, on the presence and extent of discussion and related activities designed to involve students in the exploration of ideas. The positive results that we obtained suggest that the spontaneous scaffolding or support for developing ideas that are generated during open discussions is a powerful tool for learning. This conclusion parallels one from the National Reading Panel review of comprehension strategy instruction (Langenberg, 2000), which found particular strength in approaches that involved a variety of strategies embedded in the natural flow of classroom discussion of difficult texts, because skilled reading "involves an ongoing adaptation of multiple cognitive processes" (p. 4.47). (p. 722)

A recent meta-analysis of classroom studies that more specifically examines the capacity of discussion-based approaches to promote "high-level comprehension of text (i.e., critical literacy)" (Murphy, Wilkinson, Soter, Hennessey, & Alexander, 2009, p. 741) suggests that a variety of discussion-based approaches, whether critical-analytic, efferent, or aesthetic/expressive, can specifically improve reading comprehension:

> High-level comprehension requires that students engage with text in an epistemic mode to acquire not only knowledge of the topic but also knowledge about how to think about the topic and the capability to reflect on one's own thinking (cf. Chang-Wells & Wells, 1993)....
>
> ...In the context of discussion, students make public their perspectives on issues arising from the text, consider alternative perspectives proposed by peers, and attempt to reconcile conflicts among opposing points of view. (p. 741)

Much literacy research to date that draws on sociocognitive and sociocultural work of theorists such as Vygotsky (1978) and Bakhtin (1981) assumes a strong link between talk and learning, and some have extended this idea to consider how talk about text specifically improves reading comprehension, thinking, and reasoning (Murphy et al., 2009). Echoing Bakhtin, Murphy et al. point out that "reasoning is necessarily a response to what has been said or experienced as well as an anticipation of what will be said in response. The underlying presupposition is that reasoning is dynamic and relational" (p. 741). Despite differing goals across discussion formats and approaches, Murphy and colleagues conclude "that discussions about and around text have the potential to increase student comprehension, metacognition, critical thinking, and reasoning, as well as students' ability to state and support arguments" (p. 743). Although less teacher talk and more student talk are not guarantees of enhanced student comprehension, Murphy et al. note that successful discussion approaches encourage "teachers to yield the floor to students...while mindfully attending to the nature of the discourse" (p. 761). It is this last point that we think is in part responsible for the ERWC's success. The curriculum inspires deep engagement through a wide range of literacy practices centered on high-interest texts from varied genres while simultaneously scaffolding sophisticated conversational practices (cf. Applebee, 1996; Applebee et al., 2003; Cazden, 2001; Langer, 1995; Nystrand, 1997) about text that are eventually taken up by students, informing and shaping their subsequent reading and writing.

How do talking, thinking, and writing shape one another? Collins and Madigan's (2010) Writing Intensive Reading Comprehension (WIRC) research suggests that

> comprehension and expression happen together and coconstructively—comprehension contributes to expression, and expression contributes to comprehension. This is true of all language activities; talking and writing and even thinking in words help to construct meaning by capturing ideas and images in language. In this manner, comprehension and communication of meaning happen together because meaning is actively constructed as we use words to understand ideas and images. (p. 106)

Like many of the ERWC's rhetorical literacy activities, Collins and Madigan's interactive thinksheets (see also Englert & Raphael, 1989) engage students in what these authors call "'two-handed reading.' [Students] write with one hand on the book they are writing about and one hand on the thinksheet they are using" (p. 110). Such "targeted reading"—efferent, scaffolded reading for a particular purpose (or a series of different purposes)—focuses students' "attention on specific areas of text to answer a question or respond to a writing task" (p. 110). Importantly, thinksheets, graphic organizers, and other questioning and annotation strategies externalize the reading process, making assistance, modeling, and scaffolding easier for teachers to design. As Collins and Madigan astutely point out, "Having students write their way through reading comprehension problems may be better than only talking them through the same problems because [writing about reading] records the effects of the dialogue students have with teacher, peers, and text"; such writing also ensures "that every student contributes to the work of building an understanding of the selection; this is often not the case with class discussion" occurring minus any writing (p. 114).

Like the work of Collins and Madigan (2010), the kinds of questions that the ERWC poses are not solely content based (nor are they typical test questions); students are regularly invited to reflect on their own rhetorical purposes for writing and organizing responses to text that attend to language structure and disciplinary discourse conventions. The ERWC goes a significant step further by asking students of varied proficiency levels to carefully examine and explain the rhetorical tools employed by a text's author. The collaborative unpacking of rhetorical literacies that regularly and repeatedly occurs throughout the ERWC (through both talk and writing in conjunction with reading guided by teacher modeling and assistance from classmates) ultimately enables students to understand how texts are constructed (considering not only what they say, mean, and do but also how they do it) at a level of detail that fosters reading comprehension on the one hand and students' writing on the other. As students become more skilled at integrating complex rhetorical purposes and linguistic structures into their own prose, they gain rhetorical strength and literate independence.

The ERWC creates structured yet open-ended conversational and textual opportunities for students to become deeply engaged in the content, meaning, and structure of varied genres, gradually releasing responsibility (Duke et al., 2011; Fisher & Frey, 2008; Pearson & Gallagher, 1983) to students, who then make independent, strategic choices about which rhetorical tools to deploy based on their own judgment of a given text's particular characteristics. This is authentic and deep learning in action.

The Roles of Engagement and Motivation in the ERWC's Rhetorical Literacy Approach

Increasing student motivation and engagement to improve adolescent literacy achievement has become a frequent recommendation offered by policy reports and research syntheses (Biancarosa & Snow, 2006; Duke et al., 2011; Kamil et al., 2008; Torgesen et al., 2007). The need to improve motivation and engagement to enhance reading comprehension, literacy, and academic achievement are well established, and various frameworks for fostering motivation and engagement have emerged (Brozo & Flynt, 2008; Gambrell, 2011; Guthrie, Hoa, et al., 2007; Guthrie, McRae, & Klauda, 2007; Kamil et al., 2008; Naceur & Schiefele, 2005; Reed et al., 2004; Schoenbach & Greenleaf, 2009; Turner & Paris, 1995). Evaluation studies of the ERWC cite increases in motivation and engagement as common responses to questions on the effects of the ERWC in student, teacher, and administrator surveys and interviews. Teachers and administrators report that the course effects changes in students' attitudes about their own academic identities, as well as about literacy learning more generally, and their desire to pursue postsecondary education.

It is rare in the world of evaluation research on classroom teaching to encounter such terms as "*passion*," "*excitement*," "*desire*," "*motivation*," "*enjoyment*," or "*engagement*" when describing how a professional development program has impacted students (Box 1). When asked what benefits the ERWC course had on their students' reading and writing skills and on their enjoyment of English, the teacher respondents described common student responses to the ERWC experience as "*liking*" or "*loving*" the course. Teachers reported that students displayed higher interest in the subject matter of the course. (Hafner, Joseph, & McCormick, 2010, p. 15)

Box 1

Student Attitudes
Enjoy = 27
Interest = 20
Engaged = 18
Like = 7
Connection = 7
Love = 5
Relate to = 5
More confident = 4
Comfort = 2
Less threat = 2
Motivation = 2
Buy-in = 2

Grassroots support for the ERWC from high school teachers is due in large part, we believe, to the response of high school students to the reading selections and themes of the course modules. Teachers at ERWC professional development workshops comment that their students "like" and "succeed" with the materials in ways they have not experienced with other programs. Although the module themes and texts were deliberately selected to be interesting to adolescents, other features of the curriculum support student motivation and engagement as well.

The ERWC fits well with several constructs and frameworks for motivation and engagement. Two programs with documented records of success, which emphasize engagement, are CORI and Reading Apprenticeship. CORI employs six key instructional practices: goals for learning, hands-on or real-world learning, interesting texts, choices or autonomy support, social collaboration, and strategy instruction (Guthrie, McRae, & Klauda, 2007; Swan, 2004). The Reading Apprenticeship model, grounded in the learning theories of Vygotsky, incorporates four dimensions (social, personal, cognitive, and knowledge-building) that intersect through metacognitive conversations, which cultivate adolescent reading development (Schoenbach et al., 1999). More recently, Schoenbach and Greenleaf (2009) discuss learning opportunities that help students develop the following:

1. Dispositions for engagement in academic tasks.
2. Text-based problem-solving capacities.
3. Discipline-based literacy practices.
4. Resilient learner identities. (p. 99)

Interest and intrinsic motivation can lead to long-term and deeper levels of text-based learning (Naceur & Schiefele, 2005) and, like the ERWC, both CORI and Reading Apprenticeship harness authentic interest and inquiry to encourage students to invest personally in literacy tasks (Alexander & Fox, 2011; Alexander & Murphy, 1998; Schiefele, 1999).

The reading selections for the ERWC modules represent topics or themes of interest to adolescents (e.g., fast food and obesity, workplace discrimination based on looks, racial profiling, juveniles charged as adults) and powerful rhetorical strategies and models of language that students can discuss and analyze deeply. Most importantly, the issues addressed in the modules are relevant to the lives of young adults and are truly debatable—a fact that is reflected by the inclusion of multiple perspectives in the readings. By not promoting one right answer or a particular position, the modules provide autonomy support. Students choose their positions relative to the topic at hand and interact in many different ways with the text, their peers, and the teacher to establish their thinking. Using Aristotelian rhetoric to analyze, discuss, and write about the readings, students gain insight into how authors use language strategically and subtly to convey not only ideas (content) but also their positions about those ideas (purpose). Students learn to discern how authors shape the text to accomplish particular results (e.g., building logical arguments, establishing author's credibility, appealing to the emotions of the reader). By analyzing text in this fashion (through annotation, questioning, predicting, summarizing, and many other reading–writing activities), over time, students develop a sense of power over the text, moving from understanding what a particular text says to what it does and deciding how they will respond.

As students come to exert greater control over the reading process as well as the writing they do in response to the readings, their perceptions of themselves as autonomous learners and thinkers grow. In the writing rhetorically stage of the ERWC, students "consider the importance of audience, purpose, ethos, message, and genre to affect readers in particular ways, and they...make an active contribution to the conversation of voices and texts they have been interacting with while reading" (California State University, in press). As the tables turn and students come to understand how writers exert control over their readers, students in turn begin to understand how to exert control over their readers. Importantly, we think, the power dynamics in the classroom also shift as students collaborate with peers and the teacher to genuinely discover what they think and, subsequently, negotiate and elaborate their positions. Valued now as coconstructors in thinking and analysis, students eventually become more autonomous in the teaching–learning exchange, enabling teachers to gradually step back, releasing responsibility for learning to students.

Many literacy researchers have distilled the research on engagement and motivation into lists of key practices. For example, Gambrell (2011) offers seven rules of engagement for reading: relevance, wide range, sustained reading, choices, social interaction, strategies for success with challenging texts, and appropriate incentives. Brozo and Flynt (2008) propose six principles for motivating students to read: self-efficacy, interest in new learning, out-of-school literacies connected with in-school literacies, abundance of interesting texts, expanded choices and options, and structured collaboration.

Most of the items in these lists are integral to the ERWC; specifically, the prior discussion illustrates the roles of interest and autonomy in the course. Another important component in motivating and engaging students in the ERWC is self-efficacy (Bandura, 1997; Pajares, 2003; Schunk, 2003). Schunk describes self-efficacy as "beliefs about [one's] capabilities to learn or perform behaviors at designated levels" (p. 159). Because of the historical and traditional focus on narrative forms, many students and teachers have few strategies for accessing expository text and analyzing it at deeper levels. The ERWC structures the reading of texts by giving students reasons to return to the text many times for various purposes. Students learn to dissect the text in terms of organizational structure and rhetorical purpose, understand new vocabulary, analyze stylistic choices, consider grammatical features, and evaluate arguments. Often without realizing it, students read a text multiple times, come to understand both its content and purpose, and critically analyze the writing's rhetorical and linguistic features. Although considerable flexibility exists within the course to adjust instruction according to the needs of students, the structure of the curriculum, as outlined in the assignment template (see Figure 2), moves students to competence at high levels of cognitive complexity while simultaneously engaging them through interest, autonomy support, and self-efficacy.

In addition to enthusiasm and interest, engagement also involves persistence, effort, and attention (National Research Council & Institute of Medicine, 2004), and persistence and effort are susceptible to students' perceptions of self-efficacy (Dweck, 2006). In the ERWC, students must sustain effort to read and analyze texts, establish a position based on evidence, negotiate their own position in relation to those of the authors they have read, and construct an effective argument in writing. Sustained attentiveness or cognitive engagement, described by Csikszentmihalyi (1990) as flow, is the ideal state; whether or not students in the ERWC achieve flow, they have opportunities to sustain effort over time to accomplish high-level literacy tasks and goals. Although some may contend that autonomy support and teacher-provided structure are incompatible, Jang, Reeve, and Deci (2010) argue otherwise, suggesting

> that teachers might want to initiate learning activities by involving students' inner motivational resources, communicating in noncontrolling and informational ways and acknowledging students' perspectives and negative feelings when motivational (e.g., listlessness) and behavioral (e.g., disrespectful language) problems arise. For the provision of structure, we suggest that teachers might want to initiate learning activities by offering clear and detailed expectations and instructions, offering helpful guidance and scaffolding as students try to profit from the lesson, and providing feedback to enhance perceptions of competence and perceived personal control during a reflective postperformance period. (p. 598)

The ERWC modules support teachers as they attempt to balance deep literacy learning with matters of interest, autonomy, and self-efficacy in promoting student engagement and motivation.

As students enact rhetorical literacies in the ERWC, they are often led to new conceptions of themselves as real players in the academic conversation. Given the high-stakes testing context from which the ERWC emerged, it is significant that students, who are preparing for college, and their teachers have the tools to improve secondary academic literacy so success in postsecondary education becomes a possible reality. Our Reading Apprenticeship colleagues describe this process of developing readerly and writerly identities well:

> As adolescents explore, or try on, possible selves, teachers encourage them to try on new reader identities, to explore and expand their visions of who they are and who they can become (Davidson & Koppenhaver, 1993)....
>
> Lave and Wenger (1991) describe the process of identity formation as a negotiation of the meaning of "participative experiences" and social interpretations of these experiences; through this negotiation, we construct who we are. Feldman (2004) reminds us that "learning not only changes what we know and do, but it changes who we are" (p. 144). When we ask students to learn something new, we are asking them to become someone new. When teachers are able to provide consistent support for students to try on new ways of acting, thinking, and interacting, we have seen evidence of significant shifts in academic identity over the course of an academic year (Litman & Greenleaf, 2008). (Schoenbach & Greenleaf, 2009, p. 105)

Existing Research on the ERWC

The research support for the rhetorical literacy practices in the ERWC and the promising results of earlier nonexperimental studies suggest that effective implementation of the curriculum would yield significant benefits for students preparing for college English. Over the past seven years, the CSU has conducted a series of evaluations of the ERWC, beginning to build a research base for summative program evaluation. The studies to date have been a rich source of formative feedback to the program design team and have informed ongoing refinement of curricular design; however, summative findings of these initial studies (described next) suggest that more formal and systematic study is needed. To that end, an Investing in Innovation development grant from the federal government is helping fund a large-scale quasi-experimental study, currently underway. Next, we briefly summarize the findings of the three studies conducted between 2005 and 2010 and provide a basic overview of the Investing in Innovation grant's study design.

First Study

In 2005, a nonexperimental pilot study was conducted with a small sample of participating ERWC teachers ($n = 10$) in representative schools in California to assess the Early Assessment Program's "Professional Development in English" (California State University, 2005). The ERWC teachers were asked to identify colleagues in their schools who had not yet participated in ERWC professional development to serve as a comparison group. All teachers (ERWC and non-ERWC) administered a Reading and Composing Skills Test at the end of their students' senior year. The results indicated a positive impact for students who participated in the ERWC on the skills associated with college readiness in English. Survey results also revealed the students' enthusiasm for the course, suggesting that strong positive attitudes toward rhetorical reading, writing, and thinking and high levels of engagement in course content were additionally associated with the course.

Second Study

In 2008, a larger study was conducted to assess implementation and associated student gains in a series of implementation designs. The Reading Institute for Academic Preparation[2] was an 80-hour program of professional learning conducted over a 12-month period that also incorporated professional learning for the ERWC. In this study, 37 schools were identified and matched on characteristics of school size, socioeconomic status, and percentage of English learners. The authors reported that in the highest implementing ERWC schools, an increase in the percentage of students who gained proficiency in English was 5 times the state average and 10 times the rate found in the comparison group. The outcome measure was the grade 11 California Standards Test. Participating teachers reported high levels of satisfaction with the curriculum and the related professional development (Program Evaluation and Research Collaborative, 2008).

Third Study

In 2010, a mixed-methods evaluation of the ERWC was released (Hafner et al., 2010). The study captured a variety of survey-based findings indicating broad support for the curriculum. For example, participating teachers reported that the course had a positive impact on students' reading and writing skills, motivation, and increased time on task associated with improvements in English proficiency. Quantitative student outcomes were collected to measure the percentage of students identified as proficient in English by the CSU upon entry. The authors reported that the improvement of scores on the California Standards Test in English Language Arts from 2006 to 2010 (rate of gain) was higher for schools implementing the ERWC than the statewide average (a 7 percentage-point gain versus a 4-point gain statewide).

Taken together, these studies illustrate strong support from educational professionals on the content richness of the ERWC and the associated engagement of students. These initial nonexperimental studies and opportunistic matched-case designs suggest some promising indications of student gains associated with the intervention; however, only with a rigorous quasi-experimental or experimental design could an inferential statement on the gains associated with the ERWC curriculum be made. Such a study, currently underway, is described next.

Current Research

An Investing in Innovation development grant from the U.S. Department of Education is currently funding additional research on the efficacy of the ERWC. The project, "From Rhetoric to College Readiness: The Expository Reading and Writing Course," is a collaborative effort of the Fresno County Office of Education, the CSU, and WestEd and aims to (1) expand, update, and refine the curriculum; (2) increase the scope and effectiveness of professional development;

(3) establish intensive implementation classrooms; and (4) investigate the effectiveness of the ERWC using a rigorous, quasi-experimental research design. Approximately 6,000 students will be included in the study (3,000 in the intensive implementation classrooms). The study will follow students from their senior year of high school through their first year of college and into their second year of college. The regression–discontinuity analysis proposed for the study will permit us to reach conclusions regarding the effectiveness of the curriculum during high school and its lasting effects into college. Anticipated outcomes include the following: (1) Approximately 3,000 students will demonstrate college readiness at the end of 12th grade and subsequent success in their first and second years of college; (2) approximately 75 teachers will demonstrate the capacity to teach the ERWC effectively; and (3) district, county, and university English language arts specialists will successfully support implementing teachers through professional development and coaching. Plans for other qualitative research efforts are being developed as well. What is learned about the efficacy of the curriculum and its optimum methods of implementation will allow us to consider how the curriculum and its professional learning programs might be scaled up to support students beyond California.

Future Directions: Multimedia, Multigenre, and Multimodal Practices in the ERWC

Readers may wonder about the roles of multimedia and multimodal texts in the ERWC. In their book *Multimodal Literacy*, Jewitt and Kress (2003) define *media* as the "*technologies for making and distributing meanings as messages*" (p. 4), including print and online books, newspapers, journals, magazines, videos, films, podcasts, musical recordings, blogs, message boards, images, and social media. Such forms are used in many of the ERWC modules (and appear with greater frequency within the classrooms of many individual teachers). Although not currently addressed explicitly in the curriculum itself, we also feel that more attention should be given to representational modes, "the resources that a culture makes available as *the means for making representations and meaning*" (p. 4), which include but are not limited to image, gaze, movement, gesture, speech, music, rhythm, and sound. Jewitt and Kress explain that "modes are broadly understood to be the effect of the work of culture in shaping material into resources for representation" (p. 1). They suggest that although all modes are in some sense equal—that is, potentially "significant for meaning and communication" (p. 2)—modes are also partial: Depending on context and communicative purpose as well as on the nature of the content itself, different modes may become foregrounded.

This is certainly the case in schools and universities, where particular kinds of texts tend to be highly privileged, whereas others go largely unstudied or even acknowledged. In light of that, the heavy focus on print-based textual analysis and rhetorical reading, writing, and thinking in the ERWC accomplishes three things:

1. It provides a rigorous yet highly accessible and engaging way for high school students to become more proficient at wielding critical 21st-century literacies.
2. It offers extended professional learning opportunities for high school teachers, builds a shared sense of community, and enhances their capacity to foster the literate competencies outlined by the CCSS.
3. It exemplifies a scalable model of a statewide initiative to increase college-going readiness for high school youths in one of the world's most linguistically, socioeconomically, and culturally diverse nations.

Some of the current ERWC units (e.g., module 9: "Bring a Text to Class," described in Figure 1) invite students to explore personally meaningful out-of-school texts of their own choosing (e.g., song lyrics and spoken word, poetry, video game instructions, car or bicycle repair manuals, articles from popular magazines, online blog and social network postings). Like many other literacy scholars, we believe that if teachers can become more familiar with the texts students read voluntarily outside of school, these literacies can in turn help create connections to the types of reading and writing that are highly prized within schools.[3] The reality, though, is that because we live in an increasingly technologically complex and textually demanding world, it is imperative that we do a better job of preparing young people for colleges, universities, workplaces, civic institutions, and community organizations where it will be taken for granted that they are highly conversant with a wide range of media and able to seamlessly toggle between multiple modes of expression, including formal academic or academic-like reading and writing. It is our intention to maintain a strong—some might even say relentless—emphasis on print modalities because students taking the ERWC are preparing for a freshman year of college in which print may be the symbolic domain with which they interact and create texts most intensely. Nevertheless, the ERWC's rhetorical underpinnings also naturally lend themselves to analyzing and authoring an extremely broad range of texts, including multimodal, multimedia, and multigenre texts. In future years, we will remain committed to continuing to expand students' access to myriad literacies through the ERWC.

To date, multimodal research has contributed considerably to helping language and literacy educators and researchers reconceptualize learning in a number of crucial ways. For example, we are now aware that (1) modes almost always occur in concert, rarely alone; (2) meanings are distributed across modes in distinctive ways at different times according to social contexts and purposes; (3) modes of representation interact with media; (4) modes shape what is represented and learners' uptake of those representations; and (5) varied forms of representation and learners' abilities to take them up are greatly affected by teachers' strategic pedagogical choices, hence their vital importance (Katz, in press). We will continue to reflect on these aspects of the ERWC pedagogically and theoretically.

Also of great interest to the ERWC design team are the arguments of genre theorists who have debated for years about the best ways for individuals to gain access to academic discourse (Frankel, 2010). In Frankel's review of the competing perspectives on the place of genre in academic literacy instruction, she points to models that support explicit genre instruction as "necessary in order for traditionally underserved students to gain access to the cultures and genres of power" (p. 46). She also claims that "knowledge of the textual markers that correspond to genres of power provides access to the cultures of power to which they belong" (pp. 46–47). As it is used in the ERWC (in concert with research-based approaches to reading comprehension, composition, and literacy), a rhetorical stance constitutes a powerful tool for analyzing the textual markers and cultural dimensions of genre and other critical characteristics of texts. The curriculum's second edition will include more multigenre writing and further explore the connections between rhetoric and genre theories and practices.

The ERWC is sufficiently broad and flexible to integrate new and multiple media, modes, and genres, as well as many forms of instruction and thinking. Linking popular culture and adolescents' out-of-school interests with the rhetorical literacies of academia and power via pedagogically sound and thematically engaging curriculum, the ERWC promises to support students' development of deep literacies and literate identities—the skills, dispositions, and habits of mind that will expand young people's opportunities to engage fully, and meaningfully, in the 21st century.

QUESTIONS FOR REFLECTION

1. What kinds of gaps in students' performance during their first year in college or in the workplace have contributed to the development of the ERWC?
2. What rhetorical features has the ERWC integrated into its reading and writing curriculum?
3. What does a review of the topics and texts included in the ERWC modules (Figure 1) suggest about the content of the curriculum and the challenges it presents to high school students?
4. How does the assignment template (Figure 2) function as a model for the development of curricula that promote academic literacy?
5. What does a teacher need to do to encourage students' roles as "coconstructors in thinking and analysis"?

NOTES

[1] Even though sometimes presented as new concerns, debates regarding efficiency have haunted education reform movements since the Industrial Revolution (Ravitch, 2010).

[2] The CSU's Early Assessment Program is a major collaborative effort by three California agencies, the CSU, the California Department of Education, and the California State Board of Education. Under the program's umbrella are several components, including a professional

development effort called the Reading Institute for Academic Preparation, which has operated since 2002–2003 and has provided professional learning to thousands of California high school teachers in all disciplines.

[3] See Alvermann, 2002, 2010, 2011; Alvermann, Young, Green, & Wisenbaker, 1999; Duncan-Andrade & Morrell, 2008; Dyson, 1997; Hinchman, Alvermann, Boyd, Brozo, & Vacca, 2003; Hull & Katz, 2006; Hull & Schultz, 2002; Jiménez, 2000; Jordan, Jensen, & Greenleaf, 2001; Kamil, Intrator, & Kim, 2000; Katz, 2008, in press; C.D. Lee, 1995; Mahiri & Sablo, 1996; Moje, Dillon, & O'Brien, 2000; Moll, Amanti, Neff, & Gonzalez, 1992; Morrell, 2004; Skilton-Sylvester, 2002; and Vasudevan, DeJaynes, & Schmier, 2010.

REFERENCES

ACT. (2005). *Crisis at the core: Preparing all students for college and work.* Iowa City, IA: Author. Retrieved October 26, 2012, from www.act.org/research/policymakers/pdf/crisis_report.pdf

ACT. (2006). *Reading between the lines: What the ACT reveals about college readiness in reading.* Iowa City, IA: Author. Retrieved October 26, 2012, from www.act.org/research/policymakers/reports/reading.html

Adelman, C. (1999). *Answers in the tool box: Academic intensity, attendance patterns, and bachelor's degree attainment.* Washington, DC: U.S. Department of Education. Retrieved October 26, 2012, from www2.ed.gov/pubs/Toolbox/index.html

Adelman, C. (2006). *The toolbox revisited: Paths to degree completion from high school through college.* Washington, DC: U.S. Department of Education. Retrieved October 26, 2012, from www2.ed.gov/rschstat/research/pubs/toolboxrevisit/toolbox.pdf

Ainley, M. (2006). Connecting with learning: Motivation, affect and cognition in interest processes. *Educational Psychology Review, 18*(4), 391–405. doi:10.1007/s10648-006-9033-0

Alexander, P.A., & Fox, E. (2011). Adolescents as readers. In M.L. Kamil, P.D. Pearson, E.B. Moje, & P.P. Afflerbach (Eds.), *Handbook of reading research* (Vol. 4, pp. 157–176). New York: Routledge.

Alexander, P.A., & Murphy, P.K. (1998). Profiling the differences in students' knowledge, interest, and strategic processing. *Journal of Educational Psychology, 90*(3), 435–447.

Alliance for Excellent Education. (2006). *Paying double: Inadequate high schools and community college remediation* [Issue brief]. Washington, DC: Author. Retrieved October 26, 2012, from www.all4ed.org/files/remediation.pdf

Alliance for Excellent Education. (2011a). *Assessing deeper learning* [Policy brief]. Washington, DC: Author. Retrieved October 26, 2012, from www.all4ed.org/files/AssessingDeeperLearning.pdf

Alliance for Excellent Education. (2011b). *A time for deeper learning: Preparing students for a changing world* [Policy brief]. Washington, DC: Author. Retrieved October 26, 2012, from www.all4ed.org/files/DeeperLearning.pdf

Alliance for Excellent Education. (2011c). *Saving now and saving later: How high school reform can reduce the nation's wasted remediation dollars* [Issue brief]. Washington, DC: Author. Retrieved October 26, 2012, from www.all4ed.org/files/SavingNowSavingLaterRemediation.pdf

Alvermann, D.E. (2002). Effective literacy instruction for adolescents. *Journal of Literacy Research, 34*(2), 189–208.

Alvermann, D.E. (Ed.). (2010). *Adolescents' online literacies: Connecting classrooms, digital media, and popular culture.* New York: Peter Lang.

Alvermann, D.E. (2011). Popular culture and literacy practices. In M.L. Kamil, P.D. Pearson, E.B. Moje, & P.P. Afflerbach (Eds.), *Handbook of reading research* (Vol. 4, pp. 541–560). New York: Routledge.

Alvermann, D.E., & Moore, D.W. (1991). Secondary school reading. In R. Barr, M.L. Kamil, P. Rosenthal, & P.D. Pearson (Eds.), *Handbook of reading research* (Vol. 2, pp. 951–983). New York: Longman.

Alvermann, D.E., Young, J.P., Green, C., & Wisenbaker, J.M. (1999). Adolescents' perceptions and negotiations of literacy practices in after-school read and talk clubs. *American Educational Research Journal, 36*(2), 221–264.

American Diploma Project. (2004). *Ready or not: Creating a high school diploma that counts.* Washington, DC: Achieve. Retrieved October 26, 2012, from www.achieve.org/readyornot

Anderson, R.C., Hiebert, E.H., Scott, J.A., & Wilkinson, I.A.G. (1984). *Becoming a nation of readers: The report of the Commission on Reading.* Washington, DC: National Institute of Education, U.S. Department of Education.

Anderson, R.C., & Pearson, P.D. (1984). A schema-theoretic view of basic processes in reading comprehension. In P.D. Pearson, R. Barr, M.L. Kamil, & P. Mosenthal (Eds.), *Handbook of reading research* (pp. 255–291). New York: Longman.

Applebee, A.N. (1996). *Curriculum as conversation: Transforming traditions of teaching and learning.* Chicago: University of Chicago Press.

Applebee, A.N., Langer, J.A., Nystrand, M., & Gamoran, A. (2003). Discussion-based approaches to developing understanding: Classroom instruction and student performance in middle and high school English. *American Educational Research Journal, 40*(3), 685–730. doi:10.3102/00028312040003685

Bakhtin, M.M. (1981). Discourse in the novel (C. Emerson & M. Holquist, Trans.). In M. Holquist (Ed.), *The dialogic imagination: Four essays* (pp. 259–422). Austin: University of Texas Press.

Bandura, A. (1997). *Self-efficacy: The exercise of control.* New York: W.H. Freeman.

Bean, J.C., Chappell, V.A., & Gillam, A.M. (2004). *Reading rhetorically.* New York: Longman.

Biancarosa, G., & Snow, C.E. (2006). *Reading next—a vision for action and research in middle and high school literacy: A report to Carnegie Corporation of New York* (2nd ed.). Washington, DC: Alliance for Excellent Education.

Bill & Melinda Gates Foundation. (2010). *Why college completion?* Seattle, WA: Author. Retrieved October 26, 2012, from www.gatesfoundation.org/postsecondaryeducation/Pages/why-college-completion.aspx

Brozo, W.G., & Flynt, E.S. (2008). Motivating students to read in the content classroom: Six evidence-based principles. *The Reading Teacher, 62*(2), 172–174. doi:10.1598/RT.62.2.9

California Department of Education. (1998). *English–language arts content standards for California public schools: Kindergarten through grade twelve.* Sacramento, CA: Author.

California Department of Education. (2010). *California's common core state standards for English language arts, literacy in history/social studies, science, and technical subjects.* Sacramento, CA: Author. Retrieved October 26, 2012, from www.cde.ca.gov/re/cc

California State University, Task Force on Expository Reading and Writing. (2008). *Expository Reading and Writing Course assignment template.* Long Beach, CA: Author.

California State University, Task Force on Expository Reading and Writing. (in press). *Expository Reading and Writing Course assignment template.* Long Beach, CA: Author.

California State University, Teacher Education and Public School Programs. (2005). *Pilot study evaluation of the Early Assessment Program's professional development in English 2004–05 report.* Long Beach, CA: Author. Retrieved October 26, 2012, from www.calstate.edu/teacherED/docs/EAP_ReportFinalA.pdf

Cazden, C.B. (2001). *Classroom discourse: The language of teaching and learning* (2nd ed.). Portsmouth, NH: Heinemann.

Collins, J.L., & Madigan, T.P. (2010). Using writing to develop struggling learners' higher level reading comprehension. In J.L. Collins & T.G. Gunning (Eds.), *Building struggling students' higher level literacy: Practical ideas, powerful solutions* (pp. 103–124). Newark, DE: International Reading Association.

Committee to Improve Reading and Writing in Middle and High Schools. (2009). *A critical mission: Making adolescent reading an immediate priority in SREB states.* Atlanta, GA: Southern Regional Education Board. Retrieved October 31, 2012, from publications.sreb.org/2009/09E01_Critical_Mission_Reading_.pdf

Conley, D. (2003). *Mixed messages: What state high school tests communicate about student readiness for college.* Eugene: Center for Educational Policy Research, University of Oregon.

Csikszentmihalyi, M. (1990). *Flow: The psychology of optimal experience.* New York: Harper & Row.

Csikszentmihalyi, M. (1997). *Finding flow: The psychology of engagement with everyday life.* New York: Basic.

Deci, E.L. (1980). *The psychology of self-determination.* Lexington, MA: Heath.

Duke, N.K., Pearson, P.D., Strachan, S.L., & Billman, A.K. (2011). Essential elements of fostering and teaching reading comprehension. In S.J. Samuels & A.E. Farstrup (Eds.), *What research has to say about reading instruction* (4th ed., pp. 51–93). Newark, DE: International Reading Association.

Duncan-Andrade, J.M.R., & Morrell, E. (2008). *The art of critical pedagogy: Possibilities for moving from theory to practice in urban schools.* New York: Peter Lang.

Dweck, C.S. (2006). *Mindset: The new psychology of success.* New York: Random House.

Dyson, A.H. (1997). *Writing superheroes: Contemporary childhood, popular culture, and classroom literacy.* New York: Teachers College Press.

Education Commission of the States. (2008). *From competing to leading: An international benchmarking blueprint.* Denver, CO: Author. Retrieved October 26, 2012, from www.ecs.org/html/meetingsEvents/NF2008/resources/ECS-InternationalBenchmarking.pdf

Englert, C.S., & Raphael, T.E. (1989). Developing successful writers through cognitive strategy instruction. In J.E. Brophy (Ed.), *Advances in research on teaching* (Vol. 1, pp. 105–153). Greenwich, CT: JAI.

Fisher, D., & Frey, N. (2008). *Better learning through structured teaching: A framework for the gradual release of responsibility.* Alexandria, VA: Association for Supervision and Curriculum Development.

Flower, L., & Hayes, J.R. (1981). A cognitive process theory of writing. *College Composition and Communication,* 32(4), 365–387. doi:10.2307/356600

Frankel, K.K. (2010). *Rethinking the role of explicit genre instruction in the classroom.* Unpublished manuscript, University of California, Berkeley.

Gambrell, L.B. (2011). Seven rules of engagement: What's most important to know about motivation to read. *The Reading Teacher, 65*(3), 172–178. doi:10.1002/TRTR.01024

Greenleaf, C.L., Schoenbach, R., Cziko, C., & Mueller, F.L. (2001). Apprenticing adolescent readers to academic literacy. *Harvard Educational Review, 71*(1), 79–129.

Guthrie, J.T., Hoa, A.L.W., Wigfield, A., Tonks, S.M., Humenick, N.M., & Littles, E. (2007). Reading motivation and reading comprehension growth in the later elementary years. *Contemporary Educational Psychology, 32*(3), 282–313. doi:10.1016/j.cedpsych.2006.05.004

Guthrie, J.T., McRae, A., & Klauda, S.L. (2007). Contributions of Concept-Oriented Reading Instruction to knowledge about interventions for motivations in reading. *Educational Psychologist, 42*(4), 237–250. doi:10.1080/00461520701621087

Guthrie, J.T., Wigfield, A., Barbosa, P., Perencevich, K.C., Taboada, A., Davis, M.H., et al. (2004). Increasing reading comprehension and engagement through Concept-Oriented Reading Instruction. *Journal of Educational Psychology, 96*(3), 403–423. doi:10.1037/0022-0663.96.3.403

Guthrie, J.T., Wigfield, A., & Klauda, S.L. (2012). *Adolescents' engagement in academic literacy* (Report No. 7). College Park: University of Maryland, College Park. Retrieved October 26, 2012, October 31, 2012, from www.corilearning.com/research-publications/2012_adolescents_engagement_ebook.pdf

Guthrie, J.T., Wigfield, A., & Perencevich, K.C. (Eds.). (2004). *Motivating reading comprehension: Concept-Oriented Reading Instruction.* Mahwah, NJ: Erlbaum.

Hafner, A., Joseph, R., & McCormick, J. (2010). *Assessing the impact of English professional development on teaching practices, student learning and readiness for college: An evaluation of the Expository Reading and Writing Course: FIPSE final report.* Los Angeles: California State University.

Hidi, S., & Harackiewicz, J.M. (2000). Motivating the academically unmotivated: A critical issue for the 21st century. *Review of Educational Research, 70*(2), 151–179.

Hinchman, K.A., Alvermann, D.E., Boyd, F.B., Brozo, W.G., & Vacca, R.T. (2003). Supporting older students' in- and out-of-school literacies. *Journal of Adolescent & Adult Literacy, 47*(4), 304–310.

Hull, G.A., & Katz, M.-L. (2006). Crafting an agentive self: Case studies of digital storytelling. *Research in the Teaching of English, 41*(1), 43–81.

Hull, G., & Schultz, K. (Ed.). (2002). *School's out! Bridging out-of-school literacies with classroom practice.* New York: Teachers College Press.

Intersegmental Committee of the Academic Senates of the California Community Colleges, the California State University, and the University of California. (2002). *Academic literacy: A statement of competencies expected of students entering California's public colleges and universities.* Sacramento, CA: Author.

Jang, H., Reeve, J., & Deci, E.L. (2010). Engaging students in learning activities: It is not autonomy support or structure but autonomy support and structure. *Journal of Educational Psychology, 102*(3), 588–600. doi:10.1037/a0019682

Jewitt, C., & Kress, G. (2003). *Multimodal literacy.* New York: Peter Lang.

Jiménez, R.T. (2000). Literacy and the identity development of Latina/o students. *American Educational Research Journal, 37*(4), 971–1000.

Joftus, S. (2002). *Every child a graduate: A framework for an excellent education for all middle and high school students.* Washington, DC: Alliance for Excellent Education.

Jordan, M., Jensen, R., & Greenleaf, C. (2001). "Amidst familial gatherings": Reading apprenticeship in a middle school classroom. *Voices From the Middle, 8*(4), 15–24.

Kamil, M.L. (2003). *Adolescents and literacy: Reading for the 21st century.* Washington, DC: Alliance for Excellent Education.

Kamil, M.L., Borman, G.D., Dole, J., Kral, C.C., Salinger, T., & Torgesen, J. (2008). *Improving adolescent literacy: Effective classroom and intervention practices* (NCEE 2008-4027). Washington, DC: National Center for Education Evaluation and Regional Assistance, Institute of Education Sciences, U.S. Department of Education.

Kamil, M.L., Intrator, S.M., & Kim, H.S. (2000). The effects of other technologies on literacy and literacy learning. In M.L. Kamil, P.B. Mosenthal, P.D. Pearson, & R. Barr (Eds.), *Handbook of reading research* (Vol. 3, pp. 771–788). Mahwah, NJ: Erlbaum.

Katz, M.-L. (2008). Growth in motion: Supporting young women's embodied identity and cognitive development through dance after school. *Afterschool Matters*, 7(Spring), 12–22.

Katz, M.-L. (Ed.). (in press). *Moving ideas: Multimodality and embodied learning in communities and schools.* New York: Peter Lang.

Kintsch, W. (2004). The construction–integration model of text comprehension and its implications for instruction. In R.B. Ruddell & N.J. Unrau (Eds.), *Theoretical models and processes of reading* (5th ed., pp. 1270–1328). Newark, DE: International Reading Association. doi:10.1598/0872075028.46

Kirst, M.W. (2004). The high school–college disconnect. *Educational Leadership, 62*(3), 51–55.

Kucer, S.B. (1985). The making of meaning: Reading and writing as parallel processes. *Written Communication, 2*(3), 317–336. doi:10.1177/0741088385002003006

Kucer, S.B. (2009). *Dimensions of literacy: A conceptual base for teaching reading and writing in school settings* (3rd ed.). New York: Routledge.

Langer, J.A. (1995). *Envisioning literature: Literary understanding and literature instruction.* New York: Teachers College Press.

Langer, J.A. (2000). *Beating the odds: Teaching middle and high school students to read and write well* (CELA Research Report No. 12014; 2nd ed. rev.). Albany: National Research Center on English Learning & Achievement, University at Albany, State University of New York.

Langer, J.A., & Flihan, S. (2000). Writing and reading relationships: Constructive tasks. In R. Indrisano & J.R. Squire (Eds.), *Perspectives* on writing: Research, theory, and practice (pp. 112–139). Newark, DE: International Reading Association.

Lee, C.D. (1995). A culturally based cognitive apprenticeship: Teaching African American high school students skills in literary interpretation. *Reading Research Quarterly, 30*(4), 608–630. doi:10.2307/748192

Lee, J.M., Jr., Edwards, K., Menson, R., & Rawls, A. (2011). *The college completion agenda: 2011 progress report: Executive summary.* New York: College Board. Retrieved October 31, 2012, from completionagenda.collegeboard.org/sites/default/files/reports_pdf/Progress_Executive_Summary.pdf

Lemke, J.L. (1992). Intertextuality and educational research. *Linguistics and Education, 4*(3/4), 257–267. doi:10.1016/0898-5898(92)90003-F

Lewis, L., & Farris, E. (1996). *Remedial education in higher education institutions in fall 1995* (NCES 97-584). Washington, DC: National Center for Education Statistics, Office of Educational Research and Improvement, U.S. Department of Education.

Lumina Foundation. (2010). *Raising the bar on college completion.* Indianapolis, IN: Author. Retrieved October 26, 2012, from www.luminafoundation.org/newsroom/newsletter/archives/2010-10.html

Mahiri, J., & Sablo, S. (1996). Writing for their lives: The non-school literacy of California's urban African American youth. *The Journal of Negro Education, 65*(2), 164–180. doi:10.2307/2967311

Manguel, A. (2010). *A reader on reading.* New Haven, CT: Yale University Press.

Mansfield, W., & Farris, E. (1991). *College-level remedial education in the fall of 1989* (NCES 91-191). Washington, DC: National Center for Education Statistics, Office of Educational Research and Improvement, U.S. Department of Education.

Mills, K. (2004). Preparing for success in college: California State University is working closely with high schools to improve English and math skills. *National CrossTalk, 12*(4). Retrieved October 26, 2012, from www.highereducation.org/crosstalk/ct0404/news0404-preparing.shtml

Moje, E.B., Dillon, D.R., & O'Brien, D. (2000). Reexamining roles of learner, text, and context in secondary literacy. *The Journal of Educational Research, 93*(3), 165–180. doi:10.1080/00220670009598705

Moll, L.C., Amanti, C., Neff, D., & Gonzalez, N. (1992). Funds of knowledge for teaching: Using a qualitative approach to connect homes and classrooms. *Theory Into Practice, 31*(2), 132–141. doi:10.1080/00405849209543534

Morrell, E. (2004). *Linking literacy and popular culture: Finding connections for lifelong learning.* Norwood, MA: Christopher-Gordon.

Murphy, P.K., Wilkinson, I.A.G., Soter, A.O., Hennessey, M.N., & Alexander, J.F. (2009). Examining the effects of classroom discussion on students' comprehension of text: A meta-analysis. *Journal of Educational Psychology, 101*(3), 740–764. doi:10.1037/a0015576

Naceur, A., & Schiefele, U. (2005). Motivation and learning—the role of interest in construction of representation of text and long-term retention: Inter- and intraindividual analyses. *European Journal of Psychology of Education, 20*(2), 155–170. doi:10.1007/BF03173505

NASBE Study Group on Middle and High School Literacy. (2005). *Reading at risk: The state response to the crisis in adolescent literacy.* Alexandria, VA: National Association of State Boards of Education.

National Commission on Excellence in Education. (1983). *A nation at risk: The imperative for educational reform.* Washington, DC: Author.

National Commission on Writing in America's Schools and Colleges. (2003). *The neglected "R": The need for a writing revolution.* New York: College Entrance Examination Board. Retrieved October 26, 2012, from www.nwp.org/cs/public/print/resource/2523

National Governors Association. (2010). *Complete to compete.* Washington, DC: Author. Retrieved October 26, 2012, from www.nga.org/files/live/sites/NGA/files/pdf/10GREGOIREBROCHURE.PDF

National Governors Association Center for Best Practices & Council of Chief State School Officers. (2010a). *Common core state standards for English language arts and literacy in history/social studies, science, and technical subjects.* Washington, DC: Authors. Retrieved October 26, 2012, from www.corestandards.org

National Governors Association Center for Best Practices & Council of Chief State School Officers. (2010b). *Common core state standards for English language arts and literacy in history/social studies, science, and technical subjects: Appendix A: Research supporting key elements of the standards.* Washington, DC: Authors. Retrieved October 26, 2012, from www.corestandards.org/assets/Appendix_A.pdf

National Governors Association Center for Best Practices & Council of Chief State School Officers. (2010c). *Mission statement.* Washington, DC: Authors. Retrieved October 26, 2012, from www.corestandards.org

National Research Council & Institute of Medicine. (2004). *Engaging schools: Fostering high school students' motivation to learn.* Washington, DC: National Academies Press.

Nystrand, M. (1986). Introduction. In *The structure of written communication: Studies in reciprocity between writers and readers* (pp. 1–20). Orlando, FL: Academic.

Nystrand, M. (with Gamoran, A., Kachur, R., & Prendergast, C.). (1997). *Opening dialogue: Understanding the dynamics of language and learning in the English classroom.* New York: Teachers College Press.

Office of the Press Secretary, The White House. (2009, July 14). *Excerpts of the president's remarks in Warren, Michigan and a fact sheet on the American Graduation Initiative.* Retrieved October 26, 2012, from www.whitehouse.gov/the_press_office/Excerpts-of-the-Presidents-remarks-in-Warren-Michigan-and-fact-sheet-on-the-American-Graduation-Initiative

Organisation for Economic Co-operation and Development. (2010). *PISA 2009 results: What students know and can do: Vol. I. Student performance in reading, mathematics and science.* Paris: Author. Retrieved October 26, 2012, from dx.doi.org/10.1787/9789264091450-en

Pajares, F. (2003). Self-efficacy beliefs, motivation, and achievement in writing: A review of the literature. *Reading & Writing Quarterly, 19*(2), 139–158. doi:10.1080/10573560308222

Parker, T.L., Bustillos, L.T., & Behringer, L.B. (2010). *Remedial and developmental education policy at a crossroads.* Boston: Policy Research on Preparation Access and Remedial Education, Getting Past Go, University of Massachusetts Boston. Retrieved October 26, 2012, from www.gettingpastgo.org/docs/Literature-Review-GPG.pdf

Parsad, B., & Lewis, L. (2003). *Remedial education at degree-granting postsecondary institutions in fall 2000: Statistical analysis report* (NCES 2004-010). Washington, DC: National Center for Education Statistics, Institute of Education Sciences, U.S. Department of Education. Retrieved October 26, 2012, from www.nces.ed.gov/pubs2004/2004010.pdf

Pearson, P.D. (2011a, November). *What will the future bring? A narrow window of opportunity to get comprehension instruction right!!! (A confluence of opportunity).* PowerPoint presentation presented at the annual meeting of the California Reading Association, Vacaville. Retrieved October 30, 2012, from www.scienceandliteracy.org/research/pdavidpearson

Pearson, P.D. (2011b, December). *Supporting reading comprehension: Transforming reading comprehension: 10 research-based principles.* PowerPoint presentation presented to elementary principals and literacy coaches from Providence, RI. Retrieved March 28, 2012, from www.scienceandliteracy.org/research/pdavidpearson

Pearson, P.D., & Gallagher, M.C. (1983). The instruction of reading comprehension. *Contemporary Educational Psychology, 8*(3), 317–344. doi:10.1016/0361-476X(83)90019-X

Pressley, M. (2000). What should comprehension instruction be the instruction of? In M.L. Kamil, P.B. Mosenthal, P.D. Pearson, & R. Barr (Eds.), *Handbook of reading research* (Vol. 3, pp. 545–561). Mahwah, NJ: Erlbaum.

Pressley, M. (2002). *Reading instruction that works: The case for balanced teaching* (2nd ed.). New York: Guilford.

Program Evaluation and Research Collaborative. (2008). *Evaluating the impact of reading and writing professional development on student reading and writing outcomes: Evaluation report.* Los Angeles: Charter College of Education, California State University.

RAND Reading Study Group. (2002). *Reading for understanding: Toward an R&D program in reading comprehension.* Santa Monica, CA: RAND.

Ravitch, D. (2010). *The death and life of the great American school system: How testing and choice are undermining education.* New York: Basic.

Reed, J.H., Schallert, D.L., Beth, A.D., & Woodruff, A.L. (2004). Motivated reader, engaged writer: The role of motivation in the literate acts of adolescents. In T.L. Jetton & J.A. Dole (Eds.), *Adolescent literacy research and practice* (pp. 251–282). New York: Guilford.

Rosenblatt, L.M. (1994). *The reader, the text, the poem: The transactional theory of the literary work.* Carbondale: Southern Illinois University. (Original work published 1978)

Ruddell, R.B., & Unrau, N.J. (2004). Reading as a meaning-construction process: The reader, the text, and the teacher. In R.B. Ruddell & N.J. Unrau (Eds.), *Theoretical models and processes of reading* (5th ed., pp. 1462–1521). Newark, DE: International Reading Association.

Ryan, R.M., & Deci, E.L. (2000). Intrinsic and extrinsic motivations: Classic definitions and new directions. *Contemporary Educational Psychology, 25*(1), 54–67. doi:10.1006/ceps.1999.1020

Ryan, R.M., & Deci, E.L. (2002). An overview of self-determination theory: An organismic-dialectical perspective. In E.L. Deci & R.M. Ryan (Eds.), *Handbook of self-determination research* (pp. 3–33). Rochester, NY: University of Rochester Press.

Schiefele, U. (1999). Interest and learning from text. *Scientific Studies of Reading, 3*(3), 257–279. doi:10.1207/s1532799xssr0303_4

Schoenbach, R., & Greenleaf, C. (2009). Fostering adolescents' engaged academic literacy. In L. Christenbury, R. Bomer, & P. Smagorinsky (Eds.), *Handbook of adolescent literacy research* (pp. 98–112). New York: Guilford.

Schoenbach, R., Greenleaf, C., Cziko, C., & Hurwitz, L. (1999). *Reading for understanding: A guide to improving reading in middle and high school classrooms.* San Francisco: Jossey-Bass & WestEd.

Schunk, D.H. (2003). Self-efficacy for reading and writing: Influence of modeling, goal setting, and self-evaluation. *Reading & Writing Quarterly, 19*(2), 159–172. doi:10.1080/10573560308219

Shanahan, T. (2006). Relations among oral language, reading, and writing development. In C.A. MacArthur, S. Graham, & J. Fitzgerald (Eds.), *Handbook of writing research* (pp. 171–183). New York: Guilford.

Skilton-Sylvester, E. (2002). Literate at home but not at school: A Cambodian girl's journey from playwright to struggling writer. In G. Hull & K. Schultz (Eds.), *School's out! Bridging out-of-school literacies with classroom practice* (pp. 61–90). New York: Teachers College Press.

Smith, F. (1983). Reading like a writer. *Language Arts, 60*(5), 558–567.

Smith, F. (1984). Reading like a writer. In J.M. Jensen (Ed.), *Composing and comprehending* (pp. 47–56). Urbana, IL: ERIC Clearinghouse on Reading and Communication Skills & National Conference on Research in English.

Strong American Schools. (2008). *Diploma to nowhere.* Washington, DC: Author. Retrieved October 26, 2012, from www.deltacostproject.org/resources/pdf/DiplomaToNowhere.pdf

Swan, E.A. (2004). Motivating adolescent readers through Concept-Oriented Reading Instruction. In T.L. Jetton & J.A. Dole (Eds.), *Adolescent literacy research and practice* (pp. 283–303). New York: Guilford.

Thompson, B.A. (2009). *International benchmarking toolkit.* Denver, CO: Education Commission of the States. Retrieved October 26, 2012, from www.ecs.org/IB/IBtoolkit3-26-09.pdf

Tierney, R.J., & Shanahan, T. (1991). Research on the reading–writing relationship: Interactions, transactions, and outcomes. In R. Barr, M.L. Kamil, P. Mosenthal, & P.D. Pearson (Eds.), *Handbook of reading research* (Vol. 2, pp. 246–280). Mahwah, NJ: Erlbaum.

Torgesen, J.K., Houston, D.D., Rissman, L.M., Decker, S.M., Roberts, G., Vaughn, S., et al. (2007). *Academic literacy instruction for adolescents: A guidance document from the Center on Instruction.* Portsmouth, NH: RMC Research Corporation, Center on Instruction.

Turner, J., & Paris, S.G. (1995). How literacy tasks influence children's motivation for literacy. *The Reading Teacher, 48*(8), 662–673.

U.S. Department of Education. (2011). *College completion tool kit.* Washington, DC: Author. Retrieved October 26, 2012, from www.whitehouse.gov/sites/default/files/college_completion_tool_kit.pdf

Vasudevan, L., DeJaynes, T., & Schmier, S. (2010). Multimodal pedagogies: Playing, teaching and learning with adolescents' digital literacies. In D.E. Alvermann (Ed.), *Adolescents' online literacies: Connecting classrooms, digital media, and popular culture* (pp. 5–25). New York: Peter Lang.

Vygotsky, L.S. (1978). *Mind in society: The development of higher psychological processes* (M. Cole, V. John-Steiner, S. Scribner, & E. Souberman, Eds. & Trans.). Cambridge, MA: Harvard University Press.

Wilkinson, I.A.G., & Son, E.H. (2011). A dialogic turn in research on learning and teaching to comprehend. In M.L. Kamil, P.D. Pearson, E.B. Moje, & P.P. Afflerbach (Eds.), *Handbook of reading research* (Vol. 4, pp. 359–387). New York: Routledge.

Williams, P.L., Reese, C.M., Campbell, J.R., Mazzeo, J., & Phillips, G.W. (1995). *NAEP 1994 reading: A first look: Findings from the National Assessment of Educational Progress* (Rev. ed.). Washington, DC: National Center for Education Statistics, Institute of Education Sciences, U.S. Department of Education. Retrieved October 26, 2012, from nces.ed.gov/nationsreportcard/pubs/main1994/rchpt1.asp

Reading as a Motivated Meaning-Construction Process: The Reader, the Text, and the Teacher

Robert B. Ruddell, University of California, Berkeley

Norman J. Unrau, California State University, Los Angeles

Reading as a meaning-construction process enables us to create carefully reasoned as well as imaginary worlds filled with new concepts, creatures, and characters. The complexity of the process, however, is largely hidden from our view, and over the centuries, it has taken on the aura of the magical and mysterious. A central goal of our model is to provide insight into the nature of the process that Huey (1908/1968) described early in the 20th century as the "most remarkable specific performance that civilization has learned in all its history" (p. 6).

The challenge, then, is to explain what we do when we read and comprehend printed language in sociocultural contexts. This challenge is complicated by our belief that such an explanation needs to account for how the process is acquired and used not only from the perspective of the reader but also from the perspective of the teacher. It is the teacher who frequently assumes major responsibility for facilitating meaning negotiation within the social environment of the classroom.

Our first goal and a major emphasis of this discussion is to provide an explanation of how the reading process occurs in the classroom context involving reader, text, and teacher. A second goal is to create a model that is productive, that will provide explanations and predictions useful to both teachers and researchers. In effect, it should allow us to generate hypotheses that will explain new phenomena encountered in the reading process. Our third goal is to develop a model that has utility not only in connecting current and past research but also in charting future research directions.

The construction of an abstract representation of reading and language processing is really an attempt to create a metaphor that resembles or suggests the nature of the process. However, there is still much to learn about the nature of reading and its representation in a sociocognitive model. This is especially true if we are to take into account the complex roles of reader, text and classroom context, and teacher.

Our explanation of the reading process has evolved over the years as new knowledge has accrued from various disciplines. Readers who are familiar with

This chapter is adapted from "Reading as a Meaning-Construction Process: The Reader, the Text, and the Teacher," in *Theoretical Models and Processes of Reading* (5th ed., pp. 1462–1521), edited by R.B. Ruddell and N.J. Unrau, 2004, Newark, DE: International Reading Association.

the earlier models (Ruddell, 1974; Ruddell & Kern, 1986; Ruddell & Speaker, 1985) will recognize the influence of work in many fields, ranging from anthropology and sociolinguistics to cognitive psychology and literary theory. In effect, the creation of this model has relied on what Beach (1992) referred to as "adopting multiple stances." Because of our interest in incorporating the reader, the text and classroom context, and the teacher into the model, we have drawn on research and theory that accounts for textual, social, cultural, and field/disciplinary perspectives. We have been especially sensitized to the importance of the social context of the classroom and the influence of the teacher on the reading process through our research and writing on teaching effectiveness (Fleming, Unrau, Cooks, Farnan, & Grisham, 2007; Quirk et al., 2010; Ruddell, 1994; Ruddell & Boyle, 1989; Ruddell, Draheim, & Barnes, 1990; Ruddell & Harris, 1989; Ruddell & Ruddell, 1994; Ruddell & Unrau, 2004; Unrau, 2008a, 2008b; Unrau & Schlackman, 2006), classroom observations, and direct teaching of students at a variety of levels.

Several key assumptions underlie the model. These are implicit in the research supporting the model's components and the interactions between and among components. They are as follows:

1. Readers—even beginning readers—are active theory builders and hypothesis testers.
2. Language and reading performance are directly related to the reader's sociocultural environment.
3. The driving force behind language performance and reading growth is the reader's need to obtain meaning.
4. Oral and written language development, which affect thinking processes, contributes directly to the development of reading ability.
5. Readers construct meanings not only of printed manuscripts but also of events, speech, and behaviors as they "read" gestures, images, symbols, signs, and signals that are embedded in a social and cultural environment.
6. Texts are constantly reinvented as readers construct different understandings for them over time. Meanings for texts are dynamic, not static, as individuals, texts, and contexts change and interact.
7. The role of the teacher is critical in negotiating and facilitating meaning construction in the text and social context of the classroom.

The remainder of our discussion will be devoted to four areas designed to illuminate the nature of the model:

1. A brief overview of the three major components of the model
2. A detailed discussion of the rationale and research foundation underlying each of the three major components
3. A discussion of the model components illustrating strategy-based instruction and meaning negotiation in the classroom
4. Our conclusion, with implications for practice and new research directions

The Reader, the Text, and the Teacher: A Brief Overview

For our sociocognitive interactive model, reading is conceptualized as a meaning-construction process in the instructional context of the classroom. A brief survey of the model reveals three major components (as depicted in Figure 1). These consist of the *reader*, *text and classroom context*, and *teacher*. As the reading process occurs, these three components are in a state of dynamic change and interchange while meaning negotiation and meaning construction take place.

The *reader*, the first major model component as shown on the left side of Figure 1, conceptualizes the student's previous life experiences as prior beliefs and knowledge. This reader component consists of two major interrelated parts. The first, *affective conditions*, includes a range of factors extending from the motivation to read to personal sociocultural values and beliefs about reading and schooling. The second, *cognitive conditions*, accounts for such areas as background knowledge of language, word recognition and identification skills, text-processing strategies, and understanding of classroom and social interaction.

The reader's ability to construct, monitor, and represent meaning is housed under *knowledge use and control*. As the *knowledge-construction* process proceeds, it is guided by purposes and plans while drawing on the reader's reservoir of prior beliefs and knowledge. A *text representation* begins to form in the reader's mind; it reflects the reader's meaning interpretation based on the text and is influenced by other factors, such as discussion with peers and the teacher. This representation is overseen and monitored by the *reader executive and monitor*. Prior beliefs and knowledge are used to help confirm, reject, or suspend judgments of new interpretations.

The *outcomes of meaning construction* demonstrate the kinds of understanding that have been created in the reader's mind through the text and classroom interaction. These outcomes may take a variety of forms, ranging from new semantic or lexical knowledge to interpretation of texts to changes in motivation, values, and beliefs.

At first glance, the *teacher*, the second major model component as shown on the right side of Figure 1, appears to be a mirror image of the reader component. This is only partially the case. The teacher's prior beliefs and knowledge account for previous affective and cognitive conditions based on life experiences. Affective conditions include instructional beliefs and philosophy and involve such things as motivation to engage students and instructional orientation, which reflects personal sociocultural values and beliefs. In addition, the teacher's cognitive conditions include conceptual and instructional knowledge that includes understanding the reader's meaning-construction process, teaching strategies, and personal and world knowledge.

The teacher's *knowledge use and control* includes the *instructional decision-making process* that forms general instructional purposes based on prior beliefs, prior knowledge, and concurrent classroom conditions. This general purpose directs the flow and conduct of instruction through specific purpose setting, planning and organizing, and strategy construction.

Figure 1. Reading as a Meaning-Constructed Process: The Reader, the Text, and the Teacher

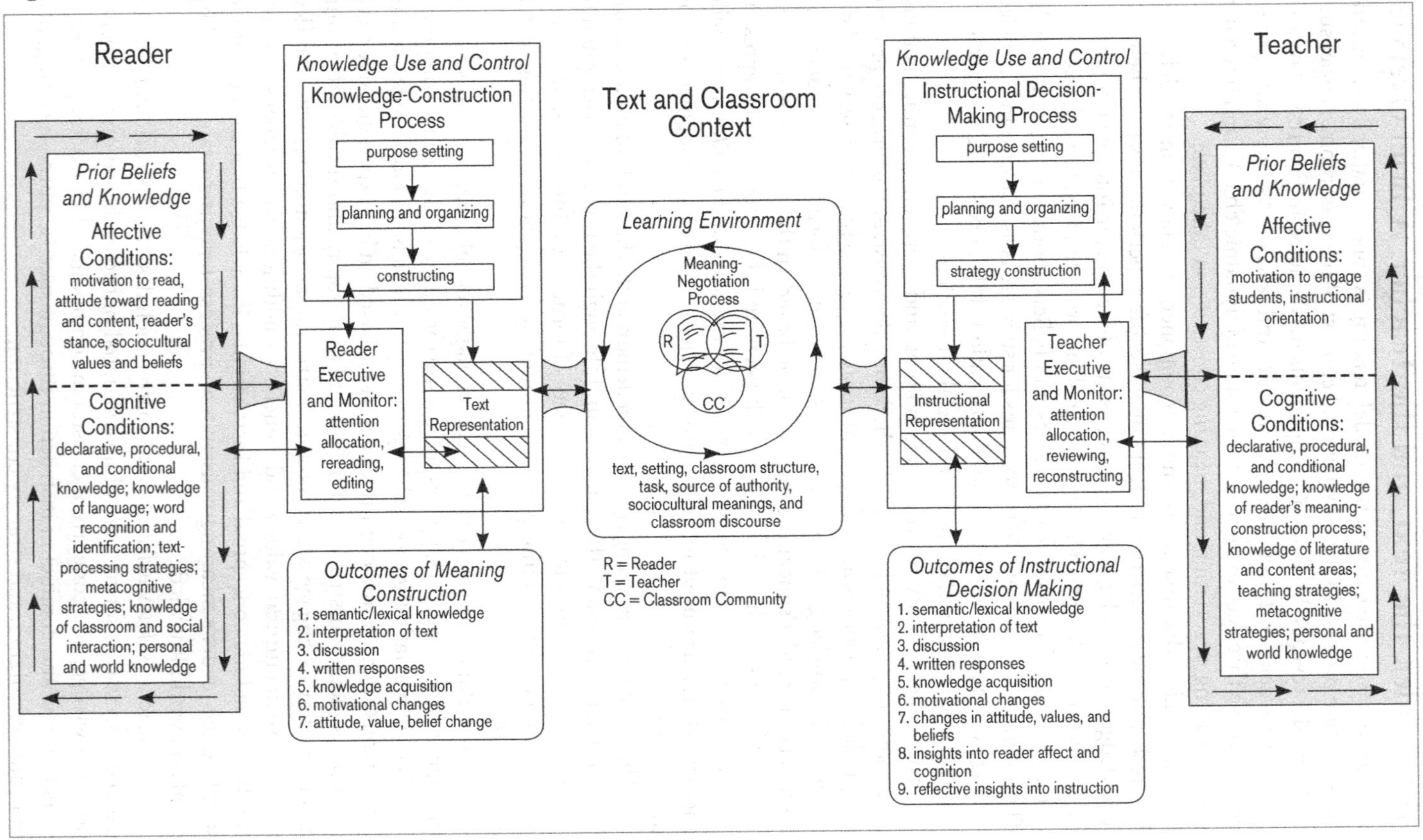

As teaching begins, the *instructional representation* emerges in the teacher's mind and reflects such features as classroom activities, instructional strategies, management techniques, and meaning construction. The *teacher executive and monitor* controls and oversees the purpose and representation. The teacher's prior beliefs and knowledge provide information that ranges from motivation and instructional orientation to teaching strategies and understanding of the student's meaning-construction process. The process continues if instruction is proceeding according to purpose and plan; if it is not, the original purpose and plan may be adjusted or changed entirely. The *outcomes of instructional decision making* for the teacher range from forming new semantic/lexical knowledge and interpretation of text to insights into reader affect and cognition and reflective insights into instruction.

The *text and classroom context*, the third major model component, is shown in the center of Figure 1. It accounts for the *learning environment* in which the *meaning-negotiation process* occurs. This process begins when the reader first interacts with the text (symbolized by the book at the center of Figure 1) and represents a fusion of meaning between reader, teacher, and classroom community. Here we are attempting to describe the reading process in the responsive classroom context where teacher and students build understandings through meaning negotiation. This requires that the teacher be attuned to student understandings of several types of meaning: *text*, *setting*, *classroom structure*, *task*, *source of authority*, *sociocultural meanings*, and *classroom discourse*.

It is within the text and classroom context that the true orchestration of instruction occurs. Here, both student and teacher initiate the process of meaning construction. They negotiate purposes and plans (*knowledge use and control*) and draw on background knowledge (*prior beliefs and knowledge*) to form text and instructional representations while simultaneously monitoring the meaning-construction process. This meaning negotiation directly influences outcomes of meaning construction for the reader and outcomes of instructional decision making for the teacher.

Our detailed discussion of the model begins with the reader component, for the reader is at the center of meaning construction. We then examine the teacher component as instructional decision making proceeds. Next, we discuss the text and classroom context as we explore the meaning-negotiation process that occurs when reader, teacher, and classroom community interact. We then apply this process to a high school English class as students negotiate and construct meaning of a short story. We conclude with selected implications for research and practice.

The Reader

As we consider various factors that contribute to the reader's meaning-construction process, we should keep in mind that these factors function in a simultaneous and integrated manner. This is reflected in the circular flow of arrows surrounding prior beliefs and knowledge in Figure 2, and in the two-way arrows connecting various reader components.

Figure 2. The Reader

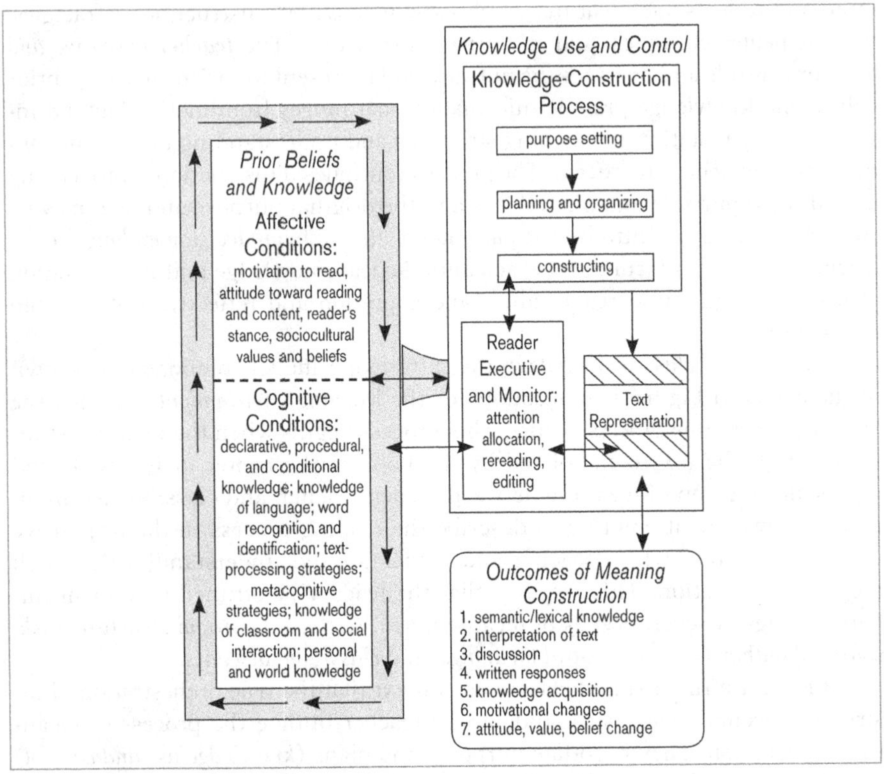

Prior Beliefs and Knowledge

Prior beliefs and knowledge consist of preexisting factors, both *affective* and *cognitive*, that influence the reader's comprehension and construction of meaning. Beliefs include opinions, assumptions, and convictions—some of which may be thoroughly grounded in reason, and some of which may be based on the reader's life experience but are wholly unexamined. Nevertheless, these beliefs constitute part of the foundation the reader uses to construct meaning through interaction with text. Furthermore, beliefs influence and shape affective conditions critical to the reader's meaning-construction process. These conditions consist of *motivation to read*, *attitude toward reading and content*, *reader's stance*, and *sociocultural values and beliefs*.

Knowledge is commonly conceived to be justified belief; however, in the model, we interpret knowledge to include concepts, procedures, and even unconscious or unattended knowledge forms that influence the meaning-construction process. Some forms of knowledge are acquired in a deliberate and purposeful manner. For example, we come to know that E.B. White created the delightful story *Charlotte's Web* based on his farm experiences and observations in rural

Maine, USA. Our personal interpretation of the story characters leads to an understanding of Charlotte's nurturing and protective nature and Wilbur's childlike attitude toward life as the two become friends. But other forms of knowledge related to reading may not be consciously learned, as is the case with the reader's potential syntactic knowledge, which is innate and activated through interaction with other language users early in life. Knowledge in our model exerts strong influence on the cognitive conditions, *declarative*, *procedural*, and *conditional* knowledge forms. These include our mental representation of concepts, language, word recognition and identification, text-processing strategies, metacognitive strategies, classroom and social interaction procedures, and personal and world knowledge.

Our discussion begins with specific affective conditions, followed by consideration of cognitive conditions, which together constitute the reader's prior beliefs and knowledge. We must emphasize, however, that although we describe and explore affective and cognitive conditions separately, these two sets of conditions are interdependent and interactive. For example, the reader's motivation, attitude toward content, and values will most certainly influence the often simultaneous acquisition of new concepts, text interpretation, and use of text-processing and metacognitive strategies.

Affective Conditions. Affective conditions directly influence the reader's decision to read. This decision is shaped by reasons for reading, what is to be read, and how the reading will occur. Motivation to read and attitude toward reading and content shape the direction and intensity of the reader's interest in reading. As the reader engages the text, one of several stances may be adopted that will have a formative effect on focus of attention, reading purpose, and level of understanding (Many, 2004; Rosenblatt, Chapter 35 this volume). Focus may be directed toward gathering information, becoming enmeshed in the narrative, grasping a writer's situation and intention, or some combination of these. The reader's sociocultural values and beliefs, which have their roots in the reader's family, community, and to some degree, the school, influence both the decision to read and the reading goals.

Motivation to read springs from each reader's motivational system, which we view as potentials for activation and engagement. These motivational potentials can be brought to life through mechanisms and processes both within readers and in their environment. Viewing motivational potential within a motivational system for reading engagement offers us the opportunity to integrate multiple motivational resources and to understand how they may interact and complement one another as individuals operate in their social contexts.

During the 1990s, research on motivation at the National Reading Research Center was grounded in an engagement perspective integrating cognitive, motivational, and social aspects of reading with achievement motivation theory (Guthrie, Wigfield, Metsala, & Cox, 2004; Taboada, Tonks, Wigfield, & Guthrie, Chapter 24 this volume). That work eventuated in the development of an engagement model of reading (Guthrie & Wigfield, 2000) that illustrates how instructional processes impact engagement processes, which ultimately influence reading and learning outcomes. Instructional processes in the model have nine variables that contribute to the context in which instruction occurs: teacher involvement, evaluation, rewards and praise, collaboration, strategy instruction, interesting texts, real-world interactions, autonomy support, and learning and knowledge goals. These processes may overlap and interact in any instructional context, creating greater instructional cohesion that theoretically could augment engagement, conceptual mastery, and reading achievement. Engagement processes include social interactions, conceptual knowledge, strategy use, and motivation. According to the model, reading engagement processes mediate the effects of instructional context on student outcomes. Thus, the instructional context does not directly influence reading outcomes; rather, the effects of the instructional context depend on levels of student engagement. Finally, positive reading achievement, knowledge, and practices are the focal outcomes in the model, which might take the form of standardized test results, knowledge in the form of student portfolios of work, and practices in the form of amount of independent reading.

We drew from and synthesized similar research, including that generated through the National Reading Research Center, to construct an integrated vision of motivation to read. We envisioned an array of factors shaping the intention to read and reading engagement. Our motivational model (Ruddell & Unrau, 2004), which reveals parallels between a reader's motives to read and a teacher's motives to design instruction, depicts the motivational system of an optimally self-regulated reader.

Although a reader's reading and a teacher's instructional planning yield different outcomes, they share three major motivational components:

1. *A developing self* that includes an identity and self-schema, a sense of self-efficacy and self-worth, expectations, an experiential self, and self-knowledge
2. *An instructional orientation* that includes achievement goals, task values, sociocultural values and beliefs, and stances
3. *Task-engagement resources* that include text-processing resources for readers or instructional design resources for teachers

The Developing Self. Although a full description of the developing self in relation to students as readers and learners and teachers as instructors and guides is beyond our scope, we can provide an overview of components of the developing self in relation to literacy and learning. The developing self comprises those aspects of the reader's or teacher's self-system that shape purpose and meaning, especially for us in relation to the life of the literacy classroom.

Identity and Self-Schema. According to the developmental psychologist Erik Erikson (1968), core identity includes two aspect of self: (1) a sense of self garnered from the integration of many selves or aspects of those selves that have been assumed, played out, rejected, or embraced; and (2) a sense of self as an organizing agency that enables self-representation. The first sense of self in past, present, and future arises from self-schema. Students and teachers access past, present, and future self-schemata as aspect of their self-system. Those lived, remembered, and possible selves influence the motivation and behavior of every student and teacher. The second organizing agency of our identity Erikson referred to as our ego-identity, the "actually attained but forever-to-be-revised sense of reality of the self within social reality" (p. 211). Students' and teachers' lives can be viewed as psychohistories that, if closely examined, reveal the outcomes of various crises through which they have passed on their way to their current role and identity as a student or teacher.

Self-Efficacy and Self-Worth. What we believe ourselves capable of doing or learning constitutes our self-efficacy. The self-efficacy of a student predicts his or her motivation for engagement in reading. A student with high self-efficacy will usually work harder, longer, and more willingly than one with low self-efficacy (Schunk & Zimmerman, 1997). Teaching students to be more efficacious and persuading them that they are efficacious improves their performance (Schunk, 1991, 1994). Self-worth may be viewed as a reflection of self-efficacy. According to self-worth theory, students' highest concern is to protect their sense of ability (Covington, 1992). Thus, a reader's motivation to engage in reading may depend on his or her perception of the impact of that reading event on self-esteem. If students do not engage in reading tasks for school, they may be avoiding them because they are motivated by a paramount concern: esteem preservation. The concept of self-worth applies to teachers as well. What teachers judge themselves capable of accomplishing in their classrooms has a determining effect on their motivation for teaching a particular lesson and the learning environments they construct.

Expectations. Expectation as a motivational construct related to self-efficacy (Schunk, 1994) influences a learner's focus of intention. Covington (1992) has explored the relations between ability attributions and expectation and notes that students' personal expectations influence their level of aspiration. That level of aspiration, in turn, can be shaped or limited by the expectations of others, especially teachers. We also know that teachers communicate different expectation messages to students whom the teacher considers to have high or low expectations (Good, 1987). Teachers are more likely to call on high-expectation students more often and wait longer for answers than they would for low-expectation students. In addition, a strong relationship between teachers' beliefs about their own efficacy to motivate and teach students and students' beliefs about their own abilities and chances for success has been identified and verified (Midgley, Feldlaufer, & Eccles, 1989).

Experiential Self. The experiential self (Epstein, 1994) processes imagery, narratives, and metaphors that give us a sense of the meaning of our experiences. Although it parallels other features of the self-system we've described, it is less conscious and rational in function. It is where seasoned teachers have stored their teaching stories that contribute to their history and identity as teachers. They refer, often unconsciously, to these narratives to help them make classroom instructional decisions. Students also store in their experiential self their school narratives that contribute to their motivation and engagement in reading. The experiential self continually interacts with and influences the more rational structures that compose the developing self-system. The extent of that influence depends on the power of internalized narratives, imagery, and metaphors contained in the experiential self.

Self-Knowledge. A student's or teacher's self-knowledge includes all that the student or teacher knows about his or her own self-system, instructional orientation, and task engagement resources. Students who have begun to gain some degree of self-knowledge often are able to use that knowledge in their reading and discussion of texts to gain deeper self-understanding (Rosenblatt, 1938/1995). The assumptions that self-knowledge enables improvements in a teacher's performance and that the inclination to gain self-knowledge should extend throughout a teacher's professional life form the foundation for reflective teaching and the development of more reflective teachers (Schon, 1987; Vigil, 1992). We suspect that the more teachers have looked at their own behavior in various settings, especially in classroom interactions, and the more they know about themselves as teachers and how they function, the more they will be able to construct productive learning relationships with their students and learning environments for themselves (Unrau, Ragusa, & Bowers, 2011).

In summary, the constructs of the developing self-system, including identity and self-schema, self-efficacy and self-worth, expectations, the experiential self, and self-knowledge, interact as they contribute to a student's or teacher's engagement and orientation toward reading and learning in the social environment of the classroom. Furthermore, the constructs of both the reader's and the teacher's developing self interact with task engagement resources and features that make up a teacher's instructional orientation, which we will explain when we describe the role of the teacher's affective conditions later in this chapter.

Together with these motivational elements that can start and sustain a reader's engagement in reading, affective conditions also include the reader's attitude toward reading and text content, reader's stance, and sociocultural values and beliefs.

The reader's *attitude toward reading and text content* plays a critical role in the reading process by influencing intention to read. Mathewson (2004) views attitude as being shaped by reader values and self-concept. Attitude is defined by three elements: (1) prevailing feelings about reading, (2) action readiness toward reading, and (3) evaluative beliefs about reading. These interacting elements directly influence the intention to read. The reader's intention to read and continue reading is further influenced by such factors as the reader's internal emotional state and external purpose, incentives, and norms, as well as by the instructional setting provided by the teacher.

It is important to note that our earlier discussion of motivation to read is closely connected to attitude toward reading through intention. In effect, motivation is designed to enhance a positive attitude toward reading and, in turn, increase the reader's intention to read and continue reading. Readers will persevere with and comprehend text that is above their instructional reading level if they have high interest in its content (Shnayer, 1969). We are also aware that several text variables, including the presence of images and author's writing style, affect the reader's prevailing feelings, action orientation, and evaluative beliefs toward reading.

While *reader's stance* refers to the reader's perspective and orientation toward a given text, *instructional stance* refers to the teacher's perspective and orientation toward the teaching of a text. By guiding the reader's purpose, the teacher's instructional stance also influences a reader's motivation to read. Theorists and researchers (Beach & Hynds, 1990; Langer, 1990; Rosenblatt, 1978) have described several different stances that readers and teachers may adopt.

Reader's stance serves to direct the reader's focus of attention and purpose in reading (Rosenblatt, 1978) and thus influences motivation, attitude, and intention to read. The reader's perspective and orientation are influenced by the nature of the text and the desired interaction with the text. The stance assumed in directing attention is, to varying degrees, under the reader's control and can be influenced by the teacher in the classroom context.

Although several stance systems have been developed to capture the range of orientations toward a text that readers may adopt, Rosenblatt (1938, 1978, 1985, Chapter 35 this volume) presented the view that readers experience texts through two stances: efferent and aesthetic. In efferent reading, the reader focuses on ideas and concepts to be taken away from the text; in aesthetic reading, the reader becomes absorbed in a text world of imagination and feelings in which "attention is focused on what [the reader] is living through during the reading-event" (Rosenblatt, 1985, p. 38). These stances are not strict categories but reside on a continuum along which the degree of emphasis may change as the reader progresses through a text. Furthermore, the efferent and aesthetic stances are integrated in varied proportions (Rosenblatt, Chapter 35 this volume).

With both literary and nonliterary texts, Langer (1990) found that readers can use four stances that offer a range of meaning-making choices to develop understandings. First, readers can be outside but step into an envisionment as they attempt to form a context for meaning making. Second, readers can be inside an envisionment and move through it to further build meaning. Third, readers can step back and reflect on what is known. And fourth, readers can step outside the text and objectify the reading experience, a stance often taken on completion of a reading as readers judge or comment on it.

The *sociocultural values and beliefs* that the reader acquires through family, peer group, and community interaction have a profound and pervasive effect on school success in general and reading development in particular. According to Gee (2012), reading is embedded or situated in complex sociocultural systems that shape and support reading and its emergence in children. Literacy events are composed not only of a text that needs to be "read" but also of a social language, a Discourse, and a cultural world in which the text exists. Literacy and languages have no meaning outside their particular cultural world.

Children become socialized into what Gee (2012, Chapter 4 this volume) calls Discourses (with a capital *D* to set it apart from discourse as plain language). While Discourses always involve language, they include how we use words in talking, writing, interacting, believing, valuing, and feeling to situate ourselves socially and culturally. As identity kits, Discourses reflect who we are and how we behave as a student or a teacher or in a wide range of other social roles.

While we become socialized into a Discourse, we also develop an accompanying cultural model about the world that is shared by people who are socialized into that Discourse. That cultural model (Gee, 1999, 2012) provides people with information about what the world looks like from the viewpoint of a particular Discourse. Gee points out that theories and beliefs about childhood development and early literacy within a cultural model provide guidelines for children's early reading, writing, speaking, and listening. In Heath's (1983) investigation of language use in Trackton, Roadville, and Gateway, we see the profound influence of these cultural models and the development of Discourse they inform.

The influence of family and cultural values on schooling is clearly depicted in Heath's (1983, Chapter 8 this volume) research. She describes literacy development in three communities: Trackton (a black mill community), Roadville (a white mill community), and Gateway (a "mainstream" urban community). Trackton children experienced a social environment in which the community shared in teaching and in uniting the youngsters with the community. Children, especially boys, were expected to respond creatively to challenging questions. Stories they created were designed to exaggerate "truth," glorify self, and entertain the listener. Few children's books or book-reading activities were found in the homes. Roadville children were reared in an environment where parents talked with their babies, modified their language to involve their children, and used interactional patterns that included answering questions, labeling, and naming objects. The children were expected to accept the power of print through association with alphabet letters and workbook-like activities. Stories were characterized by truthfulness and carried a moral message. In Gateway, a high value was placed on schools and schooling for both black and white children. From an early age, families nurtured their children's interest in books. Parents frequently asked their children information-type questions and developed book-sharing routines. The children often saw parents and siblings reading for a variety of purposes. Heath concluded that the Gateway children acquired values about reading and writing that the Trackton and Roadville children found strange. The Gateway children were not only familiar with book-reading routines but with comprehension strategies as well. The discourse and literacy practices of the Trackton and Roadville children needed to be bridged by the school.

Sociocultural values and beliefs constitute an important aspect of the reader's affective conditions for learning. As we will see later in this discussion, the teacher must exercise understanding and sensitivity to these values and beliefs if the reader's potential for success is to be enhanced.

Cognitive Conditions. The reader's cognitive conditions play a vital role in the reading process. Again, however, we must emphasize that in meaning construction, the cognitive conditions are socially embedded and interact with the affective conditions just discussed. Furthermore, we assume that these cognitive conditions not only serve as a reader's text processing resources but also contribute to the reader's motivation and engagement in reading (Ruddell & Unrau, 2004).

We now turn to cognitive conditions and the role of declarative, procedural, and conditional knowledge in the meaning-construction process. Declarative knowledge includes the reader's "what" knowledge of facts, objects, events, language, concepts, and theories about the world. The reader's procedural knowledge consists of how-to skills and strategies for using and applying knowledge, ranging from using a context strategy in identifying a new word to the use of a text organization strategy in reading a chapter. Conditional knowledge accounts for the reader's awareness of knowledge use. This may be viewed as "when" and "why" knowledge, which provides for application of declarative and procedural knowledge forms. Conditional knowledge thus accounts for understanding the social context in which reading is taking place and for the reader's intent (Paris, Lipson, & Wixson, 1983).

The reader's declarative, procedural, and conditional knowledge forms are stored and represented in memory and include a variety of knowledge essential to meaning construction. As noted in Figure 2, they include knowledge of language, word recognition and identification skills, text-processing strategies, metacognitive strategies, classroom and social interaction, and self and world. Before discussing the specific knowledge forms, we first briefly examine how these forms are represented in memory. In the model, we assume that the reader's declarative, procedural, and conditional knowledge forms are stored in knowledge structures known as schemata. Furthermore, we assume that those schemata are not merely in-the-head information structures but were acquired in social contexts and are socioculturally embedded (McVee, Dunsmore, & Gavelek, Chapter 20 this volume). Schemata can be thought of as information packets or knowledge modules, each of which is used to organize a particular class of concepts formed from our experience (Adams & Collins, 1985). As described in work by Rumelhart and his associates (Rumelhart, 1980, 1981; Rumelhart & Ortony, 1977), schemata may be seen as generic patterns or abstract representations of knowledge. These knowledge structures are composed of "slots" to be filled with specific information when a problem is to be solved or a text is to be processed. As knowledge is stored in memory, these structures set up expectations for the reader when new information is encountered for interpretation. If new information fits the slots of an existing schema so that it becomes filled with concrete instances—a condition called *instantiation*—that schema may exert control over the reader's meaning-construction process (Anderson, 1975, Chapter 19 this volume; Rumelhart, 1980).

The reader may ignore important information because it does not fit the expected conditions, or distort information so it does fit those expected slots.

The explanatory power of schema theory is found in the idea that the first level of any schema provides for an abstraction and conceptual framework for all of the particular events that fall below it but are within its domain. For example, a schema such as "going to the grocery store" may represent an overarching knowledge module that a grocery store is a business establishment where one purchases food to take home to use in meal preparation. Below this global concept are more specific schemata such as going to a large food market or to a small corner store.

Schemata have a number of important meaning-construction functions. They aid in memory searches, provide for inference making, allow text content to be reorganized and reconstructed, and are valuable in summarizing content (Anderson & Pearson, 1984). A reader's schema appears to function by using the following properties: (1) procedural information that allows the schema to become activated and instantiated by interaction with the text; (2) inheritance, which simply means that a subschema may acquire knowledge from a higher level schema; (3) default values that provide for inferences based on the text; and (4) a hierarchical organizational structure, such as that exemplified by the previous example of the "going to the grocery store" schema.

The view of schemata as monolithic, rigid knowledge structures used to direct the comprehension of texts has been expanded to include an alternative perspective that views schemata as knowledge resources for the building of new knowledge structures (Spiro, Coulson, Feltovich, & Anderson, Chapter 22 this volume). In this less linear and mechanistic, more organic and flexible perspective, the reader does not fill slots but takes chunks of knowledge from existing knowledge structures and assembles new meanings to represent a text far more complex than any one hierarchically designed knowledge structure. The reader takes pieces of knowledge from several different hierarchically designed but in some way related knowledge structures and assembles them to form a novel representation of the complex text. The newly constructed and purpose-sensitive schema allows for more elaborate interconnections than does any one hierarchical schema. This purpose-sensitive schema accounts for more effective problem solving and meaning construction than does the hierarchical schema that provides for a sole meaning representation.

Several researchers (Alba & Hasher, 1983; Sadoski & Paivio, 2001, Chapter 34 this volume; Sadoski, Paivio, & Goetz, 1991) have challenged the schema theory perspective of knowledge representation in memory, posing instead a dual coding theory of a verbal and nonverbal knowledge representation. The nonverbal imagery system, which is separate but connectable to the verbal system, includes all sensory modes, such as sight, smell, and sound, and has the capacity to evoke in the reader strong emotion and meaning through images. Such imagery often contributes to the aesthetic and thematic dimensions of our response to literature—for example, as Hester Prynne's *A* in *The Scarlet Letter* acts as an image that carries her anguish and consolidates meaning for many readers. Furthermore, research suggests that imagery plays an important role in the comprehension and long-term recall of both narrative and expository texts. At this time, however, schema theory provides strong explanatory power in accounting for the reader's knowledge representation and the role of this knowledge in the meaning-construction process (McVee et al., Chapter 20 this volume).

In the model, schemata hold the key to explaining the top-down perspective of reading as an interactive process. The reader's schemata are probably best understood as networks of associated knowledge that are activated and instantiated or as knowledge clusters that can be tapped for pieces of information that the reader reassembles to form new schemata. Thus, the reader builds a weblike representation rather than a fixed formula of slots that the reader fills, or tries to fill. We now turn to specific knowledge forms critical to the reader's meaning-construction process.

Reading is a linguistically based process that requires *language knowledge* to construct meaning. That knowledge consists of schemata that represent orthographic, phonological, syntactical, and lexical information. These knowledge forms are well developed for most children long before the start of formal schooling (Cox, Fang, & Otto, 2004; Heath, 1983). The syntactical and lexical features, however, continue to increase in complexity throughout the school years (Juel & Minden-Cupp, 2004; Ruddell & Ruddell, 1994).

Phonological knowledge is internalized and represented by about age 4 (Gibson & Levin, 1975). Children at this age choose words that conform to English phonology, in contrast to sound clusters that do not follow these phonological rules—*klec* versus *dlek*, for example (Morehead, 1971). Upon entry into kindergarten or first grade, this system is near completion (Ervin & Miller, 1963).

Syntactical knowledge is also well developed before children begin to read. The fundamental capacity to understand and generate language is innate (Chomsky, 1959, 1965) but requires a social support system for development. In Bruner's (1983, 1986) terms, the language acquisition device with which we are born requires a language acquisition support system provided by the social world. This support system may develop in many different social settings (Gee, 2012; Vygotsky, 1962/1986). But it appears that if young children do not get early social interaction and language stimulation (as occurs in rare cases of childhood isolation), normal language development does not occur (Curtiss, 1977; Rymer, 1992a, 1992b). Without language interaction, the capacity to achieve syntactic sophistication and to understand and form grammatical sentences fails to develop.

The development of syntactic knowledge previous to and during school years is well documented. Scollon (1979) discerned subtle syntactic forms before children begin to speak in two-word utterances, while Dore (1979) demonstrated that preschoolers have a significant command of conversational skills and what can be done with language. The close connection between syntactical complexity and reading comprehension has also been established (Ruddell, 1965). Together, these studies demonstrate that potential for developing syntactic knowledge appears to be inborn, that its manifestations begin early in the socially stimulated language environment, and that it directly affects the ability to read.

Lexical knowledge, which is closely related to the reader's personal and world knowledge, refers to knowledge of words and word meanings. Words representing concepts are clustered in categories that are hierarchically arranged (Johnson, Toms-Bronowski, & Pittelman, 1981). These categories are, in turn, connected to other concept structures.

Lexical knowledge is also directly related to comprehension and meaning construction as demonstrated by a range of vocabulary research (Anderson & Freebody, 1981; Beck & McKeown, 1991). Estimates indicate that children expand their vocabulary at the rate of 2,700 to 3,000 words per year—or about seven words a day (Beck & McKeown, 1991; see also Nagy & Scott, Chapter 18 this volume). That vocabulary and reading comprehension are positively related is not surprising (see Kuhn & Stahl, Chapter 15 this volume; Stanovich, 1986). Efficient meaning construction requires a knowledge of concepts, and the reader must rely on an internal mental dictionary as a resource. The larger the lexicon, the larger will be the reader's capacity to comprehend what is read. Furthermore, the reader's speed of access to lexical knowledge is related to processing efficiency and meaning construction. Poor readers usually have slower lexical access speeds than good readers have (Samuels & Naslund, 1994). This is explained by the rapid and nearly automatic access of concept knowledge stored in the schemata of the skilled reader.

Knowledge of *word recognition and identification* provides information that enables the reader to transform visual symbols in print to representational forms for meaning construction. This knowledge base expands from preschool experiences with print to the later grades where skills are used in the conscious analysis of new words and in automatic processing of known words (Ehri, 1987, 1988; Samuels, Chapter 28 this volume). In the early grades, the reader extends understanding of the relationship between print and its oral language counterpart. The beginning reader must develop and refine the idea that print represents language and, in turn, meaning (Strickland & Feeley, 1991). This concept enables the reader to make print predictions using language knowledge already possessed.

There is strong support for the idea that the reader progresses through several developmental phases in acquiring word knowledge (Frith, 1985; Mason, Herman, & Au, 1991), regardless of the instructional methodology used. Ehri's (1991, 1994; see also Ehri & McCormick, Chapter 12 this volume) extensive research review posits and describes five such phases: (1) pre-alphabetic (uses visual, contextual, or graphic cues), (2) partial-alphabetic (uses letter–sound associations in a limited way), (3) full-alphabetic (uses letter–sound relationships), (4) consolidated-alphabetic (uses predictable letter patterns and word parts), and (5) automatic-alphabetic (uses multiple sources to verify word recognition and support automaticity). These developmental phases account for children's gradual use of larger perceptual patterns that possess a high degree of predictability in specific "orthographic neighborhoods."

Thus, as the reader becomes more skilled in word knowledge, progress is made from learning how the spelling system symbolizes phonemes in speech to orthographic pattern processing of increasingly predictable letter combinations and eventually to the automatic recognition of many words. The word knowledge acquired consists of alphabetic and orthographic principles that enable the reader to recode unfamiliar word spellings phonologically. This recoding in turn provides for access to the meanings of words in the mental lexicon.

As the reader progresses developmentally and automatically recognizes many words, phonologically recoded information may not need to be activated. The spelling of specific words in memory may thus serve to represent pronunciation, and if the word is recognized, the mental lexicon is accessed directly (Ehri, 1991, 1994; Samuels, 1985, Chapter 28 this volume). When a word is not recognized, conscious processing using alphabetic and orthographic knowledge and phonological recoding is required to provide for lexical access. The development and use of word identification and recognition knowledge in meaningful contexts enables the discovery of correct word meaning.

The preceding perspective would hold that orthographic, phonological, and semantic processing are integrated, parallel processes that occur simultaneously and in coordinated networks (McClelland, Rumelhart, & Hinton, 1986; McClelland, Rumelhart, & the PDP Research Group, 1986). It would seem that for skilled readers, letter, sound, and meaning are interdependent and interacting events in the reading process.

The role of *text-processing strategies* in the model is critical as the reader responds to and interprets narrative or expository text. These strategies are stored in the form of mental schemata and hold the key to understanding text pattern organization. Narrative text structure, often referred to as "story grammar," accounts for setting, characters, plot structure, climax, and resolution. Schemata for expository writing account for structures such as comparison–contrast, cause–effect, problem–solution, thesis–support, or enumeration of ideas. The concept of flexible knowledge assembly posited by Spiro (1988) can be used to extend this text-processing view. Spiro's concept, as previously discussed, calls for a purpose-sensitive schema that provides for interconnections between schemata and the assembly of new meanings that go beyond a single hierarchical text schema.

At the preschool and kindergarten levels, children develop an understanding of story construction that moves through several stages, from picture-governed attempts in which the story is not formed to print-governed reading in which the story closely follows the print (Sulzby, 1985). For beginning readers, the development of a concept of story structure evolves from unorganized lists of events to full narrative forms (Applebee, 1978). This progression culminates in the understanding that the printed text is the critical source of meaning and that stories follow an organizational pattern (Hiebert & Martin, 2004).

Through experience with narrative reading, the reader develops a sense of story pattern that provides for expectations and predictions useful in constructing meaning. The more-important information, such as setting, initiating events, and consequences, is more likely to be recalled than less-important information, such as a character's response or reaction (Nezworski, Stein, & Trabasso, 1982).

The understanding of these text patterns, in effect, enables the reader to form a plan for reading. The plan for narrative text structures enables the reader to direct attention in making inferences and memory searches using prior knowledge (Anderson & Pearson, 1984; Rumelhart, 1975, 1980) and to predict text features useful in the comprehension process (Rumelhart & Ortony, 1977).

Expository reading also relies on the reader's awareness of text organization. The identification and use of the organizational plan of a text leads to more-effective understanding (Meyer, 1984). For example, the reader encountering a text that explores cause–effect relationships reads and comprehends the text better by using a cause–effect text schema. The research evidence suggests that instruction can assist students in identifying organizational structures in expository text and in using these structures to more effectively construct meaning (Bartlett, 1978; Meyer, Brandt, & Bluth, 1980; Meyer & Freedle, 1979; see also Meyer & Poon, 2004).

Although both narrative and expository text organization schemata can set up expectations for readers that lead to misreadings of text (Garner, 1987; Rumelhart, 1980), knowledge of text organization also enables highly efficient top-down text processing in the meaning-construction process. More-skilled readers are highly effective in using text structure strategies in immediate and delayed recall of text information. Poorer readers appear not to have developed these important meaning-construction strategies or are unable to apply them in the comprehension of text (Hiebert, Englert, & Brennan, 1983; McGee, 1982; Whaley, 1982).

In the model, the reader's *metacognitive strategies* provide for the self-monitoring and self-correcting routines used in the meaning-construction process. Following years of research, educators (Baker, 2005; Griffith & Ruan, 2005; Hacker, 2004) widely agree that the concept of metacognition includes (1) knowledge of one's own knowledge and cognitive processes and (2) the ability to monitor and regulate one's knowledge and cognitive processes. Metacognitive strategies while reading include monitoring levels of text difficulty, depth and relevance of background knowledge, problems in comprehension, meaningful text processing, and progress toward setting and reaching reading goals (Afflerbach & Cho, 2010; Pressley & Afflerbach, 1995). The reader executive directs interactive processing as needed, drawing on prior knowledge forms such as language, word recognition and identification skills, and text-processing strategies (Garner, 1987).

The emergence of the reader's metacognitive control appears to take place in the preschool years. Several researchers have noted that literacy-related metacognitive strategies such as planning, monitoring, checking, evaluating, and revising are found in the utterances of 4- and 5-year-olds in pretend reading of favorite storybooks (Cox, 1994; Rowe, 1989). Earlier research (A. Brown, 1980, 1982; Ruddell & Speaker, 1985) indicates that skilled readers, in contrast to poor readers, are more aware of the meaning-construction process and the need to take corrective action when meaning difficulties are encountered.

There is some evidence to suggest that less-skilled readers use the same metacognitive decision-making strategies as do more-skilled readers but that the strategies are used less often and less efficiently (Goetz, Palmer, & Haensly, 1983). Poorer readers appear to have more difficulty identifying the sources or causes of problems while reading more-complex text (McGee, 1982). This may be attributed, in part, to attention allocation during word recognition and identification. These findings suggest that less-skilled readers who possess knowledge and strategies to make metacognitive decisions are unable to use them effectively.

To effectively use text in the classroom, the reader must have *knowledge of classroom and social interaction* patterns. As Dyson (1984; Dyson & Genishi, Chapter 6 this volume) and Gee (Chapter 4 this volume) have emphasized, literacy is centered in social activity and is much more than skills and strategies. Interaction patterns used in the classroom are largely under the control of the teacher (Green & Harker, 1982). Features of these patterns include message form, message content, addressor, addressee, audience, outcomes, tone, and manner (Hymes, 1974). The reader must internalize these features of classroom dialogue if appropriate and meaningful interaction is to occur.

The reader must acquire the communicative competence that provides for successful classroom interaction (see Forman & Cazden, Chapter 7 this volume). This includes the ability to respond not only to texts (Mosenthal & Na, 1980) and to teachers (DeStefano, Pepinsky, & Sanders, 1982) but also to the complex social network of the classroom community (Moll, 1992; Santa Barbara Classroom Discourse Group, 1992). As will be discussed later, the teacher must be aware of and sensitive to the reader's understanding of the ways language can be used during classroom discussion and interaction.

Personal and world knowledge includes socially embedded schemata representing a wide range of experiences and understandings that have been acquired both in school and out. This knowledge includes declarative forms (e.g., exemplified by historical information acquired during a field trip to the local museum), procedural forms (e.g., how to activate a self-directed museum display), and conditional forms (illustrated by understanding the appropriate time to pose questions to the docent). Personal knowledge is stored in the reader's episodic memory as images of personal experience (Tulving, 1983, 1986). World knowledge is represented in schemata formed from the reader's life experiences and includes facts and assumptions, actions and procedures, and understanding of appropriate conditions for knowledge use. Activation of schemata from world knowledge directly affects the interpretation of a text. Two readers with different world knowledge schemata may read an ambiguous text and provide very different interpretations (Anderson & Pichert, 1978; Hull & Rose, 2004; Pichert & Anderson, 1977). Thus, the reader's background knowledge schemata are directly related to meaning construction and text interpretation.

Intertextual references frequently influence the meanings that readers construct as they read (Hartman, 1990, 1991). Intertextuality is the process of connecting current texts with past texts to construct meaning (de Beaugrande, 1980).

Those past texts are part of the reader's world knowledge. In the model, the meaning of text is expanded to include not only printed texts but also the text of events, communication, and cultures (Bloome & Bailey, 1992). These "texts" range from art and music to ritual and gesture. Intertextuality is thus more broadly conceived as the acknowledged interaction between the text being read and the "texts" based on our experiences. These texts have an important influence on the reader's construction of meaning.

The use of personal and world knowledge has a strong influence on the meaning-construction and comprehension process. The reader who has a rich knowledge base and flexible access to that base can more effectively assemble a coherent and meaningful text representation. The reader's intertextual links to "texts" outside the primary text also facilitate and enrich the meaning-construction process.

Knowledge Use and Control

The knowledge use and control component of the model directs the reader's meaning-construction process. As noted in Figure 2, this component is linked to and interactive with the reader's prior knowledge and beliefs. Knowledge use and control consists of three components: the knowledge-construction process, text representation, and reader executive and monitor.

Knowledge-Construction Process. The reader's knowledge-construction process serves to set the purpose for reading and to integrate prior beliefs and knowledge through planning, organizing, and constructing meaning. We will show later in the discussion that as meaning is formed, it is reflected in text representation. The reading executive and monitor oversees this entire process based on the original purpose and, if necessary, prompts reconstruction of purpose and meaning.

Purpose setting is initiated as the reader creates a goal or, more commonly, multiple goals when the text is encountered. This process reflects the reader's motivation or intent and is influenced by the affective and cognitive conditions noted in Figure 2. For example, the reader's stance may be aesthetic and reflect the intent of savoring the pleasure of constructing and entering an imaginary world of romance, intrigue, or interstellar space, or the reader may take a predominantly efferent stance to learn more about dinosaurs, jellyfish, or electromagnets. The reader may also adopt multiple stances to experience a text from many different perspectives (Beach, 1992; see also Galda & Beach, 2004).

The learning environment created by the teacher will also have a strong influence on the purpose setting of the reader (see Alvermann, Young, Green, & Wisenbaker, 2004). Assignments may be given that request the student to read efferently and attend to particular aspects of a text, such as imagery used to evoke a certain mood or the claims used to support a thesis. By contrast, the teacher may focus attention on pleasure reading designed to encourage an aesthetic transaction with the text and to evoke the reader's feelings and attitudes toward key characters (Many, 2004).

As the reader's original goals are realized, subsequent goals may take their place as the focus of attention. Thus, purpose setting for the reader is usually in flux as goals, both conscious and unconscious, are made and met.

As the reading purpose is established, a simultaneous process of *planning and organizing* takes place. The plans that readers make as they interact with text are of at least two types: (1) a structured text plan of events, concepts, or claims in the form of a text pattern and (2) a path of action, or strategies and approaches, used to meet a goal.

The reader begins to form a text structure plan and a plan of action to achieve the reading purpose. The reader's text structure plans may have a top-down or expectation-driven influence on the text-construction process as textual schemata become activated and influence or shape meaning construction. For example, a narrative text structure plan may be used to integrate story features, or a cause–effect plan may be invoked in reading and interpreting a science experiment. However, not every text activates textual schemata that might influence comprehension in a top-down fashion. Some texts, especially technical prose, are far better constructed and understood from the bottom up, a process that will be examined when we address text construction in the next section. Frequently, the reader builds meaning in a simultaneous and interactive manner using both top-down and bottom-up processing.

The reader's awareness of text organizational structures plays an important planning and organizing role in creating meaning. Bruner (1986) has postulated two separate ways to order experience and construct meaning. The first, the narrative mode, creates imaginative worlds through stories. Its "truth" is wrung from its imitation of reality—in effect, its likeness to real-life experience. The second, the paradigmatic, is scientific and relies on logical proof and evidence for verification of claims. As the reader interacts with texts, experience in reading both modes will assist in understanding which mode the author has used to order the experience and which must be used to reconstruct the meaning the text embodies.

Reading is a process of *constructing*, of knowledge integration, of building meaning. The goals that the reader forms, the plans adopted or created, and the organizing that occurs as text is processed and interpreted contribute to the text-constructing process. For some kinds of texts (especially narrative), the reader often constructs meaning as schemata are activated and instantiated. But that top-down process alone is often not sufficient, especially for complex narrative forms.

The cognitive components of comprehension presented here rely on both bottom-up and top-down processes interacting. *Bottom-up processing* refers to cognitive activities stimulated by a reader's perceptions of printed words on a page. Some of these activities, such as orthographic processing, phonological recoding (decoding), and word recognition and identification, have been explored previously. However, these perceptions and word activations from the bottom up contribute to the formation of propositions in the reader's mind. They represent meaningful clauses and sentences to the reader. A proposition is a basic unit of meaning. Kintsch (1998, Chapter 32 this volume) defined an atomic proposition as a linguistic unit made up of a predicate and one or more concepts. For example, "The ball is round" as an atomic proposition becomes [ROUND, BALL]. Essentially, it is the smallest unit of knowledge that can be put to a test of being true or false (Bauer, 1994). However, the propositions that are formed bottom up, together with a reader's purposes for reading and schemata from the reader's long-term memory, which come "top down," combine to form a network of activated ideas in working and long-term memory. "Top-down" information refers to many forms of knowledge held in long-term memory and activated as a result of information entering the mind bottom up. For example, we have schemata related to the word *ball*, including the knowledge that balls are round, which is activated when we construct even an atomic proposition like "The ball is round." That "top-down" information includes schemata related to the text being read and to knowledge about language, text structure, and genre that contribute to a reader's construction of meaning for a text. The constructed plasma of propositions and activated memories, some relevant and some less so, may be quite chaotic. The elements contributing to that chaos are eventually sorted out so relevant features remain activated in working memory or at a threshold state in long-term memory while irrelevant features fade away. As chaotic conditions subside, the emerging pattern of activated meanings soon becomes stabilized into what the reader experiences as comprehension. This proposition-construction process followed by the integration of features that must satisfy certain relevancy constraints is similar to Kintsch's (1998, Chapter 32 this volume) construction–integration (or CI) theory. However, the model of reading presented here, while drawing upon Kintsch's work, also draws upon the research and perspectives of many other reading researchers and theorists.

Text Representations Constructed. As the interactive bottom-up and top-down process of creating meaning proceeds, readers construct multiple forms of representation. While struggling readers may have trouble constructing even the most basic of text representations, such as a textbase, proficient readers are often facile negotiators of multiple representations. The features composing three forms of representation range from surface code to situation model.

1. *Surface code*: The literal experience of the text on the page represented by letters, words, clauses, and sentences
2. *Textbase*: The meaning of clauses derived or "translated" directly from the surface code into propositions
3. *Situation or "landscape" model*: Personal interpretation of a text created through knowledge and experience activated from long-term memory and integrated with the textbase to provide a landscape representation of the text. This representation includes intra- and intertextual connections as well as genre and text structure awareness.

Research has taught us much about moving from surface codes to a textbase by developing propositions to represent underlying features of a text and its organization, and we have begun to learn more about the larger mental structure for a text's representation as a situation model. Schmalhofer, McDaniel, and Keefe (2002) developed an example to show how a network of propositions is constructed in the mind of the reader and then integrated through spreading activation to form the textbase that is composed of propositions. That textbase then articulates at significant points of meaning with associated knowledge networks activated from long-term memory as schemata. Important to visualize in this example is the linkage among surface structure, textbase, and situation model. Thereby, a phrase or sentence in the surface structure is linked to propositions in the textbase that subsequently link to activated schemata in the situation model. Consider, for example, the following sentence: "There's much to be said about a round, red ball rolling down a cobblestone street in autumn." Such a sentence presents not only a surface structure and a textbase for its reader but also the potential for a situation model that could represent a reader's personal interpretation of the sentence's symbolic meanings.

The exact nature of text representation—whether a set of propositions, a network of concepts, an image, or some combination—remains in question (see Coté & Goldman, 2004; Kintsch, Chapter 32 this volume; Sadoski et al., 1991). Although imagery may be part of the symbolic text-in-the-head representation of the text on the page, it seems likely that the bulk of text representation for ongoing meaning construction is in the form of propositions that have been "chunked" into a coherent textbase and embellished into an elaborated situation model.

Reading Executive and Monitor. Managing and overseeing the meaning-construction process is the reader executive and monitor. As shown in Figure 2, it is linked by two-way arrows with knowledge use and control, text representation, and prior knowledge and beliefs. Although the functions of the central executive during cognitive processes such as reading have yet to be fully explicated, researchers and theorists (Baddeley, 2007; Sesma, Mahone, Levine, Eason, & Cutting, 2009) have found that the executive focuses, divides, and switches attention; integrates information in working and long-term memory; oversees knowledge manipulation; and conducts planning and sequencing of multistep tasks while keeping track of major concepts in a field of details. These functions are carried out by drawing on affective and cognitive conditions in prior beliefs and knowledge. The conditions range from establishing purposes for reading and the stance to be taken to selecting text-processing and metacognitive strategies to be applied. Time allocated to reading the text is also determined by this component. Skilled readers, for example, have been shown to adjust their reading rates and time allocation in relation to the reading purpose (Reynolds, Standiford, & Anderson, 1979; Rothkopf & Billington, 1979) and comprehension difficulty of the text (Wagner & Sternberg, 1987).

The reader executive and monitor evaluates the ongoing process of meaning construction as text representation is formed. This self-monitoring draws on metacognitive strategies in prior knowledge and beliefs and evaluates the "fit" between purpose and the meaning constructed in text representation. The monitor and executive, as part of the evaluative function, may intervene to allocate attention to the repair of meaning breakdowns when they are detected. This may require the search for and accessing of additional information in prior knowledge and beliefs, shifts of attention to reread parts of the text, shifts in reading stance, or even altering the reading purpose.

During class discussions, the reader interacts not only with the text but also with the teacher's discourse and classmates' responses. Under these conditions, more cognitive functions are activated and more attention management is required than during individual text reading. Because of the range of tasks, the reader's executive and monitor must make decisions about which cognitive tasks—or distractions—will be given priority. As text-meaning construction is represented in the mind of the reader, that representation undergoes a reviewing process that is under the control of the reading executive and monitor. The reader's text representation may be reviewed depending on the difficulty of the text, and that review may result in further planning, organizing, and reconstructing until the reader creates a text representation that is coherent and meaningful.

In summary, the knowledge use and control component of the model has as its central task the construction of meaning. The reader uses the knowledge-construction process to set purposes, activate and construct plans, organize knowledge, and formulate a text representation. While the knowledge-construction process progresses, the reader executive and monitor allocates attention during the process, evaluates the text representation based on purpose, and assists in editing and reconstructing meaning when misunderstandings arise.

Outcomes of Meaning Construction

During and after reading, the reader develops a number of text-related outcomes. These outcomes are identified in Figure 2.

While reading, the reader employs word-analysis and language knowledge to develop *semantic and lexical knowledge*, which includes the learning of new words, their range of meanings, and their use. Often context assists the reader in deciding which meanings are appropriate for the text being read. *Interpretation of text* based on prior knowledge and beliefs may be the central goal for the reader. Most readings of text in classroom settings will lead to *discussion* of the text. Certainly, discussion is a valuable outcome for teacher and readers as they explore responses to the text and expand their understanding and knowledge base. *Written response* offers the reader an opportunity to understand, synthesize, and clarify what has been learned from the text reading and discussion. A wide range of written responses to text is possible, extending from expression of the reader's feelings and emotions to the creation of new works that expand on the reader's understanding. *Knowledge acquisition* includes specific domain knowledge, such as categories, concepts, and processes. While readers learn to read, they read to learn. *Motivational changes* can influence the reader's attitude toward reading and the reader's intention to continue to read. If the reader reads because of an internally driven desire or if meaningful learning accompanies reading, *motivation* to read—and to learn—is likely to increase. However, motivation can diminish if enjoyment and expectations are not fulfilled. The final outcome of the meaning-construction process shown in the model is the reader's *attitude, value, and belief change*. Rich and rewarding personal experiences with books can change the way a reader feels, acts, and perceives the world. Through reading, students can experience new and enchanting narrative worlds, discover new and tantalizing subjects, and gain new knowledge of themselves and others.

The Reader: A Summing Up

In our attempt to explain the mysterious process that enables the reader to construct meaning, we have identified a number of interacting components, as shown in Figure 2. Prior beliefs and knowledge include affective and cognitive conditions that influence and shape meaning construction. Knowledge use and control are at the heart of the knowledge-construction process through purpose setting, planning and organizing, and constructing meaning in the form of text representation. The meaning-construction process is directed by the reader executive and monitor and guided by purpose as attention is allocated and rereading, reconstruction, and editing occur. Although the mystery of the process is far from solved, we have explored a number of critical clues that begin to help us understand it. However, much remains to be discovered about this process as we turn to the role of the teacher in facilitating the reader's construction of meaning.

The Teacher

Interest in how skillful teachers function in the learning environment is not new. Five centuries before the birth of Christ, Confucius (as cited in Müller & Legge, 1885) observed that when we know the causes that make instruction successful and those that have no effect, we can become successful teachers: "Opening the way and not conducting to the end makes [the learner] thoughtful" (p. 87). Accordingly, the teacher engages the student in a collaborative process of inquiry and self-improvement in which both teacher and student seek to refine respective skills and knowledge. The goal of teaching, then, is to model thought in action and allow the student to discover answers for himself or herself (Ruddell & Kern, 1986; Unrau, 2008b).

Teachers who have been influential in the academic and personal lives of students (Ruddell, 2004, 2009) possess a number of common characteristics. These teachers consistently use clearly formulated instructional strategies that embody focused goals, plans, and monitoring for student feedback. They possess in-depth knowledge of reading and literacy processes as well as content knowledge, and they understand how to teach these processes effectively to students. They also frequently tap internal student motivation, stimulate intellectual curiosity, explore students' self-understanding, and encourage engagement in problem solving. But these influential teachers reveal something else about their instruction that promoted motivation to learn: They are warm, caring, and flexible, while having high expectations of themselves and their students. Furthermore, they are concerned about their students as individuals in the social context of the classroom.

The teacher orchestrates instruction and the meaning-construction process, as shown in Figure 3. The teacher components of the model parallel those of the reader components. As noted earlier, the teacher's prior knowledge and beliefs extend far beyond those of the reader, accounting for more extensive life experience, academic and professional preparation, and teaching experience. The teacher's knowledge use and control draw on prior knowledge and beliefs in the instructional decision-making process as purpose, plan, and strategy construction are created with the goal of involving students in active meaning

Figure 3. The Teacher

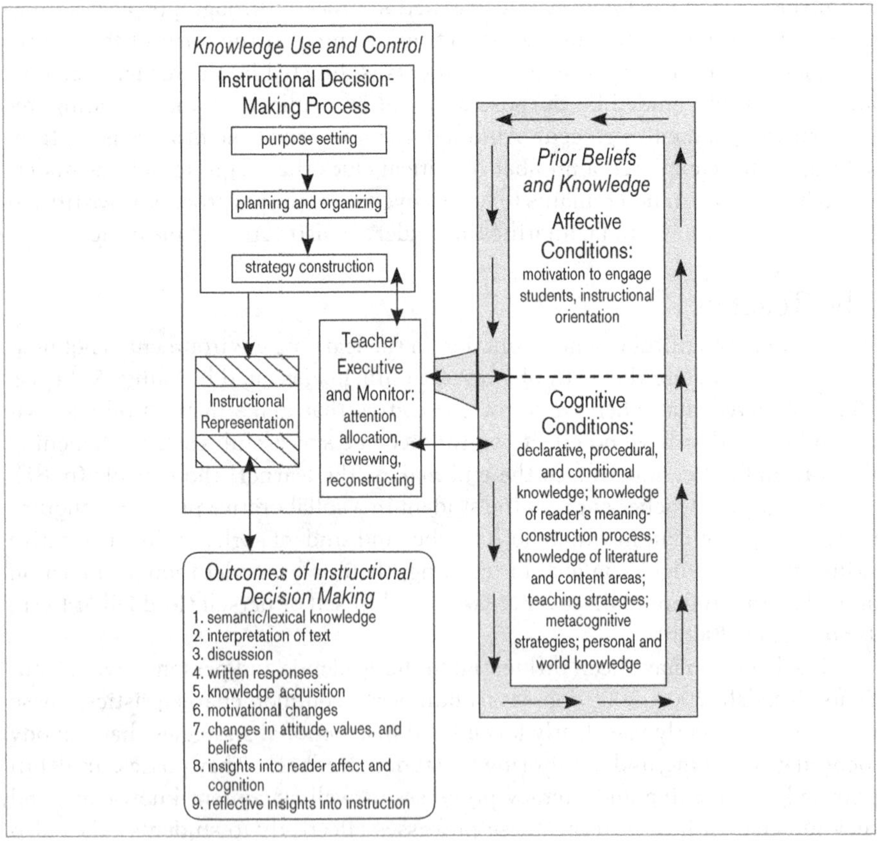

construction. As instruction is initiated, an instructional representation begins to form in the teacher's mind. The teacher executive and monitor serves to direct the instructional process based on the instructional purpose setting. These processes directly influence and shape the outcomes of instructional decision making, ranging from text interpretation to attitude, value, and belief changes. In the following sections, we briefly explore these teacher components.

Prior Knowledge and Beliefs

The teacher's prior knowledge and beliefs consist of affective and cognitive conditions based on and shaped by a wide range of life experiences. These conditions have a strong influence on knowledge use and control, instructional decision making, and instructional outcomes in the learning environment.

Affective Conditions. The teacher, like the reader, holds beliefs based on opinions, assumptions, and convictions. Teacher beliefs, however, have a direct impact on the affective conditions that influence and shape the teacher's instructional purpose, plan, and strategy construction. The teacher's *motivation to engage students* is shaped by the same three components discussed earlier that influence a reader's intention to engage in reading: a developing self, an instructional orientation, and task engagement resources. The teacher's purpose in accounting for these motivation factors is driven by the desire to create an optimal learning environment where students will participate fully and persist in meaning construction. In this process, the fit among text content, text difficulty, and the student's interests and reading ability is of central importance. In the following discussion, we focus specifically on a teacher's instructional orientation and its components.

Instructional orientation, or the alignment of teacher and student with a teaching or learning task, affects motivation and engagement. Several critical factors make up instructional orientation and contribute to motivation: achievement goals, task values, sociocultural values and beliefs, and stance.

Achievement Goals. Achievement-goal theory stresses the engagement of the learner in selecting, structuring, and making sense of achievement experience. Meece (1994) pointed out that research has focused on two kinds of achievement goals: mastery (or task-oriented goals) and performance (or ego-oriented goals). Readers and learners seeking mastery goals are intrinsically motivated to acquire knowledge and skills that lead to their becoming more competent. Readers and learners who are pursuing performance goals are eager to seek opportunities to demonstrate their skills or knowledge in a competitive, public arena.

Perceptions of ability have been shown to be one critical factor that influences patterns of achievement (Meece, 1994). If individuals believe they can become better readers or teachers by making an effort, they are more likely to embrace a mastery-goal orientation. They see themselves as able to improve over time by making an effort to master challenging tasks. By making the effort to acquire knowledge and skills, the teacher's or student's feelings of self-worth and competence are likely to increase, as is their intrinsic motivation (Ryan & Deci, 2009).

Task Values. Several interacting components that make up an individual's perception of task values, such as those related to reading tasks, have been identified and investigated (Wigfield, 1994). These components include attainment value (the importance an individual attributes to a task), intrinsic-interest value (the task's subjective interest to an individual), utility value (the usefulness of a task in light of a person's future goals), and the cost of success (the "disadvantages" of accomplishing a task, e.g., experiencing stress). Both students and teachers commonly evaluate a task's values before undertaking it. While students are likely to ask themselves how a reading assignment might contribute to their understanding of a topic in which they are interested, teachers may consider the value of redesigning a reading lesson in terms of its usefulness as a vehicle to improve student performance.

Sociocultural Values and Beliefs. A teacher's sociocultural values and beliefs, what Gee (2012) would refer to as their Discourse and its related cultural model, have a profound effect on the relationships with students, instructional decision making, and the interpretation of texts. Students are vulnerable to breakdowns in communication if their sociocultural values and beliefs do not match those of the teacher or if the teacher is not responsive to cultural differences (Hull & Rose, 2004). As Heath (1983) discovered, teachers can also positively affect students who enter school cultures that are divergent from those in which they grew up. Through the building of relationships, reflection, and self-exploration, teachers can become more responsive to students' sociocultural backgrounds and design classroom instruction that takes divergent perspectives into consideration, a move that is likely to enhance students' motivation and engagement.

Stance. Stance pertains to the perspective that a reader adopts toward the reading of a particular text and has the capacity to influence motivation. By guiding the reader's focus of attention and purpose, the teacher's instructional stance also influences a reader's intention to read. Rosenblatt (1978) has strongly influenced the field, as we have seen, with her identification and elaboration of two stances, efferent and aesthetic, that lie on a continuum along which the degree of emphasis may change. To varying degrees, the teacher and the reader can control stance. While progressing through a text, the teacher may encourage a stance that guides readers toward the integration of both efferent and aesthetic stances in varied proportions. An overemphasis on efferent readings may, in some instances, reduce the value and enjoyment of students' transactions with literature—and thus their level of motivation. On the contrary, an emphasis on efferent responses may enable students to develop analytical skills. Nevertheless, influential teachers tend to emphasize aesthetic responses over efferent ones (Ruddell, 1994).

In addition to the factors we have described that contribute to instructional orientation and teacher motivation are several instructional design resources that teachers draw upon to create engaging curriculum and instruction. These factors include knowledge of students and their meaning-construction processes, knowledge of literature and the content areas, pedagogical knowledge including instructional strategies, world knowledge, and metacognitive knowledge (Ruddell & Unrau, 2004).

Cognitive Conditions. The teacher's cognitive conditions are specific knowledge forms stored as *declarative knowledge* ("what"), *procedural knowledge* ("how to"), and *conditional knowledge* ("when" and "why"). These cognitive knowledge forms are highly interactive with one another and with the affective conditions, as illustrated by the broken line separating them in Figure 3. The cognitive conditions consist of knowledge of the reader's meaning-construction process, literature and content areas, teaching strategies, metacognitive strategies, and personal and world knowledge.

The teacher's *knowledge of the reader's meaning-construction process* is essential to instruction and instructional decision making. We assume the teacher constructs meaning from text by relying on the same processes. This knowledge is discussed in depth in our earlier exploration of the reader component. That discussion assumes a constructivist perspective that views the creation of meaning as an active comprehension process in the social context of the classroom. This active comprehension process must account for the reader's prior knowledge and beliefs as knowledge construction occurs and text representation is formed under the control of the reader's executive and monitor. Meaning negotiation in the classroom social context among teacher, reader, and classroom community is an important part of this meaning-construction process, as we shall see in our later discussion.

Knowledge of literature and content areas constitutes a store of information critical to instruction. This knowledge, largely declarative in nature, is acquired through academic experiences and enriched through personal and world knowledge. Knowledge of this type ranges from familiarity with the accepted literary canon to an understanding of important concepts in science, mathematics, and the social sciences. It also includes an understanding of the organization of both narrative and expository text and related text-processing strategies. The teacher selects literary works that are likely to engage students and to move them toward deeper understandings of various literary forms and techniques or chooses expository prose to provide students with opportunities for optimum growth in understanding discourse structures and rhetorical approaches commonly used in persuasive or content area texts, such as history or science (Unrau, 2008a).

Knowledge of teaching strategies is critical to the teacher's instructional decision making and helps implement the selected instructional purpose. Teaching-strategy knowledge may consist of understanding that provides for general problem solving or of strategies that can be used in reaching specific instructional goals. Such strategies are illustrated by the following: the Directed Reading–Thinking Activity (DRTA; Stauffer, 1976), designed to establish reader predictions, confirmations, and conclusions in narratives; the Prereading Plan (PREP; Langer, 1981), which serves to activate and assess reader background knowledge before reading narrative or expository material; the Question–Answer Relationship (QAR) strategy

(Raphael, 1982), which serves to assist the reader in connecting reading purpose to text and to personal information sources; the reciprocal teaching strategy (see A. Brown, Palincsar, & Armbruster, Chapter 27 this volume), which uses teacher modeling to clarify and summarize meaning, develop student predictions, and generate questions; Students Achieving Independent Learning (SAIL; R. Brown, Pressley, Van Meter, & Schuder, 2004), which provides low-achieving second graders with multiple-strategies instruction; and Thesis Analysis and Synthesis Key (TASK; Unrau, 2008b), which guides students through the process of analyzing argumentative expository texts. Knowledge of and ability to use strategies such as these contribute to effective comprehension instruction (Raphael, George, Weber, & Nies, 2010) and the growth of students' metacognitive knowledge and skills (Israel, Block, Bauserman, & Kinnucan-Welsch, 2005).

An important part of the teacher's strategy knowledge resides in understanding and using informal assessments of the reader during instruction. Such information provides immediate feedback to the reader and insight into the reader's meaning-construction process for follow-up instruction.

Metacognitive strategies provide a resource for self-monitoring and self-correction of meaning construction during and after instruction just as they do for readers' reading. Those resources are used by the teacher executor and monitor, guided by the instructional purpose, and interactive with other cognitive and affective conditions. Teachers who work in the dynamic and complex social context of classrooms must think on their feet and think about their thinking at the same time—clearly a description of metacognition.

To activate and apply their metacognitive strategies, the teacher needs to have an independent spirit, what Duffy (2005) called "visioning," to construct and execute instruction in reading. While visioning, the teacher uses strategies to monitor, evaluate, regulate, and adjust instruction so optimum conditions for learning prevail in the classroom. As instruction proceeds, the teacher must attend to a wide range of factors, including student responses, content of the lesson, instructional strategies employed, time constraints, and use of text and materials. The teacher must also be aware of communication breakdowns and possible ways to clarify meaning and alter instructional strategies to improve the meaning-negotiation process. Acute metacognitive awareness and skills are required to detect meaning difficulties, shift attention to understand the problem, and draw on specific strategies to correct the problem during instruction.

The teacher also learns what is working for students by reflecting on classroom interaction after instruction. Research has shown that by mentally replaying events, keeping a journal, or videotaping, the experienced teacher is able to reflect on the quality and productivity of the learning relationship with students. This reflection represents an attempt to discover what could be changed to improve instruction (Borko, Shavelson, & Stern, 1981).

The teacher's *personal and world knowledge* represents those experiences acquired through life outside of school and academic experiences. Personal knowledge, formed from these experiences and bound by time and situation, is stored in episodic memory; world knowledge is represented by schemata in semantic memory.

The teacher's personal and world knowledge directly affect the construction of meaning and interpretation of text, as with the reader. However, the teacher's knowledge base may have developed over a longer time or from a wider range of personal and world experiences.

As we noted earlier, the meaning of text as used in the model is expanded to include the "texts" from areas such as art, music, and cultural rituals. In this sense, the teacher's personal and world knowledge provide for interaction between the "texts" based on experience and the text being read. The extensive intertextual knowledge often held by the teacher can provide an important resource in instructional decision making and assist the reader to negotiate and construct meaning.

Knowledge Use and Control

The teacher's knowledge use and control component directs the instructional decision-making process, provides a mental instructional representation, and evaluates instructional purpose through the teacher executive and monitor. This component is closely connected to and interactive with prior knowledge and beliefs, as shown in Figure 3.

Instructional Decision-Making Process. The instructional decision-making process establishes *purpose setting* for instruction that reflects the teacher's instructional intent. The affective and cognitive conditions, as shown under prior beliefs and knowledge in Figure 3, help influence and shape this intent. For example, the teacher's purpose may be to elicit students' responses in the form of feelings and attitudes toward a main character. This decision, in turn, may result in the rise of a predominantly aesthetic instructional stance.

The *planning and organizing* to support this aesthetic stance draws on the teacher's knowledge of literature and content areas and of the reader's meaning-construction process. This may be reflected in the teacher's selection of a story or novel appropriate to the reader's interest and achievement level.

Strategy constructing accounts for decisions made about teaching strategies designed to implement the selected instructional stance. For example, if stance toward a text is to be aesthetic and designed to focus reader responses on personal feelings and attitudes, question prompts will need to be more open ended than would be the case with an efferent stance—for example, "How would you have felt and reacted had you been the first person to see 'SOME PIG!' written in Charlotte's web in the barnyard that foggy morning?" In addition, the use of a reader response journal would provide opportunities for the students to record their responses and to share their ideas and reactions in small-group discussions. The teacher's personal and world knowledge may be drawn on in such discussions to provide intertextual personal experiences to illuminate understandings related to the text.

Instructional Representation. An instructional representation is created in the teacher's mind during instructional planning as the lesson's purpose, organization, and strategies are considered. As instruction is initiated with the students, the original representation begins to unfold and change with the ongoing instructional process. This representation is conceived of as an "instructional world" that reflects the meaning structure and record of the instructional interaction with the students (de Beaugrande, 1981; Ruddell & Speaker, 1985).

Teacher Executive and Monitor. The teacher executive and monitor provides for managing and monitoring the instructional decision-making process and meaning construction. As noted in Figure 3, it is in a central position and linked to instructional representation, instructional decision making, and prior knowledge and beliefs.

The executive and monitor controls *attention allocation* during instruction, *review* of interactions and content discussed, and guidance for *reconstructing* of inferences and conclusions. In effect, the executive and monitor evaluates the ongoing instructional process reflected in instructional representation. This teacher-monitoring process draws on metacognitive strategies to evaluate the relationship among the original instructional purpose, plan, strategy use, and meaning construction reflected in instructional representation. Assuming the classroom interaction and meaning-negotiation process are successful and aligned with the original purpose and plan, instruction proceeds; if they are not, a shift in plan and strategy may be necessary to achieve the original purpose more effectively.

Outcomes of Instructional Decision Making

Based on the instructional plan, the teacher often has expectations that students will acquire knowledge or have experiences of a particular kind (Ames, 1992). The nature of the meaning-negotiation process, shaped by the teacher, will also strongly influence instructional outcomes, as we shall see later in our discussion. The teacher will often obtain two kinds of outcomes arising from instruction. The first includes the teacher's perceptions of the readers' understandings, and the second consists of the teacher's own understandings and insights.

During instruction, the teacher gains an understanding of the *semantic and lexical knowledge* that readers acquire. The teacher learns of the readers' new word knowledge through direct instruction, meaning negotiation in large- and small-group discussions, student self-directed use of classroom resources, or text-based contextual inference.

The reader's *interpretation of text* depends heavily on the instructional stance and strategies used by the teacher. Certainly, the teacher recognizes that the reader's prior beliefs and knowledge exert a strong influence on the text interpretation that is constructed (see Hull & Rose, 2004). The teacher's interpretation of text may also shift as a result of interaction in the classroom community.

During classroom *discussion*, the reader's personal response and understandings of the text are expressed. The discussion may also alter the teacher's response to the text based on insights derived from the reader's and the classroom community's perspective.

Written responses to text provide the teacher with an understanding of the reader's text representation and interpretation. Responses range from straightforward summaries and syntheses to journal writing that reveals the reader's underlying beliefs and emotions evoked by the text. Again, the teacher's understanding of the text may be enhanced through reflection on the reader's written responses.

The reader's *knowledge acquisition* is evident to the teacher through the reader's use of new concepts and fresh insights. This acquisition will be heavily influenced by engagement of the reader's interests and motivation through active comprehension. The teacher's acquisition of new knowledge will be influenced in a similar manner.

While the teacher expects to observe *motivational changes* in the reader, these expectations may not always be realized. The teacher's knowledge of the reader's key interests and internal motivations, such as intellectual curiosity or self-understanding, makes possible the connection of the reader with high-interest text. In addition, the teacher may derive new insights into motivation to engage students based on reader response during instruction.

The teacher may recognize the reader's *attitude, value, and belief change* through the reader's discourse involving text interpretations, discussions, and written responses. These activities enable the reader to examine closely held attitudes, values, and beliefs. In addition, the teacher may experience attitude, value, and belief change related to the text content based on the social interaction with students. The teacher's attitude toward readers may also change as a result of reader responses in the instructional setting.

A key instructional outcome for the teacher is found in *insight into reader affect and cognition.* Direct classroom observation of the reader as he or she constructs meaning and formative assessments provide "a window on the mind" that can lead to important insights. These may range from understanding of personal motivations and interests to conceptual knowledge and text-processing strategies.

Closely connected to these reader insights is the outcome of *reflective insight into instruction.* As the teacher gains understanding of the reader in the context of instruction, reflective insight can provide opportunities for refining instruction. This may include use of specific reader motivation and interests, employment of a variety of active comprehension strategies, or incorporation of an instructional stance that recognizes the importance of active reader response.

Text and Classroom Context

Our model takes a constructivist perspective of learning in which the teacher creates a learning environment that engages the reader in active comprehension through confronting and solving authentic problems in a social context. In the text and classroom context, shown in Figure 4, this environment includes a meaning-negotiation process that accounts for text, task, source of authority, and sociocultural meanings.

Figure 4. The Text and Classroom Context

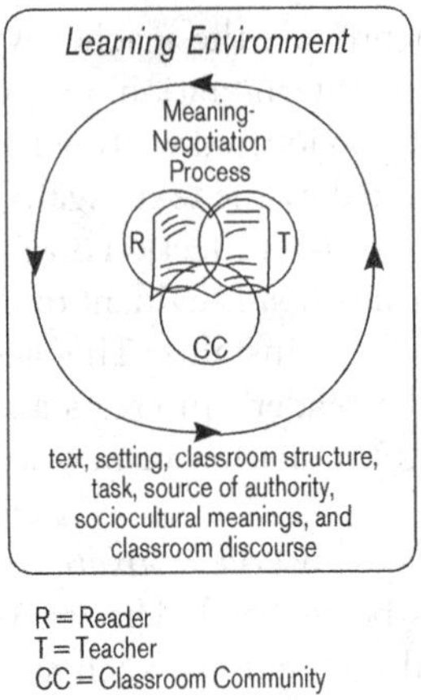

The Learning Environment

The learning environment has a powerful influence on students' motivation to engage in learning (Langer, 2004; Marshall, 1992). How teachers structure text-related tasks, who carries the power of authority, and concern for sociocultural meanings can make major differences in the goals that readers attempt to achieve and the way readers feel about themselves, their classmates, and their accomplishments (Alvermann et al., 2004).

The learning environment influences not only the reader's decision to engage with a text but also the ways in which the text is engaged. We can expect the reader's engagement with reading, interaction with teacher and peers, and participation in the meaning-negotiation process if the reader is motivated to read and to learn, if prior beliefs and knowledge are activated, if tasks are personally relevant, and if active meaning construction is involved. The teacher who incorporates these features in the learning environment is considered to be mastery-goal oriented and is much more likely to produce productive learning in students (Ames, 1992; Covington, 1992; Maehr, 1984; Pintrich & De Groot, 1990).

Furthermore, the reader's motivation to achieve is enhanced if social goals and a constructivist view of learning have been integrated into the learning environment (Blumenfeld, 1992). These social goals include the influence of teachers and parents on children and the impact of cultural expectations on learning.

The Meaning-Negotiation Process. As shown in Figure 4, the meaning-negotiation process involves interaction among text (shown in the shaded background representing a printed text), the reader (R), the teacher (T), and the classroom community (CC). During negotiation for meanings related to texts, readers bring their own meanings to the interaction, teachers bring their understanding of the story as well as their understanding of the reading process, and members of the class interact with the text to shape—and reshape—meanings. Students and the teacher read much more than the written text during this process. Texts have gone far beyond the traditional book in a book bag. In effect, students and teacher read several "texts"—if we take "texts" to mean events, situations, behavioral scripts, and other symbolic processes that require interpretation (Bloome & Bailey, 1992). In accord with the French philosopher Jacques Derrida (1982), everything is a text. Many philosophers and literacy specialists (Barthes, 1977; Derrida, 1982; Eco, 1976; Moje, Dillon, & O'Brien, 2000) now view texts as an organized network of meanings, including the self or selves that interact with other texts. Of course, students and teacher read the text on the page, but students in particular also need to "read" the task, the authority structure, the teacher (including the teacher's intentions and expectations), the sociocultural setting, and the classroom discourse; in addition, they must "read" the social dynamics of the group, which include the group's rules, such as turn taking and question–answer response patterns (Mehan, 1980).

While some critics and theorists have taken the position that the meaning of a text is located in the text itself and that the text is an object that can be objectively described, others (Bleich, 1980; Culler, 1980; Fish, 1982; Iser, 1980; Rosenblatt, 1978, Chapter 35 this volume) have argued that the meaning of a text is a more subjective construct. This construct is to be found in the reader's mind, perhaps to be authorized by the interpretive community but certainly not by an objective text. We hold, in the model, that meaning results from the reader's meaning-construction process. That meaning is not entirely in either the text or the reader but is created as a result of the interactions among reader, text, teacher, and classroom community.

But, given the multitude of interpretations that readers construct for a particular text, which one is to be accepted as correct or valid? The work of both students and teachers is to confirm that interpretations are grounded in the actual text and in the readers' response to textual features. This does not mean that the ultimate meaning is only in the text but that interpretations should be reasonably supportable with reference to events, statements, or claims that occur there and in relation to concepts or impressions evoked in the reader's mind. As Rosenblatt (1938/1976) has observed,

> Fundamentally, the process of understanding the work implies a recreation of it, an attempt to grasp completely the structured sensations and concepts through which the author seeks to convey the quality of his sense of life. Each must make a new synthesis of these elements with his own nature, but it is essential that he evoke these components of experience to which the text actually refers. (p. 113)

The authority of a classroom community has also been taken as a standard for validity (Fish, 1982). In this case, the meaning that is constructed as students and teacher interact in the classroom is the only meaning that counts. Intersubjective negotiation without adherence to textual content becomes paramount in such classrooms. Although this view certainly frees readers from adherence to an objective standard—namely, the text—it creates other problems. First, how is one's membership in an interpretive community to be confirmed? And second, how does an independent evaluator identify which text has been interpreted? These problems are of such a magnitude that in spite of efforts to solve them, we find Rosenblatt's (1938/1976) constraint upon interpretations through the principle of "warranted assertability" most tenable for our model—that is, interpretation should be grounded in experiences "to which the text actually refers."

Nevertheless, classroom community negotiation of meaning is imperative, even if that negotiated meaning does not always reside as the ultimate authority for validation. The readers and the teacher share meanings in the classroom community so that through dialogue, a community of readers comes to hold a possible range of meanings. In Figure 4, the three overlapping circles symbolize the interactive nature of the meaning-negotiation process for teacher (T), reader (R), and classroom community (CC). However, that process overlaps the real text upon which the dialogue is based. Thus, the text itself is not the sole object carrying meaning; instead, meanings arise from transactions with the text.

It is also important to note that in Figure 4, the circle with arrowheads that surrounds the meaning-negotiation process symbolizes that texts and that their interpretations exist in a hermeneutic circle. Thus, meaning construction and negotiation are viewed as fundamentally circular. While the meanings we create for whole texts influence the construction of parts, our understanding of parts influences understandings of wholes (Dilthey, 1900/1976). Furthermore, as readers and teacher voice their views about the meaning of the text, a circle of hypothesizing and validation proceeds. In reading and discussing literature, students should discover that interpretations need not be seen as ultimate or final but as constantly reinvented as discourse, dialogue, disagreement, and debate continue. In the words of Ricoeur (1979), "It is always possible to argue for or against an interpretation, to confront interpretations, to arbitrate between them, and to seek for an agreement, even if this agreement remains beyond our reach" (p. 91).

Thus, meanings are negotiated in classrooms among readers and between readers and teacher. Meanings are open, not closed or fixed, although they need to be grounded in text. Classrooms form interpretive communities that may share common understandings; however, those understandings are not then fixed forever. Meanings are shaped and reshaped in the hermeneutic circle. As the reader's knowledge changes, as the reader interacts with other readers and with the teacher in a social context, constructed meanings can be expected to change. In a sense, while a text may be fixed, its meanings for the reader are always becoming.

Interacting Variables in the Meaning-Construction Process. In the model's learning environment, the meaning-negotiation process involves interplay across texts, setting, classroom structure, tasks, source of authority, sociocultural meanings, and classroom discourse. We will briefly examine the role each of these plays in meaning construction.

Text meanings arise from the reader's meaning-construction process described earlier. Because the teacher and student bring different affective and cognitive conditions to the construction of a text representation, we must expect different interpretations for a text. For this reason, the classroom necessarily becomes a forum for the articulation and negotiation of meanings. These meanings are negotiated and negotiable in the hermeneutic circle. Those meanings shared by the entire class become part of the classroom community's intersubjective understanding of a text. However, even those shared meanings are also open for reinterpretation as the meaning-negotiation process continues in the context of classroom interaction.

The *classroom setting* refers to the immediate environment in which students and teachers interact. It includes the configuration of the classroom itself, the arrangement of desks, the location of windows, its wall mountings, posters, pictures, examples of students' work, signs, bookcases, cabinets, displays, quotations, supplies, and materials. For example, significantly different messages may be conveyed by a room whose desks are arranged in a circle, in several groups of three or four, or in rows with the teacher's desk facing the rows. While reading the setting, we ought to be asking ourselves why the classroom has been organized for the presentation it makes. Just as we are likely to do when reading a novel, we should be asking ourselves what effects the setting is likely to have on the characters and actions that take place within that setting. Just as reading affects learning, the environment affects learning as well. The way a classroom's objects are arranged and displayed can affect students' interest in learning and their interests in topics.

Classroom structure conveys information about the kinds of knowledge delivery and generation that are valued or preferred. Among the elements of classroom structure are a teacher's daily routines, lesson plans, instructional strategies, management practices, behavioral expectations, and grade policies. Readers can determine, after just a few classes, whether the teacher structures lessons for knowledge transmission, for knowledge construction, or for some mix of modes. If lectures and recitation are dominant, the teacher's pedagogical preference may be read, with some foundation in evidence, as transmission oriented. If small-group discussions with open-ended questions and whole-class conversations with lots of student input and teacher "uptake" predominate, the teacher probably prefers a constructivist pedagogy that encourages students to discover or build knowledge in social contexts. Which of these pedagogies a teacher expresses can have far-reaching consequences for students' levels of engagement and styles of interaction. Comprehending what theory or principles of learning form the foundation of a teacher's instruction and expectations can go a long way toward a student's academic adjustment and success in classrooms.

Task meanings, the interpretations assigned to tasks, have both an academic and social content (Erickson, 1982; Harris, 1989). Academic meanings include understanding the goals for an activity, knowledge of subject matter, text structure, instructions, and knowing what will count as a completed task. Social meanings consist of understanding the relationship between teacher and reader and understanding what rules will guide participation.

The interpretation of tasks, those structured activities designed or selected by the teacher and related to the text, may differ between teacher and reader. Interpretation differences are closely connected to students' success in the classroom (Dyson, 1984; Harris, 1989; Murphy, 1988). The negotiation and interpretation of task meanings are important aspects of instruction.

Flower (1987) found that college students frequently interpret an assignment quite differently from one another and from the teacher. She discovered that the process was more problematic and perplexing for students than teachers thought. What teachers, as established members of a discourse community, may not realize is that forms of response that may be instructionally transparent to them—such as asking students to analyze their responses to a story—may be very difficult for students to construe. If a task is complex and less well known to the reader, it may require elaborate interpretation to provide structure and meaning. For example, some tasks, such as writing a summary after reading, are represented automatically if the reader has a well-structured summary schema in cognitive conditions. If the reader lacks such a schema, the task may require elaborate interpretation to give it structure. It is thus important that the reader and the teacher construct and negotiate task meanings and also monitor those meanings.

Source of authority meanings refers to a negotiated understanding of where and in whom authority for constructed meanings resides. In classrooms, teachers and their students inevitably arrive at an understanding of who is the authority regarding the legitimacy of an interpretation through multiple opportunities to read and interpret events in classrooms. That authority could reside solely in the text, solely in the meanings that students construct as they interact with the text, solely with the teacher, or in a negotiated meaning arising from interaction of texts, students' meanings, and teacher's interpretations all within the classroom community. That is, the final arbiter of the source of authority for the meaning of a text could arise from the interactions among all the potential sources of authority as meanings are negotiated in a classroom context. Reading these sources can yield information about who or what has been invested with power and how that power is exercised.

First, some educators, literary critics, and literacy specialists have taken the position that an "objective" meaning is embodied in a text, referring usually to a literary text, such as a poem or a novel. Accordingly, in some classrooms, the text itself may appear to have the ultimate position of authority. Assuming this position, a reader could not attribute to a text an intended meaning that the reader believed the author rendered, nor could a reader's reaction to the text be a valid indicator of the text's meaning. With these precautions to the reader in place, the text becomes an autonomous work that is independent of both the author's and the reader's attributions of meaning. If the text holds the position as ultimate source for authority in the classroom, a reader's interpretation could easily be invalidated because it fails to correspond with close readings of literary critics, or perhaps teachers, who have established themselves as authorities. These invalidations of meaning may occur even though we know that readers construct unique meanings because of their personal background knowledge.

Second, although some educators believe an objective meaning exists in a text, others (Bleich, 1980; Culler, 1980) have argued that the meaning of a text is a more personal response to be found in the reader's mind. This perspective aligns quite closely with Rosenblatt's articulation of reader-response theory. According to Rosenblatt (1978, Chapter 35 this volume), every act of reading is a transaction between a particular reader and a particular text at a particular time in a particular context. The reader and the text compose a transactional moment. The meaning does not preexist in the text or in the reader but results from the transaction between reader and text. Meaning is the result of the reader's meaning construction that engages his or her unique background knowledge and cognitive processing.

Third, in "traditional" classrooms, students commonly identify the teacher as the source of authority. When questions about the meaning or interpretation of a text arise during students' learning or classroom discussions, the teacher's understanding of the text is the meaning students usually accept, perhaps as truth. In these classrooms, students have interpreted the learning environment in such a way that the teacher is the source of authority. Some students may question the "truths" that teachers transmit in those classrooms, but many students continue to perceive the teacher as the final arbiter of accuracy. After all, who gives and grades the tests? Many teachers have had to resist placing the radiant crown of authority on their heads when a student implores, "Will you just give us the answer?"

Advocates of a fourth approach readily accept the assumption that reader and text interact to construct meaning but expand the circle of influence to include other agents that contribute to meaning negotiation. With this interpretive community orientation (Fish, 1982), meaning is not entirely in either the text or the reader but evolves from interactions among reader, text, teacher, classroom community, and broader institutional contexts. This approach takes into account and integrates multiple social sources that influence a more broadly negotiated construction of meaning.

Teachers usually decide for their classrooms how much time and thought will be given to negotiation over the source of authority for text meanings. To a significant degree, the content area in which we teach will influence our decisions about appropriate sources of authority. Some of us may find that the text speaks loudest, some may decide that a teacher's understandings should have most significant authority, some will encourage their students to exercise textual authority, and some will continually negotiate the proper source of authority on different occasions. Just as the meanings of a printed text need not be fixed forever in a specific meaning, the source of authority for a text's meaning is always negotiable.

Thoughtful consideration of sources of authority and how they are exercised in classrooms is more than warranted. It is essential. What decisions are made about sources of authority in classrooms and how those decisions are made can have quite far-reaching effects on individual students as they read and respond to those sources. The effects may be observed not only in how students engage in classroom interactions but also in how and how much students learn.

Sociocultural meanings are influenced by the school and community ethos as well as the unique conglomeration of attitudes and values that arise in classrooms. The student and the teacher not only bring their own sociocultural values from prior beliefs and knowledge into the classroom, they also interpret the social life and culture they find there. Furthermore, each student and teacher may "read" various aspects of that sociocultural setting differently. While some students may believe that the culture of their school is supportive of their growth and development, other students—even ones in the same class—may be convinced that the school's culture is suffocating them and their identities. Teachers, like their students, may also have a range of sociocultural interpretations. In addition, some understandings of the social and cultural life of a school or classroom may be shared by most, if not all, participants.

Classroom discourse creates an abundance of oral texts that students and the teacher interpret. The origins of those texts, whether they come from the teacher or from fellow students in discussion about text-in-print or other issues, can mean the difference between transmission of knowledge or its social construction. The origins of the discourse can also send important messages about who or what is a source of authority for the truth or correctness of textual interpretations. However, participants must also read what is said and how it is said. Comprehending the content of discourse, whether it issues from the teacher as lecturer or from students in small-group or whole-class discussions, is central to participation in any significant classroom conversation.

As important as what is said—and sometimes even more important—is how participants talk. For example, does the teacher create oral texts that support the transmission of content, or does the teacher generate questions that extend dialogue and discovery among students as they explore other texts? Student talk can also convey much more than an understanding of basic concepts. It can send information about the student's level of belief in that content and attitudes toward the content. Some teachers are exceptionally good readers of subsurface messages that students broadcast, picking up deep levels of conviction to an interpretation or cynical disavowal delivered with subtlety.

In summary, the meaning-negotiation process involves a matrix of meanings that influences meaning construction. Meanings for the text, the classroom setting, classroom structure, tasks, sources of authority, sociocultural elements, and classroom discourse are brought to the negotiation process by both reader and teacher. Furthermore, the classroom community negotiates and acquires group meanings that become influential in confirming validity upon interpretations. The teacher, meanwhile, assumes a critical role in the orchestration and negotiation of meaning in the text and classroom context.

Meaning Negotiation in the Classroom Context: An Example

We will now examine the meaning-negotiation process as we apply these model-based concepts to the reality of instruction in a high school English class where students come to read and understand a short story.

A class of 11th graders taught by Norman Unrau had read J.D. Salinger's *Catcher in the Rye* and was about to begin reading a short story entitled "The Laughing Man," also by Salinger (1949). It's a love story seen through the eyes of a 9- or 10-year-old boy as he watches at a distance his baseball coach, John Gedsudski, weave through a relationship with his girlfriend—perhaps his fiancée—Mary Hudson. The coach, a law student whom the young baseball players called "the Chief," has a talent for storytelling and imparts the tale of a "Laughing Man" who covers his disfigured face with a mask and combats evil in the underworld. The story of the Laughing Man reflects symbolically the course of the coach's relationship with his girlfriend and its ultimate end. The young baseball player and his teammates, who hear the story while traveling to and from games, suffer as they hear about the Laughing Man's death, which echoes the end of the coach's relationship with his girlfriend. To gather data on the process, Unrau maintained a teaching log, detailed observational notes, and photocopies of students' log entries over several days of instruction. The learning environment was shaped in part by the instructional decision-making process used by Unrau. One of these decisions was his selection of the text, "The Laughing Man." The meaning-negotiation process for reader, teacher, and classroom community included not only text but also task, source of authority, and sociocultural meanings.

Tasks for the readers included a prediction strategy (similar to Stauffer's Directed Reading–Thinking Activity) designed to activate background knowledge and arouse expectations. As an initial task to activate knowledge and heighten motivation, readers were asked to predict the story's content based on its title. They were then asked to read the story with the intent of forming a text representation that would become part of the meaning-negotiation process. Subsequent tasks for the students called for writing first meanings in their response logs, sharing these in small groups, participating in whole-class discussions, and then writing about newly negotiated meanings in their logs.

The source of authority for the validity of text interpretations was distributed among class members—including Unrau. Authority was structured with the intent of placing a large portion of responsibility on students for sharing and shaping meanings while Unrau tried to encourage the expression of those meanings that students had constructed.

The sociocultural meaning for the setting could be described as that of a mainstream English class composed mostly of college-bound students, including some with English as a second language, some with learning disabilities, and some from minority cultures, who were embedded in the broader culture of a suburban U.S. academic high school with high expectations for reading and writing. The teacher and even the majority of the classroom community might view the sociocultural backdrop in this way. However, an individual reader might "read" it quite differently, perhaps as an externally imposed experience through which he or she must suffer until finally released after graduation, or as a useless exercise in a consumption-crazed, class-conscious, cliquish, and conforming culture. Whatever their understanding of the sociocultural setting, participants in the learning enterprise were affected directly or indirectly by it.

After discussing predictions about the story, reading it, and writing about what the story meant to them, students met in small groups to share their interpretations. Each group's reporter presented ideas to the whole class. Several students said that reading and discussing other students' interpretations and commentaries in their groups made them think in new ways about the story's significance. As groups reported, Unrau encouraged the expression and elaboration of meanings, not only of each group within the classroom community but also of the individual meanings of readers within those groups. Concern was also given not only to meanings for the whole story but also to meanings for specific objects in the story. For example, during the discussion, several students expressed different interpretations of a vial of eagle's blood, a vital food for the Laughing Man, which he crushes in despair before he dies:

Erica: We thought it represented his love for Mary Hudson.

Unrau: How would that work out?

Erica: When their relationship was going well, the Laughing Man survived by drinking the blood. But when Mary and the Chief broke up, the Laughing Man crushed the vial, and he died along with his love for Mary.

Unrau: Sort of his life blood being crushed?

Erica: Yeah, something like that.

Unrau: What other explanations for the crushed vial came up in your small-group discussions?

Mark: I thought it stood for children in the Comanche Club [the baseball team's name].

Unrau: How does that work?

Mark: I don't know. Just seems that way.

Unrau: But we need to tie the meaning to something: events in the story, ideas you had when reading it, something so it makes sense.

Mark: Seemed to me that the children of the Comanche tribe were keeping the Laughing Man alive.

Alison: I thought it was the baseball game.

Katie: Someone in our group said it stood for a false lifestyle.

Unrau: Does anyone want to explain how those meanings would make sense in the context of the story?

Katie: I don't know about baseball, but I thought there was something false about how the Chief was living or about his relationship with Mary and that when the truth was out, the relationship died.

John: I'm not absolutely sure what the vial is, but if it has a deep meaning, I'm sure it isn't baseball or the kids because they are not really deep issues. I can see the false lifestyle, but there are inconsistencies in the story because the Chief doesn't have a false life but a different life than the kids see. The mask would be more appropriate.

Unrau: So what do you think the vial represents?

John: I'd have to agree with Erica. The vial would be Mary and the Chief's love.

Unrau explored these and other meanings with the students. He frequently asked them to explain how an interpretation could be grounded in the text and how it made sense in relation to the whole story. But he tried not to impose his own "reading" of the story on the students, favoring interaction among them and with the text. The whole-class discussion gave students an opportunity to create a classroom community meaning for the story or parts of it. One student wrote, "The discussion changed my view of the story completely. I never saw any link between the Coach's life and his bizarre stories. I didn't understand that the Laughing Man's death meant anything."

A few days after the small-group discussions, students were asked to write their current understanding of the story and describe how and why their interpretation changed, if it had. Most students reported that they had formed or reformed the meanings they had given to the story during or after the small-group and class discussions. Mira, who said she did not really have an understanding when she first read the story, arrived at a meaning that went significantly beyond that initial summary. She wrote,

> I think that the story of the Laughing Man that the Chief would tell the Comanches was in a sense the way he saw himself. The Laughing Man was an alter ego of John Gedsudski, the Chief. Both were not handsome and shunned by the society and peers. Both had a band of loyal followers who looked up to them. For the Chief, it was the kids; for the Laughing Man, it was a dwarf, a Mongolian, and a beautiful Eurasian girl. At around the time that the Laughing Man is held captive by Dufarge, the Chief is having problems with Mary Hudson. When the Laughing Man gets shot, it is at the same time the Chief and Mary break up. This just enforces my theory that the Chief and Laughing Man are one in the same. The Chief takes the installments from his own day-to-day life, but he enhances them and makes them more exciting.

Students such as Mira contributed to what became a classroom community meaning for the relationship between the Chief and the Laughing Man; that is, the two paralleled each other in many ways. As for the vial of eagle's blood that could have saved the Laughing Man, Mira wrote that it "represents the Chief's love for Mary."

Emily, whose initial and rather stock response to the story was "You can't judge a book by its cover," later wrote that the story was "tragic." She thought that the Chief was so hurt and depressed by the breakup of his relationship with Mary that he "took it out on the players." She wrote,

> That night, driving home on the bus, John began telling the story of the Laughing Man once again. In this final story, John killed the Laughing Man because Mary left him, and because his love was taken away from him, he did the same to the Comanches. They loved the Laughing Man, so John took him away from them.

Although Emily interprets the meaning of Laughing Man's death quite differently from Mira, she wrote that the vial of eagle's blood, which might have saved Laughing Man, represented John's crushed love for Mary.

In summary, many readers—the initially "clueless" as well as those who offered early interpretations—began to share a community interpretation of the story. Almost everyone agreed that a close correspondence existed between the Chief's life and that of Laughing Man. Many came to think that the trouble the Chief was having in his relationship with Mary translated into the death of Laughing Man. Nevertheless, many readers still held divergent meanings about several aspects of the story.

Being in an environment that allowed alternative or unconventional readings was important to several students. As one student, Sarah, wrote,

> Too many teachers think that their understanding is the only correct one....Now I understand that a story can mean so many things, and as long as you can back it with at least some good thought, it's right for yourself. Now I feel I can just put more of my thoughts out there even if other people don't agree. I basically think that's the way my interpretation of "The Laughing Man" has changed. I think I have a little more freedom to say what I think.

What is important about "The Laughing Man" example for our discussion is not only the divergent readings of the story by different readers but also the dialogue, the meaning-negotiation process, that occurred among students and teacher. The meaning-negotiation process enabled readers of the story to engage their prior beliefs and knowledge in the meaning-construction process to develop a text representation of "The Laughing Man." This representation was strongly influenced by the negotiation of text, task, source of authority, and sociocultural meanings.

Although this example is from the high school level, the key model components can also be readily applied to the elementary school learning environment (Ruddell et al., 1990; Ruddell, 2009) as well as to that of the college classroom (Hull & Rose, 2004).

Our model thus takes a constructivist perspective of learning. The teacher creates an instructional environment in which students are involved in active comprehension as they confront and solve authentic problems. This environment places an emphasis on meaningful dialogue, negotiated meaning, and understanding.

Implications for Practice and New Research Directions

The major focus of our discussion and our first goal in this chapter centered on an explanation of the reading process within the classroom context involving the reader, the text and classroom context, and the teacher. It is our belief that this explanation has enabled us to achieve our second goal, that of developing a productive model that can serve researchers and teachers in better understanding the nature of the meaning-construction process. Our third goal, that of utility, is achieved by providing the following implications for practice and new research directions based on the review of a wide body of discipline-based research.

Our explanation of reading as a meaning-construction process is not only a theory but also a reality-based, classroom-centered model and accounts for interactions that involve the reader, the text and classroom context, and the teacher. Specific instructional implications that derive from the model include the following:

1. Activation of the reader's prior beliefs and knowledge relative to the text is of central importance to effective meaning construction.
2. Mobilization of reader motivation, attitudes, values, and beliefs related to the text content is critical to attention focus, persistence, and the comprehension process.
3. Creation of a purpose to guide and focus meaning construction provides for higher interest in the reading comprehension process.
4. Recognition that meaning construction is a purposeful, interactive, and strategic process contributes significantly to the effective comprehension of narrative and expository texts.
5. Use of metacognitive strategies that assist in monitoring, rereading, and checking meaning construction is essential to the comprehension process.
6. Awareness of the most appropriate reader stance and teacher stance relative to the text and reading purpose serves to develop higher levels of motivation and comprehension.
7. Understanding and using varied classroom community sociocultural values and beliefs by readers and teacher will provide more opportunities for active meaning negotiation in the classroom.
8. Sharing authority in the meaning-negotiation process allows readers to seek verification or validity for their interpretations within the classroom community rather than depending upon the sole authority of the teacher.

9. Encouraging readers to accept the premise that meanings evolve for both teacher and reader facilitates students' active meaning construction in the classroom.
10. Engaging readers in understanding and reflecting upon divergent meanings will increase the richness of interpretation within the classroom community.
11. Designing instructional activities that foster comprehension, discussion, and inclusion builds readers' perceptions that they are part of a classroom community.
12. Helping readers understand that they construct meanings not only of printed text but also of tasks, sources of authority, and their sociocultural environment furthers the understanding and creation of a context for learning that actively involves the reader and classroom community.

While reflecting on the design of our model of reading as a meaning-construction process, a number of specific research implications have emerged. These implications are intended to contribute to a fuller understanding of the processes that involve the reader, the teacher, and meaning negotiation of the text within the classroom context. We will briefly sample these research implications for each of the three major areas of the model.

Our discussion of the reader's prior knowledge and beliefs demonstrates that further research is needed to enable us to better understand the affective conditions that influence the reading process. We know, for example, that motivation to read changes as children progress through the grades, usually resulting in less independent pleasure reading in older children. Although we know that intrinsically motivated readers engage more frequently and for longer periods of time in reading, what constellation of motivational variables contributes to intrinsic motivation for reading, and how could those variables be developed in classrooms? Sociocultural background has been found to shape classroom discourse, but how do differences in sociocultural values and beliefs shape interpretations of texts?

Several compelling issues are related to the reader's cognitive conditions and need further research. Implications for research in cognitive conditions arise from differing views of text processing. For example, to what degree can text-processing strategies improve comprehension of reading across content areas? There is also a significant need for further research on metacognition, especially in meaning construction for early readers.

Research on processes that occur in the reader's knowledge use and control is also needed. For example, what effect on reading comprehension and discussion do students' self-selected purposes together with teacher support for student autonomy have in comparison with teacher-selected purposes? Do conscious and deliberate plans of action change reading outcomes? A number of intriguing issues need exploration to better understand the reader's executive and monitor. For instance, which functions and resources engaged during knowledge construction are most and which are least subject to direct control of an executive? Which functions and processes occur automatically? If they do operate automatically, what conditions enable those automatic functions to develop? Because neurological correlates underlie psychological processes described in our model, we believe it is important to further investigate the relationship between the psychological description of knowledge construction while reading and the underlying neurological processes.

Future research pertaining to the reader's outcomes of meaning construction needs to explore and explain the way in which reading can significantly change motivation, attitudes toward reading, and value or belief systems. Further study is also needed to explore the impact of different kinds of writing, such as summary and analysis, on text comprehension and interpretation. Although we know that certain kinds of writing can improve reading comprehension (Graham & Hebert, 2010), we know little about the effects of writing instruction on reading processes. For example, does explicit instruction in formulating a thesis or in planning and organizing an expository essay contribute to improvements in comprehending expository prose?

Implications for research arising from our representation of the teacher component are clearly present. In regard to the teacher's prior beliefs and knowledge, future research needs to further define the role of affective conditions in instruction. The most pressing work needs to address the influence of instructional stance on the teacher's instructional decision-making process. What kinds of stances do teachers encourage readers to adopt? In regard to cognitive conditions, the influence of teacher-created, expectation-driven schemata on the reader's comprehension needs to be explored. Do teachers' schemata lead to misinterpretations or "misreadings" of students, their responses, and patterns of student interactions in the classroom context? The teacher's knowledge use and control constitute an important area also needing further exploration. For example, how do novice and expert teachers differ in creating instructional plans, in selecting instructional strategies, and in making "in-flight" instructional decisions?

Several areas of research would augment our understanding of the teacher's use of outcomes of instructional decision making. What, for example, do novice and expert teachers gain from observing the outcomes of the knowledge-construction process in the reader? What kinds of teacher observation and feedback would encourage the development of reflective teaching for preservice teachers and for practicing teachers?

Many research issues emerge from the text and classroom context in our model. The issue of meaning negotiation is central among these. For example, what reader motivational profile promotes highly successful engagement in the meaning-negotiation process? What kinds of texts and tasks support a reader's involvement or openness during meaning negotiation? Do different instructional stances and different sources of authority have a differential impact on the negotiation process? For example, do "authoritative teachers" have a different impact on meaning negotiation than those teachers oriented toward more openness with the classroom community? Additional knowledge related to questions like these holds high potential for better understanding the role of meaning negotiation in the meaning-construction process.

In conclusion, our model of reading as a meaning-construction process draws on and integrates knowledge from a wide range of disciplines. Central to our discussion, however, is the role of the social context of the classroom and the influence of the teacher on the reader's meaning negotiation. Our understanding of this negotiation is of vital importance if we are to meet the challenge set forth by Huey (1908/1968) early in the 20th century—that of understanding how the reader constructs meaning.

QUESTIONS FOR REFLECTION

1. How do top-down and bottom-up types of processing interact to contribute to meaning construction?
2. What personal teaching goals might you develop from looking at the teacher component of the model?
3. What things must a teacher "read" in the classroom in order to help students grow as constructors of meaning?

REFERENCES

Adams, M.J., & Collins, A. (1985). A schema-theoretic view of reading. In H. Singer & R.B. Ruddell (Eds.), *Theoretical models and processes of reading* (3rd ed., pp. 404–425). Newark, DE: International Reading Association.

Afflerbach, P., & Cho, B. (2010). Determining and describing reading strategies. In H.S. Waters & W. Schneider (Eds.), *Metacogntion, strategy use, and instruction* (pp. 201–225). New York: Guilford.

Alba, J.W., & Hasher, L. (1983). Is memory schematic? *Psychological Bulletin*, 93(2), 203–231. doi:10.1037/0033-2909.93.2.203

Alvermann, D.E., Young, J.P., Green, C., & Wisenbaker, J.M. (2004). Adolescents' perceptions and negotiations of literacy practices in after-school read and talk clubs. In R.B. Ruddell & N.J. Unrau (Eds.), *Theoretical models and processes of reading* (5th ed., pp. 870–913). Newark, DE: International Reading Association.

Ames, C. (1992). Classrooms: Goals, structures, and student motivation. *Journal of Educational Psychology*, 84(3), 261–271. doi:10.1037/0022-0663.84.3.261

Anderson, R.C. (1975). The notion of schemata and the educational enterprise: General discussion of the conference. In R.C. Anderson, J. Osborn, & R.J. Tierney (Eds.), *Schooling and the acquisition of knowledge* (pp. 415–431). Hillsdale, NJ: Erlbaum.

Anderson, R.C., & Freebody, P. (1981). Vocabulary knowledge. In J.T. Guthrie (Ed.), *Comprehension and teaching: Research reviews* (pp. 77–117). Newark, DE: International Reading Association.

Anderson, R.C., & Pearson, P.D. (1984). A schema-theoretic view of basic processes in reading comprehension. In P.D. Pearson, R. Barr, M.L. Kamil, & P. Mosenthal (Eds.), *Handbook of reading research* (pp. 255–291). New York: Longman. doi:10.1017/CBO9781139524513.007

Anderson, R.C., & Pichert, J.W. (1978). Recall of previously unrecallable information following a shift in perspective. *Journal of Verbal Learning and Verbal Behavior*, 17(1), 1–12. doi:10.1016/S0022-5371(78)90485-1

Applebee, A. (1978). *The child's concept of story: Ages two to seventeen.* Chicago: University of Chicago Press.

Baddeley, A. (2007). *Working memory, thought, and action.* Oxford, UK: Oxford University Press. doi:10.1093/acprof:oso/9780198528012.001.0001

Baker, L. (2005). Developmental differences in metacognition: Implications for metacognitively oriented reading instruction. In S.E. Israel, C.C. Block, K.L. Bauserman, & K. Kinnucan-Welsch (Eds.), *Metacognition in literacy learning: Theory, assessment, instruction, and professional development* (pp. 61–79). Mahwah, NJ: Erlbaum.

Barthes, R. (1977). *Image, music, text.* New York: Hill and Wang.

Bartlett, B.J. (1978). *Top-level structure as an organizational strategy for recall of classroom text.* Unpublished doctoral dissertation, Arizona State University, Tempe.
Bauer, J. (1994). *Schools for thought.* Cambridge, MA: MIT Press.
Beach, R. (1992). Adopting multiple stances in conducting literacy research. In R. Beach, J. Green, M. Kamil, & T. Shanahan (Eds.), *Multidisciplinary perspectives on literacy research* (pp. 91–110). Urbana, IL: National Council of Teachers of English.
Beach, R., & Hynds, S. (1990). *Developing discourse practices in adolescence and adulthood.* Norwood, NJ: Ablex.
Beck, I., & McKeown, M. (1991). Conditions of vocabulary acquisition. In R. Barr, M.L. Kamil, P. Mosenthal, & P.D. Pearson (Eds.), *Handbook of reading research* (Vol. 2, pp. 787–814). White Plains, NY: Longman.
Bleich, D. (1980). Epistemological assumptions in the study of response. In J.P. Tompkins (Ed.), *Reader-response criticism: From formalism to post-structuralism* (pp. 134–163). Baltimore: The Johns Hopkins University Press.
Bloome, D., & Bailey, F. (1992). Studying language and literacy through events, particularities, and intertextuality. In R. Beach, J. Green, M. Kamil, & T. Shanahan (Eds.), *Multidisciplinary perspectives on literacy research* (pp. 181–210). Urbana, IL: National Council of Teachers of English.
Blumenfeld, P.C. (1992). Classroom learning and motivation: Clarifying and expanding goal theory. *Journal of Educational Psychology, 84*(3), 272–281. doi:10.1037/0022-0663.84.3.272
Borko, H., Shavelson, R.J., & Stern, P. (1981). Teachers' decisions in the planning of reading instruction. *Reading Research Quarterly, 16*(3), 449–466. doi:10.2307/747411
Brown, A. (1980). Metacognitive development and reading. In R. Spiro, B. Bruce, & W. Brewer (Eds.), *Theoretical issues in reading comprehension* (pp. 453–481). Hillsdale, NJ: Erlbaum.
Brown, A. (1982). Learning how to learn from reading. In J.A. Langer & M.T. Smith-Burke (Eds.), *Reader meets author/bridging the gap: A psycholinguistic and sociolinguistic perspective* (pp. 26–54). Newark, DE: International Reading Association.
Brown, R., Pressley, M., Van Meter, P., & Schuder, T. (2004). A quasi-experimental validation of transactional strategies instruction with low-achieving second-grade readers. In R.B. Ruddell & N.J. Unrau (Eds.), *Theoretical models and processes of reading* (5th ed., pp. 998–1039). Newark, DE: International Reading Association.
Bruner, J. (1983). *Child's talk.* New York: Norton.
Bruner, J. (1986). *Actual minds, possible worlds.* Cambridge, MA: Harvard University Press.
Chomsky, N. (1959). A review of B.F. Skinner's *Verbal Behavior. Language, 35*(1), 26–58. doi:10.2307/411334
Chomsky, N. (1965). *Aspects of the theory of syntax.* Cambridge, MA: MIT Press.
Coté, N., & Goldman, S.R. (2004). Building representations of informational text: Evidence from children's think-aloud protocols. In R.B. Ruddell & N.J. Unrau (Eds.), *Theoretical models and processes of reading* (5th ed., pp. 660–683). Newark, DE: International Reading Association.
Covington, M. (1992). *Making the grade: A self-worth perspective on motivation and school reform.* Cambridge: Cambridge University Press. doi:10.1017/CBO9781139173582
Cox, B.E. (1994). Young children's regulatory talk: Evidence of emerging metacognitive control over literary products and processes. In R.B. Ruddell, M.R. Ruddell, & H. Singer (Eds.), *Theoretical models and processes of reading* (4th ed., pp. 733–756). Newark, DE: International Reading Association.
Cox, B.E., Fang, Z., & Otto, B.W. (2004). Preschoolers' developing ownership of the literate register. In R.B. Ruddell & N.J. Unrau (Eds.), *Theoretical models and processes of reading* (5th ed., pp. 281–312). Newark, DE: International Reading Association.
Culler, J. (1980). Literary competence. In J.P. Tompkins (Ed.), *Reader-response criticism: From formalism to post-structuralism* (pp. 101–117). Baltimore: The Johns Hopkins University Press.
Curtiss, S. (1977). *Genie: A psycholinguistic study of a modern-day "wild child."* New York: Academic.
de Beaugrande, R. (1980). *Text, discourse, and process.* Norwood, NJ: Ablex.
de Beaugrande, R. (1981). Design criteria for process models of reading. *Reading Research Quarterly, 16*(2), 261–315. doi:10.2307/747559
Derrida, J. (1982). *Margins of philosophy.* Chicago: University of Chicago Press.
DeStefano, J., Pepinsky, H., & Sanders, T. (1982). Discourse rules for literacy learning in classrooms. In L. Wilkinson (Ed.), *Communicating in the classroom* (pp. 101–130). New York: Academic.
Dilthey, W. (1976). The development of hermeneutics. In H. Rickman (Ed. & Trans.), *Selected writings* (pp. 247–263). Cambridge, UK: Cambridge University Press. (Original work published 1900)
Dore, J. (1979). Conversation and preschool language development. In P. Fletcher & M. Garman (Eds.), *Language acquisition* (pp. 337–361). Cambridge, UK: Cambridge University Press.
Duffy, G.G. (2005). Developing metacognitive teachers: Visioning and the expert's changing role in teacher education and professional development. In S.E. Israel, C.C. Block, K.L. Bauserman, & K. Kinnucan-Welsch (Eds.), *Metacognition in literacy learning: Theory, assessment, instruction, and professional development* (pp. 299–314). Mahwah, NJ: Erlbaum.
Dyson, A.H. (1984). Learning to write/learning to do school: Emergent writers' interpretations of school literacy tasks. *Research in the Teaching of English, 18*(3), 233–265.

Eco, U. (1976). *A theory of semiotics*. Bloomington: Indiana University Press.
Ehri, L.C. (1987). Learning to read and spell words. *Journal of Reading Behavior, 19*(1), 5–31.
Ehri, L.C. (1988). Movement into word reading and spelling: How spelling contributes to reading. In J.M. Mason (Ed.), *Reading and writing connections* (pp. 65–81). Boston: Allyn & Bacon.
Ehri, L.C. (1991). Development of the ability to read words. In R. Barr, M.L. Kamil, P. Mosenthal, & P.D. Pearson (Eds.), *Handbook of reading research* (Vol. 2, pp. 383–417). White Plains, NY: Longman.
Ehri, L.C. (1994). Development of the ability to read words: Update. In R.B. Ruddell, M.R. Ruddell, & H. Singer (Eds.), *Theoretical models and processes of reading* (4th ed., pp. 323–358). Newark, DE: International Reading Association.
Epstein, S. (1994). Integration of cognitive and psychodynamic unconscious. *American Psychologist, 49*(8), 709–724. doi:10.1037/0003-066X.49.8.709
Erickson, F. (1982). Taught cognitive learning in its immediate learning development. *Anthropology & Education Quarterly, 13*(2), 148–180.
Erikson, E. (1968). *Identity: Youth and crisis*. New York: Norton.
Ervin, S.M., & Miller, W.R. (1963). Language development. In H. Stevenson (Ed.), *Child psychology* (62nd yearbook of the National Society for the Study of Education, pp. 108–143). Chicago: University of Chicago Press.
Fish, S. (1982). *Is there a text in this class? The authority of interpretive communities*. Cambridge, MA: Harvard University Press. doi:10.2307/1772220
Fleming, D.M., Unrau, N.J., Cooks, J., Farnan, N., & Grisham, D. (2007). A California State University initiative to improve adolescent reading in all content areas. *Teacher Education Quarterly, 34*(3), 5–17.
Flower, L. (1987). *The role of task representation in reading to write* (Tech. Rep. No. 6). Berkeley, CA: Center for the Study of Writing.
Frith, U. (1985). Beneath the surface of developmental dyslexia. In K.E. Patterson, J.C. Marshall, & M. Coltheart (Eds.), *Surface dyslexia* (pp. 301–330). Hillsdale, NJ: Erlbaum.
Galda, L., & Beach, R. (2004). Response to literature as a cultural activity. In R.B. Ruddell & N.J. Unrau (Eds.), *Theoretical models and processes of reading* (5th ed., pp. 852–869). Newark, DE: International Reading Association. doi:10.1598/RRQ.36.1.4
Garner, R. (1987). *Metacognition and reading comprehension*. Norwood, NJ: Ablex.
Gee, J.P. (1999). *An introduction to discourse analysis: Theory and method*. London: Routledge.
Gee, J.P. (2012). *Social linguistics and literacies: Ideology in discourses* (4th ed.). London: Routledge.
Gibson, E.J., & Levin, H. (1975). *The psychology of reading*. Cambridge, MA: MIT Press.
Goetz, E.T., Palmer, D.J., & Haensly, P.A. (1983). Metacognitive awareness of text variables in good and poor readers. In J.A. Niles & L.A. Harris (Eds.), *Searches for meaning in reading, languages processing, and instruction* (32nd yearbook of the National Reading Conference, pp. 129–134). Chicago: National Reading Conference.
Good, T. (1987). Teacher expectations. In D. Berliner & B. Rosenshine (Eds.), *Talks to teachers* (pp. 159–200). New York: Random House.
Graham, S., & Hebert, M.A. (2010). *Writing to read: Evidence for how writing can improve reading. A Carnegie CorporationTime toAct Report*. Washington, DC: Alliance for Excellent Education.
Green, J.L., & Harker, J.O. (1982). Reading to children: A communicative process. In J.A. Langer & M.T. Smith-Burke (Eds.), *Reader meets author/bridging the gap: A psycholinguistic and sociolinguistic perspective* (pp. 196–221). Newark, DE: International Reading Association.
Griffith, P.L., & Ruan, J. (2005). What is metacognition and what shold be its role in literacy instruction? In S.E. Israel, C.C. Block, K.L. Bauserman, & K. Kinnucan-Welsch (Eds.), *Metacognition in literacy learning: Theory, assessment, instruction, and professional development* (pp. 3–18). Mahwah, NJ: Erlbaum.
Guthrie, J.T., & Wigfield, A. (2000). Engagement and motivation in reading. In M.L. Kamil, P.B. Mosenthal, P.D. Pearson, & R. Barr (Eds.), *Handbook of reading research* (Vol. 3, pp. 403–422). Mahwah, NJ: Erlbaum.
Guthrie, J.T., Wigfield, A., Metsala, J.L., & Cox, K.E. (2004). Motivational and cognitive predictors of text comprehension and reading amount. In R.B. Ruddell & N.J. Unrau (Eds.), *Theoretical models and processes of reading* (5th ed., pp. 929–953). Newark, DE: International Reading Association. doi:10.1207/s1532799xssr0303_3
Hacker, D.J. (2004). Self-regulated comprehension during normal reading. In R.B. Ruddell & N.J. Unrau (Eds.), *Theoretical models and processes of reading* (5th ed., pp. 755–779). Newark, DE: International Reading Association.
Harris, P.J. (1989). *First grade children's constructs of teacher-assigned reading tasks in a whole language classroom*. Unpublished doctoral dissertation, University of California, Berkeley.
Hartman, D.K. (1990). *8 readers reading: The intertextual links of able readers using multiple passages*. Unpublished doctoral dissertation, University of Illinois, Urbana-Champaign.
Hartman, D.K. (1991). The intertextual links of readers using multiple passages: A post-modern/semiotic/cognitive view of meaning making. In J. Zutell & S. McCormick (Eds.), *Learner factors/teacher factors: Issues in literacy research and instruction* (40th yearbook of the National Reading Conference). Chicago: National Reading Conference.
Heath, S.B. (1983). *Ways with words*. Cambridge, UK: Cambridge University Press.
Hiebert, E.H., Englert, C.S., & Brennan, S. (1983). Awareness of text structure on recognition and

production of expository discourse. *Journal of Reading Behavior, 15*(4), 63–79.
Hiebert, E.H., & Martin, L.A. (2004). The texts of beginning reading instruction. In R.B. Ruddell & N.J. Unrau (Eds.), *Theoretical models and processes of reading* (5th ed., pp. 390–411). Newark, DE: International Reading Association.
Huey, E.B. (1968). *The psychology and pedagogy of reading*. Cambridge, MA: MIT Press. (Original work published 1908)
Hull, G., & Rose, M. (2004). "This wooden shack place": The logic of an unconventional reading. In R.B. Ruddell & N.J. Unrau (Eds.), *Theoretical models and processes of reading* (5th ed., pp. 268–280). Newark, DE: International Reading Association.
Hymes, D. (1974). *Foundations in sociolinguistics: An ethnographic approach*. Philadelphia: University of Pennsylvania Press.
Iser, W. (1980). The reading process: A phenomenological approach. In J.P. Tompkins (Ed.), *Reader-response criticism: From formalism to post-structuralism* (pp. 50–69). Baltimore: The Johns Hopkins University Press.
Israel, S.E., Block, C.C., Bauserman, K.L., & Kinnucan-Welsch K. (Eds.). (2005). *Metacognition in literacy learning: Theory, assessment, instruction, and professional development*. Mahwah, NJ: Erlbaum.
Johnson, D.D., Toms-Bronowski, S., & Pittelman, S.D. (1981). *A review of trends in vocabulary research and the effects of prior knowledge on instructional strategies for vocabulary acquisition*. Madison: Wisconsin Center for Educational Research.
Juel, C., & Minden-Cupp, C. (2004). Learning to read words: Linguistic units and instructional strategies. In R.B. Ruddell & N.J. Unrau (Eds.), *Theoretical models and processes of reading* (5th ed., pp. 313–364). Newark, DE: International Reading Association. doi:10.1598/RRQ.35.4.2
Kintsch, W. (1998). *Comprehension: A paradigm for cognition*. New York: Cambridge University Press.
Langer, J.A. (1981). From theory to practice: A prereading plan. *Journal of Reading, 25*(2), 152–156.
Langer, J.A. (1990). The process of understanding: Reading for literary and informative purposes. *Research in the Teaching of English, 24*(3), 229–260.
Langer, J.A. (2004). Beating the odds: Teaching middle and high school students to read and write well. In R.B. Ruddell & N.J. Unrau (Eds.), *Theoretical models and processes of reading* (5th ed., pp. 1040–1082). Newark, DE: International Reading Association.
Maehr, M.L. (1984). Meaning and motivation: Toward a theory of personal investment. In R. Ames & C. Ames (Eds.), *Research on motivation in education* (Vol. 1, pp. 39–73). San Diego, CA: Academic.
Many, J.E. (2004). The effect of reader stance on students' personal understanding of literature. In R.B Ruddell & N.J. Unrau (Eds.), *Theoretical models and processes of reading* (5th ed., pp. 914–928). Newark, DE: International Reading Association.
Marshall, H. (1992). Associate editor's introduction to centennial articles on classroom learning and motivation. *Journal of Educational Psychology, 84*(3), 259–260. doi:10.1037/h0092684
Mason, J.M., Herman, P.A., & Au, K.H. (1991). Children's developing knowledge of words. In J. Flood, J.M. Jensen, D. Lapp, & J.R. Squire (Eds.), *Handbook of research on teaching the English language arts* (pp. 721–731). New York: Macmillan.
Mathewson, G.C. (2004). Model of attitude influence upon reading and learning to read. In R.B. Ruddell & N.J. Unrau (Eds.), *Theoretical models and processes of reading* (5th ed., pp. 1431–1461). Newark, DE: International Reading Association. doi:10.1598/0872075028.50
McClelland, J.L., Rumelhart, D.E., & Hinton, G.E. (1986). The appeal of parallel distributed processing. In D.E. Rumelhart, J.L. McClelland, & PDP Research Group (Eds.), *Parallel distributed processing: Exploration in the microstructures of cognition, Vol. 1. Foundations* (pp. 3–44). Cambridge, MA: MIT Press.
McClelland, J.L., Rumelhart, D.E., & the PDP Research Group (Eds.). (1986). *Parallel distributed processing: Exploration in the microstructures of cognition: Vol. 2. Psychological and biological models*. Cambridge, MA: MIT Press.
McGee, L.M. (1982). Awareness of text structure: Effects on children's recall of expository text. *Reading Research Quarterly, 17*(4), 581–590. doi:10.2307/747572
Meece, J.L. (1994). The role of motivation in self-regulated learning. In D.H. Schunk & B.J. Zimmerman (Eds.), *Self-regulation of learning and performance: Issues and educational applications* (pp. 25–44). Hillsdale, NJ: Erlbaum.
Mehan, H. (1980). The competent student. *Anthropology & Education Quarterly, 11*(3), 131–152.
Meyer, B.J.F. (1984). Organizational aspects of text: Effects on reading comprehension and applications for the classroom. In J. Flood (Ed.), *Promoting reading comprehension* (pp. 113–138). Newark, DE: International Reading Association.
Meyer, B.J.F., Brandt, D.M., & Bluth, G.J. (1980). Use of top-level structure in text: Key for reading comprehension of ninth grade students. *Reading Research Quarterly, 16*(1), 72–103. doi:10.2307/747349
Meyer, B.J.F., & Freedle, R. (1979). *The effects of different discourse types on recall*. Princeton, NJ: Educational Testing Service.
Meyer, B.J.F., & Poon, L.W. (2004). Effects of structure strategy training and signaling on recall of text. In R.B. Ruddell & N.J. Unrau (Eds.), *Theoretical models and processes of reading* (5th ed., pp. 810–851). Newark, DE: International Reading Association.

Midgley, C., Feldlaufer, H., & Eccles, J. (1989). Change in teacher efficacy and student self- and task-related beliefs in mathematics during the transition to junior high school. *Journal of Educational Psychology, 81*(2), 247–258.

Moje, E.B., Dillon, D.R., & O'Brien, D.G. (2000). Re-examining the roles of the learner, the text, and the context in secondary literacy. *The Journal of Educational Research, 93*(3), 165–180. doi:10.1080/00220670009598705

Moll, L.C. (1992). Literacy research in community and classrooms: A sociocultural approach. In R. Beach, J. Green, M. Kamil, & T. Shanahan (Eds.), *Multidisciplinary perspectives on literacy research* (pp. 211–244). Urbana, IL: National Council of Teachers of English.

Morehead, D.M. (1971). Processing of phonological sequences by young children and adults. *Child Development, 42*(1), 279–289. doi:10.2307/1127082

Mosenthal, P., & Na, T. (1980). Quality of text recall as a function of children's classroom competence. *Journal of Experimental Child Psychology, 30*(1), 1–21. doi:10.1016/0022-0965(80)90071-5

Müller, F.M. (Series Ed.), & Legge, J. (Vol. Ed.). (1885). *Sacred books of the East: Part 28. The texts of Confucianism.* Oxford, UK: Clarendon.

Murphy, S. (1988). *Making sense of school: An ecological examination of students' definitions of reading tasks.* Unpublished dissertation, Virginia Polytechnic Institute & State University, Blacksburg.

Nezworski, T., Stein, N.L., & Trabasso, T. (1982). Story structure versus content in children's recall. *Journal of Verbal Learning and Verbal Behavior, 21*(2), 196–206. doi:10.1016/S0022-5371(82)90561-8

Paris, S.G., Lipson, M.Y., & Wixson, K.K. (1983). Becoming a strategic reader. *Contemporary Educational Psychology, 8*(3), 293–316. doi:10.1016/0361-476X(83)90018-8

Pichert, J.W., & Anderson, R.C. (1977). Taking different perspectives on a story. *Journal of Educational Psychology, 69*(4), 309–315. doi: 10.1037/0022-0663.69.4.309

Pintrich, P.R., & De Groot, E.V. (1990). Motivational and self-regulated learning components of classroom academic performance. *Journal of Educational Psychology, 82*(1), 33–40. doi:10.1037/0022-0663.82.1.33

Pressley, M., & Afflerbach, P. (1995). *Verbal protocols of reading: The nature of constructively responsive reading.* Hillsdale, NJ: Erlbaum. doi:10.2307/358808

Quirk, M., Unrau, N., Ragusa, G., Rueda, R., Lim, H., Velasco, A., et al. (2010). Teacher beliefs about reading motivation and their enactment in classrooms: The development of a survey questionnaire. *Reading Psychology, 31*(2), 93–120. doi:10.1080/02702710902754051

Raphael, T.E. (1982). Question–answer strategies for children. *The Reading Teacher, 36*(2), 186–190.

Raphael, T.E., George, M., Weber, C.M., & Nies, A. (2010). Approaches to teaching reading comprehension. In S.E. Israel & G.G. Duffy (Eds.), *Handbook of research on reading comprehension* (pp. 449–469). New York: Routledge.

Reynolds, R.E., Standiford, S.N., & Anderson, R.C. (1979). Distribution of reading time when questions are asked about a restricted category of text information. *Journal of Educational Psychology, 71*(2), 183–190. doi:10.1037/0022-0663.71.2.183

Ricoeur, P. (1979). The model of a text: Meaningful action considered as a text. In P. Rabinow & W. Sullivan (Eds.), *Interpretive social science: A reader* (pp. 73–101). Berkeley: University of California Press. doi:10.2307/468410

Rosenblatt, L.M. (1938). *Literature as exploration.* New York: Appleton-Century. (Reprinted 1968, 1976, 1983, 1995)

Rosenblatt, L.M. (1978). *The reader, the text, the poem: The transactional theory of the literary work.* Carbondale: Southern Illinois University Press.

Rosenblatt, L.M. (1985). The transactional theory of the literary work: Implications for research. In C.R. Cooper (Ed.), *Researching response to literature and the teaching of literature* (pp. 33–53). Norwood, NJ: Ablex.

Rothkopf, E.Z., & Billington, M.J. (1979). Goal guided learning from text: Inferring a descriptive processing model from inspection times and eye movements. *Journal of Educational Psychology, 71*(3), 310–327. doi:10.1037/0022-0663.71.3.310

Rowe, D.W. (1989). Preschoolers' use of metacognitive knowledge and strategies in self-selected literacy events. In S. McCormick & J. Zutell (Eds.), *Cognitive and social perspectives for literacy research and instruction* (38th yearbook of the National Reading Conference, pp. 65–76). Chicago: National Reading Conference.

Ruddell, R.B. (1965). Effect of the similarity of oral and written language structure on reading comprehension. *Elementary English*, 42, 403–410.

Ruddell, R.B. (1974). *Reading-language instruction: Innovative practices.* Englewood Cliffs, NJ: Prentice Hall.

Ruddell, R.B. (1994). The development of children's comprehension and motivation during storybook discussion. In R.B. Ruddell, M.R. Ruddell, & H. Singer (Eds.), *Theoretical models and processes of reading* (4th ed., pp. 281–296). Newark, DE: International Reading Association.

Ruddell, R.B. (2004). Researching the influential literacy teacher: Characteristics, beliefs, strategies, and new research directions. In R.B. Ruddell & N.J. Unrau (Eds.), *Theoretical models and processes of reading* (5th ed., pp. 979–997). Newark, DE: International Reading Association.

Ruddell, R.B. (2009). *How to teach reading to elementary and middle school students.* Boston: Allyn & Bacon.

Ruddell, R.B., & Boyle, O.F. (1989). A study of cognitive mapping as a means to improve summarization and comprehension of expository text.

Reading Research and Instruction, 29(1), 12–22. doi:10.1080/19388078909557992
Ruddell, R.B., Draheim, M., & Barnes, J. (1990). A comparative study of the teaching effectiveness of influential and non-influential teachers and reading comprehension development. In J. Zutell & S. McCormick (Eds.), *Literacy theory and research: Analyses from multiple paradigms* (pp. 153–162). Chicago: National Reading Conference.
Ruddell, R.B., & Harris, P. (1989). A study of the relationship between influential teachers' prior knowledge and beliefs and teaching effectiveness: Developing higher order thinking in content areas. In S. McCormick & J. Zutell (Eds.), *Cognitive and social perspectives for literacy research and instruction* (pp. 461–472). Chicago: National Reading Conference.
Ruddell, R.B., & Kern, R.G. (1986). The development of belief systems and teaching effectiveness of influential teachers. In M.P. Douglas (Ed.), *Reading: The quest for meaning* (pp. 133–150). Claremont, CA: Claremont Graduate School Yearbook.
Ruddell, R.B., & Ruddell, M.R. (1994). Language acquisition and literacy processes. In R.B. Ruddell, M.R. Ruddell, & H. Singer (Eds.), *Theoretical models and processes of reading* (4th ed., pp. 83–103). Newark, DE: International Reading Association.
Ruddell, R.B., & Speaker, R.B. (1985). The interactive reading process: A model. In H. Singer & R.B. Ruddell (Eds.), *Theoretical models and processes of reading* (3rd ed., pp. 751–793). Newark, DE: International Reading Association.
Ruddell, R.B., & Unrau, N.J. (2004). The role of responsive teaching in focusing reader intention and developing reader motivation. In R.B. Ruddell & N.J. Unrau (Eds.), *Theoretical models and the processes of reading* (5th ed., pp. 954–978). Newark, DE: International Reading Association. doi:10.1598/0872075028.35
Rumelhart, D.E. (1975). Notes on a schema for stories. In D.G. Bobrow & A.M. Collins (Eds.), *Representations and understanding: Studies in cognitive science* (pp. 185–210) New York: Academic.
Rumelhart, D.E. (1980). *An introduction to human information processing*. New York: Wiley.
Rumelhart, D.E. (1981). Schemata: The building blocks of cognition. In J.T. Guthrie, (Ed.), *Comprehension and teaching: Research reviews* (pp. 3–26). Newark, DE: International Reading Association.
Rumelhart, D.E., & Ortony, A. (1977). The representation of knowledge in memory. In R.C. Anderson, R.J. Spiro, & W.E. Montague (Eds.), *Schooling and the acquisition of knowledge* (pp. 99–136). Hillsdale, NJ: Erlbaum.
Ryan, R.M., & Deci, E.L. (2009). Promoting self-determined school engagement. In K.R. Wentzel & A. Wigfield (Eds.), *Handbook of motivation at school* (pp. 171–195). New York: Routledge.
Rymer, R. (1992a). A silent childhood—Part I. *The New Yorker*, pp. 41–81.
Rymer, R. (1992b). A silent childhood—Part II. *The New Yorker*, pp. 43–77.
Sadoski, M., & Paivio, A. (2001). *Imagery and text: A dual coding theory of reading and writing*. Mahwah, NJ: Erlbaum.
Sadoski, M., Paivio, A., & Goetz, E.T. (1991). A critique of schema theory in reading and a dual coding alternative. *Reading Research Quarterly*, 26(4), 463–484. doi:10.2307/747898
Samuels, S.J. (1985). Word recognition. In H. Singer & R.B. Ruddell (Eds.), *Theoretical models and processes of reading* (3rd ed., pp. 256–275). Newark, DE: International Reading Association.
Samuels, S.J., & Naslund, J. (1994). Individual differences in reading: The case for lexical access. *Reading & Writing Quarterly*, *10*(4), 285–296.
Santa Barbara Classroom Discourse Group. (1992). Constructing literacy in classrooms: Literate action as social accomplishment. In H. Marshall (Ed.), *Redefining learning: Roots of educational reform* (pp. 119–150). Norwood, NJ: Ablex.
Schmalhofer, F., McDaniel, M.A., & Keefe, D. (2002). A unified model for predictive and bridging inferences. *Discourse Processes*, *33*(2), 105–132. doi:10.1207/S15326950DP3302_01
Schon, D.A. (1987). *Educating the reflective practitioner*. San Francisco: Jossey-Bass.
Schunk, D.H. (1991). Self-efficacy and academic motivation. *Educational Psychologist*, *26*, 207–231.
Schunk, D.H. (1994). Self-regulation of self-efficacy and attributions in academic settings. In D.H. Schunk & B.J. Zimmerman (Eds.), *Self-regulation of learning and performance: Issues and educational applications* (pp. 75–99). Hillsdale, NJ: Erlbaum.
Schunk, D.H., & Zimmerman, B.J. (1997). Developing self-efficacious readers and writers: The role of social and self-regulatory processes. In J.T. Guthrie & A. Wigfield (Eds.), *Reading engagement: Motivating readers through integrated instruction* (pp. 34–50). Newark, DE: International Reading Association.
Scollon, R. (1979). A real early stage. In E. Ochs & B.B. Schieffelin (Eds.), *Developmental pragmatics* (pp. 215–227). New York: Academic.
Sesma, H.W., Mahone, E.M., Levine, T., Eason, S.H., & Cutting, L.E. (2009). The contribution of executive skills to reading comprehension. *Child Neuropsychology*, *15*(3), 232–246. doi:10.1080/09297040802220029
Shnayer, S.W. (1969). Relationships between reading interests and reading comprehension. In J.A. Figurel (Ed.), *Reading and realism* (pp. 698–702). Newark, DE: International Reading Association.
Spiro, R.J. (1988). *Cognitive flexibility theory: Advanced knowledge acquisition in ill-structured domains* (Tech. Rep. No. 441). Champaign: University of Illinois, Center for the Study of Reading.
Stanovich, K.E. (1986). Matthew effects in reading: Some consequences of individual differences

in the acquisition of literacy. *Reading Research Quarterly, 21*(4), 360–407.
Stauffer, R.B. (1976). *Teaching reading as a thinking process*. New York: Harper.
Strickland, D.S., & Feeley, J.T. (1991). The learner develops: Development in the elementary school years. In J. Flood, J.M. Jensen, D. Lapp, & J.R. Squire (Eds.), *Handbook of research on teaching the English language arts* (pp. 286–302). New York: Macmillan.
Sulzby, E. (1985). Children's emergent reading of favorite storybooks: A developmental study. *Reading Research Quarterly, 20*(4), 458–481.
Tulving, E. (1983). *Elements of episodic memory*. Oxford, UK: Oxford University Press.
Tulving, E. (1986). What kind of hypothesis is the distinction between episodic and semantic memory? *Journal of Experimental Psychology. Learning, Memory, and Cognition, 12*(2), 307–311. doi:10.1037/0278-7393.12.2.307
Unrau, N. (2008a). *Content area reading and writing: Fostering literacies in middle and high school cultures* (2nd ed.). Upper Saddle River, NJ: Pearson.
Unrau, N. (2008b). *Thoughtful teachers, thoughtful learners: A guide to helping students think critically*. Scarborough, ON, Canada: Pippin.
Unrau, N., Ragusa, G., & Bowers, E. (2011). *Witnessing identities: Bonds that motivate reading*. Research poster session presented at the International Reading Association annual conference, Orlando, FL.
Unrau, N.J., & Schlackman, J. (2006). Motivation and its relationship with reading achievement in an urban middle school. *The Journal of Educational Research, 100*(2), 81–101. doi:10.3200/JOER.100.2.81-101
Vigil, J.D. (Ed.). (1992). Gangs, social control, and ethnicity: Ways to redirect. In S.B. Heath & M.W. McLaughlin (Eds.), *Identity and inner-city youth: Beyond ethnicity and gender* (pp. 94–119). Albany: State University of New York Press.
Vygotsky, L.S. (1986). *Thought and language*. Cambridge, MA: MIT Press. (Original work published 1962)
Wagner, R.K., & Sternberg, R.J. (1987). Executive control in reading comprehension. In B.K. Britton & S.M. Glynn (Eds.), *Executive control processes in reading* (pp. 1–22). Hillsdale, NJ: Erlbaum.
Whaley, J.F. (1982). Readers' expectations for story structures. *Reading Research Quarterly, 17*(1), 90–114.
Wigfield, A. (1994). The role of children's achievement values in the self-regulation of their learning outcomes. In D.H. Schunk & B.J. Zimmerman (Eds.), *Self-regulation of learning and performance: Issues and educational applications* (pp. 101–124). Hillsdale, NJ: Erlbaum.

LITERATURE CITED

Salinger, J.D. (1949, March 19). The Laughing Man. *The New Yorker*, p. 27.

SECTION FOUR

Literacy's New Horizons: An Emerging Agenda for Tomorrow's Research and Practice

As the title suggests, we seek in this last section to catch a glimpse of tomorrow's literacy perspectives, practices, policies, and promising research. Judging from the section's contents, it could be said that crossing social and cultural divides is of paramount interest to 21st-century researchers, at least among the authors represented here—so much so, in fact, that we are reminded of a story told about a time in American history (around the 1940s) when the line between high culture and popular culture was beginning to blur. This blurring has since been captured in the memorable image that film critic Neal Gabler (2011) used in his historical tracing of cultural authority in the United States. In Gabler's account, a telling moment in the breakdown of unbending distinctions between high culture and popular culture occurred when the classical conductor Leopold Stokowski shook hands with Mickey Mouse in Walt Disney's production of *Fantasia*—a symbolic gesture, yes, but as the anecdote demonstrates, not even an icon of high culture was interested in maintaining an arbitrary cultural divide of earlier times.

The extent to which this story applies to contemporary and future literacy research is, of course, arguable. On the one hand, there are numerous examples of literacy practices that have morphed across previously firm disciplinary boundaries, some of which are illustrated in the chapters that follow. On the other hand, some paradigmatic parameters are as unyielding as ever, with little or no sign of bending. In each instance, context plays a role, and the authors in Section Four are particularly adept at teasing out the underlying assumptions that are relevant to their particular situations.

In the first chapter in this section, "Adolescent Literacy Instruction and the Discourse of 'Every Teacher a Teacher of Reading'" (Chapter 39), Donna Alvermann and Elizabeth Birr Moje provide a brief overview of the key issues and individuals that have influenced models of adolescent literacy instruction from the early 20th century to the present. Then, using a Foucaultian genealogy as their analytic, they disrupt assumptions about the naturalness or inevitability of "every teacher a teacher of reading" and conclude with a call for a relational model of adolescent literacy instruction, one that uses both a theory of action and a theory in action.

In "Literacy Research in the 21st Century: From Paradigms to Pragmatism and Practicality" (Chapter 40), Deborah Dillon, David O'Brien, and Elizabeth Heilman urge researchers to move beyond political affiliations with paradigms that can result in endless debate to practical intervention in education issues that matter in the lives of students and teachers on an everyday basis. Specifically, the authors advance pragmatism as a viable alternative to paradigmatic reasoning. They believe their recommended stance offers several significant benefits that advance research in the field of literacy

A targeted critique by David Pearson and Elfrieda (Freddy) Hiebert (Chapter 41) of the 2008 National Early Literacy Panel (NELP) finds limitations in the report's usefulness, despite the care and precision with which it was produced. The authors argue that NELP's findings fail to take into account data from other large-scale federal initiatives, such as Reading First and Early Reading First, and descriptive studies of early literacy, a research category excluded from the panel's considerations. These omissions increase the likelihood that NELP's findings could be misconstrued, such as teaching phonemic awareness and letter recognition at the expense of engaging young children in meaning-making activities—a result the authors describe as a "basic-skills conspiracy of good intentions."

In a dual theory of new literacies, Donald Leu, Charles Kinzer, Julie Coiro, Jill Castek, and Laurie Henry (Chapter 42) describe how the educational challenges presented by shifting social needs and forces influence how people communicate with one another. Literacy today is deictic, multiple, multimodal, and multifaceted. The popularity of the Internet and social media has changed how we think about knowledge; for example, transmission of knowledge is no longer top-down, thus allowing for the enrichment of lives and the exploration of new domains and perspectives. The ability to navigate relatively unregulated founts of information to construct new knowledge is available to those who can afford access to the Internet, which in turn creates a need for new forms of critical literacy.

In their chapter on the social practice of multimodal reading, Jennifer Rowsell, Gunther Kress, Kate Pahl, and Brian Street (Chapter 43) offer for the first time an integrated perspective on new literacies and a social semiotic approach to multimodality. Situated within these two complementary approaches, reading and writing (particularly in digital environments) involve navigating through multiple forms of textual representation in various social settings. The authors discuss data from their studies of early childhood literacies, youth literacies, and adult academic literacies to account for their perspective on reading (and writing, although reading is the focus of this chapter). A concluding section draws implications of their integrated perspective on the social practice of multimodal reading for pedagogy and policy.

In a fascinating study of online reading and authoring, Glynda Hull, Amy Stornaiuolo, and Laura Sterponi (Chapter 44) explore the strategies students use to create hospitable texts. The importance of intercultural communication in a digital world makes it necessary to understand how semiotic decisions can influence meaning making, especially in terms of how youths develop an awareness of audience and purpose. Using the data they gathered, the authors developed a new taxonomy of textual strategies that invite participation in online communication, namely, designfulness, overture, reciprocity, and resonance.

In the last of this section's chapters, Robert Rueda (Chapter 45) explores cultural, linguistic, and motivational concerns that confront 21st-century educators. He takes into account the new and multiple literacies needed in an interconnected global economy in which information-driven work environments depend on an individual's ability to adapt quickly and creatively while simultaneously attending to factors that influence a reader's motivation to read and write (e.g., continuously changing times, diversity of texts, and audience needs), not unlike those described in the three previous chapters. The degree to which schools, teachers, and teacher education programs address these issues will determine in no small measure how prepared students are for a rapidly changing workforce in an increasingly diverse, global society.

REFERENCE

Gabler, N. (2011, January 29). Everyone's a critic now. *The Observer.* Retrieved July 2, 2011, from www.guardian.co.uk/culture/2011/jan/30/critics-franzen-freedom-social-network

CHAPTER 39

Adolescent Literacy Instruction and the Discourse of "Every Teacher a Teacher of Reading"

Donna E. Alvermann, The University of Georgia

Elizabeth Birr Moje, University of Michigan

The endless task of conducting and interpreting studies aimed at improving literacy instruction for young people at the middle and high school levels has demanded the attention of researchers of adolescent literacy teaching and teacher education to recent large-scale national and international reform efforts (e.g., Garbe, Holle, & Weinhold, 2010; National Governors Association Center for Best Practices & Council of Chief State School Officers [NGA & CCSSO], 2010). In an era marked by today's neoliberal perspectives on how literacy should function in a society, no discourse (or way of doing life) is left untouched—politically, educationally, or otherwise. For example, in the United States, organizations such as the National Governors Association (n.d.) exist for the express purpose of ensuring that "[its members'] views are represented in the shaping of federal policy" (para. 1). Even among professional organizations that represent literacy councils at the international, national, state, and local levels, the prevailing sense is that adolescent literacy teachers and teacher educators must attend to the 21st century's rapidly changing conditions and their impact on "how adolescents engage with text" (International Reading Association, 2012a, p. 2). Practically speaking, how such changes are to be communicated and enacted is often left up to age-old discourses that may or may not be in sync with the times.

Our purpose in this chapter is to examine the conditions that have enabled the discourse of "every teacher a teacher of reading" to exist for nearly a century, yet without widespread implementation in American secondary schools. We examine this phenomenon in two ways: first, through a brief chronological overview of the key issues and individuals that have influenced models of adolescent literacy instruction in the past; and second, through Foucault's (1984/1988, 1971/1998) historical analytic, genealogy, which is a means by which to disrupt assumptions about the naturalness or inevitability of discourses such as every teacher a teacher of reading. We conclude with a call for a relational model of adolescent literacy instruction, one that uses both a theory *of* action and a theory *in* action.

First, however, three terms need clarifying: *discourse*, *adolescent*, and *adolescent literacy*. Bové (1995), a noted authority on Foucaultian concepts, defined *discourse* in terms of its functions:

> Discourses produce knowledge about humans and their society. But since the "truths" of these discourses are relative to the disciplinary structures, the logical framework in which they are institutionalized, they can have no claim upon us except that derived from the authority and legitimacy, the power, granted to or acquired by the institutionalized discourses in question. (p. 56)

Thus, the discourse of every teacher a teacher of reading produces its own truth value and its subjects (content area teachers) to the extent that the logical framework in which adolescent literacy instruction resides has the institutional authority to make that discourse seem natural and inevitable—as if the discourse itself is indispensable to adolescent literacy instruction.

Regarding the parameters of *adolescent* and *adolescent literacy*, we reject definitions in the dominant discourse that position young people as belonging to a group determined largely by chronological age and associated age-driven factors (e.g., irresponsibility, emotionality). Rather than view adolescents as isolatable from the adult population, we favor arguments in the literature that show how claims of hierarchical positioning and sameness often preclude accounting for data that support generational interdependency. For example, Hagood, Stevens, and Reinking's (2002) review of cross-generational research revealed concrete instances in which adolescents' proficiencies in some literacy practices exceeded those of adults engaged in the same practices (see Barton, 2000; Green, Reid, & Bigum, 1998). The sameness principle, which would attribute to all youths the coming-of-age syndrome portrayed in books and popular media, is both limiting and regularly challenged by researchers who view adolescence as a culturally constructed concept (Lesko, 2001; Vadeboncoeur & Stevens, 2005). We use the term *adolescent literacy* not solely as a label that depends on arbitrary age categorizations but rather as a descriptor for the vast array of literate practices that young people bring to schooled learning, as well as take away from such learning. Depending on a writer's preference and the period of time in which one was writing, the term *adolescent literacy* has been linked to teaching or instruction using various descriptors: secondary or content area reading instruction, content literacy instruction, and disciplinary literacy instruction. Our decision to use *adolescent literacy instruction* was a conscious choice, based largely on its prevalence in the literature at the time of writing.

A Chronological Overview of Adolescent Literacy Instruction

Two overarching and competing models of literacy instruction have dominated the field of adolescent literacy instruction in the United States up to now: the autonomous and the ideological models (Street, 1984, 1995). The autonomous model assumes that reading and writing are neutral processes, irrespective of context and larger social, historical, cultural, and political influences. It also assumes that a universal set of cognitive skills, when properly taught, can account for individual variations in a person's literacy achievement and interpretations of texts. By contrast, the ideological model, which draws from Street's anthropological fieldwork in Iran in the 1970s and from Scribner and Cole's (1981) research among the Vai in Africa, assumes that reading and writing processes, while locally situated (contextualized), are simultaneously subject to power relations and ideological struggle regardless of how hidden or absent that struggle may seem. For example, Heath's (1983) early work in the Carolina Piedmont demonstrated that it is *how* children are socialized into different literacies (what she called their different ways with words) and whether those ways matched a school's approach to literacy instruction were important sociocultural factors in literacy teaching and learning.

To varying degrees, both the autonomous and ideological models of literacy have influenced the field of adolescent literacy instruction since its inception (Alvermann, 2009). What this looks like, time-wise, is captured in the following brief chronology of the major issues and people leading up to the present, and specifically to the reader–text–activity–context (RTAC) model (RAND Reading Study Group, 2002) that framed the U. S. Department of Education's research agenda on reading comprehension in 2002 and continues to inform funding criteria at the federal level (e.g., the 2010 Striving Readers Comprehensive Literacy Program formula grants, the 2011 discretionary grants under Race to the Top legislation; see U.S. Department of Education, n.d.).

Influences of the Autonomous Model

The transition from oral reading instruction and rote drills to silent reading instruction marked what Smith (1934/2002), the grande dame of American reading instruction, viewed as the field's initial "emphasis on scientific investigation in reading" (p. 149). She attributed this transition to Huey's (1908) influential research on reading for meaning (comprehension), or what he described as readers' "thought-getting and thought manipulating" (p. 359) while reading silently. The instructional model associated with silent reading focused largely on the development of remedial reading techniques and the materials necessary for supporting the model once several standardized silent reading tests, which had been published in the years leading up to 1918, were made available for sorting students on the grounds of test performance (Smith, 1934/2002). Concerned for students' welfare on such tests, Gray (1925) advised that "each teacher who makes reading assignments [in her or his content area] is responsible for the direction and supervision of the reading and study activities that are involved" (p. 71).

In a review of the literature on teaching young people to read in the content areas, Moore, Readence, and Rickelman (1983) identified a major issue for 20th-century Progressivist educators, namely, whether reading skills would continue to be taught separate from the subject area in which they were embedded or as an integrated part of that instruction. Although Zirbes (as cited in Moore et al., 1983), an early Progressivist educator from Columbia University, did not develop a model per se, it is worth noting that her 1928 comparative analysis of techniques for improving teaching yielded support for simultaneous instruction in reading skills and subject matter. Like her contemporary at Columbia University, Strang was also instrumental in identifying ways of improving reading instruction in the content areas (Lapp, Guthrie, & Flood, 2007). However, it was likely LaBrant's influence as president of the National Council of Teachers of English in the mid-1950s and her tireless advocacy for teaching reading as a part of all subject area courses that influenced Herber to initiate a program of applied research at Syracuse University in the mid-1960s. Findings from that research and the subsequent federally funded Network of Secondary School Demonstration Centers for Teaching Reading in Content Areas resulted in two editions of *Teaching Reading in Content Areas* (Herber, 1970, 1978). For the first time, with the publication of Herber's book, secondary school teachers and teacher educators had access to a research-based curricular model for teaching reading processes (skills and strategies) simultaneously with course content (Alvermann, 2010).

The cognitive processes that underlie reading strategies became a focus of research beginning in 1976 when the Center for the Study of Reading at the University of Illinois was funded by the U.S. Department of Education to conduct basic research on reading comprehension, including prior knowledge activation, vocabulary development, and metacognitive monitoring. Yet, despite a significant and sizable body of basic research conducted mainly on college-age students' comprehension processing of researcher-prepared texts that is still relevant, the center's findings had limited ecological validity for adolescent literacy instruction, especially with its dependence on mass-produced texts for a curriculum that is taught in highly contextualized secondary classrooms (Alvermann, Fitzgerald, & Simpson, 2006; Alvermann & Moore, 1991; Bean, 2000; Moje, Dillon, & O'Brien, 2000; Moore, 1996). As cognitive psychology's information processing era (see Alexander & Fox, Chapter 1 this volume) began to wane, so did the emphasis on the autonomous model of adolescent literacy instruction and its assumption that a universal set of cognitive skills, when properly taught, can account for an individual student's motivation and literacy achievement. By the mid- to late 1980s, researchers were increasingly influenced by the writings of social and cultural anthropologists (e.g., Heath, 1983; Street, 1984), social linguists (Gee, 1988), and sociocultural theory (Vygotsky, 1986). It was the beginning of what Alexander and Fox refer to as a move away from the individual to the group—the era of sociocultural and contextual influences on learning and instruction.

Influences of the Ideological Model

Following a major synthesis of the qualitative research on adolescent literacy instruction, Moore (1996) concluded that the type of content area literacy strategy taught is less important than the nature of the context in which it is taught, including the opportunities students experience (or not) for motivated learning, the freedoms and constraints teachers encounter when attempting to implement research-based practices, and the situated nature of those practices. Moore's findings provide an apt introduction to this section, which focuses on the RTAC model of reading comprehension. But first, a cursory review of the literature leading up to the RTAC model is in order.

In an invited review of the research literature on adolescent literacy instruction for the third edition of the *Handbook of Reading Research* (Kamil, Mosenthal, Pearson, & Barr, 2000), Bean (2000) remarked on the growing trend among literacy researchers in the 1990s to design qualitative research studies that put "classroom social contexts in the forefront" (p. 639). He interpreted this trend as indicative of the field's attempt to overcome, at least partially, the ecological limitations outlined in earlier reviews of the research conducted under the autonomous model of literacy instruction. Despite what he viewed as an encouraging trend, Bean also noted his concern that findings from the qualitative research studies of the 1990s were still dependent on teacher-centered content instruction and single-textbook adoptions. This led him to conclude that despite the trend toward contextualized research designs, some of the same limitations that Alvermann and Moore (1991) had documented nearly a decade earlier in their review of the quantitative research literature on adolescent literacy instruction were still prevalent. As with Bean's findings, Anders, Hoffman, and Duffy's (2000) substantive review of the literature on literacy teacher education documented a growing interest in context and the use of diverse research methodologies. They decried, however, the lack of a sufficient research base that would provide answers to questions "about how best to prepare reading teachers" (p. 734) at the preservice and inservice levels.

At approximately the same time that the literacy field's interest in context and professional development was growing, the National Academy of Science charged the RAND Corporation, working in collaboration with the U.S. Department of Education's Office of Educational Research and Improvement, to appoint a panel of literacy experts whose goal would be to develop a definition of reading comprehension and set a national research agenda for improving classroom instruction in comprehension (RAND Reading Study Group, 2002). That panel, the RAND Reading Study Group (RRSG), subsequently conducted an extensive review of the literature on reading comprehension that covered three previous decades of mostly experimental and quasi-experimental research devoted to studying cognitive processes in higher order learning. Based on their review, the RRSG reached a consensus on a model of reading comprehension that consisted of three elements:

> The *reader* who is doing the comprehending
> The *text* that is to be comprehended
> The *activity* in which comprehension is a part. (p. 11)

Those three elements were viewed as essential to "the process of simultaneously extracting and constructing meaning through interaction and involvement with written language" (p. 11). Guided by sociocultural theories of learning and literacy that were prevalent at the time, the panel acknowledged that reading comprehension "occurs within a larger *sociocultural context* that shapes and is shaped by the reader and that interacts with each of the three elements" (p. 11). The resulting RTAC model of reading comprehension has dominated the adolescent literacy field for the last decade, serving researchers investigating differences in comprehending texts comprised of print versus pixels (Hartman, Morsink, & Zheng, 2010), learners with reading disabilities (Gaskins, 2003), and adolescent literacy instruction and the achievement gap (Snow & Biancarosa, 2003).

Although the RTAC model and the three earlier reviews of the research literature (Anders et al., 2000; Bean, 2000; RRSG, 2002) called for embedded literacy instruction in subject area classrooms, especially in social studies, science, English language arts, and mathematics classrooms, they made no specific mention of the discourse of every teacher a teacher of reading and its assumptions about cross-disciplinary instruction. Explicit mention would not come until a decade later when Dillon, O'Brien, Sato, and Kelly (2011) sounded the following caveat in their far-reaching review of the literature on literacy teacher education:

> Positioning secondary content teachers as resistant to incorporating literacy practices is problematic. It assumes that literacy teacher educators' pedagogical knowledge can complement pedagogical knowledge constructed by faculty within the disciplines. And, since instructional strategies adopted by literacy educators are often recommended without benefit of conceptual understanding and socio-historical contexts of disciplinary knowledge and practices generated within disciplines, the idea that generic literacy strategies can be as important or more important than pedagogies that originate in disciplines is questionable (cf. Conley, 2008; Moje, 2007). This assumption of relative importance of literacy frameworks is embodied in the phrase "every teacher a teacher of reading" which, from a pragmatic view, is embraced as a call for all teachers to collectively contribute to help all students with reading. But from the view of teachers in various disciplines, the call is often seen as an unfair demand on their time given their lack of expertise in reading; moreover, it is counter to the institutionalized practices within disciplines (Bean, 2000; O'Brien et al., 1995). (p. 639)

Thus, Dillon et al.'s caveat suggests the usefulness of a genealogical analysis of every teacher a teacher of reading if for no other reason than to examine the enabling conditions that make this discourse thinkable, especially in relation to the RTAC model of reading comprehension when applied across disciplines. Of course, such an analysis must be premised on more than the enabling conditions that make a discourse thinkable. Also needed is an analytic for discerning any power relations inherent in those enabling conditions.

A Genealogical Analysis: Heuristics and Guidelines

Foucault (1971/1998) described genealogy as "gray, meticulous, and patiently documentary" (p. 569)—a description befitting an analytic that depends on an accumulation of historical source material written in words that take on slightly different meanings meant to appeal to different ways of thinking over time and context. Genealogy requires relentless attention to details that might otherwise escape notice when reading documents such as scholarly arguments, essays, research reports, legislative records, and policy statements. Unlike history's chronological listing of events in time-order fashion, genealogy is not a search for the origin of a concept, discourse, or the like. Instead, in Foucault's words (1984/1988), a genealogy begins with "a question posed in the present" (p. 262). Engaging in a genealogical analysis of the enabling conditions that make the discourse of every teacher a teacher of reading seems commonsensical and inevitable does not assume an originating event; nor does it assume that the discourse as it presently exists is the logical result of a series of events that followed a cause–effect order without discontinuities, errors, or chance—quite the contrary, as will become evident in the analysis that we present here.

It is important to keep in mind that a genealogy's focus on how something functions in the present does not preclude looking to the past (Foucault, 1971/1998); it merely negates, as noted previously, the existence of a single originating event and a lock-step progression of events that explain the present. In further distinguishing his historical analytic from traditional historiography, Foucault employed a heuristic that he called descent. This heuristic guides a genealogist to seek multiple events (external to any cause–effect progression toward an ending point) and to remain "sensitive to their recurrence, not in order to trace the gradual curve of their evolution but to isolate the different scenes where they engaged in different roles" (p. 569). As Foucault used the term,

> Genealogy does not resemble the evolution of a species and does not map the destiny of a people. On the contrary, to follow the complex course of descent is to maintain passing events in their proper dispersion; it is to identify the accidents, the minute deviations—or conversely, the complete reversals—the errors, the false appraisals, and the faulty calculations that gave birth to those things that continue to exist and have value for us; it is to discover that truth or being does not lie at the root of what we know and what we are, but the exteriority of accidents. (p. 574)

Discovering how such accidents are inherently complex networks of power relations (involving domination, submission, and resistance) rather than natural, linear progressions is genealogy's project, and in our case, the means by which to disrupt assumptions about the commonsensical notion of every teacher a teacher of reading.

Genealogy, or the analysis of descent, is also concerned with emergence, a concept derived from the German word *entstehung*, which means "the moment of arising," made possible by a network of events (Foucault, 1971/1998, p. 576). Worth keeping in mind, however, is that just as it is incorrect to search for uninterrupted continuity in descent, so too it is wrong to associate emergences with origins. Indeed, a genealogist searching for patterns of repetition and the adjacency of events, "that is, their simultaneity within ostensibly different fields" (Bové, 1995, p. 60), is not looking for causal influences among events. Instead, the relations of power embedded in those networked events are what capture a genealogist's attention and make possible the disruption of perceived ideas about the naturalness or inevitable progression of a discourse or concept.

That power relations are important to a genealogist is made explicit in Prado's (2000) portrayal of emergence as "an appearance or advent enabled by a collision of forces, some of which enhance, nullify, or redirect others, and some of which combine with others to form new forces" (p. 37). In our genealogy of every teacher a teacher of reading, we trace lines of descent to those emergences, or discontinuities, that disrupt assumptions about the discourse's naturalness or inevitability. We do so not for the purpose of bringing this discourse to its knees, but rather to explore possibilities for its future. This is in keeping with a Foucaultian genealogy's interest in neither beginnings nor endings—only becomings.

Perceived Crises in Adolescent Literacy Instruction

The discourse of every teacher a teacher of reading emerges in times of crisis and then fades to relative obscurity until the next crisis is declared. Tracing this pattern of repetition and the power relations embedded in networked events across seemingly disparate contexts is a way of analyzing how every teacher a teacher of reading is both thinkable and yet difficult to implement. It is a discourse that has been with us for nearly a century. As noted earlier, influenced by applied psychology's statistical procedures for measuring the efficiency of schools by testing, Gray (1925) called attention to the comprehension difficulties that older students were experiencing in their efforts to read teacher-assigned textbooks. Today, the discourse of every teacher a teacher of reading shows no sign of abating, especially if one takes seriously ACT's (2010) call for subject area teachers "to help all students achieve sufficient literacy skills in history/social studies and in science and technical subjects, as well as in English language arts" (p. 5). In its 2010 report entitled *A First Look at the Common Core and College and Career Readiness*, ACT further specified that "states must *ensure that teachers in these subject areas use their unique content knowledge to foster students' ability to read, write, and communicate in the various disciplines*" (p. 5).

Tracing Lines of Descent

For the first time in several iterations of the call for every teacher a teacher of reading, English language arts teachers at the middle and high school levels are specifically directed by ACT (2010), a nonprofit organization offering standardized high school achievement/college admission tests working hand in hand with the Common Core State Standards Initiative (NGA & CCSSO, 2010), to incorporate substantially more literary nonfiction (e.g., essays; speeches; opinion pieces; biographies; other documents of journalistic, historical, and scientific importance) into their curriculum than has been typical of the traditional curriculum, comprised largely of stories, poems, and plays. Ostensibly to create buy-in for the standards by negating potential criticism, the Common Core State Standards Initiative designed a webpage titled "Myths vs. Facts" (NGA & CCSSO, 2012). Two examples aimed at deflecting potential resistance to the Common Core English language arts standards appear below:

> **Myth:** English teachers will be asked to teach science and social studies reading materials.
>
> **Fact:** With the Common Core ELA *Standards*, English teachers will still teach their students literature as well as literary non-fiction. However, because college and career readiness overwhelmingly focuses on complex texts outside of literature, these standards also ensure students are being prepared to read, write, and research across the curriculum, including in history and science. These goals can be achieved by ensuring that teachers in other disciplines are also focusing on reading and writing to build knowledge within their subject areas. (paras. 26–27)
>
> **Myth:** No teachers were involved in writing the *Standards.*
>
> **Fact:** The common core state standards drafting process relied on teachers and standards experts from across the country. In addition, there were many state experts that came together to create the most thoughtful and transparent process of standard setting. This was only made possible by many states working together. (paras. 30–31)

In the first instance, phrases such as *college and career readiness*, *complex texts*, and *these standards...ensure* are presumed to carry sufficient rationale and weight for "ensuring that teachers in other disciplines are also focusing on reading and writing to build knowledge within their subject areas" (NGA & CCSSO, 2012, para. 27). In contrast to the specificity of the intended audience in the first instance (disciplinary teachers), phrases alluding to the involvement of teachers in the second instance are vague (*relied on teachers and standards experts*, *state experts*; NGA & CCSSO, 2012, para. 31).

Networked Events

The fact that ACT (2011), by its own admission, played a significant role in the wording of the Common Core and that it regularly provides benchmarks on the students it tests—for example, nationwide only 30% of the high school students tested in 2011 met the College Readiness Benchmark in science—would seem to point to an adjacency of events (Bové, 1995), including the proclaimed crisis in adolescent literacy, that make the discourse of every teacher a teacher of reading thinkable. At the same time, according to Prado (2000) a genealogical analysis of the relations of power embedded in networked events makes it possible to discern "a collision of forces, some of which enhance, nullify, or redirect others, and some of which combine with others to form new forces" (p. 37). Thus, in a second and closer analysis of the near-simultaneously released documents produced by Common Core State Standards Initiative and ACT, and written in words that take on slightly different meanings meant to support different purposes for writing, we were able to map how competing forces (e.g., the Common Core webpage "Myths vs. Facts" previously discussed) within networked events attempted to redirect or even nullify ideas deemed harmful to the naturalness or inevitability of every teacher a teacher of reading.

Emergences and the RTAC Model

Unlike the Common Core's (NGA & CCSSO, 2010) weighty documentation and online resources that spell out specific guidelines for teaching the English language arts, ACT's (2010) much heralded report *A First Look at the Common Core and College and Career Readiness* barely mentions the role of non–English language arts teachers in helping students comprehend complex texts: "Teachers in other subject areas should use their own subject-area expertise to help students learn to read, write, and communicate effectively in their specific field" (p. 5). To supplement its brief and vaguely worded directive to teachers outside the English language arts, ACT adds,

> The Common Core State Standards in reading are explicitly modeled on the idea of shared responsibility for students' literacy development. States and districts should therefore prepare middle and high school content-area teachers for this role by providing professional development opportunities that build the reading instruction capacity of content-area specialists. (p. 5)

Here it is worth noting that on the same page and within contiguous paragraphs, ACT (2010) seems to have reversed (or at least been unclear about) its stance on the discourse of every teacher a teacher of reading. For example, is it the case that teachers in disciplines other than English language arts are free to use their own subject area expertise to teach students how to read, write, and communicate, or must they participate in professional development opportunities aimed at building their knowledge of literacy instruction, such as that spelled out in the Common Core's College and Career Readiness Anchor Standards for Reading and Writing? Whether merely a difference in wording meant to appeal to different audiences or a collision of forces working to enhance the implementation of every teacher a teacher of reading, there is room for potential misinterpretation. At the very least, a misreading of either document stands to destabilize the discourse of every teacher a teacher of reading.

Tracing lines of descent for other proclaimed crises in adolescent literacy instruction offers a rare glimpse into similar patterns of networked events that have made every teacher a teacher of reading a tenable but difficult discourse to enact. For instance, the RRSG panel charged with producing a literacy research agenda for the United States at the close of the 20th century argued in its executive summary that the country was experiencing still another crisis in teaching adolescents to comprehend complex texts. At that point in time, the crisis was equated to scores on tests that showed students in the United States were "performing increasingly poorly in comparison with students in other countries" (RRSG, 2002,

p. xi). The panel went on to explain, "Little direct attention has been devoted to helping teachers develop the skills they need to promote reading comprehension...[and] ensure content learning through reading" (pp. xi–xii). Worth noting is the similarity of the language and the crisis mentality apparent in the discourse of every teacher a teacher of reading at the close of the 20th century and today.

Then, as now, the RTAC model of reading comprehension prevailed, at least among those engaged in literacy teacher education. This model, which purportedly can address a crisis marked by growing numbers of struggling readers who potentially will leave high school before graduating, was supported by yet another panel of experts who designed the document *Reading Next—A Vision for Action and Research in Middle and High School Literacy* (Biancarosa & Snow, 2004). In the second edition of that report, Biancarosa and Snow (2006) stressed that the 15 key elements of effective adolescent literacy programs, which the *Reading Next* panel had identified based on their interpretation of the existing research, would be for naught if middle and high school teachers did not implement those elements across disciplinary lines. Although a commonsensical assessment, the second edition of *Reading Next* once again implicated teachers in reform efforts that may not have aligned well with their disciplinary understandings. In this particular instance, the discourse of every teacher a teacher of reading was invoked but without a strategic plan for making such implementation happen, much less a systematic way of evaluating its validity if it indeed were implemented. From a Foucaultian (1971/1998) perspective on genealogy, such an oversight quite literally ensures that every teacher a teacher of reading would continue to exist—a mere slogan that could be called up the next time a crisis in adolescent literacy presents itself.

Rival Views of the Subject Area Teacher and the Teaching Process

Important as they were to identifying several enabling conditions of every teacher a teacher of reading, the patterns of networked events and emergences associated with that discourse in times of perceived crises in adolescent literacy instruction did not account for all that we learned from the genealogical analysis. We also uncovered several historical discontinuities—what Foucault (1971/1998) called "accidents" (p. 574)—in the assumed legitimacy of every teacher a teacher of reading. Three such accidents are the focus of this section. But first, definitions are in order for two Foucaultian concepts: power and discursive practice.

According to Foucault (1976/1980), "power is neither given, nor exchanged, nor recovered, but rather exercised, and...it only exists in action" (p. 89). "In other words, individuals are the vehicles of power, not its points of application" (p. 98). By tracing actions visible in discursive practices—or what Foucault defined as "historically and culturally specific set[s] of rules for organizing and producing different forms of knowledge" (O'Farrell, 2007, para. 18)—we were able to document specific instances in which every teacher a teacher of reading did not seem a natural and inevitable fit with the discursive practices associated with subject area teachers and their teaching.

"Accidents" and the Subject Area Teacher

Foucault (1971/1998) maintained that in tracing lines of descent, the genealogist is "identify[ing] the accidents, the minute deviations—or conversely, the complete reversals—the errors, the false appraisals, and the faulty calculations that gave birth to those things that continue to exist and have value for us" (p. 574). In the following, we describe a series of accidents known not for producing any cause–effect actions but simply for being present in seemingly unrelated discursive practices, which over time reveal patterns disruptive of every teacher a teacher of reading.

The first accident consists of deviations in communicating the discursive practices that regulate a subject area teacher's sense of professionalism and identity. For example, there is a discourse that implies all teachers can be teachers of reading simply by using their expertise and focusing on language that is meaningful to their disciplines. Then, there is another discourse that suggests subject matter teachers can only double as reading teachers if they use a repertoire of comprehension strategies (identified by acronyms) and focus students' attention on close reading. These two discourses are oppositional, and worse, neither is very appealing to subject matter teachers who wonder why they should focus on language and literacy skills when telling students through lectures or engaging them in multimediated activities can accomplish the same goal in far less time. The accident is that these two discourses have been promulgated as a way to convince disciplinary teachers that this kind of instruction is within their reach. At the very least, mixed messages about a subject matter teacher's professional identity could be construed as detrimental to enacting the discourse of every teacher a teacher of reading.

A second accident of considerable significance for a subject matter teacher's sense of professional identity arises each time researchers and policymakers make decisions that will ultimately affect teachers, yet do not directly involve them in meaningful ways prior to expecting their cooperation in the implementation process. A case in point is the role that teachers were supposed to assume once the RTAC model of reading comprehension (RRSG, 2002) was rolled out. Unlike an earlier sociocognitive-processing model of instruction developed by Ruddell and Unrau (1994), which viewed the teacher along with the reader and the text as integral components in the comprehension process, the RTAC model did not take the teacher into account, or if it did, the teacher was more implied than explicit. For instance, in addressing the role of subject area teachers in implementing the RTAC model, members of the RRSG (2002) issued this statement: "Effective teachers of comprehension enact practices that reflect the orchestration of knowledge about readers, texts, purposeful activity, and contexts for the purpose of advancing students' thoughtful, competent, and motivated reading" (pp. 29–30). In choosing to delegate to teachers, in general, the responsibility for orchestrating and enacting what the research on reading comprehension suggested, the RTAC model's designers arguably misjudged disciplinary teachers' sense of professional identity, and thus the degree to which they would willingly take up (or not) the discourse of every teacher a teacher of reading. Specifically, this lack of attention to the role of teachers as human actors—complete with their own domain-specific and socioculturally mediated discourses, knowledges, identities, and practices coming to bear on the teaching of reading—may have undermined the very discourse that the RTAC model's designers were trying to engender.

A third accident exemplifies a complete reversal of what Alexander and Fox (Chapter 1 this volume) describe as an era of engaged learning. Lasting just over a decade, from 1995 to 2006, this era was conceived by Alexander and Fox as being a time in which teachers felt relatively free to include texts in their instruction that were outside the traditional curriculum but which students were motivated to read and write. It was also a time in which the adolescent reader was viewed as someone capable of being actively engaged by subject area teachers who subscribed to a model of disciplinary learning through the teaching of cognitive strategies (Alexander, 2003; Alexander & Jetton, 2000), such as those supported by the RTAC model of reading comprehension (Valencia, Pearson, & Wixson, 2011). However, during the engagement era, a rival view of the learner and the learning process inserted itself. According to Alexander and Fox, the "rival stance was invested in the identification, teaching, and remediation of the subskills or components underlying reading acquisition…[with a focus] on beginning or struggling readers who had yet to master these reading fundamentals" (p. 24). A reversal of the engagement era, in concert with the country's swing toward neoliberal politics and discursive practices that value individual learning over group learning (see, e.g., Spear-Swerling's discussion of the Response to Intervention model, Chapter 16 this volume), dealt a serious blow to whatever aspirations remained for encouraging subject area teachers to take up the mantra of every teacher a teacher of reading.

Disruptions of a Discourse in Subject Area Teaching

Although discourses take on lives of their own, filled with historical contingencies that are neither predictable nor inevitable, a genealogical analysis is open to disrupting, at least temporarily, discourses that are assumed commonsensical and inescapable. As we noted earlier and underscore here,

> Discourses produce knowledge about humans and their society. But since the "truths" of these discourses are relative to the disciplinary structures, the logical framework in which they are institutionalized, they can have no claim upon us except that derived from the authority and legitimacy, the power, granted to or acquired by the institutionalized discourses in question. (Bové, 1995, p. 56)

With this as background, we offer two examples of research-based disruptions to the discourse of every teacher a teacher of reading. Each is best understood by (a) recalling that while relations of power are inherent in all discourses, it is simultaneously the case that power "only exists in action" (Foucault, 1976/1980, p. 89); and (b) "individuals are the vehicles of power, not its points of application" (p. 98). The first example draws from data gathered in a participatory action research project that focused on redefining roles in subject area teacher education courses, and the second from a qualitative case study of an online literacy course that attempted to fuse reading and science instruction for preservice subject area teachers.

Redefining Roles in Subject Area Teacher Education. In describing a two-year collaboration involving herself and three other teacher educators from the same university but different disciplines (music, theater, and mathematics), Draper (2008) recounts how biweekly, one- to two-hour discussions with her colleagues following observational data gathering in their classrooms enabled her to reconsider and reconceptualize her role as a content area literacy instructor. Basically, she relied on field notes and transcriptions of her class visits, conversations, and interviews with each of her colleagues to learn what they, in their roles as content experts, enacted in the name of literacy instruction. To illustrate, the mathematics teacher insisted that students in his class explain in writing the algorithms they used to solve an equation. Mere descriptions and definitions that would have satisfied Draper in her role as a content area literacy instructor were not acceptable in the mathematics classroom. In the music professor's classroom, Draper noted a pattern of instruction that required students to produce, not consume, texts. A similar pattern was noted in the theater professor's modeling of what she calls "invisible literacy instruction" (p. 72; e.g., identifying objectives and tactics while acting out a play's script). In summarizing the action research project, Draper concluded the following about her participants:

> [Each] came to the collaboration with a clear sense of the aims of their disciplines and, thus, the practices that should be implemented in classrooms to reach those aims....Moreover, each of them, while open to my ideas about content-area literacy, had the wherewithal to challenge my views, particularly those related to instructional practices. As we worked together, each of them was firm without being resistant, gentle without being condescending....However, their knowledge, practice, and questions offered me a way to critically reconsider my own position, understanding, and practice. Specifically, this has required me to question the aims of content-area literacy instruction and the efficacy of content-area instructional practices to the extent that they are generic across all disciplines. (p. 69)

Moje's (2007) review of the literature on disciplinary literacy teaching offered a similar critique of literacy teacher educators' reliance on generic comprehension strategies. Despite support for these strategies by both the National Reading Panel (National Institute of Child Health and Human Development, 2000) and the RRSG (2002), they do not necessarily align well with the disciplinary structures that inform subject matter teachers' expertise. Examples of such structures include the forms of reasoning a history teacher might employ (as contrasted to those that a mathematics teacher might use) or the themes and devices that an

English teacher might favor (as contrasted to what a teacher of drama might find acceptable). These structural differences coupled with subject matter teachers' awareness of how symbolic representations vary by discipline are but two realities that supporters of every teacher a teacher of reading have yet to address.

Finding One's Identity as a Preservice Science Teacher. Alvermann, Rezak, Mallozzi, Boatright, and Jackson (2011) conducted a semester-long case study of how a preservice science teacher learned to identify with her discipline as she simultaneously attempted to integrate knowledge of her subject area with the generic reading strategies that she was expected to apply in an online content literacy course. Two of the researchers were teacher educators in the same college: Jackson, a science educator, had taught the preservice science teacher in an earlier on-campus course, and Alvermann, a literacy educator, was the instructor for the online course. Although they had no previous knowledge that the preservice student, who had taken a science methods course with the science teacher educator, would enroll in the online literacy methods course that was part of a larger research project in which both of these researchers were involved, this unanticipated event lent itself well to a fine-grained analysis of disciplinary differences (e.g., the natural sciences, linguistics, literary studies, psychology, sociology, anthropology) that informed each of their separate fields of study. Data sources included the preservice teacher's four intervention lesson plans (prepared for a middle-grades struggling reader) and e-mails containing reflections on the effectiveness of those plans by the preservice teacher, her classroom cooperating teacher, and members of the research team. The data were analyzed using a four-step process: (1) coding key sources, (2) writing analytic memos using deductive and inductive methods, (3) matching instances of planning and reflecting with each data source, and (4) applying Gee's (1999) Discourse analysis to interpret written reflections by the preservice teacher, the cooperating teacher, and members of the research team. The contradictory discursive practices encountered in attempting to fuse reading and science instruction in one course to which both the content literacy educator and the science educator had input is reflected in the following excerpts from e-mails exchanged among Rezak (the literacy teaching assistant for the online course), the preservice science teacher, and Jackson (the science teacher educator).

Lacking confidence in choosing appropriate texts for her middle-grades struggling reader, the preservice teacher (PST) enlisted the literacy teaching assistant's (LTA) advice, as well as that of the science teacher educator (STE):

> PST: "So am I supposed to use the same text as before? I know I need to shorten it based on [my cooperating teacher's] reflection, but should I just shorten and use basically the same text and use it for this different activity?...Sorry I keep bugging you, but I just feel like I am in a constant state of confusion with this."

LTA: "Give yourself leeway with the text. What's most important is implementing (and learning) the strategy."

STE: [responding to one of PST's e-mailed reflections] "At [Student X's] age/level of learning, I would prefer that a text and/or teacher speak of plants and their chloroplasts 'capturing/collecting light, which plants need to grow and function,' or some such wording, rather than the language used here of energy conversion (the conversion is into chemical energy, a very advanced concept)." (Alvermann, Rezak, et al., 2011, pp. 45–46)

This response by the science teacher educator was but one of several exchanges he had with the preservice science teacher throughout the semester.

In a separate instance, but one that was again related to the preservice teacher's difficulty in selecting appropriate texts, the science teacher educator wrote,

> Maybe I am just 'not seeing the forest for the trees' overall, in that I am so used to the way information is structured in a well-written science text, that it is transparent and unproblematic for me in a way that it is not for either students or for teachers in other disciplines. (Alvermann, Rezak, et al., 2011, p. 48)

His response suggests he was aware that the discourse of every teacher a teacher of reading assumes parity in subject matter knowledge, when in fact little or none may exist. Although both the literacy teacher educator and the literacy teaching assistant were intent on helping the preservice science teacher fuse reading and science instruction, their combined knowledge of the subject matter was not on par with the science teacher educator's knowledge and expertise. This same pattern surfaced in subsequent multisite case studies (Alvermann, Friese, Beckmann, & Rezak, 2011; Marsh, Lammers, & Alvermann, 2012) that involved preservice mathematics teachers.

In sum, when disciplinary knowledge is inadequate, and contradictory discursive practices prevail, every teacher a teacher of reading seems less natural and inevitable than it might appear on first glance. This is not to claim that a discourse that has weathered the discontinuities of nearly a century is of little or no value to the field of adolescent literacy education. Rather, it is to acknowledge that the complexities of adolescent literacy instruction increase substantively when variables of interest include disciplinary and classroom/social structures and practices that exceed what designers of earlier models took into account. It is also to recognize the value of reconceptualizing every teacher a teacher of reading as a discourse that has neither origins nor endings (in a linear sense), but only becomings.

Call for an Adolescent Literacy Model That Uses Theory *of* and *in* Action

With the genealogical analysis of the discourse of every teacher a teacher of reading in mind, we now turn to an analysis of the prevailing adolescent literacy (reading comprehension) model to examine how it has both supported and undermined this discourse, thus making it difficult for teachers to take action in implementing it. In the process of examining the prevailing model, we offer new ways to think about literacy theories and models in general, and the RTAC model in particular.

For all its dominance, the RTAC model has fallen short of being carried into practice in sustained or systematic ways. Moreover, despite general acceptance of the model as representing the theory of how reading comprehension is produced as an interaction of reader, text, activity, and context, most attempts to affect change in adolescent literacy teaching continue to focus on the reader. In part, the failure is due to the lack of an identified theory of action embedded in or implied by the model. That is, the current model is one of how reading comprehension or literate practice occurs. It does not represent a theory of action for how to teach reading comprehension or literate practice.

The RTAC model does not provide a theory *of* action in large part because it does not represent theory *in* action across multiple activity systems, activities, and actors. The RTAC model is a static and singular model of a dynamic, multilayered, and relational process. Although the model is a powerful representation of the interactive process of meaning making for a given individual in a given activity at a given moment in time within a given context (see Figure 1) and has guided our own work extensively, it does not translate to adolescent literacy teaching practice. That is, nothing in the model provides a theory of action for teachers who would seek to engage a range of youths across a range of classes focused on one subject matter in reading for meaning, which is the task of secondary school teachers across multiple disciplines, if the discourse of every teacher a teacher of reading is to be taken seriously.

Thus, because the RTAC model overlooks the complex roles of other people, activities, goals, and contexts as features of reading comprehension, the model fails to guide practice. In that sense, then, the RTAC model could be said to undermine the take-up of the notion that every teacher should take responsibility for teaching the reading processes and practices of their own domain. If we can build a model that more completely specifies the complex and dynamic nature of adolescent literacy, then we might be better able to engage in translational work that guides the teaching of adolescent literacy and thus invite teachers of a range of domains to see themselves as doing the work of literacy teaching to enhance learning in their subject domains. We unpack these ideas in more detail in what follows, beginning with the idea of making a more dynamic and activity-based representation of the current learning model of reading comprehension. Throughout this analysis, we offer variations on the RTAC model and suggest a possible, metaphoric model to guide the building of a theory *in* action. The theory in action is not, in itself, enough to inform the translation of adolescent literacy theory and research in the practice of every teacher a teacher of reading. However, clarifying the dynamic nature of adolescent literacy could help to generate a theory *of* action for adolescent literacy teaching.

Figure 1. A Heuristic for Thinking About Reading Comprehension

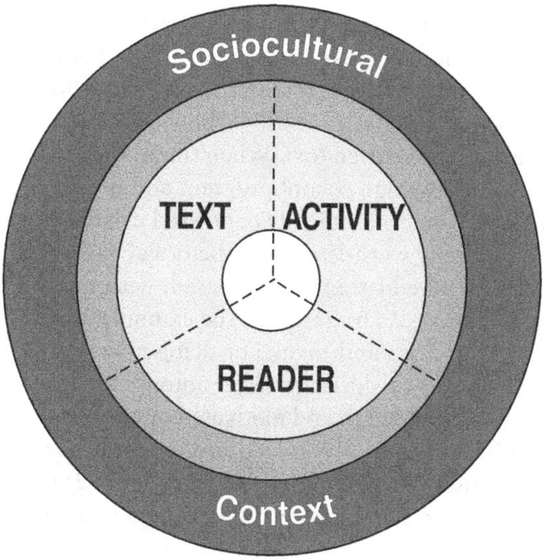

Note. Reprinted from *Reading for Understanding: Toward an R&D Program in Reading Comprehension* (p. 12), by RAND Reading Study Group, 2002, Santa Monica, CA: RAND. Copyright © by RAND. Reprinted with permission.

Building a Theory in Action of Adolescent Literate Practice/Literacy Learning

Theory and model building focused on human activity needs to recognize and situate the dynamic and context-bound nature of that activity. Not only does the process of comprehension or meaning making from text change continually, but everything around the model is also always changing. Moreover, the RTAC model has not accounted for or translated the multiple actors involved in the practice and processes of reading in any given classroom. In other words, the RTAC model is one of a cognitive process, not an enactment of teaching. It is an enormously valuable model in helping the field understand the process of reading, but it does not theorize the process of teaching reading. We expand on this point in what follows.

Readers bring something to text comprehension, but that interaction is immersed in, indeed mediated by, the activities and purposes for which acts of reading are engaged and the particular contexts in which those activities occur (Moje et al., 2000; Scribner & Cole, 1981). Readers employ their skills and knowledge from various past experiences as mediating tools (Vygotsky, 1978; Wertsch, del Río, & Alvarez, 1995) for certain goals and in particular ways that are dependent on the activities for which the reading task is being carried out. Activities, moreover, are mediated by the multiple and intersecting contexts in which they are carried out. These differences produce reading—or literacy—*practices*, that is, ways of reading and writing, together with ways of using reading and writing *skills* to achieve particular goals in those practices. For example, the literacy practices of an academic writing a research paper demand that basic skills of word knowledge and syntax be framed by knowledge of audience, appropriate register, and purpose of the written text. When that same academic turns to write a press release about a new high school program and must appeal to youths and their parents who live in an economically depressed urban setting, he or she must engage (or learn) different word-level and rhetorical skills because the textual and literate practice is embedded in an interaction with people engaged in a particular activity and context. As hinted at in the example, texts serve as tools that can further mediate activities and invoke or demand certain kinds of practices. The point here is that literacy skills are never autonomously engaged (see Street, 1984), but are always embedded in and motivated by the need to carry out certain literacy practices, which are socially and culturally produced and mediated. Thus, we offer this modification of the RTAC model (see Figure 2) to further specify the complexity of the dynamic relationship among a reader, a text, an activity, and a context.

Figure 2. Expanded Reader–Text–Activity–Context Model

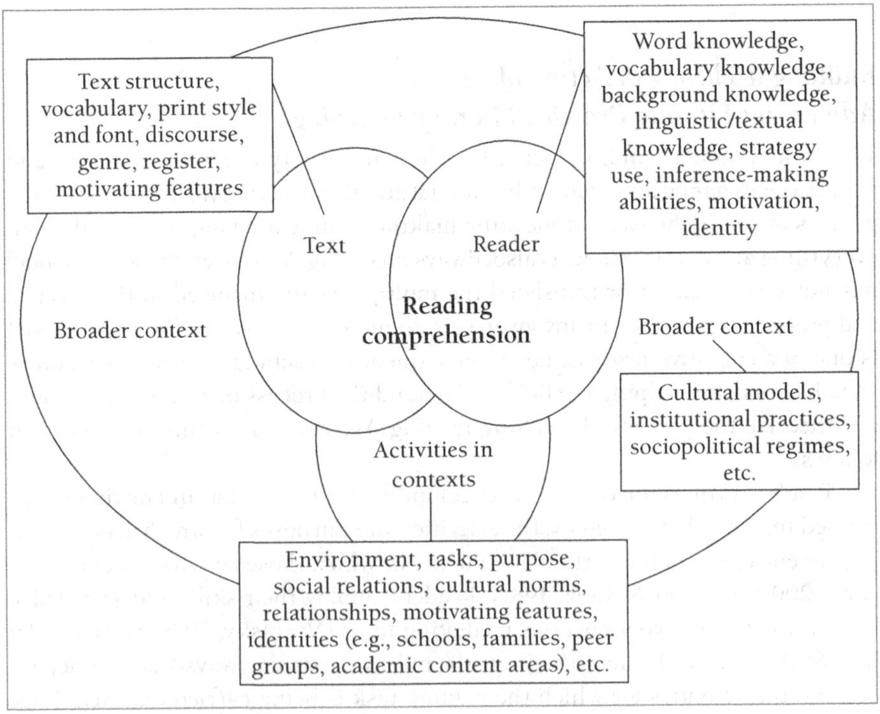

Even this representation, however, is inadequate, because the model represents the process of *one* reader's interactions with text and activity, all situated in dimensions represented as discrete examples of context. However, multiple readers inhabit classrooms and other learning spaces, and multiple dimensions of context are in play and overlap, inform, and contest one another in any given literacy event. Moreover, readers bring contexts into spaces based on their different histories of participation in other contexts. Finally, those various contexts that are both actively present in classrooms and brought into classrooms as students' histories of participation can intersect in powerful ways. For example, consider that the experience of reading an article from *Science* on genetic therapies would be experienced differently by a student who loves to read anything related to life sciences, reads regularly with parents, and works in a hospital part time and whose family medical history includes a genetically transmitted disorder. That student brings contextual knowledge based on histories of participation to the act of reading the *Science* passage. Now consider how the context of the classroom itself might interact with those varied contextual histories of the student by imagining the difference between a context in which the *Science* article is read as preparation for a debate on a controversial gene therapy and prior to a visit from a geneticist at a nearby university. That in-classroom context would set up a very different reading experience from that of a context in which the students are assigned the article to read and asked to simply write individual summaries to be submitted the next day in class. Although that student might possess the agency to extract necessary information from the article as a result of her various histories and passions, she is likely to make very different meanings from the two different reading interactions. That same student's reading experiences would also be shaped by the particular text on genetic therapies (e.g., the difference between the text of a *Science* article and one from a 10-line textbook callout designed to engage and interest grade 9 readers who have a Lexile level of 1200).

Finally, the reader's experiences would be mediated by the purpose for and activity in which they were reading any given text, whether the *Science* article or the textbook callout. Additionally, that purpose could shift not only from day to day but also from hour to hour. Students preparing for mandated state tests or college entrance examinations during one part of the school year might engage with classroom literacy experiences differently from the way they engage when the test pressure is diminished. Students might read a piece on gene therapy in a particular way if they heard a news report on the ethics of gene therapy on the way to school that morning. Students might read an article on gene therapy, or any other subject, in yet again a different way if they had a fight with a friend just before entering the classroom.

Finally, the same individual student might read the *Science* article on gene therapy differently in science class from the way she reads it in language arts or civics class, in part because the student may recognize the disciplinary or classroom differences at work; in part because the teacher may make different reading purposes or have developed different activities (e.g., a debate on the ethics of gene therapy vs. a follow-up laboratory activity on genetic mutations). Moje et al. (2004) attempted to link these two ideas together with a model of skilled content literacy practice, as illustrated in Figure 3.

Although this model attempts to signal the critical nature of disciplinary knowledge and the role of contexts and activity systems outside of school (via Moll, Veléz-Ibañéz, & Greenberg's, 1989, terminology of funds of knowledge), it falls short of providing a theory *in* or *of* action because it remains a static representation of a single reader's process. It cannot model the enactment of content literacy teaching practice, only what is happening as a single reader engages with a single text in a single classroom activity embedded in a nebulously identified context.

This kind of dynamic difference is certainly hinted at in the model, but the complexity of those various possible interactions is implicit and depends on the interpreter of the model having either extensive teaching experience or expertise

Figure 3. Skilled Content Literacy: A Model

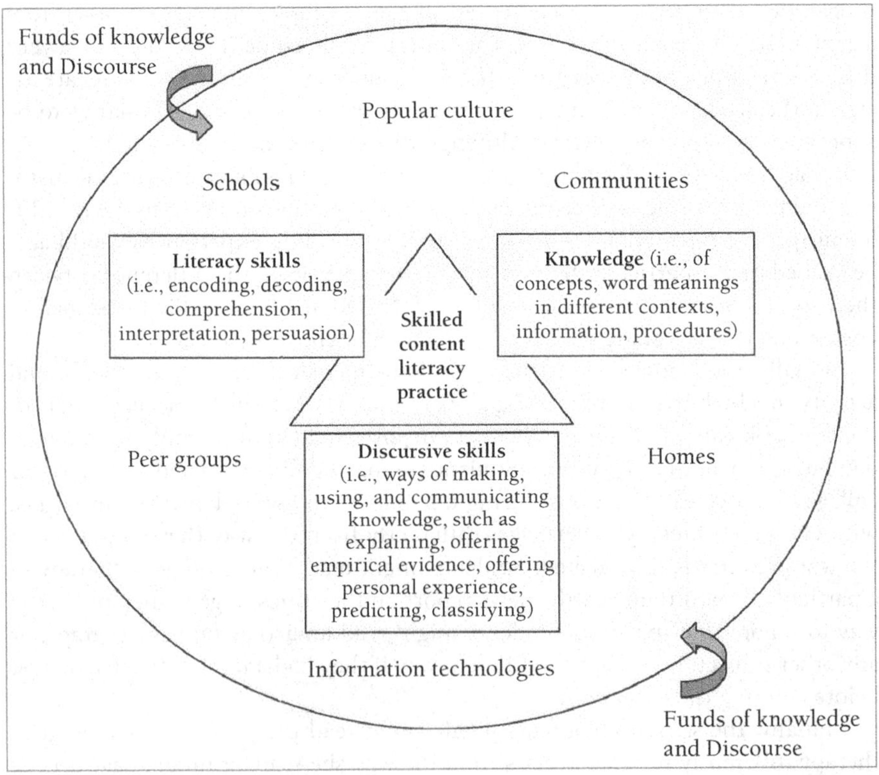

Note. Reprinted from "Working Toward Third Space in Content Area Literacy: An Examination of Everyday Funds of Knowledge and Discourse," by E.B. Moje, K.M. Ciechanowski, K.E. Kramer, L.M. Ellis, R. Carrillo, and T. Collazo, 2004, *Reading Research Quarterly*, 39(1), p. 46. Copyright © 2004 by the International Reading Association.

in reading research and theory. Moreover, the model is not adequate to the task of representing or theorizing the experience of even a single secondary student, who moves through all of those spaces in a given day. Specifically, the experience of secondary school students could be conceptualized as one of navigating (Moje, in press) different learning spaces as they move across the school day. These learning spaces are circumscribed by multiple differences in both physical and social spaces, including subject area/discipline, learning goals, teacher qualities, physical location of the classroom, student–student relationships, and time of day. Successful students appear to navigate these spaces with relative ease, picking up on cues regarding the literacy practices (among other social practices) necessary to be successful in each space, whereas less successful students appear to struggle to adapt their literacy and other social practices to the requirements of the space. These navigational acts require not only the ability to move across and integrate (or distill) the many different subject area classroom demands (which are more or less informed by disciplinary practices, depending on the teacher) but also the integration or distillation of the many contexts, activity systems, and activities of everyday life (see Figure 4).

The model in Figure 4 may be useful in indexing the contexts at play in adolescent literacy practice and reading comprehension and also in terms of

Figure 4. A Navigating Model of Secondary School Literacy

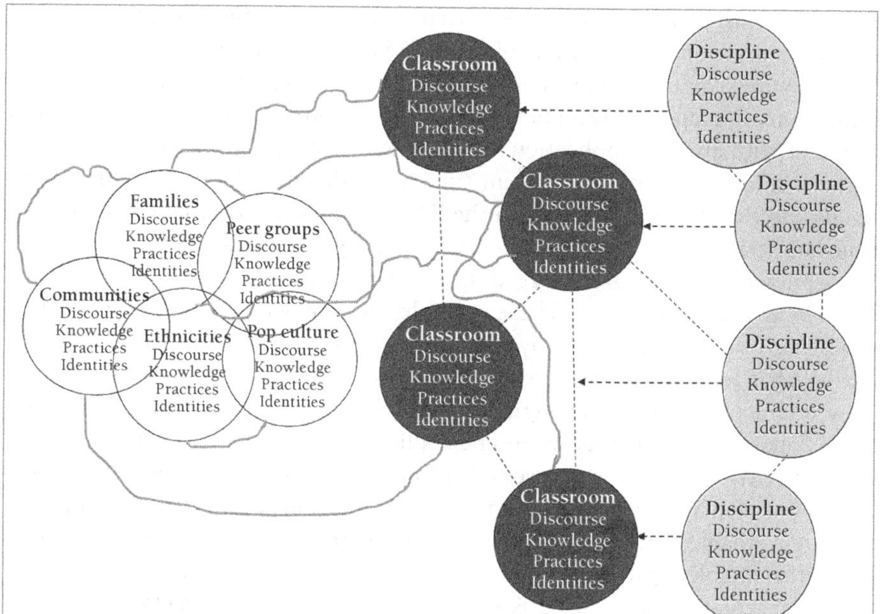

Note. Reprinted from *Developing Disciplinary Discourses and Identities: What's Knowledge Got to Do With It?* by E.B. Moje, April 2008, paper presented at the Conference on Discourse, Identity, and Educational Practices, Universidad Autónoma de Baja California, Ensenada, Mexico.

understanding the navigating acts that secondary school students must engage in, but it does not necessarily make a tight connection to the RTAC model. One is a model of the navigating work of a student, a representation of social practice; the other is a model of the act of reading comprehension of a student, a cognitive process. Each hints at the other, but neither makes clear the relationship between the social practices of a student navigating multiple everyday and school contexts and the cognitive processes of reading comprehension. Additionally, both models leave out the role of the teacher. We need to develop a model that integrates these aspects of reading comprehension and, more to the point of adolescent literacy teaching, of how to teach literate practice across a range of domains. Whatever new model we develop needs also to move past the linearity of relationship and activity represented in these past models.

Indeed, all the one-dimension models (i.e., flat drawings on paper) that we consulted or constructed fell short of our goal of representing a dynamic theory in action because they were unable to capture the dynamic and multilayered/multiactor nature of adolescent reading processes and practices, let alone represent the complexity necessary to guide a theory of action for secondary school literacy teaching.

It may be more productive, then, to employ an analogy or metaphor as a way of theorizing a dynamic theory in action of adolescent literacy. What better metaphor for a 21st-century model than one drawn from the most recent advances in technology, the smartphone? In particular, we invoke the image of Apple's iPhone, whose interface makes a particularly useful metaphor for the dynamic nature of reading comprehension. Any one of the apps is present and available at all times. With a swipe of a finger, one enters the world of a particular application, whether music, e-mail, maps, or even phone calling. Each application has the potential to intersect with another application: The calendar feature allows the user to place a phone number on an appointment time, thus allowing the user to simply tap the link to the phone number when the iPhone's clock signals that the appointed time has arrived. The phone number can be easily downloaded into the contacts list. Contacts can be shared, tagged, liked, and even memorialized with a photo taken by the phone's camera. These multiple and interacting applications are like the many features that routinely connect, overlap, and at times, interfere with one another in young people's reading practice. Indeed, all systems are dynamically interacting and ever changing. Thus, what is especially compelling about the iPhone metaphor is that when one application is in focus, the other applications still exist, and users can access them simultaneously with other applications. Moreover, when one zeroes in on an icon, new tools, ideas, images, and information are available that we could not see on the original interface. Also compelling is the completely dynamic and interconnected nature of iPhone applications. This representation, when used as a model for envisioning the practice of literacy, helps push the way we think about the RTAC model because it provides a way to consider the multiple and intersecting variables in the operation of any dynamic system.

A question arises in employing this metaphor, however, when considering the way one changes applications on the iPhone. For those unfamiliar with it, to add an application, the user installs it with a click of a button (and a swipe of a credit card, as applicable) from the iTunes store or some other source. To delete the application, the user presses and holds the on/off button until the icons begin to wiggle and an X shows up in the corner of the icon. A simple tap of the X makes the icon disappear. What is the parallel in a model of reading comprehension? Is it possible to delete an aspect of reading practice? A more likely scenario is that the applications or variables in the reading comprehension/literate practice equation never disappear but that they do shift, change, or grow. They can certainly be updated, but rarely would the variables of literate practice simply disappear. Thus, the iPhone model of comprehension/literate practice has limitations in the sense that iPhone applications/variables are either present or absent rather than dynamically evolving.

The iPhone metaphor is a useful one for breaking free from one-dimensional modeling and allows for a representation that takes the ever-changing nature of the multiple variables of reading into account. Like the models that preceded it, however, this metaphor remains a representation of a single system and does not translate the representation into the work of a teacher who would be responsible for supporting students in navigating the different applications (texts, activities, and contexts). Thus, we turn to the second part of our theory and model-building work in this chapter: the task of building a theory of action for adolescent literacy teaching.

Building a Theory of Action for Adolescent Literacy Teaching

Although useful work for expanding a working model of adolescent literacy, reconceptualizing the RTAC model to more fully account for the cognitive processes and social practices involved in literate practice did not help translate what we know from the model into a model for teaching practice. One key principle is critical to crafting a model of adolescent literacy teaching: Everything changes. Reading and literate practice are dynamic and relational, and the dynamism is magnified in secondary school settings where young people move from space to space, relationship to relationship, and across multiple knowledge/practice domains. People change, conditions of reading and learning change, activities change, and activity systems change.

To ground these points in the empirical world, recall the example of the adolescent reader of the *Science* article on genetic therapies from the previous section. Imagine adding a second student to the adolescent literacy model, in this case, one who loves to read about the life sciences but has little background or personal motivation and whose previous biology teachers taught biology as a lecture with no assigned print text reading of any kind. The student's meaning making of the article would be shaped in particular and very different ways even before knowing what the teacher expected him to do with the text in the classroom.

The translational challenge to the RTAC model is that those two types of readers featured are two among an average of 30 (or more) in a typical secondary school classroom. Each of those readers draws from histories of participation in communities, families, ethnic groups, popular cultures, and peer groups to bring knowledge, identities, and discursive and literacy skills into a given classroom. Additionally, the classroom is likely to be one among five or six class periods a teacher attends every day. Moreover, the social relationships of those two students, and of all 30 students and their one teacher (who rightly remains invisible in the RTAC model because it is a model of comprehension or learning, not a model of teaching), will also mediate the ways the students and the teacher engage in the activity, the purposes for which they read, and the sense they make of the texts they are given or choose to read. These complexities are not represented in any way in the RTAC model or the variants we have considered. Finally, when considering the larger picture of secondary school reading or literacy development, all of this is further complicated by the fact that those 30 students are one set of many that every subject area teacher called to be a teacher of reading will see each day while trying to ensure that he or she meets all the subject area content standards demanded in state and national guidelines. In sum, the RTAC model, although exceedingly useful for thinking about a moment of reading process for one person situated in one context, is not as useful for translational research that seeks to encourage every teacher to be a teacher of reading (while also teaching mathematics, natural sciences, literature, social sciences, art, music, physical education, or world languages) because the model is focused on comprehension instead of on *teaching* comprehension, discipline-specific comprehension, or the broader set of literacy practices one must master to navigate the complex worlds of schooling and everyday life, and of the life of a working citizen beyond the school years, including family, work, citizenship, and leisure.

A translational model for adolescent literacy teaching, then, needs to recognize the dynamic nature of the RTAC model and apply the singular RTAC model to a site in which hundreds of readers come together in multiple spaces with varied goals and purposes to read an enormous number of texts over roughly 180 days every year. The tentative—and messy—model offered in Figure 5 represents our first step at a one-dimensional treatment of the model.

In this model, we have tried to show, within the confines of the print page, the complexity of teaching literate practice when multiple young people (represented by the smallest circles) bring histories of participation in varied contexts (only loosely represented by phrases such as *popular culture* or *ethnicities*) into classroom spaces. Each youth brings a slightly different variation of these discourse communities, which further complicates the matter. These youths walk into classrooms with teachers who craft their own discursive practices, disciplinary and world knowledge, and identities together with the discourses of teaching, the discipline, and of schooling. Additionally, each different subject area is informed or shaped by a different discipline with its own traditions. Some are more aligned with classroom practice than are others (and the alignment can vary

Figure 5. A Model of Adolescent Literacy Teaching

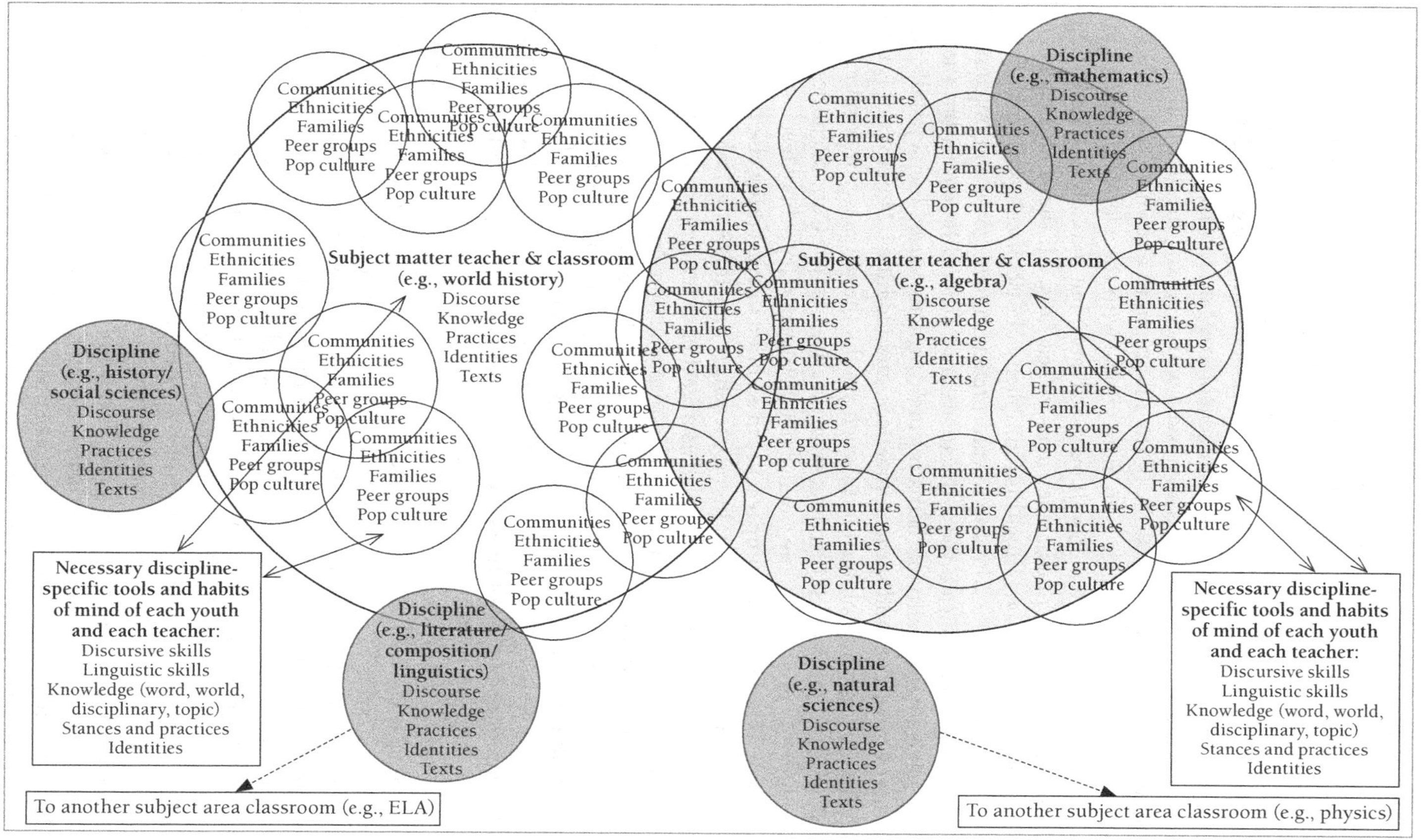

by particular school context or teacher knowledge/background). Thus, we have placed the circles that represent the disciplines in different places relative to the classroom circles. Some disciplines sit more on the fringes of classroom practice, whereas others are more central to the classrooms, depending on the kind of disciplinary knowledge and practice teachers bring to their teaching, the level of the subject, the timing and structures of the school day (e.g., block scheduling vs. shorter periods), and the views of the school in regard to what counts as valid pedagogical practice. The teachers are tasked with teaching the discursive practices, knowledge, and linguistic skills of the discipline to anywhere from 100 to 180 students a year, a task made even more critical with the adoption of the Common Core State Standards, which will make valuable, but in many cases only vaguely defined, disciplinary practice demands on teachers. All the while, teachers, like their students, are navigating this multiplicity of discourses, practices, identities, and knowledge while working toward predetermined goals and outcomes. Not only must they navigate these discursive and other differences, but they must also navigate the reality of their students' distinctly varied literacy skills, subject matter knowledge, and stances, practices, and identities. Moreover, it is the subject matter teacher's obligation to teach youths the necessary discipline-specific knowledge, linguistic skills, discursive practices, stances, and identities signaled in Figure 5's boxes. Is it any wonder that few secondary school teachers are eager to take on the label of reading teacher in addition to everything else they must do?

This model of adolescent literacy teaching may make the task of encouraging every teacher to see him- or herself as a teacher of reading seem hopeless, but we see the model as opening a space for informed action. No longer should policy be aimed solely at fixing a reader who measures below grade level on a single assessment, because the model of disciplinary literacy teaching represented in Figure 5, which draws from and extends the RTAC and other models of comprehension we have reviewed, makes clear that far more than skill shapes the demonstration of comprehension or of literate practice writ large. No longer should secondary school teachers be asked to teach reading in any generic way, because the model situates reading inside particular disciplinary discourses, practices, knowledge domains, texts, and tools. No longer should teachers be expected to do this work armed with sets of cognitive strategies alone, because the model clarifies the role of multiple social practices in the work of teaching and the various discourse communities and funds of knowledge youths bring into secondary school subject matter classrooms. In short, no longer should teachers be asked to be teachers of reading in simple terms, because the model makes clear that there is nothing simple about this work. The development of discipline-specific literacy practices, habits of mind, and skills needs to be situated not just in what one reader brings to one act of reading in one moment in time and in one classroom but also in the multiplicity of a reader's experience. The act of teaching literate practice to adolescents at the secondary level, then, is as much about teaching youths to navigate the texts, discourses, identities, and knowledge of different subject areas, classrooms, and relationships (see Moje, in press) as it is about teaching word-level skills, discipline-specific vocabulary, or even disciplinary habits of mind. This kind of teaching requires that teachers name discourse and practice in explicit ways (e.g., Bain, 2008; Lee, 2007; Warren, Ballenger, Ogonowski, Rosebery, & Hudicourt-Barnes, 2001; Wineburg & Martin, 2004), make visible how language functions to accomplish certain purposes (e.g., Coffin, 2004, 2006; Schleppegrell, Achugar, & Oteíza, 2004), and engage youths in practicing reading, writing, and speaking in the ways valued in the discipline (e.g., Lee & Spratley, 2006; Lemke, 1990; Moje, 2007, 2008b; Moje & Speyer, 2008). This kind of teaching requires that teachers begin such work with a recognition of many different histories of participation and the discourses and knowledge accompanying them that even one student may bring to a classroom, and to surface and discuss those discourses across the different students. The model we propose makes clear that a key next step in these efforts is to bring together the various interventions cited here (and many more like them) into a unified set of practices that guide teachers' practices across and within disciplines. The model also demands that both researchers and policymakers take seriously the challenges of doing this work and call a halt to simplistic policy initiatives that demand practices from teachers without providing the resources of planning and teaching time, as well as sustained professional learning opportunities to support their learning to be teachers of literacy in their separate disciplines.

For some, the lack of a linear pathway in our model will call into question whether we have indeed outlined a theory of action. We argue that what we have outlined is a theory of action for a process in action. Reading is among the most complex of human processes, situated in myriad human practices. No simple, linear model will explain it, and no simple, linear model will successfully guide its teaching. Standards can help, but only if the standards make a space for the complexity of literate practice and the even greater complexity involved in teaching literacy to many different people at the same time. This kind of teaching is difficult. It is even more difficult to assess. Additionally, it is among the most essential of human endeavors. In point of fact, the International Reading Association (2012b) issued a press release (as we sat at our computers revising this last paragraph) stating that it had developed a set of guidelines for the purpose of clarifying misperceptions and possible misapplications of the English Language Arts Common Core State Standards. The guidelines (International Reading Association Common Core State Standards Committee, 2012c) state explicitly that disciplinary literacy calls for more than teaching reading and writing across the curriculum: "Disciplinary literacy focuses on the specialized ways that reading, writing, and language are used within each discipline and attempts to introduce students to these specialized ways of thinking, problem-solving, and communication" (pp. 3–4). In the end, every teacher *is* a teacher of reading, but settling on what that discourse looks like is no simple matter; nor will it be accomplished in the same way, using the same steps, in different disciplines by different teachers interacting with different students in different classroom contexts having different social structures.

QUESTIONS FOR REFLECTION

1. In what ways do perceived crises in adolescent literacy instruction relate to the discourse of every teacher a teacher of reading? Provide at least two examples.
2. Why has this discourse survived for nearly a century despite limited implementation among secondary subject area teachers?
3. How would a teacher's adoption of either an autonomous or an ideological approach to adolescent literacy instruction contribute to what an observer would see (or not see) during instruction in a middle or high school classroom?
4. Why is the RTAC model of reading comprehension inadequate to the task of adolescent literacy instruction?
5. In your own words, how would you explain Figure 5 in terms of building a theory of action for adolescent literacy teaching?

REFERENCES

ACT. (2010). *A first look at the Common Core and college and career readiness.* Iowa City, IA: Author. Retrieved November 6, 2012, from www.act.org/research/policymakers/reports/firstlook.html

ACT. (2011). *The condition of college and career readiness.* Iowa City, IA: Author. Retrieved November 6, 2012, from www.act.org/research/policymakers/cccr11/pdf/ConditionofCollegeandCareerReadiness2011.pdf

Alexander, P.A. (2003). Profiling the developing reader: The interplay of knowledge, interest, and strategic processing. In C.M. Fairbanks, J. Worthy, B. Maloch, J.V. Hoffman, & D.L. Schallert (Eds.), *The 52nd yearbook of the National Reading Conference* (pp. 47–65). Oak Creek, WI: National Reading Conference.

Alexander, P.A., & Jetton, T.L. (2000). Learning from text: A multidimensional and developmental perspective. In M.L. Kamil, P.B. Mosenthal, P.D. Pearson, & R. Barr (Eds.), *Handbook of reading research* (Vol. 3, pp. 285–310). Mahwah, NJ: Erlbaum.

Alvermann, D.E. (2009). Sociocultural constructions of adolescence and young people's literacies. In L. Christenbury, R. Bomer, & P. Smagorinsky (Eds.), *Handbook of adolescent literacy research* (pp. 14–28). New York: Guilford.

Alvermann, D.E. (2010). The teaching of reading. In E. Lindemann (Ed.), *Reading the past, writing the future: A century of American literacy education and the National Council of Teachers of English* (pp. 55–90). Urbana, IL: National Council of Teachers of English.

Alvermann, D.E., Fitzgerald, J., & Simpson, M. (2006). Teaching and learning in reading. In P.A. Alexander & P.H. Winne (Eds.), *Handbook of educational psychology* (2nd ed., pp. 427–455). Mahwah, NJ: Erlbaum.

Alvermann, D., Friese, E., Beckmann, S., & Rezak, A. (2011). Content area reading pedagogy and domain knowledge: A Bourdieusian analysis. *Australian Educational Researcher, 38*(2), 203–220. doi:10.1007/s13384-011-0024-x

Alvermann, D.E., & Moore, D.W. (1991). Secondary reading. In R. Barr, M.L. Kamil, P. Mosenthal, & P.D. Pearson (Eds.), *Handbook of reading research* (Vol. 2, pp. 951–983). White Plains, NY: Longman.

Alvermann, D.E., Rezak, A.T., Mallozzi, C.A., Boatright, M.D., & Jackson, D.F. (2011). Reflective practice in an online literacy course: Lessons learned from attempts to fuse reading and science instruction. *Teachers College Record, 113*(1), 27–56.

Anders, P.L., Hoffman, J.V., & Duffy, G.G. (2000). Teaching teachers to teach reading: Paradigm shifts, persistent problems, and challenges. In M.L. Kamil, P.B. Mosenthal, P.D. Pearson, & R. Barr (Eds.), *Handbook of reading research* (Vol. 3, pp. 719–742). Mahwah, NJ: Erlbaum.

Bain, R.B. (2008). Into the breach: Using research and theory to shape history instruction. *Journal of Education, 189*(1/2), 159–168.

Barton, D. (2000). Researching literacy practices: Learning from activities with teachers and students. In D. Barton, M. Hamilton, & R. Ivanič

(Eds.), *Situated literacies: Reading and writing in context* (pp. 167–179). New York: Routledge.

Bean, T.W. (2000). Reading in the content areas: Social constructivist dimensions. In M.L. Kamil, P.B. Mosenthal, P.D. Pearson, & R. Barr (Eds.), *Handbook of reading research* (Vol. 3, pp. 629–644). Mahwah, NJ: Erlbaum.

Biancarosa, C., & Snow, C.E. (2004). *Reading next—a vision for action and research in middle and high school literacy: A report to Carnegie Corporation of New York*. Washington, DC: Alliance for Excellent Education.

Biancarosa, G., & Snow, C.E. (2006). *Reading next—a vision for action and research in middle and high school literacy: A report to Carnegie Corporation of New York* (2nd ed.). Washington, DC: Alliance for Excellent Education. Retrieved November 6, 2012, from www.all4ed.org/publication_material/reports/reading_next

Bové, P.A. (1995). Discourse. In F. Lentricchia & T. McLaughlin (Eds.), *Critical terms for literary study* (2nd ed., pp. 50–65). Chicago: University of Chicago Press.

Coffin, C. (2004). Learning to write history: The role of causality. *Written Communication, 21*(3), 261–289. doi:10.1177/0741088304265476

Coffin, C. (2006). Learning the language of school history: The role of linguistics in mapping the writing demands of the secondary school curriculum. *Journal of Curriculum Studies, 38*(4), 413–429. doi:10.1080/00220270500508810

Dillon, D.R., O'Brien, D.G., Sato, M., & Kelly, C.M. (2011). Professional development and teacher education for reading instruction. In M.L. Kamil, P.D. Pearson, E.B. Moje, & P.P. Afflerbach (Eds.), *Handbook of reading research* (Vol. 4, pp. 629–660). New York: Routledge.

Draper, R.J. (2008). Redefining content-area literacy teacher education: Finding my voice through collaboration. *Harvard Educational Review, 78*(1), 60–83.

Foucault, M. (1980). Power/knowledge: Selected interviews and other writings, 1972–1977 (C. Gordon, Ed.; L. Marshall, J. Mepham, & K. Soper, Trans.). New York: Pantheon. (Original work published 1976)

Foucault, M. (1988). *Politics, philosophy, culture: Interviews and other writings, 1977–1984* (L.D. Kritzman, Ed.; A. Sheridan, Trans.). New York: Routledge. (Original interview published 1984)

Foucault, M. (1998). Nietzsche, genealogy, history (R. Hurley, Trans.). In J.D. Faubion (Ed.), *Aesthetics, method, and epistemology* (Vol. 2, pp. 369–391). New York: New. (Reprinted from *Hommage à Jean Hyppolite*, pp. 145–172, D.F. Brouchard & S. Simon, Trans., 1971, Paris: Presses Universitaires de France)

Garbe, C., Holle, K., & Weinhold, S. (Eds.). (2010). *ADORE: Teaching struggling adolescent readers in European countries*. New York: Peter Lang.

Gaskins, I.W. (2003). Taking charge of reader, text, activity, and context variables. In A.P. Sweet & C.E. Snow (Eds.), *Rethinking reading comprehension* (pp. 141–165). New York: Guilford.

Gee, J.P. (1988). The legacies of literacy: From Plato to Freire through Harvey Graff. *Harvard Educational Review, 58*(2), 195–212.

Gee, J.P. (1999). *An introduction to Discourse analysis: Theory and method*. New York: Routledge.

Gray, W.S. (1925). A modern program of reading instruction for the grades and for the high school. In G.M. Whipple (Ed.), *24th yearbook of the National Society for the Study of Education: Part 1. Report of the National Committee on Reading* (pp. 21–73). Bloomington, IL: Public School.

Green, B., Reid, J.-A., & Bigum, C. (1998). Teaching the Nintendo generation? Children, computer culture and popular technologies. In S. Howard (Ed.), *Wired-up: Young people and the electronic media* (pp. 18–40). London: UCL Press.

Hagood, M.C., Stevens, L.P., & Reinking, D. (2002). What do THEY have to teach US? Talkin' 'cross generations! In D.E. Alvermann (Ed.), *Adolescents and literacies in a digital world* (pp. 68–83). New York: Peter Lang.

Hartman, D.K., Morsink, P.M., & Zheng, J. (2010). From print to pixels: The evolution of cognitive conceptions of reading comprehension. In E.A. Baker (Ed.), *The new literacies: Multiple perspectives on research and practice* (pp. 131–164). New York: Guilford.

Heath, S.B. (1983). *Ways with words: Language, life, and work in communities and classrooms*. New York: Cambridge University Press.

Herber, H.L. (1970). *Teaching reading in content areas*. Englewood Cliffs, NJ: Prentice-Hall.

Herber, H.L. (1978). *Teaching reading in content areas* (2nd ed.). Englewood Cliffs, NJ: Prentice-Hall.

Huey, E.B. (1908). *The psychology and pedagogy of reading*. New York: Macmillan.

International Reading Association. (2012a). *Adolescent literacy* [Position statement] (Rev. 2012 ed.). Newark, DE: Author.

International Reading Association. (2012b). *Literacy implementation guidance for the ELA Common Core State Standards* [Press release]. Retrieved November 6, 2012, from www.reading.org/general/AboutIRA/white-papers/ela-common-core-standards.aspx

International Reading Association Common Core State Standards Committee. (2012c). *Literacy implementation guidance for the ELA Common Core State Standards* [White paper]. Retrieved November 6, 2012, from www.reading.org/Libraries/association-documents/ira_ccss_guidelines.pdf

Kamil, M.L., Mosenthal, P.B., Pearson P.D., & Barr, R. (Eds.). (2000). *Handbook of reading research* (Vol. 3). Mahwah, NJ: Erlbaum.

Lapp, D., Guthrie, L.A., & Flood, J. (2007). Ruth May Strang (1895–1971): The legacy of a reading sage. In S.E. Israel & E.J. Monaghan (Eds.), *Shaping the reading field* (pp. 347–373). Newark, DE: International Reading Association.

Lee, C.D. (2007). *Culture, literacy, and learning: Taking bloom in the midst of the whirlwind*. New York: Teachers College Press.
Lee, C.D., & Spratley, A. (2006). *Reading in the disciplines: The challenges of adolescent literacy*. New York: Carnegie Corporation of New York.
Lemke, J.L. (1990). *Talking science: Language, learning, and values*. Norwood, NJ: Ablex.
Lesko, N. (2001). *Act your age! A cultural construction of adolescence*. New York: RoutledgeFalmer.
Marsh, J.P., Lammers, J.C., & Alvermann, D.E. (2012). Quality assurance in online content literacy methods courses. *Literacy Research and Instruction, 51*(3), 233–253. doi:10.1080/19388071.2011.568670
Moje, E.B. (2007). Developing socially just subject-matter instruction: A review of the literature on disciplinary literacy teaching. In G.J. Kelly, A. Luke, & J. Green (Eds.), *Review of research in education* (Vol. 31, pp. 1–44). Washington, DC: American Educational Research Association. doi:10.3102/0091732X07300046
Moje, E.B. (2008a, April). *Developing disciplinary discourses and identities: What's knowledge got to do with it?* Paper presented at the Conference on Discourse, Identity, and Educational Practices, Universidad Autónoma de Baja California, Ensenada, Mexico.
Moje, E.B. (2008b). Foregrounding the disciplines in secondary literacy teaching and learning: A call for change. *Journal of Adolescent & Adult Literacy, 52*(2), 96–107. doi:10.1598/JAAL.52.2.1
Moje, E.B. (in press). Hybrid literacies in a post-hybrid world: Making a case for navigating. In K. Hall, T. Cremin, B. Comber, & L.C. Moll (Eds.), *International handbook of research on children's literacy, learning and culture*. Oxford, UK: Wiley-Blackwell.
Moje, E.B., Ciechanowski, K.M., Kramer, K.E., Ellis, L.M., Carrillo, R., & Collazo, T. (2004). Working toward third space in content area literacy: An examination of everyday funds of knowledge and discourse. *Reading Research Quarterly, 39*(1), 38–70. doi:10.1598/RRQ.39.1.4
Moje, E.B., Dillon, D.R., & O'Brien, D.G. (2000). Reexamining roles of learner, text, and context in secondary literacy. *The Journal of Educational Research, 93*(3), 165–180. doi:10.1080/00220670009598705
Moje, E.B., & Speyer, J. (2008). The reality of challenging texts in high school science and social studies: How teachers can mediate comprehension. In K.A. Hinchman & H.K. Sheridan-Thomas (Eds.), *Best practices in adolescent literacy instruction* (pp. 185–211). New York: Guilford.
Moll, L.C., Veléz-Ibañéz, C., & Greenberg, J. (1989). *Year one progress report: Community knowledge and classroom practice: Combining resources for literacy instruction*. Tucson: University of Arizona.
Moore, D.W. (1996). Contexts for literacy in secondary schools. In D.J. Leu, C.K. Kinzer, & K.A. Hinchman (Eds.), *Literacies for the 21st century: Research and practice* (pp. 15–46). Chicago: National Reading Conference.
Moore, D.W., Readence, J.E., & Rickelman, R.J. (1983). An historical exploration of content area reading instruction. *Reading Research Quarterly, 18*(4), 419–438. doi:10.2307/747377
National Governors Association Center. (n.d.). *NGA Office of Federal Relations*. Retrieved November 6, 2012, from http://www.nga.org/cms/federalrelations
National Governors Association Center for Best Practices & Council of Chief State School Officers. (2010). *Common Core State Standards for English language arts and literacy in history/social studies, science, and technical subjects*. Washington, DC: Authors.
National Governors Association Center for Best Practices & Council of Chief State School Officers. (2012). *Myths vs. facts*. Retrieved November 7, 2012, from www.corestandards.org/about-the-standards/myths-vs-facts
National Institute of Child Health and Human Development. (2000). *Report of the National Reading Panel. Teaching children to read: An evidence-based assessment of the scientific research literature on reading and its implications for reading instruction* (NIH Publication No. 00-4769). Washington, DC: U.S. Government Printing Office.
O'Farrell, C. (2007). *Key concepts*. Retrieved November 7, 2012, from www.michel-foucault.com/concepts/index
Prado, C.G. (2000). *Starting with Foucault: An introduction to genealogy* (2nd ed.). Boulder, CO: Westview.
RAND Reading Study Group. (2002). *Reading for understanding: Toward an R&D program in reading comprehension*. Santa Monica, CA: RAND.
Ruddell, R.B., & Unrau, N.J. (1994). Reading as a meaning-construction process: The reader, the text, and the teacher. In R.B. Ruddell, M.R. Ruddell, & H. Singer (Eds.), *Theoretical models and processes of reading* (4th ed., pp. 996–1056). Newark, DE: International Reading Association.
Schleppegrell, M.J., Achugar, M., & Oteíza, T. (2004). The grammar of history: Enhancing content-based instruction through a functional focus on language. *TESOL Quarterly, 38*(1), 67–93. doi:10.2307/3588259
Scribner, S., & Cole, M. (1981). *The psychology of literacy*. Cambridge, MA: Harvard University Press.
Smith, N.B. (2002). *American reading instruction*. Newark, DE: International Reading Association. (Original work published 1934 by Silver Burdett)
Snow, C.E., & Biancarosa, G. (2003). *Adolescent literacy and the achievement gap: What do we know and where do we go from here?* New York: Carnegie Corporation of New York.
Street, B.V. (1984). *Literacy in theory and practice*. New York: Cambridge University Press.

Street, B.V. (1995). *Social literacies: Critical approaches to literacy in development, ethnography and education*. London: Longman.
U.S. Department of Education. (n.d.). *Striving Readers Comprehensive Literacy Program*. Retrieved November 6, 2012, from www2.ed.gov/programs/strivingreaders-literacy/awards.html#ppt
Vadeboncoeur, J.A., & Stevens, L.P. (Eds.). (2005). *Re/constructing "the adolescent": Sign, symbol, and body*. New York: Peter Lang.
Valencia, S.W., Pearson, P.D., & Wixson, K.K. (2011, February). *Assessing and tracking progress in reading comprehension: The search for keystone elements in college and career readiness*. Paper presented at the Invitational Research Symposium on Through-Course Summative Assessments, Center for K–12 Assessment and Performance Management at ETS, Atlanta, GA.
Vygotsky, L.S. (1978). *Mind in society: The development of higher psychological processes* (M. Cole, V. John-Steiner, S. Scribner, & E. Souberman, Eds. & Trans.). Cambridge, MA: Harvard University Press.
Vygotsky, L.S. (1986). Thought and language (Rev. ed.; A. Kozulin, Ed.). Cambridge, MA: MIT Press.
Warren, B., Ballenger, C., Ogonowski, M., Rosebery, A.S., & Hudicourt-Barnes, J. (2001). Rethinking diversity in learning science: The logic of everyday sense-making. *Journal of Research in Science Teaching, 38*(5), 529–552. doi:10.1002/tea.1017
Wertsch, J.V., del Río, P., & Alvarez, A. (1995). Sociocultural studies: History, action, and mediation. In J.V. Wertsch, P. del Río, & A. Alvarez (Eds.), *Sociocultural studies of mind* (pp. 1–34). New York: Cambridge University Press. doi:10.1017/CBO9781139174299.002
Wineburg, S.S., & Martin, D. (2004). Reading and rewriting history. *Educational Leadership, 62*(1), 42–45.

CHAPTER 40

Literacy Research in the 21st Century: From Paradigms to Pragmatism and Practicality

Deborah R. Dillon and David G. O'Brien, University of Minnesota

Elizabeth E. Heilman, Michigan State University

"Ideologies separate us. Dreams and anguish bring us together."

Eugène Ionesco, French (Romanian-born) Absurdist dramatist, 1909–1994

A little more than 10 years ago, we wrote an article for *Reading Research Quarterly* (Dillon, O'Brien, & Heilman, 2000), later reprinted in the fifth edition of the *Theoretical Models and Processes of Reading* (*TMPR*–5). In the article, we reviewed and reflected on what we had learned about the conduct of our inquiry in the field to consider future directions for literacy research. This chapter in *TMPR*–6 provides an opportunity to revisit and update this work. The foci of this new chapter are to (a) examine broadly how inquiry paradigms have been defined, (b) critique how paradigms are used in inquiry in literacy and to question their usefulness, (c) consider pragmatism as a perspective that may be more useful in helping us decide what we study and how we engage in inquiry, and (d) discuss the future of literacy inquiry.

Our current chapter is set within a new context of events that have occurred over the past 10 years. These events, associated primarily with political agendas resulting in new policy changes, have had profound implications for what research was conducted in the field, what findings were valued and taken up by researchers and policymakers, and the impact of the nature of both the research and policies on practices associated with K–12 students' learning. It is interesting to note that a caution we offered in 2000 about the danger of getting stuck in one paradigm did, in fact, play out during this time period. This "getting stuck" did not occur by choice, however, and many literacy researchers lived with the consequences of what happens when one research paradigm is valued over all others, particularly if these researchers need federal funding to engage in scholarship.

This chapter is adapted from "Literacy Research in the Next Millennium: From Paradigms to Pragmatism and Practicality," in *Theoretical Models and Processes of Reading* (5th ed., pp. 1530–1556), edited by R.B. Ruddell and N.J. Unrau, 2004, Newark, DE: International Reading Association.

To begin, research in the early 2000s was impacted by several pivotal events that shaped what inquiry would be valued and how it would be used to impact policy, research, and practices. A definition of scientific research was constructed to determine programs that could be used by the Reading Excellence Act (REA) of 1999 grant awardees. This action began a process in which policy shaped the educational services that could be funded under particular initiatives. In addition, the National Reading Panel (NRP) report, published in 2000 by the National Institute of Child Health and Human Development (NICHD), had a profound impact on what research was deemed worthy of including in a policy document that eventually had tremendous bearing on practice in U.S. schools, as well as having an impact on federally funded research projects that followed. That is because the panel of experts who compiled the report decided to include research that met particular parametric and statistical standards for validity and generalizability, leaving out a large body of scholarship—much of which was qualitative.

Shortly thereafter, federal education policies such as the No Child Left Behind (NCLB) Act of 2001 and the Education Sciences Reform Act (ESRA) of 2002 were published and used the term *scientifically based research*, promoting the following methods as exemplary: randomized controlled experiments for primary research studies, and meta-analyses as the standard for combing results and drawing conclusions across studies. It should be noted that the definitions of scientifically based research included in the reauthorization by the Office of Educational Research and Improvement (OERI; e.g., H.R. 4875 in 2000, H.R. 3801 in 2002, and ESRA in 2002) outlined the types of educational research that could be funded by the new Institute of Education Sciences (IES). Thus, these policies greatly affected the kinds of inquiry literacy researchers might undertake. In addition, during the George W. Bush presidency, several high-profile positions were awarded to individuals from positivist research perspectives (e.g., the director of the IES, and the chief of the Child Development and Behavior Branch within the NICHD at the National Institutes of Health). These appointments added to the already mounting concerns scholars were expressing about how particular agencies and individuals were crafting narrow definitions of scientific research in education. Before long, educational researchers were also faced with proposed legislation that would define the nature of rigorous scientific methods for conducting education research.

At this same moment, and in response to a request from the National Educational Research Policy and Priorities Board, a National Research Council (NRC) committee was commissioned in 2000 by the National Academy of Sciences. This group engaged in work resulting in the *Scientific Research in Education (SRE) Study* (NRC, 2002). The committee was given the charge to "'review and synthesize recent literature on the science and practice of scientific educational research and consider how to support high quality science in a federal education research agency'" (NRC, 2002, p. 1). The overall goal for this group of scholars and policymakers was to clarify the definition of scientific inquiry in education and speculate how the federal government could endorse and foster research that leads to evidence-based education policy and practice. The definition that emerged from the *SRE* report positioned research in education as akin to that in the sciences, noting that research

> is a continual process of rigorous reasoning supported by a dynamic interplay among methods, theories, and findings...[that] builds understandings in the form of models or theories that can be tested...[and] progresses as a result of a not-so-invisible hand of professional skepticism and criticism. (p. 2)

The definition goes on to state that "multiple methods, applied over time and tied to evidentiary standards, are essential to establishing a base of scientific knowledge..." (p. 2). Six guiding principles were posited as forming a foundation for all scientific inquiry:

1. "Pose significant questions that can be investigated empirically"
2. "Link research to relevant theory"
3. "Use methods that permit direct investigation of the question"
4. "Provide a coherent and explicit chain of reasoning"
5. "Replicate and generalize across studies"
6. "Disclose research to encourage professional scrutiny and critique" (pp. 3–5)

The report's authors acknowledged that the field of education is challenging to study because it has multiple layers, is always changing, is highly value laden, involves a number of people from different walks of life, and requires "attention to the physical, social, cultural, economic, and historical environments in the research process because these contextual factors often influence results in significant ways" (p. 5). The authors stated an important idea that

> the design of a study does not make the study scientific. A wide variety of legitimate scientific designs are available for education research. They range from randomized experiments of voucher programs to in-depth ethnographic case studies of teachers to neurocognitive investigations of number learning using positive emission tomography brain imaging. (p. 6)

The authors' goal was not to provide the federal government with a definition of what constitutes scientific research on education, but rather to provide six design principles to foster a "scientific culture" within the agency (e.g., design principle #3: "Insulate the agency from inappropriate political interference," p. 8).

Despite the reasonable ideas expressed in the report and the numerous and insightful critiques written in response to the call for a *scientific culture* as an alternative to the hard-and-fast narrow definition of research created by other reports and policy brokers (see the November 2002 issue of *Educational Researcher*), in January 2002, right after the *SRE* report was released, NCLB was passed into law. NCLB included a definition of scientifically based research that privileged testing hypotheses and using experimental and quasi-experimental designs only, including a preference for random assignment. This definition also specified what would count as evidence to justify the use of federal program dollars. However, it was stated as a restriction to the *programs* used within research initiatives (e.g., Reading First), not the *kinds* of educational research that might be funded by the federal government. Nonetheless, the research questions and proposals taken up by funding agencies narrowed, and particular research paradigms were embraced while others were rejected. One indicator of the types of studies and the resulting claims that would be honored at the federal level came in the form of the What Works Clearinghouse (WWC), an entity that was the result of a five-year $18.5 million contract with the OERI. The charge of the WWC site was to

> assess and report evidence with respect to what works in education in multiple topic areas. More specifically, it will provide easily accessible and searchable online databases that characterize the strength and nature of scientific evidence on the effectiveness of different educational programs, products, and practices (labeled interventions) claimed to enhance important student outcomes. Claims of effectiveness will be assessed with respect to the quantity, quality, and relevance of evidence, and the magnitude of effects, as determined through reviews of research. (www2.ed.gov/about/offices/list/os/technology/evaluation.html, para. 4)

The implicit message was that educational research outside of this narrow band, often referred to as the "gold standard," would not be funded, and the results would not be taken up by practitioners who were guided to the WWC site. In time, the voices of educational researchers created changes in the WWC criteria for reviewing and accessing the research that could be included to support particular programs and materials reviewed on the website.

Despite some movement toward a broader set of criteria for assessing research, Eisenhart and Towne (2003) noted that many researchers were "deeply troubled by the prominence of experimental designs and the positivist epistemology that sometimes underlies them" (p. 31), and other researchers worried that critiques of positivism would be ignored and that other ways of knowing (e.g., philosophical, historical, cultural, affective, postmodern, practice-oriented) would be rejected by funding agencies. Literacy researchers were among the most vocal critics in this educational policy arena, primarily based on their experiences in seeking REA and Reading First grants, their concerns over the NRP report and its impact on the field, and their frustration with the narrow range of literacy studies funded by IES grant monies. But many literacy researchers who did not pursue large grants to fund their research watched what occurred and maintained a low profile, often plugging away on topics of interest to themselves and/or problems of practice within local university and school and community settings.

We reviewed the critical influence of politics, policies, and funding on educational research over the past 10 years because it sets the stage for revisiting our ideas about the types of research literacy scholars are engaged in, the theoretical frameworks they use, and the role pragmatism plays in the milieu. For example, we observed an increase in experimental and quasi-experimental research published in literacy journals, and there have been more qualitative–quantitative mixed design studies and formative or design-based papers published. That said, multiple genres of qualitative research studies still enjoy a prominent role in literacy journals and books.

We also contend that since our original article was published in 2000, there are still three types of literacy scholars: career driven, project driven, and ethics driven. To recap: The first group tries to anticipate the newest research topic, methodology, and paradigm. These individuals look intently ahead with less attention to historical grounding for a simple reason: In higher education, where most of the research is supported and conducted, researchers are rewarded for carving out new directions, generating articles and grant proposals, and positioning themselves as leaders in the field. The second group of researchers achieves credibility and enjoys career-long success by introducing a single groundbreaking idea, mapping out a portion of some new territory, or working consistently on a set of problems within a given paradigm over time. The third group of scholars is motivated by a position or an issue and is philosophically and ethically driven to find an answer. These researchers focus on collaboratively identifying a problem with participants in a community and working together over time to generate theories and explanations that can be used in local settings. Researchers in all three groups have generated valuable literacy research findings. Nevertheless, debates still exist that challenge the credibility of various paradigms (e.g., quantitative vs. qualitative, cognitive vs. socially constructed) in which research questions have been grounded, and critique the appropriateness of questions posed for inquiry as well as the impact of inquiry on practice.

Paradigms and Inquiry

In this chapter, we posit that the political affiliation with paradigms and the continued preoccupation with debates have resulted in literacy research that has made less difference than it could in practice. We offer pragmatism, and the discourse from which it is constructed, as an attractive alternative—one that has been around for many years. The field of literacy, like the broader field of education, has begun to draw upon pragmatism but has not fully embraced it as a common approach to literacy research. This is due in part to the fact that some researchers do not have a strong knowledge base in this tradition, while others have characterized pragmatists as individuals who fail to take a firm stance one way or the other on a given issue. However, some approaches to research, such as action research and teacher self-study, are intrinsically pragmatic because they focus on locally created questions and knowledge that is actionable and meaningful in specific contexts. And many forms of research can potentially be employed with a pragmatic approach because the defining characteristic is not on the paradigms, theories, or methodologies through which research is conducted, but rather on why research is conducted, who asks research questions, and what research creates as praxis. As Juuti and Lavonen (2006) described, pragmatism creates research that is *for* education rather than research *about* education. Through the lens of pragmatism, knowledge and "research results" are simply that which is used and thoughtfully understood to be useful to real people in real contexts.

In the next section, we define paradigms and critique their usefulness in literacy inquiry. The following questions organize our discussion: What are paradigms? What do paradigms mean to inquiry in literacy? Has the multiplicity of paradigms we draw from helped or hindered our inquiry? What paradigms could make a difference in our inquiry, and why? Following this discussion, we present information about pragmatism and why we value it as an alternative to paradigmatic perspectives.

Paradigms: A Plethora of Perspectives

Prior to the previous version of this chapter, discussions of the so-called "paradigm wars" were rooted in the notions that quantitative and qualitative *methods*, the respective questions each posed, and designs and procedures for collecting and analyzing data within each were based in philosophically distinct and incompatible *methodologies*. Although these paradigm wars have subsided, the term *research methods* is still simplistically and erroneously used as synonymous with the term *paradigm*, and methodologists and researchers constantly weigh paradigms in discussing research methodologies. Further, the plethora of paradigms has increased since methodologists speak of a third paradigm called "mixed methods" (Johnson & Onwuegbuzie, 2004). In retrospect, it appears that our original 2000 discussion of the historical and philosophical foundation of paradigms that follows in this section has had little influence on the oversimplified method–paradigm symbiosis.

The term *paradigm* is used in so many ways that it is meaningless to talk about it without selecting a definition prior to discussing its usefulness. For example, Patton (2002), a research methodologist, defined a paradigm as a "worldview—a way of thinking about and making sense of the complexities of the real world" (p. 69). The term has been used to refer to a philosophical position, a research tradition or theoretical framework, and a methodology perspective.

Scholars across the disciplines have looked to philosophers of science for help in defining the term *paradigm*. Like other researchers who have struggled with the concept over the past 20 years, we perused Kuhn's (1970) postpositivist position on inquiry in science and scientific revolutions, realizing that he also proliferated multiple meanings for the term in his classic work. Drawing from Kuhn's work, we defined a paradigm to be a conceptual system, clearly separate from other conceptual systems, with a self-sustaining, internal logic, constituted as a set of epistemological rules directed at solving problems matched to the logic and rules.

Kuhnian perspectives often focus on paradigm shifts. Shifts involve a process in which researchers, in the act of doing normal science (the day-to-day pursuit of problems within a chosen paradigm), are confronted with problems they cannot solve or assimilate, and thus adopt new paradigms following a period of crisis. Kuhn (1970) has characterized these shifts as developmental processes. A new paradigm, perhaps more technical or esoteric than the last, is viewed as a sign of scholarly maturity and development in a field. Yet, a certain amount of snobbery accompanies membership in the community aligned with a new paradigm. As new paradigms are accepted, old paradigms are rejected by the dominant research faction (e.g., Mosenthal, 1985, 2002).

Polkinghorne (1983) characterized Kuhn's notion of paradigm shifts as an "irrational, discontinuous jump, not an evolutionary or developmental change" (p. 113). Polkinghorne believes that research, when practiced day to day *within* a paradigm, can lead to progress, albeit progress constrained by the constitutive rules and questions permitted within the paradigm. Hence, progress in research is made not only by shifting to *better*, more comprehensive paradigms but also within the conduct of normal science (Kuhn, 1970). That is, cumulative progress means continuing to do research within existing paradigms by choosing problems that are solvable, that the community agrees are worth solving, and that the community encourages its members to undertake. However, members of a paradigm may insulate themselves culturally and politically from other paradigmatic communities (Mosenthal, 1985, 2002; Tierney, 1992), satisfied to make progress within a paradigm and to buttress it against other paradigms.

In its broadest sense, a paradigm refers to a fully realized worldview that suggests not only a research methodology but also a value system or axiology, and ontological and epistemological premises. For example, paradigms as diverse as empiricism, behaviorism, progressivism, existentialism, capitalism, Marxism, feminism, romanticism, and postmodernism can be considered to be philosophical worldviews. Philosophical worldviews offer fully realized theoretical systems for understanding the world. Traditions, however, are distinct from philosophical worldviews. Traditions are disciplines from which we glean theories that guide our research methodologies (often referred to as theoretical frameworks). These traditions often reflect a worldview as well as a methodology, although the dominant worldviews and methodologies are subject to change as the research tradition or discipline changes. For example, anthropology is a discipline within which social and cultural theoretical frameworks are used to guide research; social psychology traditions are linked with symbolic interactionism; from psychology comes cognitive psychology and constructivism; and from theology, philosophy, and literary criticism comes hermeneutics. Both traditions and theoretical worldviews guide methodologies and yet commonly are referred to as paradigms; they are important philosophical choices in research.

For instance, researchers who want to study the social organizations in classrooms and how these affect learning and teaching could draw upon the discipline of anthropology, the theoretical perspectives of cultural and social theories, and the methodology of ethnography. *By methodology*, we mean ways of undertaking research including frames of reference (e.g., theoretical frameworks), models, concepts (e.g., conceptual frameworks), methods, and ideas that shape the selection of a particular set of data-collection techniques and analysis strategies. The methodology chosen would dictate the types of data collected and how these data are analyzed. The assumptions undergirding the selected theoretical perspectives would affect the interpretation of the analysis, which also would be heavily influenced by a researcher's philosophical worldviews. Research typically involves many layers of paradigms, including a philosophical worldview, a tradition or discipline, and a methodology. Further, each of these paradigms typically makes or implies ontological, epistemological, and axiological claims. (For expanded explanations of these elements, see Hitchcock & Hughes, 1989; Lincoln & Guba, 1985; and Scheurich & Young, 1997.)

A more narrow interpretation of a paradigm may focus on one or more of the epistemological, axiological, methodological dimensions. For example, literacy researchers may work primarily from a methodological paradigm and may not feel that a philosophical worldview, complete with ethical or ontological concerns, is necessary. Other researchers, such as postmodern and poststructuralist inquirers, eschew the very authority of scientism that supports assumptions, preferring to work unbound by these perceived constraints. Alternatively, one could argue that any research suggests ontological, epistemological, and axiological concerns, even if researchers do not explicitly acknowledge these assumptions.

Critical, then, to understanding the nature of paradigms is knowing the assumptions, values, shared beliefs, and practices held by communities of inquirers. Literacy researchers seldom address these ontological, epistemological, or axiological assumptions explicitly (if at all) in their writings or their research practices, although methodologies are addressed. Yet, many researchers embrace the paradigmatic assumptions as crucial to an internally cohesive, quality research project. Others argue that specific philosophical paradigmatic allegiance, grounded in the assumptions, is neither critical nor even necessary; in fact, opponents argue that philosophical debates over such esoteric matters keep us from the real work we should be doing (e.g., Patton, 2002). The latter group of individuals is more interested in finding new ways to solve problems or in re-creating and subsequently shifting the field in the direction of new paradigms (see Tierney, 1992, for an interesting discussion of the role of "ways of knowing" and its impact on research). When discussing methodological issues, Patton notes,

> [Paradigms are] deeply embedded in the socialization of adherents and practitioners. Paradigms tell us what is important, legitimate, and reasonable. Paradigms are also normative, telling the practitioner what to do without the necessity of long existential or epistemological consideration. But it is this aspect of paradigms that constitutes both strength and weakness—a strength in that it makes action relatively easy, a weakness in that the very reason for action is hidden in the unquestioned assumptions of the paradigm. (p. 69)

Patton (2002) is concerned that a great deal of our inquiry is based on the ways we have previously conducted research rather than attending to the needs of particular situations with appropriate methodologies. He reminds us that paradigmatic blinders constrain methodological flexibility and creativity: Instead of being concerned about shifting from one paradigm to another, we may adhere rigidly to the tenets of a paradigm, perhaps because of philosophical arguments about adherence to assumptions underlying our worldview, rather than adjust the paradigm to meet the challenges of new issues and problems we encounter in research.

We have cited Patton (2002) throughout our discussion of paradigms because he is a self-proclaimed pragmatist. His stance is that researchers do not need to shift to a new paradigm when the existing one is not broad enough for researchers' needs; nor do they need to stay trapped within the philosophical constraints of a particular worldview. Instead, he urges researchers to "supersede one-sided paradigm allegiance by increasing the concrete and practical methodological options available to researchers" [and to] "eschew methodological orthodoxy in favor of *methodological appropriateness*...recognizing that different methods are appropriate for different situations" (pp. 71–72). He differs from Polkinghorne (1983), who suggested that one should work within an existing paradigm and adjust research questions within it. Rather, Patton suggested that researchers work within a paradigm but bring in new frameworks, methods, and tools—whatever is needed—to better address the research questions at hand. To build upon these ideas, we discuss the use and usefulness of paradigmatic reasoning to literacy inquiry.

Paradigms in Literacy Inquiry: Have They Been Useful?

As in the case of mixed methods, a few years after our piece was originally published, the American Educational Research Association's (AERA) Design-Based Research Collective (2003) affirmed that educational research is often divorced from "problems and issues of everyday practice" (p. 5). Design-based research methods, which the group labeled as a paradigm, unlike the sort of technical, empirical, or heuristic pragmatism of mixed methods, focus on the pragmatism of addressing problems in specific, authentic learning environments looking at interactions among materials, teachers, and learners, and accommodating emergent changes in settings, usually in collaboration with participants over time. Shavelson, Phillips, Towne, and Feuer (2003) refer to these characteristics as *utility-oriented* approaches that ultimately take the form of human science rather than positivist or postpositivist science. Here, the practical design emerges after studying, over time, an existing design in an authentic context and redesigning it based on that inquiry, and ultimately applying it to educational practice. Such design-based research has been diminished by some, including federal policymakers and funding entities that have been proponents of "evidence-based" scientifically based research, even though the validity of experimental replicated studies could be questioned because of, for example, evidence that effect sizes decrease over time and across replications (Reinking, 2010). An advocated basis for both mixed-design studies and design-based research grounded in pragmatism is that research questions precede and dictate methodology (Shavelson et al., 2003). In order to answer practical questions, posed to solve problems in the real world in authentic environments, one must be free to select from a range of data types and use a variety of analytical strategies.

Recent research in literacy, as in other fields, has been influenced by broad shifts in approaches to both natural and social science research. Earlier educational research can be characterized by the use of classical empirical scientific paradigms, which were grounded in a nearly utopian belief in the possibilities of science. Scientific methods were understood to be capable of capturing truth about reality and phenomena that were not available through ordinary discourse and observation. Research was driven by epistemological concerns. A scientific epistemology was thought to reveal ontological certainty upon which actions should be based. For example, the scientific positivist study of literacy was thought to reveal unequivocal universal truths about learners and learning that would allow for the unequivocally scientific application of teaching.

Researchers in both natural and social sciences, however, have become increasingly aware of the role of context, subjectivity, interpretation, and social values in all aspects of what was earlier understood to be an objective research process. What is observed and the meaning that is made of inquiry both are understood to be deeply influenced by the theoretical assumptions of researchers. This recognition has underscored the value of research approaches that shed light on the complexity of learners, researchers, and research settings. This includes paradigms such as sociolinguistics, various qualitative approaches, and phenomenological and hermeneutical interpretations as well as the critical and postmodern. These paradigms are increasingly being pursued not only because of their intrinsic capacity to help clarify complexity, or in the case of critical theory, to champion the perceptions of the oppressed and underserved, but also because of their popularity in some settings.

A historical glance shows clearly that the field of literacy is not one that has evolved through the adoption, adaptation, and rejection of successive paradigms generated from within. Rather, paradigms in literacy research have been borrowed from various fields that have richly informed research topics and methods, albeit with arguments both supporting and criticizing the multiplicity of paradigms.

A Variety of Paradigms Can Enrich Literacy Inquiry

The diversity of fields and their accompanying paradigms that have informed literacy research can be viewed as enriching our perspectives and methods of inquiry (Beach, 1994; Beach, Green, Kamil, & Shanahan, 1992; Harris, 1969; Pearson & Stephens, 1994; Ruddell, 1999). Pearson and Stephens noted that about 30 years ago, scholarship in the field of reading consisted primarily of the study of perceptual processes. They stated that the field was transformed suddenly in the mid- to late 1960s not because of paradigm shifts from within the community of reading researchers but because scholars in other fields (e.g., linguistics, psycholinguistics, cognitive psychology, sociolinguistics) had become interested in reading. Each of these fields defined the reading process using descriptive and operational definitions, constitutive rules, and research methods that fit their individual paradigms. The field of reading (and indeed the broader field of literacy as we define it) is what Pearson and Stephens referred to as a transdisciplinary field that permits scholars to solve myriad problems using a variety of perspectives.

Pearson and Stephens's retrospect is validated by Harris (1969), who summarized the field of reading as he saw it at the time. In his chapter called "Reading" in the fourth edition of the *Encyclopedia of Educational Research*, he viewed reading research as a mirror image of research in the broader educational community, a field he characterized as being influenced by other disciplines. Harris traced reading research in this century from an early focus on perception (1910); to case studies (1920s); to evaluation and behaviorism (1930s); to reading comprehension defined by psychometrics and factor analysis (1940s); to experimental research with accompanying hypothesis testing and statistical tests (1950s and 1960s); to the most current work by scholars in other disciplines, including psychology, linguistics, sociology, and medicine, "who bring conceptual and experimental tools to bear on reading phenomena" (p. 1069). Harris took the perspective that researchers in the reading field should try to mirror the quality of the research being conducted in the multiplicity of fields informing the education field. He positioned the research methodology affecting reading research from outside the field proper as a standard to attain.

A Variety of Paradigms Can Hamper Literacy Inquiry

The notion of paradigm incommensurability (Donmoyer, 1996), if taken literally, means that fields such as literacy, informed by a range of disciplines, remain a set of subcommunities with incompatible assumptions and methodologies and little common language. The pragmatic stance, which we will discuss later, allows for compatibility. But we will explore the literal argument that the field has been hampered in its progress because of the multiplicity of voices emanating from incompatible paradigms (Clay, 1994; Mosenthal, 1985, 1999; Weintraub & Farr, 1976).

Mosenthal, who drew partly from Kuhn's (1970) work on paradigms, discussed the progress of educational research in general (Mosenthal, 1985) and reading research in particular (Mosenthal, 1984, 1988). He explored three different approaches to defining progress in research: (1) *literal approaches* in which researchers work diligently within a chosen paradigm to refine existing theories, find new features and examples compatible with the theory's higher order features (normal science), or discover anomalies leading to the creation of recombinant theories more inclusive than that developed within the paradigm supported by normal science (extraordinary science); (2) *interpretive approaches* in which researchers abandon the preoccupation with the fit between empirical definitions and reality in favor of the belief that reality is constructed; and (3) *evaluative approaches* in which ideological implications of inquiry for society are central to the researcher's work. After careful discussion of these idealized ways of making progress, Mosenthal stressed that each group of researchers, or speech communities, embraces and advances members' respective beliefs and abides by the rules that support definitions, cementing members' solidarity with discursive practices that promote each definition as the normative one. Hence, progress, he contended, is defined not by a systematic testing and reconceptualizing of theoretical perspectives but by political dominance and power of one speech community over others (Mosenthal, 1999). This is a less optimistic view of multiple paradigms and transdisciplinary research perspectives.

We can demonstrate further the negative side of positioning and repositioning of paradigms in literacy by drawing on multiple sources in which scholars synthesized research and discussed trends in the field. More than three decades ago, Weintraub and Farr (1976) noted that research in reading was being conducted using the classical empirical design because of what they referred to as "methodological incarceration" (p. 4). They contended that the model was used even though it was inappropriate for some of the research questions posed in the field. Weintraub and Farr also posited that reading researchers adhered to this paradigm to prove to allied professions, particularly psychology, that reading researchers could conduct quality research in that era of classical experimental studies. Although literacy research conducted within this paradigm has been valuable and moved the field forward, one could argue that the self-imposed methodological incarceration limited methodological vision.

In the first decade of the 21st century, methodological incarceration became a hallmark of reading research. Approaches to educational research and to reading in particular became increasingly narrowed and polarized after the publication of the NICHD's (2000) NRP report. This report, emanating from the medically oriented National Institutes of Health, claimed authority through association with science—more specifically, with "hard science." A similar artificial narrowing of what counts as worthwhile research was used in research reviews in many other disciplines, including the Abell Foundation report *Teacher Certification Reconsidered: Stumbling for Quality* (Walsh, 2001). Reading research in the United States thus underwent a profound change as part of a larger set of political reforms, including the privatization of public education, school competition and choice, centralized curriculum, and auditing through high-stakes standardized tests. Federal money and foundation grant support for a narrowing range of types and foci of reading research over the first decade of the 21st century was widely characterized as both an undemocratic misuse of power emanating from the private sector and neoconservatives and an unwise approach to complex issues in education. As Lather (2004) observes, the NCLB policy rejects particular methodologies, evidence, values, and politics:

> Human volition and program variability, cultural diversity, multiple disciplinary perspectives, the import of partnerships with practitioners, even the ethical considerations of random designs: all are swept away in a unified theory of scientific advancement with its mantra of "science is science is science" across the physical, life, and social sciences. (p. 19)

Reading researchers responded with thoughtful and complex repudiations of this narrowing of research paradigms through top-down state and federal demands for curricular change and by funding only a very narrow set of research questions and research paradigms, as did the wider research community (see the November 2002 issue of *Educational Researcher* for numerous and insightful critiques and, for a specific example, see Freeman, deMarrais, Preissle, Roulston, & St. Pierre, 2007). Nonetheless, career-driven researchers enacted this agenda, project-driven researchers sought to connect their work to these demands, and the field of reading research changed. Reading research became more centralized, privatized, commodified, and capitalized.

While this policy context led to a proliferation of macrofocused large-scale studies reporting aggregate trends and microfocused work in areas such as brain activity during reading—which was often conducted by researchers outside of the field of reading or literacy education—our interest is in exploring why certain paradigms dominate and what they do and do not accomplish. From a Marxian point of view, when times are tough, when contradictions are sharpened, more change is possible. For example, the New Deal would not have been enacted without the Great Depression. This policy context sharpened the increasing contradiction between the academic character of research production on the one hand and the private capital interests and federal power on the other. While there is no doubt that large grant funding effectively promotes and discourages certain types of research, abuses of power and situations of crisis also precipitate change. Researchers and research associations tend to avoid taking risks, good or bad, during times of prosperity and calm. However, with no hope of gaining funding, some researchers embraced unique approaches in research by approaching foundations for support and by forming collaborations across institutions to support larger-scale studies (see Vagle, Dillon, Davison-Jenkins, LaDuca, & Olson, 2006, for an example of a multisite study of reading teacher education reform, supported by the Bush Foundation).

Paradigms That Could Have Made a Difference but Did Not

As the earlier review of recent trends illustrates, the field of literacy has always been one microcosm illustrating the systematic positioning and repositioning of paradigms and their inherent communities. For example, in the first three editions of *Theoretical Models and Processes of Reading* (Singer & Ruddell, 1970, 1976, 1985), each table of contents maps out the dominant research communities. Unsurprisingly, the contents of these texts include mostly psychological studies of processes of reading wherein authors have attached operational definitions of various systems such as phonological systems, lexical systems, decoding, recoding, and visual perceptual span. The section on models in the second edition is divided into four types of models (types based on substantive theories in psychology), tested against theories using methodology grounded in positivist science. Editors Singer and Ruddell hoped that the volume would enhance further theorizing and research productivity, resulting in better reading instruction in the United States.

Embedded within the predominantly psychological perspectives in the 1976 volume is a piece written by Ray McDermott (1976) in a section called "Cultural Interaction." In his chapter, McDermott drew on anthropological theories and methods to look at the social reproduction of minority-community pariah status among poor children in school and how this pariah–host (black children–white teacher) relationship plays out in the social organization of reading instruction. At the time most literacy researchers first acquired *TMPR–2*, they were interested in the dominant psychological paradigm. Few individuals seem to have noticed the unobtrusive McDermott piece, which fell clearly outside the dominant paradigm. In today's current context of interpretive research, significantly influenced by anthropological theories and methods, we can historically situate McDermott as a scholar who was ahead of his time.

In reviewing our own literacy research careers, we wonder what would have happened if we had embraced McDermott's 1976 work instead of the dominant psychological paradigm. Might we have engaged in research at the beginning of our careers (in the early 1980s) that would be retroactively viewed as groundbreaking? However, like most of our colleagues, we overlooked McDermott because the dominant paradigm in the early 1980s was reading comprehension research, grounded in cognitive science using positivist and postpositivist methodologies. And even though we both studied qualitative research methodology and conducted such research starting in 1982, it was not readily embraced by our research community at conferences or by journal editors until years later. Hence, paradigms, although useful if considered in their broadest sense, have restricted the potential of research by limiting vision and polarizing competing research communities. Pragmatism, we contend, is a viable alternative.

Implications for the Future: Pragmatism and Practical Discourse

To meet the challenges that literacy researchers and practitioners will face in this millennium, we look outside the field of literacy to a broader perspective in education: pragmatism (Dewey, 1916, 1919/1993b; James, 1907/1991; Rorty, 1982, 1991). In the following section, we define pragmatism and discuss why it is a useful alternative to paradigmatic reasoning.

Pragmatism is a distinctive American branch of philosophy that began in the context of late-19th-century critiques of both hard science and social science. James described pragmatism as "an attitude of looking away from first things, principles, 'categories,' supposed necessities; and of looking towards last things, fruits, consequences, facts" (as cited in Menand, 1997, p. 98). In its inception, pragmatism was considered highly controversial, but it interested many scholars because

> like modernism, it reflects the break-up of cultural and religious authority, the turn away from any simple or stable truth [truth is provisional, grounded in history and experience or context, not fixed in the nature of things], the shift from totalizing systems and unified narratives to a more fragmented plurality of perspectives. (Dickstein, 1998, pp. 4–5)

The label *pragmatism*, like other vague terms, has been avoided by leading educational philosophers and researchers because it is overused and misconstrued and a "terminological lightning rod" (Boisvert, 1998, p. 11). Even Dewey, who considered himself a pragmatist, left the term out of his texts, noting, "Perhaps the word lends itself to misconception...so much misunderstanding and relatively futile controversy have gathered about the word that it seemed advisable to avoid its use" (as quoted in Boisvert, 1998, p. 11).

In this chapter, we use *pragmatism* to support what Bernstein (1983) called "radical critiques of the intellectually imperialistic claims made in the name of method" (p. xi). In calling for pragmatism, we are not advocating the approach of one or another theorist who is identifiable as a pragmatist; instead, we are advocating the spirit of the pragmatic tradition, which asserts that conducting inquiry to useful ends takes precedence over finding ways to defend one's epistemology. It is important to remember, as Dewey noted, that pragmatism does not mean "if it works then it's true" (as quoted in Boisvert, 1998, p. 31), even though the term had been so cast.

The value of inquiry using the "pragmatic method" (James, 1907/1991, p. 23) is in looking at the practical consequences of a notion (a method or perspective of inquiry) before deciding to employ it. James argued that when comparing alternative views of science, one must examine the differences these views would make in the world if each were true. Within this stance, ideas, which are based in our experiences, are true only insofar as they help us relate to other facets of our experience and achieve our goals. Paradigms, or theories developed within paradigms, each may contribute something useful, but ultimately the usefulness in summarizing, synthesizing, and using existing ideas in ways that lead to new ideas or good actions (rather than the theoretical purity) is what is important. Similarly, Dewey (1938/1981) noted that the value of scientific research must be considered in terms of the projected consequences of activities—the end in view. Dewey identified genuine problems that were part of actual social situations, as those researchers should address. These problems (from practice), he stated, should be identified and carefully defined before inquiry is undertaken. In fact, this latter point—the need to convert a problematic situation into a set of conditions forming a definite problem—was recognized by Dewey as a weakness of much inquiry (i.e., researchers selected a set of methods without a clear understanding of the problem). After the problem or subject matter (the phenomenon under study) was identified and the dimensions clearly defined, he recommended that the issue be investigated from various perspectives, depending on the purpose or objective of the inquiry. Finally, as Dewey stated, "the ultimate end and test of all inquiry is the transformation of a problematic situation (which involves confusion and conflict) into a unified one" (p. 401). For Dewey, all inquiry should be focused on transformation and evaluation of the features of situations in which we find ourselves (Biesta & Burbules, 2003).

Thus, the pragmatism developed by Holmes, James, Pierce, and Dewey, according to Menand (2001), offers that

> ideas are not "out there" waiting to be discovered, but are tools—like forks and knives and microchips—that people devise to cope with the world in which they

> find themselves...(and) since ideas are provisional responses to particular and irreproducible circumstances, their survival depends not on their immutability but on their adaptability. (p. xi)

In addition, the usefulness of pragmatic inquiry, as conceived by Dewey, also should be considered in terms of its capacity to contribute to a democratic life, broadly defined. Dewey observed that democracy "has not been adequately realized in any time" (as quoted in Boisvert, 1998, p. 299), and the goal of democracy is the "creation of a freer and...more humane experience in which all contribute" (Dewey, 1939/1993a, p. 245). Similarly, Rorty (1982) stated,

> Our identification with our community—our society, our political tradition, and our intellectual heritage—is heightened when we see this community as ours rather than nature's, shaped rather than found, one among many which men have made. In the end, the pragmatists tell us what matters is our loyalty to other human beings, clinging together against the dark, not our hope of getting things right. (p. 166)

Because the problems that pragmatists address are to contribute to a more democratic way of life characterized by the creation of a freer and more humane experience, the identification of problems for inquiry is particularly important. Democracy is not simply a set of political institutions. For Dewey, democracy is most centrally a way of life, and also a way of inquiry. Dewey wrote, "Apart from the social medium, the individual would never 'know himself'; he would never become acquainted with his needs and capacities" (1908/1978, p. 388) and "Apart from the ties which bind him to others, he is nothing" (1932/1985, p. 323). Dewey (1932/1985, 1929/1987) emphasized the inherently social nature of all problem posing, and he believed that people cannot understand themselves, or develop their practical reasoning, in isolation from others. Therefore, problems need to be socially situated and identified to be legitimate foci of inquiry. Dewey believed that all inquiry is "natural, situational, grounded in problems, interrogations of theory and practice and evaluative." Further, "The integration of particular nonexpert experience, fostered by the establishment of interaction and discussion, enables the community to better use the insights" (Campbell, 1995, p. 199). The inquiry process suggested by a pragmatic stance is quite different from traditional inquiry in which a researcher establishes a question or problem and proceeds without the integration of nonexpert opinion. In fact, for some researchers, the integration of nonexpert opinion, which was key to Dewey, is understood as a sign of methodological weakness. The importance of dialogue and listening in inquiry requires new roles for researchers and also for the community of learners and practitioners, or what traditional research would call the subjects of research.

A pragmatic approach to knowledge in general and to research results in particular is completely different from how research is usually understood. In fact, it flips generalizability and specificity upside down. Research should be focused toward the usable and the specific rather than the generalizable and abstract. As Biesta and Burbules (2003) explained, pragmatists see the point of doing educational research as not only to find out what might be possible or achievable, but also to deal with the question of whether what is possible and achievable is *desirable*—and more specifically, whether it is desirable from an educational point of view. (p. 109)

Pragmatism explicitly critiques the dangers of decontextualized knowledge and of actions and ideological positions that stem from it. It calls for a personal commitment to revision, reflection, and inquiry, which is not only more important than the latest "scientific truth," but also pragmatists argue that it leads to the only sort of truth that is both useful and justifiable.

In *Pragmatism and Educational Research*, Biesta and Burbules (2003) explained that subjectivism does not lead to relativism because as people work and live together, they develop shared meanings and build an intersubjective understanding of the world. "Intersubjective truths have value as they support ongoing solution of problems in the real world; they are always open to revision when they do not have the expected practical consequences" (Floden, 2009, p. 487). The impossibility of unequivocally grounding our assumptions about knowledge and value in research-based "truth" deprives us of authoritative external assumptions by which to judge our actions, but not of the possibility of useful informed critique because critique *makes use* of the principles and values, even as we question and explore their meaning. What is true in a democracy and what is true in science must always be considered, reconsidered, and contested. Yet, this isn't a hopeless or endless task. We always have existing grounds upon which to examine, explore, and reconsider. The following section further explores the implications of these issues for literacy inquirers.

Using a Pragmatic Stance for Literacy Inquiry in the Future

Scrutiny from within and outside the field of literacy has forced internal examination of our research and the ways that we engage in inquiry. As Chall (1998) noted, the public "seems to place less confidence now than in the past in the power of research and analysis to find better solutions" (pp. 21–22). And although we have a proliferation of research that informs practice, "it has also contributed to the loss of faith in its use. Perhaps it is too vast and confusing and not sufficiently interpreted and synthesized" (pp. 21–22). Chall commented on the unorganized plethora of research findings that seem to have little impact on pedagogy or on solving current literacy problems, whereas Ruddell (1999) emphasized that in a time when our theoretical frameworks and methods are more diverse than at any time in our scholarly history in literacy, policymakers, politicians, and others who inform them have marginalized important forms of inquiry. This marginalization has occurred because research does not conform to the accepted, albeit narrow, politically correct paradigm. Moreover, Ruddell contended that the denial of a multiplicity of inquiry paradigms by politically visible national panels and policymakers is an attempt to force compliance to a "Party Line" (p. 4). The party line requires us to disavow our allegiance to paradigms outside of the canon of research rooted in developmental psychology and traditional scientism. Specifically, researchers who address questions generated in local settings and use interpretive methods to understand how particular teachers and students work together to support learning are positioned as being less scientific and, hence, less credible in terms of their processes and results (see Freeman et al., 2007).

Alternatively, literacy researchers who have conducted research projects that would be characterized by their peers as "scientific" (e.g., use large samples of children in multiple settings with experimental designs to measure growth or impact of programs or strategies) also feel marginalized in the literacy research community and often feel more comfortable within organizations like the Society for the Scientific Study of Reading. Accepted by those in power in governmental agencies (e.g., national boards created to study why we have low reading scores in the United States), these researchers are often positioned even further away from their colleagues whose research is not deemed scientific enough.

Thus, political entities in government and elsewhere, the struggle for resources (grant monies) and jobs (tenure and promotion at universities), and a human need to feel that one has made a mark in the field have all contributed to a preoccupation with paradigm debates resulting in literacy research that has not made the difference it could in practice. Literacy researchers continue to struggle with these issues today. As a community, it would be useful to keep pooling our considerable intellectual resources. Difficult questions must be asked about why we engage in inquiry and who benefits from or is affected by the results of our efforts.

Further, pragmatism stresses the need for research to produce usable "truth" not immutable, transcendental, and universal truth findings. Large-scale studies report aggregate trends. They aim toward the universally true. It is quite possible to empirically determine which reading strategy produces the greatest gain among large groups of children. The problem is that this information—in and of itself—is often not deemed useful by practitioners because it does not provide instructional specificity. Teaching reading requires *specific knowledge of specific children* because there are many different ways that children can have struggles and strengths in reading (e.g., Valencia & Buly's 2005 study). In summarizing the intervention research, Frankel, Pearson, and Nair (2011) noted, "Emphasis must be on the individual student. To assume otherwise masks the different instructional approaches that individual students require to become more proficient readers" (p. 225). A teacher must help a group of 25 children with diverse and specific needs to read. What works for 10,000 students has little bearing on the child with visual decoding struggles, the child with phonemic storage and retrieval struggles, the child who decodes but does not comprehend, and the child who reads just fine but happens to dislike fiction. For Peirce (1992), scientific research clarifies the meaning of certain concepts or ideas through investigating their relationship with practice. A meaningful research statement, according to Peirce, is only one that has practical and experiential consequences. Biesta and Burbules (2003) agreed when they noted that

> teachers and other educators are not simply passive consumers of educational knowledge, but are as much the creators of educational knowledge, even when they are drawing from research conducted by others, because their very act of problem solving is a process of inquiry. (p. 111)

Dimensions of Literacy Inquiry for the Future

Although it is difficult to change particular large systems or structures (e.g., university systems, government agencies) and their value systems, we can begin to make changes as individuals and as a research community. We believe that a pragmatic perspective offers literacy researchers a way to approach inquiry that will enable us to agree to disagree, to address the important work of defining the literacy problems we need to solve, to determine how best to solve these problems, and to ensure that the results inform practice (Mosenthal, 1999). As Vagle (2009) related in his research as a teacher educator, we need to really listen to our participants, be reflexive in our work, and learn to become "strategic idealists" (p. 370). In the next section, we move in this direction by presenting dimensions of literacy inquiry that we believe must continue to be defined, articulated, put into practice, and evaluated.

Dimension 1: Building Communities of Inquiry

Dewey reminded us that from a pragmatic perspective, it is critical that we reconceptualize how inquiry is conducted, who we involve in the inquiry process, and the roles various participants assume within the process. For example, several years ago, the National Association of State Universities and Land-Grant Colleges published a report by the Kellogg Commission on the Future of State and Land-Grant Universities (1999). This document presents a key issue relating to the reconceptualization of how inquiry is conducted. The report challenges university personnel to work toward organizing staff and resources to better serve local and national needs in meaningful and coherent ways. The Kellogg Commission noted that university personnel must go beyond traditional notions of outreach and service to what is termed *engagement* (for an extended discussion of these ideas, see Dillon, O'Brien, & Heilman, 2000).

The idea of engagement is consonant with Dewey's pragmatic conception of social inquiry. Clearly, a commitment to engagement is necessary in forming partnerships. Strong leadership, coupled with support by administrators, promotion and tenure committees, and funding agencies, is also necessary. Communities must be open to diverse solutions to problems and varying roles of persons involved in partnerships. Challenges to this new concept of engagement and social inquiry revolve around logistical and accountability issues: How will communities of inquiry come together and function? Who will ultimately be responsible for the success or failure of partnerships? Will personnel be supported and rewarded for their efforts in both the short and long term? How do we know that people in communities of inquiry have the critical skills needed to deliberate problems? How will we mediate power and get along?

These challenges of pragmatism highlight what Bernstein (1983) understood to be a "paradox of praxis": "The type of solidarity, communicative interaction, dialogue, and judgment required for the concrete realization of praxis already presupposes incipient forms of community life that such praxis seeks to foster" (p. 175). Similarly, Dewey (1927/1993c) observed, "A class of experts is inevitably so removed from common interests as to become a class with private interests and private knowledge, which in social matters is not knowledge at all" (p. 187). It is difficult to conduct pragmatic inquiry that relies on communication and dialogue when teachers, community members, and researchers are not accustomed to working together; when literacy researchers are often separated by paradigmatic boundaries reinforced by power interests; and when researchers are similarly unaccustomed to communicative dialogue and interaction across disciplines both within education and across the academy.

Dewey (1916) envisioned communities of inquiry as communities that internally reflect "numerous and varied interests" and "full and free interplay with other forms of association" (p. 83). This conception is opposite our usual conception of independent research or academic communities in which interests and memberships are explicitly narrow. As Foucault (1975/1977, 1980) delineated, disciplinary practices with distinct types of knowledge and knowledge makers are disciplined and understood as systems of power and authority. The suggestion of a more inclusive notion of research participants and academic communities through pragmatism implicates deeply entrenched notions of power and authority.

Research partnerships are critical. A desire to work collaboratively to identify and solve problems is key to the formation of partnerships among school-based personnel, literacy researchers, and community members. This stance requires a form of advocacy by members of the partnership, what Rorty (1982) called "loyalty to other human beings" (p. 162) to promote "the creation of a freer and more humane experience" (Dewey, 1939/1993a, p. 245). For instance, partners might take up the cause of students who have been tracked using limited assessment measures. As an example of the dynamics of such advocacy that is often in stark contrast to education, one can turn to medical research, which often shows how a pragmatic perspective, with participants in the role of advocate for themselves and others, influences research and practice (see Dillon et al., 2000, for an elaborated example of this concept). A challenging question for educators is why we see little need for advocacy with such a large number of stakeholders, including researchers, teachers, parents, students, and citizens. Pragmatists would seek to develop partnerships where engagement is central to the work, where university- and school-based educators as well as students and community members bring their respective expertise to bear during deliberations, and where all stakeholders advocate for themselves to identify educational problems and inquiry designs. Ultimately, all stakeholders would be advocates for student learning. An example of a project that adheres to several of these ideals focuses on preparing elementary reading teachers on site in an urban school setting, where the principal, parents, and K–6 teachers are partnering with university literacy educators to identify key knowledge, dispositions, and skills needed by new teachers to work with the diverse learners in this urban neighborhood (Israelson, Dillon, & Brodeur, 2012).

Dimension 2: Moral Obligation in the Selection of Research Problems

Currently, many educational researchers are stepping back from their inquiry projects and the philosophical debates about the conduct of research to ask themselves these questions: Why do I engage in educational research? How meaningful is my research? Who benefits from my work? Dewey (1938/1981) would urge literacy researchers to consider problems we face in light of the institutional, social, political, and contextual influences surrounding the problems. From this pragmatic perspective, more time must be spent talking about the problem with participants and other constituents, defining the contours and the ways that addressing one feature of a problem may contribute to understanding another, and thinking about the concerns and implications associated with our decisions. This stage is what Dewey (1929/1987) characterized as "enjoying the doubtful" (p. 182). The effort at the inception of the study can result in stronger, richer efforts along the way. Particular discernment for identifying what might be a useful focus of inquiry or a problem to solve usually rests with the researcher, or what Dewey called the expert. A pragmatic perspective requires that researchers share this power with participants; researchers come to the table with expertise, but other stakeholders also bring their knowledge and experience. Within this context, researchers are charged with teaching community members about methodological options available to understanding and solving problems. The sort of democratic dialogue Dewey envisioned in such a setting helps foster both understanding and community. Dewey (1927/1993c) observed that "the essential need...is the improvement in methods and conditions of debate, discussion, and persuasion" (p. 187). Such dialogue is an important skill, which is equally appropriate for citizens, researchers, and students. Within this process, researchers lose some freedom in the formulation of problems, the way problems are addressed, and what is reported from the research. However, the sharing of power is worthwhile when inquiry is viewed as responsive, meaningful, and credible to all participants.

Along with broadening the collective of persons associated with inquiry and redefining the roles that persons might assume within this process, there is a need to reconsider how we develop research agendas, identify problems, and craft studies. We propose a literacy inquiry agenda spanning three foci: (1) developing a set of critical problems, generated by a diverse group of stakeholders, that are foundational to large-scale research projects with multiple sites and community inquiry teams; (2) developing a set of critical problems generated at the local level by community inquiry teams; and (3) collectively identifying problems that interest individual researchers and that can be parsed into various facets to be addressed by individual expertise. Consistent with a pragmatic stance, we believe that on an international, national, local, and personal level, researchers should consider Dewey's vision of inquiry as collectively generating research problems from actual social situations (practices) as identified by all stakeholders through practical discourse.

As we think about reenvisioning the conduct of research, we are faced with the realization that researchers themselves pose the biggest challenge to taking a pragmatic stance in developing multiple, interconnected research foci. That is because these scholars often research issues they enjoy or feel passionately about and/or because they want to position themselves professionally, socially, and culturally to fit into acknowledged trends and to be acknowledged by respectable communities. Dewey and other pragmatists oppose the perspective of research as a personal matter, noting that research agendas should be public and socially grounded in intent and process. Inquiry not so grounded fails to serve the purpose of democratic reconstruction. Embedded within the challenge of public versus personal research agendas is the question of how the nature of research is influenced by the way researchers are positioned by the social, cultural, and historical contexts in which they conduct inquiry. For example, researchers are valued in university settings for the innovative knowledge they generate and, like it or not, productivity in the form of quantity of articles in prestigious journals. This situation has not changed over the past 10 years. Add to this narrow conceptualization of productivity the continuing institutional pressure to reform teacher education programs, and a situation is created in which scholars actually have less time to be scholarly. In such a climate, research is often quickly conceived; small data sets are collected, analyzed, and interpreted in a cursory manner; and reports of research are written in bits and pieces when time permits in outlets that university promotion and tenure committees find acceptable (but persons engaged in practice may not read). Thus, much of this research may have little effect on the practices of K–12 educators or on learners' lives. There is evidence that this institutional culture continues to remain a formidable force that affects the character and quality of literacy inquiry.

In sum, few literacy scholars or prospective advocates of scholarship have clearly identified a broad set of issues that deserve unified, convergent efforts, despite the urging of scholars such as Dillon who argued that literacy scholars need to "work with school-based colleagues and other stakeholders to formulate pragmatic, important, and researchable questions and create appropriate research designs to collect data to address these questions—including mixed research designs" (as quoted in Falk-Ross et al., 2007, p. 14). Some exceptions exist. For example, Risko and colleagues (2008) and Dillon, O'Brien, Sato, and Kelly (2010) completed large-scale literature reviews of literacy teacher preparation, enabling us to understand where the field currently stands in terms of research questions posed, methodologies used, research findings, and directions for future inquiry. In addition, a multisite study was designed and enacted to identify the characteristics of effective elementary reading teacher preparation programs. This elementary reading teacher program study was funded by the International Reading Association (IRA; Hoffman & Roller, 2001; Hoffman et al., 2005). In this particular case, literacy researchers and IRA crafted a coherent plan, a process, and engaged literacy leaders to initiate such efforts. This scholarship—and the spin-off studies from it—created the foundation for major teacher education reform in elementary reading teacher preparation nationwide. A pragmatic stance to the formation of multiple yet connected research agendas could facilitate this effort, as evidenced by the IRA collaborative research initiative. Despite the identified need for a shared research agenda, most literacy researchers also believe that opportunities must be provided for innovative, unconventional research that advances the field. This tension among large-scale and local research agendas, shared and individual agendas, and the role of research paradigms can be managed productively with considerable thought, effort, dialogue, and organization.

Finally, in maintaining a pragmatic stance, the selection and design of studies in the literacy field should be developed with the end in view. Traditionally, this end in view is a post hoc entity we call implications or recommendations rather than an a priori design issue. Pragmatic research conversations would begin with these questions: What do we hope to achieve at the conclusion of the study? Why is this end result important for learners? Conversation about the end results could help participants better define problems and improve the design of studies, and this conversation could help participants focus on the specific social, cultural, and other contextual aspects that affect a particular inquiry. Despite its apparent usefulness, an end-in-view perspective, grounded in social responsibility and democratic purposes, presents a challenge in conducting research. In beginning a study, researchers typically review related research, carefully crafting hypotheses or guiding research questions, developing a design that best addresses questions, collecting and analyzing data, theorizing, and interpreting the results. It is possible that the end-in-view fixation may cause researchers to lose sight of the research process, including methodological possibilities, or of certain structural considerations as a project unfolds (Thompson, 1997).

Dimension 3: Reconsidering Traditions, Methodologies, and How We Communicate Findings

To move forward in the field of literacy research, we believe that scholars need to continue to think about the research traditions in which they operate and the rationale behind these choices. Technical expertise and theoretical and methodological purity have been the hallmarks of quality in paradigmatically driven research. Researchers believe that if they attend to these elements, more credible findings will result. From a pragmatic stance, using a variety of methodologies can either strengthen a study or lead to its downfall. The use of multiple methodologies can add breadth and depth and numerical, pictorial, and narrative data to support themes, assertions, or findings. But these studies must still evidence the tenets of quality research. Many researchers are careful to ground their work in substantive theories from the field of literacy; nevertheless, these same scholars can sometimes be criticized for neglecting to use and exhibit understanding about the theoretical frameworks undergirding their methodologies. In addition, although the title Doctor of Philosophy is reminiscent of the days in which a broad education was more valued, academe, as already noted, currently does not support the development of broadly educated researchers. Neither does the academy support the development of inquiry communities with school and community collaborators, or with the potentially diverse groups of colleagues that pragmatic inquiry needs to thrive. Again, Foucault (1975/1977, 1980) reminded us that the ways in which we structure knowledge in academe serve to create regimes of truth and structures of power and authority. Thus, a pragmatic turn in inquiry provides us with compelling challenges not only to the ways in which ideas are conceived and pursued but also to the ways in which power and authority are structured among intellectuals, and society in general. The change we suggest has both philosophical and political ramifications.

Concurrent with the need for new knowledge is an awareness of what knowledge bases we draw upon and which ones we inadvertently overlook. We urge literacy researchers to continue to consider new traditions and methodologies, even as we develop expertise (and a level of comfort) with a few. For example, some literacy researchers have taken up Scheurich and Young's (1997) discussion of race-based paradigms constructed via cultural and historical contexts. These authors argued that all current epistemologies and accompanying tensions (e.g., issues of qualitative vs. quantitative methodologies, objective vs. subjective reality, validity and paradigmatic issues in general) rise out of the social history of the dominant white race, thus reflecting and reinforcing that social history and racial group. We need to extend paradigms to address "epistemological racism," recognizing that dominant and subordinate racial groups "do not think and interpret realities in the same way as White people because of their divergent structural positions, histories, and cultures" (Stanfield, 1985, p. 400). Scheurich and Young argued that even critical approaches (critical theory, feminism, lesbian/gay orientations, and critical postmodernism), where racism has been a focus, have been racially biased. A pragmatic perspective beckons literacy researchers to attend to how various racial groups select issues for inquiry, conceptualize research, interpret phenomena, and record results. This is an epistemological issue that is critical to understanding literacy events currently and in the future (for a discussion of these issues, see Parker, 2002; for examples of research in action, see the work of Kris Gutiérrez, Carol Lee, and Gloria Ladson-Billings).

Finally, a pragmatic stance requires that literacy researchers consider how we communicate the findings from our inquiry to other communities of inquirers, researchers within and across paradigmatic lines and disciplines, and individuals outside the research context (e.g., policymakers, the general public). Writing for multiple audiences and writing about ideas that others find useful (keeping the end in mind as one constructs a study) are important goals. The typical article format for sharing work should change to better illuminate complex concepts for a range of readers and to meet the needs of policymakers in terms of brevity (e.g., through the use of executive summaries), clarity, and elimination of jargon. A shift in the expectations of journal editors and editorial review boards is also needed to promote the publication of concise research reports while recognizing the value of longer articles that detail theory and methodology. An example of how new publication formats have played out is the journal *Educational Researcher*, published by the AERA. Under the previous editorship (Yussen, Dillon, Harwell, & Hearn, 2010), this journal began to accept feature articles that present important new research results of broad significance and are about 5,000 words. The methodology needs to be carefully presented to warrant results, but information can also be included in supplementary online materials to further support the paper's conclusions. Reviews/essays describe new developments of broad significance and highlight unresolved questions and future directions yet are research-based and aim to convey new developments in the state of the knowledge and its implications, whether theoretical, empirical, or methodological. These papers are about 4,000 words. Briefs are short analyses focusing on a specific topic or policy question using new or existing data, with text totaling no more than 1,000 words. Methods are included in supporting online material. As indicated in the aforementioned *Educational Researcher* description, technology options for publishing research have exploded in the past 10 years, offering new forms of representation that display and explicate concepts that heretofore have been represented with flat text. We believe that published accounts of research in new concise formats and in more accessible venues (e.g., online) have the potential to reach larger audiences and inform practice, policy, and future inquiry efforts.

Conclusions

Many complex questions relating to how learners become and remain literate and how teachers can support this process remain uninvestigated. However, our past practices in selecting questions and formulating inquiry approaches must continue to be adapted to address current and future questions about teaching and learning. An individual researcher's beliefs and expertise no longer can be the sole rationale for the research questions selected and pursued. Instead, the complexity of problems and social situations that affect practice and concern local constituents must be key to the creation of shared research agendas.

We continue to propose pragmatism as a stance for academics and communities of inquirers. Pragmatism is not a paradigm adapted from those that are currently popular; rather, it is a revolutionary break in our thinking and practice relating to inquiry. As a literacy community, we need to challenge ourselves to step back and think collectively and individually about the inquiry in which we are engaged. Is our research meaningful, credible, and prone to making a difference in students' learning and teachers' pedagogy? Does our inquiry work toward concrete alternatives for students and teachers? As Rorty (1982) explains, "For the pragmatists, the pattern of all inquiry—scientific as well as moral—is deliberation concerning the relative attractions of various concrete alternatives" (p. 164). We see the goal of research at its best as practical rationality serving moral concerns with social justice at its core. Pragmatic research can be a practical and hopeful inquiry, which avoids the arrogance of modernist empiricism and the angst of postmodern deconstructions. We believe this approach seeks to understand yet also to inform, change processes, and empower marginalized individuals.

In their column "What Can We, as Americans Do Together?" two politicians from different parties reflect together on what's missing from solving today's social problems (Horner & Penny, 2012). We take a lesson from them: the need for leadership to move forward. Embracing the idea of a pragmatic paradigm that could be viewed as uniting instead of dividing the research community requires courageous and responsible leadership. Many educational researchers are taking personal and professional risks to step out of their comfort zones and up to the challenges of today's educational world. These leaders realize that solutions to vexing educational issues require finding common ground instead of polarizing positions to address the real and necessary problems facing students, teachers, schools, families, and communities. The question becomes, On the big issues facing us in education, where will you find common ground with those who have different ideologies and research perspectives? Are we ready to listen, to learn, to reflect, and to hold ourselves to a higher standard? The NRC (2002) report described in the opening of this chapter offers a parting word of advice:

> Ultimately, policy makers and practicing educators will have to formulate specific policies and practices on the basis of values and practical wisdom as well as education research. Science-based education research will affect, but typically not solely determine, these policies and practices. (p. 17)

Our recent history as educational researchers has been fraught with anxiety, anguish, and despair. But there have been moments of enlightenment. Perhaps one might be an adaptation of Eugène Ionesco's quote: Ideologies *need not* separate us. Dreams of *what could be* can bring us together.

QUESTIONS FOR REFLECTION

1. If you were to write a summary of the impact of 21st-century federal legislation on reading research, what would you highlight as being the most significant development? Be sure to identify your stance (e.g., that of a researcher, teacher, policymaker, student, or parent).
2. What, if any, evidence exists to suggest that pragmatism—the recommended approach to literacy research in the author's chapter in *TMPR–5*—was taken up by researchers in 2000 and beyond?
3. The authors claim that a diversity of paradigms can enrich or hamper research. Can you think of a research question in reading that could be fruitfully explored with multiple theories and methodologies? Can you think of another question that is best researched with just one theory or methodology?
4. How would you apply the pragmatic orientation that the authors advocate to the investigation of a problem you have identified in the field of literacy?

REFERENCES

Beach, R. (1994). Adopting multiple stances in conducting literacy research. In R.B. Ruddell, M.R. Ruddell, & H. Singer (Eds.), *Theoretical models and processes of reading* (4th ed., pp. 1203–1219). Newark, DE: International Reading Association.

Beach, R., Green, J., Kamil, M.L., & Shanahan, T. (Eds.). (1992). *Multidisciplinary perspectives on literacy research*. Urbana, IL: National Conference on Research in English & National Council of Teachers of English.

Bernstein, R. (1983). *Beyond objectivism and relativism: Science, hermeneutics and practice*. Philadelphia: University of Pennsylvania Press.

Biesta, G.J., & Burbules, N.C. (2003). *Pragmatism and educational research*. Lanham, MD: Rowman & Littlefield.

Boisvert, R.D. (1998). *John Dewey: Rethinking our time*. Albany: State University of New York Press.

Campbell, J. (1995). *Understanding John Dewey*. Chicago: Open Court.

Chall, J.S. (1998). My life in reading. In E.G. Sturtevant, J.A. Dugan, P. Linder, & W.M. Linek (Eds.), *Literacy and community* (pp. 12–24). Commerce, TX: College Reading Association.

Clay, M.M. (1994). Foreword. In R.B. Ruddell, M.R. Ruddell, & H. Singer (Eds.), *Theoretical models and processes of reading* (4th ed., pp. ix–xiii). Newark, DE: International Reading Association.

Design-Based Research Collective. (2003). Design-based research: An emerging paradigm for educational inquiry. *Educational Researcher, 31*(1), 5–8.

Dewey, J. (1916). *Democracy and education: An introduction to the philosophy of education*. New York: Macmillan.

Dewey, J. (1978). *The middle works, 1899–1924: Vol. 5: 1908. Ethics* (J.A. Boydston, Ed.). Carbondale: Southern Illinois University Press. (Original work published 1908)

Dewey, J. (1981). Social inquiry. In J.J. McDermott (Ed.), *The philosophy of John Dewey* (pp. 397–420). Chicago: University of Chicago Press. (Original work published 1938)

Dewey, J. (1985). *The later works, 1925–1953: Vol. 7: 1932. Ethics* (J.A. Boydston, Ed.). Carbondale: Southern Illinois University Press. (Original work published 1932)

Dewey, J. (1987). *The later works, 1925–1953: Vol. 4: 1929. The quest for certainty* (J.A. Boydston, Ed.). Carbondale: Southern Illinois University Press. (Original work published 1929)

Dewey, J. (1993a). Creative democracy—The task before us. In D. Morris & I. Shapiro (Eds.), *John Dewey: The political writings* (pp. 240–245). Indianapolis, IN: Hackett. (Original work published 1939)

Dewey, J. (1993b). Philosophy and democracy. In D. Morris & I. Shapiro (Eds.), *John Dewey: The political writings* (pp. 38–47). Indianapolis, IN: Hackett. (Original work published 1919)

Dewey, J. (1993c). The public and its problems. In D. Morris & I. Shapiro (Eds.), *John Dewey: The political writings* (pp. 173–191). Indianapolis, IN: Hackett. (Original work published 1927)

Dickstein, M. (1998). Introduction: Pragmatism then and now. In M. Dickstein (Ed.), *The revival of pragmatism: New essays on social thought, law, and culture* (pp. 1–18). Durham, NC: Duke University Press.

Dillon, D.R., O'Brien, D.G., & Heilman, E. (2000). Literacy research in the next millennium: From paradigms to pragmatism and practicality. *Reading Research Quarterly, 35*(1), 10–26. doi:10.1598/RRQ.35.1.2

Dillon, D.R., O'Brien, D.G., Sato, M., & Kelly, C.M. (2010). Professional development and teacher education for reading instruction. In M.L. Kamil, P.D. Pearson, E.B. Moje, & P. Afflerbach (Eds.), *Handbook of reading research* (Vol. 4, pp. 629–659). Mahwah, NJ: Erlbaum.

Donmoyer, R. (1996). Educational research in an era of paradigm proliferation: What's a journal editor to do? *Educational Researcher, 25*(2), 19–25.

Eisenhart, M., & Towne, L. (2003). Contestation and change in national policy on "scientifically based" education research. *Educational Researcher, 32*(7), 31–38. doi:10.3102/0013189X032007031

Falk-Ross, F., Sampson, M.B., Fox, B.J., Berger, A., Lewis, J., Cassidy, J., et al. (2007). Stepping forward together: Voicing the concerns of teacher educators through practical applications and collaborative actions. *Reading Research and Instruction, 46*(1, Supp.), 1–18.

Floden, R.E. (2009). Empirical research without certainty. *Educational Theory, 59*(4), 485–498. doi:10.1111/j.1741-5446.2009.00332.x

Foucault, M. (1977). *Discipline and punish: The birth of the prison* (A. Sheridan, Trans.). New York: Pantheon. (Original work published 1975)

Foucault, M. (1980). Truth and power. In C. Gordon (Ed.), *Power/knowledge: Selected interviews and other writings, 1972–77* (pp. 109–133). New York: Pantheon.

Frankel, K.K., Pearson, P.D., & Nair, M. (2011). Reading comprehension and reading disability. In A. McGill-Franzen & R.L. Allington (Eds.), *Handbook of reading disability research* (pp. 219–231). London: Routledge.

Freeman, M., deMarrais, K., Preissle, J., Roulston, K., & St. Pierre, E.A. (2007). Standards of evidence in qualitative research: An incitement to discourse. *Educational Researcher, 36*(1), 25–32. doi:10.3102/0013189X06298009

Harris, T.L. (1969). Reading. In R.L. Ebel (Ed.), *Encyclopedia of educational research: A project of the American Educational Research Association* (4th ed., pp. 1069–1108). Toronto, ON, Canada: Macmillan & American Educational Research Association.

Hitchcock, G., & Hughes, D. (1989). *Research and the teacher: A qualitative introduction to school-based research*. New York: Routledge.

Hoffman, J.V., Roller, C., Maloch, B., Sailors, M., Duffy, G., & Beretvas, S.N. (2005). Teachers' preparation to teach reading and their expectations and practices in the first three years of teaching. *The Elementary School Journal, 105*(3), 267–287. doi:10.1086/428744

Hoffman, J.V., & Roller, C.M. (2001). The IRA Excellence in Reading Teacher Preparation Commission's report: Current practices in reading teacher education at the undergraduate level in the United States. In C.M. Roller (Ed.), *Learning to teach reading: Setting the research agenda* (pp. 32–79). Newark, DE: International Reading Association.

Horner, T., & Penny, T. (2012, May 20). What can we, as Americans do together? *Star Tribune*, p. OP3.

Israelson, M., Dillon, D.R., & Brodeur, K. (2012, December). *A study of preservice elementary literacy teachers' development of culturally sustaining knowledge in practice*. Paper presented at the annual meeting of the Literacy Research Association, San Diego, CA.

James, W. (1991). *Pragmatism*. Buffalo, NY: Prometheus. (Reprinted from *Pragmatism: A new name for some old ways of thinking*, by W. James, 1907, Cambridge, MA: Harvard University Press)

Johnson, R.B., & Onwuegbuzie, A.J. (2004). Mixed methods research: A research paradigm whose time has come. *Educational Researcher, 33*(7), 14–26. doi:10.3102/0013189X033007014

Juuti, K., & Lavonen, J. (2006). Design-based research in science education: One step towards methodology. *Nordic Studies in Science Education, 2*(4), 54–68.

Kellogg Commission on the Future of State and Land-Grant Universities. (1999, February). *Returning to our roots: The engaged institution*. Washington, DC: National Association of State Universities and Land-Grant Colleges.

Kuhn, T. (1970). *The structure of scientific revolutions* (2nd ed.). Chicago: University of Chicago Press.

Lather, P. (2004). This is your father's paradigm: Government intrusion and the case of qualitative research in education. *Qualitative Inquiry, 10*(1), 15–34. doi:10.1177/1077800403256154

Lincoln, Y.S., & Guba, E.G. (1985). *Naturalistic inquiry*. Newbury Park, CA: Sage.

McDermott, R.P. (1976). Achieving school failure: An anthropological approach to illiteracy and social stratification. In H. Singer & R.B. Ruddell (Eds.), *Theoretical models and processes of reading* (2nd ed., pp. 389–428). Newark, DE: International Reading Association.

Menand, L. (1997). *Pragmatism: A reader*. New York: Knopf Doubleday.

Menand, L. (2001). *The metaphysical club: A story of ideas in America*. New York: Flamingo.

Mosenthal, P. (1984). The problem of partial specification in translating reading research into practice. *The Elementary School Journal, 85*(2), 199–227.

Mosenthal, P.B. (1985). Defining progress in educational research. *Educational Researcher, 14*(9), 3–9.

Mosenthal, P.B. (1988). Research views: The simplicity approach to solving reading research puzzles. *The Reading Teacher, 41*(8), 818–821.

Mosenthal, P.B. (1999). Critical issues: Forging conceptual unum in the literacy field of pluribus: An agenda-analytic perspective. *Journal of Literacy Research, 31*(2), 213–254. doi:10.1080/10862969909548045

Mosenthal, P.B. (2002). Reading research as an agenda-setting enterprise: Bringing science to art, and art to science. In D.L. Schallert, C.M. Fairbanks, J. Worthy, B. Maloch, & J. Hoffman (Eds.), *The 51st yearbook of the National Reading Conference* (pp. 1–15). Oak Creek, WI: National Reading Conference.

National Institute of Child Health and Human Development. (2000). *Report of the National Reading Panel. Teaching children to read: An evidence-based assessment of the scientific research literature on reading and its implications for reading instruction* (NIH Publication No. 00-4769). Washington, DC: U.S. Government Printing Office.

National Research Council. (2002). *Scientific research in education* (R.J. Shavelson & L. Towne, Eds.). Washington, DC: National Academy Press.

Parker, L. (2002). What's race got to do with it? Critical race theory's conflicts with and connections to qualitative research methodology and epistemology. *Qualitative Inquiry, 8*(1), 7–22.

Patton, M.Q. (2002). *Qualitative evaluation and research methods* (3rd ed.). Newbury Park, CA: Sage.

Pearson, P.D., & Stephens, D. (1994). Learning about literacy: A 30-year journey. In R.B. Ruddell, M.R. Ruddell, & H. Singer (Eds.), *Theoretical models and processes of reading* (4th ed., pp. 22–42). Newark, DE: International Reading Association.

Peirce, C.S. (1992). In C.J.W. Kloesel & N. Houser (Eds.), *The essential Peirce* (Vol. I). Bloomington: Indiana University Press.

Polkinghorne, D. (1983). *Methodology for the human sciences*. Albany: State University of New York Press.

Reinking, D. (2010). Beyond the laboratory and lens: New metaphors for literacy research. In P. Dunston, L. Gambrell, K. Headley, S.K. Fullerton, P.M. Stecker, V.R. Gillis, & C.C. Bates (Eds.), *60th yearbook of the Literacy Research Association* (pp. 1–17). Oak Creek, WI: National Reading Conference.

Risko, V.J., Roller, C.M., Cummins, C., Bean, R.M., Block, C.C., Anders, P.L., et al. (2008). A critical analysis of research on reading teacher education. *Reading Research Quarterly, 43*(3), 252–288. doi:10.1598/RRQ.43.3.3

Rorty, R. (1982). *Consequences of pragmatism*. Minneapolis: University of Minnesota Press.

Rorty, R. (1991). *Objectivity, relativism, and truth*. New York: Cambridge University Press.

Ruddell, M.R. (1999). Of stand-up comics, statisticians, storytellers, and small girls walking backward: A new look at the discourses of literacy research. In T. Shanahan & F.V. Rodriguez-Brown (Eds.), *The 48th yearbook of the National Reading Conference* (pp. 1–16). Oak Creek, WI: National Reading Conference.

Scheurich, J.J., & Young, M.D. (1997). Coloring epistemologies: Are our research epistemologies racially biased? *Educational Researcher*, 26(4), 4–16.

Shavelson, R.J., Phillips, D.C., Towne, L., & Feuer, M.J. (2003). On the science of education design studies. *Educational Researcher*, 32(1), 25–28. doi:10.3102/0013189X032001025

Singer, H., & Ruddell, R.B. (Eds.). (1970). *Theoretical models and processes of reading*. Newark, DE: International Reading Association.

Singer, H., & Ruddell, R.B. (Eds.). (1976). *Theoretical models and processes of reading* (2nd ed.). Newark, DE: International Reading Association.

Singer, H., & Ruddell, R.B. (Eds.). (1985). *Theoretical models and processes of reading* (3rd ed.). Newark, DE: International Reading Association.

Stanfield, J.H., II. (1985). The ethnocentric basis of social science knowledge production. *Review of Research in Education*, 12(1), 387–415.

Thompson, A. (1997). Political pragmatism and educational inquiry. In F. Margonis (Ed.), *Philosophy of education* (pp. 425–434). Urbana, IL: Philosophy of Education Society.

Tierney, R. (1992). On matters of subjectivity, knowledge claims, art, and ethics in literacy research. In C. Kinzer & D. Leu (Eds.), *Literacy research, theory, and practice: Views from many perspectives* (41st yearbook of the National Reading Conference, pp. 1–16). Oak Creek, WI: National Reading Conference.

Vagle, M.D. (2009). Lessons in contingent, recursive humility. *Journal of Adolescent & Adult Literacy*, 54(5), 362–370. doi:10.1598/JAAL.54.5.6

Vagle, M.D., Dillon, D.R., Davison-Jenkins, J., LaDuca, B., & Olson, V. (2006). Redesigning literacy preservice education at four institutions: A three-year collaborative project. In J.V. Hoffman, D.L. Schallert, C.M. Fairbanks, J. Worthy, & B. Maloch (Eds.), *The 55th yearbook of the National Reading Conference* (pp. 324–340). Milwaukee, WI: National Reading Conference.

Valencia, S.W., & Buly, M.R. (2005). Behind test scores: What struggling readers *really* need. In S.J. Barrentine & S.M. Stokes (Eds.), *Reading assessment: Principles and practices for elementary teachers* (2nd ed., pp. 134–146). Newark, DE: International Reading Association.

Walsh, K. (2001). *Teacher certification reconsidered: Stumbling for quality*. Baltimore: Abell Foundation.

Weintraub, S., & Farr, R. (1976). Introduction. In R. Farr, S. Weintraub, & B. Tone (Eds.), *Improving reading research* (pp. 1–7). Newark, DE: International Reading Association.

Yussen, S.R., Dillon, D.R., Harwell, M.R., & Hearn, J.C. (2010). A new ambition for the journal. *Educational Researcher*, 39(1), 3–4. doi:10.3102/0013189X09360515

National Reports in Literacy: Building a Scientific Base for Practice and Policy

P. David Pearson, University of California, Berkeley

Elfrieda H. Hiebert, TextProject & University of California, Santa Cruz

In this article we have combined our independent invitations to provide reviews of the report of the National Early Literacy Panel (NELP; 2008), *Developing Early Literacy* (available at http://www.nifl.gov/earlychildhood/NELP/NELPreport .html), for two reasons: (a) because we agree on so many of the virtues and issues of the report and (b) because, by avoiding redundancy between us, we can cover a wider range of issues. Another feature of this response, which may be related to our long personal histories in reading research (Pearson is a decade up on Hiebert, however), is that we take a decidedly historical stance toward this document by reminding readers of the many syntheses of early reading that came before the NELP report and by asking, very pointedly, whether that report adds value to our cumulative knowledge, wisdom, and insight about early reading instruction.

The History

Research syntheses have become an academic art form over the past half-century. By 1960, educational scholars had completely embraced the classic literature review that has been a staple of the field (as evidenced in *Review of Educational Research*, the yearbooks of the National Society for the Study of Education, and the obligatory dissertation chapter that serves as an initiation fee for entry into the academy), and we were starting down the road to what has now become something of an education cottage industry—producing the increasingly ubiquitous *Handbook of X* (where *X* is a variable whose values embrace the entire landscape of educational scholarship). The classic methodology was to empower (or require) a scholar to conduct an exhaustive, critical, and interpretive review of a given piece of the education research landscape. Gene Glass (1976) made his contribution to this art form by bringing us meta-analysis and the powerful convenience of treating each and every statistical test in each and every experimental study of a phenomenon as a "subject" in a grand experiment as an alternative to the classic literature review synthesis. And like the handbook chapter phenomenon, meta-analysis has become its own independent entity, with an ever-growing literature, its own methodological debates, and a broad programmatic presence in all fields of scholarship (Cooper & Hedges, 1994; Shanahan, 2000).

The Special Case of Reading Research

From time to time, these reviews are blessed with the aegis of professional and/or governmental authority, usually through a commission (sometimes called a panel, task force, or even a committee) that is a part of an effort to promote consensus within fields. And no field has witnessed more synthesis/consensus-seeking efforts than reading, particularly early reading research. For reading, it all began in the 1960s when Jeanne Chall (1967), under the aegis of the Carnegie Corporation, brought us *Learning to Read: The Great Debate* to settle once and for all the question of how to teach beginning reading. Chall made many recommendations, most notable among them a return to an early emphasis on the code; moreover, curriculum developers in the educational publishing industry attended to many of Chall's recommendations as they developed new programs in the 1970s (Pearson, 1999).

Chall's (1967) book came out within weeks of the publication of the First-Grade Studies (Bond & Dykstra, 1967), the most ambitious large-scale collaborative effort undertaken by the Cooperative Research Branch of the Office of Education up to that time. And although the First-Grade Studies were not presented as a synthesis, they served that role whether they wanted to or not—precisely because they brought the lens of empirical evaluation to the competing set of "best practices" for teaching early reading. And for a decade or so, things seemed to settle down as phonics made a return to a dominant position in reading pedagogy in the post-Chall years.

The next substantial synthesis came in the middle 1980s when Richard Anderson and his colleagues (Anderson, Hiebert, Scott, & Wilkinson, 1985) offered *Becoming a Nation of Readers* as a National Academy of Education–sponsored response to the frontal assault on educational policy and practice served up by *A Nation at Risk* (National Commission on Excellence in Education, 1983). It made a strong recommendation for early emphasis on phonics but focused the bulk of its energy on convincing educators and the lay public to embrace the messages of meaning and comprehension that had dominated reading research between the publication of Chall's book and the release of *A Nation at Risk*.

Still (apparently) not content with the synthesis reached in the mid-1980s, the Office of Educational Research and Improvement, under some pressure from congressional mandate (Zorinsky, 1986), directed the Center for the Study of Reading to conduct a more focused synthesis of beginning reading; this led eventually to the publication of Marilyn Adams's (1990) *Beginning to Read: Thinking and Learning About Print*. Adams emerged as a strong code-emphasis proponent but an even stronger proponent for sticking to the evidence. So she hedged on providing an unqualified endorsement of early phonics as the unadorned answer to America's reading problems. She contextualized her endorsement of an early code emphasis by unpacking all of the other rich details and practices that must be present to make a program successful, including lots of reading, writing, and talking about stories and print.

Next in line was the National Academy of Education report *Preventing Reading Difficulties in Young Children* (*PRD;* Snow, Burns, & Griffith, 1998). *PRD* was jointly funded and sponsored by the Office of Special Education Programs in the Department of Education, the Office of Educational Research and Improvement (Early Childhood Institute) in the Department of Education, and the National Institute of Child Health and Human Development (NICHD)–Human Learning and Behavior Branch. Like its predecessors, *PRD* came out squarely for early phonics. However, it added a new element to the early reading mix—an even earlier emphasis (preschool, kindergarten, or early Grade 1) on phonemic awareness (PA) instruction as a prerequisite or corequisite to early phonics instruction. And then, like its predecessors, it went on to suggest that even the most ambitious and effective of early code-emphasis programs must be surrounded and supported by all of the "rich" aspects of oral and written language known to promote the development of comprehension and meaning making. Again, a strong endorsement—but no silver-bullet status—for phonics.

In 1997, Congress asked the director of the NICHD, in consultation with the secretary of education, to convene a national panel to assess the status of research-based knowledge of early reading development, including the effectiveness of various approaches to teaching children to read. This panel, dubbed the NRP (for National Reading Panel), was charged with providing a report that

> should present the panel's conclusions, an indication of the readiness for application in the classroom of the results of this research, and, if appropriate, a strategy for rapidly disseminating this information to facilitate effective reading instruction in the schools. If found warranted, the panel should also recommend a plan for additional research regarding early reading development and instruction. (NICHD, 2000, p. 1)

The NRP used the most "scientific" review approaches (i.e., meta-analysis, wherever it could) to distill from existing research what was known about the efficacy of teaching PA, phonics, fluency (instantiated as either guided reading instruction or independent reading), comprehension, and vocabulary; in addition, the panel investigated the status of the research base on teacher education and professional development and attempted to review research on technology and literacy. The findings from the NRP (NICHD, 2000) were straightforward: Teach PA in K–1, phonics first and fast, comprehension strategies through explicit instruction, vocabulary through a range of approaches, and fluency through oral reading practices. The panel declined to make substantial recommendations about silent reading (claiming the research base was too weak to draw any credible conclusions about its efficacy) and made very modest claims about technology and teacher education. Unlike its ancestral cousins in the synthesis enterprise (save Chall's book), the report of the NRP has proved to be amazingly influential in shaping policy and practice at both the federal level (through the Reading First provisions of No Child Left Behind) and the state level (by virtue of policies designed by states to be aligned with No Child Left Behind–Reading First).

So where does the NELP (2008) report fit in this long tradition of reading research syntheses? The answer to that question constitutes the remainder of this review. We hope to convince readers that the following claims about the report's efficacy and usefulness are warranted by the evidence and arguments we will bring forward:

- The NELP report adds little new knowledge or insight about teaching reading to young children, but it does serve the function, intentional or not, of strengthening the validity of the recommendations emerging from other syntheses, most notably *PRD* and the NRP report.
- Because the scope of the NELP review did not allow examination of its findings in relation to key contemporary research and evaluation efforts (e.g., the implementation and evaluation of Reading First and Early Reading First and the Early Childhood Longitudinal Study [ECLS]), it does not provide insights or recommendations that can move the field of early literacy instruction ahead. To the contrary, it simply reinforces practices that have already been widely implemented without resounding success.

The Review

NELP Adds Weight and Strength to Earlier Reviews

The findings of NELP focus on two issues: (a) those skills or abilities that, measured early in children's development, predict later literacy proficiency and (b) the effects of interventions (i.e., specific preschool or kindergarten programs, specific instructional emphases in preschool or kindergarten literacy programs such as a code focus or shared reading, home and parent programs, and language enhancement interventions) on supporting those skills or abilities directly. Although the panel provided a chapter for each of five interventions, we believe, for purposes of clarity and brevity, that these programmatic efforts can be clustered together. Regardless of the context (i.e., home, preschool, kindergarten) or content focus (e.g., language, code, shared reading), the studies in each of the reviews described a form of intervention. That is, unlike analyses of the effects of attending *any* kindergarten (e.g., Prince, Hare, & Howard, 2001) or preschool (e.g., V. E. Lee, Brooks-Gunn, Schnur, & Liaw, 1990), the studies in these five chapters of the NELP report analyzed the effects of some form of intervention in preschools, kindergartens, or homes. For convenience in the rest of this review, we summarize the key findings of NELP in Table 1.

Predictors of Later Literacy Proficiency. With respect to early indicators of later success, the panel identified 11 variables that have proved to be moderate to strong predictors of later literacy proficiency. Six of these variables, the panel concluded, served as the "best" (i.e., strongest and most consistent) predictors. Of these 6 variables, 2—alphabet knowledge (which the panel defined to

Table 1. Key Findings From the National Early Literacy Panel Report

Category	Variable	Finding
Predictors	Precursor literacy skills: • Alphabet knowledge (knowledge of letters and sounds associated with printed letters) • Phonological awareness • Rapid automatic naming (RAN) of letters or digits • RAN of objects or colors • Writing or writing name • Phonological memory	Medium to large correlations with later conventional literacy skills
	Additional early literacy skills: • Concepts about print • Print knowledge • Reading readiness • Oral language • Visual processing	Moderate correlations with at least one measure of later literacy achievement
Interventions	Code-focused instruction	Moderate to large effects across a broad spectrum of early literacy outcomes
	Book-sharing interventions	Moderate effects on children's print knowledge and oral language skills
	Home and parent programs	Moderate to large effects on children's oral language skills and general cognitive abilities
	Preschool and kindergarten programs	Moderate to large effects on spelling and reading readiness
	Language-enhanced interventions	Large effects on children's oral language skills

include letter–sound as well as letter–name correspondences) and phonological awareness—proved to be the best of the best. This "double bill" is long-standing in the literature, having been reported as part of federal initiatives for more than 40 years, beginning with the First-Grade Studies (Bond & Dykstra, 1967) and even earlier in the work of Durrell and Murphy (1953). The addition of early writing performance to the list of strong predictors verifies optimistic but ill-substantiated observations made in earlier national summaries (Adams, 1990; Snow et al., 1998); the NELP is the first to offer a substantial database to warrant claims that previously fell into the category of informed expert judgment.

The inclusion of rapid automatic naming (RAN) of all sorts of phenomena (i.e., letters, digits, objects, or colors) on a list of strong predictors is unique to this synthesis. Whether this addition represents a contribution of the report remains to be seen because, unlike most of the other strong predictors (letter knowledge, PA, writing, and perhaps phonological memory), RAN has not made the transition from "early indicator" to causally related factor through randomized or even natural experiments. For some reason, in the culture of education research and development, we seem unable to resist the temptation to believe that *predictors* are prime candidates to be transformed into *causes* of learning and achievement. To those who develop curriculum, pedagogy, and professional development, we offer the classic cautionary tale, "Don't confuse correlation with causation," but we fear that the inclusion of RAN in a list of predictors in a national report—especially when that list appears as the first finding of the report—has potential for egregious, unwarranted, and untested translation to practice. We only hope that we have the collective wisdom to wait for the experiments that can settle the question of their pedagogical significance. This caution seems even more appropriate in light of the weak body of evidence documenting "teaching to" speeded tests of many of the important skills of early reading (Paris, 2005).

Effects of Interventions. The review of interventions, from our perspective, represents the strongest potential contribution of the NELP report. But this sort of initiative—synthesizing what we know about various interventions or programmatic elements—is not new, so what is the value added by NELP? We think its value lies in the breadth, depth, and precision of the review. Earlier national syntheses have identified these categories of interventions as useful in developing students' literacy background and capacity for benefiting from instruction (Adams, 1990; Snow et al., 1998). In the case of the *PRD*, supportive research on book-sharing or oral language programs was presented as part of a narrative commentary. However, no previous effort has collected *all* of the available evidence on *all* of these programs and examined it through the lens of meta-analysis. It is genuinely useful to know that five programmatic initiatives—namely, code-focused instruction, shared reading interventions, parent and home programs, preschool and kindergarten programs, and language enhancement interventions—all make a consistent difference in profiles of student achievement on outcomes that we value as indicators of reading competence. Even more interesting is that these five general programmatic categories tended to influence different sorts of outcomes, suggesting a kind of "specificity" of effects. For example, language enhancement programs influenced oral language skills but not necessarily code-based knowledge.

This is not to say that the previous efforts did not highlight the benefits of one or more of these types of programs; they did. In fact, in every single synthesis since Chall's (1967) book, the virtues of early phonics have been solidly proclaimed along with the obligatory caution that phonics should be surrounded by a rich curriculum in other areas. But of these five program types, code-focused instruction is the only one to have achieved the gold standard prior to the NELP report. Thus, on the value-added dimension, the NELP report offers us the possibility of insights that can inform policy and practice by expanding the preschool toolkit available to educators and policy makers.

But alas! After tempting us with the expanded toolkit, NELP panel members leave us hanging—exactly what might be a next step? We're never told. They have not embraced the mantle of expertise offered by the data—interpreting, asking questions, weighing the contributions of different types of interventions, considering their combined effects; there is no suggestion of what choices might provide the greatest leverage, and not much building on the accumulated body of evidence from earlier synthesis efforts. Granted, the panel provides the facts. But without an authoritative interpretive and comparative lens, the usefulness of the facts is not at all clear. And why are there no illustrative examples from the research to give the reader a more vivid sense of what might matter? We have no idea of what a successful home program looks like. We have no idea of what differentiates a language-enhanced intervention from business-as-usual practices in a preschool classroom.

What makes this failure to assume the mantle of expertise all the more surprising is that this was one of the explicit goals stated in the NELP (2008) report's introduction:

> to synthesize research to contribute to decisions in educational policy and practice that affect early literacy development and to determine how teachers and families could support young children's language and literacy development. In addition, this evidence would be a key factor in the creation of literacy-specific materials for parents and teachers and staff development for early childhood educators and family-literacy practitioners. (p. iii)

If that was, indeed, panel members' goal, they have failed themselves and us. And, in the case of code-focused instruction, they have taken a step backward from the immediate predecessor, the NRP (NICHD, 2000).

We base this claim on the comprehensive review conducted by the NRP (NICHD, 2000) on code-focused instruction. The NELP (2008) states that the NRP did not examine the implications of instructional practices used with children from birth through age 5 (p. v.). In the case of alphabetics (NRP's term to encompass PA and phonics instruction), that observation is simply inaccurate. The subgroup on alphabetics defined the scope of its review as "preschoolers, kindergartners, 1st graders, or 2nd through 6th graders" (NICHD, 2000, pp. 2–3). Our point is that there was an existing national database for the NELP. Not only did the NELP not build on the NRP's analysis, but the NELP's conclusions fail to go as far as those of the NRP. The generous interpretation of this failure is that the NELP found more to be cautious about than did the NRP; an alternative interpretation is that the NELP failed to exercise its scholarly prerogative in taking the next step in the interpretation of the evidence. The conclusions of the NRP had been quite sophisticated, even nuanced—at the level where useful information is provided to policy makers, practitioners, parents, and publishers (the stated goal of the NELP—p. iii). Not only did the NELP not build on the findings of the NRP, but the NELP's conclusions fail to extend or even verify the findings of the NRP even though the panel reviewed some of the same studies (a core set of 17). The NRP provided information that, indeed, could be used to guide practice—the stated goal of the NELP. We compare the two sets of recommendations about PA in Table 2.

With respect to PA, the voice of scholars experienced in classrooms and in policy arenas comes through in the NRP in its observations regarding diminishing returns, the need to contextualize PA with letters and to work with young children on particular PA skills consistently, the need to instruct in small groups, the need to start earlier rather than later, and the appropriateness of teachers' providing instruction. The tenor of these recommendations indicates that the NRP had considered the consequences of potential misinterpretations (e.g., too much, too many, too late).

By contrast, the NELP's conclusions on PA (Lonigan, Schatschneider, & Westberg, 2008) are ambiguous and generic: Activities should involve higher level PA skills. PA training can occur alone or in combination with print knowledge. Instruction should be either individual or in small groups. There is no point along the developmental continuum when PA instruction is not beneficial. And there is no evidence of teachers' efficacy at providing PA instruction. Such broad and general findings are ripe for misinterpretations and overextensions in practice. When Congress asks a group of scholars who are content specialists to synthesize research to "contribute to decisions in educational policy and practice," scholars are obligated to provide more than technical skill at selecting studies and conducting statistical analyses. Technical quality is assumed. The value added of a panel or commission of the field's most reputable scholars is their ability (and license) to provide the best answers currently available to guide policy and practice. In this task, the NELP took a step back from the answers provided by the NRP, at least with respect to code-based instruction for young readers.

NELP Should Have Examined Contemporary Large-Scale Research Efforts

Surprisingly absent from the NELP report is any mention of an important group of federal initiatives in early childhood literacy, namely, Reading First (which includes kindergarten; Gamse, Jacob, Horst, Boulay & Unlu, 2008), Early Reading First (which targets the same age group as NELP; Jackson et al., 2007), and the ECLS (Denton & West, 2002). Across several careful readings of the NELP report we could not find a single mention of Reading First or of Early Reading First; we did find two, albeit cursory, references to the ECLS. These other reports were clearly available before the official publication of the NELP report. This is particularly the case with reports related to kindergarten from the ECLS (Denton & West, 2002). In the case of the Reading First and Early Reading First reports, the NELP reviewing team had likely completed their meta-analyses before the reports' appearance. But at the very least the NELP team should have compared their results with these reports in an introductory or ending interpretive perspective.

Table 2. Conclusions of the NRP and the NELP on Phonemic Awareness/Code-Focused Instruction

Issue	National Reading Panel (NRP)	National Early Literacy Panel (NELP)
Activities	"Effect sizes were larger when children received focused and explicit instruction on one or two PA [phonemic awareness] skills than when they were taught a combination of three or more PA skills" (National Institute of Child Health and Human Development [NICHD], 2000, pp. 2–4).	"Interventions should include PA training with activities involving higher-level PA skills, such as actively engaging in analysis or synthesis of words at the syllable, onset-rime, or phoneme level with feedback on correct and incorrect responses" (NELP, 2008, p. 119).
Connection to graphemes	"Instruction that taught phoneme manipulation with letters helped normally developing readers and at-risk readers acquire PA better than PA instruction without letters" (NICHD, 2000, pp. 2–4).	"Some form of PA training, either alone or in combination with more or less complex instruction related to print knowledge (i.e., letter-name instruction, instruction in early decoding skills) is likely to yield growth in children's skills related to later reading and writing achievement" (NELP, 2008, p. 118).
Size of group	"When children were taught PA in small groups, their learning was greater than when they were taught individually or in classrooms" (NICHD, 2000, pp. 2–4).	"The majority of the code-focused interventions summarized by this meta-analysis were conducted as either individual-level or small group-level interventions. There was no evidence that whole-class or large-group code-focused interventions will produce similar-sized effects on children's reading-related skills" (NELP, 2008, p. 119).
Length of time	"The length of time spent teaching children was influential, with treatments lasting from 5 to 18 hours producing larger effect sizes than shorter or longer treatments" (NICHD, 2000, pp. 2–4).	"These findings indicate that there is not a point along either an age or a developmental continuum at which code-focused interventions become more or less beneficial to children's early literacy skills" (NELP, 2008, p. 119).
Individual differences	"Preschoolers exhibited a much larger effect size on reading than did students in the other grade levels....The effects of PA training on reading outcomes were also influenced by SES [socioeconomic status], with mid-to-high SES associated with larger effect sizes than low SES" (NICHD, 2000, pp. 2–4).	"Importantly, there was no evidence that the effectiveness of code-focused interventions was influenced by age or development level of the children. That is, the impacts of code-focused interventions were observed in children whether they were preschool age or kindergarten age, and these interventions were equally successful across a range of levels of prior literacy knowledge (from minimal AK [alphabet knowledge] to being able to read)" (NELP, 2008, pp. 118–119).
Efficacy of classroom teachers	"Classroom teachers were very effective in teaching PA to children" (NICHD, 2000, pp. 2–4).	"The majority of interventions included in these analyses were designed and implemented by researchers" (NELP, 2008, p. 119).

By ignoring these initiatives, the NELP report fails to acknowledge the elephant in the room, namely, that the code-based variables the report identifies as both predictive and causative of success are neither new nor untested; to the contrary, (a) the evidence for their effectiveness is at least as old as Adams's *Beginning to Read* volume in 1990, and (b) they *have been* the driving force of the American early childhood literacy curriculum over at least the past decade, perhaps longer. Federal policies and large-scale initiatives have promoted a particular kind of code-centric curriculum in kindergarten through Reading First and for 4-year-olds through Early Reading First. Further, the national kindergarten curriculum has been heavily influenced by the code-driven textbook mandates of California and Texas (California English/Language Arts Committee, 1999; Texas Education Agency, 1997) that almost always determine what is available to the remainder of the country. To assert, as the NELP report does, that the NELP's definitive findings should point the way to reform represents an implicit denial of the reality of early reading pedagogy in the United States at the present time.

We understand why these national reports were excluded from the main NELP analysis: They do not meet the prima facie "peer reviewed journal" test. That is well and good, but it forces the NELP panel to face a curious risk: The panel might include a minor small-*n* study that passed peer review in a third-tier regional journal while excluding a large-*n* federally supported, peer-advised, and well-designed study that was, for reasons of heft, never submitted to a journal. At the very least, the panel might have discussed its findings in relationship to these other national efforts, attempting to explain any similarities and differences in findings or implications for policy.

Recent federal and state initiatives have escalated code-focused instruction in kindergarten (Goldstein, 2007; Hiebert, 2008). In many kindergarten contexts (as well as preschool ones), young children are involved with instruction that aims to promote at least two of the code-based predictor variables identified in the NELP report—letter naming and phonological awareness. In the Executive Summary, Lonigan and Shanahan (2008) state, "Most young children develop few conventional literacy skills before starting school" (p. vii). This is simply not the case, as is evident in the findings of the ECLS (Denton & West, 2002). Although the NELP report does not acknowledge Early Reading First and Reading First, the existence of the ECLS is recognized, albeit in passing. NELP refers to the ECLS report as evidence that there is a substantial amount of variance in conventional literacy within a cohort. About the variance in the ECLS cohort, the panel is right. But there is more to be garnered from ECLS: Differences in the literacy proficiencies of a cohort of young children notwithstanding, the ECLS also indicates that on the strongest predictor variable—alphabet knowledge—the target cohort (class of 2010, since students entered kindergarten in 1998) left kindergarten quite knowledgeable. Data from the ECLS are presented in Table 3. According to the ECLS, 67% of the class of 2010 could recognize letter names at the *beginning* of kindergarten, rising to 95% at the end.

Table 3. Percentage of Students in a Cohort Attaining Particular Skills on the Early Childhood Longitudinal Study

Outcome	Fall (Kindergarten)	Spring (Kindergarten)	Spring (Grade 1)
Letter recognition	67	95	100
Beginning sounds	31	74	98
Ending sounds	18	54	94
Sight words	3	14	83
Words in context	1	4	48

Note. From Denton and West, 2002, Figure 2, p. viii.

Verification that the ECLS accurately captured the performance of a modern kindergarten cohort comes from the work of Invernizzi, Justice, Landrum, and Booker (2004) when they measured all of the kindergartners in Virginia at the *beginning* of kindergarten. Of the 83,099 children who entered Virginia's kindergartens in 2003, 17,792 (21.4%) needed intervention based on an average letter-naming score of 5.36 (SD = 5.28), whereas the remainder did not need intervention, exhibiting a mean letter-naming performance of 20.85 (SD = 4.36). The 79% level of competence in Virginia is higher than the 67% reported by the ECLS, but given that Virginia ranked sixth in the latest state-by-state fourth-grade National Assessment of Educational Progress (NAEP) comparison (75% of its students were at or above basic on NAEP, compared with 65% nationally; J. Lee, Grigg, & Donahue, 2007), the Virginia–nation discrepancy at kindergarten entry seems comparable.

Is it just an eerie coincidence that the percentage of fourth graders scoring below basic on the NAEP nationally—35% compared with 25% in a state such as Virginia—mirrors almost precisely the percentage of children who have *not* mastered letter naming on entry into kindergarten—33% nationally versus 21% in Virginia? We do not have sufficient evidence—or space in this essay—to explore this connection. So we will simply note the coincidence. The typical argument is that the NAEP is far too distal a measure of achievement to relate to kindergarten entry performance. On the other hand, the consistency with which first graders' reading achievement predicts achievement in subsequent grades is well established (e.g., Alexander, Entwisle, & Horsey, 1997; Ensminger & Slusarcick, 1992; Juel, 1988).

If kindergarten letter naming is a predictor of first-grade performance, it could be argued that simply getting students to letter naming by the end of kindergarten is not doing the trick. Once students in a cohort have started to read, measures of reading itself become the standard. On reading words in context, the ECLS data (see Table 3) suggest that the cohort of students in the longitudinal sample is not doing particularly well—even though most have alphabet knowledge under control. In other words, relative high competence in alphabet knowledge was not associated with strong word-reading performance. If the relatively high alphabet knowledge scores of this cohort do indeed reflect an increased emphasis of alphabet instruction in prekindergarten and kindergarten, then that instruction seems not to have paid off much in the way of word-reading dividends for these children in kindergarten. This finding suggests that there is little evidence that the literacy trajectories of students who enter school with "below-basic" proficiencies show progress on tasks that really matter as a result of an ever-increasing emphasis on the code.

Could it be that what these knowledgeable kindergarteners need is greater attention to word reading and writing rather than to their prerequisites? There is evidence—not included in the NELP report—that appropriate reading instruction in kindergarten can result in positive and meaningful differences in reading proficiency throughout a school career (Hanson & Farrell, 1995). Even in the NELP report, evidence points to facilitative effects of the various interventions (i.e., code focus, book sharing, home/parent, preschool/kindergarten, language focus) on young children's reading—even when that instruction is not focused directly on reading acquisition. Because the NELP does not engage in interpretive commentary, the panel's findings on word learning are not considered in depth.

In lieu of this information, we studied the report for data on word reading. Of the five interventions on which the NELP conducted meta-analyses, only shared reading—the very intervention that would be predicted to support reading acquisition—did not include any studies with assessments of reading. Effects sizes for reading, alphabet knowledge, and PA in the various interventions reviewed by the NELP are presented in Table 4. The effect sizes for reading were consistently the highest of any of the three measures. Further, as shown in Table 3.3 of the NELP (2008) report, effects were evident for preschoolers (.75, $p < .01$) as well as kindergartners (.43, $p < .0001$). Students who had little alphabet knowledge showed benefits for reading that were as high as (or higher than) those for alphabet knowledge and PA: reading (.92, $p < .05$), AK (.86, $p < .01$), and PA (.99, $p < .01$; Table 3.4 of the report). In only one of the chapters do the authors refer to the phenomenon of learning to read. Molfese and Westberg (2008), the authors of the NELP chapter on preschool/kindergarten, state the following about the effect size of .75 for reading: "Although, again, this difference did not reach statistical significance, the size of the difference is so large as to be of educational importance. These findings suggest that kindergarten and preschool programs can have an impact on children's reading development" (p. 199).

We end this section by considering the consequences of ignoring what students know at the beginning and end of kindergarten *and* what they have not learned as a result of efforts that have emphasized the code (the modest if not disappointing findings of the Early Reading First report). Consequential validity has become an increasingly critical consideration in weighing the impact of initiatives in assessment, pedagogy, and policy (Messick, 1989). We need to think of the consequential validity of this report for all students but especially for the two groups of students who anchor the ends of our distribution of competence—those who are among the 33% who begin kindergarten without conventional literacy (i.e., not knowing letter names or letter–sound matching) and the approximately

Table 4. Effect Sizes for Measures of Alphabet Knowledge (AK), Phonemic Awareness (PA), and Reading Across Five Types of Interventions

Type of Intervention (Table in NELP)	Measure	Effect Size	*n* of Studies	*p*
Code focused (3.1)				
	AK	.38	24	.0002
	PA	.82	51	< .0001
	Reading	.44	36	< .0001
Shared reading (4.1)[a]				
	AK	−.06	2	.78
	PA	.11	2	.42
Home and parent (5.1)				
	AK	−.03	1	.81
	PA	.21	2	.21
	Reading	.28	1	.17
Preschool/kindergarten (6.1)				
	AK	.23	4	.27
	PA	.08	2	.49
	Reading	.75	9	.19
Language enhancement (7.1)				
	AK	NA	NA	NA
	PA	.57	2	.05
	Reading	.36	2	.343

Note. From National Early Literacy Panel (NELP), 2008.
[a]None of the studies of shared reading included a measure of reading.

31% who begin kindergarten close to mastery of two of the most prominent skills in the typical code-based kindergarten curriculum (i.e., matching initial sounds with letters and recognizing letters).

Consider the first group of students, those in the bottom third of the performance distribution: When this report makes its way into the policy arena, those students will be subjected to an even more aggressive curriculum of "pieces" of language. As Perkins (2008) describes it, they will be faced with "elementitis," where skills are broken into elements and taught discretely, where playing the whole game of reading is put off until later, once the pieces are in place. They are at risk of falling victim to what we have called the basic-skills conspiracy of good intentions: "First things first, then we'll get to the good stuff," so the conspiracy goes. "We won't dwell long on the code, but surely it must be in place before we get to reading." Or, "First, let's make sure they get the letters and words right before we get to the 'what ifs' and 'I wonder whats' of the curriculum." This focus on molecular, rather than molar, aspects of the curriculum has surfaced again and again in our history. As far back as 1975, Johnson and Pearson (1975) described the psycholinguistic naïveté of conceptualizing reading as a string of minute behavioral objectives, and as recently as 2005, Paris pointed out the mischief that is done when constrained skills (i.e., finite skills that can be easily mastered, such as alphabet knowledge) prevail over unconstrained skills (i.e., indefinite sets that permit continuous growth such as comprehension or vocabulary breadth). Reading researchers seem to resist the idea that, somewhere in the reading curriculum, students must learn to orchestrate a wide range of these specific subskills in order to engage in the genuinely skilled practice of reading for meaning.

The more diverse our population becomes, the more we seem to have reified the conventional literacy curriculum, and the NELP report is no exception. However, the evidence suggests that even with high performances on alphabet knowledge (in the data from the ECLS, 95% of a cohort leaves kindergarten with alphabet mastery—see Table 3), students are not doing better on the task of reading as a result of this widespread code-focused curriculum. A long-standing observation that goes back to at least the 1940s (e.g., Gates, 1940) suggests one possible reason: that strong predictors like letter naming are really proxies for a host of other causative variables with which letter-naming scores are naturally correlated—early home or preschool reading experience, book sense, orthographic awareness, even language skill.

Because the NELP report looked only at experimental and predictive research (and excluded largely descriptive work), it tells us nothing about how the students in the top third got to know what they know. A substantial body of evidence supports the view that young children learn a great deal about print and literacy (acquire letter names, grasp the alphabetic principle, and even learn a handful of words) through activities that are fairly typical in some homes but not in others—manipulating magnetic letters, writing words, singing alliterative songs, playing rhyming games, and writing messages to extended family members (e.g., Frijters, Barron, & Brunello, 2000). Call it incidental learning if you like, but asking students to engage in activities that require them to orchestrate many of the components of print literacy (which could be taught and measured separately) does actually result in improvements in these "enabling" skills as well as in students' capacity to orchestrate them in an integrated performance, which we might even call "reading." Somehow, in our fascination with all the pieces and predictors, we seem to have lost sight of the goal to which their mastery is linked.

The Likely Legacy of the NELP Report

So, where is the news in NELP? And what will we do differently in our schools as a result of its addition to the long tradition of national syntheses of early reading research? There is some news in NELP, and the big question is how the various strands in the findings will play out in the press and in policy circles. For example, there is some encouraging news for those who would like to see more "meaning-oriented" variables and activities incorporated into the early literacy curriculum. NELP is the first report that has provided gold-standard evidence (i.e., in a meta-analysis) for language predictors, putting them into the second tier in terms of magnitude, just behind the traditional leaders of the pack, alphabet knowledge and PA. And on the intervention side, there is gold-standard evidence to support language and more meaning-based programs, albeit alongside code-focused programs. In fact, the surprising finding about the interventions is how many, not how few, programmatic elements seem to make a difference.

And that brings us to the question of impact and legacy. On both the predictor side and the programmatic side, there is evidence that might lead a policy maker to say, "Well, it's balance! Both code and meaning predict and shape reading performance." But having seen how the NRP was used to rationalize a "first among equals" emphasis on phonics and PA, so that fluency, comprehension, and vocabulary had to wait their turn in the curricular queue, and having seen the persistence of code emphasis in the wake of disappointing evidence about its efficacy in reports on Reading First (Gamse et al., 2008) and Early Reading First (Jackson et al., 2007), we are not sanguine about the capacity of the NELP report to move us toward the kind of balance that its findings would warrant. We wish that the NELP had contextualized its findings both historically and contemporaneously. The historical grounding would have allowed the panel to assess the value added of its report. Had the panel achieved a contemporary grounding, in light of the trends available in the literature on ECLS, Reading First, and Early Reading First, it might have concluded that balance, not focus, is what the research supports. And who knows, the panel might have concluded, as do we, that in moving back to balance as a curricular metaphor, it is high time for the field to reject the pendulum swing, or even the fulcrum, metaphor in favor of an ecological metaphor that argues for, to paraphrase the author of Ecclesiastes (3:1), a time for every curricular purpose under heaven.

QUESTIONS FOR REFLECTION

1. What do the authors caution regarding the translation of the NELP report's predictive findings into classroom practice?
2. What do the authors feel are shortcomings of the NELP report's findings on phonemic awareness/code-focused instruction regarding recommendations for teacher practice?
3. What are the implications of the data in Table 4 for classroom practice and/or future research?

REFERENCES

Adams, M. J. (1990). *Beginning to read: Thinking and learning about print.* Cambridge, MA: MIT Press.

Alexander, K. L., Entwisle, D. R., & Horsey, C. S. (1997). From first grade forward: Early foundations of high school dropout. *Sociology of Education, 70*(2), 87–107.

Anderson, R. C., Hiebert, E. H., Scott, J. A., & Wilkinson, I. A. G. (1985). *Becoming a nation of readers: The report of the Commission on Reading.* Champaign, IL: Center for the Study of Reading.

Bond, G. L., & Dykstra, R. (1967). The cooperative research program in first-grade reading instruction. *Reading Research Quarterly, 2*, 5–142.

California English/Language Arts Committee. (1999). *English-language arts content standards for California public schools (kindergarten through grade twelve).* Sacramento: California Department of Education.

Chall, J. S. (1967). *Learning to read: The great debate.* New York: McGraw-Hill.

Cooper, H. M., & Hedges, L. V. (Eds.). (1994). *The handbook of research synthesis*. New York: Russell Sage Foundation.

Denton, K., & West, J. (2002). *Children's reading and mathematics achievement in kindergarten and first grade*. Washington, DC: U.S. Department of Education, Office of Educational Research and Improvement.

Durrell, D. D., & Murphy, H. A. (1953). The auditory discrimination factor in readiness and reading ability. *Education, 73*, 556–560.

Ensminger, M. E., & Slusarcick, A. L. (1992). Paths to high school graduation or dropout: A longitudinal study of a first-grade cohort. *Sociology of Education, 65*(2), 95–113.

Frijters, J. C., Barron, R. W., & Brunello, M. (2000). Direct and mediated influences of home literacy and literacy interest on prereaders' oral vocabulary and early written language skill. *Journal of Educational Psychology, 92*, 466–477.

Gamse, B. C., Jacob, R. T., Horst, M., Boulay, B., & Unlu, F. (2008). *Reading First Impact Study final report*. Washington, DC: National Center for Education Evaluation and Regional Assistance, Institute of Education Sciences, U.S. Department of Education.

Gates, A. I. (1940). A further evaluation of reading-readiness tests. *Elementary School Journal, 40*(8), 577–591.

Glass, G. V. (1976). Primary, secondary, and meta-analysis of research. *Educational Researcher, 5*(10), 3–8.

Goldstein, L. S. (2007). Beyond the DAP versus standards dilemma: Examining the unforgiving complexity of kindergarten teaching in the United States. *Early Childhood Research Quarterly, 22*(1), 39–54.

Hanson, R. A., & Farrell, D. (1995). The long-term effects on high school seniors of learning to read in kindergarten. *Reading Research Quarterly, 30*, 908–933.

Hiebert, E. H. (2008). The (mis)match between texts and students who depend on schools to become literate. In E. H. Hiebert & M. Sailors (Eds.), *Finding the right texts for beginning and struggling readers: Research-based solutions* (pp. 1–21). New York: Guilford.

Invernizzi, M., Justice, L., Landrum, T., & Booker, K. (2004). Early literacy screening in kindergarten: Widespread implementation in Virginia. *Journal of Literacy Research, 36*(4), 479–500.

Jackson, R., McCoy, A., Pistorino, C., Wilkinson, A., Burghardt, J., Clark, M., et al. (2007). *National evaluation of Early Reading First: Final report*. Washington, DC: U.S. Department of Education, Institute of Education Sciences.

Johnson, D. D., & Pearson, P. D. (1975). Skills management systems: A critique. *Reading Teacher, 28*(8), 757–764.

Juel, C. (1988). Learning to read and write: A longitudinal study of fifty-four children form first through fourth grades. *Journal of Educational Psychology, 80*, 437–447.

Lee, J., Grigg, W. S., & Donahue, P. L. (2007). *The nation's report card: Reading 2007* (NCES 2007–496). Washington, DC: National Center for Education Statistics, Institute of Education Sciences, U.S. Department of Education.

Lee, V. E., Brooks-Gunn, J., Schnur, E., & Liaw, F. (1990). Are Head Start effects sustained? A longitudinal follow-up comparison of disadvantaged children attending Head Start, no preschool, and other preschool programs. *Child Development, 61*(2), 495–507.

Lonigan, C. J., Schatschneider, C., & Westberg, L. (2008). Impact of code-focused interventions on young children's early literacy skills. In National Early Literacy Panel, *Developing early literacy: Report of the National Early Literacy Panel* (pp. 107–151). Washington, DC: National Institute for Literacy. Available at http://www.nifl.gov/earlychildhood/NELP/NELPreport.html

Lonigan, C. J., & Shanahan, T. (2008). Executive summary of the report of the National Early Literacy Panel. In National Early Literacy Panel, *Developing early literacy: Report of the National Early Literacy Panel* (pp. v–xii). Washington, DC: National Institute for Literacy. Available at http://www.nifl.gov/earlychildhood/NELP/NELPreport.html

Messick, S. (1989). Validity. In R. L. Linn (Ed.), *Educational measurement* (3rd ed., pp. 13–103). New York: Macmillan and the American Council on Education.

Molfese, V., & Westberg, L. (2008). Impact of preschool and kindergarten programs on young children's early literacy skills. In National Early Literacy Panel, *Developing early literacy: Report of the National Early Literacy Panel* (pp. 189–209). Washington, DC: National Institute for Literacy. Available at http://www.nifl.gov/earlychildhood/NELP/NELPreport.html

National Commission on Excellence in Education. (1983). *A nation at risk: The imperative for educational reform*. Washington, DC: U.S. Government Printing Office.

National Early Literacy Panel. (2008). *Developing early literacy: Report of the National Early Literacy Panel*. Washington, DC: National Institute for Literacy. Available at http://www.nifl.gov/earlychildhood/NELP/ NELPreport.html

National Institute of Child Health and Human Development. (2000). *Report of the National Reading Panel. Teaching children to read: An evidence-based assessment of the scientific research literature on reading and its implications for reading instruction* (NIH Pub. No. 00–4769). Washington, DC: U.S. Government Printing Office.

Paris, S. G. (2005). Reinterpreting the development of reading skills. *Reading Research Quarterly, 40*(2), 184–202.

Pearson, P. D. (1999). Essay book reviews: A historically based review of *Preventing Reading Difficulties in Young Children*. *Reading Research Quarterly*, 2(34), 231–246.

Perkins, D. N. (2008). *Making learning whole: How seven principles of teaching can transform education.* San Francisco: Jossey-Bass.

Prince, D. L., Hare, R. D., & Howard, E. M. (2001). Longitudinal effects of kindergarten. *Journal of Research in Childhood Education, 16*(1), 15–27.

Shanahan, T. (2000). Research synthesis: Making sense of the accumulation of knowledge in reading. In M. L. Kamil, P. B. Mosenthal, P. D. Pearson, & R. Barr (Eds.), *Handbook of reading research* (Vol. 3, pp. 209–226). Mahwah, NJ: Lawrence Erlbaum.

Snow, C. E., Burns, M. S., & Griffin, P. (1998). *Preventing reading difficulties in young children.* Washington, DC: National Academy Press.

Texas Education Agency. (1997). *Proclamation of the State Board of Education advertising for bids on textbooks.* Austin, TX: Author.

Zorinsky, E. (1986). *Amendment #2202 to the Human Services Reauthorization Act (Public Law 99–425).* Washington, DC: U.S. Congress.

CHAPTER 42

New Literacies: A Dual-Level Theory of the Changing Nature of Literacy, Instruction, and Assessment

Donald J. Leu, University of Connecticut

Charles K. Kinzer, Teachers College, Columbia University

Julie Coiro, University of Rhode Island

Jill Castek, Portland State University

Laurie A. Henry, University of Kentucky

Literacy as Deixis

Today, the nature of literacy has become deictic. This simple idea carries important implications for literacy theory, research, and instruction that our field must begin to address. *Deixis* is a term used by linguists (Fillmore, 1966; Murphy, 1986; Traut & Kazzazi, 1996) to define words whose meanings change rapidly as their context changes. *Tomorrow*, for example, is a deictic term; the meaning of "tomorrow" becomes "today" every 24 hours. The meaning of literacy has also become deictic because we live in an age of rapidly changing information and communication technologies, each of which requires new literacies (Leu, 1997, 2000). Thus, to have been literate yesterday, in a world defined primarily by relatively static book technologies, does not ensure that one is fully literate today where we encounter new technologies such as Google docs, Skype, iMovie, Contribute, Basecamp, Dropbox, Facebook, Google, foursquare, Chrome, educational video games, or thousands of mobile apps. To be literate tomorrow will be defined by even newer technologies that have yet to appear and even newer discourses and social practices that will be created to meet future needs. Thus, when we speak of new literacies, we mean that literacy is not just new today; it becomes new every day of our lives.

How should we theorize the new literacies that will define our future, when literacy has become deictic? The answer is important because our concept of literacy defines both who we are and who we shall become. But there is a conundrum here.

This chapter is adapted from "Toward a Theory of New Literacies Emerging From the Internet and Other Information and Communication Technologies," by D.J. Leu Jr., C.K. Kinzer, J.L. Coiro, & D.W. Cammack, in *Theoretical Models and Processes of Reading* (5th ed., pp. 1570–1613), edited by R.B. Ruddell and N.J. Unrau, 2004, Newark, DE: International Reading Association.

How can we possibly develop adequate theory when the object that we seek to study is itself ephemeral, continuously being redefined by a changing context? This is an important theoretical challenge that our field has not previously faced. The purpose of this chapter is to advance theory in a world where literacy has become deictic. It suggests that a dual-level theory of New Literacies is a useful approach to theory building in a world where the nature of literacy continuously changes.

We begin by making a central point: Social contexts have always shaped both the function and form of literate practices and been shaped by them in return. We discuss the social context of the current period and explain how this has produced new information and communication technologies (ICTs), and the new literacies that these technologies demand. Second, we explore several lowercase new literacies perspectives that are emerging. We argue that a dual-level New Literacies theory is essential to take full advantage of this important and diverse work. Third, we identify a set of principles, drawn from research, that inform an uppercase theory of New Literacies. Then, we present one lowercase theory of new literacies, the new literacies of online research and comprehension, to illustrate how a dual-level theory of New Literacies can inform new literacies research that takes related but different theoretical perspectives. We conclude by considering the implications of a dual-level theory of New Literacies for both research and practice.

Literacy in Today's Social Context

Literacy has always changed. Historical analyses demonstrate that both the forms and functions of literacy have been largely determined by the continuously changing social forces at work within any society and the technologies these forces often produce (Boyarin, 1993; Diringer, 1968; Gee, 2007b; Illera, 1997; Manguel, 1996; Mathews, 1966; N.B. Smith, 1965). This story began in Sumeria with the invention of cuneiform tablets, the first system of writing, during the fourth century B.C. (Boyarin, 1993; Diringer, 1968; Manguel, 1996). It continues to the present day.

Often, we lose sight of these historic roots. We need to remember that social forces, and the technologies they produce, often define the changing nature of literacy today just as they have in the past. Clearly, the social forces in the present context will exert similar changes. Thus, attempts to develop any theory of literacy must begin by exploring the critical social forces at work today.

What are the important social forces at work today that frame, and are framed by, the changes to literacy we are experiencing? We believe they include the following:

1. Global economic competition within economies based increasingly on the effective use of information and communication.
2. The rapid appearance of the Internet in both our professional and personal lives.
3. Public policy initiatives by nations that integrate literacy and the Internet into instruction.

Global Economic Competition Within Economies Based Increasingly on the Effective Use of Information and Communication

The world of work has been undergoing fundamental transformation (Kirsch, Braun, Yamamoto, & Sum, 2007; Organisation for Economic Co-operation and Development & the Centre for Educational Research and Innovation, 2010; Rouet, 2006; M.C. Smith, Mikulecky, Kibby, Dreher, & Dole, 2000). Indeed, it is this social context that prompts many of the changes to ICTs and to literacy that we experience, making the effective use of Internet technologies a central component of the literacy curriculum.

Traditionally, industrial-age organizations were organized in a vertical, top-down fashion where most decisions were made at the highest levels and then communicated to lower levels (see Figure 1). This wastes large amounts of intellectual capital within an organization and results in lower productivity. Today, global economic competition requires organizations to abandon these traditional command and control structures to leverage all of their intellectual capital, operate more productively, and become more competitive.

In a postindustrial economy (Reich, 1992), organizations seeking to achieve greater productivity and become more competitive reorganize themselves horizontally. Instead of all decisions emanating from the top of an organization, teams within lower levels of organizations are empowered to identify and solve important problems that generate new knowledge and lead to better ways of producing goods or providing services. These high-performance workplaces seek to use the intellectual capital of every employee to increase effective decision making and increase productivity. The effective use of information to solve problems allows a horizontally organized workplace to become much more productive and competitive (see Figure 2).

Figure 1. The Typical Organizational Structure of Industrial-Age Workplaces

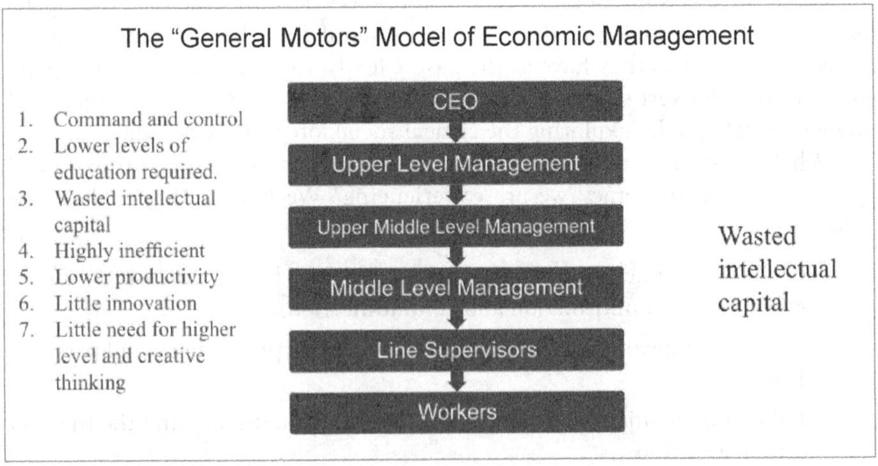

Figure 2. The Typical Organizational Structure of Postindustrial Workplaces

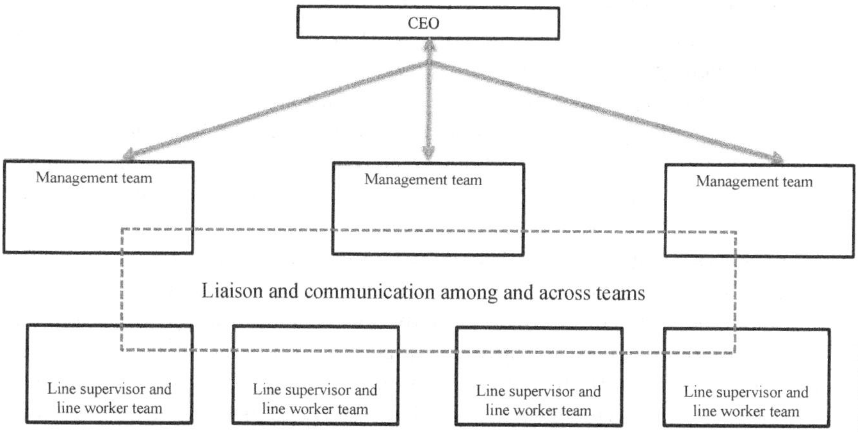

The figure shows new management and communication structures. Communication occurs in both directions at all levels, both horizontally and vertically, as indicated by the dashed box that shows teams communicate and work with one another across teams within a horizontal level but can also draw team members and communicate with teams vertically. Teams are often composed of members from all levels through liaison and communication, which occurs largely through information and communication technologies. The importance of communication and cross-team liaison/membership shows that new literacies are required for this structure to occur.

This change has had a fundamental effect on the nature of literacy within organizations. At the broadest level, members of these teams must:

- Quickly identify important problems in their work
- Locate useful information related to the problems they identify
- Critically evaluate the information they find
- Synthesize multiple sources of information to determine a solution
- Quickly communicate the solution to others so everyone within an organization is informed
- Monitor and evaluate the results of their solutions and decisions and modify these as needed

How do teams do this? Often they rely upon the Internet. Many economists have concluded that productivity gains realized during the past several decades have been due to the rapid integration of the Internet into the workplace, enabling units to better share information, communicate, and solve problems (Matteucci, O'Mahony, Robinson, & Zwick, 2005; van Ark, Inklaar, & McGuckin, 2003). Internet use in U.S. workplaces, for example, increased by nearly 60% during a single year (2002) among all employed adults 25 years of age and older (U.S. Department of Commerce, Economic and Statistics Administration & National Telecommunications and Information Administration, 2002).

The Rapid Appearance of the Internet in Our Professional and Personal Lives

It is not surprising that the Internet and other ICTs have appeared and become such a prominent part of our lives during the transition from an industrial to a postindustrial society. These new information and communication tools allow horizontally organized workplaces to identify important problems, address them, and nimbly modify and customize solutions as contexts and technologies change. In many cases, all of this is accomplished with team members situated in different locations around the globe.

This analysis suggests that competence with the new literacies required by the Internet and other ICTs is a crucial determinant of an engaged life in an online age of information and communication. However, it is important to recognize that these skills are not limited to simply creating more productive workers and workplaces. Even more important, the information resources and opportunities available on the Internet provide individuals with opportunities to make their personal lives richer and more fulfilling. This happens while advocating for social justice, refinancing a home, selecting a university to attend, managing a medical question, purchasing books, or any one of the hundreds of other tasks important to daily life. We also see this happening as citizens in some parts of the world use these skills and new technologies to overthrow corrupt and undemocratic political systems. Preparation in the new literacies required to use the Internet and other ICTs enables individuals to have more fulfilling personal as well as professional lives.

Public Policy Initiatives by Nations That Integrate Literacy and the Internet Into Instruction

Previously, we reported on public policies in nations beginning to recognize how the Internet was changing the nature of literacy (Leu & Kinzer, 2000; Leu, Kinzer, Coiro, & Cammack, 2004). At that point, however, public policies about literacy and the Internet often traveled on separate but parallel tracks. Today, we are beginning to see the evolution of these parallel public policies as they slowly become more integrated in nations such as Australia, Canada, and the United States.

In Australia, for example, the Australian Curriculum, Assessment and Reporting Authority (ACARA; n.d.) has developed the Australian Curriculum. This Australian initiative integrates literacy and the Internet *within* the English curriculum, not outside of it as it had been previously. As indicated in the Australian Curriculum:

> ICT competence is *an important component of the English curriculum* [italics added]. Students develop the skills and understanding required to use a range of contemporary technologies. In particular, they explicitly develop increasingly sophisticated word-processing skills to enhance text construction. Students also progressively develop skills in using information technology when conducting research, a range of digital technologies to create, publish and present their learning, and communication technologies to collaborate and communicate with others both within and beyond the classroom. (ACARA, n.d., General Capabilities, Information and Communication Technology Competence section, para. 2)

The English curriculum integrates this capability into each year's statement of the content standards. Evidence of this integration also appears in the "Elaborations" of the English curriculum such as this one from Year 4 English (ELBE900): "Participating in online searches for information using navigation tools and discussing similarities and differences between print and digital information." In Australia, literacy and the Internet are becoming integrated with new literacies.

In another example, this time from Canada, the province of Manitoba has developed an educational framework called Literacy With ICT Across the Curriculum (Minister of Manitoba Education, Citizenship, and Youth, 2006). This initiative outlines skills and includes standards required in the 21st century in all aspects of their curriculum:

> Identifying appropriate inquiry questions; navigating multiple *information networks* [italics added] to locate relevant information; applying critical thinking skills to evaluate information sources and content; synthesizing information and ideas from multiple sources and networks; representing information and ideas creatively in visual, aural, and textual formats; crediting and referencing sources of information and intellectual property; and communicating new understandings to others, both face to face and over distance. (p. 18)

In the United States, the Common Core State Standards Initiative (National Governors Association Center for Best Practices & Council of Chief State School Officers, 2010) has sought to establish more uniform standards across states to prepare students for college and careers in the 21st century. One of their key design principles, research and media skills, shows that literacy and new technologies are beginning to be considered together:

> To be ready for college, workforce training, and life in a technological society, students need the ability to gather, comprehend, evaluate, synthesize, and report on information and ideas, to conduct original research in order to answer questions or solve problems, and to analyze and create a high volume and extensive range of print and non-print texts in media forms old and new. The need to conduct research and to produce and consume media is embedded into every aspect of today's curriculum. (p. 4)

This design principle, however, is implemented most directly in the Common Core State Standards for writing than for reading (Leu et al., 2011). Consider, for example, these two (of 10) Anchor Standards (A.S.) in Writing:

> A.S. 6. Use technology, including the Internet, to produce and publish writing and to interact and collaborate with others.

> A.S. 8. Gather relevant information from multiple print and digital sources, assess the credibility and accuracy of each source, and integrate the information while avoiding plagiarism. (National Governors Association Center for Best Practices & Council of Chief State School Officers, p. 41)

In the Anchor Standards in Reading, we find a focus on the higher level thinking skills required while reading and conducting research online (Leu, Forzani, et al., in press).

Although these changes are more evolutionary than revolutionary, it is clear that literacy and Internet use are beginning to slowly become more integrated into the public policies and curricula of nations in ways that have a direct impact on literacy education. Because of global economic competition, even nations with a long tradition of local school control, such as Australia and the United States, are beginning to develop important national initiatives to raise literacy levels and prepare students for the use of the Internet.

A Dual-Level Theory of New Literacies

That the Internet changes the nature of literacy can be seen in the common ways that nations are trying to prepare students for these changes. It can also be seen by the fact that many scholars recently have been attracted to studying this problem and have sought to describe the changes taking place (e.g., Gee, 2007c; Kress, 2003; Lankshear & Knobel, 2006; Lemke, 2002; New London Group, 1996; Street, 1995, 2003). Many use the term *new literacies* to describe their work. *New literacies*, however, means many different things to many different people.

Some people use the term *new literacies* to capture the new social practices of literacy that are emerging (Street, 1995, 2003). Rather than seeing new social practices emerging from new technologies, they tend to see new technologies emerging from new social practices. Others use the term *new literacies* to describe important new strategies and dispositions that are essential for online research and comprehension (Castek, 2008; Coiro, 2003; Henry, 2006; International Reading Association, 2009). Still others see new literacies as new discourses (Gee, 2007b) or new semiotic contexts (Kress, 2003; Lemke, 2002). Others see literacy as differentiating into multiliteracies (Cope & Kalantzis, 1999; New London Group, 1996) or multimodal contexts (Hull & Schultz, 2002), and some see a construct that juxtaposes several of these orientations (Lankshear & Knobel, 2006). When one includes terms such as *ICT literacy* (International ICT Literacy Panel, 2002) or *informational literacy* (Hirsh, 1999; Kuiper & Volman, 2008), the construct of new literacies becomes even broader.

How are we to solve the conundrum posed earlier, where the nature of literacy changes even faster than we can develop adequate theory, especially within a context where there are so many competing theoretical perspectives that have emerged to direct separate lines of research? We believe the answer to this question is not to privilege one theoretical framework over another, but rather to take advantage of multiple perspectives, and new ones that will ultimately emerge, to capture the full range of the complexities defining literacy during a period in which literacy continually changes. In short, we see the separate lines of work taking place within a context that rapidly changes as an opportunity and not as a problem.

Lowercase and Uppercase New Literacies

Just as economic units have found it more productive to restructure from a command and control mentality to take advantage of everyone's intellectual capital, we must do the same in the literacy research community. We must find ways to bring all of our intellectual capital to the important task of understanding the extraordinary complexities that now define literacy as it continually changes and becomes richer and more complex. We can no longer afford to work in separate theoretical worlds, ignoring others and privileging our own. Recognizing that changes to literacy are taking place at many levels, and being dissatisfied with isolated attempts to capture those changes, we believe that a collaborative approach to theory building is essential, one that takes advantage of the power of multiple perspectives (Labbo & Reinking, 1999). This approach suggests that the best solutions result from collaborative groups who bring diverse, multiple perspectives to problems (Page, 2007). New Literacies theory takes an "open-source" approach, inviting everyone who studies the Internet's impact to contribute to theory development and to benefit from others' contributions. This includes more traditional theoretical and research traditions as well as those specific to new literacies because both old and new elements of literacy are layered in complex ways, and the nature of this layering and commingling is yet to be understood.

To account for the continuous changes taking place to literacy as well as the growing multiplicity of perspectives that are emerging, we frame new literacies theory on two levels: lowercase (new literacies) and uppercase (New Literacies). Lowercase theories explore a specific area of new literacies and/or a new technology, such as the social communicative transactions occurring with text messaging (e.g., Lewis & Fabos, 2005). Lowercase theories also include those that explore a focused disciplinary base, such as the semiotics of multimodality in online media (e.g., Kress, 2003) or a distinctive conceptual approach such as new literacy studies (Street, 1995, 2003). These lowercase theories are better able to keep up with the rapidly changing nature of literacy in a deictic world because they are closer to the specific types of changes that are taking place and interest those who study them within a particular heuristic. Lowercase theories also permit our field to maximize the lenses we use and the technologies and contexts we study. Every scholar who studies new literacy issues is generating important insights for everyone else, even if we do not share a particular lens, technology, or context. How, though, do we come to understand these insights, taking place in many different fields from many different perspectives? For this, we require a second level of theory, an uppercase New Literacies theory.

What defines this broader theory of New Literacies? New Literacies, as the broader, more inclusive concept, includes those common findings emerging across multiple, lowercase theories. New Literacies theory benefits from work taking place in the multiple, lowercase dimensions of new literacies by looking for what appear to be the most common and consistent patterns being found in lowercase theories and lines of research. This approach permits everyone to fully explore their unique, lowercase perspective of new literacies, allowing scholars to maintain a close focus on many different aspects of the shifting landscape of literacy during a period of rapid change. At the same time, each of us also benefits from expanding our understanding of other, lowercase, new literacies perspectives. By assuming change in the model, everyone is open to a continuously changing definition of literacy, based on the most recent data that emerges consistently, across multiple perspectives, disciplines, and research traditions. Moreover, areas in which alternative findings emerge are identified, enabling each to be studied again, from multiple perspectives. From this process, common patterns emerge and are included in a broader, common, New Literacies theory.

This process enables the broader theory of New Literacies to keep up with consistent elements that will always define literacy on the Internet while it informs each of the lowercase theories of new literacies with patterns that are being regularly found by others. We believe that when literacy is deictic and multifaceted, a dual-level theory of New Literacies is not only essential but also provides a theoretical advantage over any single-dimensional approach to theory building and research. We are richer for working together and engaging in common research and theoretical conversations, something we believe happens too rarely.

Central Principles of an Uppercase Theory of New Literacies

Although it is too early to define a complete uppercase theory of New Literacies emerging from the Internet and other ICTs, we are convinced that it is time to begin this process by identifying the central principles upon which it should be built. Our work is pointing us to these principles of New Literacies that appear to be common across the research and theoretical work currently taking place:

1. The Internet is this generation's defining technology for literacy and learning within our global community.
2. The Internet and related technologies require additional new literacies to fully access their potential.
3. New literacies are deictic.
4. New literacies are multiple, multimodal, and multifaceted.
5. Critical literacies are central to new literacies.
6. New forms of strategic knowledge are required with new literacies.
7. New social practices are a central element of New Literacies.
8. Teachers become more important, though their role changes, within new literacy classrooms.

The Internet Is This Generation's Defining Technology for Literacy and Learning Within Our Global Community

From a sociolinguistics perspective, Gee (2007b) and the New London Group (2000) have argued that literacy is embedded in and develops out of the social practices of a culture. We agree. We have argued that the Internet and related technologies now define the new literacies that increasingly are a part of our literacy lives. Put simply, a central principle of New Literacies theory is that the Internet has become this generation's defining technology for literacy in our global community.

We can see this in several data points. More than a decade ago, 90% of adolescent students in the United States with home access to the Internet reported using the Internet for homework (Pew Internet & American Life Project, 2001). Over 70% of these students used the Internet as the primary source for information on their most recent school report or project, while only 24% of these students reported using the library for the same task. Four years later, in 2005, we reached the "tipping point year" for online reading among adolescents in the United States. For the first time, students ages 8–18 reported spending more time reading online, 48 minutes per day, than reading offline, 43 minutes per day (Kaiser Family Foundation, 2005). More recently, the first international assessment of online reading among 15-year-olds took place in 2009. The PISA International Assessment of Reading (Organisation for Economic Co-operation and Development, 2011) provided important information about online research and comprehension to public policymakers around the world who were demanding it (see also R.E. Bennett, Persky, Weiss, & Jenkins, 2007).

Perhaps the most compelling evidence, though, for this claim may be found in usage. According to one of the most systematic evaluations of worldwide Internet use, over 2.4 billion individuals now use the Internet—more than one third of the world's population (Internet World Stats, 2011). Moreover, at the current rate of growth, Internet use will be ubiquitous in the world within the next decade. Never in the history of civilization have we seen a new technology adopted by so many, in so many different places, in such a short period of time, with such powerful consequences for both literacy and life.

The Internet and Related Technologies Require Additional New Literacies to Fully Access Their Potential

New technologies such as the Internet and other ICTs require additional social practices, skills, strategies, and dispositions to take full advantage of the affordances each contains. Typically, new literacies build upon foundational literacies rather than replace them completely. Foundational literacies include those traditional social practices of literacy and the elements of literacy required for traditional text reading and writing, such as word recognition, vocabulary, comprehension, inferential reasoning, the writing process, spelling, response to literature, and others required for the literacies of the book and other printed material. However, foundational literacies will be insufficient if one is to make full use of the Internet and other ICTs (Hartman, Morsink, & Zheng, 2010; International Reading Association, 2009). Reading, writing, and communication will take new forms as text is combined with new media resources and linked within complex information networks requiring new literacies for their use (Dalton & Proctor,

2008; Wyatt-Smith & Elkins, 2008). During this process, new online and traditional offline literacies are often layered in rich and complex ways.

New Literacies Are Deictic

We began this chapter by suggesting that literacy has become deictic. The rapid transformations in the nature of literacy caused by technological change is a primary source for the deictic nature of literacy; new technologies regularly and repeatedly transform previous literacies, continually redefining what it means to become literate.

The deictic nature of literacy is also caused by a second source: the envisionments we construct as we create new social practices with new technologies. Envisionments take place when individuals imagine new possibilities for literacy and learning, transform existing technologies and practices to construct this vision, and then share their envisionment with others (Knobel & Wilber, 2009; Lankshear & Knobel, 2006; Leu, Karchmer, & Leu, 1999).

Finally, rapid transformations in the nature of literacy are produced because the Internet and other ICTs permit the immediate exchange of new technologies and social practices. Because we can immediately download a new technology from the Internet or send it to millions of individuals with just a keystroke, the changes to literacy derived from new technologies happen at a pace faster than ever before. In short, the Internet and other ICTs not only change themselves but also provide the central vehicle for exchanging new technologies for information and communication and new social practices. Thus, the already rapid pace of change in the forms and functions of literacy is exacerbated by the speed with which new technologies and new social practices are communicated (Leu, 2000).

New Literacies Are Multiple, Multimodal, and Multifaceted

New literacies are multiple, multimodal, and multifaceted, and as a result, our understanding of them benefits from multiple points of view. From a sociolinguistic perspective, the New London Group (2000) has defined *multiliteracies* as a set of open-ended and flexible multiple literacies required to function in diverse social contexts and communities. We believe the same multiplicity of literacy has also emerged because of multiple technological contexts. The Internet and other ICTs require that we develop a systematic understanding of the multiple literacies that exist in both new literacies practices (Lankshear & Knobel, 2006) and in the skills, strategies, and dispositions that are required with new technologies (Leu et al., 2004). This multiplicity of new literacies is apparent on at least three levels.

First, meaning is typically represented with multiple media and modalities. Unlike traditional text forms that typically include a combination of two types of media—print and two-dimensional graphics—Internet texts integrate a range of symbols and multiple-media formats, including icons, animated symbols, audio, video, interactive tables, and virtual reality environments (Callow, 2010; Lemke, 2002; Walsh, 2010). As a result, we confront new forms and combinations of texts and images that challenge our traditional understandings of how information is represented and shared with others (Jewitt & Kress, 2003; Unsworth, 2008). Semiotic perspectives on new literacies (e.g., Kress, 2003) allow an especially rich understanding of changes taking place in these areas.

Second, the Internet and other ICTs also offer multiple tools. Literate individuals will be those who can effectively determine, from the Internet's multiple offerings, a combination of tool(s) and form(s) that best meet their needs (American Association of School Librarians, 2007). Thus, New Literacies theory includes research that is taking place with multiple forms of online meaning and content construction. It assumes that proficient users of the Internet must understand how to construct meaning in new ways as well as construct, design, manipulate, and upload their own information to add to the constantly growing and changing body of knowledge that defines the Internet.

A final level of multiplicity consists of the new social practices and skills that are required as we encounter information with individuals from a much wider range of social contexts (Hull, Stornaiuolo, & Sahni, 2010; Hull, Zacher, & Hibbert, 2009). The global sharing of information permitted by the Internet introduces new challenges as we interpret and respond to information from multiple social and cultural contexts that share profoundly different assumptions about our world (Fabos & Young, 1999; Flanagin, Farinola, & Metzger, 2000). These multiple contexts for new literacies have important implications for educators preparing students to critically understand and interpret the meanings they find on the Internet and to communicate with others (see Hull et al., 2010).

In a world of exploding technologies and literacy practices, it becomes increasingly difficult to think of literacy as a singular construct that applies across all contexts. As a result, we benefit from the complexity that multiple theoretical perspectives provide (Labbo & Reinking, 1999). Any research study in new literacies benefits when multiple theoretical frameworks inform the research questions and results. It also suggests that new literacies are best studied in interdisciplinary teams as questions become far too complex for the traditional single-investigator model.

Critical Literacies Are Central to New Literacies

New Literacies demand new forms of critical literacy and greater dependency on critical thinking and analysis. Open networks, such as the Internet, permit anyone to publish anything; this is one of the opportunities this technology presents. It is also one of its limitations; information is much more widely available from people who have strong political, economic, religious, or ideological stances that profoundly influence the nature of the information they present to others. As a result, we must assist students to become more critical consumers of the information they encounter (Bråten, Strømsø, & Britt, 2009; Clemitt, 2008; Flanagin & Metzger, 2010; Metzger & Flanagin, 2008). Although the literacy curriculum has always included items such as critical thinking and separating fact from propaganda, more instructional time devoted to more complex analytic skills will need to be included in classrooms where the Internet and other ICTs play a more prominent role (Hobbs, 2010). As we begin to study the new literacies of the Internet, we will depend greatly on work from the communities of critical literacy and media literacy to provide us with the best research in this area.

New Forms of Strategic Knowledge Are Required With New Literacies

New technologies for networked information and communication are complex and require many new strategies for their effective use. Hypertext technologies, embedded with multiple forms of media and unlimited freedoms of multiple navigational pathways, present opportunities that may seduce some readers away from important content unless they have developed strategies to deal with these seductions (Lawless & Kulikowich, 1996; Lawless, Mills, & Brown, 2002). Other cognitive and aesthetic changes to text on the Internet presents additional strategic challenges to comprehension (Afflerbach & Cho, 2010; Coiro, 2003; Hartman et al., 2010; Spires & Estes, 2002), inquiry (Eagleton, 2001), and information seeking (Rouet, Ros, Goumi, Macedo-Rouet, & Dinet, 2011; Sutherland-Smith, 2002). Thus, new literacies will often be defined around the strategic knowledge central to the effective use of information within rich and complexly networked environments.

New Literacy Practices Are a Central Element of New Literacies

It is increasingly clear that new literacy practices are a central feature of New Literacies. Work by Lankshear and Knobel (2006) show us how two important elements of the changing nature of literacy generate additional, new literacies practices. First, new digital technologies enable new ways of constructing, sharing, and accessing meaningful content. Second, the collaborative, distributed, and participatory nature of these digital spaces enable the generation of what Lankshear and Knobel call a *distinctive ethos* and what Jenkins (2006) refers to as *engagement in participatory culture*. As a result, continuously new social practices of literacy will emerge, often within new discourse communities, and serve to redefine literacy and learning.

New social practices will be needed in classrooms to interact within increasingly complex technologies for information and communication (Jonassen, Howland, Moore, & Marra, 2003; Kiili, Laurinen, Marttunen, & Leu, 2011). Models of literacy instruction, for example, have often focused on an adult whose role was to teach the skills he or she possessed to a group of students who did not know those skills. This is no longer possible, or even appropriate, within a world of multiple new literacies. No one person can hope to know everything about the expanding and ever-changing technologies of the Internet and other ICTs. In fact, today, many young students possess higher levels of knowledge about some of these new literacies than most adults.

Consequently, effective learning experiences will be increasingly dependent upon new social practices, social learning strategies, and the ability of a teacher to orchestrate literacy learning opportunities between and among students who know different new literacies (Erstad, 2002). This will distribute knowledge about literacy throughout the classroom, especially as students move above the stages of foundational literacy. One student, for example, may know how to edit digital video scenes, but another may know how best to compress the video so it can function optimally in a Web-based environment. This social learning ability may not come naturally to all students, however, and many will need to be supported in learning *how* to learn about literacy from one another (Labbo, 1996; Labbo & Kuhn, 1998).

Teachers Become More Important, Though Their Role Changes, Within New Literacy Classrooms

The appearance of the Internet and other ICTs in school classrooms will increase the central role that teachers play in orchestrating learning experiences for students. Teachers will be challenged to thoughtfully guide students' learning within information environments that are richer and more complex than traditional print media, presenting richer and more complex learning opportunities for both themselves and their students (Coiro, 2009).

In a world of rapidly changing new literacies, it will be common for some students to be more literate with some technologies than their teacher is (Erstad, 2002; Harper, 2006). As a result, teachers will increasingly become orchestrators of learning contexts rather than dispensers of literacy skills. By orchestrating opportunities for the exchange of new literacies, both teachers and students may enhance their literacy skills and their potential for effective communication and information use (O'Brien, Beach, & Scharber, 2007; Schulz-Zander, Büchter, & Dalmer, 2002). Because teachers become even more important to the development of literacy and because their role changes, an expanded focus and greater attention will need to be placed on teacher education and professional development in new literacies.

The New Literacies of Online Research and Comprehension: A Lowercase Theory of New Literacies

The new literacies of online research and comprehension (Leu, Everett-Cacopardo, Zawilinski, McVerry, & O'Byrne, in press; Leu, Forzani, et al., in press) is one example of a lowercase new literacies theory. This frames online reading comprehension as a process of problem-based inquiry and includes the new skills, strategies, dispositions, and social practices that take place as we use information on the Internet to conduct research to solve problems and answer questions. It describes how students conduct research and read online to learn. A more formal definition is as follows:

> The new literacies of online research and comprehension include the skills, strategies, dispositions, and social practices necessary to successfully use and adapt to the rapidly changing information and communication technologies and contexts that continuously emerge and influence all areas of our personal and professional lives. Online research and comprehension is a self-directed process of constructing texts and knowledge while engaged in several online reading practices: identifying

important problems, locating information, critically evaluating information, synthesizing information, and communicating information. Online research and comprehension can take place individually, but often appears to be enhanced when it takes place collaboratively.

What do we know about the new literacies of online research and comprehension? We are beginning to uncover many elements of this aspect of new literacies. They include the following:

1. Online research and comprehension is a self-directed process of text construction and knowledge construction.
2. Five practices appear to define online research and comprehension processing: (1) identifying a problem and then (2) locating, (3) evaluating, (4) synthesizing, and (5) communicating information.
3. Online research and comprehension is not isomorphic with offline reading comprehension; additional skills and strategies appear to be required.
4. Online contexts may be especially supportive for some struggling readers.
5. Adolescents are not always very skilled with online research and comprehension.
6. Collaborative online reading and writing practices appear to increase comprehension and learning.

Online Research and Comprehension Is a Self-Directed Process of Text Construction and Knowledge Construction

Readers choose the online texts that they read through the links that they follow as they gather information and construct the knowledge needed to solve a problem. Each reader typically follows a unique informational path, selecting a unique sequence of links to information and sampling unique segments of information from each location (see, e.g., Canavilhas, n.d.; McEneaney, Li, Allen, & Guzniczak, 2009). Thus, in addition to constructing knowledge in their minds, readers also physically construct the texts they read online (Afflerbach & Cho, 2008; Coiro & Dobler, 2007). While this is also possible during offline reading, of course, it always takes place during online reading (see Hartman et al., 2010). As a result, seldom do two readers read the same text to solve the same problem during online reading.

Five Processing Practices Appear to Define Online Research and Comprehension Processing

At least five processing practices occur during online research and comprehension: (1) reading to identify important questions, (2) reading to locate information, (3) reading to evaluate information critically, (4) reading to synthesize information, and (5) reading to communicate information. Within these five practices reside the skills, strategies, and dispositions that are distinctive to online reading comprehension as well as to others that are also important for offline reading comprehension (Leu, Reinking, et al., 2007).

Reading to Identify Important Questions. We read on the Internet to solve problems and answer questions. How a problem is framed or how a question is understood is a central aspect of online research and comprehension. Work by Taboada and Guthrie (2006) within traditional texts suggests that reading initiated by a question differs in important ways from reading that is not.

Reading to Locate Information. A second component of successful online research and comprehension is the ability to read and locate information that meets one's needs (Broch, 2000; Eagleton, Guinee, & Langlais, 2003; Guinee, Eagleton, & Hall, 2003; International ICT Literacy Panel, 2002; Sutherland-Smith, 2002). The reading ability required to locate information on the Internet may very well serve as a gatekeeping skill; if one cannot locate information, one will be unable to solve a given problem. New online reading skills and strategies may be required, for example, to generate effective keyword search strategies (Bilal, 2000; Guinee et al., 2003; Kuiper & Volman, 2008), to read and infer which link may be most useful within a set of search engine results (Henry, 2006), and to efficiently scan for relevant information within websites (McDonald & Stevenson, 1996; Rouet, 2006; Rouet et al., 2011).

Reading to Evaluate Information Critically. Critically evaluating online information includes the ability to read and evaluate the level of accuracy, reliability, and bias of information (Center for Media Literacy, 2005). Although these skills have always been necessary to comprehend and use offline texts, the proliferation of unedited information and the merging of commercial marketing with educational content (Fabos, 2008; Federal Trade Commission, 2002) present additional challenges that are quite different from traditional print and media sources. Tillman (2003), for example, contends that promotional efforts and related advertising may be more difficult to differentiate on the Internet than in print and other mass media forms (see also Fabos, 2008). Others (Britt & Gabrys, 2001) cite the lack of uniform standards and cues regarding document type in online text environments as necessitating a renewed interest in how students evaluate online information. Without explicit training in these new literacy skills, many students become confused and overwhelmed when asked to judge the accuracy, reliability, and bias of information they encounter in online reading environments (Graham & Metaxas, 2003; Sanchez, Wiley, & Goldman, 2006; Sundar, 2008). Consequently, as more students turn primarily to the Internet for their information (Pew Internet & American Life Project, 2005), these critical evaluation strategies become more relevant than ever before (Bråten et al., 2009; Bråten, Strømsø, & Salmerón, 2011).

Reading to Synthesize Information. Successful Internet use also requires the ability to read and synthesize information from multiple online sources (Jenkins, 2006). Synthesis requires the reader to bring together an awareness of the reading processes and an underlying understanding of the text. The Internet introduces additional challenges to coordinate and synthesize vast amounts of information presented in multiple media formats, from a nearly unlimited and disparate set of sources (Gilster, 1997; Jenkins, 2006; Rouet, 2006). This presents important challenges to online readers as they determine what to include and what to exclude.

Reading to Communicate Information. A fifth component of successful online research and comprehension is the ability to communicate via the Internet to seek information or share what one has learned (Britt & Gabrys, 2001). The interactive processes of reading and writing have become so intertwined on the Internet that they often happen simultaneously during communication. Moreover, each specific communication tool on the Internet is constituted differently and presents a range of new skills, strategies, and social practices to use them effectively (Coiro, Knobel, Lankshear, & Leu, 2008). New types of strategic knowledge are required, for example, to effectively participate and communicate in social networking environments such as e-mail, blogs, wikis, and instant messaging (Castek, 2008; Lewis & Fabos, 2005).

Online Research and Comprehension Is Not Isomorphic With Offline Reading Comprehension

Findings from several studies suggest that online research and comprehension appears not to be isomorphic with offline reading comprehension; additional reading comprehension skills seem to be required (Coiro, 2011; Coiro & Dobler, 2007; Leu et al., 2005; Leu, Zawilinski, et al., 2007). One study, among sixth-grade students proficient at using the Internet (Coiro & Dobler, 2007), found that online research and comprehension shared a number of similarities with offline reading comprehension but was also more complex and included notable differences. A second study found no statistically significant correlation between scores on a state reading comprehension assessment and an assessment of online research and comprehension with good psychometric properties (Leu et al., 2005). A third study (Coiro, 2011) found that offline reading comprehension and prior knowledge contributed a statistically significant amount of variance to the prediction of online research and comprehension, but an additional 16% of independent variance was contributed by knowing students' online research and comprehension ability. These data suggest that additional skills are required for online research and comprehension beyond those required for offline reading comprehension.

Similarly, Afflerbach and Cho's (2010) review of 46 studies involving think-aloud protocols that focused on reading strategy use during Internet and hypertext reading found evidence of strategies that "appeared to have no counterpart in traditional reading" (p. 217). Many of these strategies clustered around a reader's ability to apply new strategies to reduce levels of uncertainty while navigating and negotiating appropriate reading paths in a shifting problem space (see also Afflerbach & Cho, 2008; Cho, 2010; Zhang & Duke, 2008). Hartman et al. (2010) also offer examples of how Internet research and comprehension places many more processing demands on the reader that amount to a host of new cognitive reading challenges for comprehending online texts. Finally, case studies and videos of online research show that students who perform at a low level on state reading assessments sometimes perform at unexpectedly high levels on tasks of online research and comprehension (Castek, Zawilinski, McVerry, O'Byrne, & Leu, 2011; Leu, Zawilinski, et al., 2007). Together, these results support the claim that additional skills and strategies may be required during online research and comprehension beyond those required for offline reading and comprehension.

Although differences appear to exist, we do not fully understand how and why offline reading comprehension and online research and comprehension are not isomorphic. Several explanations are possible. Current results, showing a lack of correlation between the two, may be because online research and comprehension is a problem-based task, while offline reading includes a wider range of comprehension tasks (cf. Taboada & Guthrie, 2006). Or it may be that the reading skills required to locate information online are such "bottleneck" skills that students who lack this ability perform poorly online, even though they may be high-performing offline readers. Or the fact that greater levels of critical evaluation are typically required online may be the source of the difference. Finally, differences may be due to the new communication tools that are often used.

It is also likely that we can increase or decrease statistical relationships between offline reading comprehension and online research and comprehension by simply varying the nature of the online research task. Online assessments that require richer, more complex use of online tools (search engines, e-mail attachments, blogs, wikis), or more complex information spaces, may generate less of a relationship with offline reading comprehension compared with online assessments that simply require the reader to read information on a single website. So it is still early to claim that the lack of isomorphism between online and offline reading is either strong or weak. That it can be demonstrated appears to be the case, but we require much more work to be able to fully understand the conditions under which the two contexts for reading require different skills and strategies.

We also do not know very much about the relative contribution of various elements of online research and comprehension to successful online research outcomes. It is likely that skill areas often required earlier in the process (defining a problem, locating information, and evaluating information) may be more determinative of successful performance than other areas are, but we have not yet evaluated this claim.

Online Contexts May Be Especially Supportive for Some Struggling Readers

It is surprising to find that some struggling readers do very well with online research and comprehension. Why might this be the case? Units of text are typically shorter online as readers follow informational links from one location to another, seeking information that will help them solve their informational problem. Shorter units of text are easier for struggling readers to process. In addition, online readers construct their own texts to read, as they choose different paths to follow. This increases engagement and makes it more likely that readers find their way to texts appropriate for their abilities. Also, online texts contain multimedia, a traditionally supportive context for struggling readers. Finally, each webpage is really a graphic image, and struggling readers are often quite skilled readers of information presented graphically. Sometimes, too, these readers use a new literacies skill, the use of Command + F, to quickly scan for information on a webpage with extensive amounts of text.

Adolescents Are Not Always Very Skilled With Online Research and Comprehension

Although adolescent "digital natives" may be skilled with social networking, texting, video downloads, MP3 downloads, or mash-ups, they are not always as skilled with online research and comprehension, including locating (Bilal, 2000; Eagleton et al., 2003) and critically evaluating information (S. Bennett, Maton, & Kervin, 2008; Sutherland-Smith, 2002; Wallace, Kupperman, Krajcik, & Soloway, 2000). In fact, adolescents tend to overgeneralize their ability to read online information effectively, informed by their ability to engage successfully with online social networking, texting, and video games (Kuiper, 2007).

Collaborative Online Reading and Writing Practices Appear to Increase Comprehension and Learning

Emerging work suggests that collaborative online reading and writing may yield important gains in literacy and learning. Work by Kiili et al. (2011) suggests that collaborative reading of online information about a controversial issue can lead to important learning gains. Comparing individual reading (Kiili, Laurinen, & Marttunen, 2008) with collaborative online reading (Kiili et al., 2011), individual readers concentrated on gathering facts, whereas the collaborative reading context offered additional opportunities for deeper exploration of ideas and different perspectives. Greater collaborative online reading also appears to lead to greater meaning construction and knowledge construction (Kiili et al., 2011).

Work by Everett-Cacopardo (2011), Zawilinski (2011), O'Byrne (2011), and Coiro, Castek, and Guzniczak (2011) also explores the importance of framing online research and comprehension as a collaborative, social practice. Everett-Cacopardo discovered that a number of teachers find it highly effective to have their students engage in collaborative, online projects with students in other nations. Zawilinski found that collaborative blogging in social studies between students in first and fifth grades led to important gains in understanding and communication. O'Byrne found that collaborative development of spoof sites led to greater skill with the critical evaluation of information related most closely to the elements students focused on in the creation of their webpages. Coiro et al. found that opportunities to co-construct meaning and responses to prompts that require students to read on the Internet may foster more efficient and productive comprehension of online informational texts—even among readers who are skilled at comprehending online texts independently. Thus, we are beginning to see this area of new literacies research consider more fully the important collaborative dimensions of online research and comprehension.

New Literacies Theory: Implications

New Literacies theory tells us that the Internet and other continuously emerging ICTs will be central to both our personal and professional lives and that these technologies require new literacies to effectively exploit their potential (International Reading Association, 2009; Kinzer & Leander, 2002). It also suggests that we must begin to integrate these new literacies into classrooms if we hope to prepare all students for the literacy futures they deserve. Most important, it suggests that continuous change will define the new literacies of the Internet and other ICTs (Cammack, 2002; Leu, 2000). Because of this rapid and continuous change, misalignments in assessment and instruction are likely to appear until we begin to recognize that literacy has become deictic, and take action not to fall behind the more contemporaneous realities of literacy. These misalignments are likely to create important problems for any educational system unable to keep up with the changes.

Consider, for example, the consequences that result from our current literacy assessments, such as the National Assessment of Educational Progress or any of the state assessments of reading in the United States. None of these assessments include any elements of new literacies. This misalignment with the contemporaneous realities of literacy may result in increasing existing gaps in reading achievement between rich and poor. How does this happen? The poorest students in any nation have the least access to the Internet at home (Cooper, 2004). Unfortunately, it is often the case that the poorest schools are also under the greatest pressure to raise scores on reading tests that have nothing to do with new literacies (cf. Henry, 2007). In poorer schools, there is often little incentive to teach the new literacies of online research and comprehension simply because they are not tested (Leu, O'Byrne, Zawilinski, McVerry, & Everett-Cacopardo, 2009). Thus, students in our poorest schools become doubly disadvantaged; they have less access to the Internet at home, and schools do not prepare them for new literacies at school.

In contrast, most children from advantaged communities have broadband Internet connections at home. As a result, teachers feel greater freedom to integrate the Internet into their curricula (Henry, 2007). Thus, students in richer districts become doubly privileged: They have greater access to the Internet at home, and they integrate it more often at school. It is a cruel irony that students who most need to be prepared at school for an online age of information are precisely those who are being prepared the least. This situation must change. We cannot afford to help the rich get richer and the poor get poorer through misalignments in our assessment instruments.

During a period of rapidly changing new literacies, we will need to adapt to the continuously changing nature of literacy in several areas. These include research, assessment, and professional development and teacher education.

Research

Research might begin by focusing on two major issues: (1) What are the social practices, skills, strategies, and dispositions essential to the acquisition of new literacies? and (2) How might we best support the development of these aspects of new literacies within both real and virtual learning contexts? As we develop answers to the first question, we should keep in mind that any answers will be in continuous evolution, as even newer technologies will require additional skills, strategies, dispositions, and social practices for their effective use. We should begin now to conceptualize this problem from a deictic perspective, perhaps with a research focus on how students and teachers continually adapt to the changes that will be a part of our lives. Research on how students and teachers learn how to learn may be far more important than a listing of specific skills and strategies within the continuously changing landscape of literacy that will define our future.

Answers to the second question are likely to take place within a context of problem-based learning (see Dochy, Segers, Van den Bossche, & Gijbels, 2003; Hmelo-Silver, 2004) because we have argued that new literacies are often used to solve problems and communicate solutions with online information. One instructional model has been developed for 1:1 computing classrooms in the Teaching Internet Comprehension to Adolescents project (Leu & Reinking, 2005) and described by Leu et al. (2008).

This project focused on inquiry-based learning around diverse informational texts that students encountered on the Internet while engaged in a series of curriculum-based information challenges. A three-phase approach to instruction was designed, called Internet reciprocal teaching (IRT). Over a 20-week period, with about 40 hours of instruction, this approach resulted in significant effects on online research and comprehension among typically low-achieving readers in seventh-grade language arts classrooms in rural South Carolina and urban Connecticut school districts (Leu & Reinking, 2009).

There is some indication that a more sustained period of IRT instruction can yield an even greater effect size. Castek (2008) found positive effects for fourth and fifth graders who were instructed using IRT and laptops. Students in the experimental group showed significantly greater gains in online research and comprehension than did control students: $t(52) = 5.79, p < .001$), with a large effect size (Cohen's $d = 1.58$). This study took place in self-contained classrooms rather than the rotating, 40-minute classes typical of middle schools, providing more time each day for instruction. From these results, it appears that a longer period of time, more than 40 hours, may be necessary to generate high levels of online research and comprehension.

Another area in which important research is taking place is online gaming. Several people have noted that literacy practices and literacy-related learning activities occur within online game play (Gee, 2007a; Squire, 2008, 2011; Steinkuehler, 2006). Leander and Lovvorn (2006), for example, note how an adolescent from the United States learned Finnish and various communication strategies as a result of collaborative video game play experiences. Yet, schools continue to emphasize traditional text-based literacy practices while doing little to integrate the potentials of gaming into the school curriculum.

We also need to consider broader sources of meaning beyond text. Work by Kress, Hull, and others (Hull & Schultz, 2002; Jewitt & Kress, 2003; Kress, 2003) tell us that we must understand more fully the roles of semiotics and multimodal forms if our students are to use the affordances of tools now required in informal as well as high-performance workplace and academic settings. We must begin to shift from a focus mainly on text comprehension strategies to the interaction among text, graphics, and other content (Kinzer, Hoffman, Turkay, Gunbas, & Chantes, 2011; Kinzer et al., in press), especially during out-of-school contexts (Kleifgen & Kinzer, 2009).

These and other areas of research that need to be explored may not be able to keep up with the rapidly changing landscape of literacy if traditional research paradigms are used; important aspects of literacy are likely to change before a body of consistent research findings can be gathered. Because new literacies continuously change, we require new epistemologies and research practices that keep up with the rapid changes we anticipate. How, for example, can we keep up with new ideas about what to teach and how to teach within research and dissemination paradigms that require five years or more between the conception of a research problem and the wide dissemination of results through research journals? How can we assess students on their ability to use the Internet and other ICTs when the very skills we assess will change as soon as new technologies appear? While a New Literacies perspective does not provide complete answers to these questions, it suggests that these are critical questions to ask.

The answers may emerge in the new models of research likely to appear among those who understand the changes we are experiencing. Those who develop digital curricula, for example, may come to realize that their most important resource is not the digital curriculum they provide to schools but rather the data they obtain from students who use the curriculum. With a network that both delivers curricular activities and assesses learning each day, data could be used to conduct immediate research on the design of lesson activities, revising a different element each night to obtain immediate results on the effects of that change the next day. Anyone with access to these data, and with the appropriate resources, will be able to conduct research on a scale and with a speed that we have not previously experienced. It is quite possible that the assumptions we currently have about how, when, where, and why instructional research is conducted will change rapidly in an age of new literacies.

Assessment

We currently lack valid, reliable, and practical assessments of new literacies to inform instruction and help students become better prepared for an online age of information and communication. As a result, new literacies are not often integrated into reading or language arts instruction (Hew & Brush, 2007) and are, instead, typically viewed as an optional add-on rather than a vital component (O'Brien & Scharber, 2008). Until we develop valid, reliable, and practical assessments of new literacies to inform instruction, their integration into the classroom will always be delayed. Developing these assessments will be an important challenge in the years ahead.

Dynamic, online texts and their associated literacy practices require dynamic assessments that are sensitive to the diverse, multiple, and rapidly changing ways in which learners read, write, learn, and communicate information in the 21st century (Churches, 2009; International Reading Association & National Council of Teachers of English, 2010; Knobel & Wilber, 2009). Similarly, a range of social networking and information-sharing tools (e.g., Facebook, Twitter, Skype) continue to emerge and give rise to new means of communication and ways of connecting and sharing with wider and more diverse groups of individuals than ever before (Greenhow, Robelia, & Hughes, 2009; Johnson, Levine, Smith, & Smythe, 2009). Consequently, authentic assessments of new literacies should incorporate the information and communication tools used in the workforce and in students' daily lives (e.g., interactive blogs, wikis, e-mail) to pose and answer questions, reflect on and synthesize new learning, and collaborate across classrooms.

Assessments of new literacies should also document students' evolving dispositions toward participation in globally networked communities (Coiro, 2009; Popham, 2009). This includes assessments that document the ability to work productively as a team, appreciate differences in cultural practices and work patterns, demonstrate flexibility and perseverance during online inquiry, and respond appropriately to peer feedback (Afflerbach, 2007; American Association of School Librarians, 2007; O'Byrne & McVerry, 2009). Finally, we require better assessments of online research and comprehension, ones that are both reliable and valid and also practical. The ones we currently have appear to be valid and reliable but require extensive time to reliably score (Castek & Coiro, 2010).

Current work taking place in the Online Research and Comprehension Assessment (ORCA) project seeks this broader objective (Leu, Kulikowich, Sedransk, & Coiro, 2009). This project has developed 24 assessments that present authentic problems to students in science with text messages and collects data on both process and product aspects of the research they conduct online. The task concludes with students using their result to revise a classroom wiki or e-mailing a school board president about the results they discovered. A video of one assessment may be viewed by linking to this URL: neag.uconn.edu/orca-video-ira/. The ORCAs are currently being piloted and validated with representative state samples of nearly 2,800 seventh-grade students in Connecticut and Maine.

The most prominent challenge, perhaps, is that literacy assessments, to date, are always assessments of an individual working alone. Given the importance of social learning and collaborative meaning construction on the Internet and other ICTs, we will need to assess how well students can learn new literacies from others and how well they can co-construct meaning and collaborate in constructing written information with others. Learning how to learn from others and learning how to collaboratively construct meaning will be increasingly important in the years ahead. It seems clear that new technologies will require new approaches to both what is assessed and how we go about doing so (Coiro & Castek, 2010; Kinzer, 2010; National Research Council, 2001).

Professional Development and Teacher Education

Perhaps the greatest challenge that we face lies in professional development. It is safe to say that our educational systems have never before faced the professional development needs that will occur in our future. Current professional development models are often short in duration, with a focus on technology as a tool (Warschauer, 2006), despite the fact that studies of laptop integration universally conclude that extensive professional development on higher level learning with technology is required before gains can be realized (Penuel, 2006; Silvernail & Buffington, 2009; Silvernail & Gritter, 2007; Silvernail & Lane, 2004; Warschauer, 2006). The continuous changes that lie ahead for literacy will require continuous professional development.

It is likely that new models of professional development will require more extended commitments from school leadership teams, over longer periods of time, than we are used to. It is well established that professional development with technology integration takes longer than other areas of classroom instruction do, as much as two to three times as long to produce the expected effects (Becta, 2003; McKenzie, 2001; Saylor & Kehrhahn, 2003). This is because training requires teachers to develop more than new instructional strategies. They also have to develop proficiency with new technologies, an even greater challenge for some.

Emerging work (Spires, Hervey, & Watson, 2012; Spires, Zheng, & Pruden, 2011) has found Mishra and Koehler's (2006) TPACK model to be a useful framework for helping educators understand the complex relationships among technology, content, and pedagogy to facilitate teacher growth in new literacies (see also Lohnes Watulak & Kinzer's, 2013, argument for an extension of this model). However, we need more research and clear data on the efficacy of these and other new models to direct us in this area.

Our colleagues who conduct research on teacher education also need to apply their finest heuristics, helping us to better understand how to prepare new and experienced teachers to support children in the new literacies of ICTs in the classroom. This will require an understanding of new literacies by academic institutions and teacher educators, who will need to implement changes in our college and university preservice programs.

What seems certain is that Internet resources will increase, not decrease, the central role teachers play in orchestrating learning experiences for students as literacy instruction converges with Internet technologies. The richer and more complex information environments of the Internet will challenge teachers to thoughtfully support student learning in these new literacies contexts (Coiro &

Fogleman, 2011). This alone should make professional development and teacher education important priorities.

The Challenges of Change: Theory Building in a Deictic World of New Literacies

We believe that we are on the cusp of a new era in literacy theory, research, and practice, one in which the nature of reading, writing, and communication is being fundamentally transformed by the Internet. It will be up to each of us to recognize these changes and develop a richer understanding of them as we seek to prepare students for the new literacies of the Internet and other ICTs that define their future. They deserve nothing less.

To help us begin this journey, we have argued that one way to understand the changes taking place to literacy is to build theoretical models around change itself. We have outlined a dual-level theory of New Literacies, a perspective that provides a useful starting point to inquiry in this area and one that is both close to the continuous changes taking place at the lowercase level and also provides an understanding of the generalized principles that are common to all of the many contexts at the uppercase level.

Our own work tells us that each of us will be challenged in many ways as we enter this new world of new literacies. We will be challenged to conduct and publish research before the very issues that we study have changed as even newer literacies have appeared. We will be challenged to use collaborative models of research because so many of us work in institutions that still privilege the single-investigator model for dissertations, tenure, and promotion. We will be challenged to gain access to school classrooms when schools are under intense pressure to raise test scores, with assessments that exclude the new literacies we seek to study, and have little time for anything other than what is on their test. We will be challenged by the shift to centers of research where curriculum developers have access to massive amounts of daily data and rapidly change the classroom contexts for instruction in literacy and learning.

The most important challenge for each of us, though, may be of looking beyond our own lowercase theoretical framework to include findings taking place in other, related, new literacies work. We must begin to think in ways that do not simply privilege our own work but embrace the many other perspectives that can enrich our own understanding. By looking across multiple, lowercase, new literacies, we will develop a far richer understanding of the important work that each of us is conducting.

This chapter has explored emerging theoretical perspectives in new literacies and explained why we believe a dual-level, New Literacies theory is especially useful to understand the changes that are taking place. We hope that by sharing this perspective and the many challenges that we face, you will be encouraged to bring your own expertise to the important research that lies ahead. Nothing is more important to our collective future.

QUESTIONS FOR REFLECTION

1. What are some examples of new literacies that have arisen or will arise in the Internet age?
2. How can you apply the recommendation for "collaborative online reading and writing practices [that] appear to increase comprehension and learning"?
3. With respect to new literacies, what can schools of education do to avoid "misalignments" of assessment and instruction?

NOTES

Portions of this material are based on work supported by the U.S. Department of Education under Award Nos. R305G050154 and R305A090608. Opinions expressed herein are solely those of the authors and do not necessarily represent the position of the U.S. Department of Education, Institute of Educational Sciences.

REFERENCES

Afflerbach, P. (2007). *Understanding and using reading assessment*. Newark, DE: International Reading Association.

Afflerbach, P.A., & Cho, B.Y. (2008). Identifying and describing constructively responsive comprehension strategies in new and traditional forms of reading. In S. Israel & G. Duffy (Eds.), *Handbook of reading comprehension research* (pp. 69–90). Mahwah, NJ: Erlbaum.

Afflerbach, P.A., & Cho, B.Y. (2010). Determining and describing reading strategies: Internet and traditional forms of reading. In H.S. Waters & W. Schneider (Eds.), *Metacognition, strategy use, and instruction* (pp. 201–255). New York: Guilford.

American Association of School Librarians. (2007). *Standards for the 21st-century learner*. Retrieved fromwww.ala.org/ala/mgrps/divs/aasl/guidelinesandstandards/learningstandards/standards.cfm

Australian Curriculum, Assessment and Reporting Authority. (n.d.). *The Australian Curriculum* (Version 1.2). Retrieved from www.australiancurriculum.edu.au/Home

Becta. (2003). *What the research says about barriers to the use of ICT in teaching*. Retrieved October 29, 2012 from www.mmiweb.org.uk/publications/ict/Research_Barriers_TandL.pdf

Bennett, R.E., Persky, H., Weiss, A.R., & Jenkins, F. (2007). *Problem solving in technology-rich environments: A report from the NAEP technology-based assessment project*. Retrieved from nces.ed.gov/pubsearch/pubsinfo.asp?pubid=2007466

Bennett, S., Maton, K., & Kervin, L. (2008). The digital natives debate: A critical review of the evidence. *British Journal of Educational Technology, 31*(9), 775–786.

Bilal, D. (2000). Children's use of the Yahooligans! Web search engine: Cognitive, physical, and affective behaviors on fact-based search tasks. *Journal of the American Society for Information Science, 51*(7), 646–665. doi:10.1002/(SICI)1097-4571(2000)51:7<646::AID-ASI7>3.0.CO;2-A

Boyarin, J. (Ed.). (1993). *The ethnography of reading*. Berkeley: University of California Press. doi:10.1525/california/9780520079557.001.0001

Bråten, I., Strømsø, H.I., & Britt, M.A. (2009). Trust matters: Examining the role of source evaluation in students' construction of meaning within and across multiple texts. *Reading Research Quarterly, 44*(1), 6–28. doi:10.1598/RRQ.44.1.1

Bråten, I., Strømsø, H.I., & Salmerón, L. (2011). Trust and mistrust when students read multiple information sources about climate change. *Learning and Instruction, 21*(2), 180–192. doi:10.1016/j.learninstruc.2010.02.002

Britt, M.A., & Gabrys, G.L. (2001). Teaching advanced literacy skills for the World Wide Web. In C.R. Wolfe (Ed.), *Learning and teaching on the World Wide Web* (pp. 73–90). San Diego, CA: Academic. doi:10.1016/B978-012761891-3/50007-2

Broch, E. (2000). Children's search engines from an information search process perspective. *School Library Media Research*, 3. Retrieved from www.ala.org/arasl/ aaslpubsandjournals/slmrb/slmrcontents/volume32000/childrens

Callow, J. (2010). Spot the difference: The changing nature of page-based and screen-based texts. *Screen Education, 58*, 106–110.

Cammack, D. (2002). Literacy, technology, and a room of her own: Analyzing adolescent girls' online conversations from historical and technological literacy perspectives. In D. Shallert, C. Fairbanks, J. Worthy, B. Maloch, & J. Hoffman (Eds.), *Fifty-first yearbook of the National Reading Conference* (pp. 129–141). Chicago: National Reading Conference.

Canavilhas, J. (n.d.). *Web journalism: From the inverted pyramid to the tumbled pyramid*. Retrieved from www.bocc.ubi.pt/pag/canavilhas-joao-inverted-pyramid.pdf

Castek, J. (2008). *How do 4th and 5th grade students acquire the new literacies of online reading comprehension? Exploring the contexts that facilitate learning*. Unpublished doctoral dissertation, University of Connecticut, Storrs.

Castek, J., & Coiro, J. (2010, April). *Measuring online reading comprehension in open networked spaces: Challenges, concerns, and choices*. Alternative poster session presented at the annual meeting of the American Educational Research Association, Denver, CO.

Castek, J., Zawilinski, L., McVerry, G., O'Byrne, I., & Leu, D.J. (2011). The new literacies of online reading comprehension: New opportunities and challenges for students with learning difficulties. In C. Wyatt-Smith, J. Elkins, & S. Gunn (Eds.), *Multiple perspectives on difficulties in learning literacy and numeracy* (pp. 91–110). New York: Springer.

Center for Media Literacy. (2005). *Literacy for the 21st century: An overview and orientation guide to media literacy education. Part 1 of the CML medialit kit: Framework for learning and teaching in a media age*. Retrieved from www.medialit.org/cml-medialit-kit

Cho, B.-Y. (2010, December 3). *A study of adolescents' constructive strategy use in a critical Internet reading task*. Paper presented at the annual meeting of the Literacy Research Association, Fort Worth, TX.

Churches, A. (2009). *Bloom's digital taxonomy*. Retrieved from edorigami.wikispaces.com/Bloom%27s+Digital+Taxonomy

Clemitt, M. (2008). Internet accuracy. *CQ Researcher, 18*(27), 625–648.

Coiro, J. (2003). Reading comprehension on the Internet: Expanding our understanding of reading comprehension to encompass new literacies. *The Reading Teacher, 56*(5), 458–464.

Coiro, J. (2009). Promising practices for supporting adolescents' online literacy development. In K.D. Wood & W.E. Blanton (Eds.), *Literacy instruction for adolescents: Research-based practice* (pp. 442–471). New York: Guilford.

Coiro, J. (2011). Predicting reading comprehension on the Internet: Contributions of offline reading skills, online reading skills, and prior knowledge. *Journal of Literacy Research, 43*(4), 352–392.

Coiro, J., & Castek, J. (2010). Assessment frameworks for teaching and learning English language arts in a digital age. In D. Lapp & D. Fisher (Eds.), *Handbook of research on teaching the English language arts* (3rd ed., pp. 314–321). New York: Routledge.

Coiro, J., Castek, J., & Guzniczak, L. (2011). Uncovering online reading comprehension processes: Two adolescents reading independently and collaboratively on the Internet. In P.J. Dunston, L.B. Gambrell, K. Headley, S.K. Fullerton, & P.M. Stecker (Eds.), *60th yearbook of the Literacy Research Association* (pp. 354–369). Oak Creek, WI: Literacy Research Association.

Coiro, J., & Dobler, E. (2007). Exploring the online comprehension strategies used by sixth-grade skilled readers to search for and locate information on the Internet. *Reading Research Quarterly, 42*(2), 214–257. doi:10.1598/RRQ.42.2.2

Coiro, J., & Fogleman, J. (2011). Capitalizing on Internet resources for content-area teaching and learning. *Educational Leadership, 68*(5), 34–38.

Coiro, J., Knobel, M., Lankshear, C., & Leu, D.J. (2008). Central issues in new literacies and new literacies research. In J. Coiro, M. Knobel, C. Lankshear, & D.J. Leu (Eds.), *Handbook of research on new literacies* (pp. 1–22). Mahwah, NJ: Erlbaum.

Cooper, M. (2004). *Expanding the digital divide and falling behind on broadband: Why telecommunications policy of neglect is not benign*. Washington, DC: Consumer Federation of America. Retrieved from www.consumerfed.org/pdfs/digitaldivide.pdf

Cope, B., & Kalantzis, M. (Eds.). (1999). *Multiliteracies: Literacy learning and the design of social futures*. New York: Routledge.

Dalton, B., & Proctor, P. (2008). The changing landscape of text and comprehension in the age of new literacies. In J. Coiro, M. Knobel, C. Lankshear, & D.J. Leu (Eds.), *Handbook of research on new literacies* (pp. 297–324). Mahwah, NJ: Erlbaum.

Diringer, D. (1968). *The alphabet: A key to the history of mankind*. New York: Funk & Wagnalls.

Dochy, F., Segers, M., Van den Bossche, P., & Gijbels, D. (2003). Effects of problem-based learning: A meta-analysis. *Learning and Instruction, 13*(5), 533–568. doi:10.1016/S0959-4752(02)00025-7

Eagleton, M. (2001). *Factors that influence Internet inquiry strategies: Case studies of middle school students with and without learning disabilities*. Paper presented at the annual meeting of the National Reading Conference, San Antonio, TX.

Eagleton, M., Guinee, K., & Langlais, K. (2003). Teaching Internet literacy strategies: The hero inquiry project. *Voices From the Middle, 10*(3), 28–35.

Erstad, O. (2002). Norwegian students using digital artifacts in project-based learning. *Journal of Computer Assisted Learning, 18*(4), 427–437. doi:10.1046/j.0266-4909.2002.00254.x

Everett-Cacopardo, H. (2011). *Classrooms without borders: How online collaboration can connect*

adolescents to literacy and learning around the world. Manuscript submitted for publication.
Fabos, B. (2008). The price of information: Critical literacy, education, and today's Internet. In J. Coiro, M. Knobel, C. Lankshear, & D.J. Leu (Eds.), *Handbook of research on new literacies* (pp. 839–870). Mahwah, NJ: Erlbaum.
Fabos, B., & Young, M.D. (1999). Telecommunications in the classroom: Rhetoric versus reality. *Review of Educational Research, 69*(3), 217–259.
Federal Trade Commission. (2002, April). *Protecting children's privacy under COPPA: A survey on compliance.* Retrieved from www.ftc.gov/os/2002/04/coppasurvey.pdf
Fillmore, C. (1966). Deictic categories in the semantics of 'come.' *Foundations of Language, 2*(3), 219–227.
Flanagin, A.J., Farinola, W.J., & Metzger, M.J. (2000). The technical code of the Internet/World Wide Web. *Critical Studies in Media Communication, 17*(4), 409–428. doi:10.1080/15295030009388411
Flanagin, A.J., & Metzger, M.J. (2010). *An empirical examination of youth, digital media use, and information credibility.* Cambridge, MA: MIT Press.
Gee, J.P. (2007a). *Good video games and good learning: Collected essays on video games, learning and literacy.* New York: Peter Lang.
Gee, J.P. (2007b). *Social linguistics and literacies: Ideology in discourses.* London: Routledge.
Gee, J.P. (2007c). *What video games have to teach us about learning and literacy* (2nd ed.). New York: Macmillan. doi:10.1145/950566.950595
Gilster, P. (1997). *Digital literacy.* New York: John Wiley.
Graham, L., & Metaxas, P.T. (2003). Of course it's true: I saw it on the Internet! *Communications of the ACM, 46*(5), 71–75.
Greenhow, C., Robelia, B., & Hughes, J. (2009). Web 2.0 and classroom research: What path should we take now? *Educational Researcher, 38*(4), 246–259. doi:10.3102/0013189X09336671
Guinee, K., Eagleton, M.B., & Hall, T.E. (2003). Adolescents' Internet search strategies: Drawing upon familiar cognitive paradigms when accessing electronic information sources. *Journal of Educational Computing Research, 29*(3), 363–374. doi:10.2190/HD0A-N15L-RTFH-2DU8
Harper, D. (2006). *Generation YES (Youth and Educators Succeeding)—Vision to action: Adding student leadership to your technology plan.* Retrieved from www.genyes.com/media/programs/how_to_include_students_in_tech_plan.pdf
Hartman, D.K., Morsink, P.M., & Zheng, J. (2010). From print to pixels: The evolution of cognitive conceptions of reading comprehension. In E.A. Baker (Ed.), *The new literacies: Multiple perspectives on research and practice* (pp. 131–164). New York: Guilford.
Henry, L. (2006). SEARCHing for an answer: The critical role of new literacies while reading on the Internet. *The Reading Teacher, 59*(7), 614–627. doi:10.1598/RT.59.7.1
Henry, L.A. (2007). *Exploring new literacies pedagogy and online reading comprehension among middle school students and teachers: Issues of social equity or social exclusion?* Unpublished doctoral dissertation, University of Connecticut, Storrs.
Hew, K.F., & Brush, T. (2007). Integrating technology into K–12 teaching and learning: Current knowledge gaps and recommendations for future research. *Educational Technology Research and Development, 55*(3), 223–252. doi:10.1007/s11423-006-9022-5
Hirsh, S.G. (1999). Children's relevance criteria and information seeking on electronic resources. *Journal of the American Society for Information Science, 50*(14), 1265–1283. doi:10.1002/(SICI)1097-4571(1999)50:14<1265::AID-ASI2>3.0.CO;2-E
Hmelo-Silver, C.E. (2004). Problem-based learning: What and how do students learn? *Educational Psychology Review, 16*(3), 235–266. doi:10.1023/B:EDPR.0000034022.16470.f3.
Hobbs, R. (2010). *Digital and media literacy: A plan of action. A white paper on the digital and media literacy recommendations of the Knight Commission on the information needs of communities in a democracy.* Washington, DC: The Aspen Institute. Retrieved from www.knightcomm.org/digital-and-media-literacy/
Hull, G., & Schultz, K. (2002). *School's out: Bridging out-of-school literacies with classroom practice.* New York: Teachers College Press.
Hull, G., Stornaiuolo, A., & Sahni, U. (2010). Cultural citizenship and cosmopolitan practice: Global youth communicate online. *English Education, 42*(4), 331–367.
Hull, G., Zacher, J., & Hibbert, L. (2009). Youth, risk, and equity in a global world. *Review of Research in Education, 33*(1), 117–159. doi:10.3102/0091732X08327746
Illera, J.L.R. (1997). De la lectura en papel a la lectura de multimedia [From reading on paper to reading multimedia]. In Fundalectura (Ed.), *Lectura y nuevas tecnologías: 3er congresso nacional de lectura* [Reading and new technologies: 3rd National Congress of Reading] (pp. 69–88). Bogotá, Colombia: Fundación para el Fomento de la Lectura.
International ICT Literacy Panel. (2002, May). *Digital transformation: A framework for ICT literacy.* Retrieved from www.ets.org/Media/Tests/Information_and_Communication_Technology_Literacy/ictreport.pdf.
International Reading Association. (2009). *New literacies and 21st century technologies* (Position statement). Newark, DE: Author. Available from: www.reading.org/General/AboutIRA/PositionStatements/21stCenturyLiteracies.aspx
International Reading Association & National Council of Teachers of English. (2010). *Standards for the assessment of reading and writing* (Rev. ed.). Newark, DE, & Urbana, IL: Authors. Retrieved from www.reading

.org/General/CurrentResearch/Standards/AssessmentStandards.aspx.
Internet World Stats. (2011). *Internet users in the world: Distribution by world regions.* Retrieved July 1, 2011, from www.internetworldstats.com/stats.htm
Jenkins, H. (2006). *Convergence culture: Where old and new media collide.* New York: New York University Press.
Jewitt, C., & Kress, G.R. (2003). *Multimodal literacy.* New York: Peter Lang.
Johnson, L., Levine, A., Smith, R., & Smythe, T. (2009). *Horizon report: 2009 K–12 edition.* Austin, TX: The New Media Consortium.
Jonassen, D.H., Howland, J., Moore, J., & Marra, R.M. (2003). *Learning to solve problems with technology: A constructivist perspective* (2nd ed.). Columbus, OH: Merrill/Prentice-Hall.
Kaiser Family Foundation. (2005). *Generation M: Media in the lives of 8–18 year-olds.* Retrieved from www.kff.org/entmedia/7251.cfm
Kiili, C., Laurinen, L., & Marttunen, M. (2008). Students evaluating Internet sources: From versatile evaluators to uncritical readers. *Journal of Educational Computing Research, 39*(1), 75–95. doi:10.2190/EC.39.1.e
Kiili, C., Laurinen, L., Marttunen, M., & Leu, D. J. (2011). *Working on understanding: Collaborative reading patterns on the Web.* Manuscript submitted for publication.
Kinzer, C.K. (2010). Considering literacy and policy in the context of digital environments. *Language Arts, 88*(1), 51–61.
Kinzer, C.K., Hoffman, D.L., Turkay, S., Gunbas, N., & Chantes, P. (2011). Exploring motivation and comprehension of a narrative in a video game, book and comic book format. In P.J. Dunston, L.B. Gambrell, K. Headley, S.K. Fullerton, & P.M. Stecker (Eds.), *60th Yearbook of the Literacy Research Association Yearbook* (pp. 263–278). Oak Creek, WI: Literacy Research Association.
Kinzer, C.K., Turkay, S., Hoffman, D.L., Gunbas, N., Chantes, P., Chaiwinij, A., et al. (in press). Examining the effects of text and images on story comprehension: An eye tracking study of reading in games and comics. In P.J. Dunston & S.K. Fullerton (Eds.), *61st yearbook of the Literacy Research Association.* Chicago: Literacy Research Association
Kinzer, C.K., & Leander, K. (2002). Technology and the language arts: Implications of an expanded definition of literacy. In J. Flood, D. Lapp, J.R. Squire, & J.M. Jensen (Eds.), *Handbook of research and teaching the English language arts* (pp. 546–566). Mahwah, NJ: Erlbaum.
Kirsch, I., Braun, H., Yamamoto, K., & Sum, A. (2007). *America's perfect storm: Three forces changing our nation's future.* Princeton, NJ: Educational Testing Service. Retrieved from www.ets.org/Media/Research/pdf/PICSTORM.pdf
Kleifgen, J., & Kinzer, C.K. (2009). Alternative spaces for education with and through technology. In H. Varenne & E. Gordon (Eds.), *Comprehensive education explorations, possibilities, challenges* (pp. 139–186). Lewiston, NY: Ewin Mellen.
Knobel, M., & Wilber, D. (2009). Let's talk 2.0. *Educational Leadership, 66*(6), 20–24.
Kress, G. (2003). *Literacy in the new media age.* London: Routledge. doi:10.4324/9780203164754
Kuiper, E. (2007). *Teaching Web literacy in primary education.* Retrieved from dare.ubvu.vu.nl/bitstream/1871/10836/1/7533.pdf.
Kuiper, E., & Volman, M. (2008). The Web as a source of information for students in K–12 education. In J. Coiro, M. Knobel, C. Lankshear, & D.J. Leu (Eds.), *Handbook of research on new literacies* (pp. 241–246). Mahwah, NJ: Erlbaum.
Labbo, L. (1996). A semiotic analysis of young children's symbol making in a classroom computer center. *Reading Research Quarterly, 31*(4), 356–385. doi:10.1598/RRQ.31.4.2
Labbo, L., & Kuhn, M. (1998). Electronic symbol making: Young children's computer-related emerging concepts about literacy. In D. Reinking, M. McKenna, L.D. Labbo, & R. Kieffer (Eds.), *Handbook of literacy and technology: Transformations in a post-typographic world* (pp. 79–92). Mahwah, NJ: Erlbaum.
Labbo, L.D., & Reinking, D. (1999). Negotiating the multiple realities of technology in literacy research and instruction. *Reading Research Quarterly, 34*(4), 478–492. doi:10.1598/RRQ.34.4.5
Lankshear, C., & Knobel, M. (2006). *New literacies* (2nd ed.). Maidenhead, UK: Open University Press.
Lawless, K.A., & Kulikowich, J.M. (1996). Understanding hypertext navigation through cluster analysis. *Journal of Educational Computing Research, 14*(4), 385–399. doi:10.2190/DVAP-DE23-3XMV-9MXH
Lawless, K.A., Mills, R., & Brown, S.W. (2002). Children's hypermedia navigational strategies. *Journal of Research on Computing in Education, 34*(3), 274–284.
Leander, K.M., & Lovvorn, J.F. (2006). Literacy networks: Following the circulation of texts, bodies, and objects in the schooling and online gaming of one youth. *Cognition and Instruction, 24*(3), 291–340. doi:10.1207/s1532690xci2403_1
Lemke, J.L. (2002). Travels in hypermodality. *Visual Communication, 1*(3), 299–325. doi:10.1177/147035720200100303
Leu, D.J., Jr. (1997). Caity's question: Literacy as deixis on the Internet. *The Reading Teacher, 51*(1), 62–67.
Leu, D.J., Jr. (2000). Literacy and technology: Deictic consequences for literacy education in an information age. In M.L. Kamil, P. Mosenthal, P.D. Pearson, & R. Barr (Eds.), *Handbook of reading research* (Vol. 3, pp. 743–770). Mahwah, NJ: Erlbaum.
Leu, D.J., Castek, J., Hartman, D., Coiro, J., Henry, L., Kulikowich, J., et al. (2005). *Evaluating the development of scientific knowledge and new forms*

of reading comprehension during online learning. Final report presented to the North Central Regional Educational Laboratory/Learning Point Associates. Retrieved from www.newliteracies.uconn.edu/ncrel.html

Leu, D.J., Coiro, J., Castek, J., Hartman, D., Henry, L.A., & Reinking, D. (2008). Research on instruction and assessment in the new literacies of online reading comprehension. In C.C. Block & S. Parris (Eds.), *Comprehension instruction: Research-based best practices* (pp. 321–345). New York: Guilford.

Leu, D.J., Everett-Cacopardo, H., Zawilinski, L., McVerry, J.G., & O'Byrne, W.I. (in press). The new literacies of online reading comprehension. In C.A. Chapelle (Ed.), *The encyclopedia of applied linguistics.* Oxford, UK: Wiley-Blackwell.

Leu, D.J., Forzani, E., Burlingame, C., Kulikowich, J., Sedransk, N., Coiro, J., et al. (in press). The new literacies of online research and comprehension: Assessing and preparing students for the 21st century with Common Core State Standards. In S.B. Neuman, L.B. Gambrell (Eds.), & C. Massey (Assoc. Ed.), *Reading instruction in the age of Common Core Standards.* Newark, DE: International Reading Association.

Leu, D.J., Jr., Karchmer, R., & Leu, D.D. (1999). The Miss Rumphius effect: Envisionments for literacy and learning that transform the Internet. *The Reading Teacher, 52*(6), 636–642.

Leu, D.J., Jr., & Kinzer, C.K. (2000). The convergence of literacy instruction and networked technologies for information and communication. *Reading Research Quarterly, 35*(1), 108–127. doi:10.1598/RRQ.35.1.8

Leu, D.J., Jr., Kinzer, C.K., Coiro, J., & Cammack, D. (2004). Toward a theory of new literacies emerging from the Internet and other information and communication technologies. In R.B. Ruddell & N.J. Unrau (Eds.), *Theoretical models and processes of reading* (5th ed., pp. 1570–1613). Newark, DE: International Reading Association. doi:10.1598/0872075028.54

Leu, D.J., Kulikowich, J., Sedransk, N., & Coiro, J. (2009). *Assessing online reading comprehension: The ORCA project.* Research grant funded by the U.S. Department of Education, Institute of Education Sciences.

Leu, D.J., McVerry, J.G., O'Byrne, W.I., Kiili, C., Zawilinski, L., Everett-Cacopardo, H., et al. (2011). The new literacies of online reading comprehension: Expanding the literacy and learning curriculum. *Journal of Adolescent & Adult Literacy, 55*(1), (pp. 5–14). doi:10.1598/JAAL.55.1.1

Leu, D.J., O'Byrne, W.I., Zawilinski, L., McVerry, J.G., & Everett-Cacopardo, H. (2009). Expanding the new literacies conversation. *Educational Researcher, 38*(4), 264–269. doi:10.3102/0013189X09336676

Leu, D.J., & Reinking, D. (2005). *Developing Internet comprehension strategies among adolescent students at risk to become dropouts.* Research grant project funded by the U.S. Department of Education, Institute of Education Sciences.

Leu, D.J., & Reinking, D. (2009). *Final report: Developing Internet comprehension strategies among poor, adolescent students at risk to become dropouts.* Research grant funded by the U.S. Department of Education, Institute of Education Sciences.

Leu, D.J., Reinking, D., Carter, A., Castek, J., Coiro, J., & Henry, L.A. (2007, April 9). *Defining online reading comprehension: Using think-aloud verbal protocols to refine a preliminary model of Internet reading comprehension processes.* Paper presented at the American Educational Research Association, Chicago. Available from: docs.google.com/Doc?id=dcbjhrtq_10djqrhz

Leu, D.J., Zawilinski, L., Castek, J., Banerjee, M., Housand, B., & Liu, Y. (2007). What is new about the new literacies of online reading comprehension? In L. Rush, J. Eakle, & A. Berger (Eds.), *Secondary school literacy: What research reveals for classroom practices* (pp. 37–68). Urbana, IL: National Council of Teachers of English.

Lewis, C., & Fabos, B. (2005). Instant messaging, literacies, and social identities. *Reading Research Quarterly, 40*(4), 470–501. doi:10.1598/RRQ.40.4.5

Lohnes Watulak, S., & Kinzer, C.K. (2013). Beyond technology skills: Toward a framework for critical digital literacies in pre-service technology education. In J. Ávila & J.Z. Pandya (Eds.), *Critical digital literacies as social praxis: Intersections and challenges* (pp. 127–153). New York: Peter Lang.

Manguel, A. (1996). *A history of reading.* New York: Viking.

Mathews, M. (1966). *Teaching to read: Historically considered.* Chicago: University of Chicago Press.

Matteucci, N., O'Mahony, M., Robinson, C., & Zwick, T. (2005). Productivity, workplace performance and ICT: Industry and firm-level evidence for Europe and the US. *Scottish Journal of Political Economy, 52*(3), 359–386. doi:10.1111/j.0036-9292.2005.00349.x

McDonald, S., & Stevenson, R.J. (1996). Disorientation in hypertext: The effects of three text structures on navigation performance. *Applied Ergonomics, 27(1),* 61–68. doi:10.1016/0003-6870(95)00073-9

McEneaney, J.E., Li, L., Allen, K., & Guzniczak, L. (2009). Stance, navigation, and reader response in expository hypertext. *Journal of Literacy Research, 41*(1), 1–45. doi:10.1080/10862960802695081

McKenzie, J. (2001). *Planning good change with technology and literacy.* Bellingham, WA: FNO.

Metzger, M.J., & Flanagin, A.J. (Eds.). (2008). *Digital media, youth, and credibility.* Cambridge, MA: MIT Press.

Minister of Manitoba Education, Citizenship, and Youth. (2006). *A continuum model for literacy with ICT across the curriculum: A resource for developing computer literacy*. Retrieved from www.edu.gov.mb.ca/k12/tech/lict/resources/handbook/index.html

Mishra, P., & Koehler, M.J. (2006). Technological pedagogical content knowledge: A framework for teacher knowledge. *Teachers College Record, 108*(6), 1017–1054. doi:10.1111/j.1467-9620.2006.00684.x

Murphy, S.M. (1986). Children's comprehension of deictic categories in oral and written language. *Reading Research Quarterly, 21*(2), 118–131. doi:10.2307/747840

National Governors Association Center for Best Practices & Council of Chief State School Officers. (2010). *Common Core State Standards for English language arts and literacy in history/social studies, science, and technical subjects*. Washington, DC: Authors.

National Research Council. (2001). *Knowing what students know: The science and design of educational assessment*. Washington, DC: National Academy Press.

New London Group. (1996). A pedagogy of multiliteracies: Designing social futures. *Harvard Educational Review, 66*(1), 60–92.

New London Group. (2000). *Multiliteracies: Literacy learning and the design of social futures*. London: Routledge.

O'Brien, D., Beach, R., & Scharber, C. (2007). "Struggling" middle schoolers: Engagement and literate competence in a reading writing intervention class. *Reading Psychology, 28*(1), 51–73. doi:10.1080/02702710601115463

O'Brien, D., & Scharber, C. (2008). Digital literacies go to school: Potholes and possibilities. *Journal of Adolescent & Adult Literacy, 52*(1), 66–68. doi:10.1598/JAAL.52.1.7

O'Byrne, W.I. (2011). *Facilitating critical evaluation skills through content creation: Empowering adolescents as readers and writers of online information*. Unpublished doctoral dissertation, University of Connecticut, Storrs.

O'Byrne, W.I., & McVerry, J.G. (2009). Measuring the dispositions of online reading comprehension: A preliminary validation study. In K.M. Leander, D.W. Rowe, D.K. Dickinson, M.K. Hundley, R.T. Jimenez, & V.J. Risko (Eds.), *58th yearbook of the National Reading Conference Yearbook* (pp. 362–375). Oak Creek, WI: National Reading Conference.

Organisation for Economic Co-operation and Development. (2011). PISA 2009 results: Students on line. *Digital technologies and performance* (Volume VI). Available from dx.doi.org/10.1787/9789264112995-en

Organisation for Economic Co-operation and Development & the Centre for Educational Research and Innovation. (2010). *Trends shaping education 2010*. Paris: OECD.

Page, S.E. (2007). *The difference: How the power of diversity creates better groups, firms, schools and societies*. Princeton, NJ: Princeton University Press.

Penuel, W.R. (2006). Implementation and effects of one-to-one computing initiatives: A research synthesis. *Journal of Research on Technology in Education, 38*(3), 329–348.

Pew Internet & American Life Project. (2001). *The Internet and education: Findings of the Pew Internet & American Life Project*. Retrieved from www.pewInternet.org/reports

Pew Internet & American Life Project. (2005). *Teens and technology*. Retrieved from www.pewinternet.org/topics.asp?c=4

Popham, W.J. (2009). Assessing student affect. *Educational Leadership, 66*(8), 85–86.

Reich, R. (1992). *The work of nations*. New York: Vintage.

Rouet, J.-F. (2006). *The skills of document use: From text comprehension to Web-based learning*. Mahwah, NJ: Erlbaum.

Rouet, J.-F., Ros, C., Goumi, A., Macedo-Rouet, M., & Dinet, J. (2011). The influence of surface and deep cues on primary and secondary school students' assessment of relevance in Web menus. *Learning and Instruction, 21*(2), 205–219. doi:10.1016/j.learninstruc.2010.02.007

Sanchez, C.A., Wiley, J., & Goldman, S.R. (2006). Teaching students to evaluate source reliability during Internet research tasks. In S.A. Barab, K.E. Hay, & D.T. Hickey (Eds.), *Proceedings of the seventh international conference on the learning sciences* (pp. 662–666). Bloomington, IN: International Society of the Learning Sciences.

Saylor, P., & Kehrhahn, M. (2003). Teacher skills get an upgrade. *Journal of Staff Development, 24*(14), 48–53.

Schulz-Zander, R., Büchter, A., & Dalmer, R. (2002). The role of ICT as a promoter of students' cooperation. *Journal of Computer Assisted Learning, 18*(4), 438–448. doi:10.1046/j.0266-4909.2002.002.x

Silvernail, D.L., & Buffington, P.J. (2009). *Improving mathematics performance, using laptop technology: The importance of professional development for success*. Retrieved from www.usm.maine.edu/cepare/pdf/Mathematics_Final_cover.pdf

Silvernail, D.L., & Gritter, A.K. (2007). *Maine's middle school laptop program: Creating better writers*. Gorham: Maine Education Policy Research Institute, University of Southern Maine.

Silvernail, D.L., & Lane, D. (2004). *The impact on Maine's one-to-one laptop program on middle school teachers and students*. Gorham: Maine Education Policy Research Institute, University of Southern Maine.

Smith, M.C., Mikulecky, L., Kibby, M.W., Dreher, M.J., & Dole, J.A. (2000). What will be the demands of literacy in the workplace in the next millennium? *Reading Research Quarterly, 35*(3), 378–383. doi:10.1598/RRQ.35.3.3

Smith, N.B. (1965). *American reading instruction*. Newark, DE: International Reading Association.

Spires, H.A., & Estes, T.H. (2002). Reading in Web-based learning environments. In C.C. Block & M. Pressley (Eds.), *Comprehension instruction:*

Research-based best practices (pp. 115–125). New York: Guilford.
Spires, H.A., Hervey, L., & Watson, T. (2012). Scaffolding the TPACK framework in reading and language arts: New literacies, new minds. In C.A. Young & S. Kadjer (Eds.), *Research on technology in English education* (pp. 33–61). Charlotte, NC: Information Age.
Spires, H.A., Zheng, M., & Pruden, M. (2011). New technologies, new horizons: Graduate student views on creating their technological pedagogical content knowledge (TPACK). In K. Moyle & G. Wijngaards (Eds.), *Student reactions to learning with technologies: Perceptions and outcomes* (pp. 23–41). Hershey, PA: IGI Global.
Squire, K. (2008). Open-ended video games: A model for developing learning for the interactive age. In K. Salen (Ed.), *The ecology of games: Connecting youth, games, and learning* (pp. 167–198). Cambridge, MA: MIT Press.
Squire, K. (2011). *Video games and learning: Teaching and participatory culture in the digital age*. New York: Teachers College Press.
Steinkuehler, C. (2006). Massively multiplayer online videogaming as participation in a Discourse. *Mind, Culture, and Activity, 13*(1), 38–52. doi:10.1207/s15327884mca1301_4
Street, B. (1995). *Social literacies*. London: Longman.
Street, B. (2003). What's new in new literacy studies? *Current Issues in Comparative Education, 5*(2), 1–14.
Sundar, S.S. (2008). The MAIN model: A heuristic approach to understanding technology effects on credibility. In M.J. Metzger & A.J. Flanagin (Eds.), *Digital media, youth, and credibility* (pp. 73–100). Cambridge, MA: MIT Press.
Sutherland-Smith, W. (2002). Weaving the literacy web: Changes in reading from page to screen. *The Reading Teacher, 55*(7), 662–669.
Taboada, A., & Guthrie, J. (2006). Contributions of student questioning and prior knowledge to construction of knowledge from reading information text. *Journal of Literacy Research, 38*(1), 1–35. doi:10.1207/s15548430jlr3801_1
Tillman, H.N. (2003). *Evaluating quality on the Net*. Retrieved September 14, 2009, from www.hopetillman.com/findqual.html
Traut, G., & Kazzazi, K. (1996). *Dictionary of language and linguistics*. New York: Routledge.
Unsworth, L. (2008). Multiliteracies and metalanguage: Describing image/text relations as a resource for negotiating multimodal texts. In J. Coiro, M. Knobel, C. Lankshear, & D.J. Leu (Eds.), *Handbook of research on new literacies* (pp. 377–405). Mahwah, NJ: Erlbaum.
U.S. Department of Commerce, Economic and Statistics Administration & National Telecommunications and Information Administration. (2002). *A nation online: How Americans are expanding their use of the Internet*. Washington, DC: Author.
van Ark, B., Inklaar, R., & McGuckin, R.H. (2003). ICT productivity in Europe and the United States: Where do the differences come from? *CESifo Economic Studies, 49*(3), 295–318. doi:10.1093/cesifo/49.3.295
Wallace, R.M., Kupperman, J., Krajcik, J., & Soloway, E. (2000). Science on the Web: Students on-line in a sixth-grade classroom. *Journal of the Learning Sciences, 9*(1), 75–104. doi:10.1207/s15327809jls0901_5
Walsh, M. (2010). Multimodal literacy: What does it mean for classroom practice? *The Australian Journal of Language and Literacy, 33*(3), 211–239.
Warschauer, M. (2006). *Laptops and literacy: Learning in the wireless classroom*. New York: Teachers College Press.
Wyatt-Smith, C., & Elkins, J. (2008). Multimodal reading and comprehension in online environments. In J. Coiro, M. Knobel, C. Lankshear, & D.J. Leu (Eds.), *Handbook of research on new literacies* (pp. 899–942). Mahwah, NJ: Erlbaum.
Zawilinski, L. (2011). *An exploration of a collaborative blogging approach to literacy and learning: A mixed method study*. Unpublished doctoral dissertation, University of Connecticut, Storrs.
Zhang, S., & Duke, N.K. (2008). Strategies for Internet reading with different reading purposes: A descriptive study of twelve good Internet readers. *Journal of Literacy Research, 40*(1), 128–162. doi:10.1080/10862960802070491

CHAPTER 43

The Social Practice of Multimodal Reading: A New Literacy Studies–Multimodal Perspective on Reading

Jennifer Rowsell, Brock University

Gunther Kress, Institute of Education, University of London

Kate Pahl, University of Sheffield

Brian Street, King's College London

The aim of this chapter is to situate reading within two complementary approaches: New Literacy Studies (NLS) and a social semiotic approach to multimodality (SSMM). We use the term *reading* both as a fairly neutral description of an activity (as in, "what are you reading now?") and as a topic for theoretical attention (as in, "how can we understand reading in contemporary environments?"). In the latter sense, we argue that *reading* appears differently when it is viewed in the frame of social practices and environments and in the perspective of modally complex compositions than it does in other approaches. As concepts, reading and writing—making meaning in and with texts—name practices and processes today that differ in many respects from those some 30 or 40 years ago. At the same time, there are constants about reading and about writing as composition that provide a strong enough reason for us to look at reading from these two fields of research and theory, both of which focus on meaning making as located in social environments. Whereas the emphasis of NLS leans more toward an attention to understanding and describing social environments (where meaning is made and by whom), that of SSMM leans more toward semiotic factors (how meaning is made, by what agents, with what principles of and resources for making meaning), or in other words, toward the (material) realization of meanings.

This chapter is organized in five parts. First, we develop a view of reading through the lens of NLS and SSMM and show how these two approaches may be integrated. In the second, third, and fourth parts, we present ages and stages of reading, from early childhood literacies to youth literacies to adult academic literacies, and try to account for reading in different social settings. In the final section, we conclude with a discussion of ways forward with literacy, pedagogy, and policy. Throughout the chapter, we offer an integrated model of reading and of the reading process rooted in an epistemology that draws on both NLS and SSMM as a viable frame for thinking about reading in new times.

Why Reading Is Different Today

Children read—that is, make meaning from an engagement with—a vast range of aspects of the tangible world long before they are drawn into schooling and schooled practices, when, for instance, from a young age, they make what they regard as texts in what seems to be drawing more than writing (Kress, 1997). It is also the case when children make meaning in representing their world in any number of other ways: enacting aspects of the world in mimed movement, in gesture and facial expression, or combining existing or newly made three-dimensional objects with verbal commentary and movement in complex, sequentially staged tableaux. Such meaning making tends to be named play, and that naming acts as a potent means of deterring serious investigation of the relation of principles of composition in one domain—say, of drawing or building—with those in another, in this case with writing or reading in a conventional sense.

Such bracketing out of specific, early composition and reading has led to a profound, unrecognized problem in studies of early meaning making and its relation to reading and writing. This problem is compounded when we add, as we must, even at the earliest stages of more formal reading, the need to understand the communicational practices that form the taken-for-granted mainstream of children's communicational world. The possibilities that have arisen with the media of digital technologies, such as browsing screens, scrolling and scanning multiple websites, clicking, following and reading hyperlinks, communicating through social networks, and the associated forms of producing texts, present potentials for making meaning in both reading and writing, which are quite unlike those that existed until, say, 30 or 40 years ago. Given that, it becomes essential to consider what reading and writing involve now, what they are, and how they can be thought about and theorized.

While learning to read in its more narrow sense has always meant learning to make sense of texts, making sense of texts has always been multimodal. Even traditional books, of whatever kind, have pictures, gutters, trim sizes, fonts, and illustration styles with color or in black and white. Choices from among these meaningful resources—modes for making meaning—signal decisions to match a message and the practices used to make a message meaningful to an audience and, at the same time, to signal aesthetic choices related to audience and purpose. To capture some of the principles underlying old and new texts, Figures 1 and 2 are two contrasting examples.

Figure 1 is a page from a 1939 children's book called *Raggedy Ann in the Magic Book* by Johnny Gruelle (1939). The written text describes two rag dolls, Andy and Ann, with their stuffed arms around each other on a walk in the deep, deep woods. They suddenly encounter a Fuzzywump, which is a little gnome, sitting on a rock, and they then engage in a whimsical conversation. The text is typical of a mid-20th-century reader with pictures that supplement or complement written

Figure 1. A Page From *Raggedy Ann in the Magic Book* by Johnny Gruelle

Chapter One

THE Deep, Deep, Woods always filled with cool, blue-green shadows and patches of golden, sparkling sunlight is surely a wonderful place for fairies, elves, gnomes and magical, teeny weeny creatures to live.

Raggedy Ann and Raggedy Andy each with a rag arm around the other's shoulder, stood for a moment listening to the gentle whispering of the wind through the hemlocks.

"Let us follow the Tumbling Brook!" Raggedy Andy suggested, "We will surely meet with wonderful adventures along its mossy banks. And we shall enjoy its cheery, tinkling, laughter, as we go along."

"Yes!" agreed Raggedy Ann, "Let us follow the tinkling, tumbling, laughing brooklet."

So, the two kindly rag dolls, their cotton stuffed heads filled with pleasant thoughts, walked along the mossy bank of the tumbling brooklet until they met a funny little creature who said he was a Fuzzywump.

7

Note. From *Raggedy Ann in the Magic Book* (p. 7), by J. Gruelle, 1939, New York: Atheneum. Copyright © 1939 by Atheneum. Reprinted with permission.

text, but the pictures are visual supports without a substantive function. As the story continues, most of the illustrations that support the written text are black-and-white, smaller format line drawings (in fact, there are 34 black-and-white illustrations compared with 20 color illustrations).

Figure 2 shows the first page of a 2008 reader, designed for a similar reading level to that of the 1939 reader. There is a privileging of black-and-white line drawings with speech bubbles and cells for each character's part in the dialogue. The title of the Scholastic text by Terry Deary (2008) is *Horrible Histories: Savage Stone Age*. There is a distinct and immediately discernible difference between the 1939 text and this one. The 1939 reader resembles a classic storybook genre. It begins, "The Deep, Deep, Woods always filled with cool, blue-green shadows" and ends with "The adventure through the Fuzzywump's magic book had ended, very happily. THE END." It closely follows the convention of "Once upon a time...

Figure 2. A Page From *Horrible Histories: Savage Stone Age* by Terry Deary

Introduction

History can be horrible. And the further back in time you go, the more horrible it becomes in some ways! Of course, not everyone believes this! Some people would quite like the idea of time travel. They'd like to go back in time and live in another age. An age without homework, global warming and mad cow disease.

So the past isn't so attractive as it seems in the school books.

5

Note. From *Horrible Histories: Savage Stone Age* (p. 5), by Terry Deary, 2008, London: Scholastic. Copyright © 1999 by Terry Deary and Martin Brown. Reprinted with permission by Scholastic.

and they all lived happily ever after." The 2008 book, by comparison, seems more journalistic in genre with frequent editorializing comments: "History can be horrible. And the further back in time you go, the more horrible it becomes." The book ends with "Someone helped him, someone shared their hard-earned food, someone tended his wounds. Someone *cared.* The savage Stone Age?" The cartoon accompanying the text shows an upwardly mobile couple discussing living in the Stone Age and some of the realities of Stone Age life, such as no teachers, no policemen, no soft toilet paper, and dying from a rotten tooth. The visual image is no longer supplementary but an integral part of the text. The book exploits multiple points of view, including age-appropriate tropes and themes to address its audience, such as toilet humor, overgeneralizations, irony, and commentary on contemporary social trends, and it contrasts and compares these with rites and practices typical of (cartoon) representations of Stone Age people.

In their modal instantiation, the two books differ: In the first one, the images frame and embellish, whereas in the second book, they are interwoven entirely with the verbal text. Of course, all modes present in a multimodal ensemble always contribute meaning, but it is fair to say that the 2008 text could not exist without the images while the text from 1939 could, even though it would be less attractive.

In the 2008 book, meaning is made through the close integration of visual and verbal elements: through illustration, speech bubbles, font style, sizes, shading, color. In its use of modes, it employs a specific logic: What is best done by writing (standing in for speech) is done by writing; what is best done by image (standing in for the visually accessible world) is done by image. So much is different about the meaning, the logic and tone (i.e., matter of fact in the 1939 text, irony and sarcasm in the 2008 text), and the modal dominance of the 1939 book (privileging printed word) and the 2008 book (privileging visuals), but although reading may have changed significantly over time, we see a different kind of picture emerge when we view these texts across cultural and social contexts.

Texts take their meanings from contexts and the discourses and practices that circulate in that context. To illustrate our point, we return to Figures 1 and 2 as examples. If we move both of these texts to a very different context in another part of the world, such as Asunción, Paraguay, the content of the text and reading practices used to make the text meaningful impact what gets comprehended. In the 1939 reader, the characters are white, typically middle-class constructs, and even the 2008 reader depicts white, middle-class individuals and their experiences. Teachers and students using these same books in an English learner class in Paraguay would have to contextualize the examples, explain the humor and irony, and frame what these same meanings translate to in local terms. In other words, these two readers have limited applicability for many readers because they do not reflect their everyday, lived experiences. Concepts such as book sharing and read-alouds do not align with other cultures and religions, and in many ways, they promote a deficit model of literacy development. Researchers and theorists such as Compton-Lilly, Rogers, and Lewis (2012) refer to these paradigms as modernist projects. Looking across cultures, religions, and races, book sharing is one way to approach reading, but it is not the only way. In what follows, we look at how NLS perspectives came into being and how they challenge the efficacy of such reading processes as shared reading, picture books, and other common reading interventions.

Reading Perspectives in NLS

NLS combines such disparate fields as anthropology, semiotics, sociology, and linguistics to look at situated language as value-laden and shaped by contexts. NLS was and is rooted in issues of power and differentials in power. It has not explicitly focused on reading and reading processes, but rather on oral and written languages and the tools used for social practices within diverse settings.

Thinking about NLS in terms of reading demands revisiting researchers who are associated with the field as a domain of theory and practice. Anthropologist and folklorist Hymes (1974) looked at oral narratives within Native American communities, acknowledging and documenting how language shifts across cultural practices. During his career, he formulated an ethnography of speaking to account for poetic structures and narratives within languages as signaling communicative competence existing within communities as opposed to a universalized notion of communicative competence.

A student of Hymes, Heath (1983) similarly documented a 10-year ethnography of literacy practices in the homes of children and their families living in three different communities. Her book *Ways With Words: Language, Life, and Work in Communities and Classrooms* describes the different language and literacy practices of two rural communities and one urban community in the Piedmont Carolinas in the 1970s. Heath contrasted a black community (Trackton) to a working-class community (Roadville), paying close attention to the ways parents in these two communities spoke to their children and raised them and how the children interacted with their parents. Then she looked at what happened when the children went to school. In the cases of both Trackton and Roadville children, there was a disjuncture between their home literacy practices and their school literacy practices.

This was in sharp contrast to the children from the third community, a town Heath called Maintown. The children in Maintown were primarily teachers' children, who had been raised and talked to in ways that echoed the norms of school literacy. To understand how different ways of interacting contributed to different outcomes in literacy, Heath (1983) focused her study around the concept of literacy events, which she defined as "any action sequence, involving one or more persons, in which the production and/or comprehension of print plays a role" (p. 92). This concept enabled Heath to understand in a contrastive way by isolating specific instances of the different events and practices around literacy.

Heath (2012) has since published a follow-up to her *Ways With Words* study, in which she tracks three generations of families from Trackton and Roadville as they moved across the United States in search of work, responding to the larger economic and social changes in the country across this period. She documents the older generation's responses to her accounts of their earlier literacy practices and relates these to the current practices of their children and grandchildren in their new environments.

Shortly after Heath's original study, Brian Street (1984) examined literacy practices in different parts of the same community in Iran, finding correspondingly that literacy practices are shaped by context and identity. He introduced an ideological view of literacy that takes into account not only practices, concepts, texts, identities, and the contexts in which they take place but also how these relate to issues of power. His study demonstrated how Standard English, which was seen as happening in school, had rendered outside literacy practices as less powerful and less relevant.

Since that time, Street has extended the NLS perspective to accounts of literacy practices in other settings, such as the United States (B. Street, 1993; J.C. Street & Street, 1991), Ethiopia (Gebre, Openjuru, Rogers, & Street, 2009), and the United Kingdom (B. Street, 1997, 2011). With regard to how NLS might apply to the actual practices of education at both school and university levels, Street and colleagues (Ivanič, 1998; Jones, Turner, & Street, 1999; Lea, 2004; Lea & Street, 1998, 2006; Lillis & Scott, 2008; B. Street, 1996, 2009; Wingate, 2009; Wingate & Tribble, 2012) have developed the notion of academic literacies as a way of both analyzing what is going on in these contexts and proposing strategies for pedagogy that take account of these new perspectives. The academic literacies approach has been applied particularly in higher education in the United Kingdom but also has relevance to schooling and links with debates in the United States regarding writing across the curriculum and writing in the disciplines and rhetoric (see Prior, 1998; Russell, 1991; Russell, Lea, Parker, Street, & Donahue, 2009).

On the whole, NLS signified a social turn away from a focus on minds and a psychology of reading to a focus on social practice and interaction. Born out of several movements, from the ethnography of speaking (Gumperz, 1982; Hymes, 1974) to sociohistorical psychology with the work of Vygotsky (1978), to cultural models (Holland, Lachicotte, Skinner, & Cain, 1998), to linguistics (Gee, 1996), to composition theory (Bazerman, 1988) and sociological theory (Bourdieu, 1991), NLS offers literacy education broadly and reading specifically an alternative way of viewing reading processes and theoretical models. Stemming from different disciplines, NLS has pushed the field of literacy education to view literacy practices, such as reading a basal reader, as always situated within specific social practices and within specific Discourses (Gee, 1996). NLS has enabled researchers to think about the social practices and interactions that take place around reading events in ways that take account of all the modes involved in an increasingly complex and varied semiotic landscape.

Reading in the Perspective of Multimodal Social Semiotics

The contemporary textual landscape is marked by intense diversity. There is the relatively well-understood, hitherto usual plethora of textual (written and spoken) genres, reflecting social organizations of a more traditional kind. Additionally, there is now an increasing and increasingly normalized diversity of means for making texts due to the ever more insistent appearance of multimodality. More and more, contemporary texts draw on a number of modes: speech, image (still or moving), writing, music, and action. More and more, the dominant site of appearance for texts is the screen, or rather, screens of all kinds.

These factors are giving rise to a pronounced difference in kinds of text linked to generations. Those below, say, the age of 30 tend to have a distinctly different position in social organization and arrangements and hence a different stance toward texts, compared with those above that age group. That is the case both in the production of texts and in practices of reading. In other words, the present communicational landscape is one of a seemingly considerable confusion:

traditional texts coexist with texts produced with different means of production, digital being foremost; with different resources for representation, one major factor being that of multimodality; and last, using different principles of composition, with one prominent change being a move from linearly organized texts to texts organized on principles of modular composition. All of these can be traced back to different assumptions and givens about the social order, power, hierarchy, authority, and therefore, rights and forms of authorship.

Given the differences in stance in and to the social, there are correspondingly different genres. All of these features mark a social, generational, technological, and semiotic/representational divide. Traditional texts are typified by the means and technologies of their production, usually involving single authorship and print with its various means of dissemination as collections of pages, such as newspapers, magazines, and books. The more recent, but also now contemporary, texts are likewise typified by the means and technologies of their production, involving often multiple, continuously fluid authorship; word processing; the potential to be open and unconstrained (by comparison with print media such as the book); unlimited digital means of dissemination as screens (rather than as pages) of various kinds; and new or transformed genres, such as e-mail, websites, blogs, and so forth. These texts are based on differently organized and differently (un)constrained social arrangements and on digital technologies as the means of production and dissemination and as the sites of display.

This contrast of traditional and contemporary can be described in many ways: socially and semiotically. Socially, the major change is about structures of authority/power, leading to changes in the position of readers and forms and practices of reading. Other major changes involve the fraying of formerly firm frames and the move to quite different kinds of framing, a change in notions of canonicity, and changes in forms of subjectivity and identity in line with these changes. Semiotically, the change can be described in terms of, as mentioned earlier, a contrast of traditional pages to contemporary screens, as a shift from linearity to modularity, by a move from the centrality of speech and writing to multimodal arrangements, by changes in sites of appearance, and by the different principles of composition. All of these differences add up to distinct kinds of textual organization that habituate readers to distinct forms of reading.

NLS and Multimodality as Complementary Perspectives

Possibilities for the shaping of identity are completely interlinked with textual features, whether in making text for disseminations (outward production) or in engaging with texts in transformation (inward production). In each case, there is an accommodation to the principles that are evident in the shape of the text and, over time, a habituation to the social and semiotic characteristics that have given rise to the features of texts in their ontological and epistemological potentials and in their affordances for access to and participation in social life. Consequently, practices of reading, forms of readership, and kinds of readers—just three of the many possible aspects of identity—are shaped in encounters with texts in production through the possibilities of their dissemination and in the encounters of reading.

In the frame of SSMM, as much as in that of NLS, these factors are taken to be the effects of social organizations and practices. For example, different kinds of textual coherence can be taken as pointing to different kinds of social organization. Cohesion and coherence are signs, or semiotic indicators, of social phenomena. A tightly organized social group with strong social framing is likely to produce tightly framed, integrated, cohesive and coherent texts. A society that is less tightly integrated, that is characterized by porous boundaries and frames, is likely to produce texts that are less integrated, with fewer and weaker cohesive markers and hence less or differently coherent (Bezemer & Kress, 2008, 2009; Halliday & Hasan, 1976).

As one example, we might point to what is by now a quite common shift from presenting some material—say, an introduction to a text—in an integrated, syntactically and textually coherent paragraph to the appearance of similar material now as a bullet-point list of items, to do what might be regarded as a similar task. In the paragraph, the author provides the ordering and integration of the material; in the bullet-point list, the maker of the text provides relevant material but leaves it up to the reader to establish his or her sense of coherence from the items in the list. In the paragraph, one cannot take the sentences that make up the paragraph and put them in a different order. In the bullet-point list, it often does not make a great difference to change the order of the points.

In Figure 3a, for example, is the introductory and framing paragraph for a poem, John Milton's "L'Allegro," from an English textbook of the 1930s. In Figure 3b is a similar introductory and framing textual element for Denise Levertov's "What Were They Like?," a poem about the war in Vietnam, from an English textbook from the year 2000. Examples of this kind can be multiplied in relation to different features—continuous, running text replaced now by layout devices of various kinds, by the use of color, and so on.

Habitual and extended engagement with texts leads to settled expectations of what different texts are like and to assumptions and practices of how they are to be read. These assumptions in turn lead to dispositions that respond to and enact the characteristics and organization of the texts, overtly or implicitly. A text organized linearly suggests that the reader should follow the ordering of the textual entities as established by an author: an order of words in sequence; the order of syntax, which in writing becomes the ordering of sentences; of paragraphs, themselves an ordered arrangement of sentences; and of whole texts, in which all of these elements find their overall order. A temporally sequenced text, such as the one in Figure 1, or a narrative, such as an Agatha Christie murder mystery, is best read in the linear order of the genre set out by the author.

By contrast, the text of a website, as a modular arrangement, suggests no such reading. In that case, it is the interest of the individual that determines the order of reading the text. The generic features of the website text itself are, as with all texts, the expression of the larger level social order, although one entirely

Figure 3. English Textbook Introductions to Poetry

(a) For John Milton's "L'Allegro" in the 1930s

'L'ALLEGRO.'

The Elizabethan age was succeeded by a period of religious and political strife, which culminated in the triumph of Puritanism under Oliver Cromwell. Therefore the expansive development of literature was restricted, and thought mainly concentrated on one particular book—the Bible. The dominating figure of this age is John Milton, the great Puritan poet; but he is so supremely an artist that he blends the perfection of ancient art, as learnt from the Renaissance, with the religious turmoil of his time, which has had so profound an effect on his work. His most famous poem is the epic *Paradise Lost*, which relates the story of 'man's first disobedience and its fruit.' He also wrote many shorter poems, of which the following is an example.

(b) For Denise Levertov's "What Were They Like?" in 2000

Some details:

- The war lasted from 1959 to 1975.
- Communist North Vietnam was fighting South Vietnam.
- Fearing the growth of Communism, the US supported the South for the last ten years.
- 543 000 American troops were there at the height of the conflict.
- The war involved ferocious jungle fighting, intense air strikes and civilian casualties.
- 3–4 million Vietnamese died.
- 58 000 Americans died, and anti-war protests at home eventually contributed to the American withdrawal and defeat.

different to that of the narrative. While the narrative strongly insists on one kind of reading and, in that, implicitly suggests a particular social order, the website is the product of a rhetorician's assumptions about the varied interests of a diverse audience, and it is designed to allow the interest of any one reader to shape the coherence of the text resulting from his or her interested engagement. Texts, if read as they are meant to be, habituate their readers to a certain stance to text, to reading practices and to meaning, to authorial authority or to the reader's exercise of individual interested agency, and to the social writ large.

The characteristics of a text are the effect of a closely integral relation of reading, readership, and identity, which forms the basis of the SSMM approach to reading. Active semiotic work—the agency of individuals—is entailed in producing texts, whether in outward or inward production. The production is the semiotic work of engaging with an aspect of the world seen as text. That work entails selection of what is to be attended to and an interpretation/transformation of that, as shaped by resources brought by the reader to the text. An NLS approach complements this semiotic work in that it functions as a constant reminder that reading practices cannot be separated from the social, cultural, and ideological contexts that give rise to them.

What follows from our integrated approach is that the first step in reading is to frame what is to be read and then locate that in the wider social landscape: Where in the textual landscape does this text have its origins? Where does it belong? Answers will determine the reader's approach and engagement with the text. Of course, this does not assume that the reader is similarly located in the textual landscape as is the maker of the text. Nor does it determine whether, having made such an assessment, the (potential) reader will actually engage with the text, that is, that he or she will become a reader.

NLS, with its focus on situated concepts of literacy in homes and communities, has opened up a much broader concept of what literacy and, thereby, reading is as a social practice (Barton & Hamilton, 1998; B. Street, 1993). This perspective has enabled researchers to provide alternative languages of description for literacy. These alternative scripts enable a postmodern understanding of literacy practices that acknowledges diversity and builds on existing multilingual and multimodal literacy practices within families (Compton-Lilly et al., 2012; Gregory, 2008). In particular, much of the research on reading has not fully recognized the impact of digital technologies on reading development (Levy, 2011). Given that many research studies of home literacy practices have acknowledged the importance of the digital in the communicational landscape of young children, it is urgent and important to develop a theoretical model of the processes and practices of reading that acknowledges these changes (Marsh, 2011).

Young children do not have access to a community's principles of recognition and so establish their own, and these in turn are constantly checked by them against the world engaged with or represented. The process of socialization can be seen, in that way, as a constant process of increasing approximation to a community's principles of recognition, or to put it a different way, its rules. In what follows, we demonstrate how an NLS–multimodal perspective allows us to analyze instantiations of these processes in reading events in the early years. In the next two sections, the author team singles out the voices of researchers who conducted the research, but the chapter is very much a jointly authored piece.

Reading and Early Childhood Literacies

In this section, I (Kate) describe the contexts for young children's experience of reading. I particularly look at the landscapes of the home (Pahl, 2002, 2004) in constructing particular affordances for reading. I focus on the idea of reading as an interpretative social practice that is at once cultural, that is, making something meaningful and effective; critical, that is, understanding that reading is situated within relations of power; and operational—that is, reading is something that requires "knowing what to do to make 'it' work" (Green, 1998, p. 43). Aligning myself with early researchers, such as Ferreiro and Teberosky (1982), who recognized the plethora of print that lies outside schooling, I consider how this landscape of print constructs reading practices and how these practices can be understood as culturally located. I also recognize the layered nature of reading. Mackey (2010) has described how early reading can be understood in relation to affect (the emotion associated with being read to or reading) and location (e.g., home, church, play) when reading. These factors have to be understood as critical when considering young children's reading.

Landscapes of Home Reading Practices

By landscapes of the home, I mean the materially situated world in which young children are immersed, as described by anthropologists such as Miller (2008, 2010). This landscape includes the sensory and the embodied, which is where, as Heath (1983) observed, children learn their "ways with words." This landscape, however, has changed radically since Heath's research and now includes the digital and, increasingly, a situation in which print seeps across a wide range of technological and immaterial practices. I therefore acknowledge, with researchers such as Marsh (2011), the ways in which young children's literacy practices in the home are both embodied and situated and then flicker across the screens of the home in ways that defy a situated concept of literacy. Reading is a practice that can involve scanning a game as it comes up on the screen, locating print within a message coming up on the screen, and then composing a reply.

Levy (2011) suggests that the concept of reading as solely being associated with books can be critiqued. She draws on the work of Carrington (2005) and Marsh (2005), who have identified the plethora of new media and popular cultural literacy resources in home settings. Many scholars (e.g., Compton-Lilly et al., 2012; Marsh, 2005) have critiqued the assumption that literacy practices in the home can be mapped onto a largely middle-class model of literacy, which equates early literacy with sharing picture books. Instead, many researchers have identified a number of literacy practices that are much more diverse, including oral storytelling, multilingual storytelling, using different languages and scripts, engaging in digital and popular-culture texts, and employing different modalities for reading and writing script. For example, in her study of Hispanic families and their home literacy practices, Zentella (2005) offers the following:

> My sister and I never saw our parents read a full-length book in English or Spanish, although they read letters from Puerto Rico and Mexico, the *New York Daily News* and *El Diario*, and *mami* had prayer books. But there were no novels, no bookshelves, no magazines on coffee tables, and least of all cookbooks. I did not get books as gifts, nor did I consider a book a desirable present, and was not read to. The library books I brought home were never the topic of family discussions, and I did my homework alone. *Mami* used to yell at me to stop reading late into the night. She said that so much reading was bad for me; it could *volverme loca*, that is, drive me crazy. (p. 14)

Researchers of intergenerational home literacy practices in multilingual households have identified, much as Heath (1983) did in the Trackton and Roadville communities, a plethora of practices associated with print and with reading that are incongruent with the reading practices offered in school settings (González, Moll, & Amanti, 2005; Gregory, Long, & Volk, 2004; Kenner, 2004). Keating (2005) has described the ways in which Portuguese women who were migrants in London used popular magazines in Portuguese to support their identities. She considered how their engagement with these magazines offered an escape to other worlds and represented a "complex interaction between people's inner motivations and the ways they handle the ideologies at play in the contexts in which they have been socialized" (p. 116). Moreover, Keating argues, "When relating to social practices of literacy, these women seemed to *repeat*, to *recognise*, to *reflect* upon and to *recombine* ways with literacy and, in this process, *reinvent* these practices for themselves" (p. 114). These processes of reflecting, recombining, and ultimately transforming, as applied to reading, require also a radical rethinking of the concept of reading as a culturally available trope that often calls up the image of the book, the story, and the home with books as a signifier for cultural capital.

Learning to Read in New Worlds

In her book *Young Children Reading: At Home and at School*, Levy (2011) identifies the study of reading with a number of different perspectives, including a cognitive-psychological perspective that focuses on reading as a staged process with phonics as the central focus of research and practice. However, there are concerns voiced by early years' educators that this approach can be reductive and lead to an assumption that reading is simply a matter of decoding letters. In a recent study of eight families in Sheffield, England, funded by Book Trust, different constructs associated with a variety of perspectives were identified in relation to home reading practices (Pahl, Lewis, & Ritchie, 2010). One type of perspective, which we called skills focused, was associated with families who saw reading as being about decoding and the acquisition of the skills used to read a book independently. However, these families often missed the connectivity and emotional depth of sharing home literacy practices across a range of modalities. Levy's own study identified how all the children in her research came to associate reading as being the ability to decode words in books, despite their home literacy practices including a much wider range of literacies (p. 109).

Levy (2011) also suggests that there are a number of researchers who focus on reading and use a more psycholinguistic perspective, which considers the context of reading and the whole-language approach as involving reading for meaning. However, she argues that both this approach and the cognitive-psychological perspective "fail to acknowledge the complexity of issues surrounding the ways in which children learn to read and become readers of a variety of different texts" (p. 13). Part of the difficulty of using these approaches for a conceptualization of reading is that the concept of reading is associated primarily with printed texts rather than texts on-screen. Kress (2003) argues that the concept of "reading path" is important in locating a concept of reading across modalities:

> Reading paths in writing (as in speech) are set with very little or no leeway; in the image they are open. Reading across modes is a different concept and something that requires a close analysis of both image and text. (p. 157)

Levy (2011) argues for a sociopolitical perspective of reading and maintains that schools have the power to determine what is meant by *reading*. She combines this perspective with a sociocultural perspective that argues for the importance of broadening a conception of literacy and print to include a variety of text types and modalities. This might also include extending the reach of how reading can be defined. If reading is understood as being a culturally situated social practice, young children's engagement with reading can be differently mapped, and the sites and spaces where young children experience print and engage with reading can be understood as pertaining to the activity that is called reading.

In the study of home book-sharing practices, described previously, young children experienced reading differently according to how parents understood reading. Some parents, who were identified as skills focused, saw reading as a skill that young children could acquire through reading on their own, separately, away from parents. This model, like many school-based models of print, focuses on how children would acquire reading as an independent skill. Other parents in the study equated book sharing with connectivity, including emotional closeness, oral storytelling, and the use of gesture and drama to make stories come alive. Book sharing could take place in many different places, including on the bus and in outdoor settings. As mentioned earlier, the cultural and interpretative schemata that accompanied the concept of a picture book is embedded within cultural frames of reference (Rogoff, 2003) and can be understood to be something that varies across cultures.

However, certain reading practices have become more culturally salient in Western cultures than in others. Just as Kress (2003) argues that print literacy is more salient than other multimodal communicative practices, home reading practices have become mapped onto the concept of home book sharing rather than considering the role of reading in a number of other complex cultural practices. For example, Rosowsky (2008) describes how children learn to decode text in Arabic while learning the Koran at mosque school in quite different ways to the way children are taught to read at school. Much of the Koran learning involved recitation and pure phonics without reading for meaning. Other forms of reading involve constructing oral stories, but using script to capture the stories so they could be read later. Oral storytelling can involve writing a story that is new so it may be read aloud to younger siblings.

Reading can involve reading the messages in the online role-playing game Club Penguin (Marsh, 2011) and also learning the instructions on a computer. As Marsh elaborates in her study of children's interaction with Club Penguin, "The ability to navigate a complex multimodal screen was...a primary skill required to engage in Club Penguin" (p. 108). The affordances of the screen require an attention to multimodality, that is, an awareness of the way in which meaning is represented in a multiplicity of modes on-screen. A multimodal approach means that all aspects of the screen combine together to make meaning (Kress, 2003). The concept of multimodality can aid an understanding of situated reading practices. Marsh argues, therefore, that a multiplicity of modes is involved when looking at children's reading practices online, including the importance of sound and animation. By understanding reading as embedded within a wider frame of interaction, it becomes a social practice with complex links across domains of practice.

Looking Closely at Home Reading Practices

In my own study of home writing practices, called "Writing in the Home and in the Street," funded by the Arts and Humanities Research Council (U.K.), I considered the range of reading materials available in two homes: a British Asian family whose grandparents migrated from Pakistan to the north of England and a white working-class family. Both families lived in Rotherham in northern England. The families made films and took photographs of their home reading practices over the period of one year. In the case of the British Asian household, which involved a study of two girls, ages 8 and 12 at the time of the data described here, I logged a range of literacy practices, including Arabic script as inscriptions on walls and within Koranic literature, script embedded in toys and within decorations, embroidery, and script within books and reading matter, such as notebooks in which the young girls wrote. Their images of home reading practices reflected this range. In Figure 4 we see this instantiated within an image taken by the eldest girl of her home literacy practices.

These practices include a toy keyboard, a globe, a set of books, toys, and other small objects that include aspects of print. Ethnographic work in this home revealed that the girls wrote stories in notebooks to read to their younger sibling at night. Writing was therefore undertaken in order to produce read-alouds. The production of writing was also intertwined with the family's cultural heritage across generations. Making textiles was a strong part of this family's heritage. The girls recorded a video of the making of a piece of embroidery with the youngest child's name on it (see Figure 5). I asked the girls' aunt, with whom I was also in contact, about this, and she e-mailed me back (August 2010):

Figure 4. A 12-Year-Old British Asian Girl's Photograph of Her Home Literacy Practices

Figure 5. A Still From a British Asian Girl's Video of Embroidery Making

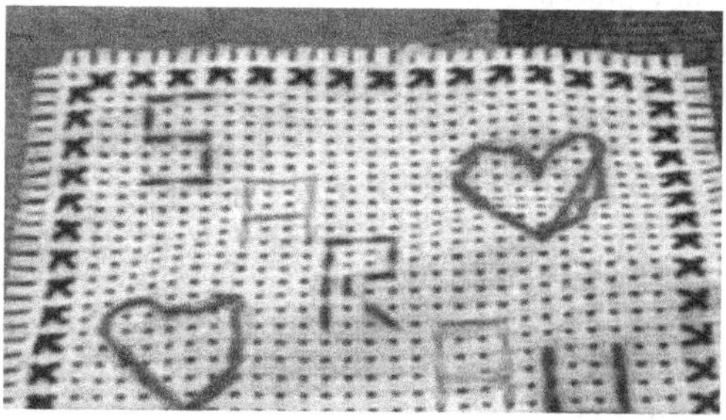

> The textile side of our heritage comes from the women in the family. We have older relatives that do appliqué, crochet, embroidery, sewing and knitting (from the girls' mother's side their grandmother's sister and cousin and from their father's side, his two cousins who live close by). My younger sister loves craft type of activities and buys the girls a lot of resources to do sewing and fabric work especially on birthdays, Christmas and Eid.

Here, reading is a process of depicting meaning embedded within wider cultural practices of using embroidery and as an example of an identity, or name.

Reading in the Street

The process of learning to read is about understanding the reading ecologies that exist in homes and communities. When investigating writing in the home and in the street, these ecologies are found to be linked to the play spaces, both inside and outside the home and both online and off-line, that create a sense of affect for the child. Ingold (2007) discusses the entanglements that occur when making pathways through the worlds. These can be understood as lines and traces of real knowledge. Mackey (2010) talks about "reading the city" (p. 326) as being a process of coming to know that could also be mapped onto her process of coming to read the signs and symbols around her. In a series of community walks as part of the "Writing in the Home and in the Street" research project, a group of 10–11-year-old children described the experience of reading the neighborhood to me. The children talked about how they felt when they encountered graffiti in their homes and surroundings:

> Kate: When you see a nasty word, do you think it is good or bad?
>
> Marianne: Bad. We have got one on our gates someone wrote it! When I first moved into my house, there was graffiti all over the wall, and they had had a paintball fight. You can still see it. It were black, and it were white, and it was hard to get off. Me granddad had to do that. (audio recording, June 2011)

Marianne lived in a home where what she read on the walls constructed her experience of home literacy practices.

Literacies in community contexts are nested within the cultural, economic, and social forces that surround them. In poor neighborhoods, literacy is often less visible, as shops are closed down and resources withheld because of economic constraints (Neuman & Celano, 2001). Local literacies are linked to the sounds, the accents, and the smells of a neighborhood. Reading a community is about reading the social worlds of the children brought up in that neighborhood. It is also about the layered nature of experience and the ways in which children come to experience the world through print. For example, a conversation with Luke showed a layered quality to his experience:

> Kate: I want to know what you think of the graffiti on this slide?
>
> Luke: It's all rude! We should spray it. It's not fair on young children.

Reading signs in the community can be hurtful and problematic. The children commented on the racist nature of some graffiti and how the everyday reading matter in the environment was damaging their sense of their community (see Figure 6).

Reading the linguistic landscape is a process of acquiring what Mackey (2010) calls "an embodied understanding of the local world" (p. 329), a world that is discovered through pathways, through walls and boundaries, through the lines that are taken, from home to school and back again, and also through the lines that are presented to children in the form of words and symbols on the street. For young children, reading is sensory and embodied (Pink, 2009). Letters and print are inscribed within material objects (Miller, 2010). The small embodiments that are

Figure 6. Image by a Child of a Community Artwork Damaged by Graffiti

present in everyday cultural life (Hoggart, 1957) make up the experience of reading. Reading can be about following the lines of graffiti on the street (Ingold, 2007), and it is also about the feeling a child gets when he or she notices some racist graffiti or an obscene word. Reading is a process that is in place (Comber, 2010) and linked to the landscape of childhood in ways that are profound and highly local (Barton & Hamilton, 1998). In the next section, we contrast this landscape of early childhood reading to the landscape of adolescent and teenage reading practices.

Reading and Youth Literacies

In this section, I (Jennifer) explore adolescents and teenagers and their reading practices. I begin with some facts about high school students and reading. Approximately two-thirds of 8th- and 12th-grade students read at less than the proficient level on the National Assessment of Educational Progress (Rampey, Dion, & Donahue, 2009). About 1.2 million U.S. students drop out of school annually, and their literacy skills are lower than most industrialized nations (Laird, Kienzl, DeBell, & Chapman, 2007). These statistics miss out on so many subtleties and idiosyncrasies of readers, but they do tell a story.

Adolescent literacies refer to the literacy practices of youths "who act provisionally at particular times" (Alvermann, 2006, p. 40). Alvermann talks about the everyday lives of adolescents as encompassing "the performative, visual, aural, and semiotic understandings necessary for constructing and reconstructing print and nonprint-based texts" (Alvermann, 2002, p. viii). Research in the area of adolescents' out-of-school digital literacy practices (Davies, 2006; Williams & Merten, 2008; Yi, 2008) is a growing area of research and inquiry. One of the most cited articles in this area is by Lewis and Fabos (2005), who examined the ways in which students manipulate and play with vernacular conventions, Standard English grammar, and electronic typography in sophisticated ways when they communicate. The researchers interviewed teenagers about their private instant-messaging practices and observed teens while they were engaged in this practice. Lewis and Fabos's research demonstrates the level of sophisticated rhetorical and discursive devices exhibited by students: "The young people we interviewed were conscious of choosing different tones and language styles depending on whom they were IMing" (p. 484). When students felt free to play with language code, they were not only more willing to write, but they also organically understood the significance of tone and syntax. Although their texts may not have satisfied the requirements of an English assignment, they demonstrated a reflective understanding of the nuances of language and, more specifically, situated language.

In my observations, interviews, and work with youths, reading is a fluid practice that involves movement across multiple genres of texts and that draws on multiple modes to comprehend texts. To gather information today demands reading across hybrid texts and finding the information in a sea of words, visuals, and hyperlinks. This is, again, a very different kind of reading from that involved in the 1939 reader presented in Figure 1. First of all, the production and reception of texts, as well as the possibility of moving between different genres of texts, is more fluid and frequent than it has ever been. Digital domains facilitate such mobility across time and space to understand a concept or to complete a text. To create mobility in digital texts, reading relies on converged texts in multimedia formats.

When the adolescents and teenagers with whom I work read, they read for interest, purpose, function, and perhaps the strongest reading practice of all, so they can remake a text into something else. Contemporary readers often read in snippets of information from multiple genres on multiple devices (mostly mobile devices for quick information). Adolescent and teenage readers expect hyperlinks, they expect color and images, they expect to go through different kinds of texts to find different kinds of information, and they expect to remix such information into another reading text. Nevertheless, a key ingredient often missing from their consumption of texts is comprehension and critical framing.

To illustrate, I draw on a two-year study in an urban, highly diverse secondary school in Toronto where the grade 11 teacher, Evelyn (pseudonym) is taking a design approach to the teaching of literature and media. In the study, funded by an IRA Elva Knight Research Grant and entitled "The Producers: Design Literacies in Action," I examine the literacy practices of the 11th-grade students. The study approaches English teaching and learning from a design perspective by asking students as rhetoricians to choose the best possible mode for a task.

By *design*, I am referring to a view of communication as designed compositions made up of visual, audio, spatial, and linguistic modes. The New London Group (1996) argues for a pedagogy based on the notion of design, claiming that to be literate today, meaning makers draw on multimodal resources as available designs that can be redesigned. The classroom teacher and I teach together, and we adopt a design-based epistemology for our study of English literature and media studies. A component of the study deals with comprehending and critically framing student reading practices. One unit of study in the research focuses on media and popular culture. For each lesson within the unit, students are presented with media and popular-culture texts. The example I offer here to illustrate teenage reading is a lesson on analyzing and critically framing language and visual features in gossip magazines, such as *Life & Style* and *Us*. To read these genres of texts critically entails a degree of scrutinizing, interrogating, and generally calling information into question, as well as actively identifying and elucidating stereotypes.

A key reading practice for a good reader of a gossip magazine is to analyze pictures, read, and critically frame written text. To promote critical reading strategies, Evelyn and I spent an hour and a half on oppositional readings of gossip magazines and popular-culture texts. We asked the students to read each gossip magazine in stages. For the first 15 minutes, the students read for information, locating new information and listing it on sticky notes that they placed throughout the print media. Then, Evelyn and I interrogated different examples of print media to illustrate what it means to do an oppositional reading of a text. We drew on media studies theory and practices that interrogate and challenge content for stereotypes, embedded assumptions, and preferred readings. After modeling the process of oppositional reading, the students selected one gossip magazine to interrogate for meanings and stereotypes. In Figure 7 are two examples of their readings of photographs and their commentaries.

The third stage in the lesson moved from oppositional readings of print media to moving-image media to foster a differentiation between mediums and media. The class watched YouTube videos of advertising that exhibit similar stereotypes and hidden messages. During viewing, the class completed a chart that asked them to comment on preferred reading of text and oppositional reading of text. We watched the commercial once with sound and then another time without sound to offer different versions of the reading experience. For the final stage of the lesson, the students were asked to create their own gossip, popular-culture text and then critically frame the process of composition and the completed text.

The 90-minute lesson identified students' perceived understandings of stereotypes and subliminal messages, and we provided some ways to critically frame these readings. Moving across genres from print to moving-image media compelled students to think about how different media converge messages through common and different techniques. For instance, some students noted that vectors (Kress & van Leeuwen, 1996) are present in both print and moving images, but sound, voice, and melody modulate the tone of the message in subtle and nuanced—or as we said earlier, modular—ways. In other words, the students recognized that increasing the number and quality of modes within a text shifted its

Figure 7. Two 11th Graders' Oppositional Reading Notes of Popular-Culture Texts

meaning. The students could only identify that shift by reading/viewing moving-image texts in different ways: with sound, without visuals and with sound, and so forth.

When they produced their own vernacular, print media texts, students were able to layer language and visuals with more connotations and discursive devices and with vectors to elicit a preferred reading. By moving from neutral readings to oppositional readings to remixing these texts into their own versions and then demonstrating the converging of different values, stereotypes, and hidden messages in visuals and written text, the students acquired a meta-awareness of rhetorical devices and visual and discursive strategies that influence readings of texts. As we demonstrate in the next section, reading shifts yet again as readers move into adulthood and institutions of higher learning, or what Lea and Street (1998) call an academic literacies model.

Reading and Adult, Academic Literacies

The academic literacies model was developed by Lea and Street (1998), drawing on the theoretical framework of NLS (Gee, 1990; B. Street, 1984; Lea & Street, 1998). The model recognizes academic writing as a set of social practices within a given institutional and disciplinary context and (perhaps more than the U.S. writing-in-the-disciplines approach) highlights the influence of factors such as power and authority on student reading and writing. In the development of this model, Lea and Street conducted an empirical research project in two very different universities in the United Kingdom, in which they examined student writing against a background of institutional practices, power relations, and identities. Rather than frame their work in terms of good and poor writing, they suggested that any explanation needed to examine faculty and student expectations around writing without making any judgments about which practices were deemed most appropriate. Findings from the research suggested fundamental gaps between student and faculty understandings of the requirements of student writing, providing evidence of conflicts of understanding at the level of epistemology and authority and contestation over knowledge, rather than at the level of technical skill, surface linguistic competence, and cultural assimilation.

Based on analysis of their research data, Lea and Street (1998) explicate three models of student writing, which they term study skills, academic socialization, and academic literacies. The study skills model is primarily concerned with the surface features of text and is based on the assumption that mastery of the correct rules of grammar and syntax, coupled with attention to punctuation and spelling, will ensure student competence in academic writing. By contrast, the academic socialization model assumes that students need to be acculturated into the discourses and genres of particular disciplines and that making the features and requirements of these explicit to students will result in their becoming successful writers. The third model, academic literacies, is concerned with meaning making, identity, and power and authority, and it foregrounds the institutional nature of what counts as knowledge in any particular academic context.

The academic literacies model is similar in many ways to the academic socialization model except that the former views the processes involved in acquiring appropriate and effective uses of literacy as more complex, dynamic, nuanced, situated, and involving both epistemological issues and social processes, including power relations among people and institutions and social identities. In some respects, the third model, academic literacies, subsumes many of the features of the other two. Lea and Street (1998) point out that the models are not mutually exclusive and that each should be seen as encapsulating the other. Nevertheless, the researchers argue that the academic literacies model is best able to take account of the nature of student writing in relation to institutional practices, power relations, and identities—in short, to consider the complexity of meaning making that the other two models fail to provide.

The explication of the three models proposed by Lea and Street (1998) has been drawn on in the literature on teaching and learning across a range of higher education contexts (e.g., Thesen & van Pletzen, 2006, on South Africa) and calls for a more in-depth understanding of student reading and writing, and their relationship to learning across the academy, thus offering an alternative to deficit models of learning and literacy based on autonomous models of literacy. Academic literacies, for instance, has been a useful critical frame for identifying shortcomings in the current provision at U.K. universities (Lea & Street, 2006; Lillis, 2006, p. 33). However, there is still much to do in developing the pedagogic implications of these research and theoretical approaches (cf. Lillis, 2006; Lillis & Scott, 2008; Wingate, 2006, 2008), including developing the reading dimension of such approaches given that they have tended to focus mainly on writing. A social practice perspective on both writing and reading, then, moves outside of school and reconceptualizes school as itself a specific social practice among many, rather than a single uniform skill.

NLS and Multimodal Reading: Implications for Literacy, Pedagogy, and Policy

How all of this applies specifically to reading is an issue currently being debated in the field. As we indicated in this chapter, adopting a social perspective on reading draws attention to the fact that reading in the contemporary era may involve more and different semiotic skills than it has traditionally, when the emphasis was more on decoding skills. For instance, as we noted, attention to the social practices associated with reading leads us to recognize that children read long before they engage in schooling practices. Children engage in social relations around reading that include their parents, notably the bedtime story as Heath (1983) has indicated; with peers as they listen to and repeat readings that they hear in their own and others' homes; in their everyday exposure to public signage, posters, and shopping; and in their involvement in communicative technologies, such as browsing screens, scrolling and scanning multiple websites, clicking, following and reading hyperlinks, communicating through social networks, and so forth.

Although the main goal of this chapter was to view reading through an integrated NLS and multimodal social semiotic lens, we might also begin to move beyond just the theoretical and methodological implications that a chapter in such an important volume highlights and also develop pedagogical principles. The theory and method that we have outlined certainly lead us to recognize that current reading processes and theoretical models need to broaden definitions of reading, which are quite narrow at present, and expand these definitions beyond the word and book-sharing notions of reading. What is clear from observing any student in school, or person on the street, is that reading has gone through a transformation since the last century. There is the sheer vastness of technology and digital worlds that have dramatically shifted what we read (modes) and how we read (practices), not to mention dramatic shifts in cultural and linguistic diversity. Although there are larger debates about new approaches and methodologies for reading, the field of reading demands radical changes in policy and pedagogy so extant research and innovations can inform current accepted reading processes and theoretical models.

What might be the implications of these broader accounts of reading for pedagogy, for how teachers work to help their students acquire the reading (and writing) practices needed at different stages of the education system? If we take Heath's (1983) starting point in *Ways With Words* and her new rich account of the experience of subsequent generations in the contemporary world of diversity in social and communicative practices (Heath, 2012), then we might as educationalists take more account of how people actually make use of reading and writing in their everyday lives—the local communities and interpersonal relations of parents, children, peers, and then those in community organizations associated with them, such as the churches, second-hand stores, and dance clubs that Heath described. This could then lead policymakers in education as well as teachers to build into their pedagogy the growing literature that applies such a social practice perspective in educational contexts.

We might, then, begin to bring together the fields reviewed here, combining New Literacy Studies and multimodality with the standard views of education that, as we have suggested, have not always recognized these new developments so continue to focus on narrower conceptions of reading, text, grammar, and so on. Such a bridging position would argue that social literacy practices learned in the world of work and play are what learners at school need to know about as they enter formal education and that teachers could and should build on these in their classroom practice. Yet, at the same time, schooling can help articulate these everyday literacies and perhaps bring together a greater variety of them than students are likely to encounter in their own everyday lives. Moreover, perhaps some explicit marking of the features of the different genres and modes, following the directions pointed out previously, can be helpful in learning and enhancing these practices, notably those features that remain hidden partly because of the narrow view of literacy frequently adopted in educational contexts. If this chapter helps us move in this direction, as both theorists and as practitioners, then it will, we hope, have fulfilled the main aims of this volume as a whole.

QUESTIONS FOR REFLECTION

1. What is the import of the authors' observation that a 2008 book published in the United States may have limited frames of reference for children in other countries?
2. What different genres have arisen in response to the development of multimodal approaches to text, where different methods of production, different representations, and different principles of composition are employed?
3. What suggestions in this chapter are important for teachers of early readers? What suggestions are important for parents?
4. What can teachers do to foster multimodal literacy, building on children's cultural and literacy backgrounds?

NOTE

Thank you to Tara McGowan for her assiduous editorial skills and reading of the manuscript.

REFERENCES

Alvermann, D.E. (Ed.). (2002). *Adolescents and literacies in a digital world.* New York: Peter Lang.

Alvermann, D.E. (2006). Ned and Kevin: An online discussion that challenges the 'not-yet-adult' cultural model. In K. Pahl & J. Rowsell (Eds.), *Travel notes from the new literacy studies: Instances of practice* (pp. 19–38). Tonawonda, NY: Multilingual Matters.

Barton, D., & Hamilton, M. (1998). *Local literacies: Reading and writing in one community.* New York: Routledge.

Bazerman, C. (1988). *Shaping written knowledge: The genre and activity of the experimental article in science.* Madison: University of Wisconsin Press.

Bezemer, J., & Kress, G. (2008). Writing in multimodal texts: A social semiotic account of designs for learning. *Written Communication, 25*(2), 166–195. doi:10.1177/0741088307313177

Bezemer, J., & Kress, G. (2009). Visualizing English: A social semiotic history of a school subject. *Visual Communication, 8*(3), 247–262. doi:10.1177/1470357209106467

Bourdieu, P. (1991). *Language and symbolic power* (J.B. Thompson, Ed.; G. Raymond & M. Adamson, Trans.). Cambridge, UK: Polity Press.

Carrington, V. (2005). New textual landscapes, information and early literacy. In J. Marsh (Ed.), *Popular culture, new media and digital literacy in early childhood* (pp. 10–20). New York: RoutledgeFalmer.

Comber, B. (2010). Critical literacies in *place*: Teachers who work for just and sustainable communities. In J. Lavia & M. Moore (Eds.), *Cross-cultural perspectives on policy and practice: Decolonizing community contexts* (pp. 43–57). New York: Routledge.

Compton-Lilly, C., Rogers, R., & Lewis, T.Y. (2012). Analyzing epistemological considerations related to diversity: An integrative critical literature review of family literacy scholarship. *Reading Research Quarterly, 47*(1), 33–60.

Davies, J. (2006). Escaping to the borderlands: An exploration of the Internet as a cultural space for teenaged Wiccan girls. In K. Pahl & J. Rowsell (Eds.), *Travel notes from the new literacy studies: Instances of practice* (pp. 57–71). Tonawonda, NY: Multilingual Matters.

Ferreiro, E., & Teberosky, A. (1982). *Literacy before schooling* (K.G. Castro, Trans.). Exeter, NH: Heinemann.

Gebre, A.H., Openjuru, G., Rogers, A., & Street, B. (2009). *Everyday literacies in Africa: Ethnographic studies of literacy and numeracy practices in Ethiopia.* Addis Ababa, Ethiopia: Fountain.

Gee, J.P. (1990). *Social linguistics and literacies: Ideology in Discourses.* New York: Falmer.

Gee, J.P. (1996). *Social linguistics and literacies: Ideology in Discourses* (2nd ed.). New York: Falmer.

González, N., Moll, L.C., & Amanti, C. (2005). *Funds of knowledge: Theorizing practices in households, communities, and classrooms.* Mahwah, NJ: Erlbaum.

Green, B. (1998). The new literacy challenge? *Literacy Learning: Secondary Thoughts, 7*(1), 36–46.

Gregory, E. (2008). *Learning to read in a new language: Making sense of words and worlds*. Thousand Oaks, CA: Sage.
Gregory, E., Long, S., & Volk, D. (Eds.). (2004). *Many pathways to literacy: Young children learning with siblings, grandparents, peers and communities*. New York: RoutledgeFalmer.
Gumperz, J.J. (1982). *Discourse strategies*. New York: Cambridge University Press.
Halliday, M.A.K., & Hasan, R. (1976). *Cohesion in English*. London: Longman.
Heath, S.B. (1983). *Ways with words: Language, life, and work in communities and classrooms*. New York: Cambridge University Press.
Heath, S.B. (2012). *Words at work and play: Three decades in family and community life*. New York: Cambridge University Press.
Hoggart, R. (1957). *The uses of literacy*. London: Penguin.
Holland, D., Lachicotte, W., Jr., Skinner, D., & Cain, C. (1998). *Identity and agency in cultural worlds*. Cambridge, MA: Harvard University Press.
Hymes, D. (1974). *Foundations in sociolinguistics: An ethnographic approach*. Philadelphia: University of Pennsylvania Press.
Ingold, T. (2007). *Lines: A brief history*. New York: Routledge.
Ivanič, R. (1998). *Writing and identity: The discoursal construction of identity in academic writing*. Philadelphia: John Benjamins.
Jones, C., Turner, J., & Street, B. (Eds.). (1999). *Students writing in the university: Cultural and epistemological issues*. Philadelphia: John Benjamins.
Keating, M.C. (2005). The person in the doing: Negotiating the experience of self. In D. Barton & K. Tusting (Eds.), *Beyond communities of practice: Language, power and social context* (pp. 105–138). New York: Cambridge University Press.
Kenner, C. (2004). *Becoming biliterate: Young children learning different writing systems*. Sterling, VA: Trentham.
Kress, G. (1997). *Before writing: Rethinking the paths to literacy*. New York: Routledge.
Kress, G. (2003). *Literacy in the new media age*. New York: Routledge.
Kress, G., & van Leeuwen, T. (1996). *Reading images: The grammar of visual design*. New York: Routledge.
Laird, J., Kienzl, G., DeBell, M., & Chapman, C. (2007). Dropout rates in the United States: 2005 (NCES 2007-059). Washington, DC: National Center for Education Statistics, Institute of Education Sciences, U.S. Department of Education.
Lea, M.R. (2004). Academic literacies: A pedagogy for course design. *Studies in Higher Education*, *29*(6), 739–756. doi:10.1080/0307507042000287230
Lea, M.R., & Street, B.V. (1998). Student writing in higher education: An academic literacies approach. *Studies in Higher Education*, *23*(2), 157–172.
Lea, M.R., & Street, B.V. (2006). The "academic literacies" model: Theory and applications. *Theory Into Practice*, *45*(4), 368–377.
Levy, R. (2011). *Young children reading: At home and at school*. Thousand Oaks, CA: Sage.
Lewis, C., & Fabos, B. (2005). Instant messaging, literacies, and social identities. *Reading Research Quarterly*, *40*(4), 470–501. doi:10.1598/RRQ.40.4.5
Lillis, T. (2003). Student writing as "academic literacies": Drawing on Bakhtin to move from "critique" to "design." *Language and Education*, *17*(3), 192–207.
Lillis, T., & Scott, M. (2008). Defining academic literacies research: Issues of epistemology, ideology and strategy. *Journal of Applied Linguistics*, *4*(1), 5–32.
Mackey, M. (2010). Reading from the feet up: The local work of literacy. *Children's Literature in Education*, *41*(4), 323–339. doi:10.1007/s10583-010-9114-z
Marsh, J. (2005). Introduction: Children of the digital age. In J. Marsh (Ed.), *Popular culture, new media and digital literacy in early childhood* (pp. 1–8). New York: RoutledgeFalmer.
Marsh, J. (2011). Young children's literacy practices in a virtual world: Establishing an online interaction order. *Reading Research Quarterly*, *46*(2), 101–108. doi:10.1598/RRQ.46.2.1
Miller, D. (2008). *The comfort of things*. Malden, MA: Polity.
Miller, D. (2010). *Stuff*. Malden, MA: Polity.
Neuman, S.B., & Celano, D. (2001). Access to print in low-income and middle-income communities: An ecological study of four neighborhoods. *Reading Research Quarterly*, *36*(1), 8–26. doi:10.1598/RRQ.36.1.1
New London Group. (1996). A pedagogy of multiliteracies: Designing social futures. *Harvard Educational Review*, *66*(1), 60–92.
Pahl, K. (2002). Ephemera, mess and miscellaneous piles: Texts and practices in families. *Journal of Early Childhood Literacy*, 2(2), 145–166. doi:10.1177/14687984020022002
Pahl, K. (2004). Narratives, artifacts and cultural identities: An ethnographic study of communicative practices in homes. *Linguistics and Education*, *15*(4), 339–358. doi:10.1016/j.linged.2005.07.002
Pahl, K., Lewis, M., & Ritchie, L. (2010). *Book sharing in the home: An ethnographic study*. Unpublished report, Book Trust.
Pink, S. (2009). *Doing sensory ethnography*. Thousand Oaks, CA: Sage.
Prior, P.A. (1998). *Writing/disciplinarity: A sociohistoric account of literate activity in the academy*. Mahwah, NJ: Erlbaum.
Rampey, B.D., Dion, G.S., & Donahue, P.I. (2009). *NAEP 2008 trends in academic progress* (NCES 2009-479). Washington, DC: National Center for Education Statistics, Institute of Education Sciences, U.S. Department of Education.

Rogoff, B. (2003). *The cultural nature of human development*. New York: Oxford University Press.
Rosowsky, A. (2008). *Heavenly readings: Liturgical literacy in a multilingual context*. Tonawanda, NY: Multilingual Matters.
Russell, D.R. (1991). *Writing in the academic disciplines, 1870–1990: A curricular history*. Carbondale: Southern Illinois University Press.
Russell, D.R., Lea, M., Parker, J., Street, B., & Donahue, T. (2009). Exploring notions of genre in "academic literacies" and "writing across the curriculum": Approaches across countries and contexts. In C. Bazerman, A. Bonini, & D. Figueiredo (Eds.), *Genre in a changing world: Perspectives on writing* (pp. 395–423). Fort Collins, CO: WAC Clearinghouse; West Lafayette, IN: Parlor.
Street, B.V. (1984). *Literacy in theory and practice*. New York: Cambridge University Press.
Street, B.V. (1993). *Cross-cultural approaches to literacy*. New York: Cambridge University Press.
Street, B.V. (1996). Academic literacies. In D. Baker, J. Clay, & C. Fox (Eds.), *Challenging ways of knowing: In English, maths and science* (pp. 96–122). London: Falmer.
Street, B. (1997). The implications of the "new literacy studies" for literacy education. *English in Education, 31*(3), 45–59.
Street, B.V. (2009). "Hidden" features of academic paper writing. *Working Papers in Educational Linguistics, 24*(1), 1–17.
Street, B. (2011). NLS1 and NLS2: Implications of a social literacies perspective for policies and practices of literacy education. In A. Goodwyn & C. Fuller (Eds.), *The great literacy debate: A critical response to the Literacy Strategy and the Framework for English* (pp. 106–116). New York: Routledge.
Street, J.C., & Street, B. (1991). The schooling of literacy. In D. Barton & R. Ivanič (Eds.), *Writing in the community* (pp. 143–166). Thousand Oaks, CA: Sage.
Thesen, L., & van Pletzen, E. (Eds.). (2006). *Academic literacy and the languages of change*. New York: Continuum.
Vygotsky, L.S. (1978). *Mind in society: The development of higher psychological processes* (M. Cole, V. John-Steiner, S. Scribner, & E. Souberman, Eds. & Trans.). Cambridge, MA: Harvard University Press.
Williams, A.L., & Merten, M.J. (2008). A review of online social networking profiles by adolescents: Implications for future research and intervention. *Adolescence, 43*(170), 253–274.
Wingate, U. (2006). Doing away with "study skills." *Teaching in Higher Education, 11*(4), 457–469.
Wingate, U. (2009). Enhancing students' transition to university through online preinduction courses. In R. Donnelly & F. McSweeney (Eds.), *Applied e-learning and e-teaching in higher education* (pp. 178–200). Hershey, PA: Information Science Reference.
Wingate, U., & Tribble, C. (2012). The best of both worlds? Towards an EAP/academic literacies writing pedagogy. *Studies in Higher Education, 37*(5), 157–172.
Yi, Y. (2008). Relay writing in an adolescent online community. *Journal of Adolescent & Adult Literacy, 51*(8), 670–680. doi:10.1598/JAAL.51.8.6
Zentella, A.C. (Ed.). (2005). *Building on strength: Language and literacy in Latino families and communities*. New York: Teachers College Press; Covina: California Association for Bilingual Education.

CHILDREN'S LITERATURE CITED

Deary, T. (2008). *Horrible histories: Savage Stone Age*. London: Scholastic.
Gruelle, J. (1939). *Raggedy Anne in the magic book*. New York: Atheneum.

CHAPTER 44

Imagined Readers and Hospitable Texts: Global Youths Connect Online

Glynda Hull, University of California, Berkeley

Amy Stornaiuolo, University of Pennsylvania

Laura Sterponi, University of California, Berkeley

In our radically interconnected world, with its global and digital flows of people, capital, and information, texts can rapidly circulate far and wide, across cultural, geographic, and linguistic borders. These texts require of those who would communicate effectively the flexible capacity to make meaning across an increasingly complex range of textual forms that integrate multiple semiotic modalities (Alvermann & McLean, 2007; Hull & Nelson, 2005; Leander & Lewis, 2008; Leu, 2000). These texts also require an ethical capacity to imagine one's literate responsibilities as author and reader in a global world (Hull, Stornaiuolo, & Sahni, 2010; Silverstone, 2007; Smith & Hull, 2012). Carrying their meanings multimodally through language, sound, and image, these texts compel us to consider how authorship and readership are shifting in a networked world. Indeed, authors and audiences now interact in ways previously unimagined (Warschauer & Grimes, 2007), as digital platforms increasingly include social media components that facilitate rapid and widespread sharing, and communication regularly requires interaction with audiences distant and unfamiliar.

In this chapter, we explore the new textuality of a digital and global age by examining how adolescent youths around the world engaged in one kind of reading practice—reading an audience—whereby they imagined projected readers who were potentially different from themselves geographically, culturally, linguistically, and ideologically. Our larger interest is in dimensions of authorship that entail sensitivity to the range of possible interpretations and responses to one's texts, as well as reflexive and hospitable dispositions toward a distant readership. In effect, we wish to explore the ethics of literate practice in a global world.

Although concerns over audience have long been considered a central part of the composing process (e.g., Ede & Lunsford, 1984), we suggest that relationships between authors and audiences have now become more fluid, less bounded, and ever more salient (Lunsford & Ede, 2009). No longer can we separate composing from reading, if ever we could, nor can we assume the division of author from audience in time and space. Instead, composing texts for online audiences involves both imagining a reader of one's assembled artifacts and messages and interacting with that reader.[1] Young people—and indeed, all respondents—will need to become adept at constructing projected readers and in communicating and/or collaborating with those readers, particularly in transnational and intercultural contexts that require imaginative authorial and readerly leaps across potential geographic, linguistic, and ideological differences (cf. Appadurai, 1996). Thoughtful authors and responsive audiences adept at moving between those roles, we believe, are the quintessential literate identities of a global and digital age (cf. Brandt, 2009).

We demonstrate in this chapter that the youths in our study who were most adept at taking up these roles thoughtfully and artfully were highly strategic in the ways that they did so. Further, we argue that such a capacity to be hospitable readers and writers (cf. Silverstone, 2007)—and to be able to be both simultaneously—is an important ethical dimension of being literate in the 21st century (cf. Coiro, 2012; James, 2009). While much of the ethical impulse around online communication has arisen from concerns regarding bullying or privacy management (cf. Davis, Katz, James, & Santo, 2010; Livingstone & Brake, 2010; Mishna, Cook, Gadalla, Daciuk, & Solomon, 2010), we have found that interpersonal challenges and opportunities to communicate and interact ethically were in fact deeply embedded in small gestures of online communication: greetings, responses, the design of online artifacts to share (Stornaiuolo, Hull, & Sahni, 2011). In this chapter, we describe participants' strategic moves in becoming audience-alert reader/writers online, and in so doing, we also reveal the fortitude with which our young people persisted in the face of daunting challenges—a rhetorical and ethical stance that is consistent with the practice of cosmopolitan citizenship in a global age (cf. Hansen, 2011; Hull et al., 2010; Rizvi, 2009; Stornaiuolo, Hull, & Sahni, 2011).

Reading Online in a Global World

Literacy researchers have argued the importance of determining what it means to read digitally, on the screen, including how such reading differs from engagement offline with paper texts (Leu et al., 2007). Such scholarship is just beginning, but it is indeed promising, as is complementary work in media studies that has demonstrated the relationship between media literacy and academic performance, including reading comprehension (e.g., Hobbs, 2007). Readers bring more and different strategies to bear in comprehending online texts than they do in reading print-based texts (e.g., Castek et al., 2008; Leu Kinzer, Coiro, & Cammack, 2004; Naumann, Richter, Christmann, & Groeben, 2008; Salmerón & García, 2011). Reading online also requires increased self-regulation and inferential reasoning strategies (Coiro & Dobler, 2007) tied to readers' purposes (Zhang & Duke, 2008) and interests (Steinkuehler, Compton-Lilly, & King, 2010). Readers must recruit additional strategies because of the complexity of reading online, in no small part because they are required to engage in self-directed text construction as they chart their own paths through hyperlinked texts (Coiro & Dobler, 2007). Such research on self-directed text construction helps us see reading online as a kind of composing process (Tierney & Pearson, 1983), with readers actively charting their own paths through online texts via their decisions about which hyperlinks to follow and click. In this way, which the research on online reading has made clear, readers' online communicative practices involve intertwined reading and writing processes that are both active and strategic.

Online communicative practices thereby offer readers new opportunities for interacting with diverse texts, especially multimodal ones that layer together written language with images, sound, and video (Burke & Rowsell, 2008; Rowsell & Burke, 2009). In multimodal texts, the relationships between modes (e.g., between music and image) multiply meaning potentials and provide qualitatively new systems of signification in which the whole is not reducible to its component parts (Hull & Nelson, 2005). Research into adolescents' digital literacies has illustrated the ways that such texts can serve as resources for meaning making (e.g., Black, 2009; Chandler-Olcott & Mahar, 2003; Lewis & Fabos, 2005; Ranker, 2007). For instance, they can offer multiple access points for readers, as young people use their familiarity or facility with one mode, such as music, to scaffold or augment their understanding of the whole. In this way, multimodal texts can offer "potentials for learning" (Bezemer & Kress, 2008, p. 168), affording youths the opportunity to build "rich intertextual landscapes" (Ranker, 2008, p. 229). Multimodal texts can also serve as resources for remixing content across multiple contexts, providing new authoring possibilities and generating textual innovation (Bearne, 2009; Erstad, Gilje, & de Lange, 2007; Forte & Bruckman, 2009; Lam, 2006). However, what we understand about the nature of online composing and reading, including the effects of increasingly multimodal digital textual practices, is still rudimentary, leaving unanswered fundamental questions. How do young people and teachers design "potentials for learning"? How do readers bring particular strategies to bear for making meaning with multimodal texts?

Similarly, we require a more nuanced understanding of how online reading practices are shaped by the interactive possibilities for readers (cf. McKenna, Conradi, Lawrence, Jang, & Meyer, 2012). As readers are more readily able to comment back to authors, read others' comments, create response texts, and otherwise engage with authors and other audience members interactively, to read means not only to decode, to comprehend, and to interpret texts but also to alter and shape them and to communicate about them (Das, 2011). Scholars investigating how young people make meaning in such interactive contexts have argued that socially networked environments in particular afford new textual possibilities for youths to develop an expanded communicative repertoire (Beach & Doerr-Stevens, 2011; Beach, Hull, & O'Brien, 2011; DePew, 2011; Dowdall, 2009; Hull et al., 2010; Reid, 2011; Richards & Gomez, 2010; Stornaiuolo, Hull, & Sahni, 2011). Although these studies indicate that people can extend their strategic repertoires by virtue of reading and writing in the company of others in networked, interactive contexts, we are still at the beginning of understanding how this interactivity shifts relationships between authors and audiences and demands new interpretive strategies for making meaning with interlocutors from around the world, who may in fact appear and disappear from our screens unpredictably (Kushner, 2011). Our study addresses questions about the roles of multimodality and interactivity in online reading, which we characterize as a semiotic practice with profound ethical implications for communication and understanding in a radically interconnected world.

A Multimodal, Social Semiotic Approach

We ground this study in a conception of reading as sign making, a semiotic approach to reading that understands it to be a culturally situated and fundamentally dialogic process (Kress, 2003; Smagorinsky, 2001). As a socially situated practice, reading involves the active construction of meaning from culturally shaped materials in a particular social and cultural context. We make meaning of the world around us via a variety of culturally available sign systems and in relation to our personal, social, and cultural histories. Signs, as culturally codified representations, hold different meanings for different readers depending on the cultural resources that they bring to bear on the interpretive situation. Smagorinsky (2011) offered an example of how different readers—a white South Carolina senator, a black South Carolina resident, a resident of a small Indonesian island, and a meteorologist—might differently understand the meaning of the Confederate battle flag, depending on its context and the histories that the individual readers bring to bear. Signs are inherently polysemous and multifunctional in that they can serve as icon, index, or symbol in different contexts or simultaneously (Houser & Kloesel, 1992; The Peirce Edition Project, 1998). Texts, as configurations of signs, are inherently multivoiced (Bakhtin, 1981, 1986) and oriented both to the past (containing echoes of historical discourses) and the future (in conversation with potential audiences). It follows that the readers in our project, who hailed from, in most cases, dramatically different cultural, linguistic, and national backgrounds, would of necessity employ varied reading practices as they engaged in semiotic work online within a range of modes and genres.

Reading, from this point of view, always entails an iterative relationship between the socially situated reader and the culturally and historically embedded texts being read. As the shape of what we read and the contexts in which reading takes place continue to shift, so too must our definition of reading (Kress, 2003). Kress importantly argued that viewing reading as a semiotic design practice is now essential in light of "the increasingly and insistently more multimodal forms of contemporary texts" (p. 140). As young people engage with multimodal texts made easily available by virtue of digital and mobile technologies, they have opportunities to engage in new kinds of meaning-making practices that have implications for online reading. In this study, we found that most young people were eager to communicate multimodally. Focusing on those who seemed most proficient at this process, we investigated their strategic repertoires in navigating the complexities of making meaning in the globally oriented, interactive space of the social network, as well as the ethical stances that they enacted in and through their textual practices.

While reading and writing multimodal texts with global audiences online indeed afford new kinds of opportunities, it is simultaneously the case that authors and audiences also bear responsibility to one another to take into account diverse meaning-making trajectories made possible by interconnected, multimodal contexts. In an ethical media space, authors are compelled to imagine audiences for their texts, ideally creating texts that are respectful, open, and welcoming of a diverse readership. Readers become obligated to listen and respond generously, hospitably, and sensitively. We have been particularly interested in such ethical dimensions of young people's semiotic work, especially in the ways that they develop hospitable dispositions as they communicate across difference. In this chapter, we explore the ways that young people embraced authorial responsibilities in relation to their readers by looking at the degree to which they engaged in hospitable semiotic practices. That is, we wanted to know whether and how young people accepted the ethical obligation to "welcome the stranger" (Silverstone, 2007, p. 136).[2] Silverstone, whose project was to theorize the desired relationship between media and morality in today's global world, argued that hospitality "begins in the recognition of the other and in the sound of his or her voice" (p. 148). Thus, we examined the extent to which young people recognized others through their semiotic work. How did our participants imagine their readers and hear others' voices? How did young people take into account readers and viewers who would bring different personal and cultural histories to bear?

In thinking about the ways that young people created a hospitable semiotic environment, we found Eco's (1979) notion of textual openness particularly valuable. A central characteristic of media hospitality is "opening [one's] space to the stranger" (Silverstone, 2007, p. 148), and we drew on Eco's work on open texts to theorize what a hospitable opening of the space of the network might look like. Eco defined an open text as one that encourages a multiplicity of readings and offers readers invitations to work together with the author. We might say, then, that an open text embeds strategies of welcome while maintaining sufficient ambiguity to allow readers room to imagine multiple interpretations sensitive to their own meaning-making histories. Eco argued that open texts provide an array of textual cues that guide (and scaffold) the reader (e.g., direct appeals, the presupposition of intertextual competence). Yet, at the same time that open texts offer helpful guidance, they are also flexible in validating a range of interpretive proposals. That is, open texts are sufficiently ambiguous to be generative but not so ambiguous that they can "afford whatever interpretation" (p. 8).

Data Collection and Analysis

Our chapter draws from a three-year design research project linking youths in four countries—India, the United States, South Africa, and Norway—via a private social network called Space2Cre8. Although participants could view the site in English, Hindi, Africaans, or Norsk and use those languages to communicate within and across sites, most exchanges occurred in English, which served as the de facto lingua franca of the network. Like commercially available social networks,

Space2Cre8 allowed participants to design their online profiles, make friends, chat, blog, share media, and exchange messages. However, our network differed from commercial sites in that it was private and educationally focused, connecting adolescents ages 12–18 from around the world who did not already know each other and who were able to shape the design of the network. It was also unique in that young people met together in small groups off-line with a teacher who guided them in creating digital artifacts to share and in communicating on the network. In these class sessions, some during the school day and some after school, which were called the Kidnet program, young people created a wide range of new media artifacts that they could post online—digital stories, documentaries, dramatizations, photo collages, poems—as well as personalized profile pages by means of which to introduce and represent themselves on the network. We collected a variety of data, both qualitative and quantitative, over three years of the project. This data collection was greatly facilitated by a custom analytics program that we built, which archived all of the content data that the youths generated, their browsing and viewing histories, and statistical information about their online participation patterns. We also collected ethnographic data on the youths' participation in the project, including field notes and audio and video recordings of class sessions, participant interviews, and creative artifacts.

In light of our interest in the ethical dimensions of reading in a global world, we set out in this study to understand how young people create hospitable texts that welcome readers standing at the figurative door. By *hospitable text*, we mean a semiotic ensemble that offers a perspective on the world, self, and/or other that invites or welcomes a reader's or audience's response. We began by examining one of the most ubiquitous features of the network, the personal profile page, as a window into how youths marshaled different semiotic resources in imagining their readers and creating hospitable texts for them. We reasoned that the personal profile page represented the most common entry point into the network for members, who often began their sessions by viewing others' profile pages. On these pages, young people performed elaborate presentations of self, shaped for fellow members of the community, by customizing their pages to the extent possible on the network. Each page allowed users to post media content (e.g., avatar, music, videos, images) as well as written text (e.g., status messages, "About Me" text, wall messages, blogs). In one of the most popular features, users could change the background of their pages by choosing a solid color, a pattern, or an image to display as digital wallpaper. Members could see all the content on one another's pages, and they could comment on media or leave messages publicly on one another's walls. As the hub of interaction online, these designed profile pages functioned as important texts in and of themselves while also operating as entry points into other texts, such as videos and blogs, that were embedded within the pages.

We theorized that hospitable texts in this networked context would be open ones (Eco, 1979) that invited readers in, not just to decode or comprehend but also to respond. Thus, we looked to our data to see how young people constructed open profile pages. We began our analysis by examining the most-viewed profile pages of the network between September 2009 and March 2011, a time of intense activity on the network. We surmised that these top-viewed profile pages would reveal a rich corpus of hospitable semiotic strategies that users had employed to invite readers to continue viewing and exploring. From the 355 users who signed on to the network during that period, we analyzed the top 10% of the most-viewed profiles (35), believing that this sample size would provide rich evidence of youths' interpretive performances (see Table 1 for a list of these 35 users). Using a constant comparative method (Glaser & Strauss, 1967), we looked

Table 1. Most-Viewed Profile Pages of Youths on Space2Cre8, September 2009–March 2011

Rank	Name	Profile Views	Site
1	Meryem	481	Norway
2	Bhakti	373	India
3	Nelson	332	United States (California)
4	Lillith	328	Norway
5	Usree	319	India
6	Nakida	288	United States (New York)
7	Isabella	276	United States (New York)
8	Susie	274	United States (New York)
9	Nadra	270	Norway
10	Supriya	225	India
11	Paloma	217	United States (New York)
12	Saravati	211	India
13	Emily	187	South Africa
14	Shushma	184	India
15	Sabina	169	India
16	Padma	168	India
17	Julian	167	United States (New York)
18	Kayla	166	South Africa
19	Luisa	161	United States (New York)
20	Selena	159	United States (New York)
21	Rachel	154	South Africa
22	Adira	151	United States (New York)
23	Laurel	145	South Africa
24	Diamond	143	United States (New York)
25	Ronan	142	South Africa
26	Gabriel	142	United States (New York)
27	Olina	142	Norway
28	Monica	138	United States (California)
29	Reggie	137	United States (California)
30	Colette	135	South Africa
31	Annisha	135	United States (California)
32	Aamira	134	Norway
33	Rahim	130	Norway
34	Willie	128	United States (New York)
35	Adele	128	South Africa

Note. All names are pseudonyms.

across the 35 most-viewed profiles, examining how authors implied their readers in composing them (Bakhtin, 1981) and the degree to which the profile pages employed open design elements. For each of these 35 adolescents, we further examined the visible traces that readers left on their pages, such as wall postings and comments, ascertaining not only how actual readers engaged with content on the profile pages but also how the authors in turn responded to their readers.

The 35 young people whose profiles we analyzed participated in six program sites: one in Lucknow, India; one in Oslo, Norway; one in the Western Cape of South Africa; and three in the United States—two in New York City and one in Oakland, California. At all the sites, this project represented a rare opportunity for the teens to access digital technologies and practices not generally available to them. In India, for example, our participants were a group of Hindi-speaking girls who worked to support their families in the mornings, attended school in the afternoons, and had never before used social media (for more information about this site, see Hull et al., 2010). In South Africa, the participants were Afrikaans-speaking eighth graders in a small farming village in the Western Cape who had never used computers prior to the project and did not know anyone, at the start of our study, who used e-mail. In Norway, the group of eighth-grade students, many of whom were children of immigrant parents living in Norway and speaking English as a third or fourth language, were familiar with computers but not necessarily with communicating online or creating media projects to share. The California participants were seventh- and eighth-grade students, primarily of Latino and African American heritage, who generally had access to computers only in school and were not experienced in creating media. In the two New York sites, the participants were adolescents in grades 9–12, many of them children of immigrant parents, who were familiar with computers and social media but often did not have access at home. All of these young people struggled with challenges in coming of age in a rapidly changing world, but they experienced markedly different lifeworlds and everyday realities, which they discovered as they communicated over time on the Space2Cre8 network.

To help us trace in more detail how students engaged with others on and off the network, we turned to an in-depth analysis of the students who had the top three most-viewed profiles: Nelson from the United States, Bhakti from India, and Meryem from Norway.[3] In addition to having the most-viewed profiles, these three participants were also the most prolific users of the site, with the greatest number of friends, activities, and postings (Stornaiuolo, Frankel, & Hull, 2011). To understand how they both imagined and interacted with others on- and offline, we analyzed their various creative artifacts, composed collaboratively or individually; their interactional patterns across the network, including participation in other collaborative spaces and communication with others via both public and private channels; and their interviews about their creative work and their participation in the Space2Cre8 community, including their design decisions in creating their pages. We used the qualitative analysis software Atlas TI during this case study analysis (Yin, 2003) as we inductively developed codes that helped us trace participation across spaces and texts over time (Bogdan & Biklen, 2007). This in-depth analysis of the three adolescents' interactions on the network over time enabled us to generate new insights about the strategies that the 35 youths used in composing open texts for imagined audiences.

These questions guided the study: (1) In what ways did youths mobilize semiotic resources to design their profile pages for local and global communities? (2) How did these young people display hospitable orientations toward their projected readers through their semiotic practices over time? and (3) How did youths enact readings of one another through various textual artifacts? We address these questions in the subsequent sections, first by exploring the central strategies that the youths used in creating open texts, and then turning to our three case study students, Nelson, Bhakti, and Meryem, to illustrate the different kinds of roles that young people took up as authors and audiences and the strategic repertoires that they developed in doing so.

Creating Open Texts: Audience-Sensitive Strategies

We found that all 35 top-viewed profile pages were highly designed, with youthful composers spending considerable effort to craft texts that were sensitive to and mindful of audiences from diverse linguistic and cultural backgrounds. For example, some adolescents added contextual information in their wall postings (e.g., explaining that Norway was in Europe), and others blended emoticons and other images with written text to amplify their message (e.g., "HELLO friends!!!!☺"). In characterizing the ways that these texts welcomed diverse audiences, we classified the features that indexed their openness. Following Eco (1979), we identified open texts as those that invited audiences to coordinate with the text in particular ways but that, at the same time, were open to multiple interpretations. Open texts thus offered guidance for readers, providing textual cues and invitations for audiences to read the authors as friendly interlocutors open to further exchange. Yet, open texts also afforded audiences flexible reading paths (Kress, 2003), with multiple ways to engage with a text. We turn to an example of one open text to illustrate how such profile pages provided guidance while also offering flexible reading paths for readers. Nakida, a 17-year-old from New York, took advantage of all available means to customize her profile page, creating an open text by virtue of her choices (see Figure 1).

The social network offered different ways of designing spaces, and the youths creatively took up those affordances (Gibson, 1986; Richards & Gomez, 2010). Because there were three primary options for customizing pages within the template of the social network, we attended closely to the ways that participants changed their profile pages, using these three options over time. First, users could add written text in predetermined fields, such as a statement about themselves under the heading "About Me," a short status message about themselves that appeared under their screen name, and wall postings and comments that appeared near the bottom of the page. On Nakida's profile page, for example, under her screen name of Fashionicon, she posted a status message that directly addressed

Figure 1. Partial Screenshot of Nakida's[a] Profile Page on the Space2cre8 Network

[a]Pseudonym of a 17-year-old girl from New York.

her readers: "What do you think of my song?" She also offered information about herself in the right column, listing her hometown as "bronx new york" and writing about herself, in part: "i love fashion an i love learning new things about people an i am very friendly. And also love questions =)."[4] At the bottom of the page (not visible in Figure 1), she posted a number of messages on her public wall. By taking advantage of the opportunity to add written text in all of the possible predetermined areas, Nakida presented herself as a welcoming interlocutor—providing information that would help others find common ground with her, characterizing herself as a friendly person who welcomed questions, and inviting others to pursue a conversation with her.

The second way that participants could customize their profiles was via image and color in three areas of the page: an avatar image, the background, and the font color. On Nakida's page, for example, she added a close-up picture of herself as her avatar image, editing it to add a white border that coordinated with the white stripe in her scarf. She wallpapered the page with an image of a fashion model on a runway, repeating the image in a checkerboard pattern across the entire page. To contrast with the reds and pinks in the background image, she chose a bold, navy blue font for the text. The final way that users could customize their profile pages was by embedding other texts within the page. Students could post four kinds of embedded texts: music, blogs, videos, and photos. For example, Nakida posted a song to play as background music so that anytime someone came to her page, the song she called "Who are you?" played (her status message referred to this song and invited others to comment on it). Students could also post a blog entry (which could include customized written text, video, emoticons, or photos) that would be previewed on their pages along with a link to the whole entry. Similarly, students could post videos and images (uploading their own or ones from a video or image-sharing site) that would appear as a clickable thumbnail image near the middle of their profile pages. Nakida posted all four kinds of embedded texts on her page.

In customizing their pages—via predetermined text fields, multimodal design elements, and embedded mixed media—the young people offered readers guidance in interpreting their texts. For example, Nakida invited readers to comment on her choice of song by asking audiences to listen to it, and she welcomed readers to ask her questions about her interests, especially fashion. At the same time, these multimodal textual designs offered readers a flexible means of navigating through the texts. For example, Nakida's readers could concentrate on getting to know her through her avatar or background images, or they could choose to read her wall comments or listen to her music—all possible entry points for readers. In these ways, the students customized their profile pages for audiences, creating hospitable texts that welcomed readers into the cross-cultural meaning-making enterprise with them. Examining the central ways that authors created these open texts, we created a taxonomy of textual strategies (see Table 2) that we organized in terms of the four primary approaches that the youths employed: designfulness (cf. Kress, 2003; The New London Group, 1996), overture, reciprocity, and resonance (cf. Du Bois, 2007).

All 35 young people whose profile pages we examined employed at least one of these four approaches in designing open texts, and the majority of them mixed several approaches to demonstrate a wide variety of audience-sensitive strategies. The most widely used approach was designfulness, as young people altered, appropriated, and hybridized multimodal content to communicate to their audiences that they were welcoming and interesting interlocutors. For example, Nakida chose an image of herself to share with her readers, a close-up of her face framed by an added border, that she coordinated with a navy blue font and an appropriated image of a fashion model. While these strategic choices were primarily designful, she also engaged in the second most popular approach of making overtures to her audiences. Her choice of avatar photo was also a way of disclosing information about herself to others, and she invited others to interact with her by soliciting comments on her posted song. Even the title that she added to that song was an overture, a question about her audience's identity. Many of the young people with the most-viewed profiles engaged in a similar kind of mixing of approaches, although when we traced the authors' design decisions over time, we found that the participants favored one approach more heavily than others. For example, while Nakida spent time designing her page for aesthetic appeal, she often made those changes to reach out to others. Her preferred means of creating

Table 2. Strategies for Creating Open Texts

General Approach	Description of Approach	Textual Strategies
Designfulness	Authors who took a designful approach were those who artfully and carefully crafted texts across multiple modes. Authors employing designful strategies made an effort to compose texts via multiple modes in order to create a welcoming environment for audiences.	• Appropriation: The author appropriated material for new purposes. • Alteration: The author edited texts to visibly alter color, perspective, line, shape, texture, form, value, or space. • Hybridization: The author edited two or more elements together to form a new design. • Synesthesia: The author layered multiple modes together to form a meaningful whole greater than the sum of the individual parts. • Symbolism: The author used something to stand for something else.
Overture	Authors who took an overture approach invited others to participate with them in the interpretive process either implicitly or explicitly.	• Direct address (e.g., "You, you all") • Greetings (e.g., "Hello!!") • Inclusive language (e.g., *we, our, let's*) • Gambits (e.g., "I like your page!") • Questions (e.g., "Do you like school?") • Invitations (e.g., "Come check out my page") • Self-disclosure (e.g., "I am a foster child") • Offering information (e.g., "I have two sisters") • Referencing shared information (e.g., "all Bieber lovers") • Boundary marking (e.g., "Only cool people should join")

(continued)

hospitable texts was the overture approach—regularly changing her status messages to invite others to talk to her and embedding media that reached out.

Like Nakida, we found that the 35 authors whose pages we examined used these first two approaches the most often in creating open texts. Many students also used a number of reciprocal strategies when interacting with others: answering questions, elaborating responses, and offering extensions, connections, and repairs to keep conversations moving and maintain intersubjectivity. However, these reciprocity strategies were not as widely used as strategies of designfulness and overture, and only a handful of students took a reciprocity approach as their central one. It is plausible that students engaged in fewer responsive strategies for a number of reasons, the most salient being that it was difficult work to sustain a conversation with unknown others across time zones, languages, and cultural and ideological

Table 2. Strategies for Creating Open Texts (*Continued*)

General Approach	Description of Approach	Textual Strategies
Reciprocity	Authors who took a reciprocal approach used responsive strategies to reciprocate a conversational move and encourage further conversation or interaction.	• Assumption of intertextual competence: The author referenced shared text or context (e.g., posting a picture that the author assumed an interlocutor would recognize). • Prediction: The author predicted what others knew (e.g., assuming an interlocutor did not know that Norway was in Europe). • Answer: The author answered a question, often part of an adjacency pair (e.g., replying yes when asked if he or she likes school). • Elaboration: The author offered additional information when asked a question (e.g., replying "I like my teachers" when asked if he or she likes school). • Extension: The author used a variety of back-channel or phatic responses to continue an exchange (e.g., "uh huh," "☺," or "lol"). • Repair: The author repaired a potential breakdown (e.g., saying, "Sorry if I offended u!"; correcting an error: "*Norway, not No way"). • Connection: The author synthesized information to talk about a similarity or difference (e.g., "India has a high level of poverty similar to parts of the US").
Resonance	Authors who used a resonance approach echoed other authors' design choices, language, or ideas. Often achieved through parallelism in conversation, resonance builds affinity between interlocutors by highlighting connections.	• Syntactic parallelism: The author repeated part of another author's syntax during an exchange (e.g., when one partner shifted in chat from writing "to you" to echoing the partner's use of "2 u"). • Semantic parallelism: The author repeated key phrases or ideas during an exchange (e.g., repetition of the term *random* in messages). • Symbolic resonance: The author echoed others' uses of symbols (e.g., several girls took photographs in which they used their hands to frame a photo of something, e.g., the sun, a flower, a person). • Iconic resonance: The author echoed others' uses of iconic images (e.g., an author posted a picture of his home in response to another student's posting of a picture of her home).

differences. None of our 35 young people took a resonance approach as their primary approach for engaging with others, although about half of the students did engage in resonance strategies, often to powerful effect. For example, we noted that several girls chose a series of images that echoed one another; that is, in each photo, the photographer had framed the subject of the photo with her hands. In one such image, a female student in India posted an avatar photo of herself framed by the photographer's cupped hand, which echoed the avatar photo of a young woman in Norway who posted an image of the sun framed by the photographer's index finger and thumb. Other kinds of parallelism, such as the echoing of vocabulary or syntax of an interlocutor, were prevalent but not used as often as other strategies.

During our case study analysis of the students with the top three most-viewed profile pages, we found that each of the three used the full strategic repertoire over time. In the subsequent sections, we describe how each of these students used a wide repertoire of audience-sensitive strategies in ways very different from one another. We demonstrate through our analysis how highly strategic these three young people were in designing open texts and presenting themselves as welcoming and hospitable authors and potential interlocutors and the different approaches they took in doing so.

A Designfulness Approach: Taking Advantage of Multimodal Resources

To explore the ways in which youths strategically mobilized semiotic resources on the social network, we first turn to Nelson, an energetic and thoughtful eighth grader, as the Space2Cre8 user who capitalized on the varied multimodal resources of the network most vividly and frequently. An articulate 12-year-old boy, Nelson was young for his eighth-grade class but a popular figure with kids of all ages, on and off the network. Regularly sporting a wide grin and a sharp wit, Nelson often bounded into the computer lab after school, dropping his backpack on the ground and dramatically announcing, "I'm here!" He had grown up his whole life in West Oakland, an urban area in the East Bay of San Francisco, as an only child who was part of an extended African American family living all around the neighborhood. On Space2Cre8, Nelson was one of the most prolific and popular users, with hundreds of friends and numerous postings across the network. In an early blog titled "My Cool Life," he described himself:

> My life is interesting. I am 12 years old and in the 8th Grade. I like to play video games and I like to go out doors. Once, I hiked all day on the Castro Valley Mountains. I like to play adventurous, shooting, and puzzling games. I like to play football, basketball, and soccer. I am really good at basketball. I was on a team last year. (blog, 9/18/09)

This blog was posted on his profile page along with numerous other artifacts that he layered there carefully. For Nelson, the profile page was his communicative window into the networked space, and he spent a considerable amount of time designing it.

Although Nelson used many different strategies to design hospitable texts and engage with others across the networked community, he generally preferred the designfulness approach, integrating multimodal design and aesthetic attention into every interaction possible. Like many of his peers on the network, Nelson used images, music, video, icons, and text in strategic ways to aesthetically design the spaces he participated in online, what Kress (2003) or Nelson (2006) might call synesthetic design, an emergent process of making meaning across multiple copresent semiotic modes so the sense of the whole is greater than the sum of its parts. We can call 12-year-old Nelson a synesthetic designer, someone who artfully arranges different modalities for amplified and coordinated effect. He did this design work across all the artifacts he created for the social network, whether it was the groups he sponsored, the videos he edited, or the messages he exchanged. Nowhere was his designed aesthetic more apparent than his profile page, which he changed by posting 15 different background images and nine different avatars in various combinations over the school year. Almost all the images he chose for the background involved a space theme, coordinated with the theme of the network ("A Space to Create") in a playful way (see Figure 2).

Nelson displayed a space photo that he repeated vertically down his page, setting the font color to a bright blue that could be seen against the gray and black color scheme of the image. His status message echoed the space scene in calling out, "Hello world!!!" This enthusiastic greeting (made clear by three exclamation marks) referenced the world displayed on his page's background as well as the members of the Space2Cre8 community around the world reading his message. His avatar was a self-portrait, an image he snapped while posing in front of a desktop computer at school. Nelson almost always used a picture of himself as his avatar,

Figure 2. Partial Screenshot of Nelson's[a] Profile Page on the Space2cre8 Network

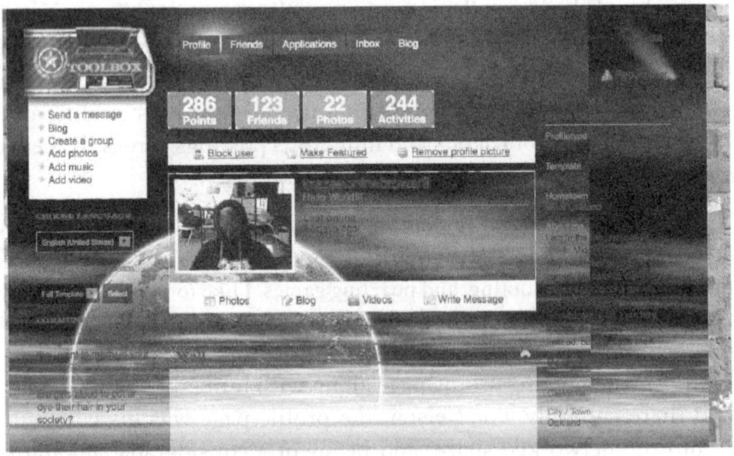

[a]Pseudonym of a 12-year-old boy from California.

and he, like many others on the site, preferred using his own photo to represent himself online. He expressed this opinion in an exchange of private messages with Colette in South Africa, who had used a photo of a popular singer as her avatar:

> Colette: hey hey i really like you and would like to be your friend. can you pretty please tell me your real name!!!
>
> Nelson: [Nelson], wat is yours???? Show a picture of yourself!!
>
> Colette: mine is [Colette]...Don't worry you'll soon see the real me!

In this message, he exhorted Colette to show herself via a personal photo, and reciprocally, he regularly pointed people to his profile page to see pictures of himself. Interestingly, in this case, Nelson's preference for personal profile pictures seems to have been activated through the coconstruction of resonance across conversational turns. Colette opened with a bid for authenticity ("tell me your real name"), to which Nelson first affirmatively responded and then made a similar authenticity bid ("show a picture of yourself"). Here in miniature, then, via a brief sequence of turns, Nelson and Colette began to stipulate the ethical conditions and commitments that would underpin their textual practices and friendship.

By coordinating the texts, images, and colors on his page to send a greeting to people in the space of the network, Nelson designed his profile page as an open text that invited others to make meaning with him. Through its carefully choreographed design, his profile page as a whole created a sense of openness that invited readers to make meaning across the images and texts. Whether others responded to the use of his own photo, his greeting to the world, or his space background—or ideally, all three working in concert—his audience was invited to interact with someone who represented himself as a friendly and welcoming interlocutor across different modalities. This strategy was very useful for communicating with others who spoke different languages, and Nelson was mindful of building in multiple ways for his friends who spoke English as a second, third, or fourth language to understand him.

Nelson used this strategy of synesthetic design in almost all of his interactions on the network, not just his profile page. That is, he regularly used multiple modes to invite others to read his work and to interact with him. Even in primarily textual media like chat or private messages, Nelson incorporated emoticons or emotive punctuation to amplify or provide nuance for his message. In his status, for example, he added three exclamation marks to emphasize his greeting, and in his chat with Colette, he used repeated question and exclamation marks to both mirror her own textual enthusiasm and add affect to his messages. He also regularly used emoticons, which the site converted to images in the chat window. Nelson knew how to make all kinds of emoticons appear in chats, and people on- and off-line regularly asked him what to type to generate the smiley face with sunglasses as well as other kinds of emoticons. Nelson's chat with 14-year-old Olina in Norway was punctuated with many such emoticons from both participants, and the following excerpt illustrates how Nelson used them not just to amplify his message but also to complicate it:

Nelson: r u like a dude, who is just posing as a 14 year old girl?
Olina: No
Olina: I'm a girl
Olina: why do u think that?
Nelson: i dont know?
Nelson: i saw it happen on this TV show
Olina: Ok... But I'm a girl. read my profile...
Olina: don't u belive me?
Nelson: yea
Nelson: if i c your picture, i'll trust even more

When he asked to see Olina's picture, he included an emoticon of a wide grin to mitigate the sting of asking to see a picture because he did not fully trust her word that she was a girl. He regularly used emoticons and punctuation to similarly extend his meaning, and every message and chat that he engaged in (thousands of lines of text) were filled with these multimodal layerings. As these young communicators illustrate in brief, and as we discuss in more detail later, a part of an ethics of communication is the acceptance of risk and the construction of trust (cf. Levinas, 1969).

Nelson was very serious about the idea of design and took the idea of design research to heart, regularly offering suggestions about how the network should be changed (he was an early advocate of the chat and wallpaper features). Many of the 11 groups that he created had a community orientation designed to bring a variety of opinions together in one space, and he regularly solicited peers' engagement with these groups by sending messages that requested participation. He created one group dedicated to issues of design, "Space2cre8 Students," which he described in the group description field this way: "Suggestions on what you would like the website to improve, have more of, or take off. Make suggestions in this group. All space2cre8 members can join to give your suggestions." This message was accompanied by an avatar of a finger pointing at the reader (see Figure 3).

Figure 3. Avatar for Nelson's[a] Online Group "Space2cre8 Students" on the Space2cre8 Network

[a]Pseudonym of a 12-year-old boy from California.

Like the direct address in the description, calling on readers to participate and including "all space2cre8 members" in his imperative to "make suggestions," this image amplifies that directive by addressing indexically the person viewing the page. For some viewers, the image would have additional indexical resonance, calling up via synecdoche the U.S. military's emblem for recruitment. Just as Uncle Sam demanded soldiers, Nelson wanted participants. In this way, he synesthetically designed a group space, as he did his profile page and messages, to elicit as much participation as possible in the redesign of the network space. He was strategic in how he used different available modalities to craft a message that could be heard and understood by others, including those for whom English was an emergent language.

While Nelson was highly strategic in how he approached meaning making across the network designfully, all of the students in our sample used the designfulness approach to differing degrees to communicate multimodally via strategies of appropriation, alteration, hybridization, synesthesia, and symbolism (see Table 2). The student who used this strategy most frequently in authoring her profile page was Nadra, a 13-year-old girl from Norway, who customized her page design 46 times. Nadra focused particularly on coordinating different modalities and articulating relations between them, and the comments that readers left on her page indicated that they appreciated her efforts. In an early iteration of her page, Nadra signaled her love of Justin Bieber, the Canadian pop singer, by using his image as her wallpaper, which she coordinated with a photo of herself smiling directly at the camera dressed in a traditional headscarf (see Figure 4). Additionally, she included information about herself in the "About Me" section of her page, which read,

> I am a girl who is 13 years old. my name is [Nadra] but it pronounced [Nadru]. I am from Kurdistan but live in Norway. I speak kurdish at home and norwegian with my friends and teacher. I Love JUSTIN BIEBER.

Figure 4. Partial Screenshot of Nadra's[a] Earlier Profile Page on the Space2cre8 Network

[a]Pseudonym of a 13-year-old girl from Norway.

This profile design can be considered open in nature because it revealed quite a lot about Nadra via different modalities. Through the juxtaposition of the background and profile images with her "About Me" statement, readers could surmise that she is a fan of Justin Bieber, of Kurdish nationality, a trilingual speaker, and an immigrant to Norway. These revelations invited readers to engage with her around any of these potential points of connection, and readers responded with compliments like "Nice pic!" or "*Fint bakgrunnsbildet*!" (Nice background image!).

One of the remarkable characteristics of Nadra's participation in the network was the sheer number of times that she shifted her semiotic strategy. For example, her later profile page was much less busy than her initial one (Figure 4), with a crisp white background and bright blue lettering that matched the flower in the hair of her avatar, American actress Nina Dobrev (see Figure 5). This version of her page, as a kind of blank canvas (distinct from the default blank canvas, which was beige parchment), highlighted the written text and avatar photo. Her "About Me" statement shifted as well, as she broadened her interests to include international music (while remaining a "BIIG" Justin Bieber fan):

> Hi !:D my name is [Nadra] and 14 years old. I am from Kurdistan but live in Norway. I speak kurdish at home and norwegian with my friends and teacher. Love to being with my friends and just have fun. I like to listen to Kurdish, Arabic, Turkish and English music. I am a BIIG fan of Justin BIeber.

In this iteration of her profile page, Nadra still attended to the synesthetic aspects of the design (e.g., matching the colors of the flower and font) and continued to invite readers to connect with her through popular culture, music, language, or

Figure 5. Partial Screenshot of Nadra's[a] Later Profile Page on the Space2cre8 Network

[a]Pseudonym of a 13-year-old girl from Norway.

national/ethnic background. However, she did not reveal herself quite as directly as before, shifting from using her own picture as her avatar to appropriating the image of a popular American actress. This new strategy led one girl in India to inquire, "hello why you use this photo?" For the young woman in India, Nadra's choice of avatar was apparently not intertextually meaningful, and thus she questioned Nadra's strategy in choosing it. Designing a page that allows for multiple meaning-making paths can signal an admirable and intrepid openness, we suggest, a willingness to welcome multiple interpretations and responses to textual overtures. Yet, it can also be risky, making one vulnerable to questions around representational choices, such as using a popular American actress's photo instead of a self-portrait.

Young people regularly took advantage of the multimodal capacities of the network to take a designful approach to creating open texts, especially in juxtaposing and layering texts to create meaning synesthetically. Nelson and Nadra, like other participants whose texts we examined, were strategic designers who exploited the communicative potential of multimodal composing to create open texts. These texts invited others into the meaning-making process by representing the author's stance as welcoming across all the modalities available to them (e.g., Nelson's "hello world" was written text that he coupled with the space/world theme of his background image). Yet, these texts were also open in the sense that the relationships among the modes were sufficiently ambiguous that others could construct different meanings than the author might have intended but still understand enough to communicate. That is, whether someone could read Nadra's English text about her interests or recognize Justin Bieber as a singer, that participant could still understand that Nadra was making an effort to communicate her interests to her viewers/readers. As designers, our young authors strategically coordinated various available semiotic resources to create a hospitable semiotic environment.

An Overture Approach: Creating a Welcoming Persona

All of the authors whose pages we examined also engaged to some degree in what we have called an overture approach to creating open texts. In this approach, young people strategically created openings for future communication with their audiences by threading many kinds of overtures throughout their networked communication. In this section, we explore how young people displayed orientations toward their projected readers through the ways they reached out to others over time. Many young people made direct and explicit overtures to their audiences, such as addressing readers through exhortation (e.g., "be my friend!"), greetings (e.g., "Hi everybody!"), or questions (e.g., "How are you today?"). Conversely, all of the young people in our study exercised a wide repertoire of subtle overtures to others as well, such as seeking similar interests with others, posting personal photos and videos, or using jointly oriented language (e.g., inclusive personal pronouns). Although all the students engaged in these kinds of outreach strategies at some point in their participation online, some of them seemed to prefer this approach over the others and spent considerable effort crafting messages of welcome in almost every move. One of the students with a top-viewed profile who engaged in a systematic and strategic campaign of welcome was Bhakti, a 17-year-old girl from India who displayed her orientation to readers as potential new friends and as a hospitable audience for her poems and other compositions. She might best be characterized as a Space2Cre8 ambassador, someone who embraced new members of the community through a vast repertoire of welcoming strategies in every online interaction. Again, we view such an orientation as a dimension of hospitality, one in which a host makes a welcoming overture and renders herself vulnerable via a textual offering to an unknown guest, who may embrace, misunderstand, ignore, or choose to reject that offering..

A central figure on the social network, Bhakti used many kinds of outreach tactics to connect with others and to portray herself as friend-worthy. Whereas in other writings (e.g., Hull et al., 2010), we analyzed an early digital story that Bhakti created and its impact as it circulated through the network, here we focus on her role in the online community. A slender teenager who seemed stately at a distance, Bhakti was always ready with her wide smile and a warm arm casually tossed across her friends' shoulders. Of all the girls in her program, Bhakti usually had her hand raised during class time, trying to answer a question or volunteering for a role in the activity at hand. She loved learning about computers, quickly becoming among the most expert in the room and mentoring her friends as they learned to navigate online. As the person on the site with the most friends (161), Bhakti initiated most of those friendships (141) by sending requests to people she had not yet met. Similarly, Bhakti reached out to others via private messages and chats, initiating 35 of her ongoing 55 message conversations and 82 of her 101 chats. She stated that her favorite part of going on the Space2Cre8 network was "making friends and sharing my life" (interview, 7/12/10), and clearly she used many of the outreach functions of the network to connect with others. As someone who had had to battle many obstacles to pursue her dream of an education and financial independence, Bhakti compared herself to the image of the sun that she posted on her profile page, spreading hope and warmth across the Space2Cre8 community (interview, 7/12/10).

One of the ways that Bhakti positioned herself in the community was as an open person, someone who shared personal information freely. This openness meant sharing some of her struggles, especially her efforts to make enough money to support her siblings after her mother's death while still staying in school. In frequent postings to her profile, she shared information about herself and her community through three videos, 35 photos, 12 blog posts, and 140 status and wall posts. Additionally, she provided background information about her love of school and her difficulties at home in her "About Me" statement:

> hey i am [Bhakti] from India. i like to make more friends. I am student of class 10th....I study in [Prayas] school. In school we have freedom to express our selves. Our School begins at 2:30 pm. Our Teachers Love us and they are Like OUR Friends. We get more love in school compared to our homes. We forget our troubles when we

are at school. We cannot share anythings with anyone at home. We don't get to play, dance, sing and study at HOME. We can participate in many activities at school, so our school life becomes very interesting. There is no freedom at home. We are not allowed to visit our friends. SCHOOL HAS Taught US to be independent. [Prayas] has given us dreams and courage to fulfill our dreams.

Bhakti assumed that her readers would be interested in the details of her everyday life, such as the time her school day began and her grade level, as well as her feelings about these things. By sharing her struggles and her hopes and dreams, Bhakti displayed an orientation toward others as potentially caring friends, ones worthy of her confidence and trust. In all of her postings online, she adopted this stance toward others, frequently asking others to be friends and sharing sometimes intimate parts of her life in the hopes that her interlocutors would do the same.

In addition to representing herself as an open and trustworthy person through her personal sharing, Bhakti signaled friendly intent by incorporating messages of welcome in every posting across the site. She regularly infused her messages with deep care for and awareness of her audience, writing status messages like "I LOVE YOU ALL" and "hi!!!everybody" and posting regular greetings to visitors to her page with wall posts like "hello every one how are you i miss you all." These postings conveyed a sense of openness to others through both her message (e.g., "love," "care") as well as her orthographic choices (e.g., capital letters, multiple exclamation points). Furthermore, she characterized her audience as members of a collective community (e.g., "everybody," "you all"), which positioned them in relationship with her and with one another. She wrote frequent messages like the following, posted on her wall for everyone who came to her page to read:

hello everyone how you all and how is going your kidnet class i miss you all . and what you all are doing at this time ? after 2 month ago what you all do and how you all sped your holidays. m...well i went to my grand mother house and there i was spend my holidays and enjoyed so many thing . and after i came to my house suddenly i join....this is company's name where i work. right now i am doing job so i don't have time to spend to our kidnet class . i miss my all kidnet class. this time i am feeling so bad . but there is problems so i need to do that .because this time i have so many problems at my home reply me soon about your holidays.

Anyone in the community who read this posting could be part of the "you all" she addressed here, as she solicited her readers' advice about her conflict in working instead of attending the Kidnet classes. In addition to addressing readers directly, she inquired about them as well, reciprocally asking them to "reply me soon" about how they spent their holidays. She spoke to her readers as members of a community whom she had missed, inviting them to interact with her in the role of concerned friend. Through her strategic positioning, Bhakti framed herself and her readers as reciprocal members of a supportive community, roles that readers often took up.

Through multimodal and textual means, Bhakti and others who preferred this welcoming approach regularly positioned themselves as thoughtful and hospitable authors concerned about their readers' needs. Moreover, they framed their relationships with their readers as reciprocal, positioning their audiences as participatory. Although not all of the young people in our study were willing to share personal information, some even expressing reservations about talking with others who were essentially strangers, all of the participants authored invitations for their audiences to take up participatory roles, inviting them to comment on media, to talk, to share information, to offer opinions, to be visible to one another.

A Reciprocity Approach: Extending the Conversation

When readers responded to authors, leaving messages, answering questions, and taking up invitations, the authors did not always know what to do next. How does one sustain dialogue with a distant other? What is textual hospitality, beyond the offer of a welcoming text? Participants with experience in other online venues were often practiced at deploying conversational strategies to draw out others, extend their responses, and solicit more interaction. Others were less practiced, answering in yes-or-no form or incorrectly predicting what an audience might understand (e.g., answering "sup" instead of "what's up" in response to a greeting). Regardless of their facility with these strategies, we found that participants persisted in their attempts to connect with peers whom they had never met and whose needs they had to infer. Several students, however, privileged a reciprocity approach, always seeking opportunities to extend conversations with others. We turn to one such student, 14-year-old Meryem from Norway, who had many opportunities for interaction, having the most-viewed profile page in our study (481 views). We found that by deploying a wide number of responsive strategies, Meryem supported her interlocutors and did something that few others did as systematically and comprehensively: She answered everyone. She took her responsibility to her readers seriously and assiduously answered anyone who contacted her. Like Nelson and Bhakti, Meryem created a hospitable semiotic environment and positioned herself favorably in relation to others, but her preferred approach was to employ a repertoire of responsive strategies that facilitated communication.

A social young woman in a Norwegian eighth-grade classroom, Meryem regularly talked to her classmates as she moved from desk to desk during Space2Cre8 activities. In her "About Me" statement online, which she regularly updated with new information, she emphasized her relationship with her friends and also highlighted her status as an immigrant to Norway: "My homecountry is Turkey. There I have a house and my aunts, uncles, grand-parents and my relatives lives there. My interest is to be with friends, shopping and much another things:)." With access to a computer with an Internet connection at home, Meryem was a practiced online communicator when she joined the Space2Cre8 project. She spent a considerable amount of time outside of class on the network and, thus, had the opportunity to chat with youths in other countries regularly at different hours of the day and night. Meryem also put energy into designing her page, coordinating her carefully posed and edited profile pictures with the background and font colors so they all worked in concert (the pink of the text matching the pink in her blouse, for example). She always used a carefully edited photo of herself each time she updated her profile, often with embellishments such as added text, borders, and soft back lighting. Like Nelson, she regularly asked people for photos of themselves and pointed potential viewers to her own photo as a means to get to know one another.

What most distinguished Meryem's approach from Bhakti's or Nelson's was that all of her efforts to create a hospitable communicative environment seemed designed to facilitate and sustain interchange with others. Meryem's participation on Space2Cre8 was characterized by a pattern of responsivity: She responded to every comment on her page right away, which usually led to further communication through other channels (i.e., chat, private message). Further, she often used humor and repartee to spark new exchanges and create a welcoming environment. In one example, a boy in New York posted on her wall that he wanted "2 instigate a conversation wif u." Whereas other students might have ignored this posting, written in American slang without greeting or context and using complex vocabulary and shorthand spelling conventions, Meryem answered right away: "if you are cute so." She turned the tables on this teenage boy, implying that she would talk to him only if he were cute (echoing the flirtatious undertones in his message). Her two friends later complimented Meryem on this conversational move, reinforcing to others who might be looking on at this public interaction that she was an open, responsive, and ultimately cool person. This in turn created a welcoming and hospitable environment on Meryem's page.

Other participants' postings on Meryem's wall, which were available for all to read, certainly added to the perception that she was a cool girl in the community. A case in point is Q'nisha's posting, the first on Meryem's page. Q'nisha, a 12-year-old girl from Oakland, was funny, bold, and confident, and her posting, using slang like "wats up grrl" and praising Meryem's page design, indicated to others that Meryem's page was worth viewing. Plus, in response to Q'nisha's statement that "I think we have to talk with each other," Meryem chose to answer publicly rather than via a private channel (i.e., chat, private message), agreeing that they should talk more and complimenting Q'nisha's page design as well. Nearly eight months later, miss d (username) from South Africa posted a reply on this comment thread, writing that Meryem struck her as a "nice girl" who was worthy of friendship. An author and designer who took the time to craft her online presence as well as to answer the comments of others, Meryem came across as a desirable friend.

Not only was Meryem responsive to all who contacted her, but she was also quite adept at using strategies to extend the conversation and at offering her interlocutors support. For example, when Kayla, a 13-year-old girl in South Africa commented on Meryem's wall, "hi my name is lovergirl [her username] i live in Shouth Africa," Meryem responded, "Hi, my name is [meryem] and i live in norwy who is in europe." Instead of responding like Kayla, with a fictional username,

Meryem offered her real name as well as reciprocal information about her location. Yet, rather than simply telling Kayla that she lived in Norway, Meryem offered additional information to orient Kayla, assuming that Kayla would know where Europe is, if not Norway. This kind of extension strategy provided scaffolding to global friends who may not have been as practiced at building relationships online, where one must reveal certain information to gain trust as well as infer what audiences might or might not know.

Meryem positioned herself in the role of supportive audience in many of her online interactions. That is, she transitioned from being a hospitable author/designer to a hospitable reader in her online interactions, and she did so fluidly. We see her model this ethical communicative stance in most of her conversations, such as the following chat with Jorell, a 13-year-old boy from Oakland:

Jorell: hey hey hey it is your friend here
Meryem: Hii, where do you live?
Meryem: Hii What is you'r real name?
Jorell: who wat when wher why
Jorell: united staes
Jorell: kevin
Meryem: Ok, what do you mean with (who what when where why) ???
Jorell: it is just a question
Meryem: Oooh
Jorell: lmao
Jorell: lmao
Jorell: lmao
Jorell: lmbo
Meryem: lmao ? lmbo ?
Jorell: it is saying laugh my but off
Meryem: Ok
Jorell: thanks for understanding
Jorell: i have 2 names but people call me [jorell] so just call me dat
Meryem: Ok, my name is [Meryem] in real:)
Jorell: sweet
Meryem: Ok
Jorell: thanks for understanding
Meryem: Thanx
Meryem: Thanx
Jorell: hey u r pretty
Meryem: Thank you, you too <3

Jorell began the interchange with a friendly gesture, positioning himself as Meryem's friend, although they had not communicated directly before. Meryem responded in kind, asking two questions that required him to share personal information. However, Jorell was cautious about what he revealed online, and in his next conversational turn, he was deliberately vague and a little critical. He provided the information that he lived in the United States and that his name was Kevin. His residential status was accurate, if quite general, but the second piece of information was false: Kevin was the name of another boy in his school. Jorell also retorted, "who wat when wher why," which implied that Meryem was asking too many questions too quickly. Although she was practiced with certain online exchanges in English, she did not understand Jorell's implication and so asked him to explain what he meant. When he told her the phrase was just meant as a question, she playfully stuck her tongue out at him via emoticon. He responded in kind, assuming that she would understand his acronym lmao, which glosses as laughing my ass off. However, after posting this without a response three times, Jorell changed the acronym to lmbo, the less offensive version of his earlier post, which he also needed to explain when she did not understand (laughing my butt off). He apologized when she did not answer in a reciprocal manner ("thanks for understanding"), relieved that she was not offended by his language. At this point in the conversation, Jorell revealed his real name to her, claiming that he had two names to cover up his lie and again apologizing for misleading her. Meryem, in persisting in conversing despite potential misunderstandings, modeled for Jorell how to playfully but respectfully engage in a conversational exchange. She offered personal information and encouraged him to do so, and she acknowledged each of his responses with a continuer ("Ok," "Oooh") or the provision of more information (questions, her name, compliments).

Through a range of responsive strategies, then, young people regularly found ways to elaborate, extend, and otherwise scaffold one another in conversation. More than just imagining audiences, our young people participated with their audiences across the network, which we view as a reading practice that required imagining what these unseen people might want or need to know to continue the conversation. This hospitable effort was challenging for participants, who sometimes, like Jorell, made communicative efforts that did not go so smoothly. However, young people often persisted through these difficulties, and efforts like Meryem's to create open texts that invited others to switch roles as both authors and audiences helped young people develop new communicative competencies. Even when they did not participate directly in such exchanges, the textual traces left by these public interactions proved important in inviting readers like miss d into the communicative process.

Communicating in a Global World

Social media and mobile and digital technologies now afford the rapid global circulation of texts and increasingly compel communication and literacy practices that are interculturally alert. They also set new horizons for those educators and researchers who would consequently redraw the boundaries of reading, writing, and literacy pedagogy. Our focus in this chapter has been the semiotics of reading online texts created for a global audience. We asked what it means to read in a world in which audiences have exploded, space and time are ever more compressed, and audiences and authors can interact in new ways. As the young people in our project imagined how to communicate with readers different from themselves culturally, linguistically, ideologically, and geographically, we examined one kind of reading practice in particular: reading one's audience. Especially in this international context, the presence and significance of imagined readers appeared magnified, constantly prompting participants to consider, how might I read, how might I be read, and how might I do so most generatively when to read requires meaning making across varied semiotic and cultural contexts? As readers meet in global, transnational spaces like social networks, they will surely experience a range of challenges around differences in their personal histories, cultural backgrounds, and communicative preferences and norms. While there are various ways to conceptualize and address such challenges, our approach has been to take an ethical turn, examining the ways that our youthful authors assumed responsibilities toward readers and stipulated with them joint commitments of hospitality and reciprocity. As young people predicted and inferred what their projected readers might need and desire, they stretched their imaginations to take into account their peers' experiences and knowledge, employing interpretive strategies that we argue are increasingly critical for communicating in a global world.

These strategic efforts to take into account potential and actual audiences were at heart hospitable gestures. Our adolescent participants welcomed virtual strangers into their online spaces through various semiotic practices. In this chapter, we operationalized the construct of hospitality in terms of openness, finding that youths who designed the most sought-after pages on the network engaged in these hospitable practices by creating open texts that invited readers to engage with authors and construct varied reading paths. The generative polysemy and indeterminacy of their multimodal compositions encouraged readers to construct multiple meanings in service of making friends and influencing people and featured overtures for engagement to which peer audiences regularly and positively responded. In characterizing how our participants took their global audiences into account by creating these open texts, we created a framework of four approaches that the young people in our study employed: designfulness, overture, reciprocity, and resonance. Although the youths used a wide repertoire of textual strategies across all four approaches, we found that they generally had a preferred method for presenting themselves as welcoming and hospitable interlocutors, and our three case study students, Nelson, Bhakti, and Meryem, were particularly adept at deploying a diverse strategic repertoire in different ways via these approaches.

One finding that is important to consider as we turn these digital technologies toward educational purposes is the sociocultural, sociocognitive challenge of this literate enterprise. Although teachers encouraged and supported the youths to develop hospitable stances toward others through the offline programs (cf. Stornaiuolo, 2012), this process was often bumpy and replete with communicative missteps and misunderstandings. Members of the network struggled to communicate in a language and register that others would understand, sometimes wrangling over the intended meanings of colloquial terms like *sup* and *lmao*. Moreover, the polysemy of the multimodal artifacts that offered audiences multiple reading paths (Kress, 2003) and opened interactional spaces could sometimes lead to unruly texts, with tensions and communicative breaches that undermined or interrupted an intended narrative. While the youths learned to communicate with others who were very different from themselves, they were simultaneously tasked with juggling the multiple roles required of them. They sometimes fumbled as they shifted between authorial and audience roles, and at other times, they failed to anticipate what their readers might need. It is noteworthy, then, that the young people persisted in their efforts to communicate with one another, compelled by their engagement in what they appeared to experience as a meaningful, creative, and interpersonal endeavor. As Nelson's, Bhakti's, and Meryem's efforts demonstrate, they did so generously, thoughtfully, and artfully as they turned their semiotic practices toward ethical purposes.

The literate challenges with which our youths engaged have taught us not only about their persistence and ingenuity in creating and responding to open texts but also about online literacy practices more generally. These online practices, which increasingly entail composing for and reading of unknown, heterogeneous, and culturally and linguistically diverse interlocutors, foreground and deepen our understanding of the inherent precariousness of communication as an encounter with the other (cf. Levinas, 1969). More than with face-to-face encounters, in which the other is never completely unknown or unidentified, or in print communication, in which the text, the author, and the reader are given a fixity that is significantly destabilized in the more ephemeral realm of digital textual transactions, in online literacy/communicative practices, the risks of misunderstanding and unfulfilled semiotic potential are greater. For this reason, composing and reading online take on a primary ethical meaning.

Our overarching interest in this chapter, as well as in related research on social media (Hull et al., 2010; Stornaiuolo, 2012), has been the exploration of ethical spaces for encounter and communication with others. For this purpose, we have found particularly generative the philosophical construct of hospitality. As Silverstone (2007) argued,

> Hospitality, an obligation, principally, rather than a right, is a primary ethic in a cosmopolitan world. It goes to the heart of our relationships with others. Indeed it is constitutive of such relations. The capacity, indeed the expectation, of welcoming the other in one's space, with or without any expectation of reciprocity, is a particular and irreducible component of what it means to be human. (p. 139)

Silverstone was interested especially in the ethical entailments of hospitality in a global and intensely mediatized world, where it "becomes intertwined with the requirement not just to let the other speak but the requirement that the stranger should be heard" (p. 139). Thus, he aptly captured an important dimension of digital readerships that we have hoped to illustrate in this chapter: the requirement, indeed the responsibility, to attempt to imagine, to know, to hear one's audience, and to compose accordingly. We would add, referencing the exchanges of our youths, that once having read their audience hospitably, authors next must trust their readers to be hospitable themselves. Here, then, is another important ethical dimension concerning the host and guest, self and other, author and reader relationship. In offering a wide and largely unknown audience access to one's textual creation and thereby to oneself, the composer/designer takes the risk of being misunderstood and/or rejected. We might in fact usefully think of the posting of a textual bid online as an act of trust in an assumed hospitable audience. Our data provide, we believe, striking examples of how young people took risks to create the conditions and then nurture an ethical space for encounter and communication with the other.

The ideal of hospitality—whether this hospitality would be offered by a nation in regard to its borders, an individual in relation to his home, or an author with respect to her text—is shot through with ever present relational tensions and challenges. The ethical nature of these challenges, we suggest, makes the semiotic work of readership complex in ways that are often not acknowledged or are reduced to matters of textual etiquette. Derrida's (1999, 2001) discussions of the fundamental aporia that rests at the core of hospitality are instructive here. He points out that to be hospitable, it is first necessary to have the power to host. Hospitality is therefore predicated on claims of property ownership, or in our case, textual authorship. To be hospitable, the host must have a measure of control over the guests who are being hosted—or over the boundaries of a nation, or over the meaning/interpretations of the text that is being offered to an audience/readership. Derrida's analysis offers us a provocative and cautionary perspective, one that acknowledges the complexity, challenge, and contradictions of hospitality but does not assert its impossibility. Authentic hospitality is a radical act imbued with uncertainty and risks. We believe the youths in our study strived to be radically hospitable—that is, hospitable in an unconditional and nonhegemonic way. As they composed and designed texts, they created spaces for encounter and communication. They were open to the possibility that readers would appropriate their texts in unanticipated ways, ways that blur the boundaries between author and audience, and ways that question the asymmetrical distribution of semiotic rights in meaning making between textual host and textual guest, if you will. At the same time, when taking on the role of readers, the youths displayed an orientation toward an ethic of listening and responsiveness—to wit, an ethical commitment to reciprocity. This compelled them to look for and acknowledge the other in the text, proffering a response in which their subjectivity was exposed to and engaged by the other. Such hospitable textual practices, in our estimation, constitute an overlooked but significant ethical dimension of being literate in the 21st century.

QUESTIONS FOR REFLECTION

1. Do students need direct instruction in the hospitable text strategies of designfulness, overture, reciprocity, and resonance to be successful online communicators? Why or why not?
2. How do you think students engaging in global communication can develop ambassadorial skills for interacting with others?
3. What questions might you ask students in a class discussion of authoring and audience in an online environment?
4. What discussions about communication interactions might you have with students who are finding new friends in other countries and cultures?
5. How might reading teachers capitalize on young people's interest in communicating multimodally?

NOTES

We gratefully acknowledge the support given the larger project from which this chapter grew: the Spencer Foundation; the UC Links project of the University of California; the Graduate School of Education at the University of California, Berkeley; and the Steinhard School of Culture, Education and Human Development at New York University. Special thanks are due Lauren Jones Young, P. David Pearson, and Mike Wood, whose considerable early assistance with and belief in the work made all that followed possible. We also acknowledge the members of the research, development, and teaching team of the Kidnet project: Anand Chitravanshi, Ola Erstad, Anna Floch, Matthew Hall, Adrienne Herd, Jennifer Higgs, Suenel Holloway, Garth Jones, Gary Jones, Stacy Marple, Mark Nelson, Urvashi Sahni, John Scott, Kenneth Silseth, Anna Smith, Xolani Tembu, Sean Turner, Kristin Beate Vasbø, Tracie Wallace, Duncan Winter, and Rian Whittle.

[1]We refer here to interacting with the reader in a literal sense—that is, the actual exchange between author and audience. Such an exchange does not negate the anticipated interaction that the writer had imagined and encoded in the text, but rather builds on it. In fact, in the actual exchange between reader and writer, the reader can variously reject, negotiate, subvert, or ratify the position and interpretive actions that the writer had projected.

[2]The philosophical construct of hospitality has a long lineage: Kant's (1983) work from the period of 1784–1795, Levinas (1969), Arendt (1998), and Derrida (1999, 2001). Among contemporary theorists, Silverstone (2003, 2007) has used hospitality quite powerfully to frame the moral challenge of living in an age of media saturation and radical connectivity (see also Chouliaraki & Orgad, 2011). In other work (Hull & Stornaiuolo, 2012), we have followed Silverstone in linking hospitality to the related construct of proper distance to theorize the challenges of interacting with mediated others. In that work, as in the present chapter, our interest was in exploring the digital, literate entailments of hospitable dispositions and habits of mind.

[3]All names of individuals and schools are pseudonyms. In the screenshots reproduced in this chapter, names have been erased as needed to maintain anonymity.

[4]Although teachers discussed with participants how messages might be perceived by others on the network and used the postings as learning moments, the students were free to use any

kind of writing style they chose. Therefore, postings quoted in this article may not follow conventions for standard written English. We thank Gunther Kress for helpful consultations on the nature of reading as semiotic design as well as for the inspiration of his work.

REFERENCES

Alvermann, D.E., & McLean, C.A. (2007). The nature of literacies. In L.S. Rush, J. Eakle, & A. Berger (Eds.), *Secondary school literacy: What research reveals for classroom practice* (pp. 1–20). Urbana, IL: National Council of Teachers of English.

Appadurai, A. (1996). *Modernity at large: Cultural dimensions of globalization*. Minneapolis: University of Minnesota Press.

Arendt, H. (1998). *The human condition* (2nd ed.). Chicago: University of Chicago Press.

Bakhtin, M.M. (1981). Discourse in the novel. In M. Holquist (Ed.), *The dialogic imagination: Four essays* (C. Emerson & M. Holquist, Trans.; pp. 259–422). Austin: University of Texas Press.

Bakhtin, M.M. (1986). *Speech genres and other late essays* (C. Emerson & M. Holquist, Eds.; V.W. McGee, Trans.). Austin: University of Texas Press.

Beach, R., & Doerr-Stevens, C. (2011). Using social networking for online role-plays to develop students' argumentative strategies. *Journal of Educational Computing Research*, *45*(2), 165–181.

Beach, R., Hull, G., & O'Brien, D. (2011). Transforming English language arts in a Web 2.0 world. In D. Lapp & D. Fisher (Eds.), *Handbook of research on teaching the English language arts* (3rd ed., pp. 161–167). New York: Routledge.

Bearne, E. (2009). Multimodality, literacy and texts: Developing a discourse. *Journal of Early Childhood Literacy*, *9*(2), 156–187. doi:10.1177/1468798409105585

Bezemer, J., & Kress, G. (2008). Writing in multimodal texts: A social semiotic account of designs for learning. *Written Communication*, *25*(2), 166–195. doi:10.1177/0741088307313177

Black, R.W. (2009). Online fan fiction, global identities, and imagination. *Research in the Teaching of English*, *43*(4), 397–425.

Bogdan, R.C., & Biklen, S.K. (2007). *Qualitative research for education: An introduction to theories and methods* (5th ed.). Boston: Pearson Education.

Brandt, D. (2009). Writing over reading: New directions in mass literacy. In M. Baynham & M. Prinsloo (Eds.), *The future of literacy studies* (pp. 54–74). New York: Palgrave Macmillan.

Burke, A., & Rowsell, J. (2008). Screen pedagogy: Challenging perceptions of digital reading practice. *Changing English*, *15*(4), 445–456. doi:10.1080/13586840802493092

Castek, J., Leu, D.J., Coiro, J., Gort, M., Henry, L.A., & Lima, C.O. (2008). Developing new literacies among multilingual learners in the elementary grades. In L.L. Parker (Ed.), *Technology-mediated learning environments for young English learners: Connections in and out of school* (pp. 111–153). Mahwah, NJ: Erlbaum.

Chandler-Olcott, K., & Mahar, D. (2003). "Tech-savviness" meets multiliteracies: Exploring adolescent girls' technology-mediated literacy practices. *Reading Research Quarterly*, *38*(3), 356–385. doi:10.1598/RRQ.38.3.3

Chouliaraki, L., & Orgad, S. (2011). Proper distance: Mediation, ethics, otherness. *International Journal of Cultural Studies*, *14*(4), 341–345. doi:10.1177/1367877911403245

Coiro, J. (2012). Understanding dispositions toward reading on the Internet. *Journal of Adolescent & Adult Literacy*, *55*(7), 645–648. doi:10.1002/JAAL.00077

Coiro, J., & Dobler, E. (2007). Exploring the online reading comprehension strategies used by sixth-grade skilled readers to search for and locate information on the Internet. *Reading Research Quarterly*, *42*(2), 214–257. doi:10.1598/RRQ.42.2.2

Das, R. (2011). Converging perspectives in audience studies and digital literacies: Youthful interpretations of an online genre. *European Journal of Communication*, *26*(4), 343–360. doi:10.1177/0267323111423379

Davis, K., Katz, S., James, C., & Santo, R. (2010). Fostering cross-generational dialogues about the ethics of online life. *The Journal of Media Literacy Education*, *2*(2), 124–150.

DePew, K.E. (2011). Social media at academia's periphery: Studying multilingual writers' Facebook composing strategies. *Reading Matrix*, *11*(1), 54–75.

Derrida, J. (1999). Hospitality, justice and responsibility: A dialogue with Jacques Derrida. In R. Kearney & M. Dooley (Eds.), *Questioning ethics: Contemporary debates in philosophy* (pp. 65–83). New York: Routledge.

Derrida, J. (2001). *On cosmopolitanism and forgiveness* (M. Dooley & M. Hughes, Trans.). New York: Routledge.

Dowdall, C. (2009). Impressions, improvisations and compositions: Reframing children's text production in social network sites. *Literacy*, *43*(2), 91–99. doi:10.1111/j.1741-4369.2009.00521.x

Du Bois, J.W. (2007). The stance triangle. In R. Englebretson (Ed.), *Stancetaking in discourse: Subjectivity, evaluation, interaction* (pp. 139–182). Philadelphia: John Benjamins.

Eco, U. (1979). *The role of the reader: Explorations in the semiotics of text*. Bloomington: Indiana University Press.

Ede, L., & Lunsford, A. (1984). Audience addressed/audience invoked: The role of audience

in composition theory and pedagogy. *College Composition and Communication*, *35*(2), 155–171.
Erstad, O., Gilje, Ø., & de Lange, T. (2007). Remixing multimodal resources: Multiliteracies and digital production in Norwegian media education. *Learning, Media and Technology*, *32*(2), 183–198. doi:10.1080/17439880701343394
Forte, A., & Bruckman, A. (2009). Writing, citing, and participatory media: Wikis as learning environments in the high school classroom. *International Journal of Learning and Media*, *1*(4), 23–44. doi:10.1162/ijlm_a_00033
Gibson, J.J. (1986). *The ecological approach to visual perception*. Hillsdale, NJ: Erlbaum.
Glaser, B.G., & Strauss, A.L. (1967). *The discovery of grounded theory: Strategies for qualitative research*. Chicago: Aldine.
Hansen, D.T. (2011). *The teacher and the world: A study of cosmopolitanism as education*. London: Routledge.
Hobbs, R. (2007). *Reading the media: Media literacy in high school English*. New York: Routledge.
Houser, N., & Kloesel, C. (Eds.). (1992). *Selected philosophical writings: Vol. 1 (1867–1893). The essential Peirce*. Bloomington: Indiana University Press.
Hull, G.A., & Nelson, M.E. (2005). Locating the semiotic power of multimodality. *Written Communication*, *22*(2), 224–261. doi:10.1177/0741088304274170
Hull, G. A., & Stornaiuolo, A. (2012, April). *Cosmopolitan literacies, social networks, and 'proper distance': The struggle for understanding in a global world*. Paper presented at the annual meeting of the American Educational Research Association, Vancouver, Canada.
Hull, G.A., Stornaiuolo, A., & Sahni, U. (2010). Cultural citizenship and cosmopolitan practice: Global youth communicate online. *English Education*, *42*(4), 331–367.
James, C. (with Davis, K., Flores, A., Francis, J.M., Pettingill, L., Rundle, M., et al.). (2009). *Young people, ethics, and the new digital media: A synthesis from the Good PlayProject*. Cambridge, MA: MIT Press. Retrieved July 31, 2012, from www.goodworkproject.org/research/goodplay/
Kant, I. (1983). *Perpetual peace and other essays* (T. Humphrey, Trans.). Indianapolis, IN: Hackett.
Kress, G. (2003). *Literacy in the new media age*. New York: Routledge.
Kushner, S. (2011). Virtually dead: Blogospheric absence and the ethics of networked reading, *The Communication Review*, *14*(1), 24–45.
Lam, W.S.E. (2006). Culture and learning in the context of globalization: Research directions. *Review of Research in Education*, *30*(1), 213–237. doi:10.3102/0091732X030001213
Leander, K.M., & Lewis, C. (2008). Literacy and Internet technologies. In N.H. Hornberger (Series & Vol. Ed.) & B. Street (Vol. Ed.), *Encyclopedia of language and education: Vol. 2. Literacy* (2nd ed., pp. 53–70). New York: Springer.
Leu, D.J., Jr. (2000). Literacy and technology: Deictic consequences for literacy information in an information age. In M.L. Kamil, P.B. Mosenthal, P.D. Pearson, & R. Barr (Eds.), *Handbook of reading research* (Vol. 3, pp. 743–770). Mahwah, NJ: Erlbaum.
Leu, D.J., Jr., Kinzer, C.K., Coiro, J.L., & Cammack, D.W. (2004). Toward a theory of new literacies emerging from the Internet and other information and communication technologies. In R.B. Ruddell & N.J. Unrau (Eds.), *Theoretical models and processes of reading* (5th ed., pp. 1570–1613). Newark, DE: International Reading Association. doi:10.1598/0872075028.54
Leu, D.J., Zawilinski, L., Castek, J., Banerjee, M., Housand, B., Liu, Y., et al. (2007). What is new about the new literacies of online reading comprehension? In L.S. Rush, A.J. Eakle, & A. Berger (Eds.), *Secondary school literacy: What research reveals for classroom practice* (pp. 37–68). Urbana, IL: National Council of Teachers of English.
Levinas, E. (1969). *Totality and infinity: An essay on exteriority* (A. Lingis, Trans.). Pittsburgh, PA: Duquesne University Press.
Lewis, C., & Fabos, B. (2005). Instant messaging, literacies, and social identities. *Reading Research Quarterly*, *40*(4), 470–501. doi:10.1598/RRQ.40.4.5
Livingstone, S., & Brake, D.R. (2010). On the rapid rise of social networking sites: New findings and policy implications. *Children & Society*, *24*(1), 75–83. doi:10.1111/j.1099-0860.2009.00243.x
Lunsford, A.A., & Ede, L. (2009). Among the audience: On audience in an age of new literacies. In M.E. Weiser, B.M. Fehler, & A.M. González (Eds.), *Engaging audience: Writing in an age of new literacies* (pp. 42–72). Urbana, IL: National Council of Teachers of English.
McKenna, M.C., Conradi, K., Lawrence, C., Jang, B.G., & Meyer, J.P. (2012). Reading attitudes of middle school students: Results of a U.S. survey. *Reading Research Quarterly*, *47*(3), 283–306. doi:10.1002/RRQ.021
Mishna, F., Cook, C., Gadalla, T., Daciuk, J., & Solomon, S. (2010). Cyber bullying behaviors among middle and high school students. *American Journal of Orthopsychiatry*, *80*(3), 362–374. doi:10.1111/j.1939-0025.2010.01040.x
Naumann, J., Richter, T., Christmann, U., & Groeben, N. (2008). Working memory capacity and reading skill moderate the effectiveness of strategy training in learning from hypertext. *Learning and Individual Differences*, *18*(2), 197–213. doi:10.1016/j.lindif.2007.08.007
Nelson, M.E. (2006). Mode, meaning, and synaesthesia in multimedia L2 writing. *Language Learning & Technology*, *10*(2), 56–76.
New London Group, The. (1996). A pedagogy of multiliteracies: Designing social futures. *Harvard Educational Review*, *66*(1), 60–92.

Peirce Edition Project, The. (1998). *Selected philosophical writings: Vol. 2 (1893–1913). The essential Peirce*. Bloomington: Indiana University Press.

Ranker, J. (2007). Designing meaning with multiple media sources: A case study of an eight-year-old student's writing processes. *Research in the Teaching of English, 41*(4), 402–434.

Ranker, J. (2008). Composing across multiple media: A case study of digital video production in a fifth grade classroom. *Written Communication, 25*(2), 196–234. doi:10.1177/0741088307313021

Reid, J. (2011). "We don't Twitter, we Facebook": An alternative pedagogical space that enables critical practices in relation to writing. *English Teaching: Practice and Critique, 10*(1), 58–80.

Richards, K.A., & Gomez, K. (2010). Participant understandings of the affordances of Remix World. *International Journal of Learning and Media, 2*(2/3), 101–121. doi:10.1162/ijlm_a_00052

Rizvi, F. (2009). Towards cosmopolitan learning. *Discourse: Studies in the Cultural Politics of Education, 30*(3), 253–268. doi:10.1080/01596300903036863

Rowsell, J., & Burke, A. (2009). Reading by design: Two case studies of digital reading practices. *Journal of Adolescent & Adult Literacy, 53*(2), 106–118.

Salmerón, L., & García, V. (2011). Reading skills and children's navigation strategies in hypertext. *Computers in Human Behavior, 27*(3), 1143–1151. doi:10.1016/j.chb.2010.12.008

Silverstone, R. (2007). *Media and morality: On the rise of the mediapolis*. Malden, MA: Polity.

Smagorinsky, P. (2001). If meaning is constructed, what is it made from? Toward a cultural theory of reading. *Review of Educational Research, 71*(1), 133–169. doi:10.3102/00346543071001133

Smagorinsky, P. (2011). Reading as culturally mediated, mediating, and meaningful action. In *Vygotsky and literacy research: A methodological framework* (pp. 123–159). Rotterdam, The Netherlands: Sense.

Smith, A., & Hull, G. (2012). Critical literacies and social media: Fostering ethical engagement with global youth. In J. Ávila & J.Z. Pandya (Eds.), *Critical digital literacies as social praxis: Intersections and challenges* (pp. 63–86). New York: Peter Lang.

Steinkuehler, C., Compton-Lilly, C., & King, E. (2010). Reading in the context of online games. In K. Gomez, L. Lyons, & J. Radinsky (Eds.), *ICLS '10 proceedings of the 9th International Conference of the Learning Sciences* (Vol. 1, pp. 222–229). Retrieved November 12, 2012, from dl.acm.org/citation.cfm?id=1854389

Stornaiuolo, A. (2012). *The educational turn of social networking: Teachers and their students negotiate social media*. Unpublished doctoral dissertation, University of California, Berkeley.

Stornaiuolo, A., Frankel, K., & Hull, G. (2011, March). *Ambassadors, provokers, and appraisers: Understanding the participation spectrum on an international social network*. Paper presented at the annual meeting of the Digital Media and Learning Conference, Long Beach, CA.

Stornaiuolo, A., Hull, G.A., & Sahni, U. (2011). Cosmopolitan imaginings of self and other: Youth and social networking in a global world. In J. Fisherkeller (Ed.), *International perspectives on youth media: Cultures of production and education* (pp. 263–280). New York: Peter Lang.

Tierney, R.J., & Pearson, P.D. (1983). Toward a composing model of reading. *Language Arts, 60*(5), 568–580.

Warschauer, M., & Grimes, D. (2007). Audience, authorship, and artifact: The emergent semiotics of Web 2.0. *Annual Review of Applied Linguistics*, 27, 1–23. doi:10.1017/s0267190508070013

Yin, R.K. (2003). *Case study research: Design and methods* (3rd ed.). Thousand Oaks, CA: Sage.

Zhang, S., & Duke, N.K. (2008). Strategies for Internet reading with different reading purposes: A descriptive study of twelve good Internet readers. *Journal of Literacy Research, 40*(1), 128–162. doi:10.1080/10862960802070491

CHAPTER 45

21st-Century Skills: Cultural, Linguistic, and Motivational Perspectives

Robert Rueda, University of Southern California

The purpose of this chapter is to examine the issue of 21st-century skills, focusing specifically on cultural, linguistic, and motivational aspects. The chapter begins with the current context and then moves to a focus on how current developments are likely to shape and modify educational practice, with a particular focus on literacy. A discussion follows about what we have learned from the 20th century related to these issues and focuses on the educational experiences and outcomes of students from diverse language and cultural backgrounds and the ways that schools have addressed these concerns. The chapter then moves to a focus on addressing the needs of these students from a research and policy perspective, both in terms of what has been done and what might need to be different. Given the focus of this volume, the focus is on literacy, although, as argued later in the chapter, the divisions between cognitive, affective, and social dimensions of language, literacy, and learning are less pronounced and important than once thought.

The Current and Future Context

The Work Context

It is useful to begin by considering the current context in terms of what a successful individual needed to meet societal demands both in terms of literacy and life experience during the last half century. In that work context, the normal expectations were that one would hold one or two jobs in one's lifetime, master one area of expertise or field of study, compete for jobs and resources primarily at the local level, engage in hands-on and fact-based work tasks and activities, receive an institution-based and degree-based education, and work in a top-down organization or institution (Institute of Museum and Library Services, 2009). In contrast, as the 21st century unfolds, it is more than likely that an individual will hold 10 to 15 jobs; be required to simultaneously master many rapidly changing fields; face global competition for employment; work in an interactive work setting that is technical in nature, requires completion of nonroutine tasks, and requires creative problem solving; receive education that is learner centered, lifelong, and partially or wholly delivered through technology; work in settings that are dynamic, flexible, and rarely top-down; and experience problems that are very complex and that occur in unpredictable environments.

These changes have been marked, since the last half of the 20th century, by changes in the industrial economy based on manufacturing, which has now shifted to a service economy driven by information, knowledge, and innovation. Scholars in business and economics have documented the nature of this shift. For example, in 1967, the production of material goods (e.g., automobiles, chemicals, industrial equipment) and delivery of material services (e.g., transportation, construction, retail) accounted for nearly 54% of the U.S. economic output. By the beginning of the 21st century, information services grew from 36% to 56% of the economy (Apte, Karmarkar, & Nath, 2008; Karmarkar & Apte, 2007). Of course, technology will play no small part in this continuing and dramatic change. Already, student use of computers to find information has been growing exponentially: 94% of students now use the Internet for at least some portion of their writing assignments for school (Lenhart, Arafeh, Smith, & Macgill, 2008). Although routine cognitive work and routine manual labor jobs were prevalent in the last several decades, these are the exact types of tasks that are easiest to automate with computers. Thus, jobs will increasingly emphasize expert thinking and complex communication for ill-structured problems, the kind which are more difficult for computers to handle (Levy & Murnane, 2004).

One important consideration that overlays this entire discussion and the issues raised in the remainder of the chapter is the issue of curriculum control and the purpose of education. Who or what should drive educational priorities? Is the purpose of schooling to serve as a simple training camp for industrial and corporate purposes? Or is the purpose a broader one that involves producing critical thinkers who are informed, self-regulated learners who are active and engaged citizens and community members? Is there a danger in shifting all educational priorities to fit corporate needs? How will the issue of privatization play in to the preparation of both teachers and students? What implications does this have for the diverse students who make up an increasingly large component of the U.S. population? As Dede (2010) notes, the primary barriers to altering curricular, pedagogical, and assessment practices are not conceptual, technical, or economic, but instead psychological, political, and cultural. These lenses should be kept in mind as the chapter unfolds, and the implications for teachers, students, and the larger society should be considered.

Interesting, at the same time that the shifts noted above are occurring, major changes in the makeup of the U.S. population are occurring as well. These are briefly summarized next.

The Changing Population

A recent report by the U.S. Census Bureau (2008) documents some of the changes that will take place in the United States in the near future, including the fact that the country will have an older and more diverse population. For example:

- Minorities are currently about one-third of the U.S. population. By 2042, they are expected to become the majority, and by 2050 they will compose about 54% of the population. This trend will occur earlier for children because more than half of all children will be from minority groups by 2023.

- It is projected that by 2030, the point at which baby boomers will be at least 65, they will compose about 20% of the population, more than doubling the 2008 number of 38.7 million.
- The population that is 85 and older will increase at an even faster rate, more than tripling by 2050 from 5.4 million in 2008.
- By 2049, the U.S. population is expected to reach over 400 million, and minorities will compose about 236 million of that total.
- There will only be a slight change in the non-Hispanic, single-race white population between the present time and 2050 (203.3 million vs. 199.8 million). It is expected that this group will lose about 20% of the total population share, dropping from 66% (the current level) to about 46%.
- Between now and 2050, the Hispanic population will nearly triple from the current level of 46.7 million, approximately doubling their percentage of the total population to 30% of the total. More than one-third of the population is expected to be Hispanic.
- The black population will increase only slightly by 2050, from 14% (41.1 million currently) to 15% (65.7 million).
- Asian Americans will almost double their percentage of the total population (from 5.1% to 9.2%), and their actual numbers will increase from 15.5 million to 40.6 million.
- Groups that make up a smaller percentage of the total population, such as American and Alaskan Indians, will only increase slightly (from 1.6% to 2% of the total population). Similarly, native Hawaiians and Pacific Islanders will more than double in number from 1.1 million to 2.6 million.
- An interesting demographic phenomenon is the growth of mixed-race Americans, who will more than triple their current number of 5.2 million.
- The population composition of children is changing as well. About two-thirds of the children will be from minority groups, an increase from the current level of 44%. The percentage of Hispanics in this group will increase from 22% now to 39% in 2050, while white children will decrease from 56% now to 38% then.
- By 2050, about 55% of the working age population will be minority, up from the current level of 34%. About a third of this group will be Hispanic, about 15% will be black, and about 10% will be Asian American (Campbell, 1996; U.S. Census Bureau, 2008; Vincent & Velkoff, 2010).

Language differences are a big factor in these changes as well. The number of school-age children (ages 5–17) who speak a language other than English at home more than doubled their percentage of the population from 10% to 21% in the three-decade span between 1980 and 2009 (Aud et al., 2011).

One of the interesting features of this increased diversity is the heterogeneity of the diverse populations, that is, diversity *within* diverse groups. For example, the term *English learner* is commonly used in the literature dealing with language instruction issues. Yet, examination of data from a large urban district such as Los Angeles, for example, indicates that there are over 99 different language groups (Los Angeles Unified School District, 2009). Across the United States, there are more than 400 language backgrounds among English learners (Capps et al., 2005). Although Spanish speakers represent the overwhelmingly largest language group, this group is anything but heterogeneous, as many authors have noted (Durgunoğlu & Goldenberg, 2011). This group ranges from very recent immigrants with no English skills to long-term English learners who are natives by birth but have limited literacy skills in their native language, and whose academic literacy skills in English are not as well developed as their oral skills (Callahan, 2006). Additionally, they often have backgrounds that reflect a wide range of cultural practices and understandings.

As elaborated on later, this accelerating diversification will challenge efforts to erase or improve already existing student performance and achievement gaps both within the United States as well as in the global context.

A Focus on 21st-Century Skills and New Literacies

21st-Century Skills

Given the existing and future changes that have been detailed, what are the implications for what one needs to know and be proficient at to succeed? What are the more specific proficiencies in literacy that will be required? Most often these are discussed in the context of 21st-century skills (National Research Council, 2010), or the set of skills, which many argue, that will be required to successfully navigate future life and work demands. It is clear that what was needed in the 20th century is different from what is and will be required in the 21st century primarily because of the emergence of very sophisticated information and communications technologies. However, there are different visions.

The National Research Council (2010) has elaborated the following as essential: adaptability, complex communication/social skills, nonroutine problem solving, self-management/self-development, and systems thinking. There are other conceptual frameworks that have tried to propose a vision of what 21st-century skills should look like, but perhaps the most comprehensive and frequently referred to framework comes from the Partnership for 21st Century Skills (2011). This organization has proposed a wide-ranging set of skills in a variety of domains as part of their framework. In addition to specific skills such as creativity and innovation in the domain of learning, this proposal includes a range of literacies in domains such as information and technology, and life and career.

There are several other organizations and groups that have offered similar visions, including the North Central Regional Educational Laboratory and the Metiri Group (2003), the Association of American Colleges and Universities (2007), and the Organisation for Economic Co-operation and Development (OECD; 2005). There are other groups and individuals who have tried to explicate needed skills and competencies in ICT specifically, including the revised ISTE (International Society for Technology in Education; 2000) student standards for technology in the curriculum, as well as digital literacy standards from the International ICT Literacy Panel (2002). In addition to organizations, individual scholars such as Dede (2005) have also formulated lists of literate skills for technology, apart from traditional reading, writing, and mathematics, as essential skills for the 21st century. Although a complete examination and analysis of all of these major frameworks is beyond the scope of this chapter, Dede (2010) provided a thorough comparison of these frameworks; in his thoughtful analysis, Dede concluded that there is significant overlap and consistency in the various frameworks. However, he also found that there are some differences, especially in those frameworks that are for education at all levels (from preschool through college) and those focused on business and industry. For example, business and industry frameworks include things such as students acting autonomously and student risk taking, which are not always stressed in most school curricula.

It is clear that the competencies demanded by employers and civic participation alike in the 21st century are and will be expanding to include abilities that are more interpersonal, as opposed to individual, in nature. Although individual skills such as reading, writing, computation, and information processing will be demanded at more complex levels (e.g., Carnegie Council on Advancing Adolescent Literacy, 2010), social competencies such as collaboration, adaptability, and oral communication will be increasingly required in the contexts in which those skills are applied as well (Wagner, 2008). The frameworks noted are consistent in emphasizing that ICT and technological literacy are at the core of 21st-century skills, as the rapid development of ICT requires a whole new set of competencies related to ICT. Taken as a whole, the frameworks draw on ICT demands as an argument for the need of 21st-century skills, but they also consider ICT as a tool that can support the acquisition and assessment of these skills.

New Literacies

In addition to the frameworks noted that focus on 21st-century skills in general, a parallel area of work has focused on the literacy aspects of 21st-century skills in the context of changing technology. Several authors argue that the Internet and all the dynamically changing uses and products are the defining technology for literacy and learning, and the backdrop for the range of 21st-century skills. As part of this change, the medium of literacy is beginning to change from the printed page to the electronic screen. Much of the thinking of the nature and implications of these changes is found in what has come to be called new literacies. However, even though there is a single label, there are many different perspectives under this umbrella, as Leu, McVerry, and colleagues (2009) have noted. These authors point out that some scholars focus on new social practices from a critical theory approach (Street, 2003), while others (Gee, 2003) focus on new Discourses, that is, the combination of language with other social practices (behavior, values, ways of thinking, clothes, food, customs, perspectives) within a specific group. Scholars such as Kress (2003) focus on meaning making as a social practice in specific social and cultural circumstances, while others (The New London Group, 2000) focus on multiliteracies that encompass a multiplicity of communications channels and increasing cultural and linguistic diversity or on the multimodal contexts of literacy practices (Hull & Schultz, 2002). Others take a broader perspective, which incorporates several of the elements described (Lankshear & Knobel, 2006).

Leu, Kinzer, Coiro, and Cammack (2004) have focused in particular on the new literacies created as a result of the multiple communicative and interactional affordances of the Internet. They define it as follows:

> The new literacies of the Internet and other information and communication technologies include the skills, strategies, and dispositions necessary to successfully use and adapt to the rapidly changing information and communication technologies and contexts that continuously emerge in our world and influence all areas of our personal and professional lives. These new literacies allow us to use the Internet and other information communication technologies (ICTs) to identify important questions, locate information, critically evaluate the usefulness of the information, synthesize the information to answer those questions, and then communicate the answers to others. (p. 1572)

In spite of the lack of consensus on the exact definition or focus of new literacies work, recent reviews (Coiro, Knobel, Lankshear, & Leu, 2008; Leu et al., 2007) have observed that most of the new literacies research is consistent in four aspects:

1. New literacies include the new skills, strategies, dispositions, and social practices that are required by new technologies for information and communication.
2. New literacies are central to full participation in a global community.
3. New literacies regularly change as their defining technologies change.
4. New literacies are multifaceted, and our understanding of them benefits from multiple points of view.

Recently, some scholars have attempted to refine the notion of new literacies by proposing a new literacies theory (Coiro et al., 2008; Leu, Kinzer, et al., 2004; Leu, O'Byrne, Zawilinski, McVerry, & Everett-Cacopardo, 2009). These authors suggest that the Internet is not a technology issue, as it is commonly viewed, but rather a context in which literate skills are displayed and constructed. These continually developing contexts and associated activities include a range such as personal blogs, the strategic use of search engines to solve everyday problems or answer questions, e-mail, online gaming, podcasting, videocasting, photosharing, shopping, chatting, and social networking sites.

This emerging theoretical framework includes two levels: an uppercase *New Literacies* and a lowercase *new literacies*. The capitalized New Literacies encompasses the broader and more inclusive framework, which is fed by the more specific work in a narrow area. The lowercase new literacies approach is exemplified in the active work on the narrower topic of reading comprehension in online environments by Leu and collaborators (Leu et al., 2007, 2011). These authors have argued that while the reading and literacy field has continued to focus on the key dimensions of phonemic awareness, decoding (phonics), fluency, vocabulary, and comprehension, the very nature of reading itself is changing and that online and print-based comprehension is not always equivalent. Interestingly, the RAND report on reading that has been so influential in research, policy, and practice does not focus on this dimension (RAND Reading Study Group, 2002).

As one example, Leu et al. (2007) found no significant correlation, among seventh-grade students, between performance on a measure of offline reading comprehension and a measure of online reading comprehension for adolescents, using a blog to provide prompts and record responses. Coiro (2007) has found that knowing a student's online reading ability adds significantly to predicting performance on another online reading task, over and above knowing their offline reading ability and prior knowledge of the topic. The basic argument is that these new environments demand not only extensions of existing skills but also new skills; yet, to date, it appears that little attention is given to these new skills in most classrooms or assessments (Madden, Ford, Miller, & Levy, 2005).

Coiro (2007) has found at least five different types of evaluation that occur during online reading comprehension:

1. *Evaluating understanding:* Does it make sense to me?
2. *Evaluating relevancy:* Does it meet my needs?
3. *Evaluating accuracy:* Can I verify it with another reliable source?
4. *Evaluating reliability:* Can I trust it?
5. *Evaluating bias:* How does the author shape it?

This list suggests that there may be only a partial overlap with traditional reading comprehension skills. Leu (2006) and Leu et al. (2011) have argued that the lack of attention to these critical skills in schools is especially problematic for those students who have the least access to the Internet or other technologies at home.

In sum, there is wide agreement that the social and economic context is rapidly changing, that some existing skills will be much more important than before, and that some new skills will receive more emphasis than in the past. The fundamental nature of the social contexts and social practices in which cognitive skills in general, but in literacy specifically, will be used will be different than in the past. Technology, especially the Internet, is a driving force and, at the same time, is itself characterized by dynamic change. It is clear that expertise in these areas will be required to assure participation in local as well as global networks and communities.

What Have We Learned From 20th-Century Literacy and the Educational Experiences and Outcomes of Students From Diverse Language and Cultural Backgrounds?

The literacy field is indeed complex. There are many different areas of focus and many different theoretical and paradigmatic approaches. Perhaps it is unrealistic to try to summarize lessons learned from the recent past related to the 20th-century literacy. However, there are some things worth noting that have a bearing on the topic of this chapter.

One important lesson has to do with the nature of the very phenomenon we study and centers on the distinction between reading and literacy. These two terms have often been used interchangeably in spite of the fact that various authors may hold very different meanings for them. An influential National Research Council report (Snow, Burns, & Griffin, 1998) defined *reading* as "the use of the products and principles of the writing system to get at the meaning of a written text" (p. 42). This definition reflects a perspective that focuses on the individual psychological processes involved in decoding and comprehending text. At the same time, however, other work in the field has reflected not only on these components but also more broadly on the beliefs, attitudes, and social practices that literate individuals and social groups engage in in a variety of settings and situations (P. Pearson & Raphael, 1999). This broader construct of literacy involves knowledge of the values, viewpoints, funds of knowledge (González, Moll, & Amanti, 2005), and language patterns established by members of the particular discourse group where literate practices are carried out.

While the psychological processes involved in reading (as previously defined) are most often seen as universal, literacy is often seen as much more culturally specific, opening the possibility of multiple literacies such as those discussed earlier on 21st-century skills. One of the lessons learned is that the language patterns, types and uses of text, vocabulary, syntax, and shared meanings and values in school-based literacy may be very different from those found in some home and community settings (Bloome, Katz, Solsken, Willett, & Wilson-Keenan, 2000). Some scholars have argued that whereas the cultural practices in home and community settings are normally *acquired*, the literate cultural practices associated with school are *learned* (Gee, 2000). One source of friction within the field has been that the terms *reading* and *literacy* have been used interchangeably even though they may carry very different meanings. In addition, research in one area is sometimes used to suggest pedagogy and policy in the other, a factor that may help explain some of the disagreements within the field.

Outcomes for Diverse Students

It has often been noted that students of color and students from families of low socioeconomic status generally fare less well on measures of reading and literacy, as well as in other academic outcomes (J. Lee, 2002). A recent policy document (Partnership for 21st Century Skills, 2008) notes an interesting pattern in these gaps, namely, the existence of two distinct achievement gaps: a high/low achievement gap and a global achievement gap. The high/low gap is primarily due to systematic and long-standing differences among U.S. subgroups.

These differences cut across the important content areas of math and reading. In the 2011 National Assessment of Educational Progress (NAEP) in mathematics, 384,200 U.S. students in grades 4 (209,000) and 8 (175,200) were tested (National Center for Education Statistics, 2011a). Of the fourth graders, 52% of white students scored in the proficient or advanced performance bands. However, only 24% of Hispanic students and 17% of black students scored in these bands. For grade 8, 44% of white students scored in the proficient or advanced performance bands, whereas only 21% of Hispanic students and 14% of black students scored in these bands. In a similar vein, the scale score difference between students not eligible for free or reduced-priced lunches and those who were was 24 points for grade 4 and 29 points for grade 8 (National Center for Education Statistics, 2011a).

In the 2011 NAEP in reading, 381,300 U.S. students in grades 4 (213,100) and 8 (168,200) were tested (National Center for Education Statistics, 2011b). Of the fourth graders, 44% of white students scored in the proficient or advanced performance bands. However, only 19% of Hispanic students and 16% of black students scored in these bands. Of the eighth graders, 44% of white students scored in the proficient or advanced performance bands, whereas only 21% of Hispanic students and 14% of black students scored in these bands. For grade 8, 43% of white students scored in the proficient or advanced performance bands, whereas only 19% of Hispanic students and 15% of black students scored in these bands. In terms of socioeconomic differences, the scale score difference between students not eligible for free or reduced-priced lunches and those who were was 29 points for grade 4 and 25 points for grade 8 (National Center for Education Statistics, 2011b). Similar patterns to those described for ethnicity/race and family income levels are found for eighth graders in the area of science (National Center for Education Statistics, 2012) and for eighth and 12th graders in writing (Salahu-Din, Persky, & Miller, 2008) from the 2007 assessments.

There is also what has been termed a global gap related to comparisons between top-performing students in the United States and those in international settings. This suggests that the achievement issues just noted are more apparent with students of color but go beyond specific ethnic or racial subgroups. The main pattern is that the United States is not doing well as compared with other countries. Evidence for this is found in data from international assessments such as TIMSS (Trends in International Mathematics and Science Study), which is a periodic set of assessments in mathematics and science in four-year cycles. In the results from the 2003 administration of this measure, the United States ranked above the international average but ranked only 15th of 46 countries in grade 8 mathematics and 12th of 25 countries in grade 4 mathematics. In science, the United States ranked 9th of 45 countries at the eighth-grade level and 6th of 25 countries at the fourth-grade level (Martin, Mullis, Gonzalez, & Chrostowski, 2004; Mullis, Martin, Gonzalez, & Chrostowski, 2004).

Another international assessment is the PISA (Programme for International Student Assessment), which measures the performance of 15-year-old students in the domains of reading literacy, mathematics literacy, and science literacy on a three-year cycle. In the results of the 2009 PISA, which focused on reading more intensively than in previous administrations, U.S. students ranked 24th in reading based on distributions of students across different performance bands, and their mean score was not statistically different from that of the mean of all countries combined (OECD, 2010, p. 50). Black and Hispanic students had lower and significantly different average scores than the overall OECD and U.S. average scores. In mathematics, 31 countries had a higher mean score than the United States (OECD, 2010, p. 135), and in science, 22 countries had a significantly higher mean (OECD, 2010, p. 152).

One alarming issue is that the patterns related to achievement differences take place against a backdrop of increasing diversity and increasing economic divides. A very recent report from the Pew Research Center (Kochhar, Fry, & Taylor, 2011) indicates a staggering pattern of economic differences among groups. In 2009, the median net worth of households for whites was $113,149, whereas for Hispanics and blacks it was $6,325 and $5,677, respectively. These figures represent an astounding drop in income in a relatively short period of time, from 2005 to 2009. In that period, income for whites decreased slightly but fell almost two-thirds for Hispanics and one-half for blacks (Kochhar et al., 2011). The authors attribute this pattern to two primary factors, the economic recession and the housing downturn, which both impacted the entire country. Unsurprising, these changes would be expected to impact most heavily any group with a high percentage of their wealth in their home and groups who live in areas of the country where the housing downturn was most dramatic, which was exactly the situation for many Hispanic and black families.

Access to and Use of Technology

As technology and Internet use have become a more central feature of daily life, there has been a pattern of significant inequities related to access. At the conclusion of the 20th century, data suggested that Asians and Pacific Islanders had the greatest access to technology, followed by whites, then blacks, and then Hispanics (T. Pearson, 2002). Children in the poorest school districts in the United States had the least amount of Internet access at home (Cooper, 2004). In 1999, schools with high poverty and schools with high minority enrollments were generally less likely to use computers or the Internet for instruction during class time than teachers in schools with low poverty and schools with low minority enrollment (Smerdon et al., 2000). This gap existed despite the fact that nearly all public schools had access to the Internet, regardless of poverty level (Williams, 2000).

The most recent national data expands on these patterns (DeBell & Chapman, 2006; Gray, Thomas, & Lewis, 2010). Figures 1a–c suggest that school-based

Figure 1. Percentage of Children in Nursery School and Students in Grades K–12 Using Computers at Home and at School in 2003

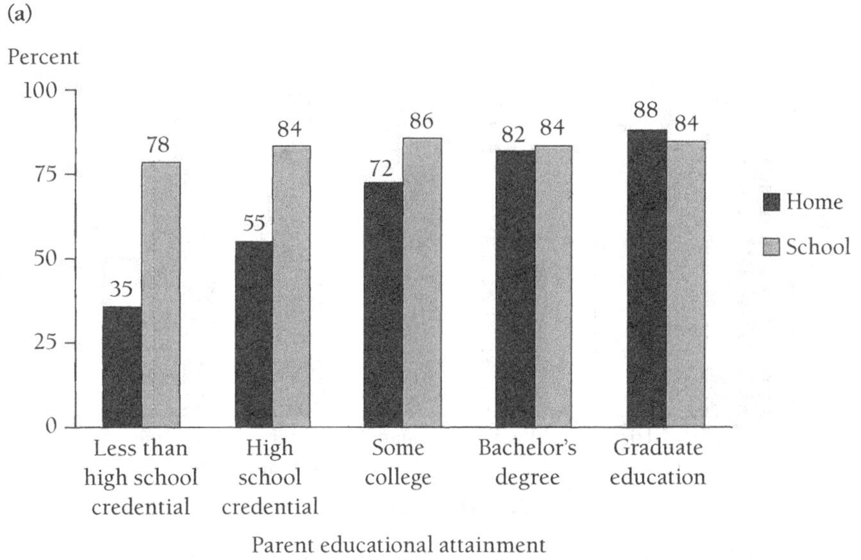

Source: U.S. Census Bureau, Current Population Survey (CPS), October 2003.

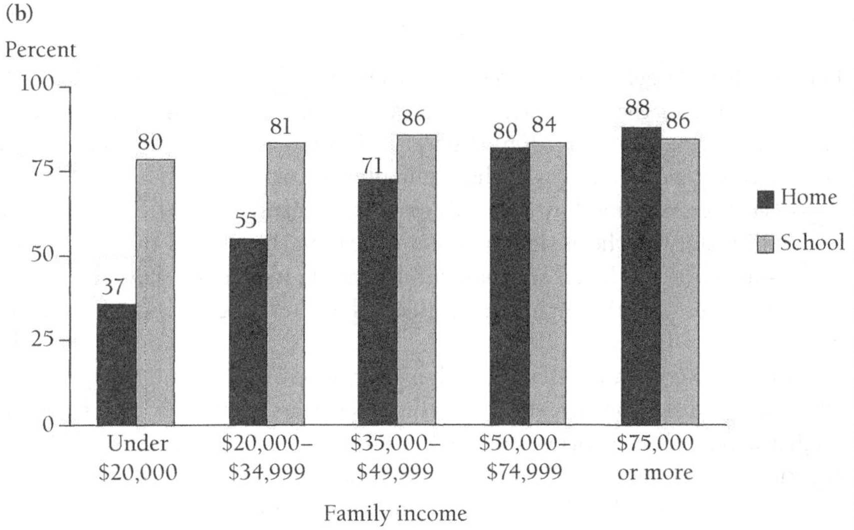

Source: U.S. Census Bureau, Current Population Survey (CPS), October 2003.

(continued)

Figure 1. Percentage of Children in Nursery School and Students in Grades K–12 Using Computers at Home and at School in 2003 (*Continued*)

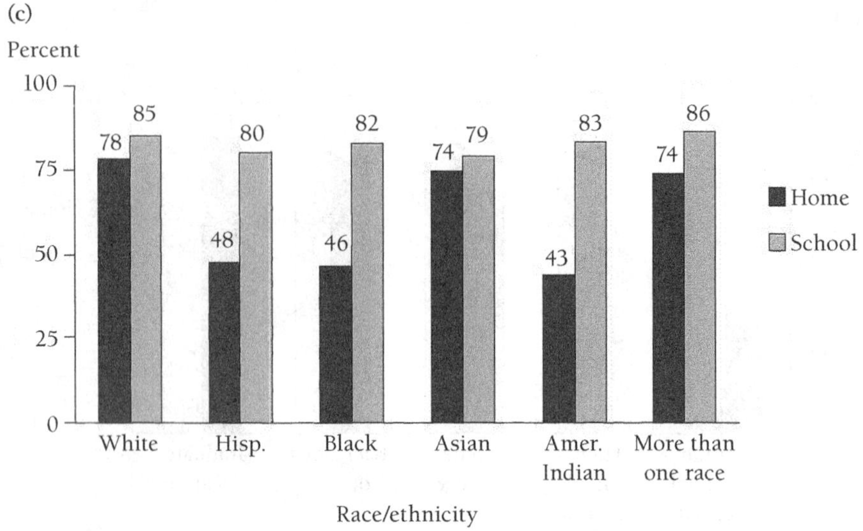

Source: U.S. Census Bureau, Current Population Survey (CPS), October 2003.

Note. From *Computer and Internet Use by Students in 2003* (NCES 2006–065, pp. 16 and 17), by M. DeBell and C. Chapman, 2006, Washington, DC: National Center for Education Statistics, Institute of Education Sciences, U.S. Department of Education.

differences have largely disappeared for students but that home-based differences exist, and some of the key patterns are tied to various sociocultural variables (DeBell & Chapman, 2005, 2006). Table 1 indicates the nature of some of these patterns. One general pattern is that computer use is relatively high across all groups, whether examined by student's grade level, gender, race/ethnicity, physical disability status, school size, parental education, household type, language, poverty status, income level, or urban/rural location. In all cases, computer usage is 80% or above, with the highest percentage characterizing 12th-grade students (97%).

There are significant differences, however, when these same categories describe Internet use. The percentage of computer users relative to Internet users is higher across all categories, but there are big differences within some of the categories. For example, 67% of whites use the Internet, whereas only 44% of Hispanics and 47% of blacks do. Also, parental education is a factor: Only 37% of students whose parent does not have a high school education use the Internet, whereas the figure is 73% if the parent has some graduate education. Some of the more striking differences are related to home language, poverty status, and family income level. The percentage of Internet users where Spanish is spoken is 28%

Table 1. Percentage of Children in Nursery School and Students in Grades K–12 Who Use Computers and the Internet, by Student and Family/Household Characteristics: 2003

Characteristic	Number of Students (in thousandths)	Percent Using Computers: Percent	Percent Using Computers: Standard Error	Percent Using the Internet: Percent	Percent Using the Internet: Standard Error
Total	58,273	91	0.3	59	0.4
Student Characteristic					
Grade level					
Nursery school	4,928	66	1.5	23	1.3
Kindergarten	3,719	80	1.4	32	1.7
1–5	20,043	91	0.4	50	0.8
6–8	12,522	95	0.4	70	0.9
9–12	17,062	97	0.3	79	0.7
Sex					
Female	28,269	91	0.4	61	0.6
Male	30,005	91	0.4	58	0.6
Race/ethnicity[1]					
White	35,145	93	0.3	67	0.5
Hispanic	10,215	85	1.2	44	1.7
Black	8,875	86	0.9	47	1.4
Asian	2,293	91	1.6	58	2.7
American Indian	346	86	4.8	47	7.0
More than one race	1,400	92	1.9	65	3.3
Physical disability status					
Disabled	646	82	3.3	49	4.3
Not disabled	47,949	91	0.3	61	0.5
School enrollment					
Public	50,653	91	0.3	60	0.5
Private	7,620	86	0.8	54	1.2
Family and Household Characteristic					
Parent educational attainment					
Less than high school credential	5,691	82	1.1	37	1.4
High school credential	13,804	89	0.6	54	0.9
Some college	16,548	93	0.4	63	0.8
Bachelor's degree	8,590	92	0.6	67	1.1
Graduate education	10,713	95	0.5	73	0.9
Family/household type					
Two-parent married household	40,987	92	0.3	62	0.5
Male householder	3,129	90	1.2	55	1.9
Female householder	13,463	89	0.6	52	0.9
Other arrangement	694	89	2.6	55	4.1

(continued)

Table 1. Percentage of Children in Nursery School and Students in Grades K–12 Who Use Computers and the Internet, by Student and Family/Household Characteristics: 2003 (*Continued*)

Characteristic	Number of Students (in thousandths)	Percent Using Computers		Percent Using the Internet	
		Percent	Standard Error	Percent	Standard Error
Household language					
Spanish-only	2,840	80	1.6	28	1.8
Not Spanish-only	55,434	91	0.3	61	0.4
Poverty status					
In poverty	10,173	84	1.1	40	1.5
Not in poverty	39,016	93	0.4	66	0.7
Family income					
Under $20,000	8,815	85	0.8	41	1.1
$20,000–$34,999	9,273	87	0.7	50	1.1
$35,000–$49,999	7,499	93	0.7	62	1.2
$50,000–$74,999	9,834	93	0.5	66	1.0
$75,000 or more	13,769	95	0.4	74	0.8
Metropolitan status					
Metropolitan, central city	13,229	88	0.6	50	0.9
Metropolitan, not central city	26,670	92	0.4	63	0.6
Non-metropolitan	10,370	91	0.7	59	1.3

Note. Detail may not sum to total because of rounding or missing data. From *Computer and Internet Use by Students in 2003* (NCES 2006–065, p. 6), by M. DeBell and C. Chapman, 2006, Washington, DC: National Center for Education Statistics, Institute of Education Sciences, U.S. Department of Education.

[1]White, Black, Asian, More than one race, and American Indian respectively indicate White, non-Hispanic; Black, non-Hispanic; Asian or Pacific Islander, non-Hispanic; More than one race, non-Hispanic; and American Indian, Aleut, or Eskimo, non-Hispanic. Hispanics may be of any race.

compared with 61% where Spanish is not spoken. With respect to poverty status, the figures are 66% for those students who do not live in poverty versus 40% for those who do. There are also dramatic effects associated with income level. The percentage of users is 41% for those from families with incomes under $20,000 and 75% for those from families with incomes of $75,000 and over. These differences are important because the Internet significantly extends the power of the computer to communicate and access information (DeBell & Chapman, 2005, 2006).

Outside-of-school technology use and access is complex and interesting as well. For example, type of technology is important because access to some forms of technology seems to be equalizing among different ethnic and racial groups. There are indications that the between-group differences seen in other areas seem to have dissipated when examining laptop ownership. For example, 55% of whites own laptops, compared with 51% of blacks and 54% of Hispanics. There is also evidence that black and English-speaking Hispanics are active users of the Web for a variety of purposes through the use of cell phones. Interesting, cell phone ownership is greater for Hispanics and blacks (87% of each group) compared with whites (80%; Smith, 2010). Moreover, the first two groups use cell phones more often than whites for communicative purposes, such as sending e-mail, sending and receiving text messages or instant messages, or accessing the Web. Blacks and Hispanics also use cell phones more often than whites do for recreational or personal uses, such as playing a game, recording a video, playing music, using a social networking site, or watching a video (Smith, 2010).

These patterns have led to questions about the effects and consequences related to how the technology is used. As the previous paragraph suggests, there is some suggestion (Washington, 2011) that recreational and social use is greater among minority youths than other groups. Thus, some have pointed out that these uses of technology are not those that might further academic goals or serve to reduce academic inequities. This is no hard evidence related to the possible consequences of this pattern, but it is an issue that deserves attention. It is reasonable to expect that technology, like other cultural tools, will be actively adapted to different ecocultural niches in ways that make sense to those who occupy them. There is no guarantee that all the things that technology may afford will be appropriated in all cases.

In sum, there are reasons to be cautious about the information just presented. There is increasing diversity along several dimensions, continuing and systematic achievement differences, and a changing world context that will demand new and more complex skills. Given that achievement differences continue to exist, it is fair to say that current approaches have not been entirely successful in addressing gaps in traditional literacy skills for diverse students. What is the likelihood that new and more complex skills will be addressed in a more favorable fashion? In light of anticipated changes, there is a very real danger that students of color and from low-income families face the threat of a double deficit, with differences continuing to surface not only in traditional literacy but also in the literate skills required in the 21st-century workplace.

The Research and Policy Context

Over the last two decades, considerable resources have been expended on trying to address literacy achievement, including the Reading Excellence Act, Early Reading First, Reading First, Even Start, Reading Is Fundamental, and Striving Readers (U.S. Department of Education, 2007, 2010). Although some progress has been made, Shanahan and Shanahan (2008) have argued that the progress has been in the area of early basic literacy, which does not automatically transfer to proficiency in more specialized disciplinary literacy as one moves up the academic ladder. They have noted that context experts in math, chemistry, and history read discipline-based texts quite differently, and the researchers thus recommend different comprehension strategies. This represents a deviation from the belief that if students are just taught to master basic strategic skills in reading, then the background knowledge that they acquire will allow them to read any type of text successfully—the so-called "vaccination" conception of teaching (Shanahan & Barr, 1995, p. 982).

Shanahan and Shanahan (2008) distinguish between basic literacy (literacy skills such as decoding and knowledge of high-frequency words that underlie virtually all reading tasks), intermediate literacy (literacy skills common to many tasks, including generic comprehension strategies, common word meanings, and basic fluency), and disciplinary literacy (literacy skills specialized to history, science, mathematics, literature, or other subject matter). Unsurprising, this suggests that different approaches, such as specialized texts, strategies and interpretive standards, thinking and analytical practices, and teachers' professional development, need to be considered. When this is superimposed on the considerable demands that will be imposed on the educational system related to helping students become proficient in 21st-century skills and new literacies, the task is daunting indeed, especially regarding those students who have fared less well traditionally.

Instructional Considerations

Although considerable investment has been made in improving literacy instruction, as noted previously, as of yet there is little that systematically targets the instruction of specialized knowledge, such as online reading comprehension and other new skills. The problem is that research in this area is in its infancy (Leu, McVerry, et al., 2009), especially for students of color (Castek et al., 2007; Parker, 2007). These and other authors have suggested that socially mediated and inquiry-based experiences may be especially useful as instructional models are developed for teaching the new literacies of online reading comprehension (Leu, Leu, & Coiro, 2004). Unfortunately, these are the kinds of educational experiences that underachieving students have traditionally received in lesser amounts.

With respect to students who are English learners, there have been several attempts to synthesize the general findings regarding literacy instruction (August & Shanahan, 2006; Genesee, Lindholm-Leary, Saunders, & Christian, 2006; Goldenberg, 2006, 2011; Goldenberg & Coleman, 2010; Rolstad, Mahoney, & Glass, 2005; Slavin & Cheung, 2005). There is relative agreement about the generalization that teaching students to read in the primary language promotes higher levels of reading in English, but that when taught in English, students require additional supports (e.g., clarifications, explanations, instructing the strategic use of cognates to aid work-attack skills and comprehension) primarily because of low English proficiency. Although these patterns likely hold for the instruction of 21st-century skills and new literacies, the research in this area is nonexistent. An additional issue for English learners is that although additive and first-language learning approaches have been recommended by many researchers in the field, there is an increasing tendency to eliminate or reduce these types of programs in favor of English-only and related restrictive language policies, with scarce theoretical or empirical justification (August, Goldenberg, & Rueda, 2010).

An interesting debate in the instructional literature focused on students of color is related to the question of universality of practices and approaches. That is, is good instruction universally applicable, or do certain groups of students profit from instruction tailored to meet their unique cultural frameworks and practices (Tharp, 1989)? While authorities in the 1960s and 1970s often considered student cultural and language differences as deficits, more recent work has come to view these as assets to be used in designing instruction (González et al., 2005; C. Lee, 2007), often lumped under the label of culturally responsive instruction. While a variety of intriguing approaches have been described in the literature, a recent review (August & Shanahan, 2006) has found a lack of systematic evidence, primarily because the issue has not been well studied, not because it has been systematically and extensively studied and found not to work. Rueda (2011) has discussed the cognitive and motivational considerations as they might influence future work in this area.

Rueda (2006) has noted that there have been important shifts related to how cultural issues have been treated in the literature. From the 1960s through the 1980s, as compared with the current context, for example, the consideration of culture in the research and writing in the areas of reading and literacy has changed from minimal treatment to more substantial treatment; from being viewed as a minor topic to a central topic; from a deficit to an instructional resource; from a focus on differences to a focus on access; from a focus on school primarily to a focus on school, home, and community; from a single literacy to multiple literacies; from a view of universal processes to a view of situated processes; and from a focus on cultural matching of teachers and students and increasing awareness and sensitivity to cultural modeling and other uses of funds of knowledge. Given the goals of this chapter, it is useful to think about a third column: what will it be like with 21st-century skills? How will this shift in the next few years given all the changes detailed earlier in this chapter? It will be important to devote attention to these issues from both a research and a policy perspective, as cultural factors and differences will be important mediators for the acquisition and use of 21st-century skills and new literacies.

Accountability and Assessment

One of the overriding factors that defines the current educational context is the press for accountability. A typical pattern is the reliance on standardized tests as the primary means of evaluating students' literacy learning (Au, 2006; Hoffman, Assaf, & Paris, 2001). As Shepard (1990) pointed out some time ago, this policy initiative is based on a simple set of arguments. First, testing helps set goals and standards to which school districts, schools, teachers, and students can aspire. Second, test data provides feedback to modify classroom instruction. Third, testing makes all actors more accountable for student learning. Finally, testing, coupled with incentives and/or sanctions, can be used to leverage changes and educational reform. However, one negative by-product of a test-based accountability approach is the incentive to play the system. As one example, Jacob and Levitt (2003) have found that a small number of teachers are more likely to cheat when faced with more accountability pressure.

Some research has attempted to examine the impact of accountability pressures specifically from a motivational perspective. Mintrop (2003) has found that accountability policies have only a mild influence on teacher motivation but a negative effect on their commitment. Although the threat of stigma resulted in increased work effort, they also resulted in compliance and anxiety. Leithwood, Steinbach, and Jantzi (2002) have found that misalignment of accountability policy with individual teachers' goals, concerns about their ability to implement the policy, concerns about inadequate time and resources, and emotions, such as frustration, all lessen teachers' motivation to implement accountability measures. The researchers have also found that accountability policies serve to challenge teachers' sense of professionalism, and the sanction of reconstituting a school has a negative effect on teachers' sense of self-worth.

Finnigan and Gross (2007) conducted a study in Chicago that drew explicitly from an expectancy–value motivation framework to examine whether teacher motivation levels changed as a result of accountability policies. They found that the value teachers placed on their professional status and their goals for students focused and increased their effort, but low morale had the potential to undercut the sustainability of teachers' responses. Of importance to the students who are the focus of this chapter, at least one study found that teachers' response to accountability policies largely depended on their beliefs about students and their own self-efficacy. Specifically, teachers did not respond to the accountability policies in ways that would lead to improved instruction and learning when they had low expectations of students' abilities or their own self-efficacy about their ability to influence learning (Abelmann & Elmore, 1999).

Apart from the motivational considerations, do these reform efforts work? This is a controversial area, although there is little evidence that accountability-based reform has served to narrow the achievement gaps (Harris & Herrington, 2006; Nichols, Glass, & Berliner, 2006). One recent national study examined the relationship between high-stakes testing pressure and student achievement across 25 states. Each state was rated as to the degree of accountability pressure, resulting in a continuum of accountability pressure from high to low. Regression and correlation analyses found no relationship between earlier pressure and later cohort achievement for math at the fourth- and eighth-grade levels on the NAEP. Further, no relationship was found between testing pressure and reading achievement on the NAEP at any grade level or for any ethnic student subgroup. It was also found that there was suggestive evidence for a relationship between high-stakes testing pressure and subsequent achievement on the national assessment tests, but only for fourth grade, noncohort achievement, and some ethnic subgroups.

The large-scale, high-stakes tests used to support accountability have been criticized for being overly narrow in content, lacking a match with curricula and instruction, neglecting higher order thinking skills, and having limited response formats. However, Leu, O'Byrne, and colleagues (2009) have noted an additional problem, notably that current assessments do not address new competencies such as online reading comprehension. Schools, especially the lowest achieving ones, are under tremendous pressure to raise scores and often tend to respond to teaching what the tests measure in a narrow fashion, thus de-emphasizing higher order and technology-related literacy skills. Thus, schools may be replicating the oft-noted pattern that those who require the most receive the least. Whether or not assessments continue to drive curricula in this way, there needs to be consideration given to a closer link to the changing nature of real-world and workplace skills and the content and formats of assessments.

The Role of Teachers

The key role of teachers in the implementation of curricular innovations has been increasingly and widely acknowledged (Lieberman & Mace, 2008). It is not only teachers' pedagogical and content knowledge that is important, but also their attitudes, beliefs, and motivational orientations are critical in the realization of effective teaching and learning environments. The negative impact of low expectations and excessive focus on real or assumed student, family, and community deficits has been well documented (Valencia, 2010).

Teachers' roles in mediating students' use of technology is an important consideration. Gray and colleagues (2010) indicate that technology is found in virtually every school in the country, but there are some interesting findings regarding how teachers use it and how these uses vary by student characteristics. For example, comparing high- and low-poverty schools, the percentage of teachers who reported that their students used educational technology sometimes or often during classes to prepare written text was 66% and 56%, respectively. In addition, there were differences related to poverty in terms of using technology to learn or practice basic skills (61% and 83%, respectively) and to develop and present multimedia presentations (47% and 36%, respectively). Other teacher differences between these types of schools (high poverty vs. low poverty) include the percentage of teachers who sometimes or often did the following: used e-mail or a listserv to send group updates or information to parents (69% vs. 39%) or to students (30% vs. 17%), used e-mail to address individual concerns with parents (92% vs. 48%) or with students (38% vs. 19%), or used a course or teacher webpage to communicate with parents (47% vs. 30%) or with students (36% vs. 18%). Interesting, not all teachers report optimal support. The percentage of teachers who reported that the following activities prepared them (to a moderate or major extent) to make effective use of educational technology for instruction are 61% for professional development activities, 61% for training provided by school staff responsible for technology support and/or integration, and 78% for independent learning. These numbers leave a wide gap from the numbers of teachers who reported not being prepared.

In terms of teacher preparation, one challenge will be to meet 21st-century educational demands with an adequate supply of qualified teachers in the face of an increasingly diverse student population and a teacher workforce that is currently more than four-fifths non-Hispanic white (Aud et al., 2011). Whereas the demographics of the student population are rapidly changing, the demographics of the teaching force are much more stable. In the case of English learners, most teachers have not been adequately trained to deal with language differences. As of 2000, for example, 41% of U.S. teachers had taught English learner students, but only 13% had received any type of specialized training (Gruber, Wiley, Broughman, Strizek, & Burian-Fitzgerald, 2002). A recent survey of 5,300 teachers in California indicated that many respondents felt unprepared to meet the challenge of teaching English learners, even when they had specialized training (Gándara, Maxwell-Jolly, & Driscoll, 2005). This does not mean that simple linguistic or ethnic/racial matching is a useful approach, as there is little evidence for this strategy with respect to student outcomes. However, it does mean that attention will need to be directed at assisting teachers in understanding how individual and interpersonal competencies are nurtured in and outside of school for students whose families are culturally (and often linguistically) different from the teachers' (Garcia, Jensen, & Cuéllar, 2006). Part of this means engineering ways to leverage the interpersonal assets found in the homes and communities of diverse students for instructional purposes (e.g., Fuller & Coll, 2010).

If it is the case that teachers are entering urban school settings with increasingly complex demands and increasingly diverse student populations, those institutions charged with preparing or advocating for teachers need to reconceptualize the roles that they play and the manner in which they provide preparation. It is not a secret that education in general, and universities' schools of education in particular, are under attack from a variety of sources. One government report portrays teacher certification requirements as a "broken system" and urges that attendance at schools of education, course work in education, and student teaching become "optional" (U.S. Department of Education, 2002, p. 19). Darling-Hammond and Sykes (2003) and Darling Hammond and Baratz-Snowden (2005) have reviewed significant evidence related to the importance of teachers in student outcomes, and how teacher preparation is complicated by unequal distribution of resources to schools, lack of support systems, inadequate compensation, and lack of coordinated state and national policies aimed at producing highly qualified teachers. Unfortunately, this set of conditions impacts most strongly those schools that are in the most needy circumstances and those with the most diverse populations, and the changing context described in this chapter makes the task that much more difficult. If preparation programs are having difficulty with addressing current needs, the new strategies, resources, and priorities will need to be leveraged to keep the United States competitive.

Motivational Considerations

In a comprehensive review of current work and issues in motivation, Pintrich (2003) outlines key motivational generalizations based on current research and theory:

- Adaptive self-efficacy and competence beliefs motivate students.
- Adaptive attributions and control beliefs motivate students.
- Higher levels of interest and intrinsic motivation motivates students.
- Higher levels of value motivate students.
- Goals motivate and direct students. (p. 672)

How will these affective dimensions play out for teachers and students from diverse backgrounds as they confront the teaching and learning of new skills and abilities surrounding 21st-century skills? In the past, work on learning and motivation has been seen as separate research areas, but more and more they are being seen as part of an integrated whole, and hot cognition has replaced the view of thinking as a cold, unfeeling set of mental processes.

When one considers that active choice, persistence, and effort are key indicators of motivation (Schunk, Pintrich, & Meece, 2008), it is striking to consider the multitude of educational issues that fall within this scope in urban schools. On the part of students, consider the issues of dropout rates, low levels of engagement, failure to complete assignments, choosing the wrong peer group, lack of clear goals, low interest, and so forth. Additionally, for teachers in urban schools, consider the low rates of persistence in the profession, burnout rates, and other concerns. What will be needed to engage an increasingly diverse group of students in mastering new and more complex sets of skills than had been required in the past?

Although the research is not yet well developed, as noted earlier, it has been hypothesized that culturally compatible instruction and culturally responsive learning environments and materials can have a significant impact on key motivational variables and thus mediate student participation in ways that help (or hinder) their reading and comprehension and ultimately achievement. Certainly, much of the descriptive research on cultural factors describes increased student engagement as a product of culturally compatible teaching (Au & Mason, 1981; Goldenberg, Rueda, & August, 2006). Although engagement is not necessarily the same as achievement, fostering engagement is not a trivial concern. There is, in fact, a robust literature from a reading engagement perspective (Guthrie & Wigfield, 2000) that has explored the motivational dimensions of reading and demonstrated the connection between reading engagement and reading outcomes. It is well established that mental effort is associated with motivational beliefs such as interest (Salomon, 1984) and that academic engagement and other achievement-related behaviors are associated with measured achievement (Fredricks, Blumenfeld, & Paris, 2004) and reading comprehension in particular (Guthrie et al., 2004, 2006).

Will teachers be motivated to incorporate new content and teaching methodologies? Again, motivational issues will be important. For example, just because teachers have access to technology, that doesn't mean they will use it. This may be mediated by the fact that not all teachers, even if motivated to use new technologies and engage students with new literacies, have the training or support to do so, as noted earlier. From the perspective of students, there are interesting motivational questions also. How well do the existing reading engagement models fit the new learning environments, content, and contexts for application that will continue to evolve? Clearly, these are issues that the field will need to tackle in the very near future.

Conclusion

The consideration of 21st-century skills in the context of reading and literacy provides an interesting challenge to the field by presenting some interesting paradoxes:

- The most rapidly increasing groups are those who are least likely to get the educational experiences that prepare them for future challenges.
- Although literacy is often included in the discussion regarding future educational considerations, it is often framed narrowly around technological literacy, at the risk of downplaying broader considerations related to literacy education and a wide range of literate cultural practices.
- In an increasingly global context, the ability to speak and write and read in more than one language will be increasingly important, yet the current trend in many schools across the country is to promote restrictive language and immigration practices and policies, including English-only approaches.
- Motivation (for students *and* teachers) is rarely emphasized in conversations around 21st-century skills, although it is critical for learning in general and for literacy specifically and may be especially important for the outcomes of the groups who are the focus of this chapter.

It is useful at this point in the discussion to return to an issue raised early on, namely, the question about who should decide what schools should produce. Whereas during earlier times that decision was left to educational professionals, the range of constituents has broadened significantly to include parents, community members, taxpayers, advocacy groups, and others. More than ever before, a corporate and business perspective is exerting influence on educational priorities, and a workable balance will need to be fashioned. Drawing on a gamelike metaphor, not only have the players changed, but the rules of the game and the goals have changed as well. It is a unique opportunity and challenge for the field.

QUESTIONS FOR REFLECTION

1. Rueda brings up an ongoing debate about the purposes of education and the control of curriculum. Where do you weigh in on this debate?
2. What kinds of assessments might be used to determine a student's online reading ability as described by the author?
3. What can schools of education do to prepare teachers to work with linguistically and culturally diverse student populations?

REFERENCES

Abelmann, C., & Elmore, R. (with Even, J., Kenyon, S., & Marshall, J.). (1999). *When accountability knocks, will anyone answer?* (CPRE Research Report No. RR-42). Philadelphia: Consortium for Policy Research in Education, University of Pennsylvania.

Apte, U.M., Karmarkar, U.S., & Nath, H.K. (2008). Information services in the U.S. economy: Value, jobs, and management implications. *California Management Review, 50*(3), 12–30.

Association of American Colleges and Universities. (2007). *College learning for the new global century.* Washington, DC: Author.

Au, K. (2006). *Multicultural issues and literacy achievement.* Mahwah, NJ: Erlbaum.

Au, K.H., & Mason, J.M. (1981). Social organizational factors in learning to read: The balance of rights hypothesis. *Reading Research Quarterly, 17*(1), 115–152.

Aud, S., Hussar, W., Kena, G., Bianco, K., Frohlich, L., Kemp, J., et al. (2011). *The condition of education 2011* (NCES 2011–033). Washington, DC: National Center for Education Statistics, Institute of Education Sciences, U.S. Department of Education.

August, D., Goldenberg, C., & Rueda, R. (2010). Restrictive state language policies: Are they scientifically based? In P. Gándara & M. Hopkins (Eds.), *Forbidden language: English learners and restrictive language policies* (pp. 139–158). New York: Teachers College Press.

August, D., & Shanahan, T. (Eds.). (2006). *Developing literacy in second-language learners: Report of the National Literacy Panel on Language-Minority Children and Youth.* Mahwah, NJ: Erlbaum; Washington, DC: Center for Applied Linguistics.

Bloome, D., Katz, L., Solsken, J., Willett, J., & Wilson-Keenan, J. (2000). Interpellations of family/community and classroom literacy practices. *Journal of Educational Research, 93*(3), 155–163. doi:10.1080/00220670009598704

Callahan, R.M. (2006). The intersection of accountability and language: Can reading intervention replace English language development? *Bilingual Research Journal, 30*(1), 1–21. doi:10.1080/15235882.2006.10162863

Campbell, P.R. (1996). *Population projections for states by age, sex, race, and Hispanic origin: 1995 to 2050.* Washington, DC: Population Division, U.S. Bureau of the Census..

Capps, R., Fix, M., Murray, J., Ost, J., Passel, J.S., & Herwantoro, S. (2005). *The new demography of America's schools: Immigration and the No Child Left Behind Act.* Washington, DC: Urban Institute.

Carnegie Council on Advancing Adolescent Literacy. (2010). *Time to act: An agenda for advancing adolescent literacy for college and career success.* New York: Carnegie Corporation of New York.

Castek, J., Leu, D.J., Coiro, J., Gort, M., Henry, L., & Lima, C.O. (2007). Developing new literacies among multilingual learners in the elementary grades. In L.L. Parker (Ed.), *Technology-mediated learning environments for young English learners: Connections in and out of school* (pp. 111–153). New York: Routledge.

Coiro, J. (2007). *Exploring changes to reading comprehension on the Internet: Paradoxes and possibilities for diverse adolescent readers.* Unpublished doctoral dissertation, University of Connecticut, Storrs.

Coiro, J., Knobel, M., Lankshear, C., & Leu, D.J. (2008). Central issues in new literacies and new literacies research. In J. Coiro, M. Knobel, C. Lankshear, & D.J. Leu (Eds.), *Handbook of research on new literacies* (pp. 1–21). New York: Erlbaum.

Cooper, M. (2004). *Expanding the digital divide and falling behind on broadband: Why a telecommunications policy of neglect is not benign.* Washington, DC: Consumer Federation of America. Retrieved May 17, 2012, from www.consumerfed.org/pdfs/digitaldivide.pdf

Darling-Hammond, L., & Baratz-Snowden, J. (Eds.). (2005). *A good teacher in every classroom:*

Preparing the highly qualified teachers our children deserve. San Francisco: Jossey-Bass.
Darling-Hammond, L., & Sykes, G. (2003). Wanted, a national teacher supply policy for education: The right way to meet the "highly qualified teacher" challenge. *Education Policy Analysis Archives, 11*(33).
DeBell, M., & Chapman, C. (2005). *Rates of computer and Internet use by children in nursery school and students in kindergarten through twelfth grade: 2003* (NCES 2005–111). Washington, DC: National Center for Education Statistics, Institute of Education Sciences, U.S. Department of Education.
DeBell, M., & Chapman, C. (2006). *Computer and Internet use by students in 2003* (NCES 2006–065). Washington, DC: National Center for Education Statistics, Institute of Education Sciences, U.S. Department of Education.
Dede, C. (2005). Planning for neomillennial learning styles: Implications for investments in technology and faculty. In D.G. Oblinger and J.L. Oblinger (Eds.), *Educating the net generation*. Boulder, CO: EDUCAUSE. Retrieved July 14, 2012, from net.educause.edu/ir/library/pdf/pub7101.pdf.
Dede, C. (2010). Comparing frameworks for 21st century skills. In J. Bellanca & R. Brandt (Eds.), *21st century skills: Rethinking how students learn* (pp. 51–75). Bloomington, IN: Solution Tree.
Durgunoğlu, A.Y., & Goldenberg, C. (Eds.). (2011). *Language and literacy development in bilingual settings*. New York: Guilford.
Finnigan, K.S., & Gross, B. (2007). Do accountability policy sanctions influence teacher motivation? Lessons from Chicago's low-performing schools. *American Educational Research Journal, 44*(3), 594–630. doi:10.3102/0002831207306767
Fredricks, J.A., Blumenfeld, P.C., & Paris, A.H. (2004). School engagement: Potential of the concept, state of the evidence. *Review of Educational Research, 74*(1), 59–109. doi:10.3102/00346543074001059
Fuller, B., & Coll, C.G. (2010). Learning from Latinos: Contexts, families, and child development in motion. *Developmental Psychology, 46*(3), 559–565. doi:10.1037/a0019412
Gándara, P., Maxwell-Jolly, J., & Driscoll, A. (2005). *Listening to teachers of English language learners: A survey of California teachers' challenges, experiences, and professional development needs*. Santa Cruz, CA: Center for the Future of Teaching and Learning.
Garcia, E.E., Jensen, B., & Cuéllar, D. (2006). Early academic achievement of Hispanics in the United States: Implications for teacher preparation. *New Educator, 2*(2), 123–147. doi:10.1080/15476880600657215
Gee, J.P. (2000). Discourse and sociocultural studies in reading. In M.L. Kamil, P.B. Mosenthal, P. David Pearson, & R. Barr (Eds.), *Handbook of reading research* (Vol. 3, pp. 195–208). Mahwah, NJ: Erlbaum.
Gee, J.P. (2003). *What video games have to teach us about learning and literacy*. New York: Palgrave/Macmillan.
Genesee, F., Lindholm-Leary, K., Saunders, W.M., & Christian, D. (Eds.). (2006). *Educating English language learners: A synthesis of research evidence*. New York: Cambridge University Press. doi:10.1017/CBO9780511499913
Goldenberg, C. (2006). Improving achievement for English-learners: What the research tells us. *Education Week, 25*(43), 34–36.
Goldenberg, C. (2011). Reading instruction for English language learners. In M.L. Kamil, P.D. Pearson, E.B. Moje, & P.P. Afflerbach (Eds.), *Handbook of reading research* (Vol. 4, pp. 684–710). New York: Routledge.
Goldenberg, C., & Coleman, R. (2010). *Promoting academic achievement among English learners: A guide to the research*. Thousand Oaks, CA: Corwin.
Goldenberg, C., Rueda, R.S., & August, D. (2006). Social and cultural influences on the literacy attainment of language-minority children and youth. In D. August & T. Shanahan (Eds.), *Developing literacy in second-language learners: Report of the National Literacy Panel on Language-Minority Children and Youth* (pp. 269–318). Mahwah, NJ: Erlbaum; Washington, DC: Center for Applied Linguistics.
González, N., Moll, L.C., & Amanti C. (Eds.). (2005). *Funds of knowledge: Theorizing practices in households, communities, and classrooms*. Mahwah, NJ: Erlbaum.
Gray, L., Thomas, N., & Lewis, L. (2010). *Educational technology in U.S. public schools: Fall 2008* (NCES 2010–034). Washington, DC: National Center for Education Statistics, Institute of Education Sciences, U.S. Department of Education.
Gruber, K.J., Wiley, S.D., Broughman, S.P., Strizek, G.A., & Burian-Fitzgerald, M. (2002). *Schools and staffing survey, 1999–2000: Overview of the data for public, private, public charter, and Bureau of Indian Affairs elementary and secondary schools* (NCES 2002–313). Washington, DC: National Center for Education Statistics, Office of Educational Research and Improvement, U.S. Department of Education.
Guthrie, J.T., & Wigfield, A. (2000). Engagement and motivation in reading. In M.L. Kamil, P.B. Mosenthal, P.D. Pearson, & R. Barr (Eds.), *Handbook of reading research* (Vol. 3, pp. 403–422). New York: Erlbaum.
Guthrie, J.T., Wigfield, A., Barbosa, P., Perencevich, K.C., Taboada, A., Davis, M.H., et al. (2004). Increasing reading comprehension and engagement through concept-oriented reading instruction. *Journal of Educational Psychology, 96*(3), 403–423. doi:10.1037/0022-0663.96.3.403
Guthrie, J.T., Wigfield, A., Humenick, N.M., Perencevich, K.C., Taboada, A., & Barbosa, P. (2006). Influences of stimulating tasks on reading motivation and comprehension.

Journal of Educational Research, 99(4), 232–246. doi:10.3200/JOER.99.4.232-246
Harris, D.N., & Herrington, C.D. (2006). Accountability, standards, and the growing achievement gap: Lessons from the past half-century. *American Journal of Education, 112*(2), 209–238. doi:10.1086/498995
Hoffman, J.V., Assaf, L.C., & Paris, S.G. (2001). High-stakes testing in reading: Today in Texas, tomorrow? *The Reading Teacher, 54*(5), 482–492.
Hull, G., & Schultz, K. (Eds.). (2002). *School's out! Bridging out-of-school literacies with classroom practice*. New York: Teachers College Press.
Institute of Museum and Library Services. (2009). *Museums, libraries, and 21st century skills* (MLS-2009-NAI-01). Washington, DC: Author.
International ICT Literacy Panel. (2002). *Digital transformation: A framework for ICT literacy*. Princeton, NJ: Educational Testing Service.
International Society for Technology in Education. (2000). *National educational technology standards for students: Connecting curriculum and technology*. Eugene, OR: Author; Washington, DC: U.S. Department of Education.
Jacob, B.A., & Levitt, S.D. (2003). Rotten apples: An investigation of the prevalence and predictors of teacher cheating. *The Quarterly Journal of Economics, 118*(3), 843–877. doi:10.1162/00335530360698441
Karmarkar, U.S., & Apte, U.M. (2007). Operations management in the information economy: Information products, processes, and chains. *Journal of Operations Management, 25*(2), 438–453. doi:10.1016/j.jom.2006.11.001
Kochhar, R., Fry, R., & Taylor, P. (2011). *Wealth gaps rise to record highs between whites, blacks and Hispanics*. Washington, DC: Pew Research Center.
Kress, G. (2003). *Literacy in the new media age*. New York: Routledge. doi:10.4324/9780203164754
Lankshear, C., & Knobel, M. (2006). *New literacies: Everyday practices and classroom learning* (2nd ed.). New York: Open University Press.
Lee, C.D. (2007). *Culture, literacy, and learning: Taking bloom in the midst of the whirlwind*. New York: Teachers College Press.
Lee, J. (2002). Racial and ethnic achievement gap trends: Reversing the progress toward equity? *Educational Researcher, 31*(1), 3–12. doi:10.3102/0013189X031001003
Leithwood, K., Steinbach, R., & Jantzi, D. (2002). School leadership and teachers' motivation to implement accountability policies. *Educational Administration Quarterly, 38*(1), 94–119.
Lenhart, A., Arafeh, S., Smith, A., & Macgill, A.R. (2008). *Writing, technology, and teens*. Washington, DC: Pew Internet & American Life Project. Retrieved May 21, 2012, from www.pewinternet.org/Reports/2008/Writing-Technology-and-Teens.aspx
Leu, D.J. (2006). New literacies, reading research, and the challenges of change: A deictic perspective. In J.V. Hoffman, D.L. Schallert, C.M. Fairbanks, J. Worthy, & B. Maloch (Eds.), *55th Yearbook of the National Reading Conference* (pp. 1–20). Oak Creek, WI: National Reading Conference.
Leu, D.J., Jr., Kinzer, C.K., Coiro, J.L., & Cammack, D.W. (2004). Toward a theory of new literacies emerging from the Internet and other information and communication technologies. In R.B. Ruddell & N. Unrau (Eds.), *Theoretical models and processes of reading* (5th ed., pp. 1570–1613). Newark, DE: International Reading Association. doi:10.1598/0872075028.54
Leu, D.J., Jr., Leu, D.D., & Coiro, J. (2004). *Teaching with the Internet K–12: New literacies for new times* (4th ed.). Norwood, MA: Christopher-Gordon.
Leu, D.J., McVerry, J.G., O'Byrne, W.I., Kiili, C., Zawilinski, L., Everett-Cacopardo, H., et al. (2011). The new literacies of online reading comprehension: Expanding the literacy and learning curriculum. *Journal of Adolescent & Adult Literacy, 55*(1), 5–14.
Leu, D.J., McVerry, J.G., O'Byrne, W.I., Zawilinski, L., Castek, J., & Hartman, D.K. (2009). The new literacies of online reading comprehension and the irony of No Child Left Behind: Students who require our assistance the most actually receive it the least. In L.M. Morrow, R. Rueda, & D. Lapp (Eds.), *Handbook of research on literacy and diversity* (pp. 173–194). New York: Guilford.
Leu, D.J., O'Byrne, W.I., Zawilinski, L., McVerry, J.G., & Everett-Cacopardo, H. (2009). Expanding the new literacies conversation. *Educational Researcher, 38*(4), 264–269. doi:10.3102/0013189X09336676
Leu, D.J., Zawilinski, L., Castek, J., Banerjee, M., Housand, B.C., Liu, Y., et al. (2007). What is new about the new literacies of online reading comprehension? In L.S. Rush, A.J. Eakle, & A. Berger (Eds.), *Secondary school literacy: What research reveals for classroom practice* (pp. 37–68). Urbana, IL: National Council of Teachers of English.
Levy, F., & Murnane, R.J. (2004). *The new division of labor: How computers are creating the next job market*. Princeton, NJ: Princeton University Press; New York: Russell Sage Foundation.
Lieberman, A., & Mace, D.H.P. (2008). Teacher learning: The key to educational reform. *Journal of Teacher Education, 59*(3), 226–234. doi:10.1177/0022487108317020
Los Angeles Unified School District. (2009). *R30 Language Census Report, Spring 2009* (Publication No. 371). Los Angeles: Planning and Assessment Division, Los Angeles Unified School District.
Madden, A., Ford, N., Miller, D., & Levy, P. (2005). Using the Internet in teaching: The views of practitioners (A survey of the views of secondary school teachers in Sheffield, UK). *British Journal of Educational Technology, 36*(2), 255–280.
Martin, M.O., Mullis, I.V.S., Gonzalez, E.J., & Chrostowski, S.J. (2004). *TIMSS 2003 international science report*. Chestnut Hill, MA: TIMSS

& PIRLS International Study Center, Lynch School of Education, Boston College.
Mintrop, H. (2003). The limits of sanctions in low-performing schools: A study of Maryland and Kentucky schools on probation. *Education Policy Analysis Archives, 11*(3), Article 3.
Mullis, I.V.S., Martin, M.O., Gonzalez, E.J., & Chrostowski, S.J. (2004). *TIMSS 2003 international mathematics report.* Chestnut Hill, MA: TIMSS & PIRLS International Study Center, Lynch School of Education, Boston College.
National Center for Education Statistics. (2011a). *The Nation's Report Card: Mathematics 2011* (NCES 2012–458). Washington, DC: National Center for Education Statistics, Institute of Education Sciences, U.S. Department of Education.
National Center for Education Statistics. (2011b). *The Nation's Report Card: Reading 2011* (NCES 2012–457). Washington, DC: National Center for Education Statistics, Institute of Education Sciences, U.S. Department of Education.
National Center for Education Statistics. (2012). *The Nation's Report Card: Science 2011* (NCES 2012–465). Washington, DC: National Center for Education Statistics, Institute of Education Sciences, U.S. Department of Education.
National Research Council. (2010). *Exploring the intersection of science education and 21st century skills: A workshop summary.* Washington, DC: National Academies Press.
New London Group, The. (2000). A pedagogy of multiliteracies designing social futures. In B. Cope & M. Kalantzis (Eds.), *Multiliteracies: Literacy learning and the design of social futures* (pp. 9–37). New York: Routledge.
Nichols, S.L., Glass, G.V., & Berliner, D.C. (2006). High-stakes testing and student achievement: Does accountability pressure increase student learning? *Education Policy Analysis Archives, 14*(1), 1–172.
North Central Regional Educational Laboratory & Metiri Group. (2003). *EnGauge 21st century skills: Literacy in the digital age.* Naperville, IL & Los Angeles: Authors.
Organisation for Economic Co-operation and Development. (2005). *The definition and selection of key competencies: Executive summary.* Paris: Author.
Organisation for Economic Co-operation and Development. (2010). *PISA 2009 results: What students know and can do: Student performance in reading, mathematics and science: Vol. 1.* Paris: Author. Retrieved July 14, 2012, from dx.doi.org/10.1787/9789264091450-en
Parker, L.L. (Ed.). (2007). *Technology-mediated learning environments for young English learners: Connections in and out of school.* New York: Routledge.
Partnership for 21st Century Skills. (2008). *21st century skills, education and competitiveness: A resource and policy guide.* Tucson, AZ: Author. Retrieved May 21, 2012, from www.p21.org/documents/21st_century_skills_education_and_competitiveness_guide.pdf
Partnership for 21st Century Skills. (2011). *Framework for 21st century learning.* Washington, DC: Author. Retrieved May 21, 2012, from p21.org/overview.
Pearson, P.D., & Raphael, T.E. (1999). Toward a more complex view of balance in the literacy curriculum. In W.D. Hammond & T.E. Raphael (Eds.), *Early literacy instruction for the new millennium* (pp. 1–21). Grand Rapids: Michigan Reading Association; Ann Arbor, MI: Center for the Improvement of Early Reading Achievement.
Pearson, T. (2002). Falling behind: A technology crisis facing minority students. *TechTrends, 46*(2), 15–20. doi:10.1007/BF02772070
Pintrich, P.R. (2003). A motivational science perspective on the role of student motivation in learning and teaching contexts. *Journal of Educational Psychology, 95*(4), 667–686. doi:10.1037/0022-0663.95.4.667
RAND Reading Study Group. (2002). *Reading for understanding: Toward an R&D program in reading comprehension.* Santa Monica, CA: RAND.
Rolstad, K., Mahoney, K., & Glass, G.V. (2005). The big picture: A meta-analysis of program effectiveness research on English language learners. *Educational Policy, 19*(4), 572–594. doi:10.1177/0895904805278067
Rueda, R. (2006). *Advances in understanding issues of socio-cultural and linguistic diversity.* Paper presented at the 56th annual meeting of the National Reading Conference, Los Angeles, November.
Rueda, R. (2011). Cultural perspectives in reading: Theory and research. In M.L. Kamil, P.D. Pearson, E.B. Moje, & P.P. Afflerbach (Eds.), *Handbook of reading research* (Vol. 4, pp. 84–103). New York: Routledge.
Salahu-Din, D., Persky, H., & Miller, J. (2008). *The Nation's Report Card: Writing 2007* (NCES 2008–468). Washington, DC: National Center for Education, Institute of Education Statistics, U.S. Department of Education.
Salomon, G. (1984). Television is "easy" and print is "tough": The differential investment of mental effort in learning as a function of perceptions and attributions. *Journal of Educational Psychology, 76*(4), 647–658. doi:10.1037/0022-0663.76.4.647
Schunk, D.H., Pintrich, P.R., & Meece, J.L. (2008). *Motivation in education: Theory, research, and applications* (3rd ed.). Upper Saddle River, NJ: Pearson/Merrill Prentice Hall.
Shanahan, T., & Barr, R. (1995). Reading Recovery: An independent evaluation of the effects of an early instructional intervention for at-risk learners. *Reading Research Quarterly, 30*(4), 958–996. doi:10.2307/748206
Shanahan, T., & Shanahan, C. (2008). Teaching disciplinary literacy to adolescents: Rethinking content-area literacy. *Harvard Educational Review, 78*(1), 40–59.

Shepard, L.A. (1990). Inflated test score gains: Is it old norms or teaching the test? *Educational Measurement: Issues and Practice, 9*(3), 15–22. doi:10.1111/j.1745-3992.1990.tb00374.x

Slavin, R.E., & Cheung, A. (2005). A synthesis of research on language of reading instruction for English language learners. *Review of Educational Research, 75*(2), 247–284. doi:10.3102/00346543075002247

Smerdon, B., Cronen, S., Lanahan, L., Anderson, J., Iannotti, N., & Angeles, J. (2000). *Teachers' tools for the 21st century: A report on teachers' use of technology* (NCES 2000–102). Washington, DC: National Center for Education Statistics, Office of Educational Research and Improvement, U.S. Department of Education. Retrieved May 21, 2012, from nces.ed.gov/pubs2000/2000102.pdf.

Smith, A. (2010). *Mobile access 2010*. Washington, DC: Pew Internet & American Life Project. Retrieved May 18, 2012, from www.pewinternet.org/Reports/2010/Mobile-Access-2010.aspx

Snow, C.E., Burns, M.S., & Griffin, P. (Eds.). (1998). *Preventing reading difficulties in young children*. Washington, DC: National Academy Press.

Street, B. (2003). What's "new" in new literacy studies? Critical approaches to literacy in theory and practice. *Current Issues in Comparative Education, 5*(2), 77–91.

Tharp, R.G. (1989). Psychocultural variables and constants: Effects on teaching and learning in schools. *American Psychologist, 44*(2), 349–359. doi:10.1037/0003-066X.44.2.349

U.S. Census Bureau. (2008). *An older and more diverse nation by midcentury*. Washington, DC: U.S. Census Bureau, U.S. Department of Commerce. Retrieved May 21, 2012, from www.census.gov/newsroom/releases/archives/population/cb08-123.html

U.S. Department of Education. (2002). *Meeting the highly qualified teachers challenge: The secretary's annual report on teacher quality*. Washington, DC: Office of Policy Planning and Innovation, Office of Postsecondary Education, U.S. Department of Education.

U.S. Department of Education. (2007). *Guide to U.S. Department of Education programs*. Washington, DC: Office of Communications and Outreach, U.S. Department of Education.

U.S. Department of Education. (2010). *Guide to U.S. Department of Education programs*. Washington, DC: Office of Communications and Outreach, U.S. Department of Education.

Valencia, R.R. (2010). *Dismantling contemporary deficit thinking: Educational thought and practice*. New York: Routledge.

Vincent, G.K., & Velkoff, V.A. (2010). *The next four decades: The older population in the United States: 2010 to 2050* (Report No. P25–1138). Washington, DC: U.S. Census Bureau, Economics and Statistics Administration, U.S. Department of Commerce.

Wagner, T. (2008). *The global achievement gap: Why even our best schools don't teach the new survival skills our children need—and what we can do about it*. New York: Basic.

Washington, J. (2011). *For minorities, new 'digital divide' seen*. Washington, DC: Pew Internet & American Life Project. Retrieved May 18, 2012, from www.pewinternet.org/Media-Mentions/2011/For-minorities-new-digital-divide-seen.aspx

Williams, C. (2000). *Internet access in U.S. public schools and classrooms: 1994–99* (NCES 2000–086). Washington, DC: National Center for Education Statistics, Office of Educational Research and Improvement, U.S. Department of Education. Retrieved May 21, 2012, from nces.ed.gov/pubs2000/2000086.pdf.

AUTHOR INDEX

B

C

D

E

F

G

H

I

J

K

L

M

P

Q

R

S

T

U

V

W

X

Y

Z

SUBJECT INDEX

A

D

E

F

G

H

I

J

K

L

M

P

Q

R

S

T

U

V

W

Z